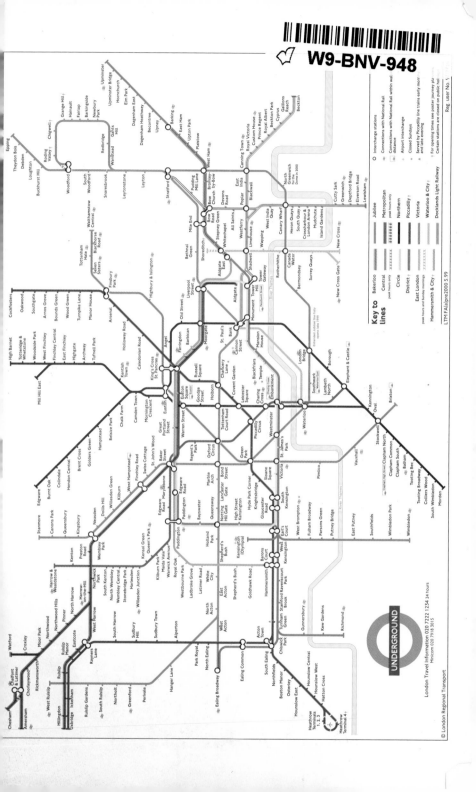

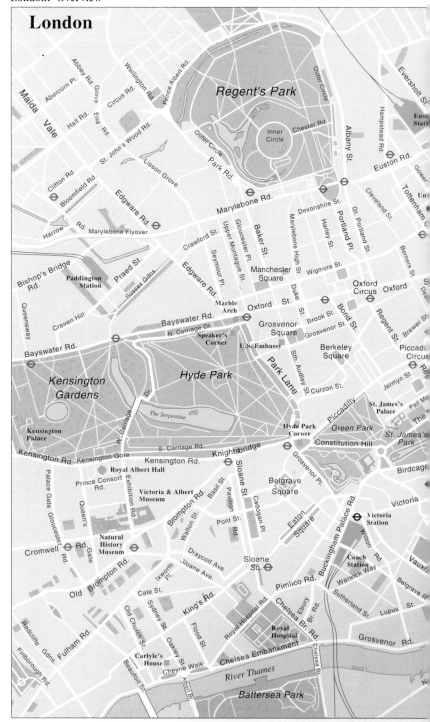

King's Cross Station

Pentonville Rd.

City Rd.

East Road

Hoxton St.

Kingsland Rd.

St. Pancras Station

King's Cross Rd.

Lever St.

Bath St.

Old St.

Gt. Eastern St.

Shoreditch High St.

Commercial St.

Gray's Inn Rd.

Judd St.

Rosebery Ave.

St. John's St.

Goswell Rd.

City Rd.

Coram's Fields

Farringdon Rd.

Aldersgate

Barbican Centre

Woburn Pl.

Guilford St.

Southampton Row

Theobalds Rd.

Clerkenwell Rd.

Charterhouse St.

Smithfield Market

London Wall

Moorgate

Liverpool St. Station

Houndsditch

Bishopsgate

British Museum

Holborn

Chancery La.

Holborn Viaduct

Old Bailey

Newgate St.

Bank of England

Cheapside

Cornhill

Leadenhall St.

Fenchurch St.

New Oxford St.

High Holborn

Kingsway

Fetter La.

St. Paul's

Queen Victoria St.

Gracechurch St.

Eastcheap

Drury La.

Aldwych

Law Courts

Fleet St.

Cannon St.

Upper Thames St.

The Tower

Charing Cross Rd.

Strand

Victoria Embankment

Blackfriars Br.

Blackfriars Station

Cannon St. Station

London Br.

Tower Hill

National Gallery

Charing Cross Stn.

National Theatre

Southwark Br.

River Thames

Tower Br.

Trafalgar Square

Whitehall

Royal Festival Hall

Stamford St.

Blackfriars Rd.

Southwark St.

Union St.

Tooley St.

St. Thomas St.

London Bridge Station

Bridge Rd.

York Rd.

The Cut

Waterloo Station

Long La.

Abbey St.

Westminster Br.

Waterloo Rd.

Borough Rd.

Borough High St.

Tabard St.

Great Dover St.

Tower Bridge Rd.

Houses of Parliament

Westminster Br. Rd.

London Rd.

Harper Rd.

Willow Walk

Westminster Abbey

Lambeth Palace Rd.

Lambeth Rd.

Imperial War Museum

New Kent Rd.

Old Kent Rd.

Millbank

Horseferry Rd.

Lambeth Br.

Black Prince Rd.

Kennington Rd.

Kennington Park Rd.

Crampton St.

Walworth Rd.

Rodney Pl.

Flint St.

East St.

Tate Gallery

Albert Embankment

Kennington La.

Manor Pl.

Portland St.

Thurlow St.

Albany Rd.

Vauxhall Br.

Vauxhall Station

Braganza St.

Kennington Oval

N

0   1/2 mile

0   1/2 kilometer

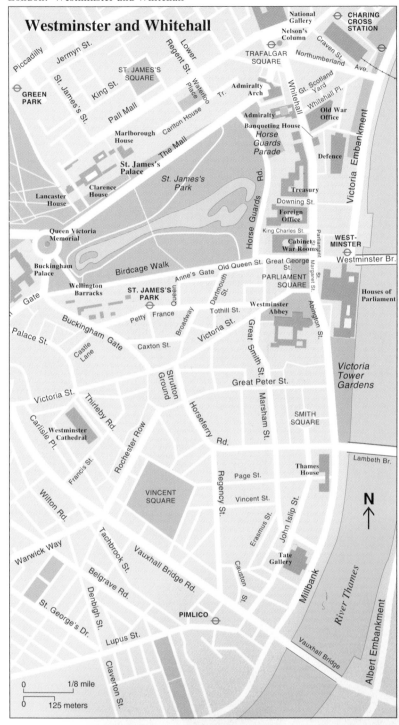

Westminster and Whitehall

National Gallery

Nelson's Column

CHARING CROSS STATION

TRAFALGAR SQUARE

Craven St.

Northumberland Ave.

Piccadilly

Jermyn St.

Lower Regent St.

Waterloo Place

ST. JAMES'S SQUARE

King St.

Admiralty Arch

Whitehall

Gt. Scotland Yard

Whitehall Pl.

GREEN PARK

St. James's St.

Pall Mall

Carlton House

Admiralty

Banqueting House

Old War Office

Marlborough House

Horse Guards Parade

Defence

St. James's Palace

The Mall

St. James's Park

Treasury

Downing St.

Lancaster House

Clarence House

Horse Guards Rd.

Foreign Office

King Charles St.

WEST-MINSTER

Queen Victoria Memorial

Cabinet War Rooms

Parliament St.

Westminster Br.

Buckingham Palace

Birdcage Walk

Anne's Gate

Old Queen St.

Great George St.

PARLIAMENT SQUARE

Margaret St.

Gate

Wellington Barracks

ST. JAMES'S PARK

Queen

Dartmouth St.

Broadway

Petty France

Tothill St.

Westminster Abbey

Abingdon St.

Houses of Parliament

Palace St.

Buckingham Gate

Caxton St.

Victoria St.

Great Smith St.

Victoria Tower Gardens

Castle Lane

Great Peter St.

Victoria St.

Thirleby Rd.

Strutton Ground

Horseferry Rd.

Marsham St.

SMITH SQUARE

Carlisle Pl.

Westminster Cathedral

Rochester Row

Lambeth Br.

Francis St.

Page St.

Thames House

Wilton Rd.

VINCENT SQUARE

Regency St.

Vincent St.

Erasmus St.

John Islip St.

N

Warwick Way

Tachbrook St.

Vauxhall Bridge Rd

Tate Gallery

Millbank

River Thames

Belgrave Rd.

St. George's Dr.

Denbigh St.

PIMLICO

Causton St.

Vauxhall Bridge

Albert Embankment

Lupus St.

Claverton St.

Victoria Embankment

0   1/8 mile

0   125 meters

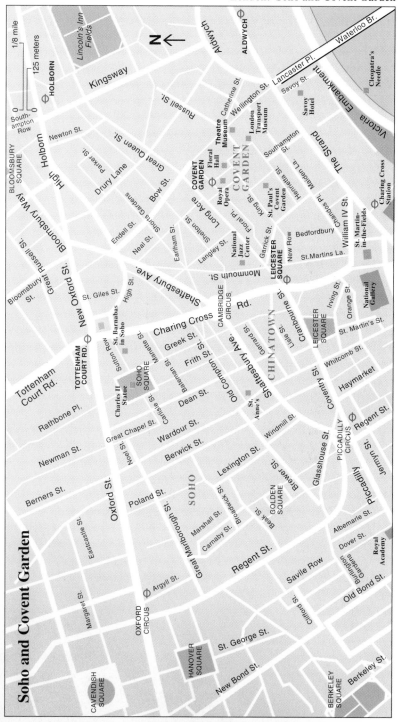

Soho and Covent Garden

1/8 mile
125 meters
Southampton Row

HOLBORN

Lincoln's Inn Fields
Kingsway
ALDWYCH
Aldwych
Waterloo Br.
Cleopatra's Needle

Holborn
High Holborn
Newton St.
Parker St.
BLOOMSBURY SQUARE
Russell St.
Catherine St.
Wellington St.
Lancaster Pl.
Savoy St.
Savoy Hotel
Victoria Embankment

Bloomsbury Way
Great Russell St.
Drury Lane
Great Queen St.
Bow St.
Shorts Gardens
Endell St.
Neal St.
Earlham St.
Station St.
Langley St.
Long Acre
Floral Pl.
COVENT GARDEN
Floral Hall
Royal Opera
Theatre Museum
London Transport Museum
Southampton St.
Henrietta St.
Maiden La.
The Strand
Charing Cross Station

Bloomsbury St.
St. Giles St.
High St.
Shaftesbury Ave.
Cambridge Circus Rd.
Monmouth St.
National Jazz Center
Garrick St.
St. Paul's Covent Garden
King St.
New Row
St.Martins La.
Bedfordbury
Chandos Pl.
William IV St.
St. Martin-in-the-Fields
St. Martin's St.
National Gallery

New Oxford St.
TOTTENHAM COURT RD.
Tottenham Court Rd.
Sutton Row
St. Barnabas in Soho
Charing Cross
Greek St.
Frith St.
Bateman St.
Manette St.
Charles II Statue
Carlisle St.
SOHO SQUARE
Dean St.
St. Anne's
Old Compton St.
Gerrard St.
Lisle St.
Cranbourne St.
LEICESTER SQUARE
CHINATOWN
Irving St.
Orange St.
Whitcomb St.
Coventry St.
Haymarket

Rathbone Pl.
Great Chapel St.
Noel St.
Wardour St.
Berwick St.
Lexington St.
Windmill St.
Brewer St.
Glasshouse St.
PICCADILLY CIRCUS
Regent St.
Piccadilly
Jermyn St.

Newman St.
Berners St.
Eastcastle St.
Oxford St.
Poland St.
SOHO
Great Marlborough St.
Marshall St.
Broadwick St.
Beak St.
GOLDEN SQUARE
Regent St.
Savile Row
Albemarle St.
Dover St.
Old Bond St.
Royal Academy
Burlington Gardens
Clifford St.

Margaret St.
OXFORD CIRCUS
Argyll St.
Carnaby St.
St. George St.
New Bond St.
HANOVER SQUARE
BERKELEY SQUARE
Berkeley St.

CAVENDISH SQUARE

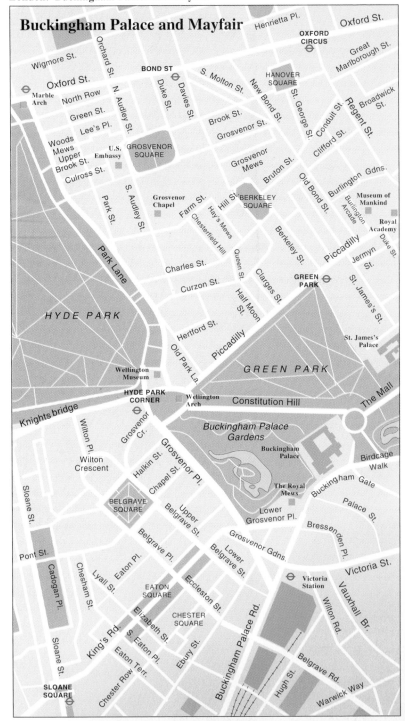

Buckingham Palace and Mayfair

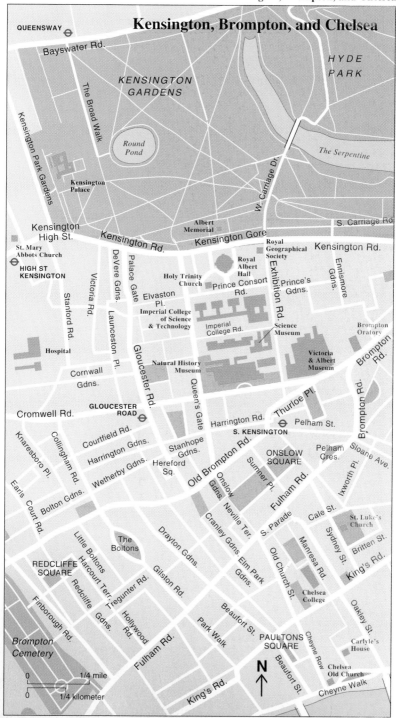

Kensington, Brompton, and Chelsea

QUEENSWAY

Bayswater Rd.

KENSINGTON GARDENS

The Broad Walk

Round Pond

Kensington Park Gardens

Kensington Palace

HYDE PARK

The Serpentine

W. Carriage Dr.

S. Carriage Rd.

Kensington High St.

St. Mary Abbots Church

HIGH ST KENSINGTON

Kensington Rd.

Albert Memorial

Kensington Gore

Kensington Rd.

Royal Geographical Society

DeVere Gdns.

Palace Gate

Holy Trinity Church

Royal Albert Hall

Prince Consort Rd.

Exhibition Rd.

Prince's Gdns.

Ennismore Gdns.

Victoria Rd.

Launceston Pl.

Elvaston Pl.

Imperial College of Science & Technology

Imperial College Rd.

Science Museum

Brompton Oratory

Stanford Rd.

Hospital

Gloucester Rd.

Natural History Museum

Victoria & Albert Museum

Brompton Rd.

Cornwall Gdns.

Queen's Gate

Brompton Rd.

Cromwell Rd.

GLOUCESTER ROAD

Thurloe Pl.

Harrington Rd.

Pelham St.

Knaresboro Pl.

Collingham Rd.

Courtfield Rd.

Harrington Gdns.

Stanhope Gdns.

S. KENSINGTON

ONSLOW SQUARE

Pelham Cres.

Sloane Ave.

Ixworth Pl.

Earls Court Rd.

Bolton Gdns.

Wetherby Gdns.

Hereford Sq.

Old Brompton Rd.

Onslow Gdns.

Sumner Pl.

Fulham Rd.

Cale St.

St. Luke's Church

Sydney St.

Britten St.

Little Boltons

The Boltons

Drayton Gdns.

Cranley Gdns.

Neville Ter.

Elm Park Gdns.

S. Parade

Old Church St.

Manresa Rd.

King's Rd.

REDCLIFFE SQUARE

Harcourt Terr.

Tregunter Rd.

Gilston Rd.

Chelsea College

Finborough Rd.

Redcliffe Gdns.

Hollywood Rd.

Fulham Rd.

Park Walk

Beaufort St.

PAULTONS SQUARE

Cheyne Row

Oakley St.

Carlyle's House

Brompton Cemetery

Chelsea Old Church

Beaufort St.

Cheyne Walk

King's Rd.

N

0   1/4 mile

0   1/4 kilometer

The City

Commercial St.
Leman St.
Mansell St.
ALDGATE EAST
Middlesex St.
Widegate St.
Minories
E. Smithfield
St. Katharine's Way
Tower Br. Approach
Tower Br.
Royal Mint St.
Houndsditch
ALDGATE
Aldgate
Fenchurch St. Station
St. Mary Axe
Liverpool St. Station
Bishopsgate
Old Broad St.
London Stock Exchange
Throgmorton St.
St. Margaret's
Bank of England
Threadneedle St.
Leadenhall St.
Lloyd's
Leadenhall Market
Lime St.
Gracechurch St.
Cornhill
Lombard St.
Fenchurch St.
Seething La.
St. Olave's
Mark La.
Mincing La.
TOWER HILL
TRINITY SQUARE
Tower Hill
All Hallows
St. Dunstan's
Gt. Tower St.
Lower Thames St.
The Tower
Tower Pier
HMS Belfast
Billingsgate Market
Sun St.
South Pl.
MOORGATE
FINSBURY CIRCUS
London Wall
Moorgate
Coleman St.
Lothbury
Princes St.
BANK
King William St.
St. Mary Abchurch
Eastcheap
St. Mary at Hill
The Monument
MONUMENT
Monument St.
St. Magnus Martyr
London Br.
Chiswell St.
Ropemaker St.
Moorfields
Basinghall Ave.
Basinghall St.
Mansion House
Poultry
St. Stephen Walbrook
Temple of Mithras
Walbrook
CANNON
Cloak La.
Cannon St. Station
Cannon St.
Queen St.
Southwark Br.
Silk St.
Fore St.
Guildhall
King St.
Gresham St.
Milk St.
Wood St.
St. Mary le Bow
Cheapside
Watling St.
St. Mary Aldermary
Bread St.
MANSION HOUSE
River Thames
Beech St.
Barbican Centre
St. Giles without Cripplegate
Museum of London
London Wall
New Change
St. Martin's-Le-Grand
St. Paul's Cathedral
Cannon St.
St. Andrew-by-the-Wardrobe
Queen Victoria St.
St. Benet's
Upper Thames St.
Aldersgate St.
St. Bartholomew the Great
Little Britain
ST. PAUL'S
Newgate St.
Puddle Dock
Blackfriars Station
BARBICAN
Long Lane
West Smithfield
Gough Gunspur St.
Holborn Viaduct Station
Old Bailey
Warwick La.
Ludgate Hill
LUDGATE CIRCUS
New Bridge St.
Blackfriars Br.
BLACKFRIARS
St. John St.
Cowcross St.
FARRINGDON
Smithfield Market
Snow Hill
Holborn Viaduct
Fleet La.
St. Bride St.
Fleet St.
GOUGH SQ.
Tudor St.
Temple Ave.
1/4 mile
1/4 km
Clerkenwell Rd.
Hatton Garden
Greville St.
Ely Pl.
Farringdon Rd.
Shoe Lane
New Fetter La.
Fetter La.
Temple Church
Middle Temple La.
The Temple
Victoria Embankment
N

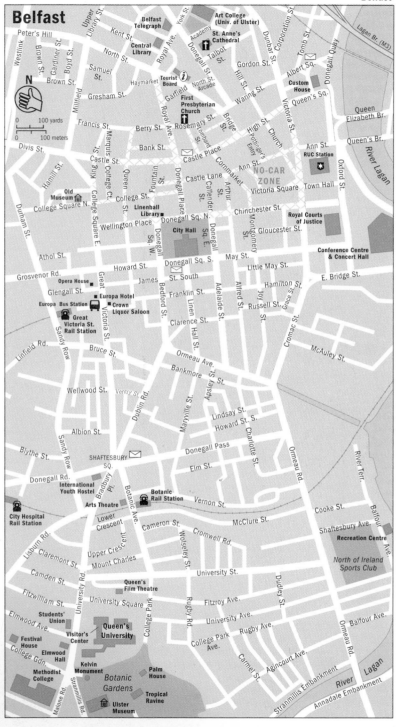

Belfast

Belfast

Peter's Hill

Westlink

Brown St.

Gardiner St.

Boyd St.

Upper Library St.

Kent St.

North St.

Samuel St.

Brown St.

Haymarket

Gresham St.

Millfield

Francis St.

Divis St.

Hamill St.

Durham St.

Marquis St.

King St.

Castle St.

College Sq. E.

College Square N.

College St.

Queen St.

Fountain St.

Wellington Place

Athol St.

Grosvenor Rd.

Howard St.

Opera House

Glengall St.

Great Victoria St.

Europa Bus Station

Europa Hotel

Crown Liquor Saloon

Great Victoria St. Rail Station

Sandy Row

Linfield Rd.

Bruce St.

Wellwood St.

Albion St.

Blythe St.

Donegall Rd.

Donegall Rd.

City Hospital Rail Station

Lisburn Rd.

Claremont St.

Camden St.

Fitzwilliam St.

Elmwood Ave.

College Gdn.

Festival House

Elmwood Hall

Methodist College

Malone Rd.

Stranmillis Rd.

University Rd.

Sandy Row

Ventry St.

Dublin Rd.

Bradbury Pl.

SHAFTESBURY SQ.

International Youth Hostel

Arts Theatre

Lower Crescent

Upper Cresc.

Mount Charles

University Square

Students' Union

Visitor's Center

Queen's University

Kelvin Monument

Botanic Gardens

Queen's Film Theatre

College Park

Botanic Ave.

Botanic Rail Station

Cameron St.

University St.

Fitzroy Ave.

Wolseley St.

Rugby Rd.

Cromwell Rd.

Vernon St.

McClure St.

Cooke St.

Shaftesbury Ave.

Recreation Centre

North of Ireland Sports Club

University Ave.

Rugby Ave.

Dudley St.

College Park Ave.

Carmel St.

Agincourt Ave.

Balfour Ave.

Ormeau Rd.

Balfour Ave.

Stranmillis Embankment

River Lagan

Annadale Embankment

Palm House

Tropical Ravine

Ulster Museum

Belfast Telegraph

Central Library

Royal Ave.

York St.

Academy St.

Donegall St.

Art College (Univ. of Ulster)

St. Anne's Cathedral

Talbot St.

Gordon St.

Dunbar St.

Corporation St.

Tomb St.

Albert Sq.

Custom House

Queen's Sq.

Donegall Quay

Lagan Br. (M3)

Tourist Board

Garfield

North Arcade

First Presbyterian Church

Royal Ave.

Berry St.

Rosemary St.

Lombard St.

Bridge St.

Hill St.

Waring St.

Victoria St.

Queen Elizabeth Br.

Queen's Br.

River Lagan

Bank St.

Castle Place

Castle Lane

Castle St.

Donegall Place

Callender St.

Cornmarket

Arthur St.

Ann St.

High St.

Church St.

Pottinger's Entry

NO-CAR ZONE

Victoria Square

Town Hall

Ann St.

RUC Station

Oxford St.

Linenhall Library

Donegall Sq. N.

City Hall

Donegall Sq. W.

Donegall Sq. E.

Chinchester St.

Gloucester St.

Royal Courts of Justice

Conference Centre & Concert Hall

Old Museum

College Square N.

May St.

Little May St.

Donegall Sq. S.

St. South

James St.

Bedford St.

Franklin St.

Linen Hall St.

Clarence St.

Adelaide St.

Alfred St.

Joy St.

Russell St.

Hamilton St.

Grace St.

Cromac St.

McAuley St.

E. Bridge St.

Montgomery St.

Howard St. S.

Ormeau Ave.

Bankmore St.

Maryville St.

Apsley St.

Lindsay St.

Howard St. S.

Charlotte St.

Donegall Pass

Elm St.

Ormeau Rd.

River Terr.

River Lagan

Victoria St.

0   100 yards

0   100 meters

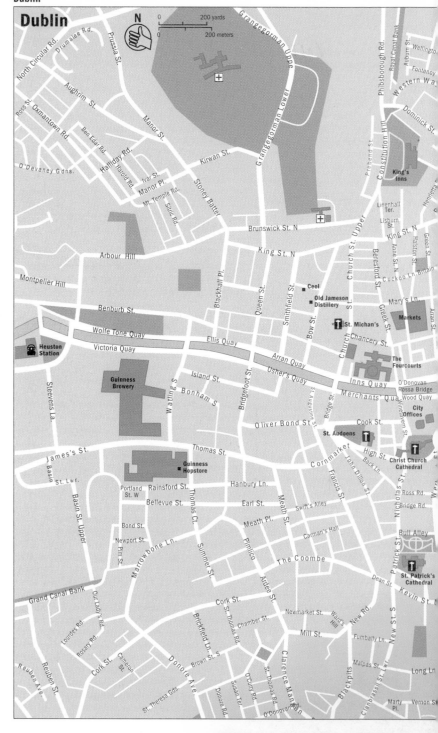

Dublin

N

0   200 yards
0   200 meters

North Circular Rd.
Prussia St.
Drumalee Rd.
Grangegorman Upper
Grangegorman Lower
Phibsborough Rd.
Royal Canal Bank
Auburn St.
Wellingto.
Fontenoy
Western Wa.
Ross St.
Aughrim St.
Oxmantown Rd.
Ben Edar Rd.
Manor St.
Kirwan St.
Constitution Hill
Dominick St.
Halliday Rd.
Harold Rd.
O'Devaney Gdns.
Ivar St.
Manor Pl.
Mt. Temple Rd.
Sluic Rd.
Stoney Batter
Prebend St.
King's Inns
Linenhall Ter.
Lisbum St.
Brunswick St. N
Church St. Upper
King St. N
King St. N
Halston St.
Green St.
Arbour Hill
Blackhall Pl.
Queen St.
Smithfield St.
Beresford St.
Cuckoo Ln.
Britain
Mary's Ln.
Montpelier Hill
Benburb St.
Ceol
Old Jameson Distillery
Bow St.
Church St.
Markets
Arran St. N
Heuston Station
Wolfe Tone Quay
Victoria Quay
Ellis Quay
Arran Quay
St. Michan's
Chancery St.
Greek St.
The Fourcourts
Guinness Brewery
Watling St.
Island St.
Bonham S
Bridgefoot St.
Usher's Quay
St. Augustine St.
Bridge St.
Winetavern St.
Inns Quay
Merchants' Quay
O'Donovan Rossa Bridge
Wood Quay
City Offices
Stevens La.
Oliver Bond St.
Cook St.
St. Audoens
High St.
Back Ln.
Christ Church Cathedral
James's St.
Basin St. Lwr.
Thomas St.
Cornmarket
John Dillon St.
Francis St.
Guinness Hopstore
Portland St. W
Rainsford St.
Hanbury Ln.
Nicholas St.
Ross Rd.
Bridge Rd.
Bellevue St.
Thomas Ct.
Earl St.
Meath St.
Swift's Alley
Bull Alley
Bond St.
Meath Pl.
Carman's Hall
Newport St.
Pim St.
Marrowbone Ln.
Summer St.
Pimlico
The Coombe
Patrick St.
St. Patrick's Cathedral
Dean St.
Kevin St.
Grand Canal Bank
Our Lady's Rd.
Lourdes Rd.
Rosary Rd.
Cork St.
Ardee St.
Cork St.
St. Thomas Rd.
Chamber St.
Newmarket St.
Ward's Hill
New Rd.
New St. S
Basin St. Upper
Cameron St.
Brickfield Ln.
Brown St. S
Mill St.
Fumbally Ln.
Malpas St. Lwr.
Long Ln.
Reuben Ave.
Reuben St.
Donore Ave.
St. Theresa Gds.
Donore Rd.
Susan Ter.
O'Curry Rd.
St. Thomas Rd.
Clarence Mangan
O'Donovan Rd.
Clanbrassil St. Lwr.
Blackpitts
Marty Pl.
Vernon St.

Cork and Galway

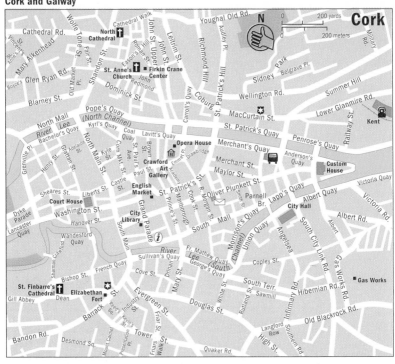

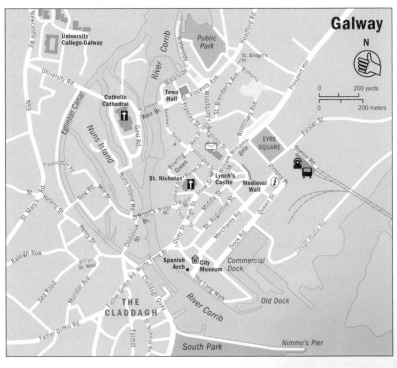

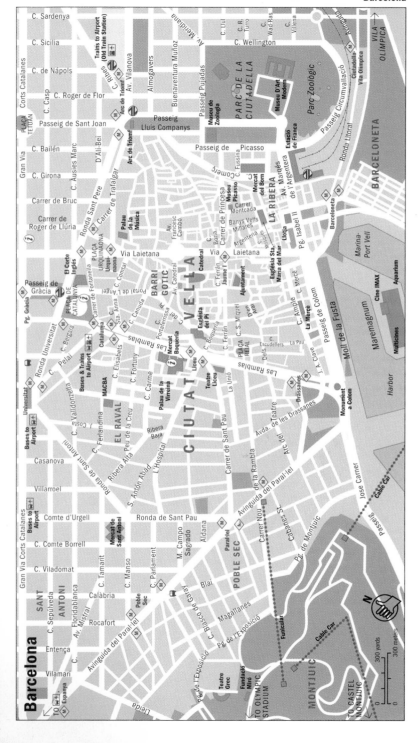

Madrid Metro

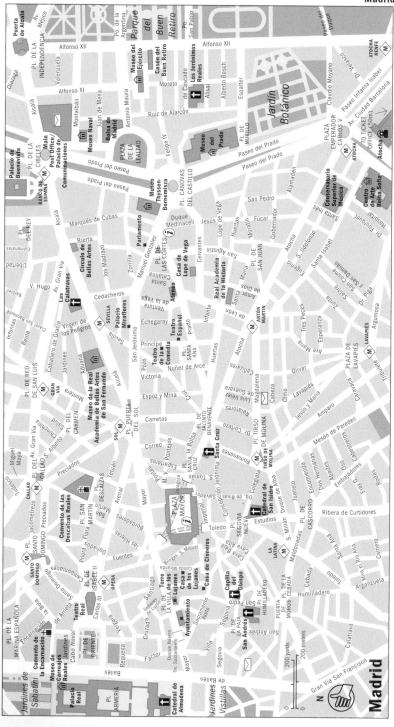

Madrid

Barcelona Metro

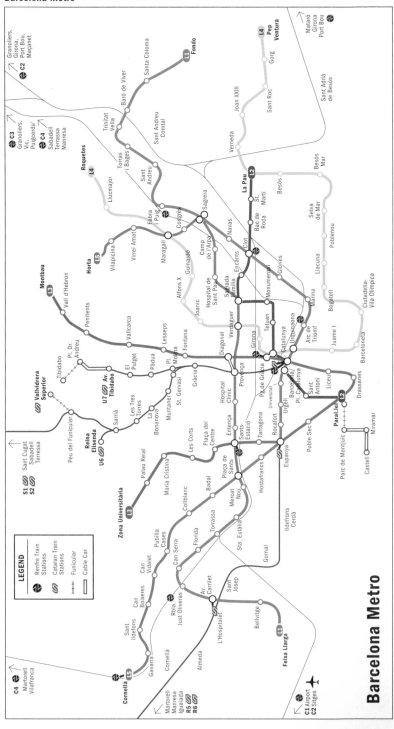

Barcelona Metro

Paris: Métro

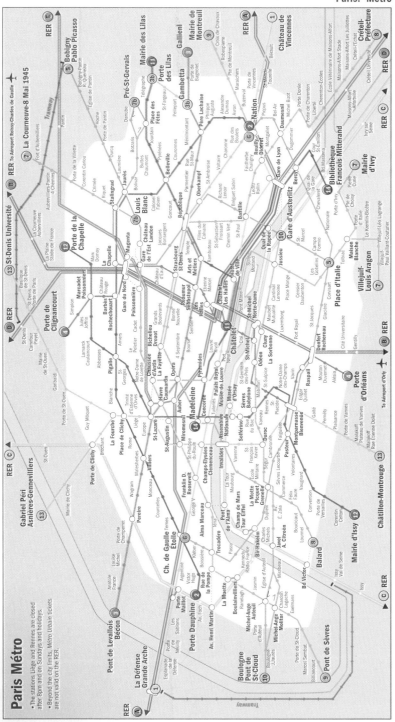

Paris: Overview and Arrondissements

1 Cimetière de Montmartre
2 Sacré Coeur Basilica
3 Parc La Villette
4 Parc des Buttes Chaumont
5 Jardins du Trocadero
6 Palais Chaillot
7 Cimetière de Passy
8 American Embassy
9 British Embassy
10 Petit Palais
11 Grand Palais
12 Arc de Triomphe
13 Madeleine
14 Gare St-Lazare
15 Parc Monceau
16 Palais de la Découverte
17 Opéra Garnier
18 Galeries Lafayette
19 Printemps
20 Gare du Nord
21 Gare de l'Est
22 Opéra Bastille
23 Palais Omnisports de Bercy
24 Ministère des Finances
25 Gare de Lyon
26 Parc de Montsouris
27 Cité Universitaire
28 Cimetière Montparnasse
29 Gare Montparnasse

30 Bureau des Objets Trouvés
   (Lost and Found)
31 Louvre
32 Palais Royale
33 Forum des Halles
34 Musée de l'Orangerie
35 Central Post Office
36 Bourse
37 Bibliothèque Nationale
38 Ecole des Arts et Métiers
39 Archives Nationales
40 Musée Carnavalet
41 Musée Picasso
42 Centre George Pompidou
43 place des Vosges
44 Musée Victor Hugo
45 Notre Dame
46 Mémorial de la Déportation
47 Université de Paris (Sorbonne)

48 Ecole Normal Supérieure
49 Musée de Cluny
50 Museum Nationale d'Histoire
   Naturelle
51 Panthéon
52 Eglise St-Etienne du Mont
53 La Mosquée
54 Jardin des Plantes
55 Jardins du Luxembourg
56 Eglise St-Sulpice
57 Théâtre Nationale de l'Odéon
58 Eiffel Tower
59 Champs de Mars

60 Ecole Militaire
61 UNESCO
62 Hôtel des Invalides
63 Assemblée Nationale
64 Musée d'Orsay
65 Cimetière de l'Est du Pere Lachaise

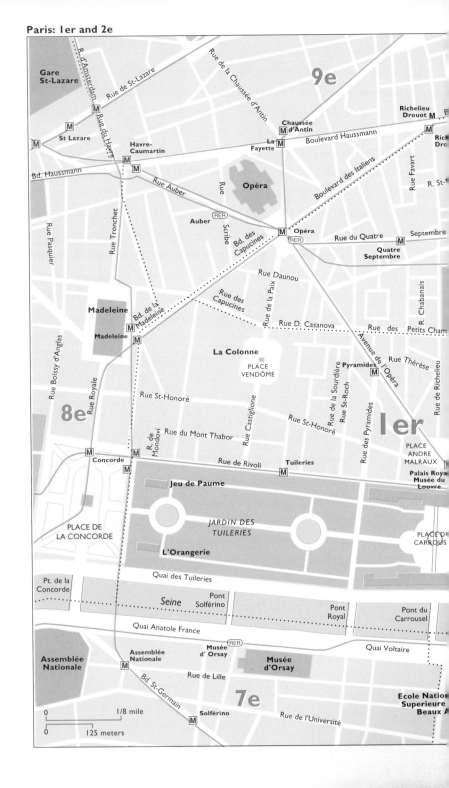

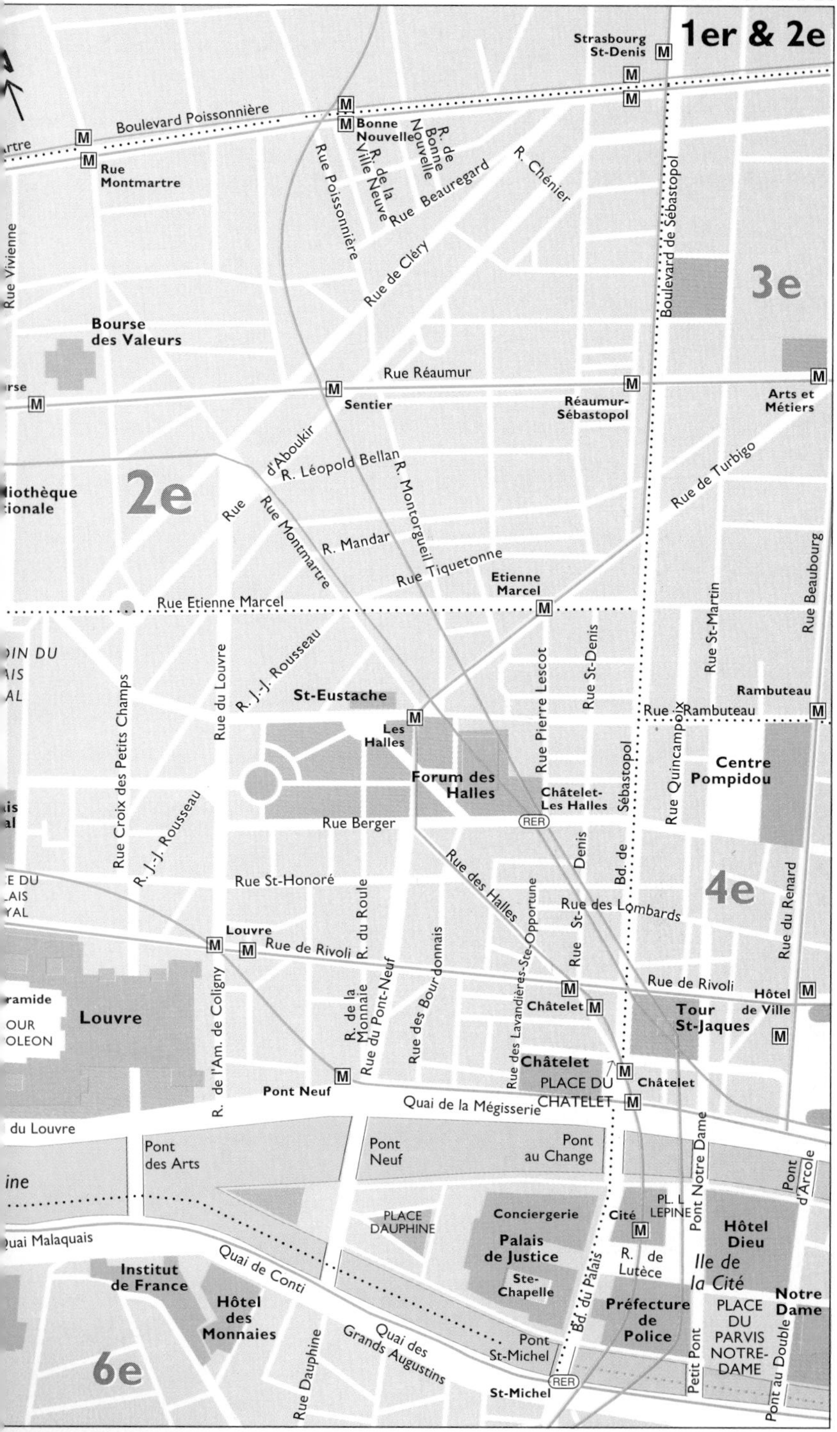

Strasbourg
St-Denis Ⓜ

Ⓜ
Ⓜ

Boulevard Poissonnière

Ⓜ Bonne
Ⓜ Nouvelle

Ⓜ
Rue
Montmartre

R. de
Bonne
Nouvelle

Rue de la
Ville Neuve

Rue Poissonnière

Rue Beauregard

R Chénier

Boulevard de Sébastopol

3e

Rue de Cléry

Rue Vivienne

**Bourse
des Valeurs**

Ⓜ rse

Rue Réaumur

Ⓜ

Ⓜ

Ⓜ Arts et
Métiers

Ⓜ Sentier

Réaumur-
Sébastopol

d'Aboukir

R. Léopold Bellan

R. Montorgueil

Rue de Turbigo

iothèque
ionale

2e

Rue

Rue Montmartre

R. Mandar

Rue Tiquetonne

Etienne
Marcel

Rue St-Martin

Rue Beaubourg

Rue Etienne Marcel

Ⓜ

Etienne
Marcel

IN DU
IS
AL

R. J.-J. Rousseau

Rue du Louvre

St-Eustache

Rue Pierre Lescot

Rue St-Denis

Rue Quincampoix

Rambuteau

ais
L

Rue Croix des Petits Champs

Ⓜ
Les
Halles

**Forum des
Halles**

Sébastopol

Rue Rambuteau

Ⓜ

**Centre
Pompidou**

is
L

R. J.-J. Rousseau

Rue Berger

Châtelet-
Les Halles

RER

Bd. de

4e

E DU
AIS
AL

Rue St-Honoré

Rue des Halles

Denis

Rue des Lombards

Rue St-

Rue du Renard

ramide

OUR
OLEON

Louvre

Rue St-Honoré

R. du Roule

R. de la
Monnaie

Rue du Pont-Neuf

Rue des Bourdonnais

Louvre
Ⓜ Rue de Rivoli

Rue des Lavandières-Ste-Opportune

Rue de Rivoli

Hôtel
de Ville Ⓜ

Ⓜ Châtelet

**Tour
St-Jaques**

Ⓜ

du Louvre

R. de l'Am. de Coligny

Pont Neuf

Ⓜ Châtelet Ⓜ

Châtelet
PLACE DU
CHATELET

Châtelet Ⓜ

Quai de la Mégisserie

Pont
des Arts

ine

Qai Malaquais

Pont
Neuf

Pont
au Change

Bd. du Palais

R. de
Lutèce

Pont Notre Dame

Pont
d'Arcole

**Institut
de France**

Quai de Conti

**Hôtel
des
Monnaies**

PLACE
DAUPHINE

Conciergerie

**Palais
de Justice**

Ste-
Chapelle

Cité Ⓜ

PL. L
LEPINE

**Hôtel
Dieu**

*Ile de
la Cité*

**Notre
Dame**

Quai des
Grands Augustins

Rue Dauphine

Pont
St-Michel

**Préfecture
de
Police**

PLACE
DU
PARVIS
NOTRE-
DAME

Pont au Double

Petit Pont

6e

St-Michel RER

Palais du Louvre

Pont Neuf

Châtelet

Quai du Louvre

1er

Pont du Carrousel

Pont des Arts

Pont Neuf

Pont au Change

Conciergerie

Cité

Ste-Chapelle

Hôte Dieu

Quai Malaquais

Quai de Conti

Pont St-Michel

Île de la Cité

Rue de la Cité

Ecole Nationale Supérieure des Beaux Arts

Institut de France

Hôtel des Monnaies

Quai des Grands Augustins

Pont St-Michel

R. Bonaparte

Rue Jacob

Rue de Seine

Rue Mazarine

Rue Dauphine

St-Michel

Rue St-Jacques

Rue des Sts-Pères

Pl. St-Michel

St-Michel

R. de l'Abbaye

PLACE ST-GERMAIN-DES-PRÉS

St-Germain Des Prés

Rue St-André des Arts

Rue Danton

Bd. St-Germain

Bd. St-Germain

St-Germain des Prés

Mabillon

Odéon

Musée du Cluny

7e

R. du Four

Rue de l'Odéon

Boulevard

Sorbonne

R. de Sèvres

R. du Vieux Colombier

R. du Saint Sulpice

Rue de Tournon

Rue Racine

PLACE DE L'ODÉON

PLACE DE LA SORBONNE

R. du Cherche Midi

PLACE ST-SULPICE

St-Sulpice

St-Michel

Rue Soufflot

R. d'Assas

R. de Rennes

St-Sulpice

Palais du Luxembourg

Bd. Raspail

Rue de Vaugirard

6e

Luxembourg

Rennes

Rue Gay-Lussac

St Placide

JARDIN DU LUXEMBOURG

Rue du Montparnasse

Notre-Dame des Champs

Rue d'Assas

Boulevard St-Michel

Rue St-Jacques

Rue Vavin

Rue Notre-Dame des Champs

Montparnasse Bienvenüe

Avenue de

Vavin

Boulevard du Montparnasse

Port Royal

R. du Départ

Boulevard Raspail

la Observatoire

14e

Edgar Quinet

Boulevard Edgar Quinet

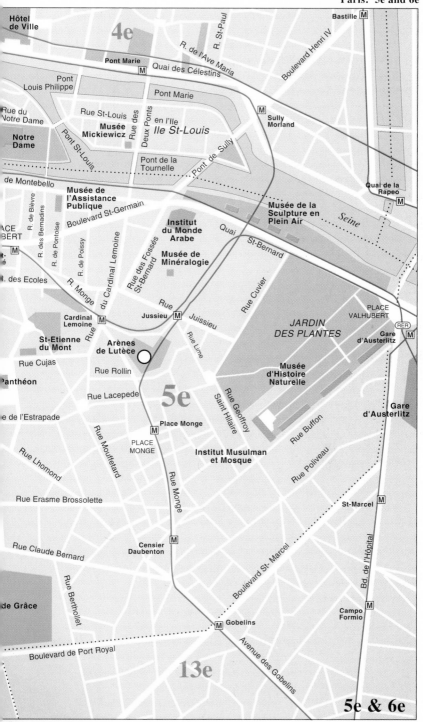

Hôtel de Ville

4e

Bastille

Pont Marie

Quai des Célestins

R. de l'Ave Maria

R. St-Paul

Boulevard Henri IV

Pont Louis Philippe

Pont Marie

Rue du Notre Dame

Rue St-Louis

Rue des Deux Ponts

en l'Ile Ile St-Louis

Sully Morland

Musée Mickiewicz

Notre Dame

Pont St-Louis

Pont de la Tournelle

Pont de Sully

de Montebello

Quai de la Rapeo

Musée de l'Assistance Publique

R. de Bièvre

R. des Bernadins

R. de Pontloise

Boulevard St-Germain

Musée de la Sculpture en Plein Air

Seine

ACE BERT

R. de Poissy

Rue du Cardinal Lemoine

Institut du Monde Arabe

Quai

St-Bernard

R. des Ecoles

R. Monge

Rue des Fossés St-Bernard

Musée de Minéralogie

Rue

Rue Cuvier

PLACE VALHUBERT

Cardinal Lemoine

Jussieu

Juissieu

Rue Lime

JARDIN DES PLANTES

Gare d'Austerlitz

RER

St-Etienne du Mont

Arènes de Lutèce

Rue Cujas

Rue Rollin

5e

Musée d'Histoire Naturelle

Gare d'Austerlitz

Panthéon

Rue Lacepede

Rue Mouffetard

Rue Saint Hilaire

Rue Geoffroy

e de l'Estrapade

Place Monge

PLACE MONGE

Institut Musulman et Mosque

Rue Buffon

Rue Lhomond

Rue Erasme Brossolette

Rue Monge

Rue Poliveau

St-Marcel

Rue Claude Bernard

Censier Daubenton

Bd. de l'Hôpital

de Grâce

Rue Berthollet

Boulevard St- Marcel

Campo Formio

Gobelins

Boulevard de Port Royal

13e

Avenue des Gobelins

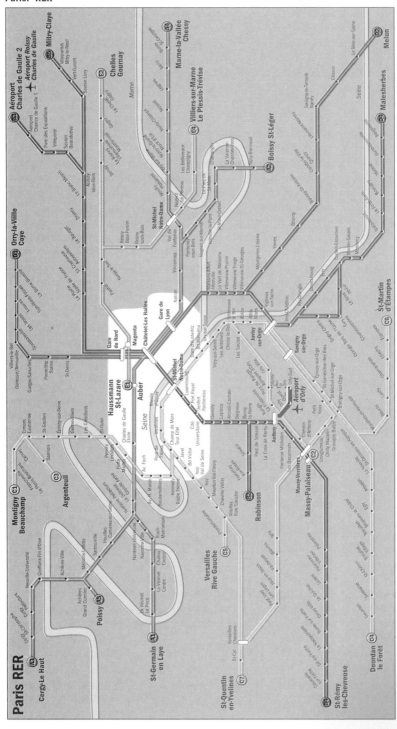

Paris: RER

◤ Let's Go writers travel on your budget.

"Guides that penetrate the veneer of the holiday brochures and mine the grit of real life."

—*The Economist*

"The writers seem to have experienced every rooster-packed bus and lunar-surfaced mattress about which they write."

—*The New York Times*

"All the dirt, dirt cheap."

—*People*

◤ Great for independent travelers.

"The guides are aimed not only at young budget travelers but at the independent traveler; a sort of streetwise cookbook for traveling alone."

—*The New York Times*

"Flush with candor and irreverence, chock full of budget travel advice."

—*The Des Moines Register*

"An indispensible resource, *Let's Go*'s practical information can be used by every traveler."

—*The Chattanooga Free Press*

◤ Let's Go is completely revised each year.

"Only *Let's Go* has the zeal to annually update every title on its list."

—*The Boston Globe*

"Unbeatable: good sightseeing advice; up-to-date info on restaurants, hotels, and inns; a commitment to money-saving travel; and a wry style that brightens nearly every page."

—*The Washington Post*

◤ All the important information you need.

"*Let's Go* authors provide a comedic element while still providing concise information and thorough coverage of the country. Anything you need to know about budget traveling is detailed in this book."

—*The Chicago Sun-Times*

"Value-packed, unbeatable, accurate, and comprehensive."

—*Los Angeles Times*

Let's Go Publications

Let's Go: Alaska & the Pacific Northwest 2000
Let's Go: Australia 2000
Let's Go: Austria & Switzerland 2000
Let's Go: Britain & Ireland 2000
Let's Go: California 2000
Let's Go: Central America 2000
Let's Go: China 2000 **New Title!**
Let's Go: Eastern Europe 2000
Let's Go: Europe 2000
Let's Go: France 2000
Let's Go: Germany 2000
Let's Go: Greece 2000
Let's Go: India & Nepal 2000
Let's Go: Ireland 2000
Let's Go: Israel 2000 **New Title!**
Let's Go: Italy 2000
Let's Go: Mexico 2000
Let's Go: Middle East 2000 **New Title!**
Let's Go: New York City 2000
Let's Go: New Zealand 2000
Let's Go: Paris 2000
Let's Go: Perú & Ecuador 2000 **New Title!**
Let's Go: Rome 2000
Let's Go: South Africa 2000
Let's Go: Southeast Asia 2000
Let's Go: Spain & Portugal 2000
Let's Go: Turkey 2000
Let's Go: USA 2000
Let's Go: Washington, D.C. 2000

Let's Go *Map Guides*

Amsterdam	New Orleans
Berlin	New York City
Boston	Paris
Chicago	Prague
Florence	Rome
London	San Francisco
Los Angeles	Seattle
Madrid	Washington, D.C.

Coming Soon: *Sydney* and *Hong Kong*

Let's Go

2000

EUROPE

Kate McCarthy
Editor

Jessica Harder
Associate Editor

Sarah Jacoby
Associate Editor

Researcher-Writers:
Ben Florman
Brina Milikowsky
Marly Ohlsson
Sarah Schauss

St. Martin's Press ✄ New York

HELPING LET'S GO

HELPING LET'S GO If you want to share your discoveries, suggestions, or corrections, please drop us a line. We read every piece of correspondence, whether a postcard, a 10-page email, or a coconut. Please note that mail received after May 2000 may be too late for the 2001 book, but will be kept for future editions. **Address mail to:**

> **Let's Go: Europe**
> **67 Mount Auburn Street**
> **Cambridge, MA 02138**
> **USA**

Visit Let's Go at **http://www.letsgo.com,** or send email to:

> **feedback@letsgo.com**
> **Subject: "Let's Go: Europe"**

In addition to the invaluable travel advice our readers share with us, many are kind enough to offer their services as researchers or editors. Unfortunately, our charter enables us to employ only currently enrolled Harvard students.

Maps by David Lindroth copyright © 2000, 1999, 1998, 1997, 1996, 1995, 1994, 1993, 1992, 1991, 1990, 1989, 1988 by St. Martin's Press.

Distributed outside the USA and Canada by Macmillan.

Let's Go: Europe Copyright © 2000 by Let's Go, Inc. All rights reserved. Printed in the United States of America. No part of this book may be used or reproduced in any manner whatsoever without written permission except in the case of brief quotations embodied in critical articles or reviews. Let's Go is available for purchase in bulk by institutions and authorized resellers. For information, address St. Martin's Press, 175 Fifth Avenue, New York, NY 10010, USA.

ISBN: 0-312-24466-5

First edition
10 9 8 7 6 5 4 3 2 1

Let's Go: Europe is written by Let's Go Publications, 67 Mount Auburn Street, Cambridge, MA 02138, USA.

Let's Go® and the thumb logo are trademarks of Let's Go, Inc.
Printed in the USA on recycled paper with biodegradable soy ink.

ADVERTISING DISCLAIMER

ADVERTISING DISCLAIMER All advertisements appearing in Let's Go publications are sold by an independent agency not affiliated with the editorial production of the guides. Advertisers are never given preferential treatment, and the guides are researched, written, and published independent of advertising. Advertisements do not imply endorsement of products or services by Let's Go, and Let's Go does not vouch for the accuracy of information provided in advertisements.

If you are interested in purchasing advertising space in a Let's Go publication, contact: Let's Go Advertising Sales, 67 Mount Auburn St., Cambridge, MA 02138, USA.

ABOUT LET'S GO

FORTY YEARS OF WISDOM

As a new millennium arrives, *Let's Go: Europe*, now in its 40th edition and translated into seven languages, reigns as the world's bestselling international travel guide. For four decades, travelers criss-crossing the Continent have relied on *Let's Go* for inside information on the hippest backstreet cafes, the most pristine secluded beaches, and the best routes from border to border. In the last 20 years, our rugged researchers have stretched the frontiers of backpacking and expanded our coverage into Asia, Africa, Australia, and the Americas. We're celebrating our 40th birthday with the release of *Let's Go: China*, blazing the traveler's trail from the Forbidden City to the Tibetan frontier; *Let's Go: Perú & Ecuador*, spanning the lands of the ancient Inca Empire; *Let's Go: Middle East*, with coverage from Istanbul to the Persian Gulf; and the maiden edition of *Let's Go: Israel*.

It all started in 1960 when a handful of well-traveled students at Harvard University handed out a 20-page mimeographed pamphlet offering a collection of their tips on budget travel to passengers on student charter flights to Europe. The following year, in response to the instant popularity of the first volume, students traveling to Europe researched the first full-fledged edition of *Let's Go: Europe*, a pocket-sized book featuring honest, practical advice, witty writing, and a decidedly youthful slant on the world. Throughout the 60s and 70s, our guides reflected the times. In 1969 we taught travelers how to get from Paris to Prague on "no dollars a day" by singing in the street. In the 80s and 90s, we looked beyond Europe and North America and set off to all corners of the earth. Meanwhile, we focused in on the world's most exciting urban areas to produce in-depth, fold-out map guides. Our new guides bring the total number of titles to 48, each infused with the spirit of adventure and voice of opinion that travelers around the world have come to count on. But some things never change: our guides are still researched, written, and produced entirely by students who know first-hand how to see the world on the cheap.

HOW WE DO IT

Each guide is completely revised and thoroughly updated every year by a well-traveled set of over 250 students. Every spring, we recruit over 180 researchers and 70 editors to overhaul every book. After several months of training, researcher-writers hit the road for seven weeks of exploration, from Anchorage to Adelaide, Estonia to El Salvador, Iceland to Indonesia. Hired for their rare combination of budget travel sense, writing ability, stamina, and courage, these adventurous travelers know that train strikes, stolen luggage, food poisoning, and marriage proposals are all part of a day's work. Back at our offices, editors work from spring to fall, massaging copy written on Himalayan bus rides into witty, informative prose. A student staff of typesetters, cartographers, publicists, and managers keeps our lively team together. In September, the collected efforts of the summer are delivered to our printer, which turns them into books in record time, so that you have the most up-to-date information available for your vacation. Even as you read this, work on next year's editions is well underway.

WHY WE DO IT

We don't think of budget travel as the last recourse of the destitute; we believe that it's the only way to travel. Living cheaply and simply brings you closer to the people and places you've been saving up to visit. Our books will ease your anxieties and answer your questions about the basics—so you can get off the beaten track and explore. Once you learn the ropes, we encourage you to put *Let's Go* down now and then to strike out on your own. You know as well as we that the best discoveries are often those you make yourself. When you find something worth sharing, please drop us a line. We're Let's Go Publications, 67 Mount Auburn St., Cambridge, MA 02138, USA (email: feedback@letsgo.com). For more info, visit our website, http://www.letsgo.com.

GOOD VALUE HOTELS IN CENTRAL LONDON

WESTPOINT HOTEL

170-172, SUSSEX GARDENS, HYDE PARK, LONDON. W2 1TP.
Tel.: 0171 402 0281 (RESERVATIONS) FAX: 0171 224 9114
e. mail: info@westpointhotel.com   Web site: www.westpointhotel.com

Popular Central London Hotel - All rooms with private showers and toilets -Elevator to All Floors.
Within Three minutes walk of Heathrow Express Rail Terminal
Two minutes walk to Lancaster Gate and Paddington
Underground and Mainline Stations
with easy access to all famous tourist attractions, shops and theatres.
CAR PARKING by arrangement - EASY access to M1, M4 & M40. Direct Bus A2 to Heathrow.

Low Season: Singles from £28 Doubles from £27. p.p. Family Rooms from £20. p.p.
High Season: Singles from £36. Doubles from £31. p.p. Family Rooms from £22. p.p.
Agency vouchers not accepted.

SASS HOUSE HOTEL

11 CRAVEN TERRACE, HYDE PARK, LONDON . W2 3QT.
Telephone: 0171 262 2325 (Reservations)   FAX: 0171 262 0889
e. mail: info@sasshotel.com   Web site: www.sasshotel.com

Budget-priced Central London, most rooms with private showers/toilets.
Easy access to all tourist attractions - walking distance form Lancaster Gate and Paddington
tube and mainline stations - Five minutes walk from Heathrow Express Rail Terminal
Low Season: Twin £23. p.p. Doubles from £22. p.p. Family rooms from £18.p.p.
High Season: Twin £26.p.p. Doubles from £25. p.p. Family Rooms from £22. p.p.
Car Parking by arrangement - Agency vouchers not accepted.

ABBEY COURT HOTEL

174 SUSSEX GARDENS, HYDE PARK, LONDON. W2 1TP.
Telephone: 0171 402 0704. Fax: 0171 262 2055
e. mail: info@abbeycourt.com   Web site: www.abbey.com

This Hotel has long been popular because of its central location
near to Hyde Park and two minutes form Paddington and Lancaster Gate
tube and main line stations. The tourist attractions of the West End,
theatres, museums and Oxford Street, are within easy reach.
Within Three minutes walk of Heathrow Express Rail Terminal
All rooms with private shower/toilets. Lift to all floors.
Car Parking by Arrangement. Direct Bus A2 to Heathrow.

Low Season: Singles from £30. Doubles from £27. p.p. Family Rooms from £20. p.p.
High Season: Singles from £38. Doubles from £31. p.p. Family rooms from £22. p.p.
Agency vouchers not accepted.

CONTENTS

MAPS

COLOR INSERTS

RESEARCHER-WRITERS

Ben Florman   *Iceland, Norway*
We immediately snapped up Ben, an old pro at the Let's Go game—this editor of
Let's Go: Alaska and the Pacific Northwest 1999 was ready for some real
northern exposure. And Ben never disappointed, as he attacked Iceland and then
Norway, filming the geysers, fjords, and armies of schoolchildren with one hand
and furiously typing up reams of flawless prose with the other. He proved his met-
tle during a brief infestation, and then met some nice folks to help him discover
the softer side of Scandinavia. Best of luck to Ben in his future adventures.

Brina Milikowsky   *Belgium, Luxembourg, Netherlands*
This editor of *Let's Go: Ireland 1999* couldn't get enough of Let's Go, and we
couldn't get enough of her. Although her arrival in the big bad world of Benelux
unfortunately coincided with a recall on Belgium-based Coca-Cola, Brina overcame the odds and continued on without her fix, getting the skinny on happening
The Hague, reporting on every inch and castle of Luxembourg, and sampling every
good there was in Amsterdam (researching for Let's Go, it's a hard life). Too bad
the Polish border police confiscated the camera—we know that Brina is a star.

Marly Ohlsson   *Sweden, Denmark*
Given her love of the outdoors and her genetic background, our own Swedish lass
seemed fated to research for us. Marly answered the call to duty like most travelers answer the call to McDonald's, transferring her dedication learned in the boathouse to her research. She inspected every "botel," deconstructed Legoland and
bogmen, and endured both an unruly bike and a stint stranded in the middle of
nowhere. Then, in her last 250m, long after most researchers lose their spunk, she
made us coo with completely reworked Copenhagen coverage.

Sarah Schauss   *Finland, Narva, Karelia*
Sarah's competition for this job was enthusiastic enough to flash us with a Finnish
flag painted on a ne'er-exposed body part. But how could we resist Sarah, with her
obsession with Scandinavia, her fluency in Finnish, and her ache to return to her
spiritual home? After exposing Finland's countless saunas and fixation on the
Moomins, she attacked the Arctic Circle, sat on Santa's lap, and still found time to
unearth the world's northernmost McDonald's. Still hungry for more, she hopped
on a mail truck and finished up researching for *Let's Go: Eastern Europe 2000*.

Michelle Aitken	*Małopolska, Slovakia*
Silas Alben	*Paris*
John Bachman	*Central Anatolia, Western Black Sea Coast, Bursa*
Judith Batalion	*Paris*
Timothy Bazzle	*England*
Sera Beak	*Western Mediterranean Coast, Konya*
David Beecher	*Estonia, Lativa, Lithuania*
Susan Biancani	*Counties Antrim, Derry, Donegal, Down, Louth*
Michelle Bowman	*Bulgaria, Moldova*
Emily Brott	*Bonn, Frankenland, Cologne, Hesse, Rhineland-Palatinate, Saxon Switzerland, Thuringia*
Whitney Bryant	*Paris*
Rick Burnes	*Belarus, Western Ukraine, Trans-Siberian*
Tova Carlin	*Brittany and western Normandy*
Penelope A. Carter	*Tuscany, Umbria*
Michelle Caswell	*Istanbul, Marmara Coast*
Craig Chosiad	*Romania*
Joshua Derman	*Vorarlberg, Tyrol, Carinthia, Styria*
Alicia DeSantis	*Hungary, Bosnia*
Katharine Douglas	*Madrid, Extremadura, the Canary Islands*
David Egan	*Cappadocia, Northern Cyprus, Eastern Mediterranean*
Nenita Ponce de León Elphick	*Provence, Lyon and the Auvergne, and Burgundy*
Holly E. Fling	*Northeastern Spain, Castilla La Mancha, and Eastern Andalucía*
Benjamin Forkner	*Northwestern Spain, Castilla y León, Northern Portugal and Granada*

Adriane Giebel	Ionian Islands, Sterea Ellada, Peloponnese
Jennifer Gootman	Emilia-Romagna
Claudia Grégoire	Allgäu, Baden-Württemberg, Frankfurt, Saarland
Brady Gunderson	Côte d'Azur, Corsica, and the Alps
Rebecca Hardiman	Bavaria
Anna Harr	Cyprus and Dodecanese
Steve Hely	Counties Cork, Kerry, Limerick, Tipperary, Waterford
Elizabeth M. Holt	Tunisia, Malta, Veneto
Lucy Ives	Berlin, Bavaria, Brandenburg, Lower Saxony, Schleswig-Holstein
Jeremy Kurzyniec	Thrace, Aegean Coast, Adana, Antakya
Brooke M. Lampley	Northern Andalucía
Claire Lewis	London, Costa del Sol (Spain)
Ollie Lewis	Counties Carlow, Dublin, Kildare, Kilkenny, Meath, Waterford, Wexford, Wicklow
Nicole López	Périgord, Languedoc-Roussillon, Aquitaine, Basque Country, and Gascony
Rochelle Kristen Mackey	Barcelona, the Balearic Islands, and the Eastern Coast
Maryanthe Malliaris	Northeast Aegean, Sporades, Evia, and Saronic Gulf Islands
Andor Meszaros	Kaliningrad, Poland
Alexander Mindlin	Calabria, Sicily
Benjamin Morgan	Hamburg, Mecklenburg-Vorpommern, Lower Saxony, North Rhine-Westphalia
Lisa M. Nosal	Venice and Padua
Johs Pierce	England, Wales
R. Hunter Pierson, III	England, Scotland
James T. Platts	Portugal and Western Andalucía
Tim Plerhoples	Southern Andalucía
Nathaniel Popper	Zurich, Schaffhausen, St. Gallen, Appenzell, Liechtenstein, Graubünden, Bernese Oberland, Central Switzerland, Bavaria (Germany)
Adam Rzepka	Eastern Black Sea Coast, Erzurum, Istanbul
Christopher M. Sahm	Vienna, Burgenland, Lower Austria, Upper Austria, Salzburg
Dana Scardigli	Czech Republic, Southwestern Poland
Charley Scott	Apulia, Basilicata, Campania, Abruzzo, Molise
Michael Seid	Crete and Central Cyclades
Katie Sigelman	Thessaly, Epirus, Macedonia, and Thrace
Ashika Singh	Champagne, Alsace-Lorraine, Franche-Comté, the North, and eastern Normandy
Daisy Stanton	Berry-Limousin, Poitou-Charente, and the Loire Valley
Gabe Struck	Caucasus, Crimea, Odessa, Volga Region
Laela J. Sturdy	England, Scotland
Jessica Temple Tardy	Counties Armagh, Clare, Fermanagh, Galway, Mayo, Monaghan, Roscommon, Sligo
Rebecca Tinio	Geneva, Neuchâtel, Basel, Solothurn, Bern, Valais, Ticino
Elizabeth M. Topp	Scotland
Yvonne Tsang	London
Ivelina Tsekova	Verona
Bonnie Tsui	Athens and Cyclades
Andrea Volfová	Croatia, Slovenia
Marc A. Wallenstein	Lombardy, Piedmont, Liguria, Sardinia
Kate Wagner	Moscow, St. Petersburg
Lano Williams	London
Filip Wojciechowski	Berlin, Kassel, Lower Saxony, Saxony, Saxony-Anhalt, Spreewald

REGIONAL EDITORS

Julie K. Smith Allen, Sarah P. Rotman	Austria and Switzerland
Daryl Sng, Alice Farmer	Britain
Melissa L. Gibson, Angus Burgin, Rich Parr	Eastern Europe
Daryush Jonathan Dawid, Valerie de Charette de la Contrie, Benjamin Lytal	France
Max Hirsh, Kirstin E. Butler, Benjamin E. Lytal	Germany
Pete Pihos, Jody Peltason	Greece
Deirdre O'Dwyer, Lillian Lew-Hailer	Ireland
J. Marshall Henshaw, Adam Waka Green, Aarup Kubal	Italy
Laura Beth Deason	London
Olivia L. Cowley, Benjamin A. Railton, Aarup Kubal	Spain and Portugal
Anna M. Schneider-Mayerson	Paris
Christina Svendsen, Dan Visel	Rome
Meredith M. Quinn, Anup Kubal	Turkey

ACKNOWLEDGMENTS

EUROPA EUROPA THANKS: First, all the Europe R-Ws, the real ones to write this book. And everyone who saved us: Elena, of course, for absolutely everything; TJ, for a bajillion things; Nick and Tom, for learning languages; Christian, for copy-room conferences and for fixing it all; DJ Sap, stud-prodass, for resurrecting files and for CD burners; Matt and Melissa, for all the graphic niftiness; Ben P., for redefining "speedy get-away"; Melissa, Rich, and Angus, for being a rock band; ITA, SPAM, TUR, GRE, GER, IRE, B&I, FRA, and A&S, for tolerating our demands; the map boys, for patience and U2; and The Wrap, Campo, and Hostess for nutrition.

KATE THANKS: sarah and jess, for all the hours of sleep you both missed. elena, for being crazy enough to take us on. mir, liz, and maria, for countless dinners. jk, for nepal and trips to come. gwen, for the email madness. amiklavc, for the life advice. k2, for the papa. anne and alexa, for being my 5 and 6. megan, for still being out there, somewhere. diet coke, for existing. and, of course, mom and dad, for wisdom and understanding; matt, for icqs; and thomas, for snowboarding. i'll come home soon, i promise.

JESSICA THANKS: Kate, for your drive and dedication. Sarah, for making us all laugh. Elena, for rescuing us. Ben, for saving my sanity countless times this summer and for always being there whenever I've needed you. Jill, for putting up with the craziness when we couldn't drive home 'til two in the morning. Liv and Lau, for being crazy smart, talented, and fun. Mom and Dad, for your unfailing love and support. Zaidi, for the walks, the airplane rides, and the berries picked early in the morning—this is for you.

SARAH J. THANKS: First off, Kate and Jess, for making it happen. Thanks always to all my college-roommates-for-life, especially Nancy and Elena for making me smile, Dov and Andy in la-la-land, Pete for being sweet, Maria, Deirdre and James for holding my hand, Anna for frying eggs, Tom for refusing to stop being my friend. Thanks to Stefa, Sem, and Rachel for being both imaginary and real, Marshall, Mike, and Sam for omelettes and more, and most of all and more than I can say and no matter what, thanks to my beloved parents and little brother, Sam.

Editor
Kate McCarthy
Associate Editors
Jessica Harder, Sarah Jacoby
Managing Editors
Elena DeCoste, Benjamin Paloff

Publishing Director
Benjamin Wilkinson
Editor-in-Chief
Bentsion Harder
Production Manager
Christian Lorentzen
Cartography Manager
Daniel J. Luskin
Design Managers
Matthew Daniels, Melissa Rudolph
Editorial Managers
Brendan Gibbon, Benjamin Paloff, Kaya Stone, Taya Weiss
Financial Manager
Kathy Lu
Personnel Manager
Adam Stein
Publicity & Marketing Managers
Sonesh Chainani, Alexandra Leichtman
New Media Manager
Maryanthe Malliaris
Map Editors
Kurt Mueller, Jon Stein
Production Associates
Steven Aponte, John Fiore
Office Coordinators
Elena Schneider, Vanessa Bertozzi, Monica Henderson

Director of Advertising Sales
Marta Szabo
Associate Sales Executives
Tamas Eisenberger, Li Ran

President
Noble M. Hansen III
General Managers
Blair Brown, Robert B. Rombauer
Assistant General Manager
Anne E. Chisholm

Europe

Honnigsvåg

Rovaniemi

Umeå
Gulf of Bothnia
FINLAND

L. Onega

L. Ladoga

Helsinki
Tallinn
St. Petersburg

Volga R.

Stockholm
ESTONIA
Nizhny Novgorod

Rīga
LATVIA
Moscow

Baltic Sea
LITHUANIA

RUSSIA
Vilnius
RUSSIA

Gdańsk
Minsk

Warsaw
BELARUS
Volgograd

POLAND
KAZAKHSTAN

Kraków
Kiev
Kharkiv

Lviv
UKRAINE
Dnieper River

SLOVAKIA
Bratislava
Caspian Sea

Budapest
MOLDOVA
Sea of Azov

HUNGARY
Chişinău
Odessa
Rostov-na-Donu

ROMANIA
Yalta
GEORGIA

Belgrade
Bucharest
Black Sea
ARMENIA

Sarajevo
YUGOSLAVIA
AZERBAIJAN

MONTENEGRO
BULGARIA

Tiranë
FYR MACEDONIA
Sofia
Istanbul
Ankara
IRAN

Thessaloniki

ALBANIA
Aegean Sea
TURKEY

Ionian Sea
Izmir
SYRIA
IRAQ

Athens

GREECE
Nicosia
LEBANON

Sea of Crete
Crete
CYPRUS

PARIS

Auberge Internationale des Jeunes

HOSTEL IN PARIS

THE BEST VALUE DOWNTOWN

- Rooms from 2 to 6 beds
- Very clean & new building
- English speaking staff
- Breakfast included
- Free luggage storage
- Free showers
- Free safes for your valuables
- Internet access in the hall
- Credit cards and travellers' cheques accepted
- Access to all sights

NO CURFEW

HOSTEL IN THE CITY CENTRE OF PARIS

81FF
from November to February

91FF
from March to October

An ideal location for young people, a lively and safe area with many cafés and pubs. Laundromats, boulangeries and supermarkets nearby.

INTERNATIONAL ATMOSPHERE

Other Hostels might be less comfortable, and more expensive...!!

10, rue Trousseau - 75011 Paris - France
Tel.: (+33) 01 47 00 62 00 - Fax : (+33) 01 47 00 33 16
Internet : http://www.aijparis.com - E-mail : aij@aijparis.com
Métro : LEDRU-ROLLIN - Line 8 (Next to Bastille station)

BOOKINGS ARE POSSIBLE BY FAX OR E-MAIL

DISCOVER
EUROPE

Ah, Europe—the second smallest of the seven continents, a land mass of 10.4 million sq. km bordered by the Atlantic, Mediterranean, Arctic, Black, and Caspian Seas and the Ural Mountains, home to roughly a seventh of the world's population and 60 native languages. About 40,000 years ago, Europe's Neanderthal population was supplanted by our dear friend *Homo sapiens*, followed just tens of millenia later by the first European settlements on Crete. Then before you knew it, the Minoans, Mycenaeans, Greeks, Etruscans, Carthaginians, Romans, Byzantines, Franks, Vikings, Holy Romans, and Ottomans had all come and gone, and pretty soon (following countless tragic wars, a few really long boat trips, and a few pinnacles of Western civilization), the year 2000 rolled around, and you decided that it was high time that you went and saw it all for yourself. So you loaded some film in the old camera, packed a change of socks, and got your mitts on a copy of *Let's Go: Europe 2000*—and you're ready to go. So go.

THE CULTURAL TAPESTRY

Europe has enough "culture" to keep you busy for a lifetime. But you don't have time to see every ornate church and crumbling Roman amphitheater in all of Europe—you want the highlights, the must-sees of art and architecture, and you want them now. **London** is one of Europe's finest museum cities (p. 139): peruse the Rosetta Stone, the Elgin Marbles, and other imperialist booty at the **British Museum;** saunter through the histories of art, design, and style at the **Victoria and Albert Museum;** and don't miss the spectacular collection of modern art at the **Tate Gallery.**

On the other side of the Chunnel, **Paris** contains a string of absolute gems (p. 292)—the *Venus de Milo* and *Mona Lisa* at the **Louvre** will stop you in your tracks; the **Musée d'Orsay** will impress and leave an impression with all that is Impressionist; and the pipes and modern art of the **Centre National d'Art et de Culture Georges-Pompidou** will wriggle their way into your heart. Stroll the streets of Paris, soaking in the city's various architectural styles; don't miss the breathtaking **Cathédrale de Nôtre-Dame.** Outside of Paris, the *châteaux* of the **Loire Valley** (p. 321) and Normandy's fortified abbey of **Mont-St Michel** (p. 317) are also must-sees.

From France, drop down to Spain to witness **Bilbao's** stunning **Museo Guggenheim** (p. 858) before continuing on to **Madrid's** stunning museums (p. 799): the **Prado** shelters the world's largest collection of paintings; the **Museo Thyssen-Bornemizsa** is practically the *Cliff Notes* of major artistic trends in painting; and the **Museo Nacional Centro de Arte Reina Sofía** harbors Picasso's *Guernica*. From there, head south to Muslim-infused southern Spain to witness the **mosque** in **Córdoba** (p. 821) and the **Alhambra** in **Granada** (p. 832). Before leaving Spain, delight in **Barcelona's** fanciful *Modernista* buildings and its museums devoted to Picasso and Miró (p. 837).

A quick train ride along the Riviera will bring you to **Italy.** First stop: **Venice** (p. 572), whose wriggling waterways encompass the Venetian art of the **Accademia** and the modern art of the **Collezione Guggenheim.** Next up: **Florence** (p. 601), home of the Renaissance; you could lounge for an entire day at the splendid **Uffizi**, then drool for another at the image of human perfection, Michelangelo's *David*, in the **Accademia.** **Rome** almost invented architecture as we know it (p. 563); can we say **Pantheon, Colosseum,** and **Forum**? Oh yeah, and Michelangelo's *Pietà* in **St. Peter's Basilica,** not to mention the **Sistine Chapel** in the **Vatican Museums,** will knock off your stinky socks.

Dive off the heel of the boot into **Greece,** where the crumbling **Acropolis,** the very foundation of Western civilization, still towers above **Athens** (p. 458). After visiting one of the foremost collections of classical art at Athens' **National Archaeological Museum,** journey to the navel of the ancient world to learn your fate from the **oracle** at **Delphi** (p. 465) or visit *the* **temple of Apollo** on **Delos** (p. 480). Skim across the Aegean to İstanbul's Byzantine **Hagia Sophia** and Ottoman **Blue Mosque** (p. 915).

Far to the north, **Moscow's Kremlin** once contained the secrets to an empire; it still holds the legendary Fabergé eggs (p. 760). The **Hermitage,** in **St. Petersburg** to the west, holds the world's largest art collection (p. 770). Head back west into Central Europe, where **Vienna** hosts the renowned **Kunsthistoriches Museum** and the Klimt-rich **Austrian Gallery** (p. 85). Cross the German border and peruse **Munich's Neue** and **Alte Pinakothek** (p. 435) before continuing north to **Weimar,** birthplace of the **Bauhaus** architectural movement (p. 398). From there, continue on to **Berlin,** the focal point for the healing of eastern and western Europe; its excellent museums will make you feel legit in a black turtleneck, too (p. 376). Believe it or not, the biggest sin you could commit in **Amsterdam** would be to miss the famed **Rijksmuseum.** Finish up with the **van Gogh Museum** and the **Hash Marijuana Hemp Museum.** Whoops, perhaps the last doesn't quite constitute culture, but hey, you deserve it (p. 655).

THE GREAT OUTDOORS

Enough urban warrior—you're ready to commune with the streams, hug a few trees, and heed the call of the wild. Although rugged hills and industrial cities make up much of its landscape, Britain is actually brimming with national parks; our favorite is the **Lake District National Park** (p. 186). For starker natural beauty, head north to the **Scottish Highlands;** the **Isle of Skye** (p. 206) and the **Outer Hebrides** (p. 206) are particularly breathtaking. Ireland's **Ring of Kerry** provides wee Irish towns (p. 534), while **Killarney National Park** features spectacular mountains (p. 533). Back on the continent in the French Alps, **Chamonix** tempts skiers with some of the world's steepest slopes (p. 352), while **Grenoble** brims with hiking opportunities (p. 352). In Spain, the **Parque Nacional de Ordesa** is set amongst the breathtaking Pyrenees (p. 851). Across the Mediterranean, the **Aeolian Islands** just north of Sicily boast its pristine beaches, belching volcanoes, and bubbling thermal springs (p. 627). Drop down to Greece and hike up to **Mt. Olympus,** where the gods used to sip ambrosia; a two-day hike will bring you to the summit (p. 474). In **Crete,** get in touch with your inner mountain goat with a trek down the **Samaria Gorge** (p. 486). Turkey's **Butterfly Valley,** near **Fethiye,** will entrance and astound (p. 933). The dramatic **Tatra** mountain range stretches across Eastern Europe; lace up your hiking boots in Slovakia's **Starý Smokovec** (p. 785) or Poland's **Zakopane** (p. 723). Austria's **Kitzbühel** (p. 107) and **Innsbruck** (p. 108) quench every hiking and skiing desire. For some fresh, Swiss Alpine air, head to the glaciers of **Grindelwald** (p. 907), make the pilgrimage to the **Matterhorn,** near **Zermatt** (p. 908), or dive into the adventure sports of **Interlaken** (p. 905). From there, disappear into Germany's buckling **Bavarian Alps** (p. 448) and then take to the hiking trails of the **Black Forest** (p. 430). After it's all over, relax your tired toes in the baths of posh **Baden-Baden** (p. 430).

OFF-THE-BEATEN-PATH...

A Eurailpass is like French kissing: it's fun at first, but eventually leaves everyone hungry for more. As in love, getting beyond that first stage in exploring Europe takes a little savvy. And like advice from a more experienced friend, here's how to get more out of Europe then just a few cheap thrills. Untouched spots still nestle in the misty forests of northwestern Spain's **Rías de Cedeira** and **Vivero.** A little bit out of the way, but certainly well worth it, are the gorgeous beaches of **Corsica** (p. 349) and the mountainous terrain of neighboring **Sardinia** (p. 629). In **Italy, Ravenna** hosts a stash of stunning Byzantine mosaics (p. 600). In the Greek Peloponnese lie the tiny, relaxing towns of **Dimitsana** and **Stemnitsa** (p. 467); on the mainland stands the exquisite, Byzantine **Osios Loukas,** the most beautiful of Greece's monasteries (p. 475). Creep inland to the surreal landscapes of Turkey's moonscape-like **Cappado-**

cia, centered on **Göreme** (p. 935), a land of fairy chimneys, cave houses, and underground cities. On the coast, **Olimpos** burns with an eternal flame (p. 933). Fishing villages and beach resorts line the Bulgarian **Black Sea Coast** (p. 218). For less beach and more culture, try Romania, where modern sculptor Constantin Brâncuşi's work is center-stage in **Târgu Jiu** (p. 751) and where the awe-inspiring **Bukovina Monasteries** litter the countryside (p. 754). To the west, Croatia's **Dalmatian Coast** bewitches with bronze beaches, beautiful old towns, and fascinating Roman ruins (p. 224).

FÊTES! FESTAS! FIESTAS! FESTIVALS!

Yes, people come to Europe to see the sights, to examine the cradle of Western civilization, to explore history, yada yada yada. But the Europeans, they throw a damn good party, too. **Cadíz** (p. 827) and **Nice** (p. 343) go crazy for **Carnaval** (Mar. 2-12), when people start dancing in the streets. Right on its toes, the Spanish city of **Valencia** sets effigies on fire and prances around wildly for **Las Fallas** (Mar. 12-19; p. 836). While waiting for the next big bash, dance your way through the mad nightlife of **Madrid** (p. 799), **Barcelona** (p. 837), and the **French Riviera** (p. 339). Next up, **Seville** steals the scene during **Semana Santa** (Apr. 17-23; Palm Sunday to Good Friday; p. 822), parading around town venerating sacred icons, then shakes loose with the **Feria de Abril** (late Apr. to early May; p. 822). **Dublin** celebrates James Joyce during **Bloomsday** with a week of celebration around June 16 (p. 521). Wild fun awaits in **London** (p. 139), but then you have a date in Scandinavia for **Midsummer Eve** (June 24), the longest day of the year, when you get to dance around bonfires and midsummer poles. Join the fun in **Rome** (p. 553) before bareback horse races take **Siena** by storm during **Il Palio** (July 2 and Aug. 16; p. 612). Drink your wine and have the time of your life when the bulls run for **San Fermines** in **Pamplona** (July 6-13; p. 852). During the concurrent **Love Parade** in **Berlin,** yes is the word (July 8-9; p. 376). The **Festival d'Avignon** brings in a crazy range of events from early July to early August (p. 336). Boogie down in **Paris** (p. 292) before crossing the Channel for the **Edinburgh International Festival,** which entertains with all things artsy (Aug. 18-Sept. 1; p. 195). The efficient Germans even party well; stop by **Cologne** (p. 411) and **Hamburg** (p. 402); then head to **Munich** for the world-famous **Oktoberfest,** which (strangely enough) starts September 16 and then goes strong until October 1 (p. 435). Rest from October to March, then begin the madness all over again.

FUN IN THE SUN

So you've seen all the sights and climbed all the mountains—now just lie back and soak up the rays. You may have guessed it, but even England hosts a tempting beach culture when it's not raining. The old artists' enclave of **St. Ives** offers sparkling beaches and blue blue water (p. 165), while **Newquay** is a surfing capital (p. 166). **Malin Head,** at Ireland's northernmost point on the **Inishowen Peninsula,** offers a beach covered with semi-precious stones (p. 542). France packs surfers onto 4km of crystalline sand in **Anglet** (p. 331), while **St-Malo** combines the beauty and history of Normandy (p. 318). Skip down to Portugal, where you can party all night and sun all day along the **Algarve,** and in **Lagos** in particular (p. 737). Along Spain's **Costa del Sol, Marbella's** beaches are lined with hip, happening clubs (p. 830), while **Tossa del Mar** along the **Costa Blanca** boasts red cliffs, small bays, and medieval alleys (p. 849). Spain's **Balearic Islands** are a must for party kids; **Ibiza** (p. 860) is manic by night. Move along to Italy and the fishing villages of **Cinque Terre,** which cling to cliffs over the bright blue sea (p. 596). Farther north in Italy, Europe's deepest lake, **Lake Como,** is peaceful perfection (p. 584). Most visitors to Italy don't venture south of Rome—a huge mistake, given the breathtaking, almost unspeakable, beauty of the **Amalfi Coast,** where you can sunbathe with the people who invented the bikini (p. 621). The **Blue Grotto** glows nearby on the island of **Capri** (p. 622). Bop down to the Greek islands: **Corfu** harbors the beautiful beach of **Agios Gordios** (p. 476); as the sun sets over volcanic sand beaches in **Santorini,** the bars salute Helios with classical music (p. 483). Drag your tanned and tired self to the **Blue Lagoon** of **Ölüdeniz,** near **Fethiye,** in **Turkey** (p. 933).

SUGGESTED ITINERARIES

There is no prescription for the perfect itinerary in Europe. Here we humbly suggest a few routes—just to give you an idea of what is possible. **The Basics** below outlines our skeletal suggestions for the best of Europe; excluding days in Great Britain (where Eurail passes are not valid), these itineraries come out to exactly one and two months, perfect for a one- or two-month unlimited Eurailpass (see **Eurailpasses,** p. 60). We've also included some regional itineraries here to help you plan a few extra forays. Since very few people have the time or cash to cover everywhere in a single trip, these other itineraries can be thought of as **Building Blocks** that you can tack onto the basic route in order to construct your ideal trip. For suggestions on how you could flesh out these skeletal itineraries to make them more in-depth, see the Discover sections in individual chapters.

THE BASICS

THE BEST OF EUROPE IN 32 DAYS (1-MONTH EURAILPASS) Start out in **London,** spinning from theater to museum to club (4 days; p. 139). Chunnel to the sights, shops, and sweets of **Paris** (4 days; p. 292), detour to glittering **Barcelona** (2 days; p. 837), then return to France for a day in festive **Avignon** (p. 336) or elegant **Aix-en-Provence** (p. 338). The party lasts all night in **Nice** (1 day; p. 343); recover in the blissful **Cinque Terre** on the Italian Riviera (2 days; p. 596). Dive into Renaissance art in **Florence** (2 days; p. 601) and pull Adam's finger in **Rome** (3 days; p. 553). Float down **Venice's** canals by goldola (2 days; p. 572) on your way to sip coffee in **Vienna** (2 days; p. 85). Join the tourist stampede to nonetheless enrapturing **Prague** (2 days; p. 229) and sample the brew in **Munich** (2 days; p. 435) before heading up to sprawling, overwhelming **Berlin** (2 days; p. 376). Indulge in the goods in **Amsterdam** (2 days; p. 655), then finish off with a day in Tintin's **Brussels** (p. 119) or beautiful **Bruges** (p. 124).

THE BEST OF EUROPE IN 9 WEEKS (2-MONTH EURAILPASS) From **London** (4 days; p. 139), get studious in **Oxford** (p. 167) or **Cambridge** (p. 175), then take to the well-worn footpaths between villages in the **Cotswolds** (1 day; p. 171). Sightsee in **Bath** (1 day; p. 174), then chunnel from London to **Paris** and gape at **Versailles** (1 day; p. 312) before rushing from museum to café in **Paris** (4 days; p. 292). Ogle the gorgeous *châteaux* of the **Loire Valley** (1 day; p. 321), proceed south to the all-night party in **Madrid** (2 days; p. 799), and marvel at the architectural gems of **Barcelona** (3 days; p. 837). After a day each in **Avignon** (p. 336), **Aix-en-Provence** (p. 338), and **Nice** (p. 343), replenish in the **Cinque Terre** (2 days; p. 596) and continue on to the orange roofs of **Florence** (2 days; p. 601). Stop at stunning **Siena** (1 day; p. 612) en route to **Rome** (3 days; p. 553), then wind through **Venice** (2 days; p. 572) on your way to posh **Milan** (1 day; p. 586) and the idyllic **Lake Region** (2 days; p. 584). Conquer the Swiss Alps around **Interlaken** (1 day; p. 905), then do high culture in **Zürich** (1 day; p. 896) before indulging your passion for *The Sound of Music* in **Salzburg** (1 day; p. 97). After **Vienna** (2 days; p. 85), soak in the baths of **Budapest** (3 days; p. 495), then head to everybody's favorite city, **Prague** (3 days; p. 229), and everybody's new favorite city, **Český Krumlov** (1 day; p. 244). Love your beer in **Munich,** then take a sobering daytrip to **Dachau** (3 days; p. 435). Head from the fairy-tale **Royal Castles** (1 day; p. 448) up the **Romantic Road** (2 days; p. 446), then cruise down the spectacular **Rhine River** (2 days; p. 411). From **Berlin** (2 days; p. 376), head north to cosmopolitan **Copenhagen** (2 days; p. 251) and continue on to **Amsterdam** (3 days; p. 655). Spend a day each in **Brussels** (p. 119) and **Bruges** (p. 124) before heading home.

BUILDING BLOCKS

THE BEST OF SPAIN AND PORTUGAL (23 DAYS)

Hop off the Paris-Madrid train at gorgeous **San Sebastián** (2 days; p. 854), then check out the new Guggenheim in **Bilbao** (1 day; p. 857) before heading to **Madrid** for urban fun (3 days; p. 799). Take a daytrip to the winding streets of **Toledo** (1 day; p. 810), then head into Portugal to marvel at the painted tiles in **Lisbon** (2½ days; p. 728). Bake in the sun along the Algarve in **Lagos** (2½ days; p. 737) before going returning to Spain for **Seville's** flower-filled plazas (2½ days; p. 822). Don't forget a daytrip to see **Córdoba's** stunning mosque (1 day; p. 818). Tan some more in **Marbella** (1½day; p. 830), then love the Alhambra in **Granada** (2 days; p. 831). Head to northeastern Spain to hit the sunny **Costa Brava** (p. 849; 2 days), the Dalí Museum in **Figueres** (1 day; p. 848), and medieval **Girona** (1 days; p. 849). Then continue with the two-month itinerary from **Barcelona** (p. 837).

THE BEST OF SCANDINAVIA (22 DAYS)

From **Copenhagen** (p. 251), be true to thine own self with a daytrip to the glorious castles of **Frederiksborg, Roskilde,** or **Elsinore** (1 day; p. 257). Cruise through **Odense** to the beautiful, quiet island of **Ærø** (3½ days; p. 261). Backtrack through Odense to Denmark's second city, **Århus** (2½ days; p. 262), then catch a ferry from Hirtshals to **Kristiansand,** Norway (1 day; p. 689). Trek up to lovely **Bergen** (2 days; p. 692) before diving into the fjords (2 days); marvel at the natural wonders that are **Sognefjord** (p. 697) and **Geirangerfjord** (p. 699). Cut across to posh **Oslo** (3 days; p. 683) and sleep your way on the night train to **Stockholm,** the jewel of Scandinavia (2 days; p. 869). Take a daytrip to **Uppsala,** home of Sweden's oldest university (1 day; p. 882). Hop on the ferry to **Helsinki** (2 days; p. 277), where east meets west, and daytrip to **Porvoo** (1 day; p. 282). After returning to Stockholm, head south to friendly **Gothenburg** (1½ days; p. 881) and then take the ferry back to Copenhagen via **Malmö** (½ day; p. 879).

THE BEST OF GREECE AND TURKEY (29-31 DAYS)

Hop off the boot from **Brindisi** (p. 624) or **Bari** (p. 623), where overnight ferries go to Greece (1 day). Get off at **Corfu** (0-2 days; p. 476), beloved by literary luminaries and partiers, or continue on to **Patras** (1 day; p. 466). Wrestle among the ruins in **Olympia** (1 day; p. 466) before beginning your Peloponnesian adventure with a survey of the ancient ruins in **Napflion, Mycenae,** and **Epidavros** (3 days; p. 469). Get initiated into the "mysteries of love" in equally ruinous **Corinth** (1 day; p. 470). On to chaotic **Athens,** a jumble of things ancient and modern (2 days; p. 458). Next stop: the Cyclades. Party all night long on **Mykonos** (p. 480), then daytrip to sacred **Delos** (p. 480) before continuing on to the earthly paradise of **Santorini** (2 days; p. 483). Catch the ferry to **Crete,** where chic **Iraklion** and **Knossos,** home to the Minotaur, await (2 days; p. 485). Base yourself in **Rethymno** or **Hania** and hike the spectacular **Samaria Gorge** (2 days; p. 485). Backtrack to Iraklion to catch the ferry to the Dodecanese to hit historical **Rhodes** (2 days; p. 489) and then start the party in **Kos** (1 day; p. 490). Cross over to **Bodrum,** Turkey, the "Bedroom of the Mediterranean" (2 days; p. 931). From there, two routes diverge depending on what you've come to Turkey to see; they both meet up in **Cappadocia** after four days. If you've come to see **ruins,** head up to **Kuşadasi** to check out the crumbling magnificence at **Ephesus** (1½ day; p. 929). Move on to the thermal springs of **Pamukkale** and **Aphrodisias** (2½ day; p. 930); then on to Cappadocia. Or, if you're more into **beaches,** head from Bodrum to **Fethiye** and serene **Ölüdeniz** (1 day; p. 933) and the eternal flame of **Olimpos** (2 days; p. 933); then head to the surreal world of **Göreme** in Cappadocia (2 days; p. 935). Sleep on an overnight bus to **Istanbul** and go a little crazy (3 days; p. 915).

THE BEST OF CENTRAL EUROPE (23 DAYS)

Link up from **Berlin** to **Gdańsk,** or skip Gdańsk and link up from **Prague** to **Warsaw.** Starting in multi-faceted **Gdańsk** (1 day; p. 714) stopping off in

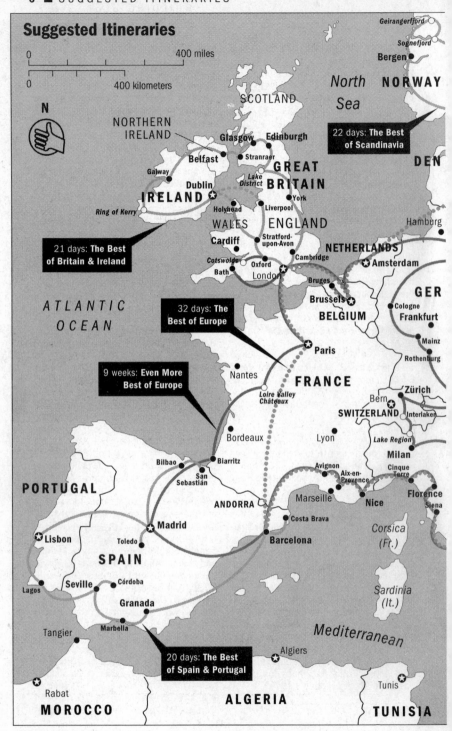

Suggested Itineraries

0 |—————————| 400 miles

0 |—————————| 400 kilometers

N

22 days: The Best of Scandinavia

21 days: The Best of Britain & Ireland

32 days: The Best of Europe

9 weeks: Even More Best of Europe

20 days: The Best of Spain & Portugal

Geirangerfjord
Sognefjord
Bergen

NORWAY

North Sea

DEN

SCOTLAND

NORTHERN IRELAND

Glasgow · Edinburgh
Belfast · Stranraer
Galway
Dublin · Lake District · York
IRELAND · GREAT BRITAIN
Ring of Kerry · Holyhead · Liverpool
WALES · ENGLAND
Cardiff · Stratford-upon-Avon
Cotswolds · Cambridge
Bath · Oxford · London

Hamburg

NETHERLANDS · Amsterdam

Bruges
Brussels · GER
BELGIUM · Cologne · Frankfurt
· Mainz
Rothenburg

ATLANTIC OCEAN

Paris

Nantes · FRANCE

Loire Valley Châteaux

Zürich
Bern · SWITZERLAND · Interlaken
Lake Region
Bordeaux · Lyon · Milan

Bilbao · Biarritz · Avignon · Cinque Terre
San Sebastián · Aix-en-Provence
ANDORRA · Marseille · Nice · Florence
Madrid · Costa Brava · Siena
Lisbon · Barcelona
Toledo · Corsica (Fr.)
SPAIN
Lagos · Seville · Córdoba
Granada · Sardinia (It.)
Marbella
Tangier · Mediterranean
Algiers
MOROCCO · Rabat · ALGERIA · Tunis
PORTUGAL · TUNISIA

Toruń, the lovely home of Copernicus (1 day; p. 716) on the way to sprawling and chaotic **Warsaw** (3 days; p. 707). Vibrant **Kraków** (3 days; p. 717) awaits, as does fabulous hiking in the Tatra Mountains surrounding **Zakopane** (1 day; p. 723). Head to vibrant **Budapest** (3 days; p. 495), then be seduced by **Lake Balaton's** warm shallow waters (2 days; p. 506). In Croatia, groove in hip, happening **Zagreb** (2 days; p. 222), then head to the delights of the Dalmatian Coast in **Dubrovnik** (3 days; p. 225) and **Split** (2 days; p. 224). Pass through delightful **Ljubljana** (2 days; p. 789) before linking back up with the two-month basic route by hopping on a train to Venice or Vienna.

THE BEST OF THE BLACK SEA (20 DAYS) From **Istanbul,** head to the the lovely beach town of **Sozopol** (2 days; p. 218) on the Bulgarian Black Sea coast. Head through Sofia to **Bucharest,** once the gem of Romania, now a ghost of itself (4 days; p. 747). Detour from Bucharest to **Târgu Jiu,** littered with marvelous Brâncuşi sculptures (2 days; p. 751), and **Braşov,** located in the heart of Transylvannia near Dracula's castle (2 days; p. 752). Truck to **Odessa,** the former USSR's party town (3 days; p. 946), then head via Simferopol to **Yalta** and its beaches (3 days; p. 946). Snooze on the night train to **Kiev,** where you can marvel at the bride industry and admire medieval castles (3 days; p. 942). Link back up with the more beaten path via transport to Moscow or Warsaw (1 day).

THE BEST OF BALTIC EUROPE (22 DAYS) Take the ferry from Helsinki or the train from Central or Eastern Europe to reach **Tallinn's** charming medieval streets (2 days; p. 268), then relax on the tranquil and secluded **Estonian Islands** (4 days; p. 272). Move on to lively **Tartu,** the oldest city in the Baltics (2 days; p.

271), before immersing yourself in the Soviet-ness of **Riga** (2 days; p. 632). Swing over to **Klaipeda** in Lithuania and relax on the dreamy beach at **Nida** (2 day; p. 642). Continue to up-and-coming **Vilnius** (3 days; p. 638), one of the many "New Pragues," then get some shut-eye on the night train to **Moscow,** where you can survey Red Square and see history in action (4 days; p. 760). Cap it off spending some time in **St. Petersburg,** home of the ornate delights of the Hermitage (3 days; p. 770).

THE BEST OF BRITAIN AND IRELAND (21 DAYS). After visiting London, Bath, the Cotswolds, and Oxford on the two-month itinerary (see above), head from from Oxford to **Stratford-upon-Avon** (1 day; p. 172), Shakespeare's hometown, also near Warwick Castle. On to **Liverpool** (2 days; p. 182), home of the Beatles; or **Conwy** and **Caernarfon** (2 days; p. 193 and p. 193), known for their castles. Depending on which route you choose, you'll cross the Irish Sea from either Liverpool or Holyhead (near Conwy and Caernafon; p. 188) to **Dublin** (3 days; p. 521), home to Joyce and Guinness. Don't forget to make a daytrip to the Wicklow Mountains (1 day; p. 530). Answer the call of rural Ireland with the **Ring of Kerry** (2½ days; p. 534). **Galway** (1½ days; p. 537), a center of Irish culture, is also close to the limestone landscape of the Aran Islands. Then on to politically divided and exciting **Belfast** (2 days; p. 542). From there it's back across the Irish Sea to **Stranraer,** then on a train to energetic **Glasgow** (1 day; p. 200) and nearby **Loch Lomond.** Then on to historic **Edinburgh** (3 days; p. 195). The **Lake District** (2 days; p. 186) offers scenic diversions; historic **York** (1 day; p. 183) and **Cambridge** (1 day; p. 175) complete the southbound journey. And return to London to kick back, maybe with a West End play or a Guinness.

ESSENTIALS

Touring through the entirety of Europe, or even just a chunk of it, can be as daunting as it is exciting. Fortunately, there are countless resources devoted to helping travelers plan a journey through Europe. All you need to do is dive in and design a trip tailored to your specific interests and needs, without losing sight of the fact that this is a vacation. Don't overplan your itinerary so that the adventure becomes one big blur; just relax and wander through Europe at your own pace.

FACTS FOR THE TRAVELER

WHEN AND WITH WHOM TO GO

Give careful consideration to when and with whom you travel. Summer is the high season for traveling in Europe. *Everything* is crowded with tourists in July and August; June or September may be a better time to go. If you're thinking about traveling with others, discuss your trip in detail with them before leaving to ensure that your interests are compatible. Traveling companions will cut down on food and lodging costs, and will also provide additional safety and comfort, but they will most likely insulate you from local culture and cut down on your freedom of movement as well. A budget travel subculture fills Europe's hostels, ensuring that even if you travel alone, you need only be as lonely as you want to be.

DOCUMENTS AND FORMALITIES

Information on European **embassies** and **consulates** at home, as well as foreign embassies and consulates in Europe, is located in individual country chapters.

PASSPORTS

REQUIREMENTS. Citizens of Australia, Canada, the Republic of Ireland, New Zealand, South Africa, the UK, and the US all need valid passports to enter most countries and to reenter their own countries. Some countries do not allow entrance if your passport expires in fewer than six months.

PHOTOCOPIES. Be sure to photocopy the page of your passport with your photo, passport number, and other identifying information, as well as any visas, travel insurance policies, plane tickets, or traveler's check serial numbers. Carry one set of copies in a safe place, apart from the originals, and leave another set at home. Consulates also recommend that you carry an expired passport or an official copy of your birth certificate in a part of your baggage separate from other documents.

LOST PASSPORTS. If you lose your passport, immediately notify the local police and the nearest mission of your government. A replacement may take weeks to process, and may be valid only for a limited time. In an emergency, ask for immediate temporary traveling papers that will permit you to reenter your home country. Your passport is a public document belonging to your nation's government; you may have to surrender it to a foreign government official, but if you don't get it back in a reasonable amount of time, inform the nearest mission of your home country.

NEW PASSPORTS. File any new passport or renewal applications well in advance of your departure date—remember that you are relying on government agencies. Most passport offices offer rush services for a steep fee. Citizens residing abroad who need a passport or renewal should contact their nearest embassy or consulate.

ESSENTIALS

FREE Student Travel Newsletter

Register at any of these great sites...

hostelcards.com

Order online! The one-stop shop for all your travel card needs.

budgetbritain.com

Travel, work and study information on Britain for students by students.

studyplanner.com

A great resource for study abroad participants.

backpackersadvantage.com

Save hundreds of $$$ in Europe on restaurants, shopping, museums and more.

Australia: Info tel. 13 12 32; www.dfat.gov.au/passports. Apply for a passport at a post office, passport office (in Adelaide, Brisbane, Canberra, Darwin, Hobart, Melbourne, Newcastle, Perth, or Sydney), or diplomatic mission. Passports AUS$126 (32-page) or AUS$188 (64-page); valid for 10 years. Children AUS$63 (32-page) or AUS$94 (64-page); valid for 5 years.

Canada: Canadian Passport Office, Department of Foreign Affairs and International Trade, Ottawa, ON K1A 0G3 (tel. (613) 994-3500 or (800) 567-6868; www.dfait-maeci.gc.ca/passport). Applications available at passport offices, missions, travel agencies, and Northern Stores. Passports CDN$60, plus CDN$25 fee; valid for 5 years (non-renewable).

Ireland: Pick up an application at a Garda station or post office, or request one from a passport office, then apply by mail to the Department of Foreign Affairs, Passport Office, Setanta Centre, Molesworth St, Dublin 2 (tel. (01) 671 16 33; www.irlgov.ie/iveagh), or the Passport Office, Irish Life Building, 1A South Mall, Cork (tel. (021) 27 25 25). Passports IR£45; valid for 10 years. Under 18 or over 65 IR£10; valid for 3 years.

New Zealand: Send applications (available from most travel agents) to the Passport Office, P.O. Box 10526, Wellington, New Zealand (tel. (0800) 22 50 50; www.govt.nz/agency_info/forms.shtml). Standard processing time is 10 working days. Passports NZ$80; valid for 10 years. Children NZ$40; valid for 5 years.

South Africa: Department of Home Affairs (www.southafrica-newyork.net/passport.htm). Passports are issued only in Pretoria, but all applications must still be submitted or forwarded to the nearest South African consulate. Processing time is 3 months or more. Passports around SAR80; valid for 10 years. Under 16 around SAR60; valid for 5 years.

United Kingdom: Info tel. (0870) 521 04 10; www.open.gov.uk/ukpass/ukpass.htm. Get an application from a passport office, main post office, or travel agent; apply by mail to or in person at a passport office (in London, Liverpool, Newport, Peterborough, Glasgow, and Belfast). The process takes about 4 weeks; the London office offers a 5-day, walk-in rush service. Passports UK£31; valid for 10 years. Under 16 UK£11; valid for 5 years.

United States: Info tel. (202) 647-0518; http://travel.state.gov/passport_services.html. Apply at any federal or state courthouse, authorized post office, or US Passport Agency (located in most major cities); see the "US Government, State Department" section of the telephone book or a post office for addresses. Processing takes 3-4 weeks. New passports US$60 (valid for 10 years); under 18 US$40 (valid for 5 years). Passports may be renewed by mail or in person for US$40.

 ONE EUROPE. With the Maastricht Treaty of 1993, the European Union came into existence. Since then, the EU has extended from its original six member-states to 15 today: Austria, Belgium, Denmark, Finland, France, Germany, Greece, Ireland, Italy, Luxembourg, the Netherlands, Portugal, Spain, Sweden, and the UK. On May 1, 1999, the Treaty of Amsterdam came into effect, incorporating the Schengen Convention (which had previously abolished internal border checks for all EU citizens between many but not all EU countries) into the EU institutional framework. With the exception of Denmark, Ireland, and the UK, visa and immigration policies are now harmonized throughout the EU, simplifying border crossings for both EU and non-EU citizens enormously. Nationals of EU member-states need only a European Identity Card to pass between Schengen countries; most non-EU nationals (including citizens of Australia, Canada, the Republic of Ireland, New Zealand, the US, and the UK) need only a passport.

VISAS, INVITATIONS, AND WORK PERMITS

VISAS. Some countries require a visa—a stamp, sticker, or insert in your passport specifying the purpose of your travel and the permitted duration of your stay—in addition to a valid passport for entrance. Most standard visas cost US$10-70, are valid for one month, and must be validated within six months to one year from the date of issue. Many countries are willing to grant double-entry visas for a premium.

East Coast <> Europe $169
West Coast <> Europe $249
Midwest <> Europe $199
other destinations cheap
discounted bus/rail passes + car rentals
EUROPE SUCKS
why spend more than $169 getting there
Air-Tech Unltd
(800)575-TECH
WWW.AIRTECH.COM

The **Center for International Business and Travel** (**CIBT**; tel. (800) 925-2428) secures visas for US citizens for travel to almost any country for a variable service charge.

The requirements in the chart below only apply to tourist stays shorter than three months. If you plan to stay longer than 90 days, or if you plan to work or study abroad, your requirements will differ. In any case, check with the nearest embassy or consulate of your desired destination for up-to-date info. US citizens can also consult www.pueblo.gsa.gov/cic_text/travel/foreign/foreignentryreqs.html.

Note that not listed in this chart are **Austria, Belgium, Croatia, Denmark, Finland, France, Germany, Greece, Iceland, Italy, Luxembourg, the Netherlands, Norway, Portugal, Slovenia, Spain,** and **Sweden.** These countries require visas of South Africans, but not of nationals of Australia, Canada, Ireland, New Zealand, the UK, or the US (for stays shorter than three months). Also not listed are the **UK, Ireland, Malta,** and **Switzerland,** which do not require visas for any of the seven nationalities listed above (including South Africans) for stays shorter than 90 days. Travelers to **Andorra** should contact a French or Spanish embassy for more info, while those going to **Liechtenstein** should contact a Swiss embassy with any enquiries.

VISA REQUIREMENTS		AUS	CAN	IRE	NZ	SA	UK	US
	BELARUS	Y³	Y³	Y³	Y³	Y³	Y³	Y³
	BOSNIA	Y	N	N	Y	Y	N	N
	BULGARIA	N¹	N¹	N¹	N¹	Y	N¹	N
	CZECH REPUBLIC	Y	N	N	N	Y	N	N¹
	ESTONIA	N	Y	N	N	Y	N	N
	HUNGARY	Y	N	N	Y	N¹	N	N
	LATVIA	Y²	Y	N	Y²	Y	N	N
	LITHUANIA	N	N	N	Y	Y	N	N
	POLAND	Y	Y	N	Y	Y	N	N
	ROMANIA	Y	Y	Y	Y	Y	Y	N¹
	RUSSIA	Y³	Y³	Y³	Y³	Y³	Y³	Y³
	SLOVAKIA	Y	N	N	Y	N¹	N	N¹
	TURKEY	N	N	Y	N	N¹	Y	Y
	UKRAINE	Y³	Y³	Y³	Y³	Y³	Y³	Y³

KEY 1 tourists can stay up to 30 days without visa; **2** tourists can stay up to 10 days without visa; **3** invitation required

INVITATIONS AND WORK PERMITS. In addition to a visa, **Belarus, Russia,** and **Ukraine** currently also require that visitors from Australia, Canada, Ireland, New Zealand, the UK, and the US obtain an invitation from a sponsoring individual or organization. Requirements change rapidly, so double-check. See individual chapters for info on how to acquire invitations. Visitors to any European country, with the exception of EU citizens in EU countries, who want the right to work will need a work permit (see **Alternatives to Tourism,** p. 73).

IDENTIFICATION

When you travel, always carry two or more forms of identification on your person, including at least one photo ID; a passport combined with a driver's license or birth certificate is usually adequate. Many establishments, especially banks, may require several IDs in order to cash traveler's checks. Never carry all your forms of ID together; split them up in case of theft or loss. It is useful to carry extra passport-size photos to affix to the various IDs or passes you may acquire along the way.

STUDENT AND TEACHER IDENTIFICATION. The **International Student Identity Card (ISIC),** the most widely accepted form of student ID, provides discounts on sights, accommodations, food, and transport. The ISIC is preferable to an institution-specific card (such as a university ID) because more likely to be recognized (and honored) abroad. All cardholders have access to an emergency helpline, and US cardholders are also eligible for insurance benefits (see **Insurance,** p. 33). Many stu-

ESSENTIALS

HOSTELS *Londons*

ESTABLISHED 1974

THE 5 FUNKIEST HOSTELS IN LONDON

Price includes:
continental breakfast • VAT • clean bed linen • cable TV
cooking facilities • hot showers • wake-up calls • fax service
free valuables lock up • NO CURFEW - PRIME LOCATIONS
and friendly staff that love to party!

SHARED ACCOM. DAILY FROM £12.50 TO £16.00 *pn*

HYDE PARK HOSTEL

Hyde Park/ Queensway/ Kensington Palace
Affordable meals, Late night Bar, Launderette – Prime Spot!
2 -6 Inverness Terrace, W2 Tel: 0171 229 5101 Fax: 0171 229 3170
Queensway   or Bayswater Underground

LEINSTER INN

Notting Hill Gate/ Portobello Market/ Bayswater
With late night bar, café & laundry on site for guests.
7 - 12 Leinster Square, W2 Tel: 0171 229 9641 Fax: 0171 221 5255
Bayswater or Queensway Underground

MUSEUM INN

British Museum/ West End/ Soho
27 Montague Street, WC1 Tel: 0171 580 5360 Fax: 0171 636 7948
Russell Square or Tottenham Court Road Underground

QUEST HOTEL

Hyde Park/ Kensington Palace/ Portobello Market
45 Queensborough Terrace, W2 Tel: 0171 229 7782 Fax: 0171 727 8106
Queensway or Bayswater Underground

VICTORIA HOTEL

Big Ben/ Tate Gallery/ River Thames
71 Belgrave Road, SW1 Tel: 0171 834 3077 Fax: 0171 932 0693
Pimlico or Victoria   Underground Station

For more info: www.scoot.co.uk/astorhostels/
E-mail: AstorHostels@msn.com or 100572.3612@compuserve.com
Astor Hostels are members of BTA and London Tourist Board.
Credit cards accepted.

ESSENTIALS

dent travel agencies issue ISICs, including STA Travel in Australia and New Zealand; Travel CUTS in Canada; USIT in the Republic of Ireland and Northern Ireland; SASTS in South Africa; Campus Travel and STA Travel in the UK; Council Travel (www.counciltravel.com/idcards/index.htm) and STA Travel in the US (see p. 51). The *ISIC Handbook* lists available discounts by country. The card is valid from September of one year to December of the following year and costs AUS$15, CDN$15, or US$20. Applicants must be degree-seeking students of a secondary or post-secondary school and must be of at least 12 years of age. Because of the proliferation of fake ISICs, some services (particularly airlines) require additional proof of student identity, such as a letter attesting to your student status, signed by your registrar and stamped with your school seal, or a school ID card. The **International Teacher Identity Card (ITIC)** offers the same insurance coverage as well as similar but limited discounts. The fee is AUS$13, UK£5, or US$20. For more info, contact the **International Student Travel Confederation (ISTC),** Herengracht 479, 1017 BS Amsterdam, Netherlands (tel. (20) 421 28 00; fax 421 28 10; email istcinfo@istc.org; www.istc.org).

YOUTH IDENTIFICATION. The International Student Travel Confederation issues a discount card to travelers who are 25 years old or under, but are not students. This one-year **International Youth Travel Card** (**IYTC;** formerly the **GO 25** Card) offers many of the same benefits as the ISIC. Most organizations that sell the ISIC also sell the IYTC (US$20).

CUSTOMS

Upon entering a country, you must declare certain items from abroad and pay a duty on the value that exceeds that country's allowance. **Duty-free** allowances were abolished for travel between EU member states on July 1, 1999, but still exist for those arriving from outside the EU. Make a list of any valuables brought from home and register them with customs before your departure to avoid import duty charges and to simplify your return. Upon returning home, you must similarly declare all articles acquired abroad and pay a duty on the value of articles in excess of your country's allowance. Keep receipts to expedite your return.

FURTHER RESOURCES ON CUSTOMS REQUIREMENTS.
Australia: Australian Customs National Information Line (tel. (01) 30 03 63; www.customs.gov.au).
Canada: Canadian Customs, 2265 St. Laurent Blvd, Ottawa, ON K1G 4K3 (tel. (613) 993-0534 or (800) 461-9999 (24hr.); www.revcan.ca).
Ireland: The Collector of Customs and Excise, The Custom House, Dublin 1 (tel. (01) 679 27 77; fax 671 20 21; www.revenue.ie/customs.htm).
New Zealand: New Zealand Customhouse, 17-21 Whitmore St, Box 2218, Weelington (tel. (04) 473 60 99; fax 473 73 70; www.customs.govt.nz).
South Africa: Commissioner for Customs and Excise, Private Bag X47, Pretoria 0001 (tel. (012) 314 99 11; fax 328 64 78).
United Kingdom: Her Majesty's Customs and Excise, Custom House, Nettleton Rd, Heathrow Airport, Hounslow, Middlesex TW6 2LA (tel. (020) 89 10 36 02 or 89 10 35 66; fax 89 10 37 65; www.hmce.gov.uk).
United States: US Customs Service, Box 7407, Washington DC 20044 (tel. (202) 927-6724; www.customs.ustreas.gov).

MONEY

CURRENCY AND EXCHANGE

Banks often use a three-letter code for national currencies (for example, NOK for Norwegian kroner). We list this code at the beginning of each country chapter along with the September 1999 exchange rates between local currency and US dollars (US$), Canadian dollars (CDN$), British pounds (UK£), Irish pounds (IR£),

ESSENTIALS

HOSTELLING INTERNATIONAL
AMERICAN YOUTH HOSTELS

The most

important

thing you'll

bring to

Europe ...

American Youth Hostels
733 15th Street, NW, Suite 840
Washington, DC 20005 USA

HOSTELLING INTERNATIONAL

Susan Smith
41 Elm Street
Anytown   MD   20902
060-3223239   11/75
                                         Date of Birth
Expires end 12/00   Adult
                                         Category
Signature   Susan Smith

(aside from your passport!)

Tuscany, Italy

Derbyshire, U.K.

Tilff-Liege, Belgium   Amsterdam, Holland   Altena, Germany   Stockholm, Sweden

Don't go abroad without your Hostelling International membership!

Here's why ...

* Access to 4,500 hostels in more than 70 countries at member rates.

* Thousands of local discounts on transportation, food, gear, local attractions and cultural amenities.

* A members-only reservation system that allows you to "book your bed ahead."

* Assurance of high-quality, budget accommodations where you can meet other travelers from around the world.

For reservations or information:
733 15th Street, N.W., Suite 840, Washington, D.C. 20005 1-202-783-6161
Fax: 1-202-783-6171 www.hiayh.org E-mail hiayhserv@hiayh.org

And it's a lot easier to get than a passport!

Call 1-202-783-6161 or order
online at www.hiayh.org

HOSTELLING INTERNATIONAL

THE EURO. On January 1, 1999, 11 members of the European Union—Austria, Belgium, Finland, France, Germany, Ireland, Italy, Luxembourg, the Netherlands, Portugal, and Spain—accepted the euro as their common currency. Euro notes and coins will gradually begin to replace notes and coins in national currencies as of January 1, 2002, and cash euros will be the only accepted form of currency starting July 1, 2002. Non-cash payments such as bank transfers, checks, and credit card payments can already be made in euros. As cash euros will not yet be in circulation in 2000, *Let's Go* still lists all prices in national currencies.

Exchange rates are fixed at 1 EUR = 40.3399 BEF (Belgian francs) = 1.95583 DEM (German marks) = 166.386 ESP (Spanish pesetas) = 6.55957 FRF (French francs) = 0.787564 IEP (Irish pounds) = 1936.27 ITL (Italian liras) = 40.3399 LUF (Luxembourgeois francs) = 2.20371 NLG (Dutch guilders) = 13.7603 ATS (Austrian schillings) = 200.482 PTE (Portuguese escudos) = 5.94573 FIM (Finnish markka). Henceforth, *bureaux de change* will be obliged to exchange eurozone currencies at these official rates and at no commission (though they may still charge a nominal service fee). For more info, see www.europa.eu.int.

Australian dollars (AUS$), New Zealand dollars (NZ$), South African Rand (SAR), and European Union euros (EUR€). Check a large newspaper or the web (e.g. finance.yahoo.com or www.bloomberg.com) for the latest exchange rates.

It is more expensive to buy foreign currency than domestic. In other words, French francs are cheaper in France than in the US. However, you should bring enough foreign currency to last for the first 24 to 72 hours of a trip to avoid being penniless should you arrive after bank hours or on a holiday. Travelers from the US can get foreign currency from the comfort of home: **Capital Foreign Exchange** (tel. (888) 842-0880) or **International Currency Express** (tel. (888) 278-6628) deliver foreign currency or traveler's checks overnight (US$15) or 2nd-day (US$12) at competitive exchange rates.

When changing money abroad, try to go only to banks or *bureaux de change* that have at most a 5% margin between their buy and sell prices. Since you lose money with every transaction, **convert large sums** (unless the currency is depreciating rapidly), **but no more than you'll need.** Some countries, such as the Czech Republic, Slovakia, and Russia, may require transaction receipts to reconvert local currency, and a few may not allow you to convert it back at all.

If you use traveler's checks or bills, carry some in small denominations (the equivalent of US$50 or less) for times when you are forced to exchange money at disadvantageous rates, but bring a range of denominations, since charges may be levied per check cashed. Store your money in a variety of forms; ideally, you will at any given time be carrying some cash, some traveler's checks, and an ATM and/or credit card. Australians and New Zealanders should also consider carrying some US dollars or German marks (about US$50 or DM95 worth), which are often preferred by local tellers. In some places (e.g. Eastern European hotels), Western currency is preferred to local, but avoid using Western money when you can; throwing dollars around is offensive, attracts theft, and invites locals to jack up their prices.

TRAVELER'S CHECKS

Traveler's checks (**American Express** and **Visa** are the most recognized) are one of the safest and least troublesome means of carrying funds. Several agencies and banks sell them for a small commission. Each agency provides refunds if your checks are lost or stolen, and many provide additional services, such as toll-free refund hotlines abroad, emergency message services, and stolen credit card assistance.

While traveling, keep check receipts and a record of which checks you've cashed separate from the checks themselves, and leave a list of check numbers with someone at home. Never countersign checks until you're ready to cash them, and always bring your passport with you to cash them. If your checks are lost or stolen, immediately contact a refund center (of the company that issued your checks) in Europe

The Thomas Cook Continental Timetable is **FREE** with rail orders over $1,000

German train station

Rail Map and Eurail Pass

The search for the perfect railpass and backpack has ended

The Backpack Traveler offers expert advice and service on railpasses, backpacks, youth hostels and travel gear

Our goal is to make your trip safe, comfortable and easy while saving you money.

With your Eurail/Europass you'll receive the lowest price available plus the following special offers:

- **Free** 2nd day shipping
- **Free** rail map
- **Free** timetable
- **Free** Eurail video
- **Free** 500 page rail guide
- **Free** Thomas Cook Continental Timetable on rail orders over $1,000

We carry a great selection of backpacks and over a hundred travel products including sleep sacks, money belts and laundry gear. Most backpacks include **free** shipping!

- When you buy a Eurail or Europass, you'll receive $20 off any Jansport backpack
- Youth hostel memberships and ISE Student Discount Cards are available
- Our entire catalog is now online at: www.europebytrain.com

Call today for a FREE catalog and railpass brochure 1-800-688-9577

The Backpack Traveler
PO Box 1386, San Juan Capistrano, CA 92693
www.europebytrain.com

Catalog and rail brochure

to be reimbursed; they may require a police report verifying the loss or theft. Less-touristed countries may not have refund centers at all, in which case you might have to wait to be reimbursed. Ask about toll-free refund hotlines and the location of refund centers when purchasing checks, and always carry emergency cash.

American Express: In Australia call (800) 25 19 02; in New Zealand (0800) 44 10 68; in the UK (0800) 52 13 13; in the US and Canada (800) 221-7282; elsewhere call US collect +1 (801) 964-6665; www.aexp.com. Traveler's checks available in 9 currencies at 1-4% commission at AmEx offices and banks, commission-free at AAA offices (see p. 64).

Citicorp: In the US and Canada call (800) 645-6556; in Europe, the Middle East, or Africa call the UK +44 (020) 75 08 70 07; elsewhere call US collect +1 (813) 623-1709. Traveler's checks available in 7 currencies at 1-2% commission. Call 24hr.

Thomas Cook MasterCard: In the US and Canada call (800) 223-7373; in the UK call (0800) 62 21 01; elsewhere call UK collect +44 (1733) 31 89 50. Checks available in 13 currencies at 2% commission. Thomas Cook offices cash checks commission-free.

Visa: In the US call (800) 227-6811; in the UK (0800) 89 50 78; elsewhere call UK collect +44 (1733) 31 89 49.

CREDIT CARDS

Where they are accepted, credit cards often offer superior exchange rates. They may also offer services such as insurance or emergency help, and are sometimes required to reserve hotel rooms or rental cars. **MasterCard** (a.k.a. EuroCard or Access in Europe) and **Visa** (a.k.a. Carte Bleue or Barclaycard) are the most welcomed; **American Express** cards work at some ATMs and at AmEx offices and major airports. However, budget travelers will probably find that few of the establishments they frequent will accept credit cards, so aside from the occasional splurge, you will probably reserve use of your credit card for financial emergencies.

Credit cards are also useful for **cash advances,** which allow you to extract local currency from associated banks and teller machines throughout Europe (particularly Western Europe) instantly. However, pricey transaction fees for all credit card advances (up to US$10 per advance, plus 2-3% extra on foreign transactions after conversion) tend to make credit cards a more costly way of withdrawing cash than ATMs or traveler's checks. In an emergency, however, the transaction fee may prove worth the cost. To be eligible for an advance, you'll need a PIN (see below).

CREDIT CARD COMPANIES. Visa (US tel. (800) 336-8472) and **MasterCard** (US tel. (800) 307-7309) are issued in cooperation with banks and some other organizations. **American Express** (US tel. (800) 843-2273) has an annual fee of up to US$55. AmEx cardholders may cash personal checks at AmEx offices abroad, access an emergency medical and legal assistance hotline (24hr.), and enjoy American Express Travel Service benefits (including plane, hotel, and car rental reservation changes, baggage loss and flight insurance, mailgram and international cable services, and held mail). **Diner's Club** (US tel. (800) 234-6377; elsewhere call US collect +1 (303) 799-1504) is also often accepted, but less preferred, across Europe.

CASH (ATM) CARDS

Cash cards—popularly called **ATM** (Automated Teller Machine) **cards**—are widespread in Europe. Depending on the system that your home bank uses, you can most likely access your personal bank account from abroad. ATMs get the same wholesale exchange rate as credit cards, but there is often a limit on the amount of money you can withdraw per day (around US$500), and computer networks sometimes fail. There is typically also a surcharge of US$1-5 per withdrawal. The two major international money networks are **Cirrus** (US tel. (800) 424-7787) and **PLUS** (US tel. (800) 843-7587). To locate ATMs around the world, call the above numbers, or consult www.visa.com/pd/atm or www.mastercard.com/atm.

©1999 Western Union Holdings, Inc. All Rights Reserved.

Money From Home In Minutes.

If you're stuck for cash on your travels, don't panic. Millions of people trust Western Union to transfer money in minutes to 165 countries and over 50,000 locations worldwide. Our record of safety and reliability is second to none. For more information, call Western Union: USA 1-800-325-6000, Canada 1-800-235-0000. Wherever you are, you're never far from home.

www.westernunion.com

The fastest way to send money worldwide.

PLEASE, SIR, MAY I HAVE SOME MORE? Most European ATMs don't have letters on their keypads, so if you have an ATM card and rely on letters to remember your **Personal Identification Number (PIN),** here's how to convert it to numeric form: the letters ABC correspond to 2; DEF to 3; GHI to 4; JKL to 5; MNO to 6; PRS to 7; TUV to 8; and WXY to 9. If your PIN is longer than four digits, ask your bank whether can just use the first four, or whether you'll need a new one. **Credit cards** in North America don't usually come with PINs, so if you intend to hit up ATMs in Europe with a credit card to get cash advances, call your credit card company before leaving to request one.

ESSENTIALS

GETTING MONEY FROM HOME

AMERICAN EXPRESS. Cardholders can withdraw cash from their checking accounts at any of AmEx's major offices and many representative offices (up to US$1000 every 21 days; no service charge, no interest). AmEx "Express Cash" withdrawals from any AmEx ATMs in Europe are automatically debited from the cardholder's checking account or line of credit. Green card holders may withdraw up to US$1000 in any seven-day period (2% transaction fee; minimum US$2.50, maximum US$20). To enroll in Express Cash, cardmembers may call (800) 227-4669 in the US; elsewhere call the US collect +1 (336) 668-5041.

WESTERN UNION. Travelers from Canada, the UK, and the US can wire money abroad through Western Union's international money transfer services. The sending fee depends on the amount to be wired as well the method of transfer. For example, transferring up to US$200 to Europe involves a US$22 fee if delivered to a Western Union location by the sendee in cash, but a US$33 fee if ordered over the phone via credit card. The money is usually available at the place to which you're sending it within an hour. In Canada call (800) 235-0000; in the UK (0800) 83 38 33; in the US (800) 325-6000. To find Western Union locations in Europe, call one of the above numbers or consult www.westernunion.com.

US STATE DEPARTMENT (US CITIZENS ONLY). In dire emergencies only, the US State Department will forward money within hours to the nearest consular office, which will then disburse it according to instructions for a US$15 fee. Contact the Overseas Citizens Service, American Citizens Services, Consular Affairs, Room 4811, US Department of State, Washington, DC 20520 (tel. (202) 647-5225; nights, Sundays, and holidays 647-4000; http://travel.state.gov).

COSTS

The cost of your trip will vary considerably, depending on where you go, how you travel, and where you stay. The single biggest cost of your trip will probably be your round-trip (return) **airfare** to Europe (see p. 49); a **railpass** would be another major pre-departure expense (see p. 59). Before you go, spend some time calculating a reasonable per-day **budget** that will meet your needs, then try to stick to it while on the road. To give you a general idea, a bare-bones day in **Western Europe** (camping or sleeping in hostels, buying food at supermarkets) would cost about US$25-35, excluding the cost of a plane ticket and railpass; a slightly more comfortable day (sleeping in hostels and the occasional budget hotel, eating one meal a day at a restaurant, going out at night) would run US$35-50; and for a luxurious day, the sky's the limit. You can expect to spend US$5-15 less per day in **Eastern Europe** or **Turkey;** similarly, if you will be traveling in **Scandinavia,** add on US$10-15 per day. If you're **camping** or traveling by campervan, knock off US$5-10, more if you plan to take advantage of free camping. For example, the typical first-time, under-26 traveler planning to spend most of his or her time in Western Europe and then tack on a quick jaunt into Eastern Europe, sleeping in hostels and traveling on a two-month unlimited Eurail pass, can probably expect to spend about US$2000, plus cost of plane fare (US$300-800), railpass (US$882), and a backpack (US$150-400). Don't forget to factor in emergency reserve funds (at least US$200).

ESSENTIALS

BUSABOUT
www.busabout.com
Europe

The Flexible Hop on Hop Off Coach Pass

30% cheaper than a rail pass

- English Speaking Driver and On-Board-Rep on every coach-Gives help and information and even arrange accommodation

NO HIDDEN COSTS

Hits 60 of Europe's hottest destinations

- Unlimited travel passes from 2 weeks to 6 months
- Flexi-passes available
- Amazing add-ons to Greece, Eastern Europe, Morrocco and more...
- Incredibly cheap London Link service
- Travel in style -Latest European Motorcoaches with stereo and video
- Travel in comfort -Air conditioned smoke free environment
- Bedabout accommodation deals from US$14 per day.

Get your brochure from your travel agent or local student travel office, or email us at our website **www.busabout.com**

TIPS FOR STAYING ON A BUDGET

Considering that saving US$5 per day for a week will fund an entire additional day of travel, the art of penny-pinching is well worth learning. Learn to take advantage of freebies: for example, **museums** in Europe will typically be free once a week or once a month, and cities often host free open-air **concerts** and/or **cultural events** (especially in the summer). Buy food in **supermarkets** instead of eating out; you'd be surprised how tasty (and cheap) simple bread can be with cheese or spread. Bring a **sleepsack** (see p. 35) to save on sheet charges in hostels, and do your **laundry** in the sink (unless you're explicitly prohibited from doing so). Split **accommodations** costs (in hotels and some hostels) with fellow trustworthy travelers; multi-bed rooms almost always work out cheaper per person than singles. The same principle will also work for cutting down on the cost of **restaurant** meals. For long trips, you can avoid accommodations costs entirely by taking **overnight trains,** though you will have to fork over extra cash if you want a couchette or sleeper (see p. 59).

With that said, don't go overboard with your budget obsession. Though US$1 may seem like a near-trivial amount at home, many travelers find that once they hit the road, their perception of that same amount becomes inflated. Though staying within your budget is important, don't do so at the expense of your sanity. After all, going to Munich without hitting a beer garden or visiting London without seeing a play simply because it's "out of your budget" defeats the purpose of your visit.

TAXES

The European Union imposes a **value-added tax (VAT)** on goods and services purchased within the EU (usually included in the sticker price). Non-EU citizens may obtain a **refund** for taxes paid on retail goods, but not those on services. As the VAT in Europe ranges from 15 to 25%, you may find it worth the hassle of filing for a refund. In order to do so, you must first obtain a Tax-free Shopping Cheque, available from shops sporting the blue, white, and silver Europe Tax-free Shopping logo, and then save the receipts from all of the purchases for which you want to be refunded. Upon leaving the last EU country on your itinerary, present your (unused) goods, invoices, and Tax-free Shopping Cheque to Customs for validation, then pick up an immediate cash refund at an ETS cash refund office or file for a refund once back home. Keep in mind that goods must be taken out of the country within three months of the end of the month of purchase, and that some stores require minimum purchase amounts to become eligible for refund. For more information on tax-free shopping, visit www.globalrefund.com.

SAFETY AND SECURITY

In 1999, the US Department of State issued **travel warnings** for Bosnia-Herzegovina, Croatia, FYR Macedonia, Moldova, Russia, and the Yugoslav provinces of Serbia and Montenegro. All of the travel warnings with the exception of Russia were at least indirectly related to the NATO bombings in Yugoslavia in the spring of 1999. Because of the bombings and at the advice of the State Department, *Let's Go* was unable to send researchers to Yugoslavia and FYR Macedonia; as a result, they are not included in this year's guide. In addition, travelers should avoid the Trans-Dniester region of Moldova, Eastern Slavonia in Croatia, the Republika Srpska in Bosnia-Herzegovina, and the Chechnya province in Russia. For more info, consult http://travel.state.gov/travel_warnings.html.

While tourists may be more vulnerable than the average individual, a few simple precautions will help you avoid problems. In countries like Russia and Turkey, you may need to take extra care. Crime in Russia, from petty robbery to murder, has been rising over the past decade, and terrorist attacks are a growing problem in Turkey. The Balkans, the former Soviet Republics, and Northern Ireland have also

ESSENTIALS

ESSENTIALS

YOUTH & STUDENT TRAVEL CENTRE

More fun... less money!

Domestic and international discount airfares

Budget accommodation

Ferries to Greece and Sardinia

Car rentals

Tours and excursions

Rail and coaches pass

✗ ROME
Via Genova, 16 - tel. 06.4620431
Corso Vittorio Emanuele II, 297- tel. 06.6872672
Telesales 06.46204385

✗ FLORENCE
Via dei Ginori, 25/R - tel. 055.289570/289721
Telesales 055.216660

✗ MILAN
Via S. Antonio, 2 - tel. 02.584751
Telesales 02.58475223-4

✗ NAPLES
Via Mezzocannone, 25 - tel. 081.5527960

✗ VENICE
Dorso Duro Ca' Foscari, 3252 - tel. 041.5205660

✗ PARIS • CTS VOYAGES
20, Rue de Carmes, 75005 Paris
tel. 0033.1. 43296094 - 43250076

✗ LONDON • CTS TRAVEL
44, Goodge St. - WIP 2AD - tel. 0044.171.5804554
Telesales
Europe 0171 636 0031 - Worldwide 0171 636 0032

More than 140 offices in Italy

WEB SITE: www.cts.it

been problem areas in recent years. Be aware that certain disgruntled groups, like the skinheads in Germany and Hungary, Basque terrorists in Spain, the Mafia in Sicily, and the *Romany* (also known as Gypsies) in Paris may pose a problem. See specific country introductions for more information.

EXPLORING. To avoid unwanted attention, try to blend in as much as possible. Respecting local customs (in many cases, dressing more conservatively) may placate would-be hecklers. Familiarize yourself with your surroundings before setting out; if you must check a map on the street, duck into a café or shop. Also, carry yourself with confidence—an obviously bewildered bodybuilder is more likely to be harassed than a confident 98-pound weakling. If you are traveling alone, be sure someone at home knows your itinerary, and **never admit that you're traveling alone.**

When walking at night, stick to busy, well-lit streets and avoid dark alleyways. Do not attempt to cross through parks, parking lots, or other large, deserted areas. Look for children playing, women walking in the open, and other signs of an active community. Keep in mind that a district can change character drastically between blocks. If you feel uncomfortable, leave as quickly and directly as you can, but don't allow fear of the unknown to turn you into a hermit. Careful, persistent exploration will build confidence and make your stay in an area that much more rewarding.

GETTING AROUND. **Trains** are very safe throughout most of Europe, and second-class travel is more than comfortable. **Overnight trains** put you at the most risk, as your vigilance is limited while you are sleeping. For tips on protecting your valuables on overnight trains and buses, see p. 27. If you are using a **car,** learn local driving signals and wear a seatbelt. Children under 40 lb. (18kg) should ride only in a specially designed carseat, available for a small fee from most car rental agencies. If you plan on spending a lot of time on the road, bring spare parts. For long drives in desolate areas, invest in a cellular phone and a roadside assistance program (see p. 64). Be sure to park your vehicle in a garage or well-traveled area, and use a steering wheel locking device in larger cities. Don't sleep in your car; it's not only dangerous, but also often illegal. *Let's Go* does not recommend **hitchhiking** under any circumstances, particularly for women (see p. 58).

SELF-DEFENSE. There is no sure-fire way to avoid all the threatening situations you might encounter when you travel. A good self-defense course will give you more concrete ways to react to different types of aggression. **Impact, Prepare, and Model Mugging** can refer you to local self-defense courses in the US (tel. (800) 345-5425) and Vancouver, Canada (tel. (604) 878-3838). Workshops (2-3hr.) start at US$50, and full courses run US$350-500. Both women and men are welcome.

TRAVEL ADVISORIES. The following government offices provide travel information and advisories by telephone, by fax, or via the web:

Australian Department of Foreign Affairs and Trade: Tel. (02) 62 61 11 11; fax 62 61 31 11. www.dfat.gov.au.

Canadian Department of Foreign Affairs and International Trade (DFAIT): Tel. (800) 267-8376, from Ottawa (613) 944-4000; auto faxback (800) 575-2500, from Ottawa (613) 944-2500. www.dfait-maeci.gc.ca.

New Zealand Ministry of Foreign Affairs: Tel. (04) 494 85 00; fax 494 85 11. www.mft.govt.nz/trav.html.

United Kingdom Foreign and Commonwealth Office: Tel. (020) 72 38 45 03; fax 72 38 45 45. www.fco.gov.uk/travel.

United States Department of State: Tel. (202) 647-5225, auto faxback (202) 647-3000. For *A Safe Trip Abroad,* call (202) 512-1800. travel.state.gov.

FINANCIAL SECURITY

PROTECTING YOUR VALUABLES. Walking down the street thumbing large wads of cash will make you an attractive target, especially when you are unfamiliar with your surroundings. First, **bring as little with you as possible.** Leave expensive

ESSENTIALS

travel

Travel helps you remember who you forgot to be.....

photograph by Jennifer Cavallaro.

Council *Travel*

Stop by one of our 65 offices
listed on
www.counciltravel.com
Or call: 1-800-2COUNCIL

watches, jewelry, cameras, and electronic equipment (like your Discman) at home; chances are you'd break it, lose it, or get sick of lugging it around anyway. Second, buy a couple small combination **padlocks** to secure them either in your pack (when it's in sight) or in a hostel or train station locker, and **never leave your pack unattended** (especially in hostels or train stations). Third, **carry as little cash as possible;** instead carry traveler's checks and/or ATM/credit cards. Leave your purse or wallet at home, and instead carry the bulk of your cash in a **money belt** along with your traveler's checks, passport, and ATM/credit or ID cards. A neck pouch is okay, but is more conspicuous (and thus less safe) than a money belt—"fanny packs" are even worse. Fourth, **keep at least one reserve separate from your primary stash.** This should entail about US$50 worth of cash (US$ or German DM is best) sewn into or stored in the depths of your pack, along with your traveler's check numbers and important photocopies.

CON ARTISTS AND PICKPOCKETS. Among the more colorful aspects of large cities are **con artists.** They often work in groups, and children are among the most effective. They possess an innumerable range of ruses. Beware of certain classics: sob stories that require money, rolls of bills "found" on the street, mustard spilled (or saliva spit) onto your shoulder to distract you while they snatch your bag. Don't ever hand over your passport to someone whose authority you question (ask to accompany them to a police station if they insist), and **don't ever let your passport out of your sight.** Similarly, don't let your bag out of sight; never trust a "station-porter" who insists on carrying your bag or stowing it in the baggage compartment, or a "new friend" who offers to guard your bag while you buy a train ticket or use the restroom. Beware **pickpockets** in city crowds, especially on public transportation. Also, be alert in public telephone booths: if you must say your calling card number, do so very quietly; if you punch it in, make sure no one can look over your shoulder.

ACCOMMODATIONS AND TRANSPORTATION. Never leave your belongings unattended; crime occurs in even the most demure-looking hostel or hotel. Bring your own **padlock** for hostel lockers, and don't ever store valuables in any locker.

Be particularly careful on **buses;** carry your backpack in front of you where you can see it, and don't trust anyone to watch your bag, even for a second. Thieves thrive on **trains;** horror stories abound about determined thieves who wait for travelers to fall asleep, or even use gas or chloroform on entire compartments in order to steal passengers' belongings. When traveling with others, sleep in alternate shifts. When alone, use good judgement in selecting a train compartment: never stay in an empty one, and use a lock to secure your pack to the luggage rack. Keep important documents and other valuables on your person, and try to sleep on top bunks with your luggage stored above you (if not in bed with you).

If traveling by **car,** don't leave valuable possessions (such as radios or luggage) in it while you are away, especially not in a visible place. If your tape deck or radio is removable, hide it in the trunk or take it with you. If it isn't, at least conceal it under something else. Similarly, hide baggage in the trunk—although savvy thieves can tell if a car is heavily loaded by the way it sits on its tires.

DRUGS AND ALCOHOL

Drug and alcohol laws vary widely throughout Europe: whereas in the Netherlands you can buy soft drugs on the open market, in Turkey and much of Eastern Europe drug possession may lead to a prison sentence. You're subject to the laws of the country in which you travel when you're abroad, so familiarize yourself with those laws before leaving. If you carry **prescription drugs,** it is vital to have both a copy of the prescriptions themselves and a note from a doctor, especially at border crossings. **Avoid public drunkenness;** it is culturally unacceptable and against the law in many countries, and can also jeopardize your safety.

ESSENTIALS

ESSENTIALS

travel

The journey *is* the reward.....

-Tao saying

Council *Travel*

Stop by one of our 65 offices
listed on
www.counciltravel.com
Or call: 1-800-2COUNCIL

HEALTH AND INSURANCE

Common sense is the simplest prescription for good health while you travel. Travelers complain most often about their feet and their gut, so take precautionary measures: drink lots of fluids to prevent dehydration and constipation, wear sturdy, broken-in shoes and clean socks, and use talcum powder to keep your feet dry.

BEFORE YOU GO

Europe, particularly Western Europe, is in general very safe health-wise, but before you go, do some research on the areas you'll be visiting to ensure that you are adequately inoculated and insured for the areas you'll be visiting. Preparation can both minimize the likelihood of contracting a disease and maximize the chances of receiving effective health care in the event of an emergency. For tips on packing a basic **first-aid kit** and other health essentials, see p. 35.

In your **passport,** write the names of any people you wish to be contacted in case of a medical emergency, and also list any allergies or medical conditions of which you would want doctors to be aware. Matching a prescription to a foreign equivalent is not always easy, safe, or possible. Carry up-to-date, legible prescriptions or a statement from your doctor stating the medication's trade name, manufacturer, chemical name, and dosage. While traveling, be sure to keep all medication with you in your carry-on luggage rather than checking it.

IMMUNIZATIONS. Travelers over two years old should be sure that the following vaccines are up to date: MMR (for measles, mumps, and rubella); DTaP or Td (for diptheria, tetanus, and pertussis); OPV (for polio); HbCV (for haemophilus influenza B); and HBV (for hepatitus B). Hepatitis A vaccine and/or immune globulin (IG) is recommended for travelers going to Eastern or Southern Europe. For more **region-specific information** on vaccinations requirements, as well as recommendations on immunizations and prophylaxis, consult the CDC (see below) in the US or the equivalent in your home country, and check with a doctor for guidance.

USEFUL ORGANIZATIONS. The US **Centers for Disease Control and Prevention** (**CDC;** tel. (888) 232-3299; www.cdc.gov/travel/travel.html) is an excellent source of information for travelers and maintains an international fax information service. To purchase the CDC's booklet *Health Information for International Travelers* (US$20), an annual rundown of disease, immunization, and general health advice for particular countries, send a check or money order to the Superintendent of Documents, US Government Printing Office, P.O. Box 371954, Pittsburgh, PA 15250-7954, or order by phone (tel. (202) 512-1800). The **US State Department** (http://travel.state.gov) compiles Consular Information Sheets on health, entry requirements, and other issues for various countries. Their *Medical Information for Americans Traveling Abroad* includes contact information for medical evacuation services and travel insurance firms (travel.state.gov/medical.html).

For detailed information on travel health, including a country-by-country overview of diseases, try the **International Travel Health Guide,** Stuart Rose, MD (Travel Medicine, US$20). Info is also available at Travel Medicine's website (www.travmed.com). For general health info, contact the **American Red Cross.** To buy the *First-Aid and Safety Handbook* (US$5), call or write the American Red Cross, 285 Columbus Ave, Boston, MA 02116-5114 (tel. (800) 564-1234).

MEDICAL ASSISTANCE ON THE ROAD. Medical care in most of Europe, particularly Western Europe, is excellent. But if you are concerned about being able to access medical support while traveling, there are special support services you may employ. The **MedPass** from **Global Emergency Medical Services (GEMS),** 2001 Westside Dr #120, Alpharetta, GA 30004 (US tel. (800) 860-1111; fax (770) 475-0058; www.globalems.com), provides 24-hour international medical assistance, support, and medical evacuation resources. The **International Association for Medical Assistance to Travelers** (**IAMAT;** US tel. (716) 754-4883; www.sentex.net/~iamat) has free member-

GET A JUMP START ON YOUR TRAVEL PLANS!

We'll help you choose the best railpasses for your travel!

EURAIL YOUTHPASSES
Under age 26, 2nd Class

- **Europass Youth** (France, Italy, Germany, Spain, Switzerland)
  5 days in 2 months-$233
  Additional countries and days may be added.
- **Eurail Youth Flexipass**
  10 days in 2 months-$458
  15 days in 2 months-$599
- **Eurail Youthpass**-15 days-$388
  21 days-$499 • 1 month-$623

EURAILPASSES-1st Class

- **Europass Saverpass** (France, Italy, Germany, Spain, Switzerland)
  (Price per person for 2 or more persons traveling together)
  5 days in 2 months-$296
  10 days in 2 months-$450
- **Eurail Flexipass**
  10 days in 2 months-$654
  15 days in 2 months-$862
- **Eurailpass**-15 days-$554
  21 days-$718 • 1 month-$890
- **Prices are subject to change**

- **No shipping fees**
- Ask for a free copy of **"Taking Off"** travel brochure

E-mail us at **edtrav@execpc.com** or call **toll free 1-800-747-5551** (9-5 Monday-Friday) to place your rail or flight order on a major credit card. Identify yourself as a *Let's Go* reader and your order will be **shipped free of charge** by UPS ground track. For **mail orders** send certified check or money order to **Educational Travel Centre, 438 N. Frances Street, Madison, WI 53703**. Indicate items needed, birthdate, address, telephone number and date of departure from the U.S.

- Hostel Memberships
- Additional Eurailpasses, Britrail and individual country passes also available!
- Student & teacher airfares to many European destinations.

Educational Travel Centre
edtrav@execpc.com
http://www.edtrav.com

ship, lists English-speaking doctors worldwide, and offers detailed info on immunization requirements and sanitation. If your regular **insurance** policy does not cover travel abroad, you may wish to purchase additional coverage (see p. 33).

Those with medical conditions (diabetes, allergies to antibiotics, epilepsy, heart conditions, etc.) may want to obtain a stainless-steel **Medic Alert** ID tag (1st year US$35, $15 annually thereafter), which identifies the condition and gives a 24-hour collect-call number. Contact the Medic Alert Foundation, 2323 Colorado Ave, Turlock, CA 95382 (US tel. (800) 825-3785; www.medicalert.org). The **American Diabetes Association**, 1660 Duke St, Alexandria, VA 22314 (US tel. (800) 232-3472), offers copies of the article "Travel and Diabetes" and a multilingual diabetic ID card.

ON THE ROAD

ENVIRONMENTAL HAZARDS

Heat exhaustion and dehydration: Heat exhaustion, characterized by dehydration and salt deficiency, can lead to fatigue, headaches, and wooziness. Avoid it by drinking plenty of fluids, eating salty foods (e.g. crackers), and avoiding dehydrating beverages (e.g. alcohol, coffee, tea, and caffeinated soda). Continuous heat stress can eventually lead to **heatstroke,** characterized by a rising temperature, severe headache, and cessation of sweating. Victims should be cooled off with wet towels and taken to a doctor.

Hypothermia and frostbite: A rapid drop in body temperature is the clearest sign of overexposure to cold. Victims may also shiver, feel exhausted, have poor coordination or slurred speech, hallucinate, or suffer amnesia. *Do not let hypothermia victims fall asleep,* or their body temperature will continue to drop. To avoid hypothermia, keep dry, wear layers, and stay out of the wind. When the temperature is below freezing, watch out for **frostbite.** If skin turns white, waxy, and cold, do not rub the area. Drink warm beverages, get dry, and slowly warm the area with dry fabric or steady body contact until a doctor is found.

High altitude: Allow your body a couple of days to adjust to less oxygen before exerting yourself. Note that alcohol is more potent and UV rays are stronger at high elevations.

INSECT-BORNE DISEASES

Many diseases are transmitted by insects—mainly mosquitoes, fleas, ticks, and lice. Be aware of insects in wet or forested areas, while hiking, and especially while camping. Use insect repellents, e.g. DEET. Wear long pants and long sleeves, and tuck long pants into socks. Soak or spray your gear with permethrin (licensed in the US for use on clothing), take vitamin B-12 or garlic pills as a natural supplement, and consider buying a mosquito net. Calamine lotion or topical cortisones (like Cortaid) may stop insect bites from itching, as can a bath with a half-cup of baking soda or oatmeal. **Mosquitoes** are most active from dusk to dawn. **Ticks**—responsible for Lyme and other diseases—can be particularly dangerous in rural and forested regions. Pause periodically while walking to brush off ticks using a fine-toothed comb on your neck and scalp. Do not try to remove ticks by burning them or coating them with nail polish remover or petroleum jelly.

Tick-borne encephalitis: A viral infection of the central nervous system transmitted through tick bites and the consumption of unpasteurized dairy products. Occurs chiefly in wooded areas of Central and Western Europe. Symptoms can range from nothing to headaches and flu-like symptoms to swelling of the brain (encephalitis). A vaccine is available in Europe, but the immunization schedule is impractical for most tourists.

Lyme disease: A bacterial infection, also carried by ticks, marked by a circular bull's-eye rash of 2 or more in. surrounding the bite. Other symptoms include fever, headache, malaise, and aches and pains. Antibiotics are effective if administered early. Left untreated, Lyme disease can cause problems in joints, the heart, and the nervous system. If you find a tick, grasp the tick's head parts with tweezers as close to your skin as possible and apply slow, steady traction. Removing a tick within 24hr. greatly reduces risk of infection.

FOOD- AND WATER-BORNE DISEASES

Prevention is the best cure: be sure that everything you eat is cooked properly and that the water you drink is clean. Unpeeled fruit and veggies and tap water should

ESSENTIALS

be safe throughout most of Europe, particularly Western Europe, but may not be in parts of Turkey, Southern Europe, or Eastern Europe. Peel your fruits and veggies and avoid tap water (including ice cubes and anything washed in tap water, like salad). Watch out for food from markets or street vendors that may have been washed in dirty water or fried in rancid cooking oil, such as juices or peeled fruits. Other culprits are raw shellfish, unpasteurized milk, and sauces containing raw eggs. Buy bottled water, or purify your own water by bringing it to a rolling boil or treating it with **iodine tablets.** Always wash your hands before eating, or bring a quick-drying purifying liquid hand cleaner. Your bowels will thank you.

Traveler's diarrhea: Results from drinking untreated water or eating uncooked foods; a temporary (and fairly common) reaction to the bacteria in new food ingredients. Symptoms include nausea, bloating, urgency, and malaise. Try quick-energy, non-sugary foods with protein and carbohydrates to keep your strength up. Over-the-counter anti-diarrheals (e.g. Imodium) may counteract the problems, but can complicate serious infections. The most dangerous side effect is dehydration; drink 8 oz. of water with ½ tsp. of sugar or honey and a pinch of salt, try uncaffeinated soft drinks, or munch on salted crackers. If you develop a fever or your symptoms don't go away after 4-5 days, consult a doctor. Consult a doctor for treatment of diarrhea in children.

Cholera: An intestinal disease caused by a bacteria found in contaminated food. A danger in Moldova, the Russian Federation, and the Ukraine. Symptoms include watery diarrhea, dehydration, vomiting, and muscle cramps. See a doctor immediately; if left untreated, you may die. Antibiotics are available, but rehydration is most important.

Hepatitis A: A viral infection of the liver acquired primarily through contaminated water, but also through sexual contact. An intermediate risk in Eastern Europe. Symptoms include fatigue, fever, loss of appetite, nausea, dark urine, jaundice, vomiting, aches and pains, and light stools. Risk is highest in rural areas and the countryside.

Parasites: Microbes, tapeworms, etc. that hide in unsafe water and food. Symptoms include swollen glands or lymph nodes, fever, rashes or itchiness, digestive problems, eye problems, and anemia. Boil water, wear shoes, avoid bugs, and eat only cooked food.

OTHER INFECTIOUS DISEASES

Hepatitis B: A viral infection of the liver transmitted via bodily fluids or needle-sharing. Symptoms may not surface until years after infection. The CDC recommends vaccinations for health-care workers, sexually-active travelers, and anyone planning to seek medical treatment abroad. The 3-shot vaccination series must begin 6 mo. before traveling.

Hepatitis C: Like Hep B, but the mode of transmission differs. IV drug users, those with occupational exposure to blood, hemodialysis patients, and recipients of blood transfusions are at the highest risk, but the disease can also be spread through sexual contact or sharing items like razors and toothbrushes that may have traces of blood on them.

AIDS, HIV, AND STDS

The virus that leads to **Acquired Immune Deficiency Syndrome (AIDS)** is most easily transmitted through direct blood-to-blood contact with an HIV-positive person, but is most commonly transmitted by sexual intercourse. *Never* share intravenous drug, tattooing, or other needles, and take precautions to avoid any blood transfusions or injections while abroad (if you do need medical care, ask to receive screened blood and sterilized equipment). Take along a supply of latex condoms, which are often difficult to find on the road. Some countries (including Lithuania, Luxembourg, Russia, Slovakia, and the Ukraine) screen incoming travelers for HIV, primarily those planning extended visits for work or study, and deny entrance to those who are HIV-positive. Contact consulates for more info, particularly if you plan an extended stay. For more info on AIDS, call the US **Centers for Disease Control** (tel. (800) 342-2437). For statistical information, contact the **World Health Organization,** Attn: UNAIDS Program, Avenue Appia 20, 1211 Geneva 27, Switzerland (tel. +41 (22) 791 21 11; www.who.int/emc-hiv). Council's brochure *Travel Safe: AIDS and International Travel* is available at Council Travel offices and their website (www.ciee.org/study/safety/travelsafe.htm).

Sexually transmitted diseases (STDs) such as gonorrhea, chlamydia, genital warts, syphilis, and herpes are easier to catch than HIV, and can be just as deadly. **Hepatitis B** and **C** are also serious STDs (see above). Though condoms may protect you from some STDs, oral and tactile contact can also sometimes lead to transmission. Warning signs for STDs include: swelling, sores, bumps, or blisters on sex organs, rectum, or mouth; burning and pain during urination or bowel movements; itching around sex organs; swelling or redness in the throat; and/or flu-like symptoms with fever, chills, and aches. If these symptoms develop, see a doctor immediately.

WOMEN'S HEALTH

Women traveling in unsanitary conditions are vulnerable to **urinary tract** and **bladder infections,** common and very uncomfortable bacterial diseases that cause a burning sensation and painful (sometimes frequent) urination. To try to avoid these infections, drink plenty of vitamin-C-rich juice and clean water, and urinate frequently, especially right after intercourse. Untreated, these infections can lead to kidney infections, sterility, and even death. If symptoms persist, see a doctor.

Vaginal yeast infections may flare up in hot and humid climates. Wearing loosely fitting trousers or a skirt and cotton underwear will help, as will over-the-counter remedies like Monostat or Gynelotrimin. Bring supplies from home if you are prone to infection, as they may be difficult to find on the road. In a pinch, some travelers use a natural alternative such as a plain yogurt and lemon juice douche.

Tampons and **pads** are sometimes hard to find when traveling, and your preferred brand may not be available, so consider bringing supplies along. Reliable **contraceptive devices** may also be difficult to find; if you're on the pill or use a diaphragm, bring enough pills or contraceptive jelly, respectively, to allow for possible loss or extended stays. Availability and quality of condoms abroad also varies, so you also might want to bring your favorite brand if you plan to be sexually active.

If you need an **abortion** while abroad, get in touch with the **International Planned Parenthood Federation,** European Regional Office, Regent's College Inner Circle, Regent's Park, London NW1 4NS (tel. (020) 74 87 79 00; fax 74 87 79 50).

INSURANCE

Travel insurance covers four basic areas: medical problems, property loss, trip cancellation/interruption, and emergency evacuation. Although your regular insurance policies may extend to travel-related accidents, you might consider travel insurance if you wouldn't be able to absorb the potential cost of trip cancellation/interruption. Prices for travel insurance purchased separately generally run about US$50 per week for full coverage, while trip cancellation/interruption may be purchased separately at a rate of about US$5.50 per US$100 of coverage.

Medical insurance (especially university policies) often covers costs incurred abroad; check with your provider. **US Medicare** does not cover foreign travel. **Canadians** are protected by their home province's health insurance plan for up to 90 days after leaving the country; check with the provincial Ministry of Health or Health Plan Headquarters for details. **Australians** traveling in the UK, the Netherlands, Sweden, Finland, Italy, and Malta are entitled to many of the services that they would receive at home as part of the Reciprocal Health Care Agreement. **Homeowners' insurance** (or your family's coverage) often covers theft during travel and loss of travel documents (passport, plane ticket, railpass, etc.) up to US$500.

ISIC and **ITIC** (see p. 13) provide basic insurance benefits, including US$100 per day of in-hospital sickness for up to 60 days, US$3000 of accident-related medical reimbursement, and US$25,000 for emergency medical transport. Cardholders have access to a toll-free 24-hour helpline for medical, legal, and financial emergencies overseas (in US and Canada call (800) 626-2427; elsewhere call US collect +1 (713) 267-2525). **American Express** (US tel. (800) 528-4800) grants most cardholders automatic car rental insurance (collision and theft, but not liability) and ground travel accident coverage of US$100,000 on flight purchases made with the card.

ESSENTIALS

Everything you ever wanted to know about backpacking in Europe

hostel reviews - where to party - packing
discussion boards - find travel friends
favourite destinations - cheap flight tactics

EUROTRIP.COM
YOUR BACKPACKIN' EUROPE SITE

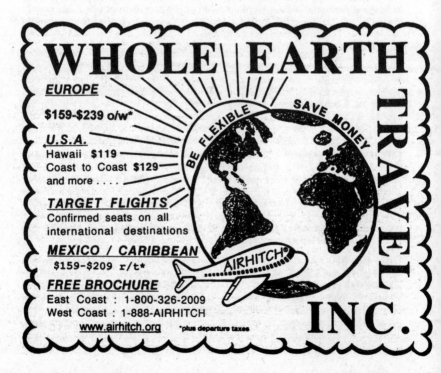

WHOLE EARTH

TRAVEL INC.

BE FLEXIBLE   SAVE MONEY

EUROPE
$159-$239 o/w*

U.S.A.
Hawaii $119
Coast to Coast $129
and more . . . .

TARGET FLIGHTS
Confirmed seats on all
international destinations

MEXICO / CARIBBEAN
$159-$209 r/t*

FREE BROCHURE
East Coast : 1-800-326-2009
West Coast : 1-888-AIRHITCH
www.airhitch.org   *plus departure taxes

AIRHITCH®

INSURANCE PROVIDERS. Council and STA (see p. 51) offer a range of plans that can supplement your basic coverage. Other private insurance providers in the US and Canada include: **Access America** (tel. (800) 284-8300); **Berkely Group/Carefree Travel Insurance** (tel. (800) 323-3149; www.berkely.com); **Globalcare Travel Insurance** (tel. (800) 821-2488; www.globalcare-cocco.com); and **Travel Assistance International** (tel. (800) 821-2828; www.worldwide-assistance.com). Providers in the UK include **Campus Travel** (tel. (01865) 25 80 00) and **Columbus Travel Insurance** (tel. (020) 73 75 00 11). In Australia, try **CIC Insurance** (tel. (02) 92 02 80 00).

PACKING

Pack light: lay out only what you absolutely need, then take half the clothes and twice the money. The less you have, the less you have to lose (or store, or carry on your back). Any extra space left will be useful for any souvenirs or items you might pick up along the way. If you plan to do a lot of hiking, also see **Outdoors,** p. 41.

LUGGAGE. If you plan to cover most of your itinerary by foot, a sturdy **frame backpack** is unbeatable. (For the basics on buying a pack, see p. 45.) Toting a **suitcase** or **trunk** is fine if you plan to live in one or two cities and explore from there, but a very bad idea if you're going to be moving around a lot. In addition to your main vessel, a **daypack** (a small backpack or courier bag) is a must.

CLOTHING. No matter when you're traveling, it's always a good idea to bring a **warm jacket** or wool sweater, a **rain jacket** (Gore-Tex® is both waterproof and breathable), sturdy shoes or **hiking boots,** and **thick socks. Flip-flops** or waterproof sandals are crucial for grubby hostel showers. You may also want to add one outfit beyond the jeans and t-shirt uniform, and maybe a nicer pair of shoes if you have the room. If you plan to visit any religious or cultural sites, remember that you'll need something besides tank tops and shorts to be respectful.

SLEEPSACK. Some hostels require that you either provide your own linen or rent sheets from them. Save cash by making your own sleepsack: fold a full-size sheet in half the long way, then sew it closed along the long side and one of the short sides.

CONVERTERS AND ADAPTERS. In Europe, electricity is 220 volts AC (240V in Britain and Ireland), enough to fry any 110V North American appliance. 220/240V electrical appliances don't like 110V current, either. **Americans** and **Canadians** should buy an **adapter** (which changes the shape of the plug) and a **converter** (which changes the voltage). Don't make the mistake of using only an adapter (unless appliance instructions explicitly state otherwise). **New Zealanders** and **South Africans** (who both use 220V at home) as well as **Australians** (who use 240/250V) won't need a converter, but will need a set of adapters to use anything electrical.

TOILETRIES. Toothbrushes, towels, cold-water soap, talcum powder (to keep feet dry), deodorant, razors, tampons, and condoms are available in Europe, but if you're attached to particular brands, bring them along. **Contact lenses,** on the other hand, may be expensive and difficult to find, so bring enough extra pairs and solution for your entire trip. Also bring a copy of your prescription and your glasses, in case you need emergency replacements. If you use heat-disinfection, either switch temporarily to a chemical disinfection system (check first to make sure it's safe with your brand of lenses), or buy a converter (about US$20) to 220/240V.

FIRST-AID KIT. For a basic first-aid kit, pack bandages, aspirin or other painkiller, antibiotic cream, a thermometer, a Swiss Army knife, tweezers, moleskin, decongestant, motion-sickness remedy, diarrhea or upset-stomach medication (Pepto Bismol or Imodium), an antihistamine, sunscreen, insect repellent, burn ointment, and a syringe for emergencies (get an explanatory letter from your doctor).

FILM. Film and developing in Europe are expensive, so consider bringing enough film for your entire trip and then developing it at home. Amateur photographers may want to bring **disposable cameras** rather than an expensive permanent one.

ESSENTIALS

Foreign Friends™
International Hosting Club

Invites You To
Stay All Over Europe
For $15 Per Night

While Enjoying

Authentic Cultural Experiences

In The Homes of European Club Members.

Foreign Friends

Is The Alternative To
Crowded Hostels and Expensive B&Bs
That Lets You
Live Like The Locals
& See Europe Through Their Eyes.

As a Club Member You Can

Choose the Age and Gender of Your Host
Make Reservations Months or Minutes In Advance
Stay in Parties of Up To 4
& Arrange It all on The Internet!

Each $19 Membership Includes One Free Night!
Visit Our Website At
www.foreign-friends.net
A Unique Addition To Your European Lodging Options

Despite disclaimers, airport security X-rays *can* fog film, so either buy a lead-lined pouch at a camera store or ask the security to hand inspect it. Always pack it in your carry-on luggage, since higher-intensity X-rays are used on checked luggage.

OTHER USEFUL ITEMS. For safety purposes, you should carry a **money belt** and bring a small **padlock.** Basic **outdoors equipment** (plastic water bottle, compass, waterproof matches, pocketknife, sunglasses, hat) may also prove useful. **Quick repairs** can be done on the road with a needle and thread; also consider bringing electrical tape for patching tears. Doing your **laundry** by hand (where it is allowed) is both cheaper and more convenient than doing it at a laundromat—bring detergent, a small rubber ball to stop up the sink, and string for a makeshift clothes line. **Other things** you're liable to forget: an umbrella; sealable **plastic bags** (for damp clothes, soap, food, shampoo, and other spillables); an **alarm clock;** safety pins; rubber bands; a flashlight; earplugs; garbage bags; and a small **calculator.**

IMPORTANT DOCUMENTS. Don't forget your **passport; traveler's checks; ATM** and/or **credit cards;** and adequate **ID** (see p. 13). Also check that you have any of the following that might apply to you: a **hosteling** membership card (see p. 37); **driver's license** (see p. 13); travel **insurance** forms; and/or **rail** or **bus pass** (see p. 58).

ACCOMMODATIONS

HOSTELS

 A HOSTELER'S BILL OF RIGHTS. Unless we state otherwise, you can assume that every hostel we list has certain standard features: no lockout, no curfew, free hot showers, secure luggage storage, and no key deposit.

Europe in the summer is overrun by young budget travelers. Hostels are the hub of this subculture, providing opportunities for young people from all over the world to meet, find travel partners, and learn about places to visit. At US$10-25 per night, only camping is cheaper. Guests tend to be in their teens and 20s, but most hostels welcome travelers of all ages. In northern Europe, many hostels have special family rooms. In the average hostel, however, you and anywhere from one to 50 roommates will sleep on bunk beds in a gender-segregated room, with common bathrooms and a lounge down the hall. The hostel warden may be a laid-back student, a hippie dropout, or a crotchety disciplinarian. Hostels sometimes have kitchens for your use, bike or moped rentals, storage areas, and/or laundry facilities.

However, some hostels close during certain daytime **lockout** hours (from morning to mid-afternoon), have a **curfew** (a distinct cramp in your style if you plan to rage in town), don't accept **reservations,** or impose a **maximum stay.** Conditions are generally spartan and crowded, and you may run into screaming pre-teen tour groups. Quality varies dramatically: some hostels are set in gorgeous castles, others in run-down barracks. Most hostels prohibit sleeping bags: you can typically rent sheets from them, or you can avoid the charge by making a sleepsack (see p. 35).

HOSTELLING INTERNATIONAL

A **hostel membership** allows you to stay at hostels throughout Europe at unbeatable prices, and you usually need not be a youth to benefit (though some German hostels are only open to those under 26). Joining the youth hostel association in your own country (listed below) automatically grants you membership privileges in **Hostelling International (HI),** a federation of national hosteling associations. HI affiliates comply with given standards and regulations and normally display a blue triangle with the symbol of the national hostel association. *Hostelling International: Europe* (UK£7 or US$11; available from national hosteling associations) lists every HI-affiliated hostel in Europe and details the **International Booking Network (IBN),** through which you can book ahead for more than 300 hostels worldwide (US$5 per hostel; V, MC, D only; maximum of 3-7 days advance notice required). To prepay

ESSENTIALS

- JET SKIS - VOLLEYBALL - BILLIARDS - INNER TUBING - WEIGHT ROOM - BASKETBALL - MOTORCYCLES - MOPEDS -

BOAT EXCURSIONS - SCUBA DIVING - WATERSKIING - BASKETBALL - JET SKIS - VOLLEYBALL - MOTORCYCLES - MOPEDS - FOOZBALL - BILLIARDS - INNER TUBING - CLIFF DIVING - WATERSKIING - BASKETBALL

BASKETBALL - BOAT EXCURSIONS - SCUBA DIVING - WATERSKIING - BOAT EXCURSIONS - FOOZBALL - BILLIARDS - SCUBA DIVING - WATERSKIING - WEIGHT ROOM - INNER TUBING - MOPEDS - MOTORCYCLES - VOLLEYBALL - JET SKIS - BASKETBALL - WATERSKIING

Take a Vacation from Your Vacation ...

Experience

THE Pink Palace

CORFU, GREECE

The World's Largest Youth Resort

Recommended
by
LET'S GO
and
FROMMERS

ONLY
$20 per night*

**Breakfast,
Dinner
& Night Club
Included**

Reservations Recommended
Call (661) 53103 / 53104
or Fax: (661) 53025

Private Rooms
Hot Showers - Laundry Service
Giant Jaccuzi - Dancing til Dawn
Breakfast til Noon - Long Distance Calling
Commission-Free Money Exchange

Get a voucher for ONE NIGHT FREE when you book your railpass from:**

Rail Connection™
THE EURAILPASS EXPERTS!
www.railconnection.com
1-888-RAIL-PASS

Council *Travel*

■ TRAVEL CUTS
VOYAGES CAMPUS

The Pink Palace accepts:

* Price in $US at time of printing.
** Based on a minimum stay of 3 nights. Voucher must be stamped by issuing office. One per person per stay. Offer may be discontinued at any time.

- CLIFF DIVING - FOOZBALL - SCUBA DIVING - INNER TUBING - WEIGHT ROOM - JET SKIS - VOLLEYBALL - BILLIARDS -

and reserve ahead from home, call (02) 92 61 11 11 in Australia; (800) 663-5777 in Canada; (1629) 58 14 18 in England and Wales; (1232) 32 47 33 in Northern Ireland; (01) 830 17 66 in the Republic of Ireland; (09) 303 95 24 in New Zealand; (541) 55 32 55 in Scotland; or (202) 783-6161 in the US (www.hiayh.org/ushostel/reserva/ ibn3.htm). If you want to make a reservation on less than three days' notice or are already in Europe, call the hostel where you want to stay directly.

Most HI hostels also honor **guest memberships**—you'll get a blank card with space for six validation stamps. Each night you'll pay a nonmember supplement (one-sixth the membership fee) and earn one guest stamp; get six stamps, and you're a member. This system works well in most of Western Europe, although in some countries you may need to remind the hostel reception. In Eastern Europe, many hostels are not HI members. Most student travel agencies (see p. 51) sell HI cards, as do all of the national hosteling organizations listed below. For more info on hostels, see www.iyhf.org, www.hostels.com, or www.budgettravel.com/hostels.htm. All prices listed below are valid for **one-year memberships** unless otherwise noted.

Australian Youth Hostels Association (AYHA), 422 Kent St, Sydney NSW 2000 (tel. (02) 92 61 11 11; fax 92 61 19 69; www.yha.org.au). AUS$44, under 18 AUS$13.50.

Hostelling International-Canada (HI-C), 400-205 Catherine St, Ottawa, ON K2P 1C3 (tel. (800) 663-5777 or (613) 237-7884; fax 237-7868; email info@hostellingintl.ca; www.hostellingintl.ca). CDN$25, under 18 CDN$12. 2-year membership CDN$35.

An Óige (Irish Youth Hostel Association), 61 Mountjoy St, Dublin 7 (tel. (01) 830 45 55; fax 830 58 08; www.irelandyha.org). IR£10, under 18 IR£4, families IR£20.

Youth Hostels Association of New Zealand (YHANZ), P.O. Box 436, 173 Cashel St, Christchurch 1 (tel. (03) 379 99 70; fax 365 44 76; email info@yha.org.nz; www.yha.org.nz). NZ$24, ages 15-17 NZ$12, under 15 free.

Hostelling International South Africa, P.O. Box 4402, Cape Town 8000 (tel. (021) 24 25 11; fax 24 41 19; www.hisa.org.za). SAR50, under 18 SAR25. Lifetime SAR250.

Scottish Youth Hostels Association (SYHA), 7 Glebe Crescent, Stirling FK8 2JA (tel. (01786) 89 14 00; fax 89 13 33; www.syha.org.uk). UK£6, under 18 UK£2.50.

Youth Hostels Association of England and Wales (YHA), 8 St Stephen's Hill, St Albans, Hertfordshire AL1 2DY, England (tel. (01727) 85 52 15 or 84 50 47; fax 84 41 26; www.yha.org.uk). UK£11, under 18 UK£5.50, families UK£22.

Hostelling International Northern Ireland (HINI), 22-32 Donegall Rd, Belfast BT12 5JN, Northern Ireland (tel. (01232) 32 47 33 or 31 54 35; fax 43 96 99; email info@hini.org.uk; www.hini.org.uk). UK£7, under 18 UK£3, families UK£14.

Hostelling International-American Youth Hostels (HI-AYH), 733 15th St NW #840, Washington, DC 20005 (tel. (202) 783-6161, ext. 136; fax 783-6171; email hiayh-serv@hiayh.org; www.hiayh.org). US$25, over 54 US$15, under 18 free.

PRIVATE HOSTELS

Privately owned hostels are found in major tourist centers and throughout some countries (e.g. Ireland and Greece). No membership is required, and there may be fewer early curfews or daytime lockouts, but quality varies. **Young Men's Christian Association (YMCA)** lodgings are usually cheaper than a hotel but more expensive than a hostel. Not all YMCA locations offer lodging; those that do are often located in urban downtowns. Many YMCAs accept women and families; some will not lodge those under 18 without parental permission.

OTHER OPTIONS

HOTELS, GUESTHOUSES, AND PENSIONS

Hotels are quite expensive in Britain, Switzerland, Austria, and northern Europe, where rock bottom for one or two people is US$25 each. Elsewhere, couples can usually get by fairly well, as can larger groups. You'll typically share a hall bathroom; a private bathroom will cost extra, as may hot showers. In Britain and Ireland, a large breakfast is often included; elsewhere a continental breakfast of a roll, jam, coffee or tea, and maybe an egg is served. Some hotels offer "full pension" (all

ESSENTIALS

C.N.N. CHANNEL

www.prettyholiday.com

FREE INTERNET ACCESS

BAR ICE CUBES

AIR CONDITIONED

PRETTY HOLIDAY
Hotels, Hostels and City Tours

Hotel Rooms from *33$ P.P.* 30 euro

Hostel dorms from *15$ P.P.* 13 euro

Tours of the city from *15$ P.P.* 13 euro

49, Via Palestro 00185 ROME - Italy

Located in the center, exit the train station TERMINI by track 1, walk straight for four blocks along via Marghera and turn left onto via Palestro, **The Pretty Holidays Office** is inside the **Hotel Romae** two blocks ahead on your left

General Manager: Francesco Boccaforno - Assistant Managers: Marco & Fabio Coppola

Ph. +39 064463554 Fax +39 064463914 - info@prettyholiday.com

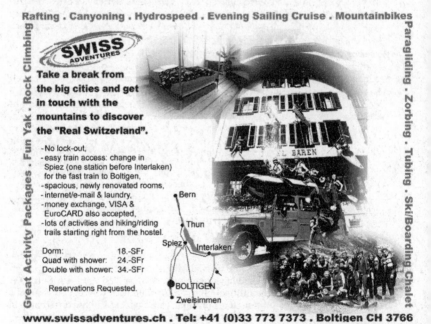

Rafting . Canyoning . Hydrospeed . Evening Sailing Cruise . Mountainbikes

Great Activity Packages . Fun Yak . Rock Climbing

Paragliding . Zorbing . Tubing . Ski/Boarding Chalet

SWISS ADVENTURES

Take a break from the big cities and get in touch with the mountains to discover the "Real Switzerland".

- No lock-out,
- easy train access: change in Spiez (one station before Interlaken) for the fast train to Boltigen,
- spacious, newly renovated rooms,
- internet/e-mail & laundry,
- money exchange, VISA & EuroCARD also accepted,
- lots of activities and hiking/riding trails starting right from the hostel.

Dorm: 18.-SFr
Quad with shower: 24.-SFr
Double with shower: 34.-SFr

Reservations Requested.

Bern
Thun
Spiez
Interlaken
BOLTIGEN
Zweisimmen

www.swissadventures.ch . Tel: +41 (0)33 773 7373 . Boltigen CH 3766

meals) and "half pension" (no lunch). Smaller **guesthouses** and **pensions** are often cheaper than hotels. If you make **reservations** in writing, indicate your night of arrival and the number of nights you plan to stay. The hotel will send you a confirmation and may request payment for the first night. Not all hotels take reservations, and few accept checks in foreign currency. Enclosing two International Reply Coupons will ensure a prompt reply (each US$1.05; available at any post office).

PRIVATE ROOMS

In nowhere-near-the-beaten-path destinations, such as parts of Eastern Europe (where hostels rarely exist outside of big cities), you may often rent a room in a private home. Although it may at first seem sketchy to a hyper-safety-concerned Westerner, going home with an old woman from the train station or knocking on doors with *Zimmer Frei* ("room free" in German; used throughout Eastern Europe) signs is absolutely legit and generally safe. Prices hover between hostel and pension prices. Tourist offices usually list private rooms, but more likely, a proprietor will flag you down at the train station first.

BED AND BREAKFASTS (B&BS)

For a cozy alternative to impersonal hotel rooms, B&Bs (private homes with rooms available to travelers, yet more formal than the private rooms described above) range from the acceptable to the sublime. Hosts will sometimes go out of their way to be accommodating by giving personalized tours or offering home-cooked meals. On the other hand, many B&Bs do not provide phones, TVs, or private baths. The British and Irish version of the B&B is extra heavy on the bacon and eggs. **Hometours International, Inc.,** P.O. Box 11503, Knoxville, TN 37939 (US tel. (800) 367-4668; http://thor.he.net/~hometour), offers catalogs of B&B listings in France, Italy, Portugal, Switzerland, Spain, and the UK, and also sells packets of B&B vouchers.

DORMS

Many **colleges** and **universities** open their residence halls to travelers when school is not in session—some do so even during term-time. These dorms are often close to student areas—good sources for information on things to do—and are usually very clean. Getting a room may take a couple of phone calls and require advanced planning, but rates tend to be low, and many offer free local calls.

HOME EXCHANGE AND RENTALS

Home exchange offers the traveler various types of homes (houses, apartments, condominiums, villas, even castles in some cases), plus the opportunity to live like a native and to cut down dramatically on accommodation fees—usually only an administration fee is paid to the matching service. Most companies have pictures of member's homes and information about the owners. Home rentals are more expensive than exchanges, but they can be cheaper than comparably-serviced hotels. Try **HomeExchange,** P.O. Box 30085, Santa Barbara, CA 93130 (US tel. (805) 898-9660; www.homeexchange.com); **Intervac International Home Exchange,** Box 12066, S-29112 Kristianstad, Sweden (UK tel. (1225) 89 22 08; US tel. (800) 756-4663; www.intervac.com); or **The Invented City: International Home Exchange,** 41 Sutter St, Suite 1090, San Francisco, CA 94104 (US tel. (800) 788-2489 or (415) 252-1141 www.invented-city.com). More exchange and rental services are listed at http://garlic.aitec.edu.au/~bwechner/Documents/Travel/lists.html.

CAMPING AND THE OUTDOORS

Organized campgrounds exist just outside most European cities, and are accessible by foot, car, and/or public transportation. Showers, bathrooms, and a small restaurant or store are common; some have more elaborate facilities. Prices are low, at US$5-15 per person, with additional charges for tents and/or cars, still making camping a much cheaper option than hosteling. **Free camping** allows you to camp in parks or public land (in some cases, such as Sweden, even on private land) for free. For information about camping, hiking, and biking, write or call the publishers and organizations listed below to receive a free catalog. Campers heading to Europe

ESSENTIALS

Flying to Europe?

YOU'LL PROBABLY TAKE THE TRAIN...

... around Europe. It's the fun and most efficient way to travel.

WE ARE EUROPEAN RAIL TRAVEL SPECIALISTS. Call us for:

- Eurail Pass, Eurail Youth Pass & Eurail Youth Flexipass
- Eurail Flexipass & Eurail Saverpass - BritRail Youth Pass
- France Rail Passes, Italian Passes, Swiss Passes

- ScanRail Passes, Spain Flexipass, Norway Railpasses
- Austrian Railpass, Benelux TourRail Pass, Gatwick Express
- All European Rail & Drive Passes
- And many more...

Thomas Cook European Timetable ...

The complete Rail travel companion featuring all European Rail Services schedules (Recommended in Let's Go Guides!)

$27.95 + $4.95 priority shipping

FREE TIMETABLE
with your Rail Order of $500 or more

ORDER TOLL-FREE · **VISIT OUR WEBSITE**
800-367-7984 · **www.forsyth.com**

FORSYTH TRAVEL LIBRARY

Serving the International rail traveler since 1976!

email:forsyth@aol.com

should consider buying an **International Camping Carnet,** which is required at a few campgrounds and provides discounts at others. It is available in North America from the Family Campers and RVers Association and in the UK from The Caravan Club (see below), but can usually also be bought on the spot.

Automobile Association, A.A. Publishing. Orders from TBS Frating Distribution Centre, Colchester, Essex, CO7 7DW (UK tel. (01206) 25 56 78; www.theaa.co.uk). Publishes *Camping and Caravanning: Europe* (UK£9) and *Camping and Caravanning: Britain & Ireland* (UK£8); also *Big Road Atlases* for Europe, France, Spain, Germany, and Italy.

The Caravan Club, East Grinstead House, East Grinstead, West Sussex, RH19 1UA (UK tel. (01342) 32 69 44; www.caravanclub.co.uk). Members receive a 700-page directory and handbook, discounts, and a monthly magazine (UK£27.50).

Family Campers and RVers/National Campers and Hikers Association, Inc., 4804 Transit Rd, Bldg. #2, Depew, NY 14043 (US tel./fax (716) 668-6242). Membership fee (US$25) includes their publication *Camping Today.*

The Mountaineers Books, 1001 SW Klickitat Way #201, Seattle, WA 98134 (US tel. (800) 553-4453 or (206) 223-6303; www.mountaineers.org).

ESSENTIALS

CAMPING AND HIKING EQUIPMENT

WHAT TO BUY... Good camping equipment is both sturdy and light. It is generally more expensive in Australia, New Zealand, and the UK than in North America.

Sleeping Bag: Most good sleeping bags are rated by season ("summer" means 30-40°F at night, while "four-season" or "winter" often means below 0°F). Sleeping bags are made either of **down** (warmer and lighter, but more expensive, and miserable when wet) or of **synthetic** material (heavier, more durable, and warmer when wet). Prices might range from US$80-210 for a summer synthetic to US$250-300 for a good down winter bag. **Sleeping bag pads** include foam pads (US$10-20), air mattresses (US$15-50), and Therm-A-Rest self-inflating pads (US$45-80). Bring a **stuff sack** to compress your bag.

Tent: The best tents are free-standing (with their own frames and suspension systems), set up quickly, and only require staking in high winds. Low-profile dome tents are the best all-around. Good 2-person tents start at US$90, 4-person tents at US$300. Seal the seams of your tent with waterproofer, and make sure it has a rain fly. Other tent accessories include a **battery-operated lantern,** a **plastic groundcloth,** and a **nylon tarp.**

Backpack: Internal-frame packs mold better to your back, keep a lower center of gravity, and flex adequately to allow you to hike difficult trails. **External-frame packs** are more comfortable for long hikes over even terrain, as they keep weight higher and distribute it more evenly. Whichever you choose, make sure your pack has a strong, padded hip-belt to transfer weight to your legs. Any serious backpacking requires a pack of at least 4000 in³ (16,000cc), plus 500 in³ for sleeping bags in internal-frame packs. Sturdy backpacks cost anywhere from US$125-420—this is one area in which it doesn't pay to economize—trust us. Fill up any pack with something heavy and walk around the store with it to get a sense of how it distributes weight before buying it. Either buy a **waterproof backpack cover,** or store all of your belongings in plastic bags inside your backpack.

Boots: Be sure to wear hiking boots with good **ankle support.** They should fit snugly and comfortably over 1-2 pairs of wool socks and thin liner socks. Break in boots over several weeks first in order to spare yourself from painful and debilitating blisters.

Other Necessities: Synthetic layers, like those made of polypropylene, and a **pile jacket** will keep you warm even when wet. A **"space blanket"** will help you to retain your body heat and doubles as a groundcloth (US$5-15). Plastic **water bottles** are virtually shatter- and leak-proof. Bring **water-purification tablets** for when you can't boil water. Although most campgrounds provide campfire sites, you may want to bring a small **metal grate** or **grill** of your own. Since virtually every organized campground in Europe forbids fires or the gathering of firewood, you'll also need a **camp stove** (the classic Coleman starts at US$40) and a propane-filled **fuel bottle** to operate it. Don't forget a **first-aid kit, Swiss Army knife, insect repellent, calamine lotion,** and **waterproof matches** or a **lighter.**

ESSENTIALS

DISCOUNTS WORLDWIDE
International Student Exchange Identity Card
ISE CARD

Airfare
Save up to 82% on airfare (major carriers).

Trains
Save $20 on train passes.

Attractions
Save up to 100% on museums and theaters (many offer free admission to ISE Cardholders).

Buses
Save up to 20% on Greyhound bus travel.

Hotels
Save up to 50% on accommodations.

Computers
Save up to 59% on computers.

With the ISE card you will receive discounts on airfare, accommodations, transportation, computer services, foreign exchange, phone calls, major attractions, and more. You will also receive basic medical and evacuation benefits when traveling outside the USA and access to 24 hour worldwide emergency assistance. Cost: $20 per year.

ise CARDS®

1-888-ISE-CARD (Toll Free)
1-888-473-2273
http://www.isecard.com

5010 East Shea Boulevard, #A-104, Scottsdale, Arizona 85254, Tel: 480-951-1177, Fax: 480-951-1216

$20.00 OFF
ANY EURAIL OR EURO PASS
ALL MAJOR CREDIT CARDS ACCEPTED
FREE EXPRESS DELIVERY
ALL HANDLING FEES WAIVED
CALL TOLL FREE
800-255-8000
Tel: 480-951-1177 Fax: 480-951-1216, www.isecard.com

...AND WHERE TO BUY IT. The mail-order/online companies listed below offer lower prices than many retail stores, but keep in mind that a visit to a local camping or outdoors store will give you a better sense of items' look and weight.

Campmor, P.O. Box 700, Upper Saddle River, NJ 07458-0700 (US tel. (888) 226-7667 or (201) 825-8300; email customer-service@campmor.com; www.campmor.com).

Discount Camping, 880 Main North Rd, Pooraka, South Australia 5095, Australia (tel. (08) 82 62 33 99; fax 82 60 62 40; www.discountcamping.com.au).

Eastern Mountain Sports (EMS), 327 Jaffrey Rd, Peterborough, NH 03458 (US tel. (888) 463-6367 or (603) 924-7231; www.emsonline.com). Also has retail outlets.

L.L. Bean, Freeport, ME 04033-0001 (US tel. (800) 441-5713 or (207) 552-6878; UK tel. (0800) 96 29 54; www.llbean.com).

Mountain Designs, P.O. Box 1472, Fortitude Valley, Queensland 4006, Australia (tel. (07) 32 52 88 94; fax 32 52 45 69; www.mountaindesign.com.au).

Recreational Equipment, Inc. (REI), Sumner, WA 98352 (US tel. (800) 426-4840 or (253) 891-2500; www.rei.com).

YHA Adventure Shop, 14 Southampton St, London, WC2E 7HA (tel. (020) 78 36 85 41).

CAMPERS AND RVS

Renting a campervan is usually more expensive than tenting or hosteling, but is cheaper than staying in hotels and renting a car (see p. 65). The convenience of bringing along your own bedroom, bathroom, and kitchen makes it an attractive option, especially for older travelers and families with children. Rates vary widely by region, season (July and Aug. are the most expensive months), and type of RV. **Auto Europe** (US tel. (800) 223-5555; UK tel. (0800) 89 98 93) rents RVs in Florence, London, Paris, Leon, Marseilles, Rotterdam (the Netherlands), Hamburg, Frankfurt, Munich, Düsseldorf, and Berlin; weekly rates for a four-passenger RV range about US$1000-2000/800-1200 in high-/low-season. For more info, try **Europe by Van and Motorhome,** David Shore and Patty Campbell (US$14; tel./fax (800) 659-5222; email shorecam@aol.com; members.aol.com/europevan).

KEEPING IN TOUCH

MAIL

SENDING MAIL TO EUROPE. Mark envelopes "airmail" or "par avion."

Australia: Allow 4-7 days for regular **airmail** to Europe. Postcards and letters up to 20g cost AUS$1; packages up to 0.5kg AUS$12, up to 2kg AUS$45. **EMS** can get a letter to Europe in 3-5 days for AUS$27. www.auspost.com.au/pac.

Canada: Allow 4-7 days for regular **airmail** to Europe. Postcards and letters up to 20g cost CDN$0.95; packages up to 0.5kg CDN$8.50, up to 2kg CDN$28.30. www.canadapost.ca/CPC2/common/rates/ratesgen.html#international.

Ireland: Allow 2-3 days for regular **airmail** to the UK, 3-4 days to the continent. Postcards and letters up to 25g cost IR£0.32 (IR£0.30 to the UK). **Swiftpost International** speeds letter for IR£2 plus normal airmail cost. www.anpost.ie.

New Zealand: Allow 6-12 days for regular **airmail** to Europe. Postcards NZ$1. Letters up to 20g cost NZ$1.80-6; small parcels up to 0.5kg NZ$15, up to 2kg NZ$39. www.nzpost.co.nz/nzpost/inrates.

UK: Allow 3 or 5-7 days for **airmail** to Western or Eastern Europe, respectively. Letters up to 20g cost UK£0.3; packages up to 0.5kg UK£2.22, up to 2kg UK£8.22. **UK Swiftair** delivers letters a day faster for UK£2.85 more. www.royalmail.co.uk/calculator.

US: Allow 4-7 days for regular **airmail** to Europe. Postcards/aerogrammes cost US$0.55/ 0.60; letters under 1 oz. US$1. Packages under 1 lb. cost US$7.20; larger packages sent by parcel post cost a variable amount (around US$15). **US Express Mail** takes 2-3 days and costs US$19/23 (0.5/1 lb.). **US Global Priority Mail** delivers small/large flat-rate envelopes to Western Europe in 3-5 days for US$5/9. http://ircalc.usps.gov.

ESSENTIALS

ESSENTIALS

Buy This

Eurail Passes
Our most popular choice for students, these passes offer unlimited travel in 17 European countries and afford maximum flexibility and great value.

	PRICE§
Eurail Youth Flexipass (2nd Class)	
10 days within 2 months	$ 458
15 days within 2 months	599
Eurail Youthpass (2nd Class)	
15 days	$ 388
21 days	499
1 month	623
2 months	882
3 months	1,089

Europasses
Ideal for students who are tight on time and know their itinerary. These passes offer less flexibility but are excellent value. Base countries are France, Italy, Germany, Spain and Switzerland.

Europass Youth (2nd Class)	BASE COUNTRIES
5 days within 2 months	$ 233
6 days within 2 months	253
8 days within 2 months	313
10 days within 2 months	363
15 days within 2 months	513

Up to 2 Additional Zones are available choose from: Belgium/Netherlands/Luxembourg; Austria/Hungary; Greece or Portugal.
1 Zone add $45; **2 Zones** add $78.

Many other pass types are available.

§ Prices subject to change without notice.
† Passengers must be under 26 years old on their first day of rail travel.

WE SHIP PASSES TO EUROPE
NO busy signals • NO lines • NO hassles

GUARANTEED BEST PRICES
Expert advice and friendly service.

And get ALL this FREE*

2,500 Discount Offers
Save on shopping, food, museums and more throughout the cities of Europe.

One FREE night at The Pink Palace
Includes breakfast and dinner at the world famous youth resort in Corfu, Greece.

FREE Eurail timetable and map

PLUS

Passes issued on the spot
Your pass is delivered to your door within 1–2 days. RUSH ORDERS are our specialty.

Toll-free help line
Call our offices toll free from Europe if you have any pass problems or questions.

* Offer good while supplies last, certain restrictions apply, call for details.

ORDER ONLINE AND GET EVEN MORE FREE STUFF!

www.railconnection.com
or Call 1-888-RAIL-PASS (1-888-724-5727)

Additionally, **Federal Express** (Australia tel. 13 26 10; US and Canada tel. (800) 247-4747; New Zealand tel. (0800) 73 33 39; UK tel. (0800) 12 38 00) handles express mail services from most of the above countries to Europe; for example, they can get a letter from New York to Western Europe in two days for US$25.50.

RECEIVING MAIL IN EUROPE. There are several ways to pick up letters sent to you abroad by friends and family:

General Delivery: Mail can be sent via **Poste Restante** (General Delivery; *Lista de Correos* in Spanish, *Fermo Posta* in Italian, and *Postlagernde Briefe* in German) to almost any city or town in Europe with a post office. Address mail to be held: Jane DOE, *Poste Restante*, London SW1, United Kingdom. The mail will go to a special desk in the central post office, unless you specify a different post office by street address or postal code. It's best to use the largest post office in the area, since mail may be sent there regardless. It is usually safer and quicker, though more expensive, to send mail express or registered. Bring your passport (or other photo ID) for pick-up; there may rarely be a small fee. If the clerks insist that there is nothing for you, have them check under your first name as well. *Let's Go* lists post offices in the **Practical Information** section for every city and most towns.

American Express: AmEx travel offices worldwide will act as a mail service for cardholders if you contact them in advance. Under this free **Client Letter Service,** they will hold mail for up to 30 days and forward upon request. Address the letter in the same manner shown above. Some offices will offer these services to non-cardholders (especially those who have purchased AmEx Travelers Cheques), but call ahead to make sure. *Let's Go* lists AmEx office locations for most large cities in **Practical Information** sections; get a complete, free list from AmEx (US tel. (800) 528-4800).

SENDING MAIL HOME FROM EUROPE. Airmail from Western Europe to North America averages seven days; from Central or Eastern Europe, allow anywhere from seven days to three weeks (although in Russia, Ukraine, and Belarus, you'll be lucky if mail leaves the post office at all). Times are more unpredictable from smaller towns. **Aerogrammes,** printed sheets that fold into envelopes and travel via airmail, are available at post offices. Most post offices will charge exorbitant fees or simply refuse to send aerogrammes with enclosures. In either case, it helps to write "airmail" (or *por avión, mit Luftpost, via aerea,* etc.) on the envelope, though *par avion* is generally understood. For exact postage for postcards and letters sent from Europe, see individual country introductions.

Surface mail is by far the cheapest and slowest way to send mail. It takes one to three months to cross the Atlantic and two to four to cross the Pacific—good for items you won't need to see for a while, such as souvenirs or other articles you've acquired along the way that are weighing down your pack.

TELEPHONES

CALLING HOME FROM EUROPE

A calling card is probably your cheapest bet. Calls are either billed collect or to your account. To **obtain a calling card** from your national telecommunications service before leaving home, contact one of the following: in **Australia,** Telstra Australia Direct (tel. 13 22 00); **Canada,** Bell Canada **Canada Direct** (tel. (800) 565-4708); **Ireland,** Telecom Éireann **Ireland Direct** (tel. (800) 25 02 50); **New Zealand, Telecom New Zealand** (tel. (0800) 00 00 00); **South Africa, Telkom South Africa** (tel. 09 03); **UK,** British Telecom **BT Direct** (tel. (800) 34 51 44); **US, AT&T** (tel. (888) 288-4685), **Sprint** (tel. (800) 877-4646), or **MCI** (tel. (800) 444-4141).

To **call home with a calling card,** contact the operator for your service provider in the appropriate country by dialing the toll-free access number provided in the Essentials chapter for each country under **Communications.** Keep in mind that phone cards can be problematic in Eastern Europe (particularly Russia, Ukraine, Belarus, and Slovenia)—double-check with your provider before setting out. You can usually make **direct international calls** from pay phones, but if you aren't using a calling card, you may need to drop your coins as quickly as your words. Where

ESSENTIALS

> **PLACING INTERNATIONAL CALLS.** To call Europe from home, to make like E.T. from Europe, or to call another country within Europe, dial:
> 1. The **international dialing prefix.** To dial out of **Australia,** dial 0011; **Canada** or the **US,** 011; **Ireland, New Zealand,** or the **UK,** 00; **South Africa,** 09. To place an international call from a **European** country, see the inside back cover or the beginning of the individual country chapter for the appropriate prefix.
> 2. The **country code** of the country you want to call. To call **Australia,** dial 61; **Canada** or the **US,** 1; **Republic of Ireland,** 353; **New Zealand,** 64; **South Africa,** 27; the **UK,** 44. To call into a **European** country, use the country code on the inside back cover or at the beginning of the appropriate country chapter.
> 3. The **city** or **area code.** For **European** cities, look for the city code either in a phone code box (in big cities) or in parentheses preceding the local number (in smaller cities). If the first digit is a zero (e.g., 020 for London), omit it when calling from abroad (e.g., dial 011 44 20 from Canada to reach London).
> 4. The **local number.**

available, prepaid phone cards (see below) and occasionally major credit cards can be used for direct international calls, but they are still less cost-efficient. Placing a **collect call** through an international operator is a more expensive alternative. You can typically place collect calls through the service providers listed above, even if you don't possess one of their phone cards.

LOCAL CALLS WITHIN EUROPE

For **local calls,** the simplest way to call within a country in Europe may be to use a coin-operated phone. However, much of Western Europe has switched to a **prepaid phone card** system, and in some countries you may have a hard time finding any coin-operated phones at all. Phone cards (usually available at newspaper kiosks and tobacco stores) carry a certain amount of phone time, measured in units.

SPECIALIZING IN

Student Travel

EURAIL PASSES
ISSUED IMMEDIATELY !
TICKETS VALID FOR UP
TO ONE YEAR !
STUDENT I.D. CARDS
AVAILABLE !

EXPERIENCED STAFF. BEST PRICES.

SCHEDULED FLIGHTS TO EUROPE AND BEYOND
Asia, Africa,
Latin America, South Pacific
and around the world.

WWW.PRISMTOURS.COM

PRISM TRAVEL

545 Fifth Ave., Suite 640, New York, NY 10017
212-986-8420 1-800-272-9676
E-mail: Staff@prismtours.com

ESSENTIALS

Investing in a phone card usually saves time and money in the long run; just use any leftover time on a call home before leaving the country. The computerized phone will tell you how much time, in units, you have left on your card. Another kind of prepaid telephone card comes with a Personal Identification Number (PIN) and a toll-free access number. Instead of inserting the card into the phone, you call the access number and follow the directions on the card. These cards can be used to make international as well as domestic calls. **Phone rates** are highest in the morning, lower in the evening, and lowest on Sundays and late at night.

TIME DIFFERENCES

Greenwich Mean Time (GMT) is five hours ahead of New York time, eight hours ahead of Vancouver and San Francisco time, two hours behind Johannesburg time, 10 hours behind Sydney time, and 12 hours behind Auckland time. Some countries (like Iceland) ignore **daylight savings time,** and fall and spring switchover times vary. See specific country introductions for more information.

GMT	GMT + 1			GMT + 2		GMT + 3
Britain	Austria	Belgium	Bosnia	Belarus	Bulgaria	Moscow
Iceland	Croatia	Czech Rep.	Denmark	Estonia	Finland	St. Petersburg
Ireland	France	Germany	Hungary	Greece	Latvia	most of Russia
Portugal	Italy	Luxembourg	Netherlands	Lithuania	Romania	
	Norway	Poland	Slovakia	W. Russia	Turkey	
	Slovenia	Spain	Sweden	Ukraine		
	Switzerland	Yugoslavia				

EMAIL AND INTERNET

Email has become the joy of backpackers worldwide, from Kathmandu to Cairo, so it's no surprise that it has become a popular and easily accessible option in Europe as well. Though in some places it's possible to forge a remote link with your home server, in most cases this is a much slower (and thus more expensive) option than taking advantage of free **web-based email accounts** (e.g., www.hotmail.com and www.yahoo.com). Travelers with laptops can call an internet service provider via a **modem.** Long-distance phone cards specifically intended for such calls can defray normally high phone charges; check with your long-distance phone provider to see if it offers this option. **Internet cafés** and the occasional free internet terminal at a public library or university are listed in the **Orientation and Practical Information** sections of major cities. For lists of additional cybercafés in Europe, check out http://cybercaptive.com or www.cyberiacafe.net/cyberia/guide/ccafe.htm.

GETTING THERE

BY PLANE

When it comes to airfare, a little effort can save you a bundle. If your plans are flexible enough to deal with complex restrictions, courier fares are the cheapest. Tickets bought from consolidators and standby tickets are also good deals, but last-minute specials, airfare wars, and charter flights often beat these fares. The key is to hunt around, to be flexible, and to ask persistently about discounts. Students, seniors, and those under 26 should never pay full price for a ticket.

DETAILS AND TIPS

Timing: Airfares to Europe peak between mid-June and early Sept.; mid-Dec. to early Jan. can also be expensive. The cheapest times to travel are Nov. to mid-Dec. and early Jan. to Mar. Midweek (M-Th morning) round-trip flights run US$40-50 less than weekend flights, but are generally more crowded and are less likely to permit frequent flier upgrades. Traveling with an "open-return" ticket can be pricier than buying a fixed-return date ticket and paying later to change it.

ESSENTIALS

✕ TRAVEL CUTS

The Student, Youth & Budget Travel Experts

- **Student Flights and Discount Airfares**
- **Rail and Bus Passes**
- **Student (ISIC) and Youth Cards**
- **Worldwide Work Abroad Programs**
- **Adventure Tours**
- **Language Courses**

**Travel CUTS London –
The Budget Travel Centre** ➜

Save on scheduled European
flights year around.

WHEN IN THE USA
The Adventure Travel Network

785 Market St, #1710
San Francisco, CA
415-247-1800
1-800-467-4595

Stanford University
Tressider Union
459 Laguita Dr., #8
Stanford, CA
650-470-0050

www.atntravel.com

**CALL our London
office for info on:**

North America 0207 255-2082
Europe 0207 255-1944
Worldwide 0207 528-6113

Travel CUTS London
295-A Regent Street
London, England W1R 7YA

WHEN IN CANADA
More than 60 offices
including:

St. John's
(709) 737-7926

Halifax
(902) 494-2054

Fredericton
(506) 472-2887

Quebec City
(418) 654-0224

Montreal
(514) 843-8511

Ottawa
(613) 238-8222

Toronto
(416) 979-2406

Winnipeg
(204) 269-9530

Regina
(306) 586-0011

Saskatoon
(306) 975-3722

Calgary
(403) 531-2070

Edmonton
(780) 488-8487

Vancouver
(604) 659-2887

Victoria
(250) 721-8352

**Check out
travelcuts.com**

Owned and operated by
the Canadian Federation
of Students

Route: Round-trip flights are by far the cheapest; "open-jaw" (arriving in and departing from different cities, e.g. London-Paris and Rome-London) tickets tend to be pricier but may make sense. Patching one-way flights together is the most expensive way to travel.

Round-the-World (RTW): If Europe is only 1 stop on a more extensive globe-hop, consider a RTW ticket. Tickets usually include at least 5 stops and are valid for about a year; prices range US$1200-5000. Try **Northwest Airlines/KLM** (US tel. (800) 447-4747; www.nwa.com) or **Star Alliance,** a consortium of 8 airlines including United Airlines (US tel. (800) 241-6522; www.star-alliance.com).

Gateway Cities: Flights between capitals or regional hubs will offer the cheapest fares. The cheapest gateway cities in Europe are typically London, Paris, Amsterdam, and Frankfurt.

Boarding: Confirm international flights by phone within 72hr. of departure. Most airlines require that passengers arrive at the airport at least 2hr. before departure. One carry-on item and 2 checked bags is the norm for non-courier flights.

BUDGET AND STUDENT TRAVEL AGENCIES

A knowledgeable agent specializing in flights to Europe can make your life easy and help you save, too, but agents may not spend the time to find you the lowest possible fare—they get paid on commission. Students and under-26ers holding **ISIC** and **IYTC** cards (see p. 13), respectively, qualify for big discounts from student travel agencies. Most flights from budget agencies are on major airlines, but in peak season some may sell seats on less reliable chartered aircraft.

Campus/Usit Youth and Student Travel, 52 Grosvenor Gardens, **London** SW1W OAG (tel. (020) 77 30 34 02, from North America call UK +44 (20) 77 30 21 01, elsewhere call UK +44 (20) 77 30 81 11; www.usitcampus.co.uk). Other offices include: 19-21 Aston Quay, O'Connell Bridge, **Dublin** 2 (tel. (01) 677 81 17; fax 679 88 33); New York Student Center, 895 Amsterdam Ave, **New York,** NY 10025 (tel. (212) 663-5435; email usitny@aol.com). Additional offices in Ireland and Greece.

Council Travel (www.counciltravel.com). In the US: Emory Village, 1561 N. Decatur Rd, **Atlanta,** GA 30307 (tel. (404) 377-9997); 273 Newbury St, **Boston,** MA 02116 (tel. (617) 266-1926); 1160 N. State St, **Chicago,** IL 60610 (tel. (312) 951-0585); 10904 Lindbrook Dr, **Los Angeles,** CA 90024 (tel. (310) 208-3551); 205 E. 42nd St, **New York,** NY 10017 (tel. (212) 822-2700); 530 Bush St, **San Francisco,** CA 94108 (tel. (415) 421-3473); 1314 NE 43rd St #210, **Seattle,** WA 98105 (tel. (206) 632-2448); 3300 M St NW, **Washington, DC** 20007 (tel. (202) 337-6464). For US cities not listed, call (800) 226-8624. Also 28A Poland St (Oxford Circus), **London,** W1V 3DB (tel. (020) 72 87 33 37), **Paris** (tel. (01) 44 41 89 89), and **Munich** (tel. (089) 39 50 22).

CTS Travel, 44 Goodge St, **London** W1 (tel. (020) 76 36 00 31; fax 76 37 53 28; email ctsinfo@ctstravel.com.uk).

STA Travel, 6560 Scottsdale Rd #F100, Scottsdale, AZ 85253 (tel. (800) 777-0112, fax (602) 922-0793; www.sta-travel.com). Ticket booking, travel insurance, railpasses, and more. In the US: 297 Newbury St, **Boston,** MA 02115 (tel. (617) 266-6014); 429 S. Dearborn St, **Chicago,** IL 60605 (tel. (312) 786-9050); 7202 Melrose Ave, **Los Angeles,** CA 90046 (tel. (323) 934-8722); 10 Downing St, **New York,** NY 10014 (tel. (212) 627-3111); 4341 University Way NE, **Seattle,** WA 98105 (tel. (206) 633-5000); 2401 Pennsylvania Ave, Suite G, **Washington, DC** 20037 (tel. (202) 887-0912); 51 Grant Ave, **San Francisco,** CA 94108 (tel. (415) 391-8407). In the UK: 6 Wrights Ln, **London** W8 6TA (tel. (020) 79 38 47 11). In New Zealand: 10 High St, **Auckland** (tel. (09) 309 04 58). In Australia: 222 Faraday St, **Melbourne** VIC 3053 (tel. (03) 93 49 24 11).

Trailfinders, 194 Kensington High St, **London,** W8 7RG (tel. (020) 79 38 39 39; www.trailfinders.com). The UK's largest independent travel agency with a wide range of services. Also 4/5 Dawson St, **Dublin** 2 (tel. (01) 677 78 88), and Australia, 8 Spring St, **Sydney** 2000, NSW (tel. (02) 92 47 76 66).

Travel CUTS (Canadian Universities Travel Services Limited), 187 College St, **Toronto,** ON M5T 1P7 (tel. (416) 979-2406; fax 979-8167; www.travelcuts.com). 40 offices in Canada. Also in the UK, 295-A Regent St, **London** W1R 7YA (tel. (020) 72 55 19 44).

ESSENTIALS

ESSENTIALS

www.railpass.com

The *ONLY* way to travel Europe!

- Over 50 European & British Railpass Choices
- Eurostar & Point-to-Point Tickets
- Rail / Drive Packages
- City Transport Cards
- Sightseeing Tours & Excursions
- Authors of *Europe by Eurail & Britain by BritRail*
- FREE Info Pak

800.722.7151

outside the U.S. call 1.614.793.7651

Rail Pass
express

ESSENTIALS

Wasteels, Victoria Station, London, UK SW1V 1JT (tel. (020) 78 34 70 66; fax 76 30 76 28; www.wasteels.dk/uk). A huge chain in Europe, with 203 locations. Sells Wasteels **BIJ** and **BIGT** discounted tickets (see p. 62). Sold only in Europe.

COMMERCIAL AIRLINES

The commercial airlines' lowest regular offer is the **APEX** (Advance Purchase Excursion) fare, which provides confirmed reservations and allows "open-jaw" tickets. Generally, reservations must be made seven to 21 days ahead, with seven-to 14-day minimum-stay and up to 90-day maximum-stay restrictions, and hefty cancellation and change penalties (fees rise in summer). Book peak-season APEX fares early; by May you will have a hard time getting your desired departure date. Use **Microsoft Expedia** (expedia.msn.com) or **Travelocity** (www.travelocity.com) to get an idea of what airlines' lowest published fares are, then use the resources we outline here to try and beat those fares. The fares listed below are **high-season** (mid-June to Aug.) fares. Low-season fares should be appreciably cheaper.

TRAVELING FROM NORTH AMERICA

Basic round-trip fares to Western Europe range from roughly US$200-750: to Frankfurt, US$300-750; London, US$200-600; Paris, US$250-700. Standard commercial carriers like American and United will probably offer the most convenient flights, but they may not be the cheapest, unless you manage to grab a special promotion or airfare war ticket. You will probably find flying one of the following "discount" airlines a better deal, if any of their limited departure points is convenient for you.

Icelandair: Tel. (800) 223-5500; www.icelandair.com. Up to 3-day stopovers in Iceland for no extra cost on most transatlantic flights. New York to Frankfurt June-Sept. US$598; Oct.-May US$350-$398.

Finnair: Tel. (800) 950-5000; www.us.finnair.com. Cheap round-trips from San Francisco, New York, and Toronto to Helsinki; connections throughout Europe.

Martinair: Tel. (800) 627-8462; www.martinairusa.com. One-way standby fares from Newark to Amsterdam (US$210; May-Sept.). Reserved seats from Newark to Amsterdam mid-June to mid-Aug. US$694; mid-Aug. to mid-June US$498.

TowerAir: Tel. (800) 348-6937; www.towerair.com. Cheap round-trip flights from Los Angeles, Miami, New York, and San Francisco to Paris, Athens, and Rome.

TRAVELING FROM THE UK AND IRELAND

Because of the myriad carriers flying from the British Isles to the continent, we only include discount airlines or those with cheap specials here. The **Air Travel Advisory Bureau** in London (tel. (020) 76 36 50 00; www.atab.co.uk) provides referrals to travel agencies and consolidators that offer discounted airfares out of the UK.

Aer Lingus: Ireland tel. (01) 886 88 88; www.aerlingus.ie. Return tickets from Dublin to Amsterdam, Brussels, Copenhagen, Düsseldorf, Frankfurt, Paris, and Zürich (IR£99-149); and from Cork, Shannon, Galway, Sligo, and Kerry to the same destinations (IR£99-199).

British Midland Airways: UK tel. (0870) 607 05 55; www.iflybritishmidland.com. Departures from throughout the UK. London to Brussels (UK£33) and Frankfurt (UK£52).

Debonair Airways: UK tel. (0541) 50 03 00; www.debonair.co.uk. Return tickets from London to Barcelona, Madrid, Munich, Nice, Paris, and Rome (UK£73-143).

easyJet: UK tel. (0870) 600 00 00; www.easyjet.com. London to Amsterdam, Athens, Barcelona, Geneva, Madrid, Nice, and Zurich (UK£36-160). Online tickets.

Go-Fly Limited: UK tel. (0845) 605 43 21; elsewhere call UK +44 (1279) 66 63 88; www.go-fly.com. A subsidiary of British Airways. From London to Edinburgh, Copenhagen, Munich, Venice, Milan, Bologna, Rome, Madrid, and Lisbon (return UK£35-120).

KLM: UK tel. (0870) 507 40 74; www.klmuk.com. Cheap return tickets from London and elsewhere to Brussels, Frankfurt, Düsseldorf, Milan, Paris, and Rome.

Ryanair: Ireland tel. (01) 609 78 00; UK (0870) 333 12 50; www.ryanair.ie. From Ireland and the UK to France, Italy, Scandinavia, and elsewhere. From UK£29.99 one-way.

ESSENTIALS

Call USTn

for the
Best Deals in
Student Travel

- **Student & Youth Tours**
- **Student Discount Airfares**
- **Eurail & BritRail Passes**
- **ISIC & Hostel Cards**

University and Student Travel Nationwide (USTN) Call or visit one of our Web sites now!

Arizona State U
Tempe (ASU)
(800) 815-6455

California State U
San Diego (CSUSD)
(800) 862-6220

U of California
Berkeley (UCB)
(510) 843-1000
Letsgo@Berkeley4
Travel.com

U of California
Irvine (UCI)
(800) 278-1132
www.outroads.uci.edu

U of California
Los Angeles (UCLA)
www.student-travel.
ucla.edu

U of Colorado
Boulder
(800) LET'S-GO-1

U of Washington
Seattle
(800) 753-6636
www.travelteam.com

We recommend only the best, including ...

The World's Biggest Travel Company For 18-35 Year Olds

www.ustn.org

TRAVELING FROM AUSTRALIA AND NEW ZEALAND

Air New Zealand: Tel. (0800) 35 22 66; www.airnz.com. Auckland to London and Frankfurt.

Qantas Air: Australia tel. 13 13 13; www.qantas.com.au. Flights from Australia and New Zealand to London for around AUS$2400.

Singapore Air: Australia tel. (02) 93 50 01 00; New Zealand tel. 379 32 09; www.singaporeair.com. Flies from Auckland, Sydney, and Melbourne to Western Europe.

Thai Airways: Australia tel. (1300) 65 19 60; New Zealand tel. (09) 377 02 68; www.thaiair.com. Melbourne, Sydney, and Auckland to Frankfurt, London, and Amsterdam.

TRAVELING FROM SOUTH AFRICA

Air France: Tel. (011) 880 80 40; www.airfrance.com. Johannnesburg to Paris; connections throughout Europe.

British Airways: Tel. (011) 441 86 00; www.british-airways.com/regional/sa. Johannesburg and Cape Town to the UK and the rest of Europe from SAR3100.

Lufthansa: Tel. (011) 484 47 11; www.lufthansa.com. To Germany and elsewhere.

AIR COURIER FLIGHTS

Those who travel light should consider being a courier. Couriers help transport cargo on international flights by using their checked luggage space for freight. Generally, couriers must travel with carry-ons only and must deal with complex flight restrictions. Most flights are round-trip only, with short fixed-length stays (usually one week) and a limit of a one ticket per issue. Most of these flights also operate only out of major gateway cities, mostly in North America. Generally, you must be over 21 (in some cases 18), have a valid passport, and procure your own visa, if necessary. In summer, the most popular destinations usually require an advance reservation of about two weeks (you can usually book up to two months ahead). Superdiscounted fares are common for "last-minute" flights (three to 14 days ahead).

TRAVELING FROM NORTH AMERICA

Round-trip courier fares from the US to Western Europe run about US$200-500. Most flights leave from New York, Los Angeles, San Francisco, or Miami in the US; and from Montreal, Toronto, or Vancouver in Canada. The first four organizations below provide their members with lists of opportunities and courier brokers worldwide for an annual fee (typically US$50-60). Alternatively, you can contact a courier broker (such as the last three listings) directly; most charge registration fees, but a few don't. Prices quoted below are **round-trip.**

Air Cargo Partners, 1983 Marcus Ave #108, Lake Success, NY 11042 (tel. (516) 358-2025 or (888) VEX-MOVE; fax (516) 358-1835). Seven US cities to Manchester and London. 90-day max. stay. Ages 18 and up. No registration fee.

Air Courier Association, 191 University Blvd #300, Denver CO 80206 (tel. (800) 282-1202; elsewhere call US +1 (303) 215-9000; www.aircourier.org). Ten departure cities throughout the US and Canada to Ireland, the UK, Copenhagen, Budapest, and throughout western Europe (high-season US$170-359). One-year US$64.

Global Delivery Systems, 147-05 176th St, Jamaica, NY 11434 (tel. (718) 995-7300). From New York to Amsterdam, Copenhagen, Rome, Milan, Dublin, and Madrid (US$250-650). Ages 18 and up. No registration fee.

International Association of Air Travel Couriers (IAATC), P.O. Box 1349, Lake Worth, FL 33460 (tel. (561) 582-8320; fax 582-1581; www.courier.org). New York to 9 western European cities. Select other cities to London only. One-year US$45-50.

Flighthound.Com, 1630 30th St #225, Boulder, CO 80301 (tel. (303) 316-8266; www.flighthound.com). Searchable online database. Eleven departure points along both coasts. Some one-way flights. One-year US$60, 2 people US$75.

NOW Voyager, 74 Varick St #307, New York, NY 10013 (tel. (212) 431-1616; fax 219-1753; www.nowvoyagertravel.com). New York to London (US$399); Amsterdam, Brussels, Copenhagen, and Dublin (US$505-535); and Paris, Madrid, Rome, and Milan (US$649-699). Usually one-week max. stay. Ages 18 and up. One-year US$50.

ESSENTIALS

ESSENTIALS

Worldwide Courier Association (tel. (800) 780-4359, ext. 441; www.massiveweb.com). From New York, San Francisco, Los Angeles, and Chicago to Western Europe, including Milan, Madrid, and London (US$300-600). One-year US$58.

FROM THE UK, IRELAND, AUSTRALIA, AND NEW ZEALAND

Although the courier industry is most developed from North America, there are limited courier flights in other areas. The minimum age for couriers from the **UK** is usually 18. **Brave New World Enterprises**, P.O. Box 22212, London SE5 8WB (email guideinfo@nry.co.uk; www.nry.co.uk/bnw) publishes a directory of all the companies offering courier flights in the UK (UK£10). The **International Association of Air Travel Couriers** (see above) often offers courier flights from London to Budapest. **Flighthound.Com** (see above) also offer flights from London and Dublin to continental Europe. **British Airways Travel Shop** (tel. (087) 06 06 11 33; www.british-airways.com/travelqa/booking/travshop/travshop.shtml) arranges return flights from London to Budapest (UK£120; specials may be as low as UK£60; no registration fee; ages 18 and up). From **Australia** and **New Zealand**, **Flighthound.Com** (see above) often has listings from Sydney and Auckland to London and occasionally Frankfurt.

STANDBY FLIGHTS

Traveling standby requires considerable flexibility in arrival and departure dates and cities. Companies dealing in standby flights sell vouchers rather than tickets, along with the promise to get to your destination (or near your destination) within a certain window of time (typically 1-5 days). You call in before your specific window of time to hear your flight options and the probability that you will be able to board each flight. You then decide which flights you want to try to make, show up at the appropriate airport at the appropriate time, present your voucher, and board if space is available. Vouchers can usually be bought for both one-way and round-trip travel. You may receive a monetary refund only if every available flight within your date range is full; if you opt not to take an available (but perhaps less convenient) flight, you can only get credit toward future travel. Carefully read agreements with any company offering standby flights, as tricky fine print can leave you in a lurch. To check on a company's service record in the US, call the Better Business Bureau (tel. (212) 533-6200). It is difficult to receive refunds, and clients' vouchers will not be honored when an airline fails to receive payment in time. One established standby company in the US is **Airhitch**, 2641 Broadway, 3rd fl., New York, NY 10025 (tel. (800) 326-2009; fax 864-5489; www.airhitch.org) and Los Angeles, CA (tel. (888) 247-4482), which offers one-way flights to Europe from the Northeast (US$159), West Coast and Northwest (US$239), Midwest (US$209), and Southeast (US$189). Intracontinental connecting flights within the US or Europe cost US$79-139. Airhitch's head European office is in **Paris** (tel. +33 01 47 00 16 30); there's also one in **Amsterdam** (tel. +31 (20) 626 32 20).

TICKET CONSOLIDATORS

Ticket consolidators, or **"bucket shops,"** buy unsold tickets in bulk from commercial airlines and sell them at discounted rates. The best place to look is in the Sunday travel section of any major newspaper (such as the *New York Times*), where many bucket shops place tiny ads. Call quickly, as availability is typically extremely limited. Not all bucket shops are reliable, so insist on a receipt that gives full details of restrictions, refunds, and tickets, and pay by credit card (in spite of the 2-5% fee) so you can stop payment if you never receive your tickets.

TRAVELING FROM NORTH AMERICA

Travel Avenue (tel. (800) 333-3335; www.travelavenue.com) rebates commercial fares to or from the US (5% for over US$550) and will search for cheap flights from anywhere for a fee. **NOW Voyager** (see above) arranges discounted flights, mostly from New York, to Barcelona, London, Madrid, Milan, Paris, and Rome. At 17% off published fares, they are often as cheap as courier fares, and are considerably more flexible. Other consolidators worth trying are **Airfare Busters** (tel. (800) 232-8783; www.af.busters.com); **Interworld** (tel. (305) 443-4929; fax 443-0351); **Pennsylvania Travel** (tel. (800) 331-0947); **Rebel** (tel. (800) 227-3235; email travel@rebeltours.com; www.rebeltours.com); **Cheap Tickets** (tel. (800) 377-1000; www.cheaptickets.com); and **Travac** (tel. (800) 872-8800; fax (212) 714-9063; www.travac.com). Yet more consolidators on the web include the **Internet Travel Network** (www.itn.com); **Surplus-Travel.com** (www.surplustravel.com); **Travel Information Services** (www.tiss.com); **TravelHUB** (www.travelhub.com); and **The Travel Site** (www.thetravelsite.com). Keep in mind that these are just suggestions to get you started in your research; *Let's Go* does not endorse any of these agencies. As always, be cautious, and research companies before you hand over your credit card number.

TRAVELING FROM THE UK, AUSTRALIA, AND NEW ZEALAND

In London, the **Air Travel Advisory Bureau** (tel. (020) 76 36 50 00; www.atab.co.uk) can provide names of reliable consolidators and discount flight specialists. Also look for ads in the Sunday papers. From Australia and New Zealand, look for consolidator ads in the travel section of the *Sydney Morning Herald* and other papers.

CHARTER FLIGHTS

Charters are flights a tour operator contracts with an airline to fly extra loads of passengers during peak season. Charters can sometimes be cheaper than flights on scheduled airlines, some operate nonstop, and restrictions on minimum advance-purchase and minimum stay are more lenient. However, charters fly less frequently than major airlines, make refunds particularly difficult, and are almost always fully booked. Schedules and itineraries may also change or be cancelled at the last moment (as late as 48hr. before the trip, and without a full refund), and check-in, boarding, and baggage claim are often much slower. Pay with a credit card if you can, and consider traveler's insurance against trip interruption.

FURTHER READING: PLANE TRAVEL.
The Worldwide Guide to Cheap Airfare, by Michael McColl. Insider Publications (US$15).
Discount Airfares: The Insider's Guide, by George Hobart. Priceless Publications (US$14).
Air Courier Bargains (US$15), *Consolidators: Air Travel's Bargain Basement* (US$8), and
  Fly Cheap (US$15) by Kelly Monaghan. Intrepid Traveler.
Courier Air Travel Handbook, by Mark I. Field. Thunderbird Press (US$10).
Consolidators FAQ: www.travel-library.com/air-travel/consolidators.html.
Air Traveler's Handbook: www.cs.cmu.edu/afs/cs.cmu.edu/user/mkant/Public/Travel/air-
  fare.html.

BY CHUNNEL FROM THE UK

Traversing 27 mi. under the sea, the Chunnel is undoubtedly the fastest, most convenient, and least scenic route from England to France.

BY TRAIN. Eurostar, 102-104 Victoria St, **London** SW1 5JL (UK tel. (0990) 18 61 86; Belgium tel. (02) 55 52 525; US tel. (800) 387-6782; elsewhere call UK +44 (1233) 61 75 75; www.eurostar.com) runs a frequent train service between London and the continent. Eight to 10 trains per day run to Paris (3hr., UK£89-145, under 26 UK£79) and Brussels (1¾hr., UK£89-125, under 26 UK£69). Both routes include stops at Ashford in England, and Calais and Lille in France. Book at major rail stations in the UK, at the office above, or by phone.

BY BUS. Both **Eurolines** and **Eurobus** provide bus-ferry combinations (see p. 63).

BY CAR. If you're traveling by car, **Eurotunnel** (UK tel. (08000) 96 99 92; www.euro-tunnel.co.uk) shuttles cars and passengers between Kent and Nord-Pas-de-Calais. Return fares for vehicle and all passengers range from UK£219-299 with car, UK£259-598 with campervan, and UK£119-299 for a trailer/caravan supplement. Same-day return costs UK£110-150, five-day return UK£139-195. Book online or via phone. Travelers with cars can also look into sea crossings by ferry (see below).

ESSENTIALS

BY BOAT FROM THE UK AND IRELAND

The following fares listed are **one-way** for **adult foot passengers** unless otherwise noted. Though standard return fares are in most cases simply twice the one-way fare, **fixed-period returns** (usually within five days) are almost invariably cheaper. Ferries run **year-round** unless otherwise noted. **Bikes** are usually free, although you may have to pay up to UK£10 in high-season. For a **camper/trailer** supplement, you will have to add anywhere from UK£20-140 to the "with car" fare. If more than one price is quoted, the quote in UK£ is valid for departures from the UK, etc. A directory of ferries in this region can be found at www.seaview.co.uk/ferries.html.

P&O Stena Line: UK tel. (087) 06 00 06 00; France tel. 08 02 01 00 20; www.posl.com. **Dover** to **Calais** (1¼hr., every 45min.-1hr., 30 per day; UK£24 or 245F). **Newhaven** to **Dieppe** (2¼-4¼hr.; June-Sept. 4 per day, Oct.-May 1 per day; 110-250F).

Hoverspeed: UK tel. (08705) 24 02 41; France tel. 03 21 46 14 54; www.hoverspeed.co.uk. **Dover** to **Calais** (35-55min., 12-20 per day, UK£25-30 or 160F) and **Ostend, Belgium** (2hr., 5-7 per day, UK£25). **Folkestone** to **Boulogne, France** (55min., 3-4 per day, UK£25 or 150F). **Newhaven** to **Dieppe, France** (2¼-4¼hr., 1-4 per day, UK£114-160 or 110-250F).

SeaFrance: UK tel. (08705) 71 17 11; France tel. 03 21 46 40 56; www.seafrance.co.uk. **Dover** to **Calais** (1½hr., 16 per day, UK£15 or 240F, with car UK£80 or 1150-1400F).

Scandanavian Seaways: UK tel. (0990) 44 43 33; www.scansea.com. **Harwich** to **Hamburg** (20hr.) and **Esbjerg, Denmark** (19hr.). **Newcastle** to **Amsterdam** (14hr.); **Hamburg** (23hr.; in summer only); **Kristiansand, Norway** (19hr.); and **Gothenburg, Sweden** (22hr.).

P&O European Ferries: UK tel. (0870) 242 49 99; France tel. 01 44 51 00 51; www.poef.com. **Portsmouth** to **Le Havre** and **Cherbourg** (both 5½hr., 1-7 per day, UK£18-32, with car UK£78-147) and **Bilbao** (35hr., 2 per week, UK£55-90, with car UK£160-295). Also **Cairnryan** to **Larne** (1-2¼hr.).

Brittany Ferries: UK tel. (0870) 901 24 00; France tel. 08 03 82 88 28; www.brittany-ferries.com. **Plymouth** to **Roscoff, France** (6hr., in summer 1-3 per day, off-season 1 per week, UK£20-58 or 140-300F) and **Santander, Spain** (24-30hr., 1-2 per week, return UK£80-145). **Portsmouth** to **St-Malo** (8¾hr., 1-2 per day, 150-320F) and **Caen** (6hr, 1-3 per day, 140-290F), France. **Poole** to **Cherbourg** (4¼hr., 1-2 per day, 140-290F). **Cork** to **Roscoff** (13½hr., Apr.-Sept. 1 per week, 340-650F).

P&O North Sea Ferries: UK tel. (01482) 37 71 77; www.ponsf.com/ponsf/index.htm. Daily ferries from **Hull** to **Rotterdam, Netherlands** (13½hr.) and **Zeebrugge, Belgium** (14hr.). Both UK£36-46, with car UK£150-188. Online bookings.

Fjord Line: Norway tel. 55 54 88 00. **Newcastle, England** to **Stavanger** (19hr.) and **Bergen** (26hr.), Norway. Also between western Norway and Denmark.

Irish Ferries: Ireland tel. (01) 638 33 33; UK tel. (0990) 17 17 17; www.irishferries.ie. **Rosslare** to **Cherbourg** (17hr., IR£45-85); **Roscoff** (14½hr., Apr.-Sept. 1-2 per week, 315-650F); and **Pembroke, England** (3¾hr.). **Holyhead, England** to **Dublin** (2-3¼hr., return IR£35-60, students IR£28-48). **Cork** to **Roscoff** (15hr.; Apr. to mid-July 1 per week, 315-650F).

Stena Line: UK tel. (0990) 70 70 70; elsewhere call UK +44 (1233) 64 70 22; www.stenaline.co.uk. **Harwich, England** to **Hook of Holland** (3¾-8½hr., UK£24-29). **Fishguard** to **Rosslare** (1-3½hr., UK£20-41). **Holyhead** to **Dublin** (4hr., UK£30-35) and **Dún Laoghaire** (1-3½hr., £20-35, students £16-28). **Stranraer** to **Belfast** (1¾-3¼hr., UK£20-27; Mar.-Jan.).

GETTING AROUND EUROPE

Fares on all modes of transportation are either **single** (one-way) or **return** (round-trip). Unless stated otherwise, *Let's Go* always lists single fares. Round-trip fares on trains and buses in most of Europe are simply double the one-way fare.

BY TRAIN

In most of Europe, trains are the fastest and easiest way to travel. Second-class travel is pleasant, and compartments, which seat two to six, are excellent places to meet fellow travelers. Trains, however, are not always safe; for safety tips, see p. 27. For long trips make sure you are on the correct car, as trains sometimes split at crossroads. Towns listed in parentheses on European train schedules require a train switch at the town listed immediately before the parentheses.

You can either buy a **railpass,** which allows you unlimited travel within a particular region for a given period of time, or rely on buying individual **point-to-point** tickets as you go. Almost all countries give students or youths (usually defined as those under 26) direct discounts on regular domestic rail tickets, and many also sell a student or youth card that provides 20-50% off all fares for up to a year.

RESERVATIONS. While seat reservations are required only for selected trains (usually on major lines), you are not guaranteed a seat without one (US$3-10). Reservations are available on major trains as much as two months in advance, and Europeans often reserve far ahead of time; you should strongly consider reserving during peak holiday and tourist seasons (at the very latest a few hours ahead). It will be necessary to purchase a **supplement** (US$10-50) or special fare for high-speed or -quality trains such as Spain's AVE, Cisalpino, Finland's Pendolino S220, Italy's ETR500 and Pendolino, Germany's ICE, and certain French TGVs. InterRail holders must also purchase supplements (US$10-25) for trains like EuroCity, InterCity, Sweden's X2000, and many French TGVs; these supplements are unnecessary for Eurailpass and Europass holders.

OVERNIGHT TRAINS. Night trains have their advantages: you won't waste valuable daylight hours traveling, and you will be able to forego the hassle and considerable expense of securing a night's accommodation. However, night travel has its drawbacks as well: discomfort and sleepless nights are the most obvious; the scenery probably won't look as enticing in pitch black, either. **Sleeping accommodations** on trains differ from country to country, but typically you can either sleep upright in your seat (for free) or pay for a separate space. **Couchettes** (berths) typically have 4-6 seats per compartment (about US$20 per person); **sleepers** (beds) in private sleeping cars offer more privacy and comfort, but are considerably more expensive (US$40-150). If you are using a railpass valid only for a restricted number of days, inspect train schedules to maximize the use of your pass: an overnight train or boat journey uses up only one of your travel days if it departs after 7pm (you need only write in the next day's date on your pass).

SHOULD YOU BUY A RAILPASS? Railpasses were conceived to allow you to jump on any train in Europe, go wherever you want whenever you want, and change your plans at will. In practice, it's not so simple. You still must stand in line to validate your pass, pay for supplements, and fork over cash for seat and couchette reservations. More importantly, railpasses don't always pay off. Consult our **railplanner** (at the front of this book) to estimate the point-to-point cost of each leg of your journey; add them up and compare the total with the cost of a railpass. If you are planning to spend extensive time on trains, hopping between big cities, a railpass would probably be worth it. But in many cases, especially if you are under 26, point-to-point tickets may prove a cheaper option.

You may find it tough to make your railpass pay for itself in Belgium, Greece, Ireland, Italy, Luxembourg, the Netherlands, Portugal, Spain, Eastern Europe, or the Balkans, where train fares are reasonable, distances short, or buses preferable. If, however, the total cost of your trips nears the price of the pass, the convenience of avoiding ticket lines may be worth the difference.

MULTINATIONAL RAILPASSES

EURAILPASS. Eurail is **valid** in most of Western Europe: Austria, Belgium, Denmark, Finland, France, Germany, Greece, Hungary, Italy, Luxembourg, the Netherlands, Norway, Portugal, the Republic of Ireland, Spain, Sweden, and Switzerland. It is **not valid** in the UK. Standard **Eurailpasses,** valid for a consecutive given number of days, are most suitable for those planning on spending extensive time on trains every few days. **Flexipasses,** valid for any 10 or 15 (not necessarily consecutive) days in a two-month period, are more cost-effective for those traveling longer distances less frequently. **Saverpasses** provide first-class travel for travelers in groups of two to five (prices are per person). **Youthpasses** and **Youth Flexipasses** provide parallel second-class perks for those under 26.

EURAILPASSES	15 days	21 days	1 month	2 months	3 months
1st class Eurailpass	US$554	US$718	US$890	US$1260	US$1558
Eurail Saverpass	US$470	US$610	US$756	US$1072	US$1324
Eurail Youthpass	US$388	US$499	US$623	US$882	US$1089

EURAIL FLEXIPASSES	10 days in 2 months	15 days in 2 months
1st class Eurail Flexipass	US$654	US$862
Eurail Saver Flexipass	US$556	US$732
Eurail Youth Flexipass	US$458	US$599

Passholders receive a timetable for major routes and a map with details on possible ferry, steamer, bus, car rental, hotel, and Eurostar (see p. 57) discounts. Passholders often also receive reduced fares or free passage on many bus and boat lines. **Eurail freebies** (excepting surcharges such as reservation fees and port taxes) include: ferries between **Ireland** (Rosslare/Cork) and **France** (Cherbourg/Le Havre); sightseeing cruises on the Rhine (Cologne-Mainz) and Mosel (Koblenz-Cochem), as well as Europabus rides down the Romantic Road (Frankfurt-Füssen; 75% off) and Castle Road (Mannheim-Heidelberg-Nuremberg), in **Germany;** ferries between **Italy** and **Sardinia** (Civitavecchia-Golfo Aranci), **Sicily** (Villa S. Giovanni-Messina), and **Greece** (Brindisi-Patras); and boat trips between **Sweden** and **Denmark** (Helsingborg-Helsingør), **Germany** (Trelleborg-Sassnitz), and **Finland** (Ůmea/Sundsvall-Vaasa).

EUROPASS. The Europass is a slimmed-down version of the Eurailpass: it allows five to 15 days of unlimited travel in any two-month period within France, Germany, Italy, Spain, and Switzerland. **First-Class Europasses** (for individuals) and **Saverpasses** (for people traveling in groups of 2-5) range from US$348/296 per person (5 days) to US$728/620 (15 days). **Second-Class Youthpasses** for those ages 12-25 cost US$233-513. For a fee, you can add **additional zones** (Austria/Hungary; Belgium/Luxembourg/Netherlands; Greece Plus, including the ADN/HML ferry between Italy and Greece; and/or Portugal): $60 for one associated country, $100 for two. You are entitled to the same **freebies** afforded by the Eurailpass (see above), but only when they are within or between countries that you have purchased. Plan your itinerary before buying a Europass: it will save you money if your travels are confined to three to five adjacent Western European countries, or if you only want to go to large cities, but would be a waste if you plan to make lots of side-trips. If you're tempted to add many rail days and associate countries, consider a Eurailpass.

SHOPPING AROUND FOR A EURAIL OR EUROPASS. Railpasses and Europasses are designed by the EU itself, and are purchasable only by non-Europeans almost exclusively from non-European distributors. These passes must be sold at uniform prices determined by the EU. However, some travel agents tack on a US$10 handling fee, and others offer certain perks with purchase of a railpass, so shop around. Also, keep in mind that pass prices usually go up each year, so if you're planning to travel early in the year, save cash by purchasing before January 1 (you have three months from the purchase date to validate your pass in Europe).

It is best to buy your Eurail- or Europass before leaving; ~~~ major European cities sell them, and at a marked-up price. Once ~~~ probably have to use a credit card to buy over the phone from a rai~~~ non-EU country (one on the North American East Coast would be c~~~ could send the pass to you by express mail. Eurailpasses are non-refunda~~~ validated; if your pass is completely unused and invalidated and you have the~~~ nal purchase documents, you can get an 85% refund from the place of purcha~~~ You can get a replacement for a lost pass only if you have purchased insurance on it under the Pass Protection Plan (US$10). Eurailpasses are available through travel agents, student travel agencies like STA and Council (see p. 51), and **Rail Europe,** 500 Mamaroneck Ave, Harrison, NY 10528 (US tel. (888) 382-7245, fax (800) 432-1329; Canada tel. (800) 361-7245, fax (905) 602-4198; UK tel. (0990) 84 88 48; www.raileu-rope.com) or **DER Travel Services,** 9501 W. Devon Ave #301, Rosemont, IL 60018 (US tel. (888) 337-7350; fax (800) 282-7474; www.dertravel.com).

INTERRAIL PASS. If you have lived for at least six months in one of the European countries where InterRail Passes are valid, they prove an economical option. There are eight InterRail **zones:** A (Great Britain, Northern Ireland, Republic of Ireland), B (Norway, Sweden, and Finland), C (Germany, Austria, Denmark, and Switzerland), D (Croatia, Czech Republic, Hungary, Poland, and Slovakia), E (France, Belgium, Netherlands, and Luxembourg), F (Spain, Portugal, and Morocco), G (Greece, Italy, Slovenia, and Turkey, including a Greece-Italy ferry), and H (Bulgaria, Romania, Yugoslavia, and Macedonia). The **Under 26 InterRail Card** allows either 14 days or one month of unlimited travel within one, two, three or all of the eight zones; the cost is determined by the number of zones the pass covers (UK£159-259). If you buy a ticket including the zone in which you have claimed residence, you must still pay 50% fare for tickets inside your own country. The **Over 26 InterRail Card** provides Unlimited second-class travel in Austria, Bulgaria, Croatia, Czech Republic, Denmark, Finland, Germany, Greece, Hungary, Republic of Ireland, Luxembourg, Netherlands, Norway, Poland, Romania, Slovakia, Slovenia, Sweden, Turkey, and Yugoslavia inclusive for either 15 days (UK£215) or one month (UK£275).

Passholders receive **discounts** on rail travel, Eurostar journeys, and most ferries to Ireland, Scandinavia, and the rest of Europe. Most exclude **supplements** for high-speed trains. For info and ticket sales in Europe contact **Student Travel Center,** 24 Rupert St, 1st fl., London W1V 7FN (tel. (020) 74 37 81 01; fax 77 34 38 36; www.stu-dent-travel-centre.com). Tickets are also available from travel agents or main train stations throughout Europe.

OTHER MULTINATIONAL PASSES. If your travels will be limited to one area, regional passes are often good values. The **ScanRail Pass,** which gives you unlimited rail travel in Denmark, Finland, Norway, and Sweden, is available both in the UK and the US (standard/under 26 passes for 5 out of 15 days of 2nd-class travel US$187/140; 10 days out of 1 month US$301/226; 21 consecutive days US$348/261). The **Benelux Tourrail Pass** for Belgium, the Netherlands, and Luxembourg is available in the UK, in the US (5 days in 1 month 2nd-class US$155, under 26 US$104; 50% discount for companion traveler), and at train stations in Belgium and Luxembourg (but not the Netherlands). The **Balkan Flexipass,** which is valid for travel in Bulgaria, Greece, the Former Yugoslav Republic of Macedonia, Montenegro, Romania, Serbia, and Turkey (5 days in 1 month US$152, under 26 US$90). The **European East Pass** covers Austria, the Czech Republic, Hungary, Poland, and Slovakia (5 days in 1 month US$205).

DOMESTIC RAILPASSES

If you are planning to spend a significant amount of time within one country or region, a national pass—valid on all rail lines of a country's rail company—would probably be more cost-effective than a multinational pass. But consider the cons as well: many national passes are limited, and don't provide the free or discounted travel on many private railways and ferries that Eurail does. However, several onal and regional passes offer companion fares, allowing two adults traveling together to save about 50% on the price of one pass. Some of these passes can be bought only in Europe, some only outside of Europe; check with a railpass agent or with national tourist offices.

NATIONAL RAILPASSES. The domestic analogs of the Eurailpass, national railpasses are valid either for a given number of consecutive days or for a specific number of days within a given time period. Usually, they must be purchased before you leave. Though they will usually frequent travelers some money, in some cases (particularly in Eastern Europe) you may find that they are actually a more expensive alternative to point-to-point tickets. Examples include the **Britrail Pass, BritIreland Flexipass, Freedom of Scotland Travelpass, Irish Explorer,** Ireland's **Emerald Isle Card** and **Irish Rover, France Flexipass, German Flexipass, Austrian Flexipass, Greek Flexipass, Italian Railpass** and **Flexipass, Swiss Railpass** and **Flexipass, Holland Flexipass, Norway Flexipass, Sweden Railpass, Finnrail Flexipass, Iberic Flexipass, Spain Flexipass, Portuguese Flexipass, Bulgarian Flexipass, Polrail Pass, Czech Flexipass, Hungarian Flexipass,** and **Romanian Flexipass.** For more info, contact Rail Europe (see p. 60).

EURO DOMINO. Like the Interrail Pass, the Euro Domino pass is available to anyone who has lived in Europe for at least six months; it differs in that it is only valid in one country (which you designate upon buying the pass). It is available for 29 European countries as well as Morocco. Reservations must still be paid for separately. The Euro Domino pass is available for first- and second-class travel (with a special rate for under 26ers), for three, five, or 10 days of unlimited travel within a one-month period. Euro Domino is not valid on Eurostar or Thalys trains. **Supplements** for many high-speed (e.g., French TGV, German ICE, and Swedish X2000) trains are included (Spanish AVE is not), though you must still pay for **reservations** where they are compulsory (e.g., about 20F on the TGV). The pass must be bought within your country of residence (except for the Euro Domino Plus pass in the Netherlands, which also includes all bus, tram, and metro rides and can be bought in the Netherlands); each country has its own price for the pass. Inquire with your national rail company for more info.

REGIONAL PASSES. Another type of regional pass covers a specific area within a country or a round-trip from any border to a particular destination and back; these are useful as supplements when your main pass isn't valid. The **Prague Excursion Pass** is a common purchase for Eurailers, whose passes are not valid in the Czech Republic; it covers travel from any Czech border to Prague and back out of the country (round-trip must be completed within 7 days; 2nd-class US$35, under 26 US$30). The **Copenhagen Pass** is valid for Europass or German railpass holders from any German or Danish border to Copenhagen and back, while the **BritRail Southeast Pass** permits unlimited travel in southeast England (3 out of 8 days US$70).

RAIL-AND-DRIVE PASSES. In addition to simple railpasses, many countries (as well as Europass and Eurail) offer rail-and-drive passes, which combine car rental with rail travel—a good option for travelers who wish both to visit cities accessible by rail and to make side trips into the surrounding areas.

DISCOUNTED TICKETS

For travelers under 26, **BIJ** tickets (Billets Internationals de Jeunesse; a.k.a. **Wasteels, Eurotrain,** and **Route 26**) are a great alternative to railpasses. Available for international trips within Europe and for travel within France as well as most ferry services, they knock 20-40% off regular second-class fares. Tickets are good for 60 days after purchase and allow a number of stopovers along the normal direct route of the train journey. Issued for a specific international route between two points, they must be used in the direction and order of the designated route and must be bought in Europe. The equivalent for those over 26, **BIGT** tickets provide a 20-30% discount on 1st- and 2nd-class international tickets for business travelers, temporary residents of Europe, and their families. Both types of tickets are available from

FURTHER READING AND WEBSITES: TRAIN TRAVEL.
Rail schedules: bahn.hafas.de/bin/db.w97/query.exe/en. A testament to German efficiency, with minute-by-minute itineraries and connection information.
Point-to-point fares: www.raileurope.com/us/rail/fares_schedules.index.htm. Allows you to calculate whether buying a railpass would save you money. For a more convenient resource, see our **railplanner** at the front of this book.
European Railway Servers: home.wxs.nl/~grijns/timetables/time.html; mercurio.iet.unipi.it/home.html. Links to rail servers throughout Europe.
Thomas Cook European Timetable, updated monthly, covers all major and most minor train routes in Europe. In the US, order it from Forsyth Travel Library (US$28; tel. (800) 367-7984; www.forsyth.com). In Europe, find it at any Thomas Cook Money Exchange Center. Alternatively, buy directly from Thomas Cook (UK£10.10; UK tel. (1733) 50 35 71; www.thomascook.com).
Info on rail travel and railpasses: www.eurorail.com; www.raileuro.com.
Guide to European Railpasses, Rick Steves. Available online and by mail. US tel. (425) 771-8303; fax (425) 771-0833; www.ricksteves.com. Free.
On the Rails Around Europe, Melissa Shales. Passport Books (US$19).
Eurail and Train Travel Guide to Europe. Houghton Mifflin (US$15).

ESSENTIALS

European travel agents, at Wasteels or Eurotrain offices (usually in or near train stations), or directly at the ticket counter in some nations. For more info, contact **Wasteels,** Victoria Station, London SW1V 1JT (tel. (020) 78 34 70 66; fax 76 30 76 28).

BY BUS

Though European trains and railpasses are extremely popular, in some cases buses prove a better option. In Spain, Hungary, and the Baltics, the bus and train systems are on par; in Britain, Greece, Ireland, Portugal, and Turkey, bus networks are more extensive, efficient, and often more comfortable; and in Iceland and parts of northern Scandinavia, bus service is the only ground transportation available. In the rest of Europe, bus travel is more of a crapshoot; scattered offerings from private companies are often cheap, but sometimes unreliable. Amsterdam, Athens, Istanbul, London, Munich, and Oslo are centers for lines that offer long-distance rides across Europe. Often cheaper than railpasses, **international bus passes** typically allow unlimited travel on a hop-on, hop-off basis between major European cities. These services in general tend to be more popular among non-American backpackers. Note that **Eurobus,** a one-time UK-based bus service, is no longer in operation.

Eurolines, 4 Cardiff Rd, Luton, Bedfordshire L41 1PP (UK tel. (0990) 14 32 19; fax (01582) 40 06 94); and 52 Grosvenor Gardens, London SW1W 0AU (tel. (020) 77 30 82 35; www.eurolines.co.uk or www.eurolines.com). The largest operator of Europe-wide coach services. Unlimited 30-day (UK£229, under 26 and over 60 UK£199) or 60-day (UK£279/249) travel between 30 major European cities in 16 countries.

Busabout, 258 Vauxhall Bridge Rd, London SW1V 1BS (tel. (020) 79 50 16 61; fax 79 50 16 62; www.busabout.com). Offers 5 interconnecting bus circuits covering 60 cities and towns in Europe. Standard/student passes are valid for 15 days (US$395/285), 21 days (US$495/380), 1 month (US$635/465), 2 months (US$875/690), 3 months (US$1145/850), or an unlimited period of time (US$1250/910).

BY CAR

Although travel by car may insulate you from backpacker culture, it will allow more flexibility and accessibility. While a single traveler won't save cash by renting a car, four typically will. Rail Europe and other railpass vendors offer rail-and-drive packages both for individual countries and all of Europe. Fly-and-drive packages are often available from travel agents or airline/rental agency partnerships. For information on preparations, see **Driving Permits and Car Insurance,** p. 64.

ESSENTIALS

Before setting off, know the laws of the countries in which you'll be driving (e.g., both seat belts and headlights must be on at all times in Scandinavia, and remember to keep left in Ireland and the UK). For an informal primer on European road signs and conventions, check out www.travlang.com/signs. Additionally, the **Association for Safe International Road Travel (ASIRT)**, 5413 West Cedar Lane #103C, Bethesda, MD 20814 (US tel. (301) 983-5252; fax 983-3663; www.asirt.org), can provide more specific information about road conditions. ASIRT considers road travel (by car or bus) to be relatively **safe** in Denmark, Ireland, the Netherlands, Norway, Sweden, Switzerland, and the UK, and relatively **unsafe** in Turkey. Scandinavians and Western Europeans use unleaded **gas** almost exclusively, but it's not available in many gas stations in Eastern Europe.

DRIVING PERMITS AND CAR INSURANCE

INTERNATIONAL DRIVING PERMIT (IDP). If you plan to drive a car while abroad, you must have an International Driving Permit (IDP), although certain countries allow travelers to drive with a valid American or Canadian license for a limited number of months. It may be a good idea to get one anyway, in case you're in a situation (e.g., if you are in an accident or stranded in a smaller town) where the police do not know English; information on the IDP is printed in 10 languages, including Spanish, French, Italian, Portuguese, Swedish, Russian, and German.

Your IDP, valid for one year, must be issued in your own country before you depart. You must be 18 years old and have a valid driver's license. An application for an IDP usually needs to include one or two photos, a current local license, an additional form of identification, and a fee.

Australia: Contact your local Royal Automobile Club (RAC) or the National Royal Motorist Association (NRMA; tel. (08) 94 21 42 98; www.rac.com.au/travel). Permits AUS$15.

Canada: Contact any Canadian Automobile Association (CAA) branch, or write to CAA, 1145 Hunt Club Rd #200, K1V 0Y3 (tel. (613) 247-0117; fax 247-0118; www.caa.ca/CAAInternet/travelservices/internationaldocumentation). Permits CDN$10.

Ireland: Contact the nearest Automobile Association (AA) office or write: The Automobile Association, International Documents, Fanum House, Erskine, Renfrewshire PA8 6BW (tel. (0990) 50 06 00). Permits IR£4.

New Zealand: Contact your local Automobile Association (AA), or write Auckland Central, 99 Albert St (tel. (09) 377 46 60; fax 302 20 37; www.nzaa.co.nz.). Permits NZ$8.

South Africa: Contact your local Automobile Association of South Africa office, or write the head office at P.O. Box 596, 2000 Johannesburg (tel. (011) 799 10 00; fax 799 10 10). Permits SAR28.50.

UK: Visit your local AA Shop. To find the location nearest you that issues the IDP, call (0990) 50 06 00; www.theaa.co.uk/motoring/idp.asp. Permits UK£4.

US: Visit any American Automobile Association (AAA) office or write to AAA Florida, Travel Related Services, 1000 AAA Dr (mail stop 100), Heathrow, FL 32746 (tel. (407) 444-7000; fax 444-7380). You don't have to be a member to buy an IDP. Permits US$10. AAA Travel Related Services (tel. (800) 222-4357) provides road maps and many travel guides free to members, and provides emergency road services and auto insurance.

CAR INSURANCE. Most credit cards cover standard insurance. If you rent, lease, or borrow a car, you will need a **green card**, or **International Insurance Certificate**, to prove that you have liability insurance. Obtain it through the car rental agency; most include coverage in their prices. If you lease a car, you can obtain a green card from the dealer. Some travel agents offer the card; it may also be available at border crossings. Verify whether your auto insurance applies abroad; even if it does, you will still need a green card to certify this to foreign officials. If you have a collision abroad, the accident will show up on your domestic records if you report it to your insurance company. Rental agencies may require you to purchase theft insurance in countries that they consider to have a high risk of auto theft (such as Italy).

ACQUIRING SOME WHEELS

RENTING A CAR. You can rent a car from a US-based firm (Alamo, Avis, Budget, or Hertz) with European offices, from a European-based company with local representatives (Europcar), or from a tour operator (Auto Europe, Europe By Car, and Kemwel Holiday Autos), which will arrange a rental for you from a European company at its own rates. Multinationals offer greater flexibility, but tour operators often strike better deals. Picking up your car in Belgium, Germany or the Netherlands is usually cheaper than renting in Paris. Expect to pay US$80-400 per week, plus tax (5-25%), for a teensy car. Reserve ahead and pay in advance if at all possible. It is always significantly less expensive to reserve a car from the US than from Europe. Always check if prices quoted include tax and collision insurance; some credit card companies cover the deductible on collision insurance, allowing their customers to decline the collision damage waiver. Ask about discounts and check the terms of insurance, particularly the size of the deductible. Rates are generally lowest in Belgium, Germany, Holland, and the UK, and highest in Scandinavia and Eastern Europe. Ask airlines about special fly-and-drive packages; you may get up to a week of free or discounted rental. Minimum age varies by country, but is usually 21 to 25. At most agencies, all that's needed to rent a car is a license from home and proof that you've had it for a year.

Car rental in Europe is available through the following agencies: **Auto Europe,** 39 Commercial St, P.O. Box 7006, Portland, ME 04101 (US tel. (888) 223-5555; fax (800) 235-6321; www.autoeurope.com); **Avis** (US and Canada tel. (800) 331-1084; UK tel. (0990) 90 05 00; Australia tel. (800) 22 55 33; www.avis.com); **Budget** (US tel. (800) 472-3325; Canada tel. (800) 527-0700; UK tel. (0800) 18 11 81; Australia tel. 13 27 27; www.budgetrentacar.com); **Europe by Car,** One Rockefeller Plaza, New York, NY 10020 (US tel. (800) 223-1516 or (212) 581-3040; www.europebycar.com); **Europcar,** 145 av. Malekoff, 75016 Paris (tel. (01) 45 00 08 06); US tel. (800) 227-3876; Canada tel. (800) 227-7368; www.europcar.com); **Hertz** (US tel. (800) 654-3001; Canada tel. (800) 263-0600; UK tel. (0990) 99 66 99; Australia tel. 13 30 39; www.hertz.com); and **Kemwel Holiday Autos** (US tel. (800) 678-0678; www.kemwel.com).

LEASING A CAR. For longer than 17 days, leasing can be cheaper than renting; it is often the only option for those ages 18 to 21. The cheapest leases are agreements to buy the car and then sell it back to the manufacturer at a prearranged price. As far as you're concerned, though, it's a lease and doesn't entail enormous financial transactions. Leases generally include insurance coverage and are not taxed. The most affordable ones usually originate in Belgium, France, or Germany. Expect to pay around US$1100-1800 (depending on size of car) for 60 days. Contact **Auto Europe, Europe by Car,** or **Kemwel Holiday Autos** (see above) before you go.

BUYING A CAR. If you're brave and know what you're doing, buying a used car or van in Europe and selling it just before you leave can provide the cheapest wheels for longer trips. Check with consulates for import-export laws concerning used vehicles, registration, and safety and emission standards. Campervans and motor homes give the advantages of a car without the hassle and expense of finding lodgings. Most of these vehicles are diesel-powered and deliver roughly 24 to 30 miles per gallon of diesel fuel, which is cheaper than gas.

BY PLANE

Though flying is almost invariably more expensive than traveling by train, if you are short on time (or flush with cash) you might consider it. Student travel agencies sell cheap tickets, and budget fares are frequently available in the spring and summer on high-volume routes between northern Europe and resort areas in Italy, Greece, and Spain; consult budget travel agents and local newspapers. For info on cheap flights from Britain to the continent, see **Traveling from the UK,** p. 53.

In addition, a number of European airlines offer coupon packets that considerably discount the cost of each flight leg. Most are only available as tack-ons to their transatlantic passengers, but some are available as stand-alone offers. Most must be purchased before departure, so research in advance.

Europe by Air: US tel. (888) 387-2479, auto faxback (512) 404-1291; Australia tel. (02) 92 85 68 11; New Zealand tel. (09) 309 80 94; www.europebyair.com. Coupons good on 14 partner airlines to 60 European cities, mostly in Western Europe but including Istanbul, Moscow, and the Balkans. Must be purchased prior to departure; available only to non-European residents (3 min., no max.). US$99 each, excluding airport tax.

Alitalia: US tel. (800) 223-5730; www.alitaliausa.com. "Europlus," available to North Americans who fly into Milan or Rome on Alitalia, allows passengers to tack on 3 coupons good for flights to 48 airports in Europe. US$299; each additional ticket US$100.

Austrian Airlines: US tel. (800) 843-0002; www.austrianair.com/specials/visit-europe-fares.html. "Visit Europe," good to cities served by AA and partner airlines, is available in the US to Austrian Airlines transatlantic passengers (3 min., 8 max.). US$130 each.

Lufthansa: US tel. (800) 399-5838; www.lufthansa-usa.com/special_offers/discover_europe.html. "Discover Europe" is available to US travelers booked on a transatlantic Lufthansa flight or flying into Germany on a US carrier (3 coupons min.). US$140/125 each in high-/low-season; additional tickets (up to 6) US$125/105 each.

SAS: US tel. (800) 221-2350; www.flysas.com/airpass.html. One-way coupons for travel within Scandinavia, the Baltics, or all of Europe US$75-155. Most are available only to transatlantic SAS passengers, but partner carrier passengers may qualify; call for details.

KLM/Northwest: US tel. (800) 800-1504; www.nwa.com/vacpkg/europe/passport1.shtml. "Passport to Europe," available to US transatlantic passengers on either airline, connects 90 European cities (mostly Western European, but including a few Eastern European and North African destinations; 3 min., 12 max.). US$100 each.

Iberia: US tel. (800) 772-4642; www.iberia.com/ibusa/special.htm#europass. "Euro-Pass" allows North American Iberia passengers to Spain to tack on at least 2 additional destinations from the 35 they serve. Most US$125 each; some US$155 each.

BY BOAT

Most European ferries are quite comfortable; the cheapest ticket typically still includes a reclining chair or couchette. Fares jump sharply in July and August. Ask for discounts; ISIC holders can often get student fares, and Eurailpass holders get many reductions and free trips (for examples of popular freebies, also see p. 60). You'll occasionally have to pay a port tax (under US$10). For more info, consult the *Official Steamship Guide International* (available at travel agents), or www.youra.com/ferry or home.wxs.nl/~grijns/seatravel/ferries.html.

ENGLISH CHANNEL AND IRISH SEA FERRIES

Ferries are frequent and dependable. The main route across the **English Channel,** from England to France, is Dover-Calais. The main ferry port on the southern coast of England is Portsmouth, with connections to France and Spain. Ferries also cross the **Irish Sea,** connecting Northern Ireland with Scotland and England, and the Republic of Ireland with Wales. For more information on sailing (or hovering) in this region, see **By Boat from the UK and Ireland,** p. 58.

NORTH AND BALTIC SEA FERRIES

Ferries in the **North Sea** are reliable and go everywhere. Those content with deck passage rarely need to book ahead. For information on ferries heading across the North Sea to and from the UK, see p. 58. **Baltic Sea** ferries service routes between Poland and Scandinavia.

Polferries: Sweden tel. +46 (40) 12 17 00; fax 97 03 70; www.polferries.se. Copenhagen (10hr.) and Malmö, Sweden (4½hr.) to Świnoujście, Poland. Also Oxelösund-Stockholm to Gdańsk (17hr.).

Color Line: Norway tel. +47 81 00 08 11; fax 83 07 76; www.colorline.com. Oslo to Kiel (19½hr.). Hirtshals, Denmark to Oslo (8½hr.), Kristiansand (2½-4½hr.), and Moss (7-9hr.), Norway. Also Frederikshavn, Denmark to Moss (6¼-11hr.).

Silja Line: Finland tel. +358 (090) 71 44 00; www.silja.com. Helsinki to Stockholm (15hr.; June-Dec.); Tallinn (3hr.; June to mid-Sept.); and Rostock, Germany (23-25hr.; June to mid-Sept.). Turku to Stockholm (10hr.). Also Vaasa, Finland to Umeå, Sweden.

Scandinavian Seaways: See p. 58. Copenhagen to Oslo (16hr.; with Eurail 50% off).

MEDITERRANEAN AND AEGEAN FERRIES

Mediterranean ferries may be the most glamorous, but they can also be the most rocky. Ferries run from Spain to Morocco, from Italy to Tunisia, and from France to Morocco and Tunisia. Reservations are recommended, especially in July and August. Bring toilet paper. Ferries run on erratic schedules, with similar routes and varying prices. Shop around, and beware of dinky, unreliable companies that don't take reservations. Ferries float across the **Adriatic** from Ancona and Bari, Italy to Split and Dubrovnik, respectively, in Croatia.

Ferries also run across the **Aegean,** from Ancona, Italy to Patras, Greece (19hr.), and from Bari, Italy to Igoumenitsa (9hr.) and Patras (15hr.), Greece. **Eurail** is valid on certain ferries between Brindisi, Italy and Corfu (8hr.), Igoumenitsa, and Patras, Greece. Countless ferry companies operate these routes simultaneously; see specific country chapters for more information.

BY BICYCLE

Today, biking is one of the key elements of the classic budget Eurovoyage. With the proliferation of mountain bikes, you can do some serious natural sightseeing. Many airlines will count your bike as your second free piece of luggage; a few charge extra (US$60-110 one-way). Bikes must be packed in a cardboard box with the pedals and front wheel detached; many airlines sell bike boxes at the airport (US$10). Most ferries let you take your bike for free or for a nominal fee, and you can always ship your bike on trains. Renting a bike beats bringing your own if your touring will be confined to one or two regions. Some youth hostels rent bicycles for low prices. In Switzerland, train stations rent bikes and often allow you to drop them off elsewhere; check train stations throughout Europe for similar deals. In addition to **panniers** in which you can pack your luggage, you'll need a good **helmet** (US$25-50) and a good U-shaped **Citadel** or **Kryptonite lock** (from US$30). For equipment, **Bike Nashbar,** 4111 Simon Rd, Youngstown, OH 44512 (US tel. (800) 627-4227; www.nashbar.com), beats all competitors' offers and ships anywhere in the US or Canada. For more country-specific books on biking through France, Germany, Ireland, or the UK, or to purchase the more general *Europe by Bike*, by Karen and Terry Whitehall (US$15), try **Mountaineers Books,** 1001 S.W. Klickitat Way #201, Seattle, WA 98134 (US tel. (800) 553-4453 or (206) 223-6303; www.mountaineers.org).

If you are nervous about striking out on your own, **Blue Marble Travel** (Canada tel. (519) 624-2494; France tel. 01 42 36 02 34; US tel. (800) 258-8689 or (973) 326-9533; www.bluemarble.org) offers bike tours for small groups for those ages 20 to 50 through the Alps, Austria, France, Germany, Italy, Portugal, Scandinavia, and Spain. **CBT Tours,** 415 W. Fullerton #1003, Chicago, IL 60614 (US tel. (800) 736-2453) or (773) 404-1710; www.cbttours.com), offers full-package one- to seven-week biking, mountain biking, and hiking tours (around US$150 per day).

BY MOPED AND MOTORCYCLE

Motorized bikes don't use much gas, can be put on trains and ferries, and are a good compromise between the high cost of car travel and the limited range of bicycles. However, they're uncomfortable for long distances, dangerous in the rain, and unpredictable on rough roads and gravel. Always wear a helmet, and never ride with a backpack. If you've never been on a moped before, a twisting Alpine road is not the place to start. Expect to pay about US$20-35 per day; try auto repair shops, and remember to bargain. Motorcycles are more expensive and normally require a license, but are better for long distances. Before renting, ask if the quoted price includes tax and insurance, or you may be hit with an unexpected additional fee. Avoid handing your passport over as a deposit; if you have an accident or mechanical failure you may not get it back until you cover all repairs. Pay ahead of time instead. For more information, try **Europe by Motorcycle,** by Gregory Frazier (Arrowstar Publishing, US$20).

BY THUMB

 Let's Go strongly urges you to consider the risks before you choose to hitch. We do not recommend hitching as a safe means of transportation, and none of the information presented here is intended to do so.

No one should hitch without careful consideration of the risks involved. Hitching means entrusting your life to a random person who happens to stop beside you on the road and risking theft, assault, sexual harassment, and unsafe driving. In spite of this, there are advantages to hitching when it is safe: it allows you to meet local people and get where you're going, especially in northern Europe and Ireland, where public transportation is sketchy.

Safety-minded hitchers avoid getting in the back of a two-door car (or any car they wouldn't be able to get out of in a hurry) and never let go of their backpacks. If they ever feel threatened, they insist on being let off immediately. Acting as if they are going to open the car door or vomit on the upholstery will usually get a driver to stop. Hitchhiking at night can be particularly dangerous; experienced hitchers stand in well-lit places, and expect drivers to be leery of nocturnal thumbers (or open-handers).

Women traveling alone, hitching is just too dangerous. A man and a woman are a safer combination, two men will have a harder time, and three will go nowhere. Where one stands is vital. Experienced hitchers pick a spot outside of built-up areas, where drivers can stop, return to the road without causing an accident, and have time to look over potential passengers as they approach. Hitching (or even standing) on super-highways is usually illegal: one may only thumb at rest stops or at the entrance ramps to highways. In the **Practical Information** section of many cities, *Let's Go* lists the tram or bus lines that take travelers to strategic hitching points. Finally, success will depend on appearance. Successful hitchers travel light and stack their belongings in a compact but visible cluster. Most Europeans signal with an open hand rather than a thumb; many write their destination on a sign in large, bold letters and draw a smiley-face under it. Drivers prefer hitchers who are neat and wholesome. No one stops for anyone wearing sunglasses.

Britain and **Ireland** are probably the easiest places in Western Europe to get a lift. Hitching in **Scandinavia** is slow but steady. Long-distance hitching in the developed countries of northwestern Europe demands close attention to expressway junctions, rest stop locations, and often a destination sign. Hitching in southern Europe is generally mediocre; **France** is the worst. In some Central and Eastern European countries, the line between hitching and taking a taxi is quite thin.

Most Western European countries offer a ride service (listed in the **Practical Information** for major cities), a cross between hitchhiking and the ride boards common at many universities, which pairs drivers with riders; the fee varies according to destination. **Eurostop International** (**Verband der Deutschen Mitfahrzentralen** in Germany and **Allostop** in France) is one of the largest in Europe. Riders and drivers can enter their names on the Internet through the **Taxistop** website (www.taxistop.be). Not all these organizations screen drivers and riders; ask in advance.

BY FOOT

Europe's grandest scenery can often be seen only by foot. Let's Go describes many daytrips for those who want to hoof it, but native inhabitants (Europeans are fervent, almost obsessive hikers), hostel proprietors, and fellow travelers are the best source of tips. Many European countries have hiking and mountaineering organizations; alpine clubs in Germany, Austria, Switzerland, and Italy, as well as tourist organizations in Scandinavia, provide simple accommodations in splendid settings.

ADDITIONAL INFORMATION

SPECIFIC CONCERNS

WOMEN TRAVELERS

Women exploring on their own inevitably face some additional safety concerns, but it's easy to be adventurous without taking undue risks. If you are concerned, consider staying in hostels which offer single rooms that lock from the inside or in religious organizations with rooms for women only. Communal showers in some hostels are safer than others; check them before settling in. Stick to centrally located accommodations and avoid solitary late-night treks or metro rides.

When traveling, always carry extra money for a phone call, bus, or taxi. **Hitching** is never safe for lone women, or even for two women traveling together. Choose train compartments occupied by other women or couples; ask the conductor to put together a women-only compartment if he or she doesn't offer to do so first. Look as if you know where you're going (even when you don't) and approach older women or couples for directions if you're lost or feel uncomfortable.

Generally, the less you look like a tourist, the better off you'll be. Dress conservatively, especially in rural areas. Trying to fit in can be effective, but dressing to the style of an obviously different culture may cause you to be ill at ease and a conspicuous target. Wearing a conspicuous **wedding band** may help prevent unwanted overtures. Some travelers report that carrying pictures of a "husband" or "children" is extremely useful to help document marriage status. Even a mention of a husband waiting back at the hotel may be enough in some places to discount your potentially vulnerable, unattached appearance.

In cities, you may be harassed no matter how you're dressed. Your best answer to verbal harassment is no answer at all; feigning deafness, sitting motionless, and staring straight ahead at nothing in particular will do a world of good that reactions usually don't achieve. The extremely persistent can sometimes be dissuaded by a firm, loud, and very public "Go away!" in the appropriate language. Don't hesitate to seek out a police officer or a passerby if you are being harassed. Memorize the emergency numbers in places you visit, and consider carrying a whistle or airhorn on your keychain. An self-defense course will not only prepare you for a potential attack, but will also raise your level of awareness of your surroundings as well as your confidence (see **Self Defense,** p. 25). Women also face some specific health concerns when traveling (see p. 33).

FURTHER READING: WOMEN TRAVELERS.

A Journey of One's Own: Uncommon Advice for the Independent Woman Traveler (US$17) and *Adventures in Good Company: The Complete Guide to Women's Tours and Outdoor Trips* (US$7), by Thalia Zepatos. Eighth Mountain Press.
Active Women Vacation Guide, by Evelyn Kaye. Blue Panda Publications (US$18).
Travelers' Tales: Gutsy Women, Travel Tips and Wisdom for the Road, by Marybeth Bond. Traveler's Tales (US$8).
A Foxy Old Woman's Guide to Traveling Alone, by Jay Ben-Lesser. Crossing Press (US$11).

TRAVELING ALONE

There are many benefits to traveling alone, among them greater independence and challenge. As a lone traveler, you have greater opportunity to interact with the residents of the region you're visiting. Without distraction, you can write a great travelogue in the grand tradition of Mark Twain, John Steinbeck, and Charles Kuralt.

On the other hand, any solo traveler is a more vulnerable target of harassment and street theft. Lone travelers need to be well-organized and look confident at all times. Try not to stand out as a tourist, and be especially careful in deserted or very crowded areas. If questioned, never admit that you are traveling alone. Maintain regular contact with someone at home who knows your itinerary.

ESSENTIALS

A number of organizations also supply information for solo travelers, and others find travel companions for those who don't want to go alone. Here are a few:

The Single Traveler Newsletter, P.O. Box 682, Ross, CA 94957 (US tel. (415) 389-0227; 6 issues US$29).

American International Homestays, P.O. Box 1754, Nederland, CO 80466 (US tel. (800) 876-2048; www.commerce.com/homestays). Lodgings with host families in E. Europe.

Connecting: Solo Traveler Network, P.O. Box 29088, 1996 W. Broadway, Vancouver, BC V6J 5C2 (Canada tel. (604) 737-7791; www.cstn.org). Membership US$25-35.

Travel Companion Exchange, P.O. Box 833, Amityville, NY 11701 (US tel. (800) 392-1256; www.travelalone.com). Newsletter links up travel partners (subscription US$48).

OLDER TRAVELERS

Senior citizens are eligible for a wide range of discounts on transportation, museums, movies, theaters, concerts, restaurants, and accommodations. If you don't see a senior citizen price listed, ask, and you may be delightfully surprised.

ElderTreks, 597 Markham St, Toronto, ON M6G 2L7 (Canada tel. (800) 741-7956 or (416) 588-5000; fax 588-9839; email passages@inforamp.net; www.eldertreks.com).

Elderhostel, 75 Federal St, Boston, MA 02110 (US tel. (617) 426-7788; www.elderhostel.org). One- to 4-week programs at universities and other institutions in Europe.

The Mature Traveler, P.O. Box 50400, Reno, NV 89513 (US tel. (800) 460-6676; www.maturetraveler.com). Soft-adventure tours for seniors. Subscription US$30.

Walking the World, P.O. Box 1186, Fort Collins, CO 80522 (US tel. (970) 498-0500; www.walkingtheworld.com). Trips to Britain, Ireland, France, Italy, Portugal, Switzerland.

FURTHER READING: OLDER TRAVELERS.
No Problem! Worldwise Tips for Mature Adventurers, by Janice Kenyon. Orca Books (US$16).
A Senior's Guide to Healthy Travel, by Donald L. Sullivan. Career Press (US$15).
Unbelievably Good Deals and Great Adventures That You Absolutely Can't Get Unless You're over 50, by Joan Rattner Heilman. Contemporary Books (US$13).

BISEXUAL, GAY, AND LESBIAN TRAVELERS

Attitudes toward bisexual, gay, and lesbian travelers are particular to each region, with acceptance generally highest in the Netherlands and particularly low in Turkey. Listed below are organizations and publishers which address those concerns.

Gay's the Word, 66 Marchmont St, London WC1N 1AB (tel. (020) 72 78 76 54; freespace.virgin.net/gays.theword). The largest gay and lesbian bookshop in the UK.

Giovanni's Room, 345 S. 12th St, Philadelphia, PA 19107 (US tel. (215) 923-2960; fax 923-0813). International feminist, lesbian, and gay bookstore with mail-order service.

International Gay and Lesbian Travel Association, 4331 N. Federal Hwy #304, Fort Lauderdale, FL 33308 (US tel. (800) 448-8550; fax (954) 776-3303; www.iglta.com). Over 1350 companies. Call for lists of travel agents, accommodations, and events.

FURTHER READING: GAY AND LESBIAN TRAVELERS.
Spartacus International Gay Guide, by Bruno Gmünder Verlag (US$33).
Damron Men's Guide, Damron's Accommodations, The Women's Traveller, and travel guides including *Amsterdam.* Damron (US tel. (800) 462-6654; www.damron.com; US$10-19).
Gay Travel A to Z, Men's Travel in Your Pocket, Women's Travel in Your Pocket, Inn Places, and guides (US$14-18) including *Gay Paris.* Ferrari Guides (US tel. (800) 962-2912; www.q-net.com).
The Gay Vacation Guide: The Best Trips and How to Plan Them, by Mark Chesnut. Citadel Press (US$15).

International Lesbian and Gay Association (ILGA), 81 rue Marché-au-Charbon, 1000 Brussels, Belgium (tel./fax +32 (2) 502 24 71; email ilga@ilga.org; www.ilga.org). Not a travel service. Provides political info, such as homosexuality laws of individual countries.

TRAVELERS WITH DISABILITIES

Countries vary in accessibility to travelers with disabilities. Some national and regional tourist boards provide directories on the accessibility of various accommodations and transportation services. If these services are not available, contact institutions of interest directly. Those with disabilities should inform airlines and hotels of their disabilities when making arrangements for travel; some time may be needed to prepare special accommodations. Call ahead to restaurants, hotels, parks, and other facilities to find out about the existence of ramps, the widths of doors, the dimensions of elevators, etc. **Guide dog owners** should inquire as to the specific quarantine policies of each destination country. At the very least, they will need to provide a certificate of immunization against rabies.

Rail is probably the most convenient form of travel for disabled travelers in Europe: many stations have ramps, and some trains have wheelchair lifts, special seating areas, and specially equipped toilets. Large stations in Britain are equipped with wheelchair facilities, and the French national railroad offers wheelchair compartments on all TGV (high speed) and Conrail trains. All Eurostar, some InterCity (IC) and some EuroCity (EC) trains are wheelchair-accessible and CityNightLine trains, French TGV (high speed) and Conrail trains feature special compartments. In general, the countries with the most **wheelchair-accessible rail networks** are: Denmark (IC and Lyn trains), France (TGVs and other long-distance trains), Germany (ICE, EC, IC, and IR trains), Italy (all Pendolino and many EC and IC trains), the Netherlands (most trains), the Republic of Ireland (most major trains), Sweden (X2000s, most IC and IR trains), and Switzerland (all IC, most EC, and some regional trains). Austria, Poland, and Great Britain offer accessibility on selected routes. Bulgaria, the Czech Republic, Greece, Hungary, Slovakia, Spain, and Turkey's rail systems have limited resources for wheelchair accessibility. Some major **car rental** agencies (Hertz, Avis, and National) may offer hand-controlled vehicles.

The following organizations either provide information or publications that might be of assistance, or arrange tours or trips for disabled travelers.

Mobility International USA (MIUSA), P.O. Box 10767, Eugene, OR 97440 (tel. (541) 343-1284 voice and TDD; fax 343-6812; www.miusa.org). Call for publications.

Moss Rehab Hospital Travel Information Service (US tel. (215) 456-9600; www.mossresourcenet.org). A telephone and internet information resource center on international travel accessibility and other travel-related concerns for those with disabilities.

Society for the Advancement of Travel for the Handicapped (SATH), 347 Fifth Ave #610, New York, NY 10016 (tel. (212) 447-1928; fax 725-8253; www.sath.org). Publishing the magazine *OPEN WORLD* (members free; nonmembers US$13) and info sheets on accessible destinations. Annual membership US$45, students and seniors US$30.

Directions Unlimited, 720 N. Bedford Rd, Bedford Hills, NY 10507 (tel. (800) 533-5343; fax (914) 241-0243; email cruisesusa@aol.com). Arranges individual and group vacations, tours, and cruises for the physically disabled. Group tours for blind travelers.

FURTHER READING: DISABLED TRAVELERS.
Access in London, by Gordon Couch. Cimino Publishing Group (US$12).
Access in Paris, by Gordon Couch. Quiller Press (US$12).
Resource Directory for the Disabled, by Richard Neil Shrout. Facts on File (US$45).
Wheelchair Through Europe, by Annie Mackin. Graphic Language Press (US tel. (760) 944-9594; email niteowl@cts.com; US$13).
Global Access: Links for disabled travelers in Europe. www.geocities.com/Paris/1502/disabilitylinks.html.

MINORITY TRAVELERS

In general, minority travelers will find a high level of tolerance in large cities; the small towns and the countryside are more unpredictable. Western Europe tends to be more tolerant than Eastern Europe, though travelers should feel more comfortable in large eastern and central cities like Budapest and Warsaw. *Romany* (Gypsies) encounter the most hostility throughout Eastern Europe, and travelers with darker skin of any nationality might be mistaken for *Romany* and face unpleasant consequences. Other minority travelers, especially those of African or Asian descent, will usually meet with more curiosity than hostility; travelers of Arab ethnicity may also be treated more suspiciously. Skinheads are on the rise in Eastern Europe, and minority travelers, especially Jews and blacks, should regard them with caution. Anti-Semitism is still a problem in many countries, including Poland and the former Soviet Union; sad to say, it is generally best to be discreet about your religion. Still, attitudes will vary from country to country and town to town; travelers should use common sense—someone who flashes money around will become a target regardless of any racial or religious differences.

TRAVELERS WITH CHILDREN

Family vacations often require that you slow your pace, and always require that you plan ahead. When deciding where to stay, remember the special needs of young children; if you pick a B&B or a small hotel, call ahead and make sure it's child-friendly. If you rent a car, make sure the rental company provides a car seat for younger children. Be sure that your child carries some sort of ID in case of an emergency or he or she gets lost. Restaurants often have children's menus and discounts. Virtually all museums and tourist attractions also have a children's rate. Children under two generally fly for 10% of the adult airfare on international flights (this does not necessarily include a seat). International fares are usually discounted 25% for children from two to 11. Finding a private place for **breast feeding** is often a problem while traveling, so pack accordingly.

FURTHER READING: TRAVELING WITH CHILDREN.
Backpacking with Babies and Small Children, by Goldie Silverman. Wilderness Press (US$10).
Take Your Kids to Europe, by Cynthia W. Harriman. Globe Pequot (US$17).
How to Take Great Trips with Your Kids, by Sanford and Jane Portnoy. Harvard Common Press (US $10).
Have Kid, Will Travel: 101 Survival Strategies for Vacationing with Babies and Young Children, by Claire and Lucille Tristram. Andrews and McMeel (US$9).
Adventuring with Children: An Inspirational Guide to World Travel and the Outdoors, by Nan Jeffrey. Avalon House (US$15).

DIETARY CONCERNS

Vegetarians should have no problem finding suitable cuisine in most of Europe. In city listings, *Let's Go* notes many restaurants that cater to vegetarians or that offer good vegetarian selections. Travelers who keep kosher should contact synagogues in larger cities for info on **kosher** restaurants. If you are strict in your observance, you may have to prepare your own food on the road. For more info, contact:

The Vegetarian Society of the UK (VSUK), Parkdale, Dunham Rd, Altringham, Cheshire WA14 4QG (tel. (0161) 928 07 93; fax 926 9182; www.vegsoc.org).

North American Vegetarian Society, P.O. Box 72, Dolgeville, NY 13329 (US tel. (518) 568-7970; email navs@telenet.com; www.cyberveg.org/navs).

The Jewish Travel Guide lists synagogues and kosher restaurants in 80 countries. Available from Vallentine-Mitchell Publishers, Newbury House 890-900, Eastern Ave, Newbury Park, Ilford, Essex IG2 7HH, UK (tel. (020) 85 99 88 66; fax 85 99 09 84); and in the US from ISBS, 5804 NE Hassallo St, Portland, OR 97213 (tel. (800) 944-6190; US$16).

FURTHER READING: DIETARY CONCERNS.
The Vegan Travel Guide: UK and Southern Ireland. Book Publishing Co. (US$15).
The Vegetarian Traveler: Where to Stay If You're Vegetarian, by Jed Civic. Larson Publishing (US$16).
Europe on 10 Salads a Day, by Mary Jane Edwards. Mustang Publishing (US$10).

ALTERNATIVES TO TOURISM

STUDYING ABROAD

The opportunities for studying in Europe are boundless: whether you seek a college semester abroad, a summer of foreign-language immersion, or a top-notch cooking school, you are sure to find a program tailored to your needs. Most American undergraduates enroll in programs sponsored by US universities. However, if your language skills are already decent, local universities can be much cheaper; enrolling directly in one usually involves passing a language-proficiency test.

Studying abroad in Europe usually requires applying for a special study **visa,** issued for a duration longer than a tourist visa. Applying for such a visa usually requires proof of admission to an appropriate university or program. In some countries, student status will affect your right to work. Information on visa and other requirements should be available from foreign embassies at home.

STUDY ABROAD ORGANIZATIONS

American Institute for Foreign Study, College Division, 102 Greenwich Ave, Greenwich, CT 06830 (tel. (800) 727-2437, ext. 6084; www.aifs.com). Organizes programs for high school and college study in universities in Austria, the Czech Republic, Russia, Britain, Ireland, France, Italy, Spain, and the Netherlands.

School for International Training, Kipling Rd, P.O. Box 676, Brattleboro, VT 05302 (US tel. (800) 336-1616; fax 258-3500; www.worldlearning.org). Runs semester- and year-long programs in Eastern Europe, France, Germany, Greece, London, and Spain (US$8200-10,300). Also operates summer programs (tel. (800) 345-2929; fax (802) 258-3428) in Britain, France, Ireland, Italy, and Spain (US$1800-5000).

Council on International Educational Exchange (CIEE), 205 East 42nd St, New York, NY 10017 (tel. (888) 268-6245; fax (212) 822-2699; www.ciee.org), sponsors work, volunteer, internships, and study abroad programs in Britain, France, Ireland, Italy, and Spain.

LANGUAGE SCHOOLS

Eurocentres, 101 N. Union St #300, Alexandria, VA 22314 (US tel. (800) 648-4809, fax 684-1495; www.eurocentres.com) or Head Office, Seestrasse 247, CH-8038 Zurich, Switzerland (tel. +41 (1) 485 50 40; fax 481 61 24), arranges language study and homestays in Eastern Europe, France, Germany, Italy, and Spain for US$1132 a month.

World Exchange, Ltd., White Birch Rd, Putnam Valley, NY 10579 (US tel. (800) 444-3924; fax 528-9187; www.worldexchange.org), offers 1- to 4-week language-based homestay programs offered in France or Spain (up to 14 days US$850; 15-28 days US$1,150).

FURTHER READING: STUDYING ABROAD.
Academic Year Abroad (US$45) and *Vacation Study Abroad* (US$40). Institute of International Education Books.
Peterson's Study Abroad Guide. Peterson's (US$30).

WORKING

There's no better way to submerge yourself in a foreign culture than to become part of its economy. **European Union citizens** can work in any EU country; if your parents were born in an EU country, you may be able to claim dual citizenship or the right to a permit (note that in some cases citizenship entails compulsory military service). Officially, **non-EU citizens** can hold a job in Europe only with a **work permit,**

ESSENTIALS

obtained by your employer, usually demonstrating that you have skills that locals lack. Working in Eastern Europe often requires both a work permit and a visa. In some countries, a particular visa called a "visa with work permit" is required, though this document (contrary to the name) actually does *not* include a work permit; in order to apply for one of these special visas (issued from the nearest consulate or embassy like any other visa), you must first acquire a work permit from the Labor Bureau of the country in question.

If you are a full-time student at a US university, the simplest way to get a job abroad in Britain, Ireland, France, or Germany is through work permit programs run by **CIEE** (see p. 51). For a US$225 application fee, Council can procure three- to six-month work permits. European friends can expedite permits or arrange work-for-accommodations swaps. You can be an au pair or advertise to teach English. Many permit-less agricultural workers go untroubled. Check with universities' foreign language departments for job opening connections, and contact the consulate or embassy of your destination country for more information.

interExchange, 161 Sixth Ave, New York, NY 10013 (US tel. (212) 924-0446; fax 924-0575; email interex@earthlink.net), provides au pair jobs in Austria, Britain, Eastern Europe, France, Germany, Ireland, Italy, Spain, and Switzerland.

Childcare International, Ltd., Trafalgar House, Grenville Pl, London NW7 3SA (tel. (020) 89 06 31 16; fax 89 06 34 61; www.childint.demon.co.uk), offers au pair positions in Austria, Belgium, France, Germany, the Netherlands, Italy, Spain, and Switzerland.

International Schools Services, Educational Staffing Program, P.O. Box 5910, Princeton, NJ 08543 (US tel. (609) 452-0990; fax 452-2690; www.iss.edu). Recruits teachers for American and English schools throughout Europe. Applicants must have a bachelor's degree and 2 years of relevant experience. Nonrefundable US$100 application fee.

Office of Overseas Schools, A/OS Room 245, SA-29, Dept. of State, Washington, DC 20522 (tel. (703) 875-7800; fax 875-7979; http://state.gov/www/about_state/schools). Keeps a list of resources for Americans who want to teach abroad.

Willing Workers on Organic Farms (WWOOF), PO Box 2675, Lewes, UK BN7 1RB (www.phdcc.com/sites/wwoof). Membership (US$10) allows you to exchange work for room and board at organic farms in Austria, Britain, Denmark, Finland, France, Germany, Hungary, Ireland, Italy, and Switzerland.

Archaeological Institute of America, 656 Beacon St, Boston, MA 02215 (US tel. (617) 353-9361; fax 353-6550; www.archaeological.org). Puts out a list of field sites in Italy, France, Greece, and Turkey (nonmembers US$16), available from Kendall/Hunt Publishing, 4050 Westmark Dr, Dubuque, IA 52002 (tel. (800) 228-0810).

VOLUNTEER

Volunteer jobs are readily available almost everywhere. You may receive room and board in exchange for your labor. You can sometimes avoid the high application fees charged by placement organizations by contacting workcamps directly.

Peace Corps, 1111 20th St NW, Washington, DC 20526 (tel. (800) 424-8580; www.peacecorps.gov). Opportunities for US citizens in a variety of fields in developing nations in Eastern Europe. Two-year commitment. A bachelor's degree is usually required.

FURTHER READING: WORKING ABROAD.

International Jobs: Where They Are, How to Get Them, by Eric Koocher. Perseus Books (US$16).

How to Get a Job in Europe, by Robert Sanborn. Surrey Books (US$22).

The Alternative Travel Directory (US$20) and *Work Abroad* (US$16), by Clayton Hubbs. Transitions Abroad.

International Directory of Voluntary Work, by Victoria Pybus. Vacation Work Publications (US$16).

Teaching English Abroad, by Susan Griffin. Vacation Work Publications (US$17).

Overseas Summer Jobs 1999, Work Your Way Around the World, and *Directory of Jobs and Careers Abroad.* Peterson's (US$17-18).

ESSENTIALS

Service Civil International Voluntary Service (SCI-VS), 814 NE 40th St, Seattle, WA 98105 (US tel./fax (206) 545-6585; email sciivsusa@igc.apc.org). Arranges placement in workcamps in Europe for those age 18 and over. Registration fee US$50-250.

Volunteers for Peace, 1034 Tiffany Rd, Belmont, VT 05730 (tel. (802) 259-2759; fax 259-2922; www.vfp.org). A nonprofit organization that arranges speedy placement in 2- to 3-week, 10- to 15-person workcamps in Europe. Registration fee US$195. Free newsletter.

OTHER RESOURCES

Let's Go tries to cover all aspects of budget travel, but we can't put *everything* in our guides. Listed below are books, travel organizations, and websites that can serve as jumping off points for your own research.

TRAVEL PUBLISHERS & BOOKSTORES

Hippocrene Books, Inc., 171 Madison Ave, New York, NY 10016 (tel. (212) 685-4371; orders (718) 454-236; fax 454-1391; www.hippocrenebooks.com). Free catalog. Publishes travel guides, as well as foreign language dictionaries and learning guides galore.

Hunter Publishing, 130 Campus Dr, Edison, NJ 08818 (US tel. (800) 255-0343; fax 417-0482; www.hunterpublishing.com). Extensive catalog of travel books, guides, language learning tapes, and quality maps, and hotel guides for throughout Europe.

Rand McNally, 150 S. Wacker Dr, Chicago, IL 60606 (tel. (800) 234-0679 or (312) 332-2009; fax 443-9540; email storekeeper@randmcnally.com; www.randmcnally.com), publishes a number of comprehensive road atlases (US$10).

Travel Books & Language Center, Inc., 4437 Wisconsin Ave NW, Washington, DC 20016 (tel. (800) 220-2665; fax 237-6022; www.bookweb.org/bookstore/travelbks). Language cassettes, dictionaries, travel books, atlases, and maps. No web orders.

Bon Voyage!, 2069 W. Bullard Ave, Fresno, CA 93711-1200 (US tel. (800) 995-9716, elsewhere call US (209) 447-8441; fax 266-6460; www.bon-voyage-travel.com), specializes in titles on Europe. Free catalog.

THE WORLD WIDE WEB

Almost every aspect of budget travel (with the most notable exception, of course, being experience) is accessible via the web. Even if you don't have internet access at home, seeking it out at a public library or at work would be well worth it; within 10min. at the keyboard, you can make a reservation at a hostel in France, get advice on travel hotspots or experiences from other travelers who have just returned from Europe, or find out exactly how much a train from Barcelona to Rome costs.

Listed here are some budget travel sites to start off your surfing; other relevant web sites are listed throughout the book. Because website turnover is high, use search engines (such as www.yahoo.com) to strike out on your own. But in doing so, keep in mind that most travel web sites simply exist to get your money.

LEARNING THE ART OF BUDGET TRAVEL

Backpacker's Ultimate Guide: www.bugeurope.com. Tips on packing, transportation, and where to go. Also tons of country-specific travel information.

Backpack Europe: www.backpackeurope.com. Helpful tips, a bulletin board, and links.

How to See the World: www.artoftravel.com. A compendium of great travel tips, from cheap flights to self defense to interacting with local culture.

TripSpot: www.tripspot.com/europefeature.htm. Good outline of the basics of backpacking through Europe, with a healthy set of links.

Rec. Travel Library: www.travel-library.com/europe/index.html. Fantastic set of links for general information on traveling in Europe as well as personal travelogues.

Shoestring Travel: www.stratpub.com. An e-zine focusing on budget travel.

COUNTRY-SPECIFIC INFORMATION

CIA World Factbook: www.odci.gov/cia/publications/factbook/index.html. Tons of vital statistics on European geography, governments, economies, and peoples.

Foreign Language for Travelers: www.travlang.com. Provides free online translating dictionaries and lists of phrases in European languages from Albanian to Yiddish.

DESTINATION GUIDES

MyTravelGuide: www.mytravelguide.com. Country overviews, with everything from history to transportation to live web cam coverage from the country of choice.

Geographia: www.geographia.com. Describes highlights and attractions of the various European countries.

Atevo Travel: www.atevo.com/guides/destinations. Detailed introductions, travel tips, and suggested itineraries.

Columbus Travel Guides: www.travel-guides.com/navigate/region/eur.asp. Helpful practical information.

LeisurePlanet: www.leisureplanet.com/TravelGuides. Good general background.

CNN: www.cnn.com/TRAVEL/CITY.GUIDES. Detailed information about services, sights, events, and nightlife in the major cities of Europe.

In Your Pocket: www.inyourpocket.com. Fantastic virtual guides to select Baltic and Eastern European cities.

LINKS TO EUROPEAN TOURISM PAGES

Everything's Travel: members.aol.com/dadeacn/dest/europe/index.htm. Thorough set of links to sites overseas, organized by country.

TravelPage: www.travelpage.com. Links to official tourist office sites throughout Europe.

Lycos: cityguide.lycos.com/europe. General introductions to cities and regions throughout Europe, accompanied by links to applicable histories, news, and local tourism sites.

PlanetRider: www.planetrider.com/Europe-index.cfm. A subjective list of links to the "best" websites covering the culture and tourist attractions of major European cities.

FURTHER READING: SURFING THE WEB.

How to Plan Your Dream Vacation Using the Web, by Elizabeth Dempsey. Coriolis Group (US$25).

Nettravel: How Travelers Use the Internet, by Michael Shapiro. O'Reilly & Associates (US$25).

Travel Planning Online for Dummies, by Noah Vadnai. IDG Books (US$25).

PRICES (US$), TRAVEL TIMES, AND DISTANCES (KM) BY TRAIN

	Amsterdam	Barcelona	Berlin	Brussels	Budapest	Copenhagen	Florence	Kraków	Madrid	Milan	Munich	Paris	Prague	Rome	Warsaw	Venice	Vienna	Zürich
Amsterdam		1773	673	246	1620	807	1530	1358	2013	1053	885	554	1044	1678	1240	1662	1249	990
Barcelona	$179; 16¾hr.[1]		2193	1531	2273	2096	1493	n/a	728	1044	1335	1219	2583	1443	2776	1358	2000	1160
Berlin	$108; 7hr.	$314 27¼hr.[1]		169	1004	280	1253	685	2582	1271	679	1123	371	1650	567	1234	772	963
Brussels	$31-37; 2½hr.	$178 15½hr.[1]	$203; 10½hr.		1191	904	1276	n/a	1919	1267	877	460	1049	1848	736	1201	1346	613
Budapest	$247; 18hr.[1]	$259; 26½hr.[1]	$104; 6¾hr.	$215; 16½hr.[1]		1260	1146	592	3112	1156	735	1653	621	1275	940	705	267	1023
Copenhagen	$141; 14hr.	n/a	$104; 6¾hr.	$173; 12hr.	n/a		1880	n/a	2575	1608	1235	1116	651	2106	847	n/a	1052	1268
Florence	$225; 18hr.[1]	$128; 19¾hr.[1]	$181; 17½hr.	$178; 12hr.[1]	$123; 14½hr.[1]	$293; 18½hr.[1]		1297	1936	316	645	1212	1084	316	n/a	257	879	663
Kraków	$145; 15½hr.[1]	n/a	$37; 8½hr.	n/a	$49; 10½hr.	n/a	$129; 18¼hr.[1]		n/a	n/a	887	698	534	n/a	320	n/a	418	1320
Madrid	$215; 17½hr.[1]	$61; 7hr.	$291; 26¼hr.[1]	$201; 15hr.[1]	$351; 31¼hr.[1]	$379; 27¾[2]	$176; 25hr.[1]	n/a		1535	2349	1459	2823	1880	2961	1806	2849	2073
Milan	$196; 14½hr.	$112; 12½hr.	$183; 17½hr.[1]	$134; 12hr.	$127; 15¾hr.[1]	$297; 21hr.	$27; 3½hr.	n/a	$170; 25¼hr.[1]		592	953	1031	632	1497	258	889	293
Munich	$154; 10hr.	$204; 16¾hr.[1]	$115; 10hr.	$148; 8½hr.	$93; 8hr.	$222; 10½hr.[1]	$71; 8hr.	$110; 11¾hr.[1]	$257; 24hr.	$68; 7½hr.		923	439	971	1201	577	469	354
Paris	$82; 4¼hr.	$110; 12½hr.	$158; 13hr.	$68; 1¾hr.	$218; 18hr.	$246; 14½hr.	$134; 10½hr.	$238; 23¼hr.[1]	$133; 13¼hr.	$117; 6¾hr.	$130; 8½hr.		1364	1585	1690	1220	1390	614
Prague	$165; 12½hr.[1]	$280; 28¼hr.[1]	$57; 5½hr.	$159; 13½hr.[1]	$59; 7¾hr.	$161; 12¼hr.	$133; 14hr.[1]	$47; 8½hr.	$319; 28¼hr.[1]	$130; 13½hr.[1]	$62; 6hr.	$186; 15hr.		1410	702	700	407	767
Rome	$262; 20hr.	$143; 21¼hr.[1]	$207; 17¾hr.[1]	$240; 18¾hr.[1]	$120; 18hr.[1]	$314; 20¾hr.[1]	$27; 1¾hr.	n/a	$192; 30½hr.[1]	$47; 4½hr.	$92; 10¼hr.	$158; 14½hr.	$154; 16¼hr.[1]		2255	570	1203	979
Warsaw	$144; 13hr.[1]	$348; 34½hr.[1]	$36; 6hr.	$174; 16½hr.[1]	$89; 11¼hr.[1]	$140; 12¾hr.[1]	n/a	$19; 2¾hr.	n/a	n/a	$112; 16½hr.[1]	$194; 19hr.[1]	$50; 10½hr.	$152; 24hr.		1303	673	1600
Venice	$222; 17hr.[1]	$141; 22hr.[1]	$255; 17hr.	$161; 15¼hr.[1]	$76; 13hr.	n/a	$24; 2¾hr.	n/a	$189; 30½hr.[1]	$24; 3hr.	$68; 7hr.	$137; 12½hr.	$110; 13½hr.	$44; 5hr.	$121; 17¼hr.[1]		630	614
Vienna	$196; 13hr.[1]	$221; 23hr.	$90; 10hr.	$214; 13½hr.[1]	$38; 3hr.	$194; 16¾hr.	$85; 11½hr.	$44; 6¾hr.	$324; 28¼hr.[1]	$89; 12¾hr.	$66; 5hr.	$191; 15hr.	$45; 5½hr.	$106; 13hr.	$51; 8¼hr.	$70; 9hr.		902
Zürich	$228; 9hr.	$133; 13hr.	$191; 8hr.[1]	$228; 8hr.	$120; 13½hr.	$262; 15hr.[1]	$84; 6hr.	$142; 16hr.[1]	$213; 21½hr.[1]	$57; 3¾hr.	$66; 4¼hr.	$80; 8¼hr.	$123; 11½hr.[1]	$105; 8¼hr.	$217; 20¼hr.[1]	$81; 8hr.	$98; 9¼hr.	

[1] Thees routes require a change of trains. Travel times do not include layover.

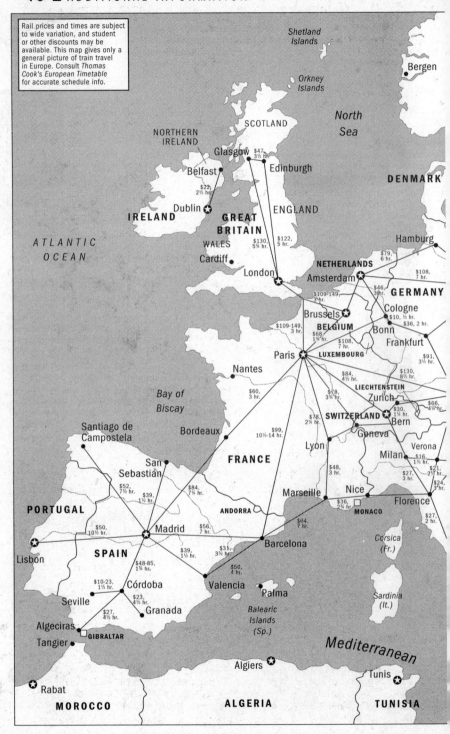

Rail prices and times are subject to wide variation, and student or other discounts may be available. This map gives only a general picture of train travel in Europe. Consult *Thomas Cook's European Timetable* for accurate schedule info.

Shetland Islands

Orkney Islands

North Sea

Bergen

SCOTLAND

DENMARK

NORTHERN IRELAND

Glasgow $47, 3½ hr.
Edinburgh

Belfast

$22, 2½ hr.

Dublin

IRELAND

ENGLAND

GREAT BRITAIN

WALES

Cardiff

$130, 5¾ hr.

$122, 5 hr.

Hamburg

$79, 6 hr.

NETHERLANDS

Amsterdam

$108, 7 hr.

GERMANY

$46, 3 hr.

London

$109-149, 3 hr.

Brussels

BELGIUM

Cologne
$10, ½ hr.
Bonn
$36, 2 hr.
Frankfurt

$109-149, 3 hr.

$68, 1¾ hr.

$108, 7 hr.

LUXEMBOURG

$91, 3½ hr.

ATLANTIC OCEAN

Paris

$84, 4½ hr.

$130, 8½ hr.

LIECHTENSTEIN

Nantes

$60, 3 hr.

$78, 3¾ hr.

Zurich

$66, 4¼ hr.

Bay of Biscay

Bordeaux

$99, 10½-14 hr.

$78, 2¼ hr.

SWITZERLAND

$30, 1¼ hr.
Bern

Geneva

Santiago de Compostela

FRANCE

Lyon

$48, 3 hr.

Verona

Milan
$16, 1½ hr.

San Sebastián

$52, 7½ hr.

$39, 1½ hr.

$84, 7¼ hr.

Marseille

$36, 2¾ hr.

Nice

MONACO

$21, 2½ hr.

$27, 3 hr.

Florence

$24, 3 hr.

PORTUGAL

$50, 10½ hr.

Madrid

$56, 7 hr.

ANDORRA

$64, 7 hr.

$27, 2 hr.

SPAIN

$39, 1½ hr.

Barcelona

Corsica (Fr.)

Lisbon

$48-85, 1¾ hr.

$31, 3½ hr.

$50, 4 hr.

$10-23, 1½ hr.

Córdoba

Valencia

Palma

Sardinia (It.)

Seville

$23, 4½ hr.

Granada

Balearic Islands (Sp.)

Algeciras

$27, 4½ hr.

GIBRALTAR

Tangier

Mediterranean

Algiers

Tunis

Rabat

MOROCCO

ALGERIA

TUNISIA

Rail Planner

ANDORRA

Embracing fewer than 500 sq. km between France and Spain in the secluded confines of the Pyrenees, pint-sized Andorra (pop. 65,000) might sell its soul, duty-free, for the right price. Tourists seeking souvenirs flock to its neon-lit streets for tax-free shopping, but outside the crowded boutiques of duty-free perfume await serene hamlets, mountain lakes, and some of the best ski slopes in Europe. Catalan is the official language, but French and Spanish are widely spoken. All establishments must accept both Spanish and French **currencies,** but *pesetas* are far more prevalent than *francs.* **Phones** require an STA *teletarjeta* (telecard) available at the tourist office, post office, or kiosk (500ptas). You cannot make collect calls, and AT&T does not have an international access code. **Directory assistance:** tel. 111. **Country code:** 376.

⌐ GETTING THERE AND GETTING AROUND. The only way to get to Andorra is by **car** or **bus,** as the country has no airport or train station. All traffic from France must enter through the town of **Pas de la Casa;** the Spanish gateway town is **La Seu d'Urgell. Andor-Inter/Samar buses** (Madrid tel. 91 468 41 90; Toulouse tel. 61 58 14 53; Andorra tel. 82 62 89) connect Andorra la Vella to **Madrid** (9hr.; departs Tu, Th, and Su; 4900ptas), while **Alsina Graells** (tel. 82 65 67) and **Eurobus** run to **Barcelona** (3-4hr., 4-6 per day, 2800ptas). To go anywhere else in Spain, take a **La Hispano-Andorra bus** (tel. 82 13 72) from Andorra la Vella to La Seu d'Urgell (30min., 5-7 per day, 340ptas) and change there for an Alsina Graells bus. Efficient **intercity buses** (90-590ptas) connect the villages; all buses make every stop in Andorra la Vella, so don't worry about finding the right bus—just look at the direction sign in the front window. For a (tiny) **map** of Andorra, consult the Spain map (see p. 794).

ANDORRA LA VELLA. Andorra la Vella (pop. 20,000), the country's capital, is little more than a narrow, cluttered road flanked by shop after duty-free shop. All buses terminate at the **Estació d'Autobusos,** on C. Bonaventura Riberaygua. To get to the **tourist office** on Av. Dr. Villanova from the bus stop on Av. Princep Benlloch, continue east (away from Spain) just past the *plaça* on your left and take Av. Dr. Villanova down to the right. (Open July-Sept. M-Sa 9am-1pm and 3-7pm; Oct.-June M-Sa 10am-1pm and 3-7pm, Su 10am-1pm.) Send mom an **email** from **Bavaria,** opposite the tourist office. (600ptas per 30min. Open daily 8:30am-1am.) Dream of duty-free cheese at **Pensió La Rosa,** Antic C. Major 18, off Av. Princep Benlloch. (Tel. 82 18 10. Singles 1700ptas; doubles 3000ptas.) The **supermarket** at **Grans Magatzems Pyrénées,** Av. Meritxell 11, has an entire aisle dedicated to chocolate bars. (Open M-F 9:30am-8pm, Sa 9:30am-9pm, Su 9:30am-7pm.)

ELSEWHERE IN ANDORRA. "Elsewhere" is where to go in Andorra. An extensive system of **hiking trails** including the *Grandes-Randonnées* traverses the tiny country; most are easy enough for even the least-seasoned outdoors enthusiasts. The masses also flock to Andorra's four outstanding **ski resorts,** all of which rent equipment; contact **SKI Andorra** (tel. 86 43 89) or pick up the tourist office's winter edition of *Andorra: The Pyrenean Country* for more info.

Ordino (pop. 2219; 1304m), 5km northeast of La Massana, is convenient for hiking and skiing adventures. An easy four-hour hike from town tours the lakes of **Tristaina.** The **tourist office** is on C. Nou Desvio. (Tel. 73 70 80. Open July-Sept. Su 9am-7pm; Oct.-June M-Sa 9am-1pm and 3-7pm, Su 9am-noon.) The homey, stone-faced **Hotel Quim** is on the *plaça.* (Tel. 83 50 13. Doubles 3000ptas.)

The tiny town of **Canillo** (pop. 952; 1400-2813m), in the center of the country, suffers from the same architectural short-sightedness as the rest of Andorra, but is surrounded by fine scenery and great **skiing. Soldeu-El Tarter** (tel. 85 11 51) occupies 840 hectares of skiable area between Andorra la Vella and Pas de la Casa, France; **free buses** transport skiers from hotels in Canillo. **Hotel Comerç,** on the road to Andorra La Vella, with bare rooms at bare prices, is the nearest budget place to snooze. (Tel. 85 10 20. Singles 1450ptas; doubles 2900ptas.)

AUSTRIA (ÖSTERREICH)

US$1 = 13.02AS (AUSTRIAN SCHILLINGS)
CDN$1 = 8.79AS
UK£1 = 20.85AS
IR£1 = 17.47AS
AUS$1 = 8.45AS
NZ$1 = 6.86AS
SAR1 = 8.59AS
EUR€1 = 13.76AS

10AS = US$0.77
10AS = CDN$1.14
10AS = UK£0.48
10AS = IR£0.58
10AS = AUS$1.18
10AS = NZ$1.46
10AS = SAR4.69
10AS = EUR€6.24

PHONE CODE	Country code: 43. International dialing prefix: 00 (from Vienna, 900).

The mighty Austro-Hungarian Empire may have crumbled after World War I, but Austria remains a complex, multi-ethnic country with a fascinating history. Drawing on centuries of Hapsburg political maneuvering, Austria has become a skillful mediator between Eastern and Western Europe, connecting Germany, Switzerland, and Italy with Slovenia, Hungary, Slovakia, and the Czech Republic. But Austria is renowned not so much for its strategic political situation as for its brilliant artists, writers, and musicians. From Gustav Klimt's *Jugendstil* paintings to Arthur Schnitzler's dark insights into imperial decadence to Beethoven's thundering symphonies, Austria has had an indelible impact on Western art and literature. Vienna was a major hub of European politics and culture from the 18th through the 20th century, culminating in an intensely introspective, apocalyptic atmosphere at the turn of the century. The lightheartedness of Strauss' waltzes succumbed to Freud's dissection of middle-class hysteria and the turbulence of two world wars.

Austria owes much of its contemporary fame to its overpowering physical beauty. The mention of Austria evokes images of onion-domed churches set against snow-capped Alpine peaks, lush meadows blanketed with wildflowers, pristine mountain lakes, dark forests, and mighty castles towering above the Danube. As a result, Austria attracts tourists year-round with its array of Alpine sports in winter, complemented by lakeside frolicking and hiking in summer.

For extensive and entertaining information on Austria's attractions, pick up a copy of *Let's Go: Austria & Switzerland 2000*.

DISCOVER AUSTRIA

Head first to Austria's capital, **Vienna,** to soak up café culture, stare down works by Klimt and other Secessionist artists, and listen to a world-famous opera or orchestra for a mere pittance (p. 85). **Salzburg** is an easy stopover between Vienna and Munich, the famous dual home of both the von Trapp family and Mozart, though some travelers find the overabundance of kitsch a tad overwhelming (p. 97). Between Vienna and Salzburg lies the newest hotspot in backpacker culture, the relaxing hostel in **Grünau** (p. 105). Go hiking around historic **Hallstatt** in the nearby **Salzkammergut** region (p. 104), or explore the natural pleasures of the **Hohe Tauern National Park,** including the the **Krimml Waterfalls** (p. 106). Farther west, **Innsbruck** is a fantastic jumping off point for skiers and hikers into the snow-capped peaks of the Tyrolean Alps (p. 108). For sunbathing try the banks of the Bodensee near **Bregenz** (p. 111); for superior superior skiing, head to **Kitzbühel** (p. 107).

GETTING THERE AND GETTING AROUND

BY PLANE. The only major international airport is **Vienna's** Schwechat Flughafen. European flights also land in **Salzburg, Graz, Innsbruck,** and **Klagenfurt.**

BY TRAIN. The **Österreichische Bundesbahn (ÖBB),** Austria's federal railroad, operates an efficient 5760km of tracks accommodating frequent, fast, and comfortable trains. The ÖBB publishes the yearly *Fahrpläne Kursbuch Bahn-Inland,* a compilation of all transportation schedules in Austria (100AS). Over 130 stations accept major credit cards and traveler's checks. **Eurail** and **InterRail passes** are valid in Austria. The **Austrian Railpass** allows three days of travel within any 15-day period on all rail lines, including Wolfgangsee ferries and private rail lines; it also entitles holders to 50% off on bike rental at train stations and on DDSG steamers between Passau, Linz, and Vienna (2nd-class US$102, up to 5 additional days US$22 each). Theone-month **Bundesnetzkarte** (National Network Pass), sold only in Austria, allows unlimited domestic train travel, including Wolfgangsee ferries and private rail lines, as well as half-price tickets for Bodensee and Danube ferries (2nd-class 4000AS, first-class 6000AS). The **Kilometer Bank,** sold only in Austria, involves prepurchasing a given number of kilometers' worth of travel, which can be used by one to six people traveling together on trips of over 70km one-way in first or second class. For **rail info,** dial 01717. For basic train lingo in German, see p. 949.

BY BUS. The efficient Austrian bus system consists mainly of orange **Bundes-Buses,** which cover areas inaccessible by train. They usually cost about as much as trains, and **railpasses** are not valid. You can buy discounted tickets, valid for one week, for any particular route. A **Mehrfahrtenkarte** gives you six tickets for the price of five. Buy tickets on-board or at a ticket office at the station. Bus stations are usually adjacent to the train station. For more bus information, dial (0222) 71101 within Austria (from outside Austria dial 1 instead of 0222).

BY FERRY. Private ferry services are offered on most lakes, while the DDSG runs boats down the Danube between Vienna and Krems, Melk, Passau, and Budapest.

BY CAR. Driving is a convenient way to see the more isolated parts of Austria. The roads are generally very good and well-marked and Austrian drivers are quite careful. Austrians drive on the right side of the road. Be aware that Austrian law tolerates only a very minimal blood-alcohol level. **Drivers** must purchase a permit/sticker at Austria's border to place on the windshield (70AS per week) at the border or face a US$130 fine. If renting a car, it is usually cheaper to do so in Germany.

BY BIKE AND BY THUMB. Bicycling is a great way to get around Austria; not only are the roads generally level and safe, but many private companies and train stations rent bikes (generally 150AS per day, 90AS with a railpass or valid train ticket from that day). If you get a bike at a train station, you can return it to any participating station. Look for the *Gepäckbeförderung* symbol (a little bicycle) on departure schedules to see if bikes are permitted in the baggage car. If your bike breaks down on the road, some auto clubs may rescue you; try the **Austrian Automobile, Motorcycle, and Touring Club (ÖAMTC)** (tel. 120) or **ARBÖ** (tel. 123).

Austria is a rough place to **hitchhike**—Austrians rarely stop, and many mountain roads are all but deserted. Generally, hitchhikers stand on highway *Knoten* (onramps) and wait. For a more certain ride, **Mitfahrzentrale** offices in larger cities match travelers with drivers heading in the same direction for a fee.

ESSENTIALS

DOCUMENTS AND FORMALITIES. For citizens of the EU, Australia, Canada, New Zealand, and the US, visas are not necessary for stays of less than three months, just a valid passport; visas are required for working and/or studying in Austria. South Africans must have a visa and a valid passport for all stays. For more information, visit www.bmaa.gv.at/embassy/uk/index.html.en).

> **Austrian Embassies at Home: Australia,** 12 Talbot St, Forrest, Canberra ACT 2603 (tel. (02) 62 95 15 33); **Canada,** 445 Wilbrod St, Ottawa, ON KIN 6M7 (tel. (613) 789-1444); **Ireland,** 15 Ailesbury Rd, Dublin 4 (tel. (01) 269 45 77; fax 283 08 60); **New Zealand,** Consular General, 22-4 Farrett St, Wellington (tel. (04) 801 9709; for visas and passports, contact the Australian office); **UK,** 18 Belgrave Mews West, London, SW1 X 8HU (tel. (020) 72 35 37 31; fax 73 44 02 92; email embassy@austria.org.uk); **US,** 3524 International Court NW, Washington DC, 20008-3035 (tel. (202) 895-6775); **South Africa,** 1109 Duncan St, Momentum Office Park, 0011 Brooklyn, Pretoria; P.O. Box 95572, 0145 Waterkloof, Pretoria (tel. (012) 46 24 83).

> **Foreign Embassies in Austria:** All foreign embassies are in **Vienna** (p. 88).

TOURIST OFFICES. Virtually every town in Austria has a **tourist office,** most marked by a green **"i"** sign. You may run into language difficulties in the small-town offices, but most brochures are available in English.

> **Tourist Boards at Home: Australia,** 1st fl., 36 Carrington St, Sydney, NSW 2000 (tel. (02) 92 99 36 21; fax 92 99 38 08); **Canada,** 2 Bloor St. East #3330, Toronto, ON M4W 1A8 (tel. (416) 967-3381; fax 967-4101); **UK,** 14 Cork St, London W1X 1PF (tel. (020) 76 29 04 61; fax 74 99 60 38); **US,** 500 Fifth Ave, #800, P.O. Box 1142, New York, NY 10108-1142 (tel. (212) 944-6880; fax 730-4568; email antonyc@ibm.net).

MONEY. The unit of currency is the **Schilling,** abbreviated AS in *Let's Go* and often simply "S" in Austria. **Exchange rates** are standardized among banks and exchange counters. Every place that exchanges currency charges a fee of at least 14AS. Many banks offer **cash advances** to Visa and MasterCard holders. **ATMs** are very convenient and usually give the best rates. Living in hostels and buying food from grocery stores will run you US$20-25 per day, excluding transport, sights, and nightlife. A little more comfort comes for about US$40-50 per day.

> **Tipping and Bargaining:** Menus will indicate whether or not service is included (*Preise inklusive* or *Bedienung inklusiv*). If it's not, tip about 10% and round up your bill to the nearest 5-10 Schillings. Don't leave tips on the table. Tell the server how much you want back; if you just say *Danke,* the server will assume that you plan to leave the change. Servers won't bring the bill until you ask for it (*Zahlen bitte;* TSAHL-en BiT-uh).

> **Taxes:** Austria has a 20-34% **value-added tax** (VAT), which is applied to all purchases of books, clothing, souvenir items, art items, jewelry, perfume, alcohol, cigarettes, etc. You can get it refunded if the total is at least 1000AS (US$95) at one store.

COMMUNICATION

> **Post:** Letters take 1-2 days within Austria. **Airmail** to North America takes 5-7 days, but it can take up to 2 weeks to Australia and New Zealand. Mark all letters and packages "mit Flugpost" or "par avion." The cheapest option is to send **aerogrammes.**

Telephone: You can usually make international calls from a pay phone, but a better option is to buy **phone cards** *(Wertkarten),* available at post offices, train stations, and *Tabak/ Trafik* (50 or 100ᴀS). The quickest and cheapest way to call abroad collect is to go to a post office and ask for *Zurückruf,* or "return call," and have your party call you back. **International direct dial** numbers include: **AT&T,** 022 90 30 11; **Sprint Global One,** 0800 20 02 36; **MCI WorldPhone Direct,** 022 90 30 12; **Canada Direct,** 0800 20 02 17; **BT Direct,** 0800 20 02 09; **Telkom South Africa Direct,** 022 90 30 27. **Police,** tel. 133. **Ambulance,** tel. 144. **Fire,** tel. 122.

Language: German. English is the most common 2nd language in Austria, but any effort to use the mother tongue will be appreciated. Outside of cities and among older residents, English is less common. *Grüss Gott* is the typical greeting. For phrases, see p. 949.

SKIING AND HIKING. Western Austria provides some of the world's best skiing and hiking; the areas around Innsbruck and Kitzbühel in Tirol are particularly well saturated with lifts and runs. High-season runs from mid-December to mid-January and from February to March. With an extensive network of hiking trails and Alpine refuges, Austria's Alps are as accessible as they are gorgeous. A membership in the **Österreichischer Alpenverein (ÖAV)** grants half-off the cost of staying at a series of mountain **huts** across the Tirol and throughout Austria, all a day's hike apart from each other. For membership info, contact Österreichischer Alpenverein, Willhelm-Greil-Str. 15, A-6010 Innsbruck (tel. (512) 58 78 28; fax 58 88 42). Membership (US$55, students under 25 US$40, plus US$10 one-time fee) also includes use of **Deutscher Alpenverein** (German Alpine Club) huts.

ACCOMMODATIONS AND CAMPING. Rooms in Austria are usually spotless; even the least appealing of Austria's **youth hostels** *(Jugendherbergen)* are quite tolerable. Most hostels charge US$8-25 a night for dorms. Many hostels are somewhat cramped and offer little privacy; hordes of school kids may also try your patience. **Hotels** are usually quite expensive. If you're on a tight budget, look instead for *Zimmer Frei* or *Privatzimmer* signs, which advertise rooms in private houses for a more reasonable 150-350AS. Otherwise, smaller pensions and *Gästehäuser* are often within the budget traveler's range. **Camping** is another popular option; prices range from 50-70AS per person and 25-60AS per tent, with a tax of 8-10AS.

FOOD AND DRINK. Loaded with fat, salt, and cholesterol, traditional Austrian cuisine is a cardiologist's nightmare, but tasty. Staple ingredients include *Schweinefleisch* (pork), *Kalbsfleisch* (veal), *Wurst* (sausage), *Eier* (eggs), *Käse* (cheese), *Brot* (bread), and *Kartoffeln/Erdäpfel* (potatoes). Austria's best-known dish is *Wienerschnitzel,* a meat cutlet (usually veal or pork) fried expertly in butter with bread crumbs. Vegetarians should look for *Spätzle* (homemade noodles), *Eierschwammerln* (tiny yellow mushrooms), or anything with the word "Vegi" in it. The best discount supermarkets are **Billa** and **Hofer,** where you can buy cheap bags of *Semmeln* (rolls) and fruits and veggies. Natives nurse their sweet tooths at *Café-Konditoreien* with *Kaffee und Kuchen* (coffee and cake). Try *Sacher Torte,* a rich chocolate pastry layered with marmalade; *Linzer Torte,* a light yellow cake with currant jam embedded in it; *Apfelstrudel;* or just about any pastry. Austrian beers are outstanding—try *Stiegl Bier,* a Salzburg brew, *Zipfer Bier* from upper Austria, and *Gösser Bier* from Graz. Austria imports lots of Budweiser beer (the famous Czech *Budvar,* not the American brew).

LOCAL FACTS

Time: Austria is 1hr. ahead of Greenwich Mean Time (GMT; see p. 49).

Hours: Most **stores** in Austria close daily noon-3pm, Sa afternoons, and all day Su. Many **museums** are closed M. **Banks** are usually open M-F 8am-12:30pm and 2-4:30pm.

Climate: Warm sweaters are the rule from Sept.-May, while summer is rainy and humid. July is usually the hottest month at up to 38°C (100°F), while February is the coldest, with temperatures down to -10°C (5°F). Mountainous areas of get cooler and wetter the higher you go. Snow cover lasts from late Dec. to Mar. in the valleys.

Holidays: New Year's Day (Jan. 1-2); Epiphany (Jan. 6); Good Friday (Apr. 2); Easter Monday (Apr. 5); Labor Day (May 1); Ascension (June 1); Whitmonday (June 12); Corpus Christi (June 22); Assumption Day (Aug. 15); Austrian National Day (Oct. 26); All Saints' Day (Nov. 1); Immaculate Conception (Dec. 8); and Christmas (Dec. 25-26).

Festivals: Just about everything closes down on public holidays, so plan accordingly. Austrians celebrate **Fasching** (Carneval) during the first 2 weeks of February. Austria's most famous summer **music festivals** are the **Wiener Festwochen** (mid-May to mid-June) and the **Salzburger Festspiele** (late July to late Aug.).

VIENNA (WIEN)

Vienna has an important cultural heritage rivaling that of Paris, thanks to its tradition of inspired musicians (Mozart, Beethoven, Schubert, Strauss, Brahms), imperial wealth, and impeccable taste in Baroque art and architecture. But it was not without reason that home-grown satirist Karl Kraus once dubbed Vienna—birthplace of psychoanalysis, atonal music, functionalist architecture, Zionism, and Nazism—a "laboratory for world destruction." Vienna's *fin de siècle* heyday carried the seeds of its own decay—at the height of the city's artistic ferment, the Viennese were already self-mockingly calling it the "merry apocalypse" as they stared down their own dissolution over coffee. The whipped cream and smooth veneer of waltz music concealed a darker reality that found expression in Freud's theories, Kafka's writings, and Mahler's music. Today, the city is busy reestablishing itself as the political, cultural, and economic gateway to Eastern Europe. Once more connecting with its turn-of-the-century identity, Vienna is again a place where experimentalism thrives, where rules of genre, style, and even structure are made and unmade in everything from music to contemporary film.

█ GETTING THERE AND GETTING AROUND

Flights: Wien-Schwechat Flughafen, 18km from Vienna's center, is the home of **Austrian Airlines** (tel. 17 89; open M-F 8am-7pm, Sa-Su 8am-5pm). The S-7 connects from the airport ("Flughafen/Wolfsthal"; every hr., 38AS; Eurail not valid) to "Wien Mitte/Landstr." on the U-3 or U-4 lines. **Vienna Airport Lines Shuttle Buses** (70AS) run from the airport to the City Air Terminal (opposite "Wien Mitte/Landstr."; every 20-30min. 24hr.).

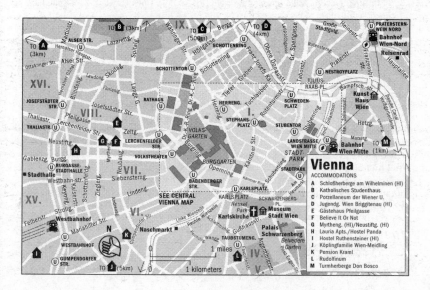

Vienna
ACCOMMODATIONS

A Schloßherberge am Wilhelminen (HI)
B Katholisches Studenthaus
C Porzellaneum der Wiener U.
D Jugendg. Wien Briggitenau (HI)
E Gästehaus Pfeilgasse
F Believe It Or Not
G Myrtheng. (HI)/Neustift. (HI)
H Lauria Apts./Hostel Panda
I Hostel Ruthensteiner (HI)
J Köplingfamilie Wien-Meidling
K Pension Kraml
L Rudolfinum
M Turmherberge Don Bosco

Trains: Info tel. 17 17 (24hr.); schedules online at www.bahn.at. Three main stations.

Westbahnhof, XV, Mariahilferstr. 132, primarily (but not exclusively) runs trains west. To: **Salzburg** (3hr., every hr., 410AS); **Budapest** (3-4hr., 9 per day, 436AS); **Munich** (4½hr., 5 per day, 788AS); **Innsbruck** (6hr., every 2hr., 660AS); **Kraków** (6½hr., 2 per day, 492AS); **Zurich** (9hr., 3 per day, 1160AS); **Amsterdam** (14hr., 1 per day, 2170AS); and **Paris** (14hr., 2 per day, 2198AS).

Südbahnhof, X, Wiedner Gürtel 1a, mostly sends trains south. To: **Bratislava** (1hr., 4 per day, 136AS); **Prague** (5hr., 3 per day, 524AS); **Rome** (14hr., 2 per day, 1230AS); and **Venice** (8hr., 5 per day, 760AS). Also to **Poland, Germany, Russia, Turkey, Greece,** and **Spain.**

Franz-Josefs Bahnhof, IX, Althamstr. 10, handles mostly commuter trains.

Ferries: Cruise the Danube with **DDSG Donaureisen** (tel. 58 88 00; www.ddsg-blue-danube.at; from 110-1880AS; 20% off with Eurail or ISIC). In summer ferries depart every Su from Schwedenplatz (take U-1, U-4, or trams 1 or 2).

Public Transportation: Info tel. 580 00 (call 790 91 05 for point-to-point directions); www.wiennet.at/efa. Excellent **U-Bahn** (subway), **bus, Straßenbahn** (tram), and **S-Bahn** (elevated train) systems cover the city. **Single-fare** 22AS if purchased on a bus (19AS in advance at ticket offices, *Tabak,* or U-Bahn station *Automaten*). The ticket includes transfers; punch it in the machine upon boarding the first vehicle of your journey and don't punch it again if you transfer or it will be invalid (fine 565AS). The following **passes** are available: **24-hour** 60AS, **3-day "rover" ticket** 150AS, **7-day** 142AS (valid from M 9am to following M 9am). The 3-day **Vienna Card** (210AS) includes unlimited public transit as well as discounts at museums and sights. Regular trams and subways stop 12:30-5am, but **nightbuses** ("N"; 25AS; passes not valid) run every 30min. along most tram, subway, and major bus routes. **Maps** (15AS) and night bus schedules are in U-Bahn stations.

Taxis: Tel. 313 00, 401 00, 601 60, 814 00, or 910 11. Stands at Westbahnhof, Südbahnhof, and Karlspl. Base fare 27AS; 14AS per km. Surcharges: 27AS Su and late nights (11pm-6am); 13-26AS for heavy luggage or taxis called by radiophone.

Hitchhiking: For Salzburg, the highway leading to the *Autobahn* is 10km past U-4: Hütteldorf. Hitchers going south ride tram 67 to the end and wait at the rotary near Laaerberg. **Mitfahrzentrale Wien,** VIII, Daung. 1a (tel. 408 22 10), off Laudong., organizes ridesharing. To **Salzburg** (210AS), **Prague** (450AS). Open M-F 8am-noon and 2-7pm, Sa-Su 1-3pm. *Let's Go* does not endorse hitching.

Bike Rental: At **Wien Nord** and the **Westbahnhof.** 150AS per day, 90AS with train ticket from day of arrival. **Pedal Power,** II, Ausstellungsstr. 3 (tel. 729 72 34). 60AS per hr., 300AS per half-day. **Bike tours** of the city (180-280AS). Open May-Oct. 8am-8pm. Pick up *Vienna By Bike* at the tourist office for info on the bike scene.

▧ ORIENTATION AND PRACTICAL INFORMATION

Vienna is divided into 23 **districts** *(Bezirke)*. The first district is the city center, *innere Stadt* or **Innenstadt** (inner city), bounded by the name-changing **Ringstraße** (once the site of the old city fortifications) and the Danube. Many of Vienna's major attractions lie along **Opernring, Kärntner Ring,** and **Kärntner Straße** in the southern section of the Ring, among them the **Kunsthistorisches Museum,** the **Rathaus,** the **Burggarten,** and the **Staatsoper** (Opera House). Districts two through nine radiate out clockwise from the center between the Ring and the larger, concentric **Gürtel** ("belt"), beyond which further districts similarly radiate out clockwise. Street signs indicate the district numbers in Roman or Arabic numerals. *Let's Go* includes district numbers before street addresses for establishments.

Vienna is a metropolis with crime like any other; be extra careful in Karlspl., home to many pushers and junkies, and at night avoid areas of the 5th, 10th, and 14th districts, as well as Landstraßer Hauptstr., Prater Park, and sections of the Gürtel (home to some of Vienna's skin trade).

TOURIST AND FINANCIAL SERVICES

Tourist Office: Main Office, I, Kärntnerstr. 38, behind the Opera House. Books 300-400AS rooms (40AS fee plus deposit). Open daily 9am-7pm. **Branch** at the **Westbahnhof. Jugend-Info Wien** (Vienna Youth Information Service), in the underground Bellaria-Pas-

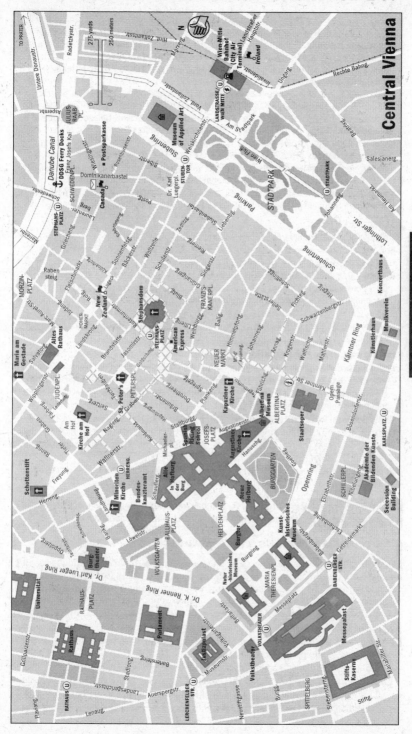

Central Vienna

AUSTRIA

sage (tel. 17 99; email jiw@blackbox.at). Enter at "Dr.-Karl-Renner-Ring/Bellaria" (tram 1, 2, 46, 49, D, or J) or U-2/U-3: Volkstheater. Get *Jugend in Wien*. Open M-Sa noon-7pm.

Embassies: Australia, IV, Mattiellistr. 2-4 (tel. 51 28 58 00), behind Karlskirche. Open M-Th 8:30am-1pm and 2-5:30pm, F 8:30am-1:15pm. **Canada,** I, Laurenzerburg 2, 3rd fl. (tel. 531 38, ext. 3000). Open M-F 8:30am-12:30pm and 1:30-3:30pm. **Ireland,** III, Hilton Center, Landstraßer Hauptstr. 21, 6th fl. (tel. 71 54 24 60; fax 713 60 04). Open M-F 9:30-11:30am and 2-4pm. **New Zealand,** XIX, Springsiedleg. 28 (tel. 318 85 05; fax 318 67 17). **South Africa,** XIX, Sandg. 33 (tel. 320 64 93). Open M-F 8:30am-noon. **UK,** III, Jauresg. 10 (tel. 71 61 30; fax 716 13 29 99), near Schloß Belvedere. Open M-F 9:15am-noon. **US,** IX, Boltzmanng. 16, off Währingerstr. (tel. 313 39; staffed M-F 8:30am-noon and 1-5pm). Open M-F 8:30am-noon.

Currency Exchange: ATMs offer excellent rates and typically accept Cirrus, V, and MC. **Banks** and **airport exchanges** offer official rates (commission on checks 65AS, cash 10AS). Most open M-W and F 8am-12:30pm and 1:30-3pm, Th until 5:30pm.

American Express: I, Kärntnerstr. 21-23, P.O. Box 28, A-1015 (tel. 515 40), down the street from Stephanspl. Mail held. Open M-F 9am-5:30pm, Sa 9am-noon.

LOCAL SERVICES

Luggage Storage: Lockers at all train stations 30-40AS per 24hr.

Bookstores: Shakespeare & Company, I, Sterng. 2 (tel. 535 50 53). Eclectic and intelligent. Open M-F 9am-7pm, Sa 9am-5pm.

Bisexual, Gay, and Lesbian Services: Rosa Lila Villa, VI, Linke Wienzeile 102 (tel. 586 81 50). Counseling, info, a library, and nightlife info. Open M-F 5-8pm. For gay info, pick up the monthly (German-language) magazine *Connect,* the monthly *Bussi* (free at any gay bar, café, or club), or the straight but hip *Falter* newspaper.

Laundromat: Schnell und Sauber, VII, Westbahnhofstr. 60 (tel. 524 64 60); U-6: Burgg. Stadthalle. Wash 60AS for 6kg. Soap included. Spin-dry 10AS. Open 24hr.

EMERGENCY AND COMMUNICATIONS

Emergencies: Police, tel. 133. **Ambulance,** tel. 144. **Fire,** tel. 122.

Medical Assistance: Allgemeines Krankenhaus, IX, Währinger Gürtel 18-20 (tel. 404 00). **Emergency care,** tel. 141. Consulates provide lists of English-speaking physicians. For info on **24-hour pharmacies,** call 15 50.

Crisis Hotlines: Rape Crisis Hotline, tel. 717 19 (24hr.). **Suicide Hotline,** tel. 713 33 74.

Internet Access: Amadeus Media Café, I, Kärntnerstr. 19, on the 5th fl. of Steffl department store. Free. Open M-F 9:30am-7pm, Sa 9:30am-5pm. **Libro,** XXII, Donauzentrum (tel. 202 52 55). Free. Open Su-F 7am-7pm, Sa 9am-5pm.

Post Offices: Hauptpostamt, I, Fleischmarkt 19. Address mail to be held: *Postlagernde Briefe* für Thomas MANN, Fleischmarkt 19, **A-1010** Wien, Austria. Open 24hr.

PHONE CODE	City code: 0222 from within Austria only. From outside Austria, dial int'l dialing prefix + 43 + 1 + local number.

▟ ACCOMMODATIONS AND CAMPING

One of the few unpleasant aspects of Vienna is the hunt for rooms in high-season (June-Sept.); reserve at least 5 days ahead, or from before 9am for a shot at a same-day spot. In July, when university dorms are converted into makeshift hostels, it might be easier; the dorms listed are open July to September. One-star *Pensionen* in the 7th, 8th, and 9th districts offer singles from 350AS and doubles from 500AS.

HOSTELS

🏠 **Believe It Or Not,** VII, Myrtheng. 10, #14 (tel. 526 46 58). From Westbahnhof, take U-6 (dir: Heiligenstadt) to "Burgg./Stadthalle," then bus 48A (dir: Ring) to "Neubaug."; backtrack a block on Burgg. and turn right on Myrtheng. (15min.). From Südbahnhof, take bus 13A (dir: Skodag./Alerstr.) to "Kellermanng."; walk left on Neustiftg. and left again on Myrtheng. Fab caretaker gives crash-course on Vienna. Easter-Oct. 160AS; Nov.-Easter 110AS. Kitchen. Reception 8am-1pm. Lockout 10:30am-12:30pm. Reserve ahead.

▩ **Hostel Ruthensteiner (HI)**, XV, Robert-Hamerlingg. 24 (tel. 893 42 02; fax 893 27 96; email hostel.ruthensteiner@telecom.at), 5min. from the Westbahnhof. Turn right as you exit, then right on Mariahilferstr., left on Haidmannsg., and right on Robert-Hammerlingg. Beautiful courtyard. Summer dorm 125AS; dorms 145-169AS; singles 245AS; doubles 470AS. Breakfast 28AS. Kitchen. **Internet.** 4-night max. stay. Reception 24hr.

Hostel Panda, VII, Kaiserstr. 77, 3rd fl. (tel. 522 53 53). From Westbahnhof, take tram 5 to "Burgg." From Südbahnhof, take tram 18 to "Westbahnhof" first. Fun and eclectic hostel in an old-fashioned Austrian apartment building. Easter-Oct. 160AS; Nov.-Easter 110AS; add 50AS for one-night stay. Kitchen. Lockers, bring a lock.

Myrthengasse (HI), VII, Myrtheng. 7, opposite Believe It or Not (see above), and **Neustift-gasse (HI)**, VII, Neustiftg. 85 (tel. 523 63 16; fax 523 58 49; email oejhv-wien-jgh-neus-tiftg@oejhv.or.at). Simple hostels around the corner from each other, 20min. from the Innenstadt. Jan.-Mar.18 and Oct. 29-Dec. 23 dorms 170-200AS. Rest of year dorms 185-215AS. Nonmembers add 40AS. Breakfast included. Laundry. Reception at Myrtheng. 7am-11:30pm. Curfew 1am. Lockout 9am-2pm. Reserve by fax or email.

Turmherberge Don Bosco, III, Lechnerstr. 12 (tel. 713 14 94). U-3: Kardinal-Nagl-Pl. The cheapest beds in town, in a barren former bell tower. 80AS. Curfew 11:45pm. Open Mar.-Nov.

Kolpingfamilie Wien-Meidling (HI), XIII, Bendlg. 10-12 (tel. 813 54 87; fax 812 21 30). U-4 or U-6: Niederhofstr.; head right on Niederhofstr. and take the fourth right onto Bendlg. Well-lit and modern, with 202 beds. Dorms 130-180AS. Breakfast 45AS. Nonmembers add 40AS. Reception 6am-midnight. Check-out 9am. Lockout midnight-4am.

Schloßherberge am Wilhelminenberg (HI), XVI, Savoyenstr. 2 (tel. 485 85 03, ext. 700; fax 485 85 03, ext. 702; email SHB@wigast.com). Take U-6 to "Thaliastr." then tram 46 (dir: Joachimsthalerpl.) to "Maroltingerg." Or take tram 44 from Schottentor to "Wilhelm-inenstr.," then bus 146B or 46B to "Schloß Wilhelminenberg" (it's to the left of the palace). Great view of the city. Dorms 220AS. Key card 25AS. Breakfast included. Laundry 65AS. Reception 7am-11pm. Lockout 9am-2pm. Curfew 11pm. Book ahead.

Jugendgästehaus Wien Brigittenau (HI), XX, Friedrich-Engels-Pl. 24 (tel. 332 82 94 or 330 05 98; fax 330 83 79), 25min. from city center. U-1 or U-4 to "Schwedenpl."; then tram N to "Floridsdorferbrücke/Friedrich-Engels-Pl." and follow signs. Dorms 145-210AS; nonmembers add 40AS. Jan.-Mar. 13 and Nov.-Dec. 23 discount 15AS. Breakfast included. 5-night max. stay. Reception 24hr. Lockout 9am-1pm. Reserve by fax or phone.

UNIVERSITY DORMS

Porzellaneum der Wiener Universität, IX, Porzellang. 30 (tel. 31 77 28 20; fax 31 77 28 30), 10min. from the Ring. From Westbahnhof, take tram 5 to "Franz-Josefs Bahnhof," then tram D (dir: Südbahnhof) to "Fürsteng." From Südbahnhof, take tram D (dir: Nuß-dorf) to "Fürsteng." Singles 190AS; doubles 380AS; quads 760AS. Reception 24hr.

Rudolfinum, IV, Mayerhofg. 3 (tel. 505 53 84; fax 50 55 38 54 50). U-1: Taubstummeng. Large rooms in a well-managed facility. Great location with MTV and CNN. Singles 270AS; doubles 480AS; triples 600AS. Breakfast included. Laundry 65AS. Reception 24hr.

Gästehaus Pfeilgasse, VIII, Pfeilg. 6 (tel. 401 74; fax 401 76 20; email acahot@academia-hotels.co.at). U-2: Lerchenfelderstr.; head right, right again on Lange Gasse, and left on Pfeilg. Singles 270AS; doubles 480AS; triples 600AS. Breakfast included. Reception 24hr. Reservations recommended. Credit cards accepted.

Katholisches Studentenhaus, XIX, Peter-Jordanstr. 29 (tel./fax 34 74 73 12). From Westbahnhof, take U-6 (dir.: Heiligenstadt) to "Nußdorferstr.," then bus 35A or tram 38 to "Hardtg.," and turn left. From Südbahnhof, take tram D to "Schottentor," then tram 38 to "Hardtg." Laid-back ambience. Singles 250AS; doubles 400AS. Reception until 10pm. Call ahead.

HOTELS AND PENSIONS

▩ **Lauria Apartments**, VII, Kaiserstr. 77, #8 (tel. 522 25 55). From Westbahnhof, take tram 5 to "Burgg." From Südbahnhof, take tram 18 to "Westbahnhof," then tram 5 to "Burgg." Modern apartments near the center and the Westbahnhof with TVs and kitchens. Dorms 160AS; singles 480AS; doubles 530-700AS; triples 700-800AS; quads 850-940AS. 2-night min. for reservations. Credit cards accepted for non-dorm rooms.

Pension Kraml, VI, Brauerg. 5 (tel. 587 85 88; fax 586 75 73), near the Innenstadt and Naschmarkt. U-3: Zierierg.; exit onto Otto-Bauerg., then take your first left and your first

AUSTRIA

right. From Südbahnhof, take bus 13A to Esterhazyg. and walk up Brauerg. Large rooms and a lounge. Singles 310AS; doubles 560-760AS; triples 720-930AS. Apartment with bath 1120-1250AS for 3-5 people. Breakfast buffet 60AS. 38 beds.

CAMPING

Wien-West, Hüttelbergstr. 80 (tel. 914 23 14; fax 911 35 94), 8km from the center. From U-4: Hütteldorf take bus 14B or 152 (dir: Campingpl.) to "Wien West." Crowded, but grassy and pleasant. July-Aug. 73AS per person, rest of year 67AS; 37-42AS per tent, 62-69AS per camper. 2-person cabins 250AS; 4-person 400-440AS. Laundry, store, and cooking facilities. Reception 7:30am-9:30pm. Open Mar.-Jan.

◖ FOOD AND COFFEE

In a world full of uncertainty, the Viennese believe that the least you can do is face it all on a full stomach. Food in the city reflects the crazy patchwork empire of the Hapsburgs: *Knödeln* (dumplings of Czech origin) and *Ungarische Gulaschsuppe* (Hungarian spicy beef stew) show Eastern European influences, and even *Wiener-schnitzel* (fried and breaded veal cutlets) probably first appeared in Milan. Vienna is renowned for sublime desserts and chocolates; though expensive, most residents maintain that the sumptuous treats are worth every *Groschen*. Gorge on *Sacher Torte, Imperial Torte, Palatschinken,* and *Apfelstrudel. Gästehäuser, Imbiße* (food stands), and *Beisln* (pubs) have cheap eats. Restaurants near **Kärntnerstr.** tend to be pricey—try north of the university near the Votivkirche (U-2: Schotten-tor), where **Universitätsstr.** and **Währingerstr.** intersect, or the area around the **Rechte** and **Linke Wienzeile** near Naschmarkt (U-4: Kettenbrückeg.). The **Naschmarkt** is full of vendors selling delicacies to snack on while shopping at Vienna's premier flea market (Sa-Su only). Supermarkets are **Billa, Hofer,** and **Sparmarkt.**

RESTAURANTS

◧ **Bizi Pizza,** I, Rotenturmstr. 4 (tel. 513 37 05), at Stephanspl. The best deal in the center. Pizza (60-75AS) or pasta (65-75AS) whipped up before your eyes. Also at Franz-Josefs-Kai; Mariahilferstr. 22-24; and X, Favoritenstr. 105. All open daily 11am-11:30pm.

◧ **Blue Box,** VII, Richterg. 8 (tel. 523 26 82). U-3: Neubaug.; turn onto Neubaug. and take your first right on Richterg. Fresh, flamboyant, and original dishes (Viennese, French, or veggie; 53-116AS). DJs pick music to match food. Open Tu-Su 10am-2am, M 6pm-2am.

OH Pot, OH Pot, IX, Währingerstr. 22 (tel. 319 42 59). U-2: Schottentor. Adorable joint with amazingly good Spanish food at rock-bottom prices. Namesake "pots" (stew-like concoctions of veggie or meat varieties) 70-85AS. Open M-F 10:30am-2:30pm and 6-11pm.

Schnitzelwirt Schmidt, VII, Neubaug. 52 (tel. 523 37 71). U-2 or U-3: Volkstheater; then take bus 49 to "Neubaug." Heaping servings of every kind of *Schnitzel* imaginable (65-115AS). Ask to wrap up the inevitable leftovers. Open M-Sa 11am-11pm.

Tunnel, VIII, Florianig. 39 (tel. 42 34 65). U-2: Rathaus; with Rathaus behind you, head right on Landesgerichtstr. and left on Florianig. A popular place prized for its dilapidated hipness, live nightly music, and affordable food (Italian, Austrian, and Middle Eastern). Lunch *Menüs* 45AS. Beer 27AS per 0.5L. Open 10am-2am.

Brezelg'wölb, I, Lederhof 9 (tel./fax 533 88 11), near Am Hof. Old-fashioned *Backstube* serving excellent, hearty cuisine that even the Viennese call *Altwiener* (old Viennese). Lunch around 100AS. Open daily 11am-1am, hot food until midnight.

Rosenberger Markt, I, Mayscderg. 2 (tel. 512 34 58), behind the Sacher Hotel. Large and chaotic subterranean buffet with a gargantuan selection of salad (29-64AS), fruit salad, waffles (55AS), antipasti, potatoes, and pasta bars. Open daily 10:30am-11pm.

COFFEEHOUSES AND KONDITOREIEN

The quintessential Viennese coffee is the *Melange,* and you can order every kind of coffee as a *Kleiner* (small) or *Grosser* (large), *Brauner* (brown, with a little milk) or *Schwarzer* (black). Most cafés also serve hot food, but don't order food and coffee together (except pastries), unless you want to be really gauche. The most serious dictate of coffeehouse etiquette is the requirement to linger. The waiter *(Herr Ober)* will serve you as soon as you sit down, and then leave you to sip, brood, and read. Vienna's *Konditoreien* are no less traditional than its coffee shops, but they focus their attention on delectable pastries rather than coffee.

MMM...COFFEE There is a steadfast rule for the Vienna coffeehouse—the drink matters, but the atmosphere *really* matters. Artists, writers, and thinkers fled poorly heated apartments to surround themselves with the dark wood and dusty velvet of the 19th-century coffeehouse. They ordered cups of coffee and stayed long into the night, composing operettas, writing books, and cutting into one another's work. The bourgeoisie followed suit, and the coffeehouse soon became the living room of the city—where Peter Altenberg, "the café writer," scribbled lines; where Kokoschka grumbled alone; where exiles Vladimir Lenin and Leon Trotsky played chess; where Theodor Herzl made plans for a Zionist Israel; where Kafka journeyed from Prague to visit the Herrenhof; and where Karl Kraus and a circle of minor writers baited Hugo von Hofmannsthal and Arthur Schnitzler. The original literary café, on the cusp of the "merry apocalypse" *fin de siècle* culture, was Café Griensteidl. After it was demolished in 1897, the torch passed first to Café Central and then to Café Herrenhof. Cafés still exist under all of these names, but only Café Central looks the way it originally did. Coffeehouses now rest partially in the past. The best places today resist massive overhauls, succumbing to a noble, comfortable decrepitude.

Café Hawelka, I, Dorotheerg. 6 (tel. 512 82 30), three blocks down Graben from the Stephansdom. With dusty wallpaper, dark wood, and red-striped velvet sofas that haven't been re-upholstered in years, this legendary café is shabby and glorious. *Buchteln* 35AS. Coffee 30-50AS. Open M and W-Sa 8am-2am, Su 4pm-2am.

Demel, I, Kohlmarkt 14 (tel. 535 17 17), 5min. from the Stephansdom down Graben. The most luxurious *Konditorei*, Demel's was confectioner to the imperial court until the empire dissolved. Chocolate made fresh every daily. Confections 40-50AS. Open 10am-6pm.

Café Central, I (tel. 533 37 63), at Herreng. and Strauchg. inside Palais Ferstel. Theodor Herzl, Sigmund Freud, Vladimir Ilych Ulianov (better known by his pen name, Lenin), and Leon Trotsky sipped coffee here. Live piano 4-7pm. Open M-Sa 9am-8pm.

Café Sperl, VI, Gumpendorferstr. 11 (tel. 586 41 58). U-2: Babenbergstr.; walk a block down Getreidemarkt and turn right on Gumpendorferstr. One of Vienna's oldest and most beautiful cafés. Coffee 30-50AS; cake 35-45AS. Open M-Sa 7am-11pm, Su 3-9pm; July-Aug. closed Su.

Café Savoy, VI, Linke Wienzeile 36, is a scruffy *fin de siècle* café with dark wood and decrepit gold trim. A large gay and lesbian crowd moves in to make this a lively nightspot on weekends. Open Tu-F 5pm-2am, Sa 9am-6pm and 9pm-2am.

SIGHTS

Viennese streets are by turns startling, scuzzy, and grandiose. The best way to see the city is simply to get lost. To wander in a more organized manner, get the brochure *Vienna from A to Z* (50AS with Vienna Card) or *Walks in Vienna*, both at the tourist office. Organized tours run 130AS, and some require additional admission fees to sites. **Vienna Bike,** IX, Wasag. (tel. 319 12 58), runs **cycling tours** (2-3hr., 280AS). Another great way to see the city is to ride around the Ring on trams 1 or 2.

INSIDE THE RING

The Innenstadt ("inner city") is Vienna's social and geographical center. With the mark of master architects on everything from palaces and theaters to tenements and toilet bowls, it's a gallery of the history of aesthetics, from Baroque to *Jugendstil*.

FROM STAATSOPER TO STEPHANSPLATZ. From the main tourist office on **Kärntnerstraße,** Vienna's café-lined grand boulevard, the first prominent building in view will be the **Staatsoper** (State Opera House). Originally completed in 1869, it was meticulously restored following heavy damage in WWII. Former directors of the Opera include Gustav Mahler, Richard Strauss, and Lorin Maazel. The cheapest way to partake of its fabulous gold, crystal, and red-velvet interior is to see an opera—standing room tickets with excellent views are only 30AS. *(Take U-1, U-2, U-4, or tram 1, 2, J, or D to "Karlsplatz" and take the Staatsoper exit. Tours July-Aug. 10, 11am, 1, 2,*

AUSTRIA

and 3pm; May-June and Sept.-Oct. 1, 2, and 3pm; Nov.-Apr. 2 and 3pm. 40AS, students 25AS.) Just to the north on Albertinapl., Alfred Hrdlicka's 1988 sculpture **Monument Gegen Krieg und Faschismus** (Memorial Against War and Fascism) recalls the suffering caused by WWII. Head north from there up Tegetthoffstr. to reach the spectacular **Neuer Markt,** where a graceful fountain and 17th-century **Kapuzinerkirche** await. The church houses an imperial **Gruft** (vault), a series of subterranean rooms whose coffins contain the remains (minus heart and entrails) of all the Hapsburg rulers since 1633. *(Open 9:30am-4pm. 30AS.)* Head down Donnerg. and north up Kärntnerstr. to see Vienna's most treasured symbol, the Gothic **Stephansdom,** whose smoothly tapered **South Tower** has become Vienna's emblem. Climb its 343 steps for a 360° view of Vienna. Photographs inside chronicle the painstaking process of reconstruction following damage suffered in WWII. Downstairs in the **catacombs,** skeletons of thousands of plague victims line the walls, while another **Gruft** (vault) stores all of the Hapsburg innards. *(U-1 or U-3: Stephansplatz. Cathedral tours in English M-Sa 10:30am and 3pm, Su 3pm; 40AS. Spectacular evening tour July-Sept. Sa 7pm; 100AS. South Tower open 9am-5:30pm; 30AS. Gruft tours M-Sa 10, 11, 11:30am, 2, 2:30, 3:30, 4, and 4:30pm; Su 2, 2:30, 3:30, 4, and 4:30pm; 50AS.)* East from Stephansdom runs **Graben,** once a moat around the Roman camp and today one of Vienna's main pedestrian streets. It shows the debris of Baroque, *Biedermeier, Jugendstil,* and postmodern trends, including the **Ankerhaus** (#10) and the red-marble **Grabenhof** by Otto Wagner.

FROM STEPHANSPLATZ TO HOHER MARKT. From Stephanspl., continue north up Rotenturmstr., bear left at Fleischmarkt onto Rabensteinerg. and turn left on Seitenstetteng. to reach the Jewish **Stadttempel,** the only synagogue of Vienna's 94 temples to escape Nazi destruction during **Kristallnacht** (Night of Broken Glass) on November 9-10, 1938; it was only spared because it stood on a residential block, concealed from the street. An armed guard now patrols the synagogue as a precaution against repeats of the 1983 terrorist attack, which killed three people. *(Seitenstetteng. 2-4. Take your passport. Open Su-F. Free.)* Continue up Seitenstetteng. to **Judengasse** (Jew Lane), a remnant of Vienna's old Jewish ghetto. Hang a left and admire the *Biedermeier*-era apartments lining the streets on your way to the **Hoher Markt,** the center of town (used as a market and execution site) during the Middle Ages. The square's biggest draw is the magnificent *Jugendstil* **Ankeruhr** (clock), which features 12 three-meter-tall historical figures (including Emperor Marcus Aurelius, Maria Theresia, and Joseph Haydn) rotating past the old Viennese coat of arms; one figure normally appears per hour, but if you show up at noon you can see them all appear in succession. The square is also the heart of the Roman encampment **Vindobona;** Roman ruins lie beneath the shopping arcade on the south side of the square. *(Open Sa-Su 11am-1pm. 25AS.)*

FROM HOHER MARKT TO AM HOF. From Hoher Markt, follow Wipplingerstr. west (right) to the impressive Baroque façade of the **Böhmische Hofkanzlei** (Bohemian Court Chancellory), the seat of Austria's Constitutional Court. The **Altes Rathaus,** directly across the street, today houses the **Austrian Resistance Museum** and various temporary exhibits. *(On Friedrich-Schmidt-Pl. Tel. 525 50. Open M, W, and Th 9am-5pm. Free. Tours M, W, and F 1pm.)* Turn left directly after the *Hofkanzlei* to get to the **Judenplatz,** the site of the city's first Jewish ghetto, behind it. On the other side of Judenpl., Drahtg. opens into the grand courtyard **Am Hof,** a medieval jousting square that now houses the **Kirche am Hof** (Church of the Nine Choirs of Angels; built 1386-1662). Roman ruins prove that Am Hof has been popular for a while.

FROM AM HOF TO MICHAELERPLATZ. Head west from Am Hof to **Freyung,** an uneven square used for public executions in the Middle Ages. Freyung is linked to **Herrengasse,** home to Vienna's nobility during the Hapsburg era, by the **Freyung-Passage.** The *Passage* (shopping arcade) leads directly through the Italianate **Palais Ferstel,** home to **Café Central** (see p. 91). Head southeast (left) down Herreng. and turn right on Landhausg. to reach the peaceful **Minoritenplatz,** home of the 14th-century **Minoritenkirche.** On the south side of the square stands the **Bundeskanzleramt** (Federal Chancery), where the Congress of Vienna met in 1815 and Chancellor Engelbert Dollfuss was assassinated in 1934. Follow Schaufterg. to the left and you'll run into **Michaelerplatz,** named for the unassuming **Michaelerkirche** on its eastern side. *(Open May-Oct. M-Sa 10:30am-4:30pm, Su 1-5pm. 25AS.)* In the middle of Michaelerpl. lie the excavated foundations of Roman Vienna—the Roman military camp called **Vindobona** where Marcus Aurelius penned his *Meditations.* A reconstructed **Café Griensteidl** is on the side of the square, inviting nostalgic visitors to imagine themselves drinking coffee alongside *fin de siècle* writers Arthur Schnitzler and Hugo von Hofmannsthal (who moved down the street to Café Central when the original café here was demolished in 1897)—although no starving artist could afford the coffee now. The square is otherwise dominated by the green, neo-Baroque, half-moon-shaped **Michaelertor,** the main gate of the Hofburg.

THE HOFBURG. The sprawling Hofburg was the Hapsburgs' winter residence until their 700-year reign ended in 1918. Over the centuries, the Hofburg experienced periods of neglect when various emperors chose to live in other palaces, such as Schönbrunn and Klosterneuburg, but it remained the symbol of the family's power. The complex today houses the office of the Austrian President.

Perhaps the best way to get an overview of the Hofburg is to walk around its perimeter. The **Stallburg** (Palace Stables), accessible via Josefspl., is home to the Royal Lipizzaner stallions of the **Spanische Reitschule** (Spanish Riding School). The cheapest way to get a glimpse of the famous steeds is to watch them train. *(Mid-Feb. to June and Nov. to mid-Dec. Tu-F 10am-noon; early Feb. M-Sa 10am-noon, except when the horses tour. Tickets sold at the door at Josefspl., Gate 2, from about 8:30am. 100AS.)* Continue down Augustinerstr. to reach the 14th-century Gothic **Augustinerkirche,** where the hearts of the Hapsburgs rest in peace in the **Herzgrüftel** (Little Heart Crypt). *(Open M-Sa 10am-6pm, Su 1-6pm).* The **Albertina,** the southern wing of the Hofburg, has a film museum and the celebrated **Collection of Graphic Arts,** with an array of old political cartoons and drawings by Dürer, Michelangelo, da Vinci, Raphael, Cézanne, and Schiele. *(Open Tu-Sa 10am-5pm. 70AS.)*

If you head back up to Michaelerpl., the wooden door on the right as you enter the Hofburg via the Michaelertor leads you to the **Kaiserappartements,** the former private quarters of Emperor Franz Josef (1848-1916) and Empress Elisabeth (1838-1898). *(Open daily 9am-4:30pm. 80AS.)* As you continue through the Michaelertor, you'll enter the courtyard **In der Burg** (within the fortress); through the red-and-black-striped **Schweizertor** (Swiss Gate) on your left and then up the stairs to the right is the Gothic **Burgkapelle,** where the heavenly voices of the **Wiener Sängerknaben** (Vienna Boys' Choir) grace Mass-goers on Sundays (see **Music,** p. 96). Just below the Burgkapelle is the entrance to the **Schatzkammer** (Treasury), where the Hapsburg jewels, the crowns of the Holy Roman and Austrian Empires, Imperial christening robes, and the **Holy Lance** that purportedly pierced Christ's side during his Crucifixion are on display. *(Open W-M 10am-6pm. 80AS, students 50AS. One tour in English per day; 30AS.)* The arched passageway at the rear of In der Burg opens up onto **Heldenplatz** (Heroes' Square). To the left is the vast **Neue Burg** (New Fortress), built between 1881 and 1926. Inside the **Österreichische Nationalbibliothek** (Austrian National Library) has an outstanding little museum of papyrus, scriptures, and musical manuscripts. *(Open May 7-Oct. 26 M-Sa 10am-4pm, Th until 7pm, Su 10am-1pm; Nov.-Apr. M-Sa 10am-1pm. May-Nov. 60AS, students 40AS; Nov.-Apr. 40AS.)*

THE RINGSTRASSE. The Hofburg's Heldenplatz gate presides over the Burgring segment of the Ringstraße. In 1857, Emperor Franz Josef commissioned this boulevard, 187 ft. wide and 2½ mi. in circumference, to replace the medieval city walls. Freud used to walk the circuit of the Ring every day during his lunch break; it took him a 2 hours. Just opposite the **Burgtor** at the back of the Hofburg stand two of Vienna's largest museums, the **Kunsthistorisches Museum** (Museum of Art History) and the **Naturhistorisches Museum** (Museum of Natural History). Head northwest on the Burgring, past the rose-filled **Volksgarten,** to reach the Neoclassical, sculpture-adorned **Parlament** (Parliament) building. Just up Dr.-Karl-Renner-Ring is the **Rathaus,** a remnant of late 19th-century neo-Gothic style. Opposite, the **Burgtheater** has frescoes by Klimt. To the north on Dr.-Karl-Lueger-Ring lies the **Universität.**

AUSTRIA

OUTSIDE THE RING

KARLSPLATZ AND RESSELPARK. *(Take the U-1, U-2. U-4, or any number of trams to "Karlsplatz" and exit toward Resselpark.)* **Karlsplatz,** within the **Resselpark,** was once a central gathering place for the Viennese and is still home to Vienna's most impressive Baroque church. The **Karlskirche,** in the southeast corner of the park, combines a Neoclassical portico with a Baroque dome; the gorgeous interior has colorful ceiling frescoes and a sunburst altar. *(Open M-Sa 9-11:30am and 1-5pm, Su 1-5pm. Free.)* The **Historisches Museum der Stadt Wien** lies to the left of the Karlskirche (see **Museums,** below), and stands across the park from the blocky yellow-and-blue **Kunsthalle** (see **Museums,** below). Above one side of the park, a terrace links the *Jugendstil* **Karlsplatz Stadtbahn Pavilions,** designed in 1899 by **Otto Wagner,** the architect primarily responsible for Vienna's *Jugendstil* face. Two of Vienna's most traditional establishments are visible to the north across Lothringerstr., between Karlsplatz and the Ring, from the pavilions: the **Künstlerhaus,** the home of Vienna's artistic community, from which the Secession artists seceded in 1897 (see **Museums,** below); and the **Musikverein,** home of the **Vienna Philharmonic Orchestra.** Northwest of the Resselpark across Friedrichstr. stands the nemesis of the Künstlerhaus, the **Secession Building,** whose white walls, restrained decoration, and gilded dome were intended to clash with the Historicist Ringstraße. The inscription above the door reads: *Der Zeit, ihre Kunst; der Kunst, ihre Freiheit* (To the age, its art; to art, its freedom). The Secession exhibits of 1898-1903, which attracted cutting-edge European artists, were led by Gustav Klimt, whose painting *Nuda Veritas* (Naked Truth) became the icon of a new aesthetic ideal.

SCHLOSS BELVEDERE. The landscaped gardens of **Schloß Belvedere,** IV, lie southeast of the center. Belvedere was originally the summer residence of **Prince Eugène of Savoy,** Austria's greatest military hero. The Belvedere summer palace, originally only the **Untere** (Lower) **Belvedere,** was ostensibly a gift from the emperor in recognition of Eugene's military prowess. Eugene later added the **Obere** (Upper) **Belvedere.** The grounds of the palace, which stretch from the Schwarzenberg Palace to the Südbahnhof, today contain three spectacular sphinx-filled gardens and an equal number of excellent museums (see **Museums,** below). *(Take tram D to "Schwarzenberg," tram 71 one stop past Schwarzenbergpl., or walk from Südbahnhof.)*

SCHLOSS SCHÖNBRUNN. Belvedere pales in comparison to **Schloß Schönbrunn,** XIII, the former Imperial summer residence. Tours of some of the palace's 1500 rooms reveal the elaborate taste of Maria Theresia's era. The frescoes lining the **Great Gallery** once observed the dancing Congress of Vienna, which loved a good party after a long day of divvying up the continent. The six-year-old Mozart played in the **Hall of Mirrors.** The **Million Gulden Room** wins the prize for excess: Oriental miniatures cover the chamber's walls. Even more impressive than the palace itself are the classical **gardens** behind it that extend nearly four times the length of the palace, designed by Emperor Josef II. The gardens include an encyclopedic orchestration of various elements, ranging from a sprawling **zoo** to the massive stone **Neptunbrunnen** (Neptune fountain) and bogus **Roman ruins.** Walk past the **flower sculptures** to reach Schönbrunn's labyrinths, rose gardens, and nature preserves. *(U-4: Schönbrunn. Apartments open daily Apr.-Oct. 8:30am-5pm; Nov.-Mar. 8:30am-4:30pm. 100AS. Audio tour 90AS, students 80AS. More worthwile grand tour 120AS, students 105AS. English tour 145AS, students 130AS. Gardens open 6am-dusk; free.)*

ZENTRALFRIEDHOF. Death doesn't get any better than at the massive Zentralfriedhof (Cemetery). Graves of the famous, infamous, and unknown spreading out from the church at the center in a grid. The cemetery is the place to pay respects to your favorite Viennese decomposer: **Tor II** (the second gate) leads to Beethoven, Wolf, Strauss, Schönberg, Moser, and an honorary monument to Mozart. (His true resting place is an unmarked pauper's grave in the **Cemetery of St. Mark,** III, Leberstr. 6-8.) **Tor I** leads to the **Jewish Cemetery** and Arthur Schnitzler's burial plot. Many of the headstones are cracked, broken, lying prone, or neglected because the families of most of the dead are no longer in Austria. Various structures throughout this por-

AUSTRIA

tion of the burial grounds memorialize the millions slaughtered in Nazi death camps. *(XI, Simmeringer Hauptstr. 234. Take tram 71 from Schwarzenbergpl., or tram 72 from Schlachthausg. The tram stops at each of the 3 main gates; Tor II is the main entrance. Or take S-7 to "Zentralfriedhof," which stops along the southwest wall of the cemetery. 38AS, Open May-Aug. 7am-7pm; Mar.-Apr. and Sept.-Oct. 7am-6pm; Nov.-Feb. 8am-5pm.)*

🏛 MUSEUMS

Vienna owes its vast selection of masterpieces to the acquisitive Hapsburgs, as well as the city's own crop of art schools and world-class artists. All museums run by the city of Vienna are free on Friday morning before noon; they are marked in the tourist office's free *Museums* brochure.

ART MUSEUMS

Kunsthistorisches Museum (Museum of Art History; tel. 52 52 40), off the Burgring. The 4th-largest art collection in the world oozes with 15th- to 18th-century Venetian and Flemish paintings, including Breughels and Rembrandts, and isn't hurting in ancient or classical art either. The Klimt mural in the lobby depicting artistic progress from the classical era to the 19th century is painted in the Historicist style he would later attack. Open Tu-Su 10am-6pm. 100AS, students 70AS. English tours in summer 11am and 3pm (30AS).

Austrian Gallery, III, Prinz-Eugen-Str. 27 (tel. 79 55 70), in the Belvedere Palace. Walk from the Südbahnhof or take tram D, 566, 567, 666, 668, or 766 to "Prinz-Eugen-Str." The **Upper Belvedere** 19th- to 20th-century Austrian art, including famous Secessionist works by Schiele, Kokoschka, and Klimt (including *The Kiss*). The **Lower Belvedere** contains the **Baroque Museum** and the **Museum of Medieval Austrian Art.** Both open Tu-Su 10am-5pm. Joint ticket 60AS, students 30AS. English guided tours 2:30pm.

Akademie der Bildende Kunst (Academy of Fine Arts), I, Schillerpl. 3 (tel. 58 81 62 25), near Karlspl. Excellent, manageable collection including Hieronymus Bosch's *Last Judgment* and works by Peter Paul Rubens. Open Tu-Su 10am-4pm. 50AS, students 20AS.

Secession Building, I, Friedrichstr. 12 (tel. 587 53 07), on the western side of Karlspl. (see p. 94). Originally built to give the pioneers of modern art, including Klimt, Kokoschka, and the "barbarian" Gauguin, space to hang artwork that didn't conform to the *Künstlerhaus'* standards. Substantial contemporary works are exhibited today. Klimt's 30km long *Beethoven Frieze*—his visual interpretation of Beethoven's *Ninth Symphony*—is also displayed. Open Tu-Sa 10am-6pm, Su and holidays 10am-4pm. 60AS, students 40AS.

Museum Moderner Kunst (Museum of Modern Art; tel. 317 69 00; www.MMKSLW.or.at) has two locations. **Liechtenstein Palace,** IX, Fürsteng. 1 (take tram D (dir: Nußdorf) to "Fürsteng."), holds work by 20th-century masters—Magritte, Picasso, Miró, Kandinsky, Pollock, Warhol, and Klee. The **20er Haus** (tel. 799 69 00), III, Arsenalstr. 1, opposite the Südbahnhof, houses ground-breaking 60s and 70s work and a great sculpture garden. Open Tu-Su 10am-6pm. 45AS, students 25AS for each; 60AS, students 30AS for both.

Künstlerhaus, Karlspl. 5 (tel. 587 96 63; see p. 94). Once the home of the Viennese artistic establishment, this museum invites temporary exhibits, usually of contemporary and non-European art. The theater hosts numerous **film festivals.** Open M-W and F-Su 10am-6pm, Th 10am-9pm. 90AS; students 60AS, M students 40AS.

OTHER MUSEUMS

Museum für Völkerkunde (tel. 53 43 00), I, in the Neue Burg on Heldenpl. U-2 or U-3: Volkstheater. Admire Benin bronzes, West African Dan heads, and Montezuma's feathered headdress, gathered by Hapsburg agents during their travels. Art and artifacts from Africa, the Americas, the Middle East, and the Far East. Open Apr.-Dec. Su-M and W-Sa 10am-4pm; Jan.-Mar. Su-M and W-Sa 10am-6pm. 80AS, students 40A. Tours Su 11am.

Historisches Museum der Stadt Wien (Historical Museum of the City of Vienna), IV, Karlspl. 5 (tel. 505 87 47), to the left of the Karlskirche. Amazing collection of historical artifacts and paintings documenting Vienna's evolution from the Roman encampment through the Turkish siege of Vienna, and the subsequent 640 years of Hapsburg rule. Open Tu-Su 9am-6pm. 50AS, students 20AS; free F 9am-noon.

Sigmund Freud Haus, IX, Bergg. 19 (tel. 319 15 96), near the Votivkirche. U-2: Schottentor; walk up Währingerstr. to Bergg. Freud's home from 1891 until the *Anschluß.* Lots of photos and documents, including the young Freud's report cards and circumcision certificate. Open July-Sept. 9am-6pm; Oct.-June 9am-4pm. 60AS, students 40AS. Tours 75AS.

♫ ENTERTAINMENT

MUSIC. The heart of Vienna beats to musical rhythms. Vienna's musical history is full of big names: Mozart, Beethoven, and Haydn wrote their greatest masterpieces in Vienna, creating the First Viennese School; a century later, Schönberg, Webern, and Berg teamed up to form the Second Viennese School. All year, Vienna presents performances ranging from the above-average to the sublime, with many surprisingly accessible to the budget traveler. The **Staatsoper** remains one of the top five companies in the world and performs about 300 times from September through June. **Standing-room tickets** give you access to world-class opera for a pittance; more expensive **last-minute student tickets** go on sale 30min. before curtain. (Standing-room tickets: balcony 20AS, orchestra 30AS. Arrive 2-3hr. early in high season. The standing-room line forms inside the side door on the western side of the Opera, by Operng. Formal dress not necessary, but no shorts. Student tickets 100-150AS. Line up to the left inside the main entrance at least 1hr. before curtain; ISIC not valid, bring a university ID.) Advance tickets (100-850AS) go on sale a week ahead at the **Bundestheaterkasse**, I, Hanuschg. 3, around the corner from the opera. (Tel. 514 44 29 60. Open M-F 8am-6pm, Sa-Su 9am-noon. ISIC not valid for student discounts, see above.) The world-famous **Wiener Philharmoniker** (Vienna Philharmonic Orchestra) has been directed by the world's finest conductors, including Gustav Mahler and Leonard Bernstein. Philharmonic performances take place in the **Musikverein**, I, Dumbastr. 3, on the northeast side of Karlspl. (Tel. 505 81 90. Box office open Sept.-June M-F 9am-7:30pm, Sa 9am-5pm. Standing-room tickets available; price varies.) The prepubescent prodigies of the famous, 500-year-old **Vienna Boys' Choir** perform Sundays at 9:15am (mid-Sept. to June only) in the **Burgkapelle** (Royal Chapel) of the Hofburg. Standing room is free, but arrive before 8am.

FESTIVALS. Vienna hosts an array of annual festivals, mostly musical; check the tourist office's monthly calendar. The **Vienna Festival** (mid-May to mid-June) has a diverse program of exhibitions, plays, and concerts. (Tel. 58 92 22; fax 589 22 49; www.festwochen.or.at/wf.) The Staatsoper and Volkstheater host the annual **Jazzfest Wien** (tel. 503 56 47; www.viennajazz.at) during the first weeks of July. Don't miss the **nightly film festival** in July and August, in the Rathauspl. at dusk, during which taped operas, ballets, and concerts enrapture audiences.

♫ NIGHTLIFE

Vienna is a great place to party, whether you're looking for a quiet evening with a glass of wine or a wild night in a disco full of black-clad Euro musclemen and drag queens. U-1 or U-4: Schwedenplatz is just blocks from the **Bermuda Dreieck** (Triangle), so dubbed both for the three-block area it covers and for the tipsy revelers who lose their way here and never make it home. If your vision isn't foggy yet, head down **Rotenturmstrasse** toward the Stephansdom, or check out the cellar bars of smooth, dark **Bäckerstraße.** Slightly outside the Ring, the streets off **Burggasse** and **Stiftgasse** in the 7th district and the university quarter (8th and 9th districts) can be good places of refuge when the summer crowd in the Bermuda Triangle feels too pubescent or touristy. Note that Viennese nightlife starts late. As usual, the best nights are Friday and Saturday, beginning around 1am or so. For the scoop on raves, concerts, and parties, grab the fliers at swanky cafés around town or pick up a copy of the indispensable *Falter* (28AS) for listings of everything from opera and theater to punk concerts to the gay and lesbian scene.

■ **Cato,** I, Tiefer Graben 19 (tel. 533 47 90). U-3: Herreng.; walk down to Strauchg., turn right, and continue on to Tiefer Graben. Laid-back, super-comfortable bar—you'll be singing songs with the friendly clientele before the end of the evening. Enjoy the music, Art-Deco decor, and delicious cocktails. Open Su-Th 6pm-2am, F-Sa 6pm-4am.

AUSTRIA

🎵 **U-4,** XII, Schönbrunnerstr. 222 (tel. 85 83 18). U-4: Meidling Hauptstr. Keeps the music fresh and the party going. Two dance areas, multiple bars, and rotating theme nights please a varied clientele. Th gay night. Cover 70-120AS. Open daily 11pm-5am.

Club Berlin, I, Gonzag. 12 (tel. 533 04 79). Vienna's bold and beautiful wind their way around the downstairs partitions of this former wine cellar—a simultaneously intimate and expansive atmosphere with great music. Open Su-Tu 6pm-2am, F-Sa 6pm-4am.

Alsergrunder Kulturpark, IX, Alserstr. 4 (tel. 407 82 14). A young Viennese crowd flocks to these beautiful grounds for the beer garden, wine bar, champagne bar, and more. All sorts of people and all sorts of nightlife. Open Apr.-Oct. daily 4pm-2am.

Chelsea, VIII, (tel. 407 93 09), Lerchenfeldergürtel under the U-Bahn between Thaliastr. and Josefstädterstr. The best place in Vienna for underground music, featuring live bands from across Europe (except in summer). Cover 50-200AS. Open daily 4pm-4am.

Objektiv, VII, Kirchbergg. 26 (tel. 522 70 42). U-2 or U-3: Volkstheater; walk two blocks down Burgg. and turn right on Kirchbergg. One of the most eclectic and strangely decorated bars in Vienna. A mellow atmosphere, lively local crowd, and cheap drinks top things off. Happy Hour daily 11pm-1am. Open M-Sa 6pm-2am, Su 6pm-1am.

Why Not, I, Tiefer Graben 22 (tel. 535 11 58). Relaxed gay and lesbian bar/disco with both a chill chatting venue and a hip-hop-happening subterranean black-box dance floor. Sa drink specials. Cover 70AS. Open F-Sa 10pm-4am, Su 9pm-2am.

🏛 EXCURSION FROM VIENNA: BADEN BEI WIEN

Only 27km from Vienna, Baden is a favorite weekend spot for Viennese and globe-trotters to rest their weary bones, thanks to the healing effects of Baden's sulfur springs. Since the days of Roman rule, these naturally heated jets of water springing from the ground have been harnessed and transformed into therapeutic spas, attracting bathers from all corners of Europe. Although the waters smell like rotten eggs, they're warm, relaxing, and good for you. The **Strandbad,** Helenenstr. 19-21, lets you simmer in the hot sulfur thermal pool and cool off in normal chlorinated pools. (Tel. (02252) 486 70. Open M-F 8:30am-7:30pm, Sa-Su 8am-6:30pm. M-F 67AS, after 1pm 57AS; Sa-Su 79AS, after 1pm 67AS.) The **Kurdirektion,** Brusattipl. 4 (tel. (02252) 445 31), is the center of all curative spa treatments, with an indoor thermal pool mainly for patients but also open to visitors (72AS). The spa has underwater massage therapy (295AS), sulfur mudbaths (305AS), and regular and sport massages (310AS). A gigantic new spa complex called the **Römertherme Baden** offers even more soothing luxuries. (Tel. (02252) 450 30. Open daily 10am-11pm.) Also be sure to smell the roses—all 20,000 of them—in Baden's **rosarium,** which extends from the center of town to the **Wienerwald** (Vienna Woods; 90,000 sq. m).

The **Badener Bahn** runs from Vienna's Karlspl., beneath the Opera House, to Baden's Josefspl. (1hr., every 15min., 57AS); **trains** also connect Vienna's Südbahnhof and Josefspl. (57AS). From Josefspl., walk toward the fountain, keep right, and follow Erzherzog-Rainer-Ring to the second tert (Brusattipl.) to reach the **tourist office,** Brusattipl. 3. In summer, the office offers free **tours** of the Altstadt (1½hr.; M 2pm and Th 10am) and the wine region (2hr.; W 3pm) as well as guided **hiking** and **mountain-biking** tours (except in Aug.). (Tel. (02252) 868 00; fax 441 47. Open May-Oct. M-Sa 9am-12:30pm and 2-6pm, Su 9am-12:30pm.) **Postal code:** A-2500.

SALZBURG

Many tourists find themselves disappointed by Salzburg, and it's not hard to see why—with the city's twin claims to fame as the birthplace of Mozart and the backdrop for *The Sound of Music,* the tourist industry's potential for (and realization of) kitschy exploitation is off the scale. But a number of qualities redeem Salzburg: wedged between mountains and dotted with church spires, medieval turrets, and resplendent palaces, it offers both attractive sights and a rich musical culture. If you stop looking for Aryan children clad in curtains running through the city singing (and ignore the hordes of tourists you *do* see doing so), and sit back to enjoy a concert or a *Mozartkugel* instead, you may be pleasantly surprised.

■ GETTING THERE AND GETTING AROUND

Trains: Hauptbahnhof, Südtirolerpl. (tel. 17 17). Frequent trains to: **Munich** (2hr., 298AS); **Innsbruck** (2hr., 350AS); **Vienna** (3½hr., 410AS); **Graz** (4½hr., 410AS); **Zurich** (6hr., 862AS); **Budapest** (6½hr., 742AS); **Venice** (6hr., 540AS); and **Prague** via Linz (7hr., 852AS). Ticket office open 24hr. **Luggage storage:** Lockers 30-50AS per 2 days; luggage check 30AS per piece per day. Open 6am-10pm.

Public Transportation: Lokalbahnhof (tel. 87 21 45), next to the train station. Tickets are cheapest from *Tabaks* (single-ride 19AS, day-pass 40AS); you can also purchase packs of 5 single-ride tickets from vending machines at bus stops for 75AS or buy single tickets on the bus. Punch your ticket when you board or face a 500AS fine. Buses usually make their last run from downtown to outer destinations at 10:30-11:30pm.

Bike Rental: Climb every mountain and ford every stream with a bicycle from the train station, counter 3 (tel. 88 87 31 63). 150AS per day, 90AS with same-day train ticket.

Hitchhiking: Hitchers headed to Innsbruck, Munich, or most of Italy allegedly take bus 77 to the German border; for Vienna or Venice, they take bus 29 (dir: Forellenwegsiedlung) or bus 15 (dir: Bergheim) to Autobahn entrances at "Grüner Wald" or "Schmiedlingerstr.," respectively.

■ ORIENTATION AND PRACTICAL INFORMATION

Just a few kilometers from the German border, Salzburg straddles the **Salzach River.** On the west bank is the **Altstadt** (old city) and the heavily touristed pedestrian district; on the east side is the **Neustadt** (new city), with the **Mirabellplatz** in the center. From the Hauptbahnhof, at the northern edge of town, head left as you exit and follow Rainerstr. all the way (under the tunnel) to Mirabellpl. (15min.).

Tourist Office, Mozartpl. 5 (tel. 84 75 68; fax 889 87 342; www.salzburginfo.or.at), in the Altstadt. From Mirabellpl., cross the Staatsbrücke and head left along the river to the next bridge (7min.). The free hotel maps are exactly the same as the 10AS city map. Tells travelers which hostels have available rooms and sells the **Salzburg Card,** good for admission to all museums and sights as well as unlimited public transport (24hr. card 200AS, 48hr. 270AS, 72hr. 360AS). Open July-Aug. 9am-8pm; Sept.-June 9am-6pm. **Branch** at platform 2a of the train station. Open M-Sa 8:45am-8pm.

Consulates: South Africa, Buchenweg 14 (tel./fax 62 20 35). Open M-F 8am-1pm and 2-5pm. **UK,** Alter Markt 4 (tel. 84 81 33; fax 84 55 63). Open M-F 9am-noon. **US,** Alter Markt 1/3 (tel. 84 87 76; fax 84 97 77), in the Altstadt. Open M, W, and F 9am-noon.

Currency Exchange: Most banks open M-F 8am-12:30pm and 2-4:30pm. **Rieger Bank,** at Alter Markt and Getreideg. Open July-Aug. M-F 9am-7:30pm, Sa 9am-6pm, Su 10am-5pm; Sept.-June M-F 9am-6pm, Sa 9am-3pm, Su 10am-5pm.

Gay and Lesbian Services: Frauenkulturzentrum (Women's Center), Elisabethstr. 11 (tel. 87 16 39). Open M 10am-12:30pm. **Homosexual Initiative of Salzburg** (HOSI), Müllner Hauptstr. 11 (tel. 43 59 27). **Café-bar** open F from 9pm and Sa from 8pm.

Laundromat: Norge Exquisit Textil Reinigung, Paris-Lodronstr. 16 (tel. 87 63 81), at Wolf-Dietrich-Str. Wash and dry 82AS, mandatory soap 28AS. Open M-F 7:30am-4pm, Sa 8-10am.

Emergencies: Police, tel. 133. Headquarters at Alpenstr. 90 (tel. 63 83). **Ambulance,** tel. 144. **Fire,** tel. 122.

Pharmacies: Elisabeth-Apotheke, Elisabethstr. 1 (tel. 87 14 84), near the train station. Pharmacies in the city center are open M-F 8am-6pm, Sa 8am-noon. There are always 3 pharmacies open for emergencies; check the list on the door of any closed pharmacy.

Medical Assistance: When the dog bites, when the bee stings, when you're feeling sad, call the **Hospital,** Dr. Franz-Rebirl-Pl. 5 (tel. 658 00).

Internet Access: Cybercafé, Gstätteng. 29 (tel. 84 26 16 22). 80AS per hr. Open M-F 2-11pm, F-Su 2pm-1am.

Post Office: Mail your brown paper packages tied up with strings or exchange money at the Hauptbahnhof (tel. 889 70). Address mail to be held: *Postlagernde Briefe* für Liesl VON TRAPP, Bahnhofspostamt, **A-5020** Salzburg, Austria. Open 6am-11pm.

| **PHONE CODE** | City code: 0662. From outside Austria, dial int'l dialing prefix (see inside back cover) + 43 + 662 + local number. |

AUSTRIA

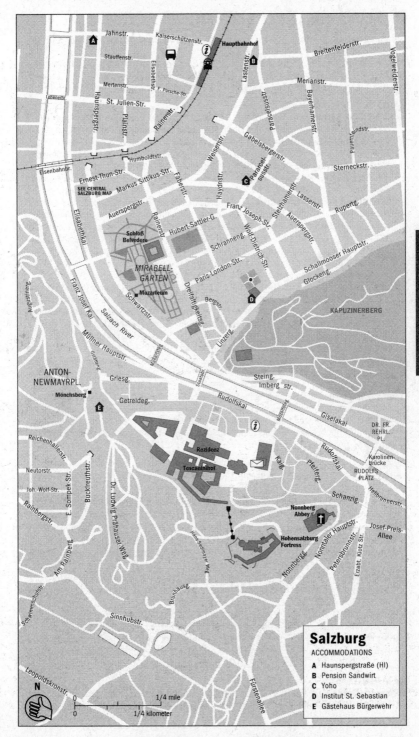

AUSTRIA

Salzburg

ACCOMMODATIONS

A Haunspergstraße (HI)
B Pension Sandwirt
C Yoho
D Institut St. Sebastian
E Gästehaus Bürgerwehr

N

0   1/4 mile
0   1/4 kilometer

ACCOMMODATIONS AND CAMPING

Salzburg has no shortage of hostels—but then, it has no shortage of tourists either. Housing in Salzburg is even more expensive than in Vienna; most affordable options lie on the outskirts of town. Ask for the tourist office's list of **private rooms** or the *Hotel Plan* (which has info on hostels). From mid-May to mid-September, hostels fill by mid-afternoon—call ahead. Reserve ahead during the *Festspiele*.

HOSTELS AND DORMS

■ **Gästehaus Bürgerwehr,** Mönchsberg 19c (tel. 84 17 29). Take bus 1 (dir: Maxglan) to "Mönchsberglift," walk a few steps down the street, pass through the stone arch on the left, and take the Mönchsberglift (elevator; runs 9am-11pm, 27AS round-trip) up. Turn right from the summit, climb the steps, and follow signs for "Gästehaus Naturfreunde-haus," for a princely view on a pauper's budget at the most scenic hostel in Salzburg. 120AS. Breakfast with a view 30AS. Showers 10AS for 4min. Sheets 20AS. Reception 8am-9pm. Curfew 1am. Only 26 beds, so reserve ahead. Open May to mid-Sept.

International Youth Hotel (YoHo), Paracelsusstr. 9 (tel. 87 96 49; fax 87 88 10), off Franz-Josef-Str. Head left from the train station, turn left on Gabelsbergerstr. through the tunnel, and take the 2nd right on Paracelsusstr. (7min.). Daily screening of *The Sound of Music* (noon). Dorms 150AS; doubles 400AS; quads 680AS. Breakfast 30-55AS. Showers 10AS for 6min. Lockers 10AS. Reception 8am-noon. Theoretical curfew 1am.

Institut St. Sebastian, Linzerg. 41 (tel. 87 13 86; fax 87 13 86 85). From the station, follow Rainerstr. left, go past Mirabellpl., turn left onto Bergstr., turn left at the end on Linzerg., and head through the arch on the left just before the church. Dorms (Oct.-June only) 180AS, with sheets 210AS; singles 330-390AS; doubles 500-680AS; triples 870AS; quads 1000-1080AS. Breakfast included. Kitchen. Laundry 40AS. Reception in summer 7:30am-noon and 1-10pm, in winter 8am-noon and 4-9pm. Reserve ahead.

Eduard-Heinrich-Haus (HI), Eduard-Heinrich-Str. 2 (tel. 62 59 76; fax 62 79 80). Fa, a long, long way to run, so take bus 51 (dir: Salzburg-Süd) to "Polizeidirektion," cross and continue down Billrothstr., turn left on the Robert-Stolz-Promenade footpath, take the 1st right, and it's up the driveway on the left. 170AS; nonmembers 210AS. Breakfast included. Reception 7-9am and 5-11pm. Lockout 9am-5pm. Curfew 11pm-midnight; ask for a key.

Haunspergstraße (HI), Haunspergstr. 27 (tel. 87 50 30; fax 88 34 77), near the train station. Walk straight out Kaiserschützenstr., which becomes Jahnstr., and turn left on Haunspergstr. Dorms 170AS; nonmembers add 40AS 1st night. Breakfast included. Laundry 80AS. Reception 7am-2pm and 5pm-midnight. Curfew 11pm. Open July-Aug. 125 beds.

HOTELS AND PENSIONS

Pensionen on **Kasern Berg** are technically outside Salzburg, so the tourist office can't officially recommend them, but they typically have personable hosts and bargain prices. All northbound regional trains run to Kasern Berg (4min., every 30min. 6:17am-11:17pm, 20AS; Eurail valid). Get off at the first stop ("Salzburg-Maria Plain") and walk uphill; all the Kasern Berg *Pensionen* lie on this road.

■ **Haus Rosemarie Seigmann,** Kasern Berg 66 (tel. 45 00 01). Bright rooms with fluffy comforters and mountain views. Doubles 380-400AS; triples 510-600AS. Breakfast included.

Germana Kapeller, Kasern Berg 64 (tel. 45 66 71). English-speaking hostess and traditional rooms. Doubles 360-400AS; triples 510-600AS. Breakfast included. Call ahead.

Haus Christine, Panoramaweg 3 (tel./fax 45 67 73). Spacious rooms with a country motif, on a gravel road set back 16m back from the main Kasern Berg street at the top of the hill. Breakfast included. Call ahead for pick-up from the station. 170-200AS per person.

Haus Matilda Lindner, Panoramaweg 5 (tel./fax 45 66 81). Matilda (Christine's sister) offers rooms with balconies. Call ahead for pick-up from the station. 170-200AS per person.

Haus Moser, Turnebuhel 1 (tel. 45 66 76), up the hidden stairs on the right side of Kasern Berg road opposite Germana Kapeller. Fur rugs and deer heads. Singles 170-200AS; doubles 340-400AS; triples 510-600AS; quads 700-800AS. Breakfast included.

CAMPING

Camping Stadtblick, Rauchenbichlerstr. 21 (tel. 45 06 52; fax 45 80 18), next to Haus Elisabeth. By car, take exit "Salzburg-Nord" off A1. On-site store. 60AS per person with

Let's Go, 15AS per tent, 25AS per card. 4-person mobile home with fridge and stove 100AS per person. Laundry 70AS. Open Mar. 20-Oct. 31.

FOOD

Blessed with fantastic **beer gardens** and **Konditoreien** (pastry shops), Salzburg begs its guests to eat outdoors. The local specialty is *Salzburger Nockerl*, a large soufflé of egg-whites, sugar, and raspberry filling baked into three mounds representing the three hills of Salzburg. World-famous **Mozartkugeln** ("Mozart balls") consist of hazelnuts covered with marzipan and nougat and dipped in chocolate. Many supermarkets line the Mirabellpl. side of the river; look for **SPAR** (the giant **EuroSpar** sprawls next to the train station and bus terminal).

Restaurant Zur Bürgerwehr-Einkehr, Mönchsberg 19c (tel. 84 17 29). Follow directions to the Gästehaus Bürgerwehr (see above). Escape the tourist throng below as you recline beneath the terrace's red umbrellas and enjoy the best views in town. One of the most reasonably priced (and tastiest) *Menüs* around. Open May-Oct. daily 10am-8:30pm.

Café im Künstlerhaus, Hellbrunnerstr. 3 (tel. 84 56 01). This low-key café is popular with students, artists, and their fans. Treat yourself to a café amaretto or a shot of tequila. Local bands play Tu and Th. Sa lesbian night. Open M-Sa 11am-11pm.

Shakespeare, Hubert Sattler. 3 (tel. 87 91 06), off Mirabellpl. Culturally schizophrenic restaurant with everything from wonton soup to Greek salad to *Wienerschnitzel*. 32-136AS. Doubles as a bar(d) with live music. Restaurant open daily 9pm-2am. V, MC.

Zum Fidelen Affen, Priesterhausg. 8 (tel. 87 73 61), off Linzerg. Phenomenal food in a dark-wood pub pleasantly crowded with locals and tourists. Drinks 30AS. Salad and main course 87-110AS. English menu available. Open M-Sa 5pm-midnight.

Café Tomaselli, Alter Markt 9 (tel. 84 44 88). Mozart's widow and her 2nd husband wrote Mozart's bio here in 1820. Sit in wood-paneled rooms with antique portraits or on the balcony overlooking the Alter Markt. Coffee 27-37AS. Open M-Sa 7am-9pm, Su 8am-9pm.

SIGHTS

THE NEUSTADT

SCHLOSS MIRABELL AND MIRABELLGARTEN. The **Schloß Mirabell** was built in 1606 by Archbishop Wolf Dietrich, who despite a vow of celibacy needed to house his mistress Salome Alt and their 10 children, and is today the seat of the city government. *(Mirabellpl. Open M-F 7am-4pm.)* Behind the palace, the manicured **Mirabellgarten** is a maze of extravagant flower beds and groomed shrubs. Students from the nearby **Mozarteum** (Salzburg's music conservatory) often perform here. If you're struck by a feeling of *déjà vu*, it's probably because Maria von Trapp and her wards once stopped here for a rousing rendition of "Do-Re-Mi." From the garden, you can see a tiny moss-covered shack called the **Zauberflötenhäuschen,** where Wolfgang Amadeus allegedly composed *The Magic Flute* in just five months.

MOZARTS WOHNHAUS. Just down the street from the Mozarteum stands the house in which the composer lived from 1773 to 1780, after moving with his family at age 17 from the Altstadt house in which he was born. The house was reopened on the composer's 240th birthday (January 27, 1996) following post-WWII renovations, with expanded displays about Mozart and his family and audio samples of his music. *(Makartpl. 8. Tel. 88 34 54 40. Open daily 10am-5:30pm. 65AS.)*

KAPUZINERKLOSTER AND SEBASTIANSKIRCHE. At the crest of the **Kapuzinerberg,** which looms to the south of the Neustadt, stands the simple **Kapuzinerkloster** (Capuchin Monastery), built by Wolf Dietrich in the late 16th century. *(From the Mirabellgarten or Mozarts Wohnhaus, follow Dreifaltigkeitsg. south to its intersection with Linzerg., head under the stone arch on the right side of Linzerg. 14, and follow the tiny stone staircase up.)* Nearby is the 18th-century **Sebastianskirche,** whose graveyard contains the gaudy mausoleum of Wolf Dietrich and the tombs of Mozart's wife Constanze and father Leopold. *(Lizerg. 41. Open Apr.-Oct. 9am-7pm, Nov.-Mar. 9am-4pm.)*

AUSTRIA

THE ALTSTADT
On the other side of the Salzach lies a labyrinth of winding pathways and 17th- and 18th-century façades. Many shops along **Getreidegasse**, one of the best-preserved streets in Salzburg, have wrought-iron signs dating from the Middle Ages.

MOZARTS GEBURTSHAUS AND UNIVERSITÄTSKIRCHE. Although Mozart eventually settled in Vienna, his **birthplace** holds the most impressive collection of his belongings: his first viola and violin, a pair of keyboardish instruments, and a supposed lock of his hair. *(Getreideg. 9. Open July-Aug. 9am-6:30pm; Sept.-June 9am-5:30pm. 70AS, students 55AS.)* Directly in Mozart's backyard stands the **Universitätskirche**, considered Fischer von Erlach's greatest masterpiece, one of the largest Baroque chapels on the continent. Its distinctive dome stands watch over Universitätspl.

TOSCANINIHOF TO THE DOM. Steps lead from **Toscaninihof**, the courtyard of **St. Peter's Monastery**, up the Mönchseberg cliffs. Adjacent to Toscaninihof, **Stiftskirche St. Peter** began as a Romanesque basilica in the 1100s and was remodeled in Rococo style in the 18th century. *(Open daily 9am-12:15pm and 2:30-6:30pm.)* Continue through the arch to the right of the church to enter the **Petersfriedhof**, a tiny cemetery dating back to the 1600s which served as the model for the cemetery where Rolf blew the whistle on the von Trapps. *(Open daily Apr.-Sept. 6:30am-7pm; Oct.-Mar. 6:30am-6pm.)* Near the far end of the cemetery against the mountains lies the entrance to the **Katakomben** (catacombs), bare cave-like rooms where Christians allegedly worshipped in secret as early as AD 250. *(Open in summer Tu-Su 10:30am-4pm; in winter W-Su 10:30am-3:30pm. 12AS, students 8AS.)* The exit at the other end of the cemetery from the Stiftskirche leads into Kapitelpl., bordered by Salzburg's immense Baroque **Dom** (cathedral), where Mozart was christened in 1756 and later worked as *Konzertmeister* and court organist.

RESIDENZ. Salzburg's ecclesiastical elite have resided in the magnificent Residenz for the last 700 years. Tours lead through stunning Baroque **Prunkräume** (state rooms), which house a three-dimensional ceiling fresco by Rottmayr. A **gallery** exhibits 16th- to 19th-century art. *(Residenzpl. 1. Tours in English May-Oct. and Dec. every 30min. 10am-4:30pm; Jan.-Apr. M-F every hr. 10am-4:00pm; 40min., 70AS, students 55AS. Gallery open Apr.-Sept. 10am-5pm; Oct.-Mar. Su-Tu and Th-Sa 10am-5pm; 50AS, students 40AS.)*

HOHENSALZBURG FORTRESS. *(Take the trail (20min.) or the Festungsbahn (funicular) up to the fortress from the Festungsg. Funicular runs every 10min. 9am-9pm; Oct.-Apr. 9am-5pm. Ascent 59AS; 69AS round-trip; includes entrance to fortress.)* Built between 1077 and 1681 by the ruling archbishops, **Festung Hohensalzburg**, which looms over Salzburg from atop Mönchsberg, is the largest preserved castle in Europe. Tours wind through torture chambers, Gothic state rooms, and an impregnable watchtower. The **Rainer Museum** in the fortress displays medieval instruments of torture. *(Fortress open July-Oct. 8:30am-7pm; Nov.-Mar. 9am-5pm; Apr.-June 9am-6pm. 35AS. Tours in English of the castle interior July-Aug. 9:30am-5:30pm; Apr.-June and Sept.-Oct. 9:30am-5pm; Nov.-Mar. 10am-4:30pm. Museum open daily 9am-5pm. Joint ticket including castle tour, museum, and fortress 75AS.)* Down the hill and to the right of the fortress, **Nonnberg Abbey** (where Maria von Trapp lived) remains a private monastic complex; you can tour the church.

THE SOUND OF MUSIC. Three remarkably similar companies run **Sound of Music Tours. Salzburg Sightseeing Tours** (tel. 88 16 16) and **Panorama Tours** (tel. 88 32 11) operate rival kiosks on Mirabellpl. *(400AS. Tours leave from Mirabellpl. daily 9:30am and 2pm.)* The renegade **Bob's Special Tours,** Kaig. 19 (tel. 84 95 11), has no high-profile kiosk, but they do have a minibus. *(350AS. Tours daily in summer 9am and 2pm; in winter 10am.)* All three companies offer free pick-up from your hotel, and all tours last four hours. The tours are generally only worth it if you're a *big* fan.

🎵 MUSICAL ENTERTAINMENT

Max Reinhardt, Richard Strauss, and Hugo von Hofmannsthal founded the renowned **Salzburger Festspiele** (Festivals) in 1920, and ever since operas, plays, films, concerts, and tourists have overrun every available public space from late July through the end of August. The festival prints a complete program of events one year in advance (10AS; available at any tourist office). To order tickets, contact **Kartenbüro der Salzburger Festspiele,** Postfach 140, A-5010 Salzburg (tel. 804 55 79; fax 804 57 60; www.salzburgfestival.at), by the beginning of January. Under-26ers can try for cheap subscription tickets (2-4 tickets for 200-300AS each) by writing eight months ahead to *Direktion der Salzburger Festspiele,* attn: Ulrich Haus-child, Hofstallg. 1, A-5020 Salzburg. Those who have no luck, or can't afford what's offered, can try the **Fest zur Eröffungsfest** (Opening Day Festival), when concerts, shows, and films are either cheap or free. Tickets for these events are available on a first-come, first-served basis the week of the opening.

Even when the *Festspiele* are not on, many other concerts and events occur around the city. The popular **Mozarteum** performs a number of concerts on a rotat-ing schedule (available at the tourist office). For tickets, contact **Kartenbüro Mozarteum,** Postfach 156, Theaterg. 2. (Tel. 87 31 54; fax 87 29 96. Open M-Th 9am-2pm, F 9am-4pm.) For a bit more money but a lot more kitsch, you can enjoy kicker-clad musicians with powdered hair performing **Mozart Serenaden** (Mozart's Serenades) in the Gothic Hall on Burgerstpitalg. 2. (Daily in summer 8:30pm, off-season 7:30pm; 200-420AS.) For info and tickets, contact **Konzertdirektion Nerat,** A-5020 Salzburg, Lieferinger Hauptstr. 136 (tel. 43 68 70; fax 43 69 70). In July and August, **outdoor opera** occasionally rings out from the historical hedge-theater of Mirabellgarten (330-560AS, students 190AS). Tickets for both series are available from the **box office** in Schloß Mirabell. (Tel. 84 85 86; fax 84 47 47. Open M-F 9am-5:30pm.) The Mirabellgarten hosts various **outdoor performances** throughout the summer, including concerts, folk-singing, and dancing. The tourist office has info, but strolling through in the evening might be just as effective.

🍸 NIGHTLIFE

Though Munich is known as the beer capital of the world, a good deal of that liquid gold flows south to Austria's beer gardens *(Biergärten).* These lager oases cluster in the center of the city by the Salzach River. Nightclubs in the Altstadt (especially along Gstätteng. and near Chiemseeg.) generally attract younger types and tourists. The other side of the river has a less juvenile atmosphere. From the Altstadt, follow the footpath from Hanuschpl. downstream, go left up the stairs past the Riverside Café, cross Müllner Hauptstr., walk uphill, and take the first left to **Augustiner Bräu,** Augustinerg. 4, a Salzburg legend; the great beer brewed by the Müllner Kloster is poured into massive steins from even more massive wooden kegs. (Tel. 43 12 46. Beer 1L 68AS (tip the tap-*meister* 4AS), 0.5L 34AS. Open M-F 3-11pm, Sa-Su 2:30-11pm.) **2 Stein,** Giselakai 9, is absolutely the funkiest bar in town, this place rocks at night. (Open M-W 6pm-4am, Th-F 6pm-5am, Sa 2pm-5am, Su 2pm-4am.) **Pub Pas-sage,** Rudolfskai 22-26, under the Radisson Hotel by the Mozartsteg bridge, is a shopping promenade for youthful bar-hopping. **Tom's Bierklinik** brags beers from all over the world; **The Black Lemon** offers Latino night every W; **Bräu zum Frommen Hell** burns with 80s music. **Hell** sells itself as a TV sports bar.

💧 EXCURSIONS FROM SALZBURG: LUSTSCHLOSS HELLBRUNN AND UNTERSBERG PEAK

Just south of Salzburg lies the unforgettable **Lustschloß Hellbrunn,** a one-time plea-sure dome for Wolf Dietrich's nephew, the Archbishop Markus Sittikus. The sprawling estate includes a large palace, fish ponds, trimmed hedge gardens, and the "I-Am-Sixteen-Going-On-Seventeen" gazebo (where Liesl and Rolf unleashed their youthful passion). To one side of the castle, the **Wasserspiele** (literally "water games") are perennial favorites—Archbishop Markus amused himself with elabo-rate water-powered figurines and a booby-trapped table that could spout water on his drunken guests. (Tel. 820 00 30. Open July-Aug. 9am-10pm; May-June and Sept. 9am-5:30pm; Apr. and Oct. 9am-4:30pm. Compulsory tours 30AS, students 20AS. Compulsory *Wasserspiele* tour 70AS, 35AS. Joint 90AS, 45AS.) Take **bus** 55 (dir: Anif) to "Hellbrunn" from the train station, Mirabellpl., or the Mozartsteg, in Salzburg, or bike 40min. down Hellbrunner Allee.

AUSTRIA

Bus 55 continues south to the luscious **Untersberg peak,** where Charlemagne supposedly rests deep beneath the ground, prepared to return and reign over Europe once again when need be. Dozens of **hikes** carve through color-soaked meadows, with mountains hovering in the distance. The **Eishöhlen** (ice caves) are only a 1½-hour climb from the peak. A **cable car** also glides over Salzburg to the summit. (Tel. (06246) 87 12 17. Runs July-Sept. Su-Tu and Th-Sa 8:30am-5:30pm, W 8:30am-8pm; Mar.-June and Oct. 9am-5pm; Dec.-Feb. 10am-4pm. Ascent 130AS, descent 110AS, 215AS round-trip.)

WESTERN AUSTRIA

THE SALZKAMMERGUT

Every summer, bands of Austrian schoolchildren, tour groups of elderly Europeans, and tourists in the know come to the smooth lakes and furrowed mountains of the Salzkammergut. The region takes its name from the salt mines that, in their glory days, underwrote Salzburg's architectural treasures; today, the white gold of the Salzkammergut is no longer salt, but pure sunshine on sparkling water in summer and tons of fresh snow in winter. The **Salzkammergut Card** (65AS at local tourist offices) grants 25% off on most local sights and attractions. The area is easily navigable, with 2000km of footpaths, 12 cable cars and chairlifts, and dozens of hostels. The mountainous area is barren of rail tracks; **buses** (dial 167 from Salzburg for schedules) are the best way to travel into and throughout the lake region.

HALLSTATT

Teetering on the banks of the **Hallstättersee** lake at the southern tip of the Salzkammergut and surrounded on all sides by the sheer rocky cliffs of the Dachstein mountains is tiny Hallstatt (pop. 1100). Declared a UNESCO World Cultural Heritage site in 1997, Hallstatt is easily the most beautiful lakeside village in the Salzkammergut, if not all of Austria. In the 19th century, it was also the site of an immense, incredibly well-preserved Iron Age archaeological find; the **Prähistorisches Museum** (Prehistoric Museum), across from the tourist office, and the smaller **Heimatmuseum** around the corner exhibit some of the treasures. (Both open May-Sept. daily 10am-6pm. Joint ticket 50AS, students 25AS.) The macabre yet fascinating parish house next to St. Michael's Chapel at the **Pfarrkirche** is a bizarre repository for skeletons, filled with remains of villagers dating from the 16th-century onwards. (Open May-Sept. daily 10am-5pm. 10AS.) Tours of the 2500-year-old **Salzbergwerke,** the oldest saltworks in the world, include a zip down a wooden mining slide on a burlap sack down to an eerie lake deep inside the mountain. To get there, climb up the path near the Pfarrkirche to the top (1hr.), or follow the black signs with the yellow eyes to the **Salzbergbahn** station at the south end of town. (Tel. 84 00 46. Open June to mid-Sept. 9:30am-4:30pm; Apr.-May and mid-Sept. to Oct. 9:30am-3pm. Tours in English 1½hr., 135AS, students 65AS. Salzbergbahn runs daily June to mid-Sept. 9am-6pm; Apr.-May and mid-Sept. to Oct. 9am-4:30pm. 60AS, round-trip 97AS.)

Buses are the cheapest way to get to Hallstatt from Salzburg (130AS). Eurailers who prefer **trains** will arrive on the opposite lake bank from downtown (210AS); **ferries** (23AS; last ferry 6:45pm) shuttle passengers across. The **tourist office,** Seestr. 169, finds rooms. (Tel. (06134) 82 08; fax 83 52; www.discover.com/hallstatt. Open July-Aug. M-F 8:30am-6pm, Sa 10am-6pm, Su 10am-2pm; Sept.-June M-F 9am-noon and 2-5pm.) To get reach **Gästehaus Zur Mühle,** Kirchenweg 36, from the tourist office, walk uphill toward the Heimatmuseum, then swing right at the end of the Platz; it's through the little tunnel on the left, by the waterfall. (Tel. (06134) 83 18. 110AS. Breakfast 40AS. Sheets 35AS. Reception 8am-2pm and 4-10pm.) **Frühstück-spension Sarstein,** Gosaumühlstr. 83, offers vistas of the lake and village. From the tourist office, head toward the ferry dock and continue along the road nearest the lake past the Pfarrkirchen steps (7min.). (Tel. (06134) 82 17. Dorms 210-300AS; add 20AS for 1-night stay. Breakfast included. Showers 10AS per 10min.) **Camping Klausner-Höll,** Lahnstr. 6, is three blocks past the bus stop on Seestr. (Tel. (06134) 83 22. 55AS per person, 40AS per tent, 30AS per car. Breakfast 100AS. Shower included.

Laundry. Open mid-Apr. to mid-Oct. Gate closed daily noon-2:30pm and 10pm-7am.) **Konsum supermarket** is by the main bus stop at the edge of town. (Open M-F 7:30am-12:30pm and 3-6:30pm, Sa 7:30am-12:30pm and 2-5pm.) **Postal code:** A-4830.

◪ DAY HIKING NEAR HALLSTATT: ECHENTAL VALLEY. Hallstatt offers spectacular **day hikes.** The tourist office has a guide (70AS) that details 38 hikes in the area, as well as a **mountain bike** map (35AS). Trails lead deep into the Echental valley, carved out millennia ago by glaciers; along the right wall, the **Gangsteig,** a slippery, nefarious, primitive stairway, is carved into the side of a cliff. Those with less gumption can visit the **Waldbachstub waterfall** or the **Glacier Gardens** in the valley. To reach the valley, go toward the Salzbergwerke and continue on Malerweg or Echenweg; about 20min. later, a sign posts the area's layout. Gangstieg is about an hour up on the right side, while the glacier gardens are about 40min. up on the left.

◪ EXCURSION FROM HALLSTATT: DACHSTEIN ICE CAVES. At the other end of the Hallstättersee in **Obertraun,** the eerily illuminated Dachstein Ice Caves give eloquent testimony to the geological hyperactivity that forged the region's natural beauty. (Tel. (06134) 84 00 46. Open May to mid-Oct. daily 9am-5pm. (Either cave 90AS, together 150AS.) From Hallstatt, take the **bus** (26AS) from near the lake, 6min. from the tourist office away from the ferry dock, to the Dachstein **cable car** station, then ride 1350m up to "Schönbergalm" (round-trip; 171AS; runs 9am-5pm).

GRÜNAU

The mountain-locked town of Grünau is not really on the way to anywhere, but it is an attractive destination in its own right. Sitting in the middle of the Totes Gebirge (Dead Mountains) is the backpacker's dream resort, ◪**The Treehouse,** Schindlbachstr. 525. Once you've settled into your room (with private shower and goosedown blankets), you're free to take advantage of the luxurious amenities. Organized adventure tours include **paragliding** (900AS), **canyoning** (650AS), **rafting** (550AS), **bungee jumping** (990AS; Sa-Su only), **mountain flights** (300AS per person; 4 person min.), and **horseback riding** (100AS per hr.). Rent a **mountain bike** (50AS per day) or ask the staff to drop you off at a nearby mountain or lake with a map so you can **hike** your way home. For winter visitors, the **ski lift** is 5min. away (lift tickets 200AS); you can borrow snow gear for free and rent skis (100AS) or a snowboard (150AS). (Tel. (07616) 84 99; email treehousehotel@hotmail.com; www.hostels.com/treehouse. Dorms 160AS; singles 200AS; doubles 400AS; bed in a triple 190AS; bed in a quad 170AS. Breakfast included. V, MC.) **Regional trains** service Grünau from Wels, on the Vienna-Salzburg rail line, every 2hr. Call ahead for pick-up from the station.

HOHE TAUERN NATIONAL PARK

The enormous Hohe Tauern National Park, the largest national park in Europe, encompasses 246 glaciers and 304 mountains over 3000m. Farmers still herd cattle over the same 2500m *Tauern* (ice-free mountain paths) once trod by Celts and Romans. The **Glocknergruppe,** in the heart of the park, has Austria's highest peak, the **Großglockner** (3798m), as well as many Alpine lakes and glaciers. The main tourist attractions are the **Krimml Waterfalls** and spectacular high mountain road **Großglocknerstraße** (a.k.a. Bundesstr. 107).

⊡ GETTING THERE AND GETTING AROUND. Two **train** lines service towns near the park: a rail line from **Zell am See** runs west along the northern border of the park, terminating in **Krimml** (1¾hr., 9 per day, 106AS); another runs from **Salzburg** to **Badgastein** in the southwest corner of the park (1½hr., every 2hr. 7:14am-8:15pm, 170AS). **Buses** connect to and traverse the park, terminating in the center at **Franz-Josefs-Höhe;** from Zell am See, take #3064 (2hr., June 19-Oct. 10 1-3 per day, 145AS). For schedules, destinations, and maps, check the brochure *Der BundesBus ist Wanderfreundlich* (available at bus stations in Zell am See). The breathtaking **Großglocknerstraße,** one of the most beautiful highways in the world, winds for 50km through silent Alpine valleys, meadows of wildflowers, tumbling waterfalls, and huge glaciers between Zell am See and Lienz (about 5hr.). Many visitors traverse the Großglocknerstr. in a **tour bus** or **rental car,** but the public **bus** service is good. Heavy snow forces the Großglockner to close from October to April. For info on road conditions, call (04824) 22 12.

FRANZ-JOSEFS-HÖHE AND PASTERZE GLACIER. Großglocknerstr. buses from Zell am See, Lienz, and Heiligenblut terminate at **Franz-Josefs-Höhe,** a large observation and tourist center above the **Pasterze glacier.** Although the area is packed with visitors, they can't detract from the sight of the glacier's icy tongue extending down the valley. In good weather, you can glimpse the summit of the **Großglockner** (3797m). The **tourist office** in the parking area has a free mini-museum and organizes daily walks around the glacier—call ahead for prices and times. (Tel. (04824) 27 27. Open daily 10am-4pm.) The **Gletscherbahn funicular** runs from Franz-Josefs-Höhe down to the glacier, where you can walk 100m across its hard-packed surface. (Runs May 21-Oct. 10 daily 9am-2pm. 98AS round-trip.) At the top of the hill at the end of the parking lot looms the **Swarovski Observation Center,** with binoculars and telescopes for viewing the surrounding terrain; keep an eye out for marmots and other animals indigenous to the park. (Open daily 10am-4pm. Free.)

KRIMML WATERFALLS AND TOWN. A sloping path leads from the small mountain town of **Krimml,** in the northwest corner of the park, to the extraordinary **Wasserfälle**—three roaring cascades totaling over 400m in height. A path running alongside the falls allows for unusually close and pulse-quickening views. The first cascade (150m) is visible past the entrance booth. It's about 30min. from the first falls to the second (100m) and another 30min. from there to the third (140m); the last is perhaps the most scenic and the least cluttered with gawking tourists. **Buses** from Zell am See (1½hr., 10 per day, 100AS) drop you at the start of the path to the falls (get off at "Maustelle Ort"). The **Pinzgauer Lokalbahn** train arrives in town from Zell am See (1½hr., 9 per day, 95AS; Swisspass and Eurail valid); catch the **bus** (19AS) across the street or walk 3km along the path to the falls. (Falls 8am-6pm 15AS; otherwise free.) **ÖAV Information** is next to the ticket booth. (Tel. (06564) 72 12. Open May-Oct. M-Sa 11am-4pm.) The **tourist office** in Krimml Town is 2min. downhill from the "Krimml Ort" bus stop. (Tel. (06564) 72 39; fax 75 50. Open M-F 8am-noon and 2:30-5:30pm, Sa 8:30-10:30am). **Bauernhof Mühleg,** Krimml 24, has big rooms with waterfall views. Head past the ADEG supermarket, continue downhill, and it's on the right (5min.). (Tel. (06564) 73 38. Doubles 220-240AS.)

HEILIGENBLUT. The cheapest, most convenient base for exploring the region is Heiligenblut, a tiny town to the south of the Großglockner. The **tourist office,** up the street from the bus stop and Hotel Glocknerhof, has info on park transport. (Tel. (04824) 20 01 21; fax 20 01 43. Open M-F 8:30am-noon and 2:30-6pm, Sa 9am-noon and 4-6pm; July-Aug. M-F 8:30am-6pm). To reach the **Jugendherberge (HI),** Hof 36, take the steep path down from the wall behind the bus stop parking lot. (Tel./fax (04824) 22 59. Dorms 180AS; members only. Breakfast included. Reception May-Sept. 7-11am and 5-9pm. Curfew 10pm; key available.) **Pension Bergkristall** has rooms with balconies. (Tel. (04824) 20 05; fax 20 05 33. In summer 300AS per person; in winter 380-420AS. Breakfast included.) **Buses** arrive from Franz-Josefs-Höhe (30min., 4 per day, 47AS) and Zell am See (2½hr., 3 per day, 145AS).

ZELL AM SEE

Surrounded by a ring of snow-capped mountains that slide into a broad turquoise lake, Zell am See (TSELL am ZAY) is a year-round resort for mountain-happy European tourists. Conquer the rugged, snow-crowned peaks surrounding Zell on one of the five **cable cars.** The BundesBus (dir: Schmittenhöhebahn/Sonnenalmbahn Talstation) goes to the **Schmittenhöhebahn,** 2km north of town on Schmittenstr. (Runs mid-July to late Oct. every 30min. 8:30am-5pm. 180AS; round-trip 235AS.) The **Zeller Bergbahn** (780-1411m) is in town, at Schmittenstr. and Gartenstr. (Mid-June to late Sept. daily 9am-5pm. 110AS; round-trip 145AS.) The Schmittenhöhe lift provides brochures detailing **hikes** ranging from casual strolls to cliff-hangers. For more hiking info, grab a *Wanderplan.* The **Zell/Kaprun Ski Pass** covers Zell and nearby Kaprun. (2-day 710-780AS, students 640-700AS. A free bus connects them every 15min. Dec. 20-Apr. 13.) The **Kitzsteinhorn** mountain (3203m) and its glacier in Kaprun offer **year-round skiing.** (Day-pass 255AS. Full rental around 255AS per day.)

Trains (tel. (06542) 73 21 43 57) arrive at Bahnhofstr. and Salzmannstr. from Kitzbühel (45min., 10 per day, 105AS); Salzburg (1¾hr., 24 per day, 150AS); and Innsbruck (2hr., 8 per day, 250AS). From the station, turn right and follow the green "i" by the stairs on the left to reach the **tourist office**, on Brucker Bundesstr. (Tel. (06542) 770; fax (06542) 720 32; zell.gold.at. Open July to mid-Sept. and mid-Dec. to Mar. M-F 8am-6pm, Sa 8am-noon and 4-6pm, Su 10am-noon; Apr.-June and Sept. to mid-Dec. M-F 8am-noon and 2-6pm, Sa 9am-noon.) To reach **Haus der Jugend (HI)**, Seespitzstr. 13, exit the train station toward the lake ("Zum See"), turn right, walk along the footpath beside the lake, and turn left at the end on Seespitzstr. (15min.). (Tel. (06542) 571 85; fax 57 18 54; email hostel-zell-se@salzburg.co.at. 165AS first night, 140AS thereafter. Breakfast included. Key deposit 300AS or passport. Reception 7-9am and 4-10pm. Check-out 9am. Lockout noon-4pm. Curfew 10pm. Open Dec.-Oct. Reserve ahead.) **SPAR supermarket** is at Brucker Bundesstr. 4. (Open M-Th 8am-7pm, F 8am-7:30pm, Sa 7:30am-1pm.) **Postal code:** A-5700.

KITZBÜHEL

Kitzbühel welcomes tourists with glitzy casinos and countless pubs, yet few visitors remain at ground level long enough to enjoy them. The mountains surrounding the city invite wealthy vacationers and poor ski bums alike.

⃠ ⃠⃠⃠ INFO, ACCOMMODATIONS, AND FOOD. Trains (tel. (05356) 640 55 13 85) arrive frequently from Zell am See (45 min., 106AS); Innsbruck (1hr., 142AS); Salzburg (2½hr., 250AS); and Vienna (6hr., 570AS). Those from Salzburg arrive at the **Hauptbahnhof,** those from Innsbruck at the **Hahnenkamm Bahnhof. Buses** stop next to both train stations. To reach the **Fußgängerzone** (pedestrian zone) from the Hauptbahnhof, head straight down Bahnhofstr. and turn left at the main road. The **tourist office,** Hinterstadt 18, is near the Rathaus in the Fußgängerzone. (Tel. (05356) 62 15 50; fax 623 07; www.kitzbuehel.com. Open July-Sept. and mid-Dec. to late Apr. M-F 8:30am-6:30pm, Sa 8:30am-noon and 4-6pm, Su 10am-noon and 4-6pm; Oct. to mid-Dec. and late Apr. to June M-F 8:30am-12:30pm and 2:30-6pm.) Wherever you stay, ask about the **guest card,** which provides discounts on local attractions. The **Hotel Kaiser,** Bahnhofstr. 2, 2min. from the Hauptbahnhof, has a terrace and inexpensive bar. (Tel. (05356) 647 09. In summer 200AS; more in winter. Laundry. V, MC, AmEx. Sometimes closed off-season; call ahead.) From the Hauptbahnhof, turn left after Hotel Kaiser, and look left for **Pension Hörl,** Josef-Pirchlstr. 60. If they have no vacancies, they'll try to put you up at their nearby **Gästehaus Hörl,** Bahnhofstr. 8. (Tel. (05356) 631 44. In summer 180-260AS; in winter add 40AS. Breakfast included.) For **Camping Schwarzsee,** Reitherstr. 24, take the train to "Schwarzsee" and follow the tracks past the bathing areas around the back of the lake; it's behind the Bruggerhof Hotel. For a long walk, head right from the tourist office, go under the archway, bear right at the Wienerwald up Franz-Reischstr., and follow the "Waldweg zum See" signs. (Tel. 62 80 60; fax 644 79. 83-90AS per person plus 7AS tax, 96AS per tent, 90-100AS per caravan.) **SPAR supermarket,** Bichlstr. 22, is at Ehrenbachg. (Open M-F 8am-6:30pm, Sa 7:30am-1pm.) **Postal code:** A-6370.

⃠ SKIING AND HIKING. The Kitzbühel **ski area,** the "Ski Circus," is one of the best in the world. A one-day **ski pass** (high-season 390-420AS) grants unlimited passage on 64 lifts and on shuttle buses that connect them. Purchase passes at any of the lifts or at the *Kurhaus* **Aquarena,** which offers a pool, sauna, and solarium. (Tel. (05356) 643 85. Open daily 9am-8pm. 80AS.) Renting downhill **ski equipment** from virtually any sports shop runs 170-500AS per day; **lessons** cost 500AS; **snowboards** 180-350AS. For summer visitors, more than 70 **hiking trails** snake up the mountains; some of the best views are from the **Kampenweg** and **Hochetzkogel** trails, accessible via the Bichlalm bus (every hr., 26AS) or a two-hour climb.

The **Kitzbüheler Hornbahn lift** (85AS) ascends to the **Alpenblumengarten,** where more than 120 different types of flowers blossom each spring. (Open late-May to mid-Oct. 8:30am-5pm.) A three-day **summer holiday pass** is valid for all cable cars, free Bichlalm bus service, and Aquarena (420AS). Guest card holders can take advantage of the tourist office's daily three- to five-hour **mountain hikes.** (Mid-May to mid-Oct. M-F at 8:45am from the tourist office. 90AS; with guest card, free except for cable car rides.) **Mountain bike trails** abound; rent a bike from **Stanger Radsport,** Josef-Pirchlstr. 42. (Tel. (05356) 25 49. 250AS per day. Open M-F 8am-noon and 1-6pm, Sa 9am-noon.) The **Schwarzsee** (Black Lake), 2.5km northwest of Kitzbühel, is famed for its healing **mud baths.** Follow the directions above to Camping Schwarzsee to float in the deep blue water and gaze at the snow-capped mountains above. (Tel. (05356) 623 81. Open 7am-8pm. 45AS, with guest card 40AS; after noon 30AS, after 4pm 15AS. Electric boats 150AS per hr., rowboats 85AS per hr.)

INNSBRUCK

Innsbruck—the site of the 1964 and 1976 Winter Olympics—is surrounded by massive, snow-capped peaks. The nearby Tyrolean Alps await skiers and hikers, while back in town, the tiny Altstadt's cobblestoned streets are peppered with fancy façades and remnants of the Hapsburg Empire.

◘ GETTING THERE AND GETTING AROUND

Trains: Hauptbahnhof, Südtirolerpl. (tel. 17 17). To: **Salzburg** (2hr., 10 per day, 350AS); **Munich** (2hr., 9 per day, 350AS, under 26 300AS); **Zurich** (4hr., 8 per day, 592AS); **Venice** (5hr., 5 per day, 402AS, under 26 284AS); and **Vienna** (5¼hr., 660AS).

Buses: Bundesbuses (tel. 58 51 55) run from Sterzingerstr., next to the Hauptbahnhof to destinations throughout Tyrol. Call 35 11 93 for schedules.

Public Transportation: The main bus station is in front of the Hauptbahnhof. Buy single-ride (21AS), 24hr. (35AS), or 4-ride (61AS) tickets from any driver or *Tabak* and punch them as you board (400AS fine for riding without a validated ticket). Most buses stop running around 10:30-11:30pm, but each night the *Nachtbus* runs east from Marktpl. at 1 and 2am, and west from Maria-Theresien-Str. at 1:30 and 2:30am.

Bike and Ski Rental: Rent **bikes** at the Hauptbahnhof (tel. 503 53 95). 90-200AS per day. Open Apr. to early Nov. Su-F 7am-6:30pm, Sa 7am-6pm. **Skischule Innsbruck,** Leopoldstr. 4 (tel. 58 17 42). Skis, boots, poles, and insurance 270AS.

◪ ORIENTATION AND PRACTICAL INFORMATION

The city center lies on the east bank of the **Inn River.** Turn right from the Hauptbahnhof on Brunecker Str., left on Museumstr., and left on Burggraben to reach the **Altstadt** and the tourist office. **Maria-Theresien-Str.,** the city's main thoroughfare, leads south from the Altstadt; Marktgraben leads west across the river to the **University district.** Most sights are clustered between the **Innbrücke** and the **Hofgarten.**

Tourist Offices: Innsbruck Information Office, Burggraben 3, 3rd fl. (tel. 598 50; fax 598 07; www.discover.com/innsbruck). Open M-F 8am-6pm, Sa 8am-noon. **Innsbruck-Information** is in the same building. Open M-Sa 8am-7pm, Su 9am-6pm. The **Innsbruck Card,** sold at both, includes many sights and unlimited transportation (24hr. 230AS, 48hr. 300AS, 72hr. 370AS). **Österreichischer Alpenverein,** Wilhelm-Greil-Str. 15 (tel. 595 47; fax 57 55 28). Mountains of info and discounts for hikers. Membership 530AS, ages 18-25 390AS. Open M-F 9am-1pm and 2-5pm.

American Express: Brixnerstr. 3 (tel. 58 24 91). Open M-F 9am-5:30pm, Sa 9am-noon.

Laundromat: Bubble Point, Andreas-Hofer-Str. 37, at the corner of Franz-Fischer-Str. Wash 45AS; soap included. Dry 5AS per 5min. Open M-F 7am-10pm, Sa-Su 7am-8pm.

Emergencies: Police, tel. 133. Headquarters at Kaiserjägerstr. 8 (tel. 590 00). **Ambulance,** tel. 144 or 142. **Fire,** tel. 122. **Mountain Rescue,** tel. 140.

Medical Assistance: University Hospital, Anichstr. 35 (tel. 50 40).

Post Office: Maximilianstr. 2 (tel. 500), a few blocks straight ahead as you exit the station. Address mail to be held: *Postlagernde Briefe* für Arthur SCHNITZLER, Hauptpostamt, Maximilianstr. 2, **A-6020** Innsbruck, Austria. Open M-F 7am-11pm, Sa 7am-9pm.

PHONE CODE City code: 0512. From outside Austria, dial int'l dialing prefix (see inside back cover) + 43 + 512 + local number.

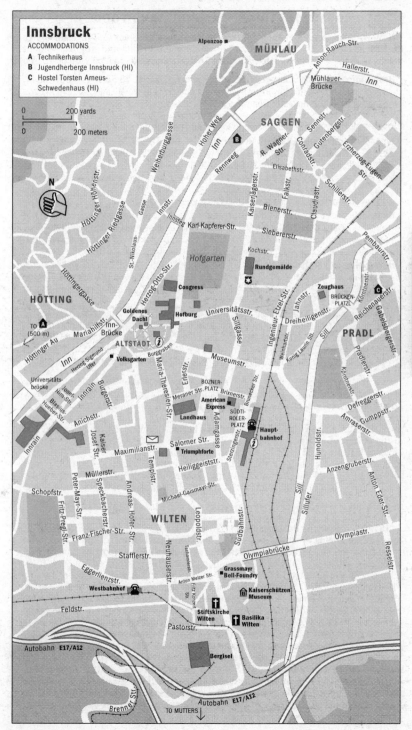

Innsbruck

ACCOMMODATIONS

A Technikerhaus
B Jugendherberge Innsbruck (HI)
C Hostel Torsten Arneus-
  Schwedenhaus (HI)

0   200 yards
0   200 meters

N

Alpenzoo ■

MÜHLAU

Anton-Rauch-Str.

Hallerstr.

Mühlauer-
Brücke

Inn

SAGGEN

Sennstr.

R. Wagner-Str.

Conradstr.

Gutenbergstr.

Erzherzog-Eugen-Str.

Schillerstr.

Weinerburggasse

Hoher Weg

Rennweg

Kaiserjägerstr.

Elisabethstr.

Falkstr.

Claudiastr.

Pembaurstr.

Bienerstr.

Innstr.

Innsteg Karl-Kapferer-Str.

Siebererstr.

Kochstr.

Hofgarten

Rundgemälde ✦

Herzog-Otto-Str.

Congress

Zeughaus

BRÜCKEN-PLATZL

C

Reichenauerstr.

Gabelsbergerstr.

Komernstr.

HÖTTING

Höttinger Höhenstr.

Höttinger Riedgasse

St.-Nikolaus

Gasse

Goldenes
Dachl

Hofburg

Universitätsstr.

Sillgasse

Ingenieur-Etzel-Str.

Dreiheiligenstr.

Jahnstr.

Weinhartstr.

PRADL

Pradlerstr.

Komernstr.

Höttingergasse

Inn-
Brücke

ALTSTADT

ⓘ

Museumstr.

König Laurin Str.

Mariahilfstr.

Herzog-Sigmund Ufer

Burggraben

Bruneckerstr.

TO A
(500 m)

Höttinger Au

Inn

Volksgarten

Maria-Theresien-Str.

Erlerstr.

BOZNER-
PLATZ

Brixnerstr.

Defreggerstr.

Universitäts-
brücke

Josef-
Hirn-Str.

Innrain

Burgstr.

Meraner Str.

American
Express

SÜDTI-
ROLER-
PLATZ

Sterzinger Str.

Hunoldstr.

Amraserstr.

Gumpptstr.

Blasius
Hueber-Str.

Anichstr.

Landhaus

Adamgasse

Haupt-
bahnhof

Sill

Anzengruberstr.

Anton-Eder-Str.

Kaiser
Josef Str.

Maximilianstr.

Salorner Str.

Triumphforte ■

Heiliggeiststr.

ⓘ

Innrain

Peter-Mayr-Str.

Müllerstr.

Templstr.

Andreas-Hofer-Str.

Michael-Gaismayr-Str.

Leopoldstr.

Südbahnstr.

Sillufer

Sill

Schopfstr.

Fritz-Pregl-Str.

Speckbacherstr.

WILTEN

Franz-Fischer-Str.

Stafflerstr.

Neuhauserstr.

Tschamlerstr.

Anton Melzer Str.

Fritz Konzert Str.

Olympiabrücke

Olympiastr.

Resselstr.

Eggerlienzstr.

Westbahnhof 🚂

Grassmayr
Bell-Foundry

Kaiserschützen
Museum

Feldstr.

Stiftskirche
Wilten ✝

Basilika
Wilten ✝

Pastorstr.

Autobahn E17/A12

Bergisel

Brenner Str.

Autobahn E17/A12

TO MUTTERS ↓

AUSTRIA

▚▞ ACCOMMODATIONS, CAMPING, AND FOOD

Hostel beds are scarce in June, when **Jugendherberge Innsbruck** and **Jugendherberge St. Niklaus** (tel. 28 65 15) are the only hostels open. In July and August, student dorms ease the crunch; try **Internationales Studentenhaus,** Recheng. 7 (tel. 50 15 92).

Hostel Torsten Arneus-Schwedenhaus (HI), Rennweg 17b (tel. 58 58 14; fax 585 81 44; email youth.hostel@idk.netwing.at). Follow the directions to the Altstadt, but turn right on Burggraben, which becomes Rennweg. 120AS. Breakfast 45AS. Sheets 20AS. Reception 6-9am and 5-10:30pm. Lockout 9am-5pm. Curfew 10:30pm; ask for a key. Open July-Aug. Reservations recommended and held until 7pm.

Jugendherberge Innsbruck (HI), Reichenauer Str. 147 (tel. 34 61 79; fax 34 61 79 12; email yhibk@tirol.com). Head right from the station and turn right on Dreiheiligenstr., which becomes Reichenauer Str. Dorms 146-176AS first night, 116-146AS thereafter. July-Aug. singles 350AS; doubles 500AS. Nonmembers add 40AS. Breakfast 85AS. Laundry 45AS. Reception 7am-12:30pm and 5-10pm. Lockout 10am-5pm. Curfew 11pm; ask for a key. Phone reservations held until 5pm.

Haus Wolf, Dorfstr. 48 (tel. 54 86 73), in Mutters. Take the Stubaitalbahn tram (26AS; last tram 10:30pm) from the third island in front of the Hauptbahnhof to "Birchfeld"; continue in the same direction down Dorfstr. (30min.). Let proprietor Titi Wolf spoil you with atten-tion and a huge breakfast. Singles 190AS; doubles 380AS; triples 570AS.

Haus Kaltenberger, Schulg. 15 (tel. 54 85 76), near Haus Wolf. Take the Stubaitalbahn (see Haus Wolf) to "Mutters"; walk toward the church, turn right on Dorfstr., and take the first left. Comfy, with well-kept rooms, attractive balconies, and mountain views. Singles 180AS; doubles 360-400AS. Breakfast included.

Camping Innsbruck Kranebitten, Kranebitter Allee 214 (tel. 28 41 80). Take bus LK from Bozner Platz (a block down Brixner Str. from the station) to "Klammstr." (20min.); at night, take bus O to "Lohbachsiedlung" and switch to the LK. Walk downhill to the right and follow the road. 68AS per person, 40AS per tent, 40AS per car; tax 7AS. Tent rental 75-110AS per person. Shower included. Laundry. Reception 8am-noon.

Gawk at the overpriced delis and *Konditoreien* on Maria-Theresien-Str., then cross the river to **Innstr.** for ethnic restaurants, *Schnitzel Stuben*, and grocers. Look for **M-Preis Supermarkets** on Maximilianstr. by the arch; at Innrain 15; and in front of the train station. (Open M-Th 7:30am-6:30pm, F 7:30am-7:30pm, Sa 7:30am-5pm.) Indulge at the ▨**Philippine Vegetarische Küche,** Templstr. 2, in the gray building at the corner of Müllerstr. (Salad bar 48-88AS. *Menü* with soup and entree 75AS. Open M-F 10am-11pm. V, MC.) **Gasthof Weißes Lamm,** Mariahilfstr. 12, 2nd fl., is pop-ular with locals for cheap Tyrolean fare. (Soup, entree, and salad 85-115AS. Open M-W and F-Su 11:30am-2pm and 6-10pm.) **Salute Pizzeria,** Innrain 35, is a popular student hangout. (Pizza 40-100AS. Pasta 60-95AS. Open daily 11am-midnight.)

▚▞ SIGHTS AND OUTDOORS

ALTSTADT. Inside the **Goldenes Dachl** (Little Golden Roof) on Herzog-Friedrich-Str. the **Maximilianeum Museum** commemorates Innsbruck's favorite emperor, who ruled from 1490 to 1519 and used his smarts (and well-timed marriages) to create an empire whose size was exceeded only by that of his nose. *(Open May-Sept. 10am-6pm; Oct.-Apr. Tu-Su 10am-12:30pm and 2-5pm. 60AS, students 30AS.)* Across Herzog-Friedrich-Str. is the 15th-century **Goldener Adler Inn,** where Goethe, Heine, Sartre, Mozart, Wagner, Camus, and even Maximilian I ate, drank, and made merry. One block behind the Goldenes Dachl rise the twin towers of the **Dom St. Jakob** (remodeled 1717-24), which contains *trompe l'oeil* ceiling murals by C.D. Asam depicting the life of St. James and an altar painting by Cranach the Elder. *(Open daily Apr.-Sept. 8am-7:30pm; Oct.-Mar. 8am-6:30pm. Free.)* Behind the Dom and to the right is the entrance to the grand **Hofburg** (Imperial Palace), whose imposing furniture and large portraits—including one of Empress Maria Theresia's youngest daughter, Marie Antoinette—fill sumptuously decorated rooms. *(Open daily 9am-5pm. 55AS, stu-dents 35AS. Tours in German 11am and 2pm.)* Across Rennweg past the Dom sits the **Hofkirche** (Imperial Church), with 28 larger-than-life bronze statues of Hapsburg saints and Roman emperors, some by Dürer. An intricate sarcophagus within is decorated with scenes from Maximilian I's life, but the monument was not completed to Maxi's wishes, so he was buried near Vienna instead. The **Tiroler Volkskunstmuseum** (Tyrolean Handicrafts Museum) shares the same building. *(Church open daily July-Aug. 9am-5:30pm; Sept.-June 9am-5pm. 30AS, students 20AS. Museum open M-Sa 9am-5pm. 60AS, students 35AS. Joint ticket 75AS, students 55AS.)* The other direction up Rennweg lies the **Hofgarten** (Imperial Garden), a beautifully manicured park complete with an outdoor chess set. Return to the Goldenes Dachl and follow Herzog-Friedrich-Str. south to **Maria-Theresien-Straße,** and its pastel-colored Baroque buildings for a view of the snow-capped mountains.

SCHLOSS AMBRAS. One of the most beautiful Renaissance castles in Austria, Schloß Ambras was built by Archduke Ferdinand of Tyrol in the late 16th century. The museum within showcases good-as-new casts of armor, paintings by Velázquez and Titian, and Archduke Ferdinand's *Wunderkammer* (Cabinet of Curiosities). The walls of the Spanish Hall, Ambras' most famous room, are covered with mythological scenes and portraits of Tyrol's princes. *(Schloßstr. 20, in a park southeast of the city. Take tram 6 (dir: Igls) to "Schloß Ambras" and follow the signs; or take the shuttle bus that departs every hr. from Maria-Theresien-Str. opposite McDonalds. Open Su-M and W-Sa 10am-5pm. 60AS, with tour 85AS; students 30AS, with tour 55AS.)*

HIKING AND SKIING. A **Club Innsbruck** membership (available at central accommodations) grants you access to a **hiking** program that provides members with guides, transportation, and equipment at no additional cost; it also provides discounts on **ski** passes and provides complimentary shuttles to suburban slopes. The **Patscherkofelbahn** in Igls takes hikers up beautiful trails to the **Alpine Garden,** the highest botanical garden in Europe. *(Runs daily 9am-4:30pm. 110AS, round-trip 180AS. Open June-Sept. 9:30am-4pm. Free.)* Ask at the tourist office about the **Innsbruck Gletscher Ski Pass,** valid for all 62 lifts in the region (3-day 1260AS, Club Innsbruck members 1020AS); **equipment rental** (Alpine 270AS per day, cross-country 160AS); and **glacier skiing** (1-day in summer 170-280AS, in winter 420AS; add 270AS for ski rental; 599AS package includes bus, lift, and rental).

🎭 ENTERTAINMENT

The **university quarter** is a mecca for late-night revelry, while the **Viaduktbögen** contains a stretch of lively theme bars along Ingenieur-Etzel-Str. Students fill **Krah Vogel,** Anichstr. 12, off Maria-Theresien-Str., a stylish bar/restaurant. (Beer 29-37AS. Open M-Sa 9:30am-1am, Su 4pm-1am.) The **Hofgarten Café,** accessible through the Hofgarten's back entrance, is a sprawling outdoor affair with networking twenty- and thirtysomethings. (Snacks 50-100AS. Beer 28-48AS. Open Sa-Th 10pm-2am, F until 4am.) **Treibhaus,** Angerzellg. 8, is Innsbruck's favorite alterna-teen club. (Open M-F 9am-1am, Sa-Su 10am-1am.) **Die Alte Piccolo Bar,** Seilerg. 2, attracts a primarily gay male crowd. (Open Th-Tu 9pm-4am.)

BREGENZ

Bregenz is a kind of tourist nirvana, and thousands come—Speedo-clad—to bathe in the gray-green waters of the Bodensee (Lake Constance), hike in the surrounding Bregenzerwald, and explore the historic buildings in the Oberstadt (Old City). The **Martinturm,** begun in 1362, rules the Oberstadt. Next door is the **Martinskirche,** with frescoes dating back to the 14th century. Hike up Schloßbergstr. to the **St. Gallus Pfarrkirche,** an 11th-century white stucco sanctuary that now glows under lavish gold ornaments and a detailed painted ceiling. The **Pfänderbahn** cable car leaves from the top of Schillerstr. and sways up the Pfänder Mountain, the tallest mountain in the Bodensee area, for a panorama spanning the Black Forest and Switzerland. (Daily 9am-7pm every 30min. Ascent 88AS, descent 63AS, round-trip 125AS.) But the main attraction of the town is the **Bodensee,** where carefully groomed waterfront paths surround fantastic playgrounds and paddleboat rental shops. Hop aboard a ferry to the **Blumeninsel Mainau** (Mainau Flower Isle) and take a tour of the island's Baroque castle, tropical palm collection, butterfly house, and gardens. (Ferries depart May-Sept. daily at 9:20, 10:20, and 11:25am; return at 2:50, 4:15, and 4:55pm. Round-trip 293AS. Admission to all sites 127AS.)

Trains go to Lindau, Germany (10min.; see p. 434); St. Gallen (45min., 134AS); Zurich (1¾hr., 378AS); and Innsbruck (3¾hr., 290AS). Local **BundesBuses** also depart from the station. For hotel reservations (30AS), head to the **tourist office,** Bahnhofstr. 14. (Tel. (05574) 495 90; fax 459 69; email tourismus@bregenz.at.) The new **Jugendgästehaus (HI),** Mehreranerstr. 3-5, offers spic-'n'-span rooms and **internet** access. From the train station, cross the bridge, pass the half-pipe, and look for yellow brick. (Tel. (05574) 428 67; fax 428 67 88; email bregenz@jgh.at. 200AS. Breakfast included.) Five minutes on foot past the hostel, the family-run **Gasthof Lamm** offers quiet rooms. (350AS per person, 50AS extra per person with bath. Breakfast included.) Next door is **Camping Lamm,** Mehrerauerstr. 50-51. (Tel. (05574) 717 01; fax 71 74 54. 45AS per person.) **Ikaros,** Deuringstr. 5, at the corner of Rathausstr. in the *Fußgängerzone* (pedestrian zone), serves up a little taste of the Mediteranneau, with Greek dishes for 55-95AS. (Open M-Sa 10am-1am.) **Postal Code:** A-6900.

SOUTHERN AUSTRIA

GRAZ

Despite its status as the second-largest city in Austria (pop. 240,000) and its dignified medieval and Baroque past, Graz remains surprisingly under-touristed. The Altstadt packs dozens of classical arches and domes into a twisting maze of cobblestoned streets; the stark, modern buildings of Technical University a few blocks away demonstrate the influence of Graz's famous School of Architecture; and the city possesses a fascinating history. Napoleon didn't manage to capture Graz's **Schloßberg** (castle hill), which had already withstood substantial battering by Ottoman Turks, until *after* he conquered the rest of Austria—when he proceeded to raze it in an infantile rage (1809). As you exit the tourist office, walk left up Herreng./Sackstr. to Schloßbergpl. and climb the **Schloßstiege,** zigzagging stone steps built by Russian prisoners during WWI, to the top of the Schloßberg (today a carefully tended park) for sweeping views. The **Landhaus** housing the tourist office below is a sight in itself, remodeled in 1557 in masterful Lombard style. The **Landeszeughaus** (Provincial Arsenal), Herreng. 16, details the history of the arsenal and the Ottoman Turk attacks and has enough spears, muskets, and armor to outfit 28,000 burly mercenaries. (Open Apr.-Oct. M-F 9am-5pm, Sa-Su 9am-1pm. 60AS, students 40AS.) The solemn 17th-century Hapsburg **Mausoleum,** on Burgg., around the corner from the cathedral, is one of the finest examples of Austrian Mannerism. (Open M-Sa 10am-12:30pm and 2-4pm. 10AS.) Down the street, Graz's **Opernhaus,** at Opernring and Burgg., sells standing-room opera tickets an hour before curtain. (Tel. (0316) 80 08. 360-1490AS; student rush 150AS, standing-room from 50AS.)

Trains (info tel. (0316) 17 17) run frequently from across the river from the center on Europapl. to Vienna (3¾hr., 310AS); Salzburg (4¼hr., 410AS); Innsbruck (6¼hr., 550AS); and Munich (6¼hr., 708AS). From there, go down Annenstr. and cross the Hauptbrücke (bridge) to reach central Hauptpl. Turn right on Herreng. to reach the **tourist office** at #16, which lists *Privatzimmer* (most 150-300AS). (Tel. (0316) 807 50; fax 807 55 15; www.graztourismus.at. Open in summer M-F 9am-7pm, Sa 9am-6pm, Su 10am-3pm; off-season M-F 9am-6pm, Sa 9am-3pm, Su 10am-3pm. Tours 2½hr., June-Sept. daily 2:30pm, Oct.-May Sa only, 75AS.) Exit the station, cross the street, head right on Eggenberger Gürtel, turn left at Josef-Huber-Gasse, and take the first right to reach the **Jugendgästehaus Graz (HI),** Idlhofg. 74. (Tel. 71 48 76; fax 71 48 76 88. Dorms 220AS; singles 320AS; doubles 540AS. Overflow mattresses 155AS. Breakfast included. Laundry. **Internet.** Reception 7am-11pm.) On the way you'll pass the **Hotel Strasser,** Eggenberger Gürtel 11, 5min. from the station on the left. (Tel. 71 39 77; fax 71 68 56. Singles 360-480AS; doubles 580-660AS; triples 840AS; quads 1000AS. Breakfast included.) Cheap student hangouts line **Zinzendorfg.** near the university. **Kebap Haus,** Jakoministr. 16, is a superior Turkish restaurant with delicious pitas and Mediterranean pizza. (Open M-Sa 11am-midnight.) The hub of after-hours activity is the so-called **Bermuda Triangle,** an area of the old city behind Hauptpl., bordered by Mehlpl., Färberg., and Prokopiag. **Postal code:** A-8010.

BELARUS (БЕЛАРУСЬ)

US$1 = 315,000BR (BELARUSSIAN RUBLES)	100,000BR = US$0.32
CDN$1 = 211,168BR	100,000BR = CDN$0.47
UK£1 = 505,291BR	100,000BR = UK£0.20
IR£1 = 424,285BR	100,000BR = IR£0.24
AUS$1 = 203,710BR	100,000BR = AUS$0.49
NZ$1 = 162,918BR	100,000BR = NZ$0.61
SAR1 = 52,408BR	100,000BR = SAR1.90
DM1 = 170,849BR	100,000BR = DM0.59

PHONE CODES Country code: 375. International dialing prefix: 810.

For as long as anyone can remember, Belarus has been the backwater of someone else's empire, and today it remains the black sheep of Eastern Europe. Flattened by the Nazis from 1941 to 1945 and exploited by the Soviets from 1946 to 1990, the country seems to have lost its sense of self. The fall of the USSR left its people grasping for a national identity but unable to find their own way. Belarus continues to suffer from the policies of a totalitarian president whose top priority has been to increase his own power, rather than to court Western economic aid. The sum of all of these troubles is a country of sprawling urban landscapes without anything resembling conventional beauty, and tiny forest villages seemingly untouched by the centuries. For those willing to endure the difficulties inherent to travel in Belarus, the country presents an interesting case study; others should avoid its trials in favor of countries better prepared for foreign consumption.

Belarus

Lift the Belarussian curtain of your mind with *Let's Go: Eastern Europe 2000*.

GETTING THERE AND GETTING AROUND

You can **fly** into Minsk on **Belavia**, Belarus' national airline, *if* you trust the old planes. **LOT** also flies from Warsaw, and **Lufthansa** has direct flights from Frankfurt. Leaving Belarus by air can be a nightmare, as customs officials are wont to rip through your bags. **Eurail** is not valid in Belarus; **railpasses** are neither available nor necessary. **Buses** and **trains** connect Brest to Warsaw, Prague, Kiev, and Lviv, and Hrodna to Warsaw, Białystok, and Vilnius. Be aware that some international train tickets must be paid partly in US dollars and partly in Belarussian rubles. All immigration and customs are done on the trains; trains between Russia and Belarus are considered domestic routes and do not stop for customs. Tickets for same-day **trains** within Belarus are purchased at the station. Info booths in the stations charge 5000BR per inquiry. **Road conditions** are poor; driving and biking aren't wise.

ESSENTIALS

DOCUMENTS AND FORMALITIES. Belarus is a useful transport link to Russia and the Baltics. If you're just passing through, 48-hour **transit visas** (US$20-30) are issued at consulates and theoretically at the border, but avoid the latter option except at Brest. For longer stays, you need an invitation and a visa. If an acquaintance in Belarus can procure you an invitation, you can get apply for a 90-day single-entry (5-day service US$50; next-day US$100) or multiple-entry (5-day service US$300; no rush service) visa. Those without Belarussian friends can turn to **Russia House** (see p. 756), which will get you an invitation and visa in five business days (US$145; rush service US$215). If you use **Host Families Association (HOFA),** 5-25 Tavricheskaya, 193015 St. Petersburg, Russia (tel./fax (812) 275 19 92; email hofa@usa.net), to find housing, they will provide invitations (homestays US$30-50). You may also obtain an invitation from a **Belintourist,** which will give you documentation after you pre-pay hotel nights. All foreigners visiting Minsk must **register passports** at OVIR (ОВИР), pr. F. Skaryny 8, #132 (tel. 220 15 05). Hotels register you automatically. To extend your visa, ask whomever provided your original invitation to apply for the extension with the Ministry of Foreign Affairs (tel. 222 26 74).

Belarussian Embassies at Home: UK, 6 Kensington Ct, London, W8 5DL (tel. (020) 79 37 32 88; fax 73 61 00 05); **US,** 1619 New Hampshire Ave NW, Washington, DC 20009 (tel. (202) 986-1604, visa tel. 986-1606; fax 986-1805).

Foreign Embassies in Belarus: All foreign embassies are in **Minsk** (see p. 115).

TOURIST OFFICES. Belintourist (Белінтуріст) hands out Soviet-era brochures and sometimes books train tickets, but does not cater to budget travelers. Hotel Belarus and Hotel Yubilyenaya in Minsk have **private travel agencies.**

MONEY. The currency is the Belarussian **ruble,** different from the Russian ruble. Because inflation is rampant, *Let's Go* lists many prices in US dollars. Expect to pay US$10 for a budget hotel room; anything nicer can balloon to US$50. Meals are very cheap (never more than US$5), even in nice restaurants. Be sure to carry hard **cash:** US dollars, Deutschmarks, and Russian rubles are preferred; other currencies, even British pounds, are problematic. There are one or two **ATM** machines in Minsk and some hotels take **credit cards,** but traveler's checks are rarely accepted. **Cash advances** on Visa and sometimes MC are available for 4% commission at **Prior Bank** (Пріор Банк), vul. V. Kharyzhan 3a (Харыжан). (Tel. 269 09 64. Open M-F 9am-6pm.) Don't leave the country with Belarussian rubles; they're impossible to exchange abroad. **Tipping** is not necessary, but 5% is always appreciated.

COMMUNICATION

Post: Avoid the unreliable **mail** system; almost everything is read by authorities.

Telephone: Local phone calls must be paid for with tokens or magnetic cards, available at the post office, train station, and some hotels. International phone calls must be placed at the post office and paid for in advance in cash. **International direct dial** numbers include: **BT Direct,** 88 00 44; **AT&T Direct,** 88 00 101; **MCI WorldPhone,** 88 00 103; **Australia Direct,** 810; **Canada Direct,** 88 00 111.

Language: Belarussians primarily speak Russian, but Polish is also fairly common in Hrodna and Brest. For the basics in Russian and Polish, see p. 949.

HEALTH AND SAFETY. The after-effects of **Chernobyl** are unlikely to harm short-term visitors, but avoid cheap dairy products and mushrooms, and drink bottled water. **Crime** seems as stagnant as anything (who wants to go to a Belarussian jail?).

ACCOMMODATIONS. There are no hostels and very few campgrounds in Belarus, and many **hotels** charge a much higher rate for foreigners. If you do stay at a hotel, keep all the slips of paper you receive to avoid paying fines on your way out of the country. **Private rooms,** often US$10 or less, are worth a shot.

LOCAL FACTS

Time: Belarus is 2hr. ahead of Greenwich Mean Time (GMT; see p. 49).

Climate: Belarus has a continental climate, with mild summers, very cold winters, and moderate precipitation year-round. Any time during Apr.-Oct. is a good time to visit.

Hours: Most **banks** are open M-F 9am-6pm.

Holidays: Orthodox Christmas (Jan. 7); International Women's Day (Mar. 8); Constitution Day (Mar. 15); Catholic Easter (Apr. 23); Orthodox Easter (Apr. 30); Labor Day (May 1); Radinitsa (Victory Day 1945) and Mother's Day (May 9); Independence Day (July 3); Dzyady (Remembrance Day; Nov. 2); October Revolution Anniversary (Nov. 7); and Catholic Christmas (Dec. 25).

MINSK (МИНСК)

If you're looking for the supreme Soviet city, skip Moscow and head to Minsk, where the fall of communism has been a reluctant shuffle rather than a wanton gallop west. Most streets have been renamed, but Lenin's statue still stands. With imaginary political reforms and concrete everywhere, everyone is asking if Belarussian authorities are really giving Minsk a new face, or just a new façade.

⌖ PRACTICAL INFO AND ACCOMMODATIONS. Trains depart from Tsentralny Vakzal (Центральный Вакзал; tel. (0172) 220 99 89; info tel. (0172) 295 54 10), on Privakzalnaya pl., for Vilnius (4½hr., 5 per day, *coupé* 2,500,000BR); Moscow (10-14hr., 13-17 per day, *coupé* 4,845,000BR); Kiev (14hr., 1-3 per day, *coupé* 3,534,000BR); Prague (1 per day, US$60 and 4,000,000BR); St. Petersburg (3 per day, *coupé* 4,173,000BR); and Warsaw (12hr., 3-5 per day, US$13 and 4,000,000BR). Buy tickets at Belintourist. **Buses** go from **Avtovakzal Tsentralny** (Автовакзал Центральный), vul. Babruyskaya 6 (Бабруйская; tel. (0172) 227 78 20), 200m left of the train station as you face it, to Vilnius (4hr., 4 per day, 3,630,000BR). From the train station, go up vul. Leningradskaya and left on Svyardlova (Свярдлова) to **pl. Nezalezhnastsi** (Independence Sq; Незалежнасці), connected by pr. F. Skaryny (Франçішка Скарыны) to pl. Peramohi (Перамогі). **Belintourist** (Белінтурісt), pr. Masherava 19 (Машэрава), is next to Hotel Yubileynaya; pr. Masherava is perpendicular to pr. F. Skaryny. (Tel. (0172) 226 97 00. M: Nemiga. Open M-F 8am-1pm and 2-8pm.) **Embassies: Russia,** vul. Staravilenskaya 48 (Старавіленская; tel. (0172) 250 36 66); **UK,** vul. Karla Marxa 37 (Карла Маркса; tel. (0172) 210 59 20); **Ukraine,** vul. Kirava 17, #306 (tel. (0172) 227 70 04); and **US,** vul. Staravilenskaya 46 (tel. (0172) 210 12 83). All **phone numbers** have 7 digits and start with a "2," so for six-digit numbers, add an initial "2"; but for some phones you have to drop the first "2" (got that?). **Gastsinitsa Svisloch** (Гасцініца Свіслочь) is at vul. Kirava 13. (Tel. (0172) 220 97 83. M-red: pl. Nezalezhnastsi (пл. Незалежнасці). Singles 3-5,200,000BR.) From M-red: Park Chelyuskintsev (Парк Челюскинцев), take a right on the street in front of you that runs perpendicular to the main road to reach **Gastsinitsa Druzhba** (Дружба), vul. Tolbukhina 3. (Tel. (0172) 266 24 81. Bed in a triple 3,000,000BR.)

▣ SIGHTS AND ENTERTAINMENT. After more than 80% of Minsk's buildings were obliterated in WWII, the city was rebuilt according to the Soviet ideal. At the southern end of the Old Town is **pl. Nezalezhnastsi,** formerly pl. Lenina, north of the train station (M-red: pl. Nezalezhnastsi; пл. Незалежнасці), a symbol of Belarussian independence. There are a few exceptions to Soviet masterpieces, including the **Church of St. Simon,** Savetskaya 15 (M-blue: Frunzenskaja; Фрунзенская). Pl. Svobody is home to the dazzling 17th-century **Cathedral of the Holy Spirit** (Svetadukha Kafedralny Sobor; Светадуха Кафедральный Собор), vul. Mefodiya 3 (M-blue: Nyamiha; Няміга). The yellow **Cathedral of St. Peter and St. Paul** (Petropavilsky Sobor; Петропавілскі Совор; vul. Rakovskaya 4 (Раковская)) is Minsk's oldest church (M-blue: Nyamiha; Няміга). The **Jewish memorial stone,** vul. Zaslavskaya, commemorates the more than 5000 Jews who were shot and buried here by the Nazis in 1941 (M-blue: Nyamiha; Няміга). Lovely city parks line the banks of the Svislac east of the Old Town; **Gorky Park** (Park Gorkoho; Парк Горкого) and **Yanka Kupala Park** (Янка Купала Парк) are on pr. F. Skaryny (M-red: pl. Peramohi; пл. Перамогі or M-red: Kastritsnitskaya; Кастрычніцкая). The grim **Museum of the Great Patriotic War** (Muzey Velikoy Otechestvennoy Voyny; Музей Великой Отечественной Войны) is at pr. Skaryny 25a. (M-red: pl. Peramohi; пл. Перамогі. Open Tu-Su 10am-5pm. 150,000BR.) The **National History and Culture Museum,** vul. K. Marxa 12 (К. Маркса) is a little happier. (M-red: pl. Nezalezhnastsi; пл. Незалежнасц. Open Th-Tu 11am-7pm. 100,000BR, students 30,000BR.) **Opera and Ballet Theater,** vul. E. Pashkevich 23 (Пашкевіч), is one of the best ballets in the former USSR. (Tel. (0172) 234 06 66. M-blue: Nyamiha; Няміга.) Buy tickets (15-20,000BR) at the **Central Ticket Office,** pr. F. Skaryny 13 (tel. (0172) 220 25 70).

BELARUS

BELGIUM
(BELGIQUE, BELGIË)

US$1 = 38.09BF (BELGIAN FRANCS) 10BF = US$0.26
CDN$1 = 25.54BF 10BF = CDN$0.39
UK£1 = 61.19BF 10BF = UK£0.16
IR£1 = 51.22BF 10BF = IR£0.20
AUS$1 = 24.56BF 10BF = AUS$0.41
NZ$1 = 19.74BF 10BF = NZ$0.51
SAR1 = 6.32BF 10BF = SAR 1.58
EUR€1 = 40.34BF 10BF = EUR€0.25

PHONE CODE | Country code: 32. International dialing prefix: 00.

Situated between France, Germany, and the Netherlands, Belgium rubs shoulders with some of Europe's most powerful cultural and intellectual traditions. But Belgium fights back: with both a charming provincialism, and a fast urbanity in its capital and commercial centers. Travelers too often mistake Belgium's subtlety for boredom, but its castle-dotted countryside provides a beautiful escape for hikers and bikers, and its cities offer some of Europe's finest art and architecture. As you enter the country by train, wondering if anything will ever punctuate the countless miles of rolling countryside, rows of poplars, and occasional small farmhouses, suddenly the swift blur of gold and green gives way to compact urban centers—Antwerp thrives with commerce, and Brussels, the capital, home to NATO and the European Union, buzzes with international decision-makers making the news you'll read about in the morning paper. Nearby, the cultural treasures of Bruges and Ghent await discovery. But if you don't get off the train, the urban bustle will vanish as quickly as it came into the wide, flat expanse of the colorful countryside.

The first stop on the military tours of many aspiring European conquerors—and still today the first stop on tours of military history buffs—Belgium bears the scars of a troubled European history. But today, Belgians have assumed a continental air—Belgium's Flemish art, French Gothic architecture, chic all-night café scene, and warm embrace of the Euro as an international currency reaffirm the border-free identity of the new Europe. Today, some tension persists between the Flemish-speaking nationalists of the northern province of Flanders, and the French-speaking area of Wallonie to the south, but the two regions have, for the most part, reconciled their differences. In any case, some things transcend political tensions: from the Ardennes forests and the white sands of the North Sea coast to the cobblestoned medieval passageways, Belgium's beauty is even richer than its chocolate.

DISCOVER BELGIUM

Many whirlwind Europe travelers pass right by Belgium on the Paris-Amsterdam train, but Belgium is a worthwhile destination all its own. Start out in the northern region of Flanders; take in the old city and diverse museums of **Brussels** (p. 119) and then spend at least two days for the real Belgian gem of **Bruges** (p. 124), a majestic town with a Gothic beauty unparalleled elsewhere in Europe. Spend a day in bustling **Antwerp** (p. 127) and a day (and definitely a night) with the students in **Ghent** (p. 128), then head south to the Wallonie region for a day or two of biking and exploration in and around **Namur** and **Dinant** (see p. 130).

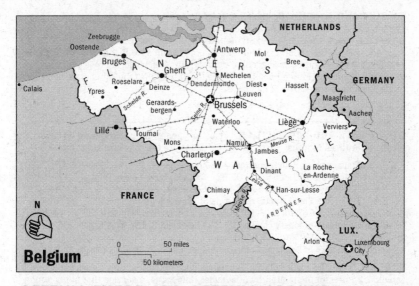

Belgium

GETTING THERE AND GETTING AROUND

BY PLANE. Several major airlines fly into **Brussels** from Europe, North America, and Africa; many offer cheap deals. **Sabena Belgian World Airlines** (Belgium tel. (02) 723 23 23; US tel. (800) 955-2000; www.sabena.com) serves many locations, including South Africa and North America, and has cheap last-minute deals.

BY TRAIN AND BY BUS. The extensive and reliable **Belgian Rail** (www.sncb.be) network traverses the country in 4hr. **Eurostar** trains connect Brussels to London's Waterloo Station (1¾hr.; call (02) 55 52 525 in Belgium for info). **Thalys** trains run from Brussels to Paris (1¼hr.) and also serve other cities in Belgium as well as parts of Germany and the Netherlands (call (08) 00 95 777 in Belgium). **Eurail** is valid in Belgium. The **Benelux Tourrail Pass** covers five days of travel in Belgium, the Netherlands, and Luxembourg in any a one-month period (3100BF, over 26 4440BF), but doesn't always make economic sense. The best deal for travelers under 26 may be the **Go Pass,** which allows 10 trips over six months in Belgium and may be used by more than one person at a time (1420BF). For travelers over 26, the **Pass 9+** allows 10 trips in Belgium after 9am (2100BF). Tourist offices sell **24-hour passes,** which cover all municipal transport in the country (150BF). Because the train network is so extensive, **buses** are used primarily for municipal transport (40-50BF); intercity buses are only slightly cheaper than trains and far less convenient.

BY FERRY. P&O European Ferries (Brussels tel. (02) 231 19 37; Ostend tel. (059) 70 76 01; Zeebrugge tel. (050) 54 22 22) cross the Channel from **Ostend,** west of Bruges, to **Dover** (2hr.; see p. 161) and **Felixstowe, England;** and from **Zeebrugge,** north of Bruges, to **Hull, England** (14hr.), near York (see p. 183). **Oostende Lines** (tel. (059) 55 99 55; fax 80 94 17) also crosses from Ostend to **Ramsgate, England,** two hours from London's Victoria Station (8 per day; July-Aug. 599BF; Sept.-June 499BF). For info on Ostend and Zeebrugge, see p. 127. For ferry prices and schedules, see p. 58.

BY CAR. Belgium honors most foreign drivers' licenses, including those from Australia, Canada, the EU, and the US. Speed limits are 120km per hr. on motorways, 90km per hr. on main roads, and 50km per hr. elsewhere. Fuel costs about 40BF per liter. For more info, or in case of breakdown, contact the **Touring Club de Belgique (TCB),** rue Joseph II 25, Brussels 1040 (tel. (02) 512 78 90), or the **Royal Automobile Club de Belgique,** rue d'Arlon 53, Brussels 1040 (tel. (02) 287 09 11).

BY BIKE AND BY THUMB. Biking is popular, and many roads have bike lanes (which you are required to use). When you see two paths next to the street, the one nearer the street is for bicycles and mopeds, while the one nearer the storefronts is for pedestrians. Bike rental is available at many train stations. Inquire at stations about **passes** that permit taking a bike on the train. **Hitchhiking** is not popular in Belgium and is not recommended as a safe means of transport, but hitchers still report a fair amount of success in some areas.

ESSENTIALS

DOCUMENTS AND FORMALITIES. Visas are generally not required for tourist stays under three months; South African citizens are the exception.

Belgian Embassies at Home: Australia, 19 Arkana St, Yarralumba, Canberra, ACT 2600 (tel. (02) 62 73 25 01; fax 62 73 33 92). **Canada,** 80 rue Elgin, Ottawa, ON K1P 1B7 (tel. (613) 236-7267; fax 236-7882). **New Zealand,** 1-3 Willeston St, Wellington (tel. (04) 472 95 58). **South Africa,** 625 Leyds St, Muckleneuk, Pretoria 0002 (tel. (012) 44 32 01; fax 44 32 16). **UK,** 103-105 Eaton Sq, London SW1W 9AB (tel. (020) 74 70 37 00; www.belgium-embassy.co.uk). **US,** 3330 Garfield St NW, Washington, DC 20008 (tel. (202) 333-6900; fax 333-3079).

Foreign Embassies in Belgium: All foreign embassies are in **Brussels** (see p. 120).

TOURIST OFFICES. Bureaux de Tourisme, marked by green-and-white signs labelled "i," are supplemented by **Info-Jeunes/Info-Jeugd,** a service that helps young people secure accommodations. For info, contact the main office of the **Belgian Tourist Board,** Grasmarkt 63, B-1000 Brussels (tel. (02) 504 03 90; fax 504 02 70; www.tourism-belgium.net). The weekly English-language *Bulletin* (85BF at newsstands) lists everything from movies to job openings.

Tourist Offices at Home: Canada, P.O. Box 760, Succursale NDG, Montréal, Quebec H4A 3S2 (tel. (514) 484-3594; fax 489-8965). **UK,** 31 Peper St, London E14 9RW (fax (020) 74 58 00 45). **US,** 780 Third Ave. 1501, New York, NY 10017 (tel. (212) 758-8130; fax 355-7675; www.visitbelgium.com).

MONEY. The unit of currency is the **Belgian franc;** bills come in 100, 200, 500, 1000, 2000 and 10,000 denominations, coins in 1, 5, 20 and 50. There are 100 centimes in one franc. Expect to pay 750-1200BF for a hotel room; 350-550BF for a hostel bed; 150-400BF for a cheap restaurant meal; and 100-300BF for a day's supermarket fare. A bare-bones day in Belgium might cost US$12-25; a slightly more comfortable day might cost US$30-40.

Tipping and Bargaining: Service charges are usually included in the price in restaurants and taxis, but tip for exceptional service. Bathroom attendants usually receive 10-20BF.

Taxes: Belgium's **VAT** (generally 21%) is always included in price; refunds (usually 17% of the purchase price) are available for a minimum purchase of 5000BF per invoice.

COMMUNICATION

Post: A **postcard** or **letter** (up to 20g) to Australia, Canada, Ireland, New Zealand, South Africa, or the US costs 34BF; to the UK, 30BF. Most post offices open M-F 9am to 4 or 7pm (sometimes with a midday break) and Sa 9 or 10am to noon or 1pm.

Telephone: Most phones require a 200BF phone card, available at PTT offices and magazine stands. Rarer coin-operated phones are more expensive and require either 5BF or 20BF coins. Calls are cheapest from 6:30pm to 8am and Sa-Su. For **operator assistance** within Benelux, dial 13 07; for **international assistance,** 13 04 (10BF). **International direct dial** numbers include: **AT&T Direct,** 0800 100 10; **MCI WorldPhone,** 0800 100 12; **Sprint Access,** 0800 100 14; **Australia Direct,** 0800 100 61, **Canada Direct,** 0800 100 19; **BT Direct,** 0800 100 24; **Ireland Direct,** 0800 110 353; **New Zealand Direct,** 0800 104 23; **Telekom South Africa Direct,** 0800 100 27.

Language: French (spoken in Brussels and Wallonie) and German. Most people, especially in Flanders, speak English. Dutch (a slightly different variety than is heard in the Netherlands) is also commonly heard. For the basics in French, see p. 949.

BELGIUM

ACCOMMODATIONS AND CAMPING. Hotels in Belgium are fairly expensive, with "trench-bottom" singles from 800BF and doubles at 1000-1100BF. Belgium's 31 **HI youth hostels,** which charge about 405BF per night, are generally modern and many boast cheap bars, but **private hostels** are often cheaper and much nicer. Pick up *Budget Holidays* or the free *Camping* at any tourist office for complete listings of hostels and campsites. **Campgrounds** charge about 130BF per night. An **international camping card** is not required.

FOOD AND DRINK. Belgian cuisine can be wonderful, but a native dish may cost as much as a night in a decent hotel. Steamed mussels *(moules),* a Belgian delicacy, are usually tasty and reasonably affordable (around 430BF per pot). Other specialities include *lapin* (rabbit) and *canard* (duck). Belgian beer is both a national pride and a national pastime; more varieties—over 500, ranging from the ordinary Jupiler to the religiously brewed Chimay—are produced here than in any other country. Try Leffe, Kwak, Duvel, cherry-flavored *kriek,* and the wheat-based *lambric doux* before you leave. Regular or quirky blonde goes for as little as 40BF, and dark beers cost about 60-90BF. Leave room for Belgium's *gaufres* (waffles)— soft, warm, glazed ones on the street (50BF) and bigger, crispier ones piled high with toppings at cafés (80-200BF)—and famous Godiva and Leonidas chocolates.

LOCAL FACTS

Time: Belgium is 1hr. ahead of Greenwich Mean Time (GMT; see p. 49).

Climate: Belgium, temperate and rainy, is best visited May to September, when temperatures average 13-21°C (54-72°F). Winter temperatures average 0-5°C (32-43°F). Bring a sweater and umbrella whenever you go.

Hours: Banks are generally open M-F 9am to 3:30pm or 4pm, sometimes with a lunch break. **Stores** are open M-Sa 10am-6pm. Most **sights** open Su but closed M except in Bruges and Tournai, where museums are closed Tu or W. Most stores close on holidays; museums stay open during all except for Christmas, New Year's, and Armistice Day.

Holidays: New Year's Day (Jan. 1); Easter (Apr. 23); Easter Monday (Apr. 24); Labor Day (May 1); Ascension Day (June 1); Whit Sunday (June 11); Whit Monday (June 12); Independence Day (July 21); Assumption Day (Aug. 15); All Saints Day (Nov. 1); Armistice Day (Nov. 11); Christmas (Dec. 25).

Festivals: Ghent hosts the **Gentse Feesten** (July 21-31) and, this year, the 500th birthday of native-born Keizer Karel (Charles V); see p. 128. Wallonie hosts a slew of quirky and creative carnival-like festivals, including the **Festival of Fairground Arts** (late May), **Les Jeux Nautiques** (early Aug.), and the **International French-language Film Festival** (early Sept.) in Namur, and the **International Bathtub Regatta** (mid-Aug.) in Dinant.

BRUSSELS (BRUXELLES, BRUSSEL)

Instantly associated with NATO and the European Union, Brussels has too often been written off by travelers as a lifeless political and economic capital. However, in the Grand-Place, the Gothic center of the old city, you'll find the essence of Belgium, from waffles to beer to the *Mannekin Pis.* Where Antwerp claims Rubens, Brussels' cultural icon is no less than Hergé's androgynous comic strip creations Tintin and his dog Snowy, who peer out from shop windows. Innovative Art Nouveau architect Victor Horta once filled the city with unique turn-of-the-century mansions; more recent architects have mingled far less interesting glass and concrete with the Gothic spires. Still, Brussels has carefully preserved its Old Town, and the city's cutting-edge culture and style lend new internationalism to the EU.

▐ GETTING THERE AND GETTING AROUND

Flights: Brussels International Airport (tel. 723 60 10). **Trains** run to the airport from Gare du Midi (25min., every 20min., 120BF); all stop at Gare Centrale and Gare du Nord.

Trains: Info tel. 555 25 55. All international trains stop at **Gare du Midi/Zuid;** most also stop at **Gare du Nord** (near the Botanical Gardens) or **Gare Centrale** (near the Grand-Place). To: **Antwerp** (30min., 195BF); **Bruges** (45min.-1hr., 380BF); **Paris** (1½hr.,

BELGIUM

2070BF, under 26 950BF); **Amsterdam** (2½hr., 1140BF, under 26 850BF); **Luxembourg City** (2¾hr., 900BF, under 26 700BF); and **Cologne/Köln** (2¾-3hr., 1200BF, under 26 900BF). **Eurostar** goes to **London** (1¾hr., from 6200BF, under 26 2100BF).

Buses: Société des Transports Intercommunaux Bruxellois (STIB), in Gare du Midi. Open M-F 7:30am-5pm, Sa 8:30am-4:30pm. Also at 20 Galeries de la Toison d'Or, 6th fl. (tel. 515 30 64). Call 515 20 00 for schedule info.

Public Transportation: Runs daily 6am-midnight. **1-hour tickets** (50BF) valid on **buses,** the **Métro (M),** and **trams. Day pass** 130BF. **10-trip pass** 350BF.

Hitchhiking: *Let's Go* does not recommend hitchhiking. Hitchers headed to **Antwerp** and **Amsterdam** take tram 52 or 92 from Gare du Midi or Gare du Nord to Heysel; **Ghent, Bruges,** and **Oostende,** bus 85 from the Bourse to the stop before the terminus, then follow E40 signs; **Paris,** tram 52, 55, or 91 to rue de Stalle, then walk toward the E19.

🔽 ORIENTATION AND PRACTICAL INFORMATION

Most major attractions are clustered around Brussels' three train stations, between the **Bourse** (Stock Market) to the west and the **Parc de Bruxelles** to the east, around the **Grand-Place.** Two **Métro** lines circle the city, and efficient trams run north to south. A **tourist passport** (300BF at the TIB and bookshops) includes two days of public transit, a map, and reduced museum prices.

TOURIST, FINANCIAL, AND LOCAL SERVICES

Tourist Offices: National, 63 rue du Marché aux Herbes (tel. 504 03 90; fax 504 02 70), 1 block from the Grand-Place. Books rooms all over Belgium and gives out the free weekly *What's On.* Open June-Sept. M-F 9am-7pm, Sa-Su 9am-1pm and 2-7pm; Oct.-May closes 6pm. **TIB (Tourist Information Brussels;** tel. 513 89 40; fax 514 45 38), on the Grand-Place, in the Town Hall, has free walking tour info and books events tickets (info tel. (0800) 212 21). Open July-Aug. M-F 9am-7pm, Sa-Su 9am-1pm and 2-7pm; May-June and Sept.-Oct. M-F 9am-6pm, Sa-Su 9am-1pm and 2-6pm; Nov.-Apr. Su only 9am-1pm.

Budget Travel: Acotra World, 51 rue de la Madeleine (tel. 512 55 40), finds cheap flights. Open M-F 8:30am-6pm. **Infor-Jeunes,** 27 rue du Marché-aux-Herbes (tel. 514 41 11). Budget travel info for young travelers. Open M-F 9:30am-5:30pm.

Embassies: Australia, 6-8 rue Guimard, 1040 (tel. 286 05 00; 230 68 02). **Canada,** 2 av. Tervueren, 1040 (tel. 741 06 11). **Ireland,** 89/93 rue Froissart, 1040 (tel. 230 53 37; fax 230 53 60). **New Zealand,** 47 bd. du Régent, 1000 (tel. 512 10 40). **South Africa,** 26 rue de la Loi (tel. 285 44 00). Generally open M-F 9am-5pm. **UK,** 85 rue Arlon (tel. 287 62 11). **US,** 25-27 bd. du Régent, 1000 (embassy tel. 512 22 10; consulate tel. 508 25 32; fax 511 96 52; www.usinfo.be). Open M-F 9am-noon.

Currency Exchange: Many exchange booths near the Grand-Place stay open until 11pm. Most banks and booths charge 100-150BF to cash checks; banks have better rates.

Gay and Lesbian Services: Call 733 10 24 for info on local events. Staffed daily 9am-9pm.

Laundromat: Salon Lavoir, 5 rue Haute, around the corner from the Jeugdherberg Bruegel. M: Gare Centrale. Wash and dry 240BF. Open M-F 8am-6pm.

EMERGENCY AND COMMUNICATIONS

Emergencies: Ambulance or **first aid,** tel. 112. **Police,** tel. 101.

Pharmacies: Neos-Bourse Pharmacie (tel. 218 06 40), bd. Anspach at rue du Marché-aux-Polets. M: Bourse. Open M-F 8:30am-6:30pm, Sa 9am-6:30pm.

Medical Assistance: Free Clinic, 154a chaussée de Wavre (tel. 512 13 14). Misleading name—you'll have to pay. Open M-F 9am-6pm. **Medical Services:** Tel. 479 18 18. 24hr.

Internet Access: Cybertheater, 4/5 av. de la Toison d'Or, has a bar and DJ. 100-150BF per 30min. Open M-Sa 10am-1am, Su 3pm-1am. **Net Surf,** 16 petite rue des Bouchers, off Marché-Aux-Herbes. 100BF per 30min. Open M-F 11am-7pm, Sa 11am-5pm.

Post Office: pl. de la Monnaie, Centre Monnaie, 2nd fl. M: de Brouckère. Address mail to be held: Ayse INAN, *Poste Restante,* Pl. de la Monnaie, **1000** Bruxelles, Belgium. Open M-F 8am-7pm, Sa 9:30am-1pm.

PHONE CODE | City code: 02. From outside Belgium, dial int'l dialing prefix (see inside back cover) + 32 + 2 + local number.

BELGIUM

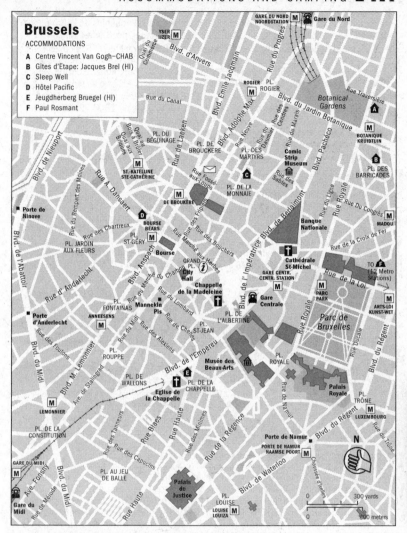

Brussels
ACCOMMODATIONS

A Centre Vincent Van Gogh–CHAB
B Gîtes d'Etape: Jacques Brel (HI)
C Sleep Well
D Hôtel Pacific
E Jeugdherberg Bruegel (HI)
F Paul Rosmant

BELGIUM

ACCOMMODATIONS AND CAMPING

Accommodations in Brussels are fairly easy to come by. In general, hotels and hostels are very well-kept; any and all will provide a good springboard to the city.

Centre Vincent Van Gogh-CHAB, 8 rue Traversière (tel. 217 01 58; fax 219 79 95; email CHAB@ping.be). M: Botanique; exit on rue Royale, head right (as you face the Jardin Botanique), and turn right on rue Traversière (5min.). Lively bar and garden. Dorms 340-475BF; singles 710BF; doubles 1120-1170BF. Laundry. **Internet.** Reception 7am-2am.

Sleep Well, 23 rue du Damier (tel. 218 50 50; fax 218 13 13; email info@sleepwell.be), near Gare du Nord. M:Rogier; go right on the bd. du Jardin Botanique and turn right on rue des Cendres, which turns into rue Damier. Dorms 330-470BF; singles 695BF; doubles 1140BF; triples 1060BF; quads 1020BF. **Internet.** Reception 24hr. Lockout 10am-4pm.

Jeugdherberg Bruegel (HI), 2 Heilige Geeststr. (tel. 511 04 36; fax 512 07 11). From the back exit of Gere Centrale, go right on bd. de l'Empereur and take the 2nd left after Pl. de la Justice. Friendly and quiet. Dorms 450BF; singles 720BF; doubles 1170BF; quads 1900BF. Sheets 125BF. Reception 7am-1am. Lockout 10am-2pm. Curfew 1am.

Gîtes d'Etape: Auberge de Jeunesse "Jacques Brel" (HI), 30 rue de la Sablonnière (tel. 218 01 87), on pl. des Barricades. M: Botanique. 15min. from Gare Centrale. Spacious, colorful rooms. Dorms 450BF; singles 720BF; doubles 1170BF; triples 1450BF; quads 1900BF. Dinner 275BF. Sheets 125BF. Reception 8am-7pm. Reserve ahead.

Hôtel Pacific, 57 rue Antoine Dansaert (tel. 511 84 59). M: Bourse; cross bd. Anspach. Excellent location and basic rooms. Singles 1100BF; doubles 1800-2250BF; triples 2550BF. Showers 100BF. Breakfast included. Reception 7am-midnight. Midnight curfew.

Camping: Paul Rosmant, 52 Warandeberg (tel. 782 10 09), in Wezembeck-Oppem. Métro 1B: Kraainem, or bus 30 to "Sint-Peterspl."; on Su, Métro 1B: Stockel, then tram 39 to "Marcelisstr." 250BF per person. Reception 9am-12:30pm and 2-10pm. Open Apr.-Sept.

⊙ FOOD

Restaurants cluster near the **Grand-Place,** but for cheap eats and small cafés, try the arcade across from the back entrance to the Central Station. (Open M-Sa 6am-5pm.) Exotic shellfish is piled on ice on **rue des Bouchers,** just north of the *place.* The small restaurants on **quai aux Briques,** in the Ste-Catherine area behind pl. St-Géry, serve cheaper seafood with a local clientele. Just south of the *place,* the **rue du Marché-aux-Fromages** is lined with Greek eateries. The abundant **Belgaufras** serves hot waffles (50-80BF). Load up at **GB supermarket,** 248 rue Vierge Noire. (M: Bourse. Open M-F 9am-7pm, Sa 10am-6pm.)

Arcadi Coffeeshop, rue d'Arenberg 1b. Small café specializing in homemade quiche (160-180BF) and lots of veggie options. Open M-F 7:30am-11pm, Sa-Su 10am-11pm.

Sole d'Italia, 67 rue Grétry. A huge serving of spaghetti with bread is only 195BF, and other specialties are only a bit more expensive. Open daily noon-late.

Zebra, St-Gèry. This chic café in the center of action serves light, tasty sandwiches and pastas (around 250BF). Open daily 11:30am-2:30am.

L'Ecole Buissonnière, 13 rue de Traversière, opposite the CHAB hostel. M: Botanique. Traditional Belgian food. Meals 165-345BF. Open M-F noon-2:30pm and 6:30-9:50pm.

Maison des Crêpes, 42 rue des Pierres. Popular among locals, this small restaurant serves specialty crêpes from 80BF; waffles from 90BF. Open daily 9am-6:30pm.

Ultième Hallutinatie, 316 rue Royale. Simple Belgian meals in an Art Nouveau house and garden. Salads, pastas, and omelettes in the **Tavern** from 155BF. Open M-F noon-2:30pm and 6pm-midnight, Sa-Su until 1am.

⊙ SIGHTS

GRAND-PLACE AND ENVIRONS. One look and you'll understand why Victor Hugo called the gold-trimmed **Grand-Place** "the most beautiful square in the world." Built in the 15th century and ravaged by French troops in 1695, the square was restored to its original splendor in only four years. A daily flower market and feverish tourist activity add color. The best sight in town is the light show, when 800 multi-colored flood lights give the **Town Hall** on the *place* a psychedelic glow accompanied by booming classical music. *(Apr.-Aug. and Dec. daily around 10 or 11pm.)* Three blocks behind the Town Hall on rue de l'Etuve at rue du Chêne is Brussels' most giggled-at sight, the **Mannekin Pis,** a statue of an impudent boy (with an apparently gargantuan bladder) steadily urinating. One story goes that a 17th-century mayor promised to build a statue in the position that his lost son was found; another says it commemorates a boy who ingeniously defused a bomb. Locals have created hundreds of outfits for him, each with a little hole for you-know-what.

ART MUSEUMS. Inside the **Musées Royaux des Beaux Arts,** the **Musée d'Art Ancien** houses a huge collection of the Flemish masters, including Brueghel the Elder's *Fall of Icarus* and works by Rubens. The other wing of the museum contains an enormous Neoclassical and contemporary collection in the **Musée d'Art Moderne,** including works by Miró, Picasso, and Brussels-based Magritte, as well as Jacque-Louis David's *Death of Marat. (Rue de la Régence 3. M: Parc or port de Namur, a block south of the Parc. Open Tu-Su 10am-5pm. 15th- to 16th- and 19th-century rooms close noon-*

1pm; 17th- to 18th- and 20th-century rooms close 1-2pm. 150BF, students 100BF. 1st W of each month free 1-5pm.) The enormous **Musées Royaux d'Art et d'Histoire** covers a wide variety of periods and parts—Roman torsos without heads, Syrian heads without torsos, and Egyptian caskets with feet. *(10 parc du Cinquantenaire. M: Mérode. Open M-F 9:30am-5pm, Sa-Su 10am-5pm.)* Early 20th-century Art Nouveau master Baron Victor Horta's graceful home, today the **Musée Horta,** is an elegant example of Brussels' architectural claim to fame. *(25 rue Américaine. M: Louise; walk down Av. Louise, bear right on rue Charleroi, and turn left on rue Américaine (15 min.). Open Tu-Su 2-5:30pm. 200BF.)*

BELGIAN COMIC STRIP CENTRE. This museum in the "Comic Strip Capital of the World" pays homage to *les bandes desineé* with hundreds of Belgian comics on display. The **museum library** features a reproduction of Tintin's rocket ship and works by over 700 artists. For Tintin souvenirs, check out the museum store or the Tintin Boutique near the Grand-Place. *(20 rue des Sables. M: Rogier. In a renovated Art Nouveau warehouse a few blocks from Sleep Well. Open Tu-Su noon–6pm. 200BF.)*

ATOMIUM AND BRUPARCK ENTERTAINMENT COMPLEX. The **Atomium,** a shining monument of aluminum and steel built for the 1958 World's Fair, represents a cubic iron crystal structure magnified 165 billion times to a height of 102m. It today houses a **science museum** featuring fauna and minerals from around the world. The Atomium towers over the **Bruparck entertainment complex,** home of the **Kinepolis cinema and Imax,** the largest movie theater in Europe. *(M: Huysel. Atomium open daily Apr.-Aug. 9am-8pm; Sept.-Mar. 10am-6:30pm. Museum 200BF. Movies from 300BF.)*

OTHER SIGHTS. Built over the course of six centuries, the magnificent **Saints Michel et Gudule Cathedral** cathedral is an excellent example of the Gothic style, and mixes in a little Romanesque and modern architecture as well. *(Pl. St-Gudule, just north of Central Station. Open daily 8am-7pm. Free.)* Wander the chic **Sablon,** home to antique markets, art galleries, and lazy cafés, around **le Grand de Balles,** where you can practice the fine art of bargaining at the morning **flea market,** and the **Schuman** area with the gleaming buildings of the **European Parliament** (called Caprice des Dieux— "Whim of the Gods"—perhaps because of their exorbitant cost). For a lazy afternoon, try the **Botanical Gardens** on rue Royale. *(Open daily 10am-10pm. Free.)*

🎵 ENTERTAINMENT

THEATER AND CONCERTS. For info on events, snag a copy of *What's On*. The flagship of Brussels' theater network is the beautiful **Théâtre Royal de la Monnaie,** on pl. de la Monnaie (M: de Brouckère; tel. 229 12 00; 250-3000BF). Renowned throughout the world for its opera and ballet, the theater had a performance of the opera *Muette de Portici* in August 1830 that inspired the audience to leave the theater early, take to the streets, and begin the revolt that led to Belgium's independence. The tourist office has schedules and tickets. Experience a distinctly Belgian art form at the **Theatre Toone,** 21 Petite rue des Bouchers, a 170-year-old puppet theater that stages marionette performances. (Tel. 511 71 37. Shows in French, German, Flemish, English. Usually Tu-Sa 8:30pm. 400BF, students 250BF.) In summer, **concerts** are on the **Grand-Place,** the **Place de la Monnaie,** and in the **Parc de Bruxelles.**

NIGHTLIFE. The scene in Brussels is casually chic and rather pricey. Note that walking from a disco in the south back to the Gare du Nord is not a good idea. The most stylish cafés surround the **Pl. St-Gèry,** behind the Bourse. At night the **Grand-Place,** the **Bourse,** and environs come to life with street performers and live concerts. The club scene changes very quickly—ask at bars and check *What's On* for the best spots. The 19th-century puppet theater **Poechenellekelder,** rue de Chêne 5, across from the Mannekin Pis, is today filled with lavishly costumed marionettes and a nice selection of Belgian beers (from 50BF). (Open daily noon-midnight, F-Sa until 1 or 2am.) **La Mort Subite,** 7 rue Montagne-aux-Herbes-Potagères, and **La Bécasse,** rue de Tabora 11, two of Brussels' oldest and best-known cafés, specialize in *lambric,* a local wheat beer. (Beer 50-90BF. Open daily 10:30am-midnight.) **L'Archiduc,** 6 rue Dansaert, is a pricey but chic Art Deco 20s jazz bar. (Open daily

4pm-late.) **Le Fuse,** 208 rue Blaes, is one of Belgium's trendiest clubs; pay homage to the gods of techno and rave. (Open daily 10pm-late.) Gay men socialize in a mellow atmosphere at **L'Incognito,** 36 rue des Pierres. (Open daily 4pm-dawn.)

▐ EXCURSION FROM BRUSSELS: WATERLOO

Napoleon was caught with both hands in his shirt at Waterloo (even ABBA couldn't escape if they wanted to), just south of Brussels. Modern residents are more likely to have their hands in your pockets, as history buffs and fans of the diminutive dictator pay for a glimpse at the town's little slice of history. **The Lion's Mound,** 5km outside of town, overlooks the battlefield; the Visitor's Center houses a panoramic painting of the battle and a brief movie about Waterloo. (Open Apr.-Sept. 9:30am-6:30pm; Oct. 9:30am-5:30pm; Nov.-Feb. 10:30am-4pm; Mar. 10:30am-5pm. Lion's Mound 40BF, with movie and panorama 305BF.) In the center of Waterloo, **Musée Wellington,** chaussée de Bruxelles 147, was Wellington's headquarters and now has artifacts from the battle. (Open daily 9:30am-6:30pm. 100BF, students 80BF.) **Buses** W and 365A leave pl. Rouppe near Brussels' Gare Midi (every 30min., 100F) and stop at Waterloo Church, opposite Musée Wellington; at a gas station near Lion's Mound, and at the train station in **Braine L'Alleud,** where trains also go to Brussels (45min., 3 per hr., 150BF). Belgian Railways offers a **B-excursion** ticket, which gives round-trip transit between Brussels and Baine L'Alleud, a bus pass from Braine L'Alleud to Waterloo, and entrance to all sights (635BF, students 585BF).

FLANDERS (VLAANDEREN)

Nearly all major Belgian cities lie in Flemish-speaking Flanders. Historically, the delta of the river Schelde at Antwerp provided the region with a major port, and the production and trade of linen, wool, and diamonds created great prosperity. Flanders' Golden Age was during the 16th century, when its commercial centers were among the largest cities in Europe and its innovative artists motivated the Northern Renaissance.Today, the well-preserved Gothic cities of Flanders, rich in art and friendly, multilingual people, hold Belgium's strongest attractions.

BRUGES (BRUGGES)

The capital of Flanders is one of the most beautiful cities in Europe, and tourists know it: the home of Jan van Eyck, famed for its lace, has become the largest tourist attraction in the country. Silver canals carve their way through rows of stone houses and lead to the breathtaking Gothic Markt. The entire city remains one of the best-preserved examples of Northern Renaissance architecture. This beauty belies the destruction this region sustained in World War I; eight decades after the war, farmers still uncover 200 tons of artillery every year as they plough their fields.

▐ GETTING THERE AND GETTING AWAY

Trains: Depart from Stationsplein (tel. 38 23 82), 15min. south of the city center. To: **Ghent** (25min., 175BF); **Antwerp** (1hr., 395BF); and **Brussels** (1hr., 380BF).

Bike Rental: At the train station; 345BF per day. **'t Koffieboontje,** Hallestr. 4 (tel. 33 80 27), off the Markt by the belfry. 250BF per day, students 150BF; 850BF per week.

Hitchhiking: Those hitching to Brussels reportedly take bus 7 to St. Michiels or pick up the highway behind the train station. *Let's Go* does not recommend hitchhiking.

▐ ORIENTATION AND PRACTICAL INFORMATION

Bruges is enclosed by a circular canal, with the train station just beyond its southern extreme. The dizzying **Belfort** (belfry) towers high at the center of town, presiding over the handsome square of the **Markt.**

Tourist Offices: Burg 11 (tel. 44 86 86; email toerisme@bruges.be; www.bruges.be), east of the Markt. Head left from the station to 't Zand square, right on Zuidzandstr., and right

BELGIUM

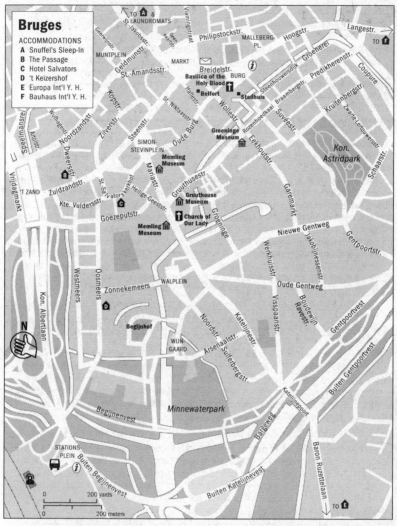

Bruges

ACCOMMODATIONS
A Snuffel's Sleep-In
B The Passage
C Hotel Salvators
D 't Keizershof
E Europa Int'l Y. H.
F Bauhaus Int'l Y. H.

on Breidelstr. through the Markt (15min.). Books rooms (400BF deposit) and sells maps (25BF). Open Apr.-Sept. M-F 9:30am-6:30pm, Sa-Su 10am-noon and 2-6:30pm; Oct.-Mar. M-F 9:30am-5pm, Sa-Su 9:30am-1pm and 2-5:30pm. **Branch** at the train station. **JAC,** Kleine Hertsbergestr. 1 (tel. 33 83 06), the 2nd right off Hoogstr. near the Burg, is a youth info center that lists cheap rooms. Open M-Tu 1-6pm, W-F 10am-6pm.

Tours: Quasimodo Tours (tel. (050) 37 04 70; fax 37 49 60), leads excellent 30km countryside bike tours to windmills, castles, and WWII bunkers. Tours depart mid-Mar. to Sept. daily 1pm from the tourist office at the Burg; 650BF, under 26 550BF. A mini-bus daytrip somberly patrols WWI battlefields; departs Su, Tu, and Th; 1400BF, under 26 1100BF.

Currency Exchange: Currency exchanges fill the streets around the Markt. **Goffin,** on Steenstr., has good rates (2% commission on traveler's checks). Open daily 10am-5pm.

Luggage Storage: At the train station; 60BF. **Lockers** at the tourist office; 15BF.

Laundromat: Belfort, Ezelstr. 51, next to Snuffel's Sleep-In. Wash 100-140BF, dry 200-300BF. Open daily 7am-10pm.

Emergencies: Tel. 100. **Police:** Tel. 101. Police station at Hauwerstr. 7 (tel. 44 88 44).

Internet Access: Brugesonline, Katelijnestr. 67 (tel. 34 93 52). 60BF per 15min. Open M-W 9:30am-noon and 1:30-9:30pm, Th-Sa 9:30am-noon and 1:30-5:30pm.

Post Office: Markt 5. Address mail to be held: Katrinka HRDY, *Poste Restante,* Recette Principale, Markt 5, **8000** Bruxelles, Belgium. Open M-F 9am-7:30pm, Sa 9:30am-12:30pm.

PHONE CODE	City code: 050. From outside Belgium, dial int'l access code (see inside back cover) + 32 + 50 + local number.

▶️ ACCOMMODATIONS, CAMPING, AND FOOD

The Passage, Dweersstr. 26 (tel. 34 02 32; fax 34 01 40). From 't Zand, go right on Zuidzandstr. and take the 1st left. Has airy rooms, an ideal location, and a restaurant and bar. Dorms 380-430BF; singles 900BF; doubles 1500BF. Breakfast 100BF. Reception 8:30am-midnight. V, MC. **The Hotel Passage** next door has funky rooms decorated with unique themes. Singles 1200BF; doubles 1800BF. Reception 8am-10pm.

Bauhaus International Youth Hotel, Langestr. 133-137 (tel. 34 10 93; fax 33 41 80; email bauhaus@bauhaus.be). Take bus 6 from the station to Kruispoort and tell the driver the destination (40BF). Great dinners and packed bar. Coastal bike trips (600BF). Dorms 380BF; doubles 950-1300BF. Breakfast 60BF. Bikes. Lockers. Reception 8am-2am.

Snuffel's Sleep-In, Ezelstr. 49 (tel. 33 31 33; fax 33 32 50; email snuffel@flanderscoast.be). From Markt, follow Sint-Jakobstr., which becomes Ezelstr. (10min.). Dorms 350-390BF; quads 1960BF. Breakfast 80BF. Kitchen. **Internet.** Reception 8am-2am.

't Keizershof, Oostmeers 126 (tel. 33 87 28; email stefaan.person@skynet.be). From the station, walk left and take the 1st right (5min.). Pretty, comfortable rooms on a quiet street. Singles 950BF; doubles 1400BF; triples 2100BF; quads 2500BF.

Europa International Youth Hostel (HI), Baron Ruzettelaan 143 (tel. 35 26 79; fax 35 37 72). Quiet, away from the Markt and the nightlife. Turn right from the station and follow Buiten Katelijnevest to Baron Ruzettelaan (15min.). 420BF; nonmembers 520BF. Breakfast included. Sheets 125BF. Key deposit 100BF. Reception 7:30-10am and 1-11pm.

Hotel Salvators, St-Salvatorsherhof 17 (tel. 33 19 21; fax 33 94 64; email salvators@skynet.be). From 't Zand, walk down Zuidzandstr. and turn right. Doubles 1800-2200BF; triples 3000BF; quads 3500BF. Breakfast included. Kitchen. **Internet.** Reception 24hr.

Camping: St-Michiel, Tillegemstr. (tel. 38 08 19; fax 80 68 24), 25min. from the Markt. Or take bus 7 from the station. 130BF per tent. Showers included. Restaurant and café.

To avoid high prices, stay away from the Markt and 't Zand, and instead look a block or two away from the center. Splurge on a pot of Belgium's famous *mosselen* (mussels), which for 450-500BF often includes appetizers and dessert, even in the Markt. Cheaper eats line **St-Amandsstr.** From Burg, turn up Hoogstr. and **Ganzespel,** Ganzestr. 37, is the 3rd right after the river with hearty portions of simple food. (Meals 285-405BF. Quiche 230BF. Open W-F noon-2:30pm and 6-10pm; Su noon-10pm.) Munch and people-watch from the terrace at **Café Craenenburg,** Markt 16. (Sandwiches 170-220BF. Salads 250-310BF. Omelettes 230-290BF. Spaghetti 250-320BF. Open daily 7am-1am.) Get veggie lunches at **The Lotus,** Wappenmakerstr. 5. From the Markt, take the 3rd left off Philipstockstr. (280-300BF. Open mid-Aug. to mid-July daily 11:45am-1:45pm.) From the Burg, cross the river and turn left to buy fresh seafood at the **Vismarkt.** For even cheaper fare, head to **Nopri Supermarket,** Noordzandstr. 4, just off 't Zand. (Open M-Th and Sa 9am-6:30pm, F 9am-7pm.)

📷 ♪ SIGHTS AND ENTERTAINMENT

Small enough to be covered by short walks, and lined with gorgeous canals and Renaissance streets, Bruges is best seen on foot. The tourist office leads **walking tours** (July-Aug. daily 3pm; 150BF). **Boat tours** also ply Bruges' canals (every 30min., 190BF); ask at the tourist office or pick up tickets at the booth on the bridge between Wollestr. and Dijver. The **museum combination ticket** covers the Gruuthuse, the Groeninge Museum, the Arentshuis, and the Memling (400BF).

MARKT AND BURG. Over the **Markt** looms the 88-meter-high medieval bell tower of the **Belfort.** Climb its dizzying 366 steps during the day for a great view; return at night when the tower serves as the city's torch. *(Open daily Apr.-Oct. 9:30am-5pm; Nov.-Mar. 9:30am-12:30pm and 1:30-5pm. 100BF, students 80BF. Bell concerts Su 2:15pm, M, W, and Sa 9pm.)* Near the Markt, the **Burg** square is dominated by the flamboyant Gothic façade of the medieval **Stadhuis** (City Hall), filled with paintings and wood carvings. *(Open daily Apr.-Sept. 9:30am-5pm; Oct.-Mar. 9:30am-12:30pm and 2-5pm. 100BF, students 80BF.)* Hidden in the corner of the Burg next to the Stadhuis, the **Basilica of the Holy Blood** houses a relic that allegedly holds the blood of Christ. *(Open daily Apr.-Sept. 9:30am-noon and 2-6pm; Oct.-Mar. 10am-noon and 2-4pm; closed W afternoon. 40BF.)*

MUSEUMS. From the Burg, follow Wollestr. left and head right on Dijver to reach the **Groeninge Museum,** Dijver 12, for a comprehensive collection of Belgian and Dutch paintings from the last six centuries, featuring works by Bruges-based Jan Van Eyck, Bruges-born Hans Memling, and the master of medieval macabre himself, Hieronymus Bosch. Next door, the **Gruuthuse Museum,** in the lavish 15th-century home of beer magnates, shelters an amazing collection of weapons, tapestries, musical instruments, and coins dating back to the 6th century. *(Dijver 17. Open Apr.-Sept. daily 9:30am-5pm; Oct.-Mar. W-M 9:30am-5pm. 130BF, students 100BF.)* Continue as Dijver becomes Gruuthusestr. and follow the curve left to reach the **Memling Museum,** Mariastr. 38, housed in St. John's Hospital, one of the oldest surviving medieval hospitals in Europe. The collection is scheduled to reopen in mid-2000.

OTHER SIGHTS. The 13th- to 15th-century **Church of Our Lady,** at Mariastr. and Gruuthusestr. near the Groeninge Museum, contains Michelangelo's *Madonna and Child,* one of his few works to have left Italy, as well as a number of medieval frescoed tombs and 16th-century mausoleums. *(Open Apr.-Sept. M-F 10-11:30am and 2:30-5pm, Sa 9-11:30am and 2:30-4pm, Su 2:30-5pm; Oct.-Mar. M-F closes 4:30pm. Church free; entrance to tombs 70BF.)* The 230-year-old windmill **Sint-Janshuismolen,** is still used to grind flour. From the Burg, follow Hoogstr., which becomes Langestr., and turn left at the end on Kruisvest. *(Open May-Sept. daily 9:30am-12:30pm and 1:15-5pm. 40BF, students 20BF.)* Between the station and the center of town, the **Minnewater** (the Lake of Love) has a less-than-romantic history as the site of ammunition dump, but you'd never know from the picnickers lounging in the beautiful park.

NIGHTLIFE. The best nighttime entertainment consists of wandering through the city's romantic streets and over its cobblestoned bridges, but if that isn't enough for you, take your pick among 300 varieties of beer at **'t Brugs Beertje,** Kemelstr. 5, off Steenstr. (Open M-Tu and Th-Sa 4pm-1am.) Next door, the **Dreiple Huis** serves tantalizingly fruity *jenever,* a flavored Dutch gin; just beware that the 15 different flavors mask the very high alcohol content. (Open daily 6pm-1am, W 4pm-1am, F-Sa 6pm-2am.) **Rikka Rock,** on 't Zand, is popular with local twenty-somethings. (Beers from 50BF. Open 24hr.) After hours, head next door to **L'ObCéDé** (The Pervert) for pulsing music. (No cover. Open daily 8pm-3am.)

⚡ EXCURSION FROM BRUGES: ZEEBRUGGE AND OSTEND

The towns along the North Sea coast of Belgium win fans largely for their **beaches. Zeebrugge** is little more than a port, but **Ostend** (Oostende) and **Knokke** have cute beaches and stores, just an hour-long bike ride from Bruges. For info on **ferries** from Zeebrugge and Ostend to the UK, see p. 58. Get ferry tickets from travel agents, at ports, or in the Oostende train station. **Trains** arrive in Zeebrugge and Ostend from Bruges (15min., 3 per hr., 150BF). To get from the Ostend train station to the **De Ploate Youth Hostel (HI),** Langestr. 82, cross the bridge, turn right on Visserkaai, follow the Promenade for 10min., and turn left on Langestr. (Tel. (059) 80 52 97. 465BF; nonmembers 565BF. Reception 7:30am-midnight. Curfew midnight.)

ANTWERP (ANTWERPEN, ANVERS)

Home of Rubens and Van Dyck and one of the world's diamond centers, 16th-century Antwerp claimed a place among the most powerful cities in Europe. Belgium's second-largest city still sparkles, with some of Belgium's finest examples of art, architecture, and literature as well as bars that stay open past dawn.

PRACTICAL INFO, ACCOMMODATIONS, AND FOOD. **Trains** go to Brussels (45min., 195BF); Rotterdam (1hr., 700BF); and Amsterdam (2hr., 970BF). To get from the station to the **tourist office,** Grote Markt 15, turn left on De Keyserlei, which becomes Meir, curve right at Meirburg on Eiermarkt, and head straight across Groenpl. around the cathedral (15-20min.). (Tel. (03) 232 01 03; fax 231 19 37. Open M-Sa 9am-6pm, Su 9am-5pm). Staying at **Globetrotter's Nest,** Vlagstr. 25, is like staying at a friend's beautiful townhouse. (Tel. (03) 236 99 28. Dorms 430BF; doubles 1100BF. Sheets 90BF. Breakfast included. Kitchen. Bikes. Open May 10-Dec.) To get to the modern **Jeugdherberg Op-Sinjoorke (HI),** Eric Sasselaan 2, take tram 2 (dir: Hoboken) to "Bouwcentrum," walk right, take first left, and follow HI signs over the bridge. (Tel. (03) 238 02 73. 385BF; nonmembers 485BF. Breakfast included. Sheets 125BF. Lockout 10am-4pm.) To get to **Scoutel,** Stoomstr. 3, from the station, turn left on Pelikaanstr., left on Langekievitstr., and right on Stoomstr. (5-10min.) (Tel. (03) 226 46 06; fax 232 63 92. Singles 1050F, under 26 950BF; doubles 1610BF, 1410BF; triples 1995BF, 1755BF. Breakfast included. Reception 8am-7pm.) **Ultimatum,** on the Grote Markt at Suiker Rui, has outdoor seating. (Sandwiches 225-295BF; pastas 300-500BF. Open daily noon-11pm.) Middle Eastern veggies are at **Mama's Garden,** at Papenstr. and Oude Korenmarkt. (Pitas 130-250BF. Open Su-Th noon-5am, F-Sa noon-7am.) **Postal code:** 2000.

SIGHTS AND ENTERTAINMENT. Many of Antwerp's best sights are free. Walk along the **Cogels Osylei** past fanciful Art Nouveau mansions built in the wealth of the city's Golden Age. **Centraal Station** itself is beautiful, and the buildings along the **Meir** are excellent examples of Antwerp old and new. The dignified Renaissance **Stadhuis** (City Hall) is in the Grote Markt in the *oude stad* (old city). (Call (03) 221 13 33 for nearly daily tour times. 30BF.) The nearby **Kathedraal van Onze-Lieve-Vrouw,** Groenpl. 21, has a showy Gothic tower and Flemish masterpieces, most notably Rubens' *Descent from the Cross.* (Open M-F 10am-5pm, Sa 10am-3pm, Su 1-4pm. 70BF.) The little-known **Mayer van den Bergh Museum,** Lange Gasthuisstr. 19, harbors Brueghel's *Mad Meg.* (Open Tu-Su 10am-5pm. 100BF, students 50BF.) Antwerp's favorite son built the stunning **Rubens Huis,** Wapper 9, off Meir, and filled it with art. (Open Tu-Su 10am-4:45pm. 100BF.) The **Royal Museum of Fine Art,** Leopold De Waelpl. 1-9, has one of the world's best collections of Old Flemish Master paintings. (Open Tu-Su 10am-5pm. 150BF, students 120BF; F free.)

Pick up *Antwerpen* at the tourist office for info on Antwerp's 300 bars and nightclubs. DJs spin house music in near-rave conditions at **Café d'Anvers,** Verversrui 15. (Cover 200BF. Open Sa-Su from midnight.) Live bands play at **Het Swingcafé,** on Suiker Rui. (Su and M. No cover. Open M-F 5pm-1am, Sa-Su later.) The streets behind the cathedral stay crowded; **Bierland,** Korte Nieuwstr. 28, is a popular student hang-out. (Open daily 8am-late.) Sample local *elixir d'Anvers* at the candle-lit **Pelgrom,** Pelgrimstr. 15. (Open daily noon-late.) Gay bars and discos cluster on **Van Schoonhovenstr.,** just north of Centraal Station. Closer to Grote Markt, a mixed crowd is at gay-friendly **in de Roscam,** Vrijdagmarkt 12. (Open daily 3pm-late.)

GHENT (GENT)

Once second only to Paris in size and prestige, modern Ghent lacks the charm of Antwerp and Bruges, but pulses with a large student population. The streets fill with puppet shows, street performers, live music, and carnival rides for the **Gentse Feesten** (Gent festivities; July 15-24, 2000) in celebration of National Day. This year, the city also celebrates the 500th birthday of Ghent-born Keizer Karel (Charles V) with year-long Charles-related art and music exhibits, performances, and festivals.

PRACTICAL INFO, ACCOMMODATIONS, AND FOOD. **Trains** run from Sint-Pietersstation (accessible by tram 1 or 12) to Bruges (20min., 175BF) and Brussels (35min.). The **tourist office** is in the belfry. (Tel. (09) 266 52 32. Open daily Apr.-Oct. 9:30am-8pm; Nov.-Mar. 9:30am-6pm.) **De Draeke (HI),** St-Widostr. 11, in the shadow of a castle, is the best place to stay in Ghent. From the station, take tram 1, 10, or 11 to "Gravensteen" (15min.); head left, then head right on Gewad and right again on St-Widostr. (Tel. (09) 233 70 50; fax 233 80 01. Dorms 495BF; singles 800BF; doubles 1170BF; nonmembers add 100BF. Breakfast included. Sheets 125BF. Reception 7:30am-11pm.) Single rooms are available at the **university;** the office is at Stalhof 6. (Tel. (09) 264 71 00; fax 264 72 96. Singles 650BF. Breakfast included. Open mid-July to mid-Sept.) To get to **Camping Blaarmeersen,** Zuiderlaan 12, walk 15 blocks or ride bus 38 northwest of Sint-Pietersstation. (Tel. (09) 221 53 99. 150BF per person, 120BF per tent. Open Mar. to mid-Oct.) Good meals run about 200BF; try around **Korenmarkt,** in front of the post office; **Vrijdagmarkt,** a few blocks from the town hall; and **St-Pietersnieuwstr.,** down by the university. The **Fritz Tearoom,** Korte Dagsteeg Walpoorstr., has hot sandwiches (150-240BF), pasta (220-235BF), and great waffles (140BF). (Open daily 8am-6:30pm.) **Postal code:** 9000.

■🎭 **SIGHTS AND ENTERTAINMENT.** Lovers of fine architecture relish a trip to Ghent. The revered **Gravensteen,** the Castle of the Counts, is a sprawling medieval fortress complete with torture instruments. (Open daily 9am-5:15pm. 200BF, students 100BF.) Wind your way up the towering **Belfort** (belfry) to experience some classic Hitchcock vertigo. (Open daily 2-5:30pm. 45BF.) The **Stadhuis** (Town Hall) is a juxtaposition of Gothic and Renaissance architecture. A block away on Limburg-str., the 14th- to 16th-century **Sint-Baafskathedraal** boasts Jan Van Eyck's *Adoration of the Mystic Lamb* (a.k.a. the *Ghent Altarpiece*). (Cathedral open daily 8:30am-6pm; free. Altarpiece open M-Sa 9:30am-4:30pm, Su 1-4:30pm; entrance and audio tour 100BF.) Head to Citadel Park for the **Museum voor Schone Kunsten's** (Museum of Fine Arts) strong Flemish collection (open Tu-Su 9:30am-5pm; 100BF, students 50BF; free during festivities) and the **Stedelijk Museum voor Actuele Kunst's (SMAK),** contemporary art (open Tu-Su 10am-6pm; 300BF, students 200BF).

From October to July 15, young scholars cavort in the cafés and discos near the university restaurant on **Overpoortstr. Vooruit.** This huge Art Deco bar on St-Pieter-snieuwstr. was once the meeting place of the Socialist Party, and later occupied by Nazis in WWII. The bar's concert hall does rock to jazz to avant-garde. (Tel. (09) 223 82 01. Open mid-Aug. to mid-July Su-Th 11:30am-2am, F-Sa 11:30am-3am.) Beer lovers flock to **Dulle Grief,** on the Vrijdagmarkt. (Open M 4:30pm-1am, Tu-Sa noon-1am, Su noon-7:30pm.) Ghent is a popular destination for gay men and women: try clubs **Parallax,** Vlannderenstr. 22, or **Dandy's,** Prinsesclementinalaar 195. During the festivities of **"10 Days Off"** (tel. (09) 269 09 45) brings 11 nights of international DJs to the Starbuilding, Rekelinge 5, near Gravensteen Castle (cover 350-400BF).

MECHELEN (MALINES)

Historically the ecclesiastical capital of Belgium, Mechelen offers a few sights for a daytrip. Mechelen's main claim to fame is its carillon (set of 49 bells) performances (M and Sa 11:30am, Su 3pm; June-Sept. also M 9:30pm). Down Consciencestr. from the station, **St. Rumbold's Tower** rises 97m over **Grote Markt,** contains two carillons. The Grote Markt is lined with early Renaissance buildings, including the **Stadhuis** (city hall) and the stately **St. Rumbold's Cathedral** (open M-Sa 8:30am-5:30pm, Su 2-5:30pm). The 18th-century military barracks used during the Holocaust as a temporary camp for Belgian and Dutch Jews en route to Auschwitz-Birkenau now houses the **Museum of Nazi Deportation and Resistance.** From the Grote Markt, head down Merodestr., left on St. Janstr. and right on Stassartstr. (10 min.). (Open Su-Th 10am-5pm, F 10am-1pm. Free.) **Trains** arrive from Brussels and Antwerp (both 15min., 120BF). The **tourist office** is n the Stadhuis. (Tel. (015) 29 76 55. Open Easter-Oct. M-F 8am-6pm, Sa-Su 9:30am-12:30pm and 1:30-5pm; June-Sept. M until 7pm; Nov.-Easter reduced hours.) **Café de York Ver-O-Peso,** Wollemarkt 4, behind the cathedral, serves great pizza. (Meals 220-400BF. Open daily 10am-late.) **Postal code:** 2800.

WALLONIE

In the third century, these dense forests marked the edge of Roman influence, and, 17 centuries later, the division remains. While Germanic tribes built the large cities of modern-day Flanders, the Romanized Celts who settled in southern Wallonie retained their French culture and language. Although Wallonie lacks the world-class cities of the north, the castle-dotted **Ardennes** offer a relaxing hideaway.

TOURNAI (DOORNIK). The first city liberated by Allied forces, Tournai's medieval old town escaped major damage in WWII. Once a Roman trading post and the original capital of France, Tournai is a peaceful town less touristy than its Flemish counterparts. The city's most spectacular sight is the Romanesque and Gothic **cathedral,** whose **treasure room** houses medieval goldware and some of St. Thomas Becket's threads. (Open Apr.-Oct. 9am-noon and 2-6pm, off-season until 4pm. Free; treasure room 30BF.) The stunning Art Nouveau building of the **Museum of Fine Arts,** Enclos Saint-Martin, houses a fine collection of Flemish paintings. (Open daily 10am-noon and 2-5:30pm. 120BF, students 80BF.) Tournai will celebrate Charles V's 500th birthday with an **international tapestry exhibit** in the summer of 2000.

To get to the **tourist office,** 14 Vieux Marché Aux Poteries, exit the station, walk straight into the city center (15min.), and go around the left side of the cathedral. (Tel. (069) 22 20 45; fax 21 62 21; email bureau.tourisme.tournai@skynet.be; www.tournai.be. Open M-F 9am-7pm, Sa 10am-1pm and 3-6pm, Su 10am-noon and 2-6pm.) The **Auberge de Tournai,** rue St-Martin, has great tapestries. Continue straight uphill from the tourist office or take bus 7 or 88 from the station (40BF). (Tel. (069) 21 61 36; fax 21 61 40; email tournai@laj.be. 420BF; nonmembers 520BF. Sheets 125BF. Reception 9-11am and 5-10pm.) Fill up at **Pita Pyramid,** 7 rue de la Tête d'Or, in the Galerie les Arcades. (Pitas 140-210BF. Open M-Th 11:30am-2pm and 5:30pm-1am, F-Su until 2am.) Party around the **Grand-Place** and the canals.

NAMUR. The quiet city of **Namur,** in the heart of Wallonie, is the last sizeable outpost before the wilderness of the Ardennes. Equipped with a hostel and pleasant nightlife, and nearby **hiking, biking, caving,** and **kayaking** options, it makes the best base for exploring the Ardennes. The foreboding **citadel,** on the top of a rocky hill to the south, was built by the Spanish in the Middle Ages, expanded by the Dutch in the 19th century, the site of a bloody battle in WWI, and occupied until 1978. Climb up, or take a **mini-bus** from the tourist office at the corner of bd. Baron Huart and rue de Grognon (every 15min., 40BF); the bus will let you off at the stadium, where you can pick up a **tour** of the fortress. (Open daily 11am-5pm. 210BF; includes train ride around the citadel and a walking tour including a portion of the casemates.)

The **tourist offices** (tel. (081) 22 28 59) a few blocks left of the train station, off pl. Léopold, and in the **Hôtel de Ville** (tel. (081) 24 64 44; fax 24 71 28; www.ville.namur.be) help plan excursions. (Both open daily 9:30am-6pm.) To reach the friendly **Auberge Félicien Rops (HI),** 8 av. Félicien Rops, take bus 3 directly to the door, or take bus 4 or 5 and ask the driver to let you off. (Tel. (081) 22 36 88; fax 22 44 12. Dorms 420-495BF; singles 620-800BF; doubles 1040-1170BF; nonmembers add 100BF. Breakfast included. Sheets 125BF. Kitchen. Laundry 240BF. Bikes 500BF per day. Reception 7:30am-1am.) To **camp** at **Les Trieux,** 99 rue des Tris, 6km away in Malonne, take bus 6. (Tel. (081) 44 55 83. 85BF per person, 85BF per tent. Cold showers free. Open Apr.-Oct.) If you're in the mood for Italian, step into the 15th-century cellar of **La Cava,** rue de la Monnaie 20. (Entrees 220-380BF. Open daily noon-11pm.) Try the regional Ardennes ham at one of the sandwich stands throughout the city, or stop at the **Match supermarket** in the city center.

DINANT. Dinant boasts a striking citadel and underground caves and is a good base for climbing and kayaking excursions. The imposing **citadel** rises over the river and the small town. Explore on your own, or ride the cable car up and try to follow along with one of the French tours. (Joint ticket 195BF. Citadel open daily 10am-6pm.) Bring a sweater to the tour of the chilly, cascade-filled caves of **La Grotte Merveilleuse,** Route de Phillippeville 142. (Tel. (082) 22 22 10. Open daily Apr.-Oct. 10am-6pm, Mar. and Nov. 11am-5pm. 200BF.) **Dakota Raid Adventure,** rue Saint Roch 17, leads **rock-climbing** and **spelunking** daytrips in the area. (Tel./fax (082) 22 32 43. Open daily 10am-5pm.) Dinant is accessible via **train** (15min., 120BF) or **bike** from Namur, or, on summer weekends, take a one-way **river cruise** on the Meuse River (tel. (082) 22 32 15; 450BF). The **tourist office,** rue Grande 37 (tel. (082) 22 28 70; fax 22 77 88; www.maison-du-tourisme.net), helps plan **kayaking** trips (1-person 650BF, 2-person 800-1000BF, 3-person 1100BF). From the train station, turn right, take your first left, cross the bridge, and turn right on rue Grand (10min.).

BELGIUM

BOSNIA-HERZEGOVINA

US$1 = 1.85KM (CONVERTIBLE MARKS, OR KM)	1KM = US$0.54
CDN$1 = 1.24KM	1KM = CDN$0.81
UK£1 = 2.96KM	1KM = UK£0.34
IR£1 = 2.48KM	1KM = IR£0.40
AUS$1 = 1.20KM	1KM = AUS$0.83
NZ$1 = 0.98KM	1KM = NZ$1.02
SAR1 = 0.31KM	1KM = SAR3.27
DM1 = 1KM	1KM = DM1
HRV KUNA1 = 0.26KM	1KM = KUNA3.89

PHONE CODES | Country code: 387. International dialing prefix: 00.

The mountainous centerpiece of the former Yugoslavia, Bosnia-Herzegovina has defied the odds and the centuries to stand as an independent nation today. Bosnia's distinction—and its troubles—spring from its self-proclaimed role as a mixing ground for Muslims, Croats, and Serbs. In Sarajevo, its cosmopolitan capital, that ideal is at least verbally maintained, but ethnic problems continue in the countryside. The country is marked by rolling hills and sparkling rivers, but its lush valleys are now punctuated with abandoned houses and gaping rooftops. The past decade has been brutal, a bloody war broadcast nightly to the world, and

much of the population became displaced. Bosnia's future is uncertain, particularly with the imminent withdrawal of NATO troops, but its resilient people are optimistic. In this period of post-Dayton peace, rebuilding is slowly underway.

Learn more about Bosnia's past and present in *Let's Go: Eastern Europe 2000*.

 In August 1999, the US Department of State reiterated its **Travel Warning** against unnecessary travel to Bosnia, particularly the Republika Srpska. For more info and the most recent updates, see travel.state.gov/travelwarnings.html.

GETTING THERE AND GETTING AROUND

Flights come from Zurich, Ljubljana, and Istanbul on **TOP Air** and **Adria Air. Croatia Airlines** (Zagreb tel. (41) 42 77 52; Split tel. (21) 36 22 02) has regular service from Zagreb. **Railways** are not an option. The only functional rail line was put out of commission by NATO bombs in Yugoslavia. Alas, **Eurail** is not accepted. **Buses**—reliable, clean, and not too crowded—run daily to Split, Dubrovnik, and Zagreb. Because of the high concentration of landmines and unexploded ordnance lacing road shoulders, poor road quality, and kamikaze Balkan driving customs, you should avoid **driving. Biking** and **hitchhiking** are also uncommon and inadvisable.

ESSENTIALS

DOCUMENTS AND FORMALITIES. Irish, British, and Americans do not require visas, but Australians, New Zealanders, and South Africans do (US$35). Upon entering, register immediately with your embassy and keep your papers on you.

Bosnian Embassies at Home: Australia, 27 State Circle, Forest, Canberra ACT 2603 (tel. (0612) 623 959 55; fax 623 957 93); **UK,** 320 Regent St, London W1R 5AB (tel. (020) 72 55 37 58; fax 72 55 37 60); **US,** 2109 E St NW, Washington, DC 20037 (tel. (202) 337-1500; fax 337-1502; email info@bosnianembassy.org).

Foreign Embassies in Bosnia: All foreign embassies are in **Sarajevo** (see p. 133).

TOURIST OFFICES. Tourist services are limited, perhaps because most travelers here are journalists and relief workers. The tourist office in Sarajevo staffs both English and German speakers. The **US Embassy** has a full-time consul and useful info. You can also go to independent tourist agencies or helpful locals for info.

MONEY. The new Bosnian **convertible mark (KM),** fixed to the **Deutschmark** 1:1, was introduced in summer 1998. Deutschmarks can be changed directly into convertible marks for no commission at most Sarajevo banks. Beware old Bosnian dinars, which are no longer valid. The Croatian **kuna** was also named an official currency in summer 1997; while not legal tender in Sarajevo, it's the only valid currency in the western (Croatian) area of divided Mostar. Change your money back to Deutschmarks when you leave; convertible marks are inconvertible outside Bosnia. **ATMs** are nonexistent. **Traveler's checks** can be exchanged at some Sarajevo banks. Accommodations are fairly pricey, at US$15-30; food, fortunately, remains affordable at US$2-5 per meal. Waitstaff are salaried and expect **tips** only for excellent service; 6% is generous. **Bargaining** is possible, particularly in clothing markets.

COMMUNICATION

Post: Post offices are marked by yellow-and-white "PTT" signs. **Postcard/letters** to Australia, Canada, Ireland, New Zealand, the UK, the US, and South Africa cost KM1 and take 1-2 weeks. **Poste Restante** is unavailable, even in Sarajevo.

Telephone: The best option is to call collect from the Sarajevo post office. Calling the UK is roughly KM3.50 per min., the US KM5. **International direct dial** numbers include: **AT&T,** 008 00 00 10. **Police,** tel. 92. **Fire,** tel. 93. **Emergency,** tel. 94.

Language: When in Bosnia, speak Bosnian. When in Croatia, Croatian. When in Serbia, Serbian. For basic phrases, see p. 949. English and German are widely spoken.

HEALTH AND SAFETY. Outside Sarajevo, **do not set foot off the pavement** under any circumstances. Even in Sarajevo, stay on paved roads and hard-covered surfaces. Do not pick up any objects on the ground. **Landmines** and **unexploded ordnance** (UXOs) cover the country, many on **road shoulders** and in **abandoned houses.** A security briefing is held every few days at the US Embassy for government officials—if you ask nicely, you may be included. **Mine Action Center (MAC),** Zmaja od Bosne 8 (tel. 66 73 10), in the gated Tito Barracks 400m past the Holiday Inn from the center, provides info that's vital if you plan travel beyond Sarajevo.

ACCOMMODATIONS AND FOOD. Until recently, lodgings were absurdly expensive, but prices are stabilizing. You can get a room in a **pension** for as little as 30KM, and **private rooms** cost about 40-60KM. There are no **hostels** or **campgrounds** in Bosnia. Almost all Bosnian **food** involves some variety of meat. If you're a vegetarian, be sure to request your meals *bez meso* (without meat).

LOCAL FACTS

Time: Bosnia is 1hr. ahead of Greenwich Mean Time (GMT; see p. 49).

Climate: Bosnia's climate is inland Mediterranean; summers are hot, winters rather cold, and fair amounts of precipitation throughout the year. Spring is the best time to visit.

Hours: Most **shops** and **banks** are open M-F 9am-6pm, with random Saturday hours.

Holidays: Bosnia celebrates many Catholic, Orthodox, and Muslim religious holidays; *Let's Go* does not include all here, as most are days of observance rather than public holidays. Catholic New Year's (Jan. 1); Orthodox Christmas (Jan.7); Eid Al Fitr (Jan. 8); Orthodox New Year's (Jan. 14); Independence Day (Mar. 1); Eid Al Adha (Mar. 17); Islamic New Year (Apr. 6); Day of the Army (Apr. 15); Catholic Easter (Apr. 23); Orthodox Easter (Apr. 30); Labor Day (May 1); Victory Day (May 4); Prophet's Birthday (June 15); Day of the Republic (Nov. 25); Catholic Christmas (Dec. 25).

SARAJEVO

Sarajevo itself defies cliché; to define the city by its bullet-holes is to reduce it to its television presence. Perhaps wary of CNN stereotyping, the city remains largely aloof to the short-term visitor, and tensions are on the rise with the recent influx of refugees. But it is just that sort of elusiveness that makes finding the real Sarajevo—the city loved so passionately by its residents—all the more rewarding.

> **!** The following outlying areas of Sarajevo are at particular risk for **mines:** Grbavica, Lukavica, Illidža, and Dobrinja. All parts of the city are considered high-risk.

▌▐█ PRACTICAL INFO, ACCOMMODATIONS, AND FOOD. Buses (tel. (071) 67 01 80) go from Kranjćevića 9, behind the Holiday Inn at the corner with Halida Kajtaza, to Dubrovnik (7hr., 2 per day, 41KM); Split (8hr., 3 per day, 37KM); Zagreb (9hr., 2 per day, 65KM); and Frankfurt, Germany (15hr., 1 per day, 200KM). Walk past the taxi stands on Kranjćevića, cross the first intersection, go downhill 20min. to the mosque at the large intersection, cross to Maršala Tita, bear right at the eternal flame, continue until you see the Catholic church on the left, turn right on Strosmajerova, and go left on Zelenih Beretki to reach the **tourist bureau** at #22a. (Tel. (071) 53 26 06. Open M-F 9am-7pm, Sa 9am-2pm.) For info on **registering,** see p. 131. **Embassies: Australians** should contact the embassy in Vienna (see p. 88); **Canada,** Logavina 7 (tel. (071) 44 79 00; open M-F 8:30am-noon and 1-5pm); citizens of **New Zealand** should contact the embassy in Rome (see p. 554); **UK,** Tina Ujevića 8 (tel. (071) 44 44 29; open M-F 8:30am-5pm); and **US,** Alipašina 43 (tel. (071) 44 57 00; open M-F 9am-1pm). **Central Profit Bank,** Zelenih Beretki 24, changes money. (Open M-F 8am-7:30pm, Sa 8am-3pm.) Relatively cheap **private rooms** (40-60KM) are all over; ask a taxi driver at the station if you arrive late. The tourist bureau also arranges rooms; call at least 3hr. before you arrive. From Maršala Tita, bear left at the eternal flame and walk two blocks past the market to get to **Prenoćište "Konak,"** Mula Mustafe Bašeskije 48, on the right. (Tel. (071) 53 35 06. Singles 40KM; doubles 60KM. Reception 7am-midnight.) For an authentic Bosnian meal, scour the Turkish Quarter for **Čevabdžinića** shops; 3KM buys a *čevapčici* (nicknamed *čevaps*), lamb sausages encased in *somun*, Bosnia's tasty, elastic flat bread. (Open M-Sa 8am-5pm, Su 8am-noon.)

▐▐ SIGHTS AND ENTERTAINMENT. The **eternal flame,** where Maršala Tita splits into Ferhadija and Mula Mustafe Bašeskije, has burned since 1945 as a memorial to all Sarajevans who died in WWII; its homage to South Slav unity now seems painfully ironic. Evidence of the city's recent four-year siege is not hard to find: the landscape is still ridden with craters. From Maršala Tita, walk toward the river to Obala Kulina Bana and turn left to find the **National Library,** at the tip of the Turkish Quarter, once the most beautiful building in the city and now an open-air structure housing piles of rubble. The glaring **treeline** up in the hills above the city clearly demarcates the front lines; Bosnians trapped in Sarajevo cut down all the available wood for winter heat. Many different religions huddle together in Central Sarajevo, indicating the best and worst of what the city represents. Walk left at the flame on Ferhadija, which becomes Sarači, to find the 16th-century **Gazi Husrev-Bey mosque,** Sarači 18, perhaps Sarajevo's most famous building. The interior is closed for repairs, but the courtyard is breathtaking. Surrounding the mosque is the picturesque **Turkish Quarter** (Baščaršija). The main Orthodox church, the **Saborna,** is also closed, but the old **Orthodox Church of St. Michael the Archangel,** on Mula Mustafe Bašeskije, remains open. (Open daily 8am-7pm.) The 1889 **Cathedral of Jesus' Heart** (Katedrala Srce Isusovo), on Ferhadija, designed by Josipa Vancasa, is the spiritual center for Bosnian Catholics. The 1892 **Sephardic Synagogue,** Hamdije Krešavljakovića 59, remains open as the base for **La Benevolencija,** the Jewish Community Center's active service organization. The corner that made Sarajevo famous is at Obala Kulina Bana and Zelenih Beretki. Near a white-railinged bridge 200m before the library, a plaque on a building wall commemorates the birthplace of WWI, where Gavrilo Princip shot Austrian Archduke Franz Ferdinand and his pregnant wife Sofia on June 28, 1914. Both the **History Museum** (Historijski Muzej), Zmaja od Bosne 5 (open M-F 9am-5pm, Sa-Su 9am-1pm; free) and the **Art Gallery of Bosnia and Herzegovina** (Umjetnička Galerija Bosne i Hercegovine), Zelenih Beretki 8 (open M-Sa 10am-4pm; free) are worth a look.

BOSNIA-HERZEGOVINA

BRITAIN

US$1 = UK£0.62 (BRITISH POUNDS)	UK£1 = US$1.61
CDN$1 =UK£0.42	UK£1 = CDN$2.39
IR£1 = UK£0.83	UK£1= IR£1.20
AUS$1 = UK£0.40	UK£1 = AUS$2.48
NZ$1 = UK£0.33	UK£1 = NZ$3.03
SAR1=UK£0.10	UK£1 = SAR9.83
EUR€1= UK£0.66	UK£1 = EUR€1.51

PHONE CODE	Country code: 44. International dialing prefix: 00.

The 20th century has not been kind to the Empire. After Britain founded modern democracy, led the Industrial Revolution, spread colonies around the globe, and, most recently, helped stave off a Nazi Europe in World War II, a former colony displaced it as the world's economic hegemon. While overseas colonies claimed independence one by one, the Empire frayed at home as well: most of Ireland won independence in 1921, and Scotland and Wales were promised regional autonomy in 1975. Today, the ongoing troubles in Northern Ireland underscore the problems of union and nationalism associated with empire. Travelers to Britain should be aware that names hold great political force. "Great Britain" refers to England, Scotland, and Wales; it's neither accurate nor polite to call a Scot or Welshman "English." The political term "United Kingdom" refers to these nations as well as Northern Ireland. Because of distinctions in laws and currency, *Let's Go* uses the term "Britain" to refer to England, Scotland, and Wales.

At first glance, anglophone Britain may not seem quite exotic enough for travelers aching to dive into the unknown. Indeed, the English language, a combination of fragmented dialects created by invaded peoples that was once considered too common for scholarship or rule, is today the world's true *lingua franca*. The sonnets of Shakespeare; the theories of Adam Smith and Isaac Newton; the philosophy of John Locke; the literature of Virginia Woolf, Charles Dickens, and George Orwell; even the lyrics of John Lennon go to show that strong British threads have been woven into the cultural and historical tapestry of the recent Western world. Despite all this, Britain is less familiar than it appears—certainly, the historic homes and quaint villages of Jane Austen and E.M. Forster movie adaptations are in abundant supply. But they are interspersed with medieval castles, rugged coasts, and eerie prehistoric monuments that hearken back to another era. Look beyond London, allowing time for sparkling lakes, small towns, and the wild islands.

For more detailed, exhilarating coverage of Britain and London, pore over *Let's Go: Britain & Ireland 2000* or *Let's Go: London 2000*.

DISCOVER BRITAIN

London is brimming with cultural wonders—wonders from other cultures, that is. The British and the Victoria & Albert Museums testify to the avarice of Empire. While in the capital, don't miss a trip to the Globe Theater to revisit the London of Shakespeare's time (p. 139). Southwest of London, **Winchester** offers a massive Norman cathedral and celebrates native daughter Jane Austen (p. 163), while prehistoric **Stonehenge** and **Avebury** (p. 164) and the massive cathedral at **Salisbury** are only a stone's throw away (p. 163). Farther west, **Newquay** in Cornwall is Britain's contribution to surfer culture (p. 166). Back toward London, **Oxford** (p. 167) and **Cambridge** (p. 175) battle to see who's smarter and prettier. Near Oxford, **Blenheim Palace** is almost oppressive in its opulence (p. 171). Walk from pretty village to pretty village in the **Cotswolds** (p. 171), then hit **Bath,** which once offered healing waters to the rich and famous of Georgian England, for a

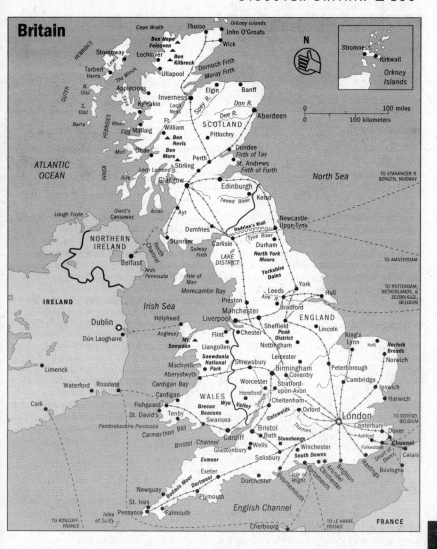

Britain

SCOTLAND

ENGLAND

WALES

NORTHERN IRELAND

IRELAND

ATLANTIC OCEAN

North Sea

Irish Sea

English Channel

FRANCE

100 miles
100 kilometers

TO STAVANGER & BERGEN, NORWAY
TO AMSTERDAM
TO ROTTERDAM, NETHERLANDS, & ZEEBRUGGE, BELGIUM
TO OSTEND, BELGIUM
TO LE HAVRE, FRANCE
TO ROSCOFF, FRANCE

Orkney Islands
Stromness
Kirkwall

combo of kitsch and excavations of the Roman city (p. 174). In nearby Wales, cavort with the sheep and commune with nature in **Snowdonia National Park** (p. 192) Back in England, **Stratford-Upon-Avon,** much like high-school English, suffers from a bit of Shakespeare overload (p. 172). Avoid slipping into permanent iambic pentameter by continuing north through the industrial heart of England—take care not to miss **Manchester's** raucous nightlife (p. 180) or **Liverpool's** kitschy Beatles mania (p. 182) along the way—to the dramatic **Lake District National Park,** filled with rugged hills and windswept fells (p. 186). Head farther north to Scotland to munch on haggis and live out your wildest *Braveheart* fantasies. Enjoy the cultural capitals of **Edinburgh** (p. 195) and **Glasgow** (p. 200), then take the low road to the bonnie, bonnie banks of **Loch Lomond** (p. 205) followed by a wee taste of the Scottish highlands on the beautiful **Isle of Skye** (p. 206) and at the famed **Loch Ness,** where Nessie awaits (p. 208).

GETTING THERE AND GETTING AROUND

BY PLANE. Most flights into Britain that originate outside Europe land at **London's Heathrow** and **Gatwick** airports. Flights from Europe also hit **Luton** and **Stansted,** near London, as well as **Cardiff, Liverpool, Manchester, Edinburgh,** and **Glasgow.**

BY TRAIN. There is no longer a single national rail company, although the various companies are often still referred to under the umbrella of "British Rail." For info, dial (0345) 48 49 50. Despite multiple providers, rail service in Britain is extensive (and expensive). The **BritRail Pass,** available to non-British travelers outside Britain, allows unlimited travel in England, Wales, and Scotland (8-day US$265, under 26 US$215; 22-day US$505, under 26 US$355). The one-year **Young Person's Railcard,** which grants 33% off most fares in addition to discounts on some ferries, is available to those ages 16 to 25 (and to full-time students at British universities over age 23; £18) at major British Rail Travel Centres in the UK. **Eurail** is not valid in Britain. For info on the **Eurostar** train to Paris and Brussels via the Chunnel, see p. 57.

BY BUS. National Express (tel. (08705) 80 80 80), Britain's principal operator of long-distance coach services, and **Bus Éireann** (tel. (01) 836 6111) offer London-Dublin and other combo bus/ferry routes. Long-distance **coach** (bus) travel in Britain is more extensive than in most European countries and is the cheapest option. **Young Persons' Discount Coach Cards,** which reduce standard coach fares by about 30%, are available to those ages 16 to 25 (£8). **Hop-on, hop-off bus tours** that cater to backpackers are good ways to get to otherwise inaccessible areas. For info on bus tours in Scotland, see p. 195. **Wales' Hairy Hog,** 22 Conduit Pl, London W2 1HS (tel. (029) 20 66 69 00 or (020) 77 06 15 39; www.hairyhog.co.uk), conducts 5-day tours of Wales out of Cardiff that take in most of the country for £119.

BY FERRY. Numerous ferry lines ply the route across the English Channel; the most popular crossing is from **Dover** to **Calais, France.** Always ask about reduced fares—an HI card or ISIC with Travelsave stamps might mean a 25 to 50% discount. Book ahead June through August. Other routes between the Continent and England include Bergen, Norway to Lerwick or Newcastle; Esbjerg, Denmark to Harwich; Göteborg, Sweden to Harwich or Newcastle; Hamburg to Harwich or Newcastle; Oostende, Belgium to Ramsgate, near Dover; and Hook of Holland to Harwich. For info on boats from **Wales** to **Dublin** and **Rosslare, Ireland,** see p. 188; from **Scotland** to **Belfast,** see p. 194; from **England** to the **Continent,** see p. 57.

BY CAR. Brits drive on the left side of the road; enter traffic circles by turning left as well. **Gas,** usually called petrol, averages about US$4 per gallon. **Roads** are generally well maintained, but parking in London is impossible and traffic is slow. In Britain, rotaries are called "roundabouts," overpasses are "flyovers," traffic jams are "tail-backs," and the breakdown lane is the "lay-by." The trunk of a car is the "boot."

BY BIKE AND BY THUMB. Much of Britain's countryside is well suited for **biking.** Many cities and villages have bike rental shops and maps of local cycle routes; ask at the tourist office. Large-scale Ordnance Survey maps detail the extensive system of long-distance **hiking** paths. Tourist offices and National Park Information Centres can provide extra information about routes. *Let's Go* does not recommend **hitchhiking**; it is illegal on motorways (roads labeled "M") and always risky.

ESSENTIALS

DOCUMENTS AND FORMALITIES. EU citizens do not need a visa to enter Britain. For visits shorter than six months, citizens of Australia, Canada, New Zealand, South Africa, and the US do not need a visa to enter.

British Embassies at Home: Australia, on Commonwealth Ave, Yarralumla, Canberra, ACT 2600 (tel. (02) 62 70 66 66; www.uk.emb.gov.au); **Canada,** 777 Bay St #2800, Toronto, ON M5G 2G2 (tel. (416) 593-1290); **France** (consulate), 9 av. Hoche 8e,

BRITAIN

Paris (tel. (01) 42 66 38 10); **Ireland,** 29 Merrion Rd, Ballsbridge, Dublin 4 (tel. (01) 205 3700); **New Zealand,** 44 Hill St, Thorndon, Wellington (tel. (04) 472 60 49; www.brithighcomm.org.nz); **South Africa,** Greystoke, 255 Hill St, Arcadia, Pretoria (tel. (012) 483 12 00); **US,** 3100 Massachusetts Ave. NW, Washington, DC 20008 (tel. (202) 462-1340; www.britain-info.org).

Foreign Embassies in Britain: Foreign embassies are all in **London** (see p. 143).

TOURIST OFFICES. There are local **tourist offices** everywhere in Great Britain; most will book a place to stay for a fee of around £2. Most offices also offer a "book-a-bed-ahead" service; for about £2.50 (less in Wales), they will reserve a room in the next town on your itinerary. Proprietors who have not paid a fee to be listed with a tourist office may be less visible. The **Scottish Tourist Board,** 19 Cockspur St, London SW1 Y5BL, has gads of info and can book train, bus, and plane tickets. (Tel. (020) 79 30 86 61. Open M-F 9am-6pm, Sa 10-5pm.) You can also visit them in Edinburgh at 23 Ravelston Terr, EH4 3EU (tel. (0131) 332 2433).

British Tourist Offices at Home: Australia, Level 16, The Gateway, 1 Macquarie Pl, Circular Quay, Sydney, NSW 2000 (tel. (02) 93 77 44 00; fax 93 77 44 99); **Canada,** 111 Avenue Rd #450, Toronto, ON M5R 3JD (tel. (416) 925-6326; fax 961-2175); **New Zealand,** 3rd fl., Dilworth Building, Queen & Customs St, Auckland 1 (tel. (09) 303 14 46; fax 77 69 65); **US,** 551 Fifth Ave #701, New York, NY 10176 (tel. (800) 462-2748).

MONEY. The pound sterling (£), the main unit of **currency** in the UK, is divided into 100 pence (p). Northern Ireland and Scotland have their own bank notes, which are identical in value to other British notes and can be used interchangeably with standard currency, although you may have difficulty using Scottish £1 notes outside Scotland. **Bank** hours across Britain are usually 9:30am to 4:30pm on weekdays, with busier locations open on Saturdays and a few hours on Sundays. If you need to **exchange** money outside of those hours, try **Thomas Cook** travel offices. Also, most banks have machines available for transactions 24 hours a day. Be aware that retailers are permitted to charge more for purchases made by **credit card**.

Tipping and Bargaining: Tip 10-15% at restaurants if service hasn't already been added to the bill. Taxis get 10-15%. Tipping the barman is a come-on.

Taxes: The UK charges a 17.5% **value-added tax** (VAT), a national sales tax on most goods and some services (not books, medicine, or food). For a VAT refund, you must ask the shopkeeper from whom you buy your goods for the appropriate form, have it later signed and stamped by customs officials, then apply for refund at Heathrow or Gatwick airports or after you get home. You must leave the UK within 3 months of purchase to get a refund.

COMMUNICATION

Post: Airmail generally arrives in Western Europe in 3 days; other destinations take 4-8 days. An airmail **postcard** costs 26p to EU destinations, 31p to the rest of Europe, and 37p to all other destinations. Post offices in most of Britain are open M-F 9am-5:30pm; main offices are also open Sa 9am-1pm.

Telephones: Pay phones charge 10p for local calls; they don't accept 1, 2, or 5p coins. Many phones only accept **Phonecards** (£2-20), available from post offices, newsagents, and John Menzies stationery shops. Calls are substantially cheaper on weekends and after 6pm on weekdays. For an **operator,** dial 100; **directory inquiries,** 192; **international directory** inquiries, 153. To make an **international call,** dial direct or call 155 for an **international operator. International direct dial numbers** include: **AT&T Direct,** 08 00 89 00 11; **Australia Direct,** 08 00 89 00 61; **Canada Direct,** 08 00 89 00 16; **Ireland Direct,** 08 00 89 03 53; **MCI WorldPhone,** 08 00 89 02 22; **New Zealand Direct,** 08 00 89 00 64. **Telkom South Africa,** 08 00 89 00 27. **Emergencies:** 999.

Languages: English and Welsh. Scottish Gaelic, though unofficial, is spoken in some parts of Scotland along with English.

ACCOMMODATIONS AND CAMPING. Britain has hundreds of **youth hostels,** both **HI** and independent. **YHA** (England and Wales) and **SYHA** (Scotland) are the national HI affiliates in Britain. Hostels here are sometimes closed from 10am to

BRITAIN

FLAKES AND SMARTIES British food has character (of one sort or another), and the traditional menu is a mad hodgepodge of candy, crisps, yeasts, and squashes. Britain has a greater variety of **candy** for sale than most countries. Brands to watch out for include Flake by Cadbury, Crunchies (made out of honeycombed magic), and the ever-popular Smarties. Watch out for the orange ones—they're made of orange chocolate. Potato chips, or **crisps** as they are known in England, are not just salted, but come in a range of flavors, including Prawn Cocktail, Beef, Chicken, Fruit 'n' Spice, and the more traditional Salt & Vinegar. All this sugar and salt can be washed down with pineapple-and-grapefruit-flavored soda Lilt or a can of Ribena, a red currant syrup which has to be diluted with water. This latter beverage belongs to a family of drinks known as **squash,** all of which are diluted before consumption. But the food that expatriate Britons miss most is **Marmite,** a yeast extract which is spread on bread or toast. If you weren't fed Marmite as a baby, you'll never appreciate it; most babies don't either.

5pm, and some impose an 11pm curfew. Some require sleep sacks; most prohibit sleeping bags. If these regulations cramp your style, stick to independent establishments. Remember, quality varies greatly. Always book ahead in high season.

The term **bed and breakfast** (B&B) generally means a small place that offers basic accommodations and breakfast at a reasonable price, often in private homes. B&Bs (usually £12-40, in London £16-60) are extremely widespread; when one is full, ask the owner for a referral. Some proprietors grant considerable rate reductions to guests who pay in advance or by the week and offer discounts between September and May. **Bed and Breakfast (G.B.),** P.O. Box 66, 94-96 Bell St, Henley-on-Thames, Oxon, England RG9 1XS (tel. (01491) 57 88 03; fax 41 08 06), covers London, England, Scotland, Wales, and Ireland (£30 deposit deducted from total price of stay). Cheap hotels, often called guest houses, can have better bargains than B&Bs.

FOOD AND DRINK. British cuisine's deservedly lackluster reputation redeems itself in a few areas. Britain is largely a nation of carnivores; the best native dishes are roasts—beef, lamb, and Wiltshire hams. And meat isn't just for dinner; the British like their famed breakfasts meaty and cholesterol-filled. Before you leave the country, you must try any of the sweet, glorious British puddings. The "ploughman's lunch" (a product of a 60s advertising campaign) consists of cheese, bread, relish, chutney, and a tomato. Fish and chips are traditionally drowned in vinegar and salt. Caffs (full meals £5-6) are the British equivalent of US diners. To escape English food, try Chinese, Greek, or especially Indian cuisine. British **"tea"** refers both to a drink and a social ritual. Tea the drink is served strong and milky; if you want it any other way, say so in advance. Tea the social can be a meal unto itself. Afternoon high tea as served in rural Britain includes cooked meats, salad, sandwiches, and pastries. Cream tea, a specialty of Cornwall and Devon, includes toast, shortbread, crumpets, scones, jam, and clotted cream.

The British **pub** is truly a social institution. Drinks (mostly beer) are generally served from 11am to 11pm, Sundays noon to 10:30pm. British beer is usually served room temperature. Lager (the European equivalent of American beer) is served colder. "Real ales" are beers naturally carbonated by an ongoing fermentation process. Traditional cider, a fermented apple juice served sweet or dry, is a potent and tasty alternative to beer. Pub grub is fast, filling, and generally cheap.

LOCAL FACTS

Discounts: Discount rates for students, seniors, children, and the unemployed are often grouped under the catch-all term "concessions."

Time: Britain is often on Greenwich Mean Time (GMT; see p. 49), but "British Summer Time" (late Mar.-late Oct.) is 1hr. ahead of GMT.

Climate: In summer, temperatures average 55-70°F (12-21°C); in winter, 36-41°F (2-7°C). The mild temperatures are often accompanied by rain. Spring is a good time to visit the countryside.

Holidays in 2000: New Year's Day (Jan. 1); Good Friday (Apr. 21); Easter Sunday and Monday (Apr. 23-24); May Day (May 1); May 29 (bank holiday); and Christmas (Dec. 25-26). Scotland also kicks back on Jan. 2 and Aug. 7 (both bank holidays).

Festivals: The largest festival in the world is the **Edinburgh International Festival** (Aug.). Manchester's Gay Village hosts **Mardi Gras** (late Aug). Muddy fun abounds at the **Glastonbury Festival. Highland Games** offer caber-tossing goodness in Edinburgh (mid-July).

ENGLAND

A land where there is the promise of a cup of tea just beyond even the darkest moor, England, for better or worse, has determined the meaning of "civilized" for many peoples and cultures. Unfortunately coasting on its Victorian domination, English civilization began to become a bit stagnant. However, its 20th-century image as the aging seat of a dying empire has made a remarkable turn-around in recent years. England is now the heart of "Cool Britannia," a young, fashionable, hip image of a country looking forward. The avant-garde has emerged from behind the sensible plaid skirts of the mainstream and taken center stage. More than ever, England is embracing its sizable immigrant communities and allowing the venerable class boat to be rocked. But traditionalists can rest easy; for all the moving and shaking in the large metropolis, around the corner there are a handful of quaint towns, dozen of picturesque castles, and a score of comforting cups of teas.

LONDON

Those who journey to London expecting friendly, tea-drinking, Royal-loving gardeners may be astounded to find that London is equally the province of black-clad slinky young things who spend their nights lounging around shadowy Soho bars. The stereotypical Londoner is almost impossible to define: both the snooty Kensington resident and the owner of an Indian takeaway in the East End hold equal claim to the title. Roman ruins stand next to thatched Shakespearean theaters, which jostle for space with glass skyscrapers and millennial landmarks. It's a dynamic, cosmopolitan city that defies simple categorization—administrative capital of Britain, financial center of Europe, and a world leader in the arts. While those who come to the city seeking a tweed domain of bobbies and Beefeaters will probably be able find it, you need only look at the array of hip restaurants or the queues in front of clubs to realize why they call it Swinging London. This dynamism comes at a price, in the form of costlier lodgings and food. Yet top-quality theater, museums, and galleries remain very much in the reach of any traveler.

For an absolutely smashing little book, peruse *Let's Go: London 2000*.

 Many area codes in the UK are changing. For long-distance calls to London (any call including the area code), both the new (020) and old (0171 or 0181) codes will work until fall 2000, after which only 020 will work. For local calls (those made without the area code), you must use the old number before April 22, 2000, and the new number starting April 22, 2000. *Let's Go* lists numbers as they will be after the change; if you are making a local call within London before April 22, drop the first digit of the eight-digit number. For more info, call the toll-free help line at (0808) 224 20 00 or try www.numberchange.org.

⌐ GETTING THERE AND AROUND

Flights: Heathrow Airport (tel. 87 59 43 21; www.baa.co.uk) is the world's busiest airport. The **Heathrow Express** (www.heathrowexpress.com) train goes between Heathrow terminals 1-4 and Paddington Station (every 15min. 5:10am-11:40pm, £10). London Transport's **Airbus** (tel. 72 22 12 34) zips from Heathrow to central points, including hotels

BRITAIN

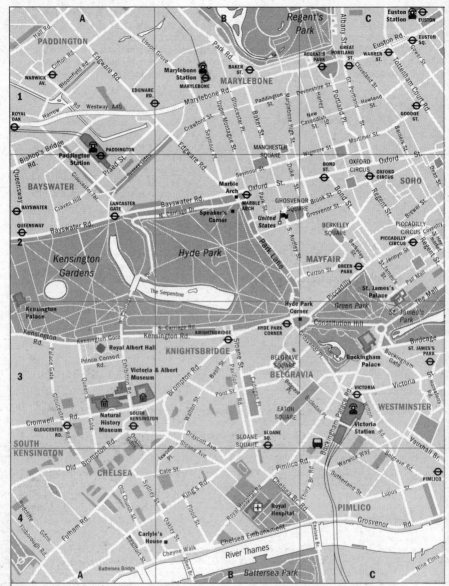

Central London: Major Street Finder
SEE COLOR INSERTS FOR MORE LONDON MAPS

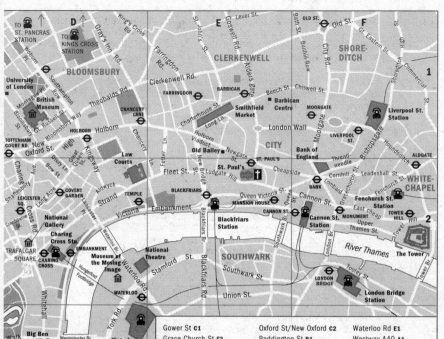

(1hr., £6). From **Gatwick Airport** (tel. (01293) 53 53 53), take the BR Gatwick Express train to Victoria Station (35min., every 15-30min. 24hr., £8.50). **National Express** (tel. (08705) 80 80 80) buses run from Victoria Station to Gatwick (1hr., every hr. 5:05am-8:20pm, £8.50). **Taxis** take twice as long and cost 5 times as much.

Trains: London has 8 major stations: **Charing Cross** (serves south England); **Euston** (the north and northwest, including Birmingham, Glasgow, Holyhead, Inverness, Liverpool, and Manchester); **King's Cross** (the north and northeast, including Cambridge, Edinburgh, Leeds, Newcastle, and York); **Liverpool St** (East Anglia, including Colchester, Ipswich, and Norwich, as well as Stansted Airport); **Paddington** (the west, including Oxford, the southwest, including Bristol, and South Wales, including Cardiff); **St. Pancras** (The Midlands, including Nottingham and Sheffield); **Victoria** (the south, including Brighton, Canterbury, Dover, and Hastings, as well as Gatwick Airport); and **Waterloo** (the south and southwest, including Portsmouth and Salisbury, and the Continent). All stations are linked by Underground. Get info at station ticket offices, tourist offices, or from the **National Rail Inquires Line** (tel. (0345) 48 49 50; www.britrail.com).

Buses: Victoria Coach Station, on Buckingham Palace Rd. Tube: Victoria. The hub of Britain's denationalized coaches. **National Express** (tel. (08705) 80 80 80) runs an expansive nationwide network. **Green Line** (tel. 86 68 72 61; www.greenline.co.uk), which serves the Greater London area, leaves frequently from Eccleston Bridge behind Victoria Station. Buy tickets from the driver. Deals include the one-day **Rover** ticket (£7, valid on Green Line coaches and London County buses M-F after 9am, Sa-Su all day).

Public Transportation: London is divided into 6 concentric transport zones; fares depend on the distance and number of zones crossed. The **24-hour help line** (tel. 72 22 12 34) helps plan subway and bus travel. The **Underground** (or **Tube**) is fast, efficient, and crowded. Open daily 6am-midnight. Buy your ticket before you board and pass it through automatic gates at both ends of your journey. The **Travelcard,** a must for budget travelers, is valid on the Underground, regular buses, British Rail (Network SouthEast), and the Docklands Light Railway. Available in 1-day, 1-week, and 1-month increments from any station; some restrictions apply. The **bus** network is divided into 4 zones. In and around central London, single fares range from £0.50-1.20, depending on the number of zones crossed. **Night buses** ("N") run frequently throughout London 11:30pm-6am; all pass through Trafalgar Sq. Pick up free maps and guides at **London Transport Information Centres** (look for the lower-case "**i**" logo on signs) at the following Tube stations: Euston, Victoria, King's Cross, Liverpool St, Oxford Circus, Piccadilly, and St. James's Park; you can also find them at Heathrow Terminals 1, 2, and 4.

Taxis: A light signifies that they're empty. Fares are steep, and 10% tip is standard.

Hitchhiking: Anyone who values safety will take a train or bus out of London. **Freewheelers** is a ride-share agency. Single-sex matching available. For more info, email freewheelers@freewheelers.co.uk or check out www.freewheelers.co.uk/freewheelers.

✦ ORIENTATION

London is a colossal aggregate of distinct villages and anonymous suburbs, of ancient settlements and modern developments. **Central London,** on the north side of the Thames, bounded roughly by the Underground's Circle Line, contains most major sights. Within Central London, the vaguely defined **West End,** south of Oxford St, incorporates the understated elegance of **Mayfair,** the shopping streets around **Oxford Circus,** the theaters and tourist traps of **Piccadilly Circus** and **Leicester Square,** bohemian **Soho,** yuppie **Covent Garden,** and London's unofficial center, **Trafalgar Square.** East of the West End lies **Holborn,** center of legal activity, and **Fleet Street,** journalists' traditional haunt. North of Oxford St are literary **Bloomsbury** and embassy-filled **Marylebone.** To the southwest are posh **Knightsbridge, Kensington,** and **Belgravia,** and to the west lie the ethnically vibrant **Notting Hill** and **Bayswater** districts. Around the southeastern corner of the Circle Line is **The City,** which refers to the ancient, and much smaller, "City of London," which covers only one of the 620 sq. mi. of today's Greater London. Today the City is the financial nerve center of London, with the Tower of London at its eastern edge and St. Paul's Cathedral nearby. Farther east is the ethnically diverse, working-class **East End.** Moving back west, along the river and the southern part of the Circle Line is the district of **Westminster,** just south of the West End, where you'll find Buckingham Palace, the **Houses of Parliament,** and Westminster Abbey. Trendy residential districts stretch to the north, including **Hampstead** and **Highgate,** with the enormous Hampstead Heath.

The most useful navigational aids are street atlases, such as *London A to Z* (the "A to Zed"), *ABC Street Atlas*, Nicholson's *London Streetfinder*, or *Let's Go Map Guide: London.* London is divided into boroughs and into postal code areas, whose letters stand for compass directions. The borough name and postal code appear at the bottom of most street signs; *Let's Go* lists postal codes in addresses.

ⓐ PRACTICAL INFORMATION

TOURIST, FINANCIAL, AND LOCAL SERVICES

Tourist Offices: London Tourist Board Information Centre, Victoria Station Forecourt, SW1 (recorded info tel. (0839) 12 34 32, £0.39-0.49 per min.; accommodations service tel. 79 32 20 20, fax 79 32 20 21). Tube: Victoria. Books plays and tours; also books rooms for £5 plus 15% deposit (cheapest rooms £22, most £25-30). Long waits around noon. Also at **Victoria Station** (open Apr.-Nov. daily 8am-7pm; Dec.-Mar. M-Sa 8am-7pm, Su 8am-5pm); **Heathrow Airport** (open daily Apr.-Nov. 9am-6pm; Dec.-Mar. 9am-5pm); and the **Liverpool St Underground Station** (open M 8:15am-7pm, Tu-Sa 8:15am-6pm, Su 8:30am-4:45pm). **City of London Information Centre,** at St. Paul's Churchyard, EC4 (tel. 76 06 30 30). Tube: St. Paul's. Open Apr.-Sept. daily 9:30am-5pm; Oct.-Mar. M-F 9:30am-5pm, Sa 9:30am-12:30pm. **British Travel Centre,** 12 Regent St, SW1. Tube: Piccadilly Circus ("Lower Regent St" exit). Run by British Tourist Authority. Changes money; books rooms (£5 plus deposit; does not book for hostels); sells maps, theater tickets, and pamphlets. Long lines. Open M-F 9am-6:30pm, Sa-Su 10am-4pm.

Tours: *Time Out* lists walks in its "Around Town" section. **The Original London Sightseeing Tour** (tel. 88 77 17 22) gives a convenient though cursory overview of London's attractions from a double-decker bus (£12). **The Original London Walks** (tel. 76 24 39 78) cover "Jack the Ripper" to "Spies and Spycatchers" (£4.50, students £3.50).

Budget Travel: Wasteels, at Victoria Station, SW1V 1JT (tel. 78 34 70 66; fax 76 30 76 28; www.wasteels.dk/uk). Sells discounted BIJ train tickets to those under 26.

Embassies and High Commissions: Australia, Australia House, The Strand, WC2 (tel. 73 79 43 34). Tube: Aldwych or Temple. Open M-F 9:30am-3:30pm. **Canada,** MacDonald House, 1 Grosvenor Sq, W1 (tel. 72 58 66 00). Tube: Bond St or Oxford Circus. **Ireland,** 17 Grosvenor Pl, SW1 (tel. 72 35 21 71). Tube: Hyde Park Corner. Open M-F 9:30am-1pm and 2:30-5pm. **New Zealand,** New Zealand House, 80 Haymarket, SW1 (tel. 79 30 84 22). Open M-F 10am-noon and 2-4pm. **South Africa,** South Africa House, Trafalgar Sq, WC2 (tel. 74 51 72 99). Tube: Charing Cross. Open M-F 10am-noon and 2-4pm. **US,** 24 Grosvenor Sq, W1 (tel. 74 99 90 00). Tube: Bond St. Phones answered 24hr.

Currency Exchange: The best rates are available walk-in at **High St** banks, including **Barclay's, Lloyd's, National Westminster (NatWest),** and **HSBC (Midland).**

American Express: Offices throughout London; call (0800) 52 13 13 for the closest one.

Gay and Lesbian Services: London Lesbian and Gay Switchboard (tel. 78 37 73 24). 24hr. advice and support service.

EMERGENCY AND COMMUNICATIONS

Emergencies: Tel. 999 or 112 (police, ambulance, and fire); no coins required.

Police: Stations in every district of London. **Headquarters,** New Scotland Yard, Broadway, SW1 (tel. 72 30 12 12). Tube: St. James's Park. **West End Central,** 10 Vine St, W1 (tel. 74 37 12 12). Tube: Piccadilly Circus.

Crisis Lines: Samaritans: (tel. 77 34 28 00). 24-hour crisis hotline.

Pharmacies: Every police station keeps a list of emergency doctors and pharmacists in its district. See listings under "Chemists" in the Yellow Pages. **Bliss Chemists,** 5 Marble Arch, W1 (tel. 77 23 61 16). Open daily (including public holidays) 9am-midnight.

BRITAIN

Medical Assistance: In an emergency, you can be treated at no charge in the Accidents and Emergencies (A&E; a.k.a. casualty) ward of a hospital. The following have 24-hour walk-in: **Royal London Hospital,** on Whitechapel Rd, E1 (tel. 73 77 70 00). Tube: Whitechapel. **Royal Free Hospital,** on Pond St, NW3 (tel. 77 94 05 00). Tube: Belsize Park. Rail: Hampstead Heath. **Charing Cross Hospital,** on Fulham Palace Rd (entrance on St. Dunstan's Rd), W6 (tel. 88 46 12 34). Tube: Baron's Court or Hammersmith. **St. Thomas' Hospital,** on Lambeth Palace Rd, SE1 (tel. 79 28 92 92). Tube: Westminster. **University College Hospital,** on Gower St (entrance on Grafton Way), WC1 (tel. 73 87 93 00). Tube: Euston or Warren St. **Eastman Dental Hospital** (tel. 79 15 10 00).

Internet Access: ■ **easyEverything,** 9-13 Wilson Rd, W1, opposite Victoria Station. Tube: Victoria. The owners of easyJet bring you this dirt-cheap internet emporium, with over 400 terminals. £1 per hr. Open 24hr. **Webshack,** 15 Dean St, W1. Tube: Leicester Sq. or Tottenham Ct Rd. £3 per 30min.; £5 per hr. Open M-Sa 10:30am-11pm.

Telephones: Most accept change and phonecards; some take only phonecards.

Post Offices: Call (0345) 22 33 44 to find the nearest one. When sending mail to the UK, be sure to include the postal district. The main office is the **Trafalgar Square Post Office,** 24-28 William IV St (tel. 930 95 80). Tube: Charing Cross. Address mail to be held: Megan <u>CHAN</u>, *Poste Restante,* Trafalgar Sq Post Office, WC2N 4DL London, UK. Open M-Th and Sa 8am-8pm, F 8:30am-8pm.

PHONE CODE	City code: 020. From outside the UK, dial int'l dialing prefix (see inside back cover) + 44 + 20 + local number.

■ ACCOMMODATIONS

Reserve rooms in advance for summer—landing in London without reservations is like landing on a bicycle with no seat. B&Bs are a bargain for groups of two or more, but hostels are the cheapest (and most social) option for small groups.

YHA/HI HOSTELS

London's YHA hostels are cheap and cheery and usually require HI membership. Reserve ahead or check for last-minute rooms through the central office (tel. 72 48 65 47; open M-Sa 9am-5pm). Bring a padlock for lockers.

Oxford Street, 14-18 Noel St, W1 (tel. 77 34 16 18). Tube: Oxford Circus. Walk east on Oxford St and turn right on Poland St. As close as possible to Soho action. Dorms £18.70; doubles £41. Laundry. Reception 7am-11pm. Reserve 3-4 weeks ahead.

City of London, 36 Carter Ln, EC4 (tel. 72 36 49 65). Tube: St. Paul's. Go left down Godliman St, take the 1st right, and look for the sign. Scrupulously clean and quiet comfort a stone's throw from St. Paul's. Luggage storage. Dorms £19-22; singles £25; doubles £49; triples £67.50; quads £57. Laundry. Currency exchange. Reception 7am-11pm.

Holland House (tel. 79 37 07 48), on Holland Walk, W8. Tube: High St Kensington. Handsome 1607 Jacobean mansion nestled in Holland Park offers lovely green views and a multilingual staff. Dorms £19.45; HI members only. Breakfast included. Laundry.

Earl's Court, Earl's Ct, 38 Bolton Gdns, SW5 (tel. 73 73 70 83; fax 78 35 20 34). Tube: Earl's Ct; exit on Earl's Ct Rd. and turn right; it's the 5th street on your left. Clean townhouse in a leafy residential neighborhood. All rooms single-sex. £18.70; nonmembers add £1.70; students £1 less. Laundry. Currency exchange. Reception 7am-11pm.

King's Cross/St. Pancras, 79-81 Euston Rd, N1 (tel. 73 88 99 98). Tube: King's Cross/ St. Pancras or Euston. Brand-spanking-new 8-story hostel with a convenient location and comfortable beds. Ask in advance about A/C. Dorms £18.65-22.15; doubles £23.50; quads £77.80; quints £97.50. Laundry. 1-week max. stay.

PRIVATE HOSTELS

■ **Ashlee House,** 261-65 Gray's Inn Rd, WC1 (tel. 78 33 94 00; email ashleehouse@tsnxt.co.uk). Tube: King's Cross/St. Pancras. From King's Cross, turn right on Pentonville Rd and right again on Gray's Inn Rd. Clean, bright rooms. Large dorms £13; smaller dorms £17-22. Breakfast included. Laundry. Reception 24hr. Check-out 10am.

BRITAIN

It's a **big world.**

And **we've got** the **network** to cover it.

Use **AT&T Direct**® Service
when you're out exploring the world.

©1999 AT&T

Global
connection
with the AT&T
Network

AT&T
direct
service

Exploring the corners of the earth? We're with you. With the world's most powerful network, **AT&T Direct® Service** gives you fast, clear connections from more countries than anyone,* and the option of an English-speaking operator. All it takes is your AT&T Calling Card. And the planet is yours.

For a list of AT&T Access Numbers, take the attached wallet guide.

AT&T

*Comparison to major U.S.-based carriers.

 AT&T

AT&T Direct® Service

AT&T Access Numbers

Austria ●	0800-200-288
Albania ●	00-800-0010
Armenia ● ▲	8◆10111
Bahrain	800-000
Belgium ●	0-800-100-10
Bulgaria ▲	00-800-0010
Croatia	0800-220111
Czech Rep. ▲	00-42-000-101
Cyprus ●	080-90010
Denmark	8001-0010

Egypt ● (Cairo)	510-0200
(Outside Cairo)	02-510-0200
Estonia	800-800-1001
Finland ●	9800-100-10
France	0-800-99-0011
Germany	0800-2255-288
Greece ●	00-800-1311
Hungary ●	00-800-01111
Ireland ✓	1-800-550-000
Israel	1-800-94-94-949

Italy ●	172-1011
Luxembourg †	0-800-0111
Macedonia, F.Y.R. of ○	
	99-800-4288
Malta	0800-890-110
Monaco ●	800-90-288
Morocco	002-11-0011
Netherlands ●	0800-022-9111
Norway	800-190-11
Poland ● ▲	00-800-111-1111
Portugal ▲	0800-800-128
Romania ●	01-800-4288

Russia ● ▲	
(Moscow) ▶	755-5042
(St. Petersburg) ▶	325-5042
Saudi Arabia ◇	1-800-10
South Africa	0-800-99-0123
Spain	900-99-00-11
Sweden	020-799-111
Switzerland ●	0-800-89-0011
Turkey ●	00-800-12277
U.K. ▲ ❖	0800-89-0011
U.K. ▲ ❖	0500-89-0011
U.A. Emirates ●	800-121

FOR EASY CALLING WORLDWIDE

1. Just dial the AT&T Access Number for the country you are calling from.
2. Dial the phone number you're calling. *3.* Dial your card number.

For access numbers not listed ask any operator for **AT&T Direct®** Service. In the U.S. call 1-800-331-1140 for a wallet guide listing all worldwide AT&T Access Numbers.
Visit our Web site at: www.att.com/traveler
Bold-faced countries permit country-to-country calling outside the U.S.
- ● Public phones require coin or card deposit.
- ▲ May not be available from every phone/payphone.
- ▶ Additional charges apply outside the city.
- ◇ Calling available to most countries.
- ◆ Await second dial tone.
- ✓ Use U.K. access number in N. Ireland.
- ❖ If call does not complete, use 0800-013-0011.
- † Collect calling from public phones.
- ○ Public phones require local coin payment through the call duration.

When placing an international call *from* the U.S., dial 1 800 CALL ATT.

© 1999 AT&T

Albert Hotel, 191 Queens Gate, SW7 (tel. 75 84 30 19; www.thealberthotel.london.co.uk). Tube: Gloucester Rd; turn right on Cromwell and left on Queen's Gate. Or take bus 2 or 70 from South Kensington. A walk from the Tube; near Hyde Park. Dorms £14-16; singles and doubles £22.50-35. Breakfast included. Laundry. Reception 24hr.

International Student House, 229 Great Portland St, W1 (tel. 76 31 83 00; fax 76 31 83 15). Across from Tube: Great Portland St, at the foot of Regent's Park. Films, concerts, discos, athletic contests, expeditions, and parties. Over 500 beds. Dorms £10; singles £28, with ISIC £21; doubles £20, £16; triples £16.50, £13. Rooms with bath and phone £4 extra. Breakfast included except for dorms. Laundry. Currency exchange.

Astor's Museum Inn (tel. 75 80 53 60), on Montague St, WC1, off Bloomsbury Sq. Tube: Holborn, Tottenham Ct Rd, or Russell Sq. Prime location compensates for standard dorms. If they're full, they'll direct you to other Astor hostels. Co-ed dorms Apr.-Sept. £14-17; Oct.-Mar. reduced. Breakfast included. Reception 24hr. Reserve 1 month ahead.

Curzon House Hotel, 58 Courtfield Gdns, SW5 (tel. 75 81 21 16; fax 78 35 13 19). Tube: Gloucester Rd; take a right on to Gloucester Rd, then turn right on Courtfield Rd, and right again on Courtfield Gdns. TV lounge. No bunk beds; single-sex rooms. 4-bed dorm £17; singles £30; doubles £44; triples £39. Breakfast included. Kitchen.

Quest Hotel, 45 Queensborough Terr, W2 (tel. 72 29 77 82; fax 77 27 81 06). Tube: Queensway; head 2 blocks right on Bayswater Rd and then turn left on Queensborough Terrace. Clean, and sociable, with a pool room. 4- to 8-bed dorms (co-ed and 1 women-only) £15; 2-bed dorm £18. Breakfast included. Kitchen. **Internet.** Check-out 10am.

Hyde Park Hostel, 2-6 Inverness Terr, W2 (tel. 72 29 51 01). Tube: Bayswater or Queensway. New and conveniently located. Travel center. Pool room/lounge. Dorms £12-16. Key deposit £5. Breakfast included. Laundry. **Internet.** Reception 24hr.

O'Callaghan's Hotel, 205 Earl's Ct Rd, SW5 (tel. 73 70 30 00; fax 73 70 26 23). Tube: Earl's Ct. Friendly management will pick you up from Victoria Station and drive you to the 2 other branches if O'Callaghan's is full. Dorms in summer £12, in winter £10; doubles £35, £30. Weekly dorms: in summer, £70, in winter £60. Reception 24hr.

Tonbridge School Clubs, Ltd (tel. 78 37 44 06), at Judd and Cromer St, WC1. Tube: King's Cross/St. Pancras; follow Euston Rd to the new British Library and go 3 blocks left on Judd. Be cautious in the area at night. No frills—blankets and foam pads £5. Students with non-British passports only. Lockout 9am-9pm. Curfew midnight.

Victoria Hotel, 71 Belgrave Rd, SW1 (tel. 78 34 30 77). Tube: Pimlico; take the "Bessborough St" exit, go left on Lupus St, and go right at St. George's Sq on Belgrave Rd. Bohemian hostel with pool room. Dorms £14-16. Breakfast included. Reception 24hr.

HALLS OF RESIDENCE

The rooms rented out by London universities are generally the cheapest singles available, particularly if you have a student ID. Rooms tend to be standard spartan student digs but clean. The halls usually offer rooms to individuals for two or three months over the summer, and during the long Easter break in the spring. Some reserve a few rooms for travelers year-round. The **King's Campus Vacation Bureau,** 127 Stanford St, SE1 (tel. 79 28 37 77), books rooms at several halls in summer.

Hampstead Campus, 23 Kidderpore Ave, NW3 (tel. 79 28 37 77; fax 74 31 44 02; email vac.bureau@kcl.ac.uk). Tube: Finchley Rd or West Hampstead, then take bus 13, 28, 82, or 113 to "Platt's Ln" on Finchley Rd; turn on Platt's Ln and turn right on Kidderpore Ave. Rooms with phone, basin, desk, and wardrobe. Kitchen and TV lounge. Singles £16.50; twins £28.50. Stays of 7 nights or more: 10% discount. Open mid-June to mid-Sept.

Stamford Street Apartments, 127 Stamford St, SE1 (tel. 78 73 29 60; fax 78 73 29 64). Tube: Waterloo; take the "Waterloo Bridge" exit, take the pedestrian "Subway to York Road," and follow it around the circle to reach Stamford St. TV lounge. 560 spacious singles with fridge and attached bath, £32.50. Stays of 7 nights or more 10% discount. Laundry. Reception 24hr. Open July-Sept.

High Holborn Residence, 178 High Holborn, WC1 (tel. 7379 5589; fax 7379 5640). Tube: Holborn; walk 10min. down High Holborn. Spacious, well-furnished singles in flats for 4-5 people. Lounge and bar. Singles £32; twins £54, with bath £65. Breakfast included. Kitchen. Laundry. Reception 7am-11pm. Reserve ahead. Open July to mid-Sept.

BRITAIN

Queen Alexandra's House (tel. 75 89 36 35; fax 75 89 31 77), at Kensington Gore, SW7. Tube: South Kensington, or take bus 9, 10, or 52 to Royal Albert Hall; it's to the right as you face the front of Royal Albert Hall. Victorian building opposite Hyde Park. No visitors 11pm-10am. **Women only.** Cozy singles £25. Breakfast included. Kitchen. Laundry.

John Adams Hall, 15-23 Endsleigh St, WC1 (tel. 73 87 40 86; fax 73 83 01 64). Tube: Euston; go right on Euston Rd, right on Gordon St, left on Endsleigh Gdns, and right on Endsleigh St. TV lounge. 124 small, simple singles; 22 doubles. Singles £22, with ISIC £20; doubles £38, 6 or more nights £35 each. English breakfast included. Laundry. Reception 8am-1pm and 2-10pm. Open July-Aug. and Easter.

BED & BREAKFASTS

The number of B&Bs in London boggles the mind. Some are dingy and indistinct; others feature unique furnishings and a warm, welcoming atmosphere. Breakfast is included (as one might guess) in all instances.

NEAR VICTORIA STATION

B&Bs around Victoria Station are close to London's attractions and transportation connections. In summer, make reservations well in advance.

■ **Melbourne House,** 79 Belgrave Rd, SW1 (tel. 78 28 35 16), past Warwick Sq. Tube: Pimlico; take the "Bessborough St (south side)" exit, go left on Lupus St and right at St. George's Sq onto Belgrave Rd. Sparkling rooms with TVs, phones, and hotpots. Singles £30-50; doubles or twins with bath £70; triples £95; quads £110. Winter discount.

■ **Luna and Simone Hotel,** 47-49 Belgrave Rd, SW1 (tel. 78 34 58 97), past Warwick St. Tube: Victoria or Pimlico. Immaculate and well-maintained. Singles £28-34; doubles £48-55, with bath £50-70; triples £90. Winter discount. 10% off for long-term stays.

Georgian House Hotel, 35 St. George's Dr, SW1 (tel. 78 34 14 38). Tube: Victoria. Spacious rooms with personality. Ask about the quieter, older annex nearby. Singles £23-46; doubles £36-62; triples £62-75; quads £62-85. Reception 8am-11pm.

Surtees Hotel, 94 Warwick Way, SW1 (tel. 78 34 71 63; fax 74 60 87 47; www.zendens.uninet.co.uk/surtees). Tube: Victoria. Cheerful hotel. Great breakfast. Rooms with shower and toilet. Singles £45; doubles £50-60; triples £60; quads £80.

Oxford House, 92-94 Cambridge St, SW1 (tel. 78 34 96 81; fax 78 34 02 25), near the church. Tube: Victoria; from St. George's Dr, turn right on Clarendon St and left on Cambridge St. Quiet area and well-prepared breakfast. Comfortable, clean rooms. Singles £36; doubles £46-48; triples £60-63; quads £80-84. Reserve 3-4 weeks ahead.

EARL'S COURT

The area feeds on the tourist trade and has a vibrant gay and lesbian population. Rooms tend to be dirt-cheap, but ask to see a room to make sure the "dirt" isn't literal. Travelers with bags will be harassed by hustlers hawking accommodations.

York House Hotel, 27-28 Philbeach Gdns, SW5 (tel. 73 73 75 19). Tube: Earl's Ct. Extraordinarily clean, with a 60s-style TV lounge and lovely garden. Low prices. Singles £32-45; doubles £50, with bath £69; triples £61, with bath £80; quads £67.

Mowbray Court Hotel, 28-32 Penywern Rd, SW5 (tel. 73 73 82 85). Tube: Earl's Ct. Fairly expensive, but with a helpful staff and clean rooms. Tours and theater bookings available. Singles £42-50; doubles £52-63; triples £66-75. Continental breakfast included.

Philbeach Hotel, 30-31 Philbeach Gdns, SW5 (tel. 73 73 12 44; fax 72 44 01 49). Tube: Earl's Ct. The largest gay B&B in England, popular with both men and women. Upscale, award-winning restaurant. Singles £45-55; doubles £60-80. Reserve ahead.

KENSINGTON AND CHELSEA

These hotels are convenient for those who wish to visit the array of museums that lines the southwest side of Hyde Park. Prices are a bit higher, but hotels are generally more comfortable than many at Earl's Ct. Most require reservations.

■ **Abbey House Hotel,** 11 Vicarage Gate, W8 (tel. 77 27 25 94), off Kensington Church St. Tube: High St Kensington. The comfort level can't be rivaled at these prices. Tea 24hr. Singles £43; doubles £68; triples £85; quads £95; quints £105. Irish breakfast included.

BRITAIN

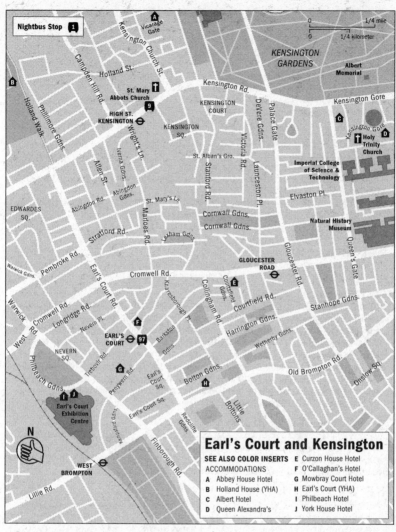

Earl's Court and Kensington

Nightbus Stop

KENSINGTON GARDENS
Albert Memorial
Kensington Gore
Kensington Rd.
St. Mary Abbots Church
HIGH ST. KENSINGTON
KENSINGTON COURT
Holy Trinity Church
KENSINGTON SQ.
St. Alban's Gro.
Imperial College of Science & Technology
Elvaston Pl.
EDWARDES SQ.
St. Mary's Lo.
Cornwall Gdns.
Cornwall Gdns.
Natural History Museum
GLOUCESTER ROAD
Cromwell Rd.
Courtfield Rd.
Stanhope Gdns.
EARL'S COURT 97
Harrington Gdns.
Wetherby Gdns.
Old Brompton Rd.
Onslow Sq.
NEVERN SQ.
Earl's Court Sq.
Bolton Gdns.
Earl's Court Exhibition Centre
WEST BROMPTON
Lillie Rd.

SEE ALSO COLOR INSERTS
ACCOMMODATIONS
A Abbey House Hotel
B Holland House (YHA)
C Albert Hotel
D Queen Alexandra's
E Curzon House Hotel
F O'Callaghan's Hotel
G Mowbray Court Hotel
H Earl's Court (YHA)
I Philbeach Hotel
J York House Hotel

Oakley Hotel, 73 Oakley St, SW3 (tel. 73 52 55 99). Tube: Sloane Sq; South Kensington; or Victoria, then take bus 11, 19, or 22. Turn left off King's Rd at the Chelsea Fire Station. Amiable staff; lovely bedrooms. Dorms (women-only) £14; singles £32; doubles £48, with bath £58; triples £63, with bath £72; quads £72; quints £80. Kitchen.

BLOOMSBURY

Despite its proximity to the West End, Bloomsbury maintains a fairly residential demeanor, with gracious, tree-filled squares and a prime location.

Arosfa Hotel, 83 Gower St, WC1 (tel./fax 76 36 21 15). Tube: Goodge St. All furnishings and fixtures are nearly new, the rooms are spacious, and the facilities are immaculate. Singles £33; doubles £46, with bath £60; triples £62, with bath £73.

Ridgemount Hotel, 65-67 Gower St, WC1 (tel. 76 36 11 41 or 75 80 70 60). Tube: Goodge St. Bright rooms with firm beds. TV lounge. Singles £31, with bath £41; doubles £46, £58; triples £60, £72. Irish breakfast included. Laundry. Call ahead.

Mentone Hotel, 54-55 Cartwright Gdns, WC1 (tel. 7387 3927). Tube: Russell Sq. Pleasant decor; newly renovated. Airport shuttle to hotel available with advance reservation. Singles £42-60; doubles £78; quads £93. Dec.-Apr. discount. Irish breakfast included.

Cosmo/Bedford House Hotel, 27 Bloomsbury Sq, WC1 (tel. 7636 4661; fax 7636 0577; email cosmo.bedford.hotel@dial.pipex.com). From Holborn Tube station, take Southampton Row, then the 2nd left onto Bloomsbury Pl; it's on the right. Comfortable rooms with TVs. Singles £36, with bath £48; doubles £58, £70; triples £75, £85.

Jesmond Dene Hotel, 27 Argyle St, WC1 (tel. 78 37 46 54; www.scoot.co.uk/jesmond-dene). Spotless rooms with TVs, sinks, and black-and-white decor. Singles £28; doubles £40-55; triples £55-70; quads £85; quints £85. Irish breakfast included. Call weeks in advance.

PADDINGTON AND BAYSWATER

🎖 **Hyde Park Rooms Hotel,** 137 Sussex Gdns, W2 (tel. 77 23 02 25 or 77 23 09 65). Tube: Paddington. Turn right as you exit the Tube station, then right on London St and left on Sussex Gdns. Family-run, with airy rooms. Outstanding value. Singles £26, with bath £38; doubles £38, £48; triples £57, £72. Reserve ahead.

Garden Court Hotel, 30-31 Kensington Gdns Sq, W2 (tel. 72 29 25 53). Tube: Bayswater. Turn left on Queensway, left on Porchester Gdns, and right on Kensington Gdns Sq. Fairly large hotel in a pleasant, leafy neighborhood. Singles £34, with bath £48; doubles £52, £76; triples £72, £86. Check-out 11am. Reserve ahead with 1 night's deposit.

Dean Court Hotel, 57 Inverness Terr, W2 (tel. 72 29 29 61). Tube: Bayswater or Queensway. Inverness is the 1st left off Bayswater Rd. Clean, functional rooms with firm mattresses. No private facilities. Dorms £14; doubles £45; twins £42; triples £60.

BELSIZE PARK

Dillons Hotel, 21 Belsize Park, NW3 (tel. 77 94 33 60; fax 74 31 79 00; email desk@dillonshotel.demon.co.uk). Tube: Belsize Park. Head right up Haverstock Hill and take the 2nd left on Belsize Ave, which becomes Belsize Park. 15 large rooms with basic furnishings. Singles £27-36; doubles £40-49; triples £46-54; quads £60. Every 7th night free. Reception daily 9am-12:30pm and 1:30-5pm. Continental breakfast included.

Buckland Hotel, 6 Buckland Crescent, NW3 (tel. 77 22 55 74; fax 77 22 55 94). Tube: Belsize Park. Head right up Haverstock Hill and take the 2nd left on Belsize Ave, which leads to Buckland Crescent. 16 clean, modern rooms with TVs. Singles £22-50; doubles £65. 4 or more £18-19 per person. Family room £90. Continental breakfast included.

🖸 FOOD AND PUBS

London presents a tantalizing range of foreign and English specialties. Indian, Lebanese, Greek, Chinese, Thai, Italian, West Indian, and African food is inexpensive and readily available. If you eat but one meal in London, let it be Indian.

THE WEST END

🎖 **Yo!Sushi,** 52 Polant St, W1. Tube: Oxford Circus. An eating experience, with conveyor-belt dining and a robotic drink cart. Inventive sushi £1.50-3. Open daily noon-midnight.

🎖 **Belgo Centraal,** 50 Earlham St, WC2, and **Belgo Noord,** 72 Chalk Farm Rd in Camden Town, NW1. Waiters in monk's cowls. Bizarre 21st-century beer-hall decor. Wild boar sausage and Belgian mash. Open M-Sa noon-11:30pm, Su noon-10:30pm.

Mandeer, 8 Bloomsbury Way. Tube: Tottenham Ct Rd. A few streets off New Oxford St, Mandeer offers some of the best Indian food around and the chance to learn about owner Ramesh Patel's Ayurvedic Science of Life. Food is fresh, organic, and vegetarian. Lunch buffet options from £3.50. Open M-Sa for lunch (self-service) noon-3pm, dinner 5-10pm.

Lok Ho Fook, 4-5 Gerrard St, W1. Busy, with good prices and welcoming atmosphere. Extensive seafood, noodles, and vegetarian dishes. Dim sum noon-6pm. Not to be confused with the nearby and expensive Lee Ho Fook. Open daily noon-11:45pm.

Neal's Yard Salad Bar, 2 Neal's Yard, WC2. Takeaway or sit outside at this simple vegetarian's nirvana. Tempting salads from £2. Open daily 11am-9pm.

The Stockpot, 18 Old Compton St, W1. Tube: Leicester Sq or Piccadilly Circus. Also at 40 Panton St. The cheapest place in Soho to soak up style. Open M-Tu 11:30am-11:30pm, W-Sa 11:30am-11:45pm, Su noon-11pm.

BRITAIN

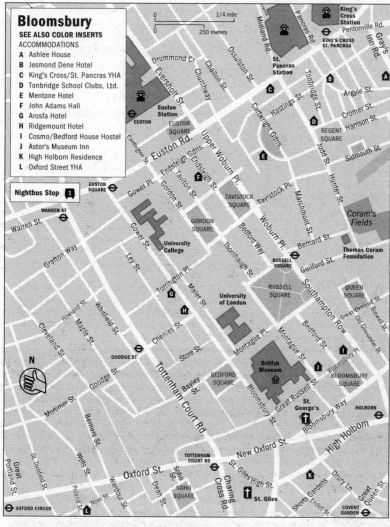

Bloomsbury

SEE ALSO COLOR INSERTS

ACCOMMODATIONS

A Ashlee House
B Jesmond Dene Hotel
C King's Cross/St. Pancras YHA
D Tonbridge School Clubs, Ltd.
E Mentone Hotel
F John Adams Hall
G Arosfa Hotel
H Ridgemount Hotel
I Cosmo/Bedford House Hostel
J Astor's Museum Inn
K High Holborn Residence
L Oxford Street YHA

Nightbus Stop 1

KENSINGTON AND CHELSEA

Ciaccio, 5 Warwick Way, SW1. Tube: Pimlico. Italian eatery whose prices and spices make it a giant for budget eaters. Pick a pasta and one of about 10 sauces, and they'll heat it in the microwave for £1.69-2.85. Open M-F 10am-7pm, Sa 9:30am-6pm.

Apadna, 351 Kensington High St, W8. Tube: Kensington High St. A 10min. walk from the Tube and an escape from the street's commercial banality. Savory kebabs in fresh-baked *naan*. Minced lamb kebab £2.80. Open daily 11am-11pm.

BLOOMSBURY AND NORTH LONDON

🏅 **Wagamama,** 4a Streatham St, WC1. Tube: Tottenham Ct Rd. Fast food: waitstaff takes your order on hand-held electronic radios that transmit directly to the kitchen. Noodles £4.50-5.70. Open M-Sa noon-11pm, Su 12:30-10pm.

Troubador Coffee House, 265 Old Brompton Rd, SW5. Tube: Earl's Ct. Live music. Snacks and sandwiches under £4. Open M-Sa 9:30am-12:30am, Su 9:30am-11pm.

BRITAIN

NOTTING HILL AND EARL'S COURT

■ **The Grain Shop,** 269a Portobello Rd, W11. Tube: Ladbroke Grove. Large array of tasty takeaway foods. Organic breads (£0.80-1.40) and groceries. Open M-Sa 9:30am-6pm.

Cockney's, 314 Portobello Rd, W10. Tube: Ladbroke Grove. "Traditional pie, mash, and eels," says the sign above the door, and they aren't joking. Eel available F-Sa. Cups of liquor only 30p. Open M-Th and Sa 11:30am-5:30pm, F 11:30am-6pm.

PUBS

The clientele of London's 700 pubs varies widely from one neighborhood to the next. For the best prices, head to the **East End.** Stylish, lively pubs cluster around the fringes of the **West End.**

■ **The Dog and Duck,** 8 Bateman St, W1. Tube: Tottenham Ct Rd. Frequent winner of the Best Pub in Soho award. Evenings bring locals, theater-goers, and some tourists. Cheap pints (£2.30). Open M-F noon-11pm, Sa 6-11pm, Su 7-10:30pm.

The Three Greyhounds, 25 Greek St, W1. Tube: Leicester Sq. This medieval-style pub provides a respite from the posturing of Soho. Open M-Sa 11am-11pm, Su noon-10:30pm.

Lamb and Flag, 33 Rose St, WC2. Tube: Covent Garden or Leicester Sq. Off Garrick St. A traditional pub, with 2 sections—the public bar for the working class and the saloon bar for the businessmen, although today the classes mix. Live jazz upstairs Su from 7:30pm. Open M-Th 11am-11pm, F-Sa 11am-10:45pm, Su noon-10:30pm.

Crown and Anchor, 22 Neal St, WC2. Tube: Covent Garden. A mellow but popular oasis in the middle of the bustle. Open M-Sa 11am-11pm, Su noon-10:30pm.

Riki Tik, 23-24 Bateman St, W1. Tube: Leicester Sq, Tottenham Ct Rd, or Piccadilly Circus. Hyped, hip, and tremendously swinging bar specializing in orgasmic flavored vodka shots (£2.60). Happy Hour W-Sa noon-8pm. Open M-Sa noon-1am. Cover after 11pm £3.

◉ SIGHTS

London's landmarks annually face an onslaught of around five million visitors. Sightseers who don't qualify for student or senior discounts may want to consider the **London for Less** card, issued by Metropolis International (tel. 89 64 42 42), which grants discounts on attractions, theaters, restaurants, and hotels, and is available at all BTA offices (2-person, 4-day card £13).

WESTMINSTER AND WHITEHALL

The city of Westminster, now a borough of London, once served as haven to a seething nest of criminals seeking sanctuary in the Abbey. For the past 1000 years, Westminster has been the center of political and religious power in England.

WESTMINSTER ABBEY. Neither a cathedral nor a parish church, Westminster Abbey is a "royal peculiar," controlled directly by the Crown instead of the Church of England. As both the site of every royal coronation since 1066 and the final resting place for an imposing assortment of sovereigns, politicians, poets, and artists, its significance extends far beyond the religious. The **Coronation Chair** has been used in the coronation ceremonies of all but two of England's monarchs since 1308; **Poet's Corner** commemorates authors from Chaucer to Byron to T.S. Eliot; and the **High Altar** has been the scene of many funerals, including Princess Diana's. *(In Deans Yard. Tube: Westminster. Open M-F 9am-4:45pm; Sa 9am-2:45pm. £5, students £3. Tours 1hr., £3; depart from the Enquiry Desk in the nave. Photography permitted W 6-7:45pm only.)*

THE HOUSES OF PARLIAMENT. Oft-imagined in foggy silhouette against the Thames, the Houses of Parliament have become London's visual trademark. The immense complex blankets eight acres and includes more than 1000 rooms and 100 staircases. It's a little-known fact that although you can hear **Big Ben,** you can't see him; he's actually neither the northernmost tower nor the clock, but rather the 14-ton bell that tolls the hours. The business of the **House of Commons Strangers' Gallery** and the **House of Lords Visitors' Gallery** is announced in a schedule by St. Stephen's Gate. Follow guards to the **Chambers of the House of Commons,** where the

BRITAIN

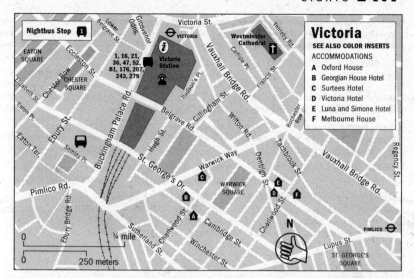

Victoria

SEE ALSO COLOR INSERTS

ACCOMMODATIONS

A Oxford House
B Georgian House Hotel
C Surtees Hotel
D Victoria Hotel
E Luna and Simone Hotel
F Melbourne House

Government party sits to the Speaker's right, and the Opposition to his or her left. To enter the Lords' Gallery, go back through the Central Lobby and pass through the mural-bedecked peers' corridor. *(On Parliament Sq. Tube: Westminster. The Houses are in recess during Easter week, from late July to mid-Oct., and for 3 weeks around Christmas. House of Commons Strangers' Gallery open M-Tu 2:30-10pm, W 9:30am-2pm, Th 11:30am-2pm, F 9:30am-3pm. House of Lords Visitors' Gallery open M-W 2:30pm-late, Th 3pm-late. For entry, wait on the left of St. Stephen's Gate for Commons, on the right for Lords. Free.)*

10 DOWNING STREET. The Prime Minister's headquarters lies just steps up Parliament St from the Houses of Parliament. The exterior of "Number Ten" is decidedly unimpressive, but behind the famous door spreads an extensive political network. The Chancellor of the Exchequer forges economic policy from 11 Downing St, while the Chief Whip of the House of Commons plans Party campaigns at #12. Tony Blair's family is too big for #10, so he's moved into #11. *(Tube: Westminster.)*

THE MALL AND ST. JAMES'S

THE MALL. Bordered by St. James's Park and Green Park to the south and Piccadilly to the north, The Mall begins at Cockspur St, off Trafalgar Sq, and leads up to Buckingham Palace. Every Sunday it is pedestrian-only. Nearby, **St. James's Street** runs into stately **Pall Mall.** *(Tube: Charing Cross, Green Park, or St. James's Park.)*

BUCKINGHAM PALACE. After a debate about the proper way to subsidize the monarchy's senselessly posh existence, Buckingham Palace finally opened to the public. Sort of—there are only two months when you can visit, and not all of the palace is open. But you can still (barring bad weather or pressing state holidays) catch the **Changing of the Guard** outside the palace, a chart-topping Kodak Moment. The "Old Guard" marches from St. James's Palace down The Mall to Buckingham Palace, where it's met by the "New Guard." The officers of the regiments then touch hands, symbolically exchanging keys, *et voilà*, the guard is officially changed. *(Tube: Victoria; walk up Buckingham Palace Rd. Open roughly Aug.-Sept. £9.50. Changing of the Guard Apr.-Aug. daily roughly 11:10am; Sept.-Mar. every other day.)*

ST. JAMES'S PALACE AND PARK. A residence of the monarchy from 1660 to 1668 and again from 1715 to 1837, **St. James's Palace** is now the home of Prince Charles, while his grandmother, the Queen Mum, bunks next door at Clarence House. The palace is closed to the public except for Inigo Jones' **Queen's Chapel,** built in 1626, open for Sunday services at 8:30 and 11am. *(Tube: Green Park. Just north of Buckingham*

BRITAIN

Palace and The Mall, up Stable Yard or Marlborough Rd.) **St. James's Park** was declared London's first royal park in 1532. Lawn chairs must be rented, but don't bother finding the attendants; sit and they'll find you (£0.70 per 4hr.).

CHRISTIE'S. Around the corner from St. James's Palace stands Christie, Manson, and Wodds Fine Art Auctioneers—better known as Christie's. Auctions, open to the public, are held weekdays at 10:30am. *(8 King St. Tube: Green Park. Tel. 839 90 60.)*

TRAFALGAR SQUARE AND PICCADILLY

TRAFALGAR SQUARE. Unlike many squares in London, Trafalgar Square, which slopes down from the **National Gallery** (see p. 156), has been public land ever since the 1830s. **Nelson's Column** commands the square, with four majestic lions guarding the base. The monument and square commemorate Admiral Nelson, killed during his triumph over Napoleon's navy at the Battle of Trafalgar. *(Tube: Charing Cross.)*

SAINT-MARTIN-IN-THE-FIELDS. This church, on the northeastern corner of the square, has its own world-renowned chamber orchestra and sponsors lunchtime and evening concerts, as well as a festival in mid-July. *(Tel. 78 39 8 362. Tube: Leicester Sq. Opposite the National Gallery. Open M-F 10am-4pm. Concerts M-Tu and F 1:05pm.)*

PICCADILLY CIRCUS. All of the West End's major arteries—Piccadilly, Regent St, Shaftesbury Ave, and the Haymarket—merge and swirl around Piccadilly Circus, a hub of lurid neon signs, hordes of tourists, and a fountain topped by a statue everyone calls **Eros.** Theaterland spans out from this hub. *(Tube: Piccadilly Circus.)*

BURLINGTON HOUSE. The only remnant of Piccadilly's stately past is this showy mansion, built in 1665. It was redesigned in the 18th century to house the burgeoning **Royal Academy of Arts** (see p. 157). The Academy consists of exhibition galleries and a school of art. *(Opposite 185 Piccadilly Circus. Tube: Piccadilly Circus or Green Park.)*

REGENT STREET. Running north from Piccadilly Circus are the grand façades of (Upper) Regent St, which lead to Oxford Circus. The buildings and street were built by John Nash in the early 19th century as part of a processional route. Today, the street is known for its elegant shopping. *(Tube: Piccadilly Circus or Oxford St.)*

COVENT GARDEN AND SOHO

The cafés, pubs, upscale shops, and slick crowds animating Covent Garden today belie the square's medieval beginnings as a literal "convent garden" where monks grew vegetables. *(Tube: Covent Garden.)* For centuries, nearby Soho was London's red-light district of prostitutes and sex shows. Today Soho overflows with artists and club kids, while the gay-owned restaurants and bars of **Old Compton Street** have turned Soho into the heart of gay London. *(Tube: Tottenham Ct Rd or Leicester Sq.)*

CARNABY STREET. Running parallel to Regent St, this notorious hotbed of 1960s sex, fashion, and Mods is the heart of "Swingin' London." Chic boutiques and bohemian stores mix with stalls of junky souvenirs. *(Tube: Oxford Circus.)*

LEICESTER SQUARE. Just south of Shaftesbury Ave, between Piccadilly Circus and Charing Cross Rd, lies this entertainment nexus of cinemas, clubs, and street entertainers. A large queue marks the **half-price ticket booth** (see p. 158) where same-day theater tickets are sold for a number of shows. *(Tube: Leicester Sq.)*

THEATRE ROYAL AND ROYAL OPERA HOUSE. These two venues represent a long tradition of theater in the Covent Garden area. The **Theatre Royal,** with an entrance on Catherine St, dates from 1812. The **Royal Opera House,** on Bow St, began as a theater for concerts and plays in 1732 and currently houses the Royal Opera and Royal Ballet companies. *(Tube: Covent Garden.)*

CHINATOWN. Cantonese immigrants first arrived in Britain as cooks on British ships, and then Chinatown swelled with immigrants from Hong Kong. The streets spout Chinese signs and pagoda-like phone booths. The vibrant **Chinese New Year Festival** takes place at the beginning of February. *(Tube: Leicester Sq.)*

BRITAIN

ROYAL COURTS OF JUSTICE. The Strand and Fleet St meet at this elaborate Gothic structure—easily mistaken for a cathedral—designed in 1874 for the Supreme Court of Judicature. At the Strand entrance, displays explain the court system. *(Tube: Temple. Tel. 79 36 60 00. Open M-F 9am-4:30pm.)*

THE STRAND AND FLEET STREET

THE STRAND. Built to connect the City with Westminster Palace and Parliament, the area is now a center of education in London. The thoroughfare curves from Trafalgar Sq past many theaters to Aldwych. *(Tube: Holborn or Charing Cross.)*

KING'S COLLEGE AND LONDON SCHOOL OF ECONOMICS. As you stroll away from the Courts of Justice on Houghton St, two of London's top educational institutions come into view. **King's College** stands opposite the prestigious **London School of Economics (LSE),** a 60s center for student radicalism. *(Tube: Holborn.)*

SOMERSET HOUSE. A magnificent Palladian structure built by Sir William Chambers in 1776, Somerset House stands on the site of a 16th-century palace. Formerly a center of the Royal Navy, the building now houses birth records as well as the exquisite Impressionist **Courtauld Collection** (see p. 157). *(On the Strand. Tube: Temple.)*

ST. CLEMENT DANES. The melodious bells of this handsome church get their 15 seconds of fame in the nursery rhyme "Oranges and lemons, say the bells of St. Clement's." Designed by Christopher Wren in 1682, today it is the official church of the Royal Air Force. *(On The Strand, east of St. Mary-le-Strand's. Tube: Temple. Tel. 72 42 82 82. Open daily 8am-5pm. Bells ring daily 9am, noon, 3, and 6pm.)*

TWINING'S TEAS. This institution of tea honors the leaf that started the American Revolution. This is both the oldest business in Britain still on its original premises and the narrowest shop in London (somebody call Ripley). *(216 The Strand, near the Fleet St end. Tube: Temple. Tel. 73 53 35 11. Open M-F 9:30am-4:30pm.)*

THE EMBANKMENT. This road runs along the Thames, parallel to the Strand. Between the Hungerford and Waterloo Bridges stands London's oldest (though not indigenous) landmark, **Cleopatra's Needle,** an Egyptian obelisk from 1450 BC, stolen by the Viceroy of Egypt in 1878. *(Tube: Charing Cross or Embankment.)*

THE CITY OF LONDON

Until the 18th century, the City of London *was* London. Today, the single-square-mile City is the financial center of Europe. When 350,000 commuters go home each weekday, they leave behind a resident population of only 6000. The City hums on weekdays, is dead on Saturdays, and seems downright ghostly on Sundays. The massive **Bank of England** controls the country's finances, and the **Stock Exchange** makes (or breaks) the nation's fortune. *(Tube: Bank.)*

ST. PAUL'S CATHEDRAL. An extraordinary Anglican spin-off of the Vatican, St. Paul's is arguably the most stunning architectural sight in London. The current edifice by Christopher Wren is the fifth cathedral to stand on the site; the Great Fire of 1666 demolished the previous version. After being topped off in 1710 with a huge Classical dome (the second-largest free-standing dome in Europe at 365 ft.), it was engulfed by fire on Dec. 29, 1940, at the height of the Blitz, but survived. Today it continues to serve as a center for state functions. The best place to head is straight up—259 steps lead to the **Whispering Gallery,** a perfect resounding chamber. *(Tube: St. Paul's. Open M-Sa 8:30am-4pm. Galleries and ambulatory open M-Sa 8:45am-4:15pm. Cathedral, ambulatory, and crypt £4, students £3.50; with galleries £7, £6.50.)*

THE TOWER OF LONDON. Palace and prison of English monarchs for over 500 years, the Tower of London is soaked in blood and stuffed with history. Its 20 towers are all connected by massive walls and gateways. The Tower and the **Crown Jewels** within are now guarded by the **Yeomen** of the Guard Extraordinary, known as the **"Beefeaters"** (derived from well-nourished domestic servants). Along the curtain wall hovers the **Bloody Tower,** the most infamous part of the fortress, where the Little Princes, the uncrowned King Edward V and his brother, were murdered by

BRITAIN

agents of Richard III. The only prisoners today are the clipped ravens hopping around on the grass outside the White Tower; legend has it that without them the Tower would crumble. *(Tube: Tower Hill. Tel. 77 09 07 65. Open M-Sa 9am-5pm, Su 10am-5pm; last entry 4pm. Mandatory tours 1hr., every 30min; £9.50, students £7.15.)*

TOWER BRIDGE. A granite-and-steel structure reminiscent of a castle with a draw-bridge, the bridge is a postcard image of the city. The **Tower Bridge Experience** explains the bridge's genesis through the eyes of its designers. *(Tube: Tower Hill; follow signs. Tel. 74 03 37 61. Open daily Apr.-Oct. 10am-6:30pm; Nov.-Mar. 9:30am-6pm. £5.70.)*

MONUMENT. Completed in 1677, the pillar's 202 ft. offer an expansive view of London. The monument stands mere feet from Pudding Ln, where the 1666 Great Fire broke out and then "rushed devastating through every quarter." *(On Fish St Hill. Tube: Monument. Open Apr.-Sept. daily 10am-5:40pm; Oct.-Mar. M-Sa 10am-5:40pm. £1.50.)*

LLOYD'S. This 1986 building supplies the most startling architectural clash in the City, with ducts, lifts, and chutes straight out of the 21st century; it seems not so much a building as a vertical street. The **Lutine Bell** is still occasionally rung—once for bad insurance news, twice for good. *(Off Leadenhall St. Tube: Monument.)*

BARBICAN CENTRE. A 37-acre brutalist masterpiece, the Barbican is a maze of restaurants, gardens, and exhibition halls, described at its 1982 opening as "the city's gift to the nation." The Royal Shakespeare Company, the Museum of London, and the Barbican Art Gallery call this complex home, as do the many politicians and actors who reside in the Barbican's apartment buildings. *(Tube: Barbican or Moorgate. Library open M and W-F 9:30am-5:30pm, Tu 9:30am-7:30pm, Sa 9:30am-12:30pm.)*

HYDE PARK AND ENVIRONS

HYDE PARK AND KENSINGTON GARDENS. The lakes and green lawns of Hyde Park and the contiguous Kensington Gardens, the "Lungs of London," sum to the largest open area (1 sq. mi.) in the city center. *(Tube: Hyde Park Corner or Marble Arch. Park open daily 5am-midnight. Gardens open daily dawn-dusk. Free.)*

KENSINGTON PALACE. At the far west of the Gardens is Kensington, originally the residence of King William III and Queen Mary II. The birthplace of Queen Victoria, and most recently home to the late Princess Diana, Kensington has moved in and out of vogue with the Royal Family. *(Tube: High St Kensington. Tel. 73 76 01 98. Mandatory tours 1¼hr., May-Sept. M-Sa every hr. 10am-5pm, £8.50, students £6.70.)*

MARBLE ARCH. Hangings at this arch, built on the site where the public gallows of Tyburn rested until 1783, once drew immense crowds to stone the criminals. *(Tube: Marble Arch. At the corner of Bayswater and Edgware Rd.)*

SPEAKERS' CORNER. On summer evenings and on Sundays, proselytizers, politicos, and flat-out crazies assemble to dispense the fruits of their knowledge to whomever will bite. *(Tube: Marble Arch. In the northeastern corner of Hyde Park.)*

NOTTING HILL AND PORTOBELLO ROAD. Simultaneously shabby and extravagant, Notting Hill pulses with chaotic energy. Genteel streets with private garden squares intersect noisy avenues and the wafting incense of large West Indian and Moroccan communities (usually no Hugh Grant, though). The **Notting Hill Carnival,** Europe's biggest outdoor festival, is held the last weekend in August. *(Tube: Notting Hill Gate.)* Portobello Rd is the commercial road that is the heart of Notting Hill's bustling activity. Antique stores and galleries line the southern end of Portobello near the Notting Hill Gate Tube station. Near Lancaster Rd and the Westway (the overhead highway), vendors sell clothing, collector's vinyl, and various trinkets. *(Tube: Notting Hill Gate; turn on Pembridge Rd from the station, and Portobello Rd is the 3rd left.)*

NORTH LONDON

221B BAKER STREET. The area's most fondly remembered resident is Sherlock Holmes who, although fictitious, still receives 50 letters per week addressed to his residence at 221b Baker St. The **Sherlock Holmes Museum**, 239 Baker St, thrills with a re-creation of the detective's lodgings. *(Tube: Baker St.)*

BRITAIN

REGENT'S PARK. North of Baker St and south of Camden Town, the wide-open Regent's Park is .78 sq. mi. full of lakes and gardens that also house the **London Zoo.** *(Tube: Regent's Park, Great Portland St, Baker St, or Camden Town. Open daily 6am-dusk.)*

CAMDEN TOWN. Regent's Park Canal flows through the zoo and into Camden Town. At the time of the canal's construction in the 19th century, Camden Town was a solid working-class district spliced with railways and covered in soot. Charles Dickens spent his childhood here; the experience served as the model for the Cratchit family in *A Christmas Carol.* Camden Town today is a stomping ground for trendy youth subcultures. At **Camden Market,** hundreds of merchants set up stands that draw swarms of bargain-seeking Londoners and bewildered tourists every weekend. *(Tube: Camden Town.)*

RUSSELL SQUARE. Directly northeast of the British Museum, Russell Square squares off as central London's second-largest, after Lincoln's Inn Fields. T.S. Eliot, the "Pope of Russell Square," hid from his emotionally ailing first wife at 24 Russell Sq. Also of note is the decadently Victorian **Russell Hotel** on the eastern side of the square, a confection of brick and terracotta. *(Tube: Russell Sq.)*

DICKENS HOUSE. Charles Dickens lived here from 1837 to 1839, scribbling parts of *Nicholas Nickleby, Barnaby Rudge,* and *Oliver Twist.* Now a four-floor museum and library of Dickens paraphernalia, the house holds an array of prints, photographs, manuscripts, and letters. *(48 Doughty St, east of Russell Sq and parallel to Gray's Inn Rd. Tube: Russell Sq or Chancery Ln. Open M-Sa 10am-5pm. £3.50, students £2.50.)*

HAMPSTEAD HEATH. The most fabulous green space in the metropolis is the perfect place to get lost in vast meadows and woodlands and forget the hustle and bustle of the city with carefree picnickers, kite-flyers, and anglers. At night the Heath, particularly West Heath, becomes one of the city's oldest gay cruising areas. On a hot day, take a dip in the murky waters of **Kenwood Ladies' Pond, Highgate Men's Pond,** or the **Mixed Bathing Pond.** *(Tube: Hampstead. Rail: Hampstead Heath. Pools open in summer 7-9:30am and 10am-7pm; off-season 7-10am. £3, students £1; free before 10am.)*

HIGHGATE CEMETERY. Magnificently creepy Highgate Cemetery is a remarkable monument to the Victorian fascination with death. Its most famous resident is Karl Marx. *(On Swain's Ln. Tube: Archway. Open M-F 10am-5pm, Sa-Su 11am-5pm; £1. Tours of western cemetery M-F noon, 2, and 4pm, Sa-Su every hr. 11am-5pm; £3.)*

THE SOUTH BANK AND LAMBETH

OXO TOWER AND GABRIEL'S WHARF. The most colorful recent changes in the South Bank landscape result from the unflagging efforts of a nonprofit development company, **Coin Street Community Builders (CSCB).** The nearby **Museum Of...** and the **gallery@oxo** are succeeding in their aim to provide a democratic artistic forum. *(Between Waterloo and Blackfriars Bridges on Barge House St. Tube: Blackfriars or Waterloo.)* **Gabriel's Wharf,** another CSCB project revolving around a designer crafts market, is not far from the Oxo Tower on Upper Ground. In summer, there are occasional free festivals. *(Tube: Blackfriars or Waterloo. Tel. 74 01 36 10. Crafts workshops Tu-Su 11am-6pm.)*

SOUTH BANK CENTRE. Behind the hulking façade of this massive performing arts center, which occupies a series of prominent modern buildings overlooking the river, lurks London's most concentrated campus of artistic and cultural activity. The complex includes the **National Film Theatre,** the modern art **Hayward Gallery,** the **Royal Festival Hall** complex for classical music, and the **Royal National Theatre.** *(Tube: Waterloo, then follow signs for York Rd; or Embankment, then cross the Hungerford footbridge.)*

LONDON AQUARIUM. The main attractions in this basement of the former County Hall are two three-story tanks; the Atlantic tank's biggest inhabitants are whopping conger eels, while the Pacific tank hosts the ever-popular sharks. *(Near Westminster Bridge, south of the Thames. Tube: Westminster. Open daily 10am-6pm. £8, students £6.50.)*

ROSE AND GLOBE THEATRES. Shakespeare's and Marlowe's plays were performed at the **Rose,** built in 1587, whose remnants were discovered during construction in 1989 and are now displayed under a new office block at Park St and

Rose Alley. The remains of Shakespeare's **Globe Theatre** were discovered just months after the Rose; the Globe was soon after reconstructed on the riverbank. *(On New Globe Walk, in Bankside. Tube: London Bridge. Tel. 79 02 14 00. Tours 45min.; May-Sept. M 9am-6pm, Tu-Su 9am-noon; Oct.-Apr. daily 10am-5pm. £6, students £5.)*

MILLENNIUM DOME. The most notable project of Millennium London may be this £758 million dome on the Greenwich Peninsula in southeast London. For all of 2000, the dome hosts **The Millennium Experience,** a high-tech circus of special effects, virtual reality, and live shows. Fourteen thematic zones aim to "challenge and amaze" visitors. The **Play Zone** encourages the inner child in you to romp around in an interactive digital environment. Over 12 million visitors are expected, so buy tickets early; beware that such fun comes at turn-of-the-new-century prices, too. *(Tube: North Greenwich. There are also plans to run a link from the East India DLR station. £20, students £16.50. Reserve by calling (0870) 606 20 00, or online at www.dome2000.co.uk.)*

RICHMOND

KEW GARDENS. The perfect antidote to central London, the Royal Botanic Gardens at Kew provide a breath of fresh air. Yet another example of the Empire's collecting frenzy, the 124-acre park houses the living bank of a research collection with millions of DNA and seeds and thousands of plants and flowers. The steamy, tropical **Palm House,** a masterpiece of Victorian engineering built in 1848, is replete with voluptuous fronds. But it's dwarfed by its younger Victorian sibling, the **Temperate House,** whose cooler climate nurtures many species, arranged according to geographic origins. *(Tube: Kew Gardens (zone 3). Rail: North London line: Kew Gardens. Boats go daily between Kew and Westminster pier. Open in summer M-F 9:30am-6:30pm, Sa-Su 9:30am-7:30pm; conservatories close at 5:30pm. £5, after 4:45pm £3.50; students £3.50. Walking tours leave Victoria Gate daily 11am and 2pm; £1, students £0.50.)*

HAMPTON COURT PALACE. Although a monarch hasn't lived here since George II moved out over 200 years ago, Hampton Court Palace continues to exude regal charm. Six miles down the Thames from Richmond, the brick palace housed over 1500 court members at its height. The 60 marvelous acres of the **Palace Gardens** are open and free, and contain celebrated amusements, including the **maze,** a hedgerow labyrinth first planted in 1714. *(Tube: Richmond (zone 4); then take bus R68 to the palace (£0.80). Rail: Trains run from Waterloo Station to Hampton Ct every 30min. (day return £4). Tel. 87 81 95 00. Open Mar.-late Oct. M 10:15am-6pm, Tu-Su 9:30am-6pm; late Oct.-Mar. M 10:15am-4:30pm, Tu-Su 9:30am-4:30pm. £10, students £7.60; maze or gardens only £2.10.)*

MARBLE HILL HOUSE. Descend Richmond Hill and cross the Thames on Bridge St (follow the signs and the tourists) to the Marble Hill House. Perched on the Thames amid vast trimmed lawns, this Palladian house was built in 1729 for Henrietta Howard, George II's mistress. The **Great Room** is lavishly decorated with gilt and carvings by James Richards and original Panini paintings of ancient Rome. Alexander Pope, the famed satirist and Howard's close friend, designed some of the gardens. *(Take bus 33, 90B, 290, H22, R68, or R70 from the Richmond station. Tel. 88 92 51 15. Open daily Apr.-Oct. 10am-6pm; Nov.-Mar. W-Su 10am-4pm. £3, students £2.30.)*

🏛 MUSEUMS

▨ **British Museum** (info tel. 73 23 82 99), on Great Russell St, WC1. Tube: Tottenham Ct Rd or Holborn. The sheer volume of the museum's collections is a fascinating document of the political, military, and economic power of the British Empire. A near-complete record of the rise and ruin of world cultures, its archaeological collections revisit the glory days of Egypt, Asia, Greece, Rome, and prehistoric and medieval Europe. Among the plunder on display are the **Rosetta Stone** (which led to the deciphering of hieroglyphics) and the **Elgin Marbles.** Open M-Sa 10am-5pm, Su 2:30-6pm. Donation £2.

▨ **National Gallery** (tel. 78 39 33 21, recorded info 77 47 28 85), on Trafalgar Sq, WC2. Tube: Charing Cross, Leicester Sq, Embankment, or Piccadilly Circus. One of the world's finest collections of 13th- to 19th-century Western European painting, especially strong in works by Rembrandt, Rubens, and Renaissance Italian painters. The Micro Gallery prints out a free personalized tour. Open M-Sa 10am-6pm, W 10am-8pm, Su noon-6pm. Free.

The Courtauld Gallery (tel. 78 73 25 26), at Somerset House, on The Strand, WC2, opposite the corner of Aldwych and The Strand. Tube: Temple, Embankment, Charing Cross, or Covent Garden. Intimate 11-room gallery with world-famous masterpieces, mostly Impressionist and post-Impressionist. Open M-Sa 10am-6pm. £4, students £2; M half-price.

Sir John Soane's Museum, 13 Lincoln's Inn Fields, WC2 (tel. 74 05 21 07). Tube: Holborn. Soane was an architect's architect, but the idiosyncratic home he designed for himself will intrigue even laypeople. Artifacts on display include Hogarth paintings, the massive sarcophagus of Seti I, and casts of famous buildings and sculptures from around the world. Open Tu-Sa 10am-5pm; free. Tours Sa 2:30pm; tickets sold from 2pm.

National Portrait Gallery, on St. Martin's Pl, WC2, opposite St.-Martin's-in-the-Fields. Tube: Charing Cross or Leicester Sq. This unofficial *Who's Who in Britain* began in 1856 to showcase Britain's most officially noteworthy citizens and includes mugs from Queen Elizabeth II to John Lennon. Open M-Sa 10am-6pm, Su noon-6pm. Free.

Tate Gallery (recorded info tel. 78 87 80 00), at Millbank, up the Thames from Parliament Sq. Tube: Pimlico. Superb collection of British works from the 16th century to the present and a distinguished ensemble of international modern art. Main galleries change frequently, with about 10-15% of the collection on display at any time. Usually includes the best of British artists, along with Monet, Dalí, Picasso, and Matisse. A must for modern art fans. Open daily 10am-5:50pm. Free. The new **Tate Gallery of Modern Art** is due to open in 2000 as the home of the Tate's foreign works; call 887 87 25 for more info.

Victoria and Albert Museum (recorded info tel. 79 38 84 41), on Cromwell Rd. Tube: South Kensington. One of the most enchanting museums in London, the V&A (a.k.a. the British Museum's attic) lets you saunter through the histories of art, design, and style. Immense galleries (58,060 sq. yards' worth) with the best Italian Renaissance sculpture collection outside Italy, the largest collection of Indian art outside India, and enough costumes for any fashion fetish. Open M noon-5:50pm, Tu-Su 10am-5:50pm. £5, students free.

Madame Tussaud's (tel. 935 68 61), on Marylebone Rd, NW1. Tube: Baker St. The classic waxwork museum, founded by an emigré aristocrat who made life-size models of French nobility. Beat horrific lines by going very early or very late. A green dome shelters the adjacent **Planetarium.** Both open in summer M-F 9am-5:30pm, Sa-Su 9:30am-5:30pm; off-season M-F 10am-5:30pm, Sa-Su 9:30am-5:30pm. £9.75, with planetarium £12.

Science Museum (tel. 79 38 80 08), on Exhibition Rd, SW7. Tube: South Kensington. Closet science geeks will be outed by their ecstatic cries as they enter this wonderland of diagrammed motors, springs, and spaceships. Introductory exhibit romps through a "synopsis" of science since 6000 BC. Numerous exhibits geared toward the under-12 sector. Open daily 10am-6pm. £6.50, students £3.50; free for all after 4:30pm.

Wallace Collection, in Hertford House in Manchester Sq, W1. Tube: Bond St. Founded by various Marquises of Hertford and the illegitimate son of the fourth Marquis, Sir Richard Wallace, this defines the adjective "sumptuous." Also home to the largest weaponry collection outside of the Tower of London. Open M-Sa 10am-5pm, Su 2-5pm. Tours M-Tu and Th-F 1pm, W and Sa 11:30am and 1pm, Su 3pm. Free.

Royal Academy of Arts (tel. 74 39 74 38), on Piccadilly, W1, opposite #185. Tube: Green Park or Piccadilly Circus. Traveling exhibits of the highest order. Annual summer exhibition (June-Aug.) is a London institution—the works of established and unknown contemporary artists festoon every square centimeter of wall space. Open daily M-Sa 10am-6pm, Su 10am-8:30pm. Advance tickets may be necessary. Average exhibition £6, students £4.

London Transport Museum (tel. 73 79 63 44, recorded info tel. 75 65 72 99), in Covent Garden, WC2, on the eastern side of the *piazza*. Tube: Covent Garden. Low-tech exhibits provide a thought-provoking cultural history: see how the expansion of the transit system increased the size of the suburbs. Open M-Th and Sa-Su 10am-6pm, F 11am-6pm; last entry 5:15pm. £5, students £3.

Design Museum (tel. 74 03 69 33, exhibition hotline 73 78 60 55), at Butlers Wharf, SE1. Tube: London Bridge; follow signs on Tooley St. Housed in an appropriately Bauhaus-like box, this museum is dedicated to mass-produced classics of culture and industry. Half filled with changing exhibitions. Open daily 11:30am-6pm. £5.50, students £4.

BRITAIN

Museum of London, 150 London Wall, EC2 (tel. 76 00 36 99, info tel. 76 00 08 07). Tube: St. Paul's or Barbican. Comprehensive is an understatement: this engrossing museum tells the story of the metropolis from its Roman origins as Londinium up through the present day. Open Tu-Sa 10am-5:50pm, Su noon-5:50pm. £5, students £3.

London Dungeon, 28-34 Tooley St, SE1 (tel. 74 03 06 06). Tube: London Bridge. An expensive and popular spectacle, with plague, decomposition, and anything else remotely connected to horror and British history thrown in. Reserve 2hr. in advance. Open daily Apr.-Sept. 10am-6:30pm; Nov.-Feb. 10am-5:30pm. £9.50, students £8.

🎭 ENTERTAINMENT

On any given day or night, Londoners and visitors can choose from the widest range of entertainment. Consult *Time Out* (£1.80), available from any newsagent.

THEATER

London theater is unrivaled. Seats cost £8-30 and up, and student standby (with an "S," "concessions," or "concs" in newspapers) puts even the best seats within reach—£7-10 just before curtain (come two hours early with ID). **Day seats** are cheap (9-10am same-day) for all; line up earlier. The **Leicester Square Ticket Booth** sells same-day half-price tickets for major plays to those willing to endure the wait. (Open M-Sa 11am-6:30pm. Fee £2. V, MC.) Standby tickets for the **Royal National Theatre** (tel. 452 34 00; Tube: Waterloo), on the South Bank Centre, go on sale 2hr. beforehand (£10-14), student tickets 45min. beforehand (£7.50). The **Barbican Theatre** (info tel. 382 72 72, reservations tel. 638 88 91; Tube: Barbican or Moorgate), London home of the Royal Shakespeare Company, has student standbys for £6 from 9am on the day of performance. For a mere £5, you can stand as a groundling and watch Shakespearean productions in the meticulously reconstructed **Globe Theatre,** on New Globe Walk, Bankside SE1. (See p. 155. For tickets, tel. 401 99 19. Tube: London Bridge. Box office open M-Sa 10am-8pm.) Exciting, cheaper performances are found on the **Fringe,** in less commercial theaters.

MUSIC

Most major classical music is staged at the acoustically superb **Royal Festival Hall** (tel. 960 42 42; Tube: Waterloo) and the **Barbican Hall.** For cheap outdoor concerts, head to **Marble Hill House** (see p. 156; tel. 413 14 43) on summer Sundays at 2pm. Londoners have been lining up for standing room in the **Royal Albert Hall's "Proms"** (BBC Henry Wood Promenade Concerts; tel. 589 82 12) for nearly a century. **Brixton Academy** (tel. 924 99 99; Tube: Brixton) is a larger venue for a variety of music including rock and reggae (advance tickets £8-25). **Ronnie Scott's,** 47 Frith St, W1 (tel. 439 07 47; Tube: Leicester Sq or Piccadilly Circus), has London's greatest jazz (cover from £15).

FILM

A Soho institution, **The Prince Charles,** on Leicester Pl, WC2, has a bar and permits drinks in the theater. Its four shows are usually second-runs (deconstructed on the amiable recorded phone message), but also include a sprinkling of classics for a mere £2-2.50. (Tel. 437 81 81. Tube: Leicester Sq. *Rocky Horror* shows every F.) Screening many cutting-edge contemporary films and an extensive list of classics, the **Institute of Contemporary Arts (ICA) Cinema,** in Nash House, The Mall, W1, shows experimental films, too (£5-6.50). ICA also has programs highlighting the works of individual directors. (Tel. 930 36 47. Tube: Piccadilly Circus or Charing Cross.) The **National Film Theatre (NFT),** in South Bank Centre, SE1 (tel. 928 32 32; Tube: Waterloo) boggles the mind with its array of film, TV, and video (most screenings £5).

BRITAIN

◩ NIGHTLIFE

CLUBS

London pounds to 100% groovy Liverpool tunes, ecstatic Manchester rave, hometown soul and house, US hip-hop, and Jamaican reggae. Many clubs host a variety of provocative one-night stands (like "Get Up and Use Me") throughout the week. Check listings in *Time Out* for the latest.

The Africa Centre, 88 King St, WC2. Tube: Covent Garden. Art center by day, psychedelic, blacklit den of funk by night. Live African music at the "Limpopo Club" most Fridays, but Saturday's "Funkin' Pussy" lets clubbers shake booty to vintage funk and hip-hop. Open F 9pm-3am, cover £5-6; Sa 9pm-3am, cover £3-7.

Bagleys Studios, at Kings Cross Freight Depot, N1. Tube: Kings Cross. From the station, walk a quarter-mile down York Way (east), on the left. Or take night bus N91. London's biggest club venue (capacity 3000). Cover £8-12. Open F 10pm-6am, Sa 10pm-7am.

Bar Rumba, 35 Shaftesbury Ave, W1. Tube: Piccadilly Circus. This small discothèque hosts brilliant nights out. Each night is something new, but a Latin influence is always present. Cover £5-12. Open M-Sa 10:30pm-3am, Su 8pm-1:30am.

The Fridge, on Town Hall Parade, Brixton Hill, SW2. Tube: Brixton. Out of the station, cross the street, walk left, walk up Brixton Hill Rd, and look for the long line. Converted cinema hosts some of the most popular nights in London. Cover £8-12. Open F-Sa 10pm-6am.

Home, 1 Leicester Sq. WC2. Tube: Leicester Sq. Brand-new superclub of the millenium aims to be the dwellingplace of clubbers worldwide. The residence of the best in DJ culture, the 8-floor abode boasts a 24-hour chill-out café/*crêperie*, a rooftop terrace, an interactive club experience and several floors of what is sure to be cutting-edge dance and house music. Cover varies. Open Th and Su until 3am, F-Sa until 6am.

Iceni, 11 White Horse St, W1, off Curzon St. Tube: Green Park. 3 beautiful floors of deep funk entertainment in this stylish Mayfair hotspot. Often wildly different beats between floors, from swing to 80s to techno. Cover £10-12. Open F 11pm-3am, Sa 10pm-3am.

Limelight, 136 Shaftesbury Ave, WC2. Tube: Leicester Sq. Converted church makes for a religious clubbing experience. A legend of the 80s with its NYC sister. Cover £5-12. Open Su-Th 10pm-3am, F 10pm-3:30am, Sa 9pm-3:30am.

Ministry of Sound, 103 Gaunt St, SE1. Tube: Elephant and Castle; take the "South Bank University" exit, turn left out of the station, walk up Newington Causeway, and Gaunt St is on the left. The grand-daddy of all serious clubbing. Cover £10-12. Open F 10:30pm-6:30am, Sa midnight-9am.

GAY AND LESBIAN NIGHTLIFE

London has a very visible gay scene, ranging from flamboyant to mainstream. *Time Out* has a section devoted to gay listings, and gay newspapers include *Capital Gay* (free, caters to men), *Pink Paper*, and *Shebang* (for women). *Gay Times* (£3) is the British counterpart to the *Advocate; Diva* (£2) is a monthly lesbian mag. Islington, Earl's Ct, and Soho (especially **Old Compton St**) are all gay-friendly areas.

Heaven (tel. 79 30 20 20), on Villiers St, WC2, underneath The Arches. Tube: Embankment or Charing Cross (Villiers is off The Strand). Still the oldest and biggest gay disco in Europe, recently remodeled and shinier than ever. Bumping garage music. Cover F £6, after 11:30pm £7.50; Sa £7, after 11:30pm £8. Open F-Sa 10pm-3am.

"G.A.Y.," at **London Astoria,** 157 Charing Cross Rd, WC2 (tel. 77 34 69 63). Tube: Tottenham Ct Rd. Pop extravaganza amidst mirrored disco balls and chrome. Clientele mixed in both gender and orientation. Open Th 10:30pm-4am, F 11pm-4am, Sa 10:30pm-5am. M £3, students and with flyer £1; Th £3, free with flyer; Sa £6, with flyer £5.

"Mis-shapes," Sundays at **Plastic People,** 37-39 Oxford St, W1 (tel. 74 39 04 64). Tube: King's Cross/St. Pancras. On Sunday this club turns into a haven for emphatically non-beautiful people: "all those misshapen types bullied at school, and rejected by the fashion/attitude side of the gay scene." Open Su 10pm-4am. Cover £4, students £2.

BRITAIN

"Popstarz," Friday at the **Leisure Lounge,** 121 Holborn Rd, EC1 (tel. 77 38 23 36). Tube: Chancery Ln. This weekly gay 1-nighter proved so popular at its inception that it moved to this venue at the Leisure Lounge. Open F 10pm-5am. £5, after 11pm £6, students £4.

SOUTHERN ENGLAND

Sprawling toward the continent, the landscape of southern England simultaneously asserts Britain's island heritage and belies a continental link deeper than the Chunnel. Early Britons settled the counties of Kent, Sussex, and Hampshire from across the English Channel, and William the Conqueror left his mark upon the downsland in the form of awe-inspiring cathedrals. But Geoffrey Chaucer, Jane Austen, Charles Dickens, E.M. Forster, and Virginia Woolf—all staples of modern British culture—also all drew inspiration from these lands. To the west, the counties of Somerset, Avon, and Wiltshire boast Salisbury's medieval cathedral, the Roman Baths at Bath, and the forever-mysterious Stonehenge. Even farther west, a mist of legends shrouds the counties of Dorset, Somerset, Devon, and Cornwall in England's West Country, home to Bronze Age barrows and King Arthur.

✖ FERRIES AND TRAINS TO FRANCE, SPAIN, AND BELGIUM

Ferries run from **Dover** (see p. 161) to **Calais, France** (see p. 369) and **Ostend, Belgium** (see p. 127). Ferries also chug from **Portsmouth** (see p. 162) to **St. Malo** (see p. 318) and **Caen, France** (see p. 314); from **Plymouth** (see p. 165) to **Roscoff, France** and **Santander, Spain;** from **Folkestone** to **Boulogne, France** (see p. 369) and from **Newhaven** to **Dieppe, France** (see p. 314). Travelers with cars can head through the **Chunnel** (from Dover to Calais) on **Le Shuttle.** For detailed info on over- and underwater transport options to the continent, see p. 57.

CANTERBURY

Six hundred years ago in his famed *Canterbury Tales*, Chaucer saw enough irony in droves of tourists to capture them in verse. His sometimes lewd, sometimes reverent tales speak of the pilgrims of the Middle Ages who flocked from London to the **Canterbury Cathedral.** Archbishop Thomas à Becket was beheaded here in 1170 after an irate Henry II asked, "Will no one rid me of this troublesome priest?" (Open Easter-Oct. M-Sa 8:45am-7pm, Su 11am-2:30pm and 4:30-5:30pm; Nov.-Easter daily 8:45am-5pm. Evensong services M-F 5:30pm, Sa-Su 3:15pm. £3, students £2. Audio tour £2.50.) **The Canterbury Tales,** on St. Margaret's St, is a museum simulating the journey of Chaucer's pilgrims; the gap-toothed Wife of Bath and her waxen companions will entertain you with an abbreviated, Modern English version of the Tales. (Open daily July-Aug. 9am-5:30pm, Mar.-June and Sept.-Oct. 9:30am-5:30pm; Nov.-Feb. Su-F 10am-4:30pm, Sa 9:30am-5:30pm. £5, students £4.25.) On Stour St, the **Canterbury Heritage Museum** tells the history of Canterbury from medieval times to WWII. (Open June-Oct. M-Sa 10:30am-5pm, Su 1:30-5pm; Nov.-May closed Su. £2.20, students £1.45.) To see two of South England's most storied castles, head 12 mi. southeast to **Deal: Deal Castle** was designed by Henry VIII as a coastal fortification; **Walmer Castle** has been converted from military bastion to elegant country estate. **Trains** leave regularly from Canterbury (£3).

For those who can't travel to Canterbury on horseback with a group of verbally gifted pilgrims, **trains** from London's Victoria Station arrive at Canterbury's **East Station,** while trains from London's Charing Cross and Waterloo Stations arrive at **West Station** (1½hr., £14.70). Stagecoach **buses** (tel. (01227) 47 20 82) leave from St. George's Ln for London's Victoria Coach Station (1¾hr., £8). The **tourist office,** 34 St. Margaret's St, stocks free mini-guides to Kent. (Tel. (01227) 76 65 67; fax 45 98 40. Open daily Apr.-Aug. 9:30am-5:30pm; Sept.-Mar. 9:30am-5pm.) Get wired at **Blockbuster Internet Bar,** 1 New Dover Rd, for £3 per 30min. **B&Bs** cluster near both train stations, on London Rd and Whitstable Rd, and on High St. The **YHA youth hostel,** 54 New Dover Rd, is ¾ mi. from East Station and ½ mi. southeast of the bus station. (Tel. (01227) 46 29 11; fax 47 07 52. £10.15. Lockers £1 plus deposit. Laundry. Recep-

BRITAIN

tion 7:30-10am and 1-11pm. Reserve ahead. Open Feb.-Dec.; call for off-season openings.) The ⌨Hampton House, 40 New Dover Rd (tel. (01227) 46 49 12), offers quiet, luxurious rooms for £20-25, while Let's Stay, 26 New Dover Rd (tel. (01227) 46 36 28), has beds for £10; both serve full English breakfasts. St. Martin's Touring Caravan and Camping Site, on Bekesbourne Ln, has good facilities. (Tel. (01227) 46 32 16. £5.20 per person; £3 per tent.) High St is crowded with pubs, restaurants, and fast-food joints. For groceries, head to Safeway supermarket, on St. George's Pl. (Open M-Th and Sa 8am-8pm, F 8am-9pm, Su 10am-4pm.) Patrick Casey's, on Butchery Ln, will warm you up with traditional Irish food and bitters. Postal code: CT1 2BA.

DOVER

The puttering of ferries, the constant hum of hovercraft, and the chatter of French families *en vacances* drown out the roar of the English Channel at Dover. However, Dover is the most vital of Britain's ports. The view from Castle Hill Rd toward Dover Castle reveals why it is famed both for its setting and its impregnability. Trains head to Dover's Priory Station from London's Victoria, Waterloo East, London Bridge, and Charing Cross stations (2hr., every 45min., £17.50). Beware when boarding—as many trains branch off en route make sure you're in the right car. National Express buses run regularly from London's Victoria Coach Station to the bus station on Pencester Rd and then on to the Eastern Docks (2¾hr., £9), where P&O Stena Line and Hoverspeed (see above) depart from the Prince of Wales Pier. Buses also make trips to Canterbury (£4). The tourist office, on Townwall St, has lodgings info and ferry and Hovercraft tickets. (Tel. (01304) 20 51 08; fax 22 54 98. Open daily 9am-6pm.) The YHA Charlton House Youth Hostel, 306 London Rd, is ½ mi. from the train station. (Tel. (01304) 20 13 14; fax 20 22 36. £10.15, students £9.15. Kitchen. Lockout 10am-1pm. Curfew 11pm.) The Victoria Guest House, 1 Laureston Pl (tel./fax (01304) 20 51 40), offers gracious Victorian lodgings for £30-56. Harthorn Farm, at Martin Mill Station off the A258, offers camping. (June to mid-Sept. £3.50 per person. Two people with car and tent June to mid-Sept. £11, Mar.-May and mid-Sept. to Oct. £6.50; plus £2 extra per person.) Cheap food fries from dawn to dusk in the fish-and-chip shops on London Rd and Biggin St. Postal code: CT16 1PB.

BRIGHTON

According to legend, the future King George IV scuttled into Brighton (pop. 250,000) for some hanky-panky around 1784. Today, Brighton is still the unrivaled home of the "dirty weekend"—it sparkles with a risqué, tawdry luster all its own. Before indulging, check out England's long-time obsession with the Far East at the excessively ornate Royal Pavilion, on Pavilion Parade, next to Old Steine. (Open daily June-Sept. 10am-6pm; Oct.-May 10am-5pm. £4.50, students £3.25.) Around the corner on Church St stands the Brighton Museum and Art Gallery, with paintings, English pottery, and a wild Art Deco and Art Nouveau collection. Leer at Salvador Dalí's sexy red sofa, *Mae West's Lips.* (Open M-Tu and Th-Sa 10am-5pm, Su 2-5pm. Free.) Before heading out to the rocky beach, stroll the Lanes, a jumble of 17th-century streets forming the heart of Old Brighton. Brighton brims with nightlife options; pick up *The Punter* or *What's On* (at music stores, newsagents, and pubs) for tips. It's also *the* gay nightlife spot in Britain outside London; pick up *Gay Times* (£2.50) or *Capital Gay.* Drink at Fortune of War, 157 King's Rd Arches (open M-Sa 10:30am-11pm, Su 11am-10:30pm), or The Squid, 78 Middle St (open M-F 5-11pm, Sa 3-11pm, Su 3-10:30pm). Paradox and Event II, on West St, are popular clubs. The Beach, 171-181 King's Rd Arches, produces some of the beachfront's biggest beats, while Casablanca, on Middle St, plays live jazz to a mostly student crowd. The converted WWII tunnels of Zap Club, on King's Rd, provide space for dirty dancing.

   Trains (tel. (0345) 48 49 50) roll to London (1¼hr., 6 per hr., £13.70) and Portsmouth (1½hr., 1 per day, day return £11.70). National Express buses (tel. (01273) 38 37 44) head to London (2hr., 15 per day, return £8). The tourist office is at 10 Bartholomew Sq. (Tel. (01273) 29 25 99. Open M-Tu and Th-F 9am-5pm, W and Sa 10am-5pm.) The rowdy ⌨Brighton Backpackers Hostel, 75-76 Middle St, is the best place for meeting other backpackers. (Tel. (01273) 77 77 17; fax 88 77 88; email

BRITAIN

stay@brightonbackpackers.com. Dorms £8; doubles £25. Sheets £1. **Internet** free.) **Baggies Back-packers,** 33 Oriental Pl, has mellow vibes and exquisite murals. Head west of West Pier along King's Rd, and Oriental Pl is on the right. (Tel. (01273) 73 37 40; www.cisweb.co.uk/baggies. Dorms £10; doubles £25.) To get to the **YHA youth hostel,** on Patcham Pl, 4 mi. away, take Patcham Bus 5 or 5A from Old Steine in front of the Royal Pavilion to the Black Lion Hotel. (Tel. (01273) 55 61 96. £10.15. Breakfast £3. Curfew 11pm.) For cheap eats, try the fish-and-chip shops along the beach or north of the Lanes, or head to **Safeway supermarket,** 5-8 St. James Pl (open M-W 8am-8pm, Th-Sa 8am-9pm). **Postal code:** BN1 1BA.

CHICHESTER

The remains of Roman walls and an imposing Norman cathedral provide the backdrop for Chichester's (pop. 30,000) superb theater, arts festivals, and gallery exhibits. The **cathedral,** begun in 1091, features a glorious stained-glass window by Marc Chagall. (Open daily in summer 8:30am-7pm; off-season 8:30am-5pm. Donation £2.) The amazingly well-preserved **Roman Palace** in nearby **Fishbourne,** dating from around AD 80, is the largest Roman residence ever excavated in Britain. From the Ave de Chartres roundabout in Chichester, head west on Westgate, which becomes Fishbourne Rd (the A259) for 1½ mi.; or take bus 11, 56, or 700 from the center of town and then walk 5min. to the palace. (Open Aug. daily 10am-6pm; Mar.-July and Sept.-Oct. daily 10am-5pm; Feb. and Nov.-Dec. daily 10am-4pm; Jan. Sa-Su 10am-4pm. £4.40, students £3.70.) Should your tastes drift to the romantic, head to the fairy-tale **castle** in nearby **Arundel** on a train or a bus (£3.40). (Tel. (01903) 88 31 36. Open Apr.-Oct. Su-F noon-5pm. £6.70.)

Trains run to Portsmouth (40min., 2-3 per hr., £4.90); Brighton (1hr., 2-3 per hr., £7.80); and London's Victoria Station (1½hr., 2 per hr., £16). **Buses** (tel. (01903) 23 76 61) depart from diagonally opposite the train station on Southgate. National Express runs to London (1 per day, period return £9); Coastline serves Brighton (bus 702; 3hr., 2 per hr., £4.60) and Portsmouth (buses 700 and 701; 1hr., 2 per hr., £3.90). To get to the **tourist office,** 29a South St, turn left as you exit the station onto Southgate, which becomes South St. (Tel. (01243) 77 58 88; fax 53 94 49. Open M-Sa 9:15am-5:15pm; July-Aug. also Su 10am-4pm.) Expect to pay £16-20 for a bed. **Hedgehogs,** 45 Whyke Ln, offers cozy rooms near the town center. (Tel. (01243) 78 00 22. Singles and doubles £18-24 per person.) **Camp** at **Southern Leisure Centre,** on Vinnetrow Rd, 15min. southeast of town. (Tel. (01243) 78 77 15. £2 per person, £8-10 per tent. Shower included. Open Apr.-Oct.) **Postal code:** PO19 1AB.

PORTSMOUTH

Set Victorian prudery against prostitutes, drunkards, and a lot of bloody cursing sailors, and there you have a basic 900-year history of Portsmouth (pop. 190,500). On the seafront, visitors relive D-Day, explore warships, and learn of the days when Britannia ruled the seas. War buffs and historians will want to plunge head first into the unparalleled **Naval Heritage Centre,** in the Naval Base, which houses a virtual armada of Britain's most storied ships. The center includes England's first attempt at a warship, Henry VIII's **May Rose.** Although Henry was particularly fond of her, she—like many women with whom Henry associated—died before her time, sinking after setting sail from Portsmouth in July 1545. Napoleon must be rolling in his little coffin to know that the **HMS Victory,** which clinched Britain's reputation as king of the waves when it defeated him at the Battle of Trafalgar in 1805, is still afloat. (Check your ticket for your tour time slot.) The five galleries of the **Royal Naval Museum** fill in the historical gaps between the three ships. Entrance is next to the tourist office on The Hard—follow the signs to Portsmouth Historic Ships. (Ships open daily 9:45am-6pm. £6 each, students £5.20.)

For info on **ferries** to France, see p. 58. **Trains** (tel. (0345) 48 49 50) run to Southsea Station, on Commercial Rd, from Chichester (40min., 2 per hr., £4.70); London's Waterloo Station (1½hr., 3 per hr., £18.60); and Salisbury (1½hr., every hr., £11-13). National Express **buses** (tel. (08705) 80 80 80) arrive from London (2½hr., 1 per hr., £10.50) and Salisbury (2hr., 1 per day, £8.25). The **tourist office** is on The

Hard; there's a **branch** next to the train station. (Tel. 92 82 67 22. Open daily 9:30am-5:45pm.) Moderately priced **B&Bs** (around £20) clutter **Southsea**, 1½ mi. east of The Hard along the coast. Take any Southsea bus and get off at The Strand to reach the **Portsmouth and Southsea Backpackers Lodge,** 4 Florence Rd. (Tel./fax 92 83 24 95. Dorms £9; twins £22; doubles £25. Kitchen. Laundry. **Internet.**) Take any bus to Cosham (including 1, 3, and 40) to the police station and follow the signs to get to the **YHA youth hostel** at Wymering Manor, on Old Wymering Ln, Medina Rd, in Cosham. (Tel. 92 37 56 61. £9.15. Lockout 10am-5pm. Curfew 11pm. Open Feb.-Aug. daily; Sept.-Nov. F-Sa.) The **Tesco supermarket,** on Craswell St, is near the center. (Open M-Th 8am-8pm, F 8am-9pm, Sa 8am-7pm, Su 10am-4pm.) **Pubs** near The Hard provide weary sailors with galley fare and bottles of gin. **Postal code:** PO1 1AA.

WINCHESTER

The glory of Winchester (pop. 31,000) stretches back to Roman times. William the Conqueror deemed the town the center of his kingdom, and Jane Austen and John Keats both lived and wrote in town. Duck through the archway, pass through the square, and behold the 900-year-old **Winchester Cathedral,** 5 The Close. Famed for its nave, the 556-foot-long cathedral is the longest medieval building in Europe; the interior holds magnificent tiles and Jane Austen's tomb. The **Norman crypt,** supposedly the oldest in England, can only be viewed in the summer by guided tour. The 12th-century Winchester Bible resides in the library. (Open daily 7:15am-6:30pm; East End closes 5pm. Tours 10am-3pm; free. Donation £2.50, students £2.) Fifteen mi. north of Winchester is the meek village of **Chawton,** where Jane Austen lived. It was in her ▉**cottage** that she penned *Pride and Prejudice*, *Emma*, *Northanger Abbey*, and *Persuasion*. Take Hampshire bus X64 (M-Sa 11 per day, return £4.50), or the London and Country bus 65 on Sundays, from the bus station; ask to be let off at the Chawton roundabout and follow the brown signs. (Tel. (01420) 832 62. Open Mar.-Dec. daily 11am-4:30pm; Jan.-Feb. Sa-Su 11am-4:30pm. £2.50.)

Trains (tel. (0345) 48 49 50) arrive at Winchester's Station Hill, at City Rd and Sussex St, from Chichester (50min., every hr., £9.50); London's Waterloo Station (1hr., 2 per hr., £16.60); and Portsmouth (1hr., every hr., £7). To get there from the train station, head down City Rd, right on Jewry St, and left on High St (10min.). National Express **buses** (tel. (08705) 80 80 80) go to London (1½hr., 7 per day, £12); Hampshire Stagecoach (tel. (01256) 46 45 01) goes to Salisbury (#68; 1½hr., 7 per day, return £4.45) and Portsmouth (#69; 1½hr., 12 per day, return £4.45). The **tourist office,** at The Guildhall, Broadway, is by the statue of Alfred the Great. (Tel. (01962) 84 05 00; fax 85 03 48. Open June-Sept. M-Sa 10am-6pm, Su 11am-2pm; Oct.-May M-Sa 10am-5pm.) The lovely home of **Mrs. P. Patton,** 12 Christchurch Rd, between St. James Ln and Beaufort Rd, is 5min. from the cathedral. (Tel. (01962) 85 42 72. Doubles £30-35; singles £22-25.) Go past the Alfred statue, across the bridge, and left before Cricketers Pub to reach the **YHA youth hostel,** 1 Water Ln. (Tel. (01962) 85 37 23. £9.15. Kitchen. Lockout 10am-5pm. Curfew 11pm. Open July-Aug. daily; mid-Feb. to June and Sept.-Oct. Tu-Sa.) **Royal Oak,** on Royal Oak Passage, next to the Godbegot House off High St, is another pub that claims to be the kingdom's oldest. (Open daily 11am-11pm.) Get **groceries** at **Sainsbury,** on Middle Brook St, off High St. (Open M-Th 8am-6:30pm, F 8am-9pm, Sa 7:30am-6pm.) **Postal code:** SO23 8WA.

SALISBURY

Salisbury (pop. 103,000) revolves around **Salisbury Cathedral,** whose spire rises a neck-breaking 404 ft. The bases of the pillars literally bend inward under the strain of 6400 tons of limestone; if a pillar rings when you knock on it, you should probably move away. (Open daily May-Aug. 8am-8:15pm, Sept.-Apr. 8am-6:30pm. Donation £3, students £2. Tours M-Sa 11:15am-2:15pm; free. Roof and tower tours M-Sa 10:30, 11:30am, 2, 3, and 6:30pm, Su 4:30pm; £2.50.) One of four surviving copies of the Magna Carta rests in the **Chapter House.** (Open Mar.-Oct. M-Sa 9:30am-5:30pm, Su 1-5:30pm; Nov.-Feb. M-Sa 11am-3pm, Su 1-3:15pm. Free.)

Trains arrive on South Western Rd from Winchester (1½hr., every hr., £10.40) and London (1½hr., every hr., £22-30). National Express **buses** (tel. 08705) 80 80 80) pull

BRITAIN

into 8 Endless St from London's Victoria Station (2¾hr., 4 per day, £11.50); Wilts & Dorset buses (tel. (01722) 33 68 55) arrive from Bath (#X4; 2hr., 6 per day, £3). The **tourist office** is on Fish Row in the Guildhall, in Market Sq; turn left on South Western Rd, bear right on Fisherton St, continue on Bridge St, cross the bridge onto High St, and walk straight on Silver St, which becomes Butcher Row and Fish Row (10-15min.). From the bus station, head left on Endless St, which (shockingly) ends and becomes Queen St, and turn right at the first old building to the right to enter Fish Row. (Tel. (01722) 33 49 56; fax 42 20 59. Open July-Aug. M-Sa 9:30am-7pm, Su 10:30am-4:30pm; June and Sept. M-Sa 9:30am-6pm, Su 10:30am-4:30pm; Oct.-May M-Sa 9:30am-5:30pm.) To get from the bus station to lodgings at **The Old Bakery,** 35 Bedwin St, head two blocks up Rollestone St, and turn left onto Bedwin St. (Tel. (01722) 32 01 00. £15-20; with full breakfast £18-25. Backpackers' cottage £15 per person; with continental breakfast £17.) From the tourist office, head left on Fish Row, right on Queen St, left on Milford St, and straight under the overpass to find the **YHA youth hostel,** in Milford Hill House, on Milford Hill. (Tel. (01722) 32 75 72; fax 33 04 46. Dorms £9.15-10.15. **Camping** £4.70 per person. Lockout 10am-1pm. Curfew 11:30pm. Call ahead.) **Sainsbury's supermarket** is at The Maltings. (Open M-Th 8am-8pm, F 8am-9pm, Sa 7:30am-7pm, Su 10am-4pm.) **Postal code:** SP1 1AB.

▶️ EXCURSION FROM SALISBURY: STONEHENGE. The 22-foot-high boulders of Stonehenge, which weigh up to 45 tons, date from about 1500 BC. Various and sundry stories attribute the monument to Druids, Phoenicians, Merlin, Mycenaean Greeks, Bjork, giants, Romans, Smurfs, Danes, and aliens. In any case, the laborers' technological capabilities were more advanced than we can imagine; their unknown methods continue to elude both archaeologists and previously failsafe supermarket tabloids. For centuries, religious devotees have come for its mystical karmic energies, building temples and leaving us to marvel at the awe-inspiring, impressive nature of the site. You can languidly admire Stonehenge for free from nearby Amesbury Hill, 1½ mi. up A303, or pay admission at the site. (Tel. (01980) 62 53 68. Open daily June-Aug. 9am-7pm; mid-Mar. to May and Sept. to mid-Oct. 9:30am-6pm; mid-Oct. to mid-Mar. 9:30am-4pm. £4, students £3.) Wilts & Dorset **buses** (tel. (01722) 33 68 55) connect from Salisbury's center and train station (40min., return £4.80).

▶️ EXCURSION FROM SALISBURY: AVEBURY. Avebury sprouts from within a **stone circle** that represents the third-largest stone henge in Europe. Avebury's sprawling titans were constructed over 500 years before Stonehenge's. Many have studied the circle, but its meaning evades all. Just outside the circle is **Silbury Hill,** built in 2660 BC; the curious manmade mound represents another archaeological mystery. Take **bus** 5 or 6 from Salisbury to Avebury (1½hr., 6 per day, £3.90). The **tourist office** is near the car park near the stone circle (follow the signs). (Tel. (01672) 53 94 25. Open W-Sa 10am-5pm, Su 10am-4pm.)

EXETER

Besieged by William the Conqueror in 1068 and flattened by German bombs in 1942, Exeter (pop. 110,000), has undergone frantic rebuilding resulting in an odd mixture of the venerable and the banal: ruins punctuate even parking lots and department store cash registers ring atop medieval catacombs. **Exeter Cathedral** was heavily damaged in WWII but nonetheless retains exquisite detail. The cathedral library's **Exeter Book** is the richest treasury of early Anglo-Saxon poetry in the world. (Cathedral open daily 7am-6:30pm; library open M-F 2-5pm. Evensong services M-F 5:30pm, Sa-Su 3pm. Free tours Apr.-Oct. M-F 11:30am and 2:30pm, Sa 11am. Donation £2.50.) Six-hundred-year-old **underground passages** are accessible from Romangate Passage next to Boots on High St. (Open July-Sept. M-Sa 10am-5:30pm; Oct.-June Tu-F 2-5pm, Sa 10am-5pm. Tours £3.50, students £2.50.)

Back in Exeter, **trains** arrive from London's Paddington and Waterloo Stations (3hr., 16 per day, £40); from St. David's Station, follow the footpath in front, turn right onto St. David's Hill (which becomes Iron Bridge and North St), and turn left on High St. National Express **buses** (tel. (08705) 80 80 80) pull into Paris St, off High

BRITAIN

St just outside the city walls, from London's Victoria Coach Station (4hr., every 1½hr., return £16) and Bath (2¾hr., 3 per day, £13); walk through the arcade to Sidwell St and turn left to reach High St. The **tourist office,** in the Civic Centre, in the City Council Building on Paris St, is opposite the rear of the bus station. (Tel. (01392) 26 57 00. Open M-Sa 9am-5pm, Su 10am-4pm.) To reach the **YHA youth hostel,** 47 Countess Wear Rd, 2 mi. away on Topsham Rd, take minibus K or T from High St to the Countess Wear Post Office (97p), follow Exe Vale Rd to the end, and turn left. (Tel. (01392) 87 33 29. £10.15. Breakfast £3.10. **Camping** about half-price. Reception 8-10am and 5-10pm.) Pack a picnic at **Sainsbury's supermarket,** in the Guildhall Shopping Centre off High St. (Open M-W and F 8am-6:30pm, Th 8am-7pm, Sa 7:30am-6pm, Su 10:30am-4:30pm.) **Postal code:** EX1 1AA.

PLYMOUTH

Plymouth is a famed port—the English fleet sailed from here to defeat the Spanish Armada in 1588, and Sir Francis Drake, Captain Cook, the Pilgrims, Lord Nelson, and millions of emigrants to the United States and New Zealand earned Plymouth a spot in the history books in their haste to escape it. Heed their age-old message. **Trains** (tel. (0345) 48 49 50) run at least every hour from Plymouth Station, on North Rd, to Penzance (1¾hr., £10.50) and London's Paddington Station (3½hr., £27-57); take Western National bus 14, 16b, 72, 83, or 84 to the city center at Royal Parade. **Buses** leave from Bretonside Station, near St. Andrew's Cross at the eastern end of Royal Parade; National Express (tel. (08705) 80 80 80) goes to London (4½hr., £20) and Stagecoach Devon runs to Exeter (X38, 1¼hr., £4.15). For **ferries** (tel. (0990) 36 03 60) departing from the Millbay Docks (take bus 33 or 34 to the docks; 15min.) for France and Spain, see p. 58. The **tourist office** is in Island House, 9 The Barbican. (Tel. (01752) 30 48 49; fax 25 79 55. Open M-Sa 9am-5pm, Su 10am-4pm.) Take bus 15 or 81 from the train station or Royal Parade to Stoke to find the **YHA youth hostel,** Belmont House, on Belmont Pl. (Tel. (01752) 56 21 89; fax 60 53 60. £10.15. Lockout 10am-5pm. Curfew 11pm. Reserve ahead.) **Plymouth Backpackers Hotel,** 172 Citadel Rd, is two blocks from the west end of the Hoe. (Tel. (01752) 22 51 58; fax 20 78 47. Dorms £8.50; singles £10; triples £27. Laundry.) **Sainsbury's,** in the Armada Shopping Centre, stocks **groceries.** (Open M-Sa 8am-8pm, Su 10am-4pm.)

THE CORNISH COAST

PENZANCE. Penzance is the very model of an ancient English pirate town: waterlogged, stealthy, and unabashed. A Benedictine monastery was built on the spot where St. Michael dropped by in AD 495, and today **St. Michael's Mount** sits offshore. The interior is unspectacular, but the grounds are more textured, and the 30-story views are captivating. (Open Apr.-Oct. M-F 10:30am-5:30pm; in summer usually also Sa-Su; Nov.-Mar. in nice weather. £4.40.) A causeway links the mount to the island; or take ferry bus 2 or 2A to Marazion (M-Sa 3 per hr., return £0.80) and catch a ferry during high tide (return £1.40). **Trains** (tel. (0345) 48 49 50) go to London (5½hr., 1 per hr., £54); Plymouth (2hr., 1 per hr., £10); and Exeter (3hr., 1 per hr., £18.60). National Express (tel. (08705) 80 80 80) **buses** go to Plymouth (3hr., 2 per hr., £6) and London (8hr., 8 per day, £27). Between the two stations is the **tourist office,** on Station Rd. (Tel. (01736) 36 22 07. Open in summer M-F 9am-5pm, Sa 9am-4pm, Su 10am-1pm; off-season M-F 9am-5pm, Sa 10am-1pm.) To get to the ✉**YHA youth hostel,** Castle Horneck, walk 30min. up Market Jew and Alverton St, then take the right fork with the signs for Castle Horneck. (Tel. (01736) 36 26 66; fax 36 26 63; email penzance@yha.org.uk. £10.15. **Camping** £5. Kitchen. Laundry. Reception 3-11pm. Lockout 10am-1pm.) **The Turk's Head,** 49 Chapel St, is a 13th-century pub (Penzance's oldest), sacked by Spanish pirates in 1595.

ST. IVES. St. Ives (pop. 11,100) perches 10 mi. north of Penzance, on a spit of land lined by pastel beaches and azure waters. Virginia Woolf too was bewitched by the energy of the Atlantic at St. Ives: her masterpiece *To the Lighthouse* is thought to refer to the Godrevy Lighthouse in the distance. Whether you seek the perfect sub-

BRITAIN

ject or the perfect strip of sand, St. Ives has it, if hidden beneath a veneer of post-cards and ice cream cones. Some **trains** (tel. (0345) 48 49 50); some (3-6 per day) go directly to Penzance, but most connect via St. Erth (10min., 2 per hr., £3). Western National **buses** go to Penzance (3 per hr., off-season M-Sa only, £2.50) and Newquay. National Express (tel. (08705) 80 80 80) stops in St. Ives between Plymouth and Penzance (6 per day). The **tourist office** is in the Guildhall on Street-an-Pol. From the stations, walk down to the foot of Tregenna Hill and turn right on Street-an-Pol. (Tel. (01736) 79 62 97. Open in summer M-Sa 9:30am-6pm, Su 10am-1pm; off-season closed Sa-Su.) **St. Ives International Backpackers,** The Stenmack, fills a renovated 19th-century Methodist church. (Tel./fax (01736) 79 94 44. £8-12. **Internet.**) Places to camp abound in nearby **Hayle;** try **Trevalgan Camping Park** (tel. (01736) 79 64 33). **Fore St** is packed with small bakeries. Many places also sell Cornish cream teas (a pot of tea with scones, jam, and Cornish clotted cream).

FALMOUTH. Seven rivers flow into the historic port of Falmouth (pop. 18,300), which is guarded by two spectacular castles. **Pendennis Castle,** built by Henry VIII to keep French frigates out of Falmouth, now features a walk-through diorama. (Open daily Apr.-Sept. 10am-6pm; Nov.-Mar. 10am-4pm. £3.80, students £2.90.) Across the channel lies another Henry VIII creation, the magnificently preserved **St. Mawes Castle.** To get there, take the ferry from the Town Pier and The Quay (20min., 2 per hr., return £3.50). (Open Apr.-Sept. daily 10am-6pm; Oct. daily 10am-5pm; Nov.-Mar. F-Tu 10am-4pm. £2.50, students £1.90.) To taste the surf, head to one of Falmouth's three **beaches. Trains** (tel. (0345) 48 49 50) arrive in town from Plymouth (2hr., 9-17 per day, return £45); Exeter (3½hr., return £40); and London (return £55). National Express (tel. (08705) 80 80 80) **buses** roll in from London (6½hr., 2 per day, £34.50). To get from inland to the **tourist office,** 28 Killigrew St, The Moor, follow signs to Killigrew St or Kimberley Park Rd, then go downhill toward the river. (Tel. (01326) 31 23 00. Open Apr.-Sept. M-Sa 9:30am-5:30pm, Su 10am-2pm.) None of the **train stations** sells tickets; get 'em at **Newell's Travel Agency,** 26 Killigrew St, The Moor, next to the tourist office. (Tel. (01326) 31 50 66. Open M-F 9am-5:30pm, Sa 9am-4pm.) The **YHA youth hostel** is in Pendennis Castle, 30min. from town. (Tel. (01326) 31 14 35; fax 31 54 73. £9.15. Reception 8:30-10am and 5-10:30pm. Curfew 11pm. Open Feb.-Sept. daily; Oct.-Nov. Tu-Sa. Reserve ahead.)

NEWQUAY. An outpost of surfer subculture, Newquay (NEW-key) lures the bald, the bleached-blond, even the blue, to its surf and pubs. Winds descend on **Fistral Beach** with a vengeance, creating what some consider the best surfing conditions in all of Europe. The enticing **Lusty Glaze Beach** beckons from the bay side. The party beast stirs around 9pm and reigns into the wee hours. Drink up at **The Red Lion,** on North Quay Hill, at Tower Rd and Fore St, then ride the wave down Fore St to **Sailors.** (Cover £4-10.) Go on and shake what your momma gave you at **Bertie's,** on East St. (Open until 1am.) From the **train station,** just off Cliff Rd, trains go to Plymouth (2hr., every hr., £8.10) and Penzance (2hr., every hr., £10.30). From the **bus station,** 1 East St, Western National runs to St. Ives (2hr., June-Sept. 1 per day, £4.90). National Express (tel. (08705) 80 80 80) buses runs to London (5¾hr., 3 per day, £26.50). Facing the street from the train station, go four blocks left to reach the **tourist office,** on Marcus Hill. (Tel. (01637) 87 13 45. Open in summer M-Sa 9am-6pm, Su 9am-4pm; off-season reduced hours.) **Newquay Backpackers International,** 69-73 Tower Rd, offers free shuttle service to its sister hostel in St. Ives. (Tel. (01637) 87 93 66; email backpacker@dial.pipex.com. £10. **Internet.**)

EAST ANGLIA AND THE MIDLANDS

The plush green farmlands and watery fens of **East Anglia** stretch northeast from London, cloaking the counties of Cambridgeshire, Norfolk, and Suffolk. Although industry is modernizing the economies of Cambridge and Peterborough, the area in between is still characterized by its sheer flatness; much of the rustic beauty that inspired the landscape paintings of natives Constable and Gainsborough remains. To the west lie the **Midlands**—the term evokes images of industrial cities, thanks to the "dark satanic mills" foreseen by William Blake that overran the area during the Industrial Revolution. But the heart of England contains its fair share of England's "must-sees"; Manchester and Liverpool are home to innovative music, arts, and nightlife scenes, while Lincoln and Chester tell many of their tales in Latin.

OXFORD

Oxford today is a scramble of rumbling trucks, screeching brakes, and pedestrians shoving past one other in the streets. But there are pockets of respite to charm and edify the academic pilgrim paying homage to more than 500 years of scholarship: the basement room of Blackwell's bookshop, the impeccable gallery of the Ashmolean Museum, and the perfectly maintained quadrangles of Oxford's 39 colleges help the town to retain an irrepressible grandeur.

▐▀ GETTING THERE AND GETTING AROUND

Trains: Depart from Park End St, west of Carfax (tel. (0345) 48 49 50, recording 79 44 22). **Thames trains** run from London's Paddington Station (1hr., every 30min., day return £13.80). Ticket office open M-F 6am-8pm, Sa 6:45am-8pm, Su 7:45am-8pm.

Buses: Depart from Gloucester Green (follow the arrows up Cornmarket St from Carfax). **Oxford CityLink** (tel. 78 54 00; open daily 6:30am-6:30pm) connects from Victoria Station (1¾hr., 1-4 per hr., next-day return £7.50, students £6.50) and from Gatwick and Heathrow. **National Express** (tel. (0990) 80 80 80) offers national routes.

Public Transportation: The **Oxford Bus Company** (tel. 78 54 00) and **Stagecoach** (tel. 77 22 50). Most local services board on the streets around Carfax. Fares are low (usually 70p). Valuable day and week passes are available from the driver or at the station.

▐ ORIENTATION AND PRACTICAL INFORMATION

Queen, High, St. Aldate's, and Cornmarket Streets intersect at **Carfax,** the town center. The colleges are all within one mi. of one another, mainly to the east of Carfax along High St and Broad St; the train and bus stations lie to the northwest.

Tourist Office: The Old School, Gloucester Green (tel. 72 68 71; fax 24 02 61), beside the bus station. A pamphleteer's paradise. Accommodations list 50p. Map £1. Books rooms for a £2.50 fee and a 10% deposit. Two-hour **walking tours** depart 2-5 times daily 11am-2pm (£4.50, children £3). Open M-Sa 9:30am-5pm, Su 10am-3:30pm.

American Express: 4 Queen St (tel. 79 20 66). Open M-Sa 9am-5:30pm, W opens at 9:30am, Sa closes at 5pm; in summer also Su 11am-3pm.

Luggage storage: Pensioners' Club in Gloucester Green (tel. 24 22 37), by the bus station. Storage for up to a few weeks. £1-2 donation requested. Open M-Sa 9am-4:45pm.

Emergency: Dial 999 (toll-free).

Police: Tel. 26 60 00. Stations at St. Aldates St and Speedwell St.

Crisis Line: Samaritans, 123 Iffley Rd (tel. 72 21 22; 24hr.); drop-in daily 8am-10pm.

Gay and Lesbian Services: Gay Switchboard, Oxford Friend (tel. 79 39 99).

Pharmacy: Boots, 6-8 Cornmarket St (tel. 24 74 61). Open M-Sa 8:45am-6pm, Su 11am-5pm.

Internet Access: Daily Information, 31 Warnborough Rd (tel. 31 00 11). £1 per 10min. Open M-Sa 9am-9pm. Call after 6pm to make sure they're open.

Post Office: 102/104 St. Aldates St (tel. 20 28 63). Open M-F 9am-5:30pm, Sa 9am-6pm. Changes money. **Postal code:** OX1 1ZZ.

PHONE CODE	City code: 01865. From outside the UK, dial int'l dialing prefix (see inside back cover) + 44 + 1865 + local number.

▐ ACCOMMODATIONS

In summer, book at least a week ahead. **B&Bs** line the main roads out of town and are reachable by Cityline buses or a 15- to 45-minute walk. More B&Bs are located in the 300s on **Banbury Rd** (take bus 2A, 2C, or 2D); cheaper ones lie in the 200s and

BRITAIN

300s on **Iffley Rd** (take bus 4), between 250 and 350 on **Cowley Rd** (take buses 51 or 52), and on **Abingdon Rd** in South Oxford (take bus 16). Expect to pay £20-25.

YHA Youth Hostel, 32 Jack Straw's Ln, Headington (tel. 76 29 97; fax 76 94 02). Take Bus 13 (4 per hr. until 11:10pm; 70p) heading away from Carfax on High St; ask the driver to stop at Jack Straw's Ln and walk 8min. up the hill. 105 beds. Kitchen, laundry, and food shop. £10.50, under 18 £6.85, students £1 less. Reserve ahead in summer.

Newton House, 82-84 Abingdon Rd (tel. 24 05 61), ½ mi. from town center; take any Abingdon bus across Folly Bridge. Affable proprietor, TVs, and dark wardrobes await Narnia fans; don't get lost. Doubles £48, with bath £58.

Bravalla, 242 Iffley Rd (tel. 24 13 26; fax 25 05 11). Six sunny rooms, all with bath and TV. Breakfast (good vegetarian options) in a conservatory; sign the breakfast board the night before. Singles £25-35; doubles £40-45. Reserve two weeks ahead in summer.

Old Mitre Rooms, 4b Turl St (tel. 27 98 21; fax 27 99 63), Lincoln College dorms with shaggy green carpet. Singles £24; twins £44, with bath £48.50; triples/family rooms £58, with bath £63. Open July to early Sept.

Heather House, 192 Iffley Rd (tel./fax 24 97 57). Take the bus marked "Rose Hill" from the bus station, train station, or Carfax Tower (70p); or walk 20min. Vivian, the Australian proprietor, keeps sparkling, modern rooms. Singles £25; doubles with bath £48.

Oxford Backpacker's Hotel, 9a Hythe Bridge St (tel. 72 17 61). Great location, between the bus and train stations. Nonstop music enlivens the common room, hallways, and bathroom. £9-11 per night. Laundry £2.50. Kitchen. **Internet** access £1.50 per 15 min.

Oxford Camping International, 426 Abingdon Rd (tel. 24 40 88), behind the Touchwoods camping store. 84 sites. £4.20 per tent, £4.50 per person; caravans £5.75. Toilet and laundry facilities. Showers 20p. Reception daily 8am-8pm. The **YHA Youth Hostel** may also offer limited camping; call to find out.

◖ FOOD

Oxford students fed up with cafeteria food sustain a market for budget eats in town. The **Covered Market** between Market St and Carfax has produce, deli goods, and breads. (Open M-Sa 8am-5:30pm.) Pick up **groceries** at **J. Sainsbury,** in the Westgate Centre mall on Queen St. (Open M-F 8am-8pm, Sa 7:30am-7pm, Su 11am-5pm.) Across Magdalen Bridge is the vegetarian-friendly **Uhuru Wholefoods,** 48 Cowley Rd. (Open M-F 10am-6pm, Sa 9:30am-5:30pm.) After hours, **kebab vans** roam around Broad St, High St, Queen St, and St. Aldates St. If you're staying across Magdalen Bridge, try restaurants along the first four blocks of **Cowley Rd.**

Café CoCo, 23 Cowley Rd (tel. 20 02 32). Lively atmosphere and a great Mediterranean menu. Don't miss their tasty bargains. Entrees £5.95-8.50. Open daily 10am-11pm.

The Nosebag, 6-8 St. Michael's St (tel. 721033). Overcomes an unfortunate name with a gourmet-grade menu served cafeteria-style. Lunch under £6, dinner under £7.50. Open M 9:30am-5:30pm, Tu-Th until 10pm, F-Sa until 10:30pm, Su until 9pm.

Chiang Mai, 130a High St (tel. 20 22 33), tucked down an alley. Popular Thai restaurant with plenty of veggie options. Entrees £5.50-9. Reserve in advance or go for lunch to beat the crowds. Open M-Sa noon-2:30pm and 6-11pm, Su noon-3pm and 6-10pm.

Heroes, 8 Ship St (tel. 72 34 59). Filled with students feeding on sandwiches, meats and cheeses, and freshly-baked breads (£1.80-3.70). Popular for takeout, but there's also a small sit-down area. Open M-F 8am-5pm, Sa 8:30am-6pm, Su 10am-5pm.

◖ SIGHTS

King Henry II founded Britain's first university in 1167; today, Oxford's alumni register reads like a who's who of British history, literature, and philosophy. The university has traditionally been a breeding ground for the country's leaders; 22 British Prime Ministers were educated here. Oxford University's three favorite sons—Lewis Carroll, C.S. Lewis, and J.R.R. Tolkien—sat near the stone-bridged waters dreaming of crossings through mirrors, through wardrobes, and through mountain passes. The tourist office's *Welcome to Oxford* guide (£2) lists the colleges' public visiting hours.

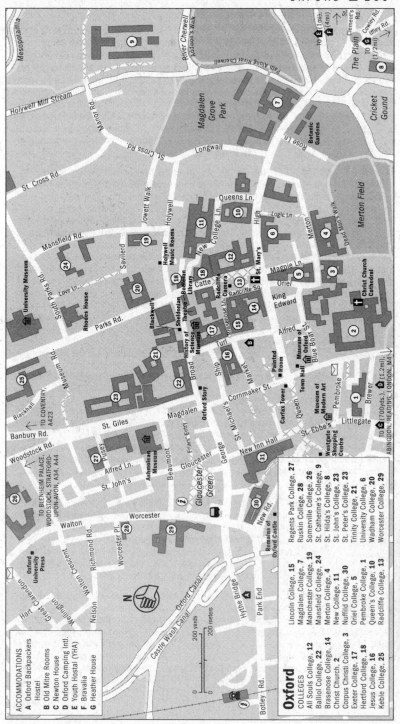

CARFAX AND SOUTH OF CARFAX. For an overview of the city, hike up the 99 spiral stairs of **Carfax Tower,** at Carfax. (Open daily Apr.-Oct. 10am-5:30pm, Nov.-Mar. 10am-3:30pm. £1.20.) Just down St. Aldates St from Carfax, **Christ Church College** has Oxford's grandest quad and its most socially distinguished students. The **Christ Church Chapel** is also Oxford's cathedral. The Reverend Charles Dodgson (better known as Lewis Carroll) was friendly with Dean Liddell of Christ Church—and friendlier with his daughter Alice. *(Open M-Sa 9am-5pm, Su 1-5pm. Church services Su 8, 10, 11:15am, 6pm; weekdays 7:30am, 6pm. £2.50, students £1.50.)* The 13th-century **University College,** on High St, welcomed Bill Clinton during his Rhodes Scholar days (his rooms at 46 Leckford Rd are an endless source of smoked-but-didn't-inhale jokes for tour guides), but expelled Percy Bysshe Shelley for writing the pamphlet *The Necessity of Atheism. (Open Jul.-Aug. daily 10am-6pm.)*

NORTH OF CARFAX. The imposing **Ashmolean Museum** houses works by Leonardo, Monet, Manet, van Gogh, Michelangelo, Rodin, and Matisse, while the **Cast Gallery,** behind the museum, exhibits over 250 casts of Greek sculptures—the finest classical collection outside London. *(Beaumont St. From Carfax, head up Cornmarket St, which becomes Magdalen St; Beaumont St is on the left. Both museum and gallery open Tu-Sa 10am-4pm, Su 2-4pm. Free.)* The **Bodleian Library** is Oxford's principal reading and research library, with over five million books; no one has ever been permitted to check one out. *(Catte St. Take High St and turn left on Catte. Open M-F 9am-6pm, Sa 9am-1pm. £3.50.)* The **Sheldonian Theatre,** beside the Bodleian, is a Roman-style jewel of an auditorium, where graduation ceremonies are conducted in Latin. The cupola of the theater affords an inspiring view of the spires of Oxford. *(Open M-Sa 10am-12:30pm and 2-4:30pm. £2.)* On Broad St you could browse for days at **Blackwell's Bookstore,** which according to Guinness is the largest room devoted to bookselling in the world. *(Open M-Sa 9am-6pm, Su 11am-5pm.)* Oscar Wilde attended **Magdalen** (MAUD-lin) **College,** considered by many to be Oxford's most handsome college. *(Open daily July-Sept. noon-6pm; Oct.-June 2-5pm; Apr.-Sept. £2, students £1; Oct.-Mar. free.)*

🎵 🎭 ENTERTAINMENT AND NIGHTLIFE

PUNTING. A more traditional pastime in Oxford is punting on the river Thames (known in Oxford as the Isis) or on the River Cherwell (CHAR-wul). Punters receive a tall pole, a small oar, and an advisory against falling into the water before venturing out in boats that look something like shallow gondolas. Don't be surprised if you suddenly come across **Parson's Pleasure,** a small riverside area where men sometimes sunbathe nude. **Magdalen Bridge Boat Co.,** Magdalen Bridge, east of Carfax along High St, rents from March to November. (Tel. 20 26 43. M-F £9 per hr., Sa-Su £10 per hr.; deposit £20 plus ID. Open daily 10am-9pm.)

CONCERTS AND THEATER. Music and drama at Oxford are cherished arts. Attend a concert or Evensong service at one of the colleges (the **New College Choir** is one of the best boy choirs around) or a performance at the **Holywell Music Rooms,** the oldest in the country. The **Oxford Playhouse,** 11-12 Beaumont St, is a venue for bands, dance troupes, and the Oxford Stage Company. (Tel. 79 86 00. Tickets from £6, standby tickets available for seniors and students.) During summer, college **theater groups** stage productions in local gardens and cloisters.

PUBS AND NIGHTLIFE. Pubs far outnumber colleges in Oxford; many even consider them the city's prime attraction. Sprawling underneath the city, the 13th-century **Turf Tavern** on Bath Pl, off Holywell St, is Oxford's unofficial student union. (Open M-Sa 11am-11pm, Su noon-10:30pm. Kitchen open noon-8pm.) **The Eagle and Child,** 49 St. Giles St, moistened the tongues of C.S. Lewis and J.R.R. Tolkien for a quarter-century; *The Chronicles of Narnia* and *The Hobbit* were first read aloud here. (Open M-Sa 11am-11pm, Su noon-10:30pm.) **The Kings Arms,** Holywell St, draws in a huge young crowd. (Open M-Sa 10:30am-11pm, Su noon-10:30pm.) Though pubs in Oxford tend to close down by 11pm, nightlife can last until 3am; grab *This Month in Oxford* at the tourist office. For starters, check out **The West-**

gate Pub, Park End St. (Dance music until 2am on F and Sa, jazz on M, comedy on Tu.) Walton St and Cowley Rd host late-night clubs, as well as a fascinating jumble of ethnic restaurants, used bookstores, and alternative shops.

▣ EXCURSION FROM OXFORD: BLENHEIM PALACE

The largest private home in England and one of the loveliest, Blenheim (BLEN-em) Palace features sprawling grounds, a lake, and a fantastic garden. While attending a party here, Winston Churchill's mother gave birth to the future Prime Minister in a closet; his grave rests appropriately near in the village churchyard of Bladon. The palace rent is a single French franc, payable each year to the Crown—not a bad deal for a palace with 187 furnished rooms. Blenheim's full glory (and fake snow) is on display in Kenneth Branagh's 4-hour film *Hamlet* (1996). (Tel. (01993) 81 10 91. Open daily mid-Mar. to Oct. 10:30am-5:30pm; grounds open year-round 9am-9pm. £8.50, students £6.50.) Blenheim sprawls in Woodstock, 8 mi. north of Oxford on the A44. Stagecoach Express buses (tel. (01865) 77 22 50) run to Blenheim Palace from Gloucester Green station in Oxford (20min., return £3.50); the same bus also goes to Stratford and Birmingham.

THE COTSWOLDS

Stretching across western England—bounded by Banbury in the northeast, Bradford-upon-Avon in the southwest, Cheltenham in the north, and Malmesbury in the south—the Cotswolds' verdant, vivid hills enfold tiny towns barely touched by modern life. These old Roman settlements and tiny Saxon villages, hewn from the famed Cotswold stone, demand a place on any itinerary, although their relative inaccessibility via public transportation will necessitate extra effort to get there.

■ GETTING THERE AND GETTING AROUND. Useful gateway cities are Cheltenham, Oxford, and Bath. Trains to Cheltenham arrive regularly from London (2½hr., every hr., £29); Bath (1½hr., every hr., £11.10); and Exeter (2hr., every 2hr., £31). National Express buses (tel. (08705) 80 80 80) also roll in from London (3hr., every hr., £10.50); Stratford-upon-Avon (1hr., 2 per day, £7.50); and Exeter (3½hr., every 2hr., £18). For connections to Oxford, see p. 167; for connections to Bath, see p. 174.

From Cheltenham, Oxford, and Bath, trains zip to Moreton-in-Marsh (from Oxford £6.70) and Charlbury (from Oxford £3.40)—the only two villages in the Cotswolds with train stations. Several bus companies cover the Cotswolds, but most routes are very infrequent (1-2 per week). Two unusually regular services run from Cheltenham; Pulham's Coaches (tel. (01451) 82 03 69) run to Moreton via Bourton-on-the-Water and Stow-on-the-Wold (50min., M-Sa 7 per day, £1.40); Castleway's Coaches (tel. (01242) 60 29 49) depart for Broadway via Winchcombe (1hr., M-Sa 9 per day, £1.45). Snag the indispensable *Connection* timetable from any bus station or tourist office, and the Cheltenham tourist office's *Getting There from Cheltenham*.

Local roads are perfect for biking; the closely spaced villages make ideal watering holes. Country Lanes Cycle Center rents bikes at the Moreton-on-the-Marsh train station. (Tel. (01608) 65 00 65. £14 per day; gear and maps included. Call ahead. Open daily 9:30am-5:30pm.) Experience the Cotswolds as the English have for centuries by treading well-worn footpaths from village to village. Cotswold Way, spanning 100 mi. from Bath to Chipping Camden, gives hikers glorious vistas of hills and dales. The *Cotswold Way Handbook* (£2) lists B&Bs along the Cotswold Way. There are hostels in Charlbury (tel./fax (01608) 81 02 02; £8.35; open Apr.-June daily, July-Aug. M-Sa, Feb.-Mar. and Sept.-Oct. W-Su, Jan. F-Su), Slimbridge, and Stow-on-the-Wold. Most campsites are close to Cheltenham; Bourton-on-the-Water, Stow-on-the-Wold, and Moreton-on-the-Marsh also have places to put your Tent-on-the-Ground. The *Gloucestershire Caravan and Camping Guide* is free at local tourist centers.

STOW-ON-THE-WOLD, WINCHCOMBE, AND CIRENCESTER. Stow-on-the-Wold is a sleepy town with fine views, cold winds, and authentic stocks. The tourist office is in Hollis House on The Square. (Tel. (01451) 83 10 82. Open Easter-Oct. M-Sa

BRITAIN

9:30am-5:30pm, Su 10:30am-4pm; Oct.-Easter M-Sa 9:30am-4:30pm.) The **YHA youth hostel** stands just a few yards from the stocks. (Tel. (01451) 83 04 97. £10.15, students £7.80. Open Apr.-Aug. daily; Sept.-Oct. M-Sa; Nov.-Dec Sa-Su.)

West of Stow-on-the-Wold and 6 mi. north of Cheltenham on A46, **Sudeley Castle**, once the manor of King Ethelred the Unready, enserfs the town of **Winchcombe.** (Open Apr.-Oct. daily 10:30am-5pm. £6.) Just 1½ mi. southwest of Sudeley Castle lies **Belas Knap,** a 4000-year-old burial mound, one piece of evidence that the area was inhabited in prehistoric times. The **tourist office** is in Town Hall, near Cheltenham. (Tel. (01242) 60 29 25. Open Apr.-Oct. M-Sa 10am-5pm, Su 10am-4pm.)

Sometimes regarded as the capital of the region, **Cirencester** is the site of Corinium, a Roman town founded in AD 49, second in importance only to Londinium. Its **Corinium Museum,** on Park St, houses a formidable collection of Roman artifacts. (Open Apr.-Oct. M-Sa 10am-5pm, Su 2-5pm; Nov.-Mar. Tu-Sa 10am-5pm, Su 2-5pm. £2.50, students £1.) On Fridays, the town turns into a mad **antique marketplace.** The **tourist office** is in Corn Hall, on Market Pl. (Tel. (01285) 65 41 80. Open Apr.-Oct. M 9:45am-5:30pm, Tu-Sa 9:30am-5:30pm; Nov.-Mar. daily 9:30am-5pm.) Your best bet is to make Cirencester and the ruins a daytrip from Cheltenham (see below).

CHELTENHAM. Although the Laura Ashley-esque spa town of Cheltenham (pop. 86,500) is a nice break from the heavily touristed Bath and Stratford, it's pricey and offers little of interest; it's best used as a launching pad into the rest of the Cotswolds. Enjoy the diuretic and laxative effects of the waters at the **Town Hall.** Sip, don't gulp. (Open M-F 9am-1pm and 2:15-5pm. Free.) Manicured gardens adorn shops and houses around town, but for a real floral fix, sunbathe at the exquisite **Imperial Gardens,** just past The Promenade away from the center of town. **Trains** run from the station on Queen's Rd. The **tourist office,** 77 The Promenade, one block east of the bus station, posts vacancies after-hours. (Tel. (01242) 52 28 78. Open July-Aug. M-Sa 9:30am-6pm, Su 9:30am-1:30pm; Sept.-June M-Sa 9:30am-5:15pm.) The well-situated **YMCA,** on Vittoria Walk, accepts both men and women. At Town Hall, turn left off Promenade and walk three blocks—Vittoria Walk is on the right. (Tel. 52 40 24; fax 23 23 65. Singles £14. Breakfast included. Reception 24hr.) **Cross Ways,** 57 Bath Rd, features home-sewn bedding and curtains, TV, and a tasty breakfast (veggie options available). (Tel. 52 76 83; fax 57 72 26; email crossways@lynch.co.uk. £20-22 per person. Credit cards accepted.) **Hamilton Guest House,** 65 Bath Rd, has comfortable rooms. (Tel. 52 77 72. £20 per person, with bath £22.) Fruit stands and bakeries dot **High St.** Down the road, **Tesco** has **groceries.** (Open M-Tu and Sa 7:30am-7pm, W-F 7:30am-8pm.) **Postal code:** GL50 1AA.

STRATFORD-UPON-AVON

Former native William Shakespeare is now the area's industry; you'll find the vaguest of connections to the Bard exploited here to their full potential. But at rare moments, beyond the "Will Power" t-shirts and the tour bus exhaust, the essence of Shakespeare does lurk in Stratford: in the groves of the once-Forest of Arden and in the pin-drop silence before a soliloquy in the Royal Shakespeare Theatre.

⊟ JOURNEY'S END. Thames **trains** roll in from London's Paddington Station (2¼hr., 7-10 per day, return £19.50); from Warwick (25 min., £2.50); and from Birmingham (1hr., £3.50). National Express runs **buses** from London's Victoria Station (3hr., 3-4 per day, return £12); Stagecoach runs from Oxford (day return £5.25); and Cambridge Coach connects to Cambridge (day return £16, students £12).

⬛ HERE CEASE MORE QUESTIONS. The **tourist office**, Bridgefoot, across Warwick Rd at Bridge St toward the waterside park, sells maps and has a free accommodations guide. (Tel. (01789) 29 31 27. Open Apr.-Oct. M-Sa 9am-6pm, Su 11am-5pm; Nov.-Mar. M-Sa 9am-5pm.) Romeo and Juliet would have lived happily ever after had they e-mail; surf the **internet** at **Java Café,** 28 Greenhill St. (£3 per 30min., £5 per hr; students £2.50 per 30min., £4 per hr.) **Postal code:** CV37 6PU.

BRITAIN

⌐ TO SLEEP, PERCHANCE TO DREAM. To B&B or not to B&B? This hamlet has tons of them (£15-26), but 'tis nobler in summer to make advance reservations. The nearest hostel is more than 2 mi. away, and the cost is comparable to many B&Bs after adding in return bus fare. Keep an eye out for B&Bs on **Grove Rd, Evesham Pl,** and **Evesham Rd. Bradbourne Guest House,** 44 Shipston Rd, is a recently redecorated Tudor-style home 8min. walk from the town center. (Tel. (01789) 20 41 78. Singles £25-30; doubles £44-48.) Warm and attentive proprietors consider **The Hollies,** 16 Evesham Pl, their labor of love. (Tel. (01789) 26 68 57. Doubles £35, with bath £45.) The **YHA youth hostel,** Hemmingford House, on Wellesbourne Rd, Alveston, has large, attractive grounds; take bus X18 from Bridge St, opposite the McDonald's (every hr., £1.70). (Tel. (01789) 29 70 93. £14.05, students £13.05. Breakfast included. Reception 7am-midnight.) **Riverside Caravan Park,** Tiddington Rd, 1 mi. east of Stratford on B4086, provides beautiful, but sometimes crowded, sunset views on the Avon. (Tel. (01789) 29 23 12. Tent and 2 people £5, each additional person £1. Open Easter-Oct.) Await what dreams may come.

⌐ FOOD OF LOVE. To get to the **Safeway supermarket** on Alcester Rd, take the Avon shuttle from the town center, or just cross the bridge past the rail station. (Open M-W and Sa 8am-9pm, Th-F 8am-10pm, Su 10am-4pm.) **Hussain's Indian Cuisine,** 6a Chapel St, has fantastic chicken *tikka masala;* keep an eye out for regular Ben Kingsley. (Lunch £6, entrees from £6. Open daily 12:30-2:30pm and 5pm-midnight.) Drink deep ere you depart at the ■ **Dirty Duck Pub,** on Waterside. (Traditional pub lunch £3-9; dinner £6-18. Open M-Sa 11am-11pm, Su noon-10:30pm.)

☉ THE GILDED MONUMENTS. Bardolatry peaks around 2pm, so try to hit any Will-centered sights before 11am or after 4pm. Die-hard fans can buy the **combination ticket** (£11, students £10) for admission to five official Shakespeare properties: Shakespeare's Birthplace, Anne Hathaway's cottage (1 mi. away), Mary Arden's House and Countryside Museum (4 mi. away), New Place and Nash's House, and Hall's Croft. For a little less of the Bard, buy a **Shakespeare's Town Heritage Trail ticket** (£7.50, students £6.50), which covers all three sights in town. **Shakespeare's Birthplace,** Henley St, is equal parts period recreation and Shakespeare life-and-work exhibition. (Open Mar. 20-Oct. 19 M-Sa 9am-5pm, Su 9:30am-5pm; Oct. 20-Mar. 19 M-Sa 9:30am-4pm, Su 10am-4pm. £4.90.) **New Place,** on High St, was Stratford's hippest address when Shakespeare bought it in 1597. Only the foundation remains—it can be viewed from **Nash's House,** which belonged to the first husband of Shakespeare's granddaughter and last descendant, Elizabeth. **Hall's Croft** and **Mary Arden's House** bank on their tenuous connections to Shakespeare's extended family. For dramatic cohesiveness, pay homage to Shakespeare's grave, his little, little grave, in the **Holy Trinity Church,** on Trinity St. (£0.60, students £0.40.)

⌐ THE PLAY'S THE THING. Get thee to a performance at the world-famous **Royal Shakespeare Company;** recent sons include Kenneth Branagh and Ralph Fiennes. Tickets (£5-49) for all three theaters—the Royal Shakespeare Theatre, the Swan Theatre, and The Other Place—are sold through the box office in the foyer of the Royal Shakespeare Theatre, on Waterside. (Reservation tel. from 9am (01789) 29 56 23, 24hr. recording 26 91 91. Open daily 9:30am-6pm, until 8pm on performance days; arrive at least 20min. before opening for same-day sales. Student and senior standbys for £11 exist in principle.)

⌐ EXCURSION FROM STRATFORD: WARWICK CASTLE. One of England's finest medieval castles, Warwick Castle makes an excellent daytrip from Stratford. Climb the 530 steps to the top of the towers of Warwick and see the countryside unfolds like a fairytale kingdom of hobbits and elves. The dungeons are filled with life-size wax figures of people preparing for battle, while "knights" and "craftsmen" talk about their trades. (Open daily Mar.-Oct. 10am-6pm; Nov.-Feb. 10am-5pm. Lockers £1. £10, students £8.50.) **Trains** arrive from Stratford (20min., day return £2.50) and Birmingham (40min., day return £3.50).

BATH

A visit to the elegant Georgian city of Bath (pop. 83,000) remains *de rigueur*, even if today it's more of a museum (or a museum gift shop) than a resort. But expensive trinkets can't conceal the fact that Bath, immortalized by Austen and Dickens, once stood second only to London as the social capital of England.

🛮🖿🖾 PRACTICAL INFO, ACCOMMODATIONS, AND FOOD. Trains head frequently to Bristol (15min., £4.70); London's Paddington Station (1½hr., £25); and Exeter (1¾hr., £21.50). National Express **buses** (tel. (08705) 80 80 80) run to Oxford (2hr., 6 per day, £12) and London's Victoria Station (3hr., 9 per day, £11.50). Both arrive near the southern end of Manvers St; walk up Manvers to the Terrace Walk roundabout and turn left on York St to reach the **tourist office,** in Abbey Churchyard. (Tel. (01225) 47 71 01; fax 47 77 87. Open June-Sept. M-Tu and F-Sa 9:30am-6pm, W-Th 9:45am-6pm, Su 10am-4pm; Oct.-May M-Sa 9am-5pm, Su 10am-4pm.)

B&Bs (from £18) cluster on **Pulteney Rd, Pulteney** and **Crescent Gardens,** and **Widcombe Hill.** The **YHA youth hostel,** on Bathwick Hill, is in a secluded mansion 20 steep minutes above the city; catch Badgerline bus 18 (dir: University) from the bus station or the Orange Grove rotary (return £1). (Tel. (01225) 46 56 74; fax 48 29 47. £10.15. Breakfast £3.10. TV, laundry.) The **International Backpackers Hostel,** 13 Pierrepont St, is up the street from the stations and is just three blocks from the baths. (Tel. (01225) 44 67 87; fax 44 63 05; email info@backpackers-uk.demon.co.uk. £12. Breakfast £1.50. Laundry. **Internet.**) To get to **Toad Hall Guest House,** 6 Lime Grove, go across Pulteney Bridge and through Pulteney Gardens. (Tel. (01225) 42 32 54. £20 per person.) To reach **Newton Mill Camping,** 2½ mi. west on Newton Rd, take bus 5 from bus station (return £1.60) to Twerton and ask to be let off at the campsite. (Tel. (01225) 33 39 09. Two people, tent, and car £11. Reserve ahead.) **Guildhall Market** is between High St and Grand Parade. (Open M-Sa 8am-5:30pm.) Try **Tilleys Bistro,** 3 North Parade Passage, for French or English fare. (Open M-Sa noon-2:30pm and 6:30-11pm, Su 6:30-10:30pm.) **The Pump Room,** in Abbey Courtyard, holds a monopoly on Bath Spa mineral water (45p). **Postal code:** BA1 1A5.

🖾🖾 SIGHTS AND ENTERTAINMENT. Once the spot for naughty sightings, the **Roman Baths** are now a must-see for all. Most of the visible complex is not actually Roman, but rather reflects Georgian dreams of what Romans might have built. The **◨Roman Baths Museum** underneath reveals genuine Roman Baths and highlights the complexity of Roman engineering, which included central heating and internal plumbing. Its recovered artifacts, scale models, and hot springs bring back to life the Roman spa city Aquae Salis—first unearthed in 1880 by sewer diggers. (Open daily Apr.-July and Sept. 9am-6pm; Aug. 9am-6pm and 7-9pm; Oct.-Mar. 9:30am-5pm. £6.70.) Penny-pinchers can view one bath in the complex by entering (for free) through the **Pump Room** on Stall St (see above). Next to the baths, the towering and tombstoned 15th-century **Bath Abbey** has a whimsical west façade with several angels climbing ladders up to heaven—and, curiously enough, two climbing down. (Open daily 9am-4:30pm. £1.50.) Head north up Stall St, turn left on Westgate St, and turn right on Saw Close to reach Queen Sq, where Jane Austen lived at #13. Continue up Gay St to **The Circus,** where Thomas Gainsborough, William Pitt, and David Livingstone once lived. To the left down Brock St is the **Royal Crescent,** a half-moon of Gregorian townhouses bordering **Royal Victoria Park.** The **botanical gardens** within nurture 5000 species of plants. (Open M-Sa 9am-dusk, Su 10am-dusk. Free.) Backtrack down Brock St and bear left at the Circus (or take a right at The Circus from Gay St) to reach Bennett St and the dazzling **Museum of Costume,** which will satisfy any fashion fetish. (Open daily 10am-5pm. £3.90; joint ticket with Roman Baths £8.70.) The laid-back **◨Paragon Wine Bar,** 1A The Paragon, is a fantastic place to kick back, while the **The Pig and Fiddle** pub, on the corner of Saracen St and Broad St, packs in a rowdy young crowd.

GLASTONBURY

The reputed birthplace of Christianity in England and the seat of Arthurian myth, Glastonbury (pop. 6900) has evolved into an intersection of Christianity and mysticism. Present-day pagan pilgrimage site **Glastonbury Tor** is supposedly the site of the mystical Isle of Avalon, where the Messiah is slated to return. To make the trek up to the Tor, turn right at the top of High St, continue up to Chilkwell St, turn left onto Wellhouse Ln, and take the first right up the hill (buses in summer 50p). On your way down, visit the **Chalice Well,** on the corner of Welhouse Ln, the supposed resting place, Indiana Jones movies aside, of the Holy Grail. (Open daily Easter-Oct. 10am-6pm; Nov.-Feb. 1-4pm. £1.50.) Back in town, the ruins of **Glastonbury Abbey,** England's oldest Christian foundation, stands behind the archway on Magdalene St. (Open daily June-Aug. 9am-6pm; Sept.-May 9:30am-6pm. £2.50, students £2.) Although no trains serve Glastonbury, Baker's Dolphin **buses** (tel. (01934) 61 60 00) run from London (3¼hr., 1 per day, return £5), while Badgerline buses (tel. (01225) 46 44 46) run from Bath (return £4.75; change at Wells). From the bus stop, turn right on High St to reach the **tourist office,** The Tribunal, 9 High St. (Tel. (01458) 83 29 54. Open Apr.-Sept. Su-Th 10am-5pm, F-Sa 10am-5:30pm; Oct.-Mar. daily 10am-4pm.) **Glastonbury Backpackers,** in the Crown Hotel on Market Pl, contributes its own splashes of color to the city's tie-dye. (Tel. (01458) 83 33 53. £9. **Internet.**) Sleep in comfort at **Blake House,** 3 Bove Town. (Tel. (01458) 83 16 80. From £18.) **Postal code:** BA6 9HG.

CAMBRIDGE

The university began a mere 791 years ago when rebels defected from nearby Oxford to this settlement on the River Cam. Today, in contrast to its sister institution, Cambridge (pop. 105,000) is steadfastly determined to remain a city under its academic robes—the tourist office "manages," rather than encourages, visitors. Most colleges close to visitors during official quiet periods in May and early June, but when exams end, cobblestoned Cambridge explodes in gin-soaked glee. May Week (in mid-June, naturally) hosts a dizzying schedule of cocktail parties.

█ GETTING THERE AND GETTING AROUND

Trains: Station Rd (tel. (0345) 48 49 50). Tickets sold daily 5am-11pm. To: **London-King's Cross** and **London-Liverpool St** (1hr., every hr., £13.50).

Buses: Drummer St. **National Express** (tel. (08705) 80 80 80) arrives from **London-Victoria Station** (2hr., 17 per day, from £7). National Express and **Stagecoach Express** buses run to **Oxford** (2¾hr., £6.55). **Cambus** (tel. 42 35 54) runs regional routes (£0.65-1.60).

Bike Rental: Mike's Bikes, 28 Mill Rd (tel. 31 25 91). £5 per day, £8 per week. Open M-Sa 9am-5:30pm, Su 10am-4pm.

⚠ ORIENTATION AND PRACTICAL INFORMATION

The main shopping street starts at **Magdalene Bridge** and changes names four times from **Bridge St** to **Hills Rd.** The main academic thoroughfare, also suffering from an identity crisis, changes names four times from **St. John's St** to **Trumpington Rd.** From the bus station, a quick walk down Emmanuel St leads to the main shopping street. From the train station, go down Station Rd and turn right onto Hills Rd.

Tourist Office: Wheeler St (tel. 32 26 40; fax 45 75 88; www.cambridge.gov.uk/leisure/tourism), just south of the marketplace. Books rooms for £3 fee plus a 10% deposit. Mini-guide 40p, maps 20p. Offers two-hour **walking tours** of the city and some colleges (£5.75). Open Apr.-Oct. M-Sa 10am-6pm, Su 11am-4pm; Nov.-Mar. M-F 10am-5:30pm, Sa 10am-5pm. Info on city events is available at **Corn Exchange Box Office,** Corn Exchange St (tel. 35 78 51), adjacent to the tourist office.

American Express: 25 Sidney St (tel. 35 16 36). Open M-F 9am-5:30pm, W 9:30am-5:30pm, Sa 9am-5pm.

Laundromat: Clean Machine, 22 Burleigh St (tel. 57 80 09). Open daily 7am-9:30pm.

BRITAIN

Emergency: Dial 999; no coins required. **Police,** tel. 35 89 66.

Medical Assistance: Addenbrookes Hospital, Hill Rd (tel. 24 51 51). Catch Cambus 95 from Emmanuel St (95p).

Post Office: 9-11 St. Andrew's St (tel. 32 33 25). Open M-Tu and Th-F 9am-5:30pm, W 9:30am-5pm, Sa 9am-12:30pm. Address mail to be held for Miss PIGGY, *Poste Restante*, 9-11 St. Andrews St Post Office, Cambridge, England **CB2 3AA.**

Internet Access: CBI, 32 Mill Rd (tel. 57 63 06), near the hostel. 10p per min. Open M-Sa 10am-8pm, Su 11am-7pm. Also at 5-7 Norfolk St. Open daily 8am-11pm.

PHONE CODE	City code: 01223. From outside the UK, dial int'l dialing prefix (see inside back cover) + 44 + 1223 + local number.

ACCOMMODATIONS, CAMPING, AND FOOD

The lesson this university town teaches is to book ahead. Many of the **B&Bs** around **Portugal St** and **Tenison Rd** are open only in July and August. Check the list at the tourist office, or pick up their guide to accommodations (50p).

YHA Youth Hostel, 97 Tenison Rd (tel. 35 46 01; fax 31 27 80). Relaxed, welcoming atmosphere. Well-equipped kitchen, laundry, TV lounge, and spiffy cafeteria. 3- to 4-bed rooms £11.15, students £9.70. In summer, call a week ahead with a credit card.

■ **Home from Home B&B,** Liz Fasano, 39 Milton Rd (tel. 32 35 55), 20min. from the center. Pricey, but worthwhile, thanks to the sparkling rooms and welcoming hostess. Singles £30; doubles £40. Full English breakfast included. Call ahead with a credit card.

Mrs. McCann, 40 Warkworth St (tel. 31 40 98). A jolly hostess offers comfortable twin rooms with TVs near the bus station. £15-18 per person. Breakfast included.

Tenison Towers Guest House, 148 Tenison Rd (tel. 56 65 11), 2 blocks from the train station. Fresh flowers grace an impeccable house. Singles £22; doubles £36.

Cambridge YMCA, Gonville Pl (tel. 35 69 98), between the train station and town center. Large, clean, industrial rooms. Singles £21.82; doubles £35.38. Breakfast included.

Highfield Farm Camping Park, Long Rd, Comberton (tel. 26 23 08). Take Cambus 118 from the Drummer St bus station. Showers, laundry. £6-6.75 per tent, £7-8.25.

Cantabrigians are too busy learning Latin to flavor their food, so try the bright pyramids of fruit and vegetables at **Market Sq.** (Open M-Sa 8am-5pm.) Students buy their gin and cornflakes at **Sainsbury's,** 44 Sidney St, the only grocery store in the middle of town. (Open M-F 8am-9pm, Sa 7:30am-9pm, Su 11am-5pm.) ■**Nadia's,** at 11 St. John's St, 9 Burleigh St, 16 Silver St, and 20 King's Parade, whips up uncommonly good bakery items at commoners' prices. (Open daily 8.30am-5pm.) **Rainbow's Vegetarian Bistro,** 9A King's Parade, is a tiny burrow with delicious veggie fare. (Open daily 9am-9pm.) **The Little Tea Room,** 1 All Saints' Passage, off Trinity St, serves a "post-tutorial tea" for £5. (Open M-Sa 10am-5:30pm, Su 1-5:30pm.) Cambridge is crazy for the jacket potatoes (£1.95-5.25) at **Tatties,** 11 Sussex St. (Open M-Sa 8:30am-7pm, Su 10am-5pm.) Foreigners and beautiful people meet for cappuccino and quiche at **Clowns Coffee Bar,** 54 King St. (Open daily 9am-midnight.) The alcohol-serving curry houses on **Castle Hill** are also popular.

SIGHTS

THE COLLEGES. Cambridge is an architect's dream—it packs some of the most breathtaking examples of English architecture into less than one sq. mi. If you are pressed for time, visit at least one chapel (preferably King's), one garden (try Christ's), one library (Trinity's is the most interesting), and one dining hall (you'll have to adopt a convincing student disguise to get in). Cambridge is most exciting during the university's three eight-week terms: Michaelmas (Oct.-Dec.), Lent (Jan.-Mar.), and Easter (Apr.-June). Most of the colleges are open daily from 9am to 5:30pm, but hours vary often. A few are closed to sightseers during the Easter term, and virtually all are closed during exams (mid-May to mid-June). **Trinity College,** the University's purse, houses the stunning **Wren Library,** which keeps such notable trea-

BRITAIN

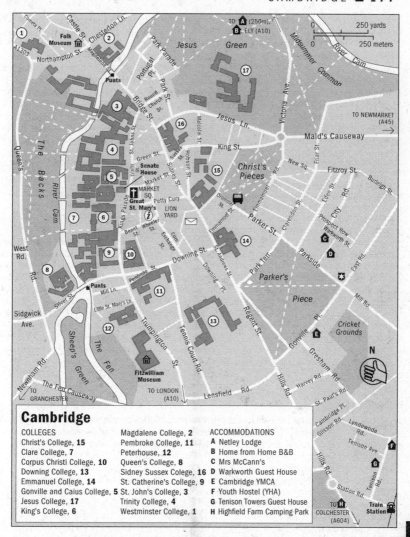

Cambridge

COLLEGES

Christ's College, **15**
Clare College, **7**
Corpus Christi College, **10**
Downing College, **13**
Emmanuel College, **14**
Gonville and Caius College, **5**
Jesus College, **17**
King's College, **6**

Magdalene College, **2**
Pembroke College, **11**
Peterhouse, **12**
Queen's College, **8**
Sidney Sussex Colege, **16**
St. Catherine's College, **9**
St. John's College, **3**
Trinity College, **4**
Westminster College, **1**

ACCOMMODATIONS

A Netley Lodge
B Home from Home B&B
C Mrs McCann's
D Warkworth Guest House
E Cambridge YMCA
F Youth Hostel (YHA)
G Tenison Towers Guest House
H Highfield Farm Camping Park

sures as A.A. Milne's handwritten manuscript of *Winnie the Pooh* and less momentous achievements by Milton, Byron, Tennyson, and Thackeray, many of whom are alums of the college. *(Trinity St. Tel. 33 84 00. Chapel and courtyard open daily 10am-5pm. Library open M-F noon-2pm. Both closed during exams. £1.75.)* **King's College,** south of Trinity, is the alma mater of E.M. Forster. Rubens' magnificent *Adoration of the Magi* hangs behind the altar of the college's spectacular Gothic chapel. *(Tel. 33 11 00. College open M-F 9:30am-4:30pm, Su 10am-5pm. Tours arranged through the Tourist Office. Chapel open M-Sa 9:30am-3:15pm, Su 1:15-2:15pm. £3, students £2.)* Across the river, **Queens' College** has the only unaltered Tudor courtyard in Cambridge. *(Tel. 33 55 11. Open Mar.-Oct. daily 10am-4:30pm; closed during exams. £1.)* **Christ's College,** back on the other side of town near the bus station, was founded as "God's house" in 1448 and today boasts gorgeous gardens. *(Off St. Andrews St. Tel. 33 49 00. College open in summer 9:30am-noon; in session M-F 9:30am-4:30pm. Free.)*

BRITAIN

OTHER SIGHTS. A welcome break from the academia of the colleges, the **Fitzwilliam Museum** boasts a hoard of Egyptian, Chinese, Japanese, and Greek treasures that only the Brits could have assembled, as well as an intimate collection of French Impressionist works. *(Trumpington St, 10min. from King's College. Tel. 33 29 00. Open Tu-Sa 10am-5pm, Su 2:15-5pm. Guided tours Sa 2:30pm. £3 donation requested. Tours £3.)* If you're searching for rejuvenation after the bustle of the college town, head to the idyllic settings of **Grantchester,** once a mecca for Cambridge literary types including Virginia Woolf, Robert Brooke, E.M. Forster, and Ludwig Wittgenstein. Today you can sip tea at **The Orchard,** Mill Way, where these same luminaries once discussed the ways of the world. Start the delightful walk there by crossing the Silver St Bridge in Cambridge and following Newnham Rd until it turns into Grantchester St; at the dead end, take a right onto Grantchester Meadows and follow it to the footpath. Pick up *The Orchard* from the tourist office for inspiration.

🎵 ENTERTAINMENT

The best source of info on student activities is the student newspaper *Varsity;* the tourist office's free *Cambridge Nightlife Guide* is also helpful. **Punts** (gondola-like boats) are a favored form of entertainment in Cambridge. Beware that punt-bombing—jumping from bridges into the river alongside a punt, thereby tipping its occupants into the Cam—has evolved into an art form. **Tyrell's,** Magdalene Bridge (tel. 35 28 47), rents boats for $8 an hour plus a $40 deposit. Even more traditional than punting is **pub-crawling;** Cambridge hangouts offer good pub-crawling year-round, though they lose some of their character (and their best customers) in summer. **The Eagle,** Benet St, is the oldest pub in Cambridge. Nobel laureates Watson and Crick once rushed into the Eagle breathlessly to announce their discovery of the DNA double helix—unimpressed, the barmaid insisted they settle their four-shilling tab before she'd serve them a toast. The **Free Press,** on Prospect Row behind the police station, is an off-the-beaten-path neighborhood pub. Students drink at the **Anchor,** Silver St, and **The Mill (The Tap and Spile),** Mill Ln. The gay crowd downs ale at **The Town and Gown,** on Poundhill just off Northhampton. Dancing rears its rocking rump at **The Junction,** Clifton Rd, off Cherry Hinton Rd. (Open F-Sa.)

NORWICH

One of England's largest and most populous cities before the Norman invasion, Norwich (rhymes with "porridge") today conceals its medieval heritage behind a modern façade. The 11th-century **Norwich Cathedral** and the 12th-century **Norwich Castle,** where King John signed the Magna Carta in 1215, reign over puzzling, winding streets. (Cathedral open daily mid-May to mid-Sept. 7:15am-7pm; mid-Sept. to mid-May 7:15am-6pm. Free. Castle closed for renovations in 2000.) **Trains** (tel. (0345) 48 49 50) arrive frequently at the corner of Riverside and Thorpe Rd from Cambridge (1½hr., $11.10) and London's Liverpool St Station (2hr., $33). National Express **buses** (tel. (08705) 80 80 80) travel from Surrey St to Cambridge (2hr., 1 per day, day return $9.50) and London (3hr., 7 per day, $13). The **tourist office,** at Guildhall, Gaol Hill, in front of city hall on the continuation of London St, has an essential map. Head right from the train station, take a left on Prince of Wales Rd, and cross the bridge to the castle. From the bus station, head left on Surrey St and then right on St. Stephen's St to the castle. (Tel. (01603) 66 60 71. Open June-Sept. M-Sa 9:30am-5pm; Oct.-May M-Sa 9:30am-4:30pm.) **The Abbey Hotel,** 16 Stracey St, is 5min. up Thorpe Rd from the train station. (Tel. (01603) 61 29 15. $18 per person.) In the heart of the city is one of England's largest and oldest open-air **markets.** (Open M-Sa 8am-4:30pm.) **Postal code:** NR1 3DD.

NOTTINGHAM

Nottingham's (pop. 261,500) age-old tradition of taking from the rich and giving to the poor lives on as modern-day Robin Hoods lure visitors to Nottingham with a tourist industry with little substance but plenty of thrill. ◼**The Galleries of Justice,** High Pavement, is an interactive museum that tries presumably innocent tourists, throws them behind bars, and lets them see the English prison system through the eyes of the convicted. (Open Tu-Su 10am-5pm. £8, students £7.) Originally constructed in 1068 by William the Conqueror, the remains of **Nottingham Castle,** atop a sandstone rise in the south of the city, now house the **Castle Museum.** (Open daily Mar.-Oct. 10am-5pm; Nov.-Feb. Sa-Th 10am-5pm, F 1-5pm. M-F free; Sa-Su £2, students £1.) From the museum entrance, enter **Mortimer's Hole,** a 100-meter-long underground passageway from the castle to the base of the cliff (£2, students £1). **Trains** (tel. (0345) 48 49 50) arrive frequently on Carrington St from Lincoln (1hr., £4.20) and London (2hr., £21.50). National Express **buses** (tel. (08705) 80 80 80) pull in between Collin and Canal St from London (3hr., 7 per day, £13). The **tourist office,** 1-4 Smithy Row, is just off Old Market Sq. (Tel. (0115) 915 53 30. Open Apr.-Oct. M-F 9am-5:30pm, Sa 9am-5pm, Su 10am-3pm; Nov.-Mar. closed Su.) To sleep at **Igloo,** 110 Mansfield Rd, take bus 90 from the train station to Mansfield Rd. (Tel. (0115) 947 52 50. £9.50.) **Ye Olde Trip to Jerusalem,** 1 Brewhouse Yard, the "Oldest Inn in England," poured its first drink in 1189. **Postal code:** NG1 2BN.

LINCOLN

Medieval streets, half-timbered Tudor houses, and a 12th-century cathedral are all relative newcomers to Lincoln (pop. 77,000), originally built as a town for retired Roman legionnaires. The King of the Hill is undoubtedly the magnificent **Lincoln Cathedral.** (Open July-Aug. M-Sa 7:15am-8pm, Su 7:15am-6pm; Sept.-May M-Sa 7:15am-6pm, Su 7:15am-5pm. £4, students £1.50.) **Lincoln Castle** houses one of the four surviving copies of the Magna Carta. (Open Apr.-Oct. M-Sa 9:30am-5:30pm, Su 11am-5:30pm; Nov.-Mar. M-Sa 9:30am-4pm, Su 11am-4pm. £2.50.) The station on St. Mary's St receives frequent **trains** from Nottingham (1hr., £4.20) and London's King's Cross Station (2½hr., £36.50). Opposite the train station, National Express **buses** (tel. (08705) 80 80 80) pull in from London (5hr., £18). From the station, walk up High St, which becomes The Strait and then Steep Hill Rd, to reach the **tourist office,** 9 Castle Hill. (Tel. (01522) 52 98 28; fax 57 90 55. Open M-Th 9am-5:30pm, F 9:30am-5pm, Sa-Su 10am-5pm.) **B&Bs** (£17-20) line Carline and Yarborough Rd, west of the castle. To get to the lovely **YHA youth hostel,** 77 South Park Ave, veer right from station, turn right on Pelham Bridge, which becomes Canwick Rd, and turn right on South Park Ave. (Tel. (01522) 52 20 76; fax 56 74 24. £9.15. Lockout 10am-5pm. Curfew 11pm. Open Feb.-Oct.) **Postal code:** LN5 7XX.

PEAK DISTRICT NATIONAL PARK

Britain's first national park, wedged between industrial giants Manchester, Sheffield, and Nottingham, serves as a 555 sq. mi. playground for its 17 million urban neighbors. In the northern Dark Peak area, deep groughs (gullies) gouge the hard peat moorland against a backdrop of gloomy cliffs, and well-marked footpaths lead over mildly rocky hillsides to village clusters. Abandoned milestones, derelict lead mines, and country homes are scattered throughout the southern White Peak.

Contact **Peak District National Park Office,** Aldern House, Barlow Rd, Bakewell DE4 5AE (tel. (01629) 81 62 00), for more info. The **National Park Information Centres** at **Bakewell** (see below), **Castleton** (tel./fax (01433) 62 06 79), and **Edale** (tel. (01433) 67 02 07) offer walking guides; you can also ask questions at **tourist offices** in **Buxton** (tel. (01298) 251 06) and **Matlock Bath** (tel. (01629) 550 82). Many farmers allow camping on their land if you leave no trace of your stay. **YHA youth hostels** in the park cost from £7.50 to £10.15 and can be found in **Bakewell** (see below), **Buxton** (tel./fax (01298) 222 87), **Castleton** (see below), **Edale** (see below), and **Matlock** (tel. (01629) 58 29 83). There are 13 **YHA Camping Barns** (£3.35 per night) throughout the park; book ahead at **Camping Barns Reservation Office** (tel. (01200) 42 83 66; fax 42 89 29), 16 Shawbridge St, Clitheroe, Lancashire, BB7 ILY. The park authority operates six **Cycle Hire Centres** (£8 per day); call **Ashbourne** (tel./fax (01335) 34 31 56) or **Hayfield** (tel. (01663) 74 62 22) for info.

■ GETTING THERE AND GETTING AROUND. The invaluable *Peak District Timetable* (£0.60; available in all Peak tourist offices) has transport routes and a map. Two **rail** lines originate in **Manchester** and enter the park from the west: one stops at **Buxton** near the park's edge (1hr., every hr.), and the other crosses the park via **Edale, Hope** (near Castleton), and **Hathersage** (1½hr., 9-15 per day) on its way to **Sheffield.** From the south, a train heads from **Nottingham** to **Matlock,** on the park's southeastern edge. Trent **bus** TP (Transpeak; tel. (01298) 230 98) serves the southern half of the park, stopping at **Buxton, Bakewell, Matlock,** and **Derby** (3hr., every 2hr.) between Manchester and Nottingham. A one-day **Wayfarer** pass (£6.60) covers unlimited train and bus travel within Greater Manchester, including most of the Peak District.

BAKEWELL, EDALE, AND CASTLETON. The Southern Peak is better served by public transportation than its northern counterpart, and is consequently more trampled. Thirty mi. southeast of Manchester, **Bakewell** is the best base for exploration. Located near several scenic walks through the White Peaks, the town is known for its Bakewell pudding, created when a flustered cook inadvertently erred while making a tart. Bakewell's **National Park Information Center** is at the corner of Bridge and Market St (tel. (01629) 81 32 27). The small and cozy **YHA youth hostel,** Fly Hill, is 5min. from the town center. (Tel./fax (01629) 81 23 13. £7.50. Open Apr.-Oct. M-Sa; Nov.-Mar. F-Sa.) **Postal code:** DE45 1EF.

The northern Dark Peak area contains some of the wildest and most rugged hill country in England. **Edale** offers little in the way of civilization other than a church, café, pub, school, and nearby **youth hostel** (tel. (01433) 67 03 02). Its environs, however, are arguably the most spectacular in northern England. The National Park Authority's *8 Walks Around Edale* (£1.20) details nearby **hiking** trails (1½-8½ mi.). Stay at the hostel (see above) or **camp** at **Fieldhead,** behind the tourist office. (Tel. (01433) 67 03 86. £3.40 per person.) From Edale, the 3½-mile hike to **Castleton** affords a breathtaking view of the dark gritstone Edale Valley (Dark Peak) and the lighter limestone Hope Valley (White Peak) to the south. Castleton's river-carved limestone engulfs several famous caverns; the gigantic **Peak Cavern** was known in the 18th century as the "Devil's Arse." (Open Easter-Oct. daily 10am-5pm; Nov.-Easter Sa-Su 10am-4pm. £4.75, students £3.75.) Stay at the excellent **YHA youth hostel** (tel. (01433) 62 02 35; £10.15; open Feb. to late Dec.) or **Cryer House,** across from the tourist office (tel. (01433) 62 02 44; doubles £38-42).

MANCHESTER

The Industrial Revolution transformed the once unremarkable village of Manchester into Britain's second-largest urban conglomeration (though still an unremarkable one). The still somewhat dodgy city has virtually no distinguishing architectural features (postcards portray mostly the fronts of trams), but its pulsing nightlife and vibrant arts scene prove two redeeming qualities.

◪ ▐▘◪ PRACTICAL INFO, ACCOMMODATIONS, AND FOOD. Trains leave **Piccadilly Station,** on London Rd, and **Victoria Station,** on Victoria St, for York (40min., 2 per hr., £13.40); Liverpool (50min., 2 per hr., £6.50); Chester (1hr., every hr., £7.30); and London's Euston Station (2½hr., every hr., £62). **Piccadilly Bus Station** consists of about 50 bus stops around Piccadilly Gardens; pick up a free route map at the tourist office. National Express **buses** (tel. (08705) 80 80 80) go from Chorlton St, two blocks south and one east of Piccadilly, to Liverpool (50min., every hr., £3.50) and London (4-5hr., 7 per day, £14.50). The **Manchester Visitor Centre,** in the Town Hall Extension, is on Lloyd St, off St. Peter's Sq. (Tel. (0161) 234 31 57; info tel. (0891) 71 55 33. Open M-Sa 10am-5:30pm, Su 11am-4pm.) **Cyberia,** 12 Oxford St, may be the UK's hippest place to check **email.** (£3 per 30min., students £2.40. Open M-W 10am-11pm, Th 10am-midnight, F-Sa 10am-1am, Su 10am-10pm.)

Take bus 33 from Piccadilly Gardens towards Wigan or walk 10min. down Liverpool Rd from the Deansgate train station to reach the sleek **YHA Manchester,** Potato Wharf, Castlefield, behind the Castlefield Hotel on Liverpool Rd. (Tel. (0161) 839 99 60; fax 835 20 54; email manchester@yha.org.uk. £17.40, students £16.40. Breakfast included. Lockers £1. Kitchen. Laundry. **Internet.** Reception 7am-11:30pm.) To get to the friendly **Woodies Backpackers Hostel,** 19 Blossom St, Ancoats, walk

BRITAIN

5min. up Newton St from Piccadilly Gardens and cross Great Ancoats St; it's just past the Duke of Edinburgh pub. (Tel./fax (0161) 228 34 56; email backpackers@woodiesuk.freeserve.co.uk. £11. Kitchen. Laundry.) **Cornerhouse Café**, 70 Oxford St, is part of the trendy Cornerhouse Arts Center. (Entrees from £3.50. Open daily 11am-8:30pm; kitchen open noon-2:30pm and 5-7:30pm; bar open M-Sa noon-11pm, Su noon-10:30pm.) **Tesco supermarket** is on Market St. (Open M-Sa 8am-8pm, Su 11am-5pm.) **Postal code:** M2 2AA.

🎦 📺 **SIGHTS AND ENTERTAINMENT.** The exception to Manchester's generally unremarkable buildings is the neo-Gothic **Manchester Town Hall**, on St. Peter's Sq, behind the tourist office. Nearby, the domed **Central Library** houses one of the largest municipal libraries in Europe, including the UK's second-largest Judaica collection. (Open M-Th 10am-8pm, F-Sa 10am-5pm.) In the **Museum of Science and Industry,** on Liverpool Rd in Castlefield, working steam engines provide a dramatic vision of Britain's industrialization. (Open daily 10am-5pm. £5, students £3.) At the **Manchester United Museum and Tour Centre,** on Sir Matt Busby Way, at the Old Trafford football stadium, you can learn all about Manchester United, England's best-known (both loved and reviled) football team. Follow the signs up Warwick Rd from the "Old Trafford" Metrolink stop. (Open daily Apr.-Oct. 9:30am-9pm, Nov.-Mar. 9:30am-5pm. £4.50. Tours £3.) One of Manchester's biggest draws is its artistic community, most notably its theater and music scenes; the **Royal Exchange Theatre,** on St. Ann's Sq, regularly puts on Shakespeare and original works. (Tel. (0161) 833 98 33. Box office open M-Sa 9:30am-7:30pm. M-Th and Sa tickets £7-23. Student tickets booked 3 days in advance £5.) Come nightfall, try the café-bar **Temple of Convenience,** 100 Great Bridgewater St, just off Oxford St. (Open daily 11am-11pm.) A couple of players in Manchester's trendsetting club scene are **Generation X,** 11/13 New Wakefield St, off Oxford St; and **Regeneration,** an *après*-clubbing Sunday chill-down. (Cover after 11pm £2. Open F-Sa until 2am, Su 3-10:30pm.) Northeast of Princess St, the **Gay Village** rings merrily at night. Drink at bars lining **Canal St;** purple **Manto's** at #46 fills with all ages, genders, and orientations with its Saturday night/Sunday morning "Breakfast Club." (Cover £2. Open daily 2-6am.)

CHESTER

With fashionable shops in faux-medieval houses, tour guides in full Roman armor, a town crier in Georgian uniform, and a Barclays bank occupying a wing of its cathedral, Chester at times resembles an American theme-park type collage of Ye Olde English Towne. Originally built by frontier-forging Romans and subsequently a base for Plantagenet royal campaigns against the Welsh, the crowded but lovely town now allows foreigners within its fortified walls while keeping a wary eye on Wales. The famous **city walls** completely encircle the town. Just outside Newgate lies the unimpressive base of the largest **Roman amphitheater** in Britain. (Open daily Apr.-Sept. 10am-6pm; Oct.-Mar. 10am-1pm and 2-4pm. Free.) Fight your way through the throngs for a visit to the brilliant stained-glass windows and cloisters of the awe-inspiring **cathedral.** (Open daily 7:30am-6:30pm. Suggested donation £2.)

Trains arrive from Manchester (1hr., every hr., £7.40) and Holyhead (2hr., every hr., £14, return £16.90). Merseyrail arrives from Liverpool (45min., every hr., £2.90); take bus 20 from the train station to Foregate St (free with rail ticket). National Express **buses** arrive on Delamere St from Manchester (1hr., 3 per day, £5.90) and London (5½hr., 5 per day, £13). From Foregate St, enter the city walls onto Eastgate St and turn right on Northgate St to reach the **tourist office,** in the Town Hall, Northgate St; from the bus station, turn left on Upper Northgate St and head through Northgate. (Tel. (01244) 40 21 11; www.chesterccc.gov.uk. Open May-Oct. M-W 9am-5:30pm, Th-Sa 9am-7:30pm, Su 10am-4pm; Nov.-Apr. M-Sa 10am-5:30pm, Su 10am-4pm.) **B&Bs** (from £13.50) cluster on **Hoole Rd,** 5min. from the train station; turn right from the exit, climb the steps to Hoole Rd, and turn right over the railroad tracks. To get to the 🏠**YHA youth hostel,** Hough Green House, 40 Hough Green, take bus 7 or 16 (1½ mi.). (Tel. (01244) 68 00 56; fax 68 12 04; email chester@yha.org.uk.

£10.85. Laundry. **Internet.** Reception 7am-10:30pm. Lockout 10am-noon. Open mid-Jan. to mid-Dec.) **Tesco supermarket** is at the end of an alley off Frodsham St. (Open M-Sa 8am-10pm, Su 11am-5pm.) Chester has 30-odd pubs along **Lower Bridge St** and **Watergate St. Postal code:** CH1 1AA.

LIVERPOOL

On the banks of the Mersey, much of Liverpool's (pop. 520,000) history is rooted in its docks. Today, Liverpool boasts two enormous cathedrals, docks transformed to attract tourists instead of ships, wild nightlife, and—oh yeah—the Beatles.

⌷ TICKET TO RIDE. Trains (tel. (0345) 48 49 50) connect Liverpool's Lime St Station to Manchester (1½hr., 2 per hr., £6); Birmingham (2hr., 1 per hr., £14.80); and London Euston (2hr., 1 per hr., £38.50). National Express **buses** (tel. (08705) 80 80 80) depart from the Norton St Coach Station for Manchester (1hr., 1 per hr., £6); Birmingham (2½hr., 6 per day, £12.50 return); and London (4-5hr., 6 per day, £15 day return, £24 return). The Isle of Man Steam Packet Company (tel. 236 20 61) runs **ferries** to and from the Isle of Man and to Dublin.

⑪ HELP! The main **tourist office,** in the Merseyside Welcome Centre in Queen Sq, sells a map guide (£1), books beds for a 10% deposit, and organizes both bus (from £4) and walking (£1) tours of Liverpool. (Tel. (0151) 709 36 31; fax 708 02 04. Open 9:30am-5:30pm.) **Phil Hughes** runs an excellent Beatles tour in an 8-seater bus. (Tel. (0151) 228 45 65. £9.) Get **internet** access upstairs at **Central Library,** William Brown St. (Open M-Sa 9am-5:30pm. £1 per 30min.) **Postal code:** L1 1AA.

⌁ HARD DAY'S NIGHT. Cheap hotels are mostly on **Lord Nelson St,** adjacent to the train station, and **Mount Pleasant,** one block from Brownlow Hill. ⚑**Embassie Youth Hostel,** 1 Falkner Sq, 15-20min. from the bus or train station at the end of Canning St, feels like a laid-back student's flat, with laundry, TV, pool table, kitchen, and all the toast and jam you can eat. (Tel. (0151) 707 10 89. £10.50.) **YHA youth hostel,** 24 Tabley St, The Wapping, is spanking new with an ideal location. From the train station, follow the signs to Albert Dock, turn left on Strand St, and it's on the left. (Tel. (0151) 709 88 88; fax 709 04 17; email liverpool@yha.org.uk. £16.40. Laundry, kitchen. V, MC.) **YWCA,** 1 Rodney St, just off Mt Pleasant, has clean, renovated rooms. (Tel. (0151) 709 77 91. £12. Kitchen.)

⌕ STRAWBERRY FIELDS FOREVER. Trendy vegetarian cafés and reasonably-priced Indian restaurants line **Bold St,** while cheap takeouts cluster on **Hardnon St** and **Berry St.** The **Kwik Save supermarket** sits at 58 Hanover St. (Open M-Tu 8:30am-6pm, W-Sa 8:30am-6:30pm.) The **Hub Café Bar,** Berry St, dishes out veggie and vegan meals (£1.50-3) in a café decorated with furniture made out of bicycle parts; the quality of the food spokes for itself. (Open M-Sa 10am-6pm.)

⌗ MAGICAL MYSTERY TOUR. Begun in 1904, the Anglican **Liverpool Cathedral** on Upper Duke St boasts the highest Gothic arches ever built, the largest vault and organ, and the highest and heaviest bells in the world. Climb to the top of the 300 ft tower for a view stretching to North Wales. (Cathedral open daily 9am-6pm; free. Tower open daily 11am-4pm; £2.) In contrast, the **Metropolitan Cathedral of Christ the King,** Mt Pleasant, with its neon-blue stained glass, looks more like a rocket launcher or a *Star Trek* set than a house of worship. (Open daily 8am-6pm; in winter Su until 5pm. Free.) **Albert Dock,** at the western end of Hanover St, is a series of Victorian warehouses transformed into a complex of restaurants and museums; drop by to see the scads of modern art at a branch of London's **Tate Gallery.** (Open Tu-Su 10am-6pm. Free; some special exhibits £3, students £1.) Also at Albert Dock, **The Beatles Story** pays tribute to the group's work with John Lennon's white piano, a recreation of the Cavern Club, and, of course, a yellow submarine. (Open daily Apr.-Oct. 10am-6pm; Nov.-Mar. 10am-5pm; £7, students £5.) The tourist office's **Beatles Map** (£2.50) will lead you to other Beatles-themed sights, including Strawberry Fields and Penny Lane. The **Beatles Shop,** 31 Matthew St, is loaded with souvenirs and memorabilia. (Open M-Sa 9:30am-5:30pm, Su 11am-4pm.)

🎵 **PLEASE PLEASE ME.** Pubs teem in almost every street in Liverpool; **Slater St** in particular brims with £1 pints. **The Jacaranda,** Slater St, site of the first paid Beatles gig, has live bands and a small dance floor. (Open M-Th 8pm-2am, F-Sa noon-2am.) John Lennon once said that the worst thing about being famous was "not being able to get a quiet pint at the Phil"; the rest of us can sip in solitude at **The Philharmonic,** 36 Hope St. (Drafts £1.60. Open M-Sa 11:30am-11pm, Su 7-10:30pm.)

Try *In Touch, Bigmouth,* or the *Liverpool Echo* for up-to-date arts and nightlife info. **Cream,** in Wolstonholme Sq off Parr St, is Liverpool's superclub. (Open Sa, plus the last F of every month. Cover £11.) **The Cavern Club,** 10 Mathew St, is on the site where the fab four gained prominence; today it plays regular club music (M and F-Sa 9pm-2am; free before 10pm) and showcases live music (Sa 2-6pm). At the end of August, a **Beatles Convention** draws pop fans from around the world.

NORTHERN ENGLAND

Cradled between the Pennines rising to the west and the North Sea to the east, the attractions of the Northeast lie primarily in calm coastal areas and in the vistas of the national parks, which include some of the most beautiful and desolate areas in England. Extensive systems of paths traverse the gray and purple moors that captured the imagination of the Brontës and the emerald green dales that figure so prominently in the stories of James Herriot. Northeast England continues to have a ruggedness about it—in its wilderness, in its sense of humor, in its endurance.

YORK

More organized than the Roman with his long spear, more aggressive than the Viking with his broad sword, more thorough than the Norman with his strong bow—she is the Tourist with her zoom camera. Unlike those before her, she invades neither for wealth or power: she comes for the history, the medieval thoroughfares, the Georgian townhouses, and the largest Gothic cathedral in Britain.

🚆🛏️🍴 **PRACTICAL INFO, ACCOMMODATIONS, AND FOOD. Trains** run from Station Rd to Newcastle (1hr., 2 per hr., £14.90); Manchester (1½hr., 2 per hr., £14.50); London's King's Cross Station (2hr., 2 per hr., £56); and Edinburgh (2-3hr., every hr., £45.50). National Express **buses** (tel. (08705) 80 80 80) depart from Rougier St for Manchester (3hr., 6 per day, £7.75); London (4hr., 6 per day, £16.50); and Edinburgh (5hr., 2 per day, £21). To reach the **tourist office,** in De Grey Rooms, Exhibition Sq, follow Station Rd, which turns into Museum St and leads over the bridge, and turn left on St. Leonards Pl. (Tel. (01904) 62 17 56. Open daily June-Oct. 9am-6pm; Nov.-May 9am-5pm.) Check your **email** at **The Gateway Internet Café,** 26 Swinegate. (£3 per 30min. Open M-Sa 10am-11pm, Su noon-4pm.)

Competition for inexpensive **B&Bs** (from £16) can be fierce in summer; try side streets along Bootham/Clifton or The Mount area (past the train station and down Blossom St). ☑**Avenue Guest House,** 6 The Avenue, ¾ mi. down Bootham/Clifton, is immaculate. From the train station, take the river footpath to the bottom of The Avenue. (Tel. (01904) 62 05 75. Singles £15-17; doubles £28-40.) **Foss Bank Guest House,** 16 Huntington Rd, follow Goodramgate/Monkgate and turn left on Huntington (¼ mi.). (Tel. (01904) 63 55 48. Singles £17-19; doubles £18.50-22.) **York Backpackers,** 88-90 Micklegate (tel./fax (01904) 62 77 20) and **York Youth Hostel,** 11-15 Bishophill Senior (tel. (01904) 62 59 04), have cheap dorms (£9-11) and friendly bars near the station. For the former, follow Station Rd left, enter the city walls via Rougier St, which becomes George Hudson St, and turn right on Mickelgate; for the latter, walk right on Queen St, turn left on Mickelgate, and turn right on Trinity Ln, which becomes Bishophill. **YHA youth hostel,** Water End, Clifton, has excellent facilities. From the tourist office, walk ¾ mi. out Bootham/Clifton and take a left at Water End. (Tel. (01904) 65 31 47. Dorms £15; singles £17.50; twins £37. Breakfast

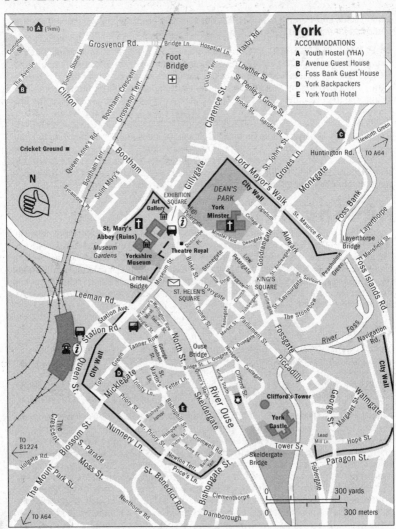

included. Reception 7am-11:30pm. Open mid-Jan. to mid-Dec.) Expensive tea rooms, mid-priced bistros, fudge shops, and cheap eateries bump elbows everywhere. Shop for produce at the **Newgate Market,** between Parliament St and the Shambles. (Open Apr.-Dec. M-Sa 9am-5pm, Su 9am-4:30pm, Jan.-Mar. M-Sa 9am-5pm.) **La Romantica,** 14 Goodramgate, serves delicious pastas and pizzas ($5-7) in candlelight. (Open daily noon-2:30pm and 5:30-11:30pm.) **Postal code:** YO1 2DA.

SIGHTS AND ENTERTAINMENT. The best introduction to the city is a 2½ mi. walk along its medieval walls; sign up for a **walking tour** at a tourist office. The **Association of Voluntary Guides** runs a good architectural tour; meet in front of the York City Art Gallery opposite the tourist office. (2-hour tours daily June-Aug. 10:15am, 2:15, and 7pm; Apr.-May and Sept.-Oct. 10:15am and 2:15pm; Nov.-Mar. 10:15am. Free.) The tourist stampede abates in the early morning and toward dusk, but everyone and everything converges at the enormous **York Minster,** built between 1220 and 1470. Half of all the medieval stained glass in England glitters here; the

Great East Window depicts the beginning and end of the world in over a hundred scenes. Climb 275 steps to the top of the **Central Tower** for a view over York's red roofs. (Cathedral open daily in summer 7am-8:30pm; off-season 7am-6pm; £2.50. Tower open daily 9:30am-6:30pm; £2.50.) The **York Castle Museum,** in Minster Yard, by the river and Skeldergate Bridge, is Britain's premier museum devoted to everyday life. (Open daily Apr.-Oct. 9:30am-5pm; Nov.-Mar. 9:30am-4:30pm. £4.95, students £3.50.) In the museum gardens, off Museum St, peacocks strut among the haunting ruins of **St. Mary's Abbey,** once the most influential Benedictine monastery in northern England. There are more pubs in the center of York than gargoyles on the east wall of the Minster; for entertainment options, pick up *What's On* or *Evening Entertainment* from the tourist office.

▛ EXCURSION FROM YORK: CASTLE HOWARD. The Baroque Castle Howard (tel. (01653) 64 83 33) presides over 1½ sq. mi. of stunning grounds, including gardens, fountains, and lakes. (Castle open mid-Mar. to Oct. daily 11am-4:45pm. Grounds open mid-Mar. to Jan. daily 10am-6:30pm. Joint ticket £7, students £6.50.) Pullman **buses** (tel. (01904) 62 29 92), based in Bootham Tower in York's Exhibition Square, run half-day trips to the castle for £4.

DURHAM CITY

Twisting medieval streets, footbridges, and restricted vehicle access make clifftop Durham pedestrian-friendly. Durham's only claim to being a "city" is the **Durham Cathedral,** England's greatest Norman cathedral; it houses the **tomb of the Venerable Bede,** author of *The Ecclesiastical History of the English People.* The view from the **tower** compensates for the 325-step climb. (Cathedral open daily May-Sept. 7:30am-8pm; Oct.-Apr. 7:30am-6pm. Tower open mid-Apr. to Sept. 9:30am-4pm; Oct. to mid-Apr. M-Sa 10am-3pm. £2.) Across the cathedral green, **Durham Castle** was once a key defensive fortress. Wander along the River Wear for tranquil shade, ambling waters, and views of the cathedral and castle; or rent a rowboat from **Brown's Boathouse Centres,** on Elvet Bridge, and do your best to dodge ducks while floating down the winding river (£2.50 per hr.).

   Trains (tel. (0191) 232 62 62) run to Newcastle (20min., 2 per hr., £2.60); York (1hr., 2 per hr., £15); and London (3hr., every hr., £63). **Buses** leave North Rd for London, Edinburgh, and Newcastle. To reach the **tourist office,** Market Pl, from the station, descend the hill on Station Approach and take the stairs to the left down to the Millburngate Bridge roundabout; cross the bridge and turn right at the first intersection into Market Pl. (Tel. (0191) 384 37 20; fax 386 30 15. Open July-Aug. daily 10am-5:30pm; June and Sept. M-Sa 10am-5:30pm; Oct.-May M-Sa 10am-5pm.) Cruise the internet at **Reality-X Durham,** 1 Framwellgate Bridge. (£3 per 30min. Open daily 11am-10pm.) A large supply of cheap and often beautiful **dormitory rooms** surrounds the cathedral. (Tel. (0191) 374 34 54. Available July-Sept. and around Christmas and Easter.) **University College** in Durham Castle has rooms (tel. (0191) 374 38 63; £20.50), and **Mrs. Koltai** runs a comfy **B&B,** 10 Gilesgate (tel./fax (0191) 386 20 26; £16). In the **Indoor Market,** off Market Pl, you'll find produce, as well as butchers, bakers, and candlestick-makers. (Open M-Sa 9am-5pm.) Starting around 11pm, head to the intersection of Crossgate and North Rd, just across Framwellgate Bridge, where pubs and clubs await with open doors. **Postal code:** DH1 3RE.

NEWCASTLE-UPON-TYNE

Hardworking Newcastle is legendary for its local pub and club scene. While you can still see straight, explore the masterful **Tyne Bridge,** neighboring **Castle Keep,** and the elegant tower of the **Cathedral Church of St. Nicholas.** (Castle open Apr.-Sept. Tu-Su 9:30am-5:30pm; Oct.-Mar. daily 9:30am-4:30pm. £1.50, students 50p. Cathedral open M-F 7am-6pm, Sa 8am-4pm, Su 7am-noon and 4-7pm. Free.) At night, the rowdy area of **Bigg Market** frowns on under-dressed student types, but milder pubs there include **Blackie Boy,** 11 Groatmarket, and **Macey's,** 31 Groatmarket. The **Quayside** (Metro: Central Station) is a slightly more relaxed, student-friendly area of town; try **The Red House,** 32 Sandhill. Revelers sway even before they've imbibed at

BRITAIN

The Tuxedo Royale, a boat/dance club under the Tyne Bridge. (Open M and W-Sa 7:30pm-2am.) Gays and lesbians flock to the corner of Waterloo and Sunderland St to drink at **The Village** and dance at **Powerhouse.** (Pub open daily noon-11pm. Club open M and Th 10pm-2am, Tu-W 11pm-1am, F-Sa 10pm-3am.)

   Trains (tel. (0191) 232 62 62) leave for Edinburgh (1½hr., 16-23 per day, £29.50) and London (3hr., every hr., £72). National Express **buses** (tel. (08705) 80 80 80) leave Percy St for Edinburgh (3hr., return £18.50) and London (6hr., return £29.50) as well. The **tourist office,** 182 Granger St, facing Grey's Monument, has essential maps. (Tel. (0191) 261 06 10. Open M-Sa 9:30am-6pm, Th 9:30am-8pm.) To get to the crowded **YHA youth hostel,** 107 Jesmond Rd, take the metro to "Jesmond" and turn left on Jesmond Rd. (Tel. (0191) 281 25 70; fax 281 87 79. £10.15, students £9.15. Breakfast £2.80. Lockout 10am-5pm. Curfew 11pm; or ask for the code. Open Feb.-Nov.) **The Brighton Guest House,** 47-51 Brighton Grove, is cheap and cheery. Take bus 10, 34-36, or 38 from the train station, or bus 12, 39, or 40 from Blackett St in the center. (Tel. (0191) 273 36 00. £16-22 per person. Breakfast included.) **Don Vito's,** 82 Pilgrim St, stands out among the many Italian eateries. (Open M-F 11:30am-2pm and 5-10pm, Sa 11:30am-11pm.) **Postal code:** NE1 7AB.

LAKE DISTRICT NATIONAL PARK

In the Lake District, quite possibly the most beautiful place in England, dramatic mountainsides plummet down to shores gently embraced by lapping waves, and water wends its way in every direction. The area's jagged peaks and windswept fells stand in desolate splendor—except for July and August, when outdoor enthusiasts outnumber water molecules. Use **Windermere, Ambleside, Grasmere,** and **Keswick** as bases from which to ascend into the hills—the farther west you go from the **A591** connecting these towns, the more countryside you'll have to yourself.

   The **National Park Visitor Centre** is in **Brockhole,** halfway between Windermere and Ambleside. (Tel. (015394) 466 01. Open Easter-Oct. daily 10am-5pm; Oct.-Easter usually Sa-Su.) **National Park Information Centres** dispense info on the camping-barn network, sell camping guides (£1), and book accommodations. While **B&Bs** line every street in every town (£15-20) and the region has the highest concentration of youth hostels in the world, lodgings do fill up in July and August; book ahead.

▣ GETTING THERE AND GETTING AROUND. Two rail lines (tel. (08457) 48 49 50) flank the park: the south-north **Preston-Lancaster-Carlisle** line skirts the park's eastern edge, while the **Barrow-Carlisle** line serves the western coast. **Oxenholme,** on the southeastern edge of the Lake District, and **Penrith,** just to the northeast, both on the former line, are accessible from **Manchester's** Piccadilly Station (2hr., 5-7 per day, £11); **Edinburgh** (2½-3hr., 8 per day, £27); and **London's** Euston Station (4-5hr., 11-16 per day, £50). From Oxenholme, a short branch line covers the 10 mi. to **Windermere** (20min., every hr., £2.70). **National Express buses** (tel. (08705) 80 8 80) go directly to Windermere from **Manchester** (3hr., 2 per day, £13) and **London** (8½hr., 2 per day, £21), and continue north through **Ambleside** and **Grasmere** to Keswick. **Stagecoach Cumberland buses** (tel. (01946) 632 22) serve over 25 towns and villages within the district; pick up the essential *Lakeland Explorer* at any tourist office. An **Explorer** ticket offers unlimited all-day travel on all area Stagecoach buses (£5.50). The Ambleside YHA Youth Hostel offers a convenient **minibus service** (tel. (015394) 323 04; £2) between hostels as well as free service from the Windermere train station to the Windermere and Ambleside hostels. Potential cyclists can get **bike rental** info at tourist offices; *Ordnance Survey Cycle Tours* (£10) has route maps.

WINDERMERE AND BOWNESS. Windermere and sidekick **Bowness-on-Windermere** (joint pop. 8500) fill to the gills with vacationers in summer, when sailboats and waterskiers swarm over Lake Windermere. **Windermere Lake Cruises** runs the **Lake Information Centre** (tel. (015394) 433 60; fax 434 68), at the north end of Bowness Pier, which provides maps, rents rowboats and motorboats, and books popular lake cruises. From Easter to October, boats sail north to Waterhead Pier in Ambleside (30min., 2 per hr., return £5.70) and south to Lakeside (40min., every hr., return

£5.90). The **train station** (tel. (01539) 72 03 97) sends off Lakeland Experience **buses** to Bowness (#599; 3 per hr., £0.80). The **tourist office** is next door. (Tel. (015394) 464 99. Open daily July-Aug. 9am-7:30pm; Easter-June and Sept.-Oct. 9am-6pm; Nov.-Easter 9am-5pm.) The local **National Park Information Centre,** on Glebe Rd, is beside Bowness Pier. (Tel. (015394) 428 95. Open July-Aug. daily 9:30am-6pm; Apr.-June and Sept.-Oct. daily 9am-5:30pm; Nov.-Mar. F-Su 10am-4:30pm.) To get to the spacious **YHA youth hostel,** on High Cross, Bridge Ln, Troutbeck, 1 mi. north of Windermere off the A591, take the Ambleside bus to Troutbeck Bridge and walk ¾ mi. uphill, or catch the YHA shuttle from the train station. (Tel. (015394) 435 43; fax 471 65; email windermere@yha.org.uk. £9.15. Bike rental. Open mid-Feb. to Dec.) To reach the social **Lake District Backpackers Hostel,** on High St, look for the sign on the right as you descend the hill from the train station (2min.) or call for free pick-up. (Tel. (015394) 463 74. £9.50. Reception 9am-1pm and 5-9pm.) **Camp** at **Limefitt Park,** 4½ mi. north of Bowness Pier on A592, just below the Kirkstone path. (Tel. (015394) 323 00. £3 per person; 2 people with tent and car £12.)

AMBLESIDE. Just under a mile north of Lake Windermere, Ambleside has adapted to the tourist influx without selling its soul to the industry. You can't go wrong **hiking** in any direction near Ambleside; however, hidden trail markings, steep slopes, and weather-sensitive visibility all necessitate a good map and compass. Excellent warden-guided **walks** leave from National Park and tourist offices. The top of **Loughrigg,** 2½ mi. from Ambleside (3½ mi. circuit descent), provides a view of higher surrounding fells. For gentler, shorter hikes, *Ambleside Walks in the Countryside* (£0.30) lists three easy walks from the town's center. Lakeslink **bus** 555 (tel. (015394) 322 31; every hr.) rolls into Kelsick Rd from Windermere, Grasmere, and Keswick. The **tourist office** is on Church St. (Tel. (015394) 325 82. Open Easter-Oct. daily 9am-5pm; Nov.-Easter Tu-Th 10am-1pm and 2-5pm, F-Sa 9am-1pm and 2-5pm.) To reach the **National Park Information Centre,** Waterside, walk south on Lake or Borrans Rd from town to the pier. (Tel. (015394) 327 29. Open mid-July to Aug. daily 9:30am-6pm; Easter to mid-July and Sept.-Oct. daily 9:30am-5:30pm; Nov.-Easter F-Su 10am-3:30pm. Bus 555 also stops in front of the superb ▨**Ambleside YHA Youth Hostel,** 1 mi. south of Ambleside and 3 mi. north of Windermere, on the northern shore of Windermere Lake. (Tel. (015394) 323 04; fax 344 08; email ambleside@yha.org.uk. £11.15. Bike rental. Nov.-Feb. curfew midnight.)

GRASMERE. The peace that Wordsworth enjoyed in the village of Grasmere is still apparent during quiet mornings. The early 17th-century ▨**Dove Cottage,** 10min. from the center of town, is where Wordsworth lived from 1799 to 1808, and remains almost exactly as he left it; next door is the outstanding **Wordsworth Museum.** (Both open mid-Feb. to mid-Jan. daily 9:30am-5:30pm. £4.80, students £4.) The six-mile **Wordsworth Walk** circumnavigates the two lakes of the Rothay River, passing the poet's grave, Dove Cottage, and ▨**Rydal Mount,** where the poet lived until his death. (Rydal Mount open Mar.-Oct. daily 9:30am-5pm; Nov.-Feb. W-M 10am-4pm. £3.50, students £3.) **Bus** 555 stops in Grasmere every hr. on its way south to Ambleside or north to Keswick; open-top bus 599 stops in every 20min. The combined **tourist office** and **National Park Information Centre** lies in town on Redbank Rd. (Tel. (015394) 352 45; fax 350 57. Open Easter-Oct. daily 9:30am-5:30pm; Nov.-Easter F-Su 9:30am-4pm.) To reach **Butterlip How (YHA),** on Easedale Rd, follow the road to Easedale for 150 yd. and turn right down the sign-posted drive. (Tel. (015394) 353 16; fax 357 98; email grasmerebh@yha.org.uk. £10.15. Open Apr.-Oct. daily; Nov.-Jan. F-Sa; Feb.-Mar Tu-Sa.) To reach **Thorney How (YHA),** follow Easedale Rd ½ mi. out of town, turn right at the fork, and look for it ¼ mi. down on the left. (Tel. (015394) 355 91; fax 358 66. £9.15. Open Apr.-Sept. daily; mid-Feb. to Mar. and Oct.-Dec. Th-M.) Sarah Nelson's famed Grasmere Gingerbread, a staple since 1854, is a steal at £0.22 in **Church Cottage,** outside St. Oswald's Church. (Open Mar.-Nov. M-Sa 9:30am-5:30pm, Su 12:30-5:30pm; Dec.-Feb. M-Sa 9:30am-5pm, Su 2-4:30pm.)

KESWICK. Between towering Skiddaw peak and the northern edge of Lake Derwentwater, Keswick (KEZ-ick) rivals Windermere as the Lake District's tourist

BRITAIN

capital, but far surpasses it in charm. One of the best ridge hikes in the Lake District begins only a mile from Keswick: ascend the **Cat Bells** from the west shore of Derwent Water at Hawes End and stroll a gentle 3 mi. atop the ridge, passing **Maiden Moor** and **Eel Crags** on the way to **Dale Head,** one of the highest peaks in the area; then descend via the saddle-shaped Honister Pass to reach Seatoller (10-12 mi. total). The **National Park Information Centre,** in Moot Hall, is behind the clock tower in Market Sq. (Tel. (017687) 726 45. Open daily Aug. 9:30am-6pm; Sept.-July 9:30am-5:30pm.) From the tourist office, bear left down Station Rd and follow the signs to reach the stellar ▨**Keswick YHA Youth Hostel,** on Station Rd. (Tel. (017687) 724 84; email keswick@yha.org.uk. £10.15. Kitchen. Curfew 11:30pm. Open mid-Feb. to late Dec.) It's worth the 2 mi. ride south on B5289 (bus 79; every hr.) to Seatoller to stay at the **Derwentwater YHA Youth Hostel,** in Barrow House, Borrowdale, where you can relax by its waterfall. (Tel. (017687) 772 46. £10.15. Open Jan.-Oct.) **Camp** at **Castlerigg Hall,** southeast of Keswick on A591. (Tel. (017687) 724 37. £2.70-3.20 per person, £1 per car. Showers £0.50. Open Apr.-Nov.)

WALES

Wales borders England, but if many of the 2.9 million Welsh people had their way, it would be floating miles away. Since England solidified its control over the country with the murder of Prince Llywelyn ap Gruffydd in 1282, relations between the two have been marked by a powerful unease. Wales clings steadfastly to its Celtic heritage, continuing a centuries-old struggle for independence. Travelers come for the miles of sandy beaches, grassy cliffs, and dramatic mountains that typify the rich landscape of this corner of Britain, or to scan the numerous castles that dot the towns, remnants of centuries of warfare with England. Enjoy the unique landscapes and cultures, and avoid calling the Welsh "English" at all costs.

▓ FERRIES TO IRELAND

Irish Ferries (tel. (0990) 17 17 17) runs to **Dublin, Ireland** from **Holyhead** (2hr.; return £35-60, students £28-48). **Stena Line** (tel. (0990) 70 70 70; www.stenaline.co.uk), runs to **Dún Laoghaire** (near Dublin), from **Holyhead** (1½hr.; £20-35/16-28). **Swansea Cork Ferries,** Ferry Port, King's Dock, Swansea SA1 8RU (tel. (01792) 456116) and 52 South Mall, Cork (tel. (021) 271166). Wales to Ireland (10hr., £22-32). **Irish Ferries** (tel. (0990) 17 17 17) runs to **Dublin, Ireland** from **Holyhead** (2hr.; return £35-60, students £28-48). Stena Line (tel. (0990) 70 70 70; www.stenaline.co.uk), runs to **Dún Laoghaire** (1½hr.; £20-35, students £16-28) and **Dublin** from **Holyhead;** and to **Belfast** from **Stranraer** (1¾-3¼hr., £20-27; Mar.-Jan.).

CARDIFF (CAERDYDD)

Cardiff (pop. 340,000) burst on the scene in the late 19th century as the main port for the shipping of Welsh coal; at its height, it was the world's busiest port. Today the buzzing capital of Wales brims with theaters and clubs as well as remnants of its past. The flamboyant **Cardiff Castle** was restored in mock-medieval style, with a different theme in each room; climb the steps of the Norman keep for a sweeping view of town. (Open daily Mar.-Oct. 9:30am-6pm; Nov.-Feb. 9:30am-4:30pm. £2.50, students £2. Tours £5, students £4.) The **National Museum and Gallery of Wales** has a collection of Western European art and an audio-visual exhibit on "The Evolution of Wales." (Open Tu-Su 10am-5pm. £4.50, students £2.65.)

National Express **buses** (tel. (08705) 80 80 80) roll to Cardiff from London's Victoria Station (3½hr., 6 per day, £13) and Manchester (5½hr., 5 per day, £24.25). **Trains** (tel. (0345) 48 49 50) arrive behind the bus station from Bath (1-1½hr., 2 per hr., £11.40) and London's Paddington Station (2hr., 1-2 per hr., £31.20). The **tourist office,** on Wood St, opposite the bus station, books B&Bs and has maps (Tel. (029) 20 22 72 81. Open Apr.-Sept. M and W-Sa 9am-6:30pm, Tu 10am-6:30pm, Su 10am-

4pm; Oct.-Mar. M and W-Sa 9am-5:30pm, Tu 10am-5:30pm, Su 10am-4pm.) **Cardiff Cybercafé** is at 9 Duke St. (£2.50 per 30min. Open M-F 11am-7pm, Sa 10am-6pm.)

The best B&Bs are off Cathedral Rd (take bus 32 or walk 15min. from the castle). To get to the colorful **Cardiff International Backpacker,** 98 Neville St, from the train station, go down Wood St, cross the river, turn right on Fitzham Embankment, and turn left at the end of the road onto Despenser St. After dark, call for pick-up from the station. (Tel. (029) 20 34 55 77; fax 20 23 04 04. Dorms £12.50; doubles £32; triples £37.50. Breakfast included. **Internet.** V, MC.) The Victorian **Central Market** is in the arcade between St. Mary St and Trinity St. (Open M-Sa 8am-5:30pm.) ◪**Celtic Cauldron Wholefoods,** 47-49 Castle Arcade, serves traditional Welsh food, including rarebit and laver-bread. (Meals £3.50-9.50. Open June-Aug. M-Sa 8:30am-9pm, Su 11am-4pm; Sept.-May M-Sa 8:30am-6pm, Su 11am-4pm.) Cardiff's specialty, **Brains S.A.** (Special Ale), known by locals as "Brains Skull Attack," is proudly served in many local pubs. Head to the **Clwb Ifor Bach** (the Welsh Club), 11 Womanby St, for dancing and the local music scene. (Cover £2-6. Open M-Th until 2am, F until 3am, Sa until 2:30am.) **Postal code:** CF10 2SJ.

WYE VALLEY

Wordsworth once came to the Wye Valley (Afon Gwy) to escape the "fever of the world"; the region's tranquility has since been disturbed by a feverish tourist trade. Even so, much of this region remains unsullied. Below Monmouth, moving past Wordsworth's "steep cliffs," "orchard tufts," and "pastoral farms," the Wye brings green to the door of even the larger towns.

🖻 **GETTING THERE AND GETTING AROUND.** The valley is best entered from the south, at Chepstow. **Trains** chug from **Cardiff** northeast to **Chepstow** (40min., 7-12 per day, £4-5.20) and **Hereford** (1hr., every hr., £13.20), the closest train station to Hay-On-Wye. Trains connect Hereford and Chepstow (13 per day, £13.20). National Express **buses** (tel. (08705) 80 80 80) run to Chepstow from Cardiff (50min., 5 per day, £3.15) and **London** (2¼hr., 5-6 per day, £16.50). Be aware that bus service in the region is rare on Sundays. Pick up the indispensable *Discover the Wye Valley on Foot and by Bus* at any Wye tourist office. Stagecoach Red and White bus 69 loops between **Chepstow, Tintern,** and **Monmouth** (4-8 per day). Stagecoach Red and White bus 39 stops at **Hay-on-Wye** as it travels between Hereford and **Brecon** (M-Sa 5 per day, £2.50-3.15; see **Brecon Beacons National Park,** p. 190); on Sundays, take **Yeoman's** bus 40 (tel. (01432) 35 62 02) instead. One-day **Roverbus** passes (£5) and week-long **Primerider** passes (£16), available from Stagecoach drivers, will save you money if you take more than one bus a day.

Hikers enjoy walks of all difficulties and lengths. The **Wye Valley Walk** heads north from Chepstow and passes the abbey at Tintern, the cathedral at Hereford, and the breathtaking vista at Symonds Yat en route to Hay-on-Wye and Prestatyn. Across the river, the **Offa's Dyke Path** run the entire length of the English-Welsh border, providing 177 mi. of hiking trails.

CHEPSTOW AND TINTERN. Chepstow's strategic position at the mouth of the river and the base of the English border made it an important fortification and commerce center in Norman times. **Chepstow Castle,** built by a fellow conqueror of William the Conqueror, is Britain's oldest stone castle, and offers awesome views of the Wye River. (Open daily Apr. to late Oct. 9:30am-6:30pm; late Oct. to Mar. M-Sa 9:30am-4pm, Su 11am-4pm. £3, students £2.) **Trains** arrive at Station Rd; **buses** stop above the town gate in front of the Somerfield supermarket. Ask about bus tickets at **Fowlers Travel,** 9 Moor St (tel. 62 30 31). The **tourist office** is in the car park of the castle. (Tel. (01291) 62 37 72; www.chepstow.co.uk. Open daily Apr.-Sept. 10am-5:45pm; Oct.-Mar. 10am-4pm.) Take bus 69 to the hostel near Tintern (see below), or stay in Chepstow at ▩ **Lower Hardwick House,** on Mt Pleasant, 300 yd. up the hill from the bus station. (Tel. (01291) 62 21 62. Singles £18; doubles £30-36; **camping** £5 per tent.) **Postal code:** NP16 5DA.

BRITAIN

Five miles north of Chepstow on A466, the haunting arches of **Tintern Abbey** shade crowds of tourists in the summer and "connect the landscape with the quiet of the sky"—a phrase from Wordsworth's famous poem, written just a few miles away. (Tel. (01291) 68 92 51. Open daily June-Sept. 9:30am-6pm, Apr.-May and Oct. 9:30am-5pm; Nov.-Mar. M-Sa 9:30am-4pm, Su 11am-4pm. £2.40, students £1.90.) Near the iron footbridge, paths lead to **Offa's Dyke** (45min.) and the **Devil's Pulpit** (1hr.). A mile north of the abbey, the **Old Station** houses the **info service.** (Tel./fax (01291) 68 95 66. Open Apr.-Oct. daily 10:30am-5:30pm.) The **YHA youth hostel,** four miles northeast of Tintern, occupies a 13th-century castle complete with dungeon. (Tel. (01594) 53 02 72; fax 53 08 49. £10.15, under 18 £6.85. Breakfast £3.10. Curfew 11:30pm. Open Feb.-Oct.) **Postal code:** NP6 6SB.

HEREFORD AND HAY-ON-WYE. Ideal for excursions into Wales, **Hereford** (pop. 60,000) also draws its own visitors with its 11th-century **cathedral** and the 13th-century **Mappa Mundi** within—a map of the world drawn on animal skin around 1290. (Cathedral open Th-Tu until Evensong at 5:30pm; W all day. Mappa Mundi shown May-Sept. 10am-4:15pm, Su 11am-3:15pm; Oct.-Apr. M-Sa 11am-3:15pm. £4, students £3.) The helpful staff at the **tourist office,** 1 King St, in front of the cathedral, books beds for a 10% deposit. (Tel. (01432) 26 84 30. Open Apr.-Sept. M-Sa 9am-5:30pm, Su 10am-4pm; Oct.-Mar. M-Sa 9am-5:30pm.) The T-junction at the end of **Bodenham Rd** hosts many of the cheaper B&Bs in town (around £16 per night). Elsewhere in town, try the B&B **Holly Tree,** 19-21 Barton Rd. (Tel. (01432) 35 78 45. Singles £17; doubles £32.) **Postal code:** HR4 9HQ.

Hay-on-Wye boasts 39 second-hand and antiquarian book shops, and hosts a 10-day **literary festival** in late May, during which luminaries like Toni Morrison and P.D. James give readings. The **tourist office,** on Oxford Rd, books beds for a £2 fee. (Tel. (01497) 82 01 44. Open daily Apr.-Oct. 10am-1pm and 2-5pm; Nov.-Mar. 11am-1pm and 2-4pm.) One hundred yards to the right of the tourist office down Oxford Rd, **1 Garibaldi Terrace** offers rooms with views of the surrounding hills. (Tel. (01497) 82 03 51. Doubles £28.) **Postal code:** HR3 5AE.

BRECON BEACONS NATIONAL PARK

The *Parc Cenedlaethol Bannau Brycheiniog*, less well-known than its sister park to the north, encompasses 519 dramatic sq. mi. of barren peaks, well-watered forests, and windswept moors. The park divides into four regions: the rugged country around the remote western **Black Mountain; Fforest Fawr**, containing the spectacular waterfalls of Ystradfellte; the **Black Mountains** to the east; and the **Beacon** peaks, where King Arthur's mountain fortress is thought to have once stood.

■ GETTING THERE AND GETTING AROUND. The market towns on the fringe of the park, particularly **Brecon**, on its northern edge, make pleasant touring bases. The **train** line (tel. (08457) 48 49 50) from **London**'s Paddington Station to South Wales runs via Cardiff to **Abergavenny**, at the park's southeastern corner, and **Merthyr Tydfil**, on its southern edge. **National Express bus** 509 (tel. (08705) 80 80 80) runs daily to **Brecon** from London (5hr., £17.50) and Cardiff (1¼hr., £2.75). **Stagecoach Red and White** (tel. (01633) 26 63 36) regularly crosses the park en route to **Brecon** from **Cardiff** via **Merthyr Tydfil** (#43, change to #X4; 1½hr., M-Sa 6 per day, £3-4); **Abergavenny** (#20 and 21, 1hr., M-Sa 5 per day; #29, Su 2 per day, £2.65); and **Hereford** and **Hay-on-Wye** (#39, 45min., M-Sa 5 per day; Yeomans #40, Su 2 per day, £3).

BRECON (ABERHONDDU). Just north of the mountains, Brecon (pop. 8000) is the best hiking base. **Buses** arrive at **The Bulwark**, the central square. The **tourist office** is in the Cattle Market Car Park (tel. (01874) 62 24 85; fax 62 52 56); walk through Bethel Sq. off Lion St. The **Brecon Beacons National Park Information Centre** is in the same building. (Tel./fax (01874) 62 31 56. open Apr.-Sept. daily 9:30am-5:30pm.) Only 3min. from town, **The Watton** is ripe with **B&Bs** (£14-17). The nearest hostel is **YHA Ty'n-y-Caeau** (tin-uh-KAY-uh), 3 mi. from Brecon. From the center, walk down The Watton, continue until you reach the roundabout, follow the branch leading to Abergavenny on A40, follow the footpath tucked away to the left to Groesffordd (grohs-FORTH), head left on the main road for 10-15min., bear left at the fork, and it's the second house on the right. The Brecon-Abergavenny bus will stop at a footpath that leads to Groesffordd if you ask the driver. (Tel. (01874) 66 52 70. Open July-Aug. daily; mid-Feb. to June and Sept.-Oct. M-Sa; Nov. to mid-Feb. F-Sa. £8.35.) **Camp** at **Brynich Caravan Park,** 1½ mi. east of town on A40, is signposted from the A40-A470 roundabout. (Tel. (01874) 62 33 25. £3.50-4 per person, £1 per car. Shower included. Laundry. Open Apr.-Oct.)

THE BRECON BEACONS. At the park's center, these mountains lure hikers with pastoral slopes and barren peaks. From the Mountain Centre, a one-hour stroll among daredevil sheep and extraordinary views leads to the remains of an **Iron-Age fort.** The most convenient route to the top of **Pen-y-Fan** (pen-uh-van; 2907 ft.) begins at **Storey Arms,** 5 mi. south of Libanus on A470, but the paths have unfortunately begun to erode. A far more pleasant hiking route starts in nearby **Llanfaes,** a western suburb of Brecon, and leads up past **Llyn Cwm Llwch** (HLIN koom hlooch), a 2000-foot-deep glacial pool. Walk 3 mi. from Llanfaes down Ffrwdgrech Rd. to the cark park (take the middle fork after the first bridge) where the trail begins.

THE WATERFALL DISTRICT (FFOREST FAWR). Forest rivers tumble through rapids, gorges, and spectacular falls near **Ystradfellte,** 7 mi. southwest of the Beacons. At **Porth-yr-Ogof** ("mouth of the cave"), less than 1 mi. from the **YHA Ystradfellte** (uh-strahd-FELTH-tuh; tel. (01639) 720301; £7.50; open mid-July to Aug. daily; Apr. to mid-July and Sept.-Oct. F-Tu), the River Mellte ducks into a cave at the base of the cliff and emerges as an icy pool. To reach the **Sgwdyr Eira** waterfall, follow the marked paths from Gwann Hepste. Near Abercrave, to the west, the huge **Dan-yr-Ogof Showcaves** (tel. (01639) 73 02 84, info tel. 73 08 01) impress with enormous stalagmites. From the YHA Ystradfellte, 10 mi. of trails pass Fforest Fawr (the headlands of the Waterfall District) on their way to the caves. (Tours every 20min. Open Apr.-Oct. 10:30am-3:30pm. Tours £6.95.) **Stagecoach Red and White** buses pause at the hostel and caves en route from Brecon.

THE BLACK MOUNTAINS. These long, lofty mountains offer 80 sq. mi. of solitude. The ridge-walks are unsurpassed; pick up the essential 1:25,000 Ordnance Survey Outdoor Leisure map 13 (£6). **Crickhowell,** on the A40 and the Stagecoach Red and White bus 21 Brecon-Abergavenny route (M-Sa every 2-3hr.), is the best base. You can also explore by bus: Stagecoach Red and White bus 39 from Brecon to Hereford descends the north side of the mountains. **Capel-y-ffin** (kap-EL-uh-fin; YHA), along Offa's Dyke Path (see p. 189), is 8 mi. from Hay-on-Wye. Take Stagecoach Red and White bus 39 from Hereford to Brecon, stop before Hay, and walk uphill. (Tel. (01873) 89 06 50. £6.80, students £4.65. **Camping.** Lockout 10am-5pm. Open July-Sept. daily; Oct. F-Tu; Nov. and Mar.-June Sa-Su.)

ABERYSTWYTH

Halfway down the sweeping Cardigan Bay coastline, the university town of Aberystwyth offers easy access to all of Wales and plenty of pubs to entertain you as you wait for your connection. The **National Library of Wales,** off Penglais Rd, on a hill east of town, houses the earliest surviving manuscript of the *Canterbury Tales* and almost every book written in Welsh or pertaining to Wales. (Open M-F 9:30am-6pm, Sa 9:30am-5pm. Free.) Aberystwyth's charming beachfront and promenade remain much as they were in Victorian times. The **train station,** on Alexandra Rd, is at the receiving end of the main rail line from England into central Wales, and sends trains throughout northern and central Wales; for destinations on the scenic Cambrian Coast to the north, change at Machynlleth (30min., £4). The **tourist office,** in Lisburne House on Terrace Rd, has info on B&Bs. (Tel. (01970) 61 21 25. Open July-Aug. daily 9am-7pm; Sept.-June M-Sa 10am-5pm.) To get to the **YHA Borth,** 9 mi. north in Borth, take the train to Borth Station (10min., 8-12 per day, £1.50) or take Crosville bus 511 or 512. (Tel. (01970) 87 14 98. £9.20. Open Apr.-Aug. daily; Sept. M-Sa; Oct. and Mar. Tu-Sa.) In town, **Mrs. E. V. Williams,** 28 Bridge St, bakes delicious Welsh cakes and offers comfortable beds. (Tel. (01970) 61 25 50. £13.50.)

BRITAIN

SNOWDONIA NATIONAL PARK

Stretching from forested Machynlleth in the south to sand-strewn Conwy in the north, the 840 sheep-dotted square miles of Snowdonia National Park, are dominated by the rough countenances of the highest mountains in England and Wales. Known in Welsh as Eryri (Place of Eagles), Snowdonia's upper reaches are as barren and lonesome as that name suggests, though the park also embrace dark pine forests, deep glacial lakes, sun-pierced coves, and shimmering estuaries. **Mount Snowdon** (3560 ft.), near Llanberis, is the highest peak in England and Wales.

Tourist offices and **National Park Information Centres** stock walk leaflets (£0.40), book lodgings, and sell Ordnance Survey Maps (£5-6), while the eight **YHA youth hostels** in the mountain area are some of the best in Wales. In the mountains, **camping** is permitted, though discouraged because of recent erosion. In the valleys, get the owner's consent. Try www.gwynedd.gov.uk for bus schedules and tourist info.

⌐ GETTING THERE AND GETTING AROUND. Trains (tel. (08457) 48 49 50) stop at several large towns on the park's outskirts, including **Bangor** (see p. 193) and **Conwy** (see p. 193). The **Conwy Valley Line** runs through the park from **Llandudno**, near Conwy, through **Betws-y-Coed** to **Blaenau Ffestiniog** (2-10 per day, return £13.80). Buses run to the interior from these towns as well as others near the edge of the park like **Caernarfon** (see p. 193). At Blaenau Ffestiniog, the Valley Conwy Line connects with the narrow-gauge **Ffestiniog Railway** (tel. (01766) 512340), which romps through the mountains to Porthmadog, meeting up with Cambrian Coaster service to **Llanberis** and **Aberystwyth** (see p. 191). Pick up the indispensable *Gwynedd Public Transport Maps and Timetables* at any tourist office.

LLANBERIS. Set amidst lakes deep in the mountains, Llanberis, the largest town in the park, serves as a great base for exploration. To reach **Ceunant Mawr,** one of Wales' most impressive waterfalls, take the footpath on Victoria Terrace by the Victoria Hotel, then your first right and first left (1 mi.). If hiking isn't your thing, the coal-fired steam locomotives of the immensely popular but immensely expensive ▓**Snowdon Mountain Railway** chug from Llanberis to Snowdon's summit. (Tel. (01286) 87 02 23. Round-trip 2hr., with a 30min. stop at the peak. £15.60, standby return £11.20.) Catch **KMP** (tel. (01286) 87 08 80) bus 77 from Bangor (40min., 5-12 per day, return £1.50.) The **tourist office** is at 41a High St. (Tel. (01286) 87 07 65; fax 87 19 51. Open Easter-Oct. daily 10am-6pm; Nov.-Easter W and F-Su 10:30am-4:30pm.) Plenty of sheep and cows keep hostelers company at the **YHA Llanberis**, a half-mile from town up Capel Goch Rd. (Tel. (01286) 87 02 80; fax 87 09 36. Tu-Sa. £8.30. Open Apr.-Aug. daily; Sept.-Oct. and Jan.-Mar.) **Snowdon Ranger,** Llŷn Cwellyn, is at the base of the **Ranger Path,** the grandest Snowdon ascent; take Sherpa bus 95 from Caernarfon. (Tel. (01286) 65 03 91; fax 65 00 93. £9.15. Open Easter-Aug. daily; Sept.-Oct. W-Su; mid-Feb. to Easter and Nov.-Dec. F-Su.)

HARLECH. On the Cambrian coast, just south of the Llŷn Peninsula and the foothills of Snowdonia, the tiny town of Harlech clings to a steep, rocky hillside. ▓**Harlech Castle,** a World Heritage Site and one of the most spectacularly located of Edward I's many fortresses, crowns a 200 ft. rock with sweeping views of Snowdonia and the bay. (Open Apr.-May and Oct. daily 9:30am-5pm; June-Sept. daily 9:30am-6pm; Nov.-Mar. M-Sa 9:30am-4pm, Su 11am-4pm. £3, students £2.) The **tourist office**, in Gwyddfor House, Stryd Fawr, doubles as a **Snowdonia National Park Information Centre**. (Tel./fax (01766) 78 06 58. Open daily Apr.-Oct. 10am-1pm and 2-6pm.) For zzz's try the **YHA Llanbedr,** 4 mi. south of town, is the closest hostel to Harlech; take the 10-minute train ride to the Llanbedr stop or ride bus 38 and ask to be let off at the hostel. (Tel. (01341) 24 12 87; fax 24 13 89. Open May-Aug. daily; mid-Feb. to Apr. and Sept.-Oct. Th-M; Jan. to mid-Feb. F-Su. £8.)

LLYN PENINSULA

The Llŷn has been a hotspot for tourism since the Middle Ages, when crowds of religious pilgrims tramped through on their way to Bardsey Island, off the peninsula's wild western tip. Now sun worshippers make the trek to the endless, sandy beaches lining the southern coast. **Porthmadog,** on the southeastern part of the peninsula, is its main gateway; Cambrian Coaster **trains** arrives from Aberystwyth to the south (3-5 per day, ₤12), while other trains arrive through the adjacent Snowdonia National Park (see above). This travel hub's principal attraction is the jolly **Ffestiniog Railway,** which runs from Harbour Station on High St into the hills of Snowdonia (1hr., 2-10 per day, ₤13.80; runs mid-Feb. to Nov.). The **tourist office** is at the opposite end of High St, by the harbor. (Tel. (01766) 51 29 81. Open daily Easter-Oct. 10am-6pm; Nov.-Easter 9:30am-5pm.) **Portmeirion,** 2 mi. east of Porthmadog, proves an eccentric landmark of Italy-fixation, with Mediterranean courtyards, pastel houses, palm trees, and exotic statues that constitute an otherworldly diversion from Wales' standard castles and cottages. (Open daily 9:30am-5:30pm. ₤4, students ₤3.30; reduced admission Nov.-Mar.) **Bus** 98 runs from Porthmadog to Minffordd, a scenic 30min. from Portmeirion (M-Sa 3 per day); some also go directly to Portmeirion (10min., 2-3 per day, ₤2 return).

NORTHERN COAST

CAERNARFON. Perched on the edge of the Menai Strait, Caernarfon (car-NARvon) lures visitors with North Wales' grandest medieval castle. Built by Edward I beginning in 1283, the ▨**Caernarfon Castle** was left unfinished when Eddie ran out of money and became distracted by unruly Scots. (Open June-Sept. daily 9:30am-6pm; Apr.-May and Oct. daily 9:30am-5pm; Nov.-Mar. M-Sa 9:30am-4pm, Su 11am-4pm. ₤4.20, students ₤3.20.) **Buses** arrive on Penllyn; Arriva Cymru (tel. (01248) 75 04 44) runs from Bangor (5, 5A, 5B, 5C, and 5X; 25min., every 10min.-1hr., ₤1.50) and Conwy (1hr., 1-2 per hr., ₤3), while KMP bus 88 zooms in from Llanberis (25min., 1-2 per hr., return ₤1.30). The **tourist office,** on Castle St, is in Oriel Pendeitsh opposite the castle gate. (Tel. (01286) 67 22 32. Open Apr.-Oct. daily 10am-6pm; Nov.-Mar. Th-Tu 9:30am-4:30pm.) Stay in comfy bunks at **Totter's Hostel,** 2 High St, at the end of the street toward the strait. (Tel. (01286) 67 29 63. ₤9.50.) Watch the sunset, pint in hand, from ▨**Anglesey Arms,** on the Promenade just below the castle. (Open M-Sa 11am-11pm, Su noon-10:30pm.)

BANGOR. Bangor is a convenient base for exploring the nearby Isle of Anglesey. The wildly opulent ▨**Penrhyn Castle** stands testament to the staggering wealth accumulated by Welsh slate barons over a century ago. To get there, walk up High St toward the pier, turn right on the A5122, and head 1 mi. north. (Open W-M July-Aug. 11am-5pm; late Mar. to June and Sept.-Oct. noon-5pm. ₤5.) **Trains** arrive on Holyhead Rd, at the end of Deiniol Rd, from Holyhead (30min., ₤5.95) and Chester (1¼hr.). **Buses** roll in on Garth Rd, down the hill from the town clock; Arriva Cymru arrives from Holyhead (#4; 1¼hr., M-Sa 2 per hr., Su 6 per day, ₤4.20) and Beaumaris (#53 and 57; 30min., M-Sa 2 per hr., Su 6 per day, ₤2.40), Arriva comes from Caernarfon (#5, 5A, 5B, 5C, and 5X; 25min., every 10min.-1hr., ₤1.50) and Conwy (#5 and 5X; 40min., M-Sa 1-2 per hr., Su 5 per day, ₤1.50), and Williams Deiniolen rolls in comes from Llanberis (#77; 40min., M-Sa every hr., Su 5 per day, return ₤1.50). The **tourist office,** in the Town Hall, is on Deiniol Rd opposite Theatre Gwynedd. (Tel. (02148) 35 27 86. Open Easter-Sept. daily 10am-1pm and 2-6pm; Oct.-Easter F-Sa 10am-1pm and 2-6pm.) To get to the **YHA Bangor,** in Tan-y-Bryn, ½ mi. from the town center, follow High St to the water and turn right at the end on A5122 (Beach Rd), then turn right again at the sign. (Tel. (02148) 35 35 16; fax 37 11 76. ₤9.15. Reception 7am-11pm. Open Jan.-Nov.)

CONWY. Farther northeast along the coast, another Edward I production, his 13th-century **castle,** solemnly guards the walled town of Conwy, a town with an agelessness that countless tourist buses can't seem to kill. (Open June-Sept. daily 9:30am-6pm; Apr.-May and Oct. daily 9:30am-5pm; Nov.-Mar. M-Sa 9:30am-4pm, Su 11am-4pm. ₤3.50, students ₤2.50.) Arriva Cymru **buses** 5 and 5X from Caernarfon and Bangor stop along the main streets in Conwy. National Express rolls in from Ches-

BRITAIN

ter (2hr., 1 per day, £5.25); Manchester (3½hr., 1 per day, £10.25); and London (7hr., 1 per day, £17.50). The **tourist office** is at entrance to the castle. (Tel. (01492) 59 22 48. Open Mar.-Oct. daily 9:30am-6pm; Nov.-Mar. daily 10am-4pm.) From Lancaster Sq, head down Bangor Rd, turn left up Mt. Pleasant, and turn right at the top of the hill to get to the ⬛YHA Conwy, Larkhill, on Sychnant Pass Rd. (Tel. (01492) 59 35 71; fax 59 35 80. £10.15. Reception from 1pm. Open mid-Feb. to Dec.)

ISLE OF ANGLESEY

The ancient Isle of Anglesey, whose Welsh name means "Mona, the mother of Wales," attracts visitors to the prehistoric ruins and eerie Celtic burial mounds set in its flat landscape. Less prehistoric is ⬛**Beaumaris Castle,** in Beaumaris, the last of Edward I's Welsh fortresses and today a World Heritage site. (Open June-Sept. daily 9:30am-6pm; Apr.-May and Oct. daily 9:30am-5pm; Nov.-Mar. M-Sa 9:30am-4pm, Su 11am-4pm. £2.20, students £1.70.) Across the Brittania Bridge from Bangor sits the longest-named village in the world, **Llanfairpwllgwyngyllgogerychwyrndrob-wllllantysiliogogogoch** (Llanfair P.G.), although there's little to see apart from the sign at the train station and Anglesey's only **tourist office.** (Tel. (01248) 71 31 77. Open Apr.-Oct. M-Sa 9:30am-5:30pm, Su 10am-5pm; Nov.-Mar. M-F 9:30am-1pm and 1:30-5pm, Su 10am-5pm.) **Bangor,** on the mainland, is probably the best hub for the island (see above). For info on **ferries** to Dublin and Dún Laoghaire, Ireland from **Holyhead,** see p. 58. Get to Holyhead via **train** (tel. (08457) 48 49 50) from Bangor (30min., £5.30); Chester (1½hr., £14); or London (6hr., £46). Some trains stop en route in Llanfair P.G. Arriva Cymru **bus** 4 (tel. (01248) 75 04 44) travels from Bangor to Holyhead via Llanfair P.G. (1¼hr., M-Sa 2 per hr., Su 6 per day, £4.20); #53 and 57 run from Bangor to Beaumaris (30min., 1-2 per hr., return £2.40).

SCOTLAND

At its best, Scotland is a world apart, a defiantly distinct nation within the United Kingdom with a culture and world view all its own. Exuberant Glasgow boasts a mind-bending nightlife, Aberdeen features grand, regal architecture, and Edinburgh is the festive epicenter of Scottish culture. A little over half the land size of England but with a tenth of its population, Scotland possesses open spaces and natural splendor its southern neighbor cannot rival. The heather-covered mountains and glassy lochs of the west coast and luminescent mists of the Hebrides demand worship; the farmlands to the south and the rolling river valleys of the east coast display a gentler beauty; and the frayed northwestern coast, cut by sea lochs and girded by islands, remains the most beautiful region in Scotland and one of the last stretches of true wilderness in Europe. While the kilts, bagpipes, and find-your-own-clan kits of Glasgow, Edinburgh, and Aberdeen may grow cloying, a visit to the less-touristed regions of Scotland will allow you to encounter inheritors of ancient traditions: a B&B proprietor talking to her grandchildren in soft Gaelic cadences, a crofter cutting peat, or a fisherman setting out in his skiff at dawn.

⬛ FERRIES TO NORTHERN IRELAND

From **Stranraer, Seacat** (tel. (0990) 52 35 23) ferries skim the water to **Belfast** (1½hr., 5 per day, £24, students £16). **Stena Line** (tel. (0990) 707070) ferries also goes from Stranraer to **Belfast** (1¾hr., 10 per day, £23).

⬛ GETTING THERE AND GETTING AROUND

National Express buses (tel. (08705) 80 80 80) connecting England with **Glasgow** and **Edinburgh** (7hr., 4 per day; single £17, return £27) are much cheaper than **ScotRail trains** (tel. (0141) 332 98 11 or (08547) 48 49 50; 6hr., return £50 return). **British Airways** (tel. (0345) 22 21 11) sells a limited number of APEX return tickets from £70. **British Midland** (tel. (0345) 55 45 54) offers a Saver fare from **London** to **Glasgow** (from

£58 return). Reserve as far ahead as possible (at least 2 weeks) for the cheapest fare. Scotland is also linked by **ferry** (see p. 136) to **Northern Ireland.**

Frequent trains and buses run throughout the **Lowlands** (south of Stirling and north of the Borders). In the **Highlands,** trains snake slowly on a few restricted routes, bypassing almost the entire Northwest region. Bus service declines in the Northwest Highlands and grinds to a standstill on Sundays. In general, **buses** are more frequent and extensive than trains and are always cheaper. **Citylink** (tel. (08705) 50 50 50) operates most inter-city service buses. The **Freedom of Scotland Travelpass** (any 4 in 8 days £64, any 8 in 15 days £93, 15 consecutive days £122) allows unlimited travel on ScotRail trains and certain ferry lines. Purchase the pass at almost any train station or order through Rail Europe (see p. 60). **Hop-on, hop-off bus tours** are often a good way to reach more inaccessible areas: try **Haggis,** 60 High St, Edinburgh EH1 1NB (tel. (0131) 557 9393; www.radicaltravel.com; unlimited 3-month travel £95, 6-day tours of Scotland £139, 3-day tours of Scotland £79); **Mac-Backpackers,** 105 High St, Edinburgh EH1 1SG (tel. (0131) 558 9900; www.macback-packers.com; 3-day £69, 5-day £89, 7-day £129); or **Go Blue Banana** (tel. 556 20 00), also based in Edinburgh.

EDINBURGH

Framed by rolling hills and the blue Firth of Forth, Edinburgh (ED-din-bur-ra; pop. 500,000) is the jewel of Scotland. The country's capital since the 12th century, the seeds of Reformation were sown in the 16th century when John Knox became the minister of the High Kirk of St. Giles. An outpouring of talent later made the city a capital of the Enlightenment: the philosopher David Hume presided over a republic of letters that fostered both Adam Smith's invisible hand and the literary wanderings of Sir Walter Scott. Today, Edinburgh Castle stands watch over a litany of literary ghosts, exuberant festivals, and the omnipresent pint of dark ale.

▌ GETTING THERE AND GETTING AROUND

Flights: Edinburgh International Airport, 7 mi. west of the city center (tel. 334 31 36). **LRT's Airlink 100** (tel. 555 63 63; £3.30) and the **Edinburgh Airbus Express** (tel. 556 22 44; £3.60) shuttle to the airport (25min.); both depart from Waverley Bridge.

Trains: Waverley Station (tel. (0345) 48 49 50), near the center of town between North and Waverley Bridges. To: **Glasgow** (1hr., every hr., £7.30); **Aberdeen** (2½hr., every hr., £32.80); and **London's** King's Cross (5hr., every 30min. 9am-3pm, £22-60).

Buses: St. Andrew Square Bus Station, on St. Andrew Sq (tel. (08705) 50 59 50), 3 blocks from the east end of Princes St. **Scottish Citylink** (tel. (0990) 50 50 50) serves: **Glasgow** (2 per hr., £4.50); **Inverness** (every hr., £12.30); and **Aberdeen** (every hr., £13). **National Express** goes to **London** twice daily (£20). For info on hop-on, hop-off backpacking tours of Scotland based in Edinburgh, see above.

Bike Rental: Edinburgh Rent-a-Bike, 29 Blackfriars St (tel. 556 55 60), off High St. Bikes £5-15 per day. Open July-Sept. 9am-9pm; Oct.-June 10am-6pm.

Hitchhiking: *Let's Go* does not recommend hitching. Those who choose to hitch to Newcastle, York, or Durham often take bus 15, 26, or 43 to Musselburgh and A1; to other points south, bus 4 or 15 to Fairmilehead and A702 to Biggar. To points north, one can take bus 18 or 40 to Barnton and the Forth Rd Bridge.

▌ ORIENTATION AND PRACTICAL INFORMATION

Princes St is the main road in the **New Town,** in the northern section of the city; the **Royal Mile** (Lawnmarket, High St, and Canongate) is the main street in the **Old Town** and connects Edinburgh Castle and Holyrood Palace. **North Bridge, Waverly Bridge,** and **The Mound** connect the Old and New Towns.

Tourist Office: Edinburgh and Scotland Information Centre, Waverley Market, 3 Princes St (tel. 473 38 00), next to Waverley Station. Sells bus and theater tickets. Open July-Aug. M-Sa 9am-8pm, Su 10am-8pm; Sept.-June closes at 7pm. Walking tours (£4-6) by **Mercat Tours** (tel. 661 45 41) leave from Mercat Cross in front of St. Giles Cathedral.

BRITAIN

Budget Travel Services: Edinburgh Travel Centre, in Potterow Union, Bristo Sq (tel. 668 22 21). Also at 92 South Clerk St (tel. 667 94 88). Both open M-W and F 9am-5:30pm, Th 10am-5:30pm, Sa 10am-1pm. **STA Travel,** 27 Forrest Rd (tel. 226 77 47). Open M-W and F 9:30am-5:30pm, Th 10am-5:30pm, Sa 11am-5pm.

American Express: 139 Princes St (tel. 225 78 81), 5 blocks from Waverley Station. Mail held. Open M-F 9am-5:30pm, Sa 9am-4pm.

Gay and Lesbian Services: Gay and Lesbian Switchboard, tel. 556 40 49. Pick up *Gay Information* at the tourist office or *Gay Scotland* at bookstores.

Emergency: Dial 999; no coins required. **Police,** 5 Fettes Ave (tel. 311 31 31).

Crisis Lines: Rape Crisis Center, tel. 556 94 37. Staffed M-W and F 7-9pm, Th 1-3pm, Sa 9:30-11am.

Hospital: Royal Infirmary of Edinburgh, 1 Lauriston Pl (tel. 536 10 00 or 536 40 40 for emergencies). From The Mound, take bus 23 or 27.

Post Office: Main office at 8-10 St. James Centre (tel. 556 95 46). Address mail to be held: Jessica SHAPIRO, *Poste Restante,* GPO, 8-10 St. James Centre, Edinburgh **EH1 3SR,** Scotland, UK. Open M-F 8:30am-5:30pm.

Internet Access: ▓**Café Cyberia,** 88 Hanover St. (tel. 220 44 03). £2.50 per 30min., students and seniors £2. Open M-Sa 10am-10pm, Su noon-7pm.

PHONE CODE	City code: 0131. From outside the UK, dial int'l dialing prefix (see inside back cover) + 44 + 131 + local number.

▚ ACCOMMODATIONS

The tourist office has free hostel lists and finds rooms ($4). In festival season (late July-early Sept.) there are few available rooms. Most of Edinburgh's countless **B&Bs** are clustered in three areas: **Bruntsfield, Newington,** and **Leith.**

▓ **Brodie's Backpacker Hostel,** 12 High St (tel. 556 67 70), at St. Mary's St. Relaxed environment. Only 50 beds, so book ahead. Sept.-July £9; higher in Aug. Laundry. Reception open 7am-midnight.

Edinburgh Backpackers, 65 Cockburn St (tel. 220 17 17, reservations 221 00 22), just off the Royal Mile. From North Bridge, turn right on High St and take the 1st right. Organizes legendary pub crawls most Tuesdays in summer. Dorms £11-13.50. Pool table, ping-pong, TV, and **internet** access (£1.50 per 15min.). Reception 24hr.

Argyle Backpackers, 14 Argyle Pl (tel. 667 99 91), south of the Meadows and the Royal Mile. From the train station, take bus 40 or 41 from The Mound to Melville Dr; or walk left and turn left on Waverley Bridge. Charming couple greets guests with tea. Rooms and lounge with TV. Dorms £10-15; doubles and twins £24-46. Check-out 10:30am.

Belford Hostel, 6-8 Douglas Gdns (tel. 225 62 09, reservations 221 00 22). Take bus 2, 26, 31, 36, 85, or 86 from Princes St to Haymarket Station, backtrack toward Princes St, turn left on Palmerston Pl; it's at the end in the converted church on the corner. Great bar area, barbeque, and TV lounge. £10.50-13, doubles £33-37.50. Reserve ahead.

Castle Rock Hostel, 15 Johnston Terr. (tel. 225 96 66). Walk toward the Castle on Royal Mile, then turn left on Johnston Terr. Gigantic hostel with views of the castle. £10.40-12. Breakfast £1.60. Laundry £2.50. **Internet** £1.80 per 30min. Reception 24hr.

Royal Mile Backpackers, 105 High St (tel. 557 61 20). Walk down High St from Cockburn St; this spiffy new hostel is directly opposite the yellow Telecom Center. Go upstairs and veer left. Free High St walking tours, pub crawls, and movies. £10.40-12. V, MC.

HAGGIS: WHAT'S IN THERE? Although restaurants
throughout Scotland produce steamin' plates o' haggis for eager tourists, we at *Let's Go* believe all should know what's inside that strange-looking bundle before taking the plunge. An age-old recipe calls for the following ingredients: the large stomach bag of a sheep, the small (knight's hood) bag, the pluck (including lungs, liver, and heart), beef, suet, oatmeal, onions, pepper, and salt. Today's haggis is available conveniently canned (!) and includes: lamb, lamb offal, oatmeal, wheat flour (healthy, no?), beef, suet, onions, salt, spices, stock, and liquor (1%).

BRITAIN

Edinburgh

ACCOMMODATIONS
A Castle Rock Hostel
B Edinburgh Backpackers
C High St. Hostel
D Brodie's
E Royal Mile Backpackers' Hostel
F Argyle Backpackers

High St Hostel, 8 Blackfriars St (tel. 557 39 84). Edinburgh's original hostel lacks a bit of the polish of the affiliated Royal Mile and Castle Rock hostels. But you can enjoy a pool table, TV, and movies. £9.90-10.50. Continental breakfast £1.60. V, MC.

Camping: Edinburgh Caravans (tel. 312 68 74), Marine Dr, by the Forth. Take bus 8A or 9A (14A after 4:30pm) from North Bridge (70p). Showers and a shop. £4 per person, £3 per tent, £1.50 per car. Open Apr.-Oct.

🍴 FOOD

You can get haggis cheap in many pubs; most offer student and hosteler discounts in the early evening. **South Clerk St** has plenty of shops offering reasonably priced Chinese or Indian takeout. For **groceries,** try **Presto's** in St. James Shopping Centre. (Open M-W and F-Sa 8am-6pm, Th 8am-8pm.)

The Basement, 10a-12a Broughton St (tel. 557 00 97). The menu changes weekly, with plenty of vegetarian options. A lively mix of students and musicians in its candle-lit, cavernous environment. Kitchen open daily noon-10pm; drinks served later.

The Black Medicine Coffee Co., 2 Nicolson Rd (tel. 622 72 09). Native American decor reflects this café's name—Black Medicine is the Native American name for coffee. Packed with sophisticated students. Open daily 8am-8pm.

The Last Drop, 72-74 Grassmarket. "Haggis, tatties, and neeps" (haggis, potatoes, and turnips) in omnivorous and veggie versions. The whole menu (save the steak) is £2.50 for students and hostelers until 6:30pm. A packed pub at night. Open daily 10am-2am.

Lost Sock Diner, 1 E. London St (tel. 557 60 97), has combined the efficiency of a laundromat with the tastiness of a café. Get a delicious meal for under £4 while your pants dry. Open M 8am-4pm, Tu-F 9am-10pm, Sa 10am-10pm, Su 11am-5pm.

Ndebele, 57 Home St (tel. 221 11 41). Women of a southern African tribe of the same name serve copious amounts of grub for under £5. Daily African special and a huge array of African and South American coffees and juices. Open daily 10am-10pm.

Kebab Mahal, 7 Nicolson Sq (tel. 667 52 14). Chicken *tikka masala* is the specialty (£5.25) but the kebabs are good, too (£2.25-4.50). Open Su-Th noon-midnight, F-Sa noon-2am; closed F for lunch.

👁 SIGHTS

THE OLD TOWN AND THE ROYAL MILE

The Royal Mile (Lawnmarket, High St, Canongate) defines the length of the Old Town. Defended by Edinburgh Castle at the top of the hill and the Palace of Holyroodhouse at the bottom, the Old Town once packed thousands of inhabitants into a few square miles—visible in the narrow shopfronts and five- to six-story slum buildings—but today the street is more the domain of tourists than slum lords.

EDINBURGH CASTLE. Crowning the top of the Royal Mile, most of the structures in the castle are the result of rebuilding from recent centuries. Inside, **St. Margaret's Chapel,** a 12th-century Norman church, is believed to be the oldest structure in Edinburgh. The castle also displays the 15th-century Scottish Crown Jewels, a royal scepter, sword, and crown. *(At the western extreme of the Royal Mile. Open daily Apr.-Sept. 9:30am-6pm; Oct.-Mar. 9:30am-5pm. £6.50.)*

ALONG THE ROYAL MILE. Everything inside the 1617 tenement **Gladstone's Land,** the oldest surviving house along the Mile, remains as it was almost 400 years ago. *(483 Lawnmarket St. Open Apr.-Oct. M-Sa 10am-5pm, Su 2-5pm. £3.20, students £2.20.)* **Lady Stair's House,** a 17th-century townhouse, contains the **Writer's Museum,** with memorabilia and manuscripts belonging to three of Scotland's greatest literary figures: Robert Burns, Sir Walter Scott, and Robert Louis Stevenson. *(Through the passage at 477 Lawnmarket St. Open M-Sa 10am-5pm; during Festival Su 2-5pm. Free.)* The **High Kirk of St. Giles** (St. Giles Cathedral), Scotland's principal church, was pressed into service as an Episcopal cathedral twice in the country's turbulent religious history. From the pulpit within, John Knox delivered the fiery Presbyterian sermons that drove Mary, Queen of Scots, into exile. *(Where Lawnmarket becomes High St, opposite Parliament. Open Easter to mid-Sept. M-F 9am-7pm, Sa 9am-5pm, Su 1-5pm; mid-Sept. to Easter M-Sa 9am-5pm, Su 1-5pm. Donation £1.)* The 17th-century chapel **Canongate Kirk** is the resting place of

BRITAIN

Adam Smith; royals also worship here when in residence. **Canongate,** the steep hill at the end of the Mile, has three museums, including a museum of children's toys. *(All 3 open M-Sa 10am-5pm; during Festival also Su 2-5pm. Free.)*

PALACE OF HOLYROODHOUSE. Once the home of Mary, Queen of Scots, this spectacular Stewart palace, which dates from the 16th and 17th centuries, is now Queen Elizabeth II's official residence in Scotland. Behind the palace lies the 12th-century abbey ransacked during the Reformation. *(At the eastern end of the Royal Mile. Open Apr.-Oct. daily 9:30am-5:15pm; Nov.-Mar. M-Sa 9:30am-3:45pm; closed during official residences in late May and late June-early July. £5.50.)*

THE NEW TOWN

Edinburgh's New Town is a masterpiece of Georgian planning. James Craig, a then 23-year-old architect, won the city planning contest in 1767 with the design you see today: the three main parallel streets (Queen, George, and Princes) form a rectangular, symmetrical gridiron linking two large squares (Charlotte and St. Andrew). The design was chosen to reflect the Scottish Enlightenment's belief in order. A crucial stop in your stroll through the New Town is the elegant **Georgian House,** a restored townhouse. *(7 Charlotte Sq. From Princes St, turn right on Charlotte St and take your 2nd left. Open Apr.-Oct. M-Sa 10am-5pm, Su 2-5pm. £4.20, students £2.80.)* The **Walter Scott Monument** is a grotesque Gothic "steeple without a church" containing statues of Scott and his dog. Climb the winding 287-step staircase for an eagle's-eye view of Princes St Gardens, the castle, and Old Town's Market St. *(On Princes St, between The Mound and Waverley Bridge. Open Apr.-Sept. M-Sa 9am-6pm; Oct.-Mar. M-Sa 9am-3pm. £2.)* The **National Gallery of Scotland** houses a superb collection of works by Renaissance, Romantic, and Impressionist masters and a fine spread of Scottish art. *(On the Mound between the two halves of Princes St. Gardens. Open M-Sa 10am-5pm, Su 2-5pm; during Festival M-Sa 10am-6pm, Su 11am-6pm. Free.)* The **Scottish National Portrait Gallery,** 1 Queen St, north of St. Andrew Sq, mounts the mugs of famous Scots. *(Open M-Sa 10am-5pm, Su 2-5pm. Free.)* For information on Edinburgh's other (mostly free) museums, pick up the *Edinburgh Gallery Guide* at the tourist office.

🎵 ENTERTAINMENT

The summer season overflows with music in the gardens and many theater and film events around town. For details on pubs and clubs, pick up *The List* ($1.95).

THEATER AND MUSIC. The **Festival Theatre,** 13-29 Nicholson St, stages ballet and opera, while the affiliated **King's Theatre,** 2 Leven St, promotes serious and comedic fare, musicals, and opera. Same-day seats ($5.50) for the Festival Theatre go on sale daily at 10am. (Tel. 529 60 00. Box office open daily 11am-6pm.) The **Royal Lyceum Theatre,** 30 Grindlay St, presents Scottish and international productions. (Tel. 248 48 48. Box office open M 10am-6pm, Tu-Sa 10am-8pm. Tickets £7-16; students £3.50-8.) Scottish bands and country dancing abound at the **Ross Open-Air Theatre** (tel. 529 41 47), under the tent in Princes St Gardens, (from 7pm).

FESTIVALS. For a few weeks in August, Edinburgh hosts the spectacular **Edinburgh International Festival** (Aug. 13-Sept. 2 in 2000), featuring a kaleidoscopic program of music, drama, dance, and art. Tickets ($4-44) are sold beginning in April, but you can usually get tickets at the door; look for half-price tickets after 1pm on performance days. For tickets and a schedule, contact the **Festival Box Office,** 21 Market St, EH1 1BW (info tel. 473 20 01; bookings 473 20 00; fax 473 20 03; www.edinburghfestivals.co.uk). Around the festival has grown a more spontaneous **Festival Fringe** (Aug. 6-28 in 2000), which now includes over 500 amateur and professional companies presenting theater, comedy, children's shows, folk and classical music, poetry, dance, and opera events that budget travelers may find more suitable for their wallets (usually free-$5). Get brochures and tickets by mail from the **Fringe Festival Office,** 180 High St, Edinburgh EH1 1QS. (Tel. 226 52 57, bookings 226 51 38; www.edfringe.com. Box office open Aug. daily 9am-9pm; Sept.-July M-Sa 10am-6pm.) Another August festival is the **Military Tattoo**—a spectacle of military bands,

BRITAIN

GREAT TRADITIONS OF BRITISH SPORT

What golf is to St. Andrews, curling is to Edinburgh. Conceived by Flemish immigrants in the 15th century, curling quickly became a Scottish favorite, appearing in native prose and verse and surfacing in the paintings of Bruegel. Modern curling involves a heavy granite stone, several small brooms, and a long sheet of ice. Curlers compete in teams of four; one member of each team, "the Skip," tells a second curler to hurl the stone down the ice; the other two curlers hop in front of the stone, using their brooms to smooth the surface of the ice, guiding the stone to a spot chosen by the Skip. The winner is the team that gets more of its stones close to the designated spots. Sadly, Scotland has all but abandoned its brooms to Canada. Well over one million of today's curlers hail from the Commonwealth nation; the rest of the world boasts fewer than a quarter million mad sweepers.

bagpipes, and drums—considered by some to be the highlight of the month. For tickets (£7.50-16), contact the **Tattoo Ticket Sale Office,** 33-34 Market St. (Tel. 225 11 88; fax 225 86 27. Open M-F 10am-4:30pm or until the show. Shows M-Sa night.)

NIGHTLIFE. If you're on a street in Edinburgh that seems to have no pubs, you're not looking hard enough. Royal Mile pubs draw an older crowd, while students loiter in Old Town pubs around the university. **The Three Sisters,** 139 Cowgate, offers copious space for dancing, drinking, and socializing. (Open daily 9am-1am.) If you see an apparition or start hearing voices at **The Living Room,** 235 Cowgate, it isn't the alcohol talking—this traditional bar is apparently haunted by a spirit named George. (Open daily noon-1am.) **Whistle Binkie's,** 4 Niddry St, off High St, packs 'em in for live music nights. (Open daily until 3am.) **Scruffy Murphy's,** 50 George IV Bridge, near St. Giles, is a student-y, pop-culture pub. (Open M-Sa 11am-1am, Su 12:30pm-1am.) Jazz enthusiasts crowd **The Cellar Bar,** on Chambers St, and **The Jazz Joint,** 8 Morrison St. Put on your dancing shoes to go to **The Honeycomb,** 36-38a Blair St, on Sunday nights for their "Taste" party devoted mostly to house and garage. (Cover £8. Open daily 11pm-late.) The Broughton St area in New Town (better known as the **Broughton Triangle**) is the center of gay and lesbian nightlife.

GLASGOW

Although it has traditionally suffered a reputation of industrial lackluster, Glasgow, Scotland's largest city (pop. 675,000), today thrives with a reawakened energy. The millions of pounds the city has poured into the arts are reflected in its free museums, extensive galleries, and first-rate theaters; the West End oozes with trendy creativity and energy. And while it rivals its sister to the east in cultural attractions, Glasgow also remains much less touristy, infused with a flourishing economy, a passion for football, and the energy of spirited locals.

▐ GETTING THERE AND GETTING AROUND

Flights: Glasgow Airport (tel. 887 11 11), 10 mi. west in Abbotsinch. Citylink buses connect to **Buchanan Station** (20min., 2 per hr., £3).

Trains: Two main stations. **Central Station,** on Gordon St. U: St. Enoch. To: **Stranraer** (2½hr., 3-8 per day, £15.30) and **London-King's Cross** (5-6hr., 5-20 per day, £78, APEX £29). **Queen St Station,** on George Sq. U: Buchanan St. To: **Edinburgh** (50min., 2 per hr., £7.30); **Aberdeen** (2½hr., 11-24 per day, £36); and **Inverness** (3¼hr., 5 per day, £30). Bus 398 runs between the 2 stations (4 per hr., £0.50).

Buses: Buchanan Station (tel. 332 71 33), on North Hanover St, 2 blocks north of the Queen St Station. **Scottish Citylink** (tel. (08705) 50 50 50) to: **Edinburgh** (50min., 2-4 per hr., £4.50); **Oban** (3hr., 2-3 per day, £10); **Inverness** (3½-4½hr., 1 per hr., £12); and **Aberdeen** (4hr., 12-24 per hr., £13.50). **National Express** (tel. (08705) 80 80 80) buses arrive daily from **London** (8hr.; 4 per day; £20, return £30).

Public Transportation: The circular **Underground (U)** subway line, a.k.a. the "Clockwork Orange" runs M-Sa 6:30am-midnight, Su 11am-6pm. Single-fare £0.80. Wave wildly to stop **buses,** and carry exact change. Single-fare £0.45-0.95.

BRITAIN

BRITAIN

500 meters
500 yards

N

Broomhill Park

Pinkston Rd.
Corn St.
TO QUEEN'S CROSS
Craighall Rd.
Dobbie's Loan
Port Dundas
Renton
Milton St.
Stewart St.
St. George's Rd.
Great Western Rd.
ST. GEORGE'S CROSS
W. Graham St.
Buccleuch St.
Scott St.
Garnet St.
Hill St.
W. Princes St.
Grant St.
Woodlands Rd.
W. Prince's St.
Lynedoch Pl.
Woodlands Pl.
Newton Pl.
Woodside Pl.
Woodside Terr.
Somerset Pl.
Royal Terr.
Park Terr.
Park Quad.
Park Circus
KELVINGROVE PARK
River Kelvin
Hunterian Museum and Art Gallery
Glasgow University
Kelvingrove Museum and Art Gallery
TO KELVIN HALL
Kelvin Way
Kelvinhaugh St.
Gray St.
Derby St.
Minerva St.
Argyle St.
St. Vincent Crescent
Kelvingrove St.
Sauchiehall St.
Claremont St.
Berkeley St.
Kent Rd.
Elderslie St.
North St.
Cleveland St.
Granville St.
Beltane St.
Mitchell Library
Eldon St.
St. Vincent St.
Stobcross St.
Greenhill Pl.
Finnieston St.
Minerva Way
Clydeside Expwy.
River Clyde
Lancefield Quay
Anderston Quay
Hydepark St.
Washington St.
James Watt St.
McAlpine St.
Brown St.
Broomielaw
Springfield Quay
Mavisbank Gardens
BURRELL COLLECTION, GREENOCK & GLASGOW AIRPORTS

M8
Dobbie's Loan
Baird St.
Stirling Rd.
St. James's Rd.
N. Wallace St.
Kyle St.
St. Mungo Ave.
Lister St.
Kennedy St.
North Hanover St.
Taylor St.
Castle St.
Royal Infirmary
Provand's Lordship
Glasgow Cathedral
John Knox St.
CATHEDRAL SQUARE
Duke St.
High St.
TO E (600 yd.)
Gallowgate
TO PEOPLE'S PALACE
Bell St.
George St.
Campus Village
Strathclyde University
Cathedral St.
Cochrane St.
Queen St. Station
Buchanan Bus Station
Killermont St.
Royal Concert Hall
BUCHANAN ST.
NELSON MANDELA PL.
City Chambers
GEORGE SQ.
Virginia St.
Hutcheson St.
Glassford St.
Brunswick St.
Ingram St.
City Hall / Ticket Centre
Wilson St.
Albion St.
High St.
Tron Steeple, Tron Theatre
Osborne St.
Trongate
Stockwell St.
Queen St.
Princes Sq.
Argyle St. Station
ST. ENOCH SQ.
ST. ENOCH
Howard St.
Clyde St.
Jamaica St.
Bridgegate
St. Strings Library
W. Nile St.
W. George St.
W. Regent St.
St. Vincent St.
Renfield St.
Hope St.
Union St.
Central Station
Gordon St.
Wellington St.
Oswald St.
Robertson St.
York St.
Cadogan St.
Waterloo St.
Douglas St.
Blythswood St.
Holland St.
Pitt St.
Bothwell St.
Campbell St.
Anderston Cross Bus Station
Argyle St.
Anderston St.
M8
Cowcaddens Rd.
Parliamentary Rd.
Theatre Royal
COWCADDENS
Cambridge St.
Rose St.
Dalhousie St.
Glasgow Film Theater
Sauchiehall St.
Bath St.
McLellan Galleries
Glasgow School of Art
Renfrew St.
Elmbank St.
Newton St.
Maryhill Rd.

🔢 ORIENTATION AND PRACTICAL INFORMATION

George Sq is the physical center of town. Sections of **Sauchiehall St** (SAW-kee-hall), **Argyle St,** and **Buchanan St,** are pedestrian areas. **Charing Cross,** in the northwest, where Bath St crosses M8, is used as a general landmark. The vibrant **West End** revolves around **Byres Rd** and **Glasgow University,** one mile northwest of the city center. To reach the **tourist office** from **Central Station,** exit on **Union St,** turn left, walk two blocks, turn right on **St. Vincent St,** and it's 3½ blocks up on your right. From **Queen St Station,** exit onto **George St,** and cross George Sq. From the **Buchanan Bus Station,** exit on **North Hanover St** and follow it right to George Sq.

Tourist Office: 11 George Sq (tel. 204 44 00; fax 221 35 24), off George Sq. U: Buchanan St. Books rooms for £2 fee plus 10% deposit. **Walking tours** depart M-Sa 6pm, Su 10:30am (1½hr.; £5, students £4). Open July-Aug. M-Sa 9am-8pm, Su 10am-6pm; June and Sept. M-Sa 9am-7pm, Su 10am-6pm; Oct.-May M-Sa 9am-6pm.

Budget Travel: STA Travel, 184 Byres Rd (tel. 338 60 00). Open M-Tu and F 9:30am-5:30pm, W 10:30am-5:30pm, Th 9:30am-7pm, Sa 11am-5pm.

American Express: 115 Hope St (tel. 221 43 66). Open July-Aug. M-F 8:30am-5:30pm, Sa 9am-5pm; Sept.-June M-F 8:30am-5:30pm, Sa 9am-noon.

Laundromat: Coin-Op Laundromat, 39/41 Bank St (tel. 339 89 53). U: Kelvin Bridge. Open M-F 9am-7:30pm, Sa-Su 9am-5pm.

Emergency: Dial 999; no coins required. **Police:** (tel. 532 30 00), on Stewart St.

Hospital: Glasgow Royal Infirmary, 84-106 Castle St (tel. 211 40 00).

Internet Access: The Internet Café, 569 Sauchiehall St (tel. 564 10 52). £3 per 30min., students £2.50. Open M-Th 9am-11pm, F-Su 9am-7pm.

Post Office: 47 St. Vincent St. Address mail to be held: T.J. KELLEHER, *Poste Restante,* 47 St. Vincent St, **G2 5QX** Glasgow, UK. Open M-F 8:30am-5:45pm, Sa 9am-5:30pm.

PHONE CODE	City code: 0141. From outside the UK, dial int'l dialing prefix (see inside back cover) + 44 + 141 + local number.

🏠 ACCOMMODATIONS AND FOOD

Reserve B&Bs and hostels in advance, especially in August. Last-minute planners may consider calling **SYHA Loch Lomond** (see p. 205). Most B&Bs cluster on **Great Western Rd,** in the university area, or near **Westercraigs Rd,** east of the Necropolis.

Glasgow Backpackers Hostel, 17 Park Terr (tel. 332 90 99). U: St. George's Cross. Clean, friendly, and extremely social hostel. Dorms £9.90; twins £23. Open July-Sept.

SYHA Youth Hostel, 7-8 Park Terr (tel. 332 30 04; fax 331 50 07). U: St. George's Cross. From Central Station, take bus 44 or 59 from Hope St and ask for the 1st stop on Woodlands Rd, then follow the signs. TV and game rooms. From Queen St or Buchanan Stations, catch bus 11 from Bath St. £12.25-13.25. Breakfast included. Kitchen. Laundry.

Blue Sky Hostel and **Berkeley Globetrotters Hostel,** 63/65 Berkeley St (tel. 221 78 80). Same proprietors. Dorms £9.50, 3 nights £25; twins £25. Breakfast included. Kitchen.

Seton Guest House, 6 Seton Terr (tel. 556 76 54; fax 402 36 55; email passway@seton.prestel.co.uk), 20min. east of George Sq. Hop on bus 6, 6A, 8, or 41A. Kindly hosts keep large immaculate rooms. Singles £17; twins £30.

Alamo Guest House, 46 Gray St (tel. 339 23 95), opposite the Kelvingrove Museum. Kind proprietors and spacious, quiet rooms. Singles £20-22; doubles from £34.

The area bordered by **Otago St** in the west, **St. George's Rd** in the east, and along **Great Western Rd, Woodlands Rd,** and **Eldon St** brims with cheap kebab 'n' curry joints. **Byres Rd** and **Ashton Ln,** a tiny cobblestoned alley parallel to Byres Rd, thrive with cheap, trendy cafés and bistros. ◼**Insomnia Café,** 38/40 Woodlands Rd, near the hostels, is the hip place to gorge, day or night. (Café and adjoining deli open 24hr.) **The Bay Tree Vegetarian Café,** 403 Great Western Rd, at Park Rd, also near the hostels (cut through Kelvingrove Park), offers pitas with hummus and salad for $3.50-4.50. (Open M-Sa 9am-9pm, Su 10am-8pm.) **La Focaccia,** 291 Byres Rd, has excellent pizzas and sandwiches on fresh foccacia ($2.40). **The Willow Tea Room,** 217 Sauchiehall

BRITAIN

St (tel. 332 05 21), upstairs from Henderson the Jewellers, is a Glasgow landmark. Sip one of 28 kinds of tea. (£1.20-1.30 per pot. High tea £7.75. Open M-Sa 9:30am-4:30pm, Su noon-4:15pm.) **Woodlands Grocers,** 110 Woodlands Rd, is open 24hr.; there's also a **Safeway** at 373 Byres Rd (open M-Sa 8am-8pm, Su 9am-7pm).

⚑ SIGHTS

The red-paved **George Square** marks the busiest part of the city. The **City Chambers,** on the east side of the square, conceal an ornate marble interior in Italian Renaissance style. (Open M-F. Tours 10:30am and 2:30pm.) Follow George St from the square and take a left on High St, which turns into Castle St, to reach the Gothic **Glasgow Cathedral,** the only full-scale cathedral spared the fury of the 16th-century Scottish Reformation. (Open Apr.-Sept. M-Sa 9:30am-6pm, Su 2-5pm; Oct.-Mar. M-Sa 9:30am-4pm, Su 2-4pm. Free.) On the same street is the **St. Mungo Museum of Religious Life and Art,** 2 Castle St, which surveys every religion from Hindu to Yoruba. (Open M-Sa 10am-5pm, Su 11am-5pm. Free.) Behind the cathedral is the spectacular **Necropolis,** a terrifying hilltop cemetery filled with broken tombstones. (Free.) In the West End, the large, wooded **Kelvingrove Park** lies on the banks of the River Kelvin. In the southwest corner of the park, at Argyle and Sauchiehall St, sits the magnificent, spired **Kelvingrove Art Gallery and Museum,** which shelters works by van Gogh, Monet, and Rembrandt. (U: Kelvin Hall. Open M-Sa 10am-5pm, Su 11am-5pm. Free.) Farther west rises the Gothic central spire of the **University of Glasgow.** The main building is on University Ave, which runs into Byres Rd. While you're walking through the campus, which that has churned out 57 Nobel laureates, stop by the **Hunterian Museum** or the **Hunterian Art Gallery,** across the street. (U: Hillhead. Open M-Sa 9:30-5pm. Free.) Several buildings designed by Charles Rennie Mackintosh, Scotland's most famous architect, are open to the public; the **Glasgow School of Art,** 167 Renfrew St, south of the river, reflects a uniquely Glaswegian Modernist style. (Tours M-F 11am and 2pm, Sa 10:30am. £3.50, students £2.) If you tire of all that culture, shop 'til you drop at **Princes Sq,** 48 Buchanan St, a gorgeous high-end shopping mall—the classiest place to shop outside of London. If your wallet has any life in it left, hit **Sauchiehall St,** which hosts shops and art galleries as well.

♫ ENTERTAINMENT

The infamous **Byers Rd** pub crawl passes the Glasgow University area, starting at Tennant's Bar and heading toward the River Clyde. ◙**Uisge Beatha,** 232 Woodlands Rd, serves over 100 malt whiskys (£1.75-35 each). (Open M-Th 11am-11pm, F-Sa 11am-midnight, Su 12:30-11pm.) The **Cul de Sac Bar,** 46 Ashton Ln, hosts an artsy, fun crowd of pre-clubbers. (Open M-Sa 9am-midnight, Su noon-midnight.) **Russell Bar-Café,** 77 Byres Rd, is a log cabin with live DJs and meal deals. (Open Su-Th 11am-11pm, F-Sa 11am-midnight.) Look for skeletons just outside the second-floor windows of club **Archaos,** 25 Queen St. (Cover £3-9. Open Th-Su until 3am.) People of all types shake their tushies at sweating **Sub Club,** 22 Jamaica St. (Cover £3-6, Sa £8. Open Th-F and Su 11pm-3am, Sa 11pm-3:30am.)

STRANRAER

On the westernmost peninsula of Dumfries and Galloway, Stranraer (stran-RAHR) provides **ferry** access to Belfast in Northern Ireland (see p. 136). **Trains** (tel. (0345) 48 49 50) arrive from Glasgow (2½hr., 2-7 per day, £15.30), as do Citylink **buses** (#923; tel. (08705) 50 50 50; 2½hr., 2 per day, £8.50). National Express buses (tel. (08705) 80 80 80) roll in from Manchester (6½hr., 1 per day, £26) and London (9hr., 1 per day, £32). The **tourist office** is at 1 Bridge St. (Tel. (01776) 70 25 95; fax 88 91 56. Open June-Sept. M-Sa 9:30am-6pm, Su 10am-6pm; Apr.-May and Oct. M-Sa 9:30am-5pm, Su 10am-4pm; Nov.-Mar. M-Sa 10am-4pm.) If you're marooned, try the **Jan Da Mar Guest House,** 1 Ivy Pl, on London Rd. (Tel./fax (01776) 70 61 94. Singles £18; twins £32.) The **Tesco supermarket** is on Charlotte St at Port Rodie near the terminal. (Open M-F 8:30am-8pm, Sa 8am-6pm, Su 10am-5pm.)

BRITAIN

STIRLING

The third point of a strategic triangle completed by Glasgow and Edinburgh, Stirling has historically presided over north-south movement in the region; it was once said that he who controlled Stirling controlled Scotland. At the 1297 Battle of Stirling Bridge, **William Wallace** (of *Braveheart* fame) outwitted and overpowered the English army, enabling Robert the Bruce to finally overthrow the English in 1314 at **Bannockburn,** two miles south of town, and lead Scotland to a 400-year-long stretch of independence. The ◨**Stirling Castle** possesses prim gardens and superb views of the Forth Valley that belie its militant and murderous past. (Open daily Apr.-Oct. 9:30am-6pm; Nov.-Mar. 9:30am-5pm. £5. Tours free.) The castle also contains the fascinating **Regimental Museum of the Argyll and Sutherland Highlanders.** (Open Easter-Sept. M-Sa 10am-5:45pm, Su 11am-4:45pm; Oct.-Easter daily 10am-4:45pm. Free.) The 19th-century **Wallace Monument Tower,** on Hillfouts Rd, 1½ mi. from town, offers incredible views from atop a set of wind-whipped stairs. (Open daily July-Aug. 9:30am-6:30pm; June and Sept. 10am-6pm; Mar.-May and Oct. 10am-5pm; Nov.-Feb. 10:30am-4pm. £3.25, students £3.)

Trains run from Goosecroft Rd (tel. (08457) 48 49 50) to Glasgow (30min., 1-3 per hr., £4.10); Edinburgh (50min., 2 per hr., £4.80); Aberdeen (2½hr., every hr., £29.70); and Inverness (3hr., 4-8 per day, £28.60). National Express **buses** also run from Goosecroft Rd to Inverness (every hr., £10.50) and Glasgow (every hr., £3.20). The **Stirling Visitor Centre** is next to the castle. (Tel. (01786) 46 25 17. Open daily July-Aug. 9am-6:30pm; Apr.-June and Sept.-Oct. 9:30am-6pm; Nov.-Mar. 9:30am-5pm.) The **SYHA Stirling,** on St. John St, halfway up the hill to the castle, occupies the shell of the first Separatist Church in Stirling. In summer, overflow singles in the **Union St. Annexe,** known in cooler months as University of Stirling dorms, are the same prices as the hostel. (Tel. (01786) 47 34 42; fax 44 57 15. £12.25-13.25. Reception 7:30am-11pm. Curfew 2am.) **Postal code:** FK8 2BP.

ST. ANDREWS

In St. Andrews, golf is the game; the rules of the sport were even formally established here. The **Old Course,** a frequent site of the British Open, is a golf pilgrim's Canterbury. (Call (01334) 46 66 66 or fax 47 70 36 for reservations; or enter the on-the-spot lottery for starting times. £75 per round.) For the financially challenged, **Balgrove Course** offers 9 holes for £7. If you've neglected to bring your clubs along, the **British Golf Museum,** next to the Old Course, details the ancient origins of golf. (Open Easter-Oct. daily 9:30am-5:30pm; Nov.-Easter Th-M 11am-3pm. £3.75, students £2.75.) Despite the onslaught of pastel and polyester, one need not worship the wedge—or the pom-pom-bearing, hat-clad putt-putt enthusiasts whom St. Andrews attracts—to love this city; its medieval streets and castle ruins transcend even golf. Though today it's only a shell, pilgrims in the Middle Ages journeyed to **St. Andrews Cathedral** to pray at the Saint's Shrine. Nearby, **St. Andrews Castle** maintains secret tunnels, bottle-shaped dungeons, and high stone walls to keep rebellious heretics out or in. (Cathedral and castle open daily Apr.-Sept. 9:30am-6:30pm; Oct.-Mar. 9:30am-4:30pm. Joint ticket £3.50.) Scotland's oldest (Britain's third oldest) university, **St. Andrews,** founded in the 15th century, lies just west of the castle, between North St and The Scores.

Fife Scottish **buses** (tel. (01334) 47 42 38) pull in from Edinburgh (bus X58; 2hr., every hr., £5.50, students £3.60) and Glasgow (bus X24 to Dunfermlane, then transfer to X58, X59, or X60; 2hr., 12 per day, £5.50). From Aberdeen or Inverness, take a CityLink bus to Dundee (every hr., £6.50) and transfer to Fife Scottish bus 95 (£2.15) to St. Andrew's. **Trains** (tel. (0345) 55 00 33) stop 5 mi. away at **Leuchars** (from Edinburgh 1hr., every hr., £7.90), where buses (X59, X60, and 95; £1) depart for St. Andrews. To get to the marvelous **tourist office,** 70 Market St, from the bus station, slice right onto City Rd and take the first left. (Tel. (01334) 47 20 21; fax 47 84 22. Open July-Aug. M-Sa 9:30am-8pm, Su 11am-5pm; Sept.-June M-Sa 9:30am-5pm, Su 11am-5pm.) Hop on the **internet** at the **Public Library,** Church Sq. (£1.75 per 30min. M and W-F 10am-7pm, Tu and Sa 10am-5pm.) The tourist office has **B&B** lists (many B&Bs line Murray Pl and Murray Park near the bus station), but your best bet is to

BRITAIN

make St. Andrews a daytrip. The only budget option is the central **Gannochy House,** North St. From the bus station, turn right on City Rd, right on St. Mary's Pl, left on College St, and right on North St. (Tel. (01334) 46 48 70. ₤10. Reception 9-10am and 2-6pm. Open June-Aug.) **Postal code:** KY16 9UL.

LOCH LOMOND AND THE TROSSACHS

LOCH LOMOND. With Britain's largest inland freshwater body as its base, the landscape of Loch Lomond is filled with lush bays, thickly wooded islands, and bare hills. Hikers on the northeastern edge of Loch Lomond are rewarded with stunning views, quiet splendor, and small beaches. The **West Highland Way** snakes along the entire eastern side of the Loch, stretching 95 mi. from Milngavie north to Fort William. **Balloch,** at the southern tip of Loch Lomond, is the major town in the area. Across the River Leven, the **Balloch Castle Country Park** provides 200 acres of gorgeous grounds, as well as a 19th-century castle housing a **Visitor's Centre.** Look for the pixies in **Fairy Glen.** (Park open daily dawn-dusk. Visitor's Centre open Easter-Oct. daily 10am-6pm. Free.) **Sweeney's Cruises** (tel. (01389) 75 23 76; 1hr., every hr., ₤4.50) boat tour depart from the tourist office side of the River Leven.

Trains arrive on Balloch Rd, opposite the tourist office, from Glasgow's Queen St Station (45min., 2 per hr., ₤3.80). Citylink **buses** (#926, 975, and 976; tel. (08705) 80 80 80) arrive from Glasgow (3-5 per day); First Midland (tel. (01324) 61 37 77) travels from Stirling (1½hr., 2-3 per day). **Buses** arrive a few minutes down Balloch Rd, across the bridge to the left of the **tourist office,** in Old Station Building. (Tel. (01389) 75 35 33. Open daily July-Aug. 9:30am-7:30pm; June 9:30am-6pm; Sept. 9:30am-7pm; Apr.-May and Oct. 10am-5pm.) **B&Bs** congregate on **Balloch Rd. SYHA Loch Lomond,** 2 mi. north of town, is one of Scotland's largest hostels. (Tel. (01389) 85 02 26. ₤11.75-12.75. Call ahead. Open early Mar. to Oct.) To reach the **SYHA Rowardennan,** the first hostel along the West Highland Way, take the Inverberg ferry (tel. (01301) 70 23 56) across the Loch to Rowardennan (May-Sept. 3 per day, ₤4). (Tel. (01360) 87 02 59. ₤9. Curfew 11:30pm. Open Mar.-Oct.) The **Tullichewan Caravan and Camping Site,** on Old Luss Rd, is up Balloch Rd from the tourist office. (Tel. (01389) 75 94 75. Tent and 2 people ₤6.50-9, with car ₤8-12. Reception 8:30am-10pm. Open year-round.)

TROSSACHS. The gentle mountains and lochs of the Trossachs form the northern boundary of central Scotland. A road for walkers and cyclists traces the Loch's shoreline; tourists drop like flies after a half mile, leaving the Loch's joys to more hardy travelers. The **Steamship Sir Walter Scott** steams between Loch Katrine's Trossachs Pier and Stronachlachar. (Tel. (0141) 955 01 28. Apr.-Oct. 2-4 per day, ₤4-5.) Only a few buses each day link to the area's two main towns, **Aberfoyle** and **Callander.** Citylink **bus** 974 runs through Edinburgh and Stirling to Fort William, stopping in Callander (1 per day). The Trossachs Trundler is a 1950s-style bus that creaks to Callander, Aberfoyle, and Trossachs Pier in time for the sailing of the *Sir Walter Scott* (July-Sept. Su-F 4 per day, ₤8). Bus 59 from Stirling connects with the Trundler in Callander. Call the **Stirling Council Public Transport Helpline** (tel. (01786) 44 27 07) for info. **Trossachs Cycle Hire,** on the pier, rents bikes. (Tel. (01877) 38 26 14. Open Apr.-Oct. daily 10am-5:30pm. ₤12 per day.)

THE INNER HEBRIDES

FORT WILLIAM AND BEN NEVIS. With a slew of beautiful lochs and valleys, **Fort William** makes an excellent base camp for mountain excursions to **Ben Nevis** (4406 ft.), the highest peak in Britain. To ascend the well-beaten trail from Fort William to the summit, go half a mile north on A82 and follow signs (5-6hr. round-trip). **Trains** arrive in Fort William from Glasgow's Queen St Station (2-4 per day, ₤8) and London's Euston Station (12hr., 3 per day, ₤95). Skye-Ways **buses** (tel. (01463) 71 01 19) run to Glasgow (3hr., 4 per day, ₤10.50); Scottish Citylink (tel. (08705) 50 50 50) goes to Inverness (2hr., 5-6 per day, ₤6.50) and Edinburgh (6hr., 1 per day). Buses and trains leave from the northern end of High St; nearby, the **tourist office** provides info on the West Highlands. (Tel. (01397) 70 37 81. Open May-Aug. M-Sa 9am-8:30pm, Su 9am-6pm; Sept. M-Sa 9am-7pm, Su 10am-6pm; Oct.-Apr. M-Sa 10am-5pm.) By far the best place to stay within striking distance of Ben Nevis is the comfy ⌘**Farr Cottage Accommodation and Activity Center** in Corpach. (Tel. (01397) 77 23 15; fax 77 22 47. £11. Kitchen. Laundry. **Internet**.) To get there, take the train two train stops north of Fort William take the bus from High St (10min., 3 per hr., £0.75). The **Fort William Backpackers Guesthouse**, on Alma Rd, is 5min. from the Fort William train station. (Tel. (01397) 70 07 11. £10. Curfew 2am.) The **Glen Nevis Caravan & Camping Park,** on Glen Nevis Rd, is ½ mi. before the SYHA hostel. (Tel. (01397) 70 21 91. Tent and 2 people £8.70. Showers included. Open mid-Mar. to Oct.)

ISLE OF SKYE. Often described as the shining jewel in the Hebridean crown, Skye radiates unparalleled splendor from the serrated peaks of the Cuillin Hills to the rugged northern tip of the Trotternish Peninsula. Touring Skye takes effort; pick up *Public Transport Guide to Skye and the Western Isles* (£1) at a tourist office. **Buses** on the island are infrequent; **biking** and **hiking** are better options.

The **Skye Bridge** links **Kyle of Lochalsh,** the last stop on the mainland before the Isle, with Kyleakin (Kyle-ACK-in), on Skye's southeastern tail fin. On the mainland side perches the made-for-postcard **Eilean Donan Castle,** which struck a pose for the movie *Highlander*. To get there, take the bus from Kyle of Lochalsh (dir: Inverness; £2.50). (Open daily Apr.-Oct. 10am-5:30pm. £3.75, students £2.75.) Skye-Ways **buses** (tel. (01599) 53 43 28) run daily to Kyle of Lochalsh from Fort William (2hr., 3 per day, £10); Inverness (2½hr., 3 per day, £9.20); and Glasgow (4½hr., 3 per day, £16.50). **Trains** (tel. (08457) 48 49 50) arrive from Inverness (2½hr., 2-4 per day). The **train station** (tel. (01599) 53 42 05) is near the pier and the **tourist office.** (Tel. (01599) 53 42 76. Open June to early Sept. M-Sa 9:15am-7pm, Su 10am-4pm; Apr.-May and mid-Sept. to Oct. M-Sa 9:15am-5:30pm.) **Cu'chulainnsis Backpackers Hostel,** in Kyle of Lochalsh, is newly renovated. (Tel. (01599) 53 44 92. £9. Sheets £0.50.)

When you're ready to skip the mainland and dive into Skye, traverse the 1½ mi. footpath or take the **shuttle bus** (2 per hr., £0.70) across the Skye Bridge, or take the **ferry** instead (tel. (01599) 53 44 74; M-Sa every 15min., return £1.50). Over the bridge, quiet **Kyleakin** harbor is resplendent at sunset. A slippery scramble leads to the small ruins of **Castle Moil;** cross the bridge behind the SYHA hostel, turn left, follow the road to the pier, and take the gravel path. Lodgings cluster alongside the park a few hundred yards from the pier; to the right is the comfy **Skye Backpackers.** (Tel. (01599) 53 45 10. £10. Laundry. Curfew 2am.) **Nick's Tour** (tel. (01599) 53 40 87) leaves Kyleakin in minibuses daily at 10:30am (8hr., £15).

West of Kyleakin, the smooth, conical Red Cuillin and the rough, craggy Black Cuillin Hills meet in **Sligachan,** from which paths wind their way up the mountains. If you plan to scale some peaks, stay at the **SYHA Glenbrittle** in Glenbrittle near the southwest coast, where expert mountaineers can give you advice on exploring the area. (Tel. (01478) 64 02 78. £8. Open mid-Mar. to Oct.) Campers should head to **Glenbrittle Campsite.** (Tel. (01478) 64 04 04. £3.50 per person. Open Apr.-Sept.)

In northern Skye is the island's capital, **Portree** (pop. 2500). Buses run from Portree to **Dunvegan Castle,** the seat of the clan MacLeod. The castle holds the **Fairy Flag,** more than 1300 years old and swathed in clan legend, although looking rather tattered of late. (Open daily late Mar. to Oct. 10am-5:30pm; Nov.-Mar. 11am-4pm. £5.20, students £4.60.) **Buses** stop at Somerled Sq. The busy **tourist office** is in the old jail on Bank St, above the harbor. (Tel. (01478) 61 21 37. Open July-Aug. M-Sa 9am-8pm, Su 10am-4pm; Sept.-June M-Sa 9am-5:30pm.) It's 10min. from the center of town along Viewfield Rd to the **Portree Backpackers Hostel,** 6 Woodpark, Dunvegan Rd. (Tel. (01478) 61 36 41. £8.50; doubles £18. Laundry.)

THE OUTER HEBRIDES

The magical Outer Hebridean archipelago is not just extraordinarily beautiful, but, for the most part, is astoundingly ancient. Much of its exposed rock has existed for about three billion years, more than half as long as the planet, and inhabitants of the island in the distant past have left behind a rich sediment of tombs, standing stones (including the remarkable stone circle at Callanish on Lewis), and Neolithic antiquities. The vehemently Calvinist islands of Lewis and Harris observe the Sabbath strictly: all shops and restaurants close, and public transportation stops on Sundays. Television and tourism are diluting some local customs, but the islands are large and remote enough to retain much of their beauty and charm.

☐ GETTING THERE AND GETTING AROUND. Four major **Caledonian MacBrayne ferries** (tel. (01475) 650100) serve the Outer Hebrides—from **Oban** to **Barra** and **South Uist**, from **Mallaig** to **South Uist**, from **Skye** to **Harris**, and from **Ullapool** to **Lewis**. Ferries and infrequent **buses** connect the islands, and **hitchers** and **cyclists** enjoy success except during frequent rain storms. Except in bilingual Stornoway and Benbecula, all road signs are now in Gaelic only. Tourist offices often carry translation keys, and *Let's Go* lists Gaelic equivalents after English place names where necessary. For up-to-date transport information, consult the *Skye and Western Isles Public Transport Travel Guide* (£1 at tourist offices).

LEWIS AND HARRIS. The island of Lewis (Leodhas) is famous for its atmosphere: pure light and drifting mists off the Atlantic Ocean shroud the untouched miles of moorland and small lochs in quiet luminescence. The unearthly setting is ideal for exploring the island's many archaeological sites, most notably the **Callanish Stones,** an extraordinary (and isolated) Bronze Age circle. Caledonian MacBrayne **ferries** from Ullapool on the mainland serve **Stornoway** (Steornobhaigh; pop. 8000), the largest town in northwestern Scotland (M-Sa 3 per day, £12.35, return £21.35). To get from the ferry terminal to the **tourist office,** 26 Cromwell St, turn right from the ferry terminal, then hang a left on Cromwell St. (Tel. (01851) 70 30 88. Open Mar.-Sept. 9am-6pm and 8-9pm; Oct.-Feb. 9am-5pm.) For a place to lay your head and wax your board, head to the new **bunkhouse,** at the intersection of Francis and Keith St, over the surf shop. (Tel. (01851) 70 58 62. £10.)

Although **Harris** (Na Hearadh) is technically part of the same island as Lewis, it might as well be on Pluto. Lewis is mainly flat and watery, while Harris, formed by volcanic gneiss, has the ruggedness more characteristic of Scotland. Behind the barricade of the treeless **Forest of Harris** (actually a mountain range), the island's steel-grey mountains, splotched with heather, descend on the west coast to brilliant crescents of yellow beaches bordered by indigo waters and *machair*—sea meadows of soft green grass and summertime flowers. **Ferries** serve **Tarbert** (An Tairbeart), the biggest town on Harris, from Uig on Skye (1-2 per day, £8.10, return £13.80). Ask at the **tourist office,** on Pier Rd, whether the new hostel has opened up yet. (Tel. (01859) 50 20 11. Open early Apr. to mid-Oct. M-Sa 9am-5pm and for late ferry arrivals.) Effie MacKinnon's huge rooms rest in **Waterstein House,** opposite the tourist office. (Tel. (01859) 50 23 58. £15 per person.)

BARRA. Little Barra, the southern outpost of the Outer Isles, is unspeakably beautiful, a composite of moor, *machair*, and beach. On sunny days, the island's colors are unforgettable; sand dunes crown waters flecked shades of light-dazzled blue, wreathed below by dimly visible red, brown, and green kelp. **Kisimul Castle,** bastion of the old Clan MacNeil, inhabits Castlebay Harbor (boat trips out M, W, and Sa 2-5pm; £3). West of Castlebay, near **Borve** (Borgh), is one squat **standing stone** allegedly erected in memory of a Viking galley captain who lost a bet with a Barra man; archaeologists who excavated the site did indeed find a skeleton and Nordic armor. Caledonian MacBrayne **ferries** (tel. (01878) 70 02 88) stop at **Castlebay** (Bagh A Chaisteil) on Barra on their way from Oban on the mainland (5hr., Tu, Th-F, and Su 1 per day, £17.80). You can almost all of Barra in a day; inquire at the **tourist office** about the **postbus,** or rent a bike from **Castlebay Cycle Hire** (tel. (01871) 81 02 84; £8-15) and follow A888, which makes a 14 mi. circle around the rather steep slopes of **Ben Havel.** The Castlebay **tourist office,** around the bend to the right from the pier, books B&Bs. (Tel. (01871) 81 03 36. Open roughly mid-Mar. to mid-Oct. M-Sa 9am-5pm, Su 11:30am-12:30pm, and for late ferry arrivals.)

ABERDEEN

The din of students partying, the hum of a vibrant arts community, and the swish of Britain's North Sea oil industry offset the perennial grayness of Aberdeen's skies. **Old Aberdeen** and **Aberdeen University** are a short bus ride (#1-4 or 15), or a long walk along King St, from the city center. The **King's College Visitor Centre**, just off High St, greets you at the other end with an exhibit on how students used to live. (Tel. (01224) 27 37 02. Open M-Sa 10am-5pm, Su noon-5pm. Free.) Peaceful **King's College Chapel** dates from the 16th century. (Open daily 9am-4:30pm. Tours July-Aug. Su 2-5pm.) The twin-spired **St. Machar's Cathedral,** with a heraldic ceiling and stained glass, was built in the 14th century. (Open daily 9am-5pm; Su services 11am and 6pm.) The **Lemon Tree Café and Theatre,** 5 West North St (tel. (01224) 64 22 30), near Queen St, presents folk, jazz, rock, drama, and dance.

Trains and **buses** arrive on Guild St. Scotrail (tel. (0345) 55 00 33) arrives from Glasgow (1½hr., 16 per day, £36); Inverness (2hr., 10 per day, £17.60); and Edinburgh (2½hr., 17 per day, £32). Scottish Citylink buses (tel. (08705) 50 50 50) roll in from Glasgow (every hr., £13.50) and Edinburgh (every hr., £13.50); and Bluebird buses (tel. (01224) 21 22 66) come from Inverness (every hr., £9.20). Turn right on Guild St, left on Market St, right on Union St, and left on Broad St to get to the **tourist office,** in St. Nicholas House on Broad St. (Tel. (01224) 63 27 27; fax 62 04 15. Open July-Aug. M-F 9am-7pm, Sa 9am-5pm, Su 10am-noon; Sept.-June M-Sa 9am-5pm.) Take bus 14 or 15 from Union St to Queen's Rd to reach the **SYHA King George VI Memorial Hostel,** 8 Queen's Rd. (Tel. (01224) 64 69 88. £10.25-12.75. Breakfast included. Kitchen. Laundry. Check-out 9:30am. Lock-out 9:30am-1:30pm. Curfew 2am.) Tesco **supermarket** is in the court in front of the St. Nicholas Centre on Union St. (Open M-W and Sa 7:30am-7pm, Th 7:30am-9pm, F 7:30am-8pm, Su 10am-5pm.)

INVERNESS AND LOCH NESS

The charms of Inverness, like the Loch Ness monster herself, are somewhat elusive, but you won't be disappointed. In town, disillusionment awaits those who remember Inverness as the home of Shakespeare's *Macbeth*. Nothing of the "Auld Castlehill" remains; the present reconstructed **castle** looks like it was made out of pink Legos this very morning (tours £3). The **Tourist Trail Day Rover bus** (July-Aug. 3 per day, £6, students £4) allows unlimited travel to most sights near Inverness. In 1746 the Jacobite cause died on **Culloden Battlefield,** east of Inverness; take **bus** 12 from the post office (£1.10). One and a half miles south of Culloden, the stone circles and chambered cairns (mounds of rough stones) of the **Cairns of Clava** recall civilizations of the Bronze Age. The **Cawdor Castle** has been the home of the Cawdors since the 15th century; don't miss the maze. (Open May to mid-Oct. daily 10am-5:30pm. £5.50, students £4.50.) And, of course, no trip to Inverness would be complete without taking in the deep and mysterious **Loch Ness,** which guards its secrets 5 mi. south of Inverness. In AD 565, St. Columba repelled a savage sea beast as it attacked a monk; whether a prehistoric leftover, giant seasnake, or cosmic wanderer, the monster has captivated the imagination of the world ever since. **Gordon's Tours** and other tour agencies are the most convenient ways to see the loch. (Tel. (01463) 73 12 02. £11.90, students £9.90.) Even if you don't see the real monster, vendors are all too happy to sell you a cute stuffed one.

Trains (tel. (08457) 48 49 50) run from Academy St, in Station Sq, to Aberdeen, (2¼hr., 7-10 per day, £17.60); Edinburgh (3½hr., 5-7 per day, £42.20); and Glasgow (4hr., 5-7 per day, £42.20). Scottish Citylink **buses** (tel. (08705) 50 50 50) run from Farraline Park, off Academy St, to Edinburgh (4hr., 8-10 per day, £12.70); and Glasgow (4-4½hr., 10-12 per day, £12). To reach the tourist office from the stations, turn left on Academy St, right on Union St, and left on Church St; the **tourist office,** Castle Wynd, is visible from the end. (Tel. (01463) 23 43 53. Open mid-May to June M-Sa 9am-6pm, Su 9:30am-5:30pm; July to mid-Sept. M-Sa 9am-8:30pm, Su 9:30am-6pm; mid- to late Sept. M-Sa 9am-6pm, Su 10am-5pm; Oct. to mid-May M-F 9am-5pm, Sa 10am-4pm.) Facing the tourist office, go left on Bridge St and right on Castle St, which leads to Culduthel Rd and the ◨**Inverness Student Hotel,** at #8 (tel. (01463) 23 65 56; £9-10; reception 6:30am-2:30am; kitchen; laundry; check-out 10:30am); and the **Bazpackers Backpackers Hotel,** farther down at #4 (tel. (01463) 71 76 63; dorms £8.50-9; doubles £24; kitchen; reception 7:30am-midnight; check-out 10:30am).

BULGARIA (БЪЛГАРИЯ)

US$1 = 1.84LV (LEVA, OR BGL)	1LV = US$0.54
CDN$1 = 1.24LV	1LV = CDN$0.81
UK£1 = 2.96LV	1LV = UK£0.34
IR£1 = 2.48LV	1LV = IR£0.40
AUS$1 = 1.20LV	1LV = AUS$0.84
NZ$1 = 0.98LV	1LV = NZ$1.02
SAR1 = 0.30LV	1LV = SAR3.28
DM1 = 1LV	1LV = DM1

PHONE CODES | **Country code:** 359. **International dialing prefix:** 00.

From the pine-clad slopes of the mountains in the southwest to the beaches of the Black Sea, Bulgaria is blessed with a lush countryside, rich in natural resources and ancient tradition. The history of the Bulgarian people, however, does not fit with their surroundings; the crumbling Greco-Thracian ruins and Soviet-style highrises attest to centuries of oppression and struggle. Once the most powerful state in the Balkans and the progenitor of the Cyrillic alphabet and Slavic Orthodoxy, Bulgaria spent 500 years under Ottoman Turk rule. These years yielded minarets, underground monasteries, and, finally, the National Revival of the 19th century, when Bulgarians established an independent church and championed use of the Bulgarian language. This was the time when much of the majestic, very European architecture now gracing its cities was built. Today, Bulgaria struggles with a small GDP and a lack of Western attention, problems only heightened by the recent Balkan wars. As a result, the country has gone unnoticed by most travelers, and its people—only slowly crawling out from under the rubble of Communism—are finding themselves too poor to package all they have to offer for Western consumption.

For more detailed coverage of Bulgaria, grab *Let's Go: Eastern Europe 2000*.

DISCOVER BULGARIA

Bulgaria is a great stopover between Western Europe and Greece or Turkey. Start in **Sofia** (p. 212), where more than 1500 years of Orthodox Churches and cobblestoned alleyways hide among the city's vast boulevards. **Plovdiv** (p. 217) shelters

Roman ruins and fabulous art museums and is only 30min. from the splendid **Bachkovo Monastery** (p. 217). Nestled in the highest mountains on the Balkan Peninsula, **Rila Monastery** (p. 216) is the masterpiece of Bulgarian religious art. Whether you're reveling with sun-scorched discoers or lounging on deserted beaches, no visit to Bulgaria is complete without a sojourn on the **Black Sea Coast** (p. 218), a summer wonderland. On your way to the coast from western Bulgaria, be sure to stop in **Veliko Turnovo** (p. 217), the most beautiful town in the country.

GETTING THERE AND GETTING AROUND

BY PLANE. Major international airports are located in **Sofia** and **Varna. Balkan Air** flies directly to Sofia from New York and other cities. **Balkan Air** domestic fares are fairly cheap (Sofia-Varna US$41, round-trip US$71).

BY TRAIN. The national rail company is **Rila.** Bulgarian trains run to Budapest, Romania, Yugoslavia, Greece, and Turkey. Service is comprehensive but slow, crowded, and old. Trains may be *ekspres* (express; експрес); *burz* (fast; бърз); or *putnicheski* (slow; пътнически). Avoid *putnicheski* like the plague—they stop at anything that looks inhabited, even if only by goats. Arrive early for a seat. Stations are poorly marked, and often only in Cyrillic; bring a map. Useful words include: *vlak* (train; влак); *avtobus* (bus; автобус); *gara* (station; гара); *peron* (platform; перон); *kolovoz* (track; коловоз); *bilet* (ticket; билет); *zaminavashti* (departure; заминаващи); *pristigashti* (arrival; пристигащи); *ne/pushachi* (non-/smoking; не/пушачи); *spalen vagon* (sleeping car; спален вагон); *purva klasa* (first-class; първа класа); and *vtora klasa* (second-class; втора класа).

BY BUS AND BY FERRY. Buses are more comfortable, quicker, and only slightly more expensive than trains, and save up to 3hr. from Sofia to the Black Sea Coast. Western Bulgaria is more navigable by bus. For long distances, **Group Travel** and **Etap** offer modern buses with air-conditioning, bathrooms, and VCRs at prices 50% higher than trains. Buy a seat from the agency office or pay when boarding. Some buses have set departure times; others leave when full. Grueling local buses stop everywhere. Private companies have great package deals on international travel. There are frequent **ferries** from Varna and Burgas to Istanbul and Odessa.

BY CAR, BY BIKE, AND BY THUMB. Road conditions in Bulgaria are passable, although not great. All drivers are required to carry international **insurance** as well as an **International Driving Permit.** Road signs, while mostly in Bulgarian (i.e., Cyrillic), are periodically in French. In residential areas, the speed limit is 60km per hr., on expressways 120km per hr. The cheapest **rental cars** average US$70-80 per day. Yellow **taxis** are everywhere in cities. Refuse to pay in dollars and insist on a metered ride *("sus apparata");* ask the distance and price per kilometer to do your own calculations. **Biking** is uncommon as it is nearly impossible to rent a bicycle. **Hitchhiking** is risky, but some claim it yields a refreshing taste of Bulgarian *gostelyubivnost* (hospitality) to those who are cautious, polite, and patient.

ESSENTIALS

DOCUMENTS AND FORMALITIES. Americans should **register** with the consular section upon arrival in Bulgaria. Citizens of the US and the EU may visit visa-free for up to 30 days. Citizens of other countries and anyone planning to stay more than 30 days must obtain a 90-day **visa** (single-entry US$53; multiple-entry US$123; 48-hour transit US$43; double transit US$63). Visas normally take about 10 days to process (5-day rush service US$68; immediate issuance US$88; not available for multiple-entry visas). Visas may be extended at a **Bureau for Foreigners** (located in every major city) before the date of expiration. The visa price includes a US$20 border tax; those who don't need visas are required to pay it upon entering the country.

Bulgarian Embassies at Home: Australia (consulate), 1/4 Carlotta Rd, Double Bay, Sydney, NSW 2028 (tel. (0612) 327 75 92; fax 327 80 67); **Canada,** 325 Stewart St,

Ottawa, ON K1N 6K5 (tel. (613) 789-3215; fax 789-3524); **South Africa,** 1071 Church St, Hatfield, Pretoria; P.O. Box 32569, Arcadia (tel. (012) 342 37 20); **UK,** 186-188 Queensgate, London SW7 5HL (tel. (020) 75 84 94 00; fax 75 84 49 48); **US,** 1621 22nd St NW, Washington, DC 20008 (tel. (202) 387-7969; fax 234-7973).

Foreign Embassies in Bulgaria: All foreign embassies are in **Sofia** (see p. 214).

TOURIST OFFICES. With all its economic woes, bolstering tourism is hardly a priority for Bulgaria. Tourist offices, where they exist, are unhelpful and rarely speak English. **Balkantourist,** the mighty state chain under communism, has been humbled by privatization. **ORBITA,** a student/budget travel chain, has little presence outside Sofia. Both agencies exchange money and book hotel and private rooms.

MONEY. The **lev** (lv; plural *leva*) is the standard monetary unit. In July 1999, Bulgaria **devalued** its currency, knocking off three zeroes. *Let's Go* lists some prices in US dollars because of inflation. Old bills are worthless, so check carefully when receiving change. Private banks and exchange bureaus are best for exchanging money, though the latter may only change US dollars. Private bureaus and major banks like **Bulbank** and **Biohim Bank** cash **AmEx traveler's checks;** banks also give **Visa cash advances. Credit cards** are rarely accepted. **Tipping** is not obligatory, but 10% doesn't hurt, especially in Sofia, where waitstaff may expect it. A 7-10% service charge will occasionally be added; check the bill (*smetka;* смегка) or the menu to see if it's listed. An absolute bare-bones day (staying in campgrounds and shopping at grocery stores) in Bulgaria will run you about US$10; a comfortable day (staying in hostels/hotels and eating out) won't cost more than US$20.

COMMUNICATION

Post: Mailing a **postcard/letter** from Bulgaria costs 0.50lv to Australia, Canada, Ireland, New Zealand, the UK, the US, or South Africa.

Telephone: Making international telephone calls from Bulgaria is expensive and challenging. To make a **collect call** (*za tyahna smetka;* за тяхна сметка), call 01 23 for a (non-English-speaking) international operator or ask the phone office or hotel clerk to order the call. Betkom or Bulfon **direct-dial phones** with digital displays (for English, press "i") require special **phone cards** sold at kiosks, restaurants, shops, and post offices; the 400-unit, 20lv cards can make international calls anywhere. In Sofia or Varna, try the AmEx office or the post office, where you pay at a kiosk after the call. Calls to the US average US$2 per min. **International direct dial** numbers include: **AT&T Direct,** 008 00 00 10; **BT Direct,** 008 00 99 44; **Canada Direct,** 008 00 13 59; **MCI,** 008 00 00 01; **Sprint,** 008 00 10 10. **Fire,** tel. 160. **Police,** tel. 166. **Ambulance,** tel. 150.

Internet: Email is fairly common in Bulgaria's mid- to large-sized cities, where connections are available in local internet clubs for 2000-3000lv per hr.

Language: Bulgarian is most similar to Russian, which is widely understood. English is increasingly spoken by young people and in touristed areas. German is understood in many big cities and throughout the tourist industry. Bulgarian transliteration is much the same as Russian except that "x" is h, "щ" is sht, and "ъ" is either a or u (pronounced like the "u" in bug). Keep in mind that Bulgarians shake their heads to indicate "yes" and nod to indicate "no." Street names are in the process of changing; you may need both old and new names. For the basics on Bulgarian and Cyrillic, see p. 949.

HEALTH AND SAFETY. Public **bathrooms** (Ж for women, M for men) are often holes in the ground; pack a small bar of soap and toilet paper, and expect to pay 0.05-0.20lv. While Sofia is as safe as most other European capitals, the city has a certain sense of chaos. Locals generally don't trust the police, and stories circulate of people being terrorized by the local mafia. Pedestrians do not have the right of way in Bulgaria, and some drivers choose to park on sidewalks. Despite its legality, acceptance of **homosexuality** is very slow in coming.

ACCOMMODATIONS AND CAMPING. Upon crossing the border, South Africans may receive a **statistical card** to document where they sleep. Ask hotels or private room bureaus to stamp your passport or a receipt-like paper that you can show upon re-crossing the border. Although they won't necessarily ask you for it, you may face a fine if you don't have it. If you are staying with friends, you'll have to register with the **Bulgarian Registration Office**. See the consular section of your embassy for details. **Private rooms** (частни квартири), good deals for solo travelers, can be arranged through Balkantourist for US$5-15; ask for a central location. Many often offer private accommodations in train and bus stations. Bulgarian **hotels** are classified on a star system and licensed by the Government Committee on Tourism; rooms in one-star hotels are almost identical to those in two- and three-star hotels, but have no private bathrooms. Most cost US$15-50 per night, although foreigners are always charged higher prices. The majority of Bulgarian **youth hostels** are in the countryside; many give ISIC discounts. In Sofia, make reservations through **Orbita**, Hristo Botev 48 (Христо Ботев; tel. (02) 80 01 02; fax 88 58 14). Outside major towns, most **campgrounds** provide spartan bungalows and tent space.

FOOD AND DRINK. Food from **kiosks** is cheap (0.60-2lv); **restaurants** average 6lv per meal. Kiosks sell *kebabcheta* (small sausage burgers; кебабчета), sandwiches, pizzas, and *banitsa sus sirene* (cheese-filled pastries; баница със сирене). Fruits and vegetables are sold in a *plod-zelenchuk* (fruit store; плод-зеленчук), *pazar* (market; пазар), or on the street. Try *shopska salata* (шопска салата), a mix of tomatoes, peppers, and cucumbers with feta cheese. Also tasty is *tarator* (таратор), a cold soup made with yogurt, cucumber, garlic, and sometimes walnuts. You'll see "пържени" (fried) used to describe many dishes. Try *kavarma* (каварма), meat with onions, spices, and egg; *skara* (grilled; скара) are cheaper. Vegetarian options with eggs (omelettes; омлети) and cheese are everywhere. Well-stirred *ayran* (yogurt with water and ice cubes; айран) and *boza* (similar to beer, but sweet and thicker; боза) are popular drinks. Melnik produces famous red wine, and the area around the old capitals in the northeast is known for excellent white wines. On the Black Sea Coast, Albenu is a good sparkling wine.

LOCAL FACTS

Time: Bulgaria is 2hr. ahead of Greenwich Mean Time (GMT; see p. 49).

Climate: Bulgaria's climate is typically Balkan: hot summers, cold winters, and plenty of precipitation. The best time to visit the Black Sea Coast is summer. For everywhere else, spring and fall weather is ideal.

Hours: Most **businesses** open at 8 or 9am and take a 1-hour lunch break sometime between 11am and 2pm. **Banks** are open 8:30am-4pm. Tourist bureaus and **shops** stay open until 6 or 8pm; in tourist areas and big cities, shops may close as late as 10pm.

Holidays: New Year's Day (Jan. 1); Orthodox Christmas (Jan. 7); 1878 Liberation Day (Mar. 3); Good Friday (Apr. 28); Orthodox Easter (Apr. 30-May 1); Labor Day (May 1); Cyrillic Alphabet Day, St. George's Day, and Bulgarian Army Day (May 24); Day of Union (Sept. 6); Independence Day (Sept. 22); and Catholic Christmas (Dec. 24-26).

SOFIA (СОФИЯ)

To find the "culture" in Sofia (pop. 1.2 million) you may have to sift through pairs of Nikes to locate the handmade lace at a bazaar, or dodge trams and cars on the way to the theater, but it's well worth the effort. Fifteen hundred years of churches and cobblestones are not quite dwarfed by Soviet-era concrete blocks, and 19th-century elegance is weathering the fast food invasion more or less gracefully.

▐▛ GETTING THERE AND GETTING AROUND

Flights: Airport Sofia (tel. 79 62 93; domestic info tel. 72 24 14; international info tel. 79 80 35). Turn left as you exit international arrivals and take bus 84 (250lv) to the center.

Trains: Tsentralna Gara (Central Train Station; Централна Гара), north of the center on Knyaginya Maria Luiza. Trams 1 and 7 go to pl. Sv. Nedelya; trams 9 and 12 down Hristo Botev; buses 85, 213, 305, and 313 to the station. The **ticket office** (tel. 843 42 80) is downstairs in front of the entry to NDK. Open M-F 7am-7pm, Sa 7am-2pm. To: **Burgas** (7 per day, 8500lv); **Plovdiv** (19 per day, 3500lv); **Thessaloniki** (23-45,000lv); **Bucharest** (42,000lv); **Athens** (53-75,000lv); **Budapest** (72-140,000lv); and **Istanbul** (35,000lv).

Sofia
ACCOMMODATIONS
A Hotel Baldjieva
B Hotel Niky
C Hotel Tsar Asen
D Hotel Orbita

Buses: Ovcha Kupel (Овча Купел), along Tsar Boris III bul. (Цар Борис III), accessible by tram 5 or 19 away from Vitosha. Buy tickets at the **Billetni Tsentur kiosks** (Ticket Center; Биллетни Център) or on the bus. To: **Athens** (2 per day, US$26); **Budapest** (2 per day, 80,000lv); and **Istanbul** (1 per day, 47,000lv, students 30,000lv). **Private buses** leave from the parking lot opposite the Central Train Station, and are cheap and fast: **Group Travel** (tel. 32 01 22) has a kiosk in the parking lot across from the bus parking lot. To: **Burgas** (2 per day, 12,500lv) and **Veliko Turnovo** (1 per day, 8000lv); **Matpu** (Матпу), ul. Damyan Gruev 23 (Дамян Груев; tel. 52 50 04), goes to **Athens** (1 per day, 74,000lv, students 60,000lv) and **Istanbul** (6 per week, 50,000lv).

Local Transportation: Trams, trolleybuses, and **buses** cost 250lv per ride. **Day-pass** 1000lv; **5-day pass** 4400lv. Buy tickets at kiosks with signs saying "билети" (tickets; *bileti*) or from the driver, then punch them in the machines between the bus windows to avoid a 10,000lv fine. Officially run 5am-1am, but rides are scarce after 9pm.

Taxis: Softaxi (tel. 12 84), **OK Taxi** (tel. 21 21), and **INEX** (tel. 919 19). From the airport, don't pay more than US$10 to the center. Fares are 320-380lv per km (and rising with gas prices), 450lv per km after 10pm—when it's really wise to take a cab.

▐ ORIENTATION AND PRACTICAL INFORMATION

The city's center, **pl. Sveta Nedelya** (пл. Света Неделя), is marked by the green roof of the Tsurkva Sv. Nedelya, the Sheraton Hotel, and Tsentralen Universalen Magazin (TSUM). **Bul. Knyaginya Maria Luiza** (Княгиня Мария Луиза) connects pl. Sveta Nedelya to the train station. Trams 1 and 7 run from the train station through pl. Sveta Nedelya and up **bul. Vitosha** (Витоша), a main shopping and nightlife thoroughfare. Bul. Vitosha in turn links pl. Sveta Nedelya to **pl. Bulgaria** and the huge, concrete **Natsionalen Dvorets Kultura** (NDK; National Palace of Culture; Национален Дворец Култура). The monthly *Sofia City Guide* (free, sometimes at the Sheraton) is a useful English publication. Good **maps** of the city are sold in most hotels and tourist agencies, as well as at kiosks and exchange bureaus.

TOURIST, FINANCIAL, AND LOCAL SERVICES

Tourist Office: Balkan Tour, Stamboliyski bul. 27 (tel. 88 06 55; fax 88 07 95). From pl. Sv. Nedelya, walk 3 blocks up Stamboliyski. Open daily 8am-7pm.

Budget Travel: ORBITA Travel, Hristo Botev 48 (tel. 986 10 63; fax 988 58 14). From pl. Sv. Nedelya, walk up Stamboliyski and go left on Hristo Botev. Books rooms at Hotel Orbita (US$8 per night). Open in summer M-F 8:30am-7pm; off-season M-F 9am-5:30pm.

Embassies: Australians, Canadians, and **New Zealanders** should contact the British embassy. **South Africans** should contact the embassy in Athens (see p. 460). **UK,** bul. (*not* ul.) Vasil Levski 38 (tel. 980 12 20 and 980 12 21). Open M-Th 8:30am-12:30pm and 1:30-5pm, F 8:30am-1pm. Consular and visa section open M-Th 9am-noon and 2-4pm, F 9am-noon. **US,** ul. Suborna 1a (Съборна; tel. 980 52 41). Consular section at Kapitan Andreev 1 (Капитан Андреев; tel. 963 00 89). Americans should register with the consular section upon arrival in Bulgaria. Open M-F 8:30am-5pm.

Currency Exchange: Vitosha, Stamboliyski, and **Graf Ignatiev** house exchange bureaus. **Commercial Bank Biohim,** Sv. Nedelya 19 (tel. 986 54 45, ext. 213 or 304), in the yellow building next to the Sheraton, cashes traveler's checks for a 1% commission and gives MC cash advances for a 6% commission. Open M-F 8:30am-3:30pm.

American Express: Aksakov 5 (Аксаков; tel. 986 58 37; fax 980 88 89). Mail held for members. Open M-F 9am-6pm, Sa 9am-2:30pm.

Luggage Storage: Downstairs at the Central Train Station. Look for "гардероб" (*garderob*) signs. 500lv per piece. Open daily 5:30am-midnight.

EMERGENCY AND COMMUNICATIONS

Emergency: Ambulance, tel. 150. **Police,** tel. 166.

Pharmacy: Purva Chastna Apteka (Първа Частна Аптека), Tsar Asen 42. Open 24hr.

Medical Assistance: State-owned hospitals offer foreigners emergency aid free of charge. **Pirogov Emergency Hospital,** Gen. Totleben bul. 21 (Ген. Тотлебен; tel. 515 31), opposite Hotel Rodina. Take trolleybus 5 or 19 from the center. Open 24hr.

Internet Access: ICN (tel. 91 66 22 13), on the lower floor of NDK. 5000lv per hr. Open daily 9am-7pm. **Internet Center,** ul. Graf Ignatiev 6. 1800lv per hr. Open daily 9am-10pm.

Telephones: Ul. Stefan Karadzha 6 (Стефан Караджа), near the post office. Use 50lv coins for local calls. Bulgarian phone cards also sold here. Open 24hr.

Post Office: Gen. Gurko 6 (Гурко). *Poste Restante* for 200lv. Address mail to be held: Bob HOPE, *Poste Restante*, Gen. Gurko 6, Sofia **1000,** Bulgaria. Open M-F 8am-8pm.

PHONE CODE	City code: 02. From outside Bulgaria, dial int'l dialing prefix (see inside back cover) + 359 + 2 + local number.

ACCOMMODATIONS AND FOOD

Hotels are rarely worth the exorbitant price—**private rooms** are often the best option. Camping is another inexpensive choice; **Camping Vrana** (tel. 78 12 13) is 10km from the center on E-80, and **Cherniya Kos** (tel. 57 11 29) is 11km away on E-79. Check with Balkan Tour (see **Tourist Office,** above) for both options.

Hotel Niky, Neofit Rilski 16 (tel. 51 19 15; fax 951 60 91), off Vitosha. Satellite TV, billiard room, and garden restaurant. Singles US$22; doubles US$40. Check-out noon.

Hotel Tsar Asen (Цар Асен), Tsar Asen 68 (tel. 54 78 01). Walk toward the NDK on Tsar Asen, cross Patr. Evtimy, and continue 40m. Ring the doorbell at the gate. White walls and wood floors contain soft beds and thermostats for each room. Cable TV and private shower. Singles US$28; doubles US$34.

Hotel Orbita, James Baucher bul. 76 (Джеймс Баучер; tel. 639 39), on the hill. Take tram 9 south past the NDK to Anton Ivanov, three stops after the tunnel (30min.). A fading behemoth, even bigger than Stalin's ego. Singles US$25; doubles US$30. Orbita Travel arranges student rooms for US$8 per person.

Hotel Darling (Дарлинг), Yabulkova Gradina 14 (tel. 67 19 86), in **Dragalevtsi.** Fom the main square, take a left on Yabulkova. Follow it past the playground and turn left onto Angel Bukoreshtiliev; the hotel is in the huge white house. Doubles with baths, satellite TV, and terraces US$30-40.

From fast food to Bulgarian specialties, cheap meals are easy to find. Meals at nice restaurants run 10,000lv, but vendors will fill you up for 2000lv. **House** (Kushtata; Къщата), Verila 4 (Верила), off Vitosha near the NDK, offers a wide range of "dishes with character." (Entrees 3700-15,000lv; salads 1300-6600lv. Open daily noon-midnight.) Hip **Eddy's Tex-Mex Diner,** Vitosha 4, does nostalgic buffalo wings (4900lv) and fajitas (6980lv). (Tel. 981 85 58. Entrees 4500-9000lv. Live band nightly 9:30pm. Open daily 11:30am-12:30am.) At the corner of Rakovski and Moskovska, up the street from the Opera House, **Luciano,** ul. Moskovska 29 (Московска), has desserts so lovely you may almost feel inclined not to eat them (2000-4000lv). (Open daily 10:30am-11pm. Visa.) **Supermarkets** (open 24hr.) line **Vitosha.**

■ SIGHTS

PL. ALEXANDER NEVSKY. The gold-domed **Cathedral of St. Alexander Nevsky** (Sv. Aleksandr Nevsky; Св. Александр Невски), was erected from 1904 to 1912 in memory of the 200,000 Russians who died in the 1877-1878 Russo-Turkish War. In a separate entrance left of the main church, the **crypt** houses a spectacular array of painted icons and religious artifacts, the richest collection of its kind in Bulgaria. *(On Pl. Alexander Nevsky. Take trolleybus 1 or 2 to the corner of Shipka and bul. Vasil Levski; facing the Grand Hotel Sofia, turn right on Shipka, and the cathedral is on the right. Open daily 7:30am-7pm. Crypt open daily 10:30am-6:30pm. 3000lv, students free.)* To the right of the cathedral is the more modest 6th-century **St. Sofia** (Sv. Sofia; Св. София), used as a mosque in the 19th century. After a series of earthquakes repeatedly destroyed the minarets, the Ottoman rulers gave it up as their house of prayer. As of summer 1999, much of the church, including the 5th-century floor mosaic, was still under renovation. *(South wing open daily 7:30am-6pm.)* At the **market** in front of the cathedral, antiques, Soviet paraphernalia, and handmade crafts are vended; diagonally to the other side of the square, Bulgarian *babushki* offer handmade lace and embroidery.

AROUND PL. SVETA NEDELYA. The focal point of Sofia is the **Cathedral of St. Nedelya** (Katedralen Hram Sv. Nedelya; Катедрален Храм Св. Неделя), a reconstruction of a 14th-century original destroyed by a bomb in an attempt on Tsar Boris III's life in 1925; the tsar escaped, but the cupola buried 190 generals and politicians. *(Open daily 7am-6:30pm.)* In the courtyard of the Sheraton Hotel, next to the church, the 4th-century **St. George's Rotunda** (Sv. Georgi; Св. Георги), one of Sofia's most venerable churches, is accompanied by a former Roman bath. *(Open daily 8am-7pm.)* In the underpass between pl. Sv. Nedelya and TSUM, the tiny, 14th-century **Church of St. Petya of Samardzhiyska** (Tsurkva Hram Sv. Petya Samardzhiyska; Църква Храм Св. Петя Самарджийска) contains fascinating layers of frescoes on the upper walls and ceiling. *(Open M-Sa 9:30am-6:30pm, Su 9:30am-2:30pm. 5000lv, students 2500lv.)* Walk up bul. Maria Luiza from pl. Sveta Nedelya to Exarh Yosif to reach the **Central Synagogue** (Tsentralen Sinagog; Централен Синагог), where a museum upstairs outlines the history of Jews in Bulgaria. *(Exarh Yosif 16. Open Tu-Sa 10am-4:30pm.)* Across the street sits the 16th-century **Banya Bashi Mosque** (Баня Баши). *(Open daily 7:30am-6:45pm. Dress modestly; women must cover their heads. Remove shoes at the door.)*

ALONG BUL. TSAR OSVOBODITEL. Bul. Tsar Osvoboditel, the first paved street in Sofia, is weighted down on either end by the **House of Parliament** and the **Royal Palace.** Down Tsar Osvoboditel from Sv. Nedelya, the 1913 Russian **Church of St. Nicholas** (Sv. Nikolai; Св. Николай), named for the miracle-maker, has five traditional Russian Orthodox-style onion domes. *(Take trolleybus 9 to Moskovska, backtrack down Rakovski, and turn right on bul. Tsar Osvoboditel. Open daily 7am-6pm.)*

NATIONAL PALACE OF CULTURE. Opened in 1981 to celebrate Bulgaria's 13th centennial, the monstrous NDK (Natsionalen Dvorets Kultura; Национален Дворец Култура) is a barracks of culture, with restaurants, theaters, and movie halls that show subtitled American movies. Buy tickets (2000lv) from the ticket office (биллетни център) through the doors, down the outside ramp, and to the left of the main entrance. *(In Yuzhen Park. From pl. Sveta Nedelya, walk down bul. Vitosha to bul. Patriarch Evtimy and enter the park. The palace is at its far end.)*

MUSEUMS. The **National Museum of History** (Natsionalen Istoricheski Muzey; Национален Исторически Музей), bul. Vitosha 2, off pl. Sv. Nedelya, chronicles Bulgarian "history" from 200,000 BC. *(Open May-Sept. daily 10am-6:30pm; Oct.-Apr. M-F 8:30am-4:30pm. 5000lv, students 2500lv.)* The Royal Palace houses the **National Museum of Ethnography** (Natsionalen Etnograficheski Muzey; Национален Етнографически) and the **National Art Gallery** (Natsionalna Hudozhestvena Galeriya; Национална Художествена Галерийа), the best art museum in Bulgaria. *(On pl. Knyaz Batenberg. Take trolleybus 9 to Moskovska. Ethnography museum open daily 10am-6pm. 3000lv, students 1500lv. Art museum open Tu-Su 10am-6pm. 3000lv, students free; Su free.)*

🎭 ENTERTAINMENT

Seats at the opera can be as cheap as 2000lv. **Rakovski** is Bulgaria's theater hub, with six theaters along 1km. On Osvoboditel and Rakovski are the columns of the **National Opera House,** Kniaz Pondukov 30. The box office is to the right of the entrance. (Tel. 87 13 66. Open Oct.-July Tu-F 8:30am-7:30pm, Sa-M 9am-5pm.)

While nightlife in Sofia does not consume the entire city, the scene is getting wilder every year. Smartly dressed Sofians fill up the outdoor bars along **bul. Vitosha** and the cafés around the **NDK.** For the younger set, nightlife centers around the University of Sofia at the intersection of **Vasil Levski** and **Tsar Osvoboditel.** Try the expansive **Mr. Punch,** 20 Stefan Karadzha, near the post office. Pick up a swipe card at the door, use it at the bars downstairs, then pay when you leave. (Beer 850lv; mixed drinks 3500lv. Open daily noon-3pm and 6pm-late.) Disco-believers flock to **Yalta** (Ялта), on the corner of Tsar Osvoboditel and Vasil Levski. (Cover 1000lv. Open daily 11pm-4am.) From Vitosha, head toward the NDK, turn left on Alabin (Алабин), veer right on Graf Ignatiev, and turn left at pl. Slaveykov (with McDonald's) into the courtyard to reach lively **Biraria Luciano** (Бирария Лучано), Slaveykov 9 (Славейков), which has beer from seven different countries. (Open daily noon-11pm.) **Spartakus** (Спартакус), in the underpass past the pl. Narodno Subranie, leading toward Vasil Levski, keeps its gay and straight clientele happy with thumping techno. It's exclusive, though—unless you know a member, you may be out of luck. (Open daily 11pm-late.)

🏛 EXCURSION FROM SOFIA: RILA MONASTERY

Holy Ivan of Rila built the 10th-century Rila Monastery (Rilski Manastir; Рилски Манастир), the largest and most famous of Bulgaria's monasteries, as a refuge from the lascivious outer world. The monastery sheltered the arts of icon painting and manuscript copying during the Byzantine and Ottoman occupations, and remained an oasis of Bulgarian culture for five centuries. Today's monastery was built between 1834 and 1837; only a brick tower remains from the 14th-century structure. Examine the 1200 brilliantly colored **frescoes** (on the central chapel), or check out the **museum.** (Open daily 8:30am-4:30pm. 5000lv, students 3000lv. Sporadic tours in English 15,000lv.) The quickest way to get to Rila Town is to take a **bus** from Novotel Europa in **Sofia** to Blagoevgrad (2hr., 8-10 per day, 1200lv), then from Blagoevgrad to Rila Town (45min., every hr., 1000lv), and then catch the bus up to the monastery (45min., 4 per day, 1000lv). To get from the monastery to the **Hotel Rilets** (Рилец), follow the signs across the river and then turn right (20min.). (Tel. (07054) 21 06. US$15 per person.) Inquire at room 170 in the monastery about staying in a heated **monastery cell;** conditions are spartan. (Tel. (07054) 22 08. 27,500lv. Reception 9am-noon and 2-4pm; 6-9pm in room 74. Curfew midnight.)

PLOVDIV (ПЛОВДИВ)

While Plovdiv is smaller than Sofia, it is widely hailed as the cultural capital of Bulgaria. In the convoluted Old Town, National Revival houses protrude over the cobblestones below, windows stare into alleys at impossible angles, and churches and mosques hide in secluded corners.

■ ■ ■ PRACTICAL INFO, ACCOMMODATIONS, AND FOOD. Trains arrive from Sofia (2½hr., 7 per day, 3540lv) en route to Burgas; **buses** arrive from Sofia at Yug (Юг) station on the north side of Hristo Botev (Христо Ботев; 1hr., every hr., 5000lv). **Puldin Tours** (Пълдин), bul. Bulgaria 106 (България), finds rooms (US$13-16), arranges tours, and changes money. From the train station, ride trolley 2 or 102 (200lv) nine stops to bul. Bulgaria and backtrack a block. (Tel. (032) 55 38 48. Open M-F 9am-5:30pm; until 9pm during fairs.) Check your **email** at **Game Zone,** on Knyaz Aleksandr opposite McDonald's (1600lv per hr.). Located in a National Revival building listed among Plovdiv's monuments, **Hostel Touristicheski Dom** (Туристически Дом), P.R. Slaveykov 5 (П.Р. Славейков), is in the Old Town (Stari Grad; Стари Град). From Knyaz Aleksandr (Княз Александр), take Patriarch Evtimii (Патриарх Евтимий) into town, passing under Tsar Boris, and hang a left on Slaveykov. (Tel. (032) 63 32 11. 22,000lv. Curfew 11pm.) From pl. Tsentralen, walk across Tsar Boris to reach **Hotel Feniks** (Феникс), Kapitan Raicho 79, 3rd fl. (Капитан Райчо), which offers shared bathrooms and unintentionally antique furniture. (Tel. (032) 22 47 29. Singles US$15; doubles US$20. Laundry.) **Kambanata** (Камбаната), Suborna 2B, serves traditional vegetarian dishes. (2000-8000lv. Open daily 10:30am-midnight.) **The Grill** (Грил), bul. Tsar Boris III Obedinitel 8, serves up delicious Syrian dishes. (2000-5000lv. Open daily 8am-2am.) **Postal code:** 4000.

■ ■ SIGHTS AND ENTERTAINMENT. Most of Plovdiv's historical and cultural treasures are concentrated in the three hills (the **Trimontium**) of the Old Town. Take a right off Knyaz Aleksandr (Княз Александр) to Stanislav Dospevski (Станислав Доспевски), turn right at the end of the street, and take the stairs to the left to reach the 2nd-century Roman marble **amphitheater** (Antichen Teatr; Античен Театр). Return to Knyaz Aleksandr and follow it to the end at pl. Dzhumaya (Джумая), home to the **Dzhumaya Mosque** (Dzhumaya Dzhamiya; Джамия) and the ancient **Philipoplis Stadium.** From pl. Dzhumaya, turn right up Suborna (Съборна) to reach the **State Art Gallery** (Durzhavna Hudozhestvena Galeria; Държавна Художествена Галерия) to admire the work of 20th-century Bulgarian artists. (Open Tu-Su 9-11am and 1-5pm. 2000lv, students 300lv.) At the end of Suborna (Съборна), the **Museum of Ethnography** (Etnografski Muzey; Етнографски Музей) displays ancient Bulgarian artifacts. (Open Tu-Su 9am-noon and 2-5pm. 3000lv, students 200lv.) In the evening, head to the fountainside café in **Tsentralni Park** (Централни Парк), near pl. Tsentralen (пл. Централен).

■ EXCURSION FROM PLOVDIV: BACHKOVO MONASTERY. About 28km south of Plovdiv lies the 11th-century Bachkovo Monastery (Bachkovski Manastir; Бачковски Манастир), the second-largest monastery in Bulgaria. Its main treasure is the miracle-working **icon of the Virgin Mary and Child** (ikona Sveta Bogoroditsa; икона Света Богородица), kept in the **Holy Trinity Church.** (Open daily 7am-dark.) To get to Bachkovo, take a **train** from Plovdiv to Asenovgrad (25min., every hr., 800lv) and then catch a **bus** to the monastery (10min., 300lv).

VELIKO TURNOVO (ВЕЛИКО ТЪРНОВО)

Veliko Turnovo has been watching over Bulgaria for 5000 years—its residents led the national uprising against Byzantine rule in 1185, and its fortress walls and battle towers have stood since it was the capital of Bulgaria's Second Kingdom. The remains of the **Tsarevets** (Царевец), a fortress that once housed a cathedral and royal palace, stretch across a hilltop overlooking the city. (Open daily in summer 8am-7pm; off-season 9am-5pm. 4000lv, students 2000lv.) At the top is the **Church of the Ascension** (Tsurkva Vuzneseniegospodne; Църква Възнесениегосподне),

BULGARIA

restored in 1981 on the 13th centennial of the Bulgarian state. Near the fortress off ul. Ivan Vazov (Иван Вазов), the **National Revival Museum** (Muzey na Vuzrazhdaneto; Музей на Възраждането) documents Bulgaria's 19th-century cultural and religious resurgence. (Open daily 8am-noon and 1-6pm. 4000lv, students 2000lv.)

Trains go to Burgas (5 per day, 6200lv) and Sofia (8 per day, 7760lv). Most city **buses** from the station go to the town center (200lv), but you should ask *("za tsen-tur?")* to be sure. There is no tourist office, but the bookstore **Kingi** (Кинги), Rakovski 15, has good **maps** (2200lv). (Open daily 10am-6:30pm.) **Hotel Trapezitsa (HI)** (Хотел Трапезица), Stefan Stambolov 79, is an excellent hostel with clean rooms. From the center, walk down Nevvisimost toward the post office and follow the street right. (Tel. (062) 220 61. 14,000lv; nonmembers 18,000lv.) **Hotel Comfort** (Комфорт), Panayot Tipografov 5 (Панайот Типографов), has tidy rooms with baths. From Stambolov, walk left on Rakovski (Раковски), turn left on the small square, and look for the street sign. (Tel. (062) 287 28. US$15, students US$11.) **Postal code:** 5000.

BLACK SEA COAST

The Black Sea, the most popular destination in Bulgaria for foreign and native vacationers alike, bundles centuries-old, thumbnail-sized fishing villages with clear, secluded bays, energetic seaside towns, and resorts designed to suck hard currency. In between, you'll find warm, sandy beaches in the south and rockier, white-cliffed shores to the north. You're bound to run into more English speakers than in any other part of Bulgaria, along with higher—though still reasonable—prices.

BURGAS. Burgas (BOOR-gahs; Бургас) is a transport hub for the Southern Black Sea Coast. The Burgas bus and train stations are near the port at **Garov pl.** (Гаров). **Trains** go to Sofia via Plovdiv (7hr., 13 per day, 9200lv); **buses** serve the Black Sea Coast, while cheaper **minibuses** run to the coastal resorts from the opposite end of the bus station from the train station. Up **Aleksandrovska** (Александровска), the main street, and to the right, pedestrian **Aleko Bogoridi** (Алеко Богориди) leads to a beach. If you stay the night here, secure a **private room** at **Primorets Tourist,** on pl. Garov, a block to the right (with your back to the station) of Aleksandrovska, under the "Частни Квартири" sign. (Tel. (056) 84 27 27. US$5-6. Open M-F 9am-6:30pm.) Or to get to **Hotel Mirage** (Мираж), Lermontov 18; from the station, go up Aleksandrovska, take a right on Bogoridi, pass the Hotel Bulgaria, and take the first left onto Lermontov. (Tel. (056) 92 10 19. Doubles US$25-28; triples US$33.)

SOZOPOL. Sozopol (soh-ZO-pohl; Созопол), settled in 610 BC, is Bulgaria's oldest Black Sea town. Once the resort of choice for Bulgaria's artistic community, it still caters to a more creative set and is also quieter and cheaper than its neighbors. Sick of the **beach,** you say? Take a **boat cruise** (15,000lv per boat) from the seaport and have a peek at the two nearby islands, **St. Peter** and **St. Ivan** (the best time to go is around sunset). **Buses** arrive from Burgas (45min., every 2hr., 1200lv). Turn left on **Apolonia** (Аполония) to reach **Stari Grad** (Old Town). To get to **Novi Grad** (New Town), go right through the park and turn left on Republikanska (Републиканска). The tourist bureau **Lotos,** at the bus station, arranges **private rooms.** (Tel./fax (5514) 24 29. US$7 per person. Open daily 8am-8pm.) For a tasty meal, walk to **Vyaturna Melnitsa** (Вятърна Мелница), Morski Skali 27a (Морски Скали), on a street along the tip of the peninsula. (Entrees 3-12,000lv. Open daily 10am-midnight.)

CROATIA (HRVATSKA)

US$1 = 7.16KN (KUNA)	1KN = US$0.14
CDN$1 = 4.81KN	1KN = CDN$0.21
UK£1 = 11.51KN	1KN = UK£0.09
IR£1 = 9.65KN	1KN = IR£0.10
AUS$1 = 4.66KN	1KN = AUS$0.21
NZ$1 = 3.80KN	1KN = NZ$0.26
SAR1 = 1.18KN	1KN = SAR0.84
DM1 = 3.88KN	1KN = DM0.26

PHONE CODES | **Country code:** 385. **International dialing prefix:** 00.

Croatia is a land of unearthly beauty. Traced with thick forests, wispy plains, underground streams, and the translucent sea, it has served for centuries as a summer playground for residents of countries less scenically endowed. Positioned where the Mediterranean, the Alps, and the Pannonian plain converge, it has also been situated on dangerous divides—between the Frankish and Byzantine empires in the 9th century, the Catholic and Orthodox churches since the 11th century, Christian Europe and Islamic Turkey from the 15th to the 19th centuries, and its own fractious ethnic groups in the past decade. Dancing in the nightclubs of Dubrovnik or lounging on the beaches in Pula, it's easy to forget the tensions that have played out here in the past. Independent for the first time in 800 years, Croatians are finally free to enjoy the extraordinary landscape in peace.

For sparkling coverage of Croatia, refer to *Let's Go: Eastern Europe 2000*.

CROATIA

DISCOVER CROATIA

Croatia is definitely Europe's best-kept secret. With Mediterranean beaches rivaling those of the Greek Islands, mind-boggling Roman ruins, and surprisingly hip cities, Croatia is worth the extra effort it takes to get there. And despite prevalent misconceptions, the country is extremely safe. For those who can't make it down the coast, **Zagreb** (p. 222) boasts an alluring mix of Hapsburg splendor, Mediterranean relaxation, and the hippest café scene in the Balkans. Croatia's most impressive Roman ruins stand in **Pula** (p. 223), the 2000-year-old heart of Istria on the Northern Coast. The true highlight of Croatia, however, is the fabled **Dalmatian Coast** (p. 224), where pristine beaches, karst-covered coast, and azure waters mingle in one of the Mediterranean's most dazzling natural spectacles. **Split** (p. 224), on the central coast, shelters the impressive ruins of Roman Emperor Diocletian's summer palace and is the gateway to the Dalmatian archipelago, the largest in the Mediterranean. At the country's southern tip, the walled medieval center of **Dubrovnik** (p. 225) was called "paradise on earth" by George Bernard Shaw; after admiring its stunning seascapes, exploring the sandy beaches of nearby **Lopud** (p. 225), and reveling in its funky nightlife, you'll definitely agree.

GETTING THERE AND GETTING AROUND

BY PLANE. Zagreb is Croatia's main entry point. **Croatia Airlines** flies there from many cities, including Frankfurt, London, and Paris, and often continues on to Dubrovnik and Split. **Rijeka, Zadar,** and **Pula** also have international airports.

BY TRAIN, BY BUS, AND BY CAR. Trains connect Zagreb to Budapest, Ljubljana, and Vienna, and continue on to other destinations throughout Croatia. *Odlazak* means departures, *dolazak* arrivals. **Eurail** is not valid in Croatia. For domestic travel, **buses,** faster than and comparably priced with their railed counterparts, are by far the best option. Tickets are cheaper on board. You can **rent a car** in larger cities, but downtown parking can be expensive, roads in the country are in atrocious condition, and those traveling through the Krajina region and other conflict areas should be wary of off-road landmines. Seatbelts are required of all passengers. **Speed limit** in residential areas is 60km per hr., on expressways 130km per hr. Contact the **Croatian Automobile Association** (tel. (01) 464 08 00) for further info.

BY FERRY. If you're along the coast, **Jadrolinija ferries** are slower but more comfortable than buses and trains. Boats sail the Rijeka-Split-Dubrovnik route, stopping at islands along the way. Ferries also float from **Split** (see p. 224) to Ancona, Italy (see p. 616), and from Dubrovnik (see p. 225) to Bari, Italy (see p. 623).

ESSENTIALS

DOCUMENTS AND FORMALITIES. Citizens of Australia, Ireland, New Zealand, the UK, and the US do not need visas to enter Croatia. Visas are required of South African citizens; send your passport, a visa application, two passport-sized photos, a document proving your intent of tourism (i.e. invitation, voucher, or receipt of business arrangements) and a check or money order (single-entry US$29, double-entry US$37, multiple-entry US$59) to the nearest embassy or consulate. All visitors must **register** with the police within two days of arrival. Hotels, campsites, and accommodations agencies should do this for you, but those staying with friends or in private rooms must do so themselves to avoid fines or expulsion. Police may check foreigners' passports anywhere. Citizens of any country staying more than 90 days should fill out an "extension of stay" form at a local police station.

Croatian Embassies at Home: Australia, 14 Jindalee Crescent, O'Malley, Canberra, ACT 2606 (tel. (06) 286 69 88; fax 286 35 44). **Canada,** 130 Albert St, #1700, Ottawa, ON K1 P5 G4 (tel. (613) 230-7351; fax 230-7388). **New Zealand** (consulate), 131 Lincoln Rd, Henderson, P.O. Box 83200, Edmonton, Auckland (tel. (09) 836 55 81; fax 836 54

81). **South Africa,** 1160 Church St, Colbyn, Pretoria; P.O. Box 11335, Hatfield 0028 (tel. (012) 342 12 06; fax 342 18 19). **UK,** 21 Conway St, London W1P 5HL (tel. (020) 73 87 20 22; fax 73 87 09 36); **US,** 2343 Massachusetts Ave NW, Washington, DC 20008 (tel. (202) 588-5899; fax 588-8936).

Foreign Embassies in Croatia: All foreign embassies are in **Zagreb** (see p. 222).

TOURIST OFFICES. Most major cities have a branch of the **state-run tourist board** (*turistička zajednica*)*;* employees speak some English and German and are great for maps and info. **Private accommodations** are handled by private tourist agencies (*turistička/putnička agencija*)*;* the largest is **Atlas.** Agencies also exchange money and arrange excursions, including infamous fish picnics on the coast.

MONEY. Croatia's monetary unit, the **kuna** (kn)—divided into 100 **lipa**—is theoretically convertible, but proves near-impossible to exchange anywhere but Hungary and Slovenia. Most tourist offices, banks, hotels, and transportation stations offer **currency exchange** and cash traveler's checks, although neither South African rand nor Irish pounds are exchangeable in Croatia. **ATMs** (*bankomat*) are widespread on the mainland and the islands. Most banks give V/MC **cash advances,** and most hotels and restaurants accept credit cards. A basic day in Croatia runs about US$25 per day. **Tipping** is not expected, but you may round up to the nearest whole kuna; in some cases, the establishment will do it for you—check your change.

COMMUNICATION

Post: Mailing a **postcard/letter** from Croatia costs 3kn to Australia, Canada, Ireland, New Zealand, the UK, the US, or South Africa. Mail from the US arrives in 7 days or less. *Avionski* and *zrakoplovom* both mean **"air mail"** in Croatian.

Telephone: Post offices usually have **public phones;** pay after you talk. Most phones on the street require **phonecards** (*telekarta*), sold at newsstands and post offices. 50 "impulses" cost 23kn (1 impulse equals 3min. domestically, 36 seconds internationally; 50% off 10pm-7am and Su). Croatia is revamping **phone numbers,** so some numbers in this book may be outdated by summer 2000; luckily, when you call a changed number, a voice states the new number in English. **Police,** tel. 92. **Fire,** tel. 93. **Ambulance,** tel. 94. **International direct dial** numbers include: **AT&T,** 0800 22 01 11; **MCI WorldPhone Direct,** 0800 22 01 12; **Canada Direct,** 0800 00 22 01 01; **BT Direct,** 0800 22 00 44. Technically, this operator assistance is free, but some phones demand a *telekarta* card, and calls to the US are expensive (about 20kn per min.).

Internet: The internet is available in even the smallest towns.

Language: Croatian. In Zagreb and most tourist offices, some people know **English,** but the most common language on the coast is **Italian.** Most of the tourist industry speaks **German,** as do many renters of private rooms. Street designations on maps often differ from those on signs by "-va" or "-a" because of grammatical declensions.

HEALTH AND SAFETY. Although Croatia is no longer at war, travel to the Slavonia and Krajina regions remains dangerous due to **unexploded mines.** Travel to the coast and islands is considered safe. **Crime** is rare. Croatians are friendly toward foreigners and sometimes a little too friendly to female travelers; going out in public with a companion will help to ward off unwanted displays of machismo. Croatians are just beginning to accept **homosexuality;** be discreet.

ACCOMMODATIONS AND CAMPING. Two words: **private rooms.** Apart from the country's six rather shabby **youth hostels** (in Zagreb, Pula, Zadar, Sibernik, Dubrovnik, and Punatu) and **camping** (bring your own tent), they are the only affordable option. Look for *sobe* signs, especially near transport stations in small towns. Agencies generally charge 30-50% more if you stay fewer than three nights. All accommodations are subject to a 5-10kn **tourist tax.** If you opt for a hotel, call at least a day ahead in summer. Wherever you stay, hot water is ephemeral at best.

FOOD AND DRINK. *Puricas mlincima* (turkey with pasta) is the regional dish near Zagreb. The spicy *Slavonian kulen,* available everywhere, is considered one of the world's best sausages by the panel of fat German men who decide such things. Along the coast, try *lignje* (squid) or *Dalmatinski pršut* (Dalmatian smoked ham). The oysters from the Ston Bay have received a number of awards at international competitions. Vegetarians will appreciate the heavy Italian influence, especially in coastal cuisine. *Grešak varivo* (green bean stew), *tikvice va le šo* (steamed zucchini in olive oil), and *grah salata* (beans and onion salad) are meatless favorites. Mix red wine with tap water to get *bevanda*, and white wine with carbonated water to get *gemišt*. Karlovačko and Ožujsko are popular beers.

LOCAL FACTS

Time: Croatia is 1hr. ahead of Greenwich Mean Time (GMT; see p. 49).

Climate: Mild and continental around Zagreb; Mediterranean along the coast.

Hours: Banks and **shops** generally open M-F 8am to 7 or 8pm, Sa 8am-noon. Most businesses take a several-hour lunch break around noon.

Holidays: New Year's Day (Jan. 1); Epiphany (Jan. 6); Catholic Easter (Apr. 23-24); Labor Day (May 1); Statehood Day (May 30); Croatian National Uprising Day (June 22); National Thanksgiving Day (Aug. 5); Feast of the Assumption (Aug. 15); All Saints' Day (Nov. 1); and Catholic Christmas (Dec. 25-26).

Festivals: Wild **carnival celebrations**, including weekly masked balls (*maškare*), are held from mid-January to Ash Wednesday (the end of February at the latest) on Korčula. The **Festival of Sword Dances** (Festival Viteških Igara) takes place each July in Korčula, during which each town's sword dance—part of the island's unique folk tradition—are performed throughout Korčcula. During the **Dubrovnik Summer Festival** (July10- Aug. 15), the city transforms into a cultural mecca; the country's most prominent artists in theater, ballet, opera, classical music, and jazz all perform.

ZAGREB

Zagreb shocks at first, with leftover Soviet architecture and scars from ancient wars as well as recent war with Serbia. But a stroll through its blooming gardens and Austro-Hungarian architecture, combined with a few days lounging with locals at outdoor cafés, reveals Zagreb to be a rare Balkan gem.

🔢 📠 **PRACTICAL INFO, ACCOMMODATIONS, AND FOOD.** The Glavni Kolodvor **train station,** Trg kralja Tomislava 12 (domestic info tel. (01) 98 30; international info tel. 457 32 38), serves Ljubljana (2½hr., 5 per day, 60kn); Vienna (6½hr., 2 per day, 327kn); Budapest (7hr., 4 per day, 194kn); and Venice (8hr., 1 per day, 243kn). **Buses** (tel. (060) 31 33 33) head from Držićeva 66 to Ljubljana (2hr., 4 per day, 65kn); Vienna (8hr., M-F 1 per day, 180kn); and Sarajevo (9hr., 3 per day, 240kn). Exit on Držićeva, walk left toward the bridge, turn left behind it on Branimirova, and walk 10min. to reach the train station. With your back to the train station, cross the street, and walk 10min. along the left side of the park on Praška to reach the main square, **Trg bana Josipa Jelačića.** The **tourist office,** Trg J. Jelačića 11, has free maps and walking tour brochures. (Tel. (01) 481 40 54. Open M-F 8:30am-8pm, Sa 10am-6pm, Su 10am-2pm.) All foreigners staying in private accommodations must **register** with the **Department of Foreign Visitors,** Petrinjska 30, Rm 101, within two days of arrival; use Form 14. (Tel. (01) 456 31 11. Open M-F 8am-2pm.) Get 24-hour **internet** access at **Aquariusnet,** ul. k. Držislava 4 (16kn per 30min.).

Rooms in Zagreb are expensive. **Omladinski Turistićki Centar (HI),** Petrinjska 77, has a perfect location; with your back to the train station, walk right on Branimirova, and Petrinjska will be on your left. (Tel. (01) 484 12 61; fax 484 12 69. Dorms 70kn, nonmembers 75kn; singles 152-205kn; doubles 205-270kn.) Newly furnished **Hotel Ilica,** Ilica 102, has a friendly staff and modern bathrooms. From the train station, take tram 6 (dir: Črnomerec) to the fourth stop on Ilica. (Tel. (01) 377 75 22. Singles 299kn; doubles 399kn; 3-person apartments 639kn. Breakfast included.) 🍴**Boban,** Gajova 9, offers budget Italian food and has a café upstairs. (Restaurant open daily 10am-midnight; café 7am-midnight.) **Postal code:** 10000.

📷 🎭 **SIGHTS AND ENTERTAINMENT.** Start your exploration of Zagreb by riding up the funicular (*uspinjača*; 2kn), which connects Donji Grad and Cornji Grad from Tomićeva. From Trg b. Jelačića, walk up Ilica and Tomićeva is on your right. The **Strossmayerovo šetalište** on top affords a gorgeous view of the city. Ul. Ćirilometodska veers off Strossmayerovo and leads to Markov trg. The colorful tiles of Gothic **St. Mark's Church** (Crkva sv. Marka) depict the coats of arms of Croatia, Dalmatia, Slavonia, and Zagreb; the interior contains works by Croatia's most famous sculptor, Ivan Meštrovič. Follow ul. Kamenita to **Stone Gate** (Kamenita Vrata), the only original gate left from the city wall. Walk down Radićeva to **Blood Bridge** (Krvavi Most) where warring clerics and craftsmen of **Kaptol** and **Gradec** hills clashed before their union in 1850. The **Dolac market** takes place daily on Tkalšićeva. Kaptol hill is dominated by the **Cathedral of the Assumption of the Virgin Mary,** whose neo-Gothic bell towers are visible from around the city. (Open M-Sa 10am-5pm, Su 1-5pm. Free.) Zagreb's museums eagerly await visitors after several years of war-induced hiatus: the **Mimara Museum,** Rooseveltov trg 4, has a vast and varied collection, from ancient Egyptian artifacts to Rembrandt. (Open Tu-Sa 10am-5pm, Su 10am-2pm. 20kn, students 15kn.) The free *Zagreb: Events and Performances,* available at the tourist office, lists museums, galleries, plays, festivals, concerts, and sporting events. Relax at the trendy **Čvenk Caffe Bar,** Radićeva 24. (Tel. (01) 42 48 51. Open M-Sa 8am-11pm, Su 4-11pm.)

NORTHERN COAST

As you head from Zagreb toward the coast, you'll approach the islands of the **Gulf of Kvarner,** blessed by long summers and gentle coastal breezes. Rab is one of the least touristed of the bunch. Farther north along the coast lies **Croatian Istria,** home to Pula, where the Mediterranean laps at the foot of the Alps. Today, the region seems almost more Italian than Croatian in language, tradition, and culture. Perhaps this has always been the case: colorful ancient fishing ports, countless craggy coves, and the deep blue-green hues of the sea led a Roman chronicler almost 2000 years ago to remark, "In Istria, Roman patricians feel like gods."

PULA

If you only get a chance to visit one city in Istria, it should be Pula—not only for its fantastic beaches, but also for its winding medieval streets, handsome Hapsburg avenues, and breathtaking first-century Roman **amphitheater** (the fourth largest in the world). From the bus station, take a left on Istarska to get there. (Open daily 7:30am-9pm. 14kn, students 7kn.) Following Istarska in the opposite direction from the station leads to the **Arch of the Sergians** (Slavoluk obitelji Sergi), which dates from 29 BC; go through the gates and down bustling **ul. Sergijevaca** to the **Forum,** which holds the **Temple of Augustus** (Augustov hram), built between 2 BC and AD 14. Buy a bus ticket from any kiosk (8kn) and take bus 1 to the Stója campground or bus 2 toward the hostel to reach Pula's **beaches. Trains** (tel. (052) 54 11 33) roll into the station at Kolodvorska 5 from Zagreb (7hr., 4 per day, 192kn) and Ljubljana (7½hr., 1 per day, 123kn). From the station, take a right, follow Kolodvorska to the amphitheater, and then walk up Istarska, which becomes Giardini, to reach the Stari Grad (on your right). **Buses** (tel. (052) 21 90 74) run from the station, between Istarska and Carrarina, to Trieste, Italy (3¾hr., 5 per day, 90kn) and Zagreb (5-6hr., 13 per day, 100kn). The TIC **tourist office** is at Istarska 11. (Tel. (052) 21 91 97; fax 21 18 55. Open July-Aug. daily 8am-1pm and 5-8pm; Sept.-June M-F 8am-1pm.) Travel agencies help find **private rooms;** try **Arenaturist,** Giardini 4. (Tel. (052) 21 86 96; fax 21 22 77.) To get to the **Omladinski Hostel (HI),** Zaljev Valsaline 4, walk right from the bus station on Istarska, take bus 2 (dir: Veruda) from the small park on Giardini to the last stop, and follow the signs. (Tel. (052) 21 00 03; fax 21 23 94. 67.50-87.60kn. Breakfast included. Reception 9am-3pm.) **Postal code:** 521 00.

RAB

An extraordinarily beautiful town whose narrow streets and whitewashed stone houses seem to rise out of the sea, Rab just might become one of your favorite places on earth. A stroll along Gornja ul. runs from the remains of **St. John's Church** (Crkva sv. Jvana), an outstanding Roman basilica, to **St. Justine's Church** (Crkva sv. Justine), which houses a museum of Christian art. (Open M-Sa 9-11am and 8-10pm,

Su 7:30-10pm. 7kn.) At sunset, climb to the top of the 13th-century **St. Mary's Bell Tower** for a truly stupendous view. (Open daily 10am-1pm and 7:30-10pm. 5kn.) The 12th-century **Virgin Mary Cathedral** (Katedrala Djevice Marije) and nearby 14th-century **St. Anthony's Monastery** (Samostan sv. Antuna) lie farther down Gornja ul. Rab's greatest assets are its **beaches**, scattered all over the island; ask at the tourist office for transport info. **Buses** (tel. (051) 72 41 89) arrive from Zagreb (6hr., June-Sept. two per day, 108kn). The **tourist office** is on the other side of the bus station. (Tel. (051) 77 11 11. Open M-Sa 8am-10pm, Su 8am-noon and 6-8pm.) **Katurbo,** Palit 491, between the bus station and the center, arranges **private rooms.** (Tel./fax (051) 72 44 95. May-Oct. 43-65kn; 30% more for fewer than 3 nights; tourist tax 4.50-7.60kn. Open daily 8am-1pm and 3-9pm.) Walk along the bay to reach **Camping Padova,** 1km east of the bus station. (Tel. (051) 72 43 55; fax 72 45 39. 22kn per person, 20kn per tent; add 7kn fee.) A **supermarket** is in the basement of Merkur, Palit 71, across from the tourist office. (Open M-Sa 6:30am-9pm, Su 6:30-11am.) **Postal code:** 51280.

DALMATIAN COAST

Stretching from Rijeka harbor to Dubrovnik in the south, Croatia's coast is a stunning seascape of hospitable locals and unfathomable beauty. With more than 1100 islands (only 66 of which are inhabited), Dalmatia boasts not only the largest archipelago but also the cleanest and clearest waters in the Mediterranean, bronze beaches, and sun-bleached Roman ruins.

SPLIT

Split is a city of extraordinary culture and history. The **Stari Grad**, wedged between a high mountain range and palm-lined waterfront, sprawls around a luxurious **palace** where Roman Emperor Diocletian used to summer. The **cellars** of the city are located near the entrance to the Palace, under a flag just past the line of taxis on the waterfront; turn either direction to wander around this labyrinth, with its archaeological and modern art displays. (Open M-F 10am-1pm and 6-8pm, Sa 10am-1pm. 6kn.) Straight through the cellars and up the stairs is the open-air **peristyle**, a colonnaded square. The **cathedral** on the right side of the peristyle was originally the mausoleum of Diocletian, an emperor known for his violent persecution of Christians. (Open daily 7am-noon and 4-7pm.) Walk from the center along Branimirova obala and then Šetalište Ivana Meštrovica to the closest **beach** (15min.).

   Ferries (tel. (021) 35 53 99) chug from Obala kneza Domagoja 66 to Ancona, Italy (10hr., June-Sept. 5 per week, 234kn), and Dubrovnik (10hr., 72-86kn). The **train** and **bus stations** lie across from the ferry terminal on Obala kneza Domagoja. **Trains** (tel. (021) 34 74 18) go from Obala kneza Domagoja 10 to Zagreb (8hr., 3 per day, 85kn) and Ljubljana (12hr., Tu, Th, and Sa, 230kn). **Buses** (tel. (021) 34 50 47) go from next door to Dubrovnik (4½hr., 13 per day, 77kn); Zagreb (7hr., 30 per day, 81-113kn); Sarajevo (7hr., 8 per day, 140kn); and Trieste (10hr., 2 per day, 150kn). From the train or bus station, follow Obala kneza Domagoja to the waterside mouthful Obala hrvatskog narodnog preporoda, which runs roughly east-west. Daluma **tourist office,** Obala kneza Domagoja 1, sells maps and tickets, and arranges **private rooms.** (Tel. (021) 34 26 99. Singles 60-100kn; doubles 100-150kn. Open M-Sa 8am-8pm, Su 8am-12:30pm.) To get from the stations to **Prenoćište Slavija,** Buvinova 2, follow Obala hrvatskog narodnog preporoda, turn right on Trg Braće Radića, go right on Mihovilova širina, and go up the stairs in the left-hand corner. (Tel./fax (021) 59 15 58. Singles 180-220kn; doubles 210-260kn; triples 250-300kn; quads 280-360kn. Breakfast included.) There is a **supermarket** at Svačićeva 4. (Open daily 7am-10pm.) **Postal code:** 21000.

KORČULA

The central Dalmatian island of Korčula (KOR-chula), stretching parallel to the nearby mainland, is an island of exceptional grace, history, and culture. Its sacral monuments and churches date from the time of the Apostles, and its exquisite natural beauty is aromatically tousled by indigenous sage, rosemary, lavendar, mint, and marjoram. Korčula can be reached by **bus,** which board a short ferry to the mainland and head to: Dubrovnik (3½hr., 1 per day, 40kn); Sarajevo (8hr., 2 per week, 145kn); and Zagreb (11-13hr., 1 per day, 150kn). **Ferries** run to Dubrovnik (3hr., 1 per day, 54kn). To get to the **tourist office,** walk along the edge of the peninsula to Hotel Korčula; the office is next door. (Tel. (020) 71 57 01; fax 71 58 66. Open M-Sa 8am-3pm.) **Private rooms** are the only budget accommodations available; **Marko Polo,** Biline 5, will arrange one for you. (Tel. (020) 71 54 00; fax 71 58 00; email marko-polo-tours@du.tel.hr. Singles 76-136kn; doubles 100-180kn; triples 140-232kn. Tourist tax 5.50-7kn. Open daily 8am-10pm.) **Postal code:** 20260.

DUBROVNIK

George Bernard Shaw said that "those who seek Paradise on earth should come to Dubrovnik." He wasn't far off the mark—if you make it to Dubrovnik, you might never leave. The city has a chic character that's more Mediterranean than Eastern European; the local dialect blends Croatian with Italian and Latin. Nearly scarless despite recent wars, Dubrovnik captivates visitors with azure waters and copper sunsets atop 14th-century **city walls** (*gradske zidine*). The awesome walls (enter from just inside the Pile Gate on the left) stretch up to 25m high and 2km around. (Open daily 9am-7:30pm. 10kn.) The Renaissance **Franciscan Monastery** (Franjevački samostan), Placa 2, is next to the wall entrance. (Open daily 9am-2pm. 5kn, students 3kn.) Farther down Placa, Europe's second-oldest **Sephardic synagogue,** Žudioska 5, serves the city's 47 Jews. (Open Tu and F 10am-noon.) At the end of the Placa stands **St. Blaise's Church** (Crkva sv. Vlaha), consecrated to the patron saint of Dubrovnik. The **Dominican Monastery** (Dominikanski samostan), Dominikanska 4, between the city walls and the Old Port, houses monks and a religious **museum.** (Open M-Sa 9am-6pm. Museum 5kn.) The **cathedral** (riznica) dominates Držićeva Poljana. (Open daily 8am-noon and 3-8pm. 5kn.) Four thousand Bosnian Muslims pray at the tiny **Bosnian Mosque,** Miha Pracata 3, the eighth right off Placa from the Pile Gate. Just around the corner, the **Serbian Orthodox Church,** Od Puča 8, houses a **Museum of Icons** (Muzej Ikona; open M-Sa 9am-1pm; 10kn). In summer, the **Dubrovnik Summer Festival** (Dubrovački Ijetni Festival; tel. (02) 42 88 64; July 10-Aug. 15) turns the city into a cultural mecca for theater, ballet, opera, classical music, and jazz lovers. To get to one of the most beautiful **beaches** in Croatia, **Plaza Šunj,** on the island of **Lopud,** hop on a ferry from Dubrovnik to the Elafiti Islands (50min., 1-2 per day, round-trip 25kn) and walk to the other side of Lopud from the village. (Turn onto the wide path at the "Konoba Barbara" sign.)

 As tempting as it may be to stroll in the hills above **Dubrovnik** or to wander down unpaved paths on **Lopud** island, both may still be laced with **landmines;** stick to the paved paths and beach.

Jadrolinija **ferries** (tel. (020) 41 80 00) leave from opposite Obala S. Radića 40 for Korčula (3hr., 2-10 per week, 54kn); Split (8hr., 2-11 per week, 72kn); and Bari, Italy (9hr., 2 per week, 234kn). **Buses** (tel. (020) 42 30 88) go to Split (4½hr., 14 per day, 65kn); Sarajevo (6hr., 1 per day, 150kn); Zagreb (11hr., 7 per day, 135-163kn); and Trieste (15hr., 1 per day, 225kn). Facing the bus station, walk around the building, turn left on ul. Ante Starčević, and follow it until uphill to reach the Stari Grad (20min.). Or, to reach the ferry terminal, head left (with your back to the bus station) and then bear right. To get to the **tourist office,** C. Zuzorić 1/2, walk to the end of Placa, turn right at St. Blaise's Church and the coffee shop Gradska Kavana, and take the first right. (Tel. (020) 42 63 03. Open M-Sa 8am-4pm.) Women at the ferry and bus stations hawk **private rooms** (around 70kn per person—haggle), but the ◙**HI youth hostel** at b. J. Jelačića 15/17 is one of the best in Croatia. From the bus station, walk up ul. Ante Starčević, turn right after 10min. at the lights, turn right on b. J. Jelačića, and look for the hidden HI sign on your left right before #17. (Tel. (020) 42 32 41. 73-87kn. Breakfast included. Check-out 10am. Curfew 2am. Open May-Oct.) Call ahead to the cozy **Begović Boarding House,** Primorska 17, for a ride from the station. (Tel. (02) 42 85 63. 70-85kn.) Pick up provisions at **Mediator supermarket,** Od puča 4. (Open M-Sa 6:30am-8:30pm, Su 7-10am.) **Postal code:** 20000.

CZECH REPUBLIC
(ČESKÁ REPUBLIKA)

US$1 = 34.47Kč (KORUNY)	10Kč = US$0.29
CDN$1 = 23.15Kč	10Kč = CDN$0.43
UK£1 = 55.38Kč	10Kč = UK£0.18
IR£1 = 46.43Kč	10Kč = IR£0.22
AUS$1 = 22.45Kč	10Kč = AUS$0.45
NZ$1 = 18.31Kč	10Kč = NZ$0.55
SAR1 = 5.69Kč	10Kč = SAR1.75
DM1 = 18.68Kč	10Kč = DM0.53

PHONE CODES | **Country code: 420. International dialing prefix: 00.**

Culturally and politically, it has been a decade of rapid change for the Czech people. In November of 1989, following the demise of Communist governments in Hungary and Poland and the fall of the Berlin Wall, Czechs peacefully threw off the Communists and chose dissident playwright Václav Havel to lead them westward. Havel attempted to preserve the Czech-Slovak union, but on New Year's Day, 1993, after more than 75 years of relatively calm coexistence, the two nations split bloodlessly. Czechs continue to admire their playwright-president, and for the most part are embracing dizzying westernization, though the notion of self-determination is relatively new to them. From the Holy Roman Empire through the Nazis and Soviets, foreigners have driven Czech internal affairs; even the 1968 Prague Spring was frozen by the iron rumble of Soviet tanks. The Czechs, unlike many of their neighbors, have rarely fought back as countries have marched through their borders; as a result, their towns and cities remain among the best-preserved in Europe. Today, they face a different kind of invasion, as tourists sweep in to savor the magnificent capital, charming locals, and the world's best beer.

Check out the Czech Republic in *Let's Go: Eastern Europe 2000*.

DISCOVER THE CZECH REPUBLIC

Prague (p. 229), of course, is the centerpiece of the Czech Republic. Spend at least a day wandering through the medieval alleys of Staré Město and the cobblestoned hills of Malá Strana to admire the fabulous Baroque and Art Nouveau architecture, and head to Prague Castle to see the magnificent stained-glass windows in St. Vitus' Cathedral (and maybe catch a glimpse of President Václav Havel riding his tricycle). For the most authentic Prague experience, spend an evening exploring the bars and beers of the Old Town, staying out just long enough to catch sunrise from the eerily empty Charles Bridge (p. 229). An interesting (if spooky) daytrip awaits in nearby **Kutná Hora** (p. 242), where femurs and crania hang from the ceilings and chandeliers. In Western Bohemia, international hipsters flock to **Karlovy Vary** (p. 243) every summer for its film festival and its Becherovka, a local herb liqueur with "curative powers" rivaled only by those of the many local hot springs. In Southern Bohemia, **Český Krumlov** (p. 244) is everybody's favorite town. This UNESCO-protected village charms visitors with its 13th-century castle, a medieval summer festival, and the most rocking nightlife this side of the Vltava.

GETTING THERE AND GETTING AROUND

BY PLANE. Air France, British Airways, ČSA, Delta, KLM, Lufthansa, and **Swissair** are among the major carriers with flights into Prague.

BY TRAIN. The national rail company, **ČSD**, publishes the monster *Jízdní řád* (train schedule; 74Kč) prefaced by a two-page English explanation. The fastest trains are *EuroCity* and *InterCity* (*expresní;* marked in blue on schedules), which require a supplement that can as much as double the original price of the ticket. *Rychlík* trains, also known as *zrychlený vlak*, are fast domestic trains, marked in red on schedules. Avoid slow *osobní* trains, marked in white. *Odjezd* (departures) are printed in train stations on yellow posters, *příjezd* (arrivals) on white. Seat reservations (*místenka;* 10Kč) are recommended on almost all express and international trains and for all first-class seating; snag them at the counter labeled with a boxed "R." **Eastrail** is valid in the Czech Republic, but **Eurail** is valid only with a special supplement called the **Prague Excursion Pass.** Other **railpasses** include **European East Pass, Central Europe Pass,** and the **Czech Republic/Slovakia Explorer Pass.** For more info on railpasses, see p. 60.

BY BUS AND BY CAR. **Buses** are the preferred means of domestic travel, but are inefficient for crossing borders. **ČSAD** runs national and international bus lines. From Prague, buses run a few times per week to Munich, Milan, and other hubs; buses leave Brno for many destinations in Austria. All drivers in the Czech Republic must carry an International Driving Permit. **Speed limits** in residential areas are 50km per hr., on expressways 130km per hr. In an **emergency,** dial 154 or contact **Ústřední Automotoklub CSFR (UAMK),** Na Rybnicku 16, 120 76 Prague 2 (tel. (2) 24 91 18 43; open M-F 7:45am-4:45pm). For help planning your trip, contact **Autoturist,** at the same address (tel. (2) 20 33 55; open M-F 7:30am-4pm).

BY BIKE AND BY THUMB. **Biking** is common in Southern Bohemia; roads and bike trails are in good condition and motorists yield bikers the right of way. You can rent bikes from most hotels and hostels and through major tourist offices. **Hitchhikers** report that hitching still remains popular in the Czech Republic, especially during morning commuting hours (6-8am).

ESSENTIALS

DOCUMENTS AND FORMALITIES. Americans may visit the Czech Republic visa-free for up to 30 days, Irish and New Zealand citizens for up to 90 days, and Canadian and UK citizens for up to 180 days. Australians and South Africans must obtain 30-day tourist visas. Visas are available at an embassy or consulate or (for an extra US$50 fee) at one of three border crossings: Rozvadov (from Nuremberg via Waidhaus, Germany), Dolní Dvořiště (from Linz via Rainbach, Austria), and Hatě (from Vienna via Hollabrunn, Austria). Single-entry visas procured in advance run US$28 plus a US$17 processing fee for Australians; South Africans need only pay the processing fee. Two-way transit visas are also US$28, plus a US$25 fee. Ninety-day multiple-entry visas cost US$39 (180-day US$70), plus a US$28 processing fee. Apply for visa extensions up to six months ahead of time.

Czech Embassies at Home: Australia, 38 Culgoa Circuit, O'Malley, Canberra, ACT 2606 (tel. (612) 290 13 86; fax 290 00 06); **Canada,** 541 Sussex Dr, Ottawa, ON K1N 6Z6 (tel. (613) 562-3875; fax 562-3878); **Ireland,** 57 Northumberland Rd, Ballsbridge, Dublin 4 (tel. (3531) 668 11 35; fax 668 16 60); **New Zealand** (honorary consul), 48 Hair St, Wainuiomata, Wellington (tel./fax (644) 564 60 01); **South Africa,** 936 Pretorius St, Arcadia, Pretoria; P.O. Box 3326, Pretoria 0001 (tel. (012) 342 34 77; fax 43 20 33); **UK,** 26 Kensington Palace Gardens, London W8 4QY (tel. (020) 72 43 11 15; fax 77 27 96 54); **US,** 3900 Spring of Freedom St NW, Washington, DC 20008 (tel. (202) 274-9100; fax 966-8540; www.czech.cz/washington).

Foreign Embassies in Czech Republic: All foreign embassies are in **Prague** (see p. 232).

TOURIST OFFICES. CKM, junior affiliate of the communist dinosaur Čedok, is helpful for the budget and student traveler; it serves as a clearinghouse for youth hostel beds and issues ISICs and HI cards. **Municipal tourist offices** in major cities provide printed matter on sights and cultural events, as well as lists of hostels and hotels. If you're lucky, they might even book you a room. German is most widely spoken, but English is also common in touristed regions.

MONEY. The basic unit of Czech currency is the **koruna** (crown), plural *koruny* (Kč); Czech *koruny* are not valid in Slovakia. A bare-bones day in the Czech Republic (sleeping in campgrounds, shopping at grocery stores) will run US$10; a more extravagant day (hostels/hotels, eating in restaurants) costs no more than US$25. **ATMs** ("Bankomats") are everywhere and offer the best rates available. Traveler's checks can be exchanged in every town, thanks to **Komerční banka** and **Česká Spořitelna.** Visa and MC are accepted only at expensive places. To **tip,** round up the cost of your meal; if the bill comes to 322Kč, tell the waiter "330Kč." Don't just leave a few *koruny* on the table as it is considered offensive.

COMMUNICATION

Post: Mailing a **postcard/letter** to Australia, Canada, Ireland, New Zealand, the UK, the US, or South Africa costs 8Kč. The postal system is usually reliable and efficient; letters reach North America in under 10 days. For **airmail,** stress that you want it to go on a plane *(letecky).* Go to the customs office to send packages over 2kg abroad.

Telephone: Seek out the blue **cardphones** (150Kč per 50 units) rather than playing Sisyphus to a pay phone's giant boulder. **Local calls** cost 2Kč regardless of length. Calls run 31Kč per min. to the **UK;** 63Kč per min. to **Australia, Canada,** and the **US;** and 94Kč per min. to **New Zealand. International operator,** tel. 013 15. **International direct dial** numbers include: **AT&T,** 0042 004 401; **Sprint,** 0042 087 187; **MCI WorldPhone Direct,** 0042 000 112; **Canada Direct,** 0042 000 151; **BT Direct,** 0042 004 401. **Fire,** tel. 150. **Ambulance,** tel. 155. **Police,** tel. 158.

Internet: The internet has spread its spindly wires to most towns. About 2Kč per min.

Language: Many Czechs, especially students, speak at least a little **English; German** phrases go even farther, especially in Prague, but might bring a little resentment. To gain some survival-level savvy in the Czech language, see p. 949.

ACCOMMODATIONS AND CAMPING. Hostels, particularly in **university dorms,** are the cheapest option in July and August; two- to four-bed rooms run 200-300Kč per person. CKM's **Junior Hotels** (year-round hostels that give discounts to ISIC and HI cardholders) are comfortable but often full. **Private hostels** have broken the CKM monopoly, but don't always surpass its reliability. **Pensions** are the next most

THE WORLD'S MOST DIFFICULT SOUND

Not quite a Spanish "r" and simply not the Polish "rz" (e.g., the second "g" in "garage"), Czech's own linguistic blue note, the letter "ř," lies excruciatingly in between. Although many of Prague's expats would sacrifice a month of Saturdays at Jo's Bar to utter the elusive sound just once, few manage more than a strangely trilled whistle. Most foreigners resign themselves to using the "ž" (akin to the Polish "rz") in its place, but what we consider a subtle difference often confuses Czechs. For all those linguistic daredevils in the audience, here's a surefire method of tackling the randy Mr. Ř: roll your tongue and quickly follow with a "ž," then repeat. Oh, yeah—and start when you're two.

affordable option (around 600Kč, including breakfast). **Private homes** are not nearly as popular (or as cheap) as in the rest of Eastern Europe. Scan train stations for *Zimmer frei* signs. In Prague, make sure anything you accept is easily accessible by public transport. Outside Prague, **local tourist offices** and **CKM/GTS** offices book rooms, while private agencies are burgeoning around train and bus stations. **Campgrounds,** strewn throughout the countryside, run 60-100Kč per person and 50-90Kč per tent. Most are only open mid-May to September.

FOOD AND DRINK. Anyone in the mood for true Czech cuisine should start learning to pronounce *knedlíky* (KNED-lee-kee). These thick, pasty loaves of dough, feebly known in English as dumplings, serve as staples of Czech meals, soaking up *zelí* (sauerkraut) juice and other schmaltzy sauces. The Czech national meal is *vepřo-knedlo-zelo* (roast pork with sauerkraut and dumplings); but *guláš* (stew) runs a close second. Subsidies on meat and dairy have managed to strip most meals of fruits and vegetables; the main food groups seem to be *hovězí* (beef), *sekaná pečeně* (meatloaf), *klobása* (sausage), and *brambory* (potatoes). If you're in a hurry, grab a pair of *párky* (frankfurters) or some *sýr* (cheese) at a *bufet, samoobsluha,* or *občerstvení,* all variations on a food stand. **Vegetarian** restaurants serve *šopský salát* (mixed salad with feta cheese) and other *bez masa* (meatless) specialties; at most restaurants, however, vegetarians will be limited to *smažený sýr* (fried cheese). The most beloved dessert is *koláč*—a tart filled with poppyseed jam or sweet cheese. *Zmrzlina* is closer to *gelati* than American ice cream. The most prominent beer is *Plzeňský Prazdroj* (Pilsner Urquell), although many Czechs are loyal to *Budvar* or *Krušovice.*

LOCAL FACTS

Time: The Czech Republic is 1hr. ahead of Greenwich Mean Time (GMT; see p. 49).

Climate: Continental climate, with bitter-cold winters, very warm summers, and moderate precipitation. Spring and fall are the best times to visit.

Hours: Banks are open M-F 9am-5pm; most **shops** are also open Sa.

Holidays: New Year's Day (Jan. 1); Catholic Easter (Apr. 23-24); May Day (May 1); Liberation Day (May 8); Cyril and Methodius Day (July 5); Jan Hus Day (July 6); 1918 Republic Day (Oct. 28); and Catholic Christmas (Dec. 24-26).

Festivals: Prague Spring Festival, Prague, May; **Five-Petal Rose Fest,** Český Krumlov, June; **Karlovy Vary International Film Festival,** Karlovy Vary, July.

PRAGUE (PRAHA)

According to legend, Princess Libuše stood above the Vltava in the 9th century and declared, "I see a city whose glory will touch the stars; it shall be called Praha (threshold)." Medieval kings, benefactors, and architects fulfilled the prophecy, building soaring cathedrals and lavish palaces that reflected Prague's status as capital of the Holy Roman Empire. Yet legends of demons, occult forces, and mazelike alleys lent this "city of dreams" a dark side that inspired Franz Kafka's tales of paranoia. Since the fall of the Iron Curtain, hordes of Euro-trotting foreigners have flooded the capital. In summer, tourists pack some streets so tightly that crowd-surfing could become a summer pastime—and the only way off the Charles Bridge is to jump. Yet walk a few blocks from any of the major sights and you'll be lost in a maze of cobblestoned alleys, looming churches, and dark cellars; head to an outlying metro stop, and you'll find haggling *babičky,* supermodel-esque natives, and not a backpack in sight. The spell might be fading, but if you look closely enough, there's still plenty of stardust left in the cobblestoned cracks.

Prague continues to reform its phone system. Businesses often receive no more than three weeks' notice before their numbers change. The eight-digit numbers provided in these listings are the least likely to be obsolete by the time you read this—but then again, nothing is sacred.

GETTING THERE AND GETTING AROUND

Flights: Ruzyně Airport (tel. 20 11 11 11), 20km northwest of the city. Take bus 119 to Metro A: Dejvická (12Kč, plus 6Kč per piece of large luggage; runs daily 5am-midnight); buy tickets from kiosks or machines. Late at night, take night tram 1 to "Divoká Šárka," then night bus 510 to the center. **Airport buses** (tel. 20 11 42 96) go every 30min. from Nám. Republiky (90Kč) and Dejvická (60Kč). Taxis to the airport are extremely expensive.

Trains: Tel. 24 22 42 00; international info tel. 24 61 52 49. Prague has 4 terminals:

Praha hlavní nádraží: Tel. 24 22 42 00. Metro C: Hlavní nádraží. The largest station. **BIJ Wasteels** (tel. 24 61 74 54; fax 24 22 18 72), 2nd fl., to the right of the stairs, sells discounted international tickets to those under 26 and books *couchettes.* Open in summer M-F 7:30am-8pm, Sa 8-11:30am and 12:30-3pm; off-season M-F 8:30am-6pm.

Holešovice: Tel. 24 61 72 65. Metro C: Nádraží Holešovice. Services most international destinations. Buy **BIJ Wasteels** tickets from the Czech Railways Travel Agency (tel. 80 08 05). Open daily 7-11:25am, noon-5:40pm, 6:20-9:45pm, 10:35pm-2am, and 3:15-6:35am. To: **Bratislava** (5hr., 2 per day, 390Kč); **Berlin** (5hr., 6 per day, 1575Kč, Wasteels 1413Kč); **Vienna** (5hr., 4 per day, 739Kč, Wasteels 574Kč); **Kraków** (6½hr., 1 per day, 1000Kč); **Budapest** (8hr., 6 per day, 1282Kč, Wasteels 1040Kč); **Munich** (9hr., 3 per day, 2025Kč); and **Warsaw** (10hr., 3 per day, 652Kč).

Masarykovo: Tel. 24 61 72 60. Metro B: Nám. Republiky. On the corner of Hybernská and Havlíčkova. Serves domestic destinations.

Smíchov: Tel. 24 61 72 55. Metro B: Smíchovské nádraží. Opposite Vyšehrad. Also serves domestic destinations.

Buses: ČSAD has several *autobusové nádraží.* The biggest is **Florenc,** Křižíkova 4 (tel. 24 21 49 90 and 24 21 10 60). Metro B,C: Florenc. Staff rarely speaks English. Tricky timetables require some studying. Info office open M-F 6am-9pm, Sa 6am-6pm, Su 8am-8pm. Buy tickets in advance, as they often sell out. To: **Berlin** (6hr., 1 per day, 820Kč); **Vienna** (8½hr., 6 per week, 400Kč); and **Sofia** (26hr., 1 per day, 1290Kč). Students may get 10% discount. The **Tourbus** office upstairs (tel. 24 21 02 21) sells tickets for Eurolines and airport buses. Open M-F 8am-8pm, Sa-Su 9am-8pm.

Public Transportation: Buy tickets for the **metro, tram,** or **bus** from newsstands and *tabák* kiosks, machines in stations, or **DP** (*Dopravní Podnik;* transport authority) kiosks. The basic 8Kč ticket is good for 15min. (or 4 stops on the metro); 12Kč is valid for 1hr. (8pm-5am 1½hr.), with unlimited connections on the entire network in any one direction. Large bags and bikes require an extra 6Kč ticket. Validate your ticket in the machines above the escalators or face a 200Kč fine. The **metro's** 3 lines run daily 5am-midnight: A is green on the maps, B yellow, C red. **Night trams** 51-58 and **buses** run all night; look for the dark-blue signs at bus stops.

Taxis: Taxi Praha (tel. 24 91 66 66) or **AAA** (tel. 24 32 24 32). Both open 24hr. Taxi drivers are notorious rip-off artists. Check that the meter is set to zero, and ask the driver to start it (*"Zapněte taximetr"*). Always ask for a receipt (*"Prosím, dejte mi paragon"*) with distance traveled and price paid. If the driver doesn't write the receipt or set the meter to zero, you aren't obligated to pay. Set rates in Prague 25Kč, plus 17Kč per km.

CZECH REPUBLIC

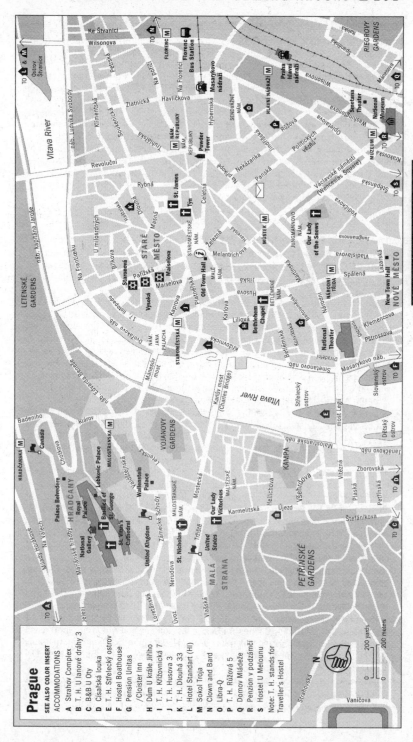

CZECH REPUBLIC

Prague

SEE ALSO COLOR INSERT

ACCOMMODATIONS
A   Strahov Complex
B   T. H. U lanové dráhy 3
C   B&B U Oty
D   Císařská louka
E   T. H. Střelecký ostrov
F   Hostel Boathouse
G   Pension Unitas
    /Cloister Inn
H   Dům U krále Jiřího
I   T. H. Křížovnická 7
J   T. H. Husova 3
K   T. H. Dlouhá 33
L   Hotel Standart (HI)
M   Sokol Troja
N   Clown and Bard
O   Libra-Q
P   T. H. Růžová 5
R   Penzion v podzámčí
S   Hostel U Melounu
Note: T. H. stands for
Traveller's Hostel

CZECH REPUBLIC

🛐 ORIENTATION AND PRACTICAL INFORMATION

Straddling the **Vltava River,** Prague is a gigantic snarl of suburbs and labyrinthine medieval streets. Fortunately, nearly everything of interest lies in the compact downtown. **Staré Město** (Old Town), centered around **Staroměstské náměstí** on the left bank of the Vltava, is the city's original medieval center, bordered to the north and west by the river, to the south by **Národní třída** and **Na Příkopě,** and to the east by **Revoluční.** The old Jewish ghetto, **Josefov,** lies in the northwestern corner of Staré Město. Surrounding Staré Město to the south and east of Staré Město is **Nové Město** (New Town), the commercial center of the city, which contains **Václavské náměstí.** Prague's main train station, **Hlavní nádraží,** and **Florenc bus station** are in Nové Město's northeastern corner. Across the Vltava sits the sprawling neighborhood of **Hradčany,** which stretches into the northern suburbs and is crowned by the giant **Prague Castle** (Pražský Hrad). At Hradčany's southern base sits the **Malá Strana** (Lesser Side), directly opposite Staré Město. All train and bus terminals are on or near the excellent **metro** system. *Tabák* stands and bookstores vend the indexed and essential *plán města* (map); the English-language weekly *The Prague Post,* is equally crucial. See also the two-page **color map** at the end of this book.

TOURIST AND FINANCIAL SERVICES

Tourist Offices: Pražská Informační Služba (Prague Info Service), in the Old Town Hall (tel. 24 48 25 62; English tel. 54 44 44). **Branches** at Na příkopě 20, Hlavní nádraží, and in the tower on the Malá Strana side of the Charles Bridge. All open in summer M-F 9am-7pm, Sa-Su 9am-6pm; off-season M-F 9am-6pm, Sa-Su 9am-5pm.

Budget Travel: CKM, Jindřišská 28 (tel. 24 23 02 18; fax 26 86 23; email ckm-prg@mbox.vol.cz). Metro A,B: Můstek. Budget air tickets for students and those under 26. Also books lodgings in Prague from 350Kč. Open M-Th 10am-6pm, F 10am-4pm.

Passport Office: Foreigner police headquarters, Olšanská 2 (tel. 683 17 39). Metro A: Flora; turn right on Jičínská with the cemetery on your right, then right on Olšanská. Or, take tram 9 from Václavské nám. toward Spojovací and get off at Olšanská. For visa extensions, get a 90Kč stamp just inside, line up in front of doors 2-12, and prepare to wait up to 2hr. Little English spoken. Open M-Tu and Th 7:30-11:45am and 12:30-2:30pm, W 7:30-11:30am and 12:30-5pm, F 7:30am-noon.

Embassies: Australia (tel. 24 31 00 71) and **New Zealand** (tel. 25 41 98) have consuls, but citizens should contact the UK embassy in an emergency. **Canada,** Mickiewiczova 6 (tel. 24 31 11 08). Metro A: Hradčanská. Open M-F 8am-noon and 2-4pm. **Hungary,** Badeního 1 (tel. 32 04 12). Metro A: Hradčanská. Open M-W and F 9am-noon. **Ireland,** Tržiště 13 (tel. 53 09 11). Metro A: Malostranská. Open M-F 9:30am-12:30pm and 2:30-4:30pm. **Poland,** Váldštejnská nám. 49 (tel. 57 32 06 78). Metro A: Malostranská. Open M-F 7am-noon. **Russia,** Pod Kaštany 1 (tel. 38 19 45). Metro A: Hradčanská. Open M, W, and F 9am-1pm. **Slovakia,** Pod Hradební 1 (tel. 32 05 07). Metro A: Dejvická. Open M-F 8:30am-noon. **South Africa,** Ruská 65 (tel. 67 31 11 14). Metro A: Flora. Open M-F 9am-noon. **UK,** Thunovská 14 (tel. 57 32 03 55). Metro A: Malostranská. Open M-F 9am-noon. **US,** Tržiště 15 (tel. 57 53 11 62; emergency tel. 53 12 00). Metro A: Malostranská. From Malostranská nám., head down Karmelitská and take a right onto Tržiště. Open M-F 8am-1pm and 2-4:30pm.

Currency Exchange: Exchange counters are everywhere with wildly varying rates. **Cheque-points** may be the only ones open when you need cash, but usually charge a 10% commission. **Komerční banka,** Na plíkopw 33 (tel. 24 02 11 11), buys notes and checks for a 2% commission. Open M-F 8am-5pm. **ATMs** ("Bankomats") are everywhere.

American Express: Václavské nám. 56, 113 26 Praha 1 (tel. 22 80 02 51; fax 22 21 11 31). Metro A,C: Muzeum. Cashes AmEx checks commission-free and grants cash advances for a 3% commission. Open July-Sept. M-F 9am-6pm, Sa 9am-2pm; Oct.-June M-F 9am-5pm, Sa 9am-noon. **Branch** near the Charles Bridge in Malá Strana, Mostecká 12. Open daily 9:30am-7:30pm.

Thomas Cook: Národní třída 28 (tel. 21 10 52 76; fax 24 23 60 77). Cashes Cook checks commission-free. Cash advances. Open M-Sa 9am-7pm, Su 10am-6pm. Also Staroměstké nám. 5 (tel. 24 81 71 73). Open M-F 9am-6pm, Sa 9am-1pm.

LOCAL SERVICES

Luggage Storage: Lockers in all train and bus stations take two 5Kč coins. If these are full, or if you need to store your special cargo longer than 24hr., use the luggage offices to the left in the basement of **Hlavní nádraží** (15-25Kč per day; open 24hr.) and halfway up the stairs at **Florenc** (10-20Kč per day; open daily 5am-11pm).

English Bookstore: The Globe Bookstore, Janovského 14 (tel. 66 71 26 10; www.globe-bookstore.cz). Metro C: Vltavská; walk right under the overpass, then right on Janovského. Open daily 10am-midnight.

Laundromat: Laundry Kings, Dejvická 16 (tel. 312 37 43), one block from Metro A: Hradčanská. Cross the tram *and* railroad tracks, then turn left on Dejvická. Wash 60Kč per 6kg; dry 15Kč per 8min. Soap 10-20Kč. Open M-F 6am-10pm, Sa-Su 8am-10pm.

EMERGENCY AND COMMUNICATIONS

Emergencies: Na Homolce (Hospital for Foreigners), Roentgenova 2 (tel. 52 92 21 46; foreign reception tel. 52 92 21 54; after-hours tel. 57 21 11 11). Open M-F 8am-4pm.

Pharmacy: "U Anděla," Štefánikova 6 (tel. 57 32 09 18). Open 24hr.

Internet Access: Prague is an internet nirvana. ▨**Terminal Bar,** Soukenická 6 (tel. 21 87 11 15). Metro B: Nám. Republiky. 120Kč per hr. for members. Coffee (20Kč). Open daily 11am-1am. **Café Electra,** Rašínovo nábřeží 62 (tel. 297 038). Metro B: Karlovo nám. 80Kč per hr. Open M-F 8am-midnight, Sa-Su noon-midnight.

Telephones: Phone cards sell for 150Kč per 50 units at kiosks, post offices, and some exchange places: don't let kiosks rip you off.

Post Office: Jindřišská 14. Metro A,B: Můstek (tel. 24 22 88 56 and 24 22 85 88). Get stamps at window 16; letters and small parcels at windows 12-14; *Poste Restante* at window 17. To send a package of more than 2kg abroad, go to the **Celní stanice** (Customs Office), Plzeňská 139. Open M-Tu and Th-F 7am-3pm, W 7am-6pm. Address mail to be held: Tamara <u>KNIGHT</u>, *Poste Restante,* Jindřišská 14, **110 00** Praha 1, Czech Republic.

PHONE CODE	City code: 02. From outside Czech Republic, dial int'l dialing prefix (see inside back cover) + 420 + 2 + local number.

◤ ACCOMMODATIONS

While hotel prices rise beyond your wildest dreams, the hostel market is glutted and prices have stabilized around 250-350Kč per night. Rooms in smaller, homey hostels must be reserved at least two days in advance. A few bare-bones hotels are still cheap, and a growing number of Prague residents are renting rooms. Sleeping on Prague's streets is too dangerous to consider.

ACCOMMODATIONS AGENCIES

The going rate for apartments hovers around 500-1000Kč, depending on proximity to the city center; you can haggle with the hawkers. This is usually safe, but if you're wary of bargaining on the street, try a private agency. Ask where the nearest tram, bus, or metro stop is, and don't pay until you know what you're getting; ask for details in writing. You can often pay in US$ or DM, but prices are lower if you pay in Kč. **Ave.,** at Hlavní nádraží, 2nd fl., next to the leftmost set of stairs, offers hundreds of rooms from 800Kč per person and books hostels from 300Kč. (Tel. 24 22 35 21; fax 57 31 29 84. Open daily 6am-11pm. V, MC, AmEx.) **Hello Travel Ltd.,** Senovážné nám. 3, between Na příkopě and Hlavní nádraží, arranges housing. (Tel. 24 21 26 47. Singles US$23-$35; doubles US$56; hostels US$10-13. Pay in Kč, DM, or with V, MC, AmEx. Open daily 10am-9pm.)

HOSTELS

If you're schlepping a backpack in Hlavní nádraží or Holešovice, you *will* be bombarded by hostel runners trying to coerce you back to their hostel. Many of these are university dorms that free up from June to August, and often you'll be offered transport to the room—an easy option for those arriving in the middle of the night without a reservation. If you prefer hostels that offer more than just a place to sleep, smaller places are a better alternative. It's best to phone the night before you arrive or at 10am when they know who's checking out in order to snag a bed. **Vinohrady** is a residential district about 15min. southeast of the city center.

■ **Penzion v podzámčí,** V podzámčí 27 (tel./fax 472 27 59), south of the center. From Metro C: Budějovická, take bus 192 to the 3rd stop—ask the driver to stop at Nad Rybníky. Eva and Michaela have the homiest hostel in Prague. Dorms 250Kč; doubles 280Kč. Kitchen. Incredible laundry service (they iron your socks!) 100Kč per 5kg.

■ **Hostel Boathouse,** V náklích 1a (tel./fax 402 10 76), south of the center. From Hlavní nádraží, Karlovo nám., Staré Město, or the Charles Bridge, take tram 3 or 17 south toward Sídliště and get off at "Černý Kůň" (20min.). From the tram stop, follow the yellow signs down to the Vltava. As Věra, the owner, says, "This isn't a hostel; it's a crazy house." Nurturing home/summer camp. Dorms 290Kč. Breakfast 50Kč. Laundry. Key deposit 100Kč. 2-night min. stay. Call ahead; if they're full, Věra might find space.

Domov Mládeže, Dykova 20 (tel./fax 22 51 25 97 and 22 51 17 77), in **Vinohrady.** Metro A: Jiřího z Poděbrad; follow Nitranská and turn left on Dykova; it's 2 blocks down on your right. So peaceful you might forget you're in Prague. Dorms 350Kč; lone double 500Kč. Breakfast included. Sister hostels: **Amadeus,** Slavojova 108/8. Metro C: Vyšehrad; descend the bridge to Čiklova, turn left, and it's on the left. **Máchova,** Máchova 11. Metro A: Nám. Míru; walk down Ruská and turn right on Máchova. **Košická,** Košická 12. Metro A: Nám. Míru. All hostels use the same phone number.

Libra-Q, Senovážné nám. 21 (tel. 24 23 17 54; fax 24 22 15 79), at Jeruzalémská, on the edge of Staré Město in **Nové Město.** Metro B: Nám. Republiky; walk down Hybernská to Senovážná. Tidy, spartan dorms. 550Kč.

Hostel U Melounu (At the Watermelon), Ke Karlovu 7 (tel./fax 24 91 83 22), 5min. from Nové Město. Metro C: I.P. Pavlova; follow Sokolská to Na Bojišti and turn left at the street's end onto Ke Karlovu. In a historic building with great facilities. 2- to 4-bed dorms 390-500Kč. 30Kč discount with ISIC, GO 25, or Euro-26. Breakfast included.

Clown and Bard, Bořivojova 102 (tel. 22 71 64 53), in **Vinohrady.** Metro A: Jiřího z Poděbrad; follow Slavíkova to Ježkova, and it's on the left at the intersection with Bořivojova. New management has set this notoriously social hostel on the right track once again. Bar with nightly music. 3- to 6-bed dorms 250-350Kč; doubles 400Kč.

Traveller's Hostels (email hostel@terminal.cz), in **Staré Město.** These summertime big-dorm specialists round up travelers at bus and train stations and herd them into one of six central hostels for lots of beds and beer. At all, breakfast is included and **internet** access is available. **Husova 3** (tel. 24 21 53 26). Metro B: Národní tlída; turn right on Spálená (which becomes Na Perštýně after Národní), and then Husova. Dorms 400Kč. **Dlouhá 33** (tel. 24 82 66 62; fax 24 82 66 65). Metro A: Staromwstské; Metro B: Nám. Republiky. In the same building as the Roxy, so it can get noisy. Dorms 350-380Kč; doubles 1100Kč; triples 1290Kč. **Střelecký ostrov** (tel. 24 91 01 88), on an island off Most Legií. Metro B: Národní tlída. 300Kč. **Křížovnická 7** (tel. 232 09 87). Metro A: Staroměstská. Dorms 230Kč. **Růžová 5** (tel. 26 01 11). Metro C: Hlavní nádraží. Dorms 220Kč. **U lanové dráhy 3** (tel. 53 31 60). Tram 6, 9, 12: Újezd. Upstairs. Dorms 200Kč.

Strahov Complex, Vaníčkova 5, west of the center. Metro A: Dejvická; then take bus 217 or 143 to Koleje Strahov. Next to the enormous stadium, Strahov is known as "hostel ghetto"—10 concrete blocks that open June-Aug. to accommodate the hordes. Not very convenient, but there's always space, and you can catch the Strahov concerts from your cubicle. Singles 300Kč; doubles 220Kč; students 180Kč for all rooms.

HOTELS AND PENSIONS

Budget hotels are now scarce. Beware of hotels that may try to bill you for a more expensive room than the one in which you stayed; some cheap establishments require reservations up to a month in advance, but many refuse reservations altogether. Call first, then confirm by fax with a credit card.

B&B U Oty (Ota's House), Radlická 188 (tel./fax 57 21 53 23; www.bbuoty.cz), west of the center. Metro B: Radlická; exit left and go right on the road; it's 400m up the slope. Charming, English-speaking Ota will make your stay a joy. Singles 500Kč; doubles 770Kč; triples 950Kč; quads 1250Kč. One-night surcharge 100Kč. Kitchen. Laundry.

Hotel Standart (HI), Přístavní 2 (tel. 875 258 and 875 674; fax 806 752), north of the center. Metro C: Vltavská; take tram 1 toward Spojavací, 3 toward Lehovec, 14 toward Vozovna Kobylisy, or 25 toward Střelničná. Continue along the street, then turn left onto Přístavní. Very quiet neighborhood. Singles 350Kč, nonmembers 620Kč; doubles 700Kč, 800Kč; triples 1050Kč, 1100Kč; quads 1400Kč. Breakfast included.

Pension Unitas/Cloister Inn, Bartolomějská 9 (tel. 232 77 00; fax 232 77 09; email cloister@cloister-inn.cz; www.cloister-inn.cz), in **Staré Město.** Metro B: Národní třída; cross Národní, head down Na Perštýně away from Tesco, and turn left on Bartolomějská. Beethoven once performed here, and Václav Havel was once incarcerated here. Singles 1020Kč; doubles 1200Kč; triples 1650Kč. Breakfast included.

Dům U krále Jiřího, Liliová 10 (tel. 22 22 09 25; fax 22 22 17 07), in **Staré Město.** Metro A: Staroměstská; exit onto Nám. Jana Palacha, walk down Křížovnická toward the Charles Bridge, turn left onto Karlova, and Liliová is the 1st right. Gorgeous rooms with private bath. Singles 1650Kč; doubles 2850Kč. Breakfast included.

CAMPING

Campsites have taken over both the outskirts and the centrally located Vltava islands. Bungalows must be reserved in advance, but tent space is generally available without prior notice. Tourist offices sell a guide to sites near the city (15Kč).

Císařská louka, on a peninsula on the Vltava. Metro B: Smíchovské nádraží; then take tram 12 (dir: Hlubočepy) to Lihovar and go toward the river. Or, take the ferry from Smíchovské nádraží. **Caravan Park** (tel. 54 09 25) is near the ferry. 110Kč per person, 90-120Kč per tent. Singles 365Kč; doubles 630Kč. **Caravan Camping** (tel./fax 54 01 29) is near the tram. 110Kč per person, 90-120Kč per tent. 4-bed bungalows 720Kč.

Sokol Troja, Trojská 171 (tel./fax 688 11 77), north of the center in the Troja district. Metro C: Nádraží Holešovice; then take bus 112 to "Kazanka," the 4th stop. Prague's largest campground. At least 4 nearly identical places line the same road. 100Kč per person, tents 80-160Kč. Dorms 250Kč; bungalows 230Kč per person.

FOOD

The basic rule is that the nearer you are to **Staroměstské nám.**, the **Charles Bridge** (Karlův most), and **Václavské nám.**, the more you'll pay; away from the center, you can get pork, cabbage, dumplings, and a half-liter of beer for 50Kč. Check your bill carefully. Go to the basement of Czech department stores for food halls and supermarkets. **Tesco,** Národní třída 26, has **groceries** right next to Metro B: Národní třída. (Open M-F 7am-8pm, Sa 8am-6pm, Su 9am-6pm.) Look for the **daily market** at the intersection of Havelská and Melantrichova in Staré Město.

RESTAURANTS

Universal, V jirchářích 6 (tel. 24 91 81 82), in **Nové Město.** Metro B: Národní třída; turn left onto Spálená and right on Myslíkova, then right on Křemencova. A transplanted California-style eatery with big, fresh salads (97-135Kč). Open daily 11:30am-1am.

Velryba (The Whale), Opatovická 24 (tel. 24 91 23 91), in **Nové Město.** Metro B: Národní třída. Relaxed café-restaurant with a chic gallery in back. International and Czech dishes (38-115Kč) and adventurous veggie platters. Open daily 11am-2am.

Lotos, Platnéřská 13 (tel. 232 23 90), in **Staré Město.** Metro A: Staroměstská; exit onto the corner of Kaprova and Valentinská., turn left down Valentinská away from the Jewish cemetery, and turn right on Platnéłská. Vegetarian restaurant with Czech food and organic menu (60-140Kč). 0.5L wheat-yeast Pilsner 30Kč. Open daily 11am-10pm.

Klub architektů, Betlémské nám. 52 (tel. 24 40 12 14), in **Staré Město.** Walk through the gates and descend to the right. A 12th-century cellar thrust into the 20th century. Veggie options 80-90Kč; meat dishes 100-150Kč. Open daily 11am-midnight.

CZEZH REPUBLIC

U Špirků, on Kožná in **Staré Město.** Metro A: Staroměstská. With the astronomical clock behind you, go down Melantrichova and make your 1st left onto Kožná, which curves to the left. Good cheap eats. Daily specials 50-60Kč. Open M-Sa 11am-midnight.

Bar bar, Všehrdova 17 (tel. 53 29 41), in **Malá Strana.** Metro A: Malostranská; follow the tram tracks down Letenská, through Malostranské nám., and down Karmelitská, then turn left on Všehrdova after the museum. A jungle jungle of salads salads with meat meat, fish fish, or just veggies veggies (64-89Kč). Pancakes pancakes—sweet sweet (22-56Kč) or savory savory (59-155Kč). Open daily noon-midnight.

Bohemia Bagel, Újezd 16 (tel. 53 10 02), in **Malá Strana.** Metro A: Malostranská. Ahhh, bagels. Open M-Th 7am-midnight, F 7am-2am, Sa 8am-2am, Su 8am-midnight.

LATE-NIGHT EATING

4:45am. Charles Bridge. Lavka's house disco beat is still pumping ferociously, but all you can hear is your stomach growling. Don't go home hungry—grab a *párek v rohlíku* (hot dog) or a *smažený sýr* (fried cheese sandwich) from a vendor on Václavské nám., or a gyro from a stand on Spálená or Vodíčkova. Or, even better, make a morning of it and uncover Prague's developing late-night eating scene. **J.J. Murphy's Breakfast Diner,** Tržiště 4, is a bar by day, night-train soul kitchen by 3am. (Metro A: Malostranská. Breakfast 80Kč. Open daily 3pm-10am.) Stay late enough sipping soup (20Kč) at **Andy's Café,** V kolkovně 3, to catch the first metro. (Metro A: Staroměstská; walk down Dlouhá and turn left on V kolkovně. Open M-F 10am-6am, Sa-Su noon-6am.)

CAFÉS

When Prague journalists are bored, they churn out yet another "Whatever happened to café life?" feature. The answer: it turned into *čajovna* (teahouse) culture.

■ **U malého Glena,** Karmelitská 23 (tel. 535 81 15). Metro A: Malostranská; then take tram 12 to Malostranské nám. With their motto "Eat, Drink, Drink Some More," they've got consumption down to a science. Killer margaritas (80Kč). Nightly jazz or blues 9pm. Cover 30-100Kč. Open M-F 10am-2am, Sa-Su 10am-3am; Su brunch 10am-4pm.

Jazz Café 14, Opatovická 14 (tel. 24 92 00 39). Metro B: Národní třída. Perpetually filled with smoke and twentysomethings. No live jazz, but photos of Louis, Miles, and others line the walls—just as good. Snacks (30Kč) and drinks (16Kč). Open daily 10am-11pm.

Unamuno Lounge, Mánesova 79 (tel. 627 77 67). Metro A: Jiřího z Poděbrad; walk 1 block down Slavíkova to Mánesova. The café is in the basement of the U Knihomola bookstore. The only place in Prague to get a real latte. Coffee 20-40Kč; carrot cake 75Kč. Open M-Th 10am-11pm, F-Sa 10am-midnight, Su 11am-8pm.

The Globe Coffeehouse, Janovského 14 (tel. 66 71 26 10). Metro C: Vltavská. Tasty, strong black coffee (20Kč), gazpacho soup (40Kč), and plenty of English speakers trying to make a love connection (priceless). Open daily 10am-midnight.

■ SIGHTS

The only Central European city left entirely unscathed by either natural disaster or WWII, central Prague is a well-preserved combination of labyrinthine alleys and Baroque buildings. The flocks of tourists might prove an amusing sight as well, but you can easily leave the packs by venturing away from Staroměstské nám., the Charles Bridge, and Václavské nám. Compact central Prague is best explored on foot. Don't leave without wandering the back alleys of Josefov, exploring the hills of Vyšehrad, and getting lost in the maze of Malá Strana's streets.

NOVÉ MĚSTO

Established in 1348 by Charles IV, Nové Město is not exactly new. Its age, however, is not readily apparent; its wide boulevards and sprawling squares seem hundreds of years ahead of their time.

WENCESLAS SQUARE (VÁCLAVSKÉ NÁMĚSTÍ). Not so much a square as a broad boulevard running through the center of Nové Město, Wenceslas Square owes its name to the equestrian statue of the Czech ruler and saint **Wenceslas** (Václav) in front of the **National Museum** (Národní muzeum). Wenceslas has presided over a century of turmoil and triumph, witnessing no fewer than five revolutions from his pedestal—the declaration of the new Czechoslovak state in 1918, Hitler's troops, the Soviet tanks in 1968, Jan Palach setting himself on fire to protest the Soviet invasion, and the 1989 Velvet Revolution. The square sweeps down from the statue past department stores, overpriced discos, posh hotels, sausage stands, and trashy casinos. At the northern end of Wenceslas Square, near the Můstek Metro station, Art Nouveau design is expressed in everything from lampposts to windowsills. The glass **Radio Prague Building**, behind the National Museum, was the scene of a tense battle during the Prague Spring, as citizens tried to protect the radio studios from Soviet tanks with a human barricade. *(Metro A,C: Muzeum.)*

FRANCISCAN GARDENS AND VELVET REVOLUTION MEMORIAL. Perhaps if the Franciscans took a break from talking to the birds, they could divulge how they managed to preserve the serene **rose garden** (Františkánská zahrada) in the heart of Prague's bustling commercial district. *(Metro A,B: Můstek; Metro B: Národní třída. Enter through the arch at Jungmannova and Národní. Open daily mid-Apr. to mid-Sept. 7 am-10pm; mid-Sept. to mid-Oct. 8am-8pm; mid-Oct. to mid-Apr. 8am-7 pm. Free.)* Under the arcades halfway down Národní třída stands a memorial to the hundreds of Prague's citizens beaten on November 17, 1989 during the **Velvet Revolution.**

MUNICIPAL HOUSE. By far the most impressive Art Nouveau building in the city, the Municipal House (Obecní dům) captures the opulence of Prague's 19th-century café culture. *(Nám. Republiky 5. Metro B: Nám. Republiky. Open daily 10am-6pm.)*

THE DANCING HOUSE. Built by American architect Frank Gehry of Guggenheim-Bilbao fame, the undulating building at the corner of Resslova and Rašínovo nábřeží is called Fred and Ginger by Anglophones and the Dancing House (Taneční dům) by Czechs. It opened in 1996, next to President Havel's former apartment building; he moved out when construction began. *(Metro B: Karlovo nám.)*

STARÉ MĚSTO

Settled in the 10th century, Staré Město remains a labyrinth of narrow roads and Old World alleys. It's easy to get lost, but doing so is the best way to appreciate the neighborhood's charm.

OLD TOWN SQUARE (STAROMĚSTSKÉ NÁMĚSTÍ). The heart of Staré Město is Old Town Square, surrounded by no fewer than eight magnificent towers. Next to the grassy knoll, **Old Town Hall** (Staroměstská radnice) is the multi-façaded building with a bit blown off the front. The building was partially demolished by the Nazis in the final week of WWII, receiving Prague's only visible damage from the war. *(Open in summer daily 9am-5:30pm. 30Kč, students 15Kč.)* Crowds gather on the hour to watch the wonderful **astronomical clock** *(orloj)* chime with its procession of apostles, a skeleton, and a thwarted Turk. They say the clockmaker's eyes were put out so he couldn't design another (something said about the man who built Moscow's St. Basil's, too). *(Metro A: Staroměstská; Metro A,B: Můstek. Clock animated until 9pm.)* The Czech Republic's most famous martyred theologian, **Jan Hus,** hovers over Old Town Square in bronze effigy. Opposite the Old Town Hall, the spires of **Týn Church** (Matka Boží před Týnem) rise above a mass of medieval homes. The famous astronomer **Tycho de Brahe** is buried inside—he overindulged at one of Emperor Rudolf's lavish dinner parties, where it was unacceptable to leave the table unless the Emperor himself did so. When poor Tycho de Brahe needed to go (you know, *go*), he was forced to stay seated, and his bladder burst.

GOLTZ-KINSKÝ PALACE. The flowery 14th-century Goltz-Kinský Palace is the finest of Prague's Rococo buildings. It is also the official birthplace of Soviet Communism in the Czech Republic: on February 21, 1948, Klement Gottwald declared communism victorious from its balcony. *(On Staroměstské nám. at the corner of Dlouhá, next to Týn Church. Open Tu-F 10am-5pm; closes early in summer for daily concerts.)*

CHARLES BRIDGE (KARLŮV MOST). Thronged with tourists and the hawkers who prey on them, this bridge is easily Prague's most recognizable landmark. Five years ago, the bridge's vendors peddled Red Army gear and dodgy black market currency deals; today, it's watercolors of the bridge and other junk. The foundation stone of the bridge was laid at 5:31am on July 9, 1357, the most significant astrological point for Leo, the mascot of Bohemia (now, incidentally, the name of a Czech porn magazine). When darkness falls, the street musicians emerge, but the penalty for requesting "Wish You Were Here" is being tied up in a goatskin and lowered into the Vltava. This same fate befell St. Jan Nepomucký when the hapless saint was tossed over the side of the bridge for faithfully guarding the queen's extramarital secrets from a suspicious King Wenceslas IV.

JOSEFOV

Metro A: Staroměstská. Tel. 231 71 91. Synagogues and museum open Su-F 9am-6pm. Closed for Jewish holidays. All sights except New Synagogue 450Kč, students 330Kč. New Synagogue 200Kč, students 140Kč. Museum only 250Kč, students 190Kč.

Prague's historic Jewish neighborhood and the oldest Jewish settlement in Europe, Josefov lies north of Staromětstské nám., along Maiselova and several sidestreets. In 1180, Prague's citizens built a 12-foot wall around the area. The closed city bred legends, many focusing on **Rabbi Loew ben Bezalel** (1512-1609), and his legendary *golem*—a mud creature that supposedly came to life to protect Prague's Jews. For the next 500 years, the city's Jews were exiled to this cramped ghetto, and were finally deported by the Nazis to Terezín and the death camps.

THE SYNAGOGUES. The **Maisel Synagogue** (Maiselova synagoga) exhibits treasures from the extensive collections of the Jewish Museum. *(On Maiselova, between Široká and Jáchymova.)* Turn left down Široká to reach the 16th-century **Pinkas Synagogue** (Pinkasova synagoga), converted in 1958 into a sobering memorial to the 77,000 Czech Jews killed in the Holocaust. Backtrack up Široká and go left on Maiselova to see the oldest operating synagogue in Europe, the 700-year-old **Old-New Synagogue** (Staronová synagoga). Further up Široká on Dušní is the ornate Moorish interior of the **Spanish Synagogue** (Španělská synagoga).

OLD JEWISH CEMETERY AND CEREMONY HALL. The **Old Jewish Cemetery** (Starý židovský hřbitov) remains Josefov's most popular attraction. Between the 14th and 18th centuries, 20,000 graves were laid in 12 layers. Rabbi Loew is buried by the wall directly opposite the entrance. *(At the corner of Široká and Žatecká.)* Originally a ceremonial hall for the Jewish Burial Society, **Ceremony Hall** (Obřadní dům) now houses the renowned exhibit, "Children's Drawings from Terezín: 1942-44"; most of the young artists died at Auschwitz. *(On Červená, just off Maiselova.)*

MALÁ STRANA

The seedy hangout of criminals and counter-revolutionaries for nearly a century, the cobblestoned streets of Malá Strana have become the most prized real estate on either side of the Vltava. The Malá Strana is centered around **Malostranské nám.** and its centerpiece, the Baroque **St. Nicholas' Cathedral** (Chrám sv. Mikuláš), whose towering dome is one of Prague's most notable landmarks. *(Metro A: Malostranská; then follow Letenská to Malostranské nám. Open daily 9am-4:30pm. 30Kč, students 15Kč.)* Along Letenská, a wooden gate opens through a 10-meter wall into the beautiful **Wallenstein Garden** (Valdštejnská zahrada), one of Prague's best-kept secrets. *(Letenská 10. Metro A: Malostranská. Open daily May-Sept. 9am-7pm; Mar. 21-Apr. and Oct. 10am-6pm.)* Opposite the Malostranská metro station, a plaque hidden in a lawn constitutes the **Charousková Memorial,** the only monument to those slain in the 1968 Prague Spring. It commemorates **Marie Charousková,** a graduate student who was machine-gunned by a Soviet soldier for refusing to remove a black ribbon protesting the invasion. Unlike other

CZEZH REPUBLIC

churches in Prague, the modest **Church of Our Lady Victorious** (Kostel Panna Marie Vítězná) is not notable for its exterior but for the famous wax statue of the **Infant Jesus of Prague** inside, said to bestow miracles on the faithful. *(Metro A: Malostranská; then follow Letenská through Malostranské nám. and continue onto Karmelitská. Open daily in summer 7am-9pm; off-season 8am-8pm. Free.)*

PRAGUE CASTLE (PRAŽSKÝ HRAD)

Metro A: Hradčanská. Open daily Apr.-Aug. 9am-5pm; Sept.-Mar. 9am-4pm. Buy tickets opposite St. Vitus' Cathedral, inside the castle walls. Three-day ticket valid at Royal Crypt, Cathedral and Powder Towers, Old Royal Palace, and Basilica of St. George. 120Kč, students 60Kč.

Prague Castle has been the seat of the Bohemian government and the center of its politics since its founding 1000 years ago. From the metro station, cross the tram tracks and turn left onto Tychonova, which leads to the newly renovated **Royal Summer Palace** (Královský letohrádek). The **castle entrance** is at the other end of the 1534 **Royal Garden** (Královská zahrada) in front of the palace, across the **Powder Bridge** (Prašný most). Before touring the castle, pass through the main gate to explore the **Šternberský Palace,** home of the National Gallery's European art collection. *(Open Tu-Su 10am-6pm. 45Kč, students 25Kč.)*

ST. VITUS' CATHEDRAL. Inside the castle walls stands Prague Castle's centerpiece, the colossal St. Vitus' Cathedral (Katedrála sv. Víta), which may look Gothic but in fact was only finished in 1929—600 years after construction began. The cathedral's stained-glass windows were created by some of the most gifted Czech artists; Alphonse Mucha's brilliant depiction of St. Ludmila and Wenceslas is the most recognizable and haunting. To the right of the high altar stands the **tomb of sv. Jan Nepomucký** (of Charles Bridge fame), 3m of solid, glistening silver that weighs 1800kg. In the main church, the walls of **St. Wenceslas's Chapel** (Svatováclavská kaple) are lined with precious stones and a painting cycle depicting the legend of this saint. Climb the 287 steps of the **Cathedral Tower** for the best view of the city.

OLD ROYAL PALACE. The Old Royal Palace (Starý královský palác), to the right of the cathedral behind the Old Provost's House and the statue of St. George, houses the lengthy expanse of the **Vladislav Hall,** which once hosted jousting competitions. Upstairs is the **Chancellery of Bohemia,** where on May 23, 1618, angry Protestants flung two Hapsburg officials (and their secretary) through the windows, triggering Europe's extraordinarily bloody Thirty Years' War.

ST. GEORGE'S BASILICA AND AROUND. Behind the cathedral and across the courtyard from the Old Royal Palace stand the Romanesque St. George's Basilica (Bazilika sv. Jiří) and its adjacent convent. The convent houses the **National Gallery of Bohemian Art** (Klášter sv. Jiří), with art ranging from Gothic to Baroque. *(Open Tu-Su 10am-6pm. 50Kč, students 15Kč; 1st F of each month free.)* The palace street **Jiřská** begins to the right of the basilica. Halfway down, the tiny **Golden Lane** (Zlatá ulička) heads off to the right; alchemists once worked here, and Kafka later lived at #22. Back on Jiřská, after passing out of the castle between the two armed sentries, peer over the battlements on the right for a fine cityscape.

OUTER PRAGUE

The city's outskirts are packed with greenery, nifty churches, and panoramic vistas, all peacefully tucked away from the tourist hordes. **Petřín Gardens** (Petřínské sady), the largest in Prague, provide some of the most spectacular views of the city. A cable car from just above the intersection of Vítězná and Újezd goes to the top. *(8Kč; look for lanová dráha signs. Open daily 11am-6pm and 7-11pm.)* At the summit is a small Eiffel tower and a wacky labyrinth of mirrors at **Bludiště.** *(Open Tu-Su 10am-7pm. 20Kč, students 10Kč.)* **Vyšehrad** is the former haunt of Prague's 19th-century Romantics; quiet walkways wind between crumbling stone walls to one of the Czech Republic's most celebrated sites, **Vyšehrad Cemetery** (home to the remains of Dvořák). Even the **Metro C: Vyšehrad** stop has a movie-sweep vista of Prague.

CZECH REPUBLIC

MUSEUMS

Prague's magnificence isn't best reflected in its museums, which often have striking façades but mediocre collections. But the city is victim to many rainy days, and it has a few public museums that shelter interesting and quirky collections. ■**House of the Golden Ring** (Dům u zlatého prstenu), Týnská 6, behind Týn Church, houses an astounding collection of 20th-century Czech art. *(Tel. 24 82 80 04. Metro A: Staromwstská. Open Tu-Su 10am-6pm. 100Kč, students 50Kč; 1st Tu of each month free.)* The **National Gallery** (Národní galerie) is spread around nine different locations; the notable **Šternberský palác** and **Klášter sv. Jiří** are in the **Prague Castle** (see p. 239). **St. Agnes' Cloister** (Klášter sv. Anežky) is the other major branch of the National Gallery, well worth seeing for its collection of 19th-century Czech art. *(U milosrdných 17. Metro A: Staromwstská. Tel. 24 81 06 28.)* The **Trade Fair Palace and the Gallery of Modern Art** (Veletržní palác a Galerie moderního umění) displays 20th-century Czech art. *(Dukelských hrdinů 47. Metro C: Vltavská. Tel. 24 30 11 11. Both open Tu-W and F-Su 10am-6pm, Th 10am-9pm. 70Kč, students 40Kč.)* The **Czech Museum of Fine Arts** (České muzeum výtvarných umění), Celetná 34, itself one of Prague's best examples of Cubist architecture, contains a complementary collection of Czech Cubism. *(Tel. 24 21 17 31. Metro A: Nám. Republiky. Open Tu-Su 10am-6pm. 25Kč, students 10Kč.)*

▇ ENTERTAINMENT AND NIGHTLIFE

For concerts and performances, consult *The Prague Post, Threshold,* or *Do města-Downtown* (the latter two are free at many cafés and restaurants). Between mid-May and early June, the **Prague Spring Festival** draws musicians from around the world. For tickets (300-2000Kč), try **Bohemia Ticket International,** Malé nám. 13, next to Čedok. (Tel. 24 22 78 32. Open M-F 9am-6pm, Sa 9am-4pm, Su 10am-3pm.) The **National Theater** (Národní divadlo), Národní třída 2/4, features drama, opera, and ballet. (Tel. 24 90 14 19. Metro B: Národní třída. Tickets 100-1000Kč. Box office open M-F 10am-6pm, Sa-Su 10am-12:30pm and 3-6pm, and 30min. before performances.) **Estates Theater** (Stavovské divadlo), Ovocný trh 1 (tel. 24 91 34 37; Metro A,B: Můstek), left from the pedestrian Na Příkopě, where *Don Giovanni* premiered many years ago, now performs mostly classic theater. Head to the box office of the National Theater, or turn up 30min. before the show.

The most authentic way to experience Prague at night is in an alcoholic fog. With some of the best beers in the world on tap, pubs and beer halls are understandably the city's favorite form of nighttime entertainment. These days, however, authentic pub experiences are restricted to the suburbs and outlying metro stops; nearly everything in central Prague has been overrun by tourists. Prague is not a clubbing city, although there are enough dance clubs pumping out ABBA and techno to satisfy any Eurotrash cravings; more popular are the city's many excellent jazz and rock clubs. Otherwise, you can always retreat to the Charles Bridge to sing along with aspiring Britpop guitarists into the wee hours. The monthly *Amigo* (15Kč) is the most thorough guide to gay life in the Czech Republic.

BARS

▇ **U Fleků,** Křemencova 11 (tel. 24 91 51 18). Metro B: Národní třída; turn right on Spálená, away from Národní, right on Myslíkova, and right on Křemencova. The oldest brewhouse in Prague (1491). A steep 50Kč per 0.4L of beer. Open daily 9am-11pm.

▇ **Kozička** (The Little Goat), Kozí 1 (tel 24 81 83 08). Metro A: Staroměstské nám.; take Dlouhá from northeast corner of the square, bear right onto Kozí, and look for the iron goat. This giant cellar bar is always packed, and you'll know why after your first 0.5L of *Krušovice* (25Kč). Open M-F noon-4am, Sa-Su 4pm-4am.

Vinárna U Sude, Vodičkova 10 (tel. 16 07 31 93). Metro A,B: Můstek; cross Václavské nám. to Vodičkova, follow the curve left, and it's on your left. Infinite labyrinth of cavernous cellars. Red wine 100Kč per 1L. Open M-F 11am-midnight, Sa-Su 2pm-midnight.

ABSINTHE BUT NOT FORGOTTEN

Shrouded in Bohemian mystique and taboo, this translucent turquoise fire-water is a force to be reckoned with. Although absinthe has been banned in all but three countries this century due to allegations of opium-lacing and fatal hallucinations, Czechs have had a long love affair with the liquor. It has been the mainstay spirit of the Prague intelligentsia since Kafka's days, and during WWII every Czech adult was rationed 0.5 liters per month. Today, backpackers, who apparently will drink anything, have discovered the liquor, which at its strongest can be 160 proof. The bravest and most seasoned expats sip it on the rocks, but for the most snapshot-worthy ritual douse a spoonful of sugar in the alcohol, torch it with a match until the sugar caramelizes and the alcohol burns off, and dump the residue into your glass.

Café Marquis de Sade, a.k.a. **Café Babylon,** Templová 8 (cellular tel. (0602) 25 59 37). Metro B: Nám Republiky. Between Nám. Republiky and Staroměstské nám. Republiky. Band does 80s pop or jazz. Beer 25Kč. Open M-F noon-2am, Sa-Su 3pm-2am.

Újezd, Újezd 18 (tel. 53 83 62). Metro B: Národní třída; exit onto Národní, turn left toward the river, cross the Legií bridge, continue straight on Vítězná, turn right on Újezd. Mecca of mellowness. DJ or live acid jazz 3 times a week. Open daily 6pm-4am.

Molly Malone's, U obecního dvora 4. Metro A: Staroměstská; turn right on Křižonvická away from the Charles Bridge, turn right after Nám. Jana Palacha on Široká, which veers left and becomes Vězeňská, and turn left at the end. *Staropramen* 30Kč; pint of Guinness 70Kč (cheaper than in Ireland). Open Su-Th noon-1am, F-Sa noon-2am.

Jáma (The Hollow), V jámě 7 (tel. 24 22 23 83). Metro A,C: Muzeum. Hidden off Vodičkova. The closest thing Prague has to a real sports bar, Jáma attracts a diverse but largely foreign crowd. Happy Hour 3-6pm. Open daily 11am-1am.

CLUBS AND DISCOS

Roxy, Dlouhá 33 (tel. 231 63 31). Metro B: Nám. Republiky; walk up Revoluční toward the river and turn left on Dlouhá. Hip locals and in-the-know tourists come here for experimental DJs and endless dancing. Cover from 50Kč. Open Tu-Su 8pm-late.

Radost FX, Bělehradská 120 (tel. 25 69 98). Metro C: I.P. Pavlova. Heavily touristed, but still plays bad-ass techno, jungle, and house music to a full house. *Staropramen* 35Kč. Cover from 50Kč. Open daily 8pm-dawn. Restaurant upstairs open until 5am.

Lávka, Novotného lávka 1 (tel. 24 21 47 97). Tourists from around the world make Prague memories under the Charles Bridge. Cover from 50Kč. Open daily 10pm-5am.

U staré paní, Michalská 9 (tel. 24 23 06 71). Metro A,B: Můstek; walk down Na můstku at the end of Václavské nám. (continue on Melantrichova), turn left on Havelská, then right on Michalská. Some of Prague's finest jazz vocalists in a dark and classy venue. Shows nightly 9pm-midnight. Cover 160Kč, includes a free drink. Open daily 7pm-4am.

U střelce, Karolíny Světlé 12 (tel. 24 23 82 78). Metro B: Národní třída. Under the archway on the right. Gay club that pulls a diverse crowd for its F and Sa night cabarets. Beer 25Kč. Cover 100Kč. Open Tu and Th 9pm-midnight, W and F-Sa 9:30pm-5am.

A Club, Milíčova 25. Metro C: Hlavní nádraží. Take tram 5 toward Harfa, 9 toward Spojovací, or 26 toward Nádraží Hostivař; get off at Lipanská. Walk back down Seifertova and turn right on Milíčova. A nightspot for lesbians, but men come too. Disco in the back starts at 10pm, but don't come before midnight. Beer 20Kč. Open daily 7pm-dawn.

⊠ EXCURSIONS FROM PRAGUE

KARLŠTEJN. A patriotic gem of the Bohemian countryside, Karlštejn is a walled and turreted fortress built by Charles IV to house his crown jewels and holy relics. (Tel. (0311) 684 617. Open Tu-Su July-Aug. 9am-6pm; Apr. and Sept.-Oct. 9am-4pm; Mar. 9am-3pm; May-June 9am-5pm. Tours in English every 2hr., 200Kč, students 100Kč.) The **Chapel of the Holy Cross** is decorated with more than 2000 inlaid precious stones and 128 apocalyptic paintings by medieval Master Theodorik. (Open

Tu-Su 9am-5pm. Tours in English 90Kč.) Ask at tourist info in Prague if they've finished restoring the chapel before setting out. Karlštejn is most easily reached by train from **Hlavní nádraží** or **Praha-Smíchov** (45min., 20Kč). Turn right out of the train station, take a left over the modern bridge, and walk 2min. to the village.

TEREZÍN (THERESIENSTADT). In 1941 Terezín became a concentration camp for Jews—by 1942, the entire pre-war civilian population had been evacuated. Jews were deported here from all over the *Reich*. Nazi propaganda films successfully touted the area as an almost idyllic spa resort where Jews were "allowed" to educate their young, partake in arts and recreation, and live a "fulfilling" life. In reality, 35,000 died here, some of starvation and disease, others at the hands of brutal guards; 85,000 others were transported to death camps in the east, primarily Auschwitz. The **Ghetto Museum,** on Komenského, in the town itself, sets Terezín in the wider Nazi context. (Tel. (0416) 782 577. Open daily May-Sept. 9am-6pm; Oct.-Apr. 9am-5:30pm. 100Kč, students 70Kč; including Small Fortress 120Kč, 80Kč. Tours in English 240Kč.) East of the town and across the river sits the **Small Fortress** (Malá Peunost), which you can explore freely. (Open daily May-Sept. 8am-6pm; Oct.-Apr. 8am-4:30pm.) The furnaces and autopsy lab at the **Jewish cemetery** and **crematorium** are as they were 50 years ago, with the addition of tributes left by the victims' ancestors. Men should cover their heads in respect. (Open Mar.-Nov. Su-F 10am-5pm.) The **bus** from **Prague's Florenc station** (1hr., every 1-2hr., 20Kč) stops by the central square, where the **tourist office** sells a map (25Kč). (Open daily until 6pm.)

KUTNÁ HORA. East of Prague, the former mining town of Kutná Hora (Mining Mountain) has a history as morbid as the bone church that has made the city famous. After 13th-century monks sprinkled soil from the Biblical Golgotha Cemetery on Kutná Hora's own cemetery, the rich and superstitious grew quite keen to be buried there, and it soon became overcrowded. Neighbors started to complain about the stench by the 15th century, so the Cistercian order built a chapel and started cramming in bodies. In a fit of whimsy, the monk in charge began designing flowers out of pelvi and crania. He never finished, but the artist František Rint eventually completed the project in 1870 with flying butt-bones, femur crosses, and a grotesque chandelier made from every bone in the human body. (Open daily Apr.-Sept. 8am-noon and 1-6pm, Oct. 9am-noon and 1-5pm, Nov.-Mar. 9am-noon and 1-4pm. 35Kč, students 20Kč.) Take a **bus** (1½hr.) from Prague's Florenc station, then walk or take a local bus to Sedlec Tabák (2km) and follow the signs.

ČESKÝ RAJ NATIONAL PRESERVE. The sandstone **Prachou rocks** (Prachovské skály) in the 2.4 sq. km Český Raj National Preserve were formed by the sedimentation of sandstone, marl, and slate on the bottom of the Mesozoic sea. High, narrow towers and pillars separated by deep, cramped gorges make for stellar climbing and hiking and stunning views. The rocks also boast the ruins of the 14th-century rock castle **Pařez.** (Open daily 9am-5pm; swimming in rock pond May-Aug. 20Kč, students 10Kč.) **Buses** run from Prague's Florenc station to Jičin (1½hr., every hr., 50Kč), from which other buses go to **Prachovské skály** and **Český Ráj** (30min., every hr., 17Kč). You can also walk 8km to the park along a fairly easy yellow trail that starts at the Runcjas Motel in Jičin. From Valdštejn nám., turn onto Palackého, go left on Jiraskova (which turns into Kollárova), bear right at the bus stop at Prachovské skály, and walk 10min. to the ticket office by the rocks.

BOHEMIA

Bursting at the seams with curative springs, West Bohemia is the Czech mecca for those in search of a good bath. Over the centuries, emperors and intellectuals have soaked in the waters of Karlovy Vary (Carlsbad in German). South Bohemia is a rustic Eden, a scenic ensemble of scattered villages, unspoiled brooks, virgin forests, and castle ruins. Low hills and plentiful attractions have made the region a favorite for wildlife-watching, castle-traipsing, *Budvar*-guzzling cyclists.

KARLOVY VARY

A stroll into Karlovy Vary's spa district or up into the hills reveals why this lovely town developed into one of the great "salons" of Europe, frequented by Johann Sebastian Bach, Peter the Great, Sigmund Freud, and Karl Marx. It was once a vacation spot for Holy Roman Emperor Karel IV; these days, older Germans seeking the therapeutic powers of the springs are the main vacationers.

⚡︎❲❳ PRACTICAL INFO, ACCOMMODATIONS, AND FOOD. Trains go from **Horní nádraží,** on the west side of town, to Prague (4½hr. plus a 1-2hr. layover in Chomutov, 5 per day, 126Kč). From the station, take bus 11 or 13 (6Kč) to the end. Faster **buses** zoom from **Dolní nádraží,** on Západní, to Prague (2½hr., 25 per day, 100Kč). Buy tickets at the **ČSAD office,** just before Západní runs into Nám. Republiky. (Open M-F 6am-6pm, Sa 7:30am-12:30pm.) To get to the center from the bus station, turn left on Západní, continue past the Becher building, and bear right on Masaryka, which runs parallel to Bechera, the other main thoroughfare. **City-Info,** in a white booth on Masaryka across from the post office, books **private rooms** from 450Kč. (Tel. (017) 322 33 51; fax 322 57 61. Open M-F 9am-12:45pm and 1:30-5pm, Sa 8am-12:45pm and 1:30-5pm, Su 10am-12:45pm and 1:30-4pm.) **Karlovarský Autorent,** Nám. Dr. Horákové 18, books doubles in private homes for 900Kč. (Tel. (017) 322 28 33. Open in summer M-F 9am-5pm, Sa 9am-noon; off-season closed noon-1pm.) Follow the directions from the bus and train stations to T.G. Masaryka and bear right at the post office to find **Pension Kosmos,** Zahradní 39, in the center of the spa district. (Tel./fax (017) 322 31 68. Singles 440-750Kč; doubles 720-1340Kč.) Luxurious **Pension Romania,** Zahradní 49, is next to the post office at the intersection with T.G. Masaryka. (Tel. (017) 322 28 22. 895Kč per person, students 717Kč. Breakfast included.) Try the sweet *oplatky* (spa wafers) for which Karlovy Vary is known at a street vendor (8Kč). The almost ▨ **Vegetarian Restaurant,** I.P. Pavlova 25, has great veggie dishes. (Tel. (017) 322 90 21. Goulash and dumplings 40Kč; beer from 9Kč. Open daily 11am-9pm.) A **supermarket,** Horova 1, is in the large building with the "Městská tržnice" sign over the local bus station. (Open M-F 6am-7pm, Sa 7am-5pm, Su 10am-6pm. V, MC.) **Postal code:** 360 01.

▨❐ SIGHTS AND ENTERTAINMENT. The spa district officially begins with the Victorian **Bath 5** (Lázně 5), Smetanovy Sady 1, across the street from the post office and marked by flowers displaying the numerical date. Thermal baths (300Kč) and underwater massages (420Kč) are among the blessings offered. (Open M-F 8am-9pm, Sa 8am-6pm, Su 10am-6pm. Massages M-F 3-9pm, Sa-Su 10am-6pm.) The pedestrian **Mlýnské nábř.** meanders alongside the Teplá beneath shady trees. **Bath 3** lies to the right, just before **Freedom Spring** (Pramen svobody). Next door, the imposing **Mill Collonade** (Mlýnská kolonáda) shelters five different springs. Crossing the Teplá to the steps of the Baroque **Church of St. Mary Magdalene** gets you a good view of the **Zawojski House,** Trižiště 9, now the Živnostenská Banka, a gorgeous cream-and-gold Art Nouveau building. Also across the river, the **Vřídlo spring** (*Sprudel* to the Germans) inside the **Vřídlo Collonade** (Vřídelni kolonáda) shoots 30L of 72°C water into the air each second. Follow Stará Louka until signs point you to the **funicular,** which leads up to the 555-meter-high **Diana Observatory** (Rozhledna) and a magnificent panorama of the city. (Funicular runs every 15min. 9am-6pm; 25Kč, round-trip 40Kč. Tower closes 6:30pm; 10Kč.) **Propaganda,** Jaltská 5, off Bechera, attracts Karlovy Vary's hippest and youngest crowd with live music and a trendy blue-steel interior. (Drinks from 20Kč. Open M-Th 5pm-3am, F-Sa 5pm-6am, Su 5pm-2am.)

ČESKÉ BUDĚJOVICE

No amount of beer will ever help you correctly pronounce České Budějovice (CHESS-kay BOOD-yeh-yoh-vee-tsay). The town was known as Budweis in the 19th century, when it inspired the name of the popular but pale North American Budweiser, which bears little relation to the malty local *Budvar*. Surrounded by Renaissance and Baroque buildings, cobblestoned **Náměstí Přemysla Otakara II** is the largest square in the country. The 72m **Black Tower** (Černá věž) in one corner looms over the town. Beware: the treacherous stairs are difficult even for the sober. (Open Tu-Su July-Aug. 10am-7pm; Sept.-Nov. 9am-5pm; Mar.-June 10am-6pm. 10Kč.) From the station, walk right on Nádražní, turn left at the first crosswalk and follow the pedestrian street, Lannova třída, as it becomes Kanovnická and pours into the square. Tours of the city's most famous attraction, the **Budweiser Brewery,** Karoliny Svwtlé 4, can be arranged for groups of six or more through the tourist office. Take bus 2 or 4 from the center of town to the brewery.

Trains travel to Prague (2½hr., 110Kč) and Brno (4½hr., 126Kč). The TIC **tourist office,** Nám. Otakara II 26, books central private rooms from 300Kč. (Tel./fax (038) 635 25 89. Open May-Sept. M-F 8am-6pm, Sa 8am-3pm, Su 8am-1pm; Oct.-Apr. closes 1hr. earlier.) Sip *Budvar* at **X-Files@Internet Café,** Senovážné nám. 6. (30-40Kč per 30min. Open M-F 10am-10pm, Sa-Su 2-10pm.) From the bus station, opposite and to the left of the train station, take bus 1, 14, or 17 five stops to "U parku" and continue 150m along the side street that branches off to the right behind the bus stop to get to the friendly **Penzion U Výstaviště,** U Výstavištw 17. (Tel. (038) 724 01 48. First night 250Kč, subsequent nights 200Kč.) The University of South Bohemia **dorms** on Studentská are open to tourists in July and August. Take tram 1 from the bus station five stops to "U parku"; backtrack down Husova, then take the second right on Studentská. (Tel. (038) 777 44 00. Doubles 240-340Kč.) **Večerka grocery** is at Palackého 10; enter on Hroznova. (Open M-F 7am-8pm, Sa 7am-1pm, Su 8am-8pm.) Sample Czech cuisine at **Vinárna U paní Emy,** Široká 25, near the main square. (Tábor steak 95Kč, veggie dishes 50-70Kč.) **Postal code:** 370 01.

ČESKÝ KRUMLOV

The worst part about Český Krumlov is leaving. Winding medieval streets, cobblestoned promenades, and Bohemia's second-largest castle make the gorgeous, UNESCO-protected town of Český Krumlov one of the most popular spots in Eastern Europe. Come for a day, but you're destined to stay for forty.

∎∎∎ **PRACTICAL INFO, ACCOMMODATIONS, AND FOOD.** Frequent **buses** arrive from České Budějovice (45min., 8-22 per day, 22Kč). From the station, head to the upper street (near stops 20-25), turn right (with the station to your back), follow the small dirt path that veers left and heads uphill, turn right on Kaplická, cross the highway at the light, and head straight onto Horní, which brings you to Nám. Svornosti, where the **tourist office** in the town hall books pension rooms (from 550Kč) as well as cheaper private rooms. (Tel.

THIS BUD'S FOR EU Many Yankees, having tasted the malty goodness of a *Budvar* brew, return home to find it conspicuously unavailable. That *Budvar* was the Czech Republic's largest exporter of beer in 1995 makes its absence from American store shelves even stranger. Where's the love? The answer lies in a tale of trademarks and town names. České Budějovice (Budweis in German) had been brewing its own style of lager for centuries when the Anheuser-Busch brewery in St. Louis came out with its Budweiser-style beer in 1876. Not until the 1890s, however, did the Budějovice Pivovar (Brewery) begin producing a beer labeled "Budweiser." International trademark conflicts ensued, and in 1911 the companies signed a noncompetition agreement: *Budvar* got markets in Europe and Anheuser-Busch took North America. But a few years ago, Anheuser-Busch attempted to buy a controlling interest in the makers of *Budvar*, to which the Czech government summarily replied: "nyeh." In retaliation, Anheuser-Busch didn't order its normal one-third of the Czech hop crop the following year, and is also suing for trademark infringement in Finland. Meanwhile, *Budvar* is lobbying to make the "Budweiser" a designation as exclusive as that of "Champagne," meaning that any brand sold in the EU under that name would have to come from the Budweiser region. As long as the battle continues on European fronts, there is little chance that a *Budvar* in America will be anything but an illegal alien.

(0337) 71 11 83. Open daily 9am-6pm.) Log onto the **internet** at **Europe Info Centrum**, Horní 155. (50Kč per hr. Open M-F 9am-6pm.) To get to the awesome ▨ **U vodníka**, Po vodě 55, or ▨ **Krumlov House**, Rooseveltova 68, both run by an American expat couple, follow the directions above from the station and turn left onto Rooseveltova after the light (just before the bridge). From there, follow the signs to U vodníka or continue down the street to Krumlov House. (Tel. (0337) 71 19 35; email vodnik@ck.bohem-net.cz. Dorms 200Kč; doubles 500Kč. Laundry. Bike rental.) To get to **Hostel Skippy**, Plešivecká 123, follow the directions above from the station, but turn left at the light onto the highway, cross the river, and bear right on Plešivecká. (Tel. (0337) 72 83 80. 175Kč. Laundry. Bike rental.) Get spicy gypsy goulash (53Kč) at **Cikánská jízba** (Gypsy Bar), Dlouhá 31. (Open M-Th 2-11pm, F-Sa 3-11pm.) Get **groceries** at **SPAR**, Linecká 49. (Open M-Sa 7am-6pm, Su 9am-6pm.) **Postal code:** 381 01.

▨ ▨ **SIGHTS AND ENTERTAINMENT.** The stone courtyards of the **castle**, perched high above the town, are free to the public. Two tours cover different parts of the lavish interior, including a frescoed ballroom, a splendid Baroque theater, and Renaissance-style rooms. The **galleries of the crypts** showcase local artists' sculptures and ceramics. Ascend the 162 steps of the **tower** for a fabulous view. (Castle open June-Aug. Tu-Su 9am-noon and 1-5pm; May and Sept. Tu-Su 9am-noon and 1-4pm; Apr. and Oct. Tu-Su 9am-noon and 1-3pm; one-hour tours in English 110Kč, students 55Kč. Crypts open May-Oct. Tu-Su 10am-5pm; 30Kč, students 20Kč. Tower open daily May-Sept. 9am-6pm; Apr. and Oct. 9am-5pm; 25Kč, students 15Kč.) The Austrian painter Egon Schiele (1890-1918) lived in Český Krumlov for a while—until the citizens ran him out for painting burghers' daughters in the nude. Decades later, the **Egon Schiele International Cultural Center**, Široká 70-72, displays his work along with paintings by other 20th-century Central European artists. (Open daily 10am-6pm. 120Kč, students 80Kč.) Borrow an **inner tube** from your hostel to spend a lazy day drifting down the Vltava, or hike up into the hills to go **horseback riding** at Jezdecký klub Slupenec, Slupenec 1; from the center, follow Horní to the highway, take the second left on Křížová, and follow the red trail up to Slupenec. (Tel. (0337) 71 10 53. Open Tu-Sa 9am-noon and 1:30-5:30pm. 220Kč per hr. Call ahead.) Rent a **bike** (300Kč per day) from **Globtour Vltava**, Kájovská 62, to cruise the Bohemian countryside (the 1263 monastery **Zlatá Koruna** makes a great trip). Throw 'em back at **U Hada** (Snake Bar), Rybarška 37 (open M-Th 7pm-3am, F-Sa 7pm-4am) or **Myší díra Kat** (Mousehole, a.k.a. The Boat Bar), down the steps to the river from Barbakan at Horní 29 (open in summer only).

MORAVIA

Wine-making Moravia makes up the easternmost third of the Czech Republic. Home of the country's finest folk-singing tradition and two of its leading universities, it's also the birthplace of a number of notables, including Tomáš G. Masaryk, founder and first president of Czechoslovakia, and psychoanalyst Sigmund Freud. Gregor Mendel founded modern genetics in his pea-garden in a Brno monastery.

BRNO

Second city of the Czech Republic, Brno (berh-NO) is a mecca of business and industry, and its streets show it: scores of "erotic club" sirens call out to lonely men, and restaurant prices have corporate expense accounts in mind. The city does offer an extensive array of Gothic and Baroque churches, splendidly cheap opera, and amazing ice cream. There are more exciting and beautiful places to visit in the Czech Republic, but Brno lets travelers experience a living Czech city.

▨ ▨ ▨ **PRACTICAL INFO, ACCOMMODATIONS, AND FOOD. Trains** (tel. (05) 42 21 48 03) go to Bratislava (2hr., 9 per day, 99Kč); Vienna (2hr., 1 per day, 415Kč); Prague (3hr., 12 per day, 220Kč); Budapest (4½hr., 2 per day, 768Kč); and České Budějovice (4½hr., 3 per day, 140Kč). From the main exit, cross the three tram lines on Nádražní to Masarykova to reach the main square, **Nám. Svobody. Buses** (tel. (05) 43 21 77 33) leave from Zvonařka, down Plotní from the train station, for Vienna (2½hr., 2 per day, 250Kč) and Prague (3hr., 120Kč). To get from the bus to the train station, take the pedestrian path at the far corner to the giant Tesco and under the train station. The tourist office, **Kulturní a informační centrum města Brna,** Radnická 8, off Zelný trh, books rooms (from 400Kč) and hostels (200Kč). Follow the directions above from the train station, then take a left off Masarykova on Květinářska just before Svobody. (Tel. (05) 42 21 10 90; fax 42 21 07 58. Open M-F 8am-6pm, Sa-Su 9am-5pm.) **@InternetCafé** is at Lidická 17. (2Kč per min. Open M-F 10am-10pm, Sa-Su 2-10pm.) From the train station, head up Masarykova and turn right on Josefská, which leads to Novobranská and the new **Hotel Astorka,** at #3. (Tel. (05) 42 51 03 70; fax 42 51 01 06; email astorka@jamu.cz. Bed in a double 200Kč, in a triple 150Kč.) Take tram 9 or 12 from the train station to the end at "Komárov," continue on Hněvkovského, and turn left on the unmarked Pompova (the second-to-last turn before the railroad overpass) to find **Interservis (HI),** Lomená 48. (Tel. (05) 45 23 31 65; fax 33 11 65. Dorms 230Kč, nonmembers 265Kč; with breakfast 270Kč, 315Kč; doubles 575Kč. V, MC.) A **Tesco supermarket** is behind the train station. (Open M-F 7am-8pm, Sa 7am-6pm, Su 8am-5pm.) **Postal code:** 602 00.

📷 ♫ **SIGHTS AND ENTERTAINMENT.** If you like macabre morbidity, try the **Capuchin Monastery Crypt** (Hrobka Kapucínského kláštera), just left of Masarykova from the train station, where monks have embalmed more than 100 of their 18th-century brothers. (Tel. 42 21 23 32. Open M-Sa 9am-noon and 2-4:30pm, Su 11-11:45am and 2-4:30pm. 40Kč, students 20Kč.) On Petrov Hill, just south of Zelný trh and across the square from the town hall, the bells of **Peter and Paul Cathedral** (Biskupská katedrála sv. Petra a Pavla) strike noon at 11am. Allegedly Brno was saved from the Swedish siege one day in 1645, when the besieging general told his army he would withdraw if they hadn't captured the town by noon. The folks of Brno rang the bells early, and the Swedes slunk away. The entrance to the **crypt** is around the back. (Cathedral and tower open daily 10am-6pm; tower 20Kč, students 15Kč. Crypt open daily 10am-6pm; 10Kč, 7Kč.) In the heart of Old Brno, the High Gothic **Basilica of the Assumption of the Virgin Mary** (Basilika Nanebevzetí Panny Marie) houses the 13th-century Black Madonna, the Czech Republic's oldest wooden icon, which supposedly held off the Swedes in 1645. (Open daily 5-7:15pm, Su also 7am-12:15pm.) The monastery next door was home to **Gregor Mendel,** father of modern genetics. The **Mendelianum,** Mendlovo nám. 1a, documents his life and work. (Open daily July-Aug. 9am-6pm; Sept.-June 8am-5pm. 8Kč, students 4Kč.)

🎏 **EXCURSION FROM BRNO OR ČESKÉ BUDĚJOVICE: TELČ.** The Italian aura of Telč (TELCH) is a result of the trip the town's ruler took to Genoa in 1546—and the battalion of Italian artists and craftsmen he brought back with him. As you step over the cobblestoned footbridge to the main square—flanked by long arcades of peach gables, lime-green Baroque bays, and time-worn terracotta roofs—it's easy to see why UNESCO designated the gingerbread town a World Heritage Monument. Browse the porticos for Bohemian glass figurines, watch the children from neighboring towns sing folk songs and dance in traditional Czech attire every Sunday, and definitely don't miss a tour of the castles: *trasa A* leads you through Renaissance hallways, through the old chapel, and under extravagant ceilings; *trasa B* leads through rooms decorated in later styles. (Open Tu-Su May-Aug. 9-11:30am and 1-6pm; Apr. and Sept.-Oct. 9am-noon and 1-5pm. Each tour 45min.; 50Kč, students 25Kč; foreign-language guide 100Kč.) You can rent a **rowboat** from **Půjčovná lodí,** on the shore, to view the castle and town from the swan-filled lake. (Open June 20-Aug. daily 10am-7pm. 20Kč per 30min.) **Buses** running between Brno and České Budějovice stop at Telč (2hr., 7 per day, 65-75Kč). From the station, follow the pedestrian path, turn right on Tyršova, then left on Masarykovo, and pass under the archway on the right to reach the square, Nám. Zachariáše z Hradce (5min.). The **tourist office,** Nám. Zachariáše z Hradce 1, in Mwstský uľad (town hall), books private rooms (200-400Kč).

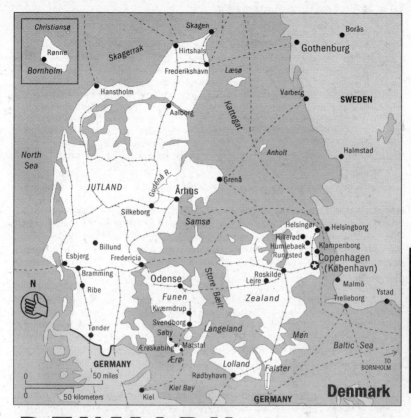

DENMARK (DANMARK)

US$1 = 7.14KR (DANISH KRONER)	10KR = US$1.40
CDN$1 = 4.86KR	10KR = CDN$2.06
UK£1 = 11.49KR	10KR = UK£0.87
IR£1 = 9.44KR	10KR = IR£1.06
AUS$1 = 4.69KR	10KR = AUS$2.13
NZ$1 = 3.82KR	10KR = NZ$2.62
SAR1 = 1.18KR	10KR = SAR8.49
EUR€1 = 7.43KR	10KR = EUR€1.34

PHONE CODE Country code: 45. International dialing prefix: 00.

Like Thumbelina, the heroine of native son Hans Christian Andersen's fairy tales, Denmark has a tremendous personality crammed into a tiny body. Danes delight in their eccentric traditions, such as burning witches in effigy on Midsummer's Eve, dancing around the Christmas tree, and eating pickled herring on New Year's Day. Although Danes are justifiably proud of their fertile farmlands, beech forests, chalk cliffs, and sand dunes, their sense of self-criticism is reflected in the Danish literary canon: the more famous voices are Søren Kirkegaard, Hans Christian Andersen, and Isak Dinesen. With its Viking past centuries behind it, Denmark now has one of the most comprehensive social welfare structures in the world (made possible by very high taxes), and liberal immigration policies in the past few decades have diversified the erstwhile homogeneous blond-haired, blue-eyed population.

Wedged between Sweden and Germany, the country is the cultural and geographic bridge between Scandinavia and continental Europe. From the 13th to 16th centuries, the Danish crown ruled an empire uniting Norway, Sweden, Iceland, and parts of Germany. Christianity, the Protestant Reformation, and the socialist movements of the late 19th century entered Scandinavia via Denmark. During WWI, Denmark remained neutral, and in 1940 the Danes capitulated to Hitler rather than risk a full invasion; however, they also smuggled 7000 Danish Jews into neutral Sweden. Today, Denmark has a progressive youth culture that beckons travelers to the pristine beaches of Funen and the hip pub scene in Copenhagen. Home to the famous beers Carlsberg and Tuborg, as well mouthwatering pastry, this just, gentle country knows how to have a good time. Contrary to the suggestion of a certain English playwright, very little seems to be rotten in the state of Denmark.

DISCOVER DENMARK

Begin to explore Denmark in chic and progressive **Copenhagen,** where you can muse about Kierkegaardian philosophy over coffee (p. 251). For the best beaches in Denmark, take a ferry over to the island of **Bornholm** (p. 259), between Sweden and Estonia. Then shoot south to **Roskilde** and the fascinating Viking Ship Museum; if you time it right, you'll hit the massive Roskilde Festival, when rock takes over the city (p. 258). Move west over the new bridge, Storebæltsbro, to the island of Funen and **Odense** (p. 260), the hometown of Hans Christian Andersen, then head south to the stunning 16th-century castle **Egeskov Slot** (p. 261). From the southern end of Funen, hop on a ferry to the idyllic island of **Ærø** (p. 261), a throwback to the Denmark of several centuries ago. Cross the Lillebælt to Jutland, where laid-back **Århus** delights with students and culture (p. 262), then play with blocks at nearby **Legoland** (p. 263). On your way back down south, stop in historic **Ribe** (p. 265).

GETTING THERE AND GETTING AROUND

BY PLANE. The airport in **Copenhagen** handles international flights from cities around the world, mostly by SAS, Delta, United, British Airways, Air France, KLM, Lufthansa, and Swissair. **Billund Airport** in Jutland handles flights to other European cities. SAS (Scandinavian Airlines; US tel. (800) 437-5804), the national airline company, offers youth, spouse, and senior discounts to some destinations.

BY TRAIN AND BY BUS. Eurail is valid on all state-run **DSB** routes. The *buy-in-Scandinavia* **Scanrail Pass** allows five days within 15 (1390kr, under 26 1040kr) or 21 consecutive days (2110kr, under 26 1585kr) of unlimited rail travel through Denmark, Norway, Sweden, and Finland, as well as many free or 20-50% discounted ferry rides. This differs from the *buy-outside-Scandinavia* **Scanrail Pass** (see p. 61). Seat reservations, compulsory on many international trains (20-68kr), can be made at central stations or by phone. For domestic info, call 70 13 14 15; for international info, 70 13 14 16. Remote towns are typically served by **buses** from the nearest train station. The national **bus** network is also very reliable and fairly cheap.

BY FERRY. Railpasses earn discounts or free rides on many Scandinavian ferries. The free *Vi Rejser* newspaper, at tourist offices, can help you sort out the dozens of smaller ferries that serve Denmark's outlying islands. For info on ferries from **Copenhagen** to **Norway, Sweden, Poland,** and **Bornholm,** see p. 251. Bornholm is also served by other international ferry routes (see p. 259). **Ærø,** reachable by boat from southern Funen (see p. 261), is connected by boat to **Kiel, Germany** (see p. 261). For more on connections from **Jutland** to **England, Sweden,** and **Norway,** see p. 262.

BY CAR. Roads are **toll-free,** except for the **Storebæltsbro** (Great Belt Bridge; 210kr). **Car rental** is generally around US$75 per day, plus insurance and a per-kilometer fee; to rent a car, you must be at least 20 years old (in some cases even 25). Speed limits are 50km per hr. (30mph) in urban areas, 80km per hr. (50mph) on highways, and 110km per hr. (68mph) on motorways. **Service centers** for motorists, called Info-terias, are spaced along Danish highways. Most **gas stations** in Denmark are open for self-service from 6 or 7am to 9pm or midnight; gas averages 6.50kr per liter. When driving, watch out for bikes, which have the right-of-way. For more info on driving in Denmark, contact the **Forenede Danske Motorejere (FDM),** Firskovvej 32, Box 500, DK-2800 Lyngby (tel. 45 27 07 07; fax 45 27 09 93; www.fdm.dk).

BY BIKE AND BY THUMB. Flat terrain, well-marked bike routes, bike paths in the countryside, and bike lanes in towns and cities make Denmark a cyclist's dream. You can **rent bikes** (40-55kr per day) from some tourist offices, rental shops, and a few train stations in North Zealand. The **Dansk Cyklist Førbund** (Danish Cycle Federation), Rømersg. 7, 1362 Copenhagen K (tel. 33 32 31 21; fax 33 32 76 83; www.dcf.dk), can hook you up with longer-term rentals. For info on bringing your bike on a train (which costs 50kr or less), pick up *Bikes and Trains* at any train station. **Hitchhiking** is legal in Denmark, but is, as usual, risky.

ESSENTIALS

DOCUMENTS AND FORMALITIES. South Africans need a **visa** to enter Denmark for tourist visits; nationals of Australia, Canada, New Zealand, and the US do not, provided they stay for fewer than three months.

Danish Embassies at Home: Australia, 15 Hunter St, Yarralumla, ACT 2600 (tel. (02) 62 73 21 95; fax 62 73 38 64); **Canada,** 47 Clarence St, #450, Ottawa, ON K1N 9K1 (tel. (613) 562-1811; fax 562-1812); **Ireland,** 121 St. Stephen's Green, Dublin 2 (tel. (01) 475 64 04; fax 478 45 36); **New Zealand,** 273 Bleakhouse Rd, Howick, P.O. Box 619, Auckland 1 (tel. (09) 537 30 99; fax 537 30 67); **South Africa,** 8th fl., Sanlam Centre, corner of Pretorius and Andries St; P.O. Box 2942, Pretoria 0001 (tel. (012) 322 05 95; fax 322 05 96); **UK,** 55 Sloane St, London SW1X 9SR (tel. (020) 73 33 02 00; fax 73 33 02 70; www.denmark.org.uk); **US,** 3200 Whitehaven St NW, Washington, DC 20008 (tel. (202) 234-4300; fax 328-1470; www.denmarkemb.org).

Foreign Embassies in Denmark: All foreign embassies are in **Copenhagen** (see p. 252).

TOURIST OFFICES. Contact the main tourist board in Denmark at Vesterbrogade 6D, 1620 Copenhagen V (tel. 33 11 14 15; fax 33 93 14 16; email dt@dt.dk). **Use It** in Copenhagen offers many excellent services (see p. 252).

Tourist Boards at Home: US, 655 Third Ave, New York, NY 10017 (tel. (212) 885-9700; fax 885-9710); **UK,** 55 Sloane St, London SW1X 9SY (tel. (020) 72 59 59 59; fax 72 59 59 55).

MONEY. The Danish unit of currency is the **kroner** (kr), divided into 100 *øre*. Like all of Scandinavia, Denmark has a high cost of living; expect to spend from US$30 (hostels and supermarkets) to US$60 (cheap hotels and restaurants) per day. Take advantage of buffet restaurants, which offer money-saving all-you-can-eat buffet lunches for around 50kr. The easiest way to get cash is from **ATMs: Cirrus** and **PLUS** cash cards are widely accepted, and many machines give advances on credit cards.

Tipping: There are no hard and fast rules, but it's always polite to round up to the nearest 10kr in restaurants and for taxis. In general, service at restaurants is included in the bill.

Taxes: Denmark has one of the highest **Value Added Taxes** in Europe, a flat 25% on just about everything except food. You can get a VAT refund upon leaving the country if you have spent at least US$95 in one store.

COMMUNICATION

Post: Mailing a **postcard/letter** to Australia, Canada, New Zealand, the US, or South Africa costs 5.50kr; to elsewhere in Europe, 4.50kr. Postage on domestic mail is 4kr.

Telephone: There are no separate city codes; include all digits for local *and* international calls. Buy **phone cards** at post offices or kiosks (30 units 30kr; 53 units 50kr; 110 units 100kr). For **domestic directory info,** call 118; **international info,** 113; **collect calls,** 141. **International direct dial** numbers include: **AT&T,** 80 01 00 10; **Sprint,** 80 01 08 77; **MCI WorldPhone Direct,** 80 01 00 22; **Canada Direct,** 80 01 00 11; **BT Direct,** 80

01 02 90; **Ireland Direct,** 80 01 03 53; **Australia Direct,** 80 01 00 61; **Telecom New Zealand,** 80 01 00 64; and **Telkom South Africa,** 80 01 00 27. **Emergency,** tel. 112.

Language: Danish. The Danish add æ (like the "e" in "egg"), ø (like the "i" in "first"), and å (sometimes written as aa; like the "o" in "lord") to the end of the alphabet; thus Århus would follow Viborg in an alphabetical listing of cities. Knowing *ikke* ("not") will help you figure out such signs as "No smoking" *(ikke-ryger); åben/lukket* (O-ben/loock-eh) means open/closed. Nearly all Danes speak flawless English, but a few Danish words might help break the ice: try *skål* (skoal), or "cheers." Danish has a distinctive glottal stop known as a *stød.* To gain limited insight into the Danish language, see p. 949.

ACCOMMODATIONS AND CAMPING. While Denmark's hotels are generally expensive (250-850kr per night), the country's 101 **HI youth hostels** *(vandrerhjem)* are cheap (less than 100kr per night; nonmembers add 25kr), well-run, and have no age limit. The one- to five-star rating system doesn't take lovely settings, friendly owners, or serendipitous encounters into account, but higher-rated hostels may have in-room bathrooms and longer opening hours. Sheets cost about 35kr more. All-you-can-eat breakfasts usually run 38kr. Reception desks normally take a break between noon and 4pm and close for the day between 9 and 11pm. Reservations are required in winter and highly recommended in summer, especially near beaches. For more info, contact the **Danish Youth Hostel Association** (tel. 31 31 36 12; fax 31 31 36 26; email ldv@danhostel.dk; www.danhostel.dk). Many tourist offices book rooms in **private homes** (125-175kr), which are often in suburbs.

Denmark's 525 official **campgrounds** (about 60kr per person) rank from one-star (toilets and drinking water) to three-star (showers and laundry) to five-star (swimming, restaurants, and stoves). You'll either need a Danish **camping pass,** available at all campgrounds and valid for one year (45kr, families 75kr, groups 120kr) or an **international camping card.** The **Danish Camping Council** *(Campingradet;* tel. 39 27 80 44) sells a campground handbook *(Camping Denmark)* and passes. The Danish Youth Hostel Association's free *Camping/Youth and Family Hostels* is also adequate. Sleeping in train stations, in parks, and on public property is illegal.

FOOD AND DRINK. A "Danish" in Denmark is a *wienerbrød* ("Viennese bread"), found in bakeries alongside other flaky treats. For more substantial fare, Danes favor small, open-faced sandwiches called *smørrebrød.* For cheap eats, look for lunch specials *(dagens ret)* and all-you-can-eat buffets *(spis alt du kan* or *tag selv buffet).* Beer *(Øl)* is usually served as a *lille* or *stor fadøl* (0.25L or 0.5L draft), but bottled beer tends to be cheaper. National brews are Carlsberg and Tuborg. The drinking age in bars in Denmark is 18, but many clubs have higher age limits; you must be 15 to buy beer and wine in stores. Many **vegetarian** *(vegetarret)* options are the result of Indian and Mediterranean influences, but salads and veggies *(grøntsaker)* can be found on most menus. For more on being veggie in Denmark, contact **Dansk Vegetarforening,** Borups Allé 131, 2000 Frederiksberg (tel. 38 34 24 48).

LOCAL FACTS

Time: Denmark is 2hr. ahead of Greenwich Mean Time (GMT; see p. 49).

Climate: Denmark's climate is more solar than polar, and more dry than wet. The four seasons are distinct and winters relatively mild.

Hours: Shop hours are normally M-Th from about 9 or 10am to 6pm, and F until 7 or 8pm; they are also usually open Sa mornings (Copenhagen shops stay open all day Sa). Regular **banking** hours are M-W and F 9:30am-4pm, Th 9:30am-6pm.

Holidays in 2000: Easter (Apr. 5); Common Prayer Day (Apr. 30); Ascension Day (May 13); Whit Sunday and Monday (May 23-24); Constitution Day (June 5); Midsummer (June 23-24); Christmas (Dec. 24-26); and New Year's Eve (Dec. 31).

Festivals: Danes celebrate **Fastelavn** (Carneval) in Feb. and Mar. In May, the **Copenhagen Jazz Festival** does a week of concerts, many free. The **Roskilde Festival** is an immense open-air music festival held in Roskilde in June (see p. 258)

COPENHAGEN (KØBENHAVN)

Despite the swan ponds and cobblestone clichés that Hans Christian Andersen's fairy-tale imagery brings to mind, Denmark's capital is a fast-paced modern city that offers cafés to rival Paris', nightlife to rival London's, and style to rival New York's—all at half the cost of Oslo or Stockholm. Some of the most beautiful (and best-dressed) people on the planet can be seen walking down Strøget, the pedestrian zone. Though studded with elaborate past and present royal palaces, Copenhagen is a cosmopolitan city where angelic blond children walk to school with their Inuit, Turkish, Greek, Vietnamese, and Ethiopian classmates. But if you are still craving Andersen's Copenhagen, the *Lille Havfrue* (Little Mermaid), Tivoli, and Nyhavn's Hanseatic gingerbread houses are also yours to discover.

 At the end of 1999, Copenhagen will change all phone numbers that begin with "31." Call toll-free 80 80 80 80 for the new numbers, but snag someone who speaks Danish to interpret the recording for you.

▐ GETTING THERE AND GETTING AROUND

Flights: Kastrup Airport (info tel. 32 47 47 47 or 32 54 17 01). S-trains connect the airport to Central Station (12min., every 20min., 16.50kr).

Trains: All trains stop at **Hovedbanegården.** For domestic schedules and reservations, call 70 13 14 15; for international travel, 70 13 14 16. To: **Hamburg** (4hr., 5 per day, 425kr, under 26 320kr); **Stockholm** (9hr., 4-5 per day, 700kr, under 26 540kr); **Oslo** (9hr., 3 per day, 740kr, under 26 530kr); and **Berlin** (9hr., 1 per day, 895kr, under 26 580kr). Seat **reservations** are required (20kr). For cheaper travel to **Gothenburg, Stockholm, Oslo,** and **Östersund, Sweden,** buy a **Scanrabat** ticket a week ahead (reservations mandatory). The **InterRail Center** in the station offers a lounge, phones, showers (10kr), a stove (no utensils), maps, free luggage storage, and free condoms to BIJ, Scanrail, and Eurail holders. Open June to mid-Sept. daily 6:30-10:30am and 4-10pm.

Public Transportation: For **bus** info, dial 36 13 14 15 (daily 7am-9:30pm); for **train** info, call 33 14 17 01 (daily 7am-9pm). **Buses** and **S-trains** (subways and suburban trains; run M-Sa 5am-12:30am, Su 6am-12:30am) operate on a zone system; 2 zones cover central Copenhagen, and 7 get you to Helsingør. 2-zone **tickets** run 11kr; add 5.50kr per additional zone. The cheaper **rabatkort** (rebate card), available from kiosks and bus drivers, gets you 10 "clips," each good for one journey within a specified number of zones; clip cards in the machines at the beginning of your journey. The blue 2-zone *rabatkort* (75kr) for travel around the city can be clipped more than once for longer trips. Tickets and clips allow 1hr. of transfers. The **24-hour pass** grants unlimited bus and train transport in greater Copenhagen (70kr); buy at the Tivoli tourist office or any train station. **Railpasses,** including **Eurail,** are good on S-trains but not buses. **Night buses** run on different routes during the remaining hours and charge double fare. A North Zealand public transport map (5kr) is available at the bus info center on Rådhauspladsen. The **Copenhagen Card,** sold in hotels, tourist offices, and train stations, grants unlimited travel in North Zealand, discounts on ferries to Sweden, and free admission to most sights (24-hour 155kr, 48-hour 255kr, 72-hour 320kr), but isn't always money-saving.

Ferries: Scandinavian Seaways (tel. 33 42 33 42; fax 33 42 33 41) departs daily at 5pm for **Oslo** (16hr., 480-735kr, under 26 315-570kr; Eurail and Scanrail 50% off). Trains to **Sweden** cross over on the **Helsingør-Helsingborg** ferry at no extra charge. Hourly **hydrofoils** (tel. 33 12 80 88) to **Malmö** go from Havnegade, at the end of Nyhavn (40min., 19-49kr). Both **Flyvebådene** and **Pilen** run hourly hydrofoils to Malmö from 9am-11pm (45min., 50kr). **Polferries** (tel. 33 11 46 45; fax 33 11 95 78) set out Su, M, and W 8am, and Th and F 7:30pm from Nordre Toldbod, 12A (off Esplanaden) to **Świnoujście, Poland** (10hr., 340kr, with ISIC 285kr). **Bornholmstrafikken** (tel. 33 13 18 66; fax 33 93 18 66) goes to **Bornholm** (7hr., 1-2 per day, 189kr).

Taxis: Tel. 35 35 35 35, 38 77 77 77, or 38 10 10 10. Base fare 22kr, plus 7.70kr per km 4am-4pm (9.60kr per km 7pm-7am). From Central Station to airport costs 150kr.

DENMARK

Bike Rental: The **City Bike** program lends out bikes for free. Deposit 20kr at any of 150 bike racks citywide and retrieve the coin upon return at any rack. **Københavns Cykler,** Reventlowsgade 11 (tel. 33 33 86 13), rents for 50kr per day, 225kr per week; 300kr deposit. Open July-Aug. M-F 8am-6pm, Sa 9am-1pm, Su 10am-1pm; Sept.-June closed Su.

Hitchhiking: Try **Use It's** ride boards (see **Tourist Office,** below) instead.

⊞ ORIENTATION AND PRACTICAL INFORMATION

Copenhagen lies on the east coast of the island of **Zealand** (Sjælland), just across the sound (Øresund) from Malmö, Sweden. Copenhagen's **Hovedbanegården** (Central Station) lies near the city's heart. One block north of the station, **Vesterbrogade** passes **Tivoli** and **Rådhuspladsen** (the central square and terminus of most bus lines) and then cuts through the city center as **Strøget** (STROY-yet), the world's longest pedestrian thoroughfare. Outlying districts fan out from the center: **Østerbro** is known as affluent, while working-class **Nørrebro** draws students. **Vesterbro** is considered Copenhagen's rougher side because of its red-light district (near the train station, on Istegade). **Christianshavn** is known as "little Amsterdam" for its waterways and, in its south-central half, the hippie-hash artists' colony **Christiania.**

TOURIST AND FINANCIAL SERVICES

Tourist Office: Use It, Rådhusstræde 13 (tel. 33 73 06 20; fax 33 73 06 49; email useit@ui.dk; www.useit.dk). From the station, follow Vesterbrogade, cross Rådhuspladsen onto Frederiksberggade, and turn right on Rådhusstræde. Indispensable and superfriendly; geared toward budget travelers. Free maps and guides, a ride-sharing board, and daytime luggage storage; finds lodgings. Mail held. Open mid-June to mid-Sept. daily 9am-7pm; mid-Sept. to mid-June M-W 11am-4pm, Th 11am-6pm, F 11am-2pm.

Tours: Join the ▧**night watchman** on his rounds through medieval Copenhagen. Tours leave from Gråbrødre Toru (June-Aug. Th-Sa 9 or 10pm). Pay as you please after the tour.

Budget Travel: Wasteels Rejser, Skoubogade 6 (tel. 33 14 46 33). Youth plane fares. Open M-F 9am-7pm, Sa 10am-3pm. **Kilroy Travels,** Skindergade 28 (tel. 33 11 00 44). Low plane fares. Open M-F 10am-5:30pm, Sa 10am-2pm.

Embassies: Australia (consulate), Strand Boulevarden 122, 5th fl. (tel. 39 29 20 77; fax 39 29 60 77). **Canada,** Kristen Bernikowsgade 1 (tel. 33 48 32 00; fax 33 48 32 21). **Ireland,** Østerbanegade 21 (tel. 35 42 32 33; fax 35 43 18 58). New Zealanders should contact the **New Zealand** embassy in Brussels (see p. 120). **South Africa,** Gammel Vartovvej 8 (tel. 39 18 01 55; fax 39 18 40 06). **UK,** Kastelsvej 36-40 (tel. 35 44 52 00; fax 35 44 52 93). **US,** Dag Hammarskjölds Allé 24 (tel. 35 55 31 44; fax 35 43 02 23).

Currency Exchange: Forex, in Central Station. 25kr commission on cash, 15kr per traveler's check. Open daily 8am-9pm. Also at the **airport,** open daily 6:30am-8:30pm. Exchange bureaus on **Strøget** charge up to 10% commission. **Banks** cluster in the pedestrian district and on Vesterbrogade, near the train station; most charge 25kr commission.

LOCAL SERVICES

Luggage Storage: Free at **Use It** tourist office and most hostels. At **Central Station,** 20-35kr per 24hr. Open M-Sa 5:30am-1am and Su 6am-1am.

English Bookstores: Atheneum, Nørregade 6, has a good-sized English collection. Open M-Th 9am-5:30pm, F 9am-6pm, Sa 10am-2pm. **Use It** tourist office offers a book swap.

Laundromats: Look for *Vascomat* and *Møntvask* chains. At Borgergade 2, Nansensgade 39, and Istedgade 45. Wash and dry 40-50kr. Most open daily 7am-9pm.

Gay and Lesbian Services: National Association for Gay Men and Women, Teglgaardsstr. 13 (tel. 33 13 19 48). Small bookstore and library. Open M-F 5-7pm. The monthly *PAN Homoguide* lists clubs, cafés, and organizations, and is available at **PAN** (see p. 257).

EMERGENCY AND COMMUNICATIONS

Emergencies: Fire, ambulance, and **police,** tel. 112; no coins required. Police headquarters are at Politorvet (tel. 33 14 14 48).

Pharmacy: Steno Apotek, Vesterbrogade 6c (tel. 33 14 82 66), and **Sønderbro Apoteket,** Amagerbrogade 158 (tel. 32 58 01 40). Open 24hr.; ring the bell.

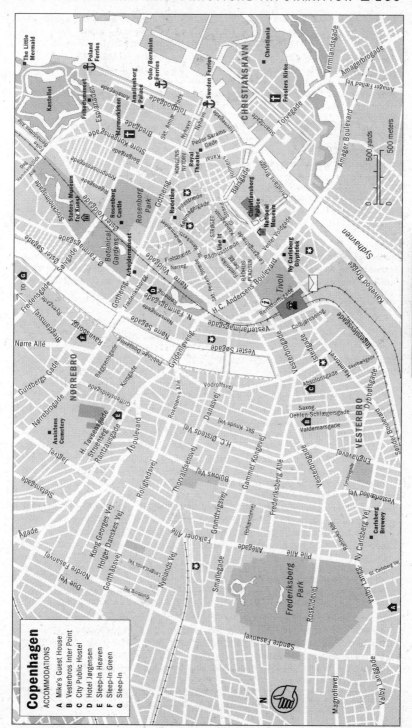

DENMARK

Copenhagen

ACCOMMODATIONS
A Mike's Guest House
B Vesterbros Inter Point
C City Public Hostel
D Hotel Jørgensen
E Sleep-In Heaven
F Sleep-In Green
G Sleep-In

Medical Assistance: Doctors on Call (tel. 33 93 63 00), open M-F 8am-4pm; after-hours, call 38 88 60 41. Visits 120-350kr. **Emergency rooms** at **Sundby Hospital,** Kastrup 63 (tel. 32 34 32 34), and **Bispebjerg Hospital,** Bispebjerg Bakke 23 (tel. 35 31 35 31).

Post Office: Tietgensgade 35-39, **1500** København V, behind Central Station. Open M-F 11am-6pm, Sa 10am-1pm. **Branch office** in Central Station. Address mail to be held to Use It: Tom DAVIDSON, Use It, **1466** København K.

Internet Access: Free at **Use It** tourist office and at **Copenhagen Hovedbibliotek** (Central Library), Krystalgade 15 (tel. 33 73 60 60; open M-F 10am-7pm, Sa 10am-2pm).

PHONE CODE	Denmark has no city codes. From outside Denmark, dial int'l dialing prefix (see inside back cover) + 45 + local number.

▌ ACCOMMODATIONS AND CAMPING

København means "merchant's port" in Danish, but the lodgings that once housed emigré merchants disappeared ages ago, leaving in their centuries-old wake lots of lovely hostels and campgrounds, but few budget hotels. HI hostels fill early with large families and school groups, despite the hostels' sometimes remote locations; excellent amenities help compensate for long commutes (bus fare 20-30kr). During holidays (such as the national vacation in early August) and the largest festivals, especially Karneval (mid-May), Roskilde (late June), and Copenhagen Jazz (late July), reserve rooms well in advance of your arrival. The lodging of choice for young travelers, city-run summertime **Sleep-In** hostels, are cheap, central, and open 24hr.

Hotel Jørgensen, Rømersgade 11 (tel. 33 13 81 86; fax 33 15 51 05), 25min. from Central Station in a quiet area. S-train: Nørreport; walk along Frederiksborggade and turn left on Rømersgade. Cramped rooms of 6-14 with TV. Central and friendly. July-Sept. dorms 115kr. Oct.-June dorms 100kr; singles 400kr; doubles from 500kr; quads 560kr. Breakfast included. Sheets 30kr. Reception 24hr. Lockout 11am-3pm. No dorm reservations.

City Public Hostel, Absalonsgade 8 (tel. 31 31 20 70; fax 31 23 51 75), in the Vesterbro Youth Center. From the station, walk away from the Rådhuspladsen on Vesterbrogade and turn left on Absalonsg. Happening lounge and BBQ. 6- to 70-bed dorms 110kr; with breakfast 130kr. Sheets 30kr. Kitchen. Reception 24hr. Open early May-late Aug.

Vesterbros Inter Point, Vesterbros KFUM (YMCA), Valdemarsgade 15 (tel. 33 31 15 74). From Central Station, walk east on Vesterbrogade and turn left. Super-friendly staff; homey atmosphere. 75kr. Breakfast 25kr. Sheets 20kr. Kitchen. Reception 8:30-11:30am, 3:30-5:30pm, and 8pm-12:30am. Curfew 12:30am. Open late June-early Aug.

Sleep-In, Blegdamsvej 132 (tel. 35 26 50 59; fax 35 43 50 58). S-train: Østerport; walk 10min. up Hammerskjölds (it's across the square from the 7-11). Near the center and Østerbro nightlife. Several hundred beds in a warehouse. 80kr. Breakfast about 30kr. Sheets 30kr. Kitchen. Reception 24hr. Open July-Aug.

Sleep-In Green, Ravnsborggade 18, Baghuset (tel. 35 37 77 77). Take bus 16 from the station. Cozy, eco-friendly 10- to 38-person dorms just outside the city center. 80kr. Organic breakfast 30kr. Sheets 30kr. Reception 24hr. Check-out noon. Open June-Sept.

Sleep-In Heaven, Struenseegade 7 (tel. 35 35 46 48; email sleepinheaven@get2net.dk), in Nørrebro. Take bus 8 (dir: Tingbjerg) 5 stops to "Rantzausgade"; continue walking in the same direction as the bus, then turn right on Kapelvej, left on Tavsensgade, and left on (poorly marked) Struenseegade. Sleep under the (painted) stars in the dorm room. Dorms 100kr; doubles about 400kr. **Internet** 20kr per 30min. Reception 24hr.

Ajax, Bavnehøj Allé 30 (tel. 33 21 24 56). S-train A: Sydhavn; walk north on Enghavevej, turn left on Bavnehøj Allé, and look for signs on the right. Dorms 60kr; hostel tent 50kr; **camp** in your own tent for 45kr. Sheets 20kr. Kitchen. TV. Open July-Aug.

København Vandrerhjem Bellahøj (HI), Herbergvejen 8 (tel. 38 28 97 15; fax 38 89 02 10; email bellahoj@danhostel.dk), in Bellahøj. Call for directions. Large, modern hostel far from the center. 6- to 12-person dorms. Lock rental 5kr. Breakfast 40kr. Sheets 30kr. Laundry 26kr. Reception 24hr. Open Mar. to mid-Jan.

København Vandrerhjem Amager (HI), Vejlandsallé 200 (tel. 32 52 29 08; fax 32 52 27 08). Take bus 46 (M-F 6am-5pm; at night, bus 96N) from Central Station or the S-train to

"Valby," then take bus 37. Far from the city center in a huge nature reserve. 2- to 5-bed dorms 85kr; nonmembers 110kr. Laundry 25kr. Kitchen. Sheets 30kr. No lockers, but free use of safe. Reception 24hr. Check-in 1-5pm. Open mid-Jan. to Nov.

Mike's Guest House, Kirkevænget 13 (tel. 36 45 65 40). 10min. by bus or train from the station; call ahead for directions. Singles 200kr; doubles 290kr; triples 400kr.

Bellahøj Camping, Hvidkildevej 66 (tel. 38 10 11 50; fax 38 10 13 32), 5km from the city center. Take bus 11 to "Bellahøj." 55kr per person. 2-person cabins 275kr, 4-person 425kr. Shower included. Kitchen. Café and market. Reception 24hr. Open June-Aug.

Absalon Camping, Korsdalsvej 132, Rødovre (tel. 36 41 06 00; fax 36 41 02 93), 9km from the city center. From Central Station, take bus 5505. 54kr per person, 7.50kr per tent. Cabins 195kr plus 54kr per person. Kitchen, laundry, and store.

◖ FOOD

The Vikings once slobbered down mutton and salted fish in Copenhagen; today you can stroll down the **Strøget** with peach juice dripping down your chin and munch pickled herring by the waterfront. Around **Kongens Nytorv,** elegant cafés serve lunchtime sandwiches (*smørrebrod*) for around 35kr. All-you-can-eat buffets (40-70kr) are popular, especially at Turkish, Indian, and Italian restaurants. **Fakta** and **Netto supermarkets** are budget fantasies; one is at Fiolstræde 7, north of Strøget (open M-F 9am-7pm, Sa 8am-5pm). Open-air **markets** provide fresh fruits and veggies; try the one at Israels Plads near Nørreport Station (open M-F 7am-6pm, Sa 7am-2pm). **Fruit stalls** line Strøget and the sidestreets to the north.

Nyhavns Færgekro, Nyhavn 5. Sit along the canal as you lunch on 10 varieties of all-you-can-eat herring (78kr). Dinners 155kr. Open daily 11:30am-11:30pm.

Crossant'er, Østergade 61. Quick, tasty food right in the center of town. Quiches 20kr. Sandwiches 30kr. Open M-F 8am-7pm, Sa 9am-5pm.

Den Grønne Kælder, Pilestræde 48. Popular, classy vegetarian and vegan dining. Hummus 18-35kr. Veggie burgers 30kr. Open M-Sa 11am-10pm.

Pilegården, Pilestræde 44. Enjoy a Danish buffet lunch (79.50kr) in a half-timbered house. Open Tu-Sa noon-5pm.

Café Norden, Østergade 61, on Strøget and Nicolaj Plads, in sight of the fountain. A French-style café with the best vantage point on Strøget. Crêpes 59-62kr; sandwiches 16-58kr; Danish and French pastries 15-40kr. Open daily 9am-midnight.

Café Europa, Amagertorv, on Nicolaj Plads opposite Café Norden. If Norden is the place to see, trendy Europa is the place to be seen. Sandwiches 23-44kr. Beer 45kr per pint. Open M-W 9am-midnight, Th-Sa 9am-1am.

Kafe Kys, Læderstræde 7, on a quiet street running south of and parallel to Strøget. Sandwiches 40-60k. Beer 35kr. Open M-Th 11am-1am, F-Sa 11am-2am, Su noon-10pm.

◉ SIGHTS

Fairly compact Copenhagen is best seen on foot or by bike; pick up a free **city bike** (see p. 252) to cruise by the city's stunning architecture. Guided and self-guided **tours** of all sorts are described in Use It's *Playtime* and in brochures at the tourist office. The squares along the lively pedestrian street **Strøget,** which divides the city center, are **Nytorv, Nicolaj Plads,** and **Kungens Nytorv.** Opposite Kungens Nytorv is **Nyhavn,** the "new port" where Hans Christian Andersen wrote his first fairy tale, lined with Hanseatic houses and sailing boats. **Nette tour boats** offers scenic tours of the waterways (late Apr. to mid-Sept. every 20min. 10am-5pm, 20kr).

CITY CENTER. Tivoli, the famed 19th-century amusement park, delights with botanical gardens, marching toy soldiers, and, of course, amusement-park rides. Wednesday and weekend nights culminate with music and fireworks. (*Vesterbrogade 3, opposite Central Station. Open late Apr. to mid-Sept. Su-Th 11am-midnight, F-Sa 11am-1am. Children's rides open 11:30am, others 12:30pm. 45kr; before 1pm 35kr. Single-ride tickets 10-20kr. Ride-pass 168kr.*) From Central Station, turn right on Bernstorffsgade and left on Tietgensgade to partake of the ancient and Impressionist art and sculpture at the beautiful **Ny Carlsberg Glyptoket.** (*Dantes Plads 7. Open Tu-Su 10am-4pm. 30kr; free W and*

DENMARK

Su or with ISIC.) Continue along Tietgensgade, which becomes Stormgade, to dive into Denmark's Viking treasures and other tidbits of its cultural history at the **National Museum.** *(Ny Vestergade 10. Open Tu-Su 10am-5pm. 40kr, students 30kr; W free.)* **Christiansborg Castle,** Prins Jørgens Gård, features subterranean ruins, royal reception rooms, and the *Folketing* (Parliament) chambers. To get there, continue down Tietgensgade from the center and continue until you cross the canal. *(Tours May-Sept. daily 11am and 3pm; June-Aug. 11am, 1, and 3pm; Oct.-Apr. Tu-Th and Sa-Su 11am and 3pm; 40kr. Ruins 20kr. Ask about the free Parliament tours.)*

CHRISTIANSHAVN. In the southern section of Christianshavn, the "free city" of **Christiania,** founded in 1971 by youthful squatters in abandoned military barracks, is inhabited by a young population of artists and "free-thinkers" trying to allow the 70s and free love to live on into the next millennium. Hash and marijuana are for sale on Pusher St (joints 20-50kr), although they're not everyone's pot of tea; also remember that all forms of cannabis are illegal in Denmark, and that possession of even small amounts could get you arrested. Always ask before taking pictures, never take pictures on Pusher St itself, and exercise caution in the area at night. Infrequent police raids rarely result in serious charges (dogs usually raise the alarm in time). *(From Central Station, turn right on Bernstorffs, left on Tietgensgade; continue along as it changes names and bear right along the water. After crossing the water, turn left on Prinsesseg.)* Climb the golden spire of **Vor Frelsers Kirke** (Our Savior's Church) for a bird's-eye view of Copenhagen. *(Sankt Annægade 29. Turn left off Prinsesseg. Church open daily Mar.-Nov. 9am-4:30pm, Dec.-Feb. 10am-2pm; free. Tower open Mar.-Nov 9am-4:30pm; 20kr.)*

FREDERIKSTADEN. Edvard Eriksen's **den Lille Havfrue** (The Little Mermaid) statue at the opening of the harbor honors favorite son Hans Christian Andersen. *(S-train: Østerport; turn left out of the station, turn left on Folke Bernadottes Allé, turn right after passing a canal, and follow it to the ocean. Open daily 6am-dusk.)* Retrace your steps and turn left to cross the moat to **Kastellet,** a 17th-century fortress-turned-park. Cross through Kastellet to the **Frihedsmuseet** (Resistance Museum), which chronicles the Nazi occupation from 1940 to 1945. The museum documents both Denmark's efforts to rescue its Jews and its period of acceptance of German "protection," when the Danish government arrested anti-Nazi saboteurs. *(At Churchillparken. Open May to early Sept. Tu-Sa 10am-4pm, Su 10am-5pm; mid-Sept. to Apr. Tu-Sa 11am-3pm, Su 11am-4pm. Free.)* From the museum, walk south down Amaliegade to reach **Amalienborg Palace;** most of the interior is closed to the public, but you can see the apartments of Christian VII. The changing of the palace guard takes place at noon on the brick plaza of the queen's palace. *(Open daily June-Aug. 10am-4pm; May and Sept.-Oct. 11am-4pm; Jan.-Apr. Tu-Su 11am-4pm. 35kr.)* The 19th-century **Marmokirken** (Marble Church), opposite the palace, features an ornate interior and an impressive dome that dwarfs the plaza. *(Church open M-Tu and Th-Sa 10:30am-4:30pm, W 10:30am-6:30pm, Su noon-4:30pm; free. Dome 20kr.)*

A few blocks north, **Statens Museum for Kunst** (State Museum of Fine Arts) displays an eclectic collection of genres and artists in an incredible building. From the church, head away from Amalienborg, go left on Store Kongensg., turn right on Dronningrnd Tværg., then take an immediate right and then left onto Sølvgade. *(Sølvgade 48-50. Open Tu-Su 10am-5pm. 40kr.)* Diagonally opposite the museum, **Rosenborg Slot** (Rosenborg Palace and Gardens) hoards royal treasures, including the crown jewels. *(Øster Volgade 4A. Open daily May-Sept. 10am-4pm; Oct. 11am-3pm; Nov.-Apr. Tu-Su 11am-2pm. 45kr.)* Nearby, the **Botanisk Have** (Botanical Gardens) provide a breath of fresh air. *(Gothersgade 128, at Øster Voldgade. Open daily late Mar.-Aug. 8:30am-6pm, Sept.-late Mar. 8:30am-4pm. Free.)*

OTHER SIGHTS. For legalized substance abuse, try the **Carlsberg Brewery.** A trip to the brewery's visitor's center will reward you with a wealth of knowledge and, perhaps even more important, free samples. *(Ny Carlsbergvej 140. Take bus 6 west from Rådhuspladsen to Valby Langgade.)* If the breweries haven't confused your senses enough, play with science at the **Experimentarium.** *(Tuborg Havnevej 7. Take bus 6 north from Rådhuspladsen. Open late June to mid-Aug. daily 10am-5pm; late Aug. to early June M and W-F 9am-5pm, Tu 9am-9pm, Sa-Su 11am-5pm. 75kr, students 61kr.)*

DENMARK

ENTERTAINMENT

For current events, consult *Copenhagen This Week* (free at hostels and tourist offices), or pick up *Use It News* from Use It. The **Royal Theater** is home to the world-famous Royal Danish Ballet. For same-day, half-price theater tickets, head to the **Tivoli ticket office,** Vesterbrog. 3. (Tel. 33 15 10 12. Open daily mid-Apr. to mid-Sept. 9am-9pm; mid-Sept. to mid-Apr. closes 7pm. Royal theater tickets available at 4 or 5pm, others at noon.) Call **Arte,** Hvidkildevej 64 (tel. 38 88 22 22), to ask about student discounts. The relaxed **Kul-Kaféen,** Teglgårdsstræde 5, is a great place to see live performers and get info on music, dance, and theater. (Open M-Sa 11am-midnight.) During the world-class **Copenhagen Jazz Festival** (July 7-16, 2000; www.cjf.dk), the city fairly drowns in excellent jazz, with many free concerts on sidewalks and squares complementing the more refined venues.

NIGHTLIFE

Copenhagen's weekends often begin on Wednesday, and nights rock until 5am. The best night to party is Thursday, when most bars and clubs have reduced covers and cheap drinks. The central pedestrian district reverberates with crowded bars and discos; **Kongens Nytorv** has fancier joints. Many buy beer at a supermarket and head to the boats and cafés of **Nyhavn** for its salty charisma. The **Scala** complex, opposite Tivoli, has many bars and restaurants. University students liven up the cheaper bars in the **Nørrebro** area. Copenhagen's gay and lesbian scene is one of Europe's best, and gay Danish men and women report equal comfort in straight establishments.

Rust, Guldbergsgade 8, in the Nørreboro. A twentysomething crowd dances the night away at this disco. Long lines by 1am. Open Tu-Su 10pm-5am. Cover 50kr.

Café Pavillionen, on Borgmester Jensens Allé, in Fælleaparken. This summer-only outdoor café has local bands 8-10pm, plus a disco W-Sa 10pm-5am. On Su, enjoy a concert 2:30-5pm, then tango lessons and dancing until midnight. No cover. Open May-Aug.

Enzo, Nørregade 41. Doll yourself up and dance with a young stylish crowd. Dress code. Ages 21 and up. Cover 60kr. Open F-Sa 10:30pm-5:30am.

Sabor Latino, Vester Voldgade 85. Groove to hot Latin beats and enjoy free salsa and merengue lessons at 10pm. Open Th 9pm-3am, F-Sa 9pm-5am. Cover 35-50kr.

IN Bar, Nørreg 1. Dance on the speakers! No, wait, drink *cheap* and then dance on the speakers! Th cover 30kr; beer and wine 10kr; open Su-Th 10pm-5am. F-Sa cover 150kr; includes open bar; open F-Sa 10pm-10am. Ages 18 and up; Th-Sa ages 20 and up.

Park, Østerbrog. 79, in Østerbro. Lose your inhibitions and your friends in this enormous club with 2 packed dance floors, live music hall, and rooftop patio. Pints 40kr. Cover F-Sa 50kr. Open Su-W 10am-2am, Th 10am-4am, F-Sa 10am-5am.

PAN Club and Café, Knabrostræde 3. Gay café, bar, and disco. Publishes the *Homoguide*. Café opens daily 8pm, disco 11pm. Both stay open late. Cover Th 20kr; F-Sa 50kr.

Sebastian Bar and Café, 10 Hyskenstræde, off Strøget. The city's best-known gay and lesbian bar. *Homoguide* available. Beer 17-31kr. Happy Hour 5-9pm. Open daily noon-2am.

EXCURSIONS FROM COPENHAGEN

Stunning castles, white-sand beaches, and a world-class museum hide in North, Central, and South Zealand, all within easy reach of Copenhagen by train. A northern train route (every 20min.) offers easy access to many attractive daytrips that lie within an hour of Copenhagen in North Zealand.

KLAMPENBORG AND CHARLOTTENLUND. Klampenborg and Charlottenlund, on the coastal line (and at the end of S-train line C), feature **topless beaches.** Though less ornate than Tivoli, **Bakken** in Dyrehaven, Klampenborg, the world's oldest amusement park, delivers more thrills. From the Klampenborg train station, turn left, cross the overpass, and head through the park. (Tel. 39 63 73 00. Open daily Mar. 25-Aug. 11am-midnight. Rides start at 2pm; 10-25kr each.) Bakken borders the **Jægersborg Deer Park,** the royal family's former hunting grounds, still home to their **Eremitage** summer *château,* miles of wooded paths, and over 2000 red deer.

DENMARK

RUNGSTED AND HUMLEBÆK. In North Zealand, the quiet harbor town of **Rungsted** (7th stop; 30min., 38.50kr or 4 clips on the blue *rabatkort*), where Isak Dinesen wrote *Out of Africa*, houses the author's abode at the **Karen Blixen Museum,** Rungsted Strandvej 111. (Open May-Sept. daily 10am-5pm; Oct.-Apr. W-F 1-4pm, Sa-Su 11am-4pm. 30kr.) A path from the gardens leads to Blixen's tree-shaded grave. **Humlebæk** (10th stop; 45min., 38.50kr or 4 clips), farther up the coast, distinguishes itself with the spectacular **Louisiana Museum of Modern Art,** named for the three wives (all named Louisa) of the estate's original owner. The museum contains works by Picasso, Warhol, Lichtenstein, Calder, and other 20th-century masters, but the building and its sculpture-studded grounds are themselves well worth the trip. Follow signs 1.5km north from the Humlebæk station or snag bus 388 (10kr). Classical music concerts ring out on Wednesday evenings in summer (90kr includes museum); call 49 19 07 19 for info. (Open Th-M 10am-5pm, W 10am-10pm. 55kr, students 47kr.)

HELSINGØR AND HORNBÆK. At the end of the northern line lies **Helsingør** (1hr.), evidence of the Danish monarchy's fondness for lavish architecture. In a region famous for castles, the most famous is undoubtedly the 15th-century **Kronborg Slot** in Helsingør, also known as **Elsinore,** the setting for Shakespeare's *Hamlet*. Viking chief Holger Danske is buried in the castle's dungeon; legend has it that he still rises to face any threat to Denmark's safety. The castle also houses the **Danish Maritime Museum,** which contains the world's oldest sea biscuit, from 1853. (Open May-Sept. daily 10:30am-5pm; Apr. and Oct. Tu-Su 11am-4pm; Nov.-Mar. Tu-Su 11am-3pm. 45kr.) The **tourist office,** inside **Kulturhuset,** to the left of the station exit, books rooms (25kr fee). (Tel. 49 21 13 33; fax 49 21 15 77. Open mid-June to Aug. M-F 9am-6pm, Sa 10am-4pm; Sept. to mid-June M-F 9am-4pm, Sa 10am-1pm.) To reach the waterfront **Villa Moltke (HI),** Ndr. Strandvej 24, take bus 340 from the station. (Tel. 49 21 16 40; fax 49 21 13 99. 74kr; nonmembers 84kr. Breakfast 40kr. Sheets 40kr. Kitchen. Reception 8am-noon and 4-9pm. Open Feb.-Nov.)

Hornbæk offers beautiful beaches where you can catch some rays and glimpse the well-to-do. City-weary urbanites flock to the beach in summer—come to see Danes at their most beautiful. There's a wild **harbor party** on the fourth weekend in July. Bus 340 and the train run from Helsingør to Hornbæk (20min., 20kr).

HILLERØD AND FREDENSBORG. A different northern route brings you to **Hillerød** (at the end of S-train lines A and E via Lyngby; 40min., 42kr), home of the moated **Frederiksborg Slot,** arguably the most impressive of North Zealand's castles, with exquisite gardens and brick ramparts. The **National Historical Museum** within displays portraits of prominent Danes. Free concerts are given weekly on the famous 1610 **Esaias Compenius organ** in the chapel. (Castle open daily Apr.-Oct. 10am-5pm; Nov.-Mar. 11am-3pm. 40kr, students 10kr. Concerts Th 1:30pm; call 48 26 04 39 for info.) A final stop on the northern castle tour is **Fredensborg Castle,** on the rail line connecting Hillerød and Helsingør, at the Fredensborg stop. Built in 1722, the castle still serves as the spring and fall royal residence. (Castle open July daily 1-5pm; 10kr. Park open year-round; free.) Sleep with (well, near) the royals and enjoy a fantastic palace garden view at **Fredensborg Youth Hostel (HI),** Østrupvej 3, 1km from the train station. (Tel. 48 48 03 15; fax 48 48 16 56. 93kr; nonmembers 118kr. Sheets 45kr. Reception 7am-9pm.)

ROSKILDE. In Central Zealand, Roskilde (25-30min., 38.50kr or 4 clips) served as Denmark's first capital when King Harald Bluetooth built the country's first Christian church here in 980; 38 other Danish monarchs repose in the ornate sarcophagi of **Roskilde Domkirke** (cathedral). (Open Apr.-Sept. M-F 9am-4:45pm, Sa 9am-noon, Su 12:30-4:45pm; Oct.-Mar. M-F 9am-4:45pm, Sa 12:30-3:45pm. Concerts June-Aug. Th 8pm. 12kr.) The **Viking Ship Museum,** on Strandengen, along the harbor, houses remnants of five trade ships and warships sunk circa 1060; in the outside harbor are their less-skeletal reconstructions and a working Viking-era shipyard. Book a ride on a Viking longboat (June 15-Aug.), but be prepared to take an oar—Viking conquest is no spectator sport. (Open daily May-Sept. 9am-5pm; Oct.-Apr. 10am-4pm. May-Sept. 50kr; Oct.-Apr. 42kr.) Near Roskilde, the open-air museum at **Lejre**

Research Centre, Slangealleen 2, reconstructs Viking agrarian life. Take the S-train from Copenhagen to **Lejre,** then bus 233 to Lejre Experimental Centre. (Open May to mid-June and mid-Aug. to mid-Sept. Tu-Su 10am-5pm; mid-June to mid.-Aug. daily 10am-5pm. 60kr.) Roskilde hosts one of Europe's largest **music festivals** (tel. 46 36 66 13; www.roskilde-festival.dk; June 29-July 2, 2000), drawing over 90,000 fans with bands such as REM, U2, Radiohead, Smashing Pumpkins, and Metallica.

The **tourist office,** Gullandsstræde 15, sells festival tickets and books rooms for a 25kr fee. (Tel. 46 35 27 00. Open Apr.-June M-F 9am-5pm, Sa 10am-1pm; July-Aug. M-F 9am-6pm, Sa 9am-3pm, Su 10am-2pm; Sept.-Mar. M-Th 9am-5pm, F 9am-4pm, Sa 10am-1pm.) The **HI youth hostel,** Hørhusene 61, has beach access but is booked during the festival. Take bus 601 from train station to Låddenhøj, then walk 800m. (Tel. 46 35 21 84; fax 46 32 66 90. 90kr; nonmembers 115kr. Reception 9am-noon and 4-8pm. Open Feb.-Dec.) To camp by the beach at **Roskilde Camping,** Baune-højvej 7, 4km north of town, take bus 603 towards Veddelev. (Tel. 46 75 79 96; fax 46 75 44 26. 50kr per person. Reception 8am-10pm. Open Apr. to mid-Sept.)

MØN. To see what Andersen called one of the most beautiful spots in Denmark, travel 2hr. south of Copenhagen to the white cliffs of the isle of Møn. Take the train to Vordingborg, bus 62 or 64 to Stege, and then bus 54 to Møn Klint. Plan carefully: only three buses go out and back each day, and the last often leaves Møn before 4pm. For more info, contact the **Møns Turistbureau,** Storegade 2, in Stege. (Tel. 55 81 44 11; fax 55 81 48 46. Open June 15-Aug. M-F 10am-6pm, Sa 9am-6pm, Su 10am-noon; Sept.-June 14 M-F 10am-5pm, Sa 9am-noon.)

BORNHOLM

Gorgeous Bornholm island gets the most sun and the least rain in Denmark, luring vacationers to its beaches and pleasant fishing villages. Ideal for avid bikers and nature-lovers, its red-roofed cliffside villas may seem southern European, but the flowers and half-timbered houses are undeniably Danish. Bornholm's unique **round churches** were both places of worship and fortresses for waiting out pirate attacks.

⊟ GETTING THERE AND GETTING AROUND. The sandiest and longest **beaches** are at **Dueodde,** on the island's southern tip. Of the four towns, **Østerlars** is the largest, and **Nylors** the best-preserved. Ferries arrive in **Rønne,** Bornholm's capital, from Denmark, Sweden, Germany, and Poland. **Bornholmstrafikken** (Rønne tel. 56 95 18 66; Copenhagen tel. 33 13 18 66; Ystad tel. +46 (411) 180 65; Sassnitz tel. +49 (38392) 352 26; Rønne fax 56 91 07 66; www.bornholmferries.dk) offers combo bus/ferry routes from **Malmö, Sweden** (4½hr., 190kr) and **Copenhagen** (5½hr., 190kr); ferries from **Ystad, Sweden,** 1hr. southeast of Malmö (1 per day, 2½hr., 98-122kr; with Scanrail 50% off); and ferries from **Sassnitz-Mukran** in **Germany** (2hr., 50-100kr). In July and August, **Polferries** sails between Rønne and **Świnoujście, Poland.** (Tel. 56 95 10 69; fax 56 95 89 10. Departs Rønne W, departs Świnoujście Sa. 6hr., 180kr.) Bornholm has an efficient local BAT **bus** service. (30kr to Gudhjem or Sandvig-Allinge, 37.50kr to Svaneke; 24-hour pass 90kr). There are numerous **cycling** paths; pick up a guide at the tourist office in Rønne. Reserve rooms well in advance.

RØNNE. Amid cafés and cobblestoned streets, tiny Rønne, on the southwest coast, is Bornholm's principal port of entry. Walking through, it's hard to imagine the devastation wrought by relentless bombing in WWII. Rent a **bike** from **Bornholms Cyke-ludlejning,** Ndr. Kystvej 5. (55kr per day. Open May-Sept. daily 7am-4pm and 8:30-9pm.) The **tourist office,** Nordre Kystvej 3, a mirrored-glass building behind the gas station by the Bornholmstrafikken terminal, books private rooms (150-200kr fee). (Tel. 56 95 95 00. Open mid-June to mid-Aug. M-Sa 9am-5:30pm, Su noon-5:30pm; mid-Aug. to mid-June M-F 9am-4pm, Sa 11:30am-2:30pm.) If the hostel isn't open when you get in, store your bag at **Café Ventesal.** (20kr. M-F 8am-10pm, Sa 10am-2pm.) The **HI youth hostel,** Arsenalvej 12, is in a quiet, wooded area. From the ferry terminal, walk along Munch Petersens Vej, left on Skansevej, left on Zahrtmanns-vej, right at the roundabout onto Søndre Allé, right on Arsenalvej; then follow the signs. (Tel. 56 95 13 40; fax 56 95 01 32. 100kr. Laundry. Kitchen. Call ahead.) **Galløkken Camping** is at Strandvejen 4. (Tel. 56 95 23 20; fax 56 95 37 66. 52kr per person. Open mid-May to Aug.) Get groceries at **Kvickly,** in the Snellemark Centret opposite the tourist office (open M-Th 9:30am-6pm, F 9:30am-7pm, Sa 9:30am-2pm), or visit the 2nd-floor cafeteria (open M-F 9am-7pm, Sa 9am-4pm). **Postal code:** 3700.

SANDVIG-ALLINGE. On the tip of the spectacular northern coast, this smaller town's white-sand beaches attract bikers and bathers. Down Hammershusvej, **Hammershus** is northern Europe's largest castle ruin. The **Nordbornholms Turistbureau,** Kirkeg. 4, is in Allinge. (Tel. 56 48 00 01; fax 56 48 02 26. Open June-Aug. M-F 9am-5pm, Sa 10am-3pm; Sept.-May closes Sa noon.) Just outside Sandvig is the **Sandvig Vandrerhjem (HI),** Hammershusvej 94. (Tel. 56 48 03 62; fax 56 48 18 62. 100kr. Members only; sells HI cards. Reception 9:30-11am and 4:30-5:15pm. Open Apr.-Oct.) **Sandvig Familie Camping,** Sandlinien 5, has sites on the sea. (Tel. 56 48 04 47; fax 56 48 04 57. 45kr per person, 10kr per tent. Reception 8am-10pm. Open Apr.-Oct.)

FUNEN (FYN)

Situated between the island of Zealand to the east and the Jutland Peninsula to the west, Funen is Denmark's garden. This remote bread basket is no longer isolated from the rest of Denmark—a bridge and tunnel now connect it to Zealand. Pick up maps of the bike paths covering the island at Funen tourist offices (75kr).

ODENSE

Visiting this hometown of Hans Christian Andersen, who once said, "To travel is to live!", may reveal the roots of his belief. Although it hosts a few interesting museums, Odense (OH-n-sa), Denmark's third-largest city, warrants only a short visit.

⚡️🐷📷 **PRACTICAL INFO, ACCOMMODATIONS, AND FOOD.** Buses depart from behind the train station (11kr). Ask the driver for an *omstigning,* a ticket valid for 1hr. The **tourist office,** on Rådhuspladsen, books rooms for a 25kr fee (125-175kr per person) and sells the 24-hour **Odense Eventyrpas,** good for discounts on museums and transit (50kr). From the train station, take Nørreg., which turns into Asylgade, turn left at the end on Vesterg., and it'll be on your right. (Tel. 66 12 75 20; fax 66 12 75 86; email otb@odenseturist.dk. Open June 15-Aug. M-Sa 9am-7pm, Su 10am-5pm; Sept.-June 14 M-F 9:30am-4:30pm, Sa 10am-1pm.) The **library** in the station has free **internet.** (Open May-Sept. M-Th 10am-7pm, F 10am-4pm, Sa 10am-2pm; Oct.-Apr. M-Th 10am-7pm, F-Su 10am-4pm.) To get from the train station to the **Vandrerhjem Kragsbjerggården (HI),** Kragsbjergvej 121, 2km away, take bus 61, 62, 63, or 64. (Tel. 66 13 04 25; fax 65 91 28 63. 89kr; nonmembers 114kr. Reception 8am-noon and 4-8pm. Open mid-Jan. to Nov. Reserve ahead.) To camp next to the Fruens Boge park at **DCU Camping,** Odensevej 102, take bus 41 or 81. (Tel. 66 11 47 02; fax 65 91 73 43. 50kr per person. Reception 7am-10pm. Open late Mar.-Sept.) **Den Grimme Ælling** (The Ugly Duckling), Hans Jensen Stræde 1, opposite H.C. Andersens Hus, serves a "proper Danish food" lunch buffet (70kr), with an option for bottomless beer and wine (99.50kr). (Open daily 11:45am-2:30pm and 5:30-10:30pm.) **Café Biografen,** Brandt's Passage 39-41, serves brunch (48-58kr; M-Sa 11am-2pm, Su noon-2pm) and is the front office for an art-house cinema with English films. (45-50kr. Café closes M-Th 1am, F-Sa 2am, Su midnight.) Get **groceries** at **Aktiv Super,** at Nørreg. and Skulkenborg. (Open M-F 9am-7pm, Sa 8:30am-4pm.) **Postal code:** 5000.

🎭🎟 **SIGHTS AND ENTERTAINMENT.** At **H.C. Andersens Hus,** Hans Jensens Stræde 37-45, you can learn about the author's eccentricities and see free performances of his work (June 19-July 30 11am, 1, and 3pm; in the garden behind the museum). (Open mid-June to Aug. daily 9am-7pm; Sept. to mid-June Tu-Su 10am-4pm. 30kr.) A few scraps from his ugly-duckling childhood are on display at **H.C. Andersens Barndomshjem** (Childhood Home), Munkemøllestræde 3-5. (Open mid-June to Aug. daily 10am-4pm; Sept. to mid-June Tu-Su 11am-3pm. 10kr.) You can don headphones and listen to the classical compositions of another Great Dane at the **Carl Nielsen Museum,** Claus Bergs Gade 11. (Open June-Aug. Tu-Su 10am-4pm; off-season reduced hours. 15kr.) At the other end of the pedestrian district, **Brandts Klædefabrik,** Brandts Passage 37 and 43, presents a medley of artistic expression with a modern art gallery, the **Museum of Photographic Art,** and the **Danish Press/ Graphic Arts Museum.** (Tel. 66 13 78 97. All open June-Aug. daily 10am-5pm; Sept.- May closed M. 30kr, 25kr, and 25kr, respectively; joint ticket 50kr.) The **Fyns Kunst- museum,** Jernbaneg. 13, features Danish art. (Open Tu-Su 10am-4pm. 25kr.) Take bus 42 to the **Den Fynske Landsby** (Funen Village), Sejerskovvej 20, for a collection of 18- and 19th-century buildings from around the island. (Open mid-June to mid-Aug. daily 9:30am-7pm; Apr. to mid-June and mid-Aug. to Oct. Tu-Su 10am-5pm; Nov.- Mar. Su 11am-3pm. 30kr.) **Ringe,** 30km away, hosts the rock-and-folk-music **Midtfyn Festival** (July 5-9, 2000), which has featured the Black Crowes, Sting, and Jamiro- quai. (Info tel. 65 96 25 12. 350kr per day, 625kr for F-Su. Free camping.) The Ringe **tourist office** has more info (tel. 62 62 52 23; www.mf.dk).

❷ EXCURSION FROM ODENSE: EGESKOV SLOT. About 45min. south of Odense on the Svendborg rail line is the town of **Kværndup** and its famous ◧**Egeskov Slot,** a stunning 16th-century castle that appears to float on the surrounding lake (it's actually supported by an entire forest of 12,000 oak piles). The grounds sur- rounding the opulently furnished castle include a large bamboo labyrinth. On sum- mer Sundays at 5pm, classical concerts resound in the castle's **Knight Hall.** (Open daily May-June and Aug.-Sept. 10am-5pm; July 10am-7pm. 50kr. Grounds open daily May and Sept. 10am-5pm; June and Aug. 10am-6pm; July 10am-8pm. 60kr.) To get to Egeskov, exit the Svendborg-bound train at Kværndrup; go right from the station until you reach Bøjdenvej, the main road. You can then wait for bus 920 (every hr., 11kr), or turn right and walk 2km through wheat fields to the castle.

SVENDBORG

On Funen's south coast, an hour from Odense by train, **Svendborg** is a beautiful har- bor town and a major departure point for ferries to the south Funen islands. The grounds of the regal 17th-century estate of **Valdemars Slot,** built by Christian IV for his son, hold a new **yachting museum** and a **beach.** (Open May-Sept. daily 10am-5pm; Apr. and early Oct. Sa-Su 10am-5pm. Castle 50kr, museum 25kr; joint ticket 65kr.) Bus 200 goes there (every hr., 35min. after the hr.), as do the cruises of the **M/S Helge,** which leave from Jensens Mole (tel. 62 50 25 00; 1hr., round-trip 50kr).

Ferries to Ærø (see below) leave from behind the train station. The **tourist office,** on the café-filled Centrum Pladsen, books ferries, hotel rooms, and hostels beds for free, and finds rooms in private homes for 25kr. (Tel. 62 21 09 80; fax 62 22 05 53. Open late June-Aug. M-F 9am-7pm, Sa 9am-3pm; Sept. to mid-June M-F 9:30am- 5:30pm, Sa 9:30am-1pm.) To get from the station to the five-star **HI youth hostel,** Vest- erg. 45, turn left on Jernbaneg. and turn left again on Valdemarsg., which becomes Vesterg. (20min.). (Tel. 62 21 66 99; fax 62 20 29 39. 88kr. Breakfast, sheets, and laundry 40kr each. Kitchen. Bikes 50kr per day. Reception 8am-8pm. Check-out 9:30am.) **Carlsberg Camping,** Sundbrovej 19, is across the sound on Tåsinge. (Tel. 62 22 53 84. 51kr. Reception 8am-10pm. Open May-Oct.) **Den Grimme Ælling,** Korsg. 17, serves all-you-can-eat lunch (70kr) and dinner (100kr). **Postal code:** 5700.

ÆRØ

The wheat fields, busy harbors, and cobblestoned hamlets of Ærø (EH-ruh), a small island off the south coast of Funen, quietly preserve an earlier era in Danish history. Here, cows, rather than real estate developers, lay claim to the beautiful land.

⬕ GETTING THERE AND GETTING AROUND. Several **trains** from Odense to **Svendborg** are timed to meet the **ferry** (tel. 62 52 40 00) from Svendborg to **Ærøskøbing** (1¼hr., 6 per day, 67kr, round-trip 113kr; buy tickets on board). From **Mommark,** on Jutland, **Ærø-Als** (tel. 62 58 17 17) sails to **Søby** (1hr., Apr.-Sept. 2-5 per day; Oct.-Mar.

DENMARK

Sa-Su only; 60kr), on Ærø's northwestern shore. From **Marstal,** on the eastern tip of Ærø, ferries also arrive from **Kiel, Germany** (3hr., 3 per week, 50DM). **Bus** 990 travels between Ærøskøbing and Marstal (15kr), but Ærø is best seen by **bike.**

ÆRØSKØBING. Thanks to economic stagnation followed by conservation efforts, the town of Ærøskøbing appears today almost as it did 200 years ago. Rosebushes and half-timbered houses attract tourist yachts from Sweden and Germany, as well as vacationing Danes, but you don't have to get too far out of town to find your own serene spot. The **tourist office,** opposite the ferry landing, arranges rooms in private homes (170kr). (Tel. 62 52 13 00; fax 62 52 14 36; email Turistar@post1.Tele.DK. Open June 15-Aug. M-F 9am-5pm, Sa 9am-2pm, Su 10am-noon; Sept.-June 14 M-F 9am-4pm, Sa 8:45-11:45am.) To get from the ferry to the **HI youth hostel,** Smedevejen 15, walk left on Smedeg., which becomes Nørreg., then Østerg., and finally Smedevejen (10min.). (Tel. 62 52 10 44; fax 62 52 16 44. 90kr; nonmembers 115kr. Breakfast 40kr. Sheets 35kr. Reception 8am-noon and 4-8pm. Check-in by 5pm or call ahead. Reserve ahead. Open Apr. to mid-Oct.) **Ærøskøbing Camping,** Sygehusvejen 40b, is 10min. to the right as you leave the ferry. (Tel. 62 52 18 54; fax 62 52 14 36. 46kr per person. Reception 8am-1pm and 3-9pm. Open May-Sept.) **Emerko supermarket** is at Statene 3. (Open M-Th 9am-5pm, F 9am-6pm, Sa 9am-4pm, Su 10am-4pm.) Rent a **bike** at the hostel or campground (40-50kr per day) to explore the towns of **Marstal** and **Søby,** on the more remote shores of the island.

JUTLAND (JYLLAND)

Homeland of the Jutes who joined the Angles and Saxons in the conquest of England, the Jutland peninsula is Denmark's largest landmass. Beaches and campgrounds mark the peninsula as prime summer vacation territory, while low rolling hills, marshland, and sparse forests add color and variety. Jutland may not be suitable for a whirlwind tour, but the plentiful supply of hostels will allow you to take a weekend beach fling without denting your budget.

▓ FERRIES TO ENGLAND, NORWAY, AND SWEDEN

From **Esbjerg,** on Jutland's west coast, **DFDF** sails to **Harwich, England** (18hr., 3-4 per week). Those stuck waiting for connections may try the **HI youth hostel,** Gammel Vade Vej 80. (Tel. 75 12 42 58; fax 75 13 68 33. 85kr; nonmembers 110kr. Reception 8am-noon and 4-7pm. Open Feb.-Dec.) From **Frederikshavn,** on the northern tip of Jutland, **Stena Line** ferries (tel. 96 20 02 00) leave for **Gothenburg, Sweden** (2-3¼hr., 145-160kr, round-trip 200-230kr; 50% off with Scanrail), **Oslo** (10hr., 350kr, round-trip 400kr; 50% off with Scanrail; see p. 684), and other points in Norway; **SeaCat** (tel. 96 20 32 00) offers cheaper service to **Gothenburg** (2hr., 3 per day, 110-130kr); and **Color Line** (tel. 99 56 20 00) sails to **Oslo** (316-352kr; 50% off with Scanrail). Boats also go from **Hirtshals,** also on the northern tip of Jutland, to **Oslo** (see p. 684) and **Kristiansand, Norway** (see p. 689); and from **Hanstholm,** on the northwestern coast of Jutland, to **Bergen, Norway** (see p. 692).

ÅRHUS

Århus (ORE-hoos), Denmark's second-largest and many Danes' favorite city, bills itself as "the world's smallest big city." This, along with the town's "Little Tivoli" and other Copenhagen-inspired touches, reveals a thriving rivalry with its big sibling to the east. Many travelers to this manageably sized and laid-back student and cultural center find themselves agreeing that size indeed doesn't matter.

▓▐▓ PRACTICAL INFO, ACCOMMODATIONS, AND FOOD. The **tourist office,** in the town hall, books private rooms (125-175kr; 25kr fee) and sells the **Århus Pass,** which includes unlimited public transit and admission to all sights (48-hour 110kr). Turn left as you exit the train station, take your first right, and walk to the building with the clock tower. (Tel. 89 40 67 00; fax 86 12 95 90; www.aarhus-

DENMARK

tourist.dk. Open late June-early Sept. M-F 9:30am-6pm, Sa 9:30am-5pm, Su 9:30am-1pm; reduced hours in off-season.) Most public buses leave from the train station or from outside the tourist office. The main **library**, at Mølleparken, has free **internet.** (Open May-Aug. M-Th 10am-7pm, F 10am-6pm, Sa 10am-2pm; Sept.-Apr. M 10am-10pm, Tu-Th 10am-8pm, F 10am-6pm, Sa 10am-2pm.)

The hip **Århus City Sleep-In,** Havneg. 20, is 10min. from the train station. (Tel. 86 19 20 55; fax 86 19 18 11; email sleep-in@mail1.stofanet.dk. Dorms 85kr; doubles 240-280kr. Breakfast 30kr. Sheets 30kr; deposit 30kr. Kitchen. Laundry 25kr. Key deposit 50kr. Bikes 50kr per day; deposit 200kr. Reception 24hr. Check-out noon.) The affiliated **Kutturgyngen student center,** Mejlg. 53, down the street from the Sleep-in, has a café/club. **Pavillonen (HI),** Marienlundsvej 10, rests in the Risskov forest, 3km from the city center and 5min. from the beach. Take bus 1, 6, 9, 16, or 56 to Marienlund, then walk 300m into the park. (Tel. 86 16 72 98; fax 86 10 55 60. 85kr, nonmembers 110kr; doubles 240-280kr. Breakfast 40kr. Sheets 30kr. Laundry 25kr. Reception 7:30-10am and 4-11pm.) Beautiful **Blommehavenn Camping Århus,** Ørneredevej 35, is near a beach in the Marselisborg forest and the royal family's summer residence. In summer, take bus 19 from the station directly to the grounds; in winter, take bus 6 to Hørhavevej. (Tel. 86 27 02 07; fax 86 27 45 22. In summer 50kr per person, 15kr per tent. Reception Apr.-early Sept. 7am-10pm; mid-Sept. to Mar. 8am-8pm.) Get **groceries** at **Fakta,** Østerg. 8-12. (Open M-F 9am-7pm, Sa 9am-4pm.) **Den Grønne Hjørne,** Frederiksg. 60, has an all-you-can-eat-buffet. (Before 4pm 59kr, after 4pm 79kr. Open M-Sa 11:30am-10pm, Su 5-10pm.) **Postal code:** 8100.

⬛🗗 SIGHTS AND ENTERTAINMENT. The exquisite rose garden of **Marselisborg Castle,** Queen Margarethe II's summer getaway, is open to the public. From the train station, take bus 1, 18, or 19. (Closed in July and whenever else the Queen is in residence.) At the town center, the 13th-century **Århus Domkirke** (cathedral) dominates Bispetorv and the pedestrian streets that fan out around its Gothic walls. (Open May-Sept. M-Sa 9:30am-4pm; Oct.-Apr. 10am-3pm. Free.) Next door, reclaim herstory at the **Women's Museum,** Domkirkeplads 5, where provocative, fascinating exhibits chronicle the role of women worldwide over time. (Open June-Aug. daily 10am-5pm; Sept.-May Tu-Su 10am-4pm. 20kr.) Behind the Women's Museum, the site of a former Gestapo headquarters contains the **Museet for Besættelsen** (Occupation Museum), which houses a collection of military paraphernalia. (Open daily June-Aug. 10am-4pm; Sept.-May Sa-Su 10am-4pm. 20kr.) **Åboulevarden,** lined with trendy cafés along a canal, makes a perfect mid-afternoon pitstop for beer and sunshine. The **Århus Kunstmuseum,** on Vennelystparken, has a fine collection of Danish Golden Age paintings. (Open Tu-Su 10am-5pm. 30kr.) Two millennia ago, the casualties of infighting were entombed in a nearby bog and mummified by its antiseptic acidity. Today you can visit Graballe Man, fresh out of the bog, at his newfound home in the **Moesgård Museum of Prehistory.** Take bus 6 from the train station to the end. (Open Mar.-Sept. daily 10am-5pm; Oct.-Feb. Tu-Su 10am-4pm. 35kr.) The **Prehistoric Trail** leads from behind the museum to a sandy **beach** (3km). In summer, bus 19 (last bus 10:18pm) returns from the beach to the Århus station.

The **Århus Festuge** (Sept. 1-10, 2000; tel. 89 31 82 70; www.aarhusfestuge.dk) is a rollicking celebration of theater, dance, and music. You can visit a smaller replica of Tivoli, the **Tivoli Friheden,** at Skovbrynet. Take bus 1, 4, 6, 8, 18, or 19. (Open daily June 19-Aug. 8 1-11pm; Apr. 19-June 18 and Aug. 9-15 2-10pm. 35kr.) The jazz club **Bent J,** Nørre Allé 66 (tel. 86 12 04 92), jams Monday evenings and occasionally on other weekdays as well. **Valdemar,** Store Torv 4, is a popular disco in the city center. (No cover. Open Th 11pm-5am, F-Sa 10pm-5am. Ages 23 and up.) The **Pan Club,** Jægergårdsg. 42, has a café, bar, and largely gay and lesbian dance club. (Café open M-Th 6pm-midnight, F-Su 8pm-5am. Club cover F-Sa 45kr; open W-Sa 11pm-4am.)

🗗 EXCURSION FROM ÅRHUS: LEGOLAND. Billund is renowned as the home of Legoland—an amusement park built of 40 million Lego pieces. More than just baby-babble, "Lego" is an abbreviation of *leg godt* (have fun playing). Don't skip the impressive indoor exhibitions. Unfortunately, private buses make Legoland a bit expensive. To get there, take the train from Århus to **Vejle** (45min., every hr.), then bus 912 or 44 (dir: Legoland). A joint ticket for the bus and park admission (including rides) costs 165kr. (Tel. 76 50 00 55; www.legoland.dk. Open daily late June-Aug. 10am-9pm; Apr. to mid-June and Sept.-Oct. 10am-8pm; rides close 2hr. earlier.)

AALBORG

The site of the earliest known Viking settlement, Aalborg (OLE-borg) is now Denmark's fourth-largest city. Its spotless streets and white church garnered it the title of Europe's Tidiest City in 1990. This is a far cry from their origins—the year 700 saw nearby Nørresundby inhabited by unkempt and rowdy Vikings. Check out these precursors at **Lindholm Høje**, Vendilavej 11, which has 700 graves and a museum of Viking life. To reach the site, take bus 6 (11kr) from near the tourist office. (Site open daily dawn-dusk. Museum open Apr. to mid-Oct. daily 10am-5pm; late Oct. to mid-Mar. Tu-Su 10am-4pm. 20kr.) The frescoed 15th-century **Monastery of the Holy Ghost**, on C.W. Obelsplads, is Denmark's oldest welfare institution. (Tours in English late June to mid-Aug. Tu and Th 1:30pm. 25kr.) The **Budolfi Church**, on Algade, has a brilliantly colored interior with ringing carillon. (Open M-F 9am-4pm, Sa 9am-2pm.) For serious rollercoasters, visit **Tivoliland**, on Karolinelundsvej. (Open daily May-Sept. noon to 8 or 10pm. 40kr; full-day 160kr.) From the station, cross the street and J.F.K. Plads, then turn left on Boulevarden, which becomes Østeråg, to find the **tourist office**, Østeråg. 8. (Tel. 98 12 60 22; fax 98 16 69 22. Open mid-June to mid-Aug. M-F 9am-6pm, Sa 10am-5pm; mid-Aug. to mid-June M-F 9am-4:30pm, Sa 9am-1pm.) **Aalborg Vandrerhjem and Camping (HI)**, Skydebanevej 50, is next to a beautiful fjord. Take bus 2, 8, or 9 (dir: Fjordparken) to the end. (Tel. 98 11 60 44; fax 98 12 47 11. 75kr; nonmembers 100kr. **Camping** 49kr. Laundry. Reception late June to mid-Aug. 7:30am-11pm; late Jan. to mid-June and early Aug. to mid-Dec. 8am-noon and 4-9pm.) Bars and restaurants line **Jomfru Ane Gade. Postal code:** 9000.

FREDERIKSHAVN

Despite noble efforts to showcase its admittedly charming streets and hospitality, Frederikshavn is best known for **ferry** links (see p. 262). The **tourist office**, Brotorvet 1, near the Stena Line terminal south of the rail station, reserves rooms for a 25kr fee. (Tel. 98 42 32 66; fax 98 42 12 99. Open mid-June to mid-Aug. M-Sa 8:15am-7pm, Su 11am-7pm; mid-Aug. to mid-June M-Sa 9am-4pm.) The **HI youth hostel**, Buhlsvej 6, serves a mixed crowd and is packed. From the bus or train station, walk right, then follow the signs (15min.). (Tel. 98 42 14 75; fax 98 42 65 22. 53kr; nonmembers 78kr. Reception in summer 7am-noon and 4-9pm; off-season call ahead. Open Feb.-Dec.) **Nordstrand Camping** is at Apholmenvej 40. (Tel. 98 42 93 50; fax 98 43 47 85. 52kr per person, 30kr per tent. Open Apr.-Sept.15.) **Postal code:** 9000.

SKAGEN

Perched on Denmark's northernmost tip, sunny Skagen (SKAY-en) is a beautiful summer retreat amidst long stretches of white-sand dunes and sea. The powerful currents of the North Atlantic and Baltic Seas collide at **Grenen**. Don't try to swim in these dangerous waters; every year some hapless soul is carried out to sea. To get to Grenen, take bus 99 or 79 from the Skagen station to **Gammel** (11kr) or walk 3km down Fyrvej. The spectacular **Råberg Mile** sand dunes, formed by a storm in the 16th century, migrate 15m east each year. From here, you can swim along 60km of **beaches,** whose endless summer light attracted Denmark's most famous late 19th-century painters. Their works are displayed in the wonderful **Skagen Museum**, Brøndumsvej 4. (Open June-Aug. daily 10am-6pm; off-season reduced hours. 40kr.) You can also tour the artists' homes at **Michael og Anna Archers Hus**, Markvej 2-4, and **Holger Drachmanns Hus**, Hans Baghsvej 21. Skagen has a large annual **Dixieland music festival** in late June (free-150kr); contact the tourist office for more info.

The **tourist office** is in the train station. (Tel. 98 44 13 77; fax 98 45 02 94. Open June-Aug. M-Sa 9am-5:30pm, Su 10am-2pm; Sept.-May reduced hours.) Nordjyllands Trafikselskab (tel. 98 44 21 33) runs **buses** and **trains** from Frederikshavn to Skagen (1hr., 33kr; with Scanrail 50% off). The **Skagen Ny Vandrerhjem**, Rolighedsvej

DENMARK

2, serves as a springboard for nocturnal forays in town. (Tel. 98 44 22 00; fax 98 44 22 55. Open Mar.-Nov. 75-85kr; nonmembers 100-110kr. Reception 9am-noon and 4-6pm.) Most **campgrounds** around Skagen are open late April to mid-September (55kr per person); try **Grenen** (tel. 98 44 25 46; fax 98 44 65 46) or **Østerklit** (tel./fax 98 44 31 23), not far from the city center.

RIBE

After centuries of wrestling with the North Sea, Denmark's oldest town, Ribe, is now separated from the water by flat salt meadows. The town boasts migratory seasonal birds, half-timbered medieval houses, and red-tiled roofs. For a great view, climb the 248 steps through the clockwork and huge bells of the 12th-century **cathedral** tower. (Open June-Aug. M-Sa 10am-6pm, Su noon-6pm; May and Sept. M-Sa 10am-5pm, Su noon-6pm; Apr. and Oct. daily 11am-4pm; Nov.-Mar. M-Su 11am-3pm. 10kr.) Next to the **Rådhus** (Old Town Hall), Van Støckens Plads, a former debtor's prison houses a small museum on medieval torture. (Tel. 76 88 11 22. Open June-Aug. daily 1-3pm; May and Sept. M-F 1-3pm. 15kr.) Follow the **night watchman** on his rounds for an English or Danish tour of town beginning in Torvet, the main square (35min., June-Aug. 8 and 10pm; May and Sept. 10pm; free). Ribe's **Vikinger,** Udin Plads 1, houses artifacts recovered from an excavation of the town, once an important Viking trading post. (Open Apr.-June and Sept.-Oct. daily 10am-4pm; July-Aug. daily 10am-6pm; Nov.-Mar. Tu-Su 10am-4pm. 45kr.) Two kilometers south of town, the open-air **Ribe Vikingcenter,** Lustrupvej 4, has authentic re-creations of a Viking town. (Open May-June and Sept. M-F 11am-4pm, July-Aug. daily 11am-4pm. 45kr.) The **Vadehavscentret** (Wadden Sea Center), Okholmvej 5, Vestervedsted, does tours of the local marshes. To get there, take bus 711. (Tel. 75 44 61 61. Open daily Apr.-Oct. 10am-5pm; Feb.-Mar. and Nov. 10am-3pm. 35kr.)

The **tourist office,** Torvet 3 (tel. 75 42 15 00; fax 75 42 40 78), has free maps and arranges accommodations for a 20kr fee. From the train station, walk down the street to the left of the Viking museum, and it'll be on your right in the **Torvet** (main square). (Open July-Aug. M-F 9:30am-5:30pm, Sa 10am-5pm, Su 10am-2pm; Apr.-June and Sept.-Oct. M-F 9am-5pm, Sa 10am-2pm; Nov.-Mar. M-F 9am-4:30pm, Sa 10am-1pm.) The central **Ribe Vandrerhjen (HI),** Sct. Pedersg. 16, offers bike rental (50kr per day) and a view of the flatlands. (Tel. 75 42 06 20; fax 75 42 42 88. 100kr, nonmembers 125kr. Breakfast 40kr. Sheets 36kr. Reception 8am-noon and 4-8pm; longer hours May-Sept. Open Feb.-Nov.) **Ribe Camping,** Farupvej 2, is 1.5km from the town center. (Tel. 75 41 07 77. 50kr per person; 2-person cabins 175kr). **Supermarkets** are around Seminarievej, near the hostel. **Valdemar,** Sct. Nicolajg 6, is a cozy pub with live music in summer. (Open M-Th 1pm-1am, F-Sa 11am-3am.)

ESTONIA (EESTI)

US$1 = 14.76EEK (ESTONIAN KROONS)	10EEK = US$0.68
CDN$1 = 9.91EEK	10EEK = CDN$1.01
UK£1 = 23.71EEK	10EEK = UK£0.42
IR£1 = 20.09EK	10EEK = IR£0.50
AUS$1 = 9.51EEK	10EEK = AUS$1.04
NZ$1 = 7.82EEK	10EEK = NZ$1.28
SAR1 = 2.44EEK	10EEK = SAR4.09
DM1 = 8.00EEK	10EEK = DM1.25

PHONE CODES | Country code: 372. International dialing prefix: 800.

German cars, cellular phones, designer shops, and ever more stylish youngsters indicate that Estonia is benefiting from its transition to democracy and capitalism. Happy to shuck its Soviet past, Estonia seems quick to revive its historical and cultural ties to its Nordic neighbors, much to the chagrin of the 35% ethnically Russian population. Having overcome successive centuries of domination by the Danes, Swedes, and Russians, the Estonians' serene, patient pragmatism has matured into a dynamic and—some would say—Scandinavian attitude.

Estonians can't resist a man with a copy of *Let's Go: Eastern Europe 2000*.

GETTING THERE AND GETTING AROUND

BY PLANE. The major international airport is in **Tallinn**, Estonia's capital. **Finnair** (tel. 611 09 50) connects Tallinn to Helsinki (round-trip 1700EEK), while **SAS** (tel. 631 22 40) flies to Stockholm (2180EEK).

BY TRAIN AND BUS. Eurail is not valid in Estonia; the only valid pass is the **Baltic Rail Explorer Pass.** Three **train** lines cross the Estonian border: one heads from Tallinn through Tartu to Moscow, another goes to Rīga and on to Warsaw, and the third goes through Narva to St. Petersburg. The **Baltic Express** is the only train to Poland that skips Belarus, linking Tallinn to Warsaw via Kaunas, Rīga, and Tartu (21hr., 1 per day, 477EEK, *coupé* 680EEK). Domestic **buses** are cheaper and more efficient. During the school year (Sept.-June 25), student bus tickets are half-price.

BY FERRY. It is easiest and cheapest to enter Estonia by ferry from Finland or Sweden (200-300EEK). For info on ferries to Tallinn (tel. 631 85 50), see p. 268.

BY CAR AND BY BIKE. Driving conditions are passable. Expressways—particularly the Via Baltica (M-12)—are in good condition; other roads are plagued by potholes and gravel. Night driving is particularly dangerous. In residential areas, the speed limit is 50km per hr.; on expressways, it's 112km per hr. Be sure to park in guarded lots; Estonia has high rates of auto theft. Car **rentals** are 350-900EEK. On the islands, **bike rentals** (100EEK per day) are an excellent means of exploration.

ESSENTIALS

DOCUMENTS AND FORMALITIES. Citizens of Australia, Ireland, New Zealand, and the US can visit visa-free for up to 90 days, UK citizens 180 days. Canadians and South Africans can obtain a visa at the border for 400EEK (about US$70), or use a Latvian and Lithuanian visa to enter the country. If arranged before departure, single-entry visas (good for 30 days) cost US$14, multiple-entry (valid for 1 year, but only 90 consecutive days in Estonia) US$68. Single-transit visas (48hr.) cost US$14, double-transit (96hr.) US$24. To get a visa extension, contact the visa department of the Immigration Department, Endla 4, in Tallinn (tel. 612 69 79).

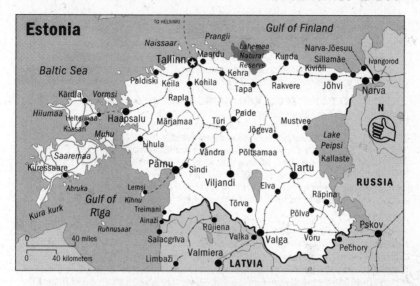

Estonian Embassies at Home: www.vm.ee. **Australia** (honorary consul), 86 Louisa Rd, Birchgrove NSW, 2041 (tel. (02) 98 10 74 68; fax 98 18 17 79); **Canada** (honorary consul), 958 Broadview Ave, Toronto, ON M4K 2R6 (tel. (416) 461-0764; fax 461-0353); **Ireland,** Merlyn Park 24, Ballsbridge, Dublin 4 (tel. (01) 269 15 52; fax 260 51 19; email asjur@indigo.ie); **South Africa** (honorary consul), 16 Hofmeyer St, Welgemoed, Belville, 7530 (tel. (021) 913 38 50; fax 913 25 79); **UK,** 16 Hyde Park Gate, London SW7 5DG (tel. (020) 75 89 34 28; fax 75 89 34 30); **US,** 2131 Massachusetts Ave NW, Washington, DC 20008 (tel. (202) 588-0101; fax 588-0108).

Foreign Embassies in Estonia: All foreign embassies are in **Tallinn** (see p. 269).

TOURIST OFFICES. Larger towns and cities in Estonia have well-equipped, English-speaking **tourist offices** that often arrange tours and make reservations. Smaller information booths, marked with a green "i," sell maps and have brochures.

MONEY. Estonia uses the **kroon** (EEK), divided into 100 **senti** and tied to the Deutschmark. **Hansapank** and **Eesti Ühispank,** the biggest and most stable banks, cash traveler's checks. Many establishments take Visa and MasterCard. **ATMs** are common. No one **tips,** although a service charge may be included in the bill.

COMMUNICATION

Post: An airmail **letter** costs 5.50EEK to Europe and the CIS, 7EEK to the rest of the world. **Postcards** run 5.20EEK to Europe and the CIS, 6.70EEK everywhere else.

Telephone: Digital **phone cards,** available at banks and newspaper kiosks, are sold in denominations of 30, 50, and 100EEK. International **long-distance** calls can be made at post offices. Calls to the Baltic states and Russia cost 8.50EEK per min. (10.50EEK with a card). Phoning the US is quite expensive (US$1-4 per min.). Estonia's recent phone reform has resulted in chaos. **There are three phone systems in Tallinn:** analog, digital, and cellular, each with its own area code. **Analog phone** numbers usually have 6 digits, with area code 22. **Digital phone** numbers have 7 numbers, the first a 6 (often mistakenly placed in parentheses); the area code is 2. For **cellular phones,** the area code is 25. To call Tallinn from outside Estonia on the old system, dial 37 22 and then the number; on the digital system, dial 372. To call a cell phone in Estonia, dial 37 25. To call out of Estonia on the old system, dial 8 and wait for the 2nd tone before dialing. From digital phones, dial 800 without waiting for a tone. For help, call the English-speaking **Ekspress Hotline** (tel. 631 32 22 in Tallinn; elsewhere, dial 8, then 11 88). **Fire,** tel. 01. **Police,** tel. 02. **Ambulance,** tel. 03. From Tallinn, preface all emergency numbers with another 0.

International direct dial numbers include: **AT&T,** 80 08 00 10 01; **Canada Direct,** 80 08 00 10 11; **BT Direct,** 810 80 01 04 41; **Australia Direct,** 800.

Internet: Access is becoming more widespread, and averages 30-60EEK per hr.

Language: Estonians speak the best English in the Baltics; most young people know at least a few phrases. German and Russian are more common among the older set. For helpful phrases in Estonian, see p. 949.

ACCOMMODATIONS, FOOD, AND DRINK. Tourist offices have listings of accommodations and can often arrange beds. There is little distinction between hotels, hostels, and guesthouses. **Homestays** are common, but aren't as cheap as most hostels. For info on HI hostels, contact the **Estonian Youth Hostel Association,** Tatari (tel. 646 14 57; fax 646 15 95; email puhkemajad@online.ee). Estonia has the same assortment of drab sausages, lifeless schnitzel, greasy bouillon, and cold fried potatoes that plague all of the former USSR. The only difference is that fish is more popular. Beer (*õlu*) is the national drink in Estonia—it is inexpensive, delicious, and high-quality. The national brand *Saku* is excellent, as is the darker *Saku Tume*.

LOCAL FACTS

Time: Estonia is 2hr. ahead of Greenwich Mean Time (GMT; see p. 49).

Climate: Winters are severe, summers temperate and pleasant.

Hours: Businesses take hour-long breaks at noon, 1pm, or 2pm; most are closed on Su.

Holidays in 2000: New Year's Day (Jan. 1); Independence Day (1918; Feb. 24); Good Friday (Apr. 21); Catholic Easter (Apr. 23-24); Spring Day (May 1); Whit Sunday (June 11); Victory Day (Battle of Võnnu, 1919; June 23); Jaanipäev (St. John's Day, Midsummer; June 24); Restoration of Independence (Aug. 20); Christmas (Dec. 25-26).

Festivals: Old Town Days (June 6-10), in Tallinn, host open-air concerts throughout Vanalinn. The first week of July provides just one more excuse (as if one were necessary) to loose the taps in Tallinn bars, as **Beersummer** celebrates all things hoppy.

TALLINN

The most renowned town of the German Hanseatic League in the 14th and 15th centuries, Tallinn is beginning to boom once again. Although its drab outskirts remain squalid, as if frozen in Soviet rule, Tallinn's cosmopolitan shops and fashionably dressed youngsters complement the ancient beauty and charming serenity of the capital. Germanic spires, Danish towers, and Russian minarets grace Tallinn's skyline, while visitors wind their way through its cobblestoned streets.

■ GETTING THERE AND GETTING AROUND

Trains: Toompuiestee 35 (tel. 615 68 51). Trams 1 and 2 connect the station to Hotel Viru. To: **Rīga** (5hr., 7 per day, 140EEK); **Vilnius** (9hr., 2 per day, 160EEK); **St. Petersburg** (10hr., 1 per day, 157EEK); and **Berlin** (11hr., 6 per week, 210-280EEK).

Buses: Lastekodu 46 (tel. 601 03 86), 1.5km southeast of Vanalinn. Take trams 2 or 4 or bus 22 to the center. Buy tickets at the station or from the driver. Buses—frequent and cheap—are the best way to travel domestically. Also to: **Rīga** (7hr., 4 per day, 132EEK); **St. Petersburg** (9hr., 2 per day, 155EEK); and **Vilnius** (9hr., 2 per day, 160EEK).

Ferries: At the end of Sadama (info tel. 631 85 50), 15min. from the center. The following chug to **Helsinki** from different terminals: **Nordic Jet Line,** Terminal B (tel. 613 70 00; fax 613 72 22; 1½hr., 432-513EEK); **Tallinn Express,** Terminal C (tel. 640 98 77; www.tallink.ee; 1¾hr., 3 per day, 405-460EEK); **Eckerö Line,** Terminal B (tel. 631 86 06; fax 631 86 61; 3½hr., 3 per day, 250-325EEK, students 150-200EEK); **Silja Line,** Terminal D (tel. 631 83 31; fax 631 82 64; 3½-8½hr., 2 per day, 270-410EEK).

Public Transportation: Buses, trams, and trolleybuses cover the entire metropolitan area 6am-midnight. Buy tickets (*talong*; 5EEK) from kiosks around town and validate them in the metal boxes on board (410EEK fine for riding without a valid ticket).

Taxis: Find a *Takso* stand, or call 612 00 00, 630 01 34, 655 60 00, or 55 79 05. Check the cab for a meter and expect to pay 4-6EEK per km.

Tallinn

ACCOMMODATIONS

A Hotell Gasthaus Eeslitall
B Hotell Küün (HI)
C Pääsu Hotell
D Merevaik (HI)

ESTONIA

ORIENTATION AND PRACTICAL INFORMATION

The ring around Tallinn's egg-shaped **Vanalinn** (Old Town) is made up of legs **Rannamäe tee, Mere pst., Pärnu mnt., Kaarli pst.,** and **Toompuiestee.** Vanalinn peaks at the fortress-rock **Toompea,** whose streets are level with the church steeples of **All-linn** (Lower Town) below. Enter Vanalinn through the 15th-century **Viru värarad,** the main gates in the city wall, 500m from **Hotel Viru,** Tallinn's central landmark. To get to Vanalinn from the **ferry terminal,** walk 15min. along Sadama, which turns into Põhja pst., and turn left on Pikk through **Paks Margareeta** (Fat Margaret) gate. From the train station, cross under Toompuiestee and continue straight on **Nunne;** turn left on Pikk and right on Kinga to get to **Raekoja pl.,** the center of All-linn.

Tourist Office: Raekoja pl. 10 (tel. 694 69 46; fax 694 69 45; www.tallinn.ee). *Tallinn in Your Pocket* 16EEK. Open M-F 9am-5pm, Sa-Su 10am-4pm. **Branch,** Sadama 5, at the **harbor** (Terminal A). Open daily 9am-6pm. The **Tallinn Card** covers a city tour, transportation, and entry to most museums (1-day 195EEK, 2-day 270EEK, 3-day 325EEK).

Embassies: Canada, Toomkooli 13 (tel. 631 79 78; fax 631 35 73). Open M-F 9am-4:30pm. **Latvia,** Tõnismägi 10 (tel. 646 13 13; fax 631 13 66). Open M-F 10am-noon. **Russia,** Pikk 19 (tel. 646 41 69; fax 646 41 78). Open M-F 9am-noon. **UK,** Kentmanni 20 (tel. 631 34 61; fax 631 33 54). Open Tu-Th 10am-noon. **US,** Kentmanni 20 (tel. 631 20 21; fax 631 20 25). Open M-F 8:30am-5:30pm.

Currency Exchange: The post office (windows 11 and 47) has some of the best rates in town. **ATM** machines can be found on nearly every street in Vanalinn.

American Express: Suur-Karja 15, EE-090 (tel. 626 62 62; fax 631 36 56). Mail held and cash advances granted for members. Open M-F 9am-6pm, Sa 10am-5pm.

Luggage Storage: Downstairs in the train station (lockers 15EEK). Also at the bus station (checked baggage 3-12EEK per day); open daily 5am-noon and 12:30-11:40pm.

Emergencies: Ambulance, tel. 003. **Fire,** tel. 001. **Police,** tel. 002.

Pharmacy: RAE Apteek, Pikk 47 (tel. 44 44 08). Open M-F 9am-6pm, Sa 10am-4pm.

Internet Access: Küber-kohvik, Gonsiori 4 (tel. 626 73 67), diagonally opposite the Hotel Viru. 60EEK per hr. Open daily 10am-midnight.

Telephones: In the post office building (see below). Public phones are available all over the city; buy a phone card (30, 50, or 100EEK) from any convenience store or kiosk.

Post Office: Narva mnt. 1, 2nd fl., opposite Hotel Viru. Open M-F 8am-7pm, Sa 9am-5pm. Address mail to be held: Allison LORENTZEN, Narva mnt. 1, Tallinn **19090**, Estonia.

PHONE CODE	From outside Estonia, dial int'l dialing prefix (see inside back cover) + 372 + city code (see p. 267) + local number.

▐▐◌ ACCOMMODATIONS AND FOOD

At the height of summer, hostels fill fast, so book ahead. In a bind, ask at the bus station about beds there (doubles 120-170EEK). **Bed & Breakfast,** Sadama 11 (tel./ fax 641 22 91), finds private rooms from 180EEK per person.

▨ Hotell Küün (The Barn; **HI**), Väike-Karja 1, 2nd fl. (tel. 631 32 52; fax 646 41 18), in Vanalinn. From Raekoja pl., follow Vanaturu kael, turn right on Vana turg, left on Suur-Karja, and bear left; the sparkling hostel is through an arch on the left. Dorms 180EEK; doubles 535EEK; nonmembers add 15EEK each. Sheets 20EEK. Laundry. V, MC.

Hotell Gasthaus Eeslitall, Dunkri 4, 2nd fl. (tel. 631 37 55; fax 631 32 10), just off Raekoja pl. Colorful, clean rooms. Singles 450EEK; doubles 585EEK. Breakfast 36EEK.

Pääsu Hotell, Sõpruse pst. 182 (tel. 52 00 34; fax 654 20 13), in Mustamäe. Take bus 4 from the train station or bus 2, 3, or 9 from the center to "Linnu tee." Backtrack and hang a left on Linnu tee, turn left on Nigri, and follow the signs. Comfortable rooms with TVs and fridges. Singles 360EEK; doubles 460EEK; triples 540EEK. Breakfast included.

Merevaik (HI), Sõpruse pst. 182, 5th fl. (tel. 52 96 04; fax 52 96 47). Enter from the messy stairwell behind the Pääsu Hotell (see above). This Russian-run hostel's sole attraction is its price. 162EEK, nonmembers 180EEK.

Merevaikus, Rahukohtu 5, on Patkuli vaateplats, boasts some of the best views of medieval Tallinn and the Baltic and is one of the best deals in town. (Crêpes, salads, soups, and herring with potatoes 30-50EEK. Open daily 11am-11pm. V, MC.) **Olematu Rüütel** (The Nonexistent Knight), Kiriku põik 4a (tel. 631 38 27), on Toompea, has everything from cheap vegetarian dishes (35-45EEK) to Indonesian pork and Atlantic salmon (120EEK). (Meals around 150EEK. *Saku* 25EEK. V, MC.) **Padakonna Kõrts,** Rüütli 28/30 (tel. 641 84 43), behind Niguliste Kirik, nestled in a corner of the lower town wall, creates medieval Tallinn with tankards of beer in a candle-lit cavern. (Meals around 150EEK. Open daily noon-midnight.) **Spar supermarket,** Aia 7, is near Viru värarad. (Open daily 9am-9pm.)

◉ SIGHTS

VANALINN. Enter the Old Town through Viru värarad; up Viru lies **Raekoja pl.** (Town Hall Square), where beer flows in outdoor cafés and local troupes perform in summer. **Old Thomas** (Vana Toomas), the 16th-century cast-iron weathervane figurine of Tallinn's legendary defender, tops the 14th-century **raekoja**. Thomas has done a good job so far; it's the oldest surviving town hall in Europe. *(Open daily 9am-5pm. Tours 30EEK.)* Head up Mündi on the north side of the square and turn right on Pühavaimu to reach 14th-century **Church of the Holy Ghost** (Pühavaimu kirik), which sports an intricate 17th-century wooden clock. *(Open M-Sa 10am-4:30pm. Free concerts M 6pm.)* Continue down Pühavaimu and turn left on Vene to satisfy your religious ardor at the **Dominican Cloister** (Dominiiklaste Klooster), founded in 1246. *(Vene 16. Open daily 11am-7pm. 25EEK.)* Continue up Vene, turn left on Olevimägi, and turn right on Pikk for a view of the medieval city's north towers. At the end of Pikk, in the squat tower known as **Fat Margaret** (Paks Margareeta), the **Maritime Museum** (Mere-muuseum) examines Tallinn's port history. *(Pikk 70. Open W-Su 10am-6pm. 7EEK, students 3EEK.)* Head to the other end of Pikk and turn left on Rataskaevu to see **St. Nicholas' Church** (Niguliste kirik) and its mighty spire. *(Open Tu 5-8pm, W noon-6pm, Th-Su 11:30am-6pm. 15EEK, students 5EEK.)* The 1475 **Peek in the Kitchen Tower** (Kiek in de Kök) offers a fun and fact-filled journey through medieval Tallinn in six floors. *(Komandandi 2. Open Tu-F 10:30am-5:30pm, Sa-Su 11am-4:30pm. 10EEK, students 5EEK.)*

TOOMPEA. From Raekoja pl., head down Kullassepa, right on Niguliste, and uphill on Lühike jalg to reach Toompea's **Castle Square** (Lossi pl.), dominated by the Russian minarets of **Aleksander Nevsky Cathedral,** begun under Tsar Alexander III and finished just in time for the Bolshevik Revolution. The exterior renovations are almost complete, and are set to rival the rich interior; inside, gold leaf climbs square pillars to the vaulted ceiling. *(Open daily 8am-7pm. Services 9am and 6pm.)* Directly behind **Toompea Castle** (the current seat of the Estonian Parliament, but closed to the public), a fluttering Estonian flag tops **Tall Hermann** (Pikk Hermann), Tallinn's tallest tower and most impressive medieval fortification. As you face the tower, turn right on Toom-Kooli and turn right at the **Dome Church** (Toomkirik) to get to the **Art Museum** (Eesti Kunstimuuseum), which displays Estonian art from the 1800s to the 1940s. *(Kiriku pl. 1. Open W-Su 11am-6pm. 10EEK, students 5EEK.)*

ROCCA-AL-MARE. On the peninsula of Rocca-al-Mare, 10km west of the city center, the **Estonian Open-Air Museum** (Vabaõhumuuseumi) recreates 18th- to 20th-century wooden mills and homesteads. Estonian folk troupes perform regularly. *(Vabaõhumuuseumi 12. From Tallinn's train station, take bus 21 or 21a (25min.). Open May-Oct. daily 10am-8pm; some buildings close 6pm. 21EEK, students 7EEK.)*

ENTERTAINMENT

Pick up *Tallinn This Week* (free) at the tourist office. **Estonia Teater,** Estonia pst. 4, offers opera, ballet, and chamber music. (Tel. 626 02 15. Tickets sold daily noon-7pm.) **Eesti Kontsert,** Estonia pst. 4, features almost nightly symphonies. (Tel. 44 31 98. Open M-F noon-7pm, Sa-Su noon-5pm. Tickets from 30EEK.) During **Old Town Days** (June 6-10), the city fills with open-air concerts. The first week of July brings **Beersummer,** a celebration of the good stuff. On summer Sundays, Tallinn converges on the **beach** of Pirita, a few km from the center (take bus 1, 1a, 8, or 114).

Bars have sprouted on almost every street of Vanalinn, and the scene moves to clubs by 11pm. **Von Krahli Teater/Baar,** Rataskaevu 10, is a bar, club, and avant-garde theater showcasing talent from Lithuanian jazz to experimental dance. (Tickets from 40EEK. Bar open Su-Th noon-1am, F-Sa noon-3am.) **Nimeta Baar** (Pub With No Name), Suur-Karja 4, draws a boisterous crowd. (Open Su-Th 11am-2am, F-Sa 11am-4am.) **Hollywood,** Vanna-Posti 8, spins house and techno. (Cover up to 100EEK. Open Tu and Su 9pm-3am, W-Th 9pm-4am, F-Sa 9pm-6am.)

TARTU

Tartu may be the oldest city in the Baltics—and Estonia's second-largest (pop. 101,900)—but it's also a fountain of youth. Tartu may slow down a bit in summer when its students run off to the coast, but enough concerts, theater, and nightlife remains to keep you entertained. The logical place to start seeing the sights is the 1775 **Raekoja plats** (Town Hall Square), the center of Tartu. Follow Ülikooli from behind the town hall to the must-see sight in Tartu, **Tartu University** (Tartu Ülikool). The main building was built in 1809 with six imposing Corinthian columns. Farther up Ülikooli (which becomes Jaani), **St. John's Church** (Jaani-kirik), Lutsu 16/24, completed in 1323, was once unique in Gothic architecture, with thousands of terracotta saints, martyrs, and other figures; most of the figures were destroyed, however, in the Russian recapture of Tartu in 1944. The central sight of **Cathedral Hill** (Toomemägi) is the majestic 15th-century **Cathedral of St. Peter and Paul** (Toomkirik); it houses the **Tartu University Museum** (Muuseum Historicum Universitatis Tartuensis). (Open W-Su 11am-5pm. 10EEK, students 5EEK.) Follow Riia uphill from the bus station and turn right on Peplen and follow it around the bend on your left as it becomes Kuperjanovi to the **Estonian National Museum** (Eesti

ESTONIA

Rahva Muuseum), J. Kuperjanov 9. (Open W-Su 11am-6pm. 5EEK, students 3EEK.)
⬛**Wilde Bar,** Vallikraavi 4, is crazy wild. (Beer 25EEK. Live music most nights.
Open Su-M noon-midnight, Tu-Th noon-1am, F-Sa noon-2am.)

Trains go from Vaksali 6 (tel. (7) 37 32 20), at Kuperjanovi and Vaksali, 1.5km from
the city center, to Tallinn (3hr., 5 per day, 70EEK) and Moscow (18hr., 1 per day,
284EEK, *coupé* 416EEK). **Buses** (tel. (7) 47 72 27) go from Turu 2, at Riia and Turu,
300m southeast of Raekoja pl. along Vabaduse, go to Tallinn (2-5hr., 40 per day,
75EEK); Rīga (5hr., 1 per day, 150EEK); and St. Petersburg (10hr., 2 per day, 160-
178EEK). Buses 5 and 6 run from the train station to the center and then to the bus
station. From the bus station follow Riia mnt. and turn right on Ülikoali to Raekoja
pl. and the **tourist office,** Raekoja pl. 14. (Tel./fax (7) 43 21 41. Open M-F 10am-6pm,
Sa 10am-3pm.) **Tartu Hotell (HI),** Soola 3, is in the center of town opposite the bus
station. (Tel. (7) 43 20 91; fax 43 30 41. 200EEK; singles 550-875EEK; doubles 640-
900EEK. Breakfast included. Sauna 140EEK per hr. Check-out noon. V, MC.)
Rotundi Kohvik, the wooden octagon in the park on Toomemägi near Angel's Bridge,
serves ample portions of Estonian favorites. (Meals 40-50EEK. Open daily 11am-
8pm.) The **supermarket,** Tartu Kaubamaja, is at Riia 2. (Tel. (7) 47 62 31. Open M-F
9am-9pm, Sa 9am-8pm, Su 10am-8pm. V, MC.) **Postal code:** 51003.

ESTONIAN ISLANDS

Worried about providing an easy escape route to the West, the Soviets once cordoned these islands off from foreigners and Estonians. As a result, they remain a
preserve for all that is distinctive about Estonia, from the outdoor museums of
Saaremaa to the exotic flora and fauna on Hiiumaa.

SAAREMAA. Saaremaa, the biggest and most-touristed island, is reckoned to be
more Estonian than Estonia itself. **Kuressaare,** its largest city and once a thriving
resort, is now making a comeback with summer influxes of young Estonians. Head
south from Raekoja pl. along Lossi, through the park, and across the moat to reach
the **Bishopric Castle** (Piiskopilinnus). Inside, the eclectic collection of the **Saaremaa
Regional Museum** chronicles the islands' history. (Open May-Aug. daily 11am-7pm;
Sept.-Apr. closed M-Tu. 30EEK, students 15EEK.) The best way to see the rest of
the island is to rent a **bike** (115EEK per day) at **Saare Autex,** Tallinna 21, and pedal
southwest to the **beaches** in southwest Saaremaa (8-12km from Kuressaare) or to
the **Kaarma Church** in east Saaremaa. Direct **buses** (tel. (245) 573 80), the easiest and
cheapest way to get from Kuressaare to the mainland, leave from Pihtla tee 2, at the
corner of Tallinna, for Tallinn (4hr., 9 per day, 110EEK). The **tourist office,** Tallinna
2, is inside the town hall. (Tel./fax (245) 331 20. Open May to mid-Sept. M-Sa 9am-
7pm, Su 10am-3pm; mid-Sept. to Apr. M-F 9am-5pm.) Sleep at **Mardi Öömaja,** Valli-
maa 5a. (Tel./fax (245) 332 85. Singles 150EEK; doubles 200EEK.) To get to **Tare
Motel and Camping,** take the Pihtla bus. (Tel. (245) 23 331. Doubles 110-190EEK.)

HIIUMAA. By restricting access to Hiiumaa (HEE-you-ma) for 50 years, the Soviets unwittingly preserved many of the island's rare plant and animal species, as well
as its unhurried way of life. The island's biggest city, **Kärdla,** contains as many
meandering creeks and trees as houses. You can **hike** or **camp** in the **West-Estonian
Islands Biosphere Reserve,** which exclusively hosts more than two-thirds of all the
plant species in Estonia. Apart from the biosphere, the most interesting sights on
the island lie along the coast; rent a **bike** (100EEK) from **Kertu Sport,** Vabrikuväljak
1, just across the bridge from the bus station in Kärdla. **Ferries** run between north
Saaremaa's Triigi port and south Hiiumaa's Sõru port (1hr., Th-Tu 2 per day,
50EEK). Direct **buses** run from Sadama 13 (tel. 320 77), north of Kärdla's main
square, Keskväljak, to Tallinn (4hr., 3 per day, 80EEK). **Postal code:** 92411.

FINLAND (SUOMI)

US$1 = 5.73MK (FINNISH MARKKA)	1MK = US$0.17
CDN$1 = 3.72MK	1MK = CDN$0.26
UK£1 = 9.23MK	1MK = UK£0.11
IR£1 = 7.55MK	1MK = IR£0.13
AUS$1 = 3.72MK	1MK = AUS$0.27
NZ$1 = 3.00MK	1MK = NZ$0.33
SAR1 = 0.94MK	1MK = SAR1.07
EUR€1 = 5.95MK	1MK = EUR€0.17

PHONE CODE | Country code: 358. International dialing prefix: 00.

Between the Scandinavian peninsula and the Russian wilderness, Finland is a land of coniferous trees, astounding summer clouds, and five million taciturn souls. Outside the Helsinki metropolitan area, nature reigns. The west coast is dotted with old wooden shacks, and the Swedish-speaking Åland Islands are a biker's paradise. The Lake District in southeast Finland also offers outdoor activities—sailing, skiing, and music festivals. Lapland, in the north, boasts rugged terrain and rolling fells, boundless wilderness, and Finland's several thousand indigenous Sami people.

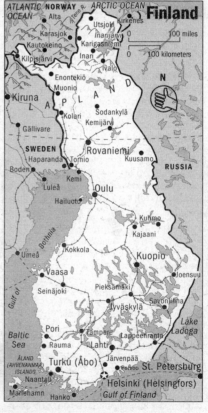

After seven centuries in the crossfire of warring Swedish and Russian empires, Finland experienced an extensive 19th-century romantic nationalistic awakening largely nurtured by the *Kalevala* folk epic, Jean Sibelius' inspirational symphonies, and Akseli Gallen-Kallela's mythic paintings. In 1917, however, the Finns fought a troubling, bitter civil war as the conservative Right completely annihilated the Social Democrats. Finland let the Nazis in to counter Russian aggression, on the principle that one's enemy's enemy is one's friend. Soon, the Finns had turned against these "allies," who were reluctant to go.

Finland is now the most active nation in the UN Peacekeeping Forces; its mediation efforts are best memorialized in Namibia, where hundreds name their children Ahtisaari in honor of the Finnish envoy who supervised the independence process. All the while, Finland has labored to maintain a delicate Nordic neutrality. Its cultural influences are felt most strongly geographically: its east tends to be more Russian, the west more Swedish.

DISCOVER FINLAND

Perched on the edge of Scandinavia and Russia, **Helsinki** (p. 277) is a melange of Orthodox cathedrals and Lutheran churches, sleek 20th-century architecture, and grand 19th-century avenues. Daytrip to oft-photographed **Porvoo** (p. 282) and seaside **Hanko** (p. 282) before heading westward to **Turku**, Finland's oldest city (p. 284). Don't forget to check out the rather unique **Moomin World** (p. 285) in nearby Naantali before ferrying over to the Swedish-speaking and lovely **Åland Islands** (p. 282) for a relaxing jaunt. **Savonlinna** in the Lake District was once a tsarist resort and is now a must-see (p. 285). Top off the adventure in Lappland, where you can sit in Santa's lap and munch at the northernmost **McDonald's** in the world in **Rovaniemi** (p. 286).

GETTING THERE AND GETTING AROUND

BY PLANE. Finnair (toll-free in Finland tel. 0800 140 160; English 24hr. info tel. 818 83 83; fax (09) 818 87 35; www.finnair.com) flies in from 50 international cities and covers the domestic market. In **Australia,** Avion House, 249-251 Pulteney St, Adelaide SA 5000 (tel. (08) 83 06 84 00; fax 83 06 84 39); in **New Zealand,** Trust Bank Building, 229 Queen St, 6th fl., Auckland (tel. (09) 379 44 55; fax 377 56 48); in the **US,** 20 Park Plaza, #912, Boston, MA 02116 (tel. (617) 482-4952 or 800-950-5000; fax (617) 482-5932). On domestic flights Finnair gives a discount of up to 50% for those ages 17-24, and has special summer and snow rates that reduce fares by up to 70%. They fly to many domestic destinations, and offer a variety of sales year-round.

BY TRAIN. Eurail is valid in Finland. The national rail company is **VR Ltd, Finnish Railways,** P.O.Box 488, 00101 Helsinki (fax (09) 707 4086; www.vr.fi/heo/english/heo.htm), which runs efficient trains north at typical Nordic prices (Turku to Helsinki 96mk, Helsinki to Rovaniemi 328mk); seat reservations (20-30mk) are not required except on the luxurious **InterCity** trains. The *buy-in-Scandinavia* **Scanrail Pass** allows unlimited rail travel through Denmark, Norway, Sweden, and Finland, as well as many free or 20-50% discounted ferry rides. (5 days within 15 days 1390kr; under 26 1040kr; 60 and over 1230kr. 21 consecutive days 2110kr; under 26 1585kr; 60 and over 1880kr.) This differs from the *buy-outside-Scandinavia* **Scanrail Pass** (see **Essentials,** p. 61). A **Finnrail Pass** gives unlimited rail travel throughout Finland during a one-month period (3 days 600mk, 5 days 810mk, 10 days 1090mk).

BY BUS. Buses cost about the same as or more than trains, and often take longer. They are, however, the only way to reach some smaller towns and to travel in northern Finland. **Onni Vilkas Ltd** (www.onnivilkas.planet.fi/pietarie.ht) runs a daily bus service between **Helsinki** and **St. Petersburg,** as well as domestic destinations. **Expressbus** covers a wide area of Finland (www.expressbus.com). For bus info anywhere in Finland, call 02 00 40 00 (6.34mk per min.). ISIC cardholders can buy a **student card** (38mk and photo required) from bus stations that ensures a 50% discount on tickets. Or try buying your ticket from the driver for a student discount with any student ID. Railpasses are valid on **VR Ltd Buses** when trains are not in service.

BY FERRY. Viking Line (in Helsinki tel. (09) 123 51, fax 17 55 51; in Stockholm tel. (08) 452 40 00, fax 452 40 75) steam nightly from **Stockholm** to **Helsinki** (15hr., 215mk, students 165mk; off-season 122mk, students 92mk), **Mariehamn** on **Åland** (6½hr., 199mk, students 169mk), and **Turku** (11-12hr., 215mk, students 165mk, off-season 110mk, students 85mk). Scanrail holders get 50% off on Viking; Eurailers ride free. **Silja Line** (in Helsinki (tel. (09) 180 41; fax 180 4402; www.silja.com/english) in Stockholm (tel. (08) 666 33 30; fax 667 86 81), in Turku (tel. (02) 335 6244) sails daily from **Stockholm** to: **Helsinki** (15hr., from 210mk, 25mk student discount); **Mariehamn** on **Åland** (5½hr., 130mk, students 120mk, off-season 70mk, students 60mk); and **Turku** (11hr., 2 per day, 90-120mk, students 65-95mk). Eurail tickets are valid on the Stockholm to Helsinki and Stockholm to Turku routes. **Birka Lines** (Mariehamn tel. (018) 170 27, in Stockholm (08) 714 55 20) launches its *Princess* daily for cruises from **Stockholm** to **Mariehamn** (24hr., 125mk).

BY CAR. Driving conditions are good, but be wary of snow and ice, as well as elk and reindeer crossings. Drive on the right side of the road. Strict drinking and driving laws result in fines and/or imprisonment for violators. **Autoliitto (Automobile and Touring Club of Finland),** Hämeentie 105A, 00550 Helsinki (tel. (09) 77 47 61; fax 77 47 64 44; www.autoliitto.fi/englishf.htm), has info. For car **rentals,** contact **Europcar** (tel. (09) 75 15 57 00; fax 75 15 54 54; www.europcar.com) or **Hertz** (tel. (09) 16 67 13 00; fax 16 67 13 82; www.hertz.com), which each charge about 2400mk per week.

BY BIKE AND BY THUMB. Finland boasts 10,000km of **cycling** paths. Some campgrounds, youth hostels, and tourist offices rent bikes. Rates average 30-70mk per day or 190mk per week. **Hitchhikers** report finding more rides in Finland than elsewhere in Scandinavia; truck drivers may be most likely to stop. As always, use your discretion, and err on the side of caution while hitchhiking.

ESSENTIALS

DOCUMENTS AND FORMALITIES. South Africans need a **visa** to enter as short-stay tourists; citizens of Australia, New Zealand, Canada, the UK, Ireland, and the US can visit for up to 90 days without a visa. This three-month period begins upon entry into any Scandinavian country; for more than 90 days in any combination of Finland, Iceland, Norway, and Sweden, you will need a visa.

Finnish Embassies at Home: Australia, 10 Darwin Ave, Yarralumla, ACT 2600 (tel. (02) 62 73 38 00; fax 62 73 36 03); **Canada,** 55 Metcalfe St, #850, Ottawa ON, K1P 6L5 (tel. (613) 236-2389; fax 238-1474; email finembott@synapse.net); **South Africa,** P.O. Box 443, Pretoria 0001 (tel. (012) 343 02 75; fax 343 30 95); **Ireland,** Russell House, Stokes Pl, St. Stephen's Green, Dublin 2 (tel. (01) 478 1344); **UK,** 38 Chesham Pl, London SW1X 8HW (tel. (020) 78 38 62 00; fax 235 36 80); **US,** 3301 Massachusetts Ave, NW, Washington, DC 20008 (tel. (202) 298-5800; fax 298-6030; www.finland.org).

Foreign Embassies in Finland: All foreign embassies are in **Helsinki** (see p. 278).

TOURIST OFFICES. The helpful and knowledgeable **Finnish tourist boards** offer a comprehensive website (www.mek.fi) and can be reached at Töölönkatu 11, PL 625, 00101 Helsinki, in Finland (tel. (09) 417 69 11; fax 41 76 93 33.)

Finish Tourist Boards at Home: Australia (Representative Office), 81 York St, Level 4, Sydney NSW 2000 (tel. (02) 92 90 19 50; fax 92 90 19 81); **Canada** (Representative Office), P.O. Box 246, Station Q, Toronto, ON M4T 2M1 (tel. (416) 964-9159; fax 964-1524); **UK,** 30-35 Pall Mall, London SW1Y 5LP (tel. (020) 78 39 40 48; fax 73 21 06 96); **US,** P.O. Box 4649, Grand Central Station, New York, NY 10163-4649 (tel. (212) 885-9700; fax 885-9710; www.travelfile.com/get/finninfo).

MONEY. The currency unit in Finland is the **markka,** also known as the Finnish mark or Finmark (mk or FIM). There are 100 *pennia* in a *markka.* Banks exchange currency, and accept ATM cards. The best exchange rates are generally found at ATMs. Orange "Otto" bank machines accept Cirrus, MC, Visa, and ATM cards. Average food costs run 60-100mk per day, depending on where you eat; restaurants are expensive. Meals generally cost at least 30mk, large beers at least 20mk.

Tipping and Bargaining: In restaurants, gratuity of 14-15% is included in the check, but leave some extra coins on the table if the service was particularly good. You need not tip taxi drivers, just round the fare up. However 5mk is a normal tip for bellhops, train porters, and sauna and cloakroom attendants.

Taxes: General **Value Added Tax** (VAT) is 22% in Finland, 17% on food and 8% on select services. For VAT refund or general info, contact **Europe Tax-free Shopping Finland Oy,** P.O. Box 460, 00101 Helsinki (tel. (09) 61 32 96 00; fax 61 32 96 75).

COMMUNICATION

Post: The mail service is fast and efficient. Post offices are open M-F from 9am until 5 or 6pm. First-class and priority postal rates for **postcards** and **letters** under 20g is 3.20mk to other EU countries; 2.70mk to non-EU countries in Europe; 6.30mk for letters and

3.40mk for postcards to places outside of Europe. Domestic letters and postcards under 50g cost 3mk. **Post Restante** can be sent to any town's main post office.

Telephones: To make a long-distance call within Finland, dial 0 followed by the number. Local and short long-distance calls within Finland usually cost 2mk; many pay phones take 1-, 5-, and 10mk coins. **Phone cards** are available from R-kiosks and post offices in 30-, 50-, 70-, and 100mk denominations. "Sonera" or "Nonstop" cards work nationwide; other cards only work in the city in which you purchase them. Some card telephones take credit cards. For **domestic information,** call 118; **emergency,** 112; **police,** 100 22. To manually make an **international call,** dial 02 02 22. For **international information** call 020 208. **International direct dialing** numbers include: **AT&T,** 0800 100 10; **Sprint,** 0800 11 02 84; **MCI WorldPhone Direct,** 08001 102 80; **Canada Direct,** 0800 11 00 11; **BT Direct,** 0800 11 04 40; **Ireland Direct,** 0800 11 03 53; **Australia Direct,** 0800 11 00 61; and **Telkom South Africa Direct,** 0800 11 02 70.

Language: Finnish and Swedish. Finnish, a Finno-Ugric language, not Indo-European, is virtually impenetrable to foreigners. Finnish is spoken by 93% of the population, while Swedish, the official second language, is spoken by 6%. Many Finns speak English, but fluency decreases in the north. Sami (Lappish) is the mother tongue of about 1700 people. Watch out for town names that modify their form on train and bus schedules due to the lack of prepositions in Finnish. For useful phrases in Finnish and Swedish, see p. 949.

ACCOMMODATIONS AND CAMPING. Finland has more than 120 **youth hostels** (retkeilymaja; RET-kay-loo-MAH-yah), 70 of which are open year-round. Prices are generally 60-150mk; non-HI-members usually add 15mk. Most have laundry and kitchen facilities; some have saunas, and rent bicycles, canoes, and ski equipment. The **Finnish Youth Hostel Association** (Suomen Retkeilymaja-järjestö-SRM) is at Yrjönkatu 38B, 00100 Helsinki (tel. (09) 693 13 47; fax 693 13 49; email info@srm.inet.fi; www.srmnet.org). Hotels are often exorbitant (over 250mk); **kesähotelli** (summer hotels) that operate June-Aug. offer accommodation for around 40-110mk. The **Finland Tourism Board** (www.finland-tourism.com/mek_page4.html) keeps a database of booking agencies for both year-round and summer hotels. **Private room** rental is not particularly common, but local tourist offices may help you find the cheapest accommodations.

Without the landowner's permission it is forbidden to **camp** outside campsites. However, throughout Finland there are about 360 well-equipped campgrounds that dapple the country, 200 of which belong to the **Finnish Travel Association's** national network (tent sites 25-90mk per night, *mökit* (small cottages) 150mk and up). Seventy are open year-round. To stay in cottages you will need a Finnish or international camping card (FICC). You can buy a membership card from any camping site (20mk per family). For more info and a guide to campgrounds, contact the **Finnish Travel Association/Camping Department,** Atomitie 5C, 00370 Helsinki (tel. (09) 622 62 80; fax 654 3 58).

FOOD AND DRINK. A *kahuila* is a café that serves food, coffee, and perhaps beer, while a *grilli* is a fast-food stand. A *ravintola* is officially a restaurant, but Finns appear not to eat in these establishments; instead, they go for a beer. Some evolve into dance spots later in the evening (covers from 15mk). You must be at least 18 years old to purchase beer and wine, and 20 for hard liquor; the age limit in bars and pubs is usually 18, but it can be as high as 25. Despite the stereotype of the drunken Finn, alcohol is no bargain. Beer *(olut)* is divided into several groups. *Olut* IV is the strongest and most expensive (at least 25mk per 0.5L). *Olut* III (the best value) is slightly weaker and cheaper (18-20mk). Outside bars and restaurants, all alcohol stronger than *Olut* III must be purchased at the state-run **Alko liquor** stores; expect lines before Midsummer. The less expensive **supermarkets** are **Alepa, Antilla, Euromarket,** and any type of **K market.** The best budget dining options are the common **all-you-can-eat lunch buffets** (35-45mk), often found at pricier restaurants. The Finns are proud of their fish; popular options include *kirjolohi* (rainbow trout), *silakka* (Baltic herring), and the favorite *lohi* (salmon) cured, pickled, smoked, poached, or baked. Finnish dietary staples include robust rye bread, potatoes, sour milk, Karelian pastries, and squirming yogurt-like *viili*. Reindeer meat, roasted or in a stew, can make an appearance on the table. If you're ready to spend a little, Finnish caviar is among the best in the world, often served with sour cream and chopped onions. In July and August, the land blossoms with blueberries, cranberries, lingonberries, and, in the far north, Arctic cloudberries. The berries are used to make desserts, wines, and vodka and other liquors. For "cheers," Finns say *"hi," "kippis,"* or the Scandinavian *"skal."* Bottoms up!

LOCAL FACTS.

Time: Finland is 2hr. ahead of Greenwich Mean Time (GMT; see p. 49).

Climate: In winter, the longest season of the year, the average temperature is 0°C (32°F), though temperatures reach significantly lower. As northernmost Finland is above the Arctic Circle, it enjoys a spell of **polar night** *(kaamos)* when the sun does not rise. This period can last for nearly 2 months and all over Finland the days are short in winter. By mid-Apr. there are 14-16hr. of daylight each day, and throughout the spring temperatures average around 10°C (50°F). Around **Midsummer** in northern Finland, the sun stays up for 2 months. In the south as well, it is never completely dark in summer. Temperatures through summer usually hover between 15-20°C (60-70°F). in fall, it is around 5°C (40°F). Rainfall is moderate year-round.

Hours: Most shops close M-F at 5 or 6pm (10pm in Helsinki; Sa around 2 or 3pm), but urban supermarkets may stay open until 9pm (Sa 6pm). Shops may also be open June-Aug. on Sundays. Kiosks sell basic food, snacks, and toiletries until 9 or 10pm. Banks are typically open M-F 9:15am-4:15pm.

Holidays in 2000: Epiphany (Jan. 6), Good Friday (Apr. 21), May Day (May 1), Ascension Day (June 1), Midsummer (June 23-24), All Saints' Day (Nov. 1), Independence Day (Dec. 6), Christmas Day (Dec. 25), and Boxing Day (Dec. 26). Many stores and museums, as well as all banks and post offices, are closed for Easter (Apr. 23-24), Christmas (Dec. 24-26), and New Year's Day. During Midsummer, when Finns party all night to the light of *kokko* (bonfires) and the midnight sun, virtually the entire country shuts down.

Festivals: The **Helsinki Festival** (mid-Aug. to early Sept.) is one of Finland's largest, with a wide variety of performances, including chamber, jazz, and rock concerts, as well as dance, theater, and opera. Savonlinna's **Opera Festival** (early July-early Aug.), is set in the beautiful Olavinlinna Castle. **Naantali** has a Chamber Music Festival (June).

HELSINKI (HELSINGFORS)

With broad avenues, grand architecture, and well-tended parks, Helsinki is a model of 19th-century city planning. But it looks forward to the next millennium as well; in 2000 it takes its place as an official European City of Culture. The city distinguishes itself with a decidedly multicultural flair: Lutheran and Russian Orthodox cathedrals stand almost face-to-face, Baltic Sea produce fills the marketplaces and restaurants, and St. Petersburg and Tallinn are but a short cruise away.

▐ GETTING THERE AND GETTING AROUND

Flights: Info tel. 96 00 81 00 (3.40mk per min.). **Buses** 615 (more direct) and 616 run frequently between the **Helsinki-Vantaa Airport** and train station square (15mk). A **Finnair bus** shuttles between the airport and the Finnair building at Asemaaukio 3, next to the train station (35min., every 20min. 5am-midnight, 25mk).

Trains: Info tel. 707 57 06. To: **Tampere** (2hr., every hr. 6am-10pm, 96mk); **Turku** (2hr., 12 per day, 96mk); **St. Petersburg** (7hr., 2 per day, 286mk); **Rovaniemi** (10hr., 8 per day, 328mk); and **Moscow** (15hr., daily at 5:32pm, 499mk). **Lockers** 10mk per day.

Buses: Info tel. 02 00 40 10. The station is between Salomonkatu and Simonkatu; from the train station, turn right and go 2 blocks up Kaivokatu. To: **Lahti** (1½hr., 2 per hr., 90mk); **Tampere** (2½hr., every hr., 94mk); and **Turku** (2½hr., 2 per hr., 109mk).

Ferries: For route options, see p. 274. **Silja Line,** Mannerheimintie 2 (tel. 980 05 26 82). **Viking Line,** Mannerheimintie 14 (tel. 123 577). **Tallink,** Erottajankatu 19 (tel. 22 82 12 11). Viking Line and **Finnjet** (contact Silja Line) depart from Katajanokka Island, east of

Kauppatori (take tram 2 or 4). Silja Line and Tallink sail from South Harbor, south of Kauppatori (take tram 3T).

Local Transportation: Info tel. 010 01 11 (2mk per min.). The metro, trams, and buses run roughly 5:30am-11pm (some major tram and bus lines, including tram 3T, continue until 1:30am). You can buy single-fare tickets on buses and trams (10mk) or from machines at the metro station (8mk); 10-trip tickets (75mk) are available at R-kiosks and at the **City Transport** office in the Rautatientori metro station (open M-Th 7:30am-6pm, F 7:30am-4pm). Tickets are valid for 1hr. (transfers free); punch your ticket on board. The **Tourist Ticket,** available at City Transport and tourist offices, provides unlimited bus, tram, metro, and local train transit (1-day 25mk, 3-day 50mk, 5-day 75mk).

❼ ORIENTATION AND PRACTICAL INFORMATION

Helsinki's main street, **Mannerheimintie,** passes between the bus and train stations as it runs toward the city's center, eventually crossing **Esplanadi.** This tree-lined promenade leads east to **Kauppatori** (Market Square) and the harbor. Both Finnish and Swedish are used on all street signs and maps.

TOURIST, FINANCIAL, AND LOCAL SERVICES

Tourist Offices: City Tourist Office, Pohjoisesplanadi 19 (tel. 169 37 57; fax 169 38 39; www.hel.fi). From the train station, walk 2 blocks south on Keskuskatu and turn left on Pohjoisesplanadi. Open May-Sept. M-F 9am-7pm, Sa-Su 9am-3pm; Oct.-Apr. M-F 9am-5pm, Sa 9am-3pm. The **Finnish Tourist Board,** Eteläesplanadi 4 (tel. 41 76 93 00; fax 41 76 93 01; www.mek.fi), has info on all of Finland. Open June-Aug. M-F 8:30am-5pm, Sa 10am-2pm; Sept.-May M-F 8:30am-4pm. **Hotellikeskus** (Hotel Booking Center; tel. 22 88 14 00; fax 22 88 14 99), in the train station, books rooms for a fee. Open June-Aug. M-Sa 9am-7pm, Su 10am-6pm; Sept.-May M-F 9am-5pm. The **Helsinki Card,** sold at the tourist office, Hotellikeskus, central R-kiosks, and most hotels, provides museum discounts and unlimited local transportation (1-day 120mk, 3-day 180mk).

Embassies: Canada, Pohjoisesplanadi 25B (tel. 17 11 41). Open M-F 8:30am-4:30pm. **Estonia,** Itäinen Puistotie 10 (tel. 622 02 80). **Ireland,** Erottajankatu 7A (tel. 64 60 06). **Latvia,** Armfeltintie 10 (tel. 476 47 20). **Lithuania,** Rauhankatu 13A (tel. 60 82 10). **Poland,** Armas Lindgrenintie 21 (tel. 684 80 77). **Russia,** Tehtaankatu 1B (tel. 66 18 76). **South Africa,** Rahapajankatu 1A 5 (tel. 65 82 88). **UK,** Itäinen Puistotie 17 (tel. 22 86 51 00). Also handles diplomatic matters for **Australians** and **New Zealanders.** Open M-F 8:30am-5pm. **US,** Itäinen Puistotie 14A (tel. 17 19 31). Open M-F 8:30am-5pm.

Currency Exchange: Exchange, Kaivokatu 6, across from the train station. No fee for cash exchange, but 10mk per traveler's check. Open M-F 8am-8pm, Sa 10am-4pm.

English Bookstore: Akateeminen Kirjakauppa (Academic Bookshop), Pohjoisesplanadi 39 (tel. 121 41). Good selection. Open M-F 9am-9pm, Sa 9am-6pm.

Laundromat: Your best bet is to use facilities at youth hostels (5-40mk). Otherwise, try **Easywash,** Runeberginkatu 47. Open M-Th 10am-8pm, F 10am-6pm, Sa 10am-4pm.

EMERGENCY AND COMMUNICATIONS

Emergencies: Tel. 112. **Police,** tel. 100 22.

Pharmacy: Yliopiston Apteekki, Mannerheimintie 96 (tel. 41 78 03 00). Open 24hr.

Medical Assistance: Aleksin lääkäriasema, Mannerheimintie 8 (tel. 77 50 84 00).

Internet Access: Sonera, Kaivokatu 2, opposite the train station, will amaze even the most computer-literate traveler. 15min. free. Open M-F 9am-7pm, Sa 10am-4pm.

Post Office: Mannerheiminaukio 1A (tel. 195 51 17). Open M-F 9am-6pm. Address mail to be held: Thomas MCCARTHY, *Poste Restante,* Mannerheiminaukio 1A, **00100** Helsinki, Finland. Open M-F 7am-9pm, Sa 9am-6pm, Su 11am-9pm.

PHONE CODE	City code: 09. From outside Finland, dial int'l dialing prefix (see inside back cover) + 358 + 9 + local number.

FINLAND

Helsinki

ACCOMMODATIONS

A Stadion Hostel
B Finnapartments Fenno
C Hostel Erottajanpuisto
D Eurohostel

ACCOMMODATIONS AND CAMPING

In June and July, it's wise to make reservations. Most hostels offer laundry facilities and provide breakfast for a fee. Extra summer hostels are open from June to August: try **Hotel Satakunta (HI)**, Lapinrinne 1A (tel. 69 58 51; fax 694 22 26), and **Academica (HI)**, Hietaniemenkatu 14A (tel. 13 11 43 34; fax 44 12 01).

Hotel Erottanjanpuisto (HI), Uudenmaankatu 9 (tel. 64 21 69; fax 680 27 57). Turn right from the train station, left onto Mannerheimintie, and right onto Erottajankatu; Uudenmaankatu is on the right. Dorms 135mk per person. In summer, singles 215mk, doubles 260mk; off-season singles 225mk, doubles 265mk; nonmembers add 15mk each. Breakfast 25-35mk. Kitchen. Reception 24hr. Reserve ahead in summer.

Finnapartments Fenno, Franzeninkatu 26 (tel. 773 16 61; fax 701 68 89). From the train station, turn left, follow Kaisaniemenkatu, and bear left onto Unioninkatu (which becomes Siltasaarenkatu); or catch the metro to Hakaniemi. Then head right on Porthaninkatu, left onto Fleminginkatu, then left again. Basic apartments, some with kitchens and bathrooms. Sauna. Singles 170-240mk; doubles 320mk.

Eurohostel (HI), Linnankatu 9, Katajanokka (tel. 622 04 70; fax 65 50 44; email euroh@icon.fi; www.eurohostel.fi), 200m from the Viking Line/Finnjet ferry terminal. From the train station, head right to Mannerheimvägen and take tram 2 or 4 (dir: Katajanokka). From Uspensky Cathedral, head down Kanavankatu, turn left on Pikku Satamankatu, and bear right on Linnankatu. The largest hostel in Finland, with bright rooms. Kitchen and café. Sauna. Singles 170mk; doubles 206mk; nonmembers add 15-17mk each. Student discounts in winter. Reception 24hr. Accepts email reservations.

FINLAND

Stadion Hostel (HI), Pohj. Stadiontie 3B (tel. 49 60 71; fax 49 64 66). Take tram 3T, 7A, or 10 from the train station to Olympic Stadium and walk to the opposite side. Kitchen, TV, pool, and nearby sauna. 150 beds. Dorms 60mk; doubles 160mk; nonmembers add 15mk each. Breakfast 25mk. Paper sheets 15mk. Laundry. Reception daily June-early Sept. 7am-2am; mid-Sept. to May 8-10am and 4pm-2am.

Rastila Camping (tel. 31 65 51), 14km east of the city center. Take the metro east to Rastila; the campsite is 100m away to the left. Toilets, showers, and washing and cooking facilities. Camping 60mk; cabins 110mk per person. Reception 24hr.

FOOD

In Finland, even groceries are expensive, but find relief at the **Alepa supermarket.** (Branch under the train station open M-Sa 8am-10pm, Su 10am-10pm.) You can buy fresh veggies, fruit, and fish at **Kauppatori** (open June-Aug. M-Sa 7am-2pm and 4-8pm; Sept.-May M-F 7am-2pm), by the port, and at the nearby **Vanha Kauppahalli** (Old Market Hall; open M-F 8am-8pm, Sa 8am-3pm). There are **food courts** in the basement of the train station and in **Forum,** at the corner of Mannerheimintie and Simonkatu (open M-F 9am-9pm, Sa 9am-6pm). If you're not traveling farther east, try one of Helsinki's excellent Russian restaurants.

Zetor, Kaivokatu 10, in Kaivopiha, opposite the train station. The very essence of Finland: food, drinks, music, dancing, and, of course, a tractor. Main dishes 40-100mk; beer 23mk. Open M 1pm-1am, Tu-Th 1pm-3am, F-Sa 3pm-3am, Su 3pm-1am.

Café Engel, Aleksanterinkatu 26. Light fare for a more serious crowd. Try the variety of coffees (from 11mk) and cakes (from 20mk). Open M-Th 7:45am-midnight, F 7:45am-1am, Sa 9:30am-midnight, Su 11am-midnight.

Golden Rax Pizza Buffet, in Forum, opposite the post office. All-you-can-eat pasta and pizza extravaganza (43mk). Open M-Sa 10:30am-10pm, Su 11:30am-10pm.

Kappeli, Eteläesplanadi 1, at the end of the park strip. Old-world charm in the middle of the city has catered to trendies since 1837. Not cheap, but a great spot for people-watching. Entrees 50-110mk. Open Su-Th 9am-2am, F-Sa 9am-3am.

Kasvis, Korkeavuorenkatu 3. Take tram 4 to partake in their elaborate vegetarian buffet. Open M-F 11am-8pm, Sa-Su noon-8pm; kitchen closes at 7:30pm.

SIGHTS

The famed Finnish architect Alvar Aalto once said of Finland, "Architecture is our form of expression because our language is so impossible." The juxtaposition of bold new designs and polished Neoclassical works in the capital, prove him right. Much of the layout and architecture of the old center, however, is the brainchild of a German. After Helsinki became the capital of the Grand Duchy of Finland in 1812, Carl Engel was chosen to design a grand city modeled after St. Petersburg. Tram 3T circles past most sights in an hour, although most sights lie within 2km of the train station—pick up *See Helsinki on Foot* from the tourist office.

SENAATIN TORI (SENATE SQUARE). The square and its **Tuomiokirkko** (Dome Church) showcase Engel's work and exemplify the splendor of Finland's Russian period. *(On the corner of Aleksanterinkatu and Unioninkatu in the city center. Open June-Aug. M-Sa 9am-6pm, Su noon-4pm; Sept.-May Su-F 10am-4pm, Sa 10am-6pm.)*

USPENSKINKATEDRAADI (USPENSKY ORTHODOX CATHEDRAL). Although it is known mainly for its red and gold cupolas and its great spires, which jut prominently out of the Helsinki skyline, it would be shame to ignore the ornate interior of this Byzantine-Slavonic creation. *(Follow Esplanadi down to Kauppatori. Interior open M and W-F 9:30am-4pm, Tu 9:30am-6pm, Sa 9am-4pm, Su noon-3pm.)*

SUOMEN KANSALLISMUSEO (NATIONAL MUSEUM OF FINLAND). The museum displays intriguing bits of Finnish culture, from Gypsy and Sami costumes to *ryijyt* (rugs), along with a magnificent roof mural by Akseli Gallen-Kallela. *(Up the street from the Finnish Parliament House. Closed until spring 2000; until then, parts of the exhibition are displayed at temporary locations. Call 94 05 01 or consult the board outside the museum.)*

OTHER MUSEUMS. Ateneum Taidemuseo, Finland's largest art museum, focuses on Finnish art from the 1700s to the 1960s. *(Kaivokatu 2, opposite the train station. Open Tu and F 9am-6pm, W-Th 9am-8pm, Sa-Su 11am-5pm. 15mk, students 10mk; special exhibits 30-35mk.)* The new museum **Kiasma** has Finnish and international art from the 1960s to 1990s. *(Mannerheiminaukio 2. Open Tu and F 9am-6pm, W-Th 9am-8pm, Sa-Su 11am-5pm. 25mk, students 20mk.)* The **Museum of Art and Design** showcases both Finnish and international design. *(Korkeavuorenkatu 23. Open M-Sa 11am-6pm. 25mk, students free.)*

FINLANDIA TALO. The magnificent white marble concert hall stands as a testament to the skill of the Finnish architect Alvar Aalto, who designed the interior and furnishings as well. *(Mannerheimintie 13E. Tel. 402 41. Tours 20mk.)*

TEMPPELIAUKIO KIRKKO. Designed in 1969 by Tuomo and Timo Suomalainen, this inspiring church is built into a hill of rock, with only the roof visible from the outside. *(Lutherinkatu 3. Walk away from the main post office near the train station on Paasikivenaudio, which becomes Arkadiagatan, then turn right on Fredrikinatu; you'll end up in the square where the church is buried. Open M-F 10am-8pm, Sa 10am-6pm, Su noon-1:45pm and 3:20-5:45pm. Services in English Su 2pm.)*

JEAN SIBELIUS MONUMENT. While looking at this monument, dedicated in 1967 by sculptor Eila Hiltunen to one of the 20th century's greatest composers, you can almost see the music. A well-touristed spot, the monument looks like a cloud of organ pipes ascending to heaven. *(On Mechelininkatu in Sibelius Park. Catch bus 24 (dir: Seurasaari) from Mannerheimintie; look for the monument on your left.)*

SUOMENLINNA. This 18th-century Swedish military fortification is five interconnected islands that were used by the Swedes to repel attacks on Helsinki. Explore old fortress' dark passageways or visit one of the island's museums; check out the model ship collection of the Ehrensvärd and the submarine Vesikko. *(Most museums open in summer daily 10am-5pm; Mar.-May Sa-Su 11am-4pm. 10mk, students 5mk; some have additional admission. Ferries depart from Market Square every hr. 8am-11pm; round-trip 25mk.)*

SEURASAARI. A quick walk across the beautiful white bridge from the mainland will bring you to the many paths of the island of Seurasaari. Old churches and farmsteads transplanted from all over the country line the paths. Visit during Midsummer to witness the *kokko* (bonfires) and Finnish revelry in its full splendor. *(Take bus 24 from Erottaja, outside the Swedish Theater, to the last stop; or, in summer, take a boat from Market Square. Open M-F 9am-3pm, Sa-Su 11am-5pm. 20mk; W free.)*

NIGHTLIFE

Sway to afternoon street music in the leafy **Esplanadi** or party on warm nights with the younger crowd at **Kaivopuisto park** or **Hietaniemi beach.** The free English-language papers *Helsinki This Week, Helsinki Happens,* and *City* list popular cafés, bars, nightclubs, and events. Finland actually enforces the drinking age—18 for beer and wine, 20 for hard alcohol—however, you'll see younger folks drinking. Many clubs have a minimum age of 22. Bouncers and cover charges usually relax on weeknights; speaking English may help. With the exception of licensed restaurants and bars, the state-run liquor store **Alko** holds a monopoly on sales of alcoholic beverages more potent than light beers. (Branch at Mannerheimintie 1. Open M-Th 10am-6pm, F 10am-8pm, Sa 9am-4pm.) Do Euro-pop at **Fennia,** Mikonkatu 17, opposite the train station. (Ages 22 and up. Cover 30mk. Open M-F 11pm-4am, Sa-Su 8pm-4am.) Sip your 80 proof on the terrace at **Vanha** (Old Students' House), Mannerheimintie 3. (Beer from 20mk. Cover 20-50mk for live bands. Open M-Sa 10am-2am, Su 10am-midnight.) **Storyville,** Museokatu 8, near the National Museum, has live jazz and blues after 10pm. (Jazz club open daily 8pm-4am. Bar upstairs open M-Sa 5pm-4am, Su 8pm-4am.) **DTM** (Don't Tell Mama), Annankatu 32, has a gay and mixed crowd. (Age 20 and up. Open Su-Th 10pm-4am, F-Sa 9pm-4am.)

EXCURSIONS FROM HELSINKI

PORVOO. Located along Old King Road, which continues from Helsinki to Russia, the cobblestoned streets and old wooden houses of Finland's second-largest town (pop. 43,000) make it one of the most photographed attractions in the country. In 1809, Tsar Alexander I granted Finland its autonomy at the Porvoo **cathedral** in the old town. (Open June-Aug. M-F 10am-6pm, Sa-Su 10am-2pm. The former home of **Johan Ludvig Runeberg,** the beloved Finnish poet who lived in Porvoo in the mid-19th century, at Aleksanterinkatu 3 is now a museum. (Open May-Aug. M-Sa 10am-4pm, Su 11am-5pm; Sept.-Apr. W-Sa 10am-4pm, Su 11am-5pm. 15mk.) Taste his wife's delicious apple pastry, *Runeberginpulla* (Runeberg's delight) at any of the cafés on Aleksanterinkatu. **Buses** roll into Porvoo from Helsinki (1hr., every 30min., 41mk). The helpful **tourist office,** Rihkamakatu 4, has free maps. (Tel. (019) 58 01 45; www.porvoo.fi. Open June-Aug. M-F 10am-6pm, Sa-Su 10am-2pm; Sept.-May M-F 10am-2:30pm, Su 10am-2pm.) **Porvoo Camping Kokonniemi,** 1.5km from the center, has a sauna, laundry, and cooking facilities. (Tel. (019) 58 19 67. 75mk per tent; cabins from 310mk. Shower included. Open June 4-Aug. 22.)

JÄRVENPÄÄ. Jean **Sibelius** tormented himself in Järvenpää, 40km north of Helsinki. The composer boozed and brooded in his home of **Ainola,** his perfectionism so exacting that he destroyed much of his late work. (Tel. (019) 28 73 22. Open June-Aug. Tu-Sa 11am-5pm. 25mk, students free.) **Buses** from platform 9, 11, or 12 at the Helsinki bus station (dir: Tuusula; 20mk) pass by the home.

HANKO. At Finland's southernmost point, the seaside resort of Hanko juts out into a beautiful rocky archipelago. The great villas lining Hanko's miles of coastland reflect the splendor and decadence of the now-vanished Russian nobility. You can pick and choose from over 30km of **beaches,** but those along Appelgrenintie are the most popular. **Buses** arrive from Helsinki (2¼hr., 7 per day, round-trip 148mk). The **tourist office,** Bulevardi 10 (tel. (019) 220 34 11; fax 248 58 21), has free maps and can help find rooms. **Ari's Snack Bar** rents **bikes;** look for the "100% Welcome" sign in the Guest Harbor. Many **guesthouses** are in former villas along Appelgrenintie; try **Villa Doris** at #23 for ocean views. (Tel. (019) 248 12 28. 110-250mk per person.) **Hanko Camping Silversand,** on Hopeahietikko, 2.5km northeast of the town center, has its own beach; follow Santalantie from town and turn left on Lähteentie. (Tel. (019) 248 55 00. 85mk per person; cabins from 365mk. Open June-Aug.) At the end of Mannerheimintie, the café at **Neljän Tuulen Tupa** (The House of the Four Winds) on Little Pine Island, once owned by Finland's great war hero, Marshal Mannerheim, is a peaceful place to grab a beer (14mk).

ÅLAND ISLANDS (AHVENANMAA)

Although they became part of the Grand Duchy of Finland in 1809, the 6500 islands that make up the Åland (OH-land) archipelago have retained a considerable degree of autonomy. In this land, which bridges Finland and Sweden culturally as well as geographically, Swedish is the language of choice, and both the Swedish and Finnish national currencies are accepted. Åland also sports its own flag, parliament, and postal system. Nonetheless, political controversy will be the last thing on your mind after you arrive—the idyllic landscape attracts all nationalities and is ideal for leisurely hiking, bike riding, and sun-soaking.

GETTING THERE AND GETTING AROUND. For info on traveling to Mariehamn on the **Viking Line** or **Silja Line,** see **By Ferry,** p. 274. **Birka Lines** (Mariehamn tel. (018) 170 27, in Stockholm (08) 714 55 20) launches its *Princess* daily from Stockholm to Mariehamn (24hr., 125mk). **Inter-island ferries** are free for foot passengers and cyclists; passengers with cars pay 20-40mk (200mk if landing on Åland, Uårdö, or the mainland). **Ferry** and **bus** schedules are available at the Mariehamn tourist office. The main island, Åland, is best explored by **bike** because of its extensive

paths and wide roads. **RoNo Rent,** facing the ferry terminal in Mariehamn and also in the Eastern harbor, rents bikes (30mk), mopeds (200mk), and boats. (Tel. (018) 128 70. Open June-Aug. daily 9am-7pm; May and Sept. call for hours.) The other islands are accessible from Mariehamn by a combo of ferries, buses, and bikes.

MARIEHAMN. On the south coast of the main island, Mariehamn (pop. 10,000) is the only town with a significant number of shops and restaurants on Åland. Stock up on groceries here—most of the island consists of small campgrounds, beaches, and a few cafés. Within sight of the ferry terminals, the moored ship **Pommern** gives visitors a feel for life on the high seas. The adjacent **Sjöfartsmuseum** takes tourists back in time with a collection of mastheads and recovered booty. (Both open May-June and Aug. 9am-5pm; July 9am-7pm. Pommern also Sept.-Oct. 10am-4pm. 20mk for either separately, 30mk combined.) The jointly housed **Åland Art Museum** and the **Åland Museum,** at Stadshusparken off Storagatan, offer a taste of Åland's historical and cultural richness. (Open W-M 10am-4pm, Tu 10am-8pm. 45mk, students 30mk.)

For maps and info, head to the **tourist office,** Storagatan 8. From the ferry terminal, head left up Hamngatan and turn right on Storagatan. (Tel. (018) 240 00; fax 242 65; www.turist.aland.fi. Open June-Aug. daily 9am-6pm; Sept.-May M-Sa 10am-4pm.) **Ålandsresor,** Torggatan 2, books rooms and cottages (from 120mk) for all the islands for a 35mk fee. (Tel. (018) 280 40; fax 283 80; www.alandsresor.fi. Open M-F 8:30am-5pm. Book ahead.) Docked at the Eastern harbor, the boat **Alida** offers sardine-sized rooms. (Tel. (018) 137 55. Doubles 80mk. Sheets 20mk. Reception 8am-10pm. Open May-Sept.) **Gröna Uddens Camping** is 10min. down Skillnadagatan from the center. (Tel. (018) 190 41. 20mk per person. Shower included. Laundry. Open mid-May to Aug.) Inflated restaurant prices make **supermarkets** all the more alluring; try **Fokus** at Torggatan 14. (Open M-F 9am-7pm, Sa 9am-4pm.) **Café Nero,** Strandgatan 12, serves up yummy baked potatoes for 30mk. (Open M-Th 10am-11pm, F 10am-midnight, Sa 11am-midnight, Su noon-10pm.) **Café Julius,** Torggatan 10, serves the island's specialty, *Ålandspannkakor* (pancakes covered with berry sauce and whipped cream), for 12mk. (Open daily 8am-10pm.) The **pub** upstairs from Café Nero has an outside terrace and dancing. (Open daily 8pm-4am.)

SUND. Northeast of Mariehamn lies the province of Sund. **Bike** (follow the cycling route to Godby) or take **bus** 4 (30min., 7 per day, 18mk) to "Kastelholm" and step back in time at the 13th-century **Kastelholms Slott** (Castle). (Open daily May-June and mid-Aug. to Sept. 10am-4pm; July to mid-Aug. 10am-5pm. 25mk, students 15mk. Includes guided tour; ask if a tour in English is possible.) Up the hill, the **Vita Björn** museum features prison cells from various centuries (open May-Sept. daily 10am-5pm; 6mk, students 4mk), and an open-air homestead museum, **Jan Karlsgården** (open daily May-Sept. 10am-5pm; free). Ten kilometers farther down the road, **Bomarsund** (bus 4; 23mk from Mariehamn, 10mk from Kastelholm) displays the ruins of a tsarist Russian fortress destroyed by British and French forces during the Crimean War. **Puttes Camping** (tel. (018) 440 16; fax 440 47), at Bomarsund, has a kitchen and laundry and rents bikes and boats.

NAKED NORTHERNERS True to the stories, the sauna is an integral part of almost every Finn's life. More than simply a place to cleanse oneself thoroughly after a shower, saunas have evolved an entire mystique and are immortalized in *Kalevala*, the Finnish national epic. They are associated with cleanliness, strength, and endurance. The country now boasts over 1.5 million saunas, or one for every three people. Modern saunas are found in every hotel, most hostels, and many campgrounds. These wooden rooms reach temperatures around 88°C, so hot that no metal parts may be exposed, or the bathers will be burned. Water thrown on heated stones brings humidity as high as 100%. Finland's electricity use skyrockets on Friday and Saturday evenings, when hundreds of thousands of saunas are heated.

ECKERÖ. Åland's second real town, Eckerö (pop. 500), in the west, is also a port of departure for **ferries** to Stockholm. Outside of town, Eckerö's humble, 12th-century stone **church** contrasts greatly with the nearby 1826 **Post and Customs House,** designed by the tsar's favorite Neoclassical architect, Carl Engel, who was also responsible for the Helsinki Senate Square. The **tourist office,** at Storby Centrum, has info on ferries, buses, fishing, and hiking. (Tel. (018) 380 95; fax 381 95. Open June-Aug. daily 10am-7pm.) **Käringsunds Camping** offers sandy beaches as well as a restaurant, pub, boat rentals, and sauna. (Tel. (018) 383 09. 40mk per tent. Shower included. Open mid-May to Aug.) **Bus** 1 runs from Mariehamn to Eckerö (24mk).

TURKU (ÅBO)

Turku (pop. 163,000), Finland's oldest city, became the country's capital in 1809 when Tsar Alexander I snatched Finland away from Sweden and granted it autonomy as a Grand Duchy. Shortly after the capital was moved to Helsinki in 1812, the worst fire in Scandinavian history devoured Turku's wooden buildings. Despite these losses, Turku remains a flourishing cultural and academic center.

⊓⌐⌐⊓ PRACTICAL INFO, ACCOMMODATIONS, AND FOOD. Trains arrive from Helsinki (2hr., 12 per day, 96mk). Viking and Silja Line **ferries** depart for the Åland Islands and continue on to Stockholm (see **By Ferry,** p. 274); to get to the terminal at the southwestern end of Linnankatu, hop on the train (3 per day) to the *satama* (harbor) or catch bus 1 along Linnankatu (10mk). The **tourist office,** Aurakatu 4, arranges accommodations. (Tel. (02) 262 74 44; fax 251 03 90; www.turku.fi. Open M-F 8:30am-6pm, Sa-Su 9am-4pm.) Check your **email** for free at the city **library,** Linnankatu 2, 2nd fl. (Open M-F 10am-7pm.)

The **Hostel Turku (HI),** Linnankatu 39, is midway between the ferry terminals and the train station. From the station, walk west three to four blocks on Ratapihankatu, take a left on Puistokatu to the river, and make a right on Linnankatu. Or, from the ferry, walk 20min. up Linnankatu. (Tel. (02) 231 65 78; fax 231 17 08. Dorms 45mk; singles 105mk; doubles 140mk; nonmembers add 15mk each. Breakfast 20mk. Sheets 30mk. Laundry.) For immaculate rooms and impeccable hospitality, stay at **Bridgettine Sisters' Guesthouse,** Ursininkatu 15A. (Tel. (02) 250 19 10. Singles 200mk; doubles 300mk.) One block from the station is **Majatalo Kultainen Turisti,** Käsityöläiskatu 11. (Tel./fax (02) 250 02 65. Singles 200mk; doubles 250mk. Breakfast included. Reception 24hr.) **Ruissalo Camping** (tel. (02) 533 46 53) on Ruissalo Island, is only open in summer. Choose from the variety of fresh foods at **Kauppatori** (open M-Sa 9am-2pm) or **Kauppahalli** (Market Hall; open M-Th 8am-5pm, F 8am-6pm, Sa 8am-2pm), on Eerikinkatu, or head to **Valintalo supermarket,** Eerikinkatu 19. (Open M-F 9am-9pm, Sa 9am-6pm.)

▣⌐ SIGHTS AND ENTERTAINMENT. The older of Turku's two universities, **Åbo Akademi,** instructs in Swedish. Opposite the university stands the impressive **cathedral** amidst the cobblestoned paths of Tuomiokirkkotori (Cathedral Square). (Open daily mid-Apr. to mid-Sept. 9am-8pm; mid-Sept. to mid-Apr. 9am-7pm.) Don't miss the 700-year-old **Turun Linna** (Turku Castle), about 3km from the center, whose **historical museum** hosts dark passageways and medieval artifacts. (Open mid-Apr.

MOOMIN MADNESS The Finn Family Moomintroll phenomenon started with just a children's book series by Jove Jansson—then entrepreneurs cashed in on the Moomins with toys, a TV cartoon, a children's clothing line, and even Moomin soda. Originally written in Swedish, the Moomins have been translated into multiple languages. They're all the rage in Japan—the Finnair (official airline of the Moomintroll) plane flying the Helsinki-Tokyo route is decorated with the smiling faces of the Moomins. To participate in Moomin madness and feel the love, head to Moomin World, a life-size creation of the Moomin's island home, complete with characters. Or go to your neighborhood library and curl up with a copy of the original *Finn Family Moomintroll.*

to mid-Sept. daily 10am-6pm; mid-Sept. to mid-Apr. M 2-7pm, Tu-Su 10am-3pm. 30mk, students 20mk.) **Luostarinmäki,** the only part of Turku to survive the 1827 fire, now houses an open-air **handicrafts museum** with over 30 workshops. (Open mid-Apr. to mid-Sept. daily 10am-6pm; mid-Sept. to mid-Apr. Tu-Su 10am-3pm. 20mk, students 15mk.) The imperial collections of the **Turan Taidemuseo** (Art Museum), including vibrant *Kalevala* paintings by Akseli Gallen-Kallela, are temporarily being housed on Vartiovuorenmaki in a building designed by Carl Engel. (Open Apr.-Sept. Tu and F-Sa 10am-4pm, W-Th 10am-7pm, Su 11am-6pm; Oct.-Mar. Tu-Sa 10am-4pm, Th until 7pm, Su 11am-6pm. 30mk, students 20mk.) The groovy bar **Downtown,** 17 Linnankatu, has live music. (Cover F-Sa from 20mk. Open Su-Tu 4pm-4am, F-Sa 4pm-5am.) **Dynamo,** Linnankatu 7, gets down to funk, soul, and ska. (Cover 20-25mk. Open W-Sa 9pm-3am.) For trance and house, try the **Morita Nightclub,** Eerikinkatu 23. (Cover 23mk. Open Tu-Sa 10pm-4am.)

📧 EXCURSION FROM TURKU: NAANTALI (NÅDENDAL). Naantali, a normally sleepy and peaceful enclave of old wooden houses 15km west of Turku, awakens each summer with an influx of vacationing Finnish families. A stroll down Mannerheiminkatu leads to the **Old Town,** where some buildings date back to the late 18th century. Visible across the harbor is the Finnish president's fortress-like summer home, **Kultaranta;** if the flag's up, keep an eye out for him. The tourist office (see below) offers tours of the home daily from late June to mid-August. (Info tel. (02) 435 08 50. Tours depart by boat from the small west harbor at 10am and 2pm; 45mk. Also from the main gate 3pm; 30mk.) The main attraction for the vacationing Finns is **Moomin World,** a harborside fantasy land. (Open early June to mid-Aug. daily 10am-7pm. 80mk, children 60mk.) The **Naantali Music Festival** (tel. (02) 434 53 63; fax 434 54 25; www.naantalinmusiikkijuhlat.fi) brings chamber music for the first two full weeks of June. Perhaps the most traditional Naantali summer event is **Sleepyhead Day** (July 27), when the residents of Naantali get up at 6am, wake anyone still sleeping, and, dressed in carnival costumes, proceed to crown the year's Sleepyhead and throw him or her into the harbor.

    Buses 11 and 110 run to Naantali from the marketplace in Turku (25min., 16mk). The **tourist office,** Kaivotori 2, helps find accommodations and provides maps. From the bus station, walk southwest on Tullikatu to Kaivokatu, go right 300m, and it's on your left. (Tel. (02) 435 08 50; fax 435 08 52; www.travel.fi/naantali. Open daily June to mid-Aug. 9am-6pm; mid-Aug. to May M-F 9am-4pm.) There is no youth hostel in town, but **Naantali camping** is 400m south of the center. (Tel. (02) 435 08 55. Year-round cabins from 140mk; summer tent sites 40mk per person.) Farther from town, **Summerhotel,** Opintie 3, has bright shiny rooms with shared kitchens and bathrooms. (Tel. (02) 445 56 60. Singles 250mk; doubles 300mk. Open June-Aug.) **Seurahuone,** Tullikatu 6B, has a filling lunch menu for 38mk. (Beer 16mk. Open May-Sept. M-Th from 3pm, F from noon, Sa-Su from 9am.)

SAVONLINNA

Perched on a chain of islands connected by picturesque bridges, Savonlinna is a must-see. The tsarist aristocracy was the first to discover Savonlinna's potential as a vacation spot, and soon turned it into a fashionable spa town. Elegant **Olavinlinna Castle,** built to strengthen the Swedish-Finnish border in 1475, impresses with towering spires and high vaulted ceilings. It stands on a rocky island just to the north of the town docks; from the Market Square, follow the docks along the water and hug Linnankatu between old wooden houses until you reach the castle. (Open daily June to mid-Aug. 10am-5pm; mid-Aug. to May 10am-3pm. Free. Multilingual tours every hr.; 25mk, students 15mk.) Both performers and spectators flock to Savonlinna's **International Opera Festival** (tel. (015) 47 67 50; www.operafestival.fi) in early July, when the castle's Great Courtyard comes to life. The **beaches** of the island of **Suolasaari** are a welcome retreat from the hordes of tourists in town. Cross the footbridge behind Market Square, walk past the baths and over another footbridge.

    Trains run to Savonlinna from Helsinki (5hr., 4 per day, 200mk); hop off at "Savonlinna-Kauppatori" in the center of town rather than the out-of-the-way "Savonlinna." The **tourist office,** Puistokatu 1, across the bridge from the market, books rooms for 50mk. (Tel. (015) 51 75 10; fax 517 51 23. Open daily June-Aug. 8am-6pm; Sept.-May M-F 9am-4pm.) **Vuorilinna Hostel (HI),** on Kylpylaitoksentie, Kasinosaari, is sandwiched between the luxurious baths and casinos of old. (Tel. (015) 739 50; fax 27 25 24. Dorms 105mk; singles 270mk; doubles 330mk; nonmembers add 15mk each. Kitchen. Reception 7am-11pm. Open June-Aug.) Bus 3 runs every hour from the bus station to **Vuohimäki Camping,** 7km out of town. (Tel. (015) 53 73 53. 80mk per person; cabins from 385mk. Open early June to late Aug.) **Ravintola Majakka,** Satamankatu 11, offers tasty Finnish entrees from 40mk. (Open daily 11am-1am.)

ROVANIEMI

Eight kilometers south of the Arctic Circle, and home to the world's favorite jolly fat man, Santa Claus, the capital of Finnish Lapland is a popular spot for tourists of all ages and nationalities. Now an entirely modern city, the old Rovaniemi is forever lost, burned to the ground by retreating German soldiers in 1944. Alvar Aalto is responsible for the design of the reconstructed city's buildings; he also conceived the plan for the city's layout (in the shape of reindeer antlers), making Rovaniemi a mecca of sorts for Aalto fanatics. To fulfill childhood (or adult) fantasies at any time of year, head to **Santa Claus's Village** to meet jolly St. Nick himself. Take bus 8 (14-17mk) to the Arctic Circle Center. (Open daily 9am-8pm.) **Arktikum** center, Pohjoisranta 4, houses the **Arctic Science Center** and the **Provincial Museum of Lapland,** a multimedia wonderland of information on Arctic peoples, culture, landscapes, and wildlife, with an incredible presentation of the Northern Lights. (Open May to mid-June and late Aug. daily 10am-6pm; mid-June to mid-Aug. daily 10am-8pm; late Aug. daily 10am-6pm; Sept.-Apr. Tu-Su 10am-6pm. 50mk, students 40mk.) The **Ranua Wildlife Park** has 3km of paths through areas of fenced-in Arctic elk, bears, and wolves. If you fell in love with the doe-eyed reindeer, skip the gift shop which sells Rudolph's fur, skin, and munchy-crunchy ribs. (Tel. (016) 355 19 21. Open daily May 10am-6pm, June to mid-Aug. 9am-8pm, mid-Aug. to Sept. 10am-6pm, Oct.-Apr. 10am-4pm. 55mk.) Ranua is also one of the best areas for cloudberry-picking—get maps at the zoo tourist office. Take **bus** 6 from Rovaniemi (1hr., 5 per day, 60mk).

Four **trains** per day roll into Rovaniemi from Helsinki (110mk). **Buses** run to destinations throughout northern Finland, with connections to Norway and Murmansk, Russia. The staff of the **tourist office,** Koskikatu 1, combs the town on yellow mopeds. If you don't spot them at the train station, head right on Ratakatu, pass the post office, go under the bridge onto Hallitustakatu, turn left on Korkalonkatu, and continue right on Koskikatu to the river (15min.). (Tel. (016) 34 62 70; fax 342 46 50; www.rovaniemi.fi. Open June-Aug. M-Sa 8am-6pm, Su 8am-4pm; Sept.-May M-F 8am-4pm.) **Lapland Safaris,** Koskikatu 1 (tel. (016) 331 12 00), leads groups up the River Ounasjoki to a reindeer farm (2½hr., 310mk) and offers cruises (1½hr., 175mk), whitewater rafting (3½hr., 350mk), and Husky and snowmobile safaris (3-6hr., 350-780mk). To get to the **HI youth hostel,** Hallituskatu 16, follow the above directions to Hallituskatu. (Tel. (016) 34 46 44. 75mk; nonmembers 95mk. Reception 6-10am and 5-9:45pm.) **Ounaskoski Camping** is across the river, next to a breezy, rocky beach. (Tel. (016) 34 53 04. 60mk. Open June-Aug.) Indulge in a Big Mac at the ▓**world's northernmost McDonald's,** Poromiehenkata 3. (Open M-Sa 10:30am-midnight, Su 11am-10pm.) Sample the sauteed reindeer and lingonberry sauce over mashed potatoes (89mk) at **Monte Rose,** Pekanata 9. (Open M 10am-11pm, Tu and Th 10am-midnight, W 10am-1am, F-Sa 10am-2am, Su 1-11pm.)

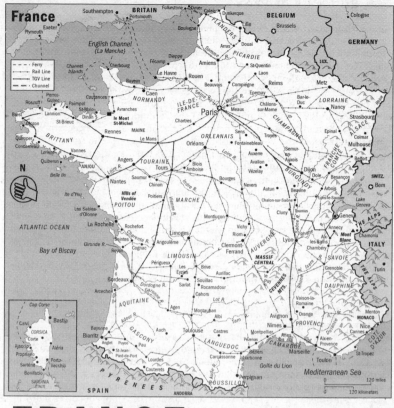

FRANCE

US$1 = 6.23F (FRENCH FRANCS)	**1F = US$0.16**
CDN$1 = 4.16F	**1F = CDN$0.24**
UK£1 = 9.94F	**1F = UK£0.10**
IR£1 = 8.33F	**1F = IR£0.12**
AUS$1 = 3.97F	**1F = AUS$0.25**
NZ$1 = 3.29F	**1F = NZ$0.30**
SAR1=1.02F	**1F = SAR0.98**
EUR€1 = 6.56F	**1F = EUR€0.15**

FRANCE

PHONE CODE	Country code: 33. **International dialing prefix:** 00.

The French celebrate the senses like no one else. Conventional preconceptions of France are steeped in such pleasures: the vineyards of Bordeaux and Burgundy, the elaborate dishes of Dijon, the sandy expanses of the Riviera, and the crisp Alpine air. Superimposed on these notions is the rationalism that has dominated French intellectual life for over 400 years. Philosopher Descartes, chemist Lavoisier, and mathematician Poincaré arose from a hotbed of methodical inquiry. These competing qualities—sensuality and reason—still meet in neighborhood brasseries and cafés, where lively conversation is enjoyed no less than wine and the *plat du jour*.

Each region of France has its own history and traditions. Normandy posed for the Impressionists and served as the springboard for English, Canadian, and

American liberators into Nazi-occupied Europe in 1944; Brittany, the Basque Country, and Corsica still cling to distinct cultural identities; the Loire Valley blossoms with *châteaux* and French Renaissance architecture; and the French Alps stretch south nearly to the Mediterranean, where the glitz and glamour of the Côte d'Azur neighbors the lavender slopes and Roman ruins of Provence.

France welcomes over 70 million visitors to its cities, *châteaux*, mountains, and beaches each year, making it the most popular tourist destination in the world. To the French, it is only natural that outsiders should flock to their beloved homeland, so steeped in history, so rich in art and architecture, and so magnificently endowed with beautiful, diverse landscapes. The fruits of France include the philosophies of Voltaire, Sartre, and Derrida; the rich literature of Hugo, Proust, and Camus; and the visionary art of Rodin, Monet, and Degas. From the trendsetting opulence of Louis XIV and Versailles to the great Revolution of 1789, from the ambition of Napoleon to the birth of existentialism and postmodernism, the French for many centuries occupied the driver's seat of history. While France no longer single-handedly controls the course of world events, it has nonetheless secured a spot as one of the most influential forces in the course of Western history, as it continues to expand its horizons. As Napoleon once quipped, "Impossible? the word is not French."

If you too are smitten by France, pick up a copy of *Let's Go: France 2000* or *Let's Go: Paris 2000* for more fact- and flavor-filled coverage.

DISCOVER FRANCE

Paris—ah, Paris. Aside from the requisite croissant-munching, elusive-smile-admiring, tower-climbing activities that occupy most visitors' time, don't miss the exquisite **Sainte Chapelle,** Gothic architecture's finest jewel (p. 292). A stroll down the **Champs-Elysées** (p. 307), through the studenty **Latin Quarter** (p. 305), or medieval **Montmartre** (p. 307) will give you a good feel for the city, with stops along the way for **Notre-Dame** (p. 304) and the **Musée d'Orsay** (p. 308). When you've had your fill of the city, be sure to squeeze in a daytrip to the epitome of Gothic style, the *cathédrale* in **Chartres** (p. 312). Northwest of Paris lies **Rouen,** home to a cathedral that so entranced Claude Monet that he painted it time and time again (p. 313). Rouen was the capital of William the Conqueror before he conquered England in 1066—the whole story unfolds on the Bayeux Tapestry in nearby **Bayeux** (p. 315), which itself serves as a good base for exploring the **D-Day beaches** of Normandy (p. 315). The majestic abbey of **Mont-St-Michel** rises from the sea above shifting sands between Normandy and Brittany (p. 317), while the *château*-studded **Loire Valley** brings visitors back to the days of royal intrigue and opulence (p. 322). The *vieille ville* of **Carcassonne,** in Languedoc-Roussillon, is surrounded by spectacular medieval ramparts (p. 334). To see Provence's **Camargue,** an untamed flatland of bulls, wild horses, and flamingoes, base yourself in **Arles,** whose picturesque streets once enchanted van Gogh (p. 337). Arles also has the largest Roman amphitheater in France, but its sister in **Nimes** is even more well-preserved (p. 337). Seven popes who called nearby **Avignon** home in the 15th century left behind an impressive palace (p. 336). Just to the south beckons the **French Riviera:** while **Nice,** with its excellent museums and nightlife, is the first stop on most itineraries (p. 343), its rocky beaches may send some to other destinations along the Riviera (p. 339-348). The main attraction at France's most famous beach towns, **Cannes** (p. 341) and **St-Tropez** (p. 340), isn't the sun—you go for the stars. For a rugged Alpine experience, strap on some boots and head to **Chamonix,** in the shadow of Mont Blanc, which features fantastic skiing and mountain climbing (p. 352). To the north, French and German culture intermingle in Alsace-Lorraine, where **Strasbourg,** home to one of France's finest Gothic cathedrals and the European Parliament, stands (p. 362).

GETTING THERE AND GETTING AROUND

BY PLANE. The two major international airports in Paris are **Charles de Gaulle** (to the north) and **Orly** (to the south). For info on cheap flights from the UK, see p. 53.

BY TRAIN. The **SNCF** (*Société Nationale de Chemins de Fer*; tel. 08 36 35 35 35; www.sncf.fr) manages one of Europe's most efficient rail networks. Timetables are complicated but well-organized, with color-designated periods: low-traffic periods are blue (*période bleue*), while peak times are white (*période blanche*) or red (*période rouge*). Traveling in blue periods makes you eligible for reductions called **tarifs Découvertes,** often up to 25%; the *Découverte 12-25* discount is available to those ages 12-25 for any blue-period travel. Tickets must be validated in the orange machine at the entrance to the platforms at the *gare* (train station). Seat **reservations,** recommended for international trips, are mandatory on EuroCity (EC), InterCity (IC), and TGV (*train à grande vitesse*) trains. All three require a ticket supplement (US$3-18; railpass-holders exempt) and reservation fee (US$2-3). **TGV** trains, the fastest in the world, run from Paris to major cities in France, as well as to Geneva and Lausanne, Switzerland. **Rapide** trains are slower, and local **Express** trains are, oddly, the slowest option. The **Eurostar** provides rapid connections to London and Brussels (see p. 57).

Eurail is valid in France. The SNCF's **France Railpass** grants three days of unlimited rail travel in France during any 30-day period (US$175; companion travelers $140 each; up to 6 extra days $30 each); the parallel **Youthpass** provides those under 26 with four days of unlimited travel within a two-month period ($158; up to 6 extra days $26 each). The **France Rail 'n' Drive pass** combines three days of rail travel with two days of car rental (US$255; companion travelers $187 each; extra rail days $30 each, extra car days $50).

BY BUS. Within France, long-distance buses are a secondary transportation choice; service is rare and infrequent relative to that in most other European countries. However, in some regions buses can be indispensable for reaching out-of-the-way towns. Bus services operated by the SNCF accept railpasses. *Gare routière* is French for "bus station."

BY FERRY. Ferries across the English Channel (*la Manche*) link France to England and Ireland. The most common route is that from **Dover** (see p. 161) to **Calais** (see p. 369), run by **P&O Stena Line, SeaFrance,** and **Hoverspeed** (tel. 03 21 46 14 54). Other ferries go from **Boulogne-sur-Mer** (see p. 369) to **Folkestone, England** on **Hoverspeed** (tel. 03 21 30 80 40); from **Cherbourg** (see p. 316) to **Rosslare, Ireland** (see p. 530) on **Irish Ferries, Portsmouth** (see p. 162) on **P&O European Ferries,** and **Poole** on **Brittany Ferries;** from **Dieppe** (see p. 314) to **Newhaven, England** on **P&O Stena Line;** from **Le Havre** (see p. 314) to **Portsmouth** (see p. 162) on **P&O European Ferries** (tel. 02 35 19 78 50); and from **Roscoff** to **Plymouth** and **Cork** (see p. 532) on **Brittany Ferries,** and **Rosslare** and **Cork** on **Irish Ferries** (tel. 02 98 61 17 17; fax 02 98 61 17 46). **Eurail** is valid on boats to Ireland (excluding 30F port tax). Students usually receive a 10% discount. For **schedules** and **prices** on English Channel ferries, see p. 58. For info on ferries from **Nice** and **Marseille** to **Corsica,** see p. 349.

BY CAR. The road system in France is extensive and well-maintained, but can be expensive, because of *autoroute* (motorway) tolls, high *essence* (gasoline) costs, and rental charges. *Autoroute à péage* indicates a toll road. Secondary national highways are denoted on maps by "N" or "RN" (*Route Nationale*) and the route number. "*Routes Départementales*" (local roads) usually have the best views; they are denoted by "D" and the route number. Driving is a nightmare at the beginning and end of August, when the French are going to and from vacation spots. Speed limits are 130km per hr. (about 80mph) on *autoroutes*, 100km per hr. (60mph) on smaller roads. Yield to cars approaching from the right. An invaluable internet resource for those planning to drive in France is **Itinéraire** (www.iti.fr), which will, given a starting point and destination, determine various routes according to speed and budget, along with estimates of driving time and toll and gas costs.

FRANCE

BY BIKE AND BY THUMB. With a wealth of well-paved minor routes, France is terrific for **cycling.** Prime regions include the Loire Valley, Normandy, Provence, the Dordogne Valley, Alsace-Lorraine, and Burgundy. SNCF's pamphlet *Guide du train et du vélo* offers details on bike-and-rail trips in France. Bike rental costs 50-70F per day. France is probably the hardest country in Europe in which to **hitch-hike.** It's slightly easier in areas where public transportation is limited and unreliable. In major cities, there are ride-sharing organizations that pair drivers and riders. **Allostop** (see p. 293) is the French division of **Eurostop International;** you can also try finding a match through **Taxistop** (www.taxistop.be).

ESSENTIALS

DOCUMENTS AND FORMALITIES. For stays shorter than 90 days, citizens of Australia, Canada, the EU, New Zealand, and the US don't require visas; South Africans do (30-day visas 165F; 90-day 195-230F). For stays longer than 90 days, all non-EU citizens require long-stay visas (650F). Non-EU nationals cannot work in France without a **work permit,** which requires a contract of employment; nor can they **study** without a **student visa,** which requires proofs of admission to a French university, financial independence, and medical insurance. For **au pair** and **teaching assistant** jobs, special rules apply; check with your local consulate.

French Embassies at Home: Australia, Consulate General, Level 26 St. Martins Tower, 31 Market St, Sydney NSW 2000 (tel. 02 926 157 79; www.france.net.au/site/administration/consulats/sydney/index.htm). **Canada,** Consulate General, 130 Bloor St W. #401, Toronto, ON M5S 1N5 (tel. (416) 925-8233; web.idirect.com/~fs1tto/index.htm); Consulate General, 1100-1130 West Pender St, Vancouver, BC V6E 4A4 (tel. (604) 681-4345; www.consulfrancevancouver.org). **Ireland,** Consulate Section, 36 Ailesbury Rd, Ballsbridge, Dublin 4 (tel. (01) 260 16 66; www.ambafrance.ie). **New Zealand,** 34-42 Manners St, P.O. Box 11-343, Wellington (tel. (04) 802 77 93; www.ambafrance.net.nz). **South Africa,** 807 George Ave, Arcadia, Pretoria 0083 (tel. (12) 429 70 30; www.france.co.za). **UK,** Consulate General, 21 Cromwell Rd, London SW7 2EN (tel. (020) 78 38 20 00; www.ambafrance.org.uk). **US,** Consulate General, 4101 Reservoir Rd NW, Washington, DC 20007 (tel. (202) 944-6000; www.france-consulat.org/dc/dc.html); Consulate General, 934 Fifth Ave, New York, NY 10021 (tel. (212) 606-3600).

Foreign Embassies in France: All embassies are in **Paris** (see p. 296). There are **UK** consulates in Bordeaux, Lille, and Marseille, and **US** consulates in Strasbourg and Marseille.

TOURIST OFFICES. The extensive French tourism support network revolves around **syndicats d'initiative** and **offices de tourisme** (in the smallest towns, the **Mairie,** the mayor's office, deals with tourist concerns), all of which *Let's Go* labels "tourist office." All three distribute maps and pamphlets, help you find accommodations, and suggest excursions to the countryside. For up-to-date events and regional info, try www.maison-de-la-france.com:8000.

MONEY. The basic unit of currency in France is the **franc français,** or French Franc (abbreviated to FF or F), divided into 100 **centimes**. The franc is available in brightly colored 50F, 100F, 200F, and 500F notes, smart two-tone 10F and 20F coins, silvery 0.50F, 1F, 2F, and 5F coins, and pale copper 5-, 10-, and 20-*centime* pieces. If you stay in hostels and prepare your own food, expect to spend anywhere from 100-140F per day. Accommodations start at about 130F per night for a double, while a basic sit-down meal with wine costs 65F.

Tipping and Bargaining: A 15% service charge is included at all restaurants, bars, and cafés in France. It is not unheard of to leave extra *monnaie* (change) at a café or bar (1-2F per drink); reward exceptional service with a 5-10% tip. Taxis get tips of 10-15%. **Bargaining** is appropriate at flea markets (*marchés aux puces*).

Taxes: All prices include a 20.6% VAT, or TVA. Non-EU residents may be eligible for a 15% **refund** on purchases of more than 1200F in a single store in a single visit, but only certain stores participate in this **vente en détaxe** refund process; ask before buying.

FRANCE

COMMUNICATION

Post: To send an **airmail letter** (up to 20g) to anywhere in the EU costs 3F (takes 3 days); South Africa 3.90F; North America 4.40F (7-10 days); Australia or New Zealand 5.20F.

Telephone: All French telephone numbers are ten digits in length; there are no city codes. When calling from abroad, drop the leading zero of the local number. To operate pay-phones, buy a *télécarte* (telephone card), available in denominations of 41F and 98F at train stations, post offices, and *tabacs*. Phone numbers starting with 0800 are toll-free; those starting with just 08 charge high rates. To call collect, tell the operator *"en PCV"* (ahn-pay-say-VAY). **Operator,** tel. 10. **Directory assistance,** tel. 12. **International operator,** tel. 00 33 11. **International direct dial** numbers include: **AT&T,** 0800 99 00 11; **Sprint,** 0800 99 00 87; **MCI WorldPhone Direct,** 0800 99 00 19; **Canada Direct,** 0800 99 00 16; **BT Direct,** 0800 99 02 44; **Ireland Direct,** 0800 99 03 53; **Australia Direct,** 0800 99 00 61; **Telecom NZ Direct,** 0800 99 00 64; and **Telkom South Africa Direct,** 0800 99 00 27. **Medical assistance,** tel. 15. **Police,** tel. 17. **Fire,** tel. 18.

Language: Contrary to popular opinion, even flailing efforts to speak French will be appreciated, especially in the countryside. Be lavish with your *Monsieurs, Madames,* and *Mademoiselles,* and greet people with a friendly *bonjour* (*bonsoir* after 6pm). For basic French vocabulary and pronunciation, see p. 949.

ACCOMMODATIONS AND CAMPING. Youth hostels *(auberges de jeunesse)* cover France, ranging from well-kept, centrally located castles to rundown barracks. For info on HI-affiliated hostels in France, contact the **Fédération Unie des Auberges de Jeunesse (FUAJ),** 4 bd. Jules ferry, 75011 Paris (tel. 01 43 57 02 60; www.fuaj.org). **Guest cards** allow nonmembers to stay at HI hostels (19F extra per night); after six stamps, they become full members. For **hotels,** you'll pay at least 110F for a single or 130F for a double. Breakfast in hotels (usually not obligatory) runs 25-40F and typically includes coffee or hot chocolate and bread and/or croissants. Hot showers sometimes cost extra (10-25F). It's illegal to **camp** in most public spaces, but organized *campings* (campsites) are common; expect to pay 50-90F per site. Most have toilets, showers, and electrical outlets, although you may have to pay extra (10-40F); cars also often require fees (20-50F). Other overnight options include **gîtes d'étapes** and mountain refuges, rural accommodations for cyclists and hikers, and **chambres d'hôtes** (bed and breakfasts; usually 200-300F per night).

FOOD AND DRINK. French chefs cook for one of the most finicky clienteles in the world. Traditionally, a complete French dinner includes an *apéritif* (pre-dinner drink), an *entrée* (appetizer), a *plat* (main course), salad, cheese, dessert, coffee, and a *digestif* (after-dinner drink). The French generally take wine with their meals; *boisson comprise* entitles you to a free drink (usually wine) with your meal. For 90F, you can splurge on a marvelous meal. In restaurants, fixed-price three-course meals *(menus)* begin at 60F. Service is usually included *(service compris)*. Be careful when ordering *à la carte; l'addition* (the check) may exceed your weekly budget. Do as the French do: go from one specialty shop to another to assemble a picnic, or find an outdoor market *(marché)*. Cafés are a forum for long chats, but you pay for the right to sit and watch the world go by: drinks and food are often 10-30% more if served in the dining room or outside rather than at the bar. *Boulangeries, pâtisseries,* and *confiseries* tempt with bread, pastries, and candy, respectively. *Charcuteries* sell cooked meats. For **supermarket** shopping, look for **Carrefour, Casino, Monoprix, Prisunic, Stoc,** and **Rallye.** Local markets are picturesque and animated, and often offer better quality than supermarkets.

LOCAL FACTS

Time: France is 1hr. ahead of Greenwich Mean Time (GMT; see p. 49).

Climate: In summer, the temperature in Paris ranges 13-24°C (55-75°F); it's cooler in the North and Alps, while southern France has scorching temperatures. Winters are generally mild near the coasts, although it rains frequently; the Alps and central France experience

FRANCE

NO PRÉSERVATIFS ADDED Having invented the French kiss and the French tickler, the speakers of the language of love have long had *savoir faire* in all things sexual—safety included. French pharmacies provide 24-hour condom (*préservatif* or *capote*) dispensers. In wonderful French style, they unabashedly adorn the sides of buildings on public streets and vending machines in the Métro. When dining out, don't ask for foods without *préservatifs* or mistake your raspberry compote for a *capote*. Funny looks will greet you, as the French have not yet caught on to the international craze for condom-eating, and will think you a bit odd.

snow and occasional frost. The best time to visit is May or Oct., when the weather is pleasant and crowds are off-peak. Aug. is not only quite hot, but all of France is on vacation for the month, leaving coastlines overcrowded and tourist facilities understaffed.

Hours: Just about everything opens at 9am, snoozes noon-2pm, and closes Su; many provincial areas also shut down M. **Banks** tend to close around 4pm. Most **shops** generally stay open until 6:30pm. **Museums** close at least one day a week, usually M or Tu. Sights run by the local government tend to close M.

Holidays: New Year's (Jan. 1); Labor Day (May 1); Easter Sunday and Monday (Apr. 23-24); Labor Day (May 1); Victory in Europe Day (May 8); Ascension Day (June 1); Whit Monday (June 11); Bastille Day (July 14); Assumption Day (Aug. 15); All Saints' Day (Nov. 1); Armistice Day (Nov. 11); Christmas (Dec. 25).

Festivals: Most festivals, like **fête du cinema** and **fête de la musique** (late June, when musicians rule the streets), are in summer. The **Cannes Film Festival** (May; www.festival-cannes.com) is mostly for directors and stars, but provides good people-watching. The **Festival d'Avignon** (July-Aug.; www.festival-avignon.com/gbindex3.html is famous for its theater. **Bastille Day** (July 14) is marked by military parades and fireworks nationwide. Although you may not be competing in the **Tour de France** (3rd or 4th Su in July; www.letour.fr), you'll enjoy all the hype. A **Vineyard Festival** (Sept., in Nice; www.nice-coteazur.org/americain/tourisme/vigne/index.html) celebrates the grape harvest with music, parades, and wine tastings. Nice and Nantes celebrate **Carnaval** in the last week or two before Ash Wednesday (culminating with Mardi Gras celebrations).

PARIS

Paris, it might be thought, needs no introduction. Once the capital of an empire that stretched from Algiers to Hanoi, Paris has many faces rooted in its 2000-year history of controversy, decadence, love, revolution, and great food. Originally home to the Gallic city of Parisii, Paris was conquered by the Romans in 52 BC and was named the capital of the Kingdom of France in AD 987. Medieval king Philippe Auguste established the city's basic geography: political and ecclesiastical institutions on the Ile de la Cité, academic on the Left Bank, and commercial on the Right. In the 1800s, under Napoleon III, the tiny, twisting cobblestoned streets of the city were ripped apart to install the sweeping *grands boulevards* that remain today.

With the City of Lights immortalized in countless films and on innumerable postcards, many simply see Paris as Notre-Dame, the Eiffel Tower, and Mona's enigmatic smile, sprinkled generously with Jean-Paul Gaultier's *haute couture* and wines so fine they can't be drunk. But the city prides itself on seamlessly melding its finest traditions with innovations in art and design, politics and economics, cuisine and *couture*. While it may be tempting to spend your days following in the footsteps of the makers of European history and your nights in the haunts of long-dead literary luminaries, equally thrilling is discovering the throbbing pulse of this most cosmopolitan of cities. With attitude, you can get away with anything in Paris.

For dazzling, detailed, definitive coverage of Paris and its environs, pick up a copy of *Let's Go: Paris 2000*.

FRANCE

⌨ GETTING THERE AND AROUND

Flights: Aéroport Roissy-Charles de Gaulle, 23km northeast of Paris. Handles most international flights. Terminal 2 serves Air France and affiliates (info tel. 01 48 62 22 80). Take the free shuttle bus from Terminal (*aérogare*) 1 (gate 28), 2A (gate 5), 2B (gate 6), or 2D (gate 6) to the Roissy train station, then ride the RER B3 into the city (45min., 48F). **Aéroport d'Orly** (tel. 01 49 75 15 15), 18km south of Paris. Handles charters and many European flights. From Orly Sud (gate H or gate I, platform 1) or Orly Ouest (arrival level gate F), take the free Orly-Rail shuttle bus to Orly train station, then the RER C2 to the center (25min., 35F), or take the shuttle to RER B4: Antony (20-25min.).

Trains: SNCF (tel. 08 36 35 35 35; 3F per min.). Guard your valuables and don't buy tickets from anyone except the uniformed personnel in the booths.

Gare du Nord: M: Gare du Nord. Serves northern France, Belgium, the Netherlands, Britain, northern Germany, Scandinavia, and the former USSR. To: **Brussels** (2hr., 287F); **Amsterdam** (5hr., 378F); **Cologne/Köln** (5-6hr., 364F); and **Copenhagen** (16hr., 1265F). The **Eurostar** (tel. 01 49 70 01 75; see p. 57) departs here for **London** (3hr., 360-740F).

Gare de l'Est: M: Gare de l'Est. To eastern France, Austria, Luxembourg, southern Germany, Hungary, and northern Switzerland. To: **Munich** (8hr., 685F) and **Vienna** (14hr., 970F).

Gare de Lyon: M: Gare de Lyon. Handles trains to southeastern France, parts of Switzerland, Italy, and Greece. To: **Geneva** (3½hr., 508F) and **Rome** (12hr., 630F).

Gare d'Austerlitz: M: Gare d'Austerlitz. Serves the Loire Valley, southwestern France, Spain, and Portugal. To: **Barcelona** (9hr., 500-800F) and **Madrid** (5-13hr., 530-850F).

Gare St-Lazare: M: Gare St-Lazare. Serves Normandy. To: **Rouen** (1hr., 103F).

Gare de Montparnasse: M: Montparnasse-Bienvenüe. Serves Brittany; also the point of departure for southbound **TGV** high-speed trains.

Buses: Gare Routière Internationale du Paris-Gallieni, 28 av. du Général de Gaulle (tel. 01 49 72 51 51), Bagnolet. M: Gallieni. Receives most international buses.

Public Transportation: The efficient **Métropolitain,** or **Métro (M),** runs 5:30am-12:30am. Lines are numbered but are generally referred to by their final destinations; connections are called *correspondences*. **Single-fare tickets** within the city 8F; **carnet** (packet) of 10 52F. Buy extras for times when ticket booths are closed (after 10pm) and hold on to your ticket until you exit. The **RER** (Réseau Express Régional), the commuter train to the suburbs, serves as an express subway within central Paris; changing to and getting off the RER requires sticking your validated ticket into a turnstile. Watch the signboards next to the RER tracks and check that your stop is lit up before riding. **Buses** use the same 8F tickets (bought on the bus; validate in the machine by the driver), but transfer requires a new ticket. Buses run 7am-8:30pm, *Autobus du Soir* until 1am, and *Noctambus* (3-4 tickets) every hr. 1:30-5:30am at stops marked with the bug-eyed moon between the Châtelet stop and the *portes* (city exits). The **Paris Visite** pass grants unlimited travel on the Métro, RER, and buses along with other discounts (2-day 70F). The **Mobilis** pass covers the Métro, RER, and buses only (1-day 32F). To qualify for a weekly (*hebdomadaire*) **Coupon Vert,** valid from M (75F), bring a photo ID to the ticket counter to get the necessary **Carte Orange.** Refer to this book's **color maps** of Paris' transit network.

Taxis: Tel. 01 47 39 47 39 or 01 45 85 85 85. Cab stands are near train stations and major bus stops. 3-person max. Taxis are pricey (13F plus 4-8F per km), and even pricier if you don't speak French. The meter starts running when you phone.

Hitchhiking: Traffic at *portes* is too heavy for cars to stop. **Allostop-Provoya,** 8 rue Rochambeau, 9ème (tel. 01 53 20 42 42). M: Cadet. Matches drivers and riders. To: **Geneva** (188F) and **Frankfurt** (about 197F). Open M-F 9am-7:30pm, Sa 9am-1pm and 2-6pm.

✳ ORIENTATION

The **Ile de la Cité** and **Ile St-Louis** sit at the geographical center of the city, while the **Seine,** flowing east to west, splits Paris into two large expanses: the **Rive Gauche** (Left Bank) to the south and the **Rive Droite** (Right Bank) to the north. The Left Bank, with its older architecture and narrow streets, has traditionally been considered bohemian and intellectual, while the Right Bank, with its grand avenues and designer shops, is more chi-chi. Administratively, Paris is divided into 20

FRANCE

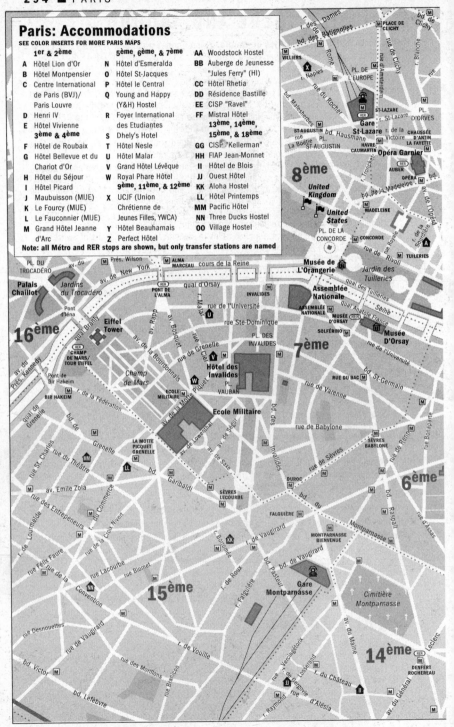

Paris: Accommodations

SEE COLOR INSERTS FOR MORE PARIS MAPS

1er & 2ème
- A Hôtel Lion d'Or
- B Hôtel Montpensier
- C Centre International de Paris (BVJ)/ Paris Louvre
- D Henri IV
- E Hôtel Vivienne

3ème & 4ème
- F Hôtel de Roubaix
- G Hôtel Bellevue et du Chariot d'Or
- H Hôtel du Séjour
- I Hôtel Picard
- J Maubuisson (MIJE)
- K Le Fourcy (MIJE)
- L Le Fauconnier (MIJE)
- M Grand Hôtel Jeanne d'Arc

5ème, 6ème, & 7ème
- N Hôtel d'Esmeralda
- O Hôtel St-Jacques
- P Hôtel le Central
- Q Young and Happy (Y&H) Hostel
- R Foyer International des Etudiantes
- S Dhely's Hotel
- T Hôtel Nesle
- U Hôtel Malar
- V Grand Hôtel Lévêque
- W Royal Phare Hôtel
- X UCJF (Union Chrétienne de Jeunes Filles, YWCA)
- Y Hôtel Beauharnais
- Z Perfect Hôtel

- AA Woodstock Hostel
- BB Auberge de Jeunesse "Jules Ferry" (HI)
- CC Hôtel Rhetia
- DD Résidence Bastille
- EE CISP "Ravel"
- FF Mistral Hôtel

13ème, 14ème, 15ème, & 18ème
- GG CISP "Kellerman"
- HH FIAP Jean-Monnet
- II Hôtel de Blois
- JJ Ouest Hôtel
- KK Aloha Hostel
- LL Hôtel Printemps
- MM Pacific Hôtel
- NN Three Ducks Hostel
- OO Village Hostel

9ème, 11ème, & 12ème

Note: all Métro and RER stops are shown, but only transfer stations are named

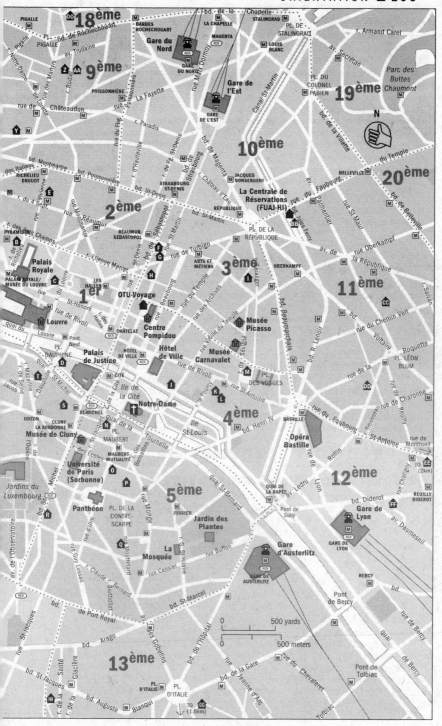

arrondissements (districts) that spiral clockwise around the Louvre. Areas of interest are compact and central, and sketchier neighborhoods tend to lie on the outskirts of town. Refer also to this book's **color maps** of the city.

RIVE GAUCHE (LEFT BANK). The **Latin Quarter,** encompassing the 5ème and parts of the 6ème around the **Sorbonne** and the **Ecole des Beaux-Arts,** has been home to students for centuries; the animated **bd. St-Michel** is the boundary between the two *arrondissements*. The area around east-west **bd. St-Germain,** which crosses bd. St-Michel just south of pl. St-Michel in the 6ème, is known as **St-Germain des Prés.** To the west, the gold-domed **Invalides** and the stern Neoclassical **Ecole Militaire,** which faces the **Eiffel Tower** across the **Champ-de-Mars,** recall the military past of the 7ème and northern 15ème, now full of traveling businesspeople. South of the Latin Quarter, **Montparnasse,** in the 14ème, eastern 15ème, and southwestern 6ème, lolls in the shadow of its tower. The glamorous **bd. du Montparnasse** belies the more residential districts around it. The eastern Left Bank, comprising the 13ème, is the city's newest up-and-coming hotspot, centered on the **pl. d'Italie.**

RIVE DROITE (RIGHT BANK). The **Louvre** and **rue de Rivoli** occupy the sight- and tourist-packed 1er and the more business-oriented 2ème. The crooked streets of **Marais,** in the 3ème and 4ème, escaped Baron Haussmann's redesign of ancient Paris and now support many diverse communities. From **pl. de la Concorde,** at the western end of the 1er, **av. des Champs-Elysées** bisects the 8ème as it sweeps up toward the **Arc de Triomphe** at **Charles de Gaulle-Etoile.** South of the Etoile, money old and new chinks in the exclusive 16ème, bordered to the west by the **Bois de Boulogne** park and to the east by the Seine and the **Trocadéro,** which faces the Eiffel Tower across the river. Back toward central Paris, the 9ème, just north of the 2ème, is defined by the sumptuous **Opéra.** East of the 9ème, the 10ème hosts cheap lodgings and the **Gares du Nord** and **de l'Est.** The 10ème, 3ème, and the happening 11ème (which peaks with the nightlife of **Bastille**) meet at **pl. de la République.** South of Bastille, the 12ème surrounds the **Gare de Lyon,** petering out at the **Bois de Vincennes.** East of Bastille, the party atmosphere gives way to the quieter, more residential 20ème and 19ème, while the 18ème is home to **Montmartre,** capped by the **Sacré-Cœur.** To the east, the 17ème starts in the red-light district of **Pigalle** and bd. de Clichy, growing more elegant toward the Etoile, the **Opéra Garnier,** and the 16ème. Continuing west along the *grande axe* defined by the Champs-Elysées, the skyscrapers of **La Défense,** Paris' newest quarter, are across the Seine from the Bois de Boulogne.

▉ PRACTICAL INFORMATION

TOURIST AND FINANCIAL SERVICES

Tourist Offices: Bureau d'Accueil Central, 127 av. des Champs-Elysées, 8ème (tel. 08 36 68 31 12; 23F per min.). M: Charles-de-Gaulle-Etoile. English-speaking and mobbed. Open daily 9am-8pm. **Branches** at Gare de Lyon (open M-Sa 8am-8pm) as well as the Orly (open daily 6am-11:30pm) and Charles de Gaulle (open daily 7am-10pm) airports.

Budget Travel: Office de Tourisme Universitaire (OTU), 119 rue St-Martin, 4ème (tel. 01 40 29 12 12), opposite the Centre Pompidou. M: Rambuteau. Sells ISICs and discounted student plane, train, and bus tickets; books hostel and hotel rooms for a 10F fee. Open M-F 10am-6:30pm, Sa 10am-5pm. Also at 139 bd. St-Michel, 5ème (tel. 01 44 41 74 74). M: Port-Royal. Open M-F 10am-6:30pm. **Council Travel,** 1 pl. Odéon, 6ème (tel. 01 44 41 89 80). M: Odéon. Sells plane tickets, train tickets (including BIJ/Eurotrain), and ISICs to students and under-26ers. Open M-F 9:30am-6:30pm, Sa 10am-5pm.

Embassies: Australia, 4 rue Jean-Rey, 15ème, 75015 (tel. 01 40 59 33 00; www.austgov.fr). M: Bir-Hakeim. Open M-F 9:15am-noon and 2-4:30pm. **Canada,** 35 av. Montaigne, 8ème, 75008 (tel. 01 44 43 29 00). M: Franklin-Roosevelt or Alma-Marceau. Open M-F 9am-noon and 2-5pm. **Ireland,** 12 av. Foch, 16ème (tel. 01 44 17 67 48). M: Argentine. Open M-F 9:30am-noon. **New Zealand,** 7ter rue Léonard de Vinci, 16ème, 75116 (tel. 01 45 00 24 11). M: Victor-Hugo. Open M-F 9am-1pm and 2-5:30pm. **South Africa,** 59 quai d'Orsay, 7ème, 75007 (tel. 01 53 59 23 23). M: Invalides. Open M-F 9am-noon. **UK,** 35

FRANCE

rue du Faubourg-St-Honoré, 8ème (tel. 01 44 51 31 00). M: Concorde. Open M-F 9:30am-12:30pm and 2:30-5pm. Consulate Section, 18bis rue d'Anjou, 75008 (tel. 01 44 51 31 02; www.amb-grandebretagne.fr). Open M-F 9:30am-12:30pm and 2:30-5pm. **US,** 2 av. Gabriel, 8ème (tel. 01 43 12 22 22). M: Concorde. Open M-F 9am-6pm. Consulate General, 2 rue St-Florentin, 75008 (tel. 01 43 12 22 22). Open M-F 9am-3pm.

Currency Exchange: Hotels, train stations, and airports offer poor rates but have extended hours; Gare de Lyon, Gare du Nord, and both airports have booths open 6:30am-10:30pm. Most **ATMs** accept **Visa** ("CB/VISA") and **MasterCard** ("EC"). Crédit Lyonnais ATMs take **AmEx;** Crédit Mutuel and Crédit Agricole ATMs are on the **Cirrus** network; and most Visa ATMs accept **PLUS**-network cards. **PLUS** card bearers can also head to Crédit Commercial de France, Banque Populaire, Union de Banque à Paris, Point Argent, Banque Nationale de Paris, Crédit du Nord, Gie Osiris, and many post offices.

American Express: 11 rue Scribe, 9ème (tel. 01 47 77 79 33), opposite the rear of the Opéra. M: Opéra. Poor rates; long lines. Mail held for cardholders and AmEx Travelers Cheques holders; otherwise 5F per inquiry. Open M-F 9am-6:30pm, Sa 10am-5:30pm.

LOCAL SERVICES

Bookstores: Shakespeare and Co., 37 rue de la Bûcherie, 5ème, across the Seine from Notre-Dame. M: St-Michel. No relation to Sylvia Beach's 1920s bookstore. Quirky, wide-ranging selection of new and used books. Open daily noon-midnight. **Gibert Jeune,** 5 pl. St-Michel, 5ème. M: St-Michel. The best bookstore in town, with several departments along bd. St-Michel. Books in all languages for all tastes. Open M-Sa 9:30am-7:30pm.

Gay and Lesbian Services: Centre Gai et Lesbien, 3 rue Keller, 11ème (tel. 01 43 57 21 47). M: Ledru Rollin. Info hub of all gay services and associations in Paris. English spoken. Open M-Sa 2-8pm, Su 2-7pm. **Les Mots à la Bouche,** 6 rue Ste-Croix-de-la-Bretonnerie, 4ème (tel. 01 42 78 88 30). M: St-Paul or Hôtel-de-Ville. Gay/lesbian bookstore with info on current goings-on. Open M-Th 11am-11pm, F-Sa 11am-midnight, Su 2-8pm.

Laundromats: Most *laveries* charge about 5F for 8-12min. in the dryer *(séchoir)* and 2-5F for detergent. **LaveauClaire,** 119 rue Charenton, 11ème. Wash 18F per 6kg. Open daily 7am-9pm. **Lavage,** 69 rue de Bac, 6ème. Wash 25F per 6kg. Open daily 7:30am-9pm. **Lav' Club,** 19 rue Pergolese, 16ème. Wash 27F per 9kg. Open daily 7:30am-9pm. **Laverie Primus,** 87 rue Didot, 14ème. Wash 25F per 7kg.

EMERGENCY AND COMMUNICATIONS

Emergencies: Ambulance, tel. 15. **Fire,** tel. 18. **Police,** tel. 17. For non-emergencies, head to the local *gendarmerie* (police force) in each *arrondissement.*

Crisis Lines: Rape, SOS Viol (tel. (0800) 05 95 95). Call free anywhere in France for counseling (medical and legal too). Open M-F 10am-7pm. **SOS Friendship** (tel. 01 47 23 80 80). For depressed, lonely English-speakers. Open daily 3-11pm.

Pharmacies: Pharmacie Dhéry, 84 av. des Champs-Elysées, 8ème (tel. 01 45 62 02 41). M: George V. **Grande Pharmacie Daumesnil,** 6 pl. Félix-Eboué, 12ème (tel. 01 43 43 19 03). M: Daumesnil; visible as you exit the Métro. All open 24hr.

Medical Assistance: Hôpital Americain, 63 bd. Victor Hugo (tel. 01 46 41 25 25), in the suburb of Neuilly. M: Porte Maillot; then take bus 82 to the end of the line. English-speaking, but much pricier than French hospitals. The full gamut of specialists, including state-of-the-art facilities and dental services. **Hôpital Franco-Britannique de Paris,** 3 rue Barbès, Levallois-Perret (tel. 01 46 39 22 22), also in a suburb. M: Anatole-France. Considered a French hospital. Has some English-speakers, but don't count on it.

Post Office: 52 rue du Louvre, 1er. M: Châtelet-les-Halles. Open almost 24hr. (daily 7am-6:20am). For postal info, call 01 40 28 20 40. Address mail to be held: Alex PAYNE, *Poste Restante,* 52 rue du Louvre, **75001** Paris, France. **Postal code:** 750xx, where "xx" is the *arrondissement* (e.g. 75003 for any address in the 3ème).

Internet Access: WebBar, 23 rue de Picardie, 3ème. M: République. 40F per hr., 300F per 10hr. Open M-F 8:30am-2am, Sa-Su 11am-2am. **Cyber Cube,** 5 rue Mignon, 6ème. 1F per min. Students 200F per 5hr., 300F per 10hr. Open M-Sa 10am-10pm. Also 12 rue Daval, 11ème. M: Bastille. **Luxembourg Micro,** 83 bd. St-Michel, 5ème. RER: Luxembourg. 0.75F per min., 23F per 30min., 45F per hr. Open M-Sa 9am-9pm.

FRANCE

Telephones: Paris has as many phones as lovers. Most don't accept coins; buy a **phone card** (télécarte) at post offices, Métro stations, and tabacs. For **directory info,** call 12.

PHONE CODE	France has no city codes. From outside France, dial int'l dialing prefix + 33 + local number (drop the leading zero).

⚡ ACCOMMODATIONS

High season in Paris falls around Easter and from May to October, peaking in July and August. Most hostels and foyers (student dorms) include the **taxe de séjour** (1-5F per person per day) in their listed prices, but many hotels do not.

ACCOMMODATIONS SERVICES

If you haven't made a reservation in advance, tourist offices (see p. 296) and some organizations can help find and book rooms.

La Centrale de Réservations (FUAJ-HI), 4 bd. Jules Ferry, **11ème** (tel. 01 43 57 02 60; fax 01 40 21 79 92). M: République; follow rue du Fbg. du Temple away from pl. de la République, cross the park that divides bd. Jules Ferry, and it's a half-block up on your left. Offers same-day reservations in affiliated hostels (115F) and budget hotels. Show up early. Also arranges excursions and sells plane/bus tickets. Open 24hr.

OTU-Voyage, 119 rue St-Martin, **4ème** (tel. 01 40 29 12 12), across the pedestrian mall from the Pompidou. Guarantees same-day "decent and low-cost lodging" (10F fee). Full price due with reservation. English spoken. Open Sa 10am-5pm. Also at 2 rue Malus, **5ème** (tel. 01 44 41 74 74). M: Place Monge. Open M-F 10am-6:30pm.

HOSTELS AND FOYERS

Paris' hostels skip many standard restrictions—sleep sheets, curfews, and the like—but they do tend to have (flexible) maximum stays. The six HI hostels within the city are for members only. The rest of Paris' dorm-style beds are either private hostels or foyers, often quieter and more private than regular hostels.

Hôtel des Jeunes (MIJE; tel. 01 42 74 23 45; fax 10 40 27 81 64; www.mije.com), **4ème**. Books beds in Le Fourcy, Le Fauconnier, and Maubuisson (see below), 3 small hostels in old Marais residences. Picturesque and best-located youth hostels. Ages 18-30 only. Dorms 140F; singles 220F; doubles 340F; triples 450F. Breakfast included. 7-day max. stay. Reception 7am-1am. Lockout noon-3pm. Curfew 1am. Open M-F 11:30am-1:30pm and 6:30-8:30pm. Reserve a month ahead; arrive before noon.

Centre International de Paris (BVJ)/Paris Louvre, 20 rue J.-J. Rousseau, **1er** (tel. 01 53 00 90 90; fax 01 53 00 90 91). M: Louvre or Palais-Royal. From M: Louvre, take rue du Louvre away from the river, turn left on rue St-Honoré, and turn right on rue J.-J. Rousseau. Bright rooms. English spoken. 120F. Breakfast included. Reception 24hr. Make Sa-Su reservations (by phone only) up to a week in advance. Call if you'll be late.

Young and Happy (Y&H) Hostel, 80 rue Mouffetard, **5ème** (tel. 01 45 35 09 53; fax 01 47 07 22 24), in the student quarter. M: Place Monge; cross rue Gracieuse and take rue Ortolan to rue Mouffetard. Lively hostel with cheap beer. Clean, cheerful rooms. Dorms in summer 117F, doubles 137F; off-season 97F, 117F. Breakfast included. Sheets 15F. Lockout 11am-5pm. Curfew 2am. Reserve with 1 night's deposit or show up at 8am. V, MC.

Foyer International des Etudiantes, 93 bd. St-Michel, **6ème** (tel. 01 43 54 49 63). RER: Luxembourg. Opposite the Jardin du Luxembourg. Spacious rooms, some with balconies. Library and TV lounge. July-Sept. co-ed; Oct.-June women-only. Dorms 120F; singles 170F. Breakfast included. Kitchenettes. Laundry. Reserve in writing 2 months ahead. 300F deposit if confirmed. Call ahead or arrive at 10am to check for no-shows.

UCJF (Union Chrétienne de Jeunes Filles, YWCA), 22 rue Naples, **8ème** (tel. 01 53 04 37 47; fax 01 53 04 37 54). M: Europe; take rue de Constantinople and turn left on rue de Naples. Spacious, quiet rooms. **Women only.** Singles 155F; doubles 280F; triples 420F. Cheaper weekly. Members only. Breakfast and dinner included. Kitchen. Laundry.

FRANCE

June-Aug. 3-day min. stay. Reception M-F 8am-12:30am, Sa-Su 9am-12:30pm and 1:30pm-12:30am. Curfew 12:30am; key available. Also at 168 rue Blomet, **15ème** (tel. 01 56 56 63 00; fax 01 56 56 63 12). M: Convention. Men can try the **YMCA Foyer Union Chrétienne de Jeunes Gens,** 14 rue de Trévise, **9ème** (tel. 01 47 70 90 94).

Woodstock Hostel, 48 rue Rodier, **9ème** (tel. 01 48 78 87 76; fax 01 48 78 01 63). M: Anvers or Gare du Nord; or take bus 85. Walk against traffic on pl. Anvers, right on av. Trudaine, and left on rue de Rodier. Or, with your back to Gare du Nord, turn right on rue Dunkerque, veer left at pl. de Roubaix on rue de Maubeuge, then right on rue Condorcet and left on rue Rodier (15min.). Near Sacré-Cœur. Clean and quiet. Apr.-Oct. 4-bed dorms 97F, doubles 214F; Sept.-May 87F, 97F. Call ahead. V, MC.

📷 **Auberge de Jeunesse "Jules Ferry" (HI),** 8 bd. Jules Ferry, **11ème** (tel. 01 43 57 55 60), next to pl. de la République. M: République; walk east on rue du Fbg du Temple and turn right on the far side of bd. Jules Ferry. Lively hostel. Dorms 120F; doubles 250F. Breakfast included. Lockers 10F. Sheets 5F. Laundry. **Internet** 1F per min. Flexible 4-night max. stay. Reception 24hr. Lockout 10am-2pm. No reservations; arrive by 8am. V, MC.

Résidence Bastille, 151 av. Ledru Rollin, **11ème** (tel. 01 43 79 53 86; fax 01 43 79 35 63). M: Voltaire; cross pl. Léon Blum and head south onto av. Ledru Rollin. Fairly subdued. Ages 18-30. Mar.-Oct. 125F; Nov.-Feb. 110F. Students and under-26ers 10% off. Breakfast included. Lockers 20F. **Internet.** 5-night max. stay. Reception 7am-10pm. Lockout noon-4pm. Flexible curfew 1am. Reserve by fax 10-15 days ahead. V, MC.

Centre International du Séjour de Paris (CISP) "Ravel," 6 av. Maurice Ravel, **12ème** (tel. 01 44 75 60 00; fax 01 43 44 45 30). M: Porte de Vincennes; walk east on cours de Vincennes, then right on bd. Soult, left on rue Jules Lemaître, and right on av. Maurice Ravel (15min.). Dorms 143F; singles 191F; doubles 322F. Breakfast included. **Internet.** Reception 7:30am-1:30am. Curfew 1:30am. Reserve ahead by phone. V, MC.

CISP "Kellerman," 17 bd. Kellerman, **13ème** (tel. 01 44 16 37 38; fax 01 44 16 37 39; email 100616.2215@compuserve.com) M: Porte d'Italie; cross the street and turn right. Impeccably clean. Cafeteria. 2- to 8-bed dorms 100-125F; singles 142-173F; doubles 248-285F. Laundry. A good place to try for last-minute reservations. V, MC.

FIAP Jean-Monnet, 30 rue Cabanis, **14ème** (tel. 01 43 13 17 00; fax 01 43 13 17 07). M: Glacière; go down bd. Auguste-Blanqui, left on rue de la Santé, and right on rue Cabanis. Night buses stop at the Denfert-Rochereau Métro. Mostly groups. Well-furnished rooms with toilet and shower. Specify dorms or you'll get a single. 50F deposit per night in check/credit card. Dorms 133F; singles 287F; doubles 376F; triples 492F; quads 656F. Breakfast included. Curfew 2am. Reserve 2-4 weeks ahead. V, MC.

📷 **Three Ducks Hostel,** 6 pl. Etienne Pernet, **15ème** (tel. 01 48 42 04 05; fax 01 48 42 99 99). M: Félix Faure; walk against traffic on the left side of the church and look to the left. Aimed at young Anglophone fun-seekers. 2- to 8-bed dorms Mar.-Oct. 117F; Nov.-Feb. 97F. Breakfast included. Sheets 15F. Towels 5F. Kitchen. Laundry nearby. Curfew 2am. Reserve several days ahead in summer with credit card. V, MC.

Aloha Hostel, 1 rue Borromée, **15ème** (tel. 01 42 73 03 03; fax 01 42 73 14 14). M: Volontaires; walk against traffic on rue de Vaugirard and turn right on rue Borromée. Café/bar. Mar.-Nov. dorms 107F, doubles 127F; Dec.-Feb. 97F, 117F. Breakfast included. Sheets 15F. Towels 10F. Reception 8am-2am. Lockout 11am-5pm. Curfew 2am. Reserve 1 week ahead in summer with credit card. V, MC.

Village Hostel, 20 rue d'Orsel, **18ème** (tel. 01 42 64 22 02; fax 01 42 64 22 04). M: Anvers; go uphill on rue Steinkerque and right on rue d'Orsel. Dorms 120-150F; doubles 294-310F. Same-day reservations only—call at 7:30am. V, MC.

HOTELS

Hotels may be the most practical accommodations for the majority of travelers. They have no curfews or school groups, afford total privacy, and often have concerned managers. Groups of two to four may also find hotels more economical than hostels. Expect to pay at least 150F for a single, 200-400F for a double. In cheaper hotels, few rooms have private baths; hall showers can cost 15-25F per use. Rooms fill quickly after morning check-out (generally 10am-noon), so arrive early or reserve ahead. Most hotels accept reservations with a one-night credit card deposit.

FRANCE

LOUVRE-PALAIS ROYAL: 1ER AND 2ÈME

Central to the **Louvre**, the **Tuileries**, the **Seine**, and the ritzy **pl. Vendôme**, this area still has a few budget hotels. Avoid rue St-Denis.

◪ **Hôtel Montpensier,** 12 rue de Richelieu, **1ᵉʳ** (tel. 01 42 96 28 50; fax 01 42 86 02 70). M: Palais-Royal; walk around the left side of the Palais-Royal to rue de Richelieu (directly ahead). Spacious, clean rooms, most with showers. Singles and doubles 310-510F. Extra bed 80F. Breakfast 37F. Shower 25F.

Henri IV, 25 pl. Dauphine, **1ᵉʳ** (tel. 01 43 54 44 53). M: Cité; head toward the Conciergerie, right on bd. du Palais, left on quai de l'Horloge, and left at the front of the Conciergerie. Well-located and attractive. Singles 125-160F; doubles 170-205F, with shower 250F; triples 240-265F; quads 290F. Showers 15F. Reserve a month ahead.

Hôtel Lion d'Or, 5 rue de la Sourdière, **1ᵉʳ** (tel. 01 42 60 79 04; fax 01 42 60 09 14). M: Tuileries; walk down rue du 29 Juillet away from the park, right on rue St-Honoré, then left. Quiet, carpeted rooms with phone and TV. English spoken. Singles 230-350F; doubles 450-480F; extra bed 60F. Breakfast 35F. 5% off stays of more than 3 nights.

◪ **Hôtel Vivienne,** 40 rue Vivienne, **2ᵉᵐᵉ** (tel. 01 42 33 13 26; fax 01 40 41 98 19). M: Rue Montmartre; walk with traffic on bd. Montmartre, pass the Théâtre des Variétés, and turn left on rue Vivienne. Gracious living at budget rates. Singles and doubles with shower or bath 370-450F. 3rd person 30% extra. Breakfast 40F.

THE MARAIS: 3ÈME AND 4ÈME

The Marais' 17th-century mansions now house budget hotels close to the **Centre Pompidou**, the **Ile St-Louis**, and bars (both gay and straight). Convenient for sampling nightlife further afield, Paris' night buses converge in the 4ᵉᵐᵉ at M: Châtelet.

◪ **Hôtel du Séjour,** 36 rue du Grenier St-Lazare, **3ᵉᵐᵉ** (tel. 01 48 87 40 36). M: Etienne Marcel; follow traffic on rue Etienne Marcel, which becomes rue Grenier St-Lazare. Under renovation; ask for a new room. Singles 180F; doubles, some with showers, 260-320F; extra bed 150F. Showers 20F. Reception 7am-10:30pm; call ahead for later arrivals.

Hôtel de Roubaix, 6 rue Greneta, **3ᵉᵐᵉ** (tel. 01 42 72 89 91; fax 01 42 72 58 79). M: Réaumur-Sébastopol; walk against traffic on bd. de Sébastopol then turn left. Very clean rooms, some noisy, with shower and toilet. Singles 305-330F; doubles 370-410F; triples 415-480F; quads 500F; quints 525F. Breakfast included.

Hôtel Bellevue et du Chariot d'Or, 39 rue de Turbigo, **3ᵉᵐᵉ** (tel. 01 48 87 45 60; fax 01 48 87 95 04). M: Etienne Marcel; walk against traffic on rue Turbigo. Lovely rooms with toilet, bath, and TV. Singles 315F; doubles 350F; triples 425; quads 460F. Breakfast 35F. Reserve 2 weeks ahead by fax.

Hôtel Picard, 26 rue de Picardie, **3ᵉᵐᵉ** (tel. 01 48 87 53 82; fax 01 48 87 02 56). M: Temple; walk down rue du Temple, turn left on rue Béranger, right on rue de Franche-Comté, then left. Centrally located. Singles 210-260F; doubles 250-330F; triples 520F. 10% off with *Let's Go*. Breakfast 30F. Showers 20F. Apr.-Sept. reserve a week ahead.

◪ **Grand Hôtel Jeanne d'Arc,** 3 rue de Jarente, **4ᵉᵐᵉ** (tel. 01 48 87 62 11; fax 01 48 87 37 31; www.hoteljeannedarc.com). M: St-Paul; walk against traffic on rue de Rivoli, turn left on rue de Sévigné, then turn right. Rooms with TVs, toilets, and showers. Singles 300-400F; doubles 305-500F; triples 540F; quads 600F. Breakfast 35F. Reserve 2 months ahead.

THE LATIN QUARTER AND ST-GERMAIN-DES-PRÉS: 5ÈME AND 6ÈME

The lively *quartier latin* and St-Germain-des-Prés offer proximity to the **Notre-Dame**, the **Panthéon**, the **Jardin du Luxembourg**, and the bustling student café-culture.

◪ **Hôtel d'Esmeralda,** 4 rue St-Julien-le-Pauvre, **5ᵉᵐᵉ** (tel. 01 43 54 19 20; fax 01 40 51 00 68). M: St-Michel; walk along the Seine on quai St-Michel toward Notre-Dame and turn right at Parc Viviani. Friendly staff and homey rooms. Singles 160-320F; doubles 420-490F; triples 550F; quads 600F. Breakfast 40F.

◪ **Hôtel St-Jacques,** 35 rue des Ecoles, **5ᵉᵐᵉ** (tel. 01 44 07 45 45; fax 01 43 25 65 50). M: Maubert-Mutualité; turn left on rue des Carmes, then left on rue des Ecoles. Regal rooms with balconies and TVs. English spoken. Singles 250F, with shower and toilet 480F; doubles 420-580F; triples 560-650F. Breakfast 35F. V, MC, AmEx.

FRANCE

Hôtel le Central, 6 rue Descartes, **5ème** (tel. 01 46 33 57 93). M: Maubert-Mutualité; walk up rue de la Montaigne Ste-Geneviève. Near rue Mouffetard and the Panthéon. Newly painted rooms, all with showers. Singles 160-213F; doubles and triples 236-266F.

▨ **Hôtel Neslé,** 7 rue du Neslé, **6ème** (tel. 01 43 54 62 41). M: Odéon; walk up rue de l'Ancienne Comédie onto rue Dauphine and turn left. Fantastic and sparkling, with a warm management. Singles 175F; doubles 350-500F. No reservations; arrive around 10am.

Dhely's Hotel, 22 rue de l'Hirondelle, **6ème** (tel. 01 43 26 58 25; fax 01 43 26 51 06). M: St-Michel. Modern, pretty rooms with TV and phone. Quiet location. Singles 200F; doubles 290F, with shower 380F; triples 370F, with shower 490F. Extra bed 100F. Breakfast 35F. Hall showers 25F. Reserve in advance with deposit. V, MC, AmEx.

EIFFEL TOWER, INVALIDES, MUSÉE D'ORSAY, MUSÉE RODIN: 7ÈME

▨ **Grand Hôtel Lévêque,** 29 rue Cler (tel. 01 47 05 49 15; fax 01 45 50 49 36; www.interresa. ca/hotel/leveque). M: Ecole Militaire; walk on av. de la Motte-Picquet and turn left. Completely renovated. Singles 270F; doubles 380-450F; triples 515F. Breakfast 30F.

Hôtel Malar, 29 rue Malar (tel. 01 45 51 38 46; fax 01 45 55 20 19). M: Latour Maubourg; follow traffic on bd. de la Tour Maubourg, turn left on rue St-Dominique, then turn right. Classy area. Singles 295-370F; doubles 400-450F. Extra bed 100F. Breakfast 32F.

Royal Phare Hôtel, 40 av. de la Motte-Picquet (tel. 01 47 05 57 30; fax 01 45 51 64 41), right next to M: Ecole Militaire. Small, tidy, colorful rooms with TV and phone. Singles 320-415F; doubles 365-440F. Extra bed 100F. Reserve 1 week ahead with deposit.

OPÉRA: 9ÈME

The northern part of the 9ème mixes pumping nightlife with a red-light district; avoid M: Pigalle, M: Barbès-Rochechouart, and bd. de Clichy.

▨ **Hôtel Beauharnais,** 51 rue de la Victoire (tel. 01 48 74 71 13). M: Le Peletier; follow traffic on rue de la Victoire and look for flower boxes (there's no sign). Elegant rooms with antiques and showers. Prices with *Let's Go:* doubles 320F; triples 490F. Breakfast 30F.

Perfect Hôtel, 39 rue Rodier (tel. 01 42 81 18 86; fax 01 42 85 01 38). M: Anvers; walk against traffic on pl. Anvers, turn right on av. Trudaine, then left on rue Rodier. Or, from M: Gare du Nord, go right on rue Dunkerque, left at pl. de Roubaix on rue de Maubeuge, right on rue Condorcet, and left on rue Rodier. Clean rooms with phones. Singles and doubles with hall shower 180-205F; triples with bath 265F. V, MC, AmEx.

PLACE DE LA BASTILLE AND RÉPUBLIQUE: 11ÈME AND 12ÈME

Convenient to hopping nightlife, although the area can get a little bit sketchy at night.

Hôtel Rhetia, 3 rue du Général Blaise, **11ème** (tel. 01 47 00 47 18; fax 01 48 06 01 73). M: Voltaire; take av. Parmentier, turn right on rue Rochebrune, and turn left on rue du Général Blaise. Calm neighborhood. Singles 180-220F; doubles 200-240F; triples 240-290F. Breakfast 15F. Hall showers 10F. Reception 7:30am-10pm.

Mistral Hôtel, 3 rue Chaligny, **12ème** (tel. 01 46 28 10 20; fax 01 46 28 69 66). M: Reuilly-Diderot; go west on bd. Diderot, then left. Singles 205-250F; doubles 210-290F; triples 320F; quads 500F. Breakfast 35F. Hall showers 15F. Reserve 1 week ahead.

MONTPARNASSE: 14ÈME AND 15ÈME

Just south of the Latin Quarter, Montparnasse mixes bohemian, intellectual charm with thriving commercial centers and venerable cafés.

▨ **Hôtel de Blois,** 5 rue des Plantes, **14ème** (tel. 01 45 40 99 48; fax 01 45 40 45 62). M: Mouton-Duvernet; turn left on rue Mouton Duvernet and left at its end. Singles and doubles 230-360F; triples 360F. Breakfast 27F. Reserve at least 10 days in advance.

Ouest Hôtel, 27 rue de Gergovie, **14ème** (tel. 01 45 42 64 99; fax 01 45 42 46 65). M: Pernety; walk against traffic on rue Raymond Losserand and turn right. Clean and friendly. Singles and doubles 120-230F. Breakfast 20F. Hall showers 20F.

Hôtel Printemps, 31 rue du Commerce, **15ème** (tel. 01 45 79 83 36; fax 01 45 79 84 88). M: La Motte-Picquet-Grenelle. Clean, cheap rooms near shops and restaurants. Singles and doubles 150-230F. Breakfast 20F. Hall showers 15F. Reserve 3-4 weeks ahead.

FRANCE

Pacific Hôtel 11 rue Fondary, **15ème** (tel. 01 45 75 20 49; fax 01 45 77 70 73). M: Dupleix or av. Emile Zola. 2-star quality at 1-star prices. Elegant hotel on a quiet street, near laundry (rue Violet). Singles 200-262F; doubles 260-318F; triples 370F. V, MC.

◘ FOOD

For most Parisians, life is about eating. Eating establishments range from the famous repositories of *haute cuisine* to corner *brasseries*. Inexpensive bistros and *crêperies* offer the breads, cheeses, wines, pâtés, *pôtages*, and pastries central to French cuisine. *Gauche* or gourmet, French or foreign, you can find just about anything to eat here. **CROUS (Centre Regional des Oeuvres Universitaires et Scolaires),** 39 av. Georges Bernanos, 5ème, has info on university restaurants. (Tel. 01 40 51 37 10. M: Port-Royal. Open M-F 9am-5pm.) To assemble a picnic, visit the specialty shops of the **Marché Montorgeuil,** 2ème, **rue Mouffetard,** 5ème, or the **Marché Bastille,** on bd. Richard-Lenoir (M: Bastille; open Th and Su 7am-1:30pm).

RESTAURANTS

LOUVRE-PALAIS ROYAL AND THE CHAMPS-ELYSÉES: 1ER, 2ÈME, AND 8ÈME

Cheap options surround **Les Halles,** 1er and 2ème, but the area can be sketchy at night. Near the **Louvre,** the small streets of the 2ème teem with traditional bistros.

▩ **Papou Lounge,** 74 rue J.-J. Rousseau, **1er** (tel. 01 44 76 00 03). M: Les Halles; walk toward the church St-Eustache, take a right on rue Coquillère, then another right. This Tahitian/French café serves gourmet hamburgers (48-55F), salmon burgers (52F), and cold beer (16-20F). Daily special 55F. Open daily 10am-2am. V, MC.

▩ **Le Dénicheur,** 4 rue Tiquetonne, **2ème** (tel. 01 42 21 31 01). M: Etienne-Marcel; walk against traffic on rue de Turbigo and turn left on rue Tiquetonne. Decorated with bric-a-brac, this restaurant has lawn gnomes and excellent food. Three-course *menu* with coffee 70F. Sunday brunch 80F. Open daily noon-3:30pm and 7:30pm-2am.

Antoine's: Les Sandwichs des 5 Continents, 31 rue de Ponthieu, **8ème** (tel. 01 42 89 44 20). M: Franklin D. Roosevelt; walk toward the Arc de Triomphe on the Champs-Elysées, turn right on av. Franklin D. Roosevelt, and left on rue de Ponthieu. This sandwich shop offers up a 35F meal (*panini,* yogurt, and a drink) on bread that is probably worth 35F on its own. An incredible deal for the 8ème. Open M-Sa 8am-7pm.

THE MARAIS: 3ÈME AND 4ÈME

The Marais offers chic bistros, kosher delis, and same-sex cafés, serving *brûnch,* invented by gay men in the 7th century.

▩ **Chez Omar,** 47 rue de Bretagne, **3ème** (tel. 01 42 72 36 26). M: Arts et Métiers; walk down rue Réamur, away from rue St-Martin. Heaps of Middle Eastern food in an Art Deco restaurant. Open M 7:30-11:30pm, Tu-Su noon-3pm and 7:30-11:30pm.

Le Divin, 41 rue Ste-Croix-de-la-Bretonnerie, **4ème** (tel. 01 42 77 10 20). M: Hôtel-de-Ville or Rambuteau; walk away from the Hôtel de Ville on rue du Temple and turn right. Fabulous *provençal* specialties. *Menu* 89F. Open July-Aug. Tu-Su 7:30-11pm, Sept.-June Tu-Sa noon-2pm and 7:30-11:30pm, Su 7:30-11pm. V, MC, AmEx.

THE LATIN QUARTER, ST-GERMAIN-DES-PRÉS, EIFFEL TOWER, AND CHAMP DE MARS: 5ÈME, 6ÈME, AND 7ÈME

Tiny restaurants with rock-bottom *menus* crowd the area bounded by bd. St-Germain, bd. St-Michel, and the Seine in the 6ème. Restaurants in the 7ème are a bit pricey, but they make for a great splurge.

Le Jardin des Pâtes, 4 rue Lacépède, **5ème** (tel. 01 43 31 50 71) M: Jussieu; walk up rue Linné and turn right. Bright restaurant with organic gourmet pastas like *pâtés de seigle* (ham, white wine, and sharp *comté* cheese; 56F). Open daily noon-2:30pm and 7-11pm.

Restaurant Perraudin, 157 rue St-Jacques, **5ème** (tel. 01 46 33 15 75). M: Luxembourg; take rue Collard to rue St-Jacques. Classic *bistro* with traditional dishes like Burgundy beef stew (59F). Open M and Sa 7:30-10:15pm, Tu-F noon-2:15pm and 7:30-10:15pm.

FRANCE

Così, 54 rue de Seine, **6ème** (tel. 01 46 33 35 36). M: Mabillon. Produces enormous, tasty, cheap sandwiches for around 40F. Desserts 20F. Open daily noon-midnight.

La Varangue, 27 rue Angereau, **7ème** (tel. 01 45 05 51 22). M: Ecole Militaire; from av. de la Bourdonnais, turn right on rue de Grenelle, then left. Near the Eiffel Tower, with super-fresh offerings. Dinner *menus* 77-98F. Open M-F noon-10pm, Sa 6:30-10pm.

OPÉRA, BASTILLE, AND RÉPUBLIQUE: 9ÈME, 10ÈME, AND 11ÈME

The 9ème and 10ème host a high concentration of ethnic restaurants. Restaurants in the 11ème fill to capacity with pretty young things; try to reserve ahead.

Haynes Bar, 3 rue Clauzel, **9ème** (tel. 01 48 78 40 63). M: St-Georges; take rue Notre-Dame-de-Lorette uphill and turn right on rue H. Monnier, then right again. The first African-American-owned restaurant in Paris (1947) was once a center for expats such as Armstrong, Baldwin, and Wright. Big plates of soul food like fried chicken and fresh corn bread (70F). Jazz F nights. Open Tu-Sa 7pm-midnight. Closed Aug. V, MC, AmEx.

Paris-Dakar, 95 rue du Faubourg St-Martin, **10ème** (tel. 01 42 08 16 64). M: Gare de l'Est. Senegalese cuisine. Lunch and dinner *menus* (59-179F) feature *tiébou dieune* (fish with rice and veggies). Open Tu-Th and Sa-Su noon-3pm and 7pm-2am, F 7pm-2am.

Café Moderne, 19 rue Keller, **11ème** (tel. 01 47 00 53 62). M: Ledru-Rollin; walk up av. Ledru Rollin, turn left on rue de Charonne and right on rue Keller. Meat galore and coucous (70-98F). Open M-F noon-2:30pm and 7-11:30pm, Sa-Su 7-11:30pm.

BUTTE AUX CAILLES AND MONTPARNASSE: 13ÈME, 14ÈME, AND 15ÈME

Restaurants and bars in the **Butte aux Cailles,** 13ème, fill with the young and high-spirited. At the turn of the century, Bretons brought their specialty crêpes to **Montparnasse** (the 14ème and 15ème).

Café du Commerce, 39 rue des Cinq Diamants, **13ème** (tel. 01 53 62 91 04). M: Pl. d'Italie; take bd. Auguste Blanqui and turn left. Dinner *menus* 65-120F. Open daily 11:30am-3pm and 7pm-2am. Reservations recommended Sa-Su. V, MC, AmEx.

Crêperie de Josselin, 67 rue du Montparnasse, **14ème** (tel. 01 43 20 93 50). M: Edgar Quinet. On a street full of *crêperies,* locals come here for sweet and savory numbers (22-70F). Open Tu-F noon-2pm and 6-11:45pm, Sa-Su noon-midnight.

Sampieru Corsu, 12 rue de l'Amiral Roussin, **15ème**. M: Cambronne; walk into pl. Cambronne, turn left on rue de la Croix Nivert, then left again. Eat your fill of roast chicken and pay according to your means, but the suggested price for the 3-course *menu* (with pâté, cheeses, and wine) is 45F. Open M-F 11:45am-1:30pm and 6:30-9:30pm.

MONTMARTRE: 18ÈME ARRONDISSEMENT

During the siege of Paris in 1814, Russian cossacks occupied **Montmartre;** the restaurants where they grabbed quick bites between battles became known as bistros (Russian for "quick"). The Russians are gone, but the tourists are here in force, particularly around **pl. du Tertre** and **pl. St-Pierre.** Charming bistros and cafés are common between **rue des Abbesses** and **rue Lepic.**

Chez Ginette, 101 rue Caulaincourt, **18ème** (tel. 01 46 06 01 49). Upstairs from M: Lamarck-Caulaincourt. Inventive and inexpensive French cooking, like eggplant stuffed with goat cheese (50F). More conventional meat and fish dishes 78-98F. Omelettes and salads 38-55F. Open M-Sa noon-2:30pm and 7:30pm-2am. Open Sept.-June. V, MC.

CAFÉS

French cafés conjure up images of writers and long afternoons. Popular drinks include coffee, wine, *citron pressé* (fresh-squeezed lemon juice), tea, and spring, mineral, and soda water. Cafés also serve affordable light lunches and snacks. It's cheaper at the counter (*comptoir* or *zinc*) than in the seating area.

Le Marais Plus, 20 rue des Francs-Bourgeois, **3ème** (tel. 01 48 87 01 40). Wacky toys and knick-knacks. Divine cappuccino 25F. Salads 60F. Open daily noon-6:30pm.

Café Beaubourg, 100 rue St-Martin, **4ème** (tel. 01 48 87 63 96). M: Hôtel-de-Ville. This simple, sleek cavern draws models, tourists, and comrades. Legendary bathrooms. Coffee 16F; hot chocolate 26F. Brunch 110F. Open daily 8am-1am. V, MC, AmEx.

FRANCE

Café de la Mosquée, 39 rue Geoffrey St-Hilaire, **5ᵉᵐᵉ** (tel. 01 43 31 38 20). M: Censier Daubenton. Incredible *mahgrebin* pastries 10F. Open daily 10am-midnight.

Aux Deux Magots, 6 pl. St-Germain-des-Prés, **6ᵉᵐᵉ** (tel. 01 45 48 55 25). M: St-Germain-des-Prés. *Café* and pastries (12-24F) drew Sartre and Beauvoir. Open daily 7am-1:30am.

La Coupole, 102 bd. du Montparnasse, **14ᵉᵐᵉ** (tel. 01 43 20 14 20). M: Vavin. The Art Deco interior has hosted Lenin, Stravinsky, Hemingway, and Einstein. Coffee 11F. *Croque monsieur* 28F. Open M-Th 7:30am-2am, F 9:30pm-4am, Sa 3-7pm and 9:30pm-4am.

▨ **Le Sancerre,** 35 rue des Abbesses, **18ᵉᵐᵉ** (tel. 01 42 58 08 20). M: Abbesses. Classic Montmartre café serves interesting entrees (25-80F). Open daily 7am-2am.

👁 SIGHTS

In a few hours, you can walk from the heart of the Marais in the east to the Eiffel Tower in the west, passing most major monuments along the way. Try to reserve a day for wandering; you don't have a true sense of Paris until you know how close medieval Notre-Dame is to the modern Centre Pompidou, or the *quartier latin* of students to the Louvre of kings. After dark, spotlights illuminate everything from the Panthéon to the Eiffel Tower, Notre-Dame to the Obélisque.

ILE DE LA CITÉ AND ILE ST-LOUIS

ILE DE LA CITÉ. If any place could be called the heart of Paris, it is this island in the river. In the 3rd century BC, when it was inhabited by the *Parisii*, a Gallic tribe of hunters, sailors, and fishermen, the Ile de la Cité was all there was to Paris. Although the city has expanded in all directions, all distance-points in France are measured from *kilomètre zéro*, a sundial on the ground in front of Notre-Dame.

CATHÉDRALE DE NOTRE-DAME DE PARIS. This 12th- to 14th-century cathedral, begun under Bishop Maurice Sully, is one of the most famous and beautiful examples of medieval architecture. After the Revolution, the building fell into disrepair and was even used to shelter livestock until Victor Hugo's 1831 novel *Notre-Dame-de-Paris* (a.k.a. *The Hunchback of Notre Dame*) inspired citizens to lobby for restoration. Architect Eugène Viollet-le-Duc made subsequent modifications, including the addition of the spire and the gargoyles. The intricately carved, apocalyptic façade and soaring, apparently weightless walls (effects produced by brilliant Gothic engineering and optical illusions) are inspiring even for the most church-weary. The cathedral's biggest draws are its enormous stained-glass **rose windows** that dominate the north and south ends of the transept. A claustrophobic staircase inside the towers leads to a spectacular perch from which weather-worn gargoyles survey the city. *(M: St-Michel-Notre-Dame; exit on the island side. From the Left Bank, cross the Pont au Double and turn right. Open M-F 8am-6:45pm, Sa-Su 8am-7:45pm. Towers open Apr.-Sept. 10am-6pm; Oct.-Mar. 10am-5pm; free. Treasury open M-Sa 9:30am-6pm; 15F, students 10F. Crypt open daily Apr.-Sept. 10am-6pm; Oct.-Mar. 10am-5pm; 35F, students 23F. Tours in English leave from the booth to the right of the entrance; W and Th noon, Sa 2:30pm; free.)*

STE-CHAPELLE AND CONCIERGERIE. Within the courtyard of the **Palais de Justice,** which has harbored Paris' district courts since the 13th century, the opulent, Gothic **Ste-Chapelle** was built by Saint Louis (Louis IX) to house his most precious possession, Christ's crown of thorns (now in Notre-Dame). The chapel contains some of the most beautiful stained-glass in the world. *(M: Cité; take rue du Lutèce away from Notre-Dame to bd. du Palais. Open daily Apr.-Sept. 9:30am-6:30pm; Oct.-Mar. 10am-5pm. 35F; joint ticket with Conciergerie 50F, under 26 23F.)* The **Conciergerie,** around the corner from Ste-Chapelle, was one of Paris' most famous prisons; Marie-Antoinette and Robespierre were imprisoned here during the Revolution. *(1 quai de l'Horloge. M: Cité. Tel. 01 53 73 78 50. Open daily Apr.-Sept. 9:30am-6:30pm; Oct.-Mar. 10am-5pm. 35F, students 23F. Guided tours in French 11am and 3pm; free. For tours in English, call in advance.)*

ILE ST-LOUIS. The Ile St-Louis is home to some of Paris' most privileged elite, such as the Rothschilds and Pompidou's widow, and former home to other super-famous folks, including Voltaire, Baudelaire, and Marie Curie. At night, the island glows in the light of cast-iron lamps and candlelit bistros. Look for Paris' best ice cream at Ile St-Louis' **Berthillon,** 31 rue St-Louis-en-Ile. *(Across the Pont St-Louis from Notre-Dame; also across the Pont Marie from M: Pont Marie. Berthillon open Sept.-July 14; take-out W-Su 10am-8pm; eat-in W-F 1-8pm, Sa-Su 2-8pm. Also closed 2 weeks in both Feb. and Apr.)*

THE LATIN QUARTER AND ST-GERMAIN-DES-PRÉS

The autumn influx of Parisian students is the prime cultural preservative of the *quartier latin,* so named because prestigious *lycées* and universities taught in Latin until 1798. Since the violent student riots in protest of the outmoded university system in May 1968, many artists and intellectuals have migrated to the less expensive outer *arrondissements,* and the *haute bourgeoisie* has moved in. The 5ème still presents the most diverse array of bookstores, cinemas, bars, and jazz clubs in the city. Designer shops and fascinating galleries line **St-Germain-des-Prés.**

CAFÉS. Cafés along bd. St-Germain have long been gathering places for literary and artistic notables such as Hemingway and Mallarmé. **Aux Deux Magots,** 6 pl. St-Germain-des-Prés, named for two porcelain figures that adorned a store selling Chinese silk and imports on the same spot in the 19th century, quickly became a favorite hangout of Verlaine and Rimbaud, later attracting Breton, Artaud, and Picasso as well. The **Café de Flore,** 172 bd. St-Germain, established in 1890, was made famous in the 1940s and 50s by literati Sartre and Camus, who favored its wood-burning stoves over their cold apartments. *(M: St-Germain-des-Prés.)*

BOULEVARD ST-MICHEL AND ENVIRONS. At the center of the Latin Quarter, bd. St-Michel, which divides the 5ème and 6ème, is filled with cafés, restaurants, bookstores, and clothing stores. **Place St-Michel,** at its northern tip, is filled with students, often engaged in typically Parisian protests, and lots of tourists. *(M: St-Michel.)*

JARDIN DU LUXEMBOURG. South along bd. St-Michel, the formal French gardens of the Jardin du Luxembourg are fabulous for strolling, reading, and watching the famous *guignol* puppet theater. *(RER: Luxembourg; exit onto bd. St-Michel. The main entrance is on bd. St-Michel. Open daily Apr.-Oct. 7:30am-9:30pm; Nov.-Mar. 8:15am-5pm.)*

PANTHÉON. The **crypt** of the Panthéon, which occupies the highest point on the Left Bank, houses the tombs of Voltaire, Rousseau, Victor Hugo, Émile Zola, Jean Jaurès, and Louis Braille; you can spy each tomb from behind locked gates. The **dome** features uninspiring Neoclassical frescoes. *(On pl. du Panthéon, east of the Jardin du Luxembourg. M: Cardinal Lemoine; follow rue du Cardinal Lemoine uphill and turn right on rue Clovis. Or, from RER: Luxembourg, head north on bd. St-Michel and turn right on rue Soufflot. Open daily 10am-6:30pm; last admission 5:45pm. 35F, students 23F.)*

EGLISE ST-GERMAIN-DES-PRÉS. Scarred by centuries of weather, revolution, and war, the Eglise St-Germain-des-Prés, which dates from 1163, is the oldest standing church in Paris. *(3 pl. St-Germain-des-Prés. M: St-Germain-des-Prés. Open daily 8am-7:45pm.)*

JARDIN DES PLANTES. Opened in 1640 to grow medicinal plants for King Louis XIII, the garden now features natural science museums and a **zoo,** one which Parisians raided for food during the Prussian siege of 1871. *(On pl. Valhubert. M: Jussieu; follow rue Jussieu southeast along the university building.)*

MERDE! The French have a love affair with their dogs, and nearly 500,000 pooches call Paris home. According to official figures, the dogs of Paris leave over 11 tons of *déjections canines* on Paris' streets per day. Sidewalks are veritable minefields; experienced Parisians keep one eye on the ground. Since 1977, the Paris government has been campaigning—under the title *"La lutte contre les polutions canines"* (The Fight Against Canine Pollution)—to encourage people to have their best friends defecate in street gutters. Inspiring slogans include "Teach him the gutter" and "If you love Paris, don't let him do that!" Clean-up efforts are now aided by a technological triumph called the *Caninette,* or more informally the *Motocrotte* (crapmobile), hybrid motorcycle/vacuum cleaners. If you have the misfortune of stepping into some *crotte de chien,* hope it's with your left foot; according to Parisian superstition, it's good luck.

FRANCE

MOSQUÉE DE PARIS. The cool courtyards and ornate archways of this mosque provide a soothing setting for prayer, mint tea, or an afternoon in the *hammam*. *(On pl. du Puits de l'Ermite. M: Jussieu; take rue Linné, turn right on rue Lacépède, and left on rue de Quatrefages. Open June-Aug. Sa-Th 9am-noon and 2-6pm. Tours 15F, students 10F.)*

THE EIFFEL TOWER AND INVALIDES

EIFFEL TOWER. Built in 1889 as the centerpiece of the World's Fair, the Tour Eiffel has come to symbolize the city. Despite criticism, tacky souvenirs, and Gustave Eiffel's own sentiment that "France is the only country in the world with a 300m flagpole," the tower is unfailingly elegant and commands an excellent view of the city. At night, it will impress even the most jaded tourist. *(M: Bir Hakeim; follow bd. de Grenelle to the Seine and turn right on quai Branly. Or, from RER: Champ de Mars-Tour Eiffel, follow quai Branly. Open daily June-Aug. 9am-midnight; Sept.-May 9:30am-11pm. Lift closes 10:30pm; to 1st fl. 21F, 2nd fl. 43F, 3rd fl. 60F. Stairs to 1st and 2nd floors 15F.)*

INVALIDES. The tree-lined **Esplanade des Invalides** runs from the grand **Pont Alexandre III** to the gold-leaf dome crowning the **Hôtel des Invalides**. The Hôtel, built under Louis XIV for veterans, now houses the **Musée de l'Armée** and **Napoleon's Tomb**. Nearby, on rue Varenne, is the **Musée Rodin.** *(M: Invalides, Latour Maubourg, or Varenne.)*

THE LOUVRE, THE OPÉRA, THE MARAIS, AND THE BASTILLE

AROUND THE LOUVRE. World-famous art museum and former residence of kings, the **Louvre** (see p. 308) occupies about one-seventh of the 1er *arrondissement.* **Le Jardin des Tuileries,** at the western foot of the Louvre, was commissioned by Catherine de Médici in 1564 and improved by André Le Notre (designer of the gardens at Versailles) in 1649. Three blocks north along rue de Castiglione, **Place Vendôme** hides 20th-century offices and luxury shops behind 17th-century façades. Look out for Napoleon on top of the column in the center of the *place* (he's the one in the toga). *(M: Tuileries or Concorde.)* The **Palais-Royal** was commissioned in 1632 by Cardinal Richelieu, who gave it to Louis XIII. In 1784, the elegant buildings enclosing the palace's formal garden became *galeries*, the prototype of a shopping mall. The revolutions of 1789, 1830, and 1848 all began with angry crowds in the same garden. *(M: Palais-Royal/Musée du Louvre or Louvre-Rivoli.)*

OPÉRA. North of the Louvre, Charles Garnier's grandiose **Opéra** was built under Napoleon III in the eclectic style of the Second Empire. Gobelin tapestries, gilded mosaics, a 1964 Marc Chagall ceiling, and a six-ton chandelier adorn the magnificent interior. *(M: Opéra. Open daily in summer 10am-6pm; off-season 10am-5pm. 30F, students 20F. Tours in English in summer daily at noon; off-season varies; 60F, students 45F.)*

MARAIS. This area, made up of the 3ème and 4ème *arrondissements*, became the most chic place to live with Henri IV's construction of the elegant **place des Vosges** at the beginning of the 17th century; several remaining mansions now house museums. Today, the small streets of the Marais house the city's Jewish and gay communities as well as fun, hip restaurants and shops. At the confluence of the 1er, 2ème, 3ème, and 4ème, the **Centre Pompidou** looms like a colorful factory over the vast cobblestoned *place*, where artists, musicians, and pickpockets gather. Linger in the day, but be cautious at night. *(M: Rambuteau; take rue Rambuteau to Pl. Georges Pompidou. Or, from M: Chatelet-Les Halles, take rue Rambuteau or rue Aubry le Boucher.)*

BASTILLE. Farther east, Charles V built the Bastille prison to guard the eastern entrance to his capital. When it became a state prison under Louis XIII, it housed religious heretics and political undesirables. On July 14, 1789, revolutionaries stormed the Bastille, searching for gunpowder and political prisoners. By 1792, nothing was left of the prison but its outline on the *place*. On July 14, 1989, François Mitterrand inaugurated the glittering **Opéra Bastille** to celebrate the destruction of Charles' fortress. *(120 rue de Lyon. M: Bastille. Tours daily 1pm. 50F, students 30F.)*

FRANCE

CHAMPS-ELYSÉES, BOIS DE BOULOGNE, AND LA DÉFENSE

PLACE DE LA CONCORDE. Paris' most famous public square lies at the western edge of the Tuileries. Constructed between 1757 and 1777 to hold a monument to Louis XV, the area soon became the *place de la Révolution*, site of a guillotine that severed 1343 necks. After the Reign of Terror, the square was optimistically renamed (*concorde* means "peace"). The huge, rose-granite, 13th-century BC **Obélisque de Luxor** depicts the deeds of Ramses II. Given to Charles X by the Viceroy of Egypt in 1829, it is Paris' oldest monument. *(M: Concorde.)*

ARC DE TRIOMPHE. Stretching west, the **avenue des Champs-Elysées** is lined with luxury shops, *haute couture* boutiques, cafés, and cinemas. The avenue is the work of Baron Haussmann, who was commissioned by Napoleon III to convert Paris into a grand capital with broad avenues, wide sidewalks, new parks, elegant housing, and sanitary sewers. Napoleon commissioned the **Arc de Triomphe,** at the western terminus of the Champs-Elysées, in 1806 in honor of his Grande Armée. In 1940, Parisians were brought to tears as Nazis goose-stepped through the Arc; on August 26, 1944, British, American, and French troops liberating the city from Nazi occupation marched through to the roaring cheers of thousands. The terrace at the top has a fabulous view. *(On pl. Charles de Gaulle. M: Charles-de-Gaulle-Etoile. Open daily Apr.-Sept. 9:30am-10:30pm; Oct.-Mar. 10am-6pm. 40F, under 26 25F.)*

BOIS DE BOULOGNE. Avenue Foch, one of Haussmann's finest creations, runs from the Arc de Triomphe to the Bois de Boulogne. Though popular by day for picnicking, the park is a risky choice at night (until recently it was home to many drug dealers and prostitutes). *(16ème. M: Porte Maillot, Sablons, Pont de Neuilly, or Porte Dauphine.)*

LA DÉFENSE. Outside the city limits, the skyscrapers and modern architecture of La Défense make up Paris' newest (unofficial) *arrondissement*, home to the headquarters of 14 of France's top 20 corporations. The **Grande Arche,** inaugurated in 1989, completes the *axe historique* running through the Louvre, pl. de la Concorde, and the Arc de Triomphe. There's yet another stunning view from the top. Trees, shops, and sculptures by Miró and Calder line the esplanade. *(M: La Défense, zone 2; RER, zone 3. Open daily 10am-7pm; last entrance 6pm. 43F, students 33F.)*

MONTMARTRE AND PÈRE-LACHAISE

BASILIQUE DU SACRÉ-COEUR. The Basilique du Sacré-Coeur crowns the **butte Montmartre** like an enormous white meringue. Its onion dome is visible from almost anywhere in the city, and its 112m bell tower is the highest point in Paris, offering a view that stretches up to 50km. *(35 rue du Chevalier de la Barre, 18ème. M: Château-Rouge, Abbesses, or Anvers. From Anvers, take rue de Steinkerque off bd. de Rochechouart and climb the steps. Open daily 7am-11pm; free. Dome and crypt open daily 9am-6pm; each 15F, students 8F.)* Nearby, **place du Tertre** features touristy outdoor cafés and sketch artists.

CIMETIÈRE PÈRE-LACHAISE. The Cimetière Père-Lachaise holds the remains of Balzac, Colette, Seurat, Danton, David, Delacroix, La Fontaine, Haussmann, Molière, Proust, and Sarah Bernhardt within its peaceful, winding paths and elaborate sarcophagi. Foreigners buried here include Chopin, Modigliani, Gertrude Stein, and Oscar Wilde, but the most visited grave is Jim Morrison's. French Leftists make ceremonious pilgrimage to the **Mur des Fédérés** (Wall of the Federals), where 147 revolutionary *Communards* were executed and buried. *(16 rue du Repos, 20ème. M: Père-Lachaise. Open Mar.-Oct. M-F 8am-6pm, Sa 8:30am-6pm, Su 9am-6pm; Nov.-Feb. M-F 8am-5:30pm, Sa 8:30am-5:30pm, Su 9am-5:30pm. Free.)*

🏛 MUSEUMS

For updated info, check the bimonthly *Paris Museums and Monuments*, available at the Champs-Elysées tourist office. The weekly *Pariscope* and *L'Officiel des Spectacles* list museum hours and temporary exhibits. The **Carte Musées et Monuments** grants entry to 65 Paris museums without waiting in line; it is available at major museums and Métro stations (1-day 80F, 3-day 160F, 5-day 240F).

FRANCE

ABSINTHE MAKES THE HEART GROW FONDER

The liquor absinthe made a big emerald splash on the Paris scene in the 19th century. Dégas' *L'absinthe* (1876) features the green concoction being downed at a café in Pigalle. Van Gogh, some think, owed much of his inspiration (and madness) to it. Like Baudelaire and Verlaine, Hemingway wrote about absinthe, calling it "that opaque, bitter, tongue-numbing, brain-warming, stomach-warming, idea-changing liquid alchemy." Picasso, Toulouse-Lautrec, and hordes of Parisians loved and drank it fanatically. First distilled in 1792 from the wormwood plant *(Artemisia absinthium)* and the chlorophyll that makes it green, the 120-proof, licorice-like drink was initially used by French soldiers in Algeria to ward off dysentery. They returned to France in the 1830s with a taste for the stuff, and soon it seemed that all of Paris was riding the green wave. Bars had *l'heure vert* (green hour), where water was poured onto a sugar cube and into the clear green liquor, turning it a darker, cloudy hue. Drinkers talked about the *fée verte* (green fairy—she's all over Art Nouveau posters) that stole the drinker's soul, while others warned of *le peril vert,* and in 1915 absinthe was outlawed in France. Most countries followed suit, although it's still available in Spain and the Czech Republic. "After the first glass," wrote Oscar Wilde, "you see things as you wish they were. After the second, you see things as they are not. Finally you see things as they really are, and that is the most horrible thing in the world."

■ **Musée du Louvre, 1ᵉʳ** (tel. 01 40 20 50 50). M: Palais-Royal/Musée du Louvre. A short list of its masterpieces includes the Code of Hammurabi, the *Venus de Milo,* the *Winged Victory of Samothrace,* Vermeer's *Lacemaker,* and Delacroix's *Liberty Leading the People.* Oh, yeah, and there's that lady with the mysterious smile, too. Enter through I.M. Pei's **Pyramid** in the Cour Napoléon, or skip lines by entering directly from the Métro. M and W evenings are quiet. Open M and W 9am-9:45pm, Th-Su 9am-6pm. Before 3pm 45F, after 3pm and Su 26F; 1st Su of each month free. Tours in English M and W-Sa 17F.

■ **Musée d'Orsay,** 62 rue de Lille, 7ᵉᵐᵉ (tel. 01 40 49 48 48). RER: Musée d'Orsay. While it's considered the premier Impressionist museum, the museum is dedicated to presenting all major artistic movements between 1848 and WWI. Highlights include Manet's *Déjeuner sur l'Herbe,* Monet's *Gare St-Lazare* and *Rouen Cathedral,* Dégas' *L'absinthe,* and Whistler's *Mother,* as well as works by Rodin, Renoir, Cézanne, van Gogh, Toulouse-Lautrec, Gaugin, and Seurat. Open June 20-Sept. 20 Tu-W and F-Su 9am-5:45pm, Th 9am-9:30pm; Sept. 21-June 19 opens 10am. 40F, under 26 and Su 30F.

Centre National d'Art et de Culture Georges-Pompidou (Palais Beaubourg), 4ᵉᵐᵉ (tel. 01 44 78 12 33). M: Rambuteau. This inside-out building has inspired debate since its inauguration in 1977. Its exhibit halls, library, and superb museum collections (including the **Musée National d'Art Moderne**) are scheduled to reopen in January 2000; hours were unavailable at press time. The exterior is a sight, with chaotic colored piping and ventilation ducts (blue for air, green for water, yellow for electricity, red for heating).

Musée Rodin, 77 rue de Varenne, 7ᵉᵐᵉ (tel. 01 44 18 61 10). M: Varenne; take bd. des Invalides away from the Seine and turn left on rue de Varenne. The elegant 18th-century Hôtel Biron holds hundred of sculptures by Auguste Rodin (and his lover, Camille Claudel), including the *Gates of Hell, The Thinker,* the *Burghers of Calais,* and *The Kiss.* Open Tu-Su Apr.-Sept. 9:30am-5:45pm; Oct.-Mar. 9:30am-4:45pm. 28F, students and Su 18F.

Musée Picasso, 5 rue de Thorigny, 3ᵉᵐᵉ (tel. 01 42 71 63 15). M: Chemin-Vert; from bd. Beaumarchais, take rue St-Gilles, which becomes rue du Parc Royal, then bear right at pl. de Thorigny. Catalogs Picasso's life and career from his early work in Barcelona to his Cubist and Surrealist years in Paris and his Neoclassical work on the Riviera. Open W-M Apr.-Sept. 9:30am-6pm; Oct.-Mar. 9:30am-5:30pm. 30F, under 26 and Su 20F.

Musée de Cluny, 6 pl. Paul-Painlevé, 5ᵉᵐᵉ (tel. 01 43 25 62 00). M: Cluny-Sorbonne; follow bd. St-Michel away from the Seine and turn left on rue P. Sarrazin. One of the world's finest collections of medieval art, housed in a medieval monastery built on top of Roman baths. *La Dame et La Licorne* (The Lady and the Unicorn) is one of the most beautiful extant medieval tapestry series. Open W-M 9:15am-5:45pm. 30F, under 25 and Su 20F.

The Invalides Museums, Esplanades des Invalides, 7ème (tel. 01 44 42 37 72). M: Invalides. The resting place of Napoleon also hosts the **Musée de l'Armée,** which celebrates French military history, and the **Musée de l'Ordre de la Libération** (entrance on bd. de Latour-Maubourg), which tells the story of those who fought for the liberation of France. Open daily Apr.-Sept. 10am-6pm; Oct.-Mar. 10am-5pm. 38F, students under 26 28F. In the *cour d'honneur,* the **Musée d'Histoire Contemporaine** (tel. 01 44 42 54 91 or 01 44 42 38 39) probes current events. 30F, students 20F.

La Villette, 19ème. M: Porte de la Villette or Porte de Pantin. From Porte de Pantin, take Galerie de la Villette. A vast urban renewal project that encloses a landscaped park, a huge science museum (open M-Sa 10am-6pm, Su 10am-7pm; 50F), an Omnimax cinema (57F), a conservatory, a jazz club, a concert/theater space, and a high-tech music museum (open Tu-Th noon-6pm, F-Sa noon-7:30pm, Su 10am-6pm; 35F, students 25F).

Musée d'Art Moderne de la Ville de Paris, 11 av. du Président Wilson, in the Palais de Tokyo, 16ème (tel. 01 53 6740 00). M: Iéna; from pl. d'Iéna, take av. du Président Wilson to pl. de Tokyo. Paris' second-best collection (after the Pompidou) of 20th-century art, with works by Matisse *(The Dance)* and Picasso *(The Jester);* temporary exhibits vary. Open Tu-F 10am-5:30pm, Sa-Su 10am-6:45pm. 30-45F, students 20-35F.

Institut du Monde Arabe, 23 quai St-Bernard, 5ème (tel. 01 40 51 38 38). M: Jussieu; take rue Jussieu away from rue Linné and turn right on rue des Fossés St-Bernard, which leads to quai St-Bernard. Features art from the Maghreb and the Near and Middle East. The riverside façade is shaped like a boat, representing the migration of Arabs to France; the opposite side has camera-lens windows with Arabic motifs that open and close to control the amount of sunlight in the museum. Open Tu-Su 10am-6pm. 25F.

Musée Marmottan Monet, 2 rue Louis-Boilly, 16ème (tel. 01 44 96 50 33). M: La Muette; follow Chaussée de la Muette (av. du Ranelagh) through the Jardin (park) du Ranelagh, turn right on av. Raphaël, then left on rue L. Boilly. This hunting-lodge-turned-stately-mansion features an eclectic collection of Empire furniture, Impressionist Monet and Renoir canvases, and medieval illuminations. Open Tu-Su 10am-5pm. 40F, students 25F.

Musée de l'Orangerie, 1er (tel. 01 42 97 8 16). M: Concorde. Houses Renoirs, Cézannes, Rousseaus, Matisses, and Picassos, but is most famous for Monet's 8 gigantic *Water Lilies.* **Closed until spring 2001.** Open W-M 10am-5pm. 30F, under 25 18F.

Musée Carnavalet, 23 rue de Sévigné, 3ème (tel. 01 42 72 21 13). M: Chemin-Vert; take rue St-Gilles, which becomes rue du Parc Royal, to rue de Sévigné. In a 16th-century *hôtel particulier,* Carnavalet traces Paris' history from its origins to the present and guards Voltaire and Rousseau's writing supplies. Open Tu-Su 10am-5:40pm. 30F, students 20F.

Galérie Nationale du Jeu de Paume, 1er (tel. 01 47 03 12 50), opposite the Musée de l'Orangerie in the Tuileries. M: Concorde. Hosts changing contemporary art exhibitions. Open Tu noon-9:30pm, W-F noon-7pm, Sa-Su 10am-7pm. 38F, students under 26 28F.

🎞 ENTERTAINMENT

Paris' cabarets, cinemas, theaters, and concert halls can satisfy all tastes and desires. The bibles of Paris entertainment, the weekly **Pariscope** (3F) and the **Officiel des Spectacles** (2F), on sale at any kiosk or *tabac,* have every conceivable listing. Pariscope includes an English-language pull-out section. When going out, remember that some popular nightlife areas, such as **Pigalle, Gare St-Lazare,** and **Beaubourg,** are not always safe. To avoid expensive late-night taxis, keep an eye on the time and hop on the Métro before it closes at 12:30am.

THEATER

Theater tickets can run high, but reduced student rates are nearly always available, and some theaters sell rush tickets an hour before curtain. Most theaters close in August. Go directly to theaters, or try the **Kiosque-Théâtre,** 15 pl. de la Madeleine, 8ème, for half-price, same-day tickets. (16F. M: Madeleine or M: Châtelet-Les Halles. Open Tu-Sa 12:30-7:45pm, Su 12:30-3:45pm.) **Alpha FNAC: Spectacles,** 136 rue de Rennes, 6ème (M: Montparnasse-Bienvenüe; tel. 01 49 54 30 00), Forum des Halles, 1-7 rue Pierre Lescot, 1er (tel. 01 40 41 40 00; M: Châtelet-Les Halles), and 71 bd. St-

Germain, 5ème (M: Cluny-La Sorbonne; tel. 01 44 41 31 50), sells tickets for theater, concerts, and festivals. (Open M-Sa 10am-7:30pm.) **La Comédie Française**, 2 rue de Richelieu, 1er, features classic comedies by Molière. (70-190F, remainders for under 27 60-70F, rush tickets 30F. M: Palais Royal. Tel. 01 44 58 15 15.) The **Odéon Théâtre de l'Europe**, 1 pl. Odéon, 6ème, offers productions from the classics to the avant-garde. (30-180F, student rush 60F. M: Cluny-La Sorbonne. Tel. 01 44 41 36 36.) The **Théâtre de la Huchette**, 23 rue de la Huchette, 5ème, still performs Ionesco's *La Cantatrice Chauve (The Bald Soprano)* and *La Leçon.* (Each 100F, students M-F 80F. Both shows 160F, 120F. M: St-Michel. Tel. 01 43 26 38 99. M-Sa at 7 and 8pm, respectively.) *Café-théâtres* like **Au Bec Fin**, 6 rue Thérèse, 1er (80F; M: Palais-Royal or Pyramides; tel. 01 42 96 29 35), perform low-budget, high-energy skits that require good French-language skills to understand.

CINEMA

Auguste and Louis Lumière's short film "Leaving the Lumière Factory in Lyon" was the world premiere of cinema. It showed to an audience of 35 at the Grand Café (14 bd. des Capucines) on March 19, 1895. Today, Paris, of all the cities in the world, probably airs the greatest number of films each week. Cinemas offer a range of discounts, especially on Mondays and Wednesdays. Check *Pariscope* for listings. The notation "v.o." *(version originale)* means that the film has French subtitles but is in its original language; "v.f." *(version française)* means that it has been dubbed. **Action Christine**, 4 rue Christine, 16ème, plays eclectic international art and cult films from the 40s and 50s, all original-language. (M: Odéon. Tel. 01 43 29 11 30. 40F, early show (6 or 7pm) 25F; M and students 30F.) **Cinémathèque Française**, in pl. du Trocadéro, 16ème, at the Musée du Cinéma in the Palais de Chaillot (enter through the Jardins du Trocadéro), shows two to three classics (or soon-to-be classics) per day, usually original-language. (M: Trocadéro. Info tel. 01 47 04 24 24. Tel. 01 45 53 21 86. Open W-Su 5-9:45pm. 28F, students 17F.)

■ NIGHTLIFE

The primary leisure pastime of Parisians, as they would have it, is fomenting revolution and burning buildings. Actually, their nighttime pleasures tend more toward drinking, relaxing, and people-watching. For those new to the town, the exclusive nightlife scene will probably feel like a tough nut to crack, but there are definitely alternatives to the mega-trendy and mega-expensive.

Those looking for live music, especially jazz, are in for a heavenly time. Those on the prowl for dancing may be at first frustrated by Paris' rather closed (and sometimes downright nasty) club scene, but *Let's Go* tries to list places that are tolerant of non-models. If you'd rather just drink and watch the world go by, Parisian bars and the cafés that blend into bars at sundown won't disappoint. For gay and lesbian nightlife, Paris is tops.

JAZZ

Ever since the arrival of American expatriate jazz musicians in the 30s and 40s, Paris has become one of the jazz capitals of the world. Frequent summer festivals sponsor free or near-free concerts. French mags *Jazz Hot* (45F), *Jazz Magazine* (35F), and *LYLO* (*Les Yeux, Les Oreilles;* free) have the most complete listings.

Au Duc des Lombards, 42 rue des Lombards, **1er** (tel. 01 42 33 22 88). M: Châtelet; from pl. J. du Bellay, take rue Ste-Opportune and go left on rue des Lombards. A hip crowd fills the dark, smoky interior and partakes of the best in French jazz, occasional American soloists, and hot items in world music. Cover 80-100F, music students 50-80F. Drinks 28-55F. Music starts at 8:30 or 10pm and ends at 3am (F-Sa 4am). Visa.

Caveau de la Huchette, 5 rue de la Huchette, **5ème** (tel. 01 43 26 65 05). M: St-Michel; from the Seine, take the first left off bd. St-Michel. Watch and dance the jitterbug, bebop, swing, and jive in this extremely popular jazz club. The caves served as prison and execution rooms for Danton and Robespierre in the Revolution; in the 40s, the club moved in to find 2 skeletons chained together, dancing. Drinks 26-35F. Cover Su-Th 60F, F-Sa 75F; students 55F. Open Su-Th 9:30pm-2:30am, F-Sa 9:30pm-3:30am.

BARS, PUBS, AND LOUNGES

Chez Richard, 37 rue Vieille-du-Temple, **4ème** (tel. 01 42 74 31 65). M: Hôtel-de-Ville; take rue de Rivoli a few blocks east, then turn left on rue Vieille-du-Temple; it's inside a courtyard off the street. This super-sexy bar/lounge screams drama but is actually fun and friendly. Drinks 22-60F. Open daily 5pm-2am. V, MC.

Lizard Lounge, 18 rue du Bourg-Tibourg, **4ème** (tel. 01 42 72 81 34). M: Hôtel-de-Ville; take rue de Rivoli east and turn left at pl. du Bourg-Tibourg. Drinks 20-55F. Happy Hour in the cellar 8-10pm (cocktails 25F). Open daily 11am-2am. V, MC.

Le Reflet, 6 rue Champollion, **5ème** (tel. 01 43 29 97 27). M: Cluny-La Sorbonne; take bd. St-Michel away from the river, turn left on rue des Ecoles, and take the 1st right. Dark, smoky bar-café-restaurant, packed with *académes* on weekend nights. Beer 11-16F, cocktails 12-32F at bar. Open M-Sa 10am-2am, Su noon-2am. V, MC.

Le Bar Dix, 10 rue de l'Odéon, **6ème** (tel. 01 43 54 87 68). M: Odéon; from beside pl. H. Mondor take rue de l'Odéon uphill. Classic student hangout where you might be forced to eavesdrop on existentialist discussions. No matter; after enough sangria (15F per glass), you'll feel okay about being condemned to freedom. Open daily 5:30pm-2am.

DANCE AND ROCK CLUBS

Rex Club, 5 bd. Poissonnière, **2ème** (tel. 01 42 36 10 96). M: Bonne-Nouvelle. A casual, non-selective club with international DJs playing cutting-edge techno, break beats, and hip-hop fusion. Drinks 60-80F. Cover 70F. Open Tu-Sa 11:30pm-6am. V, MC.

Le Queen, 102 av. des Champs-Elysées, **8ème** (tel. 01 53 89 08 90). M: George V. The fiercest funk in town, with drag queens, superstars, models, moguls, and buff Herculean go-go boys. Extremely fashionable. M disco (50F cover plus 50F drink); W "Respect" (no cover); Th house (no cover); F-Sa house (80F cover plus 50F drink); Su 80s retro (no cover). Drinks 50F. Open daily midnight-dawn. Pray to Madonna that you get in.

Folies Pigalle, 11 pl. Pigalle, **9ème** (tel. 01 48 78 25 56). M: Pigalle. Frequented by both gay and straight clubbers. The former strip joint now spins mostly house and techno. Open Tu-Sa 11pm-7am, Su 3-8pm. Cover 100F. Drinks 50F. V, MC, AmEx.

Le Cithéa, 114 rue Oberkampf, **11ème** (tel. 01 40 21 70 95). M: Parmentier; take av. de la République to rue Oberkampf. Hip, club-like bar with live music. Lots of jazz, hip-hop, and free jack fusion bands, as well as occasional DJs spinning drum 'n' bass. Drinks 25-60F. Cover F-Sa 50F; includes 1-2 drinks. Open daily 9:30pm-5:30am. V, MC.

GAY AND LESBIAN NIGHTLIFE

Paris' gay and lesbian life centers on the **Marais** (3ème and 4ème), with most establishments clustering around **rue Vieille-du-Temple, rue Ste-Croix de la Bretonnerie,** and **rue des Archives.** For the most comprehensive listing of gay and lesbian establishments and services, consult *Guide Gai* (79F at any kiosk) or *Pariscope*.

Banana Café, 13-15 rue de la Ferronerie, **1er** (tel. 01 42 33 35 31). M: Châtelet. Around the corner from Les Halles. Piano bar and legendary theme nights. Beer before 10pm 20F, after 10pm 30-35F; drinks half-price 4:30-7pm. Open daily 4:30pm-dawn. V, MC.

Le Champmeslé, 4 rue Chabanais, **2ème** (tel. 01 42 96 85 20). M: Pyramides; take rue de Ventadour from av. de l'Opéra, turn right on rue des Petits Champs, then left on rue Chabanais. Paris' oldest and most famous lesbian bar. Mixed crowd in the front, but women-only in back. Drinks 30-45F. Open M-W 5pm-2am, Th-Sa 5pm-5am. V, MC.

Les Scandaleuses, 8 rue des Ecouffes, **4ème** (tel. 01 48 87 39 26). M: St-Paul; walk with traffic along rue de Rivoli and turn right on rue des Ecouffes. Ultra-hip lesbian bar set to techno beats. Men accompanied by women are welcome. Open daily 6pm-2am.

Open Café, 17 rue des Archives, **4ème** (tel. 01 42 72 26 18). M: Hôtel-de-Ville. The most popular of the Marais gay bars. Grit your teeth, grip your handbag, and bitch your way onto the terrace. Drinks 18-35F. Su brunch 70-105F. Open daily 10am-2am. V, MC.

FRANCE

⚡ EXCURSIONS FROM PARIS

VERSAILLES. Louis XIV, the Sun King, built and held court at Versailles' extraordinary palace and gardens, 12km west of Paris. The incredibly lavish *château* embodies the extravagance of the Old Regime. Louis XVI and Marie Antoinette held fabulous *fêtes* in the *château*'s **Hall of Mirrors, Grand** and **Petit Trianons,** and faux **Hameau.** Le Notre's geometric **gardens** are studded with fountains, which spurt to music every Sunday from May through September. Take any **RER C5** train beginning with a "V" from M: Invalides to the Versailles Rive Gauche station (30-40min., every 15min., round-trip 28F). Buy your RER ticket before getting to the platform; a Métro ticket will not get you through the RER turnstiles at Versailles. (*Château* open May-Sept. Tu-Su 9am-6:30pm; Oct.-Apr. 9am-5:30pm. 45F, after 3:30pm and under 26 35F (entrance A). Audio (1hr., 25F) and guided tours (1-2hr., 25-50F) available at entrances C and D, respectively. Gardens open dawn-dusk; free.)

CHARTRES. The Chartres' stunning **Cathédrale Notre-Dame** is one of the most beautiful surviving creations of the Middle Ages. Arguably the finest example of early Gothic architecture in Europe, the cathedral retains several of its original 12th-century stained-glass windows; the rest of the windows and the magnificent sculptures on the main portals date from the 13th century. Take a **train** from Paris' Gare Montparnasse (1hr., every hr, round-trip 142F, under 26 108F). From the station, walk straight ahead, turn left into the pl. de Châtelet, turn right on rue Ste-Même, then turn left on rue Jean Moulin. (Open Apr.-Sept. M-Sa 9am-7pm, Su 9:30am-5:30pm; Oct.-Mar. M-Sa 10am-6pm, Su 10am-1pm and 2:30-4:30pm. Tours in English Apr.-Jan. M-Sa noon and 2:45pm; 1¼hr.; 30F, students 20F.)

DISNEYLAND. It's a small, small world, and Disney seems bent on making it even smaller. When EuroDisney opened, it was met by the jeers of French intellectuals and the popular press. Resistance to the park has subsided since it was renamed Disneyland Paris; a touch of class goes a long way. From Paris, take **RER A4** "Marne-la-Vallée" to the last stop, "Marne-la-Vallée/Chessy" (45min., every 30min., round-trip 76F); the last train back leaves at 12:22am but arrives after the Métro closes. Eurailers can take the TGV from Roissy/Charles de Gaulle Airport to the park in 15min. (Open in summer daily 9am-11pm; in winter hours vary. Buy *passeports* (tickets) on Disneyland Hotel's ground floor, at the Paris tourist office, or at any major station on RER line A. Apr.-Sept. and Dec. 23-Jan. 7 220F; off-season 175F.)

NORTHWEST FRANCE

Since the beginning of history, the fate of northwestern France has been caught up with that of its neighbor across the Channel. Even today, although Gauls, Celts, Franks, and Normans no longer clash in battle over the region's treasures, waves of peaceful invaders continue to flock to the *châteaux* of the Loire Valley, the craggy cliffs of Brittany, and the D-Day beaches and incomparable Mont-St-Michel in Normandy. But beyond these must-see sights lie a wealth of small towns, rugged coastline, and idyllic islands that have yet to succumb to the lures of mass tourism.

NORMANDY (NORMANDIE)

Fertile Normandy is a land of gently undulating fields, tiny fishing villages along a jagged coastline, and soaring cathedrals. Vikings seized the region in the 9th century, and invasions have twice secured Normandy's place in military history: in 1066, when William of Normandy conquered England, and on D-Day, June 6, 1944, when Allied armies began the liberation of France here. In the intervening centuries, Normandy exchanged its warlike reputation for a quiet agricultural role, far removed from the border wars that raged between France and its neighbors.

ROUEN

Best known as the city where Joan of Arc was burned and Emma Bovary was bored, Rouen (pop. 400,000) is no provincial hayseed town. The city enjoyed prosperity and status from the 10th through 12th centuries as the capital of the Norman empire, and was later immortalized in Monet's multiple renditions of the cathedral.

🔼🔣☕ PRACTICAL INFO, ACCOMMODATIONS, AND FOOD. Trains chug to Paris (1½hr., every hr., 103F) and Lille (3hr., 2 per day, 159F). From the station, walk down rue Jeanne d'Arc and turn left to reach pl. de la Cathédrale and the **tourist office,** 25 rue du Gros Horloge. (Tel. 02 32 08 32 40; fax 02 32 08 32 44. Open Apr.-Sept. M-Sa 9am-7pm, Su 9:30am-12:30pm and 2:30-6pm; Oct.-Mar. M-Sa 9am-6:30pm, Su 10am-1pm.) Check your **email** at **Place Net,** 37 rue de la République, near the Eglise St-Maclou. (37F per hr. Open M 1-9pm, Tu-Sa 11am-9pm.) To reach the **Hôtel Normandya,** 32 rue du Cordier, head straight down rue Jeanne d'Arc from the station and left on rue Donjon to rue du Cordier. (Tel. 02 35 71 46 15. Singles and doubles 110-150F. Shower 10F. Reception 8am-8pm.) **Hôtel des Arcades,** 52 rue de Carmes, is comfy but pricier. (Tel. 02 35 70 10 30; fax 02 35 70 08 91. Singles and doubles 150-245F. Reception 7am-8pm. V, MC, AmEx.) **Camping Municipal de Déville,** on rue Jules Ferry in Déville-lès-Rouen, is 4km from Rouen; take bus 2 from the station to "Mairie." (Tel. 02 35 74 07 59. 24F per person, 8F per tent or car. Open May-Sept.) Cheap eateries crowd **pl. du Vieux-Marché** and the **Gros Horloge** area. **◾Natural Gourmand'grain,** 3 rue du Petit Salut, off pl. de la Cathédrale, has organic veggie food. (*Menu* 69F. Open Tu-Sa noon-2pm and 7-9pm. V, MC.) **Monoprix supermarket** is at 73-83 rue du Gros Horloge. (Open M-Sa 8:30am-9pm.) **Postal code:** 76000.

📷🎭 SIGHTS AND ENTERTAINMENT. The most famous of Rouen's "hundred spires" are those of the **Cathédrale de Notre-Dame,** in pl. de la Cathédrale, with the tallest tower in France (151m). The façade incorporates nearly every style of Gothic architecture; don't miss the stained glass in its **Chapelle St-Jean de la Nef.** (Open M-Sa 8am-8pm, Su 8am-6pm.) Behind the cathedral, the flamboyant **Eglise St-Maclou,** in pl. Barthélémy, features an elaborately carved pipe organ. (Open M-Sa 10am-noon and 2-5:30pm, Su 3-5:30pm.) A poorly marked passageway at 186 rue de Martainville leads to the **Aitre St-Maclou,** which served as the church's charnel house and cemetery through the later Middle Ages; a 15th-century frieze depicts the plague years. Visitors gape at the cadaver of a cat entombed alive to exorcise spirits. (Open daily 8am-8pm. Free.) Head down rue du Gros Horloge with the cathedral to your left to see the charmingly inaccurate 14th-century **Gros Horloge** (Big Clock). Joan of Arc died on **place du Vieux Marché,** to the left as you exit the station on rue du Donjon. A cross marks the spot near the unsightly **Eglise Ste-Jeanne d'Arc,** designed to resemble an overturned Viking boat. A block up rue Jeanne d'Arc, the **Musée des Beaux-Arts,** on pl. Verdrel, houses an excellent collection of European masters from the 16th to 20th centuries, including Monet and Renoir. (Open W-Su 10am-6pm. 20F, ages 18-25 13F.) If you're ill from Monet overdose, be happy that you won't be treated at the **Musée Flaubert et d'Histoire de la Médecine,** 51 rue de Lecat, far west of the art museum in pl. de la Madeleine next to the Hôtel-Dieu hospital, which showcases a gruesome array of pre-anaesthesia medical instruments, including gallstone crushers and a battlefield amputation kit. Writer Gustave Flaubert's possessions are also on display. (Open Tu 10am-6pm, W-Sa 10am-noon and 2-6pm. 12F, students free.)

🔼 EXCURSION FROM ROUEN: GIVERNY. Impressionist Claude Monet and his eight children settled in Giverny in 1883, and by 1887 John Singer Sargent, Paul Cézanne, and Mary Cassatt had placed their easels beside Monet's and turned the village into an artists' colony. Today the **Fondation Claude Monet,** 84 rue Claude Monet, maintains the artist's gardens and his collection of 18th- and 19th-century Japanese prints. (Open Apr.-Oct. Tu-Su 10am-6pm. 35F, students 25F.) **Buses** run to the museum from **Vernon** (10min., 4-6 per day, round-trip 20F), accessible by **train** from Rouen (40min., 9-10 per day) and Paris (40min.-1hr., 10-16 per day).

FRANCE

NORMANDY COAST

DIEPPE. In 1942, Allied (mostly Canadian) forces struggled to retake Dieppe's (pop. 36,000) **beach;** today, tourists flock to the long pebbly stretch and to the 15th-century **château** that rises from the cliffs to the west. Courtesy buses run from the tourist office to the Stena **ferry terminal** (tel. 08 02 01 00 20), where ferries depart for Newhaven, England (see p. 58). **Trains** (tel. 02 35 06 69 33) leave from bd. Clemenceau for Rouen (45min., 7-9 per day, 55F); Paris (2½hr., 6-10 per day, 138F; change at Rouen); and Caen (145F; change at Rouen). From the station, turn right and take a left on quai Duquesne to reach the **tourist office,** on pont Jehan Ango, on the waterfront in the *centre ville* (10min.). (Tel. 02 32 84 16 92; fax 02 32 14 40 61. Open July-Aug. daily 9am-1pm and 2-8pm; May-June and Sept. M-Sa 9am-1pm and 2-7pm, Su 10am-1pm and 3-6pm; Oct.-Apr. M-Sa 9am-noon and 2-6pm.) The **auberge de jeunesse (HI),** 48 rue Louis Fromager, has clean, spacious rooms. Take bus 2 (dir: Val Druel) from the Chambre du Commerce, 200m down quai Duquesne from the train station, to "Château Michel," backtrack a bit, and take the first left. (Tel. 02 35 84 85 73. 67F. Sheets 17F. Reception 8-10am and 5-10pm.)

FÉCAMP. The port town of Fécamp (pop. 20,000) is one of the jewels of the High Normandy coast, with a scenic beach and two architectural marvels. The magnificent, Renaissance-inspired **Palais Bénédictine,** 110 rue Alexandre Le Grand, houses impressive collections of medieval and Renaissance religious artifacts and is famous for its monk-produced after-dinner liqueur. (Open daily May 13-Sept. 5 9:30am-6pm; Sept. 6-May 12 reduced hours. 29F.) The 12th- to 13th-century **Abbatiale de la Trinité** houses an even rarer liquid: the relic of the *précieux-sang,* a fig trunk that allegedly carried a few drops of Christ's blood to the shores of Fécamp in the 6th century. **Trains** arrive from Rouen (1¼hr., 7 per day, 68F) and Paris (2½hr., 17 per day, 146F). The **tourist office,** 113 rue Alexandre Le Grand, books rooms for a 10F fee. From the station, head right on rue St-Etienne as it becomes rue de Mer and then left at Palais Bénédictine; it's opposite the entrance. (Tel. 02 35 28 51 01; fax 02 35 27 07 77. Open July-Aug. M-F 10am-6pm, Sa-Su 10am-noon and 2-6pm; Sept.-June M-Sa 9am-12:15pm and 1:45-6pm.) **Hôtel Martin,** 18 pl. St-Etienne, has cheery rooms. (Tel. 02 35 28 23 82; fax 02 35 28 61 21. Singles and doubles 150-200F. Reception 7:30am-11pm, closed Su night and M. V, MC, AmEx.) **Marché supermarket** is at 83 quai Berigny. (Open M-Sa 7am-9pm, Su 9am-1pm.)

LE HAVRE. An elegy to reinforced concrete, Le Havre (pop. 197,000) can boast of being the largest transatlantic port in France and little else—get in, get out, and no one gets hurt. For information on **ferries** to Portsmouth, see p. 289. **Trains** leave from cours de la République (tel. 02 35 98 50 50) for Fécamp via Etretat (45min., 5 per day, 43F); Paris (1hr., 7-9 per day, 150F); and Rouen (1hr., 9-12 per day, 71F). If you must stay in town, **Hôtel Jeanne d'Arc,** 91 rue Emile Zola, offers homey rooms with TVs and phones. (Tel. 02 35 21 67 27; fax 02 35 41 26 83. Singles 140-150F; doubles 160-165F; triples 230F. Breakfast 20F. V, MC.) Stock up for the ferry ride at **Nouvelles Galeries supermarket,** on quai George V. (Open M-Sa 8:30am-7pm. V, MC.)

CAEN

Although Allied bombing leveled three quarters of its buildings in WWII, Caen has since restored its architectural treasures and revitalized its tourist industry. Its biggest draw is the powerful **Mémorial de Caen,** in the northwestern corner of the city, which includes footage of WWII, displays on pre-war Europe and the Battle of Normandy, and a short but haunting testimonial to the victims of the Holocaust. Take bus 17 to "Mémorial." (Open daily July-Aug. 9am-8pm; Feb. 15-June and Sept.-Oct. 9am-7pm; Nov.-Jan. 4 and Jan. 20-Feb. 14 9am-6pm. 72F, students 63F, veterans free.) The city's twin abbeys, **Abbaye aux Hommes** and the **Abbatiale St-Etienne,** both off rue Guillaume le Conquérant, were financed by William the Conqueror as penance for marrying his distant cousin despite the Pope's interdiction. (Tours of Abbaye aux Hommes in French daily 9:30, 11am, 2:30, and 4pm. 10F, students 5F.

FRANCE

Abbatiale St-Etienne open daily 8:15am-noon and 2-7:30pm.) Opposite the tourist office sprawl the ruins of William's **château**. Inside, the **Musée des Beaux-Arts** contains a fine selection of 16th- and 17th-century Flemish works and 19th-century Impressionist paintings. (*Château* open daily May-Sept. 6am-1am; Oct.-Apr. 6am-7:30pm. Museum open W-M 9:30am-6pm. 25F, students 15F; W free.)

Trains (tel. 08 36 35 35 35) run to Rouen (2hr., 4 per day, 113F); Paris (2½hr., 5-7 per day, 152F); Rennes (3hr., 2 per day, 163F); and Tours (3½hr., 6 per day, 168F). CTAC city **buses** (6.20F) run from the station to near pl. St-Pierre, where the **tourist office** sells maps (2-24F) and books rooms (10F fee). (Tel. 02 31 27 14 14; fax 02 31 27 14 18. Open July-Aug. M-Sa 9:30am-7pm, Su 9:30am-1pm and 2-5pm; Sept.-June M-Sa 10am-1pm and 2-6pm, Su 10am-1pm.) The clean and popular **auberge de jeunesse (HI)**, 68bis rue Eustache-Restout, is at Foyer Robert Reme. Take a right from the train station, take your second right on rue de Vaucelles, walk one block, and catch bus 5 or 17 (dir: Fleury or Grâce de Dieu) from the stop on your left to "Lycée Fresnel." (Tel. 02 31 52 19 96; fax 02 31 84 29 49. 62F. Sheets 15F. Reception 5-10pm.) For great rooms near the *centre ville*, try ⬛**Hôtel de la Paix**, 14 rue Neuve-St-Jean. (Tel. 02 31 86 18 99; fax 02 31 38 20 74. Singles 140-175F; doubles 160-195F; triples 240-260F. Breakfast 28F. V, MC.) **Terrain Municipal**, on rte. de Louvigny, has riverside **campsites**. Take bus 13 (dir: Louvigny) to "Camping." (Tel. 02 31 73 60 92. 20F per person, 14F per tent, 11F per car. Reception 8am-9pm. Open May-Sept.) Ethnic restaurants, *crêperies*, and *brasseries* line the **quartier Vaugueux** near the *château* as well as the streets between **Eglise St-Pierre** and **Eglise St-Jean**. Get your grocery fix at **Monoprix supermarket**, 45 bd. du Maréchal Leclerc. (Open M-Sa 8am-8:30pm.) Caen's old streets pulsate by moonlight, especially around **rue de Bras, rue des Croisiers**, and **rue St-Pierre. Postal code:** 14000 (specify "Gambetta" for *Poste Restante*).

BAYEUX

An ideal base for exploring the D-Day beaches, Bayeux (pop. 15,000) is renowned for its **Tapisserie de Bayeux** (Bayeux Tapestry). The 70m of embroidery depict the Norman conquest of England in 1066, when William the Conqueror (né "the Bastard") earned himself a suaver nickname. The tapestry is displayed in the **Centre Guillaume le Conquérant**, on rue de Nesmond. (Open daily May-Aug. 9am-7pm; mid-Mar. to Apr. and Sept. to mid-Oct. 9am-6:30pm; mid-Oct. to mid-Mar. 9:30am-12:30pm and 2-6pm. 38F, students 16F. Audio tour in English 5F.) The **Musée de la Bataille de Normandie**, on bd. Fabian Ware, recounts the summer of 1944 through old newspaper clippings, photographs, films, and uniforms. (Open daily May to mid-Sept. 9:30am-6:30pm; mid-Sept. to Apr. 10am-12:30pm and 2-6pm. 30F, students 15F.)

Trains (tel. 02 31 92 80 50) arrive from Caen (20min., 12 per day, 33F); Cherbourg (50min., 4 per day, 78F); and Paris (2½hr., 5 per day, 164F). Turn left on the highway (bd. Sadi-Carnot), bear right, follow the signs to the *centre ville*, and follow rue Larcher to rue St-Martin to reach the **tourist office**, on pont St-Jean (10min.). (Tel. 02 31 51 28 28; fax 02 31 51 28 29. Open June-Sept. 15 M-Sa 9am-noon and 2-6pm, Su 9:30am-noon and 2:30-6pm; Sept. 16-May closed Su.) To get from the station to **Centre d'Accueil Municipal**, 21 rue des Marettes, follow bd. Sadi-Carnot and bear left at the rotary onto bd. Maréchal Leclerc, which becomes bd. Fabien Ware. (Tel. 02 31 92 08 19. Singles 75F. Breakfast 15F. Reception 7am-8pm.) The central **Hôtel Notre-Dame**, 44 rue des Cuisiniers, is opposite the cathedral. (Tel. 02 31 92 87 24; fax 02 31 92 67 11. Singles and doubles 180-280F. Breakfast 35F. Shower 5F. V, MC.) Follow rue Genas Duhomme and head straight on av. de la Vallée des Prés for **Camping Municipal**, on bd. d'Eindhoven. (Tel. 02 31 92 08 43. 14F per person, 17F per tent and car. Open Mar. 15-Nov. 15.) Get **groceries** at **Proxi**, on pl. St-Patrice. (Open Tu-Sa 7:30am-12:30pm and 2:30-7:30pm, Su 9am-12:30pm. V, MC.) **Postal code:** 14400.

D-DAY BEACHES

On June 6, 1944, over a million Allied soldiers invaded the beaches of Normandy—code-named Utah and Omaha (American), Gold and Sword (British), and Juno (Canadian). Today, the record of the battle can be clearly seen in sobering gravestones, remnants of German bunkers, and the pockmarked landscape.

FRANCE

The beaches/sights lie from west to east as follows: **Utah Beach, Pointe du Hoc, Omaha Beach, Arromanches/Gold Beach** (just northeast of Bayeux), **Juno Beach,** and **Sword Beach** (just north of Caen). Most of the region is accessible by **bus** from Caen or Bayeux. **Bus Fly** runs informative tours of the area in English. (Tel. 02 31 22 00 08. Half-day 160F, students 140F; full-day 300F, students 280F. Reserve ahead.)

UTAH BEACH. At Utah Beach, the Americans headed the western flank of the invasion. The **Musée du Débarquement** shows how 836,000 troops, 220,000 vehicles, and 725,000 tons of equipment came ashore. (Tel. 02 33 71 53 35. Open July-Aug. daily 9:30am-7:30pm; June daily 9:30am-7pm; Apr.-May daily 9:30am-6:30pm; Dec.-Mar. Sa-Su 9:30am-6:30pm. 27F, students 22F.) The beach and museum are accessible only by car or by foot from **Ste-Mère-Eglise.** Take a **train** from **Bayeux** to **Caretan** (20min., 5-6 per day) and then a **bus** from Caretan (1 per day) to Ste-Mère-Eglise.

POINTE DU HOC, OMAHA BEACH, AND GOLD BEACH. The most difficult landing was that of the 1st US Infantry Division at **Pointe du Hoc.** The grassy area beyond the cliffs is still marked by deep pits; one of the still-extant German bunkers has been turned into a memorial. Next to **Colleville-sur-Mer** and east of the Pointe du Hoc at **Omaha Beach,** memorialized in the American movie *Saving Private Ryan* (1998), almost 10,000 graves stretch over the 172-acre **American Cemetery.** (Open daily Apr.-Nov. 8am-6pm; Dec.-Mar. 9am-5pm.) Ten kilometers north of Bayeux and just east of Omaha is **Arromanches,** a small town at the center of **Gold Beach,** where the British built the artificial **Port Winston** in a single day to provide shelter while the Allies unloaded their supplies. The **Musée du Débarquement** on the beach houses relics and photos of the Allied landings. (Tel. 02 31 22 34 31. Open daily Apr.-May 5 9-11:30am and 2-6pm; May 6-Sept. 5 9am-6:30pm; Sept. 6-Mar. 9-11:30am and 2-5:30pm. Sept.-May opens Su 10am. 32F, students 27F.) The **Arromanches 360°** **Cinéma** combines images of modern Normandy with those of D-Day. Turn left on rue de la Batterie from the museum and follow the steps up. (Tel. 02 31 22 30 30. Open daily June-Aug. 9:10am-6:40pm; May and Sept. 10:10am-5:40pm; Oct.-Dec. and Feb.-Apr. 10:10am-4:40pm. 22F, students 19F.) **Bus Verts 70** (M-Sa 3 per day) runs from **Bayeux** to Pointe du Hoc, the American Cemetery, and Arromanches.

JUNO BEACH AND SWORD BEACH. East of Arromanches lies **Juno Beach,** the landing site of the Canadian forces. The **Canadian Cemetery** is at **Bény-sur-Mer-Reviers.** In **Ouistreham,** the **No. 4 Commando Museum,** on pl. Alfred Thomas, tells the story of British and French troops who participated in the attack on Sword Beach. (Tel. 02 31 96 63 10. Open Mar. 15-Oct. 3. 25F, students 15F.) **Bus Verts line 20** links **Caen** to Bény-sur-Mer-Riviers, while **line 1** runs from Caen to Ouistreham.

CHERBOURG

On the northern tip of the Cotentin peninsula, Cherbourg (pop. 28,000) was WWII's "Port de la Libération." Today **ferries** connect to Portsmouth, Poole, and Rosslare (see p. 58). Follow bd. Maritime northeast from the *centre ville* to reach the **ferry** terminal. The **train station** at the base of the Bassin du Commerce, 25min. (or a 6F shuttle) from the ferry terminal, serves Bayeux (1hr., 6 per day, 78F); Caen (1½hr., 9 per day, 97F); Rouen (3hr., 2 per day, 177F); and Paris (3½hr., 6 per day, 218F). From the station, to reach the **tourist office,** at the northern end of the Bassin du Commerce near the Pont Tournant, take a left and an immediate right onto quai Alexandre III and walk four blocks. Or, from the ferry terminal, turn right on bd. Felix Amiot, go straight at the rotary, and head right over the canal (20min.). (Tel. 02 33 93 52 02. Open in summer M-Sa 9am-6:30pm; off-season M-F 9am-noon and 2-6pm, Sa 9am-noon.) To get from the tourist office to the new **auberge de jeunesse (HI),** 55 rue de l'Abbaye, walk left on rue de Port, pass through pl. de la Mairie, continue on the pedestrian rue de la Paix, and bear left at the fork (25min.). (Tel. 02 33 78 15 15; fax 02 33 78 15 16. 51F. Sheets 17F. Kitchen. Reception 8am-noon and 6-11pm.) Stock up at the **Continent supermarket,** on quai de l'Entrepôt, next to the station. (Open M-Sa 8:30am-9:30pm.) **Postal code:** 50100.

MONT-SAINT-MICHEL

Rising abruptly from the sea, the island of Mont-St-Michel is visible for miles. The Mont is a dazzling labyrinth of stone arches, spires, and stairways that climb (and keep climbing) up to the **abbey,** balanced precariously on the jutting rock. To reach the abbey entrance (which is the departure point for tours), climb several flights of stairs up from the winding **Grande Rue,** a pedestrian street below filled with souvenir stands and restaurants. (1hr., 6 tours in English per day, free). (Open daily May-Sept. 9:30am-5pm; Oct.-Apr. 9:30am-4:30pm. 40F, under 26 25F. Audio tour 30F. Mass daily 12:15pm; free.) The descent to the frigid **crypts** beneath the church leads to its dark, chilly foundations, where walls are up to 2m thick. **La Merveille,** an intricate 13th-century cloister, encloses a seemingly endless web of passageways and chambers. The Mont is most stunning at night, particularly from the causeway entrance, but there is no late-night public transport off the island. Mont-St-Michel is best visited as a daytrip via Courriers Bretons **bus** (tel. 02 33 60 11 43) from St-Malo (1½hr., 2-4 per day, 53F) or Rennes (1½hr., 1-3 per day, 63F); CAT/TV buses (tel. 02 96 39 21 05) also roll in from Dinan (July-Aug. 1-2 per week, round-trip 105F).

BRITTANY (BRETAGNE)

Lined with spectacular beaches, misty, almost apocalyptic headlands, and cliffs gnawed by the sea into long crags and inlets, the peninsula of Brittany has always tugged away from mainland France, self-consciously maintaining its Celtic traditions. Present-day Breton culture has its roots in the 5th to the 7th centuries, when Britons fled Anglo-Saxon invaders; in the centuries that followed, they fought for and retained their independence from Frankish, Norman, French, and English invaders, uniting with France only after the last Duchess ceded it to her husband in 1532. Traditions are fiercely guarded, and lilting *Brezhoneg* (Breton) is spoken energetically at pubs and ports in the western part of the province.

RENNES

The administrative center of Brittany and home to two major universities, Rennes (pop. 209,000) combines Parisian sophistication with traditional Breton charm. A 1720 fire destroyed much of the city, but the lovely *vieille ville* remained intact and today teems with hip cafés and bars. A popular stopover between Paris and Mont-St-Michel, Rennes also makes for a packed weekend excursion of its own.

🛈🚆🍴 PRACTICAL INFO, ACCOMMODATIONS, AND FOOD. Trains (tel. 02 99 29 11 92) arrive on the south side of the river, opposite the town center, from St-Malo (1hr., every hr., 53-69F); Nantes (1¼-2hr., 10 per day, 85-112F); Paris (2hr., every hr., 213-286F); and Caen (3hr., 2 per day, 123-163F). **Buses** (tel. 02 99 30 87 80) leave from the left of the station (as you face it) for Angers (3hr., 1-2 per day, 96F). The **tourist office,** 11 rue Saint-Yves, has free maps and events listings. From the station, take av. Jean Janvier, turn left on quai Chateaubriand and walk along the river, turn right on rue George Dottin, and then right on rue Saint-Yves. (Tel. 02 99 67 11 11; fax 02 99 67 11 10. Open M-Sa 9am-7pm, Su 11am-6pm.) Surf the **internet** at **Cyberspirit,** 2D rue de la Visitation. (30F per 30min., 5F per sent email. Open M 2-7pm, Tu noon-7pm, W-F noon-midnight, Sa 2pm-midnight.)

To get to the **auberge de jeunesse (HI),** 10-12 Canal St-Martin, take bus 20 (M-F bus 1, Sa-Su bus 18; dir: Centre Commercial Nord) to "Hôtel Dieu"; continue down the road, turn right on rue de St-Malo, walk over the canal, and it's on the right. (Tel. 02 99 33 22 33; fax 02 99 59 06 21. Dorms 89F; singles 130F. Breakfast included. Reception 7am-11pm.) **Hôtel Venezia,** 27 rue Dupont des Loges, off quai Richemont, is in a great location; take av. Jean Janvier from the train station and turn right on rue Dupont des Loges. (Tel. 02 99 30 36 56; fax 02 99 30 78 78. Singles and doubles 160-220F.) From rue Gambetta, turn right on rue Victor Hugo, which becomes rue de Paris; from there take bus 3 to **Camping Municipal des Gayeulles,** in Parc les Gayeulles. (Tel. 02 99 36 91 22; fax 02 99 35 32 80. 14F per person, 15.50F per tent, 5F per

FRANCE

car. Shower 5F.) Rennes is a *gourmand*'s dream—seek out your fancy on **rues St-Malo, St-Georges, Ste-Melaine,** or in **pl. St-Michel.** There is a **supermarket** in the Galeries-Lafayette on quai Duguay-Trouin. (Open M-Sa 9am-8pm.) **Postal code:** 35000.

📷 🎵 **SIGHTS AND ENTERTAINMENT.** The **Musée des Beaux-Arts,** 20 quai Emile Zola, houses a small but eclectic collection, from Picassos to Egyptian pottery. (Open W-M 10am-noon and 2-6pm. Tours July-Aug. W and F 2:30pm. 30F, students 15F.) Sculptures and fountains grace the labyrinthine **Jardin du Thabor,** reputedly one of the most beautiful gardens in France. (Open June-Sept. daily 7am-9:30pm.) In the *vieille ville*, the **Cathédrale St-Pierre** boasts a magnificent chandeliered ceiling. (Open daily 9am-noon and 2-5pm.) Across the street from the cathedral, down rue Porte Mordelaise, stands the **Porte Mordelaise,** the last remaining piece of the city's medieval wall. In early July, the **Tombées de la Nuit** festival (tel. 02 99 67 11 11; fax 02 99 30 88 88; www.ville-rennes.fr) brings nine days of nonstop music, dance, partying, and theater. *Rennais* nightlife centers around **pl. Ste-Anne** and **pl. St-Michel.** The club **Le Zing,** 5 pl. des Lices, picks up at 1am and goes strong until 3am.

ST-MALO

St-Malo is the ultimate oceanside getaway—unfortunately, everybody knows it. Tourists converge on its miles of warm, sandy **beaches** and crystalline blue waters as well as its historic *centre ville*. The best view of St-Malo is from its **ramparts**—enter the walled city through the Porte St-Vincent and follow the stairs up on the right. **Trains** run from pl. de l'Hermine to Dinan (1hr., 8 per day, 46F); Rennes (1hr., 8-12 per day, 68F); and Paris (5hr., 3 per day, 294F). As you exit the station, cross bd. de la République and follow av. Louis-Martin straight to the **tourist office,** on esplanade St-Vincent, near the entrance to the old city (10min.). (Tel. 02 99 56 64 48. Open July-Aug. M-Sa 8:30am-8pm, Su 10am-7pm; Sept.-June reduced hours.) **Auberge de Jeunesse/Centre de Rencontres Internationales (HI),** 37 av. du Révérend Père Umbricht, is three blocks from the beach. Follow bd. de la République right from the station, turn right on av. Ernest Renan, turn left on rue Guen (which becomes av. de Moka), turn right on av. Pasteur (which turns into av. du Révérend Père Umbricht), and keep right (30min.). (Tel. 02 99 40 29 80; fax 02 99 40 29 02. Dorms 74-80F; singles 87F. Reception closed noon-2pm. Lockout 10am-5pm.) For **Hôtel Gambetta,** 40 bd. Gambetta, head toward the hostel and look for bd. Gambetta off av. Pasteur. (Tel. 02 99 56 54 70. Singles 110-150F; doubles 140-220F. Showers 16F. V, MC.) **Stoc supermarket,** on av. Pasteur, is near the hostel. (Open M-F 8:30am-12:30pm and 2:30-7:30pm, Sa 8:30am-7:30pm, Su 9:30am-noon. V, MC.) **Postal code:** 35400.

DINAN

Walking through beautiful Dinan (pop. 11,600) is like walking into the pages of a history text. Perhaps the best-preserved medieval town in Brittany, the cobblestoned streets in the *vieille ville* are lined with 15th-century houses inhabited by traditional artisans. Take the **Promenade des Petits-Fossés** along the ramparts to the 13th-century **Porte du Guichet,** the entrance to the **Château de la Duchesse Anne.** Climb the steps to the terrace to look out over the town, or inspect the galleries of the **Tour de Coëtquen,** which includes a spooky subterranean room full of tomb sculptures. (Complex open June to mid-Oct. daily 10am-6:30pm; mid-Oct. to May W-M reduced hours. 26F, students 11F.) As you enter the *vieille ville* from the port, you'll pass through the **Porte du Jerzual,** formerly the main gate to the city; climb up onto the **ramparts** for a breathtaking view. Re-entering the *vieille ville* through Porte St-Louis and turning right on rue du Général de Gaulle will lead you to the Promenade de la Duchesse Anne, flanked by the stately **Jardin Anglais** and the pale sandstone façade of the 12th-century **Basilique St-Sauveur.**

Trains run to Rennes (1¼hr., 6 per day, 92F) and Paris (5hr., 6 per day, 512F). To get from the station to the **tourist office,** 6 rue de l'Horloge, bear left across the plaza onto rue Carnot, turn right on rue Thiers, head left at the rotary (pl. Duclos) through the Porte de Brest onto rue du Marchix and rue de la Ferronnerie, turn left at pl. du Champ on rue Ste-Claire, and turn left on rue de l'Horloge. (Tel. 02 96 39 75

40; fax 02 96 39 01 64. Open June-Sept. M-Sa 9am-7pm, Su 10am-noon and 3-5pm; Oct.-May M-Sa 8:30am-12:30pm and 2-6pm. Walking tours July-Aug. daily 10am and 3pm; 25F.) To walk to the wonderful **auberge de jeunesse (HI),** on Moulin du Méen in Vallée de la Fontaine-des-Eaux, turn left as you exit the station, head left across the tracks, turn right, follow the tracks and signs downhill, and turn right after 1.5km onto a wooded lane (30min.). (Tel. 02 96 39 10 83; fax 02 96 39 10 62. 49F. Sheets 16F. Breakfast 18F. **Camping** 26F. Reception 9-11am and 3-11pm.) Hôtel du Théâtre, 2 rue Ste-Claire, is opposite the tourist office. (Tel. 02 96 39 06 91. Singles 80-120F; doubles 110-150F; triples 200F. Breakfast 22F.) Get **groceries** at **Monoprix,** on rue de la Ferronnerie. (Open M-F 9am-12:30pm and 2:30-7:30pm, Sa 9am-7pm.) Inexpensive *brasseries* lie near **rue de la Ferronnerie** and **pl. des Merciers. Postal code:** 22100.

CÔTE D'EMERAUDE AND THE CÔTE DE GRANITE ROSE

There's not much to see in **St-Brieuc,** but situated between the Côte d'Emeraude and the Côte de Granite Rose, it's a perfect base for daytrips to the scenic countryside. **Trains** arrive from Dinan (1hr., 2-3 per day, 54F) and Rennes (1hr., 15 per day, 83F). From the station, walk straight down rue de la Gare and bear right at the fork to reach the pl. de la Résistance and the **tourist office,** 7 rue St-Gouéno. (Tel. 02 96 33 32 50. Open July-Aug. M-Sa 9am-7pm, Su 10am-1pm; Sept.-June M-Sa 9am-noon and 2-6:30pm.) The **auberge de jeunesse (HI)** is in a 15th-century house outside of town; take bus 3 (dir: le Village). (Tel. 02 96 78 70 70. 70F. Call ahead. V, MC.)

Northeast of St-Brieuc, the rust-hued cliffs of **Cap Fréhel**—what landscape artists must dream of—mark this northern point of the Côte d'Emeraude. Catch a CAT **bus** from St-Brieuc (July-Aug. 3 per day, 1½hr., 42F) and follow the red-and-white-striped markers along the well-marked **GR34 trail** on the edge of the peninsula. The 13th-century **Fort La Latte** boasts drawbridges and a hair-raising view of the Cap (1½hr.). To reach the barracks-like **Auberge de Jeunesse Cap Fréhel (HI),** in la Ville Hadrieux, in Kerivet, walk toward Plévenon on the D16, then follow the inconspicuous signs with the fir-tree hostel symbol (35min.). (May-Sept. 15 tel. 02 96 41 48 98; Sept. 16-Apr. tel. 02 98 78 70 70. 45F. Sheets 17F. **Camping** 25F. Breakfast 19F. Lockout noon-5:30pm. Open May-Sept.) If you ask at St-Brieuc's hostel, you can leave a rented **bike** (45F per half-day) at Cap Fréhel, or vice-versa.

Paimpol, northwest of St-Brieuc at the end of the Côte de Granite Rose, offers access to nearby islands, beaches, and hiking. **Buses** run to the dramatic pink granite **Pointe de l'Arcouest** (12min., 7-8 per day, 10F), 6km north of Paimpol, where boats depart in summer for the tranquil beaches of the tiny **Ile de Bréhat** (10min., 40F round-trip). **Trains** (1hr., 4-5 per day, 60F) and CAT **buses** (1¼hr., 3-7 per day, 42F) arrive in Paimpol from St-Brieuc. From the station, go straight on rue du 18 Juin and turn right on rue de l'Oise, which becomes rue St-Vincent, to reach the **tourist office,** on pl. de la République. (Tel. 02 96 20 83 16. Open July-Aug. M-Sa 9am-7:30pm, Su 10am-1pm; Sept.-June reduced hours.) To get to the **auberge de jeunesse/gîte d'étape (HI),** turn left on av. Général de Gaulle, turn right at the first light and left at the next one, follow rue Bécot, bear right on rue de Pen Ar Run, and turn left at the end (20min.). (Tel. 02 96 20 83 60. 47F. **Camping** 25F. Breakfast 18F. Sheets 17F. Check-in until 9pm.)

BREST

Although it is often used simply as a base for exploring northwest Brittany, Brest (pop. 220,000) is a lively home to boisterous sailors and students who attend Brittany's second largest university. Brest's **château** was the only building to survive WWII and is now the world's oldest active military institution, as well as home to a museum on local maritime history. To get there, turn left out of pl. de la Liberté onto av. de Georges Clemenceau; then right on rue de Château, and follow it to its end. (29F, students 19F. Open W-M 9:15am-noon and 2-6pm.) The impressive **Océanopolis Brest,** at port de Plaisance, has space-age exhibits devoted to marine life, biodiversity, and conservation. Take bus 7 from diagonally across from the station to "Océanopolis." (Bus every 30min. until 8pm, 6F. Open June-Aug. daily 9:30am-6pm; Sept.-May M 2-5pm, Tu-F 9:30am-5pm, Sa-Su 9:30am-6pm.)

FRANCE

Trains (tel. 02 98 31 51 72) arrive from Rennes (1½hr., 5-6 per day, 161F plus 10F for TGV) and Nantes (4hr., 6 per day, 210F). From there, av. Georges Clemenceau leads to the pl. de la Liberté, at the intersection of the main rues de Siam and Jean Jaurès, and the **tourist office.** (Tel. 02 98 44 24 96; fax 02 98 44 53 73. Open mid-June to mid-Sept. M-Sa 9:30am-12:30pm and 2-6:30pm, Su 10am-noon and 2-4pm; mid-Sept. to mid-June M-Sa 10am-12:30pm and 2-6pm.) To get to the **auberge de jeunesse (HI),** on rue de Kerbriant, 4km away, take bus 7 from diagonally opposite the station to "Port de Plaisance" (6F; last bus M-Sa 7:30pm, Su 6pm); facing the port, take your first right, then another right, and it's on the right. (Tel. 02 98 41 90 41; fax 02 98 41 82 66. 69F. Reception M-F 7-9am and 5-8pm, Sa-Su 7-10am and 5-8pm. Lockers 5F. Curfew July-Aug. midnight; Sept.-June 11pm; ask for a key.) **Camping du Goulet** is 6km from Brest and 1km from the sea; take bus 14 to "Le Cosquer" or bus 7, 11, 12, or 26 to "Route de Conquest." (Tel. 02 98 45 86 84. 18F per person, 21F per tent. Shower included. Laundry.) For **groceries,** try the **Monoprix,** on rue de Siam. (Open M-Sa 8:30am-7:30pm.) **Postal code:** 29200 (29279 for *Poste Restante*).

CROZON PENINSULA

With spectacular scenery, rugged terrain, and few inhabitants, the Crozon Peninsula *(Presqu'île de Crozon)* merits the effort required to get there, especially for hikers and bikers seeking a challenge. **Crozon** is a good base from which to explore the peninsula; from Brest, take a Vedettes Armoricaines combo **boat/shuttle** (tel. 02 98 44 44 04; Apr.-Oct. 3 per day, 56F) or Pouget **bus** (tel. 02 98 27 02 02; 1¼hr., 1-3 per day, 68F). Buses stop at the **tourist office.** (Tel. 02 98 27 07 92. Open July-Aug. M-Sa 9:15am-7pm, Su 10am-7pm, Sept.-June M-Sa 9:30am-noon and 2-6pm.) **Presqu'île Loisirs,** across the street, rents indispensable **bikes.** (Tel. 02 98 27 00 09. 40F per half-day, 60F per day, 390F per week. Open July-Aug. M-Sa 9am-noon and 2-7pm, Su 9am-noon; Sept.-June Tu-Sa 9am-noon and 2-7 pm.) **ULAMIR** (tel. 02 98 27 01 68) has info on the peninsula's four **gîtes d'étape** (hostels; 45F). **Hôtel du Clos St-Yves,** 61 rue Alsace Lorraine, has decent rooms. From the bus stop, with the tourist office on your right, go left on rue St-Yves and right on rue Alsace Lorraine. (Tel. 02 98 27 00 10; fax 02 98 26 19 21. Doubles 184-300F; 60-80F per extra person. Breakfast 35F.)

From Crozon, you can take a **bus** to Camaret (2-3 per day, 11F). Just a few minutes on D8 from Camaret by bike or foot (look for signs to the left of the Hôtel le Styvel) stand the **Alignements de Lagatjar,** rocky monoliths believed to have been sun-worshiping sites from 2500 BC. Behind them, the ruins of **Château de St-Pol Roux** afford a magnificent view of the bay. A path winds to the **Pointe de Penhir,** 3.5km away on D8. A view of the isolated rock clusters of the **Tas de Pois** rewards those who climb to the edge. On the other side of town, D355 leads to another dramatic promontory, the **Pointe des Espagnols.** From the bus stop, take a left and backtrack to the **tourist office,** in the Gendarmerie next to pl. de Gaulle. (Tel. 02 98 27 93 60. Open July-Aug. M-Sa 9am-7pm, Su 9am-noon and 2-6pm; Apr.-May and Sept. M-Sa 9:15am-noon and 2-6:30pm, Su 9am-noon and 2-6pm; Oct.-Mar. M-F 9:15am-noon and 2-6pm.) **Hôtel le Styvel** (tel. 02 98 27 93 06) and **Hôtel Vauban** (tel. 02 98 27 91 36), next to each other on quai du Styvel, offer rooms (singles and doubles 160-250F).

To get to **Morgat** from Crozon, you can walk or bike the 3km or wait for the infrequent Vedettes Armoricaines shuttle (10F). To walk from the Crozon bus stop to Morgat, take a left onto rue St-Yves, a right on rue Alsace Lorraine, and another left on bd. de la France Libre. You'll pass splendid beaches as you walk from Crozon into the tiny *centre ville*. Along this path is the **tourist office** on the right. (Tel. 02 98 27 29 49. Open June-Sept. Tu-Sa 10am-noon and 3-6pm.) Ask at the tourist office about **tours** of Morgat's famous **marine caves** (45min., 30-45F; May-Sept.). Hikers can take the 14km path along the cliffs overlooking the ocean from Morgat port to Cap de la Chèvre for breathtaking ocean views. **Camping du Bouis** is 1.5km out of town on the way to the Cap. (Tel. 02 98 26 12 53. 1 person 35F, 2 people 62F; 15F per additional person. Showers 5F. Reception Easter-Sept. 8am-11pm.)

NANTES

Although Nantes (pop. 500,000) lies in the Pays de la Loire, most *Nantais* feel a cultural allegiance to Brittany. While there aren't many must-see sights, its ideal location, year-round festivals, and vibrant nightlife make Nantes a smart stop between Brittany and points south. It was in the heavily fortified **Château des Ducs de Bretagne** that Henri IV composed the Edict of Nantes, granting considerable religious liberties to the Huguenots in 1598. Although the *château*'s museums are closed until 2008, the interim **Musée du Château des Ducs de Bretagne** hosts temporary exhibits. (*Château* open daily July-Aug. 10am-7pm; Sept.-June 10am-noon and 2-6pm. Free. Museum open daily July-Aug. 10am-noon and 2-6pm; Sept.-June W-M 10-11:50am and 2-5:50pm. 20F, students 10F; free after 4:30pm.) Go inside the **Cathédrale St-Pierre** to gape at Gothic vaults which tower 38m and the largest stained-glass window in the country. (Open daily 8:45am-7pm.) A reminder of the late 19th century, **La Cigale**, 4 pl. Graslin, is considered one of the most beautiful *brasseries* in France, with art nouveau mosaics, gold detail, and huge mirrors. *Menus* are expensive, but snacks are available all day for under 50F. (Tel. 02 51 84 94 94; www.lacigale.com. Open daily 7:30am-12:30am; reserve for dinner. V, MC.)

Trains (tel. 08 36 35 35 35) run to La Rochelle (2hr., 8-11 per day, 125F); Rennes (2hr., 3-10 per day, 117F); Paris (2-4hr., 17-20 per day, 222-358F); and Bordeaux (4hr., 6-8 per day, 226F). The **tourist office** is on pl. du Commerce. Take the north exit *(accès nord)* from the station onto allée du Charcot, which turns into cours John Kennedy, pass the *château*, cross cours des 50 Otages, and the *place* is on the right (20min.). (Tel. 02 40 20 60 00; fax 02 40 89 11 99. Open M-Sa 10am-7pm.) To get from the *place* to the **Foyer des Jeunes Travailleurs, Beaulieu (HI)**, 9 bd. Vincent Gâche, take bus 24 (dir: Beaulieu) to "Albert." (Tel. 02 40 12 24 00; fax 02 51 82 00 05. 60F. Breakfast 12F. Sheets 16F. Reception 8am-midnight.) The central **Hôtel St-Daniel**, 4 rue du Bouffay, is just off pl. du Bouffay. (Tel. 02 40 47 41 25; fax 02 51 72 03 99. Singles 150F; doubles 150-220F. Breakfast 24F. V, MC.) To reach **Camping du Val de Cens**, 21 bd. du Petit Port, take tram 2 from pl. du Commerce to "Marhonnière" (10min.). (Tel. 02 40 74 47 94. 18F per person, 35F per tent and car. Shower included. Reception 8am-10pm.) You'll find many a morsel to suit your fancy behind **pl. du Bouffay**—the *crêperies* are great. **Monoprix supermarket** is at 2 rue de Calvaire. (Open M-Sa 9am-9pm.) For nightlife info, check the weekly *Nantes Poche* (3F at any *tabac*). The **rue Scribe** is full of bars and cafés. **Postal code:** 44000.

LOIRE VALLEY (VAL DE LOIRE)

Between Paris and Brittany is the fertile valley of the Loire, France's longest and most celebrated river. The valley seems to overflow with *châteaux*, which range from dilapidated medieval fortresses to elegant Renaissance homes. Although some date back to the 9th century, most were built in the 16th and 17th centuries, when French monarchs left Paris for the countryside around Tours to mix business with pleasure; here they could simultaneously hunt and attend to state duties.

Tours is the region's best **rail** hub, although the *châteaux* Sully-sur-Loire, Chambord, and Cheverny aren't accessible by train. Infrequent public transit from larger cities can strand travelers. Train stations distribute the invaluable *Les Châteaux de la Loire en Train Eté* and *Châteaux pour Train et Vélo* with train schedules and **bike** and **car** rental info, which are the best ways to experience the region.

ORLÉANS

Orléans (pop. 200,000), with its fairy-tale castle, expansive vineyards, and rich forests, has been besieged by jealous foreigners for millennia—today, its prominence is gradually waning as nearby Tours steals the show. Come to Orléans to get better acquainted with Joan of Arc or to explore the nearby *châteaux*. The stained-glass windows of the stunning **Cathédrale Ste-Croix**, in pl. Ste-Croix, depict Joan's dramatic story, from her liberation of the city to the flames that consumed her. (Open daily July-Aug. 9:15am-noon and 2:15-7pm; May-June and Sept. closes 6pm; Oct.-Apr. closes 5pm.) The **Musée des Beaux-Arts**, on rue Ferdinand Rabier 1, has a fine

FRANCE

collection of Italian, Flemish, Dutch, and French works spanning the last five centuries. (Open Th-Sa 10am-6pm; Tu and Su 11am-6pm; W 10am-8pm. 21.50F, students 11F.) The **Maison de Jeanne d'Arc,** 3 pl. de Gaulle, off pl. du Martroi, celebrates the life and times of Orléans' favorite liberator. (Open May-Oct. Tu-Su 10am-noon and 2-6pm; Nov.-Apr. Tu-Su 2-6pm. 14F, students 7F.) A pleasant daytrip down the Loire lies the region's second-oldest castle, the imposing 14th-century fortress **Sully-sur-Loire,** accessible by bus from the bus station (1hr., 57F).

Trains arrive from Blois (30min., 104F); Tours (1hr., 178F); and Paris (1¼hr., 180F). To get to the **tourist office,** on pl. Albert 1er, from the station, ascend into the mall, turn right, and it's on the left as you exit the mall. (Tel. 02 38 24 05 05. Open July-Aug. M-Sa 9am-7pm, Su 9:30am-12:30pm and 3-6:30pm; Apr.-June and Sept. M-Sa 9am-7pm, Su 10am-noon; Oct.-Mar. M-Sa 9am-6:30pm, Su 10am-noon.) To get to the **auberge de jeunesse (HI),** 1 bd. de la Motte, take bus RS (dir: Rosette) or SY (dir: Concyr/La Bolière) from pl. d'Arc to "Pont Bourgogne"; head straight down bd. de la Motte and it's on the right at the end. (Tel. 02 38 53 60 03. 61F.) For **groceries,** head to **Monoprix,** 46 rue de Faubourg Bannier. (Open M-Th 8:30am-12:45pm and 2:30-7:30pm, F 8:30am-8pm, Sa 8:30am-7pm. V, MC.) **Postal code:** 45000.

BLOIS

Blois (pop. 55,000) relishes its position as gateway to the Loire Valley, and welcomes visitors with bucolic charm. Home to monarchs Louis XII and François I, Blois' **château** was the Versailles of the late 15th and early 16th centuries; today it houses museums. (Open daily July-Aug. 9am-8pm; mid-Mar. to June and Sept. 9am-6:30pm; Oct. to mid-Mar. 9am-12:30pm and 2-5:30pm. 35F, students 20F.)

Trains run to Orléans (30min., 14 per day, 53F) and Paris (1¾hr., 8 per day, 121F), but not to most *châteaux*. **Point Bus,** 2 pl. Victor Hugo (tel. 02 54 78 15 66), sends buses to Chambord and Cheverny (65F, students 50F; reduced admission with bus pass) and other *châteaux*. Or rent a **bike** from **Atelier Cycles,** 44 Levée des Tuileries (tel. 02 54 74 30 13), and pedal for an hour. The **tourist office,** 3 av. Jean Laigret, can point the way. (Tel. 02 54 90 41 41; www.chambordcountry.com. Open May-Sept. M-Sa 9am-7pm, Su 10am-7pm; Oct.-Apr. M-Sa 9am-12:30pm and 2-6pm, Su 9:30am-12:30pm.) Five kilometers west is the **auberge de jeunesse (HI),** 18 rue de l'Hôtel Pasquier. To get there from the tourist office, follow rue Porte Côté and then rue Denis Papin to the river, and take bus 4 (dir: Les Grouets) to the end. (Tel./fax 02 54 78 27 21. First night 61F, each additional night 44F. Reception 6:45-10am and 6-10:30pm. Lockout 10am-6pm. Curfew 10:30pm. Open Mar.-Nov. 15.) The rustic **Auberge de Jeunesse Verte (HI),** convenient for Chambord visitors, is 11km away in Montivault; take TLC bus 1 (dir: Beaugency). (Tel. 02 38 44 61 31. 45F. **Camping** 27F. Open July-Aug.) **Le Pavillon,** 2 av. Wilson, has clean, bright rooms. (Tel. 02 54 74 23 27. Singles 115-135F; doubles 220F.) Sumptuous *pavé du roi* (chocolate-almond cookies) and *malices du loup* (orange peels in chocolate) entice pedestrians from *pâtisseries* along **rue Denis Papin.** For those who cling foolishly to the dinner-before-dessert convention, ☕**La Mesa,** 11 rue Vauvert, serves tempting Franco-Italian fare in a secluded romantic courtyard. **Postal code:** 41000.

🖪 EXCURSIONS FROM BLOIS: CHAMBORD AND CHEVERNY. Built to satisfy François I's egomania, **Chambord** is the largest and most extravagant of the Loire *châteaux*. Seven hundred of François I's trademark stone salamanders are stamped throughout this petite "hunting lodge," whose 440 rooms kept the king and his hounds warm with 365 fireplaces. A double-helix staircase dominates the center of the castle. (Tel. 02 54 50 40 00. Open daily July-Aug. 9am-6:45pm; Apr.-June and Sept. 9:30am-6:15pm; Oct.-Mar. 9:30am-5:15pm. 41F, under 26 26F.) Take TLC **bus** 2 from Blois (45min., 20F); hop on the TLC **Chambord-Cheverny bus circuit** (50-65F to both *châteaux* plus reduced admission); or **bike** from Blois (1hr.; take D956 south 2-3km, then go left on D33).

Cheverny, accessible by bus (see above) or bike from Blois (take D956 south), soothes with manicured grounds and a magnificent interior: Spanish leather walls, delicate Delft vases, and an elaborate royal bedchamber still await the visit of their first French king. (Tel. 02 54 79 96 29. Open daily June to mid-Sept. 9:15am-6:45pm; Apr.-May 9:15am-6:30pm; late Sept. 9:30am-noon and 2:15-6pm; Mar. and Oct. closes 5:30pm; Nov.-Feb. closes 5pm. 34F, students 22F.)

AMBOISE

The battlements of the 15th-century *château* at **Amboise** stretch out protectively across the hill above the town. Two of the four kings who lived here also met their end here: the four-foot-tall Charles VIII bumped his head on a *really* low door and died a few hours later, and the equally clumsy Charles V tripped over a torchbearer and burned himself alive. Today, the jewel of the grounds is the late 15th-century **Chapelle St-Hubert;** a plaque inside marks **Leonardo da Vinci's** final resting place. (Open daily July-Aug. 9am-8pm; Apr.-June 9am-6:30pm; Mar. 15-30 and Sept.-Oct. 9am-6pm; Nov.-Jan. 9am-noon and 2-5pm; Feb.-Mar. 13 9am-noon and 2-5:30pm. 37F, students 30F.) After being invited to France by François I, Leonardo spent his last four years at **Clos Lucé** manor. Today, its main attraction is a collection of 40 of his inventions, built with the materials that would have been available to da Vinci at the time. (Tel. 02 47 57 62 88. Open July-Aug. 9am-8pm, Apr.-June and Sept.-Oct. 9am-7pm; Nov.-Mar. daily 9am-6pm; Jan. 10am-5pm. 38F, students 29F. V, MC.) **Trains** run to Blois (15min., 15 per day, 32F); Tours (20min., 14 per day, 28F); and Paris (2¼hr., 5 per day, 140F). The **Centre International de Séjour (HI) Charles Péguy,** on Ile d'Or, sits on an island in the middle of the Loire. (Tel. 02 47 57 06 36. 50F; members only. Reception M-F 3-8pm. Call ahead.) **Postal code:** 35400.

TOURS

Tours is the urban centerpiece of the Loire region, and boasts fabulous nightlife, diverse population, and great food, but not many sights. The **Cathédrale St-Gatien,** on rue Jules Simon, has dazzling stained glass. (Open daily Easter-Sept. 8:30am-noon and 2-8pm; Oct.-Easter 8:30am-noon and 2-5:30pm.) At the **Musée du Gemmail,** 7 rue du Murier, *gemmail*-works (in which shards of brightly colored glass and enamel are fused) by Picasso and Braque glow in rooms of dark velvet. **Trains** run to Paris (1-2¼hr., 12-13 per day, 160-261F) and Bordeaux (2½hr., 6 per day, 226F). The **tourist office,** 78/82 rue Bernard Palissy, books rooms and leads a historical tour. (Tel. 02 47 70 37 37; fax 02 47 61 14 22. Open June-Aug. M-Sa 8:30am-6pm, Su 2:30-5pm; Sept.-May M-Sa 8:30am-6pm.) **Hotel Foch,** 20 rue du Maréchal Foch, has a marvelous location and a friendly proprietor. (Tel. 02 47 05 70 59; fax 02 47 20 95 10. Singles 130-220F; doubles 150-300F; triples 240-380F; quads 330-380F.) **Hotel Regina,** 2 rue Pimbert, is near the happening rue Colbert. (Tel. 02 47 05 25 36; fax 02 47 66 08 72. Singles 110-175F; doubles 140-240F.) **Pl. Plumereau** is your best bet for great restaurants, cafés, and bars. ☒**Charolais Chez Jean Michel,** 123 rue Colbert, makes *haute cuisine* affordable. (*Menus* 60-72F. Open M 7:30-10:30pm, Tu-Sa noon-2pm and 7:30-10:30pm.) **Le Dépanneur,** 108 rue du Commerce, has 15F half-pint beer, while a young crowd frequents the alternative, techno-pop, and jazz nights at **Rhythm and Blues,** 19 rue Petit Soleil (cover 30-50F; open daily 11pm-4am). **Postal code:** 37000.

☒ EXCURSIONS FROM TOURS: VILLANDRY, LOCHES, CHENONCEAU, AND AZAY-LE-RIDEAU. Villandry maintains fantastic gardens with waterfalls, vine-covered walkways, and over 120,000 plants, but the *château* itself is of less historical interest than its regal cousins. (Tel. 02 47 50 02 09. Gardens open daily June-Aug. 8:30am-8pm; Sept.-May 9am-dusk. *Château* open daily June to mid-Sept. 9am-6:30pm; mid-Feb. to May and mid-Sept. to Nov. 11 9:30am-5:30pm. Ticket 48F.) Villandry is hard to get to; take the **train** from Tours to Savonnières (10min., 4 per day, 17F) and walk 4km along the Loire. **Cyclists** and **drivers** follow the D16.

The walled medieval town of **Loches** surrounds its grand *château*, which has two distinct structures at opposite ends of a hill. To the south, the 11th-century **donjon** (keep) and watchtowers went from keeping enemies out to putting them up when Charles VII turned it into a state prison, complete with suspended cages. To the north, the **Logis Royal** housed French kings from the 12th to 15th centuries. (Open

FRANCE

daily July to mid-Sept. 9am-7pm; mid-Mar. to June and late Sept. 9:30am-1pm and 2:30-7pm; Feb. to mid-Mar. and Oct. 9:30am-1pm and 2:30-6pm. Joint ticket 32F, students 22F.) **Buses** run from the Tours train station to Loches (50min., 4 per day, 47F; pay on board); nine **trains** also make the trip (1hr., 47F).

A series of women created the exquisite beauty of *château* **Chenonceau:** first Catherine, the wife of a royal tax collector, then Diane de Poitier, the lover of Henri II, and then his widowed wife, Catherine de Médici. The bridge over the river Cher that connects two sections of the *château* also marked the border between annexed and Vichy France during WWII. Chenonceau's beautiful setting makes it the most touristed of the *châteaux.* (Tel. 02 47 23 90 07. Open mid-Mar. to mid-Sept. daily 9am-7pm; call for off-season hours. 45F, students 30F.) **Trains** from Tours roll into the station 2km away (45min., 3 per day, 36F).

Lounging on an island in the Indre, **Azay-le-Rideau** gazes peacefully at its reflection. Intended to rival Chambord in beauty and setting, Azay succeeded so well that François I seized the *château* before its third wing was completed. Azay's flamboyant style is apparent in the ornate second-floor staircase. (Tel. 02 47 45 42 04. Open daily July-Aug. 9am-7pm; Apr.-June and Sept.-Oct. 9:30am-6pm; Nov.-Mar. 9:30am-12:30pm and 2-5:30pm. 35F, under 26 23F. Audio guides in English 26F.) **Trains** run from Tours to Azay-le-Rideau town, 2km away (30min., 3 per day, 28F). **Buses** run from Tours' train station to the tourist office, 1km from the train station (45min.; M-Sa 3 per day, Su 1 per day; one-way 29F; pay on the bus).

SAUMUR

Saumur (pop. 35,000) is a delight to the senses—its wines and *champignons* (mushrooms) will tickle your taste buds, and its enchanting old quarter will soothe your eyes. The 14th-century **château,** built by Charles V's brother, Louis I of Anjou, looms over the city and contains the **Musée des Arts Décoratifs,** with plentiful porcelain, and the **Musée du Cheval's** gear-and-tackle collection. (All open July-Aug. Su-Tu and Th-F 9:30am-6pm; W and Sa 9:30am-6pm and 8:30-10:30pm; June and Sept. 9:30am-6pm; Oct.-Mar. W-M 9:30am-noon and 2-5:30pm; Apr.-May daily 9:30am-noon and 2-5:30pm. 37F, students 26F.) **Gratien et Meyer,** on rte. de Chinon, gives tours of its wine *cave* and offers *dégustations* (tastings). Take bus D from pl. Bilange to "Beaulieu." (Tel. 02 41 83 13 32. Open Apr.-Sept. daily 9am-6:30pm; Oct.-Mar. M-F 9am-noon and 2-6pm, Sa-Su 10am-12:30pm and 3-6pm. 15F; 1-hour *dégustation* 50F.) The **Musée de Champignon,** on rte. de Gennes, in St-Hilaire-St-Florent, is a mushroom *cave* that offers grilled hors d'oeuvres outside the exhibit. (Tel. 02 41 50 31 55. Open daily mid-Feb. to mid-Nov. 10am-7pm. 38F, students 30F.)

Trains run frequently to Angers (30min., 42F) and Tours (45min., 56F). The **tourist office,** on pl. Bilange, just off the pont Cessart (bridge), books beds (5F fee). Exit to the right of the station on av. David d'Angers, turn right onto pont des Cadets, continue straight on av. de Général de Gaulle, and it'll be on your left (15min.). (Tel. 02 41 40 20 60. Open mid-May to mid-Oct. M-Sa 9:15am-7pm, Su 10:30am-12:30pm and 3:30-6:30pm; mid-Oct. to mid-May M-Sa 9:15am-12:30pm and 2-6pm.) The modern **Centre International de Séjour,** on rue de Verden, on Ile d'Offard, has a superb view of the *château.* From the station, follow the directions above to pont des Cadets, and turn left immediately after crossing it toward the hostel. (Tel. 02 41 40 30 00. Dorms 82F; doubles 216F. Reception 8am-8pm.) Stock up on fungi at the indoor **market** at the end of pl. St-Pierre (daily until 1pm), or more mass-produced goods at **Atac supermarket,** 6 rue Franklin D. Roosevelt, inside a shopping center. (Open M-F 9am-7:30pm, Sa 8:45am-7:30pm. V, MC.) **Postal code:** 49400.

■ EXCURSION FROM SAUMUR: FONTEVRAUD ABBEY. The **Abbaye de Fontevraud,** the largest existing monastic complex in Europe, has left nine centuries of visitors in awe. The 12th-century abbey church serves as a Plantagenêt necropolis; **Eleanor of Aquitaine,** who lived out her days here after being repudiated by her second husband, **Henry II** of England, now lies next to him along with their son **Richard the Lionheart.** Outside, the **gardens** host patches of legumes, tubers, greens, and medicinals; they bloom behind the abbey **kitchen,** whose spire-like chimney led

19th-century restorers to take it for a chapel. (Tel. 02 41 51 71 41. Open daily June-Sept. 17 9am-6:30pm, Sept. 18-Oct. 9:30am-noon and 2-5:30pm; Nov.-Mar. 7 9:30-noon and 2-5pm or dusk; Mar. 8-May 9:30am-noon and 2-6pm. 32F, students 21F.) **Bus 16** travels the 14km from Saumur's train station (25min., 3 per day, 14F).

ANGERS

From behind the massive stone walls of the 15th-century **Château d'Angers,** on pl. Kennedy, the Dukes of Anjou ruled the surrounding countryside and an island across the Channel (known today as Britain); Henry II held court in Angers (pop. 220,000) as often as in London. The 14th-century **Tapisserie de l'Apocalypse** within, the world's largest tapestry masterpiece, depicts the Book of Revelations. (Open daily June to mid-Sept. 9:30am-7pm; mid-Sept. to Oct. and Lent-May 10am-6pm; Nov.-Lent 10am-5pm. 35F, students 23F.) Angers' second woven masterpiece, the **Chant du Monde** ("Song of the World"), in the **Musée Jean Lurçat,** 4 bd. Arago, illustrates a symbolic journey through human destiny. (Open mid-June to mid-Sept. daily 9am-6:30pm and mid-Sept. to mid-June Tu-Su 10am-noon and 2-6pm. 20F.)

Trains roll out to Nantes (1hr., 5 per day, 75F); Tours (1hr., 7 per day, 88F); Orléans (3-4hr., 6 per day, 166F); and Paris' Austerlitz station (4hr., 3per day, 242F). **Buses** run to Rennes (3hr., 2 per day, 97F). To get from the station to the **tourist office,** on pl. Kennedy, exit straight onto rue de la Gare, turn right on rue Talot, turn left on bd. du Roi-René, and continue until you hit the plaza. (Tel. 02 41 23 51 11; fax 02 41 23 51 66. Open June-Sept. M-Sa 9am-7pm, Su 10am-1pm and 2-6pm; Oct.-May M-Sa 9am-12:30pm and 2-6:30pm.) To get to **Auberge de Jeunesse Darwin (HI),** 3 rue Darwin, take bus 8 (dir: Beaucouzé; 20min.) to "Essca Technopole" or bus 1 (dir: Belle Beille) to its end. (Tel. 02 41 22 61 20; fax 02 41 48 51 91. 62F, nonmembers 72F. Breakfast 17F. Sheets 20F. Kitchen. **Internet.** Reception until 10pm.) The family-run **Royal Hôtel,** on rue d'Iéna, off pl. de la Visitation, has spacious rooms. (Tel. 02 41 88 30 25; fax 02 41 81 05 75. Singles 100-210F; doubles 150-240F. Breakfast 28-32F. V, MC, AmEx.) Grab **groceries** in the basement of **Galerie Lafayette,** at the corner of rue d'Alsace and pl. du Ralliement. (Open M-Sa 9am-7pm.) ■**La Soufflerie,** 8 pl. du Pilori, has great sweet and savory soufflés (36-53F). (Open Tu-Sa noon-2:30pm and 7-10pm.) **Postal code:** 49052 (specify "Angers-Ralliement" for *Poste Restante*).

SOUTHWEST FRANCE

Caught between the wild Atlantic surf and the calm brilliance of the Mediterranean, southwestern France holds a hand full of aces beneath its demure poker face. Gastronomes will delight in the wines of Bordeaux and the delicacies of Gascony, paleontologists will rejoice in the prehistoric surplus of Perigord, hikers will thrill to the vistas of the Pyrénées, and heat-seekers will find sun throughout the vast expanses of sand and surf on both coasts. The most geographically diverse of France's four corners, the Southwest is equally diverse culturally, with Basques in the west and Cataláns in the east proudly guarding their ancient traditions.

POITOU-CHARENTES

Although little-known outside France, Poitou-Charentes offers sun-drenched beaches, sedate canals, craggy cliffs, fertile plains, and a rich history. The Côte d'Azur may be tops in topless beaches, and the Loire Valley may be the king of *châteaux*, but no other region of France has so impressive a collection of both. Poitou-Charentes is a brilliant collage of pristine natural sights and coastal towns tucked away on the western shore of France.

LA ROCHELLE

With beautiful beaches, refined 14th-century architecture, and popular festivals, La Rochelle (pop. 100,000) is vacation heaven. Climb around the fortifications of the 14th-century towers **Tour St-Nicolas** and **Tour de la Chaîne,** to the left as you face the

harbor. (Open daily Apr.-Sept. 10am-7pm; Oct.-Mar. 10am-12:30pm and 2-5:30pm.
25F, students 15F.) From the last week in June until the first week in July, the city
hosts the **Festival International du Film de la Rochelle.** (Tel. 01 48 06 16 66; fax 01 48 06
15 40. Three films 90F.) In the third week of July, the massive **FrancoFolies** music
festival features performing Francophones from around the world. (Tickets 55-
175F; ask at the tourist office.) **Ile de Ré,** an island known for its 70km of white sand
beaches, lies 10km from La Rochelle. Get to the island by bike, ferry (30F), or bus 1
or 50 (dir: La Pallice; depart from pl. de Verdun; 10F). **Trains** go to Poitiers (2hr., 8
per day, 109F); Bordeaux (2hr., 5 per day, 133F); and Nantes (2hr., 5 per day, 129F).
The **tourist office,** on pl. de la Petite Sirène, is in the quartier du Gabut. (Tel. 05 46 41
14 68; fax 05 46 41 99 85. Open July-Aug. M-Sa 9am-8pm, Su 11am-5pm; June and
Sept. M-Sa 9am-7pm, Su 11am-5pm; Oct.-May M-Sa 9am-noon and 2-6pm, Su 10am-
noon.) Take bus 10 (dir: Port des Minimes) to "Auberge de Jeunesse" or take the
waterside footpath to reach **Centre International de Séjour, Auberge de Jeunesse (HI),**
on av. des Minimes. (Tel. 05 46 44 43 11; fax 05 46 45 41 48. Dorms 72F; singles 107F.
Breakfast included. Lockout 10am-2pm. Reception 8am-12:30pm, 1:30-7:30pm, and
8:30-10pm.) **Postal code:** 17000 (17021 for *Poste Restante;* specify "Hôtel de Ville").

POITIERS

Poitiers' (pop. 120,000) churches are a stunning reminder of Christianity's lasting
influence in the region. Façades in the 12th-century Romanesque **Notre-Dame-la-
Grande,** on pl. de Gaulle, off Grand Rue, display the story of Christianity, while the
massive **Cathédrale St-Pierre,** in pl. de la Cathédrale, off rue de la Cathédrale, still
boasts some of its original 12th-century stained-glass windows. Nearby is the 4th-
century **Baptistère St-Jean,** on rue Jean Jaurès, the oldest Christian edifice in France.
(Open July-Aug. daily 10am-12:30pm and 2-7pm; Apr.-June and Sept.-Nov. W-M
10:30am-12:30pm and 3-6pm; Dec.-Mar. W-M 2:30-4:30pm. 4F.)

    Trains (tel. 08 36 35 35 35) run to Tours (1hr., 5 per day, 92F); La Rochelle (1¾hr.,
8 per day, 117F); Bordeaux (2hr., 9 per day, 168F); and Paris (2½hr., 5 per day, 198-
310F). To get from the train station to the **tourist office,** 8 rue des Grandes Ecoles, go
up bd. Solférino and up the stairs, turn left at pl. Leclerc, and turn left on rue des
Grandes Ecoles (10min.). (Tel. 05 49 41 21 24; fax 05 49 88 65 84. Open June 21-Sept.
20 M-F 9am-7pm, Sa 9:45am-6:45pm, Su 9:45am-1pm and 2:45-6pm; Sept. 21-June 20
M-Sa 9am-noon and 1:30-6pm.) For the **auberge de jeunesse (HI),** 1 allée Tagault,
catch bus 3 (dir: Pierre Loti) from the traffic light in front of the station to "Cap
Sud." Or head right as you exit the station, follow bd. du Pont Achard as it curves
around to av. de la Libération, bear right on rue B. Pascal, turn right on rue de la
Jeunesse, and turn left on Roger Tagault (35min.). (Tel. 05 49 58 03 05; fax 05 49 30
09 79. 51-65F; members only. Breakfast 19F. Reception M-Sa 8-10am, noon-2pm,
and 7-11pm; Su 8-10am and 7-11pm.) **Postal code:** 86000.

ANGOULÊME

Angoulême (pop. 50,000) affords magnificent views of the surrounding countryside. This 17th-century hotbed of the French paper industry is now the capital of
French comic strips. In the **CNBDI,** 121 rue de Bordeaux, the **Musée de la Bande Dess-
inée** explores the history of comics. (Tel. 05 45 38 65 65. Open July-Aug. Tu-F 10am-
7pm, Sa-Su 2-7pm; Sept.-June Tu-F 10am-6pm, Sa-Su 2-6pm. 30F, students 20F.)
Cathédrale St-Pierre, in pl. St-Pierre, was an important stepping-stone in 12th-cen-
tury architecture. (Open daily 9am-7pm.) Amble through the flowers and waterfalls
of **Jardin Vert** and climb the town's 4th-century **ramparts** for spectacular views.

    Trains run to Poitiers (1hr., 5 per day, 91F); Bordeaux (1-1½hr., 10-12 per day, 100-
109F); Périgueux (2hr., 4 per day, 116F); and Paris (2¾hr., 7 per day, 300-399F). To
get from the station to the **tourist office,** 7bis rue du Chat, follow av. Gambetta uphill
to pl. G. Perrot, continue up the rampe d'Aguesseau, turn right on bd. Pasteur, and
left on rue de Chat. (Tel. 05 45 95 16 84; fax 05 45 95 91 76. Open July-Aug. M-Sa
9:30am-7pm, Su 10am-noon and 2-5pm; Sept.-June M-F 9:30am-7pm.) Pick up a map
from the **kiosk** by the station before you depart. Access the **internet** at **Café de Limo-
ges** in the CNBDI (see above). (Open M-F 10am-6pm. Students 20F per hr.) To get to

the **auberge de jeunesse (HI),** on Ile de Bourgines, turn left from the station onto av. de Lattre de Tassigny, left again on bd. du 8 Mai 1945, left yet again on bd. Besson Bey, and cross the bridge (20min.). (Tel. 05 45 92 45 80. 51F. Breakfast 19F. Sheets 16F. Call ahead.) Stock up at the **Stoc Supermarket,** 19 rue Périgueux. (Open M-Sa 8:30am-7:15pm, Su 9am-noon. V, MC.) **Postal code:** 16000.

⁊ NEAR ANGOULÊME: LA ROCHEFOUCAULD. La Rochefoucauld has been home to the aristocratic Foucaulds for over a millennium. The present **château,** the "pearl of Angoumois," was built by Duke Francis II in 1528 on a feudal-era foundation with twin towers, a medieval fortress, and an elegant chapel. (Tel. 05 45 62 07 42. Open May-Sept. daily 10am-7pm; Oct.-Easter Su and holidays 2-7pm. Call for details about the *Son et lumière* show. 40F.) **Trains** run from Angoulême (M-Sa 5 per day, Su 3 per day; 29F), while **Château transport** (tel. 05 45 84 14 86) rolls buses out of Angoulême's Champ de Mans (30min., 19F; M-Sa 11:30am).

PERIGORD AND AQUITAINE

The images presented by Périgord and Aquitaine are seductive: green countryside splashed with yellow sunflowers, white chalk cliffs, golden white wine, plates of black truffles, and the smell of warm walnuts. First settled 150,000 years ago, the area around Les Eyzies-de-Tayac has turned up more stone-age artifacts—tools, bones, weapons, cave paintings, and etchings—than any other place on earth.

PÉRIGUEUX

Encircled by the river Isle, Périgueux (pop. 37,700) preserves significant architecture in both the medieval-Renaissance and Gallo-Roman halves of the town. The city is also a good base for visiting local prehistoric caves. The *vieille ville* sports Renaissance architecture, and the multi-domed **Cathédrale St-Front** combines the styles of several eras. (Open daily 8am-7:30pm.) The **Tour de Vésone** is a remarkable Roman ruin; it was a *cella*, the holiest place and center of worship of a temple. (Open daily Apr.-Sept. 7:30am-9pm; Oct.-Mar. 7:30am-6:30pm.)

    Trains run to Bordeaux (1½hr., 97F); Toulouse (4hr., 179F); and Paris (5-7hr., 271-368F; change at Limoges). The **tourist office,** 26 pl. Francheville, has free walking tour maps. From the station, turn right on rue Denis Papin, bear left on rue des Mobiles-de-Coulmierts (which becomes rue du Président Wilson), pass rue Guillier (which leads to the Roman ruins), take the next right, and it's on the left. (Tel. 05 53 53 10 63; fax 05 53 09 02 70. Open July-Aug. M-Sa 9am-7pm, Su 9:30am-5:30pm; Sept.-June M-Sa 9am-6pm.) To reach the **Foyer des Jeunes Travailleurs Résidence Lakanal,** off bd. Lakanal, from the tourist office, turn left down cours Fénélon, take a right on bd. Lakanal, and look for the Municipal Bridge and Billiard Club after the intersection with bd. Bertran de Born; it's on the left side of the club. (Tel. 05 53 53 52 05; fax 05 53 54 37 46. Dorms 73F; singles 88F. Breakfast included. Reception M-F 4-8pm, Sa-Su 7-8pm.) **Monoprix supermarket** is on pl. de la République. (Open M-Sa 8:30am-8pm.) **Postal code:** 24070 (24017 for *Poste Restante*).

SARLAT

Even with the dense mobs swarming Sarlat (pop. 10,700) in summer, the town's remarkable *vieille ville* of golden sandstone merits a mosey. Sarlat's movie-set medieval perfection has attracted the gaze of more than a few cameras—*Cyrano de Bergerac* and *Manon des Sources* were filmed here. Today, its narrow 14th- and 15th-century streets fill with flea markets, dancing violinists, and purveyors of *gâteaux aux noix* (cakes with nuts) and golden Monbazillic wines. **Trains** go to Bordeaux (2½hr., 2 per day, 116F) and Périgueux (3hr., 1 per day, 73F). Stop by the **tourist office,** on pl. de la Liberté. (Tel. 05 53 59 27 67. Open M-Sa 9am-noon and 2-7pm, Su 10am-noon and 2-6pm.) Sarlat's **auberge de jeunesse,** 77 av. de Selves, is 30min. from the train station but only 5-10min. from the *vieille ville*. Go straight along rue de la République (which becomes av. Gambetta), bear left at the fork onto av. de Selves, and it's on your right. (Tel. 05 53

FRANCE

59 47 59. 45F. Sheets 16F. **Camping** 30F. Open mid-Mar. to Nov. Reserve ahead.) **Champion supermarket** is near the hostel on rte. de Montignac (continue following av. de Selves away from the *centre ville*). (Open M-Sa 9am-7:30pm, Su 9am-noon. V, MC.) **Postal code:** 24200.

⚑ EXCURSIONS FROM SARLAT AND PÉRIGUEUX: CAVE PAINTINGS. The most spectacular cave paintings yet discovered hide in the **caves of Lascaux,** near the town of **Montignac,** 25km north of Sarlat. Discovered in 1940 by a few teenagers and their dog, the caves were closed in 1963 after it was found that the oohs and aahs of millions of tourists had fostered algae and micro-stalactites, ravaging the paintings. **Lascaux II** duplicates every inch of the original cave, in the same pigments used 17,000 years ago. Although the reproduction may lack ancient awe and mystery, the caves—filled with paintings of five-meter-tall bulls, horses, and bisons—nevertheless manage to inspire a wonder all their own. (Caves open May-Aug. daily 9am-7pm; Apr. and Sept.-Oct. Tu-Su 9am-7pm; Jan. 26-Mar. and Nov.-Jan. 4 Tu-Su 10am-12:30pm and 1:30-5:30pm. 48F.) The automatic machine near the **tourist office** (tel. 05 53 51 82 60), on pl. Bertram-de-Born, sells tickets. They go fast, so reserve a week or two ahead for the 45-minute tours (in French or English). One **bus** for Montignac leaves Périgueux each night (1½hr., 37F); one CFTA bus per day runs each morning from Sarlat (July-Aug. 2 per day, 30min., 23F) and returns in early evening.

At the **Grotte de Font-de-Gaume,** 1km outside **Les Eyzies-de-Tayac** on D47, 15,000-year-old horses, bison, reindeer, and woolly mammoth cavort along the cave walls. (Tel. 05 53 06 90 80. Open Tu-Th Apr.-Sept. 9am-noon and 2-6pm; Mar. and Oct. 9:30am-noon and 2-5:30pm; Nov.-Feb. 10am-noon and 2-5pm. 35F, under 26 21F, artists and art students free.) **Grotte du Grand Roc,** 1.5km northwest of town, contains millions of stalactites, stalagmites, and *eccentriques* (small, crooked calcite accretions). (Open July-Aug. daily 9:30am-7pm; Apr.-June and Sept.-Nov. 10 daily 9:30am-6pm; Feb. 9-Mar. and Nov. 11-Jan. 10 Su-F 10am-5pm. 35F.) For both caves in summer, call at least two weeks in advance to get tickets. The town is served by trains from Périgueux (30min., 40F) and Sarlat (1hr., 45F; change at Le Buisson).

⚑ EXCURSION FROM SARLAT: THE DORDOGNE VALLEY. Steep, craggy cliffs and poplar tree thickets overlook the slow-moving turquoise waters of the Dordogne River, 15km south of Sarlat. Numerous *châteaux* keep watch over tourists in canoes, on bikes, and in cars; by avoiding the major towns, it's also possible to find solitude. Ten kilometers southwest of Sarlat, the town of **Castelnaud-La Chapelle** snoozes in the shadow of its crumbling, pale-yellow-stone *château*, a fortress of the 12th to 15th centuries, and now the most visited castle in Aquitaine. **Domme,** the best-defended of the Dordogne Valley's villages, was built by King Philippe III (Philippe the Bold) in 1280 on a high dome of solid rock. *Chambres d'hôte* provide cheap, farmhouse **accommodations** near the historic sites; ask at any tourist office for lists of *hôtes* and campgrounds. To get to and around the valley, you'll need to rent a car or be prepared for a good bike workout—the hills are steep but manageable. You can reach *châteaux* by **excursion buses** leaving Sarlat. **Hep!** (tel. 05 53 28 10 04), on pl. Pasteur, and **CFTA Périgord,** 21 rue de Cahors (tel. 05 53 59 01 48), run convenient but expensive **buses** each day.

BORDEAUX

Enveloped by emerald vineyards, Bordeaux (pop. 700,000) toasts the deep, violet wine that made it famous. A temple to wine connoisseurs, the city itself is also a treasure. The local government has scrubbed Bordeaux's splendid mansions, Gothic cathedrals, and *places* clean; today, nightclubs, art galleries, concerts, and some of the best food in France reflect the diversity of the *Bordelais.*

FRANCE

⚆⚆⚆ PRACTICAL INFO, ACCOMMODATIONS, AND FOOD. Trains depart for Toulouse (2½hr., 10 per day, 163F); Paris (3hr., 10-20 per day, 345F, TGV 330-380F); and Nice (9½hr., 4 per day, 421F). From the train station, take bus 7 or 8 (dir: Grand Théâtre) to pl. Gambetta and walk toward the Monument des Girondins to the **tourist office,** 12 cours du 30 Juillet, which arranges winery tours (see below). (Tel. 05 56 00 66 00; fax 05 56 00 66 01; www.bordeaux-tourisme.com. Open May-Sept. M-Sa 9am-8pm, Su 9am-7pm; Oct.-Apr. M-Sa 9am-7pm, Su 9:45am-6pm.) **Wasteels,** opposite the station, sells BIJ tickets. (Tel. 08 03 88 70 22. Open M-F 9am-noon and 2-7pm, Sa 9am-1pm and 2-6pm.) **American Express** is at 14 cours de l'Intendance. (Tel. 05 56 00 63 36. Open M-F 8:45am-noon and 1:30-5:30pm.) Get **internet** access at **Cyberstation,** 23 cours Pasteur. (Tel. 05 56 01 15 15. Open M-Sa 11am-2am, Su 2pm-midnight.) **Postal code:** 33065.

The **auberge de jeunesse (HI),** 22 cours Barbey, is scheduled to reopen after renovation in June 2000; call ahead to make sure. From the station, follow cours de la Marne and turn left on cours Barbey; women may feel uncomfortable walking alone. (Tel. 05 56 91 59 51; fax 05 56 94 02 98. 56F. Breakfast included.) The clean, airy **Hôtel la Boétie,** 4 rue de la Boétie, between pl. Gambetta and the Musée des Beaux-Arts, has rooms with showers, toilets, TVs, and phones. (Tel. 05 56 81 76 68; fax 05 56 81 24 72. Singles 120F; doubles 135-160F; triples 180F. Breakfast 20F. Reception 24hr. V, MC, AmEx.) The same family runs 11 other nearby hotels. For the **Hôtel Boulon,** 22 rue Boulon, take bus 7 or 8 from the train station to the cours d'Albret; turn left before the Irish pub on the corner; the hotel is on the right. (Tel. 05 56 52 23 62; fax 05 56 44 91 65. Singles 100F, with shower 120F; doubles 110-200F, with shower 140F. Breakfast 20F. Reception 24hr. V, MC.) Pitch a tent at **Camping les Gravières,** on pont de la Maye in Villeneuve d'Ornon. (Tel. 05 56 87 00 36. 19F, children 12F; tent 22F, tent and car 30F. Reception 8am-12:30pm and 5-8pm.)

Living in the *région de bien manger et de bien vivre* (region of fine eating and living), *Bordelais* take their food as seriously as their wine. Hunt around **av. St-Remi** and **pl. St-Pierre** for splendid regional specialties, including oysters, *foie gras*, beef braised in wine sauce, and *canelé de Bordeaux* (a cake created in 1519). Descend into the cool cellar of **Baud et Millet,** 19 rue Huguerie, off pl. Tourny, for all-you-can-eat cheese (105F). (Tel. 05 56 79 05 77. Open M-Sa 9am-midnight. V, MC, AmEx.) The helpful English-speaking waitstaff at the elegant and romantic **La Casuccia,** 49 rue St-Rémi, serves French and Italian delicacies from 65F. (Tel. 05 56 51 17 70. Open daily for lunch from 11:30am, for dinner 4pm-midnight. V, MC.) Stock up at **Auchan supermarket,** at the Centre Meriadeck on rue Claude Bonnier. (Tel. 05 56 99 59 00. Open M-Sa 8:30am-10pm.)

⚅⚄ SIGHTS AND ENTERTAINMENT. Nearly 900 years after its consecration by Pope Urban II, the stunning **Cathédrale St-André,** in pl. Pey-Berland, remains Bordeaux's Gothic masterpiece. The 18th-century **Grand Théâtre,** near the tourist office, often hosts operas, concerts, and plays (30F, students 25F). In the Entrepôt Laine gallery, 7 rue Ferrère, near the river, the **Musée d'Art Contemporain** (tel. 05 56 00 81 50) and the **Arc en Rêve Centre d'Architecture** (tel. 05 56 52 78 36) exhibit modern painting, sculpture, and photography. (Open Tu and Th-Su 11am-6pm, W 11am-8pm. 30F, students 10F, seniors free; 1st Su of each month all museums free.) *Clubs and Concerts* (free at the tourist office) and *Bordeaux Plus* (2F at any *tabac*) provide an overview of nightlife.

Bordeaux is, of course, famous for its wine. The most efficient and comprehensive way to get a glimpse (and taste) is through the tourist office's guided **wine tour,** which alternates between les Côtes de Bourge et de Blaye, L'Entre-Deux-Mers, Graves et Sauternes, Médoc, and St-Emilion. (May-Oct. daily, Nov.-Apr. W and Sa; 1:30pm. 160F, students 140F.) The **Maison du Vin/CIVB,** 1 cours du 30 Juillet, opposite the tourist office, offers a two-hour "Initiation to Wine Tasting" course which allows you to sample some of the most outstanding (and expensive) wines of the region. (Tel. 05 56 00 22 66. Course June-Aug. twice weekly, 100F. Open M-Th 8:30am-6pm, F 8:30am-5:30pm.) For a cheaper taste, head to **Vinothèque,** 8 cours du 30 Juillet. (Tel. 05 56 52 32 05. Open M-Sa 9:15am-7:30pm.)

FRANCE

THE BASQUE COUNTRY

In the southwest corner of France, bordering Spain and the Pyrénées, the Basque Country is home to the mysterious *Euzkadi*, or Basque, people. For millennia, since before the arrival the Celts in Europe, the Basques have lived in this triangle between the Pyrénées and the Atlantic, speaking a language that linguists are still at a loss to classify. Long renowned as fierce fighters, the Basques continue to struggle today, striving to win independence for their long-suffering homeland.

BAYONNE

Bayonne (pop. 43,000) is a grand port with small-town appeal. The 13th-century **Cathédrale Ste-Marie,** with twin steeples needling the sky, intimidates from afar and impresses from within. (Open M-Sa 10am-noon and 3-6pm, Su 3:30-6pm.) Highlights of the **Musée Bonnat,** 5 rue Jacques Laffitte, in Petit-Bayonne, include works by Rubens, El Greco, and Goya. (Open W-Th and Sa-M 10am-noon and 3-6:30pm, F until 8:30pm. 20F, students 10F.) Free traditional Basque **concerts** are at the gazebo in pl. de Gaulle (July-Aug. Th at 9:30pm).

Trains depart from the station in pl. de la République, running to Bordeaux (1½-2½hr., 8 per day, 130-189F) and Toulouse (4hr.) as well as San Sebastián, Spain (1½-2hr.; change at Hendaye). Trains run between Bayonne and Biarritz (10min., 10-22 per day, 13F), but the local **bus** network provides more comprehensive (and usually cheaper) regional transit. Local STAB **buses** depart from the Hôtel de Ville, running to Anglet and Biarritz (every 30-40min., last bus M-Sa 8pm, Su 7pm). Tickets are good for 1hr. and cost 7.50F. Packets of 10 cost 62F (students 52F during school year only). The **tourist office,** on pl. des Basques, has maps and finds rooms. From the train station, take the middle fork onto pl. de la République, veer right over pont St-Esprit, pass through pl. Réduit, cross pont Mayou, turn right on rue Bernède (which becomes av. Bonnat), and turn left on pl. des Basques (15min.). (Tel. 05 59 46 01 46; fax 05 59 59 37 55. Open July-Aug. M-Sa 9am-7pm, Su 10am-1pm; Sept.-June M-F 9am-6:30pm, Sa 10am-6pm.) Decent lodgings dot the area around the train station and pl. Paul Bert, but the closest **hostel** is in Anglet. The **Hôtel Paris-Madrid,** on pl. de la Gare, has cozy rooms. (Tel. 05 59 55 13 98; fax 05 59 55 07 22. Singles and doubles 95-170F. Breakfast 25F. Reception July-Sept. 24hr.; Oct.-June 6am-12:30am. V, MC.) To get to **Camping de la Chêneraie,** take bus 1 from the station to Leclerc supermarket; walk or catch the bus (5 per hr.) for the remaining 2km. (26F per person, 58F per tent or car. Reception Easter-Sept. 8am-10pm.) Huge portions of delicious regional specialties are served at the elegant **Le Bistrot Ste-Cluque,** 9 rue Hugues, opposite the station. (*Menu* 55F. Open daily noon-2pm and 7-11pm.)

🎇 **EXCURSION FROM BAYONNE: ST-JEAN-PIED-DE-PORT.** The Pyrenean village of St-Jean-Pied-de-Port (pop. 1600) epitomizes the spicy splendor of the Basque interior. The narrow, cobblestoned streets ascend through the *haute ville* to the dilapidated fortress, and down below, the calm Nive hides acrobatic trout among shimmering rocks. This medieval capital of Basse-Navarre still hosts a continual procession of pilgrims on their way to Santiago de Compostela, Spain, 900km away. **Trains** arrive from Bayonne (1hr., 7 per day, 45F). **Rent bikes** at **Garazi Cycles,** 1 pl. St-Laurent. (Tel. 05 59 37 21 79. 120F per day, 150F per weekend. Passport deposit. Open M-Sa 8:30am-noon and 3-6pm.) From the station, turn right on av. Renaud, follow it up the slope until it ends at av. de Gaulle, and turn right to reach the **tourist office,** 14 av. de Gaulle. (Tel. 05 59 37 03 57; fax 05 59 37 34 91. Open July to mid-Sept. M-Sa 9am-12:30pm and 2-7pm, Su 10:30am-12:30pm and 3-6pm; mid-Sept. to June M-F 9am-noon and 2-7pm, Sa 9am-noon and 2-6pm.)

BIARRITZ

Biarritz (pop. 29,000) is not a budgeteer's dream, but its free **beaches** make a daytrip *de luxe*—you too can sunbathe where Napoleon III, Bismarck, and Queen Victoria summered. At the **Grande Plage,** you'll find a wealth of surfers and bathers, and just to the north at the less-crowded **plage Miramar,** bathers repose *au naturel*. A short

FRANCE

hike to **Pointe St-Martin** affords a priceless view. In summer, **BASC Subaquatique,** near Plateau de l'Atalaye (tel. 05 59 24 80 40), organizes **scuba** excursions in summer for 155F. **Trains** roll into **Biarritz-la-Négresse,** 3km out of town; hop on blue bus 2 (dir: Bayonne via Biarritz) or green bus 9 (dir: Biarritz HDV) to get to the *centre ville.* Or, get off the train in Bayonne and hop on STAB **bus** 1 or 2 to the central Hôtel de Ville (30min.). The **tourist office,** 1 sq. d'Ixelles, helps with finding accommodations and dispenses events listings. (Tel. 05 59 22 37 10. Open daily June-Sept. 8am-8pm, Oct.-May 9am-6:45pm.) The **auberge de jeunesse (HI),** 8 rue de Chiquito de Cambo, has a friendly staff and lakefront location. From the train station, turn left up the hill, turn left at the rotary, and follow rue de Movettes to the right; the hostel is across the street at the bottom. (Tel. 05 59 41 76 00; fax 05 59 41 76 07. 82-90F; members only. Breakfast included. Sheets 35F.) **Hôtel Barnetche,** 5bis rue Charles-Floquet, has homemade croissants for breakfast. (Tel. 05 59 24 22 25; fax 05 59 24 98 71. Dorms 100F, doubles 260-350F, triples 420F, quads 560F. Obligatory breakfast for non-dormers 35F; in Aug., obligatory half-pension 90F. Reception 7:30am-11pm. Open May-Sept.) **Codec Supermarket,** 2 rue du Centre, just off rue Gambetta, has typical supermarket fare and selection of local wines. (Open July-Aug. M-Sa 8:45am-12:25pm and 3-7:10pm, Su 8:45am-1pm; Sept.-June closed Su.)

ANGLET

Anglet's *raisons d'être* are its nine beaches of fine-grained white sand, from the perfect waves of the **plage Les Cavaliers** to the rocky jetty of the **Chambre d'Amour.** Anglet hosts a number of professional surfing championships during the summer (free to spectators), including the **O'Neill Surf Challenge** and the **Europe Surfing Championship.** The **Rainbow Surfshop,** 19-21 av. Chambre d'Amour, rents boards (half-day 40-60F, full-day 100F; 1000-2000F deposit) and wetsuits (half-day 30F, full-day 50F; 1000F deposit), and arranges surfing lessons. (Tel. 05 59 03 54 67. Open Apr.-Oct. daily 9:30am-8pm.) STAB **buses** connect Anglet to Bayonne and Biarritz. The **tourist office,** 1 av. de Chambre d'Amour, in pl. Leclerc, has info on summer surfing contests. (Tel. 05 59 03 77 01. Open July-Sept. M-Sa 9am-7pm; Oct.-June M-F 9am-12:15pm and 1:45-6pm, Sa 9am-12:15pm.) The carefree **auberge de jeunesse (HI),** 19 rte. de Vignes, is right uphill from the beach. (Tel. 05 59 58 70 00; fax 05 59 58 70 07. 73F; camping 56F. Breakfast included. Sheets 23F. Reception 8:30am-10pm.) From the Hôtel de Ville in Biarritz, take bus 4 (dir: Bayonne Sainsontain) to "Auberge." From pl. de la République or pl. de Réduit in Bayonne, take bus 4 to "La Barre," then take bus 9 to "Auberge." The centrally located **Camping Fontaine Laborde,** 17 allée Fontaine Laborde, caters to young surfers. Take bus 4 to "Fontaine Laborde." (Tel. 05 59 03 48 16. 27F per person, 25F per site, 18F per car.) The restaurants along the **Sables d'Or** feature international cuisine at affordable prices.

GASCONY AND THE PYRÉNÉES

South of Aquitaine, the forests recede and the mountains of Gascony begin, shielded from the Atlantic by the Basque Country. Both Gascons and Basques are descended from the people the Romans called *Vascones.* They differ in that Gascony was more amenable to outside influences, and Gascons have long considered themselves French. Today, people come to Gascony to be healed; millions of believers descend on Lourdes hoping for miracle cures while thousands of others undergo scarcely more scientific treatments in the many *thermes* of the Pyrénées.

LOURDES

In 1858, 14-year-old Bernadette Soubirous saw the first of what would total 18 visions of the Virgin Mary in the Massabielle grotto in Lourdes (pop. 16,300). "The Lady" made a healing spring appear, and today five million rosary-toting faithful make pilgrimages here annually. To get from the tourist office to the **Caverne des Apparitions (La Grotte)** and the two **basilicas** above, follow av. de la Gare, turn left on bd. de la Grotte, and follow it across the river (10min.). **Processions** depart daily from the grotto at 3:30pm and 8:45pm. (Grotto open daily 5am-midnight. Dress modestly. Basilicas open daily Easter-Oct. 6am-7pm; Nov.-Easter 8am-6pm.)

FRANCE

Lourdes is accessible by **train** via Bayonne (2hr., 5 per day, 104F); Toulouse (2½hr., 8 per day, 122F); and Bordeaux (3hr., 7 per day, 170F). To get to the **tourist office**, on pl. Peyramale, from the station, turn right on av. de la Gare, bear left on av. Marasin, and keep an eye out to the right (5min.). (Tel. 05 62 42 77 40; fax 05 62 94 60 95; email lourdes@sudfr.com. Open May to mid-Oct. M-Sa 9am-7pm, Su 10am-6pm; mid-Oct. to mid-Mar. M-Sa 9am-noon and 2-6pm; mid-Mar. to Apr. daily 9am-12:30pm and 1:30-7pm.) To find the clean and comfortable **Hôtel-Restaurant Saint-Sylve**, 9 rue de la Fontaine, turn right just before the tourist office on rue des 4 Frères Soulas and then right again on rue Basse; rue de la Fontaine will be the second street on the left. (Tel./fax 05 62 94 63 48. Singles 75F, with shower 110F; doubles 140F, with shower 170F; triples 205F; quads 260F. Breakfast 25F. Shower 15F. Call ahead if arriving late. Open Apr.-Oct.) **Camping de la Poste**, 26 rue de Langelle, is just a few minutes from the center of town. (Tel. 05 62 94 40 35. 14F per person, 14-19F per site. Shower 8F. Open Mar. 28-Oct. 15.) Save a few francs by heading to **Prisunic supermarket**, 9 pl. du Champ-Commun. (Open M-Sa 8:30am-12:30pm and 2-7:30pm, Su 8am-noon.) **Postal code:** 65100.

CAUTERETS

Nestled in a narrow, breathtaking valley on the edge of the **Parc National des Pyrénées Occidentales** is tiny Cauterets. Romans first discovered the therapeutic effects of Cauterets' hot sulfuric *thermes*, but most visitors today come to take advantage of the skiing (Dec.-Apr.; passes 115-138F per day) and hiking. Head to the **tourist office**, on pl. Foch, for info on sights in town. (Tel. 05 62 92 50 27; fax 05 62 92 59 12; www.cauterets.com. Open daily July-Aug. 9am-7pm; Sept.-June 9am-12:30pm and 2-6:30pm.) For good **hiking info** and **maps**, head to **Parc National des Pyrénées**, in Maison du Parc, on pl. de la Gare (tel. 05 62 92 52 56; fax 05 62 92 62 23). **Skilys**, rte. de Pierrefitte (tel. 05 62 92 52 10), pl. de la Gare, has guides for hire and rents **bike, mountain,** and **ski equipment. Postal code:** 65110.

SNCF **buses** (Eurail valid) run from Lourdes to Cauterets (50min., 3-6 per day, 39F). The sparkling white **Gîte d'Etape: Le Pas de l'Ours**, 21 rue de la Raillère, is a few blocks up the street opposite the tourist office. (Tel. 05 62 92 58 07; fax 05 62 92 06 49. 65F per person. Triples 270F. Breakfast 40F. Laundry 50F. Reception 8am-noon and 2-11pm. Open Dec. to mid-Apr. and mid-May to Oct. V, MC.) The covered **Halles market**, in the center of town on av. du Général Leclerc, has fresh produce. (Open daily 8:30am-12:30pm and 2:30-7:30pm.)

🎿 **EXCURSIONS FROM CAUTERETS: LUZ AND THE PYRÉNÉES.** One of seven French national parks, the **Parc National des Pyrénées** soothes with sulfur springs, frustrates with unattainable peaks, and awes visitors with mountain biking, hiking, and skiing opportunities. It is crucial to procure a good map before setting off on a trail. Pick up maps for intermediate hikes at sporting goods stores, or go to the friendly and helpful **Parc National des Pyrénées** (see above) which has *Promenades en Montagne* maps (40F) of 15 different trails beginning and ending in Cauterets, all labeled with estimated duration (from 1hr. to 2 days) and difficulty.

From Cauterets, the **Grand Randonée 10 (GR 10)** meanders across the Pyrénées, connecting to **Luz-St-Saveur** just over the mountain and then on to **Gavarnie**, another day's hike up the valley. Circling counterclockwise from Cauterets to Luz-St-Sauveur, the **Refuges Des Oulettes** (2152m) is the first shelter past the **Lac de Gaube**, which you can find on the IGN map. (Tel. 05 62 92 62 97. 80F. Open June-Sept.) Dipping into the **Vallée Lutour**, the **Refuge Estom** rests peacefully near **Lac d'Estom.** (In summer, call 05 62 92 72 93, off-season 05 62 92 75 07. 60-70F.) The **Refuge Jan Da Lo** is in **Gavarnie**, near the loop's halfway mark. (Tel. 05 62 92 40 66. 48F.)

Luz-St-Sauveur is actually two villages: Luz caters mostly to skiers, while St-Sauveur deals in close encounters of the thermal kind. Set in the wide, grassy **Vallée du Toy**, Luz itself offers few challenging hikes in the immediate vicinity, but its proximity to Gavarnie and Bagnées and its accessibility via the SNCF **bus** from Lourdes (6 per day, 39F) and Cauterets (6 per day, 39F) make it an excellent launching pad into the Pyrénées. The **tourist office**, pl. du 8 Mai 45, will provide you with a rough map and a list of hotels and send you to the **Maison de la Vallée** for everything else. (Tel. 05 62 92 30 30; fax 05 62 92 87 19. Open M-Sa 9am-noon and 2-6:30pm.) In winter, the **Bureau des Guides, l'Ecole de Ski Français,** on pl. Clemenceau (tel. 05 62 92 55 06), provides ski guides and assistance. Many nearby skiing towns are accessible by SNCF buses from Cauterets or Lourdes.

LANGUEDOC-ROUSSILLON

Languedoc and Roussillon, rugged lands whose peoples' origins are as much Spanish as French, have never been comfortable with Parisian authority. Once, an immense region called Occitania (today Languedoc) stretched from the Rhine to the foothills of the Pyrénées. Its people spoke the *langue d'oc*, not the *langue d'oïl* spoken in northern France (which evolved into modern French). The region was eventually integrated into the French kingdom, and the Cathar religion, popular among Occitanians, was severely persecuted by the Crown and Church. The *langue d'oc* faded, and in 1539, the *langue d'oïl* became official. Latent nationalism lingers on, however: many speak Catalán, a relative of the *langue d'oc*, and look to Barcelona, rather than Paris, for guidance.

TOULOUSE

Just when all of France starts to look alike, Toulouse's (pop. 350,000) eclectic architecture and squares provide a breath of fresh air. Gardens and gurgling fountains abound, from the old-school grandeur of pl. du Capitole to the café chit-chat of the student quarter. Once a center for the bloody persecution of Protestants by the French kings—culminating in the St. Bartholomew's Day Massacre of 1572—today Toulouse is the prosperous capital of the French aerospace industry, and its economic prosperity is reflected in its clean streets and shining edifices.

⚑ ▚▞ PRACTICAL INFO, ACCOMMODATIONS, AND FOOD. Trains (tel. 08 36 35 36 15) head to Bordeaux (2¼hr., 8 per day, 160F); Marseille (4½hr., 11 per day, 234F); Lyon (6hr., 6 per day, 295F); and Paris (7hr., 9 per day, 425F). To reach the **tourist office,** at Donjon du Capitôle, on rue Lafayette, in sq. Charles de Gaulle, from the station, turn left along the canal, turn right on the broad allée Jean Jaurès, bear right around pl. Wilson, turn right on rue Lafayette; it's in a park near rue d'Alsace-Lorraine. (Tel. 05 61 11 02 22; fax 05 61 22 03 63; www.mairie-toulouse.fr. Open May-Sept. M-Sa 9am-7pm, Su 10am-1pm and 2-6:30pm; Oct.-Apr. M-F 9am-6pm, Sa 9am-12:30pm and 2-6pm, Su 10am-12:30pm and 2-5pm.) **Cybercopie** has two locations, 18 rue des Lois and 5 pl. de Deyrou, both just off pl. Capitole, which offer **internet** access. (25F per 30min., 45F per hr. Open June-Sept. M-F 9am-noon and 2-7pm; Oct.-May M-Th 8:30am-7pm, Sa 10am-noon and 2-7pm.)

To reach the spacious and well-located **Hôtel des Arts,** 1 bis rue Cantegril, at rue des Arts near pl. St-Georges, take the Métro (dir: Basso Cambo) to "Pl. Esquirol"; follow rue du Metz away from the river and turn left after three blocks. (Tel. 05 61 23 36 21; fax 05 61 12 22 37. Singles 80-140F; doubles 125-160F; triples and quads 150-180F. Breakfast 25F. Shower 15F. Reserve ahead. V, MC.) **Hôtel du Grand Balcon,** 8 rue Romiguières, in pl. du Capitole, has a prime location, and some rooms have balconies. (Tel. 05 61 21 48 08. Singles 110-150F; doubles 130-190F; triples and quads 150-210F. Breakfast 25F. Shower 10F. Closed first 3 weeks of Aug.) **Camp** at **Pont de Rupé,** 21 chemin du Pont de Rupé, at av. des Etats-Unis. Take bus 59 (dir: Camping) to "Rupé" or drive north on N20. (Tel. 05 61 70 07 35; fax 05 61 70 00 71. 50F; 2 people 60F; 16F per additional person. Restaurant. Laundry.) **Markets** line **pl. des Carmes, pl. Victor Hugo,** and **bd. de Strasbourg** (open Tu-Su 6am-1pm); inexpensive eateries line **rue du Taur** and **pl. Wilson. Le Bar à Pâtes,** 8-10 rue Tripière, off rue St-Rome, has delicious pasta for 39F. (Open M-Sa noon-2pm and 7:15-11:30pm, Su 7:15-11:30pm. Bar in basement. V, MC.) **Postal code:** 31000.

◉ ♫ SIGHTS AND ENTERTAINMENT. Just up rue du Taur from pl. du Capitole is the **Eglise Notre-Dame-du-Taur,** so named because it marks the spot where the priest Saturninus died in AD 250 after being tied to the tail of a wild bull by disgrun-

FRANCE

tled pagans. (Open daily July-Sept. 9am-6:30pm; Oct.-June 8am-noon and 2-6pm.) Continuing north on rue du Taur leads to the **Basilique St-Sernin**, the longest Romanesque structure in the world; its **crypt** houses ecclesiastical relics gathered from Charlemagne's time. (Open July-Sept. M-Sa 9am-6:30pm, Su 9am-7:30pm; Oct.-June M-Sa 8:30-11:45am and 2-5:45pm, Su 9am-12:30pm and 2-7:30pm. Tours July-Aug. 2 per day; 35F. Crypt 10F.) Backtrack to the pl. du Capitole, take a right on rue Romiguières, and turn left on rue Lakanal to get to the 13th-century **Les Jacobins**, an excellent example of the southern Gothic style. A modest crypt inside its **cloister** contains the ashes of St. Thomas Aquinas. (Open daily June-Sept. 10am-6:30pm; Oct.-May 10am-noon and 2-6pm. Cloister 10F.) Continue down rue Lakanal, turn right on rue Gambetta, and continue straight to rue de Metz. The newly restored **Hôtel d'Assézat**, at pl. d'Assézat on rue de Metz, houses the **Fondation Bemberg**, with an impressive collection of Bonnards, Dufys, Pisarros, and Gauguins. (Open Tu and Th-Su 10am-6pm, W 10am-9pm. 25F, students 18F.) Follow rue de Metz away from the river past pl. Esquirol to the **Musée des Augustins**, 21 rue de Metz, for an unsurpassed collection of Romanesque and Gothic sculptures. (Open Th-M 10am-6pm, W 10am-9pm. 12F, students free.) **La Cité de l'Espace** is a new park devoted to Toulouse's space programs. Take bus 19 to pl. de l'Indépendance and follow the signs. (Open Tu-Sa mid-June to mid-Sept. 9:30am-7pm; mid-Sept. to mid-June 9:30am-6pm. 50F. Planetarium 10F.)

Toulouse has something to please almost any nocturnal whim, although nightlife is liveliest when students are in town. Numerous cafés flank **pl. St-Georges** and **pl. du Capitole,** and late-night bars line **rue St-Rome** and **rue des Filatiers.** La Ciguä, 6 rue de Colombette, just off bd. Lazare Carnot, is a friendly gay bar and a great place to ask about discos. (Open Tu-F and Su 9pm-2am, Sa 9pm-4am.)

CARCASSONNE

Carcassonne (pop. 45,000) has had a rough go of it. Attacked at various times by Romans, Visigoths, and Moors, Europe's largest fortress has come to exemplify stalwart opposition in the face of the enemy. The backdrop for the movie *Robin Hood: Prince of Thieves* (1991), the *cité* is still bombarded by day, but only by tourists. Constructed as a palace in the 12th century, the **Château Comtal** was transformed into a citadel following submission to royal control in 1226. (Open daily July-Aug. 9am-7:30pm; June and Sept. 9am-7pm; Oct.-May 9:30am-12:30pm and 2-6pm. 35F, under 26 23F.) The **Musée de l'Inquisition**, 5 rue du Grand Puits, displays the objects of gentle persuasion used by the Catholics to show Cathar heretics the light. (Open daily July-Aug. 9am-11pm; Sept.-June 10am-7pm. Explanations in English. 40F, students 30F.) At the other end of the *cité*, the beautiful **Basilique St-Nazaire**, in pl. de l'Eglise, is the coolest place in the city on a sultry summer afternoon. (Open July-Aug. 9am-7pm; Sept.-June 9:30am-noon and 2-5:30pm.) Although nightlife is limited, several bars and cafés along **rue Omer Sarraut** and **pl. Verdun** offer some excitement. Locals dance until dawn at **La Bulle,** 115 rue Barbacane.

Trains arrive from Toulouse (50min., 24 per day, 53F); Nîmes (2½hr., 12 per day, 135F); Marseille (3hr., every 2hr., 195F); and Nice (6hr., 5 per day, 288F). Shops, hotels, and the train station are located in the *basse ville;* walk a steep 30min. uphill or catch the *navette* in front of the station (every 40min.) to reach the *cité* or the campsite. Or take bus 4 to pl. Gambetta and switch to bus 2 or 8 (every 30min. until 7pm, 5.40F). To reach the **tourist office,** 15 bd. Camille Pelletan, pl. Gambetta, from the train station, walk over the canal on rue Clemenceau, turn left on rue de la Liberté, then turn right on bd. Jean Jaurès. (Tel. 04 68 10 24 30; fax 04 68 10 24 38. Open July-Aug. 9am-7pm; Sept.-June 9am-12:15pm and 1:45-6:30pm.) The **auberge de jeunesse (HI),** on rue de Vicomte Trencavel, is in the middle of the *cité*. (Tel. 04 68 25 23 16; fax 04 68 71 14 84. 74F; members only. Breakfast included. Sheets 17F. Laundry 40F. Reception 24hr. V, MC.) The **Hôtel Astoria**, at the corner of rues Montpellier and Tourtel, has pleasant rooms. From the station, turn left after crossing the bridge and turn right on rue Montpellier. (Tel. 04 68 25 31 38; fax 04 68 71 34 14. Singles and doubles 100-200F. Breakfast 20F with *Let's Go*. Shower 10F. Reception 7:30am-9pm. V, MC, AmEx.) **Le Cathare,** 53 rue Jean Bringer, has cozy, bright rooms.

FRANCE

(Tel. 04 68 25 65 92. Singles and doubles 117-170F; triples 185F. Breakfast 27F. English spoken. V, MC.) **Camping de la Cité**, on rte. de St-Hilaire, across the Aude 2km from town, has a pool and grocery store. (Tel. 04 68 25 11 77. 83F for tent and 1 person; 53F per additional person. Open Apr.-Sept.) The regional food speciality is *cassoulet* (a stew of white beans, herbs, and meat). On **rue du Plo**, 55-60F *menus* abound, but save room for dessert at one of the many outdoor *crêperies* in **pl. Marcou. Postal code:** 11000 (11012 for *Poste Restante*).

PERPIGNAN

Comfortably cradled between the Mediterranean and the Pyrénées, Perpignan (pop. 108,000) has bounced between French and Spanish ownership as the former capital of the counts of Roussillon and the kings of Mallorca. While the unexpected palm trees, immense Citadel, and quiet cafés of the *quai* give Perpignan a Mediterranean allure, its best advantage is its proximity to Collioure and Céret. A short walk from the action, the **citadelle** is both formidable and *formidable*, with beautifully intact walls rising up from the residential area below. Within the citadel lies the 13th-century **Palais des Rois de Majorque,** the city's most impressive sight, with an immense arcaded courtyard and two curiously superimposed chapels. The courtyard now serves as a concert hall, and theater. (Palace tel. 04 68 34 48 29. Enter from av. Gilbert Brutus. Open daily June-Sept. 10am-6pm; Oct.-May 9am-5pm. 20F, students 10F.) The **Musée Hyacinthe Rigaud,** 16 rue de l'Ange, contains 13th-century Spanish and Catalán paintings; canvases by Rigaud, court artist to Louis XIV; and works by Ingres, Picasso, Miró, and Dalí. Check out the **Collection de Maître Rey** on the top floor, with walls packed with a tiny but diverse set of paintings created for local writer Rey by his artist friends. (Tel. 04 68 35 43 40. Open W-M noon-7pm. 25F, students 10F.)

   Trains trundle from Carcassonne (2hr., 10 per day, 140F); Toulouse (3hr., 15 per day, 140F; some change at Narbonne); Nice (6hr., 3 per day, 289F); and Paris (6-10hr., 4 per day, 418-484F). To get from the station to the **tourist office,** 7 quai de Lattre de Tassigny, walk straight up av. Général de Gaulle, turn right at pl. Catalogne onto cours Lazare Escarguel, cross the canal, turn left on quai de Barcelone, which becomes quai de Lattre de Tassigny, and look right (15min.). (Tel. 04 68 34 29 94. Open July-Aug. M-F 9am-12:30pm and 2-7pm, Sa 9am-noon and 2-6pm; Sept.-June M-F 9am-noon and 2-6:30pm, Sa 9am-noon and 2-6pm.) The **Auberge de Jeunesse La Pépinière (HI),** on rue Marc-Pierre, is on the edge of town, between the highway and police station. From the train station, turn left on rue Valette, right on av. de Grande Bretagne, left on rue Claude Marty (rue de la Rivière on some maps), and right on rue Marc Pierre (10min.). It offers squat toilets and hot showers. (Tel. 04 68 34 63 32; fax 04 68 51 16 02. 70F; members only. Breakfast included. Sheets 18F. Lockout 11am-4pm. Check-out 11am. Open Jan. 21-Dec. 19.) The **Hôtel de l'Avenir,** 11 rue de l'Avenir, 5min. straight ahead from the station, has balconies and a rooftop terrace. (Tel. 04 68 34 20 30; fax 04 68 34 15 63. Singles 90F, with shower 125F; doubles 100-125F, with shower 160-220F; triples and quads 220-250F. Shower 15F. Breakfast 23F. Call ahead in summer, when prices rise. V, MC, AmEx.) The local specialties are *cargolade* (snails grilled and smothered in garlic sauce) and *touron* (nougat available in many flavors). **Casino supermarket,** on bd. Félix Mercader, stockpiles food. (Tel. 04 68 34 74 42. Open M-Sa 8:30am-8pm.)

🖪 **EXCURSIONS FROM PERPIGNAN: COLLIOURE AND CÉRET.** Where the Pyrénées finally tumble into the Mediterranean, tiny Collioure (pop. 2770) captured the fancy of Greeks and Phoenicians long before enrapturing Fauvists and Surrealists such as Dalí, Picasso, and Matisse. And it's easy to see why—its stony beaches, lighthouse, and enchanting harbor, flooded with aspiring artists and their easels, continue to cast a spell over the artistic eye. **St-Laurent** (tel. 04 68 81 43 88) offers daily **boat** excursions. **Trains** (tel. 04 68 82 05 89) roll in from Perpignan (21F) as well as Barcelona (5 per day, 75F). The **tourist office,** on pl. du 18 Juin, has info on **day hikes** (1-7hr.) and coastal bus routes. (Tel. 04 68 82 15 47; www.little-france.com/collioure. Open July-Sept. daily 9am-8pm; Oct.-June M-Sa 9am-noon and 2-7pm.)

FRANCE

Hôtel Triton, 1 rue Jean Bart, sits on the waterfront 10min. from the *centre ville* and 20min. from the station. (Tel. 04 68 98 39 39; fax 04 68 82 11 32. Doubles 180-320F. Breakfast 35F. Reserve ahead. V, MC, AmEx.)

Céret (pop. 8000) prides itself on its cherry trees, celebrated in a yearly spring festival, yet it is another flowering that puts this proud Catalán village on the map. Around 1910, the warm wind in the trees, the ochre sunlight, and the narrow streets of the town inspired Picasso, Chagall, Manolo, and Herbin, creating a "Cubist Mecca." The works they left to the town are housed in the seemingly graffiti-bedecked **Musée d'Art Moderne,** 8 bd. Maréchal Joffre—look carefully and you'll see the building's name spray-painted on the side. (Tel. 04 68 87 27 76. Open July-Sept. daily 10am-7pm; May-June and Oct. daily 10am-6pm; Nov.-Apr. W-M 10am-6pm. 35F, students 20F.) Car Inter 66 (tel. 04 68 35 29 02) runs **buses** from Perpignan (35min., 1 per hr., 34F). From the bus stop on av. George Clemenceau, the **tourist office,** 1 av. Clemenceau, is two blocks up the hill on the right. If you're let off outside town at "Céret-pont," follow the signs to the *centre ville,* turn left at the end of rue St-Ferréol on bd. Maréchal Joffre, then left again on av. Clemenceau. The office offers a tour of the spots that inspired Picasso. (Tel. 04 68 87 00 53. Open July-Aug. M-Sa 9am-12:30pm and 2-7pm, Su 10am-12:30pm; Sept.-Oct. M-F 10am-noon and 2-5pm, Sa 10am-noon. Tours Nov.-June F around 3pm. 15F.)

SOUTHEAST FRANCE

Heavy with the fragrance of lavender and wild herbs, the air in the southeast of France brings a piercing vitality to the landscape, a sense of eternal youth that today draws aging movie stars just as once it drew artists like van Gogh and Cézanne. A panacea for the weary traveler, southeastern France has it all, from some of the best skiing and hiking in the world to the most glamorous beach resorts, from unspoiled villages and natural parks to astoundingly well-preserved reminders of earlier ages.

PROVENCE

At the southern end of the Rhône River, where it cascades into the Mediterranean, the Rhône Valley towns of Provence are among France's best destinations. From the Roman arena and cobblestoned grace of Arles to the formidable Palais des Papes of Avignon to the lingering footsteps of Cézanne in Aix-en-Provence, life unfolds along Provence's shaded promenades like an endless game of *pétanque* or a bottomless glass of *pastis.*

AVIGNON

The city of Avignon (pop. 100,000) has danced with cultural and artistic brilliance ever since it snatched the papacy away from Rome for almost 70 years some 700 years ago. Film festivals, street musicians, and Europe's most prestigious theatrical gathering keep this university town shining. The 14th-century **Palais des Papes** is the most stunning fortified Gothic palace extant. Each year, May through September, it hosts an art exhibition. (Open daily May-June and Oct. 9am-7pm; July 9am-9pm; Aug.-Sept. 9am-8pm; Nov.-Mar. 9:30am-5:45pm. Palace or exhibition 45F; combined ticket 55F. English audio tour included.) During the **Festival d'Avignon** (also known as the **IN;** early July-early Aug.), Gregorian chanters rub shoulders with all-night *Odyssey*-readers and African dancers. (Tickets free-200F per event. Reservations accepted from mid-June; tickets are also on sale at each venue 45min. before shows. Call 04 90 14 14 26 for tickets or info.)

From the train station, walk through porte de la République onto cours Jean Jaurès to reach the **tourist office** at #41. (Tel. 04 90 82 65 11; www.avignon-tourisme. com. Open Apr.-Sept. M-F 9am-1pm and 2-6pm, Sa-Su 9am-1pm and 2-5pm; Oct.-Mar. closed Su; during festival M-F 10am-7pm and Sa-Su 10am-5pm.) Access the

FRANCE

Don't let anyone tell you where to go.

EUROPE ON TRACK
is your one stop station for:

- Eurailpass
- BritRail Pass
- Europass
- Eurailpass/Drive
- BritRail/Drive
- Europass/Drive

RAIL PASSES
for most European countries:

Austria / Belgium / Finland / France
Germany / Hungary Italy
Luxembourg / Netherlands
Norway / Spain / Sweden
Switzerland

Visit Eurails award winning website
www.europeontrack.com

Call for more information about
Europe on Track SPECIALS

- Receive a Free Eurail Guide Book
- Free Reservations (trains w/supplements not included)
- Free Pass Protection
- Free Shipping
- Free Eurail Map and Travelers Guide
- Draws for Free Eurailpass

Specials are offered at designated times of the year, call for details.

Go where you want with...

EUROPE ON TRACK

Fax 519.645.0682 • Toll Free 1.888.667.9734 • email: europrail@eurail.on.ca
Visit us on the web: www.europeontrack.com

Bring this page and get **50% OFF** 3ʳᵈ NIGHT when booking 2 activities at Balmer's!

BALMER'S *herberge*

INTERLAKEN ✠ SWITZERLAND

BALMER'S HERBERGE • GUESTHOUSE • TENT • *Hauptstrasse 23–25 • CH-3800 Interlaken/Switzerland*

Phone ++41 (0)33 822 19 61 • Fax ++41 (0)33 823 32 61 • E-mail: balmers@tcnet.ch • http://www.balmers.com

STOP *here for excitement—*
FOR GREAT TIMES AND THE BEST DEALS!

RIVER RAFTING • CANYONING • FUN YAK • BUNGY JUMPING • PARAGLIDING
SKY DIVING • ROCK CLIMBING • FLYING FOX • GLACIER FLIGHTS • SCENIC FLIGHTS

Tel. ++41 (0)33 826 77 11 • Fax ++41 (0)33 826 77 15
Internet: http://www.adventureworld.ch • e-mail: info@adventureworld.ch

internet at **Cyberdrome,** 68 rue Guillaume Puy. (50F per hr. Open M-Sa 7am-1am, Su 2pm-1am.) The **Foyer YMCA/UCJG,** 7bis chemin de la Justice, is across the river in Villeneuve. From the station, turn left and follow the city wall, cross the second bridge (pont Daladier), and turn left on chemin de la Justice (30min.). Or take bus 10 (dir: Les Angles-Grand Angles) to "Général Leclerc" or bus 11 (dir: Villeneuve-Grand Terme; 6.50F) to "Pont d'Avignon." (Tel. 04 90 25 46 20; fax 04 90 25 30 64; email ymca@avignon.packwan.net. 56-150F. Breakfast 25F. Reception 8:30am-8pm.) To get to **Foyer Bagatelle,** on Ile de la Barthelasse, follow the directions above, cross pont Daladier, and it's on the right (15min.); or take bus 10 or 11 (same directions as above) to "La Barthelasse." (Tel. 04 90 86 30 39; fax 04 90 85 78 45. 62F. Breakfast 20F. **Camping** 18-24F per person, 10-13F per tent. V, MC.) **Codec supermarkets** are on rue de la République. (Open M-Sa 8:30am-8pm.) **Postal code:** 84000.

NÎMES

Established as a Roman colony, Nîmes (pop. 132,000) is the home of a durable textile once imported by Lévi-Strauss for Californian gold-diggers; its name is a truncated version for the French phrase "de Nîmes" (from Nîmes): denim. The magnificent **Les Arènes** (Roman amphitheater) was built in the first century AD for gory animal and gladiatorial combats; it's open for visits, but the best way to experience it is to attend a bullfight or concert held there. (Open daily in summer 9am-6:30pm; off-season 9am-noon and 2-5pm. 28F, students 20F.) The exquisitely sculpted **Maison Carré** (Square House) is actually a rectangular temple, built in the first century BC. (Open daily in summer 9am-noon and 2:30-7pm; off-season 9am-12:30pm and 2-6pm. Free.) Across the square, Norman Foster's ultra-modern **Carré d'Art** houses the eclectic collection of the **Musée d'Art Contemporain.** (Open Tu-Su 10am-6pm. 28F, students 20F.) If you're tired or hot, head down pl. Foch to the left along the canals from the Maison to relax by the beautiful fountains of the **Jardins de la Fontaine,** which also house the Roman ruins of the **Temple de Diane** and the **Tour Magne.** (Garden and Temple de Diane open daily June 15-Sept. 15 7am-11pm; Apr.-June 14 and Sept. 16-Oct. 8am-9pm; Nov.-Mar. 8am-7pm. Free. Tour Magne open daily July-Aug. 9am-6:30pm; Sept.-June 9am-5pm. 15F, students 12F.)

Trains chug from bd. Talabot to Arles (30min., 10 per day, 41F); Marseille (1¼hr., 10 per day, 95F); and Toulouse (3hr., 12 per day, 181F). **Buses** (tel. 04 66 29 52 00) depart from behind the train station for Avignon (1¼hr., 2-8 per day, 42F). To get from the stations to the **tourist office,** 6 rue Auguste, follow av. Feuchères, veer left around the park, and clockwise around the arena, then head straight on bd. Victor Hugo, and it's just off pl. Comédie. (Tel. 04 66 67 29 11; fax 04 66 21 81 04. Open July-Aug. M-F 8am-8pm, Sa-Su 9am-7pm; Sept.-June M-F 8am-7pm, Sa 9am-7pm, Su 10am-6pm.) Access the **internet** at **Cybersnack Le Vauban,** 34 rue Clérisseau. (30F per 30min. Open daily 10am-10pm.) The relaxed **auberge de jeunesse (HI),** on chemin de l'Auberge de la Jeunesse, off chemin de la Cigale, 3.5km from the station, is scheduled to reopen in March 2000; call ahead. Take bus 2 (dir: Alès or Villeverte) to "Stade, Route d'Alès" and follow the signs uphill (after buses stop running, call for pickup). (Tel. 04 66 23 25 04; fax 04 66 23 84 27. 48F; members only. Breakfast 19F. Sheets 17F. **Camping** 28F. Reception 24hr. V, MC.) **Hôtel de France,** 4 bd. des Arènes, faces the arena. (Tel. 04 66 67 23 05; fax 04 66 67 76 93. Singles 110F; doubles 150F; triples and quads 180F. Breakfast 25F. Reserve ahead. V, MC.) Stock up at **Marché U supermarket,** 19 rue d'Alès, downhill from the hostel. (Open M-Sa 8am-12:45pm and 3:30-8pm.) **Postal code:** 30000 (30006 for *Poste Restante*).

ARLES

Roman grandeur haunts the sun-baked remnants of Arles' (pop. 35,000) **arènes,** the largest surviving amphitheater in France (15F, students 9F), and the **Théâtre Antique,** an evocatively ruined theater strewn with carved stone (15F, students 9F); both are still in use, the former for bullfights, the latter for plays. The city's Roman past is brought back to life in the brand-new **Musée d'Arles Antique,** on Av. de la 1ère DFL. (Tel. 04 90 18 88 88. Open W-M Apr.-Sept. 9am-7pm; Oct.-Mar. 10am-6pm. 35F, students 25F, children 5F.) A medieval gem is the calming courtyard of the **Cloitre**

FRANCE

St-Trophime (cloister; 20F, students 14F). The passion of Arles' *corridas* (bullfights) lured Picasso here, while van Gogh spent two years (and an ear) in Arles; both have left enduring impressions (and post-impressions) on the city. *Arles et Vincent* (5F at the tourist office) explains the markers around the city at the spots where van Gogh's easel once stood. The **Fondation Van Gogh,** 26 Rond-Point des Arènes, houses tributes to the master by artists, poets, and composers. (Open daily in summer 10am-7pm; off-season reduced hours. 30F, students 20F.) The last weekend in June and the first in July, the city celebrates the **Fête d'Arles** in local costume.

Trains roll to Avignon (30min., M-Sa 13 per day, 35F); Nîmes (30min., M-Sa 6 per day, 41F); Marseille (1hr., M-Sa 8 per day, 71F); and Aix-en-Provence (1¾hr., 93F). Next to the station, **buses** (tel. 04 90 49 38 01) depart for the 30km of beaches at **Les Stes-Maries-de-la-Mer** (1hr., 7 per day, 36.50F). To get to the **tourist office,** on esplanade Charles de Gaulle at bd. des Lices, turn left from the station, walk to pl. Lamartine, turn left and follow bd. Emile Courbes (10min.), then cross and turn right on bd. des Lices. (Tel. 04 90 18 41 20; fax 04 90 18 41 29. Open Apr.-Sept. daily 9am-7pm; Oct.-Mar. M-Sa 9am-6pm, Su 10am-noon.) To get from the tourist office to the **auberge de jeunesse (HI),** on av. Maréchal Foch, cross bd. des Lices, walk down av. des Alyscamps, and follow the signs (20min.). (Tel. 04 90 96 18 25; fax 04 90 96 31 26. First night 80F, each additional night 65F. Breakfast included. Reception 7-10am and 5pm-midnight. Lockout 10am-5pm. Curfew 11:30pm, during festival 1-2am. Call ahead Apr.-June.) Or, try the sweet-smelling **Hôtel Gauguin,** 5 pl. Voltaire (tel. 04 90 96 14 35; fax 04 90 18 98 87; singles and doubles 160-220F; triples 260F), and friendly **Hôtel le Rhône,** 11 pl. Voltaire (tel. 04 90 96 43 70; fax 04 90 93 87 03; singles and doubles 130-200F). Take bus (dir: Pont de Crau) from bd. des Lices to "Graveaux" to reach **Camping-City,** 67 rte. de Crau. (Tel. 04 90 93 08 86. 23F per person and per site, 16F per car. Open Apr.-Sept.) **Monoprix supermarket** is on pl. Lamartine, near the station. (Open M-Sa 8:30am-7:30pm, F 8:30am-8pm.) Try cafés in **pl. du Forum** or **pl. Voltaire,** which has music on summer Wednesdays. **Postal code:** 13200.

▐ EXCURSION FROM ARLES: THE CAMARGUE. Between Arles and the Mediterranean coast stretches the Camargue. Pink flamingoes, black bulls, and the famous white Camargue horses roam freely across this flat expanse of protected wild marshland. Aspiring botanists and zoologists should stop at the **Centre d'Information de Ginès** along D570, which distributes info on the region's unusual flora and fauna. (Tel. 04 90 97 86 32. Open Apr.-Sept. daily 9am-6pm; Oct.-Mar. Sa-Th 9:30am-5pm.) Next door, the **Parc Ornithologique de Pont de Gau** provides paths through the marshland and offers views of birds and grazing bulls. (Tel. 04 90 97 82 62. Open daily Apr.-Sept. 9am-dusk; Oct.-Mar. 10am-dusk. 35F.) The best way to see the Camargue is on **horseback;** call the **Association Camarguaise de Tourisme Equestre** for more info. (Tel. 04 90 97 84 72. 80F per hr., 200-230F per 3hr., 350F per day.) **Jeep safaris** (tel. 04 66 70 09 65; 200F per 2hr., 230F per 4hr.) and **boat trips** (tel. 04 90 97 84 72; 1½hr., 60F) are also great ways to see the area, and while many trails are only for horseback riders, **bicycle touring** is also an option. **Trail maps** indicating length, level of difficulty, and dangerous spots are available from the Les Stes-Maries-de-la-Mer **tourist office,** 5 av. Van Gogh (tel. 04 90 97 82 55). From Arles, take a **bus** (dir: Stes-Maries-de-la-Mer) to "Pont du Gau" (1hr., 7 per day, 36.50F).

AIX-EN-PROVENCE

Famous for its festivals and fountains, Aix (EX; pop. 150,000) marks the spot as the cultural core of Provence. Once home to artists Cézanne and Vasarely as well as the novelist Emile Zola, today an international student population lends a frenzied intellectual energy to the city. The leaflet *In the Footsteps of Cézanne,* from the tourist office, leads you along the **Chemin de Cézanne,** which transforms the city into an open-air museum of the artist's life and haunts, including his studio at 9 av. Paul Cézanne. (Open daily Apr.-Sept. 10am-noon and 2:30-6pm; Oct.-Mar. 10am-noon and 2-5pm. 25F, students 10F.) The **Fondation Vasarely,** on av. Marcel-Pagnol, in quartier du Jas de Bouffan, designed in the 1970s by Hungarian-born artist Victor Vasarely, is a must-see for modern art fans. (Open in summer M-F 10am-1pm and 2-

FRANCE

7pm, Sa-Su 10am-7pm; off-season 9:30am-1pm and 2-6pm. 35F, students 20F.) **Cathédrale St-Sauveur,** on rue Gaston de Saporta, is a dramatic melange of additions and carvings. (Open W-M 8am-noon and 2-6pm.) Aix's **International Music Festival,** June through July, features operas and concerts. (Tel. 04 42 17 34 34. Tickets 100-350F.) Aix also hosts a two-week **Jazz Festival** (end of June to early July; tickets 80-150F) and a two-week **Dance Festival** (end of July to early Aug.; tickets 90-150F, students 60-120F). The **Comité Officiel des Fêtes** (tel. 04 42 63 06 75), on cours Gambetta at bd. du Roi René, has festival info. When the sun sets, Aix's students party. Bars line the **Forum des Cardeurs,** behind the Hôtel de Ville. **Le Scat,** 11 rue Verrerie, is a club with live music. (Open M-Sa 11pm to whenever.) **Bistro Aixois,** 37 cours Sextius, off La Rotonde, packs in students. (Open daily 6:30pm until 3 or 4am.)

Trains run almost exclusively to Marseille (35min., every hr. until 9:53pm, 37F). **Buses** run to Marseille (30min., 2 per hr., 26F) and Avignon (2hr., 4 per day, 80F). From the train station, follow av. Victor Hugo (bear left at the fork) to the pl. du Général de Gaulle (La Rotonde) to reach the municipal bus station and the **tourist office,** 2 pl. du Général de Gaulle, which books rooms for free and has city maps and guides. (Tel. 04 42 16 11 61; fax 04 42 16 11 62. Open daily July-Aug. 8:30am-10pm; May-June and Sept. 8:30am-9pm; Oct.-Apr. 8:30am-7pm.) You can surf the **internet** at **Hublot Cyber Café,** 17 rue Paul Bert. (Tel. 04 42 21 37 31; email hublet@wanadoo.fr. 30F per 30min., 50F per hr.) To get to the **auberge de jeunesse (HI),** 3 av. Marcel Pagnol, in quartier du Jas de Bouffan, follow av. de Belges from La Rotonde, turn right on av. de l'Europe, bear left at the first rotary after the overpass, climb the hill, and it's on the left (35min.). Or take bus 4 (bus A on weekends; every 15-30min. until 8pm; 7F) from La Rotonde to "Vasarely." (Tel. 04 42 20 15 99; fax 04 42 59 36 12. 69F. Breakfast included. Sheets 11F. Laundry 35F. Reception before noon or after 5pm. Lockout 9am-4pm. Curfew midnight.) **Hôtel des Arts,** 69 bd. Carnot, has compact rooms with phones. (Tel. 04 42 38 11 70. Singles and doubles 180-205F. V, MC.) To **camp** at **Arc-en-Ciel,** on pont des Trois Sautets, on rte. de Nice, 2km from the town center, take bus 3 from La Rotonde to "Trois Sautets." (Tel. 04 42 26 14 28. 34F per person, 35F per tent.) Eating around **pl. des Cardeurs** or **pl. Ramus** will be kinder to your wallet than **cours Mirabeau** to the south. Stock up at a **Casino supermarket,** 3 cours d'Orbitelle. (Open M-Sa 8am-1pm and 4-8pm.) **Postal code:** 13100.

FRENCH RIVIERA (CÔTE D'AZUR)

Paradises are made to be lost. Between Marseille and the Italian border, the sun-drenched beaches and warm waters of the Mediterranean form the backdrop for this fabled playground of the rich and famous—F. Scott Fitzgerald, Cole Porter, Picasso, Renoir, and Matisse are among those who flocked to the coast in its heyday. The area today is crammed with as many low-budget tourists as high-handed millionaires, but the Riviera's seductive loveliness has been its undoing, as shrewd developers have turned the coast's beauty into big business. Many French condemn the Riviera as a mere shadow of its former self.

 Every woman who has traveled on the Riviera has a story to tell about men in the big beach towns. Unsolicited pick-up techniques range from subtle invitations to more, uh, bare displays of interest. Brush them off with a biting *"laissez-moi tranquille!"* ("leave me alone") or stony indifference, but don't be shy about enlisting the help of passersby or the police to fend off Mediterranean Don Juans.

MARSEILLE

France's third-largest city, Marseille (pop. 900,000) is like the *bouillabaisse* soup for which it is famous: steaming hot and pungently spiced, with a little bit of everything mixed in. A mix of wild nightclubs, beaches, islands, gardens, and big-city adventure, Marseille bites its thumb at the manicured nails of Monaco and struts a gritty urban intensity as well as a rare and astounding cultural melange.

FRANCE

■ ■ ■ **PRACTICAL INFO, ACCOMMODATIONS, AND FOOD. Trains** run to Nice (2¾hr., every hr., 148F); Lyon (3½hr., 16 per day, 205F); and Paris (4¾hr., 12 per day, 406F). **Buses** serve Avignon (2hr., 5 per day, 89F, 134F round-trip); Cannes (2¼-3hr., 4 per day, 122F); and Nice (2¾hr., 4 per day, 136F). SNCM, 61 bd. des Dames (tel. 08 36 67 95 00), runs **ferries** to Corsica (see p. 349) and Sardinia. From the train station, descend the stairs and follow bd. d'Athenes, which becomes bd. Dugommier, and turn right on La Canebière to reach the **tourist office**, 4 La Canebière. (Tel. 04 91 13 89 00; fax 04 91 13 89 20. Open July-Aug. daily 9am-8pm; Oct.-June M-Sa 9am-7pm, Su 10am-5pm.) The tourist office **annex** is at the train station. (Tel. 04 91 50 59 18. Open daily July-Aug. 10am-6pm; Sept.-June M-F 10am-1pm and 1:30-6pm.) Check **email** at Le Rozo, 28 cours Julien. (40F per hr. Open M-Sa 10am-7pm.) To reach the **Auberge de Jeunesse de Bois-Luzy (HI),** on allée des Primevères, take bus 6 from cours J. Thierry at the top of La Canebière (or take night bus T) to "Marius Richard" and follow the signs. (Tel./fax 04 91 49 06 18. 45F, 65F including breakfast; **camping** 26F. Laundry. Reception 7:30-10am and 5-10:30pm. Lockout 10:30am-5pm. Curfew 10:30-11pm.) ■**Hôtel du Palais,** 26 rue Breteuil, has large rooms. From the *vieux port,* head down quai des Belges, which turns into cours J. Ballard and then rue Breteuil. (Tel. 04 91 37 78 86. Singles and doubles 185F; triples 280F. Breakfast 20F. V, MC.) **Hôtel Le Provençal** is at 32 rue Paradis. (Tel. 04 91 33 11 15. Singles 120F; doubles 170F; triples 200F. V, MC.) For the city's famed seafood and North African fare, poke around the *vieux port,* especially **pl. Thiars** and **Honoré d'Estienne d'Orvies.** For a more artsy crowd and cheaper fare, head up to **cours Julien,** northeast of the harbor; ■**Ce Soleil Donne,** 70 cours Julien, has exotic dishes like kangaroo and bananas for 59F. You can pick up **groceries** at BAZE, on La Canebière. (Open M-Sa 8:30am-8pm.) Nightlife centers around cours Julien and pl. Thiars. **Trolleybus,** 24 quai de Rive Neuve, is a mega-club. (Cover Sa 60F. Open Th-Sa 11pm-7am.) **Postal code:** 13001.

■ ■ **SIGHTS AND ENTERTAINMENT.** To truly experience Marseille, wander through its neighborhoods of mind-boggling cultural diversity. **La Canebière** separates the city into east and west, funneling into the *vieux port* to the south. West of the *vieux port* and north of bd. République, working-class residents of varied ethnicities pile onto the hilltop neighborhood of **Le Panier,** where the original Greek city stood. North of Le Panier, the dilapidated buildings of the **Belsunce Quarter** (between cours Belsunce and bd. Athens) house the city's Arab and African communities. East of La Canebière and near the *vieux port,* **rues de Rome, St-Ferreol,** and **Paradis** and nearby squares contain large shops and upscale restaurants. Past rue de Rome near La Canebière, narrow streets teem with peerless intensity in the colorful African markets. Farther northeast, **cours Julien** is a funky neighborhood whose book and music stores and eclectic restaurants converge to create a definitive counterculture feel. After exploring Marseille's neighborhoods, follow rue Breteuil from the *vieux port,* turn right on bd. Vauban, and turn right again on rue Fort du Sanctuaire to reach the majestic 19th-century **Basilique de Notre Dame de la Garde,** which perches on a hill above the city. (Open daily in summer 7am-8pm; off-season 7am-7pm. Free.) The imposing **Abbaye St-Victor,** on rue Sainte at the end of quai de Rive Neuve, evokes the ascetic beginnings of Christianity. (Open daily 8:30am-6:30pm. Crypts 10F.) **Musée Cantini,** 19 rue Grignan, exhibits Fauvist to present-day art. (Open Tu-Su June-Sept. 11am-6pm; Oct.-May 10am-5pm. 10F, students 5F.) Bus 83 (dir: Rond Pont du Prado) from the *vieux port* runs to Marseille's **beaches;** get off just after the statue of David (25min.).

ST-TROPEZ

Nowhere does the glitz and glamour of the Riviera seem more apparent than in the former fishing hamlet of St-Tropez. While other towns along the coast cling to past glories, *St-Trop d'Aise* (St. Too-Much-Luxury) religiously devotes itself to the holy trinity of sun, sand, and big boats. The "St-Tropez-Ramatuelle" Sodetrav **bus** line stops along the beach from the *gare routière* (M-Sa 3 per day, 9F, 10min.), stopping at the **plage Tahiti, plage des Salins,** and **plage de Pampelonne.** If public transit cramps your style, rent **wheels** from **Louis Mas,** 3-5 rue Quarenta. (Bikes 50-80F per day; deposit 1000-2000F. Mopeds 110F; deposit 2500-5000F. Open Easter to mid-Oct. M-Sa 9am-7pm, Su 9am-5pm.)

Sodetrav **buses** (tel. 04 94 97 88 51) head to St-Tropez from St-Raphaël (1½-2¼hr., 15 per day, 48F). The **boat** ride from St-Raphaël is faster and more scenic (50min., July-Aug. 5 per day, Sept.-June 2 per day, round-trip 100F; Fréjus hostel guests 80F); in July, you can also catch a ferry from Cannes (tel. 04 93 39 11 82; departs Tu, Th, and Sa 9:30am, returns 6:30pm; 100F). The **tourist office,** on quai Jean Jaurès, is on the waterfront. (Tel. 04 94 97 45 21; fax 04 94 97 82 66. Open daily 9:30am-1:30pm and 3:30-11pm.) Budget hotels do not exist in St-Tropez, and the closest youth hostel is in Fréjus. **Camping** is the cheapest option, but you'll need reservations; try **La Croix du Sud,** on rte. des Plages, in Ramatuelle (tel. 04 94 79 80 84; fax 04 94 79 89 21; 1-2 people 85F, 3 people 120F; open Easter-Sept.), or **Kon Tiki** (tel. 04 94 79 80 17; 2 people, car, and tent 113F), both behind Pampelonne beach. The **vieux port** and the streets behind the waterfront are the hub of culinary activity. To be charmingly rustic and do it yourself, duck into **Prisunic supermarket,** 7 av. du Général Leclerc. (Open in summer M-Sa 8am-8pm, Su 8:30am-1pm and 3-8pm; off-season M-Sa 8am-8pm.) In summer, **Le Pigeonnier,** 13 rue de la Ponche, and **La Plage,** 11 rue de la Ponche, move to the beat of perfect tans and money to burn (cover 100F).

ST-RAPHAËL AND FRÉJUS

Bearing neither the charm of the Riviera's smaller towns, nor the liveliness of its more cosmopolitan centers, the twin cities of St. Raphaël and Fréjus (5min. apart by train, yet impossible to traverse by foot) are of dubious appeal except as a great (read: cheap) base from which to visit **St-Tropez** (see above) as a daytrip. There's also evidence that the Romans dropped by while building their empire; an **amphitheater,** on rue Henri Vadon, in Fréjus, marks the spot. (Open daily Apr.-Sept. 9:30-11:45am and 2-6:15pm; Oct.-Mar. 9-11:45am and 2-4:15pm. Free.)

St-Raphaël sends **trains** every 30min. to Cannes (25min., 34F) and Nice (1hr., 56F). **Buses** leave from behind the train station in St-Raphaël for Fréjus (26min., every hr., 6.50F); Cannes (70min., 8 per day, 33F); and St-Tropez (1½hr., 15 per day, 49F). The **tourist office** in St-Raphaël is opposite the train station. (Tel. 04 94 19 52 52; fax 04 94 83 85 40. Open July-Aug. daily 8:30am-7pm; Sept.-June M-Sa 9am-12:30pm and 2-6:30pm.) The excellent **Auberge de Jeunesse de St-Raphaël-Fréjus (HI),** on chemin du Counillier, is 4km from the St-Raphaël train station. A direct shuttle bus runs from quai 7 of the *gare routière* to the hostel at 6pm (6.50F), with return shuttles at 8:30am, 6, and 7pm. (Tel. 04 94 53 18 75; fax 04 94 53 25 86. Dorms 66-82F; **camping** 32F. Breakfast included. Sheets 17F. Lockout 10am-6pm. Curfew 11pm. Ask about bike rental and boat discounts.) Exit right from the train station in St-Raphaël and take your third left to get to **Le Touring,** 1 quai Albert 1er. (Tel. 04 94 95 01 72; fax 04 94 95 86 09. Singles and doubles 150-260F; twin beds 290-350F. Open mid-Dec. to mid-Nov.) **Monoprix supermarket** is on bd. de Félix Martin, off av. Alphonse Karr near the St-Raphaël train station. (Open daily July-Aug. 8:30am-8:30pm; Sept.-June 8:30am-7:30pm.) **Postal codes:** St-Raphaël 83700; Fréjus 83600.

CANNES

All stereotypes of the French Riviera materialize in Cannes (pop. 78,000), a favorite stopover for the international jet-set. Less exclusive than St-Tropez, Cannes still allows even ungroomed budget travelers to tan like the stars. In May, the spotlights turn on and the red carpets roll out for the **Festival International du Film** which imports Hollywood's *crème de la crème.* None of the festival's 350 screenings is open to the public, but the sidewalk show is free. The best window-shopping along the Riviera lies along **rue d'Antibes** and **bd. de la Croisette.** Farther west, the **Castre Cathédrale** and its courtyard stand on the hill on which *vieux Cannes* was built. Of Cannes' three **casinos,** the most accessible is **Le Casino Croisette,** 1 jetée Albert Eduoard, next to the Palais des Festivals, with slots, blackjack, and roulette. (Gambling daily 5pm-4am; open for slots at 10am. No shorts. Ages 18 and up.) If your luck sours, you can lose your shirt in a different locale when the focus shifts to

Palm Beach at the eastern edge of Cannes, where **Mocambo** and **Whisky à Go Go** rev it up by night. Dance until dawn at **Jane's,** 38 rue des Serbes, in the Hôtel Gray d'Albion. (Cover and 1 drink Th 50F, F-Su 100F; F before midnight 50F; Su before 1am women free.) **Le Loft,** on rue du. Doc. Monod, sports no cover and a lively dance floor. At the Irish pub 🌑**Morrison's,** 10 rue Teisseire, enjoy a Guinness to live music after 10pm (W Irish trad, Th blues and rock).

Coastal **trains** run every 30min. west to St-Raphaël (25min., 34F) and Marseille (2hr., 129F; TGV connects through Marseille to Paris, 463F); and east to Antibes (15min., 14F); Nice (35min., 32F); and Monaco (50min., 46F). The **tourist office,** 1 bd. de la Croisette, gives accommodations advice. (Tel. 04 93 39 24 53; fax 04 92 99 84 23. Open July-Aug. daily 9am-7pm; Sept.-June M-Sa 9am-6:30pm.) Access the **internet** at **Asher MCS,** 44 bd. Carnot. (10F per 15min. Open M-Th 9am-7pm and F-Su 9am-noon.) Hostels are 10-20min. farther from the beach and nightlife than other lodgings, but are the cheapest option in town. Take the stairs that lead to a passageway under the station and follow the signs left to the **Auberge pour la Jeunesse-Le Chalit,** 27 av. Maréchal Galliéni (5min.; tel./fax 04 93 99 22 11; 90F; sheets 17F; reception 8:30am-12:30pm; lockout 12:30-5pm); or right (veer left at the pl. du Cdt. Maria) to the **Auberge de la Jeunesse de Cannes (HI),** 35 av. de Vallauris (10min.; tel./fax 04 93 99 26 79; 70-80F; reception 8am-noon and 3-10pm; curfew midnight). **Hotel Cybelle,** 14 rue du 24 Août, is between the station and beach. (Tel. 04 93 38 31 33; fax 04 93 38 43 47. Singles 120-140F; doubles 200-250F. V, MC, AmEx.) **Camp** at **Le Grand Saule,** 24 bd. Jean Moulin, in nearby Ranguin; take bus 9 (dir: Grasse; 7F) from pl. de l'Hôtel de Ville. (Tel. 04 93 90 55 10. 2 people and tent 124F. Open Apr.-Oct.) Save your francs at **Monoprix supermarket,** in Champion 6, on rue Meynadier. (Open M-Sa in summer 8:45am-8pm; off-season 8:45am-7:30pm.) Reasonably priced restaurants abound in the pedestrian zone around **rue Meynadier. Postal code:** 06400.

ANTIBES-JUAN-LES-PINS

Although joined as one in the city of Antibes-Juan-les-Pins (pop. 70,000), Antibes and Juan-les-Pins are 3km apart and use separate train stations and tourist offices. **Antibes** is quieter and more serene than Nice; the beaches are sandy, the museums are close by, and the city is clean and pleasant. After lounging in the sun, retreat to the charming *vieille ville.* The **Musée Picasso,** in the Château Grimaldi, on pl. Mariejol, displays works by the master and his contemporaries. (Open Tu-Su June-Sept. 10am-6pm; Oct.-May 10am-noon and 2-6pm. 30F, students 18F.) **Trains** go to Juan-les-Pins (5min., every 30min. until 12:25am, 7F); Cannes (10min., every 30min., 14F); and Nice (18min., every 30min., 22F). Exit the station, turn right on av. Robert Soleau, and follow the "Maison du Tourisme" signs to the **tourist office,** 11 pl. de Gaulle. (Tel. 04 92 90 53 00. Open July-Aug. daily 8:45am-7:30pm; Sept.-June M-Sa 9am-noon and 2-6pm.) To get to the **Hôtel Jabotte,** 13 av. Max Maurey, follow bd. Albert 1er from pl. de Gaulle to its end, turn right on Mal. Leclerc, and walk along the beach for 10min.; or take the *bus gratuit* (free), which leaves every hour and stops at the beach. (Tel. 04 93 61 45 89; fax 04 93 61 07 04. Singles and doubles 180-370F; triples 350-520F. Breakfast 30F. V, MC, AmEx.) **Postal code:** 06600.

Juan-les-Pins is Antibes' younger, hipper, and more hedonistic sibling. Boutiques remain open until midnight, cafés until 2am, and nightclubs until past dawn. The streets are packed with seekers of sea, sun, and sex (the order varies), and nightclubs pulse with promises of decadence. The cafés are much cheaper and almost as lively, so even the most miserly traveler can be included in the nightly bash. *Discothèques* are generally open from 11pm to 5am (covers around 100F; includes 1 drink). **Le Village,** 1 bd. de la Pinède, is notorious for its lively dance floor. Check out the psychedelic **Whiskey à Go Go,** on la Pinède, and newcomer **Vertigo,** at the intersection of av. Maupassant and bd. Wilson, or join the crowds piling onto the patio of hip **Che Café,** 1 bd. de la Pinède. **Trains** arrive from Cannes (10min., every 20min., 12F) and Nice (30min., every 20min.). To get from Antibes' pl. du Général de Gaulle to Juan-les-Pins by foot, follow bd. Wilson, which runs right into the center of town (about 1.5km). Rather than make the post-party trek back to Antibes, take a right out of the train station and sack out at **Hôtel Trianon,** 14 av. de L'Estérel. (Tel. 04 93 61 18 11. Singles 200F; doubles 200-300F; triples 350F. Breakfast 30F. V, MC.)

FRANCE

NICE

Cosmopolitan and chic, sun-drenched and spicy, Nice sparkles as the unofficial capital of the Riviera—a rite of passage for young travelers. The city's pumping nightlife, top-notch museums, and bustling beaches enhance the native *Provençal* charms: flowery, palm-lined boulevards, casual affluence, and soothing sea breezes. During its **Carnaval** (the second half of February), the visitors and *Niçois* alike ring in the spring with wild floral revelry, grotesque costumes, and raucous song and dance. Prepare to have more fun than you'll remember.

▐ GETTING THERE AND GETTING AROUND

Trains: Gare SNCF Nice-Ville (tel. 04 92 14 81 62), on av. Thiers. Info office open M-Sa 8am-6:30pm, Su 8:30-11:15am and 2-6pm. To: **Monaco** (25min., 2-6 per hr., 20F); **Antibes** (25min., 1-2 per hr., 26F); **Cannes** (40min., 1-4 per hr., 32F); **Marseille** (2¾hr., 1-2 per hr., 148F); and **Paris** (TGV; 7hr., 4-7 per day, 420-522F, reservation 20F).

Buses: 5 bd. Jean Jaurès (tel. 04 93 85 61 81). Tickets sold M-Sa 6:30am-8pm and on most buses. To: **Monaco** (25-45 min., 17-20F) and **Cannes** (1¼hr., 30F).

Ferries: SNCM (tel. 04 93 13 66 66), on quai du Commerce. Take bus 1 or 2 (dir: Port) from pl. Masséna. To **Corsica** (see p. 349). Open M-F 8am-7pm, Sa 8am-noon.

Public Transportation: Sunbus, 10 av. Félix Faure (tel. 04 93 16 52 10), near pl. Leclerc and pl. Masséna. 8F per ride; 10-ticket *carnet* 72F. Bus passes (day pass 24F, 5-day 88F, 7-day 115F) are well worth it; buy them at the office (open M-F 7am-7pm, Sa 7am-6pm) or at the info kiosk at sq. Leclerc (open M-F 6:30am-9:30pm). Bus 12 runs between the train station, pl. Masséna, and the beach every 12min.

Bike and Scooter Rental: JML Location, 34 av. Auber, opposite the train station. Bikes 60-80F per day, 300-390F per week. Scooters 130-310F per day, 1850F per week; credit card required for deposit. Open M-F 8am-1pm and 2-6:30pm, Sa 8am-1pm.

▐ ORIENTATION AND PRACTICAL INFORMATION

As you exit the train station, **av. Jean-Médecin** to the left and **bd. Gambetta** to the right run directly to the beach. **Pl. Masséna** is 10min. down av. Jean-Médecin. Along the coast, **Promenade des Anglais** is a people-watching paradise. To the southeast, past av. Jean Médecin and toward the bus station, pulsates **Vieux Nice**. Women should avoid walking alone after sundown, and everyone should exercise caution at night around the train station, in *Vieux Nice*, and on the Promenade des Anglais.

Tourist Office: (tel. 04 93 87 07 07; fax 04 93 16 85 16; email otc@nice-coteazur.org; www.nice-coteazur.org), on av. Thiers, beside the train station. Books rooms; line up before 8am if you want one. Essential city maps as well as bus maps and schedules. Open daily mid-June to mid-Sept. 7:30am-8pm; mid-Sept. to mid-June 8am-7pm.

Currency Exchange: Cambio, 17 av. Thiers (tel. 04 93 88 56 80), opposite the train station. No commission. Open daily 7am-midnight.

American Express: 11 promenade des Anglais (tel. 04 93 16 53 53; fax 04 93 16 53 42), at rue des Congrès. **ATM** machine. Open daily 9am-9pm.

Luggage Storage: At the train station. 30F per day. Open daily 7am-10pm. Lockers 15F.

Laundromat: Laverie Automatique, on rue de Suisse, near hotels around the station. Wash 20F per 6kg, 40F per 15kg. Dry 2F per 5min. Soap 2F. Open daily 7am-9pm.

Emergency: Tel. 17. **Medical emergency:** Tel. 15.

Police: Tel. 04 93 17 22 22. At the far end of bd. M. Foch from bd. Jean Médecin.

Pharmacy: 7 rue Masséna (tel. 04 93 87 78 94). Open 24hr.

Post Office: 23 av. Thiers (tel. 04 93 82 65 22), near the train station. Open M-Tu and Th-F 8am-7pm, W 8:30am-7pm, Sa 8am-noon. 24-hour **ATM**. Address mail to be held: Melissa GIBSON, *Poste Restante*, Recette Principale, Nice **06000,** France.

Internet Access: Organic Café, 16 rue Paganini. Mention *Let's Go* and pay 10F per 15min.; 35F per hr. Open M-Sa 10am-10pm, Su 2-8pm. **Web Nice,** 25bis Promenade des Anglais. 30F per 30min., 50F per hr. Open Tu-Su 10am-8pm.

FRANCE

PHONE CODE	France has no city codes. From outside France, dial int'l dialing prefix + 33 + local number (drop the leading zero).

ACCOMMODATIONS

To sleep easy, come to Nice with reservations. Affordable places surround the train station, but without reservations (made 3-5 days ahead), you'll be forced to join the legions outside the train station, which moonlights as one of the largest and most dangerous bedrooms in France.

Hôtel Les Orangiers, 10bis av. Durante (tel. 04 93 87 51 41; fax 04 93 82 57 82). Bright rooms, most with showers and fridges. English spoken. Free beach-mat loan and luggage storage. In summer, dorms 85F; singles 100F; doubles 210F; triples 285F; quads 360F. Off-season 10F less. Breakfast 20F. Open Dec.-Oct. V, MC.

Hôtel Baccarat, 39 rue d'Angleterre (tel. 04 93 88 35 73; fax 04 93 16 14 25). Large, well-kept rooms with showers. Friendly staff creates a homey ambience. Dorms 84-90F; singles 174F; doubles 217F. Off-season 10-20F less. Breakfast 15F. V, MC.

Hôtel des Flanders, 6 rue de Belgique (tel. 04 93 88 78 94; fax 04 93 88 74 90). Large rooms with phones and big bathrooms. Friendly owners will negotiate prices for longer stays. Beautiful TV parlor. Dorms 90F; singles 200F; doubles 220-250F; triples 340F; quads 360-400F. Extra bed 60F. Breakfast 25F. V, MC.

Hôtel St François, 3 rue St-Francois (tel. 04 93 85 88 69; fax 04 93 85 10 67). Incredible location—the only cheap rooms in *Vieux Nice.* Just a short stumble from the city's best nightlife. Singles 95-135F; doubles 158F; triples 215-240F. Showers 15F.

Relais International de la Jeunesse "Clairvallon," 26 av. Scudéri (tel. 04 93 81 27 63; fax 04 93 53 35 88), in Cimiez, 4km out of town. Take bus 15 (dir: Rimiez; 20min.; every 10min.) from the train station or pl. Masséna to "Scudéri"; then head uphill to the right and take your 1st left. You and 160 buddies in the luxurious villa of a dead marquis. Tennis and basketball courts. Lovely TV and dining rooms. 72F. Breakfast included. Check-in 5pm. Lockout 9:30am-5pm. Curfew 11pm.

Hôtel Belle Meunière, 21 av. Durante (tel. 04 93 88 66 15), on a street facing the train station. Hostelers hang out in the hallways and gardens. Co-ed dorms 76-101F; doubles 160-275F; triples 243-330F. Breakfast included. Luggage storage 10F.

Hôtel Meublé Drouot, 24 rue d'Angleterre (tel. 04 93 88 02 03). Well-run hotel with English-speaking owner. Singles 130-150F; doubles 220-240F; triples 270F; quads 350F. Hall bathrooms. Some kitchenettes. Free luggage storage.

Auberge de Jeunesse (HI) (tel. 04 93 89 23 64; fax 04 92 04 03 10), on rte. Forestière du Mont Boron, 4km out of town. From the train station, take bus 17 and tell the driver you need to switch to the 14 Sunbus (dir: Mont Boron; M-F every 15min., Sa-Su every 30min., both until 7:30pm) to "l'Auberge." From the train station, turn left, then right on av. Jean Médecin, then left on bd. Jaurès, then right on rue Barla, and follow the signs (50min.). 68F. Breakfast included. Kitchen. Lockout 10am-5pm. Curfew 12:30am.

Hôtel Notre Dame, 22 rue de la Russie (tel. 04 93 88 70 44; fax 04 93 82 20 38), at the corner of rue d'Italie, 1 block west of av. Jean Médecin. Spotless, quiet rooms with phones and pleasant decor. If full, they will shuttle you to one of their other hotels nearby. Elegant singles 200F; doubles 240F; triples 300F. Apartments 350F for 4 people; each additional person 85F. Breakfast 20F. Shower 10F. V, MC, AmEx.

Hôtel Lyonnais, 20 rue de la Russie (tel. 04 93 88 70 74; fax 04 93 16 25 56). Popular with backpackers thanks to pleasant rooms, all with phones and some with marble balconies. Singles 145-200F; doubles 160-260F; triples 240-290F; quads 300-390F. Off-season *Let's Go* discount 10%. Breakfast 22F. Shower 15F per 10min. V, MC, AmEx.

FOOD

Nice offers a smorgasbord of seafood, Asian cuisine, and Italian gastronomic delights. *Vieux Nice* is crowded and touristy, but good eats are easy to find. Stock up at the **Prisunic supermarket,** 42 av. Jean Médecin, or at a **Casino supermarket,** on rue Deudor, behind the Nice Etoile on av. Jean Médecin, and on av. Gloria, behind Espace Magnan. (All 3 supermarkets open M-Sa 8:30am-8pm.)

Nice

ACCOMMODATIONS

A Hôtel Belle Meunière
B Hôtel Les Orangiers
C Hôtel Baccarat
D Hôtel des Flanders
E Hôtel Notre Dame &
Hôtel Lyonnais
F Relais International dela
Jeunesse "Clairvallon"
G Hôtel St François
H Auberge de Jeunesse (HI)

FRANCE

Baie des Anges

Port

Nissa Socca, 5 rue Ste-Réparate (tel. 04 93 80 18 35). Practically a town landmark. Famous for its 35F *niçois* dishes and homey aura. Open M-Sa noon-2pm and 7-11pm.

Acchiardo, 38 rue Droite (tel. 04 93 85 51 16) Wonderful, simple *niçois* dishes. Popular with a loyal local clientele. *Menu* from 36F. Open M-F noon-1:30pm and 7-9:30pm.

Lou Pilha Leva, 10 rue du Collet (tel. 04 93 80 29 33). A wonderful way to try a lot for a little. Pizzas, *socca* (a fresh, olive-oil-flavored chickpea bread), and *pissaladière* (anchovy and olive pizza) all 10-15F. Hard-to-resist *moules* (mussels) 40F. Open daily 8am-11pm.

La Casa Della Pasta, 9 rue du Pont Vieux. Typical *Vieux Nice* fare, but large portions and hard-to-beat prices. Pizzas and pastas from 35F. V, MC, AmEx.

■ SIGHTS

Nice's **Promenade des Anglais,** along the waterfront, is a sight in itself. Private beaches crowd the water between bd. Gambetta and the Opéra, but plenty of public space remains. Whatever dreams you've had about Nice's beach, the hard reality is an endless stretch of smooth rocks; bring a beach mat. Sprawling southeast from bd. Jean Jaurès, **Vieux Nice's** labyrinthine streets contain buildings of considerable historical significance. Promenade des Anglais leads east to **Le Château,** a flowery hillside park crowned with the remains of an 11th-century cathedral. (Open daily 7am-8pm.) **Eglise St-Martin,** on pl. St Augustin, the city's oldest church, was visited by Luther, and a few centuries later saw Italian revolutionary Giuseppe Garibaldi's baptism. (Open daily 9am-noon and 2-6pm.) Far to the northwest, the gorgeous **Cathédrale Orthodoxe Russe St-Nicolas,** 17 bd. du Tzarevitch, west of bd. Gambetta near the train station, is a reminder of the days when the Côte d'Azur was a favorite retreat for Russian nobility. (Open daily June-Aug. 9am-noon and 2:30-6pm; Sept.-May 9:30am-noon and 2:30-5pm. 12F.)

Even burn-hard sunbathers will have a hard time passing by Nice's excellent museums. The **Musée des Beaux-Arts,** 33 av. Baumettes, off bd. François Grosso just north of the Promenade des Anglais, exhibits the work of Fragonard, Monet, Sisley, Bonnard, and Degas, and also features sculptures by Rodin and Carpeaux. Take bus 38 from the train station to "Chéret," or bus 12 to "Grosso." (Open Tu-Su 10am-noon and 2-6pm. 25F, students 15F.) The elegant **Musée National Marc Chagall,** on av. du Dr. Ménard, a 15-minute walk northeast of the station or a short ride on bus 15 (dir: Rimiez and Les Sources; 9F), is a true joy to visit. (Open W-M July-Sept. 10am-5:40pm; Oct.-June 10am-4:50pm. 30-38F, students 20-28F.) If the Chagall museum provides a religious experience, then the **Musée Matisse,** 164 av. des Arènes de Cimiez, proves a truly transcendental one. Matisse lived and worked in Nice from 1917 until his death in 1954; although he was best known for his paintings, the museum emphasizes other forms of his artistry, including his sketches. Take bus 15, 17, 20, or 22 to "Arènes." (Open W-M Apr.-Sept. 10am-6pm; Oct.-Mar. 10am-5pm. 25F, students 15F.) Finally, the **Musée d'Art Moderne et d'Art Contemporain,** on promenade des Arts, at the intersection of av. St-Jean Baptiste and Traverse Garibaldi near *Vieux Nice,* features over 400 French and American avant-garde pieces from 1960 to the present. Take bus 5 (dir: St-Charles) from the station to "Garibaldi." (Open Su-M and W-Th 11am-6pm, F 11am-10pm.)

■ ENTERTAINMENT

Nice's **Jazz Festival,** in mid-July at the Parc et Arènes de Cimiez near the Musée Matisse, attracts world-famous jazz and non-jazz musicians. (Tel. 04 93 21 68 12; fax 04 93 18 07 92. Tickets 50-250F.) The **FNAC,** 24 av. Jean Médecin, in the Nice Etoile shopping center, sells tickets for performances around town.

Nice guys do finish last—here the party crowd swings long after the folks in nearby St-Tropez and Antibes have called it a night. The bars and nightclubs around rue Masséna and *Vieux Nice* rollick with dance, jazz, and rock. However, the areas around *Vieux Nice* and the Promenade des Anglais can be dangerous at night.

Wayne's, 15 rue de la Préfecture (tel. 04 93 13 46 99), is popular with young Anglophones on the prowl, with live music every night in summer and Sunday karaoke. Undubbed episodes of "The Simpsons" on Su nights.

De Klomp, 6 rue Mascoinat (tel. 04 93 92 42 85), a Dutch pub with a kitschy brothel theme. Try one of their 40 whiskeys (from 35F) or 18 beers on tap (pint 40F). Live music nightly from salsa to jazz. Big-time musicians are known to slurp suds here.

Le Tapas, 2bis rue de l'Abbaye (tel. 04 93 62 27 46). Although this bar resembles a French Revolution secret meeting spot, the only plotting involved will be how you'll get home after braving their meter-long box of shots (100F; 0.5m 60F). Live music M-Th.

Subway, 19 rue Droite, at rue Rosetti in *Vieux Nice*. Tucked in a narrow alley, this club plays a mélange of music to a touristy crowd. Cover 40-50F. Open Th-Su.

THE CORNICHES: NICE TO MONACO

Rocky shores, pebble beaches, and luxurious villas glow along the coast between hectic Nice and high-rolling Monaco. More relaxing than their glam-fab neighbors, these tiny towns are like freshwater pearls—similar in brilliance, yet gratifyingly unique, with interesting museums, architectural finds, and breathtaking country-side. The train offers a good glimpse of the coast up close, while bus rides on the high roads provide bird's-eye views of the steep cliffs and crashing sea below.

▣ GETTING THERE AND GETTING AROUND. Trains run between Nice and Monaco hourly and stop at (from west to east): Villefranche-sur-Mer (7min., 8F); Beaulieu-sur-Mer (10min., 9F); Eze-sur-Mer (16min., 11F); and Cap D'Ail (20min., 13F). **RCA buses** (tel. 04 93 85 64 44), which depart from Nice's *gare routière*, run the route more frequently; **RCA 100** leaves every 15-40min. (M-Sa 6:45am-7:45pm, Su 8:10am-7:45pm) for Villefranche-sur-Mer (10min., 8F50); Beaulieu-sur-Mer (20min., 12F); Eze-Le-Village (25min., 13F50); Cap D'Ail (30min., 16F50); Monaco-Ville (40min., 20F); and Monte Carlo (45min., 20F). **RCA 111** and **117** also heads to Ville-franche-sur-Mer; RCA 111 continues on to St-Jean-Cap-Ferrat (14.50F). **RCA 112** runs between Nice and Monte Carlo, stopping in Eze-Le-Village.

VILLEFRANCHE-SUR-MER. Narrow streets and pastel houses have enchanted Aldous Huxley, Katherine Mansfield, and a bevy of other writers. Strolling from the train station along quai Ponchardier, a sign to the *vieille ville* points toward the spooky and dungeonesque 13th-century **rue Obscure,** which has been layered with so many homes and shops that the only light comes from iron chandeliers hanging from the street's "ceiling." The **tourist office,** on Jardin François Binon, gives out free maps and info on sights. (Tel. 04 93 01 73 68; fax 04 93 76 63 65. Open July-Aug. daily 9am-8pm; mid-Sept. to June M-Sa 9am-noon and 2-6pm.)

ST-JEAN-CAP-FERRAT. A lovely town with an even lovelier beach, St-Jean-Cap-Ferrat is the trump card of the Riviera. Consider taking the bus or train to Beaulieu and then walking to St-Jean-Cap-Ferrat (25min.); the walk leads you along a seaside path full of lavish villas secluded rocky beaches. The **Fondation Ephrussi di Roths-child**—a stunning Italianate villa with an impressive, eclectic collection of art-work—is the town's main draw, and the best sight between Nice and Monaco. (Open mid-Feb. to Oct. daily 10am-6pm; Nov. to mid-Feb. M-F 2-6pm, Sa-Su 10am-6pm. 46F, students 35F.) The town's beautiful and untouristed **beaches** merit the area's nickname *Presqu'ile des Rêves* (Peninsula of Dreams), and are mostly fre-quented by local families.

EZE-LE-VILLAGE. The most colorful of the towns from Nice to Monaco, this imposing medieval town (the center of the larger Eze-sur-Mer) features the **Porte des Maures,** which served as a portal for a surprise attack by the Moors, and the newly renovated Baroque **Eglise Paroissial,** decorated with a combination of Chris-tian and Egyptian symbols. (Open daily 9am-noon and 2-6pm.) The best views go to those who venture 40min. up the **Sentier Friedrich Nietzsche,** a windy trail whose namesake found inspiration here for the third part of *Thus Spake Zarathustra;* the trail begins in Eze Bord-du-Mer, 100m east of the train station and tourist office, and ends near the base of the medieval city, by the Fragonard *parfumerie.*

FRANCE

CAP D'AIL. With 3km of cliff-framed foamy seashore, Cap d'Ail's (pop. 5000) **Les Pissarelles** draws hundreds of nudists, while **plage Mala** is frequented by more modest folk. Free maps and lists of daytrips are available from the **tourist office,** 104 av. de 3 Septembre. Walk uphill from the train station, turn right at the village, continue on av. de la Gare, and turn right on rue du 4 Septembre (20min.). (Tel. 04 93 78 02 33; fax 04 92 10 74 36. Open M-F 9am-noon and 2-6:30pm, Sa 9am-noon and 1-6pm.) The **Relais International de la Jeunesse,** on bd. de la Mer, has an amazing beachfront location. (Tel. 04 93 78 18 58 70F. Breakfast included. 3-night max. stay when busy. Lockout 9:30am-5pm. Curfew midnight.)

MONACO / MONTE-CARLO

Wealth and casual luxury drip from every ornate street lamp and newly scrubbed sidewalk of sumptuous Monaco, the world's playground for the rich and famous. The money and mystery of the Monte-Carlo *quartier* revolve around the Casino, where Mata Hari shot a Russian spy and Richard Burton wooed Liz Taylor.

PHONE CODE	**Country code:** 377. **International dialing prefix:** 00.

🛈🖐🗺 PRACTICAL INFO, ACCOMMODATIONS, AND FOOD. Trains (tel. 08 36 35 35 35) run to Nice (25min., every 30min., 19F); Antibes (45min., every 30min., 38F); and Cannes (1¼hr., every 30min., 46F). From the station, turn right on av. du Port and left on bd. Albert 1er, overlooking the harbor; on the right is the *quartier* of **Monaco-Ville,** with its *vieille ville* and the palace, and to the left rises the fabled *quartier* of **Monte-Carlo** and the casino. The **tourist office,** 2a bd. des Moulins, near the casino, has maps and reserves rooms. (Tel. (377) 92 16 61 16; fax 92 16 60 00. Open M-Sa 9am-7pm, Su 10am-noon.) Access the **internet** at **Stars N' Bars,** on quai Antoine 1er. (40F per hr. Open daily 11am-1:30am.) To afford a room in Monaco, you'll either need to seduce royalty or win big. Try the **Centre de Jeunesse Princesse Stéphanie,** 24 av. Prince Pierre, 100m uphill from the station. (Tel. (377) 93 50 83 20; fax 93 25 29 82. 80F. Breakfast included. Must be age 16-26, or under 31 with student ID. 7-night max. stay. Laundry 30F. Reception July-Aug. 7am-1am, Sept.-June 7am-midnight.) Have your chauffeur drop you by the fruit and flower **market** in pl. d'Armes, at the end of av. Prince Pierre. (Open daily 6am-1pm.) **Carrefour supermarket** is in Fontvieille's *centre commercial* (shopping plaza). To get there walk right from the station, turn right on rue de la Colle; at pl. du Canton, cross and go down one level. (Open M-Sa 8:30am-10pm.) **Postal code:** 06500.

📷🎭 SIGHTS AND ENTERTAINMENT. The **Monte-Carlo Casino** is ablaze with red velvet curtains, gilded ceilings, and gold-and-crystal chandeliers. If you feel lucky, the slot machines open at 2pm, while blackjack, craps, and roulette (25F minimum) open at 3pm. If you need your gambling fix before noon, head next door to **Café de Paris,** where admission to the main room is free, but a peek at the high-stakes *salons privés* costs 50-100F. (Open daily from 10am.) At all casinos you must be over 21 to gamble, and no shorts, sneakers, sandals, or jeans are permitted. After losing your shirt in Monte Carlo, walk west to Monaco where you can admire the royal robes at the **Palais Princier,** the sometime home of Prince Rainier and his family. When the flag is down, the prince is away and visitors can tour the lavish palace. (Open daily June-Sept. 9:30am-6pm; Oct. 10am-5pm. 30F, students 20F.) Next door is the stately **Cathédrale de Monaco,** 4 rue Colonel Bellando de Castro, where former Princes of Monaco are buried. Grace Kelly's tomb, behind the altar, is simply marked "Patritia Gracia." (Open daily 9am-12:30pm and 1:30-4:30pm. Free.) The **Exhibition of H.S.H. the Prince of Monaco's Private Collection of Classic Cars,** on les Terraces de Fontvieille, features 105 of the sexiest and most stately cars ever made. (Open daily Dec.-Oct. 10am-6pm. 30F, students 15F.) Once run by Jacques Cousteau, the stunning **Musée Océanographique,** on av. St-Martin, houses thousands of species of marine animals. (Open daily July-Aug. 9am-8pm; Apr.-June and Sept. 9am-7pm; Mar. and Oct. 9:30am-7pm; Nov.-Feb. 10am-6pm. 60F, students 30F.)

FRANCE

CORSICA (LA CORSE)

A story told to Corsican children goes something like this: and on the sixth day, God made Corsica. He mixed the turquoise waters of the Mediterranean, the snow-capped splendor of the Alps, and the golden sunshine of the Riviera in order to create the island the Greeks called *Kallysté* (the most beautiful).

⊟ GETTING THERE AND GETTING AROUND. **Air France** (tel. 04 91 39 36 36) and **Air Inter** (tel. 04 95 29 45 45) fly to **Bastia, Ajaccio,** and **Calvi** from **Nice** (1037F, students 737F); **Marseille** (1155F, students 815F); **Paris** (2200F, students 1200-1900F); and **Lyon** (2400F, students 1700F). Or fly from **Lille** to **Bastia** (3600F, students 1500F). **Ferries** to Corsica can be rough and aren't much cheaper than flights. The **Société National Maritime Corse Méditerranée (SNCM)** sails to **Bastia, Calvi,** and **Ajaccio** from **Marseille** (8½hr., 6 per week, 305-360F, under 25 265-305F) and **Nice** (4hr., night ferry 10hr., 1-2 per day, 260-305F, under 25 235-260F). **Corsica Ferries** (tel. 04 95 32 95 95) travels from **Livorno** and **Savona,** Italy to **Bastia** (140-200F). Ferries also bridge the gap from **Bonifacio,** at the southern tip of the island, to **Sardinia, Italy.**

Train service in Corsica is slow and limited to the half of the island north of Ajaccio; **railpasses** are not valid. **Eurocorse Voyages buses** (tel. 04 95 21 06 30) are neither cheaper nor more frequent, but provide more comprehensive service. **Hiking** is the best way to explore the island's mountainous interior. The longest marked route, **GR20,** is a difficult 13- to 15-day trail (160km) traversing the island. The **Parc Naturel Régional de la Corse,** 2 rue Major-Lambroschini, in Ajaccio (tel. 04 95 51 79 10; fax 04 95 21 88 17), publishes maps and a guide to *gîtes d'étapes*.

AJACCIO

Ajaccio (pop. 60,000) swings like nowhere else on the island. Napoleonophiles find Ajaccio's sights better than another 100 days. Start at the **Musée National de la Maison Bonaparte,** on rue St-Charles, between rue Bonaparte and rue Roi-de-Rome, containing everything from Napoleon's baby pictures to his death mask. (Tel. 04 95 21 43 89. Open M 2-6 pm, Tu-Su 10am-noon and 2-6pm. 22F, ages 18-25 15F, under 18 free.) Napoleon's uncle Fesch piled up a stash of money as a merchant during the Revolution. When he renounced his worldly goods for the Church, the new cardinal used the booty to amass Renaissance art. Inside the **Musée Flesch,** 50-52 rue Cardinal Fesch, you'll find a collection including works by Raphael, Botticelli, and Titian. Within the complex is the **Chapelle Impériale,** the final resting place of most of the Bonaparte family—though Napoleon himself is buried in a modest Parisian tomb. (Tel. 04 95 21 48 17. Open June 15-Aug. Tu-Th 10am-5:30pm, F 10am-6:30pm and 9:30pm-midnight, Sa-Su 10am-4:30pm; Sept.-June 14 Tu-Sa 9:15am-12:15pm and 2:15-5:15pm. Museum 25F, students 15F; with chapel 39F, students 20F.) The closest beach to the town center is **plage St-François,** beyond the citadel.

Buses (tel. 04 95 51 43 23) shuttle between the **airport** and bus station (every hr., 20F). **Trains** (tel. 04 95 23 11 03) run from rue Jean-Jérôme Levie, between cours Napoléon and bd. Sampiero, to Bastia (4hr., 4 per day, 118F) and Calvi via Ponte Leccia (5hr., 2 per day, 138F). From quai l'Herminier (tel. 04 95 21 28 01), Eurocorse Voyages **buses** (tel. 04 95 21 06 30) go to Bastia (3hr., 2 per day, 105F) via Corte (1½hr., 60F), while Autocars SAIB (tel. 04 95 22 41 99) runs to Calvi (6hr., 2 per day, 130F) via Porto (2¾hr., 65F). The **tourist office** is at 3 bd. du roi Jérôme. (Tel. 04 95 51 53 03; fax 04 95 51 53 01. Open mid-June to Aug. M-Sa 8am-8:30pm, Su 9am-1pm; Sept. to mid-June M-Sa 8am-6pm and Su 9am-1pm. Call ahead.) **Hôtel Kallisté,** 51 cours Napoléon, is serene. (Tel. 04 95 51 34 45; fax 04 95 21 79 00. Singles 200-300F; doubles 250-340F; triples 360-450F; quads 400-560F. V, MC.) **Hôtel Bella Vista** is on bd. Lantivy. (Tel. 04 95 21 07 97; fax 04 95 21 81 88. Singles 190-240F; doubles 210-270F; triples 260-330F; quads 380F. V, MC, AmEx.) **Monoprix supermarket** is at 31 cours Napoléon. (Open M-Sa 8:30am-7:15pm.)

CALVI

With its sandy beaches, warm aquamarine waters, misty mountains, and nearly 2400 hours of sunshine per year, Calvi could well be paradise—although no benevolent god would charge these rates. Visit the alluring **citadel** at the end of the day and bask in the setting sun. Gorgeous sand and water stretch as far as the eye can see; 6km of **public beaches** dotted by rocky coves wind around the coast. Les Beaux Voyages **buses** (tel. 04 95 65 15 02), on av. Wilson, runs to Bastia (2¼hr., 1 per day, 80F). **Trains** (tel. 04 95 65 00 61) go from pl. de la Gare, at the end of Corso di la Repubblica near Port de Plaisance, to Bastia (3hr., 2 per day, 93F). **Buses** stop at pl. Porteuse d'Eau Agence. To reach the **tourist office**, at Port de Plaisance, exit from the back of the train station, turn left (facing the beach), and follow the signs. (Tel. 04 95 65 16 67; fax 04 95 65 14 09. Open daily July-Aug. M-Sa 9am-7pm, Su 9am-1pm and 2:30-7pm; Sept.-June M-Sa 9am-noon and 2-6pm.) To hoof it to the isolated but beautiful **Relais International de la Jeunesse U Carabellu**, exit the station, turn left on av. de la République, turn right at rte. de Pietra-Maggiore, follow the signs 5km up the mountain, continue straight past Bella Vista camping, and bear right at the stop sign. (Tel. 04 95 65 14 16. 75F. Breakfast included. Sheets 20F. Open May-Sept.) **BVJ Corsotel** is on av. de la République. (Tel. 04 95 65 14 15; fax 04 95 65 33 72. 120F. Breakfast included. Reception 24hr. Open late Mar.-Oct.) **Camp** at **International**, on RN 197, close to the beach past Super U and Hotel L'Onda. (Tel. 04 95 65 01 75. 20-27F per person, 12-15F per tent, 8-10F per car. Open Apr.-Oct.)

BASTIA AND CAP CORSE

Corsica's second largest city, Bastia (pop. 45,000) seems content with its role as a transport hub. The 18th-century **Eglise St-Jean Baptiste**, on pl. de l'Hôtel de Ville, is the stunning centerpiece of the photogenic port. The **Citadel**, also called Terra Nova, was the spot from which the Genovese projected their power over the island and now houses several museums. Trek 1km to the beautiful **beaches** of **L'Arinella** at **Montesoro** via the road just beyond the Citadel. **Buses** connect to the **airport** from pl. de la Gare (30min., 38F), where **trains** (tel. 04 95 32 80 61) also depart for Calvi (3hr., 2 per day, 96F) and Ajaccio (4hr., 5 per day, 122F). Eurocorse **buses** (tel. 04 95 21 06 30) also run to Ajaccio (3hr., 2 per day, 114F). The **tourist office** is on pl. St-Nicholas. (Tel. 04 95 55 96 96; fax 04 95 55 96 00. Open M-Sa June-Aug. 8am-8pm, Sept.-May 8am-6pm.) **Hôtel Central**, 3 rue Miot, is inviting. (Tel. 04 95 31 71 12; fax 04 95 31 82 40. Singles 200-280F; doubles 250-380F; triples 330-440F; quads 460F; each additional person 60F. Breakfast 30F. V, MC, AmEx.) Beachside **Les Orangiers camping** is 4km north in Miomo. (Tel. 04 95 33 24 09. 24F per person, 12F per tent. Open May-Sept.) **SPAR supermarket** is at 14 rue César Campinchini. (Open M-Sa 7:30am-1pm and 6-9pm, Su 7:30am-1pm.)

The **Cap Corse** peninsula stretches north from Bastia, a necklace of tiny former fishing villages connected by a narrow road of perilous curves and breathtaking views. Mountains rise 1000m above the sleepy, rocky shores. **Transports Michéle** (tel. 04 95 35 61 08) offers full-day tours of the Cap, departing from 1 rue de Nouveau Port in Bastia (runs July-late Sept. M-Sa 9am; 84F), but the cheapest way to see Cap Corse is to take **bus** 4 from pl. St-Nicolas in Bastia; nicely ask the driver to drop you off wherever you feel the urge to explore (1-2 per hr., 15F). The bus also goes to **Erbalunga** (25min., 11F), which you will never want to leave.

CORTE

"The heart of Corsica," Corte is enfolded amidst huge sheer cliffs and snow-capped peaks, appearing from a distance like a fairy-tale illustration. Corsica's intellectual center, Corte houses the island's only university, and students (2600 of its 6000 residents) keep prices fairly low. The town's *vieille ville*, with its steep, inaccessible topography and stone citadel, has always been a bastion of fierce Corsican patriotism. At the top of the *vieille ville*, the focus of the **Citadel** is the brand new **La Musée de la Corse**. The museum also provides entrance to the higher fortifications of the citadel. (Tel. 04 95 45 25 45. Museum open June 16-Aug. daily 10am-8pm; Sept.-June 15, M-Sa 10am-noon and 2-5:45pm. Citadel closes 1hr. earlier than museum. Citadel 20F; museum and citadel 35F, students 25F.) Countless trails through the area's mountains and valleys are nothing short of spectacular. Choose from **hiking** (tel. 04 95 21 56 54 for maps and trail info; tel. 04 95 51 79 10 for weather conditions), **biking** (if you can procure one—there are no rentals in town), and **horse riding** (tel. 04 95 46 24 55; 90F per hr., 200F per half-day, 400F per day).

Trains run to Bastia (1¾hr., 4 per day, 58F); Calvi via Ponte-Leccia (2½hr., 2 per day, 78F); and Ajaccio (2½hr., 4 per day, 66F). Eurocorse Voyages (tel. 04 95 31 03 79) runs **buses** to Bastia (1¼hr., 3 per week, 55F) and Ajaccio (45min., M-Sa 2 per day, 65F). From the train station, turn right on D14 (a.k.a. av. Jean Nicoli), cross two bridges, and follow the road until it ends at **cours Paoli**. To reach the citadel, turn left onto cours Paoli until you reach **pl. Paoli**, the pizzeria *place* to be. Struggle up the steep **rue Scoliscia** until you faint at the citadel's gates and the **tourist office.** (Tel. 04 95 46 26 70. Open July-Aug. M-F 9am-1pm and 2-7pm, Sa 10am-1pm and 3-7pm; Sept.-June M-F 9am-noon and 2-6pm.) In the summer, students can stay in university housing for 60F per night; contact **CROUS,** 7 av. Jean Nicoli. (Tel. 04 95 45 21 00; fax 04 95 61 01 57. Office open M-F 9am-noon and 2-3:30pm.) The **Gîte d'Etape: U Tavignanu,** on chemin de Balari, offers a lovely converted farmhouse and gorgeous **campsites.** Turn left out of the station and bear right when the road forks, first following allée du 9 Septembre and then the signs at the base of the Citadel (20min.). (Tel. 04 95 46 16 85; fax 04 95 61 49. 80F with breakfast; half-pension 160F. Camping 20F per person, 10F per tent.) The huge **Casino supermarket** is on allée du 9 Septembre. (Open M-F 8:30am-12:30pm and 3-7:30pm, Sa 8:30am-7:30pm.)

PORTO VECCHIO

On an island full of memorable beaches, those on the Golfe de Porto Vecchio are something to write home about. Reaching them is no easy task, but despite inaccessibility and high prices, dedicated sunseekers will not be disappointed. **Palombaggia** is about a mile long, and summer crowds thin out the farther you walk from the parking lot. Farther south, **Santa Giulia** wins both congeniality and swimsuit competitions. Beaches north of Porto Vecchio also provide stunning spectacles of sand and ocean. **Punta di Benedettu** is the first you get to, but it's worth continuing on. **San Cipriano** is fairly laid-back, attracting anchored sailboats into its calm cove. From July to September, Trinitours **buses** (tel. 04 94 95 70 13 83) go to **Palombaggia** and **San Cipriano** (1 per day, one-way 20F); updated schedules are posted on the tourist office wall, but are rarely convenient for beachgoers.

Eurocorse **buses** (Ajaccio info tel. 04 95 21 06 30) run to Ajaccio (3¼hr.; July-Aug. M-Sa, Sept.-June M-F 1 per day; 110F), while Autocars Rapides-Bleus (tel. 04 95 31 03 79) goes to **Bastia** (3hr., M-Sa 2 per day, 115F). The **tourist office** is around the corner from pl. de la République. (Tel. 04 95 70 09 68. Open June-Sept. M-Sa 9am-8pm, Su 9am-1pm; Oct.-May M-F 9am-noon and 2-6pm.) There are few budget hotels in town, so be sure to call ahead. **Le Modern,** 10 cours Napoleon, has simple blue rooms with a Mediterannean flair, but only one shower to share between bathroomless rooms. (Tel. 04 95 70 06 36. Doubles 200-550F. Open early Apr. to mid-Oct. V, MC.) **Hôtel Panorama,** 12 rue Jean-Nicoli, is just outside the citadel walls on the way to Bonifacio. (Tel. 04 95 70 07 96; fax 04 95 46 78. Doubles 240F, with shower 280F, with shower and toilet 330F. Breakfast 40F. Open Apr.-Sept. V, MC.)

THE ALPS

Natural architecture is the real attraction of the Alps. The curves of the Chartreuse Valley rise to rugged crags in the Vercors range and ultimately crescendo into Europe's highest peak, Mont Blanc. **Hiking trails** are clearly marked, and winter **skiers** enjoy some of the most challenging slopes in the world; make arrangements in advance. The cheapest months for skiing are January, March, and April; most resorts close in October and November. **FUAJ** (tel. 01 43 57 02 60; www.fuaj.org), the French Youth Hostel Federation, offers skiing and sports packages.

TGV **trains** will whisk you from Paris to Grenoble or Annecy; from there, it's either slow trains, special slow mountain trains, or more often, torturously slow **buses.** The farther into the mountains you want to get, the harder it is to get there, although service is at least twice as frequent in ski season (Dec.-Apr.).

GRENOBLE

Grenoble (pop. 160,000) hosts the eccentric cafés, dusty bookshops, and shaggy radicals you'll find in any university town, but it also boasts the snow-capped peaks and sapphire-blue lakes cherished by hikers, skiers, bikers, and aesthetes alike.

⚡ ⌂ ◄ PRACTICAL INFO, ACCOMMODATIONS, AND FOOD. Trains (tel. 08 36 35 35 35) arrive in Grenoble from Lyon (1½hr., 16 per day, 96F); Annecy (2hr., 9 per day, 89F); Marseille (3½hr., 14 per day, 222F); Paris (4hr., 11 per day, 362F); and Nice (6½hr., 8 per day, 316F). **Buses** leave from the left of the station for Geneva (2¾hr., 1 per day, 150F) and Chamonix (3hr., 1 per day, 159F). From the station, turn right into pl. de la Gare, take the third left on av. Alsace-Lorraine, and follow the tram tracks on rue Félix Poulat and rue Blanchard to reach the **tourist office**, 14 rue de la République (10min.). (Tel. 04 76 42 41 41; fax 04 76 51 28 69. Open M-Sa 9am-6pm, Su 10am-1pm.) To get from the station to the **auberge de jeunesse (HI)**, 10 av. du Grésivaudan, 4km away in Echirolles, follow the tram tracks down av. Alsace-Lorraine, turn right on cours Jean Jaurès, and take bus 8 (dir: Pont Rouge) to "La Quinzaine"; it's behind the Casino supermarket. (Tel. 04 76 09 33 52; fax 04 76 09 38 99. 68F. Breakfast included. Sheets 17F. Kitchen. Laundry. Reception M-Sa 7:30am-11pm, Su 7:30-10am and 5:30-11pm. V, MC, AmEx.) From the tourist office, follow pl. Ste-Claire to pl. Notre-Dame and take rue du Vieux Temple on the far right to reach **Le Foyer de l'Etudiante**, 4 rue Ste-Ursule, near pl. Notre-Dame. (Tel. 04 76 42 00 84; fax 04 76 44 36 85. Dorms 50F; singles 80F; doubles 140F. Shower and sheets 15F for dorms. Kitchen. Laundry. Reception 24hr. Open mid-June to mid-Sept. for short-term stays.) **Hôtel de L'Europe**, 22 pl. Grenette, is in the *vieille ville*. (Tel./fax 04 76 46 16 94. Singles from 140F; doubles from 160F. Reception 24hr.) To reach **Camping Les 3 Pucelles**, in Seyssins, take tram A to "Fontaine," then bus 51 (dir: Les Nalettes) to "Mas des Iles." (Tel. 04 76 96 45 73. 30F per person and tent. Call ahead.) ▣**La Galerie Rome**, on rue du Vieux Temple, has flawless cuisine. (Open Tu-Su for lunch and dinner. V, MC, AmEx.) **Prisunic**, opposite the tourist office, stocks **groceries**. (Open M-Sa 8:30am-7:30pm.) **Postal code:** 38000.

▣ SIGHTS. Téléphériques (lifts) depart from quai Stéphane-Jay (every 10min., July-Aug. M 11am-12:30am, Tu-Su 9am-12:30am; off-season shuts down earlier) for the 16th-century **Bastille**, a fort which hovers above town. Enjoy the views from the top, then descend via the **Parc Guy Pape**, which criss-crosses through the fortress and deposits you just across the river from the train station. The **Musée Dauphinois**, 30 rue Maurice Gignoux, toward the bottom of the Bastille hill on the north bank of the Isère, has futuristic exhibits. (Open May-Oct. W-M 10am-7pm; Nov.-Apr. 10am-6pm. 20F, students 10F; W free after 2pm.) Grenoble's major attraction is its proximity to the slopes. The biggest and most developed **ski areas** lie in the **Oisans** to the east; the **Alpe d'Huez** (tel. 04 76 80 30 30) boasts 220km of trails (lift tickets 189F per day). The **Belledonne** region, northeast of Grenoble, lacks the towering heights of the Oisans but is cheaper. **Chamrousse** is its biggest and most popular ski area (lift tickets 125F per day), and has a **youth hostel** (tel. 04 76 89 91 31). Only 30min. from Grenoble by **bus** (49F), the resort makes an ideal daytrip in summer.

FRANCE

CHAMONIX

In other Alpine towns, the peaks provide harmless backdrops; in Chamonix (pop. 20,000), daggers of mammoth glaciers seem to reach down and menace the village. Just west of Mont Blanc, Europe's highest peak (4807m), this site of the first Winter Olympics (1924) has exploited its surroundings since 19th-century gentleman-climbers scaled the peaks in crewneck sweaters.

⚡ ⌂ ◄ PRACTICAL INFO, ACCOMMODATIONS, AND FOOD. Trains (tel. 04 50 53 00 44) go to Annecy (2½hr., 6 per day, 106F); Geneva (2½hr., 4 per day, 108F); Lyon (5hr., 4 per day, 184F); and Paris (8hr., 1 per day, 373F). Société Alpes Transports **buses** (tel. 04 50 53 01 15) depart from the train station for Geneva (2hr., 2 per day, 148-188F); Annecy (2¾hr., 2 per day, 98F); and Grenoble (3½hr., 1 per day,

156F). **Local buses** connect with ski slopes and hiking trails (7.50F). From the station, follow av. Michel Croz, turn left on rue du Dr. Paccard, and take the first right to reach the pl. de l'Eglise and the **tourist office**, 85 pl. du Triangle de l'Amitié (5min.). (Tel. 04 50 53 00 24; fax 04 50 53 58 90. Open daily July-Aug. and during winter vacation 8:30am-7:30pm; Sept.-June 8:30am-12:30pm and 2-7pm.) **Maison de la Montagne**, on pl. de l'Eglise, will help plan **hiking** adventures (tel. 04 50 53 22 08; open daily in summer 8:45am-12:30pm and 2:30-6:15pm; off-season closed Sa-Su); while the **Compagnie des Guides** (tel. 04 50 53 00 88) downstairs and the **Ecole du Ski** next door and will help plan a **ski trip.**

Chamonix's *gîtes* (mountain hostels) and dorms are a budget traveler's dream if you can get a bed; call in advance. The **auberge de jeunesse (HI),** 127 montée Jacques Balmat, in Les Pélerins at the base of the Glacier de Bossons, offers all-inclusive winter **ski packages** (2500-3500F per week). Take the bus from pl. de l'Eglise (dir: Les Houches) to "Pélerins Ecole" (7F) and follow the signs uphill, or take the train to "Les Pélerins" and follow the signs. (Tel. 04 50 53 14 52; fax 04 50 55 92 34. Dorms 76F; singles 98F; doubles 170F. Breakfast included. Sheets 19F. Bike rental. Reception 8am-noon, 4-7:30pm, and 8:30-10pm. V, MC.) ■**Red Mountain Lodge,** 435 rue Joseph-Vallot, is friendly and cozy. (Tel. 04 50 53 94 97. Dorms 100F; doubles and triples 120-160F. Breakfast included.) To reach the popular **Le Chamoniard Volant,** 45 rte. de la Frasse, from the station, turn right, go under the bridge, and turn right across the tracks, left on chemin des Cristalliers, and right on rte. de la Frasse. (Tel. 04 50 53 14 09; fax 04 50 53 23 25. Dorms 62F with *Let's Go*. Sheets 20F. Reception 10am-10pm.) Turn left from the base of the Aiguille du Midi *téléphérique*, continue 5min. past the main intersection, and look right to **camp** at **L'Ile des Barrats,** on rte. des Pélerins. (Tel. 04 50 53 51 44. 27F per person, 22F per tent, 12F per car. Reception May-June and Sept. 9am-noon and 4-7pm; July-Aug. 8am-noon and 2-8pm. Closed Oct.-Apr.) The **Super U,** 117 rue Joseph Vallot, has groceries. (Open M-Sa 8:15am-7:30pm, Su 8:15am-12:15pm.) **Postal code:** 74400.

⚡ **HIKING AND OUTDOORS.** Whether you've come to climb up the mountains or to ski down them, you're in for a challenge. The **Téléphérique de l'Aiguille du Midi** (tel. 04 50 53 30 80; reservations tel. 04 50 53 40 00; runs daily July-Aug. 6am-5pm; Apr.-June and Sept. 9am-3pm) offers a pricey but knuckle-whitening ascent over forests and snow-covered cliffs to a needlepoint peak at the top. The first stop isn't really worth it, but the second and last (1½hr., round-trip 180F), reveals a fantastic panorama from 3842m. If you bring your passport, you can continue by gondola to **Helbronner, Italy** for great views of three countries, the **Matterhorn,** and **Mont Blanc,** as well as the opportunity to picnic on a glacier (round-trip additional 96F). In summer, you can **hike** 2hr. to **La Mer de Glace,** a glacier that slides 30m per year. Special **trains** (tel. 04 50 53 12 54) also run from the small station next to Chamonix's main *gare* (round-trip 73F; runs May-Sept. daily 8:30am-5:30pm). A web of **hiking trails** wraps around the town. The tourist office sells a **hiking map** (25F).

Sunken in a valley, Chamonix is surrounded by skiable mountains. To the south, **Le Tour-Col. de Balme** (tel. 04 50 54 00 58), above the village of **Le Tour,** cuddles up to the Swiss border and provides sunny intermediate slopes (lift tickets 120F per day). On the northern side of the valley, **Le Brevent** (tel. 04 50 53 13 18), a proving ground for experts, has also expanded its slopes for beginners and intermediates (lift tickets 230F per day). Wherever you go, be cautious—one person a day on average dies on Chamonix's mountains.

ANNECY

With narrow cobblestoned streets, winding canals, and a turreted castle, all bordering the purest lake in Europe, Annecy appears more like a fairy-tale fabrication than a modern city. The **Palais de l'Isle** is a 12th-century fortress that originally served as home of the de l'Isle family. The grassy **Champ de Mars,** opposite the tourist office, stretches to the lake. **Plage des Marquisats,** to the south down rue des Marquisats, is a crowded beach. A 12th-century **château** is a short, steep climb from the *vieille ville.* (Open June-Aug. daily 10am-6pm; Sept.-May W-M 10am-noon and 2-

FRANCE

6pm. 30F, students 10F; grounds free.) Although it may be hard to tear yourself away from the city's cosmetic charms, a **bike ride** or **hike** through nearby Alpine forests will prove that Annecy is also a natural beauty. One of the best hikes begins at the Basilique, near the hostel. Ten kilometers west of Annecy, waterfalls roar over the cliffs of the glacier-carved **Gorges du Fier.** To get there, take the **bus** to Lovagny (10min., 3-4 per day, 12F) and walk 800m. (Open daily mid-June to Sept. 10 9am-6pm; mid-Mar. to mid-June and Sept. 11 to mid-Oct. 9am-noon and 2-5pm. 24F.)

Trains (tel. 08 36 35 35 35) arrive in Annecy from Lyon (2hr., 9 per day, 113F); Grenoble (2hr., 9 per day, 89F); Chamonix (2¼hr., 7 per day, 106F); Paris (4hr., 10 per day, 375F); and Nice (8hr., 2 per day, 352F). Voyages Frossard **buses** (tel. 04 50 45 73 90) leave from next to the station for Geneva (1hr., 6 per day, 52F) and Lyon (3hr., 2 per day, 92F). From the train station, take the underground passage to rue Vaugelas, follow the street left for four blocks, and enter the modern Bonlieu shopping mall to reach the **tourist office,** 1 rue Jean Jaurès, in pl. de la Libération. (Tel. 04 50 45 00 33; fax 04 50 51 87 20. Open daily July-Aug. 9am-6:30pm; Sept.-June M-Sa 9am-noon and 1:45-6:30pm, Su 3-6pm.) In summer, you can reach the **Auberge de Jeunesse "La Grande Jeanne" (HI),** on rte. de Semnoz, via minibus 91 (dir: Semnoz) from the station (7F); otherwise, take bus 1 (dir: Marquisats) from the station to "Hôtel de Police" and follow D41 and signs pointing to Semnoz (10min.). (Tel. 04 50 45 33 19; fax 04 50 52 77 52. 74F. Breakfast included. Sheets 17F. Kitchen. Laundry. Reception 7am-midnight. Reserve ahead.) From the station, exit left, walk around the station to av. Berthollet, and turn left again on av. de Cran to reach the **Hôtel Savoyard** at #41. (Tel. 04 50 57 08 08. Singles and doubles 100-180F.) **Camp** at 8 rte. de Semnoz, near the youth hostel. (Tel. 04 50 45 48 30; fax 04 50 45 55 56. 60F for tent and 2 people, 17F per car. Laundry. Reception Apr.-Aug. daily 8am-10pm; off-season ring the bell. V, MC. Open mid-Dec. to mid-Oct.) A **Prisunic supermarket** fills the better part of pl. de Notre-Dame. (Open M-Sa 8:30am-7:30pm.) **Postal code:** 74000.

CENTRAL FRANCE

Central France is often overlooked by tourists speeding south from Paris toward the attractions of the coasts. Thanks to the benign neglect engendered by its smokestack reputation, most of the region has escaped the deleterious effects of mass tourism; still continuing in its traditional lifestyle, it is here that cliché meets reality. With medieval abbeys, *grands vins*, outstanding cuisine, unspoiled countryside, and magnificent *châteaux*, this is France in all its preconceived glory.

LYON

France's second-largest city is second in little else. With industrial and culinary *savoir faire*, Lyon (pop. 1.5 million) has established itself as a cultural and economic alternative to Paris. Despite its historical reputation for bourgeois snobbery, Lyon is friendlier and more relaxed than Paris. And unlike so many other European cities, Lyon focuses on the present: its best art collections are contemporary, and the entire metropolis overflows with a dynamic creativity.

▐◤ GETTING THERE AND GETTING AROUND

Flights: Aéroport Lyon-Satolas (tel. 04 72 22 72 21), 25km east of Lyon. **Satobuses** (tel. 04 72 68 72 17) shuttle to Perrache, Part-Dieu, and the "Jean Mace," "Grange-Blanche," and "Mermoz Pinel" Métro stops (50min., every 20min. until 9pm, 48.50F).

Trains: Two major stations: **Perrache,** between the Saône and Rhône rivers, is more central; but more trains stop at **Part-Dieu,** in the business district on the east bank of the Rhône. TGV trains to Paris stop at both (reservations tel. 08 36 35 35 35). SNCF info and reservation desk at Perrache open M-Sa 8am-7:30pm; at Part-Dieu open M-F 9am-7pm, Sa 9am-6:30pm. To: **Paris** (2hr., 20 TGVs per day, 312-388F); **Geneva** (2hr., 8 per day, 118F); **Marseille** (3hr., 13 per day, 205F); and **Nice** (6hr., 15 per day, 299F).

FRANCE

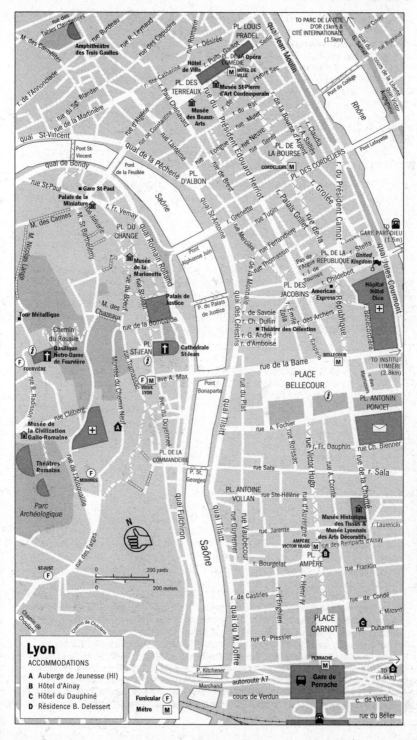

FRANCE

Lyon

ACCOMMODATIONS

A Auberge de Jeunesse (HI)
B Hôtel d'Ainay
C Hôtel du Dauphiné
D Résidence B. Delessert

Funicular Ⓕ
Métro Ⓜ

Buses: Station on the bottom floor of the **Perrache** train station. **Cars Faure** (tel. 04 78 96 11 44) goes to **Annecy** and **Grenoble.** International bus terminal across the hall.

Public Transportation: TCL (tel. 04 78 71 80 80), at both train stations and major Métro stops. **Single-fare tickets** good for 1hr. including transfers (8F per ticket; 10-ticket *carnet* 68F, students 58F). The full-day *Ticket Liberté* (24F), good for unlimited public transport, is sold at tourist and TCL offices. The Métro runs 5am-midnight. **Buses** run 5am-9pm (a few until midnight), later on theater performance nights.

Taxis: Taxi Radio de Lyon (tel. 04 72 10 86 86). Airport to either station 200-280F.

Hitchhiking: Travelers find that *autoroute* ramps to Paris are hard places to find a ride, but offer longer hauls; some find it easier to pick up a shorter ride by taking bus 2, 5, 19, 21, 22, or 31 and standing past Port Mouton at the intersection with the N6.

🛈 ORIENTATION AND PRACTICAL INFORMATION

Lyon is divided into nine **arrondissements** (districts). The **Saône** (to the west) and the **Rhône** (to the east) rivers run north-south through the city. West of the Saône, **Four-vière Hill** and its basilica overlook *vieux Lyon* (5ème). Between the two rivers lies the *centre ville*, home to the **Perrache** train station and **pl. Bellecour** (2ème) as well as the old **Terraux** neighborhood (1er); the **Croix-Rousse** (1er and 4ème) lies farther north. East of the Rhône (3ème and $6\text{-}8^{ème}$) lies the **Part-Dieu** train station (3ème), its commercial complex, and most of the city's population.

From Perrache, it's a straight shot from pl. Carnot in front of the station down rue Victor Hugo to pl. Bellecour (15min.); from Part-Dieu, exit by the fountains, turn right, turn left after three blocks on cours Lafayette, cross pont Lafayette, continue as the street changes to pl. des Cordeliers, and turn left on rue de la République, which pours into pl. Bellecour (30min.). The Métro is quicker; take line A from Perrache to "Bellecour," or take line B and transfer to A at "Part-Dieu."

Tourist Office: At Pl. Bellecour (tel. 04 72 77 69 69; fax 04 78 42 04 32), in the Pavilion, 2ème. M: Bellecour. Maps with museum listings (4F), hotel reservation office, SNCF desk, and city tours (50-60F, students 25-35F). The *Lyon City Card* (90F) grants admission to 7 museums and 1 day of public transport. Open M-Sa 10am-7pm, Su 10am-6pm. **Annex,** on av. Adolphe Max, near the cathedral, 5ème. Open mid-June to mid-Sept. M-F 9am-7pm, Sa 9am-6pm; mid-Sept. to mid-June M-F 9am-1pm and 2-6pm, Sa 9am-5pm.

Budget Travel: Wasteels (tel. 04 78 37 80 17), in Perrache's Galerie Machande. BIJ tickets. Long lines. Open M-F 9am-12:30pm and 2-6:15pm, Sa 9am-noon. V, MC.

Consulates: Canada, 21 rue Bourgelat, 2ème (tel. 04 72 77 64 07). M: Ampere. Open M-F 9am-noon. **Ireland,** 58 rue Victor Lagrange, 7ème (tel. 06 85 23 12 03). Open M-F 9am-noon. **UK,** 24 rue Childebert, 2ème (tel. 04 72 77 81 70). M: Bellecour. Open M-F 9am-12:30pm and 2-5:30pm.

English Bookstore: Eton, 1 rue du Plat, 2ème (tel. 04 78 92 92 36), between pl. Bellecour and the Saône. *Let's Go* discount 5%. Open M 2-7pm, Tu-Sa 10am-12:30pm and 2-7pm.

Laundromat: Lavadou, 19 rue Ste-Hélène, near pl. Ampère, 2ème. Open daily 7:30am-8:30pm.

Emergencies: Tel. 17. **Police:** 47 rue de la Charité (tel. 04 78 42 26 56). **Medical emergency:** tel. 15.

Medical Assistance: Hôpital Edouard Herriot, 5 pl. Arsonval (tel. 04 72 11 73 11). M: Grange Blanche. Best equipped for serious emergencies. More central is **Hôpital Hôtel-Dieu,** 1 pl. de l'Hôpital, 2ème (tel. 04 72 41 30 00), near quai du Rhône.

Post Office: (tel. 04 72 40 65 22), on pl. Antonin Poncet, 2ème, near pl. Bellecour. **Currency exchange** and **internet.** Open M-F 8am-7pm, Sa 8am-noon. M-Sa 8am-midnight, Su 8am-2pm. Address mail to be held: Angus KHAN, *Poste Restante*, pl. Antonin Poncet, **69002** Lyon, France. **Postal codes:** 69000-69009; last digit indicates *arrondissement.*

Internet Access: Station-Internet, 4 rue du President Carnot, 2ème. 50F per hr. Open M-Sa 10am-7pm. Also at the **post office** (see above).

PHONE CODE	France has no city codes. From outside France, dial int'l dialing prefix + 33 + local number (omit the first zero).

FRANCE

ACCOMMODATIONS AND CAMPING

As a financial center, Lyon has few empty beds during the work week but openings on the weekends. Off-season here is actually July and August. Inexpensive hotels cluster just east of pl. Carnot near Perrache and just north of pl. des Terreaux.

Auberge de Jeunesse (HI), 41/45 Montée du Chemin Neuf, **5ème** (tel. 04 78 15 05 50; fax 04 78 15 05 51). M: Vieux Lyon. Or walk west from pl. Bellecour, cross pont Bonaparte, turn right at pl. St-Jean and left on rue de la Bombarde, follow the hairpin left turn on Montée du Chemin Neuf, and climb for a room with a view (15min.). 71F; members only. Breakfast included. Sheets 17F. Bar, kitchen. **Internet.** Reception 24hr.

Résidence Benjamin Delessert, 145 av. Jean Jaurès, **7ème** (tel. 04 78 61 41 41; fax 04 78 61 40 24). M: Jean Macé. From Perrache, you can also take bus 11 or 39 to "J. Macé," walk under the tracks, and look left after 3 blocks. Singles 90F, with shower 95F. TV, laundry. **Internet** 60F per 100min. Reception 24hr. Reserve ahead.

Hôtel d'Ainay, 14 rue des Remparts d'Ainay, **2ème** (tel. 04 78 42 43 42; fax 04 72 77 51 90), near Perrache on top of pl. Ampère. M: Ampère-Victor Hugo. Sparkling and sunny, but somewhat bland. English spoken. Singles from 139F, with shower from 208F; doubles 175F, with shower 235F. Breakfast 25F. Shower 15F. Reception 7am-11pm. V, MC.

Hôtel du Dauphiné, 3 rue Duhamel, **2ème** (tel. 04 78 37 24 19; fax 04 78 92 81 52), near Perrache. Comfortable rooms with showers. Rooms over 205F have TV. Singles from 135F; doubles from 205F; triples from 280F; quads 300F. Breakfast 27F. Reception 24hr. V, MC.

Camping Dardilly (tel. 04 78 35 64 55), 10km from Lyon. Take bus 19 (dir: Ecully-Dardilly) from the Hôtel de Ville to "Parc d'Affaires." 60F per tent and car. Reception mid-June to mid-Sept. 8am-noon and 4-9pm; mid-Sept. to mid-June 8am-11pm. Open year-round.

FOOD

The galaxy of *Michelin* guide stars adorning Lyon's restaurants confirms the city's reputation as the culinary capital of Western civilization. Cozy *bouchons*, descendants of inns, serve *andouillettes* (sausages made of cow intestines) and other local treats in the **Terreaux** district, 1*er*, and along **rue Mercière,** 2*ème*. Finish off your dinner with *torte tatin* (think upside-down apple pie) or *cocons* (chocolates wrapped in marzipan). Ethnic restaurants cluster off **rue de la République,** 2*ème*. The market at **Les Halles,** 102 cours Lafayette, 3*ème*, counts Paul Bocuse—the culinary messiah—as well as mere mortals among its patrons. (Open Tu-Th 7am-noon and 3-7pm, F-Sa 7am-7pm, Su 7am-noon.) **Prisunic supermarket** is on rue de la République, in pl. des Cordeliers, 2*ème*. (Open M-Sa 8:30am-8:30pm.)

Chez Mounier, 3 rue des Marronniers, **2ème** (tel. 04 78 37 79 26). This tiny place satisfies a discriminating local clientele with generous traditional specialties. 4-course *menus* 59-93F. Open Tu-Sa noon-2pm and 7-10:30pm, Su noon-2pm.

Comptoir du Bœuf, 3 pl. Neuve St-Jean, **5ème** (tel. 04 78 92 82 35). *Lyonnais* cuisine with an unusually light, imaginative twist. Specialties include lamb sautéed in ginger chutney. *Menus* 89-119F. Open daily noon-2pm and 7pm-midnight. V, MC.

L'Acteur, 5 Charles Dullin, **2ème** (tel. 04 78 92 88 53). Innovative, delicious French cuisine. Menu changes frequently, but recent features include rabbit pâté and smoked salmon salad. Lunch *menu* 75F; dinner from 82F. Open M-Sa noon-2pm and 7-11pm. V, MC.

Chabert et Fils, 11 rue des Marronniers, **2ème** (tel. 04 78 37 01 94). One of the better known *bouchons* in Lyon. *Museau de bœuf* (snout of cattle) and *andouillettes* make it to the 99F *menu*. Lunch *menus* 61-71F. Open daily noon-2pm and 7-11pm. V, MC.

Chez Carlo, 22 rue du Palais Grillet, **2ème** (tel. 04 78 42 05 79). Locals call it the best pasta and pizza in town (40-55F). Open Tu-Sa noon-2pm and 7-11pm, Su noon-2pm. V, MC.

SIGHTS

VIEUX LYON. (M: Vieux Lyon.) Along the Saône at the bottom of the Fourvière Hill, the cobblestoned streets of *vieux Lyon* are lined with lively cafés and magnificent medieval and Renaissance townhouses. The most distinguishing features of the townhouses are the *traboules*, decorated tunnels that lead from the street through

FRANCE

a maze of courtyards (peek in for a look). Colorful *hôtels particuliers*, with delicate carvings, shaded courtyards, and ornate turrets, are the result of wealth accrued from the silk and publishing industries over 400 years. The 12th-century **Cathédrale St-Jean** is where Henri IV met and married Marie de Médici in 1600. *(On pl. St-Jean. Open M-F 8am-noon and 2-7:30pm, Sa-Su 2-5pm. Free.)*

FOURVIÈRE AND ROMAN LYON. *(M: Fourvière.)* From the corner of rues du Bœuf and de la Bombarde, northwest of the cathedral, ascend the stairs and then follow the rose-lined **chemin de la Rosarie** up the **Fourvière Hill,** the nucleus of Roman Lyon. You can also take the **funiculaire** (runs until 10pm; 8F) from the head of av. Max, off pl. St-Jean, to the top of the hill. From there you can admire the view from the **Esplanade Fourvière,** where a model of the cityscape points out local landmarks. Behind the Esplanade is the **Basilique Notre-Dame de Fourvière,** with multicolored mosaics, gilded pillars, and elaborate carvings. If you walk left down the hill as you exit the church, you'll see signs for the **Musée Gallo-Romain,** which displays mosaics, helmets, swords, jewelry, and a bronze tablet inscribed with a speech by Lyon native Emperor Claudius. *(17 rue Cléberg. Open W-Su 9:30am-noon and 2-6pm. 20F, students 10F.)* Next door in the **Parc Archéologique** is the 2000-year-old **Théâtre Romain** and the smaller **Odeon,** still used during the festival *Nuits de Fourvière*. *(Park open daily Apr. 15-Sept. 15 7am-9pm; Sept. 16-Apr. 14 7am-7pm. Free.)*

LE PRESQU'ÎLE AND LES TERREAUX. Monumental squares, statues, and fountains are the trademarks of the **Presqu'île,** the lively area between the Rhône and the Saône. The heart of the area is **place Bellecour,** a barren expanse of red gravel fringed with shops and flower stalls and crowned by an equestrian statue of Louis XIV. The movie theaters, FNAC, and rushing crowds along **rue de la République,** which runs north from pl. Bellecour, establish the street as the urban aorta of Lyon. It terminates at **pl. Louis Pradel** in the 1er, at the tip of the **Terreaux** district. Opposite the spectacular 17th-century **Hôtel de Ville** (town hall), on pl. Louis Pradel, stands the **Musée des Beaux-Arts,** with a collection of French paintings, works by Spanish and Dutch masters, an Italian Renaissance wing, and a sculpture garden. *(On pl. des Terreaux. Open M 1-6pm, W-Su 10:30am-noon and 1:05-6pm. 25F, students 13F.)*

LA CROIX-ROUSSE AND THE SILK INDUSTRY. Historically, Lyon dominated the European silk industry, and by the 18th century, 28,000 looms operated in the city, mainly in the **Croix-Rousse** district on a hill in the 1er. Although the silk industry is now based elsewhere, namely China, an extraordinary collection of silk and embroidery remains at the **Musée Historique des Tissus.** *(34 rue de la Charité. Open Tu-Su 10am-5:30pm. 30F, students 15F.)* **La Maison des Canuts** (silk workers) demonstrates the weaving techniques of the *canuts Lyonnais*. *(10-12 rue d'Ivry, 4ème. Open M-F 8:30am-noon and 2-6:30pm, Sa 9am-noon and 2-6pm. 20F, students 15F.)*

EAST OF THE RHÔNE AND MODERN LYON. The **Centre d'Histoire de la Résistance et de la Déportation** has documents, photos, and films of the Lyon-based resistance to the Nazis. *(14 av. Bertholet, 7ème. From Perrache, walk east over pont Gallieni; or take bus 11, 26, 32, or 39. Open W-Su 9am-5:30pm. 25F, students 15F.)* The **Musée d'Art Contemporain,** in the futuristic Cité Internationale de Lyon, has an extensive collection. *(On quai Charles de Gaulle, 6ème. M: Masséna or bus 4. Open W-Su noon-7pm. 25F, students 13F.)* The Cité is a sight itself; the super-modern complex houses offices, shops, theaters, and—don't jaywalk—Interpol's world headquarters. Far to the north lies the massive **Parc de la Tête d'Or,** a 1.05 sq. km park with a zoo, botanical garden, and beautiful rose garden. *(Open daily Apr.-Sept. 6am-11pm; Oct.-Mar. 6am-9pm.)*

ENTERTAINMENT AND NIGHTLIFE

THEATER AND FILM. Lyon's major theater is the **Théâtre des Célestins,** 4 rue Charles Pullin, 2ème. (Tel. 04 78 42 17 67. 65-250F.) The **Opéra,** on pl. de la Comédie, 1er (tel. 04 72 00 45 45), sells last-minute student tickets (50F) 15min. before shows. Lyon, where the Lumière brothers filmed the world's first moving picture, is still a superb place to see quality film. The **Cinéma Opéra,** 6 rue J. Serlin (tel. 04 78 28 80 08), and **Le Cinéma,** 18 impasse St-Polycarpe (tel. 04 78 39 09 72), show black-and-white oldies, all in *v.o.* (original language; 34-40F). For the avant-garde (44F), try **CNP Terreaux Cinéma,** 40 rue Président Edouard Herriot, 1*er* (tel. 04 78 27 26 25).

FESTIVALS. In summer, Lyon bursts with festivals and special events. Highlights are the **Fête de la Musique** (June 21), when performers take over the city streets, and the **Bastille Day** celebration (July 14). In September and October of even-numbered years (like 2000), Lyon erupts with **Biénniale de la Danse Lyon,** at Maison de Lyon, in pl. Bellecour, 2*ème*, which draws modern-dance performers from around the world. (Tel. 04 72 41 00 00. Tickets 40-240F.) **Les Nuits de Fourvière** is a two-month summer festival held in the ancient Théâtre Romain, featuring both pop and classical concerts and plays. (Buy tickets at the FNAC shop on rue de la République.)

NIGHTLIFE. Nightlife in Lyon is fast and furious. Pound 10F tequilas with the crowd at **L'Abreuvoir,** 18 rue Ste-Catherine. (Open Su-Th 6pm-1am, F-Sa 6pm-2am.) **Le Chantier,** 20 rue Ste-Catherine, is a bit classier; slip down the spiral slide to reach the dance floor downstairs. (Live music W-Sa. Nominal cover. Open M-Sa 7:30pm-3am.) The city's best and most accessible late-night spots are a strip of **riverboat dance clubs** by the east bank of the Rhône. **Le Fish,** opposite 21 quai Augagneur, has theme nights with salsa, jungle, house, and disco in a swank floater. (60-80F includes 1 drink; free before 10pm. Open Th 7pm-4:30am, F-Sa 10pm-6am.) Next door, **La Marquise** draws big-name DJs for jungle and house. (Occasional 30-40F cover. Open W-Sa 10:30pm-dawn.) For gay spots, try the 1*er*, where a mixed gay and lesbian crowd schmoozes over drinks at **Le Verre à Soi,** 25 rue des Capucins. (Drinks half-price until 8pm. Open M-F 11am-3am, Sa 5pm-3am.)

BURGUNDY (BOURGOGNE)

Drunk on the power of their Duchy, the rulers of Burgundy made so bold as to challenge the French monarchy during the 15th century. Shifting alliances during the Hundred Years' War brought them lands as far north as the Netherlands, but Louis XI took advantage of the death of the last duke, Charles the Bold, to annex Burgundy to France. Today, Burgundy's fame rests on more peaceful foundations, as the home of some of the world's finest wines. Even cheaper wines can be superb, and dishes like *coq au vin* and *bœuf bourguinon* have made this region a capital in the hearts of Epicureans both in France and elsewhere.

DIJON

Dijon (pop. 160,000) is renowned for its snobbery in France, and for its mustard everywhere else. The city is also richly endowed with late medieval and early modern architecture, myriad museums, a marvelous culinary tradition, and fine wines. The diverse **Musée des Beaux-Arts** occupies the east wing of the colossal **Palais des Ducs de Bourgogne,** in pl. de la Libération at the center of the *vieille ville.* (Open W-M 10am-6pm. 22F, students free; Su free for all.) At the **Eglise Notre-Dame,** in pl. Notre-Dame, admire the façade of gargoyles and rub the owl on the left side of the exterior for good luck. The Renaissance façade of the **Eglise St-Michel,** in pl. St-Michel, has been beautifully restored. The brightly tiled **Cathédrale St-Bénigne,** in (surprise) pl. St-Bénigne, has a spooky circular crypt (7F). Next door, in the cloisters of the cathedral's former monastery, the **Musée Archéologique,** 5 rue Dr. Maret, features Gallo-Roman sculpture and neolithic housewares. (Open June-Sept. W-M 9:30am-6:30pm; Oct.-May W-M 9am-noon and 2-6pm. 14F, students 7F; Su free.) A trip to the **Grey Poupon** store, 32 rue de la Liberté, where *moutarde au vin* has been made since 1777, should be more than a mere condiment to any Dijon excursion.

Trains chug to Lyon (1½hr., 9 per day, 132F) and Paris (1¾hr., 12 per day, 222F). The **tourist office,** on pl. Darcy, is a straight shot down av. Maréchal Foch from the station (5min.). (Tel. 03 80 49 11 44. Open daily July-Aug. 9am-8pm; Sept.-June 9am-7pm.) Check **email** at **Station Internet,** in the bus station next to the train station. (Open M-F noon-8pm, Sa noon-5pm. 40F per hr.) Students can call CROUS (tel. 03 80 40 40 40) for info on **university housing.** To get to the huge **auberge de jeunesse (HI),** 1 av. Champollion, take bus 5 (bus A at night; dir: Epirey) from pl. Grangier to

FRANCE

"Epirey." (Tel. 03 80 72 95 20; fax 03 80 70 00 61. Dorms 52F; singles 130F; doubles and triples 144F. Reception 24hr.) **Hôtel Montchapet**, 26-28 rue Jacques Cellerier, north of av. Première Armée Française off Pl. Darcy, is spotless. (Tel. 03 80 53 95 00; fax 03 80 58 26 87. Singles 150-215F; doubles 230-235F; triples 320F; quads 370F. Breakfast 32F. Reception 6am-midnight. V, MC, AmEx.) **Rues Berbisey** and **Monge** host a wide variety of low- to mid-priced restaurants. Get your Grey Poupon fix at the **supermarket** downstairs in the **Galeries Lafayette**, 41 rue de la Liberté. (Open M-Sa 9am-7:15pm.) **Postal code:** 21000 (21031 for *Poste Restante*).

🖪 **EXCURSIONS FROM DIJON: BEAUNE AND CLUNY.** The well-touristed town of **Beaune**, just south of Dijon on the Lyon rail line (25min., 21 per day, 38F), has poured out wine for centuries. Surrounded by the famous Côte de Beaune vineyards, the town itself is packed with wineries offering free *dégustations* (tastings). The largest of the cellars belongs to **Patriarche Père et Fils**, 5-7 rue du Collège; stairs descend from the altar of an 18th-century chapel to a labyrinth of 5km of corridors packed with ten million bottles. (Tel. 03 80 24 53 78. Open daily 9:30-11:30am and 2-5:30pm. 50F.) The **tourist office**, on rue de l'Hôtel-Dieu, lists *caves* in the region offering tours. (Tel. 03 80 26 21 30; fax 03 80 26 21 39. Open mid-June to mid-Sept. M-Sa 9am-8pm, Su 9am-7pm; mid-Sept. to mid-June M-Sa 9am-8pm, Su 9am-6pm.)

   Cluny (pop. 5000) has not grown since the abbey controlled 10,000 monks, 1200 monasteries, 11 popes, and a few kings in the Middle Ages before succumbing to the blows of the Reformation and Revolution. The **Musée d'Art et d'Archéologie** houses a reconstruction of the abbey and some religious art which escaped destruction. (Tel. 03 85 59 23 97. Open July-Aug. 9am-7pm., Sept.-June 10am-noon and 2-6pm. 32F, under 25 21F.) The Romanesque abbey church, **Cluny III**, is the third church on the site and was the largest in the world until the construction of St. Peter's in Rome. A mental reconstruction of its scale requires some effort, but its wealth can still be easily glimpsed in the ornamentation of the façade. To get to Cluny, take the **train** to Mâcon from Dijon (1¼hr., 6 per day, 94F) or **Lyon** (1hr., 13 per day, 61F), and transfer to the SNCF **bus** (40min., 5 per day, 25F).

SEMUR-EN-AUXOIS

Legend attributes Semur-en-Auxois' founding to Hercules. Often called the "Athens of Burgundy," the *vieille ville*'s stunning towers and ramparts crown this unspoiled regional treasure of cobblestones and archways that overlook the Armençon river. Deep in the medieval town, down rue Buffon, gargoyles sneeringly menace the eastern *place* from the 15th-century façade of the **Collégiale Notre-Dame**. Facing rue Notre-Dame is the 13th-century tympanum on the **porte des Bleds**; on the left pillar, two sculpted snails slime their slippery way to the feet of St. Thomas—*escargot* zealously seeking divine intervention from their likely fate as a buttery, garlicky *entrée*. (Open in summer 9am-noon and 2-6pm; off-season closes 5pm.) The mighty, noble **Tour de l'Orle d'Or**, along the castle walls, has a collection on the medieval history of Semur. (Open daily in July-Aug. 10am-6pm. 10F.)

   TRANSCO **buses** (tel. 03 80 42 11 00) go to Dijon (1½hr., 1-3 per day, 58.80F). The **tourist office**, on pl. Gaveau, is by the gates of the old town. (Tel. 03 80 97 05 96. Open mid-June to mid-Sept. M-Sa 9am-9pm, Su 10am-noon and 3-6pm; mid-Sept. to mid-June M-Sa 8:30am-noon and 2-6:30pm.) The **Foyer des Jeunes Travailleurs**, 1 rue du Champ de Foire, is off rue de la Liberté about 300m away from the tourist office. (Tel. 03 80 97 10 22; fax 03 80 97 36 97. 100F. Breakfast 10F, meals 48F. Reception M-F 9am-8pm, Sa-Su 11am-2pm and 6-8pm.) **Camping Municipal du Lac de Pont** is 3km south of Semur on a scenic lake with a beach, with a laundry and minimart. (Tel. 03 80 97 01 26. 20F per person, 10F per site, 8F per car. Electricity 13F. Reception 9am-noon and 4-8pm. Open May-Sept. 15.) For **groceries**, head a few blocks down rue de la Liberté to **Intermarché**, on av. du Général Maziller. (Open M-Th 9am-12:15pm and 2:30-7:15pm, F 9am-7:45pm, Sa 9am-7:15pm.)

FRANCE

BOURGES

In 1433, Jacques Coeur, financial minister to Charles VII, chose Bourges (pop. 76,000) as the site for one of his many *châteaux*. In 45 minutes, you'll see more of the unfurnished **Palais Jacques-Coeur** than he ever did; he was imprisoned years before its completion. (Tours in French roughly every hr. from 9:15am; last tour July-Aug. 6:10pm; Apr.-June and Sept. 5:10pm; Oct.-Mar. 4:10pm. 32F, ages 18-24 21F. English text available.) The **Cathédrale St-Etienne,** across town near the tourist office, is graced with stunning 13th-century handiwork in the cathedral, **tower,** and **crypt,** including a dramatic Gothic façade and bright stained-glass windows. (Open daily July-Aug. 8am-9pm, June and Sept. 8:30am-7:30pm; Oct.-May 8:30am-6:30pm. Combined ticket for all three 30F.) As you exit the cathedral, head right on rue des 3 Maillets and turn left on rue Molière to find the intimate **promenade des Remparts,** between rues Bourbonnoux and Molière, which offers a quiet stroll past Roman ramparts and flower-filled back gardens.

Trains leave for Tours (1½hr., 15 per day, 123F) and Paris (2½hr., 4 per day, 153F). Follow av. H. Laudier (which turns into av. Jean Jaurès) from the station, bear left onto rue du Commerce, and continue straight on rue Moyenneto to reach the **tourist office,** 21 rue Victor Hugo (15min.). (Tel. 02 48 23 02 60; fax 02 48 23 02 69. Open July-Sept. M-Sa 9am-7:30pm, Su 10am-7:30pm; Oct.-June M-Sa 9am-6pm, Su 10am-12:30pm.) To get to the **auberge de jeunesse (HI),** 22 rue Henri Sellier, follow the above directions to rue du Commerce, then bear right on rue des Arènes (which becomes rue Fernault), cross at the intersection to rue René Ménard and follow it to the right, and turn left at rue Henri Sellier (25min.). (Tel. 02 48 24 58 09. 49F. Reception M-F 8am-noon and 2-11pm, Sa-Su 8am-noon and 5-10pm.) To reach the skateboard mecca of Europe, otherwise known as the **Centre International de Séjour, "La Charmille,"** 17 rue Félix-Chédin, cross the footbridge from the station over the tracks and head up rue Félix-Chédin (5min.). (Tel. 02 48 23 07 40. Singles 99F; for three or more people 73F per person.) Outdoor tables pack **pl. Gordaine** and **rue des Beaux-Arts,** and sandwich shops line **rues Moyenne** and **Mirebeau.** The huge **E. Leclerc** **supermarket** is on rue Prado off bd. Juraville. (Open M-F 9:15am-7:20pm, Sa 8:30am-7:20pm.) For late-night relaxing, try the pedestrian core of the *centre ville.* **Postal code:** 18000 (18012 "Bourges Cedex" for *Poste Restante*).

EASTERN FRANCE

Commonly ignored by travelers except as a rest stop between France and the rest of Europe, the "frontier regions" of the northeast represent the last outpost of French tourism. Sprawling clockwise from the Chunnel terminus to the mountainous Swiss border, the regions of Flanders, Champagne, Alsace, Lorraine, and Franche-Comté have been memorialized as battlefields since the Middle Ages, and for many travelers the northeast is of interest for primarily historical reasons. Yet the fields and cellars of Champagne, the wine towns surrounding Strasbourg, and the splendid hiking trails in the Jura mountains suggest other motives for visiting the area. Furthermore, the bloody history of these regions has done more than leave behind solemn monuments—it has left behind a culturally independent region, as fascinating as any in France.

ALSACE, LORRAINE, AND FRANCHE-COMTÉ

Heavily influenced by its tumultuous history, the northeastern frontier of France has been defined by its place as the prize in the ceaseless border wars between France and Germany. The entire region maintains a fascinating blend of local dialects, cuisine, and architecture. Germanic influences are most apparent in its cuisine, which pairs baguettes and fine wine with sauerkraut and heavy German meats, bringing an element of heartiness to traditional delicacies.

FRANCE

STRASBOURG

Just a few kilometers from the Franco-German border, Strasbourg (pop. 260,000) has spent much of its history being annexed by one side or another. Today the city is seen as a symbol of French-German détente: German is heard on its streets almost as often as French, and as many *winstubs* line its squares as *pâtisseries*. Strasbourg is also joint center of the European Union, along with Brussels. With half-timbered houses and flower-lined canals, the city makes a fantastic stopover.

🛈 🍴 **PRACTICAL INFO, ACCOMMODATIONS, AND FOOD.** Strasbourg is a major European rail hub. **Trains** (tel. 03 88 22 50 50) go to Germany's Black Forest; Luxembourg City (2½hr., 6 per day, 167F); Frankfurt (3hr., 12 per day, 237F); Zurich (3hr., 12 per day, 265F); and Paris (4hr., 16 per day, 235F). The **tourist office,** 17 pl. de la Cathédrale, has maps (3-24F) and makes hotel reservations (10F). (Tel. 03 88 52 28 28. Open June-Sept. M-Sa 9am-7pm, Su 9am-6pm; Oct.-May daily 9am-6pm.) You can rent **bikes** at **Vélocation,** at the train station. (Tel. 03 88 21 06 38. 20F per half-day, 30F per day.) Hop on the **internet** at **Le Midi-Minuit,** 5 pl. de Corbeau. (30F per 30min. Open, oddly enough, M-W 7am-7pm, Th-Sa 7am-10pm, Su 8am-7pm.)

Make reservations or arrive early to find reasonable accommodations. **CIARUS (Centre International d'Accueil de Strasbourg),** 7 rue Finkmatt, boasts sparkling rooms, a social atmosphere, a TV, and **internet** access. From the station, take rue du Maire-Kuss to the canal, turn left, and follow quais St-Jean, Kléber, and rue Fink-matt; turn left on rue Finkmatt, and it's on the left (15min.). (Tel. 03 88 15 27 88; fax 03 88 15 27 89; email ciarus@media-net.fr. Dorms 92-124F; singles 206F. Breakfast 20F. Reception 24hr. Check-in 3:30pm. Check-out 9am. Curfew 1am. V, MC, AmEx.) **Auberge de Jeunesse René Cassin (HI),** 9 rue de l'Auberge de Jeunesse, 2km from the station, has clean but slightly worn rooms in a beautiful setting. From the station, go up rue de Maire-Kuss, turn right on quai St-Jean (which becomes quai Altoffer), and turn right on rue Ste-Marguerite to get to the bus station. From "Ste-Marguerite," take bus 3 (dir: Holtzheim-Entzheim Ouest) or 23 (dir: Illkirch) to "Auberge de Jeunesse." (Tel. 03 88 30 26 46; fax 03 88 30 35 16. Dorms 73F; singles 149F; doubles 200F; nonmembers add 19F per person. Sheets for dorms only 18F. Camping 42F. Breakfast included. Reception 7am-12:30pm, 1:30-7:30pm, and 8:30-11pm. Curfew 1am. Open Feb.-Dec.) **Hôtel Michelet,** 48 rue du Vieux Marché aux Poissons, around the corner from the cathedral, has tidy rooms. (Tel. 03 88 32 47 38. Singles 145-210F; doubles 170-255F. Breakfast 25F. Reception 7am-8pm. V, MC.)

Winstubs are informal places traditionally affiliated with wineries that serve Alsatian specialties such as *choucroute garnie* (spiced sauerkraut served with meats)—look in the **La Petite France** neighborhood, especially along rue des Dentelles and petite rue des Dentelles. Try **pl. de la Cathédrale, rue Mercière,** or **rue du Vieil Hôpital** for restaurants, and **pl. Marché Gayot,** hidden off rue des Frères, for lively cafés. For **groceries,** swing by the **ATAC Supermarket,** 47 rue des Grandes Arcades, off pl. Kléber. (Open M-Sa 8:30am-8pm.) **Poêles de Carottes,** 18 rue de la Krutenau, has tempting vegetarian options. (Lunch *menu* 50F; dinner *menu* 98F. Open M-Sa noon-2:30pm and 7-10:30pm. V, MC.) **Postal code:** 67000 (67074 for *Poste Restante*).

📷 🎭 **SIGHTS AND ENTERTAINMENT.** The ornate, Gothic **Cathédrale de Strasbourg** sends its tower 142m skyward. Inside, the **Horloge Astronomique** demonstrates the wizardry of 16th-century Swiss clockmakers. While you wait for the clock to strut its stuff—apostles troop out of the clockface while a cock crows to greet St. Peter (daily at 12:30pm)—check out the **Pilier des Anges** (Angels' Pillar), a masterpiece of Gothic sculpture. You can climb the **tower** in front of the clock to follow in the footsteps of young Goethe, who scaled its 330 steps regularly to cure his fear of heights. (Cathedral open M-Sa 7-11:45am and 12:45-7pm, Su 12:45-6pm. Tickets for the clock go on sale at 11:30am at the south entrance; 5F. Tower open daily 9am-6:30pm; 20F.) **Palais Rohan,** 2 pl. du Château, houses a trio of small museums: the **Musée des Beaux-Arts, Musée des Arts Décoratifs,** and **Musée Archéologique** (20F each; combined ticket for all three 40F, students 20F). Next door, **Maison de l'Oeuvre Notre-Dame,** 3 pl. du Château, houses some of the cathedral's statues and reconstructed stained glass. (Open Tu-Sa 10am-noon and 1:30-6pm, Su 10am-5pm. 20F, students 10F.) Take bus 23, 30, or 72 to "L'Orangerie" to see, predictably, **l'Orange-**

rie, Strasbourg's largest park, designed by Le Notre after cutting his teeth on Versailles; there are free concerts in summer (Th-Tu 8:30pm) at the Pavillion Josephine. Across the canal from La Petite France, the spectacular collection of the new **Musée d'Art Moderne et Contemporain**, 1 pl. Hans Jean Arp, ranges from Impressionist to avant garde (30F, students 20F).

LA ROUTE DU VIN

Since the High Middle Ages, the wines of Alsace have been highly prized—and highly priced—across Europe. The vineyards of Alsace flourish along a corridor of 170km known as La Route du Vin (Wine Route) that begins at **Strasbourg** and stretches south along the foothills of the Vosges, passing through (from north to south) Molsheim, Obernai, Barr, Sélestat, Kintzheim, Riquewihr, Kaysersberg, Colmar, Eguisheim, and Guebwille along the way to **Mulhouse**. Hordes of tourists are drawn each year to explore the beautifully preserved medieval villages along the route—and, of course, for the free *dégustations* (tastings) along the way.

Colmar and Sélestat offer excellent bases and fascinating sights of their own; but don't miss out on smaller, less-touristed villages. The most accessible towns from Strasbourg are **Molsheim**, a medieval university center, and **Barr**, with an intricate old town and a vineyard trail that leads up through the hills. The more famous towns lie to the south: the most visited sight in Alsace, the **Château de Haut Koenigsbourg**, towers over **Kintzheim**; and the 16th-century walled hamlet of **Riquewihr**, the Route's most touristed village, is home to many of Alsace's best-known wine firms.

If you're in Strasbourg and are contemplating a detour along the Wine Route, drop by the **Departmental Tourist Office**, 9 rue du Dôme, for more info. (Tel. 03 88 15 45 80. Open M 10am-noon and 2-6pm, Tu-F 9:30am-noon and 2-6pm, Sa 10am-1pm and 2-6pm.) Great info on regional *caves* can be found in Colmar at the **Centre d'Information du Vin d'Alsace**, 12 av. de la Foire aux Vins (tel. 03 89 20 16 20; fax 03 89 20 16 30), at the Maison du Vin d'Alsace.

🗲 GETTING THERE AND GETTING AROUND. Strasbourg, the northern terminus of the Wine Route, is a major rail hub, easily accessible from France, Germany, and Luxembourg. Trains from Strasbourg hit many of the towns along the northern half of the Route, including **Molsheim** (20min., 21F); **Barr** (45min., 33F); and **Sélestat** (30min., 41F). If you're short on time, you can go directly from Strasbourg to **Colmar** (30min., 57F), although wine lovers are more likely to get there via train from Sélestat (20min., 24F). **Bus** lines pepper the southern half of the Route, running from Colmar to **Kaysersberg** (30min., 14 per day, 12F60); **Riquewihr** (30min., 6 per day, 15-20F); and many other small towns on the Route. Trains from Colmar run south to **Mulhouse** (30min., 41F), the southern terminus of the Route. From Mulhouse, leap into Switzerland from nearby **Basel** (30min., 6 per day, 83F); hop over the border to **Freiburg**, a perfect gateway into Germany's Black Forest (see p. 430); return to Strasbourg (1hr., 22 per day, 81F); or go to Paris (4½hr., 9 per day, 260F).

Bus tours of the region are also available; try **Astra** between April and October (tel. 03 88 21 52 40; departs Sa 9am; 160F). For the experienced, **biking** is a viable option as trails and turn-offs are well-marked, although the many rolling hills can be tiring.

SÉLESTAT. Sélestat (pop. 17,200), an imperial city of the German Empire from the year 1217 and a center of humanism in the 15th century, has avoided the touristed fate of larger towns such as Colmar and Strasbourg. Founded in 1452, the **Bibliothèque Humaniste**, 1 rue de la Bibliothèque, contains a fascinating collection of ancient documents, including the 16th-century *Cosmographie Introductio*, the first book to call the New World "America." (Tel. 03 88 92 03 24. Open July-Aug. M and W-F 9am-noon and 2-6pm, Sa-Su 2-7pm; Sept.-June closed Sa-Su. 20F.) The **tourist office**, 10 bd. Gén. Leclerc, in the Commanderie St-Jean, has good, free maps and rents **bikes** (35F per 2hr., 50F per half-day, 80F per day). (Tel. 03 88 58 87 20; fax 03 88 92 88 63; www.ville-selestat.fr. Open May-Sept. M-F 9am-12:30 pm and 1:30-7pm, Sa 9am-noon and 2-5pm, Su 9am-3pm.) The **Hôtel de l'Ill**, 13 rue des Bateliers, off bd. des Thiers, has cheerful rooms in a lovely white stucco building. (Tel. 03 88 92 91 09. Singles 150F; doubles 180-240F; triples 350F. Breakfast 28F. Reception daily 7am-10pm. V, MC, AmEx.) **Camping Les Cigognes** is outside the ramparts on the

FRANCE

south edge of the *vieille ville*. (Tel. 03 88 92 03 98. 15.30F per person, 15.30F per site. Reception 7:30am-noon and 2-10pm.) For tasty treats try **rue des Chevaliers** and **rue de l'Hôpital. Postal code:** 67600.

COLMAR. Colmar (pop. 65,000) derives its name from the *colombes* (doves) Charlemagne kept at his estate along the Lauch river. The town teems with packs of tourists in summer, but its crooked lanes and pretty pastel houses manage to retain a measure of untouched, bucolic charm. The collection is at the **Musée Unterlinden,** 1 rue d'Unterlinden, ranges from Romanesque to Renaissance—its crown jewel, Grünewald's *Issenheim Altarpiece*, justifies a visit in itself. (Open Apr.-Oct. daily 9am-6pm; Nov.-Mar. W-M 10am-5pm. 35F, students 25F.) The **Eglise des Dominicains,** on pl. des Dominicains, houses Colmar's other major masterpiece, Schongauer's *Virgin in the Rose Bower*. (Open daily 10am-12:45pm and 3-5:45pm. 8F, students 6F.) A friendly welcome and a great selection of local wines await at **Robert Karcher et Fils,** 11 rue de l'Ours, in the *vieille ville*. (Tel. 03 89 41 14 42. White wines 26-200F per bottle, reds from 50F. Open daily 8am-noon and 2-7pm.)

To get to the **tourist office,** 4 rue des Unterlinden, from the train station, turn left on av. de la République (which becomes rue Kléber) and follow it to the right to pl. Unterlinden. (Tel. 03 89 20 68 92; email accueil@ot-colmar.fr. Open July-Aug. M-Sa 9am-7pm, Su 9:30am-2pm; Apr.-June and Sept.-Oct. M-Sa 9am-6pm, Su 10am-2pm; Nov.-Mar. M-Sa 9am-noon and 2-6pm, Su 10am-2pm.) To reach the **auberge de jeunesse (HI),** 2 rue Pasteur, take bus 4 (dir: Logelbach) to "Pont Rouge." (Tel. 03 89 80 57 39. Dorms 68F; singles 92F; doubles 184F. Members only. Breakfast included. Sheets 20F. Lockout 9am-5pm. Curfew midnight. Reception 7-10am and 5pm-midnight. Open mid-Jan. to mid-Dec.) Take bus 1 (dir: Horbourg-Wihr) to "Plage d'Ill" for **Camping de l'Ill,** on rte. Horbourg-Wihr. (Tel. 03 89 41 15 94. 17F per person, 20F per site, 10F per tent. Reception M-F 7am-9pm, Sa-Su 8am-9pm. Open May-Sept.) Stock up at **Monoprix supermarket,** on pl. Unterlinden. (Open M-F 8:30am-8:25pm, Sa 8am-7:55pm.) *Brasseries* with canal-side terraces abound in **La Petite Venise** and the **Quartier des Tanneurs. Postal code:** 68000.

MULHOUSE. If Colmar constitutes the heart of Alsace and Strasbourg serves as the mind, then prosperous Mulhouse (pop. 110,000) provides the muscle. The town's industrial heritage has endowed it with a host of first-rate museums, including the **Musée Français du Chemin de Fer,** 2 rue Alfred de Glehn, which has a stunning collection of gleaming engines and railway cars. (Open daily Apr.-Sept. 9am-6pm, Oct.-Mar. 9am-5pm. 45F, students 20F, children 10F.) The **tourist office,** 9 av. Foch, is two blocks from the train station. (Tel. 03 89 35 48 48. Open July-Aug. M-Sa 9am-7pm, Su 10am-1pm; Sept.-June closed Su.) To get to the cheerful **auberge de jeunesse (HI),** 37 rue d'Ilberg, take bus 2 (bus S1 after 8:30pm; dir: Loteaux) to "Salle des Sports." (Tel. 03 89 42 63 28. 48F; members only. Breakfast 19F. Sheets 17F. Reception daily in summer 8am-noon and 4pm-midnight; off-season closes 11pm.) Hunt for inexpensive food on **rue de l'Arsenal,** or buy **groceries** at **Monoprix,** on the corner of rue du Sauvage and rue des Maréchaux. (Open M-F 8:15am-8pm, Sa 8:15am-7pm.) **Postal code:** 68100 (68074 for *Poste Restante*).

BESANÇON

Besançon (pop. 120,000) has been around since Julius Caesar founded a military post here in 58 BC. Now a university town, Besançon is a base for nearby Alpine ski slopes, *promenades* by day, and crowds into bars and sweaty discos by night.

◼◼◼◻ **PRACTICAL INFO, ACCOMMODATIONS, AND FOOD. Trains** chug to the station, on av. de la Paix (tel. 08 36 35 35 35), from Dijon (1hr., 9 per day, 73F); Paris' Gare de Lyon station (2hr., 7 per day, 263-309F); and Strasbourg (3hr., 10 per day, 180F). From the station, head downhill and cross onto Av. Marechal Foch, then continue downhill and to the left (as it becomes av. de l'Helvétie) until you reach pl. de la Première Armée Française. The *vieille ville* is across the pont de la République; the **tourist office,** 2 pl. de la 1ère Armée Française, is in the park to the right. (Tel. 03 81 80 92 55; fax 03 81 80 58 30; www.besancon.com. Open Apr.-Sept. M 10am-7pm, Tu-Sa 9am-7pm; mid-June to mid-Sept. also Su 10am-noon and 3-

FRANCE

5pm.) Surf the **internet** at **Rom Collection,** 22 rue du Lycée. (1F per min., 50F per hr.) **Postal code:** 25000 (25031 "Besançon-Cedex" for *Poste Restante*).

To get to **Foyer Mixte de Jeunes Travailleurs (HI),** 48 rue des Cras, turn left from the station on av. de la Paix (which becomes rue de Belfort) and left again on rue Marie-Louise (which turns into rue des Cras); the hostel is uphill on the right (total 25min.). Or take bus 7 from pl. Flore off rue de Belfort on av. Carnot (dir: Orchamps; 3 per hr.) to "Oiseaux." (Tel. 03 81 40 32 00; fax 03 81 40 32 01. Singles 90F; doubles 180F. Breakfast and sheets included. Reception 9am-8pm. No reservations; arrive early.) An eclectic group of student-oriented restaurants line **rue Claude-Pouillet.** Pick up **groceries** at **Monoprix,** 12 Grande Rue. (Open M-Sa 8:30am-8pm.) ▨ **La Boîte à Sandwiches,** 21 rue du Lycée, off rue Pasteur, serves scrumptious sandwiches (11-30F) and salads (15-35F). (Tel. 03 81 81 63 23. Open M-F 11:30am-2:30pm and 6:30pm-midnight, Sa noon-2:30pm.)

⛅🖪 **SIGHTS AND ENTERTAINMENT.** The elegant Renaissance buildings gracing the *vieille ville* provide plenty of eye candy for a casual stroll around town, but the city's true delights lie high above in the **citadel,** designed by Louis XIV's architect, Vauban. It's a grueling trek uphill from town, but the view and the three museums inside are worth it. The **Musée de la Résistance et de la Déportation** chronicles the Nazi rise to power and the German occupation of France via letters, artifacts, and photographs; other sights include a natural history museum, a zoo, and a folk arts museum. Access to the first level, including manicured lawns and a breathtaking panorama, is free. (At the end of rue des Fusilles de la Résistance. Tel. 03 81 65 07 50. Grounds open daily July-Aug. 9am-7pm, Apr.-June and Sept.-Oct. 9am-6pm, Nov.-Mar. 10am-5pm. Museums open daily in summer 9am-6pm, off-season 10am-5pm. Admission to inner fortress and all museums 40F, students 30F.) The **Cathédrale St-Jean,** perched on the hill beneath the citadel, mixes architectural styles from the 12th to the 18th centuries and is crowned by the intricate 19th-century **Horloge Astronomique** clock. (Open W-M 9am-7pm. Free. Tours of clock 15F, children 9F.) The **Musée des Beaux-Arts,** on pl. de la Révolution, houses an exceptional collection ranging from ancient Egyptian treasures to Picassos. (Open W-M 9:30am-6pm. 21F, students free; Su and holidays free for all.) Small bars and *brasseries* line **rues Pasteur** and **Bersot.** Local students pack bars and discos into the wee hours every night of the week. Dancing queens can strut their stuff at **Le Queen,** 8 av. de Chardonnet. (Open W-Th 10:30pm-4am, F-Sa 10:30pm-5am.)

🏲 **EXCURSION FROM BESANÇON: PONTARLIER AND THE JURA.** The quiet town of **Pontarlier** (840m), makes a good base from which to reach even greater heights in the Haut-Jura mountains. The Jura are most famed for their cross-country **skiing;** over 60km of trails wind around the city (day pass 30F, under 17 20F). The closest Alpine ski area is **Le Larmont** (tel. 03 81 46 55 20). **Sport et Neige,** 4 rue de la République (tel. 03 81 39 04 69), rents skis (45F per day). In summer, **fishing, hiking,** and **mountain biking** are the sports of choice. Rent a **bike** (80F per day) from **Cycles Pernet,** 23 rue de la République. (Tel. 03 81 46 48 00. Open Tu-Sa 9am-noon and 2-7pm.) **Monts Jura buses,** 9 rue Proudhon in Besançon (tel. 03 81 39 19 54), run to Pontarlier (55min., 6 per day, 51F). The **tourist office,** 14bis rue de la Gare, has info on outdoors activities and sells hiking and topographical maps. (Tel. 03 81 46 48 33; fax 03 81 46 83 32. Maps 12-58F.) **L'Auberge de Pontarlier (HI),** 2 rue Jouffroy, is clean and central. (Tel. 03 81 39 06 57; fax 03 81 39 24 34. 49F. Breakfast 19F. Sheets 17F. Reception 8am-noon and 5:30-10pm. Reserve ahead.) **Postal code:** 25300.

NANCY

Nancy (pop. 100,000) is a model of 18th-century classicism, with broad plazas, wrought-iron grillwork, and cascading fountains. But more than just a pretty face, the city also reigns as the cultural and intellectual heart of Lorraine. The **place Stanislas** wraps Baroque gilded-iron arms around a statue of the "Good Duke" Stanislas Lesczynski, a dethroned Polish king relocated to Lorraine by his son-in-law Louis XV. The **Musée des Beaux-Arts,** 3 pl. Stanislas, has an excellent collection spanning from the 14th century to the present day. (Open W-M 10:30am-6pm. 30F, students 15F; W students free.) Pass through the five-arch **Arc de Triomphe** to the

FRANCE

tree-lined pl. de la Carrière, whose northern end segues into the relaxing **Parc de la Pépinière.** The park's aromatic **Roseraie** beckons with roses from around the world.

Trains roll frequently to Metz (40min., 51F); Strasbourg (1hr., 109F); and Paris (3hr., 206F). Head left from the station and right on rue Raymond Poincaré, which leads straight to pl. Stanislas and the **tourist office.** Ask for the invaluable *Le Fil d'Ariane* guide. (Tel. 03 83 35 22 41. Open June-Sept. M-Sa 9am-7pm; Su 10am-5pm; Oct.-May M-Sa 9am-7pm, Su 10am-noon.) Access the **internet** at **Voyager** on rue St-Jean. (35F per 30min. Open M-Sa 9am-midnight, Su 2-11pm.) **Centre d'Accueil de Remicourt (HI),** 149 rue de Vandoeuvre, is in Villers-lès-Nancy, 4km away. From the station, take bus 26 (dir: Villiers Clairlieu; 2 per hr.; last bus 8pm) to "St-Fiacre"; head downhill from the stop, turn right on rue de Vandoeuvre, walk uphill, and follow the signs. (Tel. 03 83 27 73 67; fax 03 83 41 41 35. Bed in a double 95F; bed in a triple or quad 80F. Members only. Breakfast included. Reception 9am-10:30pm. V, MC.) **Hôtel de l'Académie,** 7 rue des Michottes, is between the station and pl. Stanislas. (Tel. 03 83 35 52 31; fax 03 83 32 55 78. Singles 130-150F; doubles 150-180F. Breakfast 20F. Reception 24hr. V, MC.) Restaurants cluster around **rue des Maréchaux. Postal code:** 54000 (54039 "Nancy-RP" for *Poste Restante*).

METZ

Modern Metz (pronounced MEZ; pop. 200,000) reflects its mixed Franco-German parentage. The city maintains classic fountains, sculptured gardens, verdant canals, and golden cobblestoned streets without mobs of tourists. Only two other cathedrals in France have naves that soar higher than that of the **Cathédrale St-Etienne,** which dominates the pl. d'Armes. Marvel at its 6500m of stained-glass windows, including some by Marc Chagall. (Free. Tours in French May-Sept. daily 10am, 2, and 6pm; 15-25F.) At the other end of the rue des Clercs from pl. d'Armes lies the **Esplanade,** a patchwork of gardens and promenades. Down the steps from the Esplanade, shady paths wind their way through wooded parkland along the **Lac aux Cygnes.** In summer (June 18-Sept. 5), watch the brightly lit fountains dance to music from J.S. Bach to Louis Armstrong on weekends (F-Su at dusk). Afterward, teeter and sway yourself to the student-packed bars and cafés in **pl. St-Jacques.**

Trains arrive frequently from Nancy (40min., 51F); Strasbourg (1½hr., 115F); and Paris (3hr., 209F). They also hop the French border to nearby Luxembourg City (45min., 15 per day, 84F; see p. 645) and Germany's Mosel Valley (see p. 424). Head right from the station, left on rue des Augustins, straight through pl. Quartier and pl. St-Louis, left at pl. St-Simplice on the pedestrian rue de la Tête d'Or, and right on rue Fabet to reach the **tourist office,** on pl. d'Armes. (Tel. 03 87 55 53 76. Open July-Aug. M-Sa 9am-9pm, Su 10am-1pm and 2-5pm; Sept.-June M-Sa 9am-7pm.) Surf the **internet** at **Net Café,** 1-3 Rue Paul Bezanson, near the cathedral. (Students 30F per 30min. Open M-Sa 1-6pm.) Take bus 3 (dir: Metz-Nord) or 11 (dir: St-Eloy) to "Pontiffroy" to reach the well-run **auberge de jeunesse (HI),** 1 allée de Metz Plage. (Tel. 03 87 30 44 02; fax 03 87 33 19 80. 49F; members only. Breakfast 19F. Reception 7:30-10am and 5-10pm.) For the **Association Carrefour/auberge de jeunesse (HI),** 6 rue Marchant, take the minibus from the station to "Ste-Ségolène" and take a left up the hill. (Tel. 03 87 75 07 26; fax 03 87 36 71 44. Dorms 71F; singles 82F; doubles 164F. Members only. Breakfast included. Reception 24hr.) Cheap eateries cluster near the hostel on **rue du Pont des Morts** and toward the station on **rue Coisin.** The **ATAC supermarket** is in the Centre St-Jacques, off pl. St-Jacques. (Open M-Sa 8:30am-7:30pm.) **Postal code:** 57000 (57037 for *Poste Restante*).

CHAMPAGNE AND THE NORTH

John Maynard Keynes once remarked that his major regret in life was not having consumed enough champagne; a trip through the rolling vineyards and fertile plains of Champagne promises many opportunities not to repeat his mistake. The moniker *champagne* is fiercely guarded; the name can only be applied to wines made from regional grapes and produced according to a rigorous, time-honored method. Farther north, a different sparkling drink holds sway; in Flanders, by the Belgian border, beer is the order of the day, to be quaffed with lots of mussels. The northern corner of the country is the final frontier of tourist-free France, perhaps because of the scars the Channel coast bears from WWII and its aftermath. But as you flee the ferry ports, don't overlook the hidden treasures of the North, including the intriguing Flemish culture of Arras and the world-class art collections of Lille.

REIMS

Reims (pop. 185,000) delights with the bubbly champagne of its fabulous *caves* as well as the beauty of architectural masterpieces. The famed **Cathédrale de Notre-Dame,** built with golden limestone quarried in the Champagne *caves*, features a set of sea-blue stained-glass windows by Marc Chagall. (Open daily 7:30am-7:30pm. Tours July-Aug. daily 10:30am (Su 11am), 2:30, and 4:30pm; Mar.-June and Sept.-Oct. less frequently; 35F, under 26 15F.) Enter the adjacent **Palais du Tau** through the cathedral for a dazzling collection including reliquaries from as far back as Charlemagne. (Open daily July-Aug. 9:30am-6:30pm; Sept. to mid-Nov. and mid-Mar. to June 9:30am-12:30pm and 2-6pm; mid-Nov. to mid-Mar. M-F 10am-noon and 2-5pm, Sa-Su 10am-noon and 2-6pm. 32F, students 21F.) Four hundred kilometers of *crayères* (Roman chalk quarries) wind underground through the countryside around Reims, along with more recently dug tunnels sheltering bottles emblazoned with the great names of Champagne—Pommery, Piper-Heidsieck, Mumm, and Taittinger. The tourist office (see below) has a list of *caves* open to the public; many offer tours by appointment only, so call ahead. The most elegant tour is at **Pommery,** 5 pl. du Général Gouraud. (Tel. 03 26 61 62 55. By appointment Apr.-Oct. daily 10am-5:30pm; Nov.-Mar. M-F 10am-4:30pm. 40F, students 20F.) For a taste of bubbly, order a *coupe de champagne* at any bar in town (25-30F) or look for sales at wineshops (from 70F per bottle of the good stuff). **Pl. d'Erlon** is crowded with cafés and bars open until 3am; try **Jour et Nuit,** 81 pl. d'Erlon.

Trains (tel. 08 36 35 35 35) serve Paris (1½hr., 9 per day, 116F). To get to the **tourist office,** 2 rue Guillaume de Machault, from the station, follow the right-hand curve of the rotary to pl. d'Erlon, turn left on rue de Vesle, turn right on rue du Tresor, and it's on the left before the cathedral. (Tel. 03 26 77 45 25; fax 03 26 77 45 27. Open July-Aug. M-Sa 9am-8pm, Su 9:30am-7pm; Easter-June and Sept. M-Sa 9am-7:30pm, Su 9:30am-6:30pm; Oct.-Easter M-Sa 9am-6:30pm, Su 9:30am-5:30pm.) To get to the **auberge de jeunesse (HI),** on chaussée Bocquaine, from the station, cross the park, turn right on bd. Général Leclerc, cross the first bridge (pont de Vesle), and take your first left (15min.). (Tel. 03 26 40 52 60; fax 03 26 47 35 70. Singles 85F; bed in a double or triple 69F. Breakfast 15F. Reception 7am-midnight. V, MC.) **Au Bon Accueil,** 31 rue Thillois, is off pl. d'Erlon. (Singles 80-140F; doubles 120-170F. Breakfast 25F. Reception 24hr. V, MC.) **Pl. d'Erlon** brims with *boulangeries*, cheap cafés, and restaurants. **Monoprix supermarket** is at the corner of rue de Vesle and rue de Talleyrand. (Open M-Sa 8:30am-9pm.) **Postal code:** 51100.

▓ EXCURSION FROM REIMS: EPERNAY. Unlike the more metropolitan Reims, neighboring Epernay (pop. 30,000) strips away all urban distractions and devotes itself heart and soul to the production of the bubbly. **Avenue de Champagne,** one of the richest streets in the world, is distinguished by its mansions, lush gardens, and monumental champagne firms. **Moët & Chandon,** 20 av. de Champagne, produces the king of all wines: Dom Perignon. (Tel. 03 26 51 20 20. Open Mar. 15-Nov. 19 daily 9:30-11:30am and 2-4:30pm; Nov. 20-Mar. 14 closed Sa-Su. Tours 40F.) **Mercier,** 70 av. de Champagne, is the self-proclaimed most popular champagne in France, and gives fascinating 30-minute tours in roller-coaster-like cars. (Tel. 03 26 51 22 22. Open Mar.-Nov. M-Sa 9:30-11:30am and 2-4:30pm, Su 9:30-11:30am and 2-5pm; Dec.-Feb. closed Tu-W. Tours 30F.) Frequent **trains** arrive from Reims (20min., 15 per day, 33F). From the station, walk straight through pl. Mendès and one block up rue Gambetta to reach the town center at pl. de la République; from there, turn left on av. de Champagne to reach the **tourist office** and the myriad *caves*.

TROYES

Modern Troyes (pop. 60,000) bears little resemblance to its grape-crazy northern neighbors. It has no *caves*, and the downtown area's nickname—*bouchon de champagne* (champagne cork)—stems from the shape of its *vieille ville*, not the success of its wine. Medieval and Renaissance churches comprise the premier

FRANCE

attractions of the *vieille ville*. Troyes has also preserved whole tracts of 16th-century houses and spiced them up with teeming cafés and strong collections of modern art. The **Musée de l'Art Moderne**, on pl. St-Pierre, is the jewel of Troyes' crown, with over 2000 modern sculptures, drawings, and paintings by French artists, including Rodin, Degas, Courbet, Seurat, and Picasso. (Open W-M 11am-6pm. 30F, students 5F; W free.) Movie theaters, arcades, and pool halls rub elbows with chic boutiques on **rue Emile Zola.** On warm evenings, *Troyers* swarm the cafés and taverns of **rues Champeaux** and **Mole** near pl. Alexandre Israel.

Trains chug west to Paris' Est station (1½hr., 12 per day, 115F) and east to Mulhouse (3hr., 4 per day, 191F). The **tourist office,** 16 bd. Carnot, near the station, offers free walking tour maps and reserves rooms for 15F. (Tel. 03 25 82 62 70. Open M-Sa 9:30am-8:30pm, Su 10am-noon and 2-5pm.) To get to the **auberge de jeunesse (HI),** 2 rue Jules Ferry, 7km away, take bus 6 (dir: Chartreux) to the final stop; then either take bus 24 (4-5 per day) to the hostel, or ask directions for the 2.2km walk down a country road. (Tel. 03 25 82 00 65. 48F. Breakfast 20F. Sheets 17F. Kitchen. Reception 8am-10pm.) **Camping Municipal,** 2km from Troyes, has showers, laundry, and TV. Take bus 1 (dir: Pont St-Marie) and ask to be let off at the campground. (Tel. 03 25 81 02 64. 25F per person, 30F per tent or car. Open Apr. to mid-Oct.) Inviting restaurants and inexpensive *crêperies* line **rue Champeaux** in quartier St-Jean. On the other side of the *vieille ville*, reasonably priced international eateries can be found on **rue de la Cité,** near the cathedral. Try the creamy *fromage de Troyes* or the *andouillette de Troyes*, a tasty sausage. Stock up at **Prisunic supermarket,** 78 rue Emile Zola. (Open M-Sa 8:30am-8pm.) **Postal code:** 10000.

LILLE

With a rich Flemish ancestry, a duo of fine museums, and an exuberant nightlife scene, the unsullied and largely untouristed Lille (pop. 175,000) flaunts big-city charm without any big-city hassle. One of France's most respected museums, the **Musée des Beaux-Arts,** on pl. de la République (M: République), boasts an encyclopedic collection of 15th- to 20th-century French and Flemish masters. (Open M 2-6pm, W-Th and Sa-Su 10am-6pm, F 10am-7pm. 30F, students 20F.) The **Musée d'Art Moderne,** 1 allée du Musée, showcases Cubist and postmodern art. (Open W-M 10am-6pm. 25F, students 15F.) The beautiful **Vieille Bourse** (Old Stock Exchange), on pl. Général de Gaulle, epitomizes the Flemish Renaissance and today houses flower and book markets. Head down rue de Paris from there to reach the 14th- to 19th-century **Eglise St-Maurice** (M: Rihour). (Open M-Sa 9am-6pm, Su 2-6pm.) After a long day, head to the pubs and bars lining **rues Solférino** and **Masséna.**

Trains leave from **Gare Lille Flandres,** on pl. de la Gare (tel. 08 36 35 35 35; M: Gare Lille Flandres), for Paris (1hr., 199F) and Brussels (1½hr., 94F). **Gare Lille Europe,** on rue le Corbusier (tel. 03 20 87 30 00; M: Gare Lille Europe), is a stopover point for **Eurostar** trains en route to London, Brussels, and Paris; it also sends TGVs to the south of France. From Gare Lille Flandres, walk straight down rue Faidherbe and left through pl. du Théâtre and pl. de Gaulle to reach the **tourist office** (M: Rihour), in Palais Rihour just beyond pl. de Gaulle. (Tel. 03 20 21 94 21. Open M 1-6pm, Tu-Sa 9:30am-6:30pm, Su 10am-noon and 2-5pm.) To reach the **auberge de jeunesse (HI),** 12 rue Malpart, from Gare Lille Flandres, head counterclockwise (left) around the station, follow rue du Molinel, turn left on rue de Paris, and take your third right. (Tel. 03 20 57 08 94; fax 03 20 63 98 93. Dorms 73F; singles 113F. Breakfast included. Sheets 18F. Reception 7am-noon and 2pm-1am. Check-out 10:30am. Curfew 2am. Open Feb.-Dec. 17.) Restaurants and cafés pepper the fashionable pedestrian area around **rue de Béthune;** try the mussels, *maroilles* cheese, or *genièvre* (juniper berry liqueur). **Monoprix supermarket** is on rue du Molinel. (Open M-Sa 8:30am-8pm.) **Postal code:** 59000 (59035 "Lille Cedex" for *Poste Restante*).

🔁 **EXCURSIONS FROM LILLE: ARRAS AND VIMY.** The town hall of **Arras** is built directly over the eerie **Les Boves tunnels,** which have sheltered medieval chalk miners and British WWI soldiers alike (ask about daily tours at the tourist office). Arras' two central squares, **Grand'Place** and **Petit'Place (pl. des Héros),** are framed by nearly identical houses; Grand'Place, flanked by Flemish façades, was once divided by barbed wire, when French and German forces occupied opposite sides during

WWI. **Trains** arrive every 45min. from Lille (54F); walk straight across pl. Foch from the station onto rue Gambetta, turn right on pedestrian rue Ronville, and turn left on rue de la Housse to reach the **tourist office**, on pl. des Héros, on the ground floor of the Hôtel de Ville. (Tel. 03 21 51 26 95. Open May-Sept. M-Sa 9am-6:30pm, Su 10am-1pm and 4:30-6:30pm; Oct.-Apr. M-Sa 9am-noon and 2-6pm, Su 10am-12:30pm and 3-6:30pm.) Spend the night at the central **auberge de jeunesse (HI)**, 59 Grand Place. (Tel. 03 21 22 70 02. 48F. Sheets 17F. Breakfast 19F. Reception 7:30-noon and 5-11pm. Lockout 10am-5pm. Curfew 11pm. Open Feb.-Nov.)

The gouged and cratered countryside surrounding Arras (which witnessed heavy fighting in WWI) is dotted with war cemeteries and unmarked graves. The monument of **Vimy**, 12km from Arras, honors the more than 66,000 Canadians killed in WWI. The kiosk near the trenches is the starting point for an underground tour of the crumbling chalk-walled tunnels dug by British and Canadian soldiers to facilitate access to the front. (Memorial open dawn-dusk. Free tours of the tunnels Apr. to mid-Nov. 10am-6pm.) Several **buses** and **trains** (each 12F) run from Arras to Vimy daily, but you must hike 3km down N17 from town to get to the memorial; the best way to get there is to pool funds for a **taxi** from Arras (100F).

CALAIS

Ever since Richard the Lionheart and his crusaders passed through, Calais has been the continent's primary portal to Britain. If you're here for any length of time (most aren't), duck over to the flamboyant, faux-Gothic Hôtel de Ville at bd. Jacquard and rue Royale, where Rodin's famous sculpture **The Burghers of Calais** awaits, or watch the white ships glide by from one of the town's wide, gorgeous beaches. Most **ferries** dock at the Car Ferry Terminal (tel. 03 21 46 80 00); for schedules and prices to Dover, England, see p. 58. During the day, free **buses** connect the hoverport, ferry terminal, and **train station**, on bd. Jacquard, where trains leave for Boulogne (30min., 19 per day, 44F); Lille (1¼hr., 12 per day, 84F); and Paris (1½-3hr., 10 per day, 198-265F). To reach the **tourist office**, 12 bd. Clemenceau, cross the street from the station, turn left, and cross the bridge; it's on your right. (Tel. 03 21 96 62 40; fax 03 21 96 01 92. Open M-Sa 9am-7pm, Su 10am-1pm.) The **Centre Européen de Séjour (HI)**, on av. Maréchal Delattre de Tassigny, is a block from the beach. From the station, turn left, follow the main road past pl. d'Armes, cross the bridge, go left at the rotary onto bd. de Gaulle, and turn right on rue Alice Marie. From the ferry, take the shuttle bus to pl. d'Armes; your first right down the bus route is the main road (rue Royale). (Tel. 03 21 34 70 20; fax 03 21 96 87 80. 80F; nonmembers add 10F for 1-night max. stay. Breakfast included. Sheets 14F. Reception 24hr.) **Hotel Bristol**, 13 rue du Duc de Guise, is off rue Royale. (Tel./fax 03 21 34 53 24. Singles 130-200F; doubles 150-220F. Breakfast 25F. Reception 24hr. V, MC.) **Match supermarket** is on pl. d'Armes. (Open M-Sa 8:30am-7:30pm, Su 10am-7pm.) **Postal code:** 62100.

BOULOGNE-SUR-MER

The most attractive of the Channel ports, Boulogne combines modern bustle and ages-old charm. Legend has it that a boat carrying a statue of the Virgin Mary washed onto the beach in 636, making the town a pilgrimage site. The massive **Château-Musée**, on rue de Bernet, houses an eclectic but impressive art collection. (Open M and W-Sa 10am-12:30pm and 2-5pm; Su 10am-12:30pm and 2:30-5:30pm. 20F.) Just down rue de Lille, the towering 19th-century **Basilique de Notre-Dame** sits above labyrinthine 12th-century crypts, housing precious religious objects. (Open M-Sa 9am-noon and 2-6pm. Crypt and basilica 10F.) For info on **ferries** to Folkstone, England, see p. 58. **Trains** go to Calais (30min., 19 per day, 44F); Lille (2½hr., 12 per day, 102-135F); and Paris (2-2¾hr., 8 per day, 161-280F). From the station, turn right on bd. Voltaire, follow bd. Danou left to pl. Angleterre, and look left for the **tourist office,** on quai de la Poste, in Forum Jean Noël, off pl. Frédéric Sauvage. (Tel. 03 21 31 68 38; fax 03 21 33 81 09. Open July-Aug. M-Sa 9am-7pm, Su 10am-12:30pm and 2-5:30pm; Sept.-June M-Sa 8:45am-6pm, Su 9:30am-1pm and 2:30-5:30pm.) The fantastic **auberge de jeunesse (HI)**, 56 pl. Rouget de Lisle, is opposite the station. (Tel. 03 21 99 15 30; fax 03 21 80 45 62. 72F; nonmembers 91F. Breakfast included. **Internet.** Reception 8:30am-1am. Check-in 5pm. Curfew 1am. V, MC.) **STOC supermarket** is at 54 rue Daunou. (Open M-Sa 8:30am-8pm.) **Postal code:** 62200.

FRANCE

GERMANY
(DEUTSCHLAND)

US$1 = DM1.84 (DEUTSCHMARKS)
CDN$1 = DM1.23
UK£1 = DM2.97
IR£1 = DM2.48
AUS$1 = DM1.17
NZ$1 = DM0.97
SAR1= DM0.30
EUR€1= DM1.96

DM1 = US$0.55
DM1 = CDN$0.82
DM1 = UK£0.34
DM1 = IR£0.40
DM1 = AUS$0.86
DM1 = NZ$1.03
DM1 = SAR3.32
DM1 = EUR€0.51

PHONE CODE | Country code: 49. International dialing prefix: 00.

A decade after the fall of the Berlin Wall, Germans are still trying to fashion them-selves a new identity for the 21st century. After centuries of war, fragmentation, occupation, and division, Germany now finds itself a wealthy nation at the fore-front of both European and global politics. Yet the nation's story is a parable for life in the modern era—its history encapsulates all of the promises and betrayals of the 20th century and exposes the fissures beneath Western civilization's veneer.

Germany has always been a wellspring of revolutionaries and innovators—for better and for worse. One of the first heroes of German history, Charlemagne (Karl der Große), unified post-Roman Europe under relatively enlightened rule. Martin Luther went from small-town German monk to one of the most influential figures in Western history with his *95 Theses*, which started the Protestant Reformation. Karl Marx and Friedrich Engels equipped the revolutionary groundswell of 19th-century Europe with an ideology that precipitated the major conflicts of the latter half of the 20th century. One of the most horrifying figures in history, Adolf Hit-ler—whose influence will perhaps always elude explanation—forever tainted Ger-many's name with his dreams of nationalist expansionism and his genocidal theories. This last image has, of course, indelibly colored German history; Ger-mans must grapple with the fact that the cradle of Bach, Beethoven, Goethe, Kant, and Nietzsche, also spawned Dachau and Buchenwald.

While combatting this incongruous legacy, modern Germans must also come to terms with the problems brought on by the country's remarkably quick reunifica-tion. In the wake of Europe's most recent revolutions, Germany's pivotal role between East and West is even more important than it was during the Cold War, yet efforts to provide leadership on the Continent have been hampered by Ger-many's internal identity crises. Nevertheless, Germany assumes an increasingly assertive role in the global community, and as it enters the next millennium, it remains the dominant economic power on the Continent.

For more comprehensive coverage, treat yourself to *Let's Go: Germany 2000*.

DISCOVER GERMANY

Berlin's myriad cultural and historical treasures, not to mention its chaotic night-life, sprawl over an area eight times the size of Paris (see p. 376). **Dresden** is nearly as intense, with a jumping nightlife and exquisite palaces and museums (see p. 392). The buckling hills and tiny villages of **Saxon Switzerland** are an easy stopover from Dresden en route to Prague, and are a surefire way to satisfy your *Wander-lust* (see p. 396). **Weimar** rests solidly on the cultural heritage of Goethe, the Bau-haus movement, and Germany's first liberal constitution (see p. 398). To the north, reckless **Hamburg,** Germany's second-largest city, fuses the burliness of a port town with cosmopolitan flair (see p. 402), while **Cologne,** near the Belgian and

Germany

N

North Sea

NETHER-
LANDS

BEL.

LUX.

FRANCE

SWITZERLAND

North
Frisian
Islands

Sylt

East
Frisian
Islands

Norden

Cuxhaven

Bremerhaven

Oldenburg

Bremen

Hamburg

Lüneburg

Lüneburger
Heide

Celle

Hannover

Hameln

Hildesheim

Braunschweig

Wolfenbüttel

Magdeburg

DENMARK

Flensburg

Schleswig

Kiel

SCHLESWIG-
HOLSTEIN

Lübeck

Travemünde

Wismar

Schwerin

Plauersee

Muritzsee

Fehmarn

Rostock

Greifswald

Stralsund

Sassnitz
Rügen

Baltic Sea

MECKLENBURG-VORPOMMERN

Neubrandenburg

LOWER SAXONY

Osnabrück

Münster

Bielefeld

TEUTOBURG
FOREST

Detmold

NORTH RHINE-WESTPHALIA

Essen

Dortmund

Düsseldorf

Wuppertal

Solingen

Cologne
(Köln)

Aachen

Bonn

Koblenz

Eifel Masif

Trier

Mosel

RHINELAND-
PALATINATE

SAARLAND

Saarbrücken

Mannheim

Speyer

Worms

Mainz

Wiesbaden

Darmstadt

Frankfurt-am-Main

Main

Würzburg

Bamberg

Bayreuth

Fürth

Nüremberg
(Nürnberg)

BAVARIA

Marburg

HESSE

Fulda

Frankenberg

Kassel

Göttingen

Goslar

Harz Mountains

Quedlinburg

Dessau

SAXONY-ANHALT

Halle

Naumburg

Leipzig

Wittenberg

Lübben

SPREEWALD

Cottbus

Bautzen

Dresden

Meissen

SAXONY

Chemnitz

Zwickau

Plauen

Erz Mountains

Prague

CZECH
REPUBLIC

THURINGIA

Eisenach

Erfurt

Weimar

Jena

Gera

Gotha

THURINGIAN FOREST

BRANDENBURG

Brandenburg

Berlin

Potsdam

Bernau

Frankfurt
a.d. Oder

Oder

POLAND

Neisse

Ruhr

Rhine

Limburg

Oder

BAVARIAN FOREST

Regensburg

Straubing

Landshut

Passau

Danube

Inn

Rothenburg

Heilbronn

Dinkelsbühl

Schwäbisch
Gmünd

Danube

Augsburg

Ulm

Swabian Jura

Tübingen

Freudenstadt

BADEN-
WÜRTTEMBERG

BLACK FOREST

Baden-Baden

Pforzheim

Karlsruhe

Stuttgart

Strasbourg

Breisach

Freiburg

Konstanz

Lake Constance
(Bodensee)

Wangen

Lindau

Ammersee

Starnbergersee

Garmisch-
Partenkirchen

Bavarian Alps

Füssen

Munich
(München)

Chiemsee

Berchtesgaden

AUSTRIA

Schwerin

Heidelberg

0   50 miles

0   50 kilometers

Dutch borders, is home to Germany's largest and perhaps most poignant cathedral and a pounding nightlife (see p. 411). Just to the south, **Koblenz** is the gateway to the castles and wine towns of the **Rhine** (see p. 422) and **Mosel** (see p. 424) **Valleys.** A bit south, Germany's oldest, most prestigious, and most scenic university sits below the brooding ruins of **Heidelberg's** castle (see p. 425). Head farther south to live out your favorite Brothers Grimm fairy tales in the **Black Forest,** from the winding alleys of **Freiburg** to the mountain-top lakes of **Titisee** and **Schluchsee** (see p. 430). Or work your way south instead via the so-called **Romantic Road** (see p. 446), which snakes along the western edge of Bavaria from **Würzburg** to **Füssen** and is epitomized by the kitschy yet fascinating medieval city of **Rothenburg** (see p. 446). At the southern end of the trail lies the fairy-tale triumvirate of Mad King Ludwig's **Royal Castles** (see p. 448). And no trip to Germany would be complete without visiting the Bavarian capital of **Munich,** which takes bucolic merriment to a frothy head with its excellent museums and jovial beer halls (see p. 435).

GERMANY

GETTING THERE AND GETTING AROUND

BY PLANE. Most flights to Germany land in **Frankfurt,** although **Berlin, Munich,** and **Hamburg** also have major international airports. **Lufthansa,** Germany's national airline, has the most flights in and out of the country, though they're not always the cheapest. For cheap fares, look into **Icelandair** flights to neighboring Luxembourg; Cologne is only 3hr. away by train, Frankfurt 4hr. Flying within Germany is usually more expensive and less convenient than taking the train.

BY TRAIN. "In Germany, the trains run on time." It may be said jokingly, and it's not infallibly true, but it brings up an important truth about getting around in Germany. Averaging 120km per hr., the **Deutsche Bahn (DB)** network is Europe's best, and also one of the most expensive. Check out **schedules** and **prices** at http://bahn.hafas.de. **RE** (RegionalExpress) and slightly slower **RB** (Regionalbahn) trains include rail networks between neighboring cities. **IR** (InterRegio) trains cover larger networks between cities. **D** trains are foreign trains serving international routes. **EC** (EuroCity) and **IC** (InterCity) trains zoom along between major cities every hr. 6am-10pm. The futuristic **ICE** (InterCityExpress) trains run at speeds up to 280km per hr. You must purchase a **Zuschlag** (supplement) to ride an ICE, IC, or EC train (DM7 from the station, DM9 on the train). For basic train **lingo,** see p. 949.

The **German Railpass** allows unlimited travel for four to 10 days within a four-week period. Non-Europeans can purchase German Railpasses in their home countries and in major German train stations (2nd-class 5-day US$196, 10-day US$306). The **German Rail Youth Pass** is for tourists under 26 (5-day US$156, nine-day US$198). Contact DB through their web page (www.bahn.de), or, once in Germany, via their toll-free hotline (tel. (0180) 599 66 33). Travelers under 26 can also purchase **TwenTickets,** which knock 20-60% off fares over DM10; be sure to let your ticket agent know your age. **Schönes-Wochenende-Tickets** grant up to five people unlimited travel on any of the slower trains (i.e., not ICE, IC, EC, D, or IR) from 12:01am Saturday until 2am on Monday for DM35. **Guten-Abend-Tickets** entitle holders to travel anywhere in Germany (although not on InterCityNight or CityNight-Lines) between 7pm and 2am of one night (2nd-class DM59, with ICE surcharge DM69; 1st-class DM99, with ICE surcharge DM109; F and Su add DM15).

Urban **public transit** is excellent throughout Germany, consisting of **U-Bahn** (subway), **S-Bahn** (commuter rail), **Straßenbahnen** (streetcars), and **buses.** Throughout this chapter, U- and S-Bahn lines are abbreviated following German convention: "S2" indicates S-Bahn line 2, "U6" indicates U-Bahn line 6, etc. Note that a double-digit U- or S-Bahn line, such as "U75" in Berlin, usually indicates nighttime combined service of two lines, in this example the U7 and U5 lines. Consider purchasing a day card *(Tageskarte)* or multiple-ride ticket *(Mehrfahrkarte)* for unlimited public transit. Validate your ticket in the *Entwerter* (validation machine) on subway platforms before boarding, or on buses immediately upon boarding, or face a a DM60 on-the-spot fine. **Eurail** is valid in Germany and provides free passage on the S-Bahn in cities and DB bus lines, but not on the U-Bahn.

BY BUS. Bus service between cities and to outlying areas run from the local **Zentralomnibusbahnhof (ZOB),** which is usually close to the main train station. Buses are often slightly more expensive than trains for comparable distances. **Railpasses** are not valid on any buses other than a few run by Deutsche Bahn.

BY FERRY. Ferries run from port cities along the northern coast of Germany—Hamburg, Kiel, Travemünde, Rostock, and Saßnitz—to Scandinavia, the UK, Ireland, Poland, the Baltics, and Russia. See p. 401 for more detailed info.

BY CAR. With the exception of a few secondary roads in the former East that have yet to be renovated, German road conditions are in general excellent. Yes, there is no set speed limit on the **Autobahn,** or highway, though authorities only recommend driving up to 130km per hr. (81mph). The Autobahn is indicated by an

GERMANY

"A" on signs; secondary highways, where the speed limit is usually 100km per hr., are accompanied by signs bearing a "B." Germans drive on the right side of the road, and it is illegal to pass on the right, even on superhighways. In cities and towns, speeds hover around 30-60 km per hr. (31mph). Germans use unleaded gas almost exclusively; prices run around DM7 per gallon, or about DM1.80 per liter.

BY BIKE AND BY THUMB. Germany makes **biking** easy with a wealth of trails and bike tours. Cities and towns usually have designated bike lanes. For info on bike routes, regulations, and maps, contact **Allgemeiner Deutscher Fahrrad-Club,** Postfach 10 77 47, 28077 Bremen. A bike tour guidebook, including extensive maps, is available from **Deutsches Jugendherbergswerk (DJH)** (tel. (05231) 740 10). Although *Let's Go* does not recommend **hitchhiking** as a safe means of transportation, it is permitted and quite common on the Autobahn. Hitchers may stand only at rest stops *(Raststätten)*, gas stations, and in front of Autobahn signs at on-ramps. **Mitfahrzentralen** pair up drivers and riders, who pay the agency a commission and then directly negotiate expenses with drivers. These agencies are indicated in the **Getting There and Getting Around** sections of individual cities.

ESSENTIALS

DOCUMENTS AND FORMALITIES. Germany requires visas of South Africans, but not of nationals of Australia, Canada, the EU, New Zealand, or the US, for stays of shorter than three months. All embassies in Germany moved back to Berlin in summer 1999. For up-to-date info, call the **Auswärtiges Amt** at (030) 20 18 60.

German Embassies at Home: Australia, 119 Empire Circuit, Yarralumla, Canberra, ACT 2600 (tel. (02) 62 70 19 11; fax 62 70 19 51); **Canada,** 1 Waverly St, Ottawa, ON K2P OT8 (tel. (613) 232-1101; fax 594-9330). **Ireland,** 31 Trimleston Ave, Booterstown, Blackrock, Co. Dublin (tel. (012) 69 30 11; fax 269 39 46). **New Zealand,** 90-92 Hobson St, Thorndon, Wellington (tel. (04) 473 60 63; fax 473 60 69). **South Africa,** 180 Blackwood St, Arcadia, Pretoria, 0083 (tel. (012) 427 89 00; fax 343 94 01). **UK,** 23 Belgrave Sq, London SW1X 8PZ (tel. (020) 78 24 13 00; fax 78 24 14 35). **US,** 4645 Reservoir Rd NW, Washington, D.C. 20007 (tel. (202) 298-4000; fax 298-4249).

Foreign Embassies and Consulates in Germany: For all foreign **embassies** (in Berlin), see **p. 380**. The remainder of listings on this page are all **consulates. Australia: Frankfurt,** Grunebrückweg 58-62, 60311 (tel. (069) 273 90 90). **Canada: Düsseldorf,** Benrataer-str. 8, 40213 (tel. (0211) 172 170); **Hamburg,** ABC-Str. 45, 20354 (tel. (040) 35 55 62 95); **Munich,** Tal 29, 80331 (tel. (089) 219 95 70). **Ireland: Hamburg,** Feldbrunner-str. 43, 20148 (tel. (040) 44 18 62 13); **Munich,** Mauerkircherstr. 1a, 81679 (tel. (089) 98 57 23). **New Zealand: Hamburg,** Zürich-Dom-Str. 19, 20095 (tel. (040) 442 55 50). **South Africa: Frankfurt,** Cerberstr. 33 (tel. (069) 719 11 30); **Munich,** Sendlinger-Tor-Pl. 5, 80336 (tel. (089) 231 16 30). **UK: Düsseldorf,** Yorckstr. 19, 40476 (tel. (0211) 944 80); **Frankfurt,** Bockenheimer Landstr. 42, 60323 (tel. (069) 170 00 20); **Hamburg,** Harvestehuder Weg 8a, 20148 (tel. (040) 448 03 20); **Munich,** Bürkleinstr. 10, 80538 (tel. (089) 21 10 90); **Stuttgart,** Breite Str. 2, 70173 (tel. (0711) 16 26 90). **US: Düsseldorf,** Kennedydamm 15-17, 40476 (tel. (0211) 47 06 10); **Frankfurt,** Siesmayerstr. 21, 60323 (tel. (069) 753 50); **Hamburg,** Alsterufer 27, 20354 (tel. (040) 41 17 10); **Leipzig,** Wilhelm-Seyfferth-Str. 4, 04107 (tel. (0341) 21 38 40); **Munich,** Königinstr. 5, 80539 (tel. (089) 288 80).

TOURIST OFFICES. Every city in Germany has a **tourist office,** usually located near the main train station (Hauptbahnhof) or central market square (Marktplatz). All are marked by a thick lowercase **"i"** sign. The offices provide city maps and info on cycling routes and local sights and often book rooms for a small fee.

MONEY. The **deutsche Mark** or **Deutschmark** (DM) is one of the most stable and respected currencies in the world, typically regarded along with US dollars as one of the world's two "hard currencies." One DM equals 100 *Pfennige* (Pf). Coins come in 1, 2, 5, 10, and 50Pf, and DM1, 2, and 5 denominations. Bills come in DM5,

GERMANY

10, 20, 50, 100, 200, 500, and 1000 denominations, though DM5 bills are now rare. **Credit cards** are generally accepted in Germany, and major credit cards—**Master-Card** and **Visa**—can be used to extract cash advances in *Deutschmarks* from associated banks and teller machines throughout Germany. **Eurocard,** which is affiliated with MasterCard, is preferred in Germany, and is more widely accepted than Visa. **24-hour ATMs** (Automated Teller Machines) are widespread in Germany.

Tipping and Bargaining: Germans generally round up DM1-2 to tip, but typically only in restaurants and bars, or for services such as taxi rides. Tips aren't left on the table, but are handed directly to the server when paying. If you don't want any change, say *das stimmt so* (DAS shtimt zo). Germans rarely bargain, except at flea markets.

Taxes: The marked prices on goods and services bought in Germany already include a Value Added Tax (VAT), or *Mehrwertsteuer (MwSt),* of 15%. For more on the VAT, see p. 23.

COMMUNICATION

Post: Mailing a postcard or letter from Germany costs DM1/1.10 to destinations within Europe, DM2/3 beyond Europe. Mail can be sent **Postlagernde Briefe,** German for *Poste Restante* (see p. 47*),* to almost any city or town with a post office.

Telephone: Public phones *(Telefonzellen)* are located in all post offices, as well as at train and bus stations, on ICE trains, and on nearly every street corner. Most only accept **Telefonkarten** (telephone cards), although restaurants and bars sometimes have coin-operated phones. You can buy phone cards (DM12, DM24, or DM50) at post offices, newsstands, and major train stations. **Local calls** cost DM0.12-0.18 per 3min., depending on time of day and type of phone. To place **inter-city calls,** dial the *Vorwahl* (area code), including any leading zero, and then the *Rufnummer* (local number). For **national information,** dial 118 33. For **international information,** dial 118 34. **AT&T:** Tel. (0800) 2255 288. **Sprint:** Tel. (0800) 8880 013. **MCI WorldPhone Direct:** Tel. (0800) 888 8000. **Canada Direct:** Tel. (0800) 888 0014. **BT Direct:** Tel. (0130) 80 0144. **Ireland Direct:** Tel. (0800) 180 0027. **Australia Direct:** Tel. (0130) 80 0061. **Telecom New Zealand Direct:** Tel. (0130) 80 0064. **Telkom South Africa Direct:** Tel. (0800) 180 0027. In case of an **emergency,** call the **police** at 110; **fire** or **ambulance** at 112.

Language: English language ability is common in Western Germany, but far less so in the East. The letter ß is equivalent to a double s. For German tips, see p. 949.

Violent crime is less common in Germany than in most countries, but it exists, especially in big cities like Frankfurt and Berlin, as well as in economically depressed regions of Eastern Germany. Most neo-Nazis and skinheads subscribe to a traditional uniform of flight jackets, white short-sleeved shirts, and tight jeans rolled up high over high-cut combat boots. Skinheads also tend to follow a shoe-lace code, with white supremacists and neo-Nazis wearing white laces, while anti-gay skinheads wear pink laces. Left-wing, anti-Nazi "S.H.A.R.P.s" (Skinheads Against Racial Prejudice) also exist; they favor red laces.

ACCOMMODATIONS AND CAMPING. A German schoolteacher founded the world's first youth hostel in 1908, and the country today has more than 600 *Jugendherbergen.* **Deutsches Jugendherbergswerk (DJH)** (tel. (05231) 740 10; fax 74 01 49; www.djh.de) oversees hosteling in Germany and publishes *Deutsches Jugendherbergen in Deutschland* (DM14.80), a guide to all federated German hostels available at bookstores, at many newsstands, and through DJH. Dorm rates ates hover around US$8-20. DJH **Jugendgästehäuser,** or youth guesthouses, are slightly more expensive, have more facilities, and attract slightly older guests. Keep in mind that hostels in Bavaria do not accept guests over the age of 26.

The cheapest hotel-style accommodations include the words **Pension, Gasthof, Gästehaus,** or **Hotel-Garni.** Breakfast is almost always included. Rock-bottom singles cost DM30, doubles DM40-45; in big cities, expect to pay at least DM50 for a single or DM90 for a double. Your best bet for a cheap bed will often be a **private room** *(Privatzimmer)* in a home, which will cost DM20-50 per person; you can reserve through the local tourist office or through a private **Zimmervermittlung** (room-booking office), either for free or for a DM2-8 fee.

GERMANY

There are about 2600 **campgrounds** in Germany, about 400 of which are open in winter. Prices run about DM3-10 per person, with additional charges for tents and vehicles. For more info, contact the **Deutscher Camping-Club (DCC)**, Mandlstr. 28, 80802 München (tel. (089) 380 14 20), or the **Allgemeiner Deutscher Automobil-Club (ADAC)**, Am Westpark 8, 81373 Munich (tel. (089) 767 60).

FOOD AND DRINK. Although German cuisine is neither as sophisticated as French cooking nor as sultry as Italian food, *Deutsche Küche* has a robust charm, especially satisfying for meat-and-potato lovers. German delights include *Schnitzel* (a lightly fried veal cutlet), *Spätzle* (a southern noodle), and *Kartoffeln* (potatoes). The typical German **Frühstück** (breakfast) consists of coffee or tea with *Brötchen* (rolls), bread, *Wurst* (cold sausage), and cheese. The main meal of the day, **Mittagessen** (lunch), consists of soup, broiled sausage or roasted meat, potatoes or dumplings, and a salad or *Gemüsebeilage* (vegetable side dish). **Abendessen** or **Abendbrot** (dinner) is a reprise of breakfast, only beer replaces coffee and the selection of meats and cheeses is wider. Many older Germans indulge in a daily ritual of **Kaffee und Kuchen** (coffee and cakes) at 3 or 4pm.

With few exceptions, **restaurants** expect you to seat yourself. In traditional restaurants, address waiters as *Herr Ober* and waitresses as *Fräulein* (FROY-line); in an informal setting, just say *hallo*. Ask for the **check** by saying *Zahlen, bitte* (TSAH-len, BIT-teh). If you ask for *Wasser*, you get pricey mineral water; for tap water, ask for *Leitungswasser* and expect funny looks. **Tax** and **tip** are included, but it is customary to leave a little something extra (see **Tipping**, p. 374). To eat on the cheap, stick to the daily *Tagesmenü*, buy food in **supermarkets**, or, if you have a student ID, head to a university **Mensa** (cafeteria). Fast-food *Imbiß* stands also provide cheap fare; try the delicious Turkish *Döner*, something like a gyro.

The average German **beer** is maltier and more "bread-like" than Czech, Dutch, or American beers; an affectionate German slang term for beer is *flüßiges Brot* ("liquid bread"). Among the exceptions is **Pils**, or Pilsner, popular in the north, whose clarity and bitter taste come from extra hops. From the south comes **Weißbier,** also known as **Weizenbier**, a smooth, refreshing wheat beer. **Hefeweizen** is wheat beer with a layer of yeast in the bottom. Also try the largely overlooked German **wines**, particularly the sweet (*lieblich* or *süß*) whites of the Rhine and Mosel Valleys.

LOCAL FACTS

Time: Germany is 1hr. ahead of Greenwich Mean Time (GMT). For more info, see p. 49.

Climate and When to Go: Germany's climate is temperate, with rain year-round (especially in summer). Temperatures range between -1-2°C (30-36°F) in deep winter to 12-25°C (55-77°F) in July and Aug. The cloudy, temperate months of May, June, and Sept. are the best time to go, as there are fewer tourists and the weather is pleasant. Germans head to vacation spots en masse with the onset of school vacations in early July. Winter sports gear up Nov.-Apr.; high-season for skiing is mid-Dec. to Mar.

Hours: Bank hours are often quite bizarre; a typical work week might be M-W and F 9am-12:30pm and 2:30-4pm, Th 9am-12:30pm and 2:30-5pm. **Store hours** are usually M-F 9am-6:30pm, Sa 9am-2pm. Some stores remain open until 8:30pm on Th and until 4pm on the 1st Sa of each month. In larger cities, shops inside train stations are open longer. Many smaller shops take a midday break from noon to 2pm.

Holidays: Epiphany (Jan. 6), Ash Wednesday (Mar. 8), Good Friday (Apr. 21), Easter Sunday and Monday (Apr. 23-24), Labor Day (May 1), Ascension Day (June 1), Whit Sunday (June 11), Whit Monday (June 12), Corpus Christi (June 22), Assumption Day (Aug. 15), Day of German Unity (Oct. 3), Reformation Day (Nov. 1), All Saint's Day (Nov. 1), and Christmas (Dec. 25-26). Expect reduced hours in establishments.

Major Festivals: Fasching in Munich (Jan. 7-Mar.7), Berlinale Film Festival (Feb. 9-20), Karneval in Cologne (Mar. 2-7), Hafensgeburtstag in Hamburg (May 5-7), Expo 2000 in Hannover (June-Oct.), International Film Festival in Munich (late June), Christopher St Day in Berlin and other major cities (late June to early July), Love Parade in Berlin (early July), Bach Festival in Leipzig (July 21-30), Wagner Festspiele in Bayreuth (July 25-Aug. 28), Wine Festival in Stuttgart (Aug. 24-Sept. 3), Oktoberfest in Munich (Sept. 16-Oct. 1), and Christmas Market in Nuremberg (Dec. 24-27).

GERMANY

BERLIN

While plans are underway to transform Berlin from a decentralized city into a sparkling and whole metropolis that will do Germany's capital justice, what has always made Berlin remarkable is its ability to flourish in times of adversity. Raised in the shadow of global conflict, post-WWII Berliners responded with a storm of cultural activity and the type of free-for-all nightlife you might expect from a population with its back against a Wall. The fall of the physical and psychological division between East and West Berlin in 1989 symbolized the end of the Cold War, and Berlin was officially reunited (along with the rest of Germany) to widespread celebration on October 3, 1990. But the task of uniting Berlin's twin cities has proven no easier than that of stitching together both halves of the country; it seems that Eastern and Western Berliners don't really like each other as much as they once imagined they might. As Karl Zuckmayer once wrote, "Berlin tasted of the future, and for that one happily accepted the dirt and the coldness as part of the bargain." A kaleidoscope of GDR apartment blocks and gleaming office complexes, Berlin today still balances its gritty melancholy with exhilarating cutting-edge intensity.

◰ GETTING THERE AND GETTING AROUND

Flights: Info tel. (0180) 500 01 86 for all airports. **Flughafen Tegel** is Western Berlin's main airport. Take express bus X9 from Bahnhof Zoo, bus 109 from U7: Jakob-Kaiser-Platz, or bus 128 from U6: Kurt-Schumacher-Platz. **Flughafen Tempelhof** handles domestic and European flights. U6: Platz der Luftbrücke. **Flughafen Schönefeld,** southeast of Berlin, handles intercontinental flights and those to the former USSR and developing countries. Take S9 or S45 to "Flughafen Berlin Schönefeld," or bus 171 from U7: Rudow.

Trains: Info tel. (0180) 599 66 33. Most trains arrive at both **Zoologischer Garten (Bahnhof Zoo)** in the West and **Ostbahnhof** in the East, though some from the former GDR only stop at the latter. Many connect to **Schönefeld** airport, some via **Potsdam.** To: **Dresden** (2hr., every hr., DM59); **Hamburg** (2½hr., every hr., DM88); **Frankfurt** (4hr., 2 per hr., DM207); **Cologne/Köln** (4¼hr., every hr., DM190); **Prague** (5hr., 4 per day, DM127); **Warsaw** (6hr., 4 per day, DM49); **Amsterdam** (6½hr., 4 per day, DM203); **Copenhagen** (7½hr., 4 per day, DM188); **Brussels** (7½hr., 6 per day, DM217); **Munich** (7½hr., 2 per hr., DM249); **Kraków** (10½hr., 4 per day, DM51); and **Paris** (11hr., 5 per day, DM287).

Buses: ZOB (Central Bus Station; tel. 301 80 28), by the *Funkturm* near Kaiserdamm. U2: Kaiserdamm or S4, S45, or S46: Witzleben. Buses, while uncomfortable, are often cheaper than trains. To **Paris** (10hr., DM109) and **Vienna** (10½hr., DM79).

Hitchhiking: *Let's Go* does not recommend hitchhiking as a safe mode of transportation. It's illegal to hitch at rest stops or on the highway. Those heading west and south take bus 211 to the Autobahn entrance ramp from S1 or S7: Wannsee. Those heading north walk 50m to the bridge on the right from S25: Hennigsdorf. **Mitfahrzentralen: City Netz,** Joachimstaler Str. 17 (tel. 194 44), arranges **ride-sharing.** U9 or U15: Kurfürstendamm. To Hamburg DM12, Frankfurt DM17, Munich DM18. Open M-F 9am-8pm, Sa-Su 9am-7pm.

Public Transit: BVG (Berliner Verkehrsbetriebe; info tel. 194 49), in the bus parking lot outside Bahnhof Zoo (tel. 25 62 25 62). While it is impossible to tour Berlin on foot, the **bus, Straßenbahn** (streetcar), **U-Bahn** (subway), and **S-Bahn** (surface rail) systems are extensive and efficient. Berlin is divided into 3 transit zones: **Zone A** (downtown Berlin); **Zone B** (almost everywhere else); and **Zone C** (outlying areas including Potsdam and Oranienburg). The *Liniennetz* map is free at any tourist office or subway station. U- and S-Bahn lines generally do not run 1-4am, though most S-Bahn lines run every hr. on weekend nights and the U9 and U12 run all night F and Sa. **Night buses** (designated "N") run about every 20-30min.; pick up the free *Nachtliniennetz* map at the BVG. A single **ticket** (*Langstrecke* AB or BC, DM3.90; or *Ganzstrecke* ABC, DM4.20) is good for 2hr., but passes are usually better values. A **Tageskarte** (AB DM7.80, ABC DM8.50) is valid until 3am the next day. A **Gruppentageskarte** (AB DM20, ABC DM22.50) allows up to 5 people to travel together on the same ticket. The **WelcomeCard** (DM29) is valid on all lines for 72hr. The **7-Tage-Karte** (AB DM40, ABC DM48) is good for 7 days of travel. Buy tickets from *Automaten* (machines), bus drivers, or ticket windows in the U- and S-Bahn sta-

GERMANY

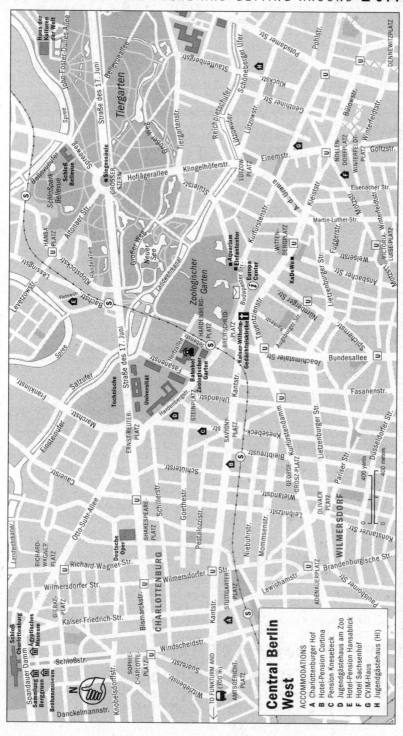

GERMANY

Central Berlin West

ACCOMMODATIONS
A Charlottenburger Hof
B Hotel-Pension Cortina
C Pension Kresebeck
D Jugendgästehaus am Zoo
E Hotel-Pension Hansablick
F Hotel Sachsenhof
G CVJM-Haus
H Jugendgästehaus (HI)

tions. Validate your ticket in the **validation box** marked *"hier entwerten"* before boarding, or face a steep fine (DM60).

Taxis: tel. 26 10 26, 21 02 02, or 690 22. Call at least 15min. in advance. Women may request a female driver. Trips within the city usually cost less than DM20.

Car Rental: The **Mietwagenservice**, counter 21 in Bahnhof Zoo's *Reisezentrum*, represents Avis, Europacar, Hertz, and Sixt. Open daily 4:45am-11pm. Also at Tegel airport.

Bike Rental: Hackescher Markt Fahrradstation, downstairs at S3, S5, S7, S9, S75: Hackescher Markt. Also try the red trailer off the **Lustgarten**. DM5 per day. Same S-Bahn stop.

🔄 ORIENTATION

Berlin is an immense conglomeration (eight times the size of Paris) of two once-separate cities: the former East, which contains most of Berlin's landmarks, historic sites, and cookie-cutter concrete socialist architectural monsters, and the former West, which functioned for decades as an isolated Allied protectorate and still remains the commercial heart of united Berlin.

The commercial district of Western Berlin lies southwest of the huge **Tiergarten** park, centered around **Bahnhof Zoo** and the renowned and reviled **Kurfürstendamm (Ku'damm).** Southeast of the Ku'damm, **Schöneberg** is a pleasant residential neighborhood renowned for its café culture and as the traditional nexus of the city's gay and lesbian community. North of Ku'damm, **Charlottenburg** is home to cafés, restaurants, and *Pensionen*. The grand, tree-lined **Straße des 17. Juni** runs east from Charlottenburg through the Tiergarten to the triumphant **Brandenburg Gate** on the other side, opening onto **Unter den Linden,** Berlin's most famous boulevard. The broad, tree-lined throughway cuts through **Mitte** and empties into **Alexanderplatz,** the center of Eastern Berlin's growing commercial district and the home of Berlin's most visible landmark, the **Fernsehturm (TV tower).** The west-east Spree river splits between Mitte and Alexanderpl., forming the **Museumsinsel** (Museum Island), Eastern Berlin's cultural epicenter. Heading south from the Brandenburg Gate and the nearby **Reichstag,** Ebertstraße runs haphazardly through the construction sites to **Potsdamer Platz.** Southeast of Potsdamer Pl. lies **Kreuzberg,** a district home to an incongruous mix of radical leftists, Turks, punks, and homosexuals. Northeast of the city center, **Prenzlauer Berg,** a former working-class-suburb-turned-squatter's-paradise, rumbles with as-yet-unrestored pre-war structures and a sublime café culture. Southeast of Mitte, **Friedrichshain** is emerging as the center of Berlin's counterculture and nightlife, though the area suffers from a high concentration of prefabricated apartment complexes.

The blue-and-yellow **Falk Plan** (available at most kiosks and bookstores) is an indispensable and convenient city map that includes a street index and unfolds like a book (DM11). Dozens of streets and subway stations in Eastern Berlin were named after Communist heroes and heroines. Many, but not all, have been renamed in a process only recently completed; be sure that your map is up-to-date.

> ❗ Although Berlin is by far the most tolerant city in Germany, the economic chaos caused by reunification has unfortunately unleashed a new wave of right-wing extremism. While it is unlikely that you will come into contact with neo-Nazis, people of color as well as gays and lesbians should take precautions in the eastern suburbs or on the S-Bahn late at night (avoid **Bahnhof Lichtenberg** in particular). Also be aware that if you run into gangs of shaved-head, leather-toting types in Schöneberg or Kreuzberg, they're more likely to be radical leftists or homosexuals.

🔢 PRACTICAL INFORMATION

TOURIST AND FINANCIAL SERVICES

Tourist Offices: www.berlin.de. Most tourist offices sell city maps (DM1) and book same-day hotel rooms (from DM50, plus DM5 fee). 🔲 **Euraide** is in Bahnhof Zoo, to the left and

Berlin Mitte

ACCOMMODATIONS
A Circus
B Clubhouse Hostel

Volkspark Friedrichshain

Friedenstr.

Palisadenstr.

Karl-Marx-Allee

Lichtenberger Str.

Singerstr.

Ostbahnhof

Schillingbrücke

400 yards
400 meters

Blumenstr.

STRAUSBERGER PLATZ

Karl-Marx-Allee

Singerstr.

Spree

Michaelkirchstr.

Prenzlauer Berg

Otto-Braun-Str.

Mollstr.

Grunerstr.

Alexanderstr.

Holzmarktstr.

Brückenstr.

Köpenicker Str.

MICHAEL-KIRCHPLATZ

Torstr.

ROSA-LUXEMBURG-PLATZ

ALEXANDER-PLATZ

Fernsehturm

Marienkirche

Rotes Rathaus

Nikolaikirche

Ephraim-Palais

Knoblauchhaus

Märkisches Museum

Jannowitzbrücke

Spree

Mühlendamm

Fischerinsel

Alte Jakobstr.

Sebastianstr.

Waldeckpark

Heinrich-Heine-Str.

ROSENTHALER PLATZ

Rosenthaler Str.

Alter Jüdischer Friedhof

Dircksenstr.

HACKESCHER MARKT

Karl-Liebknecht-Str.

MARX-ENGELS-FORUM

Sandauer Str.

NIKOLAIVIERTEL

Breite Str.

Werderstr.

Staats-rat

Gertraudenstr.

Former Berlin Wall

Lindenstr.

Gr. Hamburger Str.

Neue Synagoge

Oranienburger Str.

Nicolaikirche

Alte Nationalgalerie

Pergamon-Museum

Berliner Dom

Palast der Republik

SCHLOSSPLATZ

Zeughaus

Neue Wache

Oberwallstr.

HAUSVOGTEI-PLATZ

Leipziger Str.

Zimmerstr.

Kochstr.

Augustr.

Bode-museum

Altes Museum

Humboldt-Universität

Unter den Linden

Deutsche Staatsoper

Französische Str.

Deutscher Dom

Markgrafenstr.

Checkpoint Charlie

Oranienburger Str.

Johannisstr.

B

Tucholskystr.

Georgenstr.

Charlottenstr.

Deutsche Staatsbibliothek

Deutsche Guggenheim Berlin

St.-Hedwigs-kathedrale

Bibliothek

GENDARMEN-MARKT

Französische Str.

Friedrichstr.

Linienstr.

Torstr.

Friedrichstr.

Friedrichstr.

Charlottenstr.

Russia

Behrenstr.

Glinkastr.

Mauerstr.

Konzert-haus

Mohrenstr.

Abgeordnetenhaus von Berlin

Niederkirchnerstr.

Martin-Gropius-Bau

Chausseestr.

Bertolt-Brecht-Haus

Dorotheen-städtischer Friedhof

Hannoversche Str.

Oranienburger Str.

Albrechtstr.

Reinhardtstr.

Marienstr.

Schiffbauerdamm

A

Dorotheenstr.

Wilhelmstr.

Voßstr.

Stresemannstr.

PLATZ VOR DEN NEUEN TOR

Luisenstr.

Schumannstr.

Reichstagufer

PARISER PLATZ

Brandenburger Tor

Hotel Adlon

Führerbunker

Infobox

Friedrich-Ebert-Str.

POTSDAMER PLATZ

Linkstr.

Hamburger Bahnhof

Heidestr.

Humboldt-hafen

Former Berlin Wall

Invalidenstr.

Reichstag

PLATZ DER REPUBLIK

Scheidemannstr.

Sowjetisches Ehrenmal

Straße des 17. Juni

John-Foster-Dulles-Allee

Entlastungstr.

Tiergarten

KEMPERPLATZ

Kongreßhalle

Spree

Moltkestr.

Alt-Moabit

Kunst-gewerbe-museum

Musik-instrumenten-museum

Philharmonie

Kulturforum

Gemälde-galerie

Neue National-galerie

Staats-bibliothek

Sigismundstr.

Potsdamer Str.

N

GERMANY

down the passage on your right as you face the *Reisezentrum*. Open daily 8am-noon and 1-6pm. **Europa-Center** has an entrance on Budapester Str. From Bahnhof Zoo, walk along Budapester Str. past the Kaiser-Wilhelm-Gedächtniskirche and it's on the right (5min.). Open M-Sa 8am-10pm, Su 9am-9pm.

Tours: Berlin Walks (tel. 301 91 94) offers a range of English-language walking tours, including **Infamous Third Reich Sites, Jewish Life in Berlin,** and the **Discover Berlin Walk** (2-3hr.; tours depart at 10am from the taxi stand in front of Bahnhof Zoo; Discover Berlin Walk in summer also 2:30pm; all tours DM15). **Insider Tour** provides a thorough historical narrative and hits all the major sights (3½hr.; departs from the McDonald's by Bahnhof Zoo late Mar. to Nov. daily at 10am and 2:30pm; DM15).

Budget Travel: STA, Goethestr. 73 (tel. 311 09 50). U2: Ernst-Reuter-Platz. Open M-W and F 10am-6pm, Th 10am-8pm. **Kilroy Travels,** Hardenbergstr. 9 (tel. 313 04 66), 2 blocks northwest of Bahnhof Zoo. Open M-F 10am-6pm, Sa 11am-1pm.

Embassies: Due to construction, the locations of embassies and consulates remain in a state of flux; for up-to-date info, call 20 18 60. **Australia,** Friedrichstr. 200, 10117 (tel. 880 08 80). U2 or U6: Stadtmitte. Open M-F 9am-noon. **Canada,** Friedrichstr. 95, International Trade Center, 12th fl., 10117 (tel. 20 31 20; fax 20 31 25 90). S1, S2, S3, S5, S7, S9, S75, or U6: Friedrichstr. Open M-F 8:30am-12:30pm and 1:30-5pm. **Ireland,** Ernst-Reuter-Pl. 10, 10587 (tel. 34 80 08 22; fax 34 80 08 63). U2: Ernst-Reuter-Platz. Open M-F 10am-1pm. **New Zealand,** Friedrichstr. 60, 10117. U6: Oranienburger Tor. **South Africa,** Friedrichstr. 60, 10117. U6: Oranienburger Tor. Open M-F 9am-noon; (consulate) Douglasstr. 9, 14193 (tel. (030) 82 50 11). **UK,** Unter den Linden 32-34, 10117 (tel. 20 18 40; fax 20 18 41 58). S1, S2, S3, S5, S7, S9, S25, S75, or U6: Friedrichstr. Open M-F 8:30am-5pm. **US Citizens Service,** Clayallee 170 (tel. 832 92 33; fax 831 49 26). U1: Oskar-Helene-Heim. Open M-F 8:30am-noon. **US,** Neustädtische Kirchstr. 4-5 (tel. 238 51 74; fax 238 62 90). S1, S2, S3, S5, S7, S9, S25, S75, or U6: Friedrichstr.

Currency Exchange: Wechselstube, Joachimstaler Str. 1-3, near Bahnhof Zoo. Good rates and no commission. Open M-F 8am-8pm, Sa 9am-3pm. **Geldwechsel,** Joachimstaler Str. 7-9. Decent rates and no commission. **ATMs** at **Berliner Sparkasse** and **Deutsche Bank** usually grant credit card advances (V, MC). There are **24-hour ATMs** at Kurfürstendamm 72, Wittenbergpl. 1, Wilmersdorfer Str. 133, and Karl-Marx-Allee 153.

American Express: Uhlandstr. 173 (tel. 88 45 88 21). U15: Uhlandstr. Mail held. No commission on AmEx traveler's checks. Open M-F 9am-5:30pm, Sa 9am-noon.

LOCAL SERVICES

Luggage Storage: In **Bahnhof Zoo** and **Ostbahnhof.** Lockers DM2-4 per day; 72hr. max. Also at **Bahnhof Lichtenberg** and **Alexanderplatz.** Lockers DM2 per day; 24hr. max.

English Bookstores: Marga Schoeler Bücherstube, Knesebeckstr. 33 (tel. 881 11 12), at Mommsenstr., between Savignyplatz and the Ku'damm. Open M-W 9:30am-7pm, Th-F 9:30am-8pm, Sa 9:30am-4pm. **British Bookshop,** Mauerstr. 83-84 (tel. 238 46 80), by Checkpoint Charlie. U6: Kochstr. Open M-F 10am-7pm, Sa 10am-4pm.

Laundromat: Wasch Centers, Leibnizstr. 72, in **Charlottenburg** (U7: Wilmersdorfer Str.); Wexstr. 34, in **Schöneberg** (U9: Bundesplatz); Bergmannstr. 109, in **Kreuzberg;** Behmstr. 12, in **Mitte** (S1, S2, S25, or U8: Gesundbrunnen). Wash DM6 per 6kg; soap included. Dry DM2 per 30min. All open daily 6am-11pm.

EMERGENCY AND COMMUNICATIONS

Emergency: Police, tel. 110. Station at Platz der Luftbrücke 6. **Ambulance** and **fire,** tel. 112.

Crisis Lines: English spoken at most crisis lines. **American Hotline** tel. (0177) 814 15 10. Crisis and referral service. **Sexual Assault Hotline,** tel. 251 28 28. Open Tu and Th 6-9pm, Su noon-2pm. **Schwules Überfall** (gay bashing), tel. 216 33 36. Hotline and legal help. Open daily 6-9pm. **Frauenkrisentelefon** (women's crisis line), tel. 615 42 43. Open M and Th 10am-noon, Tu-W and F 7-9pm, Sa-Su 5-7pm.

Pharmacies: Europa-Apotheke, Tauentzienstr. 9-12 (tel. 261 41 42), near the Europa-Center and Bahnhof Zoo. Open M-F 9am-8pm, Sa 9am-4pm. For information about **late-night pharmacies,** call 011 89.

GERMANY

Medical Assistance: The American and British Embassies have a list of English-speaking doctors. **Emergency Doctor** (tel. 31 00 31) and **Emergency Dentist** (tel. 89 00 43 33).

Internet Access: Alpha, Dunckerstr. 72 (tel. 447 90 67), in Prenzlauer Berg. U2: Eberswalder Str. DM12 per hr. Open daily 3pm-midnight. **Cyberb@r,** Joachimstaler Str. 5-6, near Bahnhof Zoo on the 2nd fl. of Karstadt Sport department store. DM5 per 30min. **Info Box** on Potsdamer Platz. Free.

Post Office: Budapester Str. 42, opposite the Europa-Center near Bahnhof Zoo. Address mail to be held: *Postlagernde Briefe* für Jordan <u>KNIGHT</u>, Postamt in der Budapester Str. 42, **10787** Berlin, Germany. Open M-Sa 8am-midnight, Su 10am-midnight.

PHONE CODE	City code: 030. From outside Germany, dial int'l dialing prefix (see inside back cover) + 49 + 30 + local number.

■ ACCOMMODATIONS AND CAMPING

Same-day accommodations aren't impossible to find even in summer, though as always it's best to call ahead. If arriving on a weekend or during the **Love Parade,** book ahead. For DM5, **tourist offices** find rooms in hostels, *Pensionen*, and hotels (singles from DM70; doubles from DM100), as well as *Privatzimmer* (private rooms; singles DM80; doubles DM100; add DM5 for single-night stay).

HOSTELS AND DORMS

HI hostels can be a great, cheap sleep, but they often fill quickly with school groups and usually impose a curfew, which might cramp your style. Most are also for members only, but you can usually get a guest stamp (DM6 per night). Large, well-equipped **private hostels** typically cater to more party-ready crews and are usually located near train stations or nightlife centers. **Smaller independent hostels,** though often less central and with fewer amenities, often offer the most relaxed atmospheres. The hostels listed below have **no curfew** unless otherwise specified.

MITTE AND KREUZBERG

Circus, Rosa-Luxemburg-Str. 39-41 (tel. 28 39 14 33; fax 28 39 14 84; email circus@mind.de), near Alexanderpl. U2: Rosa-Luxemburg-Platz. A heroic effort at hostel hipness, with cheap **internet** and a disco ball in the lobby. 5- to 6-bed dorms DM25-35; 4-bed DM27; 3-bed DM30; 2-bed DM35; single DM45. Sheets DM3. Bikes DM12 per day. Reception 24hr. Reserve ahead and reconfirm a day before.

Clubhouse Hostel, Johannisstr. 2 (tel. 28 09 79 79). S1, S2, or S25: Oranienburger Str., or U6: Oranienburger Tor. Great location in the center of the Oranienburger Str. club and bar scene. 8- to 10-bed dorms DM25; 5- to 7-bed DM30; 2-bed DM40. Breakfast DM5. **Internet** DM1 per 5min. Reception 24hr. Call 2-3 days ahead.

The Backpacker/Mitte, Chausseestr. 102 (tel. 262 51 40; fax 28 39 09 35; email backpacker@snafu.de; www.backpacker.de). U6: Zinnowitzer Str. An English-speaking haven filled with whirlwind-tourers. Eager staff with tips on sightseeing and nightlife. 5- to 6-bed dorms DM25-29; 4-bed DM31; 3-bed DM33; 2-bed DM38. Sheets DM5. Laundry DM5. Bikes DM10-12 per day. Reception 7am-10pm.

Die Fabrik, Schlesische Str. 18 (tel. 611 71 16; fax 617 51 04; email info@diefabrik.com). U1 or U15: Schlesisches Tor, or night bus N65: Taborstr. Within walking distance of Kreuzberg's mad nightlife. 15-bed dorms DM30; 4-bed DM36; 3-bed DM40; 2-bed DM47; single DM66. Breakfast DM10. Bikes DM20 per day. Reception 24hr. Reserve or call ahead. Curfew? Rage all night, little pumpkin.

SCHÖNEBERG–TIERGARTEN–BAHNHOF ZOO

Jugendgästehaus (HI), Kluckstr. 3 (tel. 261 10 97; fax 265 03 83). From Bahnhof Zoo, take bus 129 (dir: Hermannplatz) to "Gedenkstätte"; or take U1 to "Kurfürstenstr.," then head up Potsdamer Str., left on Pohlstr., and right on Kluckstr. HI's most magnificent fortress. 4- and 5-bed dorms DM43, under 27 DM34. Breakfast included. Laundry. Key deposit DM10. Bikes DM10-15 per day. **Internet.** Reception 24hr. Curfew midnight; stragglers admitted at 30min. intervals. Lockout 9am-1pm. Reserve ahead.

GERMANY

Jugendgästehaus am Zoo, Hardenbergstr. 9a, 5th fl. (tel. 312 94 10; fax 401 52 83), within spitting distance of Bahnhof Zoo (back exit). Classy, though perhaps a little worse for wear. 4- to 8-bed dorms DM40, under 27 DM35; 2-bed DM95, DM85; singles DM52, under 27 DM47. Reception 9am-midnight. Check-in 10am. Check-out 9am. Lockout 10am-2pm. No reservations, but call ahead.

Studentenhotel Berlin, Meininger Str. 10 (tel. 784 67 20; fax 788 15 23). U4: Rathaus Schöneberg; walk toward the Rathaus on Freiherr-vom-Stein-Str., cross Martin-Luther-Str., and turn right on Meininger Str. Call from the station to ask about same-day rooms. 4-bed dorms DM37; 2-bed DM43; single DM59. Breakfast included. Reception Th-M 8am-10pm, Tu-W 8am-midnight. Check-in by 10pm.

Jugendgästehaus Feurigstraße, Feurigstr. 63 (tel. 781 52 11; fax 788 30 51). U7: Kleist-park, or take bus 204 or 348 to "Kaiser-Wilhelm-Platz." Close to Schöneberg nightlife. 4- to 6-bed dorms DM38 (DM27 after Aug.); 2-bed DM45; single DM55. Breakfast included. Sheets DM5 for fewer than 3 nights. Reception 24hr. Call ahead.

FRIEDRICHSHAIN AND PRENZLAUER BERG

Odyssee, Grünberger Str. 23 (tel. 29 00 00 81; www.hostel-berlin.de). U5: Frankfurter Tor, or S3, S5, S6, S7, S9, S75, U1, or U15: Warschauer Str. 8-bed dorms DM24; 6-bed DM28; 4-bed DM32; 2-bed DM36. Breakfast DM5. **Internet.** Reception 24hr. Reserve ahead.

Frederik's Hostel, Str. der Pariser Kommune 35 (tel. 29 66 94 50; fax 29 66 94 52; email hostel@frederiks.de; www.frederiks.de). Exit U5: Weberwiese on Karl-Marx-Allee and turn left on Str. der Pariser Kommune. Or, from S3, S5, S7, S9, or S75: Ostbahnhof, walk to the farthest exit along the train tracks, go straight along Str. der Pariser Kommune, and it's on the left (10min.). 7-bed dorms DM22; 4-6 bed DM25-27; 3-bed DM29; 2-bed DM35; single DM49. Sheets DM4. Kitchen. **Internet.** Reception 24hr.

Lette'm Sleep Hostel, Lettestr. 7 (tel. 44 73 36 23; fax 44 73 36 25). U2: Eberswalder Str. Redefines the expressions "laid-back staff" and "relaxed atmosphere." 3-6 bed dorms DM26-35. Kitchen. **Internet** DM1 per 5min. Call ahead.

TEGEL

Jugendgästehaus Tegel, Ziekowstr. 161 (tel. 433 30 46; fax 434 50 63). S25: Tegel or U6: Alt-Tegel; then bus 222 or N22 to "Titusweg." 3-8 bed dorms DM37.50. Breakfast included. Reception 7:30am-11pm. No English spoken. Reserve ahead.

Backpacker's Paradise, Ziekowstr. 161 (tel. 433 86 40), next to the Jugendgästehaus Tegel (see above). The next best thing to rolling a doobie in your VW van. DM10 gets you a blanket and thermal pad under a tent; add DM3 for a cot. Campfire every night. Officially under 27 only, but rules are made for conformists. Breakfast DM3. Wash DM5. Reception 24hr. No reservations needed. Open late June-Aug.

HOTELS AND PENSIONEN

Many small *Pensionen* and hotels are within budget range, particularly those amenable to **Mehrbettzimmer,** where extra beds are moved into a large double or triple. Most affordable hotels are in Western Berlin. The best place to find cheap rooms is **Charlottenburg,** especially around Savignyplatz and Wilmersdorfer Str.

CHARLOTTENBURG

Pension Berolina, Stuttgarter Pl. 17 (tel. 32 70 90 72; fax 32 70 90 73). S3, S5, S7, S9, S75: Charlottenburg or U7: Wilmersdorfer Str. Simple, spartan rooms, but the prices get two thumbs up. Singles DM50; doubles DM60; triples DM70; quads DM80; quints DM90. Shared bathrooms. Breakfast DM8. Reservations recommended.

Hotel-Pension Cortina, Kantstr. 140 (tel. 313 90 59; fax 31 73 96). S3, S5, S7, S9, or S75: Savignyplatz. Bright, convenient, and hospitable. Dorms DM35-60; singles DM60-90; doubles DM90-150. Breakfast included. Reception 24hr.

Pension Knesebeck, Knesebeckstr. 86 (tel. 312 72 55; fax 313 95 07), just north of the park. S3, S5, S7, S9, or S75: Savignyplatz. Large *Alt-Berliner* rooms with faux Baroque and couches. Singles DM75, with shower DM85; doubles DM110-120, with shower DM130-140; big *Mehrbettzimmer* DM50-60 per person. Cheaper in winter. Breakfast included. Laundry DM8. Reception 24hr. Confirm phone reservations by fax or letter.

GERMANY

Charlottenburger Hof, Stuttgarter Pl. 14 (tel. 32 90 70; fax 323 37 23). S3, S5, S7, S9, S75: Charlottenburg (across the street) or U7: Wilmersdorfer Str. Slick *Pension* with Miró, Klee, and Dalí on the walls. Spotless rooms with phones and TVs. Singles DM80-120; doubles DM110-160; quads DM160-220. All rooms have bath and TV. Nov.-Dec. 20-30% less. Breakfast DM6. Laundry DM5.

SCHÖNEBERG—WILMERSDORF

Hotel Sachsenhof, Motzstr. 7 (tel. 216 20 74; fax 215 82 20). U1, U2, U4, or U15: Nollendorfpl. Small but well-furnished. Singles DM57, with shower DM65; doubles DM99-116, with bath DM126-156; DM30 per extra bed. Breakfast DM10. Reception 24hr.

Hotel-Pension München, Güntzelstr. 62, 3rd fl. (tel. 857 91 20; fax 85 79 12 22). U9: Güntzelstr. Bright *Pension* with balconies and art by contemporary Berlin artists. Clean, white-walled rooms with TVs and phones. Singles DM66-70, with shower DM95-110; doubles DM80-90, with bath DM115-130. Breakfast DM9.

KREUZBERG

Pension Kreuzberg, Großbeerenstr. 64 (tel. 251 13 62; fax 251 06 38). U6, U7, or bus N19: Mehringdamm. Small but well-decorated rooms. Singles DM75, doubles DM98, *Mehrbettzimmer* DM44 per person. Breakfast included. Reception 8am-10pm.

Hotel Transit, Hagelberger Str. 53-54 (tel. 789 04 70; fax 78 90 47 77). U6, U7, or bus N19: Mehringdamm. Party hard and crash gently in this stylin' *Pension*. Big-screen MTV lounge and bar. Singles DM90; doubles DM105; triples DM140; quads DM180. Share a *Mehrbettzimmer* for DM33. Breakfast included. Reception 24hr.

CAMPING

Dreilinden (tel. 805 12 01). S7: Griebnitzsee; then walk back between the station and lake. Surrounded by the vestiges of the Berlin Wall. The bar is an old border checkpoint. DM9.70 per person, DM7.20 per tent, DM12.70 per trailer. Open Mar.-Oct.

Kladow, Krampnitzer Weg 111-117 (tel. 365 27 97). U7: Rathaus Spandau; then bus 135 (dir: Alt-Kladow) to the end. Switch to bus 234 to "Krampnitzer Weg/Selbitzerstr." DM9.70 per person, DM7.20 per tent, DM12.70 per trailer. Store. Open year-round.

◨ FOOD

Berlin's most notable home-grown option is the sweet **Berliner Weiße mit Schuß,** a concoction of wheat beer with a shot of syrup. A lot of typical Berlin food is Turkish, and almost every street has its own Turkish *Imbiß* or restaurant. The *Döner Kebab*, a sandwich of lamb and salad, has cornered the fast-food market, with falafel running a close second (each DM3-5). The leisurely breakfast is a gloriously civilized institution in Berlin cafés, often served well into the afternoon.

Aldi, Plus, Edeka, and **Penny Markt** are the cheapest supermarket chains, followed by the pricier **Bolle, Kaiser's,** and **Reichelt.** Supermarkets are usually open Monday to Friday 9am-6pm, Saturday 9am-4pm, though some chains like Kaiser's are open until as late as 8pm on weekdays. At Bahnhof Zoo, **Ullrich am Zoo,** below the S-Bahn tracks, and **Nimm's Mit,** near the *Reisezentrum,* have longer hours. (Open daily 6am-10pm.) The best **open-air market** fires up Saturday mornings on Winterfeldtplatz, though almost every neighborhood has one. For cheap vegetables and enormous wheels of *Fladenbrot,* check out the **Turkish market** in Kreuzberg, along Maybachufer on the Landwehrkanal (U-Bahn 8: Schönleinstr.), on Fridays.

MITTE AND ORANIENBURGER STRASSE

Käse-König, under the *Fernsehturm.* S3, S5, S7, S9, S75, U2, U5, or U8: Alexanderplatz. Serves cheap German food in a GDR-style canteen to a mix of students and hard-hats. *Bockwurst* (DM1), Schnitzel (DM2.70). Open M-F 9am-6:30pm, Sa 9am-6pm.

Trattoria Ossena, Oranienburger Str. 65 (tel. 283 53 48). Ossena serves more substantial fare than most cafés in the area. Delicious Italian pastas and enormous pizzas. Most meals under DM20, many large enough for 2. Open daily from 5pm.

Mendelssohn, Oranienburger Str. 39 (tel 281 78 59). S1, S2, or S25: Oranienburger Str. Macedonian fare in a candlelit setting. Open M-F from 11am, Sa-Su from 9am.

GERMANY

CHARLOTTENBURG—KU'DAMM—WILMERSDORF

Mensa TU, Hardenbergstr. 34 (tel. 311 22 53), 10min. northeast of Bahnhof Zoo. Cheap, decent food. Meals DM4-5 for students, others DM6-7. Open M-F 11:15am-2:30pm.

Café Hardenberg, Hardenbergstr. 10 (tel. 312 33 30), opposite the TU *Mensa*, but with more atmosphere. Funky music and artsy interior. Order sizzling breakfasts (DM5-12) day or night. Salads and pasta DM5-13. Open M-F 9am-1am, Sa-Su 9am-2am.

Website, Joachimstaler Str. 41 (tel. 88 67 96 30; www.vrcafe.de). U9 or U15: Kurfürsten-damm. Berlin's trendiest cybercafé caters to cyber-hip Germans and homesick Americans (DM7 per 30min.). Snacks DM5-7. Open M-Sa 10am-late.

Restaurant Marché, Kurfürstendamm 14-19 (tel. 882 75 78). Styles itself as a French marketplace, with a colorful cafeteria full of fresh produce, salads, grilled meats, pour-it-yourself wines, and hot pastries (DM12-25). Open daily 8am-midnight.

Café Voltaire, Stuttgarter Platz 14 (tel. 324 50 28). S3, S5, S7, S9, or S75: Charlotten-burg, or U7: Wilmersdorfer Str. Café-bistro-gallery with an extensive menu of salads, omelettes, and baguettes. Great breakfasts DM6-8 (served 5am-3pm). Open 24hr.

SCHÖNEBERG

Baharat Falafel, Winterfeldtstr. 37. U1, U2, U4, or U15: Nollendorfplatz. Perhaps the best falafel in Berlin (DM5-6). Juice DM3-6. Open daily 11am-2am. Closed last week in July.

Café Belmundo, Winterfeldtstr. 36 (tel. 215 20 70), opposite Baharat Falafel. U1, U2, U4, or U15: Nollendorfplatz. Nights are for the young; days for a slightly older, newspa-per-wielding clientele. Sunday breakfast buffet (DM14) until 3pm. Open daily 9am-1am.

KREUZBERG

Amrit, Oranienstr. 202-203 (tel. 612 55 50). U1 or U15: Görlitzer Bahnhof. Possibly Ber-lin's best Indian restaurant. Fabulous vegetarian dishes like Palak Paneer (DM11) as well as delectably spicy meat entrees. Open Su-Th noon-1am, F-Sa noon-2am.

Die Rote Harfe, Oranienstr. 13 (tel. 618 44 46), on Heinrichplatz. U1 or U15: Görlitzer Bahnhof. Leftists and grizzled types eating solid German food. Menu changes daily; most meals DM5-17, salads DM9-12. Open daily 2pm-late.

Café V, Lausitzer Pl. 12 (tel. 612 45 05). U1 or U15: Görlitzer Bahnhof. Berlin's oldest veg-gie restaurant. Pizzas DM10.50-13, salads from DM8.50. Open daily 10am-2am.

PRENZLAUER BERG

Die Krähe, Kollwitzstr. 84 (tel. 442 82 91), off Kollwitzpl. U2: Senefelderplatz. Changing weekly menu; breakfasts under DM10, crunchy salads DM12. Sunday buffet DM13.50. Open M-Th 5:30pm-2am, F-Sa 5:30pm-3am, Su 10:30am-2am.

Ostwind, Husemannstr. 13 (tel. 441 59 51). U2: Senefelderplatz. Prenzlauer hipsters indulge in the dim sum or *Shao-Lin Min* (noodles with tofu, lotus, broccoli, and carrots; DM13.90). Open M-Th 6pm-1am, F-Sa 10am-1am.

Café-Restaurant Miró, Raumerstr. 29 (tel. 44 73 30 13). U2: Eberswalder Str. Generous portions of delectable Mediterranean cuisine. Breakfast DM7-11. Soups DM5, large appetizers DM8.50-15.50, salads DM7.50-16. Open 10am-midnight.

🔍 SIGHTS

It's impossible to see all of sprawling Berlin on foot, but many major sights lie along the route of **bus 100,** which travels from Bahnhof Zoo to Prenzlauer Berg via the Siegessäule, Brandenburg Gate, Unter den Linden, Berliner Dom, and Alexander-platz. To add an element of thrill, climb up to the second floor of the double-decker bus and sit in the very first row: the view is unbeatable, and you'll feel like you're on an amusement park ride (day pass DM7.80, 7-day pass DM40).

Though the sights below are organized by *Bezirk* (district), exhausting each dis-trict one by one is not necessarily the most time-efficient way to see Berlin. If you're interested in seeing all of the major sights, the following is perhaps the most time-efficient way to do so; keep in mind that completing the entire circuit would take several days at least. If you walk (or hop on and off bus 100) from through the

Tiergarten to Alexanderplatz via **Under den Linden,** stopping at **Museuminsel** (home to the fantastic **Pergamonmuseum** and **Altes Museum;** see p. 388) en route, you can then take the U2 from "Alexanderplatz" to "Stadtmitte" to see **Checkpoint Charlie** before hopping back on the U2 to "Potsdamer Platz." The **East Side Gallery** and former **Stasi headquarters** are also easy excursions from "Alexanderplatz" via S3, S5, S7, S9, or U5, respectively. Either way, pick up at Potsdamer Platz, where you can admire the cranes and shiny new highrises, check your email at the Info box, and then stop by a museum or two (the **Gemäldegalerie** and **Neue Nationalgalerie** are the most famed; see p. 388). Then catch the U2 to "Wittenbergplatz," ooh and aah at **KaDeWe** and other wonders of the capitalist world on **Ku'damm,** and catch bus 145 from Bahnhof Zoo or U7 from "Adenauer Platz" down Ku'damm to the **Schloß Charlottenburg.** There you can partake not only in the palace, but also of museums like the **Galerie der Romantik,** the **Ägyptisches Museum,** and the **Sammlung Berggruen.**

MITTE

Formerly the heart of Imperial Berlin, much of Mitte languished and fell into disrepair during the days of the GDR. Today the district is beginning to once again live up to its name ("center"), as embassies and national institutes pour back into the area's rapidly renovating streets. **Unter den Linden,** once one of Europe's best-known boulevards and the spine of old Berlin, runs east from the Brandenburg Gate to Alexanderplatz via Bebelplatz. The remainder of sights in this section lie between Under den Linden and the former Berlin Wall to the south.

BRANDENBURGER TOR. At the eastern edge of the Tiergarten, the Brandenburg Gate became *the* symbol of the East-West division during the Cold War, and was for decades a barricaded gateway to nowhere. But when the Wall came down in 1989, images of East and West Berliners dancing together atop the embedded Gate portion of the Wall—the only section with a flat top—were broadcast around the world, and today the Brandenburg Gate stands as the most powerful emblem of reunited Berlin. The gate opens east onto **Pariser Platz,** site of landmark public addresses. *(S1, S2, or S25: Unter den Linden.)*

BEBELPLATZ. On May 10, 1933 Nazi students burned nearly 20,000 books by "subversive" authors such as Heinrich Heine and Sigmund Freud, both Jews. A plaque in the center of the square is engraved with Heine's eerily prescient 1820 quote: *Nur dort wo man Bücher verbrennt, verbrennt man am Ende auch Menschen* ("Wherever books are burned, ultimately people are burned as well"). The building with the curved façade is the **Alte Bibliothek,** once the royal library. Opposite the library is the handsome **Deutsche Staatsoper,** fully rebuilt after the war. The distinctive blue dome at the end of the square belongs to the **St.-Hedwigs-Kathedrale.** *(U2: Französische Str. or S1, S2, or S25: Unter den Linden.)*

LUSTGARTEN AND MUSEUMINSEL. Continuing east on Unter den Linden, the thoroughfare passes over the **Museuminsel** (Museum Island), home to four major museums (see **Museums,** p. 388) and the **Berliner Dom,** next to the Altes Museum. The cathedral, built during the reign of Kaiser Wilhelm II, recently emerged from 20 years of restoration after suffering severe damage in a 1944 air raid. *(Open daily 9am-7:30pm. Cathedral DM5, students DM3. Joint ticket for cathedral, tower, and galleries DM8, students DM5. S3, S5, S7, S9, or S75: Hackescher Markt, or bus 100: Lustgarden.)*

ROTES RATHAUS AND NIKOLAIVIERTEL. Following Karl-Liebnecht-Str. (the continuation of Unter den Linden) farther east and turning right on Spandauer Str. will bring you to the **Nikolaiviertel,** the carefully reconstructed Altstadt. Full of narrow, winding streets, its name is from the **Nikolaikirche,** whose twin spires mark Berlin's oldest building. *(Centered around Poststr. U2: Klosterstr.)* Just east of the Nikolaiviertel lies the **Rotes Rathaus,** home to East Berlin's city government between 1949 and *die Wende* (reunification); since 1990, the mayor and senate of the unified city have had their seats here. *(Jüdenstr. 1-9. Open Tu-W and F 9am-4pm, Th 4-6pm. Free.)*

GERMANY

ALEXANDERPLATZ AND FERNSEHTURM. Head back up to Karl-Liebknecht-Str. and continue east to the end of the famed boulevard at the monolithic **Alexanderplatz.** Formerly the frantic heart of Weimar Berlin, the plaza was transformed in East German times into an urban wasteland of fountains and pre-fab office buildings. The buildings surrounding the square include some GDR concrete-block classics, including the **Hotel Forum.** *(S3, S5, S7, S9, S75, U2, U5, or U8: Alexanderplatz.)* Just south of Alexanderpl. rises the awkward **Fernsehturm (TV tower),** the tallest structure in Berlin (365m), intended to show off the new heights achieved through five-year plans. Take the elevator up for a spectacular view from the top (the spherical node 203m up the spike). *(Open daily Mar.-Oct. 9am-1am; Nov.-Feb. 10am-midnight. DM9.)*

SCHEUNENVIERTEL. Northwest of Alexanderpl. lies the Scheunenviertel, once the center of Berlin's Orthodox Jewish community. Today, the area is better known for its outdoor cafés and punk clubs than for its historical significance. The **Neue Synagoge,** a huge "oriental-style" building designed by the famous Berlin architect Knoblauch, was destroyed by bombing. The temple's beautiful gold-laced domes have been reconstructed, and two first-class exhibits are housed here. The interior houses an exhibit chronicling the synagogue's history in addition to temporary exhibits on the history of Berlin's Jews. *(Oranienburger Str. 30. S1, S2, or S25: Oranienburger Str. or U6: Oranienburger Tor. Tel. 28 40 13 16. Open M-Th and Su 10am-6pm, F 10am-2pm. Museum DM5, students DM3. Dome DM3, students DM2.)*

GENDARMENMARKT. Berlin's most impressive ensemble of 19th-century buildings is a few blocks south of central Unter den Linden on the Gendarmenmarkt, also known as the French Quarter—it was the main settlement for Protestant Huguenots in the 18th century. *(U2: Französische Str., or U2 or U6: Stadtmitte.)*

POTSDAMER PLATZ AND FÜHRERBUNKER. Heading south along Ebertstr. from the Brandenburg Gate will bring you to **Potsdamer Platz,** at the southeast corner of the Tiergarten. Caught in the death strip between the two walls during the Cold War, the Platz gained notoriety in the 1990s as the world's largest construction site. Current plans aim to restore Potsdamer Platz to its position as the commercial heart of reunited Berlin by 2004. To find out more about the future of the square, visit the **Infobox,** the shiny red structure near the subway station. *(Leipziger Pl. 21. S1, S2, S25, or U2: Potsdamer Platz. Open daily 9am-7pm. Tours every hr. 10am-4pm. Free.)* Near Potsdamer Platz lies the unmarked and inconspicuous site of the **Führerbunker,** where Hitler married Eva Braun and later ended his life. In macabre irony, the actual bunker site is now a playground (behind the record store at Wilhelmstr. 92); tourists looking for it often mistakenly head for the visible bunker at the southern edge of Potsdamer Platz.

TIERGARTEN

The lush Tiergarten in the center of old Berlin stretches from Bahnhof Zoo to the Brandenburg Gate and is bisected by **Straße des 17. Juni;** the vast park was formerly used by Prussian monarchs as a hunting and parade ground. The 70m **Siegessäule** (Victory Column) in the heart of the park, topped by a gilded statue of winged victory, commemorates Prussia's humiliating defeat of France in 1870. Climb the monument's 285 steps to the top for a panorama of the city. *(Take bus 100, 187, or 341 to "Großer Stern." Open Apr.-Nov. M 1-6pm, Tu-Su 9am-6pm. DM2, students DM1.)*

THE REICHSTAG. Just north of the Brandenburg Gate in the Tiergarten sits the former seat of the parliaments of the German Empire and the Weimar Republic. When the Reichstag became the fractured center of the economically troubled Republic during the late 20s and early 30s, Nazi members gradually started showing up to sessions here in uniform, and on February 28, 1933, a month after Hitler became Chancellor, fire mysteriously broke out in the building, providing a pretext for Hitler to declare a state of emergency and seize broad powers to arrest and intimidate opponents before the upcoming elections. The infamous Enabling Act soon after established Hitler as legal dictator and abolished democracy. In the summer of 1995, the Reichstag metamorphosed when husband-and-wife team **Christo** and **Jeanne-Claude** wrapped the dignified building in 120,000 yards of shimmery

GERMANY

metallic fabric. Most recently, the long-awaited return of Germany's *Bundestag* (parliament) from Bonn to Berlin was completed in 1999.

KU'DAMM—CHARLOTTENBURG—SCHÖNEBERG

The borough of Charlottenburg, one of the wealthiest areas in Berlin, includes the area between the Ku'damm and the Spree river. During the city's division, West Berlin centered around **Bahnhof Zoo,** the only train station in the world to inspire a rock album stadium tour (the U2 subway line runs through the station). The station is surrounded by a tourism-oriented district of currency exchange booths, drunks, peep shows, and department stores. Stretching several kilometers east from Bahnhof Zoo, **Ku'damm** is Berlin's biggest and fanciest shopping strip, lined with designer boutiques, department stores, and pricey hotels. South of the Ku'damm, Schöneberg is a pleasant, middle-class residential district noted for its shopping streets, lively cafés, and good restaurants.

KAISER-WILHELM-GEDÄCHTNISKIRCHE. A sobering reminder of the destruction caused during WWII, the church's decapitated tower, its jagged edges silhouetted against the sky, is one of Berlin's most striking sights. Built in 1852 in a Romanesque/Byzantine style, the church has an equally striking interior, with colorful mosaics and deep blue stained-glass windows. The ruins house an exhibit showing what the church used to look like, as well as photos of the entire city in ruins just after the war. *(Exhibit open M-Sa 10am-4pm. Church open daily 9am-7pm.)*

KADEWE. This largest department store in mainland Europe (an abbreviated version of *Kaufhaus des Westens,* or "Department Store of the West") is the high temple of the consumerist religion in commercial Berlin. For the tens of thousands of product-starved former East Germans who flooded Western Berlin in the days following the fall of the Wall, KaDeWe *was* the West— prompting warnings such as, "OK now, we're going in. Just act normal," as intrepid children stood on the threshold of consumerism. The food department, sixth floor, has to be seen to be believed. *(Wittenbergpl. at Tauentzienstr. 21-24. Open M-F 9:30am-8pm, Sa 9am-4pm.)*

SCHLOSS CHARLOTTENBURG. The broad, bright Baroque palace commissioned by Friedrich I for his second wife, Sophie-Charlotte, lies on the northern edge of Charlottenburg. The Schloß's many buildings include the **Neringbau** (or **Altes Schloß**), the palace proper, which contains many rooms filled with historical furnishings; the **Schinkel-Pavilion,** a museum dedicated to Prussian architect Karl Friedrich Schinkel; **Belvedere,** a small building housing the royal family's porcelain collection; and the **Mausoleum,** the final resting spot for most of the family. The **Galerie der Romantik,** a state museum housing Berlin's first-rate collection of German Romantic paintings, is located in a side wing (see **Museums,** p. 388). The carefully manicured **Schloßgarten** behind the main buildings is an elysium of small lakes, footbridges, and fountains. *(Take bus 145 from Bahnhof Zoo to "Luisenpl./Schloß Charlottenburg" or U7 to "Richard-Wagner-Platz." and walk 15min. down Otto-Suhr-Allee. Altes Schloß open Tu-F 9am-5pm, Sa-Su 10am-5pm. DM8, students DM4. Schinkel-Pavilion open Tu-Su 10am-5pm. DM3, students DM2. Belvedere open Apr.-Oct. Tu-Su 10am-5pm; Nov.-Mar. Tu-F noon-4pm and Sa-Su noon-5pm. DM3, students DM2. Mausoleum open Apr.-Oct. Tu-Su 10am-noon and 1-5pm. DM3, students DM2. Schloßgarten open Tu-Su 6am-9pm. Free. Joint admission DM15, students DM10.)*

KREUZBERG—FRIEDRICHSHAIN—LICHTENBERG

Indispensable for a sense of Berlin's famous *alternative Szene,* or counterculture, is a visit to Kreuzberg, an area loaded with cafés, clubs, and bars. Kreuzberg has long been proud of its diverse population and liberal leanings: this is the place to see anti-Nazi graffiti and left-wing revolutionary slogans (in English, Turkish, Russian, Spanish, and German). During President Reagan's 1985 visit to Berlin, authorities so feared protests from this quarter that they cordoned the whole Kreuzberg district off without warning—an utterly unconstitutional measure. Much of the area was occupied by *Hausbesetzer* (squatters) in the 1960s and 70s. A conservative city government decided to forcibly evict the illegal residents in the early 80s, provoking riots and throwing the city into total consternation.

HAUS AM CHECKPOINT CHARLIE. A strange, fascinating exhibition on the site of the famous border-crossing point with an uneasy mixture of blatant Western tourist kitsch and didactic Eastern earnestness, the Haus is one of Berlin's most popular tourist attractions. Upstairs you can find out everything you've ever wanted to know about the Wall or various ways of escaping over it (e.g., in a hot-air balloon), while studying the history of human rights struggles throughout the world. Documentaries and dramas about the Wall are screened daily. *(Friedrichstr. 44. Tel. 251 10 31. U6 or bus 129: Kochstr. Open daily 9am-10pm. DM8, students DM5. Films M-F at 5:30 and 7:30pm, Sa-Su at 4:30, 6, and 7pm.)*

EAST SIDE GALLERY. The longest remaining portion of the Wall, the 1.3km stretch of cement and asbestos slabs also serves as one of the world's largest open-air art galleries. The murals are not the remnants of Cold War graffiti, but rather the efforts of an international group of artists who gathered here in 1989 to celebrate the end of the city's division. *(Along Mühlenstr. Walk back toward the river from S3, S5, S6, S7, S9, S75, U1, or U15: Warschauer Str.)*

FORSCHUNGS- UND GEDENKSTÄTTE NORMANNENSTRASSE. In the suburb of Lichtenberg stands perhaps the most hated and feared building of the GDR regime—the headquarters of the East German secret police, the **Staatssicherheit** or **Stasi.** On January 15, 1990, a crowd of 100,000 Berliners stormed and vandalized the building to protest the continued existence of the police state. The building once contained six million individual dossiers on citizens of the GDR, a country of only 16 million people. Since a 1991 law returned the records to their subjects, the "Horror-Files" have rocked Germany, exposing informants—and wrecking careers, marriages, and friendships—at all levels of society. The exhibit displays the offices of Erich Mielke (the loathed Minister for State Security from 1957-1989), surveillance equipment employed by the Stasi, and loads of Stasi kitsch. *(Ruschestr. 103, Haus 1. Tel. 553 68 54. U5: Magdalenenstr. From the Ruschestr. exit, walk up Ruschestr. and take a right on Normannenstr.; it's Haus 1 in the complex of office buildings. Exhibits in German only. Open Tu-F 11am-6pm, Sa-Su 2-6pm. DM5, students DM3.75.)*

🏛 MUSEUMS

Berlin is one of the world's great museum cities, with collections encompassing all subjects and eras. The **Staatliche Museen Preußischer Kulturbesitz (SMPK)** runs the four major museum complexes: **Museuminsel** (S3, S5, S7, S9: Hackescher Markt, or bus 100: Lustgarden); **Tiergarten-Kulturforum,** on Matthäikirchplatz at the eastern end of the Tiergarten (walk up Potsdamer Str. from S1, S2, S25, or U2: Potsdamer Platz); **Charlottenburg** (walk 15min. down Otto-Suhr-Alle from U7: Richard-Wagner-Platz, or take bus 145 from Bahnhof Zoo to "Luisenpl./Schloß Charlottenburg"; see p. 387); and **Dahlem** (U2: Dahlemdorf). Museuminsel's **Alte Nationalgalerie,** Bodestr. 1-3, and **Bodemuseum,** Monbijoubrücke, will remain closed for renovations until 2001 and 2004, respectively. SMPK admission **prices** are standardized (each DM4, students DM2). A one-day *Tageskarte* (DM8, students DM4) is valid for all SMPK museums; a *Wochenkarte* (DM25, students DM12.50) is valid for an entire week. The first Sunday of the month is free.

Pergamonmuseum, Kupfergraben (tel. 203 55 00), on Museuminsel. One of the world's great ancient history museums, thanks to Heinrich Schliemann, who traversed the world, pillaged the debris of ancient civilizations, and reassembled it at home. Mind-boggling exhibits: the entire Babylonian Ishtar Gate, the Roman Market Gate of Miletus, and the Pergamon Altar of Zeus. Also extensive collections of Greek, Assyrian, Islamic, and Far Eastern art. Open Tu-Su 9am-6pm. *Tageskarte* required. Free audio tours.

Altes Museum, at the far end of the Lustgarten on Museuminsel. Permanent collection of ancient Greco-Roman decorative art. Also temporarily houses the Alte Nationalgalerie's greatest 19th-century German and French Impressionist works. Open Tu-Su 9am-6pm. *Tageskarte* valid as long as the Alte Nationalgalerie collection remains. Free audio tour.

■ **Gemäldegalerie** (Painting Gallery; tel. 20 90 55 55), Tiergarten-Kulturinform. Rightly one of Germany's most famous museums. Stunning and enormous collection by Dutch, Flemish, German, and Italian masters, including works by Rembrandt, Bruegel, Vermeer, Raphael, Titian, Botticelli, and Dürer. Open Tu-Su 10am-6pm. SMPK ticket.

Neue Nationalgalerie, Potsdamer Str. 50 (tel. 266 26 62), Tiergarten, just past the Kulturinform. Sleek van der Rohe building contains a collection of large works—the first 2 floors are enough to make Atlas cry. SMPK ticket will get you into permanent collection including Kokoschka, Kirchner, and Beckmann, but special exhibits occupy two-thirds of the building (DM12, students DM6). Open Tu-F 10am-6pm, Sa-Su 11am-6pm.

Galerie der Romantik, in the *Neuer Flügel* (new wing) of the Schloß Charlottenburg (tel. 20 90 55 55). Holds the Prussian crown's dynamic collection of 19th-century art, including landscapes by Caspar David Friedrich. Open Tu-F 10am-6pm, Sa-Su 11am-8pm. SMPK prices.

Ägyptisches Museum, Schloßstr. 70 (tel. 20 90 55 55), across Spandauer Damm from Schloß Charlottenburg. Collection of dramatically lit ancient Egyptian art, including the 3300-year-old bust of Queen Nefertiti. Open Tu-Su 10am-6pm. SMPK prices.

Sammlung Berggruen, Schloßstr. 1 (tel. 326 95 80), across the street from the Ägyptisches Museum. Five floors of a spiral staircase provide a comprehensive overview of Picasso's life's work and influences. Open Tu-F 10am-6pm, Sa-Su 11am-6pm. SMPK prices.

Brücke Museum, Bussardsteig 9 (tel. 831 20 29). U1 or U7: Fehrbelliner Pl., then take bus 115 (dir: Neuruppiner Str.) to "Pücklerstr." (30min.). Along with the *Neue Nationalgalerie*, this is *the* Expressionist museum in Berlin, with wildly colorful works by the Expressionist *Brücke* school. Open M and W-Su 11am-5pm. DM6, students DM3.

Martin-Gropius-Bau, Niederkirchnerstr. 7 (tel. 25 48 60), near Potsdamer Platz. S1, S2, or S25: Anhalter Bahnhof or U2: Mendelssohn-Bartholdy-Park. Museum for the industrial arts. The building alone is worth the price of admission. Millenium-related exhibits in 2000. Open Tu-Su 10am-8pm. Admission varies.

Topographie des Terrors (tel. 25 48 67 03), at the corner of Niederkirchnerstr. and Wilhelmstr. near Martin-Gropius-Bau. Comprehensive exhibit details the Nazi rise to power and war-time atrocities. English guides DM2. Open Tu-Su 10am-6pm. Free.

Bauhaus Archiv-Museum für Gestaltung, Klingenhöferstr. 13-14. Take bus 100 or 187 to "Stülerstr." Exhibit on the **Bauhaus** movement in a building designed by founder Walter Gropius. Open M and W-Su 10am-5pm. DM5, students DM2.50; M free.

Deutsches Historisches Museum (tel. 20 30 40), temporarily housed in the Kronprinzenpalais, across from its usual home in the Zeughaus at Unter den Linden 2. S3, S5, S7, or S9: Hackescher Markt. Permanent displays spanning Neanderthals to Nazis; rotating exhibits on last 50 years. Lots of "happy worker" GDR art. Th-Tu 10am-6pm. Free.

🎦 ENTERTAINMENT

Berlin has one of the most vibrant cultural scenes in the world: exhibitions, concerts, plays, and dance performances abound. Reservations can be made by calling the box office directly. Most theaters and concert halls offer student discounts of up to 50% off, but only if you buy at the *Abendkasse* (evening box office), which generally opens one hour before performance. Most major theaters and operas close from mid-July to late August. **Hekticket,** on Hardenbergstr. next to the Zoo-Palast cineplex, has last-minute half-price tickets. (Tel. 230 99 30. Open M-F 9am-8pm, Sa 10am-8pm, Su 4-8pm.) **Berliner Festspiele,** Budapester Str. 48-50, sells tickets for a variety of shows, concerts, and events. (Tel. 25 48 92 50. Open M-F 10am-6pm, Su 10am-2pm.) Find theater, cinema, nightlife, and music listings in *Tip* or *Zitty* (both DM4 and in German), and the gay and lesbian *030* (free in cafés and bars).

CONCERTS AND OPERA

Look for concert listings in the monthly *Konzerte und Theater in Berlin und Brandenburg* (free) and *Berlin Programm* (DM2.80). The programs for many theaters and opera houses are also listed on posters in U-Bahn stations. **Berliner**

GERMANY

Philharmonisches Orchester, Matthäikirchstr. 1, is one of the world's finest. Check for last-minute seats an hour before curtain. (Tel. 25 48 81 32. U2, S1, S2, or S25: Potsdamer Pl., then head up Potsdamer Str. Tickets from DM14-26; sold M-F 3:30-6pm, Sa-Su 11am-2pm. Closed late June to early Sept.) **Deutsche Oper Berlin,** Bismarckstr. 35, is Berlin's best opera. (Info tel. 341 02 49, for tickets 343 84 01. U2: Deutsche Oper. Tickets DM15-140. Evening tickets available 1hr. before show. Box office open M-Sa from 11am until 1hr. before show, Su 10am-2pm. Closed July-Aug.)

THEATER AND FILM

Berlin has a lively English-language theater scene; look for listings marked *in englischer Sprache* (in English). *"O.F."* next to a movie listing means original version (i.e. not dubbed and without German subtitles), while *"O.m.U."* means original with German subtitles. **Odeon,** Hauptstr. 116, plays a mixture of mainstream American and British films with a pseudo-leftist slant. (Tel. 78 70 40 19. U4: Rathaus Schöneberg. All films in English.) **UCI Kinowelt Zoo-Palast,** Hardenbergstr. 29a (tel. 25 41 47 77), near Bahnhof Zoo, is one of the most popular cineplexes showing dubbed blockbuster Hollywood films. **Deutsches Theater,** Schumannstr. 13a, is the best theater in the country, with innovative productions of both classics and newer works. (Tel. 28 44 12 25. U6 or S1, S2, S3, S5, S7, S9, S25, or S75: Friedrichstr. Tickets DM15-25. Box office open M-Sa 11am-6:30pm, Su 3-6:30pm.) **Friends of Italian Opera,** Fidicinstr. 40 (tel. 691 12 11), is Berlin's leading English-language theater. (U6: Platz der Luftbrücke. Tickets DM15-20. Box office opens at 6:30pm. Most shows at 8pm.)

☑ NIGHTLIFE

Berlin's nightlife is madness: a teeming cauldron of debauchery that runs around the clock and threatens to inflict coronaries upon the faint of heart. Bars, clubs, and cafés typically jam until at least 3am and often stay open until daylight; on weekends, you can dance non-stop from Friday night 'til Monday morning. It's also worth mentioning that Berlin has **de-criminalized marijuana possession** of up to 8g. Smoking in public, however, has not been officially accepted, though becoming more common in some clubs. *Let's Go* does not recommend puffing clouds of hash smoke into the faces of police officers. If at all possible, try to hit (or, if you're prone to bouts of claustrophobia, avoid) Berlin during the **Love Parade,** usually held in the second weekend of July, when all of Berlin just says "yes" to everything. Though there is much speculation as to whether the Love Parade will be in Berlin next year (a move to Paris seems imminent), most cannot imagine the parade anywhere else.

In **Western Berlin,** the best nightlife venues are **Savignyplatz, Nollendorfplatz** in Schöneberg (*café-Kneipen* lie along Winterfeldtplatz, Akazienstr., and Goltzstr.), and particularly **Kreuzberg** (between U1 or U15 stops "Kottbusser Tor" and "Görlitzer Bahnhof"), where a menagerie of radically alternative clubs range from laid-back to breathtakingly salacious. But while Kreuzberg tries to defend West Berlin's reputation as the dance capital of the world, its alterna-charm has become a tad passé as clubs have fled to the east and north. Berlin's best clubs currently lie in **Eastern Berlin: Potsdamer Platz** and the intersection of **Oranienburger Str.** and **Friedrichstr.** are the clear hotspots, and the area around Mitte's **Oranienburger Str.** is also lively. Farther afield, **Prenzlauer Berg** and **Friedrichshain** (S3, S5, S6, S7, S9, S75, U1, U12, or U15: Warschauer Str.) both host Berlin's newest alternative clubs. Traditionally, the social nexus of **gay and lesbian** nightlife has centered around **Nollendorfplatz** and the surrounding *Schwuler Kiez* (gay neighborhood) of **Schöneberg.** For up-to-date events listings, pick up a copy of the amazingly comprehensive *Siegessäule* (free), named after the phallic monument.

Sage Club, Brückenstr. 1, in Kreuzberg. U8: Heinrich-Heine-Str. or bus N8. Fast-paced dance club arena corners the techno and house market in Kreuzberg. Bring your lycra and pleatherwear, or at least enough hair gel to make up for those dirty sneakers. Cover DM10-25. Get into the groove Th-Su from 11pm.

Tresor/Globus, Leipziger Str. 126a (tel. 229 06 11), in Mitte. U2 or S1, S2, S25 or bus N5, N29 or N52 to "Potsdamer Platz." One of the most rocking techno venues in Berlin. **Globus** chills with house; **Tresor** rocks to techno beats. Cover W DM5, F DM10, Sa DM15-20. Open W and F-Sa 11pm-6am.

Bibo Bar, Lychener Str. 17 (tel. 443 97 98). From U2: Eberswalder Str., walk along Danziger Str. to Lychener Str. DJs change daily, but they're always as crazy and mixed (in every sense) as the bar's clientele, who spend long nights boozing it, dancing wildly, and discussing the meaning of life on crowded sofas. Drinks DM8-12. Open daily 5pm-late.

Tacheles, Oranienburger Str. 53-56 (tel. 282 61 85). U6: Oranienburger Tor or S1, S2, S25: Oranienburger Str. or bus N6 or N84. Artists, punks, and tourists from nearby hostels converge on its art galleries, bars, and vicious raves. Open 24hr.

Hackesche Höfe, Rosenthaler Str. 40-41. S3, S5, S7, S9, or S75: Hackescher Markt. Series of interconnected courtyards with cafés, clubs, galleries, shops, and a movie theater. Low-key **Oxymoron** (tel. 28 39 18 85) within offers daily jazz concerts for a thirtysomething crowd (DM15-20). Open M and W-Sa from 11pm, Tu from 8:30pm, Su from 10pm.

S036, Oranienstr. 190 (tel. 61 40 13 06; www.S036.de), in Kreuzberg. U1, U12, U15: Görlitzer Bahnhof, bus N29 to "Heinrichplatz," or bus N8 to "Adalbertstr." Berlin's only truly mixed club, with a clientele of hip heteros, gays, and lesbians grooving to a mishmash of wild genres. M trance; Th hip-hop/reggae/punk/ska; weekends run the gamut from techno to live concerts. Cover varies. Open daily after 11pm.

Kulturbrauerei, Knaackstr. 97 (tel. 44 05 67 56). U2: Eberswalder Str. Variety of concerts and parties in enormous former brewery; call ahead for info. Cover DM3-5, more for special events. Open Tu and Th-Su after 10pm.

Insel der Jugend, Alt-Treptow 6 (tel. 53 60 80 20), on an island in the Spree river. S4, S6, S8, or S9: Treptower Park; then take bus 166, 167, 265, or N65 to "Alt-Treptow." 3 dance floors: reggae, hip-hop, ska, and house upstairs, and frantic techno in the basement. Cover Th-Sa DM5-15. Open W from 7pm, Th from 9pm, F-Sa from 10pm.

Quasimodo, Kantstr. 12a (tel. 312 80 86). S3, S5, S7, S9, or S75: Savignyplatz. This unassuming basement pub with attached *Biergarten* is one of Berlin's most integral jazz venues, drawing big names and lively crowds. Cover free-DM40. Concert tickets available from 5pm or at Kant-Kasse ticket service (tel. 313 45 54; fax 312 64 40). Open daily from 8pm.

GAY AND LESBIAN NIGHTLIFE

Café Berio, Maaßenstr. 7 (tel. 216 19 46), in Schöneberg. U1, U2, U4, or U15: Nollendorfplatz. Bright, charming café caters to an easy-going gay and lesbian crowd. Perfect for brunch or an early evening drink. Outdoor seating in summer. Open daily 8am-1am.

Schoko-Café, Mariannenstr. 6 (tel. 615 15 61). Lesbian central; a café with a cultural center upstairs, billiards, and dancing every 2nd Sa of the month (10pm). Open M-Th and Su 5pm-1am year-round, plus F-Sa from noon in the summer.

S036, Usually a mixed club (see above), but also hosts predominantly queer events: W trance and drum 'n' bass party; Su ballroom dancing and *Schlagerkarusell* at 10pm; 3rd F of month wild party for lesbians and drags (10pm-late).

Die Busche, Mühlenstr. 12, in Friedrichshain. U1, U12, U15, S3, S5, S6, S7, S9, or S75: Warschauer Str. East Berlin's largest queer disco serves up an incongruous rotation of techno, top 40, and, yes, *Schlager*. Very cruisey. Cover DM6-10. Open W and F-Su from 9:30pm. The party gets going around midnight. It *really* gets going around 3am.

⚡ EXCURSIONS FROM BERLIN: POTSDAM

Visitors disappointed by Berlin's gritty, distinctly unroyal demeanor could do no better than to head to nearby Potsdam, the glittering city of Frederick II (the Great). From 1921 through WWII, Potsdam served as Germany's "Little Hollywood," and in 1945 the Allies divided up Germany at the Potsdam Conference. The 600-acre **Park Sanssouci,** with countless marble fountains, exotic pavilions, and Baroque castles, stands as a monument to Frederick the Great's (not necessarily matching) aesthetic tastes. A **day ticket** gives you access to all of the park's four castles (DM20, students DM15). At one end of the long **Hauptallee** (central path) stands the park's main attraction, the Versailles-esque **Schloß Sanssouci,** where Frederick escaped his wife and drowned his sorrows. (Open Apr.-Oct. daily 9am-5pm; Feb.-Mar. 9am-4pm; Nov.-Jan. 9am-3pm. Tours in German every 20min.; last tour at 5pm sells out by 2pm in high-season. DM10, students DM5.) At the opposite end of the park is the largest of the four castles, the 200-room **Neues Palais,** built by Frederick to demonstrate Prussia's power (oh, and to house his guests). Its *Grottensaal* (reception room) glitters with seashells. (Open Apr.-Oct. Su-Th 9am-5pm; Nov.-Mar. Su-Th 9am-4pm. DM6, students DM4.) The most exotic of the park's pavilions is the gilded **Chinesisches Teehaus,** complete with a parasol-toting Buddha on the roof (DM2). Potsdam's second park, the **Neuer Garten,** contains several former royal residences. Built in the style of an English country manor, **Schloß Cecilienhof** hosted the signatories of the 1945 Potsdam Treaty. To get there, take **bus** 694 to "Cecilienhof." (Open Tu-Su 9am-noon and 12:30-5pm; DM6, with tour DM8, students DM4).

S7 runs to Potsdam-Stadt (in Zone C; see **Public Transportation,** p. 376) from Berlin's Bahnhof Zoo (30min., DM4.20), and hourly **trains** arrive from Leipzig (2hr., DM46). The **tourist office,** Friedrich-Ebert-Str. 5, between the "Alter Markt" and "Pl. der Einheit" streetcar stops, books rooms (DM20-40 per person) for a DM5 fee. (Tel. (0331) 27 55 80; fax 275 58 99. Open Apr.-Oct. M-F 9am-8pm, Sa 9am-6pm, Su 9am-4pm; Nov.-Mar. M-F 10am-6pm, Sa-Su 10am-2pm.)

EASTERN GERMANY

Saxony (Sachsen) is known primarily for Dresden and Leipzig, but the entire region offers a fascinating historical and cultural diversity that reveals a great deal about life in the former East. West of Saxony, Thuringia (Thüringen), the "Green Heart of Germany," is a hilly and mostly pastoral land. Echoes of Thuringia are heard throughout Europe's cultural canon: Bach, Goethe, Schiller, Luther, and Wagner all left their mark on this landscape, arguably the most beautiful in Germany. North of Thuringia and Saxony, Saxony-Anhalt's (Sachsen-Anhalt) endless grass plains offer one of the region's more tranquil landscapes. Its high unemployment rate mirrors the economic woes of Eastern Germany as a whole, but many construction sites mushrooming across the *Land* point toward the future.

DRESDEN

Dresden (pop. 500,000) pulses with an intensity that is both sublime and vicious—an emblem of everything that was and is East Germany. Allied bombings shattered the "Baroque Jewel" in 1945; today over 200 cranes assist the massive reconstruction of the city's skyline, scheduled for completion by the city's 800th birthday in 2006. But while tourists everywhere wax pretentious about "the hope of tomorrow," raw Dresden offers a vitality that transcends the process of reconstruction.

▐ GETTING THERE AND GETTING AROUND

Trains: Hauptbahnhof (tel. 194 19). To: **Leipzig** (1½hr., 34 per day, DM33); **Berlin** (2hr., 20 per day, DM52); **Prague** (3hr., 7 per day, DM38); **Frankfurt am Main** (6hr., 11 per day, DM136); **Kraków** (7hr., 3 per day, DM52); **Warsaw** (8hr., 9 per day, DM55); and **Munich** (8hr., 24 per day, DM148). Trains from **Bahnhof Dresden Neustadt,** on the other bank of the Elbe, head primarily to other cities in Eastern Germany.

Public Transportation: Dresden is sprawling—even if you only spend a few days here, familiarize yourself with the major bus and streetcar lines. **Single-ride** fare DM2.70; 4 or fewer stops DM1.60. **Day pass** DM8; **weekly pass** DM24, students DM18. Most major lines run every hr. after midnight. Buy tickets from *Automaten* in the Hauptbahnhof and cancel them in the red validating machines as you board; insert the ticket and press *hard*.

Hitchhiking: *Let's Go* does not recommend hitchhiking. Hitchers stand in front of on-ramp *Autobahn* signs. To **Berlin:** streetcar 3 or 13 to "Liststr.," then bus 81 to "Olter." To **Prague** or **Frankfurt:** bus 72 or 88 to "Luga," or bus 76, 85, or 87 to "Lockwitz."

GERMANY

🛈 ORIENTATION AND PRACTICAL INFORMATION

Dresden is bisected by the Elbe River: the **Altstadt** and the Hauptbahnhof lie on the southern side of the river, while the **Neustadt** lies to the north of the river. Most tourist attractions are centered in the Altstadt along the Elbe. From the Hauptbahnhof, heading straight down Prager Str. will bring you to the heart of the Altstadt.

TOURIST, FINANCIAL, AND LOCAL SERVICES

Tourist Office: Prager Str. (tel. 49 19 20; fax 49 19 21 16), opposite the Hauptbahnhof; and on **Theaterpl.**, in the Schinkelwache, a small building in front of the Semper-Oper. Sells the **Dresden Card** (DM26), which provides 48hr. of public transit and free or reduced entry at many museums. Both open M-F 10am-6pm, Sa-Su 10am-2pm.

Currency Exchange: ReiseBank, in the main hall of the Hauptbahnhof. 2.5-4.5% commission for currency exchange, DM7.50 for traveler's checks. Open M-F 7:30am-7:30pm, Sa 8am-noon and 12:30-4pm, Su 9am-1pm. Other banks are on Prager Str.

American Express: Hoyerswerdaer Str. 20 (tel. 80 70 30), in Neustadt near Rosa-Luxemburg-Pl. Money sent and mail held. Open M-F 7:30am-6pm.

Luggage Storage: At both train stations. Lockers DM2-4. Checked luggage DM4 per piece per 24hr. Open M-F 6am-10pm, Sa 6am-9pm.

Laundromat: Groove Station, Katharinenstr. 11-13. Wash your clothes (DM8 including a cup of coffee) while shopping for leather, tattoos, piercings, drinks, or *Erektionsbekleidung* (condoms). Open Su-F 11am-2am, Sa 10am-late.

EMERGENCY AND COMMUNICATIONS

Emergency: Police, tel. 110. **Ambulance** and **fire,** tel. 112.

Pharmacy: Apotheke Prager Straße, Prager Str. 3 (tel. 490 30 14). Open M-F 8:30am-7pm, Sa 8:30am-4pm. Sign on the door indicates night pharmacies.

Internet Access: Upd@te, Louisenstr. 30 (tel. 804 87 47), near Die Boofe (see below). DM10 per hr. Open M-F noon-8pm, Sa noon-2pm.

Post Office: Hauptpostamt, Königsbrücker Str. 21/29 (tel. 819 13 70), in Neustadt. Address mail to be held: *Postlagernde Briefe* für Speedy <u>GONZALEZ</u>, Hauptpostamt, **D-01099** Dresden, Germany. Open M-F 8am-7pm, Sa 8am-1pm.

PHONE CODE	City code: 0351. From outside Germany, dial int'l dialing prefix + 49 + 351 + local number.

📷 ACCOMMODATIONS, CAMPING, AND FOOD

New hotels and hostels are constantly being planned, built, and opened in Dresden, but it's hard to get a spot in a good location on weekends. A 110-bed ship located at **Leipziger Str. 57** is scheduled to open in September 1999, 10min. from the train station in Neustadt (DM30, under 27 DM25). For info or to reserve rooms, inquire at Rudi-Arndt (see below). The excess of available rooms also means that there are often same-day deals at some of the hotels on Prager Str.

▧ Mondpalast Backpacker, Katharinenstr. 11-13 (tel./fax 804 60 61). From Bahnhof Neustadt, walk down Antonstr., turn left on Königsbrücker Str., cross the street and turn right on Katharinenstr. (10min.). Created by backpackers for backpackers, in the heart of the Neustadt scene. Dorms DM25-27; bed in a double DM31. Breakfast DM8. Sheets DM5. **Internet** DM12 per hr. Key deposit DM10. Reception 24hr. Call ahead.

Hostel Die Boofe, Louisenstr. 20 (tel. 801 33 61; fax 801 33 62), in Neustadt. A new hostel with immaculate rooms. Dorms DM27; breakfast DM8. Doubles DM39.50 including breakfast. Sheets DM5. Bike rental DM10 per day. Reception 24hr.

Jugendherberge Dresden Rudi Arndt (HI), Hübnerstr. 11 (tel. 471 06 67; fax 472 89 59). Take streetcar 5 (dir: Südvorstadt) or 3 (dir: Plauen) to "Nürnberger Platz"; continue down Nürnberger Str. and turn right on Hübnerstr. Or, from the Hauptbahnhof, walk down Fritz-Löffler-Str., bear right on Münchener Str., turn right on Eisenstuckstr. and walk 2 blocks. Central and comfortable, with a laid-back staff. DM30, under 27 DM25; members only. Sheets DM5. Check-in 3pm-1am. Curfew 1am.

GERMANY

Jugendgästehaus Dresden (HI), Maternistr. 22 (tel. 49 26 20; fax 492 62 99). From the Hauptbahnhof, exit onto Prager Str. and turn left, following the streetcar tracks along Ammonstr. to Freiberger Str.; turn right and take a quick right onto Maternistr. Attracts lots of school groups. Dorms DM38, under 27 DM33; with shower DM45, under 27 DM40. Singles add DM15. Breakfast included. Check-in from 4pm. Check-out 9:30am.

Pension Raskolnikoff, Böhmischer Str. 34 (tel. 804 57 06). Good location in Neustadt, with spacious rooms. Doubles DM75; add DM12 per additional person. Call ahead.

Campingplatz Altfranken, Otto-Harzer-Str. 2 (tel. 410 24 00; fax 410 24 80), next to a bus stop. From the Hauptbahnhof, take streetcar 7 (dir: Gorbitz) to Tharandter Str., then bus 90 all the way to Altfranken. DM10 per tent. Reception 24hr.

Unfortunately, the surge in Dresden tourism has yielded an increase in food prices, particularly in the Altstadt. The cheapest eats are at **supermarkets** or *Imbiß* stands along Prager Str. The **Neustadt** area, between **Albertpl.** and **Alunpl.,** spawns a new bar every few weeks and packs in ethnic and student-friendly restaurants. **Raskolnikoff,** Böhmische Str. 34, hidden beneath a sign for Galerie Raskolnikow, serves Russian and Afghan fare. (Meals DM8-20. Open daily 10am-2am.) **El Perro Borracho,** Alaunstr. 70, serves tasty tapas and sangría. (Entrees DM12. Buffet breakfast Sa-Su until 4pm DM10. Open M-F 11:30am-1am, Sa-Su 10am-1am.)

👁 SIGHTS

Most of Dresden's celebrated sights are located near **Theaterpl.** The *Tageskarte* (1-day DM12, students DM7; available at any museum) covers admission to the Albertinum museums, the Schloß, most of the Zwinger, and other sights.

ZWINGER PALACE AND SEMPER-OPER. The extravagant collection of Friedrich August I, a.k.a. August the Strong, Prince Elector of Saxony and King of Poland, is housed in the magnificent **Zwinger** palace, designed by Matthäus Daniel Pöppelmann and championed as one of the most successful examples of Baroque design. Hordes of tourists flock to view the Zwinger's array of decadent gates, pavilions, and museums. The **Gemäldegalerie Alte Meister,** in the Semper Wing (through the main courtyard and to the left of the main entrance) houses a world-class collection of paintings from 1500 to 1800, including Cranach the Elder's luminous *Adam* and *Eve* paintings and Rubens's erotically charged *Leda and the Swan*. *(Open Tu-Su 10am-6pm. DM7, students DM4. Tours F and Su 4pm. DM1.)* The painstaking restoration of the famed **Semper-Oper** (Opera House), just north of the Zwinger and west of the Hofkirche, makes it one of Dresden's major attractions. *(DM9, students DM6—and worth every Pfennig. For tour times, check the main entrance or call 491 17 05.)*

DRESDENER SCHLOSS. Opposite the Zwinger, the residential palace of Sachsen's Electors and emperors (who once ruled nearly all of Central Europe) was ruined in the Allied firebombing of February 13, 1945, but its restoration is nearly complete. The 100-meter-tall **Hausmannsturm** hosts an exhibition of photographs of the destruction of the city caused by the February bombings and offers an excellent view of the city. *(Open Tu-Su 10am-6pm. DM5, students DM3.)* The **Katholische Hofkirche** (Catholic Royal Church) used to be connected to the Schloß—August the Strong converted to Catholicism to obtain the Polish crown. His heart now occupies a little case stored safely in the church's crypt. *(Open M-Th 9am-5pm, F 1-5pm, Sa 10:30-4pm, Su noon-4pm. Free.)* If you've been mistaking Friedrich the Earnest for Friedrich the Pugnacious, stop by the **Fürstenzug** (Procession of Electors) along Augustusstr. for a quick history lesson—it's a mammoth (102m) mural made of 24,000 tiles of Meißen china depicting the rulers of Saxony from 1123 to 1904.

ALBERTINUM. The ▣**Gemäldegalerie der Neuen Meister** contains a solid ensemble of German and French Impressionists, including Renoirs and Gauguins, and some Expressionist and modernist works. Upstairs, the **Grünes Gewölbe** has a dazzling collection of the completely gratuitous refinements possessed by the House of Sachsen. *(East of the Schloß. Both open F-W 10am-6pm. Joint ticket DM7, students DM4.)*

STADTMUSEUM. Although the museum details Dresden's history since the 13th century, early history just can't compete with the collection of mementos from the Communist period: Stalinist propaganda and posters of happy children flashing toothy grins abound, and the 80s fashion collection will bring tears to your eyes. Across the wall, pictures, demonstration posters, and secret police files examine the more heroic side of the Socialist era. *(Wilsdruffer Str. 2, in the Landhaus, near Pirnaischer Pl. and south of the Albertinum. Open Sa-Th 10am-6pm. DM4, students DM2.)*

NEUSTADT. Just across the magnificent **Augustus Brücke** (bridge) from the Altstadt, the cobblestoned, tree-lined pedestrian avenue **Hauptstraße** (Main Street) stretches from the Elbe past the **Goldener Reiter,** a gold-plated vision of August the Strong, to **Albertplatz,** surrounded by handsome 19th-century mansions.

SCHLACHTHOFRINGE. The Schlachthofringe (Slaughterhouse Circle) is an original 1910 housing complex in a relatively dismal part of Dresden, commandeered during WWII as a camp for prisoners of war. Novelist **Kurt Vonnegut** was imprisoned here during the bombing of Dresden, inspiring his novel *Slaughterhouse Five.* Take streetcar 9 (dir: Friedrichstadt) to the end and walk up (though not at night).

◪ NIGHTLIFE

The Neustadt is the thudding heart of this fast-paced city. At last count, over 50 bars were packed into the area bounded by Königsbrücker Str., Bischofsweg, Kamenzerstr., and Albertpl.; *Kneipen Surfer* provides a list and description of each one. Peruse the back of *SAX* (DM2.50 at the tourist office, or ask to see one at any bar) to glean info on concerts and clubs. **Scheune,** Alaunstr. 36-40, is the granddaddy of the Neustadt bar scene; its culturally eclectic dance floor invites you to disco to West African, Baltic, and Yiddish beats. (Cover varies. Club opens at 8pm.) **Down-Town,** Katharinenstr. 11-13, below the Mondpalast hostel, is *the* place to indulge in Dresden's neon techno scene—it's one of the few night venues capable of convincing skeptics that some Germans can dance. (F house and techno, Sa funk and occasional live music, gay night M. Cover DM7, students DM5. Open F-M 10pm-5am.) **Die Tonne,** Am Brauhaus 3, offers "cool drinks and hot jazz." (Cover DM8-20. Open daily 6pm-1am. Performances at 9pm.)

◪ EXCURSION FROM DRESDEN: MEISSEN

Just 30km from Dresden, Meißen is yet another testament to the frivolity of August the Strong. In 1710, the Saxon elector developed a severe case of *Porzellankrankheit* (the porcelain "bug"—an affliction that still manifests itself in tourists today) and turned the city's defunct castle into a porcelain-manufacturing base. From the station, walk straight onto Bahnhofstr., follow the riverbank to the Elbbrücke, cross the bridge, continue straight to the Markt, turn right onto Burgstr., and follow the stairs on Schloßstr. that lead to the right up to the castle and cathedral at **Albrechtsburg.** (Open daily Mar.-Oct. 10am-6pm; Nov.-Feb. 10am-5pm. DM6, students DM3.) Next door, the early Gothic **Meißener Dom** (cathedral) ensures that its visitors get their money's worth with four priceless 13th-century statues by the Naumburg Master, a triptych by Cranach the Elder, and beautiful metal grave coverings. (Open daily Apr.-Oct. 9am-6pm; Nov.-Mar. 10am-4pm. DM3.50, students DM2.50.) Although the castle porcelain factory was once more tightly guarded than KGB headquarters for fear that competitors would discover its secret techniques, today anyone can tour the **Staatliche Porzellan-Manufaktur,** Talstr. 9. The **Schauhalle** serves as a museum where visitors can peruse finished products, but the real fun lies in the high-tech tour of the **Schauwerkstatt** (show workshop), where you can see people actually manufacturing the porcelain. (Tel. (03521) 46 82 07. *Schauhalle* DM9, students DM7. *Schauwerkstatt* open daily 9am-6pm; DM5; English tapes available.) Meißen is an easy daytrip from Dresden by **train** (45min., DM7.70). The **tourist office** is at Markt 3. (Tel. (03521) 45 44 70; fax 45 82 40. Open Apr.-Oct. M-F 10am-6pm, Sa-Su 10am-3pm; Nov.-Mar. M-F 9am-5pm.)

SAXON SWITZERLAND

Formerly one of East Germany's most beloved holiday destinations, Saxon Switzerland (*Sächsische Schweiz*)—so dubbed because of its stunning, Swiss-like landscape—is now one of unified Germany's favorite national parks. Perched right on the Berlin-Dresden-Prague rail line, its sandstone cliffs, sumptuous summits, and breathtaking hikes (literally) should be reason enough to lure any lover of the outdoors off the tracks and into the hills for a few days.

E GETTING THERE AND GETTING AROUND. Dresden's S-Bahn (line 1; dir: Schöna) runs east along the Elbe River, stopping at (west to east) Pirna, Wehlen, Rathen, Königstein, and Bad Schandau. **Wanderwege** (footpaths) wind up into the hills, connecting all the towns in a spidery web. The S-Bahn stops just across the river from **Wehlen** (hop on a short ferry to get to town; DM1.30), the point of origin of two hiking trails to **Rathen.** The first climbs up onto the most famous cliffs of the area, the Bastei, and was a favorite of August the Strong; the other is shorter and easier but much less impressive (45min.). To get to **Hohnstein,** either hike from Rathen (see below) or hop off the S-Bahn at Pirna and catch bus 236 or 237 from the Bahnhof to "Hohnstein Eiche" (DM5.20). From **Bad Schandau** at the end of the line, cross the river by ferry (DM1.30) and hop on the S-Bahn back to **Dresden** (50min., every 30min., DM7.70) or continue by train to **Prague** (2hr., DM30.60).

RATHEN AND HOHNSTEIN. Rathen, on the edge of **Sächsische Schweiz National Park,** hosts hiking trails of all lengths and difficulties. It's also home to the **Felsenbühne,** one of Europe's most beautiful open-air theaters, with stone pillars looming over the stage and 2000 seats carved into a cliff. Follow the signs from town; along the way you'll pass the **Theaterkasse,** where you can buy tickets. (Tel. (035024) 77 70; fax 777 35. DM6-39.) A **tourist office** upstairs in the *Gästeamt,* 10min. from the ferry, has hiking info. (Tel./fax (035024) 704 22. Open in summer M-F 9am-noon and 2-6pm, Sa 9am-2pm; in winter closed Sa.) Sleep in a castle above the town at **Gästehaus Burg Altrathen.** (Tel. (035024) 700 37; fax 700 38. Mattress accommodations DM25; singles DM40-45; doubles DM70-90. Breakfast included.)

The small village of **Hohnstein** ("high stone" in old Sachsen), with grand forest vistas on all sides, is linked to Rathen by a gorgeous hike through one of the National Park's most stunning valleys, flanked by large sandstone boulders and magnificent rock formations. Facing the *Gästeamt* in Rathen, take a left through the parking lot and follow the path marked by the white squares with a horizontal red stripe (2hr.). The town encircles the **Naturfreundehaus Burg Hohnstein,** Am Markt 1, a fortress which holds a history and nature museum, *Aussichtsturm* (lookout tower), and **hostel.** (Tel. (035975) 812 02; fax 812 03. DM27.20-38.20, nonmembers DM34.20-38.20 including tax; add DM2 for stays shorter than 3 days. Breakfast included. Reception 7am-8pm.) The **tourist office,** Rathausstr. 10, in the Rathaus, finds rooms for free and doles out info on trails and the Burg. (Tel. (035975) 194 33; fax 868 10. Open M-F 9am-noon and 12:30-5pm, Tu until 6pm.)

KÖNIGSTEIN. Above the town of Königstein looms the fortress **Festung Königstein,** whose huge walls are built right into the same stone spires that made Saxon Switzerland famous. The unobstructed view from the fortress is worth sweating for—it's a 45-minute struggle up from town. (Open daily Apr.-Sept. 9am-8pm; Oct. 9am-6pm; Nov.-Mar. 9am-5pm. DM7, students DM5.) The **tourist office,** Schreiberberg 2, two blocks uphill from the "Festungs Express" stop, books rooms (DM25-45). (Tel. (035021) 682 61; fax 688 87. Open in summer M-F 9am-noon and 2-6pm, Sa 9am-noon; in winter M-F 9am-noon and 3-5pm, Sa 9-10:30am.) Königstein's **Naturfreundehaus,** Halbestadt 13, is nicer (but pricier) than most hostels. (Tel. (035022) 424 32. DM40-90. Breakfast included. Reception 6am-10pm.) The **campground,** in the shadow of the fortress, is on the banks of the Elbe 10min. upstream from the station. (Tel. (035021) 682 24. DM6 per tent, DM7.30 per person.)

BAD SCHANDAU. The largest town in Saxon Switzerland, Bad Schandau serves as the region's transport hub. The solar-powered **Kirnitzschtalbahn train** (May-Oct. 2 per hr., DM6) runs to the **Lichtenhain Waterfall,** not that impressive in itself, but a starting point for full-day hikes to the spectacular **Schrammsteine.** The **tourist office,** Markt 12, finds rooms (DM25-30). (Open M-F 9am-6:30pm, Sa 9am-4pm.)

GERMANY

LEIPZIG

Leipzig gained fame for its role as the crucible of *die Wende*, the sudden toppling of the GDR in 1989. The city now jumps out from the Eastern German landscape in a fiery blaze of glitzy nightlife. Over 20,000 students harken back to the days when Goethe, Nietzsche, and Leibniz stalked these ivory (well…gray) towers.

⚐⛛⚑ PRACTICAL INFO, ACCOMMODATIONS, AND FOOD. Trains run to Dresden (1-1½hr., every hr., DM26) and Berlin (2-3hr., every hr., DM46). To reach the **tourist office,** Richard-Wagner-Str. 1, walk across Willy-Brandt-Pl. in front of the station and turn left at Richard-Wagner-Str. (Tel. (0341) 710 42 60; fax 710 42 71; email lipsia@aol.com. Open M-F 8am-8pm, Sa 8am-4pm.) Check your **email** at **Café le bit,** Kohlgartenstr. 2 (30min. free, then DM2 per 15min). Budget lodgings in Leipzig are hard to find; the tourist office finds **private rooms** (singles from DM40; doubles from DM70). To reach the **Jugendherberge Leipzig Centrum (HI),** Volksgartenstr. 24, take streetcar 17, 37, or 57 (dir: Thekla or Schönefeld; 15min.) to "Löbauer Str.," walk past the supermarket along Löbauer Str., and turn right on Volksgartenstr. (Tel. 245 70 11; fax 245 70 12. DM29, under 27 DM24. Breakfast included. Sheets DM6. Reception 2:30-11pm. Curfew 1am.) **Campingplatz Am Auensee,** Gustav-Esche-Str. 5, in nearby Wahren, is a budgetary *deus ex machina* in the absence of hostels. From the station, take streetcar 11 or 28 (dir: Wahren) to "Rathaus Wahren"; turn left at the Rathaus and follow the twisting main road for 10min. (Tel. 465 16 00. DM8 per person, DM5 per car. Small 2-person hut DM30, large hut with shower DM60. Reception M-Sa 6am-9:30pm, Su 6am-8:30pm.) The Innenstadt is well-supplied with *Imbiß* stands, bistros, and restaurants. There's a **Kaiser's supermarket** on the Brühl, near Sachsenpl. (Open M-F 7am-8pm, Sa 7am-4pm.) **Postal code:** 04109.

◙ ♫ SIGHTS AND ENTERTAINMENT. The heart of the city beats in the **Marktplatz,** a colorful square guarded by the 16th-century **Altes Rathaus.** Inside the Rathaus, the **Stadtgeschichtliches Museum Leipzig** offers a straightforward look at Leipzig's history. (Open Tu 2-8pm, W-Su 10am-6pm. DM5, students DM2.50.) Just behind the Altes Rathaus at Grimmaischestr. 1-7 is the temporary home of the **Museum der Bildenden Künste Leipzig** (Museum of Fine Arts), which chronicles German art from the 18th century to the present. (Open Tu and Th-Su 10am-6pm, W 1-9:30pm. DM5, students DM2.50.) Head up Nikolaistr. to see the 800-year-old **Nikolaikirche,** which witnessed the birth of Bach's *Johannes Passion* as well as the GDR's peaceful revolution. (Open M-Sa 10am-6pm, Su after services. Free.) Backtrack down Nikolaistr. and turn right on Grimmaischestr., which turns into Thomasg., until you come upon the **Thomaskirche,** where Bach spent the last 27 years of his career. Although the church is currently undergoing massive restorations for the Bach Festival (July 21-30, 2000), it's open to the public; the **Thomascor,** one of Europe's most prestigious boys' choirs, performs here. (Open daily in summer 9am-6pm; off-season 9am-5pm. Performances F 6pm, Sa 3pm, and Su during services.) Just behind the Thomaskirche lies the **Johann-Sebastian-Bach-Museum,** Thomaskirchhof 16, which chronicles Bach's life in Leipzig from 1723-50. (Open daily 10am-5pm. DM4, students DM2.50.) Head back to Thomasg., turn left, then turn right on Dittrichring to reach Leipzig's most fascinating museum, the **Museum der "Runden Ecke,"** Dittrichring 24. Once the headquarters of the feared East German Ministry for State Security, the museum has a stunningly blunt exhibit on the history, doctrine, and tools of the SS. (Open W-Su 2-6pm. Free.)

Barfußgäschen, a street just off the Markt, serves as the see-and-be-seen bar venue for everyone from students to *schicki-micki* yuppies. **Karl-Liebknecht-Str.** is just as *Szene*-ic without being quite as claustrophobic as Barfußgäschen; take streetcar 11 (dir: Markkleeburg-Ost) to "Arndtstr." Bars along the street pour drinks for Irish-lovers (**Killiwilly** at #44), Francophiles (**Maitre** at #62), tough art-house film types (**naTo** at #46), caffeine addicts (**KAHWE** at the corner of Arndtstr. and Karl-Liebknecht-Str.), and everyone else (**Weißes Rössel** next door).

GERMANY

WEIMAR

Last year was a big year for Weimar, one of the designated Cultural Capitals of Europe in 1999. Although most of the hype has died down, it remains one of the most thoroughly rebuilt of former East German cities, and intellectual energy continues to resonate through the former home of Goethe, Schiller, and Herder. While countless towns leap at any excuse to build a memorial to Goethe (Goethe slept here, Goethe went to school here, Goethe once asked for directions here), Weimar's **Goethehaus,** Frauenplan 1, is the real deal, where he entertained, wrote, studied, and died after 50 years in Weimar. (Open mid-Mar. to mid-Oct. Tu-Su 9am-7pm; mid-Oct. to mid-Mar. Tu-Su 9am-4pm. DM8, students DM5.) Between the Frauenplan and the Marktpl. is the beginning of **Schillerstraße,** a vivacious shop-lined pedestrian zone. **Schillers Wohnhaus** at #12, where the dramatist lived for the last three years of his life, today houses original drafts and chronicles his life. (Open mid-Mar. to mid-Oct. W-M 9am-7pm; mid-Oct. to mid-Mar. W-M 9am-4pm. DM5, students DM3.) A block down Hummelstr., Schiller and Goethe are joined in bronze before the **Deutsches Nationaltheater,** Am Palais 3, which first breathed life into their stage works and from which the Weimar Constitution also emerged in 1919. Opposite the theater is the **Bauhaus-Museum,** which features works produced by the Bauhaus school of design and architecture, which originated in Weimar in 1919 before being ousted to Dessau (see p. 400). (Open Tu-Su Apr.-Oct. 10am-6pm; Nov.-Mar. 10am-4:30pm. DM5, students DM3.) The **Nietzsche-Archiv,** Humboldtstr. 36, where the philosopher spent the last three wacky years of his life (1897-1900), was founded by his sister Elisabeth, who helped the Nazis to distort her brother's philosophy. (Open Tu-Su mid-Mar. to mid-Oct. 1-6pm; mid-Oct. to mid-Mar. 1-4pm. DM4, students DM3.) On the far slopes of the Goethe-landscaped **Park an der Ilm,** on Corona-Schöfer-Str., is the poet's **Gartenhaus.** (Open W-M mid-Mar. to mid-Oct. 9am-7pm; mid-Oct. to mid-Mar. 9am-4pm. DM5, students DM2.50.) South of the center, Goethe and Schiller rest together at the **Historischer Friedhof** (cemetery). (Open Mar.-Sept. 8am-9pm; Oct.-Feb. 8am-6pm. DM4, students DM3.)

   Trains run to Erfurt (15min., 4 per hr., DM7.60); Eisenach (1hr., 3 per hr., DM19.40); Leipzig (1hr., every 2hr., DM24.40); Dresden (2½hr., every 2hr., DM65); and Frankfurt (3hr., every hr., DM78). To reach Goethepl. from the station, head down Carl-August-Allee to Karl-Liebknecht-Str. (15min.); the Markt and Herderpl. lie just east down side streets. The efficient **tourist office,** Marktpl. 10, in view of the Rathaus, books rooms for a DM5 fee and runs walking tours (daily 11am and 2pm; DM12, students DM8). (Tel. (03643) 240 00; fax 24 00 40. Open M-F 10am-7pm, Sa-Su 10am-4pm.) To get from Goethepl. to the student-run ◧**Jugendhotel Hababusch,** Geleitstr. 4, follow Geleitstr. around the sharp right to the entrance tucked in behind the statue on your left. (Tel. (03643) 85 07 37; email yh@larry.scc.uni-weimar.de. Shared bedroom DM15; doubles DM40. Kitchen. Key deposit DM20. Reception 24hr.) The **Jugendherberge Germania (HI),** Carl-August-Allee 13, is 2min. straight downhill (on the right) from the station. (Tel. (03643) 85 04 90; fax 85 04 91. DM29, under 27 DM24. Sheets DM7. Lockout 10am-2pm. Reception 24hr.) **Rewe supermarket,** on Theaterpl., is in the basement of the *Handelhaus zu Weimar.* (Open M-F 7am-8pm, Sa 7am-4pm.) **Postal code:** 99423.

 ▣ **EXCURSION FROM WEIMAR: BUCHENWALD.** Two hundred fifty thousand Jews, Gypsies, homosexuals, Communists, and political prisoners were imprisoned and murdered by the Nazis at the labor camp of Buchenwald during WWII, now the **Nationale Mahnmal und Gedenkstätte Buchenwald** memorial. Many Jews were sent here, but after 1942, most were deported to Auschwitz; the camp mostly served to detain and murder political enemies of Nazism and prisoners of war. After "liberation," Soviet authorities then used the site from 1945 to 1950 as an internment camp in which more than 28,000 Germans, mostly Nazi war criminals and opponents of the Communist regime; an exhibit detailing the Soviet abuses opened in 1997. A museum at the **KZ-Lager,** the remnants of the camp, documents the history of Buchenwald (1937-45) and the general history of Nazism, and features a moving photo exhibit by Polish artist Józef Szajna. On the other side of the hilltop from the

KZ-Lager, are the GDR-designed **Mahnmal** (memorial) and **Glockenturm** (bell tower). A path leads through the woods, emerging at a two-way fork in the road. Head right, past the parking lot and bus stop, and continue as the street curves left (20min.). Catch **bus** 6 from Weimar's train station or Goethepl.; only buses marked with a "B" or "EB" make the trip to Buchenwald (M-F every hr., Sa-Su every 2hr.). On your way back to Weimar, catch the bus by the parking lot near the Glockenturm.

ERFURT

The capital of Thüringen, Erfurt has been renovated more thoroughly and ingeniously than most towns and cities of the former East Germany. Although not a cultural powerhouse like Dresden or Eisenach, the city offers a stunning cathedral and a handful of churches. The mammoth Gothic **Mariendom,** up on **Domhügel** hill, completely dominates the view from the marketplace. Martin Luther was invested as a priest here and interrupted his first mass by hurling his Bible across the altar, claiming his target was the Devil himself, which impressed his audience if not the Bishop. (Open May-Oct. M-F 9-11:30am and 12:30-5pm, Sa 9-11:30am and 12:30-4:30pm, Su 2-4pm; Nov.-Apr. M-F 10-11:30am and 12:30-4pm, Su 2-4pm. Free.) From the Dompl., Marktstr. leads down to the **Fischmarkt,** bordered by restored guild houses sporting wildly decorated façades. The collection of myth-depicting paintings in the neo-Gothic **Rathaus** outdoes most museums and all rodent dwellings. (Open M and W-Th 9am-4pm, Tu 9am-6pm, F 9am-2pm. Free.) Farther down Markstr., the Gera River is spanned by the **Krämerbrücke,** a medieval bridge covered by small shops, some from the 12th century; in the 15th century, the bridge was part of a great trade route from Kiev to Paris. From the far side of the bridge, follow Gotthardtstr. and cut left through Kircheng. to the **Augustinerkloster,** where Martin Luther spent 10 years as a Catholic priest and Augustine monk. He ultimately had the last laugh—it now functions as a Protestant college. The **library** houses one of Germany's most priceless collections, including a number of early Bibles with personal notations by Luther. (Tours Apr.-Oct. Tu-Sa every hr. 10am-noon and 2-4pm, Su from 11am; Nov.-Mar. Tu-Sa 10am, noon, and 2pm. DM5.50, students DM4.)

Trains chug to Weimar (15min., 4 per hr., DM7.60); Leipzig (2hr., 13 per day, DM32); Frankfurt (2½hr., every hr., DM72); and Dresden (3hr., every 2hr., DM64). Head straight down Bahnhofstr. to reach the **Anger,** a wide pedestrian promenade, and then the Altstadt, then cross the river on Schlößerstr. to reach the **tourist office,** Fischmarkt 27, which books rooms (DM25-50) for a DM5 fee. (Tel. (0361) 664 00; fax 664 02 90. Open M-F 10am-7pm, Sa-Su 10am-4pm.) To get from the station to the **Jugendherberge Karl Reiman (HI),** Hochheimer Str. 12, take streetcar 5 (dir: Steigerstr.) to the last stop, backtrack a little, turn left on Hochheimer Str., and on the left at the first intersection. (Tel. (0361) 562 67 05; fax 562 67 06. DM29, under 27 DM24. Breakfast included. Sheets DM7. Reception 6-9am and 3-10pm. Curfew midnight.) **Rewe supermarket** is to the right as you exit the station. (Open M-W 6am-7pm, Th-F 6am-8pm, Sa 7am-1pm.) **Postal code:** 99084.

EISENACH

Birthplace of Johann Sebastian Bach and home-in-exile to Martin Luther, Eisenach boasts impressive humanist credentials. High above its half-timbered houses, the **Wartburg fortress** sheltered the excommunicated Luther (disguised as a noble named Junker Jörg) in 1521 while he worked on his landmark German translation of the Bible. By Luther's account, it took only the toss of an ink pot to ward off a visit from the Devil as he burned the midnight oil here (amazing how often the two crossed paths; see p. 399). From the station, stroll down Wartburgerallee and make like a pilgrim up one of the steep **footpaths** (30min.), or catch a **tour bus** (DM2.50 round-trip). (Open daily Mar.-Oct. 8:30am-5pm; Nov.-Feb. 9am-3:30pm. Mandatory tour DM11, students DM6.) En route to the fortress, a turn off Wartburgallee down Grimmelg. will bring you to the **Bachhaus,** Frauenplan 21, where Johann Sebastian stormed into the world in 1685. Regular tours include anecdotes about Bach's life and spellbinding musical interludes. (Open Apr.-Sept. M noon-5:45pm, Tu-Su 9am-5:45pm.; Oct.-Mar. M 1-4:45pm, Tu-Su 9am-4:45pm. DM5, students DM4.) The lat-

GERMANY

ticed **Lutherhaus,** Lutherpl. 8., is where young Martin lived from 1498 to 1501. (Open daily Apr.-Oct. 9am-5pm; Nov.-Mar. 10am-5pm. DM5, students DM2.)

Frequent **trains** run to Erfurt (1hr., DM15); Weimar (1hr., DM19.40); Kassel (1½hr., DM27); and Göttingen (2hr., DM35). The **tourist office,** Markt 2, offers city tours (daily 2pm; DM5), and books rooms (DM30-40) for free. From the station, walk on Bahnhofstr. through the tunnel, and bear left until you turn right on the pedestrian Karlstr. (Tel. (03691) 67 02 60. Open M 10am-12:30pm and 1:15-6pm, Tu-F 9am-12:30pm and 1-6pm, Sa-Su 10am-2pm.) The **Jugendherberge Artur Becker (HI),** Mariental 24, is expected to reopen in July 2000. From the station, take Bahnhofstr. to Wartburger Allee, which runs into Mariental, continue past the pond, and it'll be on your right (35min.). (Tel. (03691) 74 32 59; fax 74 32 60. DM26, under 27 DM22. Breakfast included. Sheets DM7. Reception 4-9pm.) **Gasthof Storchenturm,** Georgen-str. 43, fills a secluded courtyard next to a park with a restaurant, *Biergarten,* and several quiet rooms. (Tel. (03691) 21 52 50; fax 21 50 82. Singles DM45; doubles DM70. Breakfast DM7.50.) To **camp** at **Am Altenberger See,** 10km from town, catch the bus (dir: Bad Liebenstein; 3-14 per day) from the train station and tell the driver your destination. (Tel. (03691) 21 56 37; fax 21 56 07. DM7 per person, DM5 per tent, DM2 per car. Reception 8am-1pm and 3-10pm.) For **groceries,** head to the **Edeka** on Johannispl. (Open M-F 7am-7pm, Sa 7am-2pm.) **Postal code:** 99817.

WITTENBERG

The Protestant Reformation, which initiated centuries of religious conflict, began quietly in Wittenberg on October 13, 1517, when local professor and priest Martin Luther nailed his *95 Thesen* to the wooden door of the Schloßkirche. All the major sights lie along **Collegienstraße.** The **Lutherhalle** at #54 was Luther's home from 1508, and today houses a museum chronicling the history of the Reformation. (Open Tu-Su Apr.-Sept. 9am-6pm; Oct.-Mar. 10am-5pm. DM7, students DM4.) Turn right from the Lutherhalle and stroll down to Lutherstr. to behold the oak tree under which Luther defiantly burned a papal bull (a decree of excommunication, not a Catholic beast). Farther down Collegienstr., the **Schloßkirche,** crowned by a sumptuous Baroque cupola, holds a copy of the complaints that Luther nailed to its doors. (Open May-Oct. M 2-5pm, Tu-Sa 10am-5pm, Su 11:30am-5pm; Nov.-Apr. M 2-4pm, Tu-Sa 10am-4pm, Su 11:30am-4pm. Free.) **Trains** arrive from Leipzig (1hr., every 2hr., DM16.20) and Berlin (1½hr., every 2hr., DM39). Instead of disembarking at the less-than-central Hauptbahnhof, get off at Wittenberg-Elbtor; walk straight down Elbstr. and turn left on Schloßstr. to reach the Schloß. Across the street, the **tourist office,** Schloßpl. 2, books rooms (DM25-75) for a DM3 fee. (Tel. (03491) 49 86 10; fax 49 86 11. Open Mar.-Oct. M-F 9am-6pm, Sa 10am-3pm, Su 11am-4pm; Nov.-Feb. M-F 10am-4pm, Sa 10am-2pm, Su 11am-3pm.) Cross the street from the tourist office and walk straight into the castle's enclosure, then trek up the spiraling stairs to the right to reach the **Jugendherberge (HI),** housed in the castle. (Tel./fax (03491) 40 32 55. DM26, under 27 DM21. Breakfast included. Sheets DM6. Reception 5-10pm. Reserve ahead.) **City-Kauf supermarket** waits about 20m from the tourist office. (Open M-F 8am-6:30pm, Sa 8am-12:30pm.) **Postal code:** 06886.

DESSAU

Dessau, 30km west of Wittenberg, is worth a daytrip for those interested in the Bauhaus art school or in native son and musician Kurt Weill. A number of buildings in Dessau reflect the Bauhaus aesthetic. After originating in Weimar in 1919, the school was based in Dessau from 1925 to 1932, when it moved to Berlin (and was soon after exiled by the Nazis in 1933). American skyscrapers were the high point of Bauhaus, whose teachers were intrigued by the possibilities of glass and steel. Since 1977, the **Bauhaus,** Gropiusallee 38, has housed a design school for international architecture; hallways feature rotating exhibits, including works by *Bauhausmeisters* Gropius, Klee, and Kandinsky. From the station, turn left, go up the steps, head left over the tracks, then veer left on Kleiststr. and right on Bauhausstr. (Open Tu-Su 10am-5pm. DM5, students DM3.) This year's **Kurt Weill Festival** (Feb. 18-Mar. 5, 2000) celebrates the 100th anniversary of the conductor's birth.

Trains arrive from Wittenberg (35min., every 2hr., DM9.80); Leipzig (1hr., every 2hr., DM14.80); and Berlin (2hr., every hr., DM33). To reach the **tourist office,** Zerbster Str. 2c, take streetcar 1 or 2 from the station to "Hauptpost," walk toward the Rathaus-Center, veer left on Ratsg., and take the 1st right. (Tel. (0340) 204 14 42; fax 204 11 42. Open M-F 9am-7pm, Sa 9am-1pm.) To reach the **Jugendherberge (HI),** Waldkaterweg 11, exit from the station's *Westausgang* via the underground tunnel, follow Rathenaustr. left to the end, zig-zag across at the intersection, and follow Kühnauer Str. for 10min.; after crossing Kiefernweg 50m later, follow the small path on the right (25min.). (Tel. (0340) 61 94 52. DM26, under 27 DM21. Breakfast included. Sheets DM6. Reception M-F 8am-4pm and 7:30-9:30pm, Sa-Su 6-9pm. Check-out 9am.) The hip ◪**Klub im Bauhaus,** in the Bauhaus school basement, is a delightful place to indulge in angsty pretense over a light meal. (Open M-F 8am-midnight, Sa 10am-midnight, Su 10am-6pm.) **Postal code:** 06844.

NORTHERN GERMANY

Although once a favored vacation spot for East Germans, Mecklenburg-Vorpommern, the northeasternmost portion of Germany, has unfortunately suffered in recent years from economic depression. Restoration work continues to reveal dramatic Hanseatic architecture throughout the *Land*, but the presence of neo-Nazis is unfortunately palpable. Just to the west, Schleswig-Holstein, which borders Denmark, has always depended on its port towns. The region became a Prussian province in 1867 as the first step of Bismarck's unification plan, and chose after WWI to remain part of Germany, but the *Land* retains close cultural and commercial ties with Scandinavia. To the west, Bremen (along with Bremerhaven) constitutes Germany's smallest *Land*, a small pocket within Niedersachsen.

⚓ NORTH AND BALTIC SEA FERRIES

Hamburg: See p. 402. **Scandinavian Seaways** (tel. (040) 389 03 71; fax 38 90 31 41) sets sail for **Harwich, England** (20hr., from DM152); **Ireland; Copenhagen;** and **Oslo.**

Kiel: 1½hr. by train north of Hamburg (see p. 402) and Lübeck (see p. 407). **Baltic Line** (tel. (0431) 20 97 60) goes to **Sweden. Color Line** (tel. (0431) 730 03 00; fax 730 04 00) sails to **Oslo** (12½hr., departs daily 2pm, single DM114-174, double DM150-202). **Langeland-Kiel** (tel. (0431) 97 41 50; fax 945 15) ships 'em out to **Bagenkop, Denmark** (2½hr., DM7-9). Boats from Kiel also serve **Kaliningrad** and the **Baltics.**

Rostock: See below. **TT-Linie** (tel. (0381) 67 07 90; fax 670 79 80) chugs to **Trelleborg, Sweden** (5hr., 6 per day, DM50, students DM25). **Scandlines Europa GT Links** (tel. (0381) 670 06 67; fax 670 66 71) sails to **Gedser, Denmark** (2hr., 8 per day, DM5-8). **DFO** (tel. (0381) 514 06; fax 514 09) heads to Gedser and other Scandinavian ports (2hr., 8 per day, DM10-16).

Travemünde: 25min. from Lübeck by train. **TT-Linie** (tel. 80 10) toots to **Trelleborg, Sweden** from the Skandinavienkai (M-Th and Su 10am and 10pm; DM69 round-trip).

Saßnitz: On Rügen Island, northeast of Rostock (see below). Ferries leave from the *Fährhafen* in Mukran (15min. by bus from the Saßnitz train station) to: **Sweden; Bornholm** and elsewhere in **Denmark; Russia; Świnoujście, Poland;** and **Lithuania.**

ROSTOCK

Eight years ago, an event occurred that would change the way the world viewed Rostock: on August 24, 1992, neo-Nazi youths capitalized on the tension caused by a recent flood of immigrants by setting fire to a hostel for foreigners seeking political asylum in Germany. Today most natives and left-leaning students would like to put this event in the past; walls spraypainted with swastikas also carry the response *Nazis raus!* ("Nazis out!"). As Günter Grass noted, "Since Rostock, Germany has changed." Still, there is much to see in Rostock, including its 13th-century brick **Marienkirche.** (Open M-Sa 10am-5pm, Su 11am-noon.) Or wander along **Kröpeliner Straße,** Rostock's main pedestrian mall, and admire the restored buildings that reflect the city's past as a center of Hanseatic trade.

GERMANY

Trains (tel. (0381) 493 44 54) connect to Schwerin (1hr., every hr., DM22.20); Berlin (2½hr., DM53); Hamburg (3hr., DM75); and Dresden (7hr., DM118). **Ferries** leave for Scandinavia (see above) from the Überseehafen (TT-Linie and Scandlines Europa GT Links) and Warnemünde (DFO) docks. To get from the station to the **tourist office,** Schnickmannstr. 13/14, take streetcar 11 or 12 to "Lange Str.," then follow the sign to the right. (Tel. (0381) 194 33; fax 497 99 23. May-Sept. open M-F 10am-6pm, Sa-Su 10am-2:30pm; Oct.-Apr. closes 5pm.) Ride the **internet** at **Riz Café,** Wismarische Str. 44. (DM3 per hr. Open M-Sa 9am-10pm.) Both of Rostock's hostels are rather far from town and in somewhat dangerous neighborhoods, but the tourist office arranges private rooms (DM30-40 plus DM5 fee). If you must get to the boat-hostel **Jugendgästeschiff Rostock-Schmarl** (tel. (0381) 71 62 24; fax 71 40 14), take the S-Bahn (dir: Warnemünde) to "Lütten Klein," then bus 35 (dir: Schmarl Fähre; last bus 8pm) to the end of the line; follow the street to the end and board the *Traditionsschiff.* Past travelers have complained of harassment by aggressive hooligans on the way, but once inside the kind staff will make you feel at home. There's a **market** on Seinstr. (open M-F 8am-5pm, Sa 8am-1pm), and bakeries on **Kröpeliner Str.** have sandwiches. **Postal code:** 18055.

SCHWERIN

First recognized in 1018, Schwerin is the grandfather of Mecklenburg-Vorpommern's cities, and with reunification, the city regained its status as capital of the *Land.* The Altstadt brims with well-preserved townhouses and remnants of its past life as an elegant spa town. A plethora of galleries and performance spaces house dozens of art festivals and concerts throughout the year, but *haute couture* isn't all the city has to offer; it's not impossible to take in an opera and a rave in the same night, if your wardrobe can withstand the transition. Schwerin's **Schloß,** a ridiculous amalgamation of architectural styles on an island just south of the city center, is everything your mother told you a castle should be. Its gilded Baroque cupolas runneth over with luxury—the red silk wallpaper and mahogany floors pale in comparison to the gilded, marble columns of the sumptuous throne room. (Open Tu-Su 10am-6pm. DM6, students DM3.) Across from the Schloß, the **Alter Garten** was the site of mass demonstrations preceding the downfall of the GDR in 1989. Atop the stairs on the right sits the **Staatliches Museum,** which houses a good collection of 15th- to 19th-century Dutch and German works, including a few by Rembrandt, Cranach the Elder, and Rubens. (Open Tu 10am-8pm, W-Su 10am-6pm. DM5, students DM2.) Each summer, the steps of the museum are converted into an opera stage, and the throne room in the Schloß is a grand venue for monthly concerts (DM39, students DM19). The **Schelfstadt** neighborhood houses a number of galleries and performance spaces. Live bands keep the party going into the early morning at **Louis,** Wittenburger Str. 50. (Open Th-Sa from 9pm.)

Trains run to Rostock (1¼hr., every hr., DM22.20) and Lübeck (1½hr., every hr., DM19.60). To get from the station to the **tourist office,** Am Markt 1, go right on Grundthalpl., continue as it becomes Wismarsche Str., then turn left on Arsenal, right on Mecklenburgstr., and left on Schmiedestr. (Tel. (0385) 592 52 12; fax 55 50 94. Open M-F 10am-6pm, Sa-Su 10am-2pm.) To get to the **Jugendherberge (HI),** Waldschulweg 3, take bus 14 (dir: Jugendherberge) to the end of the line and walk toward the zoo; it's on the left. (Tel./fax (0385) 326 00 06. DM28, under 27 DM23. Breakfast included. Sheets DM6. Reception 9am-noon and 4-10pm. Curfew 10pm. Call ahead.) Pick up **groceries** at **Edeka,** just off the Markt on Schmiedestr. (Open M-F 8am-8pm, Sa 8am-4pm.) **Postal code:** 19053.

HAMBURG

With a fiercely activist population and a licentious, reckless sex industry, modern Hamburg is a crazy coupling of the progressive and the perverse. A proud tradition of autonomy dates back to 1618, when Hamburg gained the status of Free Imperial City, and the city today remains a politically autonomous *Land.* Restoration and riots determined the post-WWII landscape, but recently Hamburg, the largest port town in Germany, has become a harbor for lonesome sailors, contemporary artists, and revelling party-goers who absorb Germany's self-declared "capital of lust."

⎕ GETTING THERE AND GETTING AROUND

Trains: From the **Hauptbahnhof** at least hourly to **Hannover** (1½hr., DM67); **Berlin** (2¾hr., DM93); **Frankfurt** (3¾hr., DM182); and **Munich** (6hr., DM256). Also to: **Amsterdam** (5½hr., 3 per day, DM105) and **Copenhagen** (6hr., 3 per day, DM102). **Dammtor** station is near the university, and **Altona** station is in the west; frequent trains and the S-Bahn connect the 3 stations. **Lockers** DM2-4 per day.

Buses: ZOB, across Steintorpl. from the Hauptbahnhof. To: **Berlin** (8 per day, DM41) and **Copenhagen** (6hr., 2 per day, DM63). **Lockers** in the main hall (DM2).

Ferries: Scandinavian Seaways, Van-der-Smissen-Str. 4 (tel. 389 03 71; fax 38 90 31 41). S1 or S3: Königstr. Open M-F 10am-4:30pm. For route info, see p. 401.

Public Transportation: HVV runs an efficient U-Bahn, S-Bahn, and bus network. **Single-fare tickets** within downtown DM1.80. All tickets can be bought at orange *Automaten.*

▚ ORIENTATION AND PRACTICAL INFORMATION

The city center sits between the **Elbe** River and the **Außenalster** and **Binnenalster** Lakes. Most major sights lie between the **St. Pauli Landungsbrücken** port in the west and the **Hauptbahnhof** in the east. The **Hanseviertel** quarter is filled with banks, shops, and art galleries. North of the center, the **university** dominates the **Dammtor** area. West of the university, the **Sternschanze** hosts a politically active community of artists, squatters, and Turks. The **Altona** district was once an independent Danish city. Down south in **St. Pauli,** the raucous **Fischmarkt** (fish market) is juxtaposed with the equally wild **Reeperbahn,** home to Hamburg's infamous sex trade.

TOURIST, FINANCIAL, AND LOCAL SERVICES

Tourist Offices: In the **Hauptbahnhof** (tel. 30 05 12 01; fax 30 05 13 33; www.hamburg-tourism.de), near the Kirchenallee exit. Books rooms for a DM6 fee. Open daily 7am-11pm. Also at **St. Pauli Landungsbrücken** (tel. 30 05 12 00), between piers 4 and 5. Open daily 10am-7pm. Both sell the **Hamburg Card,** which provides unlimited public transport, museum admission, and tour discounts (1-day DM12.50, 3-day DM26). Up to 5 people get the same perks with the **Group Card** (1-day DM24, 3-day DM42).

Currency Exchange: ReiseBank, in the Hauptbahnhof, 2nd fl. Cashes traveler's checks and exchanges money for a DM5 fee. Open daily 7:30am-10pm. Most banks downtown open M-W and F 9am-1pm and 2:30-4pm, Th 9am-1pm and 2:30-6pm.

American Express: Ballindamm 39, 20095 (tel. 30 39 38 11 12; fax 30 90 81 30). Mail held for cardmembers; all banking services. Open M-F 9am-6pm, Sa 10am-1pm.

Gay and Lesbian Services: Magnus-Hirschfeld-Centrum, Borgweg 8 (tel. 279 00 69). U3: Borgweg. Center open M and F 2-6pm, Tu-W 7-10pm. Café open daily 5pm-midnight.

Laundromat: Schnell und Sauber, Grindelallee 158. S21 or S31: Dammtor. Wash DM6 per 6kg; soap included. Dry DM1 per 15min. Open daily 7am-10:30pm.

EMERGENCY AND COMMUNICATIONS

Emergency: Police, tel. 110. **Fire** and **ambulance,** tel. 112.

Post Office: Großer Burstah 3. Address mail to be held: *Postlagernde Briefe* für Katrin UNTERMAN, Großer Burstah 3, **20099** Hamburg, Germany. Open M-F 8am-6pm, Sa 8am-12pm. **Branch** at the Kirchenallee exit of the Hauptbahnhof.

Internet Access: Staats- und Universitätsbibliothek, Von-Melle-Park 3, 2nd fl., in the "Bibliografien" section. Open M-F 10am-7pm, Sa 10am-1pm. Free. **Cyberb@r,** in the **Karstadt** department store on Mönckebergstr., 3rd fl. DM5 per 30min.

PHONE CODE	City code: 040. From outside Germany, dial int'l dialing prefix (see inside back cover) + 49 + 40 + local number.

⌐ ACCOMMODATIONS AND CAMPING

Hamburg is expensive: single rooms start at around DM60, doubles at DM75. A slew of small, relatively cheap *Pensionen* line **Steindamm, Steintorweg, Bremer Weg,** and **Bremer Reihe** around the Hauptbahnhof. While the area is filled with drug addicts and wannabe *mafiosi,* the hotels are generally safe. Check out your hotel before you accept a room, or let the tourist office's *Hotelführer* (free) help steer you clear.

GERMANY

■ **Schanzenstern Übernachtungs und-Gasthaus,** Bartelsstr. 12 (tel. 439 84 41; fax 439 34 13; email info@schanzerstern.de). S3, S21, or U3: Sternschanze; go left down Schanzenstr., right on Susannenstr., and left on Bartelsstr. Managed by a politically and ecologically progressive cooperative. Dorms DM33; singles DM60; doubles DM90; triples DM115; quads DM140; quints DM175. Breakfast DM11. Reception 6:30am-2am.

Instant Sleep, Max-Brauer-Allee 277 (tel. 43 18 23 10; fax 43 18 23 11; email backpackerhostel@instantsleep.de). S3, S21, S31, or U3: Sternschanze; go straight on Schanzenstr. and turn left on Altonaer Str., which becomes Max-Brauer-Allee. Brand-new, spic 'n' span hostel—the best deal in Hamburg. Dorms DM29; singles DM45; doubles DM76; triples DM105. Sheets DM3. Internet. Reception 9am-2pm. Call ahead.

Hotel Alt-Nürnberg, Steintorweg 15 (tel. 24 60 24; fax 280 46 34). From the Hauptbahnhof, go right on Kirchenallee and left on Steintorweg. In a somewhat sketchy area, but clean rooms, some with TV. Singles DM60-90; doubles DM90-130. Call ahead.

Jugendherberge auf dem Stintfang (HI), Alfred-Wegener-Weg 5 (tel. 31 34 88; fax 31 54 07; email jh-stintfang@t-online.de). S1-3 or U3: Landungsbrücke. Great location near the Reeperbahn and U-Bahn, clean rooms, and harbor views compensate for the regimental rules. DM32, under 27 DM27; nonmembers add DM6. Breakfast included. **Internet.** Reception 12:30pm-1am. Lockout 9:30-11:30am. Curfew 1am. Call ahead.

Jugendgästehaus und Gästehaus Horner-Rennbahn (HI), Rennbahnstr. 100 (tel. 651 16 71; fax 655 65 16; email jgh-hamburg@t-online.de). U3: Horner-Rennbahn; walk right 10min. to the corner of Tribünenweg. Inconveniently far, but clean and safe. DM37, under 27 DM31.50; members only. Reception 7-9:30am and 12:30pm-1am. Curfew 1am.

Campingplatz Rosemarie Buchholz, Kieler Str. 374 (tel. 540 45 32). From Altona station, take bus 182 or 183 to "Basselweg" (10min.), then walk 100m with traffic. DM7 per person, DM12.50 per tent. Showers DM1.50. Reception 8am-10pm. Call ahead.

◖ FOOD

The most interesting part of town from a culinary standpoint is **Sternschanze**, where Turkish fruit stands, Asian *Imbiße*, and avant-garde cafés coexist (S3, S21, S31, or U3: Sternschanze). **Schulterblatt, Susannenstr.,** and **Schanzenstr.** host funky cafés and restaurants. Cheaper establishments abound near the **university,** especially along **Rentzelstr., Grindelhof,** and **Grindelallee.** In **Altona,** the pedestrian zone leading up to the train station is packed with ethnic food stands and produce shops. Myriad eateries in the **Mercado** mall run the gamut from sushi bars to Portuguese fast food.

■ **Noodles,** Schanzenstr. 2-4 (tel. 439 28 40), in **Sternschanze.** Serves innovative pasta creations alongside a full bar. Open Su-Th 10am-1am, F-Sa 10am-3am.

Machwitz, Schanzenstr. 121 (tel. 43 81 77), in **Sternschanze.** Join the hip student crowd in the funky angular interior or people-watch outside. Creamy soups DM6; entrees DM10-15. Occasional concerts from local bands. Open daily from 10am until everyone leaves.

Falafel-König, Schanzenstr. 113, in **Sternschanze.** Tiny Lebanese *Imbiß* is indeed the "Falafel-King" (DM5-6). Open Su-Th 11:30am-midnight, F-Sa 11:30am-3am.

Café Gasoline, on Bahrenfelder Str. near the **Altona** train station, caffeinates its customers as they relax in comfy wicker chairs. Open daily from 11am until the java runs out.

◖ SIGHTS

ALTSTADT. The pedestrian shopping zone stretches from the Rathaus to the Hauptbahnhof along **Mönckebergstraße,** and is punctuated by two spires. The first belongs to the **St. Petrikirche,** site of the oldest church in Hamburg. *(Open M-Tu and F 10am-6:30pm, W-Th 10am-7pm, Sa 10am-5pm, Su 9am-6pm. Free concerts W 5:15pm.)* The second church in the area is the **St. Jakobikirche,** known for its 14th-century Arp-Schnittger organ. *(Open daily 10am-5pm.)* Mönckebergstr. pours out into Rathausmarkt, where the copper spires of the **Rathaus** (town hall), a richly ornamented, neo-Renaissance monstrosity, rise above the city center. *(Tours in German every 30min. M-Th 10am-3pm, F-Su 10am-1pm. Tours in English every hr. M-Th 10:15am-3:15pm, F-Su 10:15am-1:15pm.)* Nearby, a zig-zagging maze of canals and bridges centered on the **Alte Börse** (old stock market)—Germany's first stock market. Buildings along the

Hamburg

ACCOMMODATIONS

A Instant Sleep
B Schanzenstern
   Übernachtungs
   und-Gasthaus
C Hotel Alt-Nürnberg
D Jugendgästehaus
   Horner-Rennbahn
E Jugendherberge

ST. GEORG

Museum für Kunst und Gewerbe

Kurt-Schumacher-Allee

Steintorwall
STEINTORPL.
Steintorweg
süd

Klosterwall
DEICHTOR PLATZ
Altländerstr.

Hauptbahnhof

Lange Mühren
STEINTOR STR.
Johannis Wall
Deichtorhallen

Ober- hafen
Oberbaumbrücke

Glockengießer-Wall
Kunsthalle
FERDINANDSTOR

Brooktorhafen

MÖNCKEBERGSTR.
Burgstr.
Jacobikirche
Steinstr.
BURCHARD PLATZ
Chilehaus
MESSBERG

Außenalster

Ballindamm
Ferdinandstr.

Petrikirche
Speersort
Kl. Reichenstr.

Kennedybrücke
Lombardsbrücke

Binnenalster

American Express
JUNGFERN- STIEG
Schmelldstr.
Domstr.
Ost-West-Str.

Katharinen-kirche

Alsterglacis
Esplanade
Neuer Jungfernstieg

RATHAUS MARKT
Alte Börse
Rathaus
Nikolaikirche
ALTSTADT

Bei den Mühren
Zollkanal
Speicherstadt

STEPHANSPLATZ

Colonnaden
Dammtorstr.
Staatsoper
GÄNSE MARKT
Hanse Viertel
Adolfsbr.

Binnenhafen
BAUMWALL

Botanischer Garten
Gorch-Fock-Wall
Neue ABC Str.
GÄNSE MARKT

RÖDINGS MARKT
Ródings-Markt
Stadthausbrücke
STADTHAUS BRÜCKE

Caffamacherreihe
Fuhlentwiete
Speckstr.
Kaiser-Wilhelm-Str.
Korntrögerg.

Stein Hof

Musikhalle
Backerbreitergasse
NEUSTADT

Kleine Wallanlagen
Gorch-Fock-Wall
KARL-MUCK-PLATZ
Poolstr.
Kohlhöfen
THIELBECK
GR. NEUMARKT

MESSEHALLEN

Neanderstr.
ENCKE PLATZ

Michaeliskirche
SCHAAR MARKT
Neustädter Neuerweg

Große Wallanlagen
Große Holstenwall
Ludwig-Erhard-Str.
Gerstackerstr.

TO FERNSEHTURM
FELDSTR.
Feldstr.

Reeperbahn
Stuntfang
Elbpark
Helgolander Allee

Windjammer Rickmer Rickmers

ST. PAULI
Heiligengeistfeld
Budapester Str.
MILLERNTOR PLATZ

LANDUNGS BRÜCKEN

Norderelbe

300 yards
300 meters

TO ALTONA (1.6km)

GERMANY

Trostbrücke to the south sport huge clipper ship models on their spires—a reminder of the significance of sea-trade in the accumulation of Hamburg's wealth. Over the bridge rest the somber ruins of **St. Nikolaikirche,** flattened by a 1943 air raid and left unrestored as a memorial to the horrors of war. From the church, turn right on Ost-West-Str. and continue on Ludwig-Erhard-Str. to reach the gargantuan 18th-century **Große Michaelskirche,** the granddaddy of all Hamburg churches, affectionately referred to as *"der Michael." (Open Apr.-Sept. M-Sa 9am-6pm, Su 11:30am-5:30pm; Oct.-Mar. M-Sa 10am-4:30pm, Su 11:30am-4:30pm. DM1.)*

ST. PAULI LANDUNGSBRÜCKEN AND FISCHMARKT. Hamburg's harbor **St. Pauli Landungsbrücken,** the largest port in Germany, lights up at night with ships from all over the world. More than 100,000 dockers and sailors work the ports, and their presence permeates Hamburg. The elevator to the **Old Elbe Tunnel** protrudes through the floor of the building behind Pier 6; with all of its machinery exposed, the building looks like a nautilus machine for the gods. Head farther west to reach the **Fischmarkt,** where charismatic vendors haul in and hawk huge amounts of fish, produce, and other goods. *(Take the U- or S-Bahn to "Landungsbrücken" or S-Bahn to "König-str." Market open in summer Su 6-10am, off-season 7-10am.)*

PLANTEN UN BLOMEN AND ALSTER LAKES. To the west of the Alster near the university, the **Planten un Blomen** park features dozens of meticulously planned and trimmed flowerbeds surrounding two lakes and a handful of outdoor cafés. From May to September, daily performances ranging from Irish step-dancing to Hamburg's police orchestra shake the outdoor **Musikpavillon; Wasserlichtkonzerte** feature lighted fountain arrangements to music. *(Wasserlichtkonzerte daily May-Aug. 10pm; Sept. 9pm.)* North of the center, the two **Alster lakes** are rimmed by tree-lined paths. Elegant promenades and commercial façades surround **Binnenalster,** while windsurfers, sailboats, and paddleboats dominate the larger **Außenalster.**

GEDENKSTÄTTE JANUSZ-KORCZAK-SCHULE. In the midst of warehouses, this school serves as a memorial to 20 Jewish children brought here from Auschwitz for "testing," murdered by the SS only hours before Allied troops arrived. Visitors are invited to plant a rose for the children in the flower garden behind the school, where plaques with the children's photographs line the fence. *(Bullenhuser Damm 92. S21: Rothenburgsort; walk north from the station, turn right on Bullenhuser Damm, and it's 200m down. School open Su 10am-5pm; flower garden open M-Sa 10am-5pm. Free.)*

MUSEUMS. The dozens of museums in Hamburg range from the erotic to the Victorian. The first-rate **Hamburger Kunsthalle** holds an extensive and dazzling collection including medieval to modern art. *(Glockengießerwall 1. Turn left from the "City" exit of the Hauptbahnhof and cross the street. Open Tu-W and F-Su 10am-6pm, Th 10am-9pm. DM15, students DM12.)* Hamburg's contemporary art scene resides in the two buildings of the **Deichtorhallen Hamburg,** whose exhibits showcase up-and-coming artists. *(Deich-torstr. 1-2. U1: Steinstr.; then follow the signs. Open Tu-Su 11am-6pm, Sa-Su 10am-6pm. Each building DM10, students DM8.)* Follow the silver sperm painted on the floor through four floors of tactful iniquity at the **Erotic Art Museum.** *(Nobistor 12 and Bernhard-Nocht-Str. 69. S1 or S3: Reeperbahn. Open Tu-Su 10am-midnight. DM15, students DM10.)*

🎵🖼 **ENTERTAINMENT AND NIGHTLIFE**

MUSIC AND THEATER. Hamburg's **Staatsoper,** Dammtorstr. 28, houses one of the best opera companies in Germany; performances tend toward the modern but also include a steady stream of Bizet and Puccini (from DM7). Take U1 to "Stephans-platz." (Tel. 35 17 21. Open M-F 10am-6:30pm, Sa 10am-2pm.) **Orchestras** abound—the Philharmonie, the Norddeutscher Rundfunk Symphony, and Hamburg Symphonia, the big three, all perform at the **Musikhalle** on Karl-Muck-Pl. (tel. 34 69 20). Take U2 to "Gänsemarkt" or "Messehallen." The **Deutsches Schauspielhaus,** Kirche-nallee 39, presents a full repertory, including Ibsen, Brecht, Fassbinder—and *Rent.* (Tel. 24 87 13. Box office open 10am-showtime. Student tickets from DM10.) In July and August, many theaters close down, but only to make way for the **Ham-**

burger Sommer arts festival; pick up a schedule at any kiosk. This year, **Carmen 2000** will grace the Hagenbeck's Tierpark stage from June to October; for information on the "modernized" Bizet opera, call 35 71 85 36. The **West Port** jazz festival (tel. 44 64 21), Germany's largest, runs July 15-24, 2000.

NIGHTLIFE. *Szene*, available at newsstands (DM5), lists events and parties. The **Sternschanze, St. Pauli,** and **Altona** areas monopolize Hamburg's crazy nightlife scene. The infamous **Reeperbahn,** a long boulevard which makes Las Vegas look like Sunday school, is the spinal cord of St. Pauli; sex shops, strip joints, peep shows, and other establishments that seek to satisfy every libidinal desire compete for space along the sidewalks. **Herbertstraße,** Hamburg's only remaining legalized prostitution strip, open only to men over 18, runs parallel to the Reeperbahn. But between the sex shops and prostitutes, many of Hamburg's best bars and clubs fill with a young crowd that leaves debauchery and degradation outside. **Mojo Club,** Reeperbahn 1, was dubbed the best club in Germany by MTV. The attached, trendy **Jazz Café** features acid jazz. (Weekend cover DM12. Open 11pm-4am.) If you're rich and pretty, you'll fit in at **La Cage,** Reeperbahn 136. (Cover DM18. Open F-Sa 11pm.) **Indra,** Große Freiheit 64, is a haven of calm, live jazz just off the adrenaline-powered Reeperbahn. (Cover DM5-10. Open W-Su from 9pm; music starts around 11pm.) **Cotton Club,** Alter Steinweg 10, gives a different jazz, swing, or skittle band a chance every night. Take U3 to "Rödingsmarkt." (Cover around DM12. Open M-Sa 8pm-midnight. Shows start at 8:30pm.)

Those trying to avoid the hypersexed Reeperbahn head north to the cafés and alternative weekend extravaganzas of the **Sternschanze** district. The graffiti-covered ▧**Rote Flora,** Schulterblatt 71, serves as the nucleus of the Sternschanze scene, with huge drum 'n' bass parties on weekends. (Café open M-F 6-10pm. Opening times vary. Weekend cover from DM8.) **Logo,** Grindelallee 5, is an informal club near the university with nightly live music. (Cover varies. Open daily from 9:30pm.) Hamburg's **gay scene** is located in the **St. Georg** area of the city, near Berliner Tor. *Hinnerk* lists gay and lesbian events. **Absolut,** Hans-Albers-Pl. 15, hosts the gay scene Saturday nights as it spins unrelenting house to a younger crowd that grooves until well past dawn. (Cover DM10. Open daily from 11pm.)

LÜBECK

With a skyline of Neoclassical townhouses punctuated by 13th-century copper spires, Lübeck is easily Schleswig-Holstein's most beautiful city. In its heyday, the city served as capital of the Hanseatic League. Between the Altstadt and the train station is the massive **Holstentor,** one of Lübeck's four 15th-century gates and the symbol of the city. The centerpiece of the Altstadt is the **Rathaus,** a 13th-century structure of glazed black and red bricks. (Open M-F 9:30am-6pm, Sa-Su 10am-2pm. Tours M-F 11am and noon; DM4, students DM2.) The **Marienkirche,** begun in the Romanesque style around 1200 but finished as a Gothic cathedral in 1350, houses the largest mechanical organ in the world. A reproduction of the church's famous **Totentanzbild** mural depicts the plague era. (Open daily in summer 10am-6pm; off-season closes 4pm; free. Organ concerts Tu 6:30pm, Th 8pm, Sa 6:30pm; DM5, students DM3.) Opposite the Marienkirche is the **Buddenbrookhaus,** Mengstr. 4, the childhood home of literary giants Heinrich and Thomas Mann and today a museum dedicated to their life and work. (Open daily 10am-5pm. DM7, students DM4.) At the **Behnhaus** and **Drägerhaus** museums, Königstr. 11, modern art clashes with the Neoclassical architecture of an 18th-century townhouse. (Open Tu-Su Apr.-Sept. 10am-5pm; Oct.-May closes 4pm. DM5, students DM3; free 1st F of each month.)

Frequent **trains** arrive from Hamburg (45min., DM17); Schwerin (1¼hr., DM20); Rostock (1¾hr., DM37); and Berlin (3¼hr., DM87). Skip absurdly expensive maps and services at the tourist office in the train station and instead try the **tourist office** in the Altstadt, Breite Str. 62 (tel. (0451) 122 54 13; fax 122 54 19; open M-F 9:30am-6pm, Sa-Su 10am-2pm). From the station, walk past the Holstentor (gate), left on An der Untertrave, right on Beckergrube (which becomes Pfaffstr. and then Glockengießerstr) to reach the ▧**Rucksack Hotel,** Kanalstr. 70, on the north side of the Alt-

GERMANY

stadt by the canal (20min.). (Tel. (0451) 70 68 92; fax 707 34 26. Dorms DM24-26; bed in a quad DM28-34; bed in a double DM40. Breakfast DM8. Sheets DM6. Kitchen. Reception 9am-1pm and 3-10pm.) To get from the station to **Sleep-In (CVJM),** Große Petersgrube 11, near the Petrikirche in the Altstadt, walk past the Holstentor, turn right on An der Obertrave, turn left on Große Petersgrube, and look to the right for the sign (10min.). (Tel. (0451) 719 20; fax 789 97. Dorms DM15; bed in a double DM20-40. Breakfast DM5. Sheets DM5. Reception M-F 8am-10pm, Sa-Su 8am-noon and 5-7:30pm.) The hip waitstaff at ◪**Tipasa,** Schlumacherstr. 12-14, serves students pizza and pasta, with a *Biergarten* out back. (Open Su-Th noon-1am, F-Sa noon-2am.) A **Co-op supermarket** is at the corner of Sandstr. and Schmiedstr. (Open M-F 8:30am-7pm, Sa 9am-4pm.) **Postal code:** 23552.

SCHLESWIG

Schleswig, at the southern end of the **Schlei inlet,** has picture-perfect fishing settlements, a 16th-century castle, and extensive museum collections. Towering over the meandering cobblestoned streets of the Altstadt is the 12th-century **St. Petri-Dom,** famous for its intricately carved wooden altarpiece. (Open May-Sept. M-Th and Sa 9am-5pm, F 9am-3pm, Su 1-5pm; Oct.-Apr. M-Th and Sa 10am-4pm, F 10am-3pm, Su 1-4pm.) Twenty minutes along the harbor from the Altstadt, the 16th-century **Schloß Gottorf** houses the **Landesmuseen,** a treasure trove of Dutch, Danish, and Art Deco pieces. On the other side of the castle, the **Kreuzstall** houses the **Museum des 20. Jahrhunderts,** devoted to artists of the Brücke school. The surrounding park holds an **outdoor sculpture museum.** (All open daily Mar.-Oct. 9am-5pm; Nov.-Feb. 9:30am-4pm. DM7, students DM3.) If long to see the remains of a civilization of tall, attractive people who seem to have made lots of combs and beautiful boats, **ferries** travel from the Stadthafen near the Dom to the **Wikinger Museum Haithabu,** next to an archaeological dig of a former **Viking settlement.** (Open Apr.-Oct. daily 9am-5pm; Nov.-Mar. Tu-Su 9am-4pm. DM4, students DM2.)

Schleswig's **train station** is 20min. south of the city center; take bus 1, 2, 4, or 5 from the stop outside the **bus terminal** (ZOB), close to the Altstadt (15min., DM1.80). Trains go hourly to Kiel and Hamburg (via Neumünster). The **tourist office,** Plessenstr. 7, is up the street from the harbor; from the ZOB, walk down Plessenstr. toward the water. (Tel. (24837) 248 78; fax 207 03. Open May-Sept. M-F 9am-12:30pm and 1:30-5pm, Sa 9am-noon; Oct.-Apr. M-Th 9am-12:30pm and 1:30-5pm, F 9am-12:30pm.) The **Jugendherberge (HI),** Spielkoppel 1, is near the center of town. With your back to the ZOB, walk right along Königstr., turn right onto Poststr. (which turns into Moltkestr.), turn left on Bellmannstr., and follow it to Spielkoppel on your left. (Tel. (24837) 238 93. DM26, under 27 DM21. Breakfast included. Sheets DM7. Reception 7am-1pm and 5-11pm. Curfew 11pm.) The **Wikinger Campingplatz,** Am Haithabu (tel. 324 50; fax 331 22), is across the inlet from the Altstadt. Try the fresh and cheap seafood at the *Imbiße* by the **Stadthafen. Postal code:** 24837.

BREMEN

Bremen's cultural flair, liberal politics, and strong desire to remain an independent *Land* have caused Germans to coin the adjective *bremisch,* which simply means "something unusual." The Altstadt revolves around the ornate **Rathaus,** which was spared during WWII by a bomber pilot who deliberately missed the target because he couldn't bear to bomb it. (DM5, children DM2.50.) Just to the left of the Rathaus is a sculpture of the Brothers Grimm's *Die Bremer Stadtmusikanten* (The Musicians of Bremen)—a donkey, dog, cat, and rooster who terrified a band of robbers with their off-key singing en route to Bremen. Also next to the Rathaus is **St. Petri Dom,** Sandstr. 10-12, with a mosaic exterior and frescoed ceilings; its first stone was laid by Charlemagne in AD 798. (Open M-F 10am-5pm, Sa 10am-1:45pm, Su 2-5pm. Free.) Bremen's sophistication is most notably on display in its museums; the **Neues Museum Weserberg Bremen,** Terrhofstr. 20, between the Klein Weser and the Weser, houses strange and beautiful installations by modern international artists. (Tel. (0421) 59 83 90. Open Tu-F 10am-6pm, Sa-Su 11am-6pm. DM8, students DM5.) For the irresistibly yeasty smell of brewing beer, head across the Weser to **Beck's Brew-**

ery, Am Deich 18/19. (Tel. (0421) 50 94 55 55. Tours every hr. Tu-Sa 10am-5pm, Su 10am-3pm. tours in English 1:30pm. DM5.)

Trains run to Hannover (1hr., 2 per hr., DM34) and Hamburg (1hr., 2 per hr., DM33). The **tourist office,** opposite the station, has museum and theater guides. (Tel. (0421) 308 00 51; fax 308 00 30. Open M-W 9:30am-6:30pm, Th-F 9:30am-8pm, Sa 9:30am-4pm.) To reach the sleek **Jugendgästehaus Bremen (HI),** Kalkstr. 6, from the station, take Bahnhofstr. to Herdentorsteinweg, go right at Am Wall, then left on Bürgermeister-Smidt-Str. and right along the water. (Tel. (0421) 17 13 69; fax 17 11 02. DM34, under 27 DM27. Breakfast included. Reception 24hr.) ☒**Hotel-Pension Garni Weidmann,** Am Schwarzen Meer 35, has plush comforters and cavernous rooms fit for royalty. Walk down Ostertorsteinweg, which becomes Am Schwarzen Meer. (Tel. (0421) 498 44 55. Singles from DM40; doubles from DM80.) To get to the local **campsite,** Am Stadtwaldsee 1, take streetcar 5 or 8 to "Külen Campf," then bus 28 to the door. (Tel. (0421) 21 20 02. DM7.50-11 per tent. DM4.50 per child. Showers included. Laundry DM8.) Bremen's renowned **Ratskeller** in the *Rathaus* is one of the oldest wine bars in Germany. (DM7-8 per 0.2L; meals DM40. Open daily 11am-midnight; kitchen open noon-2:30pm and 6-11pm.) For a cheap meal, try the open-air **market** nearby. (Open daily 8am-2pm.) **Postal code:** 28195.

CENTRAL GERMANY

Stretching from the North Sea to the hills of central Germany, Lower-Saxony has two distinct flavors: along the coast, descendants of the Frisians run their fishing boats along foggy marshland, while the majority of the *Land* is a broad, agricultural plain. Along the Dutch and Belgian borders, North Rhine-Westphalia, with 17 million inhabitants and the mighty Ruhr Valley, is the most heavily populated and economically powerful area in Germany. While the region's squalor may have inspired the philosophy of Karl Marx and Friedrich Engels, the area's natural beauty and intellectual energy of Cologne and Düsseldorf spurred the muses of Goethe, Heine, and Böll. Hesse, mainly known prior to the 20th century as a source for mercenary soldiers (many hired by King George III to put down an unruly gang of colonials in 1776), is today the busiest commercial center in the country, led by the banking metropolis of Frankfurt. Fortunately, the medieval delights and Baroque elegance of areas outside the city remain blessedly off the beaten path.

HANNOVER (HANOVER)

Despite its relatively small size, Hannover puts on a magical display of cultural and cosmopolitan charm. With great economic vigor, a wealth of museums, and a tradition of outdoor festivals, the city reigns as the political and cultural capital of Lower Saxony. To fully experience Hannover, follow the **Red Thread,** a 4-kilometer-long walking tour guided by a red line connecting all the major sights; an accompanying guide in English (DM3) is available at the tourist office. Painstakingly recreated after World War II, the modern **Neues Rathaus** offers features models of Hannover's past; climb up to the tower for a great view of the present version. (Open Apr.-Oct. M-F 9:30am-5:30pm, Sa-Su 10am-5pm. Tower DM3, students DM2.) The **Kestner-Museum,** Trammpl. 3, next to the Neues Rathaus, exhibits the decorative arts of medieval and Renaissance Europe as well as ancient Egypt, Greece, and Rome. (Open Tu and Th-Su 11am-6pm, W 11am-8pm. DM5, students DM3; F free.) The **Herrenhausen Gardens** contain exotic vegetation, Europe's highest garden fountain (80m), and the 18th-century **Herrenhausen Palace.** Take U4 (dir: Garbsen) or U5 (dir: Stöcken) to "Herrenhäusen Gärten." (Gardens open Apr.-Oct. M-Tu 8am-8pm, W-Su 8am-10pm; Nov.-Mar. daily 8am-dusk. DM3. Fountains open M-F 11am-noon and 3-5pm, Sa-Su 11am-noon and 2-5pm. DM3.) The ☒**Sprengel Museum,** on Kurt-Schwitters-Pl., is a modern-art-lover's dream come true, with works by Turrell, Dalí, Picasso, Magritte, and Antes. (Open Tu 10am-8pm, W-Su 10am-6pm. DM8.50.)

Trains arrive frequently from Hamburg (1½hr., DM50-67); Berlin (2½hr., DM78-101); Cologne/Köln (3hr., DM104); and Frankfurt (3½hr., DM140). As you exit the station, turn right (as you face the large rear of the king's splendid steed) to reach the **tourist office,** Ernst-August-Pl. 2. (Tel. (0511) 30 14 20. Open M-F 9am-7pm, Sa 9:30am-3pm.) Rooms will become scarce during **EXPO 2000** (June 1-Oct. 31; www.expo2000.de/englisch), which will highlight the cultural, technological, and economic achievements of the past decade; reserve ahead if you plan to crash. Note that the hostel and *Naturfreundehäuser* are situated in parks and woods on the outskirts of town, where walkways are deserted and poorly lit at night; use caution late at night. To reach **Jugendherberge Hannover (HI),** Ferdinand-Wilhelm-Fricke-Weg 1, take U3 or U7 (dir: Wehbergen) to "Fischerhof/Fach-hochschule"; cross the tracks, walk through the parking lot, follow the path as it curves, cross the street, go over the enormous red footbridge, and walk right for 50m. (Tel. (0511) 131 76 74; fax 185 55. DM28, under 27 DM23. Sheets DM5.70. Reception 7:30-9am and 2-11:30pm. Curfew 11:30pm.) To reach **Naturfreundehaus Stadtheim,** Hermann-Bahlsen-Allee 8, take U3 (dir: Lahe) or U7 (dir: Fasanenk-rug) to "Spannhagengarten"; backtrack 15m to the intersection, follow Hermann-Bahlsen-Allee left for 5min., and follow the sign to your right down the paved road. (Tel. (0511) 69 14 93; fax 69 06 52. DM43.80. Breakfast included. Reception 8am-noon and 3-10pm.) ◪**Uwe's Hannenfaß Hannover,** Knochenhauerstr. 36, in the center of the Altstadt, serves steaming *Niedersachsenschmaus* (potato casse-role; DM7.50) and house-brewed *Hannen Alt* (DM5.40). (Open M-Sa noon-2am, Su 3pm-2am.) **Spar supermarkets** sit by the Lister Meile and Kröpcke U-Bahn stops. (Both open M-F 8am-7pm, Sa 8am-2pm.) The student- and smoke-filled ◪**The Loft,** Georgstr. 50b, is near Kröpcke. (Open M-Th 9pm-2am, F-Sa 9pm-5am, Su 8pm-2am.) **Postal code:** 30159.

GÖTTINGEN

Home to Europe's first free university, Göttingen remains a college town to the core. Otto von Bismarck and the Brothers Grimm, as well as 41 Nobel laureates in science, including Max Planck (the father of quantum mechanics) and Werner Heisenberg (of Uncertainty Principle fame) have graduated from or taught at the **Georg-August-Universität.** The **Altes Rathaus** (Old Town Hall) at the center of the Altstadt serves as a meeting spot for the whole town. For a taste of a strumpet, kiss the little **Gänsliesel** (goose-girl) on the fountain; centuries of graduates have embraced her upon receiving their diplomas. **Bismarckturm** (Bismarck tower), Im Hainberg, commemorates the troublemaking of political giant Otto von Bis-marck and offers a splendid view of the town. Take bus A to "Bismarckstr./Reit-saal." (Open Sa-Su 11am-6pm. Free.) The **Städtisches Museum,** Ritterplan 7, gives a detailed examination of the city over the past few millennia. (Open Tu-Su 10am-5pm. DM3, students DM1.) The renowned **Deutsches Theater,** Theaterpl. 11, has world-class performances. (Tel. (0551) 49 69 11. Open M-F 10am-1:30pm and 5-7pm, Sa 10am-noon, and 1hr. before performances.)

Trains arrive at least every hr. from Hannover (1hr., DM30); Frankfurt (2hr., DM66); Hamburg (2hr., DM80); and Berlin (2½hr., DM100). From the station, cross Berliner Str., follow Goetheallee (which becomes Prinzenstr.), and turn right on Weender Str. to reach the **tourist office,** Markt 9, in the Altes Rathaus. (Tel. (0551) 540 00; fax 400 29 98; email tourismus@goettingen.de. Open Apr.-Oct. M-F 9:30am-6pm, Sa-Su 10am-4pm; Nov.-Mar. M-F 9:30am-1pm and 2-6pm, Sa 10am-1pm.) The ◪**Jugendherberge (HI),** Habichtsweg 2, puts most *hotels* to shame with immaculate rooms and many singles. Take bus 8, 10, 11, 15, or 18 to "Kornmarkt," then bus 6 (dir: Theaterpl./Klausberg) to "Jugendherberge." (Tel. (0551) 576 22; fax 438 87. DM32, under 27 DM27. Breakfast included. Reception 6:30am-11:30pm.) ◪**Shucan,** Weender Str. 11, is a hip café and bar with outdoor seating overlooking the Marktpl. (Open M-Th and Su 9am-2pm, F-Sa 10am-3am.) Pick up **groceries** at **Plus,** Prinzenstr. 13, opposite the library. (Open M-F 8am-7:30pm, Sa 8am-4pm.) **Blue Note,** Wilhelmspl. 3, is the best place to hear music and hang with students in the Altstadt. (Cover for weekly concerts DM8-30. Open daily from 8pm.) **Postal code:** 37073.

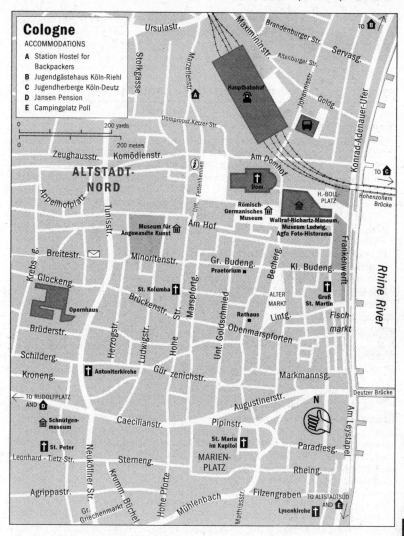

Cologne

ACCOMMODATIONS

A Station Hostel for
   Backpackers
B Jugendgästehaus Köln-Riehl
C Jugendherberge Köln-Deutz
D Jansen Pension
E Campingplatz Poll

COLOGNE (KÖLN)

Founded as a Roman colony (*colonia*, hence Köln) in AD 48, Cologne gained fame and fortune in the Middle Ages as an elite university town and an important trade hub. While most of the inner city was destroyed in WWII, the magnificent Gothic cathedral survived no fewer than 14 bombings and remains Cologne's main attraction. Today, tourists come to see this symbol of Cologne's rebirth, participate in bibulous celebrations, and indulge in the burgeoning fine arts scene.

GETTING THERE AND GETTING AROUND

Trains: From the **Hauptbahnhof** to: **Düsseldorf** (30min., 6 per hr., DM12.20); **Frankfurt** (2½hr., every hr., DM69); **Brussels** (2½hr., every 2hr., DM54); **Hamburg** (4hr., every hr., DM130); **Amsterdam** (4hr., every 2hr., DM79); **Paris** (4hr., every 2hr., DM128); **Berlin** (5½hr., every 2hr., DM190); and **Munich** (6-8hr., every hr., DM180).

GERMANY

Ferries: Köln-Düsseldorfer (tel. 258 30 11) begins its ever-popular Rhine cruises here (see p. 422). Students 50% off; most trips (excluding hydrofoils) covered by Eurail.

Public Transportation: VRS (Verkehrsverbund Rhein-Sieg) offices have free maps of the S- and U-Bahn, bus, and streetcar lines; one is downstairs in the train station near the U-Bahn. **Single-fare tickets** DM2.20-14.20; **day pass** DM9.50.

🔽 ORIENTATION AND PRACTICAL INFORMATION

The city center lies along the west bank of the **Rhine** River. The Altstadt is split into **Altstadt-Nord,** near the **Hauptbahnhof,** and **Altstadt-Süd,** south of the Severinsbrücke.

Tourist Office: Verkehrsamt, Unter Fettenhennen 19 (tel. 221 33 45; fax 22 12 33 20; www.koeln.org/koelntourismus), opposite the Dom. Open May-Oct. M-Sa 8am-10:30pm, Su 9am-10:30pm; Nov.-Apr. M-Sa 8am-9pm, Su 9:30am-7pm.

Currency Exchange: An office at the **train station** is open daily 7am-9pm, but the service charges are lower at the **post office** (see below).

Gay and Lesbian Services: Schulz Schwulen-und Lesbenzentrum, Kartäuserwall 18 (tel. 93 18 80 80), near Chlodwigpl. Info, movies, youth activities, library, and popular café.

Laundry: Eco-Express, on Richard-Wagner-Str. Wash DM6; soap included. Dry DM1 per 10min. Open M-Sa 6am-11pm.

Emergency: Police, tel. 110. **Fire** and **ambulance,** tel. 112.

Pharmacy: Dom-Apotheke, Komödienstr. 5 (tel. 257 67 54), near the station, posts a list of after-hours pharmacies outside. English spoken. Open M-F 8am-6:30pm, Sa 9am-1pm.

Post Office: Hauptpostamt, at the corner of Breite Str. and Auf der Ruhr. Address mail to be held: *Postlagernde Briefe* für Alyona IVANOVNA, Hauptpostamt, **50667** Köln, Germany. Open M-F 8am-8pm, Sa 8am-4pm.

PHONE CODE	City code: 0221. From outside Germany, dial int'l dialing prefix (see inside back cover) + 49 + 221 + local number.

🄯 ACCOMMODATIONS AND FOOD

Most hotels fill up in spring and fall when conventions come to town, and the two hostels are nearly always booked from June to September. Call ahead.

🔽 **Station Hostel for Backpackers,** Marzellenstr. 44-48 (tel. 912 53 01; fax 912 53 03; email station@t-online.de). From the station, walk 1 block along Dompropst-Ketzer-Str. and turn right on Marzellenstr. Independent hostel with impeccable rooms and a relaxed atmosphere. Dorms DM27; singles DM40; doubles DM70. Sheets DM3. Laundry DM6. **Internet** DM4 per 30min. Reception 24hr. Call by 3pm to confirm reservations.

Jugendherberge Köln-Deutz (HI), Siegesstr. 5a (tel. 81 47 11; fax 88 44 25), over the Hohenzollernbrücke. S6, S11, or S12: Köln-Deutz; from the main exit, go down Neuhöfferstr. and take the 1st right. Small but clean rooms. DM37, under 27 DM33. Breakfast included. Laundry free; soap DM1. Reception 11am-1am. Curfew 1am. Call ahead.

Jugendgästehaus Köln-Riehl (HI), An der Schanz 14 (tel. 76 70 81; fax 76 15 55), on the Rhine north of the zoo. U6 (dir: Ebertplatz/Mülheim): Boltensternstr. Or walk north along the Rhine on Konrad-Adenauer-Ufer until it becomes An der Schanz (40min.). Dorms DM38.50; singles DM63.50. Breakfast included. Reception 24hr. Call ahead.

🔽 **Jansen Pension,** Richard-Wagner-Str. 18 (tel. 25 18 75). U1, U6-7, U15, U17, or U19: Rudolfplatz; then follow Richard-Wagner-Str. to just before Brüsseler Str. Charming rooms in a Victorian townhouse. Singles DM50-60; doubles DM100. Breakfast included.

Campingplatz Poll, Weidenweg (tel. 83 19 66), on the Rhine, southeast of the Altstadt. U16: Marienburg; then cross the Rodenkirchener Brücke. DM8 per person, DM4 per tent, DM4 per car. Reception 8am-noon and 5-8pm. Open Apr.-Oct.

Cologne cuisine includes scrumptious *Rievekoochen* (potato pancakes), slabs of fried potato dunked in *Apfelmus* (applesauce), as well as smooth **Kölsch** beer. Small cafés packed and cheap restaurants line **Zülpicher Str.** (U7 or U9: Zülpicher Platz). Mid-priced ethnic restaurants lie around the perimeter of the Altstadt, particularly from **Hohenzollernring** to **Hohenstaufenring;** the city's best cheap eats are in the Turkish district on **Weideng.** Pick up **groceries** at **Mini-Mal,** Hohenstaufenring 30. (Open M-F 8am-8pm, Sa 8am-4pm.) Breakfast (from DM5.50) is served until 4pm at **☒Café Waschsalon,** Ehrenstr. 77. (Open M-Th 8am-1am, F 8am-3am, Sa 10am-3am, Su 10am-1am.) **Sushi Nara,** Friesenstr. 70, has excellent sushi at unbeatable prices. (Meals from DM10. Open M-Th noon-3:30pm and 5:30pm-midnight, F-Sa noon-midnight, Su 6-11pm.) **Café Magnus,** Zülpicherstr. 48, is popular with the university crowd. (Pizzas and salads from DM6; pasta from DM10. Open daily 8am-3pm.)

👁 🎵 SIGHTS AND ENTERTAINMENT

☒DOM. Visitors exiting Cologne's train station are immediately treated to the beauty, power, and sorrow emanating from Germany's greatest cathedral. Six centuries in the making, the cathedral was finally completed in 1880 in High Gothic style. The stunning stained-glass windows cast a harlequin display of colored light over the interior. To the right of the center altar is the **Dombild triptych,** a masterful 15th-century painting and gilded altarpiece. Look for the brightly shining **Shrine of the Magi,** a reliquary of the Three Kings in blinding gold brought to the city in 1164; the 976 **Gero crucifix,** the oldest intact sculpture of *Christus patiens* (depicting a crucified Christ with eyes shut); and Rubens' *Crucifixion of St. Peter.* A mere 509 steps lead to the top of the **Südturm** (south tower); catch your breath 400 steps up at the Glockenstube, where the 24-ton **Der große Peter,** the world's heaviest swinging bell, roosts. *(Open daily 6am-7pm; free. Tours in German M-Sa 11am and 12:30, 2, and 3:30pm, Su 2 and 3:30pm; DM6, students DM3. Tours in English M-Sa 10:30am and 2:30pm, Su 2:30pm; DM7. Tower open Mar.-Oct. 9am-5pm; Nov.-Feb. 9am-dusk; DM3, students DM1.50.)*

GROSS ST. MARTIN AND FISCHMARKT. Along with the cathedral, **Groß St. Martin** defines the legendary Rhine panorama of Cologne. The renovated church was reopened in 1985 after near-destruction in WWII. *(An Groß St. Martin 9, south of the cathedral near the Fischmarkt. Open M-Sa 10am-6pm, Su 2-4pm. Free.)* Near the church, the squares and crooked streets of the old **Fischmarkt** area open onto paths along the Rhine, and crowded cafés give way to riverside stretches of grass.

HOUSE #4711. This magic water **Eau de Cologne,** once prescribed as a drinkable curative, made the town a household name. If you're after the real thing, be sure your bottle says *Echt kölnisch Wasser* ("real Cologne water"), or look for the "4711" label. The house today is a boutique, with a small fountain continually dispensing the famous scented water. *(Glockeng, at the intersection with Tunisstr. From Hohe Str., turn right on Brückenstr., which becomes Glockeng. Open M-F 9am-8pm, Sa 9am-4pm.)*

MUSEUMS. Between the cathedral and the Hohenzollernbrücke, the cultural center on **☒Heinrich-Böll-Platz** houses three complementary collections. The **Wallraf-Richartz Museum** features masterpieces from the Italian Renaissance to the French Impressionists; the **Museum Ludwig** spans Impressionism, Picasso, Dalí, Liechtenstein, Warhol, and art where the glue has yet to dry; and the **Agfa Foto-Historama** chronicles chemical art of the last 150 years, with a rotating display of Man Ray's

---

INSULTS FOR SALE The concept of free speech in Germany does not imply *cost-free* speech—dropping insults will unload your wallet in no time. Public humiliation in Germany carries such destructive force that officials have created an insult price list; offended or drunk budget travelers should beware. The heaviest fines are incurred by mouth-flappers who put down a police officer's respectability: belting out *Trottel in Uniform* (fool in uniform) costs DM3000, while the lesser insult *Dumme Kuh* (dumb cow) requires a mere DM1200 payoff. Call any uniformed official *Idiot* and you'll be out a whopping DM3000. The budget traveler's insult, *Holzkopf* (wood-headed), goes for DM1500. Equivalent insults in English are not exempt; stories abound of policemen who've doled out thousands of *Marks* in fines to tourists who think that Germans don't understand what "asshole" means. We tell you this merely as a warning—and prices, of course, are subject to change, you idiot.

works. *(Bischofsgartenstr. 1. Open Tu 10am-8pm, W-F 10am-6pm, Sa-Su 11am-6pm. Tours Tu 6pm, W 4:30pm, Sa 11:30am, and Su 11:30am and 3pm. DM10, students DM5.)* West of the Heinrich-Böll-Platz, the **Römisch-Germanisches Museum,** built on the ruins of a Roman villa, displays the world-famous Dionysus mosaic, the tomb of Publicus, an intimidating six-breasted sphinx, and some naughty candle-holders. *(Roncallipl. 4. Open Tu-Su 10am-5pm. DM5, students DM2.50.)* Better than Willy Wonka's Chocolate Factory, the **Schokoladenmuseum** allows you to salivate at every step of the chocolate production process. Resist the urge to drool and wait for the free, but small, samples. *(Rheinauhafen 1a, near the Severinsbrücke. From the station, walk right along the Rhine, head under the Deutzer Brücke, and take the 1st footbridge. Open Tu-F 10am-6pm, Sa-Su 11am-7pm; DM10, students DM5. Tours Sa 2 and 4pm, Su 11:30am, 2 and 4pm; DM3.)*

🎵 🎬 ENTERTAINMENT AND NIGHTLIFE

Cologne becomes a living spectacle during **Karneval,** a week-long pre-Lent festival celebrated in the hedonistic spirit of the city's Roman past. The weekend builds up to a bacchanalian parade on **Rosenmontag,** the last Monday before Lent (Mar. 6, 2000), when everyone is in costume and gets and gives dozens of *Bützchen* (kisses on a stranger's cheek). Pick up the *Karneval* booklet at the tourist office.

Students congregate in the *Bermuda-Dreieck* (triangle), bounded by **Zülpicherstr., Zülpicherpl., Roonstr.,** and **Luxemburgstr.** Gay nightlife runs up **Matthiasstr.** to **Mühlenbach, Hohe Pforte, Marienpl.,** and up to **Heumarkt** by the Deutzer Brücke. **Papa Joe's Jazzlokal,** Buttermarkt 37, features high-caliber live jazz and oodles of New Orleans atmosphere. (Open M-Sa 7pm-2am, Su 3:30pm-1am.) You'll be livin' la **Taco Loco** at Zülpicherstr. 4a, with happy "hour" daily 6-8pm and tasty margaritas. (Open Su-Th 10am-2am, F-Sa 10am-3am.) Legendary *Kölsch* is brewed on the premises and at **Päffgen-Brauerei.** (Open daily 10am-midnight.) **MTC,** Zülpicherstr. 10, has everything from punk/grunge to live concerts to recorded bar tunes. (Cover DM6; includes 1 drink. Open M, W, and Su 9pm-2am, Tu and Th-Sa 9pm-3am.) 🔲**Vampire,** Rathenaupl. 5, is a gay and lesbian bar with a laid-back atmosphere and a garlic-breath-free clientele. (Open Tu-Th and Su 8pm-1am; disco F-Sa 8pm-3am.)

BONN

Derisively called the *Hauptdorf* (capital village), Bonn has been Germany's whipping boy for 50 years just because it's not Berlin. Bonn made it big by chance, because postwar chancellor Konrad Adenauer had a house in the suburbs. The Bundestag packed up and moved back to Berlin in 1999, but Bonn remains a worthy destination with several museums, a bustling Altstadt, and a respected university.

🔲🔳 **PRACTICAL INFO, ACCOMMODATIONS, AND FOOD. Trains** run to Cologne (30min., 6 per hr., DM8.90); Koblenz (1hr., 3 per hr., DM14.80); and Frankfurt (1½hr., every hr., DM59). Take the "Stadtmitte" exit from the station, walk up Poststr., and turn left on Münsterstr. to reach the **tourist office,** Münsterstr. 20, in a passageway. (Tel. (0228) 77 34 66; fax 69 03 68. Open M-F 9am-6:30pm, Sa 9am-4pm, Su 10am-2pm.) Take bus 621 (dir: Ippendorf Altenheim) to "Jugendgästehaus" to get to the **Jugendgästehaus Bonn-Venusberg (HI),** Haager Weg 42. (Tel. (0228) 28 99 70; fax 289 97 14; email jgh-bonn@t-online.de. DM39. Breakfast included. Laundry DM10. Reception 9am-1am. Curfew 1am.) **Hotel Virneburg,** Sandkaule 3a, offers an unbelievable price and location. Walk up Poststr., bear right on Acherstr. at the north end of Münsterpl., turn left on Rathausg., and turn left again on Belderberg, which runs into Sandkaule. (Tel. (0228) 63 63 66. Singles DM35-65; doubles DM65-95. Breakfast included.) To reach **Campingplatz Genienaue,** Im Frankenkeller 49, take U16 or U63 to "Rheinallee," then bus 613 (dir: Giselherstr.) to "Guntherstr."; turn left on Guntherstr. and right on Frankenkeller. (Tel. (0228) 34 49 49. DM8 per person, DM5-8 per tent. Reception 9am-noon and 3-10pm.) 🔲**Carl's Mensa-Bistro,** Nassestr. 15, has restaurant-quality meals served cafeteria-style. (Open M-Th 10:30am-10pm, F 10:30am-3pm.) There is a **supermarket** in the Kaufhof basement on Münsterpl. (Open M-F 9:30am-8pm, Sa 9am-4pm.) **Postal code:** 53111.

⌕ ⎗ SIGHTS AND ENTERTAINMENT. Bonn's old town center winds into a lively pedestrian zone littered with historic niches. The **Beethoven Geburtshaus** (birthplace), Bonng. 20, hosts a fantastic collection of his personal effects, from his primitive hearing aids to his first violin. (Open Apr.-Sept. M-Sa 10am-6pm, Su 11am-4pm; Oct.-Mar. M-Sa 10am-5pm, Su 11am-4pm. DM8, students DM6.) In its governmental heyday, the vaguely Bauhaus **Bundestag** earned the title of "least prepossessing parliament building" in the world; take U16, U63, or U66 to "Heussallee/Bundeshaus," or bus 610 to "Bundeshaus." The castles, palaces, and most museums lie just outside the inner city. The **Kurfürstliches Schloß**, a huge 18th-century palace, now serves as the center of Bonn's university. Down the Poppelsdorfer Allee promenade, the 18th-century **Poppelsdorfer Schloß** sports a French façade, an Italian courtyard, and manicured **botanical gardens.** (Gardens open May-Sept. M-F 9am-6pm, Su 9am-1pm; Oct.-Apr. M-F 9am-4pm, Su 9am-1pm. M-F free, Su DM1.) The **Bonncard** (DM24 per day from the tourist office) provides public transport and admission to most museums of the **Museum Mile** (U16, U63, or U66: Heussallee or Museum Koenig). The **Kunstmuseum Bonn,** Friedrich-Ebert-Allee 2, has superb Expressionist and contemporary German art (open Tu and Th-Su 10am-6pm, W 10am-7pm; DM5, students DM3), while the art in the **Kunst- und Ausstellungshalle der BRD,** Friedrich-Ebert-Allee 4, is so new that you can smell the paint (open Tu-W 10am-9pm, Th-Su 10am-7pm; DM10, students DM5). The futuristic ⦿**Haus der Geschichte,** Adenauerallee 250, one block from the Kunstmuseum Bonn, offers an interactive look at German history. (Open Tu-Su 9am-7pm. Free.) For cultural and entertainment listings, check out *Schnüss,* or hang at **Café Göttlich,** on Franziskanerstr. near the university. (Open M-Sa 9am-4am, Su noon-2am.)

AACHEN

Charlemagne sang the mantra of multiculturalism when he made this the capital of his Frankish empire in the 8th century, and today a flux of students and international travelers continues to renew Aachen's vibrant atmosphere. The world-famous neo-Byzantine **Dom** (cathedral) is in the center of the city. Beneath the chancel lie Charlemagne's bones. (Open daily 10am-7pm. Tours M 11am and noon; Tu-F 11am, noon, 2:30, and 3:30pm; Sa-Su 12:30, 2:30, and 3:30pm. DM3.) The 14th-century stone **Rathaus,** built on the ruins of Charlemagne's palace, looms over the wide Marktpl. and the cathedral. On the northern façade stand 50 statues of former German sovereigns, 31 of whom were crowned in Aachen. (Open daily 10am-1pm and 2-5pm. DM3, students DM1.50.) The ⦿**Ludwigforum für Internationale Kunst,** Jülicherstr. 97-109, in a converted Bauhaus umbrella factory, showcases a cutting-edge collection of current greats (Jeff Koons' gigantic sex dolls) and the soon-to-be-greats (a 3 ft. Marge Simpson stone fertility doll). (Open Tu and Th 10am-5pm, W and F 10am-8pm, Sa-Su 11am-5pm. DM6, students DM3.)

Aachen sits between Germany, Belgium, and the Netherlands. **Trains** chug to Cologne/Köln (1hr., 2-3 per hr., DM20); Brussels (2hr., every hr., DM50.80); and Amsterdam (4hr., every hr., DM102). To get from the station to the **tourist office,** on Friedrich-Wilhelm-Pl. in the Atrium Elisenbrunnen, cross the street, head up Bahnhofstr., turn left on Theaterstr., then right onto Kapuzinergraben, which leads to Friedrich-Wilhelm-Pl. (Tel. (0241) 180 29 60; fax 180 29 31. Open M-F 9am-6pm, Sa 9am-2pm.) The ⦿**Euroregionales Jugendgästehaus (HI),** Maria-Theresia-Allee 260, feels more like a hotel than a hostel. From the station, walk left on Lagerhausstr. until it intersects Kareliterstr. and Mozartstr., then take bus 2 (dir: Preusswald) to "Ronheide" or bus 12 (dir: Diepenbendem) to "Colynshof." (Tel. (0241) 711 01; fax 70 82 19. DM38.50. Curfew 1am.) Take bus 5 from the bus station to "Strangenhäuschen" to reach **ETAP-Hotel,** Strangenhäuschen 15. (Tel. (0241) 91 19 29; fax 15 53 04. Singles DM62; doubles DM74; F-Su all rooms DM62. Breakfast DM8.50. Reception 6:30-10am and 5-11pm. Lockout 10am-5pm.) **Plus,** Marienbongard 27, off Pontstr., stocks **groceries.** (Open M-F 8am-8pm, Sa 8am-4pm.) **Postal code:** 52064.

GERMANY

DÜSSELDORF

The capital of North Rhine-Westphalia and the headquarters of Germany's largest corporations and fashion industry, Düsseldorf is a stately, modern metropolis, pulsating with an energy unlike anything found in most other German cities. The city has rebounded from wartime destruction with resilience and fierce pride. By day, crowds line The Königsallee (a.k.a. the "Kö"), a one-kilometer-long fashion runway that sweeps down either side of the old town moat. At night, propriety (and sobriety) are cast aside as thousands of Düsseldorfers flock to the 500 pubs of the Altstadt, trading monocles and Rolexes for beer goggles and a good time.

▐ GETTING THERE AND GETTING AROUND

Trains: From the **Hauptbahnhof** to: **Frankfurt** (3hr., 2 per hr., DM79); **Amsterdam** (3hr., every hr., DM54.60); **Brussels** (3¼hr., every hr., DM58.80); **Hamburg** (3½hr., every hr., DM116); **Berlin** (4hr., every hr., DM103); **Munich** (4hr., 3 per hr., DM191); and **Paris** (4½hr., 7 per day, DM140). To **Aachen** or **Cologne/Köln,** the S-Bahn is cheaper.

Public Transportation: The **Rheinbahn** includes the U-Bahn, S-Bahn, streetcars, and buses. **Single-fare tickets** DM2.10-12. The **Tagesticket** (from DM11) buys 24hr. of unlimited transport for up to 5 people. Vending machines sell tickets; pick up the *Fahrausweis* brochure in the tourist office for instructions. For **schedule info,** call 582 28.

▐ PRACTICAL INFORMATION

Tourist Office: Konrad-Adenauer-Pl. (tel. 17 20 20; fax 35 04 04; www.duesseldorf.de). Walk up and to the right from the Hauptbahnhof. Open M-F 8:30am-6pm, Sa 9am-12:30pm; books rooms (from DM55) for a DM5 fee M-Sa 8am-8pm, Su 4-10pm.

Currency Exchange: Deutsche Verkehrsbank, in the train station and the airport. Open M-Sa 7am-9pm, Su 8am-9pm.

Laundromat: Wasch Center, Friedrichstr. 92, down the street from the Kirchpl. S-Bahn. Wash DM6; soap included. Dry DM1 per 15min. Open M-Sa 6am-11pm.

Post Office: Hauptpostamt, Konrad-Adenauer-Pl. Address mail to be held: *Postlagernde Briefe* für Jenny CU, Hauptpostamt, Konrad-Adenauer-Pl., **40210** Düsseldorf, Germany. Open M-F 8am-6pm, Sa 9am-2pm. Limited service M-F 6-8pm.

Internet Access: Ratin Gate, Ratinger Str. 8. DM8 per hr.; 11pm-1am DM4 per hr. Open Su-Th 1pm-1am, F-Sa 1pm-3am. **G@rden,** Rathausufer 8. DM10 per hr.

PHONE CODE	City code: 0211. From outside Germany, dial int'l dialing prefix (see inside back cover) + 49 + 211 + local number.

▐ ACCOMMODATIONS, CAMPING, AND FOOD

Corporate convention crowds make rooms scarce and costly; call at least a month ahead if possible. Most rooms go for at least DM50 per person even in off-season. Cheap hotels populate the seedy train station neighborhood.

Jugendgästehaus Düsseldorf (HI), Düsseldorfer Str. 1 (tel. 55 73 10; fax 57 25 13), just over the Rheinkniebrücke from the Altstadt. U70 or U74-77: Luegplatz; then walk 500m down Kaiser-Wilhelm-Ring. Unbeatable location makes up for the price. DM41.50, under 27 DM37.50. Reception 7am-1am. Curfew 1am, but doors open every hr. 2-6am.

Hotel Amsterdam, Stresemannstr. 20 (tel. 840 58; fax 840 50), between Oststr. and Berliner Allee. From the station, head up Graf-Adolf-Str. and right at Stresemannpl. Singles DM65, with TV and breakfast DM90; doubles from DM145. Reception 7am-midnight.

Hotel Manhattan, Graf-Adolf-Str. 39 (tel. 37 71 38; fax 37 02 47), 2 blocks from the station. Singles DM68-105; doubles DM100-150. Breakfast included. Reception 24hr.

Hotel Diana, Jahnstr. 31 (tel. 37 50 71; fax 36 49 43), 5 blocks from the station. Head left down Graf-Adolf-Str., left on Hüttenstr., and right on Jahnstr. Ugly tile, but it's clean. Singles DM65; doubles DM95, with bath DM135. Breakfast included. Reception 24hr.

GERMANY

Camping: Kleiner Torfbruch (tel. 899 20 38). S-Bahn to "Düsseldorf Geresheim," then bus 735 (dir: Stamesberg) to "Seeweg." DM7.50 per person, DM10 per tent.

Rows of pizzerias, *Döner* stands, and Chinese eateries reach from **Heinrich-Heine-Allee** to the banks of the Rhine in the **Altstadt.** The house specialties at **Zum Uerige,** Bergerstr. 1, are *Blutwurst* (blood sausages; DM4) and Mainz cheese (DM4); wash it down with a *Schlösser Alt* beer. (Open daily 10am-midnight; kitchen open M-F 6-9pm, Sa 11am-4pm.) **Galerie Burghof,** Burgallee 1-3, is somewhat touristy, but has delicious pancakes and a great view of the Rhine and the Kaiserwerth ruins. Take U79 to "Klemensplatz"; walk down Kaiserwerther Markt and turn left on the Rhine promenade. (Open daily 11am-1am; pancakes served M-F 6-10:45pm, Sa 2-10:45pm, Su 2-11pm.) **Marché,** Königsallee 60, in the Kö-Galerie mall, is cheap. (Entrees from DM7. Open M-Th and Su 9am-9pm, F-Sa 9am-10pm.) **Olto Mess supermarket** is on Karlspl. in the Altstadt. (Open M-F 8am-8pm, Sa 8am-4pm.)

■ SIGHTS AND ENTERTAINMENT

ALTSTADT AND ENVIRONS. The glitzy **Königsallee,** just outside the Altstadt, embodies the vitality and glamour of Düsseldorf. What it doesn't have in fashion-center prestige à la Milan or New York, it more than makes up for in pretentiousness. Midway up is the awesome **Kö-Galerie,** a gaudy marble-and-copper complex of one haughty store after another—even the mannequins have attitude. At the upper end of the Kö, the **Hofgarten** park is an oasis of green within urban Düsseldorf. The Neoclassical **Ratinger Tor** gate, halfway down the length of the park, opens onto Heinrich-Heine-Allee, where skylights lavish sunshine on Matisse, Picasso, Surrealists, and Expressionists at the **Kunstsammlung Nordrhein-Westfalen.** The collection of works by hometown boy Paul Klee is one of the most extensive in the world. *(Grabbepl. 5. U70, U75-76, or U78-79: Heinrich-Heine-Allee; walk north 2 blocks. Open Tu-Th and Sa-Su 10am-6pm, F 10am-8pm. Tours Su 11am and W 3:30pm. DM5, students DM3. Special exhibits DM10, students DM8.)* Across the square is the **Kunsthalle**—not a museum, mind you, but a forum for modern exhibits of every shape and size. *(Grabbepl. 4. Around DM10, students DM7. Open Tu-Su 11am-6pm.)* At the far end of the Hofgarten, where the park meets the Rhine, the **Kunstmuseum Düsseldorf** balances Baroque and Romantic art with a 20th-century collection. The **Kunstpalast** is an extension of the Kunstmuseum devoted to rotating contemporary exhibits. *(Ehrenhof 5. Open Tu-Su 11am-6pm; DM8, students DM5.)* The **ArtTicket** includes entrance to all museums. *(DM20 at the tourist office or any museum.)*

KAISERWERTH. North on the Rhine but still within Düsseldorf dwell the **ruins** of Emperor Friedrich's palace in the tiny town of Kaiserwerth. Built in 1184 and destroyed in the 1702 War of Spanish Succession, only the palace's gloomy *Kaiserpfalz* frame remains. Take U79 to "Klemensplatz," then follow Kaiserwerther Markt to the Rhine, and walk left another 150m.

NIGHTLIFE. Folklore holds that Düsseldorf's 500 pubs make up *die längste Theke der Welt* ("the longest bar in the world"). Whether or not that's true, pubs in the Altstadt are standing-room-only by 6pm, and foot traffic is shoulder-to-shoulder by nightfall—it's nearly impossible to see where one pub ends and the next begins. **Bolkerstr.** is jam-packed nightly with street performers of the musical and beer-Olympic varieties. Pick up *Prinz* (DM5) for tips on hotspots. The classic factory-turned-disco **Stahlwerk,** Ronsdorfer Str. 134, packs in 1500 of the city's most divine. (U75: Ronsdorfer Str. Cover DM10. Open F-Sa and last Su of every month after 10pm.) At **La Pocca,** Grünstr. 8, just off the Kö, a mostly twentysomething crowd showcases the day's purchases while dancing the night away to house. (Cover DM8. Open F-Sa from 10pm, sometimes also on weeknights.) The café **Unique,** Bolkerstr. 30, is a club that draws a younger, trendier crowd. (Cover DM10. Open daily 10pm-late.) Down a glass of *Schlösser Alt* at hugely popular pub **Zum Uel,** Ratinger Str. 16. (Open Su-Tu and Th 10am-1am, W and F 10am-3am.) **Café Rosa,** Oberbilker Allee 310, is the socio-cultural mecca of Düsseldorf's gay community. (Tu men only; F women only. Open Tu-Sa 8pm-1am, later on weekends.)

GERMANY

FRANKFURT AM MAIN

Known to some as "Bankfurt" or "Mainhattan," Frankfurt is a thriving financial and commercial center. Although it perhaps lacks the architectural beauty common to more traditional German cities, its integral economic role as home to the central bank of the European Union lends it a glitzy vitality. Anne Frank, Goethe, and the social theorists of the Frankfurt School have enriched the city's cultural treasury, and the city government spends more on cultural attractions and tourism than any other German city. If all this isn't enough to make you visit, the likelihood of your passing through Frankfurt's highly trafficked train station or airport probably is.

▐ GETTING THERE AND GETTING AROUND

Flights: Flughafen Rhein-Main (tel. 69 01). S-Bahn 8 connects to the Hauptbahnhof every 15min. Buy tickets (DM5.90) from the green *Automaten* (vending machines).

Trains: Info and reservations tel. (0180) 599 66 33. To: **Cologne/Köln** (2½hr., 2 per hr., DM70, under 26 DM56); **Munich** (3½-4½hr., 2 per hr., DM212); **Amsterdam** (5hr., every 2hr., DM120, under 26 DM110); **Berlin** (5-6hr., 2 per hr., DM207, under 26 DM166); **Paris** (5-6hr., every 2hr., DM140, under 26 DM108); **Hamburg** (6hr., 2 per hr., DM191, under 26 DM153); and **Rome** (15hr., every hr., DM279).

Public Transportation: Runs until about 1am. Refer to the color **subway** map in the front of this guide. **Tageskarte** passes provide unlimited transportation on the U-Bahn, S-Bahn, streetcars, and buses (valid until midnight on the day of purchase); buy from any *Automat* (DM8.20). **Single-ride** tickets are valid for 1hr. in one direction, including transfers (rush-hour DM3.60, off-peak DM3). **Eurail** valid only on the S-Bahn.

▐ ORIENTATION AND PRACTICAL INFORMATION

The Hauptbahnhof (Main Train Station) lies at the end of Frankfurt's red-light district; walk 20min. down Kaiserstr. or Münchener Str. to reach the **Altstadt** (old city) and the **Römerberg** (U4: Römer). To the north, the commercial **Zeil** stretches from **Hauptwache** (S1-6 or S8: Hauptwache) to **Konstablerwache** (1 stop farther). Students and cafés cluster in **Bockenheim** (U6-7: Bockenheimer Warte). South of the Main River, **Sachsenhausen** (U1-3: Schweizer Pl.) draws pub-crawlers and museum-goers.

Tourist Office: In the Hauptbahnhof (tel. 21 23 88 49; www.frankfurt.de). Sells maps (DM1-2) and books rooms (DM5 fee). Also sells the **Frankfurt Card** (1-day DM12, 2-day DM19), which grants unlimited travel on all trains and buses and 50% off admission to 15 museums and other attractions. Open M-F 8am-9pm, Sa-Su 9am-6pm.

American Express: Kaiserstr. 8 (tel. 21 05 01 11, 24-hour hotline (0180) 523 23 77; fax 210 52 70). No mail held. Open M-F 9:30am-6pm, Sa 9:30am-12:30pm.

English Bookstores: Süssman's Presse und Buch, Zeil 127 (tel. 131 07 51). Open M-W and F 9am-7pm, Th 9am-8pm, Sa 9am-4pm.

Laundromat: Schnell & Sauber, Wallstr. 8, near the hostel in Sachsenhausen. DM8-9. Open daily 6am-11pm. **Miele Washworld,** Moselstr. 17. DM10. Open daily 8am-11pm.

Emergency: Tel. 110. **Fire** and **ambulance,** tel. 112.

Pharmacy: Downstairs in the Hauptbahnhof (tel. 23 30 47; fax 24 27 19 16). Open M-F 6:30am-9pm, Sa 8am-9pm, Su and holidays 9am-8pm. In an emergency, call 192 92.

Internet Access: CybeRyder Internet Café, Töngesg. 31. DM5 per 30min. Open M-Th 10am-11pm, F-Sa 10am-1am, Su 3-11pm. **Cyber's,** Zeil 112-114, in the Zeil Galerie, 7th fl. DM6 per 30min. Open M-F 11am-1am, Sa 10am-1am, Su noon-midnight.

Post Office: Zeil 90 (tel. 13 81 26 21), in Hertie department store. U- or S-Bahn: Hauptwache. Address mail to be held: *Postlagernde Briefe* für Alotta FAGINA, Hauptpostamt, **60001** Frankfurt, Germany. Open M-F 9:30am-8pm, Sa 9am-4pm.

PHONE CODE	City code: 069. From outside Germany, dial int'l dialing prefix (see inside back cover) + 49 + 69 + local number.

GERMANY

Frankfurt
ACCOMMODATIONS

A Jugendherberge,
   Pension Brüns, &
   Pension Backer
B Pension Gölz

ACCOMMODATIONS

The hotel industry has adopted Frankfurt's city motto: "show me the money." However, there are a few reasonable options in the Westend/University area. If all else fails, the hostel in Mainz is less than 45min. away (take S14; see p. 422).

Jugendherberge (HI), Deutschherrnufer 12 (tel. 610 01 50; fax 61 00 15 99; www.jugendherberge_frankfurt.de). Take bus 46 from the Hauptbahnhof to "Frankensteiner Pl."; turn left at the river and it's at the end of the block. After 7:30pm M-F, 5:45pm Sa, and 5pm Su, take S2-6 to "Lokalbahnhof"; go down Darmstädter Landstr. with your back to the train bridge, bear right onto Dreieichstr., and turn left along the river. In the midst of the Sachsenhausen pub and museum district; loud and lively with schoolkids and inebriated locals. DM33, under 20 DM26. Breakfast included. Sheet deposit DM10. Reception 24hr. Check-in from 11am. Check-out 9:30am. Curfew 2am.

Pension Bruns, Mendelssohnstr. 42. (tel. 74 88 96; fax 74 88 46). From the Hauptbahnhof, head left on Düsseldorfer Str., right on Beethovenstr., and right again at the circle on Mendelssohnstr. (10-15min.). Spacious Victorian rooms with phone and TV. Doubles DM79; triples DM105; quads DM140. Breakfast included. Showers DM2. Call ahead.

Pension Backer, Mendelssohnstr. 92 (tel. 74 79 92), past Pension Bruns (see above). U6 (dir: Heerstr.) or U7 (dir: Hausen): Westend. The best value in town. Singles DM25-50; doubles DM60; triples DM78. Breakfast included. Showers DM3.

FOOD

Regional specialties include *Handkäse mit Musik* (cheese curd with raw onions—Goethe's favorite), *grüne Sosse* (green sauce with various herbs, served

GERMANY

over boiled eggs or potatoes), and *Ebbelwei* (apple wine; called *Äpfelwein* in the north). The cheapest grub surrounds the university in **Bockenheim** and nearby parts of **Westend** (U6-7: Bockenheimer Warte), and many pubs in **Sachsenhausen** (U1-3: Schweizer Pl.) serve food at a decent price. The German dishes (DM8-27) and liters of *Äpfelwein* (DM2.50 per 0.3L) at ⬛**Adolf Wagner,** Schweizer Str. 71, in Sachsenhausen, keep patrons jolly, rowdy, and loyal. (Open daily 11am-midnight.) **Zum Gemalten Haus,** Schweizer Str. 67, four doors down, has treated generations of talkative locals to a quick *Wurst, Kraut,* and home-brewed wine (DM13). (Open W-Su 10am-midnight.) The **Kleinmarkthalle,** on Haseng., between Berliner Str. and Töngeg. in a three-story warehouse, hosts cutthroat competition between bakery, butcher, and fruit and vegetable stands—and has the prices to prove it. (Open M-F 7:30am-6pm, Sa 7:30am-3pm.) For **supermarket** grub, **HL Markt,** Dreieichstr. 56, is near the hostel (open M-F 8am-8pm, Sa 8am-4pm), while **Tengelmann,** Münchener Str. 37, is near the Hauptbahnhof (open M-F 8:30am-7:30pm, Su 8am-2pm).

🔳 SIGHTS

Much of Frankfurt's historic splendor lives on only in memories and in accurately reconstructed monuments nostalgic for the time before the 1944 bombing. At the center of the Altstadt is **Römerberg** square (U-Bahn: Römer), which sports reconstructed half-timbered architecture and a medieval fountain. At the west end of the Römerberg, the gables of **Römer** have marked the site of Frankfurt's city hall since 1405. Upstairs, the **Kaisersaal,** a former imperial banquet hall, is adorned with portraits of the 52 German emperors from Charlemagne to Franz II. (Open daily 10am-1pm and 2-5pm. Obligatory tour every hr. DM3, students DM1.) East of the reconstructed Römerberg stands the only building in the city that survived the bombings: the red sandstone Gothic **Dom** (cathedral), the site of coronation ceremonies from 1562 to 1792. The **museum** within contains intricate chalices and the venerated robes of the imperial electors. (Cathedral open daily 9am-noon and 2:30-6pm. Museum open Tu-F 10am-5pm, Sa-Su 11am-5pm. DM3, students DM1.) South of the Römerberg, the **Alte Nikolaikirche** raises its considerably more modest, pinkish spires. (Open daily Apr.-Sept. 10am-8pm; Oct.-Mar. 10am-6pm. Free.) The ⬛**Museum für Moderne Kunst,** Domstr. 10, just a few blocks up the street from the Dom, is not to be missed; it houses a stunning modern art collection, including works by Claes Oldenburg, Roy Liechtenstein, and Jasper Johns. (Open Tu and Th-Su 10am-5pm, W 10am-8pm. DM7, students DM3.50; W free.) The **Museumsufer,** on the Schaumainkai along the south bank of the Main between the Eiserner Steg and the Friedensbrücke, hosts an eclectic collection of museums, including the **Deutsches Filmmuseum,** Schaumainkai 41, which presents a fun, interactive history of filmmaking. (Open Tu, Th-F, and Su 10am-5pm, W 10am-8pm, Sa 2-8pm. Tours Su 3pm. DM5, students DM2.50; W free. Films DM8, students DM6.)

🎵 ENTERTAINMENT

Frankfurt might be lacking in other areas, but it excels in the realms of entertainment and nightlife. Shows and schedules of the city's stages are detailed in several publications, including *Fritz* and *Strandgut* (free at the tourist office) and the *Journal Frankfurt* (DM3.30 at newsstands). The jazz clubs that reinvigorated the city post-WWII by drawing such legends as Duke Ellington and Ella Fitzgerald can be found on Kleine Bockenheimer Str., also known as the **Jazzgasse** (Jazz Alley). **Der Jazzkeller** at #18a is a Frankfurt instition. (Live music Th and Sa. Cover around DM8. Open Tu-Su 9pm-3am.) For a night out drinking, head to the **Alt-Sachsenhausen** district between Brückenstr. and Dreieichstr., home to a huge number of rowdy pubs and taverns specializing in *Äpfelwein.* The narrow, cobblestoned streets around **Grosse** and **Kleine Ritterg.** teem with canopied cafés, bars, and gregarious Irish pubs. Frankfurt has a number of thriving discos and prominent techno DJs, mostly in the between Zeil and Bleichstr. Wear your best dancing clothes—even the hippest jeans won't make it past most bouncers. (Covers run DM10-15.) **Nachtleben,** Kurt-Schumacher-Str. 45, on the corner of Zeil, serves as a postmodern café by day but hosts hordes of rocking twentysomethings on its red velour-draped dance floor by night. (Cover DM7-9. Open M-W and Su 11pm-2am; live concerts Th-Sa 11pm-4am. Th reggae; F hip-hop and R&B.) **The Cave,** Brönnerstr. 11, hosts independent punk rock plus some reggae and ska in a speakeasy-style underground locale. (Cover DM5. Open M-Th 10pm-4am, Sa-Su 10pm-6am. No dress code.)

KASSEL

When Napoleon III was captured by Prussian troops and brought to the Schloß Wilhelmshöhe prison in 1870, Aacheners jeered *"Ab nach Kassel"* ("off to Kassel"). Today, hordes answer the call to see this ultra-sophisticated city. From the Wilhelmshöhe station, take bus 43 (dir: Herkules) to the last stop to reach **Wilhelmshöhe,** a hillside park with one giant Greek hero, two castles, three museums, and five waterfalls. **Schloß Löwenburg** is an amazing piece of architectural fantasy, built with stones deliberately missing to make it look like a crumbling medieval castle; **Schloß Wilhelmshöhe** was the mammoth home of Kassel's rulers. (Open Tu-Su Mar.-Oct. 10am-5pm; Nov.-Feb. 10am-4pm. DM6, students DM4.) All of the park's paths lead up to the large **Riesenschloß,** topped by the figure of **Herkules,** Kassel's emblem. Hordes of art-lovers descend on Kassel every five years to take part in **documenta,** the world's preeminent contemporary art exhibition, next scheduled for 2002. The remains of previous exhibitions sprawl across the city. The **Museum Friedricianum,** Friedrichspl. 18, houses most *documenta*-related exhibitions. (Open W and F-Su 10am-6pm, Th 10am-8pm. DM12, students DM8.) Even the Hauptbahnhof gets a piece of the action—check out the **caricatura,** its "museum of bizarre art." (Open Tu-F 2-8pm, Sa-Su noon-8pm.) The **Brüder-Grimm-Museum,** Schöne Aussicht 2, in Palais Bellevue near the Orangerie, exhibits the brothers' handwritten copy of *Kinder- und Hausmärchen*, their darker-than-most collection of fairy tales, and translations into dozens of languages. (Open daily 10am-5pm. DM3, students DM2.)

The **Wilhelmshöhe station,** an ICE hub, is the point of entry to Kassel's ancient castles on the west side; the older **Hauptbahnhof** is the gateway to the Altstadt. **Trains** arrive from Frankfurt (2½hr., 2 per hr., DM54); Hamburg (2½hr., 2 per hr., DM99); and Düsseldorf (3½hr., every hr., DM170). The **tourist office** is in the Wilhelmshöhe station. (Tel. (0561) 340 54; fax 31 52 16. Open M-F 9am-1pm and 2-6pm, Sa 9am-1pm.) To reach **Jugendherberge am Tannenwäldchen (HI),** Schenkendorfstr. 18, take streetcar 4 or 6 from the Rathaus or Bahnhof Wilhelmshöhe (dir: Ottostr. or Lindenberg) to "Annastr.," continue walking up Friedrich-Ebert-Str., and make a right on Schenkendorfstr.; or, from the Hauptbahnhof, walk out the *Südausgang*, turn right on Kölnische Str., and turn right again onto Schenkendorfstr. (Tel. (0561) 77 64 55; fax 77 68 32. DM29.50, under 27 DM24.50. Sheets DM6. Breakfast included. Reception 9am-11:30pm.) To get to **Hotel Kö78,** Kölnische Str. 78, from Wilhelmshöhe, follow the directions to the Jugendherberge, walk up Annastr. from the stop, and turn right on Kölnische Str; from the Hauptbahnhof, exit through the *Südausgang*, walk up the stairs, and follow Kölnische Str. uphill and to the right. (Tel. (0561) 716 14; fax 179 82. Singles from DM59, doubles from DM93. Breakfast included. Reception M-F 6am-10pm, Sa-Su 8am-10pm.) ◪**Lohmann Biergarten,** Königstor 8, is one of Kassel's oldest and largest beer gardens. (Open daily noon-2am.) Fine fruit, bakeries, and **groceries** at **okay!,** at Bahnhof Wilhelmshöhe and Friedrich-Ebert-Str. 27. (Open M-F 8:30am-8pm, Sa 8am-2pm.) **Postal code:** 34117.

SOUTHWEST GERMANY

A trip to the Rhineland-Palatinate (Rheinland-Pfalz) to see the castles and wine towns along the Rhine is an obligatory tourist tromp. The region is a visual feast—the Mosel River curls downstream to the Rhine Gorge, a soft shore of castle-backed hills. But it also provides a literal feast; a rich agricultural tradition keeps fresh fruits and vegetables in abundance, and the vineyards of the Rhine and Mosel Valleys produce sweet, delicious wines. Two of the most prominent of German icons—the Brothers Grimm and the Mercedes-Benz—duke it out just to the south, in Baden-Württemberg, where the bucolic, traditional hinterlands of the Black Forest contrast with the region's modern, industrial cities.

GERMANY

RHINE VALLEY (RHEINTAL)

The Rhine River may run from Switzerland to the North Sea, but in the popular imagination it exists only in the 80km of the Rhine Gorge stretching from Bonn to north of Mainz. This is the Rhine of legends: sailors' nightmares, poets' dreams, and often the center of rhetorical storms of nationalism.

⊡ GETTING THERE AND GETTING AROUND. The Rhine Valley runs north from **Mainz,** easily accessible from Frankfurt, to **Bonn** (see p. 414), just south of **Cologne/ Köln** via (from south to north) **Bacharach, St. Goarshausen** and **St. Goar,** and **Koblenz.** Two different **train** lines (one on each bank) traverse this fabled stretch; the line on the west bank stays closer to the water and provides superior views. **Eurail** is valid on trips between Cologne and Mainz. If you're willing to put up with lots of tourists, **boats** are probably the best way to see the sights. **Köln-Düsseldorfer (KD) Line** (see p. 412) covers the Mainz-Koblenz stretch three times per day in summer.

MAINZ. At the heart of Mainz, the capital of the Rhineland-Palatinate, lies the colossal sandstone **Martinsdom,** the resting place of the archbishops of Mainz. (Open Apr.-Sept. M-F 9am-6:30pm, Sa 9am-4pm, Su 12:45-3pm and 4-6:30pm; Oct.-Mar. M-F 9am-5pm, Sa 9am-4pm, Su 12:45-3pm and 4-5pm. Free.) The adjacent **Diözesanmuseum** houses changing exhibitions; through April 15, 2000 it holds the **Gutenberg** exhibit. (Open Tu-Sa 9am-5pm, Su 11am-6pm. Prices vary.) After April 15, Mainz's favorite son and the father of movable type, Johannes Gutenberg, will return to being immortalized at the **Gutenbergmuseum,** Liebfrauenpl. 5, with several **Gutenberg Bibles** and a replica of his original press. (Open Tu-Sa 10am-6pm, Su 10am-1pm. DM5, students DM2.50; Su free.) On a hill several blocks south of the Altstadt, the **Stephanskirche** is noted for its stunning stained-glass windows by Marc Chagall. From the Dom, take Ludwigstr. until it ends at Schillerpl. and follow Gaustr. up to the church. (Open daily 10am-noon and 2-5pm. Free.)

Köln-Düsseldorf **ferries** (tel. 23 28 00; fax 23 28 60) depart from the wharfs on the other side of the Rathaus. The **tourist office** finds rooms (from DM50) for a DM5 fee. (Tel. (06131) 28 62 10; fax 286 21 55. Open M-F 9am-6pm, Sa 9am-1pm.) The **Jugendgästehaus (HI),** Otto-Brunfels-Schneise 4, is in Weisenau in a corner of the Volkspark; take bus 22 to "Jugendherberge/Viktorstift." (Tel. (06131) 853 32; fax 824 22. Small dorms DM29.10-38.60. Reception 7am-midnight.) Near the Dom, the **Central Café,** on the corner of Rheinstr. and Heug., cooks up traditional German fare for under DM15. (Open Su-Th 10am-1am, F-Sa 10am-2am.) **Postal code:** 55001.

BACHARACH. On the west bank of the Rhine, the gorgeous yet hidden gem of Bacharach brims with **Weinkeller** and **Weinstuben** (wine cellars and pubs) that do justice to its name—"altar to Bacchus." Find love, sweet love, at **Die Weinstube,** behind the stunning **Altes Haus** in the center of town on Oberstr. Also off Oberstr. is the 14th-century **Wernerkapelle,** ghost-like remains of a red sandstone chapel that took 140 years (1294-1434) to build but only a few hours to destroy in the Palatinate War of Succession in 1689; climb the steps next to the late-Romanesque **Peterskirche.** The **tourist office,** Oberstr. 45, in the post office, is 5min. from the station on the right. (Tel. (06743) 91 93 13; fax 91 93 14. Open Apr.-Sept. M-F 9am-5pm, Sa 10am-1pm; Oct.-Mar. M-F 9am-12:30pm and 1:30-5pm, Sa 10am-1pm.) Hostels get no better than the unbelievable ⚑**Jugendherberge Stahleck (HI),** a gorgeous 12th-century castle with a panoramic view of the Rhine Valley. From the station, turn left at the Peterskirche and take any of the marked paths leading up the hill (20min.). (Tel. (06743) 12 66; fax 26 84. DM25.20. Breakfast included. Curfew 10pm. Call ahead.) To reach **Campingplatz Bacharach,** directly on the Rhine, turn right from the station (heading downhill toward the river) and walk 10min. south. (Tel. (06743) 17 52. DM8 per person, DM5 per tent.)

LORELEI CLIFFS AND CASTLES. The section of the Rhine just north of Bacharach was so difficult to navigate that a sailors' song developed about the siren Lorelei, who seduced sailors with her intoxicating song and drew them into the rocks; the song was eventually immortalized by poet Heinrich Heine. Protected by the tinted windows of the ubiquitous Loreley Express tour buses, most visitors today avoid such grim fates as they visit St. Goarshausen and St. Goar, which sit on either side of the Rhine. **St. Goarshausen,** on the east bank, provides access by foot to the statue and the infamous cliffs. Facing the Rhine, follow Rheinstr. left past the last houses to the peninsula to reach the statue. To reach the cliffs, take the stairs across the street from the beginning of the peninsula (45min.). St. Goarshausen's **tourist office** is at Bahnhofstr. 8. (Tel. (06771) 91 00; fax 910 15. Open M-F 9am-1pm and 2-5:30pm, Sa 9:30am-noon.)

A ferry from St. Goarshausen runs across the Rhine to **St. Goar** (7 per hr., last ferry 11pm, round-trip DM2.50). The view from the cliffs on the western side is spectacular, and **Burg Rheinfels** is dazzling. Tour the sprawling, half-ruined castle and see its underground passageways by flashlight (DM5)—it doesn't get more *romantisch,* or dimly lit, than this. (Open daily 9am-6pm. DM5, students DM3.) St. Goar's **tourist office,** Heerstr. 6, is in the pedestrian zone. (Tel. (06741) 383; fax 72 09. Open M-F 8am-12:30pm and 2-5pm, Sa 10am-noon.) From the station, follow Oberstr. left (with your back to the tracks), veer left on Schloßberg, and turn right on Bismarckweg to reach the **Jugendherberge (HI)** at #17 (10min.). (Tel. (06741) 388; fax 28 69. DM22. Breakfast included. Reception 5-6pm and 7-8pm.)

KOBLENZ. The beauty of Koblenz—or perhaps its strategic position at the confluence of the Rhine and the Mosel—has attracted Roman, French, Prussian, and German conquerors for the past 2000 years. Before reunification, the city served as a large munitions dump, but now the only pyrotechnics are during the **Rhein in Flammen** (Rhine in Flames) fireworks festival (Aug. 12, 2000). The city's focal point is the **Deutsches Eck** (German Corner), a peninsula at the rivers' meeting point that purportedly saw the birth of the German nation when the Teutonic Order of Knights settled here in 1216. The tremendous **Mahnmal der Deutschen Einheit** (Monument to German Unity) on the right was erected in 1897 in honor of Kaiser Wilhelm I's forced reconciliation of the German Empire. Behind the Mahnmal, the ⊠**Museum Ludwig im Deutschherrenhaus,** Danziger Freiheit 1, mainly features contemporary French art. (Open Tu-Sa 10:30am-5pm, Su 11am-6pm. DM5, students DM3.) Most of the nearby Altstadt was flattened during WWII, but several churches have been carefully restored. The 12th-century **Florinskirche** was used as a military encampment by Napoleon in the 19th century (open daily 11am-5pm), while the stunning **Liebfrauenkirche** features oval Baroque towers, emerald- and sapphire-colored stained glass, and intricate ceiling latticework (open M-Sa 8am-6pm, Su 9am-12:30pm and 6-8pm). If ground-level viewing has you down, head for **Festung Ehrenbreitstein,** a Brobdingnagian fortress at the highest point in the city. The Prussians used it to accommodate French troops in past centuries; today, the German state uses it to accommodate you (see below; non-hostel guests DM2, students DM1).

Trains go to Mainz (50min., 3 per hr., DM24.60); Cologne/Köln (1hr., 3-4 per hr., DM24.60); Trier (2hr., every hr., DM30); and Frankfurt (2hr., 2 per hr., DM36). Take a sharp left from the station for the **tourist office,** Löhrstr. 141. (Tel. (0261) 313 04; fax 100 43 88. Open M-F 9am-8pm, Sa-Su 10am-8pm.) The **Jugendherberge Koblenz (HI),** in the Festung, yields a perfect view of Koblenz and the Rhine and Mosel Valleys. Take bus 7, 8, or 8A from opposite from the tourist office (dir: Vallendar) to "Ehrenbreitstein Bf.," continue along the Rhine side of the mountain on the main road following the "DJH" signs, and follow the steep footpath up (20min.). Or take bus 9 or 10 from the tourist office to "Obertal" and take the **chairlift** (runs Mar.-Sept. daily 9am-5:50pm; DM4). (Tel. (0261) 97 28 70; fax 972 87 30. DM24. Breakfast included. Reception 7:30am-11:30pm. Curfew 11:30pm.) **Ferries** (DM0.60) cross the Mosel to **Campingplatz Rhein-Mosel,** Am Neuendorfer Eck. (Tel. (0261) 827 19. DM6.50 per person, DM5 per tent. Reception 8am-noon and 2-8pm. Open Apr.-Oct. 15.) ⊠**Marktstübchen,** Am Markt 220, at the bottom of the hill from the hostel, serves real German food at real budget prices. (Open M-Tu, Th, and Sa-Su 11am-midnight, W 11am-2pm, F 4pm-1am.) **Plus supermarket** is at Roonstr. 49-51. (Open M-F 8:30am-7pm and Sa 8am-2pm.) **Postal code:** 65068.

GERMANY

MOSEL VALLEY (MOSELTAL)

As if trying to avoid its inevitable surrender to the Rhine at Koblenz, the Mosel meanders slowly past the sun-drenched hills, pretty towns, and ancient castles of the softly cut Mosel Valley. The valley's slopes aren't as steep as the Rhine's narrow gorge, but the arresting landscape, castles, and vineyards easily compensate.

E **GETTING THERE AND GETTING AROUND.** The Mosel Valley runs northeast from **Trier,** just 45min. from **Luxembourg City** by train (see p. 645), to **Koblenz,** where it bisects the Rhine Valley (see p. 422), passing **Beilstein** and **Cochem** en route. The best way to see the scenery is by **boat, bus,** or **bicycle;** the **train** line between Koblenz and Trier strays frequently from the river, cutting through the unremarkable countryside. Although **passenger boats** no longer make the complete Koblenz-Trier run, several companies run daily trips along shorter stretches in summer.

COCHEM AND BEILSTEIN. The wine-making village of **Cochem** has become a repository of German nostalgia, its quintessential quaintness voraciously devoured by busloads of city-dwellers. Yet the impressive vineyard-covered hills and majestic **Reichsburg** castle, perched high on a hill above town, simply can't be cheapened. The 11th-century castle was destroyed in 1689 by French troops led by Louis XIV, but was rebuilt in 1868. The view from the grounds alone warrants the 15-minute climb up Schloßstr. from the Marktpl. (Frequent 40-minute tours in German; English translations available. Open mid-Mar. to Oct. daily 9am-5pm. DM7, students DM6.) **Trains** run to Koblenz (50min., 2-3 per hr., DM12.20) and Trier (1hr., 2-3 per hr., DM16.40). The Moselbahn **bus** service links trains to the rest of the Mosel Valley in **Bullay,** one stop away from Cochem (10min., 2-3 per hr., DM4.60). From the train station, go to the river and turn right to reach the **tourist office,** Endertpl. 1. (Tel. (02671) 600 40; fax 60 04 44. Open May-June M-Th and Sa 10am-5pm, F 10am-7pm; July-Oct. M-Th and Sa 10am-5pm, F 10am-7pm, Su 10am-noon; Nov.-Apr. M-Th 10am-5pm, F 10am-7pm.) To reach the friendly, basic **Jugendherberge (HI),** Klottener Str. 9, cross the Nordbrücke to the left as you exit the station, and it's next to the bridge on the right (15min.). (Tel. (02671) 86 33; fax 85 68. DM22. Breakfast included. Reception noon-1pm and 5-10pm.) Continue down the path below the hostel for the **Campingplatz am Freizeitzentrum,** on Stadionstr. (Tel. (02671) 44 09. DM6.50 per person, DM6-12 per tent. Reception 8am-10pm. Open Easter-Oct.)

Ten kilometers upstream from Cochem lies the tiny hamlet of **Beilstein,** filled with half-timbered houses and crooked cobblestoned streets. The ruins of **Burg Metternich,** another casualty of French troops in 1689, offer a sweeping view of the valley. (Open Apr.-Oct. daily 9am-6pm. DM3, students DM2.) The Baroque **Karmelitenkirche** contains an intricately carved wooden altar and a famous 16th-century sculpture. (Open daily 9am-8pm.) **Bus** 8060 runs to Beilstein from both Cochem's Endertpl. and train station (10min., 3-12 per day, DM4.80). The **passenger boats** of Personnenschiffahrt Kolb (tel. (02673) 15 15) also travel between the two towns (1hr., May-Oct. 4 per day, DM18 round-trip).

TRIER. The oldest town in Germany, Trier was founded by the Romans during the reign of Augustus, and reached its heyday in the 4th century as the capital of the Western Roman Empire and the residence of Emperor Constantine. The city's most impressive Roman remnant is the massive 2nd-century **Porta Nigra** (Black Gate), named for the centuries of grime that have turned its originally light yellow sandstone face gray. (Open daily Palm Sunday to Sept. 9am-6pm; Oct.-Nov. and Jan. to Palm Sunday 9am-5pm; Dec. 10am-4pm. DM4, students DM2.) From here, a stroll down Simeonstr. leads to the **Hauptmarkt,** off of which the 11th-century **Dom** shelters archbishops' tombs as well as the reputed **Tunica Christi** (Holy Robe of Christ), brought from Jerusalem to Trier around AD 300 by St. Helena, mother of Emperor Constantine. (Open daily Apr.-Oct. 6:30am-6pm; Nov.-Mar. 6:30am-5:30pm. Tours daily 2pm. Free.) The **Basilika,** just south of the Dom, was originally the location of Emperor Constantine's throne room. (Open M-Sa 9am-6pm, Su 11:30am-6pm. Free.) The masses can head down Konstantinstr. and turn left on Fleischstr. to make a pilgrimage to the **Karl-Marx-Haus,** Brückenstr. 10, where young Karl first walked, talked, and dreamed of labor alienation. (Open Apr.-Oct. M 1-6pm, Tu-Su 10am-6pm; Nov.-Mar. M 3-6pm, Tu-Su 10am-1pm and 3-6pm. DM3, students DM2.) Just down Am Palastgarten from the Basilica lie the ruins of the **Kaiserthermen,** the Roman baths where Constantine once scrubbed himself; head left on Olewiger Str. from there to reach the 2nd-century **amphitheater,** which once hosted demonstrations of the most spectacular and gruesome ways to inflict pain (and death) on humans and animals—for crowds of up to 20,000. (Both same hours and admission as Porta Nigra; amphitheater closed Dec.)

Trains go to Luxembourg City (45min., every hr., DM14.80) and Koblenz (1¾hr., 2 per hr., DM30). From the station, walk down Theodor-Heuss-Allee or Christophstr. to reach the **tourist office,** in the shadow of the Porta Nigra; it offers tours in English daily at 1:30pm (DM9) and books rooms for free. (Tel. (0651) 97 80 80; fax 447 59. Open Apr.-Oct. M-Sa 9am-6:30pm, Su 9am-3:30pm; Nov.-Dec. M-Sa 9am-6pm, Su 9am-3:30pm; Jan.-Feb. M-Sa 9am-5pm; Mar. M-Sa 9am-6pm, Su 9am-1pm.) Get info on **wine tasting** in the region (and in the office) at Margaritengässchen 2a, near the Porta Nigra. (Tel. (0651) 994 05 40. Open daily 10am-7pm.) The ⬛**Jugendhotel/Jugendgästehaus Kolpinghaus,** Dietrichstr. 42, is one block off the Hauptmarkt. (Tel. (0651) 97 52 50; fax 975 25 40. Dorms DM27; singles DM39; doubles DM78. Breakfast included. Reception 8am-11pm. Call ahead.) To get from the station to the **Jugendgästehaus (HI),** An der Jugendherberge 4, follow Theodor-Heuss-Allee as it becomes Nordallee and bear right onto Lindenstr. to the bank of the Mosel (30min.). (Tel. (0651) 14 66 20; fax 146 62 30. Dorms DM27-36.50; singles DM57. Breakfast included. Reception 7am-midnight.) To get from Hauptmarkt to **Trier City Campingplatz,** Luxemburger Str. 81, follow Fleischstr. to Brückenstr. to Karl-Marx-Str., cross the Römerbrücke, head left on Luxemburger Str., and turn left at the sign. (Tel. (0651) 869 21. DM8 per person, DM5 per tent. Reception 8am-10pm. Open Apr.-Oct.) **Kaufmarkt supermarket** is at the corner of Brückenstr. and Stresenanstr. (Open M-F 8am-8pm, Sa 8am-4pm.) **Postal code:** 54292.

HEIDELBERG

Believe the tourist propaganda—Heidelberg truly shines. In 1386, the sages of Heidelberg turned from illuminating manuscripts to illuminating young German minds when they founded Germany's first and greatest university. Set against wooded hills along the Neckar River, the town and its crumbling *Schloß* have exerted a magnetic pull over numerous writers and artists, including Mark Twain, Goethe, and Hugo, and today draw thousands of shutter-clicking tourists daily.

▐ GETTING THERE AND GETTING AROUND

Trains: To **Stuttgart** (1hr., 2 per hr., DM38) and **Frankfurt** (1hr., 3 per hr., DM30).

Public Transportation: Single-ride tickets DM3.30. **Day passes** are valid for up to 5 people on all streetcars and buses (DM10); buy them at the tourist office.

Hitchhiking: *Let's Go* does not recommend hitchhiking. Hitchers are said to walk to the western end of Bergheimer Str. **Mitfahrzentrale,** Bergheimer Str. 125 (tel. 246 46), organizes ride-sharing. To Cologne/Köln DM28, Hamburg DM54, Paris DM51. Open Apr.-Oct. M-F 9am-5pm and Sa 9am-noon; Nov.-Mar. closed Sa.

▐ ORIENTATION AND PRACTICAL INFORMATION

Most of Heidelberg's attractions are clustered in the eastern part of the city, along the southern bank of the Neckar. To get from the train station to the **Altstadt,** take any bus or streetcar to "Bismarckpl.," then walk east down **Hauptstraße,** the city's spine, to the center. The two-day **Heidelberg Card** includes unlimited of public transit as well as admission to most sights (DM19.80 from the tourist office).

Tourist Office: Tourist Information (tel. 142 20; fax 14 22 22; www.heidelberg.de/cvb), in front of the station. Books **rooms** for a DM5 fee and a 7% deposit. Pick up *Meier* (DM2) or *Heidelberg Aktuell* (DM1) for events info. Open Mar.-Dec. M-Sa 9am-7pm, Su 10am-

GERMANY

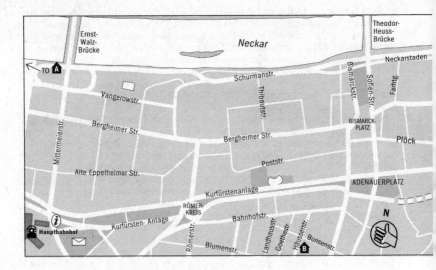

6pm; Jan.-Feb. closed Su. **Branches** at the Schloß (tel. 211 44; open in summer daily 9am-5pm) and at Neckarmünzpl. (open in summer daily 9am-6:30pm).

Currency Exchange: Change cash at the **Sparkassen** on Universitätspl. and Bismarckpl., or try the exchange office in the train station. Open M-Sa 8am-8pm, Su 9am-1pm.

American Express: Brückenkopfstr. 1 (tel. 450 50; fax 41 03 33), at the northern end of Theodor-Heuss-Brücke. Mail held. Open M-F 10am-6pm, Sa 10am-1pm.

Emergency: Tel. 110. **Police,** Römerstr. 2-4 (tel. 990). **Fire** and **ambulance,** tel. 112.

Internet Access: Café Gecko, Bergheimer Str. 8 (tel. 60 45 20). Must order a drink for access. DM4 per 30min. Open Su-Th 9am-1am, F 9am-2am, Sa 9am-3am.

Post Office: Sofienstr. 6-10 (tel. 91 24 12). Address mail to be held: *Postlagernde Briefe* für Jon STEIN, Filiale Heidelberg 12, Sofienstr. 6-10, **69115** Heidelberg, Germany. Open daily 9am-7:30pm.

PHONE CODE	City code: 06221. From outside Germany, dial int'l dialing prefix (see inside back cover) + 49 + 6221 + local number.

ACCOMMODATIONS, CAMPING, AND FOOD

In summer, reserve ahead or arrive early in the day. If you get stuck, try the **youth hostels** in nearby **Neckargemünd** (10min.; tel. (06223) 21 33); **Mannheim** (20min.; tel. (0621) 82 27 18); and **Eberbach** (25min.; tel. (06271) 25 93).

Jeske Hotel, Mittelbadg. 2 (tel. 237 33). From the station, take bus 33 (dir: Ziegelhausen) or 11 (dir: Karlstor) to "Rathaus/Kornmarkt"; Mittelbadg. is the 2nd left off the square. The best value in Heidelberg in an unbeatable location. Reservations only accepted 1hr. ahead. Doubles DM48. Breakfast DM10. Open Feb. to mid-Nov.

Jugendherberge (HI), Tiergartenstr. 5 (tel. 41 20 66; fax 40 25 59). From Bismarckpl. or the station, take bus 33 (dir: Zoo-Sportzentrum) to "Jugendherberge." Calling less than a week ahead rarely works; fax your reservation. DM28, under 27 DM23; members only. Sheets DM5.50. Reception until 11pm. Lockout 9am-1pm. Curfew 11:30pm.

Hotel-Pension Elite, Bunsenstr. 15 (tel. 257 33 or 257 34; fax 16 39 49). From Bismarckpl., follow Rohrbacher Str. away from the river, turn right on Bunsenstr., and it's on the left. Nice rooms with high ceilings, bath, and TV. With *Let's Go:* single DM75-85; doubles DM95-100; DM15 per extra person. Breakfast included. DM5 credit card surcharge.

GERMANY

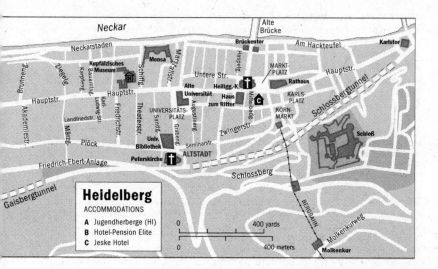

Camping Haide (tel. (06223) 21 11), between Ziegelhausen and Neckargemünd. Take bus 35 to "Orthopädisches Klinik," cross the river, turn right, and it's on the right. DM14.50-20 per person, DM6-12 per tent, DM2 per car. Cabins DM14.50-20. Reception 8am-noon and 4:30-7:30pm. Open Apr.-Oct.

Get cheap grub at **Handelshof supermarket,** Kurfürsten-Anlage 60, 200m straight down from the station on the right. (Open M-F 7:30am-8pm, Sa 7:30am-4pm.) There is a **fruit market** on Marktpl. on Wednesdays and Saturdays. Appetizing aromas of Chinese food emanate from **Großer Wok,** Bergheimer Str. 1a, near Bismarckpl. (Entrees DM4-12. Open Su-Th 11am-11pm, F-Sa 11am-midnight.) Although most traditional German dishes at **Goldener Anker,** Untere Neckar 52, near the river and the Alte Brücke, are fairly expensive, some are affordable (DM8-15). (Open M-Sa 6pm-midnight.)

👁 SIGHTS

HEIDELBERGER SCHLOSS. The ramparts of Heidelberg's aging castle, the jewel in the crown of an already striking city, preside over the Altstadt. After 1329, it served as the home of the prince electors, but was later thrice destroyed—twice by war (1622 and 1693) and once by lightning (1764). The castle's regal state of disrepair is best viewed from the **Philosophenweg** across the Neckar. *(Walk uphill from the base of the castle, or take the Bergbahn cable car from the "Bergbahn/Rathaus" bus stop (round-trip DM4.70). Tel. 53 84 14. Mandatory tour DM4, students DM2. tours in English daily at 11:30am, 2, and 3:45pm. Grounds open daily 8am-dusk; DM3, students DM1.50.)*

MARKTPLATZ AND UNIVERSITÄT. The Altstadt centers on the cobblestoned **Marktplatz,** where accused witches and heretics were burned at the stake in the 15th century; today, tourists recline on legions of plastic chairs and admire **Hercules' Fountain.** The two oldest structures in Heidelberg border the square. The bordering 14th-century **Heiliggeistkirche** (Church of the Holy Spirit), where residents hid during Louis XIV's invasion, and **Haus Zum Ritter,** opposite the church, are the two oldest structures in Heidelberg. *(Church open M-Th and Sa 11am-5pm, F 1-5pm, Su 1:30-5pm. Free.)* Five blocks down Hauptstr., a stone-lion fountain oversees the oldest remaining buildings of the **Alte Universität** (Old University), established in 1368. It was here that Clemens Brentano compiled *Des Knaben Wunderhorn,* a collection of folk poetry that led to the Brothers Grimm's prose compilation, and that sociology became a legitimate academic subject under Max Weber.

GERMANY

KURPFÄLZISCHES MUSEUM. The museum is crammed with artifacts such as the jawbone of an unfortunate *homo Heidelbergensis*, a.k.a. "Heidelberg man," one of the oldest humans ever discovered. Elsewhere in the museum stand well-preserved works of art by Dürer and a spectacular archaeology exhibit. *(Hauptstr. 97. Open Tu and Th-Su 10am-5pm, W 10am-9pm. DM5, students DM3; Su DM3, students DM2.)*

PHILOSOPHENWEG. A stroll across the elegant **Karl-Theodor-Brücke** to the northern bank of the Neckar, opposite the Altstadt, finds a statue of the Prince-Elector himself (commissioned by Theodor as a symbol of his modesty). From the far end of the bridge, clamber up the **Schlangenweg,** a winding stone stairway, to the **Philosophenweg** ("philosopher's path"), where Hegel and Max Weber indulged in afternoon promenades. Atop the **Heiligenberg** (mountain) lie the ruins of the 9th-century **St. Michael Basilika,** the 13th-century **Stefanskloster,** and an **amphitheater,** built under Hitler in 1934 on the site of an ancient Celtic gathering place. *(Take streetcar 1 or 3 to "Tiefburg," a castle in neighboring Handschuhsheim, and hike upward.)*

■ NIGHTLIFE

The **Marktplatz, Unter Straße** (on the Neckar side of the Heiliggeistkirche), and **Hauptstraße** are the main venues for nightlife action. **Zum Sepp'l,** Hauptstr. 213, hosts a loud crowd that's been partying since 1634. (Meals DM12-25. Beer DM4.80. Open daily 11am-midnight.) **Cave 54,** Krämergasse 2, keeps a somewhat older crowd jumping with live jazz every Sunday; other nights reggae, funk, and soul. (Cover M and W-Sa DM5, Tu and Su DM12. Open daily 10pm-3am.) **O'Reilly's,** on the corner of Brückenkopfstr. and Uferstr. (turn right after you cross Theodor-Heuss-Brücke) is a hopping Irish pub popular with a young crowd. (Open M-F 4pm-1am, Sa-Su noon-1am.) College students converge after midnight to chill among the vintage 1950s ads to partake of cheap food and drinks at **VaterRhein,** Untere Neckarstr. 20-22, close to the river near the *Stadthalle*. (Pilsner DM4.40. Open daily 8pm-3am.)

■ EXCURSIONS FROM HEIDELBERG: THE NECKAR VALLEY

The Neckar Valley (Neckartal), a scenic stretch of narrow, thickly wooded ridges along the Neckar River, encompasses several medieval **castles** and small, untouristed towns from **Heilbronn** to **Heidelberg.** At the northern end of the valley, 14km upstream from Heidelberg, **Neckarsteinach** is renowned for its four 12th- to 13th-century medieval castles, all within 3km of one another along the northern bank of the Neckar River. The two westernmost castles stand in ruins, while the two to the east stand in splendor. Although the latter two are not open to the public, the beautiful views make for a great daytrip. The castles are accessible via the **Burgenweg** (castle path); from the Neckarsteinach **train station** (15min. from Heidelberg), turn right on Bahnhofstr., turn left on Hauptstr., follow the bend in the road, then the brick *Schloßsteige* (castle steps) that lead up to the right. The **tourist office,** Hauptstr. 7, inside the Rathaus, is on the way to the *Schloßsteige*. (Open M-W 8am-noon and 1:30-3:30pm, Th 8am-noon and 1:30-5pm, F 8am-noon.)

Until the recent influx of tour buses, **Bad Wimpfen,** just downstream from Heilbronn, was one of the best-kept secrets in southwest Germany. Set against the ruins of a Roman imperial **castle,** it nonetheless still manages to cast a fairy-tale spell over the valley from high above the river. Easily accessible points on the ancient battlements along the northern side of the old castle walls offer incredible views of the valley and the surrounding countryside. The friendly **tourist office** is in the train station. (Tel. (07063) 972 00. Open M-F 9am-1pm and 2-5pm, Sa-Su 10am-noon and 2-4pm.) From the station, follow Karl-Ulrich-Str. to reach the Altstadt (10min.).

STUTTGART

Blown to bits in WWII, the former seat of the kings of Württemberg had nowhere to aim but the future. The city was rebuilt in an uninspiring, functional style and has aggressively pursued modernization. Today the home of Porsche and Daimler-Benz and the capital of Baden-Württemberg is a blissfully livable metropolis, boasting one of the most verdant settings of any major German city.

GERMANY

🔢🔢 PRACTICAL INFO, ACCOMMODATIONS, AND FOOD. Trains (tel. (0180) 599 66 33) run from Stuttgart, the transportation hub of southwest Germany, to Frankfurt (1½hr., every hr., DM88); Munich (2½hr., every hr., DM73); Basel (3hr., every hr.); Berlin (6hr., every 2hr., DM249); and Paris (6hr., 3 per day). **Single-ride** tickets for **public transportation** (U-Bahn, S-Bahn, streetcars, and buses) run DM3.20-9.60; a 3-day **tourist pass** is valid on the U-Bahn (DM13) or entire transit system (DM20). Buy passes at the **tourist office, I-Punkt,** Königstr. 1, in front of the escalator down to the Klett-Passage. (Tel. (0711) 222 80; fax 222 82 53. Open May-Oct. M-F 9:30am-8:30pm, Sa 9:30am-6pm, Su 11am-6pm; Nov.-Apr. opens Su 1pm.) For info on youth travel or the Stuttgart youth scene head to **tips 'n' trips,** Rotebühlpl. 26/1, in the U-Bahn passage at Theodor-Heuss-Str. and Fritz-Elsas-Str. (Tel. 222 27 30; fax 222 27 33. **Internet** DM5 per hr. Open M-F noon-7pm, Sa 10am-4pm.) To reach the spotless **Jugendgästehaus Stuttgart,** Richard-Wagner-Str. 2, take streetcar 15 (dir: Heumaden) to "Bubenbad," continue in same direction on the right side of the street, veer right immediately, and it's on the right. (Tel. (0711) 24 11 32. Singles DM35-55; DM35-45 per extra person. Breakfast included. Key deposit DM20. Reception M-F 9am-10pm, Sa-Su 11am-8pm.) To get to the **Jugendherberge Stuttgart (HI),** Haußmannstr. 27, take the "ZOB" exit from the Klett-Passage, continue through the Schloßgarten, and follow signs uphill. (Tel. (0711) 24 15 83; fax 236 10 41. DM28, under 27 DM23. Breakfast included. Sheets DM5.50. Reception 7-9am and noon-11pm. Lockout 9am-noon. Curfew 11:30pm. Call ahead.) Take U6 (dir: Gehrlingen) to "Sportpark Feuerbach" and cross the tracks toward the sport park to get to the **Tramper Point Stuttgart,** Wiener Str. 317. (Tel. (0711) 817 74 76. Cot in a dorm DM13. Breakfast included. Wool blanket DM1.50. Reception 5-11pm. Ages 16-27 only. Open late June to early Sept.) At **Weinhaus Stetter,** Rosenstr. 32, you can choose from an incredible wine selection (DM5-7) to wash down Swabian specialties (DM7-9). Take the U-Bahn to "Charlottenplatz," walk down Esslinger Str., and take a left onto Rosenstr. (Open M-F 3-11pm, Sa 10am-3am.) For **groceries,** head to the basement of **Kaufhof,** two blocks from the station. (Open M-F 9am-8pm, Sa 9am-4pm.) **Postal code:** 70001.

🔢🔢 SIGHTS AND ENTERTAINMENT. At Stuttgart's core lies an enormous pedestrian zone, centered on **Königstraße** and **Calwerstraße,** with shops and restaurants stretching as far as the eye can see. The main municipal park, the tranquil **Schloßgarten,** runs south from the station to the elegant Baroque **Neues Schloß.** The north end of the park contains the **Rosensteinpark** and **Wilhelma,** Stuttgart's famous zoo and botanical garden. (Open daily Mar.-Oct. 8:15am-5pm; Nov.-Feb. 8:15am-4pm. DM14, students DM7; Nov.-Feb. reduced.) Across from the Schloßgarten is the superb **◼Staatsgalerie Stuttgart,** Konrad-Adenauer-Str. 30-32, containing works by Picasso, Kandinsky, Beckmann, and Dalí. Take U1, U4, U9, or U11 to "Staatsgalerie." (Open W and F-Su 10am-5pm, Tu and Th 10am-8pm. DM5, students DM3.) For artistry of a different sort, the **Mercedes-Benz Museum** covers the history of the luxury automobile from its creation to modern experimental models. Take S1 to "Neckarstadion," go left under the bridge, and turn left at the next intersection. (Open Tu-Su 9am-5pm. Free.) The **Porsche Museum** tells a similar story with curvier cars. Take S6 (dir: Weil-der-Stadt) to "Neuwirtshaus." (Open M-F 9am-4pm, Sa-Su 9am-5pm. Free.) The recently reopened 58-meter-high **clock tower** in the Hauptbahnhof has a great view of the city. (Open M-F until 9pm, Sa until 2pm. Free.)

The soothing waters of Stuttgart's **mineral baths** are an ideal remedy for budget travel exhaustion. The **Mineralbad Leuze,** Am Leuzebad 2-6, has spectacular facilities. (Tel. (0711) 216 42 10. Open daily 6am-9pm. Day card DM15.50, students DM10.50.) Once refreshed, join the crowd for drinks at **Palast der Republik,** Friedrichstr. 27 (beer DM4-6; open M-W 11am-2am, Th-Sa 11am-3am, Su 3pm-2am; in winter M-W 11am-1am, Th-Sa 11am-2am, Su 3pm-1am), or music and foosball at **Oblomow,** Torstr. 20 (open daily 4pm-5am). Or put on your dancing shoes and head to **Zap,** Hauptstätterstr. 40, in the Schwabenzentrum, for hip-hop, house, and soul. (Cover DM8-15. Tu 9pm-3am, W-Su 10pm-4am.)

GERMANY

BADEN-BADEN

Anyone who ever wanted to lead the life of a pampered Old World aristocrat will have a ball in Baden-Baden. Although the spa town has declined somewhat since its 19th-century heyday, it still remains primarily a playground for minor royalty and the well-to-do, who convene here to bathe in the curative mineral spas and drop fat sums of money in the casino. Backpackers may feel a bit out of place, but the haughtiness may be worth tolerating, if only to experience the incredible baths.

🚆🛏🍴 **PRACTICAL INFO, ACCOMMODATIONS, AND FOOD.** The **train station** is 7km out of town; walk 1½hr. along the park path or take **bus** 204, 205, 216 (dir: Stadtmitte) or 201 (dir: Oberbeuren) to "Augustapl." to reach the **tourist office,** Augustapl. 8, next to the Kongresshaus. (Tel. (07221) 27 52 00; fax 27 52 02; www.baden-baden.de. Open May-Oct. M-F 9:30am-6pm, Sa 9:30am-3pm; Nov.-Apr. closes M-F 5pm.) Check your **email** at **Café Contact,** Eichstr. 5, near Augustapl. (Open W-M 2pm-midnight.) The **Werner-Dietz-Jugendherberge (HI),** Hardbergstr. 34, is halfway between the station and the center; take bus 201, 205, or 216 to "Große-Dollen-Str." (6th stop) and follow the signs uphill. (Tel. (07221) 522 23; fax 600 12. DM28, under 27 DM23; members only. Sheets DM5.50. Reception 5-11pm. Curfew 11:30pm.) Most rooms in the center are ritzy and expensive, but the **Hotel am Markt,** Marktpl. 18, has reasonable prices and a great location uphill from the main pedestrian area. (Tel. (07221) 270 40; fax 27 04 44. Singles DM54-90; doubles DM110-145; *Kurtaxe* DM5. Breakfast included. Reception 7am-10pm.) Most restaurant prices aren't budget-priced, but daily specials often run for under DM12. Slurp affordable pasta (DM10-15) at the **Pizzeria Roma,** Gernsbacherstr. 14, or stock up at the **Pennymarkt** at the "Große-Dollenstr." bus stop near the hostel (open M-W 8:30am-6:30pm, Th-F 8:30am-7pm, Sa 8:30am-2pm).

🎰 **LOSING YOUR SHIRT.** Baden-Baden's history as a resort goes back nearly two millennia, when the Romans started soaking themselves in the town's first **thermal baths.** The **Friedrichsbad,** Römerpl. 1, is a beautiful 19th-century bathing palace where visitors are parched, steamed, soaked, scrubbed, doused, and pummeled by trained professionals for three hours. Not a stitch of clothing is permitted. (Open M-Sa 9am-10pm, Su noon-8pm; last entry 3hr. before closing. Baths are co-ed Tu and F 4-10pm and all day W and Sa-Su. Standard Roman-Irish bath DM36, with soap and brush massage DM48.) The more modest or budget-minded can head next door to the beautiful **Caracalla-Thermen,** Römerpl. 11, which offers placid soaking—in bathing suits. (Open daily 8am-10pm. DM19 for 2-3hr.) To lose your shirt all over again, head to the **casino,** where Marlene Dietrich and Fyodor Dostoevsky once tried their luck. The lavish decor was modeled after Versailles. To gamble, you must be 21 and wear semi-formal attire. (Open Su-Th 2-11pm, F-Sa 2pm-midnight. DM5 min. Tours Apr.-Sept. 9:30am-noon; Oct.-Mar. 10am-noon; DM6.)

⛰ **HIKING: THE BLACK FOREST.** When you've had enough of Baden-Baden, take **bus** 204 or 205 from Leopoldpl. to "Merkurwald" and ride the Bergbahn to the top, where a slew of trails plunge into the **Black Forest** (see below). The Bergbahn station at the bottom is also crossed by the **Panoramaweg,** which connects to the best lookout points near Baden-Baden and is marked by white signs with green circles. Pick up a Panoramaweg map from the tourist office before you go (DM3).

BLACK FOREST (SCHWARZWALD)

The German cultural consciousness has always dreamt of the dark, from early fairy tales to Franz Kafka's disturbing fiction. Nowhere are such nightmarish thoughts more legitimated than in the Black Forest, a tangled expanse in southwestern Baden-Württemberg that owes its name to the eerie gloom that prevails under its evergreen canopy. One-time inspiration for the tale of Hänsel and Gretel, the region now attracts hikers and skiers with more than just bread crumbs.

⊏ GETTING THERE AND GETTING AROUND. The main entry points to the Black Forest are **Freiburg** in the center (see p. 432); **Baden-Baden** to the northwest (see above); **Stuttgart** to the east (see p. 428); and **Basel, Switzerland** to the southwest (see p. 903). Only one **train** penetrates the interior; **bus** service is more thorough, albeit slow and less frequent. The **Freiburg tourist office** (tel. (0761) 368 90 90; fax 37 00 37) is the best place to gather information about the Black Forest.

TITISEE AND SCHLUCHSEE. The more touristed **Titisee** (TEE-tee-zay) is only 30min. by train from Freiburg via the scenic Höllental (Hell's Valley). The **tourist office,** Strandbadstr. 4, dispenses maps of 130km of nearby hiking trails (DM1-15). From the station, turn right on Parkstr., turn left, and and make a quick right around the pink house. (Tel. (07651) 980 40; fax 98 04 40. Open July-Sept. M-F 8am-6pm, Sa 9am-noon and 3-5pm, Su 10am-noon; Oct.-June M-F 9am-noon and 1:30-5:30pm.) **Hiking trails** start in front of the office; consider the placid **Seeweg,** or keep going along Strandbadstr. and turn right on Alte Poststr. for more challenging trails.

Schluchsee, to the south, is home to a slew of first-rate **hiking trails.** The **Seerundweg** circumvents the lake (18km, about 4hr.); more difficult trails depart from the **Sportplatz** parking lot, 15min. up Dresselbacher Str. **Trains** run from Titisee to Schluchsee (30min., every hr.). From the station, turn right, walk through the underpass, and turn left on Kirchsteige to reach the **tourist office,** at the corner of Fischbacher Str. and Lindenstr. (Tel. (07656) 77 32; fax 77 59. Open July-Aug. M-F 8am-6pm, Sa 10am-noon and 4-6pm, Su 10am-noon; Sept.-Oct. and May-June M-F 8am-noon and 2-6pm, Sa 10am-noon; Nov.-Apr. closed Sa-Su.) The **Jugendherberge Schluchsee-Wolfsgrund (HI),** Seeweg 28, has stunning lake views. From the station, cross the tracks, hop the fence, and follow the path right (over the bridge). (Tel. (07656) 329; fax 92 37. DM28, under 27 DM23. May-Oct. DM1-2 *Kurtaxe.* Laundry. Reception closed 2-5pm. Curfew 11pm.) Walk left up Bahnhofstr., continue on Freiburger Str., turn left on Sägackerweg, go past Am Waldrain, and take another left to reach **Campingplatz Wolfsgrund.** (Tel. (07656) 77 32 33. DM8.50 per person, DM10 per tent.) Get **groceries** at **Schmidt's Markt,** Im Rappennest 2.

ST. PETER AND ST. MÄRGEN. North of Titisee and 17km east of Freiburg, twin villages **St. Peter** and **St. Märgen** lie between cow-speckled hills in the High Black Forest. **Bus** 7216 runs from Freiburg to St. Märgen via St. Peter; you can also take any **train** on the Freiburg-Neustadt line to "Kirchzarten" (3rd stop) and then take bus 7216 to St. Peter (only half continue to St. Märgen; check with the driver). An easy but very scenic 8km path leads from **St. Peter,** surrounded by cherry orchards, to St. Märgen; follow the blue diamonds of the **Panoramaweg.** From the front of the St. Peter's **Klosterkirche,** make a sharp right alongside it (don't cross the stream and the main road), heading for Jägerhaus, and cross the highway. The **tourist office,** in the Klosterhof, lists rooms from DM25. Get off the bus at "Zähringer Eck"; it's right in front of the church. (Tel. (07660) 91 02 24; fax 91 02 44. Open June-Oct. M-F 8am-noon and 2-5pm, Sa 11am-1pm; Nov.-May closed Sa.)

With links to all major Black Forest trails and a number of gorgeous day hikes, **St. Märgen** rightfully calls itself a *Wanderparadies* (hiking paradise). One of the more challenging trails leads to the **Zweibach waterfall;** follow the yellow signs with a black dot (16km, 4hr.). To reach the trail, walk downhill along Feldbergstr., turn left on Landfeldweg, and follow signs for Rankmühle. The **tourist office,** in the Rathaus, 100m from the "Post" bus stop, has good hiking and biking maps (DM5), and finds rooms for free. (Tel. (07669) 91 18 17; fax 91 18 40. Open M-F 8am-noon and 2-5pm; June-Aug. also Sa 10am-noon; Nov.-Dec. closed M-F 2-5pm.)

TRIBERG. The residents of touristy **Triberg** brag about the **Gutacher Wasserfall,** the highest **waterfall** in Germany, a series of bright cascades tumbling 163m down moss-covered rocks. The idyllic hike through the lush pine trees makes up for the unimpressive trickle. In the park you can also follow signs to the **Wallfahrtskirche,** continue on Kroneckweg, and follow the Panoramaweg signs for an excellent view of the Black Forest valley. (Park admission DM2.50, students DM2.) **Trains** chug to Triberg from Freiburg (1¾hr., every hr., DM32). To get from the station to the **tourist**

GERMANY

office, in the Kurhaus, cross the bridge, go under it, bear right up steep Fréjusstr. (which turns into Hauptstr.), pass the Marktpl. (10min.), and turn left at the Hotel Pfaff. (Tel. (07722) 95 32 30; fax 95 32 36. Open May-Sept. M-F 9am-5pm, Sa 10am-noon; Oct.-Apr. closed Sa.) The town's sparkling **Jugendherberge (HI),** Rohrbacher Str. 35, requires a masochistic climb up Friedrichstr. (which becomes Rohrbacher Str.) from the tourist office (30min.). (Tel. (07722) 41 10; fax 66 62. DM27, under 27 DM22. Sheets DM5.50. Reception 5-7pm and at 9:45pm. Call ahead.) The **Hotel Zum Bären,** Hauptstr. 10, is closer to the center and the park entrance. (Tel. (07722) 44 93. Singles DM37-45; doubles DM66-84. Breakfast included.)

FREIBURG IM BREISGAU

Freiburg may be the "metropolis" of the Schwarzwald, but it has yet to succumb to the hectic rhythms of city life. Its relaxed air results not only from persistent French influence (its genial citizens flout the dour German stereotype), but also from the surrounding hills, which brim with greenery and fantastic hiking trails.

▨ ▨▨ PRACTICAL INFO, ACCOMMODATIONS, AND FOOD. Trains arrive from Basel, Switzerland (45min., 1-2 per hr.); Stuttgart (1½hr., every hr., DM67); and Strasbourg, France (1¾hr., every hr.). The **tourist office,** Rotteckring 14, is two blocks down Eisenhahnstr. from the station. (Tel. (0761) 388 18 82; fax 388 18 87. Open M-F 9:30am-8pm, Sa 9:30am-2pm, Su 10am-noon.) Check your **email** at **Web-SPIDERcafé,** Molketstr. 28. (DM2.50 per 15min. Open M-Sa 9am-8pm.) To reach the **Jugendherberge (HI),** Kartäuserstr. 151, take S1 (dir: Littenweiler) to "Römerhof," cross the tracks, backtrack 20m, walk 10min. down Fritz-Geiges-Str., cross the stream, and follow the footpath right. (Tel. (0761) 676 56; fax 603 67. DM29, under 27 DM24; members only. Reception 7am-9am and 1-10pm. Curfew 1am.) **◪Hotel Zum Löwen,** Breisgauer Str. 62, doesn't feel like a budget hotel. Take S1 to "Padua-Allee," backtrack 30m along the tracks, and walk 5min. down Breigauerstr. (Tel. (0761) 809 72 20; fax 840 23. Singles DM50-60; doubles DM90-110. Breakfast included.) To get from the station to **Hotel Schemmer,** Eschholzstr. 63, take the overpass at the end of track 1, go past the church, and turn left. (Tel. (0761) 27 24 24; fax 220 10. Singles DM65-75; doubles DM90-95. Breakfast included.) **◪Brennessel,** Eschholzstr. 17, is a plucky student tavern with funk, jazz, and cheap chow. (Open M-Sa 6pm-1am, Su 5pm-1am.) Or load up at **Edeka ActivMarkt,** Eisenhahnstr. 39. (Open M-F 7:30am-8pm, Sa 8am-4pm.) **Postal code:** 79098.

▨ ▨ SIGHTS AND ENTERTAINMENT. Freiburg's pride and joy is the majestic 13th- to 16th-century **Münster,** a stone cathedral with a 116m spire and a tower with the oldest bell in Germany. (Cathedral open M-Sa 10am-6pm, Su 1-6pm. Tower open May-Oct. M-F 9:30am-5pm, Su 1-5pm; Nov.-Apr. Tu-Sa 9:30am-5pm, Su 1-5pm; DM2.50, students DM1.50.) Two medieval gates—the **Schwabentor** and the **Martin-stor**—stand within a few blocks of one another in the southeast corner of the Alts-tadt. From the Schwabentor, take the pedestrian overpass across the heavily trafficked Schloßbergring to climb the **Schloßberg** for an excellent view of the city. The **Museum für Neue Kunst** (Museum of Modern Art), Marienstr. 10a, near the Schwabentor, displays the work of 20th-century German artists such as Otto Dix. Borrow the helpful English-language guide to brush up on modern German art. (Open Tu-Su 10am-5pm. Free.) You may notice a set of narrow streams as you run around town—these **Bächle** served as swift-flowing gutters in medieval times.

Call ahead to get in on a one-hour tour at the **Brauerei Ganter,** Schwarzwaldstr. 43 (tel. (0761) 218 51 81); the tours track the production process of the malt beverage, and the grand finale consists of food and lots of beer atop one of the factory build-ings (Tu and Th 1:30pm; free). For less structured entertainment, Freiburg's night-life revolves around the **Martinstor** near the university. Despite its inhospitable name, **Exit,** Kaiser-Josef-Str. 248, inspires people to do just the opposite. (Open M and W-Th 10pm-3am, F-Sa 10pm-4am; Th and Sa students free.) **Jazzhaus,** Schnewl-ingstr. 1, features live performances almost every night (cover from DM10), while **Greiffenegg-Schlößle,** Schloßbergring 3, offers beer (DM5-7) on a hillside terrace.

GERMANY

TÜBINGEN

Tübingen is a bookish city, and proud of it; nearly half of its residents are affiliated with the 500-year-old university. In addition to being populated by students, the Altstadt is also surprisingly devoid of tourists, allowing independent travelers a chance for solo exploration. The chancel of the 15th-century **Stiftskirche**, the focal point of the Altstadt's winding alleys and gabled houses, contains the tombs of 14 members of the former House of Württemberg; climb the tower for an amazing view of the city. (Church open daily 9am-5pm. Chancel and tower open daily Aug.-Sept. 10:30am-5pm; Apr.-July and Oct. F-Su 10:30am-5pm. Joint ticket DM2, students DM1.) Head down Kirchg. to the old market square to see the ornate painted façade of the **Rathaus**. A few blocks left (as you face the Rathaus) on Kronenstr. stands the **Tübingen Evangelisches Stift**, which was built as an Augustinian monastery but later became a seminary that housed such academic luminaries as Kepler, Hegel, Schelling, and Mörike. Down Bursag. is the **Bursa**, where roommates Hegel and Schelling dozed through dull theology lectures. Their third roommate, the great 18th- and 19th- century Friedrich Hölderlin, lived the last 36 years of his life in the nearby **Hölderlinturm** in a state of clinical insanity. (Museum open Tu-F 10am-noon and 3-5pm, Sa-Su 2-5pm. DM3, students DM2.) On top of the hill that divides the university from most of the city is the **Schloß Hohentübingen**, which dates from 1078 and commands the best views; inside, an ethnographic **museum** has the purported oldest surviving example of handiwork, a 35,000-year-old sculpted ivory horse. (Open W-Su May-Sept. 10am-6pm; Oct.-Apr. 10am-5pm. DM4, students DM2.)

Trains arrive from Stuttgart (1hr., every 30-45min.) on the other side of the Neckar River from the Altstadt. Turn right from the station and left on Karlstr. to reach the **tourist office** on the Neckarbrücke, which books rooms (DM30-100) for free. (Tel. (07071) 913 60; fax 350 70. Open M-F 9am-7pm, Sa 9am-5pm, Su 2-5pm; Oct.-Apr. closed Su.) To get from the station to the **Jugendherberge (HI)**, Gartenstr. 22/2, cross the Neckarbrücke and make a right (12min.). (Tel. (07071) 230 02; fax 250 61. DM28, under 27 DM23; members only. Breakfast included. Reception 5-8pm and 10-11pm. Lockout 9am-5pm. Curfew 10pm.) To **camp** at **Rappernberghalde**, on the river, head upstream from the Altstadt, or turn left from the station, cross the Alleenbrücke, turn left, and follow the blue signs (20-25min.). (Tel. (07071) 431 45; fax 350 70. DM9.50 per person, DM5.50-7 per tent. Laundry. Reception 8am-12:30pm and 2:30-10pm. Open Mar. to mid-Oct.) ⊠**Tübingen Ratskeller**, Haagg. 4, with an entrance on Rathausg., serves up Swabian specialties and veggie platters (DM12-16). (Open M-Sa 6-11:30pm, Su 6-11pm.) Buy bread and Nutella at **Pfannkuch**, Karlstr. 3, next to the tourist office. (Open M-F 8:30am-7:30pm, Sa 8am-2pm.) **Postal code**: 72072.

LAKE CONSTANCE (BODENSEE)

Germany has long suffered from a Mediterranean complex, and the single strip of land along the Bodensee in southern Baden-Württemberg provides an opportunity for Italian fantasies to be enacted and Grecian longings to be satisfied with a thoroughly un-German casualness. With the snow-capped Swiss and Austrian Alps in the background, the Bodensee is one of Germany's most stunning destinations.

KONSTANZ. Narrow streets in the elegant university city of Konstanz, among the few German cities to have escaped Allied bombing in WWII, wind around the beautifully painted Baroque and Renaissance façades in the town center. The **Münster** has a 76m soaring Gothic spire and a display of ancient religious objects, although the tower is unfortunately being renovated through 2003. (Open daily 10am-5pm. Free.) Wander down **Seestraße**, near the yacht harbor on the lake, or down **Rheinsteig**, along the Rhine, for two picturesque waterside promenades, or rent a **paddleboat** or **rowboat** at Am Gondelhafen. (Open Apr.-Oct. daily 10am-dusk. DM12-16 per hr.). Take bus 5 to reach **Strandbad Horn**, Konstanz's most popular **public beach**, with a nude sunbathing section modestly enclosed by hedges. Twentysomethings frolic at the beach near the university; take bus 4 to "Egg" and walk past the *Sporthalle* and playing fields, or walk 10min. from the Konstanz hostel.

GERMANY

Trains arrive from Zürich (1¼hr.); Freiburg (2½hr., DM43); and Stuttgart (3hr., DM56). The **tourist office,** Bahnhofspl. 13, is in an arcade to the right of the train station. Ask about the one-day **Gästekarte,** which provides unlimited bus transit in Konstanz and reduced admission to some sights. (Tel. (07531) 13 30 30; fax 13 30 60;. Open May-Oct. M-F 9am-8pm, Sa 9am-4pm, Su 10am-1pm; Nov.-Mar. M-F 9:30am-12:30pm and 2-6pm.) Reserve ahead for the marvelous ⬛**Jugendherberge Kreuzlingen (HI),** Promenadenstr. 7, which is actually in Switzerland but is closer to downtown Konstanz than the other hostel. From the station, turn left, cross the metal bridge over the tracks, turn right, go through the parking lot to checkpoint "Klein Venedig," continue along Seestr., continue straight on the gravel path instead of following the sharp curve right, go past the gate and goats, then head right through the castle parking lot and up the hill (20min.). (Tel. +41 (71) 688 26 63; fax 688 47 61. SFr23/DM28. Breakfast included. Reception 8-9am and 5-9pm. Curfew 11pm. Open Mar.-Nov.) **Jugendherberge "Otto-Moericke-Turm" (HI),** Zur Allmannshöhe 18, is less luxurious, but has a great view. Take bus 4 from the station to "Jugendherberge" (7th stop), backtrack, and head straight up the hill. (Tel. (07531) 322 60; fax 311 63. DM35, under 27 DM30; members only. Breakfast and dinner included. Sheets DM5.50. Reception Apr.-Oct. 3-10pm; Nov.-Mar. 5-10pm. Curfew 10pm. Lockout 9:30am-noon. Call ahead.) Get **groceries** at **Tengelmann,** at Münzg. and Brotlaube. (Open M-F 8:30am-8pm, Sa 8am-4pm.) **Postal code:** 78462.

LINDAU IM BODENSEE. Tourists come to soak in Lindau's balmy climate and wander among the 14th-century gabled houses along **Maximilianstr.** The **Cavazzen-Haus** in the Marktpl. houses the **Stadtmuseum.** (Open Apr.-Oct. Tu-Su 10am-noon and 2-5pm. DM5, students DM3.) Roulette wheels spin and wallets thin at the **Spielbank** (casino) by the Seebrücke. (Open daily 3pm-4am. DM5 and a passport. Must be 21 No jeans.) Lindau's biggest **beach** is **Eichwald,** 30min. right (as you face the harbor) along Uferweg. (Open M-F 9:30am-7:30pm, Sa-Su 9am-8pm. DM5.) To reach the quieter **Lindenhofbad,** take bus 1 or 2 to "Anheggerstr." and then bus 4 to "Alwind." (Open M-F 10:30am-7:30pm, Sa-Su 10am-8pm. DM4, students DM3.)

Trains (2hr., DM13) and **ferries** run to Konstanz (3hr., 3-6 per day. DM18.80, under 24 DM11.20); trains also hop the border to Bregenz, Austria (10min.; see p. 111). You can rent a **boat** from 50m to the left of the casino, next to the bridge. (Open mid.-Mar. to mid.-Sept. daily 9am-9pm. Rowboats DM10-18; paddleboats DM14-18 per hr.) The **tourist office,** Ludwigstr. 68, is across from the train station. (Tel. (08382) 26 00 30; fax 26 00 26. Open mid-June to early Sept. M-Sa 9am-1pm and 2-7pm; May to mid-June and Sept. M-F 9am-1pm and 2-6pm, Sa 9am-1pm; Apr. and Oct. M-F 9am-1pm and 2-5pm, Sa 9am-1pm; Nov.-Mar. M-F 9am-noon and 2-5pm.) The spectacular **Jugendherberge,** Herbergsweg 11, lies across the Seebrücke off Bregenzer Str. (20min.). (Tel. (08382) 967 10; fax 496 71 50. DM28 including *Kurtaxe;* under 27 and those with small children only. Breakfast included. Reception 7am-midnight. Curfew midnight. Call ahead.) **Campingplatz Lindau-Zech,** Frauenhofer Str. 20, is 3km south of the island on the mainland; take bus 1 or 2 to "Anheggerstr.," then bus 3 (dir: Zech) to the end. (Tel. (08382) 722 36; fax 26 00 26. DM9.50 per person, DM4 per tent; *Kurtaxe* DM1.50. Shower included. Open May-Oct.) Pick up **groceries** at **Plus,** in the basement of the department store at the corner of In der Grub and Cramerg. (Open M-F 8:30am-6:30pm, Sa 8am-1pm.) **Postal code:** 88131

BAVARIA (BAYERN)

Bavaria is the Germany of Teutonic myth, Wagnerian opera, and fairy tales. From the Baroque cities along the Danube to Mad King Ludwig's castles perched high in the Alps, the region beckons to more tourists than any other part of the country. Indeed, when most foreigners conjure up images of Germany, they imagine Bavaria, land of beer gardens, oom-pah-pah bands, and *Lederhosen.* This largest of Germany's federal states, mostly rural, Catholic, and conservative, contrasts greatly with the rest of the country, and its unique traditions and dialect are insistently preserved: residents have always been Bavarians first and Germans second.

REMINDER. HI-affiliated hostels in Bavaria do not admit guests over age 26, although an exception is usually made for those accompanied by young children.

MUNICH (MÜNCHEN)

The capital and cultural center of Bavaria, Munich is a sprawling, relatively liberal metropolis in the midst of solidly conservative southern Germany. The two cities of Munich and Berlin are emblematic of the two poles of German character: Munich's sensual air of merriment—most obvious during the wild Fasching and the legendary Oktoberfest—contrasts with Berlin's dizzying reconstruction and sense of fragmented avant-garde. Since falling from the Bavarian Golden Age of the 18th and 19th centuries and being shattered in WWII (when less than 3% of the city was left intact), Munich has proved resilient, and today basks unabashedly in Western German postwar economic glory: world-class museums, handsome parks and architecture, and a rambunctious arts scene collide to create a city of astonishing vitality.

▐ GETTING THERE AND GETTING AROUND

Flights: Flughafen München (tel. 97 52 13 13). S8 connects to the Hauptbahnhof (50min., every 20min., DM14 or 8 strips on the *Streifenkarte*).

Trains: Hauptbahnhof (tel. 22 33 12 56). To: **Salzburg** (1¾hr., every hr.); **Innsbruck** (2hr., every hr.); **Frankfurt** (3½hr., every hr., DM113); **Zürich** (5hr., every 2hr., DM110); **Vienna** (5hr., every hr., DM103); **Cologne/Köln** (6hr., every hr., DM173); **Hamburg** (6hr., every hr., DM224); **Berlin** (7½hr., every hr., DM183); **Prague** (8½hr., 6 per day, DM97); **Amsterdam** (9hr., every hr., DM245); and **Paris** (10hr., DM193). For schedules or reservations, call (0180) 599 66 33. **EurAide** (see below) provides info in English.

Public Transportation: MVV runs M-F 5am-12:30am, Sa-Su 5am-2:30am. **Single-fare** DM3.50 (valid 3hr.); **Kurzstrecke** (short-trip; 2 stops on U- or S-Bahn or 4 on streetcar or bus) DM1.80. **Streifenkarte** (11-strip ticket) DM15; cancel 2 strips in the city center (1 strip for a *Kurzstrecke*), plus 2 strips per zone beyond the center. Buy tickets at the blue *MVV-Fahrausweise* machines and validate them in "E" boxes before entering the platform, or face a DM60 fine. **Eurail** and **InterRail** valid on S-Bahn only. **Single-Tageskarte** (single-day ticket; valid until the following 6am) DM9; **3-Day Pass** DM21. Buy passes at the MVV office behind tracks 31 and 32 in the Hauptbahnhof. Pick up a **transit map** at the tourist office, EurAide, or at MVV counters near the U-Bahn entrance in the station.

Taxis: Taxi-Zentrale (tel. 216 11 or 194 10) has large stands in front of the train station and every 5-10 blocks in the central city. Women can request a female driver.

Bike Rental: Radius Bikes (tel. 59 61 13), in the Hauptbahnhof, behind the lockers opposite tracks 30-31. DM30 per day. Deposit DM100, passport, or credit card. Students and Eurailpass holders 10% off. Open Apr. to early Oct. daily 10am-6pm.

Hitchhiking: *Let's Go* does not recommend hitchhiking. Hitchers try Autobahn on-ramps; those who stand behind the blue sign with the white auto may be fined. Hitchers to Salzburg reportedly take U1-2 to "Karl-Preis-Platz"; to Stuttgart, streetcar 17 to "Amalienburgstr."; to Nuremberg or Berlin, U6 to "Studentenstadt," near the Frankfurter Ring; to Switzerland, U4-5 to "Heimeranpl.," then bus 33 to "Siegenburger Str." **McShare Treffpunkt Zentrale**, Klenzestr. 57b and Lämmerstr. 4 (tel. 194 40), matches McDrivers and McRiders. To Heidelberg DM34, Frankfurt DM41, Berlin DM54. Open daily 8am-8pm.

▐ ORIENTATION AND PRACTICAL INFORMATION

Most sights lie within the main traffic **Ring,** which changes names as it bounds around the center. The east-west and north-south thoroughfares cross at the city's center, the **Marienplatz,** and meet the Ring at **Karlsplatz** ("Stachus") in the west, **Isartorplatz** in the east, **Odeonsplatz** in the north, and **Sendlinger Tor** (gate) in the south. **Ludwigstraße** stretches north from the **Residenz** palace and Odeonspl. to the university district, then continues farther north as **Leopoldstraße,** which brushes the student country known as **Schwabing** ("Schwabylon") to the west. To the east of Schwabing sprawls the **Englischer Garten;** to the west is the **Olympiazentrum** complex. Farther

GERMANY

west lies the **Schloß Nymphenburg.** Southwest of Marienpl., **Sendlinger Straße** leads past shops to the Sendlinger Tor. From there, Lindwurmstr. proceeds to Goetheplatz, from which Mozartstr. leads to **Theresienwiese**, site of the Oktoberfest, southwest of the Hauptbahnhof.

The **Hauptbahnhof** (main train station) is west of Karlspl., just beyond the Ring. From there it's a straight shot down Schützenstr., Neuhauserstr., and Kaufingerstr. to Marienpl. (15-20min.); or take S1-8 two stops to "Marienpl." Pick up the monthly *Munich Found* from any newsstand or bookshop for info on events and museums; the bi-weekly *in München* (free) for movie, theater, and concert schedules; or the hip monthly *Prinz* for tips on shopping, art, music, film, concerts, and food.

TOURIST AND FINANCIAL SERVICES

Tourist Offices: Fremdenverkehrsamt (tel. 23 33 02 57; fax 23 33 02 33; www.munich-tourist.de), in front (east) of the Hauptbahnhof. Books rooms for free with a 10-15% deposit; sells maps (DM0.50), the youth-oriented *München Infopool* (DM1), and the **München Welcome Card,** which provides unlimited transit and discounts on many sights (1-day DM12; 3-day DM29, up to 5 people DM42). **Branches** in the Neues Rathaus on Marienpl. (tel. 23 33 02 72). ■ **EurAide in English** (tel. 59 38 89; fax 550 39 65; www.cube.net/kmu/euraide.html), in the Hauptbahnhof along track 11, is the savior of frazzled English-speaking tourists. Books rooms (DM7 fee), gives free train info, and offers castle tours. Open June-Sept. daily 7:45am-noon and 1-6pm; Oct.-Apr. M-F 7:45am-noon and 1-4pm, Sa 7:45am-noon; May daily 7:45am-noon and 1-4:30pm.

Tours: Munich Walks (tel. (0177) 227 59 01) leads daily walking tours of the major sights (May-Aug. 10:30am, also M-Sa 2:30pm; Apr. and Oct. 10:30am; Nov. to late Dec. 10am) and special tours emphasizing Nazi history (May-Aug. Tu, Th, and Sa 10:30am; Sept.-Oct. Tu, Th, and Sa 2:30pm; Apr. Sa 2:30pm). Tours 2½hr., DM12-15; depart from EurAide (see above). **Mike's Bike Tours** (tel. 651 42 75) survey the sights and stop at a *Biergarten.* Daily tours leave from the Altes Rathaus by the Spielzeugmuseum. Tours 4hr.; Apr. to early Oct. 11:30am and 4pm; Mar. and late Oct. 12:30pm; DM31.

Budget Travel: Council Travel, Adalbertstr. 32 (tel. 39 50 22), near the university, sells ISICs. Open M-F 10am-1pm and 2-6:30pm.

Currency Exchange: ReiseBank (tel. 551 08 37), in front of the Hauptbahnhof on Bahnhofpl. (open daily 6am-11pm) and around the corner from EurAide at track 11 (open M-Sa 7:30am-7:15pm, Su 9:30am-12:30pm and 1-4:45pm). Pick up *Inside Track* at EurAide for 50% off commission on exchanges of least US$50 in US traveler's checks. All cash transactions DM5. Western Union services.

American Express: Promenadepl. 6 (tel. 29 09 00), in the Hotel Bayerischer Hof. Mail held. Cashes traveler's checks. Open M-F 9am-5:30pm, Sa 9:30am-12:30pm.

LOCAL SERVICES

Luggage Storage: At the **Hauptbahnhof** (*Gepäckaufbewahrung*; tel. 13 08 50 47). DM4 per piece per day. Open daily 6am-11pm. **Lockers** DM2-4 per 24hr.

English Bookstore: ■ **Anglia English Bookshop,** Schellingstr. 3 (tel. 28 36 42). U3 or U6: Universität. Open M-F 9am-6:30pm, Sa 10am-2pm.

Gay and Lesbian Services: Gay services information (tel. 260 30 56). **Lesbian information** (tel. 725 42 72). Phones staffed F 6-10pm.

Laundromat: City SB-Waschcenter, Paul-Heyse-Str. 21, near the Hauptbahnhof. Wash DM6; dry DM1 per 10min. Open daily 7am-11pm. **Münz Waschsalon,** Amalienstr. 61. Wash DM6.20 (soap DM1); dry DM1 per 10min. Open M-F 8am-6:30pm, Sa 8am-1pm.

EMERGENCY AND COMMUNICATIONS

Emergency: Police, tel. 110. **Ambulance** and **fire,** tel. 112. **Medical emergency,** tel. 59 44 75.

Pharmacy: Bahnhof-Apotheke, Bahnhofpl. 2 (tel. 59 41 19 or 59 81 19), outside the station. Open M-F 8am-6:30pm, Sa 8am-2pm. Call 59 44 75 for night pharmacy info.

Medical Assistance: Klinikum Rechts der Isar, across the river on Ismaninger Str. U4 or U5: Max-Weber-Platz. UK and US consulates have lists of English-speaking doctors.

Internet Access: Times Square Internet Café, Bayerstr. 10a, on the south side of the station. DM4.50 per 15min.

Munich

ACCOMMODATIONS

A Pension Utzelmann
B CVJM Jugendgästehaus
C Pension Schillerhof
D Jugendhotel Marienberge
E Hotel Helvetia
F Pension Locarno
G Pension Hungaria

GERMANY

Post Office: On Bahnhofpl. (tel. 59 90 87 16), across from the station. Address mail to be held: *Postlagernde Briefe* für Sonesh CHAINANI, Hauptpostamt, München **80335,** Germany. Open M-F 7am-8pm, Sa 8am-4pm, Su 9am-3pm. **Postamt 31** (tel. 552 26 20), upstairs in the station, sells stamps and phone cards and mails letters, but doesn't mail packages or exchange money. Open M-F 7am-8pm, Sa 8am-4pm, Su 9am-3pm.

PHONE CODE	City code: 089. From outside Germany, dial int'l dialing prefix (see inside back cover) + 49 + 89 + local number.

▟ ACCOMMODATIONS AND CAMPING

Munich's accommodations usually fall into one of three categories: seedy, expensive, or booked solid. During Oktoberfest, all three may apply. Don't even think of sleeping in any public area, including the Hauptbahnhof; police patrol frequently all night long. If you're in a pinch, consider taking a train to the hostel in Augsburg (30-45min., 2-3 per hr. until 11:20pm, DM10; see p. 448), or throw your luggage into a locker, party until 5am, and return to re-evaluate the hotel lists afterward.

HOSTELS

🏕 **Jugendlager Kapuzinerhölzl** ("The Tent"), In den Kirschen 30 (tel. 141 43 00; fax 17 50 90). Take streetcar 17 from the station (dir: Amalienburgstr.) to "Botanischer Garten" (15min.), go straight on Franz-Schrank-Str., and turn left on In den Kirschen. Sleep with 400 new buddies under a circus tent on a foam pad (DM14) or bed (DM18). **Camping** DM7 per person, DM7 per tent. Rent a *Grüne Karte* transport pass (DM4 per day) or a *Partner-Tageskarte* good for 5 people (DM13 per day). Reception 24hr. Kitchen. Laundry. **Internet.** Free city tours (W 9am). Passport deposit. Rarely full. Open mid-June to Aug.

🏕 **Euro Youth Hotel,** Senefelderstr. 5 (tel. 59 90 88 11; fax 59 90 88 77). From the "Bahnhofspl." station exit, turn right on Bayerstr. and left on Senefelderstr. Outlandishly friendly and well-informed English-speaking staff. DM29; doubles and triples DM36-45. Breakfast DM8. Laundry DM3. Reception 24hr.

Jugendherberge München (HI), Wendl-Dietrich-Str. 20 (tel. 13 11 56; fax 167 87 45). U1 (dir: Westfriedhof): Rotkreuzplatz; cross toward Kaufhof and go down Wendl-Dietrich-Str. The most "central" HI hostel (3km from the center). Big dorm (men only) DM24; smaller co-ed dorms DM29. Breakfast included. Key deposit DM20. Safe deposit DM50. Check-in from 11am, but lines form by 9am. Reception 24hr.

Jugendherberge Pullach Burg Schwaneck (HI), Burgweg 4-6 (tel. 793 06 43; fax 793 79 22), in a castle 12km from the center. S7 (dir: Wolfratshausen): Pullach (20min.); walk down Margarethenstr. toward the field and follow the signs (8min.). Clean, quiet rooms. 6- to 8-bed dorms DM22; singles DM36.50; doubles DM34.50; quads DM25. Breakfast included. Reception 4-11pm. Curfew 11:30pm.

4 you münchen, Hirtenstr. 18 (tel. 552 16 60; fax 55 21 66 66). From the station, go left on Arnulfstr., right on Pfefferstr., and left on Hirtenstr. Ecological hostel with bar and hang-out areas. 12-bed dorms DM24; 4- to 8-bed DM29; 2-bed DM38; singles DM54. Over 27 add 15%. Key deposit DM20. Breakfast DM7.50. Sheets DM5. Reserve ahead.

Jugendgästehaus Thalkirchen, Miesingstr. 4 (tel. 723 65 50; fax 724 25 67; email Bine-Munich@aol.com). U3 (dir: Fürstenrieder West): Thalkirchen ("Thalkirchner Pl." exit); follow Schäftlarnstr. toward Innsbruck, bear right around the curve, follow Frauenbergstr., and follow Münchner Str. left. Dorms DM31.50; singles DM36.50. Breakfast included. Reception 7am-1am. Check-in 2pm-1am. Curfew 1am. Reserve ahead.

Jump In, Hochstr. 51 (tel. 48 95 34 37). S1-8: Rosenheimer Platz ("Gasteig" exit); walk left on Hochstr. (10min.). Private hostel founded by a brother and Pointer Sister tired of impersonal institutions. Disorganized and spartan rooms, but friendly. Mattresses on floor DM29; beds DM35; doubles DM39. Reception 10am-1pm and 5-10pm.

Jugendhotel Marienberge, Goethestr. 9 (tel. 55 58 05; fax 55 02 82 60). Take the "Bayerstr." exit from the station and walk down Goethestr. Staffed by merry nuns. 6-bed dorms DM30; 3-bed DM30; 2-bed DM35; singles DM40. Breakfast included. Kitchen. Laundry. Reception 8am-midnight. Curfew midnight. **Women under 26 only.**

CVJM Jugendgästehaus, Landwehrstr. 13 (tel. 552 14 10; fax 550 42 82; email muenchen@cvjm.org). Take the "Bayerstr." exit from the station, head down Goethestr. or Schillerstr., and turn left on Landwehrstr. 3-bed dorms DM40; 2-bed DM43; singles DM50. Over 27 add 16%. Breakfast included. Reception 8am-12:30am. Curfew 12:30am. Reserve by mail, phone, fax, or email. Closed for Easter and Dec. 20-Jan. 7.

Haus International, Elisabethstr. 87 (tel. 12 00 60; fax 12 00 62 51). Take U2 (dir: Feld-moching) to "Hohenzollernplatz," then streetcar 12 (dir: Romanplatz) or bus 33 (dir: Aid-enbachstr.) to "Barbarastr." It's the 5-story beige building behind the BP gas station. 5-bed dorms DM40; 4-bed DM43; 3-bed DM46; 2-bed DM52-72; singles DM55-85. Small beer garden, TV room, and disco. Reception 24hr. Reserve ahead.

HOTELS AND PENSIONEN

Hotel Helvetia, Schillerstr. 6 (tel. 590 68 50; fax 59 06 85 70), to the right as you exit the station. The friendliest hotel in all of Munich. 10-bed dorms DM22; 4- to 6-bed DM26. Singles DM55-65; doubles DM68-90; triples DM99-120. Breakfast included. Add 10-15% during Oktoberfest. Breakfast DM7. Sheets DM4. Laundry DM8.50. Reception 24hr.

Hotel-Pension Utzelmann, Pettenkoferstr. 6 (tel. 59 48 89; fax 59 62 28). From the station, walk 4 blocks down Schillerstr. and go left on Pettenkofer to the end (10min.). Elegant rooms. Singles DM50-125; doubles DM95-145; triples DM123-175; quads DM180. Showers DM5 for cheapest rooms. Breakfast included. Reception 7am-10pm.

Hotel Kurpfalz, Schwanthaler Str. 121 (tel. 540 98 60; fax 54 09 88 11; email hotel-kur-pfalz@munich-online.de). From the station, go 5-6 blocks right down Bayerstr., veer left on Holzapfelstr., and turn right on Schwanthaler Str. (10min.). Or take streetcar 18 or 19 to "Holzapfelstr." (3 stops). Rooms with TV, phone, and bath. Singles from DM79; doubles from DM99; triples DM165. Breakfast included. Free **internet.** Reception 24hr.

Pension Locarno, Bahnhofpl. 5 (tel. 55 51 64; fax 59 50 45). From the main exit of the station, walk left across Arnulfstr. past the U-Bahn exit and look left. Helpful owners and plain rooms with TV and phone. Singles DM55-75; doubles DM85; triples DM125; quads DM140. Breakfast included. *Let's Go*ers DM5 off. Reception 7:30am-midnight.

Pension Schillerhof, Schillerstr. 21 (tel. 59 42 70; fax 550 18 35). Exit onto Bahnhofpl. from the train station, turn right, and walk 2 blocks down Schillerstr. Unpretentious, tidy rooms with TV. Singles DM60-80, doubles DM90-120. Extra bed DM20. Oktoberfest surcharge DM25-40 per person. Breakfast included. Reception 6am-10pm.

Pension Hungaria, Briennerstr. 42 (tel. 52 15 58). From the station, go left on Dachauer Str., right on Augustenstr., and right on Briennerstr. (10min.). Oriental rugs and comfy furnishings. Singles DM58; doubles DM85; triples DM110; quads DM120. Breakfast included. Showers DM3. Add DM10 during Oktoberfest. Reception 24hr.

Pension Central, Bayerstr. 55 (tel. 543 98 46; fax 543 98 47), 5min. from the station's "Bayerstr." exit. The unattractive exterior belies the qualities within—just like Quasimodo. Singles DM50-85; doubles DM85-115, with bath DM120-130. Reception 24hr.

Pension Frank, Schellingstr. 24 (tel. 28 14 51; fax 280 09 10; www.city-netz.com/pen-sionfrank). U3 or U6: Universität ("Schellingstr." exit); take the 1st right on Schellingstr. A mix of backpackers, students, and dolled-up fashion models. 3- to 6-bed dorms DM40; singles DM55-65; doubles DM95. Breakfast included. Reception 7:30am-10pm.

Pension am Kaiserplatz, Kaiserpl. 12 (tel. 34 91 90). U3 or U6: Münchener Freiheit; take the escalator to Herzogstr., turn left, and go left on Viktoriastr. to the end (10min.). Sweet owner and elegant *Pension.* Singles DM59; doubles DM85-95; add DM40 per additional person; 6-bed rooms DM160-170. Breakfast included. Reception 7am-9pm.

Pension Geiger, Steinheilstr. 1 (tel. 52 15 56; fax 52 31 54 71). U2: Theresienstr. ("Augustenstr. S.O." exit); go down Theresienstr. toward Kopierladen München, right on Enhuberstr., and left on Steinheilstr. (5min.). Singles DM50-75; doubles DM90-98. Showers DM2. Reception 8am-9pm. Arrive by 6pm or call. Closed Dec. 24-Jan.

CAMPING

Campingplatz Thalkirchen, Zentralländstr. 49 (tel. 723 17 07; fax 724 31 77). Take U3 to "Thalkirchen" and change to bus 57 (20min.); from the stop, cross the street on the left and turn right on the footpath. Groceries. DM8.40 per person, DM5.50-7 per tent, DM8.50 per car. Showers DM2. Laundry. Curfew 11pm. Open mid-Mar. to late Oct.

GERMANY

FOOD

To sink your fangs into an authentic Bavarian lunch, grab a *Brez'n* (pretzel) and spread on *Leberwurst* or cheese (DM4-5), or try *Weißwürste* (white veal sausages served with sweet mustard and a soft pretzel on the side). Munich's gastronomic center is the vibrant **Viktualienmarkt,** 2min. south of Marienpl., with a rainbow of bread, fruit, meat, pastry, cheese, wine, vegetable, and sandwich shops. (Open M-F 9am-6:30pm, Sa 9am-2pm.) The university district off **Ludwigstr.** (U3 or U6: Universität) features cheap and lively restaurants and cafés—hunt around **Schellingstr., Amalienstr.,** and **Türkenstr.** Pick up **groceries** from **Tengelmann,** Bayerstr. 5, straight ahead from the main station (open M-F 8:30am-8pm, Sa 8am-4pm), or **HL Markt,** on Rotkreuzpl. (open M-F 8:30am-8pm, Sa 8am-4pm).

CAFÉS AND RESTAURANTS

■ **Valentinmusäum Café** (tel. 22 32 66), in the Valentinmusäum in the Isartorturm. S1-8: Isartor. Hot milk with honey (DM4.20) and savory *Apfelstrudel* a la mode (DM9.40). Must pay museum admission. Open M-Tu and F-Sa 11am-5:30pm, Su 10am-5:30pm.

Türkenhof, Türkenstr. 78 (tel. 280 02 35). Popular with low-key students. Creative pseudo-Turkish entrees DM10-15. Open M-Th and Su 11am-1am, F-Sa 11am-2am.

Schelling Salon, Schellingstr. 54 (tel. 272 07 88). Lenin, Rilke, and Hitler have racked balls at this pool joint, founded in 1872. Breakfast DM5-9, *Wurst* DM6-7; also serves Bavarian *Knödel*. Restaurant and billiard museum open M-Tu and Th-Su 6:30am-1pm.

News Bar, Amalienstr. 55 (tel. 28 17 87), at Schellingstr. Trendy café teeming with young 'uns. Crêpes DM12-14, pasta with pesto DM12. Open daily 7:30am-1am.

Shoya, Orlandostr. 5 (tel. 29 27 72), opposite the Hofbräuhaus. Japanese rice dishes (DM13-19), teriyaki (DM8-16), and sushi (DM5-30). Open daily 10:30am-midnight.

Beim Sendlmayr, Westenriederstr. 6 (tel. 22 62 19), off the Viktualienmarkt. Anyone craving a *Weißwurst* will love this slice of Bavaria. Specials DM7-25. Beer DM5.60 per 0.5L. Open daily 9am-10pm. Kitchen open M-F 11am-9pm, Sa 8am-4pm.

Marché, Altheimer Eck 14 (tel. 23 08 79 19), between Karlspl. and Marienpl. Monstrous eatery on the top floor has cafeteria-style food and a make-your-own-pizza bar. Downstairs, customers are given food cards before entering a mini-Munich filled with buffet and food stations where chefs prepare every food imaginable. Top floor open daily 11am-10pm, bottom floor open daily 8am-11pm.

BEER, BEER, AND MORE BEER

To most visitors, Munich means beer. The six great Munich labels are Augustiner, Hacker-Pschorr, Hofbräu, Löwenbräu, Paulaner, and Spaten-Franziskaner. **Helles** and **Dunkles** indicate standard but delicious light and dark beers; **Weißbier** is a cloudy, blond beer made from wheat instead of barley; and **Radler** ("cyclist's brew") is half-beer and half-lemon soda. *"Ein Bier, bitte"* will get you a *Maß* (liter; DM8-11); many establishments only serve *Weißbier* in 0.5L sizes. The longest beer festival in the world, Munich's **Oktoberfest** runs, ironically, during the last two weeks in September (Sept. 16-Oct. 1, 2000). The touristy Hofbräu tent at **Theresienwiese** ("Wies'n"; U4-5: Theresienwiese) is the rowdiest—fights often break out.

■ **Hirschgarten,** Hirschgarten 1 (tel. 17 25 91). U1: Rotkreuzplatz; then take streetcar 12 to "Romanplatz" and walk straight to the end of Guntherstr. The largest beer garden in Europe, boisterous and pleasant but somewhat remote. Entrees DM7-25. *Maß* DM8.60. Open daily 9am-midnight. Restaurant closed Mondays Nov.-Feb.

Augustinerkeller, Arnulfstr. 52 (tel. 59 43 93), at Zirkus-Krone-Str. S1-8: Hackerbrücke. Viewed by most Müncheners as the finest beer garden in town. Tasty, enormous *Brez'n* (pretzels; DM5.20), but the real attraction is the delicious, sharp Augustiner beer. *Maß* DM11. Meals DM10-28. Open daily 10am-1am; hot food until 10pm.

Hofbräuhaus, Am Platzl 9 (tel. 22 16 76), 2 blocks from Marienpl. Munich's world-famous beer hall was once reserved for royalty and guests; now it seems reserved for frat boys and drunken tourists. 15-30,000L of beer sold per day. Hitler was proclaimed the first Nazi party chair in the *Festsaal*. *Maß* DM10.40. Open daily 9:30am-midnight.

GERMANY

Augustiner Bräustuben, Landsberger Str. 19 (tel. 50 70 47). S1-8: Hackerbrücke. Heaps of delicious Bavarian food (DM6-20). Beer DM4 per 0.5L. Open daily 10am-midnight.

Chinesischer Turm, (tel. 383 87 27), in the Englischer Garten next to the pagoda. U3 or U6: Giselastr. A fair-weather tourist favorite. *Maß* DM9.50. Open daily 10am-11pm.

👁 SIGHTS

MARIENPLATZ AND ENVIRONS. Numerous sacred stone edifices prickle the area around **Marienplatz,** the social nexus of the city. The **Mariensäule,** an ornate 17th-century column dedicated to the Virgin Mary, was built to commemorate the fact that the powerful Swedes did not destroy the city during the Thirty Years War. The **Glockenspiel** of the neo-Gothic **Neues Rathaus** chimes with jousting knights and dancing coopers daily at 11am, noon, and 5pm; at 9pm, a mechanical watchman marches out and the Guardian Angel escorts the *Münchner Kindl* (Munich Child, the town symbol) to bed. To the right of the Neues Rathaus, the face of the **Altes Rathaus** tower features Munich's changing coats of arms from throughout history, with one notable exception: the post-WWII local government refused to include the swastika-bearing one from the Nazi era. The onion-domed towers of the 15th-century **Frauenkirche,** just northeast of Marienpl., are some of Munich's most notable landmarks. *(Towers open Apr.-Oct. M-Sa 10am-5pm. DM4, students DM2.)*

SOUTH OF MARIENPLATZ. Baroque elements were added to the golden interior of the 11th-century **Peterskirche,** just south of Marienpl., in the 18th century. More than 300 steps scale the tower, dubbed *"Alter Peter"* by locals. *(Rindermarkt and Peterspl. Open M-Sa 9am-7pm, Su 10am-7pm. DM2.50, students DM1.50.)* Mad King Ludwig (of crazy castle fame) rests peacefully with 40-odd other Wittelsbachs in the crypt of the 16th-century Jesuit **Michaelskirche.** *(On Neuhauser Str. Crypt open M-F 9:15am-4:45pm. DM2, students DM1.)* Farther south along Sendlinger Str. lies the Rococo **Asamkirche,** named after the Asam brothers, who promised God that they would build a church if they survived a shipwreck. *(Sendlinger Str. 32.)*

RESIDENZ. The richly decorated rooms of the **Residenz** palace, built from the 14th to 19th centuries, form the material vestiges of the Wittelsbach dynasty. The grounds now contain several museums, the beautiful **Hofgarten,** and a jewel- and crown-filled **Schatzkammer** (treasury). The **Residenzmuseum** comprises the former Wittelsbach apartments and State Rooms, a collection of European porcelain, and a 17th-century court chapel. The walls of the **Ahnengalerie** are hung with 120 "family portraits" that trace the royal lineage in an unusual manner. *(Max-Joseph-Pl. 3. U3-6: Odeonsplatz. Open Tu-Su 10am-4:30pm; DM6, students DM4. Residenzmuseum tours Su and W 11am, Tu and Sa 2pm; DM8, Su DM10. Schatzkammer open Tu-Su 10am-4:30pm; DM6, students DM4. Joint ticket to Schatzkammer and Residenzmuseum DM10, students DM8.)*

SCHLOSS NYMPHENBURG. After 10 years of trying for an heir, Ludwig I celebrated the birth of son Maximilian in 1662 by erecting an elaborate Baroque summer playroom to mimic Louis XIV's. The palace hides a number of treasures, including a two-story granite marble hall, frescoes, and a Chinese lacquer cabinet. Check out Ludwig's "Gallery of Beauties"—whenever a woman caught his fancy, he would have her portrait painted. *(Take streetcar 17 (dir: Amalienburgstr.) to "Schloß Nymphenburg." Palace open Apr.-Sept. Tu-Su 9am-12:30pm and 1-5pm; Oct.-Mar. 10am-12:30pm and 1:30-4pm; DM6, students DM4. Entire complex DM8, students DM5.)*

ENGLISCHER GARTEN. On sunny days, all of Munich turns out to bike, go horseback-riding, or sunbathe at this sprawling park. Nude sunbathing areas (designated "FKK") + *Bratwurst*-fed population = consider yourself warned. **Beer gardens** pepper the park, including one at the **Chinesischer Turm** (see p. 443). Head to the stone bridge on Prinzregentenstr., near the Staatsgalerie Moderner Kunst, to watch Müncheners surf the whitewater rapids of the artificial Eisbach river.

GERMANY

MUSEUMS

Munich is a supreme museum city, and many of the city's offerings would require days for exhaustive perusal. A day pass for entry to all of Munich's museums is sold at the tourist office and at many larger museums (DM30).

KÖNIGSPLATZ (U2: KÖNIGSPLATZ)

Alte Pinakothek, Barerstr. 27 (tel. 23 80 52 16). Commissioned by King Ludwig I, the last of the passionate Wittelsbacher art collectors, this world-renowned hall houses Munich's most precious collection—including works by Titian, da Vinci, Raphael, Dürer, Rembrandt, and Rubens. Open Tu-W and F-Su 10am-5pm, Th 10am-8pm. DM7, students DM4.

Neue Pinakothek, Barerstr. 29 (tel. 23 80 51 95), next to the Alte Pinakothek. Contains sleek space for 18th- to 20th-century works by van Gogh, Klimt, Cézanne, and Manet. Same hours and admission costs as the Alte Pinakothek.

Lenbachhaus, Luisenstr. 33 (tel. 23 33 20 00), around the corner from the Glyptothek. Exhibits Munich cityscapes as well as works by Kandinsky, Klee, and the *Blaue Reiter* school. Open Tu-Su 10am-6pm. DM8, students DM4.

Glyptothek, Königspl. 3 (tel. 28 61 00). Another manifestation of Ludwig I's dream to make Munich a cultural mecca, this museum features 2400-year-old pediment figures from the Temple of Aphaea as well as Etruscan and Roman sculptures. Open Tu-W and F-Su 10am-5pm, Th 10am-8pm. DM6, students DM3.50.

Antikensammlung, Königspl. 1 (tel. 59 83 59), across from the Glyptothek. Flaunts a first-rate flock of vases and the other half of Munich's finest collection of ancient Ancient Greek and Etruscan pottery and jewelry. Open Tu and Th-Su 10am-5pm, W 10am-8pm. DM6, students DM3.50. Joint ticket with Glyptothek DM10, students DM5.

ELSEWHERE IN MUNICH

Deutsches Museum (tel. 217 91), on the Museumsinsel. S1-8: Isartor. One of the world's best museums of science and technology; the planetarium and electrical show will warm any physicist's heart. Open daily 9am-5pm. DM10, students DM4. Planetarium DM3.

Staatsgalerie Moderner Kunst, Prinzregentenstr. 1 (tel. 21 12 71 37), in the Haus der Kunst at the southern tip of the Englischer Garten. U4-5: Lehel. This gallery celebrates 20th-century art from the colorful palettes of the Expressionists to the spare canvases of the Minimalists. Open Tu-W and F-Su 10am-5pm, Th 10am-8pm. DM6, students DM3.50.

Museum für Erotische Kunst, Odeonspl. 8 (tel. 228 35 44). U3-6: Odeonsplatz. For those lonely days when you're 5000km from your beloved (or those uninspired days when you're right next to your beloved), this museum covers all four bases around the world and through time. Open Tu-Su 11am-7pm. DM8, students DM6.

ENTERTAINMENT AND NIGHTLIFE

Munich's streets erupt with bawdy beer halls, rowdy discos, and cliqueish cafés every night. The most zealous parties are **Fasching** (Jan. 7-Mar. 7, 2000), Germany's equivalent of Mardi Gras, and the legendary **Oktoberfest** (see below).

THEATER AND MUSIC

Stages sprinkled throughout the city run from dramatic classics at the **Residenztheater** and **Volkstheater** to comic opera at the **Staatstheater am Gärtnerplatz** to experimental works at the **Theater im Marstall** in Nymphenburg. Small fringe theaters, cabaret stages, art cinemas, and artsy pubs populate **Schwabing.** The *Monatsprogramm* (DM2.50) lists schedules for all of Munich's stages, museums, and festivals. Munich's **Opera Festival** (in July) is held in the ■**Bayerische Staatsoper,** Max-Joseph-Pl. 2, accompanied by a concert series in the Nymphenburg and Schleissheim palaces. (Tel. 21 85 19 20. Standing-room and student tickets DM6-20. Box office open M-F 10am-6pm, Sa 10am-1pm. No performances Aug. to mid-Sept.)

Gasteig Kulturzentrum, Rosenheimerstr. 5, hosts diverse musical performances on the former site of the Bürgerbräukeller, where Adolf Hitler launched his abortive Beer Hall Putsch. (Tel. 48 09 80. Box office in the Glashalle (tel. 54 89 89) open M-F 10am-6pm, Sa 10am-2pm, and 1hr. before curtain.)

GERMANY

NIGHTLIFE

Munich's nightlife is a curious collision of Bavarian *Gemütlichkeit* and trendy *Schicki-Mickis*, club-going German yuppies—expensively dressed, coiffed and sprayed, beautiful, blonde specimens of both sexes. The odyssey begins at Munich's beer gardens and beer halls in the early evenings (see **Beer, Beer, and More Beer**, p. 440). The alcohol keeps flowing at cafés and bars until 1am, when discos and dance clubs take over and throb relentlessly until 4am. A few tips: no tennis shoes, no shorts, and no sandals. **Münchener Freiheit** is the most famous (and most touristy) bar/café district; more low-key is the southwestern section of **Schwabing.** The center of Munich's gay nightlife scene lies within the **"Golden Triangle"** defined by Sendlinger Tor, the Viktualienmarkt/Gärtnerpl. area, and Isartor. Pick up the free, extensive booklet *Rosa Seiten* at **Max und Milian Bookstore,** Ickstattstr. 2, for info on gay nightlife. (Tel. 260 33 20. Open M-F 10:30am-2pm, Sa 11am-4pm.)

Günther Murphy's, Nikolaistr. 9a (tel. 39 89 11). U3 or U6: Giselastr. Good ol' Irish cheer accompanies each serving of scrumptious British and American food (DM9-30). and mug of Guinness (DM5-7.50). Open M-F 5pm-1am, Sa 2pm-3am, Su noon-1am.

Reitschule, Königstr. 34. U3 or U6: Giselastr. Above a club, with windows overlooking a horseback-riding school. Marble tables and a sleek bar. Also a café with a beer garden out back. Very relaxed. *Weißbier* DM6. Breakfast served all day. Open daily 9am-1am.

■ **Kunstpark Ost,** Grafinger Str. 6 (tel. 490 43 50). U5 or S1-8: Ostbahnhof. This huge complex with 20 different venues swarms with young people hitting clubs, concerts, and bars—and dancing the night away. Hours and cover vary—call 49 00 29 28 for info.

Nachtwerk and Club, Landesberger Str. 185 (tel. 578 38 00). Take streetcar 18-19 or bus 83 to "Lautensackstr." These sister clubs spin dance tunes for sweaty crowds. Beer DM4.50 at both places. Open daily 10pm-4am. Cover DM10 for both.

Club Morizz, Klenzestr. 43 (tel. 201 67 76). U1-2: Fraunhofer Str. Reminiscent of certain Casablanca scenes, this relaxed café and bar is frequented by gay men. Cocktails DM13.50-16. Entrees DM18-26. Open M-Th and Su 7pm-2am, F-Sa 7pm-3am.

▍⊁ EXCURSION FROM MUNICH: DACHAU

"Once they burn books, they will end up burning people," wrote German poet Heinrich Heine in 1820. This eerily prophetic statement is posted at the former concentration camp at Dachau, first German concentration camp and the model for the network of 3000 Nazi work and concentration camps, next to a photograph of one of Hitler's book burnings. The camp walls, gas chamber, and crematorium have been restored in a chillingly sparse memorial to the 206,000 prisoners who were interned here from 1933 to 1945. The **museum** examines pre-1930 anti-Semitism, the rise of Nazism, and the lives of prisoners through photographs, documents, and artifacts. Most exhibits are accompanied by short captions in English. (Open Tu-Su 9am-5pm. Films 22min.; screened in English 11:30am and 3:30pm.) Excellent **tours** in English leave from the museum (July daily 12:30pm, Aug.-June Sa-Su 12:30pm; DM5 donation). From Munich, take **S2** (dir: Petershausen) to "Dachau" (20min., DM7), then **bus** 724 (dir: Kraütgarten) or 726 (dir: Kopernikusstr.) from the front of the station to "KZ-Gedenkstätte" (20min., DM1.80).

NUREMBERG (NÜRNBERG)

Although few visible scars remain, Nuremberg is a city inextricably bound to a darker past. The city served as site of the massive annual Nazi party rallies (1933-38) and lent its name to the 1935 Racial Purity Laws; Allies later chose it as the site of the post-WWII war crimes trials in order to foster a sense of justice. Although 90% of the city was reduced to rubble in 1945, the city today is a model of postwar prosperity, known as much for its toy fair and Christmas market, sausages and gingerbread, and association with Albrecht Dürer as for its ties to Nazism.

▍▎▍⊡ PRACTICAL INFO, ACCOMMODATIONS, AND FOOD. Trains chug to

Regensburg (1hr., every hr., DM27-36); Würzburg (1hr., 2-3 per hr., DM28-42); Munich (2hr., 2-3 per hr., DM54-74); Frankfurt (2hr., every hr., DM66-80); Stuttgart

GERMANY

(2½hr., 6 per day, DM35-54); Prague (5hr., 2 per day); and Berlin (5½-6hr., 1-2 per hr., DM137-149). The **tourist office** is in the train station. (Tel. (0911) 233 60; fax 23 36 16 11; www.nuernberg.de. Open M-Sa 9am-7pm.) Check **email** at **Café M@x,** Färberstr. 11, 3rd fl. (Before 3pm DM5 per hr.; after 3pm DM5 per 30min., DM9 per hr. Open M-Sa noon-1am, Su 4pm-midnight.) The friendly **Jugendgästehaus (HI),** Burg 2, is perched in a castle above the city. From the station, cross Frauentorgraben, turn right, walk along the outside of the city walls to Königstor, follow Königstr. through Lorenzerpl. over the bridge to the Hauptmarkt (10min.), head toward the golden fountain on the far left, bear right on Burgstr., and huff and puff up the hill (20min.). (Tel. (0911) 230 93 60; fax 23 09 36 11. 2-bed dorm DM35; singles DM58. Reception 7am-1am. Curfew 1am. Reserve ahead.) Take U2 (dir: Hernhütte) to the end, then bus 21 to "Zum Zelsenkeller" to reach **Jugend-Hotel Nürnberg,** Rathsbergstr. 300. (Tel. (0911) 521 60 92; fax 521 69 54. Singles DM37; doubles DM58; triples DM75. Breakfast DM8. Reception 8am-10pm. Call ahead.) For **Campingplatz im Volkspark Dutzendteich,** Hans-Kalb-Str. 56, behind the stadium, take S2 (dir: Freucht) to "Frankenstadion." (Tel. (0911) 81 11 22. DM9 per person, DM5-10 per tent, DM5 per car. Reception 2-10pm. Open May-Sept. Call ahead.) Nuremberg is famous for its *Rostbratwurst* (sausage); try some at the crowded **Bratwurst Häusle,** Rathauspl. 1, next to the Sebalduskirche. (Open M-Sa 10am-9:30pm.) **Aldi,** near the station on Königstr., has **groceries.** (Open M-F 8:30am-6pm, Sa 8am-2pm.) **Postal code:** 90402.

◪ 🎵 SIGHTS AND ENTERTAINMENT. Allied bombing left little of Nuremberg for posterity; its churches, castle, and buildings have all been reconstructed since the war. The closest part of the Altstadt to the train station is the walled-in **Handwerkhof,** a cottage- and shop-filled tourist trap masquerading as a historical attraction; head up **Königstraße** for the real sights. The Gothic **Lorenzkirche** on Lorenzpl. features a 20-meter-high **tabernacle** whose delicate stone tendrils curl up into the roof vaulting. (Open M-Sa 9am-5pm, Su 1-4pm. Tours in summer M-F 11am and 2pm; in winter M-F 2pm.) Across the river on Hauptmarktpl. are the **Frauenkirche** (open M-Th 8am-6pm, F 8am-5pm, Sa 8am-7:30pm, Su 10am-8pm) and the **Schöner Brunnen** (Beautiful Fountain), with 40 imaginatively carved figures. Walk uphill from the fountain to the **Rathaus,** built between 1616 and 1622 in early Baroque style, with a little Renaissance Classicism thrown in. The **Lochgefängnisse** (dungeons) beneath contain medieval torture instruments. (Open Apr. to mid-Oct. and Dec. M-F 10am-4:30pm, Sa-Su 10am-1pm. Required tour every 30min.; English translation available. DM4, students DM2.) Across from the Rathaus is the Catholic **Sebalduskirche,** which houses the remains of St. Sebaldus for 364 days a year; on the 365th, they're paraded around town. (Open daily June-Aug. 9:30am-8pm; Mar.-May and Sept.-Dec. 9:30am-6pm; Jan.-Feb. 9:30am-4pm.) Atop the hill, the **Kaiserburg** (Emperor's fortress), Nuremberg's symbol, offers the best vantage point of the city. Every Holy Roman Emperor after Konrad III spent at least his first day in office here. (Open daily Apr.-Sept. 9am-noon and 12:45-5pm; Oct.-Mar. 9:30am-noon and 12:45-4pm. Required tours in German 45min., every 30min.; DM9, students DM8. Ask at the tourist office about English-language tours.)

The ruins of **Dutzendteich Park,** site of the Nazi Party Congress rallies of 1934 and 1935 (which each drew more than 500,000 citizens), remind visitors of a darker time in German history. **Zeppelinfield** sits on the far side of the lake, near the massive marble platform from which Hitler addressed throngs. The poles along the field, which once stationed enormous banners, were made famous in Leni Riefenstahl's film *Triumph des Willens* (Triumph of the Will), which immortalized the 1935 rally in one of the most terrifying and enduring depictions of the Fascist aesthetic. The exhibit *Faszination und Gewalt* (Fascination and Terror), in the **Golden Hall** at the rear of the Tribüne, covers the rise of the Third Reich and the war crimes trials. (Open mid-May to Oct. Tu-Su 10am-6pm. DM5, students DM4.) To reach the park, take S2 (dir: Freucht) to "Dutzendteich," take the middle exit, head down the stairs, turn left, turn left 200m later after Strandcafé Wanner, and follow the path.)

Cine Città, Gewerbemuseumspl. 3, packs seven cafés, 12 cinemas, and a disco into a multimedia megaplex. (Open M-Th and Su until 3am, F-Sa until 4am.) **Treib-**

haus, Karl-Grillenberger-Str. 28, in the west part of the Altstadt, south of Westtor, draws an older crowd with killer cocktails and *Milchkaffee* (milk coffee). (Open M-W 8am-1am, Th-F 8am-2am, Sa 9am-2am, Su 9am-1am.)

BAMBERG

Packed with sights but largely overlooked by travelers, this little city on the Regnitz River boasts one of the most beautiful Altstadts in Bavaria. The residents of Bamberg are proud of their picturesque home, and they celebrate by drinking an astounding amount of beer—330 liters per capita annually, the highest consumption rate in the world. The 15th-century **Altes Rathaus** guards the middle of the river like an anchored ship. Stand on one of the two bridges to gaze at the half-timbered, half-Baroque façade with a Rococo tower in between. (Open Tu-Su 9:30am-4:30pm.) Across the river and up the hill, the 11th-century **Dom** (cathedral) contains the 13th-century equestrian statue of the **Bamberger Reiter** (Bamberg Knight), which embodies the chivalric ideal of the medieval warrior-king. (Open Apr.-Oct. daily 8am-6pm; Nov.-Mar. 8am-5pm. Museum DM4, students DM2.) Opposite the cathedral, the **Neue Residenz** boasts lavish furnishings and a primrose garden. Entry to the museum (which houses art from the period of the palace's construction, 1600-1703) includes a tour of the palace's parade rooms. (Open daily Apr.-Sept. 9am-noon and 1:30-5pm; Oct.-Mar. 9am-noon and 1:30-4pm. Last entry 30min. before closing. DM5, students DM4.) As you pass by the 18th-century Baroque houses on your way from the Rathaus to the cathedral, admire the bay window of **Pfahl-plätzchen,** the pink house on the corner of Judenstr., from which the philospher Hegel once peered while editing the proofs of *Phenomenology of Spirit.*

Trains arrive from Nuremberg (1hr., 2-4 per hr., DM8.20); Würzburg (1¼hr., 2 per hr., DM28); and Munich (2½-4hr., 1-2 per hr., DM71-90). To reach the Altstadt from the station, walk down Luitpoldstr., cross the canal, walk straight on Willy-Lessing-Str., turn right at Schönleinspl. onto Lange Str., turn left on Obere Brückestr., which leads through the archway of the Rathaus and across the Regnitz (25-30min.). Once through the Rathaus, take two lefts and recross the Regnitz on the wooden footbridge; the **tourist office,** Geyerwörthstr. 3, is on the right under the arches. (Tel. (0951) 87 11 61; fax 87 19 60. Open Apr.-Oct. M-F 9am-6pm, Sa 9am-3pm, Su 10am-2pm; Nov.-Mar. closed Su.) To reach the **Jugendherberge Wolfsschlucht (HI),** Oberer Leinritt 70, take bus 18 to "Am Regnitzufer" (every 20min., DM1.50). (Tel. (0951) 560 02; fax 552 11. DM20. Breakfast included. Sheets DM5.50. Reception 5-10pm. Curfew 10pm. Reserve ahead. Open Feb. to mid-Dec.) To get from the station to ▓**Maisel-Bräu-Stübl,** Obere Königstr. 38, turn left off Luitpoldstr. before the river (10min.). (Tel./fax (0951) 255 03. Singles DM39; doubles DM70. Breakfast included. Reception 9am-midnight.) **Tengelmann,** Lange Str. 14, has **groceries.** (Open M-F 8:30am-6:30pm, Sa 7:30am-4pm.) **Postal code:** 96052.

BAYREUTH

Once you've turned off Tristanstr. onto Isoldenstr. and passed Walküreg., there will be little doubt that you're in Bayreuth (Buy-ROIT), the adopted home of **Richard Wagner.** Every summer from July 25 to August 28, thousands pour in for the **Bayreuth Festspiele,** a vast and bombastic—in a word, Wagnerian—celebration of the artist himself. Tickets go on sale three years in advance and sell out almost immediately (DM40-300; write to Bayreuther Festspiele, 95402 Bayreuth). The avid fan can tour Wagner's house (Haus Wahnfried), now the **Richard Wagner Museum,** Richard-Wagner-Str. 48. (Open daily Apr.-Oct. 9am-5pm, Tu and Th until 8pm; Nov.-Mar. 10am-5pm. DM4, students DM2.) Bayreuth is an easy daytrip by **train** from Nuremberg (1hr., every hr., DM24.60). The **tourist office,** Luitpoldpl. 9, about four blocks to the left from the station, provides maps and hotel listings. (Tel. (0921) 885 88. Open M-F 9am-6pm, Sa 9:30am-1pm.) To reach the friendly but regimented **Jugendherberge (HI),** Universitätsstr. 28, past the Hofgarten, from the city center, walk down Ludwigstr., turn left on Friedrichstr., veer left on Jean-Paul-Str., which merges with Universitätsstr. (Tel. (0921) 25 12 62; fax 51 28 05. DM20. Breakfast included. Sheets DM5.50. Reception 7am-noon and 5-9:30pm. Lockout 9:30-11am. Strict curfew 10pm. Open Mar. to mid-Dec.) **Postal code:** 95444.

ROMANTIC ROAD (ROMANTISCHE STRASSE)

Between Würzburg and Füssen lies a beautiful countryside of colorful castles, walled cities, elaborate churches, and dense forest. Sensing opportunity, the German tourist industry christened these bucolic backwaters the Romantic Road in 1950, and the region has since become the most visited in Germany.

⌐ GETTING THERE AND GETTING AROUND. Although Deutsche Bahn's **Europabus** is the most popular way to see the Romantic Road, it's also one of the most inflexible—there is only one bus in each direction per day. There are two Europabus routes: the **Frankfurt-Munich** route runs via (from north to south) Würzburg, Rothenburg ob der Tauber, Dinkelsbühl, Nördlingen, and Augsburg; the **Dinkelsbühl-Füssen** route picks up from Dinkelsbühl and makes stops en route at (from north to south) Augsburg, Wieskirche (northbound only), and Hohenschwangau and Neuschwanstein. Pick up schedules at any tourist office. The Europabus is relatively expensive (Frankfurt to Munich DM116; Dinkelsbühl to Hohenschwangau or Füssen DM66), but students and under 26ers get 10% off, while Eurailers get 75% off.

A more economical way to travel the Romantic Road is on the faster and much more frequent **trains,** which run to every town except Dinkelsbühl. The route also provides an excellent opportunity for a **bike** journey, with campgrounds located 10 to 20km apart; drop by any tourist office for cycling maps and campground info.

WÜRZBURG. Surrounded by vineyard slopes and bisected by the Main River, Würzburg is a famous university town and the bustling center of the Franconian wine region as well as a scenic portal to the Romantic Road. The striking 12th-century **Marienburg Fortress,** the symbol of the city, keeps vigil high on a hillside across the Main. Inside, artifacts from the lives of the prince-bishops and a display on the destruction of Würzburg at the end of WWII grace the **Fürstenbau Museum.** Outside the walls of the main fortress is the Baroque castle arsenal, which now houses the **Mainfränkisches Museum,** with statues by Tilman Riemenschneider, the Master of Würzburg. Climb the footpath to the fortress, which starts a short distance from the statue-lined **Alte Mainbrücke,** or take bus 9 from the train station. (Tours depart from the main courtyard Tu-F 11am, 2, and 3pm, Sa-Su every hr. 10am-4pm. Fürstenbaumuseum open Apr.-Sept. Tu-Su 9am-12:30pm and 1-5pm; Oct.-Mar. Tu-Su 10am-12:30pm and 1-4pm; DM4, students DM3. Mainfränkisches Museum open Tu-Su 10am-5pm; Nov.-Mar. closes 4pm; DM3.50, students DM2.) The **Residenz** palace, on Residenzpl., which served as base camp for Würzburg's prince-bishops during the Enlightenment, is a Baroque masterpiece housing the largest ceiling fresco in the world. The **Residenzhofkirche** is simply astounding: the gilded moldings and pink marble place the little church at the apex of Baroque fantasy. (Palace open Tu-Su Apr.-Oct. 9am-5pm; Nov.-Mar. 10am-4pm; DM8, students DM6. Church same hours, except closed daily noon-1pm; free.)

Trains roll in from Rothenburg (1hr., every hr., DM17); Frankfurt (2hr., every hr., DM38); and Munich (2½hr., every hr., DM76). **Europabuses** also go to Rothenburg (DM27) and Munich (DM84). The **tourist office** is in front of the station. (Tel. (0931) 37 24 36. Open M-Sa 10am-6pm.) The ☒**Jugendgästehaus (HI),** Burkarderstr. 44, is across the river from downtown; take streetcar 3 (dir: Heidingsfeld) or 5 (dir: Heuchelhof) to "Löwenbrücke," backtrack, go down the stairs with the *Jugendherberge/Kapelle* sign, turn right, go through the tunnel, and it's on the left. (Tel. (0931) 425 90; fax 41 68 62. DM29. Breakfast included. Reception 8am-10pm. Check-in 2-5:15pm and 6:30-10pm.) **Gasthof Goldener Hahn,** Marktg. 7, is right off the Markt. (Tel. (0931) 519 41; fax 519 61. Singles DM40-80; doubles DM140. Showers DM3.) For **groceries,** hit **Kupsch,** at the end of Kaiserstr. (Open M-F 8:30am-8pm, Sa 8am-4pm.) To sample the region's distinctive wines, contact **Haus des Frankenweins Fränkischer Weinverband,** Krankenkai 1 (tel. (0931) 120 93). **Postal code:** 97070.

ROTHENBURG OB DER TAUBER. Although Rothenburg ob der Tauber is *the* Romantic Roadstop, touched by everyone—and we mean *everyone*—it's probably your only chance to see a walled medieval city without a single modern building, thanks to strict preservation laws. The lantern- and iron-spear-bearing ☜**"night watchman"** leads a nightly **tour** in English that's more entertaining than educational; meet at the Rathaus at 8pm (DM6). On the Marktpl. stands the Renaissance **Rathaus,** whose 60m tower affords a nice view of town. (Rathaus open daily 8am-6pm; free. Tower open Apr.-Oct. daily 9:30am-12:30pm and 1-5pm; Nov.-Mar. M-F 9:30am-12:30pm, Sa-Su noon-3pm; DM1.) The **Jakobikirche,** Klosterg. 15, is famed for its altar by Tilman Riemenschneider, its 5500-pipe organ, and its 14th-century stained-glass windows. (Open Apr.-Oct. M-F 9am-5:30pm, Su 10:30am-5:30pm; Dec. noon-2pm and 4-5pm. DM2.50, students DM1.) The disturbing yet incredibly fascinating **Medieval Crime Museum,** Burgg. 3, houses exhibits on torture instruments and "eye for an eye" jurisprudence. (Open daily Apr.-Oct. 9:30am-6pm; Nov. and Jan.-Mar. 2-4pm; Dec. 10am-4pm. DM5, students DM4.) Head to Käthe Wohlfahrt's **Christkindlmarkt** (Christ Child Market), Herrng. 2, and **Weihnachtsdorf** (Christmas Village), Herrng. 1, to explore Rothenburg's obsession with Christmas. (Open M-F 9am-6pm, Sa 10am-4pm; Easter-Dec. also Su 10am-6pm.)

Trains arrive at Steinach from Würzburg (30min., every hr., DM15) and Munich (2hr., every hr., DM60); change there for Rothenburg (15min.). The **Europabus** leaves from the Hotel Rothenburg Hut, across the street from the station. To reach the **tourist office,** Marktpl. 2, go left from the station and bear right on Ansbacher Str. (15min.). (Tel. (09861) 404 92; fax 868 07. Open May-Sept. M-F 9am-12:30pm and 1-6pm, Sa-Su 10am-3pm; Nov.-Apr. M-F 9am-12:30pm and 1-5pm, Sa 10am-1pm.) To get from the tourist office to the fantastic **Jugendherberge Rossmühle (HI),** Mühlacker 1, go left down Obere Schmiedg. and look for the small, white *Jugendherberge* sign to the right (10min.). (Tel. (09861) 941 60; fax 94 16 20; email jhrothen@aol.com. DM22-27. Breakfast included. Sheets DM5.50. Check-in until 10pm.) You're almost obligated to try Rothenburg's heart-stopping *Schneeballen* (snowballs), large balls of sweet dough fried and then dipped in chocolate, nuts, and powdered sugar, with sweet marzipan or amaretto centers. Wash them down with milk from **Kapsch supermarket,** on Röderg., inside the city wall as you enter town. (Open M-F 8:30am-6:30pm, Sa 8am-1pm.) **Postal code:** 91541.

DINKELSBÜHL AND NÖRDLINGEN. Forty kilometers south of Rothenburg, the historic town of **Dinkelsbühl** boasts medieval half-timbered houses, a climbable 16th-century church tower, and a navigable town wall with gateways, towers, and moats. Regional **buses** go from the town's main stop at Am Stauferwall to Rothenburg (M-F 9 per day, Sa-Su 1-3 per day; transfer at Dombühl or Feuchtwangen) and Nördlingen (M-F 7 per day, Sa-Su 4-5 per day); the **Europabus** (see p. 446) also serves Dinkelsbühl. From the stop, walk right toward the city walls and turn right on Nördlinger Str. to reach the **tourist office,** on the Marktpl. (Tel. (09851) 902 40; fax 902 79. Open Apr.-Nov. 7 M-F 9am-noon and 2-6pm, Sa 10am-1pm and 2-4pm, Su 10am-1pm; Nov. 8-Mar. M-F 9am-noon and 2-5pm, Sa 10am-1pm.) From there, head right up Nördlinger Str., right on Bahnhofstr., and left on Koppeng. to snooze at the **Jugendherberge (HI),** Koppeng. 10. (Tel. (09851) 95 09; fax 48 74. DM18. Breakfast included. Sheets DM5.50. Reception 5-10pm. Curfew 10pm. Open Mar.-Oct.)

The only town in Germany whose original walls are complete and can be navigated in their entirety, **Nördlingen** is built on the spot where a meteorite crashed some 15 million years ago. Climb up the 90m Gothic bell tower **Daniel** for a hawk's-eye view of the town below. (Open daily Apr.-Oct. 9am-8pm; Nov.-Mar. 9am-5:30pm. DM3.) **Trains** arrive from Augsburg (1hr., DM19.40) and Nuremberg (1¾hr., DM35); change at Donauwörth for both. **Buses** also run from Dinkelsbühl to Nördlingen (45min., 8 per day, DM7.90). The **Europabus** (see p. 446) also stops daily at Nördlingen's Rathaus. The **tourist office** finds rooms for free. (Tel. (09081) 43 80; fax 841 13. Open M-Th 9am-6pm, F 9am-4:30pm, Sa 9:30am-12:30pm.) The **Jugendherberge,** Kaiserwiese 1, is just outside the city walls on the north side of town. From the station, turn right on Bgm. Reigerstr., take your first left through the city walls, and head right on Bödingerstr. from the Marktpl. out of the city walls; it's on your right in the parking lot one cross-street beyond the walls. (Tel. (09081) 841 09; after 8pm 79 93 90. DM18. Reception 8-10am and 4:30-7pm.)

GERMANY

AUGSBURG. Founded by Caesar Augustus in 15 BC, Augsburg was the financial center of the Holy Roman Empire and a major commercial city by the end of the 15th century. The town owed its success and prestige mainly to the Fuggers, an Augsburg banking family; Jakob Fugger "the Rich," personal financier to the Hapsburg Emperors, founded the **Fuggerei** quarter, the first welfare housing project in the world, in 1519; elderly residents today still only pay the equivalent of a "Rhine Guilder" (DM1.72) in rent annually. To reach the Fuggerei from the Rathaus, walk behind the Perlachturm tower on Perlachberg, which becomes Barfüsserstr. and finally Jakoberstr., and turn right under the archway. Fugger was also responsible for building the **Fugger Haus**, Maximilianstr. 36-38, where the 1518 dispute between Martin Luther and Cardinal Cajetan ensured church schism. Luther stayed in the **St. Anna Kirche**, on Annastr. near Königspl., where he convinced Prior Frosch to pioneer the Reformation in Augsburg. **Bertolt Brecht's** birthplace was renovated in 1998, on the 100th anniversary of his birth; the **museum** within chronicles his life through photos, letters, and poetry. From the station, head up Prinzregentenstr. and turn right on tiny Schmiedg. (Open daily 10am-5pm. DM2.50, students DM1.50.)

Trains arrive from Munich (30min., 3 per hr., DM25); Stuttgart (1¾hr., 2 per hr., DM66); Nuremberg (2hr., 2 per hr., DM45); and Würzburg (2hr., every hr., DM76). The infamous **Europabus** (see p. 446) stops at the train station. The **tourist office**, Bahnhofstr. 7, 300m in front of the station, books rooms (DM30-40) for a DM3 fee. (Tel. (0821) 50 20 70; fax 502 07 45. Open M-F 9am-6pm.) On weekends, head to the **branch** on Rathauspl.; from the station, walk to the end of Bahnhofstr., turn left at Königspl. on Annastr., take the third right, and Rathauspl. is on the left. (Tel. (0821) 502 07 24. Open M-F 9am-6pm, Sa 10am-4pm, Su 10am-1pm.) To get from the station to the **Jugendherberge (HI)**, Beim Pfaffenkeller 3, walk up Prinzregentenstr. as it curves to the right, turn left at Karolinenstr., turn right at the cathedral on Innere Pfaffeng., and bear left on Beim Pfaffenkeller. (Tel. (0821) 339 03; fax 15 11 49. DM25, under 27 DM20. Reception 7-9am and 5-10pm. Curfew 1am. Open Feb.-Dec. Call ahead). Stock up on **groceries** at **Penny Markt,** Maximilianstr. 71, to the left of the Rathaus. (Open M-F 8:30am-7pm, Sa 8am-2pm.) **Postal code:** 86150.

BAVARIAN ALPS (BAYERISCHE ALPEN)

Visible on a clear day from Munich are a series of snow-covered peaks and forested slopes spanning from southeastern Germany across Austria and into Italy. It was in this rugged and magical terrain that Ludwig II of Bavaria, the certifiably batty "Fairy Tale King," chose to build his dramatic castles; it's also here that even today people authentically, even nonchalantly, wear *Lederhosen.*

FÜSSEN. Curled up at the base of the Alpine foothills at the southern end of the Romantic Road, Füssen provides easy access to Mad King Ludwig's famed **Königsschlösser** (royal castles). Reminders of the prince-bishop's medieval reign linger in Füssen's architectural wonders. The inner walls of the **Hohes Schloß** (High Castle) courtyard scream royalty with arresting *trompe l'oeil* windows and towers. The **Staatsgalerie** in the castle shelters a collection of regional late Gothic and Renaissance art. (Open Tu-Su Apr.-Oct. 11am-4pm; Nov.-Mar. 2-4pm. DM3, students DM2.) Just below the castle rests the 8th-century Baroque **St. Mangkirche,** with a frescoed 10th-century subterranean crypt. (Tours July-Sept. Tu and Th 4pm, Sa 10:30am; May-June and Oct. Tu 4pm and Sa 10:30am; Jan.-Apr. Sa 10:30am.) Inside the **Annenkapelle,** macabre skeleton-decked panels depict the *Totentanz* (death dance), a public frenzy of despair that overtook Europe during the plague. Northeast of Füssen, torrents of light bathe the splendid Rococo pilgrimage church **Wieskirche** (Church in the Meadows). (Open daily 8am-7pm.) **Buses** run to the Wieskirche from the Füssen station (50min., 3 per day, round-trip DM15.20).

Trains arrive in Füssen from Munich (2hr., every hr., DM35) and Augsburg (2hr., every 2hr., DM21). To get from the station to the **tourist office,** Kaiser-Maximilian-Pl. 1, walk the length of Bahnhofstr. and head straight on Luitpoldstr. to the big yellow building. (Tel. (08362) 938 50; fax 93 85 20; www.fuessen.de. Open M-F 8am-

LUD-WIGGING OUT After Queen Marie bore Maximilian II two healthy sons, there was no reason to expect the fall of the Bavarian royal family—but it was soon to come. Otto, the younger son, developed schizophrenia as a young adult, leaving Ludwig to carry on the family name. In 1864, Ludwig assumed the throne at the tender age of 18, a shockingly handsome lad naïve in the world of politics. A zany visionary and fervent Wagner fan, he squandered his private fortune (and bankrupted Bavaria) creating majestic castles that soared into the Alpine skies, physical manifestations of his own fantasyland. In 1886, a band of upstart nobles and bureaucrats deposed Ludwig in a coup d'état and imprisoned him in Schloß Berg on the Starnberger See. Three days later, the King and a loyal advisor were found dead in the lake amidst mysterious circumstances—suicide? murder? a failed escape attempt? The enigma of Ludwig's life, death, and self-fashioned dream-world continues to captivate the imagination. You can step into Ludwig's batty mind at Schloß Neuschwanstein (see p. 449), Schloß Linderhof (see p. 449), and Schloß Herrenchiemsee (see p. 449).

6pm, Sa 9am-noon.) The **Jugendherberge (HI)**, Mariahilferstr. 5, is blessed by a lovely location and friendly staff. Turn right from the station and follow the railroad tracks (10min.). (Tel. (08362) 77 54; fax 27 70. DM20; add DM1.50 tax. Sheets DM5.50. Reception 7-9am, 5-7pm, and 8-10pm. Reserve ahead. Open Dec.-Oct.) Pick up cheap grub at **Plus supermarket,** on the corner of Bahnhofstr. and Luitpoldstr. (Open M-F 8:30am-7pm, Sa 8am-2pm.) **Postal code:** 87629.

NEUSCHWANSTEIN AND HOHENSCHWANGAU. Ludwig II's desperate building spree across Bavaria peaked with the glitzy ■**Schloß Neuschwanstein,** built from 1869 to 1886, now Germany's most clichéd tourist attraction and the inspiration for Disneyland's Cinderella Castle. The young Ludwig II lived a mere 173 days within the extravagant edifice. The completed chambers (63 remain unfinished) include a Byzantine throne room, a small artificial grotto, and an immense *Sängersaal* (singer's hall) built expressly for Wagnerian opera performances. Ludwig grew up in (and watched his own creation of Neuschwanstein being created from) the bright-yellow, neo-Gothic **Schloß Hohenschwangau** across the way. Hohenschwangau is a bit less touristed than its cousin, but the rooms actually appear to have been lived in. The castle houses Wagner's piano and a loaf of bread from the 1830s. (Both open Apr.-Sept. 9am-5:30pm, Oct.-Mar. 10am-4pm. Mandatory tours of each castle 30min., DM12, students DM9. Frequent tours in German; tours in English commence whenever 20 English speakers build up.) Consider spending the rest of the day **hiking** around the spectacular environs. For the fairy godmother of all views, hike up path 33 from Neuschwanstein to the **Marienbrücke,** which spans the dramatic **Pöllat gorge** behind the castle (10min.). Continue uphill from here for a knockout overview of the castle and nearby lake (1hr.).

Buses run to the castles (dir: Königsschlösser) from Füssen's train station (every hr., DM2.50). Separate paths lead up from the drop-off point to each castle. The less-touristed route to Hohenschwangau is path 17, which starts from the left side of the information booth and meanders through the moss-covered forest (10min.). Path 32 from Car Park D is the shortest but steepest trail up to Neuschwanstein (25min.). A *Tagesticket* (DM13) entitles castle-hoppers to unlimited bus travel on regional buses (including the ride to Linderhof); buy it from the bus driver.

LINDERHOF. East of Neuschwanstein and Hohenschwangau lies the exquisite Schloß Linderhof, Ludwig II's compact hunting palace, which (like Schloß Herrenchiemsee) reflected Ludwig's obsession with France's Louis XIV (the Sun King). Although the castle lacks Neuschwanstein's pristine exterior, it's bathed in gold. The royal bedchamber, the largest room in the castle, is unbelievably lush, with gold leaf and a colossal, 454kg crystal chandelier. Even more impressive than the palace is the surrounding **park.** Paths originating at the swan lake at the park entrance weave through the ornately landscaped grounds, which include an enormous, artificial **grotto** swathed in red and blue floodlights (good taste was per-

GERMANY

> **HYPERTRAVEL TO THE CASTLES.** Seeing all three of the Royal Castles during a daytrip from Munich requires some fancy footwork and luck with connections (and can only be done M-F). Take the 6:50am train from Munich to Buchloe, then transfer to the 7:46am to Füssen. After arriving in Füssen at 8:57am, hop on the 9:35am bus to the Königsschlösser. Arriving at 9:43am, you'll have 3½hr. to fight through the lines at Hohenschwangau and Neuschwanstein before catching bus 1084 at 1:13pm to Schloß Linderhof (change at Steingaden and Oberammergau). Indulge in the surrounding opulence until 5:05pm, when it'll be time to catch bus 9606 (dir: Füssen) to "Oberammergau Post/Bahnhof." At 5:25pm, you'll arrive at the Oberammergau train station with plenty of time to catch the 6:07pm train to Murnau, where you'll change at 6:58pm and hopefully grab a *Löwenbräu* at 7:55pm back in Munich. Double check your schedule with a timetable before departing. A simpler and more advisable option, particularly if you don't have a railpass, is to sign on with EurAide for a castle tour (see p. 436).

haps not one of Ludwig's strengths) and the **Hunding-Hütte,** modeled after a scene in Wagner's *Die Walküre.* (Castle open Apr.-Sept. daily 9am-12:15pm and 12:45-5:30pm; Oct.-Mar. 10am-12:15pm and 12:45-4pm. Apr.-Sept. DM9, students DM6; Oct.-Mar. DM7, students DM4. Park free.) **Bus** 9606 connects to Linderhof from Oberammergau (20min., every hr. 9:45am-6:15pm, round-trip DM9.20; last return bus 6:45pm). Oberammergau is accessible by **bus** from Füssen (1½hr.) and by **train** from Munich (1¾hr., 1-2 per hr., DM24; change at Murnau).

BERCHTESGADEN. At the easternmost point of the Bavarian Alps, Berchtesgaden profits from a sinister and overtouristed attraction—Hitler's mountaintop **Kehlsteinhaus,** dubbed "Eagle's Nest" by the American troops who occupied it after WWII. Although it's little more than a restaurant up top, the view from the 1834m peak is spectacular on a clear day. Take the "Oversalzburg, Kehlstein" bus 9538 (June-Oct. every 45min., off-season less regularly; DM5.80) from the train station to "Oversalzburg, Hintereck"; while waiting for bus 9549 to "Kehlstein Parkpl., Eagle's Nest" at Hintereck, buy your combined ticket for the second leg of the bus ride and the elevator ride up at the other end (every 30min. 9:30am-4pm, DM20). Reserve your spot for the return bus when you get off (allow at least an hour to wander around on top). A 35-minute English-language **tour** (DM6) is available daily at 10:30am; meet at the tunnel entrance to the elevator. Back in the Altstadt, the Berchtesgaden **Schloß,** a monastic priory until Bavarian rulers appropriated the property, now houses a mixture of art and weaponry. (Open Su-F 10am-noon and 2-4pm; Oct.-Easter M-F 10am-1pm and 2-5pm; last entry 4pm. DM7, students DM3.50.)

Hourly **trains** (tel. (08652) 50 74) arrive from Salzburg (1hr., DM12.20) and Munich (2½hr., DM48); change at Freilassing. The **tourist office,** Königsseerstr. 2, opposite the station, has tips on trails in the Berchtesgaden National Park. (Tel. (08652) 96 71 50; fax 633 00. Open M-F 8am-5pm, Sa 9am-noon.) To get from the station to the rowdy **Jugendherberge (HI),** Gebirgsjägerstr. 52, take bus 9539 (dir: Strub Kaserne; DM2.40) to "Jugendherberge." Or head right from the station, left for 15min. on Ramsauer Str., right on Gmündbrücke, and left up the steep gravel path following the signs. (Tel. (08652) 943 70; fax 94 37 37. DM23. Breakfast included. Sheets DM5.50. Reception 8am-noon and 5-7pm. Check-in until 10pm. Curfew midnight. Closed Nov.-Dec. 26.) Pick up **groceries** at **Edeka Markt,** Königseer Str. 22. (Open M-F 7:30am-6pm, Sa 7:30am-noon.) **Postal code:** 83471.

⚡ HIKING NEAR BERCHTESGADEN: KÖNIGSSEE AND RAMSAU. From Berchtesgaden, the 5.5km path to the **Königsee**—which winds through fields of flowers, across bubbling brooks, and past several beer gardens—affords a heartstopping view of the Alps. From the Berchtesgaden train station, walk across the street, take a right and then a quick left over the bridge, turn left at the stone wall onto the gravel path, and follow the signs. Alternatively, take bus 9541 (round-trip DM6.80) from near the train station to Königsee. Once you arrive, walk down

Seestr. and look for the **Nationalpark Informationstelle** to your left, which has hiking info. Continue down Seestr. to reach the dock, where **Bayerische Seen Schiffahrt** cruises depart for points throughout the Königssee (DM22.50). From **Ramsau,** 20km southwest of Berchtesgaden, a vast network of well-marked hiking trails radiates throughout the surrounding Alpine landscape and into the **Berchtesgaden National Park.** The **tourist office,** Im Tal 2, has trail maps and hiking info. (Tel. (08657) 98 89 20; fax 772. Open M-F 8am-noon and 1:15-5pm, Sa 9am-noon.) From Berchtesgaden, bus 9546 (DM3.80) runs hourly to Ramsau.

THE CHIEMSEE

For almost 2000 years, artists and musicians have marveled at the picturesque islands, mountains, and forests of the Chiemsee region. **Herreninsel** and **Fraueninsel** are the two inhabited islands on Lake Chiem; the former is home to **Königsschloß Herrenchiemsee,** the third and last of Mad King Ludwig's "fairy-tale castles."

PRIEN AM CHIEMSEE. Prien, on the northwestern corner of the Chiemsee, is a good base from which to see the islands. **Trains** arrive from Salzburg (40min., every hr., DM26.40) and Munich (1hr., every hr., DM36). The **tourist office,** Alte Rathausstr. 11, finds private rooms (DM30-45) for free. (Tel. (08051) 690 50; fax 69 05 40. Open M-F 8:30am-6pm, Sa 9am-noon.) To get to the **Jugendherberge (HI),** Carl-Braun-Str. 66, from the station, head right on Seestr. and turn left on Staudenstr., which turns into Carl-Braun-Str. (15min.). (Tel. (08051) 687 70; fax 68 77 15. DM25. Breakfast included. Sheets DM5.50. Reception 8-9am, 5-7pm, and 9:30-10pm. Lockout 9am-1pm. Curfew 10pm. Open early Feb. to Nov.) For **Campingplatz Hofbauer,** Bernauer-str. 110, turn left on Seestr. from the station, turn left at the next intersection, and follow Bernauerstr. out of town (30min.). (Tel. (08051) 41 36; fax 626 57. DM10.50 per person, DM10 per tent and car. Showers included. Open Apr.-Oct.) Grab **groceries** at **HL Markt,** Seestr. 11. (Open M-F 8am-8pm, Sa 8am-4pm.)

HERRENINSEL AND FRAUENINSEL. On **Herreninsel** (Gentlemen's Island), the **Königsschloß Herrenchiemsee** is as fabulously overwrought as only King Ludwig II could manage. Ludwig bankrupted Bavaria building this place—a shameless attempt to be bigger, better, and more extravagant than Versailles. A few stark, barren rooms (abandoned after the cash ran out) contrast greatly with the lavish, excessively ornate completed portion of the castle. (Open daily Apr.-Sept. 9am-5pm; Oct.-Mar. 10am-4pm. Obligatory tour DM8, students DM5. German tours every 10min.; tours in English 10:30, 11:30am, 2, 3, and 4pm.) **Fraueninsel** (Ladies' Island), home to the still-extant nunnery that complemented the former monastery on Herreninsel, offers subtler pleasures. Its miniature world has no room for cars; only footpaths wander through this village of fishermen and nuns. The 8th-century Merovingian **Cross of Bischofhofen** is on display above the **Torhalle** (Gate), the oldest surviving part of the cloister. (Open mid-June to Sept. daily 11am-6pm; Oct. to mid-June closed Su. DM4, students DM1.50.) **Ferries** run from Prien to Herreninsel and Fraueninsel (every hr. 6:40am-7:30pm, DM10-12.50). To get to the ferry port, hang a right from the main entrance of the Prien train station and follow Seestr. for 20min., or hop on the green *Chiemseebahn* steam train from the station (departs 9:40am-6:15pm, round-trip DM5.50, round-trip including ship passage DM17).

REGENSBURG

The first capital of Bavaria, the administrative seat of the Holy Roman Empire, and later the site of the first German parliament, Regensburg is packed with history. The impotent (Holy Roman) Imperial Parliament, the first of many similar bodies in German history, lives on in the **Reichstagsmuseum** within the Gothic **Altes Rathaus.** (Tours in German every 30min.-1hr. Tours in English May-Sept. M-Sa 3:15pm. DM5, students DM2.50.) The high-Gothic **Dom St. Peter,** just a few blocks away on Dompl., dazzles with richly colored stained glass. Inside the cathedral, the **Domschatz** contains a priceless collection of gold and jewels purchased by the Regensburg bishops back in the days of indulgences and economic exploitation by the clergy.

GERMANY

(Cathedral open daily Apr.-Oct. 6:30am-6pm; Nov.-Mar. 6:30am-5pm; free. Tours 1¾hr.; May-Oct. M-Sa 10, 11am, and 2pm, Su noon and 2pm; Nov.-Apr. M-Sa 11am, Su noon; DM4, students DM2. Domschatz open Apr.-Nov. Tu-Sa 10am-5pm, Su noon-5pm; Dec.-Mar. F-Sa 10am-4pm, Su noon-4pm; DM3, students DM1.50.)

Trains chug to Nuremburg (1-1½hr., 1-2 per hr.); Passau (1-1½hr., every hr.); and Munich (1½hr., every hr., DM38). To get from the station to the **tourist office,** in the Altes Rathaus on Rathauspl., walk down Maximilianstr., turn left on Grasg. (which turns into Obermünsterstr.), turn right at the end on Obere Bachg., and continue on Untere Bachg. (Tel. (0941) 507 44 10; fax 507 44 19. Open M-F 8:30am-6pm, Sa 9am-4pm, Su 9:30am-2:30pm; Apr.-Oct. open Su until 4pm.) To get from the station to the **Jugendherberge (HI),** Wöhrdstr. 60, walk to the end of Maximilianstr., turn right at the *Apotheke* on Pflugg., turn immediately left at the *Optik* sign on tiny Erhardig., take the steps down at the end, walk left over the Eiserne Brücke (bridge), and continue on Wöhrdstr. (25min.). (Tel. (0941) 574 02. DM28; under 27 only. Breakfast included. Reception 6am-11:30pm.) ▧**Wurstküche,** Thundorfer Str., next to the Steinerne Brücke, is a great beer garden. (Open M-Sa 9am-6pm, Su 10am-6pm.) **Tengelmann supermarket,** Untere Brückg. 2, is on the way to the tourist office from the train station. (Open M-F 8am-8pm, Sa 7:30am-4pm.) **Postal code:** 93047.

PASSAU

At the confluence of the Danube, Inn, and Ilz Rivers, this beautiful Baroque *Dreiflüssestadt* (three-river city) embodies the ideal Old World European city. Its Baroque architecture peaks in the sublime **Stephansdom** (St. Stephen's Cathedral), where hundreds of cherubs sprawl across the ceiling and the world's largest **church organ** (17,774 pipes) looms above the choir. (Open M-Sa 8-11am and 12:30-6pm. Free. Organ concerts May-Oct. M-Sa noon; DM4, students DM2. Also Th 7:30pm; DM10, students DM5.) Behind the cathedral, the **Domschatz** (cathedral treasury) of the **Residenz** houses an extravagant collection of gold and tapestries. (Open May-Oct. M-Sa 10am-4pm. DM2, students DM1.) The 13th-century Gothic **Rathaus** contains a stunning *Trunksaal* (Great Hall). (Open Apr.-Oct. 10am-4pm. DM2, students DM1.) Over the Luipoldbrücke (bridge) is the former palace of the Bishopric, the **Veste Oberhaus** (open early Apr.-Oct. Tu-Su 9am-5pm), now home to the **Cultural History Museum** (open Mar.-Jan. Tu-F 9am-5pm, Sa-Su 10am-6pm; DM7, students DM4).

Trains (tel. (0851) 194 19) arrive from Regensburg (1-2hr., every hr., DM32); Nuremberg (2hr., every 2hr., DM60); Munich (2hr., every hr., DM52); Vienna (3hr., 1-2 per hr.); and Frankfurt (4½hr., every 2hr., DM74-131). To get to the **tourist office,** Rathauspl. 3, walk right down Bahnhofstr., downhill across Ludwigspl. to Ludwigstr., which becomes Rindermarkt, Steinweg, and finally Große Messerg.; continue straight on Schusterg. and turn left on Schrottg. to reach Rathauspl. The **branch** across from the station has maps. (Tel. (0851) 95 59 80; fax 351 07. Open Apr.-Oct. M-F 8:30am-6pm, Sa-Su 10am-2pm; Nov.-Mar. M-Th 8:30am-5pm, F 8:30am-4pm.) The **Jugendherberge (HI),** Veste Oberhaus 125, is in a medieval castle perched high above the Danube. Cross the suspension bridge just downstream of the Rathaus, *ignore* the sign pointing up the steps and instead continue right along the curve through the lefthand tunnel (skeptics will pay an extra 20min. of steep hell for their disbelief), head up the steep cobblestoned driveway to your left, bear left, and take a right to the hostel. (Tel. (0851) 413 51; fax 437 09. DM22. Breakfast included. Sheets DM5.50. Check-in 4-11:30pm. Curfew 11:30pm.) The **Rotel Inn** has wide beds in tiny rooms overlooking the Danube. Walk down the steps in front of the station and through the tunnel toward the blue head of this hotel, built in the shape of a sleeping man. (Tel. (0851) 951 60; fax 951 61 00. Singles DM30; doubles DM50. Breakfast DM8. Reception 24hr.) Grab cheap grub at **Tengelmann supermarket,** on Ludwigstr. at Grabeng. (Open M-F 8am-8pm, Sa 7:30am-4pm.) **Postal code:** 94032.

GERMANY

GREECE (Ελλας)

US$1 = 310.14DR (GREEK DRACHMAS)	100DR = US$0.34
CDN$1 = 209.44DR	100DR = CDN$0.48
UK£1 = 498.64DR	100DR = UK£0.20
IR£1 = 414.36DR	100DR = IR£0.24
AUS$1 = 201.02DR	100DR = AUS$0.50
NZ$1 = 163.92DR	100DR = NZ$0.61
SAR1 = 50.71DR	100DR = SAR1.97
EUR€1 = 326.11DR	100DR = EUR€0.31

PHONE CODE | Country code: 30. International dialing prefix: 00.

Greece is known to its celebrants less as a place than as a state of soul. The land and light of Greece fueled and inspired the imaginations of its ancient poets and philosophers, upon whose genius much of Western civilization was founded—the Western imagination hasn't been the same since, sometime between Homer and Plato, they came upon the notion of the human soul. Today, this mixture of art and essence, at once timeless and heavy with millennia of history, calls countless visitors to commune with the unearthed temples, theaters, palaces, and stadia of lost civilizations.

Over the centuries, Greece has occupied a unique position at the crossroads of Europe and Asia. The relics of Crete's Minoan civilization betray the influence of flowering contemporary cultures in Egypt and Babylon. The Byzantine era saw the preservation—in the bushy beards and long black robes of Orthodox priests—of the mores of an Eastern empire. Four hundred years under the Ottoman Turks left a certain spice in Greek food, an Oriental flair in the strains of its *bouzouki* music, and a skyline of minarets. Greece emerged independent in 1821 under the dual veneer of Classical Athens and Imperial Byzantium, but Ottoman folkways persist.

The culture that brought us the Doctrine of the Mean is today a land of extremes: old meets new, east meets west, and monk meets hedonist. The memory of Dionysus, god of the vine, still fuels the island circuit—a blur of sun, sand, and sex, framed in the blues of the clear sky and the golds of the endless beach. Back from the shore, in Greece's austere hills, monks and hermits live the old life in structures that have aged a millennium.

Greece harbors one of the heaviest tourist industries in Europe, surrounding many of its treasured sights with camera-flashing hordes and cheap junkshops. Today, as the country moves toward the European Monetary Union and overhauls its infrastructure in preparation for the 2004 Summer Olympics in Athens, development has accelerated at a blistering pace. Still, when you climb above the resorts and whirring tour buses—when you hear the wind's lonely, persistent whistle—you'll know that Greece remains oracles' ground.

For unparalleled coverage of Greece, look into the ancient writings of Pausanias; the only thing better is *Let's Go: Greece 2000*.

DISCOVER GREECE

Launch your Greek adventure in the urban sprawl of **Athens** (p. 458), with visits to the Acropolis and the National Museum, a daytrip to Cape Sounion, a sunset atop Lycavittos, and a night out clubbing. Then swing south into the Peloponnese and get dramatic at the theater of **Epidavros** (p. 469) before strolling amongst the mansions of **Nafplion** (p. 469). Dash west to **Olympia** (p. 466) to wrestle amongst the ruins, and then ferry from Patras to **Corfu** (p. 476), an isle lovingly immortalized by both cultural luminaries (Edward Lear, Oscar Wilde) and intrepid party-goers. Back on the continent, soak up culture in Greece's second city, **Thessaloniki** (p. 470), where trendy shops neighbor some of Byzantium's most precious ruins. Climb the cliffside monasteries of the **Meteora** (p. 474), then switch gears to commune with the gods of **Mt. Olympus** (p. 474). Forget the psychic hotline: find your fate at the **Oracle of Delphi** (p. 465). Ferry from Athens all the way down to **Crete**, home to the mythical Minotaur (**Knossos;** p. 485), Europe's largest gorge, **Samaria** (see p. 486), and some of the Mediterranean's most beautiful beaches. Then hop over to the Cyclades for a rest on **Santorini** (p. 483), whose white cliffside buildings are modern Greece's most singularly iconic image. Party for days and nights on **Mykonos** (p. 480), then repent your sins with a visit to the Temple of Apollo on **Delos** (p. 480).

GETTING THERE AND GETTING AROUND

BY PLANE. Olympic Airways, Syngrou 96-100, 11741 Athens (tel. (01) 926 72 51), is Greece's national airline. In recent years, Olympic's domestic *(esoteriko)* service has increased appreciably; from Athens, an hour's flight (US$60-90) can get you to almost any island in Greece. Even in low-season, more remote destinations (Limnos, Hios) are serviced several times weekly, while more developed areas (like Thessaloniki and Crete) may have several flights per day. Those under 24 enjoy a 25% discount. Make sure to reserve tickets one week in advance.

BY TRAIN. Greece is served by a number of international train routes that connect Athens, Thessaloniki, and Larissa to most European cities. However, the Greek rail system is one of Europe's most antiquated and least efficient. **Hellenic Railways Organization (OSE)** connects Athens to other major Greek cities, but service is limited and sometimes uncomfortable, and no lines go to the western coast. Greece's new, express, air-conditioned intercity trains, although slightly more expensive and rare, are worth the higher price. **Eurail** is valid in Greece.

BY BUS. The long-distance bus networks of Greece are more extensive, efficient, and often more comfortable than trains. Most buses are run through **KTEL**. Smaller towns may use cafés as bus stops; ask for a schedule. Confirm your destination with the driver, as many signs are mislabeled. Along the road, little blue signs marked with white buses or the word "ΣΤΑΣΗ" indicate stops, but drivers usually stop anywhere if you flag them down. Let the driver know ahead of time where you want to get off, but if you see your stop fly by unheeded, just shout "*Stasi!*"

BY FERRY. The most popular way to get to Greece is by ferry from **Italy**. Boats (mostly night boats) travel primarily from **Ancona, Bari,** and **Brindisi** (some also from **Trieste** and **Venice**) to **Corfu** and **Cephalonia** (see p. 476) as well as **Patras** (see p. 466). The trip to or from Brindisi is free for **Eurail** holders on ADN/HML ferries (excluding US$6.25 port tax year-round and a US$12 supplement in high-season).

There is frequent **ferry** service between mainland Greece and the various Greek island groups. Ferries run from **Peiraias,** just south of Athens (see p. 465), to the **Cyclades, Dodecanese Islands, Northeast Aegean Islands,** and **Crete.** Most ferries to the **Sporades** depart from **Agios Konstantinos** or **Kimi** (see p. 477), while those headed for the **Ionian Islands** (see p. 476) depart from Patras. In general, ferries trace a four- or five-port route; a round-trip "split" ticket allows you to decide how many days to spend at each stop. Ferry schedules are irregular and exasperating; don't expect steadfast routes, prices, or schedules. In some places, fierce competition will keep one ferry agent silent about another ferry line's schedule; head to government tourist offices for unbiased ferry info. For *very* tentative advance planning, you can try the Greek Travel Page Online (www.gtpnet.com), but check schedules at tourist offices, with the **limenarcheio** (port police), or at the dock. Make reservations, and check in at least two hours in advance to confirm your seat. If you sleep on deck, bring warm clothes and a sleeping bag. **Flying dolphins** (hydrofoils) are twice as fast but twice as expensive as ferries, and run most of the same routes.

Those continuing east from the islands can reach **Turkey** via the Dodecanese and Northeast Aegean Islands: ferries run from **Lesvos** and **Hios** to **Çesme; Samos** to **Kuşadası; Rhodes** to **Marmaris;** and **Kos** to **Bodrum.** For more info on ferries to Turkey, see p. 487. Research and plan your trip to Turkey before arriving in Greece, as info on Turkey in Greece is sketchy at best.

BY CAR. Driving in Greece can be dangerous; roads, especially on the islands, are narrow and of poor quality. Greece's mountainous terrain means twisting, winding roads, many of which do not have barriers along the curves. Signs in Greek appear roughly 100m before the transliterated versions. Foreign drivers are required to have an **International Driver's License** and an **International Insurance Certificate** to drive in Greece (see p. 64). The **Automobile and Touring Club of Greece (ELPA),** Messogion 2, Athens 11527 (tel. 779 74 01), provides assistance and offers reciprocal membership to foreign auto club members. They also have 24-hour **emergency road assistance** (tel. 104) and an **info line** (tel. 174).

BY BIKE AND BY THUMB. The mountainous terrain and unpaved roads make **cycling** in Greece difficult. *Let's Go* does not recommend hitchhiking; in any case, Greeks are not eager to pick up foreigners, and sparsely populated areas have little or no traffic. Visitors who choose to **hitchhike** write their destination on a sign in both Greek and English, and hitch from turn-offs rather than along stretches of straight road. Women should *never* hitch alone.

ESSENTIALS

DOCUMENTS AND FORMALITIES. Citizens of Australia, Canada, New Zealand, the EU, and the US do not require visas for stays of fewer than three months. South Africans need a visa; apply to stay longer at least 20 days prior to the three-month expiration date at the **Aliens Bureau,** 175 Alexandras Ave., Athens 11522 (tel. (011) 30 642 3094), or check with a Greek embassy or consulate.

GREECE

Greek Embassies at Home: Australia, 9 Turrana St, Yarralumla, **Canberra,** ACT 26000 (tel. (02) 62 73 30 11; fax 62 73 26 20); **Canada,** 80 MacLaren St, **Ottawa,** ON K2P 0K6 (tel. (613) 238-6271; fax 238-5676); **Ireland,** 1 Upper Pembroke St, **Dublin** 2 (tel. (01) 67 67 25 45; fax 661 88 92); **South Africa,** 1003 Church St Athlone, Arcadia, 0083, **Pretoria** (tel. (012) 437 35 13; fax 43 43 13); **UK,** 1a Holland Park, **London** W113TP (tel. (020) 72 29 38 50; fax 72 29 72 21); **US,** 2221 Massachusetts Ave NW, **Washington, DC** 20008 (tel. (202) 939-5800; fax 939-5824).

Foreign Embassies in Greece: All embassies are located in **Athens** (see p. 460).

TOURIST OFFICES. Tourism in Greece is overseen by two national organizations: the **Greek National Tourist Organization (GNTO)** and the **tourist police** *(touristiki astinomia)*. The **GNTO,** known as **EOT** in Greek, can supply general information about sights and accommodations throughout the country. The main office is at 2 Amerikis St, Athens (tel. (01) 322 41 28). The **tourist police** (Athens tel. 171, elsewhere 922 77 77) deals with more local and immediate problems: bus schedules, accommodations, lost passports, etc. They are open long hours and are willing to help, although their English is often limited.

GNTO Offices: Australia, 3rd fl., 51 Pitt St, Sydney, NSW 2000 (tel. (02) 92 41 16 63; fax 92 35 21 74). **Canada,** 1300 Bay St, Toronto, ON M5R 3K8 (tel. (416) 968-2220; fax 968-6533; www.aei.ca/gntomtl); 1170 Place du Frére André, Suite 300, Montréal, PQ H3B 3C6 (tel. (514) 871-1535; fax 871-1498). **UK,** 4 Conduit St, London W1R DOJ (tel. (020) 77 34 59 97; fax 72 87 13 69; www.antor.com). **US,** Olympic Tower, 645 Fifth Ave, 5th fl., New York, NY 10022 (tel. (212) 421-5777; fax 826-6940).

MONEY. Greek *drachmas* are issued in paper notes (100, 200, 500, 1000, 5000, and 10,000dr) and coins (5, 10, 20, 50, and 100dr). If you're carrying more than US$1000 in cash when you enter Greece, you must declare it upon entry. No more than 20,000dr can be taken out of the country when you leave. Banks charge a 2% commission (50dr min., 4500dr max.) on cashing traveler's checks.

Tipping and Bargaining: Service is included in all but the ritziest restaurants; rounding up to the nearest denomination; several hundred drachmas for a several thousand drachma meal is usually sufficient. You should haggle in souvenir shops, clothing and jewelry stores, and *domatia* (especially on weekdays in off-season), and negotiate prices with taxi drivers before getting in. Don't waste time bargaining for toothpaste or souvlaki. If in doubt, hang back and watch someone else buy. Merchants with any pride in their wares will refuse to sell to someone who has offended them in the negotiations.

Taxes: The Value Added Tax (VAT) refund threshold for non-EU citizens is 40,000dr.

COMMUNICATION

Post: Post offices are generally open M-F 7:30am-2pm. Airmail **postcards** to other European countries cost 150dr; domestic and other international destinations cost 120dr. **Letters** within Europe cost 200dr (up to 50g); anywhere else in the world costs 240dr (up to 150g). Expect airmail within 4-14 days. For express mail, ask for *katepeegon;* to register a letter, *systemeno;* for air mail, *aeroporikos,* and write "air mail" on the envelope.

Telephone: OTE offices usually open 7:30am-3pm in villages, 7:30am-10pm in towns, and 24hr. in larger cities. **International direct dial** numbers include: **AT&T,** 00 800 13 11; **Sprint,** 00 900 14 11; **MCI WorldPhone Direct,** 00 800 12 11; **Canada Direct,** 00 800 16 11; **BT Direct,** 00 800 44 11; **Ireland Direct,** 155 11 74; **Australia Direct,** 13 22 00; **Telecom NZ Direct,** 0800 00 00 00; **Telkom South Africa Direct,** 09 03. **Police,** tel. 100. **First aid,** tel. 166. **Fire,** tel. 199. **Hospital,** tel. 106. **Tourist police,** 171 in Athens, 922 77 77 elsewhere. **US citizens' emergency,** (01) 722 36 52.

Language: Although many Greeks (particularly the young) in Athens and other heavily touristed areas speak English, off the beaten path you'll probably have to stumble around a bit in Modern Greek. To avoid misunderstandings, it is also important to know Greek body language: to say no, Greeks lift their heads back abruptly while raising their eyebrows; to indicate yes, they emphatically nod once. A hand waving up and down that seems to say "stay there" actually means "come." For help in deciphering and transliterating the Greek alphabet, as well as basic phrases in Modern Greek, see p. 949. Keep in mind that there are exceptions—for instance, Φ and φ are often spelled *ph*.

ACCOMMODATIONS AND CAMPING. Lodging in Greece is a bargain. At the time of publication, **Hostelling International (HI)** had yet to reach an agreement with Greek hostels, and they endorse only one hostel in the entire country (in Athens). However, hostels that are not currently endorsed by HI are in most cases still safe and reputable. Hotel prices are regulated, but proprietors may try to push you to take the most expensive room. Check your bill carefully, and threaten to contact the tourist police if you think you are being cheated. **GNTO offices** usually have a list of cheap accommodations. In many areas, **domatia** (rooms to let) are an attractive and perfectly dependable option. Although you may sacrifice some amenities, talking to your proprietor about local life often compensates. Often you'll be approached by locals offering rooms to let as you enter town or disembark from your boat; this practice is technically illegal and occasionally unsafe. Greece hosts plenty of official **campgrounds,** and discreet freelance camping is common in July and August, although it is illegal and may not be the safest way to spend the night.

FOOD AND DRINK. Greek food is simple and healthy. A restaurant is known as either a *taverna* or *estiatorio*, while a grill is a *psistaria*. Breakfast can be bread, *tiropita* (cheese pie), or a pastry with *marmelada* (jam) or *meli* (honey), plus a cup of coffee (*elliniko* is powerful Turkish-style, *Nescafé* instant coffee, and *frappé* is a frothy iced drink). Lunch, the largest meal of the day, is eaten in the mid- to late afternoon. Dinner is typically served after 8pm, as late as 1am, during the summer in the larger cities. Greek restaurants divide food into two categories: *magiremeno* (cooked—generally cheaper) and *tis oras* (grilled meat). The latter includes *moskari* (veal), *arni* (lamb), or *kotopoulo* (chicken), served with *tiganites patates* (french fries), *rizi* (rice), or *fasolia* (beans). The former includes *moussaka* (chopped meat and eggplant mixed with a cheese and tomato paste), *pastitsio* (a lasagna-like dish of thick noodles covered with a rich cream sauce), *yemista* (stuffed tomatoes and peppers), *dolmadhes* (stuffed grape leaves), and *youvrelakia* (meatballs in egg and lemon sauce). You can hardly avoid *souvlaki*, a large skewer of steak, generally pork or lamb. A *souvlaki pita*, the budget food of the masses, is a pita crammed full of skewered meat and fillings (about 300dr). Fast-food stands sell *gyros*, a savory mixed meat (about 350dr). A favorite snack is *mezes*—tidbits of cheese, sausage, cakes, and octopus—with *ouzo*, a distilled spirit to which anise is added, giving it a licorice taste.

One of the great arts in Greece is **wine-making,** and every region has its own specialty. Long ago, the Greeks discovered that when wine was stored in pine pitch-sealed goatskins, it developed a fresh, sappy flavor. After much deduction, and perhaps after a nagging disgust at drinking out of a carcass, they discovered that adding pine resin in varying amounts during fermentation achieved the same result. The resulting wine became known as *retsina*. Resinated wines now come in three varieties: white, rosé, and red (*kokkineli*).

LOCAL FACTS

Time: Greece is 2hr. ahead of Greenwich Mean Time (GMT). For more info, see p. 49.

Climate: The islands are a bit milder than the mainland, and northern Greece's high altitude areas are cooler. Summer is sunny and sticky—it's almost impossible to escape the heat and humidity without A/C or a beach. Winter temperatures hover around 50°C; Oct.-Mar. is the rainy season.

Hours: Normal **business hours** in Greece include a break from about 2pm until 6pm or so. Hours vary from place to place. **Banks** are normally open M-F 8am-1:30pm, and also 3:30-6pm in some larger cities.

Holidays: All banks and shops and most museums are closed on Greece's major national holidays: New Year's Day (Jan. 1); Epiphany (Jan. 6); the first Su in Lent (Mar. 12); Independence Day (Mar. 25); Easter Sunday (Apr. 30); Labor Day (May 1); The Assumption of the Virgin Mary (Aug. 15); *Ohi* day, which celebrates resistance to Italy in WWII (Oct. 28); Christmas (Dec. 25); and St. Stephen Day (Dec. 26).

Festivals: Greeks take a good 3 weeks to get ready for the Lenten Fast, feasting and dancing throughout Carnival (Jan. 31-Feb. 22); Patras and Cephalonia celebrate with particular zest. Apr. 23 is **St. George's Day**, when Greece—especially Limnos and Hania—honor the dragon-slaying knight with horse races, wrestling matches, and dances. The **Feast of St. Demetrius** (Oct. 26), is celebrated with particular enthusiasm in Thessaloniki, coinciding with the opening of new wine.

ATHENS (Αθηνα)

The course of Greek history has patched together a busy mosaic in modern Athens: the Acropolis looms over the city that has grown up at its feet; Byzantine churches remind of a time when the city waned in power and was forgotten; and strip malls and outdoor *tavernas* confirm that Athens has since grown into thorough contemporaneity. The city is a dense, polluted, and crowded concrete jungle—the type of place where you might find yourself stuck in traffic at 2am on a Tuesday. Modern Athenians recognize that modernity cannot stand on teetering ruins, but even as they dig subway tunnels in preparation for the 2004 Olympic Summer Games, they carefully pick their way amongst the antiquities and springs of lost ancient rivers residing quietly beneath the city—looking forward while treasuring their rich past.

▐ GETTING THERE AND GETTING AROUND

Flights: The airport's **East Terminal** handles all flights by international carriers; the **West Terminal** receives all Olympic Airways flights; and the **New Charter Terminal** handles charter flights. Express **buses** (bus 091 from the center, bus 092 from the airport; 35min.; every 20min. 7:10am-9pm, 12 per night 9:50pm-6:45am; 250dr, after 11:30pm 500dr) connect to Pl. Syndagma and Stadiou near Pl. Omonia. A **taxi** costs 2500-4000dr (add 50dr for heavy luggage and a 300dr surcharge from the airport).

Trains: Info tel. 145 or 147; www.ose.gr. **Larissis Train Station** (tel. 529 88 37) serves northern Greece and Europe. To: **Thessaloniki** (7½hr., 10 per day, 4100-5850dr); **Sofia** (16hr., 1 per day, 12,000dr); **Istanbul** (24hr., 1 per day, 20,000dr); and **Budapest** (40,000dr). Trolley bus 1 runs from the station to Panepistimiou in Pl. Syndagma (every 10min., 120dr). **Peloponnese Train Station** (tel. 513 16 01) serves **Patras** (1600dr) and the Peloponnese. To get to the station from Larissis, exit to your right and go over the footbridge; from Panepistimiou, take bus 057 (every 15min., 120dr).

Buses: Terminal A, Kifissou 100 (tel. 512 49 10). To: **Patras** (3hr., 30 per day, 3650dr); **Thessaloniki** (7½hr., 6 per day, 8200dr); and the Peloponnese. Take blue bus 051 (every 15min., 120dr) from the corner of Zinonos and Menandrou near Pl. Omonia. **Terminal B,** Liossion 260 (M-F tel. 831 71 53), serves central Greece. Take blue bus 024 from Amalias and Panepistimiou. From the **Peloponnese Train Station** (see above), **Hellenic Railway (OSE;** tel. 362 44 02) buses run to **Sofia** and **Istanbul.**

Ferries and Hydrofoils: Ferries serving Crete and the Cyclades, Northeast Aegean, and Dodecanese Islands dock at the Athenian suburb of **Peiraias** (tel. 422 60 00). **Hydrofoils** serving the mainland, Sporades, and Cyclades also depart from Peiraias. See **Peiraias,** p. 465. For info on ferries to other destinations, see **By Ferry,** p. 455.

Public Transportation: Purchase tickets for the blue **buses** (designated by 3-digit numbers; every 15min. 5:30am-11:30pm) or yellow **trolleys** (1-2 digits) from any street kiosk (120dr) and validate them in the orange machines on board. The current single line of the **metro** (every 5min. 5am-midnight) extends 20 stops from Peiraias Harbor to Kifissia in northern Athens; buy tickets at booths or automatic machines (120dr). Hold onto your ticket, or face a 1500dr fine for riding without a valid ticket.

Taxis: Hail your taxi by shouting your destination—not the street address, but the area (e.g. "Kolonaki"). Base fare 250dr, plus 66dr per km within the city limits, 130dr outside. Be sure the meter is turned on, and ask how much the fare will be in advance.

▐ ORIENTATION AND PRACTICAL INFORMATION

Pl. Syndagma is the center of modern Athens. Budget travel offices, eateries, and hostels line **Nikis** and **Filellinon,** which run south from Pl. Syndagma into the eastern

GREECE

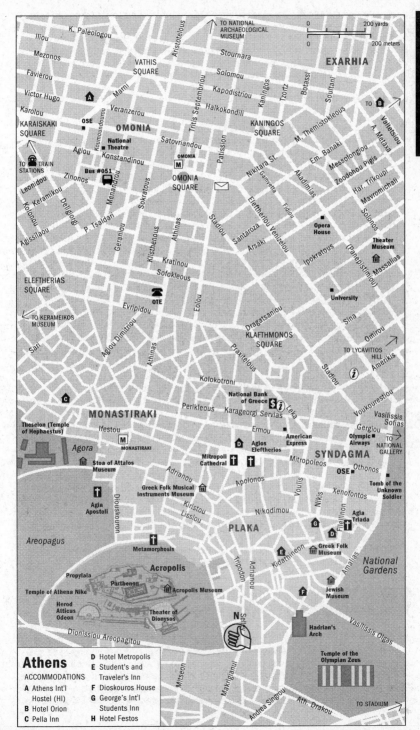

0   200 yards
0   200 meters

TO NATIONAL ARCHAEOLOGICAL MUSEUM

K. Paleologou
Iliou
Mezonos
Favierou
Victor Hugo
Karolou
KARAISKAKI SQUARE
Leonidou
Keramikou
Kolonou
Agissilaou
Sari
ELEFTHERIAS SQUARE
TO KERAMEIKOS MUSEUM

VATHIS SQUARE
Aristotelous
Stournara
Solomou
Kapodistriou
Halkokondili
Tritis Septembriou
OMONIA
Satovriandou
OMONIA
OMONIA SQUARE
Stadiou
Eoliou
Agiou Dimitriou
Athinas
Klisthenous
Kratinou
Sofokleous
Evripidou
OTE

EXARHIA
KANINGOS SQUARE
Kaningos
Tzortz
Botassi
Soultani
M. Themistokleous
Em. Banaki
Messolongiou
Zoodohou Pigs
Har. Trikoupi
Mavromichali
Solonos
Nikitara St.
Gamveta
Fidiou
Akadimias
Ipokratous
Sina
Omirou
Amerikis
TO LYCAVITTOS HILL
Opera House
University
Theater Museum
Massalias
(Panepistimiou)
KLAFTHMONOS SQUARE
Dragatsaniou
Praxitelous
Kolokotroni
Perikleous
Karageorgi Servias
Leka
Stadiou
Voukourestiou
Vasilissis Sofias
Gergiou
National Bank of Greece
American Express
Olympic Airways
SYNDAGMA
TO NATIONAL GALLERY
Ermou
Agios Eleftherios
Mitropoleos
Othonos
OSE
Tomb of the Unknown Soldier
Mitropoli Cathedral
Adrianou
Apolonos
Voulis
Nikis
Xenofontos
Filellinon
Amalias
Agia Triada
Greek Folk Musical Instruments Museum
Kiristou
Lissiou
Nikodimou
PLAKA
Kidathineon
Greek Folk Museum
National Gardens
Jewish Museum
MONASTIRAKI
Ifestou
Theseion (Temple of Hephaestus)
Agora
Stoa of Attalos Museum
Dioskouron
Agia Apostoli
Areopagus
Metamorphosis
Acropolis
Propylaia
Parthenon
Temple of Athena Nike
Herod Atticus Odeon
Theater of Dionysos
Acropolis Museum
Dionissiou Areopagitou
Tripodon
Adrianou
Hadrian's Arch
Temple of the Olympian Zeus
Vasilissis Olgas
Mitseon
Makrigianni
Andrea Singrou
Ath. Drakou
TO STADIUM

OMONIA
OSE
National Theatre
Bus #051
Agiou
Konstandinou
Koumoundourou
Menandrou
Zinonos
Veranzerou
Marni
Agiou
TO TRAIN STATIONS
Deligiori
Geraniou
P. Tsaldari
KANINGOS SQUARE
Eleftheriou Venizelou
Santaroza
Arsaki
Patision

Athens

ACCOMMODATIONS

A Athens Int'l
  Hostel (HI)
B Hotel Orion
C Pella Inn

D Hotel Metropolis
E Student's and
  Traveler's Inn
F Dioskouros House
G George's Int'l
  Students Inn
H Hotel Festos

part of **Plaka** (bounded by the Acropolis to the southwest and the Temple of Olympian Zeus to the southeast), the center of the old city and temporary home to most tourists. **Monastiraki,** mostly known for its hodge-podge flea market, lies west of Pl. Syndagma. Northwest of Pl. Syndagma, **Pl. Omonia** (which has become increasingly unsafe) is the site of the city's main subway station. North of Pl. Syndagma and northeast of Pl. Omonia, hip **Exharia** brims with students, while northeast of Pl. Sydagma lies the glitzy area of **Kolonaki.** Southwest of Pl. Syndagma is large, quiet **Pangrati;** to the south is **Glyfada,** a seaside suburb where the bacchanalians party. Be aware that Athenian streets often have multiple spellings or names.

TOURIST, FINANCIAL, AND LOCAL SERVICES

Tourist Office: Hellenic Tourism Organization Information, Amerikis 2 (tel. 331 05 61; fax 325 28 15; www.areianet.gr/infoxenios/GNTO), off Stadiou near Pl. Syndagma. Detailed city maps and transportation info. Open M-F 9am-9pm, Sa-Su 10am-9pm.

Budget Travel: Magic Travel Agency, Filellinon 20 (tel. 323 74 71; fax 322 02 19). Extremely competent, English-speaking staff. Open M-F 9am-6pm, Sa 10am-2pm.

Embassies: Australia, D. Soutsou 37 (tel. 645 04 04). Open M-F 8:30am-12:30pm. **Canada,** Ioannou Genadiou 4 (tel. 727 34 00). Open M-F 8:30am-12:30pm. **Ireland,** Vas. Konstandinou 7 (tel. 723 27 71). Open M-F 9am-3pm. **South Africa,** Kifissias 60 (tel. 680 66 45). Open M-F 8am-1pm. **Turkey,** Vas. Georgiou B. 8 (tel. 724 59 15). Open M-F 8:30am-12:30pm. **UK,** Ploutarchou 1 (tel. 723 62 11), at Ypsilantou. **US,** Vas. Sofias 91 (tel. 721 29 51; www.usisathens.gr). Open M-F 8:30am-5pm.

Currency Exchange: National Bank of Greece, Karageorgi Servias 2, on Pl. Syndagma. Open for currency exchange M-Th 3:30-6:30pm, F 3-6:30pm, Sa 9am-3pm, Su 9am-1pm. 24-hour **ATMs** are available all over the city, including Pl. Syndagma.

American Express: Ermou 2, P.O. Box 3325 (tel. 324 49 75), above McDonald's in Pl. Syndagma. Mail held for members. Open M-F 8:30am-4pm, Sa 8:30am-1:30pm.

Luggage Storage: At the **airport** 1000dr per piece per day; hang on to your ticket stub. Also at several offices on **Nikis** and **Filellinon** for 500dr per piece per day.

English Bookstore: Eleftheroudakis Book Store, Panepistimiou 17 (tel. 331 41 80). Open M and W 9am-4pm, Tu and Th-F 9am-8:30pm, Sa 9am-3pm.

Laundromats: The Greek word for laundry is *plinitirio,* but most signs say "Laundry." Try **Angelou Geront 10** in Plaka (2000dr) or **Kolokinthous 41 and Leonidou** (2300dr).

EMERGENCY AND COMMUNICATIONS

Emergencies: Ambulance, tel. 166. **Police,** tel. 100. **Tourist Police,** tel. 171.

Pharmacies: Check the daily *Athens News* (300dr) for the night pharmacy schedule.

Medical Assistance: The Greek word for hospital is *nosokomio.* A **public hospital** is at Evangelismou 45-47 (tel. 722 01 01; fax 729 18 08), near Kolonaki.

Telephones: OTE, Patission 85 (tel. 821 44 49). Overseas collect calls. Open M-F 7am-9pm, Sa 8am-3pm, Su 9am-2pm. Most **phone booths** require **telephone cards,** sold at OTE offices, street kiosks, and tourist shops (denominations of 1000, 1700, 7000, or 11,500dr). Push the "i" button on the phones for instructions in English.

Internet Access: ▧ **Sofokleous.com Internet Café,** Stadiou 5, just up Stadiou from Pl. Syndagma. 2000dr per hr., students 1500dr per hr. Open daily 10am-10pm.

Post Office: Pl. Syndagma (tel. 322 62 53), on the corner of Mitropolis. Address mail to be held: Pete PIHOS, Pl. Syndagma Post Office, Athens, Greece **10300.** Open M-F 7:30am-8pm, Sa 7:30am-2pm, Su 9am-1:30pm.

PHONE CODE	City code: 01. From outside Greece, dial int'l dialing prefix (see inside back cover) + 30 + 1 + local number.

▌ ACCOMMODATIONS

Although some hawkers at the train station represent decent places near the station, others lure tourists to expensive dumps far from town; if you're inclined to go with one, be sure to set a price and to have the place pointed out on a map before departing. Men arriving by bus should beware "friendly barkeepers" who may lead them to a brothel. Many budget options cluster in central Plaka and Syndagma, though women will have to ward off Plaka's catcalling *kamakia* (literally "octopus spears"). Noisy Monastiraki is central and is known for its bustling markets. Cheap lodgings abound in Omonia, but the area is not very safe at night. Lively Exahria is packed with students. **The prices quoted below are valid for summer;** you can typically subtract around 500-1000dr per person for off-season (Sept.-May) lodgings. Prices, like much else in Greece, are highly flexible; don't expect these figures to be exact. Also note that hotel owners can legally add a 10% surcharge to your bill if you stay fewer than three nights. Athens proper has no camping.

■ **Pella Inn,** Ermou 104 (tel. 325 05 98; fax 325 05 98), in **Monastiraki,** 10min. from Pl. Syndagma and 2 blocks northwest of the Monastiraki subway station (entrance on Karaiskaki). Breathtaking views of the Acropolis. Dorms 2500dr; singles 6000dr; doubles 8-10,000dr; 20% *Let's Go* discount. Breakfast 800dr. Check-out 11am.

■ **Student's and Traveler's Inn,** Kidatheneon 16 (tel. 324 48 08; fax 321 00 65; email Students-inn@ath.forthnet.gr), in **Plaka.** Good locale, friendly staff, and outdoor courtyard. Doubles 10,000dr; triples 14,000dr; quads 14,000dr. Students, youth, and hostel card-holders 10% off. **Internet** 1500dr per 30min. Reception 24hr. Check-out 11am.

Hotel Metropolis, Mitropoleos 46 (tel. 321 78 71 or 321 74 69), opposite Mitropoli Cathedral, in **Plaka.** Newly renovated. A step up from others in the area at a great price. Singles with bath 9000dr; doubles 8000dr, with bath 12,000dr. Check-out noon.

Dioskouros House, Pitakou 6 (tel. 324 8165), in **Plaka,** opposite Hadrian's Arch, near the southwest corner of the National Gardens. Nifty outdoor bar. Singles 9000dr; doubles 10,000dr; triples 15,000dr. Breakfast 500dr. Reception 24hr. Check-out 10am.

George's International Students Inn, Nikis 46 (tel. 322 64 74), in **Syndagma.** Head up Othonos from Pl. Syndagma and take your 2nd left. Huge windows and balconies. Dorms 3000dr; singles 5000dr; doubles 7000dr; triples 9000dr. Reception 24hr. Check-out 10am. Curfew 1:30am; ring bell after hours. Usually closed Jan.-Feb; call.

Hotel Festos, Filellinon 18 (tel. 323 24 55; email consolas@hol.gr), in **Syndagma.** Hires travelers as desk and lounge workers. Cable TV. Dorms 3000dr; doubles 8000dr; triples 12,000dr; quads 14,000dr. A/C. Reception 24hr. Check-out 10am. V, MC.

Athens International Hostel (HI), Victor Hugo 16 (tel. 523 41 70; fax 523 40 15), in **Omonia.** From Pl. Omonia, walk up Tritis Septembriou and turn left on Veranzerou, which becomes Victor Hugo. 1750-1800dr, nonmembers add 700dr (or buy an HI card for 4200dr). Breakfast 900dr. Kitchen. Laundry 1500dr. Call ahead in summer.

Hotel Orion, Em. Benaki 105 (tel. 382 73 62; fax 380 51 93), in **Exarhia.** Go all the way up Em. Benaki from Pl. Omonia, or take bus 230 from Syndagma. Rooftop TV lounge. Singles 8000dr; doubles 12,000dr; triples 14,400dr. Breakfast 1500dr. Laundry.

◖ FOOD

Athens offers a melange of stands, open-air cafés, side-street *tavernas,* and intriguingly dim restaurants. Cheap fast food abounds in Syndagma and Omonia—try *souvlaki* (250-400dr), served either on a *kalamaki* (skewer) or wrapped in *pita; tost* (a grilled sandwich of variable ingredients, usually ham and cheese, 300-600dr); *tiropita* (hot cheese pie, 300dr); or *spanakopita* (hot spinach pie, 300dr). A *koulouri* (a doughnut-shaped, sesame-coated roll) makes for a quick breakfast (50-100dr). Pick up basic **groceries** at a minimarket on **Nikis.**

■ **Eden Vegetarian Restaurant,** Lissiou 12 (tel. 324 88 58), in **Plaka.** Head down Kidatheneon from Filelinon, turn right on Tripidon, and bear left on Lissiou. Huge portions. Eggplant salad or hummus 900dr. Spinach special 2200dr. Open daily noon-midnight.

O Platanos, Diogenous 4 (tel. 322 06 66), on a street parallel to Adrianou in **Plaka.** Popular, friendly, and one of the oldest restaurants around. Lamb is the specialty, served with potatoes, rice, or *fricase* for 1800dr. Open M-Sa noon-4:30pm and 8-11pm.

Oinéas, Essopou (Aisopou) 9 (tel. 321 56 14), off Karaiskaki in **Monastiraki.** Adorned with an impressive array of Greek nostalgia, but the experimental, delicious food is just as interesting. *Tzatziki* 800dr. Salads 2000-2500dr. Open Tu-Su 11am-2am.

Pluto, Plutarchou 38 (tel. 724 47 13), in **Kolonaki.** A one-of-a-kind restaurant with a warm ambience and fine international menu. Be sure to try one of Chef Constantine's specialties (the seafood risotto is divine). Open daily 1-5pm and 9pm-2:30am.

Apokentro Pizzeria and Crêperie, Deinokratous 2 (tel. 725 19 82), in **Kolonaki.** From Vas. Sofias, walk up Karaoli-Dimitriou (which turns into Loukianou), then right on Deinokratous. Delicious crêpes and pizzas 1250-1600dr. Open Su-F noon-12:30am.

O Barba Giannis, Em. Benaki 94 (tel. 330 01 85), in **Exarhia.** From Pl. Syndagma, walk up Stadiou and turn right on Em. Benaki. Cheap and delicious. Fish and veggie dishes from 950dr. Salads 650-1000dr. Open in summer M-Sa 9am-1am; off-season also open Su.

SIGHTS

THE ACROPOLIS

The main entrance is on the west side of the Acropolis. Areopagitou to the south and Theorias in western Plaka (follow the sporadic signs) both lead to the entrance. Alternatively, exit the Agora (see below) to the south, following the path uphill, and then turn right. Tel. 321 02 19. Open in summer 8am-6:30pm; off-season 8am-2pm. 2000dr, students 1000dr; includes the Acropolis Museum. The marble can be slippery, so wear shoes with good traction.

Perched on a rocky plateau above the city, the Acropolis has been Athens' highlight since the 5th century BC. At the center, the Parthenon towers over the Aegean and the Attic Plains, the ultimate achievement of Athens' classical glory. Although each Greek *polis* had an *acropolis* ("high city"), Athens' magnificent example has effectively monopolized the name. Today, the hilltop's remarkable (if scaffolded) ruins grace otherwise rubble-strewn grounds.

BEULÉ GATE AND PROPYLAEA. The ramp that led to the Acropolis in classical times no longer exists; today's visitors make the five-minute climb to the ticket window, enter through the crumbling Roman **Beulé Gate** (added in the 3rd century AD), and continue through **Propylaea,** which formed the towering entrance in ancient times. The middle gate of the Propylaea opened onto the **Panathenaic Way,** an east-west route cutting across the middle of the Acropolis that was once taken by Panathenaic processions venerating the goddess Athena.

ATHENA NIKE AND ATHENA PROMACHOS. On the right after leaving the Propylaea, the tiny **Temple of Athena Nike,** at the cliff's edge, was built during a respite from the Peloponnesian War, the so-called Peace of Nikias (421-415 BC). It once housed a winged statue of the goddess; allegedly, however, frenzied Athenians who feared that their deity (and peace) would flee the city one day clipped the statue's wings. In a similar vein, the foundation to your left as you continue along the Panathenaic Way after leaving the Temple once hosted a **statue of Athena Promachos;** when the statue lost its spear hundreds of years later, the inhabitants interpreted her outstretched hand as an invitation to invaders, so they smashed it to pieces.

THE ERECHTHEION. The Erechtheion, to the left as you continue down the Panathenaic Way, was finished in 406 BC, just prior to Athens' defeat by Sparta. The unique two-level structure once housed the cults of Athena, Poseidon, and Erechtheus. Its southern portico, facing the Parthenon, is supported by six much-photographed (albeit reproduced) **caryatids,** columns sculpted in the shape of women.

THE PARTHENON. Looming over the hillside, the Parthenon ("Virgin's Apartment") keeps vigil over the city. The crowning glory of the **Periclean project** to beautify Athens, it was designed by the architect Aktinos, who added two extra columns to the usual six in the front row of the Doric order. The temple also featured other subtle irregularities: the upward bowing of the temple's *stylobate* (pedestal) and the slight swelling of its columns compensated for the optical illusion by which, from a distance, straight lines appear to bend. Its elegance reflected the ancient Greek obsession with proportion: it was built such that everything from the layout to the details of the entablature respected a four-to-nine ratio.

THE ACROPOLIS MUSEUM. Footsteps away from the Parthenon, the museum contains a superb collection of sculptures, including five of the original Erechtheion Caryatids (the sixth is in the British Museum). Most treasures date from the period of transition between Archaic and Classical Greek art (550-400 BC), a development reflected in the faces of the statues: compare the stylized, entranced faces and static poses of Archaic sculptures such as the famous **Moschophoros** (calf-bearer) to the more naturalistic (if idealized) figures of classical art, epitomized in the perfect balance of the curvaceous **Kritias** boy. Unfortunately, only a few pieces from the Parthenon are here—Lord Elgin helped himself to the rest. *(Open M noon-6:30pm, Tu-Su 8am-6:30pm; in winter M 11am-2pm; Tu-Su 8am-2pm.)*

SOUTHERN SLOPE. From the southwest corner of the Acropolis, you can look down on the reconstructed **Odeon of Herodes Atticus,** a still-functioning theater dating from the Roman Period (AD 160). Admire the ruins of the classical Greek **Asclepion** and **Stoa of Eumenes II** as you continue east to the **Theater of Dionysus,** which dates from the 4th century BC and once hosted dramas by Aeschylus and Sophocles as well as comedies by Aristophanes for audiences of up to 17,000. *(Main entrance on Dionissiou Areopagitou, but you can also enter from the Acropolis, just above the Herodes Atticus theater. Open Tu-Su 8:30am-2:30pm. 500dr, students 250dr.)*

ANCIENT AGORA. The **Athenian Agora,** at the foot of the Acropolis, was the administrative center and marketplace of Athens from the 6th century BC to the late Roman Period (5th-6th centuries AD). The **Temple of Hephaestos,** on a hill in the northwest corner, is one of the best-preserved Classical temples in Greece, especially notable for its friezes depicting the tales of Hercules and Theseus. To the south, the elongated **Stoa of Attalos,** a multi-purpose building for shops, shelter, and gatherings, was rebuilt between 1953 and 1956 and now houses the **Agora Museum,** which contains a number of relics from the site. *(Enter from Pl. Thission, from Adrianou, or as you come down from the Acropolis. Open Tu-Su 8:30am-2:30pm. 1200dr, students 600dr.)*

HADRIAN'S ARCH AND THE TEMPLE OF OLYMPIAN ZEUS. Hadrian's Arch marked the 2nd-century boundary between the ancient city of Theseus and the new city built by Hadrian. Next to the arch, fifteen majestic columns are all that remain of the **Temple of Olympian Zeus,** the largest temple ever built in Greece. *(Vas. Olgas at Amalias, southwest of the National Gardens. Open Tu-Su May-Oct. 8am-2:30pm; Nov.-Apr. 8:30am-2:30pm. 500dr, students 300dr.)*

MUSEUMS. One of the world's finest collections of classical sculpture, ceramics, and bronzework lies in the **National Archaeological Museum.** The *Mask of Agamemnon* from Heinrich Schliemann's Mycenae digs and the huge bronze statue of Poseidon are must-sees. *(Patission 44, also called Oktovriou 28. Walk from Pl. Syndagma up Stadiou and turn right on Patission (20min.). Open Apr.-Oct. M 12:30-7pm, Tu-Su 8am-5pm; Nov.-Mar. M 11am-5pm, Tu-F 8am-5pm, Sa-Su 8:30am-3pm. 2000dr, students 1000dr; free Su and holidays.)* The **National Gallery** (Alexander Soutzos Museum) exhibits works by Greek artists, including El Greco, supplemented by periodic international displays. *(Vas. Konstandinou 50. Open M and W-Sa 9am-3pm, Su 10am-2pm. 1000-1500dr, students 500dr.)*

PANATHENAIC OLYMPIC STADIUM. This site of the first modern Olympic Games (1896) will host the opening ceremonies for the 2004 Summer Olympics (the actual Games will be held in the new stadium). The original Classical stadium was destroyed during the Byzantine era and restored in 1895. Run a lap and feel the glory. *(On Vas. Konstandinou, between the National Gardens and Pangrati. From Pl. Syndagma, walk 15min. down Amalias and turn left on Vas. Olgas. Open daily 8am-8:30pm. Free.)*

NEAR PLATEIA SYNDAGMA. Walk along the tranquil paths of the pleasant **National Gardens,** adjacent to Pl. Syndagma. *(Open daily dawn-dusk. Women should avoid coming here alone.)* Don't miss the changing of the guard in front of the **Parliament** building. Unlike their British equivalents, *evzones* occasionally wink, smile, or even say "I love you" to tourists. *(Two sets of guards perform every hr. on the hr. Catch a more pomp-filled version—with a complete troop of guards and a band—on Sundays at 10:45am.)*

LOOKOUT POINTS. For a spellbinding 360° view of Athens at night, head to **Pnyx Hill** opposite the Acropolis. Formerly the meeting place of the ancient Athenian assembly, the hill now serves to join locals with tourists for guitar-strumming by the city lights. Also, don't miss the view from the top of **Mt. Lycavittos,** the biggest of Athens' seven hills. The best time to ascend is sunset, when you can catch a last glimpse of Athens in daylight and watch the city light up. Using the Acropolis as your point of reference, observe Monastiraki, Omonia, and Exarhia to your right, then continue spinning clockwise to delight in the flashy lights and music of Lycavittos Theater, several parks, the Panathenaic Olympic Stadium, the National Gardens, and the Temple of Olympian Zeus. *(Hike 15min. to the top, or take the funicular from near the end of Ploutarchou in Kolonaki. Departs every 10-15min., round-trip 1000dr.)*

🎵 🎭 ENTERTAINMENT AND NIGHTLIFE

FESTIVALS. The **Athens Festival** runs annually from June until September, featuring classical theater groups at the Odeon of Herodes Atticus, at the Lycavittos Theater, and in Epidavros. The Greek Orchestra plays during this festival regularly, and visiting artists have ranged from the Bolshoi Ballet to B.B. King. The **Festival Office**, Stadiou 4 (tel. 322 20 35), sells student tickets for 3000-5000dr.

MARKETS. The bazaar-like **Athens Flea Market**, adjacent to Pl. Monastiraki, offers a potpourri of second-hand junk, costly antiques, and everything in between. (Open M, W, and Sa-Su 8am-3pm, Tu and Th-F 8am-8pm.) On Sundays, the flea market overflows the square and fills Athinas, and a huge indoor-outdoor **food market** lines the sides of Athinas between Evripidou and Sofokleous. The **meat market** is huge, and certainly not for the faint of heart. (Open M-Sa 8am-2pm.)

FILM, CAFÉS, AND BARS. Enjoy your own *cinema paradiso* at the open-air movie theater 🎬**Cine Paris,** Kidatheneon 22 (tel. 322 20 71). Check *Athens News* (300dr) for showtimes (tickets 1900dr). For a livelier night, head to **Kolonaki,** with plenty of café-by-day-bar-by-night type establishments. The bar 🎷**Jazz in Jazz,** Deinokratous 10, in Kolonaki, lures mellow Athenian Bacchants with endless old jazz records and spontaneous swing dancing. In Pl. Exarhia, the **Café Floral** is lit with paper lanterns. In Plaka, colorful **Bretto's,** Kidatheneon 41, distills its own liqueur. **Bee,** at Miaoli and Themidos, off Ermou in Monastiraki, is a player on the hip Athenian artistic scene. (Drinks 700-2000dr. Open daily noon-3am.)

CLUBS. In summer, hip Athenians head to the seaside clubs in **Glyfada** (past the airport). Go for glam; no shorts pass through these doors. Cover ranges from 3000-5000dr, and drinks are ridiculously pricey (cheap beers 1500-2000dr; cocktails 2000-3000dr). Bars and cafés line Vouliagmenis, Glyfada's main drag; clubs are just down the beach. Good hotspots include **King Size** and **Bedside,** Poseidonos Beach 5; **Camel Club,** Pergamon 25, for rock; and **+ Soda,** on Poseidonos Beach, for after-hours (post-3am) fun. For **gay clubs** (primarily male), try the northern end of Singrou or Lembessi (off Singrou). To get to Glyfada, bus A3 (240dr) from Pl. Syndagma to the last stop and then cab it to your club of choice. Taxi fare back is 2000-2500dr.

🔍 EXCURSIONS FROM ATHENS

TEMPLE OF POSEIDON. The **Temple of Poseidon** has for centuries been a dazzling white landmark for sailors out at sea, and also offers fantastic views of the blue, blue Aegean. The original temple was constructed around 600 BC, destroyed by the Persians in 480 BC, and rebuilt by Pericles in 440 BC. The 16 remaining Doric columns sit on a promontory at **Cape Sounion** (Ακρωτηριο Σουνιο), 65km from Athens. (Tel. 393 63. Open daily 10am-dusk. 800dr, students 400dr, EU students free.) Two **bus** routes run to Cape Sounion from Athens; the shorter and more scenic route commences from the Mavromateon 14 stop near Areos Park in Athens (2hr., every hr. 6:30am-6:30pm, 1150dr). The last bus back is around 8-9pm.

MARATHON. In 490 BC, when the Athenians defeated the Persians at the bloody battle of Marathon (Μαραθωνας), the messenger Pheidippides ran 42km to announce the victory and then collapsed dead from exhaustion. Although modern marathoners regularly repeat this feat *(sans* fatal collapse), twice annually on Pheidippides' very route, others choose to reach Marathon by bus from Mavromateon 29 by Areos Park in Athens (1hr., every hr. 5:30am-10:30pm, 700dr). Although the town itself isn't that inspiring, the five rooms of the **Archaeological Museum of**

THE IRONY OF ORACLES

The Delphic Oracle was famed for giving obscure, deceptively metaphorical answers. Many a suppliant went home more confused than he came, having failed to draw meaning from the answer—or, worse still, having drawn the wrong meaning from it. In the 6th century BC, King Croesus of Sardis, ruler of most of Asia Minor, came to the Oracle to ask about the threat the Persians posed to his kingdom. The Oracle's answer: "A great empire will be destroyed." Croesus returned to Sardis thinking that he would conquer the Persian Empire; it was not until he watched his own kingdom and capital fall that he realized that the empire to which the Oracle had been referring had been his own. Later, Themistocles, leader of Athens during the first Persian War, asked the Oracle how to prepare for the approaching war. When he was told to "build wooden walls," most took this to indicate that wooden walls should be built around the city, but Themistocles instead set to work building a fleet of ships. It was only after Athens' decisive victory over the Persians at the great naval battle of Salamis that Themistocles' great wisdom was recognized. Such stories show that the nature of the Oracle was not simply to answer questions, but rather, as the exhortation once inscribed on the Temple of Apollo said, to "know thyself."

Marathonas are packed with exciting archaeological finds. Ask the driver to let you off at the sign ("Mouseion and Marathonas"), then follow the signs 2km through farmlands (bear right at the one unlabeled fork in the road) to the end of the paved road, 114 Plateion. (Tel. (0294) 551 55. Open Tu-Su 8am-3pm. 500dr, students 250dr, EU students and classics or archaeology students free.)

DELPHI. Troubled denizens of the ancient world journeyed to the Oracle of Apollo at Delphi (Δελφοι; pop. 2500), where the Pythia (priestess of Apollo) gave them profound, if cryptic, advice. If modern Delphi is the center of anything, it's the tour-bus circuit—visit early in the morning. Despite the tourists, truly fascinating ruins make Delphi a rewarding daytrip. **Buses** leave Athens for Delphi from the station at Liossion 260 (3½hr., 5 per day, 3000dr). Railpass holders can take the **train** to Livadia and catch the bus (7 per day, 800dr). From the bus station, at the western end of Delphi, walk east on Pavlou toward Athens (with the mountain edge on your right) to reach the **tourist office,** 12 Friderikis, in the town hall. (Open M-F 7:30am-2:30pm.) Continue east down Pavlou to reach the Oracle site.

FERRIES FROM ATHENS: PEIRAIAS PORT

A far cry from the charm of Plato's *Republic*—set in Peiraias (Πειραιας), then at the height of Athenian power—modern Peiraias is best appreciated only as a point of departure to the Greek isles. **Ferries** go to nearly all Greek islands (except the Sporades and Ionians): **Mykonos** (6hr., 2 per day, 4800dr); **Naxos** (6hr., 4 per day, 4800dr); **Paros** (6hr., 4 per day, 4800dr); **Ios** (7½hr., 5090dr); **Santorini** (9hr., 5636dr); **Hios** and **Lesvos** (9-11hr., 7pm, 5400dr); **Iraklion** (10hr., departs 7:45 and 8am, 6400dr), **Hania** (10hr., departs 8:30pm, 5400dr), and **Rethymno** (10hr., departs 7:30am, 6500dr) on Crete; **Rhodes** (16hr., departs 2 and 4pm, 8000dr); and **Limassol, Cyprus.** Minoan Flying Dolphins (tel. 428 00 01) **hydrofoils,** roughly twice as fast and twice as expensive as ferries, depart for the mainland, Sporades, and Cyclades islands from the port of **Zea** on the opposite site of the peninsula, 10min. down any of the roads off Akti Miaouli. Long-distance **trains** for **Patras** and the **Peloponnese** leave daily from the train station on **Akti Kalimassioti,** while trains bound for northern Greece (Larissis) leave daily from the station on **Ag. Dimitriou** across the harbor.

From Athens, take the **metro** to the last southbound stop (20min.). The **tourist office** in the metro station offers ferry advice and sells tickets. (Tel. (01) 412 11 81. Open daily 6am-8pm.) From the stop, head left (as you face the water) down Akti Kalimassioti, which becomes Akti Poseidonos, and bear right onto Akti Miaouli. Small **ferries** depart from Akti Poseidonos; larger ferries dock at Akti Miaouli; and international ferries are at the end of Akti Miaouli toward the Customs House.

THE PELOPONNESE (Πελοποννησος)

Connected to the mainland by the narrow isthmus of Corinth, the Peloponnese contains the majority of Greece's best archaeological sites, including Olympia, Mycenae, Messene, Corinth, Mystra, and Epidavros; it also offers some of the country's most stunning landscapes, from the barren crags of the Mani to the forested peaks and flowered fields of Arcadia. The beautiful and sparsely populated Peloponnese is also a bastion of the disappearing Greek village life.

✕ FERRIES TO ITALY AND CRETE

Boats go from **Patras** to **Brindisi** (20hr., 6000-8000dr, plus 2200dr port tax), **Trieste, Bari, Ancona,** and **Venice, Italy.** The trip to or from Brindisi is free for **Eurail** holders on certain ferry lines. Check the travel offices on Iroon Polytechniou and Othonas Amplias in Patras to consult about tickets, and ask about discounts for those under 25. Ferries also sail from **Gythion** to **Crete** (7½hr., 2 per week, 4700dr).

PATRAS (Πατρας)

Sprawling Patras, Greece's third-largest city, serves primarily as a transport hub, but the port becomes one big dance floor during **Carnival** (mid-Jan. to Ash Wednesday). During the rest of the year, spend your layover heading inland from town on Ag. Nikolaou and climbing the steps to the 13th-century Venetian **castle** (open daily 8am-7pm; free), then continuing west to the **Ancient Odeum,** a restored Roman theater (open Tu-Su 8:30-2:30; free). Follow the water to the west end of town to reach **Agios Andreas,** the largest Orthodox cathedral in Greece, which holds magnificent frescoes and an unusual relic—St. Andrew's head. (Open daily 9am-dusk.) Sweet black grapes are transformed into *Mavrodaphne* wine at the **Achaïa Clauss winery,** the most famous in the country. Check with tourist office for a schedule of daily tours, then take bus 7 from the intersection of Kolokotroni and Kanakari.

KTEL **buses** (tel. (061) 62 38 86) go from on Othonos Amalias, between Aratou and Zaïmi, to Kalamata (1hr., 2 per day, 4100dr); Athens (3hr., 26 per day, 3650dr); Ioannina (4 per day, 4400dr); Tripoli (4hr., 2 per day, 3100dr); and Thessaloniki (3 per day, 8250dr). **Trains** (tel. (061) 27 36 94) also go from Othonos Amalias to Kalamata (4½hr., 2 per day, 1500dr); Athens (8 per day, 1580dr-2600dr; reserve ahead); and Olympia (2hr., 8 per day, 820dr-1220dr) via Pyrgos. Daily **ferries** go to Ithaka (3¾hr., 3500dr) via Cephalonia (3hr., 3200dr) as well as to Corfu (night ferry 6-8hr., 5800dr). For info on ferries to **Italy,** see above. From the docks, turn right after leaving Customs and follow Iroon Polytechniou, which becomes Othonos Amalias, to reach the center of town. If you have a **Eurail** pass, head to **HML** (tel. (061) 45 25 21), on Iroon Polytechniou near Customs, for your ferry ticket. **Strintzis Tours,** Othonas Amalias 14, is also helpful. (Tel. (061) 62 26 02. Open daily 9am-11pm.) The **tourist office** is on the waterfront at the entrance to Customs. (Tel. (061) 62 22 49. Open M-F 8:30am-8pm.) **Rocky Raccoon Online Café,** Gerokostopoulou 56, is open late (1500dr per hr.). Hotels are scattered on **Ag. Andreas,** one block up from the waterfront. **Pension Nicos,** Patreos 3, is two blocks from the water. (Tel. (061) 22 16 43. Singles 5000dr; doubles 7000dr.) **Postal code:** 26001.

OLYMPIA (Ολυμπια)

The site was settled in the 3rd millennium BC, but beginning in 776 BC, leaders of rival city-states in ancient Greece shed their armor every four years and congregated to enjoy the Olympic games and make offerings to the gods. Today, the remains of a gymnasium, palaestra, stadium, and several temples and treasures remain scattered around **Ancient Olympia,** although they are not labeled or particularly well-preserved. Follow the main road 5min. out of town to reach the ruins and museum. Dominating the site is the gigantic **Temple of Zeus,** which once held a statue of the god by Phidias so beautiful that it was considered one of the **seven wonders of the ancient world.** On the north edge of the Altis lie the remains of the 7th-century BC **Temple of Hera,** the ruins' best-preserved structure and the site of the quadrennial lighting of the **Olympic flame.** Opposite the site, the **New Museum** houses a vast array of sculpture, including the Nike of Paionios, the Hermes of Praxiteles, the pedimental sculptures from the Temple of Zeus, and fun military spoils. (Site open daily 8am-7pm. Museum open M noon-7pm, Tu-Su 8am-7pm. Joint ticket 2000dr; separately 1200dr each, students 600dr; EU students free.)

In New Olympia, **buses** run from opposite the tourist info booth to Tripoli (4hr., 3 per day, 2350dr). The **tourist office,** on Kondili, is on the east side of town, toward the ruins. (Tel. (0624) 231 00. Open daily in summer 8am-10pm; off-season 11am-5pm.) The conveniently located **youth hostel** is at Kondili 18. (Tel. (0624) 255 80. 1700dr. Breakfast 600dr. Check-out 10am. Lockout 10:30am-noon.) **Camping Diana** is farther uphill on Kondili from Pension Poseidon. (Tel. (0624) 223 14. 1600dr per person, 1200-1600dr per tent, 1000dr per car.) ■**Pension Poseidon,** two blocks uphill on Kondili from the National Bank, has rooms and serves Greek food. (Moussaka 1500dr; salad 900dr. Singles 5000dr; doubles 7000dr.) **Postal code:** 27065.

TRIPOLI (Τριπολη)

Although you may have to dodge wild motorists while crossing the perilous streets of Urban Tripoli, the transport hub of Arcadia, the town provides pleasant squares and cafés for those awaiting the next bus out. The **Archaeological Museum,** on Evangelistrias, exhibits pottery, jewelry, and weaponry from the neolithic to the Mycenaean periods. **Buses** arrive at Pl. Kolokotronis, east of the center. From the station, follow Georgiou to Pl. Ag. Vasiliou; as you face the Church of Agios Vasiliou, take a left and head north on Ethnikis Antistasis to reach Pl. Petrinou. **Buses** go to Sparta (1hr., 10 per day, 1000dr); Kalamata (2hr., 12 per day, 1550dr); and Athens (3hr., 14 per day, 3000dr). Four **trains** per day go to Corinth (2½hr., 900dr); Kalamata (2½hr., 840dr); and Athens (4hr., 1500dr). The **tourist office,** on Ethnikis Antistasis, is past Pl. Petrinou in the town hall. (Tel. (071) 23 18 44. Open M-F 7am-2pm.) Crash at **Hotel Alex,** Vas. Georgios 26, between Pl. Kolokotronis and Pl. Agios Vasiliou. (Tel. (071) 22 34 65. Singles 5500dr; doubles 8000dr; triples 9000dr.) **Postal code:** 22100.

■ EXCURSIONS FROM TRIPOLI: DIMITSANA AND STEMNITSA. West of

Tripoli, the enticing villages of Dimitsana (Δημητσανα) and Stemnitsa (Στεμνιτσα) are good bases for **hiking** excursions into the idyllic, rugged countryside. **Dimitsana** has been a center of Greek learning and revolutionary activity since the 16th century. **Buses** pull in on Labardopoulou from Tripoli (1½hr., 1-3 per day, 1200dr). Buses to Tripoli and Olympia make frequent stops in Karkalou, 20min. away by taxi (1000dr). Let a room in town or head to the luxurious ■**Domatia Kousteni.** Ask at the Teythis Café, beside the OTE, on the right as you walk to the town from the bus stop. (Tel. (0795) 315 50. Rooms for 1-3 10,000dr. Breakfast included.) From Dimitsana, a beautiful 11km stroll along the road (or a 1000dr taxi ride) will bring you to to **Stemnitsa,** whose narrow, irregular cobblestoned streets betray its medieval roots. Many consider the town to be the most beautiful in Greece. The splendid **Hotel Triokolonion** is on the left side of the main road from Dimitsana. (Tel. (0795) 812 97. Singles 7000dr; doubles 9000dr.)

KALAMATA (Καλαματα)

Kalamata, the Peloponnese's second-largest city, is a fine base for exploring the southwestern coast. The well-preserved ruins of **Ancient Messene** in nearby **Mavromati** constitute one of Greece's most impressive archaeological sites. Buses run to to Mavromati from Kalamata (1hr., depart M-Sa 5:40am and 2pm, 500dr; return bus 2:30pm). (Open daily 8:30am-3pm. 500dr, students 300dr, EU students free.) **Buses** arrive in Kalamata from Sparta (2hr., 2 per day, 1100dr); Tripoli (2hr., 1550dr); Corinth (3hr., 3000dr); Patras (4hr., 2 per day, 4150dr); and Athens (4hr., 11 per day, 4250dr). From the bus station, go down Artemidos, turn right on Iatropoulou just before the post office, and follow it to Aristomenous; to the left is the old town and to the right is the waterfront. **Trains** run from Sideromikou Stathmou to Tripoli (2½hr., 840dr); Olympia (3hr., 900dr); Corinth (5¼hr., 1700dr); Patras (5½hr., 1500dr); and Athens (7hr., 4 per day, 2400dr). Turn right on Frantzi at the end of Pl. Georgiou and walk a few blocks to reach the town center. To get to **Hotel Nevada,**

Santa Rosa 9, take bus 1 and get off as soon as it turns left along the water. (Tel. (0721) 824 29. Singles 3500dr; doubles 5000dr; triples 7000dr.) **Postal code:** 24100.

⚡ EXCURSIONS FROM KALAMATA: PYLOS AND METHONI. Beautiful **Pylos** (Πυλος) offers beaches, a palace, two fortresses, and unspoiled charm. **Nestor's Palace,** where Nestor met Telemachus in Homer's *Odyssey,* was built in the 13th century BC. To see the site, still under excavation, take the bus to Kyparissia and get off at the palace (40min., 300dr). **Buses** arrive in Pylos from Kalamata (1½hr., 9 per day, 950dr). Look for **"Rooms to Let"** signs as the bus descends into town (singles 4000-6000dr; doubles 5000-8000dr). Buses continue to nearby **Methoni** (Μεθωνη; 15min., 7 per day, 220dr), where hibiscus-lined streets wind around the impressive **Venetian fortress,** a 13th-century mini-city. (Open M-Sa 8am-8pm, Su 9am-8pm. Free.) The **Hotel Alex** has air-conditioned rooms. (Tel. (0723) 312 19. Singles 6000dr; doubles 8000dr; triples 10,000dr; ask about student discounts.)

SPARTA AND MYSTRA (Σπαρτη, Μυστρας)

While **Ancient Sparta** has been immortalized in the annals of military history, the modern version is noted mostly for its olive oil and orange trees and serves best as a base for visits to the now-more-impressive Mystra, 6km away. **Buses** arrive in Sparta from Gythion (1hr., 6 per day, 800dr); Tripoli (1hr., 1000dr); Areopolis (1½hr., 4 per day, 1250dr); Corinth (2hr., 2350dr); Monemvassia (2hr., 3 per day, 1800dr); Kalamata (2hr., 2 per day, 1100dr); and Athens (3½hr., 9 per day, 3700dr). To reach the town center from the bus station, walk 10 blocks west on Lykourgou; the **tourist office** is to the left of the town hall in the *plateia.* (Tel. (0731) 248 52. Open daily 8am-2pm.) The minimalist **Hotel Panellinion, on** Paleologou, is just south of Lykourgou. (Tel. (0731) 280 31. Singles 4000dr; doubles 6000dr.)

Once the religious center of Byzantium and the locus of Constantinople's rule over the Peloponnese, **Mystra's** extraordinary ruins reveal a veritable city of Byzantine churches, chapels, and monasteries. Don't miss the beautiful **Metropolis of St. Demetrios** on the lower tier, with its flowery courtyard and museum of architectural fragments. At the extreme left of the lower tier, every inch of the **Church of Peribleptos** is bathed in exquisitely detailed religious paintings; despite Ottoman vandalization, the church is still Mystra's most stunning relic. (Open daily 8am-7pm; in winter 8:30am-3pm. 1200dr, students 600dr, EU students free. Dress modestly.) **Buses** from Sparta to Mystra stop at the corner of Lykourgou and Kythonigou (every 1½hr., 220dr), two blocks past the town *plateia* away from the main bus station.

GYTHION AND AREOPOLIS (Γυθειο, Αρεοπολη)

Formerly plagued by violent family feuds and savage piracy, the sparsely settled **Mani** (Μανη) province derives its name from *manis,* Greek for wrath or fury, and history has affirmed its etymological roots many times. Today, the fire behind Maniot fury has been cooled by a coastal breeze, and the Maniots play excellent hosts to the visitors who stay in their traditional gray-stone tower houses, seeking beautiful beaches and views. **Gythion,** the "Gateway to the Mani," is the liveliest town in the region, near beautiful sand and stone beaches. A tiny causeway connects to the island of **Marathonisi,** where Paris and Helen consummated their ill-fated love; to reach it, follow the harbor road to the right. **Buses** arrive at the north end of the waterfront from Sparta (1hr., 800dr); Tripoli (2¼hr., 1800dr); Kalamata (2 per day, 2020dr); Corinth (3hr., 3000dr); and Athens (4hr., 6 per day, 4500dr). **Ferries** sail from the quay near **Pl. Mavromichali,** in the middle of the waterfront (see p. 466). To explore the hard-to-reach parts of Mani, rent a **moped** at **Rent-A-Moped,** on the waterfront near the causeway. (4500dr per day. Open 9am-noon and 5-7:30pm.) **⚡Xenia Karlaftis Rooms,** on the water 20m from the causeway, offers spacious rooms. (Tel. (0733) 227 19. Singles 3000dr; doubles 5000dr; triples 6000dr. Higher prices July-Aug. Kitchen. Laundry.) To get to **Meltemi Camping,** 4km south of town toward Areopolis, take a city bus (3-4 per day, 230dr). (Tel. (0733) 228 33. 1400dr per person, 1200dr per tent, 800dr per car.) **Postal code:** 23200.

GREECE

From **Areopolis,** along the western coast of Mani, you can daytrip to the spectacular **Glyfatha Cave** (Spilia Dirou or Pyrgos Dirou), 4km from town. The 30-minute **boat ride** through the cave, which is believed to extend all the way to Sparta, down a subterranean river passes a forest of stalagmites. The bus to the caves leaves Areopolis at 11am and returns at 12:45pm (230dr). (Open daily June-Sept. 8am-5pm; Oct.-May 8am-2:45pm. 3500dr.) **Buses** stop in Areopolis' main *plateia* from Gythion (30min., 500dr); Sparta (1½hr., 4 per day, 1250dr); Kalamata (3 per day, 1600dr); and Athens (6hr., 4 per day, 4950dr). To stay at **Tsimova,** turn left at the end of Kapetan Matapan. (Tel. (0733) 513 01. Singles 5000dr; doubles 6000dr; triples 12,000dr.)

GEFYRA AND MONEMVASSIA (Μονεμβασια)

The island of Monemvassia, one of the major tourist sights on the Peloponnese, has an other-worldly quality. No cars or bikes are allowed on the island; pack horses bear groceries into the city, and narrow streets hide stairways, child-sized doorways, and flowered courtyards. From Monemvassia gate, a cobblestoned main street winds up past tourist shops and restaurants to the town square. At the edge of the cliffs perches the oft-photographed 12th-century **Agia Sofia;** to get there, navigate through the maze of streets to the edge of town farthest from the sea, where a path climbs the side of the cliff to the tip of the rock. Stay in modern and cheaper **Gefyra;** from there, it's a 20-minute walk down 23 Iouliou along the waterfront to the causeway, from which an orange **bus** connects to the Monemvassia gate (July-Aug. every 10min., free). **Buses** leave Gefyra twice daily from 23 Iouliou for Sparta (2½hr., 1750dr); Tripoli (4hr., 2800dr); and Corinth (5hr., 4100dr). **Private rooms** line the waterfront (doubles 5000-8000dr). **Hotel Sophos** is beside the National Bank on a side street. (Tel. (0732) 613 60. Singles 7000dr; doubles 9000dr.) **Camping Paradise** is 3.5km along the water on the mainland. (Tel. (0732) 611 23. 1400dr per person, 900-1200dr per tent, 950dr per car.) **To Limanaki,** beside the harbor on the mainland, serves exceptionally tasty Greek favorites.

NAFPLION (Ναυπλιο)

Nafplion is the perfect base for playing archaeologist, and its beautiful old town, Venetian architecture, fortresses, *plateias,* and pebble beach may even entice you to spend time away from the ruins. The town's crown jewel is the 18th-century **Palamidi Fortress,** with spectacular views of the town. To get there, walk the 3km road; or take a grueling 999 steps up from Arvanitias, across the park from the bus station. (Open M-F 7:45am-7pm, Sa-Su and off-season 8:30am-3pm. 800dr, students 400dr, EU students free.) **Buses** arrive on Singrou, off Pl. Kapodistrias, from Corinth (2hr., 1150dr) and Athens (3hr., 15 per day, 2500dr). To reach Bouboulinas along the waterfront, walk left from the station as you exit and follow Singrou to the harbor—everything to your left along the way is the old town. Buy tickets two days in advance for the **ferry** to Peiraias/Athens (4hr., 1 per day Tu-Su, 9300dr). The **tourist office** is on 25 Martiou. (Tel. (0752) 244 44. Open daily 9am-1pm and 4-8pm.) To enjoy the rooftop views of **Dimitris Bekas' Domatia** in the old town, turn up the stairs on Kokinou, and follow the sign for rooms off Staikopoulou; climb to the top, turn left, and go up another 50 steps. (Tel. (0752) 245 94. Singles 4500dr; doubles 6500dr.) In the new town, try **Hotel Artemis** on Argos. (Tel. (0752) 278 62. Singles 4000dr; doubles 6000dr.) **Taverna O Vasiles,** on Staikopoulou, serves a rabbit (1650dr) that will delight even the most avid Beatrix Potter fans. **Postal code:** 21100.

EXCURSIONS FROM NAFPLION: MYCENAE AND EPIDAVROS. Greece's supreme city from 1600 to 1100 BC, **Mycenae** (Μυκηνες) was once ruled by Agamemnon, leader of the Greek forces during the Trojan War (as gorily detailed in Homer's *Iliad*). Most of the site's treasures are in Athens, but the remaining **Lion's Gate** and the **Treasury of Atreus** are among the most-celebrated modern archaeological finds. (Open daily Apr.-Sept. 8am-7pm; Oct.-Mar. 8am-5pm. 1500dr, students 800dr, EU students free. Keep your ticket or pay again at Agamemnon's tomb.) Join the illustrious ranks of Heinrich Schliemann, Virginia Woolf, Claude Debussy, William Faulkner, Agatha Christie, Himmler, and Allen Ginsberg, who have all stayed at

Belle Helene Hotel; it also serves as a bus stop on the main road. (Tel. (0751) 762 25. Singles 7000dr; doubles 8000dr; triples 12,000dr.) **Buses** roll in from Nafplion (30min., 4 per day, 600dr); others from Athens (2½hr., 15 per day, 1750dr) stop at Fihtia, 1.5km away. **Trains** run from Athens to Fihtia via Corinth (5 per day). From Fihtia, take the Corinth-Argos road and follow the sign to Mycenae to reach the site.

The grandest structure at the ancient site of **Epidavros** (Επιδαυρος) is the **theater**, built in the early 2nd century BC, with a capacity of 14,000 at its height. Henry Miller wrote that he heard "the great heart of the world" beat here; the incredible acoustics allow you to stand at the top row of seats and hear a *drachma* drop on stage. Near the theater and ruins of the sanctuary is Epidavros' **museum.** (Open in summer M noon-7pm and Tu-Su 7:30am-7pm; off-season M noon-5pm and Tu-Su 8am-5pm. 1500dr, students 800dr, EU students free.) From late June to mid-August, the **Epidavros Theater Festival** brings performances of classical Greek plays (in modern Greek, but it'll all be Greek to you) on Friday or Saturday nights. Shows are at 9pm; purchase tickets at the site or in advance in Athens, at the Athens Festival Box Office (tel. (01) 322 14 59), or at Nafplion's bus station (tickets 4000-6000dr, students 2000dr). **Buses** arrive in Epidavros from Nafplion (1hr., 5 per day, 600dr).

CORINTH (Κορινθος)

Most visitors to the Peloponnese stop first at New Corinth, where a green bus drives 7km from Koliatsou, near Kolokotroni, to the ruins of **Ancient Corinth** (every hr. 6am-9pm, 20min., 300dr), which stand at the base of the **Acrocorinth.** Columns, metopes, and pediments lie around the courtyard of the excellent **museum** in fascinating chaos. As you exit the museum, the 6th-century BC **Temple of Apollo** is down the stairs to the left. The **fortress** at the top of Acrocorinth is a tough 1½-hour walk, but the summit holds the surprisingly intact remains of a **Temple to Aphrodite,** where disciples were initiated into the "mysteries of love." (Museum and site open daily in summer 8am-8pm; off-season 8am-5pm. Together 1200dr; students 600dr; free Su.) Hired **taxis** (tel. (0741) 314 64) from New Corinth will wait at the site for an hour (4000dr). Frequent **buses** stop in New Corinth two blocks inland, at Ermou and Koliatsou, from Mycenae (40min., 700dr); Athens (1¼hr., 1600dr); and Nafplion (1¼hr., 1150dr). **Trains** go to Athens (2hr., 15 per day, 800dr); Tripoli (2hr., 4 per day, 900dr); Patras (2½hr., 8 per day, 1000dr); and Kalamata (5hr., 4 per day, 1640dr). To get to the waterfront from the train station, turn right as you exit on Demokratias and right again on Damaskinou. **Hotel Akti,** 3 Ethnikis Antistasis, is near the waterfront. (Tel. (0741) 233 37. Singles 4000dr; doubles 8000dr.) To get to **Camping Korinth Beach,** 3km away, catch a bus (every 30min., 210dr) on Kollatsou, near Kolokotroni, and get off at the signs. (Tel. (0741) 279 20. 1400dr per person, 850dr per tent.)

NORTHERN AND CENTRAL GREECE

A bastion of Greek culture under 19th-century Ottoman rule, the provinces of Thessaly, Epirus, Macedonia, and Thrace offer forgotten regions threaded with mountain goat paths leading to some of Greece's freshest springs, glorious mountaintop vistas, and precious Byzantine treasures. Following these gems will lead you through a varied landscape of silvery olive groves, fruit-laden trees, and patchwork farmland.

THESSALONIKI (SALONICA; Θεσσαλονικη)

Thessaloniki's elusive character is a jumble of ancient, Byzantine, European, Turkish, Balkan, and contemporary Greek cultural and historical debris—utility, frilly beauty, and tasteless chintz all mingle together here. The Byzantine-Turkish fortress oversees the old town, while the city rests its feet among the tree-lined, congested avenues. Byzantine churches are encircled by modernity, masking interiors of glimmering gold mosaics, masterful frescoes, and floating domes.

GETTING THERE AND GETTING AROUND

Trains: Main Terminal (tel. 51 75 17), on Monastiriou in the western part of the city. Take any bus down Egnatia (100dr). To: **Athens** (6-8hr., 9 per day, 4100dr); **Sofia, Bulgaria** (7hr., 1 per day, 5500dr); and **Istanbul, Turkey** (12hr., 1 per day, 12,500dr). **OSE** (tel. 51 81 13), at Aristotelous and Ermou, has tickets and schedules. Open M-Sa 8am-2:30pm.

Buses: Most **KTEL** buses depart from between the port and railway station or from north of the railway. To: **Athens** (6hr., 20 per day, 8200dr), from along Monastiriou; **Ioannina** (7hr., 5 per day, 6000dr), from Giannitsa 39 (tel. 51 24 44); **Corinth** (7½hr., 1 per day, 8950dr), from Monastiriou 69 (tel. 52 72 65); **Patras** (8hr., 2 per day, 8250dr), from Monastiriou 87 (tel. 52 52 53). **International buses** (tel. 59 91 00) leave from the train station for **Sofia** (6hr., 4 per day, 5600dr) and **Istanbul** (12hr., 1 per day, 24,300dr).

Ferries and Hydrofoils: Buy tickets at **Karacharisis Travel and Shipping Agency,** Koundouriotou 8 (tel. 52 45 44; fax 53 22 89), on the corner. Open M-F 9am-9pm, Sa 9am-3pm. To: **Limnos** (7hr., departs W and Su 1am, 5300dr); **Lesvos** (9hr., departs W and Su 1am, 8300dr); **Samos** (14hr., departs W 4pm, 9600dr); **Mykonos** (16hr., departs M 2pm and F 7pm, 9200dr); and **Hios** (21hr., departs W and Su 1am, 8300dr). **Flying Dolphins:** June-Sept. daily 8am and Th-M (usually) 4:30pm. To: **Skiathos** (3¾hr., 8500dr); **Skopelos** (4½hr., 9300dr); and **Skyros** (6hr., 13,400dr). **Crete Air Travel,** Dragoumi 1 (tel. 54 74 07), opposite the port, sells tickets. Open M-F 8:30am-9pm, Sa 8:30am-3pm, Su 9am-3pm.

Public Transportation: Extensive **buses** (100dr) traverse the city. Buses 8, 10, 11, and 31 run up and down Egnatia. Buy tickets at kiosks or ticket booths at major stations.

ORIENTATION AND PRACTICAL INFORMATION

Running from the shore inland parallel to the water, the main streets are **Nikis, Mitropoleos, Tsimiski, Ermou, Egnatia,** and **Agios Dimitriou.** Intersecting these streets and running from the water into town are (west to east) **Dragoumi, El. Venizelou, Aristotelous, Agios Sophias,** and **Eth. Aminis.** Tsimiski, Mitropoleos, Ag. Sophias, and smaller streets between Aristotelous and Ipodromiou are the main shopping streets. The roads north of Ag. Dimitriou get smaller and steeper and lead up into the **old town.** Facing inland, go left on Mitropoleos to reach the **Ladadika** district.

Tourist Office: EOT, Pl. Aristotelous (tel. 27 18 88; fax 26 55 04), 1 block from the water. Open M-F 9am-9pm, Sa 10am-6pm, Su 10am-5pm; reduced hours in winter.

Currency Exchange: Banks and **24-hour ATMs** line Timiski, including **National Bank,** Tsimiski 11 (tel. 53 86 21). Open M-F 7:45am-2pm and 6-8pm.

American Express: Memphis Travel, Aristotelous 3, 1st fl. (tel. 28 23 51). Cashes traveler's checks and exchanges currency. Open M-F 9:30am-3:30pm and Sa 9am-2pm.

Consulates: Bulgaria, N. Manou 12 (tel. 82 92 10). Open M-F 10am-noon. **Cyprus,** L. Nikis 37 (tel. 26 06 11). Open M-F 9am-1pm. **Turkey,** Ag. Dimitriou 151 (tel. 24 84 52). Open M-F 9am-noon. **UK,** Venizelou 8 (tel. 27 80 06). Open M-F 8am-1pm. **US,** Tsimiski 43 (tel. 24 290 0). Open M, W, and F 9am-noon.

Laundromat: Bianca, L. Antoniadou 3 (tel. 20 96 02), behind the church to your right as you face the Arch of Galerius. 1400dr for wash, dry, and soap. Open M-Sa 8am-3pm.

Tourist Police: Dodekanissou 4, 5th fl. (tel. 55 48 70 or 55 48 71). Open 24hr. For the **general police,** call 55 38 00 or 100.

Hospital: Ippokration Public Hospital, A. Papanastasiou 49 (tel. 83 79 20).

Internet Access: The Web, Gonata 4 (tel. 23 70 31), 1 block south of Svolou, near Pl. Navarino between Ipodromiou and Gounari. 700-900dr per hr. Open 24hr.

Telephones: OTE, Karolou Diehl 27 (tel. 22 18 99), at the corner of Ermou, 1 block east of Aristotelous. Open daily 7:15am-9:30pm.

Post Office: On Aristotelous, just before Egnatia. Open M-F 7:30am-8pm, Sa 7:30am-2pm, Su 9am-1:30pm. Address mail to be held: Scary SPICE, *Poste Restante,* **54101** Thessaloniki, Greece.

| PHONE CODE | City code: 031. From outside Greece, dial int'l dialing prefix (see inside back cover) + 30 + 31 + local number. |

📷 ACCOMMODATIONS AND FOOD

Most less-expensive hotels are clustered along the western end of Egnatia, between Pl. Dimokratias (500m east of the train station) and Pl. Dikastiriou. Egnatia can be noisy and gritty, but you'll have to pay more elsewehere.

📷**Hotel Augustos,** Elenis Svoronou 4 (tel. 52 29 55; tel./fax 52 25 00). From Egnatia, turn north at the Argo Hotel and it's straight ahead. The best budget deal in town. Some rooms with bath. Singles 5000-7000dr; doubles 7000-10,500dr; triples 13,000dr.

Youth Hostel, Alex. Svolou 44 (tel. 225 946; fax 262 208). Take tram 8, 10, 11, or 31 on Egnatia and get off at "Kamara" (Arch of Galerius), walk toward the water, and turn left on Svolou. 1800dr; nonmembers 2000dr. 3-night max. stay; nonmembers 1-night if full. Reception 8:30-11am and 7-11pm. Lockout 11am-6:30pm. Open Mar.-Nov.

Hotel Acropolis, Tantalidou 4 (tel. 536 170). From Pl. Dimokratias, take the 2nd right off Egnatia after Dodekanissou. Quiet. Singles 5000dr; doubles 6000dr; triples 7000dr.

Hotel Averof, L. Sofou 24 (tel. 538 840; fax 543 194), at Egnatia. Friendly staff and communal TV room. Singles 6000-9000dr; doubles 8000dr, with bath 12,000dr.

Hotel Emporikon, Singrou 14 (tel. 525 560 or 514 431), at Egnatia. Basic rooms. Singles 5000dr; doubles 8000dr, with shower 10,000dr; triples 12,000dr.

Most food can be found east of Aristotelous, on several streets a block south of Egnatia; the innovative places a block down from Egnatia between Dragoumi and El. Venizelou cater to a younger clientele. There are **open-air markets** on Vati Kioutou, just off Aristotelous between Irakliou and Egnatia. **📷Rogoti,** Venizelou 8, on the corner, has been serving up *soutzoukakia* (meatballs; 1650dr) since 1928. **O Loutros,** Komninon 15, near the corner of Irakliou, has tasty fish (entrees 1000-2800dr). East of Aristotelous, a block south of Egnatia, **Mesogeios,** Balanou 38, is the largest *ouzeri* in the area (entrees 1200-2200dr).

👁️ 🎵 SIGHTS AND ENTERTAINMENT

Salonica was an important city in the Byzantine Empire, and the era left it with enough churches to keep devout old women crossing themselves at a truly aerobic rate on the buses down Egnatia alone. Over the centuries, earthquakes, fire, and Muslim appropriations have severely damaged most of its 90 churches, but many are still worth a visit. Come early and dress modestly. **Agios Dimitrios,** north of Aristotelous, is the city's oldest and most famous church. (Open daily 8am-8pm.) The **Roman Forum,** on Egnatia behind the Pl. Dikastiriou bus station, although not terribly spectacular (it's still under excavation), was the center of public life from the 2nd to 3rd centuries AD. The domed 7th-century **Agia Sophia,** on Ag. Sophia, erected on the site of an earlier 5th-century basilica, served as Thessaloniki's cathedral from the 8th century until it returned to mosquehood in 1523-24. (Open daily 7am-1pm and 5-7pm.) Across the street, **Panagia Achirpoeitos,** is chock full of mosaics. (Open daily 7:30am-12:30pm and 6-9pm.) Originally designed as an emperor's mausoleum, the **Rotunda** became a church named **Agios Georgios;** the walls of the enormous, cylindrical Rotunda are plastered with some of the city's most lavish mosaics. (Open daily 7am-2:30pm.) A colonnaded processional once led south from the Rotunda to the **Arch of Galerius,** at the intersection of Egnatia and Gounari, and the **Palace of Galerius,** south of the Arch on Dragoumi near Pl. Navarino.

The **Archaeological Museum** is packed with Macedonian gold, grand mosaics, and Roman heads. Restorations on the **Derveni Papyrus,** the only papyrus to have survived Greece's humid climate, may be completed by 2000. Take bus 3 from the train station to Pl. Hanth. (Open M 12:30-7pm, Tu-Su 8am-7pm; reduced in winter. 1500dr, students 800dr, EU students free.) Behind the archaeological museum across Septembriou 3, the **Museum of Byzantine Culture** features mosaic fragments salvaged from the 1917 fire at Ag. Demetrius, 3rd- and 4th-century frescoed tombs, and the assortment of Byzantine fish-hooks, tableware, belt buckles, and dice. (Open M 12:30-8pm, Tu-Su 8am-7pm; reduced in winter. 1000dr, students 500dr, EU students free. Joint ticket with Archaeological Museum 2000dr.) The **White Tower,** at the far eastern end of Nikis, is all that remains of a 15th-century Venetian seawall. It once

GREECE

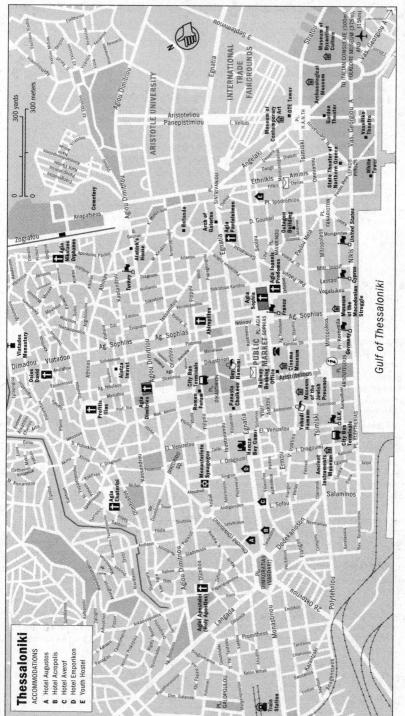

Thessaloniki

ACCOMMODATIONS
A Hotel Augustos
B Hotel Acropolis
C Hotel Averof
D Hotel Emporikon
E Youth Hostel

Gulf of Thessaloniki

served as an Ottoman "Death Row," where an elite corps of Ottoman soldiers carried out gruesome executions; it now houses the **Museum of Early Christian Art.** (Open Tu-Su 8am-2:30pm. Free.) The **Museum of Jewish Presence,** Irakliou 26, chronicles the city's Jewish community from the 15th century to the present. (Open M-F 10am-1:30pm; ring the bell if the door is closed. Free.)

There are three main hubs for late-night fun: the bars and cafés of the **Ladadika** district (once the city's red-light district), the waterfront, and the big open-air discos that throb near the airport exit (2000-2500dr by taxi). **Mylos,** Andreou Georgiou 56 (tel. 52 59 68), in the far west of the city (take bus 31 or a taxi), is a massive entertainment complex with art exhibits, bars, and live shows. You might have thought it died with the 80s, but disco fever lives forever at ▧Tataboo Disco, right at the airport exit (cover 2000dr). You can also dance the night away at **Theatron** (tel. 47 11 60) and **Ipnovates** (tel. 47 21 59), next to each other, 11km east of the city along the main highway (cover 1500-3000dr; includes 1 drink.)

MOUNT OLYMPUS (Ορος Ολυμπος)

Erupting out of the Thermaic Gulf, the impressive height (nearly 3000m) and formidable slopes of Mt. Olympus once so awed the ancients that they named it the divine dwelling place of their gods. A network of well-maintained **hiking** trails now makes the summit accessible to just about anyone with sturdy legs and a taste for adventure, although you may yearn for a pair of Hermes' winged sandals. Two approaches to the peaks begin near **Litohoro** (280m), one at **Prionia** (1100m), 18km from the village, and one at **Diastavrosi** (also called **Gortsia;** 1300m), 14km away. There is no bus to the trailheads from Litohoro, so you'll have to walk, hitch, or drive the asphalt road. A **taxi** will cost you about 6000dr to Prionia or 1500dr to Diastavrosi. You'll want to make your ascent between May and October, when Persephone returns to Olympus from the Underworld and her mother, Demeter, warms the earth. **Mytikas,** the tallest peak, is inaccessible without special equipment before June. There are three **refuges** near the summits where you can find lodgings. The EOS-run **Spilos Agapitos** ("Refuge A"; 2100m) is about 800m below Skala and Mytikas peaks. In addition to offering accommodations, the English-speaking staff also happily dispenses hiking info over the phone to prospective hikers, and can also help you reserve nights in other EOS refuges. (Tel. (0352) 818 00. 2500dr; members of any mountain club 2000dr; camping 500dr. Open mid-May to late October.)

Trains (tel. (0352) 225 22) run from Athens (7hr., 3 per day, 3400dr) and Thessaloniki (1½hr., 5 per day, 830dr) to the Litohoro station; from there walk 1km to the **bus stop** to catch a 5km ride into town (20min., 13 per day, 220dr). A **taxi** from the train station should cost around 2000dr. Or take a direct KTEL **bus** (tel. (0352) 812 71) from Athens (6hr., 3 per day, 7250dr) or Thessaloniki (1½hr., 16 per day, 1700dr); they'll arrive at the station opposite the church in Litohoro's main *plateia*. Opposite the bus stop is the town's **tourist office.** (Tel. (0352) 831 00. Open 8:15am-9:45pm.) The most affordable hotel is the **Hotel Park,** Ag. Nikolaou 23, about 10m down from the *plateia*. (Tel. (0352) 812 52. Singles 6500dr; doubles 8000dr; triples 9000dr.) **Camp** at **Olympus Zeus** (tel. (0352) 221 15) or **Olympus Beach** (tel. (0352) 221 12 or 221 13), on the beach about 5km from town.

METEORA (Μετεωρα)

Southwest of Olympus lie the majestic, iron-gray pinnacles of the Meteora rock formations, bedecked by 24 exquisite, gravity-defying Byzantine monasteries. (All open Apr.-Sept. Sa-Su and W 9am-12:30pm and 3:20-6pm; staggered schedules during the rest of the week. 500dr per monastery. Dress modestly; women must wear skirts. No photography allowed.) The **Grand Meteoron Monastery** is the oldest, largest, and most important of the monasteries, with brilliant frescoes of the Roman persecution of Christians. The chapel of **Varlaam Monastery** contains 16th-century frescoes, including a particularly disturbing rendition of the Apocalypse. The most popular base for exploring Meteora is the town of **Kalambaka** (Καλαμπακα). There will be **no train service** to Kalambaka through 2000 due to construction of new rail lines, but **buses** arrive from Thessaloniki (3hr., 6 per day, 3600dr); Ioannina (3hr., 2 per day, 2350dr); Athens (5hr., 8 per day, 5400dr); and Patras (6hr., 2 per week, 5600dr). From the bus station, walk uphill to reach the town's small central square, at the intersection of the town's major thoroughfares. Local buses depart from Kalambaka for Meteora (20min., 2 per day, 230dr); a **taxi** will run you there for about 1500dr. Most people walk the 6km downhill back to town, visiting the monasteries along the way. ▓**Koka Roka** offers an awe-inspiring view of Meteora; from the central square, follow Vlachara uphill until it ends, then bear left and follow the signs to Kanari (15min.). (Tel. (0432) 245 54. 3500dr per person without bath. With bath, singles 6000dr; doubles 8000dr; triples 10,000dr.) **Postal code:** 42200.

OSIOS LOUKAS (Οσιος Λουκας)

The 10th- to 11th-century Byzantine monastery, still in use today, is absolutely exquisite: overlooking Boeotia and Phokis from the verdant slopes of Mt. Elikon more than 1700m above sea level, it contains golden mosaics, vibrant frescoes, and intricate brick- and stonework. Osios Loukas is the most famous and probably the most beautiful of Greece's monasteries. Dress modestly (long skirts for women, long pants for men, no bare shoulders). Two churches are at the site: the **katholikon**, on the right after the museum, built in AD 1011 and dedicated to the monastery's founding saint, Osios Loukas, is the most impressive of the monastery's jewels; the smaller **Church of Panagia** holds the dried body of the saint himself in a glass coffin, as well as a **crypt** with stunning frescoes that are not to be missed. (Tel. (0267) 22 797. Open daily May to mid-Sept. 8am-2pm and 4-7pm; mid-Sept. to Apr. 8am-5pm. 800dr, students 400dr, seniors 600dr, EU students free.) Without a car or a lot of faith in the *very* sporadic traffic to the monastery (*Let's Go* does not recommend hitchhiking), you must hire a **taxi** (tel. (0267) 22 322; 5000-6000dr one-way) or walk along the hilly, narrow road from the town of Distomo, 9km west.

IOANNINA (Ιωαννινα)

On the shores of Lake Pamvotis lies Ioannina, the capital of and largest city in Epirus. The city has not yet escaped the intriguing, half-legendary historical presence of Ali Pasha, who was the Ottoman governor of Epirus before the Greek War of Independence and rebuilt the Byzantine walls of his dreamed-of capital of a Greek-Albanian empire. The walled **Frourio** (also known as the Castro), which juts regally over the lake, contains the old city. Enter on Karamanli; just inside the facing wall is a **synagogue,** Ioustinianon 16. Follow signs to the **Its Kale** (Inner Acropolis), which encloses the 18th-century **Fethiye Camii** (Victory Mosque) and the **tomb of Ali Pasha.** The smaller of the walled inner areas contains the **Municipal Museum,** housed in the lovely **Aslan Pasha Camii** (mosque). (Open daily July-Sept. 8am-8pm; Oct.-May 8am-3pm. 700dr, students 300dr.) Off Averof near the city center, the **Archaeological Museum** has tablets on which puzzled ancients wrote angsty queries to that divine Dear Abby, the oracle in nearby Dodoni. (Open Tu-Su 8am-2pm. 500dr, students free.) Catch a frequent **boat** (10min.; 150dr) across the lake to the cleverly named **To Nisi** (The Island) to explore **Byzantine monasteries.** Follow the signs to Averof's end at the waterfront, and veer left at the walls on Karamanli to reach the dock.

Buses run regularly from Zossimadon 4 to Athens (7hr., 7250dr) and Thessaloniki (7hr., 6050dr). If you walk uphill from the station to the intersection and continue uphill along M. Botsari on the left (as you face the Agricultural Bank), the right fork leads to Napoleonda Zerva and the **tourist office.** (Tel. (0651) 250 86; fax 721 48. Open daily in summer 8am-2:30pm and 5:30-8pm; in winter 8am-2:30pm.) **Café Internet and Ioannina Club,** Stoa Sarka 31-32, is past the tourist office, to the left off Nap. Zerra. (1000dr per hr. Open daily 10am-1am.) To get to **Hotel Paris,** Tsirigoti 6, walk uphill from the station and look left at the bank. (Tel. (0651) 205 41. Singles 6000-8000dr; doubles 9-10,000dr.) **Hotel Metropolis,** Kristali 2, is on the corner of Averof toward the waterfront. (Tel. (0651) 262 07. Singles 5000-6000dr; doubles 8-10,000dr.) Eat on the waterfront or in the old town. **Postal code:** 45221.

🖪 **EXCURSION FROM IOANNINA: DODONI.** Ancient Dodoni (Δωδωνη), the site of mainland Greece's oldest oracle, is at the base of a mountain 22km southeast of Ioannina. According to myth, Zeus resided in Dodoni as the roots of a giant oak while courting a nearby cypress tree (don't ask). Although the oracle no longer exists, the well-preserved **amphitheater** remains. (Open daily in summer 8am-7pm; in winter 8am-5pm. 500dr; students free.) Dodoni is difficult to visit; if you take the 4:30pm **bus** from Ioannina's small station (30min., M-F, 400dr), you can explore for 30min. before catching the bus back at 5:30pm. Or **cab** it (at least 5000dr round-trip).

IONIAN ISLANDS (Νησια Του Ιονιου)

The Ionian Islands have followed a historical path distinct from mainland Greece. Situated on the country's western edge, the islands escaped Ottoman occupation, and were instead conquered at various times by the Venetians, British, French, and Russians. Each of the Ionians' uninvited visitors left a lasting cultural, commercial, and architectural imprint. The islands also enjoy the company of hundreds of ferry-hopping backpackers, who make the short trip from Italy.

✈ FERRIES TO ITALY

If you want to catch a ferry to **Italy,** buy your ticket at least a day ahead in high-season; be sure to find out if the port tax (1500-2000dr) is included. Ferries run to **Corfu** from **Brindisi** (8hr., 4 per day, 7500-19,500dr); **Bari** (10hr., 3-4 per week, 9000dr); **Ancona** (21hr., 1 per day, 10,550-16,750dr); **Trieste** (24hr., 2 per week, 14,500-19,400dr); and **Venice** (26hr., 1-2 per day, 10,450-21,800dr). **Catamarans** also go to **Corfu** from **Brindisi** (3¼hr., 9am, 17,800-27,000dr, under 28 5-10,000dr less). In summer, ferries connect **Cephalonia** to **Brindisi, Venice,** and **Ancona.**

CORFU (KERKYRA; Κερκυρα)

Since Odysseus washed ashore and praised the lush beauty of Corfu, the seas have brought Crusaders, conquerors, and colonists to this verdant Ionian Island. Sadly, its enchanting beauty has often captivated too many, leading to the degradation of many of its beaches. But those who stray from **Corfu Town** (mainly a transport hub) and the beaten path are greatly rewarded. **Paleokastritsa beach,** where Odysseus supposedly washed ashore, lies west of Corfu Town; take a KTEL **bus** to Paleokastritsa (45min., 10 per day, 650dr). A 90-minute walk from there will bring you to the white mountaintop monastery **Panagia Theotokos** and the fort of **Angelokastro** (Castle of the Holy Angels), which jut out over the sea. South of Paleokastritsa is **Pelekas Town;** walk 30min. downhill to reach **Pelekas beach.** The more touristed **Glyfada beach,** 5km from Pelekas Town, is accessible by free **shuttles** from Pelekas and by KTEL **buses** from Pl. Sanrocco in Corfu Town. The isolated beach **Moni Myrtidon** and the unofficial nude beach **Myrtiotissa** are also nearby. **Agios Gordios,** 10km south of Pelekas, offers impressive rock formations, a good beach, and the immensely popular (and frat-like) **Pink Palace Hotel.** On weekends, wild toga parties at the "palace" conjure up scenes from *Animal House.* (Tel. (0661) 530 24; fax 530 25. 6000dr includes breakfast, dinner, ferry pick-up and drop-off, and nightclub.) Blue **buses** run to Agios Gordios from Pl. Sanrocco (45min., 7 per day, 300dr).

　Ferries run from Corfu Town to Italy; Cephalonia (5hr., departs Sa 11am, 5200dr); and Patras (9hr., 1-2 per day, 5580-5800dr). KTEL runs two **bus/ferry** combos daily to Thessaloniki (9hr., 8000dr) and Athens (9hr., 8150dr). KTEL inter-city **green buses** depart from just off I. Theotaki; **blue buses** (municipal buses) leave from Pl. Sanrocco. From the customs house at the new port, cross the intersection and walk uphill on Avramiou, which becomes I. Theotoki, to reach Pl. Sanrocco (1km). The **tourist office** is at the corner of Rizospaston Voulefton and Iak. Folila. (Tel. (0661) 375 20. Open May-Sept. M-F 8:30am-2:15pm, Tu and Th-F 5:30-9pm; Oct.-Apr. M-F 5:30-8:30pm.) A branch is in the customs house at the new port. **Tourist agencies** along Arseniou and Stratigou, also by the new port, help find singles (from 5000dr) and doubles (from 6000dr). To get to **Hotel Europa,** Giantsilio 10, from the customs house, cross the main street and make a right; Giantsilio is a tiny road on your left just after the road turns and becomes Napoleonta. (Tel. (0661) 393 04. Singles 4000-5000dr; doubles 6000-7000dr; triples 8000dr.) **Hotel Ionian,** Xen. Sratigou 46, is at the new port. (Tel. (0661) 399 15. Singles 6000-7000dr; doubles 8-10,000dr.) There are **supermarkets** on I. Theotaki and in Pl. Sanrocco. **Postal code:** 49100.

GREECE

CEPHALONIA (Κεφαλονια)

Dubbed "The Island of Peculiarities" for its disparate but beautiful beaches, subterranean caves, rugged mountains, and shady forests, Cephalonia is ideal for a longer stay. **Argostoli** (Αργοστολι), the capital and transport hub of Cephalonia and Ithaka, is a busy, noisy city with palm-lined, traffic-filled streets. **Ferries** sail to Ithaka (1hr., 3 per day, 480dr) and Patras (3hr., 1 per day, 3200dr). **Buses** (tel. (0671) 222 81) leave from the station at the southern end of the waterfront. The **tourist office** is at the port beside the port authority. (Tel. (0671) 222 48. Open in summer M-Sa 8am-2:30pm and 5-9pm; off-season M-F 7:30am-2pm.) To get from the waterfront to the main *plateia*, follow 21 Maiou (to the right of the station as you face inland) up two blocks. To get from the waterfront to **Villa Aspasia Rooms To Let,** follow the left edge of the *plateia* up the hill on Lassi, turn right past the garden, and it'll be on your left. (Tel. (0671) 235 11. Doubles July-Aug. 9000dr; Sept.-June 6000dr.)

A small pretty town on a harbor surrounded by steep, lush hills, **Sami** (Σαμη), 24km from Argostoli, offers white-pebble beaches, proximity to **Melissani Lake** and **Drograti Cave,** and a break from the hustle and bustle of Argostoli. **Buses** arrive from Argostoli (4 per day, 500dr). **Hotel Kyma,** in the main *plateia*, has spectacular views. (Tel. (0674) 220 64. Singles 6000dr; doubles 10,000dr.)

ITHAKA (ITHAKI; Ιθακη)

The least-touristed and perhaps the most beautiful of the Ionian Islands, Ithaka (Ith-ah-KEE) is all too often passed over for the tourist havens of Lefkada and Cephalonia. Those who do come discover the island's pebbled, rocky hillsides and terraced olive groves. According to Homer, Ithaka was the kingdom that **Odysseus** left behind, while **Penelope** faithfully waited 20 years for his return. Ithaka's largest town and capital, **Vathy,** wraps around a circular bay skirted by steep, green hills. Those of poetic bent and sturdy footwear can climb up to the **Cave of the Nymphs,** where Odysseus supposedly hid the treasure that the Phoenicians bestowed upon him. (Open July-Aug. 200dr. Bring a flashlight.) **Ferries** connect Vathy to Sami on Cephalonia (3hr., 1040dr) and Astakos on the mainland (4hr., 1910dr). Boats also go from Piso Aetos (10min. taxi ride) on the southern side of Ithaka, to Sami on Cephalonia (1hr., 620dr). **Ferry** schedules vary; check with **Delas Tours** (tel. (0674) 321 04; open daily 9am-2pm and 4-10pm) or **Polyctor Tours** (tel. (0674) 331 20; open daily 9am-1:30pm and 5-9pm), both in the main square right off the water. Your best bet for accommodations is to find a private *domatia* (6000-8000dr in summer). **Camping** at **Dexa Beach,** Odysseus' mythological landing point, is free. **Taverna To Trexantiri** is the hands-down favorite among locals. **Postal code:** 28300.

The island's only **bus** runs north from Vathy, passing through the scenic villages of Lefki, Stavros, Platrithiai, Frikes (1hr., 350dr), and Kioni. Schedules are erratic, but buses usually run three times daily in high-season. **Frikes** and **Kioni,** both with small, crystal-blue harbors on the northern coast of the island, are exceptionally beautiful. **Stavros** is high in the mountains on the way to Frikes and Kioni and was allegedly once home to **Odysseus' Palace;** the site is now a small museum filled with excavated items from the site. (Open July-Aug. Free; small tip expected.)

THE SPORADES (Σποραδες)

The Sporades seem like a fairy-tale family. Greece's second-largest island, Evia, is the queen, and the Northern Sporades are her three princesses: quietly sophisticated Skopelos is the eldest, home to artists and jazz-filled harbors; Skiathos is the middle child, in a hurry to grow up and the best party scene for miles; and innocent Alonissos, the youngest, is a land of pristine wilderness and hiking trails. Skyros, in the east, is the vaguely enchanted granny, the keeper of the Old Ways.

■ GETTING THERE AND GETTING AROUND

To get to most of the Sporades from **Athens,** take the daily bus from the station at Liossion 260 to **Agios Konstantinos** (2½hr., 16 per day, 2650dr), where **Nomikos/Gou-**

tos Lines ferries run to **Skiathos** (3½hr., 1-2 per day, 3300dr); **Skopelos** (4hr., 2 per day, 4085dr); and **Alonissos** (5½hr., 3 per day, 4300dr). To reach **Skyros**, take a bus from Athens to **Kimi** (3½hr., 2 per day, 2600dr), between Evia and Linaria, and take a direct ferry (1¾hr., 2300dr, 2 per day; high-season only). Nomikos/Goutos also runs ferries from **Thessaloniki** to **Skopelos** (6hr., 3 per week, 4800dr) and **Alonissos** (6hr., 1 per week, 5630dr). **Flying Dolphins hydrofoils** follow nearly the same routes, and in general cost twice as much and are twice as fast.

Ferries and hydrofoils also connect the various islands. **Nomikos/Goutos ferries** (Skiathos tel. (0427) 222 09; Skopelos tel. (0424) 223 63) run from **Skiathos** to **Skopelos** (1-1½hr., 2-5 per day, 1400-1800dr) and **Alonissos** (2hr., 1-3 per day, 1800-1900dr) as well as between **Skopelos** and **Alonissos** (30min., 1-2 per day, 1100dr); again, **Flying Dolphins hydrofoils** are generally twice as fast and twice as expensive. **Skyros** is only accessible from the other Sporades by Flying Dolphins (4-8 per week): to **Alonissos** (1¼hr., 7300dr); **Skopelos** (1¾hr., 6800dr); and **Skiathos** (2¼hr., 8300dr).

SKIATHOS (Σκιαθος)

Ski-A-Thos. To the Greeks it's Sporadic and to the Halkydians it's Little Mykonos, but to the middle-aged Brits who come here to let their hair down, it's Disco Heaven. Package tourists pack the streets of **Skiathos Town,** while budding writers follow Papadiamantis to the beautiful beaches and nature preserves. Buses leave the port in Skiathos Town for the southern **beaches** (every 15min., 280dr), including **Megali Ammos, Nostros, Platanias,** and **Vromolimnos.** The road and bus route end in **Koukounaries,** where the more secluded beaches begin, including the lovely, pine-wooded **Biotrope of Koukounaries;** the yellow, curved **Banana Beach;** and the nude, gay-friendly **Little Banana Beach. Private rooms** abound, particularly on Evangelista, but in a pinch head to the **Rooms to Let Office,** in the wooden kiosk by the port. (Tel. (0427) 229 90. Open daily 8:30am-midnight.) **Pension Danaos,** in an alley off Papadiamantis opposite the OTE, packs in a young backpacker crowd. (Tel. (0427) 228 34. 1- to 4-person rooms 5000-10,000dr. Open May-Sept.) **Camping Koukounaries** is on the bus route to Koukouniares between stops 20 and 21 (get off at 21). (Tel. (0427) 49 250. 1700dr per person, 1000dr per tent.) Eat at **Gyro Gyro Oli,** just off Papadiamantiou to the left, a block inland, last in the string of fast-food stands. (*Gyros* 400dr. *Souvlaki* 250dr. Open daily noon-late.) Indulge yourself at the countless bars in **Pl. Papadiamantis** or along **Polytechniou** or **Evangelista,** and then dance all night long at the clubs on the far right side of the coast.

SKOPELOS (Σκοπελος)

Relaxed Skopelos sits between the glitzy Bacchanalia of Skiathos and the largely untouched wilderness of Alonissos. The pious head to the hills, where the island's monasteries and shrines hide in the woods, still heady with the fading sounds of *rembetika* (folk songs). About eight **buses** per day leave from the stop left of the waterfront (as you face inland) for **beaches** near **Stafylos, Agnondas, Milia,** and **Loutraki. Hiking trails** wind through the terrain to monasteries and beaches. The Thalpo **tourist agency,** on the 2nd fl. behind Restaurant Akteon, is up on everything from Flying Dolphins tickets to catching octopi. (Tel. (0424) 229 47. Open daily M-Sa 10am-9pm, Su 10am-2pm.) Decent offers for rooms come at the dock; otherwise, try the **Rooms and Apartments Association of Skopelos,** in the small wooden building near the dock. (Tel. (0424) 245 67. Open 10am-2pm and 6-10pm.) ◪**Pension Sotos,** 10m left of Thalpos Travel, is a well-located gem. (Tel. (0424) 225 49; fax 236 68. Doubles 6500-10,000dr; triples 9-15,000dr; quads 11-16,500dr.) You can find 350dr *gyros* on **Pl. Platanos,** but for the good stuff, put on your walking shoes: walk 10min. up the white-washed steps at the far right of the harbor (facing inland) to reach ◪**Anatoli,** where one of the world's last great *rembetika* singers, Giorgos Xintaris, sings the old songs nightly (usually a little before midnight; meals 600-3000dr).

ALONISSOS (Αλοννησος)

Of the islands comprising Greece's recently christened **National Marine Park,** only Alonissos is inhabited. Most of the 25 small, remaining islets can be visited only by organized tour boats in summer; trips are advertised and sold along the harbor (usually 1-2 days; from 12,000dr in high-season). Alonissos' unexplored northern coast defines a clear and white-sanded boundary against the sea, and **hiking trails** lace the high heartland; check the kiosk next to the ferry dock in **Patitiri**, for all intents and purposes the only town on the island, for an overview of walking routes. **Alonissos Travel,** in the center of the waterfront, books excursions and sells ferry tickets. (Tel./fax (0424) 655 11. Open daily 9am-midnight.) Inquire at **Boutique Mary,** on the right side of Pelasgon, about rooms at the **Dimakis Pension** next door. (Tel. (0424) 652 94. Singles 5000-7000dr; doubles 6000-8000dr.) **Camping Rocks** is 1km away off Pelasgon; follow the signs. (Tel. (0424) 654 10. 1000dr per person, 500dr per tent.) Tiny **Artolicoudies,** marked by the yellow sign inland on Pelasgon, serves delicious olive bread (400dr) and traditional pastries. (Open daily 7am-2pm and 6pm-10pm.)

Hikers may find the beautiful **Old Town** (Hora; Χωραατ) a more convenient spot to snooze than Patitiri. The island's only **bus** runs between Hora and Patitiri (10min., 12 per day, 250dr); alternatively, walk uphill on Pelasgon from Patitiri and continue on the main road (1hr.). No dancing hippopotami await at **Fantasia House,** but it's just up from the bus stop on the left. (Tel. (0424) 651 84. Doubles 7000dr-10,000dr.)

SKYROS (Σκυρος)

Crayola-bright and gorgeous, Skyros protected itself first against pirates, and then against modern culture, with its huge cliffs, long sandy beaches, pine woods, and cleverly hidden villages. Stark-white, cubist **Skyros Town** (Horio) is a relic of prewar Greek life; old men sew sandals by porch light late into the evening and women embroider patterns learned from pirates. Above Skyros Town, the 1000-year-old **Monastery of St. George** and the **Castle of Licomidus** command magnificent views of Skyrian sunsets. (Open daily Mar.-Aug. 7am-10pm, Sept.-Feb. 7:30am-6pm. Free.) **Ferries** arrive in the tiny western port of Linaria (2 per day), and are met by **buses** to Skyros Town (20min., 250dr); tell the driver where you're going. The superb **Faltaits Museum,** up the stairs from Pl. Rupert Brooke in Skyros Town, boasts an incredible folk art collection. (Open daily 10am-1pm and 6-9pm. 500dr.) To reach the **tourist office,** take the first right after the street with the post office. (Tel./fax (0222) 927 89. Open daily July-Aug. 9am-3pm and 6:30-10:30pm; Sept.-June 8:30am-2:30pm.) **Skyros Travel,** past the central *plateia* on Agoras, organizes boat excursions and rents mopeds (3500dr per day). (Tel. (0222) 911 23. Open daily 9:15am-2:15pm and 6:30-10pm.) For a genuine experience, bargain to stay in a traditional Skyrian house; the thick-walled treasure troves are brimming with Delft ceramics and Italian linens, purchased from pirates who conveniently looted much of the known world. If you're chicken, **Hotel Elena,** next to the post office, offers plain rooms. (Tel. (0222) 917 38. Singles 5000dr; doubles 8000dr; triples 10,000dr.) The incredible **O Pappas Kai Ego** ("Grandpa and me") serves brilliant Skyrian specialties (entrees 800-2000dr).

THE CYCLADES (Κυκλαδες)

When people wax rhapsodic about the Greek islands, chances are they're talking about the Cyclades. Whatever your idea of Greece—peaceful cobblestoned streets and whitewashed houses, breathtaking sunsets, scenic hikes, night-long revelry—you'll find it here. Although each island has quiet villages and untouched spots, in summer most are mobbed by backpackers convening for the post-Eurail party.

▐ GETTING THERE AND GETTING AROUND

Ferries from **Peiraias/Athens** toot to **Mykonos** (6hr., 2-3 per day, 5100dr); **Naxos** (7hr., 4-8per day, 5000dr); **Paros** (6hr., 4 per day, 4950dr); **Ios** (8hr., 4-6 per day, 5500dr); and **Santorini** (9hr., 6090dr). Ferries from **Crete** connect to **Ios** (5hr., 1 per week, 4300dr) and **Naxos** (7hr., 2 per day, 4960dr). Ferries also run to **Paros** from **Samos** (6hr., 5 per week, 4050dr) and **Rhodes** (16hr., 4 per week, 6950dr). Faster but more expensive Flying Dolphin **hydrofoils** ply the same routes. The Cycladic islands are interconnected by ferries and hydrofoils as well.

MYKONOS (Μυκονος)

Coveted by pirates in the 18th century for its blond beaches, chic Mykonos is still lusted after by those seeking revelry and bacchanalian excess amidst a rich history. Social life, both gay and straight, certainly abounds, but it's not cheap—you'll need a wallet thicker than your *Let's Go* to afford all the festivities. Mingle with the *kosmopolitikos* and then savor the beaches and labyrinthine streets of **Mykonos Town.** Losing yourself in the colorful alleyways at dawn or dusk is one of the easiest, cheapest, and most exhilarating ways to experience the island; at every corner you're bound to stumble upon a miniature church or a quiet corner glowing in ethereal Cycladic light. All of Mykonos' beaches are technically nudist, but the degree of bareness varies; the most daring are **Plati Yialos, Paradise Beach, Super Paradise Beach,** and **Elia. Buses** run from South Station to Plati Yialos (2 per hr., 230-290dr), where you can catch *kaïkia* to the other three (around 400dr); direct buses also run to Paradise from South Station (2 per hr., 250dr) and to Elia from North Station (9 per day, 320dr). At night, *everyone* passes through the **Skandinavian Bar,** near Niko's Taverna, where mellowness winds into madness around midnight. (Beer 800dr, shots 900dr, cocktails 1500dr. Open Su-F 8:30pm-3am, Sa 8:30pm-4am.) ■**Caprice Bar,** on the water in Little Venice, is popular, crowded, and fruit-filled. (Open Su-Th 6:30pm-3:30am, F-Sa 6:30pm-4:30am.) Step into a Toulouse-Lautrec painting at **Montparnasse Piano Bar,** Agion Anargyron 24, in Little Venice. (Open daily 7pm-3am.) On Matogianni, **Pierro's,** reputedly the most happening place on Mykonos, was the first gay bar in Greece (beer 1500dr, cocktails 2500dr).

Ferries run to Tinos (45min., 3 per day, 1200dr); Paros (2hr., 1-2 per day, 1750dr); Naxos (3hr., 1-2 per day, 1850dr); Ios (4hr., 1 per day, 3200dr); and Santorini (6hr., 1 per day, 3400dr). The helpful **tourist police** await at the ferry landing. (Tel. (0289) 22 482. Open daily 8am-11pm.) Hawking is a full-blown industry on Mykonos; if you're aggressive and undaunted, you may find a good deal. Otherwise, push past the solicitors at the port, bear right 10m along the water, and head straight to the **hotels** (tel. (0289) 245 40), **Rooms to Let** (tel. (0289) 248 60), or **camping** (tel. (0289) 235 67) office. **Hotel Apollon,** on the waterfront, is the best deal in town. (Tel. (0289) 222 23. Singles 9-13,000dr; doubles 11,500-15,000dr; triples 15-18,000dr.) **Zoris Hotel,** N. Kalogera 30, is the nicest around Kalogera. (Tel. (0289) 221 67. Doubles 18-22,000dr.) **Paradise Beach Camping** is 6km from the village; take the **bus** (round-trip 380dr) or the free shuttle from the port. (Tel. (0289) 228 52. 1800dr per person, 1000-1300dr per tent. Bungalows 3500dr per person; singles 4000dr.) You'll have to wait for a table at the ■**Dynasty Thai Chinese Restaurant,** on Pl. Lymni, by the cinema on Meletopoulou, but it's worth it. (Entrees 1600-2500dr. Open daily 6:30pm-12:45am.) **Niko's Taverna,** inland from the excursion boat docks, hops with more traditional Greek cuisine. (Open daily noon-2am.) **Postal code:** 84600.

☒ EXCURSION FROM MYKONOS: DELOS. Delos (Δηλος), the sacred navel around which the Cyclades whirl, is not to be missed, even by those with little interest in mythology or history. Delos claims the most famous sanctuary in the Cyclades, *the* **Temple of Apollo,** built to commemorate the birthplace of the god and his twin sister, Artemis. After several centuries of inhabitation, Delos went native by the end of the 2nd century AD, taken over by legions of leaping lizards, huge spiderwebs, and members of the French School of Archaeology (well, the last just since 1873). The archaeological site, which occupies much of the small island, takes several days to explore completely, but highlights can be seen in under 3hr. From the dock, head straight to the **Agora of the Competaliasts;** continue in the same direction and turn left onto the wide **Sacred Road** to reach the **Sanctuary of Apollo,** a collection of temples built in the god's honor from Mycenaean times to the 4th century BC. The famous **Great Temple of Apollo,** or **Temple of the Delians,** was completed at the end of the 4th century BC. Continue 50m straight past the end of the Sacred Road to the beautiful **Terrace of the Lions.** The **museum,** next to the cafeteria, contains an assortment of archaeological finds. From there, a path leads to the summit of **Mt. Kythnos,** where Zeus watched the birth of Apollo. (Open daily Tu-Su 8am-3pm. 1200dr, students 600dr, EU students free.) Delos is most accessible as a daytrip from Mykonos. **Boats** leave from the dock near town, not the dock for large ferries (25min.; depart Tu-Su every 30-45min. 8:30-11:30am, return 11am-3pm; round-trip 1900dr).

TINOS (Τηνος)

In southern Tinos, tree-dotted hills gently cascade into the clear sea; wildflowers line the road with brilliant color; and a bit of exploration yields quiet, secluded beaches. The island is a popular destination for Greek travelers, but remains virtually undiscovered by others. In **Tinos Town (Chora)**, the most visited part of the island, the **Panayia Evangelistira Church** houses the miraculous **Icon of the Annunciation,** one of the most sacred relics of the Greek Orthodox Church. On August 15 and March 25, the church is the final destination of a massive pilgrimage. (Open daily 7am-8pm. Free. Dress modestly.) **Beaches** surround Tinos Town; **Tinos** and **Stavros** are fairly crowded, while **Agios Fokas,** closer but equally crowded, is just a short walk east of town. To get to beautiful **Porto,** take the KTEL bus. For the spectacular **Kardianis,** take the Pyrgos bus to Kardiani and travel down from the main road to the bay to see 2000 beautifully latticed medieval **dovecotes.** Many hikes lead up **Mt. Exóbourgo,** 14km north of Tinos Town, the site of the Venetian fortress **Xombourgo.**

    Ferries arrive at the main dock, next to the bus depot; walk left to get to the center of town, where Megalochares begins and leads uphill to the Church. Ferries travel to Mykonos (30min., 4-5 per day, 1100dr). In high-season, a ferry goes once a week to Paros (1700dr). A **catamaran** (Goutos Lines) sails daily to: Mykonos (30min., 2275dr); Paros (1¼hr., 3385dr); and Naxos (1¾hr., 3750dr). **Buses** (3-5 per day) depart from left of the National Bank for Tinos' smaller towns of Pyrgos (750dr) and Porto (230dr); check the schedule in the KTEL ticket agency opposite the bus depot. **Malliaris Travel** (tel. (0283) 242 41), left of the KTEL bus office, handles ferry and sea-jet services. Rent a **car** (6-15,000dr) or **moped** (2000-3000dr) and chat about Tinos at **Jason's** (tel. (0283) 245 83), on the waterfront just before Alavanou. **Giannis,** at the far right end of the waterfront, has airy rooms. (Tel. (0283) 250 89. Singles 5000dr; doubles 7000dr; triples 8-12,000dr.) **Tinos Camping** is 10min. from the waterfront to the right (follow the signs). (Tel. (0283) 223 44. 1000-1200dr per person, 700-800dr per tent.) There's a **supermarket** on the far right end of the waterfront, facing inland. (Open M-Sa 8am-9:30pm, Su 9am-1:30pm.) **Postal code:** 84200.

PAROS (Παρος)

Paros, famed throughout antiquity for its pure white marble (slabs of which were used for the Venus de Milo), is today a favorite for its golden beaches and tangled whitewashed villages. The island has struck a careful balance between New-World nightlife and Old-World dignity, and gracefully absorbs hordes of summer tourists. Behind the commercial façade of **Paroikia,** Paros' port and largest city, flower-filled streets wind through archways and past windmills and a historic basilica. Byzantine architecture buffs will be enraptured by **Panagia Ekatontapiliani** (Church of Our Lady of 100 Gates), which looms over Paroikia's *plateia* and houses three separate churches, cloisters, and a peaceful courtyard. Tradition holds that only 99 of the church's 100 doors can be counted—when the 100th appears, Constantinople will once again belong to the Greeks. (Open 7am-11pm. No shorts.) Ten kilometers south of town is the cool, spring-fed **Valley of the Butterflies** *(Petaloudes)*, home to an enormous swarm of brown-and-white-striped winged insects. Take the bus from Paroikia toward Aliki and ask to be let off at the *petaloudes* (10min., 12 per day, 200dr); then follow the signs 2km up the steep, winding road to the entrance. (Open M-Sa 9am-8pm, Su 9am-1pm and 4-8pm. 400dr.)

    Ferries sail to Folegandros (3 per week, 1950dr); Ios (2½hr., 5-7 per day, 2450dr); and Santorini (3½hr., 6-9 per day, 3080dr). The **tourist office** is to the right of the windmill as you leave the port. (Tel. (0284) 238 64. Open daily in summer 9:30am-2:30pm and 5:30-9:30pm.) From the dock, walk straight past the windmill into the left *plateia*, continue straight with the church on your left, turn right at the dead end, and follow the sign to reach **Festos Pension.** (Tel. (0284) 216 35; fax 241 93. Doubles 3000-6000dr. Breakfast July-Aug. 700dr; Sept.-June included. Laundry. Check-out 10am. Reserve ahead.) Turn left from the dock and take a right after the ancient cemetery ruins to get to **Rena Rooms.** (Tel./fax (0284) 222 20. Doubles 6000dr; triples 9000dr; 20% *Let's Go* discount.) Shuttles run from the port to **Parasporos Camping,** 1.5km south of town. (Tel. (0284) 222 68. 1400dr; tent rental 600dr per person.) Psychedelic ◼**Happy Green Cow,** a block inland off the *plateia* behind the National Bank, serves tasty veggie fare. (Open daily 1-3pm and 7pm-midnight.) ◼**Pirate Blues and Jazz,** is tucked away in the old town half a block from Apollon Garden Restaurant. (Beer 700dr. Open daily 7pm-3am.) **Postal code:** 84400.

NAXOS (Ναξος)

Naxos, where Cretan princess Ariadne was deserted by Theseus (for reasons that remain mythologically unclear) and fell in love with Dionysus, boasts more than just a rich history. Old **Naxos Town** lies behind waterfront shops, on the hill leading up to the **Venetian Castle.** The **Archaeological Museum** is in the former Collège Français, where Nikos Kazantzakis (author of *Zorba the Greek*) studied. (Open Tu-Su 8am-2:30pm. 500dr, students 300dr; Su free.) The marble, 6th-century BC **Portara** archway, visible from the waterfront, is one of the few archaeological sites in Greece that you can climb all over—*Let's Go* recommends it for midnight starwatching. Buses run from the port (every 30min., 300dr) to **beaches** near town; of **Ag. Georgios, Ag. Prokopios, Agia Anna,** and **Plaka,** the last is the hands-down favorite for nude frolicking. Chill the heat of a Naxian night with some smooth Billie Holliday at the **Lakridi Jazz Bar,** in Old Naxos on Old Market. (Open daily 8pm-4am.) **Super Island Bar and Club,** along the water along the road next to the bus depot, is where to see and be seen. (Cover 1500dr; includes 1 drink. Open daily 11pm-3:30am.) To properly experience the island, explore the stunning interior; **buses** run from Naxos Town to the small fishing village of **Apollonas,** on the northern tip, via a gorgeous coastal road (2hr., 3 per day, 1100dr). The most exhilarating aspects of the interior, such as the **Tragea** highland valley (a vast green olive grove), however, are not serviced by buses; ask for **hiking** info at the tourist office.

Ferries go to Paros (1hr., 6-8 per day, 1400dr); Ios (1½hr., 6 per day, 2200dr); Mykonos (2hr., 5 per week, 2000dr); Tinos (2½hr., 2-3 per day, 1900dr); and Santorini (3hr., 6 per day, 2910dr). The **tourist office** is 300m up from the waterfront (past the private agencies) by the bus station. (Tel. (0285) 243 58; fax 252 00. Open daily 8am-midnight. The **Rental and Internet Center** is in Pl. Protodikiou. (2500dr per hr. Open daily 8:30am-11pm.) ◼**Irene Studios** is in newer Naxos, up the hill from Galini Restaurant, 300m from Ag. Georgios Beach. (Tel. (0285) 231 69. Doubles 10,000dr; triples 12,000dr; quads 15,000dr.) **Hotel Dionysus,** in Old Naxos (follow the red hand signs), is cheap and popular with backpackers. (Tel. (0285) 252 01. Dorms 2000dr; singles 4000-5000dr; doubles and triples 5000-6000dr. Reception 10am-6pm and 10pm-midnight.) Take a shuttle from the ferry or one of the frequent buses to Ag. Anna beach (2 per hr., 300dr) for **Maragas Camping.** (Tel. (0285) 42 552. 900-1200dr per person; 300dr for tent rental. Doubles 6000-8000dr.) **Postal code:** 84300.

IOS (Ιος)

Ios can be summed up in three words: frat party run amok (all right, so that was four, but after a week on Ios, you won't be able to count either). It has everything your mother warned you about—people swimming less than 30min. after they've eaten, wine being swilled from the bottle at 3pm, drinking games all day long, men and women dancing madly in the streets, and oh-so-much more. The **port** (Yialos) is at one end of the island's paved road; the **village** (Hora) sits above it on a hill (you can do most of your "serious" business within 5min. of the village bus stop on the paved road opposite the blue domed church); and crowded **Mylopotas beach** rests 20min. downhill on the other side of the village. **Buses** shuttle between the port, village, and beach (every 10-20min., 230dr). Follow the main pedestrian path as it curves left through the *plateia* to reach ◼**Blue Note,** where you can **get drunk**—down seven shots and earn a free t-shirt. Start your pub crawl by **getting drunk** at **Dubliner,** next to the bus stop (Guinness 500dr; open daily 8:30pm-3:30am), then migrate with the masses to nearby **Sweet Irish Dream,** near the "donkey steps," to **get drunk** and dance on tables after 2am (no cover before 1am). You can **get drunk** on "tequila slammers" (900dr) at packed **The Slammer Bar,** just uphill from the *plateia*. At **Red Bull,** in the *plateia*, **get drunk** on the Red Bull and Vodka "energy special" (1700dr). Find techno techno a go go at **Scorpion Disco,** on the edge of town on the way to the beach (cover after 1am 1000dr). Take some aspirin in the morning and head down to the beach, where three **Mylopotas Water Sports Center** shacks along the beach offer free **windsurfing, water-skiing,** and **snorkelling lessons** with rental. (2000-5000dr per hr. Open Apr.-Oct. daily.)

Ferries go to Santorini (1¼hr., 4-6 per day, 1700dr); Naxos (1½hr., 6 per day, 2100dr); Paros (2½hr., 5-6 per day, 2600dr); Mykonos (4-5hr., 1 per day, 3300dr); and Crete (5hr., 1 per week, 4300dr). Frequent **buses** shuttle between the port, village, and beach (every 10-20min. 7am-midnight, 230dr). The **Tourist Information Center** is next to the bus stop. (Tel. (0286) 911 35. Open daily 7:45am-1am.) To sleep near the port, try **Pension Irene,** on the waterfront (tel./fax (0286) 918 82; doubles 8000dr; triples 12,000dr), or **Camping Ios** (tel. (0286) 913 29; 1200dr per person; 500dr for tent rental; open June-Sept.). In the village, take the uphill steps to the left (with your back to the bank) in the *plateia* and take the first left to reach ◪**Francesco's,** where you can **get drunk** at the terrace bar (tel./fax (0286) 912 23; dorms 3000dr; doubles 6000-8000dr; triples 9-12,000dr), or walk past the OTE and take the white archway to ◪**Kolitsani View,** then **get drunk** at the poolside bar (tel. (0286) 910 61; fax 922 61; doubles 8000dr; triples 10,500dr). On the end of Mylopotas Beach, **Far Out Camping** has a bar and parties where you can **get drunk.** (Tel. (0286) 923 01; fax 923 03. 1200dr per person; 300dr for tent rental. Cabins 1500-2000dr; bungalows 2000-3000dr. Open Apr.-Sept.) A **supermarket** is in the *plateia.* **Lordos Byron,** uphill from the National Bank on the tiny street below the main drag, has exquisite Greek cuisine. (Open daily 7pm-midnight.) **Postal code:** 84001.

FOLEGANDROS (Φολεγανδρος)

For respite from bacchanalian excess, commune with the serene, spectacular landscape of Folegandros, laden with jagged cliffs and narrow cobblestoned streets. The locals are fiercely protective of their island, and you'll have to shell out a bit more for the privilege of sharing it with them, but it's well worth it. Don't miss the view from the **Church of Panagia,** above the town on Paliokastro hill, at sunset; take the path from the right of the bus stop. **Agali beach,** accessible by foot (1hr.), is lined with several *tavernas;* climb up past the first *tavernas* on the right and continue on the rocky trail to reach **Agios Nikolaos beach** (30min.), or continue along the main road to get to the tiny old settlement of **Ano Maria,** where you'll find Ottoman artifacts at the superb **Folklore Museum.** (Open June-Aug. daily 5-8pm.) **Ferries** usually connect daily to Ios (1500dr); Santorini (1700dr); Paros (1900dr); and Naxos (2300dr). **Buses** run from the port of **Kararostassi** to the main town, **Hora** (every 2hr., 240dr). Near the bus stop is the **Sottovento tourist office.** (Tel. (0286) 414 44; fax 414 30. Open daily 10am-2pm and 5:30pm-midnight.) Down toward the port about 300m from the post office are **Pavlo's Rooms.** (Tel. (0286) 412 32. 2000-3000dr per person; doubles 10-12,000dr.) To get to the new **Meltemi Hotel,** take the road leading to Panagia and it's on your right, 30m from Pl. Pounta. (Tel. (0286) 413 28. Doubles 15,000dr; triples 17,000dr.) **Postal code:** 84011.

SANTORINI (Σαντορινη)

Santorini's landscape is as dramatic as the cataclysm that helped shape it—a massive volcanic eruption around 1450 BC buried the island in lava and pumice, leading some to believe it was Plato's lost island of Atlantis. Despite all the kitsch in touristy **Fira,** the island's capital (in the central western part of the island), nothing can destroy the pleasure of wandering its narrow, cobblestoned streets, inspecting its craft shops, and taking in the stunning sunsets from its western edge. On the southwestern part of the island, the fascinating excavations at **Akrotiri,** a late Minoan city, are preserved virtually intact under layers of volcanic rock; **buses** run to Akrotiri from Fira (370dr). (Open Tu-Su 8am-7pm. 1200dr, students 600dr.) Frequent **buses** also run from Fira to the black-sand **beaches** of Perissa (390dr) and Kamari (240dr) in the southeast. The former route stops along the way in **Pyrgos;** from there, you can hike to the **Profitias Ilias Monastery** (45min.) and continue to the ruins of **ancient Thira** (an additional 2hr.), near Kamari. The theater, church, and forum of ancient Thira, the island's old capital, remain visible. (Open Tu-Su 8am-2pm.)

GREEK CHIC So you've just spent a long day visiting ancient temples and Byzantine churches or cavorting on beaches. Now it's nighttime, and you're wondering what to wear. Let's Go recommends the following for Greek chic. **Men:** Greek fashion doesn't allow you much room for creativity; you *must* wear asphyxiatingly tight jeans and an equally skin-tight short-sleeved shirt (preferably V-necked), tucked in all the way beneath a big black belt. Your pants should be white, blue, or black and your shirt white, grey, or black. Important: Your hair must be oiled back. **Women:** You can improvise a bit more; pretty much anything goes, as long as it's tight enough to make breathing difficult. Tight black pants with tighter shirts and skimpy, scandalous dresses are currently *de mode*. The **bottom line:** whether male or female, banish that baggy attire to the bottom of your pack. If you have any further questions, refer back not to ancient Greece but to John Travolta's *Grease*, and you'll be a hit on summer nights.

Ferries run to Ios (1½hr., 4-8 per day, 1700dr); Naxos (4hr., 4-8 per day, 3090dr); Iraklion (4hr., 3 per week, 3700dr); Paros (4½hr., 4-8 per day, 3200dr); Mykonos (7hr., 1 per day, 3600dr); and Rhodes (16hr., 3 per week, 6400dr). Most land at **Athinios** harbor; frequent **buses** (30min., 370dr) connect to Fira. Share homemade wine with Petros at the ▨**Pension Petros;** follow the signs for Santorini Camping one block east from Fira's main *plateia*, or catch the free shuttle from the port. (Tel. (0286) 225 73; fax 226 15. Doubles and triples 16,000dr.) Head 300m north from the *plateia* for the **Thira Youth Hostel** (tel. (0286) 223 87; dorms 1600-2000dr; doubles 10,000dr; reception 24hr.; open Mar.-Nov.), or follow the blue signs east from it for **Santorini Camping** (tel. (0286) 229 44; 1500dr per person, 800dr per tent; reception 24hr.; open Apr.-Oct.). If you plan to spend substantial time baking on the black sand, take the bus from Fira to Perissa and stay at the **Youth Hostel Perissa-Anna,** 500m on the road out of town. (Dorms 2000dr; private rooms 2000-4000dr. Sheets 200dr.) Back in Fira, the menu at ▨**Nikolas Taverna** may be all Greek to you, but you can't go wrong; head uphill from the northwestern corner of the *plateia* and take the first right at Hotel Tataki. Afterward, cross the street to the **Kira Thira Jazz Club.** (Open 9pm-late.) **Postal code:** 84700.

CRETE (Κρητη)

Greece's largest island embraces an infinite store of mosques, monasteries, mountain villages, gorges, grottoes, and beaches. Since 3000 BC, Crete has maintained an identity distinct from the rest of Greece, first expressed in the language, script, and architecture of the ancient Minoans. While the resort towns of Crete's eastern half seem to have sprung from the brains of British booking agents, the mountainside-gripping highway that winds from Malia to Agios Nikolaos and Sitia is absolutely spectacular; meanwhile, the vacation spots of Western Crete have grown naturally around towns with rich histories and distinctive characters.

▐ GETTING THERE AND GETTING AROUND

Olympic Airways and **Air Greece** connect **Athens** to **Sitia** (2-3 per week; 23,200dr) in the east; **Iraklion** (45min., 7 per day, 21,900dr) in the center; and **Hania** (3 per day, 20,000dr) in the west. **Ferries** arrive in **Iraklion** from **Santorini** (4hr., 4 per week, 3700dr); **Naxos** (7hr., 3 per week, 5200dr); **Mykonos** (8½hr., 2 per week, 6000dr); **Paros** (9hr., 4 per week, 5200dr); and **Athens/Peiraias** (14hr., 2 per day, 7000dr). As usual, **hydrofoils** service most destinations in half the time, but at double the price.

Buses from **Iraklion** run west along the northern coast to **Rethymno** (1½hr., 8 per day, 1550dr) en route to **Hania** (from Iraklion 17 per day, 2900dr; from Rethymno 1hr., 1500dr). Buses run from **Rethymno, Hania,** and **Iraklion** south to the **Samaria Gorge** (from Hania 4 per day, round-trip 2700dr). Buses also run east from **Iraklion** to **Heronissos** (40min.); **Malia** (from Iraklion 1hr., 750dr; from Heronissos 20min., 2-4 per hr., 240dr); and **Agios Nikolaos** (from Iraklion 1½hr., 26 per day, 1400dr; from Malia 1½hr., 26 per day, 750dr). Buses from **Agios Nikolaos** continue east to **Sitia** (1½hr., 6 per day, 1500dr; from Iraklion 3¼hr, 6 per day, 2850dr).

IRAKLION (Ηρακλιο)

As Crete's capital and the fifth-largest city in Greece, Iraklion sports a chic native population, a more diverse nightlife than nearby resorts, and an ideal location as a base for a cultural tour of Crete. Off Pl. Eleftherias, the phenomenal **Archaeological Museum** has appropriated the major finds from all over the island and presents a comprehensive island history from the Neolithic period to Roman times. (Open M noon-7pm and Tu-Su 8am-7pm. 1500dr, students 800dr; EU students free.)

Travel Hall Travel Agency, Hatzimihali Yiannari 13, has info on **flights** to Athens and elsewhere. (Tel. (081) 34 18 62. Open M-F 9am-4pm and 5:30-9pm.) **Boat** offices line 25 Augustou. KTEL **Terminal A,** between the old city walls and the harbor near the waterfront, sends buses to Agios Nikolaos and Malia; to reach the **Hania-Rethymno terminal,** walk down 25 Augustou to the waterfront, turn right, and walk about 500m. The **tourist office,** Xanthoudidou 1, is opposite the Archaeological Museum in Pl. Eleftherias. (Tel. (081) 22 82 03. Open M-F July-Aug. 8am-7pm, Sept.-June 8am-2:30pm.) The **tourist police** is at 10 Dikeosinis. (Tel. (081) 28 31 90. Open daily 7am-11pm.) Check your **email** at **Polykentro,** on Androgeou, off 25 Augustou. (500dr per hr. Open Su-Th 9am-1am, F-Sa 10am-2am.) ◪**Rent a Room Hellas,** Handakos 24, is two blocks from El Greco Park. (Tel. (081) 28 88 51. Dorms 1800dr; singles 3500-4000dr; doubles 4500-6000dr.) To get from the bus station to the **youth hostel,** Vyronos 5, take a left (with the water on your right) on 25 Augustou and a right on Vyronos. (Tel. (081) 28 62 81; fax 22 29 47. Dorms 1800dr; doubles 3000-4000dr. Check-out 10am. Curfew midnight.) The best show in town is the **open-air market** on **1866** street, starting near Pl. Venizelon. Walk down D. Beaufort for dancing at **Privilege Club** and **Yacht,** next door. **Postal code:** 71001.

🢒 EXCURSION FROM IRAKLION: KNOSSOS. At Knossos, the most famous archaeological site in Crete, excavations have revealed the remains of a Minoan city that thrived here 3500 years ago. Sir Arthur Evans, who financed and supervised the excavations, eventually restored large parts of the **palace** in Knossos; his work often crossed the line from preservation to artistic interpretation, but the site is impressive nonetheless. (Open daily Apr.-Oct. 8am-7pm; Nov.-Mar. 8am-5pm. 1500dr, students 800dr; Nov.-Mar. Su free.) To reach Knossos from Iraklion, take **bus** 2 from 25 Augustou or Pl. Eleftherias (every 20min., 240dr) and look for the signs.

RETHYMNO AND HANIA (Ρεθυμνο, Χανια)

Nowhere in Western Crete are the manifestations of the island's turbulent occupations as mingled or as magical as in **Rethymno's** old city, not far from the cave that is famed as Zeus' mythological birthplace. Arabic inscriptions lace the walls of the narrow streets, minarets highlight the skyline, and the 16th-century **Venetian fortress** (open Tu-Su 8am-8pm; 800dr) guards the scenic harbor and hosts a lively **Renaissance Festival** (June-Sept.). The **Rethymno-Hania bus station** (tel. (0831) 22 212) is south of the fortress on the water. Climb the stairs behind the bus station, turn left on Igoum Gavril, which becomes Kountouriotou, and turn left on Varda Kallergi to reach the waterfront. The **tourist office** is on El. Venizelou, by the waterfront. (Tel. (0831) 291 48. Open M-Sa 8am-2pm.) Check your **email** at **Café Galero** at Rimondi Fountain. (800dr per 30min. Open daily 7am-3am.) To get from the station to the cheerful **youth hostel,** Tombazi 41-45, walk down Igoum Gavril, take a left at the park traffic light, walk through the gate, and take your second right. (Tel. (0831) 228 48. 1500dr per person. Sheets 150dr. Reception 8am-noon and 5-9pm.) **Olga's Pension,** Souliou 57, is off Antistassios. (Tel. (0831) 532 06. Singles 5000-7000dr; doubles 7000-9000dr; triples 10-11,000dr.) Buses (170dr) shuttle from the station to **Elizabeth Camping,** 3km east of town. (Tel. (0831) 286 94. 1500dr per person, 1300dr per tent. Open mid-Apr. to Oct.) **Postal code:** 74100.

Narrow Venetian buildings and Ottoman domes mingle in the lively harbor town of **Hania. Ferries** arrive in **Souda** from Peiraias/Athens (9½hr., 1 per night, 5900-8600dr); buses connect to Hania's Municipal Market (15min., 240dr). **Buses** arrive at the station (tel. (0821) 933 06) on the corner of Kidonias and

Kelaidi; walk right on Kidonias and turn left on Pl. 1866 to reach the **tourist office,** Kriairi 40, just off Pl. 1866. (Tel./fax (0821) 926 24. Open M-F 7:30am-2:30pm.) To get to **Hotel Fidias,** Sarpaki 6, walk toward the harbor on Halidon and turn right at the far end of the cathedral. (Tel. (0821) 524 94. Dorms 2000dr; singles 2000-4000dr; doubles 3000-4500dr; triples 4500-6000dr.) The **harbor** is the place for late night fun. **Postal code:** 73100.

⚡ HIKING NEAR RETHYMNO AND HANIA: SAMARIA GORGE. The most popular excursion from Hania, Rethymno, and Iraklion is the 5- to 6-hour hike down the 16km Samaria Gorge, a spectacular ravine through the White Mountains worn by rainwater over 14 million years. The gorge retains its allure despite having been trampled by thousands of visitors: rare and endemic plants peek out from sheer rock walls, wild Cretan goats climb the hills, and endangered griffon vultures and golden eagles soar overhead. (Open daily May-Oct. 15 6am-4pm. 1200dr.) For gorge info, call **Hania Forest Service** (tel. (0821) 922 87). The trail starts at **Xyloskalo;** take the 6:15, 7:30, or 8:30am **bus** from Hania to Xyloskalo (1½hr., 1300-1400dr), the 6:15 or 7am bus from Rethymno to Omalos (just north of Xyloskalo; 2450dr), or the 5:30am bus from Iraklion to Omalos (3750dr). The trail ends in the town of **Agia Roumeli,** on the southern coast, where you can hop on a **boat** to Hora Sfakion (1¼hr., 4 per day, 1500dr; last ferry 6pm) and catch a waiting bus back to Hania (2hr., 1500dr); Rethymnon (1500dr); or Iraklion (3000dr).

MALIA (Μαλια)

Although Malia's pubs and Guinness taps come closer to evoking the pages of Joyce than those of Homer, and the town is overrun by young nightlife-seeking Brits, the palatial Minoan site at Malia still merits a visit. The **Minoan Palace,** one of the three great cities of Minoan Crete, lacks the labyrinthine architecture and magnificent interior decoration of Knossos and Phaistos, but it's still imposing. Follow the road east to Agios Nikolaos for 3km and turn left toward the sea. (Open daily 8am-3pm. 800dr, students 400dr, EU students free.) Walking east toward Agios Nikolaos, past the point where the bus drops you off on the main road, make a right onto 25th Martiou for **Pension Menios** (tel. (0897) 313 61); continue down 25th Martiou and take a left on Konstantinou for **Pension Aspasia** (tel. (0897) 312 90); both have singles (2000-3000dr) and doubles (4000-6000dr). **Postal code:** 70007.

THE NIGHT I SPENT WITH A BULL AND THE MINOTAUR AFTER
The story of **King Minos,** one of the most complex and resonant myths in all Greek mythology, begins with a simple crime of ingratitude. When Minos withheld the sacrifice of a fine white bull that Poseidon had granted him for that exclusive purpose, Aphrodite was dispatched to exact a twisted retribution, and the tricky goddess gave Minos' queen **Pasiphaë** a burning lust for the bull. To woo the bull, Pasiphaë hired master engineer **Daedalus** to build a sexy cow costume that might rouse the bull's affections. After a roll in the hay (so to speak), Pasiphaë gave birth to the **Minotaur,** a fearsome beast with the head of a bull, the body of a man, and a taste for human flesh. The Minotaur was kept in an inescapable **labyrinth** designed by Daedalus, and to feed his queen's child Minos imposed an annual tax of seven maidens and seven youths upon mainland Greece. A dashing Athenian prince named **Theseus** put a stop to this when he volunteered for the sacrifice and, once inside the labyrinth, slew the Minotaur. With a ball of string he'd gotten from Minos' daughter **Ariadne,** who had conspired with Daedalus to save her Athenian main squeeze, Theseus retraced his path and escaped by ship. He took Ariadne with him, promising marriage, but later he forgot and left her on the beach of Naxos to be swept off by Dionysus. Meanwhile, Minos imprisoned Daedalus and his son **Icarus** for their role in the whole mess. Resourceful Daedalus made himself and his son wings of wax, with which they went for the ultimate jailbreak. With freedom in sight, hubristic Icarus soared to close to the sun: his wings melted, and he plummeted to his death.

AGIOS NIKOLAOS (Αγιος Νικολαος)

An intense nightlife, a diverse selection of intriguingly glamorous tourists, and remnants of the indigenous Cretan culture make Agios Nikolaos a lively concoction—a town that moves, yet doesn't project the sense that it has been chewed up and spit out by tourists. **Boats** (3000-4000dr) depart from the tourist office for the small but striking **Spinalonga island**, formerly a leper colony. From Agios Nikolaos, **ferries** go to Peiraias (12hr., 7500dr), Rhodes (12hr., 6250dr); Sitia (1hr., 1600dr); and Karpathos (7hr., 3950dr). **Buses** (tel. (0841) 222 34) depart from Pl. Atlantidos, on the opposite side of town from the harbor. With your back to the station, head right and make your first right; follow Venizelou and then R. Koundourou to the harbor, then head to the left and across the bridge to reach the **tourist office,** S. Koundourou 21A. (Tel. (0841) 223 57; fax 825 34. Open Apr.-Oct. daily 8:30am-9:45pm.) To get to **The Green House,** Modatsou 15, climb Kapetan Tavila (to your left as you stand with your back to the bus station), which turns into Modatsou. (Tel. (0841) 220 25. Singles 3500dr; doubles 5000dr. Laundry.) For nocturnal fun, stroll around the harbor on **I. Koundourou** or walk up **25 Martiou. Postal code:** 72100.

SITIA (Σητεια)

A winding drive east from Agios Nikolaos brings you to the fishing and port town of Sitia, where the wave of tourism slows to a trickle and pelicans walk the streets at dawn. The town's **beach** extends 3km to the east, while the hilltop **fortress** provides views of the town and bay. **Ferries** leave Sitia for Karpothos (5hr., 3400dr); Rhodes (12hr., 2 per week, 6000dr) and Peiraias/Athens (16-17hr., 5 per week, 7600dr) via Agios Nikolaos (1½hr., 1600dr). With your back to the **bus station** (tel. (0843) 222 72), walk right, take your first right and then your first left, and follow Venizelou to the waterfront. A new **tourist office** has opened on the waterfront; from Bolytechiou Sq, head right along the water. (Tel. (0843) 283 00. Open M-F 9:30am-2pm and 5-9pm, Sa-Su opens 10am.) To get to the **youth hostel** at Therissou 4, walk right from the bus station, take your first right and then your first left, turn left at the first big street, and bear left onto Therissou; or call for a ride from the station. (Tel. (0843) 226 93. Dorms 1500dr; singles 2500dr; doubles 3500-4000dr; triples 5000dr. Sheets 100dr. Reception 9am-noon and 6-9pm. Call ahead.) **Venus Rooms to Let** is at Kondilaki 60; walk up on Kapetan Sifi from the main square and make your first right after the telephone office. (Tel. (0843) 243 07. Singles 3000-4000dr; doubles 3500-8000dr; triples 8400dr.) ▨**Cretan House,** K. Karamanli 10, off the *plateia*, serves Cretan classics for 700-850dr. (Open 9am-1:30am.) Head to **Hot Summer,** way down the road to Palaikastro by the beach, after midnight (cover 1000dr). **Postal code:** 72300.

EASTERN AEGEAN ISLANDS

The intricate, rocky coastlines and unassuming port towns of the **Northeastern Aegean Islands** enclose thickly wooded mountains that give way to unspoiled villages and beaches. Just miles from the Turkish coast, they have a sizable military presence, but nonetheless provide a rare taste of undiluted Greek culture. The landscapes of the **Dodecanese** (Twelve Islands), southeast of the Northeastern Aegean Islands, reflect changes in Greek history, from the rise of Christianity to the influence of Mussolini's architectural style. In summer, tourists flock to Rhodes and Kos for raucous nightlife, while the other islands are best for peaceful relaxation.

▰ FERRIES TO TURKEY

Ferries run to **Çesme** from **Lesvos** (45min., 3 per week, 9000dr) and **Hios** (45min., 2 per day, 11-12,000dr); to **Kuşadası** from **Samos** (2hr., depart 8am and 5pm, 8000dr; those who stay the night have to pay the tax twice); to **Marmaris** from **Rhodes** (10,000dr, round-trip 12,000dr); and to **Bodrum** from **Kos** (round-trip 12-15,000dr). **Visas** must be bought at the border if you are staying the night in Turkey (citizens of the US US$45, the UK UK$10, Ireland IR$15). **Port taxes** are typically 3000dr in Turkey and 5000dr in Greece.

SAMOS (Σαμος)

Although it is perhaps the most beautiful and certainly the most-touristed island in the Northeast Aegean, many simply stop here en route to **Kuşadası** and the ruins of **Ephesus** on the Turkish coast (see p. 929). With its quiet inland streets, palm trees, red-roof-covered hillside, and engaging archaeological museum, **Samos Town** (Vathy) is among the Northeast Aegean's most attractive port cities. The phenomenal ▩**Archaeological Museum** is behind the municipal gardens. (Open Tu-Su 8am-2:30pm. 800dr, students 400dr, EU students free.) The beach town of **Pythagorion**, the island's ancient capital, is 14km south of Samos Town. Near the town are the magnificent remains of Polykrates' 6th-century BC engineering projects: the **Tunnel of Eupalinos**, which diverted water from a natural spring to the city, a 40-meter-deep **harbor mole**, and the **Temple of Hera**. (Tunnel open Tu-Su 8:15am-2pm. 500dr, students 300dr, EU students free. Temple open Tu-Su 8am-2:30pm. 800dr, students 400dr.) Hourly **buses** arrive in Pythagorion from Samos Town (20min., 280dr).

Ferries arrive in Samos Town from Naxos (6hr., 4-7 per week, 4900dr) via Paros (4370dr); Mykonos (6hr., 5 per week, 5100dr); Lesvos (8hr., 1 per week, 4090dr); and Peiraias (12hr., 2-3 per day, 6700dr) via Ikaria (2100dr). **ITSA Travel,** on the waterfront at the dock, is the most helpful resource in town. (Tel. (0273) 236 05; fax 279 55. Open daily 6am-midnight.) Turn right at the end of the ferry dock on E. Stamatiadou, before the Hotel Aiolis, then turn right on Manoli Kalomiri and left on Areos to get to the **Pension Avli,** Areos 2. (Tel. (0273) 229 39. Doubles 5000-7000dr. Open in summer only.) Or walk 10min. along the waterfront away from town to reach the **Pythagoras Hotel.** (Tel. (0273) 286 01; fax 288 93. Singles 4000-5000dr; doubles 5000-7000dr.) **Postal code:** 83100.

LESVOS (Λεσβος)

Once home to the sensual poet Sappho, Lesvos is still something of a mecca for lesbians paying homage to their legendary etymological roots. Huge and geographically diverse, the island is known for its horse-breeding, serious *ouzo* drinking, and leftist politics. Most travelers pass through the modern **Mytilini**, the capital and central port city. The enormous **Church of St. Therapon** presides benignly over the fish market, while the **Archaeological Museum,** Argiri Eftalioti 7, houses an impressive collection of the island's archaeological finds (open Tu-Su 8:30am-3pm; 500dr). **Ferries** go to Hios (3hr., 1 per week, 3250dr); Limnos (5hr., 4 per week, 3600dr); Peiraias (12hr. 1 per day, 71,000dr); and Thessaloniki (12hr., 2 per week, 8300dr). Book **ferries** at **NEL Lines,** Pavlou Koudoutrioti 67 (tel. (0251) 222 20), along the waterfront. The **tourist police,** in the northwest corner of the ferry dock, offers maps and advice. (Tel. (0251) 227 76. Open daily 9am-9pm.) The **Rooms to Let** office is one block inland from the center of the waterfront. (Singles 5000-6000dr; doubles 7000-8000dr. Open M-Sa 9am-1pm.) Take an intercity **bus** from the station behind Agios Irinis Park, southwest of the harbor, to reach the artist colonies of **Petras** and **Molyvos** (1½hr., 4 per day, 1300dr) on the northern coast. The **Petra Women's Cooperative,** in the main square, or the **Molyvos tourist office** (tel. (0253) 713 47), just up from the bus stop, respectively, can help you find a room. The monastery of **Agios Rafael** remains a major pilgrimage site; travelers can stay two nights for free. Take the bus from Mytilini (45min., every 2hr., 360dr). **Postal code:** 81100.

HIOS (Χιος)

When the mythical hunter Orion drove all the wild beasts from Hios, grand pine, cypress, and mastic trees sprouted on the vast mountainsides. As its striking volcanic beaches and medieval villages become more accessible, Hios is rising to a new fame. **Pirgi,** high in the hills 25km from Hios Town, is one of Greece's most striking villages, because of the fantastic black-and-white geometrical designs covering its buildings; take a **bus** from Hios Town (1-7 per day, 600dr). Farther south lies **Emborio,** where beige volcanic cliffs contrast with the black stones and deep-blue water below; **buses** run from Hios Town (4 per week, 700dr). **Ferries** go to Lesvos (3hr., 1 per day, 3600dr); Samos (4hr., 3 per week, 2800dr); and Piraeias (overnight, 1 per day, 5800dr); Patmos; Kos; and Rhodes. To reach Hios Town's **tourist office,** Kanari

11, turn off the waterfront onto Kanari, walk toward the *plateia*, and look for the "i" sign. (Tel. (0271) 443 44. Open May-Sept. M-F 7am-2:30pm and 6:30-9:30pm, Sa-Su 7-10pm; Oct.-Apr. M-F 7am-2:30pm.) **Hatzelenis Tourist Agency,** immediately to the left of the ferry dock (at the far right end of the waterfront as you face inland), can hook you up with **Hios Rooms.** (Agency tel. (0271) 267 43. Open M-Sa 7am-1:30pm and 6-9pm, Su 10am-1pm and 6-9pm; also often open when boats arrive at night. Doubles 4000-6000dr; triples 9,000dr; quads 12,000dr.) **Postal code:** 82100.

RHODES (Ροδος)

Although Rhodes is the undisputed tourism capital of the Dodecanese, the sandy beaches along its east coast, the jagged cliffs skirting its west coast, and the green mountains freckled with villages in the interior have still retained their serenity. The island's most famous sight is one that doesn't exist, and perhaps never existed; the **Colossus of Rhodes,** a 35m bronze statue of Helios and one of the **seven wonders of the ancient world,** supposedly straddled the island's harbor but was allegedly destroyed by an earthquake in 237 BC. The beautiful, still-extant **City of Rhodes** has been the island's capital for over 20 centuries. The **Old Town,** surrounded by remnants of the 14th-century occupation (by the Knights of St. John), lends the city a medieval flair. Begin exploring the Old Town in the **Plateia Symi,** inside the **Eleftherias Gate** at the base of the waterfront. In nearby Pl. Argykastrou, the beautiful former **Hospital of the Knights** is now the **Archaeological Museum.** (Open Tu-Su 8:30am-2:30pm. 800dr, students 400dr.) At the top of the hill, a second archway leads to Pl. Kleovoulou; to the right sits the pride of the city, the **Palace of the Grand Master,** with 300 rooms, moats, drawbridges, watchtowers, and colossal battlements. (Open M noon-7pm, Tu-Su 8am-7pm. 1200dr, students 600dr.) The **New Town** is a mecca for nightlife; **Orfanidou** is popularly known as **Bar Street.** Daytrips to **Lindos,** south of the City of Rhodes and known for its rowdy drinkers, leave on **excursion boats,** stopping along the way in **Faliraki,** perhaps the island's most picturesque town, with narrow vine-lined streets, courtyards carpeted by pebble mosaics, and whitewashed houses clustered beneath a castle-capped acropolis. See schedules and prices on the dock along the lower end of the Mandraki (from 3500dr). **Buses** also run to Faliraki (20 per day, 300dr) and Lindos (13 per day, 1000dr).

Ferries arrive in the City of Rhodes from Karpathos (3 per week, 4400dr); Kos (2-3 per day, 4000dr); Patmos (1-2 per day, 5400dr); Mykonos (1 per week, 6800dr); Paros (1 per week, 6900dr); Hios (7000dr); Samos (2 per week, 6500dr); Santorini (1 per week, 5100dr); Crete (1 per week, 6200dr); and Peiraias/Athens (14hr., 1-4 per day, 9000dr). Walk to the base of the waterfront and head one block inland along the park on the New Town side to reach the **tourist office,** in Pl. Rimini. (Tel. (0241) 359 45. Open M-Sa 8am-9pm, Su 8am-3pm.) The **Greek National Tourist Office (EOT)** is up Papgou a few blocks from Pl. Rimini, at Makariou. (Tel. (0241) 232 55. Open M-F 7:30am-3pm.) Walk up Ag. Fanouriou from Sokratous in the Old Town to reach either ▧ **Rooms Above Mango Bar,** Pl. Dorieos 3 (tel. (0241) 248 77; singles 5000dr; doubles 7000dr; triples 9000dr), or the **Rodos Youth Hostel,** Ergiou 12 (tel. (0241) 304 91; dorms 2000dr; private suites 7000dr; check-out 10am). Or snooze in the New Town at the **New Village Inn,** Konstantopedos 10. (Tel. (0241) 349 37. Singles 5000dr; doubles 8000dr.) **Yiannis,** Apellou 41, just off Sokratous away from the New Town, serves huge portions of Greek delights (1100-1800dr).

KARPATHOS (Καρπαθος)

The midpoint between Rhodes and Crete, friendly Karpathos often receives no more than a passing glance from the deck of an overnight ferry, but the charming port town and its gorgeous surroundings are worth a stop. Words can't convey the isolation of the town of **Olympus,** whose preservation of centuries-old customs has kept ethnologists and linguists in a tizzy. **Chrisovalandu Lines** and **Karpathos 1** run daily excursions to **Olympus** (depart 8:30am, return 6pm; 5000dr); find them near the ferry docks, or make reservations through Karpathos or Possi Travel. **Ferries** arrive in **Karpathos Town** (Pigadia) from Rhodes (5hr., 2 per week, 4175dr); Iraklion (6hr., 2 per week, 3500dr); and Santorini (12hr., 2 per week, 4860dr). From the bus station, turn right (as you face inland) and take the first left to get to ■**Harry's Rooms to Rent.** (Tel. (0245) 221 88. Singles 3500dr; doubles 5000dr; triples 5500dr.)

KOS (Κως)

Although it rivals Rhodes in sheer numbers, Kos tends to draw a younger, louder, and more intoxicated crowd. Don't be dismayed by the raucous bars and mammoth hotels lining the golden beaches: perseverance rewards those who take the time to explore Kos' quiet nooks and discover its ruins. In **Kos Town,** minarets of Ottoman mosques rise amongst grand Italian mansions, the massive walls of a Crusader fortress, and scattered ruins. The ancient sanctuary of **Asclepion,** 4km west of Kos Town, is dedicated to the god of healing. In the 5th century BC, Hippocrates opened the world's first medical school here to encourage the development of a precise medical science. Most ruins at the Asclepion actually date from the 3rd century BC. From the lowest level *(andiron)*, steps from the 3rd century BC lead to the 2nd-century AD **Temple of Apollo** and 4th-century BC **Minor Temple of Asclepios.** Sixty steps lead to the third *andiron*, with the forested remains of the **Main Temple of Asclepios** and a view of the ruins, Kos Town, and the Turkish coast. The site is also easily reached by **bus** (15min., 16 per day). (Open June-Sept. Tu-Su 8:30am-7pm. 800dr, students 400dr.) The island's best **beaches** stretch along Southern Kos up to Kardamene; the **bus** will let you off at any of them.

Ferries run to Patmos (4hr., 1-2 per day, 2800dr); Rhodes (4hr., 2 per day, 3500dr); Peiraias/Athens (11-15hr., 2-3 per day, 7536dr); and the Cyclades. Walk left (facing inland) from the harbor to reach Vas. Georgios; the **tourist office** is at #1 (tel. (0242) 244 60; fax 211 11). It's best to find your own room, but if your boat docks in the middle of the night, you may have no choice but to go with hawkers. Take the first right off Megalou Alexandrou, on the back left corner of the first intersection, to get to ■**Pension Alexis,** Herodotou 9. (Tel. (0242) 287 98. Doubles 5500-7000dr; triples 7500dr). **Hotel Afendoulis,** Evrilpilou 1, is right down Vas. Georgiou near the beach. (Tel./fax (0242) 253 21. Doubles 7500-9000dr.) **Rooms to Let Nitsa,** Averof 47, is near the beach north of town. (Tel. (0242) 258 10. Doubles 7000dr; triples 9000dr.) Most bars are located either in **Exarhia,** between Akti Koundouriotou and the ancient *agora*, or around Vas. Pavlou; the second area contains the more subdued **Porfiriou,** in the north near the beach. **Fashion Club,** Kanari 2, is huge and bumpin'. (Cover 2500dr; includes 1 drink.) **Heaven,** on Zouroudi along the waterfront, is loud and popular. (Cover 2000dr; includes 1 drink.) **Postal code:** 85300.

PATMOS (Πατμος)

The holy island of Patmos balances a weighty religious past with excellent beaches and traces of an artistic community. The white houses of **Hora** and the majestic walls of the sprawling **Monastery of St. John the Theologian** above are visible from all over the island. (Monastery and treasure museum open M, W, and F-Sa 8am-1:30pm, Tu and Th 8am-1pm and 4-6pm, Su 8am-noon and 4-6pm. Treasury 1000dr; monastery free.) Hora is 4km from the colorful port town of **Skala;** take a **bus** (10min., 11 per day, 200dr) or **taxi** (1000dr) from Skala (walk left and follow the signs from the bus/taxi station) or tackle the steep hike. Halfway between the two is the turn-off for the **Apocalypsis Monastery,** which houses the natural **Sacred Grotto of the Revelation,** where St. John dictated the *Book of Revelation* (the last book of the New Testament). (Open M, W, and F 8am-1:30pm, Tu and Th 8am-1pm and 4-6pm, Su 8am-noon and 4-6pm. Free. Dress modestly.) **Ferries** arrive in Skala from Samos (4 per week, 1700dr); Kos (4hr., 2700dr); Mykonos (2 per week, 4000dr); Rhodes (10hr., 5600dr); and Peiraias/Athens (10hr., 6500dr). The **tourist office** is opposite the dock. (Tel. (0247) 316 66. Open M-F 9am-3:30pm and 4-10:30pm, Sa 11am-1:30pm and 6:30-8pm.) **Jason's Rooms** are near the OTE, on the other side of the street. (Tel. (0247) 318 32. Singles 7000dr; doubles 8000-9000dr.) To get to **Flower Stefanos Camping at Meloi,** walk right along the waterfront (facing inland) and follow the signs (2km), or catch the free shuttle from the port. (Tel. (0247) 318 21. 1500dr per person, 750dr per tent; 750dr for tent rental. Open mid-May to mid-Oct.)

HUNGARY
(MAGYARORSZÁG)

US$1 = 241 FORINTS (FT, OR HUF)
CDN$1 = 162FT
UK£1 = 386FT
IR£1 = 324FT
AUS$1 = 157FT
NZ$1 = 128FT
SAR1 = 39FT
DM1 = 130FT

100FT = US$0.42
100FT = CDN$0.62
100FT = UK£0.26
100FT = IR£0.31
100FT = AUS$0.64
100FT = NZ$0.78
100FT = SAR2.51
100FT = DM0.77

PHONE CODES | **Country code:** 36. **International dialing prefix:** 00.

Communism was a mere blip in Hungary's 1100-year history of repression and renewal. Today, the nation appears well at ease with its new-found capitalist identity. Budapest remains Hungary's social and economic keystone, though it by no means has a monopoly on cultural attractions. Intriguing provincial capitals lie within a three-hour train ride. Nonetheless, with luscious wine valleys hidden in the northern hills, a rugged cowboy plain in the south, and a bikini-worthy beach resort in the east, the beauty of the countryside should not be forsaken for a whirlwind tour of the capital. Otherwise, you'll have seen the heart of Hungary, but missed its soul entirely.

For everything Hungarian, ask to dance with *Let's Go: Eastern Europe 2000.*

DISCOVER HUNGARY

Quickly being discovered as Central Europe's hippest and most cosmopolitan city, **Budapest** is the vibrant, fast-paced heart of Hungary. By day, explore the city's art collections (some of Eastern Europe's best) or indulge in a hedonistic Turkish bath. For an authentic Budapest evening, dine at one of Pest's sinful restaurants, masquerade as a Habsburg at the opulent Opera House, or imbibe with the ex-pats at Fat Mo's Speakeasy (p. 495). Afterward, mosey on over to

491

the relaxed, nearby villages of the **Danube Bend** (p. 504) and linger a while. You'll then be in a prime position to strike out and experience the alcohol-flavored giddiness of Northern Hungary, a region laden with fine vineyards. While **Eger** is home to one of Hungary's most important castles, its Bull's Blood wine and the nearby Valley of the Beautiful Women attract international visitors (as well as the region's most discriminating drunks; p. 505). **Lake Balaton,** capital of the Hungarian summer, boasts the kitschiest beach scene this side of Corfu. An escape from the thonged throngs of **Siófok's** Baywatch-esque Strand, **Keszthely**—on the lake's western end—shelters a stunning palace and the world's largest radioactive thermal bath (p. 506).

GETTING THERE AND GETTING AROUND

BY PLANE. Hungary's national airline, **Malév,** has daily direct flights from New York to Budapest's **Ferihegy airport.**

BY TRAIN. Hungarian **trains** *(vonat)* are reliable and inexpensive, although theft is frequent on the Vienna-Budapest line. **Eurail** is valid in Hungary; other railpasses include Eastrail, European East Pass, and Central Europe Pass. *Személyvonat* trains are excruciatingly slow; *gyorsvonat* (listed on schedules in red) cost the same and move at least twice as fast. Large provincial towns are accessible by the blue *expressz* lines. Air-conditioned *InterCity* trains are fastest. A seat reservation *(potegy)* is required on trains labeled "R." Purchasing the reservation on board will double the price of a ticket. Students and travelers under 26 are sometimes eligible for a 30% discount on train fares; inquire ahead and be persistent. An **ISIC** commands discounts at IBUSZ, Express, and station ticket counters. Flash your card and repeat "student," or the Hungarian, *"diák"* (DEE-ahk). Book international tickets in advance. Some basic vocabulary will help you navigate the rail system: *érkezés* (arrival), *indulás* (departure), *vágány* (track), and *állomás* or *pályaudvar* (station, abbreviated *pu.*).

BY BUS. The cheap, clean, and crowded **bus** system links many towns that have rail connections only to Budapest. The **Erzsébet tér** bus station in Budapest posts schedules and fares. *InterCity* bus tickets are purchased on board (arrive early if you want a seat). In larger cities, tickets for **local transportation** must be bought in advance from a newsstand and punched when you get on; there's a fine if you're caught without a ticket. In smaller cities, you pay when you board (usually 60Ft).

BY FERRY. The Danube **hydrofoil** goes to Vienna via Bratislava (12,700Ft); Eurailpass holders get 50% off.

BY CAR. International Driving Permits, third-party insurance, and green cards are required of all non-Hungarian drivers. It is illegal to use a mobile phone while driving, unless you use a speakerphone. The speed limit in residential areas is 50kph, on expressways 120kph. For general road and traffic information in Hungarian, call 322 22 38. The **Hungarian Automobile Club** (tel. 188) operates the "Yellow Angels" breakdown service 24hr. a day. The national motorists' club is **Magyar Autóklub (MAK),** II, Rómer Flóris u. 4/a, 1024 Budapest (tel. (1) 212 39 52; open M-Th 7:30am-4pm, F 7:30am-3pm.) For 24-hour MAK breakdown service, call 169 18 31.

BY BIKE AND BY THUMB. IBUSZ and Tourinform can provide brochures about **cycling** in Hungary that include maps, suggested tours, sights, accommodations, bike rental locations, repair shops, and border-crossings. Write the **Hungarian Tourist Board,** 1065 Budapest, Bajcsy-Zsilinszky út 31, or the **Hungarian Cycling Federation,** 1146 Budapest, Szabó J. u. 3, for more info. Hitchhiking is uncommon; *Let's Go* does not recommend hitchhiking as a safe means of transportation.

ESSENTIALS

DOCUMENTS AND FORMALITIES. Citizens of Canada, Ireland, the UK, and the US can visit Hungary without visas for 90 days, provided that their passports are not within six months of expiring. Australians, New Zealanders, and South Africans must obtain 90-day tourist visas from a Hungarian embassy or consulate; no border-control posts issue visas. For US residents, visas cost: single-entry US$40, double-entry US$75, multiple-entry US$180, 48-hour transit US$38. Non-US residents pay US$65, US$100, US$200, and US$50. Visa processing takes one day and requires proof of transportation (such as plane ticket). Visa extensions are rare; apply at Hungarian police stations.

Hungarian Embassies at Home: Australia (consulate): Edgecliff Centre 203-233, #405, Head Rd, Edgecliff, Sydney, NSW 2027 (tel. (02) 93 28 78 59); **Canada,** 299 Waverley St, Ottawa, ON K2P 0V9 (tel. (613) 230-2717; fax 230-7560); **Ireland,** 2 Fitzwilliam Pl, Dublin 2 (tel. (01) 661 29 03; fax 661 28 80); **South Africa,** 959 Arcadia St, Hatfield, Arcadia; P.O. Box 27077, Sunnyside 0132 (tel. (012) 43 30 20; fax 43 30 29); **New Zealand,** Wellington, 151 Orangi Kaupapa Rd 6005 Z (tel. (644) 475 85 74; fax 475 35 55); **UK,** 35 Eaton Pl, London SW1X 8BY (tel. (020) 72 35 52 18; fax 78 23 13 48); **US,** 3910 Shoemaker St NW, Washington, DC 20008 (tel. (202) 362-6730; fax 686-6412).
Foreign Embassies in Hungary: All foreign embassies are in **Budapest** (see p. 495).

TOURIST OFFICES. Tourinform has branches in every county, and is generally the most useful tourist service in Hungary. They can't make reservations, but they'll check on vacancies, usually in university dorms and private *panzió*. Tourinform should be your first stop in any Hungarian town, as they always stock maps and tons of local info. **IBUSZ** offices throughout the country book private rooms, exchange money, sell train tickets, and charter tours, although they are generally better at helping with travel plans than at providing information about the actual town. Snag the pamphlet *Tourist Information: Hungary* and the monthly entertainment guides *Programme in Hungary* and *Budapest Panorama* (all free and in English). Regional agencies are most helpful in the outlying areas. **Tourist bureaus** are generally open in summer Monday through Saturday 8am-8pm.

MONEY. The national currency is the **forint,** divided into 100 **fillérs,** which are quickly disappearing from circulation. Make sure to keep some US dollars or Deutschmarks on hand for visas, international train tickets, and (less often) private accommodations. New Zealand and Australian dollars, as well as South African rand and Irish pounds, are not exchangeable in Hungary. Rates are generally poor at exchange offices with extended hours. **American Express** offices in Budapest and **IBUSZ** offices around the country convert **traveler's checks** to cash for a steep 6% commission; head instead to **OTP Bank** and **Postabank** offices. **Cash advances** are available at most OTP branches, but with the already abundant and ever-increasing number of **ATMs,** many banks no longer give them. Major **credit cards** are accepted at expensive hotels and many shops. Currency exchange machines are popping up all over and have excellent rates. A basic day in Hungary (hostels, eating in budget restaurants) runs about US$25. Rounding up the bill as a **tip** is standard for a job well done—especially in restaurants. Remember in restaurants to hand the tip to the server when you pay, as it's rude to leave it on the table. Waiters expect foreigners to tip 15%. Bathroom attendants get 30Ft.

COMMUNICATION

Post: Mailing a **postcard/letter** from Hungary costs 120Ft to Australia, Canada, Ireland, New Zealand, the UK, the US, or South Africa. The mail service is perfectly reliable; airmail *(légiposta)* to the US takes 5-10 days. Hungarians put the family name first; hence Poste Restante or a phone directory would list "GABOR, Zsa Zsa."

Internet: Access is increasing throughout the country, and is ubiquitous in Budapest and major provincial centers. However, be prepared to go without access at Lake Balaton or in Szombathely and Kecskemét.

Telephone: Almost all phone numbers have six digits. For intercity calls, wait for the tone and dial slowly; "06" goes before the phone code. **International calls** require red phones or new, digital-display blue ones. Though the blue phones are more handsome than their red brethren, they tend to cut you off after 3-9min. Phones increasingly require **phone cards** (telefonkártya), available at kiosks, train stations, and post offices in denominations of 800Ft and 1600Ft. Direct calls can also be made from Budapest's phone office. To **call collect,** dial 190 for the international operator. To make a **direct call,** put in a 10 and a 20Ft coin (which you get back), dial 00, wait for the second dial tone, then finish dialing. **International direct dial** numbers include: **AT&T,** 80 00 11 11; **Sprint,** 80 00 18 77; **MCI WorldPhone Direct,** 80 00 14 11; **Canada Direct,** 80 00 12 11; **BT Direct,** 80 00 44 11. **Ambulance,** tel. 104. **Fire,** tel. 105. **Police,** tel. 107.

Language: Hungarian belongs to the Finno-Ugric family of languages. After German and Hungarian, English is the country's very distant third language. Bond with your fellow Bohemian souls by brushing up on your Hungarian (see p. 949).

ACCOMMODATIONS AND CAMPING. Many travelers stay in **private homes** booked through a tourist agency. Singles are scarce—it's worth finding a roommate, as solo travelers must often pay for a double room. Outside Budapest, the region-specific (e.g. EgerTourist in Eger) will often make advance reservations for your next stop. After staying a few nights, you can make arrangements directly with the owner, thus saving yourself the agencies' 20-30% commission. **Panzió,** run out of private homes, are the next most common option, although not necessarily the cheapest. Some towns have cheap **hotels,** but most are disappearing. Hostels are usually large enough to accommodate summer crowds, and **HI cards** are increasingly useful. Sheets are rarely required. Many hostels can be booked through Express, the student travel agency, or sometimes the regional tourist office. From June through August, university **dorms** become hostels. Locations change annually; inquire at Tourinform and always call ahead. More than 300 **campgrounds** are sprinkled throughout Hungary; most sites stay open from May through September. Tourist offices offer the annual booklet *Camping Hungary* for free.

FOOD AND DRINK. Paprika, Hungary's chief agricultural export, colors most dishes red. In Hungarian restaurants (*vendéglő* or *étterem*), begin with *halászlé*, a deliciously spicy fish stew. The Hungarian national dish is *bográcsgulyás*, a stew of beef, onions, green pepper, tomatoes, potatoes, dumplings, and plenty of paprika. *Borjúpaprikás* is veal with paprika and potato-dumpling pasta. Vegetarians can find recourse in the tasty *rántott sajt* (fried cheese) and *gombapörkölt* (mushroom stew) on most menus. In general Hungarian food is fried, and fresh vegetables other than peppers and cabbage are a rarity. A *csárda* is a traditional inn, a *bisztró* an inexpensive restaurant, and an *önkiszolgáló étterem* a cheap cafeteria. *Salátabárs* vend deli concoctions. Fresh fruit and vegetables abound on stands and in produce markets. For pastry and coffee, look for a *cukrászda*, where you can fulfill relentless sweet-tooth desires for dangerously few forints. Hungarians are justly proud of their wines; most famous are the red *Egri Bikavér* (Bull's Blood) and the sweet white *Tokaji*.

LOCAL FACTS

Time: Hungary is 1hr. ahead of Greenwich Mean Time (GMT; see p.49).

Climate: Hungary suffers the extremes of very cold winters and very hot summers; fortunately, precipitation is very low.

Hours: Business hours in Hungary are M-F 9am-5pm (grocers 7am-7pm). **Banks** close around 3pm on F. Museums are open Tu-Su 10am-6pm, with Tu an occasional free day.

Holidays: New Year's Day (Jan. 1); National Day (Mar. 15); Catholic Easter (Apr. 23-24); Labor Day (May 1); Whit Sunday (June 11); Whit Monday (June 12); Constitution Day (St. Stephen's Day; Aug. 20); Republic Day (1956; Aug. 23); Christmas (Dec. 25-26).

Festivals: The best of all worlds come together in the last two weeks of March for the **Budapest Spring Festival,** a showcase of Hungary's premier musicians and actors. Óbudai island in Budapest hosts the week-long **Sziget Festival** (mid-Aug.), Europe's biggest open-air rock festival. An international folk-dance festival, **Eger Vintage Days,** is held daily in the beginning of September.

BUDAPEST

A cosmopolitan capital and the stronghold of Magyar nationalism, Budapest awakened from 40 years in a Communist cocoon with the same pride that rebuilt the city from the rubble of WWII and endured the Soviet invasion of 1956. No toyland Prague, the city is endowed with an architectural majesty befitting the Hapsburg Empire's number-two city, and the grace of its buildings is matched only by the energy running through its streets. Although neon lights and legions of tourists may have added a new twist to the Budapest rhapsody, the city remains one of Eastern Europe's most sophisticated tunes.

HUNGARY

🛈 ORIENTATION AND PRACTICAL INFORMATION

The formerly separate cities of Buda and Pest (PESHT), separated by the **Duna** (Danube) river, have combined to form modern Budapest. On the west bank, **Buda** inspires countless artists with its hilltop citadel, trees, and cobblestoned **Castle District,** while **Pest,** on the east bank, is the heart of the modern city. Three bridges link the two halves: **Széchenyi lánchíd;** slender, white **Erzsébet híd;** and green **Szabadság híd. Moszkva tér** (Moscow Square), just down the northern slope of the Castle District, is Budapest's bus and tram transportation hub. One metro stop away toward Örs vezér tere, **Batthyány tér,** on the west bank opposite the **Parliament** (Országház) building, is the starting point of the **HÉV commuter railway.** Budapest's three **Metro** lines (M1, M2, and M3) converge at **Deák tér,** at the core of Pest's loosely concentric boulevards, next to the main international bus terminal at **Erzsébet tér.** Two blocks west toward the river lies **Vörösmarty tér.** As you face the statue of Mihály Vörösmarty, the main pedestrian shopping zone, **Váci u.,** is to the right.

Budapest is divided into 23 **districts;** "I" indicates Central Buda, while "V" means downtown Pest. Because many streets have shed their Communist labels, an up-to-date **map** is essential; pick up a free one at American Express or Tourinform, or buy the *Belváros Idegenforgalmi Térképe* at any Metro stop (199Ft).

⬛ GETTING THERE AND GETTING AROUND

Flights: Ferihegy Airport (tel. 267 43 33; info tel. 357 71 55). Terminal 1 is for most foreign airlines and Malév flights to New York and Vienna; terminal 2 is for all other Malév flights, Lufthansa, and Air France. **Volánbusz** runs to both terminals from Erzsébet tér (20-30min., every 30min., 5:30am-9pm, 500Ft).

Trains: Tel. 461 54 00. Most international trains arrive at **Keleti pu.;** some from Prague end at **Nyugati pu.,** which also serves eastern Hungary. **Déli pu.** serves western Hungary. To: **Vienna** (3hr., 11 per day, 7150Ft plus 700Ft reservation); **Prague** (EC train 6hr., 3 per day, 13,564Ft plus 800Ft reservation; night train 9hr., 1 per day, 12,064Ft); **Warsaw** (11hr., 2 per day, 12,857Ft plus 2000Ft reservation); **Berlin** (13hr., 2 per day, 23,577Ft plus 3000Ft reservation; night train 12hr., 1 per day, 37,337Ft); and **Bucharest** (14hr., 6 per day, 12,220Ft). The daily **Orient Express** stops on its way from **Paris** to **Istanbul.** Students and under 26 33% off on international tickets; indicate *diák* (DEE-ak; student). **International Ticket Office,** Keleti pu. Open daily 7am-6pm. **MÁV Hungarian Railways,** VI, Andrássy út 35 (tel./fax 322 84 05), and at all stations. Open M-F 9am-6pm. V, MC.

Buses: Tel. 117 29 66. Most buses to Western Europe leave from **Volánbusz main station,** V, Erzsébet tér (international ticket office tel. 317 25 62; fax 266 54 19). M1-3: Deák tér. Open June-Sept. 15 M-F 6am-7pm; Sept. 16-May M-F 6am-6pm, Sa-Su 6:30am-4pm. V, MC. Most buses to the **Czech Republic, Poland, Romania, Slovakia, Turkey, Ukraine,** and **eastern Hungary** depart from **Népstadion,** Hungária körút 48/52 (tel. 252 18 96). M2: Népstadion. To: **Vienna** (3½hr., 5 per week, 5190Ft); **Prague** (8½hr., 6 per week, 9900Ft); and **Berlin** (14½hr., 3 per week, 16,110Ft).

Public Transportation: Subway, buses, and **trams** are inexpensive, convenient, and easy to navigate. The **Metro** has three lines: yellow (M1), red (M2), and blue (M3). Most tourist maps include Metro lines, but pick up the *Budapest közlekedési hálózata* (Network Map of Budapest Transport; 250Ft) at any Metro station to navigate the buses. **Night transit** ("E") runs midnight-5am along major routes; bus 7E and 78E follow the M2 route.

Blue **single-fare tickets** for all public transport (one-way on one line 90Ft) sold in Metro stations, in *Trafik* shops, and by some sidewalk vendors; punch them in the orange boxes at the gate of the Metro or on buses and trams and punch a new ticket when you change lines, or face a 1200-3000Ft fine. **10-trip booklet** (*tíz jegy*) 810Ft; **20-trip booklet** 1500Ft. **1-day passes** 700Ft; **3-day** 1400Ft; **1-week** 1750Ft.

Taxis: Often a rip-off; check that the meter is on, and negotiate a price ahead of time. **Budataxi** (tel. 233 33 33) has the best rates. 90-100Ft per km.

TOURIST & FINANCIAL SERVICES.

Tourist Offices: All sell the **Budapest Card** (Budapest Kártya), which provides unlimited public transport, museum admission, and discounts at shops and restaurants (2-day 2450Ft, 3-day 2550Ft). **Vista Travel Center,** VI, Andrássy út 1 (tel. 267 86 03). MI-3: Deák tér; exit onto Bajcsy-Zsilinszky út. The multilingual staff arranges lodgings and books train, plane, and bus tickets. Open M-F 9am-6:30pm, Sa 9am-2:30pm. Also at V, Apaczai u. 1. (tel. 318 48 48). Open 24hr. **IBUSZ,** V, Ferenciek tér 10 (tel. 337 09 39; fax 318 49 83). M3: Ferenciek tér. Books discounted tickets and sightseeing packages and finds lodgings. Open M-F 8:15am-6pm, Sa 9am-1pm. V, MC, AmEx.

Embassies and Consulates: Australia, XII, Királyhágo tér 8/9 (tel. 201 88 99). M2: Déli pu.; then take bus 21. Open M-F 9am-noon. **Canada,** XII, Budakeszi út 32 (tel. 275 12 00). Take bus 158 from Moszkva tér to the end. Open M-F 9am-noon. **South Africa,** VII, Rákóczi út 1/3 (tel. 266 21 48). **UK,** V, Harmincad u. 6 (tel. 266 28 88), off the corner of Vörösmarty tér. M1: Vörösmarty tér. Open M-F 9:30am-noon and 2:30-4pm. **US,** V, Szabadság tér 12 (tel. 267 45 55; in emergency 266 93 31). M2: Kossuth Lajos; walk two blocks down Akademia and turn on Zoltán. Open M and W 8:30-11am, Tu and Th-F 8:30-10:30am. **New Zealand** and **Irish** nationals should contact the UK embassy.

Currency Exchange: Magyar Külkereskedelmi Bank, V, Szent István tér 11 (tel. 269 09 22). M1-3: Deák tér, at the basilica's entrance. One of the few to grant V/MC cash advances (no commission; go inside if you don't have a PIN) and cash traveler's checks in US$ (2% commission, minimum $20). **ATM.** Open M-Th 8am-4:30pm and F 8am-3pm.

American Express: V, Deák Ferenc u. 10, H-1052 (tel. 235 43 30; fax 267 20 28), next to Hotel Kempinski. M1: Vörösmarty tér. No commission on traveler's checks cashed in Ft; variable commission on those cashed in US$. AmEx cash advances in Ft. Mail held for members and checkholders. **AmEx ATM.** Open June-Sept. M-F 9am-6:30pm, Sa-Su 9am-1pm; Oct.-May M-F 9am-5:30pm, Sa 9am-2pm. Currency desk open daily 9am-6:30pm.

LOCAL SERVICES

Luggage storage: Lockers at all three **train stations** 200Ft. Nyugati pu. also has a luggage desk in the waiting room; 140-280Ft per day.

English Bookstore: Bestsellers KFT, V, Október 6 u. 11 (tel./fax 312 12 95), near the intersection with Arany János u. M1-3: Deák tér or M1: Vörösmarts tér. Lit, pop novels, magazines, and travel guides. Open M-F 9am-6:30pm, Sa 10am-6pm, Su 10am-4pm.

Gay and Lesbian Services: Gay Switchboard Budapest (tel. (0630) 32 33 34; http://our-world.compuserve.com/homepages/budapest), provides a comprehensive gay guide on the internet and a daily Info-Hotline service to assist gay tourists in Budapest.

Laundromats: Irisz Szalon, V, Városház u. 3/5 (tel. 317 20 92). M3: Ferenciek tére. Wash 1100Ft per 7kg; dry 450Ft per 15min. Open M-F 7am-7pm, Sa 7am-1pm.

EMERGENCY AND COMMUNICATIONS

Police: tel. 107. **Ambulance,** tel. 104. **Fire,** tel. 105.

Tourist Police: Kulföldiket Elenörzö Osztály (KEO), VI, Városligeti fasor 46/48 (tel. 343 00 34). M1: Hősök tere; go 3 blocks up Dózsa György út and turn right. Open Tu 8:30am-noon and 2-6pm, W 8:30am-1pm, Th 10am-6pm, F 8:30am-12:30pm.

Pharmacies: II, Frankel L. út 22 (tel. 212 44 06); III, Szentendrei út 2/A (tel. 388 65 28); IV, Pozsonyi u. 19 (tel. 389 40 79); VII, Rákóczi út 39 (tel. 314 36 95); IX, Boráras tér 3 (tel. 217 07 43); X, Liget tér 3 (tel. 260 16 87); XII, Alkotás u. 1/B (tel. 355 46 91). At night, call the number on the door or ring the bell; you will be charged a slight fee.

Medical Assistance: Falck Személyi Olvosi Szolgálat KFT, II, Kapy út 40/B (tel. 200 01 00). First aid free for foreigners. Open 24hr. US embassy lists English-speaking doctors.

HUNGARY

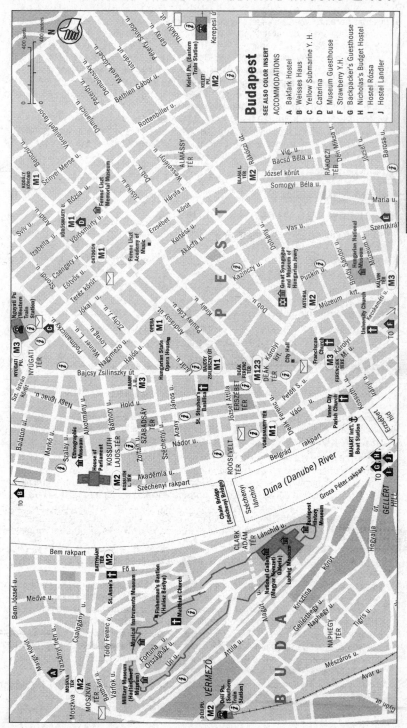

Budapest

SEE ALSO COLOR INSERT

ACCOMMODATIONS

A Bakfark Hostel
B Weisses Haus
C Yellow Submarine Y. H.
D Caterina
E Museum Guesthouse
F Strawberry Y.H.
G Backpacker's Guesthouse
H Nicholas's Budget Hostel
I Hostel Rózsa
J Hostel Landler

HUNGARY

Internet Access: Cybercafés litter the city, but reserve well ahead of time and avoid peak afternoon hours; or try a wired hostel. **Telefon**, Petőfi Sándoru. M1-3: Deák tér. Expect to wait at least 1hr. 500 Ft per hr. Open M-F 8am-8pm, Sa 9am-3pm. **Vista Travel Center** (see above). Shorter wait. 11Ft. per min. Open M-F 8am-10pm, Sa-Su 10am-10pm.

Telephones: Most phones use **phone cards**, available at newsstands, post offices, and Metro stations. 50-unit card 800Ft, 120-unit card 1800Ft. **Telefon**, V, Petőfi Sándor u. 17. M1-3: Deák tér. Phones, faxes, and **internet** (500Ft per hr.). Open M-F 8am-8pm, Sa 9am-3pm. **Local operator**, tel. 01; **international operator**, tel. 09.

Post Office: V, Városház u. 18 (tel. 318 48 11). Address mail to be held: SKYWALKER, Anakin, *Poste Restante,* V, Városház u. 18, **1052** Budapest, Hungary. Open M-F 8am-8pm, Sa 8am-2pm. **Branches** at Nyugati pu., VI, Teréz krt. 105/107; and Keleti pu. VIII, Baross tér 11/C. All open M-F 8am-9pm, Sa 8am-2pm.

PHONE CODE	City code: 1. From outside Hungary, dial int'l dialing prefix (see inside back cover) + 36 + 1 + local number.

⛏ ACCOMMODATIONS AND CAMPING

In summer, call ahead or stash your pack while you seek out a bed for the night to save yourself blisters. Travelers arriving at Keleti pu. enter a feeding frenzy as hawkers elbow their way to tourists; take their promises with a grain of salt.

ACCOMMODATION AGENCIES

Private rooms, slightly more expensive than hostels (2000-5000Ft per person, depending on location and bathroom quality), usually offer what hostels can't: peace, quiet, and private showers. Arrive early, bring cash, and haggle stubbornly.

Budapest Tourist, V, Roosevelt tér 5 (tel. 317 35 55; fax 318 60 62), near Hotel Forum, 10min. from M1-3: Deák tér. on the Pest end of Széchenyi lánchíd. Singles in Central Pest 2500-3300Ft; doubles 4000-6000Ft; triples 5000-7000Ft. Off-season prices considerably lower. Also rents flats for stays longer than four days. Open M-F 9am-5pm.

IBUSZ, V, Ferenciek tére 10 (tel. 337 09 39; fax 318 49 83). M3: Ferenciek tére. Rents rooms at a base price plus 1050Ft per day. 2-bed room 3500Ft; 3-bed 4500Ft; 4-bed 5000Ft. Open M-F 8:15am-6pm, Sa 9am-1pm.

Non-Stop Hotel Service, V, Apáczai Csere J. u. 1 (tel. 318 48 48; fax 317 90 99), M1: Vörösmarty tér. Private doubles in Pest from 7500Ft during in summer, off-season 6000Ft; triples and quads from 8000Ft, off-season 7000Ft. Open 24hr.

YEAR-ROUND HOSTELS

Budapest's hostels are generally social centers, with no curfews and beer- and music-filled common rooms that often prove more alluring than the city's bars and clubs. Most, including university dorms, operate under the auspices of the Hungarian Youth Hostel Association; representatives wear HI t-shirts. Beware theft in hostels; always keep your belongings in lockers, or take all valuables with you. Unless otherwise noted, all have luggage storage, kitchens, and TV in the common room.

▨ Backpacker's Guesthouse, XI, Takács Menyhért u. 33 (tel. 385 89 46; fax 209 84 06; email backpackguest@hotmail.com), in **Buda,** 12min. from Central Pest. From Keleti pu., take bus 7 or 7A toward Buda, get off at Tétenyi u. (five stops past the river), walk back under the railway bridge, turn left, and it's on the 3rd street on the right. Graffitied rooms, weekly spelunking trips, and Gen-X slacker-guests who never leave the kitchen. Superb CD and video collections, **internet** (15ft per min), cheap beer at reception, satellite TV, and laundry. 5- to 8-bed dorms 1200Ft; small dorm 1500Ft; double1800Ft.

Nicholas's Budget Hostel, XI, Takács Menyhért u. 12 (tel. 385 48 70), in **Buda.** Follow the directions to the Backpacker's Guesthouse and continue half a block farther. Quieter and smaller than the local competition. Musty dorm, but bright doubles. 12-bed dorm 1200Ft; doubles 4000Ft. Sheets 600Ft. Laundry 700Ft per 5kg.

Station Guest House (HI), XIV, Mexikói út 36/B (tel. 221 88 64; email station@mail.hatav.hu), in **Pest.** From Keleti pu., take bus 7 one stop to Hungária Körút, walk under the railway pass, take an immediate right on Mexikói út, walk 2 blocks, and look for the HI logo. Provides paints for guests to graffiti the walls. Common room rages with billiards, satellite TV, liquor, and live music twice a week. Ask for a 3rd floor room if you plan on sleeping. 6- to 8-bed 1600F; 4-bed 2000Ft; 2- to 3-bed dorms 2400Ft; nonmembers add 200Ft. Breakfast 250Ft. **Internet** 400Ft per 30min. Laundry 350Ft per 4kg. Reserve 2 days ahead or end up on an attic mattress (1200Ft).

Yellow Submarine Youth Hostel, VI, Teréz Körút 56, 3rd fl. (tel./fax 296 43 54), opposite Nyugati pu. in **Pest.** Bright rooms and friendly staff. Weekly fest with goulash and free booze. 8- to 10-bed dorms 1800Ft; 4-bed 2500Ft; 2-bed 3000Ft; HI members 10% less. Breakfast included. Laundry 1000Ft. Check-out 9am. V, MC.

SUMMER HOSTELS

Many university dorms, mostly near Móricz Zsigmond Körtér, morph into hostels in July and August. They typically have kitchens and a common room TV.

Bakfark Hostel, I, Bakfark u. 1-3 (tel. 201 54 19 and 340 85 85), in **Buda.** M2: Moszkva tér; walk along Margit krt. with Burger King to your right, and take the first (unmarked) street after Mammut. Some of the most comfortable hostel rooms in town. 4- to 6-bed dorms 2200-2400Ft; HI members 200Ft less. Check-out 9am. Reserve ahead.

Hostel Landler, XI, Bartók Béla út. 17 (tel. 463 36 21), in **Buda.** Take bus 7 or 7A across the river, get off at Géllert, and follow Bartók Béla útaway from the river. Singles 4100Ft; doubles 2600Ft; triples and quads 2475Ft; HI members 10% less. Some English spoken. Check-out 9am. Open July 5-Sept. 5.

Hostel Rózsa, XI, Bercsényi u. 28/30 (tel. 463 42 50), in **Buda.** M2: Blaha Lujzatér; take tram 4 and get off three stops after the river. Basic accommodations. Doubles 2900Ft; HI members 10% less. Free transport from bus or train station. Open July 1-Sept. 5.

Strawberry Youth Hostels, IX, Ráday u. 43-45 (tel. 218 47 66), and Kinizsi u. 2/6 (tel. 217 30 33), in **Pest.** M3: Kálvin tér. Doubles 2600Ft; triples and quads 2300Ft; HI members 10% less. Free Keleti pick-up. Check-out 10am. Open June 29-Sept. 1.

GUESTHOUSES

Guesthouses and rooms in private homes lend a personal touch for about the same price as hostels. Owners prowl for guests in Keleti pu., but often carry cell phones for reservations.

◾ Museum Guesthouse, VIII, Mikszáth Kálmán tér 4 (tel. 318 95 08), in **Pest.** M3: Kálvin tér; take the left exit, walk straight down Baross ut., keep left onto Reviezky u., go to the far right corner when you reach the square, and ring the buzzer at gate 4. In the heart of a hopping bar scene. Run by young, hostel-style management. 1800Ft. 500Ft locker and key deposit. **Internet** 1000Ft per hr. Laundry. Reserve the morning of your stay.

Caterina, V, Andrássy út 47, 3rd fl., #48 (tel. 291 95 38; mobile tel. (0620) 34 63 98), in **Pest.** M1: Oktogon; or take tram 4 or 6. In a century-old building on Andrássy just minutes from central Pest. Run by "Big" Caterina and daughter "Little" Caterina. TV. 18-bed dorm 1500Ft; double 2300Ft. Laundry 800Ft per 5kg. Check-out 10am. Call ahead.

Weisses Haus, III, Erdőalja út 11 (tel./fax 387 82 36; mobile tel. (0620) 34 36 31), 30min. from the center. M3: Árpád hid; take tram 1 to the HÉV Árpád híd station; then take bus 137 (last bus 11:30pm) to Erdőalja. A family-owned villa in a classy neighborhood. Doubles 3000Ft per person. Laundry. German and some English spoken.

CAMPING

Zugligeti "Niche" Camping, XII, Zugligeti út 101 (tel./fax 200 83 46). Take bus 158 from "Moszkva tér" to the end. 850Ft per person, 500-900Ft per tent; 700Ft per car; V, MC.

Római Camping, III, Szentendrei út 189 (tel. 368 62 60; fax 250 04 26). M2: Batthyány tér; then take the HÉV to "Római fürdő" and walk 100m toward the river. 1950Ft per tent; bungalows 1350-2000Ft; HI members 10% less. Kitchen. Open mid-Apr. to mid-Oct.

◻ FOOD

Even the most expensive restaurants in Budapest may fall within your budget, but eating at family joints can be tastier and more fun. A 10% tip is generally expected; another 10% if your meal is accompanied by live music. Seek out the *kifőzés* or *vendéglő* in your neighborhood for a taste of Hungarian life. For the less adventurous, the **world's largest Burger King** is on Oktogon. The **Central Market,** V, Kőzraktár tér u. 1 (M3: Kelvin tér), near Szabadság híd, is a vast indoor collection of competing vendors. **Hold utca piac,** V, Hold u. 13, off Szabadság tér in central Pest, boasts two floors of fresh food. (Open M 6:30am-5pm, Tu-F 6:30am-6pm, Sa 6:30am-2pm.)

RESTAURANTS

Marcello's, XI, Bartók Béla út 40 (tel. 466 62 31), just before Móricz Zsigmond Körtér, on the river side in **Buda.** Tasty pizzas 480-630Ft. Open M-Sa noon-10pm.

Paksi Halászcsárda, II, Margit Körút 14 (tel. 212 55 99), in **Buda.** Take tram 4 or 6 to Margit Híd. Well-executed Hungarian standbys run 790-2900Ft. Open daily noon-midnight.

Söröző a Szent Jupáthoz, II, Dékán u. 3 (tel. 212 29 29), in **Buda.** M2: Moszkva tér. Enter on Retek u. An exhaustive menu and generous portions. Entrees 595-1709Ft. Open 24hr.

Remiz, II, Budakeszi út 8 (tel. 275 13 96), in **Buda.** Take bus 122 from "Moszkva tér" three stops to "Szépilona." Famous outdoor BBQ ribs and steak prepared on "lavastones" (hot rocks). Entrees 980-1780Ft. Open daily 9am-1am; BBQ May-Sept. only. V, MC, AmEx.

🍽 **Fatâl Restaurant,** V, Váci út 67 (tel. 266 26 07), in **Pest.** Giant, hearty Hungarian meals. Very popular. Entrees from 980Ft. Reservations required. Open daily 11am-11pm.

🍽 **Marquis de Salade,** VI, Hajós u. 43 (tel. 302 40 86), at the corner of Bajcsy-Zsilinszky út, 2 blocks from M3: Arany János in **Pest.** Chic waiters and cosmopolitan cuisine; dishes from India, Azerbaijan, and Georgia. Entrees 700-2200Ft. Open daily noon-midnight.

Korona Passage, V, Kecskeméti u. 14 (tel. 317 41 11), in **Pest.** M3: Kálvin tér. Across from the Mercure Korona Hotel. Watch as giant Hungarian crêpes (*palacsinta*) are prepared to order. Sweet and savory crêpes 420-590Ft. Open daily 10am-10pm.

CAFÉS

A café in Budapest is a living museum of a bygone era, once the pretentious haunts of Budapest's literary, intellectual, and cultural elite, the cafés now cater to customers with simpler tastes, offering cheap and absurdly rich pastries.

🍽 **Művész Kávéház,** VI, Andrássy út 29 (tel. 352 13 37), diagonally across from the Opera. M1: Opera. The name means "artist café," and—unlike most remaining Golden Age coffee houses—the title fits. *Művész torta* 170Ft; cappuccino 180Ft. Open daily 9am-midnight.

Café New York, VII, Erzsébet krt. 9-11 (tel. 322 38 49). M2: Blaha Lujza tér. This symbol of the *fin-de-siècle* Golden Age fell into disrepair under communism, but has been restored in exquisite velvet, gold, and marble. Ice cream and coffee delights priced accordingly (700-1200Ft). Cappucino 280Ft. Open daily 10am-midnight. V, MC, AmEx.

Ruszwurm, I, Szentháromság u. 7 (tel. 375 52 84), just off the square on Várhegy in the Castle District. The sweets that once attracted the Hapsburgs now draw packs of tourists. Ice cream 60Ft per scoop; chocolate cake 200-280Ft. Open daily 10am-7pm.

🔲 SIGHTS

In 1896, Hungary's 1000th birthday bash prompted the construction of what are today Budapest's most prominent sights—a testament to the optimism of a capital on the verge of its Golden Age. Among the works commissioned by the Hapsburgs were **Heroes' Square** (Hősök tere), **Liberty Bridge** (Szbadság híd), and **Vajdahunyad Castle** (Vajdahunyad vár). The domes of **Parliament** (Országház) and **St. Stephen's Basilica** (Szent István Bazilika) are both 96m high—references to the historic date.

BUDA

Buda is older, more conservative, and more disjointed than its sister, but with the city's best parks, lush hills, and Danube islands, it is no less worth exploring. The **Castle District** lies atop **Castle Hill** and contains the bulk of Buda's sights. South of Castle Hill, also on the banks of the Danube, lies **Gellért Hill.**

CASTLE DISTRICT. Towering above the Danube, the **Castle District** has been razed three times in its 800-year history, most recently in 1945. With its winding, statue-filled streets, breathtaking views, and magnificent hodge-podge of architectural styles, the UNESCO-protected district now appears much as it did in Hapsburg times (though today it's much more touristed). Though bullet holes in the **castle**

LIKE A TROUBLED BRIDGE OVER WATER

The citizens of Budapest are justly proud of the bridges that bind Buda to Pest. The four great lions that have guarded the Széchenyi lánchíd (Széchenyi Chain Bridge) since 1849 make the bridge one of the most recognizable. These beasts were created by János Marschalkó in a naturalistic style, with the tongues resting far back in their gaping mouths. The anatomical correctness of their new mascots did not impress Budapestians—distraught by public laughter over the seemingly missing tongues, Marschalkó jumped from the bridge to his death. Another version of the story has the king reprimanding Marschalkó, with the same result. *Let's Go* does not recommend sculpting lions without visible tongues.

façade still recall the 1956 Uprising, the reconstructed palace today houses a number of fine museums (see **Museums,** below). *(I, Szent György tér 2, on Castle Hill. M2: Moszkva tér; walk up to the hill on Várfok u. and enter the castle at Vienna Gate (Becsi kapu). Alternatively, take the cable car (sikló) from the Buda side of the Széchenyi Chain Bridge. Cable car runs daily 7:30am-10pm; closed 1st and 3rd M of each month; ascent 300Ft, descent 250Ft. The upper lift station sits inside the castle walls near the National Gallery.)*

MATTHIAS CHURCH AND FISHERMAN'S BASTION. The multi-colored roof of the neo-Gothic **Matthias Church** (Mátyás templom), which was converted into a mosque when Ottoman armies seized Buda in 1541 (and re-converted 145 years later when the Hapsburgs defeated the Turks), is one of the most-photographed sights in Budapest. Descend the stairway to the right of the altar to enter the **crypt** and **treasury.** *(On Castle Hill. From the Vienna Gate, walk straight down Fortuna u. From the cable car, turn right on Színház and veer left on Tárnok u. High mass with full orchestra and choir Su 7, 8:30, 10am, noon, and 8:30pm. Treasury open daily 9:30am-5:30pm; 150Ft.)* Behind St. Matthias Church is the grand equestrian monument of King Stephen bearing his trademark double cross in front of the **Fisherman's Bastion** (Halászbástya). The view across the Danube from the squat, fairy-tale **tower** is stunning. *(Tu-Su 200Ft; M free.)*

GELLÉRT HILL. The Pope sent Bishop Gellért to the coronation of King Stephen, the first Christian Hungarian monarch, to assist in the conversion of the Magyars; those unconvinced by his message gave the hill its name (Gellért-hegy) by hurling the good bishop to his death from the top. The **Liberation Monument** (Szabadság Szobor), created to honor Soviet soldiers who died "liberating" Hungary, looks over Budapest from atop the hill. The view from the top of the adjoining **Citadel,** built as a symbol of Hapsburg power after the foiled 1848 revolution, is especially spectacular at night. At the base of the hill sits the **Gellért Hotel and Baths** (see **Baths,** p. 503), Budapest's most famous Turkish Bath. *(To ascend the hill, take tram 18 or 19 to Hotel Gellért; follow Szabó Verjték u. to Jubileumi Park, continuing on the marked paths to the summit. Or, take bus 27 to the top; get off at Búsuló Juhász and walk 5min. to the peak.)*

PEST

The winding streets of Pest were constructed in the 19th century and today host European chain stores, corporations and banks, and myriad monuments. The old **Inner City** (Belváros), rooted in the pedestrian **Váci u.** and **Vörösmarty tér,** is a crowded tourist strip with street vendors hawking overpriced wares.

PARLIAMENT. Pest's riverbank sports a string of luxury hotels leading up to its magnificent Neo-Gothic **Parliament** (Országház), modeled after Britain's. The massive structure has always been too big for Hungary's government; today, the legislature uses only 12% of the building. *(M2: Kossuth Lajos tér. Tours in English available M and W-Su 10am; 900Ft, students 500Ft. Purchase tickets at gate 10 and enter at gate 12.)*

ST. STEPHEN'S BASILICA. The city's largest church (Sz. István Bazilika) was decimated by Allied bombs in WWII. Its neo-Renaissance façade remains under reconstruction, but the ornate interior continues to attract both tourists and worshippers. The **Panorama Tower** offers an amazing 360° view, but the highlight is the **Basilica Museum,** where St. Stephen's mummified right hand, one of Hungary's most revered religious relics, sits on public display. For the devout and the macabre, a 100Ft donation dropped in the box will light up the religious relic for 2min. of closer inspection. *(M1-3: Deák tér. Basilica and museum open Apr.-Sept. M-Sa 9am-5pm, Su 1-5pm; Oct.-Mar. M-Sa 10am-4pm, Su 1-5pm. Tower open daily June-Aug. 9:30am-6pm; Sept.-Oct. 10am-5:30pm; Apr.-May 10am-4:30pm; 400Ft, students 300Ft.)*

SYNAGOGUE. Much of the artwork in Pest's Moorish synagogue (zsinagóga), the largest active synagogue in Europe and the second-largest in the world, is unfortunately blocked from view, as it has been under renovation since 1988. In back is the **Holocaust Memorial,** an enormous metal tree that sits above a mass grave for thousands of Jews killed near the end of WWII. *(M2: Astoria. At the corner of Dohány u. and Wesselényi u. Open M-Sa 10am-2:30pm, Su 10am-1:30pm. 400Ft, students 200Ft.)*

ANDRÁSSY ÚT & HEROES' SQUARE. Hungary's grandest boulevard, Andrássy út, extends from **Erzsébet tér** in downtown Pest to **Heroes' Square** (Hősök tere) to the northeast. Perhaps the most vivid reminder of Budapest's Golden Age is the **Hungarian National Opera House** (Magyar Állami Operaház), whose 24-carat gilded interior glows on performance nights. If you can't see an opera, make sure to take a tour. *(Andrássy út 22. M1: Opera. Tel. 353 01 70. Tours in English daily 3 and 4pm. 900Ft, students 450Ft.)* At the Heroes' Square end of Andrássy út, the **Millenium Monument** (Millenniumi emlékmű) commemorates the nation's most prominent leaders. Right off Heroes' Square is the **Museum of Fine Arts** (see **Museums,** below).

CITY PARK. The **Városliget** is home to a zoo, a circus, a run-down amusement park, and the lake-side **Vajdahunyad Castle** (Vajdahunyad Vár), whose Disney-esque collage of Romanesque, Gothic, Renaissance, and Baroque styles is intended to chronicle the history of Hungarian architecture. Outside the castle broods the hooded statue of **Anonymous,** the secretive scribe to whom we owe much of our knowledge of medieval Hungary. Rent a **rowboat** or **ice skates** on the lake next to the castle, or a **bike-trolley** to navigate the paths. *(M1: Széchenyi Fürdɒ. Boat and bike-trolley rented June to mid-Sept. M-F 10am-8pm, Sa-Su 9am-8pm; ice skates rented Nov.-Mar. daily 9am-1pm and 4-8pm. Boats 400Ft per 30min.; ice skates and bike-trolleys 300Ft per 30min.)*

🏛 MUSEUMS

Buda Castle (tel. 375 75 33), on Castle Hill (see above). ▩ **Wing A** contains the **Museum of Contemporary Art** (Kortárs Művészeti Múzeum) and the **Ludwig Museum** upstairs, devoted to Warhol, Lichtenstein, and other modern masters. **Wings B-D** hold the **Hungarian National Gallery** (Magyar Nemzeti Galéria), a hoard of Hungarian paintings and sculptures. Artifacts from the 1242 castle revealed by WWII bombings lie in the **Budapest History Museum** (Budapesti Történéti Múzeum) in **Wing E.** Wings A-D open Tu-Su 10am-6pm. Wing A 200Ft, students 100Ft. Wings B-D 300Ft together, students 100Ft; tours in English 300Ft. Wing E open May 16-Sept. 15 daily 10am-6pm; Sept. 16-Oct. 31 and Mar.-May 15 W-M 10am-6pm; Nov.-Feb. 28 W-M 10am-4pm; 100Ft, students 50Ft.

▩ **Museum of Fine Arts** (Szépművészeti Múzeum), XIV, Dózsa György út 41 (tel. 343 97 59). M1: Hősök tere. A simply spectacular collection. From Raphael to Rembrandt, Gaugin to Goya, these are the paintings you've never seen but shouldn't miss. Open Mar. 16-Dec. Tu-Su 10am-5:30pm; Jan.-Mar. 15 Tu-Su 10am-4pm. 500Ft, students 200Ft.

Museum of Applied Arts (Iparmˌvészeti Múzeum), IX, Üllői út 33-37 (tel. 217 52 22). M3: Ferenc körút. Exhibits Tiffany glass, furniture, and Fabergé eggs. Open Mar. 15-Dec. Tu-Su 10am-6pm; Dec. 14-Mar. 11 Tu-Su 10am-4pm. 200Ft, students 50Ft; Tu free.

Jewish Museum (Zsidó Múzeum), VII, Dohány út 2 (tel. 342 89 49). M2: Astoria. Juxtaposes a celebration of Hungary's rich Jewish past with haunting photographs and documents from the Holocaust. Open Apr.-Oct. M-F 10am-3pm, Su 10am-2pm. Tours 1200Ft.

Hungarian National Museum (Magyar Nemzeti Múzeum), VIII, Múzeum krt. 14/16 (tel. 338 21 22). M3: Kálvin tér. Exhibits from the Hungarian Crown Jewels to Soviet propaganda guarded by a cheery Stalin. Open Mar. 15-Oct. 15 Tu-Su 10am-6pm; Oct. 16-Mar. 14 Tu-Su 10am-5pm. 400Ft, students 150Ft. Tour 600Ft, students 200Ft.

🎵 ENTERTAINMENT

Programme in Hungary and *Budapest Panorama* (available at tourist offices) are the best English-language guides to entertainment; also try "Style" section of the weekly English-language *Budapest Sun*.

THEATER, MUSIC, AND DANCE. The **Central Theater Booking Office**, VI, Andrássy út 18 (tel. 312 00 00), next to the Opera House (open M-Th 9am-6pm and F 9am-5pm), and at Moszkva tér 3 (tel. 212 56 78; open M-F 10am-6pm), sells commission-free tickets to most performance. For less than US$5, you can enjoy an opera in the splendor of the gilded, neo-Renaissance ▓**State Opera House** (Magyar Allami Opera-haz), VI, Andrássy út 22. The box office on the left side of the building sells cheaper, unclaimed tickets 30min. before showtime. Take M1 to "Opera." (Box office tel. 353 01 70. Open Tu-Sa 11am-1:45pm and 2:30-7pm, Su 10am-1pm and 4-7pm.) The **Philharmonic Orchestra**, Vörösmarty tér 1, has equally grand music (concerts Sept.-June almost nightly) in a slightly more modest venue. The ticket office is on the side of the square farthest from the river; look for the Jegyroda sign. (Tel. 317 62 22. Open M-F 10am-6pm, Sa-Su 10am-2pm. Tickets 1200-1700Ft; less on the day of show.)

THERMAL BATHS. To soak away weeks of city grime and crowded trains, sink into a **thermal bath,** the quintessential Budapest experience. The baths were first built in 1565 by a Turkish ruler who feared that a siege of Buda would prevent the population from bathing. Thanks to him, you get to dive in, too, and the services—from mud baths to massages—are cheap enough to warrant indulgence without guilt. ▓**Gellért**, XI, Kelenhegyi út 4/6, has indoor thermal baths segregated by sex, a roof-top sundeck, a huge outdoor pool, mudbaths, ultrasound, and new "Thai massage" (6500Ft; reserve ahead). The staff is accustomed to tourists—this is the only spa with English signs. Take bus 7 or tram 47 or 49 to Hotel Gellért, at the base of Gellért Hill. (Tel. 466 61 66. Thermal bath 800Ft; with pool 1500Ft. 15-minute massage 1000Ft. Open May-Sept. M-F 6am-7pm, Sa-Su 6am-4pm; Oct.-Apr. M-F 6am-7pm, Sa-Su 6am-2pm. Pools also open Sa-Su until 6-7pm.) Indoor baths and an outdoor swimming pool attract the city's gentry to **Széchenyi Fűrdő**, XIV, Állatkerti u. 11/14. (Tel. 321 03 10. M1: Hősök tere. Swimsuit required. 500Ft, after 5pm 400Ft. Massage 1000Ft per 15min. Open May-Sept. daily 6am-7pm; Oct.-Apr. M-F 6am-7pm, Sa-Su 6am-5pm. Baths men-only July-Aug. M, W, and F; women-only Tu, Th, Sa.)

🎭 NIGHTLIFE

After a few drinks in Budapest amongst the global-village alterna-teens, you may forget you're in Hungary. A virtually un-enforced drinking age and cheap drinks may be the only cause for culture shock, though cover prices are rising. To find out what's going on where and when, pick up *Budapest Week* (126Ft). Gay life in Budapest is just beginning to make itself visible; it is safer to be discreet.

▓ **Undergrass,** VI, Liszt Ferenc tér 10 (tel. 322 08 30). M1: Oktogon. Or take tram 4 or 6. The hottest spot in Pest's trendiest area. Busy bar; an equally-packed disco spins out 80s hits and pop standards. Open daily 7pm-4am; disco starts at 10pm.

Old Man's Pub, VII, Akácfa u. 13 (tel. 322 76 45). M2: Blaha Lujza tér. Despite the name, the crowd is still in the larval phase of yuppie-dom. Lively, clean-cut, and hip, this is the place to be for the horn-rimmed glasses set. Live blues and jazz. Open M-Sa 3pm-dawn.

Fat Mo's Speakeasy, V, Nyári Pal u. 11 (tel. 267 31 99). M3: Kálvin tér. "Spitting prohibited" in this Depression-era bar; luckily, drinking ain't. Lots of beer (260-280Ft per 0.5L). Th-Sa DJ from 11:30pm, Su-Th live jazz. Open M-F noon-3am, Sa-Su 6pm-3am.

Morrison's Music Pub, VI, Révay u. 25 (tel. 269 40 60). M1: Opera. Jostling nightspot with a bar and dance floor. June-Aug. cover 400Ft. Open M-Sa 8:30pm-4am.

The Long Jazz Club, VII, Dohány u. 22/24 (tel. 322 00 06). Billiards-and-darts bar with nightly jazz (10pm). Cover M-Th and Su 300Ft, F-Sa 500Ft. Open daily 6pm-2am.

Capella Café, V, Belgrád rakpart 23 (tel. 318 62 13). With glow-in-the-dark grafitti and an underground ambience, this popular gay hangout draws a mixed crowd for a line-up that varies from transvestite lip-synchs to W night strip-teases. Nightly shows at midnight. Cover 500Ft; 500Ft min. consumption. Open Tu-Su 9pm-5am. Women welcome.

HUNGARY

THE DANUBE BEND

North of Budapest, the Danube sweeps in a dramatic arc called the Danube Bend (Dunakanyar), deservedly one of the greatest tourist attractions in Hungary.

SZENTENDRE. By far the most tourist-thronged of the Danube Bend towns, Szentendre's (sen-TEN-dreh) delights with narrow cobblestoned streets, upscale art galleries, and bite-size museums. Start your visit by heading up **Church Hill** (Templomdomb), above the town center in Fő tér, home to a 13th-century Roman Catholic church. Just across Alkotmány u., the museum at the Baroque **Serbian Orthodox Church** (Szerb Ortodox Templom) displays religious art. (Open W-Su 10am-5pm. 80Ft.) The popular **Margit Kovács Museum,** Vastagh György u. 1, exhibits work by the 20th-century Hungarian artist Margit Kovács. (Open mid-Mar. to Oct. Tu-Su 10am-6pm; Nov. to mid-Mar. Tu-Su 10am-4pm. 250Ft, students 150Ft.) The real thriller of **Szabó Marzipan Museum,** Dumtsa Jenő u. 7, is the larger-than-life chocolate statue of Michael Jackson. (Open daily 10am-6pm. 150Ft, students 100Ft.)

The HÉV commuter train and bus station is 10min. from Fő tér; descend the stairs outside the bus station, go through the underpass, and head up Kossuth u. At the fork in the road, bear right onto Dumsta Jenő út, which leads to the 1763 **Plague Cross** in the town center. **HÉV** travels to Budapest's Batthyány tér (45min., every 20-30min., 240Ft). **Buses** run from Budapest's Árpád híd station (30min., every hr., 146Ft), many going on to Esztergom (1½hr., 408Ft). **MAHART boats** leave from a pier north of the center; with the river on your right, walk along the water until you see the sign (15min.). Mid-May to August, boats float to Budapest (3 per day, 600Ft) and Esztergom (2 per day, 650Ft). **Tourinform,** Dumsta Jenő u. 22, is between the center and the station. (Tel. (26) 31 79 65. Open in summer M-F 10am-5pm, Sa-Su 10am-2pm; in winter M-F 10am-5pm; closed 1-1:30pm.) **IBUSZ,** Bogdányi u. 15, finds **rooms** (doubles 3000Ft). (Tel. (26) 361 81; fax 31 35 97. Open M-F 9am-4pm, Sa-Su 10am-3pm.) **Ilona Panzió,** Rákóczi Ferenc u. 11, is in the center of town. (Tel. (26) 31 35 99. 3200Ft for 1 person; 4400Ft for 2. Breakfast included.) A **supermarket** is by the train station. (Open M-F 9am-7pm, Sa-Su 10am-5pm.)

ESZTERGOM. If you can't find the Esztergom (ESS-ter-gom) **cathedral,** you're either in the wrong town or too close; step back and look up. Hungary's largest church, consecrated in 1856, is responsible for the town's nickname "The Hungarian Rome." Climb to the top of the cathedral cupola (100Ft) for the best view of the bend, then descend into the **crypt** to honor the remains of Hungary's archbishops. (Open daily 9am-4:45pm. 50Ft.) The **Cathedral Treasury** (Kincstáv), to the right of the main altar, has Hungary's most extensive ecclesiastical collection. (Open daily 9am-4:30pm. 200Ft, students 100Ft; English-language guide 80Ft.) On a smaller scale, the red marble **Bakócz Chapel,** to the left of the altar, is a masterwork of Renaissance Tuscan craftsmanship. Beside the cathedral stands the 12th-century **Esztergom Palace** with a museum inside. (Open Tu-Su in summer 9am-4pm; in winter 10am-3:30pm. 160Ft, students 60Ft.) At the foot of the cathedral's hill, the **Christian Museum** (Keresztény Múzeum), Berenyi Zsigmond u. 2, houses exceptional religious art. (Open Tu-Su 10am-5:30pm. 200Ft, students 100Ft.)

Trains also to Budapest (1½hr., 10 per day, 408Ft). With the station to your back, turn left on the main street, then right on Kiss János Altábornagy út, which becomes Kossuth Lajos u., to reach the square. Catch **buses** three blocks away from Rákóczi tér, on Simor János u., to Budapest (1¼hr., 2 per hr., 350-440Ft) and Szentendre (1½hr., every hr., 252Ft); the bus from Budapest departs from Budapest's M3: Árpád híd." From the bus station in Esztergom, walk up Simor János u. toward the street market to reach Rákóczi tér. **Grantours,** Széchenyi tér 25, at the edge of Rákóczi tér, will help locate central **panzió rooms** (doubles 4000-7500Ft) or cheaper **private rooms** (1550Ft). (Tel./fax (33) 41 37 56. Open July-Aug. M-F 8am-6pm, Sa 9am-noon; Sept.-June M-F 8am-4pm, Sa 9am-noon.) **Platán Panzió,** Kis-Duna Sétány 11, is between Rákóczi tér and Primas Sziget. (Tel. (33) 41 13 55. Singles 2000Ft; doubles 4000Ft. Breakfast included. Check-out 10am.) **Gran Camping,** Nagy-Duna Sétány, is in the middle of Primas Sziget, a park on the banks of the

Danube. (Tel. (33) 40 25 13. 250Ft per person, 380Ft per tent.) **Julius Meinl,** just off Rákóczi tér, sells **groceries**. (Open M-F 6:30am-6:30pm, Sa 6:30am-1pm.)

EGER

The siege of Eger Castle and the subsequent defeat of an entire attacking Ottoman army by locals figures prominently in Hungarian lore. The key to victory: local "bull's blood" wine. The legacy remains alive today in lively wine cellars; other attractions include magnificent Baroque monuments and gypsy musicians.

⁊▐▚▐ PRACTICAL INFO, ACCOMMODATIONS, AND FOOD. Trains bound for Budapest-Keleti (2hr., 5 per day, 1050Ft) split in Hatvan; make sure you're in the right car. From the train station, turn right on Deák u., right on Kossuth Lajos u., left on Széchenyi u., and right on Érsek u. to get to **Dobó tér** (main square; 20min.). **Tourinform,** Dobó tér 2, has maps and lodgings info. (Tel./fax (36) 32 18 07. Open M-F 9am-5:30pm, Sa-Su 10am-1pm.) **OTP,** Széchenyi u. 2, grants credit card advances, cashes AmEx traveler's checks commission-free, and has a 24-hour ATM. (Tel. 31 08 06. Exchange open M-Th 7:45am-1:45pm, W also 2:30-3:30pm, F until 11:45am.) Surf the **internet** at **PC Club,** Mecset u. 2. (480Ft per hr. Open daily 10am-10pm.)

The best accommodations are **private rooms;** look for *Zimmer Frei* signs outside the center, particularly on Almagyar u. and Mekcsey u. near the castle. **Eger Tourist,** Bajcsy-Zsilinszky u. 9, arranges private rooms for around 3000Ft per person. (Tel. (36) 41 17 24. Open M-F 9am-5pm.) It also runs the very basic **Tourist Motel,** Mekcsey u. 2. (Tel. (36) 42 90 14. Doubles 2800-3600Ft; triples 3450-4350Ft.) Take bus 5, 11, or 12 north for 20min. to get to **Autós Caravan Camping,** Rákóczi u. 79; get off at the Shell station and look for signs. (320Ft per person, 250Ft per tent. Open mid-Apr. to mid-Oct.) **HBH Bajor Söház,** Bajcsy-Zsilinsky u. 19, off Dobó tér, is a Bavarian beer house serving Hungarian fare such as cold brains, ham knuckles, and goose liver. (Tel. (36) 31 63 12. Entrees 599-1499Ft.) In the Valley of the Beautiful Women, **Kulacs Csárda Borozó's** vine-draped courtyard keeps the crowds coming. (Tel. (36) 31 13 75. Main dishes 720-1100Ft. Open Tu-Su noon-10pm.) **Postal code:** 3300.

▨▐ SIGHTS AND ENTERTAINMENT. Hungarians revere the medieval **Eger Castle,** where Dobó István and his 2000 men successfully repelled the attacking Ottoman army. The Castle includes subterranean barracks, catacombs, a crypt, and a wine cellar. One ticket covers a picture gallery; the **Dobó István Castle Museum,** which displays excavated artifacts and an impressive array of weapons; and the **Dungeon Exhibition,** a collection of torture equipment that will inspire sadists and masochists alike. (Castle open daily 8am-8pm; museums open Tu-Su 9am-5pm. Castle 100Ft, students 50Ft. Museums 300Ft, students 150Ft. Tours in English 300Ft.) The yellow **basilica,** the second-largest church in Hungary, often hosts exquisite organ and soprano concerts. (Concerts held May to mid-October M-Sa 11:30am, Su 12:45pm. 300Ft, under 18 100Ft.) The nearby Rococo **Lyceum,** at the corner of Kossuth Lajos u. and Eszterházy tér, houses a **camera obscura** that projects a live picture of the surrounding town onto a table, providing a god-like view of the world. (Open Tu-F 9:30am-1pm, Sa-Su 9:30am-noon. 200Ft, students 100Ft.)

In **Szépasszonyvölgy** (Valley of the Beautiful Women), 25 of the cellars dug into the hills are open for **wine tasting.** Most open after 10am and close around 6pm; the best time to visit is late afternoon. Samples are free, 0.1L shots run 30-50Ft, and 1L of wine costs about 300Ft. To reach the wine cellars, start on Széchenyi u. with Eger Cathedral to your right. Turn right on Kossuth Lajos u., left on Deák u. (contrary to the directions on the sign), right on Telekessy u. (which becomes Király u.); continue for about 10min., then bear left onto Szépasszonyvölgy. Try **Cellar #3** for a thorough and entertaining introduction to the area's wines. (Open 3pm-late.)

In summer, the city's **open-air baths** offer a desperately needed respite from the sweltering city. (Open May-Sept. M-F 6am-7pm, Sa-Su 8am-7pm, Oct.-Apr. daily 9am-7pm. Full day 280Ft, students and seniors 170Ft; either 6-8am or 4:30-8:30pm only 100Ft.) Eger revels in its heritage during the **Baroque Festival,** held for two weeks in late July and early August. Nightly performances of operas, operettas, and medieval and Renaissance court music are held around the city. You can buy tickets (300Ft, students 100ft) at the site of the performance.

◪ **EXCURSION FROM EGER: SZILVÁSVÁRAD.** Szilvásvárad (SEAL-vash-vahrod), a perfect daytrip from Eger, attracts horse and nature lovers alike. **Horse shows** (400Ft) kick into action on most weekends in the arena on Szalajka u. **Lipicai Stables** is the stud farm for the town's famed Lipizzaner breed. Walk away from the park entrance on Egri út, turn left on Enyves u., and follow signs to the farm. (Tel. 35 51 55. Open daily 8:30am-noon and 2-4pm. 80Ft.) Many farms offer **horseback riding**, especially in July and August. **Péter Kovács,** Egri út 62 (tel. (36) 35 53 43), rents horses (1500Ft per hr.) and two-horse carriages (4500Ft per hr.). **Hikers** should head to the nearby **Bükk mountains** and **Szalajka valley.** A 45-minute walk along the green trail will lead you to the park's most popular attraction, the **Fátyol waterfall;** a further 30-minute hike from the falls leads to the **Istálósk cave,** the Stone Age home to a bear-worshipping cult. **Buses** (45min., every hr., 246Ft) and **trains** (1¼hr., 8 per day, 202Ft) run to Szilvásvárad from Eger. From the train station, follow Egri út to Szalajka u. directly to the national park. There is no actual bus station in town; simply get off at the second stop in Szilvásvárad (it's the next town after passing the concrete factories of Bükkszentmárton), on Egri út near Szalajka u. Nor is there a tourist office in town, so stop by **Eger Tourinform** (see above) before heading out.

LAKE BALATON

The warm and shallow Lake Balaton has become one of the most coveted vacation spots in Central Europe. Villas first sprouted along its shores under the Romans, and when a railroad linked the lake to its surrounding towns in the 1860s, the area became the summer playground of the Central European elite. Be aware that storms roll in over the lake quickly; amber lights on tall buildings give weather warnings: one revolution per second means swimmers must be within 100m.

SIÓFOK. The fact that more tourist offices per sq. km congregate in Siófok than in any other Hungarian city says something about the number of surf-starved tourists who descend upon this town annually. Most attractions in Siófok pale in comparison with the **Strand,** a series of park-like lawns running to an extremely un-sandy concrete shoreline. There are public and private sections, the latter about 150Ft per person. **Nightclubs** of varying degrees of seediness line the lakefront. Amphibious lounge lizards frolic to ABBA and the Bee Gees aboard MAHART **disco boats.** Music ranges from disc jockeys to live pop. (Cover 800Ft. Departs July 9-Aug. 21 nightly 7-9:30pm.) If you don't spot the yellow convertible throwing flyers, just follow the spotlights scoping the sky to **Flört Disco,** Sió u. 4. (Cover 600Ft. Open daily 9pm-5am.) From **Fő u.,** the town's main drag, **trains** go to Budapest (2½hr., every hr., 904Ft); **express buses** (gyorsjárat) also head to Budapest (2½hr., 6 per day, 1227Ft). **Tourinform,** Fő u. 41, in the base of the wooden water tower across from the train station, helps find rooms. (Tel. (84) 31 53 55. www.siofok.com. Open July-Aug. M-Sa 8am-8pm, Su 10am-noon; Sept.-June M-F 9am-4pm.) To get to comfy **Tuja Panzió,** Szent László u. 74, turn left as you leave the train station, cross the tracks as soon as you can, hang an immediate right onto Ady Endie u., turn left on Tátra u. and right on Szent László. (Tel. (84) 31 49 96. 3000Ft per person.) With your back to the train station, go right onto Fő u. and right again onto Mártirok u. just before the Fő u. bridge; take the first left onto Indóhúz u. and cross the bridge on the other side of the tracks, then follow the street as it curves right to become Vitorlás u. and go left on Erkel Ferenc u. to find the huge **Hunguest Hotel Azúr,** Vitorlás u. 11. (Tel. (84) 31 20 33; fax 31 21 05. Doubles with bath 2400Ft. Reserve well in advance.)

TIHANY. With its green hikes, luxurious homes, and extensive panoramas, the Tihany (TEE-hain) peninsula is known as the pearl of Balaton. The attraction that draws over a million visitors a year is the magnificent **Benedictine Abbey** (Bencés Apátság). Luminous frescoes and intricate Baroque altars make the interior distinctly photo-worthy; with so many blinding flashes going off at once, you might need to take a picture to see it properly. (Open daily 9am-5:30pm. 180Ft, students

90Ft.) Follow the "Strand" signs along the Promenade behind the church to descend to the **beach** (open daily 7am-7pm; 200Ft), or continue a along the panoramic walkway to **Echo Hill**. MAHART **ferries** are the fastest way to reach Tihany from **Siófok** (80min., every hr., 500Ft). To reach the town from the ferry pier and neighboring Strand, walk towards the elevated road. Pass underneath and follow the "Apátság" signs up the steep hill to the abbey.

KESZTHELY. Sitting at the lake's western tip, Keszthely's (KESS-tay) pride is the ☙**Helikon Palace Museum** (Helikon Kastélymúzeum) in the **Festetics Palace** (Kastély). Built by one of the most powerful Austro-Hungarian families of the period, the storybook palace does Baroque architecture proud, housing the 90,000-volume, wood-paneled **Helikon Library,** an exotic arms collection, and an exhibit of the Festetics elaborate porcelain pieces. The **English park** around the museum provides a vast strolling ground. Follow Kossuth Lajos u. from Fő tér toward the Tourinform office until it becomes Kastély u. (Open Tu-Su 9am-6pm; ticket office closes at 5:30pm. 1000Ft, students 600Ft. Tours 2000Ft.) The rocky and swampy **Strand,** on the coast to the right as you exit the train station, still attracts the crowds. From the center, walk down Erzsébet u. as it curves right into Vörösmarty u.; go through the park on the left after the train tracks to reach the beach beyond (200Ft). **Express trains** (expressz) run between Keszthely and Budapest (3hr., 5 per day, 1080Ft). To reach the main square from the train station, walk straight up **Mártirok u.,** which ends in Kossuth Lajos u., and walk 5min. right to Fő tér. **Tourinform,** Kossuth Lajos u. 28, sits on the palace side of Fő tér. (Tel./fax (83) 31 41 44. Open July-Aug. M-F 9am-6pm, Sa-Su 9am-1pm; Sept. and Apr.-June M-F 9am-5pm, Sa 9am-1pm; Oct.-Mar. M-F 8am-4pm, Sa 9am-1pm.) **IBUSZ,** Fő tér 6/8, books private rooms. (Tel. (84) 31 43 20. Open June-Aug. M-Sa 8am-6pm; Sept.-May M-F 8am-4pm.) Pitch a tent at **Castrum Camping,** Móra Ferene u. 48. (Tel. (84) 31 21 20. July-Aug. 990Ft per person, 620Ft per tent. Sept.-June 480Ft per tent, plus 690Ft per person. Tax 240Ft.)

GYŐR

The cobblestoned streets of Győr's (DYUR) inner city wind peacefully around a wealth of religious monuments, well-kept museums, and prime examples of 17th- and 18th-century architecture. Most sights lie near the center of town. With McDonald's to your right, walk up Baross Gabor u. and turn left on Kazinezy u. to reach Bécsi Kapu tér, the site of the yellow, 18th-century **Carmelite church** (Karmelita-templom) and the remains of a **medieval castle** built to defend the town from the Ottomans. Further up Baross Gabor u. on the left, the striking **Ark of the Covenant** (Frigylada szobov) statue marks the way to **Chapter Hill** (Káptalandomb). At the top, the **Episcopal Cathedral** (Székesegyház) has suffered constant additions since 1030. Legend has it that the **Weeping Madonna of Győr** within wept blood and tears in compassion for persecuted Irish Catholics on Saint Patrick's Day 1697. (Closed M-Sa noon-2pm, Su 1-3pm.) Across the river from the town center, thermal springs serve as the basis for a **water park,** Cziráky tér and Tőltésszev u. 24. Cross the main bridge from the city center at Jedlik Ányos, take a left on the other side, and walk along the sidewalk until you come to another footbridge on the left—cross and the park is to the left. (Open M-F 6am-8pm, Sa-Su 7am-6pm. 400Ft, students 300Ft.)

The **train station** lies 5min. from the inner city; the underpass that links the rail platforms leads back to the **bus station.** Frequent trains and buses go to Budapest (2½hr., 910Ft); trains also head to Vienna (2hr., 6 per day, 5116Ft). To reach the center, head out of the train station, go right until you come to the bridge., turn left just before the underpass, and cross the big street to pedestrian **Baross Gabór u.** The **Tourinform kiosk,** Árpád u. 32, at the corner of Baross Gabór u., finds rooms. (Tel. (96) 31 17 71. Open June-Aug. M-F 8am-8pm, Sa 9am-3pm, Su 9am-1pm; Sept.-May M-Sa 9am-4pm.) **Hotel Szárnyaskerék,** Révai Miklós u. 5, is right across the street from the train station. (Tel. (96) 31 46 29. Doubles 3750Ft-5500Ft.) For a Guinness (450Ft) after a look at the Madonna, head to **Dublin Gate Irish Pub,** Bécsikapu tér 8, across from the Carmelite Church. (Open daily noon-midnight.) **Kaiser's Supermarket** is at the corner of Arany János u. and Aradi Vértanúk. (Open M 7:30am-7pm, Tu-F 6:30am-7pm, Sa 6:30am-2pm.) **Postal code:** 9001.

ICELAND (ÍSLAND)

US$1 = 73.21IKR (ICELANDIC KRÓNUR)
CDN$1 = 49.64IKR
UK£1 = 118.54IKR
IR£1 = 96.42IKR
AUS$1 = 47.70IKR
NZ$1 = 39.01IKR
SAR1 = 12.10IKR
EUR€1 = 75.94IKR

100IKR = US$1.36
100IKR = CDN$2.01
100IKR = UK£0.84
100IKR = IR£1.04
100IKR = AUS$2.10
100IKR = NZ$2.56
100IKR = SAR8.25
100IKR = EUR€1.32

PHONE CODE	Country code: 354. International dialing prefix: 00.

Forged by the massive power of still active volcanoes, raked and scarred by the slow advance and retreat of glaciers, and whipped by seemingly never-ending wind, rain, and snow, Iceland's landscape is uniquely warped and contorted. Nature, in its primeval fury, is Iceland's greatest attraction: moonscapes, geysers, and icecaps dominate the territory. Vegetation stands little chance, and the twisted shadows of the few existing trees provide mute evidence of the environment's brute power.

Today, the forces of nature which once ravaged the land have been turned to the benefit of mankind, and yet it is clear that Iceland's environment is largely untamed. The geothermal power that provides hot water and electricity to Iceland's settlements is also the cause of numerous earthquakes. Roads are carved through the inhospitable terrain, but not even 30% of them are paved, and many are impassable during winter. Planes battle the whipping winds, often in vain, and are grounded. People have made a powerful mark on Iceland, yet much of the island remains virtually unchanged from how it was found by the first Irish monks around 700 AD. Although cell phones and trendy fashions are omnipresent in Reykjavík (and testament to the fact that the country is only as insulated as it wants to be), customs and laws have kept Iceland separate. Strict immigration laws and physical isolation have resulted in a country girded by a deep sense of community, a strong economy, a booming tourist industry, and a pollution-free environment.

GETTING THERE AND GETTING AROUND

BY PLANE. Icelandair (US tel. (800) 223-5500) flies to **Reykjavík** year-round from throughout the US and Europe. Icelandair charges no extra airfare for transatlantic travelers who stop over up to three days in the country in the Awesome Iceland Stopover Package—also ask about their "Take-A-Break" special offers. **SAS** from Copenhagen and **Lufthansa** from Frankfurt also fly to Iceland. **Flugfélag Islands** (the domestic service) flies between Reykjavík and major towns; **Flugfélag Norðurlands** out of Akureyri; and **Flugfélag Austurlands** among towns in the east. The **Four Sector Icelandair Pass** provides for four flights, whether those flights are used for two round-trips or in a three-destination loop from Reykjavík (18,800Ikr). The **Five** and **Six Sector Icelandair Passes** allow for five and six flights, respectively; all three passes are valid on the regional airlines. Another option is the **Air/Bus Rover** (fly one way, bus the other), offered by Icelandair and BSI Travel (June-Sept.; Reykjavík to Akureyri 8760Ikr). Icelandair has some student discounts, including half-price on standby flights. Weather can ground flights; leave yourself time for delays.

BY BUS. Iceland has no trains, and although flying is faster and more comfortable, **buses** are usually cheaper and provide a close-up look at the terrain. Within Iceland, one tour company, **BSI Travel** (tel. 552 23 00; fax 552 99 73), with offices in the Reykjavík bus terminal, coordinates all schedules and prices. Schedules are available at hostels and tourist offices. The *Iceland 99* brochure lists selected bus schedules as

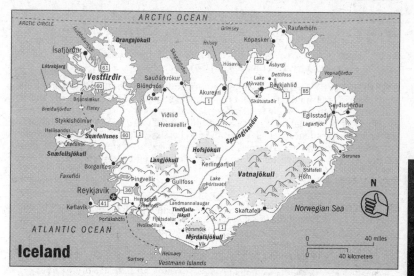

Iceland

well as tours and ferry routes; the *Leiðabók* lists all bus schedules and is a must for anyone traveling the **Ring Road;** a loop that circles Iceland, mainly following the 1411km **Highway 1,** with occasional arms radiating toward the coast. Buses run daily on each segment from mid-June through August, but frequency drops dramatically off-season. Be warned, the going is slow; though most of Highway 1 is paved, much less of the other roads is paved. The circle can be completed in three days, but to adequately explore plan for a ten-day journey. Tickets are sold in the stations (*umferðarmiðstöð*) in Reykjavík and Akureyri, or from the driver.

BSÍ sells passes that simplify bus travel greatly. The **Full Circle Passport** (14,600Ikr) lets travelers circle the island at their own pace on the Ring Road (available mid-May to Sept.). It only allows for continuous directional travel, so a traveler must continue either clockwise or counter-clockwise around the country. For an extra 7000Ikr, the pass (which has no time limitation) provides access to the Westfjords in the island's extreme northwest. The **Omnibus Passport** (available all year) gives a period of unlimited travel on all scheduled bus routes including non-Ring roads (1-week 16,800Ikr, 2-weeks 24,400Ikr); prices drop in off-season as there are fewer routes. Both passes give 5% discounts on many ferries, campgrounds, farms, *Hótel Edda* sleeping-bag dorms, and guided bus tours. Neither pass covers the interior, but BSÍ has a **Highland Pass** for inland exploration.

BY FERRY. The best way to feel the sea wind off Iceland's rugged shores is on the car and passenger ferry, *Norröna* (tel. 562 63 62 in Reykjavík), which circles the North Atlantic via Seyðisfjörður, East Iceland; Tórshavn in the Faroe Islands; Bergen, Norway; and Esbjerg, Denmark. Between the months of June and September, *Norröna* docks every Thursday at Seyðisfjörður, moves on to Tórshavn in the Faroe Islands (18hr., 14,640Ikr), and from there continues to Hanstholm, Denmark (32hr. from Tórshavn, 24,480Ikr). The ferry then returns to Tórshavn before continuing to Bergen and Esbjerg. Those journeying to Bergen and Esbjerg therefore have a three-day layover in the Faroe Islands. Students get a 25% discount on all trips. **Eimskip** (tel. 525 70 00) offers more expensive ferry rides on cargo ships from Reykjavík to Immingham, Rotterdam, and Hamburg.

BY CAR. In Iceland, travelers using **cars** (preferably 4-wheel-drive) have the most freedom. The country is fairly overflowing with car rental (*bílaleiga*) companies. Prices average about 4500Ikr per day and 30Ikr per km after the first 100km (ask about special package deals). Some companies also require the purchase of insurance that can cost from 750-2000Ikr. **Geysir-Gullfoss,** Dugguvogur 10 (tel. 568 88 88, fax 588 18 81), offers the lowest rates (2500 per day, 22Ikr per mi. after 100 mi., and a 1000Ikr insurance fee). You are required to keep your headlights on at all times, wear a seatbelt, and drive only on marked roads. A **Green Card** or other proof of insurance is mandatory. Gas runs about US$1.16 per liter.

BY BIKE AND BY THUMB. Cycling is becoming more popular, but ferocious winds, driving rain, and nonexistent road shoulders make the going difficult. Buses will carry bikes for a 500Ikr fee. **Trekking** is extremely arduous; well-marked trails are rare, but several suitable areas await the truly ambitious. Determined **hitchers** try the roads in summer, but sparse traffic and harsh weather exacerbate the inherent risks of hitching. Nevertheless, for those who last, the ride usually does come (easily between Reykjavík and Akureyri; harder in the east and the south).

ESSENTIALS

DOCUMENTS AND FORMALITIES. South Africans need a **visa** for stays of any length. Citizens of Australia, New Zealand, Canada, the UK, Ireland, and the US can visit for up to 90 days without one, but this three-month period begins upon entry into any Scandinavian country; for more than 90 days in any combination of Finland, Iceland, Norway, and/or Sweden, you will need a visa.

Icelandic Embassies at Home: Canada (consulate), 485 Broadview Ave, Ottawa, ON K2A 2L2 (tel. (613) 724-5982; fax 724-1209); **UK,** 1 Eaton Terr, London SW1W 8EY (tel. (020) 75 90 11 00; fax 730 16 83; www.iceland.org.uk); **US,** 1156 15th St NW Suite 1200, Washington DC 20005 (tel. (202) 265-6653; fax 265-6656; www.iceland.org).

Foreign Embassies in Iceland: All foreign embassies are in **Reykjavík** (p. 512).

TOURIST OFFICES. Tourist offices in large towns have schedules, maps, and brochures; check at hotel reception desks in smaller towns for local info. Must-haves are the free brochures *Around Iceland* (accommodation, restaurant, and museum listings for every town), *The Complete Iceland Map,* and the *Leiðabók* (with bus schedule). The tourist office in Iceland is at Ban Kasteeli 2, Rejkjavík (tel. 562 30 45; fax 562 30 57; www.icetourist.is).

Tourist Boards at Home: UK, 172 Tottenham Court Rd, London W1P, 9LG; (tel. (020) 73 88 53 46; fax. 387 57 11); **US,** 655 Third Ave, New York, NY 10017 (tel. (212) 885-9700; fax 885-9710; www.goiceland.org).

MONEY. The primary Icelandic monetary unit is the **króna,** which equals 100 **aurar.** Coins come in denominations of 100Ikr, 50Ikr, 10Ikr, 5Ikr, and 1Ikr; notes are in denominations of 5000Ikr, 2000Ikr, 1000Ikr, and 500Ikr. Costs are sky-high: on average, a night in a hostel might cost you US$70-95; a night in a budget hotel, US$20; a budget restaurant meal, US$12; and a day's worth of supermarket food, US$25.

Tipping: Not customary in Iceland.

Taxes: Value-added tax is included in all posted prices. **VAT refunds** (of up to 15% of the retail price) are given if departing Iceland within 30 days after purchase. The amount bought must be at least 4,000 Ikr (VAT included) per receipt; goods must be unopened.

COMMUNICATION.

Post Mailing a **postcard/letter** from Iceland cost 75Ikr to Australia, Canada, New Zealand, the US, or South Africa. To Ireland and the UK 50Ikr. Post offices *(póstur)* are generally open M-F 8:30am to 4:30pm. Post offices and hostels hold mail.

Telephone: Telephone *(sími)* offices are often in the same building as post offices. Pay phones take **phone cards** or 10 or 50Ikr pieces; local calls are 20Ikr. For the best prices, make calls from telephone offices; next best is a prepaid phone card. Before making an international call, deposit at least 10Ikr or insert a phone card (at the tourist office; 100 units 500Ikr). To reach the **operator,** call 115, and for **information,** call 114. **International direct dial numbers** include: **AT&T,** 800 90 01; **Sprint,** 800 90 03; **MCI World-**

Phone Direct, 800 90 02; **Australia Direct,** 900 90 61; **Canada Direct,** 800 90 10; **BT Direct,** 800 90 44; **Ireland Direct,** 800 93 53; **Telecom New Zealand Direct,** 800 90 64. In case of **emergency,** dial 112.

Language: Icelandic; the language has changed little from Old Norse. They also follow the Viking tradition of using patronymics rather than surnames; that is, an Icelander's first name is followed by his or her father's name and the suffix *son* or *dottir.* Icelandic has two extra letters: Þ (lowercase þ) as in *thorn;* Ð (lowercase ð) as in *them.* Most young people and many adults speak English, but knowing a few phrases may endear you to them. Other languages are also widely spoken, including Danish.

ACCOMMODATIONS AND CAMPING. Iceland's 28 **HI youth hostels,** invariably clean and always with kitchens, are uniformly priced at 1050Ikr for members, 1350Ikr for nonmembers. Pick up the free *Hostelling in Iceland* brochure at tourist offices. **Sleeping-bag accommodations** *(svefnpokapláss),* available on farms, at summer hotels, and in guesthouses *(gistiheimili),* are competitively priced (most often you get at least a mattress). In early June, many schoolhouses become *Hótel Eddas,* which offer sleeping-bag accommodations from 900 to 1450Ikr (no kitchens, 5% discount for bus pass holders). Most of these places also offer breakfast and beds (both *quite* expensive). Staying in a tiny farm or hostel can easily be the highlight of a trip, but the nearest bus may be 20km away and run once a week. Many remote lodgings offer to pick up tourists in the nearest town for a small fee. In cities and nature reserves, **camping** is permitted only at designated campsites. Outside of official sites, camping is free but discouraged; watch out for *Tjaldstœði bönnuð* (No Camping) signs, and *always* ask at the nearest farm before you pitch a tent. Use gas burners; Iceland has no firewood, and it is illegal to burn the sparse vegetation. Always pack your trash out. **Official campsites** (summer only) range from rocky fields with cold water taps to the sumptuous facilities in Reykjavík. Upper-crust sites may cost 500Ikr per person; more basic ones start at about 250Ikr. Many offer discounts for students and bus pass holders.

FOOD AND DRINK. Icelandic cuisine celebrates animals foreigners might normally envision in a zoo or at their local aquarium. Traditional foods include *lundar* (puffin), *rjúpa* (ptarmigan), and *selshreifar* (seal flippers). You can stick to fish and lamb, or bust out and try *svið* (singed and boiled sheep's head), *hrútspungur* (ram's testicles), or *hákarl* (rotten, years-old shark). But there's Italian, American, and Chinese food for the cowards. If you just can't get that last bite of puffin down, rejoice: Iceland has some of the purest water in Europe. Beer costs 350-600Ikr at most pubs, cafés, and restaurants. The national drink is *Brennivín,* a type of schnapps known as "the Black Death." The rarely-enforced drinking age is 20. Grocery stores are the way to go; virtually every town has a **Kaupfélag** (cooperative store) and often also a fast-food kiosk. Gas stations sell snacks, too. Grocery stores sometimes close for an hour at noon, especially outside Reykjavík. **Bonus** and **Netto** are cheaper alternatives to the ubiquitous **Hagkaup.** Food is very expensive in Iceland; a *cheap* restaurant meal will cost at least 600Ikr.

LOCAL FACTS

Time: Iceland is even with Greenwich Mean Time (GMT; see p. 49).

Climate: Tourist season starts in mid-June, but it really isn't high-season until July, when the interior opens up, snow almost disappears, and all the bus lines are running. In summer, the sun dips below the horizon for a few hours each night, but it never gets truly dark, and it's warm enough to camp and hike. The off-season tourist industry is picking up such that with warm clothing you could travel as late as October, but in winter there is very little sun. It rarely gets hotter than 60°F (16°C) in summer or dips below 20°F (-6°C) in winter.

Hours: Regular hours are M-F 9am-5pm (6pm in summer) and Sa mornings.

Holidays: New Year's (Jan. 1); Good Friday (Apr. 21); Easter (Apr. 23-24); Labor Day (May 1); Ascension Day (June 1); National Day (June 17); Whit Sunday and Monday (June 11-12); Commerce Day (Aug. 7); Christmas Eve and Day (Dec. 24-25); Boxing Day (Dec. 26); New Year's Eve (Dec. 31).

ICELAND

REYKJAVÍK

Geothermal steam heats the houses of Iceland's capital (pop. 105,000), home to nearly half of the country's population. Reykjavík's charm more than makes up for its modest size; bold, modern architecture complements the backdrop of snow-dusted purple mountains, and the city's refreshingly sweet and clear air is matched by its sparkling streets and gardens (thanks to legions of youngsters who are required to work on municipal beautification projects in summer). But don't conclude that Reykjavík is a natural wonder untouched by civilization—its cell-phone-toting, pedal-pusher- and platform-shoe-donning inhabitants pride themselves on their modernity. Inviting and virtually crime-free, Reykjavík's only weaknesses are its often blustery weather and its high cost of living.

▐ GETTING THERE AND GETTING AROUND

Flights: Keflavík Airport, 55km from Reykjavík. **Flybuses** (tel. 562 10 11; 700lkr) depart 45min. after each arrival for the domestic **Reykjavík Airport** and the adjacent Hótel Loftleiðir, just south of town. From there walk 15min. or take **bus** 1 (every 30min., 120lkr) to Lækjartorg Square downtown. Flybuses pick up passengers from the Hótel Loftleiðir (2hr. before each flight departure) and the Grand Hotel Reykjavík (2½hr. before); June-Aug. also from the youth hostel (4:45am and 1:15pm). The Omnibus Pass (but not Full Circle Passport) covers the Flybus; you can get a refund for your ride into town at BSÍ Travel (see below) or Reykjavík Excursions (in the Hotel Loftleiðir; 24hr.).

Buses: Umferðarmiðstöð (local; also known as **BSÍ Station**), Vatnsmýrarvegur 10 (tel. 552 23 00), off Hringbraut near Reykjavík Airport. Open daily 7am-11:30pm; tickets sold 7:30am-10pm. Upstairs, **BSÍ Travel** (tel. 552 23 00; fax 552 99 73) sells bus passes and numerous tour packages. Open June-Aug. Su-F 7:30am-7pm, Sa 7:30am-2pm.

Public Transportation: Strætisvagnar Reykjavíkur (SVR; tel. 551 27 00) operates yellow city buses (120lkr). Tickets are sold at 5 terminals; the main 2 are Laekjartorg (open M-F 9am-6pm) and Hlemmur (open M-F 8am-6pm, Sa-Su noon-8pm). If you have exact change, you can also buy tickets on the bus. Ask the driver for a free transfer ticket (*skip-timiði;* valid for 30-45min.). *Around Reykjavík* has a map and schedule. Buses run M-Sa 7am-midnight, Su and holidays 10am-midnight, every 20-30min. Some night buses (rare and tricky to find) with limited routes run until 4am on weekends.

Taxis: BSR, Skolatröð 18 (tel. 561 00 00). 24-hour service. Tipping not customary.

Bike Rental: BSÍ Travel (see above) rents mountain bikes for 1400lkr per day, 8000lkr per week. 20/50% off for Full Circle/Omnibus Passport holders. Reservations required. The **youth hostel** also rents bikes (600lkr per hr., 1200lkr per day).

Hitchhiking: Those hitching take buses 15, 10, or 110 to the east edge of town, then stand on Vesturlandsvegur to go north or Suðurlandsvegur to go southeast.

▐ ORIENTATION AND PRACTICAL INFORMATION

Lækjartorg is the main square of old Reykjavík. South of Lækjartorg are **Tjörnin** (the pond), the long-distance bus station, and the Reykjavík Airport. Extending east and west from Lækjartorg square is the main thoroughfare, which becomes from (west to east) **Austurstræti, Bankastræti,** and **Laugavegur.** Pick up *Around Reykjavík* at the tourist office or around town (free).

TOURIST AND FINANCIAL SERVICES

Tourist Office: Upplýsingamiðstöð Ferðamála í Íslandi, Bankastr. 2 (tel. 562 30 45), at Lækjartorg and Bankastr. Open mid-May to mid-Sept. daily 8:30am-7pm; mid-Sept. to mid-May M-F 9am-5pm, Sa-Su noon-6pm. **Branch** at the **airport.**

Budget Travel: Ferðaskrifstofa Stúdenta (tel. 561 56 56; fax 551 91 13), Hringbraut, next to National Museum. Sells ISICs, railpasses, and bus passes. Open M-F 9am-5pm.

Embassies: Canada, Suðurlandsbraut 10, 3rd fl. (tel. 568 08 20; fax 568 09 80). Open M-F 8am-4pm. **Ireland,** Kringlan 7 (tel. 588 66 66; fax 588 65 64). Open M-F 8am-4pm. **South Africa,** P.O. Box 916 (tel. 520 33 00; fax 520 33 99). Open M-F 9am-5pm. **UK,** Laufásvegur 31 (tel. 550 51 00; fax 550 51 05). Open M-F 9am-noon. **US,** Laufásvegur 21 (tel. 562 91 00; fax 562 91 23). Open M-F 8am-12:30pm and 1:30-5pm.

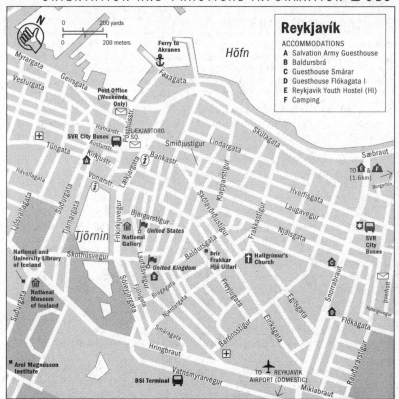

Reykjavík

ACCOMMODATIONS
A Salvation Army Guesthouse
B Baldursbrá
C Guesthouse Smárar
D Guesthouse Flókagata I
E Reykjavik Youth Hostel (HI)
F Camping

Currency Exchange: Banks charge no commission; many are located on Austurstr and Laugavegur. Most open M-F 9:15am-4pm.

LOCAL SERVICES

Camping Equipment: Sport Leigan (tel. 551 98 00), next to the BSÍ station. Open M-F 9am-6pm, F 9am-7pm, Sa 10am-3pm. **Útivistarbúðin** (tel. 551 98 05), Laugeveguri 25. Sleeping bags start at 3000lkr; tents 39,000lkr. Open M-F 10am-6pm, Sa 10am-4pm.

Luggage Storage: At the HI hostel for 50lkr per day, 300lkr per week, even for non-guests. Also at the BSÍ terminal for 150lkr per day, 400lkr per week.

English Bookstore: Mál og Menning, Laugavegur 18 (tel. 515 25 00). Books on Iceland and a large selection of fiction, non-fiction, and poetry. Open daily 9am-11pm.

Laundromat: Many hostels do laundry. **Þvoið Sjálf,** Barónsstígur 3 (tel. 552 74 99), below Hverfisg. 1000lkr per load, students 900lkr. Open M-F 8am-7pm, Sa 10am-6pm.

EMERGENCY AND COMMUNICATIONS

Emergencies: Tel. 112. **Police:** tel. 569 90 00; after-hours call 369 90 11.

Pharmacies: Haaleitis Apótek, Haaleitisbraut 68 (tel. 581 21 01; 24hr.). **Laugevegur Apótek,** Laugevegur 16 (tel. 552 40 45). Open M-F 9am-6pm, Sa 10am-2pm.

Medical Assistance: Sjukrahus Reykjavíkur (City Hospital; tel. 525 17 00), on Slettuve-gur, has a 24-hour emergency ward. From the center of town, take bus 3.

Internet Access: City Library, Ðineholtsstr. 29A. Sign up for free one-hour slots. Open June-July M-Th 9am-9pm, F 9am-7pm, Sa 1-4pm; Aug.-May closed Sa.

Telephones: Landssiminn, opposite Kirkjustr. 8. Open M-F 9am-6pm.

Post Office: ÍSLANDSPÓSTUR, Pósthússtr. 5, at Austurstr. (tel. 550 70 10). Address mail to be held: Gwen SHEN, Poste Restante, ÍSLANDSPÓSTUR, Pósthússtr. 5, 101 Reykjavík, Iceland. Open M-F 8am-4:30pm.

ICELAND

ACCOMMODATIONS AND CAMPING

Many guesthouses offer "sleeping-bag accommodations" (a nice room and a nice bed with neither sheets nor blanket). A cheap hotel will cost at least 5000Ikr. Breakfast costs an extra 550-600Ikr; take advantage of Iceland's cheap cereal and yogurt instead. From mid-June through August, call ahead for reservations.

▨ **Hjálpræðisherinn Gisti-og Sjómannaheimili** (Salvation Army Guest and Seamen's Home), Kirkjustr. 2 (tel. 561 32 03), in a pale yellow house near the pond. Filled with backpackers enjoying the fantastic location and the extremely friendly staff. Sleeping-bag accommodations 1400Ikr. Singles 2900Ikr; doubles 3900Ikr. Sheets 400Ikr. Laundry 750Ikr. Reception 7am-1am; after-hours ring the bell. Reserve ahead.

Guesthouse Flókagata 1, Flókag. 1 (tel. 552 11 55; fax 562 03 55; email guesthouse@skyrr.is), entrance on Snorrabraut. Take bus 1 from BSÍ terminal. Pristine rooms. Sleeping-bag accommodations 1300Ikr; singles 4200Ikr; doubles 6400Ikr. Breakfast 1900Ikr; included with singles and doubles. Reception 24hr.

Reykjavík Youth Hostel (HI), Sundlaugavegur 34 (tel. 553 81 10; fax 588 92 01). Take bus 5 from Lækjarg. to Sundlaugavegur. Clean and comfortable. A bit far, but happily located next to a huge geothermal pool. 1200Ikr; 1450Ikr for non-members. Luggage storage 50Ikr per day. Sleeping bags allowed; sheets 400Ikr. Kitchen. Bike rental. Reception 8am-midnight, Sa-Su closed 11am-4pm; ring the bell after hours.

Baldursbrá, Laufásvegur 41 (tel. 552 66 46; fax 562 66 47; email heijfis@centrum.is), 5min. from BSÍ. Jacuzzi and sauna (200Ikr). May-Aug. singles 5000Ikr, doubles 7000Ikr; Sept.-Apr. singles 2500Ikr, doubles 5000Ikr. Kitchen.

Guesthouse Smárar, Snorrabraut 52 (tel. 562 33 30; fax 562 33 31). Spacious. Sleeping-bag accommodations 1600Ikr. Singles 3900Ikr; doubles 5300Ikr; triples 7000Ikr. Kitchen. Laundry 400Ikr.

Camping Reykjavík (tel. 568 69 44), behind the Reykjavík youth hostel. Take bus 5 from the center. Great, with geothermal pool (200Ikr). 500Ikr per tent, 300Ikr per person; 2-bed cabins 3000Ikr. Showers 50Ikr per 5min. Laundry. Open mid-May to mid-Sept.

FOOD

Hunting down affordable cuisine in Reykjavík can be a challenge. A real experience of Icelandic cuisine (which consists primarily of seafood and lamb) will cost you at least 1000Ikr. The cafés of Reykjavík transform from quiet places for an early breakfast to boisterous bars by night. *What's On in Reykjavík* lists live café shows. **Nykaup,** Laugavegur 59, has **groceries.** (Open M-Sa 10am-7:30pm, Su noon-7:30pm.) Smaller convenience stores typically stay open until 10pm.

▨ **One Woman Restaurant,** Laugavegur 20B, at the intersection with Klapparstígur. Vegetarian fare in an environment as soothing as its food is tasty. Different cuisine daily (700Ikr; F and Sa usually Pakistani and Indian). Dinner buffet 900Ikr. Open M-F 11:30am-2pm and 6-10pm, Sa 11:30am-9pm, Su 6-10pm.

Jómfrúin, Laekjarg. 4. Danish restaurant serving delectable open-faced sandwiches (500-1300Ikr). Beer 200-650Ikr. Open daily 11am-10pm.

Kebab Húsiþ, on the corner of Laekjarg. and Austurstr. Hearty kebabs on pita-like bread (500-750Ikr). Open M-Th 11:30am-midnight, F-Sa 11:30am-5am, Su 1pm-midnight.

Kaffi Barinn, on Bergstatastr. near Laugavegur. Intimate, largely local crowd. Packed on weekend nights, especially after the DJ shows up on F and Sa. Coffee 160-250Ikr, beer 500-600Ikr. Open M-F 11am-1am, Sa noon-3am, Su 3pm-1am. Kitchen closed Sa-Su.

Sólon Íslandus, Bankastr. 7a. Students, literati, and wannabes congregate in this hip yet stately café. Often live jazz upstairs in summer (cover 1000Ikr). Coffee 220Ikr, beer 450-650Ikr, entrees around 900Ikr. Open May-Sept. M-Th 10am-1am, F-Sa 10am-3am, Su noon-3am; Sept.-May M-Th 11am-1am, F-Sa 11am-3am, Su 2pm-midnight.

◆ ⚠ SIGHTS AND HIKING

The **Reykjavík Card,** available at the tourist office, allows unlimited public transportation, entrance to the geothermal pools around Reykjavík, and admission to many sights (1-day 600Ikr, 2-day 800Ikr, 3-day 1000Ikr).

MUSEUMS. The **Þjóðminjasafn Íslands** (National Museum of Iceland) exhibits national historical artifacts. *(At Hringbraut and Suðurg., near the university. Scheduled to reopen following renovations in Aug. 2000.)* The **Ásmundur Sveinsson Sculpture Museum** celebrates Sveinsson's sculptures and huge concrete monuments to the working man. *(On Sigtún. Open daily June to mid-Sept. 2-5pm; mid-Sept. to May 1:30-4pm. 200Ikr.)* The **Listasafn Íslands** (National Gallery of Iceland) is a stunning construction of glass, marble, and stainless steel that outdoes the collection. *(Fríkirkjuvegur 7, on the east shore of Tjörnin; enter on Skálholtsstígur. Open Tu-Su 11am-5pm. 300Ikr; W free.)* The **Árbaer Open-Air Folk Museum** has exhibits chronicling Icelandic history. *(On Ártúnsholt. Take bus 10 or 110. Open Tu-F 9am-5pm, Sa-Su 10am-6pm. 300Ikr, students 150Ikr.)*

OUTDOORS AND HIKING. For a terrific view of Reykjavík and the surrounding ocean and mountains, hike up Skólavörðustígur to **Hallgrímskirkja** (Hallgrímur's Church). The church's design was inspired by Iceland's natural basalt columns, and the soaring steeple is easily the highest point in Reykjavík. *(Open M-F 9am-6pm, Sa-Su 10am-6pm in summer; daily 10am-6pm in winter. 200Ikr.)* The outdoor **Laugardalslaug** is the largest of Reykjavík's geothermally heated pools, with a giant slide. *(On Sundlaugavegur next to the campground. Open M-F 6:50am-10pm, Sa-Su 8am-8pm. 200Ikr.)* Well-marked trails lead to the salmon-filled Elliðaár river. Follow the river to **Lake Elliðavatn** and the **Heiðmörk reserve,** a popular picnic spot and photo stop.

Ferries run regularly to **Viðey Island,** which on a hypothetically sunny, warm, and non-windy day provides excellent opportunities for hiking and picnicking. The island has been inhabited since the 10th century and boasts Iceland's second-oldest church. Across the bay from Reykjavík looms **Mt. Esja,** which you can ascend via a well-kept trail in two to three hours. While the trail is not difficult, in summer hikers are often assaulted by icy rain, hail, and snow. *(Take bus 10 or 110 to Artún and transfer to bus 20, exiting at Mógilsá. Bus 20 runs less frequently; consult a schedule before setting out.)*

⚊ NIGHTLIFE

Though Reykjavík's summer nights are brief, the sun sets around midnight and rises around 2am, there's still fun to be had; unfortunately, you'll have to pay for your fun—cover charges can run 500-1000Ikr, and beer costs 400-650Ikr. The city's cafés are the hottest nightspots (see above), although Reykjavík has its fair share of pubs and discos as well. **Gaukur á Stöng,** Tryggvag. 22, is Iceland's first pub. (Live music M-F 11pm, Sa-Su midnight. Open Su-Th 6pm-1am, F-Sa until 3am.) **22,** Laugavegur 22, is an artsy hangout that attracts a large gay crowd on weekends with its upstairs disco. (Tel. 551 36 28. Open M-Th noon-1am, F noon-3am, Sa 6pm-3am, Su 6pm-1am.) A younger, magnificently dressed crowd packs into **Astro,** Austurstr. 22 (tel. 552 92 22). Stay a while and your eyes will begin to sting, though it's hard to tell whether the tears are caused by the hazy smoke or the fact that everyone inside is so much more beautiful than you are.

⫸ EXCURSIONS FROM REYKJAVÍK

Buses traverse the terrain from Reykjavík to various surrounding sights (mostly within an hour or two of downtown), but many opt for comprehensive scheduled tours instead. BSÍ's eight-hour **Golden Circle** guided bus tour departs from Hotel Lofteiðir in Reykjavík daily at 9am and covers Hveragerði, Kerið, Skálholt, Geysir, Gullfoss, and Þingvellir National Park (4800Ikr; May-Sept.). Book ahead with **Reykjavík Excursions** (tel. 562 10 11). BSÍ also provides free pickup for customers at a number of other hotels and hostels around Reykjavík.

ÞINGVELLIR NATIONAL PARK. Fifty kilometers east of Reykjavík, this park straddles both the European and North American tectonic plates. This prime location causes the park to spread 2cm each year, and massive rifts and fissures abound (watch your step). The river Öxará slices through lumpy lava fields and jagged fissures on its way to the **Drekkingarhylur** (Drowning Pool), where convicted witches were once drowned, and to **Lake Þingvallavatn,** the largest lake in Iceland. The river purportedly foreshadows doom by changing into blood, and changes mysteriously into wine for one hour each year. If possible, have your visit coincide with this particular hour. The legendary river of wine once brought more than just tourists to the park; the site commemorates the world's first parliamentary democracy and the site of Iceland's ancient parliament, the Alþing. For almost nine centuries, Icelanders gathered once a year in the shadow of **Lögberg** (Law Rock) to discuss matters of blood, money, and justice. The **bus** runs daily from Reykjavík to Þingvellir (departs May 20-Sept. 10 1:30pm, return 5pm; 570Ikr). The **tourist office** sells maps (100Ikr). (20min. north of drop-off point. Tel. 482 26 60. Open May-Sept. daily 8:50am-10pm; Oct.-Apr. 10am-5pm.) There are **campgrounds** by the info center and the lake (450Ikr per person; no showers); the grounds farther north are cheaper (300Ikr).

GEYSIR. The bus from Reykjavík traverses lush green valleys and bright red clay paths to the **Geysir** area, a rocky, rugged tundra, with steaming pools of hot water every few meters. Most merely bubble, and the Geysir itself, the etymological parent of the word "geyser" and one of the world's largest (the spray used to reach 80m high), is now inactive. A few steps away, the smaller **Strokkur** erupts with energetic frequency (every 5-10min.). Look for the water beginning to swell, and then take cover. You can also find azure and rust-colored boiling mud baths near the geysers—but at over 120°C they're a little too hot for a dip. The **bus** runs from Reykjavík to Geysir. (1210Ikr. Departs May-Sept. daily at 9am; mid-June to Aug. also at 11:30am. Returns May-Aug. at 2:30pm; mid-June to Aug. also at 5pm.) A **tourist shop** sells all you'll need. (Open daily 10am-7pm.) Across the road from the geyser, **Hotel Geysir** has a pool and panoramic views. (Tel. 486 89 15; fax 486 87 15. Sleeping-bag accommodations 650-1400Ik, sleeping-bag doubles 2800Ikr. Singles 3000Ikr; doubles 4200Ikr. **Camping** 250Ikr per person, 250Ikr per tent; bus pass discounts.)

GULLFOSS (GOLDEN FALLS). Nine kilometers past Geysir cascades Gullfoss. The glacial river drops 30m in two tiers through a gorge, shooting billowing mist into the air. An outcropping of rock allows extremely close access, but at such proximity the enchanting mist seems more like a torrential downpour. Nearby, a small museum/info-shack details the geology of the falls. The **bus** runs daily from Reykjavík to Gullfoss. (1290Ikr. Departs May-Sept. at 9am, mid-June to Aug. also at 11:30am. Returns May to mid-June at 12:45pm, mid-June to Aug. also at 4:15pm.)

BLUE LAGOON. Southwest of Reykjavík lies a vast hot pool of geothermally heated water in the middle of a lava field. The lagoon's water is the run-off from a power plant that provides Reykjavík with electricity and heat by using the steam of the geothermal water to turn turbines. In no way dangerous, some claim that the lagoon's unique concentrations of silica, minerals, and algae can heal skin diseases such as psoriasis. Mystical, tourist-trap powers aside, the Blue Lagoon offers a magnificent chance at heat-bathed relaxation in a way that is uniquely Icelandic. The **bus** runs from Reykjavík to the Blue Lagoon. (1330Ikr. Departs daily at 10:30am and 6pm; July-Aug. also 1:30pm. Returns to Reykjavík at 12:35pm and 7:50pm; July-Aug. also 4:05pm.)

REPUBLIC OF IRELAND

AND NORTHERN IRELAND

US$1 = IR£0.76 (IRISH PUNT OR POUNDS)
CDN$1 =IR£0.52
UK£1 =IR£1.20
AUS$1 =IR£0.50
NZ$1 =IR£0.41
SAR1=IR£0.13
EUR€1 = IR£0.79

IR£1 = US$1.32
IR£1 = CDN$1.94
IR£1 = UK£0.83
IR£1 = AUS$2.00
IR£1 = NZ$2.48
IR£1 = SAR7.96
IR£1 = EUR€1.27

PHONE CODES **Country codes:** 353 (Republic); 44 (Northern; dial 08 from the Republic). **International dialing prefixes:** 00.

! Although the Republic of Ireland and Northern Ireland are grouped together in this chapter for geographical reasons, no political statement is intended. For info on Northern Ireland's currency exchange rates and the like, see **Britain,** p. 134.

Literary imaginations have immortalized Ireland's natural scenery since the ancient times of Celtic bards. Travelers who come to Ireland with this poetic imagery in mind won't be disappointed: this largely agricultural and sparsely populated island has experienced little physical change over thousands of centuries. Spectacular, windswept scenery wraps around the coast, and small mountain chains punctuate interior expanses of bogland. Pockets of civilization dot the landscape, ranging from one-street villages to handfuls of cities. Dublin and Belfast have flowered into cosmopolitan urban centers, suffusing sophistication into their orbits. The Irish language lives on in small, secluded areas known as *gaeltacht,* in national papers, and in a growing body of modern literary works. Today's Ireland promises an old-world welcome along with the edge of urban counter-cultures.

Current tensions and conflicts on the island continue centuries-old disputes. Following the Reformation in England, the defiant Catholic population was suppressed by the English, and the negligence of the English government during the Potato Famine of the late 1840s exacerbated tensions. After turn-of-the-century Nationalists agitated for home rule, fighting degenerated into civil war. The island was provisionally partitioned into the Irish Free State and Northern Ireland, which remained part of the UK. In 1949, the Free State officially proclaimed itself the independent Republic of Ireland (officially Éire), while the British retained control of the area now called Northern Ireland. By the end of the 1960s, the tension in Northern Ireland between Catholic Nationalists, who considered themselves Irish, and Protestant Unionists, who considered themselves British, again erupted into violence. For years, the British and Irish governments' attempts to defuse the situation only led to sectarian attacks by paramilitaries on both sides of the debate. In the spring of 1998, the British and Irish governments formulated a peace accord, which was adopted by popular vote. 1999 has seen the accord's fate fall into uncertainty, but negotiations continue in hopes of a lasting peace.

For more detailed coverage of Ireland, snag a copy of *Let's Go: Ireland 2000.*

DISCOVER IRELAND

Ireland's small area is well-stocked with activities to suit the whims of hikers, bikers, aesthetes, poets, birdwatchers, musicians, and drinkers. Land in **Dublin** (p. 521) and spend several days exploring this thousand-year-old city, a bastion of literary history and, these days, the stomping-ground of international hipsters as well. Take the train up to **Belfast** (p. 542) and contemplate its complex history, then catch the bus to **Giant's Causeway** (p. 547), a strange formation of rocks called by some the earth's eighth natural wonder. Ride the bus to **Donegal Town,** spend a night at the pub and loving the trad, before climbing **Slieve League** (p. 541), the tallest seacliffs in Europe. Next up is **Sligo** (p. 540), once the beloved home of W.B. Yeats. From there, head to **Galway** (p. 537), an artsy student town that draws the island's best musicians to its pubs. Relax in the picture-perfect **Ring of Kerry** (p. 534) and the **Killarney National Park** (p. 533), with its exquisite mountains, lakes, and wildlife. On your way back to Dublin, take a detour to **Kilkenny** (p. 530) and visit Ireland's oldest brewery.

GETTING THERE AND GETTING AROUND

BY PLANE. British Airways, British Midlands, and **Manx Air** offer **flights** from Britain (including Gatwick, Heathrow, Manchester, Birmingham, Liverpool, and Glasgow) and other cites to **Dublin, Shannon, Cork, Galway, Sligo, Waterford, Belfast,** and **Derry.** For info on cheap flights to Britain and the continent, see p. 53.

BY TRAIN. Trains run by **Iarnród Éireann** (Irish Rail) branch out from Dublin to larger cities, but service is limited. Pick up an *InterCity Rail Traveler's Guide* (IR₤0.50), available at most train stations, for schedules. By far the most useful student travel pass in Ireland is the **TravelSave stamp,** available to ISIC holders from USIT (see p. 523) for IR₤8. Affixed to your ISIC, this stamp decreases fares by about 50% on rail lines and 15% on bus services in Ireland (except fares less than IR₤1). **Eurail** is valid on trains in the Republic but not in Northern Ireland.

Northern Ireland Railways (tel. (01232) 89 94 11; www.nirailways.co.uk) covers much of the northeast coastal area as well. The main line goes from Dublin to Belfast (UK₤17, round-trip UK₤26), where lines run to Bangor and Larne. There is a **TravelSave stamp** (UK₤7) in Northern Ireland similar to the one offered in the Republic of Ireland. The **Freedom of Northern Ireland** ticket allows unlimited travel by train and Ulsterbus for seven days (UK₤7), three days (UK₤25), or one day (UK₤10).

BY BUS. Buses in the Republic of Ireland reach many more destinations than trains. **Bus Éireann,** the national bus company, operates **Expressway** buses, which link larger cities, and **local** buses, which serve the countryside and smaller towns. The bus timetable book (IR₤1) is available at Busáras Station in Dublin and many tourist offices. Ireland has **Rambler** tickets, offering unlimited bus travel in Ireland for three out of eight days (IR₤28), eight out of 15 days (IR₤68), or 15 out of 30 days (IR₤98)—you have to move fast to make them pay off.

Ulsterbus, Laganside, Belfast (tel. (01232) 33 30 00; email feedback@ulsterbus.co.uk; www.ulsterbus.co.uk), the North's version of Bus Éireann, runs extensive and reliable routes throughout Northern Ireland, where there are no private bus services. Coverage expands in summer, when several buses running a purely coastal route, and full- and half-day tours leave for key tourist spots from Belfast. Pick up a timetable free at any station. Again, the bus passes won't save you much money: a **Freedom of Northern Ireland** bus and rail pass offers unlimited travel for one day (UK₤10), or consecutive days (3-day UK₤25; 7-day UK₤37).

BY FERRY. Ferries journey between Britain and Ireland several times per day; tickets usually range IR₤20-35. Traveling mid-week at night promises the cheapest fares. **An Óige (HI) members** receive up to a 20% discount on fares from Irish Ferries and Stena Sealink. **ISIC cardholders** with the **Travel Stamp** (see above) receive a 15% discount from Irish Ferries and an average 17% discount (variable among four routes) on StenaLine ferries. Ferry passengers from the Republic are taxed an addi-

Ireland:
Republic of Ireland and Northern Ireland

0 ————— 30 miles
0 ————— 30 kilometers

N

SCOTLAND

Giant's Causeway Rathlin I.

Carndonagh Portrush Ballycastle

Tory I. L. Swilly Inishowen Peninsula

North Channel

Aranmore I. Letterkenny Derry

DONEGAL Strabane DERRY ANTRIM Larne

Dungloe TYRONE Omagh Belfast Bangor Ards Peninsula

Glencolmcille Donegal Ballyshannon NORTHERN IRELAND L. Neagh Portadown DOWN Downpatrick

Donegal Bay Enniskillen FERMANAGH Armagh ARMAGH Newcastle Mourne Mts.

Inishmurray SLIGO N16 Monaghan MONAGHAN Newry Dundalk Cooley Peninsula

Belmullet Bangor Sligo LEITRIM CAVAN LOUTH IRISH SEA

Ballina Carrick-on-Shannon Drogheda

MAYO N5 ROSCOMMON LONG-FORD Mullingar Hill of Tara

Clare I. Clew Bay Westport N17 Roscommon Athlone WESTMEATH MEATH Dublin

Inishturk L. Mask Cong L. Corrib GALWAY OFFALY KILDARE Dún Laoghaire

Inishbofin Connemara Clifden Galway Galway Bay REPUBLIC OF IRELAND Kildare Enniskerry HOLYHEAD, WALES

ATLANTIC OCEAN ARAN ISLANDS Kinvara The Burren Slieve Bloom Mts. LAOIS WICKLOW Wicklow

Lisdoon-varna Portlaoise Wicklow Mts.

Cliffs of Moher CLARE L. Derg KILKENNY Carlow Arklow

Ennis Shannon Airport TIPPERARY CARLOW N11

Kilrush Shannon R. Limerick Tipperary Kilkenny WEXFORD Enniscorthy

KERRY LIMERICK N20 Cashel N25 Rosslare Harbor

Tralee N21 Clonmel Wexford TO FISHGUARD, WALES, PEMBROKE, WALES, & ROSCOFF, FRANCE

Dingle Dingle Peninsula CORK WATERFORD Waterford St. George's Channel

Killarney Ring of Kerry Macroom N25 Youghal

Waterville Iveragh Peninsula Cork Kinsale

Bantry Clonakilty TO SWANSEA, WALES

Beara Peninsula Schull Skibbereen

Mizen Head Cape Clear I.

TO ROSCOFF, FRANCE TO CHERBOURG & LE HAVRE, FRANCE

IRELAND

tional IR£5 when travelling from England to Éire. Ferries run from **Cork** to **South Wales** and **Roscoff, France** (see p. 531) and from **Rosslare Harbour** to **Pembroke, Wales** and **Roscoff** and **Cherbourg, France** (see p. 529). For more info, see p. 58.

BY CAR. Drivers in Ireland use the left side of the road, and place their steering-wheel on the right side of the car. Gas prices are high. Be particularly cautious at roundabouts (rotary interchanges)—give way to traffic from the right. Irish drivers speed along narrow, twisting, pot-holed, poorly lit back roads. Irish law requires drivers and passengers to wear seat belts—these laws are enforced. The general speed limit in the Republic is 90km per hr. (55 mph) on the open road and either 50km per hr. (30 mph) or 65km per hr. (40 mph) in town. The North's speed limits are 97km per hr. (60 mph) on single carriageways (non-divided highways), 113km per hr. (70 mph) on motorways (highways) and dual carriageways (divided highways), and usually 48km per hr. (30 mph) in urban areas. People under 21 cannot rent, and those under 23 often encounter difficulties. Prices range from IR£100-300 (plus VAT) per week with insurance and unlimited mileage.

BY BIKE, BY FOOT, AND BY THUMB. Much of Ireland's countryside is well suited for **cycling,** and towns throughout the island offer bike rental outlets. Ireland offers rugged hills and small mountains to its **hikers.** The best hiking maps are the **Ordnance Survey** series (IR£4.20 each), available at tourist offices. Irish drivers are astoundingly **hitchhiker**-friendly, though *Let's Go* does not recommend hitching.

ESSENTIALS

DOCUMENTS AND FORMALITIES. Citizens of Australia, Canada, European Union countries, New Zealand, South Africa, the United Kingdom, and the United States, do not need **visas** to visit Ireland for stays shorter than three months.

Irish Embassies at Home: Australia, 20 Arkana St, Yarralumla ACT 2600 (tel. (02) 62 73 30 22; fax 62 73 37 41); **Canada,** 130 Albert St, #1105, Ottawa, ON K1P 5G4 (tel. (613) 233 62 81; fax 233 58 35); **South Africa,** Tubach Centre, 1234 Church St, 0083 Colbyn, Pretoria (tel. (012) 342 50 62; fax 342 45 72); **UK,** 17 Grosvenor Pl, London SW1X 7HR (tel. (020) 72 35 21 71; fax 72 45 69 61); **US,** 2234 Massachusetts Ave, NW, Washington, DC 20008 (tel. (202) 462-3939; fax 232-5993; www.irelandemb.org/contact.html). **New Zealanders** should contact the embassy in Australia.

Foreign Embassies in Ireland: All embassies for the Republic of Ireland are in **Dublin** (see p. 523). The US has a consulate in **Belfast** (see p. 544).

TOURIST OFFICES. Bord Fáilte (Irish Tourist Board) operates a nationwide network of offices. Most tourist offices book rooms for a small fee (IR£1-3) and a 10% deposit, but many fine hostels and B&Bs are not "approved," so the tourist office can't tell you about them. In Ireland the **Irish Tourist Board** can be reached at PO Box 273 IRL-Dublin 8 (tel. (01) 602 40 00; 602 41 00; www.iol.ie/~discover/itb.htm).

Tourist Boards at Home: Australia, Carrington St, 5th level, Sydney, NSW 2000 (tel. (02) 299 61 77); **Canada,** 160 Bloor St East #1150, Toronto, ON M4W 1B9 (tel. (416) 929-2777; fax 929-6783); **UK,** 150 New Bond St, GB-London W1Y 0AQ (tel. (020) 74 93 32 01); **US,** 345 Park Ave, New York, NY 10154 (tel. (212) 418-0800; fax 371-9052).

MONEY. In the Irish Republic the currency is the **pound** or punt (POONT), divided into 100 pence; *Let's Go* uses "IR" to differentiate it from the UK pound. Northern Ireland uses British pounds (see p. 542). If you stay in hostels and prepare your own food, expect to spend anywhere from US$18-30 per day. Accommodations start at about UK£8-10 for a single bed, while the cost for a basic sit-down **meal** begins around UK£6. Transport and beer will increase your budget significantly.

Tipping and Bargaining: Some restaurants in Ireland figure a service charge into the bill; the menu often indicates whether this is the case (ask if you're not sure). If the tip isn't included (more common in cities), leave 10-15%. For waiter service in a bar or lounge, IR£0.20 will do. Cab drivers are usually tipped 10%. Never tip the barman.

Taxes: Both Ireland and Northern Ireland charge a **value-added tax** (VAT) on most goods and some services. In Ireland, the VAT ranges from 0% on food and children's clothing to 17% in restaurants to 21% on other items. The rate in Northern Ireland is 17.5% on many services and on all goods (except books, medicine, and food).

COMMUNICATION

Post: To send a **postcard** to an international destination within Europe costs 32p; to any other international destination, 45p. Domestic postcards require IR£0.30.

Telephones: For an **international operator,** dial 114 in the Republic or 153 in the North; **operator,** 190; **directory,** 1190 in the Republic, 192 in the North. **International direct dial** numbers include: **AT&T,** 1800 55 00 00; **Sprint,** 1 800 55 20 01; **MCI WorldPhone Direct,** 1800 55 10 01; **Canada Direct,** 800 656 47 08; **BT Direct,** 800 34 51 44; **Ireland Direct,** 800 25 02 50; **Australia Direct,** 13 22 00; **Telecom New Zealand Direct,** 800 00 00 00; **Telkom South Africa Direct,** 09 03. **Emergency,** tel. 999.

HEALTH AND SAFETY. Both the Republic of Ireland and Northern Ireland are very safe by European standards. However it's best to avoid traveling in Northern Ireland during **Marching Season** (July 4-July 12). Vacation areas are less affected by the parades. As always be sensitive; use common sense in conversation, and be respectful of locals' religious and political perspectives (see p. 542).

ACCOMMODATIONS AND CAMPING. Hosteling is the way to go. **An Óige,** the Irish Hostelling International affiliate, runs 37 hostels that are often relatively bare and somewhat out of the way. The North's HI affiliate is **YHANI** (Youth Hostel Association of Northern Ireland), which operates nine nicer hostels. The *An Óige Handbook* lists and details all An Óige and YHANI hostels; its standard pricing system isn't always followed by every hostel listed. A number of hostels in Ireland belong to the **Independent Holiday Hostels (IHH);** they have no lockout or curfew (with a few exceptions), accept all ages, don't require membership, and are all Bord Fáilte-approved. **B&Bs** provide a luxurious break from hosteling; expect to pay IR£20-25 for singles and IR£25-36 for doubles. "Full Irish breakfasts" are often filling enough to get you through to dinner. **Camping** in Irish State Forests and National Parks is not allowed; camping on public land is permissible only if there is no official campsite nearby. Most caravan and camping parks are open April through October, although some are open year-round. Pick up the *Caravan and Camping Ireland* guide from any Bord Fáilte office for info on camping in the Republic.

FOOD AND DRINK. Food in Ireland is expensive. The basics are simple and filling. "Take-away" (takeout) fish and chips shops are quick, greasy, and very popular. Many pubs serve food as well as drink; typical pub grub includes Irish stew, burgers, soup, and sandwiches. Soda bread is delicious and keeps well, and Irish dairy products are addictive. Pubs in Ireland are the forum for banter, singing, and *craic* (a good time). In the evening, many pubs play impromptu or organized traditional music (trad). Guinness, a rich, dark stout, is the most revered brew in Ireland. Irish whiskey (with an "e") is sweeter and more stinging than its Scotch counterpart. **Pubs** are usually open Monday to Saturday 10:30am to 11 or 11:30pm, Sunday 12:30 to 2pm and 4 to 11pm (in the North Su 12:30-2:30pm and 7-10pm).

LOCAL FACTS

Time: Ireland is even with Greenwich Mean Time (GMT; see p. 49).

Hours: Most **banks** are open M-F 9am-4:30pm, sometimes later on Th. In big cities, **shop** hours are much longer.

Climate: Weather in Ireland is temperate (summer averages 15-18°C, or 60-65°F) yet tempermental. Keep a poncho or umbrella handy and carry a sweater.

Holidays: Much of Southern Ireland closes for holidays on January 1, St. Patrick's Day (Mar. 17), Good Friday, Easter (Apr. 13-15), June 1, August 3, October 26, and Christmas (Dec. 25-26). Northern Ireland adds on May Day (May 1), Spring or Whitsun Holiday (May 25), Orange Day (June 12), August 31, and Christmas.

Festivals: All of Ireland goes green for **St. Patrick's Day** (Mar. 17th). On **Bloomsday** Dublin (June 16) traipses about revering James Joyce (see p. 527).

DUBLIN

In a country known for its quiet and lackadaisical pace, Dublin stands out for its style and energy. Although many Irish citizens residing outside of Dublin worry that it has taken on the characteristic vices of big cities everywhere, it's as friendly a major city as you'll find. The city and its suburbs, home to one-third of Ireland's population, are at the vanguard of the country's rapid social change; countercultures flourish here in a way the rest of the Emerald Isle would summarily reject, and cutting-edge, world-renowned music bursts from the city's pub doors. Despite Dublin's progressive pace and rocking nightlife, old Ireland still courses through its citified veins. Statues of great writers like Joyce, Swift, Burke, and Beckett pepper the streets, and beneath the urban bustle, majestic cathedrals and quaint pubs welcome visitors with Ireland's trademark friendliness and zeal.

IRELAND

▐ GETTING THERE AND GETTING AROUND

Flights: Dublin Airport (tel. 844 49 00). Catch Dublin bus 41, 41B, or 41C (every 20min., IR£1.10) to Eden Quay in the city center. **Airport Express buses** (tel. 844 42 65) run to the Central Bus Station and O'Connell St (30min., every 15-30min. 7am-11pm, IR£2.50). **Airlink** (buses 747 and 748; every 10-15min. 6:30am-11:45pm) shuttles to the Central Bus Station and O'Connell St (30-40min., IR£3) as well as Heuston Station (50min., IR£3.50). A **taxi** to the city center costs IR£12-15.

Trains: Most inter-city trains arrive at **Heuston Station** (tel. 703 21 32), just south of Victoria Quay and well west of the city center. Buses 26, 51, and 79 go to the center. To: **Limerick** (2¼hr., 9 per day, IR£25); **Galway** (2½hr., 4-5 per day, IR£15-21); **Waterford** (2½hr., 3-4 per day, IR£12); **Cork** (3½hr., 6-11 per day, IR£32); and **Tralee** (4½hr., 4-7 per day, IR£33.50). The other main terminus is **Connolly Station** (tel. 836 33 33), on Amiens St near the Central Bus Station. To: **Belfast** (2¼hr., 5-8 per day, IR£17); **Wexford** and **Rosslare** (3hr., 3 per day, IR£10.50); and **Sligo** (3½hr., 3-4 per day, IR£13.50). **Pearse Station** is east of Trinity College. **Irish Rail Information,** 35 Lower Abbey St (tel. 836 62 22). Open M-F 9am-5pm, Sa 9am-1pm; recording after hours.

Buses: Busáras Central Bus Station (tel. 836 61 11), on Store St, next to Connolly Station, sends off most inter-city buses. **Bus Éirann** runs to: **Belfast** (3hr., 4-7 per day, IR£10.50); **Rosslare Harbour** (3hr., 7-10 per day, IR£9); **Limerick** (3¼hr., 13 per day, IR£10); **Galway** (4hr., 14 per day, IR£8); and **Cork** (4½hr., 3-4 per day, IR£12).

Ferries: Stena Line pulls into **Dún Laoghaire,** a Dublin suburb, from **Holyhead, England;** DART shuttles incoming passengers to Connolly Station, Pearse Station, or Tara St (IR£1.30). **Irish Ferries** (tel. (1890) 31 31 31; www.irishferries.ie) arrive from Holyhead at the Dublin Port (tel. 607 56 65), right in town. Buses 53 and 53A run from the Dublin Port to the Central Bus Station (every hr., IR£0.80); Dublin Bus also runs from the city to meet outgoing ferries (IR£2-2.50). **Irish Rail** (see above) handles bookings for all of the above. **Merchant Ferries** runs a Dublin-Liverpool route (8hr., 2 per day, IR£40, with car IR£150-170); book through **Gerry Feeney,** 19 Eden Quay (tel. 819 29 99).

Public Transportation: Dublin Bus, 59 Upper O'Connell St. Distressingly lime green. Fares IR£0.55-1.10. Buses run every 8-45min. daily 5am-11:30pm. Their **NiteLink** runs express routes to the suburbs (Th-Sa every hr. 12:30-3:30am; IR£2.50, no passes valid). Timetables (IR£1.50) available from newsagents and above office. **Dublin Area Rapid Transportation (DART)** serves coastal suburbs from Howth to Greystones from Connolly Station (IR£0.55-1.10). Runs daily 6:30am-11:30pm. Timetables available at many stations (IR£0.50). **Travel Wide passes** offer unlimited bus transportation (1-day IR£3.30; 1-week IR£13, students IR£10; valid Su-Sa inclusive no matter when you buy the ticket). Other passes allow unlimited bus and suburban rail/DART transport.

Car Rental: Budget, 151 Lower Drumcondra Rd (tel. 837 96 11), and at the airport. In summer from IR£35 per day, IR£165 per week; in winter IR£30, IR£140. Ages 23-75.

Bike Rental: Raleigh Rent-A-Bike (tel. 626 13 33), on Kylemore Rd. IR£10 per day, IR£40 per week; deposit IR£50. Limited one-way rental system for IR£10 surcharge.

▐ ORIENTATION AND PRACTICAL INFORMATION

The **River Liffey** cuts central Dublin in half from west to east. Better food and the more famous sights reside on the **South Side,** although hostels and the bus station inhabit the less expensive **North Side.** When streets split into "Upper" and "Lower" sections, "Lower" generally indicates closer proximity to the Liffey's mouth (east). Most attractions are in the area circumscribed by North and South Circular Rd, both of which frequently change names. **O'Connell St,** three blocks west of the Central Bus Station, is the primary link between north and south Dublin; south of the Liffey, it becomes Westmoreland St, passes **Trinity College Dublin (TCD),** and then becomes Grafton St. TCD functions as the nerve center of Dublin's cultural activity. **Dame St** heads west from TCD to **Temple Bar** (literally a street but used more generally to describe an area), Dublin's liveliest nightspot. The **North Side** has the reputation of being a rougher part of town; avoid walking in unfamiliar areas at night. Although Dublin is fairly compact, street names change often. The color map in the back of this book was updated for this edition. Collins' superb *Handy Map of Dublin* (IR£4.64) can be purchased at the tourist office.

TOURIST, FINANCIAL, AND LOCAL SERVICES

Tourist Offices: Dublin Tourist Centre, Suffolk St (tel. (1850) 23 03 30; www.visitdublin.com). From Connolly Station, walk left down Amiens St, turn right after the Central Bus Station, make a left over O'Connell Bridge, go past TCD, and Suffolk St is on the right. Finds rooms for IR£1 plus 10% booking deposit. Maps IR£4.50-4.60. Open July-Aug. M-Sa 9am-7pm, Su 10:30am-2:30pm; Sept.-June M-Sa 9am-6pm.

Budget Travel: Usit NOW (Irish Student Travel Agency), 19-21 Aston Quay (tel. 679 88 33), near O'Connell Bridge. ISICs, HI cards. Many discounts, especially for students and those under 26. Open M-W and F 9am-6pm, Th 9am-8pm, Sa 10am-5:30pm.

Embassies: Australia, 2nd fl., Fitzwilton House, Wilton Terr. (tel. 676 15 17). Open M-Th 8:30am-12:30pm and 1:30-4:30pm, F 9am-noon. **Canada,** 65 St. Stephen's Green South (tel. 478 19 88). Open M-F 9am-1pm and 2-4:30pm. **New Zealanders** should contact their embassy in London (tel. +44 (020) 79 30 84 22). **South Africa,** 2nd fl., Alexandra House, Earlsfort Centre (tel. 661 55 53; fax 661 55 90). Open M-F 8:30am-5pm. **UK,** 29 Merrion Rd (tel. 269 52 11). Open M-F 9am-5pm. **US,** 42 Elgin Rd, Ballsbridge (tel. 668 87 77). Open M-F 8:30am-5pm.

American Express: 61-3 South William St (tel. 677 55 55; fax 677 55 77), at the back of Grafton St. Client mail held. Open M-F 9am-5:30pm.

Luggage Storage: Connolly, Heuston, and **Central Bus Stations.** IR£1.50-3.50 per day.

Gay and Lesbian Services: Gay Switchboard Dublin (tel. 872 10 55). Open Su-F 8-10pm. **Outhouse,** 65 William St (tel. 670 63 77), has a library and café. Get the monthly *Gay Community News* for info on gay life and nightlife (free around Temple Bar).

Laundromat: The Laundry Shop, 191 Parnell St (tel. 872 35 41), is nearest the Central Bus Station and hostels. Wash and dry IR£4.20. Open M-F 8am-7pm, Sa 9am-6pm.

EMERGENCY AND COMMUNICATIONS

Emergency: Dial 999 for **police, fire,** or **ambulance;** no coins required.

Crisis Lines: Samaritans, 112 Marlborough St (tel. (1850) 60 90 90). Staffed 24hr. **Rape Crisis Centre,** 70 Lower Leeson St (tel. (1800) 77 88 88).

Pharmacy: O'Connell's, 55 Lower O'Connell St (tel. 873 04 27). Open M-Sa 8am-10pm, Su 10am-10pm.

Internet Access: Global Internet Café, 8 Lower O'Connell St. IR£1.25 per 15min., students IR£1. Open M-Sa 10am-11pm, Su noon-10pm. **Central Cybercafé,** 6 Grafton St. IR£1.25 per 15min., students IR£1. **Planet Cyber Café,** 23 South Great Georges St. IR£1.50 per 15min. Open Su-W 10am-10pm, Th-Sa 10am-midnight.

Telephones: On every corner. Use phonecards, available at most newsstands, or coins.

Post Office: General Post Office (GPO; tel. 705 70 00), O'Connell St. *Poste Restante* at the *bureau de change* window. Open M-Sa 8am-8pm, Su 10am-6:30pm. Address mail to be held: Matt MCCARTHY, *Poste Restante,* GPO, **Dublin 1,** Republic of Ireland.

PHONE CODE	City code: 01. From outside Republic of Ireland, dial int'l dialing prefix (see inside back cover) + 353 + 1 + local number.

ACCOMMODATIONS

Dublin's accommodations overflow, especially during Easter, holidays, and summer—reserve ahead. Dorms range from IR£7-15 per night. Quality **B&Bs** blanket Dublin and the surrounding suburbs, although prices have risen with housing costs (most charge IR£16-30 per person); many cluster along Upper and Lower Gardiner St, on Sherriff St, and near Parnell Sq. Phoenix Park may tempt the desperate, but camping there is dangerous. Dublin Tourism's annual *Dublin Accommodation Guide* (IR£3) lists approved B&Bs and other accommodations.

HOSTELS AND CAMPING

The Brewery Hostel, 22-23 Thomas St (tel. 453 86 00; fax 453 86 16; email breweryh@indigo.ie), next to Guinness, 20min. from Temple Bar. Follow Dame St (which becomes High and Cornmarket St) past Christ Church, or take bus 123. Social scene with patio, kitchen, and comfy TV lounge. All rooms with bath. Dorms IR£10-12; singles IR£15; bed in a double IR£22; bed in a quad IR£15. Breakfast included. Laundry.

Avalon House (IHH), 55 Aungier St (tel. 475 00 01; fax 475 03 03; email info@avalon.ie), within stumbling distance of Temple Bar. Turn off Dame St onto Great Georges St, which becomes Aungier St (10min.). Co-ed bathrooms and dorms. June-Sept. dorms IR£11-13.50; doubles IR£32; cheaper off-season. Breakfast included. **Internet.**

Abbey Hostel, 29 Bachelor's Walk, O'Connell Bridge (tel. 878 07 00 or 878 07 19; email info@abbey-hostel.ie). Well-kept hostel in a great location. All rooms with bath. June-Sept. dorms IR£14-17; doubles IR£40-60; cheaper off-season. **Internet** IR£1 per 7min.

Barnacle's Temple Bar House, 19 Temple Ln (tel. 671 62 77; fax 671 65 91; email templeba@barnacles.iol.ie). A new hostel right in Temple Bar. All rooms with bath. June-Sept. dorms IR£11-15; doubles and twins IR£20; cheaper off-season. Breakfast included.

Abraham House, 82-3 Lower Gardiner St (tel. 855 06 00; fax 855 05 98; email abraham@indigo.ie). Well-kept hostel. June-Sept. dorms IR£8.50-12.50; doubles IR£30; cheaper off-season. Laundry IR£5. Breakfast included. **Internet.**

Jacob's Inn, 21-28 Talbot Pl (tel. 855 56 60; fax 855 56 64; email jacob@indigo.ie), on a north-south street between the Central Bus Station and Talbot St. Reception area with a café. The pub next door has abnormally cheap pints. Apr.-Oct. dorms IR£10.95-16.50; doubles IR£39; cheaper off-season. Bed lockout 11am-3pm. Laundry.

Globetrotter's Tourist Hostel (IHH), 46-7 Lower Gardiner St (tel. 873 58 93; fax 878 87 87; email gtrotter@indigo.ie). Comfortable beds and excellent bathrooms. TV room. July to mid-Sept. IR£15; off-season IR£12. Great breakfast included. **Internet.**

Celts House, 32 Blessington St (tel. 830 06 57; email res@celtshouse.iol.ie). Comfy bunkbeds in a brightly painted, friendly atmosphere 15min. from the city center. Dorms IR£9-10.50; doubles IR£32. Sheets IR£1.50. Key deposit IR£5. **Internet.**

Mount Eccles Court (M.E.C.), 42 North Great Georges St (tel. 878 00 71; fax 874 64 72; email meccles@iol.ie). Walk up O'Connell, turn right on Parnell St, and take the first left. This former convent seems impossibly spacious. Kitchen, TV lounge. Apr.-Sept. dorms IR£8.50-11.50; bed in a twin IR£16; cheaper off-season. Breakfast included.

Morehampton House Tourist Hostel, 78 Morehampton Rd, Donnybrook (tel. 668 88 66; fax 668 87 94), at the intersection with Herbert Pk. Take bus 10 or 46A (10min.) or walk 20min. Clean, light, and comfy, if a bit cramped. Kitchen, TV room, and garden. June-Sept. dorms IR£8-14; doubles IR£35-37; cheaper off-season.

Camac Valley Tourist Caravan & Camping Park (tel. 464 06 44; fax 46 40 643; email camacmorriscastle@tinet.ie), on Naas Rd, in **Clondalkin**, near Corkagh Park. Take bus 69 from the city center (35min., IR£1.10). Store, TV room, laundry, and kitchen. Tent and 1 person IR£3-4, each additional person IR£1; caravans IR£9-11. Showers IR£0.50.

BED & BREAKFASTS

Parkway Guest House, 5 Gardiner Pl (tel. 874 04 69), just off Gardiner St. Rooms are plain but high-ceilinged and immaculate, and the location is excellent. Young, friendly proprietor. Singles IR£21; doubles IR£35, with bath IR£44.

Charles Stewart Budget Accommodation, 5-6 Parnell Sq (tel. 878 03 50; email cstuart@iol.ie). In summer, singles IR£20-37; twin bunks IR£40; double IR£50. Off-season 10% less. Full Irish breakfast included. Laundry IR£3.

Marian B&B, 21 Upper Gardiner St (tel. 874 41 29). Brendan and Cathrine McElroy provide lovely, comfortable rooms with TVs. Singles IR£20; doubles IR£40.

Mona B&B, 148 Clonliffe Rd (tel. 837 67 23). Walk up O'Connell St, turn right on Dorset St, and turn right on Clonliffe (10min.). The proprietress, Mrs. Kathleen Greville, would "never refuse anyone tea and cakes!" Singles IR£17; doubles IR£32. Open May-Oct.

Rita and Jim Casey, Villa Jude, 2 Church Ave (tel. 668 49 82), off Beach Rd in Sandymount, near Dublin Port. Take bus 3 from Clery's on O'Connell St to the first stop on Tritonville Rd and backtrack a few yards. Mrs. Casey has nourished 7 children with her strapping Irish breakfasts. Immaculate rooms with TVs. Singles IR£17; doubles IR£30.

Dublin Accommodations

SEE ALSO COLOR INSERT

A Celts House
B MEC Hostel
C Abraham House
D Globetrotter's Hostel
E Jacob's Inn
F Abbey Hostel
G Barnacle's Temple Bar Hostel
H The Brewery Hostel
I Avalon House

IRELAND

FOOD

Head to the open-air **Moore St Market,** between Henry St and Parnell St, to pick up fresh, cheap veggies. (Open M-Sa 7am-5pm.) The cheapest **supermarkets** are the **Dunnes Stores,** at St. Stephen's Green Shopping Centre; at the ILAC Centre, off Henry St; and on North Earl St, off O'Connell. (All open M-W and F-Sa 9am-6pm, Th 9am-8pm.) The **Temple Bar** area has creative eateries for every budget.

Café Irie (tel. 672 50 90), on Fownes St, above the colorful Sé Sí Progressive. Probably the best value in Temple Bar: lip-smackingly good sandwich concoctions at unbeatable prices (under IR£3). Open M-Sa 9am-8pm, Su noon-5:30pm.

La Mezza Luna (tel. 671 28 40), 1 Temple Ln, at Dame St. The food is celestial. Roast-pepper-and-chicken crêpe IR£8.50. IR£5 lunch specials noon-3pm. Scrumptious desserts IR£3.50. Open M-Th noon-11pm, F-Sa noon-11:30, Su noon-10:30pm.

Bad Ass Café (tel. 671 25 96), on Crown Alley, off Temple Bar. Gimmicky, touristy café where Sinéad O'Connor once worked, but the food makes up for it. Lunch IR£4-7. Medium pizza IR£5.15-7.75. Student menu IR£7.30. Open daily 9am-late.

Poco Loco, 32 Parliament St (tel. 679 19 50), between Grattan Bridge and City Hall. Fast, friendly service and the cheapest Mexican food in town. Meals IR£5.75-7. Open M-Tu 5-11pm, W-Th 5-11:30pm, F-Sa 5pm-midnight, Su 5-10pm.

Cornucopia, 19 Wicklow St (tel. 677 75 83). This vegetarian horn of plenty overflows with huge portions and crunchy friendliness. Snacks around IR£1.50, meals around IR£5. Take-away, too. Open M-W and F-Sa 9am-8pm, Th 9am-9pm.

Chez Jules, 16a D'Olier St (tel. 677 04 99). Their seafood specialties and red-checkered tables attract people of all ages. Veggie dish of the day IR£7. Two-course lunch IR£5.90. Open M-F noon-3pm and 6-11pm, Sa 1-3:30pm and 6-11pm, Su 5-10pm.

Leo Burdock's, 2 Werburgh St (tel. 454 03 06), uphill from Christ Church Cathedral. Take-out only, but even eating and walking shouldn't deter you from the religious experience of consuming their fish and chips (IR£4.20). Open M-Sa noon-midnight, Su 4pm-midnight.

Bewley's Cafés. A Dublin institution, with dark wood paneling, marble table tops, and mirrored walls. Wildly complex pastries (IR£1), outstanding coffee, and plain but inexpensive meals. Drop by branches at 78 Grafton St (tel. 635 54 70), with a room for its most famous patron, James Joyce (open daily 7:30am-11pm); 12 Westmoreland St (tel. 677 67 61; open M-Sa 7:30am-7:30pm, Su 9:30am-8pm); and Mary St, past Henry St (open M-W 7am-9pm, Th-Sa 7am-2am, Su 10am-10pm).

◉ SIGHTS

Dublin is a walkable city; most of the sights lie less than a mile from O'Connell Bridge. The tourist office sells *Dublin's Top Visitor Attractions* (IR£2.50) and *Heritage Trails: Signpost Walking Tours of Dublin* (IR£2.50). The **Historical Walking Tour** is a two-hour crash course in Dublin's history, from the Celts to the present. (Tel. 878 02 27. May-Sept. M-F 11am and 3pm; Sa-Su 11am, noon, and 3pm; Oct.-Apr. F-Su noon. Meet at Trinity's front gate. IR£5, students IR£4.)

TRINITY COLLEGE TO ST. STEPHEN'S GREEN. Sprawling at the center of Dublin, **Trinity College** is the *alma mater* of Jonathan Swift, Thomas Moore, Samuel Beckett, and Oscar Wilde. The **Old Library**, built in 1712, houses the *Book of Kells* (c. AD 800), an illuminated four-volume edition of the Gospels; each page holds a dizzyingly intricate lattice of Celtic knotwork and scrollwork interwoven with text. *(Open June-Sept. M-Sa 9:30am-5pm, Su noon-4:30pm; Oct.-May M-Sa 9:30am-5pm, Su noon-4:30pm. IR£4.50, students IR£4.)* South of the college, on the block between Kildare St and Upper Merrion St, Irish history and culture reign. The **National Museum** protects the Ardagh Hoard, the Tara Brooch, and other artifacts from the last two millennia. *(Kildare St. Open Tu-Sa 10am-5pm, Su 2-5pm. Free. Tours 2:15, 3:15, and 4:15pm. IR£1.)* Portraits of Lady Gregory, Eliza O'Neill, Joyce, Shaw, and Yeats line the **National Gallery's** staircase; the museum also houses works by Brueghel, Caravaggio, Vermeer, Rembrandt, and El Greco. *(Just down Merrion St West. Open M-Sa 10am-5:30pm, Th 10am-8:30pm, Su 2-5pm. Donation IR£2. Free tours Sa 3pm, Su 3 and 4pm.)* Kildare, Dawson, and Grafton St all lead south from Trinity to **St. Stephen's Green.** Bequeathed to the city by the Guinness clan, this 22-acre park boasts arched bridges, a lake, fountains, gazebos, and a waterfall. On summer days, half of Dublin fills the lawns, and outdoor music and productions are held by the old bandstand. *(Open M-Sa 8am-dusk, Su 10am-dusk.)*

TEMPLE BAR, DUBLIN CASTLE, AND THE CATHEDRALS. West of Trinity, between Dame St and the Liffey, the **Temple Bar** area bustles with cheap cafés, hole-in-the-wall theaters, rock venues, and used clothing and record stores. Next to this hipster scene is **Dublin Castle,** built in 1204 by King John on top of the first Viking settlement in Dubh Linn; it was the seat of English rule in Ireland for the next 700 years. *(At the west end of Dame St, where it meets Parliament St and Castle St. State Apartments open M-F 10am-5pm, Sa-Su 2-5pm. IR£3, students IR£2; rest of castle free.)* Both of Dublin's two official cathedrals, **Christ Church Cathedral** and **St. Patrick's Cathedral,** are owned by the Church of Ireland, not the Catholic Church; since the Anglo-Irish aristocracy no longer exists, today they are considered more works of art than centers of worship. *(Christ Church is on Dame St. Open daily 10am-5:30pm. IR£2. St. Patrick's is down Nicholas St, which becomes Patrick St. Open Apr.-Sept. M-F 9am-6pm, Sa 9am-5pm, Su 9:30-11am, 12:45-3pm, and 4:15-5pm; Oct.-Mar. hours slightly reduced. IR£2.)*

GUINNESS BREWERY. Those craving alcoholic ambrosia are drawn to the giant Guinness Brewery. The **Hopstore** perpetuates the Guinness mystique and accompanies tours with a complimentary pint of dark and creamy goodness. *(St. James Gate. The Hopstore is on Crane St off James St. Take bus 68A or 78A from Aston Quay or bus 123 from O'Connell St. From Christ Church Cathedral, follow High St west as it changes names to Cornmarket, Thomas and then James. Open Apr.-Sept. M-Sa 9:30am-5pm, Su 10:30am-4:30pm; Oct.-Mar. M-Sa 9:30am-4pm, Su noon-4pm. IR£5, students IR£4.)*

KILMAINHAM GAOL. "The cause for which I die has been rebaptized during this past week by the blood of as good men as ever trod God's earth," wrote Sean Mac-Diarmada in a letter as he awaited execution for participating in the 1916 Easter Rising. He, along with most rebels who fought in Ireland's struggle for independence from 1792 to 1921, was imprisoned at Kilmainham Gaol. Today the prison houses a museum tracing the history of penal practices. *(20min. west of the city center on foot. Take bus 51 or 79 from Aston Quay, or bus 51A from Lower Abbey St. Open Apr.-Sept. daily 9:30am-4:45pm; Oct.-Mar. M-F 9:30am-4pm, Su 10am-4:45pm. IR£3, students IR£1.25.)*

THE NORTH SIDE. On the North Side, the **Dublin Writer's Museum** introduces visitors to the city's rich literary legacy with manuscripts, memorabilia, and caricatures of pen-wielding Dubliners. *(18 Parnell Sq North. Open June-Aug. M-F 10am-6pm, Sa 10am-5pm; Sept.-May M-Sa 10am-5pm. IR£3, students IR£2.55.)* At the heart of the up-and-coming Smithfield neighborhood is the **Old Jameson Distillery,** which offers tours more entertaining and less commercial than Guinness'. The experience ends with a glass of the Irish whiskey of your choice; be quick to volunteer in the beginning and you'll get to sample a whole tray of different whiskeys. Feel the burn. *(Bow St. From O'Connell St, turn onto Henry St and continue as it turns into Mary St, Mary Ln, and finally May Ln; the warehouse is on a cobblestoned street to the left. Tours daily 9:30am-5pm. IR£4, students IR£3.)*

ENTERTAINMENT

The *Event Guide* (free at the tourist office and Temple Bar restaurants) and *In Dublin* (IR£1.95) detail a smorgasbord of events. Hostel workers are also a good, if sometimes biased, source of information on entertainment options. *Hot Press* (IR£1.50) has the most up-to-date music listings, particularly for rock. Traditional music (trad) is an important element of the Irish culture and the Dublin music scene. Some pubs in the city center have trad sessions nightly, others almost every night. **Whelan's** (see **Pubs,** below) is one of the hottest spots in Dublin. Big deal bands frequent the **Baggot Inn,** 143 Baggot St (tel. 676 14 30). The **National Concert Hall,** Earlsfort Terr., is the venue for classical music. (Tel. 671 15 33. Concerts July-Aug. 8pm. IR£6-12, students half-price.) Part of the National Theater, the **Abbey Theatre,** 26 Lower Abbey St, was founded in 1904 by Yeats and Lady Gregory to promote Irish culture and modernist theater. (Tel. 878 72 22. Box office open M-Sa 10:30am-7pm. Tickets IR£10-16; student rate M-Th and Sa matinee IR£8.)

Dublin pretty much owns two days of the year. **St. Patrick's Day** (Mar. 17) and the half-week leading up to it host a city-wide carnival of concerts, fireworks, street theater, and intoxicated madness (tel. 676 32 05; fax 676 32 08; www.paddyfest.ie). The city returns to 1904 on **Bloomsday** (June 16), the day on which the action of Joyce's *Ulysses* takes place. Festivities are held all week long. The **James Joyce Cultural Center** (tel. 873 19 84) sponsors a reenactment of the funeral and wake, a lunch at Davy Byrne's, and a breakfast with Guinness.

■ NIGHTLIFE

PUBLIN

The **Dublin Literary Pub Crawl** (tel. 670 56 02) traces Dublin's liquid history in reference to its literary one. Meet at **The Duke,** 2 Duke St. (Tours depart Easter-Oct. M-Sa 7:30pm, Su noon and 7:30pm; Nov.-Easter Th-Sa 7:30pm, Su noon and 7:30pm. IR£6.50, students IR£5.50. Book at the door or at the Suffolk St. tourist office for IR£0.15 extra.) *Let's Go* recommends beginning your personal journey at the gates of Trinity College, moving onto Grafton St, stumbling onto Camden St, teetering down South Great Georges St, and crawling (triumphantly if soused) into the Temple Bar area. Be sure not to miss the following gems along the way.

Mulligan's, 8 Poolbeg St, behind Burgh Quay off Tara St. A bit off the pub crawl route, but reputed to serve one of the finest pints of Guinness in Dublin. Mainly attracts middle-aged men. A taste of the typical Irish pub: low key and nothing fancy. Really.

Whelan's, 25 Wexford St, down South Great Georges St. A hotspot for live rock and trad. Cover IR£5-8; ladies free Sa before midnight and Su. Open Th-Su until 1:30am.

KNOW YOUR WHISKEY

Anyone who drinks his whiskey as it's meant to be drunk—"neat," or straight—can tell you that there's a huge difference between Irish whiskeys (Bushmills, Jameson, Power and Son, and the like), Scotch whiskys (spelled without an e), and American whiskeys. But what makes an Irish whiskey *Irish?* The basic ingredients in whiskey—water, barley (which becomes malt once processed), and heat from a fuel source—are always the same; it's the quality of these ingredients, the way in which they're combined, and the manner in which the combination is stored that gives each product its distinct flavor. The different types of whiskey derive from slight differences in this production process. American whiskey is distilled once and is often stored in oak, bourbon is made only in Kentucky, scotch uses peat-smoked barley, and Irish whiskey is triple distilled. After this basic breakdown, individual distilleries will claim that their further variations on the theme make their product the best of its class. The best way to understand the distinctions between brands is to taste the various labels in close succession to one another—line up those shot glasses, sniff and then taste each one (roll the whiskey in your mouth like a real pro), and have a sip of water between each brand. **"But I don't have the money to buy a shot of each brand,"** our budget-traveling readers murmur. Well, then, get thee to a distillery tour and squeal, "Me! Me!" when the tour guide asks for volunteers. "Irish Whiskey Tasters" get to try no less than five kinds of Irish, two kinds of scotch, and one bourbon whiskey under the supervision of their highly trained tour guides.

The Globe, 11 South Great Georges St. Perhaps the clientele's a little pretentious, but it's a fine spot for relaxing with a Guinness or a frothy cappuccino. Meet the regular cast of amicable if somewhat freakish characters—if you're hair's not dyed, you might want to bleach it. Attached to the **Rí Rá** nightclub (see below).

Hogan's, 35 South Great Georges St. Attracts a trendy crowd, heroes all. Bizarre mix of old and new decor. DJ action Su from 4pm. Late bar Th-Sa until 1:30am.

The Stag's Head, 1 Dame Ct. Beautiful Victorian pub with stained glass, mirrors, and yes, a stag's head. The crowd dons everything from t-shirts to tuxes and spills out into the alleys. Truly excellent grub. Late bar Th-F until 12:30am.

The Porter House, 16-18 Parliament St. This microbrewery has the largest selection of world beers in the country, and brews 8 different kinds of porter, stout, and ale itself. Late bar Th-F until 1:30am, Sa until midnight. Occasional trad, blues, and rock gigs.

The Palace, 21 Fleet St, behind Aston Quay. This classic neighborhood pub has old-fashioned wood paneling and close quarters; head for the comfy seats in the back room.

CLUBLIN

Clubs open at 10:30 or 11pm, but the action typically gets moving only after 11:30pm, when pubs start closing. Covers run IR£4-10, pints IR£3.

The Kitchen, The Clarence Hotel, Wellington Quay, Temple Bar. With 2 bars and a dance floor, this U2-owned club is the coolest spot in town. Often hard to get in with the VIPs; dress to fit in with the rocker/model crowd. Cover IR£8-10; students IR£3-4 on Tu.

Rí-Rá, 1 Exchequer St, in the back of The Globe pub. Generally good music that steers clear of the pop and house extremes. Two floors and several bars. Open daily 11pm-2:30am. Cover IR£6; women free on W.

POD, 35 Harcourt St. Spanish-style decor meets hard-core dance music. Up there with The Kitchen in terms of trendiness. The truly brave venture upstairs to **The Red Box,** a separate, more intense club. A warehouse atmosphere with brain-crushing music. Cover IR£8-10; ladies free before midnight on Th; Th and Sa students IR£5.

Club M, Blooms Hotel, Anglesea St, Temple Bar. One of Dublin's largest clubs; attracts a diverse crowd. Multiple stairways and a few bars in the back. Cover around IR£6.

■ EXCURSIONS FROM DUBLIN

HOWTH. The peninsula of Howth (rhymes with "both") dangles from the mainland in Edenic isolation, less than 10 mi. from Dublin. A three-hour **cliff walk** rings the

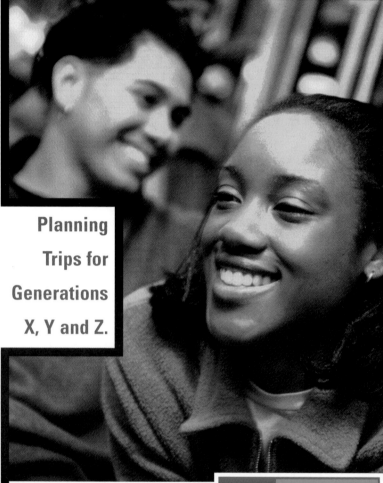

STUDENT TRAVEL

Planning Trips for Generations X, Y and Z.

(800) 777-0112

STA TRAVEL

We've Been There.

BOSTON   NEW YORK   SEATTLE   CAMBRIDGE   WASHINGTON   MIAMI   AUSTIN
CHICAGO   LOS ANGELES   ORLANDO   BERKELEY   MINNEAPOLIS   ANN ARBOR
SAN FRANCISCO   SAN DIEGO   PHILADELPHIA   TEMPE   PALO ALTO   GAINSVILLE
TUCSON   CHAMPAIGN   CHARLOTTESVILLE   TAMPA   BATON ROUGE   MADISON

www.statravel.com

Buy 1 of These

And Get ALL this FREE

2,000 Discount Certificates

Save hundreds of dollars on shopping, restaurants, museums and more.

One FREE night at The Pink Palace

Includes breakfast and dinner at the world famous youth resort in Corfu Greece.

Toll-free emergency help line

Call our offices toll free from Europe if you have any pass problems or questions.

FREE Eurail timetable and map

Passes issued on the spot

Your pass is delivered to your door within 1-2 days. RUSH ORDERS are our specialty.

PLUS

NO handling fees • NO busy signals • NO lines • NO hassles

GUARANTEED BEST PRICES

Expert advice and friendly service with over 15 YEARS of helping European Rail Travelers.

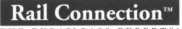

ORDER ONLINE AND GET EVEN MORE FREE STUFF!

www.railconnection.com

or Call 1-888-RAIL-PASS (1-888-724-5727)

Call and ask about

peninsula, passing heather and thousands of seabird nests. The best section of the walk is a one-hour hike between the harbor and the lighthouse at the southeast tip of the peninsula. To get to the trailhead from town, turn left at the DART station and follow Harbour Rd around the coast (20min.); or hike downhill from the lighthouse. In town, the ruins of the 14th-century **St. Mary's Abbey** stand peacefully in a cemetery at the bend in Church St. Get the key from the caretaker, Mrs. O'Rourke, at 13 Church St. To reach the private **Howth Castle,** an awkwardly charming patchwork of styles, turn right as you exit the DART station and then left after a quarter-mile, at the entrance to the Deer Park Hotel. Farther up the hill, a vague path goes around the right side of the Deer Park Hotel to the fabulous **Rhododendron Gardens.** At the top, you emerge into an astounding floral view overlooking Howth and Dublin. To get to Howth, take a northbound DART **train** to the end (30min., 6 per hr., IR£1.15). Turn left out of the station to get to the **tourist office,** in the Old Courthouse on Harbour Rd. (Open May-Aug. M-Tu and Th-F 11am-5pm, W 11am-1pm.) **Gleann na Smól** is on the left at the end of Nashville Rd, off Thormanby Rd, which forks off upper Main St. (Tel. 832 29 36. Singles IR£25; doubles IR£36-40.) Bus 31B runs to **Hazelwood** at the end of the cul-de-sac in the Thormanby Woods estate, 1 mi. up Thormanby Rd. (Tel. 839 13 91. Singles IR£30; doubles IR£42.)

BOYNE VALLEY. The thinly populated Boyne Valley safeguards Ireland's greatest archaeological treasures. Along the curves of the river between Slane and Drogheda lie no fewer than 40 mind-boggling passage-tombs constructed by the Neolithics around the 4th millenium BC, including **Newgrange, Dowth,** and **Knowth.** The first, built over 5000 years ago using stones believed to have been carted from Wicklow 40 mi. away, is the most spectacular, covered with elaborate patterns and symbols that continue to mystify archaeologists. You can only enter Newgrange through the ■**Brú na Bóinne Visitor Centre,** near Donore on the south side of the River Boyne, across from the tombs; be prepared to wait. (Tel. (041) 988 03 00. Open Mar.-Apr. 9:30am-5:30pm; May 9am-6:30pm; June to mid-Sept. 9am-7pm; late Sept. 9am-6:30pm; Oct. 9:30am-5:30pm; Nov.-Feb. 9:30am-5pm. Center and 1-hour tour IR£3, students IR£1.25.) **Bus Éireann** shuttles to the Visitor Centre from Dublin (1½hr., 4-5 per day, return IR£7). From prehistoric times until at least the 10th century, **Hill of Tara** was the political and often religious center of Ireland. Take any local (not express) bus from Dublin to **Navan** (1hr., 7-15 per day, IR£5.50) and ask the driver to let you off at the turn-off; the site is a mile straight uphill. A flock of enormous, well-preserved Norman castles, including **Trim Castle,** which Mel Gibson sacked 800 years later for a scene in *Braveheart,* overlook **Trim** on the River Boyne. **Bus Éireann** stops on Castle St. in front of the castle en route to **Dublin** (1½hr.; M-Sa 8 per day, Su 3 per day; IR£5). The **tourist office** is on Mill St. (Tel. (046) 371 11. Open daily 10am-1pm and 2-5pm.)

SOUTHEAST IRELAND

Historically the power base of the Vikings and then the Normans, the influence of the Celts is faintest in southeast Ireland. Beaches are the most fruitful of the Southeast's tourist attractions. Continue your hunt for raging nightlife south from Dublin through Kilkenny and Waterford; the daylight hours are most enjoyably spent exploring the pretty paths through Glendalough and the Wicklow Mountains.

■ FERRIES TO FRANCE AND BRITAIN

Irish Ferries sails from Rosslare Harbour to Pembroke, Wales (4hr.), Roscoff, France (14½hr.); and Cherbourg France (17hr.). Eurail is valid on passage on ferries to France. For specific schedules and fares contact them at **Rosslare Harbour** (tel. (053) 331 58; Dublin info tel. (01) 661 07 15; email info@irishferries.ie; www.irishferries.ie). **Stena Line** ferries go from Rosslare Harbour to Fishguard, South Wales, and Pembroke, Wales (3½-3¾hr.). For info, contact **Ferry Check** (tel. (01) 204 7799; email david@seaview.co.uk; www.seaview.co.uk/Stena.html).

IRELAND

THE WICKLOW MOUNTAINS. Over 2000 ft. high, covered by heather, and pleated by rivers, the Wicklow summits are home to grazing sheep and a few villagers. Smooth glacial valleys embrace the two lakes and the monastic ruins. The lush, blessed valley of **Glendalough** draws a steady summertime stream of coach tours filled with hikers and ruin-oglers. For more affordable food, B&Bs, and groceries, head to **Laragh** (LAR-a), 1 mi. up the road (10min. from the Wicklow Way). St. Kevin's **Bus** Service (tel. (01) 281 81 19) runs from Dublin's St. Stephen's Green West (2 per day; IR£6, return IR£10) and returns from the glen in the evening (2-3 per day). The **tourist office** is across from the Glendalough Hotel. (Tel. (0404) 456 88. Open mid-June to Sept. Tu 11am-1pm and 2-6pm, W-Su 10am-1pm and 2-6pm.) The **National Park Information Office,** between the two lakes, is the best source for hiking advice. (Tel. (0404) 454 25. Open May-Aug. daily 10am-6pm; Apr. and Sept. Sa-Su 10am-6pm.) The **Glendaloch Hostel (An Óige/HI)** is 5min. past the Glendalough tourist office. (Tel. (0404) 453 42. Dorms IR£11-12.50; doubles IR£30; off-season IR£1-2 less. Laundry. **Internet.** Bike rental.) Laragh has tons of **B&Bs,** as well as the **Wicklow Way Hostel.** (Tel. (0404) 453 98. Dorms IR£7; twins IR£25.)

ROSSLARE HARBOUR. Although Rosslare offers little in the way of Irish charm, it serves as an important transportation link to Wales, France, and the Irish coast. **Trains** run from the ferry port to Waterford (1¼hr., 1-2 per day, IR£6); Limerick (2½hr., 1-2 per day, IR£12); and Dublin (3hr., 3 per day, IR£10.50). **Buses** run twice per day via Waterford (IR£8.80) to Galway (IR£16); Killarney (IR£15); and Tralee (IR£16); as well as to Cork (M-Sa 4 per day, IR£13); Limerick (2-3 per day, IR£13); and Dublin (3hr., 7-10 per day, IR£9). The Rosslare-Kilrane **tourist office** is 1 mi. from the harbor on Wexford Rd in Kilrane. (Tel. (053) 336 22. Open daily 10:15am-5pm and 5:30-8pm.) If you must stay overnight before catching a ferry, try the **Rosslare Harbour Youth Hostel (An Óige/HI),** Goulding St. Take a right at the top of the cliff, head left around the far corner of the Hotel Rosslare, and it's past the **SuperValu supermarket,** on the left. (Hostel tel. (053) 333 99; fax 336 26. IR£6.50-7.50. Members only; buy a membership card for IR£1. Sheets IR£1.50. Midnight curfew. Supermarket open M-F 8am-7pm, Sa 8am-6pm, Su 9am-1pm.)

KILKENNY. The best-preserved medieval town in Ireland, Kilkenny offers rocking nightlife, too—nine churches share the streets with 78 pubs. Thirteenth-century **Kilkenny Castle** housed the Earls of Ormonde from the 1300s until 1932. (Open June-Sept. daily 10am-7pm; Apr.-May daily 10:30am-5:30pm; Oct.-Mar. Tu-Sa 10:30am-12:45pm and 2-5pm, Su 11am-12:45pm and 2-5pm. Mandatory guided tour IR£3, students IR£1.50.) **Tynan Walking Tours** provide the down-and-dirty on Kilkenny's folkloric tradition in about an hour. (Tel. (056) 659 29. IR£3, students IR£2.) After the tour, climb up the thin, 100-foot tower of **St. Canice's Cathedral,** up the hill off Dean St, for a panoramic view of the town and its surroundings. (Open Easter-Sept. M-Sa 9am-1pm and 2-6pm, Su 2-6pm.) **Trains** (tel. (056) 220 24) and **buses** (tel. (056) 649 33) stop at Kilkenny Station on Dublin Rd; buses also stop on Patrick St in the city center. Trains go to Dublin (2hr., IR£11) and Waterford (45min., IR£5). Buses go to Cork (3hr., 3 per day, IR£9); Dublin (4-5 per day, IR£7); Galway (mid-June to mid-Sept.; IR£12); Rosslare Harbour (daily mid-June to mid-Sept.); and Waterford (1 per day, IR£5). From Kilkenny Station, turn left on John St to reach The Parade, dominated by the castle to your left. The **tourist office,** Rose Inn St, has free maps and info on B&Bs (around IR£19). (Tel. (056) 515 00; fax 639 55. Open July-Aug. M-Sa 9am-8pm, Su 11am-1pm and 2-5pm; May-June and Sept. M-Sa 9am-6pm, Su 11am-1pm and 2-5pm; Apr. M-Sa 9am-6pm; Oct.-Mar. M-Sa 9am-5pm.) Check your **email** at **Compustore,** in the Market Cross shopping center off High St. (IR£2 per 15min.; IR£5 per hr. Open M-W and Sa 10am-6pm, Th-F 10am-8pm.) **Kilkenny Tourist Hostel (IHH),** 35 Parliament St, is always brimming with activity. (Tel. (056) 635 41; fax 233 97; email kilkennyhostel@tiniet.ie. Dorms IR£8; doubles IR£21. Oct.-Apr. IR£1 less. Laundry IR£3.) The biggest **grocery** in town is **Superquinn,** also in the Market Cross shopping center. (Open M-Tu and Sa 9am-7pm, W-F 9am-9pm.) **Maggie's,** St. Kieran St, is a superb wine cellar (hosts trad Tu-Th).

WATERFORD. Behind an industrial façade of metal silos and cranes, Waterford charms with winding, narrow streets filled with pubs and shops. The town highlight is the **Waterford Crystal Factory,** 1 mi. away on the N25 (Cork Rd). One-hour tours allow you to witness the transformation of molten glass into polished crystal. Admire the finished products—and their outrageous prices—in the gallery. Catch bus 1 (dir: Kilbarry-Ballybeg; 2 per hr., IR£0.75) across from the Clock Tower in Waterford. (Tel. (051) 37 33 11. Showroom open daily Apr.-Oct. 8:30am-6pm, tours every 15min. until 4pm; Nov.-Mar. 9am-5pm, tours every 15min. until 3:15pm; Jan.-Feb. showroom only 9am-5pm. IR£3.50, students IR£2.) One-hour **Walking Tours of Historic Waterford** depart from the front of the Granville Hotel on the Quay. (Tel. (051) 87 37 11. Departs Mar.-Oct. daily at noon and 2pm. IR£3.)

Trains (tel. (051) 87 62 43) leave from across the bridge from the Quay; the **bus** station (tel. (051) 87 90 00) is on the Quay by the bridge. **Trains** run to Kilkenny (40min., 3-5 per day, IR£5); Limerick (2¼hr., M-Sa 2 per day, IR£10); Dublin (2½hr., 3-5 per day, IR£12-15); and Rosslare Harbour (1hr., M-Sa 2 per day, IR£6.) **Buses** depart for Kilkenny (1hr., 1-2 per day, IR£5); Limerick (2½hr., 4-5 per day, IR£9.70); Cork (2½hr., 5-8 per day, IR£9); Rosslare Harbour (1¼hr., 3-4 per day, IR£8.80); Galway (4¾hr., 5-8 per day, IR£13); and Dublin (2¾hr., 4-7 per day, IR£7). The **tourist office,** in The Granary at the intersection of the Quay and Hanover St, has maps. (Tel. (051) 87 58 23. Open Apr.-Oct. M-Sa 9am-6pm, July-Aug. also Su 11am-5pm; Nov.-Mar. M-Sa 9am-5pm.) Check your **email** at **Voyager Internet Café,** in a mall where Parnell and John St meet. (Open M-W 8:30am-12:15am, Th-Su 8:30am-3:30am. IR£1.50 per 15min.) A friendly staff awaits at **Barnacle's Viking House (IHH),** Coffee House Ln, Greyfriars, the Quay. Follow the Quay east past the Clock Tower and a block past the post office. (Tel. (051) 85 38 27; fax 87 17 30. Dorms IR£7.50-8.50; doubles IR£13.50-15.50. Breakfast included.) Get **groceries** at **Treacy's,** on the Quay near the Granville Hotel. (Open daily 9am-11pm.) **Pubs** cluster on the Quays and on John St.

CASHEL. Cashel sprawls at the foot of the commanding 300 ft. **Rock of Cashel** (a.k.a. **St. Patrick's Rock**), a huge limestone outcropping topped by medieval buildings. (Open daily mid-June to mid-Sept. 9am-7:30pm; mid-Sept. to mid-June reduced hours. IR£3, students IR£1.25.) The two-towered **Cormac's Chapel,** consecrated in 1134, holds semi-restored Romanesque paintings. Down the cow path from the Rock lie the ruins of **Hore Abbey,** built by Cistercian monks who were fond of arches; the abbey is presently inhabited by nonchalant sheep. **Bus Éireann** (tel. (062) 621 21) leaves from Bianconi's Bistro, on Main St, for Cork (1½hr., 2-3 per day, IR£8); Limerick (4 per day, IR£8.80); and Dublin (3hr., 4 per day, IR£9). The **tourist office** is in the City Hall on Main St. (Tel. (062) 613 33. Open daily May-June and Aug.-Sept. 9:30am-5pm; July 9:30am-6pm.) Just down Dundrum Rd from town lies the stunning **O'Brien's Farmhouse Hostel** (5min.) (Tel. (062) 610 03. Dorms IR£8.50; private rooms IR£10-12.50; **camping** IR£3.50. Laundry.) **Cashel Holiday Hostel (IHH),** 6 John St, is just off Main St. (Tel. (062) 623 30. Dorms IR£7.50-9, private rooms IR£10-12.50. Laundry. Key deposit IR£3. Internet.) **Centra Supermarket** is on Friar St. (Open daily 7am-11pm.) The *craic* is nightly at **Feehan's,** on Main St.

SOUTHWEST IRELAND

The southwest's astonishing landscape, from ocean-battered cliffs to mystic stretches of lakes and mountains are matched by a momentous history. Outlaws and rebels once lurked in hidden coves and glens now frequented by visitors and ruled over by publicans. If the tourist mayhem is too much for you, it's easy to retreat to the more quiet stretches along the Dingle Peninsula and Cork's southern coast.

FERRIES TO FRANCE AND BRITAIN

Cork-Swansea Ferries sails between **Cork** and **Swansea, South Wales** (10hr., 1 per day, IR£44-64, with car IR£170-358). Contact them at 52 South Mall, Cork (tel. (021) 27 11 66; fax 27 50 61; email scs.iol.ie). **Brittany Ferries** (www.brittany-ferries.com) sails from **Cork** to **Roscoff, France** (13½hr.).

CORK CITY

Cork (pop. 150,000), Ireland's second-largest city, serves as the center of the southwest's sport, music, and arts scenes. Despite a tumultuous history, Cork has regularly rebuilt itself, and today a stroll along its pub-lined streets reveals grand architecture juxtaposed with many new commercial and industrial developments.

◪◪◪ PRACTICAL INFO, ACCOMMODATIONS, AND FOOD. Trains leave from Kent Station, Lower Glanmire Rd (tel. (021) 50 67 66), for Limerick (1½hr., IR£15.50); Killarney (2hr., IR£15.50); and Dublin (3hr., IR£32). **Buses** depart from Parnell Pl (tel. (021) 50 81 88), along Merchants' Quay, to Rosslare Harbor (4hr., IR£13); Dublin (4½hr., IR£12); and Belfast (7½hr., IR£17). **Irish Ferries** (tel. (021) 55 19 95) arranges **ferry** service to Swansea, England; buses run to Ringaskiddy Terminal, 8 mi. south of the city (30min., IR£3). Pick up a map and sights guide (IR£1.50) at **Tourist House,** Grand Parade. (Tel. (021) 27 32 51. Open July-Aug. M-Sa 9am-7pm, Su 10am-5pm; June M-Sa 9am-6pm; Sept.-May M-Sa 9:30am-5pm.) Bring IR£1 coins to surf the **internet** at **The Favourite,** 122 Patrick St. (Open daily 9am-10:30pm.)

Sheila's Budget Accommodation Centre (IHH), 3 Belgrave Pl, by the intersection of Wellington Rd and York St, lures visitors with a huge kitchen and a sauna. (Tel. (021) 50 55 62. Dorms IR£7-8.50; doubles from IR£21. Breakfast IR£1.50. Sheets IR£0.50. **Internet** IR£2 per 20min. Reception 24hr.) To get to the ultra-relaxed **Cork City Independent Hostel,** 100 Lower Glanmire Rd, from the train station, turn right, walk 300 ft., and keep an eye out on the left. (Tel. (021) 50 90 89. Dorms IR£7; doubles IR£17. Kitchen. Laundry IR£3.50.) **Cork City International Hostel, An Oige (HI)** is in a stately Victorian house at 1-2 Redclyffe, Western Rd. Take bus 8, which stops across the street, or walk 15min. from Grand Parade. (Tel. (021) 54 32 89. Dorms IR£6-8; doubles with bath IR£12.50. Breakfast IR£2. Reception 8am-midnight.) Prepare to be pampered at the B&B **Garnish House,** Western Rd. (Tel. (021) 27 51 11. Singles from IR£25; doubles from IR£40. Breakfast included. Free laundry.) **Blarney Camping and Caravan Park,** Stone View Rd, is 5 mi. from the city. (Tel. (021) 38 51 67. Tents IR£6; IR£2 extra per person. Showers included.) Restaurants and cafés cluster near the city center, especially between **Patrick St, Paul St,** and **Oliver Plunkett St. Tesco Supermarket** on Paul St is the biggest grocery store in town. (Open M-W and Sa 8:30am-8pm, Th-F til 10pm.) The burgers, pizza, and grilled chicken at ◪ **Scoozi,** in the alley just off Winthrop Ave, will instill wild abandon in you. (Open M-Sa 9am-11pm, Su noon-10pm.) Scrumptious vegetarian delights await at the **Quay Co-op,** 24 Sullivan's Quay. (Open M-Sa 9am-9pm.)

◪◪ SIGHTS AND ENTERTAINMENT. Downtown Cork is located on the tip of an arrow-shaped island in the River Lee; bridges link the island to Cork's residential south side and less affluent north side. Across the river to the north, walk up Shandon St, then take a right down unmarked Church St to reach Cork's most famous landmark, **St. Ann's Church.** The church earned the nickname of "the four-faced liar" because the four tower clocks are notoriously out of sync with one another. (Open M-Sa 9:30am-5:30pm. IR£3, students IR£2.50.) Do not pass go before heading to the **Cork City Gaol,** where multimedia tours of the former prison await; cross the bridge at the western end of Fitzgerald Park, turn right on Sunday's Well Rd, and follow the signs. (Open daily Mar.-Oct. 9:30am-6pm; Nov.-Feb. 10am-5pm. IR£4.50, students IR£3.) After visiting the jail, taste liberty by wandering the grounds of the nearby **University College Cork,** on the riverbank along Western Rd. The **Crawford Municipal Art Gallery,** Emmet Pl, boasts Irish paintings and traveling exhibitions. (Open M-Sa 10am-5pm. Free.)

Cork is the proud producer of both **Murphy's** and **Beamish,** which you can enjoy in the myriad of pubs along **Oliver Plunkett St, Union Quay,** and **South Main St. An Spailpín Fánac,** 28 South Main St, is a popular traditional pub. **The Lobby,** 1 Union Quay, arguably the most famous venue in Cork, gave some of Ireland's biggest folk acts their big breaks; it features live music nightly. (Tel. (021) 31 93 07. Occasional cover IR£3-5.) **The Western Star,** Western Rd, lures a huge student crowd with its outdoor patio and free Friday and Saturday barbecues. **Gallaghers,** MacCurtain St, holds backpacker nights on Mondays and Tuesdays (3-pint pitchers IR£6). **Loafer's,** 26 Douglas St, is Cork's sole gay and lesbian pub. When the pubs close, the spotlight shifts to Cork's nightclubs. **Gorbys,** Oliver Plunkett St, features young groovers grinding. (Open W-Sa. Cover IR£2-5.) **Sir Henry's,** South Main St, is popular, crowded, and intense. (Open W-Sa. Cover IR£2-11.)

⊠ EXCURSION FROM CORK CITY: BLARNEY. Busloads of tourists eager for quintessential Irish scenery and a cold kiss head 5 mi. northwest of Cork to see **Blarney Castle** and its legendary **Blarney Stone,** which confers the gift of gab upon those who manage to smooch it while leaning over backwards. While crowds awaiting this opportunity can clog the dank passageways, the top of the castle provides an airy and stunning view of the countryside. (Open June-Aug. M-Sa 9am-7pm, Su 9:30am-5:30pm; May and Sept. M-Sa 9am-6:30pm, Su 9:30am-dusk; Oct.-Apr. M-Sa 9am-sundown, Su 9:30am-sundown. IR£3.50, students IR£2.50.) **Bus Éireann** runs buses from Cork (10-16 per day, return IR£2.50.)

KINSALE

Each summer, affluent tourists come to swim, fish, and eat at Kinsale's famed and pricey twelve restaurants known as the "Good Food Circle"; but luckily the town's best attractions are cheap. The star-shaped, 17th-century **Charles Fort** offers spectacular views of the town and its watery surroundings; follow the coastal **Scilly Walk** from the end of Pearse St (30min.). (Open mid-June to mid-Sept. daily 9am-6pm; mid-Apr. to mid-June and mid-Sept. to mid-Oct. M-Sa 9am-5pm, Su 9:30am-5:30pm. IR£2, students IR£1.) Across the harbor, the grass-covered ruins of **James Fort** delight with panoramic views. (Open 24hr. Free.) **Buses** arrive at the Esso station on the pier from **Cork** (40min., 3-10 per day, return IR£3.80). The **tourist office,** Emmet Pl, is on the waterfront. (Open Mar.-Nov. daily 9am-6pm.) To get to the **Castlepark Marina Centre (IHH),** across the harbor, walk along the pier away from town for 10min., turn left to cross Duggan Bridge, take a left just past the bridge, and follow the road back toward the harbor (40min.). (Tel. (021) 77 49 59. Dorms IR£8-9; doubles IR£10. Open mid-Mar. to Dec.) **Dempsey's Hostel (IHH),** Cork Rd, is 2min. from town. (Tel. (021) 77 21 24. Dorms IR£6; doubles IR£8.)

SCHULL AND THE MIZEN HEAD PENINSULA

The seaside hamlet of **Schull** is an ideal base for exploring the craggy, windswept, and beach-laden southwest tip of Ireland. In summer, it's also a jumping-off point to the striking island of **Cape Clear** (June.-Sept. 1-3 ferries per day, return IR£8; call (028) 391 35 for ferry info). A calm harbor and numerous shipwrecks make a **diver's** paradise; the **Watersports Centre** rents gear. (Open M-Sa 9:30am-8:30pm.) Pick up the excellent *Schull Guide* from any store in town (IR£1.50). The immaculate **Schull Backpackers' Lodge (IHH),** Colla Rd, has **hiking** and **biking** maps and info. (Tel. (028) 286 81. Dorms IR£8; doubles IR£24-26.) **Spar Market** is on Main St. (Open M-Sa 7am-9pm, Su 8am-8pm.) **Buses** arrive in Schull from Cork (1-3 per day, IR£13 return) and Killarney (June-Sept.1 per day). The Mizen becomes more scenic and less populated the farther west you go from Schull. Once you've reached Schull, there's no further public transportation on the peninsula besides a Bus Éireann bus to Goleen (2 per day). **Betty's Bus Hire** offers tours of the Mizen via the scenic coast road. (Tel. (028) 284 10. IR£5. Departs Schull June-Aug. Tu and Th 11am.) Those who choose to accept the risks of **hitching** often try to avoid poor public transport by waiting at the crossroads on Goleen Rd outside of town. Confident **cyclists** can daytrip to Mizen Head (18 mi. from Schull).

KILLARNEY AND KILLARNEY NATIONAL PARK

The town of Killarney is tourist-infested, but for good reason—it's just minutes from some of Ireland's most extraordinary natural scenery. The 37 sq. mi. **national park** outside town blends forested mountains with the famous lakes of Killarney. **Muckross House,** 3 mi. south of Killarney on Kenmare Rd, is a massive 19th-century manor with a garden that blooms brilliantly each summer. A path from the House leads up to the 60-foot **Torc Waterfall.** (House open daily July-Aug. 9am-7pm; Sept.-

IRELAND

June 9am-6pm. IR£3.80, students IR£1.62.) You can also walk or drive to the 14th-century **Ross Castle**, a right on Ross Rd off Muckross Rd, 2 mi. from Killarney, but the numerous footpaths from Knockreer (out of town on New St) are more scenic (15min.). (Open daily June-Aug. 9am-6:30pm; May-Sept. 10am-6pm; Oct. 9am-5pm. Obligatory tour IR£2.50, students IR£1.) Bringing a bike along with you will facilitate a trip to the top of the **Gap of Dunlow**, which borders **Macgillycuddy's Reeks**, Ireland's highest mountain range. You can hop on a **boat** from Ross Castle to the head of the Gap (IR£7; book through the tourist office). Head left over the stone bridge from Lord Brandon's Cottage, continue 2 mi. to the church, follow the hairpin turn, and huff the 1½ mi. to the top; your reward will be a 7 mi. coast downhill through the park's most breathtaking scenery. The 8 mi. ride back to Killarney (bear right after Kate Kearney's Cottage, turn left on the road to Fossa, and turn right on Killorglin Rd) passes the ruins of **Dunloe Castle**, demolished by Cromwell's armies.

Trains arrive at the station off East Avenue Rd, near Park Rd, from Cork (2hr., 5 per day, return IR£9.50); Limerick (3hr., 3-4 per day, IR£15); and Dublin (3½hr., 4 per day, IR£33.50). **Buses** rumble from Park Rd to Cork (2hr., 3-5 per day, IR£8.50). You won't be able to walk five feet without tripping over a **bike rental** place. The **tourist office** is on Beech St, off New St. (Tel. (064) 316 33. Open July-Aug. M-Sa 9am-8pm, Su 9am-1pm and 2:15-6pm; June and Sept. M-Sa 9am-6pm, Su 10am-6pm; Oct.-May M-Sa 9:15am-5:30pm.) From the bus or train station, turn left on College St and take your first right to reach **The Súgán (IHH)**, Lewis Rd (2min.). (Tel. (064) 331 04. IR£9.) The immense **Neptune's (IHH)**, Bishop's Ln, is up the first walkway off New St on the right. (Tel. (064) 352 55. Dorms IR£7.50-8.50; doubles IR£20. Breakfast IR£1.50-3.50.) Call ahead to get a ride from either station to the **Bunrower House Hostel (IHH)**, next to the park. (Tel. (064) 339 14. Dorms IR£7-8; doubles IR£18; **camping** IR£3.50.) Pick up **groceries** at **Quinnsworth**, in an arcade off New St. (Open M-W and Sa 8am-8pm, Th-F 8am-10pm, Su 10am-6pm.) **Yer Mans**, Plunkett St, is the only pub in the world licensed to sell Guinness in jam jars (IR£1.25).

RING OF KERRY

The Southwest's most celebrated peninsula holds wee villages, fabled ancient forts, and rugged mountains—the romantic scenery most visitors come to Ireland seeking. Although noxious, air-conditioned tour buses often hog the roads, greater rewards await those who take the time to explore the landscape on foot or by bike.

▐ GETTING THERE AND GETTING AROUND. The term "Ring of Kerry" is usually used to describe the entire **Iveragh Peninsula**, though it more technically refers to the ring of roads circumnavigating it. Prepackaged private bus tours from **Killarney** stop in **Killorglin, Glenbeigh, Kells, Cahersiveen, Waterville, Caherdaniel, Sneem**, and **Moll's Gap** (IR£8 through a hostel; students IR£12 with one-night stopover). Freer souls hop on the no-frills circuit run by **Bus Éireann**, which stops at the major towns on the Ring (June-Sept. 2 per day): **Killorglin; Cahersiveen** (from Killorglin 50min., IR£5); **Waterville; Caherdaniel** (from Cahersiveen 1½hr., IR£3.10); **Sneem;** and **Killarney** (from Caherdaniel 1½hr., IR£7.30; from Cahersiveen 2½hr., IR£9).

CAHERSIVEEN. Cahersiveen (car-si-VEEN) is best known in Ireland as the birthplace of patriot Daniel "The Liberator" O'Connell, who won Catholic representation in Parliament in 1829. Two miles northwest of town across the bridge are the ruins of the **Ballycarbery Castle**, once held by O'Connell's ancestors. Two hundred yards past the castle turn-off, you can walk along the 10-foot-thick walls of **Cahergall Fort** or visit the small stone dwellings of **Leacanabuaile Fort**. The **tourist office** is in a former barracks on the road to the castle. (Tel. (066) 947 25 89. Open May to mid-Sept. M-Sa 10am-6pm, Su 1-6pm.) The friendly **Sive Hostel (IHH)** is at 15 East End, Main St. (Tel. (066) 947 27 17. Dorms IR£7; doubles IR£18; **camping** IR£4 per person. **Internet** IR£5 per hr.) Equally fabulous is **Mortimer's Hostel**, Main St. (Tel. (066) 947 23 38. IR£6.) Cahersiveen's 30 **original pubs** may seem like a lot, but residents wistfully recollect when there were 52.

A fantastic daytrip is to quiet ◨**Valentia Island,** where shady country roads link a handful of beehive huts, *ogham* stones, and small ruins. The views in between, across to the mountainous mainland, and out over Dingle Bay, would be reason enough to come to Ireland. You can **bike** to the island, connected by bridges on either end to the mainland, or take a comically short **ferry** (3min., every 10min. Apr.-Sept. 8:15am-10:30pm, IR£3) from **Reenard Point,** 3 mi. west of Cahersiveen; a taxi to the ferry dock from Cahersiveen runs IR£4. Another great daytrip is to the **Skellig Rocks,** a stunning mass of natural rubble about 8 mi. off the shore of the Iveragh Peninsula. From your boat, **Little Skellig** will at first appear snow-capped, but it's actually just covered with 22,000 crooning birds. Climb the vertigo-inducing 650 steps past puffins, kittiwakes, gannets, and petrels (birds to you) to reach a **monastery** built by 6th-century Christian monks, whose beehive-like dwellings are still intact. The hostels and campground in Cahersiveen will all arrange the stomach-churning **ferry** ride (45-90min.) for IR£20, including a ride to the dock.

CAHERDANIEL. There's little in the village of **Caherdaniel** to attract the Ring's droves of buses, but nearby **Derrynane Strand,** 1½ mi. away in Derrynane National Park, delights with 2 mi. of gorgeous beach ringed by picture perfect dunes. **Derrynane House,** signposted just up from the beach, was the cherished residence of Irish patriot Daniel O'Connell (see above). (Open May-Sept. M-Sa 9am-6pm, Su 11am-7pm; Apr. and Oct. Tu-Su 1-5pm; Nov.-Mar. Sa-Su 1-5pm. IR£2, students IR£1.) Guests have the run of the house at ◨**The Travellers' Rest Hostel.** (Tel. (066) 947 51 75. Dorms IR£7.50-8; singles IR£9-9.50 per person. Breakfast IR£2.50.)

DINGLE PENINSULA

For decades the Ring of Kerry's undertouristed counterpart, the gorgeous Dingle Peninsula remains more congested with ancient sites than tour buses. The Ring's tourist blitz has only just begun to encroach upon the spectacular cliffs and sweeping beaches of the Irish-speaking peninsula. A *gaeltacht* to the west of Dingle Town preserves centuries-old Irish heritage.

◧ **GETTING THERE AND GETTING AROUND.** The best base for exploring the peninsula, which lies just across the Dingle Bay from the Ring of Kerry to the south, is **Dingle Town,** most easily reached from Tralee (1¼hr., 4-6 per day, IR£5.90; see below) or Killarney (2hr., 3-6 per day, IR£8.50; see p. 533). From **Dingle Town, Bus Éireann** runs west to **Ballydavid** (20min., Tu and F 3 per day, return IR£3.15) as well as **Dunquin** and **Ballyferriter** (20-30min., in summer 1-4 per day, IR£2.30). In summer, additional buses also tour the south of the peninsula from Dingle (June-Sept. M-Sa 2 per day). If you only have time for a daytrip, a prepackaged **Dingle/Slea Head** tour runs from **Killarney** (M-Sa 2 per day, IR£9.70).

DINGLE TOWN. Lively Dingle Town, adopted home of **Fungi the Dolphin** (now a major focus of the tourist industry), serves as a good regional base. **Sciúird Archaeology tours** (tel. (066) 915 16 06) take you from the pier on a 3-hour whirlwind bus tour of the area's ancient spots (2 per day, IR£8; book ahead). **Morans** (tel. 91 51 55) runs great tours to Slea Head that stop by historical sites, film sets, and majestic views. The **tourist office** is on the corner of Main and Dykegate St. (Tel. (066) 915 11 88. Open June-Aug. M-Sa 9am-6pm, Su 10am-6pm; Sept.-Oct. and mid-Mar. to May M-Sa 9am-5pm.) ◨**Ballintaggart Hostel (IHH),** 25min. east on Tralee Rd in a stone mansion, is supposedly haunted by the wife of the Earl of Cork, whom he strangled here. (Tel. (066) 915 14 54. Dorms IR£7-10; twins and doubles IR£14 per person; off-season IR£1-2 less. **Camping** IR£3.50. Breakfast IR£2-4. Free shuttle to town.) The laid-back **Grapevine Hostel** is on Dykegate St, off Main St. (Tel. (066) 915 14 34. IR£7-8.50.) The pub **An Droichead Beag,** Lower Main St, has the best trad around. From Dingle Town, a winding cliff-side road runs north by way of the 1500 ft. **Connor Pass.** As the road twists downhill, a waterfall marks the base of **Pedlars Lake.**

SLEA HEAD AND DUNQUIN. Glorious Slea Head impresses with its jagged cliffs and crashing waves. Green hills, interrupted by rough stone walls and occasional sheep, suddenly break off into the foam-flecked sea. *Ryan's Daughter* and parts of *Far and Away* were filmed in this appropriately melodramatic scenery. By far the best way to see Slea Head and Dunquin in a day or less is to bike along the predominantly flat **Slea Head Drive.** Past Dingle Town towards Slea Head sits the village of **Ventry** (Ceann Trá), home to a sandy beach and the brand-new **Ballybeag Hostel;** a regular shuttle runs to Dingle Town. (Tel. 915 98 76; email balybeag@iol.ie. IR£7.50-9. **Bike rental.** Laundry.) The ■**Celtic and Prehistoric Museum,** farther down the road, is a must-see. (Tel. 915 99 41; www.kerryweb.ie. Open daily June-Sept. 10am-5pm, other times call ahead. IR£3.) North of Slea Head, the scattered settlement of **Dunquin** (Dún Chaoin) boasts **Kruger's,** purportedly the westernmost pub in Europe. (Tel. 915 61 27. Entrees around IR£5.) Its adjacent **B&B** has comfortable rooms (IR£16). Just outside of Dunquin on the road to Ballyferriter, **Blasket Centre** has outstanding exhibits about the isolated Blasket Islands. (Open daily July-Aug. 10am-7pm; Easter-June and Sept.-Nov. 10am-6pm. IR£2.50, students IR£1.)

TRALEE

While tourists see Killarney as the core of County Kerry, residents are proud to identify Tralee (pop. 20,000) as its economic center. Ireland's second-largest museum, ■**Kerry the Kingdom,** Ashe Memorial Hall, Denny St, showcases a high-tech history of Ireland from 8000 BC to the present. (Open daily Mar.-Oct. 9am-6pm; Nov.-Dec. noon-4:30pm. IR£5.50, students IR£4.75.) During the last week of August, the nationally-known **Rose of Tralee Festival** brings a maelstrom of entertainment to town as lovely Irish lasses compete for the "Rose of Tralee" title. **Trains** go to Killarney (40min., 4-5 per day, IR£5.50); Cork (2½hr., 3-5 per day, IR£17); and Galway (3 per day, IR£33.50). **Buses** rumble off to Killarney (40min., June-Sept. 5-14 per day, IR£4.40); Limerick (2¼hr., 7 per day, IR£9); Cork (2½hr., 3-6 per day, IR£9.70); and Galway (4-6 per day, IR£13). To get to the **tourist office,** Ashe Memorial Hall, from either station, head into town on Edward St, then hang a right on Castle St and a left on Denny St. (Tel. (066) 712 12 88. Open July-Aug. M-Sa 9am-7pm, Su 9am-6pm; May-June and Oct. M-Sa 9am-6pm; Oct.-Apr. M-F 9am-5pm.) The well-located **Finnegan's Hostel (IHH),** 17 Denny St, is in a majestic 19th-century townhouse containing part of the old town castle. (Tel. (066) 712 76 10. Dorms IR£9; doubles IR£20.) Call for pick-up to the ■**Collis-Sandes House (IHH).** (Tel. (066) 712 86 58; www.col-sands.com. Dorms IR£8; doubles from IR£20; **camping** IR£4.)

WESTERN IRELAND

Even Dubliners will tell you that the west is the "most Irish" part of Ireland. The area hardest hit by the 19th-century potato famine, this land is miserable for farming, but it's a boon for hikers and bikers who enjoy the isolation of brilliantly mountainous landscapes. Western Ireland's gorgeous desolation and enclaves of traditional culture are now its biggest attractions.

LIMERICK CITY

Although Limerick's 18th-century Georgian streets and parks remain regal and elegant, later industrial developments and hard economic times give the city a duller, urban feel. To reach the requisite local castle, **King John's Castle,** on Nicholas St, walk across the Abbey River and turn after St. Mary's Cathedral. (Open Mar.-Dec. daily 9:30am-6pm. IR£4.20, students IR£3.30.) **Trains** (tel. (061) 31 55 55) leave Parnell St for Dublin (2hr., 8-9 per day, IR£25); Waterford (2hr., M-Sa 1-2, IR£12); and Cork (2½hr., 6-7 per day, IR£13.50). **Buses** (tel. (061) 31 33 33) leave the train station for Cork (2hr., 6 per day, IR£9); Galway (2hr., 7 per day, IR£9); Tralee (2hr., 6 per day, IR£9); Waterford (2½hr., 5-6 per day, IR£9.70); and Dublin (3hr., 5-8 per day, IR£10). The **tourist office** is on Arthurs Quay, in the space-age glass building. From the station, walk straight down Davis St, right on O'Connell St, and left just before Arthurs Quay Mall. (Tel. (061) 31 75 22. Open July-Aug. M-F 9am-7pm, Sa-Su 9am-

6pm; May-June and Sept.-Oct. M-Sa 9:30am-5:30pm; Nov.-Apr. M-F 9:30am-5:30pm, Sa 9:30am-1pm.) Snooze at **Clyde House,** St. Alphonsus St, right off Henry St. (Tel. (061) 31 47 27. Dorms IR£11.50; singles IR£20; twins IR£35.) From the bus station, cross Parnell St and head up Daris St for one long block. Take a left on Pery St and walk two blocks to Harstoye St to **Finnegan's (IHH),** 6 Pery Sq. (Tel. (061) 31 03 08. Dorms IR£7.50; private rooms IR£10. Laundry.) Get **groceries** at **Tesco** in Arthurs Quay Mall. (Open M-W and Sa 8:30am-8pm, Th-F 8:30am-10pm.)

CLARE COAST

Europe's best traditional Irish music, highest cliffs, and strangest landscapes are to be found on the superlative coast of County Clare. **Ennis** is the main rail hub in the region. **Bus Éireann** (tel. (065) 682 41 77) runs south-north from Kilkee to Galway; a **West Clare** line goes south-north from Kilkee to Milltown Malbay and Doolin. **Kilkee** features the spectacular **Westend Cliff Walk** and a famously fun pub crawl. The **Kilkee Hostel (IHH),** among the pubs on O'Curry St, makes friends of strangers. (Tel. (065) 562 09. IR£7. Sheets IR£0.50. Laundry IR£4.) Just 20 mi. north of Kilkee and 2 mi. inland from Spanish Point beach is **Milltown Malbay,** the best place to be for Irish music. During **Willie Week** in early July, musicians and *craic* addicts converge in Milltown for a week of recitals, lectures, and nonstop sessions. The **Station House,** at the old railway station, has huge beds. (Tel. (065) 840 08. IR£17.) Just north of Milltown, the tiny seaside resort of **Lahinch** sits on smooth sand in a crook of the bay. The comfortable **Lahinch Hostel,** on Church St, has a central, waterfront location. (Tel. (065) 708 10 40. Dorms IR£7.50; doubles IR£24. Laundry IR£2. Bikes IR£7 per day.) A 20-minute bus ride continues around the coast to the extraordinary **Cliffs of Moher,** justifiably one of Ireland's most famous sights. Standing 700 ft. above the Atlantic spray, you'll peer below onto gulls circling limestone spires. Eight miles north up the coast, **Doolin** (pop. 200) is a rural backpackers' mecca. Its lower village is a handful of buildings near the sea; the tiny upper village is a mile up the road. Fifteen years ago, Doolin was the trad capital, and its three legendary pubs—**McDermott's** and **McGann's** in Upper Village and **O'Connor's** in the Lower— still have fantastic sessions and tasty food. By the river between the two villages is the **Aille River Hostel (IHH),** a small cottage with a groovy ambience. (Tel. (065) 707 42 60. July-Aug. IR£7.50-8; Sept.-May IR£7-8; **camping** IR£3.50. Open mid-Mar. to mid-Nov.) Doolin is an easy bike ride from the Burren and the Cliffs; the **Doolin Bike Store** rents bikes. (Tel. (065) 707 42 82. IR£7 per day. Open daily 9am-8pm.)

THE BURREN

If there were wild orchids, cantakerous cows, and B&Bs on the Moon, it would probably look a lot like the Burren. Its land comprises nearly 100 sq. mi. and almost one-third of Co. Clare's coastline. The lunar beauty of the Burren sees jagged gray hills resembling skyscrapers turned to rubble, hidden depressions that open up into labyrithian caves, ruined churches and castles, thousands of miles of stone walls, ancient megaliths, and wildflowers indigenous found only in this region. It's notoriously difficult to get around the Burren. Yellow arrows mark a 26 mi. **hiking** trail from Liscannor to Ballyvaughan; Doolin and Kinvara are the best bases for **biking** tours. All of the surrounding **tourist offices** (at Ennis, the Cliffs of Moher, and Kinvara) have good maps of the region and other info. Although cars plow right through town on their way from Galway to the Burren, **Kinvara** (pop. 2300) is a fairly well-kept secret with a vibrant artistic community, pubs with character, and a well-preserved medieval castle. **Johnston's Hostel (IHH),** on Main St. (tel. 37164), uphill from the Quay, is a relaxing haven. (Tel. (091) 371 64. Dorms IR£7.50; **camping** IR£4.50. Sheets IR£1. Showers IR£0.50. Laundry. Curfew 12:30am. Open June-Sept.)

GALWAY CITY

In the past few years, Galway's (pop. 60,000) reputation as Ireland's cultural capital has brought young Irish flocking to the city like Elvis fans to Graceland. Mix in over 13,000 students, a transient population of twenty-something Europeans, and droves of backpackers, and you have one happening college town.

IRELAND

⊓⌐⌐ PRACTICAL INFO, ACCOMMODATIONS, AND FOOD. Direct **trains** (tel. (091) 56 14 44) run to Dublin (3hr., 4-5 per day, IR£15-21); transfer at Athlone (IR£7.50-13.50) for all other cities. **Bus Éireann** (tel. (091) 56 20 00) leaves for Dublin (7-9 per day, IR£8); Cork (5 per day, IR£12); and Belfast (1-3 per day, IR£17). The main **tourist office**, Victoria Pl, is a block southeast of the bus and train stations at Eyre Sq. (Tel. (091) 56 30 81. Open July-Aug. daily 8:30am-7:45pm; May-June and Sept. daily 8:30am-5:45pm; Oct.-Apr. Su-F 9am-5:45pm, Sa 9am-12:45pm.) Check your **email** at **Net Access**, the Old Malte Arcarde, High St (IR£4-5 per hr.). The ▨**Salmon Weir Hostel**, 5min. west of Eyre Sq on St. Vincent's Ave, is friendly and sucks you into group pub-hopping excursions. (Tel. (091) 56 11 33. Dorms IR£7-9; doubles IR£18-22. Curfew 2-3am.) **Great Western House (IHH)**, Eyre Sq, across from the station, approaches hostel heaven with its sauna and pool room. (Tel. (091) 56 11 50. July-Aug. dorms IR£10-12.50; singles IR£18; doubles IR£32; cheaper off-season. Breakfast included. Bike rental. **Internet.** Reception 24hr.) **Kinlay House (IHH)**, Merchant's Rd, across from the tourist office, is modern, spotless, secure, and big. (Tel. (091) 56 52 44. July-Sept. dorms IR£8.50-12.50; off-season cheaper; 10% ISIC discount. Breakfast included. **Internet.**) **Woodquay Hostel**, 23-24 Woodquay, is cute, comfy, and clean to boot. (Tel. (091) 56 26 18. Dorms IR£7.50-10; singles IR£12; twins IR£10.) **Barnacle's Quay Street Hostel (IHH)**, Quay St (farther down Shop St), has a fabulous location in pub central. (Tel. (091) 56 86 44. Dorms IR£7-12; doubles IR£24-9.) For cheap eats, head to the east bank; try **Abbeygate St** and the short blocks around **Quay, High,** and **Shop St.** Pick up **groceries** at **Supervalu**, in the Eyre Sq mall. (Open M-W and Sa 9am-6:30pm, Th-F 9am-9pm.)

⊙▯ SIGHTS AND ENTERTAINMENT. The town's main attractions are its night-life and setting—it's a convenient base for trips to the Clare coast or the Conne-mara. You can rent a **rowboat** from **Frank Dolan's**, 13 Riverside, Woodquay, and row/drift down the Corrib for great views of the city, the countryside, and nearby castles (IR£3 per hr.). Otherwise, occupy your days with leisurely strolls around town and rest up for the long nights ahead. Choosing from Galway's endless list of fantastic pubs is a difficult challenge even for residents (nightclubs lag far behind in quality and value). Generally speaking, the beautiful pubs along **Quay St** cater to tourists and students; try **Seaghan Ua Neachtain** (called **Knockton's**), one of the oldest and most genuine pubs in the county, which hosts nightly trad; or the popular **The Quays**, built with the carved wood and stained-glass windows of an old church. (Cover IR£5. Open daily 10pm-1:30am.) Also in the Quay area, **Buskar Browne's/The Slate House**, between Cross St and Kirwin's Ln, was a nunnery for 300 years before turn-ing to the Dark Side; the medieval-themed **King's Head,** High St, has nightly live music and several bars; and **Taaffe's,** Shop St, packs 'em in for booze and trad. Pubs along **Dominick St** (across the river from the Quay) are popular with locals; check out **Roisín Dubh** (The Black Rose), where big-name Irish and international musicians light up the stage. In **Eyre Sq,** the packed **The Hole in the Wall** hosts a hip late-night crowd, while the huge **Skeffington Arms** is a pub crawl unto itself.

ARAN ISLANDS (OILEÁIN ÁRANN)

The harsh limestone landscapes of the Aran Islands guard the entrance to Galway Bay. Awesome Iron Age forts sit atop the stark cliffs while mazes of stone walls divide deserted fields. The islands are discovered each summer by throngs of visi-tors but islanders still fish, speak Irish, and produce traditional sweaters and *cur-raghs* (tar-bottomed boats), maintaining the lifestyle they've had for centuries. **Island Ferries** (tel. (091) 56 17 67) leaves from **Rossaveal** (return IR£15; return bus from Galway IR£4) and **O'Brien Shipping/Doolin Ferries** (tel. (091) 56 72 83) leaves from the Galway pier (return IR£12, students IR£9) and Doolin (return IR£15-20); both have booths in the Galway tourist office.

Of the dozens of ruins, forts, churches, and holy wells which rise from the stony terrain of Inishmore (Inis Mór; pop. 900), the most amazing is the **Dún Aengus** ring fort, where a small semicircular wall surrounds a sheer 300-foot drop. Inishmore is still fairly isolated despite an increase in tourists. Ferries land at **Kilronan,** where the **tourist office** holds bags (IR£0.75) and changes money. (Tel. (099) 612 63. Open Feb.-Nov. daily 10am-6:15pm.) Beds at **Kilronan Hostel** come with a spotless kitchen, ocean views, and a TV lounge. (Tel. (099) 612 55. IR£8-9.) A free hostel minibus meets the ferries. The **Spar Market,** past the hostel, seems to be the island's social center. (Open M-Sa 9am-8pm, Su 10am-6pm.) Windswept **Inishmaan** (Inis Meáin; pop. 300) elevates solitude to its greatest form. **Inisheer** (Inis Oírr; pop. 300) the smallest island, is least rugged and most budget-friendly. The **Brú Hostel (IHH)** is clean, spacious, and a limestone slab's throw from the pier. (Tel. (099) 750 24. Dorms IR£7.50; singles and doubles IR£10-11 per person. Breakfast IR£4.)

CONNEMARA

Connemara, a largely Irish-speaking region, comprises a lacy net of inlets and islands, a rough gang of mountains, and some bogs in between. This thinly popu-lated western arm of County Galway harbors some of Ireland's most desolate yet breathtaking scenery. The jagged southern coastline teems with sinuous estuaries, safe beaches for camping, and tidal causeways connecting to rocky islands.

CLIFDEN (AN CLOCHÁN). Busy English-speaking Clifden has more amenities and modernities than its old-world, Irish-speaking neighbors. Clifden's proximity to the scenic bogs and mountains of the region attracts crowds of tourists, who enjoy the frenzied pub scene, shop in its ubiquitous arts and crafts studios, and use it as a base for exploring the region. The **Connemara Walking Center,** on Market St, runs tours of the bogs (much more interesting than you'd guess). (Tel. (095) 213 79. Open Mar.-Oct. M-Sa 10am-6pm. Easter-Oct. 1-2 tours daily. IR£8-20.) **Bus Éireann** goes from the library on Market St to Westport via Leenane (1½hr., late June to Aug. 1-2 per day) and Galway via Oughterard (2hr., 1-5 per day, IR£6.50); Michael Nee runs a bus from the courthouse to Galway (June-Sept. 3 per day, IR£5). Rent a **bike** at **Mannion's,** Bridge St. (Tel. (095) 211 60. IR£7 per day, IR£40 per week; deposit IR£10. Open M-Sa 9:30am-6:30pm, Su 10am-1pm and 5-7pm.) The **tourist office** is on Market St. (Tel. (095) 211 63. Open July-Aug. M-Sa 9:45am-5:45pm and Su noon-4pm; May-June and Sept. M-Sa 9:30am-5:30pm.) **B&Bs** litter the streets (IR£18-20). The excellent **Clifden Town Hostel (IHH)** is on Market St. (Tel. (095) 210 76. Dorms IR£8; doubles IR£24; triples IR£30; quads IR£36; off-season IR£1-2 less.) Head straight past the bottom of Market St to find **Brookside Hostel,** Hulk St. (Tel. (095) 218 12. Dorms IR£7-8; private rooms IR£8-9. Laundry IR£4.) Tranquil **Shana-heever Campsite** is a little over 1 mi. outside Clifden on Westport Rd. (Tel. (095) 210 18. IR£8 for 2 people and tent; IR£3 per additional person.) **O'Connor's SuperValu** is on Market St. (Open M-F 8:30am-8pm, Su 9am-7pm.) Shake your booty and down a few pints along **Market St,** in **The Square,** and on **Church Hill.**

CONNEMARA NATIONAL PARK. Connemara National Park occupies 7¾ sq. mi. of mountainous countryside that thousands of birds call home. The far-from-solid terrain of the park comprises bogs thinly covered by a screen of grass and flow-ers—be prepared to get muddy. The **Snuffaunboy Nature Trail** and the **Ellis Wood Trail** are easy hikes. More experienced hikers head for the **Twelve Bens** (*Na Benna Beola,* a.k.a. the Twelve Pins), a rugged range that reaches 2400 ft. There are no proper trails, but Jos Lynam's guidebook (IR£5) meticulously plots out 18 fantastic hikes through the Twelve Bens and the Maamturks. A tour of all 12 Bens takes experienced walkers about 10hr. Biking the 40 mi. circle through Clifden, Letter-frack, and the Inagh Valley is breathtaking, but only appropriate for fit bikers.

Tiny **Letterfrack** is the gateway to the park. The Galway-Clifden **bus** (M-Sa mid-June-Aug. 11 per week, Sept. to mid-June 4 per week) and the summertime Clifden-Westport bus (1-2 per day) stop at Letterfrack. The **Visitors Centre** excels at explain-ing the fascinating differences between blanket bogs, raised bogs, turf, and heath-land. Guides lead free two-hour **walks** over the hills and through the bogs. (Tel. (095) 410 54. Open daily July-Aug. 9:30am-6:30pm; June 10am-6:30pm; May and Sept. 10am-5:30pm. IR£2, students IR£1. Tours July-Aug. M, W, and F 10:30am.)

IRELAND

Uphill from the intersection in Letterfrack, the ⬛**Old Monastery Hostel** is one of Ireland's finest. (Tel. (095) 411 32. Dorms IR£8-10. Breakfast included. Laundry. Bike IR£7 per day. **Internet.**) The turn-off to the **Ben Lettery Hostel (An Óige/HI)**, in Ballinafad, is 8 mi. east of Clifden. (Tel. (095) 511 36. IR£5.50-6.)

WESTPORT. One of the few planned towns in the country, Westport (pop. 4300) still looks marvelous in its Georgian-period costume. Tourists savor its thriving pub life, drink tea at dapper cafés, and shop for snow-globes. **Trains** arrive at the Altamont St Station (tel. (098) 252 53), 5min. up North Mall, from Dublin via Athlone (2-3 per day, IR£15). **Buses** leave from the Octagon on Mill St for Galway (M-F 6 per day, IR£8.80). **Breheny & Sons,** on Castlebar St, rents **bikes.** (Tel. (098) 250 20. IR£5-7 per day, IR£35 per week; IR£30 deposit.) The **tourist office** is at North Mall. (Tel. (098) 257 11. Open Apr.-Oct. M-Sa 9am-12:45pm and 2-5:45pm, July-Aug. also Su 10am-6pm.) **B&Bs** are on the Castlebar and Altamont Rd off North Mall (IR£18-20). ⬛**The Granary Hostel,** 1 mi. west of town on Louisburgh Rd, is near the entrance to Westport House on Westport Quay. (Tel. (098) 259 03. IR£6. Open Jan.-Nov.) **Old Mill Holiday Hostel (IHH),** James St, is between The Octagon and the tourist office. (Tel. (098) 270 45. IR£7. Sheets IR£1. Laundry. Kitchen.) **SuperValu supermarket** is on Shop St. (Open M-W and Sa 8:30am-7:30pm, Th-F 8:30am-9pm, Su 10am-6pm.)

Nearby, conical **Croagh Patrick** rises 2510 ft. over Clew Bay. The summit has been revered as a holy site for thousands of years. St. Patrick worked it here in AD 441, praying and fasting for 40 days and nights, arguing with angels, and then banishing snakes from Ireland. Climbers start their excursion from the 15th-century **Murrisk Abbey,** several miles west of Westport on R395 toward Louisburgh (4hr. round-trip). **Buses** go to Murrisk (July-Aug. M-F 3 per day, Sept.-June M-Sa 2 per day), but **cabs** (tel. (098) 271 71) for several people are cheaper and more convenient.

NORTHWEST IRELAND

The farmland of the upper Shannon spans northward into County Sligo's mountains, lakes, and ancient monuments. A mere sliver of land connects County Sligo to County Donegal, the most remote of the Republic's counties, with its most spectacular scenery. Donegal's *gaeltacht* is a storehouse of genuine Irish tradition.

SLIGO. Since the beginning of the 20th century, Sligo has been a literary pilgrimage for William Butler Yeats fanatics; the poet spent summers in town as a child, and set many of his poems around Sligo Bay. The county remains as beautiful today as it was when Yeats wrote his odes. **Sligo Town,** the commercial center of the county, does business by day but goes wild at night with one of Ireland's most colorful pub scenes, and is an excellent base from which to explore Yeat's haunts. Most Yeatsian sights are at least a mile from the town center. In town, the 13th-century **Sligo Abbey,** on Abbey St, is well-preserved. (Open daily in summer 9:30am-6:30pm. IR£1.50, students IR£0.60.) **The Niland Gallery,** Stephen St, houses one of the finest collections of modern Irish art along with some first editions of Yeats works. (Open Tu-Sa 10am-noon and 2-5pm. Free.) Yeats is buried per his instructions in **Drumcliffe churchyard,** on the N15, 4 mi. northwest of Sligo. His grave is to the left of the church door. **Buses** from Sligo to Derry stop at Drumcliff (10min.; in summer 1-3 per day, off-season M-Sa 3 per day; return IR£2.60).

Trains (tel. (071) 698 88) go from Lord Edward St to Dublin via Carrick-on-Shannon and Mullingar (3 per day; IR£13.50, students IR£10.50). From the same station, **buses** (tel. (071) 600 66) fan out to Galway (2½hr., 3-4 per day, IR£11); Westport (2½hr., 1-3 per day, IR£9.70); Derry (3hr., 3-6 per day, IR£10); Dublin (4hr., 3 per day, IR£9); and Belfast (4hr., 1-3 per day, IR£12.40). Turn left on Lord Edward St, then follow the signs right on Adelaid St and around the corner to Temple St to find the **tourist office,** on Temple St at Charles St. (Tel. (071) 612 01. Open M-Tu 10am-7pm, W-F 10am-9pm, Sa 10am-6pm.) **B&Bs** cluster on **Pearse Rd,** on the south side of town. **Harbour House,** Finisklin Rd, is 10min. from the station. (Tel. (071) 715 47. Dorms IR£8; private rooms IR£10. Bikes IR£7.) Follow signs from the station to **Rail-**

way Hostel, 1 Union St. (Tel. (071) 445 30. Dorms IR£6.50; private rooms IR£8 per person.) "Faery vats / Full of berries / And reddest stolen cherries" are not to be found in Sligo today; but **Quinnsworth Supermarket,** O'Connell St, sells packaged berries. (Open M-Tu 9am-7pm, W-F 9am-9pm, Sa 9am-6pm.)

DONEGAL COAST AND SLIEVE LEAGUE. Tourists are likely to feel a bit out of place in this most remote and least Anglicized of Ireland's "scenic" provinces. Donegal escaped the widespread deforestation of Ireland; vast wooded areas engulf many of Donegal's mountain chains, while the coastline alternates beautiful beaches with majestic cliffs. Many travelers use **Donegal Town** as the gateway to the county. **Bus Éireann** (tel. (073) 211 01) runs to Sligo (1hr.; M-Sa 7 per day, Su 3 per day); Dublin (4hr., 3-6 per day, IR£10); and Galway (4hr., 2-3 per day, IR£8.80). Buses stop outside the Abbey Hotel on The Diamond; turn right with your back to the hotel to reach the **tourist office,** on Quay St, just outside of The Diamond on Sligo Rd. (Tel. (073) 211 48; www.donegaltown.ie. Open July-Aug. M-Sa 9am-8pm, Su 9am-1pm; Sept.-Nov. and Easter-June M-F 9am-5pm.) ⬛**Donegal Town Hostel (IHH)** is a half-mile out on Killybegs Rd. (Tel. (073) 228 05. Dorms IR£7; doubles IR£17; **camping** IR£4 per person. Laundry. Reserve ahead.)

To the west of Donegal Town lies the **Slieve League Peninsula,** with some of the most stunning scenery in Ireland and the highest sea cliffs in Europe. The sheer face of its 2000-foot drop into the Atlantic is spectacular, and its rugged, wild appearance shows little evidence of human habitation. The few villages on the peninsula all lie along busy N56, which leads from Donegal Town and turns into R63 as it approaches the western tip of the peninsula. **Bus Éireann** runs from Donegal Town to Glencolmcille, stopping in tiny **Kilcar** (3-4 per day), the gateway to Donegal's *gaeltacht* and a commercial base for many Donegal tweed weavers. Most Slieve League hikers stay in Kilcar, from which they can comfortably drive, bike, or walk (about 6hr. round-trip) to the mountain. Nearly 2 mi. out on the coast road from Kilcar to Carrick is the fabulous ⬛**Derrylahan Hostel (IHH);** call for pick-up. (Tel. (073) 380 79. Dorms IR£7; private rooms IR£10; **camping** IR£4. Laundry IR£4.50.) On the western top of the Slieve League peninsula, **Glencolmcille** (glen-kaul-um-KEEL) is renowned for its rolling hills, sandy coves between huge seacliffs, and handmade sweaters. On sunny days, trips to the **Silver Strand** reward with stunning views of the gorgeous beach and surrounding rocky cliffs; from here, you can start the trek along the Slieve League. McGeehan's **buses** leave from Biddy's Bar for Kilcar and Letterkenny (1-2 per day). **Bus Éireann** has services to Kilcar. Snooze at the just peachy ⬛**Dooey Hostel (IHO).** (Dorms IR£6.50; doubles IR£14; **camping** IR£3.50.)

DERRYVEAGH MOUNTAINS. Here, the Donegal Gaeltacht—Irish language, music, and dance—is lived, not practiced. Expansive, sandy beaches are isolated by the eerie stillness of the **Derryveagh Mountains.** On the eastern side of the mountains, **Glenveagh National Park** is 37 sq. mi. of forest glens, bogs, and mountains. The coastal road N56 twists and bends along the jagged edges where Donegal meets the sea, leading through spectacular scenery to **Croll.** From Croll, Feda O'Donnell (tel. (075) 481 14) has a daily **bus** to Galway and Donegal Town via Letterkenny; John McGinley Coaches (tel. (074) 352 01) go to Dublin; and O'Donnell Trans-Ulster Express (tel. (075) 483 56) goes to Belfast. In Croll, just past Paddy Oig's pub, a sign will point you toward ⬛**Screagan an Iolair Hill Hostel** (SCRAG an UH-ler; tel. (075) 485 93), 4 mi. up a mountain road at **Tor** in the national park; turn left off the coastal road at the sign and follow Tor Rd straight there. (Dorms IR£7.50; private rooms IR£9. Laundry IR£3. Call ahead Nov.-Feb.) Trails wind from the hostel up into the the pristine heath lands of the **Derryveagh Mountains,** inhabited by red deer.

LETTERKENNY. Letterkenny is the center of action in Donegal, but that's not saying much. Nonetheless, it's a lively place to make bus connections to the rest of Donegal, the Republic, and Northern Ireland. **Buses** leave from the junction of Port and Derry Rd in front of the Quinnsworth Supermarket. Bus Éireann (tel. (074) 213 09) runs to Derry (40min., 3-10per day, IR£4); Sligo (2hr., 3 per day, IR£9); and Donegal Town (50min., IR£4.80). Feda O'Donnell Coaches (tel. (075) 481 14 or

(091) 761 656) drive to Galway (IR£9) via Donegal Town (2-3 per day, IR£4) and to Croll (IR£4). Lough Swilly Buses (tel. (074) 228 63) head north toward the Fanad Peninsula (M-Sa 2 per day, IR£6) to Derry (M-Sa 9 per day, IR£4). McGeehan's Bus (tel. (074) 461 01) goes twice a day to Glencolmcille (IR£8). The **Chamber of Commerce Visitors Information Centre** is at 40 Port Rd. (Tel. (074) 248 66. Open M-F 9am-5pm.) From the bus station, head up Port Rd toward town and turn right up the lane marked "Covehill House B&B"; continue past the playground, through the parking lot, and up the road to find the **Manse Hostel (IHH),** on High Rd. (Tel. (074) 252 38. Dorms IR£7; doubles and twins IR£16. Dorm sheets IR£0.50.)

INISHOWEN PENINSULA AND MALIN HEAD. It would be a shame to leave Ireland without seeing the Inishowen Peninsula, an untouristed mosaic of pristine mountains, forests, meadows, and white-sand beaches that reaches farther north than "the North." Inishowen's unusual inland landscape is outdone only by its striking northern and western shores. The clearly posted **Inish Eoghin 100** road navigates the peninsula's perimeter, exactly 100 mi. The peninsula's most popular attraction is **Malin Head,** remarkable for its rocky, wave-tattered coast and sky-high sand dunes, reputedly the highest in Europe (up to 100 ft.). The scattered town of Malin Head includes **Bamba's Crown,** the northernmost tip of Ireland, a tooth of dark rock rising up from the ocean spray. The raised beaches around Malin Head are covered with semi-precious stones; walkers sifting through the sands may find jasper, quartz, small opals, or amethysts. Lough Swilly **buses** (Buncrana tel. (077) 613 40; 1½hr.; M, W, and F 1 per day, Sa 3 per day) and Northwest Buses (tel. (077) 826 19; M-Sa 2 per day) run from Derry, the nearest city to Inishowen, to points on the the peninsula including Malin Head. To reach the ■**Sandrock Holiday Hostel (IHO),** Port Ronan Pier, take the left fork off the Inish Eoghin 100, just before the Crossroads Inn (also a bus stop). (Tel. (077) 702 89. IR£6.50. Sheets IR£1. Laundry. Bikes IR£5-7 per day.)

NORTHERN IRELAND

The predominantly calm tenor of life in the North has been overshadowed overseas by media headlines concerning politics and bombs. Northern Ireland's natural beauty includes the Glens of Antrim's pockets of green and Giant's Causeway, one of the world's strangest geological sights. The ceasefires of recent years have allowed Belfast and Derry to develop into hip, pub-loving cities. Pub culture, urban neighborhoods, and tiny villages show everyday life in a divided but mostly peaceful society. The support of the 1998 Peace Agreement raises hopes for a resolution to the struggles that have divided the island for centuries, but the events of 1999 show that the success of the agreement is not yet secure.

The **currency** in Northern Ireland is the British pound. Northern Ireland has its own bank notes, equal in value to English and Scottish notes of the same denominations. Although this currency is *not* accepted outside Northern Ireland, both English and Scottish notes are accepted in the North; currency from the Republic of Ireland is generally not accepted in the North, with the exception of some border towns. It's best to avoid traveling in Northern Ireland during Marching Season (July 4-12), although vacation areas are less affected by the parades. Overall, Northern Ireland has one of the lowest tourist-related crime rates in the world. Border checkpoints have been removed, and armed soldiers and vehicles are less visible in Belfast and Derry. Do not take **photographs** of soldiers, military installations, or vehicles. Unattended luggage is always considered suspicious and worthy of confiscation. It is still generally unsafe to **hitch** in Northern Ireland.

BELFAST

The second-largest city on the island, Belfast (pop. 330,000) is the center of the North's cultural, commercial, and political activity. Acclaimed writers and the annual arts festival in November maintain Belfast's reputation as a thriving artistic center. West Belfast's famous sectarian murals are perhaps the most informative source on the effects of the Troubles (sectarian strife) on the city. The bar scene, a mix of Irish and British pub culture, entertains locals, foreigners, and students. Despite Belfast's reputation as a terrorist-riddled metropolis, the city feels more neighborly than most international—and even Irish—visitors expect.

▶ GETTING THERE AND GETTING AROUND

Flights: Belfast International Airport (tel. 90 42 28 88) in Aldergrove. **Airbus** (tel. 90 33 30 00) goes to the Europa (Glengall St) bus station (M-Sa every 30min., Su every hr.; UK£5). From **Belfast City Airport,** at the harbor, **trains** connect to Central Station (UK£0.90).

Trains: Central Station, East Bridge St (tel. 90 89 94 11). To: **Derry** (2½hr., 3-7 per day, UK£6.70) and **Dublin** (2½hr., 5-8 per day, UK£17).

Buses: Europa (Glengall St) Station (tel. 90 33 30 00) serves the west and the Republic. To: **Dublin** (3-8 per day, UK£10.50) and **Derry** (6-15 per day, UK£6.50). **Laganside Station** serves buses to Northern Ireland's east coast.

Ferries: Belfast SeaCat terminal (tel. (01345) 52 35 23; 3hr.) and **Stena Line ferries** (tel. (01) 204 77 99; www.seaview.co.uk/Stena.html; 1½hr.) go to **Stanraer, Scotland.**

Local Transportation: The red **Citybus Network** (info tel. 90 24 64 85) is supplemented by **Ulsterbus's** "blue buses" to the suburbs. Single-fare within the city center UK£0.50. **Centrelink** green buses traverse the city (every 15min. M-F 7:15am-8:30pm, Sa 8:35am-8:30pm; UK£0.50, free with bus or rail ticket). Late **Nightline** bus tickets (UK£2.50) must be bought in advance from ticket units in Shaftesbury Sq.

Taxis: City Cab (tel. 90 24 20 00). Residents of West and North Belfast utilize the huge **black cabs** that follow set routes. Standard UK£0.60 charge.

▶ ORIENTATION AND PRACTICAL INFORMATION

Buses arrive at the Europa bus station on **Great Victoria St.** To the northeast is the City Hall in **Donegall Sq.** South of the bus station, Great Victoria St meets **Dublin Rd** at **Shaftesbury Sq;** this stretch of Great Victoria St between the bus station and Shaftesbury Sq is known as the **Golden Mile. Botanic Ave** and **Bradbury Pl** (which becomes University Rd) extend south from Shaftesbury Sq into the **Queen's University area,** where cafés, pubs, and budget lodgings await. To get to Donegall Sq from Central Station, turn left, walk down East Bridge St, turn right on Victoria St, and turn left after two blocks on May St, which runs into Donegall Sq South. Or take the Centrelink bus service (free with rail ticket). Divided from the rest of Belfast by the Westlink Motorway, the working-class **West Belfast** area is more politically volatile. The city center, Golden Mile, and the university area are relatively safe.

Belfast: Accommodations
SEE ALSO COLOR INSERT
A EYHANI
B The Ark
C Arnie's Backpackers

IRELAND

Tourist Office: 59 North St, St. Anne's Court (tel. 90 24 66 09). 24-hour computerized info kiosk outside. Open July-Aug. M-F 9am-7pm, Sa 9am-5:15pm, Su noon-4pm; Sept.-June M 9:30am-5:15pm, Tu-Sa 9am-5:15pm.

Travel Agency: USIT, 13b The Fountain Centre, College St (tel. 90 32 40 73), near Royal Ave. Open M and W-F 9:30am-5:30pm, Tu 10am-5:30pm, Sa 10am-4pm.

Consulates: US, Queen's House, Queen St (tel. 90 32 82 39). Open M-F 1-4pm.

Luggage Storage: For security reasons, there is no luggage storage at airports or stations.

Gay and Lesbian Services: Rainbow Project NI (tel. 90 31 90 30). Open M-F 10am-4pm.

Laundry: Duds & Suds, Botanic Ave (tel. 90 24 39 56). Wash UK£1.95, dry £UK1.95; students UK£1.80 each. Open M-F 8am-9pm, Sa 8am-6pm, Su noon-6pm.

Emergency: Dial 999; no coins required. **Police:** 65 Knock Rd (tel. 90 65 02 22).

Hospitals: Belfast City Hospital, 9 Lisburn Rd (tel. 32 92 41).

Internet Access: Belfast Central Library, on Royal Ave. UK£2 per hr. Open M and Th 9:30am-8pm, Tu-W and F 9:30am-5:30pm, Sa 9:30am-1pm.

Post Office: Central Post Office, 25 Castle Pl (tel. 90 32 37 40). Open M-Sa 9am-5:30pm. Address mail to be held: Tom DAVIDSON, *Poste Restante*, CPO, 25 Castle Pl, Belfast **BT1 1NB,** Northern Ireland.

PHONE CODE	The regional code for all of Northern Ireland is 028. From outside Northern Ireland, call int'l dialing prefix (see inside back cover) + 44 (from the Republic, 08) + 28 + local number.

■ ☼ ACCOMMODATIONS AND FOOD

Nearly all of Belfast's budget accommodations are near Queen's University, south of the city center. You can catch a **Centrelink** bus to Shaftesbury Sq, or bus 59, 69-71, 84, or 85 from Donegall Sq East to areas to the south. B&Bs occupy every other house between Malone and Lisburn Rd, just south of Queen's University.

Arnie's Backpackers (IHH), 63 Fitzwilliam St (tel. 90 24 28 67). From Europa bus station on Great Victoria St, turn right away from the Grand Opera House, bear right at Shaftesbury Sq on Bradbury Pl, bear left on University Rd, and Fitzwilliam St is on your right across from the university (15min.). Relaxed atmosphere. Dorms UK£7.50. Key deposit UK£2.

The Ark, 18 University St (tel. 90 32 96 26). Follow directions to Arnie's; University St is the 3rd left off University Rd. A hard place to leave. Dorms UK£6.50-7.50; doubles UK£28. Laundry UK£2.50. **Internet** UK£3.50 per hr. Sony playstation. Curfew 2am.

The Linen House Youth Hostel (IHH), 18-20 Kent St (tel. 90 58 64 00; email info@belfasthostel.com). From Europa bus station, head 2 blocks left on Great Victoria St, 2nd right on Howard St, left on Donegall Pl (opposite the main entrance to City Hall), which becomes Royal Ave, and turn left on Kent St. Dorms UK£6.50-8.50; singles UK£12; doubles and twins UK£20. Laundry UK£3. **Internet** UK£5 per hr. Key deposit UK£5.

Macpackers, 1 Cameron St (tel. 90 22 04 85), just off Botanic Ave. Social atmosphere in a basic setting. 4- to 6-bed dorms UK£7.50.

The George, 9 Eglantine Ave (tel. 90 68 32 12). Immaculately clean B&B in a Victorian row-house. Rooms with shower and TV. Singles UK£20; doubles UK£40-44.

Dublin Rd, Botanic Rd, and the **Golden Mile** have Dublin's highest concentration of restaurants. Munch on ethnic foods from Thai to Cajun at ■**The Other Place,** 79 Botanic Ave, 133 Stranmillis Rd, and 537 Lisburn Rd. (All open M-Sa 8am-11pm.) **Bookfinders,** 47 University Rd, is a super-cool yet relaxed bookstore/café. (Soup, bread, and sandwiches UK£2-3. Open M-Sa 10am-5:30pm.) Get your meat and potatoes in fast-food form at **Spuds,** 23 Bradbury Pl. (Most spuds around UK£2. Open M-W 9am-2am, Th-Sa 9am-3am, Su 9am-1am.) **Spar Market,** at the top of Botanic Rd, is open nearly 24hr. (Open M 6am-Su 3am.)

SIGHTS

DONEGALL SQUARE. The **Belfast City Hall** is the administrative and geographical center of Belfast. Its green copper dome (173 ft.) is visible from any point in the city. *(Tel. 90 32 02 02, ext. 2346. Mandatory tours 1hr.; June-Sept. M-F 10:30, 11:30am, and 2:30pm, and Sa 2:30pm; Oct.-May M-Tu and Th-F 2:30pm, W 11:30am; free.)* One of Belfast's oldest establishments is the **Linen Hall Library,** which contains many Christmas cards, posters, hand bills, and newspaper articles related to Northern Ireland. *(17 Donegall Sq. Open M-W and F 9:30am-5:30pm, Th 9:30am-8:30pm, Sa 9:30am-4pm.)*

CORNMARKET AND ST. ANNE'S CATHEDRAL. Just north of the city center, a shopping district envelops eight blocks around Castle St and Royal Ave. This area has been a marketplace since Belfast's early days. Wander the **entries,** or tiny alleys, around the area, relics of old Belfast. **St. Anne's Cathedral,** also known as the **Belfast Cathedral,** was begun in 1899. Each of the cathedral's interior pillars name Belfast's 10 fields of professionalism, including Science, Agriculture, Shipbuilding, Freemasonry, and Womanhood (a nice enough profession, but the pay is lousy). *(On Donegall St, near the tourist office a few blocks from the city center. Open daily 9am-5pm.)*

THE GOLDEN MILE. This strip along Great Victoria St contains many of Belfast's jewels, including the city's pride and joy, the **Grand Opera House,** which was cyclically bombed by the IRA, restored to its original splendor at enormous cost, and then bombed again. If there's not a rehearsal in progress, they'll give you a tour. *(Ticket office open M-Sa 9:45am-5:30pm.)* The National Trust has restored the highly frequented **Crown Liquor Saloon,** 46 Great Victoria St, to a showcase of carved wood, gilded ceilings, and stained-glass. Damaged by 32 bombs in its history, the **Europa Hotel** has the dubious distinction of being "Europe's most bombed hotel."

QUEEN'S UNIVERSITY AREA. The Queen's University Belfast was designed in 1849, modeled after Oxford's Magdalen College. You can bask in Belfast's occasional sun behind the university at the meticulously groomed **Botanic Gardens.** *(Open daily 8am-dusk. Free.)* The **Ulster Museum,** within the gardens, contains a lovely hodgepodge. *(Off Stranmillis Rd. Open M-F 10am-5pm, Sa 1-5pm, Su 2-5pm. Free.)*

WEST BELFAST AND THE MURALS. Separated from the rest of the city by the Westlink motorway, the neighborhoods of West Belfast have historically been at the heart of the political tensions in the North. Residents of West Belfast provide the best introduction to the city's sectarian neighborhoods; **Black Cab** tours give a fascinating, if biased, commentary. (Arrange tours through hostels; UK£6-7.) The Catholic area centers on **Falls Rd,** while the Protestant neighborhood centers on the **Shankill;** a gray wall known as the **peace line** separates the two. As you wander among the houses, you'll pass by numerous political murals on the streets.

ENTERTAINMENT AND NIGHTLIFE

Belfast's many cultural events and performances are covered in the monthly *Arts Council Artslink* (free at the tourist office). Belfast's **theater** season runs from September to June. The **Grand Opera House,** on Great Victoria St, shows operas, ballets, musicals, and dramas. Buy tickets at the box office, 2-4 Great Victoria St. (Info tel. 24 91 29. Tickets from UK£8; M-Th student rush tickets 50% off after noon.) During the **Queens University Belfast Festival** in November, the city reigns supreme in the art world. (Tel. 90 66 76 87. Tickets UK£2.50-25.)

Pubs close early; start crawling while the sun's still up. In Cornmarket, begin with an afternoon pint at Belfast's oldest pub, **White's Tavern,** Winecellar Entry, off Lombard and Bridge St, which has been serving drinks since 1630. Near the Golden Mile, check out **Katie Daly's** and **The Limelight,** 17 Ormeau Ave, a hip bar/nightclub complex (cover UK£3). Lively **Robinson's,** 38-40 Great Victoria St, houses a Fibber McGees with nightly trad sessions. Put on your dancing shoes and head to **The Fly,** 5-6 Lower Crescent, or swing by **The Eglantine Inn** (the "Egg"), 32 Malone Rd, in the Queen's University area, almost an official extra-curricular. (Open until 1am.)

IRELAND

▶ EXCURSION FROM BELFAST: ULSTER FOLK MUSEUM

In **Holywood,** the **Ulster Folk Museum** and **Transport Museum** stretch over 176 acres. Established by Act of Parliament in the 1950s, the ◪**Folk Museum,** which aims to preserve the way of life of Ulster's farmers, weavers, and craftspeople, contains over 30 buildings from the past three centuries. The **Transport Museum** and the **Railway Museum** are across the road. (Tel. 90 42 84 28. Open July-Aug. M-Sa 10:30am-6pm, Su noon-6pm; Apr.-June and Sept. M-F 9:30am-5pm, Sa 10:30am-6pm, Su noon-6pm; Oct.-Mar. M-F 9:30am-4pm, Sa-Su 12:30-4:30pm. UK£4, students UK£2.50.) Frequent **buses** (45min.) and **trains** (30min.) stop by en route to Bangor.

DERRY (LONDONDERRY)

Modern Derry's determined effort to cast off the legacy of the Troubles has been largely successful. Although the Derry landscape was once razed by years of bombings, and although violence still erupts occasionally during the Marching Season (July 4-12), recent years have been relatively peaceful and today's rebuilt city looks sparklingly new. Derry's **city walls,** 18 ft. high and 20 ft. thick, erected between 1614 and 1619, have never been breached, hence Derry's nickname "the Maiden City." The stone tower along the southeast wall past New Gate was built to protect **St. Columb's Cathedral,** off Bishop St, the symbolic focus of the city's Protestant defenders. (Open M-Sa Apr.-Oct. 9am-5pm, Nov.-Mar. 9am-4pm. Donation UK£1; chapterhouse UK£0.50.) At Union Hall Place, just inside Magazine Gate, the **Tower Museum's** engaging exhibits relay Derry's long history. (Open July-Aug. M-Sa 10am-5pm, Su 2-5pm; Sept.-June Tu-Sa 10am-5pm. UK£3.75, students UK£1.25.) West of the city walls, Derry's residential neighborhoods, both the Catholic **Bogside** as well as the Protestant **Waterside** and **Fountain Estate,** display brilliant murals. After dark, roll by **Peadar O'Donnell's,** 53 Waterloo St, and **The Gweedore Bar,** 59-61 Waterloo St, which have been connected since Famine times.

Trains (tel. 71 34 22 28) arrive on Duke St, Waterside, on the east bank, from Belfast (2½hr., 3-7 per day, UK£6.40). A free **Rail-Link bus** connect the train station and the **bus station,** on Foyle St, between the walled city and the river. Ulsterbus (tel. 71 26 22 61) goes to Belfast (1½-3hr., 8-15 per day, UK£6.80) and Dublin (2-5 per day, UK£10.50). The **tourist office** is at 44 Foyle St. (Tel. 71 26 72 84. Open July-Sept. M-F 9am-7pm, Sa 10am-6pm, Su 10am-5pm; Oct.-Easter M-Th 9am-5:15pm, F 9am-5pm; Easter-June M-Th 9am-5:15pm, F 9am-5pm, Sa 10am-5pm.) Go down Strand Rd and turn left on Asylum Rd just before the RUC station to reach the **Derry City Independent Hostel (Steve's Backpackers),** 4 Asylum Rd. (Tel. 71 37 79 89. UK£7.50. Key deposit UK£2. Laundry. **Internet.**) **Oakgrove Manor (YHANI/HI)** is on Magazine St. (Tel. 71 28 41 00. Dorms UK£7.50-8.50; B&B with bath UK£15. Laundry. Check-out 10am. Reception 24hr.) **Tesco supermarket** is on Strand Rd, in the Quayside Shopping Center. (Open M-Sa 8:30am-9pm, Su 1-6pm.) **Postal code:** BT48 6AA.

GLENS OF ANTRIM

Nine lush green valleys, or "glens," slither from the hills and high moors of County Antrim down to the seashore. **Ulsterbus** (Belfast tel. 90 32 00 11, Larne tel. 28 27 23 45) #162 goes from Belfast to Waterfoot, Cushendall, and Cushendun (3-5 per day). You can also **bike** along the shore.

GLENARIFF. Antrim's broadest (and arguably most beautiful) glen, Glenariff, lies 4 mi. south of Waterfoot along Glenariff Rd in the large **Glenariff Forest Park.** Bus 150 between Cushendun and Ballymena stops at the official park entrance (M-Sa 3-5 per day), but if you're walking from Waterfoot, you can enter the park 1½ mi. downhill of the official entrance by taking the road that branches left toward the Manor Lodge Restaurant. The stunning **Waterfall Trail** follows the cascading, fern-lined Glenariff River from the park entrance to the Manor Lodge. (Tel. 21 75 87 69. Park open daily 10am-8pm. UK£3 per car or UK£1.50 per pedestrian.)

CUSHENDALL. Cushendall is the best place to base yourself in the Glens. **Ulsterbus** 150 runs from Glenariff to Cushendall (M-Sa 3-5 per day); from July to August, the **Antrim Coaster** (#252) runs through Cushendall toward Belfast (2 per day). The **tourist office,** 25 Mill St, is near the bus stop at the Cushendun end of town. (Tel. 21 77 11 80. Open July-Sept. M-F 10am-1pm and 2-5:30pm, Sa 10am-1pm; Oct. to mid.-Sept. and Mar.-June Tu-Sa 10am-1pm.) **Cushendall Youth Hostel (YHANI/HI),** 42 Layde Rd, is a half-mile from town; take the left-hand (uphill) fork from Shore Rd. (Tel. 21 77 13 44. UK£8.25. Laundry. Bike rental. Reception 7:30am-10:30am and 5-11pm.) Or sleep at ▨**Glendale,** run by Mrs. Mary O'Neill, 46 Coast Rd. (Tel. 21 77 14 95. UK£16.)

CUSHENDUN. This miniscule, picturesque seaside village is 5 mi. (an easy bike ride) north of Cushendall on A2. This white-washed and black-shuttered set of buildings lies by a beach with wonderful, dark **caves** carved within red sea cliffs. **Mary McBride's,** 2 Main St, used to be the *Guinness Book of World Records'* "smallest bar in Europe" until it expanded. **Buses** stop in Cushendun en route to Waterfoot via Cushendall (June-Sept. 3-9 per day; Oct.-May 1-7 per day).

CAUSEWAY COAST

Past Cushendun, the northern coast shifts from lyrical into dramatic mode. Sea-battered, 600-foot-tall cliffs tower over white wave-lapped beaches and give way to spectacular **Giant's Causeway,** a spillage of 40,000 black and red hexagonal stone columns formed by volcanic eruptions 65 million years ago.

In good summer weather, **Bushmills Bus** (Coleraine tel. (01265) 70 43 33 34) outlines the coast between Coleraine, 5 mi. south of Portrush, and Giant's Causeway (July-Aug. 5 per day). In the summer, the Antrim Coaster (Belfast tel. 90 33 30 00) runs up the coast from Belfast to Portstewart via every town listed here (late June to early July M-Sa 2 per day; early July to late Sept. daily 2 per day).

BALLYCASTLE AND ENVIRONS. The Causeway Coast leaves the sleepy glens behind when it hits this bubbly seaside town, popular with Giant's Causeway-bound tourists. **Ulsterbus** rides to Cushendall via Cushendun (50min., M-F 1 per day) and Belfast (3hr., M-Sa 4-6 per day). The **tourist office** is in Sheskburn House, 7 Mary St. (Tel. 20 76 20 24. Open July-Aug. M-F 9:30am-7pm, Sa 10am-6pm, Su 2-6pm; Sept.-June M-F 9:30am-5pm.) Snooze at **Castle Hostel (IHH),** 62 Quay Rd (tel. 20 76 23 37), or **Ballycastle Backpackers Hostel,** 4 North St (tel. 70 26 36 12), next to the Marine Hotel. (Dorms UK£6; private rooms UK£7.50 per person.)

Just off the coast at Ballycastle, beautiful, bumpy, boomerang-shaped **Rathlin Island** ("Fort of the Sea") is the ultimate in escapism for 20,000 puffins, the odd golden eagle, and 100 human beings. Caledonian MacBrayne **ferries** run to the island from the pier at Ballycastle, up the hill from Quay Rd on North St. (45min., 2-4 per day, return UK£7.80); pick up schedules from the Ballycastle tourist office.

Five miles from Ballycastle, the modest village of **Ballintoy** attracts the crowds on their way to itsy-bisty teeny-tiny **Carrick-a-rede Island.** Cross the shaky, 4-inch-wide, 67-foot fishermen's rope bridge over the dizzying 100-foot drop to rocks and sea below; **be extremely careful in windy weather.** A sign marks the turn-off from the coastal road a half-mile east of Ballintoy.

GIANT'S CAUSEWAY. Advertised as the eighth natural wonder of the world, Giant's Causeway is Northern Ireland's most famous sight. A spillage of 40,000 hexagonal columns of basalt form a 60-million-year-old honeycomb path from the foot of the cliffs far into the sea. Many paths loop to and from the Causeway. The **Giant's Causeway Visitors Centre,** which sits at the entrance to the Causeway from the car park, runs a bus to the columns (every 15min., return UK£1). (Tel. 20 73 18 55. Open daily June 10am-6pm; July-Aug. 10am-7pm; Mar.-May and Sept. 10am-5pm; Nov.-Feb. 10am-4:30pm.)

IRELAND

ITALY (ITALIA)

US$1 = L1833 (LIRE)	L1000 = US$0.55
CDN$1 = L1240	L1000 = CDN$0.79
UK£1 = L2940	L1000 = UK£0.34
IR£1 = L2458	L1000 = IR£0.41
AUS$1 = L1195	L1000 = AUS$0.84
NZ$1 = L973	L1000 = NZ $1.03
SAR1 = L300	L1000 = SAR3.33
EUR€1 = L1936	L1000 = EUR€0.51

PHONE CODE   Country code: 39. International dialing prefix: 00.

In the span of time between the stabbing of Julius Caesar and the acceptance of Italy into the European Monetary Union, the boot-shaped land-mass has undergone numerous transformations. Toward the end of the last two millennia, the former city-states were mashed together under the red, white, and green flag of Mother Italy; but prior to and since that time, the provinces have hit dizzying highs, terrifying lows, and creamy middles. Italy—both as separate regions and as one nation—has run the gamut in economic prosperity, cultural respectability, and military might. Throughout its long, convoluted history, Italy has commanded the center stage of world events: first as the base for the ambitious Roman empire; later, as persecutor and popularizer of an upstart religion called Christianity; next as the hub of the artistic and philosophical Renaissance; and finally as a world power that has changed governments more than 50 times since World War II. Italy has long been a prized international possession, both for its terrain and its key position. Countless invasions have left the land rich with examples of nearly every artistic era. Egyptian obelisks, Etruscan huts, Greek temples, Augustan arches, Byzantine mosaics, Renaissance *palazzi*, Baroque fountains, and Fascist superstructures sprawl across the 19 regions. The fusion of these Italian regions under one Viva Italia creates a vibrant patchwork of dialects, dress, customs, and artistic styles that separate the prosperous, industrialized north from the poorer, agricultural south.

In the Board Meeting of the World, Italy may be viewed as the jaded senior member: "Been there, done that," he says, slumping on the couch of the Mediterranean, "let's break for lunch." Through its history, Italy has learned to enjoy the finer things in life, like sumptuous culinary delights. From the meats of the Veneto to the cheeses of Sardinia and from perfect pasta to the creation pizza, Italy has found that the best way to a country's happiness is through its stomach. But when Italy isn't eating, it's loving. The Italian language has been the trademark of romance—its mellifluous syllables inspiring passionate lovers to proclaim their *amore* from the rooftops of the world. But whatever your tastes, Italy is sure to please.

Glean fistfuls of informative tips from *Let's Go: Italy 2000*.

DISCOVER ITALY

The inevitable place to begin an Italian voyage is in **Rome,** where you can view the rubble of the toga-clad empire, the cathedrals of high Christianity, and the art of the Renaissance, then whizz around wildly on a moto (p. 553). Shoot north to shun worldly wealth a la St. Francis in **Assisi** (p. 615), before checking out the black-and-white *duomo* of stunning **Siena** (p. 612) and the medieval towers of **San Gimignano** (p. 613). Continue the northward jaunt to be enchanted by **Florence,** where burnt-orange roofs shelter incredible works by Renaissance grandmasters (p. 601). Make a quick stop to prop up the Leaning Tower in **Pisa** (p. 614) before reaching pastel houses clinging to mountain cliffs in the five bright fishing villages of **Cinque Terre** on the Italian Riviera (p. 596). Leave the coast for oh-so hip **Milan** (p. 586), and then

Italy

relax on the achingly beautiful shores of **Lake Como** (p. 584). Afterwards, start moving south to indulge your Shakespeare fetish in **Verona** (p. 581). In romantic **Venice** misty mornings give way to mystical *palazzi* (p. 572). For a change of pace, head to glittering **Ravenna**, a Byzantine treasure chest on the east coast (p. 600) and move inland to sample **Bologna's** culinary delights (p. 597). Haul way down to **Naples**, home to the world's best pizza and pickpockets (p. 617). Take a daytrip to **Pompeii** and check out randy Roman remains buried in AD 79 (p. 620). Next is captivating **Capri** (p. 622) and the **Amalfi Coast** (p. 621), framed by crystal-blue waters. Return to Naples and board the ferry to vibrant **Palermo** (p. 625), the perfect start to Sicily. Take in the stunning Arab-Romanesque art of nearby **Monreale** (p. 626) and temple hop to **Agrigento** (p. 626). From there, continue to **Syracuse**, which boasts a theater and beautiful grottoes (p. 626). A cliff city of unsurpassed beauty, **Taormina** (p. 627) is the perfect next stop. Round out your tour of Sicily (and Italy) at the spectacular **Aeolian Islands** (p. 627), with beaches of ebony sand, and a gurgling volcano.

GETTING THERE AND GETTING AROUND

BY PLANE. **Rome's** international airport (known as both Fiumicino and Leonardo da Vinci) is served by most major airlines. You can also fly into **Milan's** Malpensa or Linate Airports or **Florence's** international airport. **Alitalia** (US tel. (800) 223-5730) is Italy's national airline and may offer off-season youth fares.

BY TRAIN. The **Ferrovie dello Stato (FS)** (national info tel. 147 88 80 88; www.fs-online.com), the Italian State Railway, runs more or less on time and its network is comprehensive. A *locale* train stops at nearly every station; the *diretto* goes faster but serves fewer stations, while the *espresso* stops only at major stations. The *rapido*, an InterCity (IC) train, zips along but costs a bit more. If you plan to travel extensively in Italy and are under 26, the **Cartaverde** should be your first purchase (L40,000, valid for 1 year) which gives a 20% discount on any state rail fare. **Eurail** is accepted within Italy, but if you are planning on extensive domestic travel you can look into the two-week **Italian Rail Pass**, a cheaper alternative to the Eurail Pass. But since regular fares are cheap, these railpasses are seldom cost-effective. For more information, contact the **Italian State Railways**, 666 Fifth Ave, 5th fl., New York, NY 10103 (tel. (212) 730 2121).

BY BUS. Intercity buses are often more convenient for shorter hauls off the main rail lines, and they serve countryside points inaccessible by train. For **city buses**, buy tickets in *tabacchi*, newsstands, or kiosks, and validate them on board.

BY FERRY. Ferry services in the port towns of **Bari** (p. 617), **Brindisi** (p. 624), and **Ancona** (p. 616) connect Italy to **Greece.** Unless you have a Eurailpass (honored only at Brindisi), the ferries from Bari and Ancona are preferable—they're cheaper and less crowded. Boats from **Trieste** (see p. 582) serve the Istrian Peninsula as far south as **Croatia's** Dalmatian Coast. Ferries also connect Italy's islands to the mainland. For **Sardinia**, catch a boat in **Genoa** (p. 593), **La Spezia** (p. 597), or **Naples** (p. 617). **Sicily**-bound travelers should take the ferry from **Naples** or **Reggio di Calabria** (p. 625).

BY CAR. An *Autostrada* (super-highway) is a worthy successor to the Appian Way, but tolls are prohibitive, and Italian driving is frightening. Driving can be particularly challenging in Rome, Milan, and Naples; congested traffic is more common in cities and in the north. There is an extensive network of smaller highways: *strade statali* (national), *provinciali* (provincial), and *communali* (municipal). On three lane roads, be aware that the center lane is for passing. Helpful words include: gasoline *(benzina)*, entrance *(entrata)*, exit *(uscita)*, one-way *(senso unico)*, and 'no parking' *(vietato parcheggiare)*. Gas is about US$4 per gallon. It is possible to drive into Italy from Austria, France, Slovenia, or Switzerland. From Switzerland, take the Simplon Pass through the Alps and into Italian wine country (Zurich to Milan, about 5hr.). Some mountain passes close in winter; check ahead. Ljubljana, Slovenia, is only an hour east of Trieste. From Chamonix, France, Milan is a three-hour drive; from Nice to Genoa is about 2hr. From Innsbruck, Austria, to Verona about 4hr.; from Trieste to Graz about 5hr.; Salzburg is a bit farther.

Mopeds (L40-60,000 per day) can be a great way to see the islands and the more scenic areas of Italy, but can be disastrous in the rain and on rough roads.

BY BIKE AND BY THUMB. Bicycling is a popular national sport, but bike trails are rare, drivers often reckless, and, except in the Po Valley, the terrain challenging. Although hitchhiking is relatively common, *Let's Go* urges travelers to consider the safety risks. Women should never hitchhike alone.

ESSENTIALS

DOCUMENTS AND FORMALITIES. Citizens of Australia, Canada, Ireland, New Zealand, South Africa, the UK, and the US need valid passports to enter Italy and to re-enter their own country. British, Irish, and EU citizens need only carry a valid passport to enter Italy, and they may stay in the country for as long as they like. Citizens of Australia, Canada, New Zealand, South Africa, and the US do not need visitor visas for up to three months. Those wishing to stay in Italy for more than three months must apply for a *permesso di soggiorno* (residence permit) at a police station *(questura)*. For more info, contact the Italian embassy in your country.

Italian Embassies at Home: Australia, 12 Grey St, Deakin, A.C.T. 2601; P.O. Box 360, **Canberra City** A.C.T. 2601 (tel. (02) 62 73 33 33; fax 62 73 42 23); **Canada,** 275 Slater St, 21st fl., Ottawa, ON K1P 5H9 (tel. (613) 232-2401; fax 233-1484; www.trytel.com/~italy); **Ireland,** 63/65 Northumberland Rd, Dublin 4 (tel. (3531) 660 17 44; fax 668 27 59; email italianembassy@tinet.ie); **New Zealand,** 34 Grant Rd, Wellington (tel. (04) 473 53 39; fax 472 72 55; email ambwell@xtra.co.nz); **South Africa,** 796 George Ave, Arcadia 0083, Pretoria (tel. (012) 43 55 41; fax 43 55 47; www.smartnet.co.za/ambital); **UK,** 14 Three Kings Yard, London W1Y 2EH (tel. (020) 73 12 22 00; fax 73 12 22 30; www.embitaly.org.uk); **US,** 1601 Fuller St NW, Washington, DC 20009 (tel. (202) 328-5500; fax 462-3605; www.italyemb.org).

Italian Embassies in Italy: All embassies are in **Rome** (see p. 554).

TOURIST OFFICES. In provincial capitals, look for the **Ente Provinciale per il Turismo (EPT)** or **Azienda di Promozione Turistica (APT)** for info on the entire province and the town. Local tourist offices, **Informazione e Assistenza ai Turisti (IAT)** and **Azienda Autonoma di Soggiorno e Turismo (AAST),** are generally the most useful. Also keep an eye out for **Pro Loco, Centro Turistico Studentesco e Giovanile (CTS),** and **Compagnia Italiana Turismo (CIT).**

Italian Government Tourist Boards (ENIT) at Home: Australia, Level 26, 44 Market St, Sydney NSW 2000 (tel. (02) 92 62 16 66; fax (02) 9262 57 45); **Canada,** 1 pl. Ville Marie #1914, Montréal, Québec H3B 2C3 (tel. (514) 866-7668; fax 392-1429; email initaly@ican.net); **UK,** 1 Princess St, London WIR 9AY (tel. (020) 74 08 12 54; fax 74 93 66 95; email Enitlond@globalnet.co.uk); **US,** 630 Fifth Ave #1565, New York, NY 10111 (tel. (212) 245-5618; fax 586-9249; www.italiantourism.com).

MONEY. The **currency** in Italy is the lira. Banks tend to offer the best exchange rates. A thrifty traveler staying in a hostel, preparing meals from supermarket supplies, and visiting few sights can get by on L55-60,000 a day. Travelers who indulge, staying in more luxurious spots, could make it on L100,000 a day.

Tipping and Bargaining: Italian tipping customs are complicated and vary by region. In touristed areas, a service charge will probably be added to restaurant and hotel bills; leave an additional 5-10%. In cafés, leave L500 if you sat at a table, and L100-200 if you stood at the counter. Maids, bellhops, and valets get L1-2000 tip per day. Give taxi drivers 10%. Tour guides get L2000 tip for a half-day tour.

Taxes: The value added tax in Italy (known as IVA) ranges from 12-35%. Upon departure from the EU, non-EU citizens can get a refund of the VAT for purchases over L650,000.

COMMUNICATION

Post: Airmail letters under 1 oz. between North America and Italy take 4 to 7 days and cost US$0.90 or CDN$1.35. Allow at least 10 days from Australia (postage AUS$1.52 for up to 1oz.) and at least 6 days from Britain (postage UK£0.64 for up to 1 oz.). Envelopes should be marked "air mail" or "par avion." Since Italian mail is notoriously unreliable, it is usually safer and quicker (but more expensive) to send mail express *(espresso)* or registered *(raccomandata)*. *Fermo Posta* is Italian for *Poste Restante*. When picking up your mail, bring a form of photo ID, preferably a passport.

Telephone: Some take only coins—put more in than you think you'll need, or risk getting cut off. *Scatti* calls (often available only from telephone offices) are made from a phone run by an operator. A meter records the cost of the call, and you pay when you finish. Check first for a service fee. The most common type of phone accepts phone cards (L5000, L10,000, or L15,000 from *tabacchi*, newsstands, bars, post offices, and the occasional machine). A collect call is a *contassa a carico del destinatario* or *chiamata collect*. **International direct dial** numbers include: **AT&T,** 172 10 11; **Sprint,** 172 18 77; **MCI World-**

ITALY

Phone Direct, 172 10 22; **Canada Direct,** 172 10 01; **BT Direct,** 172 00 44; **Ireland Direct,** 172 03 53; **Australia Direct,** 172 10 61; **Telecom New Zealand Direct,** 172 10 64; **Telkom South Africa Direct,** 172 10 27. In an **emergency,** call the **police** at 112, **fire department** at 115, **medical help** at 113, and English-speaking **operator** at 170.

Language: Any knowledge of Spanish, French, Portuguese, or Latin will help you understand Italian. The tourist office staff usually speaks some English. For a traveler's survival kit of basic Italian, see p. 949.

SAFETY AND CUSTOMS. Italy's cathedrals and churches are religious institutions and not museums. Don't visit during mass, and *cover your knees and shoulders;* the more conservative your appearance, the more likely you are to see what you came for. Italian men, in general, have earned their tarnished reputation.

ACCOMMODATIONS AND CAMPING. Associazione Italiana Alberghi per la Gioventù (AIG), the Italian **hostel** federation and an affiliate of Hostelling International (HI), operates dozens of youth hostels *(ostelli per la gioventù)* across the country, especially in the north. A complete list is available from most **EPT** and **CTS** offices and from many hostels. Prices average about L50-55,000 per night, including breakfast. Hostels are the best option for solo travelers (single rooms are relatively scarce in hotels), but curfews, lockouts, out-of-the-way locations, and less than perfect security detract from their appeal. For more information on hostels in Italy, contact the **AIG office,** V. Cavour, 44 (tel. 06 487 11 52), in Rome.

Italian hotel rates are set not by private owners but by the state; hotel owners will need your passport to register you, don't be afraid to hand it over for a while (usually overnight), but ask for it as soon as you think you will need it. One-star *pensioni* are the best options. Prices fluctuate by region, but singles usually start around L45,000, doubles L70,000. By law, the price must be posted in each room; if it isn't, get it in writing. Always check to see if breakfast and showers are additional and/or mandatory. A room with a private bath *(con bagno)* usually costs 30-50% more. A new breed of tourist office, the **Azienda di Promozione Turismo (APT),** provides list of hotels that have paid to be listed; some of the hotels we recommend may not be on the list. **Affittacamere** (rooms to let in private residences) can be significantly less. Try to reach your destination and begin looking for accommodations before noon, especially in summer. If you must arrive late, call and reserve a day ahead. **Camping** sites tend to be loud and modern and cost around L8000 per person (or tent) plus L7000 per car, much more near big cities.

FOOD AND DRINK. *"Mangia, mangia!"* For simple, hearty, and inexpensive eating, try *alimentari* stores; they often prepare *panini* (sandwiches) with cold cuts and cheese: *Bel Paese, provolone, La Fontina,* or *mozzarella. Rosticcerie* sell hot food to take out and are often the cheapest option for a filling dinner. A *tavola calda* is a cheap, sit-down option. *Osterie, trattorie,* and *ristoranti* are, in ascending order, fancier and more expensive. They are usually open 12:30-2pm and 7-11pm (later in the south). Pizza can be sold by the *etto* (100g) or the *fetta* (slice) in a *pizza a taglio* place. In a sit-down pizzeria, you can order a whole round pizza. Menus in smaller restaurants are often incomplete or nonexistent; ask for the *piatti del giorno* (daily specials). A *menù turistico,* when offered, might run only L15-25,000 for a full meal, but variety is limited. Sit-down establishments often charge *pane e coperto* (bread and cover charge), usually around L2-3000. Check whether service is included *(servizio compreso).* A full meal consists of an *antipasto* (appetizer), a *primo* (pasta or soup), a *secondo* (meat or fish) occasionally with a *contorno* (vegetable), and usually salad, fruit, and/or cheese. In the north, butter and cream sauces dominate. Rome and central Italy are notoriously spicy regions. Farther south, tomatoes play an increasingly significant role. Pastries also become sweeter toward the south. Coffee is another rich and varied focus of Italian life; espresso is to shoot, cappuccino is the breakfast beverage. *Caffè macchiato* ("spotted") is espresso with a touch of milk, while *latte macchiato* is milk with a splash of coffee. Wines from the north of Italy, such as the Piedmont's *Asti Spumante* or Verona's *Soave,* tend to be heavy and full-bodied; stronger, fruitier wines come from the hotter climate of south Italy and the islands. In almost every Italian town you can find numerous shops selling Italy's greatest contribution to civilization: *gelato* (ice cream).

LOCAL FACTS

Time: Italy is 1hr. ahead of Greenwich Mean Time (GMT; see p. 49).

Climate: Summers are humid and hot in the north, drier and hotter in the south. Winters are ferocious in the Alps and cold and damp in Venice and Florence, but Sicilian waters are swimmable year-round. Mid-Apr. to mid-June or mid-Sept. to Oct. may be the best times to visit, when temperatures are moderate and the crowds are not at their peak.

Hours: Nearly everything closes from around 1 to 3 or 4pm for siesta. Most museums are open 9am-1pm and 3-6pm; some are open through lunch, however. Monday is often their *giorno di chiusura* (day of closure). Food shops have a different *giorno di chiusura* from province to province.

Holidays: Italy closes on the following holidays: New Year's Day (Jan. 1); Epiphany (Jan. 6); Easter Sunday and Monday (Apr. 23-24); Liberation Day (Apr. 25); Labor Day (May 1); Assumption of the Virgin (Aug. 15); All Saints' Day (Nov. 1); Immaculate Conception (Dec. 8); Christmas Day (Dec. 25); and Santo Stefano (Dec. 26). August is vacation month for Italians; the cities shut down and empty out.

Festivals: The most common excuse for a local festival is the celebration of a religious event—a patron saint's day or the commemoration of a miracle. Most of these festivals include parades, music, wine, obscene amounts of food, and general boisterousness. Though **Jubilee 2000** will take place during the entire year, smaller local festivities add a unique flavor to any vacation. **Carnevale,** held in February during the 10 days before Lent, energizes Italian towns; in Venice, costumed Carnevale revelers fill the streets and canals (see p. 572). During **Scoppio del Carro,** held in Florence's P. del Duomo on Easter Sunday, Florentines set off a cart of explosives, following a tradition dating back to medieval times. On July 2 and Aug. 16, the **Palio** hits Siena (see p. 612), which celebrates the event with a horse race around the central *piazza*.

ROME (ROMA)

Rome is a sensory overload, rushing down the hills of Lazio to knock you flat on your back, gasping for air, and dying for more. Even today, its glory is not dimmed, its head not bowed, its ruins not—well, ruined. Augustus boasted that he had found a Rome a city of brick and left it one of marble, but his work was only the start. For 2000 years, Caesars and popes built forums, churches, temples, palaces, and *piazze*, all testifying to monumental ambitions and egos. This capital of kingdoms and republics, this home of the Roman Empire and the Catholic Church, and the cities under its control dictated over 2000 years of world history, politics, art, architecture, and literature. The city contains so much to see, hear, eat, smell, and absorb that it feels at once exhilarating and overwhelming, as if it's impossible to experience everything, or even anything. Pilgrims who try to conquer Rome often find themselves wearied by its twisting, hot alleyways and multilayered design. But why worry about what has been missed? In *bella Roma*, everything is beautiful, and everything tastes good. Liberate your senses from the pollution eroding the monuments and from the maniacal crush of motorcyclists, and enjoy the dizzying paradox that is the *Caput Mundi*, the Eternal City, Rome.

For more detailed information about Rome, curl up with *Let's Go: Rome 2000*.

■ GETTING THERE AND GETTING AROUND

Flights: Leonardo da Vinci International Airport (tel. 06 659 51), known as **Fiumicino,** handles most flights. The Termini **train** line runs nonstop to Termini Station (30min., every hr. 8am-10pm, L16,000). When trains aren't running, take the blue COTRAL **bus** to Tiburtina (2 per hr., L15,000); buy tickets on the bus. From Tiburtina, take bus 40N to Termini Station. Most charter and a few domestic flights arrive at **Ciampino** airport (tel. 06 79 49 41); a COTRAL bus runs to Ciampino (every 30min., L2000) from Anagnina on Metro A.

ITALY

Trains: The main station is **Termini. Railway Info,** at the front entrance facing P. dei Cinquecento, houses the **Eurail Office.** Open daily 7am-10pm. To: **Naples** (2-2½hr., L29,500); **Florence** (2-3hr., L38,500); **Venice** (5hr., L66,000); and **Milan** (5-6hr., L58,000). Trains arriving midnight-5am may arrive at **Stazione Tiburtina** or **Stazione Ostiense;** take the 40N or 20N-21N buses, respectively, to Termini.

Public Transit: The 2 **Metropolitana** subway lines meet at Termini and run 5:30am-11:30pm. **Buses** run 6am-midnight; board only at the front or back doors, and validate your ticket in the machine at the back. Buy subway and bus **tickets** (L1500) at *tabacchi,* newsstands, and machines in stations; they are valid for 1 ride on the Metro or unlimited bus travel within 1¼hr. of validation (no transfers between the Metro and bus networks). **B.I.G. daily tickets** (L8000) and **C.I.S. weekly tickets** (L32,000) allow unlimited bus or train travel everywhere in the *Comune di Roma,* including Ostia but not Fiumicino.

Taxis: Prontotaxi (tel. 06 66 45); **Societa Cooperativa Autoradio Taxi** (tel. 06 35 70); **Cosmos la Capitale** (tel. 06 49 94). From the city center to the airport L70,000. Base fare L4500. Surcharges: night L5000; Su L2000; luggage L2000; airport L14,000.

Bike Rental: In summer, there are bike rental stands in P. S. Lorenzo at V. del Corso, and at V. di Pontifici and V. del Corso. Open daily 10am-7pm. **Scooters For Rent,** V. della Purificazione 84 (tel. 06 488 54 85), off P. Barberini, rents bikes (L20,000 per day) and mopeds (L50,000 per day). Open daily 9am-7pm. V, MC, AmEx.

■ ORIENTATION

From the train station, **Termini,** the arrival point for most visitors to Rome, **Via Nazionale** is the central artery connecting **Piazza della Repubblica** with **Piazza Venezia,** home to the immense **Vittorio Emanuele II Monument.** West of P. Venezia, **Largo Argentina** marks the start of C. Vittorio Emanuele II, which leads into **Centro Storico,** the tangle of sights around the **Pantheon, Piazza Navona, Campo dei Fiori,** and **Piazza Farnese.** From P. Venezia, V. dei Fori Imperiale leads southeast to the **Forum** and **Colosseum,** south of which are the ruins of the **Baths of Caracalla** and the **Appian Way. Via del Corso** stretches from P. Venezia north to **Piazza del Popolo.** East of the Corso, chic streets border the **Piazza di Spagna** and, above P. del Popolo, the **Villa Borghese.** South and east are the **Fontana di Trevi, Piazza Barberini,** and the **Quirinal Hill.** Across the **Tiber River** to the north is **Vatican City** and the crenelated **Castel Sant'Angelo.** To the south is **Trastevere,** the best neighborhood for wandering. Across the Tiber from Trastevere is the old **Jewish Ghetto.** South of the Ghetto and the Ancient City are the **Aventine Hill** and the working-class **Testaccio** district.

Some people say that it's impossible to navigate the winding streets of Rome without a map. These people are, in fact, correct. Try to pick up the official **Jubileum** map at tourist offices. For more detail, refer to this book's myriad **color maps** of the city.

■ PRACTICAL INFORMATION

TOURIST AND FINANCIAL SERVICES

Tourist Offices: EPT (tel. 06 487 12 70), in Termini, in the middle of the main concourse. Long lines. Open M-Sa 8:15am-7pm. **Central Office,** V. Parigi 5 (tel. 06 48 89 92 55; fax 06 48 89 92 28). From Termini, cross P. Cinquecento diagonally to the left, cross P. della Repubblica, and take V. Parigi from the other side of the church, near the Grand Hotel. Open M-Sa 8:15am-7pm. **Enjoy Rome,** V. Varese 39 (tel. 06 445 18 43; fax 06 445 07 34; www.enjoyrome.com). From Termini, cross V. Marsala, walk 3 blocks on V. Milazzo, and turn right on V. Varese. Arranges lodgings as well as walking and biking tours. Open M-F 8:30am-2pm and 3:30-6:30pm, Sa 8:30am-2pm.

Budget Travel: Centro Turistico Studentesco (CTS), V. Genova 16 (tel. 06 462 04 31), off V. Nazionale. Other branches elsewhere. Open M-F 9am-1pm and 2-6pm.

Embassies and Consulates: Australia, V. Alessandria 215 (tel. 06 85 27 21; fax 85 27 23 00). Consular and passport services around the corner at C. Trieste 25. Open M-Th 8:30am-12:30pm and 1:30-4:30pm, F 8:30am-1:15pm. **Canada,** V. De Rossi 27, 5th fl. (tel. 06 44 59 81; fax 44 59 89 12). Open M-F 9am-noon and 2-4pm. **Ireland,** Largo

Rome: Around Termini Station

ACCOMMODATIONS

A Hotel Virginia
B Pensione Papa Germano
C M&J Place
D Hotel Lachea & Hotel Dolomiti
E Hotel Des Artistes
F Hotel Continentale
G Pensione Fawlty Towers
H Hotel Magic
I Hotel Giugiu
J Hotel San Paolo
K Pensione Sandy
L Hotel Orlanda
M Pensione di Rienzo
N Pensione Cortorillo
O Hotel Kennedy

Nazareno 3 (tel. 06 678 25 41). **New Zealand,** V. Zara 28 (tel. 06 441 71 71; fax 440 29 84). Open July-Aug. M-Th 8am-12:30pm and 1-4pm, F 8am-1pm; Sept.-June M-F 8:30am-12:45pm and 1:45-5pm. **South Africa,** V. Tanaro 14 (tel. 06 85 25 41; fax 06 85 25 43 00). **UK,** V. XX Settembre 80A (tel. 06 482 54 41; fax 06 48 90 30 73). Open Sept. to mid-July M-F 9:15am-1:30pm and 2-4pm; mid-July to Aug. M-F 8am-1pm. **US,** V. Veneto 119A (tel. 06 467 41; fax 06 46 74 22 17). Open M-F 8:30am-noon and 2-4pm.

American Express: P. di Spagna 38 (tel. 06 67 64 13). Mail held. Good exchange rates and great free maps; long lines. Open Aug. M-F 9am-6pm, Sa 9am-12:30pm; Sept.-July M-F 9am-7:30pm, Sa 9am-3pm.

Thomas Cook: P. Barberini 21A (tel. 06 482 80 82). Cashes Thomas Cook traveler's checks free; all others 3% commission. Sells phone cards and Metro tickets. Open M-Sa 9am-8pm, Su 9:30am-5pm.

LOCAL SERVICES

Luggage Storage: In Termini, at track 22. L5000 per 12hr. Open daily 5:15am-12:20am.

English Bookstores: Libreria Feltrinelli International, V. V. E. Orlando 84/86 (tel. 06 482 78 78), near P. della Repubblica. Open daily 9am-7:30pm. V, MC, AmEx. **Anglo-American Bookshop,** V. della Vite 102 (tel. 06 679 52 22), south of the Spanish Steps. Open daily 9am-7:30pm. V, MC, AmEx.

Gay and Lesbian Services: ARCI-GAY, V. Primo Acciaresi 7 (tel. 06 855 55 22), off V. Tiburtina. Open M-F 3-7pm, Sa 4:30-7:30pm.

Laundromat: OndaBlu, V. G. de Mattheis 7 (tel. 06 44 25 14 91), at P. Bologna. Rome's first self-serve laundromat chain. "Almost a nightclub." Wash or dry L6000 per 6.5kg; soap L2000. Open daily 8am-10pm. **Aqua & Sapone,** V. Montebello 66, near Termini.

EMERGENCY AND COMMUNICATIONS

Police: Tel. 113. **Carabinieri:** Tel. 112. **Ufficio Stranieri (Foreigners' Office):** V. Genova 2 (tel. 06 46 86 28 76), around the corner from Questura. Open 24hr.

Pharmacies: Farmacia Internazionale, P. Barberini 49 (tel. 06 487 11 95), west of Termini. V, MC. **Farmacia Piram,** V. Nazionale 228 (tel. 06 488 07 54). V, MC. All open 24hr.

Hospital: Rome-American Hospital, V. E. Longoni 69 (tel. 06 225 51).

Internet Access: Internet Café, V. dei Marrucini 12 (tel./fax 06 445 49 53; www.internetcafe.it), in San Lorenzo, 15min. from Termini. L8-10,000 per hr. Open M-F 9am-2am, Sa-Su 5pm-2am. **Marco's (Evergreen Cultural Center),** V. Varese 33 (tel. 06 44 70 35 91), 3 blocks north of Termini. L7000 per hr. Open daily 10am-2am.

Telephones: Though there are coin-operated phones, most use **phone cards** (L5000, L10,000, or L15,000), sold at *tabacchi,* newsstands, bars, post offices, and machines in stations. At the **Telecom** office in the main concourse of Termini you can make metered calls *(telefoni a scatti).* Open daily 8am-9:45pm. **English-speaking operator:** tel. 170.

Post Office: Main Office, P. S. Silvestro 19, south of P. di Spagna; take bus 56, 60, 71, or 492. Address mail to be held: Melissa GIBSON, Palazzo delle Poste, *In Fermo Posta,* Roma **00186,** Italy. **Branch,** V. delle Terme di Diocleziano 30 (tel. 06 48 64 76), next to Termini. Open M-F 9am-6pm, Sa 9am-2pm. **Postal codes:** 00100 to 00200.

PHONE CODE	Italian city codes are included in local numbers. From outside Italy, dial int'l dialing prefix + 39 + local number.

☝ ACCOMMODATIONS AND CAMPING

Rome swells with tourists around Easter, from May through July, and in September. Termini is swarming with hotel scouts; some have legitimate IDs issued by the tourist office, but most don't. In general, more charming places are near the Centro Storico (historical center), but cheaper lodgings are near Termini. The tourist offices in Rome will scrounge to find you a room; **Enjoy Rome** is much more helpful.

AROUND TERMINI

Reasonably priced *pensioni* and hotels are just a five- to 15-minute walk from Termini. Once somewhat rundown, this area has recently experienced a renaissance of sorts. The **Esquiline** area, south of Termini, can sometimes be seedy.

NORTH OF TERMINI

🛏 **Pensione Fawlty Towers,** V. Magenta 39 (tel./fax 06 445 03 74; www.enjoyrome.it/ftytwhtl.htm). Exit Termini and cross V. Marsala, walk 1 block along V. Marghera, and turn right on V. Magenta. Charming, English-speaking staff and flower-filled terrace provide peaceful respite from the panic of Termini. Frequently full. Some rooms with bath. Dorms L25-30,000; singles L60-75,000; doubles L90-125,000; triples with shower L120-130,000. **Internet.** Check-out 9am for dorms, 10am for private rooms.

🛏 **Hotel Des Artistes,** V. Villafranca 20 (tel. 06 445 43 65; fax 06 446 23 68). Exit Termini and turn left on V. Marsala, right on V. Vicenza, and left on V. Villafranca (the 5th street). Impeccable 3-star service. Dorms L35,000; singles L60,000; doubles L100-170,000; triples L120-210,000. In winter 20-30% off. Breakfast included for rooms with bath. **Internet.** Reception 24hr. Check-out 10:30am. V, MC, AmEx.

ITALY

Hotel Dolomiti and **Hotel Lachea,** V. San Martino della Battaglia 11 (tel. 06 495 72 56 or 06 49 10 58; fax 06 445 46 65; www.hotel-dolomiti.it), near "Castro Pretorio" Metro stop. Aged exterior belies sparkling interior. Lachea is plainer and cheaper; both have **internet,** breakfast (L10,000) and 11am check-out. **Dolomiti:** Singles L85,000; doubles L130-160,000; triples L150-210,000; quads L200-230,000. V, MC. **Lachea:** Singles L65-75,000; doubles L85-120,000; triples 110-160,000; quads L140-220,000.

Pensione Papa Germano, V. Calatafimi 14A (tel. 06 48 69 19; fax 06 478 812 81; www.hotelpapagermano.it). Exit Termini, turn left on V. Marsala (which becomes V. Volturno), and turn right. Will help you find another place if full. Singles L45-50,000; doubles L72-90,000; triples L99-110,000; quads L108-120,000. Check-out 11am. V, MC.

Hotel Virginia, V. Montebello 94 (tel. 06 445 76 89; fax 06 488 17 86). Exit Termini and turn left on V. Marsala, which becomes V. Volturno; V. Montebello is on the right. Singles L45-50,000; doubles L60-120,000; triples L75-90,000. Laundry. Check-out noon.

Hotel Continentale, V. Palestro 49 (tel. 06 445 03 82; fax 06 445 26 29). Exit Termini, cross V. Marsala, and walk up V. Marghera to V. Palestro. All rooms with shower or bath, some with balconies. Singles L60-80,000; doubles L130-160,000; triples L180-210,000. 20% off with *Let's Go*. Breakfast included. Check-out 11am. V, MC, AmEx.

M&J Place, V. Solferino 9 (tel./fax 06 446 28 02; www.micanet.it/mejplace). Exit Termini, turn left on V. Marsala, then turn right on V. Solferino. Owners Mario and Luigi are twin brothers who save the princess, and make sure guests have a rollicking good time. Dorms Apr.-Sept. L30,000; Oct.-Mar. L20,000. Doubles Apr.-Sept. L100,000; Oct.-Mar. L80,000. Ask about *Let's Go* discounts. Reception 24hr. Check-out 10am.

Hotel Magic, V. Milazzo 20 (tel./fax 06 495 98 80). Exit Termini and cross V. Marsala to V. Milazzo; it's upstairs from Hotels Galli and Fenicia. All 3 hotels are competitive, each with its own special amenities and services. Alacazam! Singles L80-100,000; doubles L100-130,000; triples L140-160,000; quads L200-220,000. V, MC.

SOUTH OF TERMINI (ESQUILINO)

🔲 **Pensione di Rienzo,** V. Principe Amedeo 79A (tel. 06 446 71 31). Exit Termini and turn right on V. Giolitti; turn left on V. Manin and walk 2 blocks away from the station. Tranquil retreat with spacious, newly renovated rooms, some with balconies and baths. Singles L50-86,000; doubles L40-98,000. Check-out 10am. V, MC.

🔲 **Hotel Kennedy,** V. Filippo Trati 62/64 (tel. 06 446 53 73; fax 06 446 54 17). Exit Termini on V. Giolitti and go straight 1 block on V. Cattaneo. Very classy. Singles L65-120,000; doubles L85-199,000; triples L120-249,000; quads L150-360,000. 10% off with *Let's Go*. Breakfast included. Check-out 11am. V, MC, AmEx.

Pensione Cortorillo, V. Principe Amedeo 79A, 5th fl. (tel. 06 446 69 34; fax 06 445 47 69). Exit Termini, turn right on V. Giolitti, then left on V. Gioberti. Singles L70-120,000; doubles L90-220,000. Breakfast L5000 for singles. Check-out 10am. V, MC, AmEx.

Hotel Orlanda, V. Principe Amedeo 76, 3rd fl. (tel. 06 488 01 24; fax 06 488 01 83; www.traveleurope.it/h24.htm), at V. Gioberti. Take the stairs on the right in the vestibule. Singles L45-120,000; doubles L70-180,000; triples L90-220,000.

WEST OF TERMINI

🔲 **Hotel San Paolo,** V. Panisperna 95 (tel. 06 474 52 13 or 06 474 52 17; fax 06 474 52 18; email hsanpaolo@tin.it). From Termini, follow V. Cavour to V. S. Maria Maggiore and bear right after the Church of S. Maria Maggiore. Far from Termini, in the older Rioni Monti. Tranquil rooms; most have frescoes. Singles L70,000; doubles L90-135,000; triples L165,000. Breakfast L10,000. Check-out 10:30am. V, MC, AmEx.

Pensione Sandy, V. Cavour 136 (tel. 06 488 45 85; www.sandyhostel.com), near S. Maria Maggiore. From Termini, take V. Cavour to this centrally located *pensione*. No sign; next door to Hotel Valle. In summer L30,000 per person; off-season L25,000. **Internet.**

Hotel Giugiu, V. del Viminale 8 (tel. 06 482 77 34; fax 06 48 91 26 16), 2 blocks from Termini. From Termini, head right on V. Giovanni Giolitti and left on V. del Viminale. Large, quiet rooms. Singles L60,000; doubles L75-100,000; triples L135,000; quads L160,000. *Let's Go* discount. Breakfast L10,000. Check-out 10am.

ITALY

CENTRO STORICO

Il centro storico (the historical center) is the ideal, if expensive, place to do as the Romans do. Most major sights and the market at Campo dei Fiori are within walking distance. Reservations are a necessity, especially in summer.

Hotel Navona, V. dei Sediari 8 (tel. 06 686 42 03; fax 06 68 21 13 92). From P. Navona, cross C. del Rinascimento to V. dei Sediari. This 16th-century Borromini building has been a *pensione* for over 150 years. Renovated with Versace's help. Singles L100-140,000; doubles L180-205,000; triples L240,000. Breakfast included. Check-out 10am.

Albergo della Lunetta, P. del Paradiso 68 (tel. 06 686 10 80; fax 06 689 20 28), off C. Vittorio Emanuele II, near the Church of S. Andrea della Valle. Great location between Campo dei Fiori and P. Navona. Singles L80-100,000; doubles L120-160,000; triples L165-210,000; quads L200-260,000. Reserve by credit card or check. V, MC.

Albergo Pomezia, V. dei Chiavari 12 (tel./fax 06 686 13 71), off C. Vittorio Emanuele II. Ask to stay on the renovated first floor. Mar.-Oct. singles L100-150,000; doubles L150-200,000; triples L180-270,000; Nov.-Feb reduced. Breakfast included. V, MC, AmEx.

Hotel Mimosa, V. S. Chiara 61 (tel. 06 68 80 17 53; fax 06 683 35 57), off P. della Minerva behind the Pantheon. Spacious. Singles L95,000; doubles L130-150,000; triples L195,000; quads L240,000. 10% off in winter. Curfew 1am; key available.

PIAZZA DI SPAGNA AND ENVIRONS

Sure, the accommodations in this area might run a few thousand more *lire* per day, but can you really put a price tag on living a scant few steps away from Prada?

▨ **Pensione Panda,** V. della Croce 35 (tel. 06 678 01 79; fax 06 69 94 21 51), between P. di Spagna and V. del Corso. Arched ceilings and neo-Roman reliefs in some hallways. Singles L60-90,000; doubles L110-170,000; triples L130-180,000; quads L160-200,000. *Let's Go* discount with cash. Check-out 11am. Reserve ahead. V, MC, AmEx.

Pensione Jonella, V. della Croce 41 (tel. 06 679 79 66), between P. di Spagna and V. del Corso. Bird's-eye view of V. della Croce. Singles L60,000; doubles L100,000; triples L120,000; quads L140,000. No reception; call ahead. Reserve ahead.

Hotel Pensione Suisse S.A.S., V. Gregoriana 54 (tel. 06 678 36 49; fax 06 678 12 58), off P. di Trinità dei Monti. Turn right at the top of the Spanish Steps. Near the wisteria-hung Steps, but far from the hubbub. Singles L125-145,000; doubles L155-215,000; triples L285,000; quads L340,000. Breakfast included. Curfew 2am. V, MC for half of bill.

Hotel Marcus, V. del Clementino 94 (tel. 06 68 30 03 20; fax 06 68 30 03 12). From the Spanish Steps, head toward the Tiber River on V. dei Condotti, which becomes V. della Fontanella di Borghese and then V. del Clementino. Singles L130-170,000; doubles L200-210,000. Breakfast included. V, MC, AmEx.

Hotel Boccaccio, V. del Boccaccio 25 (tel. 06 488 59 62; www.webeco.it/hotelboccaccio), off V. del Tritone down from P. Barberini. 8 spacious rooms with unique furnishings. Singles L80,000; doubles L100-130,000; triples L120-165,000. V, MC, AmEx.

BORGO AND PRATI (NEAR VATICAN CITY)

The *pensioni* across the Tiber aren't Rome's cheapest, but they tend to be comfortable and spotless. Those in Prati, near the Vatican, are attractive for their proximity to popular sights and a quiet residential area. Bus 64 from Termini ends at St. Peter's; nearby stops on the Metro A line are "Lepanto" and "Ottaviano."

▨ **Pensione Ottaviano,** V. Ottaviano 6 (tel. 06 39 73 72 53 or 06 39 73 81 38; www.pensioneottaviano.com). Metro A: Ottaviano; go a few blocks toward P. del Risorgimento. English-speaking hostel-style backpacker haven with TV, fridge, and microwave. In summer dorms L30,000, doubles L90,000; off-season L25,000, L60,000. **Internet.**

▨ **Hotel Pensione Joli,** V. Cola di Rienzo 243, 6th fl. (tel. 06 324 18 54; tel./fax 06 324 18 93), at V. Tibullo, *scala* A, near P. dell'Unita. Nice beds and gorgeous views of the Vatican. All rooms with bath and phone. Singles L80,000; doubles L120,000; triples L160,000; quads L200,000. Breakfast included. Curfew 1am. V, MC.

Hotel Florida, V. Cola di Rienzo 243, 2nd and 3rd fl. (tel. 06 324 18 72 or 06 324 16 08; fax 06 324 18 57). Friendly management and abundant flora greet happy travelers. Sin-

ITALY

gles L70-120,000; doubles L105-160,000; triples with bath L190,000. Breakfast L7000. Call ahead to reserve and ask about discounts. Breakfast L7000. V, MC, AmEx.

Hotel Lady, V. Germanico 198, 4th fl. (tel. 06 324 21 12; fax 06 324 34 46), between V. Fabbio Massimo and V. Paolo Emilio near P. di Quiriti. Small, peaceful *pensione*. Common room with couches and an electronic keyboard. Rooms with phones. Singles L104-130,000; doubles L120-150,000, with bath L160-200,000.

Ostello del Foro Italico (HI), Vle. delle Olimpiadi 61 (tel. 06 323 62 67 or 06 323 62 79; fax 06 324 26 13). Take Metro A to Ottaviano and exit onto V. Barletta (away from Vatican City), then take bus 32 (in the middle of the street) to Cadorna. Get off at the 7th stop as soon as you see the pink Foro Italico; the entrance is across the street. 6- to 12-bed dorms L25,000; nonmembers L30,000. HI cards L30,000. Breakfast included. Reception 2pm-midnight. Check-out 7-9am. Lockout 9am-2pm. Curfew midnight.

CAMPING

Camping on beaches, roads, and inconspicuous plots is illegal but not uncommon. Always ask permission before bedding down.

Seven Hills, V. Cassia 1216 (tel. 06 30 36 27 51 or 06 303 31 08 26; fax 06 303 31 00 39), 8km north of Rome. Take bus 907 from P. Risorgimento to V. Cassia, or 201 from Flaminio. Ask where to get off; walk 3-4km past the big GRA highway, then follow the country road 1km (look for the sign). The bar, market, restaurant, pizzeria, pool, and disco don't accept cash—instead, buy a Seven Hills card for charges. L13,000 per person, L8000 per tent, L7000 per car. Camper L14,000; bungalow L80-130,000. Daily Vatican shuttles at 8 and 9:30am (round-trip L6000). Check-in 7am-11pm. Open late Mar.-Oct.

○ FOOD

Ancient Roman writers reported on the erotica, exotica, and excess at the Imperial dinner table: peacocks, flamingos, and herons were served with their full plumage, and acrobats and fire-eaters distracted guests between courses of camels' feet and goat ears. Meals in Rome are still important, if not as spectacular, affairs. Restaurants tend to close from 3 to 7pm. **Cover prices** are the charges for bread.

Get a taste of local produce and local haggling techniques at Rome's many outdoor **markets;** the largest are at P. Campo dei Fiori, P. Vittorio Emanuele II, and P. S. Cosimato in Trastevere. **STANDA supermarkets** are at V. Cola di Rienzo 173 (near the Vatican), and V. di Trastevere 62. If you're fed up with pasta, head to **Castroni,** V. Cola di Rienzo 196/198 (tel. 06 687 43 83), a great ethnic food market.

RESTAURANTS

AROUND TERMINI

There is no reason to subject yourself to the gastronomic nightmare of the tourist-trap restaurants around Termini. Still, after a long day of travel, they're convenient.

Trattoria da Bruno, V. Varese 29 (tel. 06 49 04 03), between V. Milazzo and V. Castro Pretorio. The grilled *calamari* excels (L15,000), as does the homemade *gnocchi* (L10,000). Open daily noon-3:30pm and 7-10:15pm. Open Sept.-July. V, AmEx.

La Cantinola da Livio, V. Calabria 26 (tel. 06 42 82 05 19). Take V. Piave off V. XX Settembre, then take the 4th left onto V. Calabria. Specializes in seafood; the *spaghetti alla cantinola* (with Veraci clams and caviar; L12,000) is to die for. Cover L1500. Open M-Sa 12:30-3pm and 7:30-11:30pm. Open late Aug.-July. V, MC, AmEx.

CENTRO STORICO

There are plenty of fabulous *trattorie* and pizzerias near **Piazza Navona,** but you won't find them in the *piazza* itself. Wander along sidestreets for delicious deals.

Pizzeria Baffetto, V. del Governo Vecchio 114 (tel. 06 686 16 17), at V. Sora. Once a meeting place for 60s radicals, Baffetto now overflows with hungry Romans. Protest yourself a pizza for L8-14,000. *Vino* L6000. Cover L1000. Open M-F 10am-noon and 7:30pm-1am, Sa-Su 10am-noon and 7:30pm-2am.

■ **Filetti di Baccalà,** Largo dei Librari 88 (tel. 06 686 40 18). From Campo dei Fiori, take V. dei Giubbonari to Largo dei Librari on the left. The best *filetti di baccalà* (fried cod fillets) in Rome L5000. Cover L1500. Open Sept.-July M-Sa 5:30-11:10pm.

Pizzeria Pentola, V. Metastasio 21 (tel. 06 68 80 26 07), off P. Firenze. A short walk from the Pantheon is long enough to escape its tourist traps. Pizza L8-15,000. *Pizza dello chef* (spinach and parmesan) L13,000. Open daily noon-11pm. V, MC.

L'Insalata Ricca, Largo di Chiavari 85 (tel. 06 68 80 36 56), off C. Vittorio Emanuele II near P. S. Andrea della Valle and Campo dei Fiori. Coming here and not eating a salad is like going to the Colosseum and not looking at the Colosseum. Salads L10-15,000. Also at P. Pasquino 72, V. del Gazometro 62, P. Albania 3, V. Polesine 16, and P. Risorgimento 5. Cover L1500. Open daily 12:30-3:15pm and 6:45-11:15pm. **Branches** at P. Pasquino 72, V. del Gazometro 62, P. Albania 3, V. Polesine 16, and P. Risorgimento 5.

Ristorante da Giggetto, V. del Portico d'Ottavio 21/22 (tel. 06 686 11 05), near Teatro di Marcello. A great value in the heart of the historic Jewish Ghetto. *Carciofi alla giudia* (fried artichokes) L10,000. Cover L3000. Open Tu-Su 12:30-3pm and 7:30-11pm.

Ristorante Il Portico 16, V. del Portico d'Ottavio 16 (tel. 06 68 30 79 37), around the corner from the Teatro di Marcello. Fresh veggies and flavorful pastas. *Rigatoni al pomodoro verde* (with green tomatoes) L12,000. *Menù* with house *antipasto* and pizza L18,000. Cover L2500. Open W-M 12:30-3pm and 7:30-11pm. V, MC, AmEx.

PIAZZA DI SPAGNA AND ENVIRONS

The high prices in this flashy district are no guarantee of quality. If you're after bargains, start walking—the best values are away from the monuments on the other side of V. del Corso, toward the Pantheon and the Ara Pacis.

■ **Margutta Vegetariano RistorArte,** V. Margutta 118 (tel. 06 32 65 05 77), off V. del Babuino, near P. del Popolo. Even if you haven't eaten veggies in years and don't recall what they look like, you'll be happy here. Dress decently. Su 11am-3pm all-you-can-eat brunch L30,000. Open Sept.-July M-Sa 1-3:30pm and 7:40-11:40pm. V, MC, AmEx.

Trattoria da Settimio all'Arancio, V. dell'Arancio 50/52 (tel. 06 687 61 19). From P. di Spagna, take V. dei Condotti, cross V. del Corso, continue on V. della Fontanella Borghese, take the first right after V. del Corso, then make an immediate left. The grilled *calamari* (L18,000) may be Rome's best. Cover L2000. Fresh fish Tu and F. Open M-Sa 12:30-3pm and 7:30-11:30pm. Reservations accepted. V, MC, AmEx.

THE ANCIENT CITY

Despite its past glory, this area has yet to discover the noble concept of "affordable food." But along **V. dei Fori Imperiali,** several restaurants offer decent prices.

■ **Taverna dei Quaranta,** V. Claudia 24 (tel. 06 700 05 50). Shaded by the trees of the Celian Park, outdoor dining at this *taverna* is a must. Outstanding, ever-changing menu. Wine L4-5000 per 0.5L. Open daily noon-3pm and 8pm-midnight. V, MC, AmEx.

■ **I Buoni Amici,** V. Aleardo Aleardi 4 (tel. 06 70 49 19 93). From the Colosseum, take V. Labicana, turn right on V. Merulana, and turn left on V. Aleardo Aleardi. The cheap, excellent food is worth the walk. It's hard to go wrong with *linguine all'astice* (L10,000) or *risotto con i funghi* (L8000). Open M-Sa noon-3pm and 7-11:30pm. V, MC, AmEx.

Pizzeria Imperiale, Largo Carlo Ricci 37 (tel. 06 678 68 71), at the start of V. Cavour, opposite the entrance gate to the Roman Forum. Tasty pizza. Open daily 11am-5pm and 7pm-midnight; off-season 11am-3:30pm and 7pm-midnight. V, MC, AmEx.

TESTACCIO

Testaccio provides food for people who want to get a true taste of Rome; take Metro B to Piramide to reach this area south of the ancient city.

■ **Pizzeria Ficini,** V. Luca della Robbia 23 (tel. 06 574 30 17). Take V. Luigi Vanvitelli off V. Marmorata, then take the 1st left. Cheap, delicious pizzas L6-8000. *Calzone* L8000. Wine L6000 per liter. Open Sept.-July Tu-Su 6-11:30pm.

Osteria dei Tempi Nostri, V. Luca della Robbia 32/34. A tiny 5-table *osteria* overflowing with bottles of wine and excellent food. Try the *gnocchi* (L10,000) or salmon (L18,000). Crêpes L10-12,000. Open M-Sa noon-3pm and 7-11pm. V, MC.

TRASTEVERE

Just across the river from the Centro Storico and down the river from the Vatican, Trastevere is home to raucous beer parlors and hopping pizza joints.

▓ **Pizzeria Panattoni,** Vle. di Trastevere 53/59 (tel. 06 580 09 19). Excellent pizzas (L8-13,000), fantastic appetizers (L5-9000), and the "fabulous fancy salad," which includes just about everything you could imagine (L9800). Open Th-Tu 6pm-2:30am.

Ristorante da Gildo, V. da Gildo 31, at the base of V. Garibaldi. Start with the *pâté d'olive* (L10,000 serves 2) and move on to the *fettucine italia* (with tomatoes, spinach, and radicchio, L13,000). Open Tu-Su noon-3pm and 7-11pm.

BORGO AND PRATI (NEAR VATICAN CITY)

Just blocks away from the museums hide some real treasures: tiny bakeries, family-run restaurants, and a huge indoor market on V. Cola di Rienzo.

▓ **Armando,** V. Plauto 38/39 (tel. 06 68 30 70 62), off Borgo Angelico, which is near P. A. Capponi. Inside the neighborhood restaurant, the *Let's Go* traveler looked around. The waitress eyed him. Armando's wife. Had to be. Somewhere in the back of the simply decorated white-walled bistro, a man coughed. The traveler took a seat under the low-speed fan. He knew what he wanted. The *lasagne con porcini* (L10,000). Cover L2500. Open Th-Tu 12:30-3pm and 7-11pm. And in the background, soft rock played. V, MC, AmEx.

Ristorante Max, P. dell'Unita 26/27 (tel./fax 06 322 31 13), at V. dei Gracchi and V. C. Mario, just east of P. del Risorgimento; look for the pink neon MAX. Pizza L8-12,000. *Bruschetta* with olive spread L2000. Open Tu-Su noon-3pm and 7-11pm. V, MC, AmEx.

DESSERTS

Save your pennies for *gelato*—more flavors than in your childhood dreams. In many places, it's one price to stand at the bar and up to twice that for a table.

▓ **Giolitti,** V. degli Uffici del Vicario 40 (tel. 06 699 12 43). From the Pantheon, follow V. del Pantheon (at the northern end of the *piazza*) to the end, then V. della Maddelena to the end, and turn right. Enter the gates of creamy heaven to this St. Peter's of ice cream shops. Cones L2500-4000. Open May-Oct. daily 7am-1am; Nov.-Apr. Tu-Su 7am-1am.

Da Quinto, V. di Tor Millina 15 (tel. 06 686 56 57), off V. dell'Anima, a block west of P. Navona. Every combo of ice, milk, fruit, and ice cream imaginable (L2500-12,000). Open daily noon-2am; off-season Th-Tu noon-2am.

San Crispino, V. Acaia 56 (tel. 06 70 45 04 12), off V. Satrico south of the city center, in Appio. Walk down V. Magna Grecia (15min.). Many Romans call this the best *gelateria* in the city. Cups only; L3000. Open W-M 11am-11pm.

Palazzo del Freddo Giovanni Fassi, V. Principe Eugenio 65/67 (tel. 06 446 47 40), off P. Vittorio Emanuele II, southeast of Termini. Cones L2500-5000. Open in summer daily noon-12:30am; off-season Tu-Su noon-12:30am. Also at V. Vespasiano 57.

Gelateria della Palma, V. della Maddalena 20 (tel. 06 68806752), off P. della Rotonda. A sweet shop extraordinaire. Cones L2500-5000. Open daily 8am-2:30am.

Il Fornaio, V. dei Baullari 5-7 (tel. 06 68 80 39 47), opposite P. San Pantaleo, south of P. Navona. Masses of irresistible baked goodies. Open daily 7am-8:30pm.

WINE BARS

Roman wine bars are in the corners of *piazze* or on small side streets.

▓ **Cul de Sac,** P. Pasquino 73 (tel. 06 68 80 10 94), just west of P. Navona. The best of the wine bars. Open M 6:30pm-12:30am, Tu-Su 12:30-3pm and 6:30pm-12:30am.

Bar Da Benito, V. dei Falegnami 14, off P. Mattei in the Jewish Ghetto. Most authentic award. A tiny 1-room shop lined with wine bottles and hordes of hungry workmen. Meals around L16,000. Lunch served noon-3:30pm. Open M-Sa 7am-8pm. Open Sept.-July.

⬛ SIGHTS

Rome wasn't built in a day, and it's not likely that you'll see any substantial portion of it in 24 hours, either. Ancient temples and forums, Renaissance basilicas, 280 fountains, and 981 churches cluster together in a city bursting with masterpieces from every era of Western civilization. From Etruscan busts to modern canvases, there is more than enough in Rome to captivate visitors for years on end.

THE ANCIENT CITY

⬛THE ROMAN FORUM

Take Metro A to "Colosseo" or a bus (56, 60, 64, 75, and more) to P. Venezia; V. dei Fori Imperiali runs between the two. Open in summer M-Sa 9am-7pm, Su 9am-1pm; off-season closes 1hr. before dusk, may close M-F by 3pm, Su and holidays by noon. Free. Archaeologist-led tour L6000; audio tour L7000.

The people who would soon be known as the Romans founded a thatched-hut shantytown on the site of the Forum in 753 BC, when Romulus and the Sabine leader Titus Tatius, met to end the war triggered by the famous rape of the Sabine women. Now mostly in crumbling ruins, the Forum bears witness to many centuries of civic buildings, most excavated at random and in a confusing jumble. The entrance ramp to the Forum leads to the **Via Sacra,** the oldest street in Rome.

THE CIVIC FORUM. The **Basilica Aemilia,** on the left, built in 179 BC, housed the guild of the money-changers that operated the first *cambiomat* in the city. Next to the Basilica Aemilia stands the **Curia** (Senate House), one of the oldest buildings in the Forum. The broad space in front of the Curia was the **Comitium** (assembly place), where male citizens came to vote and representatives of the people gathered for public discussion. Bordering the Comitium is the large brick **Rostrum** (speaker's platform), erected by Caesar in 44 BC just before his death. Julia, Augustus' rebellious daughter, reputedly voiced her dissenting opinion here by engaging in amorous activities with some of her father's enemies (e.g. getting it on with Marc Antony's son). The hefty **Arch of Septimius Severus,** to the right of the Rostrum, was dedicated in AD 203 to celebrate Augustus' victories in the Middle East.

LOWER FORUM. The three great temples of the lower Forum have been closed off during excavations and restoration; however, the eight columns of the early 5th-century BC **Temple of Saturn,** next to the Rostrum, have at last shed their scaffolding cloak. Around the corner, rows of column bases are all that remain of the **Basilica Julia,** a courthouse built by Julius Caesar in 54 BC. At the far end, three white marble columns and a shred of architrave mark the massive podium of the recently restored **Temple of Castor and Pollux,** built to celebrate the Roman defeat of the Etruscans. The circular building next to it is the **Temple of Vesta,** which dates back to the time of the Etruscans. In this temple, the Vestal Virgins tended the city's eternal, sacred fire, keeping it lit for more than a thousand years.

THE UPPER FORUM. The **House of the Vestal Virgins,** shaded by the Palatine Hill, occupied the sprawling complex of rooms and courtyards behind the Temple of Vesta. For 30 years, the six virgins who officiated over Vesta's rites lived in seclusion here, starting from the ripe old age of seven. As long as they kept their vows of chastity, they remained among the most respected people in ancient Rome. This esteem, however, had its price; a virgin who strayed was buried alive with a loaf of bread and a candle, which would allow her to survive long enough to contemplate her sins. Near here, V. Sacra runs over the **Cloaca Maxima,** the ancient sewer that still drains water from the otherwise marsh-like valley.

THE VELIA. V. Sacra continues out of the Forum proper on to the gargantuan **Basilica of Maxentius** (also known as the Basilica of Constantine). The middle apse of the basilica once contained a gigantic statue of Constantine—the body was bronze, the head, legs, and arms marble. The uncovered remains, including a two-meter-long foot, are on exhibit at the **Palazzo dei Conservatori** on the Capitoline Hill (see p. 569).

V. Sacra leads to an exit on the other side of the hill to the Colosseum; the path that crosses before the **Arch of Titus** heads to the Palatine Hill.

THE PALATINE HILL

Take Metro A to "Colosseo" or any bus to P. Venezia (56, 60, 64, 75, and more). Buy tickets at the Forum info booth or at the entrance on V. di San Gregorio, 100m south of the Colosseum. Open in summer M-Sa 9am-7pm, Su 9am-1pm; in winter closes 1hr. before dusk; may close M-F by 3pm, Su by noon. L12,000.

The best way to attack the Palatine is from the access stairs near the Arch of Titus in the Forum, which ascend to the **Farnese Gardens.** The hill, actually a plateau between the Tiber and the Forum, was home to the she-wolf that suckled Romulus and Remus. Throughout the garden complex are terraces with breathtaking views. Farther down, excavations continue on the 9th-century BC village. The long, spooky **Cryptoporticus** connected Tiberius' palace with nearby buildings. The short end of the tunnel, the path around the House of Augustus, leads to the vast ruins of a giant palace built by Domitian (AD 81-96). The solemn **Domus Augustana** half was the private space for the emperors; adjacent is the other wing and the sprawling **Domus Flavia,** whose courtyard was once occupied by a gigantic octagonal fountain.

FORI IMPERIALI. Opposite the ancient Roman Forum is the Fori Imperiali, a vast conglomeration of temples, basilicas, and public squares. Built between AD 107 and 113, the **Forum of Trajan** celebrated the emperor's victorious Dacian campaign (in modern-day Romania). At one end of the now-decimated forum stands the almost perfectly preserved spiral of ▨**Trajan's Column,** one of the greatest specimens of Roman relief-sculpture ever found. Down the street, the three-floor **Markets of Trajan** provide a glimpse of the first shopping mall and retail warehouses in Rome. *(Down the street from the Forum. Entrance at V. IV Novembre 94, up the steps in V. Magnanapoli, to the right of the 2 churches behind Trajan's column. Open in summer Tu-Sa 9am-6:30pm, Su 9am-1:30pm; in winter closes earlier. L3750, students L2500.)* Across the V. dei Fori Imperiali, the gray tufa wall of the **Forum of Augustus** commemorates Augustus' vengeful victory over the murderers of Julius Caesar at the Battle of Philippi in 42 BC. The only remnant of **Vespasian's Forum** is the mosaic-filled **Church of Santi Cosma e Damiano.** *(Across V. Cavour, by the entrance to the Roman Forum. Open daily 9am-1pm and 3-7pm.)*

▨**THE COLOSSEUM AND ARCH OF CONSTANTINE.** The **Colosseum** stands as the enduring symbol of the Eternal City—a hollowed-out ghost of travertine marble that dwarfs every other ruin in Rome. In its heyday, the Colosseum hosted its share of gory spectacles for as many as 50,000 crazed spectators—within the first 100 days of operation, some 5000 wild beasts perished in the bloody arena (from the Latin word for sand, *harena*, which was put on the floor to absorb blood); the slaughter continued for three more centuries. Between the Colosseum and the Palatine Hill lies the **Arco di Costantin,** one of the latest and best-preserved imperial monuments in the area. *(Metro B: Colosseo. Ground level open M-Tu and Th-Sa 9am-7pm, W and Su 9am-2pm; in winter closes 1hr. before dusk. Upper level closes 2hr. before dusk. L8000.)*

THE VELABRUM. The Velabrum lies in a flat flood plain of the Tiber, between the Palatine and Capitoline hills. At the bend of V. del Portico d'Ottavia, a shattered pediment and a few ivy-covered columns in the shadow of the **Teatro di Marcello** are all that remain of the once magnificent **Portico d'Ottavia.** One block farther south is the **Chiesa di Santa Maria in Cosmedin,** which harbors some of Rome's most beautiful medieval decoration as well as the famed **Bocca della Verità** (in the portico). According to legend, the hoary face will chomp on the hand of a liar. *(Take any bus to P. Venezia, head down V. del Teatro di Marcello (to the right of the Vittorio Emanuele II Monument), walk past and around the Theater of Marcellus, go right on V. del Foro Olitorio to P. di Monte Savello, and walk toward the back of the Theater of Marcellus to V. del Portico d'Ottavia. Portico open daily 9am-5pm. Church open daily 10am-1pm and 3-5pm.)*

THE CAPITOLINE HILL. The **Campidoglio,** Rome's original capitol, still serves as the seat of the city's government. Around the spacious **Piazza di Campidoglio,**

designed by Michelangelo, stand the twin Palazzo dei Conservatori and Palazzo Nuovo, now the home of the **Capitoline Museums** (see **Museums,** p. 569). At the far end, opposite the stairs, the turreted **Palazzo dei Senatori** houses the offices of Rome's mayor. *(From P. Venezia, face the Vittorio Emanuele II Monument, walk around to the right to P. d'Aracoeli, and take the stairs uphill.)*

CIRCUS MAXIMUS AND BATHS OF CARACALLA. Boxed in the valley between the Palatine and Aventine Hills, today's **Circo Massimo** offers only a grassy shadow of its former glory. After its construction around 600 BC, the circus drew more than 300,000 Romans, who gathered to watch as chariots careened around the quarter-mile track. The remains of the **Baths of Caracalla,** in which some 1500 Romans once sponged themselves off, are the largest and best-preserved in the city. Beautiful floor mosaics line the proto-health club; check out the ones in the **Apodyteria** (dressing rooms). *(Metro B: Circo Massimo. To get to the baths from P. di Porta Capena at the eastern end of the Circus, follow V. delle Terme di Caracalla. Baths open Su-M 9am-2pm, Tu-Sa 9am-7pm; in winter closes 1hr. before dusk. L8000.)*

CENTRO STORICO

PIAZZA VENEZIA AND VIA DEL CORSO. The **Via del Corso,** which runs over 2km between P. del Popolo and P. Venezia along the line of the ancient V. Lata, takes its name from its days as Rome's premier racecourse. **Piazza Venezia,** a glorified traffic circle, is dominated by the wedding-cake-like **Vittorio Emanuele II Monument.** On the right as you face the monument is the crumbling **Palazzo Venezia,** one of the first Renaissance *palazzi* built in the city. Mussolini used it as an office and delivered some of his most famous speeches from its balcony. *(Most buses stop at or near P. Venezia, including 56, 57, 60, 64, 75, and 170.)*

THE PANTHEON AND ENVIRONS. With its granite columns and pediment, bronze doors, and a soaring domed interior, the famed ▨**Pantheon** has stood remarkably the same since the day it was erected nearly 2000 years ago on Hadrian's orders. The dome, a perfect half-sphere, was constructed entirely from poured concrete, without the support of vaults, arches, or ribs. *(From P. Venezia, go north on V. del Corso, then left after 3-4 blocks on V. Seminario to P. della Rotonda, more commonly known as P. del Pantheon. Open June M-Sa 9am-6pm, Su 9am-1pm; July-Aug. M-Sa 9am-6:30pm, Su 9am-1pm; Oct.-May M-Sa 9am-4pm, Su 9am-1pm. Free.)* Around the left side of the Pantheon, an obelisk supported by Bernini's winsome elephant statue marks the center of tiny **Piazza Minerva.** On the *piazza*, the **Chiesa di Santa Maria Sopra Minerva** hides some Renaissance masterpieces, including Michelangelo's *Christ Bearing the Cross* and the famous **Cappella Carafa,** with a brilliant fresco cycle by Filippo Lippi. *(Open M-Sa 7am-7pm, Su 7am-1pm and 3:30-7pm.)* The **Chiesa di San Luigi dei Francesi,** the French National Church in Rome, is home to three of Caravaggio's most famous ecclesiastical paintings. *(From the upper left-hand corner of P. della Rotonda, take V. Giustiniani north to where it intersects with V. della Scrofa and V. della Dogana Vecchia, halfway to C. del Rinascimento. Open F-W 7:30am-12:30pm and 3:30-7pm, Th 7:30am-12:30pm.)*

PIAZZA NAVONA. The *piazza*, opened as a stadium in AD 86, housed wrestling matches, javelin and discus throws, foot and chariot races, and even mock naval battles (the stadium was flooded and filled with fleets sailed by convicts). The towering rippling bodies of Bernini's **Fontana dei Quattro Fiumi** (Fountain of the Four Rivers) commands the center. One story holds that Bernini designed the Nile and Plata statues on the fountain to block the view of the **Church of Sant'Agnese in Agone,** created by Bernini's great rival, Borromini. *(From P. Venezia, follow V. del Corso and go left on V. Seminario past P. della Rotonda, across C. del Rinascimento, and into P. Navona.)* West of P. Navona, V. di Tor Millina intersects V. della Pace just steps from the charming semi-circular porch of the **Chiesa di Santa Maria della Pace,** whose Chigi chapel contains Raphael's gentle *Sibyls*. *(May be closed for renovations.)* Off the *piazza* on C. del Rinascimento, the **Chiesa di Sant'Ivo's** corkscrew cupola hovers over the **Palazzo della Sapienza,** the original home of the University of Rome.

CAMPO DEI FIORI AND AROUND

CAMPO DEI FIORI. During papal rule, the area was the site of countless executions; now the only carcasses that litter the *piazza* are those of the fish in the colorful **market,** which springs up with plenty of fresh fruit, veggies, and flowers. *(From P. Venezia, go west on V. del Plebiscito, which becomes C. Vittorio Emanuele II, and turn left on V. Biscione or V. della Cancelleria. Market open M-Sa 6am-2pm.)*

PALAZZO FARNESE AND VIA GIULIA. The huge, stately **Palazzo Farnese** dominates P. Farnese, several streets south of the *campo* on V. Farnese. Alessandro Farnese, a major Counter Reformation pope (1534-1549), commissioned the best architects of his day to design his dream abode, the greatest of Rome's Renaissance *palazzi*. Since 1635, the French Embassy has rented the *palazzo* for one *lira* a year. As part of his campaign to clean up Rome in the early 1500s, Pope Julius II commissioned Bramante to construct a straight road leading directly to the Vatican. His efforts gave birth to **Via Giulia,** behind the palace—an elegant, even revolutionary, contrast with Rome's narrow, winding medieval streets.

THE JEWISH GHETTO. The Jewish community in Rome is the oldest in all of Europe—the first Israelites came to Rome in 161 BC as ambassadors from Judas Maccabee, asking for imperial help against invaders. Today, of the 40,000 Jews who live in Italy, 16,000 call the Eternal City home. The Ghetto, where Pope Paul IV confined Jews from the 16th to the 19th centuries, bridges the Centro Storico to the west and north and the ancient ruins of the Tiber's flood plain and the Capitoline Hill to the south and east. With the 16th-century **Fontana delle Tartarughe** (Tortoise Fountain) by Taddeo Landini, **Piazza Mattei** marks the center of the lowland Ghetto. *(From the Campo dei Fiori, take bus 64. Or, from P. Venezia, head south downhill on V. del Teatro di Marcello, turn right into P. Campitelli, and follow it to P. Mattei.)* The **Sinagoga Ashkenazita** (1874-1904) incorporates Persian and Babylonian architectural devices and today houses the **Jewish Museum.** Guards have searched and questioned all visitors ever since a 1982 attack on the synagogue. *(Between V. Catlana and Lungotevere dei Cenci. From P. Mattei, take V. S. Ambrogio toward the river, bear right, continue on V. del Templo, and turn left on V. Catalana. Tel. 06 687 50 51. Open for services or by tour through the Jewish Museum.)*

PIAZZA DI SPAGNA AND ENVIRONS

PIAZZA DEL POPOLO. Cleared in 1525 by Pope Clement VII, **People's Square** was once a favorite venue for publicly executing heretics. Augustus brought back the 3200-year-old **Obelisk of Pharaoh Ramses II** at the center of the square from Egypt in the first century BC. Behind a simple early Renaissance façade, the **Chiesa di Santa Maria del Popolo** contains several Renaissance and Baroque masterpieces. The **Cappella Cerasi** houses Caravaggio's exquisite *The Conversion of St. Paul* and *Crucifixion of St. Peter.* Raphael designed the Cappella Chigi for the Sienese banker Agostino "il Magnifico" Chigi, said to have been the world's richest man at the time. *(From Metro A: Flamino, walk south on V. Flamino. Open daily 7am-noon and 4-7pm.)*

MAUSOLEUM OF AUGUSTUS AND ARA PACIS. The circular brick mound of the **Masoleo d'Agosto** once housed the funerary urns of Rome's imperial family. *(On P. Augusto Imperatore. From P. del Popolo, follow V. di Ripetta south toward the Tiber. Open sporadically for tours.)* To the west (the right as you come from P. del Popolo) of the mausoleum stands the glass-encased **Ara Pacis** (Altar of Augustan Peace), completed in 9 BC to celebrate Augustus' successful achievement of peace after years of civil unrest and war. *(Open Tu-Sa 9am-7pm, Su 9am-1pm. L3750.)*

THE SPANISH STEPS. Designed by an Italian, paid for by the French, named for the Spaniards, occupied by the British, and currently under the sway of American ambassador-at-large Ronald McDonald, the **☒Scalinata di Spagna,** in the aptly named **Piazza di Spagna,** exude an international air. A small plaque on the side of the pink house to the right of the Spanish Steps marks the home where Keats died in 1821. The second floor now houses the **Keats-Shelley Memorial Museum** (see **Museums,** p. 570). *(Metro A: Spagna. Or, from P. del Popolo, follow V. del Babuino to the piazza.)*

THE FOUNTAIN OF TREVI. Nicolo Salvi's (1697-1751) extravagant and now sparkling ▨**Fontana di Trevi** emerges from the back wall of **Palazzo Poli**, dwarfing the already narrow *piazza* and fascinating crowds with its rumbling cascades. Anita Ekberg took a dip in the fountain in Federico Fellini's film *La Dolce Vita*. Legend has it if you throw a coin into the fountain, you're ensured a speedy return to Rome; another coin, and you'll also fall in love in Rome. *Let's Go* recommends falling in love in Rome. *(From P. del Popolo, follow V. del Corso and turn left on V. delle Muratte. From P. Spagna, go down V. due Macelli, turn right on V. del Tritone, and bear left on V. d. Stamperia.)*

VILLA BORGHESE. In celebration of becoming a cardinal, Scipione Borghese built the lush **Villa Borghese** park, home to three notable art museums: the world-renowned **Galleria Borghese;** the stark, white **Galleria Nazionale d'Arte Moderna;** and the intriguing **Museo Nazionale Etrusco** in Villa Giulia (see **Museums,** p. 569). *(Metro A: Flaminio. Tram 19 also passes the villa. Enter from P. del Popolo, outside the Porta del Popolo, and walk up Vle. George Washington. Or cut across the switchback road that begins at the eastern end of the piazza and ascend the steps.)*

AROUND TERMINI

BATHS OF DIOCLETIAN AND PIAZZA DELLA REPUBBLICA. From AD 298 to 306, 40,000 Christian slaves were kept busy building these baths, the grandest community center of ancient Rome. The public baths, which had a capacity of 3000, included a heated marble public toilet with 30 seats. In 1561, Michelangelo's last architectural endeavor involved converting the ruins into the **Chiesa di Santa Maria degli Angeli.** The **sundial** between the east transept and the altar has provided the standard time for Roman clocks for hundreds of years. *(Metro A: Repubblica.)*

PIAZZA BARBERINI. Rising from the modern hum of a busy traffic circle at the end of V. del Tritone, Bernini's **Fontana del Tritone,** which marks the fulcrum of Baroque Rome, and his **Fontana delle Api** (Bee Fountain) spout streams of water over the droning buzz of traffic. Maderno, Borromini, and Bernini all had a hand in the designing the **Palazzo Barberini,** which houses 11th- to 18th-century paintings in the **Galleria Nazionale d'Arte Antica** (see **Museums,** p. 569). *(V. delle Quattro Fontane 13. Metro A: Barberini. Or, from P. della Repubblica, walk northwest across V. XX Settembre and bear left on V. Barberini.)* **Via Vittorio Veneto,** once lined with grand mansions, and now with embassies and airline offices, stretches north. Nearby, the **Chiesa di Santa Maria della Concezione,** built in 1626, houses the tomb of Antonio Barberini. The **Capuchin Crypt** downstairs contains the macabre, morbid, yet artfully arranged bones of 4000 Capuchin friars. *(Open F-W 9am-noon and 3-6pm. L1000 min. donation.)*

PIAZZA DEL QUIRINALE AND VIA XX SETTEMBRE. At the southeast end of V. del Quirinale, P. Quirinale lies at the summit of the tallest of Rome's seven hills. The President of the Republic officially resides in the imposing **Palazzo del Quirinale,** a Baroque creation by Bernini, Maderno, and Fontana. *(From P. Barberini, walk southeast on V. delle Quattro Fontane and go right down V. del Quirinale to P. Quirinale. Or, from P. della Repubblica, walk northwest to V. XX Settembre and go right as it becomes V. del Quirinale.)* Farther along the street lies the marvelous façade of Borromini's **Chiesa di San Carlo alle Quattro Fontane,** often called **San Carlino.** *(Open M-F 9:30am-12:30pm and 4-6pm, Sa 9am-12:30pm. If the interior is closed, ring at the convent next door.)* Four fountains grace the buildings at the four corners of the intersection of V. del Quirinale and **V. delle Quattro Fontane.** From here, V. del Quirinale becomes V. XX Settembre and leads to the **Chiesa di Santa Maria della Vittoria,** which contains Bernini's fantastic *Ecstasy of St. Theresa of Ávila. (Open daily 7:30am-12:30pm and 4-6:30pm.)*

TRASTEVERE AND JANICULAN

Trastevere, which became part of Rome under Augustus, has a proud independent vitality. *(Take bus 75 or 170 from Termini to V. Trastevere.)* Tourists flock to **Piazza Sonnino,** on V. Trastevere, for restaurants, bars, and movie houses. On the left is the **Casa di Dante,** which hosts readings of the *Divine Comedy* (Nov.-Mar. Su). On V. di Santa Cecilia (behind the cars, through the gate, and beyond the courtyard) is the **Basilica di Santa Cecilia in Trastevere,** which shelters Stefano Maderno's famed statue of

Santa Cecilia. *(Open Tu and Th 10am-noon and 4-5:30pm.)* From P. Sonnino, V. della Lun-garetta leads west to P. di S. Maria in Trastevere, home to the **Chiesa di Santa Maria in Trastevere**, whose beautiful mosaics date from AD 337-352. *(Open daily 7:30am-7pm.)* Rome's beautiful **Botanical Gardens** are on the **Janiculan Hill.** *(From P. Sonnino, take V. della Lungaretta, pass the piazza, bear right on V. della Scala, and go left up medieval V. Garibaldi (10min.).)* The **Isola Tiberina** (Tiber Island), between Trastevere and Centro Storico, has been continuously inhabited for nearly 3000 years. From V. Trastevere, walk to the river and jog right along it to the **Ponte Cestio**. The bridge going to the east bank of the river, the **Ponte Fabricio,** known as the **Ponte dei Quattro Capi** (Bridge of Four Heads), is the oldest in the city, built in 62 BC.

THE SOUTH AND SOUTHEAST

ESQUILINE HILL AND LATERAN. As one of the five churches in Rome granted extraterritoriality, **Basilica di Santa Maria Maggiore,** which crowns the Esquiline Hill, is officially part of Vatican City. Glowing mosaics celebrate the Council of Ephesus' 4th-century ruling of Mary as the Mother of God. To the right of the altar, a slab marks the tomb of Bernini. *(Four blocks down V. Cavour from Termini. Open daily 7am-6:50pm. L5000.)* The immense **Basilica di San Giovanni in Laterano,** founded by Constantine in AD 314, is the oldest Christian basilica in the city. It holds the heads of St. Peter and St. Paul and the finger used by St. Thomas to probe Christ's wounds. *(Metro A: San Giovanni. Open daily 7am-6:45pm; in winter 7am-6pm. Dress code enforced.)*

THE OPPIAN HILL. Chiesa di San Pietro in Vincoli (St. Peter in Chains) is home to an unfinished fragment of Michelangelo's *Tomb of Julius II* and an imposing **statue of Moses.** The goat horns protruding from Moses' head come from a medieval misin-terpretation of the Bible—the Hebrew word "rays" was read as "horns." *(From Termini, follow V. Cavour until you reach a set of steps on the left and head up the archway of V. S. Francesco di Paola. Open daily 7am-12:30pm and 3:30-7pm.)*

THE APPIAN WAY AND THE CATACOMBS. Because burial inside the city walls was forbidden in ancient times, fashionable Romans made their final resting places along V. Appia. At the same time, early Christians secretly dug maze-like **catacombs** under the ashes of their persecutors. **San Callisto** is the largest cata-comb in Rome, comprising almost 22km of subterranean paths. Its four serpentine levels once held 16 popes, 7 bishops, and some 500,000 other early Christians. *(V. Appia Antica 110. Take bus 218 at Domine Quo Vadis; walk up the path between V. Appia Antica and V. Ardeatina. Open Mar.-Jan. Th-Tu 8:30am-noon and 2:30-5:30pm; in winter 8:30am-noon and 2:30-5pm.)* **Santa Domitilla** is acclaimed for its paintings, including a 3rd-century portrait of Christ and the Apostles. *(V. delle Sette Chiese 282. Take bus 218 to S. Callisto at the far gates; cross V. Ardeatina and turn right on V. delle Sette Chiese. Open Feb.-Dec. W-M 8:30am-noon and 2:30-5:30pm; in winter 8:30am-noon and 2:30-5pm.)* **San Sebastiano's** claim to fame is that it serves as the temporary home for the bodies of Peter and Paul. *(V. Appia Antica 136. Take bus 660 from Colli Albani to "San Sebastiano." Open Dec.-Oct. M-Sa 8:30am-noon and 2:30-5:30pm; in winter 8:30am-noon and 2:30-5pm. Each L8000.)*

EUR. South of the city stands a monument to a Roman empire that never was. The zone is called **EUR** (pronounced AY-oor), an Italian acronym for Universal Exposi-tion of Rome, the 1942 World's Fair that Mussolini meant to be a showcase of Fas-cist and Imperial Roman achievements. The new, modern Rome was to shock and impress the rest of the world with its futuristic ability to build several square build-ings that all looked the same. **Via Cristoforo Colombo,** EUR's main street, runs roughly north to south and is the first of many internationally ingratiating names like "Viale Asia" and "Piazza Kennedy." *(Take Metro A or bus 714 to "EUR Fermi.")*

VATICAN CITY

*Metro A: Ottaviano; walk south on V. Ottaviano toward the distant colonnade. Or take bus 64 or 492 from Termini, 62 from P. Barberini, or 23 from Testaccio. For a general orientation, refer to this book's delightful **color map** of Vatican City.*

Occupying 108.5 independent acres entirely within the boundaries of Rome, Vati-can City, the last foothold of the Catholic Church, once wheeled and dealed as the mightiest power in Europe. The Lateran Treaty of 1929, which allowed the Pope to maintain all legislative, judicial, and executive powers over this tiny theocracy, required the Church to remain neutral in Italian national politics and Roman municipal affairs. As the spiritual leader for millions of Catholics around the world, however, the Pope's influence extends far beyond the walls of this tiny domain. The nation preserves its independence by minting *lire* coins with the Pope's face, running a postal system, and maintaining an army of Swiss Guards.

Papal audiences are held Wednesdays, usually at 10am. To attend, stop by the **Prefettura della Casa Pontificia,** beyond the bronze doors to the right of the basilica, on the previous day to pick up tickets; look at the beginning of the colonnade, just past the Swiss Guards. Audiences are held in the Aula behind the colonnade, to the left of the basilica. Wear appropriate clothing; cover those ungodly knees and shoulders. (Tel. 06 69 88 30 17. Open M-W 9am-1pm. Free.)

ST. PETER'S BASILICA. As you enter the P. S. Pietro, Bernini's colonnade draws you toward the **Basilica di San Pietro.** Mussolini's broad V. della Conciliazione, built in the 1930s to connect the Vatican to the rest of the city, opened a wider view of St. Peter's than Bernini had ever intended. Round disks set in the pavement between each fountain and the obelisk mark the spots where you should stand so that the quadruple rows of Bernini's colonnades visually resolve into one perfectly aligned row. The basilica itself, whose overwhelming interior measures 186m by 137m, rests on the reputed site of St. Peter's tomb. To the right, Michelangelo's **Pietà** has been protected by bullet-proof glass since 1972, when an axe-wielding fiend attacked it, smashing Christ's nose and breaking Mary's hand. The crossing under the dome is anchored by four niches with statues of saints—Bernini's **San Longinus** is to the northeast. In the center of the crossing, Bernini's bronze **baldacchino** rises on spiral columns over the marble altar. In the apse is Bernini's **Cathedra Petri,** a Baroque reliquary housing St. Peter's original throne in a riot of bronze and gold. *(Open daily Apr.-Sept. 7am-6pm; Oct.-Mar. 7am-5pm; free. Dome closes 1hr. earlier and may be closed when the pope is in the basilica on W morning; on foot L7000, by elevator L8000.)*

Below the statue of St. Longinus, steps lead down to the **Vatican Grottoes,** the final resting place of innumerable popes and saints. The exit from the grottoes is by the entrance to the **cupola;** you can take an **elevator** to the walkway around the interior of the dome or ascend 350 claustrophobic stairs to the outdoor top ledge, which affords a great view of the basilica's roof, the *piazza,* and the Vatican Gardens.

VATICAN MUSEUMS. The Vatican Museums constitute one of the world's greatest collections of art—a vast storehouse of ancient, Renaissance, and modern statuary, paintings, and sundry papal odds and ends. If you have limited time, plan your tour before you go—the design of the museum makes it hard to retrace your steps. A good place to start your tour is the sublime **Museo Pio-Clementino,** the world's greatest collection of antique sculpture. From here, the Simonetti Stairway climbs past galleries to where the long trudge to the Sistine Chapel (see below) begins. On the way, a door leads into the first of the four **Stanze di Rafaele,** apartments built for Pope Julius II in the 1510s that contain many of Raphael's masterpieces. From here, one staircase leads to the brilliantly frescoed **Borgia Apartments,** while another goes to the Sistine Chapel. After the Sistine Chapel is the **Pinacoteca,** with one of the best painting collections in Rome. *(Major galleries open Oct. 31-Mar. 15 M-Sa 8:45am-1:45pm. Mar. 16-Oct. 30 M-F 8:45am-4:30pm, Sa 8:45am-1:45pm; L18,000, students L12,000. Museums also open the last Su of each month 8:45am-1:45pm; free.)*

■**THE SISTINE CHAPEL.** Ever since its completion in the 16th century, the Sistine Chapel (named for its founder, Pope Sixtus IV) has served as the chamber in which the College of Cardinals meets to elect a new pope. The ceiling, which is actually flat but appears vaulted, gleams as a result of recent restoration. The frescoes on the side walls predate Michelangelo's ceiling. The simple compositions and vibrant colors of Michelangelo's masterpiece hover above, each section depicting a story from Genesis. The scenes are framed by the famous *ignudi,* young nude males.

CASTEL SANT'ANGELO. Built by the Emperor Hadrian (AD 117-138) as a mausoleum for himself and his family, this mass of brick and stone has served the popes as a fortress, prison, and palace. When the city was wracked with plague in AD 590, Pope Gregory the Great saw an angel sheathing his sword at the top of the complex; when the plague abated soon after, the edifice was rededicated to the angel. Outside, the marble **Ponte Sant'Angelo,** lined with statues of angels designed by Bernini, leads across the river. *(Down V. della Conciliazione from St. Peter's. Open in summer Tu-F 9am-10pm, Sa-Su 9am-8pm; in winter Tu-Su 9am-2pm. L10,000.)*

🏛 MUSEUMS

Etruscans, emperors, popes, and *condottiere* have been busily stuffing Rome's belly full of artwork for several millennia, leaving behind a city teeming with galleries. The most heavily touristed are the **Vatican Museums** (see above). Museums are generally closed on holidays, on Sunday afternoons, and all day Monday.

🖼 **Capitoline Museums** (tel. 06 67 10 20 71), on top of the **Capitoline Hill.** Among the largest collections of ancient sculpture in the world; breathtaking frescoes. Fragments of the **Colossus of Constantine** and the **Capitoline Wolf,** an Etruscan statue that has symbolized the city of Rome since ancient times. The **pinacoteca** has an incredible array of 16th- to 17th-century Italian paintings. Open Tu-Su 9am-7pm. L10,000, students L5000.

🖼 **Galleria Borghese,** P. le Scipione Borghese 5 (tel. 06 854 85 77), in the **Villa Borghese;** take bus 910 from Termini and get off at V. Pinciana, or take Metro A to "Spagna," follow the Villa Borghese exit signs, and head left up the road. The exquisite museum has reopened its doors at long last. Come and get it—Bernini! Caravaggio! Raphael! Rubens! Titian! Open Tu-Sa 9am-7pm, Su and holidays 9am-1pm. L10,000. Tickets may be reserved in advance and do sell out; visitors are admitted for 2-hour periods.

🖼 **Villa Farnesina,** V. della Lungara 230, in **Trastevere,** opposite the Palazzo Corsini off the Lungotevere Farnesina. Bus 23 parallels the river, a street to the east. Chigi (see p. 565) lived here sumptuously and eccentrically. To the right of the entrance lies the breathtaking **Sala of Galatea,** mostly painted by the architect, Baldassare Peruzzi, in 1511. The masterpiece of the room is Raphael's **Triumph of Galatea.** Open M-Sa 9am-1pm. L8000.

🖼 **Galleria Nazionale d'Arte Moderna,** Vle. delle Belle Arti 131 (tel. 06 32 29 81). Metro A: Flaminio; enter **Villa Borghese** and walk up Vle. George Washington. Tram 19 also passes the villa. The Palazzo delle Belle Arti houses the city's principal modern art treasures, by Cézanne, van Gogh, Degas, Rodin, Monet, Klimt, Modigliani, Giacometti, Mondrian, Braque, and Duchamp. Open Tu-Su 9am-7pm; holidays 9am-2pm. L12,000.

Galleria Spada, P. Capo di Ferro 13 (tel. 06 32 81 01), in Baroque **Palazzo Spada.** Take bus 64 past S. Andrea della Valle and walk south through Campo dei Fiori. The 17th-century Cardinal Bernardino Spada commissioned these opulent rooms to house his fantastic paintings and sculpture. Open Tu-Sa 9am-6:30pm, Su 9am-12:30pm. L10,000.

Museo Nazionale Etrusco di Villa Giulia, P. Villa Giulia 9 (tel. 06 320 19 51), in Villa Borghese. Take bus 19 from P. Risorgimento or 52 from P. San Silvestro. Built under Pope Julius III. Etruscan extravaganzas. Open Tu-Su 9am-7pm; holidays 9am-2pm. L8000.

Museo Nazionale d'Arte Antica, V. delle Quattro Fontane 13, near the **Barberini** stop on Metro A. National collection of 12th- through 18th-century art in 2 buildings. **Palazzo Barberini** has paintings from the medieval through Baroque periods. The main floor is undergoing restoration, but you can still see Raphael, El Greco, and Caravaggio. Open Tu-Sa 9am-2pm, Su 9am-1pm. L8000. The **Galleria Corsini,** V. della Lungara 10, on the corner of V. Corsini, opposite the Villa Farnesina in **Trastevere,** holds a fine collection of 17th- and 18th-century paintings. Open Tu-F 9am-7pm, Sa 9am-2pm, Su 9am-1pm. L8000.

Galleria Colonna, V. della Pilotta 17 (tel. 06 679 43 62), north of P. Venezia in the **Centro Storico;** take any bus to P. Venezia. Designed in the 17th century for the express purpose of flaunting the family goods in a dazzling central gallery lined with ancient statues. Ivory reliefs of Michelangelo's famous *Last Judgment* adorn the ebony desk in the next room. Open Sa 9am-1pm. L10,000, students L8000.

ITALY

Galleria Doria Pamphilj, P. del Collegio Romano 2 (tel. 06 679 73 23), in Palazzo Doria Pamphilj, off V. del Corso near the **Pantheon.** Take any bus to P. Venezia. Stunning private collection, in the family's palatial home; includes Titian's *Spain Succouring Religion* and *Salome With the Head of St. John the Baptist* and Caravaggio's *Mary Magdalene.* Open F-W 10am-5pm. L13,000, students L9000. The attached **private apartments** have more art and tapestries. Open F-W 10:30am-12:30pm. Mandatory tour L5000

Museo Nazionale Romano, P. dei Cinquecento (tel. 06 48 90 35 00), in the Palazzo Massimo, across the street from Termini. Main branch of 4 associated museums. Art from villas owned by the likes of Nero and the Empress Livia as well as several important patrician collections of antiquities and other Greco-Roman art. Open Tu-Sa 9am-9:45pm, Su 9am-1pm. Oct.-May Tu-Sa 9am-2pm, Su 9am-1pm. L12,000, last Su of month free.

Keats-Shelley Memorial Museum, P. di Spagna 26 (tel. 06 678 42 350). Metro A: Spagna. Immediately to the right of the Spanish Steps. Keats memorabilia, deathbed correspondence, and copies of original manuscripts. Extensive books about Keats, Shelley, and Byron. Open May-Sept. M-F 9am-1pm and 3-6pm, Sa 11am-2pm and 3-6pm; Oct.-Apr. M-F 9am-1pm and 2:30-5:30pm. Closed 2nd and 3rd weeks of Aug. L5000.

🎦 ENTERTAINMENT

The classical scene in Rome goes wild in summer. The smaller festivals that run from mid-May to August are just parts of the larger **Roma Estate** (www.romaestate.com), which starts with the **Festa Europea della Musica,** a weekend of concerts at the end of June. In July, the **Accademia Nazionale di Santa Cecilia** holds concerts in the **Villa Giulia,** P. della Villa Giulia 9; for concert info and schedules, head to the **ticket office** in Villa Borghese. (Tel. 06 361 10 64. Open Tu-Sa 10am-2pm, Su 10am-1pm, and on the day of the performance.) The **Theater of Marcellus,** V. del Teatro di Marcello 44, near P. Venezia, hosts summer evening concerts organized by the **Associazione Il Tempietto** (L30,000). Roman theaters, although not on par with those in other major European cities, still generate a number of quality productions; for info, see www.musical.it or www.comune.rome.it. Considered the most important theater in Rome, **Teatro Argentina,** V. di Torre Argentina 52, also runs many drama and music festivals in Rome; take bus 64 from Termini. (Tel. 06 68 80 46 01. Box office open M-F 10am-2pm and 3-7pm, Sa 10am-2pm. V, MC, AmEx.) **Cineclubs** show foreign films, golden oldies, and an assortment of original-language favorites. A "v.o." or "l.o." in any listing means *versione originale* or *lingua originale* (i.e., not dubbed). In summer, huge screens come up in various *piazze* for **outdoor film festivals;** for info, see www.alfanet.it/welcomeItaly/roma/default.html. Check out the weekly *Roma C'è* (which has an English-language section) or *Time Out* for a comprehensive list of concerts, plays, clubs, and movies.

🎵 NIGHTLIFE

MUSIC CLUBS, DISCOS, AND JAZZ

Although Italian discos can make for a thrilling, flashy, sweaty good time, travelers must overcome several obstacles before donning their dancing shoes. The really cool club scene changes as often as Roman phone numbers, and bigger clubs flee beachward to **Fregene, Ostia,** or **San Felice Circeo** during Rome's steaming summer.

Il Santo, V. Galvani 46-48 (tel. 06 574 79 45), near V. di Monte Testaccio. One of Rome's most popular discos. 2 floors: heaven and hell—choose wisely (but heaven's fun, too). Cover L30,000; includes 1 drink. Open Tu-Su 10:30pm-4am. Closed in summer.

Alexanderplatz Jazz Club, V. Ostia 9 (tel. 06 39 74 21 71), near Vatican City. Metro A: Ottaviano; head west on Vle. Giulio Cesare, right on V. Leone IV, then left on V. Ostia. Night buses to P. Venezia and Termini go from Ple. Clodio. Smoky jazz scene. Guests must buy a *tessera* (L12,000). Open Sept.-June daily 9pm-2am. Shows start 10:30pm.

Akab/The Cave, V. di Monte Testaccio 69 (tel. 06 574 44 85), in Testaccio. DJs spin retro and hip-hop; live bands. Open M-Sa 10pm-4am. Cover around L15,000; includes 1 drink.

ITALY

Alien, V. Velletri 13/19 (tel. 06 84 12 12). One of the biggest discos in Rome attracts a well-dressed, well-mixed, and, well, drunk crowd. Moves to Fregene during the summer. Open Tu-Sa 11pm-4am. Cover around L30,000; includes 1 drink.

Charro Café, V. di Monte Testaccio 73 (tel. 06 578 30 64). Look what happens—1 tequila, 2 tequila, 3 tequila, floor. A little taste of Tijuana in Rome. Home of the **Museo del Tequila** (L5000 per shot). Open M-Sa 8:30pm-3:30am. Cover L10,000; includes 1 drink.

Hangar, V. in Selci 69 (tel. 06 488 13 97). Metro B: Cavour; or take any bus down V. Cavour from Termini or the Colosseum. Hotspot for gay nightlife in Rome; mainly men. Open W-M 10:30pm-2am. Closed 3 weeks in Aug. *Tessera* needed to get in (L10,000).

Muccassassina, c/o Alpheus, V. del Commercio 36. Gays, lesbians, and straights get down to house, retro, and pop in one of Rome's biggest clubs. 3 huge dance floors and lots and lots of beautiful people. Open F only 10:30pm-4am.

PUBS

If the ubiquitous bottles of Peroni and Nastro Azzuro littering the streets of Rome have you longing for the days of the organized, indoor drunkenness of your native land, your only recourse might be found in the dark, cramped confines of Rome's pubs. Drink prices often increase after 9pm.

◩ Jonathan's Angels, V. della Fossa 16 (tel. 06 689 34 26), west of P. Navona. Take V. del Governo Vecchio from Campo dei Fiori, turn left at the Abbey Theatre on V. Parione, then left again toward the lights. Look what happens—you replace Charlie in the finest American TV show of the 1980s and you get a pub named after you. The finest bathroom in Rome, nay, Italy. Cocktails/long drinks L15,000. Open daily 4pm-2am.

Trinity College, V. del Collegio Romano 6 (tel. 06 678 64 72), off V. del Corso near P. Venezia. Look what happens—you're a renowned British university and you get a pub named after you. You'll pray for an acceptance letter from this school, where the Health Department offers degrees in diverse curricula such as Guinness, Harp, and Heineken. Tuition L6-9000. Classes held daily 7:30pm-3am.

The Drunken Ship, Campo dei Fiori 20/21 (tel. 06 68 30 05 35). Look what happens—you're the Exxon Valdez and you get a pub named after you. Because you're tired of meeting Italians. Because you have an earnest desire to share experiences with others in the hosteling set. Because you feel the need to have an emotion-free fling with someone else who feels the same way. Happy hour 5-9pm. Open daily 5pm-2am.

Julius Caesar, V. Castelfidardo 49, just north of Termini near P. dell'Indipendenza, on the corner of V. Solferino. Packed with backpackers and locals. Live music, cheap drinks, and good times. During happy hour (9-10pm), beer and sandwich L10,000. Pitchers L15,000; cocktails L10,000. Ask about *Let's Go* discounts. Open daily 9pm-3am.

▊ EXCURSIONS FROM ROME

Surrounding Rome, ancient cities maintain traces of their original cultures. Romans, Etruscans, Latins, and Sabines all settled here, and their contests for supremacy over the land make up some of the first pages of Italy's recorded history. When the Eternal City's traffic and mayhem overwhelm you, the sanctuary of the Lazio countryside beckons.

TIVOLI. Horace, Catullus, Propertius, Maecenas, and many others retreated to villas lining the ravine in Tivoli. Spectacular terraces and fountains abound in the gardens of the ◨**Villa d'Este,** a castle-garden, particularly the rows of grotesque faces spouting watery plumes, the **Grotto of Diana,** and the **Fontana della Civetta.** From P. Garibaldi, sneak your way through the gauntlet of souvenir stands in P. Trento down the path to the Villa on your left. (Open daily May-Aug. M-Sa 9am-6:45pm and Su 9am-5:15pm; Sept.-Apr. M-Sa 9am-1hr. before dusk, Su 9am-2½hr. before dusk. L8000.) Follow V. di Sibilla across town to reach the **Villa Gregoriana,** a park with paths descending through scattered grottoes carved by rushing water, and walk past a series of lookouts over the cascades to the ancient **Temple of Vesta.** (Open June-Aug. Tu-Su 10am-7:30pm; Sept.-May Tu-Su 9:30am-1hr. before dusk. L3500.)

ITALY

From Rome, take the Metro B to "Rebibbia" and exit the station to the COTRAL terminal above. Tickets to Tivoli (L3000) are sold here, and the **buses** leave from Capolinea (3-5 per hr.). The bus climbs to the center of Tivoli, making a stop slightly beyond P. Garibaldi at P. delle Nazioni Unite. On the street leading away from P. Garibaldi, a big "I" on a round shack marks the information center and **tourist office.** (Tel. 0774 31 12 49; fax 0774 33 12 94. Open M-Sa 9:45am-3pm).

From Tivoli proper, it's a short trip to the vast remains of the **Villa Adriana.** Either return to Largo Garibaldi and take orange bus 4 from the newsstand (L1400; buy 2 tickets, as they often run out at the villa), or take the COTRAL bus (dir: Giudonia) from Largo Massimo (10min., every hr., L2000). The villa is the largest and most expensive ever built in the Roman Empire. Emperor Hadrian designed its buildings in the 2nd century AD in the styles of monuments he had seen in his travels. (Open daily 9am-1½hr. before dusk. L8000.)

OSTIA ANTICA. The settlement at Ostia, the first Roman colony, was a commercial port and naval base during the 3rd and 2nd centuries BC, but fell into disuse. Mud immersed the brick site and preserved it remarkably well, far better than the monumental marble precincts of Rome. A necropolis, extensive baths, ancient laundry shop, and the ☒**Piazzale delle Corporazioni** (Forum of the Corporations), which held offices of shipping agents from all over the Roman world, await discovery. (Open daily in summer 9am-7pm; in winter 9am-5pm. L8000.) To reach the **archaeological site,** take Metro B to "Piramide" or "Magliana," change to the Lido train, and disembark at Ostia Antica (same ticket for both legs of the trip). Cross the overpass, turn left when the road ends, and follow the signs.

THE VENETO

From the rocky foothills of the Dolomites to the fertile valleys of the Po River, the Veneto region has a geography as diverse as its historical influences. Once loosely linked under the Venetian Empire, these towns retained their cultural independence, and visitors are more likely to hear regional dialects than standard Italian when neighbors gossip across their geranium-bedecked windows. The sense of local culture and custom that remains strong within each town may surprise visitors lured to the area by Venice, the *bella* of the north.

VENICE (VENEZIA)

It is with good reason that Venetians call their city *La Serenissima* (the most serene); they awaken each morning to a refreshing absence of cars and mopeds, instead making their way on foot or by boat through an ancient maze of narrow streets and winding canals. The serenity is broken only by tourists, who swarm in Venice's *campi* (squares) and thoroughfares, searching out the city's wealth of museums and landmarks. Two worlds collide as they cross paths with the locals living in the sparsely populated back streets of Cannaregio and the Ghetto; uniting them are the architectural gems of the city's glorious past and the intertwining canals, still the true arteries of this slowly sinking city.

▐ GETTING THERE AND GETTING AROUND

The **train station** is on the northwest edge of the city; be sure to get off at Santa Lucia and *not* Mestre (on the mainland). **Buses** and **boats** arrive at Ple. Roma, just across the Grand Canal from the train station. To get from either station to **Piazza San Marco** or the **Rialto Bridge,** take *vaporetto* 82 or follow the signs (and the crowds) for the 40min. walk (exit left from the train station onto Lista di Spagna).

Flights: Aeroporto Marco Polo (tel. 041 260 61 11; www.veniceairport.it), 5 mi. north of the city. Take the **ACTV local bus** 5 (20min., 2 per hr. 5:30am-12:30am, L1500) or the **ATVO shuttle** (tel. 041 520 55 30; 30min., every 45min. 5:30am-8:40pm, L5000).

Trains: Stazione Venezia Santa Lucia. To: **Bologna** (2hr., 2 per hr., L22,500); **Florence** (3hr., every 2hr., L22-44,000); **Milan** (4hr., 1-2 per hr., L22-34,000); **Rome** (5hr., 5 per

ITALY

Central Venice

SEE ALSO COLOR INSERT

ACCOMMODATIONS

A Antica-Locanda Montin
B Cà Foscari
C Domus Civica (ACISJF)
D Albergo Adua
E Casa Gerotta/Hotel Calderan
F Albergo San Samuele
G Hotel Bernardi-Semenzato
H Al Gambero
I Hotel Noemi
J Foresteria Valdese
K Locanda Canal & Locanda Silva
L Pensione Casa Vererdo
M Locanda Corona
N Ostello Venezia
O Suore Cannosiano

Vaporetti Stops

100 yards
100 meters

Canal Grande

day, L64-75,000); **Innsbruck** (5hr., 2 per day); **Ljubljana** (5½hr., 1 per day, L51,000); **Zagreb** (8hr., 2 per day, L77,000); **Zurich** (8hr., 1 per day, L150,000); and **Vienna** (8-9hr., 4 per day, L157,000). For Rome and Florence, it's generally cheaper to change at Bologna. **Luggage Storage** by platform 7; L5000 per 12hr.

Buses: ACTV, P. Roma (tel. 041 528 78 86), runs local buses and boats. **ACTV long distance carrier** buses run to nearby cities. Ticket office open daily 7am-11:30pm.

Public Transportation: The **Grand Canal** can be crossed on foot only at the *ponti* (bridges) of Scalzi, Rialto, and Accademia. Most **vaporetti** (water buses) run 24hr. (less frequently after 11pm). **Single-ride** L6000; **round-trip** L10,000; **24-hour** *biglietto turistico* pass L18,000; **3-day** *biglietto turistico* L35,000 (L25,000 for Rolling Venice Cardholders; see **Tourist Offices,** below). Buy tickets from booths in front of *vaporetto stops*, automated machines at the ACTV office in Ple. Roma or at the Rialto stop, or the conductor; pick up some extra *non timbrati* (non-validated) tickets so you don't get stuck when the booths aren't open (validate them yourself before you board). The **fine** for riding without a valid ticket is L26,000 but is often not enforced. **Lines 82** (faster) and **1** (slower) run from the station down the Grand and Giudecca Canals; **line 52** goes from the station through the Giudecca Canal to Lido and along the city's northern edge; and **line 12** runs from Fondamente Nuove to Murano, Burano, and Torcello.

■ ORIENTATION AND PRACTICAL INFORMATION

Venice spans 118 bodies of land in a lagoon and is connected to the mainland by a thin causeway at its northwestern edge. The Grand Canal snakes through the city, dividing it up into **sestieri** (sixths, or districts; see the **color map** at the back of this book): **Cannaregio** includes the train station, Jewish Ghetto, and Cà d'Oro; **Castello** extends east from Cannaregio toward the Arsenal; **San Marco** fills in the area between P. S. Marco and the Grand Canal (and constitutes about three-quarters of our adjacent "Central Venice" map); **Dorsoduro** is just across the Accademia bridge from S. Marco, swinging from the Salute church out to Giudecca and up to Cà Rezzonico; **San Polo** runs north from Dorsoduro to the Rialto Bridge; and **Santa Croce** lies between S. Polo to the east and the train station to the west. There are no individual street numbers within each *sestiere*—door numbers form one long, haphazard set. If *sestiere* boundaries are too nebulous, Venice's **parrochie** (parishes) provide a more defined idea of where you are, and *parrochia* signs, like *sestiere* signs, are painted on the sides of buildings. There are also **yellow signs** throughout the city directing pedestrians to the certain landmarks: the **Rialto Bridge** (at the center, between S. Marco and S. Polo); **Piazza San Marco** (south central, in S. Marco); the **Accademia** (southwest, in Dorsoduro), **Ferrovia** (the train station; northwest, in Cannaregio); and **Piazzale Roma** (directly south of the station, in S. Croce).

Venice is notoriously impossible to navigate; navigating Venice is like playing pin-the-tail-on-the-donkey with more water and fewer donkeys. The city will twist and turn and confound you, and then deposit your dazed self at a dead end. Unglue your eyes from your map and go with the flow—it's only by getting lost that you'll discover some of the unexpected surprises that make Venice spectacular.

TOURIST AND FINANCIAL SERVICES

Tourist Offices and Tours: APT, P. S. Marco 71/f (tel. 041 520 89 64), opposite the Basilica. Open daily 9am-1pm and 1:30-5pm. **Branches** at the train station (tel./fax 041 71 90 78; open daily 8am-7pm) and in the **Lido,** Gran Vle. 6a (tel. 041 526 57 21; open in high-season M-Sa 10am-1pm). **Rolling Venice,** S. Marco 1529 (tel. 041 274 76 50; fax 041 274 76 42), on Corte Contarina. Exit P. S. Marco opposite the Basilica, turn right, follow the road left, continue through the building, look for the yellow "Comune di Venezia" signs, take a left, turn right, and go into the courtyard. Sells the **Youth Discount Card** (L5000), which provides discounts at hotels, restaurants, and museums, as well as the 3-day **Rolling Venice vaporetto pass** (L25,000). Open M, W, and F 9:30am-1pm, Tu and Th 9:30am-1pm and 3-5pm. **Branch** (tel. 041 524 28 52) at the train station. Open July-Sept. 8am-8pm. **Enjoy Venice** (tel. 800 27 48 19 or 06 445 18 43) offers informative walking tours covering the major sights. L30,000, under 26 L25,000. Tours leave in summer M-Sa at 10am (call for winter hours) from Thomas Cook by the Rialto Bridge.

ITALY

Budget Travel: CTS, Dorsoduro 3252 (tel. 041 520 56 60; fax 041 523 69 46). From Campo S. Barnaba, cross the bridge nearest the church, then turn right at the end, left through the *piazza*, and left at the foot of the large bridge. Open M-F 9:30am-1:30pm and 3-7pm. **Transalpino** (tel./fax 041 71 66 00), next to the station, sells international train tickets. Open M-F 8:30am-12:30pm and 3-7pm, Sa 8:30am-12:30pm.

Currency Exchange: Banks and 24-hour **ATMs** line **Calle Larga XXII Marzo** (between P. S. Marco and the Accademia) and **Campo San Bartomoleo** (near the Rialto bridge).

American Express: Sal. S. Moise, S. Marco 1471 (tel. 800 87 20 00). Exit P. S. Marco away from the basilica, to the left. No commission; mediocre rates. Mail held for members and traveler's check customers. Open M-F 9am-5:30pm, Sa 9am-12:30pm.

Bookstore: Libreria Studium, S. Marco 337 (tel./fax 041 522 23 82). From P. S. Marco, head left along the basilica. Open M-Sa 9am-6:30pm. V, MC, AmEx.

EMERGENCY AND COMMUNICATIONS

Emergency: Tel. 113. **Police,** tel. 112. **First Aid,** tel. 118.

Police: Carabinieri, Castello 4693/a (tel. 041 520 47 77), in Campo S. Zaccaria.

Pharmacy: Farmacia Italo Inglese, Calle della Mandola, S. Marco 3717 (tel. 041 522 48 37), off Campo Manin. Open M-F 9am-12:30pm and 4:45-7:30pm, Sa 9am-12:30pm. Check the door of any pharmacy for night and weekend pharmacies.

Hospital: Ospedale Civile (tel. 041 529 41 11), Campo SS. Giovanni e Paolo.

Internet Access: Omniservice, Fond. d. Tolentini, S. Croce 220 (tel. 041 71 04 70). From the station, cross the Scalzi bridge, take a right, and turn left on Fond. d. Tolentini. L4000 per 15min. Open M-F 8:30am-1pm and 3-6:30pm, Sa 9:30am-12:30pm.

Post Office: S. Marco 5554 (tel. 041 271 71 11), on Salizzada Fontego dei Tedeschi, off Campo S. Bartolomeo. The building (palace) itself merits a visit. *Fermo Posta (Poste Restante)* at window 4. Address mail to be held: Marshall HENSHAW, *In Fermo Posta*, Fontego dei Tedeschi, S. Marco 5554, **30124** Venezia, Italia. Open M-Sa 8:15am-7pm.

PHONE CODE	Italian city codes are included in local numbers. From outside Italy, dial int'l dialing prefix + 39 + local number.

▐ ACCOMMODATIONS AND CAMPING

Rooms in Venice cost slightly more than elsewhere in Italy. Dorms are sometimes available without reservations, even in high-season, but single rooms vanish quickly (make reservations up to a month in advance). In *pensioni*, watch out for L12,000 breakfasts and other rip-offs. Always agree on what you will pay before you take a room. **AVA,** in the train station (open daily 8am-10pm) and at Ple. Roma 540d near the bus station (open daily 9am-10pm), books rooms for L1000 (call 041 522 22 64 for advance reservations), but proprietors are more willing to bargain in person. If you get desperate, ask the tourist office for info about the campgrounds at Mestre or head to the hostel in nearby Padua (see p. 580) or even Verona (see p. 581).

Cannaregio offers budget accommodations and a festive atmosphere, though the area is a 20- to 30-minute ride from most major sights. Accommodations in **San Marco,** surrounded by luxury hotels and Venice's main sights, are prime choices—if you can get a reservation. **Dorsoduro** is a lively, less-touristed area between the Accademia and the Frari church. **Castello** provides lodging near the Rialto and the center of town, a bit removed from the tourist hordes. **Guidecca** lies just across the Canale della Giudecca, south of Dorsoduro.

HOSTELS AND DORMITORIES

Ostello Venezia (HI), Fondamenta Giudecca Zitelle 86 (tel. 041 523 82 11), on **Giudecca.** *Vaporetto* 82 or 52: Zitelle. Institutional but friendly. Dorms L27,000. Members only; HI cards sold. Breakfast included. Reception 7-9am and 1-11pm. Lockout 9:30am-1:30pm. Curfew 11:30pm. IBN reservations only (see p. 37). 250 beds. V, MC.

Foresteria Valdese, Castello 5170 (tel. 041 528 67 97; fax 041 241 62 38; email valdesi@doge.it). From the Rialto Bridge, head to Campo S. Bartolomeo, left to Salizzada S. Lio, and left on Calle Mondo Novo; enter Campo S. Maria Formosa and take Calle

Lunga S. Maria Formosa over the 1st bridge. Amiable management and dazzling frescoed ceilings. Private rooms with TV. Dorms L30-31,000; doubles L84-120,000; quads L160,000. Breakfast included. Reception 9am-1pm and 6-8pm, Su 9am-1pm. Lockout 10am-1pm. No dorm reservations. 49 beds. Closed 2 weeks in Nov. V, MC.

Domus Civica (ACISJF), S. Polo 3082 (tel. 041 524 04 16), between the Frari and Ple. Roma. From the station, cross the Scalzi bridge, turn right, hang a left on Fond. dei Tolentini, head left through the courtyard on Corte Amai, and it's a few blocks down on the right. Church-affiliated student housing that offers rooms to tourists from mid-June to Sept. Ping-pong, TV, and piano. Singles L45,000; doubles L80,000. 20% off with Rolling Venice or ISIC. Check-in 7:30am-11:30pm. Curfew 11:30pm. 100 beds.

Suore Cannosiano, Fondamenta del Ponte Piccolo, **Giudecca** 428 (tel. 041 522 21 57). *Vaporetto* 82: Giudecca/Palanca; walk left over the bridge to get thee to this nunnery, managed by non-English-speaking nuns. Women only. Large dorms L21,000. Check-out 7:30-8:30am. Lockout 9am-3pm. Strict curfew 10:30pm. 35 beds.

HOTELS

■ **Casa Gerotto/Hotel Calderan,** Campo S. Geremia 283 (tel. 041 71 55 62; tel./fax 041 71 53 61), in **Cannaregio.** Turn left from the station (2min.). The city's best bargain and a backpacker's haven. Wonderful owners and huge, bright rooms, some with TV. Dorms L30,000; singles L50-60,000; doubles L80-130,000; triples L90-160,000; quads L135-200,000. Check-out 10am. Curfew 12:30-1am. 34 rooms.

■ **Hotel Bernardi-Semenzato,** Campo SS. Apostoli, **Cannaregio** 4366 (tel. 041 522 72 57; fax 041 522 24 24). *Vaporetto* 1: Cà d'Oro; turn right on Strada Nuova, left onto Calle del Duca, and right on Calle di Loca. The most gorgeous, luxurious budget digs in Venice. Prices with *Let's Go:* singles L60-75,000; doubles L85-110,000; triples L130-150,000; quads L150-170,000. Breakfast included. TV L5000 per day. Check-out 10:30am. Flexible curfew 1am. 25 rooms. V, MC, AmEx.

Albergo Adua, Lista di Spagna, **Cannaregio** 233a (tel. 041 71 61 84; fax 041 244 01 62). Clean, attractive rooms in a sunny building. Curfew midnight. Breakfast L10,000. Singles L65,000, with bath L100,000; doubles L95,000, with bath L170,000. Breakfast L10,000. Curfew midnight. V, MC, AmEx. 24 rooms.

Albergo San Samuele, S. Marco 3358 (tel./fax 041 522 80 45). Follow Calle delle Botteghe from Campo S. Stefano (near the Accademia) and turn left on Salizzada S. Samuele. Traditional Venetian flooring, elegant bedspreads, and flowers galore. Singles L80,000; doubles L130-190,000. Breakfast L3-7000. Reserve ahead. 10 rooms.

Hotel Noemi, Calle dei Fabbri, **S. Marco** 909 (tel. 041 523 81 44; fax 041 277 10 05; email hotelnoemi@tin.it). Take the 2nd archway from the Basilica di S. Marco and follow Calle dei Fabbri left (1min.). Singles L110,000; doubles L150,000; triples L180,000. Cash only for 1-night stays. Reservations in writing with credit card. V, MC. 15 rooms.

Al Gambero, Calle dei Fabbri, **S. Marco** 4687 (tel. 041 522 43 84; fax 041 520 04 31; email hotgamb@tin.it). Past Hotel Noemi (see above; 2min.). Friendly staff. Singles L85,000; doubles L140,000, with bath L210,000. Breakfast included. 30 clean rooms.

Antica Locanda Montin, Fondamenta del Borgo, **Dorsoduro** 1147 (tel. 041 522 71 51; fax 041 520 02 55), on a picturesque canal. *Vaporetto* 1: Cà Rezzonico; head straight to Campo S. Barnaba, then turn left under the archway, right at the iron sign, and left at the canal. Some rooms with terraces. Doubles L150-190,000. 10 rooms.

Cà Foscari, Calle della Frescada, **Dorsoduro** 3887b (tel. 041 71 04 01; fax 041 71 08 email Valtersc@tin.it). *Vaporetto* 1 or 82: S. Tomà; turn left at the dead end, cross the bridge, turn right, and take a left into the alleyway. Little touches give rooms a homey feel. Singles L85,000; doubles L105-140,000; triples L138-177,000; quads L168-208,000. Breakfast included. Curfew 1am. Rooms held until 2pm. Open Feb.-Nov.

■ **Pensione Casa Verardo, Castello** 4765 (tel. 041 528 61 27; fax 041 523 27 65). *Vaporetto:* S. Zaccaria; take Calle degli Albanese to Campo SS. Filippo e Giacomo, cross the *campo*, and continue down Rimpetto la Sacrestia. Gorgeous, luxurious rooms. Singles L100-150,000; doubles L160-200,000; triples L250,000; 4-person suite L320,000. Reserve with a one-night deposit. 3-night min. stay to use V, MC. 9 rooms.

Locanda Canal, Fondamenta del Remedio, **Castello** 4422c (tel. 041 523 45 38). From S. Marco, head under the clock tower, right on C. Larga S. Marco, left on Ramo dell'Anzolo, over the bridge, and left on Fondamenta del Remedio. Large rooms in a converted *palazzo*. Doubles L120-170,000; triples L150-210,000; quads L180-250,000. Breakfast included. Shower L4000. Reserve with one-night deposit. 7 rooms.

Locanda Silva, Fondamenta del Remedio, **Castello** 4423 (tel. 041 522 76 43; fax 041 528 68 17), next to the Locanda Canal (see above). Basic rooms are cheery and clean, all with phone and a communal cat. Singles L70,000; doubles L110-165,000; triples L140-210,000; quads L240,000. Breakfast included. 25 rooms. Open Feb. to mid-Nov.

Locanda Corona, Calle Corona, **Castello** 4464 (tel. 041 522 91 74). *Vaporetto:* S. Zaccharia; take Calle degli Albanese to Campo SS. Fillipo e Giacomo, continue on Rimpetto la Sacrestia, take the 1st right, and turn left on Calle Corona. Singles L59,000; doubles L85,000; triples L106,000. Breakfast is a hefty extra. Closed Feb.-Dec.

CAMPING

Camping Miramare, Punta Sabbioni (tel. 041 96 61 50; fax 041 530 11 50). Take *vaporetto* 14 from P. S. Marco to "Punta Sabbioni" (40min.), then walk 700m along the beach to your right. In high season L9600 per person, L20,500 per tent; 4-person bungalow L60,000, 5-person L95,000. 3-night min. stay. Open Mar. to mid-Oct.

Campeggio Fusina, V. Moranzani 79 (tel. 041 547 00 55), in Malcontenta. From Ple. Roma, take bus 2 to the "Fusino" stop of S. Marta (1hr., L1500) or boat 16 from "Zattere." L10,000 per person, L7000 per tent, L20,000 per tent and car. Call ahead.

FOOD

Restaurant prices are steeper in Venice than in the rest of Italy. For cheap eats, head to small side streets, or visit any *osteria* or *bacaro* and create a meal from the vast display of *cicchetti* (chee-KET-ee; snacks), including meat- and cheese-filled pastries, tidbits of seafood, rice, and meat, and *tramezzini* (white bread with filling). Venetian cuisine is highly distinct from other Italian fare; try the local seafood, which may include calamari, *polpo* (octopus), or shrimp.

The internationally renowned **Rialto markets,** once the center of trade for the Venetian Republic, abound on the S. Polo side of the Rialto Bridge every morning Monday through Saturday. Smaller **fruit and vegetable markets** set up in Cannaregio, on **Rio Terra S. Leonardo** by the Ponte delle Guglie, and in many *campi* throughout the city. **STANDA supermarket,** Strada Nuova, Cannaregio 3650, is near Campo S. Felice. (Open M-Sa 8:30am-7:20pm, Su 9am-7:20pm. V, MC, AmEx.) Across town on the Zattere, **Billa** at Dorsoduro 1491 is one of the largest and most affordable **supermarkets** in Venice. (Open M-Sa 8:30am-8pm, Su 9am-8pm.)

Oasi, Calle degli Albanesi, **S. Marco** 4263/a (tel. 041 528 99 37), between the Prisons and the Danieli Hotel. Enormous salads and delectable *frulatti* and juices. Salads L9-15,000, *panini* L4-6000. Open Feb. to mid-Dec. M-Sa 8am-6pm.

Vino, Vino, Ponte delle Veste, **S. Marco** 2007a (tel. 041 523 70 27). From Calle Larga XXII Marzo, turn onto Calle delle Veste. Wine bar with delicious, aromatic food. *Primi* L8000, *secondi* L15,000. Cover L1000. 10% off food with Rolling Venice card. Open for drinks W-M 10am-11:30pm; for food W-M 11:30am-3pm and 6:30-11:30pm.

Rosticceria San Bartomoleo, Calle della Bissa, **S. Marco** 5424/a (tel. 041 522 35 69). Follow the neon sign under the last archway on the left from Campo S. Bartolomeo. Pasta L6500-8500, entrees L12-23,000. Open Tu-Su 9:30am-9pm. V, MC, AmEx.

Due Colonne, Campo S. Agostin, **S. Polo** 2343 (tel. 041 524 06 85). Cross the bridge away from the Frari, turn left and cross into Campo S. Stin, turn right on Calle Dora, and cross the bridge. The best pizza in Venice (L6-13,000). Cover L1500. Open Sept.-July M-F noon-3pm and 7-11:30pm, Sa 7-11:30pm.

Do Mori, Calle dei Do Mori, **S. Polo** 429 (tel 041 522 54 01), near the Rialto markets. Venice's oldest wine bar and an elegant place to grab a glass of local wine (L3-5000) or a few *cicchetti* (from L2000). Standing room only. Open M-Sa 8:30am-9pm.

ITALY

Taverna San Trovaso, Fondamenta Nani, **Dorsoduro** 1016 (tel. 041 520 37 03). Young, enthusiastic staff serves great pastas and pizzas. *Primi* L10-15,000, *secondi* L16-24,000, pizzas L7500-11,000. Cover L3000. Open W-Su noon-2:30pm and 7-9:45pm.

Ristorante da Poggi, Campo della Maddalena, **Cannaregio** 2103 (tel. 041 524 07 58). Left from the station and cross 2 bridges. Popular college hangout. *Primi* and *secondi* L16-30,000. 15% discount with *Let's Go.* Open Tu-Su noon-3pm and 6:30pm-midnight.

GELATERIE

🐌 **La Boutique del Gelato,** Salizzada S. Lio, **Castello** 5727 (tel. 041 522 32 83). Go. Go NOW. Enormous cones from L1500. Open Feb.-Nov. daily 10am-8:30pm.

Gelati Nico, Zattere, **Dorsoduro** 922 (tel. 041 522 52 93). Try *gianduiotto* (chocolate-hazelnut ice cream dunked in whipped cream). L2-4000. Open F-W 6:45am-11pm.

▓ SIGHTS

Many churches enforce a strict dress code: shoulders and knees must be covered.

PIAZZA SAN MARCO TO THE RIALTO BRIDGE. Piazza San Marco is the city's pigeon-infested, *campanile*-punctuated nucleus. In contrast to Venice's narrow, maze-like streets, the *piazza* is an expanse of light and space, framed all around by museums and medieval buildings. Construction of the **Basilica di San Marco** began in the 9th century, when two Venetian merchants stole St. Mark's remains from Alexandria and hid them in a barrel of pork to sneak past Arab officials. The basilica's main treasure is the **Pala d'Oro** that rests behind the altar—a Veneto-Byzantine gold bas-relief encrusted with over 3000 precious gems. *(Basilica open in summer M-Sa 9am-5pm; off-season only illuminated 11:30am-12:30pm. Free. Pala d'Oro open M-Sa 9:30am-4:30pm, Su 2-4:30pm. L3000, reduced L1500.)* The 15th-century **Torre dell'Orologio** (clock tower) to the left of S. Marco indicates the hour, lunar phase, and ascending constellation. The brick **campanile** (bell tower; 96m) across the *piazza* originally served as a watchtower and lighthouse, and was rebuilt after a failed 1902 restoration project turned it into a pile of bricks. *(Elevator open daily 9am-7pm. L8000, reduced L4000.)* To the right of the Basilica stands the **Palazzo Ducale** (Doge's Palace), once the home of Venice's mayor and today the site of one of Venice's finest museums. Rebuilt in the 14th century after a fire, the palace epitomizes the Venetian Gothic with elegant arcades and light-colored stone cladding. *(Tel. 041 522 49 51. Open daily Apr.-Sept. 9am-7pm; Oct.-Mar. 9am-5pm; last ticket sold 1½hr. before closing. Joint ticket to Biblioteca Marciana and Museos Correr, Archeologico, Vetrario di Murano, and del Merletto di Burano L18,000, students L10,000.)* Facing the palace are Sansovino's masterpieces, the elegant **Libreria** and the **Zecca** (coin mint). The main reading room of the **Biblioteca Marciana,** on the second floor, is adorned with frescoes by Titian and Tintoretto. *(Entrance at P. S. Marco 12.)*

The Gothic-Renaissance **Chiesa di San Zaccaria** holds one of the masterpieces of the Venetian Renaissance, Giovanni Bellini's *Virgin and Child Enthroned with Four Saints* (1505)—it's the second altar on the left. *(Vaporetto: S. Zaccaria. Or, from P. S. Marco, turn left along the water, cross the bridge, and turn left under the sottoportico. Open daily 10am-noon and 4-6pm. Free.)* The **Rialto Bridge** (1588-91) arches over the middle of the **Grand Canal,** whose lacy, delicate *palazzi* testify to the city's wealthy history. To survey the main façades, ride *vaporetto* 82 from the station to P. S. Marco (the view at night, with dazzling reflections of light, is particularly impressive).

SAN POLO. The Gothic ▓**Basilica di Santa Maria Gloriosa dei Frari (I Frari),** begun in 1330, houses a moving wooden sculpture of St. John by Donatello, Bellini's *Madonna and Saints,* and Titian's famous *Assumption*—as well as the remains of Titian himself. *(Vaporetto: S. Tomà; follow the signs back to Campo dei Frari. Open M-Sa 9am-6pm, Su 1-6pm. L3000.)* The *scuole* of Venice, a cross between guilds and religious fraternities, erected ornate "clubhouses" throughout the city; the most illustrious is the **Scuola Grande di San Rocco.** To view its 56 Tintorettos (which took him 23 years to paint) in chronological order, start on the second floor in the Sala dell'Albergo and follow the cycle downstairs. *(Behind I Frari in the Campo S. Rocco. Open daily in summer 9am-5:30pm; off-season 9am-4pm. L9000, reduced L7000.)*

DORSODURO. The theatrical **Chiesa di Santa Maria della Salute,** poised at the tip of Dorsoduro facing S. Marco, is a prime example of the Venetian Baroque. Survey the city from the doors of the old **customs house** next door, where ships sailing into Venice were once required to stop and pay duties. Its bell tower provides the best view of Venice. *(Vaporetto: Salute. Open daily 9am-5:30pm. Free.)* The ▨**Accademia** is a must-see for lovers of Venetian art; its world-class collection includes the superb Bellini *Pala di San Giobbe,* Giorgione's enigmatic *La Tempesta,* and Titian's last work, a brooding *Pietà. (Vaporetto: Accademia; or walk across the Ponte dell'Accademia from S. Marco. Tel. 041 522 22 47. Open in summer M 9am-2pm, Tu-F 9am-9pm, Sa 9am-11pm, Su 9am-8pm; off-season M 9am-2pm, Tu-Sa 9am-9pm, Su 9am-8pm. L12,000.)* The ▨**Collezione Peggy Guggenheim,** housed in her former Palazzo Venier dei Leoni, houses works by Brancusi, Kandinsky, Picasso, Magritte, Rothko, Ernst, Pollock, and Dalì. *(Dorsoduro 701. Vaporetto: Accademia; turn left and follow the yellow signs to Calle S. Cristoforo. Tel. 041 240 54 11. Open W-M 11am-6pm. L12,000, students L8000.)*

NORTHERN VENICE. The **Chiesa di Santissimi Giovanni e Páolo (San Zanipolo),** the largest Gothic church in the city, was built by the Dominican order from the mid-13th- to mid-15th centuries. The church contains a wonderful polyptych by Bellini, and outside stands a dignified equestrian statue, designed in 1479 by Verrochio, da Vinci's teacher. *(Vaporetto: Fond. Nuove; turn left and then right onto Fond. d. Mendicanti. Open M-Sa 8am-12:30pm and 3-6pm, Su 3-5:30pm. Free.)* In 1516, the Doge forced Venice's Jewish population into the old cannon-foundry area, coining the modern usage of the word "ghetto" (Venetian for "foundry"). Several **synagogues** remain open for tours; one shares a building with the **Museo Comunità Ebraica** (Jewish Museum). *(Vaporetto: S. Marcuola; follow the signs straight ahead and then left into Campo d. Ghetto Nuovo. The museum is at Cannaregio 2899/b. Open Su-F June-Sept. 10am-7pm; Oct.-May 10am-4:30pm. L5000, reduced L3000. Obligatory tours for synagogues 40min., every hr. on the half-hour. Museum and tour L12,000, students L9000.)*

GIUDECCA, SAN GIORGIO MAGGIORE, AND THE LAGOON. Many of Venice's most beautiful churches are a short boat ride away from S. Marco. The **Chiesa di San Giorgio Maggiore,** an austere church of simple dignity, is across the lagoon on the island of the same name. *(Vaporetto 52 or 82: S. Giorgio Maggiore. Tel. 041 522 78 27. Open M-Sa 10am-12:30pm and 2:30-6:30pm, Su 9:30-10:30am and 2:30-6:30pm.)* On the adjoining island of Giudecca is his famous **Redentore,** a church built reflecting mathematical harmonies that were intended to glorify God (with their beauty) and man (for his impressive ability to understand said mathematics). During the pestilence of 1576, the Venetian Senate swore that they would build this devotional church and make a yearly pilgrimage here if the plague would leave the city. *(To make your own pilgrimage, take Vaporetto 82 from S. Zaccharia to "Redentore." Open M-Sa 10am-5pm, Su 1-5pm. Expected to reopen following renovations in January 2000. L3000.)*

North of Venice stretches the **lagoon. San Michele** is Venice's cemetery island and the resting place of Ezra Pound, Igor Stravinsky, and Sergei Diaghilev. *(Vaporetto: Cimitero.)* **Murano** has been famed for its glass-blowing since 1292; **Burano** remains a traditional fishing village with bewitching colored façades; and rural **Torcello** boasts an enchanting Byzantine cathedral with magnificent medieval mosaics. *(For Murano, Burano, or Torcello, catch Vaporetto 12 or 52 from S. Zaccaria or Fond. Nuove to "Faro.")* The **Lido** is Venice's beach island as well as the setting for Mann's *Death in Venice. (Vaporetto 1, 41, 52, or 82: Lido.)*

🎵 ENTERTAINMENT AND NIGHTLIFE

ENTERTAINMENT. Mark Twain may have called the **gondola** "an inky, rusty canoe," but it's a canoe only the gentry can afford; the minimum authorized rate starts at L120,000 for 45min. and increases after sunset. However, Venice was built to be traveled by gondola, and you won't have a true sense of the city until you quietly slide down its canals and pass by the front doors of its houses and *palazzi.* Rates are negotiable, but if you still can't afford it, try one of the city's *traghetti* (ferry gondolas that cross the Grand Canal at six points; L700).

ITALY

The weekly *A Guest in Venice*, free at hotels and tourist offices, lists current festivals, concerts, and gallery exhibits. **Vivaldi** concerts occur almost nightly; talk to any of the people wearing almost-authentic period costume scattered throughout town. During the 10 days before Ash Wednesday, Venice's famous **Carnevale** brings masked figures, camera-happy tourists, and outdoor concerts to the city. The famed **Biennale di Venezia** (tel. 041 241 10 58; www.labiennale.org), drowns the city with provocative contemporary international art every odd-numbered year.

NIGHTLIFE. Venetian nightlife is much quieter than that of other major cities. Even the most hopping places close around 1:30am. Students congregate in **Campo Santa Margherita** in Dorsoduro and around **Fondamenta della Misericordia** in Cannaregio. **Paradiso Perduto**, Fondamenta della Misericordia 2540, is a bar, jazz club, and restaurant well-known among locals and tourists; from Strada Nuova, cross Campo S. Fosca, and head straight over three bridges. (Open daily 7pm-2am.) **Bar Salus**, Campo S. Margherita, Dorsoduro 2963, is popular with both Venetian and international students. (Open M-Sa 7am-midnight.) If you're starved for a *discoteca*, slink into **Casanova** and let modern-day Latin lovers show you their moves; if the scene doesn't impress, follow the precedent set by the establishment's namesake and make a daring early escape. (Cover varies. Open daily 7pm-4am.)

PADUA (PADOVA)

Brimming with art and student life, Padua is a treasury of strident frescoes, sculpture-lined *piazze*, and ethereal nighttime festivals. Art escapes the canvas, covering churches floor to ceiling, and high culture blends with a lively university scene.

🛇🚆🛏 PRACTICAL INFO, ACCOMMODATIONS, AND FOOD. Trains depart at least hourly from P. Stazione for Venice (30min., L4100); Verona (1hr., L7900); Bologna (1½hr., L10,100-25,000); and Milan (2½hr., L20-31,500). The **bus station,** P. Boschetti (tel. 049 820 68 11), serves Venice (45min., L5200). The **tourist office** is in the train station. (Tel. 049 875 20 77; fax 049 875 50 88. Open M-Sa 9:15am-5:45pm, Su 9am-noon.) The **Ostello Città di Padova (HI)**, V. Aleardi 30, near Prato della Valle, has an English-speaking staff. Take bus 3 or 8 from the station. (Tel. 049 875 22 19; fax 049 65 42 10. L23,000. Breakfast included. Reception 7-9:30am and 2:30-11pm. Lockout 9:30am-4pm. Curfew 11pm. Reserve a week ahead. V, MC.) **Hotel Al Santo**, V. Santo 147, near the Basilica, has airy, well-kept rooms with phones. (Tel. 049 875 21 31; fax 049 875 21 31. Singles L45-60,000; doubles with shower L80,000; triples with shower L105,000. Open Feb. to mid-Dec.) Women under 26 can stay in the modern, tiny rooms at **Opera Casa Famiglia (ACISJF)**, V. Nino Bixio 4, off P. Stazione. Walk right as you exit the station and turn left just before Hotel Monaco. (Tel. 049 875 15 54. Doubles L60,000; triples L90,000; quads L120,000. Kitchen. Curfew 10:30pm.) Join a rollicking crowd for late-night dinner (creative pizzas from L11,000) on the terrace at **Pizzeria Al Borgo**, V. L. Belludi 56, near the Basilica di S. Antonio. The Lancelot salad, with *radicchio* and spinach, cures a broken or adulterous heart. (Cover L2500. Open W-Su noon-3pm and 7-11:30pm. V, MC.) Or, try **Alexander Bar**, V. S. Francesco 38, near the university, for an immense range of sandwiches (*panini* L6-10,000). (Open M-Sa 8:30am-2am.) **Postal code:** 35100.

📷🎭 SIGHTS AND ENTERTAINMENT. The one-year **Biglietto Unico** is valid at most of Padua's museums (L15,000, students L10,000; buy at the tourist office and participating sights). The ◪**Cappella degli Scrovegni** (Arena Chapel) contains Giotto's breathtaking floor-to-ceiling fresco cycle, illustrating the lives of Mary, Jesus, and Mary's parents. Buy tickets at the adjoining **Musei Civici Eremitani,** which itself features a restored Giotto crucifix. (Open Tu-Su Feb.-Oct. 9am-7pm; Nov.-Jan. 9am-6pm. Chapel open M Feb.-Dec. L10,000, students L7000.) Thousands of pilgrims are drawn to see St. Anthony's jawbone and well-preserved tongue at the **Basilica di Sant'Antonio**, in P. del Santo, a medieval conglomeration of eight domes filled with devastatingly beautiful frescoes. (Open daily 6:20am-7pm.) In the center of P. del Santo stands Donatello's bronze equestrian **Gattamelata statue** of Erasmo da Narni (a.k.a. Gattamelata or Calico Cat), a general remembered for his agility and ferocity. Next door to the **duomo**, in P. Duomo, lies the 12th-century **Battistero**, perhaps the most beautiful of Padua's structures. (Open daily in summer 9:30am-1:30pm and 3-7pm; off-season 9:30am-1pm and 3-6pm. L3000, students L2000.) The fascinating yet somewhat bizarre **Palazzo della Ragione** (Law Courts), built in 1218, retains most of its original shape. Astrological signs line the walls, and to the right of the entrance sits the **Stone of Shame,** upon which partially clad debtors were forced to sit and repeat *"Cedo bonis"* (I renounce my property). (Open Tu-Su Jan.-Oct. 9am-7pm; Nov.-Dec. 9am-6pm. L7000, students L4000.) Buildings of the ancient **university** are scattered throughout the city, but are centered in Palazzo Bó.

The tourist office pamphlet *Where Shall We Go Tonight?* lists restaurants and bars; or, just head to the central *piazza*. **Lucifer Young,** V. Altinate 89, is a hip bar whose decorator may have mortgaged his soul for decorating tips from the *Divine Comedy*'s lowest circle. (Open Su-Tu and Th 7pm-2am, F-Sa 7pm-4am.)

VERONA

After traversing the old Roman Ponte Pietra on a summer's evening, with the gentle rush of the Adige River below and the illuminated towers of churches and castles glowing above, it becomes clear that Verona deserved *Romeo and Juliet*. The city's monumental gates and ancient amphitheater memorialize its Roman past, while the Scaligeri bridge and tombs hark back to its Gothic glory.

🔢 ⌗ PRACTICAL INFO, ACCOMMODATIONS, AND FOOD. Trains (tel. 045 800 08 61) go from P. XXV Aprile to Venice (1¾hr., every hr., L12,000); Milan (2hr., every hr., L13,000); and Bologna (2hr., every 2hr., L10,100). The **tourist office,** in Cortile del Tribunale, is adjacent to P. dei Signori. From P. Bria, take V. Mazzini to V. Cappello, and turn left; it's on the right. (Tel. 045 806 86 80; fax 045 800 36 38. Open Tu-Su 10am-7pm.) Access the **internet** at the record shop **Diesis,** V. Sottoriva 15, to the left of the Ponte Nuovo, under the arches. (L4000 per 15min. Open M-Th 11am-11pm, F-Sa 11am-midnight, Su 3-8pm.) Reserve lodgings ahead, especially in opera season (June 26-Aug. 30). The **⊠Ostello della Gioventù (HI),** "Villa Frances-catti," Salita Fontana del Ferro 15, in a renovated 16th-century villa with gorgeous gardens; from the station, take bus 73 or night bus 90 to P. Isolo, turn right, and follow the yellow signs uphill. (Tel. 045 59 03 60; fax 045 800 91 27. Dorms L22,000; **camping** L8000. Breakfast included. 5-night max. stay. Check-in 5pm. Check-out and rebooking 7-9am. Lockout 9am-5pm. Curfew 11pm; flexible for opera-goers. No reservations.) Women can also try the beautiful **Casa della Giovane (ACISJF),** V. Pigna 7, 3rd fl., in the historic center of town. (Tel. 045 59 68 80. Dorms L22,000; singles L32,000; doubles L50,000. Reception 9am-11pm. Curfew 11pm; flexible for opera-goers.) To get to **Locanda Catullo,** Vco. Catullo 1, walk to V. Mazzini 40, turn onto V. Catullo, and turn left on Vco. Catullo. (Tel. 045 800 27 86. Singles L60,000; doubles L90-110,000; triples L130-160,000; quads L170-210,000. July-Sept. 3-night min. stay. Reserve ahead.) Verona is famous for its wines—its dry white *soave* and red *valpolicella*, *bardolino*, and *recioto*. Prices in **P. Isolo** are cheaper than those in P. delle Erbe. For a large sampling, try **Oreste dal Zovo,** Vco. S. Marco in Foro 7/5, off C. Porta Borsari. **Cantore,** V. A. Mario 2, a block from the Arena near V. Mazzini, has Verona's best pizza-ambience combo. (Tel. 045 803 43 69. Open M-Tu and Th-Su 9am-3pm and 6pm-midnight.) **Supermercato Vivo** is in Piazzetta Pescheria. (Open M-Sa 8:30am-1pm and 4:15-7:45pm; closed W afternoon.) **Postal code:** 37122.

📷 🎵 SIGHTS AND ENTERTAINMENT. The physical and emotional heart of Verona is the majestic, pink-marble, first-century **⊠Arena,** in P. Brà. (Open Tu-Su 9am-7pm; in opera season 8am-3:30pm. L6000, students L4000.) From P. Brà, V. Mazzini leads to the markets and stunning medieval architecture of **Piazza delle Erbe,** the former Roman forum. The 83m **Torre dei Lambertini,** down V. Capello from P. Erbe, offers perhaps the most stunning view of Verona. (Open Tu-Su 9:30am-6pm. Elevator L4000. Stairs L3000; students L2000.) The **Giardino Giusti,** V. Giardino Giusti 2, is a magnificent 16th-century garden with a labyrinth of mythological stat-

ITALY

ues. (Open daily Apr.-Sept. 9am-8pm; Oct.-Mar. 9am-dusk. L7000, students L3000.) The della Scala fortress, the **Castelvecchio,** down V. Roma from P. Brà, is filled with walkways, parapets, and an extensive art collection including Pisanello's *Madonna and Child.* (Open Tu-Su 9am-7pm. L6000, students L4000; 1st Su of each month free.) Thousands of tourists have falsely immortalized **Casa di Giulietta** (Juliet's House), V. Cappello 23, where the dal Capello (Capulet) family never really lived. Avoid wasting *lire* to stand on the balcony and view the few paintings inside. (Open Tu-Su 9am-7pm. L6000, students L4000; 1st Su of each month free.) From late June to late August, Verona resounds with arias, as tourists and singers from around the world descend on the Arena for the annual **Opera Festival.** (Info tel. 045 805 18 11. For tickets, call 045 800 51 51.)

FRIULI-VENEZIA GIULIA

Friuli-Venezia Giulia traditionally receives less than its fair share of recognition. James Joyce lived in Trieste for 12 years, during which he wrote most of *Ulysses;* Ernest Hemingway drew part the plot for *A Farewell to Arms* from the region's role in WWI; and Freud and Rilke both worked and wrote here. Trieste attracts more tourists, however, as home to the cheapest beach resorts on the Adriatic.

TRIESTE (TRIEST)

In the post-Napoleonic real estate market, the Austrians snatched Trieste (pop. 230,000), a city once rival to Venice; after a little more ping-pong, the city became part of Italy in 1954, but still remains divided between its Slavic and Italian origins. Trieste's past lingers in the its Neoclassical architecture, in the Slavic nuances of its local cuisine, and in the Slovenian still heard in its streets. The grid-like 19th-century **Città Nuova,** between the waterfront and the Castello di S. Giusto, centers on the **Canale Grande.** Facing the canal from the south is the striking Serbian Orthodox **Chiesa di San Spiridione.** The ornate **Municipio** complements the **Piazza dell'Unità d'Italia,** the largest *piazza* in Italy. Trieste's Neoclassical architecture contrasts with its narrow, twisting alleys, reminiscent of its medieval and Roman history. The 15th-century Venetian **Castello di San Giusto** presides over **Capitoline Hill,** south of P. Unità, the city's historical center. (Castle open daily 9am-dusk.) Hilltop **Piazza della Cattedrale** overlooks the sea and downtown Trieste; from P. Goldoni, you can ascend the hill by way of the daunting 265 **Scala dei Giganti** (Steps of the Giants). The archaeological **Museo di Storia e d'Arte,** V. Cattedrale 15, is down the other side of the hill past the *duomo.* (Open Tu-Su 9am-1pm. L3000.)

　Trains (tel. 040 441 14) go from P. della Libertà 8, down C. Cavour from the quays, to Venice (2hr., 2 per hr., L14,000); Ljubljana (4 per day, L35,000); Milan (5hr., 1 per hr., L34,500-50,000); and Budapest (11hr., 2 per day, L117,000). Trains and **buses** also go daily to elsewhere in Slovenia and to Croatia. Less-frequent **ferries** service the Istrian Peninsula as far south as Croatia's Dalmatian Coast. The **tourist office** is near the exit in the train station. (Tel. 040 42 01 82; fax 040 41 68 06. Open M-Sa

HOLY SHROUD, BATMAN! Called a hoax by some and a miracle by others, the holy shroud of Turin (a 1m by 4.5m piece of linen) was supposedly wrapped around Jesus' body in preparation for burial after his crucifixion. Although radiocarbon dating places the piece in the 12th century AD, the shroud's uncanny resemblance to Christ's dissuades its immediate dismissal. Visible on the cloth are outflows of blood: around the head (supposedly from the Crown of Thorns), all over the body (from scourging), and most importantly, from the wrists and feet (where the body was nailed to the cross). Scientists agree that the shroud was wrapped around the body of a 5'7" man who died by crucifixion, but whether it was the body of Jesus remains a mystery. For Christian believers, however, the importance of this relic is best described by Pope Paul VI's words: "The Shroud is a document of Christ's love written in characters of blood."

9am-7pm, Su 10:30am-1pm and 4-7pm.) To get from the station to **Ostello Tegeste (HI)**, V. Miramare 331, on the seaside, take bus 36 (L1400) from across V. Miramare, the street on the left of the station as you exit, and ask the driver for the ostello. From the stop, walk back down the road toward Trieste and take the seaside fork toward the castle. (Tel./fax 040 22 41 02. L20,000; members only. Reception noon-midnight. Breakfast included. Check-out 9am. Lockout 9am-noon. Curfew midnight.) Take the tram to Opicina from platform 2 in P. Oberdan, near Hotel Posta, (30min., every 20min., L1400) to sleep at **Valeria**, V. Nazionale 156. (Tel. 040 21 12 04. Singles L35,000; doubles L60,000.) It wouldn't be Italy without a **STANDA**, on V. XX Settembre. Thanks to Viennese influence, coffee is an art form in Trieste; try ▓**Antico Caffè San Marco**, V. Battisti 18. (Open in summer Tu-F and Su 7am-midnight, Sa 7am-1am; off-season Tu-Su 7am-1am.) **Postal code:** 34100.

PIEDMONT (PIEMONTE)

Piedmont has been a politically influential region for centuries, as well as a fountainhead of fine food, wine, and nobility. After native-born Vittorio Emanuele II and Camillo Cavour united Italy, Turin served as the capital from 1861 to 1865.

TURIN (TORINO)

Turin, which will host the Winter Olympics in 2006, is today primarily known as home to the Fiat Auto Company as well as one of the strangest relics of Christianity. The **Cattedrale di San Giovanni**, behind the Palazzo Reale, houses the **Holy Shroud of Turin.** While the chapel is closed for restorations until August 2000, there is a lifesize canvas copy of the shroud on display. (Open daily 7am-noon and 3-7pm.) The **Museo Egizio**, in the **Palazzo dell'Accademia delle Scienze,** V. dell'Accademia delle Scienze 6, boasts a collection of Egyptian artifacts second only to the British Museum. (Open Tu-F 9am-9pm, Sa 9am-noon, Su 9am-8pm. L12,000.) One of Guarini's great Baroque palaces, the **Museo Nazionale del Risorgimento Italiano,** in the **Palazzo Carignano,** V. dell'Accademia delle Scienze 5, at various times housed both the first Italian parliament and the cradle of Prince Vittorio Emanuele. Today the museum details the unification of Italy, from 1800 to the early 20th century. (Tel. 011 562 37 19. Open Tu-Sa 9am-7pm, Su 9am-1pm. L8000. Tours Su 10:30am-noon; free.)

Trains roll to Milan (2hr., every hr., L16,000); Genoa (2hr., every hr., L14,000); and Venice (4½hr., 10 per day, L34,000). The **tourist office**, P. Castello 165, has free maps. (Tel. 011 53 51 81. Open daily 8:30am-7:30pm.) To get to the clean, comfortable, and bright-orange **Ostello Torino (HI)**, V. Alby 1, take bus 52 (bus 64 on Su) from Stazione Porto Nuova to the third stop after crossing the river. Go back up V. Thoveu, bear left onto V. Curreno, and turn left onto V. Gatti, which branches off onto V. Alby. (Tel. 011 660 29 39; fax 011 660 44 45. L20,000. Breakfast and sheets included. Laundry L10,000. Oct.-Apr. heat L2000 per day. Reception 7-10am and 3:30-11pm. Curfew 11pm. Open Feb.-Dec.) To **camp** at **Campeggio Villa Rey**, Strada Superiore Val S. Martino 27, take bus 61 north from the right side of the Porta Nuova across the Emanuele bridge. Get off at the Porta Margherita bridge, then take bus 54 or walk up C. Gabetti away from the river to the right and follow the signs. (Tel. 011 819 01 17. L7000 per person; L4-7000 per tent. Showers L1000.) The open-air **market** sets up on P. della Repubblica. (Open M-F 8am-1pm, Sa 8am-6pm.) **Postal code:** 10100.

THE LAKES AND THE DOLOMITES

When Italy's monuments and museums all start to blur together, you can escape to the natural beauty of the country's lakes and mountains. The Lake Country fueled Stendhal's drippiest descriptions of lakes, flowers, and mountains. The Dolomites dominate the landscape in the province of Trentino-Alto Adige, rising from Austrian-influenced valley communities to lofty peaks perfect for skiing and hiking. The Lake Country lends itself to relaxation, whether by the lakeside or in the nightclubs. Windsurfing and pensive reflection are also popular in the region.

LAKE COMO (LAGO DI COMO)

Although an unworldly magnificence lingers over the northern reaches of Europe's deepest lake (410m), peaceful Lake Como is not a figment of your imagination. Bougainvillea and lavish villas adorn the lake's craggy backdrop, warmed by the sun and cooled by lakeside breezes.

⌐ GETTING THERE AND GETTING AROUND. The only town on the lake accessible by train is its largest urban outpost, **Como,** on the southwestern tip of the lake. **Trains** roll in from Milan (1hr., every hr., L10,000), while **buses** ply the route from Bergamo (2hr., every 2hr., L8200). From Como, hourly **buses** run to towns in the **Central Lago** area, where the three prongs of the forked lake meet. **Bellaggio** (1hr., L5000), on the southern shore of the Centro Lago, is the favorite lake town of upper-crust Milanese society; steep streets lead to sidewalk cafés, silk shops, and the villas of Lombard aristocrats. **Varenna,** on the eastern shore, is far more peaceful and scenic. The C10 bus runs along the western shore of the lake to **Menaggio** (1hr., L4700; see below) and **Tremezzo,** which boasts the enormous azaleas and sculptures of **Villa Carlotta** (L9000, L5000 through the hostel; open Mar.-Nov.) but is otherwise quiet. Once you've found a place to stay, you can spend the day zipping between the stores, gardens, villas, and wineries of the remaining towns on the lake by **ferry;** a partial **lake pass** is good for travel throughout the Centro Lago (L15,000), while a full lake pass is good for travel on the entire lake (L21,000).

COMO. For excellent hiking and stunning views, take the *funicolare* from the far end of Lungo Lario Trieste (every 15-30min.; round-trip L7200, through the hostel L5000) up to **Brunate.** To get from the station to the **tourist office,** P. Cavour 16, walk down the steps to V. Gallio, which becomes V. Garibaldi and leads to P. Cavour via P. Volta. (Tel. 031 26 20 91. Open M-Sa 9am-12:30pm and 2:30-6pm, Su 9am-1pm.) **Ostello Villa Olmo (HI),** V. Bellinzona 2, offers clean rooms, great food, and discounts on various sights in Como. From the station, walk 20min. left down V. Borgovico, which becomes V. Bellinzona. (Tel. 031 57 38 00. L17,000. Breakfast included. Reception daily 7:30-10am and 4-11pm. Lockout after 10am. Call ahead. Open Mar.-Nov.) Picnickers will appreciate the **G.S. supermarket,** on the corner of V. Recchi and V. Fratelli Roselli. (Open M 2-8pm, Tu-Sa 8am-8pm, Su 10am-6pm.)

MENAGGIO. Menaggio is home to historic streets and unbelievable scenery. A one- to two-hour hike will reward you with the spectacular **Sass Corbee waterfalls;** inquire at the tourist office for directions. To get to the jolly, resort-like ⌕**Ostello La Prinula (HI),** V. IV Novembre 86, from the bus stop or ferry port, face the water, turn right, and walk along the shore to the main thoroughfare; just past the gas station, walk up the less steep incline to the right. (Tel. 0344 323 56; fax 0344 316 77; email menaggiohostel@mclink.it. L17,000. Breakfast included. Bike and kayak rental L17,000 per day. Laundry L5000. **Internet** L4000 per 15min. Lockout 10am-5pm. Curfew 11:30pm. Call ahead. Open mid-Mar. to early Nov.) If the hostel happens to be full, hop on the bus heading north and get off at "Rezzonico"; **Hotel Lauro** (tel. 0344 500 29) has singles for L30-35,000 and doubles for L52-60,000.

DOMASO. The tiny town of Domaso boasts perfect windsurfing. Though the **Ostello della Gioventù (HI),** V. Case Sparse 12, will remain closed partway into 2000 for renovations (tel. 0344 960 94; call ahead), Domaso has 12 **campsites,** including **Europa,** near the hostel. (Tel./fax 0344 960 44. L8000 per person; L18,000 per tent.)

LAKE MAGGIORE (LAGO MAGGIORE)

Lacking only the frenzy of its eastern neighbors, Lake Maggiore cradles the same temperate mountain waters and idyllic shores. The charming resort town of **Stresa,** only an hour from Milan by **train** (every hr., L8200, IC supplement L6000), is the most convenient base for exploring the area. To get to Lake Maggiore from Lake Como, take a train from Como to Laveno (L4800; change at Saronna), on the eastern shore of Lake Maggiore, then take a ferry to elsewhere on the lake. To get from the Stresa train station to the **tourist office,** V. Principe Tommaso 70/72, turn right and walk down the hill on V. Carducci, which becomes V. Gignous; V. Tommaso is on the left. (Tel. 0323 301 50. Open M-F 8:30am-12:30pm and 3-6:15pm.) To get to **Orsola Meublé**, V. Duchessa di Genova 45, turn right from the station, walk downhill, and turn left at the intersection. (Tel. 0323 310 87. Singles L50-70,000; doubles L80-100,000. Breakfast included. V, MC, AmEx.)

Alternatively, to get to the new and much cheaper **Ostello Verbania Internazionale** from Stresa, take a ferry across the lake to **Pallanza**. After disembarking the ferry, walk to the right along the water to V. Vittorio Veneto, turn left on V. Panoramica, and walk up the hill, around the bend, and take your last right; the hostel is on the left. (L23,000. Breakfast included. Reception 8-11am, 4-5:30pm, 10-11pm. Kitchen.) The **tourist office**, on V. Zanitello, is located between the port and the hostel.

⚑ EXCURSION FROM LAKE MAGGIORE: BORROMEAN ISLANDS. Stresa and Pallanza are perfect stepping stones to the gorgeous **Borromean Islands**. Daily excursion tickets (L14,800; L17,400 including travel to Laveno's train station) allow you to hop back and forth between either Stresa and Pallanza and the three islands (**Isola Bella, Isola Superiore dei Pescatori,** and **Isola Madre**). The islands boast lush and manicured botanical gardens, elegant villas, and an opulent Baroque palace.

LAKE GARDA (LAGO DI GARDA)

Garda—the ultimate resort destination for many German families—has staggering mountains and breezy summers. **Desenzano,** the lake's southern transport hub, lies on the Milan-Venice line, 30min. from Verona, 1hr. from Milan, and 2hr. from Venice. From Desenzano, the other lake towns are easily accessible by bus and boat.

SIRMIONE. Along the lake's shore, Sirmione, with beautifully situated medieval castle and extensive Roman ruins, can fill a leisurely day or a busy afternoon. **Buses** arrive hourly from Desenzano (20min., L2500) and Verona (1hr., L5000). *Battelli* (water steamers) run to Desenzano (20min., L4400); Gardone (1¼hr., L9900); and Riva (4hr., L13,900). The **Albergo Grifone**, V. Bisse 5, has a prime locale by the castle. (Tel. 030 91 60 14; fax 030 91 65 48. Singles L65,000; doubles L90,000; L27,000 per additional bed. Reserve ahead.)

GARDONE RIVIERA. The town prides itself on the mansion of famous author, and latter-day Casanova, Gabriele D'Annunzio. Quirky **Ⅱl Vittoriale** sprawls above Gardone, off V. Roma and V. dei Colli. (Villa open Apr.-Sept. Tu-Su 10am-12:30pm and 2:30-6pm; gardens open Oct.-Mar. Tu-Su 8:30am-8pm.) **Buses** (tel. 0365 210 61) run to Desenzano (30min., 6 per day, L3900) and Milan (3hr., 2 per day, L15,100). The **APT tourist office**, V. Repubblica 39, is in the center of Gardone Sotto. (Tel./fax 0365 203 47. Open Apr.-Oct. M-Sa 9am-12:30pm and 4-7pm; Nov.-Mar. M-W and F 9am-12:30pm and 3-6pm, Th 9am-12:30pm.)

RIVA. Riva has few sights, but the town is livelier, the crowd younger, and the prices lower than other places on the lake; it's the best place to base yourself. Travelers **swim, windsurf, hike,** and **climb** in the most stunning portion of the lake, where Alpine cliffs crash into the water. Riva is accessible by **bus** (tel. 0464 55 23 23) from Trent (1¼hr., 6 per day, L6000) and Verona (2hr., 11 per day, L9300). **Ferries** (tel. 030 914 95 11), on P. Matteoti, head to Gardone (L12,200). The **tourist office**, Giardini di Porta Orientale 8, is near the water. (Tel. 0464 55 44 44; fax 0464 52 03 08. Open M-Sa 9am-noon and 4-6pm.) Snooze at the fabulous **Ostello Benacus (HI)**, P. Cavour 9, in the center of town; from the bus station, walk down V. Trento, take V. Roma, turn left under the arch, and follow signs. (Tel. 0464 55 49 11; fax 0464 55 65 54. L22,000. Breakfast included. Reception 7-10am and 4pm-midnight. Reserve ahead.)

THE DOLOMITES

Limestone spires shoot skyward from pine forests in the Dolomites. These amazing peaks—fantastic for hiking, skiing, and rock climbing—start west of Trent and extend north and east to Austria. With their sunny skies and powdery, light snow, the mountains offer very popular year-round downhill skiing.

TRENT. Inside the Alpine threshold, yet connected to the Veneto by a long, deep valley, Trent is worth a stop for its sampling of northern Italian life and engaging walks set against a backdrop of dramatic limestone cliffs. The **Piazza del Duomo,** Trent's center and social heart, contains the city's best sights. The **Fontana del Nettuno** stands, trident in hand, in the center of the *piazza*. Nearby is the **Cattedrale di San Vigilio,** named for the patron saint of Trent. (Open daily 6:40am-12:15pm and 2:30-7:30pm.) Walk down V. Belenzani and head right on V. Roma to reach the well-preserved **Castello del Buonconsiglio.** (Open Apr.-Sept. Tu-Su 9am-noon and 2-5:30pm; Oct.-Mar. Tu-Su 9am-noon and 2-5pm. L9000, students L5000.) **Monte Bondone** rises majestically over Trent, begging a pleasant daytrip or overnight excursion. Catch the **cable car** (L1500) from Ponte di S. Lorenzo, between the train tracks and the river, to **Sardagna.**

Trains (tel. 0461 82 10 00) head to Bolzano (50min., every hr., L5200); Verona (1hr., every hr., L8500); Venice (2½hr., L14,400); and Bologna (2½-3hr., 8 per day, L18,000). Atesina **buses** go from V. Pozzo, next to the train station, head to Riva del Garda (1hr., every hr., L5500). From the train station, turn right on V. Pozzo and left on V. Torre Vanga to reach the **tourist office,** V. Alfieri 4. (Tel. 0461 98 38 80; www.apt.trento.it. Open M-Sa 9am-6pm, Su 9am-1pm.) From the station, turn right on V. Pozzo and left on V. Torre Vanga to get to **Ostello Giovane Europa (HI),** V. Manzoni 17. (Tel. 0461 23 45 67; fax 0451 25 84 34. Dorms L21,000; singles L30,000. Breakfast included. Reception 3:30-11pm. Check-out 9:30am. Curfew 11:30pm. Reserve ahead.) **Hotel Venezia** is at P. Duomo 45. (Tel./fax 0461 23 41 14. Singles L62,000; doubles L88,000. Breakfast L8000. V, MC.)

BOLZANO. In the tug-of-war between Austrian and Italian cultural influences, Bolzano pulls the Austrian side of the rope. The town's hybrid culture and prime location beneath vineyard-covered mountains makes it a splendid stopover en route to the Dolomites. With its prickly spined tower and a diamond-patterned roof, the Gothic **duomo,** on P. Walther, is a dark and awesome sight. Aside from that, the best "sights" in town are found by exploring the winding streets and admiring the façades. (Open daily 6am-noon and 2:30-6pm.) **Castel Ronacolo** sits on the hills above town. From the bus stop, wind up the path for a spectacular view of the city en route to the frescoes in the castle. (Open Mar.-Nov. Tu-Sa 10am-5pm; frescoes close 4pm. L2000.) **Trains** (tel. 0471 97 42 92) go to Trent (1-2hr., 1-2 per hr., L9000); Verona (2hr., 1-2 per hr., L12,100); and Milan (3½hr., 3 per day, L23,500). Walk up V. Stazione from the train station, or V. Alto Adige from the bus stop, to reach the **tourist office,** P. Walther 8. (Tel. 0471 30 70 00; fax 0471 98 01 28. Open M-F 9am-6:30pm, Sa 9am-12:30pm.) The **Provincial Tourist Office for South Tyrol,** P. Parrocchia 11, near P. Walther opposite the *duomo*, is a must for those heading into the mountains. (Tel. 0471 99 38 08. Open M-F 9am-noon and 2-5pm.) **Croce Bianca,** P. del Grano (Kornpl.) 3, is around the corner from P. Walther. (Tel. 0471 97 75 52. Singles L40,000; doubles L60-78,000; triples L90,000. Breakfast L8000. Reserve ahead.)

LOMBARDY (LOMBARDIA)

Over the centuries, Roman generals, German emperors, and French kings have vied for control of Lombardy's fertile soil. In the recent past, increases in employment and developments in industry have made Lombardy an even more vibrant cornerstone of the Italian economy. Cosmopolitan Milan may drive the mighty engine of progress, but don't let its exhaust fumes blind you to the beauty of Bergamo, Mantua, or the nearby foothills of the Alps.

MILAN (MILANO)

Briefly the capital of the western half of the Roman Empire, modern Milan retains few reminders of its distinguished pedigree. The city has embraced modernity with more force than any other major Italian city, creating a fast-paced life—even the requisite *siesta* is shorter. Although success has also brought petty crime and drugs, Milan remains a vibrant city on the cutting edge of high finance and fashion.

GETTING THERE AND GETTING AROUND

Flights: Info tel. 02 74 85 22 00. **Malpensa Airport,** 45km away, handles intercontinental flights. **Malpensa Express** connects to MM1,2: Cadorna (45min., L15,000). **Linate Airport,** 7km away, covers Europe. Take bus 73 from MM1: P. San Babila (L1500).

Trains: Stazione Centrale, P. Duca d'Aosta (tel. 01 47 88 80 88), on MM2. To: **Genoa** (1½hr., every hr., L24,000); **Turin** (2hr., every hr., L24,500); **Florence** (2½hr., every hr., L40,000); **Venice** (3hr., every hr., L36,000); and **Rome** (4½hr., every hr., L71,000). Info office open daily 7am-9:30pm. **Luggage storage** L500 per 12hr.

Buses: Stazione Centrale (see **Trains** above). Intercity buses tend to be less convenient and more expensive than trains. **SAL, SIA, Autostradale,** and other carriers leave from P. Castello and nearby (MM1: Cairoli) for Turin, Lake Country, and Bergamo.

Public Transportation: The **subway** (Metropolitana Milanese, or **MM**) runs 6am-midnight. **ATM** (tel. 167 01 68 57 toll-free), in the MM1,3: Duomo station, handles local transportation. Single-fare tickets (L1500) are good for 75min. of surface transportation. Day passes L5000, 2-day L9000. Info and ticket booths open M-Sa 7:15am-7:15pm.

ORIENTATION AND PRACTICAL INFORMATION

Milan's layout resembles a giant target, encircled by remnants of concentric ancient city walls. The **duomo** and **Galleria Vittorio Emanuele II** comprise the bull's-eye. From the train station, a scenic ride on bus 60 or quick commute on metro line 3 will take you downtown. See our **color map** at the front of this book.

TOURIST, FINANCIAL, AND LOCAL SERVICES

Tourist Office: APT, V. Marconi 1 (tel. 02 72 52 43 00; fax 02 72 52 43 50), in the Palazzo di Turismo, to the right of the *duomo*. Useful museum guide (in Italian) and map. No room reservations, but will check for vacancies. Pick up *Milano: Where, When, How* and *Milano Mese* for info on activities and clubs. Open M-F 8:30am-8pm, Sa 9am-1pm and 2-7pm, Su 9am-1pm and 2-5pm. **Branch** at Stazione Centrale (tel. 02 72 52 43 70). Open M-Sa 9am-6pm, Su 9am-12:30pm and 1:30-6pm.

Budget Travel: CIT (tel. 02 86 37 01), in Galleria Vittorio Emanuele. Open M-F 9am-7pm, Sa 9am-1pm and 2-6pm. **CTS,** V. S. Antonio 2 (tel. 02 58 30 41 21). Open M-F 9:30am-12:45pm and 2-6pm, Sa 9:30am-12:45pm. **Transalpino Tickets** (tel. 02 67 16 82 28; www.transalpino.com), next to the info office in Stazione Centrale. Discounts for those 26 and under. Open M-Sa 8am-9pm, Su 9am-1pm and 2-8pm.

Currency Exchange: Banca di San Paolo, at Stazione Centrale, has standard rates and charges a L6000 fee. Open M-Sa 8:30am-12:30pm and 2-7:30pm.

American Express: V. Brera 3 (tel. 02 72 00 36 93), on the corner of V. dell'Orso. Holds mail free for AmEx members for 1 month and receives wired money (L2500 fee if over US$100). Open M-Th 9am-5:30pm, F 9am-5pm.

Laundromat: Vicolo Lavandai, V. Monte Grappa 2 (MM2: Garibaldi). Wash or dry L5000 for 7kg. Open daily 8am-10pm.

EMERGENCY AND COMMUNICATIONS

Emergency: Tel. 113. **Police,** tel. 112. **Ambulance,** tel. 118.

Pharmacy: In Stazione Centrale (tel. 02 669 07 35). 24hr.

Hospital: Ospedale Maggiore di Milano, V. Francesco Sforza 35 (tel. 02 550 31).

Internet Access: Bronx Lab in the **Università Statale,** Ospedale Maggiore on V. Festa del Perdono. Free. Open M-F 8:15am-6pm. **Hard Disk Café,** C. Sempione 44 (tel. 02 33 10 10 38). L10-15,000 per hr.; free if you eat there 1-2pm. Open M-Sa 9am-2am.

Post Office: V. Cordusio 4 (tel. 02 869 20 69), near P. del Duomo. Address mail to be held: Jessica WANG, *In Fermo Posta,* Ufficio Postale Centrale di Piazza Cordusio 4, Milano **20100,** Italia. Open M-F 8:30am-7:30pm, Sa 8:30am-1pm.

Telephones: In Galleria Vittorio Emanuele. Open daily 8am-7:30pm. Phones are also available in Stazione Centrale. Open daily 8am-9:30pm.

PHONE CODE	Italian city codes are included in local numbers. From outside Italy, dial int'l dialing prefix + 39 + local number.

ITALY

▮ ACCOMMODATIONS AND CAMPING

It's always high season in Milan, except August, when mosquitoes outnumber human inhabitants. A single room in a decent place for under L60,000 is a real find. Try east of the train station or the southern periphery of the city for the best deals.

▧ Hotel San Tomaso, V. Tunisia 6, 3rd fl. (tel./fax 02 29 51 47 47; email hotelsantomaso@tin.it). MM1: Porta Venezia; take the C. Buenos Aires exit and turn left at McDonald's. The exuberant proprieter runs the hotel *come sua casa.* Clean, renovated rooms with phone and TV. English spoken. **Internet** in 2000. Singles L60,000; doubles with shower L100,000, with bath L120,000; triples L135,000; quads L200,000.

Ostello Pietra Rotta (HI), V. Salmoiraghi 1 (tel. 02 39 26 70 95). MM1: QT8; walk to the right (so the round church is across the street and to your back) for 5min., and it's on your right. Modern facilities and 350 beds. L26,000. Members only; HI cards L30,000. Breakfast included. 3-day max. stay. Reception 7-9am and 3:30pm-midnight, but no morning check-in. Curfew 11:30pm. Open Jan. 13-Dec. 20.

Hotel Ca' Grande, V. Porpora 87 (tel./fax 02 26 14 40 01), 7 blocks in from P. Loreto. MM1,2: Loreto, then take tram 33 to V. Ampere, 60m from the hotel. Wonderful proprietors and clean rooms with phones, though the street below can be noisy. Singles L60-80,000; doubles L90-100,000. Breakfast included. Reception 24hr. V, MC.

Hotel Kennedy, V. Tunisia 6, 6th fl. (tel. 02 29 40 09 34), above Hotel San Tomaso. MM1: Porta Venezia. Pristine rooms. Some English spoken. Singles L50-70,000; doubles L70-130,000; triples L120,000; quads L160,000. Check-out 10am. Ask for keys if you want to go out late. Reserve ahead. V, MC, AmEx.

Hotel Aurora, C. Buenos Aires 18 (tel. 02 204 79 60; fax 204 92 85). MM1: Porta Venezia; exit onto C. Buenos Aires, walk straight for 5min., and it's on the right. Spotless rooms with phone and TV. Enthusiastic, English-speaking owner. Singles L70-90,000; doubles L120-130,000; triples L170,000. Reception 24hr. V, MC, AmEx.

Hotel Casa Mia, Vle. Veneto 30 (tel./fax 02 657 52 49). MM1: Porta Venezia or Repubblica. More upscale. 15 rooms, all with phone, TV, hair dryer, bath, and A/C. English spoken. Singles L85-100,000; doubles L120-150,000; triples L170-200,000. Discounts for *Let's Go* readers. Great continental breakfast included. V, MC.

Hotel Due Giardini, V. B. Marcello 47 (tel. 02 29 52 10 93; fax 02 29 51 69 33). MM1: Lima; walk along V. Vitruvio and turn left onto V. Marcello. Deep red carpet and winding staircase. Quiet neighborhood. 12 rooms, all with phone and TV. Some English spoken. Singles L80-100,000; doubles L130-150,000. Breakfast L7000.

Albergo Brasil di Ramella Luisa, V. G. Modena 20, 4th fl. (tel./fax 02 749 24 82). MM1: Palestro; or bus 60 from Stazione Centrale. From Palestro, take V. Serbelloni and turn left onto V. Cappuccini, which becomes V.F. Bellotti and then V. G. Modena. In a Belle Epoque building. Large rooms and a kind proprietress. Singles L60-85,000; doubles L80-110,000. Reception closes at 12:30am; ask for keys to go out late. V, MC, AmEx.

Camping di Monza (tel. 039 38 77 71), in the park of the Villa Reale in Monza. Take a train or bus from Stazione Centrale to Monza, then a city bus. L5000 (L8000 in Sept.) per person and per tent. Hot showers L500. Open Apr.-Sept. Call ahead.

▮ FOOD

Like its fine *couture*, Milanese cuisine is sophisticated and overpriced. Specialties include *risotto giallo* (rice with saffron), *cotoletta alla milanese* (breaded veal cutlet with lemon), and *cazzouela* (a mixture of pork and cabbage). The largest **markets** are around V. Fauché and Vle. Papiniano on Saturdays and Tuesdays, and along P. Mirabello on Mondays and Thursdays. The **Fiera di Sinigallia,** a 400-year-old market extravaganza, occurs on Saturdays on the banks of the Darsena, a canal in the Navigli district (V. d'Annunzio). Splurge on a local pastry at **Sant'Ambroeus,** a Milanese culinary shrine, under the arcades at C. Matteotti 7. (Open daily 8am-8pm.) Pick up **groceries** near the *duomo* at the **Standa supermarket,** V. Torino 45, in the basement of the department store. (Tel. 02 86 67 06. Open M 1-7:30pm, Tu-Sa 9am-7:30pm.) Nearer to C. Buenos Aires is **Supermarket Regina Giovanna,** 34 V. Regina Giovanna. (Tel. 02 45 83 90 11. Open M-Sa 9am-6pm.)

ITALY

Milan

SEE ALSO COLOR INSERT

ITALY

PIAZZA ASCOLI

Viale dei Mille
Viale Piceno
Viale Umbria

Via Bronzetti

Stazione Porta Vittoria

TO LINATE AIRPORT (6KM)

Corso XXII Marzo

Via Anfossi
Via Campionesi
Via Spartaco
Via Lazio

PIAZZALE LIBIA

Viale Piave
Viale Premuda
Viale B. Maria

Luigi Maino

Via Belotti
Via Carlo Goldoni

Via Mozart

300 yards
300 meters

N

PORTA ROMANA

Museo di Storia Naturale
PALESTRO
Via Palestro
Galleria d'Arte Moderna
Palazzo del Senato
Via Senato
Museo di Milano

Corso Monforte
Via Conservatorio
Conservatorio

Viale Reg. Margherita
Nero
Via Monte
Vle. L. Lazio
Via Caldara

Corso di Vittoria
Via della Pace
Corso di Porta Romana
Viale Filippetti

Via Fatebenefratelli
Via della Spiga
Via Manzoni
Via Monte Napoleone
Via Bigli
MONTE NAPOLEONE
Museo Poldi-Pezzoli

Damiano
S. Babila
Via Borgogna
Via Cavallotti
Corso Matteotti
Via F. Sforza
Via San Barnaba
Via d. Commenda
Policlinico
CROCETTA
Corso di Porta Romana
Corso Porta Vignetina

Pinacoteca di Brera
Via Brera
American Express
Via Monte di Pietà
La Scala
Via Verdi
Via Mercanti
PIAZZA DELLA SCALA
Galleria V. Emanuele II
United Kingdom
Duomo
Palazzo Arcivescovado
Teatro Lirico
Via Festa del Perdono
Ospedale Maggiore (University)
San Nazaro

Via Pontaccio
Via Mercado
PIAZZA CAIROLI
LANZA
CAIROLI
Via Dante
Via Meravigli
PIAZZA CORDUSIO
CORDUSIO
DUOMO
Orefice
Via Spadari
Pinacoteca Ambrosiana
Via Torino
PIAZZA DEL DUOMO
Palazzo Reale
Via Mazzini
MISSORI
Via Paola
Via Larga
Corso di Porta Romana
San Lorenzo
Via S. Sofia
Corso Italia
Via Savola

Via Amedei
PIAZZA VETRA
San Eustorgio
PORTA TICINESE
Corso Porta Ticinese

Via Meravigli
Via Goretti
Via Olona
Via Stampa
Via San Vito
Via Vetere

Castello Sforzesco
Buses to Malpensa Airport
Foro Buonaparte
CADORNA
Stazione Nord
Santa Maria delle Grazie
Basilica di Sant'Ambrogio
S. AMBROGIO
Via Lanzone
Via Edmondo de Amicis
Via Arena
PIAZZALE XXIV MAGGIO

PARCO SEMPIONE
Via Gadio
Via Pagano
Palazzo dell'Arte
Via Vincenzo Monti
Via Boccaccio
Corso Magenta
Via Togni
Via San Vittore
Museo Nazionale della Scienza e della Tecnica "da Vinci"
S. AGOSTINO
Via Olivetani
Via Valeria
CARCERI

PARCO SOLARI
Via Papiniano
Viale Conti Zugna
Stazione Porta Genova
PORTA GENOVA
Via Vigevano
Via Gorizia
PIAZZA CANTORE
Colombo C. di porta Genova
Via Ariberto
Via Cristoforo Colombo
Viale G. d'Annunzio
Viale Col di Lana
Viale Beatrice d'Este
Via Beatrice d'Este

Via L. Mascheroni
CONCILIAZIONE
Via Ariosto
Viale Vercellina
Viale Vercelli
Via Solari
Via Savona
Via Tortona

Via Pagano
Via G. Carducci

■ **Brek,** V. Lepetit 20 (tel. 02 670 51 49), near Stazione Centrale; 2nd location in P. Cavour. Elegant self-serve restaurant. Fresh ingredients cooked into tasty dishes before your eyes. *Secondi* around L7500. Open M-Sa 11:30am-3pm and 6:30-10:30pm.

Pizzeria Grand'Italia, V. Palermo 5. Massive pizzas (L7-10,000), are worth the wait. Open daily 12:15-2:45pm and 7pm-1:15am; Sept.-July closed Tu.

Ristorante "La Colubrina," V. Felice Casati 5 (tel. 02 29 51 84 27). MM1: Porta Venezia. A neighborhood restaurant with pizza from L6000 and specials from L9000. Cover L2000. Open Sept.-July Tu-Su noon-2:30pm and 7-11:30pm; closed Tu and Su lunch.

Le Briciole, V. Camperio 17 (tel. 02 87 71 85), near the *duomo*. MM1: Cairoli. Young clientele. Pizza L9-16,000. Spectacular *antipasto* buffet L13-22,000. Cover L3000. Open daily 12:15-2:30pm and 7:15-11:30pm; closed Sa lunch. V, MC, AmEx.

Il Fondaco dei Mori, V. Solferino 33 (tel. 02 65 37 11). MM2: Moscova; walk north to P. XXV Aprile, turn right onto B. Porta Nuova, and take your 2nd right onto V. Solferino. No sign; ring the bell. First Middle Eastern restaurant in Italy. Vegetarian lunch menu L14,000. Delicious dinner buffet L20,000. Try the mango or guava juice, or the excellent ginger coffee. Cover L3000. Open daily 12:30-3pm and 7:30pm-midnight.

La Crêperie, V.C. Correnti 21 (tel. 02 837 57 08). MM1: S. Ambrogio. Fruit crêpes L6000; liqueur L4000; savory other types L5-7000. Open daily 11am-1am.

◉ SIGHTS

AROUND THE DUOMO. The Gothic **duomo** is the geographical and spiritual center of Milan. More than 3400 statues, 135 spires, and 96 gargoyles grace this third-largest church in the world. *(On P. del Duomo. Open daily June-Sept. 7am-5pm; Oct.-May 9am-4pm. Free. Roof access L6000, with elevator L8000.)* The **Museo d'Arte Contemporanea,** in Palazzo Reale to the right of the *duomo*, holds a fine permanent collection of 20th-century Italian art and a few Picassos. *(Open daily 9:30am-5:30pm. Free.)* Follow V. Torino from P. del Duomo, take a right on V. Spadari, and turn left on V. Cantù to get to the tiny but lovely **Pinacoteca Ambrosiana,** which houses 15th- to 17th-century art, including works by Botticelli, Leonardo, Raphael, Brueghel, and Caravaggio. *(P. Pio XI 2. Open Tu-Su 10am-5:30pm. L12,000.)* Backtrack to the P. del Duomo and head into the **Galleria Vittorio Emanuele II,** to the left as you face the *duomo*, a four-story arcade of cafés and shops with mosaic floors. Meander through this beautiful gallery to the P. della Scala on the other side, home to the **Teatro alla Scala (La Scala),** the world's premier opera house, where Maria Callas, among other opera titans, became a legend. Enter the lavish hall through the **Museo Teatrale alla Scala,** which includes such opera memorabilia as Verdi's famous top hat. *(Open daily 9am-noon and 2-5:30pm. L6000.)* From La Scala, V. Verdi leads to V. Brera, another charming street lined with small, brightly-colored palaces and art galleries. The 17th-century **Pinacoteca di Brera** presents perhaps the most impressive collection of paintings in Milan, with works by Caravaggio, Bellini, and Raphael. *(Open Tu-F 9am-9:45pm, Sa 9am-11:40pm, Su 9am-8pm. L8000.)* Backtrack to La Scala and head up V. Manzoni and you'll stumble upon the **Museo Poldi-Pezzoli,** which contains an outstanding private art collection; its signature piece is Antonio Pollaiolo's *Portrait of a Young Woman.* *(V. Manzoni 12. Open daily 10am-6pm. L10,000.)*

AROUND CASTELLO SFORZESCO. Restored since heavy bomb damage in 1943, the enormous **Castello Sforzesco,** northeast of the *duomo*, is one of Milan's best-known monuments. It houses Michelangelo's unfinished last work, *Pietà Rondanini*, and other excellent pieces. *(MM1: Cairoli. Open Tu-Su 9:30am-5:30pm. Free.)* The **Chiesa di Santa Maria delle Grazie** contains Leonardo da Vinci's *Last Supper*. The immensely famous fresco captures the apostles' reaction to Jesus' prophecy: "One of you will betray me." *(MM1,2: Cadorna; head down V. Carducci away from Castello Sforzesco and turn right on C. Magenta. Open Tu-F 9am-9pm, Sa 9am-midnight, Su 9am-8pm. L12,000. Arrive early or late to beat the crowds.)* From the church, head down V. Togni and turn left on V. S. Vittore to explore more da Vinci genius at the **Museo Nazionale della Scienza e della Tecnica "Leonardo da Vinci,"** which houses wooden models of the master's most ingenious and visionary inventions. *(V. S. Vittore 21, off V. Carducci. MM1: San Ambrogio. Open Tu-F 9:30am-4:50pm, Sa-Su 9:30am-6:20pm. L10,000.)*

CORSO PORTA TICINESE AND THE NAVIGLI. Head southeast on V. Torino from the *duomo* and left on C. Ticinese to reach the 4th-century **Chiesa di San Lorenzo Maggiore,** the oldest church in Milan. *(C. Ticinese. MM3: Missori or MM2: S. Ambrogio. Open daily 7:30am-6:45pm.)* To the right of the church lies the **Cappella di Sant'Aquilino,** which contains a 5th-century mosaic of a beardless Christ among his apostles. *(L2000.)* Farther down C. Ticinese stands the **Chiesa di Sant'Eustorgio,** founded in the 4th century to house the bones of the Magi, later taken to Cologne in 1164. *(MM2: Porta Genova; walk down V. Vigevano and turn left on C. Ticinese. Open daily 8am-noon and 3-7pm.)* Near the front of the church is the 12th-century neoclassical **Arco di Porta Ticinese,** which serves as the northeastern gateway to the **Navigli** district. This Venice of Lombardy, complete with canals, small footbridges, open-air markets, and cafés, constituted part of a canal system (whose original locks were designed by Leonardo da Vinci) once used to transport tons of marble to build the *duomo* and link Milan to various northern cities and lakes.

GIARDINI PUBBLICI AND ENVIRONS. From the *duomo*, follow C. Vittorio Emanuele II and then C. Venezia northeast to reach the **Giardini Pubblici** (Public Gardens). The **Galleria d'Arte Moderna,** next to the gardens in the neoclassical Villa Comunale, displays important modern Lombard art and works by Impressionists. Napoleon lived here when Milan was capital of the Napoleonic Kingdom of Italy (1805-14). *(V. Palestro 16. MM2: Palestro. Open Tu-Su 9am-6:30pm. Free.)* The **Museo Civico di Storia Naturale** (Museum of Natural History) in the gardens holds extensive geology and paleontology collections. *(C. Venezia 55. Open M-F 9am-6pm, Sa-Su 9:30am-6:30pm. Free.)*

🎵 ENTERTAINMENT

While seats at the famed **La Scala** (tel. 02 72 00 37 44) are expensive on average, gallery seats may cost as little as L30,000, and 200 standing-room tickets go on sale 45min. before the show (L10,000). (Opera season is Dec.-June; fewer shows July-Sept. Box office open daily noon-6pm.) If you've come to Milan to (window) **shop,** the city's most elegant boutiques are between the *duomo* and P. Babila, especially on **V. Monte Napoleone** and off P. S. Babila at V. della Spiga. Wander like a pauper among the marble and brass racks of designer merchandise.

The nocturnal scene varies with the hour and the locale. A safe, chic, and very touristed district lies by **Via Brera,** northwest of the *duomo* and east of MM1: Cairoli, where you'll find art galleries, small clubs, restaurants, and an upscale thirtysomething crowd. Younger Milanese migrate to the areas around **C. Porta Ticinese** and **P. Vetra** (near Chiesa S. Lorenzo) to sip beer at one of the many *birrerie* (pubs). The highest concentration of bars and youth can be found into the wee hours of the morning in the **Navigli district.** (MM2: Porta Genova; then walk along V. Vigevano until it ends and veer right onto V. Naviglio Pavese.)

Tunnel, V. Sammartini 30 (tel. 02 66 71 13 70), near Stazione Centrale, is frequented by post-punk, hard-core, ska, reggae, minimalist sci-fi-surf, kraut-rock, rockabilly, and various indie bands. L3-12,000. Hours vary; check the paper.

Lollapaloosa, C. Como 15 (tel. 02 655 56 93). Attracts an energetic crowd that will have you dancing on the tables in no time. Great rock 'n' roll. Open daily 7pm-2am.

Grand Café Fashion (tel. 02 89 40 07 09), C. di Porta Ticinese, on the corner of V. Vatere. A bar/restaurant/dance club with a stunningly beautiful crowd and velour leopard print couches. Open Tu-Sa noon-3pm, 8pm-midnight.

Café Rhodania (tel. 02 832 26 68), V.A. Sforza near V. Lagrange. Live jazz F and Su, and rock Th. Mixed drinks L6-11,000. Open M, W-Sa 10pm-2am, Su 3:30pm-2am.

Uiti Bar, V. Monvisa 14 (tel. 02 331 59 96). Attracts a mixed gay/straight crowd. Open Tu-Su 8:30pm-2am.

ITALY

WALK LIKE AN ITALIAN Italians have an uncanny ability to pick tourists out of a crowd. Perhaps it is because every American tourist is wearing khaki shorts, a white t-shirt, and a pair of Tevas. If you want to avoid this phenomenon, and you're ready to make the leap into Euro-chic, add this simple starter kit of must-haves to your wardrobe.

Adidas Shirt: Preferably flourescent stripes on black. Buy one that is too tight, and while you're at it get the matching windpants with chrome buttons from mid-shin down, to accomodate extremely large boots.

Really tight jeans: Dark, with untapered leg. Ouch.

Really tight cargo pants: Thus negating the utility of all those pockets.

Invicta backpack: Who knew that neon yellow went with neon pink? It does when the word "Invicta" is plastered on the back in alternating neon blue, fuschia, and mint green. Make sure all your friends sign it in permanent ink. If your shoulders ache, try walking kangaroo-style, with the straps running down your back.

Telefonino: A mobile phone is essential. If you can't afford one, no one will stop you from pretending. Buy a fake from a wandering cigarette-lighter salesman.

MANTUA (MANTOVA)

Mantua owes its literary fame to its most famous son, the poet Virgil. The driving force that built the city's *centro storico*, however, was not the punning crafter but the Gonzaga family. After ascending to power in 1328, the family persistently altered Mantua's small-town image by importing well-known artists and cultivating local talent. Lined with grand *palazzi* and graceful churches, Mantua also provides easy passage to the surrounding lakes. The cobblestoned **Piazza Sordello** marks the center of a vast complex built by the Gonzaga family. The huge ⚅**Palazzo Ducale,** which towers over the *piazza*, has over its history absorbed the Gothic Magna Domus *(duomo)* and Palazzo del Capitano. Inside, check out frescoes, tapestries, gardens, you name it. Outside the *palazzo*, signs point to the formidable **Castello di San Giorgio** (1390-1406). Underneath the Castello di S. Giorgio dwells a dank prison, home to the **Museo degli Strumenti di Tortura's** instruments of torture. (Palazzo open Tu-F and Su 9am-7pm, Sa 9am-7pm and 9-11pm; L12,000. Museum open Apr.-Oct. daily 10am-1pm and 3:30-6:30pm; Mar. and Nov.-Dec. Sa-Su 10am-1pm and 3:30-6:30pm; L5000.) At the far south of the city, down V. P. Amedeo through P. Veneto and down Largo Parri, the opulent **Palazzo del Te,** built by Giulio Romano in 1534 as a suburban retreat for Francesco II Gonzaga, is widely considered the finest building in the Mannerist style. (Open M 1-6pm, Tu-Su 9am-6pm. L12,000, students L5000.) Opposite **Piazza delle Erbe,** just south of P. Sordello, is Alberti's **Chiesa di Sant'Andrea,** Mantua's most important Renaissance creation.

Trains (tel. 0376 32 16 47) go from P. Don Leoni to Verona (40min., every hr., L3900) and Milan (2hr., 9 per day, L15,000). From the station, head left on V. Solferino, through P. S. Francesco d'Assisi to V. Fratelli Bandiera, and right on V. Verdi to find the **tourist office,** P. Mantegna 6, next to Sant'Andrea's church; ask them about **agriturismo.** (Tel. 0376 32 82 53; fax 0376 36 32 92. Open M-Sa 8:30am-12:30pm and 3-6pm.) Shmancy **Hotel ABC,** P. Don Leoni 25, is opposite the station. (Tel. 0376 32 33 47; fax 0376 32 23 29. Breakfast included. Singles L70-90,000; doubles L90-130,000; triples L140,000. V, MC.) ⚅**Antica Osteria ai Ranari,** V. Trieste 11, down V. Pomponazzo near Porta Catena, is a friendly place specializing in regional dishes. (*Primi* L8000, *secondi* L9-15,000. Cover L2000. Open mid-Aug. to late July. Tu-Su noon-2:30pm and 7:15-11:30pm. V, MC, AmEx.) **Postal code:** 46100.

BERGAMO

An entire medieval city glistens from the hills over Bergamo, complete with palaces, churches, and a huge stone fortification. **Via Pignolo,** in the *città bassa* (lower city), winds past a succession of handsome 16th- to 18th-century palaces. Turning right on V. S. Tomaso brings you to the astounding **Galleria dell'Accademia Carrara,** one of the most important galleries in Italy, with works by virtually every Italian notable as well as Breughel, van Dyck, and El Greco. (Open W-M 9:30am-12:30pm and 2:30-5:30pm. L5000; Su free.) From there, the terraced **Via Noca** ascends to the *città alta* (upper city) through Porta Sant'Agostino. Continue down V. Porta Dipinta to V. Gambito, which ends in **Piazza Vecchia,** a majestic ensemble of medieval and Renaissance buildings flanked by restaurants and cafés at the heart of the *città alta.* Climb the **Torre Civica** (L2000) for a marvelous view of Bergamo and the hills. Under the archway is **Piazza del Duomo,** with the multicolored marble façade of the 1476 **Cappella Colleoni.** (Open daily Apr.-Oct. 9am-noon and 2-6:30pm; Nov.-Mar. 9am-noon and 2:30-4:30pm.) To the right of the chapel is an octagonal **baptistery,** whose stark Romanesque exterior contrasts sharply with its breathtakingly ornate Baroque interior. (Open M-Sa 8:30am-noon and 3-6pm, Su 10am-noon and 3-6pm.)

The train and bus stations and many budget hotels are in the *città bassa.* **Trains** (1hr., L6000) and **buses** (L7300) pull into P. Marconi from Milan. To get to the **tourist office,** Vco. Aquila Nera 2, in the *città alta,* take bus 1 or 1a to the funicular, then follow V. Gambito to P. Vecchia and turn right. (Tel. 035 23 27 30; fax 035 24 29 94. Open daily 9am-12:30pm and 2-5:30pm.) Take bus 14 from Porto Nuova to "Leonardo da Vinci" and walk uphill to reach the **Ostello Città di Bergamo (HI),** V. G. Ferraris 1. (Tel. 035 34 30 38; fax 035 36 17 24. L25,000; singles L35,000; doubles L60,000; members only. Breakfast included. **Internet.) Locanda Caironi,** V. Torretta 6B, off V. Gorgo Palazzo, is in a beautiful residential neighborhood. Take bus 5 or 7 from V. Angelo Maj, or walk for 20min. (Tel. 035 24 30 83. Singles L25,000; doubles L45,000.) **Trattoria Casa Mia,** V. S. Bernardino 20, off V. Zambonate, offers a full "home-style" meal for L15-20,000. (Tel. 035 22 06 76. Open Sept.-July M-Sa noon-3:30pm and 6pm-midnight.) The prison-turned-communist-café **Circolino Cooperativa Città Alta,** V. S. Agata 19, features *bocce* and a view, as well as sandwiches, pizza, and salads for under L7000. (Open Th-Tu 11am-2:30pm and 7:30pm-2:20am.)

ITALIAN RIVIERA (LIGURIA)

The Italian Riviera stretches 350km along the Mediterranean between France and Tuscany, forming the most famous and touristed area of the Italian coastline. Genoa divides the sandy crescent-shaped strip into the more dramatic Riviera di Levante ("rising sun") to the east and the Riviera di Ponente ("setting sun") to the west. The elegant coast beckons with lemon trees, almond blossoms, and turquoise sea. Especially lovely is the **Cinque Terre** area, just to the west of La Spezia.

▐ GETTING THERE AND GETTING AROUND

All the coastal towns are linked by the main **rail** line, which runs west from Genoa to Ventimiglia (near the French border) and east to La Spezia (near Tuscany), but slow local trains can make short distances take hours. Frequent intercity **buses** pass through all major towns, and local buses run to inland hill-towns. **Boats** connect most resort towns. **Ferries** go from Genoa to Olbia, Sardinia and Palermo, Sicily.

GENOA (GENOVA)

Urban, gritty Genoa has little in common with its picture-perfect resort neighbors. But flourishing trade in this port town in the 13th century allowed for the construction of parks and lavish palaces, and its financial glory was soon matched by the repute of its citizens, including Chistopher Columbus and Giuseppe Mazzini. Since falling into decline in the 18th century, modern Genoa has turned its attention from industry to the restoration of its former grandeur.

⚄⌂ PRACTICAL INFO, ACCOMMODATIONS, AND FOOD. Trains go to Turin (2hr., 22 per day, L17,500-24,000) and Rome (6hr., 14 per day L57-78,000). Most international trains arrive at **Stazione Principe,** on V. Acquaverde, northwest of center; take bus 41 to reach the central P. Ferrari, or walk down V. Balbi to V. Cairoli (which becomes V. Garibaldi) and turn right on V. XXV Aprile. From **Stazione Brignole,** on P. Verdi (east of the city center), take bus 40 to P. Ferrari; or head right from the station, left on V. Fiume, and right on C. XX Settembre to reach P. Ferrari. Pick up a map (L9000) at any newsstand. **Ferries** (see above) depart from the Ponte Assereto arm of the port; buy tickets from the Stazione Marittima (tel. 010 25 66 82). The APT **tourist office** is at Porto Antico, in P. Santa Maria. From P. Matteotti, adjacent to P. Ferrari, walk all the way down V. S. Lorenzo, and the office is through the gate, to the left of the aquarium. (Tel. 01 02 48 71; fax 01 02 46 76 58. Open daily 9am-6:30pm.) Log on at **Internet Village**, at V. Brigata Bisagno and C. Buenos Aires, near Stazione Brignole. (L15,000 per hr. Open 9am-1pm and 2-7pm.)

Ostello per la Gioventù (HI), V. Costanzi 120, has a bar and TV. From Stazione Principe, walk down V. Balbi to P. della Nunziata and catch bus 40 (also runs directly from Brignole; every 10min.), and tell the driver your destination. (Tel./fax 01 02 42 24 57. L22,000. Members only; sells HI cards. Breakfast included. Laundry L7-12,000. Reception 7-9am and 3:30pm-12:30am. Curfew midnight.) **Albergo Balbi**, V. Balbi 21/3, has massive rooms with ornate ceilings. (Tel. 01 02 47 21 12. Singles L35-50,000; doubles L70-80,000; less with *Let's Go*. Breakfast L6,500.) A beautiful palazzo on V. Gropallo houses **Pensione Mirella**, 4/4 (tel. 01 08 39 37 22; doubles L67,000), and **Albergo Carola**, 4/12 (tel. 01 08 39 13 40; singles L45,000; doubles L65-75,000). To **camp** at **Villa Doria**, 15 V. al Campeggio Villa Doria, take the train or bus 1-3 from P. Caricamento to Pegli, then walk up V. Vespucci. (Tel. 01 06 96 96 00. L8000 per person, L9-15,000 per tent.) Genoa is famous for its *pesto* and *focaccia*. **La Locanda del Borgo**, V. Borgo Incrociati 47r, behind Stazione Brignole, has a tasty L15,000 *menù*. (Open daily 8am-4pm and 7pm-12:30am.) **Postal code:** 16100.

◙ SIGHTS. The 18th-century **Palazzo Reale**, V. Balbi 10, in the university quarter near Stazione Principe, is filled with rococo rooms bathed in gold and upholstered in red velvet. (Open Su-Tu 9am-1:45pm, W-F 9am-7pm. L8000.) Follow V. Balbi through P. della Nunziata and continue to L. Zecca, where V. Cairoli leads to **Via Garibaldi**, the most impressive street in Genoa, bedecked with elegant *palazzi* constructed by Genoa's wealthiest families in the 17th century. The **Galleria di Palazzo Bianco**, V. Garibaldi 11, exhibits Ligurian, Dutch, and Flemish paintings. Across the street, the 17th-century **Galleria Palazzo Rosso**, V. Garibaldi 18, has magnificent furnishings in a lavishly frescoed interior. (Both open Tu and Th-F 9am-1pm, W and Sa 9am-7pm, Su 10am-6pm. L6000 each, L10,000 together; Su free.) The Palazzo Rosso faces the Renaissance façade of the **Palazzo Municipale** (City Hall), V. Garibaldi 9, where you can ask the guards to see Nicolò Paganini's violin. (Open M-F 8:30am-4:30pm. Free.) The **Villetta Di Negro**, on the hill to your left, features waterfalls, grottos, and terraced gardens. At the summit is the **Museo d'Arte Orientale**. (Open Tu and Th-Su 9am-1pm. L6000.) From P. Corvetto, V. Roma continues to P. Ferrari, and V. Boetto then leads to P. Matteotti and the **Palazzo Ducale**, where the city's rulers once lived; on the opposite corner stands the ornate **Chiesa del Gesù**. (Open daily 7:30am-10:30am and 3-6pm.) Head past the Chiesa del Gesù down V. di Porta Soprana to V. Ravecca to reach the medieval twin-towered **Porta Soprana**, the supposed boyhood home of Christopher Columbus (his father was the gatekeeper). Through the archway to the left rest the ruins of the 12th-century **Cloister of San'Andrea**. Backtrack to P. Matteotti and go down V. S. Lorenzo to see the **duomo**, which has a Gothic façade and a carved central portal with lions, sirens, and vines (oh my!). (Open M-Sa 8am-noon and 3-6:30pm, Su noon-6:30pm. Free.) The *duomo* lies on the southern edge of the **centro storico** (the historical center of town), a tangled web of alleys bordered by the port to the east, V. Garibaldi to the north, P. Ferrari to the southeast. The region is home to some of Genoa's most memorable monuments, but is only safe for tourists during the day. Head down Salita all'Arcicovato from behind the *duomo*, left on V. Campetto, right on V. Soziglia (which turns into V. Bianchi), and right at P. Bianchi on V. S. Luca, continue past the **Chiesa di San Mateo**, and bear right onto V. S. Siro to reach the ▨ **Chiesa di San Siro**, Genoa's first cathedral, with majestic, vaulted ceilings and ornate paintings. (Open M-F 4-6pm. Free.)

RIVIERA DI PONENTE
AND RIVIERA DI LEVANTE

FINALE LIGURE. A prime spot to vacation from your vacation, Finale Ligure welcomes weary backpackers with soft sands, the turquoise sea, and plenty of *gelato*. The city is divided into three sections: **Finalborgo** (the old city) to the west (1km left up V. Bruneghi from the station), **Finalpia** to the east, and **Finalmarina** (with the train station and most sights) in the center. You'll have to work for the hike up to the ruined 13th-century **Castel Govone**, but you'll be rewarded with spectacular views. To avoid being squished like a sardine on the beach across from Hotel Boncardo, walk east along V. Aurelia through the first tunnel and hang a quick right down to a less populated **free beach.** Near Finale Ligure, tiny and refreshingly tourist-free **Borgo Verezzi** (L1800) delights with cool, peaceful streets. Borgo Verezzi and other beachside towns are accessible via SAR **buses** from the front of the train station.

Trains head to Genoa (1hr., every hr., L6500). The IAT **tourist office,** V. S. Pietro 14, gives out maps and personal advice. (Tel. 019 68 10 19; fax 019 68 18 04. Open in summer M-Sa 9am-12:30pm and 3:30-7pm, Su 9am-noon.) Though it's a tough hike up to ◪**Castello Wuillerman (HI),** on V. Generale Caviglia, the sweat is well worth it. From the station, take a left onto V. Mazzini, which becomes V. Torino, turn left on V. degli Ulivi, and trudge up the seemingly endless 321 steps. (Tel./fax 019 69 05 15. L19,000. Breakfast included. Reception 7-10am and 5-10pm. Strict check-in 5pm. Curfew 11:30pm. No phone reservations. Open mid-Mar. to mid-Oct.) To get to **Albergo San Marco,** V. della Concezione 22, walk straight down V. Saccone from the station and turn left on V. della Concezione. (Tel. 019 69 25 33. Singles L50,000; doubles L75-85,000. Breakfast included. Closed Oct.-Feb. V, MC, AmEx.) To reach **Camping Tahiti,** on V. Varese, take the bus from P. Vittorio Veneto (dir: Calvisio) to the Boncardo Hotel, C. Europa 4, then walk up the river on the left side to V. Varese after passing beneath the train tracks. (Tel./fax. 019 60 06 00. L12,000 per person, L11,000 per tent; off-season reduced. Showers L1000. Reception 8am-8pm. Open Easter-Sept.) Cheap restaurants lie inland along **V. Rossi** and **V. Roma. Simpatia Crai supermarket** is at V. Bruneghi 2a. (Open M-Sa 8am-12:30pm and 4:30-8pm.)

CAMOGLI. The postcard-perfect town of Camogli cascades with color. Sun-faded peach and yellow houses crowd the hilltop, red-and-turquoise boats bob in the water, piles of fishing nets cover the docks, and bright umbrellas cover the dark stone beaches. To reach the **beach,** turn left down the steep stairs 100m away from the station (where a large blue sign points to Albergo Camogliese), which lead to V. Garibaldi, then turn right off V. Garibaldi into the alley. **Trains** run on the Genoa-La Spezia line to Santa Margherita (10min., 24 per day, L2000); Genoa (20min., 32 per day, L2400); and La Spezia (1½hr., 19 per day, L6400). Golfo Paradiso **ferries,** V. Scalo 3 (tel. 01 85 77 20 91), near P. Colombo, go to Portofino (1 per week, L13,000, round-trip L20,000) and Cinque Terre (July-Aug. 3 per week, L20,000); buy tickets on the dock. Head right from the station to find the **tourist office,** V. XX Settembre 33, which can help find rooms. (Tel. 01 85 77 10 66. Open June-Sept. daily 8:30am-12:30pm and 3-7pm; Oct.-May M-Sa 9am-noon and 4-7pm, Su 9am-1pm.) Exit the station, walk down the long stairway to the right, and look for the sign to reach the joyful ◪**Albergo La Camogliese,** V. Garibaldi 55. (Tel. 01 85 77 14 02; fax 01 85 77 40 24. Singles L70-90,000; doubles L90-120,000. Breakfast L10,000. 10% off for *Let's Go*-ers paying in cash. Reserve ahead. V, MC, AmEx.)

SANTA MARGHERITA LIGURE. Santa Margherita Ligure led a calm existence as a fishing village from the 12th century to the early 20th century, when it fell into favor with Hollywood stars. Today, grace and glitz paint the shore, Art-Deco lighting softens the pastel walls, and palm trees line the harbor. But the serenity of the town's early days still lingers. While in town, note especially the stunning *Relaxation* by Placid Waters and *Calming Atmosphere* by Soothing Beach. Or check out the gold-and-crystal Rococo **Basilica di Santa Margherita. Trains** along the Pisa-Genoa line go from P. Federico Raoul Nobili, at the top of V. Roma, to Genoa

(40min., 2-3 per hr., L3100) and La Spezia via Cinque Terre (2 per hr., L6800). Tigullio **buses** (tel. 01 85 28 88 34) go from P. Vittorio Veneto to Portofino (20min., 3 per hr., L1900) and Camogli (30min., every hr., L2000). Tigullio **ferries**, V. Palestro 8/1b (tel. 01 85 28 46 70), chug to Portofino (7 per day; L6000, round-trip L10,000) and Cinque Terre (July-Sept. 2 per day, Oct.-June Sa-Su; L25,000, round-trip L35,000). Turn right from the train station on V. Roma, turn left on C. Rainusso, and take a hard right onto V. XXV Aprile from Largo Giusti to find the **tourist office**, V. XXV Aprile 2b, which arranges rooms. (Tel. 01 85 28 74 85. Open M-Sa 9am-12:30pm and 3:30-6:30pm, Su 9:30am-12:30pm.) ◪**Hotel Nuova Riviera**, V. Belvedere 10, is in a garden near P. Mazzini. (Tel./fax 01 85 28 74 03. Singles L85-115,000; doubles L95-140,000.) **Hotel Terminus**, P. Nobili 4, to the left as you exit the station, has lovely views. (Tel. 01 85 28 61 21. Singles L70,000; doubles L140,000. Breakfast included. V, MC, AmEx.) ◪**La Piadineria and Creperia**, V. Giuncheto 5, off P. Martiri della Libertà, serves huge sandwiches (L7-9000) and more. (Open daily afternoon-late.)

PORTOFINO. Secluded and exclusive, tiny Portofino—a great daytrip from Santa Margherita—has long been a playground for the financially advantaged. Yachts fill the harbor and chic boutiques line the streets, but both princes and paupers can enjoy the shore's curves and tiny bay. A one-hour walk along the ocean road offers the chance to scout out small rocky **beaches**. The beach at **Paraggi** (where the bus stops) is the area's only sandy beach. In town, follow the signs uphill from the bay to escape to the cool interior of the **Chiesa di San Giorgio**. A few minutes up the road toward the **castle** is a serene garden with sea views. (Open daily in summer 10am-6pm; off-season 10am-5pm. L3000.) To get to town, take the bus to Portofino Mare (*not* Portofino Vetta). From P. Martiri della Libertà, Tigullio **buses** go to Santa Margherita (3 per hr., L1900); buy tickets at the green kiosk in P. Martiri della Libertà. **Ferries** also go from Portofino to Santa Margherita (every hr. 9am-7pm, L6000) and Camogli (2 per day, L13,000). The **tourist office**, V. Roma 35, is en route to the waterfront from the bus stop. (Tel. 01 85 26 90 24. Open in summer daily 9:30am-1:30pm and 2-7pm; off-season 9:30am-12:30pm and 2:30-5:30pm.)

CINQUE TERRE. The five bright fishing villages of Cinque Terre cling to a stretch of terraced hillsides and steep crumbling cliffs, while a dazzling turquoise sea laps against their shores. Savage cliffs and lush tropical vegetation surround the stone villages. You can **hike** through all five—Monterosso, Vernazza, Corniglia, Manarola, and Riomaggiore—in a few hours. **Monterosso** is the most developed, with sandy beaches and exciting nightlife; **Vernazza** is immediately charming, with colorful buildings, a harbor full of parked boats, and a sandy beach covered with sunbathers; **Corniglia** floats high above the sea; **Manarola** is a small, beautiful village with a spectacular swimming cove; and **Riomaggiore** has a tiny harbor and lots of rooms to rent. The best views are from the narrow goat paths that link the towns, winding through vineyards, streams, and dense foliage dotted with cacti and lemon trees. The best hike lies between Monterosso and Vernazza (1½hr.), while the trail between Vernazza and Corniglia (2hr.) leads through spectacular scenery. There are only two public **beaches** in the area, one on the south side of Monterosso (to the left through the tunnel as you face the harbor) and the other between Corniglia and Manarola. **Guvano Beach**, a pebbly strip frequented by nudists, is through the tunnel at the base of the steps leading up to Corniglia (L5000). Tiny trails off the road to Vernazza lead to hidden coves popular with locals.

The Genoa-La Spezia rail line connects the five towns; Monterosso is the most accessible. From the station on V. Fegina, at the north end of town, **trains** run to La Spezia (20min., every 30min., L2500); Genoa (1½hr., every hr., L7300); Pisa (2½hr., every hr., L8200); Florence via Pisa (3½hr., every hr., L14,000); and Rome (7hr., every 2hr., L32,400). Trains also connect the five towns (5-20min., every 50min., L1800). **Ferries** run from Vernazza to Camogli (1½hr., 2-4 per week; L20,000, round-trip L33,000) and Santa Margherita Ligure (2hr., 2 per day, L25,000, round-trip L35,000); Ferries from Monterosso go to Manarola and Riomaggiore (5 per day; L10,000, round-trip L15,000); Vernazza (5 per day; L4000, round-trip L6000); and La

Spezia (1hr., 2 per day, L33,000). Reserve rooms at least several weeks in advance. **Private rooms** *(affittacamere)* are the cheapest, most plentiful options. To find Manarola's hostel, the 🏠**Albergo Della Gioventù-Ostello "Cinque Terre,"** V. B. Ricco-baldi 21, turn right from the train station and go uphill (300m) to discover more incredible, fabulous amenities than can be listed in the space allotted. (Tel. 01 87 92 02 15; fax 01 87 92 02 18; email ostello@cdh.it. L25,000. Breakfast L5000. Reception mid-Sept. to May 7-10am and 4pm-midnight; June to mid-Sept. 7-10am and 5pm-1am. Laundry. **Internet.** Reserve 2 weeks ahead.) In Vernazza, ask in Trattoria Capi-tano about **Albergo Barbara,** P. Marconi 30, top floor, at the port. (Tel. 01 87 81 23 98. Singles L85,000; doubles L95-115,000; triples L130,000.) In Monterosso, try the **tour-ist office** (tel. 01 87 81 75 06) or **Hotel Souvenir,** V. Gioberti 24, the best deal in town. (Tel. 01 87 81 75 95. L45,000. Breakfast L10,000.) To arrange private rooms in Riom-aggiore, call **Robert Fazioli,** V. Colombo 94 (tel. 01 87 92 09 04; L25-40,000 per per-son).

LA SPEZIA. A departure point for Corsica and an unavoidable transport hub for Cinque Terre, La Spezia is probably Italy's most beautiful port, with regal palms lin-ing the promenade and parks filled with glorious citrus trees. La Spezia lies on the Genoa-Pisa **train** line. **Corsica Ferries** (tel. 01 87 77 80 97) go to Bastia, Corsica (5hr., Apr. 3 per week, May-Sept. 1 per day, L36-48,000). Ferries run by Navigazione Golfo dei Poeti, V. Mazzini 21 (tel. 01 87 210 10), stop in each Cinque Terre village (1 per day; L20,000, round-trip L33,000); Capri (July-Aug. 1 per day, Apr.-Aug. Su only, round-trip L70,000); and Elba (July W and Sa, round-trip L80,000). The **tourist office** (tel. 01 87 77 09 00) is at the port at V. Mazzini 45. To reach **Albergo Terminus,** V. Pale-ocapa 21, turn left out of the train station. (Tel. 01 87 70 34 36; fax 01 87 71 49 35. Singles L35-45,000; doubles L50-70,000; triples L70,000. Breakfast L5000.)

EMILIA-ROMAGNA

Go to Florence, Venice, and Rome to sightsee, come to Emilia-Romagna to eat. Italy's wealthiest wheat- and dairy-producing region covers the fertile plains of the Po River Valley, fostering the finest culinary traditions on the Italian Peninsula. Gorge yourself on Parmesan cheese and *prosciutto,* Bolognese fresh pasta and *mortadella,* and Ferrarese *salama* and *grana* cheese. Complement these dishes with such regional wines as Parma's sparkling red *lambrusco.*

BOLOGNA

With just one forkful of Bologna's *tortellini,* it becomes clear that the city appreci-ates the better things in life. Bright façades lean on 700-year-old porticoes and cob-blestoned roads twist by churches, but the city's appeal extends far beyond aesthetics. Blessed with prosperity and Europe's oldest university, Bologna has developed an open-minded character; minority and gay political activism is strong. Apart from a formidable list of its university's graduates—including Dante, Petrarch, and Copernicus—the city prides itself on its great culinary heritage.

🔢📶 PRACTICAL INFO, ACCOMMODATIONS, AND FOOD. At the heart of northern Italy, Bologna is a rail hub for all major Italian cities and the Adriatic coast; **trains** go to Florence (1½hr., every 2hr., L8200-13,500); Venice (2hr., every hr., L14,000); Milan (3hr., 2-3 per hr., L18,000); and Rome (4hr., 1-2 per hr., L35,000). Arrive during the day, as the area near the station is not the safest. Buses 25 and 30 run between the station and the historic center at **P. Maggiore** (L1800). The **tourist office,** P. Maggiore 6, is next to the Palazzo Comunale. (Tel. 051 23 96 60; fax 051 23 14 54; www.comune.bologna.it. Open M-Sa 9am-7pm, Su 9am-2pm.) Check **email** at **Crazy Bull Café,** V. Montegrappa 11/e, off V. dell'Indipendenza near P. Maggiore. (L9000 per hr. Open Tu-Sa 10am-2am, Su 7:30pm-2am. Open Sept.-July.) Take V. Ugo Bassi from P. Maggiore and take the third left to find sparkling 🏠**Albergo Pan-orama,** V. Livraghi 1, 4th fl. (Tel. 051 22 18 02; fax 051 26 63 60. Singles L70,000; dou-bles L95-120,000; triples L120-135,000. V, MC, AmEx.) **Albergo Minerva,** V. dé Monari

ITALY

EAT YOUR HEART OUT, CHEF BOYARDEE

For Italians, the desecration of pasta is a mortal sin. Pasta must be chosen correctly and cooked *al dente* (firm, literally "to the tooth"). To avoid embarrassment, get to know the basics. The s*paghetti* family includes all variations that require twirling, from hollow cousins *bucatini* and *maccheroni* to the more delicate *capellini*. Flat *spaghetti* include *fettuccini, taglierini,* and *tagliatelle*. Short pasta tubes can be *penne* (cut diagonally and occasionally *rigate,* or ribbed), *sedani* (curved), *rigatoni* (wider), or *cannelloni* (usually stuffed). *Fusilli* (corkscrews), *farfalle* (butterflies or bow-ties), and *ruote* (wheels) are fun as well as functional. Don't be alarmed if you see pastry displays labeled "pasta"; the Italian word refers to anything made of dough.

3, is off V. dell'Indipendenza near P. Maggiore. (Tel. 051 23 96 52. Singles L50,000; doubles L100,000.) Follow V. Rizzoli past the towers to V. S. Vitale to reach **Hotel San Vitale,** V. S. Vitale 94. (Tel. 051 22 59 66; fax 051 23 93 96. Singles L90,000; doubles L110,000; triples L150,000.) To get to **Ostello due Torre San Sisto (HI),** V. Viadagola 5, off V. San Donato in the Località di San Sisto (6km from the center), walk down V. dell'Indipendenza from the station, turn right on V. della Mille, catch bus 93 (every 30min.) on the left side of the road, ask the driver for "San Sisto," cross the street, and it's on the right. On Sunday, take bus 301 from the station (6 per day). (Tel./fax 051 50 18 10. L21,000; nonmembers L26,000. Breakfast included. Laundry. Reception 7am-midnight. Lockout 10am-3:30pm. Curfew midnight.)

Bologna's namesake dish, *spaghetti alla bolognese*, has a hefty meat and tomato sauce. Scout **V. Augusto Righi, V. Piella,** and **V. Saragozza** for traditional *trattorie*. A **supermarket PAM,** V. Marconi 26, is near V. Riva di Reno. (Open M-W and F-Sa 7:45am-7:45pm, Th 7:45am-1pm.) Locals chat over regional dishes like *tagliatelle* at ◙**Trattoria Da Maro,** V. Broccaindosso 71d, off Strada Maggiore. (Lunch *primi* L8000, *secondi* L9000; dinner L10-12,000. Cover L3000. Open M-Sa noon-2:30pm and 8-10:15pm. V, MC, AmEx.) Savor hearty food at **Antica Trattoria Roberto Spiga,** V. Broccaindosso 21a. (*Primi* L8000, *secondi* L12-18,000. Cover L2000. Open Sept.-July M-Sa noon-3pm and 7:30-10pm.) **Trattoria Da Danio,** V. S. Felice 50, off V. Ugo Bassi, is an authentic *trattoria* with an appetizing menu. (*Primi* L7-15,000, *secondi* L7-25,000. *Menù* L13,500. Cover L3000. Open M-Sa 11:30am-4pm and 7:30-10pm. V, MC, AmEx.) **Il Gelatauro,** V. S. Vitale 82/b, will stop my scream, your scream, our collective scream for ice cream. (From L3000. Open June-Aug. daily 11am-midnight, Sept.-May Tu-Su 11am-midnight.)

◙ ◪ **SIGHTS AND ENTERTAINMENT.** Twenty-five miles of porticoed buildings line the streets of Bologna. In the 14th century, porticoes offered a solution to the housing crisis of a growing city; buildings expanded into the street but left room for mounted riders below. Tranquil **Piazza Maggiore** flaunts both Bologna's historical and modern-day wealth. **Basilica di San Petronio,** the city's *duomo,* designed by Antonio da Vincenzo in 1390, was meant to be larger than Rome's St. Peter's, but the jealous Church ordered that the funds be instead used to build the nearby Palazzo Archiginnasio. The pomp and pageantry of the exercises at the church allegedly drove a disgusted Martin Luther to reform religion in Germany. (Open M-Sa 7:15am-1:30pm and 2:30-6:30pm, Su 7:30am-1pm and 2:30-6:30pm. Sacristy open daily 8am-noon and 4-6pm.) ◙**Palazzo Archiginnasio,** behind the church, was once a university building; the upstairs theater was built in 1637 to teach anatomy to students. (Palazzo open M-F 9am-7pm, Sa 9am-2pm. Theater open M-Sa 9am-1pm. Both closed 2 weeks in Aug. Free.) ◙**Pinacoteca Nazionale,** V. delle Belle Arti 56, off V. Zamboni, traces the progress of Bolognese artists. (Open Tu-Sa 9am-1:50pm, Su 9am-12:50pm; June-Aug. Sa 9pm-midnight. L8000.) On the northern side of P. Maggiore is **Palazzo de Podestà,** remodeled by Fioravanti's son Aristotle, who later designed Moscow's Kremlin. Next to P. Maggiore, **Piazza del Nettuno** contains Giambologna's famous 16th-century fountain Neptune and Attendants. From P. Nettuno, go down V. Rizzoli to **Piazza Porta**

ITALY

Ravegana, where seven streets converge to form Bologna's medieval quarter. Two towers that constitute the city's emblem rise magnificently from the *piazza;* you can climb the **Torre degli Asinelli.** (Open daily in summer 9am-6pm; off-season 9am-5pm. L3000.) Follow V. S. Stefano from V. Rizzoli to P. Santo Stefano, where four of the original seven churches of the Romanesque **Piazza Santo Stefano Church Complex** remain. Bologna's patron saint, San Petronio, lies buried under the pulpit of the **Chiesa di San Sepolcro** in the center. (Open daily 9am-noon and 3:30-6pm.) Take Strada Maggiore to P. Aldrovandi to reach the Gothic, remarkably intact **Chiesa di Santa Mari del Seru,** whose columns support an unusual combination of arches and ribbed vaulting.

Bologna's hip student population ensures raucous nighttime fun. Call ahead for hours and covers. ◪**Cassero,** in the Porta Saragozza, at the end of V. Saragozza, is a lively gay bar is packed with men and women livin' *la vida loca.* (Tel. 051 644 69 02. Open daily 10pm-2am.) **Cluricaune,** V. Zamboni 18/b. (Tel. 051 26 34 19. Pints L8000. Happy hour 5-8:30pm. Open daily 5pm-2am.) **Made in Bo** (tel. 051 53 38 80; www.madeinbo.it) raves from mid-March to July with three open-air discos and multi-layered bars on a mystical, floodlit hill; take bus 25 (taxi L10-50,000).

PARMA

Parma's loyalties lie with its excellent food. The *Parmigiani* craft silky-smooth *prosciutto crudo*, sharp and crumbly *parmigiano* cheese, and sweet, sparkling white Malvasia wine. Parma's artistic excellence goes beyond the kitchen, too: Giuseppe Verdi lived here while composing some of his greatest works. From P. Garibaldi, follow Strada Cavour toward the train station and take the third right on Strada al Duomo to reach the 11th-century Romanesque ◪**duomo,** in P. del Duomo, one of the country's most vibrant, filled with masterpieces. Most spectacular is the **dome,** where Correggio's *Virgin* ascends to a golden heaven in a spiral of white robes, pink *putti*, and blue sky. The pink-and-white marble **baptistery** was built between the Romanesque and Gothic periods. (*Duomo* open daily 9am-noon and 3-7pm. Baptistery open daily 9am-12:30pm and 3-7pm. L5000, students L3000.) Behind the *duomo* is the frescoed dome of the **Chiesa di San Giovanni Evangelista,** designed by Correggio. (Open daily 6:30am-noon and 3:30-8pm.) From P. del Duomo, follow Strada al Duomo across Strada Cavour, continue one block down Strada Piscane, and cross P. della Pace to reach the monolithic **Palazzo della Pilotta,** Parma's artistic treasure chest, constructed in 1602, which today houses the excellent **Galleria Nazionale.** (Open daily 9am-1:45pm. L8000.)

Parma is on the Bologna-Milan rail line; **trains** go from P. Carlo Alberto della Chiesa to Milan (1½hr., every hr., L12,100); Bologna (1hr., 2 per hr., L7400); and Florence (3hr., 7 per day, L25,500). Walk left from the station, right on V. Garibaldi, and left on V. Melloni to reach the **tourist office**, V. Melloni 1b. (Tel./fax 05 21 23 47 35. Open M-Sa 9am-7pm, Su 9am-1pm.) From the station, take bus 9 (L1300) and get off when the bus turns left on V. Martiri della Libertà (10min.) to get to the modern **Ostello Cittadella (HI),** on V. Passo Buole, in a corner of a 15th-century fortress. (Tel. 05 21 96 14 34. L16,000; members only. 3-night max. stay. Lockout 9:30am-5pm. Curfew 11pm. **Camping** L11,000 per person, L18,000 per site; open Apr.-Oct.) **Locanda Lazzaro,** Borgo XX Marzo 14, is off V. della Repubblica, upstairs from the restaurant of the same name. (Tel. 05 21 20 89 44. Singles L55-65,000; doubles L90,000. Reserve ahead. V, MC, AmEx.) Native *parmigiano* cheese, *prosciutto*, and sausages fill the windows of the *salumerie* along **V. Garibaldi.** Malvasia is the wine of choice. **Le Sorelle Picchi,** Strada Farini 27, near P. Garibaldi, is one of the best *trattorie* in town. (*Primi* L10-11,000, *secondi* L12-14,000. Cover L3000. *Trattoria* open M-Sa noon-3pm. V, MC.) ◪**K2,** at Borgo Cairoli and Borgo Coreggio, next to the Chiesa di San Giovanni Evangelista, has great *gelato.* (L2500. Open Th-Tu 11am-midnight.) **Supermarket 2B** is at V. XXII Luglio 27c. (Open M-W and F-Sa 8:30am-1pm and 4:30-8pm, Th 8:30am-1pm.) **Postal code:** 43100.

ITALY

RAVENNA

Tired of fresco cycles? Come to Ravenna to get byzy...uh, Byzantine and enter a world of golden mosaics. Ravenna's 15 minutes of historical superstardom came and went 14 centuries ago, when Justinian and Theodora, rulers of the Byzantine Empire, headquartered their campaign to restore order in the anarchic west here. Take V. Argentario from V. Cavour to reach the 6th-century ◧**Basilica di San Vitale,** V. S. Vitale 17. An open courtyard overgrown with greenery leads to the brilliant, glowing mosaics inside; those of the Emperor and Empress adorn the lower left and right panels of the apse, respectively. Behind S. Vitale, the city's oldest and most interesting mosaics cover the glittering interior of the **Mausoleo di Galla Placidia.** (Both open Apr.-Sept. daily 9am-7pm; Oct.-Mar. daily 9:30am-4:30pm. Joint ticket L6000.) Take bus 4 or 44 from opposite the train station (L1300) to Classe, south of the city, to see the astounding mosaics at the ◧**Chiesa di Sant'Apollinare in Classe.** (Open daily 9am-7pm. L4000.) Much to Florence's dismay, Ravenna is also home to the **Tomb of Dante Alighieri,** its most popular sight. In the adjoining **Dante Museum,** his heaven and hell come alive in etchings, paintings, and sculptures. From P. del Popolo, cut through P. Garibaldi to V. Alighieri. (Tomb open daily 9am-7pm; free. Museum open Apr.-Sept. Tu-Su 9am-noon and 3:30-6pm; Oct.-Mar. Tu-Su 9am-noon. L3000.) One ticket (L10,000, students L8,000 at participating sight) is valid at multiple sights including the S. Vitale, S. Appolinare, and the Mausoleo. After looking at mosaics all day, buy some tiles from ◧**Colori-Belle Arti,** P. Mameli 16 (tel. 0544 373 87), off Vle. Farini, and try your own hand at it.

   Trains (tel. 0544 21 78 84) connect through Bologna to Florence; Venice (1hr., every 1-2hr., L7400); and Ferrara (1hr., every 2hr., L6700). The train station is in P. Farini, at the east end of town. Follow Vle. Farini from the station to V. Diaz, which runs to the central P. del Popolo and the **tourist office,** V. Salara 8. (Tel. 0544 354 04; fax 0544 48 26 70. Open daily 8:30am-7pm; in winter 8:30am-6pm.) Walk down V. Farini and turn right at P. Mameli to find **Albergo Al Giaciglio,** V. Rocca Brancaleone 42. (Tel. 0544 394 03. Singles L35-45,000; doubles L50-65,000; triples L80-90,000. Breakfast L5000. Closed 2 weeks in Dec. or Jan. V, MC.) Take bus 1 or 70 from V. Pallavicini at the station (30min., L1300) to reach **Ostello Dante (HI),** V. Nicolodi 12. (Tel./fax 0544 42 11 64. Dorms L22,000. Breakfast included. **Internet.** Reception 2-11pm. Lockout noon-3:30pm. Curfew 11:30pm. V, MC.)

FERRARA

Rome has its mopeds, Venice its boats, and Ferrara its bicycles. Old folks, young folks, and babies perched precariously on handlebars whirl through Ferrara's jumble of major thoroughfares and twisting medieval roads inaccessible to automobiles. **Bike** the tranquil, wooded concourse along the city's 9km, well-preserved **medieval wall,** which begins at the far end of C. Giovecca. Towered, turreted, and moated, **Castello Estense** stands precisely at the center of town. C. della Giovecca lies along the former route of the moat's feeder canal, separating the medieval section from the part planned by the d'Este's architect, Biagio Rosetti. (Open Tu-Su 9:30am-5:30pm. L8000, students L6000.) From the *castello*, take C. Martiri della Libertà to P. Cattedrale and the **duomo,** which contains the **Museo della Cattedrale.** (Cathedral open M-Sa 7:30am-noon and 3-6:30pm, Su 7:30am-12:30pm and 4-7:30pm. Museum open Tu-Sa 10am-noon and 3-5pm, Su 10am-noon and 4-6pm.) From Castello Estense, cross Largo Castello to C. Ercole I d'Este and walk to the corner of C. Rossetti to reach the **Palazzo Diamanti,** built in 1493, which outshines all other ducal residences. Inside, the **Pinacoteca Nazionale** contains many of the best works of the Ferrarese school. (*Pinacoteca* open Tu-Sa 9am-2pm, Su 9am-1pm. L8000.) Follow C. Ercole I d'Este behind the *castello* and turn right on C. Porta Mare to find the Palazzo Massari, C. Porta Mare 9, which now houses both the **Museo d'Arte Moderna e Contemporanea "Filippo de Pisis"** and, upstairs, the spectacular **Museo Ferrarese dell'Ottocentro/Museo Giovanni Boldini.** (Both open daily Oct.-Feb. 8am-6pm; Mar.-May 8am-8pm; June-Sept. 7:30am-midnight. Joint ticket L10,000.) From the *castello*, head down C. Giovecca, turn left on V. Montebello, and continue to V. Vigne to find the **Cimitero Ebraico** (Jewish Cemetery), where a monument commemorates Ferrarese Jews murdered at Auschwitz.

Ferrara is on the Bologna-Venice rail line; **trains** go to Bologna (30min., 1-2 per hr., L4700); Ravenna (1hr., 1-3 per hr., L6700); Padua (1hr., every hr., L7500); Venice (2hr., 1-2 per hr., L10,100); and Rome (3-4hr., 7 per day, L38-65,500). To get to the town center, head left from the station and then right on Vle. Costituzione, which becomes Vle. Cavour and runs to the Castello Estense at the center of town (1km). ACFT (tel. 0532 59 94 92) and GGFP **buses** go from V. Rampari S. Paolo (most also leave from the train station) to Ferrara's beaches (1hr., 12 per day, L7600-8400) and Bologna (1½hr., 3-15 per day, L5000). The **tourist office** is in Castello Estense. (Tel. 0532 20 93 70; www.comune.fe.it. Open daily 9am-1pm and 2-6pm.) From the *duomo*, head down C. Porta Reno, left on V. Ragno, and left on V. Vittoria to get to **Casa degli Artisti,** V. Vittoria 66, in the historic center near P. Lampronti. (Tel. 0532 76 10 38. Singles L30,000; doubles L56-80,000.) **Albergo Nazionale,** C. Porta Reno 32, is right off the *duomo*. (Tel. 0532 20 96 04. Curfew 12:30am. Singles L65-L75,000; doubles L110,000; triples L145,000. Reserve ahead for July-Sept.) For wine, try the slightly sparkling *Uva D'Oro* (Golden Grape), compliments of the slightly insane Renata Di Francia, who brought the grapes from France for her 16th-century marriage to Duca D'Ercole II D'Este. Note that all food stores in Ferrara are closed on Thursday afternoons. Try delicious *panini* (L5000) with one of 600 varieties of wine at the oldest *osteria* in Italy, ⬛**Osteria Al Brindisi,** V. G. degli Adelardi 9b. (*Menù* L30,000. Open Tu-Su 8:30am-1am. V, MC.) Get **groceries** at the **Mercato Comunale,** on V. Mercato, off V. Garibaldi next to the *duomo*. (Open M-W 7am-1:30pm and 4:30-7:30pm, Th and Sa 7am-1:30pm, F 4:30-7:30pm.) In July and August, a free **Discobus** (tel. 0532 59 94 11) runs every Saturday night between Ferrara and the hottest clubs; pick up flyers in the station. **Postal code:** 44100.

TUSCANY (TOSCANA)

Tuscany is the stuff of Italian dreams (and more than one Brits-in-Italy movie). With rolling hills covered in olive groves and grapevines, bright yellow fields of sunflowers, and inviting cobblestoned streets, it's hard not to wax poetic. Tuscany's Renaissance culture became Italy's heritage, while its regional dialect, the language of Dante, Petrarch, and Machiavelli, has developed into modern textbook Italian. After a tumultuous medieval period of strife, Tuscany came under the astute (and despotic) rule of the Medici family, who commissioned huge *palazzi* and incredible art. Eventually, the ever-cavalier Tuscans watched their region decline into a cultural and political non-entity. Today, protected by centuries of relative serenity, the cities and towns of Tuscany remain virtually unchanged and their eminence has returned with a thriving tourism industry.

FLORENCE (FIRENZE)

Surveying the glow of the setting sun over a sea of burnt-orange roofs and towering domes prompts the realization that perhaps no other city offers so high a concentration of beauty in such a small area. The city evolved from a busy 13th-century wool- and silk-trading town plagued by civil strife into a center of political experimentation and artistic rebirth. Under Medici rule, Florentine Renaissance culture peaked in a flurry of splendid productivity: in the mid-15th century the city was the unchallenged European capital of art, architecture, commerce, and political thought. Present-day Florence works hard to preserve its cultural legacy, but it's far from a lifeless museum: street graffiti quotes Marx and Malcolm X, cell-phone-toting businessmen whiz by on Vespas, children play soccer against the *duomo*, and even the loneliest of back alleys hides some scintillating jewel.

▐ GETTING THERE AND GETTING AROUND

Flights: Amerigo Vespucci Airport (tel. 055 37 34 98), in the suburb of Peretola. Mostly domestic and charter flights. Orange ATAF **bus** 62 connects to the train station (L1500).

ITALY

Galileo Galilei Airport (tel. 050 50 07 07), in Pisa, has an info booth at platform 5 in the Florence train station. The **airport express** runs from the station to Pisa (1hr., L7500).

Trains: Santa Maria Novella Station (tel. 055 27 87 85), northwest of the center. Info open daily 7am-9pm; take a number from the machine. After-hours go to ticket window 20. Trains depart hourly to: **Bologna** (1hr., L14,200); **Rome** (2½hr., L35-40,000); **Venice** (3hr., L34,100); and **Milan** (3½hr., L39,000). Also to: **Vienna** (10hr., 4 per day) and **Frankfurt** (12hr., 3 per day). **Luggage storage** (track 16) L5000 per 12hr.

Buses: LAZZI, P. Adua 1-4r (tel. 055 21 51 55). To: **Pisa** (L11,100) and **Rome** (L24,000). **SITA,** V. S. Caterina da Siena 15r (tel. 055 48 36 51). To: **Siena** (1¼-2hr., L11,000).

Public Transportation: ATAF, outside the train station, runs orange city buses 6am-1am. **One-hour tickets** L1500, packet of 4 L5800; **3-hour** L2500; **24-hour** L6000; and **3-day** L11,000. Buy tickets at any newsstand, *tabacchi,* or automated ticket dispenser before boarding. Validate your ticket using the orange machine on board or risk a L70,000 fine. One-hour tickets are sold on the bus from 9pm-6am for L3000.

Taxis: Tel. 055 43 90, 055 47 98, or 055 42 42. Stands outside the train station.

Bike and Moped Rental: MotoRent, V. S. Zanobi 9r (tel. 055 49 01 13). Mountain bikes L5000 per hr., L30,000 per day; mopeds from L10,000 per hr., L50-75,000 per day.

Hitchhiking: Hitchers take the A-1 north to Bologna and Milan or the A-11 northwest to the Riviera and Genoa. Buses 29, 30, or 35 run from the station to the feeder near Peretola. For the A-1 south to Rome and the extension to Siena, they take bus 31 or 32 from the station to Exit 23 ("Firenze Sud"). *Let's Go* does not recommend hitchhiking.

▣ ORIENTATION AND PRACTICAL INFORMATION

From the train station, it's a short walk down V. de' Panzani and a left on V. de' Cerretani to the *duomo*, at the northern edge of the city center (which stretches south to the Arno River, east to the Bargello, and west to the Palazzo Strozzi). Major arteries radiate from the *duomo* and its two *piazze:* **Piazza del Duomo** surrounds the cathedral and **Piazza San Giovanni** encircles the baptistery just to the west. **Via dei Calzaiuoli** runs south from the *duomo* to **Piazza della Signoria.** The parallel **Via Roma** to the west leads from P. S. Giovanni through **Piazza della Repubblica** to the **Ponte Vecchio,** which crosses the Arno to the **Oltrarno** district. To the east of and parallel to V. Roma, **Via del Proconsolo** runs south to the **Bargello. Borgo S. Lorenzo** (opposite V. Roma) runs north from P. S. Giovanni to **Piazza San Lorenzo,** and V. dei Servi leads northeast from P. del Duomo to the **Galleria dell'Accademia.**

Sights are scattered throughout Florence, but few lie beyond walking distance. **Florence's streets are numbered in red and black sequences.** Red numbers indicate commercial establishments and black (or blue) numbers denote residential addresses (including most sights and hotels). Black addresses appear in *Let's Go* as a numeral only, while red addresses are indicated with a subsequent "r." If you reach an address and it's not what you're looking for, you've probably got the wrong color—just take a step back and look for the other sequence. See the **color map** at the front of this book for an overview of Florence and its sights.

TOURIST, FINANCIAL, AND LOCAL SERVICES

Tourist Offices: Consorzio ITA (tel. 055 28 28 93), in the train station by track 16. If you show up and suggest a price range, they will find you a room (although often not the best value) for L3-10,000 commission. Bulletin board for travelers. Open daily 8:30am-8:30pm. **Informazione Turistica** (tel. 055 21 22 45), in P. della Stazione, in the round glass-and-concrete building outside the train station (exit by track 16). Info on entertainment and cultural events. Open daily Apr.-Oct. 8:15am-7:15pm; Nov.-Mar. 8:15am-2pm.

Tours: Enjoy Florence (tel. 800 274 819 or 06 445 18 43) gives fast-paced, informative walking tours of the old city center, focusing on the history and culture of medieval and Renaissance Florence. Tours meet in summer M-Sa at 10am in front of the Thomas Cook office at the Ponte Vecchio; reduced hours in winter. L30,000, under 26 L25,000.

Consulates: UK, Lungarno Corsini 2 (tel. 055 28 41 33). Open M-F 9:30am-12:30pm and 2:30-4:30pm. **US,** Lungarno Vespucci 38 (tel. 055 239 82 76), at V. Palestro, near the station. Open M-F 8:30am-noon and 2-4pm. **Canadians, Australians,** and **New Zealanders** should contact consulates in Rome or Milan.

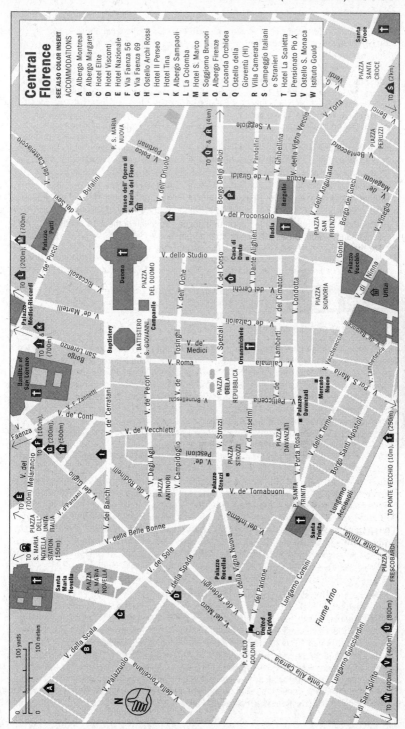

Central Florence

SEE ALSO COLOR INSERT

ACCOMMODATIONS

- A Albergo Montreal
- B Albergo Margaret
- C Hotel Elite
- D Hotel Visconti
- E Hotel Nazionale
- F Via Faenza 56
- G Via Faenza 69
- H Ostello Archi Rossi
- I Hotel Il Perseo
- J Hotel Tina
- K Albergo Sampaoli
- L La Colomba
- M Hotel S. Marco
- N Soggiorno Brunori
- O Istituto Gould
- P Locanda Orchidea
- Q Ostello della Gioventù (HI)
- R Villa Camerata
- S Campeggio Italiani e Stranieri
- T Hotel La Scaletta
- U Pensionato Pio X
- V Ostello S. Monaca
- W Istituto Gould

ITALY

Currency Exchange: Local banks offer the best rates. Most are open M-F 8:20am-1:20pm and 2:45-3:45pm, some also Sa morning. **ATMs** are everywhere–withdraw away.

American Express: V. Dante Alighieri 20-22r (tel. 055 509 81). From the *duomo*, walk down V. dei Calzaiuoli and turn left on V. dei Tavolini. Mail held; free for card- and check-holders, otherwise L3000 per inquiry. Open M-F 9am-5:30pm, Sa 9am-12:30pm.

Bookstores: Paperback Exchange, V. Fiesolana 31r (tel. 055 247 81 54), swaps books. Open M-Sa 9am-1pm and 3:30-7:30pm; July closed Sa afternoons; mid-Nov. to mid-Mar. closed M. Closed 2-3 weeks in Aug. **After Dark,** V. de' Ginori 47r (tel. 055 29 42 03). New books in English. Open M-F 10am-1:30pm and 3-7pm, Sa 10am-1:30pm.

Laundromat: Launderette, V. Guelfa 55r. Wash and dry L12,000. Open daily 8am-10pm.

EMERGENCY AND COMMUNICATIONS

Emergencies: Tel. 113. **Medical Emergency,** tel. 118. **Fire,** tel. 115. **Police,** tel. 112.

Pharmacies: Farmacia Comunale (tel. 055 28 94 35), in the train station by track 16. **Molteni,** V. dei Calzaiuoli 7r (tel. 055 28 94 90). Both open 24hr.

Internet Access: Get on the **Internet Train** at V. Guelfa 24a (tel. 055 21 47 94); V. dell'Orivolo 25r (tel. 055 263 89 68); and Borgo S. Jacopo (tel. 055 265 79 35), near the Ponte Vecchio. L12,000 per hr., students L10,000 per hr. With membership (free after 1st 2hr.) L2000 less per hr. Open M-F 10am-11pm, Sa 12:30-7:30pm, Su 3-7pm.

Post Office: V. Pellicceria (tel. 055 21 61 22), off P. della Repubblica. Send packages from V. dei Sassetti 4. Address mail to be held: Kelsey DOUB, *In Fermo Posta*, L'Ufficio Postale, V. Pellicceria, Firenze, **50100** Italy. Open M-F 8:15am-7pm, Sa until 12:30pm.

PHONE CODE	Italian city codes are included in local numbers. From outside Italy, dial int'l dialing prefix + 39 + local number.

▐ ACCOMMODATIONS

Florence abounds with one-star *pensioni* and private *affitta camere*. If you arrive late in the day, consult the accommodations service at the tourist office in the train station. Make reservations *(prenotazioni)* at least 10 days in advance if you plan to visit during Easter or summer. As a courtesy to hotel owners and fellow travelers, immediately cancel any reservations you decide not to keep; hotel owners are disgruntled by no-shows, and many no longer accept reservations for this reason. **Expect prices higher than those listed here;** rates uniformly increase by 10% or so every year. Don't embarrass hotel owners or yourself by insisting on the infallibility of the figures below, gathered in late summer 1999.

The budget accommodations around the **Piazza Santa Maria Novella,** near the train station, are excellently located near the *duomo*. Although the **Old City** (the center) is flooded by tourists, budget accommodations often provide great views of Florence's monuments or reside in Renaissance *palazzi*. Inexpensive budget hotels on and around **Via Nazionale,** off P. della Stazione in front of the station, cater to the disoriented; the area isn't big on ambience, but it's filled with cheap rooms. The area near **Piazza San Marco** is considerably calm and tourist-free given its proximity to the center; to get there, turn right from the station, left on V. Nazionale, right on V. Guelfa, and left on V. Cavour. **Oltrarno,** across the river from the *duomo* (10min.), offers a break from Florence's hustle and bustle.

HOSTELS

▩ **Ostello Archi Rossi,** V. Faenza 94r (tel. 055 29 08 04; fax 055 230 26 01). Exit left from the station on V. Nazionale and turn left on V. Faenza. Floor-to-ceiling graffiti, TV, and patio brimming with young travelers. Dorms L20-35,000, with bath L25-40,000. Breakfast L3-5000. Laundry L10,000. Lockout from noon 9:30am, from hostel 11am. In summer, arrive before 11am. Curfew 12:30am. No phone or fax reservations.

▩ **Istituto Gould,** V. dei Serragli 49 (tel. 055 21 25 76; fax 055 28 02 74), in the **Oltrarno.** Exit the station by track 16, head right to P. della Stazione, walk along the left side of the church, and continue straight through the P. S. Maria Novella and down V. dei Fossi, which turns into V. dei Serragli after the bridge (15min.). Sunny, spotless rooms in a cool, cavernous *palazzo* with a large courtyard. Singles L48-55,000; doubles L72-78,000; triples L78-105,000; quads with bath L132,000. Reception M-F 9am-1pm and 3-7pm, Sa 9am-1pm. No check-in or check-out Sa afternoons or Su.

Ostello Santa Monaca, V. S. Monaca 6 (tel. 055 26 83 38; fax 055 28 01 85; email info@ostello.it; www.ostello.it), off V. dei Serragli (see above) in the **Oltrarno.** Crowded high-ceilinged dorms L25,000. Kitchen. Laundry L12,000. 7-night max. stay. Reception 6am-1pm and 2pm-1am. Curfew 12:30am. Reserve in writing. V, MC.

Pensionato Pio X, V. dei Serragli 106 (tel./fax 055 22 50 44), past the Istituto Gould in **Oltrarno.** Quiet, clean rooms and comfortable lounges. L25-30,000; L22,000 for multiple-night stays. Arrive before 9am. Check-out 9am. Curfew midnight. No reservations.

Ostello della Gioventù Europa Villa Camerata (HI), V. Augusto Righi 2-4 (tel. 055 60 14 51; fax 055 61 03 00). Take bus 17 from P. del Duomo or P. dell'Unità near the train station (25min.); ask the driver where to get off. Tidy and popular, in a gorgeous villa with *loggia* and gardens. Nightly English-language movie. L25,000; nonmembers L30,000. Breakfast included. Laundry L10,000. Reception 1-11pm. Strict midnight curfew. Reserve in writing. If they're full, sleep on a cot in their outdoor tent for L17,500.

OLD CITY (NEAR THE DUOMO)

🦉 **Locanda Orchidea,** Borgo degli Albizi 11 (tel. 055 248 03 46), a left off V. Proconsolo from the southeast corner of P. del Duomo. Dante's wife was born in this 12th-century *palazzo.* Some of the graceful rooms open onto a garden. Singles L60,000; doubles L90,000; triples L130,000. Reservations recommended. Closed 2 weeks in mid-Aug.

Soggiorno Brunori, V. del Proconsolo 5 (tel. 055 28 96 48), off P. del Duomo. Friendly, English-speaking staff provides advice on excursions. Singles L50-64,000; doubles L88-112,000; triples L119-152,000; quads 150-190,000. Curfew 12:30am.

Hotel Il Perseo, V. de Cerretani 1 (tel. 055 21 25 04; fax 055 28 83 77), en route to the *duomo* from the station, opposite the Feltrinelli bookstore. Enthusiastic owners and bright, immaculate rooms with fans. Bar and TV lounge. Singles L80,000; doubles L125-160,000; triples L180-200,000. Breakfast included. V, MC, AmEx.

Albergo Firenze, P. dei Donati 4 (tel. 055 21 42 03 or 055 26 83 01; fax 055 21 23 70). From the *duomo,* walk down V. del Proconsolo and head right on V. del Corso to the *piazza.* Central and tranquil rooms with TV and bath in a beautiful *palazzo.* Singles L90,000; doubles L130,000; triples L180,000; quads L225,000. Breakfast included.

AROUND PIAZZA SANTA MARIA NOVELLA

Albergo Montreal, V. della Scala 43 (tel. 055 238 23 31; fax 055 28 74 91). Exit east from the station (left as you face the tracks), walk down V. degli Orti Oricellari, and turn left on V. della Scala. Cozy TV lounge and ebullient staff. Singles L70,000; doubles L85-100,000; triples L140,000; quads L170,000. Curfew 1:30am.

Hotel Visconti, P. Ottaviani 1 (tel./fax 055 21 38 77). From P. S. Maria Novella, follow V. de' Fossi 1 block. Pseudo-Neoclassical decor, bar, and TV lounge. Singles L73,000; doubles with bath L126,000. Delicious breakfast in roof garden included.

Hotel Elite, V. della Scala 12 (tel. 055 21 53 95; fax 055 21 38 32), past the Albergo Montreal (see above). Bubbly reception gives advice on sightseeing, eating, and playing in Florence. Singles L90-110,000; doubles L120-140,000. Breakfast L10,000.

Albergo Margaret, V. della Scala 25 (tel. 055 21 01 38), past the Albergo Montreal (see above). Serene decor, kind staff, and beautiful rooms. June-Aug. singles L80,000; doubles L100-120,000; Sept.-May reduced. Curfew midnight.

AROUND PIAZZA SAN MARCO

🦉 **Hotel Tina,** V. S. Gallo 31 (tel. 055 48 35 19; fax 055 48 35 93). From P. S. Marco, follow V. XXII Aprile and turn right on V. S. Gallo. *Pensione* with high ceilings, new furniture, and amicable owners. Singles L80,000; doubles L100,000, with bath L120,000; triples with bath L140,000; quads with bath L160,000.

Albergo Sampaoli, V. S. Gallo 14 (tel. 055 28 48 34), before the Hotel Tina (see above). Proprietress makes her *pensione* a backpacker's "home away from home." Singles L90-100,000; doubles L110-160,000; extra bed L56,000. Call the night before you arrive.

La Colomba, V. Cavour 21 (tel. 055 28 91 39; fax 055 28 43 23; email info@hotelcolomba.it), right off P. S. Marco. Clean rooms with phones, TVs, A/C, and fridges. Singles L100,000; doubles L170-210,000. Breakfast included. Flexible curfew 1:30am. V, MC.

Hotel San Marco, V. Cavour 50 (tel./fax 055 28 42 35), right off P. S. Marco. Modern, airy rooms. Singles L80-100,000; doubles L110,000, with bath L140,000; triples with bath L150,000. Breakfast included. Curfew 1:30am; ask for a key. V, MC.

VIA NAZIONALE AND ENVIRONS

Hotel Nazionale, V. Nazionale 22 (tel. 055 238 22 03), near P. della Indipendenza. Comfy beds in sunny rooms. Singles L80-90,000; doubles L120-140,000; triples L160-190,000. Breakfast included. Curfew midnight; ask for a key. V, MC, AmEx.

Via Faenza 56 houses 6 separate *pensioni,* among the best budget lodgings in the city. From the station, head up V. Nazionale and turn left on V. Faenza. **Pensione Azzi** (tel. 055 21 38 06). Styles itself as a *locanda degli artisti* (an artists' inn), but all travelers enjoy the large, immaculate rooms and relaxing terrace. Singles L70-90,000; doubles L120-140,000. Breakfast included. V, MC, AmEx. **Albergo Anna** (tel. 055 239 83 22). Lovely rooms with frescoes and fans. Singles L65,000; doubles L110,000. 8 rooms. **Locanda Paola** (tel. 055 21 36 82). Minimalist doubles, some with views of Fiesole and the surrounding hills. Doubles L110,000. Curfew 2am. **Albergo Merlini** (tel. 055 21 28 48; fax 055 28 39 39). Some rooms with *duomo* views. Singles L70,000; doubles L100-120,000. Breakfast L9000. Curfew 1:30am. V, MC, AmEx. **Albergo Marini** (tel. 055 28 48 24). Spotless. Singles L60-70,000; doubles L80-100,000; triples L110-130,000; quads L120-140,000. Breakfast L10,000. Curfew 1am. **Albergo Armonia** (tel. 055 21 11 46). Bedecked with American film posters. Singles L60,000; doubles L100,000; triples L130,000; quads L150,000. Breakfast L8000.

Via Faenza 69 houses 4 accommodations under 1 roof. **Hotel Soggiorno d'Errico,** 4th fl. (tel./fax 055 21 55 31). Small rooms with hill views. Singles L55,000; doubles L75,000; triples L95,000; quads L110,000. Kitchen. **Locanda Giovanna,** 4th fl. (tel. 055 238 13 53). Basic, well-kept rooms, some with garden views. Singles L50,000; doubles L75,000. **Locanda Pina** and **Albergo Nella,** 1st and 2nd fl. (tel. 055 265 43 46). Basic rooms and friendly proprietors. Singles L60,000; doubles L90-110,000. Free **internet.**

IN THE OLTRARNO

■ **Hotel La Scaletta,** V. Guicciardini 13b (tel. 055 28 30 28; fax 055 28 95 62; email lascaletta@italyhotel.com). From the southwest corner of P. del Duomo, head down V. Roma, which becomes V. Guicciardini after crossing the Ponte Vecchio. Beautiful rooms with antique furniture and rooftop terraces with spectacular views of the Boboli gardens. Singles L80-140,000; doubles L140-200,000; triples L160-240,000; quads L260,000. Breakfast included. 10% off for cash-wielding *Let's Goers.* V, MC.

CAMPING

Campeggio Italiani e Stranieri, V. Michelangelo 80 (tel. 055 681 19 77), beneath Ple. Michelangelo. Take bus 13 from the station (15min.; last bus 11:25pm). Popularity leads to crowding, but offers a spectacular panorama of Florence. L10,000 per person; L8000 per tent; L6000 per car; L4000 per motorcycle. Reception 6am-midnight. Open Apr.-Nov.

Villa Camerata, V. A. Righi 2-4 (tel. 055 60 03 15; fax 055 61 03 00), outside the HI hostel (see p. 604). L8000 per person, L6800 with camping card; L8000 per small tent, L16,000 per large tent. Reception 1pm-midnight. Check-out 7-10am. Open year-round.

◖ FOOD

Florence's hearty cuisine originated in the peasant fare of the surrounding countryside. Specialties include the Tuscan classics *minestra di fagioli* (a delicious white bean and garlic soup), *ribollita* (a hearty bean, bread, and black cabbage stew), and *bistecca alla Fiorentina* (thick sirloin steak). Wine is a Florentine staple, and genuine *chianti classico* commands a premium price; a liter of house wine costs L7-10,000 in Florence's *trattorie,* while stores sell bottles for as little as L5000. The local dessert is *cantuccini di prato* (almond cookies made with egg yolks) dipped in *vinsanto* (a rich dessert wine made from raisins). *Gelato* is said to have been invented centuries ago by Florence's own Buontalenti family; as a tourist, it's your duty to sample the creamy manifestation of the city's culture.

For lunch, visit a *rosticceria gastronomia,* peruse the city's pushcarts, or pick up fresh produce or meat at the **Mercato Centrale,** between V. Nazionale and S.

Lorenzo. (Open June-Sept. M-Sa 7:30am-2pm; Oct.-May Sa 7am-2pm and 4-8pm.) To get to **STANDA supermarket**, V. Pietrapiana 1r, follow V. del Proconsolo from the *duomo*, turn left on Borgo degli Albizi, and continue straight through P. G. Salvemini to V. Pietrapiana. (Open Tu-Sa 8:30am-8pm, Su 8:30am-1:30pm.)

OLD CITY (THE CENTER)

▧ **Acqua al Due,** V. Vigna Vecchia 40r (tel. 055 28 41 70), behind the Bargello. Serves Florentine specialties. Popular with young Italians. Their *assaggio* (L13,000) demands a taste. *Primi* L9-12,000; *secondi* from L12,000. Cover L2000. Open June-Sept. daily 7:30pm-1am; Oct.-May Tu-Su 8pm-1am. Reserve ahead. V, MC, AmEx.

▧ **Le Colonnine,** V. dei Benci 6r (tel. 055 23 46 47), north of the Ponte alle Grazie. Delicious traditional fare (pasta L9-10,000; *secondi* from L11,000). Famous *paella* "for 2" could feed a small army (L30,000). Open Tu-Su noon-2pm and 7pm-1am. V, MC.

I Latini, V. Palchetti 6r, just north of the Ponte alla Carraia. Be prepared to wait for its delicious Tuscan classics such as *ribollita* (L8000). *Primi* L8-12,000; *secondi* L15-20,000. Cover L2500. Open Tu-Su 12:30-2:30pm and 7:30-10:30pm.

PIAZZE SANTA MARIA NOVELLA AND DEL MERCATO CENTRALE

Trattoria da Zà-Zà, P. del Mercato Centrale 26r (tel. 055 21 54 11). Food Gabor—er, galore—in a hopping *trattoria;* try the *tris* (veggie soup; L9000) or the *tagliatelle al tartufo* (L12,000). Cover L2000. Open M-Sa noon-3pm and 7-11pm. V, MC, AmEx.

Trattoria da Garibaldi, P. del Mercato Centrale 38r (tel. 055 21 22 67). The food is fresh, tasty, and cheap. Daily *menù* L15,000. Cover L2000 for meals outside the *menù.* Open daily noon-3pm and 7-10pm; in winter M-Sa noon-3pm and 7-10pm. Visa.

Trattoria Contadino, V. Palazzuolo 71r (tel. 055 238 26 73). Filling, home-style meals. Lunch *menù* L16,000; dinner *menù* L20,000. Open M-Sa noon-2:30pm and 6-11pm.

Trattoria da Giorgio, V. Palazzuolo 100r. Generous portions and a daily *menù* (L15,000); the homemade *fettuccine alfredo* is to die for. Open M-Sa 11am-3pm and 7pm-midnight.

THE OLTRARNO

▧ **Il Borgo Antico,** P. S. Spirito 6r (tel. 055 21 04 37). An array of creative, tasty, and filling dishes. *Primi* L10,000; *secondi* L15-25,000. Cover L3000. Open daily 12:45-2:30pm and 7:45pm-midnight. Reservations recommended. V, MC, AmEx.

Oltrarno Trattoria Casalinga, V. Michelozzi 9r (tel. 055 21 86 24), near P. S. Spirito. Delicious Tuscan specialties like *pasta al pastore* (L10,000) with *famiglia. Primi* L6-10,000; *secondi* L8-18,000. Cover L2000. Open M-Sa noon-2:30pm and 7pm-midnight.

GELATERIE

▧ **Vivoli,** V. della Stinche 7 (tel. 055 29 23 34), behind the Bargello. The most renowned Florentine *gelateria,* with the self-proclaimed "best ice cream in the world." Huge selection. Cups from L3000. Open Tu-Su Feb.-July 8am-1am; Aug.-Jan. 8am-midnight.

Perchè No?, V. Tavolini 19r (tel. 055 239 89 69), off V. dei Calzaiuoli. Florence's oldest *gelateria*—try the *nocciolosa.* From L3000. Open in summer daily 9am-8:30pm.

◔ SIGHTS

Florence's museums have recently doubled their prices (now L6-12,000 per venue) and no longer offer student discounts. In summer, watch for **Sere al Museo,** evenings when certain museums are free from 8:30 to 11pm. Additionally, don't miss Florence's churches, many of which are free treasuries of great art.

PIAZZA DEL DUOMO

DUOMO. The red brick of Florence's **duomo,** the **Cattedrale di Santa Maria del Fiore,** at the center of P. del Duomo, is visible from virtually every part of the city. Filippo Brunelleschi dreamed up the ingenious technique that made building the sublime dome—the world's largest at the time—possible: his revolutionary method of double-shelled construction utilized self-supporting interlocking bricks. Climb the 463 steps inside the dome to the **lantern,** or cupola, which offers an unparalleled view of the city. *(Open M-F 10am-5pm, Sa 10am-4:45pm, Su 1-5pm; 1st Sa of each month closes 3:30pm. Mass daily 7-10am and 5-7pm. Lantern open M-Sa 8:30am-7pm. L8000.)* A climb to the top of the 82m-high **campanile** next to the *duomo* earns ineffably beautiful views. *(Open daily Apr.-Oct. 9am-6:50pm; Nov.-Mar. 9am-5:30pm. L8000.)*

BATTISTERO. The **battistero** (baptistery) next to the *duomo*, built between the 5th and 9th centuries, was the site of Dante's christening; years later, its Byzantine-style mosaics inspired the details of the author's *Inferno*. The baptistery's famous **bronze doors** were a product of intense competition between Florentine artists: when Brunelleschi (then 23) and Ghiberti (then 20) were asked to collaborate on the doors in 1401, Brunelleschi was unwilling to compromise, so Ghiberti completed the project on his own in 1425. His work was so admired that he was immediately commissioned to forge the last set of doors, which he finished in 1452. The products—the ■**Gates of Paradise,** as Michelangelo reportedly dubbed them—were nothing like his two earlier portals; they abandoned his earlier 28-panel design for 10 large, gilded squares, each of which employed mathematical perspective to create the illusion of deep space. They have been under restoration since a 1966 flood and will soon be housed in the Museo dell'Opera del Duomo (see below). *(Open M-Sa 1:30-6pm, Su 9am-12:30pm. Mass 10:30 and 11:30am. L3000.)*

MUSEO DELL'OPERA DEL DUOMO. Most of the *duomo*'s art resides behind the cathedral in the Museo dell'Opera del Duomo. Up the first flight of stairs is a late *Pietà* by Michelangelo, who according to legend destroyed Christ's left arm with a hammer in a fit of frustration; soon after, a diligent pupil touched up the work, leaving visible scars on parts of Mary Magdalene's head. When the museum reopens, it will house the entire collection of frames from the baptistery's *Gates of Paradise*. *(P. del Duomo 9. Due to reopen following construction in 2000. Open M-Sa in summer 9am-6:50pm; off-season 9am-6:20pm. L10,000. Tours in English in summer W-Th 4pm.)*

PIAZZA DELLA SIGNORIA AND ENVIRONS

From P. del Duomo, the bustling **Via dei Calzaiuoli,** one of the city's oldest streets, runs south through crowds and chic shops to P. della Signoria.

PIAZZA DELLA SIGNORIA. The *piazza*, a vast space by medieval standards, came into being in the 13th century. In 1497, religious leader and social critic Savonarola convinced Florentines to light the **Bonfire of the Vanities,** a grand roast that consumed some of Florence's best art, in the square. A year later, disillusioned citizens sent Savonarola up in smoke on the same spot, marked today by a granite disc. Monumental sculptures cluster in front of the *palazzo*, including Michelangelo's *David* (a copy now stands in place of the original). The awkward *Neptune* to the left of the Palazzo Vecchio so revolted Michelangelo that he insulted the artist: "Oh Ammannato, Ammannato, what lovely marble you have ruined!" The graceful 14th-century **Loggia dei Lanzi,** built as a stage for civic orators, became a misogynistic sculpture gallery under the Medici dukes.

PALAZZO VECCHIO. At the far end of the *piazza*, the area around the Palazzo Vecchio forms Florence's civic center. Arnolfo del Cambio designed this fortress-like *palazzo* in the late 13th century as the seat of the *comune*'s government. It later became the Medici family home, and in 1470 Michelozzo decorated the **courtyard** in Renaissance style. Inside are works by Michelangelo, da Vinci, and Bronzino. *(Open M-W and F-Sa 9am-7pm, Th 9am-2pm, Su 8am-1pm. L10,000; courtyard free.)*

■**THE UFFIZI.** Vasari designed this palace in 1554 for the offices *(uffizi)* of the administration of Duke Cosimo; today, it houses more first-class art per square inch than any other museum in the world. A few rooms in the Uffizi are closed to the public while reconstruction progresses (a 1993 terrorist bomb killed five people in nearby buildings and destroyed priceless works of art), but the museum still displays an unparalleled collection of Renaissance art. Botticelli, da Vinci, Michelangelo, Raphael, Titian, Giotto, Fra Angelico, Caravaggio, Bronzino, Cimabue, della Francesca, Bellini, even Dürer, Rubens, and Rembrandt—you name it, they have it. *(Extends from P. della Signoria to the Arno River. Tel. 055 21 83 41. Open Tu-F 8:30am-9pm, Sa 8:30am-midnight, Su 8:30am-8pm. L12,000. Advance tickets spare hours of waiting (L13,600); call 055 29 48 83 to reserve with a credit card, or visit the tourist office in the train station.)*

PONTE VECCHIO. From the Uffizi, follow V. Georgofili left and turn right along the river to reach the nearby Ponte Vecchio (Old Bridge), the oldest bridge in Florence, which replaced an older Roman version in 1345. In the 1500s, the Medici kicked out the butcheries and tanneries that lined the bridge—apparently, the odor of pig's blood and intestines offended powerful bankers on their way to work—and proceeded to install goldsmiths and diamond-carvers. Social criticism aside, the view of the bridge from the neighboring Ponte alle Grazie at sunset is heart-stopping.

PIAZZA DELLA REPUBBLICA. This *piazza* replaced the Mercato Vecchio (Old Market) as the site of the town market in 1890. A single column remains from the Mercato Vecchio, topped off by a statue representing *Abundance*. The pricey, decadent **Gilli,** Florence's most famous coffeehouse (established in 1733), and the nearby **Giubbe Rosse,** once the haunt of Communists, artists, and Futurist writers, are two of the city's most popular cafés. *(West of V. Calzaiuoli. From the Ponte Vecchio, walk straight up V. Por S. Maria, which turns into V. Calimala and pours into the piazza.)*

THE BARGELLO AND ENVIRONS

BARGELLO. The heart of medieval Florence lies at this 13th-century fortress, between the *duomo* and P. della Signoria. Once the residence of the chief magistrate, later a brutal prison that held public executions in the courtyard, it was restored in the 19th century and now houses the sculpture-filled **Museo Nazionale.** Donatello's bronze ▨*David*, the first free-standing nude since antiquity, stands opposite the two bronze panels of the *Sacrifice of Isaac*, submitted by Ghiberti and Brunelleschi in the baptistery door competition. *(In P. San Firenze. From P. della Signoria, follow V. della Ninna east and take a left on V. dei Leoni. Open daily 9am-1:30pm; closed on the 1st, 3rd, and 5th Su and the 2nd and 4th M of each month. L8000.)*

PIAZZA SANTA CROCE. Follow V. Ghibellina east from the Bargello and turn right on V. Giuseppe Verdi to reach the P. Santa Croce, home to the Franciscan **Chiesa di Santa Croce.** Despite the stark asceticism of the Franciscans, it's quite possibly the most splendid church in the city, with some impressive Giotto frescoes. Among the all-star Florentines buried here are Michelangelo, Macchiavelli, and Galileo. *(Open daily 8am-6:30pm.)* Cool *pietra serena* pilasters and statues of the evangelists by Donatello grace Brunelleschi's small **Cappella Pazzi,** at the end of the cloister next to the church. *(Enter through Museo dell'Opera. Open Th-Tu 10am-12:30pm and 2:30-6:30pm; off-season Th-Tu 10am-12:30pm and 3-5pm. L8000.)*

NORTH OF THE DUOMO

CHIESA DI SANTA MARIA NOVELLA. The wealthiest merchants in Florence built their chapels in this 13th- and 14th-century church. Renaissance frescoes covered the interior until the Medici commissioned Vasari to paint new ones over them; fortunately, he spared Masaccio's powerful *Trinity*, the first painting to use geometric perspective. Keep your eyes peeled for works by Ghirlandaio and Filippo Lippi. *(P. S. Maria Novella, south of the station. Open M-Sa 7am-12:15pm and 3-6:30pm, Su 3-5pm.)*

BASILICA DI SAN LORENZO. In 1419, Brunelleschi designed the spacious **Basilica di San Lorenzo.** The Medici, who lent the city the funds to build the church, retained artistic control over its construction. The family cunningly placed Cosimo's grave in front of the high altar, making the entire church his personal mausoleum. Michelangelo designed the church's exterior, but (disgusted by Florentine politics) abandoned the project and ran off to Rome to study architecture. *(Northwest of the duomo. From the P. dell'Unità Italiana near the Chiesa di S. Maria Novella, follow V. del Melarancio two blocks east. Open daily 8am-noon and 3:30-5:30pm.)* The basilica's still-unadorned façade complements the **Palazzo Medici,** diagonally across the *piazza*, which hosts rotating exhibits. *(Open Th-Tu 9am-12:45pm and 3-5:45pm. L6000.)*

To reach the ▨**Cappelle dei Medici** (Medici Chapels), walk around to the back entrance on P. Madonna degli Aldobrandini. The **Cappella dei Principi** (Princes' Chapel) is a rare moment of the Baroque in Florence, while the **Sacrestia Nuova** (New Sacristy; 1524) reveals Michelangelo's study of Brunelleschi and holds two Medici tombs. *(Open M-Sa 8:30am-5pm, Su 8:30am-1:50pm; closed the 2nd and 4th Su and*

ITALY

the 1st, 3rd, and 5th M of each month. L13,000. Ask for a free ticket to the Sacrestia Nuova at the window.) The **Laurentian Library** next door contains one of the most valuable manuscript collections in the world, while the portico and staircase exemplify Michelangelo's graceful, innovative designs. *(Open M-Sa 9am-1pm. Free.)*

■**ACCADEMIA.** Michelangelo's triumphant *David* stands in self-assured perfection in a rotunda designed specifically for it. In the hallway stand Michelangelo's four *Prisoners;* the master left these intriguing statues intentionally unfinished, chipping away just enough to liberate the "living stone." *(V. Ricasoli 60. From P. S. Lorenzo, take V. de' Ginori, turn right on V. Guelfa, and turn left on V. Ricasoli. Open Tu-Sa 8:30am-6:15pm, Su 8:30am-2pm. L12,000.)*

■**MUSEO DELLA CHIESA DI SAN MARCO.** Remarkable works by Fra Angelico adorn the Museo della Chiesa di San Marco; climb the stairs to see his famous *Annunciation.* Every monastery cell contains its own Fra Angelico fresco, painted in flat colors and with sparse detail to facilitate somber meditation. The convent's patron, Cosimo I, retired here (look for the largest cell). *(P. S. Marco. Open daily 8:30am-1:50pm; closed the 1st, 3rd, and 5th Su and the 2nd and 4th M of each month. L8000.)*

THE OLTRARNO

Historically disdained by downtown Florentines, the far side of the Arno remains a lively, unpretentious quarter, even in high season.

PALAZZO PITTI. Luca Pitti, a nouveau-riche banker of the 15th century, built his *palazzo* east of Santo Spirito against the Boboli hill. The Medici acquired the *palazzo* and the hill in 1550 and enlarged everything possible. Today, it houses six museums, including the ■**Galleria Palatina.** The Galleria was only one of a few public galleries when it opened in 1833, and today houses Florence's second most important art collection (after the Uffizi). Works by Raphael, Titian, Andrea del Sarto, Caravaggio, and Rubens line the walls. Other museums display Medici family treasures, costumes, porcelain, carriages, and *Apartamenti Reale* (royal apartments)—lavish reminders of the time when the *palazzo* was the royal House of Savoy's living quarters. *(V. Guicciardini leads from Ponte Vecchio to the palazzo. Galleria Palatina open Su-F 8:30am-9pm, Sa 8:30am-midnight; L12,000. All other museums open 8:30am-1:50pm; closed on the 1st, 3rd, and 5th M and the 2nd and 4th Su of the month; L4000. Apartamenti Reale open Tu-Sa 8:30am-7pm, Su 8:30am-2pm; L12,000.)*

BOBOLI GARDENS. With geometrically sculpted hedges, contrasting groves of holly and cypress trees, and bubbling fountains, the elaborate gardens are an exquisite example of stylized Renaissance landscaping. You'll want to get lost (or picnic) in this sea of green, which stretches from behind the Palazzo Pitti all the way up the hill to the **Forte di Belvedere,** built for Grand Duke Ferdinand I and once the Medici fortress and treasury. The fort, a star-shaped construction by Buontalenti with a central *loggia* designed by Ammannati, now hosts summer exhibitions and tanning exhibitionism. *(From P. Santa Felicità, to the right as you face the Ponte Vecchio from the Palazzo Pitti, ascend Costa di S. Giorgio to reach the fortress. Gardens open daily Apr.-Oct. 9am-8pm; Nov.-Feb. 9am-4:30pm; Mar. 9am-5:30pm. Closed 1st and last M of the month. L4000. Fort open daily 9am-10pm; in winter 9am-5pm.)*

OTHER SIGHTS. The **Brancacci Chapel** inside the **Chiesa di Santa Maria del Carmine** holds, in glorious restored form, Masaccio's stunning and influential 15th-century frescoes—declared masterpieces even in their own time. With such works as the *Tribute Money,* this chapel became a school for many artists, including Michelangelo. *(Open M and W-Sa 10am-5pm, Su 1-5pm. L5000.)* The splendid view of Florence from **Forte di Belvedere** is only equalled by the picture-perfect panorama from **Piazzale Michelangelo,** itself filled with marble copies of its namesake's statues. Go at sunset for the most spectacular lighting of the city. *(Take bus 13 from the station or from the Ponte Vecchio on the fort side, follow V. de' Bardi (go right at the fork after the piazza) and continue uphill as it becomes V. di S. Niccolò, V. S. Miniato, and finally V. del Monte alle Croci. A staircase to your left heads directly to the piazzale.)* From Ple. Michelangelo, climb the stairs to ■**San Miniato al Monte** for a glorious survey of the city. The inlaid marble façade and

13th-century mosaics hint at the incredible della Robbia terra-cottas inside the **Chapel of the Cardinal of Portugal.** *(Ask the sacristan for admittance to the chapel. Church open daily 8am-12:30pm.)*

⚡ ENTERTAINMENT

Every June, the various *quartieri* of Florence turn out in costume to play their own medieval version of soccer, known as **calcio storico.** Two teams of 27 players face off over a wooden ball in one of the city's *piazze.* Tickets (from L20,000) are sold at the **Chiosco degli Sportivi** (tel. 055 29 23 63), on V. dei Anselmi.

The **Festival of San Giovanni Battista** (June 24) features a tremendous fireworks display in Ple. Michelangelo (easily visible from the Arno) that starts around 10pm. May starts the summer music festivals with the classical **Maggio Musicale.** The **Estate Fiesolana** (June-Aug.) fills the Roman theater in nearby Fiesole with concerts, opera, theater, ballet, and film; contact **Biglietteria Centrale** (tel. 055 21 62 53) or **Universalturismo** (tel. 055 21 72 41) for tickets. September brings the **Festa dell'Unità,** a concert series at Campi Bisenzia (take bus 30). The **Florence Film Festival** (tel. 055 24 07 20) is usually held in December. On the **Festa del Grillo** (Festival of the Cricket; the 1st Sunday after Ascension Day), crickets in tiny wooden cages are hawked in the Cascine park to be released into the grass.

🎵 NIGHTLIFE

For info on what's hot and what's not in the nightlife scene, consult the monthly *Firenze Spettacolo* (L2700). Begin your nighttime *passeggiata* along V. dei Calzaiuoli and end it with coffee or *gelato* in a ritzy café on P. della Repubblica, where singers prance about the stage in front of **Bar Concerto.** In the Oltrarno, **P. San Spirito** has plenty of bars and restaurants, and regular live music in summer.

Amadeus, on V. dei Pescioni, down V. de' Pecori from the *duomo.* The "best German beer at the best price in town" is served here to a relaxed crowd. Open daily 4pm-1am.

Dolce Vita, in P. del Carmine. Open-air bar with tables on the beautiful *piazza.* Hip local *giovani* come for occasional live music. Open M-Sa 10pm-1:30am, Su 5pm-1:30am.

The William, V. Magliabechi 7/9/11r. New, trendy pub for Italians and tourists in the know. Rowdy and packed on weekends; mellower on weeknights. Open M-Sa 6pm-1am.

Angie's Pub, V. dei Neri 35r. Very Italian (despite the name) pub catering mostly to students. Imported beer and cider from L4000. Open Tu-Sa 12:30-3pm and 7pm-1am.

The Lion's Fountain, in P. G. Salvemini. Head down V. Proconsolo from the *duomo* and left on Borgo degli Albizi. Friendly late-night, English-speaking crowd. Open daily 5pm-2am.

Meccanò, V. degli Olmi 1, near Parco delle Cascinè. The most popular of Florence's discos among locals and tourists alike. Take bus 17c from the *duomo* or train station. Cover L30,000; includes 1 drink. Subsequent drinks L10,000. Open Tu-Sa 11pm-4am.

Central Park, in Parco delle Cascinè. Open-air dance floor pulses with hip-hop, jungle, reggae, and something Italians call "dance rock." Open daily.

🏛 EXCURSION FROM FLORENCE: AREZZO

Petrarch, Michelangelo (born in the surrounding countryside), and, most recently, Roberto Benigni (who wrote and acted in the award-winning film *Life is Beautiful*) have all found inspiration in the streets of Arezzo. The town's most famous treasure is Piero della Francesca's magnificent fresco cycle *Leggenda della Vera Croce* (Legend of the True Cross), which portrays the story of the wood used for Christ's cross. It is housed in the spiritual and physical center of Arezzo, the 14th-century **Basilica di San Francesco,** P. S. Francesco, up V. G. Monaco from the train station. (Open daily 8:30am-noon and 2:30-6:30pm. L10,000.) Seven 20-foot-high circular stained-glass windows let light into the massive **duomo,** in P. del Duomo. **Piazza Grande** showcases Arezzo's most impressive examples of architecture, including the spectacular **Chiesa di Santa Maria della Pieve.** (Open M-Sa 8am-noon and 3-7pm, Su 8:30am-noon and 4-7pm.) Two **trains** arrive in Arezzo hourly from Florence (1½hr., L7600). The **tourist office,** P. della Repubblica 22, is to the right as

ITALY

you exit the station. (Tel. 0575 37 76 78. Open Apr.-Sept. M-Sa 9:15am-1:15pm and 3-7pm, Su 9:15am-1:15pm; Oct.-Mar. M-Sa 9:15am-1:15pm and 3-6:30pm.) **Ostello Villa Severi,** V. Redi 13, is a bit of a hike from town, but is well worth it. Take bus 4 (L1200) from P. G. Monaco and get off 2 stops after the Ospedale Vecchio (7min.). (Tel. 0575 29 90 47. L20,000. Reception 9am-1pm and 6-11:30pm.)

SIENA

After centuries of intense, sometimes violent, rivalry with neighboring Florence, a period of blossoming as a cultural and bureaucratic center during the Renaissance, and the destruction of half the population in the Black Death, Siena today shines peacefully beside its more-touristed sibling in astounding aesthetic harmony.

⛊⛊⛊ PRACTICAL INFO, ACCOMMODATIONS, AND FOOD. From P. Rosselli, **trains** (tel. 05 77 28 01 15) go to Florence (1½hr., every hr., L8800) and Rome via Chiosi (2½hr., every hr., L22,000). Take **TRA-IN** bus 4, 7-10, 14, 17, or 77 across the street from the station to the central P. del Campo (L1400); buy tickets from vending machines. Express **TRA-IN/SITA buses** (tel. 05 77 20 42 45) link P. S. Domenico 1, near the heart of the city, with Florence (every hr., L11,000) and other Tuscan towns. The central **tourist office** is at Il Campo 56. (Tel. 05 77 28 05 51; fax 05 77 27 06 76. Open in summer M-Sa 8:30am-7:30pm, Su 8:30am-2pm; off-season M-Sa 8:30am-1pm and 3-7pm.) **Prenotazioni Alberghiere,** in P. S. Domenico, finds rooms for L3000. (Tel. 05 77 28 80 84. Open in summer M-Sa 9am-8pm; off-season M-Sa 9am-7pm. Call ahead.) Check **email** at **Internet Train,** V. Pantaneto 54. (Open M-F 10am-11pm, Sa 10am-1pm, Su 6-11pm.) Tasteful **Albergo Tre Donzelle** is at V. Donzelle 5. (Tel. 0577 28 03 58. Singles L50,000; doubles L80-100,000. Flexible curfew 1am.) Take bus 15, 35, or 36 from P. Gramsci, opposite the station, to reach the **Ostello della Gioventù "Guidoriccio" (HI),** V. Fiorentina 89, in Località Lo Stellino (20min.). (Tel. 05 77 522 12; fax 05 77 561 72. L30,000. Breakfast included. Curfew 11:30pm. Call ahead.) **Locanda Garibaldi,** V. Giovanni Dupré 18 is behind the Palazzo Pubblico and P. del Campo. (Tel. 05 77 28 42 04. Singles L45,000; doubles L85,000; triples L110,000. Breakfast L10,000. Curfew midnight. Reserve ahead.) To **camp** at **Colleverde,** Strada di Scacciapensieri 47, take bus 3 or 8 from P. Gramsci. (Tel. 0577 28 00 44. L13,000 per person, car, and tent. Open mid-Mar. to mid-Nov.) Siena specializes in rich pastries such as *panforte,* a concoction of honey, almonds, and citron; indulge at **Bar/Pasticceria Nannini,** V. Banchi di Sopra 22-24. From P. del Duomo, take V. del Capitano to P. della Postierla and turn left on V. di Stalloreggi for **Osteria il Tamburino** at #11. (*Primi* L8-13,000, *secondi* L10-18,000. Open M-Sa noon-2:30pm and 7-9:30pm.) **Consortio Agrario supermarket,** V. Pianigiani 5, is off P. Salimberi. (Open M-F 7:45am-1pm and 4:30-8pm, Sa 7:45am-1pm.) **Postal code:** 53100.

⛊⛊ SIGHTS AND ENTERTAINMENT. The salmon-colored ⛊**Piazza del Campo** (Il Campo) is the focus of Sienese life; the **Fonte Gaia** is fed by the same aqueduct that Siena used in the 1300s. At the bottom, the **Torre del Mangia** clock tower looms over the graceful Gothic **Palazzo Pubblico.** (Palazzo open July-Aug. daily 10am-11pm; Mar.-June and Sept.-Oct M-Sa 9:30am-6pm, Su 9am-1:30pm; Nov.-Feb. daily 9am-4pm; L8000, students L6000. Tower open in summer M-Sa 9:30am-6:30pm, Su 9:30am-1:30pm; off-season M-Sa 10am-5pm; L7000.) Inside, the **Museo Civico** contains excellent Gothic and early Renaissance painting; the **Sala del Mappamondo** and the **Sala della Pace** contain stellar works. (Same hours as the *palazzo.* L8000, students L6000.) Siena's Gothic ⛊**duomo** was built on the edge of a hill; the apse would have been left-hanging in mid-air if not for the construction of the baptistery below. The **baptistery** is lavishly decorated, with carvings by Ghiberti and Donatello. (Duomo open daily Jan. to mid-Mar. and Nov.-Dec. 7:30am-1:30pm and 2:30-5pm; mid-Mar.-Oct. 9am-7:30pm. Free. Open daily mid-Mar. to Sept. 9am-7:30pm; Oct. 9am-6pm; Nov. to mid-Mar. 10am-1pm and 2:30-5pm; L3000.) The lavish **Libreria Piccolomini,** off the left aisle, holds frescoes and exquisite 15th-century musical scores. (Open mid-Mar. to Oct. 9am-7:30pm; Nov. to mid-Mar. 10am-1pm and 2:30-5pm. L2000.) To reach the *duomo,* face the Palazzo Pubblico and take the stairs nearest the Palazzo on the right; cross V. di Città and continue on the same twisting street. The **Museo dell'Opera della Metropolitana** next to the cathedral, houses its overflow art. (Same hours as baptistry. L6000.) The **biglietto cumulativo** covers the baptistery, Piccolomini library, and Museo dell'Opera Metropolitana (L9500; in winter L8500).

The central event of the **Palio di Siena** (July 2 and Aug. 16) is a traditional bare-back horse race around the packed P. del Campo. Get there three days early to watch the rambunctious horse selection in the *campo* (10am) and to pick a *con-trada* (neighborhood) for which to root. For tickets and a list of rooms to let, write the tourist office by March; arrive without a reservation and you'll be on the streets.

⚄ EXCURSION FROM SIENA: SAN GIMIGNANO.

Only an hour from Siena by bus (every hr., L8800) stretch the medieval towers of **San Gimignano.** The towers and the walled *centro* testify to 13th-century conflicts between San Gimignano's wealthiest families; the towers (originally 72, now 14) were used to store grain for sieges. Scale the **Torre Grossa,** the tallest remaining tower, attached to **Palazzo del Popolo,** for a panorama of Tuscany. (Torre open Mar.-Oct. daily 9:30am-7:30pm; Nov.-Feb. Tu-Su 9:30am-12:30pm and 1:30-4:30pm; L8000, students 6000. Palazzo open Tu-Su 9am-7:30pm.) In the shadow of the Torre Grossa, the **Museo Civico** houses an amazing collection of Sienese and Florentine works. (Open same hours as the tower. L7000, students 5000.) From the bus station, pass through the *porta,* climb the hill, and follow V. San Giovanni to the central P. della Cisterna and P. del Duomo. *Affitte camere* (doubles; around L75,000) are a good alternative to over-priced hotels. Get a list from the **tourist office,** P. del Duomo 1 (tel. 05 88 94 00 08; open daily 9am-1pm and 3-7pm), or the **Associazione Strutture Extralberghiere,** P. della Cisterna 6 (tel. 05 77 94 31 90; open daily Mar.-Nov. 9:30am-7:30pm). For the **Ostello di San Gimignano,** V. delle Fonti 1, turn off V. S. Matteo onto V. XX Settembre and fol-low the signs. (Tel. 05 58 07 70 09. L20-24,000. Breakfast included. Reception 7-9am and 5-11:30pm. Curfew 11:30pm. Open Mar.-Oct. V, MC, AmEx.) **Albergo/Ristorante Il Pino,** V. S. Matteo 102, is quiet and rustic. (Tel./fax 05 77 94 04 15. Singles L60-70,000; doubles L80-90,000. Breakfast L8000. Call ahead. V, MC, AmEx.) **Camp** at **Il Boschetto,** at Santa Lucia, 2.5km downhill from Porta S. Giovanni; buses run from town (L1500). (Tel. 0577 94 03 52. L10,000 per person, L8500 per small tent. Recep-tion 8am-1pm, 3-8pm, and 9-11pm. Open Apr.-Oct. 15.) A **market** is at V. S. Matteo 19. (Open M-Sa Mar.-Oct. 8am-8pm; Nov.-Feb. 8am-1pm and 4-7pm.)

ELBA

According to legend, the enchanting island of Elba grew from a precious stone that slipped from Venus' neck into the azure waters of the Tyrrhenian Sea. Napo-leon, able was he saw Elba, spent his exile here. **Ferries** go from **Piombino Mar-ittima** (a.k.a. Piombino Porto) to **Portoferraio,** Elba's largest city. Although **trains** on the Genoa-Rome line travel go to Piombino Marittima, most stop at Campiglia Marittima (from Florence, change at Pisa), where a a *pullman* (intercity bus; 30min., L2500) meets trains and connects to ferries in Piombino Marittima. Both Toremar (tel. 0565 311 00; 30min.-1hr., L12-24,000; summer only) and Moby Lines (1hr., L12,000) run frequently to Elba. **Portoferraio** isn't that picturesque, but if you have time to spare, stroll along the cobblestoned streets and browse the assorted Napoleon sights. **APT,** Calata Italia 26, 1st fl., across from the Toremar boat land-ing, helps with rooms and transport. (Tel. 05 65 91 46 71. Open daily 9am-1pm and 2:30-7:30pm; in winter 9am-1pm and 3-7pm.) **Ape Elbana,** Salita Cosimo de' Medici 2, overlooks the main *piazza* of the *centro storico.* (Tel./fax 05 65 91 42 45. Sin-gles L90,000; doubles L120,000.) Smart kiddies head onto the strip of pebbles that borders **Marciana Marina's** waterfront; take the **bus** from Portoferraio (1hr., L3500). The **tourist office,** V. Scali Mazzini 13, finds **rooms** for free. (Tel. 05 65 90 40 81. Open in summer daily 9am-11pm; off-season M-Sa 9am-12:30pm and 3:30-7pm, Su 9am-12:30pm.) In Marciana Marina, **Casa Lupi,** V. Amedeo is just uphill from the beach. (Tel. 05 65 991 43. Singles L50-75,000; doubles L75-110,000.)

ITALY

PISA

Tourism hasn't always been Pisa's prime industry: during the Middle Ages, the city was a major port with an empire extending to Corsica, Sardinia, and the Balearics. But when the Arno River silted up and the tower started leaning, the city's power and wealth declined accordingly. Today the city seems resigned to welcoming tourists and myriad t-shirt and ice cream vendors to the **Piazza del Duomo,** also known as the **Campo dei Miracoli** (Field of Miracles), a grassy expanse enclosing the tower, duomo, baptistery, and Camposanto. An **all-inclusive ticket** to the Campo's sights costs L18,000. To reach the Campo from the train station, take bus 1 (L1500); or walk straight up V. Gramsci, through P. Vittorio Emanuele, and down C. Italia across the Arno, continue on V. Borgo Stretto, turn left on any street branching west, and continue through the old town. Begun in 1173, the famous ▨**Leaning Tower** had reached a height of 10m when the soil beneath suddenly shifted; the tower continues to slip 1-2mm every year. Visitors are no longer allowed to enter the tower. The dazzling **duomo,** also on the Campo, is a treasury of fine art. (Open M-Sa 10am-7:45pm.) Next door is the **baptistery,** whose precise acoustics allow an unamplified choir to be heard 2km away. (Open daily in summer 8am-7:30pm; off-season 9am-4:40pm.) The adjoining **Camposanto,** a cloistered cemetery, has a series of haunting frescoes by an unidentified 14th-century artist known only as the "Master of the Triumph of Death." (Open daily in summer 9am-5:40pm; off-season 9am-4:40pm.) The **Museo delle Sinopie,** across the *piazza* from the Camposanto, displays preliminary fresco sketches discovered during post-WWII restoration. Behind the tower is the **Museo dell'Opera del Duomo.** (Both open daily in summer 8am-7:45pm; off-season 9am-12:30pm and 3-4:30pm. Joint ticket L10,000, EU citizens free.) From the Campo, walk down V. S. Maria and over the bridge to the Gothic **Chiesa di Santa Maria della Spina,** whose bell tower allegedly holds a thorn from Christ's crown.

Trains (tel. 05 04 13 85) go from P. della Stazione, in the southern part of town, to Florence (1hr., every hr., L7200); the main coastal line serves Genoa (2½hr., L16,200) and Rome (3hr., L27,400). The **tourist office** is to the left as you exit the station. (Tel. 05 04 22 91; www.turismo.toscana.it. Open M-Sa 8am-8pm, Su 9am-1pm.) The **Centro Turistico Madonna dell'Acqua** hostel, V. Pietrasantina 15, is 1km from the Tower. Take bus 3 from the station (4 per hr.) and ask for the *ostello.* (Tel. 050 89 06 22. Dorms L23,000; doubles L70,000; triples L89,000; quads L115,000. Sheets L2000. Kitchen. Reception 6-11pm. Check-out 9am. V, MC.) The **Albergo Gronchi,** P. Archivescovado 1, just off P. del Duomo, has frescoed ceilings. (Tel. 050 56 18 23. Singles L35,000; doubles L56,000; triples L75,000. Curfew midnight. Reserve ahead.) Follow the signs (1km) from P. Manin to **Campeggio Torre Pendente,** V. delle Cascine 86. (L12,000 per person, L3500-6000 per tent. Open June-Aug.) ▨**Marcovaldo,** V. S. Martino 47, has superb food but no table service. (*Primi* L7000, *secondi* L10,000. Open M-Sa noon-2pm and 6-10:30pm.) Get **groceries** at **Superal,** V. Pascoli 6, just off C. Italia. (Open M-Tu and Th-Sa 8am-8pm, W 8am-1:30pm.) **Postal code:** 56100.

UMBRIA

Umbria is known as the "Green Heart of Italy," a land rich in natural beauty, encompassing wild woods and fertile plains, craggy gorges and tiny cobblestoned villages. This irresistible, landlocked region wedged between the Adriatic and Tyrrhenian coasts has long been a cherished and greatly contested prize. One conqueror, Christianity, transformed Umbria's architecture and regional identity, turning it into a breeding ground for saints and religious movements; it was here St. Francis of Assisi shamed the extravagant church with his humility.

PERUGIA

The extremely polite residents of Perugia may be trying to make up for two millennia of excessive nastiness, during which their ancestors regularly stoned each other and even threw tree-hugging St. Francis of Assisi into a dungeon. The city earns more dubious fame as the birthplace of the Flagellants, who wandered Europe whipping themselves, and as the site of two popes' deaths by poisoning.

But Perugia now lures visitors with steep medieval streets and a mellow university atmosphere. The city's most visited sights frame **Piazza IV Novembre.** The façade of Perugia's austere Gothic **duomo,** on the *piazza,* was left unfinished when the *Perugini* were forced to return the marble they had stolen to build it. The *duomo* houses the Virgin Mary's purported wedding ring. The **Fontana Maggiore** in the center is adorned with sculptures and bas-reliefs by Nicolà and Giovanni Pisano. The 13th-century **Palazzo dei Priori** presides over the *piazza* with the immense collection of the **Galleria Nazionale dell'Umbria,** C. Vannucci 19. (Open M-F 9am-7pm, Sa 9am-7pm and 9pm-midnight, Su 9am-8pm; closed 1st M of each month. L8000.) The ▧**Basilica di San Pietro,** on C. Cavour, at the end of town past the Porta S. Pietro, maintains its original 10th-century basilica layout; at its far end is an exquisitely manicured garden with incredible views. (Open daily 8am-noon and 3:30pm-dusk.)

The **FS train station,** P. V. Veneto, serves Assisi (25min., every hr., L3500); Siena (every hr., L14,000); Florence (2½hr., every hr., L24,900); and Rome (2½hr., L26,000; direct 2½hr., L26,900). From the station, take bus 6, 7, or 9 to the central P. Italia (L1200), then take C. Vannucci to P. IV Novembre and the **tourist office,** in P. IV Novembre. (Tel. 07 55 72 33 27. Open M-Sa 8:30am-1:30pm and 3:30-6:30pm, Su 9am-1pm.) To get from there to ▧**Ostello della Gioventù/Centro Internazionale di Accoglienza per la Gioventù,** V. Bontempi 13, pass the *duomo* and P. Dante, take the farthest street right through P. Piccinino, and turn right on V. Bontempi. (Tel. 075 572 28 80; email ostello@edisons.it. L16,000. Sheets L2000. Kitchen. Lockout 9:30am-4pm. Curfew midnight. Open mid-Jan. to mid-Dec.) **Albergo Anna,** V. dei Priori 48, off C. Vannucci, has clean, cool 17th-century rooms with great views. (Tel. 075 573 63 04. Singles L45-60,000; doubles L70-90,000; triples L95-120,000.) To **camp** at **Paradis d'Eté,** 5km away in Colle della Trinità, take bus 36 from the station. (Tel. 075 517 21 17. L7000 per person, L6000 per tent, L3000 per car.) ▧**Trattoria Dal Mi Cocco,** C. Garibaldi 12, up from the University for Foreigners, offers an extremely generous L25,000 *menù.* (Open Tu-Su 1-2:30pm and 8:15-10:30pm.) The **COOP,** P. Matteoti 15, has **groceries.** (Open M-Sa 9am-8pm.) **Postal code:** 06100.

ASSISI

Assisi's serenity originates with the legacy of monk St. Francis, who preached poverty, obedience, and love eight centuries ago. After his death in 1226, Florentine and Sienese painters decorated the **Basilica di San Francesco** with spectacular frescoes illustrating his life. From P. del Commune, take V. Portica. (Tel. 075 81 22 38. Call for free tour in English. Upper church open daily dawn-dusk; may be closed for restorations. Lower level open M-Sa 9:30am-noon and 2-6pm. L3000.) The dramatic fortress **Rocca Maggiore** towers above town, offering a shady perch and tremendous views. From P. S. Rufino, go left of the *duomo* up the cobblestoned street. (Open daily in good weather 10am-dusk. L5000, students L3500.) Take C. Mazzini from P. del Commune to reach the **Basilica of Santa Chiara,** where St. Francis attended school and St. Clare now rests. (Open M-F 10am-noon and 3:30-5:30pm, Sa-Su 9:30-11:30am and 3:30-5:30pm.) Many of Assisi's sights were badly damaged in the 1997 earthquake and may be temporarily closed; however, restorations are proceeding rapidly in preparation for the Jubilee Year 2000 of the Catholic Church.

From the station near the Basilica Santa Maria degli Angeli, **trains** go to Ancona (L12,100); Florence (2 per day, L17,000); and Rome (1 per day, L25,500); more frequent trains go to Rome via Foligno and to Florence via Ternotola. ASP **buses** run from P. Matteoti to Perugia (1½hr., 7 per day, L4900) elsewhere in Umbria. From P. Matteotti, follow V. del Torrione, bear left in P. S. Rufino, and take V. S. Rufino to the town center. The **tourist office,** P. del Comune 12, is down V. Mazzini. (Tel. 075 81 25 34; fax 075 81 37 27. Open M-F 8am-2pm and 3:30-6:30pm, Sa 9am-1pm and 3:30-6:30pm, Su 9am-1pm.) For ▧**Ostello della Pace (HI),** V. di Valecchi 177, turn right out of the station, then left at the intersection on V. di Valecchi (30min.). (Tel./fax 075 81 67 67. L22,-27,000. Breakfast included. Laundry. Reception 7-9:15am and 3:30-11:30pm. Check-out 9:30am. Reserve ahead. V, MC.) Peaceful **Camere Annalisa Mar-**

tini, V. S. Gregorio 6, is in the medieval core of Assisi. (Tel. 075 81 35 36. Singles L38-40,000; doubles L58-60,000; triples L80,000. Laundry.) For well-made *panini* and staples, try **Micromarket AMICA,** V. Fortabella 61, near P. Unità and San Francesco. (Open M-Sa 7:30am-2pm and 3:30-8pm, Su 7:30am-2pm.) **Postal code:** 06081.

THE MARCHES (LE MARCHE)

In the Marches, green foothills separate the gray shores of the Adriatic from the Apennine mountains, and the traditional hill-towns from the umbrella-laden beaches. Inland towns, easily accessible by train, rely on agriculture, and preserve the region's historical legacy in the architectural remains of Gauls and Romans.

URBINO

Urbino's fairy-tale skyline, scattered with humble stone dwellings and an immense turreted palace, has changed little over the past 500 years. The city's most remarkable monument is the looming Renaissance **Palazzo Ducale** (Ducal Palace), in P. Rinascimento, though its façade is more thrilling than its interior. The enclosed **courtyard** is the essence of Renaissance balance and proportion; to the left, stairs lead to the former private apartments of the Duke, which now house the packed **National Gallery of the Marches.** Check out the Duke's study, where inlaid panels give the illusion of real books and the underground baths, kitchen, and washroom. (Open M 9am-2pm, Tu-F 9am-7pm, Sa 9am-7pm and 9pm-midnight, Su 9am-8pm. L8000.) Raphael's birthplace, **Casa di Rafaele,** V. Raffaello 57, is now a vast and delightful museum; his earliest work, a fresco, *Madonna e Bambino,* hangs in the *sala.* (Open Mar.-Oct. M-Sa 9am-1pm and 3-7pm, Su 10am-1pm. L5000.)

Bucci **buses** (tel. 0721 324 01) go from Borgo Mercatale to Rome (5hr., 2 per day, L34,000). SAPUM **buses** runs along the Bologna-Lecce **rail** line along the Adriatic coast. From there, a short walk uphill on V. G. Mazzini leads to **P. della Repubblica,** the city center. The **tourist office,** P. Rinascimento 1, is opposite the palace. (Tel. 07 22 26 13; fax 07 22 24 41. Open in summer M-Sa 9am-1pm and 4-7pm, Su 9am-1pm; off-season M-Sa 9am-1pm and 3-6pm.) Reserve ahead to get a room. **Pensione Fosca,** V. Raffaello 67, top floor, has charming, high-ceilinged rooms. (Tel. 07 22 32 96 22. Singles L50,000; doubles L60,000.) The **Hotel San Giovanni,** V. Barocci 13, has a restaurant downstairs. (Tel. 07 22 28 27. Singles L35-53,000; doubles L50-80,000. Open Aug.-June.) **Camping Pineta,** on V. San Donato, is 2km away in Cesane; take bus 4 or 7 from Borgo Mercatale and ask to get off at "camping." (Tel./fax 07 22 47 10. L10,000 per person, L20,000 per tent. Reception 9-11am and 3-10pm. Open Apr. to mid-Sept.) Many *paninoteche, gelaterie,* and burger joints are in or near **P. della Repubblica. Margherita supermarket** is at V. Raffaello 37. (Open M-Sa 7:30am-2pm and 4:30-8pm.) At night, **The Bosom Pub,** on V. Budassi, is stacked with fun.

ANCONA

Ancona is the center point of Italy's Adriatic Coast—a major port in a small, whimsical, and largely unexplored city. **Piazza Roma** is dotted with yellow and pink buildings, and **Piazza Cavour** is the heart of the town. **Ferries** go to Greece and Croatia; **Adriatica** (tel. 071 20 49 15), **Jadrolinija** (tel. 071 20 45 16), and **SMC Maritime Co.** (tel. 071 552 18) go to Croatia (from L57-70,000); ANEK (tel. 071 207 32 22) and **Strintzis** (tel. 071 207 10 68) go to Greece (from L62-82,000); and Strintzis also sends ferries to Venice. Ferry schedules and tickets are available at the Stazione Marittima; reserve ahead in July or August. **Trains** arrive at P. Rosselli from Bologna (2½hr., 1-2 per hr., L18,000); Rome (3-4hr., 9 per day, L23,500-40,000); Milan (5hr., 24 per day, L18,000); and Venice (5hr., 3 per day, L31,000). Take bus 1 or 1/4 along the port past **Stazione Marittima** and up C. Stamira to reach P. Cavour. Bus 1 and 1/4 also go to the **tourist office,** V. Thaon de Revel 4. (Tel. 071 35 89 91. Open M-Sa 8am-8pm, Su 8am-2pm.) ⊠**Pensione Euro,** C. Mazzini 142, 2nd fl., has airy rooms. (Tel. 071 207 22 76. Singles L30-40,000; doubles L60-70,000; triples L75,000.) **SIDIS supermarket** is at V. Matteotti 115. (Open M-W and F-Sa 8:15am-12:45pm and 5-7:30pm, Th 8:15am-12:45pm.)

ITALY

SOUTHERN ITALY

South of Rome, the sun gets brighter, the meals longer, and the passion more intense. The introduction to the *mezzogiorno* (Italian South) begins in Campania, the fertile crescent that cradles the Bay of Naples and hugs the Gulf of Salerno. In the shadow of Mount Vesuvius lie the famous Roman ruins of Pompeii, frozen in time in a bed of molten lava. In the Bay of Naples, Capri is Italy's answer to Fantasy Island, while the Amalfi Coast cuts a dramatic course down the lush Tyrrhenian shore. Though long subject to the negative stereotypes and prejudices of the more industrialized North, the region remains justly proud of its open-hearted populace, strong traditions, classical ruins, and relatively untouristed beaches.

NAPLES (NAPOLI)

Italy's third-largest city is also its most chaotic: shouting merchants flood markets, stoplights serve as mere suggestions, and traffic jams clog the broiling city in summer. But despite Naples' notorious pickpockets and poverty, the city is improving rapidly. The city's color and vitality, evident in the markets off V. Toledo and in the world's best pizza, defy stereotypes of the city. In recent years, aggressive restoration of monuments and art treasures has opened them to the public for the first time. If you're patient with Naples' rough edges, you'll be rewarded by the exquisite churches, artisan's workshops, and colorful *trattorie* in the narrowest of alleys.

▐ GETTING THERE AND GETTING AROUND

Trains: Ferrovie dello Stato goes from **Stazione Centrale** to **Rome** (2hr., 38 per day, L18,000); **Brindisi** (5hr., 5 per day, L35,000); and **Milan** (8hr., 13 per day, L95,000). **Circumvesuviana** (tel. 08 17 72 24 44) also leaves Stazione Centrale for local destinations.

Ferries: Depart from **Molo Angioino** and **Molo Beverello,** at the base of P. Municipio. From P. Garibaldi, take tram 1; from P. Municipio, take the R2 bus. **Caremar,** Molo Beverello (tel. 08 15 51 38 82), goes frequently to **Capri** and **Ischia** (both 1-1½hr., L9500-18,000). **Tirrenia Lines,** Molo Angioino (tel. 08 17 20 11 11), goes to **Palermo, Sicily** (11hr., 1 per day, L80,500) and **Cagliari, Sardinia** (15hr., 1-2 per week, L98,000). L10,000 port tax. Schedules and prices change; check *Qui Napoli.*

Public Transportation: *Giranapoli* tickets (1½-hour L1500; full-day L4500) are valid on **buses, Metropolitana** (subway), **trams,** and **funiculars.**

Taxis: Cotana (tel. 08 15 70 70 70) or **Napoli** (tel. 08 15 56 44 44). Take metered taxis.

▐ ORIENTATION AND PRACTICAL INFORMATION

The main train and bus terminals are in the immense **Piazza Garibaldi,** on the east side of Naples. From P. Garibaldi, broad **Corso Umberto I** leads southwest to **Piazza Bovi,** from which **Via De Pretis** leads left to **Piazza Municipio,** the city center, and **Piazza Trieste e Trento** and **Piazza Plebiscito.** Below P. Municipio lie the **Stazione Marittima** ferry ports. From P. Trieste e Trento, **Via Toledo** (a.k.a. **Via Roma**) leads through the Spanish quarter to **Piazza Dante.** Make a right into the historic **Spaccanapoli** ("splitting Naples") district, which follows **Via dei Tribunali** through the middle of town. While violence is rare in Naples, petty theft is relatively common (unless you're in the Mafia, in which case the opposite is true). Always be careful.

Tourist Offices: EPT (tel. 081 26 87 79; fax 081 20 66 66), at Stazione Centrale. Help with hotels and ferries, but long lines. Grab a map and *Qui Napoli.* Open M-Sa 9am-8pm. **Branches** at P. dei Martiri 58, Stazione Mergellina, and the airport.

Consulates: South Africa, C. Umberto I (tel. 081 551 75 19). **UK,** V. Crispi 122 (tel. 081 66 35 11). M: P. Amedeo. Open July-Aug. M-F 8am-1:30pm; Sept.-June M-F 9am-12:30pm and 2:30-4pm. **US** (tel. 081 583 81 11; in emergency 03 37 94 50 83), in P. della Repubblica at the west end of Villa Comunale. Open M-F 8am-5pm.

Currency Exchange: Thomas Cook, P. Municipio 70 (tel. 081 551 83 99) and at the airport. Open M-F 9:30am-1pm and 3-6:30pm.

Emergencies: Tel. 113. **Ambulance:** Tel. 081 752 06 96.

Hospital: Cardarelli (tel. 081 747 11 11), north of town on the R4 bus line.

Police: Tel. 113 or 081 794 11 11. **Carabinieri:** Tel. 112. English spoken.

Internet Access: Internet Café, V. Giancardo Tramontano 12. Go right onto V. Duomo from P. Nicola Amore, then right onto V. Tramontano. L3000 per hr. Open M-Sa 10am-2pm and 4pm-1am, Su 8pm-1am.

Post Office: P. Matteotti, at V. Diaz (R2 line). Address mail to be held: Vanilla ICE, *In Fermo Posta*, P. Matteotti, Naples **80100**, Italy. Open M-F 8:15am-6pm, Sa 8:15am-noon.

PHONE CODE	Italian city codes are included in local numbers. From outside Italy, dial int'l dialing prefix + 39 + local number.

▮◌ ACCOMMODATIONS AND FOOD

The gritty area near **P. Garibaldi** is packed with hotels; many solicit customers at the station. Be careful: while some are safe but noisy, many are noisy and worse. Rooms are scarce in the historic district between P. Dante and the *duomo*. In all cases, don't give your passport until you've seen the room; agree on the price *before* unpacking; be alert for unexpected costs; and gauge how secure it seems.

▨ **Casanova Hotel,** V. Venezia 2 (tel./fax 081 26 82 87; email hcasanov@tin.it). From P. Garibaldi, follow V. Milano and turn left at the end. Ivied front, clean, airy rooms, and a rooftop terrace. Prices with *Let's Go:* Singles L35,000; doubles L60-70,000; triples L95,000; quads L110,000. Breakfast L8000. Reserve ahead. V, MC, AmEx.

Hotel Eden, C. Novara 9 (tel. 081 28 53 44). From the train station, turn right and continue down the street; it's on the left. Large and friendly. Prices with *Let's Go:* singles L42,000; doubles L66,000; triples L90,000; quads L108,000. Breakfast L5000. V, MC, AmEx.

Hotel Ideal, P. Garibaldi 99 (tel. 081 26 92 37 or 081 20 22 23; fax 081 28 59 42; email ideal@export.it). Prices with *Let's Go:* singles L40-50,000; doubles L60-90,000; triples L80-100,000. Breakfast included. **Internet.** Call ahead. V, MC, AmEx.

Ostello Mergellina (HI), V. Salita della Grotta 23 (tel. 081 761 23 46; fax 081 761 23 91). M: Mergellina; make 2 sharp rights on V. Piedigrotta, a left on V. Salita della Grotta, and a right on the driveway after the overpass (before the tunnel). Dorms L24,000; doubles L60,000. Breakfast included. Lockout 9am-3pm. Curfew 2:30am. Reserve ahead.

Soggiorno Imperia, P. Miraglia 386 (tel. 081 45 93 47). Take the R2 from the train station, walk up V. Mezzocannone through P. S. Domenico Maggiore, and enter the 1st set of green doors to the left on P. Miraglia. Bright rooms in a 16th-century *palazzo*. Singles L30,000; doubles L50-60,000; triples L75,000. Call ahead.

Pizza-making is an art born in Naples; you can't go wrong. ▨**Pizzeria Di Matteo,** V. Tribunali 94, near V. Duomo, was visited by President Clinton during the 1994 G-7 Conference. He denies ever having had relations with the pizza. (*Margherita* L9000. Open M-Sa 9am-midnight.) To get from P. Garibaldi to **Antica Pizzeria da Michele,** V. Cesare Sersale 1/3, walk up C. Umberto and take the first right. Michele makes only two traditional pizzas, and he makes them right; *marinara* (tomato, garlic, oregano, and oil) and *margherita* (tomato, mozzarella, and basil). (L5000. Open M-Sa 8am-11pm.) According to the *New York Times*, the best pizza in Naples is found at **Pizzeria Trianon da Ciro,** V. Pietro Colletta 42/44/46, a block off C. Umberto I. (L5500-12,500; 15% service. Open daily 10am-4:30pm and 6:30pm-midnight.) If you tire of pizza (who are we kidding?), head to the side streets around **P. Amadeo.**

◉▮ SIGHTS AND ENTERTAINMENT

▨**MUSEO ARCHEOLOGICO NAZIONALE.** This world-class collection houses exquisite treasures from Pompeii and Herculaneum, including the outstanding "Alexander Mosaic." The sculpture collection is also impressive. (*From M: P. Cavour, turn right and walk 2 blocks. Open M and W-F 9am-7:30pm, Sa-Su 9am-8pm. L12,000.*)

MUSEO AND GALLERIE DI CAPODIMONTE. This museum, in a royal *palazzo*, is surrounded by a pastoral park of woods and sprawling lawns. You can inspect the plush royal apartments, but the true gem is the **Farnese Collection,** with works by

ITALY

Naples

ACCOMMODATIONS
A Ostello Mergellina (HI)
B Soggiorno Imperia
C Hotel Ideal
D Casanova Hotel
E Hotel Eden

0   200 yards
0   200 meters

Corso Meridionale
Corso Novara
Corso A. Lucci
Corso
Via G. Pica
Via G. Agresti
Via F. Agresti
Via San Cosmo
Fuori Porta Nolania
Via Padre Rocc
Via E. Cosenz
Stazione Circumvesuviana
Via Nuova Marina
Corso Garibaldi
PIAZZA G. PEPE
PIAZZA NOLANA
Via Nolania
Via Lavinaio
PIAZZA DEL CARMINE
Via San Eligio
PIAZZA MERCATO
Via Giacomo Savarese
Via Nuova Marina
Via San Spaventa
PIAZZA GARIBALDI
M GARIBALDI
Naples Central Railroad Station
Via G. Riccardi
Via Bologna
Via Firenze
Via Torino
Via Milano
Via Venezia
Corso
Novara
E
Corso Genova
PIAZZA PRINCIPE UMBERTO
Corso Garibaldi
Via Carreira Grande
Via A. Poerio
P. S. Mancini
Via Maddelena
Via Ranieri
B
PIAZZA SAN FRANCESCO
Porta Capuana
PIAZZA DE NICOLA
Castel Capuano
Via Or. Costa
Via Carbonara
Via P. Colletta
Via Forcella
Corso Umberto
Chiesa di San Giorgio Maggiore
Ospedale delle Bambole
Via Duomo
Palazzo Cuomo
Via S. Baldachini
PIAZZA NICOLA AMORE
Via Duomo
Corso Umberto
Via del Tribunali
Vicaria Vecchia
Duomo
Via Duomo
San Lorenzo Maggiore
Monte di Pietà
Al Libral
Via del G. Archivio
San Paolo Maggiore
PIAZZA SAN GAETANO
Palazzo Marigliano
San Blagio
Via Pisanelli/ Anticaglia
Vico Gigante
Vico San Paolo
Vico dei Maiorani
Vico San Severino
University
Cappella di San Severo
Via Nilo
PIAZZA SANT'ANGELO
Via Mezzocannone
Via Luigi
Via Settembrini
Via Atri
Via S. D. Maggiore
PIAZZA MIRAGLIA
San Domenico Maggiore
Via Sedile di Porto
Viale L. de Crecchio
PIAZZA BELLINI
Chiesa di San Domenico Maggiore
Via San Sebastiano
Via Benedetto Croce
Chiesa di Santa Chiara & Convent of the Clarisse
Via Santa Chiara
PIAZZA CAVOUR
M CAVOUR
Via Santa Maria Di Constantinopoli
Museo Archeologico Nazionale
M MUSEO
PIAZZA MUSEO NAZIONALE
Via Santa Teresa degli Scalzi
Via Port'a
Via E. Pessina
Via Bellini
M DANTE
PIAZZA DANTE
Via Roma
SPACCANAPOLI
Chiesa di Gesù Nuovo
PIAZZA GESÙ NUOVO
Chiesa di Sant'Anna dei Lombardi
PIAZZA MONTEOLIVETO
Via Montoliveto
Via Toledo
PIAZZA CARITÀ
Via Salvatore
Via Maddaloni
V. Scura

TO CAPODIMONTE (1km)
TO PALAZZO REALE (600m)
TO (450m)
TO (2.5km)
TO (600m) CASTEL NUOVO (600m)

N

Bellini and Caravaggio. *(Take bus 110 from P. Garibaldi to Parco Capodimonte. Enter by Portas Piccola or Grande. Open Tu-F 10am-7pm, Sa 10am-midnight, Su 9am-8pm. L9500.)*

PALAZZO REALE AND CASTEL NUOVO. The 17th-century **Palazzo Reale** contains the **Museo di Palazzo Reale**, opulent royal apartments, and a fantastic view from the terrace of the **Royal Chapel**. The **Biblioteca Nazionale** of 1.5 million volumes, includes the scrolls from the **Villa dei Papiri** in Herculaneum. The **Teatro San Carlo** is reputed to have better acoustics than La Scala in Milan. *(Take the R2 bus from P. Garibaldi to P. Trieste e Trento and go around to the P. Plebiscito entrance. Open M-Tu and Th-F 9am-8pm. L8000.)* From P. Trieste e Trento, walk up V. Vittorio Emanuele III to P. Municipio; it's impossible to miss the five-turreted **Castel Nuovo,** built in 1286 by Charles II of Anjou. The double-arched entrance commemorates the arrival of Alphonse I of Aragon in Naples. Inside, admire the **Museo Civico.** *(Open M-Sa 9am-7pm. L10,000.)*

DUOMO. The main attraction of the 14th-century *duomo* is the **Capella del Tesoro di San Gennaro** on the right. A beautiful 17th-century bronze grille protects the high altar, which possesses a gruesome reliquary with the saint's head and two vials of his coagulated blood. Supposedly, disaster will strike if the blood does not liquefy on the celebration of his *festa* (twice a year); miraculously, it always does. *(3 blocks up V. Duomo from C. Umberto I. Open M-F 9am-noon and 4:30-7pm, Sa-Su 9am-noon. L5000.)*

SPACCANAPOLI. This renowned east-west neighborhood, which "splits" the city in two (reflected in its name) and is replete with gorgeous architecture, merits at least a 30-minute stroll. Don't lose track of yourself while gawking at picturesque churches, *palazzi*, and alleys, or you'll soon find yourself staring at the wrong end of a *motorino* buzzing toward you. From P. Dante, walk through Porta Alba and P. Bellini before turning down V. dei Tribunali, which follows the location and direction of an old Roman road. Along V. dei Tribunali, you'll see the churches of **San Lorenzo Maggiore** and **San Paolo Maggiore.** Take a right on V. Duomo and another on V. San Biago into the heart of the area; you'll meander past the **University of Naples** and the **Chiesa di San Domenico Maggiore,** where a painting once spoke to St. Thomas Aquinas. *(In P. S. Domenico Maggiore. Open daily 7:15am-12:15pm and 4:15-7:15pm.)*

NIGHTLIFE. P. Vanvitelli in Vomero (take the funicular from V. Toledo or the C28 bus from P. Vittoria) is where the cool kids go. Outdoor bars and cafés are a popular choice in **P. Bellini** (near P. Dante). If you're in the mood for imbibing, try **Green Stage,** P. S. Pasquale 15. From P. Amedeo, take V. Vittorio Colonna to V. S. Pasquale. **1799,** P. Bellini 70, mixes eerie trance music with dark decor. (Open Tu-Th 10am-1am, F-Su 10am-3am.) **Camelot,** V. Petrarca 101, in Posillipo, is a typical disco, with pop, house, and dance. (Open Oct.-May F-Sa midnight-4am. Cover L25,000.) **Tongue,** V. Manzoni 207, in Posillipo, features visiting DJs. (Take nightbus 404d from P. Garibaldi. Open Oct.-May F-Sa 11pm-4am. Cover L25,000.) **ARCI-Gay/Lesbica** (tel. 081 551 82 93) has information on gay and lesbian nights at local clubs.

⚡ EXCURSION FROM NAPLES

Mount Vesuvius, the only active volcano on the European continent, looms over the area east of Naples. Its infamous eruption in AD 79 buried the nearby Roman city of **Herculaneum** (Ercolano) in mud, and neighboring **Pompeii** (Pompei) in ashes.

POMPEII. Excavations, which began in 1748, have unearthed a stunningly well-preserved picture of Roman daily life. The site hasn't changed much since then, and neither have the victims, whose ghastly remains were partially preserved by plaster casts in the hardened ash. Walk down V. D. Marina to reach the ◪**Forum,** surrounded by a colonnade and once the commercial, civic, and religious center of the city. Exit the Forum through the upper end, by the cafeteria, and head right on V. della Fortuna to reach the ◪**House of the Faun,** where a bronze dancing faun and the spectacular Alexander Mosaic (today in the Museo Archeologico Nazionale) were found. Continue on V. della Fortuna and turn left on V. dei Vettii to reach the **House of the Vettii,** on the left, and the most vivid frescoes in Pompeii. Back down V. dei Vetti, cross V. della Fortuna to V. Storto, turn left on V. degli Augustali, and take a quick right to reach a small **brothel** (the Lupenar). After 2000 years, it's still the most popular place in town; you may have to wait in line. V. dei Teatri, across the street, leads to oldest-standing **amphitheater** in the world (80 BC), which once held up to 12,000 spectators. To get to the **⌘Villa of the Mysteries,** the complex's best-preserved villa, go all the way west on V. della Fortuna, right on V. Consolare, and all the way up Porta Ercolano. (Complex open daily in summer roughly 9am-7pm; off-season 9am-3pm. L12,000.) Take the Circumvesuviana **train** from Naples or Sorrento to "Pompeii Scavi/Villa dei Mistert" (about L3000). To reach the site, head downhill and take your first left to the west (Porta Marina) entrance. To get to the **tourist office,** P. Porta Marina Inferiore 12, walk right from the station and continue to the bottom of the hill. (Open M-F 8am-3:30pm, Sa 8am-2pm.) Bring lunch and water.

HERCULANEUM. Herculaneum is 500m downhill from the "Ercolano" stop on the Circumvesuviana Line train (from Naples 20min., L2200). Stop at the **tourist office,** V. IV Novembre 84, en route to pick up a free **map.** Less of the city has been excavated, but the 15-20 houses open to the public were so neatly dug up that the tour feels like an invasion of privacy. (Site open daily 9am-1hr. before dusk. L12,000.)

MT. VESUVIUS. You can peer into the only active volcano on mainland Europe at Mt. Vesuvius. Trasporti Vesuviani **buses** (L6000; buy tickets on the bus) and taxis/minibuses (L12,000) run from outside the Ercolano Circumvesuviana station up to the crater. Although Vesuvius hasn't erupted since March 31, 1944 (scientists say volcanoes should erupt every 30 years), experts deem the trip safe.

AMALFI COAST

Although the beauty of the Amalfi Coast cannot be captured in words, we provide in this section a humble attempt. Steep cliffs along the coast plunge down into the bright blue sea, and little towns are wedged into the narrow ravines. The picturesque villages provide stunning panoramas, delicious food and throbbing nightlife.

▐ **GETTING THERE AND GETTING AROUND.** The coast is accessible from Naples, Sorrento, Salerno, and the islands by **ferry** and blue SITA **bus.** The harrowing bus ride along the Amalfi coast is unforgettable: narrow roads wind along the mountainsides, yielding spectacular views of the cliffs and the sea; sit on the right side of the bus heading south (from Sorrento to Amalfi) and the left heading back. **Trains** run directly to Salerno from Naples (45min., 8 per day, L5000); Naples (45min., 32 per day, L5100-17,100); Rome (2½-3hr., 18 per day, L22-43,000); Florence (5½-6½hr., 7 per day, L49-79,500); and Venice; and go on to Paestum (40min., 9 per day, L4700). From Salerno Travelmar (tel. 089 87 31 90) runs **ferries** to Amalfi (1hr., 3 per day, 7:30-8:30am, L9000) via Positano (40min., L7000). Trains also run to Sorrento from Naples (1hr., L4700) and from Sorrento's port, accessible from P. Tassi by bus (L1700), Linee Marittime Partenopee (tel. 081 878 14 30) **ferries** run to Amalfi (45min., 2 per day, L16,000) via Positano (30min., L15,000); and Capri (50min., L8000); from Amalfi they service Salerno (30min., 9 per day, L16,000) Hydrofoils also link the Almafi Coast and Capri and Ischia. Sita **buses** run from Postitano to Amalfi (L2000), Sorrento (L2200), and from Amalfi to Salerno (L3100) and Ravello (L1700). Buses also link Paestum and Salerno (1hr., every hr., L4700).

AMALFI AND ATRANI. A small coastal ravine hides **Amalfi,** which exudes noise and chaos worthy of a city many times its size. Visitors crowd the waterfront, visit the surrounding coastal hills, and admire the elegant, Moorish-influenced 9th-century **duomo,** rebuilt in the 19th century. **A'Scalinatella,** P. Umberto 12, lets hostel beds and regular rooms all over Atrani and Amalfi. (Tel. 089 87 19 30. Dorms L20-35,000; doubles L50-120,000; **camping** L15,000 per person.) **Pensione Proto** is at Salita dei Curiali 4. (Tel. 089 87 10 03. Doubles from L60,000.) **Trattoria La Perla,** Salita Truglio 5, has good seafood. To get to **Atrani,** a tiny ravine town unaltered by tourism, walk 10min. around the bend from Amalfi. Spectacular **hikes** lead up from Amalfi and Atrani through lemon groves and across mountain streams.

RAVELLO. Capping a promontory 330m above Amalfi, Ravello is ideal for quiet contemplation. The Moorish cloister and meandering gardens of **Villa Rufolo** (off P. Duomo) inspired Boccaccio's *Decameron* and Wagner's *Parsifal.* (Open daily 9am-dusk. L5000.) On the small road to the right, signs lead to the especially impressive **Villa Cimbrone,** where floral walkways and gardens hide temples and statued grottoes. Frequent **classical music concerts** shatter Ravello's tranquility, especially in summer. **Hike** 2hr. up to Ravello from Amalfi for spectacular views; **buses** carry the weary and the lazy (20min., L1700). The best rooms are at **Hotel Villa Amore.** (Tel. 089 85 71 35. In summer, doubles L120,000; off-season L110,000.)

POSITANO. Cliffside homes and idiosyncratic locals began luring writers, artists, and actors to Positano in the early 1900s. Not surprisingly, the invention of the bikini here in 1959 heralded a marked increase in tourism. Soon afterwards, its artsy cachet and skimpy swimwear made it a popular destination for high-rollers. To see the large *pertusione* (hole) in **Montepertuso,** one of three perforated mountains in the world (the other two in India), hike 45min. uphill or take the bus (every hr., L1500) from any stop. Positano's **beaches** are also popular, and although boutiques may be a bit pricey, no one charges for window shopping. The **tourist office** (tel. 089 87 50 67) is below the *duomo.* **Ostello Brikette,** V. G. Marconi 358, 100m up the main coastal road to Sorrento from Vle. Pasitea, has incredible views from two large terraces. (Tel./fax 089 87 58 57. Dorms L35,000; singles L35,000; doubles L100,000. Breakfast included.) **Pensione Maria Luisa,** V. Fornillio 40, has seaside terraces. (Tel. (089) 87 50 23. Singles L50,000; doubles L80-90,000.) Prices in the town's restaurants reflect the high quality of the food. For a sit-down dinner, thrifty travelers head toward Fornillo.

SORRENTO. The largest, most heavily touristed town on the peninsula, lively and charming Sorrento, makes a convenient base for daytrips around the Bay of Naples. Caremar **ferries** (tel. 08 18 07 30 77) go to Capri (50min., 3 per day, L9000), while a local **bus** (L1700) shuttles between P. Tasso and the port. Halfway to the **free beach** at Punta del Capo on bus A, ◪**Hotel Elios,** V. Capo 33, has comfy rooms. (Tel. (081) 878 18 12. Singles L35,000; doubles L70,000.) For extensive services, stay at **Hotel City,** C. Italia 221; turn left on C. Italia from the station. (Tel. (081) 877 22 10. Singles L65-70,000; doubles L95-100,000.) It's easy to find good, affordable food in Sorrento. At **Ristorante Giardiniello,** V. Accademia 7, off V. Giuliani, eat Mamma Luisa's *gnocchi* in a peaceful garden. (Cover L1500. Open June-Sept. daily 11am-2am; Oct.-May F-W 11am-2am.) ◪**Davide,** V. Giuliani 39, off C. Italia two blocks from P. Tasso, has divine gelato and masterful mousse (55-80 flavors daily). After 10:30pm, a crowd gathers upstairs in the rooftop lemon grove above **The English Inn,** C. Italia 56.

SALERNO AND PAESTUM. Industrial **Salerno** is best used as a base for daytrips to nearby **Paestum,** the site of three spectacularly preserved ◪**Doric buildings:** including the **Temple of Ceres,** the **Temple of Poseidon,** and the **basilica.** (Temples open daily 9am-1hr. before dusk. Closed 1st and 3rd M of each month. L8000.) **Trains** (35min.) and **buses** (1hr.) head south from Salerno to Paestum daily (L4700). Sleep in Salerno at the cheerful **Ostello della Gioventù "Irno" (HI),** V. Luigi Guercio 112; go left from the station on V. Torrione, then left under the bridge on V. Mobilio. (Tel. 089 79 02 51. L17,500. Breakfast included. Lockout 10:30am-3:30pm. Curfew 2am.)

BAY OF NAPLES ISLANDS

CAPRI. The sheer bluffs, divine landscapes, and azure waters of **Capri** have beckoned wayfarers from the mainland since Roman times. **Capri town** is above the ports, while **Anacapri** sits higher up the mountain. From P. Umberto in Capri Town, V. Roma leads up to Anacapri; buses also make the trip until 1:40am (taxi L20,000). The ◪**Grotta Azzurra** (Blue Grotto) is a must-see—light enters the cavern through a hole in the rock under the water, causing the whole grotto to glow a fantastic neon-blue. (Open Apr.-Oct. in good weather.) Take the bus from Capri to Anacapri and a second bus to the Grotto (L1700), or go by boat from Marina Grande (L8000).

Upstairs from P. Vittoria in Anacapri, **Villa San Michele** has lush gardens, ancient sculptures, and a remarkable view of the island. (Open daily 9:30am-1hr. before dusk. L8000.) To appreciate Capri's Mediterranean beauty from higher ground, take the **chairlift** up **Monte Solaro** from P. Vittoria. (Open daily 9:30am-1hr. before dusk. Round-trip L8000.) From P. Umberto in Capri take V. Longano, which becomes V. Tiberio, to **Villa Jovis** (1hr.), the most magnificent of the 12 villas that the emperor Tiberius scattered throughout Capri. (Open daily 9am-1hr. before dusk. L4000.)

Caremar **ferries** run from Marina Grande to Naples (1hr., 11 per day, L9500-18,000) and Sorrento (45min., 3 per day, L10,000). Linee Lauro sends **hydrofoils** to Ischia (40min., 1 per day, L20,000) and Sorrento (20min., 12 per day, L13,000); LineaJet hydrofoils go to Naples (40min., 11 per day L16,000.) The Capri **tourist office** (tel. 081 837 06 34) is at the end of Marina Grande; in Anacapri, at V. Orlandi 19a (tel. 081 837 15 24), to the right from the P. Vittoria bus stop. (Both open June-Sept. M-Sa 8:30am-8:30pm and Oct.-May 9am-1:30pm and 3:30-6:45pm.) In Anacapri, beautiful ◨**Villa Eva**, V. La Fabbrica 8, will pick you up from P. Vittoria. (Tel. 081 837 15 49; email villa.eva@capri.it. Singles L50,000; doubles from L80,000; triples from L105,000; quads from L140,000. Breakfast included. Reserve ahead. V, MC.) From the last bus stop, follow the signs up the stairs to **Il Girasole**, V. Linciano 47. (Tel. 081 837 23 51; fax 081 837 38 80. Prices with *Let's Go*: doubles from L90,000; triples L150,000. **Internet.**) In Capri, **Pensione Stella Maris**, V. Roma 27, is opposite the bus stop. (Tel. 081 837 04 52; fax 081 837 86 62. Singles L50-70,000; doubles L80-120,000. V, MC.) Get **groceries** at **STANDA** in Capri; head right at the fork at the end of V. Roma. (Open M-Sa 8:30am-1:30pm and 5-9pm, Su 9am-noon.) At night, beautiful, dressed-to-kill Italians come out for Capri's *passegiatta;* bars in the streets around **P. Umberto** keep the music pumping late. Anacapri is cheaper and still loads of fun.

ISCHIA. Across the bay from overrun Capri, larger, less glamorous Ischia (EES-kee-yah) offers luscious beaches, natural hot springs, ruins, forests, vineyards, and lemon groves. Buses 1, CD, and CS (every 20min., L1700, day-pass L5000) follow the coast in a circular route from **Ischia Porto,** a port formed by the crater of an extinct volcano, to **Casamicciola Terme,** with a crowded beach and legendary thermal waters; **Lacco Ameno,** the oldest Greek settlement in the western Mediterranean; and well-touristed **Forio,** whose streets house popular bars. Take bus 5 from Porto to the beautiful beach at **Maronti.** Caremar **ferries** (tel. 081 98 48 18) arrive from Naples (1-1½hr., 14 per day, L8-10,000). **Linee Marittime Partenopee** (tel. 081 99 18 88) runs hydrofoils from Sorrento (L18,000). SEPSA **buses** run from P. Trieste (one-way L1700, full-day L5000). Stay in Ischia Porto only if you want to be close to the ferries—most *pensioni* are in Forio. In Forio, the floral **Pensione Di Lustro,** V. Filippo di Lustro 9, is near the beach. (Tel. 081 99 71 63. Doubles L80-110,000. Breakfast included.) The new **Ostello "Il Gabbiano" (HI),** Strada Statale Forio-Panza 162, between Forio and Panza, is accessible by bus 1, CS, or CD and has beach access. (Tel. 081 90 94 22. Around L28,000. Breakfast included. Lockout 9am-3pm. Curfew 12:30am. Open Apr.-Sept.) **Camping Internazionale** is at V. Foschini 22, 15min. from the port. Take V. Alfredo de Luca from V. del Porto; bear right on V. Michele Mazzella at P. degi Eroi. (Tel. 081 99 14 49; fax 081 99 14 72. L15,000 per person, L10,000 per tent. 2-person bungalows L8000. Open mid-Apr. to mid-Oct.)

BARI

Most tourists only stay in Bari long enough to buy a ferry ticket to Greece, but Apulia's capital is a vibrant city, with a university, historical sights, and the world's most organized backpacker-welcoming committee. If it receives its funding for 2000, **Stop-Over in Bari,** V. Nicolai 47 (tel. 080 621 45 38), will continue to lure backpackers with irresistible amounts of **free stuff,** including campsites with tents and showers, bike rentals, excursions (including daytrips to the stunning, octagonal **Castel del Monte**), "big-name" Eastern European speed-metal concerts, and **internet.** Near Bari, on the Ferrovie del Sud Est **train** line, **Alberobello's** famous *trulli* (mortarless conical roofs; 1½hr.) and the spectacular **Castellana Grotte** ("Grotte di Castellana Grotte" stop; 1hr.) are worth a daytrip.

Trains go to Brindisi (1-1¾hr., 27 per day, L10,100-25,100); Naples (4½hr., 1 per day, L25,500); and Rome (5-7hr., 6 per day, L47-65,500). **Eurail** holders get **no discounts** on **ferries** from Bari (see **Brindisi**, below), but some ferries have student rates. **Poseidon Lines**, C. de Tullio 36/40 (tel. 080 521 00 22; window 11 at the port) goes to Turkey and Israel; **Ventouris Ferries**, V. Piccinni 133 (tel. 080 521 76 99; windows 7-10) goes to Corfu (11hr., June 27-Sept. 29 1 per day, L53-73,000, students L47-67,000); Igoumenitsa (13hr., in summer 1 per day, L53-73,000, students L47-67,000); Cephalonia (15hr., July 26-Aug. 21 every other day, L63-83,000, students L57-77,000); and Patras (18hr., 1 per day, L63-83,000, students L57-77,000); and **Marlines** (tel. 080 523 18 24) goes to Igoumenitsa (13hr., 2-4 per week, L50-70,000). The area around the port can be extremely intimidating, so take a bus rather than walking the 2km through the old city. **Pensione Romeo**, V. Crisanzio 12 (tel. 080 521 63 52; fax 080 523 72 53; singles L45-55,000; doubles L95,000), offers cheaper rooms than its star-crossed love upstairs **Pensione Giulia** (tel. 080 521 66 30; fax 080 521 82 71; singles L70-80,000; doubles L90-110,000; off-season L15-20,000 less).

BRINDISI

Every year, about a million Eurailers and InterRailers get off the train at Brindisi, walk to the port, pay a port tax, and get on a boat to Greece. If you're one of them, arrive in the afternoon, as ferries leave in the evening. In August, consider arriving early or departing from Ancona or Bari instead. **Trains** arrive from Rome (6-9hr., 4 per day, L49-79,500); Naples (7hr., 5 per day, L31,000); and Venice (11hr., 7:50pm, L67,500). **Ferries** leave for Corfu (8hr.); Igoumenitsa (10hr.); Cephalonia (16½hr.); and Patras (17hr.). **Adriatica**, C. Garibaldi 85/87 (tel. 08 31 52 38 25) and **Hellenic Mediterranean Lines**, C. Garibaldi 8 (tel. 08 31 52 85 31), **the only two ferry lines on which InterRail and Eurail are valid,** offer free deck passage on a space-available basis (a seat inside costs L29,000 extra), not including port tax (Adriatica L10,000, HML L12,000; June 10-Sept. Eurailers add L19,000 fee). Those without railpasses will have to shop for cheap fares—tickets are usually L30-60,000. Contrary to what you might see, Brindisi has no official Eurail or InterRail offices. Three of the more reliable companies are **Strintzis Lines**, C. Garibaldi 65 (tel. 08 31 56 22 00), **Fragline**, C. Garibaldi 88 (tel. 0831 59 01 96), and **Med Link Lines**, C. Garibaldi 49 (tel. 08 31 52 76 67). Board the ferry 2hr. in advance, and bring warm clothes or a sleeping bag.

Corso Umberto, a jumble of ferry offices and restaurants, runs 1km from the station to the port, becoming **Corso Garibaldi** halfway down. The *stazione marittima* is on the right at the end of V. Regina Margherita. (Tel. 08 31 52 30 72. Open in summer M-Sa 8am-7pm; off-season M-F 9am-1pm and 4-6pm.) **Ostello della Gioventù**, 2km from the train station, in the Casale area, rents beds for a day (L9000). After they've picked you up, do laundry while you nap before being driven back to the port. (Tel. 08 31 41 31 23. Stay the night for L18,000. Breakfast included.) In town, try **Hotel Altair**, V. Giudea 4. (Tel./fax 0831 56 22 89. Singles L25-60,000.) Stock up for the ferry ride at **Maxis Sidis supermarket**, C. Garibaldi 106, near the port.

SICILY (SICILIA)

With a history so steeped in chaos, catastrophe, and conquest, it's no wonder that the island of Sicily possesses such passionate volatility. Greek, Roman, Arab, Norman, and Aragonese conquerors all transformed Sicily's landscape, but none thwarted its independent spirit. Today, Sicilians speed unchecked toward the future, installing condom vending machines in front of medieval cathedrals and demonstrating against their own well-known Mafia. The tempestuousness of Sicilian history and political life is matched only by the island's dramatic landscapes, dominated by craggy slopes. Entire cities have been destroyed in seismic and volcanic catastrophes, but those that have survived have lived up to the cliché and grown stronger; Sicilian pride is a testament to resilience during centuries of occupation and destruction.

LA FAMIGLIA Pin-striped suits, machine guns, horse heads, and the Godfather are a far cry from the reality of the Sicilian Mafia. The system has its roots in the *latifondi* (agricultural estates) of rural Sicily, where land managers and salaried militiamen (a.k.a. landlords and bouncers) protected their turf and people. Powerful because people owed them favors, strong because they supported one another, and feared because they did not hesitate to kill offenders, they founded a tradition that has dominated Sicilian life since the late 19th century. Since the mid-80s, the Italian government has worked to curtail Mafia influence, with visible results. Today Sicilians shy away from any Mafia discussion, referring to the system as *Cosa Nostra* (our thing). Unfortunately, "their thing" expanded to include a rigid structure of national politics, drug-smuggling, and assassination. But hey, *Ch' t' le dich'à fa'*.

▐ GETTING THERE AND GETTING AROUND

Tirrenia ferries (Palermo tel. 091 33 33 00) offers the most extensive and reliable service. From southern Italy, take a **train** to **Reggio di Calabria**, then the NGI or Meridiano **ferry** (40min., 12 per day, L1000) or Ferrovie Statale **hydrofoil** (tel. 0965 86 35 40; 25min., 6-16 per day, L5000) to **Messina**, Sicily's transport hub. Ferries also go to **Palermo** from **Cagliari, Sardinia** (14hr., L38-66,500); **Naples** (11hr., 1 per day, L55-90,500); and **Genoa** (20hr., 6 per week, L123-181,000). **SAIS Trasporti** (tel. 091 617 11 41) and **SAIS** (tel. 091 616 60 28) buses serve destinations throughout the island, including Corleone (perhaps you've seen *The Godfather?*). **Trains** also chug to **Messina** directly from **Naples** (4 per day, L38,500) and **Rome** (9hr., 4 per day, L53,000). Trains continue west to **Palermo** (3½hr., 16 per day, L19,500) via **Milazzo** (L4500) and south to **Syracuse** (3hr., 12 per day, L16,000) via **Taormina** (45min., L5500).

PALERMO

As Sicily's capital, Palermo is notorious as the cradle of Italian organized crime. Recently the city has begun cleaning up its politics and revitalizing its historic district, much of which was destroyed in WWII. Although Palermo has its share of sketchy neighborhoods, it is also sports the attractions of a modern metropolis. The city's fast-paced streets present life as an amalgamation of old and new as horse-drawn carriages compete with Fiats, and pious nuns hold their own against wantonly dressed women. From the Quattro Canti, C. Vittorio Emanuele heads away from the harbor toward the historic district, passing the striking exuberance of Palermo's **cattedrale** en route. Begun by the Normans in 1185, it gained turrets, domes, and arches of every architectural style from the 13th through 18th centuries. (Open daily 7am-noon and 4-6pm. Treasury, crypts, and sarcophagi L1000.) Farther up C. Vittorio Emanuele, the Palazzo dei Normanni contains the ⊠**Cappella Palatina**, with a carved wooden stalactite ceiling, and an incredible cycle of golden Byzantine mosaics. In the morbid **Cappuchin Catacombs**, in P. Cappuccini, 8000 bodies dressed in their moth-eaten Sunday best line the tunnels, and the virgins get a room of their own. To get there, take bus 109 or 318 from the central station to P. Indipendenza and then hop on #327. (Open M-Su 9am-noon and 3-5:30pm. L2500.)

Direct **trains** run from P. Cesare, on the eastern side of town, to Rome (11½hr., 4 per day, L71,000) and Milan (17½hr., 3 per day, L89,000). SAIS Trasporti **buses** depart V. Balsamo 16, by the train station, for Rome (14hr., 1 per day, L75,000, students L65,000.) From the port, C. Vittorio Emanuele runs west through central Palermo and intersects with V. Maqueda. The **tourist office**, P. Castelnuovo 34, is 2km up V. Maqueda opposite Teatro Politeama; turn right from the station or take bus 101 or 102. (Tel. 09 16 05 83 51. Open M-F 8:30am-2pm and 2:30-6pm, Sa 8:30am-2pm.) Homey **Hotel Regina**, C. Vittorio Emanuele 316, is near V. Maqueda. (Tel. 091 611 42 16. Singles L30,000; doubles L55-70,000. Kitchen.) To reach the **Petit Hotel**, V. Principe di Belmonte 84, take V. Roma from the train station, walk six blocks (past V. Cavour), and turn left. (Tel. 091 32 36 16. Single L35,000; doubles L65,000; triples L90,000. AmEx.) Take bus 101 from the station to P. de Gasperi, then take

ITALY

bus 628 to V. Sferracavallo; walk one block down, turn right on V. dei Manderini after the post office, and **Campeggio dell'Ulivi**, on V. Pegaso, is on the right (35min.). (Tel. 091 53 30 21. One person and tent L9000.) Palermo's specialty is *rigatoni alla palermitana* (with a sauce of meat and peas); indulge at ◨**Lo Sparviero,** V. Sperlinga 23, a block from the Teatro Massimo. (Entrees from L9000. Open M-W and F-Su 11am-2pm and 7:30pm-midnight.) **STANDA supermarket** is at V. Roma 59. (Open M 4-8pm, Tu and Th-Su 9am-1pm and 4-8pm, W 9am-1pm.) **Postal code:** 90100.

▓ EXCURSIONS FROM PALERMO

MONREALE. Ten kilometers southwest, Monreale's magnificent Norman-Saracen cathedral **Santa Maria la Nuova** (c. 1174) displays 6430 sq. meters of mosaics, 130 panels of gold and colored glass tiles. The church features incredible mosaics and intricate arches; the **cloister** next door houses a renowned collection of Sicilian sculpture. (Cathedral open daily 8am-noon and 3:30-6pm; free. Cloister open M-Sa 9am-1pm and 3pm-6:30pm, Su 9am-12:30pm; L4000. Roof L3000. Treasury L4000.) **Bus** 389 runs from Palermo's P. Indipendenza (15min., 3 per hr., L1500).

CEFALÙ. Cefalù guards a cache of Arab, Norman, and medieval architecture. In P. Duomo, off C. Ruggero, is the town's 11th-century Norman **duomo.** Inside, Byzantine and Roman columns support superb capitals, while elegant horseshoe arches and a huge mosaic dazzle. (Open 8:30am-noon and 3:30-6:30pm. Dress modestly.) For city views, walk up the **Rocca** by way of the Salita Saraceni; from near P. Garibaldi, off C. Ruggero, follow the signs for *"pedonale Rocca"* (30min.). On the mountain, ancient walls and crumbling cisterns lead to the 9th-century BC **Tempio di Diana.** From the station, V. Moro eventually leads to the old town and to the **tourist office,** C. Ruggero 77. (Tel. 092 12 10 50; fax 092 12 23 86. Open June-Sept. M-Sa 8am-2pm and 3:30-8pm, Su 9am-1pm; Oct.-May M-F 8am-2pm and 4-7pm, Sa 8am-2pm.). Take the **train** from Palermo (1hr., 18 per day, L7000).

AGRIGENTO

Among Sicily's classical remains, the **Valle dei Tempii** at Agrigento shares top honors with those at Syracuse; take bus 1 or 2 from the train station (L1000). The **Tempio della Concordia,** one of the world's best-preserved Greek temples, owes its survival to consecration by St. Gregory of the Turnips. One kilometer uphill from the ruins, the **Museo Nazionale Archeologico di San Nicola** houses Greek odds and ends, including a huge *telamones*, a statue used to support the temple's weight. (Open M-Sa 8am-12:30pm. L8000.) Revisit modern fashion and convenience at the **centro storico,** a cobblestoned web of animated shops and eateries. **Trains** arrive from Palermo (1½hr., L11,500). The **tourist office,** V. Battista 13, is the first left off V. Atenea. (Open in summer M-F 9am-2pm and 4:30-7pm, Sa 9am-2pm.) **Hotel Bella Napoli,** P. Lena 6, off V. Bac from V. Atenea, has a terrace overlooking the valley. (Tel./fax 092 22 04 35. Singles L25-40,000; doubles L55-75,000.) Take the first left off V. Imera and follow signs uphill to reach **Hotel Concordia,** V. San Francesco 11. (Tel. 09 22 59 62 66. Singles L30-35,000; doubles L60-70,000.) ◨**Trattoria Atenea,** V. Ficani 32, the fourth right off V. Atenea from P. Moro, has a quiet courtyard and extensive seafood offerings. (*Calamari* L9000. Open M-Sa noon-3pm and 7pm-midnight.)

SYRACUSE (SIRACUSA)

Founded in 734 BC by Greeks, ancient Syracuse cultivated such luminaries as Pindar, Archimedes, and Theocritus. The city hasn't been the same since the Romans sacked it in 211 BC, but some ancient monuments remain. Cross the bridge on C. Umberto to the island of **Ortigia** to pay homage to the **Temples of Apollo** and **Athena**. The latter, now part of the city's cathedral, has an embellished façade added over several centuries. From P. Duomo, a trip down V. Picherale leads to the spring-fed **Fonte Aretusa** (pond). Syracuse's larger monuments are in or near the **Archaeological Park,** on the north side of town, which contains an enormous ancient **Greek theater** where Aeschylus premiered his *Persians*. The exceptional acoustics of the **Orec-**

chio di Dionigi (Ear of Dionysius) spawned the legend that the tyrant Dionysius put prisoners here to eavesdrop on them. To see the 2nd-century **Roman amphitheater**, once the workplace of Roman gladiators and the wild animals who loved them, follow C. Gelone until it meets V. Teocrito, then walk left down V. Augusto. (Open daily 9am-2hr. before dusk. L4000.) Near the tourist office is the **Catacombe di San Giovanni.** (Open daily Mar. 15-Nov. 14 9am-12:30pm and 2-5pm; Nov. 15-Mar. 14 9am-1pm; L4000.) Those who prefer tans to temples should bus 18km to **Fontane Bianche** (bus 21, 22, or 24; L600), which is a silken beach home to outdoor nightclubs.

Trains go to Messina (3hr., 3 per day, L16,000) and Rome (11hr., 2 per day, L67,500), **buses** to Palermo (3¼hr., 7 per day, L21,500) and Taormina (2hr., 1 per day, L12,500). Solo travelers should beware the train station area at night. To get from the train station to the **tourist office,** V. S. Sebastiano 43, turn right at the end of C. Gelone on V. Teocrito and left at the sanctuary. (Tel. 093 16 77 10. Open in summer M-Sa 8:30am-1:45pm and 3:30-6:30pm, Su 9am-1pm; off-season M-Sa 8:30am-2pm and 3:30-6:30pm, Su 8:30am-2pm.) From the station, follow signs from C. Gelone to find the **Pensione Bel Sit,** V. Oglio 5. (Tel. 093 16 02 45. Singles L40,000; doubles L50-65,000. Book ahead for July-Aug.) **Albergo Aretusa,** V. Francesco Crispi 73, also near the train station, has marble-tiled rooms in an old *palazzo*. (Tel./fax 093 12 42 11. Singles L35-45,000; doubles L60-75,000; triples L80-100,000. Breakfast L5000. Reserve ahead for Aug. AmEx.) **Spaghetteria do Scugghiu,** V. D. Sciná 11, off P. Archimede, on Ortigia, serves 18 delicious kinds of spaghetti. (Most L7000. Open Tu-Su noon-3pm and 5pm-midnight.) For budget eats, try **Ortigia** or **FAMILA supermarket,** V. Teracati 34. (Open M-Tu and Th-Sa 8:30am-1:45pm and 4:30-8:15pm, W 8:30am-1:45pm.)

TAORMINA

Clifftop mansions and local flora punctuate a hazy blue coastline in Taormina, a city of unsurpassed beauty. The 3rd-century **Greek theater,** at cliff's edge, is one of the most dramatic spots in Italy. To get there, walk up V. Teatro Greco, off C. Umberto I at P. Vittorio Emanuele. (Open daily 9am-dusk. L4000.) Opposite the Greek theater, the Church of S. Caterina hides the small **Roman Odeon** theater. Descend V. di Giovanni and follow the signs to the sculpted English garden of the **Villa Comunale.** A short trip away is **Gole Alcantara,** a haven of gorgeous gorges, freezing waterfalls, and crystal rapids. (Entrance L4000. Wetsuit L13,000.) Six **buses** run there daily, but the only return bus is at 2pm (round-trip L8500).

Reach Taormina from Messina by **bus** (L5-6000) or take the more frequent **train** (L4700) to its less central station. The **tourist office,** in P. S. Caterina, is at P. V. Emanuele in P. Corvaia off C. Umberto. (Tel. 0942 232 43; fax 0942 249 41. Open M-F 8am-2pm and 4-7pm, Sa 9am-1pm and 4-7pm, Su 9am-1pm.) **Pensione Svizzera,** V. Pirandello 26, has gorgeous coastal views and clean rooms. (Tel. 0942 237 90. Singles L80,000; doubles 130,000; triples 175,000. Open Feb.-Nov. Reserve ahead.) Nearby **Inn Piero,** V. Pirandello 20, has small, colorful rooms that also overlook the sea. (Tel. 0942 231 39. Singles L84,000; doubles L120,000. Half-pension L93,000; required in high-season. Reserve ahead.) Dining can be expensive; stock up at **STANDA supermarket,** V. Apollo Arcageta 49, at the end of C. Umberto. (Open M-Sa 8:30am-1pm and 5-9pm.) **Bella Blu,** V. Pirandello 28, has huge portions and a stupendous view. (L20,000 tourist menù. *Primi* from L6000, *secondi* from L10,000. Cover L2000. Open daily 10am-3:30pm and 6pm until the last person leaves.)

AEOLIAN ISLANDS (ISOLE EOLIE)

Home of the wind god Aeolus and the Sirens, the Aeolian (or Lipari) Islands, with their long, rocky beaches, boast some of Italy's last few stretches of unspoiled seashore. Volcanoes belching fire and smoke are often an easy hike from sea level.

◧ GETTING THERE AND GETTING AROUND. The archipelago lies off the Sicilian coast, north of **Milazzo,** the principal and least expensive embarkation point. Hop off a **train** from **Messina** (40min., 18 per day, L4500; see p. 625) or **Palermo** (3hr.,

L15,500) and onto an orange AST **bus** for the port (10min., every hr., L600). There, Siremar (tel. 090 928 32 42) and Navigazione Generale Italiana (NGI; tel. 090 928 40 91) **ferries** depart for **Lipari** (2hr., L10,500-12,500); **Vulcano** (1½hr., L10-12,000); and **Stromboli** (5hr., L16,500-18,500). Siremar and SNAV (tel. 090 928 45 09) **hydrofoils** (*aliscafi*) make the trip in half the time but cost almost twice as much. All three have ticket offices on V. Dei Mille facing the port in Milazzo. **Ferries** leave for the islands less frequently from **Naples'** Molo Beverello port. Ferries between Lipari and Vulcano cost L2500; between Lipari and Stromboli, L25,500.

LIPARI. Lipari, the largest and most developed of the islands, makes a great base, with cheap hostels, great beaches, and hopping nightlife. The small promontory is crowned by the walls of a medieval **castello,** the site of an ancient Greek acropolis. The fortress shares its hill with an **archeological park,** the **San Bartolo church,** and the superb **Museo Archeologico Aeoliano,** where English captions explain Lipari's history and artifacts, including a series of grotesque Greek funerary masks. (Tel. 090 988 01 74. Open daily May-Oct. 9am-1:30pm and 4-7pm; rest of year 9am-1:30pm and 3-6pm. L8000.) Rent a bike to explore the **beaches** or **pumice mines,** or find a fisherman willing to ferry you to the island's even tinier beaches. The popular **Spiaggia Bianca** and **Spiaggia Porticello** beaches are often the spot for nude (or semi-nude) sunbathing; to get there, take the Lipari-Cavedi bus to Canneto.

The AAST **tourist office,** C. Vittorio Emanuele 202, is up the street from the ferry dock. (Tel. 090 988 00 95; fax 090 981 11 90; email infocast@netnet.it. Open July-Aug. M-Sa 8am-2pm and 4-10pm, Su 8am-2pm; Sept.-June M-F 8am-2pm and 4:30-7:30pm, Sa 8am-2pm.) Next to the museum, **Ostello Lipari (HI),** V. Castello 17, makes up for its barracks-like interior with a location overlooking Lipari and the sea. (Tel. 090 981 15 40, off-season 090 981 25 27. L15,000. Breakfast L3000. Reception 7-10am and 6pm-midnight. Check-out 10am. Strict midnight curfew. Open Mar.-Oct.) **Hotel Europeo,** C. Vittorio Emanuele 98, has bright, bare rooms in a great location. (Tel. 090 981 15 89. Singles L25-55,000; doubles L70-110,000.) **Camp** at **Baia Unci,** V. Marina Garibaldi 2, 2km from Lipari at the entrance to the hamlet of Canneto. (Tel. 090 981 19 09; fax 090 981 17 15. L14,500 per person; L18,000 for 1 person and tent. Open mid-Mar. to mid-Oct. Reserve in Aug.) Stock up at **UPIM supermarket,** C. Vittorio Emanuele 212. (Open M-Sa 8am-3:20pm and 4-11pm. V, MC, AmEx.) **Discoteca Turmalin,** P. Giuseppe Mazzini, hugs the walls above the ocean, just seconds away from the youth hostel. (Cover L12,000. Open daily 10pm-2am.) **Postal code:** 98055.

VULCANO. This island makes an intriguing daytrip for its thermal springs, black beaches, and bubbling mudbaths; the pervading smell of sulphur makes it less attractive for longer stays. A steep one-hour **hike** to the inactive **Gran Cratere** (Grand Crater) snakes between the volcano's smoke-belching fumaroles. On a clear day, you can see all the other islands from the top, like the god you are. The supposedly therapeutic **Laghetto di Fanghi** (Mud Pool) is just up V. Provinciale from the port. If you would prefer not to bathe in dirt, you can step gingerly into the scalding waters of the **acquacalda,** where underwater volcanic outlets make the sea percolate like a jacuzzi, or visit the crowded beach and clear waters of **Sabbie Nere,** just down the road from the *acquacalda,* instead; follow the signs off V. Ponente through the black sand. For more info, the **tourist office** is at V. Provinciale 41. (Tel. 090 985 20 28. Open July-Aug. daily 8am-1:30pm and 3-5pm.)

STROMBOLI. Tired of hearing that this or that mild-looking hill destroyed the surrounding countryside back when your ancestors were still learning to oppose their thumbs? Sigh no more. Those disappointed by Vulcano will enjoy Stromboli's active **volcano,** which spews orange cascades of lava and molten rock nightly (roughly every 10min.). From July to September, however, forget finding a room unless you have a reservation. **Hiking** the *vulcano* on your own is illegal and dangerous, but **Guide Alpine Autorizzate** offers tours. (Tel. 090 98 62 11. Tours depart from P. Vincenzo M, W, and Sa-Su 5:30pm; return midnight. L35,000.) Bring sturdy shoes, a flashlight, snacks, water, and warm clothes. If you do ignore the law and head up alone (3hr.), latch onto a GAA group for the more dangerous descent. And finally, when hiking down the volcano at night, always use the same path you took up; the professional guides' shortcuts are tempting but infinitely easier to get lost on.

SARDINIA (SARDEGNA)

According to Sardinian legend, when God finished making the world, he tossed a handful of leftover dirt into the Mediterranean and stepped on it, creating Sardinia. The contours of that divine foot formed spectacular landscapes; the savage coastline, lush green valleys, and pink and yellow mountains inspired D.H. Lawrence to declare that the island had "escaped the net of European civilization." Its most fascinating archaeological finds are its more than 7000 *nuraghe*, cone-shaped fortified tower-houses assembled 3500 years ago without any mortar.

⊡ GETTING THERE AND GETTING AROUND. Tirrenia **ferries** (tel. 1678 240 79) run from **Civitavecchia** (3½-7½hr., 1-4 per day, L18-110,000), just north of Rome, and **Genoa** (6-13½hr., 1-2 per day, L34-171,000) to **Olbia** on the northern tip of Sardinia. They also chug from Civitavecchia (15½hr., 1 per day, L31-70,000); **Palermo** (13½hr., 1 per week, L30-66,500); and **Naples** (15½hr., Jan.-Sept. 1 per week, L28-71,000) to **Cagliari** on the southern tip. **Trains** run from Cagliari to Olbia (4hr., L23,500) via Oristano (1½hr., L8200), branching off between Oristano and Olbia for **Alghero** (from Cagliari 1hr., L8200; from Olbia 4hr., L16,000). PANI **buses** connect major cities (Cagliari to Oristano 1½hr., 11,300); ARST handles local routes.

CAGLIARI. Cagliari gracefully combines the vigor of a bustling city and the rich history of a medieval town. Its Roman ruins, Carthaginian fortifications, and *nuraghe* fortress-cities contrast with tree-lined streets and flamingo-populated beaches. From the **tourist office,** on P. Matteotti (tel. 070 66 92 55; open in summer M-Sa 8am-8pm; off-season 8am-1:30pm), climb Largo Carlo Felice to the cramped medieval quarter to reach the impressive **duomo,** whose dazzling gold mosaics top each entryway. (Open daily 8am-12:30pm and 4-8pm.) If you prefer to worship the sun, take city **bus** P, PQ, or PF to the **Il Poetto beach** (20min., L1300), with pure white sand and turquoise water. The elegant family-run **⊠Pensione Vittoria** is at V. Roma 75. (Tel. 070 65 79 70. Singles L55-60,000; doubles L85-100,000.)

ALGHERO. A leisurely walk through the *centro storico* of Alghero reveals tiny alleyways, half-hidden churches, and ancient town walls. At the nearby **⊠Grotte di Nettuno,** an eerie stalactite-filled cavern complex best reached by ferry (1hr., 1-3 per day, round-trip L6300), you can descend a memorable 654 steps between massive white cliffs into the sea. (Open daily Apr.-Sept. 9am-7pm; Oct. 10am-5pm; Nov.-Mar. 9am-2pm. L13,000.) The **tourist office,** P. Porta Terra 9, is to the right from the bus stop and park. (Tel. 079 97 90 54. Open May-Sept. M-Sa 8am-8pm, Su 9am-1pm; Oct.-Apr. M-Sa 8am-2pm.) To get to the **⊠Ostello dei Giuliani (HI),** V. Zara 3, 7km away in Fertilia but near the beach, take the orange AF city bus from V. La Marmora next to the train station (25min., every hr., L1100); from the stop, follow the street to the left as you face the church and turn right on V. Zara. (Tel./fax 079 93 03 53. L14,000. Breakfast L2500. Showers L1500. Call ahead.)

ORISTANO. Although somewhat dull on its own, Oristano is a good base for excursions to nearby **beaches** and **archaeological sites.** From the train station, follow V. Vittorio Veneto straight to P. Mariano, then take V. Mazzini to P. Roma to reach the center (25min.). Rent a moped from **Marco Moto,** V. Cagliari 99/101 (open M-F 8:30am-1pm and 3:30-8pm, Sa 8:30am-1pm) and explore the stark white cliffs, deep blue water, and ancient ruins of the mystical **Sinis Peninsula.** At the tip, 17km west of Oristano, lie the ruins of the ancient Phoenicians port of **Tharros.** ARST **buses** (dir: Is Arutas) also serve the tip; get off at "San Giovanni di Sinis" (45min., L2200). Hop back on the bus and continue to the end of the line to reach the gorgeous white-quartz sands of **Is Arutas.** The **tourist office,** V. Cagliari 278, 6th fl., is back in Oristano (Tel. 0783 731 91. Open M-F 8am-2pm, Tu-W also 4-8pm.) Snooze at **Piccolo Hotel,** V. Martignano 19. (Tel. 0783 715 00. Singles L50,000; doubles L100,000.)

LATVIA

(LATVIJA)

US$1 = 0.59LS (LATS)	1LS = US$1.70
CDN$1 = 0.40LS	1LS = CDN$2.52
UK£1 = 0.95LS	1LS = UK£1.06
IR£1 = 0.79LS	1LS = IR£1.26
AUS$1 = 0.38LS	1LS = AUS$2.61
NZ$1 = 0.31LS	1LS = NZ$3.21
SAR1 = 0.10LS	1LS = SAR10.25
DM1 = 0.32LS	1LS = DM3.13

PHONE CODES	Country code: 371. International dialing prefix: 00.

Except for a brief period of independence that ended with WWII, Latvia was ruled by Germans, Swedes, and Russians from the 13th century until 1991. A half-century of Soviet occupation resulted in a mass exodus of Latvians and a huge influx of Russians. With the smallest majority of natives of the three Baltic States, Latvia remains the least affluent and developed. Attitudes toward the many Russians who still live in the country are softening, but evidence of national pride abounds, from patriotically renamed streets with crimson-and-white flags to a rediscovery of native holidays predating Christian invasions. Rīga is a westernizing capital luring more and more international companies. The rest of the country is mostly a provincial expanse of green hills dominated by tall birches and pines.

Latvia is covered in delightful detail in *Let's Go: Eastern Europe* 2000.

GETTING THERE AND GETTING AROUND

Flights to Latvia arrive via the Rīga Airport. **Air Baltic, SAS, Finnair, Lufthansa,** and others serve Rīga. **Trains** link Latvia to most Eastern European capitals. Trains are cheap and efficient, but stations aren't well-marked. The **suburban rail** system renders the entire country a suburb of Rīga. **Eurail** is not accepted. Latvia's long-distance **bus** network reaches Prague, Tallinn, Vilnius, and Warsaw. Buses are quicker than trains for travel within Latvia. **Ferries** run to Rīga from Stockholm and Kiel, Germany, but are slow and expensive. **Roads,** while not ideal, are passable, especially expressways. **Hitchhiking** is common, but hitchers may be expected to pay.

ESSENTIALS

DOCUMENTS AND FORMALITIES. Irish, UK, and US citizens don't require a visa for stays of fewer than 90 days without a visa. Citizens of Australia, Canada, New Zealand, and South Africa require 90-day visas, obtainable at Latvian consulates and the Rīga airport. Single-entry visas cost US$15, multiple-entry US$30; 24-hour rush processing costs US$60 and US$90, respectively. Standard processing takes 10 days. For visa extensions, apply to the Department of Immigration and Citizenship in Rīga, Raiņa iela 5 (tel. 721 91 81).

Latvian Embassies at Home: Australia, P.O. Box 457, Strathfield NSW 2135 (tel. (02) 97 44 59 81; fax 97 47 60 55); **Canada,** 112 Kent St, Place de Ville, Tower B, #208, Ottawa, ON K1P 5P2 (tel. (613) 238-6014; fax 238-7044); **UK,** 45 Nottingham Pl, London W1M 3FE (tel. (020) 73 12 00 40; fax 73 12 00 42); **US,** 4325 17th St NW, Washington, DC 20011 (tel. (202) 726-8213; fax 726-6785).

Foreign Embassies in Latvia: All foreign embassies are located in **Rīga** (see p. 632).

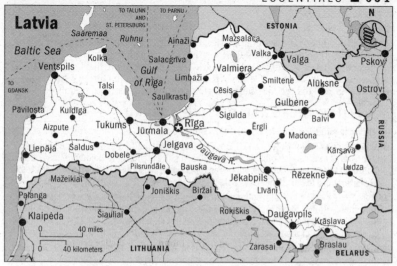

TOURIST OFFICES. Private tourist offices are more helpful than the old state-owned bureaus, marked by a green "i." In Rīga, **Patricia** is a stand-out.

MONEY. The currency is the **Lat** (abbreviated Ls), divided into 100 *santīmi*. There are many V, MC, and Cirrus **ATMs** in Rīga. Larger businesses, restaurants, and hotels accept V and MC. **Traveler's checks** are harder to use; both AmEx and Thomas Cook can be converted in Rīga. If a **tip** is expected in a restaurant, it will be included in the bill. Hostel beds run US$7-10, hotels US$10-15, and meals US$5-7.

COMMUNICATION

Post: Latvia's postal system is fairly reliable, with air mail taking 10-14 days to reach Canada, Ireland, and the US, slightly longer to reach Australia, New Zealand, and South Africa. International air mail from Latvia costs 0.20Ls per letter.

Telephone: Phone cards (2, 3, 5, or 10Lt) are available at post offices, telephone offices, and large state stores. Make international calls from a telephone office. There is no way to make a free call on a Latvian phone to an international operator. To call abroad from an analog phone, dial 1, then 00 to call out; from a digital phone, just dial 00. **International direct dial** numbers include: **AT&T Direct,** 700 70 07 in Rīga, 827 00 70 07 elsewhere; **MCI,** tel. 724 50 05. **Fire,** tel. 01. **Police,** tel. 02. **Ambulance,** tel. 03.

Language: Latvian. Russian is hated but spoken. German is relatively common, and English is among students. For a useful set of phrases in Latvian, see p. 949.

ACCOMMODATIONS AND FOOD. College dorms, open to travelers in summer, are the cheapest places to sleep. In Rīga, **Patricia** provides English info and arranges homestays and apartments for US$15 per night (see p. 632). Latvian food is heavy, starchy, and greasy. Big cities offer foreign cuisine, and Rīga is an easy place to be a vegetarian. Latvian beer is stellar, particularly *Porteris*. Latvians claim that Rīga tap water is drinkable, but boil it for 10min. or buy bottled water to be safe.

LOCAL FACTS

Time: Latvia is 2hr. ahead of Greenwich Mean Time (GMT; see p. 49).

Climate: Being so far north, Latvia suffers severe winters. Fortunately, summers are temperate and pleasant, making it the best time to visit.

Hours: Shops are usually open M-F 9am-7pm except for 1-2hr. between noon and 3pm.

Holidays: New Year's Day (Jan. 1); Good Friday (Apr. 22); Catholic Easter (Apr. 23-24); Labor Day (May 1); Mother's Day (2nd Su in May); Ligo (Midsummer Festival; June 23); Jāni (St. John's Day; June 24); National Day (1918; Nov. 18); Ziemsvetki (Christmas; Dec. 25-26); and New Year's Eve (Dec. 31).

RĪGA

The self-proclaimed capital of the Baltics, Rīga (pop. 826,500) feels strangely out of proportion as the capital of small, struggling Latvia. Although more Westernized and cosmopolitan than the rest of the Baltic cities, it feels more like Las Vegas than Paris, with 24-hour casinos on every street, showgirls parading through posh hotels and cabarets, and the tell-tale tinted windows of German luxury automobiles.

⌐ GETTING THERE AND GETTING AROUND

Flights: Lidosta Rīga (tel. 20 70 09), 8km southwest. Take bus 22 from Gogol iela.

Trains: Stacijas laukums (tel. 23 21 34), east of Vecrīga and north of the canal. Long-distance trains in the larger building to the left facing the station. The Baltic Express goes to **Berlin** and **Warsaw** via **Vilnius**. All prices for *coupés*. To: **Vilnius** (8hr., 1 per day, 11Ls); **St. Petersburg** (13hr., 1 per day, 23Ls); and **Moscow** (17hr., 2 per day, 28Ls).

Buses: Tel. 721 36 11. 200m south of the train station along Prāgas iela, across the canal from the central market. To: **Tallinn** (5-6hr., 7 per day, 6-7Ls); **Vilnius** (6hr., 5 per day, 3.50-6Ls); and **Minsk** (10hr., 2 per day, 6.20-6.90Ls). **Eurolines** (tel. 721 40 80), at the bus station right of the ticket windows, goes to **Warsaw** (14hr., 1 per day, 15Ls).

Ferries: Transline Balt Tour, Eksporta iela 1a (tel. 732 23 11), 1km north of Rīga Castle at the passenger port. To: **Stockholm** (17hr., departs M, W, and F 6pm; deck space 20Ls).

⚇ ORIENTATION AND PRACTICAL INFORMATION

The city is neatly divided in half by **Brīvības bulvāris,** which leads from the outskirts to the **Freedom Monument** in the center, continuing through **Vecrīga** (Old Rīga) as **Kaļķu iela.** With the trains behind you, turn left on the busy Marijas iela and right on any of the small streets beyond the canal to reach Vecrīga. For good **maps** and tons of info, pick up *Riga in Your Pocket* 0.60Ls from a kiosk, hotel, or travel agency.

Tourist Offices: Patricia, Elizabetes iela 22-26, 3rd fl. (tel. 728 48 68; fax 728 66 50; www.rigalatvia.com), 2 blocks from the train station. Arranges homestays in Vecrīga (US$15 per person) and can help with Russian visas (6-day US$80). Open M-Sa in summer 9am-9pm; off-season 9am-6pm. The **tourist office,** Skārņu iela 22 (tel. 722 17 31; fax 722 76 80; email tourinfo@latnet.lv), behind St. Peter's Church, is more central.

Embassies: Belarus, Jēzusbaznīcas 12 (tel. 732 25 50; fax 73 22 89). Open M-F 9am-1pm. **Canada,** Doma laukums 4, 4th fl. (tel. 722 63 15). Open M-F 9am-5:30pm. **Russia,** Antonijas iela 2 (tel. 721 25 79). Open M-F 10am-1pm. **Ukraine,** Kalpaka bulv. 3 (tel. 33 29 56). Open M-F 10am-1pm. **UK,** Alunāna iela 5 (tel. 733 81 26). Open M-F 9am-5pm. **US,** Raiņa bulv. 7 (tel. 721 00 05). Open M-F 9am-noon and 2-4pm.

Currency Exchange: At any of the many *Valutos Maiņa* kiosks in the city. **Unibanka,** Kaļķu iela 13, gives cash advances for a 4% commission and cashes AmEx and Thomas Cook traveler's checks for a 3% commission. Open M-F 9am-9pm, Sa 9am-6pm.

Luggage Storage: In the bus station, on guarded racks near the Eurolines office (0.20Ls per 2hr. for 10kg). Open daily 6:30am-10:30pm. At the train station, **lockers** (0.60Ls) are in the tunnel under the long-distance tracks. Open daily 5am-1am.

Pharmacies: Mēness aptieka, Brīvības 121. Open 24hr.

Internet Access: Latnet, Raiņa 29 (tel. 721 12 41). 0.22Ls per hr. Open M-Th 9am-6pm, F 9am-5pm. **Audalūzijas Suns,** Elizabetes iela 83/85 (tel. 724 28 26). 1.80Ls per hr.

Telephones: Brīvības bulv. 19 (tel. 733 12 22). Smaller office at post office by the train station. Open 24hr. V/MC/Cirrus **ATM.**

Post Offices: Stacijas laukums 1 (tel. 701 88 04), near the train station. *Poste Restante* at window 2. Open M-F 8am-8pm, Sa 8am-4pm, Su 8am-4pm. Address mail to be held: Vincent PLANEL, *Poste Restante,* Stacijas laukums 1, Riga, **LV-1050** Latvia.

| PHONE CODE | City code: 2 for all six-digit numbers; none for seven-digit numbers. From outside Latvia, dial int'l dialing prefix (see inside back cover) + 371 + (2 or none) + local number. |

(margin) LATVIA

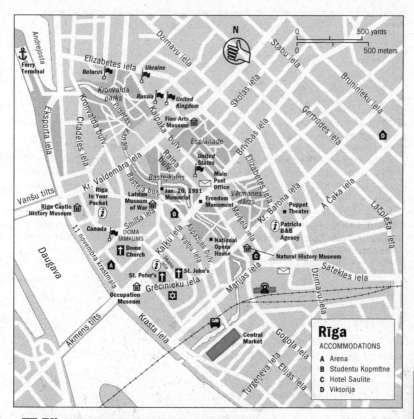

Map legend:

Rīga

ACCOMMODATIONS

A Arena
B Studentu Kopmītne
C Hotel Saulite
D Viktorija

🔲🔲 ACCOMMODATIONS AND FOOD

Rīga's prices for decent rooms are generally the highest in the Baltics. If you are interested in a **private room,** try your luck with **Patricia** (see **Tourist Offices,** above).

■ **Arena,** Palasta iela 5 (tel. 722 85 83). Unmarked building by Dome Cathedral; the cheapest place in town. Open Apr.-Oct. (Nov.-Mar. circus performers live here). 3Ls per person.

Studentu Kopmītne (Student Dormitories), Basteja bulv. 10 (tel. 721 62 21). From the bus station, cross under the railroad tracks and take the pedestrian tunnel under the highway. Bear right on Aspazijei bul., which becomes Basteja bul, and enter through the Europcar Interrent office on the edge of Vecrīga. 3-7Ls per person. Call ahead.

Saulite, Merķeļa iela 12 (tel. 22 45 46), directly opposite the train station. Emerald spiral staircase branches off to clean halls, rooms, and communal toilets. Singles 6-16Ls; doubles 10-20Ls; triples 9-25Ls. Shared shower 0.40Ls. English spoken. V, MC.

Viktorija, Čaka iela 55 (tel. 701 41 11; fax 731 06 29). 8 blocks from the trains on Marijas iela (which becomes Čaka iela), or 2 stops on trolleybus 11 or 18. More expensive, newly renovated rooms and old, cheaper rooms. Singles 8-26Ls; doubles 10-38Ls. V, MC.

Look for 24-hour food and liquor stores along **Elizabetes** and **Gertrūdes iela. Interpegro,** Raiņa bulv. 33, stocks lots o' stuff. (Tel. 722 90 44. Open 24hr.) The **Centrālais Tirgus** (Central Market) is one of the largest markets in Europe. (Open M-Sa 8am-5pm, Su 8am-3pm.) Descend from the entrance on Arsenāla to ■ **Alus Arsenāls,** Pils Laukums 4, to partake of its excellent, inexpensive Latvian cuisine. (Entrees 3-4.50Ls. Open daily 11am-midnight.) **LuLu Pizza,** Gertrūdes iela 27, has the best pizza in town. (Slices 0.69-.95Ls; pizzas 2.50-5.50Ls. Open daily 8am-midnight. V, MC.) **Kirbis**

LATVIA

(Pumpkin), Doma laukums 1, directly across from the Dome Cathedral, serves up veggie delights. (Entrees 2-4Ls. Open M-F 9am-11pm, Sa-Su 10am-11pm.)

👁 SIGHTS

VECRĪGA. From the top of the dark, 103m spire of **St. Peter's Church's** (Sv. Pētera baznīca; 1209-1408), you can see the entire city and the Baltic. *(On Kungu iela, off Kaļķu iela. Open Tu-Su 10am-7pm. Church free. Tower 1.50Ls, students 1Ls.)* Follow Skārņu iela, opposite the church, to Jāņa iela and the small **St. John's Church** (Sv. Jāņa baznīca); an alleyway on the left leads to **St. John's Courtyard** (Jāņa sēta), the oldest populated site in Rīga, where the first city castle stood. *(Church open Tu-Su 10am-1pm.)* Follow Kungu iela across Kaļķu iela, and take a right on Jauniela into cobblestoned **Dome Square,** the home of Rīga's centerpiece, **Dome Cathedral** (Doma baznīca), begun in 1226. *(Open Tu-F 1-5pm, Sa 10am-2pm. 0.50Ls, students 0.20Ls. Concerts W and F 7pm.)* Follow Jēkaba iela to Smilšu iela to eight floors of fun (covering the Middle Ages to the present) at the ■**Latvian Museum of War** (Latvijas kara muzejs), Smilšu iela 20, inside the red brick walls of the **Powder Tower,** Rīga's most interesting military site. *(Open Tu-Su 10am-6pm. 0.50Ls, students 0.25Ls. Foreign-language tours 3Ls.)*

FREEDOM MONUMENT AND ENVIRONS. In the center of the city stands the beloved **Freedom Monument** (Brivibas Piemineklis; affectionately known as "Milda"). It was dedicated in 1935, during Latvia's brief tenure as an independent republic. To survive the subsequent 1940-41 occupation, it had to become a Soviet symbol; it represented Mother Russia supporting the three Baltic states. *(At the corner of Raiņa bul. and Brīvības iela.)* Continuing along Kaļķu iela from the Freedom Monument toward the river, you'll see three granite soldiers guarding the square **Latviešu strēlnieku laukums,** one of the few Soviet monuments not torn down. Rising behind the statues are the black walls of the ■**Occupation Museum** (Okupācijas muzejs), Strēlnieku laukums 1, perhaps the finest museum in the Baltics. The initial Soviet occupation is depicted so vividly that you can almost hear the Red Army marching through the streets of Rīga. *(Open daily 11am-5pm. Free.)*

BASTEJKALNS. The central park of the ring near the old city moat **Pilsētas kanāls,** Bustejkalns houses ruins of the old city walls. Across and around the canal, five red stone slabs stand as **memorials** to the dead of January 20, 1991, when Soviet special forces stormed the Interior Ministry on Raiņa bul. At the north end of Bastejkalns, on Kr. Valdemāra iela, sits the **National Theater,** where Latvia first declared its independence on November 18, 1918. *(Open M-F 10am-7pm, Sa-Su 11am-6pm.)*

🎵 ENTERTAINMENT

Summer is the off-season for ballet, opera, and most of the theaters around town; otherwise, purchase tickets at Teātra 10/12. (Tel. 722 57 47. Open daily 10am-7pm.) The **Latvian National Opera** performs in the magnificent 19th-century Opera House on Aspazijas bul., where Richard Wagner once presided as director. After July, the **Latvian Symphony Orchestra** has frequent concerts in the Large and Small Guilds off Filharmonija laukums, while smaller local and foreign ensembles perform throughout the summer in **Vāgnera zāle,** Vāgnera iela. (Tel. 722 48 50. Open daily noon-7pm.) The ticket office, Amatu iela 6 (tel. 22 36 18), on the first floor of the Large Guild, sells tickets for nearly all concerts in Rīga. The **Rīga Ballet** carries on the proud dancing tradition of native star Mikhail Baryshnikov.

■**Paddy Whelan's,** Grēcineku iela 4, is Rīga's first Irish pub. (Guinness 1.20Ls. Open M-Th and Sa-Su 10am-1am, F 10am-2am.) At night, trendy youngsters pack the backlit steel bridge at **Pulkuedim Neviens Neraksta** (Nobody Speaks to the Colonel), Peldu 26/28. (Cover after 9pm F 2Ls, Sa 1Ls. Open Su-Th noon-3am, F-Sa noon-5am.) Shiny ■**Vernisāža,** Terbātas 2, is set to carry its nightlife into the 21st century. (Cover 5Ls. Open W-Su 11pm-6am.) **Hamlet Club,** Jāņa Sēta 5, in the heart of Vecrīga, does jazz. (M-Su at 9pm. Tel. 722 99 38. Call ahead for a table. Open daily 7pm-5am.)

LATVIA

LIECHTENSTEIN

A recent Liechtenstein (pop. 31,000) tourist brochure unfortunately mislabeled the already tiny 160 sq. km country as an even tinier 160 sq. m. However, this is approximately how much most tourists see of the world's only German-speaking monarchy; they pause only long enough to hastily record the visit in a passport and buy some postage stamps (the sales of which incidentally generate almost a quarter of the country's income). But the cliff-hanging roads dotted with luxury cars are gateways to unspoiled mountains, a world away from the southern tourist traps. **Biking** is a dream in flatter areas, and an efficient and cheap **postal buses** link all 11 villages (most trips 2.40SFr; 1-week pass 10SFr, students 5SFr; Swisspass valid). To enter the principality, catch a bus from Sargans or Buchs in Switzerland, or from Feldkirch just across the Austrian border (20min., 3.60SFr). German is the official **language,** but many residents also speak English, French, and an Alemannic dialect. The **currency** is the Swiss franc (SFr). **Country code:** 41. **Area code:** 075 (nationwide). **International dialing prefix:** 00. For the **police,** call 117, and for **medical emergencies,** call 144. **Postal code:** FL-9490. For a (tiny) **map,** see the Switzerland chapter.

VADUZ

More a hamlet than a national capital, Vaduz is not a budget-friendly place. Tourists travel in packs, scrambling furiously to find something worthy of a photo opportunity. Your best bet for a Kodak moment is the 12th-century **Schloß Vaduz,** regal home to Hans-Adam II, Prince of Liechtenstein, above the town. Philatelists (that's stamp collectors to you) flock to the **Briefmarkenmuseum** (Stamp Museum). (Open daily Apr.-Oct. 10am-noon and 1:30-5:30pm; Nov.-Mar. closes at 5pm. Free.)

Liechtenstein's **national tourist office,** Städtle 37, up the hill from the Vaduz-Post bus stop, stamps passports (2SFr) and gives advice on hiking, cycling, and skiing. (Tel. 392 11 11. Open June-Oct. M-F 8am-noon and 1:30-5:30pm, Sa 9am-noon and 1-4pm, Su 10am-noon and 1-4pm; Nov.-May closed Sa-Su.) Take bus 1 (dir: Schaan) to get to the budget-friendly **Hotel Post** in nearby **Schaan,** behind the post office; the welcoming staff makes up for the simple rooms. (Tel. 232 17 18. Singles 35-45SFr; doubles 70-90SFr. Breakfast included. Reception 6am-noon.) Liechtenstein's lone **Jugendherberge (HI),** Untere Rütig. 6, also in Schaan, is less service-oriented. Take bus 1 to "Mühleholz"; then turn left down Marianumstr. (Tel. 232 50 22; fax 232 58 56. Dorms 26.30SFr; doubles 64.60SFr; family quads 113.20SFr. Members only. Breakfast included. Laundry. Reception M-Sa 7-9:30am and 5-10pm, Su 7-9:30am and 6-10pm. Lockout 9:30am-5pm. Curfew 10pm. Open Mar.-Nov. 15.) **Camping Mittagspitze,** between Triesen and Balzers on the road to Sargans, is easily accessible by postal bus. (Tel. 392 26 86. Reception 8-10am and 4-8pm. 5SFr per tent, 8.50SFr per person.) Buy **groceries** at **Migros,** Aulestr. 20, across from the tour bus parking lot. (Open M-F 8:30am-1pm and 1:30-6:30pm, Sa 8am-4pm.)

UPPER LIECHTENSTEIN. With gorgeous views and great hiking, the villages in the upper country are far more rewarding for visitors than Vaduz. **Triesenberg** (take bus 10), the principal town, was founded in the 13th century by the Walsers, who were fleeing overpopulation, religious intolerance, and natural disaster—the usual. The **tourist office** (tel. 262 19 26) is in the same building as the **Walser Heimatmuseum.** For a spectacular Alpine **hike** with views of the Rhine, take bus 30 (dir: Gaflei). From the bus stop, cross the street to the gravel road and the trail is on the left. **Malbun,** the hippest spot in the country, offers great **hiking** and affordable **skiing** on the other side of the mountain from Triesenberg (day pass 33SFr, 6-day 136SFr). Contact the **tourist office** for info. (Tel. 263 65 77. Open May-Oct. and Dec.-Apr. M-F 9am-noon and 1:30-5pm, Sa 9am-noon and 1-4pm.) Sleep in the excellent chalets, **Hotel Alpen** and **Hotel Galina;** reception for both is at the former. (Tel. 263 11 81; fax 263 94 46. Singles and doubles 40-65SFr per person. Breakfast included. Open mid-May to Oct. and mid-Dec. to mid-Apr.

LITHUANIA (LIETUVA)

US$1 = 4.00LT (LITAI)	1LT = US$0.25
CDN$1 = 2.69LT	1LT = CDN$0.37
UK£1 = 6.43LT	1LT = UK£0.16
IR£1 = 5.39LT	1LT = IR£0.19
AUS$1 = 2.60LT	1LT = AUS$0.38
NZ$1 = 2.12LT	1LT = NZ$0.47
SAR1 = 0.66LT	1LT = SAR1.51
DM1 = 2.17LT	1LT = DM0.46

PHONE CODES | Country code: 370. International dialing prefix: 810.

Once the largest country in Europe, stretching into modern-day Ukraine, Belarus, and Poland, Lithuania has since faced oppression from tsarist Russia, Nazi Germany, and Soviet Russia. The first Baltic nation to declare its independence from the USSR in 1990, Lithuania has become more Western with every passing year. Its spectacular capital city of Vilnius welcomes hordes of tourists into the largest old town in Europe, recently covered in a bright new coat of paint from city-wide renovations. In the other corner of the country, the mighty Baltic Sea washes up against Palanga and Kuršių Nerija also called Curonian Spit.

Tune in to *Let's Go: Eastern Europe 2000* for more madcap Lithuanian info.

GETTING THERE AND GETTING AROUND

Flights arrive at the Vilnius airport. **Air Baltic, SAS, Finnair, Lufthansa,** and others make the hop to Vilnius from their respective hubs. **Eurail** is not valid in Lithuania, but the **Baltic Rail Explorer Pass** is. Vilnius, Kaunas, and Klaipėda are the main centers of rail travel in Lithuania and are easily reached from Belarus, Estonia, Latvia, Poland, and Russia. Two major rail lines cross Lithuania: one runs north-south from Latvia through Šiauliai and Kaunas to Poland, and the other runs east-west from Belarus through Vilnius and Kaunas to Kaliningrad, or on a branch line from Vilnius through Šiauliai to Klaipėda. Domestically, **buses** are faster, more common, and only a bit more expensive than the crowded **trains. Driving** conditions, while not ideal, are passable. Expressways—particularly the Via Baltica (M-12)—are in good condition; other roads, however, are plagued by potholes and gravel. Night driving is particularly dangerous. In residential areas, the speed limit is 60km per hr.; on expressways, it's 112km per hr. Both **hitchhiking** and **biking** are uncommon.

ESSENTIALS

DOCUMENTS AND FORMALITIES. Citizens of Australia, Canada, Ireland, the UK, and the US don't need a visa for visits up to 90 days. Citizens of New Zealand and South Africa who have visas from Estonia or Latvia can use those to enter Lithuania; otherwise, regular 90-day visas are required. Obtain visas through your nearest embassy or consulate. Single-entry visas cost US$20; multiple-entry visas US$40; transit visas (good for 48hr.) US$5; double-transit visas US$15. Regular service takes two weeks; rush service costs US$20 extra for 24hr. or US$15 extra for 72-hour service. Obtaining a visa extension may be a wild goose chase, but start at the Immigration Dept. in Vilnius, Virkių g. 3 #6 (tel. 75 64 53).

Lithuanian Embassies at Home: Australia (honorary consul), 40B Fiddens Wharf Rd. Killara NSW 2071 (tel. (2) 949 825 71); **Canada**, 130 Albert St, #204, Ottawa, ON K1P 5G4 (tel. (613) 567-5458; fax 567-5458); **New Zealand** (honorary consul), 28 Heather St, Parnell Auckland (tel. (9) 379 66 39; fax 307 29 11); **South Africa** (honorary consul), Killarney Mall, 1st fl., Riviera Rd, Killarney Johannesburg; P.O. Box 1737,

Houghton, 2041 (tel. (011) 486 36 60; fax 486 36 50); **UK,** 84 Gloucester Pl, London W1H 3HN (tel. (20) 74 86 64 01; fax 74 86 64 03); **US,** 2622 16th St NW, Washington, DC 20009-4202 (tel. (202) 234-5860; fax 328-0466; www.ltembassyus.org).

Foreign Embassies in Lithuania: All foreign embassies are in **Vilnius** (see p. 638).

TOURIST OFFICES. Tourist offices are knowledgeable. **Litinterp,** in most towns, is the most helpful; they will reserve accommodations, usually without a surcharge.

MONEY. The unit of **currency** is the **Litas** (1Lt=100 centu), plural Litai. Since March 1994, it has been fixed to the US dollar at US$1 = 4Lt. **ATMs** are readily available in most cities. **Traveler's checks** can be cashed at most banks (for a 2-3% commission). **Cash advances** on **Visa** cards can be obtained with minimum hassle. **Vilniaus Bankas,** with outlets in major cities, accepts credit cards and traveler's checks for a small commission. Hostel beds run US$6-8, hotels US$15-20, and meals US$4-6.

COMMUNICATION

Post: Airmail *(oro pastu)* **letters** abroad cost 1.35Lt. Airmail **packages** weighing up to 250g cost 4.80Lt plus a 1Lt registration fee. **EMS** international mail takes 3-5 days.

Telephone: There are two kinds of **public phones:** the rectangular ones accept magnetic strip cards; the rounded ones accept chip cards. Both are sold at phone offices and kiosks (3.54Lt, 7.08Lt, or 28.32Lt). Calls to **Estonia** and **Latvia** cost 1.65Lt per min., to **Europe** 5.80Lt, to the **US** 7.32Lt. Dial 8, wait for the 2nd tone, dial 10, then enter the country code and number. For countries to which direct dialing is unavailable, dial 8, wait for the 2nd tone, and dial 194 or 195 for English-speaking operators. **Fire,** tel. 01. **Police,** tel. 02. **Ambulance,** tel. 03. **International direct dial** numbers include: **AT&T,** (8) 196; **BT Direct,** (8) 192; **Canada Direct,** (8) 80 09 10 04; **Sprint Express,** (8) 197.

Languages: Lithuanian is one of the only two languages left in the Baltic branch of Indoeuropean tongues (Latvian is the other). **Polish** is helpful in the south, **German** on the coast, and **Russian** most places, although it is not as prominent as in Latvia. For Lithuanian, Polish, German, and Russian phrases, see p. 949.

ACCOMMODATIONS AND CAMPING. Lithuania has several **youth hostels,** with plans for more to open. HI membership is nominally required, but an LJNN guest card (US$3 at any of the hostels) will suffice. Their *Hostel Guide* is a handy booklet with info on bike and car rentals, reservations, and maps to various hostels. Outside Vilnius, **Litinterp** is the best option for hunting down a budget room.

FOOD AND DRINK. Lithuanian cuisine is heavy and greasy. Keeping a vegetarian or kosher diet will prove near impossible. *Karbonadas* is fried pork fillet, and *koldunai* are meat dumplings. Restaurants serve various types of *blynai* (pancakes) with *mèsa* (meat) or *varske* (cheese). Lithuanian beer is excellent, with *Kalnapis* and *Baltijos* reigning supreme. Lithuanian vodka *(degtinx)* is also very popular.

LOCAL FACTS

Time: Lithuania is 2hr. ahead of Greenwich Mean Time (GMT; see xref).

Climate: Being so far north, Lithuania suffers severe winters. Fortunately, summers are temperate and pleasant, making it the best time to visit.

Hours: Most **shops** are open M-F 8am-2pm and 3pm-7 or 8pm, Sa 9am-6pm. **Department stores** are also open Su 10am-6pm. **Banks** are open M-F 9am-12:30pm and 2:30-5pm.

LITHUANIA

Holidays in 2000: New Year's Day (Jan. 1); Independence Day (1918; Feb. 16); Restoration of Lithuanian Statehood (Mar. 11); Catholic Easter (Apr. 23-24); Labor Day (May 1); Rasos Šventi (Midsummer Night; June 23); Day of Statehood (Mindaugas Day; July 6); All Saints' Day (Nov. 1); All Souls' Day (Nov. 2); Christmas (Dec. 25).

VILNIUS

Once a major Eastern European political and intellectual center, Vilnius (pop. 586,000) today is a small-feeling city of Baroque and Classical architecture, vast stretches of greenery, and a vibrant international community. By the 19th century, Vilnius was one of the world centers of Jewish scholarship (along with Warsaw and New York); sadly, nearly all of Vilnius' Jews were killed during WWII at the Paneriai death camp. After resisting Sovietization and healing from war wounds, Vilnius is on the up and up. With the Old Town's cafés frequented more and more by beer-guzzling ex-pats and hostel beds quickly snatched up by the backpacking masses, time is running out to get in on the Vilnius secret.

▟ GETTING THERE AND GETTING AWAY

Flights: The airport *(oro uostas)*, Rodūn×s Kelias 2 (tel. 63 55 60), is 5km south. Take bus 1 from the station, or bus 2 from the Sparta stop of trolley bus 16 on Kauno g.

Trains: Geležinkelio g. 16 (tel. 63 00 86). Tickets for all trains are sold in the yellow addition left of the main station; windows 3 and 4 are specifically for trains to western Europe. All international trains (except those heading north) pass through Belarus; for visa info, see p. 113. To: **Minsk** (5hr., 3 per day, *coupé* 52Lt); **Rīga** (7½hr., 1 per day, *coupé* 67Lt); **Warsaw** (11hr., 1 per day, *coupé* 115Lt); **Moscow** (17hr., 3 per day, *coupé* 128Lt); **St. Petersburg** (18hr., 2 per day, *coupé* 108Lt); and **Berlin** (22hr., 1 per day, 309Lt).

Buses: Autobusų Stotis, Sodų g. 22 (tel. 26 24 82 and 26 24 83; reservations tel. 26 29 77), opposite the train station. **Tarpmiestinė Salė** covers long-distance buses; windows 13-15 serve destinations outside the former Soviet Union. Open daily 7am-8pm. To: **Minsk** (5hr., 8 per day, 19Lt); **Rīga** (6½hr., 5 per day, 25-40Lt); **Warsaw** (9½hr., 4 per day, 60-65Lt); and **Tallinn** (10hr., 2 per day, 81Lt).

▐ ORIENTATION AND PRACTICAL INFORMATION

From the **train** or **bus stations,** which are directly across from each other, walk east on **Geležinkelio g.** (right with your back to the train station), and turn left at its end. This is the beginning of **Aušros Vartų g.,** which leads downhill through the gates of **Senamiestis** (Old Town) and changes its name first to **Didžioji g.** and then **Pilies g.,** before reaching the base of Castle Hill. Here, **Gediminas Tower** presides over **Arkikatedros aikštė** (Cathedral Square) and the banks of the river **Neris. Gedimino pr.,** the commercial artery, leads west from the square in front of the cathedral's doors.

Tourist Offices: Tourist Information Centre, Pilies str. 42 (tel./fax 62 07 62; www.vilnius.lt). Open M-F 9am-7pm, Sa noon-6pm.

Budget Travel: Lithuanian Student and Youth Travel, V. Basanavičiaus g. 30, #13 (tel. 22 13 73). Great deals for travelers under 27. Open M-F 8:30am-6pm, Sa 10am-2pm.

Embassies: Australia (consulate), Radvilaitės 4 (tel./fax 22 33 69). **Belarus,** P. Klimo g. 8 (tel./fax 26 34 43); visas at Muitinės g. 41 (tel. 63 06 26). Open M-Tu and Th-F 10am-4:30pm. **Canada,** Gedimino pr. 64 (tel. 22 08 98; fax 22 08 84). Open M-F 10am-1pm. **Russia,** Latvių g. 53/54 (tel. 72 17 63; visa tel. 72 38 93). Open M-Tu and Th-F 10am-1pm. **Ukraine,** Turniškių g. 22 (tel./fax 76 36 26); visas at Kalvarijų 159, 2nd fl. (tel. 77 84 13). Open M-Tu and Th-F 10am-1pm. **UK,** Antakalnio g. 2 (tel. 22 20 70). Open M-F 9:30am-12:30pm. **US,** Akmenų g. 6 (tel. 22 30 31). Open M-Th 8:30am-5:30pm.

Currency Exchange: Geležinkelio 6 (tel. 33 07 63), to the right from the train station. Open 24hr. **Vilniaus Bankas,** Gedimino pr. 12, gives cash advances and has **ATMs.**

Laundromat: Slayana, Latvių g. 31 (tel. 75 31 12), in Žvėrynas, 5min. west of Senamiestis across the Neris River. Take tram 7 from the train station or tram 3 from Senamiestis. Do-it-yourself wash and dry 12Lt; full service 20Lt. Detergent 3Lt. Open M-F 8am-3pm.

LITHUANIA

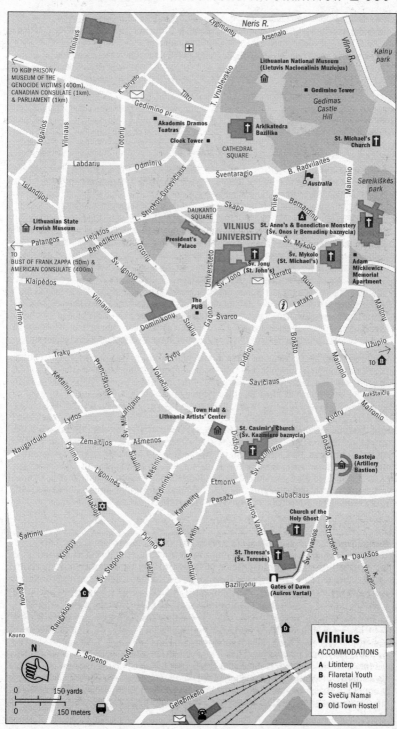

Neris R.

Zygimantu

Arsenalo

Vilna R.

Kalnų park

Vilniaus

Lithuanian National Museum
(Lietuvis Nacionalinis Muziejus)

Gedimino Tower

Gedimas Castle Hill

TO KGB PRISON/
MUSEUM OF THE
GENOCIDE VICTIMS (400m),
CANADIAN CONSULATE (1km),
& PARLIAMENT (1km)

K. Sirydo

Tilto

T. Vrublevskio

Gedimino pr.

Akademis Dramos
Teatras

Clock Tower

Arkikatedra
Bazilika

CATHEDRAL
SQUARE

St. Michael's
Church

Jogailos

Totoriu

Odminiu

Vilniaus

Labdariu

Šventaragio

B. Radvilaitės

Sereikiškės park

Islandijos

L. Stuokos-Gucevičiaus

Australia

Bernardinu

Lithuanian State
Jewish Museum

DAUKANTO
SQUARE

Skapo

Pilies

St. Anne's & Benedictine Monstery
(Šv. Onos ir Bernadinų baznycia)

Patangos

Benediktinu

Liejyklos

VILNIUS
UNIVERSITY

Šv. Mykolo

Šv. Mykolo
(St. Michael's)

TO
BUST OF FRANK ZAPPA (50m) &
AMERICAN CONSULATE (400m)

Šv. Ignoto

Totoriu

President's
Palace

Universiteto

Sv. Jono
(St. John's)

Literatu

Rusu

Adam
Mickiewicz
Memorial
Apartment

Klaipėdos

Šv. Jono

Pylimo

Vilniaus

The
PUB

Gaono

Švarco

Lalako

Latako

Malunu

Dominikonų

Stiklių

Žydu

Didžioji

Bokšto

Užupio

TO

Traku

Kedainiu

Pranciškonu

Vokiečiu

Savičiaus

Aukštaičiu

Maironio

Lydos

Šv. Mikalojaus

Ašmenos

Town Hall &
Lithuania Artists' Center

Kudrų

Naugarduko

Žemaitijos

Šiauliu

Didžioji

St. Casimir's Church
(Šv. Kazimiero baznycia)

Šv. Kazimiero

Bokšto

Basteja
(Artillery
Bastion)

Pylimo

Ligoninės

Mesiniu

Rodininku

Etmonu

Subačiaus

Plačioji

Karmelitu

Pasažo

Aušros Vartu

Church of the
Holy Ghost

Šaltiniu

Kruopu

Pylimo

Visu

Arkliu

Šv. Dvasios

A. Strazdelio

M. Daukšos

St. Theresa's
(Šv. Teresės)

Aguonu

Raugyklos

Šv. Stepono

Gėliu

Šventu

Bazilijonu

Gates of Dawn
(Aušros Vartai)

K. Vanaglio

C

D

Kauno

N

0   150 yards

0   150 meters

F. Šopeno

Sodu

Geležinkelio

LITHUANIA

Vilnius

ACCOMMODATIONS

A Litinterp
B Filaretai Youth
   Hostel (HI)
C Svečių Namai
D Old Town Hostel

Pharmacy: Gedimino Vaistinė, Gedimino pr. 27 (tel. 61 01 35). Open 24hr.

Medical Assistance: Baltic-American Medical & Surgical Clinic, Antakalnio g. 124 (tel. 34 20 20), at Vilnius University Hospital. Open 24hr.

Internet Access: Soros Foundation, Šv. Jono g. 3/5. Free. Open M-F noon-8pm.

Post Office: Centrinis Paštas, Gedimino pr. 7 (tel. 61 67 59), west of Arkikatedros aikštė. Address mail to be held: Alice FARMER, Centrinis Paštas, Gedimino pr. 7, Vilnius **LT-2000,** Lithuania. Open M-F 7am-7pm, Sa 9am-4pm.

PHONE CODE	City code: 822. From outside Lithuania, dial int'l dialing prefix (see inside back cover) + 370 + 22 + local number.

📇 ACCOMMODATIONS AND FOOD

Old Town Hostel (HI), Aušros vartų g. 20-15a (tel. 62 53 57; fax 22 03 05; email livijus@pub.osf.lt), 100m from the "Gates of Dawn" in the Old Town. With your back to the train station, turn right on Geležinkelio and left on Aušros Vartų; it's through the arch on the right. Dorms 32-34Lt; singles and doubles 40-60Lt. **Internet** free. Laundry.

Litinterp, Bernardinų 7, #2 (tel. 22 38 50; fax 22 35 59; email litinterp@post.omnitel.net). With your back to the train station, turn right on Geležinkelio g., take the 3rd left on Aušros Vartv g., cross the square, follow Didžiolji g. as it turns into Pilies g., and turn right on Bernardinų. Singles 70-100Lt; doubles 120-140Lt. Apartment 200Lt per night. Breakfast included. Reception M-F 9am-6pm, Sa 9am-4pm. Reserve ahead.

Filaretai Youth Hostel (HI), Filaretų g. 17 (tel. 25 46 27; fax 22 01 49; email filareta@post.omnitel.lt). Take bus 34, which leaves from the right of the station (across from McDonald's) to the 7th stop (10min.). Cozy and comfy. Dorms 24-29Lt; nonmembers 26-31Lt. Laundry 10Lt. Reception 7am-midnight. Curfew 1am.

Svečiv Namai, Šv. Stepono 11 (tel. 26 02 54). With your back to the train station, head down Stoties and turn left on F. Šopeno, then right on Šv. Stepono. 40Lt per person.

A full meal can be as cheap as US$4-6, but quality and price are closely correlated. Check out translated menus and take notes before hitting a less-touristed joint. A **supermarket** is at Žirmūnų g. 2, just across the Žirmunv bridge. (Open M-Sa 9am-10pm, Su 9am-8pm.) ▥ **Ritos Slėptuvė** (Rita's Hideaway), A. Goštauto g. 8, west of Senamiestis along the Neris, is *the* place to go. "No sweat-suits allowed" is a subtle ban on the local mafia. Come before 4pm, when the place becomes a **bar.** (Meal 10Lt. Live music Su nights; disco F and Sa. Open M-Th 7am-2am, F 7am-6am, Sa 8am-6am, Su 8pm-2am.) **Stikliai Aludė** (Beer Bar), Gaono g. 7, is cozy, folksy, and yummy. (Entrees 16-28Lt. Excellent local brew 3-4.50Lt. Open daily noon-midnight.) **Prie Parlamento,** Gedimino pr. 46, has "the best lasagna in Lithuania" for 12.50Lt. (Open M-F 8am-midnight, Sa-Su 10am-2pm.) Head to **Užupio Kavinė,** Užupio g. 2, between Senamiestis and the Filaretų hostel, for great potato pancakes with mushroom sauce for 9.10Lt. (Open daily 11am-2am.)

👁 SIGHTS

With the largest Old Town in Eastern Europe, Vilnius has no shortage of architectural wonders or historic spots. The moment you reach the end of Geležinkelio g. and turn left, the 16th-century **Gates of Dawn** (Aušros Vartai), the only surviving portal of the old city walls, welcomes you in. Take a map, or just enjoy getting lost.

SENAMIESTIS (OLD TOWN). Through the gates, enter the first door on the right to ascend the 17th-century **Chapel of the Gates of Dawn** (Aušros Vartų Koplyčia), packed with locals praying to the icon and selling holy paraphernalia. Head back to the street and through the doorway at the building's end to reach **St. Theresa's Church** (Šv. Teresės bažnyčia), known for its Baroque sculptures, multicolored arches, and frescoed ceiling. A few steps farther down, a gateway leads to the bright 17th-century **Church of the Holy Ghost** (Šv. Dvasios bažnyčia), seat of Lithuania's Russian Orthodox Archbishop. Didžioji g. continues north past **St. Nicholas' Church** (Šv. Mikalojaus bažnyčia), Šv. Mikalojaus g. 4, Lithuania's oldest church. The street merges with the pedestrian **Pilies g.** and leads to the main entrance to

LITHUANIA

Vilnius University (Vilniaus Universitetas), at Pilies g. and Šv. Jono g. Founded in 1579, the **library,** Universiteto g., remains one of Europe's largest with more than five million volumes. Continue north on Pilies g. or Universiteto g. to **Cathedral Square** (Arkikatedros aikštė), depicted on the 50Lt note. Behind the cathedral, walk up the path of Castle Hill to **Gedimino tower** for a great view of Vilnius's spires. Off Pylimo, between Kalinausko 1 and 3, shoots up the most random monument on the continent, capped by a **bust of Frank Zappa** (installed in 1995).

THE OLD JEWISH QUARTER AND GENOCIDE MEMORIAL. Vilnius was once a center of Jewish life comparable to Warsaw and New York, with a Jewish population of 100,000 (in a city of 230,000) at the outbreak of World War II. Nazi persecution left only 6000 survivors. Only one of prewar Vilnius's 96 **synagogues** remains, at Pylimo g. 39. The **Lithuanian State Jewish Museum,** housed in two buildings at Pylimo g. 4, offers a variety of exhibits testifying to the vitality of Yiddish culture in Lithuania and the tragedy of the Holocaust. *(Open M-Th 9am-5pm, F 9am-4pm. Donation requested.)* The **Genocide Memorial,** Agrastų g. 15, is only 10-15min. away by train in **Paneriai** (2Lt). Exit the train tracks on the left side and follow Agrastų g. straight to the memorial. Between 1941 and 1944, 100,000 people, including 70,000 Jews, were shot, burned, and buried here. Paved paths connect the pits that served as mass graves. *(Open M and W-Sa 11am-6pm.)* For information on locating ancestors or on the Jewish Quarter, visit the **Jewish Cultural Centre.** *(Šaltiniv g. 12. Tel. 41 88 09.)*

▧MUSEUM OF GENOCIDE VICTIMS. Don't miss the Museum of Genocide Victims (Genocido Aukų Muziejus), in the **old KGB prison.** One of the tour guides, G. Radžius, was once a prisoner in its cells; find someone to translate what he says. Originally constructed in 1899 to serve as a Russian court, the Nazis turned it into a Gestapo headquarters during WWII. When the Soviets came to town, the building became Vilnius' KGB headquarters. *(Gedimino pr. 40. Enter around the corner at Aukv g. 4. Tel. 62 24 49. Open Tu-Su 10am-4pm. Tours in Lithuanian and Russian, captions in English.)*

🎵 ENTERTAINMENT

In summer, music and dance festivals and pop concerts come to town; pick up *Vilnius in Your Pocket.* New discos, bars, and clubs spring up daily to entertain the influx of foreigners and the city's younger crowd. Lithuanian hipsters Eduardas and Vladimiras organize a **gay disco** every Saturday night at a different venue; call for info. (Tel. 63 30 31. Cover 15Lt. Usually open F-Sa 10pm-6am.) **The Pub (Prie Universiteto),** Dominikonų g. 9, in the heart of Senamiestis, is a traditional English pub with a heavy wooden interior and a cozy, 19th-century dungeon. (W night jazz. Cover 8Lt. Open daily 11am-2am.) Mingle with the locals at **Amatininskv Užeiga,** Didžiogi g. 19, #2. (Open M-F 8am-5am, Sa-Su 11am-5am.) **Ultra,** Goštauto g. 12, is young and groovy. (Cover 5Lt. Open Th-Sa 8pm-5am.) Think about 1993 and start dancing; you'll fit right in at **Ministerija,** Gedimino pr. 46, in the basement of Prie Parlamento. (Cover 5Lt. Age 20 and up. Open M-Th 6pm-2am, F-Sa 6pm-5am.)

IT'S A SMALL GULAG AFTER ALL
Apart from bringing freedom and opportunity for advancement to the millions formerly under its yoke, the fall of communism has left former Soviet states with a slew of statues to the leaders of the glorious revolution and no where to put them. Enter Viliumas Malinaukas, a Lithuanian entrepreneur (dare we say "beeznessman?") who wants to collect them all for a massive Soviet theme park. His plan to place the statues in a strip of filled bog land has already won the grace of the government, but not of all of the country. The older generation, which actually lived through communism, is particularly enraged at this plan to package their repression for tourists. And while Malinaukas claims that the park is meant to be educational, whether it's in good taste is another matter. Take, for example, the planned entrance to Leninland: a replica of the Vilnius train station from which thousands of Lithuanians were shipped to Siberia. Ooh-la-la.

KLAIPĖDA

Guarding the Curonian Lagoon with its fortress on the tip of the Neringa peninsula, Klaipėda (klai-PAY-da; pop. 201,500), Lithuania's third-largest city, may be a little too strategically located for its own good. Briefly the Prussian capital in the 17th century, the town went to France in the 1919 Treaty of Versailles and served as a German U-boat base in WWII before being industrialized by the Soviets after the war. On mainland Klaipėda, the **Clock Museum** (Laikrodživ Muziejus), Liepv g. 12, is just the place for the perennially late. From S. Daukanto g., turn right on H. Manto and left on Liepv g. (Open Tu-Su 9am-5:30pm. 4Lt, students 2Lt. Tours 20Lt, foreign-language 40Lt.) **Klaipėda Theater** (Klaipėdos Dramos Teatras), Teatro aikštė, on the other side of Manto g., dominates the Old Town center. Built in 1857, the theater is famous as one of Wagner's favorite haunts. (Tel. (026) 21 25 89. Open Tu-Su 10am-2pm and 4-6pm.) **Smiltynė**, across the lagoon, houses the excellent **Maritime Museum and Aquarium** (Jurv muziejus ir Akvariumas), Tomo g. 10, in an 1860s fortress. (Open June-Aug. Tu-Su 10:30am-6:30pm; May and Sept. W-Su 10:30am-6:30pm; Oct.-Apr. Sa-Su 10:30am-5:30pm. 5Lt, students 3Lt.) The ■**Dolphinarium** next door stages shows at noon, 2, and 4pm (12Lt, students 6Lt). Both aquatic attractions are located in **Kopgalis,** at the head of the Spit, 1.5km from the ferry landing. Forest paths lead west about 500m to the **beaches.** Imbibe aboard the permanently moored ■**Meridianas,** Dauès Krautinė (river bank). (Cover 20-30Lt. Open daily 3pm-5am.)

Trains (tel. (026) 21 46 14) go from Priestočio g. 7 to Vilnius (5hr., 3 per day, 38Lt). **Buses** (tel. (026) 21 48 63) chug from Butkv Juzès 9 to to Nida (2hr., 2 per day, 8Lt) and Vilnius (4-7hr., 10 per day, 30-37Lt). With your back to the bus station, turn left on Priestoties and left again on S. Nèries g. Follow S. Nèries g. away from the train station and turn right on S. Daukanto g., which intersects with S. Šimkaus g. on the left. **Litinterp,** S. Šimkaus g. 21/8, arranges **rooms** (singles 60Lt; doubles 100Lt). (Tel. (026) 31 14 90; fax 21 98 62. Open M-F 8:30am-5:30pm, Sa 10am-3pm.) Centrally located **Hotel Viktorija,** S. Šimkaus g. 2, is on the corner of Vytauto g. (Tel. (026) 21 36 70. Singles 45Lt; doubles 60-120Lt. Shower 3.50Lt.) To get to **Klaipėda Traveller's Guesthouse (HI),** Turgaus 3/4, in the Old Town, walk left from the train station (right from the bus station) down Trilapio, turn right on Liepu, and turn left on H. Manto, which crosses the river; Turgaus is the second left after the bridge. (Tel. (026) 21 49 35; email oldtown@takas.lt. 32Lt; nonmembers 34Lt. Free beer and bike rental if you reserve by email.) ■**Skandalas,** Kanto 44, serves American eats and has dancing after 8pm. (Lunch 25-35Lt. Open daily noon-3am. V, MC.) **IKI supermarket** is at Mažvyado 7. (Open daily 9am-10pm.) **Postal code:** LT-5800.

🎯 EXCURSION FROM KLAIPĖDA: NIDA. The magical rise of wind-swept, white-sand dunes has long drawn summer vacationers to Nida (pop. 2000), only 3km north of the Kaliningrad region on the Curonian Spit. From an immense sundial, you can look down on the summer home of Thomas Mann and beyond, to where the dunes shelter the lagoon from the Baltic. Walk along the beach or through forest paths to reach steps leading to surreal mountains and plains of white sand blowing gracefully into the sea from 100m above. From the center of town, walk along the promenade by the water and bear right on Skruzdynės g. to reach the renovated **Thomas Mann House** (Thomo Manno Namelis) at #17. Mann built the cottage in 1930 and wrote *Joseph and His Brothers* here, but had to give it up when Hitler invaded. From Naglių 18, **microbuses** (tel. (8259) 523 34) run to Smiltynė (1hr., 7Lt); buy tickets on board. The last one (11:45pm) should get you there to catch the 12:45am ferry back to mainland **Klaipėda.** The **Tourist Information Center,** Taikos g. 4, opposite the bus station, arranges **bed-and-breakfasts** (30-50Lt per person) for a 5Lt service charge. (Tel. (8259) 523 45; fax 523 44. Open M-Sa 9am-noon and 1-7pm, Su 9am-2pm.)

LUXEMBOURG

US$1 = 38.00LUF (FRANCS)	10LUF = US$0.26
CDN$1 = 25.51LUF	10LUF = CDN$0.39
UK£1 = 60.94LUF	10LUF = UK£0.16
IR£1 = 51.22LUF	10LUF = IR£0.20
AUS$1 = 24.53LUF	10LUF = AUS$0.41
NZ$1 = 19.73LUF	10LUF = NZ$0.51
SAR1 = 6.31LUF	10LUF = SAR1.58
EUR1 = 40.34LUF	10LUF = EUR0.25

PHONE CODE | Country code: 352. International dialing prefix: 00.

Too often overlooked by budget travelers, the tiny (2586 sq. km) Grand Duchy of Luxembourg possesses impressive fortresses and castles, as well as miles of beautiful hiking trails. Founded in AD 963, the Duchy was first named *Luclinburhuc*, or "little castle." By the time successive waves of Burgundians, Spaniards, French, Austrians, and Germans had receded, the little castle had become a bristling armored mountain, and the countryside was saturated with fortresses. Only after the last French soldier returned home in 1867 and the Treaty of London restored its neutrality did Luxembourg begin to cultivate its current image of peacefulness. Today the wealthy little nation, with 420,000 residents, is an independent constitutional monarchy, a member of the European Union, and a tax haven for investors worldwide. From the wooded and hilly Ardennes in the north to the fertile vineyards of the Moselle Valley in the south, the country's unspoiled rural landscapes provide a sharp contrast to the high-powered banking in the small capital city.

Luxembourg

DISCOVER LUXEMBOURG

Luxembourg is a charming stopover between France or Belgium and Germany. The surprisingly striking **Luxembourg City,** though a rare stop on most travelers' grand tour, is arguably one of Europe's most beautiful capitals (p. 645). After spending a day or two in the capital, your next stop should be **Vianden,** whose gorgeous *château* and possibilities for outdoors activities make it well worth an overnight stay (p. 648). If you have extra time, consider daytripping to **Diekirch** (p. 649) or hiking or biking around **Echternach** and **Grevenmacher** (p. 649).

GETTING THERE AND GETTING AROUND

The Luxembourg City **airport** is serviced by Luxair (tel. 479 81, reservations tel. 0800 20 00) and British Airways (tel. 43 86 47) with flights from the UK and throughout the continent. Cheap last-minute flights on Luxair are available at www.luxair.lu. A **Benelux Tourrail Pass** allows five days of unlimited **train** travel in a one-month period in Belgium, the Netherlands, and Luxembourg (4400LF, under 26 3300LF). The **Billet Réseau** (160LF) is good for one day of unlimited bus and train travel; even better is the **Luxembourg Card** (see p. 644), which covers unlimited transportation and most entrance fees. International gateways to Luxembourg include Liège (2½hr.) and Brussels (see p. 119), Belgium; Metz, France (see p. 366); and Koblenz (2¼hr.; see p. 423) and Trier (see p. 424), Germany. **Hiking** and **biking trails** run between Luxembourg City and Echternach, from Diekirch to Echternach and Vianden, and elsewhere. **Bikes** aren't permitted on buses, but are allowed on many trains for 40LF. **Ettelbrück** (1hr.) and **Clervaux** (30min.) lie on the Luxembourg City-Liège-Belgium rail line; to get to **Vianden,** take a bus from Ettelbrück. The towns of Grevenmacher, Echternach, Diekirch, and Vianden are all 15- to 40-minute bus rides from one another; there are usually also direct buses from Luxembourg City.

ESSENTIALS

DOCUMENTS AND FORMALITIES. Citizens of Australia, Canada, the EU, New Zealand, and the US need only a valid passport for stays of up to three months. South Africans require a short-stay visa.

Luxembourg Embassies at Home: Australia (consulate), Level 3, 345 George St, Sydney NSW 2000 (tel. (02) 93 20 02 55; fax 92 62 40 80); **Canada** (consulate), 3877 Draper Ave, Montreal, PQ H4A 2N9 (tel. (514) 849-2101); **South Africa** (consulate), P.O. Box 782922, Sandton 2146 (tel. (011) 463 17 44; 463 32 69); **UK,** 27 Wilton Crescent, London SW1X 8SD (tel. (020) 72 35 69 61; fax (020) 72 35 97 34); **US,** 2200 Massachusetts Ave NW, Washington, DC 20008 (tel. (202) 265-4171; fax 328-8270).

Foreign Embassies in Luxembourg: All located in **Luxembourg City** (see p. 646). Foreign embassies in **Brussels** also have jurisdiction over Luxembourg (see p. 118).

TOURIST OFFICES. The **Luxembourg Card,** available from Easter to October at tourist offices, hostels, and many hotels and public transportation offices, provides unlimited transportation on national trains and buses and includes admission to 32 tourist sites (1-day 350LF, 2-day 600LF, 3-day 850LF). For more info, contact the **Luxembourg National Tourist Office,** P.O. Box 1001, 1010 Luxembourg (tel. (352) 42 82 82 20; fax 42 82 82 30; email tourism@ont.smtp.etat.lu; www.etat.lu/tourism).

Tourist Boards at Home: UK, 122 Regent St, London W1R 5FE (tel. (020) 74 34 28 00; fax 77 34 12 05; www.luxembourg.co.uk); **US,** 17 Beekman Pl, New York, NY 10022 (tel. (212) 935-8888; fax 935-5896; www.visitluxembourg.com).

MONEY. The currency is the Luxembourg **franc,** subdivided into 100 centimes. Luxembourg *francs* are worth the same as Belgian *francs;* you can use Belgian money in Luxembourg, but not vice versa. Expect to pay 800-1500LF for a hotel room, 435-650LF for a hostel bed, and 280-400LF for a restaurant meal. **Service** (15-20%) is generally included in the price; tip taxi drivers 10%. The **value-added tax** is already included in most prices. Luxembourg's **VAT refund threshold** (US$85) is lower than most other EU countries; refunds are usually 13% of the purchase price.

COMMUNICATION

Post: Mailing a **postcard** or a **letter** (up to 20g) from Luxembourg costs 16LF to the UK and 25LF to the US, Canada, Australia, New Zealand, and South Africa.

Telephone: There are no **city codes;** just dial 352 + local number. **International direct dial** numbers include: **AT&T Direct,** 0800 01 11; **Sprint Access,** 0800 01 15; **MCI World-Phone,** 0800 01 12; **Australia Direct,** 0800 00 61; **Canada Direct,** 0800 01 19; **BT Direct,** 0800 00 44; **Ireland Direct,** 0800 89 35 30 **NZ Direct,** 0800 57 84.

Languages: French, German, and, since a popular referendum in 1984, *Letzebuergesch*, a unique mixture of the other two that sounds a bit like Dutch. French is most common in the city, where most people also speak English. For basic phrases, see p. 949.

ACCOMMODATIONS AND CAMPING. Luxembourg's 12 **HI youth hostels** *(Auberges de Jeunesse)* are generally not filled in summer; hostels are busiest in late spring and early fall with school groups. Prices range from 435-650LF, under 27 355-650LF; nonmembers pay about 110LF extra. Breakfast is included, and a packed lunch costs 125LF, and dinner 260LF. Sheets are 125LF. Half of the hostels close from mid-November to mid-December, and the other half close from mid-January to mid-February. Several hostels are planning major renovations, so be sure to check with the tourist board or the **Centrale des Auberges de Jeunesse Luxembourgeoises** (tel. 22 55 88, fax 46 39 87, email information@youthhostels.lu) before going. **Hotels** advertise 800-1500LF per night but have been known to try to persuade tourists to take more expensive rooms. **Campgrounds** abound, and most have hot showers. Two people with a tent will typically pay 250-300LF per night.

FOOD AND DRINK. Restaurants will devour your budget, but moderately priced **brasseries** can usually be found easily. Luxembourgeois cuisine is close to that of the neighboring Lorraine region of France, and sliced Ardennes ham is the national specialty. The sparkling **wines** of the Moselle Valley will please most gourmets.

LOCAL FACTS

Time: Luxembourg is 1hr. ahead of Greenwich Mean Time (GMT; see p. 49).

Climate: Luxembourg enjoys a temperate climate with less moisture than Belgium. Anytime between May and mid-Oct. is a good time to visit.

Hours: Most **banks** are open M-F 9am-4:30pm; most **shops** are open M 1-6pm and Tu-Sa 9:30am-6pm, though many close at noon for 2hr., especially in the countryside.

Holidays: New Year's Day (Jan. 1); Carnival (Feb. 24-26); Shrove Monday (Mar. 6); Easter (Apr. 23); Easter Monday (Apr. 24); May Day (May 1); Ascension Day (June 1); Whit Sunday and Monday (June 11-12); National Holiday (June 23); Assumption Day (Aug. 15); All Saints Holiday (Nov. 1); Christmas (Dec. 25); and Boxing Day (Dec. 26).

LUXEMBOURG CITY (VILLE DE LUXEMBOURG)

Rising above the ramparts of its medieval fortress and overlooking two lush river valleys, the 1000-year-old Luxembourg City (pop. 80,000) is one of the most attractive and dramatic capitals in Europe. Though it is home to thousands of foreign business executives due to its status as both an international banking capital and the center of the European Community, most visitors find it surprisingly relaxed.

▐ GETTING THERE AND GETTING AROUND

Flights: Findel International Airport, 6km from the city. **Bus 9** (40LF plus a rarely enforced 40LF for baggage) is cheaper than the Luxair bus (150LF) and runs the same airport-hostel-train station route more frequently (every 20min.).

Trains: Info tel. 49 90 49 90 (toll-free); see schedules at www.cfl.lu. **Gare CFL,** av. de la Gare, near the foot of av. de la Liberté, 10min. south of the city center. To: **Brussels** (2¾hr., 930LF, under 26 540LF); **Paris** (3½-4hr., 1550LF); **Frankfurt** (5hr., 1710 LF, under 26 1520 LF); and **Amsterdam** (5¾hr., 1660LF, under 26 1230LF).

Buses: Buy a **billet courte distance** (short-distance ticket) from the driver (single-fare 40LF, full-day 160LF), or pick up a package of 10 (320LF) at the train station.

Taxis: Tel. 48 22 33. 32LF per km. 10% premium 10pm-6am; 25% premium on Su. 700-800LF from the city center to the airport.

Bikes: Rent from **Velo en Ville,** 8 rue Bisserwé (tel. 22 27 52). Open M-F 1-8pm, Sa-Su 9am-noon and 1-8pm. 215LF per half-day, 400LF per day. 20% discount if under 26.

🔢 ORIENTATION AND PRACTICAL INFORMATION

The entire city is tiny by European capital standards. The old city is home to most museums, restaurants, and bars. Ten minutes away, the area south of the Pétrusse Valley contains the train station and the happening rue de Hollerich; cheaper hotels crowd the area, though the area is a little unsafe.

Tourist Offices: Grand Duchy National Tourist Office, in the train station (tel. 42 82 82 20; fax 42 82 82 30; www.etat.lu/tourism). Open 9am-7pm. **Municipal Tourist Office,** pl. d'Armes (tel. 22 28 09; fax 46 70 70). Open Apr.-Sept. M-Sa 9am-7pm, Su 10am-6pm; Oct.-Mar. M-F 9am-6pm, Su 10am-6pm.

Budget Travel: SOTOUR, 15 pl. du Théâtre (tel. 46 15 14). Sells BIJ and other discount tickets; makes plane, train, and hotel reservations. Open M-F 9am-6pm, Sa 9am-noon.

Embassies: Ireland, 28 rue d'Arlon (tel. 45 06 10; fax 45 88 20). Open M-F 9am-12:30pm and 2-5pm. **UK,** 14 bd. Roosevelt (tel. 22 98 64; fax 22 98 67). Same hours as Irish Embassy. **US,** 22 bd. E. Servais (tel. 46 01 23; fax 46 14 01). Open M-F 8:30-11:30am; visas M-Tu and Th-F 3:30-4:30pm, W 2-4pm. **Australians, Canadians, New Zealanders,** and **South Africans** should contact embassies in France or Belgium.

American Express: 34 av. de la Porte-Neuve (tel. 22 85 55). Exchange rates slightly better than banks. Open M-F 9am-1pm and 2-5:30pm, Sa 9:30am-noon.

Luggage Storage: At the **station** 100LF per day (1-month max.); 2-day **lockers** 100LF.

Laundromat: Quick Wash, 31 rue de Strasbourg, near the station. Wash and dry 390F. Open M-Sa 8:30am-6:30pm. Doing your laundry is cheaper at the HI hostel (350F).

Emergencies: Police, tel. 113. **Ambulance,** tel. 112.

Pharmacy: Pharmacie Goedert, 5 pl. d'Armes (tel. 22 23 99). Open M 1-6pm, Tu-F 8am-6:15pm, Sa 8am-12:30pm. Check any pharmacy window for night pharmacy info.

Internet Access: CDROMWORLD, 41 rue de la Gare (tel. 26 48 03 12; fax 26 48 03 13), in the Galerie Mercure. One hour 200LF, HI members 150LF. Also see **Chiggeri** below.

Telephones: Outside post offices and at the train station. Coin-operated phones are rare; buy a 50-unit **phone card** at either place (each good for 50 local calls; 250LF).

Post Office: 38 pl. de la Gare, across the street and to the left of the train station. Open M-F 6am-7pm, Sa 6am-noon. Address mail to be held: Adam PASCAL, *Poste Restante*, Recette Principale, **L-1009** Luxembourg City, Luxembourg.

PHONE CODE	Luxembourg has no city codes. From outside Luxembourg, dial int'l dialing prefix + 352 + local number.

📷 ACCOMMODATIONS, CAMPING, AND FOOD

Inexpensive hotels jam the streets near the train station, but become increasingly pricey and posh as you move north of the ravine. Campgrounds surround the city.

Auberge de Jeunesse (HI), 2 rue du Fort Olisy (tel. 22 68 89; fax 22 33 60; email luxembourg@youthhostels.lu). Take bus 9 and ask to be let off at the hostel stop; head under the bridge and turn right down the steep path. Dorms 520-580F, under 27 435-485LF; doubles 1340LF, under 27 1140LF; nonmembers add 110LF. Breakfast included. Sheets 125LF. Laundry 350LF. Reception 7am-2am. Lockout 10am-1:30pm. Curfew 2am.

Hotel Carlton, 9 rue de Strasbourg (tel. 48 48 02; fax 29 96 64; email carlton@pt.lu). From the station, walk up av. de la Liberté and turn left on rue de Strasbourg. Beautiful lobby and friendly staff. Singles 750LF; doubles 1400LF, with bath 1700LF. Renovated singles 2500LF; doubles 3000LF. Breakfast included. Reception 24hr. V, MC.

Bella Napoli, 4 rue de Strasbourg (tel. 48 46 29; fax 49 33 54), opposite Hotel Carlton. Clean, sparse, yet pretty rooms, all with showers and toilets. Singles 1500LF; doubles 1800LF; triples 2400LF. Breakfast included. V, MC.

Camping: Kockelscheuer (tel. 47 18 15). Bus 2 to "Cloche d'Or/Kockelscheuer" from the station. 120LF per person, 140LF per tent. Showers included. Open Easter-Oct.

The area around **Pl. d'Armes,** blanketed with outdoor terraces and frequent live music, teems with fast-food options and pricey restaurants. The brasserie **Le Beaujolais,** at the corner of rue Genistre, has tasty pastas and pizzas (250-390LF). **Restau-**

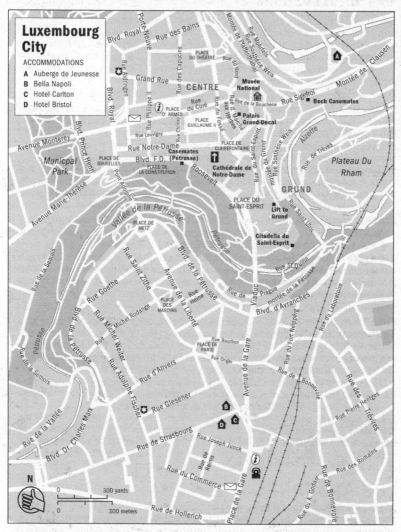

Luxembourg City

ACCOMMODATIONS

A Auberge de Jeunesse
B Bella Napoli
C Hotel Carlton
D Hotel Bristol

rant Bacchus, 32 rue Marché-aux-Herbes, down the street from the Grand Ducal palace, serves up excellent pizza and pasta for 250-400LF. (Open Tu-Su noon-10pm.) **Giorgio,** 11 rue du Nord, has veggie options for 330LF. (Open M-Th 11:45am-2:30pm and 6:30pm-midnight, F-Sa 1:45-2:30pm and 6:30pm-12:30am.) **Maybe Not Bob's,** 107 rue de la Tour Jacob, complements its veggie fare (340-425LF) with burgers (305LF) and spare ribs (355LF). Stock up at **Nobilis supermarket,** 47 av. de la Gare. (Open M-F 9am-7:30pm, Sa 8:30am-6pm, Su 9am-1pm.)

👁 SIGHTS AND ENTERTAINMENT

FORTRESSES AND THE OLD CITY. The 10th-century **Boch Casemates** fortress, part of Luxembourg's original castle, looms imposingly over the Alzette River Valley and offers a fantastic view of the Grund and the Clausen. The strategic stronghold was closed in 1867 when Luxembourg signed an act of neutrality, but was used during WWII to shelter 35,000 people while the rest of the city was pounded. *(Entrance on rue*

Sigefroi just past the bridge leading to the hostel. Open Mar.-Oct. daily 10am-5pm. 70LF.) The **Pétrusse Casemates** were built by the Spanish in the 1600s and were later improved by the Austrians. *(On pl. de la Constitution. Open July-Sept. 70LF, children 40LF. Tours every hr. 11am-4pm.)* The tourist office has info on self-guided **walking tours** through the historic city center and around its medieval ramparts. The guided **Wenzel Walk** leads through 1000 years of history in 100min., winding around the walls of the old city and down into the casemates. *(Easter-Oct Sa 3pm. Reservations tel. 22 28 09. 240LF.)*

MUSEUMS. The **Luxembourg Card** (see p. 644) covers entrance to all museums in the city. The **All-in-One Ticket** covers five museums in two days (250LF at the Municipal Tourist Office). The eclectic collection at the **Musée National d'Histoire et d'Art** reflects the influences of the various European empires that have ruled over Luxembourg. *(Marché-aux-Poissons, at rues Boucherie and Sigefroi. Open Tu-Su 10am-5pm. 100LF. Will partially close for renovations in 2000.)* The **Musée d'Histoire de la Ville de Luxembourg** features multimedia exhibits that allow you to excavate the history of the city through archived photographs, films, and music clips; borrow an English-language guide. *(14 rue du St-Esprit. Open Tu-Th 2-6pm, F-Su 10am-6pm. 200LF, students 150LF.)*

OTHER SIGHTS. Built as the city hall in 1574, the Renaissance **Grand Ducal Palace** became the official city residence of the Grand Duke in 1890. *(Tours mid-July to mid-Aug. M-Sa; inquire at the Municipal Tourist Office. 200LF.)* Nearby, the 7th-century **Notre Dame Cathedral,** which incorporates features of the Dutch Renaissance and early Baroque styles, houses the tombs of John the Blind, the 14th-century King of Bohemia and Count of Luxembourg, and other members of the Grand Ducal family. *(Entrance at bd. Roosevelt. Open Easter-Oct. M-F 10am-5pm, Sa 8am-6pm, Su 10am-6pm; Nov.-Easter M-F 10-11:30am and 2-5pm, Sa 8-11:30am and 2-5pm, Su 10am-5pm. Free.)*

ENTERTAINMENT. Pick up *La Semaine à Luxembourg* at the tourist office for a list of events. In summer, there are free **concerts** on the pl. d'Armes almost nightly. On the Grand Duke's birthday (June 23), the city shuts down to host a large military and religious procession; the night before, the city erupts in street parties. There are a few cafés and clubs in the old city center, but nocturnal debauchery centers on the valley in the **Grund** (reachable by the lift on pl. du St-Esprit), on **rue de Hollerich** near the train station, and in the **Clausen** neighborhood by the Mousel brewery. Check the monthly *Nightlife.lu*, available at most cafés and newsstands. Warm up for the night with an older crowd in the Grund at the candle-lit piano bar **Café des Artistes,** 22 montée du Grund, or grab a Guinness with a younger crowd across the river at **Scott's Pub. Chiggeri,** 11 rue de Nord, which has cool decor and free internet access and serves drinks until 3am on weekends. Backpackers flock to **Pula-Pula,** rue de Sigefroi (DJ on W, F, Sa). The hippest club in town is **Pulp,** bd. d'Avranches.

THE ARDENNES

In 1944 the Battle of the Bulge mashed Luxembourg into slime and mud. Now, more than 50 years later, the forest is verdant again, and its quiet towns, looming castles, and sobering WWII monuments provide a powerful draw to the region.

VIANDEN. Hidden in the greenery of the dense Ardennes (ar-DEN) woods, the small, steep village of Vianden (pop. 1600), home to one of the most impressive castles in Western Europe, is not to be missed. Vianden was the ancestral home of the Orange-Nassau dynasty, rulers of Holland and, thanks to William III's marriage to Mary, England as well. While wealthy Europeans on weekend getaways whiz down Vianden's curvy streets in antique sportscars, backpackers **hike, kayak** on the Sûre River, or **bike** to Diekirch (15-20min.) or Echternach (30min.). The **château,** a mix of Carolingian, Gothic, and Renaissance architecture, is now filled with medieval armor, 16th-century furniture, and 17th-century tapestries. (Open daily Apr.-Sept. 10am-6pm.; Mar. and Oct. 10am-5pm; Nov.-Feb. 10am-4pm. 180LF, students and HI members 130LF.) For a great view of the *château*, ride the **télésiège** (chairlift), 39 rue de Sanatorium, down the hill and across the river from the *château*. From the tourist office, cross the river, turn left on rue Victor Hugo, and turn left again on rue de Sanitorium. (Open Easter-Oct. daily 10am-5pm. 90LF; round-trip 160LF.)

Buses arrive from Echternach and Ettelbrück via Diekirch roughly hourly. The **tourist office,** 1 rue du Vieux Marché, next to the main bus stop, has info on kayaking and private rooms (singles 800LF; doubles 1000LF). (Tel. 83 42 57; fax 84 90 81. Open Easter-Oct. daily 8am-noon and 1:30-5:30pm; Oct.-Easter closed Sa-Su.) Rent **bikes** from **Beltendorf René.** (Tel. 84 92 22. 550LF per day.) To reach the **HI youth hostel,** 3 montée du Château, from the bus stop or tourist office, follow the Grande Rue away from the river and head most of the way up the hill; branch off onto montée du Château and follow the signs (10-15min.). (Tel. 83 41 77; fax 84 94 27; email vianden@youthhostels.lu. 455LF, under 26 375LF. Sheets 125LF. Reception 5-9pm. Lockout 10am-5pm. Curfew 11pm. Open mid-Mar. to mid-Nov.) **Camp op dem Deich,** 5min. downstream from the tourist office, is in the shadow of the *château.* (130LF per person and per tent. Open Easter-Aug.) Food in Vianden is good, cheap, and plentiful, with a strong Germanic influence. Get **groceries** at **Economart,** 1 rue de la Gare. (Open M-Sa 8am-6pm and Su 10am-noon.)

DIEKIRCH. Between Vianden and Echternach lies Diekirch. The **National Museum of Military History,** 10 Bamertal, around the corner from the tourist office, presents a powerful and comprehensive exhibition of relics from WWII's Battle of the Bulge. (Open daily Apr.-Nov. 10am-6pm, Dec.-Mar. 2-6pm. 220LF, students and HI members 120LF.) Around the corner from the 15th-century **Eglise Saint-Laurent,** the **Municipal Museum,** on pl. Guillaume, houses three Roman mosaics. (Open Easter-Oct. F-W 10am-noon and 2-6pm. 50LF.) The **tourist office,** 1 Esplanade, is across from the church. (Tel. 80 30 23. Open mid-July to mid-Aug. Open M-Sa 9am-6pm, Sa-Su 10am-noon and 2-4pm; mid-Aug. to mid-July M-F 9am-noon and 2-5pm.)

CLERVAUX. Northwest of Vianden and Diekirch is tiny Clervaux (pop. 1000), whose **château** houses the striking **Family of Man** exhibition. This collection of over 500 pictures from 68 countries depicts every facet of human life and emotion and was compiled in 1955 by Luxembourg-born photographer Edward Steichen for a show at the Museum of Modern Art in New York. The exhibit was displayed around the world before being permanently installed in Clervaux. (Tel. 92 96 57. Open Mar.-Dec. Tu-Su 10am-noon and 1-6pm. 150LF, students 80LF.)

LITTLE SWITZERLAND (LE MULLERTHAL)

Echternach (pop. 4000) is a quiet, beautiful town next to the German border. Its monastic center was founded in the 7th century and became well known for its illuminated manuscripts. As you exit the bus station, turn left at the marketplace on rue de la Gare, take your last left, and walk past the basilica to see the 18th-century Benedictine **Abbaye,** which contains two 8th-century skeletons and a small museum detailing the monastery's history. (Open July-Aug. 10am-6pm, June and Sept. closed noon-2pm, Oct.-May 10am-noon and 2-5pm. 80LF.) The **tourist office,** on Porte St-Willibrord next to the *Abbaye,* has info on outdoor activities. (Tel. 72 02 30. Open M 2-5pm, Tu-F 9:30am-noon and 2-5pm, Sa 2-4pm.) To get from the bus station to the **youth hostel (HI),** 9 rue André Drechscher, turn left on av. de la Gare and make your last right. (Tel. 72 01 58. 455LF, under 26 375LF. Sheets 125LF. Reception 5-11pm.)

THE MOSELLE VALLEY (LA MOSELLE)

The **Moselle Valley,** with its sunny weather and fertile land, was discovered by French winemakers as a suitable substitute for the Champagne region. Today the valley is renowned not only for its sparkling wines (often marked *méthode traditionelle*), but also for its still wines such as *Riesling* and *Pinot Gris.* **Grevenmacher** is right in the center of this wine culture and makes for a pleasant afternoon visit. Begin with a tour of the **Bernard-Massard winery,** rue du Pont, to learn about the Champagne method and indulge in a glass of excellent sparkling wine. From the bus stop, turn left on rue de Treves, left on rue de la Moselle, and right on rte. du Vin, then enter the *cave* through the gate and garden just under the bridge. (Open Apr.-Oct. daily 9:30am-6pm. 100LF.) A small but spectacular **Jardin des Papillons** (Butterfly Garden) lies nearby. (Open Apr. to mid-Oct. daily 9:30am-5pm. 180LF.)

MALTA

US$1 = LM0.40 (MALTESE LIRE)   **UK£1 = LM0.65**

Malta is a fairy-tale island whose past includes knights in shining armor, pirates, and the salvation of Christian Europe. Remember the *Maltese Falcon*? Citizens of Australia, Canada, the EU, New Zealand, South Africa, and the US only require **visas** for stays of longer than three months. Malta's official **languages** are Maltese and English. The **currency** is the **lira** (Lm), divided into 100 **cents** (¢); you can't leave Malta with more than Lm25 in cash. **Directory assistance:** tel. 190. **Country code:** 356.

☐ GETTING THERE AND GETTING AROUND. Island Seaway (tel. 32 06 55) runs **ferries** from **Catania** in Sicily and **Reggio di Calabria** (at the big toe of Italy's boot) to **Valletta. Virtu** (tel. 31 70 88) sends **catamarans** to Catania and **Syracuse** (also on Sicily). **Trains** run to Reggio Calabria from **Naples** (5hr., L45,000), and to Catania and Syracuse from **Messina** (1½-3hr., L10-16,000). **Air Malta** (tel. 69 08 90) and **Alitalia** (tel. 24 67 82) fly from **Rome** (Lm100 round-trip); **NSTS Travel Service** in Valletta sells discounted fares (Lm35 one-way; see below). **Buses** 8 and 39 run between the airport and Valletta (run 6am-8pm; Lm0.11). For more info, try www.maltayellowpages.com/malta/intro.htm.

VALLETTA. Malta's capital is located on a narrow finger of land on the southeast side of the island. The ☒**Lascaris War Rooms,** St. Ursula St, were used by Winston Churchill, Dwight Eisenhower, and other Allied greats for strategic planning in WWII. Take S. Ursula St from Republic St and follow the signs. (Open M-F 9:30am-4pm, Sa-Su 9:30am-12:30pm. Lm1.60, students 85¢.) The excellent **National Museum of Archaeology** is on Republic St, in the Auberge de Provence. (Open mid-June to Sept. daily 7:45am-2pm; Oct. to mid-June M-Sa 8:15am-5pm, Su 8:15am-4:15pm. Lm1, students free.) The spectacular Baroque **St. John's Co-Cathedral** contains works by Caravaggio. From the City Gate, go down Republic St and turn right on St. John's St. (Open M-F 9:30am-12:45pm and 1:30-5:15pm, Sa 9:30am-12:45pm and 4-5pm. Lm1, students free.) Just beyond the cathedral is the opulent **Grand Master's Palace,** home of Malta's rulers since 1575. (Open mid-June to Sept. daily 9am-1pm; Oct. to mid-June M-Sa 8:15am-5pm, Su 8:15am-4:15pm. State and armory rooms each Lm1, students free. Tours M-F 10:30 and 11:30am, Sa 11:30am; Lm1.50.)

The **tourist office** is on Pope Pius V St, inside the City Gate and to the right from the bus terminal. (Tel. 23 77 47. Open Apr.-Oct. M-Sa 8:30am-6:30pm, Su 8:30am-1pm; Nov.-Mar. M-Sa 8:30am-6pm, Su 8:30am-1pm.) The **NSTS Travel Service** is at 220 St. Paul's St. (Tel. 24 49 83. Open M-Sa 9am-1pm and 3-6pm; in winter closes at 5pm.) To reach **Coronation Guest House,** 10 E. M. A. Vassalli St, turn left on South St at the City Gate and descend the steps near the Osborne Hotel. (Tel. 23 76 52. Lm4-5. Open June-Aug. and Oct.-Mar. Breakfast included.) The **Valletta Asti Guest House,** 18 St. Ursula St, is near the Upper Barracca Gardens. (Tel. 23 95 06. Lm5.50. Breakfast included.) Reserve through NSTS for the **Hibernia House (HI)** on Depiro St in **Sliema;** take Manoel Dimech St from the top of Balluta Bay and turn left on Depiro St. (Tel. 33 38 59. Lm3-3.70.) Get **groceries** at the **Wembley Store,** 305 Republic St, just inside the City Gate. (Open M-F 8am-7pm, Sa 8am-1:30pm.) ☒**Misfits,** in the White House Hotel on Triq Paceville, pulses with a techno beat. (Open daily 8pm-late.)

NEAR VALLETTA. The 9th-century fortifications in **Mdina** (em-DEE-na), once the island's capital, surround a well-preserved Baroque world. **St. Paul's Catacombs** and **St. Agatha's Catacombs** house Christian relics and labrynthine underground passages. To reach Mdina, take bus 80 or 81 from Valletta or bus 65 from Sliema. Near the end of bus route 38, boats (Lm2.50) leave the harbor for the phosphorescent **Blue Grotto.** The astonishing megalithic temples of **Hagar Qim** and **Mnajdra** are 20min. away on foot. For **beaches,** try the crowded **Golden Bay** or quieter **Gnejna Bay** along the west coast (take bus 47 from Valletta or bus 652 from Sliema), the **Marfa** peninsula in the northwest, or the **Pretty Bay** to the east (take bus 11).

The Netherlands

North Sea

TO NEWCASTLE-UPON TYME

TO HARWICH, ENG AND HULL, ENG

GERMANY

BELGIUM

0 — 25 miles
0 — 25 kilometers

THE NETHERLANDS
(NEDERLAND)

US$1 = F2.08 (GUILDERS)	F1 = US$0.48
CDN$1 = F1.39	F1 = CDN$0.72
UK£1 = F3.33	F1 = UK£0.30
IR£1 = F2.80	F1 = IR£0.36
AUS$1 = F1.34	F1 = AUS$0.75
NZ$1 = F1.08	F1 = NZ$0.93
SAR1 = F0.34	F1 = SAR2.90
EUR€1 = F2.20	F1 = EUR€0.45

PHONE CODE **Country code:** 31. **International dialing prefix:** 00.

The Dutch say that although God created the rest of the world, they created the Netherlands. The country is truly a masterful feat of engineering; since most of the country is below sea level, vigorous pumping and a series of dikes were used to create thousands of square kilometers of land known as *polders*, which now constitute most of the country's area, including Amsterdam. What was once the domain of seaweed and cod is now packed with an extraordinary number of windmills, bicycles, tulips, cheese, Vermeers, van Goghs, and the occasional wooden shoe.

During the Age of Exploration, Dutch conquerors fanned out over the globe. The Dutch East and West India Companies traded as far afield as Java, the Caribbean, and Africa, and set up a small colony called "New Amsterdam" that eventually evolved into New York. With a steady influx of wealth from the colonies, 17th-century Holland became one of Europe's most powerful commercial centers. The Dutch Golden Age supported a thriving artistic community including such masters as Rembrandt and Vermeer; at the same time, Holland served as a sanctuary for many of Europe's religious and political dissidents, cultivating an atmosphere of freedom and tolerance that spawned the philosophies of Descartes and Spinoza.

Since suffering the devastating effects of two world wars, the Dutch have rebuilt their cities under the stark, modernist influence of Mondrian's de Stijl school and the architecture of Mies van der Rohe. Since the 1960s, they've continued to push the boundaries of social frontiers, pioneering progressive policies regarding sexual identity, gender equality, birth control, and—as teenage tourists and hostile foreign drug officials know all too well—the legalization of soft drugs. The Netherlands' wealth of 17th-century and modern art, its charming, canal-lined towns, and the (ahem) uniqueness of Amsterdam's perpetual party are all reflected in the hordes of travelers that double the country's population every summer.

DISCOVER THE NETHERLANDS

Roll that shit, light that shit, then smoke that shit in **Amsterdam,** a hedonist's wet dream, with chill coffeeshops and breathtaking museums that overwhelm the senses (p. 655). After that shit is kicked (at least four days), head to rustic Dutch countryside to clear your head. The amazing **Hoge Veluwe National Park,** southeast of Amsterdam, shelters within its 30,000 wooded acres one of the finest modern art museums in Europe (p. 675). Beautifully preserved **Leiden** (p. 671) and **Utrecht** (p. 674), less than 30min. away, delight with picturesque canals. Dutch politics and museums abound in **The Hague** (p. 671); for more innovative art and architecture, step into futuristic **Rotterdam** (p. 673). An afternoon in **Delft** (p. 672) or **Gouda** (p. 674) provides a dose of small-town Dutch charm. Visit the sand dunes and isolated beaches of the tiny **Wadden Islands,** a biker's paradise (p. 677). In spring, don't miss the exploding blooms of the **Keukenhof gardens** near **Lisse** (p. 671).

GETTING THERE AND GETTING AROUND

BY PLANE. KLM Royal Dutch Airlines, Martinair, Continental, Delta, Northwest, United, and Singapore Airlines serve **Amsterdam's** Schiphol Airport. Amsterdam is a major hub for cheap transatlantic flights (see p. 49).

BY TRAIN. The national rail company is the efficient **Nederlandse Spoorwegen** (NS; Netherlands Railways; info tel. (09) 00 92 92; www.ns.nl). Train service tends to be faster than bus service. *Sneltreins* are the fastest; *stoptreins* make the most stops. One-way tickets are called *enkele reis;* normal round-trip tickets, *retour;* and day return tickets (valid only on day of purchase, but cheaper than normal round-trip tickets), *dagretour.* **Day Trip (Rail Idee)** programs, available at train stations, has reduced-price combo transportation/entrance fees. **Eurail** and **InterRail** (see p. 61) are valid in the Netherlands. The **Holland Railpass** (US$52-98) is good for three or five travel days in any one-month period. Although available in the US, the Holland Railpass is cheaper in the Netherlands at DER Travel Service or RailEurope. The **Euro Domino Holland** card similarly allows three (f130, under 26 f100), five (f200, f150), or 10 days (f350, f275) of unlimited rail travel in any one-month period, but is only available to those who have lived in Europe for at least six months and cannot be bought in the Netherlands (see p. 62). **One-day train passes** cost f71.50; an option on many passes offers use of trams and other services for an extra f18-47. The **Meerman's Kaart** grants one day of unlimited travel for two to six people (f108-186).

BY BUS. A nationalized fare system covers city buses, trams, and long-distance buses. The country is divided into zones; the number of strips on a **strippenkaart**

(strip card) required depends on the number of zones through which you travel. The base charge within a city is two strips, and travel between towns costs from five to 20 strips. On buses, tell the driver your destination and he or she will cancel the correct number of strips; on trams and subways, stamp your own *strippenkaart* in either a yellow box at the back of the tram or in the subway station. Bus and tram drivers sell two- (f3.50), three- (f4.75), and eight-strip tickets (f12), but they're *much* cheaper in bulk, available at public transit counters, tourist offices, post offices, and some tobacco shops and newsstands (15-strip f11.75, 45-strip f34.50). **Dagkaarten** (day tickets) are available for one to nine days (one-day f16). Riding without a ticket can result in a f60 fine plus the original cost of the ticket.

BY FERRY. Ferries traverse the North Sea, connecting **England** to the Netherlands. Boats arrive in **Hook of Holland** (3¾-8½hr.), near Delft and The Hague, from **Harwich,** northeast of London; in **Rotterdam** from **Hull** (13½hr), near York (p. 183); and in **Amsterdam** from **Newcastle-upon-Tyne** (14hr.; p. 185). For more info, see p. 58.

BY CAR. The Netherlands has well-maintained roadways. North Americans and Australians need an International Driver's License; if your insurance doesn't cover you abroad, you'll also need a green insurance card. On maps, a green "E" indicates international highways; a red "A," national highways; and small yellow signposts and "N," other main roads. Speed limits are 50km per hr. in towns, 80km outside, and 120km on highways. Fuel prices per liter average about f2.30. The **Royal Dutch Touring Association** (ANWB) offers roadside assistance to members (tel. (06) 08 88). For more info, contact the ANWB at Wassenaarseweg 220, 2596 EC The Hague (tel. (070) 314 71 47), or Museumsplein 5, 1071 DJ Amsterdam (tel. (020) 673 08 44).

BY BIKE AND BY THUMB. Cycling is the way to go in the Netherlands—distances between cities are short, the countryside is absolutely flat, and most streets have separate bike lanes. Bikes run about f8 per day or f30 per week plus a f50-100 deposit (railpasses will often earn you a discount). Call the station a day ahead to reserve; phone numbers are listed in the free *Fiets en Trein.* For info try www.visitholland.com/find/rental/bike.html. Hitchhiking is somewhat effective, but on the roads out of Amsterdam there is cutthroat competition. *Let's Go* does not recommend hitchhiking. The **International Lift Center,** Oudezijds Achterburgwal 169, in Amsterdam (tel. (020) 622 43 42), matches riders and drivers for destinations all over Europe for a f10 membership fee and the cost of gas. (Open M-F 10am-6pm, Sa 10am-2pm.)

ESSENTIALS

DOCUMENTS AND FORMALITIES. Citizens of Australia, Canada, the EU, New Zealand, and the US do not need visas for stays shorter than three months. South Africans require visas for visits of any duration.

Netherlands Embassies at Home: Australia, 120 Empire Circuit, Yarralumba ACT 2600 (tel. (02) 62 73 31 11; fax 62 73 32 06). **Canada,** 350 Albert St, Suite 2020, Ottawa, ON K1R 1A4 (tel. (613) 237-5030; fax 237-6471). **Ireland,** 160 Merrion Rd, Dublin 4 (tel. (01) 269 34 44; fax 283 96 90). **New Zealand,** P.O. Box 840, Wellington (tel. (04) 471 63 90; fax 471 29 23). **South Africa,** P.O. Box 117, Pretoria 0001 (tel. (012) 344 39 10; fax 343 99 50). **UK,** 38 Hyde Park Gate, London SW7 5DP (tel. (020) 75 90 32 00; fax 75 81 34 58). **US,** 4200 Linnean Ave NW, Washington, DC 20008 (tel. (202) 244-5300; fax 362-3430; www.netherlands-embassy.org).

Foreign Embassies and Consulates in the Netherlands: All embassies and most consulates are located in **The Hague** (see p. 671). The **UK** and the **US** also have consulates in **Amsterdam** (see p. 655).

TOURIST OFFICES. VVV (vay-vay-vay) tourist offices are marked by triangular blue signs. They also sell **Museumkaart** passes that cover admission to most of the 800 museums in the Netherlands (f55, under 25 f25; bring a passport-size photo).

Tourist Offices at Home: Canada, 25 Adelaide St. E #710, Toronto ON H5C 1Y2 (tel. (416) 363-1577; fax 363-1470). **South Africa,** P.O. Box 781738, Sandton 2146 (tel. (11) 884 81 41; fax 883 55 73). **UK** and **Ireland,** P.O. Box 523, London SW1E 6NT (tel. (020) 79 31 06 61; fax 78 28 79 41). **US,** 355 Lexington Ave, New York, NY 10017 (tel. (888) 464-6552; fax (212) 370-9507; www.goholland.com).

MONEY. The Dutch currency is the **guilder** (**f** a.k.a. florin), made up of 100 cents. Coins include the *stuiver* (5¢), *dubbeltje* (10¢), *kwartje* (25¢), and *rijksdaalder* (f2.50). Post offices offer reasonable **currency exchange** rates; **GWK** often has the best rates and doesn't charge ISIC holders commission. Otherwise, expect a flat fee of about f5 and a 2.25% commission. A bare-bones day traveling in the Netherlands will cost US$15-25; a slightly more comfortable day will run US$30-40.

Tipping and Bargaining: A 5-10% gratuity will generally be added to your hotel, restaurant and taxi bills. An additional 5% is common for superior service.

Taxes: VAT refunds in the Netherlands are usually 13.5%, and are available on purchases of more than f300 made during a single visit to a store.

COMMUNICATION

Post: Post offices are generally open M-F 9am-5pm. Mailing a **postcard** or **letter** to the UK costs f1; to destinations outside Europe, postcards cost f1, letters (up to 20g) f1.60. Mail takes 2-3 days to the UK, 4-6 to North America, 6-8 to Australia and New Zealand, and 8-10 to South Africa.

Telephone: When making **international calls** from pay phones, **phone cards** (in denominations of f10; available at post offices) are the most economical option. For **directory assistance,** dial 06 80 08 within the Netherlands or 06 04 18 from outside the country; for **collect calls,** dial 06 04 10. **International dial direct numbers** include: **AT&T,** 0800 022 91 11; **Sprint,** 0800 022 91 19; **MCI WorldPhone Direct,** 0800 022 91 22; **Australia Direct,** 0800 022 20 61; **Canada Direct,** 0800 022 91 16; **BT Direct,** 0800 022 04 44; **Ireland Direct,** 0800 02 20 353; **NZ Direct,** 0800 022 23 13; **Telekom South Africa Direct,** 0800 022 02 27. For **police, medical,** and **fire emergencies,** dial 112.

Language: Dutch. Most natives speak English fluently, but a few words can't hurt. Fill up on *dagschotel* (dinner special), *broodje* (bread or sandwich), *bier* (beer), and *kaas* (cheese). Dutch uses a gutteral "g" sound for both "g" and "ch." "J" is usually pronounced as "y"; e.g., *hofje* is "hof-YUH." "Ui" is pronounced "ow," and the dipthong "ij" is best approximated in English as "ah" followed by a long "e." For more basic lingo, see p. 949.

ACCOMMODATIONS AND CAMPING. VVV offices supply accommodations lists and can nearly always reserve rooms in both local and other areas (fee around f4). **Private rooms** cost about two-thirds as much as hotels, but they are hard to find; check with the VVV. During July and August, many cities add approximately f2.50 tourist tax to the price of all rooms. The country's best values are the 35 **HI youth hostels,** run by the **NJHC (Dutch Youth Hostel Federation);** hostels are divided into three price categories based on quality. Most are exceedingly clean and modern and cost f28-33 for bed and breakfast, plus high-season or prime-location supplements (f1-3). The VVV has a hostel list, and the useful *Jeugdherbergen* brochure describes each one (both free). For more info, contact the NJHC at Prof. Tulppein 2, Amsterdam (tel. (020) 551 31 33; fax 623 49 86). Pick up a membership card at hostels (f30); nonmembers are charged an additional f5. **Camping** is available country-wide, but many sites are crowded and trailer-ridden in summer. An **international camping card** is not required.

FOOD AND DRINK. Dutch food is hearty and simple. Pancakes, salted herring, and pea soup are national specialties. Dutch cheeses transcend Gouda and Edam; try Leiden, the mild Belegen, and the creamy Kernhem too. A typical breakfast consists of meat and cheese on bread and a soft-boiled egg. Sweet bread toppings like *hagelslag* (chocolate sprinkles) and chocolate spread are also extremely popular. For a hearty brunch, try *uitsmijter* (OWTS-myter; literally "bouncer"), which packs in salad, ham, cheese, and fried eggs. At dinner, reap the benefits of Dutch imperialism: *rijsttafel* is an Indonesian specialty comprising up to 25 different dishes, including curried chicken or lamb with pineapple, served with rice. *Pannenkoeken* is the traditional Dutch lunch of buttery, sugary, golden brown pancakes, topped with everything from ham and cheese to strawberries and whipped cream. Wash it all down with a small, foamy glass of hometown **beer** Heineken or Amstel (f2-2.50), or order a pint (f5-6). *Jenever* (usually f3) is a strong gin.

LOCAL FACTS

Time: The Netherlands is 6hr. ahead of Greenwich Mean Time (GMT; see p. 49).

Climate: Mid-May to early October is the ideal time to visit, when the day temperatures are generally 20-31°C (70-80°F), with nights around 10-20°C (50-60°F). However, it can be quite rainy; bring an umbrella. The tulip season runs from Apr. to mid May.

Hours: Banks open M-F 10am-4pm, occasionally also Th 6-8pm or 7-9pm. **Stores** are generally open M 1-6pm, Tu-F 9am-6pm, and Sa 9am-5pm. Some stay open later Th-F.

Holidays: New Year's Day (Jan. 1); Good Friday (Apr. 21); Easter Monday (Apr. 24); Queen's Birthday (Apr. 30); Liberation Day (May 5); Ascension Day (June 11); Whit Monday (June 11-12); Christmas Day (Dec. 25); and Boxing Day (Dec. 26).

Festivals: Koninginnedag (Queen's Day; Apr. 30) features huge parties. The Hague hosts the huge **North Sea Jazz Festival** (July 14-16, 2000). The **Holland Festival** (in June) celebrates the nation's cultural diversity. **Bloemen Corso** (Flower Parade; first Sa in Sept.) runs from Aalsmeer to Amsterdam. Many historical canal houses and windmills open to the public for **National Monument Day** (2nd Sa in Sept.).

AMSTERDAM

Amsterdam—just the name conjures up more images of sugarplums in young travelers' heads than any night before Christmas could. Some people say that the best vacation to Amsterdam is the one you can't remember. True, the city lives up to its reputation as a never-never land of bacchanalian excess: the aroma of cannabis wafts from coffeeshops, and the city's infamous sex scene swathes itself in red lights. But one need not be naughty to enjoy Amsterdam. Art enthusiasts will delight in the troves of Rembrandts, Vermeers, and van Goghs, and romantics can stroll along endless cobblestoned streets and canals sparkling with reflected lights.

▛ GETTING THERE AND GETTING AROUND

Flights: Schiphol Airport (SKIP-pull; tel. (0900) 01 41; f1 per min.). **Trains** connect the airport to Centraal Station (20min., every 10min., f6.50). Interliner **buses** run from the airport to Leidsepl. (on the half-hour., 4-5 strips).

Trains: Centraal Station, Stationspl. 1, at the end of the Damrak (for international info call (0900) 92 96, domestic info (0900) 92 92; f0.50 per min.; schedules at www.ns.nl/reisplan2a.asp). To: **Brussels** (3-4hr.); **Hamburg** (5hr.); **Frankfurt** (5¼-6hr.); **Paris** (8hr.); and **Berlin** (8hr.). For international info and reservations, take a number and wait (up to 1hr. in summer). Info desk open M-F 8am-10pm, Sa-Su 9am-8pm; reservations made M-F 8am-8pm, Sa-Su 9am-5pm. **Lockers** f4-6.

Buses: Trains are quicker. The **GVB** will direct you to a bus stop for destinations not on a rail line. **Muiderpoort** (2 blocks east of Oosterpark) sends buses east; **Marnixstation** (at the corner of Marnixstr. and Kinkerstr.) west; and the **Stationsplein depot** north and south.

Public Transportation: GVB (tel. (06) 92 92), Stationspl. Tram and bus lines radiate from Centraal Station and run until around midnight; pick up a *nachtbussen* (night buses) schedule. Trams are most convenient for inner-city travel; the 2-line subway leads to farther out neighborhoods. Don't buy *dagkaart* (day passes; f12) on the bus; you'll pay dearly. The 15-strip *strippenkaart* (strip card; f11.75) is the best deal. It is available at the VVV, the GVB, and many hostels. Open M-F 7am-9pm, Sa-Su 8am-9pm.

Taxis: Tel. 677 77 77. Fares from f6 plus f2.80 per km or min. (more at night). Stands at the Dam, Spui, Nieuw Markt, Rembrantspl., Leidsepl., and Centraal Station.

Bike Rental: Beware rampant bike theft. All **train stations** rent plain ol' bikes for f12.50 per day, f30-40 per week with a train ticket. **Damstraat Rent-a-Bike,** Pieter Jacobstr. 11

(tel. 625 50 29), just off Damstr. near the Dam. Rentals f15 per day, f67 per week (plus f50 deposit and passport); used bikes sold for f185-250. Open daily 9am-6pm.

Hitchhiking: Hitching is increasingly less common in the Netherlands, but it can be done, though *Let's Go* does not recommend it. Those heading to **Utrecht,** central and southern Germany, and Belgium take tram 25 to the end and start at the bridge; **Groningen** and northern Germany, take bus 56 to Prins Bernhardpl. or the metro to Amstel and start along Gooiseweg; **The Hague,** hop on tram 16 or 24 to Stadionpl. and start on the other side of the canal on Amstelveenseweg; **Haarlem** and **Noord Holland,** take bus 22 to Haarlemmerweg and start from Westerpark. For ridesharing info, see p. 653.

✈ ORIENTATION

A series of roughly concentric canals ripple out around the **Centrum** (city center), resembling a giant horseshoe with its opening to the northeast. Emerging from Centraal Station, at the top of the horseshoe, you'll hit **Damrak,** a key thoroughfare leading to the **Dam,** the main square. Just east of Damrak in the Centrum is Amsterdam's famed **red-light district,** bounded by Warmoestr., Gelderskade, and Oude Doelenstr. Don't head into the area until you've locked up your bags, either at the train station or at a hostel or hotel. South of the red-light district but still within the horseshoe lies the **Rembrandtsplein.** The canals radiating around the Centrum (lined by streets of the same names) are **Singel, Herengracht, Keizergracht,** and **Prinsengracht.** West of the Centrum, beyond Prinsengracht, lies the **Jordaan,** an attractive residential neighborhood. Moving counterclockwise around Prinsengracht you'll hit the **Leidseplein,** which lies just across the canal from the **Museum District** and **Vondelpark.** Street names change capriciously; buy a good **map** of the city (f2.75-4) at the VVV tourist office or from a magazine stand. *Use It* (f4) includes a map, info on cheap lodgings, an index of youth agencies, and city news.

▮ PRACTICAL INFORMATION

TOURIST AND FINANCIAL SERVICES

Tourist Office: VVV, Stationspl. 10 (tel. (0900) 400 40 40, f1 per min.; fax 625 28 69), to the left and in front of Centraal Station. Hefty f5 fee plus f5 deposit for room booking. Sells maps, phone cards, museum passes, and *strippenkaart.* Pick up *What's On* (f4), a fabulous listing of events. Open daily 9am-5pm. **Branches** at Centraal Station, platform 2, Leidsepl. 1, and the airport are open daily and much less crowded.

Budget Travel: NBBS, Rokin 38 (tel. 624 09 89). Budget student flights. Open mid-May to mid-Aug. M-F 9:30am-5:30pm, Sa 10am-4pm; mid-Aug. to mid-May closes Sa at 3pm. **Budget Bus/Eurolines,** Rokin 10 (tel. 560 87 88). Open M-F 9:30am-5:30pm, Sa 10am-4pm. **Wasteels,** also on Rokin, has cheap plane tickets.

Consulates: All **embassies** and most consulates are in **The Hague** (see p. 671). Consulates: **UK,** Koninginnelaan 44 (tel. 676 43 43). Open M-F 9am-noon and 2-3:30pm. **US,** Museumpl. 19 (tel. 664 56 61). Open M-F 8:30am-noon and 1:30-4:30pm.

Currency Exchange: Best rates at **American Express** (see below). The **GWK** offices at Centraal Station and Schiphol have good rates, and charge students no commission for traveler's checks (open 24hr.). **Change Express,** Kalverstr. 150 (open daily 8am-8pm) or Leidestr. 106 (open daily 8am-midnight) has good rates and a 3% commission.

American Express: Damrak 66 (tel. 520 77 77; fax 504 87 07). Excellent rates and no commission on traveler's checks. Mail held. Open M-F 9am-5pm, Sa 9am-noon. **AmEx ATM.** Beware the pickpockets in the neighborhood. The **branch** at Van Baerlestr. 28 (tel. 671 41 41) is less crowded and in a safer area. Open M-F 9am-5pm, Sa 9am-noon.

LOCAL SERVICES

English Bookstores: Spui, near the Amsterdam University, is lined with bookstores and holds an open-air *Boekemarkt* F 10am-6pm. **American Discount Book Center,** 185 Kalverstr. 10% student discount. Open M-Sa 10am-8pm, Th 10am-10pm, Su 11am-6pm.

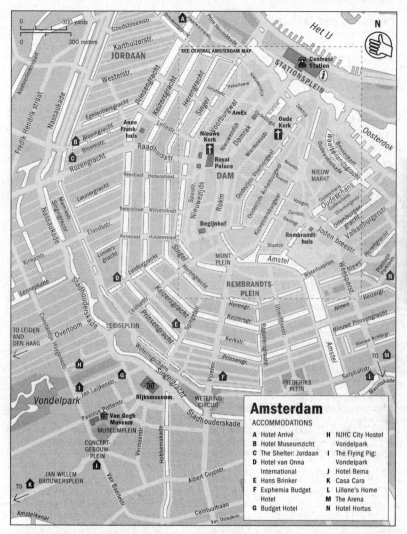

Amsterdam

ACCOMMODATIONS

A	Hotel Arrivé	H	NJHC City Hostel
B	Hotel Museumzicht		Vondelpark
C	The Shelter: Jordaan	I	The Flying Pig:
D	Hotel van Onna		Vondelpark
	International	J	Hotel Bema
E	Hans Brinker	K	Casa Cara
F	Euphemia Budget	L	Lillane's Home
	Hotel	M	The Arena
G	Budget Hotel	N	Hotel Hortus

Gay and Lesbian Services: COC, Rozenstr. 14 (tel. 626 30 87), is the main source of info. Open M-F 10am-5pm (café closed M-Tu). **Intermale,** Spuistr. 251 (tel. 625 00 09), is a gay bookstore. Open M 11am-6pm, Tu-W and F-Sa 10am-6pm, Th 11am-9pm. **Gay and Lesbian Switchboard** (tel. 623 65 65) daily 10am-10pm.

Laundry: Look for a *Wasserette* sign. **The Clean Brothers,** Kerkstr. 56. Wash f8, dry f1 per 20min. Open daily 7am-9pm.

Condoms: Find the widest variety of colors, flavors, and styles at the **Condomerie,** Warmoesstr. 141, next to the red-light district. Open M-Sa 11am-6pm.

EMERGENCY AND COMMUNICATIONS

Emergencies: Tel. 112 (police, ambulance, and fire brigade).

Police: Headquarters, Elandsgracht 117 (tel. 559 91 11).

Crisis Lines: Rape crisis hotline, tel. 613 02 45; staffed M-F 2:30am-11pm, Sa-Su 4-11pm. **Drug counseling,** Jellinek clinic (tel. 570 23 55).

Pharmacies: Most are open M-F 8:30am-5pm. When closed, each *apotheek* (pharmacy) posts a sign directing you to the nearest open one.

Medical Assistance: Tourist Medical Service, tel. 695 56 38. Open 24hr. For hospital care, call **Academisch Medisch Centrum,** Meibergdreef 9 (tel. 566 91 11), near the Holendrecht Metro stop. For free emergency medical care, visit the **Kruispost,** Oudezijds Voorburgwal 129 (tel. 624 90 31). Open M-F 6:45am-11pm. **STD Line,** tel. 623 22 52.

Internet Access: Cybercafé, Nieuwendijk 19 (tel. 623 51 46). f3 per 20min. Open Su-Th 10am-1am, F-Sa 10am-2am. **Café ZoëZo,** Vijzelgracht 63 (tel. 330 67 67). f2.50 per 15min. Open Su-Th 11am-midnight, F-Sa 11am-1am.

Telephones: Call first and pay afterward at **Telehouse,** Raadhuisstr. 48-50, near the Dam (open 24hr.), or the **TeleTalk Center,** Leidsestr. 101, near the safer Leidsepl. (open daily 10am-midnight). Most public phones require prepaid phone cards, available at the tourist office, the post office, cigarette shops, and currency change offices. Coin phones can be found in hostels, hotels, and the post office.

Post Office: Singel 250-256 (tel. 556 33 11), at Raadhuisstr. behind the Dam. Address mail to be held: Jill <u>WEADER</u>, *Poste Restante,* Singel 250-256, Amsterdam **1016 AB,** The Netherlands. Open M-F 9am-6pm, Sa 10am-1:30pm.

PHONE CODE	City code: 020. From outside the Netherlands, dial int'l dialing prefix (see inside back cover) + 31 + 20 + local number.

◤ ACCOMMODATIONS AND CAMPING

Amsterdam is packed from mid-June to mid-September; reserve ahead. You can book (and pay for) spaces in **HI hostels** from any other HI hostel (free within the Netherlands, f4 elsewhere). Many other hostels do not accept dorm reservations; call ahead and plan to arrive between 9 and 10am in summer. The single-sex dorms at **Christian hostels** are safer, more sedate, and fairly cheap, but they also tend to have earlier curfews (midnight or 1am). **Private hostels** generally charge more, but they also tend to have later curfews (or none at all) and are more laid-back. You can assume that hostels have **no curfew** unless specified otherwise. Almost all places are about f2.50 cheaper in the off season. At the station and tourist office you'll be accosted by hawkers; many are from reputable hostels, but be cautious (ask to see a printed card with address and official prices). Carry your own luggage, and never pay before you look. If you arrive at night and can't find a room, consider staying in a neighboring city (Haarlem is only 15min. away by train).

Accommodations closer to the **station** often take good security measures. Hostels and hotels in **Vondelpark** and the **Jordaan** are quieter (by Amsterdam's standards) and safer. They're also near their share of bars and coffeeshops, are close to large museums and the busy Leidsepl., and are only 15min. by foot or 2min. by train from the red-light district and city center. When you tire of Amsterdam's intensity, consider staying in nearby **Edam** or **Volendam** (about 30min. away by bus) for a good dose of the Dutch countryside. VVV offices in every town will book accommodations and **private rooms** for around f40 including booking fee.

LEIDSEPLEIN AND MUSEUMPLEIN

HOSTELS

The Flying Pig Palace, Vossiusstr. 46-47 (tel. 400 41 87; fax 400 41 05; email palace@ flyingpig.nl). Take tram 1, 2, or 5 from the station to Leidsepl., cross the canal, turn left at the Marriott, pass the Vondelpark entrance, and take the next right. This clean, bright hostel maintains a fun atmosphere in a beautiful location. From f25. Breakfast included. Kitchen, bar. Key deposit f15. Free **internet.** Reception 8am-9pm.

NJHC City Hostel Vondelpark (HI), Zandpad 5 (tel. 589 89 99; email vondelpark@ njhc.org), bordering Vondelpark. Follow directions to the Pig above, but after the turn at the Marriott, take your 2nd right, before the park entrance. A slick stainless steel hostel with clean, spacious rooms with full baths. Dorms f38; singles f85; doubles f100; quads

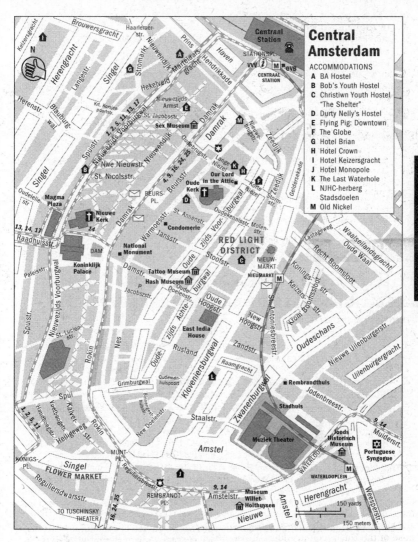

Central Amsterdam

ACCOMMODATIONS
A BA Hostel
B Bob's Youth Hostel
C Christiwn Youth Hostel "The Shelter"
D Durty Nelly's Hostel
E Flying Pig: Downtown
F The Globe
G Hotel Brian
H Hotel Crown
I Hotel Keizersgracht
J Hotel Monopole
K The Last Waterhole
L NJHC-herberg Stadsdoelen
M Old Nickel

NETHERLANDS

f158. Nonmembers add f5. Breakfast included. Lockers f3. Bike rental f10 per day. Maps f3.50. Reception 7am-midnight. Avoid the park after dark.

Hans Brinker, Kerkstr. 136 (tel. 622 06 87; fax 638 20 60; www.hansbrinker.com). Take tram 16 or 25 from the station, get off at Kerkstr., turn right, and it's 1 block down on the left. Clean, sparse, and comparatively safe, with a bar and disco (guests only). Dorms f41.50-49; singles f77-89; doubles f60-73; triples f186; quads f248. Add f2.50 for 1-night stay. Breakfast included. Key deposit f10. Reception 24hr.

International Budget Hotel, Leidsegracht 76 (tel. 624 27 84; fax 626 18 39; email ibh@budgethotel.a2000.nl). Take tram 1, 2, or 5 to Prinsengracht, head right down Prinsengracht, turn left on Leidsegracht, and it's on your right. Not the spiffiest hostel in the city, but well-located with a friendly staff and a TV lounge. Dorms f35-55; doubles f120-175. Breakfast f2.50-7. Min. 2-night stay in summer. Reception 9am-11pm.

HOTELS

The Arena, 's-Gravesandestr. 51-53 (tel. 694 74 44; fax 663 26 49; email info@hotelarena.nl). Take tram 9 from Centraal Station to "Tropenmuseum"; turn right on Mauritskade and then left on 's-Gravesandestr. (10min.). Or take tram 6, 7, or 10 from Leidsepl. Stylish rooms with fancy baths; DJs Th-Sa. Doubles f135, off-season f110; triples f190, f150; duplex quads f230, f175. Breakfast f15. Reception 24hr.

Hotel Museumzicht, Luykenstr. 22 (tel. 671 29 54; fax 671 35 97). Take tram 2 or 5 from the station to Hobbemastr. Beautiful little hotel in a quiet neighborhood with an unbelievable view of the nearby Rijksmuseum. Singles f60-80; doubles f125-165; triples f165. 10-15% cheaper off season. Breakfast included. Reception 8am-11pm.

Euphemia Budget Hotel, Fokke Simonszstr. 1-9 (tel./fax 622 90 45; email euphemia-hotel @budgethotel.a2000.nl), 10min. from Leidsepl. Take tram 16, 24, or 25 to Wetering Circuit, backtrack on Vijzelstr., cross the canal, and turn right on Fokke Simonszstr. Small, airy rooms, most with bath and TV. Singles f75-180; doubles f100-210; triples f105-255. Breakfast f8.50. Reception until 11pm. Discounts for email reservations.

Hotel Bema, Concertgebouw. 19b (tel. 679 13 96; fax 662 36 88; email postbus@hotel-bema.demon.nl), across from the Concertgebouw in a posh area. Take tram 16 from the station to Museumplein; it's a block up on the left. Singles f65-75; doubles f100-125; triples f135-150. Breakfast included. Reception 8am-midnight. No credit cards.

Casa Cara, Emmastr. 24 (tel. 662 31 35; fax 676 81 19; www.com-all.nl/hotels/casa-cara), 10min. beyond the Rijksmuseum. Take tram 2 or 16 from the station to Emmastr. Simple rooms in a quiet area. Singles f70-130; doubles f100-155; triples f155-180. Breakfast included in summer. Reception 7:30am-10:30pm. No drugs. Call ahead.

RED-LIGHT DISTRICT AND REMBRANDTSPLEIN

HOSTELS

Flying Pig: Downtown, Nieuwendijk 100 (tel. 420 68 22; fax 421 08 02; email downtown@flyingpig.nl), just off Damrak. Voted one of the most fun hostels in Europe, the Pig is what Amsterdam myths are made of. Lively bar with shoe-free smoking mats. 6- to 26-bed dorms f26.50-38.50; doubles f60; quads f41.50. f2 less in winter. Key and sheets deposit each f15. Reception 24hr. Free **internet.** Reserve at least a week ahead.

NJHC-Herberg Stadsdoelen (HI), Klovenniersburgwal 97 (tel. 624 68 32; fax 639 10 35), between Nieuwmarkt and Rembrandtspl. Take tram 4, 9, 16, 24, or 25 to Muntpl., walk down Amstel, cross the first bridge, and it's 1 block up on the right. Large dorms; a lively lounge, and a casual atmosphere. f28.75, off-season f24-26; nonmembers add f5. Breakfast included. Sheets f6.50. Locker deposit f25 or passport. Laundry f11. Kitchen. Bike rental f12.50. **Internet.** Reception 7am-12:30am. Flexible curfew 2am.

The Globe, Oudezijds Voorburgwal 3 (tel. 421 74 24; fax 421 74 23; email manager@the-globe.demon.nl). From the station, head toward Damrak, take the 2nd left on Nieuwezijds Brugsteeg and the 2nd right on Oudezijds Voorburgwal. The hostel is across the 1st bridge on your left. Lively pub (24hr. for guests) with live music F-Sa. Dorms f40, weekends f45; private rooms with bath f60-65 per person. English breakfast f7.50-15. Reception 24hr.

Christian Youth Hostel "The Shelter," Barndesteeg 21-25 (tel. 625 32 30), off the Nieuwmarkt (metro: Nieuwmarkt). Virtue amid the red lights. Cozy courtyard and religious slogans. Clean, airy single-sex dorms f25; off-season f20. Breakfast included. Key deposit f10. Lockers f1. Reception 7:30am-midnight. Curfew Su-Th midnight, F-Sa 1am.

The Last Waterhole, Oudezijds Armsteeg 12 (tel. 624 48 14; www.lastwaterhole.nl), 3min. from the station. It's a nonstop party in these brightly painted dorms above the bar. Live music. f30, weekends f35; in winter f25. Breakfast included. Reception 24hr.

Bob's Youth Hostel, Nieuwezijds Voorburgwal 92 (tel. 623 00 63; fax 675 64 46), near Centraal Station. No smoking in the rooms; you'll inhale enough on the stairs. Basic dorms and a chill atmosphere. Mattress on floor f20; dorms f26. Breakfast included. Key and locker deposit f25. Reception 8am-3am. No reservations or credit cards.

BA Hotel, Martelaarsgracht 18 (tel. 638 71 19; fax 638 88 03). From the station, cross the bridge to Damrak, take a right on Prins Henrikkade, and the first left on Martelaarsgracht. Well-located, with a friendly staff and bar. 8-12 bed dorms f25-45 depending on season. Breakfast and map included. Key deposit f25. Reception 8am-midnight.

Durty Nelly's Hostel, Warmoesstr. 115/117 (tel. 638 01 25; fax. 633 44 01; email nellys@xs4all.nl). From the station, walk 2 blocks left of the Damrak. Small hostel above an Irish pub in the middle of the red-light district. f25-35. Breakfast included. Padlock deposit f15. Reception 24hr. No reservations—arrive as close to 9am as possible.

HOTELS

Hotel Brian, Singel 69 (tel. 624 46 61; fax 416 47 85). Small rooms in a very friendly and comfortable atmosphere. On a quiet block only minutes from the center. 2-4 bed rooms Apr.-Aug. f40; Sept. f35; Oct.-Mar. f25. Breakfast included—with eggs cooked to order. TV lounge. Key deposit f25. Reception 24hr. No credit cards.

Hotel Monopole, Amstel 60 (tel. 624 62 71; fax 624 58 97; email arad@monopole.demon.nl). Gay-friendly hotel near Rembrandtspl. Spacious rooms. Singles f75; doubles f135-165, off-season f110-135; triples f185-195; larger rooms with bath f50 per person. Breakfast included. Key deposit f10. Reception 24hr.

Hotel Hortus, Plantage Parklaan 8 (tel. 625 99 96; fax 416 47 85). From the station, take tram 9 to Artis, backtrack on Plantage Middenlaan, and go left on Parklaan. Same manager as Brian. f45. Breakfast included. Key deposit. **Internet.** Reception 7:30am-11pm.

Hotel Crown, Oudezijds Voorburgwal 21 (tel. 626 96 64; fax 420 64 73; www.web2day.com). Simple, clean accommodations in the red-light district. Dorm f45; singles f80; doubles f60-70; quads f55. Off-season f10-20 less.

Old Nickel, Nieuwebrugsteeg 11 (tel. 624 19 12; fax 620 76 83). Quiet hotel in a central location just a block from the station. Singles f65; doubles f90-125; quads f160-200. Breakfast included. Reception 8am-midnight. No credit cards.

Hotel Keizersgracht, Keizersgracht 15-17 (tel. 625 13 64; fax 620 73 47). From the station, head right on Prins Hendrikkade, across and left along the Singel canal, right on Brouwersgracht, and left on Keizersgracht. Singles f90; doubles f100-134; triples f143-165; quads f180-192. Breakfast f12.50. Reception 7am-11pm. Curfew 3am.

THE JORDAAN

The Shelter: Jordaan, Bloemstr. 179 (tel. 624 47 17; fax 627 61 37; email jordaan@shelter.nl), 1 street from Rozengracht in the Jordaan (tram 13 or 17: Marnixstr.). A cheap and well-located Christian hostel. Huge single-sex dorms. f28. Few showers. Breakfast included. Age limit 15-35. Reception 7:30am-1am. Curfew 1am.

Hotel van Onna, Bloemgracht 104 (tel. 626 58 01). Take tram 13 or 17 from the station. Charming hotel, with airy rooms and immaculate bathrooms. Beautiful neighborhood. f80 per person. Breakfast included. Reception 8am-11pm. No credit cards.

Hotel Arrivé, Haarlemmerstr. 65 (tel. 622 14 39; fax 622 19 83). Head right on Prins Hendrikkade from the station, left on Buitstr., and right on Haarlemmerstr. Clean rooms with TV. Singles f80; doubles f100-120; triples 150-180; quads f200. 20-30% less in off season. Breakfast included. Reception 24hr.

CAMPING

Camping Zeeburg, Zuider-ljdijk 20 (tel. 694 44 30), next to the Amsterdam Rijncanal. Take bus 22, tram 14, or night bus 79 (15min.) and walk 3min. Backpacker-oriented. Live music regularly. f7.50 per person, f5 per tent. Showers f1.50. Reception July 8am-11pm; Apr.-June and Aug.-Mar. 9-11am and 5-9pm.

Gaaspercamping, Loosdrechtdreef 7 (tel. 696 73 26; fax 696 93 69), in Gaasper Park. Take the metro (dir: Gaasperplas) to the end; or night bus 75. f6.75 per person, f15 per tent. Showers f1.50. Laundry f13. Reception 9am-9pm. Open mid-Mar. to Dec.

⬛ FOOD

Dutch food ranges from the hopelessly bland to the oddly tasty. Dutch *pannenkoeken* (pancakes), best described as thick, unrolled crêpes, are prepared as both main courses and sweet desserts and are the most savory of Dutch cuisine. Fast fried food abounds—*Frikandel* (fried sausage) usually costs as little as f1.50, and a heaping portion of french fries at a *friteur* costs f2.50-3. **FEBO** is a reasonably priced self-service fast food chain, but the best fries are at the abundant **Vlaamse**

frites stalls. If you're feeling adventurous, stop by a fish stall in summer to try herring—raw, salted, with a squeeze of lemon, and best when swallowed whole in one mouthful. Sample Surinamese, Indonesian, Chinese, and Indian food in the red-light district around the Nieuwmarkt and off the Dam, on streets such as **Hartenstr.** Many cheap restaurants cluster around **Leidsepl., Rembrandtspl.,** and **Spui.** *Eetcafés,* especially in the Jordaan, serve cheap sandwiches (f4-9) and good meat-and-potatoes fare for f12-20. Bakeries selling inexpensive cheese croissants and magnificent breads line **Utrechtsestr.,** south of Prinsengracht.

Fruit, cheese, flowers, and sometimes even live chickens populate the **markets** on **Albert Cuypstr.,** behind the Heineken brewery. (Open M-Sa 10am-4:30pm.) The cheapest **groceries** are found at **Aldi Supermarket,** Nieuwe Weteringstr., off of Vijzelgracht, near the Heineken brewery. (Open M 11am-6pm, Tu-F 9am-6pm, Sa 8:30am-4pm.) **Albert Heijns** branches are centrally located at Koningspl. and 226 Nieuwezijds Voorburwal, besides the Magna Plaza. (Open M-Sa 8am-10pm, Su 11am-7pm.)

LEIDSEPLEIN, THE MUSEUM DISTRICT, AND THE JORDAAN

Bolhoed, 60-62 Prinsengracht, across the canal from the Anne Frank Huis. Café with delicious veggie food. Rolls f6.50. Salads and quiche f12-19. Open daily noon-10pm.

Brasserie van Gogh, Hooftstr. 28, at the corner of Hobbemastr. A large menu and a sunflower-inspired decor. Salads f18.50-22.50. Baguettes f8.50-11.50. Lasagna f18.50.

Gary's Muffins, Prinsengracht 454. Small café bakes homemade muffins (f2.50), cookies, brownies, and great bagel sandwiches (f4.25-6.75). Open M-Sa 8:30am-6pm, Su 9am-6pm. Late-night location at Reguliersdwarsstr. 53. Open until 3am, F-Sa until 4am.

Esoterica, Overtoom 409. Incredible homemade vegetarian food by the Vondelpark. Snacks and salads f4-9, meals f15-17. Open W-Su 2-10pm.

Bojo, 51 Lange Leidsedwar. Delicious, heaping Indonesian food at reasonable prices. Meals f13-21. Open M-Th 4pm-2am, F 4pm-4am, Sa noon-4am, Su noon-2am.

Lunchcafé Nielsen, Berenstr. 29, in the Jordaan. Gourmet sandwiches (f6.50-7.50) and salads (f14). Veggie options. Open Tu-Sa 8:30am-5pm, Su 9:30am-5pm.

Dionysos, Overtoom 176 (tel. 689 44 41). From Leidsepl., walk right on the Stadhouderskade and Overtoom is on the left. Tasty Greek dishes served daily from 5pm-midnight.

Café ZoëZo, Vijzelsgracht 63 (tel. 330 67 67). A small, bright **internet** café (f2.50 per 15min.). Sandwiches f6.50-12.50. Open Su-Th 11am-midnight, F-Sa 11am-1am.

New Deli, Harlemmerstr. 73 (tel. 626 27 55). See directions to Hotel Arrivé. Salads (f6-15) and sandwiches (f5.25-15) in a slick, minimalist café. Open daily 10am-10pm.

Café 't Hoekje, Frans Hals Str. From the Rijksmuseum, head down Hobbemakade and turn left on Eerst Jacob Can Campen Str. Chill here with the locals on your way from the museum to the Heineken brewery. Sandwiches f4-8. Open daily 10am-10pm.

Paviljoen de Carrousel, Weteringschans. Feast on scrumptious pancakes (f7.50-14.50) after your Heineken tour. Open daily 10am-10pm.

RED-LIGHT DISTRICT AND REMBRANDTSPLEIN

Café de Jaren, Nieuwe Doelenstr. 20-22. Borrow a magazine/newspaper and chill. Gourmet meals f12-32. Open Su-Th 10am-1am, F-Sa 10am-2am; kitchen closes 10:30pm.

Pannenkoekenhuis Upstairs, Grimburgwal 2. A tiny nook with perhaps the best pancakes in the city. Pancakes f7.50-17.50. Open M-F noon-7pm, Sa noon-6pm, Su noon-5pm.

Café Restaurant Turquoise, Wolvenstr. 30. Turkish cuisine in a classy atmosphere at unbeatable prices. Most meals f19-26. Huge menu with a few vegetarian options.

Thai Pohchana, Haarlemmerstr. 83. Each dish is prepared with exquisite care. Most meals f13-20. Open daily 1-11pm.

Sukabumi, Geelvincksteeg 2, on Singel canal. Get an outdoor table at this tiny Indonesian restaurant/market. Lunch specials f9-14; dinner f18.50. Open daily noon-11pm.

Kam Yin, Warmoesstr. 6. This Chinese/Surinamese landmark has a huge menu of cheap dishes. Meals f8-16. Open daily noon-midnight.

La Place, on Rokin near Muntpl., and at Vroom Dreesman, Kalverstr. 201. Buffet-style restaurant with piles of veggies and fresh meat. Meals around f10. Open M 11am-8pm, Tu-W 9:30am-8pm, Th 9:30am-9pm, F-Sa 9:30am-6pm, Su noon-6pm.

Cybercafé, Nieuwendijk 19. Munch on sandwiches (f5-10) and sip coffee as you log on. **Internet** f3 per 20min. Happy Hour 7-8pm. Open M-Th 10am-1am, F-Sa 10am-2am.

Keuhen Van 1870, Spuistr. 4. Serves traditional Dutch food at the cheapest prices around. Open M-F noon-8pm, Sa-Su 4-9pm.

📷 SIGHTS

Amsterdam is fairly compact, so tourists can easily explore its range of offerings, from the Rijksmuseum to the red-light district, on foot. **Circle Tram 20,** geared toward tourists, stops at 30 attractions throughout the city (runs every 10min. 9am-6pm, one-day pass f10; buy on the tram or at VVV offices). The more peaceful **Museumboot Canal Cruise** allows you to hop on and hop off along their loop from the VVV to the Anne Frank Huis, the Rijksmuseum, the Bloemenmarkt, Waterlooplein, and the old shipyard—buy tickets at any stop (departs every 30min. 10am-5pm, f25; also yields 10-50% off at all museums). Rent a **canal bike** to power your own way through the canals (2 people f19.50 per hr., 4 people f29.50, f50 deposit; same pick-up and drop-off points as the Museumboot). **Mike's Bike Tours** provide an entertaining introduction to the city's sites and the surrounding countryside (daily mid-May to Aug. 11:30am and 4pm; mid-Apr. to mid-May and Sept.-Oct. 12:30pm; f37; meet at the entrance of the Rijksmuseum). The economical **Museumkaart** grants year-long discounts or admission to museums and transportation throughout the Netherlands (f55, under 25 f25; buy at the VVV). The **Amsterdam Leisure Pass** includes a canal trip and admission to the Rijksmuseum, the Stedelijk Museum, and the Amsterdam Historical Museum (f39.50; buy at the VVV).

MUSEUM DISTRICT

RIJKSMUSEUM (NATIONAL MUSEUM). If you've made it to Amsterdam, it would be sinful to leave without seeing the Rijksmuseum's impressive collection of works by Rembrandt, Vermeer, Frans Hals, and Jan Steen. With thousands of Dutch Old Master paintings, it can be an overwhelming place—a good approach is to follow the crowds to Rembrandt's famed militia portrait **The Night Watch,** in the Gallery of Honor, and then proceed into Aria, the interactive computer room. Aria, which provides interesting historical info on specific works, can create a personalized map of the museum to help you navigate through its enormous collection. *(On Stadhouderskade. Tel. 673 21 21. Take tram 2 or 5 from the station. Open daily 10am-5pm. f15.)*

VAN GOGH AND STEDELIJK MUSEUMS. The newly renovated **Van Gogh Museum** houses the largest collection of van Goghs in the world (mostly from his family's private collection) and a varied group of 19th-century paintings by artists who influenced or were contemporaries of the master. Pick up the audio tour to learn about the artist, whose name, you will learn, was actually pronounced "Van Choch" rather than "Van Go." *(Paulus Potterstr. 2. Take tram 2 or 5 from the station. Or, from the Rijksmuseum, walk a block down Museumstr. Tel. 570 52 52. Open daily 10am-6pm. f12.50. Audio tour f8.50.)* The **Stedelijk Museum of Modern Art** showcases an outstanding collection of modern and contemporary paintings, pottery and photography. *(Paulus Potterstr. 13, next to the Van Gogh Museum. Tel. 573 27 37. Open daily 11am-5pm. f9.)*

HEINEKEN BREWERY. This former brewery is scheduled to reopen after renovations in the spring of 2000. The new and improved museum will explain the history of Heineken and the process of beer production. Admission gets you free beer, *and* the money goes to charity—so drink up. *(Stadhouderskade 78, off Ferdinand Bolstr. and just down Stadhouderskade from the Rijksmuseum. Tel. 523 96 06. Call for opening hours. f2.)*

REMBRANDTSPLEIN AND ENVIRONS

TUSCHINSKI THEATER. This fabulously ornate movie theater is one of Europe's first experiments in Art Deco. Although a group of drunk Nazis once got out of hand and started a fire in its cabaret, the theater miraculously survived WWII and has remained in operation for over 75 years. Guided tours lead through the nooks and crannies of the theater and provide interesting information about the history of the theater and its incredible design. A ticket to a screening of one of their Hollywood features allows you to explore on your own; theater 1 is the mainstage and has private boxes. *(Reguliersbreesstr., between Rembrandtspl. and Muntpl. Tours in summer Su-M 10:30am; f10. Performances f14-38.)*

JOODS-PORTUGUESE SYNAGOGUE AND JOODS HISTORISCH MUSEUM. Having been expelled from their country in the 15th century, a sizable number of Spanish and Portuguese Jews established a community in Amsterdam and in 1675 built the large, handsome **Joods-Portuguese Synagogue.** The Dutch government protected the building from the Nazis' torches by declaring it a national historic site. Across the street, the **Joods Historisch Museum (Jewish Historical Museum),** housed in three connected former synagogues, traces the history of the Dutch Jewish community. *(Jonas Daniel Meijerpl., at Waterloopl. Take tram 9 or 14. Synagogue open daily 10am-4pm; f7.50. Museum open daily 11am-5pm; f8, students f4.)*

VERZETSMUSEUM (DUTCH RESISTANCE MUSEUM). Housed in a brand-new building, this museum chronicles the experiences of Dutch Jews, Catholics, and Communists at the time of the Nazi invasion and the struggles and strategies of the Dutch Resistance Movement. *(Plantage Kerklaan 61. Take tram 7, 9, or 14 to "Artis." Or, from the Synagogue, walk down Muiderstr., which turns into Plantage Middenlaan, and turn right on Plantage Kerklaan. Tel. 620 25 35. Open Tu-F 10am-5pm, Sa-Su noon-5pm. f8, students f4.)*

TROPENMUSEUM (MUSEUM OF THE TROPICS). Thanks to the Dutch East India company, this multimedia presentation of artifacts from Asia, Africa, and Latin America has especially fine Indonesian art and an engaging children's wing. It also hosts frequent film, food, and music festivals. *(Linnaeusstr. 2. Take tram 9 to "Artis," east of Waterloopl. Tel. 568 82 15. Open M-F 10am-5pm, Sa-Su noon-5pm. f12.50, students f7.50.)*

REMBRANDTHUIS. Recently restored in 17th-century fashion, the Rembrandthuis was where the master lived, worked, and taught until the city confiscated the house for taxes. It holds 250 of Rembrandt's etchings and dry points, as well as many of his tools and plates. *(Jodenbreestr. 4-6, at the corner of the Oudeschans Canal. Take tram 9 or 14. Open M-Sa 10am-5pm, Su 1-5pm. f17.50.)*

MUSEUM WILLET-HOLTHUYSEN. Catch a glimpse of what life was like for the Dutch upper crust in this 17th-century canal house, richly decorated in 19th-century furnishings and with a peaceful, pristine garden. *(Herengracht 605, between Reguliersgracht and Vijzelstr., 3min. from Rembrandtspl. Open M-F 10am-5pm, Sa-Su 11am-5pm. f7.50. Borrow an English-language guide from the cashier.)*

RED-LIGHT DISTRICT

The red-light district, bounded by Warmoestr., Gelderskade, and Oude Doelenstr., is the vice sink of Europe; it will either repulse or excite you. Pushers, porn shops, and live sex theaters do a brisk business, though in many ways you may find it less outrageous, twisted, and seedy than you might have expected. **Sex shows** (f10-50) consist of costumed, disaffected couples repeatedly acting out your "wildest" (i.e., choreographed) dreams. Red neon marks houses of legalized ill repute, where sex workers display themselves in windows. During the day, the red-light district is comparatively flaccid, with tourists milling about and consulting their maps. As the sun goes down, the people get braver, and the area much more stimulating (or disgusting, depending on your viewpoint). Cops from the police station on Warmoestr patrol the district until midnight. Women may feel uncomfortable walking through this area, and all tourists are prime targets for pickpockets.

OUR LORD IN THE ATTIC. A secret enclave of virtue and piety hides in a 17th-century house, today known as the **Museum Amstelkring, Ons' Lieve Heer op Solder** ("Our Lord in the Attic"), where a Catholic priest, forbidden to practice his faith in public during the Reformation, established a surprisingly grand chapel in the attic. *(Oudezijds Voorburgwal 40, at the corner of Oudez. Armstr., 5min. from the station. Open M-Sa 10am-5pm, Su 1-5pm. f7.50, students f6.)*

THE VICES. For a historical, chemical, and agricultural breakdown of all the wacky tobacky you've been smelling all over town, drop by the small, informative **Hash Marijuana Hemp Museum.** The museum is not all that exciting, but a certain thrill remains in going to a museum devoted to the celebration of soft drugs. *(Open in summer daily 11am-10pm; off-season Su-W 11am-6pm, Th-Sa 11am-10pm. f8. Seeds f25-275.)* **The Tattoo Museum**—the name says it all—displays designs, rituals, and tattoo-making tools from all over the world, plus a 2000-year-old mummified and tattooed arm found in Peru. *(Oudezijds Achterburgwal 130, next to the Hash Marijuana Hemp Museum. Open Tu-Su noon-5pm. f5.)* See sex in every way you dreamed possible (and many you didn't) at the semi-tacky **Amsterdam Sex Museum,** which showcases an "only in Amsterdam" collection of erotic art and hardcore porn through the ages. *(Damrak 18, near the station. Open daily 10am-11:30pm. f6; under 17 not admitted.)*

OTHER SIGHTS. The area in and around the red-light district (the oldest part of the city) contains some of Amsterdam's most interesting buildings. Amsterdam's former town hall, **Koninklijk Palace,** may be a symbol of 17th-century commercialism, but its majesty is topped by the stunning **Magna Plaza mall** next door, the 20th-century's monument to commercialism. *(Open Su-M 11am-7pm, Tu-Sa 9:30am-7pm.)*

THE JORDAAN

When you're through with the museums, lose the hordes in the narrow streets of the **Jordaan,** built as an artisan district in the Golden Age. Bounded roughly by Prinsengracht, Brouwersgracht, Marnixstr., and Lauriersgracht, and teeming with small cafés, antique shops, and vine-laden buildings, the area is possibly the prettiest and most peaceful in the city. You can also take refuge from Amsterdam's mobbed sights and seamy streets in **Begijnhof,** a beautifully maintained grassy courtyard surrounded by 18th-century buildings that runs between Kalverstr. and the Spui. *(Open daily 10am-5pm. Free.)* For a bigger dose of nature and better people-watching, relax in the sprawling **Vondelpark.**

ANNE FRANK HUIS. The tiny space where the young journal-keeper hid with her family from the Nazis until their capture in 1944 now has video interviews with Otto Frank, Anne's father, and Miep Gies, the woman who hid with the Franks and four other Jews. A multimedia exhibit provides extensive information about the Franks and their life in the Annex, and relates the Holocaust to current human rights issues. *(Prinsengracht 263, next to the Westerkerk. Take tram 13, 14, or 17. Tel. 556 71 00. Open daily Apr.-Sept. 9am-9pm; Oct.-Mar. 9am-5pm. f10.)* While you're there, check out the **Homomonument,** in front of the Westerkerk at the banks of the canal, a memorial to those persecuted through history for their sexual orientation.

ELSEWHERE IN AMSTERDAM

GRAFFITI ART. Some of the most exciting art in Amsterdam is free—painted on doors, walls, and trams. The **Vrankrijk** building, Spuistr. 216, and the area around **Mr. Visserplein,** near Waterloopl. and the Hortus Botannicus, give evidence that graffiti is more than names and vulgar phrases. Continue the psychedelic survey at the **3D Hologram Store.** *(Grimburgwal 2. Open Su-M 1-5:30pm, Tu-F noon-6pm, Sa noon-5:30pm.)*

MARKETS. An open-air art market takes place every Sunday in the **Spui,** where local and international artists regularly present their oils, etchings, sculptures, and jewelry, and where a book market occasionally yields rare editions and 17th-century Dutch romances. *(Art market open Mar.-Dec. daily 10am-6pm. Book market open F 10am-6pm.)* Pick up ancient stamps at the **Poszegelmarkt** on **Nieuwezijds Voorburgwal** or bulbs you crave at the **Bloemenmarkt** (flower market). *(On the Singel canal, by Muntplein. Poszegelmarkt open W and Sa 1-4pm. Bloemenmarkt open M-Sa 9:30am-5pm.)* Mill with the masses at the famous flea market on **Waterlooplein,** where you can try your hand at bargaining for antiques, birds, or farm tools. *(Open M-Sa 9am-5pm.)*

NETHERLANDS

🎭 ENTERTAINMENT

Pick up the monthly *What's On* (f4) from the VVV for comprehensive cultural listings. The mini-magazine *Boom!*, free at restaurants and cafés around the city, is chock full of tourist info; also try the free monthly *UITKRANT*. The **Amsterdams Uit Buro** (AUB), Leidsepl. 26, has fliers and other info and makes reservations for any cultural event. (Tel. 621 12 11. Open daily 10am-6pm.) Also check the online www.aub.nl for "Culture in Amsterdam." The monthly *Culture and Camp* (f5) provides info on gay venues and events. The fortnightly *Queer Fish* (f2.50) catalogues less mainstream concerts and parties.

CONCERTS

In the summer, there are free performances Wednesday through Sunday at the **Vondelpark Openluchttheater** (tel. 673 14 99). Jazz and folk concerts dominate, but children's theater, rock bands, political music, and mime also grab the limelight; check posters at park entrances. The **Royal Concertgebouw Orchestra** at the Concertgebouw on Van Baerlerstr. is one of the world's finest. (Tickets from f35; student discounts around 50%. Tel. 671 83 45. Box office around the back of the building open daily 10am-7pm.) Organ concerts resound on summer Wednesdays at 8:15pm at **Westerkerk,** Prinsengracht 281, where Rembrandt is buried. Concerts also happen at **Nieuwe Kerk,** on the Dam (f5-12.50).

FILM AND THEATER

Check out the free *De Week Agenda* for movie listings. When you're in the Vondelpark, see what's on at **The Vertigo** movie theater and café. Frequent English-language performances and cabarets are given at the theater/café **Suikerhof,** Prinsengracht 381. (Tel. 22 75 71. Open M-Sa from 5pm, Su from 2pm.) Make reservations for any cultural event at the **AUB** (see p. 666) or at the VVV's theater desk, Stationspl. 10 (open M-Sa 10am-5pm). There's no escaping **Boom Chicago,** Leidepl. 12, an American comedy troupe based in the Leidseplein theater that publishes the *Boom!* and performs improv sketches. (Tel. 431 01 01. Tickets Su-Th f27.50, F-Sa f29.50; Su-F f5 off with *Boom!* Performances Su-F at 8:15pm, doors open at 6pm; F also 11:30pm. Box office open daily 10am-6pm.) The **Muziektheater,** perched over the junction of the Amstel and the Oude Schans (tel. 625 54 55), hosts the **Netherlands Opera** and the **National Ballet.**

FESTIVALS

The **Queen's Day** (April 30) turns the city into a huge carnival. On the same day is the year's largest flea market, when parrots, skulls, and glue sticks are bought and sold. The **Holland Festival** in June, with dance, drama, and music, is closely followed by the **Summer Festival** of small theater companies in July. (Tickets f10-15. Call the Balie Theatre at 623 29 04 for info.) On the first weekend in August, gay pride comes out in street parties along Warmoesstr., Amstel, Kerkstr., and Reguliersdwarsstr., and in the outrageously fun **Gay Pride Parade** (tel. 625 83 75). During **Uitmarket** weekend at the end of August, street theater, hundreds of free concerts around the Dam Square, and a book market along the Nieuwezijds Voorburgwal transform the streets of Amsterdam into a brilliant and raucous party.

COFFEESHOPS AND SMART SHOPS

Yes, the rumors are true: marijuana and hashish are legal in the Netherlands. Since soft drugs were officially decriminalized in 1996 and Mayor Patijn issued the first **coffeeshop** license, "coffeeshop" is no longer a euphemism for semi-shady spots dealing quasi-legal drugs. Coffeeshops still don't just sell coffee (unless one counts the green, leafy "mother's milk" and "super skunk" varieties) but now, like bars, come in a variety of styles and offer a range of atmospheres. Any place calling itself a coffeeshop sells pot or hash or will let you buy a drink and smoke your own stuff. You can legally possess up to 5g of marijuana or hash (the previous 30g limit was reduced in response to foreign criticism). Also legal are **smart shops,** which peddle a variety of **"herbal enhancers"** and **hallucinogens** that walk the line between soft and hard drugs. Some shops are alcohol-free and all have a strict no-hard-drugs policy. All **hard drugs** are illegal and possession is treated as a serious crime. For info on the legal ins and outs, call the **Jellinek clinic** at 570 23 55.

Hash comes in two varieties, black (like Afghani and Nepali; f10-24 per gram) and blonde (like Moroccan); black tends to be heavier and hits harder. Although Amsterdam is known as the hash capital of the world, **marijuana** is increasingly popular. The Dutch tend to mix tobacco with their pot, so joints are harsher on your lungs. Dutch marijuana is the most common and costs f12-15 per gram, f25-30 for a bag. The smaller the quantity, the smoother and more potent. Staffs at coffeeshops are used to explaining the different kinds of pot on the menu to tourists. Most places will supply rolling papers and filter tips. Almost no one smokes out of pipes, and while some places provide glass bongs, usually only tourists use them; similarly, though smoking in the streets is legal, only tourists do it. **Never buy drugs from street dealers.** Don't get too caught up in Amsterdam's narcotic quirk; use common sense, and remember that any experimentation with drugs can be dangerous. Two ubiquitous coffeeshop chains somewhat geared toward tourists are **The Grasshopper** (one is at Nieuwezijds Voorburgwal 57) and **The Bulldog** (Oudezijds Voorburgwal 90 and on Leidsepl.)—but plenty of other options await if you seek to branch out beyond this sports-bar culture. The farther you travel from the touristed spots, the better and cheaper the establishments. Pick up a free copy of the *BCD Official Coffeeshop Guide* for the pot-smoker's map of Amsterdam.

Homegrown Fantasy, Nieuwezijds Voorburgwal 87a. Bright, chill atmosphere with big windows, abstract art, and an amazing bathroom (whether on drugs or not). Free cookies. Bags f10-25, rolled joints f5, pure cannabis joints f7.50. Open daily 11am-11pm.

De Rokerij, Amstelstr. 8, in the Muntplein. A dark, untouristed coffeeshop with wrought-iron candlesticks and a blue-and-gold-painted Neoclassical ceiling and walls. Open daily noon-11pm. Also at Lange Leidsestr. 41 and Martelaasgracht 24.

Dutch Flowers, Singel 387, near the Spui. Huge menu. Winner of the coveted "Highlife" cup. Outside seating on the canal. Open M-F 10am-1am, Sa-Su 10am-2am.

The Greenhouse Effect, Warmoesstr. 53. Lime green walls and a relaxed atmosphere. Friendly, knowledgeable staff. Open M-Th 9am-1am, F-Sa 9am-3am, Su 10am-1am.

The Noon, Zieseniskade 22, 10min. from Leidsepl. Owned by Americans, this small shop with Native American decorations is one of the few to sell cannabis-only joints (f8.50). Ask the owners how they got their US flag. Open daily 11am-10pm.

Barney's Coffeeshop, Haarlemmerstr. 102. Friendly staff and amazing food. Huge breakfast options served all day and lots of veggie fare (f9-17.50). Open daily 8am-7:30pm.

La Tertulia, Prinsengracht 312. Defies any coffeeshop preconceptions: Spanish music and flowers surround an indoor waterfall. Rolled joints f5. Open Tu-Sa 11am-7pm.

The Other Side, Reguliersdwarsstr. 6 (open daily 11am-1am), and **Downtown,** Reguliersdwarsstr. 31 (open daily 10am-8pm). Small, hip coffeeshops popular with gay men.

Global Chillage, Kerkstr. 51. Trance music provides a chilled alternative to the Hendrix and Marley excess at the other coffeeshops. Open M-Sa noon-11pm.

◪ NIGHTLIFE

CAFÉS AND BARS

Amsterdam's finest cafés are the old, dark, wood-paneled *bruine kroegen* (brown cafés) of the **Jordaan,** many of which have outdoor seating lining the canal on **Prinsengracht. Leidseplein** is the liveliest nightspot, with loud coffeeshops, loud bars, and tacky clubs galore. **Rembrandtsplein** is the place to watch soccer and sing with drunk revelers. Gay bars line **Reguliersdwarsstr.,** which connects Muntpl. and Rembrandtspl., and **Kerkstr.,** five blocks north of Leidsepl. Most cafés open at 10 or 11am and close at 1am during the week and 2 to 3am on Fridays and Saturdays.

Café 't Smalle, at the corner of Prinsengracht and Egelandiersgracht. Tiny bar with intimate dark wood interior and stained-glass windows. Open Su-Th noon-1am, F-Sa noon-3am.

Café de Tuin, Tweede Tuindwarsstr. 13 (open M-Th 10am-1am, F-Sa 10am-2am, Su 11am-1am), and **Café Sas,** Marnixstr. 79 (open Su-Th noon-1am, F-Sa noon-2am), both attract a young, artsy set. Café Sas often has live music on weekends.

Grand Café Dulac, Haarlemserstr. 118. A fantastic mix of cherubs, flowers, and animal prints on the wall gives this big café the feel of a hole-in-the-wall antique junk store. Pool table and a small garden in the back. Open daily 4pm-1am or 2am.

Vrankrijk, Spuistr. 216. Revolutionary slogans, Marxist literature, punks, and cheap beer converge at an unmarked bar. First M of the month women only. Last M of the month gay night. Open Su-F 10pm-2am, Sa 11pm-3:30am.

The Sound Garden, Marnixstr. 164. Grunge café near the Christian Youth Hostel where you can recharge on angst before entering happyland. Pool table and seats out back on the canal. Open Su-Th 1pm-1am, F-Sa 3pm-3am.

Absinthe, Nieuwezijds Voorburgwal 157. Looks and feels more like a chill mini-club than typical Dutch bar. Shots of its namesake f7.50. Open Su-Th 10pm-3am, F-Sa 10pm-4am.

Saarein, Elandstr. 119. A (gay and straight) women-only bar in the Jordaan. Pool and pin-ball downstairs; books and women's magazines upstairs. Open M 8pm-1am, Tu-Th and Su 3pm-1am, F-Sa 3pm-2am.

Havana, Reguliersdwarsstr. 17-19. Glam it up in plush red velvet booths in this popular gay bar. DJs upstairs on weekends. Open Su-Th 4pm-1am, F-Sa 4pm-2am.

De Prins, Prinsengracht 124. A very lively student bar in the Jordaan. Bathed in old, dark wood—no frills, but cool. Open 11am-1am, F-Sa until 2am.

Vive La Vie, Amstelstr. 7, at the corner of Rembrandtsplein. Amsterdam's only lesbian bar is small but lively. Open Su-Th 3pm-1am, F-Sa 3pm-3am.

LIVE MUSIC

Though large clubs occasionally feature world-famous mainstream groups, the soul of the music scene lies in the wide range of music at dozens of smaller cafés and bars. The **Jazzlijn** (tel. 626 77 64) provides info on local concerts. The **AUB** (see p. 666) has the "Pop & Jazz Uitlijst" and fliers for other free concerts. Many clubs will expect you to buy an overpriced drink instead of charging a cover.

Melkweg, Lijnbaansgracht 234a (tel. 624 17 77), in a warehouse off Leidsepl. Legendary nightspot has a cutting-edge aura even with crowds. Live bands, theater, films, dance shows, and an art gallery (free W-Su 2-8pm) make for sensory overload. "Tearoom" sells leaves of choice. Bar cover about f6 plus f4 monthly fee. Club nights usually Sa 1-5am (cover f10-15). Box office open M-F 1-5pm, Sa-Su 4-6pm, and until 7:30 on showdays.

Paradiso, Weteringschans 6-8 (tel. 626 45 21; www.paradiso.nl). Some of the foremost punk, new-wave, and reggae bands play in this former church. DJs often follow concerts. Cover f10-27. Shows daily 10pm. Buy tickets in advance from AUB (see above).

Alto, Korte Leidsedwarsstr. 115. A touch of class in the Leidsepl. Live jazz and blues every night. No cover. Open Su-Th 9pm-3am, F-Sa 9pm-4am.

Bourbon Sheets Jazz & Blues Café, Leidsekruisstr. 6. Blues, jazz, or funk bands rock this crowded bar every night. Red curtains, chandeliers, and a New Orleans street gaslight keep it real. Cover around f5. Open Su-Th 10pm-4am, F-Sa 10pm-5am.

De Kroeg, Lijnbaansgracht 163. Vibrant crowds writhe to reggae, salsa, rock, and blues. Cover f5 on live music nights, f2.50 on DJ Fridays, periodic jam sessions (M and W) free. Open Su-Th 8pm-3am, F-Sa until 4am (music starts at 10pm).

The Bimhuis, Oude Schans 73-77 (www.xs4all.nl/~bimhuis), near Waterloopl. The hub of Dutch jazz. More than 200 concerts held every year. Cover around f10, students f7.50. Su-Tu free jam sessions. W-Sa concerts after 9pm.

Winston Kingdom, Warmoesstr. 127 (cover f5-10; open Su-W 8pm-2am, Th-Sa until 3am) and **The Last Waterhole,** Oudezijds Armsteeg 12 (open Su-Th until 2am, F-Sa until 4am), both in the red-light district, offer nightly live music from acid rock to disco.

CLUBS AND DISCOS

Many clubs charge a membership fee in addition to normal cover, so the tab can be obscene. Be prepared for cocky doormen who live to turn away tourists; show up early or hope the bouncer thinks you're cute. If you're really desperate, a f10-20 tip may help them overlook your imperfections. There are pricey discos aplenty on **Prinsengracht,** near **Leidsestr.,** and on **Lange Leidsedwarsstr.** Gay discos line **Amstelstr.** and **Reguliersdwarsstr.** and cater almost exclusively to men. A lesbian club called **You II,** was scheduled to open in Rembrandtsplein in late '99. Pick up a wallet-sized *Club* guide, free at cafés and coffeeshops, for a club map of the city, and *Gay and Night,* a free monthly magazine, for info on the tons of gay parties.

Time, Nieuwezijds Voorburgwal 153-55. Blue lights, textured walls, and sharks hanging from the ceilings. Chill, funky crowds. Cover f10-15. Open almost every day 10pm-4am.

MAZZO, Rozengracht 114, in the Jordaan. Artsy disco with red Victorian couches and lampshades. Constantly revolving DJs, music styles, display, and slideshow. Cover Su-Th f10, F f12.50, Sa f15. Open Su-Th 11pm-4am, F-Sa 11pm-5am.

Exit, Reguliersdwarsstr. 42 (open Th-Su 11pm-4am), and **Ministry,** Reguliersdwarsstr. 12 (open W-Su 11pm-4am). The most popular gay discos. Mostly men. Cover around f15.

The Arena, Gravesandestr. 51-53 (see p. 660). Former chapel throws fab parties. Take night bus 7. 80s, 90s dance F from 11pm; f12.50. 60s, 70s dance Sa from 10pm; f15.

Odeon, Singel 460, near Leidsestr. Men in sharp suits and women in heels come here to groove to 90s dance music. Beautiful quiet bar in front masks the serious bootyshaking inside. Open Su-Th 11pm-4am, F-Sa 11pm-5am. Cover f5, on weekends f10.

Dansen bij Jansen, Handboogstr. 11, near the Spui. Nothing particularly special, but cheap, near the university, and popular with students. Cover Su-W f2.50, F-Sa f5. Open Su-Th 11pm-4am, F-Sa 11pm-5am. Happy Hour Su-W 11pm-midnight.

COC, Rozenstr. 14 (tel. 626 30 87). See **Practical Info,** p. 656. Th night youth disco 11pm-3am. F night disco 11pm-4am. Sa girls' café (8pm-midnight) and disco (11pm-4am).

⚐ EXCURSIONS FROM AMSTERDAM

EDAM. When you tire of free-living Amsterdam, discover quaint cottages, peaceful parks, and lots of cheese and clogs in **Edam.** The 15th-century **Grote Kerk,** or St. Nicholaaskerk, is the largest three-ridged church in Europe and has exquisite stained-glass windows. (Open Apr.-Oct. daily 2-4:30pm.) Farmers still bring their famed cheese to **market** by horse and boat. (July-Aug. W 10am-12:30pm.) Rent a bike at **Ronald Schot,** Kleine Kerkstr. 9-11 (f12 per day), and head to the source yourself. At **Alida Hoeve,** Zeddewed 1, Edam cheese is still made by hand and samples are free. (Open daily 9am-6pm.) It's across the street from the bike path as you head toward Volendam (pass the first touristy cheese factory you see); bike or take bus 110 from Edam. Farther down the path stands a towering **windmill.** For f1, you can climb the ladder to the top while it's turning. (Open Apr.-Aug. daily 9am-4pm.) Edam is just outside Amsterdam; take bus 114 from Centraal Station (30min., 7 strips). The **VVV,** Kaizergracht 1, in the old town hall, can help find a **room** (f35). (Tel. (0299) 31 51 25; fax 37 42 36; email info@vvv-edam.nl. Open July-Aug. M-Sa 10am-5pm, Su 1:4:30pm; May-June and Sept. closed Sa; Oct.-Apr. M-Sa 10am-3pm.)

HOORN. A little farther from Amsterdam, Hoorn awaits on the edge of the **Ijsselmeer,** an inlet of the Atlantic that the ever-enterprising Dutch diked off in 1932 to form a freshwater sea. The town itself is charming, with frequent open-air markets and a picturesque harbor. If the weather cooperates, **swimming** and **sailing** in the Ijsselmeer can be the perfect tranquilizer after the frenzy of Amsterdam. The **tourist office,** Veemarkt 4, organizes walking tours. From the train station, turn left on Veemarkt. (Tel. (0229) 21 83 44. Open M-F 9-11:30am and 12:30-4pm.) **De Toorts (HI)** has rooms right on the water. To get there, take bus 133, 137, or 147 to "Julianaplaen." (Tel. (0229) 21 42 56. f28, nonmembers f33. Open July-Aug.)

HAARLEM

Surrounded by fields of tulips and daffodils and punctuated with Renaissance façades and placid canals, it's not hard to see how Haarlem served as inspiration for native Frans Hals and other Golden Age Dutch artists. The local 17th- and 18th-century *hofjes* (almshouses for elderly women), now private residences,

NETHERLANDS

feature elegant brickwork and idyllic courtyards. Especially noteworthy are the secluded **Hofje van Bakenes,** Wijde Appelaarsteeg 11, near the Teylers Museum, and the **Hofje van Oirschot,** where Kuisstr. becomes Barteljorisstr. (Open 10am-5pm.) From the station, Kruisweg leads to the **Grote Markt** and the glorious medieval **Stadhuis** (Town Hall), originally the hunting lodge of the Count of Holland. When the Hall of Counts is not in use, you can ask at the reception desk to sneak a peek at the lavish interior. The **Grote Kerk,** at the opposite end of the Grote Markt, houses the Müller organ at which an 11-year-old Mozart once played. (Open M-Sa 10am-4pm. f2.50, students f1.50.) From the church, follow Damstr. to the Netherlands' oldest museum, the **Teylers Museum,** Spaarne 16, which contains an eclectic assortment of scientific instruments, fossils, paintings, and drawings, including works by Raphael, Michelangelo, and Rembrandt. (Open Tu-Sa 10am-5pm, Su noon-5pm. f10.) The **Frans Hals Museum,** Groot Heiligland 62, in a 17th-century almshouse, contains work by the portraitist and a collection of modern art. (Open M-Sa 11am-5pm, Su 1-5pm. f7-8.)

Reach Haarlem from Amsterdam both by **train** (15min., f6.50) from Centraal Station and by **bus** 86 from Marnixstr., near Leidsepl. (2 per hr., 6 strips). Five **night buses** (#86; 12:42-3:20am) cruise from Leidsepl. to Haarlem's city center, 15min. from the hostel. The VVV **tourist office,** Stationspl. 1, sells maps (f4-8.50). (Tel. (0900) 616 16 00, f1 per min.; fax (023) 534 05 37; www.saturnus.nl/vvv_zk. Open M-F 9am-5:30pm, Sa 10am-2pm.) To reach the lively **NJHC-herberg Jan Gijzen (HI),** Jan Gijzenpad 3, on the banks of a canal 3km from the station, take bus 2 (dir: Haarlem-Nord) and tell the driver your destination. (Tel. (023) 537 37 93; fax 537 11 76. f26.50-35; nonmembers f31.50-35. Sheets f6.50. Key deposit f25 or passport. Reception 7:30am-midnight. Bikes f10 per day.) Haarlem apparently hasn't heard of budget hotels, but the VVV finds **private rooms** (from f35) for a f10 fee. **Hotel Carillon,** Grote Markt 27, is ideally located, if not ideally priced. (Tel. (023) 531 05 91. Singles f57.50-92.50; doubles f137. Breakfast included. Reception and bar 7:30am-1am.) To **camp** at **De Liede,** Liewegje 17, take bus 2 (dir: Zuiderpolder) and walk 10min. (Tel. (023) 33 23 63. f6 per person, f5 per tent; in summer add f2.50 tax.) **Pannekoekhuis De Smikkel,** Kruisweg 57, serves plump, buttery pancakes (f11-20; open daily 4-10pm), but try cafés in the Grote Markt for cheaper meals.

🖸 **EXCURSIONS FROM HAARLEM.** Near Haarlem, the seaside town of **Zandvoort** boasts two **nude beaches** south of town (walk left when you hit the beach), along with more modest sands for the bashful; the city is also known for its casinos and circus. The VVV **tourist office,** Schoolpl. 1, in the center, 8min. from the beach and the station, sells a lodgings guide for f2; follow signs from the station. (Tel. (023) 571 79 47; fax 571 70 03. Open mid-July to Aug., M-F 9am-7pm, Sa 9am-5pm; Sept. to mid-July M-Sa 9am-5pm.) The **Hotel-Pension Noordzee,** Hogeweg 15, is 100m from the beach. (Tel. (023) 571 31 27. Singles f55; doubles f90. Breakfast included.) **Guest House Corper,** Koninginneweg 21, 10min. from the beach, is on a quiet street. (Tel./fax (023) 571 34 49. Singles f50-60; doubles f100-120; triples f150-180. Breakfast included.) **Trains** arrive in **Zandvoort** from Haarlem (10min., round-trip f4.75).

What **Bloemendaal** lacks in nude beaches (it just has one such portion at its northern edge) it makes up for with stately mansions, peaceful sand dunes, and fields of flowers. The town is accessible by **bus** 81 from the Haarlem train station (15min., every 30min., 3 strips) or by a short **bike** ride from the Haarlem youth hostel (bikes f10 per day) or train station (bikes f9.50 per day plus f100 or passport deposit).

An international **flower auction** is held year-round in the nearby town of **Aalsmeer.** From Haarlem, take bus 140 (45min., every 30min.) from the train station. (Open M-F 7:30-11am.) The **Frans Roozen Gardens** bloom with 500 different types of flowers and plants; summer flower shows are free. Bus 90 (dir: Den Haag; 20-25min., every 30min.) stops in front of the gardens. (Tulip shows Apr.-May daily 8am-6pm.) Buses 50 and 51 run past some of Holland's famous flower fields on their way to the magnificent **Keukenhof** gardens (see **Lisse,** p. 671). Daffodils blossom in early to late April, hyacinths in mid- to late April, and tulips from late April to mid-May.

LEIDEN

Home to one of the oldest and most prestigious universities in Europe, Leiden brims with bookstores, bicycles, museums, and a few requisite windmills. Rembrandt's birthplace and the site of the first tulips, Leiden offers visitors a picture-perfect gateway to flower country. The **Rijksmuseum voor Volkenkunde** (National Museum of Ethnology), Steenstr. 1, is one of the world's oldest anthropological museums, with fantastic artifacts from the Dutch East Indies. (Open Tu-F 10am-5pm, Sa-Su noon-5pm. f10, students f7.50.) The **Rijksmuseum van Oudheden** (National Antiquities Museum), Rapenburg 28, harbors the lovingly restored Egyptian Temple of Taffeh, a gift removed from the reservoir basin of the Aswan Dam. (Open Tu-Sa 10am-5pm, Su noon-5pm. f7, free with Museumkaart.) The university's 400-year-old garden, the **Hortus Botanicus,** Rapenburg 73, is where the first Dutch tulips were grown. (Open Apr.-Sept. M-Sa 9am-5pm, Su 10am-5pm; Oct.-Mar. M-F 9am-5pm. f5.) You can inspect the innards of a functioning windmill at the **Molenmuseum "De Valk,"** 2e Binnenvestgracht 1. (Open Tu-Sa 10am-5pm. f5; included in Museumkaart.) The **Museum De Lakenhal,** Oude Singel 32, exhibits works by Rembrandt and Jan Steen. (Open Tu-F 10am-5pm, Sa-Su noon-5pm. f8; included in Museumkaart.) The small **Leiden American Pilgrim Museum,** Beschuitsleeg 9, tells the story of those who sought refuge in Leiden before sailing to America on the Mayflower. (Open W-Sa 1-5pm. f3.) The **Duke,** Oude Singel 2, has live jazz nightly at 9:30pm and jam sessions on Sundays. (Open daily 7pm-1am; in summer 2pm-1am.)

Leiden is an easy daytrip by **train** from The Hague (20min., f5) or Amsterdam (30min., f12). The VVV **tourist office,** Stationsweg 2d, sells maps (f1.25) and walking tour brochures (f1-4) and finds **private rooms** (fee f4.50). Head straight from the station and it'll be on your right after 3min. (Tel. (0900) 222 23 33; fax (071) 516 12 27; www.leiden.nl. Open M-F 9am-5:30pm, Sa 10am-2pm.) The **NJHC-herberg De Duinark (HI),** Langevelderlaan 45, 18km away in Noordwijk, is 5min. from beautiful white-sand beaches. Take bus 60 or 61 to Brink and walk 15min. following the signs to Sancta Maria. (Tel. (0252) 37 29 20. f31; nonmembers f35. Sheets f6.50. Reception 8am-midnight.) The **Hotel Pension Witte Singel,** Witte Singel 80, 5min. from the town center, has immaculate rooms overlooking gardens and canals. Take bus 43 to "Merenwijk" and tell the driver your destination. (Tel. (071) 512 45 92. Singles f57.50; doubles f85-110.) **Café de Illegale,** Hooigracht 72, serves veggie and Dutch eats. (Meals f16-22. Open daily 5pm-midnight; kitchen closes 10pm.) The **VIV supermarket** is opposite the station. (Open M-F 8am-8pm, Sa 8am-5pm.)

⚡ EXCURSION FROM LEIDEN OR HAARLEM: LISSE. Arriving in Lisse is like landing in technicolor Oz. In late spring, the **Keukenhof** gardens becomes a kaleidoscope as over five million bulbs explode into life. (Tel. (0252) 46 55 55. f15. Open late Mar. to mid-May daily 8am-7:30pm; last entry 6pm.) The **Zwarte Tulip Museum** details the history and science of tulip raising. (Open Tu-Su 1-5pm. f4.) Look for petals in motion at the April **flower parade.** Take **bus** 50 or 51 toward Lisse from the Haarlem train station; combo bus/museum tickets are available at the station (f21). The **VVV** is at Grachtweg 53. (Tel. (02522) 41 42 62. Open M noon-5pm, Tu-F 9am-5pm, Sa 9am-4pm.)

THE HAGUE (DEN HAAG)

William II moved the royal residence to The Hague, in 1248, spawning the requisite parliament buildings, museums, and sprawling parks. During the **North Sea Jazz Festival** (July 14-16, 2000), the city draws in world-class musicians and 50,000 swinging fans, but during the rest of the year it lacks the vitality of its neighbors; make it a daytrip from beachside Scheveningen.

⚡▢▢ PRACTICAL INFO, ACCOMMODATIONS, AND FOOD. Trains (tel. (0900) 92 92) serve Amsterdam (1hr., f17) and Rotterdam (30min., f7.50) from Holland Spoor; others go to Centraal Station. *Stoptrein* and trams 9 and 12 connect the two stations. The VVV **tourist office,** Kon. Julianapl. 30, in front of Centraal Station under the Hotel Sofitel books rooms (fee f4). (Info tel. (0900) 340 35 05; f0.75 per

NETHERLANDS

min. Open M-F 8:30am-5:30pm, Sa 10am-5pm; July-Aug. also Su 11am-3pm.) **Embassies: Australia,** Carnegielaan 4, 2517 KH (tel. 310 82 00; fax 310 78 63). **Canada,** Sophialaan 7, 2514 JP (tel. 361 41 11; open M-F 10am-noon, M-Tu and Th-F also 2:30-4pm); **Ireland,** 9 Dr. Kuyperstr., 2514 BA (tel. 363 09 93); **New Zealand** (consulate), Carnegielaan 10 (tel. 346 93 24; open M-F 9am-12:30pm and 1:30-5:30pm); **South Africa** (consulate), Wassenaarseweg 36, 2596 CJ (tel. 392 45 01; open daily 9am-noon); **UK,** Lange Voorhout 10, 2514 ED (tel. 364 58 00; open M-F 9am-1pm and 2:15-5:30pm); **US,** Lange Voorhout 102, 2514 EJ (tel. 310 92 09; fax 361 46 88). To get from Centraal Station to the **NJHC City Hostel,** Scheepmakerstr. 27, take tram 1 (dir: Delft), 9 (dir: Vrederust), or 12 (dir: Duindrop) to "Rijswijkseplein" (2 strips); cross to the left in front of the tram, cross the big intersection, and Scheepmakerstr. is straight ahead. From Holland Spoor, turn right, follow the tram tracks, turn right at the big intersection, and Scheepmakerstr. is on your right (3min). (Tel. (070) 315 78 78; fax 315 78 77. Dorms f33.75-38; doubles f90; nonmembers add f5. Breakfast included.)

For the pleasant 5km bike ride from The Hague to **Scheveningen** (SCHAYVE-uhn-ing-un; so difficult to say that it was used as a code word by the Dutch in WWII), rent a **bike** from Holland Spoor or Centraal Station (both f8 per day). The VVV sells cycling maps (f8), but routes and nearby towns are clearly marked along paths. The Scheveningen **branch** of the VVV, Gevers Deynootweg 1134, has info on rooms. (Tel. (0900) 340 35 05; f0.75 per min. Open July-Aug. M-Sa 9am-7pm, Su 11am-3pm; Sept.-June M-Sa 9am-5:30pm.) **Hotel Scheveningen,** Gevers Deynootweg 2, has rooms with shower and TV. (Tel. (06) 354 70 03. Singles f50; larger rooms f40 per person. Breakfast included.) Around the corner at Havenkade 3, is the bright **Hotel Pension Marion.** (Tel. (070) 350 50 50; fax (070) 352 11 89. Doubles f40.) To reach **Camping Duinhorst,** Buurtweg 135, take bus 43 from Centraal Station. (Tel. (070) 324 22 70. f8.15 per person, f4 per tent. Open Apr.-Sept.). Cafés line **Korte Poten,** on the street connecting Centraal Station with the Binnenhof.

📷 🎭 **SIGHTS AND ENTERTAINMENT.** For snippets of Dutch politics, visit the **Binnenhof,** The Hague's Parliament complex. Guided tours leave from Binnenhof 8a and visit the 13th-century **Ridderzaal** (Hall of Knights) as well as one or both of the chambers of the States General. (Open M-Sa 10am-4pm. f5-6.) Just outside the north entrance of the Binnenhof, the 17th-century **Mauritshuis** features an impressive collection of Dutch paintings, including work by Rembrandt and Vermeer. (Open Tu-Sa 10am-5pm, Su 11am-5pm. f12.50.) The impressive modern art collection at the **Gemeentmuseum** proudly displays Piet Mondrian's famous *Victory Boogie Woogie,* and a contemporary fashion exhibit. (Open daily 10am-5pm. f10, students f5.) The **Peace Palace,** the opulent home of the International Court of Justice at Carnegiepl., 10min. from the Binnenhof, was donated by Andrew Carnegie during a bout of robber baron guilt. (Tel. (070) 302 41 37. Tours M-F 10, 11am, 2, 3, and 4pm. f5. Book in advance through the tourist office.) The Netherlands' most famous buildings and bridges have been reproduced at a 1:25 scale at **Madurodam,** a mini-city that delights kids, mathematicians, and everyone in between. Take tram 7 or 8 from the center to Johan de Witlaan (2 strips). (Open daily June 9am-8pm; July-Aug. 9am-10pm; Sept.-Mar. 9am-5pm. f19.50.) The streets empty out early—head to **Muziekcafé La Valletta,** Nwe. Schoolstr. 13a, for mellow jazz. (Live shows Th 10pm. Open daily 5pm-1am.) In addition to the **North Sea Jazz Festival,** The Hague also hosts **Parkpop** (June 18, 2000), the largest free mainstream rock concert in Europe.

DELFT

To gaze out over Delft's lilied canals from one of its stone footbridges is to behold the very images that local master Jan Vermeer immortalized on canvas over 300 years ago. Tourists flock to Delft's tree-lined canals and many-hued *markts* to collect the city's signature porcelain from the source. Thursdays and Saturdays, when townspeople flood to the bustling marketplace, are the best days to visit.

🚆 🎭 **PRACTICAL INFO, ACCOMMODATIONS, AND FOOD. Trains** arrive from The Hague (15min., f4); Leiden (30min., f6.50); and Amsterdam (1hr.). For train or **bus** info, call (0900) 92 92. The VVV **tourist office,** Markt 85, has hiking and cycling maps and books rooms (f3.50 fee plus 10% deposit). From the station, cross the bridge, turn left, turn right at the first light, and follow signs to the Markt. (Tel. (015) 212 61 00. Open Apr.-Sept. M-F 9am-6pm, Sa 9am-5:30pm, Su 10am-3pm; Oct.-Mar. M-F 9am-5:30pm, Sa 9am-5pm.) Delft has few budget accommodations. To reach the unmarked **Van Leeuwen,** Achterom 143, walk out straight from the station, cross four canals, and turn right on Achterom. (Tel. (015) 212 37 16. Singles f35; doubles f70.) A few affordable hotels are around the Markt, including the **Pension Van Domburg,** Voldersgracht 24. (Tel. (015) 212 30 29. Doubles f75.) To **camp** on Korftlaan in the Delftse Hout recreation area, take bus 64 from the station to "Aan't Korft." (Tel. (015) 213 00 40. f25 per tent. Laundry. Reception May to mid-Sept. 9am-10pm; mid-Sept. to Apr. 9am-6pm.) Restaurants line **Volderstr.** and **Oude Delft. Kleyweg's Stads-Koffyhuis,** Oude Delft 133-135, with a terrace on the canal, serves sandwiches (f4-8) that were voted the best *broodje* in the Netherlands. (Omelettes and salads from f8.25. Open M-F 9am-7pm, Sa 9am-6pm.) Down the street, **Stads Pan,** Oude Delft 113-115, has savory pancakes. (f5-17. Open daily 10am-10pm.)

📷 🎵 **SIGHTS AND ENTERTAINMENT.** Delft is renowned for its **Delftware,** the blue-on-white china developed in the 16th century to compete with the newly imported Chinese porcelain. To gawk at the precious platters in the 17th-century factory **De Porceleyne Fles,** Rotterdamseweg 196, in southern Delft, take bus 63, 121, or 129 from the station to "Jaffalaan." (Open Apr.-Sept. M-Sa 9am-5pm, Su 9:30am-5pm; Oct.-Mar. M-Sa 9am-5pm. Demonstrations every hr. f5.) Built in 1381, the **Nieuwe Kerk** on the central Markt hosts the mausoleum of Dutch liberator William the Silent. The mausoleum, flanked by a statue of his dog (who starved to death out of despair after his master died), is under restoration through 2000, but a multimedia presentation offers info about William's life and the restorations. Ascend the tower, as caretakers of the 48-bell carillon have for six centuries, for a view of old Delft. (Church open Apr.-Oct. M-Sa 9am-6pm; Nov.-Mar. M-Sa 11am-4pm; f3. Tower closes 1hr. earlier; f3.) Built as a 15th-century nun's cloister, **Het Prinsenhof,** on Sint Agathapl. off Oude Singel, was William's abode until a fanatic French Catholic hired by Spain's Phillip II assassinated him in 1584; today it houses paintings, tapestries, and pottery. (Open Tu-Sa 10am-5pm, Su 1-5pm. f5.) **Rondvaart Delft,** Koormkt. 113, offers canal rides. (Tel. (015) 212 63 85. Apr.-Oct. 10am-6pm. f8.50, students f7.50.) The café **Verderop,** Westvest 9, near the station, has cheap drinks and live music. (Open M-F 10am-1am, Sa-Su 2pm-2am; July-Aug. opens daily at 3pm.)

ROTTERDAM

After Rotterdam was bombed to bits in 1940, experimental architects replaced the rubble with striking (some say strikingly ugly) buildings, creating an urban, industrial conglomerate. Artsy and innovative, yet desolate and almost decrepit in its hypermodernity, it's like the movie *Blade Runner* come alive. For a dramatic example of Rotterdam's eccentric designs (heavily influenced by the de Stijl school), check out the freaky 1984 **Kijks-Kubus** (cube houses) by Piet Blom; #70 offers tours. Take the metro to "Blaak," turn left, and look up. (Open Mar.-Dec. daily 11am-5pm; Jan.-Feb. Sa-Su 11am-5pm. f3.50.) Try to decipher the architectural madness at the **Netherlands Architecture Institute,** Museumpark 25 (open Tu-F 10am-5pm, Su 11am-5pm; f7.50, students f4), then refresh yourself with Rubens, van Gogh, and Magritte across the street at the **Museum Boijmans van Beuningen,** Museumpark 18-20 (Metro: Eendractspl., or take tram 4 or 5; open Tu-Sa 10am-5pm, Su 11am-5pm; f10, students f6.50). The powerful **Monument for the Destroyed City,** a statue of an anguished man is a memorial to the pain and terror of the 1940 bombing raid. The stately **Schielandshuis** (Historical Museum), Korte Hoogstr. 31, recounts the history of the city. (Open Tu-F 10am-5pm, Sa-Su 11am-5pm. f6.) The **Oude Haven** and **Oostplein** brim with cafés and students. Mellow coffee shops line **Oude Binnenweg** and **Nieuwe Binnenweg,** but avoid the area west of **Dijkzigt.** For less talk and more sweat, dance the night away at **Night Town,** West Kruiskade 28. (Cover f10-25 plus f5 "membership fee." Open F-Sa 11pm-late.)

Trains run to Amsterdam (1hr., f23); The Hague (20min., f7.50); and Utrecht (45min., f15). For info on **ferries** to Hull, England, see p. 653. The VVV **tourist office,** Coolsingel 67, opposite the *Stadhuis*, books rooms (fee f2.50-3.50). (Tel. (0900) 403 40 65; f0.50 per min. Open M-Th 9:30am-6pm, F until 9pm, Sa 9:30am-5pm, Su noon-5pm.) **Use It,** Conradstr. 2, to the right of the station, has free advice. (Tel. (010) 240 91 58; fax 240 91 59; www.jip.org/use-it. Open mid-May to mid-Sept. Tu-Su 9am-6pm; mid-Sept. to early May Tu-Sa 9am-5pm.) To reach the comfy **NJHC City-Hostel Rotterdam (HI),** Rochussenstr. 107-109, take the metro to "Dijkzigt"; it's to the left off the street. (Tel. (010) 436 57 63; fax 436 55 69. Dorms f30.75-33.50; doubles f85-95; nonmembers add f5. Breakfast included. Reception 7am-midnight.) The student-run **Sleep-In,** Mauritsweg 29, is cheap; to get there walk straight from the station and it's on the left (10min.). (Tel. (010) 412 14 21; fax 414 32 56. f17.50. Breakfast included. Reception 8-10am and 4pm-1am. Open mid-June to mid-Aug.) To get from the station to the **Hotel Bienvenue,** Spoorsingel 24, exit through the back, walk straight along the canal, and look right (5min.). (Tel. 466 93 94; fax 467 74 75. Singles f78; doubles f125; triples f165; quads f175. Reception M-F 7:30am-9pm, Sa-Su 8am-9pm.) Eat around **Nieuwe Binnenweg** or in the **Oude Haven. De Consul,** Westeringracht 28, draws a student crowd. (Dinner f17.50. Open Su-Tu 3pm-2am, W-Sa 3pm-4am; kitchen open daily 5:30-10pm.) Buy **groceries** at **A&P,** Nieuwe Binnenweg 30. (Open M-Th 9am-8pm, F 9am-9pm, Su 9am-6pm.)

⚐ EXCURSION FROM ROTTERDAM: GOUDA. Gouda (HOW-da) is the quintessential Dutch town, with canals, a windmill, and well-known (if mispronounced) cheese. A regional **cheese market** is held weekly in summer (late June to Aug. Th 10am-12:30pm). The monstrous, late Gothic **St. John's Church** has managed to maintain its collection of 16th-century stained-glass windows despite attacks by both lightning and Reformation iconoclasts. (Open M-Sa Apr.-Oct. 9am-5pm; Nov.-Mar. 10am-4pm. f3.50, students f2.50.) Around the corner on Oosthaven, the **Museum Catherine Gasthuis** houses Flemish art and early surgical instruments in its former chapel and adjoining torture chamber. (Open daily 8am-5pm. f4.75, students f2.75.) The **Goudse Pottenbakkerij,** Peperstr. 76, has produced the famous Gouda clay pipes since the 17th century. (Open M-Sa 9am-5pm. Free.) **Trains** roll into town from Rotterdam (15min., round-trip f12.50). From the station, cross the bridge, walk straight on Kleiweg, which turns into Hoogstr. and leads to the Markt and the VVV **tourist office** (5min.). (Tel. (0182) 51 36 66. Open M-F 9am-5:30pm, Sa 9am-5pm.)

UTRECHT

With pretty canals, a Gothic cathedral, and a prestigious university, Utrecht (OO-trekt; pop. 233,000) is popular with daytrippers from Amsterdam, but it warrants an overnight stay. Its 52,000 students bring a dynamic pulse to the seemingly quiet, picturesque old city—only in Utrecht would a traditional monument to a 17th-century Dutch hero don a tulle hot-pink scarf.

⚐ ⚐⚐ PRACTICAL INFO, ACCOMMODATIONS, AND FOOD. Those arriving by **train** from Amsterdam (25min., 3-6 per hr., day return f19.75) will find themselves trapped in the middle of the **Hoog Catharijne** mall in Utrecht; to get to the VVV **tourist office,** Vredenburg 90, exit the mall and follow the signs around the corner. (Tel. (090) 04 14 14 14; fax (030) 233 14 17; email vvv.utrecht@tref.nl. Open M-F 9am-6pm, Sa 9am-5pm.) Set in a majestic manor house, the **Jeugdherberg Ridderhofstad (HI),** Rhijnauwenselaan 14, is one of the nicest hostels in the Netherlands. Take bus 40, 41, or 43 from Centraal Station (12min., 3 strips) and tell the driver your destination; from the stop, cross the street, backtrack, turn right on Rhijnauwenselaan, and it's at the end of the road (8min.). (Tel. (030) 656 12 77; fax 657 10 65. In summer f30; off-season f28. Breakfast included. Reception 7am-12:30am.) **B&B Utrecht,** Egelandierstr. 25, has a friendly student environment. Call from the station for shuttle service. (Tel. (650) 43 48 84; email amitie@xsyall.nl. f25 per person. Laundry f5. Bikes f8. **Internet.**) To get to **Camping De Berekuil,** Ariënslaan 5-7, take bus 57 (2 strips) from the station and tell the driver where you are going. (Tel. (030) 271 38

70. f8 per person, f8 per tent.) The relaxed **Café De Baas,** Lijnmarkt 8, has big dinners for f14-18. (Open W-Sa 5:30-10:30pm; kitchen closes at 8:30.) For cheap, delicious Dutch pancakes (f9-20), head to the **Pancake Bakery "de oude muntkelder,"** Oude Gracht 112. (Omelettes f10-15. Open daily noon-9:30pm.) The chic **Toque Toque,** Oude Gracht 138, at Vinkenburgstr., serves up generous pasta dishes for f18-23. (Open M-F 10am-midnight, Sa 9am-midnight, Su noon-midnight.)

▩ ▣ SIGHTS AND ENTERTAINMENT. At the center of the old town stands the awe-inspiring, Gothic **Domkerk,** begun in 1254 and finished 250 years later. Its statues were defaced in the early 16th century by Calvinists who considered artistic representations of Biblical figures to be sacrilegious. (Open May-Oct. M-F 10am-5pm, Sa 10am-3:30pm, Su 2-4pm; Nov.-Apr. M-F 11am-4pm, Sa 10am-3:30pm, Su 2-4pm. Free.) The **Domtoren,** originally attached to the cathedral but freestanding since a medieval tornado blew away the nave, is the highest tower in the Netherlands—on a clear day you can see Amsterdam. (Open Tu-Su 10am-6pm, last entrance 5pm. f15.) The **Nationaal Museum Van Speelklok tot Pierement,** Buurkerkhof 10, traces the history of mechanical musical instruments; on the one-hour guided tour you can hear them played. (Open Tu-Sa 10am-5pm, Su noon-5pm. Tours depart on the hr. f9.) **Het Catharijneconvent,** Nieuwe Gracht 63, documents the history of Christianity in the Netherlands through Dutch religious artwork. (Open Tu-F 10am-5pm, Sa-Su 11am-5pm. f7.) **De Winkel van Sinkel,** Oude Gracht 158, by the water's edge, is a café, bar, and dance hall. (Meals f9-16. Kitchen open noon-10pm.) A mellow crowd chills at the theater-café **De Bastaard,** Jansveld 17, while students party at **Woolloo Moollo** on Lucasbolwek. (Open Tu-Su 11pm-late. Cover varies. Student ID required.) The **Homocafé Bodytalk,** Oude Gracht 64, is a popular gay hangout. (Open M-Th 8pm-3am, F-Sa 4pm-5am, Su 4pm-4am.)

HOGE VELUWE NATIONAL PARK

If you've made it to the Netherlands, you shouldn't miss the impressive **Hoge Veluwe National Park** (HO-geh VEY-loo-wuh), a 13,000-acre preserve of woods, heath, dunes, red deer, and wild boars between Arnhem and Apeldoorn that shelters one of the finest modern art museums in all of Europe. Take one of the free **bikes** from the Koperen Kop **visitor center** to explore over 33km of paths winding through woods, alongside ponds, and amidst sand dunes. (Park open daily June to mid-Aug. 8am-10pm; May and late Aug. 8am-9pm; Apr. 8am-8pm; Sept. 9am-8pm; Oct. 9am-7pm; Nov.-Mar. 9am-5:30pm. f7.) Tucked deep within the park, a 35min. walk from the nearest entrance, the **Rijksmuseum Kröller-Müller** has many van Goghs, as well as works by Seurat, Mondrian, Picasso, and Brancusi. The museum's striking sculpture garden, one of the largest in Europe, has exceptional work by Rodin, Bourdelle, and Hepworth. (Museum open Tu-Su 10am-5pm. Sculpture garden open Apr.-Oct. daily 10am-4:30pm. f7.) The **Museonder,** at the visitor center, is an underground museum about the subterranean ecosystem. (Open daily 10am-5pm. Free.)

▤ GETTING THERE AND GETTING AROUND. Arnhem and Apeldoorn (both 15km from the park) are good bases for exploration. From March to October, bus 12 (round-trip f7.85) from the **Arnhem** train station stops at the museum and visitor center; in winter, bus 107 (dir: Otterlo) stops in the park. After 6pm, you can take bus 2 to "Schaarvbergen" to pick up bikes. To reach Hoge Veluwe from **Apeldoorn,** take bus 110 from the train station (every hr. 9:40am-4:10pm, f6.75 or 4 strips).

ARNHEM. Arnhem itself offers little excitement, but the VVV **tourist office,** to the left of the station, has park info. (Tel. (090) 02 02 40 75; fax 02 64 42 26 44. Open Apr.-Sept. M 11am-5:30pm, Tu-F 9am-5:30pm, Sa 10am-4pm; Oct.-Mar. M 1-5:30pm, Tu-F 9am-5:30pm, Sa 10am-1pm.) The **Jeugdherberg Alteveer (HI),** Diepenbrocklaan 27, is clean and friendly. Take bus 3 from the station (dir: Alteveer; 10min., 3 strips) to the Rijnstate Hospital stop, turn right, take a left at the intersection, cross the road, take the brick path on your right up into the woods, turn right at the top of the path, and it will be on the right (5min.). (Tel. (026) 442 01 14. f30.75; nonmembers

NETHERLANDS

f35.75; July-Aug. add f2 tourist tax. Breakfast included. Sheets f6.50. Laundry f10. Bike rental. Key deposit f10. Reception 8am-11pm. Curfew 12:30am.) Take bus 2 (dir: Haedaveld; 20min., 3 strips) to **camp** at **Kampeercentrum Arnhem,** Kemperberg-erweg 771. (Tel. (026) 445 61 00. f13.50 for 1 person, f18.50 for 2. Open Mar.-Sept.)

APELDOORN. Apeldoorn (AH-pul-dorn) is home to the exceptional **Museum Paleis Het Loo,** the magnificent 17th- and 18th-century palace of the many King Williams of Orange. The palace's pristine gardens, featuring Neoclassical sculptures, fountains, and a colonnade, have been precisely and symmetrically trimmed for over 350 years. From the station, take bus 102 or 104 (10min., 2 strips). (Open Tu-Su 10am-5pm. f12.50.) The VVV **tourist office,** Stationstr. 72, 5min. straight ahead from the station, sells bike maps (f8.95). (Tel. (0900) 168 16 36; fax (055) 521 12 90. Open Apr.-Oct. M 9:30am-6pm, Tu-F 9am-6pm, Sa 9am-5pm; Nov.-Mar. M 9:30am-5:30pm, Tu-F 9am-5:30pm, Sa 9am-2pm.) To get to the lively **De Grote Beer (HI),** Asselsestr. 330, take bus 4 or 7 (dir: Orden) from the station. (Tel. (055) 355 31 18; fax 355 38 11. In summer dorms f31, doubles f82; off-season f27.75, f77.50. Breakfast included. Bikes f12.50 per day. Reception 8am-10pm. Flexible midnight curfew.)

MAASTRICHT

Situated on a narrow strip of land between Belgium and Germany, Maastricht (Mah-STRICT; pop. 120,000) is one of the oldest cities in the Netherlands. Home of the prestigious **Jan van Eyck Academie of Art,** Maastricht has long been known for its abundance of art galleries and antique stores. The new **Bonnefantenmu-seum,** 250 av. Ceramique, which has permanent collections of archaeological artifacts, medieval sculpture, and Northern Renaissance painting. (Open Tu-Su 11am-5pm. f12.50.) Although the city has been a hopeful symbol of European unity since the 1991 Maastricht Treaty, it's seen its share of interstate rivalries; centuries of foreign threats culminated in an innovative subterranean defense system. The **Mount Saint Peter Caves,** with a mazelike 20,000 passages, were used as a siege shelter as late as WWII and contain inscriptions and artwork by gener-ations of inhabitants. Tours in English leave from Chalet Bergrust, 71 Luiker-wegdaily. (Tours July-Aug. daily 2:15pm. f5.75.) The **Kazematten,** 10km of underground passageways constructed between 1575 and 1825, enabled locals to detect enemies and to make surprise attacks. From Vrijtmarkt, go toward Tongersepl. and follow the signs for Waldeck Bastion. (Tours Apr.-Sept. daily; Oct.-May Su only. f5.75.) Maastricht's above-ground marvels include the **Basilica of Saint Servatius,** Keizer Karelplein, which contains ornate ecclesiastical crafts, 11th-century crypts, and the country's largest bell, affectionately known as *Grameer* (Grandmother). (Open July-Aug. daily 10am-6pm; Sept.-Oct. and Apr.-May daily 10am-5pm; Dec.-Mar. Su 12:30-5pm. f4.) The **Onze Lieve Vrouwe Basiliek,** O.L. Vrouweplein, is a medieval basilica with a smaller collection of treasures. (Open Easter-Oct. M-Sa 11am-5pm, Su 1-5pm. f3.50.)

The station is on the eastern side of town, across the river from most of the action, but buses run frequently to the Markt. The VVV **tourist office,** Kleine Staat 1, is a block south of the Markt at Het Dinghuis. (Tel. (043) 325 21 21. Open May-Oct. M-Sa 9am-6pm, Su 11am-3pm; Nov.-Apr. M-F 9am-6pm, Sa 9am-5pm.) To get from the station to **Hostel Sportel de Dousberg (HI),** Dousbergweg 4, from the station, take bus 11 on weekdays, bus 8 or 18 on Saturdays, or bus 22 on Sundays and weeknights to "De Dousberg" (10min., 2-3 strips). (Tel. (043) 346 67 77; fax 346 67 55. Dorms f36-42; doubles f98. Breakfast included. Key deposit f10. Strict 1am curfew.) The **Botel Maastricht** is moored at Maas-bouleverd 95, with an on-board bar and a great view of the Bonnefantenmu-seum. (Tel. (043) 321 90 23; fax 325 79 98. Singles f57-67; doubles f88-93. Breakfast included.) **De Bobbel,** Wolfstr. 32, is the perfect stop for a light meal or sandwich (from f8). (Open M-Sa 10am-2am, Su noon-2am.) On Kesselkade, **de Kadans** serves salads (f12-20) and pumps house in the **K-Club** downstairs. (Brasserie open M-Su 10am-2am, Th-Sa until 5am. Club open usually 11pm-5am; no cover.) **Odeon,** Heggenstr., has jazz and **internet** (f2.50 per 15min.).

GRONINGEN

With 50,000 students and the nightlife to prove it, the small city of Groningen (KRO-ning-en; pop. 170,000) supports a surprising number of eccentric museums, quirky art galleries, and trendy cafés. The town's gem is the spectacular **Groninger Museum,** a unique pastel assemblage of squares, cylinders, and slag metal that forms a bridge between the station and the city center. The multicolored, steel-trimmed galleries create a futuristic laboratory atmosphere for their wild contemporary art exhibits. A loopy maze of white chiffon curtains contains a collection of 16th-century Chinese sculpture and 18th-century Dutch china. (Open Tu-Su 10am-5pm; June-Aug. also M 1-5pm. f12.) While WWII bombing left most of the city in ruins, the 500-year-old **Martinitoren** in the Grote Markt somehow weathered the German attacks. (Open Apr.-Sept. daily noon-4:30pm; Oct.-Mar. Sa-Su noon-4:30pm. f3.) Escape Groningen's gray urbanity in the serene 16th-century **Prinsenhoftuin** (Princes' Court Gardens); the entrance is on the canal behind the Martinitorin. The tiny **Theeschenkerij** within has 130 kinds of tea amidst ivy-covered trellises and towering rose bushes.

To reach the VVV **tourist office,** Ged. Kattendiep 6, turn right as you exit the station, cross the first bridge to your left, head straight through the Hereplein on Herestr., turn right at Ged. Zuderdiep, and veer left onto Ged. Kattendiep. (Tel. (0900) 202 30 50; fax (050) 311 02 58. Open June-Aug. M-F 9am-6pm, Sa 10am-5pm; Sept.-May M-F 9am-5:30pm, Sa 10am-5pm.) Surrounding lakes and forests are within easy biking distance of town; rent a **bike** (f8 per day) at the station and buy a map (f7) at the VVV. Hang out in the snack bar at the funky **Simplon Youth Hotel,** Boterdiep 73, and admire its quirky ceiling art. Take bus 1 from the station and tell the driver your destination. (Tel. (050) 313 52 21; fax 313 30 27. f21.50. Breakfast f7.50. Sheets f4.50. Laundry. Lockout noon-3pm.) Groningen's nightlife jams in a corner of the **Grote Markt** and along nearby **Poelstr.** and **Peperstr.** The intimate, candle-lit **de Spieghel Jazz Café,** Peperstr. 11, has live jazz, funk, or blues every night. (Usually no cover. Open daily 11pm-5am.) **Postal code:** 9725 BM.

WADDEN ISLANDS (WADDENEILANDEN)

Wadden means "mudflat" in Dutch, but sand is the defining characteristic of these islands: stretches of isolated beaches hide behind dune ridges with windblown manes of golden grass. Dutch vacationers keep these idyllic islands to themselves. Deserted, tulip-lined bike trails carve through vast, flat stretches of grazing land and lead to serene beaches.

▣ GETTING THERE AND GETTING AROUND. The islands arch clockwise from Amsterdam around northern Holland: Texel (closest to Amsterdam), Vlieland, Terschelling, Ameland, and Schiermonnikoog. To reach **Texel,** take the train from Amsterdam to **Den Helder** (70min., f20), bus 3 from the other end to the port, and then a ferry to Texel (20min., every hr. 6am-9pm, round-trip f11). To reach **Terschelling,** take a train from Amsterdam to **Harlingen** (3hr., f35), where **ferries** (tel. (0562) 44 21 41) depart for **Terschelling** (3 per day, round-trip f35-40). Ferries from Terschelling connect to the even tinier island of **Vlieland** (f15). In summer, ferries also link the rest of the islands. **Biking** is the easiest way to get around.

TEXEL. The southernmost and largest of the Wadden Islands, Texel (TES-sel) can be a voyeur's paradise, with two popular **nude beaches** (south of Den Hoorn and off De Cocksdorp at paal 28) and **bird watching.** You can only visit the **nature reserves** on a guided tour; book in advance from **Ecomare,** Ruyslaan 92, in De Koog, and specify English-speaking tours not requiring rubber boots. (Tel. (0222) 31 77 41. Tours 2hr.; daily 11am. f7.50.) The island's three major villages are the central **Den Burg,** the beachfront **De Koog,** and the more isolated **De Cocksdrop** to the north. Pedal between them with a **bike** rented from **Verhuurbedrijf Heijne,** across from the ferry stop at 't Horntje. (f8 per day. Open daily Apr.-Oct. 9am-9pm; Nov.-Mar. 9am-6pm.) Or, a **Texel Ticket** allows unlimited one-day travel on island's relatively inefficient bus system (runs mid-June to mid-Sept.; f6). The VVV **tourist office,** Emmaln 66, is in Den Burg. (Tel. (0222) 31 28 47; fax 31 41 29; www.vvv-wadden.nl. Open M-F 9am-6pm, Sa

9am-5pm; July-Aug. also Su 10am-1:30pm.) Both **youth hostels (HI)** are easily accessible from the ferry; tell the bus driver your destination. Take bus 29 to **Panorama,** Schansweg 7, snuggled between sheep pastures 7km from the ferry, and 3km from Den Burg's center. (Tel. (0222) 31 54 41; fax 31 38 89. In summer f31.25; off-season f29; nonmembers add f4. Sheets f6.50. Bikes f8 per day.) Bus 28 goes to **De Eyercoogh,** Pontweg 106. (Open July-Sept.; also Apr.-June and early Oct. for groups. Reserve through Panorama.) **Hotel de Merel,** Warmoestr. 22, is in the center of Den Burg. From the bus stop in Den Burg Square, turn left on Elemert and left again on Warmoerstr. (Tel. (0222) 31 31 32; fax 31 03 33. Singles from f100; doubles from f140; off-season f10-20 less. Breakfast included.) **Campgrounds** are in De Koog (f4-7); ask at the tourist office. The pub **De 12 Blacken Tavern,** Weverstr. 20 in Den Burg, specializes in *'t Jutterje,* the island's popular alcohol, blended from herbs and wheat (f2.75). (Open M-Sa 10am-2am, Su noon-2am.)

TERSCHELLING AND VLIELAND. With 80% of the island covered by a European Nature Reserve, tiny **Terschelling** (pop. 4500) offers secluded beaches that stretch around the western tip and across the northern coast of the long, narrow island. To explore the island's striking scenery, rent a **bike** from **Elslo,** Willem Baretszkade 139, on a pier 3min. from the VVV (f8 per day plus f25 deposit; hostel guests 10% off). The VVV **tourist office** is opposite the ferry landing. (Tel. (0562) 44 30 00; fax 44 28 75. Open M-Sa 9:30am-5:30pm.) A few cafés are in the main village, **Terschelling West,** but the best dinner (f17) is at the **Terschelling Hostel (HI),** van Heusdenweg 39, just out of town. With your back to the harbor, take a right, walk along the pier, continue on the bike path to "Midland," and it's straight ahead. (Tel. (0562) 44 23 38; fax 44 33 12. In summer f30; off-season f28; nonmembers add f5. Breakfast included. Sheets f6.50. Laundry f8. Reception 9am-10pm.) With only one village, **Vlieland** (Vlee-lond) is an easy daytrip from Terschelling, but the Vlieland VVV **tourist office,** opposite the ferry dock, can book rooms (f35 and f4.50 fee). (Tel. (0562) 45 11 11. Open M-F 9am-5pm, Sa 9:30am-12:30pm; Sa-Su also open to meet arriving boats.)

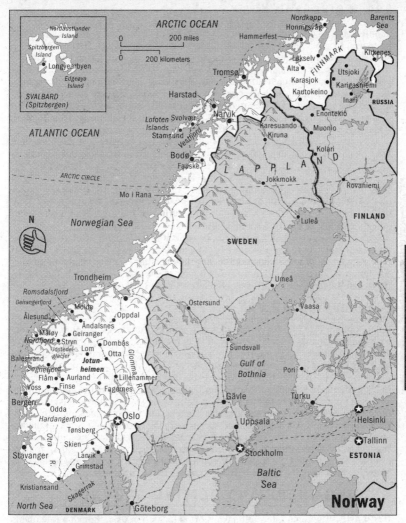

NORWAY (NORGE)

US$1 = 7.75KR (NORWEGIAN KRONER)	**1KR = US$0.13**
CDN$1 = 5.21KR	**1KR = CDN$0.19**
UK£1 = 12.57KR	**1KR = UK£0.08**
IR£1 = 10.44KR	**1KR = IR£0.10**
AUS$1 = 5.03KR	**1KR = AUS$0.20**
NZ$1 = 4.09KR	**1KR = NZ$0.24**
SAR1 = 1.27KR	**1KR = SAR0.78**
EUR€1 = 8.22KR	**1KR = EUR€0.12**

PHONE CODE Country code: 47. **International dialing prefix:** 095.

Norway is blessed with an abundance of beauty, from jagged, magnificent fjords to glacier-capped mountain ranges; from the stern, harsh beauty of the far north to stunningly turquoise rivers. Although the country's relation with the sea is today manifested through its fishing industry, the original Norwegian seafarers wandered in search of glory, gold, and blood. In the age of the Vikings, fierce Norsemen spread across the Atlantic, plundering and settling in England, Ireland, and France; their influence, at its height, extended all the way to Russia and southern Europe. Viking dominance, though dramatic, was short lived, and the pillaging party subsided altogether in the 10th century, when King Harald Hårfagre (the Fair-haired) unified the realm and Olav Haraldsson successfully imported Christianity. Rune stones, stave churches, and preserved Viking ships still survive today from the age, while sagas chronicle the Vikings' adventures in rich poetry and epics.

After the Viking twilight, Norway was annexed to Denmark and then Sweden. Even while politically dependent, the country emerged in the late 19th century as an aesthetic power, nurturing artistic luminaries from Munch to Ibsen to Grieg. Norway enjoyed over three decades of independence after gaining sovereignty in 1905 before German occupation in WWII. The psychological and physical legacies of this occupation are still felt: as the Nazis were retreating from Norway, they burned much of the country to the ground; although the destroyed towns were quickly rebuilt, their distinctive local architecture was forever lost.

In the years since WWII, Norway has developed into a modern welfare state. The result is a country with some of the highest prices and taxes in the world; but also unparalleled social services and little class stratification. With a population of only 4.5 million—and a population aware of the natural world it inhabits at that—Norway's beauty and solitude are in good hands.

DISCOVER NORWAY

Cosmopolitan **Oslo,** the first stop on most travelers' itineraries, swarms with lively cafés and museums (p. 683). After you've exhausted the capital, hop on the gorgeous Oslo-Bergen rail line (p. 691) into fjord country. At the other end lies relaxed and cultural **Bergen,** a former Hanseatic stronghold with signature pointed gables lining the wharf (p. 692). If you only have one day to see the fjords, spend it exploring **Sognefjord;** one popular daytrip from Bergen involves taking the train to **Myrdal** and then either hiking or taking the Flåm Railway down the valley, then catching a ferry on Sognefjord to nearby **Gudvangen** and a connecting bus back up to the main rail line (p. 697). If you have more time to explore the fjords, glacierwalk on the **Jostedalsbreen Glacier** (p. 698) or head to **Hardangerfjord** (p. 696). Quirky and vivacious **Trondheim,** at the northern end of fjord country, feels more authentic than tourist-oriented Bergen and Oslo (p. 700). If you have substantially more time to spend in Norway, don't miss the magical, isolated **Lofoten Islands** up north (p. 701).

GETTING THERE AND GETTING AROUND

BY PLANE. The main international airport is located in **Oslo,** though a few flights land at **Trondheim** and **Bergen. SAS** (Australia tel. (02) 92 99 98 00, South Africa tel. (8) 84 56 00, Sweden tel. (020) 72 77 27, UK tel. (0845) 60 72 77 27, US tel. (800) 221-2350, elsewhere call Sweden +46 (8) 797 50 80) fly to Norway, as do **Finnair** (US tel. (800) 950-5000) and **Icelandair** (US tel. (800) 223-5500). For those under 25 or students under 32, special youth fares make **flying** a viable option for domestic travel, often cheaper than the train. **Braathens SAFE** (tel. 67 58 60 00) and **SAS** (tel. 81 00 33 00) both offer domestic standby tickets *(chance billets).* Any trip that stays either north or south of Trondheim costs around 410kr one-way (both zones 800kr).

BY TRAIN. You'll have to collect reams of free regional schedules, or ask at travel agencies, train stations, or tourist offices for a look at *Rutebok for Norge* to figure out train transport. Trains run only as far north as Bodø, where buses take over. Trains farther north move along the Swedish rail line through Kiruna, which ends at Narvik on the Norwegian coast, on a line from Murmansk in Russia. Seat reservations are compulsory on many long-distance trains and all night trains (25kr). **Eurail** is valid on all trains. The **Norway Railpass** grants unlimited travel within the country for three (1100kr), four (1364kr), or five (2002kr) days over the course of a month. The *buy-in-Scandinavia* **Scanrail Pass** allows five days within 15 (1575kr, under 26 1190kr) or 21 consecutive days (2510kr, under 26 1815kr) of unlimited rail travel through Scandinavia, as well as free or discounted ferry rides and reduced bus fares in Norway. This differs from the *buy-outside-Scandinavia* **Scanrail Pass** (see p. 61). Foreign students sometimes get the same discounts on domestic rail travel as Norwegian students. Off-peak green trains are always discounted.

BY BUS. Buses are quite expensive (about 1kr per km), but are the only land option north of Bodø and in the fjords. **Norway Bussekspress** (tel. 23 00 24 40) operates 75% of the domestic bus routes and publishes a free, easy-to-follow book of schedules and prices called *NSB Togruter*. **Scanrail** and **InterRail** pass holders are entitled to a 50% discount on most bus routes, and students are entitled to a 25-50% discount on most routes—be insistent and follow the rules listed in the Norway Bussekspress booklet. **Bus passes** valid for one (1375kr) or two (2200kr) weeks are good deals for those exploring the fjords or the north.

BY FERRY. Car ferries *(ferjer)* are usually much cheaper (and slower) than the many **hydrofoils** *(hurtigbåte)* cruising the coasts and fjords; both often have student, Scanrail, and/or InterRail discounts. The **Hurtigruten** (the famed Coastal Steamer) takes six days for the fantastic voyage from **Bergen** to **Kirkenes** on the Russian border; there is one northbound and one southbound departure from each of its 34 stops per day. There are no railpass discounts, but students get 50% off. Generally buses and trains will be more affordable, but there are exceptions. For info on boats from **Oslo** to **Kiel, Germany; Hirtshals, Frederikshavn,** and **Copenhagen, Denmark;** and **Helsingborg, Sweden,** see p. 684. For boats from **Kristiansand** to **Hirtshals** or **Newcastle,** see p. 689. For ships connecting **Stavanger** and **Newcastle,** see p. 689. For ferries from **Bergen** to **Hanstholm, Denmark, Newcastle,** the **Faroe Islands,** the **Shetland Islands,** and **Iceland,** see p. 692. For additional info on ferries to the UK, see p. 58.

BY CAR. Roads in Norway are generally in good condition, although they can be frighteningly narrow in some places; harrowing does not even begin to describe the occasional one-lane tunnel heading into a blind curve. Driving around the fjords can be frustrating, as only Nordfjord has a road that completely circumnavigates it, but there are numerous car ferries. RVs are common; rental cars are expensive, but for groups they can be more affordable than buying separate railpasses. **Gas** is prohibitively expensive at about 10kr per liter. Cars and other vehicles are required to keep **headlights** on at all times. For road maps, ask at local tourist offices or contact the Sons of Norway in the US and Canada at (800) 945-8851.

BY BIKE AND BY THUMB. Biking is becoming increasingly common. The beautiful scenery is rewarding for cyclists, although the hilly terrain can be rough on bikes. Contact **Syklistenes Landsforening** (Oslo tel. 22 41 50 80) for more info. **Hitching** is notoriously difficult and discouraged by *Let's Go*. Some Norwegians hitch beyond the rail lines in northern Norway and the fjord areas of the west, but many others try for six hours and end up exactly where they started. Hitchers should bring several layers of clothing, rain gear, and a warm sleeping bag.

ESSENTIALS

DOCUMENTS AND FORMALITIES. Visas are not required for citizens of Australia, Canada, the EU, New Zealand, or the US for stays shorter than three months. This three-month period begins upon entry into any Scandinavian country; for more than 90 days in any combination of Finland, Iceland, Norway, and/or Sweden, you will need a visa. South Africans require a visa for stays of any length.

Norwegian Embassies at Home: **Australia,** 17 Hunter St, Yarralumla, Canberra ACT 2600 (tel. (02) 62 73 34 44); **Canada,** 90 Sparks St #532, Ottawa, ON K1P 5B4 (tel. (613) 238-6571; fax 238-2765); **Ireland,** 34 Molesworth St, Dublin 2 (tel. (01) 662 18 00); **New Zealand,** 61 Molesworth St, Wellington (tel. (04) 471 25 03); **South Africa,** P.O. Box 9843, Pretoria, 0001 (tel. (012) 323 47 90; fax 323 47 89); **UK,** 25 Belgrave Sq,

London SW1X 8QD (tel. (020) 75 91 55 00; fax 72 45 69 93); **US,** 2720 34th St NW, Washington DC 20008 (tel. (202) 333-6000; fax 337-0870; www.norway.org).
Foreign Embassies in Norway: All located in **Oslo** (see p. 684).

TOURIST OFFICES. Virtually every town, village, and pit stop has an ever-helpful **Turistinformasjon** office; look for a black lower-case **"i"** on a green sign. Try to go the night before you're planning to head out of town, as buses often leave early. In July and the first half of August, all tourist offices are open daily; most have reduced hours the rest of the year. For more info, contact the **Norwegian Tourist Board,** P.O. Box 2893 Solli, N-0230 Oslo (tel. (47) 22 92 52 00; fax 22 56 05 05; www.tourist.no).

Tourist Boards at Home: UK, Charles House, 5 Regent St, London SW1Y 4LR (tel. (020) 78 39 62 55; fax 78 39 60 14); **US,** P.O. Box 4649, Grand Central Station, New York, NY 10163-4649 (tel. (212) 885-9700; fax 885-9710).

MONEY. The Norwegian **kroner** (KR) is divided into 100 *øre.* Banks and large post offices change money, usually for a small commission and the best rates.

Tipping and Bargaining: A 15% service charge is usually included in restaurant and hotel bills. Taxi drivers are usually tipped a few kroner.
Taxes: Value-added tax refunds (10-17% of the price) are available for single-item pur-chases of more than 300kr in a single store in a single visit.

COMMUNICATION

Post: Mailing a **postcard/letter** from Norway costs 5.50kr to Australia, Canada, New Zealand, the US, or South Africa. To Ireland and the UK it costs 4.50kr.
Telephones: Phone calls are pricey. **Pay phones** take 1, 5, 10, and 20kr coins, and local calls need at least 3kr; buying a **phone card** (*telekort;* 35, 98, or 210kr at Narvesen Kiosks and post offices) is more economical. Pay phones cost twice as much as from pri-vate lines; between 10pm-8am it's 15-20% cheaper. To make **domestic collect calls,** dial 117; **international collect calls, 115. International direct dial** numbers include: **AT&T,** 800 190 11; **Sprint,** 800 198 77; **MCI WorldPhone Direct,** 800 199 12; **Austra-lia Direct,** 800 190 61; **Canada Direct,** 800 191 11; **BT Direct,** 800 199 44; **Ireland Direct,** 800 19 353, **Telecom New Zealand Direct,** 800 128 53; **Telkom South Africa Direct,** 800 199 27. **Fire,** tel. 110. **Police,** tel. 112. **Ambulance,** tel. 113.
Language: Norway is officially bilingual: the Danish-influenced **bokmål Norwegian** used in Oslo and the standardized **nynorsk Norwegian** based on the dialects of rural western Nor-way are both taught in schools. Another language, **Sami,** is spoken by the Same, the indigenous people of the north. Most Norwegians speak fluent English. For basic phrases and vocabulary in Norwegian, see p. 949.

ACCOMMODATIONS AND CAMPING. When in Norway, **camp.** Norwegian law allows free camping anywhere on public land for up to two nights, provided that you keep 150m from all buildings and fences and leave no trace behind. **Den Norske Turistforening** (DNT; Norwegian Mountain Touring Association) sells excellent maps, offers guided hiking trips, and maintains more than 300 **mountain huts** *(hyt-ter)* throughout the country. (Tel. 22 82 28 22; www.turistforeningen.no. 75-145kr per night; nonmembers add 80kr. Membership cards available at DNT offices, huts, and tourist offices; 325kr, under 25 160kr.) Staffed huts, open around Easter and from late June to early September, serve meals and have better ambience and more Norwegians than hostels. Unstaffed huts are open from late February until mid-October; you can pick up entrance keys (100kr deposit) from DNT and tourist offices. The DNT offices in Oslo (see p. 684) and Bergen (see p. 692) are particularly helpful. The useful *Vandrerhjem i Norge* brochure lists prices, phone numbers, and more for Norway's 98 **HI youth hostels** *(vandrerhjem),* run by **Norske Van-drerhjem,** Dronninggensgt. 26, in Oslo (tel. 23 13 93 00; fax 23 13 93 50). Beds run 80-170kr; another 25-60kr usually covers breakfast. Sheets typically cost 35-40kr per stay. Usually only rural or smaller hostels have curfews, and only a few are open year-round. Most tourist offices book **private rooms** (singles around 190kr, doubles

NORWAY

330kr). Official **campgrounds** charge 90-120kr per tent. Many also have two- to four-person cabins (450-800kr). Hot showers almost always cost extra.

FOOD AND DRINK. Eating in Norway is pricey; cuddle up to markets and bakeries. The supermarket chain **REMA 1000** generally has the best prices (usually open M-F 9am-8pm, Sa 9am-6pm). Join Norwegians at outdoor **markets** for cheap seafood and fruit, but be wary of the lookalike markets aimed at tourists. Many restaurants have cheap **dagens ret** (dish of the day) specials (full meal 60-70kr); otherwise, you'll rarely get away with less than 100kr. All-you-can-eat buffets and self-service *kafeterias* are other less expensive options. Fish in Norway—cod, salmon, and herring—is fresh, good, and (relatively) cheap. National specialties include cheese *(ost)*; pork and veal meatballs *(kjøtkaker)* with boiled potatoes; and, for lusty carnivores, reindeer, ptarmigan (a type of bird), as well as the controversial whale meat *(kval)*. Norway also grows divine berries. Come winter, you can also delight in dried fish *(lutefisk)*. In most Norwegian restaurants, alcohol is served only after 3pm and never on Sundays, although this is beginning to change in cities. Beer is very expensive (45kr for 0.5L in a bar). Alcohol is cheapest in supermarkets, but few towns permit the sale of alcohol outside of government-operated liquor stores.

LOCAL FACTS

Time: Norway is 1hr. ahead of Greenwich Mean Time (GMT; see p. 49).

Climate: Oslo averages 18°C (63°F) in July and -4°C (24°F) in Jan. In the north, average temperatures dip to 10°C (50°F) in summer; winter temperatures match those in the south. The north and the fjord country are wetter than the south and east. June-Sept. is the best time to visit. For a few weeks around summer solstice (June 21), the area north of Bodø basks in the **midnight sun.** You stand the best chance of seeing the **Northern Lights** in Nov.-Feb. from above the Arctic Circle (although they are occasionally visible in the south). Skiing is best just before Easter.

Hours: Business hours end early in summer, especially on Friday and in August, when Norwegians vacation. **Shop** hours are M-F 9am-5pm, Sa 9am-1pm; hours may be extended on Th. **Banks** are generally open M-W and F 8:15am-3pm, Th 8:15am-5pm.

Holidays: New Year's Day (Jan. 1); Easter Sunday and Monday (Apr. 23-24), May Day (May 1); National Independence Day (May 17); Ascension Day (June 1); Christmas Eve and Day (Dec. 24-25); Boxing Day (Dec. 26); and New Year's Eve (Dec. 31).

Festivals: The **Bergen Festival** in May offers world-class performances in music, dance, and theater. The **Norwegian Wood** (www.norwegianwood.no) rock festival in early June in Oslo features big-name rock bands, while the week-long **Quart** music festival in Kristiansund in early July attracts acts from Marilyn Manson to Ben Harper to Garbage. The mid-July **Molde Jazz Festival** pulls in the luminaries of jazz. **Midsummer Night,** June 23, on the longest day of the year, is celebrated with bonfire and partying countrywide.

OSLO

Verdant Oslo (pop. 500,000) bustles like a city twice its size, yet feels as intimate as a small town. The summer's Midnight Sun and the extraordinary blue light in winter belie the gloomy shadows found in the work of native artists Edvard Munch and Henrik Ibsen. In Oslo everything is spotless, runs on time, and costs you your immortal soul. But Oslo's urban edge—typefied by classy cafés, cool boutiques, and beautiful Norwegians in tight, trendy clothes—is softened by nearby forests, islands, and lakes that hint at the splendor to be found farther west.

☞ GETTING THERE AND GETTING AROUND

Flights: White SAS buses run every 10-15min. between **Gardermoen Airport** and the city (55min., 65kr), with pick-up/drop-off at the bus station (track 9), train station, Parliament, and National Theater. Daily to airport 6am-9:40pm; from airport 7:30am-11:30pm.

Trains: Oslo Sentralstasjon (Oslo S; tel. 81 50 08 88). Reduced fares *(minipriser)* available for M-Th and Sa to major cities if you book 5 days ahead. Several trains daily to: **Lillehammer** (2hr., 240kr); **Stockholm** (7hr., 2 per day, 675kr, under 26 525kr); **Bergen**

(7-8hr., 530kr, *minipris* 335kr); **Trondheim** (7-8hr., 610kr, *minipris* 390kr); and **Copenhagen** (10hr., 3 per day, 790kr, under 26 650kr). Mandatory reservations 65-110kr.

Buses: Norway Bussekspress, Schweigårdsgate 8 (tel. 23 00 24 40), in the Oslo Galleri Mall, behind and to the right as you exit the train station, sends buses to Bergen (580kr), throughout Norway, and across Europe. Pick up their schedule, *NSB Togruter.*

Ferries: Color Line (tel. 22 94 44 44; fax 22 83 20 96). To **Kiel, Germany** (20hr., 560-710kr) and **Hirtshals, Denmark** (12½hr., 450-580kr). 50% off with Eurail, InterRail, or Scanrail. **DFDS Scandinavian Seaways** (tel. 22 41 90 90; fax 22 41 38 38). To **Helsingborg, Sweden** (14hr.), and **Copenhagen** (16hr.) daily at 5pm (in summer 570-830kr; students 25% off, with InterRail or Scanrail 50% off). **Stena Lines** (tel. 23 17 90 00). Daily to **Frederikshavn, Denmark** (high-season 415-490kr, 50% off with Scanrail). Color Line departs from a 20min. west of the train station; DFDS and Stena from 10min. south.

Public Transportation: Trafikanten (tel. 177), in front of the train station, has info; the tourist office also has comprehensive schedules. All transit (bus, tram, subway, and ferry) 20kr per ride; fines over 500kr for traveling without valid ticket. **Dagskort** (day pass) 40kr; **7-day Card** 140kr; **Flexicard** (good for 8 trips) 115kr. The **Oslo Card** (see below) grants unlimited public transport. Late-night transportation runs midnight-5am.

Bike Rental: For info on cycling, contact **Syklistenes Landsforening** (tel. 22 41 50 80).

Hitchhiking: Oslo is not a hitchhiker's paradise; the persistent go to gas stations and ask everyone who stops. Those heading southwest (E-18 to **Kristiansand** and **Stavanger**) take bus 31 or 32 to "Maritime." Hitchers to **Bergen** take bus 161 "Skui" to the last stop; to **Trondheim,** bus 32 or 321, or Metro 5 to "Grorudkrysset"; to **Sweden,** bus 81, 83, or 85 to "Bekkeleget" or local train "Ski" to "Nordstrand."

🚩 ORIENTATION AND PRACTICAL INFORMATION

Running from Oslo south to the *Slottet* (Royal Palace), **Karl Johans gate** is Oslo's main boulevard. Virtually everything of interest is packed in the city center near the **National Theater,** at the end of the **Slottsparken** between the station and the palace. Don't be confused by the word "gate," which simply means "street" in Norwegian.

TOURIST, FINANCIAL, AND LOCAL SERVICES

Tourist Offices: Main Tourist Office, Vestbaneplassen 1 (tel. 23 11 78 84; fax 22 83 81 50; www.oslopro.no), behind the Rådhus. Sells the **Oslo Card,** which covers public transit and admission to nearly all sights (1-day 150kr, 2-day 220kr, 3-day 250kr). Open daily June-Aug. 9am-7pm; M-Sa Sept. 9am-6pm, Oct.-May 9am-4pm. Info center at **Oslo S** books rooms from 440kr. Open daily 8am-11pm. **Den Norske Turistforening,** Storgata 3 (tel. 22 82 28 22; fax 22 82 28 23). Enter around the corner on Olav V gt.; country-wide hiking info. Open M-F 10am-4pm, Th 10am-6pm, Sa 10am-2pm. **Use It,** Møllergata 3 (tel. 22 41 51 32; fax 22 42 63 71; www.unginfo.oslo.no). Turn right 4 blocks up Karl Johans gt. from the station. Youth-oriented info and invaluable *Streetwise* guide. Open M-F July-Aug. 7:30am-5pm; Sept.-June 11am-5pm.

Budget Travel: Kilroy Travels, Nedre Slottsgt. 23 (tel. 23 10 23 10; fax 22 42 97 09; www.kilroytravels.com), has airline bargains. Open M-F 10am-6pm, Sa 10am-3pm.

Embassies: Australia (consulate), Jernbanetorget 2 (tel. 22 41 44 33; fax 22 42 26 83). **Canada,** Wergelandsveien 7 (tel. 22 99 53 00; fax 22 99 53 01). **Ireland,** Kirkeveien 7, P.O. Box 5683, Briskeby, N-0209 (tel. 22 56 33 10; fax 22 12 20 71). **South Africa** (consulate), Drammensveien 88c, P.O. Box 2822 Solli, N-0204 (tel. 22 44 79 10; fax 22 44 39 75). Open M-F 9am-noon. **UK,** Thomas Heftyesgt. 8, N-0244 (tel. 22 53 24 00; fax 22 43 40 05). Open M-F 9am-4pm. **US,** Drammensveien 18, N-0244 (tel. 22 44 85 50; fax 22 44 04 36; www.usembassy.no). Consular services open 9am-noon.

Currency Exchange: Up to US$100 at AmEx. The post office exchanges 30-100kr.

American Express: Karl Johans gt. 33, N-0121 Oslo (tel. 22 98 37 20, in emergency 80 03 32 44). Open M-F 9am-6pm, Sa 10am-4pm.

Luggage Storage: Lockers at the train station. 25kr per 24hr.

Bookstore: Tanum Libris, Karl Johans gt. 37-41 (tel. 22 41 11 00), in the Paléet. Good array of English books. Open M-F and Su 8am-7pm, Tu opens at 9am, Sa 10am-5pm.

NORWAY

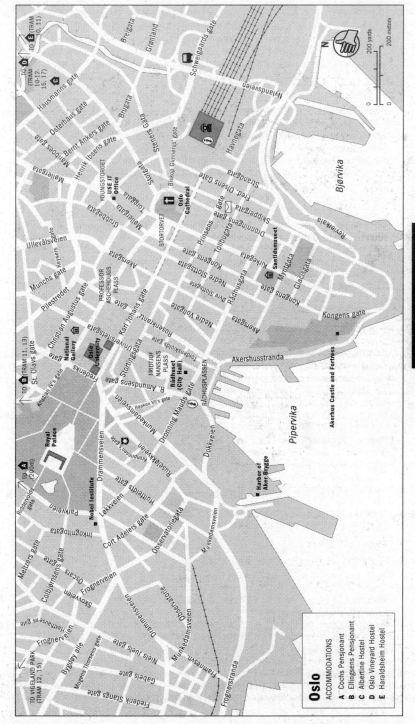

NORWAY

Oslo

ACCOMMODATIONS

A Cochs Pensjonant
B Ellingsens Pensjonant
C Albertine Hostel
D Oslo Vineyard Hostel
E Haraldsheim Hostel

Laundromat: Look for the word *Myntvaskeri*. **Selvbetjent Vask,** Ullevålsveien 15. Wash 30kr per 20min. (soap included), dry 20kr per 30min. Open daily 8am-9pm.

Gay and Lesbian Services: The **Landsforeningen for Lesbiskog Homofil fri gjøring (LLH),** 2 St. Olavs plass (tel. 22 11 05 09; fax 22 20 24 05). Pick up *Blick* (30kr), a monthly gay and lesbian newspaper with attractions and nightlife listings. Open M-F 9am-4pm.

EMERGENCY AND COMMUNICATIONS

Emergencies: Ambulance: tel. 113. **Fire:** tel. 110. **Police:** tel. 112.

Pharmacy: Jernbanetorvets Apotek (tel. 22 41 24 82), opposite the train station. 24hr.

Medical Assistance: Oslo Kommunale Legevakt, Storgata 40 (tel. 22 11 70 70). 24hr.

Internet Access: Free at the **Rådhuset** (Town Hall); sign up for free slots. Open Aug.-June M-F 10am-6pm, Sa 9am-3pm; July M-F 10am-3pm.

Post Office: Dronningens gt. 15 (tel. 23 14 78 02); enter at Prinsens gt. Address mail to be held: Angela MIKLAVCIC, *Poste Restante*, Dronningens gt. 15, N-0101 Oslo 1. Open M-F 8am-6pm, Sa 10am-3pm.

▐▘ ACCOMMODATIONS AND CAMPING

Hostels in Oslo fill up quickly in the summer—make reservations. Some of the best deals in town are the **private rooms** arranged by **Use It** (see above); though the later you show up, the farther away your room (125kr, with sleeping bag 100kr). **Pensions** *(pensjonater)* are usually cheaper than hotels. Some **hotels** offer cheaper "last-minute" prices on vacant rooms through the tourist office. In principle, the Norwegian *allmansrett* gives you the right to **free camp,** but no one really camps on private lawns. Free camping is in the forest north of town as long as you avoid public areas; try the end of the Sognsvann line. Fires are not allowed.

Albertine Hostel, Storgata 55 (tel. 22 99 72 00; fax 22 99 72 20), 15min. north of the train station. Take tram 10, 11, 12, 15, or 17 to "Hausmanns gate"; it's 100m up Storgata on the left. New and beautifully furnished. Dorms 115kr; singles 340kr; doubles 340kr; quads 560kr. Breakfast 50kr. Sheets 40kr. Reception 24hr. Open June 7-Aug. 24.

Oslo Vandrerhjem Haraldsheim (HI), Haraldsheimveien 4 (tel. 22 15 50 43 or 22 22 29 65; fax 22 22 10 25). Take tram 10 or 11, or bus F1 from the airport to "Sinsenkrysset"; follow the signs across the field and up the hill. No sleeping bags. Dorms 160kr, non-members 180kr; singles 260kr; doubles 370kr. Breakfast included. Sheets 45kr. Kitchen. Laundry. **Internet.** Reception 24hr. Lockout 10am-3pm.

Ellingsens Pensjonat, Holtegata 25 (tel. 22 60 03 59; fax 22 60 99 21). Take tram 11, 13, or 19 to "Brisky," or walk 3km from the city center. Unmarked gray building is hard to spot but is popular with backpackers. Singles 270kr; doubles 410kr; extra bed 100kr. Reception M-F 7:30am-10:30pm, Sa-Su 8am-10:30pm.

Oslo Vandrerhjem Holtekilen (HI), Michelets vei 55 (tel. 67 51 80 40; fax 67 59 12 30). Take bus 151/161, 251/252, or 261 to "Kveldsroveien" (20min.) or take the subway to "Stabekk." Popular, though a little far. Dorms 160kr; singles 260kr; doubles 420kr; non-members add 25kr. Breakfast included. Reserve ahead. Open late May to late Aug.

Cochs Pensjonat, Parkveien 25 (tel. 23 33 24 00; fax 23 33 24 10), at Hegdehaugsveien by the royal park, 20-25min. from the train station. Singles 240kr, with bath and kitchenette 430kr; doubles 480-580kr; quads 660-780kr.

OSI-Chalet (tel. 22 49 90 36), in the Nordmarka forest. Take bus 41 to "Sørhedalen School" (40min.) and walk 1hr. Students in sleeping bags doze in forest cottages. Call for directions, or get a map from Use It (see p. 684). Pack food. 125kr.

Ekeberg Camping, Ekebergveien 65 (tel. 22 19 85 68), 3km from town. Take tram 18/19 or bus 34A from the train station. Marvelous view. Cooking facilities, grocery store. Tent and 2 people 120kr, showers included; extra person 40kr. Open May 25-Aug.

Langøyene Camping (tel. 22 36 37 98), on the beach of Langøyene island. Take boat 94 from Vippetangen. Tent and 2 people 70kr; extra person 35kr. Open May-Aug.

Bogstad Camping, Ankerveien 117 (tel. 22 50 76 80), on Bogstand Lake is beautiful, if a bit far. Take bus 32 from the station (30min.). Tent and 2 people 115kr; tent and 4 people 155kr; extra person 20kr. Reception 24hr. Open year-round.

⊙ FOOD

Budget eating in Oslo entails forming a cosmic union with **grocery stores:** try **Rema 1000,** Torggata 2-G (open M-F 9am-7pm, Sa 9am-6pm), or **Kiwi Supermarket,** on Storgata (open M-Sa 8am-11pm). Take advantage of hostels' breakfast buffet.

Stortorvets Gjæstgiveru, Grensen 1. Traditional Norwegian cuisine in one of Oslo's oldest restaurant-pubs. Live jazz in summer F and Sa, sporadically in summer. Cold salmon 78kr; bowl of fresh prawns 72kr. Open M-Th 9am-midnight, F-Sa 9am-2am, Su 1-8pm.

Lord Sandwich, Prinsens Gate 18. Tiny shop serves tasty sandwiches (32kr) made even tastier by the knowledge that they're the sweetest deal in town. Open M-F 8am-5:15pm.

Coco Chalet, Prinsens Gate 21. Cozy and very popular, if somewhat pricey. Lunch 40-90kr. Salads 40-50kr. Dinner 79-149kr. Open M-Sa 11am-11pm.

Café Sult, Thorvald Meyersgt. 26, way up in the trendy 'hood of Løka north of the Albertine Hostel. Salmon with feta salad 46-72kr. Lunch 46-72kr. Dinner 118-140kr. Open Tu-F 4pm-1am, Sa 11:30am-1am, Su 1pm-midnight.

Vegeta Vertshus, Munkedamsveien 3b, off Stortings gt. All-veggies-you-can-strategically-engineer-onto-a-plate 79-114kr. 50kr for students Tu-F 3-8pm, 10% student discount at any other time. Open daily 11am-11pm; buffet closes at 10pm.

Pasta Factory, Kristian IV gate 9. Filling pasta dishes with a fishy flair (85-119kr). Open Su-Th 3pm-midnight, F-Sa 3pm-1am. Bar open M-Th until midnight, F-Sa until 2am.

Børsen Café Stock Exchange, Nedre Vollgt. 19. Drink prices change according to supply and demand—watch for the rush when the "stock exchange" crashes. **Internet** 20kr. Open W-Th 8pm-3:30am, F-Sa 8pm-5am.

⊙ SIGHTS

EDVARD MUNCH. The **Munch Museum** has an outstanding collection of Edvard Munch's unsettling paintings, lithographs, and photographs. *(Tøyengata 53. Take bus 20 to "Munch-museet," or the subway to "Tøyen," or walk 10min. east from the train station. Open June to mid.-Sept. daily 10am-6pm; mid.-Sept to May Tu-Su 10am-4pm, Th and Su until 6pm. 50kr, students 20kr.)* Another of Munch's copies of "The Scream" is at the **Nasjonal Galleriet.** *(Universitetsgaten 13. Take tram 12, 13, or 19, or the subway to "Nationaltheatret." Open M, W, and F 10am-6pm, Th 10am-8pm, Sa 10am-4pm, Su 11am-4pm. Free.)* Next door at the **University** are Munch's massive mural "Sun" paintings. *(Open M-F 9am-4pm. Free.)*

FROGNERPARKEN. Gustav Vigeland's powerful, masculine sculptures at Frognerparken, Norway's visited attraction with over one million visitors annually, depict each stage of the human life cycle. The park is a playground of grassy knolls, duck ponds, and tennis courts, and occasionally hosts large concerts. *(Entrance on Kirkeveien. Take bus 20 or tram 12 or 15 to "Vigelandsparken." Open 24hr. Free.)*

RÅDHUS. The artists who painted the interior of the towering Rådhus during WWII did so in defiance of the orders of the Nazi occupiers; they were punished by deportation to prison camps. The Nobel Peace Prize ceremony takes place here each December 10. *(South of the Nationaltheatret on Fridtjof Nansens plass. Open M-Sa 9am-4pm, Su noon-4pm. 25kr. Free tours M-F 10am, noon, and 2pm.)*

AKERSHUS CASTLE AND FORTRESS. Built in 1299, this waterfront complex was transformed into a Renaissance palace by Christian IV between 1637 and 1648. Explore the complex's dungeons, underground passages, and vast halls. *(Take bus 60 to "Bankplassen" or tram 10 or 15 to "Christianiatorv." Fortress open May to mid-Sept. M-Sa 8am-8pm, Su 10am-8pm; mid-Sept. to Apr. M-F 11am-4pm. Castle open May-June and Aug. to mid-Sept. M-F 10am-4pm, Su 12:30-6pm; July M-Th 10am-6pm, F-Sa 10am-4pm, Su 12:30-6pm; mid- to late Apr. and mid-Sept. to Oct. Su 12:30-4pm. Tours of the castle M-Sa 11am, 1 and 3pm, Su 1 and 3pm.)* The powerful **Hjemmefrontmuseet** (Resistance Museum) in the fortress documents Norway's efforts to subvert Nazi occupation. *(Open mid-June to Aug. 8 M-Sa 10am-5pm, Su 11am-5pm; Sept.-June closes 1-2hr. earlier. 20kr.)*

BYGDØY. The peninsula of Bygdøy is right across the inlet from downtown Oslo; though mainly residential, it swarms with museums and even has a few beaches.

NORWAY

The three vessels of the impressive **Viking Ship Museum** include the 9th-century ring-prowed, dragon-keeled *Oseberg* burial barge. *(Open daily May-Aug. 9am-6pm; Sept. 11am-5pm; Apr. and Oct. 11am-4pm; Nov.-Mar. 11am-3pm. 30kr.)* At the ferry's second stop, "Bygdøynes," the **Polar Ship "Fram" Museum** chronicles the Arctic and Antarctic explorations of two of the most famous Norwegian explorers, Fridtjof Nansen and Roald Amundsen. *(Open daily in summer 9am-5:45pm; in winter reduced hours. 25kr.)* The ethnologist Thor Heyerdahl's boats have their own museum, the **Kon-Tiki Museum,** featuring (surprise) the original *Kon-Tiki,* which set out in 1947 to prove that the first Polynesian settlers had enough technology at their disposal to have sailed from pre-Incan Peru. *(Bygdøynesveien 36. Open daily June-Aug. 9:30am-5:45pm; Sept. and Apr.-May 10:30am-5pm; Oct.-Mar. 10:30am-4pm. 30kr.)* The **Folkemuseum** is a massive outdoor museum with buildings from various eras and parts of the country, including the 13th-century *Stav* Church, one of the last of its kind in existence. *(Museumsveien 10. Open mid-May to mid-June and early to mid-Sept. daily 10am-5pm; mid-June to Aug. daily 10am-6pm; Jan. to mid-May and mid-Sept. to Dec. M-Sa 11am-3pm, Su 11am-4pm. 50kr.)* The popular **Huk Beach** lies 1km from the Viking Ship Museum. Or, if you think you can hang with the Norwegians, go bare at nude **Paradisbukten,** on the far side of the peninsula. *(To reach Bygdøy, take the commuter ferry Bygdøyfergene, which departs from pier 3 at Rådhusbryggen May-Sept. every 40min.; 20kr. For ferry info, call 22 20 07 15. Or, take bus 30 from Nationaltheatret to "Bygdøynes" or "Folkemuseet.")*

OTHER SIGHTS. The **Samtidsmuseet** (Museum of Contemporary Art), is near Akershus Fortress. *(Bankplassen 4. Open Tu, W, and F 10am-5pm, Th 10am-8pm, Sa 11am-4pm, Su 11am-5pm. Free.)* Though the royal residence, at the top of Karl Johans gt., is not open to the public, you can stop by the beautiful **Slottsparken** (Palace Park) nearby to see the changing of the guard, held daily at 1:30pm. *(Take tram 12, 13, or 19, or bus 30-32, or 45, to "Slottsparken.")* The **Oslo Damkirk** (cathedral), consecrated in 1697, has stained-glass windows by Emmanuel Vigeland and a wonderful ceiling mural. *(Continue down Karl Johans gt. to Stortorvet. Open daily 10am-4pm. Free.)* For a great panorama of **Oslofjord** and the city, head to the ski jump **Holmenkollen** at the **Ski Museum,** which chronicles the history of skiing. A **simulator** recreates the adrenaline rush of a four-minute, 130km-per-hour downhill ski run. *(Take subway 15 on the Frognerseteren line to "Holmenkollen." Open daily June-Aug. 9am-10pm; May and Sept. 10am-5pm; Sept.-Apr. 10am-4pm. Museum 60kr, students 35kr. Simulator 35kr, with Oslo Card 25kr.)*

♫ ENTERTAINMENT

What's on in Oslo (free at tourist offices) details Oslo's "high culture," including the opera, symphony, and theater. **Filmenshus,** Dronningsgt. 16, is the center of Oslo's art film scene, while Hollywood flicks are screened at **Saga Cinema,** Stortingsgata 28. At **Nordic Black Theater,** Olaf Ryes plass 11 (tel. 22 38 12 62), immigrant and minority Norwegians stage social critiques in English. Big-name rock concerts take place at the **Rockefeller Music Hall,** Torggata. (Tel. 22 20 32 32. 50-350kr.)

In addition to the countless bars along **Karl Johans gt.** and the **Aker Brygge** harbor complex, Oslo boasts a number of nightclubs with busy DJs and live music. Dance to the house, rock, and funk of **Barock,** Univeritetsgt. 26. (Weekend cover 50kr. Open Th-Su 9pm-3am.) **So What!,** Grensen 9, is popular with a young, indie, and beer-loving crowd. (2-3 concerts per week. Cover 50kr. Open F-Sa 9pm-3:30am.) **Sikamikanico,** 2 Møllergata, is *the* hip coffee bar in Oslo, replete with retro couches. (DJs Th-Sa. Open daily 4pm-3am.) Oslo's gay and lesbian crowd paints the town red on weekends at **Castro,** Kristian IV gt. 7, a two-story dance club, and arguably the coolest bar, gay or straight, in Oslo. (Weekend cover 50kr. Open daily 9pm-3am.)

🎭 EXCURSIONS FROM OSLO

The nearby islands of inner **Oslofjord** offer cheap, delightful daytrips. The ruins of a **Cistercian Abbey** lie on the landscaped island of **Hovedøya,** while **Langøyene** has Oslo's best **beach.** Take **bus** 29 from Oslo to **Vippetangen** (round-trip 40kr), southwest of downtown, to catch a ferry to either island. **Drøbak,** a town about an hour from Oslo by ferry, is filled by traditional wooden houses. The **ferry** to Drøbak leaves from the pier in front of the Rådhus (round-trip 100kr). **Fredrikstad's** old city is encircled by a massive wall, Norway's only fully-preserved fortified town. The town is on the Oslo **train** line toward Halden or Gothenburg (1¼hr.).

To bask in Norway's natural grandeur, take the Sognsvann subway from Nationaltheatret to the end of the line. **Use It,** the youth info center (see p. 684) provides trail maps; in winter, ask the tourist office about cross-country ski rental. **Villmarkssenteret,** Christian Krohgs gt. 16, rents canoes and kayaks on the Akerselva river. (Tel. 22 05 05 22. 270kr per 8hr., 310kr per 24hr., 530kr per weekend.)

SOUTHERN NORWAY

Norway's southern coast substitutes serenity for drama. *Skjærgard*, archipelagos of water-worn rock, hug the shore and stretch smoothly southward from Oslo to endless white beaches past Kristiansand. The coast is the premier Norwegian summer holiday destination. Fishing, hiking, rafting, and canoeing are popular in summer, while cross-country skiing reigns in winter.

KRISTIANSAND

Kristiansand attracts glacier- and winter-weary Norwegian tourists to its **beaches.** The open-air **Vest-Agder Fylkesmuseum,** Vigeveien 23b, showcases 17th-century southern Norwegian farmhouses and traditional folk dancing. (Open mid-June to mid-Aug. M-Sa 10am-6pm, Su noon-6pm; mid-Aug. to mid-June Su noon-5pm.) The remains of a Nazi bunker and a number of historical cannons are on display at the **Kristiansand Kanonenmuseum.** (Open mid-June to Aug. daily 11am-6pm; May to mid-June and Sept. closed F-Sa. 40kr.) Scramble up the walls of the 17th-century circular stone **Christiansholm Fortress** for a great view of the harbor. (Open mid-May to Sept. 9am-9pm.) Early in July, Kristiansand hosts the **Quart Festival** (www.quart.yahoo.no) which draws major hip-hop, rock, and pop acts; headliners at the '99 show included Garbage, Ben Harper, Blur, and Marilyn Manson.

Daily **trains** chug to Oslo (4½-5½hr., 430kr). Color Line **ferries** (tel. 81 00 08 11) run from **Kristiansand** to **Hirsthals, Denmark** (2½-4½hr., in summer 5 per day, 330-370kr). Ferries also run from Kristiansand to the scenic **Skerries** (tiny islands and fjords; 150kr); for more info, ask at the **tourist office,** at Henrik Wegerlandsgate and Vestre Strandsgate, opposite the train station. (Tel. 38 12 13 14. Open mid-June to Aug. M-F 8am-8pm, Sa-Su noon-8pm; Sept. to mid-June 8:30am-3:30pm.) The **Kristiansand Youth Hostel (HI),** Skansen 8, is 25min. from the station. (Tel. 38 02 83 10; fax 38 02 75 05. Dorms 160kr; singles 320kr; nonmembers add 25kr. Reception mid-June to mid-Aug. 24hr.; mid-Aug. to mid-June 5-11pm.) The noisy **Roligheden campground** is 45min. from town. (Tel. 38 09 67 22. 20kr per person, 60kr per tent. Showers 5kr per 3min. Open June-Aug.) The area around Kristiansand's main street, **Markensgata,** is full of affordable bars, cafés, and restaurants. **Husholdnings,** on Gyldenløves gt. in the old town, serves up authentic Norwegian cuisine. (Open M-F 9am-5pm.) **Munch,** Kristian IV gt. 1, is a pub far more lively than the dark art of its namesake.

STAVANGER

Stavanger is a delightful port town with colorful wooden fishing houses lining a busy pier and daily fish market. On the other side of the bustling harbor is **Gamle Stavanger,** a neighborhood restored to its prosperous 19th-century state. The Gothic **Stavanger Domkirke** (cathedral) broods in medieval solemnity in the modern town center. (Open mid-May to mid-Sept. M-Sa 10am-7pm, Su 1-6pm; mid-Sept. to mid-May M-F 10-11:45am and 12:15-2pm. Free.) The **Rogalund Kunstmuseum** (art museum) has a small but interesting collection. (Open Tu-Su 11am-4pm. 50kr, students 25kr.) Feel like a Norse god, but don't tumble over the edge of **Pulpit Rock** (Preikestolen) in nearby **Lysefjord,** one of Norway's postcard darlings. To get there, take the 8:20 or 9:15am ferry to Tau (runs June 21-Sept. 7, 40min., 25kr), catch the waiting bus (40kr), and hike 2hr. (return bus leaves at 4:15pm).

Trains pull in for Oslo (9hr., 4 per day, 630kr). **Flaggruten Catamarans** (tel. 51 86 87 80) speed to Bergen (4hr., 2-4 per day, 510kr, students 295kr; 50% off with Scanrail.)

Three Fjordline **ferries** (tel. 51 52 45 45) per week go to Newcastle, England (18hr., July-Aug. from 980kr, Sept.-June 410-790kr). The **tourist office,** Roskildetorget 1, is on the harbor next to the fish market. (Tel. 51 85 92 00; fax 51 85 92 02. Open June-Aug. daily 9am-8pm; Sept.-May M-F 9am-4pm, Sa 9am-2pm.) The **Mosvangen Vandrerhjem (HI),** Ibsensgt. 21, has a kitchen and free laundry. (Tel. 51 87 29 00; fax 51 87 06 30. 135kr; nonmembers 160kr. Reception 7-11am and 5-10pm.) Next door is **Mosvangen Camping.** (Tel. 51 53 29 71. 10kr per person, 70kr per tent. Open late May to early Sept.) To reach either from the town center, take bus 130, 78-79, or 97 (17kr). The fish and fruit **market** opposite the cathedral will satisfy your most finned or seedy culinary fantasy. (Open M-Sa 9am-5pm, Su closes earlier.) The popular jazz bar **Sting** is uphill from where Kirkegata and Breigata meet. (Open M-Sa noon-3:30am, Su 3pm-2am. Live performances W-Sa 11pm-3:30am.) **Postal code:** 4000.

EASTERN NORWAY

The faster of the two train lines that shoot north from Oslo to Trondheim heads through the **Gudbrandsdalen** valley via Lillehammer. Farther up the valley, the **Rondane** and **Dovrefjell** mountain ranges offer many decent hikes, but the truly breathtaking hikes are those in the **Jotunheimen** mountains to the west.

LILLEHAMMER

Lillehammer became a household name as host of the 1994 Winter Games. Lillehammer today still lives off its six-year-old Olympic legacy, but what a legacy it is: several billion *kroner* worth of state-of-the-art athletic facilities and new infrastructure, all constructed to harmonize with the mountainous environment. Håkons Hall, at the **Olympic Park,** the venue for the '94 ice-hockey and figure-skating competitions with a capacity of 10,000, now houses the **Norwegian Olympic Museum.** (Open mid-May to mid-Sept. daily 10am-6pm, mid-Sept. to mid-May Tu-Su 11am-4pm. 50kr, students 40kr.) In the square outside the hall, a **bobsled simulator** (40kr) gives your spinal cord a jolt. On the genuine article, 15km north at Hunderfossen (tel. 61 27 75 50), you can reach speeds of up to 105 km per hr. in a wheeled bobsled (125kr). In sight of the museum spire, the seemingly infinite steps of the Olympic **ski jumps** are open to be climbed; the ramps are used by aspiring ski-jumpers for training even during the summer. (Open daily 9am-8pm. Free.)

Daily **trains** run to Oslo (2½hr., 240kr); Åndalsnes (4hr., 350kr); and Trondheim (4½hr., 430kr). Most restaurants are on **Storgata,** parallel to the hillside two blocks uphill from the bus and train stations. The **tourist office,** Elvegata 19, off Storgata, has good info on hiking. (Tel. 61 25 92 99. Open mid-June to mid-Aug. M-Sa 9am-7pm, Su 11am-6pm; mid-Aug. to mid-June M-F 9am-4pm, Sa 10am-2pm.) **Gjeste Bu,** Gamleveien 110, is a block north of Storgata. (Tel./ fax 61 25 43 21. Sleeping bag accommodations 80kr; singles 200kr; doubles 300kr; triples 450kr. Sheets 40kr. Kitchen. Reception M-Sa 9am-11pm, Su 11am-11pm.) The comfy if simple **Lillehammer Youth Hostel (HI),** on the top floor of the train station, gives an 8am wake-up call when the station starts announcing departures. (Tel. 61 26 25 66. 170kr. Breakfast included.) Try the popular lunch (49kr; 11am-3pm) or dinner (79kr; 3-10pm) special at **Nikkers** café/pub, just before the tourist office on Elvegata.

VALDRES AND JOTUNHEIMEN

The **Valdres** valley ends in the highest mountain range in Europe north of the Alps, the jagged, reindeer-inhabited **Jotunheimen** massif. Even though only two of several hundred peaks require technical gear to climb, the weather can be harsh and it snows at higher altitudes even in July. The DNT offices in Bergen and Oslo and tourist offices in the region overflow with maps and tips on trails and huts. Consider basing yourself in **Gjendesheim,** 1hr. north of Fagernes by bus (2 per day, 60kr), at the DNT **hut,** from which you can hike across the **Besseggen,** a spectacular ridge with an emerald green lake at 984m and a deep blue one at 1200m.

FAGERNES. Though not particularly memorable, Fagernes holds is ideally located for hiking, rafting, or visiting medieval wooden stave churches in the Valdres. Reach the town by **bus** (students 25% off, with railpass 50% off) from Gol, on the Oslo-Bergen rail line (70min., 60kr); from Lillehammer (2hr., 104kr); or by *Valdresekspressen* bus from Oslo (3hr., 190kr). The **tourist office**, in the bus station, has the great *Valdres Summer Guide* or *Winter Guide*. (Tel. 61 35 94 10. Open July to mid-Aug. M-F 8am-7pm, Sa 9am-6pm, Su 10am-6pm; late Aug. to June M-F 8am-4pm.) The more rough 'n' tumble can get info on the *Vardevandring* (watchtower hikes), which wind through the valley. The **Leira Youth Hostel (HI),** Valdres Folkehøjskole, is 4km south of town. Ask the bus driver to drop you at the hostel on the way to town. (Tel. 61 36 20 25. 90kr; nonmembers 115kr. Open May 25-Aug. 9.)

LOM, BØVERDALEN, SPITERSTULEN, AND TURTAGRØ. From Otta, the trip to **Lom** involves a breathtaking bus ride over the main massif of Jotunheimen (62kr). The two highest points in Norway, **Galdhøpiggen** (2469m) and **Glittertinden** (2464m), are within distant striking distance of Lom, and can be scaled without technical gear. Lom's **tourist office** is across the bridge from the bus stop. (Tel. 61 21 29 90. Open mid-June to mid-Aug. M-F 9am-9pm, Sa-Su 10am-8pm; early June and late Aug. M-F 9am-6pm, Sa-Su 10am-5pm; May and Sept. M-F 9am-4pm, Sa-Su 11am-4pm.) Two daily **buses** toward Sogndal stop 20km from Lom in **Bøverdalen,** where there's an **HI youth hostel.** (Tel. 61 21 20 64; fax 61 21 20 64. 90kr, nonmembers 115kr. Breakfast 50kr. Reception 8am-10pm. Open May 25-Sept.) In Lom, the legendary Norwegian chef Arne Brimi prepares magnificent ptarmigan and reindeer specialties at the **Fossheim Hotel Restaurant,** considered by many to be the finest restaurant in Norway. (3-course meal 385kr, 5-course 425-495kr. Reserve ahead.)

The **tourist chalet,** about 18km off Route 55 at **Spiterstulen** (tel. 61 21 14 80), provides better access to Glittertinden (200kr, DNT members 150kr; camping 50kr). A **bus** leaves Lom daily (June 27-Aug. 16) at 8:35am and 4:25pm, returning from Spiterstulen at 10:30am and 5:25pm (round-trip 102kr). Southwest of Bøverdalen, the plateau between **Krossbu** and **Sognefjellhytta** is strewn with rock cairns tracing the way between snow-covered lakes; **cross-country skiing** is possible throughout the summer. Near **Turtagrø,** just above the tip of the Sognefjord system, is one of Norway's premier rock-climbing areas. From Sognefjellhytta, a steep five-hour path leads to **Fannaråkhytta** (2069m), the highest hut in the DNT system.

THE FJORDS AND WEST COUNTRY

Ten thousand years ago, during the last Ice Age, glaciers sliced out huge, steep gashes into Norway's coast. When the glaciers receded, the sea rushed in, creating fjords. Buses and ferries wind through this unique and scenic coastal region, from south of Bergen to Ålesund. Approaches to the fjords are infinite, and routes through them plentiful. Except for a small stretch on the Oslo-Bergen line (see below), seeing the fjords from a train is impossible.

ALONG THE OSLO-BERGEN RAIL LINE

The rail journey from Oslo to Bergen (7hr., 470km) is the most scenic in Norway. If you're coming from Oslo, there are stops along the way at **Geilo; Finse** (see below); **Myrdal,** the transfer point for the **Flåm railway** (see **Sognefjord,** p. 697); and **Voss** (see below) before finally pulling into Bergen.

FINSE. Wilderness junkies hop off at Finse and hike north for three or four beautiful days down the Aurlandsdal Valley to **Aurland,** 10km from Flåm. You can sleep warmly all the way in evenly spaced DNT *hytter*. For maps, prices, and reservations, inquire at DNT in Oslo (tel. 22 82 28 22) or Bergen (tel. 55 32 22 30).

VOSS. Stretched along a glassy lake that glimmers with the reflections of the surrounding snow-capped mountains, Voss is an adventurer's dream. In winter, skiing is plentiful; in summer there's paragliding, horseback riding, and whitewater raft-

NORWAY

ing. Book through the **Voss Adventure Center** (tel. 56 51 36 30), in a mini-golf hut behind the Park Hotel, and the **Voss Rafting Center** (tel. 56 51 05 25; www.bbb.no/ rafting). **Trains** arrive from Oslo (5 per day, 450kr) and Bergen (10 per day, 125kr). **Buses** also run from Voss to Gudvangen (70min., 4-9 per day, 64kr; 50% ISIC discount; see p. 697) on the Sognefjord. To get from the bus station to the **tourist office,** Hestavangen 10, turn left when you reach the lake and bear right at the fork by the church. (Tel. 56 52 08 00; fax 56 52 08 01. Open June-Aug. M-Sa 9am-7pm, Su 2-7pm; Sept.-May M-F 9am-4pm.) Turn right as you exit the station and walk along the lakeside road to reach to Voss's modern, well-equipped **HI youth hostel,** where you can admire the terrific view or relax in the sauna. (Tel. 56 51 20 17. 175kr; nonmembers 200kr. Canoe, rowboat, bike, and kayak rental. Reception 24hr.) To reach **Voss Camping,** head left from the station, stick to the lakeshore, and follow the road until you hit the campground pool. (Tel. 56 51 15 97. Tent and 4 people 60kr.)

BERGEN

Vaunted as the "Gateway to the Fjords," Bergen is clean, compact, and stunningly beautiful, surrounded by unblemished, forested mountains rising steeply from the fjords. Once Norway's capital and a center of trade in the Middle Ages, the city still claims a prominent commercial and intellectual standing. The lively student population and myriad international influences make Bergen much more than just another scenic spot on the Norwegian coast.

⌨ GETTING THERE AND GETTING AROUND

Trains: Tel. 81 50 08 88. Three trains daily to **Oslo** (6½-7½hr., 555kr, mandatory seat reservations 25kr) via **Voss** (1hr., 120kr) and **Myrdal** (1¾-2½hr., 175kr).

Buses: Bystasjonen, Strømgaten 8 (tel. 177, from outside Bergen 55 55 90 70). Serves neighboring areas, the **Hardangerfjord** area, **Ålesund** (470kr, students 25% off), and **Oslo** (560kr; students 25% off). Ticket office open M-Sa 7am-6pm, Sa 7am-2pm.

Ferries: The **Hurtigruten** stops along the way from **Bergen** to **Kirkenes** (leaves Bergen daily 10:30pm; full trip May-Sept. 3685kr; Oct.-Apr. cheaper; students 50% off); inquire at the tourist office. **Fjord Line,** on Skoltegrunnskaien (tel. 55 54 88 00), goes to **Hanstholm, Denmark** (15½hr., departs M, W, and F 4:30pm, 660-890kr; off-season 515kr; round-trip 10% off) and **Newcastle, England** (25hr.; departs Tu and F; in summer also Su; 980kr, in winter students 50% off). **Smyril Line,** Slottsgaten 1 (tel. 55 32 09 70; fax 55 96 02 72), departs for the **Faroe Islands** (24hr., 820-1400kr; departs June-Aug. Tu 3pm); **Iceland** (40hr., 1790-2810kr); and the **Shetland Islands** (11hr., 670-1140kr; students 25% off). International ferries depart from **Skoltegrunnskaien,** 20min. past Bryggen along the right side of the harbor.

Public Transportation: Yellow and red buses chauffeur you around the city. 8kr per ride in city center, 17kr outside; free from the bus station into the center of town.

⌨ ORIENTATION AND PRACTICAL INFORMATION

The **train station** lies at the opposite end of the city center from the harbor, 10min. away. As you face the harbor, **Bryggen** (the extension of Kong Oscars gt.) and the town's most imposing mountains are to your right; most of the main buildings are to the left. The **Torget,** Bergen's famous outdoor market, is at the harbor's tip.

Tourist Office: Bryggen 7 (tel. 55 32 14 80; fax 55 32 14 64), just past the Torget. Books rooms and has free copies of the *Bergen Guide* and suggested itineraries through the fjords. The **Bergen Card** includes museum admissions and other discounts (1-day 130kr, 2-day 200kr). Open June-Aug. daily 8:30am-10pm; May and Sept. daily 9am-8pm; Oct.-Apr. M-Sa 9am-4pm. **DNT,** Tverrgt. (tel. 55 32 22 30), off Marken, sells detailed topological maps for all of Norway. Open M-W, and F 10am-4pm, Th until 6pm.

Currency Exchange: At the post office. After hours both tourist offices will change currency at 4% worse than the bank rate. No commission.

Luggage storage: At the train station 20kr per day. Open daily 7am-11:50pm.

Emergencies: Fire: tel. 110. **Police:** tel. 112. **Ambulance:** tel. 113.

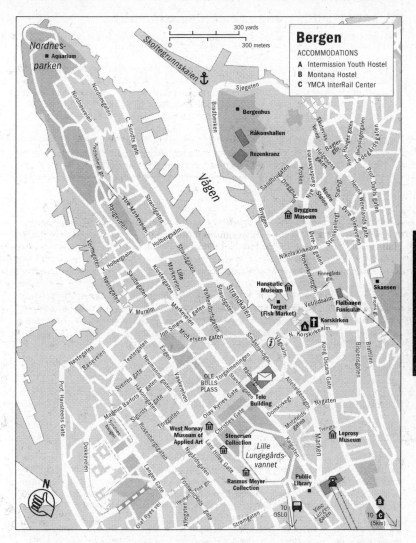

Bergen

ACCOMMODATIONS

A Intermission Youth Hostel
B Montana Hostel
C YMCA InterRail Center

Pharmacy: Apoteket Nordstjernen (tel. 55 31 68 84), on the 2nd floor of the bus station. Open M-Sa 8am-midnight, Su 9:30am-midnight.

Medical Assistance: 24-hour Accident Clinic, Vestre Strømkai 19 (tel. 55 32 11 20).

Internet Access: Free at the **public library** *(bibliotek)* at Stromgata Vestre Stromkaien, though time is officially limited to 15min. Open M and Th 9am-7pm, Tu-W and F 9am-3pm, Sa 9am-2pm. Or try **Netropolis,** Theatergaten 20. 30kr per 30min., 40kr per hr.

Telephones: Tele Building, Byparken Starrhusegate 4, across Rådhusgaten from the post office. Open M-F 9am-4pm.

Post Office: Småstrandgt. (tel. 55 54 15 00). Address mail to be held: Michael <u>WILLIAMS</u>, *Poste Restante,* **N-5014** Bergen, Norway. Open M-F 8am-6pm, Sa 9am-3pm.

PHONE CODE There is no city code. From outside Norway, dial int'l access code (see inside back cover) + 47 + local number.

⛰ ACCOMMODATIONS, CAMPING, AND FOOD

The tourist office books rooms (some with bathrooms) in private homes for a 25kr fee (40kr fee for 2 people; singles 185-210kr; doubles 295-430kr).

⛵ Intermission, Kalfarveien 8 (tel. 55 31 32 75). Head right from the train station and right down Kong Oscars gt., which becomes Kalfarveien (5min.). Friendly staff and communal atmosphere. Free sheets, blankets, ghost stories, tea and cookies, laundry, and (on M and Th nights) waffles. Co-ed dorms 95kr. Breakfast 25kr; pack a lunch for 15kr. Reception 7-11am and 5pm-midnight, F-Sa until 1am. Lockout 11am-5pm. Curfew M-Th and Su midnight, F-Sa 1am. Reserve ahead. Open mid-June to mid-Aug.

YMCA InterRail Center, Nedre Korskirkealmenningen 4 (tel. 55 31 72 52; fax 55 31 35 77). Warm, knowledgeable staff. Dorms 100-150kr. Reception 7am-midnight. Lockout noon-4pm. Kitchen. Laundry 40kr. **Internet.** Open June to mid-Sept.

Montana Youth Hostel (HI), Johan Blyttsvei 30 (tel. 55 20 80 70; fax 55 20 80 75), halfway up Mt. Ulriken, 5km from the city center. Take bus 31 (dir: Lægdene; 17kr) from the post office to "Montana." Dorms 135-170kr; doubles with bath 470kr. Breakfast included. Sheets 40kr. Kitchen. Laundry. Reception 24hr. Lockout 10am-3pm.

Camping: Bergen Camping Park, Haukås om Åsane (tel. 55 24 88 08). 15kr per person, 70kr per tent. Or **free camp** on the far side of the hills above town. Pick up a map or ask for further info at the DNT office in town.

Bergen's culinary centerpiece is the **fish market** that springs up on the Torget, by the harbor; it's unclear, however, whether fish or tourists are the main haul. (Open in summer M-F 7am-4pm, Th until 7pm, Sa until 3pm; in off-season opens later.) Grab **groceries** at **Mekka,** Marken 3. **Fellini,** Tverrgt., just off Marken, serves up Italian specialties and the best pizza in town from 59kr. (Open M-Th 1pm-midnight, F-Sa 1pm-2am, Su 2-11pm.) Enjoy Norwegian cuisine with the older set at **Kaffistova til Ervingen,** Strandkaien 2B, on the second floor next to the harbor, a cafeteria-style joint with *dagens tilbur* (daily offer) for 69kr. (Open M-F 8am-7pm, Sa 8am-5pm, Su 11am-6pm.) **Den Gode Klode,** Fosswinckelsgate 18, satisfies vegetarians in an elegant spot with outdoor seating. (Salads from 30kr. *Dagens ret* 60-70kr. Students 10% off. Open M-F 11:30am-7pm, Sa 11:30am-5pm.) **The Dromedar Kaffebar,** next door, is a classy little place. (Open M-F 10am-5pm, Sa-Su 11am-5pm.)

👁 SIGHTS

BRYGGEN AND BERGENHUS. From the Torget, gazing down the right side of the harbor yields a view of **Bryggen's** (The Wharf) pointed gables. This row of medieval buildings has survived half a dozen disastrous fires and the explosion of a Nazi munitions ship, and is today listed by UNESCO as one of the world's significant examples of the history and culture of the Middle Ages. Today, the buildings are occupied by restaurants and artsy-craftsy workshops. The **Hanseatic Museum** is contains secret compartments, mummified hanging fish, and an aura of gloom from the days when German merchants controlled trade through Europe. *(At the end of Bryggen, near the Torget. Open daily June-Aug. 9am-5pm; Sept.-May 11am-2pm. May-Sept. 35kr; Oct.-Apr. 20kr.)* **Bryggens Museum** displays old costumes, runic inscriptions, and scenes from life in old Norway. *(3 Dreggsalm, behind a small park at the end of the Bryggen houses. Open May-Aug. daily 10am-5pm; Sept.-Apr. M-F 11am-3pm, Sa noon-3pm, Su noon-4pm. 20kr, students 10kr.)* The former city fortress, **Bergenhus,** teeters at the end of the quay, and the **Rosenkrantz Tower** stands adjacent in late medieval splendor. **Håkonshallen,** built by Håkon Håkonsson in the 13th century, is all that remains of the royal residence. *(At the end of Bryggen. Hall and tower open daily mid-May to Aug. 10am-4pm; Sept. to mid-May noon-3pm. Guided tours of both every hr. in summer. 15kr.)*

ART MUSEUMS AND GALLERIES. The **Rasmus Meyer Collection** provides a extensive overview of Norwegian Naturalists, Impressionists, and Expressionists, while the **Stenersens Collection** two doors down has works by Munch and Picasso; both are branches of the **Bergen Art Museum.** *(7 and 3 Rasmus Meyers Allé, respectively. Both open mid-May to mid-Sept. daily 10am-5pm; mid-Sept. to mid-May Tu-Su 11am-5pm. Mid-May to* *mid-Sept. 35kr together; mid-Sept. to mid-May 20kr.)* The **West Norway Museum of Applied Art** highlights stunning 20th-century developments in Norwegian design. *(9 Nordahl Brunsgt. Open mid-May to mid-Sept. Tu-Su 11am-4pm; mid-Sept. to mid-May Tu-Sa noon-3pm, Th noon-6pm, Su noon-4pm. 30kr, students 20kr.)* Smaller, contemporary works line the intriguing **Galleri Nygaten.** *(Nygaten 5, off Kong Oscars gt. Open daily noon-4pm.)*

OTHER SIGHTS. The university has tastefully documented the history of the disease in a 19th-century hospital at the **Leprosy Museum.** *(Kong Oscars gt. 59. Open daily mid-May to Aug. 11am-3pm. 20kr.)* For lighter material, commune with the fishies at the **Bergen Aquarium.** *(Nordnesbakken 4, on the tip of the peninsula near the harbor entrance. Take bus 4, or walk 15min. from the city center. Open daily May-Sept. 9am-8pm; Oct.-Apr. 10am-6pm. May-Sept. 75kr, Oct.-Apr. 55kr.)* For an authentic taste of the city, explore the steep streets between the **Korskirken** church and the **Skansen** tower, and the **Sydneskleiben** and **Dragefjellsbarker** neighborhoods near the university campus. **Gamle Bergen** (Old Bergen) is a rather touristy "village" and open-air museum of wooden buildings from the last century. *(Take city bus 20, 21, 22, or any red bus going to Sandviken to the 1st stop past the 2nd tunnel (7min.) and then walk under the overpass, following the signs. Houses open May 24-Aug. 9:30am-4:30pm. Obligatory tours every hr. 40kr, students 20kr.)* **Troldhaugen** (Troll Hill) was the summer villa of Edvard Grieg, Norway's most famous composer. The house still contains many of Grieg's belongings, including his Steinway piano, which is used at summer concerts in neighboring **Troldsalen Hall.** *(Hopsbroen, 8km south of Bergen. From the Bergen bus station, take any bus to "Hopsbroen" ("Hop."), turn right, walk 200m, then turn left at Troldhaugsveien and follow the signs (20min.). Open daily Apr. 18-Sept. 9am-6pm. 40kr. Summer concerts W and Sa-Su; buy tickets at the tourist office.)*

HIKING. A vast archipelago spreads westward from Bergen, and towering mountains encroach on all three other sides. Trails surrounding the city are well-kept, easily accessible, and awe-inspiring. The **Fløibanen funicular** (lift) runs to a lookout point atop **Mt. Fløyen.** *(From the Torget, follow Vetrlidsalm. east to the funicular. Sept.-Apr. M-F 7:30am-11pm, Sa 8am-11pm, Su 9am-11pm; May-Aug. until midnight. Round-trip 40kr.)* At the summit, you can enjoy the spectacular views or join up with one of the many intersecting **hiking** trails that meander through a striking landscape dotted by massive boulders, springy moss, waterfalls, and ponds. A four-hour trail from Fløyen leads to the top of **Mt. Ulriken,** the highest peak above Bergen, and a panoramic view over the city, fjords, mountains, and nearby islands. Free concerts are held at the top of Mt. Ulriken in summer (weekdays at 6pm). A **cable car** also runs to the top of Mt. Ulriken (every 7min. daily in summer 9am-9pm; in winter 10am-dusk; round-trip 60kr). Pick up a **map** of the hills above Bergen at the DNT office.

🎵 ENTERTAINMENT

The city pulls out all the stops for the annual **Bergen International Festival** (tel. 55 21 61 50), a 12-day program of music, ballet, folklore, and drama, and the simultaneous **May Jazz Festival** in late May (tickets for both are generally expensive). The **Garage Bar,** at the corner of Nygårdsgaten and Christies gate, usually has live bands on Fridays and Saturdays (cover varies); on Wednesdays and Thursdays, check out the psychedelic dungeon. (Open daily 1-6:30pm and 10pm-3am, Su opens at 3pm.) The milder scene is on at **Café Opera,** Engen 18, a mellow café-restaurant (try the reindeer roast with mountain cranberries for 98kr) with student theater on Thursday nights; it gets funky on Fridays and Saturdays with dance music. (No cover. Open M-Th noon-2am, F noon-3am, Sa 11:30am-3am, Su 1pm-2am.) **Maxime Club,** Ole Bulls Plass, has got the bodies that rock the parties. (Cover 40-60kr. Open Th-Sa 11pm-3am.) **Rick's,** Veiten 3, has a great bar and two discos (rock and pop) upstairs. (Cover 50kr F-Sa after 10:30pm. Open 10pm-3am.)

🏞 EXCURSIONS FROM BERGEN: THE FJORDS

Virtually all of western Norway's **fjords** are accessible as daytrips from Bergen. Most **ferries** leave from the **Strandkaiterminalen** on the side of the harbor opposite Bryggen. Here we outline possibilities for daytrips to the fjords for those with a limited amount of time, but those with more luxurious schedules should see the individual fjord write-ups for suggestions on where to base extended stays.

SOGNEFJORD. for more info see p. 697. Get immersed in the infinite spaces of Sognefjord on the excellent and popular **Norway In a Nutshell** tour, which explores Sognefjord by a variety of vehicles: the stunning rail line to **Flåm** (see p. 697) connects with an awe-inspiring ferry ride through narrow fjords to **Gudvangen** (2½hr., 4 per day, 130kr, 50% discount for InterRail and ISIC—if you make it a self-guided tour), which leads to a bus ride on a series of dramatic switchbacks up to **Voss** (1¼hr., 5-8 per day, 64kr, 50% ISIC discount), where trains await to zip you to your next destination. Most people begin this full-day tour in Bergen, but you can also start from Oslo or from other points. Tours, available through tourist offices, cost 525kr round-trip from Bergen, 890kr round-trip from Oslo, or 660kr from Bergen to Oslo; railpass holders and students can get discounts on individual legs of the package, and thus may benefit from paying by segment instead of buying a full ticket. **Fylkesbaatane** (tel. 55 90 70 70) sends boats on daytrips to towns on the **Sognefjord** and back to Bergen (to Gudvangen and Stalheim 560kr; to Flåm 595kr; students 50% off). They also give day tours of Sognefjord and the Flåm valley (595kr).

HARDANGERFJORD. See p. 696 for more info. **Hardanger Sunnhordlandske Dampskipsselskap (HSD)** offers tours of the Hardangerfjord. (Tel. 55 23 87 80. Round-trip 450-595kr, discounts for students and railpass holders.)

ELSEWHERE. The **M/S Bruvik** runs an excellent day-long tour of **Osterfjord** and **Osterøy island.** (Tel. 56 39 17 00. Tours 9hr., 325kr. Tickets at the tourist office or on the boat. Departs June 21-Aug. daily 9am; Apr. 26-June 20 and Sept.-Oct. 4 Su only.) **Bergen Fjord Sightseeing** also has tours. (Tel. 55 25 90 00. Tours 4hr., 250kr; students and InterRailers 25% off. Tickets at the tourist office or fish market pier.)

HARDANGERFJORD

Slicing through one of Norway's fruit-growing regions, the steep banks of the Hardangerfjord are lined with orchards and small farms. The tourist office in Bergen and other local tourist offices distribute the free *Hardanger Guide.*

ROSENDAL. Perched at the mouth of the fjord, Rosendal is an excellent base from which to explore nearby glaciers and waterfalls for more extended stays. The town itself is home to Norway's only Barony and a beautiful rose garden. **Ferries** travel to Rosendal from Bergen (2½hr., 1 per day, 190kr). The **tourist office** can help you find a place to stay. (Tel. 53 48 42 80. Open daily June-Aug. 10am-6pm.)

JONDAL. Jondal, about halfway through Hardangerfjord and another good base for longer stays on the fjord, is quite close to the **Folgefonna Glacier,** with everything from views to walks along glacier trails. Jondal is accessible by **ferry** from Bergen (3¼hr., 1 per day, 225kr). For more info, contact the Jondal **tourist office.** (Tel. 53 66 85 31. Open mid-June to mid-Aug. M-F 9am-5pm, Sa-Su 11am-3pm.)

EIDFJORD. The thunder of stampeding hikers can be heard in beautiful Eidfjord, 45km southeast of Voss on RV13, as they pass through this main gateway to **Hardangervidda,** Norway's largest national park. **Ferries** arrive at Eidfjord from Bergen (5¾hr., 1 per day, 340kr; change at Northeimsund). Duck into Eidfjord's **tourist office** for an info refill. (Tel. 53 66 51 77. Open July M-F 9am-8pm, Sa 9am-6pm, Su 11am-8pm; late June and Aug. M-Sa 9am-6pm; Sept. to mid-June M-F 8:30am-4pm.) Walk 1km to see Vikings from AD 400-800 decaying at the **Viking Burial Place** in Hereid, or take the bus 20km to one of Norway's most famous waterfalls, the 182m **Vøringstossen.** Ask the Eidfjord tourist office to find you a bed (huts from 180kr), or try **Saebø Camping** (tel. 53 66 59 27; 35kr per tent, 10kr per person; 235kr per cabin).

SOGNEFJORD

The deep, jaggedly slender fingers of Sognefjord, the longest of the fjords (200km), penetrate all the way to the foot of the Jotunheimen Mountains. Easily accessible, Sognefjord is just a short, stunning ride north of the Oslo-Bergen rail line.

FLÅM. Deep in Sognefjord, Flåm is the only fjord town accessible by rail; the spectacular **Flåm Railway** runs from **Myrdal** (on the Oslo-Bergen line) to Flåm (50min., 11-13 per day, 50kr for railpass holders). Alternatively, a 20km **hike** (4-5hr.) on well-tended paths from Myrdal to Flåm allows for extended lingering (and free camping) amid the rainbow-capped waterfalls and snowy mountain vistas. Express **boats** also run between Flåm and Bergen (5hr., 2 per day, 435kr; 50% off with InterRail or ISIC). During the day the tiny town is heavily touristed; but in the off-season, or even once the tourists have melted away by nightfall, the stunning surroundings make Flåm a terrific, soothing place to spend a night or two. The **tourist office** is in the large building by the train station. (Tel. 57 63 21 06. Open daily mid-June to mid-Aug. 8:30am-8:30pm.) To get to **Flåm Camping and Hostel (HI)**, cross to the side of the river opposite the train station and follow the road into the valley. (Tel. 57 63 21 21; fax 57 63 23 80. 95kr; nonmembers 120kr; tent and 1 person 65kr, 2 people 90kr. Open May-Sept.) The **Heimly Pensjonat**, on the right bank of the fjord, offers sleeping bag accommodations. (Tel. 57 63 23 00. 125kr. Reception 8am-midnight.)

AURLAND. A short distance from Flåm, Aurland provides access to much the same natural splendor, but with far fewer tourists. One of the most popular **day hikes** (8-10hr. one-way) in Norway, actually the final stage of a 3- to 4-day hike starting in Finse (see p. 691), begins in nearby Østerbø and runs through the Aurlandsdal Valley to Vassbygdi. Both endpoints can be reached by bus (4 per day, 40kr) from Aurland or Flåm. There is a fantastic view of the Aurland fjord a short hike up from **Otternes Bygdetun**, a unique cluster of 17th-century houses between the two towns. (Tel. 57 63 33 00. Open mid-June to mid-Aug. 11am-6pm. 20kr.) About 2km from town, just past the campground (see below), a trail branches to the left and offers a scenic, intense four-hour hike to the top of **Prest** (1360m). **Buses** connect Aurland and Flåm (7-8 per day, 22kr), as do **ferries** (5-6 per day, 28kr). Aurland has no youth hostel, but the **tourist office**, at the highway junction, helps find rooms. (Tel. 57 63 33 13. Open June-Aug. M-F 8:30am-7pm, Sa-Su 10am-5pm; Sept.-Apr. M-F 8am-3:30pm.) Or, contact the DNT office in Bergen or Oslo to rent one of the DNT **huts** along the Aurlandsdal Valley trail. **Lunde Camping**, 1.5km from town along the river, sprouts tents and caravans. (Tel. 57 63 34 12. 15kr per person, 50kr per tent.)

BALESTRAND. On the north side of Sognefjord, midway between Bergen and Flåm, Balestrand is a groovy base for fjord and glacier excursions. Express boats whiz from Balestrand up the **Fjærlandsfjord** to Fjærland (2 per day, round-trip 290kr). From there, buses (80kr) shuttle passengers for a tour of the **Glacier Museum** (see **Fjærland,** below), whisk them to view two offshoots of the **Jostedal Glacier,** and return them to Fjærland in time to catch the boat back to Balestrand. **Hiking** in the area immediately around Balestrand is also excellent. Follow the blue-marked trail above the town to **Balastølen,** a mountain meadow with a sublime view of the fjord; get maps and info at the **tourist office,** near the quay. (Tel. 57 69 12 55. Open M-F 7:30am-9pm, Sa-Su 7:30am-6:30pm.) Hydrofoils from Bergen serve Balestrand (4hr., 2 per day, 320kr; with railpass or ISIC 50% off). The gorgeous fjord-side **Kringsjå Hotel and Youth Hostel (HI)** is 100m up the hill behind town. (Tel. 57 69 13 03. Dorms 165kr, doubles 190-230kr; nonmembers 195kr, 220-260kr. Breakfast included. Kitchen. Laundry.) **Sjøtun Camping,** 1km down the coastal road, has tent sites and huts. (Tel. 57 69 12 23. 15kr per person, 25kr per tent; 2-person hut 125kr. Reception 9-10am, 6-7pm, and 9-10pm. Open June to mid-Sept.)

■ **EXCURSIONS FROM SOGNEFJORD: FJÆRLANDSFJORD AND FJÆR-LAND.** With Balestrand perched at its mouth, Fjærlandsfjord branches off from Sognefjord in a thin northward line to the tiny town of **Fjærland,** which lies under the looming Jostedalsbreen glacier. Fjærland itself is home to a number of fine hikes, an incongruous "book town"—with fourteen multilingual used book stores—and little else. The **Glacier Museum** 3km away is ready to elucidate about all things icy. (Open daily June-Aug. 9am-7pm; Apr.-May and Sept.-Oct. 10am-4pm. 70kr.) **Ferries** from Balestrand make the run to Fjærland (2 per day, 58kr), providing a nifty way to get north of Sognefjord without having to go all the way around it. **Buses** from Fjærland to Sogndal (2-4 per day, 90kr; students 50% off) and Stryn (1-3 per day, 120kr; students 50% off) leave from stops 200m up the road from the Glacier Museum on Route 5; travelers just passing through Fjærland should take the bus to the Glacier Museum one-way (16kr) to reach the stops. The **tourist office** can solve any transport woes. (Tel. 57 69 32 33. Open May 29-Sept. 12 daily 9:30am-4pm.)

NORDFJORD AND JOSTEDALSBREEN GLACIER

Enveloping 800km of the area around **Nordfjord** in an icy cocoon, the **Jostedalsbreen Glacier** is difficult to miss as it licks its way through mountain passes in frozen cascades of luminous blue. Nordfjord itself is less impressive than Geirangerfjord and Sognefjord, to the north and south, respectively; it's really more of a geographical entity around which you'll have to navigate than an object of direct interest. Jostedalsbreen, in contrast, is becoming an increasingly popular destination, and a number of companies leading glacier walks have sprung up in recent years. Yet without a car, it's fiendishly difficult to take advantage of these tours in the space of one day. Although neither of the most accessible arms of the glacier, **Briksdalsbreen** and **Nigardsbreen**, is far from good-sized base towns, the public bus network does not yet easily accommodate backpackers wishing to explore the glacier.

It is possible to get to Geirangerfjord from Sognefjord in a day—from Balestrand to Hellesylt via Fjærland, Skei, and Stryn. But if you have any interest in probing the blue ice of Jostedalsbreen Glacier—which is truly as exciting as it sounds—linger in Stryn a while, or base yourself in Sogndal instead.

STRYN (BRIKSDALSBREENARM AND BØDALSBREEN). Stryn is wedged between the mountains near the inner end of Nordfjord, just northwest of the glacier. **Briksdal Breføring** (tel. 57 87 68 00) and **Olden Aktiv** (tel. 57 87 38 88) run a variety of tours for different fitness and skill levels (200-400kr) on the nearby **Briksdalsbreenarm** of Jostedalsbreen glacier. **Stryn Fjell-og Breførarlay** (tel. 57 87 76 59) runs longer, more intense hikes on **Bødalsbreen** (300-500kr), a different limb of the glacier. A bus (50kr, 50% off with railpass) leaves Stryn daily at 10am for **Briksdal**; the meeting point for glacier walks is a mild half-hour hike from there. All is not so rosy, however, for car-less travelers: the return bus leaves Briksdal at 2pm, meaning that anyone relying on the bus for transport back can only spend an hour actually on the ice. The determined can camp in Briksdal's campgrounds or dish out the dough for a room (from 350kr). **Buses** arrive at the edge of Stryn from Otta (205kr) via Lom (140kr) and Jotunheim, from Hellesylt in Geirangerfjord (60kr), and from Fjærland near Sognefjord (120kr); students earn 25% off all fares, while railpass holders get 50% off. To get to the **tourist office,** on Walhallengen, walk past the Esso station, bear slightly left at the rotary, then hang a right on Walhallengen. (Tel. 57 87 40 54. Open daily July 10am-8pm; June and Aug. 10am-6pm.) The comfy **youth hostel (HI)** is a hike up the hill behind town; call ahead and ask nicely for a ride. (Tel. 57 87 11 06. 160kr, nonmembers 185kr. Breakfast included. Laundry 30kr. Reception 8-11am and 4-11pm. Open June-Aug.) **Stryn Camping** is in the center of town. (Tel. 57 87 11 36. 120kr for tent and 1 person, 10kr per extra person. Reception 8am-11pm.)

SOGNDAL (NIGARDSBREEN). Southeast of Fjærland on the Sognefjord, Sogndal, though not much of a destination in itself, is another fine base from which to glacier walk. The **Nigardsbreen** arm of Jostedalsbreen is nearby, virtually begging for hikers to trek across its icy expanse. **Jostedal Breheimsenteret** (tel. 57 68 32 50) runs everything from one-hour outings to full-day jaunts (100-500kr). Buses (75kr; 50% off with railpass) leave Sogndal for the glacier at 8:10am, with a return bus at 5pm. When you've had your fill of the glacier, **buses** leave town for Fjærland (30min., 7 per day, 40kr); Stryn (3hr., 7 per day, 100kr); and Lom (3½hr., 3 per day, 140kr). The campground at Nigardsbreen also has huts. (Tel. 57 68 31 35. 30kr per tent, 10kr per person; 4-person huts 250kr.) Contact the Sogndal **tourist office** for more info. (Tel. 57 67 30 83. Open daily June 20-Aug. 20 9am-8pm; Aug. 21-June 19 M-F 9am-4pm.) The Sogndal **youth hostel (HI)** has a fjord-side spot 15min. east of the bus station. (Tel. 57 67 20 33. Dorms 95kr; singles 160kr; doubles 220kr; nonmembers add 25kr.)

GEIRANGERFJORD

Though only 16km long, Geirangerfjord's gorgeous cliffs and waterfalls make it Norway's most sublime fjord. While cruising through the green-blue water, watch the drama of the **Seven Sisters,** the spurting and gushing of the **Suitor,** and the **Bridal Veil's** mist. Geirangerfjord can be reached from the north via the famous Tollstigen road from Åndalsnes, or from the south from Stryn, Sogndal, or Fjærland, into Hellesylt. Hellesylt and Geiranger are connected by a stunning 1¼-hour ferry ride.

GEIRANGER. Ensconced on glorious Geirangerfjord's eastern terminus, and an endpoint, along with Åndalsnes, of the famous **Tollstigen** road with its spectacular views and incredibly steep inclines. Geiranger's streets are trampled by over 3000 tourists every day in summer. Even the tourists, however, can't manage to overwhelm the area, which stands at the pinnacle of fjordom. **Hiking** abounds in this charmed country; consider the hike to **Dalsnibba Mountain** (or take the daily 10am bus from the church next to the hostel; returns 12:45pm; 90kr), the path underneath the **Storseter Waterfall,** and the hikes to **Flydalsjuvet Cliff** and **Skageflå Farm.**

Buses run to Åndalsnes (3hr., 2 per day, 250kr; with railpass 50% off). The **tourist office,** up from the ferry landing, finds private rooms (from 200kr) for a 20kr fee. (Tel. 70 26 30 99. Open late May to Aug. daily 9am-7pm.) **Geiranger Camping** is by the water, 500m past the ferry dock. (Tel. 70 26 31 20. 10kr per person, 50kr per tent. Showers 5kr per 3min.) To get to the fantastic view of the fjord at **Vinjebakken Hostel,** follow the main road up the steep hill behind town (15min.). (Tel. 70 26 32 05. 130kr. Breakfast 60kr. Shower 10kr. Laundry 25kr. Checkout 11am. Reception 8-11am and 3pm-midnight. Open mid-June to mid-Aug.) **Geiranger Fjordservice** cruises the fjord's chilly waters. (Tel. 70 26 30 07. Cruises 1hr. round-trip, 5 per day June-Aug. 10am-5:30pm; June 25-July 31 also 8pm.)

HELLESYLT. Another way to see the fjord is to take the ferry connecting Geiranger with Hellesylt, the fjord's less touristy (for a reason) western base (bus 1hr., 10 per day, 33kr, 50% discount with Scanrail). To reach Hellesylt from the south, leave from Stryn (2-3 buses per day, 70kr); from the north, start from Åndalsnes or from Ålesund. Hikers head for the **Briksdal glacier** (see **Jostedalsbreen** p. 698; 3hr. round trip, glacier guides available) and the **Troll's Path.** The **tourist office,** right on the ferry landing, provides hiking maps. (Tel. 70 26 50 52. Open daily mid-June to mid-Aug. 10am-4pm.) The **Hellesylt Youth Hostel (HI),** up the steep hill along the road to Stranda, has a great view; take the path up the right side of the waterfall that thunders through town, hang a right at the top, and walk along the road 300m. If coming by bus ask the driver to let you off in front of the hostel. (Tel. 70 26 51 28; fax 70 26 36 57. 100kr; nonmembers 125kr. Reception June-July 10 and late Aug. 8am-noon and 5-11pm; July 10-Aug. 10 24hr.) Walk 1km across the bridge from the dock and left to find **Hellesylt Camping.** (Tel. 70 26 51 88. 15kr per person, 45kr per tent.)

ÅNDALSNES

Surrounded by a ring of serrated peaks, Åndalsnes is a paradise for mountaineers, rock climbers, and hikers. Daily trains split off the Oslo-Trondheim line at Dombås (from Oslo 6hr., 520kr, *minipris* 290kr) and take off onto the roller-coaster **Rauma Line,** which passes over stunning bridges and makes a U-turn inside the 1340m Stavems tunnel. The train passes Norway's ultimate mountaineering challenge, **Trollveggen**—the highest vertical rock wall in Europe—and the most notable peak in the area, **Romsdalshorn.** Dombås-Åndalsnes **buses** parallel the train. An equally awesome approach is the dizzying bus route up **Trollstigen** from Geiranger (3hr., 2 per day, 250kr; with railpass 50% off). Between the hostel and campground, the **Norsk Tindemuseum** houses legendary mountaineer Arne Randers Heen's collection of expedition paraphernalia. (Open June to mid-Aug. daily 1-5pm. 30kr.) Go **climbing** with **Tore Klokk** (tel. 71 22 55 86); go "potholing" (i.e. **spelunking**) with **Troll Tours** (tel. 90 65 04 16); or ask about **paragliding** or **hiking** at the **tourist office,** next to the train station. (Tel. 71 22 16 22; fax 71 22 16 82. Open mid-June to mid-Aug. daily 10am-7pm; mid-Aug. to mid-June M-F 10am-3:30pm.) To get to the **Åndalsnes Youth Hostel Setnes (HI),** walk up Jernbanegata, take the first left onto the bridge over the train tracks, go straight to the rotary, bear right through the tunnel, cross the river, and it's one block down on the left (30min.). (Tel. 71 22 13 82. Dorms 175kr; singles 275kr; doubles 420kr. Breakfast included. Reception 8-10am and 4-11pm. Open May 20-Sept. 10.) Follow the directions above, but turn left after crossing the bridge and continue 1.3km along the road to reach scenic **Åndalsnes Camping.** (Tel. 71 22 16 29. 15kr per person, 50kr per tent; 4-bed huts from 160kr.) **Postal code:** 6300.

ÅLESUND

The largest city between Bergen and Trondheim, Ålesund (oh-les-oond) is renowned for its Art Nouveau architecture and beautiful oceanside location. For a view of the splendid city and the distant mountains, gasp up the 418 steps to the **Aksla** mountain viewpoint. The **Sunnmøre Museum,** Borgundgavlen, displays old local fishing boats and a reconstructed Viking ship from AD 800. To get there, take bus 13, 14, 18, or 24 (10min., 5kr). (Open June 25-Aug. M-Sa 11am-5pm, Su noon-5pm; off-season reduced hours. 50kr, students 30kr.) Fishes of the North Sea commune at the new **Atlantic Sea Park,** the largest aquarium in Scandinavia, 3km west of Ålesund. (Open daily June-Aug. 10am-8pm; Sept.-May 10am-4pm. 75kr.) There's an old Viking site and 12th-century marble church on **Giske.** A hydrofoil and a bus link Ålesund and Giske (2hr., M-F 3 per day, 104kr). Ornithusiasts flock to the island of **Runde,** sanctuary to over 500,000 of our fine feathered friends. To get there, take a bus to Hareid and catch the waiting ferry (3hr., 3 per day, 109kr). Contact **Runde Vandrerhjem (HI)** (tel. 70 08 59 16) if you want to spend the night.

Buses arrive from Åndalsnes (3 per day, 142kr; with railpass 50% off) and Helle-sylt (3 per day, 124kr; with railpass 50% off); the **Hurtigruten** also docks here daily (see p. 681). The **tourist office,** on Keiser Wilhelms gt., is opposite the bus station in the city hall. (Tel. 70 15 76 00. Open June-Aug. M-F 8:30am-7pm, Sa 9am-5pm, Su 11am-5pm; Sept.-May M-F 8:30am-4pm.) The **Ålesund Vandrerhjem,** Parkg. 14, is 5min. from the bus station. (Tel. 70 11 58 30. 165kr. Breakfast included. Kitchen. Laundry.) **Hansen Gaarden,** Kongensg. 14, has spotless, spacious rooms. (Tel. 70 12 10 29. Doubles 320kr. Kitchen. Laundry 15kr. Reception 8am-9pm. Open mid-June to Aug. 20.) **Volsdalen Camping** is 2km out along the main highway next to a beach. Take bus 13, 14, 18, or 24 (11kr), turn right off the highway, follow the road down to the bottom of the stairs, cross the road, turn right and cross the overpass, and head 200m left. (Tel./fax 70 12 58 90. 10kr per person, 90kr per tent; cabins 290-490kr. Laundry 60kr. Reception 9am-9pm. Open May to mid-Sept.) **Postal code:** 6025.

TRONDHEIM

A thousand years ago, Viking kings turned Trondheim (then "Nidaros") into Nor-way's seat of power. Today, a slightly better-mannered 20,000 students give the city its flair, its (relatively) low prices, and a sense of quirkiness that other Norwe-gian cities can't quite match. Fresh from celebrating its 1000th birthday, Trond-heim will no doubt keep the good times rolling for the millennium to come.

▄▟ PRACTICAL INFO, ACCOMMODATIONS, AND FOOD. Trains come from Oslo (7-8hr., 4 per day, 590kr) and Stockholm (13hr., 2 per day, 718kr). **Long-distance buses** go from the train station. **City buses** go from Munkeg. and Dronningensg. (19kr). To get from the train station to the **tourist office,** Munkeg. 19, cross the bridge, walk six blocks down Søndreg., go right on Kongensg., and on to the square.

(Tel. 73 92 94 05 Open July M-F 8:30am-10pm, Sa-Su 10am-8pm; June and early Aug. M-F 8:30am-8pm, Sa-Su 10am-6pm; late May and late Aug. M-F 8:30am-6pm, Sa-Su 10am-4pm; Sept. to early May M-F 9am-4pm.) **DNT,** Munkeg. 64, 2nd fl., has info on huts and trails. (Tel. 73 52 38 08. Open M-W and F 9am-4pm, Th 9am-6pm.)

To get from the station to the rambunctious **InterRail Center,** Elgeseterg. 1, in the Studentersenter, cross the bridge, then head right on Olav Tryggvasonsg., left seven blocks down Prinsensg., cross the bridge, and it's on your left. Or, take bus 41, 44, 46, 48, 49, 52, or 63 (10kr) to "Samfundet." (Tel. 73 89 95 38; email tirc@stud.ntnu.no. Sleeping-bag dorms 105kr. Breakfast included. **Internet** free. Open last weekend in June to last Tu in Aug.) For more luxurious respite, walk up Lillegårdsbabakken to reach the student-run **Singsaker Sommerhotell,** Rogertsg. 1, near the Kristiansten Fortress. (Tel. 73 89 31 00; fax 73 89 32 00. Sleeping-bag dorms 125kr; singles 255kr; doubles 400kr; triples 670kr. Sheets 30kr. Breakfast included. Open early June to late Aug.) To reach the institutional **Trondheim Vandrerhjem (HI),** Weidemannsvei 41, walk 15min. from the center or ride bus 63 from the train station. (Tel. 73 53 04 90. 160kr; nonmembers 185kr. Breakfast included. Sheets 45kr.) To reach **Sandmoen Camping,** 10km south of town, take bus 44 from the bus station to Sandbakken. (Tel. 72 88 61 35. 100kr per tent. Reception in summer 24hr.; off-season 8am-10pm.) Sit for a while in **Bare Blåbær's** ("Just Blueberries") comfy couches at Nedre Bakklandet 5, in the old district. (Open daily until 1am.) Nearby, **Café Gåsa,** Øvre Bakklandet 36, has an eccentric, intimate interior and a riverside terrace (dinner from 50kr). Nightlife centers around **Nordre Gate** and along **Brattør-gata; Café 3B,** Brattørgata 3B, pulls in students and musicians. **Postal code:** 7000.

🖼️ 🎵 **SIGHTS AND ENTERTAINMENT.** The image of Olav Tryggvason, who founded Trondheim in 997, now presides over the main square, **Torget.** Local boy King Olav Haraldsson, who died fighting to introduce Christianity to his country and was quickly granted sainthood, soon became the icon of a Christian cult; the stream of pilgrims to St. Olav's grave prompted the construction of **Nidaros Cathe-dral,** the site of all Norwegian coronations and the keeper of the crown jewels. (Open mid-June to mid-Aug. M-F 9am-6pm, Sa 9am-2pm, Su 1-4pm; May to mid-June and mid-Aug. to mid-Sept. M-F 9am-3pm, Sa 9am-2pm and 1-4pm; off-season reduced hours. Cathedral 25kr. Tower 5kr.) The **Trondhjems Kunst Museum,** Bispeg. 7B, next to the cathedral, has a hallway devoted to Edvard Munch. (Open June-Aug. F-W 10am-4pm, Th 10am-6pm; Sept.-May Tu-Su noon-4pm. 30kr, students 20kr.) Also near the cathedral are the **Archbishop's Palace,** the oldest secular building in Scandinavia (open mid-June to mid-Aug. M-Sa 10am-5pm, Su noon-5pm; 25kr), and **Hjemmefrontmuseet,** which details the development of the Norwegian army and deals frankly with the issue of Nazi collaboration (open June-Aug. M-F 9am-3pm, Sa-Su 11am-4pm; Feb.-May and Sept.-Nov. Sa-Su 11am-4pm; free). Across the **Gamle Bybro** (Old Town Bridge), the **old district,** on Innherredsveien, parallel to the river, gives a taste of old Trondheim. On the hill across the river, the 1681 **Kristiansten For-tress** yields a splendid view. Borrow one of the 200 **city bicycles** parked at stations in town (deposit 20kr) and ride up the **bike lift** at the base of the Old Town Bridge (pick up a key-card at the tourist office; 100kr deposit). The monastery, **Munkhol-men** (Monks' Island), became a prison fortress in 1658 and is now a quiet beach and picnic spot (fortress 15kr). Daily **ferries** run from Ravnkloa (every hr., 33kr).

LOFOTEN ISLANDS

The Lofoten Islands' jagged emerald and slate mountains thrust dramatically up from the ocean, sheltering fishing villages, bird colonies, and happy sheep. The crystal-clear water and mild climate make the islands a magical place to spend a few days or weeks. There are many hiking trails, but the islands' charm can also be appreciated from a deck chair or cozy fireplace. As late as the 1950s, fisherfolk lived in the small *rorbuer,* yellow and red wooden shacks along the coast. Today, tourists book the *rorbuer* solid (90-250kr per person in groups of 4 or more).

NORWAY

⌨ GETTING THERE AND GETTING AROUND. Highway E10 binds the four largest islands: **Vågen, Vestvågøy, Flakstad,** and **Moskenes. Bodø** (10hr. north of Trondheim by train; 680dr; with railpass 50% off) and **Narvik** (7hr. north of Bodø by train; 330kr; with railpass 50% off) are the two best mainland springboards to the islands. **Buses** run daily from Narvik (7hr., 321kr; with railpass 50% off) and Bodø (10½hr., 440kr; with railpass 50% off) to the town of **Svolvær,** on the northernmost island of **Austvågøy.** Car **ferries** from Bodø to **Moskenes** (4hr., 4-5 per day, 112kr) stop four times per week at **Røst** (120kr) and **Værøy** (95kr). **Hydrofoils** go to Svolvær from Bodø (departs Su-F; 230kr) and Narvik (departs Tu-F and Su; 270kr; with railpass 50% off). The **Hurtigruten** (see p. 681) connects Bodø with **Stamsund** (4½hr., 216kr), on Vestvågøy, and Svolvær (6hr., 232kr) daily. **Bus** service between the major islands is frequent, but it ain't cheap. **InterRail** gives 50% off on *internal* routes within the islands; a **Scanrail** gets you a discount only if your destination town is on a rail line. Students get 50% off any route. Many long routes are in segments with connecting buses; the cheapest tickets are those to your final destination, not to individual stops. The tiny isles of craggy **Værøy** and flat, puffin-thronged **Røst** are accessible by ferry. **Værøy** has an **HI youth hostel** (tel. 76 09 53 52 85; 85kr; nonmembers 110kr) while the **tourist office** on **Røst** finds rooms (tel. 76 09 64 11; open June 16-Aug. 18 M-F 9am-noon and 6-9pm, Sa-Su 1-3pm). Try www.lofoten-info.no for more info.

MOSKENES AND FLAKSTAD. Ferries dock in **Moskenes,** the southernmost of the large Lofotens. The **tourist office,** by the ferry landing, has tours of the Maelstrom, as well as tours of Refsuika caves and their 3000-year-old drawings. (Tel. 76 09 15 99. Open June 1-18 M-F 10am-5pm; June 19-Aug. 23 daily 10am-7pm.) **Adventure Rafting Lofoten** (tel. 76 09 20 00) runs similar tours in much smaller and more challenging, rafts (290-590kr). A local **bus** whisks incoming ferry passengers 5km south to **Å** (OH), a tiny fishing village at the end of E10. Half of Å's buildings are the **Norsk Fiskeværsmuseum,** an open-air museum. (Open mid-June to mid-Aug. daily 10am-6pm; mid-Aug. to mid-June M-F 10am-3:30pm. 55kr, students 30kr.) The **Å Vandrerhjen and Rorbuer** has bunks in 19th-century buildings. (Tel. 76 09 11 21; fax 76 09 12 82. 125kr, nonmembers 150kr. *Rorbuer* 550-1000kr. Laundry. Rowboats and bikes 150kr per day. Call ahead.) To get to **Moskenes-Straumen Camping,** follow E10 until it stops at the edge of Å. (Tel. 76 09 11 48. 10kr per person, 80kr per tent. Showers 5kr.) Or just **free camp** on the shores of the snow-fed lake behind town.

To the north, the next large island is **Flakstad,** centered on the hamlet of **Ramberg.** Flakstad's **hiking** trails are perhaps the best in the islands; the **tourist office,** books doubles from 120kr. (Tel. 76 09 34 50. Open June 16-Aug. daily 10am-7pm.)

VESTVÅGØY AND AUSTVÅGØY. The next island north is **Vestvågøy,** whose magnificent **HI youth hostel,** in the hamlet of **Stamsund,** often convinces travelers to remain for weeks. (Tel. 76 08 93 34. 80kr. Laundry 30kr. Showers 5kr per 5min. *Rorbuer* 400-600kr. Fishing gear (100kr deposit) and rowboats free. Bikes. Open mid-Dec. to mid.-Oct.) A **tourist office** is 1km down the main road near the steamer dock. (Tel. 76 08 97 92. Open mid-June to mid-Aug. daily 6-9:30pm.) **Buses** run north from Å to Leknes and Stamsund (4 per day, 92kr; with InterRail 50% off) and on to Svolvær. On the road between Leknes and Svolvær is **Borg,** the site of the largest Viking building ever found; the reconstructed longhouse holds a **Viking museum** staffed by costumed Norse folk who do full-scale reenactments. (Open mid-May to Sep. 21 daily 10am-7pm. 70kr, students 56kr; Viking soup included.)

Svolvær, on the northernmost island of **Austvågøy,** is the bland hub of the beautiful Lofotens. The **tourist office** is by the ferry dock. (Tel. 76 07 30 00. Open July to mid-Aug. M-F 9am-4pm and 5-10pm, Sa 9am-8pm, Su 10am-10pm.) **Svolvær Sjøhuscamping** offers rooms on stilts above the harbor; take the third right from Torget on Vestfjordg. as you go north from the tourist office. (Tel./fax 76 07 03 36. Doubles 350kr. Reception 8am-midnight.) Further is the friendly **Marinepollen Sjøhus.** Head 15min. north along the E10 until Jektveien is on the right, or call ahead for pick up. (Tel. 76 07 18 33. 125kr. Fishing gear and rowboats free. Kitchen.) **Rimi,** at Torgg. and Storg., has **groceries.** (Open M-F 9am-8pm, Sa 9am-6pm.)

POLAND (POLSKA)

US$1 = 4.11ZŁ (ZŁOTY, OR PLN)	**1ZŁ = US$0.24**
CDN$1 = 2.76ZŁ	**1ZŁ = CDN$0.36**
UK£1 = 6.60ZŁ	**1ZŁ = UK£0.15**
IR£1 = 5.53ZŁ	**1ZŁ = IR£0.18**
AUS$1 = 2.67ZŁ	**1ZŁ = AUS$0.37**
NZ$1 = 2.18ZŁ	**1ZŁ = NZ$0.46**
SAR1 = 0.68ZŁ	**1ZŁ = SAR1.47**
DM1 = 2.22ZŁ	**1ZŁ = DM0.45**

PHONE CODES | **Country code: 48. International dialing prefix: 00.**

Poland has always been caught at the threshold of East and West, and its moments of freedom have been brief. It is easy to forget that from 1795 to 1918, Poland simply did not exist on any map of Europe, and that its short spell of independence thereafter—like so many before it—was brutally dissolved. Ravaged by World War II and viciously suppressed by Stalin and the USSR, Poland has at long last been given room to breathe, and its residents are not letting the opportunity slip by. The most prosperous of the "Baltic tigers," Poland now has a rapidly expanding GDP, a new membership in NATO, and a likely future membership in the EU. With their new wealth, the legendarily hospitable Poles have been returning to their cultural roots and repairing buildings destroyed in the wars, a trend popular with the growing legions of tourists that visit each year. Capitalism brought with it Western problems, like rising crime and unemployment, issues politicians now recognize as serious. But few Poles complain about the events of the past 10 years. Political and economic freedoms have helped this rich culture to occupy its own skin once again, even if it's now wearing a pair of Levi's.

Even the Pope sometimes kicks back with a copy of *Let's Go: Eastern Europe 2000* for the more detailed coverage of Poland therein.

DISCOVER POLAND

Over 19 million visitors flocked to Poland last year, beckoned by everything from virgin forest, beautiful beaches, and charming villages in the countryside to the spectacular castles, Old Towns, and museums in large cities. For history buffs, **Warsaw,** totally flattened in WWII, is a living testament to the effects of WWII and communism; for others, Warsaw is a wild, energetic capital with great museums, a burgeoning backpacker scene, and plenty of cheap beer (except when the Pope's in town; p. 707). Much-adored **Kraków,** however, is Poland's true darling. The only Polish city to make it to the 20th century unscathed by either natural disaster or war, Kraków now proudly flaunts its magnificent castle and perfectly-preserved Old Town. The city is doubly-blessed with UNESCO protection and the honor of being one of Europe's Cultural Capitals for 2000 (p. 717). **Gdańsk** is another of Poland's historically important towns, the site of both the start of WWII and of Poland's anti-Communist Solidarity movement in the 1980s (p. 714). It's now a favored gateway to the Baltic Coast: nearby **Sopot** shelters Poland's best beaches, while **Frombork** is home to more impressive castles (p. 716). In the south, on the border with Slovakia and in the heart of the High Tatras, the high-altitude fun of **Zakopane** pleases with ear-popping hikes, world-renowned music festivals, and a hefty dose of Tatran folk culture (p. 723). **Kazimierz Dolny** features a thriving artists' colony, a spritely-colored downtown, and stunning sunsets over the Wisła, one can easily see why (p. 723).

GETTING THERE AND GETTING AROUND

BY PLANE. LOT, British Airways, and Delta fly into Warsaw's **Okęcie Airport** from London, New York, Chicago, and Toronto (among other cities).

BY TRAIN. Eurail is not valid in Poland; Eastrail, European East Pass, and Central Europe Pass are. **Almatur** offers ISIC holders a discount of 192zł international **trains. Wasteels** tickets and **Eurotrain** passes, sold at Almatur, Orbis, and major train stations, get those under 26 40% off international train fares. For all but daytrips, **PKP trains** are preferable to and, for long hauls, usually cheaper than buses. **InterCity** and *Ekspresowy* (express) trains are listed in red with an "IC" or "Ex" in front of the train number. *Pośpieszny* (direct; also in red) are almost as fast. *Osobowy* (in black) are the slowest but are 35% cheaper than *pośpieszny*. All **InterCity,** *ekspresowy,* and some *pośpieszny* trains require seat reservations; if you see a boxed R on the schedule, ask the clerk for a *miejscówka* (myay-SOOV-ka; reservation). Buy surcharged tickets on board from the *konduktor* before he or she finds (and fines) you. Train tickets are good only for the day they're issued. Allot plenty of time for long, slow lines. Better yet, buy your ticket in advance at the station or an Orbis office. Stations are not announced and are sometimes poorly marked.

BY BUS AND BY FERRY. PKS buses are cheapest and fastest for short, local trips. As with trains, there are *pośpieszny* (direct; marked in red) and *osobowy* (slow; in black). Purchase advance tickets at the bus station, and expect long lines. However, many tickets can only be bought from the driver. In the countryside, PKS markers (steering wheels that look like upside-down, yellow Mercedes-Benz symbols) indicate bus stops, but drivers will often stop if you flag them down. Traveling with a backpack can be a problem if the bus is full, since there are no storage compartments. **Ferries** run from Sweden and Denmark to Gdańsk (see p. 66).

BY CAR. An International Driving Permit is required of all drivers in Poland. Road conditions are generally safe, except at night and harvest season when horse-drawn wagons carrying agricultural products pack the roads. Speed limits in residential areas are 60kph, on expressways 110kph. For roadside assistance, contact **Polski Zwiazek Motorowy (PZM),** 85 Solec St, 00950 Warsaw (tel. (22) 49 93 61, 49 92 12, and 49 84 49; open M-F 8am-4pm). For 24-hour PZM roadside assistance, dial 981. All PZM services are free for AAA members.

BY BIKE AND BY THUMB. Biking is relatively common throughout Poland; bicycle rentals are available through most tourist offices. Though legal, **hitchhiking** is rare and more dangerous for foreigners. Hand-waving is the accepted signal.

ESSENTIALS

DOCUMENTS AND FORMALITIES. Citizens of Ireland and the US can travel to Poland without a **visa** for up to 90 days and UK citizens for up to 180 days. Australians, Canadians, New Zealanders, and South Africans all need visas. Single-entry visas (valid for 180 days) cost US$60 (students under 26 US$45); multiple-entry visas cost US$100 (students US$75); 48-hour transit visas cost US$20 (students US$15). A visa with a **work permit** is required of everyone seeking work in Poland. It is valid for 12 months and costs US$170 (students US$128). Visas can only be obtained through an embassy or consulate; a visa with work permit also requires a work permit issued by the Labor Office or a certificate of employment. Regular visa service takes four days; 24-hour rush service costs an additional US$35. To extend your stay, apply at the local province office *(urząd wojewódzki)*.

> **Polish Embassies at Home:** www.polishworld.com/polemb. **Australia,** 7 Turrana St, Yarralumla ACT 2600 Canberra (tel. (06) 273 12 08; fax 273 31 84); **Canada,** 443 Daly St, Ottawa, ON K1N 6H3 (tel. (613) 789-0468; fax 789-1218); **Ireland,** 5 Ailesbury Rd, Dublin 4 (tel. (01) 283 08 55; fax 283 75 62); **New Zealand,** 17 Upland Rd, Kelburn, Wellington (tel. (04) 71 24 56; fax 71 24 55); **South Africa,** 14 Amos St, Colbyn, Pretoria 0083 (tel. (012) 43 26 31; fax 43 26 08; **UK,** 47 Portland Pl, London W1N 4JH (tel. (020) 75 80 43 24; fax 73 23 40 18); **US,** 2640 16th St NW, Washington, DC 20009 (tel. (202) 234-3800; fax 328-6271; email embpol@dgs.dgsys.com).
> **Foreign Embassies in Poland:** All embassies are in **Warsaw** (see p. 707); there's also a US consulate in **Kraków** (see p. 717).

TOURIST OFFICES. Travel agencies vary wildly in quality, with city-specific offices generally more helpful than bigger chains. In general, you can count on all offices to provide free info in English or German and to advise on accommodations for a small fee. **Orbis,** the state-sponsored travel bureau staffed by English speakers, sells transportation tickets for longer journeys. **Almatur,** the Polish student travel organization, sells ISICs and helps find summer dorm rooms. Both provide maps, as do **PTTK** and **IT** *(Informacji Turystycznej)* bureaus.

MONEY. The Polish **złoty**—plural *złote*—is divided into 100 *grosze*. For cash, private **kantor** offices (except for those at the airport and train stations) offer better exchange rates than banks. **Bank PKO S.A.** cashes **traveler's checks** and gives MC/ Visa **cash advances. ATMs** *(Bankomat)* are everywhere except the smallest of villages. **MC** and **Visa** are the most widely accepted ATM networks. Budget accommodations rarely, if ever, accept **credit cards,** although some restaurants and pricier shops will. In restaurants, tell the server how much change you want back, leaving the rest as a 10% **tip.** If you're paying with a credit card, give the tip in cash.

COMMUNICATION

> **Post:** Mail is becoming increasingly efficient, although there are still incidents of theft. Airmail *(lotnicza)* usually takes a week to reach the US. For *poste restante,* put a "1" after the city name to ensure that it goes to the main post office.
> **Telephone:** Phones requiring **phone cards** have become standard, even for calling long-distance access numbers; buy them at post offices and some kiosks. For **collect calls,** write

the name of the city or country and the number plus *"Rozmowa 'R'"* on a slip of paper, hand it to a post office clerk, and be patient. **International direct dial** numbers include: **AT&T,** 00 8001 11 11 11; **Sprint,** 00 8001 11 31 15; **MCI WorldPhone Direct,** 00 8001 11 21 22; **Canada Direct,** 00 8001 11 41 18; **BT Direct,** 00 8004 41 11 44. **Police,** tel. 997. **Fire,** tel. 998. **Ambulance,** tel. 999.

Language: Polish varies little across the country. The 2 exceptions are the region of Kaszuby, which has a Germanized dialect, and Karpaty, where the highlanders' accent seems thickened by the goat's milk they drink. Always try English and German before Russian, which many Poles understand but show an open aversion to speaking. Most Poles can understand slowly spoken Czech or Slovak. Students may also know French. For basic phrases in all these languages and more, see p. 949.

ACCOMMODATIONS AND CAMPING. Grandmotherly **private room** owners drum up business at the train station or outside the tourist office. Private rooms are usually safe, clean, and convenient, but can be far from city centers. Expect to pay about US$10 per person. **Youth hostels** (*schronisko młodzieżowe*) abound and average 9-25zł per night. They are often booked solid, however, by school or tourist groups; call at least a week in advance. **PTSM** is the national hostel organization. **University dorms** transform into spartan budget housing in July and August; these are an especially good option in Kraków. The Warsaw office of **Almatur** can arrange stays in all major cities. **PTTK** runs a number of hotels called **Dom Turysty,** which have multi-bed rooms as well as budget singles and doubles. **Hotels** generally cost 30-50zł per night. **Camping** averages US$2 per person (US$4 with a car). **Bungalows** are often available; a bed costs about US$5. *Polska Mapa Campingów* lists all campsites. Almatur runs a number of sites in summer; ask for a list at one of their offices.

FOOD AND DRINK. Monks, merchants, invaders, and dynastic unions have all flavored Polish cuisine—a blend of dishes from the French, Italian, and Jewish traditions. Polish food favors meat, potatoes, and butter. A Polish meal always starts with **soup,** usually *barszcz* (beet broth), *chłodnik* (a cold beet soup with buttermilk and hard-boiled eggs), *kapuśniak* (cabbage soup), *krupnik* (barley soup), or *żurek* (barley-flour soup loaded with eggs and sausage). Filling **main courses** include *gołąbki* (cabbage rolls stuffed with meat and rice), *kotlet schabowy* (pork cutlet), *naleśniki* (cream-topped crepes filled with cottage cheese or jam), and *pierogi* (dumplings with various fillings—meat, potato, cheese, blueberry). Poland bathes in **beer, vodka,** and **spiced liquor.** *Żywiec* is the most popular strong (12%) brew. *Wódka* ranges from wheat to potato. *Wyborowa, Żytnia,* and *Polonez* usually decorate private bars. The herbal *Żubrówka* vodka comes with a blade of grass from the region where the bison roam. It is sometimes mixed with apple juice *(z sokem jabłkowym)*. *Miód* and *krupnik*—two kinds of meal—are beloved by the gentry, and many grandmas make *nalewka na porzeczce* (black currant vodka).

LOCAL FACTS

Time: Poland is 1hr. ahead of Greenwich Mean Time (GMT; see p. 49).

Climate: Typically continental climate, with cold winters and very hot (bit rainy) summers. In the Tatras, anytime between Nov. and Feb. is ideal for skiing, and Aug. is the perfect hiking month. Otherwise, summer and autumn are the best times to visit.

Hours: Business hours tend to be M-F 8am-6pm, Sa 9am-2pm. Saturday hours vary, as some shops in Poland distinguish "working" *(pracująca)* Saturdays, when they work longer hours, from "free" *(wolna)* ones, when hours are shorter. Very few businesses are open on Su. **Museums** are open Tu-Su 10am-4pm. **Banks** are open M-F 9am-3 or 6pm.

Holidays: New Year's Day (Jan. 1); Catholic Easter (Apr. 23-24); Labor Day (May 1); Constitution Day (May 3); Corpus Christi (June 22); Assumption Day (Aug. 15); Independence Day (1918; Nov. 11); Christmas (Dec. 25-26).

Festivals: Kraków is Poland's festival capital, especially in summer. Some of the most notable are the **International Short Film Festival** (late May), the **Festival of Jewish Culture** (end of June), and the **Jazz Festival** (Oct.-Nov.).

WARSAW (WARSZAWA)

According to legend, Warsaw was created when a fisherman netted and released a mermaid *(syrena)* who promised that if he founded a city, she would protect it forever. However, in WWII alone, two-thirds of the population was killed and 83% of the city destroyed. Today, Warsaw is once again the world's largest Polish city (a title long held by Chicago) and is quickly throwing off its Soviet legacy to emerge as an important international business center. Skyscrapers are popping up all over, and the university infuses Warsaw with young blood, keeping energy high and the nightlife lively. All things considered, the *syrena* appears to have kept her promise.

⌐ GETTING THERE AND GETTING AROUND

Flights: Port Lotniczy Warszawa-Okęcie ("Terminal 1"), ul. Żwirki i Wigury. Take **bus** 175 (bus 611 after 11pm) to the center; buy tickets at the Ruch kiosk in the departure hall or at the *kantor* outside. 2zł, students 1zł; extra tickets required for suitcases and packs. Open M-F 7:30am-6pm. The faster **Airport-City Bus** runs daily 5:30am-11pm (2-3 per hr.). 8zł, students 4zł; buy tickets from the driver.

Trains: Warszawa Centralna, ul. Jerozolimskie 54 (tel. 825 50 00; international info 620 45 12; domestic info 620 03 61), in the center of town. English is rare; write down where and when you want to go, then ask *Który peron?* ("Which platform?"). Yellow signs list departures, white signs arrivals. To: **Gdańsk** and **Kraków** (3-4hr., 30-50zł); **Berlin** (7-8hr., 6 per day, 136zł); **Bratislava** (8hr., 2 per day, 164zł); **Budapest** (10hr., 2 per day, 201zł); **Vilnius** (12hr., 2 per day, 130zł); **Minsk** (12hr., 4 per day, 110zł); **Prague** (12-14hr., 2 per day, 153zł); **Kiev** (22-24hr., 3 per day, 136zł); **St. Petersburg** (26hr., 1 per day, 250zł); and **Moscow** (27-30hr., 2 per day, 251zł).

> **⚠ Warning:** Theft is rising on overnight trains, especially to and from Berlin and Prague, and in train stations in Poland. Protect your property, and avoid sleeping on night trains (or trade off staying awake with any travel companions).

Buses: PKS Warszawa Zachodnia, al. Jerozolimskie 144 (tel. 94 33, info 524 41 45), in the same building as the Warszawa Zachodnia train station. It sends buses to the north and west, including Western Europe. International Bus Information window sells tickets (open M-F 8am-4pm). Buses from **PKS Warszawa Stadion,** on the other side of the Wisła, head east and south. **Polski Express,** al. Jana Pawła II (tel. 630 29 67), offers fast and comfortable bus service to **Lublin** (4hr., 7 per day, 20zł); **Gdańsk** (6hr., 2 per day, 37zł); **Kraków** (6hr., 2 per day, 32zł); and Szczecin (9½hr., 1 per day, 32zł).

Public Transportation: Rides on **trams** and **buses** (including express lines) 2zł, students 1zł; night buses 4.20zł; extra ticket required for large baggage. Fine for traveling without a valid ticket 100zł (luggage with no ticket 40zł). Daily pass 6zł, students 3zł. Buy tickets at most kiosks or from the driver at night. Punch the end marked by the arrow and *tu kasować* in the machines on board. **Bus 175** runs from the airport to Stare Miasto via the central train station, the town center, and ul. Nowy Świat. **Bus 130** connects Zachodnia Station, Centralna Station, and Wilanów in the south. Warsaw's single **metro** line connects the southern border of town with the center (same prices per ride).

Taxis: MPT Radio Taxi, tel. 919. **Sawa Taxi,** tel. 644 44 44. Overcharging is still a problem; call to arrange pickup. State-run cabs with a mermaid sign are usually a safe bet. Fares start at 4zł plus 1.60zł per km; 2zł is the legal maximum per km.

⚡ ORIENTATION AND PRACTICAL INFORMATION

The busy downtown area **Śródmieście** is on the west riverbank of the **Wisła River,** which bisects the city. In the middle of it all, **Warszawa Centralna,** the central train station, lies on **al. Jerozolimskie,** between **al. Jana Pawła II** and **ul. Emilii Plater.** From the vast marketplace of **pl. Defilad** (Parade Square), a short walk along al. Jerozolimskie leads to the large intersection with **ul. Marszałkowska,** one of the city's main north-south avenues. This busy street leads north to **Ogród Saski** (Saxon Gardens); the intersection serves as a major stop for most bus and tram lines. Al. Jerozolim-

POLAND

skie continues east to the other main north-south avenue, **Trakt Królewski,** which intersects al. Jerozolimskie at **rondo Charles de Gaulle.** A left here runs north up **ul. Nowy Świat,** which becomes **ul. Krakowskie Przedmieście,** and leads directly to **Stare Miasto** (Old Town) and the Royal Palace. A right at rondo Charles de Gaulle leads to **al. Ujazdowskie,** which leads down embassy row to the Łazienki Palace.

TOURIST AND FINANCIAL SERVICES

Tourist Offices: Informacja Turystyczna (IT), al. Jerozolimskie 54 (tel. 524 51 84; fax 654 24 47), in the central train station. English-speaking staff changes money and provides maps, guides, and hotel reservations. Open daily 9am-7pm. Also **pl. Zamkowy** 1/13 (tel. 635 18 81; fax 831 04 64), by the entrance to Stare Miasto across from the Royal Palace. Open M-F 9am-6pm, Sa 10am-6pm, Su 11am-6pm. Also at **Zachodnia Station** and at the **airport.** Pick up the indispensable *Warsaw Insider* (6zł).

Budget Travel: Almatur, ul. Kopernika 23 (tel. 826 35 12; fax 826 35 07). International bus, ferry, and plane tickets at student discounts. Open M-F 9am-6pm, Sa 10am-2pm.

Embassies: Most are near ul. Ujazdowskie. **Australia,** ul. Estońska 3/5 (tel. 617 60 81). Open M-Th 8:30am-1pm and 2-5pm. **Belarus,** ul. Ateńska 67 (tel. 617 39 54). **Canada,** ul. Matejki 1/5 (tel. 629 80 51). Open M-F 8am-4:30pm. **Russia,** ul. Belwederska 49, bldg. C (tel. 621 34 53). Open W and F 8am-1pm. **South Africa,** ul. Koszykowa 54 (tel. 625 62 28). Open M-F 8am-12pm. **Ukraine,** al. Ujazdowskie 13 (tel. 629 32 01). Open M-F 10am-4pm. **UK,** al. Róż 1 (tel. 628 10 01). Open M-F 9am-noon and 2-4pm. **US,** al. Ujazdowskie 29/31 (tel. 628 30 41). Open M-F 8:30am-5pm.

Currency Exchange: Private *kantori* have the best rates. **24-hour exchange** is available at Warszawa Centralna and the airport. **Bank PKO S.A.,** pl. Bankowy 2 (tel. 637 10 61), in the blue skyscraper; ul. Mazowiecka 14 (tel. 661 25 59); and ul. Grójecka 1/3 (tel. 658 82 17), in Hotel Sobieski. AmEx/Visa **traveler's checks** are cashed into dollars or *złoty* for a 1% commission. Visa/MC **cash advances.** Open M-F 8am-6pm, Sa 10am-2pm. **ATMs** are at ul. Mazowiecka 14 and inside Hotel Sobieski, ul. Grójecka 1/3. 24hr.

American Express: ul. Krakowskie Przedmieście 11 (tel. 551 51 52; fax 828 75 56). Cash and traveler's check exchange at no commission. Address **Poste Restante** mail to "American Express Travel," PL 00-069. Open M-F 9am-6pm.

LOCAL SERVICES

Luggage Storage: At Warszawa Centralna train station, below the main hall. Lockers 6-17zł per day depending on size. In Zachodnia Station 4zł for a large pack.

English Bookstore: American Bookstore, ul. Koszykowa 55 (tel. 660 56 37; fax 660 56 38). A good but pricey selection. Open M-F 11am-7pm, Sa 11am-6pm.

Gay and Lesbian Services: Lambda Center Information Line (tel. 628 52 22). Very friendly and helpful. English spoken. Tu-W 6-9pm, F 4-10pm.

Laundromat: ul. Karmelicka 17 (tel. 831 73 17). Take bus 180 from ul. Marszałkowska toward Żoliborz, get off at ul. Anielewicza, and go back one block. Wash and dry 19.50zł. Detergent 2.50zł. Open M-F 9am-5pm, Sa 9am-1pm. Call ahead. Some English spoken.

EMERGENCY AND COMMUNICATIONS

Emergencies: Fire, tel. 998. **Ambulance,** tel. 999. **Police,** tel. 997.

Crisis Lines: Women's Crisis Line, tel. 635 47 91. Open M-F 4-8pm.

Pharmacy: Apteka Grabowski (tel. 825 13 72), at the central train station. Open 24hr.

Medical Assistance: American Medical Center, ul. Wilcza 23 m. 29 (tel. 622 04 89; 24hr. emergency tel. 0 602 24 30 24; fax 622 04 97). Provides English-language referrals. General practice clinic open M-Sa 8am-6pm.

Post Office: ul. Świętokrzyska 31/33 (tel. 826 75 11). Take a ticket at the entrance and wait in line. For stamps and letters, push "D." For packages, push "F." For *Poste Restante,* turn left into the other room, push "C" at the computer, and pick it up at window 11 or 12. **Fax** bureau (fax 30 00 21). 14.10zł for the first 3min., 0.60zł per min. thereafter. Address mail to be held: Benjamin PALOFF, *Poste Restante,* ul. Świętokrzyska 31/33, Warsaw 1, **00-001** Poland. Open 24hr.

Internet Access: Lameriada Internet Café, ul. Piękna 68A (tel. 622 33 77). 3zł per 15min., 6zł per 30min., 8zł per hr. Open M-Sa 11am-midnight, Su 1pm-midnight.

Telephones: At the post office; sells tokens and phone cards. **Directory assistance:** 913.

POLAND

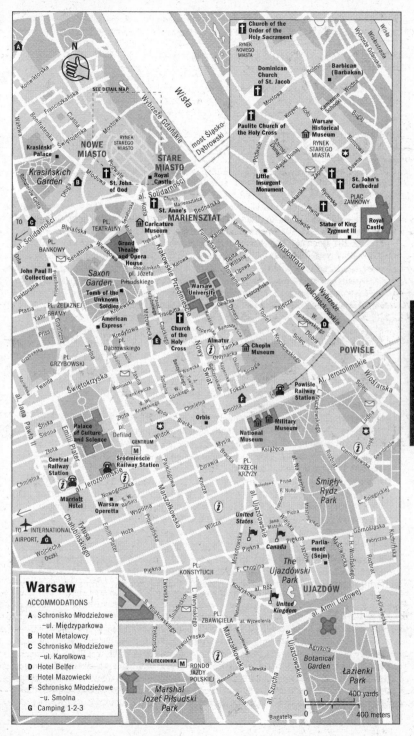

POLAND

Warsaw

ACCOMMODATIONS

- **A** Schronisko Młodzieżowe
  –ul. Międzyparkowa
- **B** Hotel Metalowcy
- **C** Schronisko Młodzieżowe
  –ul. Karolkowa
- **D** Hotel Belfer
- **E** Hotel Mazowiecki
- **F** Schronisko Młodzieżowe
  –u. Smolna
- **G** Camping 1-2-3

PHONE CODE	City code: 022. From outside Poland, dial int'l dialing prefix (see inside back cover) + 48 + 22 + local number.

ACCOMMODATIONS AND CAMPING

Prices rise and rooms become scarce in June, July, and August; call ahead, particularly for hostels. For help finding **private rooms**, check in with **Syrena**, ul. Krucza 17, off al. Jerozolimskie. (Tel. 628 75 40. Open M-Sa 9am-7pm, Su 9am-5pm. Singles from 61zł; doubles from 84zł.) City tourist offices have accommodations lists.

Schronisko Młodzieżowe (HI), ul. Karolkowa 53a (tel. 632 88 29). Take tram 22 or 24 west from al. Jerozolimskie or the train station to "Okopowa." Cross at the corner near Pizza Hut, continue down al. Solidarności, and follow the green IYH signs. Dorms often overrun by school groups. Kitchen. Doubles and triples include TV and fridge. Dorms 21zł, non-members 28zł; singles 50zł, with bath 120zł; doubles 80zł, with shower 100zł; bed in a triple or quad 38zł. Sheets 3.50zł. Lockout 10am-5pm. Curfew 11pm.

Schronisko Młodzieżowe (HI), ul. Smolna 30, top floor (tel. 827 89 52), across from the National Museum. From the train station, take any eastbound tram to the third stop, "Muzeum Narodowe." Great location, but extremely crowded all summer. Kitchen. Dorms 19.50zł, non-members 26zł; singles 40zł; bed in a double or triple 36zł. Sheets 2.50zł. 3-day max. stay. Call 2 weeks in advance. Lockout 10am-4pm. Curfew 11pm.

Schronisko Młodzieżowe (HI), ul. Międzyparkowa 4/6 (tel. 831 17 66), near the river. Take tram 2, 6, or 18 north from ul. Marszałkowska to "K.K.S. Polonia"; continue down the road and it's on your left. Mostly school groups; attracts few foreigners. 25zł, under 26 10zł. Sheets 5zł. Lockout 10am-5pm. Curfew 11pm. Open mid-Apr. to mid-Oct.

Hotel Mazowiecki, ul. Mazowiecka 10 (tel. 682 20 65 or 682 20 69; tel./fax 827 23 65). Hidden away a little more than a block from ul. Krakowskie Przedmieście off ul. Świętokrzyska. One of the poshest budget hotels downtown, with hardwood floors and colorful carpeting. Clean bathrooms. Bed in a double 65zł; bed in a triple or quad 50zł.

Hotel Metalowcy, ul. Długa 29 (tel. 831 40 20; fax 635 31 38). Take bus 175 from the train station to "pl. Krasińskich," go back to ul. Długa, and turn right. Great location. Clean rooms and passable communal bathrooms. Small singles 47zł, with private bath 56zł; roomier doubles 88zł; quads with bath 144zł.

Hotel Belfer, ul. Wybrzeże Kościuszkowskie 31/33 (tel. 625 55 62; for reservations 625 26 00; fax 625 51 85). From the train station, take any tram east to "Most Poniatowskiego," then head north (with the river to your right) along Wybrzeże Kościuszkowskie. Clean, bright, and roomy. Some rooms have rooftop views. Singles 90zł, with bath 129zł; doubles 128zł, with bath 170zł. V, MC, AmEx.

Camping "123," ul. Bitwy Warszawskiej 1920r. 15/17 (tel. 822 91 21; tel./fax 823 37 48), by the main bus station. Take bus 127 to "Zachodnia" and cross the street at the traffic circle; Bitwy Warszawskiej is to the left. Close to downtown. English spoken. 10zł per person, children 4-10 5zł. Small tent space 8zł, large 10zł.

FOOD

Food stands dot the square beneath the Palace of Culture and beneath the train station. **Milk bars** *(bar mleczny)* or proletarian-style **cafeterias** are an inexpensive and generally tasty option. There are **supermarkets** at the central train station (open 24hr.) and at **Delikatesy**, ul. Nowy Świat 53 (tel. 826 03 22; open 7am-5am).

RESTAURANTS

Pod Samsonem, ul. Freta 3/5 (tel. 831 17 88), between Stare Miasto and Nowe Miasto. Hearty Polish-Jewish cuisine to make you big and strong like Samson. Decorated with photos of pre-war Jewish life. Meals 20-30zł. Open daily 10am-10pm. AmEx.

Bong Sen, ul. Poznańska 12 (tel. 621 27 13), just south of the train station on a road parallel to al. Marszałkowska. The decidedly Polish waitstaff won't create any illusion that you're in the Far East, but the authentic Vietnamese and Chinese cuisine will sure fool your mouth. Entrees 19-30zł. Open daily 11am-10pm. V, MC, AmEx.

Restauracja Ekologiczna "Nowe Miasto," Rynek Nowego Miasta 13/15 (tel. 831 43 79). Organically grown vegetarian entrees 20-50zł. Healthy soups, a variety of crêpes, and an ensemble cast of salads. Encores of Polish beer (0.5L *Zywiec* 9zł) and German wine. Outdoor seating available. Live music nightly 7-10pm. Open daily 10am-midnight.

Bar Mleczny Familijny, ul. Nowy Świat 39. A giant version of a Polish grandmother's kitchen. Full meals 2-6zł. Open M-F 7am-8pm, Sa-Su 9am-5pm.

CAFÉS

■ **Pożegnanie z Afryka,** ul. Freta 4/6. The name of this chain means "Out of Africa," though most types of coffee are actually South American; regardless, it's the best in town. Worth the wait for one of six tables. Coffee 6-7zł. Open daily 11am-9pm.

Kawiarnia Bazyliszek, Rynek Starego Miasta 9/11/13 (tel. 831 32 35). A fancy café with relaxed outdoor seating. Great views of the restored splendor of Stare Miasto and the tourists here to see it. Tortes 3zł. Coffee 2zł. Open daily 11am-11pm.

Gwiazdeczka, ul. Piwna 40/42 (tel. 831 94 63), in Stare Miasto. The menu is full of innocent snacks and coffees (3-8zł). Beer and cocktails are ever-tempting alternatives (large *Zywiec* 5.50zł). Open daily 9am-10pm.

◉ SIGHTS

Razed beyond recognition during WWII, Warsaw was almost entirely rebuilt from the rubble. Thanks to the wonders of Soviet upkeep, though, most of the buildings look much older than their 50 years. As sights are spread out and some are quite distant from the center, the city requires time to explore.

STARE MIASTO AND NOWE MIASTO. Warsaw's postwar reconstruction shows its finest face in the narrow, cobblestoned streets and colorful façades of **Stare Miasto** (Old Town), at the very end of ul. Krakowskie Przedmieście in pl. Zamkowy. *(Take bus 175 or E3 from the city center to "Miodowa.")* At the right side of the entrance to Stare Miasto stands the impressive **Royal Castle** (Zamek Królewski). Burned down in September 1939 and plundered by the Nazis, the castle was elevated to martyrdom by Polish freedom fighters. Many Varsovians risked their lives hiding its priceless works in the hope that one day they could be returned. Reconstructed from 1971 to 1984, today the castle houses the ■**Royal Castle Museum,** which showcases the world of Poland's kings through paintings, artifacts, and the stunning Royal Apartments. *(Pl. Zamkowy 4. Tel. 657 21 78. www.zamek-krolewski.art.pl. Open M and Su 11am-6pm, Tu-Sa 10am-6pm; last entrance 5pm. 14zł, students 7zł. Tours 50zł.)* Just down ul. Świętojańska sits Warsaw's oldest church, the **Cathedral of St. John** (Katedra św. Jana), decimated in the 1944 Uprising but rebuilt after the war. *(Cathedral and crypts open daily dawn-dusk.)* Ul. Świętojańska leads to the restored Renaissance and Baroque **Rynek Starego Miasta** (Old Town Square). A stone plaque at the entrance commemorates its reconstruction, finished in 1953-54, and recalls the square's prewar history. Ul. Krzywe Koło (Crooked Wheel) starts in the northeast corner of the *rynek* and leads to the restored **barbakan,** a rare example of 16th-century Polish fortification and a popular spot for locals to rest their feet to the tune of street performers. The *barbakan* opens onto ul. Freta, the edge of **Nowe Miasto.** Despite its name, this is the city's second-oldest district; its 18th- and 19th-century buildings have enjoyed an expensive facelift since WWII. The great physicist and chemist **Maria Skłodowska-Curie,** winner of two Nobel prizes, was born at ul. Freta 16 in 1867.

TRAKT KRÓLEWSKI (ROYAL WAY). Warsaw's most attractive thoroughfare (named the Royal Way because it leads south toward Kraków, Poland's former capital) starts at **pl. Zamkowy,** at the entrance to Stare Miasto, and stretches 4km south, changing its name from **ul. Krakowskie Przedmieście** to **ul. Nowy Świat** to **al. Ujazdowskie.** On the left as you leave pl. Zamkowy, **St. Anne's Church** (Kościół św. Anny), with a large figure of Christ above the entrance and beautiful gilded altar, dates from the 15th century but was rebuilt in the Baroque style. *(Open daily dawn-dusk.)* **Fryderyk Chopin,** who spent his childhood in the neighborhood near ul. Krakowskie Przedmieście, gave his first public concert in **Pałac Radziwiłłów** (a.k.a. **Pałac Namiestnikowski**) 46/48, the building guarded

POLAND

by four stone lions; today an armed guard stands watch alongside his feline counterparts outside the now-Polish presidential mansion. **Pałac Czapskich** was Chopin's last home before he left for France in 1830; today the palace houses the **Academy of Fine Arts** and **Chopin's Drawing Room** (Salonik Chopinów). *(Ul. Krakowskie Przedmieście 5. Open M-F 10am-2pm. 3zł, students 2zł.)* Chopin died abroad at the age of 39 and was buried in Paris, but his heart belongs to Poland; it now rests in an urn in the **Holy Cross Church** (Kościół św. Krzyża). If you haven't gotten enough of the mop-topped composer, waltz on over to the **Fryderyk Chopin Museum** (Muzeum Fryderyka Chopina), which has a small collection of original letters, scores, paintings, and keepsakes, including the great composer's last piano. *(Ul. Okólnik 1; enter from ul. Tamka. Open May-Sept. M, W, and F 10am-5pm, Th noon-6pm, Sa-Su 10am-2pm. 4zł, students 2zł. Audio guides 4zł.)*

Meanwhile, the Royal Way continues down ul. Nowy Świat; turn left just after rondo Charles de Gaulle to reach Poland's largest museum, the **National Museum** (Muzeum Narodowe). *(Al. Jerozolimskie 3. Tel. 629 30 93. Open Tu-W and F 10am-4pm, Th noon-5pm, Sa-Su 10am-5pm. 7zł, students 4zł; Sa free.)* Further down, the Royal Way turns into al. Ujazdowskie and runs alongside **Łazienki Park** (on your left). Near the entrance is the **Chopin Monument** (Pomnik Chopina), site of free concerts every Sunday at noon and 4pm from spring to autumn. Farther into the park is the striking Neoclassical **Palace on Water** (Pałac na Wodzie), also called Pałac Łazienkowski, which houses galleries of 17th- and 18th-century art. *(Take bus 116 or 195 from ul. Nowy Świat or 119 from the city center south to Bagatela. Park open daily dawn-dusk. Palace open Tu-Su 9:30am-4pm. 10zł, students 7zł. Tours in English 55zł.)*

THE WARSAW GHETTO AND SYNAGOGUE. Still referred to as the Ghetto, the modern **Muranów** ("walled") neighborhood northwest of the city center holds few vestiges of the nearly 400,000 Jews—then one-third of the city's population—who lived here prior to WWII. The **Umschlagplatz,** at the corner of ul. Dzika and ul. Stawki was the railway platform where the Nazis gathered 300,000 of the Jews for transport to the death camps. *(Take tram 35 from ul. Marszałkowska to "Dzika." Or follow ul. Freta out of the Rynek Starego Miasta on foot, continue as the street turns into Zakroczymska, turn left on Konwiktorska, and turn left on Muranowska, which becomes Stawki.)* With the monument to your left, continue down Stawki and turn right on ul. DuBois, which becomes ul. Zamenhofa; you will pass a stone monument marking the location of the command bunker of the 1943 ghetto uprising. Further on, in a large park to your right stands the large **Monument of the Ghetto Heroes** (Pomnik Bohaterów). Continue along ul. Zamenhofa in the same direction (south), turn right on ul. Anielewicza, and continue for 5 blocks to reach the **Jewish Cemetery** (Cmentarz Żydowski), in the western corner of Muranów. Thickly wooded and several kilometers long, the cemetery is the final resting place of 200,000 of Warsaw's Jews. *(Or take tram 22 from the city center to "Cm. Żydowski." Open M-Th 9am-3pm, F 9am-1pm. 3zł.)* The **Museum of Pawiak Prison** (Muzeum Więzienia Pawiak) features photographic exhibits and several intact cells recalling the Gestapo's use of the building as a headquarters. Over 100,000 Poles were imprisoned here from 1939-1944; 37,000 were executed and 60,000 were transferred to concentration camps. *(Ul. Dzielna 24/26. Tel. 831 13 17. Open W 9am-5pm, Th and Sa 9am-4pm, F 10am-5pm, Su 10am-4pm. English captions. Free; donation requested.)* The beautifully reconstructed **Nożyk Synagogue** (Synagoga Nożyka), is a lasting remnant of Warsaw's Jewish life. The only synagogue to survive the war, today it serves as the spiritual home for the few hundred observant Jews who remain in Warsaw. *(Ul. Twarda 6, north of the Palace of Culture and Science (Pałac Kultury). From the central train station, take any tram north along ul. Jana Pawła II to "Rondo ONZ." Turn right on Twarda and left at the Jewish Theater (Teatr Żydowski). Or, from the tourist office, walk west down Świętokrzyska, turn right on Emilii Plater, and cross Twarda. Open M-F 10am-3pm, Sa 9am-noon. Call call 620 43 24 for a schedule of services. 5zł.)*

WILANÓW. After his coronation in 1677, King Jan III Sobieski bought the sleepy village of Milanowo, had its existing mansion rebuilt into a Baroque palace, and named the new residence Villa Nova *(Wilanów)*. Since 1805, **Pałac**

Wilanowski has functioned both as a museum and as a residence for the highest-ranking guests of the Polish state. Inside are lovely frescoed rooms, countless 17th- to 19th-century portraits, and extravagant royal apartments. You can break off from the slow-moving Polish-language tour to explore on your own (there are multilingual signs along the way). *(Tel. 842 81 01. Take bus 180, 410, or 414 from ul. Marszałkowska, or bus 130 or 519 from the train station south to "Wilanów"; cross the street and the road to the palace will be to your right. Palace open June 15-Sept. 15 M and W-Sa 9:30am-2:30pm, Su 9:30am-4:30pm; Sept. 16-June 14 9:30am-2:30pm. 15zł, students 8zł. Including tour in English 100zł, for groups of 6-35 20zł each. Garden open M and W-F 9:30am-dusk. 3zł, students 2zł.)*

ELSEWHERE IN CENTRAL WARSAW. The center of Warsaw's commercial district, southwest of Stare Miasto and near the central train station, is dominated by the 70-story Stalinist Gothic **Palace of Culture and Science** (Pałac Kultury), ul. Marszałkowska. Locals claim the view from the top is the best in Warsaw, because it's the only place from which you can't see the building; the eyesore is reviled even more as a symbol of Soviet domination than for its aesthetics. Below, **pl. Defilad** (Parade Square), Europe's largest square (even bigger than Moscow's Red Square) swarms with freelance bazaar capitalists. Adjacent to **Ogród Saski** (Saxon Garden) is the **John Paul II Collection,** with over 400 works by artists including Dalí, Titian, Rembrandt, van Gogh, Goya, Renoir, and others. *(Pl. Bankowy 3/5. Tel. 620 21 81. Open Tu-Su 10am-5pm; last entry 4pm. 5zł, children under 11 3zł.)*

🎵 ENTERTAINMENT AND NIGHTLIFE

After you've digested your dinner *pierogi* and *kiełbasa*, Warsaw is chock full o' excitement. A large variety of pubs attract big crowds and often have live music, and cafés *(kawiarnie)* around Stare Miasto and ul. Nowy Świat serve late. In the summer, large outdoor beer gardens complement the pub scene.

CONCERTS, OPERA, AND THEATER. Classical concerts fill Pałac na Wodzie in Łazienki on summer Saturdays. (Performances June-Sept. at 4pm. 15zł, students 10zł.) Inquire about concerts at the **Warsaw Music Society** (Warszawskie Towarzystwo Muzyczne), ul. Morskie Oko 2. (Tel. 849 68 56. Take tram 4, 18, 19, 35, or 36 to "Morskie Oko" from ul. Marszałkowska. Concerts Oct.-May Th at 6pm and Su at 11am. Tickets available M-F 9am-3pm and just before concerts. 5zł.) The **Warsaw Chamber Opera** (Warszawska Opera Kameralna), al. Solidarności 76B (tel. 831 22 40), hosts a Mozart festival each year during early summer, with performances throughout the city. The **Chopin Monument** (Pomnik Chopina), nearby in Łazienki Park, hosts free Sunday performances. (May-Oct. noon and 4pm.) **Teatr Wielki,** pl. Teatralny 1, Warsaw's main opera and ballet hall, offers performances almost daily. (Tel. 692 07 58; www.teatrwielki.pl. *Kassa* open M-F 9am-7pm, Su 10am-7pm, and one hour before shows. Tickets 6-90zł.) **Sala Kongresowa** (tel. 620 49 80), in the Palace of Culture and Science on the train station side with the casino, hosts serious **jazz** and **rock** concerts with famous international bands; enter from ul. Emilii Plater.

PUBS AND NIGHTCLUBS. Drinks are expensive, but many pubs compensate with live music. The nightclub and dance scene shifts frequently; check posters around town. Gay life is a bit underground here; call 628 52 22 for info. (Open Tu-W 6-9pm, F 4-10pm.) *Inaczej* and *Filo* list gay establishments. ■**Morgan's,** ul. Okólnik 1, with an entrance on ul. Tamka under the Chopin Museum, has the best "Guinness in Poland" 13zł (0.5L). (Tel. 826 81 38. Live music M and F-Sa at 9pm. Open daily 2pm-midnight.) Inside Stare Miasto, **Metal Bar,** Rynek Starego Miasta 8, this bar features, well, a metal theme. (Tel. 635 32 72. Open M-Th and Su noon-midnight, F-Sa noon-2am.) Across from the Palace of Culture; walk down the steps in front of McDonald's to find **Underground Music Café,** ul. Marszałkowska 126/134, has a bar upstairs, and dance floor downstairs. (Tel. 826 70 48; fax 826 70 47. F disco, Sa house party. Cover F 25zł, students 15zł; Sa 25zł, students 20zł; women free before 11pm. Open M-Tu 11am-1am, W-Th 11am-3am, F-Sa 11am-5am, Su 4pm-1am.)

GDAŃSK

The strategic location of Gdańsk (gh-DA-insk) on the Baltic Coast and at the mouth of the Wisła has helped it to flourish architecturally and culturally, and has also put it at the forefront of Polish history for more than a millennium. Today, Gdańsk is a multi-faceted gem, with a dizzying array of things to eat, drink, see, and do.

⌷ GETTING THERE AND AWAY

Trains: Gdańsk Główny, ul. Podwale Grodzkie 1 (info tel. 301 11 12). To: **Warsaw** (4hr., 18 per day, 32.12zł); **Berlin** (7hr., 2 per day, 123zł); **Kraków** (8hr., 10 per day, 36zł); **Prague** (17hr., 1 per day, 182zł); and **St. Petersburg** (36hr., 3 per week, 264zł).

Local Transportation: Buses and **trams** cost 0.90-2.70zł; **day-pass** 4.50zł. Prices higher at night. Students pay half-price, and baggage needs a ticket.

Taxis: Super Hallo Taxi, tel. 301 91 91. Not to be confused with **Hallo Taxi,** tel. 91 97.

⏣ ORIENTATION AND PRACTICAL INFORMATION

From the **Gdańsk Główny** train station, the city center lies a few blocks southeast, bordered on the west by **Wały Jagiellońskie** and on the east by the **Motława.** Take the underpass in front of the train station, go right, exit the shopping center, then turn left on ul. Heweliusza. Turn right on ul. Rajska and follow the signs to **Główne Miasto** (Main Town), turning left on **ul. Długa.** Długa becomes **Długi Targ** as it widens near Motława.Gdańsk has a number of suburbs, all north of Główne Miasto.

Tourist Offices: IT Gdańsk, ul. Długa 45 (tel./fax 301 91 51), in Główne Miasto. Open daily 9am-6pm.

Budget Travel: Orbis, ul. Podwale Staromiejskie 96/97 (tel. 301 21 32; fax 301 84 12). International and domestic ferry, train, and plane tickets. English tours of town. Open M-F 9am-5pm, Sa 10am-2pm. **Almatur,** ul. Długi Targ 11, 2nd fl. (tel. 301 29 31; email almatur@combidata.com.pl), in the Główne Miasto center. ISICs (32zł), info about youth and student hostels, ferries, and more. Open M-F 9am-5pm, Sa 10am-2pm.

Currency Exchange: The train station has a 24-hour *bureaux de change* and an **ATM. Bank Gdański,** Wały Jagiellońskie 14/16 (tel. 307 92 12), cashes traveler's checks for 1% commission and provides cash advances for no commission. Open M-F 8am-6pm.

Late Night Pharmacy: At the train station (tel. 346 25 40). Closed 7:30-8am.

Emergencies: Tel. 999.

Internet Access: Rudy Kot Internet Music Café, ul. Garncarska 18/20 (tel. 301 86 49). Off Podwale Staromiejskie. 2.50zł per 30min. Open daily 10am-midnight.

Post Office: ul. Długa 22/28 (tel. 301 88 53). *Poste Restante* is around the back, through a separate entrance. Address mail to be held: Frieda GLAUBERMAN, *Poste Restante,* Gdańsk 1, **80-801.** Open M-F 8am-8pm, Sa 9am-1pm.

PHONE CODE	City code: 058. From outside Poland, dial int'l dialing prefix (see inside back cover) + 48 + 58 + local number.

⌷◔ ACCOMMODATIONS AND FOOD

Try to book ahead in summer or get a **private room** through **Gdańsk-Tourist** (Biuro Usług Turystycznych), ul. Heweliusza 8, opposite the station. (Tel. 301 26 34; fax 301 63 01. Singles 37-46zł; doubles 63-76zł. Open July-Aug. daily 8am-7pm; Sept.-June M-Sa 9am-5pm.) If you don't have luck inside, try an **elderly woman** out front.

Schronisko Młodzieżowe (HI), ul. Wałowa 21 (tel. 301 23 13). Cross the street in front of the train station, head up ul. Heweliusza, turn left at ul. Łagiewniki, then right on Wałowa; the conveniently located hostel is on the left. Dorms 12.84zł; single and doubles 26.75zł; triples and quads 16.05zł; "Seaside" tax 1zł, students 0.50zł. Sheets 3zł. Kitchen. Luggage storage 1zł. Lockout 10am-5pm. Curfew 11pm.

Schronisko Młodzieżowe (HI), ul. Grunwaldzka 244 (tel. 341 41 08). Take tram 6 or 12 north from the front of the train station and get off at "Abrahama" (unmarked), 14 stops later; you will see a complex of tram garages on the left (20-25min.). Turn right on ul.

Abrahama, then right again on Grunwaldzka; the hostel is on the right. Doubles 21.40-32.10zł, nonmembers 26.75-32.10zł; with bath 32.10zł, 37.45zł; quads 13.91-16.05zł. Sheets 3zł. Luggage storage 1zł. Reception 5-9pm. Lockout 10am-5pm. Curfew 10pm.

Hotel Zaułek, ul. Ogarna 107/108 (tel. 301 41 69). Ogarna runs parallel to Długi Targ, 1 block south. Well-located but dark. Singles 50zł; doubles 65zł; triples 85zł; quads 100zł.

Hotel Dom Nauczyciela, ul. Uphagena 28 (tel. 341 55 87 and 341 91 16), in Gdańsk-Wrzeszcz. Take tram 6 or 12 north from the train station to "Miszewskiego" (7 stops). Turn right on ul. Miszewskiego and take the next right onto Uphagena; the hotel will be ahead on the left, facing the tennis courts. Singles 43-118zł; doubles 60-166zł; triples 81-90zł.

For fresh produce, try **Hala Targowa** on ul. Pańska, in the shadows of Kościół św. Katarzyny just off Podwale Staromiejskie. (Open M-F 9am-6pm, first and last Sa of the month 9am-3pm.) When in Poland do as the Polish do—that is, eat tasty Vietnamese fare at ◼**Tan Viet,** ul. Podmłyńska 1/5. (Tel. 301 33 35. Entrees 16-35zł. V, MC, AmEx.) Or do hearty, homestyle Polish food at **Bar Mleczny,** ul. Długa 33/34. (Tel. 301 49 88. Full meal 5-10zł. Open M-F 7am-6pm, Sa 9am-5pm.)

🎦 🎵 SIGHTS AND ENTERTAINMENT

GŁÓWNE MIASTO. Gdańsk was one of the first Polish cities to undergo an exhaustive postwar facelift; only a few buildings have yet to be fully restored. The handsome market square, **Długi Targ,** forms the physical and social center of Główne Miasto, where the original 16th-century façade of **Arthur's Court** (Dwór Artusa) faces out onto **Neptune Fountain** (Fontanna Neptuna). The court now houses a branch of the **Gdańsk History Museum** (Muzeum Historii Gdańska). Next to the fountain, where ul. Długa and Długi Targ meet, the 14th-century **ratusz** (town hall) houses another excellent branch of the **Gdańsk History Museum.** For an extra 2zł, you can climb the **tower** for an incredible view of the city. *(Both museums open Tu and Th noon-7pm, F-Sa 10am-5pm, Su 11am-5pm. 4zł, students 2zł. Tower also open W 8-10pm.)* One block north of Długi Targ is the city's grandest house of worship, the 14th-century **Church of the Blessed Virgin Mary** (Kościół Najświętszej Marii Panny). *(Open M-Sa 9am-5:30pm, Su 1:30-5:30pm. Donation requested.)* The cobblestoned ul. Mariacka leads to riverside ul. Długie Pobrzeże. Going left along Długie Pobrzeże leads to the huge Gothic **Harbor Crane,** part of **Central Maritime Museum** (Centralne Muzeum Morskie). *(Open daily 10am-6pm. 3zł, students 2zł.)* The flags of Lech Wałęsa's trade union *Solidarność* fly high once again at **Gdańsk Shipyard** (Stocznia Gdańska) and at the **Solidarity monument,** on pl. Solidarności, just north of the center at the end of ul. Wały Piastowskie.

GDAŃSK-OLIWA. The most beautiful of Gdańsk's many suburbs, Oliwa provides a brief respite from the big city. The fastest way there from the center of the city is by commuter rail (15min., 2zł, students 1zł). Trams 6 and 12 will get you there more slowly (30-35min.). From the Oliwa train station, go up ul. Poczty Gdańskiej, turn right on ul. Grundwaldzka, then turn left at the signs for the cathedral on ul. Rybiń skiego. To the right you'll find the lush green shade and ponds of **Park Oliwski.** *(Open daily May-Sept. 5am-11pm; Mar.-Apr. and Oct. 5am-8pm.)* Within the park's gates is the oldest church in the Gdańsk area, the 13th-century **Oliwska Cathedral** (Katedra) which houses the magnificent 18th-century Rococo organ. *(Consult "Informator Turystyczney," at the tourist office, for a complete schedule of daily tours.)*

WESTERPLATTE. When Germany attacked on September 1, 1939, the little island **fort** guarding the entrance to Gdańsk's harbor gained the unfortunate distinction of being the target of the first shots of WWII. Its defenders held out bravely for a week, until a lack of food and munitions forced them out. To get here, take bus 106 or 158 south from the train station to the last stop. **Guardhouse #1** has been converted into a museum about the fateful day. *(Open May-Sept. 9am-4pm. 1.50zł, students 1zł.)* The path beyond the museum passes the ruins of a command building and, farther up, the massive **Memorial to the Heroes of the Coast** (Pomnik Obrońców Wybrzeża).

BRZEŹNO. For some fun at the **beach,** Brzeźno—though it may not be as trendy as Sopot—is perfect. What it does have over Sopot is **Park Brzeźnieński,** a wondrous escape full of tall pine trees. Take tram 13 north from the train station to the last stop, "Brzeźno." Follow the footpath in the wooded area ahead to reach the beach.

POLAND

NIGHTLIFE. Długi Targ rages as crowds of all ages pack the pubs, clubs, and beer gardens late into the evening. Near the intersection of ul. Podwale Staromiejskie and ul. Podmłyńska, **U7**, pl. Dominikański 7, has seven attractions: bowling, billiards, a sauna, a solarium, a shooting range, a fitness center, and of course, the bar. (Open daily 9am-1am.) The popular **Jazz Club**, ul. Długi Targ 39/40, is a great spot for live music (F-Sa after 9pm). (Open daily 10am until the last guest leaves). **Cotton Club**, ul. Złotników 25/29, does jazz. (Beer 5-10zł. Open daily 4pm-late.)

▌ EXCURSIONS FROM GDAŃSK

FROMBORK. Little Frombork is closely associated with the name and work of astronomer **Mikołaj Kopernik** (Copernicus), who lived here from 1510 until his death in 1543. It was in this town that Kopernik conducted most of his research and composed his revolutionary book, *De Revolutionibus Orbium Coelestium.* The tiny waterfront village surrounds a truly breathtaking and well-maintained cathedral complex perched majestically atop a hill. Once you cross the wooden bridge, the *kasa* ahead on the right sells tickets to **Muzeum Kopernika,** which houses copies of the great book and other odds and ends, the **cathedral** and its impressive **organ,** and the **tower** *(wieża).* (Museum open Tu-Su May-Sept. 10am-5:30pm; Oct.-Apr. 9am-3:30pm; 2zł, students 1zł. Cathedral open M-Sa 9:30am-5pm. Organ concerts twice daily, usually 11am and 3pm; 2zł, students 1zł. Tower open M 9:30am-5pm, Tu-Sa 9:30am-7:30pm; 2.50zł, students 2zł.) Frombork is best reached by **bus** from Gdańsk (2hr., 6 per day, 8-12zł) that leave from behind the Gdańsk train station via the underground passageway. The main **tourist office,** Globus, ul. Elbląska 2, sits across from the cathedral in the *rynek,* at the end of the path from the train station. (Tel./fax (055) 243 73 54. Open daily 9am-7pm.)

SOPOT. Simply put, Sopot is a **beach** resort: white, sandy, big, and adorned with all manner of recreation. The most popular sands are at the end of ul. Monte Cassino, where the 512-meter **pier** (molo) begins. (M-F 1.90zł, students 0.90zł; Sa-Su 2.50zł, 1.40zł.) The **commuter rail** (SKM) connects Sopot to Gdańsk (15min., every 6-12min., 4zł, students 2zł). Ul. Dworcowa begins at the train station and leads to the pedestrian ul. Monte Cassino, which runs along the sea to the pier. **Ferries** (tel. (058) 551 12 93) go from the end of the pier to Gdańsk (1hr., 1 per day, round-trip 38zł, students 28zł). **IT,** ul. Dworcowa 4, next to the train station, arranges **rooms** (singles 43zł; doubles 72zł). (Tel. (058) 550 37 83. Open M-F 8:30am-5pm, Sa-Su 8:30am-2pm. Accommodations bureau closed Sa and Su.)

TORUŃ

Toruń sells itself as the birthplace and childhood home of Mikołaj Kopernik—a.k.a. Copernicus—the man who "stopped the sun and moved the earth." After wandering its cobblestoned medieval streets, you might wonder why he ever left. The **Old Town** (Stare Miasto), commanding the right bank of the Wisła River, was constructed by the Teutonic Knights in the 13th century. Copernicus' birthplace, **Dom Kopernika,** ul. Kopernika 15/17, where he popped out on February 19, 1473, has been meticulously restored. (Open Tu-Su 10am-4pm. 3zł, students 2zł.) The 14th-century **ratusz** (town hall), Rynek Staromiejski 1, in the center of the tourist district, now houses the **Regional Museum** (Muzeum Okręgowe). (Open Tu-Su 10am-6pm. 3zł, students 2zł; Su free.) A city-wide burghers' revolt in 1454 led to the destruction of the **Teutonic Knights' Castle,** but the ruins on ul. Przedzamcze are still impressive. The 50-foot **Leaning Tower,** Pod Krzywą Wieżą 17, was built in 1271 by a Teutonic knight as punishment for falling in love with a peasant girl. The 13th- to 15th-century **Cathedral of St. John the Evangelist** (Bazylika Katedralna pw. św. Janów), at the corner of ul. Zeglarska, is the most impressive of the tall Gothic churches dotting the skyline. From there, it's a short walk across the *rynek* to ul. Panny Marii and the beautiful stained glass of the **Church of the Virgin Mary** (Kościół Św. Marii). At the end of the day, stroll along **Bulwar Filadelfijski** (named for Toruń's sister city, Philadelphia), where fishermen and couples line the stone steps.

The **train** station, across the Wisła River from the city center, serves Gdańsk (2½hr., 6 per day, 26zł) and Warsaw (3hr., 3 per day, 36zł). Comfortable Polski Express **buses** leave from pl. Teatralny for Warsaw (3½hr., 14 per day, 23zł). The IT **tourist office,** ul. Piekary 37/39, offers helpful advice in English and helps find lodgings. From the station, take city bus 22 or 27 to pl. Rapackiego (the first stop across the river), head through the little park area, and it's on your left. (Tel./fax (056) 621 09 31; www.um.torun.pl. Open May-Aug. M and Sa 9am-4pm, Tu-F 9am-6pm, Su 9am-1pm; Sept.-Apr. closed Su.) Surf the **internet** at **Internet Club Jeremi,** Rynek Staromiejski 33. (4zł per hr. Open daily 9am until last guest leaves.) ⬛**Hotel Kopernik,** ul. Wola Zamkowa 16, by Rynek Nowomiejski, is a deal. (Tel./fax (056) 652 25 73. Singles 60-100zł; doubles 70-110zł.) To get to the distant but decent **Schronisko Młodzieżowe (HI),** ul. Św. Józefa 22/24, from the train station or pl. Rapackiego, take bus 11 (five stops from pl. Rapackiego) to "Św Józefa." (Tel. (056) 654 41 07. Dorms 14-24zł; singles 32-36zł.) There is a 24-hour **grocery store** at ul. Chełmińska 22. **Bar Mleczny,** ul. Różana 1, serves up primarily veggie traditional Polish dishes. (Open M-F 9am-7pm, Sa 9am-4pm.) **Postal code:** 87-100.

KRAKÓW

Once tucked away behind the walls of communism, Kraków (KRAH-koof) has quickly become a trendy, international city, recently earning a place as a European City of Culture for 2000. Music and chatter spill upward from a veritable underground town of cellar pubs and galleries and people mingle at all hours of the day and night amongst Kraków's architectural gems and cobblestoned streets.

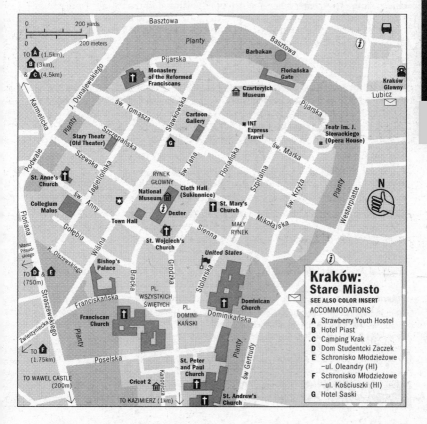

Kraków: Stare Miasto
SEE ALSO COLOR INSERT
ACCOMMODATIONS
A Strawberry Youth Hostel
B Hotel Piast
C Camping Krak
D Dom Studentcki Zaczek
E Schronisko Młodzieżowe
 –ul. Oleandry (HI)
F Schronisko Młodzieżowe
 –ul. Kościuszki (HI)
G Hotel Saski

▤ GETTING THERE AND GETTING AROUND

Flights: Balice airport (tel. 411 19 55), 15km west of the center. Connected to the main train station by northbound bus 208 (40min.) or express bus D (30min.).

Trains: Kraków Główny, pl. Kolejowy 1 (tel. 624 54 39). To: **Warsaw** (4¾hr., 9 per day, 45zł); **Bratislava** (7hr., 1 per day, 150zł); **Berlin** (8hr., 2 per day, 110zł); **Prague** (8½hr., 1 per day, 150zł); **Vienna** (9hr., 2 per day, 145zł); **Budapest** (11hr., 1 per day, 160zł); **Lviv** (10½hr., 1 per day, 60zł); and **Kiev** (22hr., 1 per day, 110zł). Some trains to southeast Poland leave from **Kraków Płaszów,** pl. Dudzinskich 1 (info tel. 933). Take the train from Kraków Główny or tram 3 or 13 from the center south to ul. Wielicka.

Buses: Info tel. 936. On ul. Worcella, directly across from Kraków Główny. **Sindbad** (tel. 266 19 21) in the main hall, sells international tickets. Open M-F 9am-5pm. To: **Warsaw** (6hr., 3 per day, 35zł); **Lviv** (10hr., 1 per day, 45zł); **Budapest** (11hr., 2 per week, 94zł); and **Prague** (11hr., 3 per week, 140zł).

Local Transportation: Stock up on tickets at kiosks near **bus** and **tram** stops (1.50zł) or on board (1.80zł); punch them on board. Large backpacks need their own tickets (0.75zł). **Night buses** 3.50zł. **Day pass** 6zł. You'll be fined if you or your pack are ticketless.

Taxis: Express Taxi (tel. 644 41 11). **Hellou** (tel. 644 42 22). **Major** (tel. 636 33 33).

▨ ORIENTATION AND PRACTICAL INFORMATION

The city fans outward in roughly concentric circles from the huge **Rynek Główny** (Main Market Square), at the heart of the **Stare Miasto** (Old Town). The **Wisła** river skims the southwest corner of **Wzgórze Wawelskie** (Wawel Hill). The **bus** and **train stations** sit opposite each other about 10min. northeast of the *rynek*. To reach the *rynek*, turn left out of the train station, turn right past the kiosks, head through the underpass to the Planty gardens, walk toward the crumbled city wall, turn left down ul. Szpitalna, and turn right at the church.

Tourist Offices: Dexter, Rynek Główny 1/3 (tel. 421 77 06; fax 421 30 36). English-speaking staff organizes tours. Open M-F 9am-6pm, Sa 9am-1pm.

Budget Travel: Orbis, Rynek Główny 41 (tel. 422 40 35; fax 422 28 85). Sells international tickets. Arranges trips to the Wieliczka and Auschwitz. English spoken. Open Apr.-Oct. M-F 8am-6pm, Sa 8:30am-3pm; Nov.-Mar. M-F 8am-6pm, Sa 8:30am-1pm.

Consulates: US, ul. Stolarska 9 (tel. 429 66 55; in emergency 422 14 00). Open M-F 8:30am-4:30pm. Observes American holidays.

Currency Exchange: At *kantory,* Orbis, and hotels. *Kantory* not around the train station have the best rates.

American Express: Rynek Główny 41 (tel. 422 91 80), in the Orbis office (see above).

Luggage Storage: Kraków Główny. 1% of luggage value plus 3.60zł per day. Open 24hr.

English Bookstore: Odeon, Rynek Główny 5 (tel. 492 12 93). Open daily 9am-9pm.

Laundromat: Ul. Piastowska 47, on the 1st floor of Hotel Piast. 3hr. drop-off. Wash 12zł; dry 12zł. Open daily July-Aug. 8am-8pm; Sept.-June 10am-7pm.

Police: Tel. 997.

Medical Assistance: Profimed, Rynek Główny 6 (tel. 421 79 97), and ul. Grodzka 26 (tel. 422 64 53). Some English spoken. Open M-F 8am-8pm, Sa 9am-1pm.

Internet Access: Available at **Club U Louisa** (see **Entertainment,** p. 721) for 5zł per hr.

Telephones: At the post office and opposite the train station, ul. Lubicz 4 (tel. 422 14 85 and 422 86 35). Both open 24hr.

Post Office: Ul. Westerplatte 20 (tel. 422 86 48; fax 422 36 06). *Poste restante* at counters 1 and 3. Open M-F 7:30am-8:30pm, Sa 9am-2pm, Su 9-11am. Address mail to be held to Ang LEE, Poste Restante, Kraków 1, **31-045,** Poland.

PHONE CODE	CIty code: 012. From outside Poland, dial int'l dialing prefix (see inside back cover) + 48 + 12 + local number.

ACCOMMODATIONS

Call a couple days ahead in summer. **Waweltur,** ul. Pawia 8, arranges **private rooms.** (Tel. 422 16 40; fax 422 19 21. Open M-F 8am-8pm, Sa 8am-2pm. Singles 64zł; doubles 96zł.) For private rooms, watch for signs or solicitors in the train station.

Strawberry Youth Hostel, ul. Ractawicka 9 (tel. 636 15 00). Take tram 4, 8, or 13 from the train station to Urzędnicza. Backtrack to the intersection and go left up ul. Urzędnicza; go left on ul. Kazimierza Wielkiego, right on Raclawicka. 40zł per person. Check-out 10am.

Schronisko Młodzieżowe (HI), ul. Oleandry 4 (tel. 633 88 22). Take tram 15 from the train station and get off when the main drag turns into ul. 3-go Maja. Take the 1st right up 3-go Maja onto Oleandry. 16-24zł. Flexible lockout 10am-5pm. Curfew midnight.

Dom Studentcki Zaczek, ul. 3-go Maja 5 (tel. 633 54 77). Opposite Hotel Cracovia, accessible by tram 15. Get off one stop after the museum at the start of ul. 3-go Maja. Well located, but the nearby disco might keep you up. Singles 55-65zł; doubles 65-99zł; triples 75-125zł. Check-out 10am.

Hotel Piast, ul. Piastowska 47 (tel. 637 49 33). Take tram 4 or 12 from the train station to "Wawel." Walk in the direction of the tram to the first intersection, then turn left. Go straight a few blocks and Piast will be on the left. Tidy rooms teem with English speakers. Singles 50-85zł; doubles 74-110zł; triples with bath 120zł.

Schronisko Młodzieżowe (HI), ul. Kościuszki 88 (tel. 422 19 51), inside a convent. Take tram 32 (dir: Salwator) from the train station and get off at the last stop (15min.). Run by nuns on the Wisła, 20min. from the center. 9.75zł, nonmembers 15zł. Sheets 2.50zł. Reception daily 6am-3pm and 5-11pm. Lockout 10am-5pm. Strict curfew 11pm.

Hotel Saski, ul. Sławkowska 3 (tel. 421 42 22; fax 421 48 30). Singles 110-200zł; doubles 145-275zł; triples 180-315zł. Check-out noon. V, MC.

Camping Krak, ul. Radzikowskiego 99 (tel. 637 21 22 and 637 29 57; fax 637 25 32). Take tram 4, 8, or 13 from the train station to "Balicka Wiaduct." If it stops at "Wesele," take bus 313 the last 2 stops, walk down to ul. Armu Krajowej, the street under the tram line, and turn left. Tents 16zł per person, cars 18zł. Open May 15-Sept. 15.

FOOD

Many restaurants and cafés are on and around the *rynek*. Grocery stores surround the bus and train stations; more can be found near the *rynek*.

Chimera, ul. św. Anny 3 (tel. 423 21 78), in the cellar and ivy garden. The oldest and most famous salad joint in town. Salad sampler costs 9zł; slightly smaller plate 6zł. Live music nightly 8pm. Open M-Tu 9am-11pm, W-Su 9am-midnight.

Camelot, ul. św. Tomasza 17 (tel. 421 01 23). Popular with students, artists, and foreigners alike. Adorned with handcrafted wooden dolls and original paintings. Salad 14-18zł. Cabaret on F in winter. Concerts every W and Sa. Open daily 9am-midnight.

Café Zakgtek, Grodzka 2 (tel. 429 57 25). Great fresh sandwiches and salads. Sandwiches 4-6zł. Breakfast 6zł. Open summer M-Sa 8:30am-10pm; winter M-Sa 9am-7pm.

Jadłodajnia u Stasi, ul. Mikołajska 16. Famous for its traditional Polish food. Open M-F 12:30pm until the food runs out—usually 4-5pm.

Balaton, ul. Grodzka 37 (tel. 422 04 69). Divine Hungarian cuisine that always attracts crowds. Entrees 6-20zł. Open daily 9am-10pm.

Restauracja Ariel, ul. Szeroka 17 (tel./fax 421 38 70), in the old Jewish district, Kazimierz, 15min. south of the *rynek*. Music nightly 8pm; cover 20zł. Open daily 9am-11pm.

Kawiarnia Jama Michalika, ul. Floriańska 45 (tel. 422 15 61). More than a century old, this is one of Kraków's most famous, and best decorated, cafés. Open daily 9am-10pm.

SIGHTS

STARE MIASTO (OLD TOWN). At the center of the Stare Miasto spreads **Rynek Główny,** complete with seas of cafés and bars, not to mention tourists and Poles alike. The two towers of **St. Mary's Church** (Kościół Mariacki) were built by two brothers with different working styles: one hurried, the other deliberate. The hasty brother realized that the work of his careful sibling would put his own to shame,

POLAND

and killed him in a fit of jealousy. The murder weapon is on display in the Cloth Hall (see below). A trumpet call blares from the towers once in each direction every hour. Its abrupt ending recalls the destruction of Kraków in 1241, when the invading Tartars are said to have shot down the trumpeter in the middle of his song. *(At the corner of the rynek closest to the train station. Open daily noon-6pm. Altar 2.50zł, students 1.50zł.)* In the middle of the *rynek*, the yellow Italianate **Cloth Hall** (Sukiennice) houses the **National Museum** (Muzeum Narodowe) upstairs. *(Open Tu-W and F-Su 10am-3:30pm, Th 10am-6pm. 5zł, students 2.50zł.)* Ul. Floriańska runs from the corner of the *rynek* closest to the train station to the **Barbakan,** the only remnant of the city's medieval fortifications. At the top of the street, **Floriańska Gate** (Brama Floriańska), the old entrance to the city, is the centerpiece of the only surviving remnant of the city wall. Walking down Grodzka from the corner of the *rynek* closest to **Wojciech's Church,** turn right one block down ul. Franciszkańska to the **Franciscan Church** (Kościół Franciszkański), which houses Stanisław Wyspiański's famed *God the Father* stained-glass window. Pope John Paul II resided across the street in the **Bishop's Palace** when he was still Cardinal Karol Wojtyła.

KAZIMIERZ. South of the Stare Miasto lies Kazimierz, Kraków's 600-year-old **old Jewish quarter.** On the eve of WWII, 64,000 Jews lived in the Kraków area, many of them in Kazimierz, but Nazi policies forced most out. All were deported by March 1943, many to the nearby Płaszów (where parts of *Schindler's List* was filmed) and Auschwitz-Birkenau concentration camps. Kazmierz today is a focal point for the 5000 Jews living in Poland, and serves as a starting place for those seeking their ancestral roots. *(The walk from the rynek leads down ul. Sienna by St. Mary's Church, and opposite the statue of Adam Mickiewicz; ul. Sienna turns into Starowiślna. After 1km, turn right on Miodowa, then take the 1st left onto Szeroka (15min.).)* The tiny **Remuh Synagogue** is surrounded by **Remuh's Cemetery,** one of Poland's oldest Jewish cemeteries, with graves dating back to the plague of 1551-52. *(Szeroka 40. Open M-F 9am-4pm. 5zł, students 2zł. Services F dusk and Sa morning.)* **Temple Synagogue** was founded by the Association of Progressive Israelis in the early 1860s; it's under renovation through 2000, but for a small donation you can usually sneak in to take a look. *(Miodowa 24.)* Poland's oldest synagogue, and the one most emblematic of Jewish architecture, **Old Synagogue** (Stara Synagoga) houses a **museum.** *(Szeroka 24. Open W-Th and Sa-Su 9am-3pm, F 11am-6pm. 5zł, students 2.50zł.)* Built in 1644, **Isaac Synagogue,** Kraków's largest and newest synagogue, offers continuous screenings of five -minute films depicting life in the district in 1936 and the Nazi evacuation. *(Ul. Kapa 18. Open Su-F and Su 9am-7pm; closed Jewish holidays. 6zł.)* **The Center for Jewish Culture,** in the former Bene Emenu prayer house, operates a library, supports restoration efforts, and arranges heritage tours. *(Rabina Meiselsa 17. Tel. 423 55 87; fax 423 50 34.)*

WAWEL CASTLE AND AROUND. ■**Wawel Castle** (Zamek Wawelski) is one of the finest pieces of architecture in Poland. Begun in the 10th century but remodeled during the 1500s, the castle contains 71 chambers, a magnificent sequence of 16th-century tapestries commissioned by the royal family, and a series of arrases depicting the story of Noah's Ark, among many other treasures. The castle is currently undergoing renovation, so not all rooms are open to the public. The **Oriental Collection** has an amazing display of 17th- and 18th-century porcelain from China and Japan. *(Open Tu and F 9:30am-4:30pm, W-Th 9:30am-3:30pm, Sa 9:30-3pm, Su 10am-3pm. Royal chambers 10zł, students 5zł; Oriental collection 5zł, students 3zł; treasury and armory 10zł, students 5zł; Apr.-Sept. W free; Oct.-Mar. Sa free.)* Poland's monarchs were crowned and buried in the **Wawel Cathedral** (Katedra Wawelska), next to the castle. Karol Wojtyła, who grew up in Kraków, was archbishop here before he became Pope. *(Cathedral open May-Sept. M-F 9am-5:15pm, Sa 9am-4:45pm, Su 12:15-5:15pm. 6zł, students 3zł.)* Climb the steep wooden stairs from the church to reach **Zygmunt's Bell** (Dzwon Zygmunta). It sounds only on major holidays, but when it does, its tones echo for miles. The entrance to **Dragon's Cave** (Smocza Jama), legendary dwelling of Kraków's special friend, hides in the complex's southwest corner. If you've descended the hill, you've passed it. *(Cave open May-Sept. daily 10am-5pm. 2zł.)*

♪ ENTERTAINMENT

The **Cultural Information Center,** ul. św. Jana 2, sells the comprehensive monthly guide *Karnet* (2zł; www.karnet.krakow2000.pl) and tickets for upcoming events. (Tel. 421 77 87; fax 421 77 31. Open M-F 10am-7pm, Sa 11am-7pm.) Festivals abound in Kraków, particularly in summer. Some to note are the **International Short Film Festival** (late May), the **Festival of Jewish Culture** (end of June), the **International Festival of Outdoor Performances** (early July), and the **Jazz Festival** (Oct./Nov.). Classical music buffs will appreciate **Filharmonia Krakowska** (tel. 422 09 58 and 422 94 77), performing regularly at ul. Zwierzyniecka 1, and the **Opera Stage,** Plac Św. Ducha 1, whose box office is at the **J. Słowacki Theater** (tel. 423 17 00).

U Louisa, Rynek Główny 13, draws a diverse crowd with good, loud jazz and blues on weekends. (Tel. 421 80 92. Beer 4-7.50zł. Cover 5-10zł. Open daily 11am until the last guest leaves.) Head under the archway, then down the stairs through the door on the right to find mellow **Free Pub,** ul. Sławkowska 4. (Beer 4.50zł. Open daily 4pm until the last guest leaves.) **Jazz Club "U Muniaka,"** ul. Floriańska 3 has concerts Th-Sa 9:30pm. (Tel. 422 26 53. 15zł at the door. Open daily 5pm-midnight, 1am for concerts.) **Student Club,** Rynek Główny 8, is a laid-back student hangout but on weekends is a loud, smoky disco. (Open daily from 9am or 10am until 3 or 4am.)

▐ EXCURSIONS FROM KRAKÓW

AUSCHWITZ-BIRKENAU. An estimated 1.5 million people, mostly Jews, were murdered—and thousands more suffered unthinkable horrors—in the Nazi concentration camps at **Auschwitz** (Oświęcim) and **Birkenau** (Brzezinka). The largest and most efficient of the death camps, their names are synonymous with the Nazi death machine. The smaller **Konzentrationslager Auschwitz I** is located within the limits of the town of Oświęcim. Tours begin at the **museum** at Auschwitz; as you walk past the remnants of thousands of lives—suitcases, shoes, glasses, and more than 100,000 lb. of women's hair—the sheer enormity of the evil committed here comes into focus. There's an English-language **film** shown every half-hour, shot by the Soviet Army that liberated the camp on January 27, 1945 (2zł). (Open daily June-Aug. 8am-7pm; May and Sept. 8am-6pm; Apr. and Oct. 8am-5pm; Mar. and Nov. to mid-Dec. 8am-4pm; mid-Dec.-Feb. 8am-3pm. Free. Guided tour in English daily at 11:30am; 3½hr., 16zł.) The starker and larger **Konzentrationslager Auschwitz II-Birkenau** lies in the countryside 3km from the original camp. A half-hour walk along a well-marked route or a quick **shuttle** ride from the parking lot of the Auschwitz museum (mid-Apr. to Oct., every hr. 10:30am-4:30pm, 1zł) will get you there. Birkenau was built later in the war, when the massive numbers of Jews, Roma, Slavs, homosexuals, disabled people, and other "inferiors" flooding Auschwitz necessitated a more "efficient" means of killing. The site today is only a small section of the original camp; the remainder was destroyed by retreating Nazis. In the right corner of the camp lies a pond, still gray from the ashes deposited there half a century ago; fragments of bone can still be found in the area near the crematoria.

Buses from Krakow's central bus station go to "Muzeum Oświęcim" in Oświęcim (1½hr., 10 per day, 7.90zł). Less convenient **trains** leave from Kraków Główny (1¾hr., 2 per day, 7.40zł) and from Kraków Plaszów, south of the center. Buses 2-5 from the Oświęcim train station then connect to "Muzeum Oświęcim"; or walk right as you exit the station, turn left after a block on ul. Więźniów Oświęcimia, and walk 1.6km to Auschwitz, which will be on the right.

WIELICZKA. A 1000-year-old ▩ **salt mine** awaits at ul. Daniłowicza 10 in the tiny town of Wieliczka, 13km southeast of Krakow. Pious Poles carved the immense 20-chapel complex 100m underground entirely out of salt; in 1978, UNESCO declared the mine one of the 12 most priceless monuments in the world. The most spectacular cavern is the 60m-by-11m **St. Kinga's Chapel,** complete with salty chandeliers, an altar, and relief works. (Tel. 278 73 02; fax 278 73 33. Open daily mid-Apr. to mid-Oct. 7:30am-6:30pm; mid-Oct. to mid-Apr. 8am-4pm. Obligatory tours 23zł, students 12zł. Cameras 6zł; video 11zł. English guide June-Aug.; 28zł per person.) **Orbis** (see

p. 718) organizes daily trips to the mine (3hr.; 100zł, students 75zł). **Trains,** a cheaper option, also make the trip from Kraków (25min., every hr., 2zł), and private **mini-buses** depart from the road between the train and bus stations (every 15min., 2zł). Look for the minibuses with "Wieliczka" on the door. Once in Wieliczka, follow the former path of the tracks and then the *"do kopalni"* signs.

LUBLIN

Long an incubator of social and religious movements, Lublin (LOO-bleen) served as the center of the Polish Reformation and Counter-Reformation in the 16th and 17th centuries. Today, despite unsightly apartment blocks on the outskirts of the city, it maintains a vibrant, bohemian flair. **Ul. Krakowskie Przedmieście** runs east from the tourist office to **Pl. Łokietka,** gateway to **Stare Miasto** (Old Town) and home to the 1827 **New Town Hall** (Nowy Ratusz). To the right along ul. Królewska is the grand, 16th-century **Cathedral of St. John the Baptist and St. John the Evangelist** (Katedra Św. Jana Chrzciciela i Jana Ewangelisty). To the left is **ul. Lubartowska,** the main artery of pre-war Lublin's Jewish district. **Victims of the Ghetto Square** (Pl. Ofiar Getta), on the left of the street, centers on the **Monument to the Murdered Jews.** Heading straight through pl. Łokietka and through the **Kraków Gate** (Brama Krakowska) onto ul. Bramowa leads to the *rynek*, with early Renaissance houses and the Neoclassical **Old Town Hall** (Stare Ratusz). Continue through the square via the 15th-century **Grodzka Gate** (Brama Grodzka) onto ul. Grodzka (which turns into ul. Zamkowa) to reach the massive **Lublin Castle** (Zamek Lubelski). Most of the structure was built in the 14th century, but was restored in the 19th century with a neo-Gothic exterior. During the Nazi occupation, the castle functioned as a Gestapo jail; the prisoners were shot en masse when the Nazis had to make a hasty retreat. The castle contains the art **Muzeum Lubelskie;** don't miss the stunning Russo-Byzantine frescoes at the attached **Holy Trinity Church.** (Open W-Sa 9am-4pm, Su 9am-5pm. Joint ticket 8zł.)

The Lublin Główny **train station,** pl. Dworcowy 1 (tel. (081) 532 02 19, info tel. 933), south of Stare Miasto, sends trains to Warsaw (2½hr., 10 per day, 22.50zł) and Kraków (4hr., 2 per day, 32.12zł). From the station, take trolley 150 or bus 13 to the city center. **Buses** leave the station at ul. Tysiąclecia 4 (tel. (081) 77 66 49; info tel. 934), near the Old Town, for Warsaw (3hr., 10 per day, 12zł). From the bus station, take bus 5, 10, or 13 into town. The IT **tourist office,** ul. Narutowicza 54, speaks some English and has maps (5zł) and brochures. (Tel. (081) 532 44 12. Open M-F 9am-5pm, Sa 10am-2pm.) **Orbis,** ul. Narutowicza 31/33, handles train and bus tickets, and books rooms at their own hotels. (Tel. (081) 532 22 56; fax 532 15 30. Open M-F 9am-6pm, Sa 9am-2pm. English spoken.) In summer, you can ask the tourist office about staying in cheap (but often far) **university dorms. Schronisko Młodzieżowe (HI),** ul. Długosza 6a, west of the center near the KUL, is clean and quiet. Walk to the end of the Ogród Saski, turn right on ul. Długosza, then turn left at the blue hostel sign. (Tel. (081) 533 06 28. Dorms 16zł, nonmembers 18zł; triples 19zł per person, 20zł. Sheets 4.50zł. Lockout 10am-5pm. Curfew 10pm.) The minimalist **ZNP Dom Nauczy-ciela,** ul. Akademicka 4, next to the KUL, is good if you want to stay out late. From the Ogród Saski bus stop, cross the street and follow ul. Łopacińskiego until it turns into ul. Akademicka. (Tel. (081) 533 82 85. Dorms 27-31zł; singles 64zł; doubles 72zł.) Eateries cluster around **ul. Krakowskie Przedmieście;** you'll find **beer gardens** outside the gate to Old Town. **Grocery** stores line ul. Krakowskie Przedmieście. The **Colosseum Club,** Radziszewskiego 8, near the University, features a great bar and disco. (Cover usually 10zł. Open 8pm-whenever.) **Postal code:** 20-930.

◪ **EXCURSIONS FROM LUBLIN: MAJDANEK. Majdanek,** the largest concentration camp after Auschwitz, is all too near Lublin, just 4km from the city center. Approximately 235,000 Jews, Poles, Danes, and other Europeans died here. **The Majdanek State Museum** (Panstwowe Muzeum na Majdanku) was founded in 1944. Because the Nazis didn't have time to destroy the camp, gas chambers, crematorium, prisoners' barracks, and chilling piles of ash and bone remain. Seeing the camp takes two hours. (Open May-Sept. Tu-Su 8am-6pm; Oct.-Nov. and Mar.-Apr. Tu-Su 8am-3pm. Free. Tours in English 100zł.) The **information center** (tel. (081) 744

26 48) shows a 25-minute documentary available in English (2zł; last showing 3pm). To get to Majdanek from Lublin, take eastbound **bus** 28 from the train station, trollies 153 or 158 from al. Racławickie, or the southbound 156 from ul Królewska.

KAZIMIERZ DOLNY

Although this lovely, picturesque town was established by Kazimierz the Great in the 14th century, it was actually named in honor of Prince Kazimierz the Just, who in 1181 donated the settlement to a nunnery near Kraków. Hike up to the **castle tower,** which used to alert the residents to passing boats on which they could levy tolls. (Open Tu-Su 10am-5pm. 2zł.) On your way down, take a left by the Zamek, cross the road, and head up the trail to **Three Crosses Hill** for an even better view (1zł). The **Museum of Goldsmithery** (Muzeum Sztuki Złotniczej) and **Kamienica Lelejoska,** ul. Senatorska 11/13, jointly exhibit sparkling jewelry, ancient relics, paintings inspired by the town, and a display on the local pre-war Jewish community.

Some **buses** stop on the way between Puławy and Lublin (1½hr., every hr., 6.30zł); others zoom to Warsaw (3½hr., 7 per day, 12zł). If you're coming from Lublin or Warsaw, Kazimierz will not be posted as the final destination—ask the driver if the bus is stopping there *("Czy ten autobus jedzie do Kazimierza?").* When leaving Kazimierz by bus, the bus may depart from across the street from the bus station, just off the cobblestoned **ul. Podzamcze.** Follow ul. Podzamcze to the *rynek* (town square). The **PTTK tourist office,** Rynek 27, sells maps of town (3.50zł) and arranges private rooms (100-140zł). (Tel. (081) 881 00 46. Open May-Oct. M-F 8am-6pm, Sa-Su 10am-5:30pm; off-season M-F 8am-3pm, Sa-Su 10am-2pm.) The conveniently-located **Youth Hostel Strażnica,** ul. Senatorska 23a, is just one block southwest of the *rynek.* (Tel. (081) 881 04 27. Dorms 15zł; doubles and triples 18zł per person. Breakfast included. Sheets 4zł.) A **grocery** store is south of the *rynek* at ul. Klasztorna 5. (Open M-F 6am-6pm, Sa 6am-3pm, Su 9am-2pm.) **Postal code:** 24-120.

ZAKOPANE

Set in a valley surrounded by jagged Tatran peaks and alpine meadows, Zakopane (ZAH-ko-PAH-neh; pop. 100,000), Poland's premier year-round resort, buzzes with hikers and skiers. The magnificent **Tatran National Park** (Tatrzański Park Narodowy) shelters outdoor opportunities. Entrances to the park lie at the trailheads. (3zł, students 1.50zł; off-season 2zł, students 1zł. Keep your ticket). For dramatic vistas, catch a bus or minibus to **Kuźnice** (every 20min., 1.50zł), south of central Zakopane. Or walk along ul. Jagiełłońska, which turns to ul. Chałubińskiego, then continue down ul. Przewodników Tatrzańskich from the train station to catch the 1955m **Kasprowy Wierch** cable car. (Open July-Aug. 7:30am-6:30pm; June and Sept. 7:30am-4pm; Oct. 7:30am-3pm. Round-trip 23zł, students 15zł.) Before hiking, pick up the map *Tatrzański Park Narodowy: Mapa turystyczna* at a kiosk or bookstore.

The **bus station** (tel. 146 03) is on the corner of ul. Kościuszki and ul. Jagiełłońska across from the **train station** (tel. (01820) 145 04). Trains go to Kraków Głowny (3½hr., 12 per day, 13.82zł) and Warsaw (8hr., 5 per day, 21.38zł). Buses go to Kraków (2½hr., 22 per day, 10zł); Warsaw (8hr., 1 per day, 33zł); and Poprad, Slovakia (2½hr., 5 per day, 12zł). Walk down ul. Kościuszki to reach the central ul. Krupówki (10-15min.). The helpful **Tourist Agency Redykołka,** ul. Kościeliska 1, secures **private rooms** (20zł) and run tours. (Tel./fax (01820) 132 53; email king@zakopane.top.pl. Open July-Aug. and Dec.-Mar. M-Sa 9am-6pm, Su 10am-3pm; Sept.-Nov. and Apr.-June M-Sa 9am-5pm, Su 10am-1pm.) When it's time to crash, look for *pokój, noclegi,* or *Zimmer* signs (25-30zł with some haggling). To get to **The Cukiers,** ul. Za Strugiem 10, convenient for hikers, from the bus station, go right up ul. Kościuszki toward the center, turn right onto ul. Krupówki, then left onto Kościeliska; ul. Za Strugiem is 10min. up the road on the left (30min.). (Tel. (01820) 666 29 or 629 20. Doubles and triples 30zł per person. Reserve 3 days ahead.) **PTTK Dom Turysty,** ul. Zaruskiego 5, is a large chalet in the center of town. Walk right down ul. Kościuszki from the bus station; it turns into ul. Zaruskiego after the intersection with Krupówki. (Tel. (01820) 632 07; fax 123 58. Dorms 17-34zł; 3zł surcharge for 1-night stays. Reception 24hr. Check-out 10am.) **Postal code:** 34-500.

POLAND

▲ HIKING NEAR ZAKOPANE. Dolina Kościeliska offers an easy and lovely hike crossing the valley of Potok Kościeliski. A bus shuttles from Zakopane to Kiry (every 30min., 2zł) and the trailhead. The mountain lake **Sea Eye** (Morskie Oko; 1406m) dazzles tourists each summer; take a bus from Zakopane's bus station (45min., 11 per day, 4zł) to Burnt Clearing (Polana Palenica), a.k.a. Bald Clearing (Łysa Polana), or take a minibus from opposite the bus station to start the 9km hike. **Valley of the Five Polish Lakes** (Dolina Pięciu Stawów Polskich) is one of the most beautiful hikes. It departs from Kuźnice and follows the blue trail to Morskie Oko; from the lake, a road travels down to Łysa Polana, which is connected to Zakopane by bus (9hr.; summer only). A shorter version of the hike (6hr.) begins at Łysa Polana. To climb Poland's highest peak, **Rysy** (2499m; 8hr.), follow the red trail from Schronisko Morskie Oko along the east lakeshore and up to Black Lake (Czarny Staw). The arduous climb to Rysy begins in the lake's southeast corner.

WROCŁAW

Since the city's elaborate post-war and post-communist reconstructions, only photographs recall Wrocław's destruction in WWII. Now, the city charms visitors with the antique grace of its many bridges, lush parks, and 19th-century buildings. The modern heart of the city, **Stare Miasto** (Old Town) centers around **Main Market Square** (Rynek Główny), the Renaissance and Gothic **ratusz** and the **History Museum** (Muzeum Historyczne). One exhibit focuses entirely on ul. Świdnicka, a central street so beautiful that the Germans tried to have its stones moved to their soil. (Open W-F 10am-4pm, Sa 11am-5pm, Su 10am-6pm. 4zł, students 3zł; free on W.) With your back to the *ratusz*, bear two blocks left on Kuznicza, bear right on Kotlarska, which becomes ul. Purkyniego, turn left over Most Pokuju, and turn left again on Kard B. Kominka to reach pl. Katedralny and the stately **Cathedral of St. John the Baptist** (Katedra św. Jana Chrzciciela) on Cathedral Island (Ostrów Tunski). Bearing right down Kapitalna brings you to the **Botanical Gardens** (Ogród Botaniczny), ul. Sienkiewicza 23. (Open M-F 8am-6pm, Sa-Su 10am-6pm. 3zł students 2zł.) The center of Wrocław's cultural life, the **University** (Uniwersytet Wrocławski), pl. Uniwersytecki 1, houses many architectural gems, the most impressive of which is **Aula Leopoldina,** an 18th-century lecture hall with magnificent frescoes. (Open Th-Tu 10am-3:30pm. 2.50zł, students 1zł.)

Trains (tel. (071) 68 83 33) go from ul. Piłsudskiego to Poznań (1hr., 18 per day, 20zł); Kraków (4hr., 14 per day, 25zł); Dresden (4½hr., 3 per day, 88zł); Warsaw (5hr., 9 per day, 29zł); Berlin (5½hr., 3 per day, 87zł); Prague (6½hr., 3 per day, 88zł); and Budapest (12hr., 1 per day, 151zł). Buses leave from behind the train station; they are, generally slower and more expensive, so you might want to avoid them. With your back to the train station, turn left on ul. Piłsudskiego, take your third right on ul. Świdnicka, and go past the Kosciuszki pl. over the Podwale river to reach the central *rynek*. **IT,** ul. Rynek 14, can help with rooms. (Tel. (071) 344 31 11; fax 44 29 62. Open M-F 9am-5pm, Sa 10am-2pm. Surf the **internet** at **Cyberkawiarnia,** ul. Kuźnica 29a. The clean **HI youth hostel,** ul. Kołłataja 20, is directly opposite the train station on the road perpendicular to ul. Piłsudskiego. Clean, safe, and spacious. (Tel. (071) 343 88 56. Dorms and doubles 13-18zł per person. Lockout 10am-5pm. Curfew 10pm. Call ahead.) **Hotel Piast,** ul. Piłsudskiego 98, is near the train station; look for the neon crown. For a quiet stay, request a room that doesn't face the street. (Tel. (071) 343 00 33. Singles 40zł; doubles 70zł; triples 90zł; quads 110zł. Breakfast 10zł. Prices higher May-June and Sept.-Oct.) **Postal code:** 50-415.

PORTUGAL

US$1 = 190.80 ESCUDOS ($)
CDN$1 = 127.52$
UK£1 = 304.65$
IR£1 = 254.56$
AUS$1 = 121.64$
NZ$1 = 100.77$
SAR1 = 31.33$
EUR€1 = 200.48$

100$ = US$0.52
100$ = CDN$0.78
100$ = UK£0.33
100$ = IR£0.39
100$ = AUS$0.82
100$ = NZ$0.99
100$ = SAR3.19
100$ = EUR€0.50

PHONE CODE	Country code: 351. International dialing prefix: 00.

The government denied Christopher Columbus' request that the country fund his legendary voyage, but Portugal soon joined the ensuing exploration melee, developing revolutionary navigational and shipbuilding techniques that allowed Vasco da Gama to sail around the Cape of Good Hope and Magellan to sail around the world. The country prospered, transforming art and architecture into the ornate Manueline style. Once a period of decline set in, though, nostalgia imbued its culture in a manner still reflected in *fado* folk ballads. By 1580, Portugal had exhausted its resources and its royal line, and the Spanish Hapsburg Felipe II easily took the Portuguese throne; independence was regained in 1640. An earthquake in 1755 reduced much of Lisbon to rubble, shaking the country's faith and economy.

Events in this century have proved no less turbulent. A parliamentary republic emerged in 1910, only to be overthrown by a 1926 military coup led by António Salazar, an economist-turned-dictator. Salazar and his successor, Marcelo Caetano, ruled the country for the next 50 years. In 1974, a bloodless coup toppled the regime, prompting mass rejoicing—every Portuguese town now has its Rua 25 de Abril to honor the day. The new government finally granted independence to Portugal's African holdings, but ensuing civil wars in Mozambique and Angola set off a rush of immigration into an already unstable Portugal.

Expo '98 spurred urban renewal that revived a flagging economy and rebuilt Lisbon's waterfront. Despite ongoing modernization in Lisbon and beyond, though, some of Portugal's age-old and rich traditions seem destined never to change—the wines of Porto are as fine as ever, pristine beaches still line the Atlantic seaboard, and the country's hard-earned character and loyal people continue to stand proud.

Let's Go: Spain & Portugal 2000 has more info on fabulous, vibrant Portugal.

DISCOVER PORTUGAL

Portugal often seems the forgotten country of Western Europe. Peaceful towns are graced with medieval castles and cobblestone *praças*, often perched a top a hill or along a winding river. Most grand tours start at vibrant **Porto,** home of port, the strong dessert wine (p. 742). From there continue on to the beach resort of **Figueira da Foz** (p. 742), then head inland for some nighttime fun in the thriving university town **Coimbra** (p. 741). Next, hit the sights, sounds, and cafés of fascinating **Lisbon** (p. 728). Climb to the castles of nearby **Sintra** (p. 734), then head south to the **Algarve** where the country's wildest nightlife swings, its most spectacular beaches entice, and **Lagos** (p. 737) is the belle of the ball. Nearby are **Sagres** (p. 739) and the glorious beach **Praia da Rocha** (p. 739).

GETTING THERE AND GETTING AROUND

BY PLANE. Most international airlines serve Lisbon; some go to Porto, Faro, and the Madeiras. Portugal's national airline **TAP Air Portugal** (in US and Canada tel. (800) 221 7370; in UK tel. (171) 828 20 92; in Lisbon tel. (1) 841 69 90; www.tap.pt) also serves international cities. The smaller **Portugália** (www.pga.pt) flies to Porto, Faro, Lisbon, major Spanish cities, and other Western European destinations. It has offices in Lisbon (tel. (1) 842 55 00) and Manchester (tel. (161) 489 50 40).

BY TRAIN. Caminhos de Ferro Portugueses is Portugal's national railway, but long-distance travel off the Porto-Coimbra-Lisbon line is much better by bus. Around Lisbon local trains and commuter rails are fast and efficient. Most trains have first- and second-class cabins, except for local and suburban routes. When you arrive in town, go to the station ticket booth to check the departure schedule; trains often run at irregular hours, and posted *horarios* (schedules) are not always accurate. Be aware that unless you use a Eurailpass, the return on round-trip tickets must be used before 3am the following day. Those riding without tickets are fined over 3500$. The Portugal Flexipass is not worth purchasing. **Eurail** is valid in Portugal.

BY BUS. Buses are cheap, frequent, and go to just about every town in Portugal. **Rodoviária** (tel. (1) 354 57 75), the national bus company, has recently been privatized. Each company name corresponds to a particular region of the country, such as **Rodoviária Alentejo** or **Minho e Douro,** with notable exceptions such as **EVA** in the Algarve. Private regional companies also operate, among them **Cabanelas, AVIC,** and **Mafrense.** Be wary of non-express buses in small regions, which stop every few minutes. *Expressos* (express coach service) between major cities is especially good; inexpensive city buses often run to nearby villages. Schedules are usually posted, but double-check with the ticket vendor to make sure they're accurate.

BY CAR. Portugal has the most automobile accidents per capita in Western Europe. The highway system (IP) is quite good, but off the main arteries, the narrow, twisting roads are hard to negotiate. Speed limits are basically ignored, recklessness is common, and lighting can be inadequate. In-city parking is difficult. Buy **gas** in super (97 octane), normal (92 octane), or unleaded; prices are high by North American standards—140-170 *escudos* (or US$0.75-0.90) per liter. The national automobile association, the **Automóvel Clube de Portugal (ACP),** R. Rosa Araújo, 49A (tel. (1) 711 23 60), provides **breakdown** and **towing service** and 24-hour **first aid.**

BY THUMB. Hitchers are rare in Portugal. Beach-bound locals occasionally hitch in summer but otherwise stick to the inexpensive bus system. Rides are easiest to come by between smaller towns. Best results are reputedly at gas stations near highways and rest stops. *Let's Go* does not recommend hitchhiking.

ESSENTIALS

DOCUMENTS AND FORMALITIES. Citizens of the US, Canada, the UK, and New Zealand can visit Portugal **visa-free** for up to 90 days. Citizens of Australia and South Africa need a visa.

Portuguese Embassies at Home: Australia, 23 Culgoa Circuit, O'Malley, ACT 2606. Mailing address P.O. Box 9092, Deakin, ACT 2600 (tel. (02) 62 90 17 33; fax 62 90 19 06); **Canada,** 645 Island Park Dr, Ottawa, ON K1Y OB8 (tel. (613) 729-0883; fax 729-4236). **South Africa,** 599 Leyds St, Mucklenuk, Pretoria (tel. (012) 341 2340; fax 341 3975). **UK,** 11 Belgrave Sq, London SW1X 8PP (tel. (020) 72 35 53 31; fax 72 45 12 87). **US,** 2125 Kalorama Rd NW, Washington, DC 20008 (tel. (202) 328-8610; fax 462-3726). **New Zealanders** should contact the embassy in Australia.

Foreign Embassies and Consulates in Portugal: Australians can use their embassy in **France** (see p. 296); all other embassies are in **Lisbon** (see p. 730). Canada's consulate is in **Faro** and the UK's is in **Porto.**

TOURIST OFFICES. The tourist board, **Direção General do Turismo (DGT),** has offices in most cities; look for the **"Turismo"** sign. They often have accommodations lists and free maps. Most offices have an English speaker. The main student travel agency is **TAGUS-Youth Student Travel.** The website www. portugal.com is helpful.

Tourist Info at Home: Portugal **website:** www.portugal.org. **Canada,** 60 Bloor St W, #1005, Toronto ON M4W 3B8 (tel. (416) 921-4925; fax 921-1354); Ireland, 54 Dawson St, Dublin 2 (tel. (353) 670 91 33; fax 670 91 41); **South Africa,** Sunnyside Ridge, 4th fl., Sunnyside Dr, Parktown, 2193 Johannesburg (tel. (27) 114 84 34 87; fax 114 84 54 16); **UK,** 22-25A Sackville St, 2nd fl., London W1X 1 DE (tel. (44) 20 74 94 14 41; fax 20 74 94 18 68); **US,** 590 Fifth Ave, 4th fl., New York, NY 10036-4704 (tel. (212) 354-4403; fax 764-6137).

MONEY. The **currency** is the *escudo* which is divided into 100 *centavos.* **Banking hours** are typically Monday through Friday 8:30am to 3pm.

Tipping and Bargaining: Tips are customary only in fancy restaurants or hotels. Some cheaper restaurants include a 10% service charge; otherwise, you can round up and leave the change. Taxi drivers only expect a tip if the trip was quite long. Bargaining is not customary, but you can try it at the local *mercado* (market) or when looking for a room.

Taxes: All prices include a 16-30% **VAT** (value-added tax). Non-EU residents may eligible for refunds on purchases over US$71.

COMMUNICATION

Post: Mail in Portugal is somewhat inefficient—**air mail** *(via aerea)* takes a week to reach Europe, at least 10 days to reach the US or Canada, and over 2 weeks to reach Australia, New Zealand, and South Africa. **Registered** or **blue mail** and **EMS** (Express Mail) arrive more quickly but cost significantly more. **Stamps** are available at post offices *(correios),* at stamp machines outside post offices, and in central locations in cities.

Telephone: International direct dial numbers include: **AT&T,** 0800 80 01 28; **Sprint,** 05 017 18 77; **MCI WorldPhone Direct,** 05 017 12 34; **Canada Direct,** 05 017 12 26; **BT Direct,** 0800 800 440; **Ireland Direct,** 05 05 03 53; **Australia Direct,** 05 017 61 10; **Telecom New Zealand Direct,** 05 017 64 00; **Telkom South Africa Direct,** 05 017 27 00. Portugal's national telephone company is **Telecom Portugal.** Coin-operated phones are essentially nonexistent in Portugal; you'll need phone cards. For both the **Credifone** and **Telecom Portugal** systems, the basic unit for all calls (and the price for local calls) is 18$. Local calls do not require dialing any portion of the city code. For **directory assistance,** dial 118. In an **emergency,** dial 112.

Language: Portuguese is a Romance language similar to Spanish. English, Spanish, and French are fairly widely spoken. To snuggle up to Portuguese and get Romantic with other members of the family, see p. 949.

ACCOMMODATIONS AND CAMPING. Movijovem, Av. Duque de Ávila 137, 1050 Lisbon (tel. (1) 313 88 20; fax 352 86 21), is the Portuguese Hostelling International affiliate. A bed in a *pousada da juventude* (not the same as plush *pousadas*) costs 1200-2900$ per night (breakfast and sheets included). To stay in an HI hostel, an **HI card** (3000$) is usually required. **Pensões,** or **residenciais,** are cheaper than hotels and only slightly more expensive (and far more common) than youth hostels. All are rated on a five-star scale and must post their category and price limits. In summer, many *pensões* do not take reservations, but for those that do, try to book at least two weeks ahead. **Quartos** are rooms in private homes (similar to *casas particulares* in Spain); they may be the only option in less-touristed, smaller towns and the cheapest one in cities. Tourist offices can help find *quartos*. Prices can be flexible, and may drop 500-1000$ with bargaining. There are over 150 **official campgrounds** *(parques de campismo)* with lots of amenities. Police have been strict about illegal camping, so don't try it—especially near official campgrounds. Tourist offices stock *Portugal: Camping and Caravan Sites,* an official campgrounds guide (free). Or, write the **Federação Portuguesa de Campismo e Caravanismo,** Av. 5 de Outubro, 15-3, 950 Lisbon (tel. (1) 842 84 80).

FOOD AND DRINK. Portuguese dishes are seasoned with olive oil, garlic, herbs, and sea salt, but few spices. Portugal has a tantalizing selection of fish, such as *chocos grelhados* (grilled cuttlefish), *linguado grelhado* (grilled sole), and *peixe espada* (swordfish). *Sopas* are **soups** and *sandes* are **sandwiches.** Vegetarians will likely eat lots of cheese sandwiches on Portugal's delectable bread. The favorite **dessert** is *pudim,* or *flan,* a caramel custard. The hearty midday meal, *almoço* (lunch), is eaten between noon and 2pm and *jantar* (dinner) between 8pm and midnight. A full meal costs 1000-2000$. **Meia dose** (half-portions) cost more than half-price but are often adequate; a full portion may satisfy two. The **prato do dia** (special of the day) or **ementa** (menu) of appetizer, bread, entree, and dessert are filling. The **ementa turista** is usually not budget-savvy—restaurants with multilingual menus probably charge steep prices. In restaurants, expect to pay 300-500$ per person for automatically served pre-meal munchies. **Vinho do porto** (port) is a dessert in itself. A six-month heating process gives **Madeira** wines a unique "cooked" flavor. Portuguese coffees are **bica** (black espresso), **galão** (coffee with milk, served in a glass), and **café com leite** (coffee with milk, served in a cup).

LOCAL FACTS

Time: Greenwich Mean Time (GMT; see p. 49).

Climate: Portugal's climate is very mild; summers are fairly hot in the south, but not too extreme and not at all humid. In winter it never gets particularly cold.

Hours: A normal workday is from about 9am-7pm with a lunch break from 1-3pm. On Saturdays most places only open in the morning; on Sundays you're on your own.

Holidays: New Year's (Jan. 1); Good Friday (Apr. 21); Liberation Day (Apr. 25); Labor Day (May 1); National Day/Camoes and Portugal Day (June 10); Corpus Christi (June 22) Assumption Day (Aug. 15); Republic Day (Oct. 15); All Saints Day (Nov. 1); Independence Day (Dec. 1); Immaculate Conception (Dec. 8); Christmas (Dec. 24-25).

Festivals: Carnival rocks the party Mar. 2-12; followed by a more serious **Holy Week,** Apr. 17-23—smack in the middle is **Senhor Ecoe Homo (Maundy Tuesday)** on Apr. 20, and **Good Friday** on Apr. 21. Early May in Coimbra students celebrate graduating during the **Queima das Lisboa** (Burning of the Ribbons; see p. 741). The 1st week in June, Santarém does the jolly **Feira Nacional de Agricultura** (Feira do Ribatejo; see p. 736).

LISBON (LISBOA)

Lisbon was once the center of the world's richest and farthest-reaching empire; today, it has risen above social and political problems of the last century to reclaim its place as one of Europe's grandest cities. Like Portugal, Lisbon preserves its traditions by renovating historic monuments and meticulously maintaining its black-and-white mosaic sidewalks, pastel façades, and cobblestoned, medieval alleys.

N

Lisbon

ACCOMMODATIONS
- A Camping Municipal
- B Pousada da Juventude de Lisboa (HI)
- C Residêncial Florescente
- D Pensão Campos
- E Casa de Hóspedes Globo
- F Pensão Moderna
- G Pensão Ninho das Águias
- H Pensão Beira-Mar
- I Pousada da Juventude de Catalazete (HI)

Rio Tejo

GRAÇA

R. Angelina Vidal
R. Damasceno Monteiro
R. Graça
R. Voz. do. Operario

Santa Engrácia
São Vicente
C. S. VICENTE

TO EXPO '98
GROUNDS (5.5km)

Estação
Santa Apolónia

Museu da
Artilharia

R. Verónica
Campo Sto. Clara

Caçada Monte
R. Lagáres
C. d Santo André
R. S. Tomé
ALFAMA

Fundação Espirítu
Santo Silva
R. Esc. Gerais
R. REMEDIOS

Dom Henrique

Castelo de
São Jorge
G
R. Costa d. Castelo
R. Milagre
R. Antonio

R. Teixeira do Trigo
Av. Infante

R. Palma
R. S. Lázaro
R. S. Bentormoso
R. Cavaleiros

MARTIM
MONIZ
M

MOURARIA

R. Bentormoso

R. Instituto Bacteriologico

R. Portas Santo Antão
C

RESTAURADORES
PR. DAS
RESTAURADORES

Teatro Nacional
M
ROSSIO
M
PR.
FIGUEIRA

R. Madalena
R. Fanqueiros
R. Prata
R. Correiros
R. Augusta
R.Aurea

BAIXA

Sé
Madalena
Casa d.
dos Bicos
R. Bacalhoeiro
R. A. Rosa

R. Alfândega
TERREIRO
DO PAÇO
(under const.)
M

Ferry
Terminal

Government
Buildings

R. Conceição
R. São Julião
PR. DO
COMÉRCIO

M AVENIDA
TO C (right at
pr. pombal, 750m)

Avenida da Liberdade

PRAÇA D.
PEDRO IV
M
M

R. Carmo
Rua Nova d. Almada

Ascensor de
Santa Justa

PR. DO
MUNICIPIO

Av. Ribeira Naus

TO A (left at pr
pombal, 14km)

Concelção Glória
Dom Pedro IV
Ascensor
Glória
R. Glória
C. da Glória

Estação
do Rossio
i

R. Nova da
Trindade
R. Teixeira
São Roque

R. Diano de Noticias
R. Texeira
BAIRRO
ALTO

Museu
Arqueológico
LARGO
CHIADO R. Garrett
PR. LUIS
D. CAMÕES
BAIRRO CHIADO
M

R. Capelo
R. A.M. Cardoso
R. Serpa Pinto
R. Alecrim

Museu Nacional de
Arte Contemporânea

R. Arsenal

Jardim
Botânico

Escola Politécnica

R. Rosa
R. Atalaia
R. Século
Caçada do Combro
R. Eduardo Coelho
R. Acad. d. Ciências

R. Flores
R. d. São Paulo
Cordeoiros

Estação Cais
do Sodré
M

CAIS DO SODRÉ
M

R. Ribeira Nova

R. São Bento
Santo Amaro
R. N. Piedade
R. São Marçal
PR. DAS
FLORES
R. Cruz Polais
R. Acad. d. Ciências
R. Polais

R. Luis I
TO MUSEU DE
ARTE ANTIGA
(600m)

Av. Dom Carlos I
Av. 24 de Julho

R. Boavista

Palácio da
Assembleia
Nacional

Rio Tejo

0   1/8 mile
0   125 meters

PORTUGAL

⊏ GETTING THERE AND GETTING AROUND

Flights: Aeroporto de Lisboa (tel. 840 20 60 or 849 63 50), on the city's northern edge. **Buses 44** and **45** (20-40min., 160$) connect to Pr. Restauradores. The express **AeroBus** (bus 91; 15min., every 20min., 430$) to Pr. Restauradores may be a better option during rush hour. A **taxi** to the downtown area costs about 1500$, plus a 300$ fee for luggage.

Trains: Estação Santa Apolónia (tel. 888 40 25), on Av. Infante D. Henrique, east of the Alfama on the river. Take bus 9, 39, or 46 to Pr. Restauradores. To: **Coimbra** (2½hr., 10 per day, 1300$); **Évora** (3hr., 6 per day, 1075$); **Porto** (4hr., 10 per day, 2000$); **Madrid** (10hr., 1 per day, 8200$); and **Paris** (23hr., 1 per day, 24,000$). **Estação Barreiro,** across the river. To **Lagos** (5½hr., every 2hr., 1700$). Ferries from the Terreiro do Paço dock, off Pr. Comércio, are included in train tickets (30min., every 30min.). **Estação Rossio,** between Pr. Restauradores and Pr. Dom Pedro IV, serves points west. **Estação Cais do Sodré,** between the Bairro Alto and the Baixa on the river. M: Cais do Sodré.

Buses: Arco do Cego, on Av. João Crisóstomo. M: Saldanha; exit on Av. República, walk 1 block from the *praça,* turn right on Av. Dunque de Ávila, and right before the McDonald's. "Saldanha" buses (36, 44, and 45) stop in the *praça* (160$). **Rede Expressos** to: **Coimbra** (2½hr., 16 per day, 1450$); **Évora** (3½hr., 15 per day, 1450$); **Porto** (4hr., 15 per day, 2800$); and **Lagos** (5hr., 10 per day, 2400$).

Public Transit: CARRIS (tel. 363 93 43) operates **buses, trams,** and **funiculars** (each 160$ per ride), and the **metro** (runs 6am-1am; 100$ per ride, 10 tickets 800$).

Taxis: Rádio Táxis de Lisboa (tel. 815 50 61), **Autocoope** (tel. 793 27 56), and **Teletáxi** (tel. 815 20 16) cluster along Av. Liberdade and Rossio. Luggage surcharge 300$.

⊓ ORIENTATION AND PRACTICAL INFORMATION

Lisbon's center is the **Baixa,** the old business center, between the **Bairro Alto** and the **Alfama.** The Baixa's grid of mostly pedestrian streets is bordered to the north by **Rossio** (a.k.a. **Praça Dom Pedro IV**), adjacent to **Praça da Figueira** and **Praça dos Restauradores; Av. da Liberdade** runs north uphill from Pr. Restauradores. At the Baixa's southern end is the **Praça do Comércio,** on the **Rio Tejo** (a.k.a. **River Tagus**). Along the river are the Expo '98 grounds, now called the **Parque das Nações** (Park of Nations), and the **Alcantara** and **Docas** (docks) regions.

TOURIST, FINANCIAL, AND LOCAL SERVICES

Tourist Office: Palácio da Foz (tel. 346 63 07), on Pr. Restauradores. M: Restauradores. Bus schedules, room listings, and a free map. English spoken. Open daily 9am-8pm.

Embassies: Canada, Av. Liberdade 144, 4th fl. (tel. 347 48 92; fax 347 64 66); **Ireland,** R. Imprensa a Estrela, 4th fl., #1 (tel. 392 94 40; fax 397 73 63); **New Zealand** (consulate), R. S. Felix 13-2, (tel. 350 96 90; fax 572 00 40); **South Africa,** Av. Luis Bivar 10 (tel. 353 50 41; fax 353 57 13); **UK,** R. São Bernardo 33 (tel. 392 40 00; fax 392 41 86); **US,** on Av. Forças Armadas (tel. 727 33 00; fax 727 91 09).

American Express: Top Tours, Av. Duque de Loulé 108 (tel. 315 58 85). M: Marquês de Pombal; walk up Av. Liberdade toward the Marquês de Pombal statue and turn right. Open M-F 9:30am-1pm and 2:30-6:30pm.

Luggage Storage: Estação Rossio, between Pr. Restauradores and Pr. Dom Pedro IV (Rossio). M: Rossio. Lockers 550$ per 48hr. Open daily 8:30am-11:30pm.

English Bookstore: Livraria Británica, R. Luis Fernandes 14/16 (tel. 342 84 72), opposite the British Institute in the Bairro Alto. Open M-F 9:30am-7pm. V, MC, AmEx.

Laundromat: Lavatax, R. Francisco Sanches 65A (tel. 812 33 92). M: Arroios. Wash, dry, and fold 1100$ per 5kg. Open M-F 9am-1pm and 3-7pm, Sa 9am-noon.

EMERGENCY AND COMMUNICATIONS

Emergency: Tel. 112. **Police:** R. Capelo 3 (tel. 346 61 41). English spoken.

Pharmacy: Tel. 118. Night pharmacy info is posted on pharmacy doors.

Medical Services: British Hospital, R. Saraiva de Carvalho, 49 (tel. 395 50 67).

Post Office: Main office (tel. 346 32 31), on Pr. Comércio. Open M-F 8:30am-6:30pm. **Branch** in Pr. Restauradores. Open M-F 8am-10pm, Sa-Su 9am-6pm. Address mail to be held: Adam STEIN, *Posta Restante,* Praça do Comércio, **1100** Lisbon, Portugal.

PORTUGAL

Internet Access: Web Café, R. Diário de Notícias 126 (tel. 342 11 81). 200$ per 15min., 700$ per hr. Open daily 6pm-2am.

Telephones: Portugal Telecom, Pr. Dom Pedro IV 68. M: Rossio. Open daily 8am-11pm **Phone cards** come in 50 units (650$), 100 units (1300$), or 150 units (1900$). Buy them here or at bookstores and stationery stores.

PHONE CODE	City code: 01. From outside Portugal, dial int'l dialing prefix (see inside back cover) + 351 + 1 + local number.

ACCOMMODATIONS AND CAMPING

Expect to pay 3000-5000$ for a single and 5000-9000$ for a double; if prices seem high, ask for a price list. Most hotels are in the town center on **Av. Liberdade,** while in the **Baixa** budget *pensões* line the **Rossio** and **R. Prata, R. Correeiros,** and **R. Ouro.** Lodgings in the **Alfama** or **Bairro Alto** are quieter and closer to sights, but cost more. If more central accommodations are full, head east along **Av. Almirante Reis.** Be cautious near the docks and near Cais de Sodné. At night, be careful in the Bairro Alto, the Alfama, and the Baixa; many streets are empty and poorly lit.

Pensão Campos, R. Jardim do Regedor 24, 3rd fl. (tel. 346 28 64), in the **Baixa.** M: Restauradores. Between Pr. Restauradores and R. Portas de Santo Antão. Comfy rooms over a pedestrian street. Singles 4000$; doubles 6000-7000$; triples 7000$. Laundry.

Pensão Moderna, R. Correeiros 205, 4th fl. (tel. 346 08 18), in the **Baixa.** M: Rossio. One block toward the water from Pr. Figueira. All 10 antique-filled rooms have large windows and balconies. Great location. Singles 3500$; doubles 6000$; triples 8000$.

Residencial Florescente, R. Portas de Santo Antão 99 (tel. 342 66 09; fax 342 77 33), in the **Baixa.** A block from Pr. Restauradores. Luxurious, with incredible views of Pr. Figueira. Doubles 5000-8000$; triples 7500-10,500$; large room 12,000$. V, MC, AmEx.

Casa de Hóspedes Globo, R. Teixeira 37 (tel. 346 22 79), in **Bairro Alto.** Take the funicular from Pr. Restauradores to the Parque São Pedro de Alcântra; from the park entrance, cross the street and turn right on R. Teixeira. Safe, convenient, and nice. Singles 2500-4500, with bath 4500$; doubles 4000-6000$. English spoken. Reserve ahead.

Pensão Ninho das Águias, R. Costa do Castelo 74 (tel. 886 70 08), in the **Alfama,** down the street from the Teatro Taborda. From Pr. Figueira, take R. Madalena to Largo Adelino Costa and head up to R. Costa do Castelo. The spectacular views are worth the hike. Singles 5000$; doubles 7000-8000$; triples 10,000$. Breakfast included. Reserve ahead.

Pensão Beira-Mar, Largo Terreiro do Trigo 16, 4th fl. (tel. 886 99 33), in the **Alfama.** In a small square off Av. Infante Dom Henrique (parallel to the Tejo). Clean, spacious rooms. Singles 2500$; doubles 4000-6000$; triples 7500-8000$. Laundry. Reserve ahead.

Pousada da Juventude de Lisboa (HI), R. Andrade Corvo 46 (tel. 353 26 96; fax 353 75 41). M: Picoas; turn right and walk 1 block. Huge and ultra-clean, but inconvenient. June-Sept. dorms 2900$, doubles with bath 5500$; Oct.-May 1900$, 4700$. Members only. Breakfast included. Lockers 250$. Reception 8am-midnight. Check-out 10:30am.

Pousada da Juventude de Catalazete (HI), on Estrada Marginal (tel. 443 06 38), in the coastal town of **Oeiras.** Take a train from Estação Cais do Sodré to Oeiras (20min., every 15min., 155$); exit through the underpass, cross the street, follow signs to Lisbon and Cascais, turn left at the intersection opposite a bus stop (no street signs), go downhill on R. Filipa de Lencastre, go straight at the underpass, and follow the signs. June-Sept. dorms 1800$, doubles 4500$; Oct.-May 1500$, 3700$. Members only. Breakfast included. Reception 8am-midnight. Curfew midnight. Reserve ahead.

Parque de Campismo Municipal de Lisboa (tel. 760 96 20), on the road to Benfica. Take bus 43 from Rossio to the Parque Florestal Monsanto. July-Aug. 800$ per person and per tent, 500$ per car; Sept.-June 560-720$, 350-450$. Reception 9am-9pm.

FOOD

Lisbon has cheap restaurants and great wine; dinner runs 1800-2000$. Top off a *prato do dia* (daily special) with a sinfully cheap and even more sinfully delicious pastry. **Baixa** near the port, the area near the **Alfama,** and the **Bairro Alto** have superior and cheap dining options. Specialties include the *bacalhau cozido com grão e batatas* (cod with chickpeas and potatoes). **Supermercado Celeiro,** R. 1 de Dezembro 65, is two blocks from Estação Rossio. (Open M-F 9am-8pm, Sa 9am-7pm.)

Restaurante Bonjardim, Tr. Santo Antão 11 (tel. 342 43 89), off Pr. Restauradores in the **Baixa.** Self-proclaimed *rei dos frangos* (king of chicken) rules the roost. Delicious roast chicken (1300$). Entrees 1000-2900$. Open daily noon-11pm. V, MC.

Restaurante João do Grão, R. Correeiros 222 (tel. 342 47 57), with a yellow sign, in the **Baixa.** Very popular and very touristy. Entrees 990-1900$. Open daily noon-10:30pm.

Confeitaria Nacional, Praça Figueira 18B (tel. 346 17 29), in the **Baixa.** Famed *pastelaría* has all kinds of Portuguese sweets (from 120). Open M-F 8am-8pm, Sa 8am-2pm.

Cervejaria da Trindade, R. Nova Trindade 20C (tel. 342 35 06), near the Igreja do São Roque in the **Bairro Alto.** Excellent food. Entrees 790-2500$; budget finds are the *sugestões do chefe* (chef's suggestions). Open daily noon-1:30am. V, MC, AmEx.

Hell's Kitchen, R. Atalaia 176 (tel. 342 28 22), in the **Bairro Alto.** From Pr. Restauradores, walk uphill on C. Glória to the top and go right on R. Atalaia. Heavenly hummus with pita 450$. Falafel and salad 1100$. Open Tu-Su 8pm-12:30am.

■ SIGHTS

BAIXA. The best place to embark upon a tour of Lisbon's Enlightenment-era center is from its heart, the **Rossio.** Once a cattle market, the site of public executions, a bullfighting arena, and a carnival ground, the *praça* is now the domain of drink-sipping tourists and heart-stopping traffic whizzing around a statue of Dom Pedro IV. Past the train station, an obelisk and a sculpture of the "Spirit of Independence" in the **Praça dos Restauradores** commemorate Portugal's independence from Spain in 1640. The *praça* is the start of **Avenida da Liberdade,** one of the city's most elegant promenades, modeled after 19th-century Parisian boulevards. On the other side of the Rossio from Pr. Restauradores, **Baixa's** grid of pedestrian streets, designed by the Marquês de Pombal after Lisbon's devastating earthquake of 1755, caters to ice-cream eaters and window-shoppers.

BAIRRO ALTO. From Baixa, walk to the *bairro* or take the historic **Ascensor de Santa Justa,** a 1902 elevator built in a Gothic wrought-iron tower. From the upper terrace, a narrow **walkway** leads under a huge flying buttress to the 14th-century **Igreja do Carmo,** whose roof was destroyed in the 1755 earthquake but which retains its dramatic Gothic arches. *(Elevator runs M-F 7am-11pm, Sa-Su 9am-11pm. Walkway usually open 7am-6pm. 80$.)* At the center of the **Chiado,** Biarro Alto's chic shopping neighborhood, **Praça Camões** joins Largo Chiado at the top of R. Garrett. *(To reach R. Garrett, turn left from the elevator, walk 1 block, and it's on the right.)* From R. Carmo in Baixa, head uphill on R. Garrett to R. Misericórdia to find the **Igreja de São Roque,** on Largo Trinidade Coelho; inside the church, the **Capela de São João Baptista** is ablaze with gems and metals. For a perfect picnic, walk up R. Misericórdia to the shady **Parque de São Pedro de Alcântara.** The European paintings at the **Museu Nacional** dates to the 12th century. *(R. Janelas Verdes, Jardim 9 Abril. Walk 30min. down Av. Infante Santo from the Ascensor de Santa Justa. Buses 40 and 60 stop to the right of the museum exit and head back to the Baixa. Open Tu 2-6pm, W-Su 10am-6pm. 500$, students 250$.)*

ALFAMA. The only neighborhood to survive the 1755 earthquake, Lisbon's medieval quarter slopes in tiers from the **Castelo de São Jorge,** facing the Rio Tejo. Between the Alfama and the Baixa is the **Mouraria** (Moorish quarter), established after the Crusaders expelled the Moors in 1147. **Scenic tram 28** (160$) winds up past most of its sights. From Pr. Comércio, follow R. Alfandega two blocks, climb up R. Madalena, turn right after the church on Largo Madalena, follow R. Santo António da Sé, and follow the tram tracks to the richly ornamented 1812 **Igreja de Santo António da Sé.** *(Open daily 8am-7pm.)* In the square beyond the church is the stolid 12th-century **Sé** (cathedral). *(Open M-Sa 10am-5pm.)* Follow yellow signs to a spectacular ocean view from the top of the Alfama to the 5th-century ■**Castelo de São Jorge,** a Visigoth castle expanded by the Moors in the 9th century. *(Open daily Apr.-Sept. 9am-9pm; Oct.-Mar. 9am-7pm. Free.)* Northeast of the Alfama, the **Convento da Madre de Deus**

houses the excellent **Museu Nacional do Azulejo**, filled with the classic Portuguese *azulejos* (tiles). *(R. Madre de Deus 4. Follow Av. Infanta Dom Henrique east along the Rio Tejo; or, from the station, take bus 13. Open W-Su 10am-6pm, Tu 2-6pm. 350$, students 180$.)*

SALDANHA. Amidst Lisbon's business affairs, this modern district has two excellent museums, both owned by the Fundação Gulbenkian. The **Museu Calouste Gulbenkian** houses the collection of oil tycoon Calouste Gulbenkian, including an extensive array of ancient art. *(Av. Berna 45. M: Palhavã or S. Sebastião. Bus 16, 31, or 46. Open Tu-Su 10am-5pm. 500$; students Su morning free.)* The adjacent **Museu do Centro de Arte Moderna** has an extensive modern art collection, as well as beautiful gardens. *(On R. Dr. Nicolau Bettencourt. Open Tu-Su 10am-5pm. 500$, students Su morning free.)*

BELÉM. More of a suburb than a Lisbon neighborhood, Belém showcases the opulence and extravagance of the Portuguese empire with well-maintained museums and historical sites. To get to Belém, take tram 15 from Pr. Comércio (20min., 160$) or bus 28 or 43 from Pr. Figueira (20min., 160$). From the bus station, head straight. The **Mosteiro dos Jerónimos** is on the banks of the Tejo behind a lush public garden; the monastery was established by King Dom Manuel I in 1502 to give thanks for Vasco da Gama's successful voyage to India. *(Open Tu-Su 10am-5pm. June-Sept. 400$, students 200$; Oct.-May 250$. Su 10am-2pm free. Cloisters open Tu-Su 10am-5pm; free.)* Take the underpass by the gardens to cross the highway to the ⬛**Torre de Belém** (10min.), on the north bank of the Tejo, surrounded by the ocean on three sides. The tower once sat right on the shoreline, but due to the receding beach it is now only accessible by a small bridge. Nevertheless, this symbol of Portuguese grandeur offers spectacular panoramic views of Belém, the Tejo, and the Atlantic. *(Open Tu-Su 10am-5pm. 400$; Oct.-May 250$, students 200$.)* Do not, repeat, do not leave Belém, without trying the heavenly *pastéis de Belém* at ⬛**Pastéis de Belém,** R. Belém 88; join the throngs buying tubes filled with warm mini custard tarts.

⬛**PARQUE DAS NAÇÕES (PARK OF NATIONS).** At the former Expo '98 grounds 6km from downtown, the park houses a mall, food options galore, worthy museums, and lots more. *(Main entrance at the Centro Vasco da Gama. Take the metro red line to its end (Linha Oriente, 100$). Tel. 891 93 33; www.parquedasnacoes.pt. Park open M-F 9:30am-1am, Sa-Su 9:30am-3am.)* The biggest attraction is the **Pavilhão dos Oceanos**, the largest oceanarium in Europe. *(Open daily 10am-7pm. 1500$.)* The famed **Museu Nacional dos Coches** moved here from its old home in Belém, with its 50 lavish carriages in tow. *(Open Tu-Su 10am-6pm. 450$, under 26 225$.)*

🎵 🎭 ENTERTAINMENT AND NIGHTLIFE

The *Agenda Cultural* and *Lisboa em*, free at kiosks in the Rossio, on R. Portas de Santo Antão, and at the tourist office, has info on arts events and bullfights. Lisbon's trademark is *fado*, an expressive art combining elements of singing and narrative poetry; *fadistas'* melancholy wailing expresses *saudade* (a feeling of nostalgia and yearning). Listeners should feel a "knife turning in their hearts." The Bairro Alto has many *fado* joints off R. Misericórdia and on streets radiating from the Museu de São Roque; prices alone may turn a knife in your heart. **Adega Machado**, R. Norte 91, is frequented by locals and tourists. (Tel. 322 46 40. Cover 3000$; includes 2 drinks. Open daily 8pm-3am.) Lisbon is home to many cafés; the famed 19th-century **A Brasileira**, R. Garrett 120/122, is in the Bairro Alto's stylish Chiado neighborhood. (Coffee 80-300$. Mixed drinks 700$. Open daily 4pm-1am.)

Lisbon rocks 'til it drops. You can't go wrong along the **Bairro Alto's** R. Norte, R. Diario Notícias, and R. Atalaia, where small clubs and bars are packed into three short blocks, making club-hopping easy. The **Rato** area near the edge of Bairro Alto has a number of gay and lesbian clubs; try **Memorial**, R. Gustavo de Matos Sequeira 42A, one block from R. Escola Politécnica in the Bairro Alto. (Cover Tu-W and F-Sa 1000$; includes 2 beers or 1 mixed drink. Open Tu-Su 11pm-4am.) A recent in-spot is the revamped **Docas de Santo Amaro,** a strip of waterfront bars and clubs. There, swing by crowded and palm-treed **Havana**, Armazem 5. (Beer 400$; mixed drinks 500$. Open M-Sa 11pm-5:30am.) Throw back a Guinness (600$) at **Celtas & Iberos**

Irish Pub, Armazem 7. (Open Tu-Su midnight-3am.) A little farther away from the Doca de Santo Amaro cluster, live salsa swivels its hips at **Salsa Latina,** at the Gare Marítima de Alcântara. (Beer 500$; mixed drinks 1000$. Open M-Th 9pm-4am, F-Sa 9pm-6am.) The popular, young, and hip line up at **Kremlin,** Escandinhas da Praia 5, off Av. 24 de Julho. (F-Sa cover 1000-2000$. Open Tu-Sa midnight-9am.) Next door are the equally trendy clubs **Kapital** and **Plateau.** While these places along the river are all along a 2.5km stretch, it's best to cab it late at night (from Rossio 500-1200$). Dress to impress and come fashionably late (after 2am).

EXCURSIONS FROM LISBON

QUELUZ. The only reason to visit Queluz, 12km west of Lisbon, is the amazing **Palácio Nacional de Queluz,** a pink-and-white Rococo wedding cake of a palace. In the mid-18th century, Dom Pedro III turned an old hunting lodge into this summer residence—check out the **Sala dos Embaixadores,** with its gilded thrones and Chinese vases, and the *azulejo*-lined canal in the garden. (Open W-M 10am-1pm and 2-5pm. Palace 500$, students 250$. Garden 100$.) Take the **train** toward Sintra from Lisbon's Estação Rossio (M: Rossio) and get off at the Queluz-Belas (not Queluz-Massomá) stop (20min., every 15min., 150$). Exit the station through the ticket office, go left on Av. Antonio Ennes, and follow the signs (10min.).

ESTORIL. Beautiful beaches, stately vistas, and a bustling casino give Estoril a reputation of opulence. **Praia Estoril Tamariz beach** greets visitors on arrival. **Casino Estoril,** Europe's largest casino, beckons those feeling lucky. (Open daily 3pm-3am. No jeans or shorts. Must be 18 for slots, 21 for game room. Foreigners must show passport.) **Trains** from Lisbon's Estação do Sodré (M: Cais do Sodré) stop in Estoril (30min., every 20min., 200$) en route to Cascais. Stagecoach **bus** 418 to **Sintra** departs from Av. Marginal, near the train station (40min., every hr., 410$). For the **tourist office,** on Arcada do Parque opposite the train station, take the tunnel under Av. Marginal. (Tel. 466 38 13; fax 467 22 80. Open M-Sa 9am-7pm, Su 10am-6pm.)

CASCAIS. Once the summer vacation resort of the royal family, Cascais still caters to a well-to-do crowd. Four popular **beaches** close to the center draw throngs of locals and tourists. **Trains** from Lisbon's Estação do Sodré head to Cascais (30min., every 20min., 200$) via Estoril. Stagecoach **bus** 417 leaves from the train station for **Sintra** (40min., every hr., 500$). Or, walk 20min. from Estoril. To get to the **tourist office,** Av. dos Combatentes 25, which books **rooms,** turn right at the fork in the promenade, follow the train tracks to the station, cross the square, and turn right at the McDonald's on Av. Valbom. (Tel. 486 82 04. Open July-Sept. 15 M-Sa 9am-8pm, Su 10am-6pm; Sept. 16-June M-Sa 9am-7pm, Su 10am-6pm.)

SINTRA. After British Romantic poet Lord Byron dubbed Sintra (pop. 20,000) a "glorious Eden," the city became a chic 19th-century destination; Sintra is still popular among tour groups drooling over its fairy-tale castles and incredible mountain vistas. **Palácio Nacional de Sintra,** in Pr. República, in the old town, **Sintra-Vila,** was once the summer residence of Moorish sultans and their harems. (Open Th-Tu 10am-1pm and 2-5pm. 400$, students 200$.) Perched above Sintra, the **Castelo dos Mouros** dates back to the 8th century. The 3km ascent (1-1½hr.) starts to the left of the tourist office; follow the blue signs up the mountain. Bus 434 also runs to the top from the tourist office (15min., 2 per hr., round-trip 500$). (Open daily 10am-7pm. Free.) One kilometer farther uphill is the fantastic **Palácio Nacional de Pena,** built in the 1840s by Prince Ferdinand of Bavaria, the husband of Queen Maria II, an amalgamation of German and Portugese styles. (Open in Tu-Su July-Sept. 10am-6:30pm; Oct.-June 2-4:30pm. May-Sept. 600$, students 400$; Oct.-Apr. 200$.)

Trains (tel. (01) 923 26 05) arrive on Av. Dr. Miguel Bombarda from Lisbon's Estação Rossio (45min., every 15min., 200$). Stagecoach **buses** leave from outside the train station for Cascais (#417; 40min., every hr., 500$) and Estoril (#418; 40min., every hr., 410$); Mafrense, down the street, goes to Mafra (50min., 11 per day, 380$). Head left out of the station, turn right downhill at the next intersection

THE MAN WHO WOULD BE KING Although Portugal's chances of returning to a monarchy are slim, if it did, the Portuguese know who'd be king. He is Dom Duarte, a direct descendant of the royal crown. If you met him on the street in his home of Sintra (near his ancestor's castle), you would not recognize his royal heritage. A whiskered man with a round tummy, Duarte has a jovial disposition, a degree in engineering, and a great love for the people. In 1995, his popularity soared when he married Isabel, a young Spanish (!) noblewoman, 22 years his junior. It was once forbidden for a Portuguese monarch to marry a Spaniard of any ilk, but this wedding was one of the grandest and most regal of the decade and was cheerfully applauded nationwide. Their eldest child, Afonso, is an adorable blond youth named for Portugal's first king. Afonso is said to have inherited his namesake's best traits; unfortunately, he will likely have to apply them in some other fashion.

and left in front of the castle-like Câmara Municipal, then follow the road uphill to reach the **tourist office,** Pr. República 23. (Tel. (01) 923 11 57; fax 923 51 76. Open daily June-Sept. 9am-8pm; Oct.-May 9am-7pm.) To get to **Pousada da Juventude de Sintra (HI),** on Sta. Eufémia, take the bus from the train station to São Pedro (180$; tell the driver your destination), turn right as you exit the station, and follow the signs (30-40min.). (Tel./fax (01) 924 12 10. Dorms 1200-1400$; doubles 3200-3600$. Reception 9am-noon and 6pm-midnight.)

MAFRA. Sleepy Mafra is home to one of Portugal's most impressive sights and one of Europe's largest historical buildings, the **Palácio Nacional de Mafra.** The massive castle incorporates a cathedral-sized church, a monastery, a library, and a palace. To get to the palace, go through the door to the right of the church exit. (Open W-M 10am-5pm. 400$, students 200$. Ask about tours in Portuguese and English.) **Trains** arrive from Sintra (1hr., every hr., 370$). If you take the train from Lisbon's Estação Sta. Apolónia you'll have a two-hour hike to town. Frequent Mafrense **buses** stop in front of the palace from Sintra (1hr., 380$) and Lisbon (1½hr., 500$).

CENTRAL PORTUGAL

Jagged cliffs and whitewashed fishing villages line **Estremadura's** Costa de Prata (Silver Coast), with beaches that rival even those in the Algarve. Nearby, the fertile region of the **Ribatejo** (Banks of the Tejo) is perhaps the gentlest and greenest you will come across in Portugal. In this region just north of Lisbon, relatively untouristed towns beckon travelers with historical sights and lush scenery.

TOMAR

For centuries, the arcane Knights Templar—made up of monks and warriors—plotted crusades from a celebrated convent-fortress high above this small town. The ◨**Convento de Cristo** complex was the Knights' powerful and mysterious headquarters. The first structure was built in 1160, but some cloisters, convents, and buildings were added later. The **Claustro dos Felipes** is one of Europe's masterpieces of Renaissance architecture. Walk out of the tourist office, take the second right, bear left at the fork, and either follow the steep dirt path to the left or follow the cars up the road. (Tel. (049) 31 34 81. Complex open June-Aug. 9am-6:30pm; Sept.-May 9am-5pm. 400$, students 200$.) The **Museu dos Fósforos** (match museum), in the Convento de São Francisco, just opposite the stations, exhibits Europe's largest matchbox collection. (Open daily 10-11am and 3-5pm. Free.) Hiking trails lead into the **Parque da Mata Nacional dos Sete Montes** from opposite the tourist office.

Trains (tel. (049) 31 28 15) go from Av. Combatentes da Grande Guerra, at the southern edge of town, to Santarém (1hr., 12 per day, 500$); Lisbon (2hr., 12 per day, 900$); Coimbra (2½hr., 9 per day, 900$); and Porto (4½hr., 5 per day, 1450$). Rodoviaria Tejo **buses** (tel. (049) 31 27 38) leave from Av. Combatentes Grande Guerra, by the train station, for Santarém (1hr., 5 per day, 750$); Lisbon (2hr., 5 per day, 1050$); Coimbra (2½hr., 3 per day, 1350$); and Porto (4hr., 2 per day, 1750$). From either station, go through the square onto Av. General Bernardo Raria, go left after four blocks on Av. Dr. Cândido Madureira, continue to the end of the street, and look right for the **tourist office**. (Tel. (049) 32 24 27. Open in summer M-F 9:30am-8pm, Sa-Su 10am-8pm; off-season closes 6pm.) **Residencial União**, R. Serpa Pinto 94, is halfway between Pr. República and the bridge. Look for the large *azulejos* outside. (Tel. (049) 32 31 61; fax 32 12 99. Singles 3500-4500$; doubles 6000-7000$; triples 8000$. Breakfast included. Call ahead July-Aug.) **Postal code:** 2300.

⚡ EXCURSION FROM TOMAR: BATALHA. The only reason (but a good one) to visit Batalha (pop. 6000) is the gigantic, flamboyant, spectacular, (insert superlative here) ⬛**Mosteiro de Santa Maria da Vitória.** Built by Dom João I in 1385 to commemorate his victory over the Spanish, the complex of cloisters and chapels remains one of Portugal's greatest monuments. To get to the monastery, enter through the church. (Open daily June-Aug. 9am-6pm; Sept.-May 9am-5pm. Monastery 400$, under 25 200$. Church free.) **Buses** run from near Pensão Vitória on Largo Misericórdia to Tomar (1½hr., 4 per day, 490$) and Lisbon (2hr., 5 per day, 2150$). The **tourist office,** on Pr. Mouzinho de Albuquerque along R. Nossa Senhora do Caminho, stands opposite the unfinished chapels of the *mosteiro*. (Tel. (044) 76 51 80. Open daily May-Sept. 10am-1pm and 3-7pm; Oct.-Apr. 10am-1pm and 2-6pm.)

SANTARÉM

Perhaps the most charming of Ribatejo's cities, Santarém (pop. 30,000) was once a flourishing medieval center as well as the capital of the Portuguese Gothic style. The austere façade of the **Igreja do Seminário dos Jesuítas** dominates Pr. Sá da Bandeira, Santarém's main square. (Open Tu-Su 9:30am-12:30pm and 2-5:30pm. Free. If closed, enter the door to the right of the main entrance and ask Sr. Domingos to unlock it.) Take R. Serpa Pinto from Pr. Sá da Bandeira to Pr. Visconde de Serra Pilar to reach the ⬛**Praça Visconde de Serra Pilar,** where Christians, Moors, and Jews gathered centuries ago. The 12th-century **Igreja de Marvilha,** off the *praça*, has a 17th-century *azulejo* interior. (Open Tu-Su 9:30am-12:30pm and 2-5:30pm. Free.) Nearby is the early Gothic purity of **Igreja da Graça;** within the chapel lies Pedro Alvares Cabral, the explorer who discovered Brazil. (Church and chapel open Tu-Su 9:30am-12:30pm and 2-5:30pm. Free.) Take R. São Martinho from Pr. Visconde to the **Museu Arqueológico de São João do Alporão,** housed in a 13th-century former church. (Open Tu-Su 9am-12:30pm and 2-5:30pm. 200$, students 100$.)

The **train station** (tel. (043) 32 11 99), 2km from town, serves Tomar (1hr., every hr., 500$); Lisbon (1hr., 10-20 per day, 650$); Coimbra (2hr., 8 per day, 1350$); and Porto (4hr., 6 per day, 1650$). Buses (10min., every 1hr., 160$) connect the train station with the **bus station** (tel. (043) 33 32 00), on Av. Brasil, near the main *praça*, Pr. Sá da Bandeira. **Buses** serves Lisbon (1-1½hr., 20 per day, 760-900$); Tomar (1½hr., 5 per day, 750-1050$); Coimbra (2hr., 4 per day, 1500$); and Porto (4hr., 4 per day, 2000$). The nearby **tourist office,** R. Capelo Ivêns 63, is nearby. (Tel. (043) 39 15 12. Open Tu-F 9am-7pm, Sa-M 10am-12:30pm and 2:30-5:30pm.) Around the corner is **Residencial Abidis,** R. Guilherme de Azevedo 4. (Tel. (043) 32 20 17. Singles 4000-5500$; doubles 4500-7000$. Breakfast included.) **Postal code:** 2000.

ÉVORA

Designated a UNESCO World Heritage site, Évora (pop. 54,000) is justly known as the "Museum City." The picture-perfect town boasts a Roman temple, an impressive cathedral, a 16th-century university, and streets that wind past Moorish arches.

⚡ 📷 PRACTICAL INFO, ACCOMMODATIONS, AND FOOD. Trains (tel. (066) 70 21 25) go from the end of R. Dr. Baronha to Lisbon (3hr., 5 per day, 1075$); Faro (4hr., 4 per day, 1650$); and Porto (6½hr., 3 per week, 2750$). From the train station, flag down bus 6 (100$) from just down the tracks or hike up R. Dr. Baronha, which becomes R. República and leads to the central Pr. Giraldo (20min.). **Buses** (tel. (066) 76 94 10) go from the continuation of R. Raimundo, 15min. downhill from Pr. Giraldo, just past the gas station, to Lisbon (2½hr., 5 per day, 1450$) and Faro (5hr., 5 per day, 1800$). The **tourist office** is at Pr. Giraldo 73. (Tel. (066) 70 26 71. Open Apr.-Oct. M-F 9am-7pm, Sa-Su 9am-12:30pm and 2-5:30pm; Nov.-Mar. daily

PORTUGAL

9am-12:30pm and 2-5:30pm.) Check **email** at ⌨**Oficin@,** R. Moeda 27, off Pr. Giraldo. (500$ per hr. Open daily Sept.-June 6pm-2am; July-Aug. 8:30pm-2am.)

Most *pensões* cluster on side streets around **Pr. Giraldo.** From the end of Pr. Giraldo, opposite the church, walk down R. República and bear left on R. Miguel Bombarda (a.k.a. R. São Vicente) to reach the excellent **Pousada de Juventude (HI),** R. Miguel Bombarda 40. (Tel. (066) 74 48 48; fax 74 48 43. Dorms 2500$; doubles 5500$. Reception 8am-midnight. Curfew midnight. Reserve ahead.) From the tourist office, walk down the street and three blocks right to get to **Casa Palma,** R. Bernando Mato 29A. (Tel. (066) 70 35 60. Singles 4500$; doubles 4500$.) Buses from Pr. Giraldo go near **Orbitur's Parque de Campismo de Évora,** on Estrada das Alcáçovas, which branches off the bottom of R. Raimundo. (Tel. (066) 70 51 90; fax 70 98 30. 620$ per person, 490$ per tent, 530$ per car. Shower included. Laundry. Reception 8am-10pm.) Many budget restaurants are near **Pr. Giraldo,** particularly along **R. Mercadores.** Try **Restaurante A Choupana,** R. Mercadores 16/20, off Pr. Giraldo. (Entrees 900-1600$; half-portions 800$. Open M-Sa 10am-2am. V, MC, AmEx.) Grab **groceries** at **Maxigrula,** R. João de Deus 130. (Open M-Sa 9am-7pm.) **Postal code:** 7000.

🔯🎵 **SIGHTS AND ENTERTAINMENT.** The city's most famous monument is the 2nd-century **Roman temple,** on Largo do Vila Flor. Facing the temple is the town's best-kept secret, the **Igreja de São João Evangelista** (1485), its interior covered with dazzling *azulejos* (tiles); ask to see the church's hidden chambers. (Open Tu-Su 10am-noon and 2-5pm. 250$.) From Pr. Giraldo, head up R. 5 de Outubro to the colossal 12th-century **cathedral;** the 12 apostles on the doorway are masterpieces of medieval Portuguese sculpture. The **Museu de Arte Sacra,** above the nave, has interesting religious artifacts. (Cathedral open daily 9am-12:30pm and 2-5pm. Museum closed M. Cloister and museum 350$. Cathedral free.) Attached to the pleasant **Igreja Real de São Francisco,** the bizarre **Capela dos Ossos** (Chapel of Bones), was built entirely out of the bones of 5000 people by three morbid Franciscan monks. From Pr. Giraldo, follow R. República; the church is on the right and the chapel around back to the right of the main entrance. (Open M-Sa 9am-1pm and 2:30-6pm, Su 10-am-1pm and 2:30-6pm; chapel closed during mass. 160$.) Although most of Évora turns in at sunset, **Kalmaria Discoteca,** R. Valdevinos 21A, the second right off R. 5 de Outubro from Pr. Giraldo, opens its doors to bar-hoppers. (Cover 1000$, includes 2 beers. Open M-Sa 10pm-5am.) The **Feira de São João** festival keeps the town up all night with a huge Portuguese-style country fair in the last week of June.

ALGARVE

Behold the Algarve—a freak of nature, a desert on the sea, an inexhaustible vacationland where happy campers from all over the world bask in the sun. Nearly 3000 hours of sunshine per year have transformed this one-time fishermen's backwater into one of Europe's favorite vacation spots. In July and August, tourists mob the Algarve's resorts in search of perfect tans and wild nights in bars and discos. In the off-season, a less intense sun presides over tranquil grotto beaches at the bases of rugged cliffs. The westernmost town of Sagres offers isolated beaches and steep cliffs, while the eastern border near Tavira features floating flamingo wetlands.

LAGOS

For as long as anyone in Lagos can remember, this modestly sized town (pop. 22,000) has played host to swarms of sun-worshipping Europeans, Australians, and North Americans. Although there isn't much more than beaches and bars, between soaking in the view from the cliffs, soaking in the sun on the beach, and soaking in drinks at the bars, you won't find anyone complaining.

📧 **GETTING THERE AND GETTING AROUND**

Trains: Tel. 76 29 87. Across the river (over the metal drawbridge) from the center. To **Évora** (6hr., 2 per day, 1850$) and **Lisbon** (6½hr., 5 per day, 1700-2175$).

Buses: EVA bus station (tel. 76 29 44), off Av. Descobrimentos, just past the train station bridge (as you leave town). To **Lisbon** (5hr., 7-10 per day, 2400$) and **Seville** (6hr.; 1 per day; 3000$). For more info on getting to Seville, ask at the hostel.

PORTUGAL

⚡ ORIENTATION AND PRACTICAL INFORMATION

Avenida dos Descobrimentos, the main road, runs along the river. From the train station, exit left, go around the pinkish building, cross the river, and hang a left on Av. Descobrimentos. From the bus station, turn right on the main thoroughfare as you exit, and follow R. Portas de Portugal, which leads to the center of the old town at **Praça Gil Eanes.** Most everything hovers near this *praça*, the adjoining **Rua 25 de Abril,** and the parallel **Rua Cândido dos Reis.** Farther down Av. Descobrimentos, on the right, closer to the **fortaleza,** is **Praça República.**

Tourist Office: Tel. 76 30 31. On R. Vasco de Gama, an inconvenient 10min. past the bus station as you on Av. Descobrimentos. Go through the rotary and past the gas station; it's on the left. Open daily 9:30am-12:30pm and 2-5:30pm.

Laundromat: Lavanderia Miele, Av. Descobrimentos 27 (tel. 76 39 69). Wash and dry 1000$ per 5kg. Open M-F 9am-1pm and 3-7pm, Sa 9am-1pm.

Emergency: Tel. 112. **Police:** On R. General Alberto Silva (tel. 76 29 30).

Medical Services: Hospital (tel. 76 30 34), R. Castelo dos Governadores.

Post Office: (tel. 77 02 50), on R. Portas de Portugal, between Pr. Gil Eanes and the river. Open M-F 9am-6pm. Address mail to be held: Thomas KELLEHER, *Posta Restante,* Estação Portas de Portugal, **8600** Lagos, Portugal.

PHONE CODE	City code: 082. From outside Portugal, dial int'l dialing prefix (see inside back cover) + 351 + 82 + local number.

⚡☕ ACCOMMODATIONS, CAMPING, AND FOOD

Reserve at least week ahead. Rooms in *casas particulares* run around 2000-3000$ per person in summer; haggle with owners at the train and bus stations.

🏠 **Pousada de Juventude de Lagos (HI),** R. Lançarote de Freitas 50 (tel./fax 76 19 70). From Pr. República, follow the small street in the back-center 1 block until it becomes R. Lançarote de Freitas. Social and friendly. July-Sept. dorms 2000$, doubles with bath 5000$; Oct.-June 1500$, 3800$. Breakfast included. Kitchen. Laundry. **Internet** 300$ per 30min. Reception 9am-1am. Check-out noon. Summer reservations only guaranteed if booked through **Movijovem** (tel. (01) 313 88 20; fax (01) 352 86 21).

🏠 **Residencial Rubi Mar,** R. Barroca 70 (tel. 76 31 65, ask for David; fax 76 77 49; rubimar01@hotmail.com), off Pr. Gil Eanes. Centrally located, quiet, and comfortable— a good deal if you can grab one of their 8 rooms. Doubles 6000-7000$; quads 10,000$. Breakfast included. Reserve 2 weeks ahead in summer.

Residencial Caravela, R. 25 de Abril 8 (tel. 76 33 61). 16 small rooms off a courtyard. In summer singles 4000$, doubles 5500-6000$; less in winter. Breakfast included.

Camping Valverde (tel. 78 92 11), on a beach 5km from Lagos. 700$ per person, 600-900$ per tent, 590$ per car. Shower included.

Parque de Campismo do Imulagos (tel. 76 00 31). Take a shuttle from either station (10min., M-F 15 per day). 900$ per person, 450-640$ per tent. Reception 8am-10pm.

Multilingual menus abound near **Pr. Gil Eanes** and **R. 25 de Abril,** but budget Portuguese is almost impossible to find. **Groceries** are at **Supermercado São Toque,** on R. Portas de Portugal, opposite the post office. (Open July-Sept. daily 9am-5pm; Oct.-June M-F 9am-8pm, Sa 9am-2pm.) **Casa Rosa,** R. Ferrador 22, is a Lagos standby; hordes of backpackers enjoy 600$ meals. (M and W all-you-can-eat pasta 999$. Open daily 7pm-2am.) Try one of the 91 titillating *piri piri* (hot-spice) dishes at **Restaurante Piri Piri,** R. Lima Leitão 15. (Entrees 990-1890$. Open daily noon-11pm.)

⚡🏄 BEACHES AND NIGHTLIFE

Lagos' beaches are seductive any way you look at them. Flat, smooth, sunbathing sands (crowded in summer, pristine in the off-season) can be found at the 4km **Meia Praia,** across the river from town. Hop on the 30-second ferry near Pr. República (60$). For beautiful cliffs hiding less-crowded beaches and caves, follow Av. Descobrimentos toward Sagres to the **Praia de Pinhão** (20min.). A tad farther, **Praia Dona Ana** features the sculpted cliffs and grottos that appear on at least half of all Algarve postcards. For other picturesque (and less populated) stretches, continue west to the **Praia do Camilo** and the cliffs of **Ponta da Piedade.**

You're tan, you're glam, now go find yourself a (wo)man. The streets of Lagos pick up as soon as the sun dips down, and by midnight the walls start to shake. The area between **Pr. Gil Eanes** and **Pr. Luis de Camões** is filled with cafés. **R. Cândido dos Reis** and the intersection of **R. 25 de Abril, R. Silva Lopes,** and **R. Soeiro da Costa** are crammed with bars. Swing by **Mullen's,** R. Cãndido dos Reis 86, a Lagos hotspot. (Kitchen open daily noon-2pm and 7-10pm. Bar open until 2am.) Down the street from the hostel is the friendly █**Taverna Velha** (Old Tavern), R. Lançarote de Freitas 34. (Happy Hour 9pm-midnight. Beer 200-400$; mixed drinks 500-700$. Open M-Sa 4pm-2am, Su 8pm-2am.) Awake and spend your second wind at **Phoenix Club,** R. São Gonçalo 29, near the Old Tavern and the hostel. (Beer 500-600$. Cover 1000$; includes 2 beers or 1 mixed drink. Open daily 1-6am.) **Whyte's Bar,** R. Ferrador 7, is packed all night long. (Beer 400$. Open daily 6pm-2am.)

▐ EXCURSIONS FROM LAGOS

SAGRES. Marooned atop a bleak desert plateau in Europe's southwesternmost corner, desolate Sagres and its cape were for centuries considered the end of the world. The windswept, barren, rugged cape plunges dramatically on all three sides into the Atlantic. Near the town lurks the **Fortaleza,** the fortress where Prince Henry stroked his beard, decided to map the world, and founded his famous **school of navigation.** (Open daily June-Aug. 10am-8:30pm; Sept.-May 10am-6:30pm. 300$, students 150$.) Six kilometers west lies the dramatic **Cabo de São Vicente,** where the second most powerful lighthouse in Europe shines over 96km out to sea. To get there, hike 1hr. or bike past the several fortresses perched atop the cliffs. (Get permission to climb up from the gatekeeper, who is there for much of the day but not noon-2pm.) The most notable **beach** in the area is **Mareta,** at the bottom of the road from the town center, a sandy crescent flanked by rock formations jutting into the ocean.

Rodoviária **buses** (tel. (082) 76 29 44) pull in from Lagos (1hr., 8 per day, 450$). The **tourist office,** on R. Comandante Matoso, is next to the bus stop. (Tel. (082) 62 48 73. Open Tu-Sa 9:30am-12:30pm and 2-5pm, Su 9:30am-noon.) The privately run **Turinfo,** on Pr. República, rents **bikes** (2000$ per day) and has info on **jeep tours** of a nearby nature preserve (6400$). (Tel. (082) 62 00 03. Open daily 10am-7pm.) Hump over to **O Dromedário Bistro,** on R. Comandante Matoso, has pizzas and veggie dishes (740-1310$). (Open Mar.-Dec. daily 10am-midnight; bar open until 3am.)

█**PRAIA DA ROCHA.** A short jaunt from Lagos, this grand **beach** is perhaps the very best the Algarve has to offer. With vast expanses of sand, surfable waves, rocky red cliffs, and plenty of secluded coves, the beach has a well-deserved reputation. From Lagos, take a **bus** to **Portimão** (35min., 10 per day, 345$), then switch at the station to the Praia da Rocha bus (10min., every 15min.). The **tourist office,** is at the end of R. Tomás Cabreina. (Tel. (082) 42 22 90. Open May-Sept. daily 9:30am-8pm; Oct.-Apr. M-F 9:30am-12:30pm and 2-6pm, Sa-Su 9:30am-12:30pm.)

ALBUFEIRA

Albufeira (pop. 22,000), the largest seaside resort in the Algarve, attracts visitors hellbent on having a good time. Sun, surf, and booze satisfy the masses, nary a Portuguese roams its cobblestoned streets, and graceful Moorish buildings fill the town…but who are we kidding? Most who can even *focus* on the buildings are just using them as reference points to navigate their way between Albufeira's beaches and bars. The town's spectacular slate of said **beaches** ranges from the popular **Galé** and **São Rafael** (4-8km toward Lagos) to the central **Baleira** and **Inatel** (the easiest to reach) to the chic **Falésia** (10km toward Faro). After a day at the beach, you could, nay, will go to a bar. Join the crowds at **Fastnet Bar,** R. Cândido dos Reis 5. (Beer 500$; mixed drinks 800$. Open daily 11am-4am.) **7½ Disco** (tel. 51 33 06), on R. São Gonçalo de Lagos, is a popular beachside club. Many of the hottest clubs are just

PORTUGAL

outside town; try **Reno's Bar, IRS Disco,** or **Kiss Disco** (taxi 500-1000$). (Open daily 2am-6am.) Head east along the coast for the mellower old town.

The **train station,** 6km inland, serves to Faro (45min., 6 per day, 300$); Lagos (1hr., 5 per day, 500$); Tavira (2hr., 6 per day, 380$); and Lisbon (4-5½hr., 5 per day, 2025-2950$). EVA **buses** (tel. (089) 57 16 16) connect to the town center (10min., every hr., 200$). The **bus station** (tel. (089) 58 97 55), on Av. Liberdade, at the entrance to town, sends buses to Faro (1hr., every hr., 600$); Lagos (1½hr., 7 per day, 870$); Tavira (1½hr., 5 per day, 760$); and Lisbon (3½-4hr., 12 per day, 2100-2550$). From the bus station, turn right and walk downhill to Largo Eng. Duarte Pacheco, turn right out of the square, then turn left on R. 5 de Outubro to get to the **tourist office,** R. 5 de Outubro 8. (Tel. (089) 58 52 79. Open daily 9:30am-7pm.) Book ahead or ask for *quartos* at the tourist office or any restaurant or bar. The modern **Pensão Albufeirense,** R. Liberdade 16, is a few blocks downhill from the bus station. (Tel. (089) 51 20 79. Singles 4000$; doubles 6000$; triples 7600$. Open May-Sept.) Weary campers can succumb to the shmancy **Parque de Campismo de Albufeira,** a few kilometers outside town toward Ferreiras. (Tel. (089) 58 76 29; fax 58 76 33. 850$ per person, per tent, and per car.)

TAVIRA

Farmers teasing police by riding their motor scooters over the **Roman pedestrian bridge** may be about as eventful as Tavira gets. But for most visitors to this relaxing haven—speckled with white houses, palm trees, and Baroque churches—that's just fine. Steps from the central **Pr. República** lead up to the **Igreja da Misericórdia.** (Open daily 10am-1pm and 3-6:30pm. Free.) Just beyond it, the remains of the city's **Castelo Mouro** (Moorish Castle) sit next to the **Santa Maria do Castelo.** (Castle open M-F 8am-5pm, Sa-Su 10am-7:30pm. Church open M-F 10am-1pm and 3-6pm, Sa 10am-1pm. Free.) Local **beaches,** such as **Pedras do Rei,** are accessible year-round. To reach the great beach on **Ilha da Tavira,** an island 2km away, take the ferry from the end of Estrada das 4 Aguas, 20min. downstream (every 15min., round-trip 150$). EVA **buses** (tel. (081) 32 25 46) leave from the station upstream from Pr. República for Faro (1hr., 10 per day, 450$). **Trains** (tel. (081) 32 23 54) also head to Faro (1hr., 6 per day, 300$). The **tourist office,** R. Galeria 9, is up the stairs off Pr. República. (Tel. (081) 32 25 11. Open M-Sa 9:30am-12:30pm and 2-5:30pm, Su 9:30am-12:30pm.) To get from Pr. República to the riverfront **Pensão Residencial Lagôas Bica,** R. Almirante Cândido dos Reis 24, cross the footbridge, continue down R. A. Cabreira, turn right, and go down one block. (Tel. (081) 32 22 52. Singles 3000$; doubles 4500-6500$; in winter 500$ less.) **Ilha de Tavira campground** is on (imagine that!) the Ilha da Tavira (follow directions above). (Tel. (081) 32 50 21. 430$ per person, 680$ per tent. Reception 8am-midnight. Showers 100$. Open May-Oct. 15). Try restaurants on **Pr. República** or opposite the garden on **R. José Pires Padinha.**

FARO

Although many begin their holidays in the Algarve's capital, largest city, and transport hub (pop. 55,000), few stay long enough to observe its **old town,** an untouristed, traditional medley of museums, handicrafts shops, and ornate churches. From Pr. Gomes, walk through the gardens to get to the entrance of the old town. **Trains** (tel. (089) 80 17 26) run from Largo Estação to Albufeira (45min., 14 per day, 300$); Lagos (2hr., 7-9 per day, 720$); Évora (5hr., 2-4 per day, 1650$); and Lisbon (5-6hr., 6 per day, 2175$). EVA **buses** (tel. (089) 89 97 00) go from Av. República to Albufeira (1hr., 14 per day, 570$); Tavira (1hr., 11 per day, 450$); Lagos (3hr., 6 per day, 680$). Renex (tel. (089) 81 29 80) goes from across the street to Lisbon (4½hr., 9 per day, 2350$) and Porto (8½hr., 9 per day, 3400$); Intersul (tel. (089) 89 97 70) runs to Seville (2600$). From the stations, turn right down Av. República along the harbor, then turn left past the garden to reach the **tourist office,** R. Misericórdia 8, at the entrance to the old town. (Tel. (089) 80 36 04. Open daily June-Aug. 9:30am-7pm; Sept.-May 9:30am-5:30pm.) If you have a layover, head down Av. República from either station to the central Pr. Gomes, and take R. 1 de Maio from the marina side to get to **Pensão Residencial Oceano,** R. Ivens 21, 2nd fl. (Tel. (089) 82 33 49. Singles

7000$; doubles 8000$; triples 10,000$; in winter 500-1000$ less. Breakfast 250$.
Visa.) While waiting for your bus to come in, enjoy some coffee and local marzipan
at one of the Algarve's best cafés, many along **R. Conselheiro Bívar**, off Pr. Gomes.

NORTHERN PORTUGAL

Although their landscapes and Celtic history invite comparison with the northwest
of Spain, the **Douro** and **Minho** regions of northern Portugal are more populated,
developed, and wealthy than Spanish Galicia. Hundreds of trellised vineyards for
porto and *vinho verde* wines beckon connoisseurs, *azulejo*-lined houses draw
visitors to charming, quiet streets. The **Three Beiras** region offers a sample of the
best of Portugal: the unspoiled Costa da Prata (Silver Coast) in the **Beira Litoral**
(coastal region) begins with the resort town of Figueira da Foz, while **Coimbra**, a
bustling university city, overlooks the region from high above the Rio Mondego.

COIMBRA

The country's only university city from the mid-16th to the early 20th century,
Coimbra serves as a mecca for the country's youth. The city's charm has long since
blotted out Coimbra's infamous dual roles as center of the Portuguese Inquisition
and the site of former dictator, António Salazar's education.

PRACTICAL INFO, ACCOMMODATIONS, AND SIGHTS. Trains (tel.
(039) 82 46 32) from other regions stop only at **Estação Coimbra-B (Velha)**, 3km northwest of town, while regional trains stop at Coimbra-B and **Estação Coimbra-A (Nova)**,
two blocks from the lower town center. Trains go to Figueira da Foz (1¼hr., 25 per
day, 290$); Porto (2hr., 12 per day, 980-1300$); and Lisbon (3hr., 19 per day, 1350$).
Bus 5 connects the two stations (5min., every 15min., 130$). **Buses** (tel. (039) 82 70
81) go from Av. Fernão Magalhães, on the university side of the river 10min. from
town, past Coimbra-A, to Porto (1½hr., 10 per day, 1300$); Lisbon (2½hr., 15 per
day, 1450$); Évora (4hr., 2 per day, 1900$); and Faro (8hr., 4 per day, 2900$). From
the bus station, go right on Av. Fernão Magalhães to Coimbra-A, then walk two
blocks upstream to Largo Portagem to find the **tourist office**, off Largo Portagem
(15min.). (Tel. (039) 85 59 50; fax 82 55 76. Open M-F 9am-7pm, Sa-Su 10am-1pm
and 2:30-5:30pm. Check **email** at **Ciber Espaço**, on Av. Sá Bandeira, on the top floor of
the Centro Comercial Avenida. (250$ per 30min. Open daily 1pm-midnight.)

To get from Coimbra-A or Largo Portagem to the ⚄**Pousada de Juventude de Coimbra (HI),** R. Henrique Seco 14, walk 20min. uphill on R. Olímpio Nicolau Rui
Fernandes to Pr. República, go up R. Lourenço Azevedo (left of the park), take the
second right, and it's on the right. Or, take bus 2, 7, 8, 29, or 46 to Pr. República and
walk (5min.). (Tel. (039) 82 29 55; fax 82 17 30. June-Aug. dorms 1700$, doubles
4500-5000$; Sept.-May 1500$, 3700$. Breakfast included. Kitchen. Laundry. Recep-
tion 9-10:30am and 6pm-midnight. Lockout 10:30am-6pm.) **Residência Moderna,** R.
Adelino Veiga 49, off Av. Fernão de Magalhães, offers private baths, A/C, and cable
TV. (Tel. (039) 82 54 13. Singles 4000-5000$; doubles 5500-8500$. Breakfast
included.) Enter the **Municipal Campground** through the arch off Pr. 25 de Abril; take
bus 5, 7, or 10 (dir: São José or Estádio) from Largo Portagem. (Tel. (039) 70 14 97.
231$ per person, 153-174$ per tent, 294$ per car. Reception Apr.-Sept. 9am-10pm;
Oct.-Mar. 8am-6pm.) The best cuisine in Coimbra lies around **R. Direita**, off Pr. 8 de
Maio; on the side streets between the river and Largo Portagem; and around **Pr.
República** in the university district. **Supermercado Minipreço**, R. António Granjo 6C, is
in the lower town center; turn left as you exit Coimbra-A and take another left.
(Open M-Sa 9am-8pm, Su 10am-1pm and 3:30-5:30pm.) **Postal code:** 3000.

SIGHTS AND ENTERTAINMENT. Take in the old town sights by climbing
from the river up the narrow stone steps to the university. Begin your ascent at the
Arco de Almedina, a remnant of the Moorish town wall, one block uphill from Largo
Portagem. At the top is the looming 12th-century Romanesque **Sé Velha** (Old Cathedral), complete with tombs, Gregorian chants, and a cloister. (Open M-Sa 10am-

noon and 2-6pm, Su 10am-noon. Cloisters 100$.) Follow signs to the late-16th century **Sé Nova** (New Cathedral), built for the Jesuits (open Tu-Sa 9am-noon and 2-6pm; free), just a few blocks from the 16th-century **University of Coimbra**. The **Porta Férrea** (Iron Gate), off R. São Pedro, opens onto the old university, whose buildings were Portugal's de facto royal palace when Coimbra was the kingdom's capital. The stairs to the right lead to the **Sala dos Capelos**, which houses portraits of Portugal's kings, six Coimbra-born. (Open daily 9:30am-12:30pm and 2-5pm. 250$.) The **university chapel** and **library** lie past the clock tower; press the library buzzer to enter the gilded halls. (Open daily 9:30am-noon and 2-5pm. 250$, students free. All university sights 500$; buy tickets from the office in the main quad.) The 12th-century **Igreja de Santa Cruz**, Pr. 8 de Maio, at the far end of R. Ferreira Borges in the lower town, has a splendid **sacristy**. (Open M-Sa 9am-noon and 2-6pm, Su 4-6pm. Cloisters 200$.) Cross the bridge in front of Largo Portagem to find the 14th-century **Convento de Santa Clara-a-Velha** and the 17th-century **Convento de Santa Clara-a-Nova**.

Nightlife in Coimbra gets highest honors. After dinner, outdoor cafés around **Pr. República** are popular; try the **Café-Bar Cartola**. (Beer from 150$. Open M-Sa 8am-2am, Su 8am-1am.) **Via Latina**, R. Almeida Garrett 1, around the corner and uphill from Pr. República, is hot in all senses of the word. (Open F-Sa midnight-8am.) **Diligência Bar**, R. Nova 30, off R. Sofia, does *fado* (10pm-2am). In early May, graduates burn narrow ribbons they got as first-years and get wide ones in return during Coimbra's famed week-long festival, the **Queima das Fitas** (Burning of the Ribbons).

FIGUEIRA DA FOZ

Figueira da Foz's best features are its 3 sq. km Sahara-like beach and its partying. Pleasure-seekers who don't mind concrete buildings come here to worship the sun and the neon sign—in Figueira, entertainment is the sight, and vice versa. Bars and clubs line **Av. 25 de Abril**, next to and above the tourist office. Most popular of all is the **casino** complex, on R. Bernardo Lopes. (Casino open daily July-Aug. 4pm-4am; Sept.-June 3pm-3am; free. Club cover 1000$; includes 2 beers. Open Oct.-June 11:30pm-6am.) **Trains** (tel. (033) 42 83 16) leave near the bridge for Coimbra (1hr., 27 per day, 290$); Porto (2¼hr., 8 per day, 1150$); and Lisbon (3½hr., 6 per day, 1450$). From there, walk with the river to your left on Av. Saraiva de Carvalho, which becomes R. 5 de Outubro and then curves into the central Av. 25 de Abril (25min.). **Buses** (tel. (033) 42 67 03) go to Lisbon (3hr., 4 per day, 1450$) and Faro (12hr., 2 per day, 2900$). Facing the church, turn right on R. Dr. Santos Rocha, walk 10min. toward the waterfront, and turn right on R. 5 de Outubro to reach the **tourist office**, Av. 25 de Abril (15min.). (Tel. (033) 40 28 27; fax 40 28 20. Open June-Sept. daily 9am-midnight; Oct.-May M-F 9am-5:30pm, Sa-Su 10am-12:30pm and 2:30-6:30pm. Most hotels and eats line **R. Bernardo Lopes,** four blocks inland from Av. 25 de Abril. ✠**Pensão Central**, R. Bernardo Lopes 36, is down the street from the casino. (Tel. (033) 42 23 08. Singles 5000$; doubles 8000$; triples 10,000$. Breakfast included.) With the beach on your left, walk up Av. 25 de Abril, turn right at the rotary on R. Alexandre Herculano, and turn left at Parque Santa Catarina to reach the **Parque Municipal de Campismo da Figueira da Foz Municipal**, on Estrada Buarcos. (Tel. (033) 40 28 10. 400$ per person, 300$ per tent and per car. Showers 100$. Reception June-Sept. 8am-8pm; Oct.-May 8am-7pm. June-Sept. parties of 2 or more only.) **Supermercado Ovo** is at R. A. Dinis and R. B. Lopes. (Open M-F 9am-1pm and 3-7pm.)

PORTO (OPORTO)

Porto is famous for its namesake—sugary-strong port wine. Magnificently situated on a gorge cut by the Douro River, just 6km from the sea, Portugal's second-largest city, one of the designated Cultural Capital of Europe for 2001, is punctuated with granite church towers, orange-tiled houses, and graceful bridges.

◨▮🖫 PRACTICAL INFO, ACCOMMODATIONS, AND FOOD. From the main train station, **Estação de Campanhã** (tel. (02) 519 13 00), east of the center, **trains** go to Coimbra (2¼hr., 12 per day, 980$) and Lisbon (4½hr., 5 per day, 2000$). Trains connect to the **Estação de São Bento** (5min., 130$), a block from the central Pr. Liberdade. Garagem Atlântico **buses** leave from R. Alexandre Herculano 366 (tel.

(02) 200 69 54) for Coimbra (1½hr., 12 per day, 1300$) and Lisbon (4hr., 10 per day, 2800$); Renex goes from R. Carmelitas 34 (tel. (02) 200 33 95) to Lagos (9½hr., 8 per day, 3400$). Get a map at the **tourist office,** R. Clube dos Fenianos 25, off Pr. Liberdade. (Open July-Sept. M-F 9am-7pm, Sa 9:30am-4:30pm, Su 10am-1pm; Oct.-June M-F 9am-5:30pm, Sa 9am-5:30pm.) Check **email** at **Portweb,** Pr. Gen. Humberto Delgado 291, by Pr. Liberdade. (100-300$ per hr. Open M-Sa 9am-2am, Su 3pm-2am.)

To get from the station to the spacious ◨**Residencial Paris,** R. Fábrica 27-9, cross Pr. Liberdade, and turn left on R. Dr. Artur de Magalhães Basto, which turns into R. Fábrica. (Tel. (02) 207 31 40; fax 207 31 49. Singles 2850-4600$; doubles 4200-6300$; triples 8200$. Breakfast included.) Take bus 35 from Estação Campanha or 37 from Pr. Liberdade to **Pousada de Juventude do Porto (HI),** R. Paulo da Gama 551; be careful in this area at night. (Tel. (02) 617 72 47. June-Aug. dorms 2500$; doubles with bath 5500$; Sept.-May 1900$, 4700$. Reception 9-11am and 6pm-midnight.) From Av. Aliados, go two blocks up R. Elísio de Melo, and turn right on R. Almada to find the small and tidy **Pensão Porto Rico,** R. Almada 237, 2nd fl. (Tel. (02) 339 46 90. Singles 4500$; doubles 7500$; triples 9000$. Breakfast included. V, MC.) Take bus 6 from Pr. Liberdade (bus 54 at night) to **camp** at **Prelada,** on R. Monte dos Burgos, in Quinta da Prelada, 2km from the center. (Tel. (02) 831 26 16. 600$ per person, 500$ per tent and per car. Reception 8am-11pm.) In pricey Porto you might want to head to **Mercado de Bolhão,** at R. Formosa and R. Sá de Bandeira. (Open M-F 8am-5pm, Sa 8am-1pm.) Doling out a more *escudos* will land you some tasty dishes; look in near the river in the **Ribeira** district, on C. Ribeira, R. Reboleira, and R. Cima do Muro. Try the city's specialty, *tripas à moda do Porto* (tripe and beans). Do coffee (200$) at ◨**Majestic Café,** R. Santa Catarina 112. (Open daily 9am-12:30am.) **Restaurante O Gancho,** Largo Terreiro 11-12, serves Portuguese classics. (Entrees 800-1200$. Open daily noon-3pm and 7:30-10:30pm.) **Postal code:** 4000.

◨ ▣ **SIGHTS AND ENTERTAINMENT.** Your first brush with Porto's rich stock of fine artwork may be the celebrated collection of *azulejos* (tiles) in the **Estação São Bento.** Walk past the station and uphill on Av. Afonso Henriques to reach Porto's pride and joy, the 12th- to 13th-century Romanesque ◨**Cathedral** (Sé). The *azulejo*-covered cloister was added in the 14th century. (Open M-Sa 9am-12:30pm and 2:30-6pm, Su 2:30-6pm. Cloister 250$.) From the station, follow signs downhill on R. Mouzinho da Silveira to R. Ferreira Borges and the ◨**Palácio da Bolsa** (Stock Exchange), the epitome of 19th-century elegance. The ornate **Sala Árabe** (Arabic Hall) took 18 years to decorate. (Open M-F 9am-6:40pm, Sa-Su 9am-12:30pm and 2-6:30pm. Tours every 30min. 750$, students 550$; main courtyard free.) Next door the Gothic **Igreja de São Francisco** glitters with an elaborately gilded wooden interior. Under the floor, thousands of human bones are stored in preparation for Judgment Day. (Open daily 9am-6pm. 500$, students 250$.) From Pr. Liberdade up R. Clérigos rises the **Torre dos Clérigos** (Tower of Clerics), adjoined to the **Igreja dos Clérigos.** (Tower open daily 10am-noon and 2-5pm; 100$. Church free.) The rotating exhibits at the **Museu de Arte Contemporânea** crown 44 acres of sculpted gardens and fountains. Take bus 78 from Pr. Dom João I and ask the driver to stop at the museum (30min., 170$). (Open Tu-Su 10am-7pm. Park closes at sundown. 800$, students 400$; Th free.) To get to Porto's rocky and polluted (but popular) **beach,** in the ritzy Foz district, take bus 7 or 78 from Pr. Liberdade (170$).

If you are only in Porto for the **port,** fine and bounteous port wines are available for tasting at 20-odd port wine lodges, usually *gratuito* (free). The lodges are all across the river in Vila Nova da Gaia—from the Ribeira district and cross the lower level of the large bridge. **Sandeman,** with its costumed guides (500$), are a good start; **Cálem,** next door, has a less-stilted tour, and the port is almost as good. At **Ferreira,** down the road, you'll learn about the illustrious *senhora* who built the Ferreira empire in the 19th century. **Taylor's** wins the tasty and inebriating, but highly unscientific, *Let's Go* poll for best port lodge in Porto. (Most open daily 10am-6pm.)

Boogie to Brazilian and Latin tunes at bars in the **Ribeira,** a few blocks downhill from the center, over the bridge from Vila Nova de Gaia. **Pr. Ribeira, M. Bacalhoeiros,** and **R. Alfândega** harbor most bars and pubs. **Discoteca Swing,** on R. Júlio Dinis near the youth hostel, has swinging action for a mixed gay-straight crowd (cover 1000$). Or try discos **Industria, Twins,** or **Dona Urraca** in the Foz beach district.

PORTUGAL

ROMANIA (ROMÂNIA)

US$1 = 16,325 LEI (ROL)	1000 LEI = US$0.06
CDN$1 = 11,026 LEI	1000 LEI = CDN$0.09
UK£1 = 26,689 LEI	1000 LEI = UK£0.04
IR£1 = 21,960 LEI	1000 LEI = IR£0.05
AUS$1 = 10,674 LEI	1000 LEI = AUS$0.09
NZ$1 = 8697 LEI	1000 LEI = NZ$0.12
SAR1 = 2682 LEI	1000 LEI = SAR0.37
DM1 = 8839 LEI	1000 LEI = DM0.11

PHONE CODES Country code: 40. International dialing prefix: 00.

Romania, devastated by the long reign of Communist dictator Nicolae Ceaușescu, now suffers under a government incapable of bridging its gaps with the West. The resulting state of flux has left the country disheartened, as the tourist industry flounders with sights packaged far less smoothly than those of its more Westernized neighbors. Bucharest, the political and cultural center, has been swallowed by concrete apartment blocks and sterile Communist squares. The joy of travel here comes in peeling the layers off to the nation's recent history to find what lies underneath. Romanians go out of their way to make visitors feel at home, and travelers daring enough to explore will find a dynamic people hopeful in spite of their past.

For more coverage of Romania, brave *Let's Go: Eastern Europe 2000*.

DISCOVER ROMANIA

Romania is blessed with sky-tickling snowy peaks, a superb chunk of Black Sea coast, and culturally rich cities—all at half the price of similar attractions in Western Europe. Vast and hectic **Bucharest,** the capital, surprises with good museums, expanses of green parks, myriad historical monuments, and an *über*-hip, *über*-Euro night scene (p. 747). The streets of tiny **Târgu Jiu** are a blessed, serene break from the breakneck pace of the city, with an impressive outdoor collection of works by internationally renowned modern sculptor Constantin Brancuși (p. 751). For a hefty dose of Transylvanian vampire mythology, visit **Bran,** home to the legendary castle of Count Dracula (p. 753). Nearby **Brașov** provides easy access to the trails and slopes of the Transylvanian Alps (p. 752). Culture is centered in **Cluj-Napoca,** Romania's student capital and the most diverse city in the country (p. 752). For a holier take on Romania, visit the secluded **Bukovina Monasteries** near Suceava; their colorful frescoes are the best examples of devotional art in Eastern Europe. After days of sacred exploration, you, too, will believe (p. 754).

GETTING THERE AND GETTING AROUND

BY PLANE. You can fly into **Bucharest** on **Air France, Alitalia, British Airways, Lufthansa,** or **TAROM** (Romanian Airlines). TAROM flies direct from Bucharest to New York and major European cities. The renovation of Otopeni International Airport has improved the ground services, but the airport is still far from ideal.

BY TRAIN. Eurail is not valid in Romania; **Interail** and the **Balkan Flexipass,** however, are. International trains head daily to Western Europe via Budapest on the Orient Express. There are also direct trains to and from Chișinău, Moscow, Prague, Sofia, Vienna, and Warsaw. To buy international tickets, go to the **CFR** (Che-Fe-Re) office in larger towns. Budapest-bound trains leave through Arad or Oradea; specify where you want to exit and show your papers. An ISIC might get you 50% off, but student discounts are technically for Romanians only. CFR sells domestic tickets up to 24hr. before departure; after that, only stations sell tickets. The timetable *Mersul Trenurilor* is in English (L12,000). Call 221 for **schedule** info in most cities.

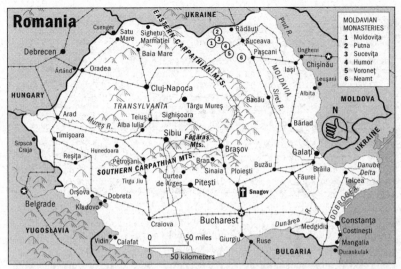

There are four types of trains: InterCity ("IC"), *rapid* (in green), *accelerat* (red), and *personal* (black). International trains (often blue) are usually indicated by "i" on timetables. InterCity trains stop only at major cities such as Bucharest, Cluj-Napoca, Iaşi, and Timişoara, and have three-digit numbers. *Rapid* trains (also 3 digits) are the next fastest; *accelerat* trains have four digits starting with "1" and are slower and dirtier. The sluggish and decrepit *personal* have four digits and stop at every station. First-class (*clasa-întîi;* wagons marked with a "1" on the side) is worth it. On overnight trains, shell out for a *vagon de dormit* (sleeping carriage).

BY BUS. Buses connect major cities to Athens, Istanbul, Prague, and various cities in Western Europe. Since plane and train tickets to Romania are often expensive, buses are a good—if slow—option. It is generally cheapest to take a domestic train to a city near the border and catch an international bus from there. Inquire at tourist agencies about timetables and tickets, but buying tickets straight from the carrier saves you from paying commission. Use the local bus system only when trains are not available. Buses are more expensive, but still as packed and poorly ventilated. Look for signs for the *autogară* (bus station) in each town.

BY CAR. While far from perfect, Romania's road conditions are passable. However, beware random spot checks from police who are authorized to collect inexplicable fines on the spot. Theft of vehicle parts and fuel shortages are common. In **speed limit** is 60km per hr. in residential areas, 90km per hr. on expressways. The **Automobil Clubul Român (ACR),** Strada Tache Ionescu 27, 70154 Bucharest 22 (tel. (01) 85 00 25 95; open M-F 8am-4pm), provides roadside assistance. In Bucharest, dial 927 for **emergency** help; in the rest of Romania, dial 123 45.

BY BIKE AND BY THUMB. Biking is neither common nor particularly safe. **Hitch-hiking,** although popular, remains risky. A wave of the hand, rather than a thumb, is the recognized sign. Some Romanians drive vans that become unofficial buses along popular routes. Big trucks, often traveling long distances, have also been reported to take passengers. The best places to hitch are at bus stops outside cities. Drivers generally expect a payment similar to the price of a train ticket.

ESSENTIALS

DOCUMENTS AND FORMALITIES. Americans do not need visas for stays of up to 30 days, while citizens of Australia, Canada, Ireland, New Zealand, South Africa, and the UK need visas for stays of any length. Single-entry visas (US$35) are good

ROMANIA

for 60 days, multiple-entry visas (US$70) for 180 days, and transit visas (US$25) for four days. Obtain a visa at a Romanian embassy or at the border (no additional fee). Get a visa extension at a local police station.

Romanian Embassies at Home: Canada, 655 Rideau St, Ottawa, ON K1N 6A3 (tel. (613) 789-5345; fax 789-4365); **South Africa,** 117 Charles St, Brooklyn Pretoria, P.O. Box 11295, Brooklyn, 0011 (tel. (012) 46 69 40; fax 46 69 47); **UK,** 4 Palace Green, Kensington, London W8 4QD (tel. (020) 79 37 96 66; fax 79 37 80 69); **US,** 1607 23rd St. NW, Washington, DC 20008 (tel. (202) 332-4848; fax 232-4748).

Foreign Embassies in Romania: All foreign embassies are in **Bucharest** (see p. 747).

TOURIST OFFICES. ONT (National Tourist Office) used to be one of the most corrupt government agencies in Romania. While you'll no longer have to bribe anyone, the information you get might not be correct. ONT also moonlights as a **private tourist agency,** providing travel packages for a commission. Get friendly locals to help.

MONEY. The Romanian unit of currency is the **leu,** plural lei (abbreviated L). The banknotes are L500, L1000, L5000, L10,000, L50,000, and the new L100,000. While many establishments accept US$ or DM, pay for everything in *lei* to avoid being ripped off and to save your hard currency for bribes and emergencies. Private **exchange bureaus** litter the country; unfortunately, not many take **credit cards** or **traveler's checks.** Most banks will cash traveler's checks into dollars or Deutschmarks, then exchange them for *lei*, at a high fee. Always keep receipts for money exchanges. **ATMs,** which generally accept Cirrus, Plus, V, and MC and offer reasonable rates, are rare outside major cities. It is customary to give (and receive) inexact change for purchases, generally rounding to the nearest L500; this suffices as a tip in restaurants. Hostel beds average US$10-12; budget hotels can range wildly from US$10-35. Meals are incredibly cheap at US$2-5.

COMMUNICATION

Post: An airmail **letter** to Australia, New Zealand, South Africa, and the US costs L8,000. Be sure to request *par avion* for airmail, which takes 10-19 days to reach North America.

Telephone: Almost all **public phones** are orange and accept **phone cards** (L50,000 at phone offices, major Bucharest Metro stops, and some post offices), although a few old blue phones take L500 coins. **International calls** run L10,000 per min. to neighboring countries, L18,000 to most of Europe, and L30,000 to North America. **Local calls** cost L500-1500 and can be made from any phone. Dial several times before giving up; a busy signal may just indicate a connection problem. It may be necessary to make a phone call *prin comandă;* that is, with the help of the operator at the telephone office, which, of course, takes longer and costs more. At the phone office, write down the destination, duration, and phone number for your call. Pay up front, and always ask for the rate per minute. **International direct dial** numbers include: **AT&T,** 018 00 42 88; **Sprint,** 018 00 08 77; **MCI WorldPhone Direct,** 018 00 18 00; **Canada Direct,** 018 00 50 00; **BT Direct,** 018 00 44 44. **Police,** tel. 955. **Ambulance,** tel. 961. **Fire,** tel. 981.

Language: Romanian. Those familiar with French, Italian, Spanish, or any other Romance language can usually decipher public signs. In Transylvania, German and Hungarian are widely spoken. Throughout the country, French is a common second language for the older generation, English for the younger. Get cuddly with Romanian on p. 949.

ACCOMMODATIONS AND CAMPING. While some **hotels** charge foreigners up to twice as much as locals, lodging is still relatively cheap. As a general rule, one-star hotels are on par with mediocre European youth hostels, so don't let the bed bugs bite—literally. Two-star places are decent, and those with three are good but expensive. In some places, going to ONT (in resorts, the *Dispecerat de Cazare*) and asking for a room may get you a price at least 50% lower than that quoted by the hotel. **Private accommodations** are good, but hosts rarely speak English; be aware that renting a room "together" means sharing a bed. Rooms run US$6-10 per person, sometimes with breakfast. See the room and fix a price before accepting. Foreign students can sometimes stay in **university dorms** at low prices. Ask at the local university rectorate or the ONT. **Campgrounds** are crowded and often have frightening bathrooms. Relatively cheap **bungalows** are often full in summer.

FOOD AND DRINK. Romanian food is fairly typical of Central Europe, with a bit of Balkan and French thrown in. Romanians rarely eat out, which explains the paucity of decent restaurants; try to wrangle a dinner invite from a local. In the mountains or resorts, peasants sell fresh fruit and cheese. On the street, you can find cheap *mititei* (a.k.a. *mici*; barbecued ground meat) or Turkish-style kebabs. "Fast food" in Romania should be regarded with suspicion. Bucharest is the only place where you'll find non-Romanian cuisine. *Garnituri*, the extras that come standard with a meal, are usually charged separately, down to that dollop of mustard. As a rule, if the waiters put it in front of you, you're paying for it.

LOCAL FACTS
Time: Romania is 2hr. ahead of Greenwich Mean Time (GMT; see p. 49).

Climate: Romania suffers hot summers and cold winters; visit in spring or autumn.

Hours: "Nonstop" cafés and kiosks can be found in cities, but their names can be misleading; shops close arbitrarily when attendants feel like it. Romanians don't take posted hours very seriously, and many businesses may be closed F afternoons.

Holidays in 2000: New Year's Day (Jan. 1-3); Epiphany (Jan. 6); Orthodox Christmas (Jan. 7); Orthodox Easter (Apr. 30-May 1); National Day (Dec. 1); and Christmas (Dec. 25-26).

BUCHAREST

Once the fabled beauty at the end of the Orient Express, Bucharest (BOO-kooresht; pop. 2 million) is fabled today only for its infamous Communist makeover under Romanian dictator Nicolae Ceauşescu, who in his 25 years in power managed to entirely undo the city's splendor. After escaping war-time destruction, Neoclassical architecture, grand boulevards, and Ottoman traces were replaced with concrete blocks and Communist monuments. Today, the metropolis is a somber ghost of its former self. Luckily, Romania's current government is slowly beginning to give Bucharest a desperately-needed face-lift.

⊑ GETTING THERE AND GETTING AROUND

Airplanes: Otopeni Airport (tel. 230 00 22), 18km from the city. Buses from the airport go to "Centru" near Hotel Intercontinental Piaţa Universităţii (M2: Piaţa Universităţii). Bus 783 to Otopeni leaves from Piaţa Unirii every 20min. Buy **international tickets** at the **CFR/TAROM office,** Str. Brezoianu 10 (tel. 646 33 46). M2: Piaţa Universităţii.

Trains: Gara de Nord (tel. 223 06 60; M3: Gara de Nord) is the principal station. L2000 to enter the station if you're not catching a train. To: **Sofia** (10hr., 3 per day, L350,000); **Budapest** (12hr., 6 per day, L470,000); **Istanbul** (20-24hr., 1 per day, L370,000); and **Kiev** (30hr., 1 per day, L568,000).

Buses: Filaret, Cuţitul de Argint 2 (tel. 335 11 40). M2: Tineretului. South of the Centru. **Fotopoulos Express** (tel. 335 82 49) goes to **Athens. Toros** and **Murat** go from outside Gara de Nord to **Istanbul. Double T** (tel. 613 36 42), affiliated with Eurail, goes you to Western Europe. International bus companies are near Piaţa Dorobanţilor.

Public Transportation: Buses, trolleys, and **trams** cost L2000. Buy tickets from a kiosk; you can't always get them on board. Validate on board or face a L50,000 fine. Beware pickpockets during peak hours. The **Metro** offers reliable, less crowded service to major points in Bucharest and runs 5am-11:30pm; hold on to your card (L4000 for 2 trips).

Taxis: Colbăcescu, tel. 945. **Getax,** tel. 953. Expect to pay at least L1600 per km, and arrange the price *(preţul)* beforehand; L30-50,000 is probably the best you'll get. Bargain harshly, and *never* pay more than US$10.

⊉ ORIENTATION AND PRACTICAL INFORMATION

Bucharest is divided into six sectors that circle clockwise around the city. **In the** northern portion are **Piaţa Victoriei** and **Piaţa Romană,** as well as the train station,

ROMANIA

Gara de Nord. In the southeast corner are what remains of Bucharest's **Old Town** and **Piaţa Unirii, Piaţa Universităţii,** and **Piaţa Revolutiei.** Gara de Nord lies along the M3 metro line just west of the Centru. Take a train (dir: Dristor II) one stop to Piaţa Victoriei, then change to the M2 line to Depoul. Take this train one stop to Piaţa Romana, two stops to Piaţa Universităţii, or three stops to Piaţa Unirii.

Tourist Offices: ONT, Bd. Magheru 7 (tel. 315 84 41; fax 312 09 15). M2: Piaţa Romană. Open M-F 8am-8pm, Sa 8am-3pm, Su 8am-1pm.

Embassies: Canada, Str. Nicolae Iorga 36 (tel. 222 98 45). M2: Piaţa Romană. Open M-F 9am-5pm. **UK,** Str. Jules Michelet 24 (tel. 312 03 03). M2: Piaţa Romană. Open M-Th 8:30am-1pm and 2-5pm, F 8:30am-1:30pm. **US,** Str. Tudor Arghezi 7/9 (tel. 210 40 42; after-hours tel. 210 01 49; fax 211 33 60). M2: Piaţa Universităţii. Consular services at Str. Nicolae Filipescu 26. Open M-Th 8-11:30am and 1-3pm, F 8-11:30am. Citizens of **Australia, Ireland,** and **New Zealand** should contact the UK embassy. Citizens of **South Africa** should contact the embassy in Budapest (see p. 496).

Currency Exchange: Exchange houses are everywhere; **ATMs,** located at major banks, always give the best rates. Don't change money on the street.

American Express: Marshall Tourism, Bd. Magheru 43, 1st fl., #1 (tel. 223 12 04). M2: Piaţa Romană. Cannot cash traveler's checks. Open M-F 9am-5pm, Sa 9am-1pm.

Luggage Storage: At Gara de Nord. Foreigners pay L4800-9600. Open 24hr.

Police: Tel. 955. **Ambulance,** tel. 961. **Fire,** tel. 981.

Pharmacies: SF, Calea Victoriei 103-5 (tel. 650 78 38). Open 24hr.

Medical Assistance: Spitalul de Urgenţă, Calea Floreasca 8 (tel. 212 19 43). M3: Ştefan cel Mare.

Internet Access: Internet Café, Bd. Carol I 25 (tel. 313 10 48). M2: Piaţa Universităţii; head east on Bd. Carol I past Piaţa Rosetti. L15,000 per 30min. Open 24hr.

Telephones: Telephone office, Calea Victoriei 37. Open M-F 7:30am-8pm, Sa 8am-2pm. Orange phone cards L20,000 or L50,000.

Post Office: Str. Matei Millo 10 (tel. 613 03 87). M2: Piaţa Universităţii. Open M-F 7:30am-8pm, Sa 7am-2pm. *Poste Restante* nearby, next to Hotel Carpati. Address mail to be held: Clark KENT, *Poste Restante,* Str. Matei Millo 10, Bucharest **70154.**

PHONE CODE	City code: 01. From outside Romania, dial int'l dialing prefix (see inside back cover) + 40 + 1 + local number.

♦☼ ACCOMMODATIONS AND FOOD

The ONT office can arrange **private rooms** or **hotel** accommodations, but tourist offices in the train station may be more objective. It's difficult to find decent rooms for less than L300-400,000 per person.

Villa Helga Youth Hostel, Str. Salcâmilor 2 (tel. 610 22 14). Take bus 86, 79, or 133 two stops from M2: Piaţa Romana or six stops from Gara de Nord to Piaţa (east along Bd. Dacia). From Bd. Dacia, take a right on Str. Gemini Lascăr, a left at the triangular green, another left onto Str. Viitorlui, and a final right on Str. Salcâmilor. Don't trust the "staffers" at Gara de Nord; they're scam artists. The real staff, however, is friendly and funny. US$12. Breakfast included. Kitchen. Laundry free.

Hanul Manuc, Str. Franceză 62/64 (tel. 313 14 15; fax 312 28 11). M1-3: Piaţa Unirii. With McDonald's behind you, walk along the square with the green on the left. Take the 1st right, then continue straight to the end of a cobblestoned street. Enter to the right. This former monastery is now a lux hotel. Doubles L630,000. Call ahead. V, MC, AmEx.

Hotel Triumf, şos. Kiseleff 12 (tel. 222 31 72; fax 223 24 11). M2: Aviatorilor. Take bus or trolley 131, 205, 301, or 331 from Piaţa Lahovari to Arcul de Triumf. From the Arcul de Triumf, walk south on şos. Kiseleff; the hotel is on the left. Singles L500-550,000; doubles L650-750,000. Breakfast included. Laundry. V, MC.

Hotel Bucegi, Str. Witing 2 (tel. 637 52 25). M3: Gara de Nord. Across from the train station. Singles L140,000; doubles L180-350,000; triples L240,000.

ROMANIA

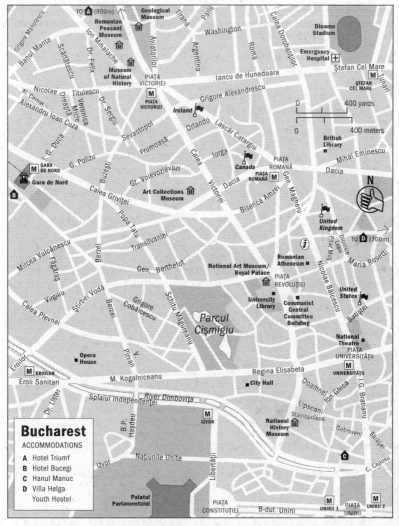

Bucharest

ACCOMMODATIONS

A Hotel Triumf
B Hotel Bucegi
C Hanul Manuc
D Villa Helga
   Youth Hostel

ROMANIA

Enjoy a light meal at artsy **Mes Amis,** Str. Lipscani 82, in a tiny alley between Lipscani and Gabroveni. (M2: Piața Unirii or Piața Universității. Meals L25-35,000. Open daily noon-2am; food served until 11pm.) For the best Romanian food in town, head east from M2: Piața Romană on Bd. Dacia to Piața Gemeni, then walk two more blocks and take a right on Toamnei; after an intersection on the right, you'll find **Nicorești,** Str. Maria Rosetti 40. (Open M-Sa 9am-10pm, Su 1-10pm.) To get to the exceptional Indian **Taj Palace,** Str. Radu Vodă 18, take the Metro to Piața Unirii," walk away from McDonald's with the green to your right and take a right on Radu Vodă (the 1st right not along the water). (Entrees 40-60,000. Open noon-10pm.) Fabulous seafood awaits at **Pescarul** ("The Fisherman"), Bd. N. Bălcescu 9 across from Hotel Intercontinental. (Entrees L40,000. M2: Piața Universității. Open M-Sa 10am-11pm.) **Open-air markets** offering all manner of veggies and more abound in Bucharest—good ones are at Piața Amzei, Piața Matache, and Piața Latină. **Vox Maris Supermarket,** at Piața Victoriei, is open 24hr.

SIGHTS

Bucharest is not a beautiful city. Once referred to as "Little Paris" and the "Pearl of the Balkans," Bucharest now lacks any traces of urban splendor. But the city is worth exploring for the omnipresence of its history, for the sobering scars left on nearly every square and building by its recent revolutions and regimes.

CIVIC CENTER. In order to create his perfect Socialist capital, Ceauşescu destroyed five sq. km of Bucharest's historic center, demolishing over 9000 19th-century houses and displacing more than 40,000 Romanians. The result is today's **Centru Civic,** completed in 1989 just in time for his overthrow. Its centerpiece, the **Parliamentary Palace** (Palatul Parlamentului), is the world's third-largest building (after the Pentagon in Washington, DC and the Potala in Tibet); Romanians still refer to it as the "Madman's Palace." *(M1,3: Izvor. For a more spectacular view, approach the palace from Piaţa Unirii. For tours, enter at entrance A1. Open daily 10am-6pm. Tours L30,000.)* Although he destroyed the rest of Piaţa Unirii, Ceauşescu inexplicably spared **Dealul Mitropoliei,** the hill on its southwest side, and atop it the **Romanian Orthodox Church.** *(M2: Piaţa Unirii. Head up Aleea Dealul Mitropoliei. Open M-Su 8am-7pm.)*

SIGHTS OF THE REVOLUTION. Bucharest is as marked by its 1989 revolution as it is by its 24 years under Ceauşescu. Streets and squares are marked with crosses and plaques commemorating the *eroilor revoluţiei Române,* or heroes of the 1989 revolution. **Piata Universităţii** houses memorials to victims of both the 1989 and June 1990 revolutions. Demonstrators perished fighting Ceauşescu's forces here on December 21, 1989, the day before his fall. Students had been protesting the new ex-Communist government in the small Piaţa 22 Decembrie 1989, opposite Hotel Intercontinental, since April, when in June over 10,000 Romanian miners were bussed in to violently squash the protesters and 21 students were killed. *(M2: Piaţa Universităţii.)* Walk up Bd. Bratianu, which turns into to Bd. Balcescu, from the Metro and turn left on Str. Rosetti to reach **Piaţa Revoluţiei,** where the first shots of the revolution were fired on December 21, 1989.

PARKS. One of Bucharest's few remaining beauties is its extensive park system. Sprawling and beautiful **Herăstrău Park** is just north of downtown. Within the park lies Bucharest's largest lake, meandering peacocks, and a small Island of Roses. *(M2: Aviatorilor; or take bus 301, 331, or 131 from Piata Lahovari. Open daily 9am-8pm.)* One of Bucharest's oldest parks, the **Cişmigiu Gardens,** is filled with elegant paths and a small lake where you can rent paddleboats. *(M2: Piaţa Universităţii. Just west of Piaţa Universităţii on Bd. Regina Elisabeta. Open daily 8am-8pm. Paddleboats L25,000 per hr.)*

OTHER SIGHTS. If you're in the mood for something truly Romanian, visit the huge **market** at the "Obor" Metro stop. Among many other things, you're likely to find eggs, raw wool, rusty nails, Bulgarian cigarettes, Turkish Levis, shower heads, ceramic plates, and ducks. *(M3: Obor.)* Several of modern Bucharest's most fashionable streets are sights in and of themselves; be sure to stroll along **Calea Victoriei, şos. Kiseleff, Bd. Aviatorilor,** and **Bd. Magheru.** The sidestreets just off Piaţa Victoriei and Calea Dorobanţilor, with names like Paris, Washington, and Londra, brim with villas and houses typical of the beautiful Bucharest that once was.

MUSEUMS. Bucharest's museums vary in quality, but all are a welcome break from the grim specter of Bucharest's streets. The **Museum of the Romanian Peasant** (Muzeul Tăranului Român), şos. Kiseleff 3, is Bucharest's museum star. *(M2,3: Piaţa Victoriei. Open Tu-Su 10am-6pm. L10,000, students L3000.)* The **Jewish History Museum of Romania** (Muzeul de Istorie a Comunitaţilor Evreieşti din România), Str. Mămulari 3, focuses on the history and contributions of Romania's Jewish community. The central sculpture mourns the 350,000 Romanian Jews deported and killed by the Nazis. *(M2: Piata Unirii. Head up Bd. Corneliu Coposu from Piata Unirii, near Unirea. Take the 1st right across a parking lot between Unirea and the KMO store and turn left at the end; it's on the right in the Great Synagogue. Open W and Su 9am-1pm. L5000.)* In Piaţa Revolutiei, the **National Art Museum** (Muzeul Naţional de Artă), Calea Victoriei 49/53, is in the Royal Palace. The permanent collection remains closed for renovations after damages sustained in the 1989 revolution, but the rest houses temporary exhibits. *(Tel. 313 30 30. M2: Piata Universitatii. Open W-Su 10am-6pm. Each building L10,000, students L5000.)*

🎭 ENTERTAINMENT

THEATER AND OPERA. Bucharest hosts some of the biggest **rock festivals** this side of Berlin; guests include rising indie groups and falling stars like Michael Jackson (who from the balcony of the Parliamentary Palace responded to screaming fans with "Hello, Budapest!") or Metallica; ask at the tourist office. **Theater** and **opera** are cheap diversions in Bucharest. (No shows June-Sept.). Try the **Teatrul Naţional,** Bd. N. Bălcescu 2 (tel. 613 91 75; M2: Piaţa Universităţii), also home to **Teatrul de Operetă** (tel. 313 63 48). **Ateneul** (tel. 315 68 75; M2: Piaţa Revoluţiei) holds excellent classical music concerts. **Opera Română,** Bd. M.L. Kogălniceanu 70 (tel. 313 18 57; M1,3: Eroilor) stages top-notch opera for ridiculously cheap prices.

NIGHTLIFE. For nighttime debauchery, pack a map (streets are poorly lit) and cab fare. Walk down Bd. Brătianu and take the third right to find **Club A,** Str. Blanari 14, run by the University of Bucharest's School of Architecture and always packed by 11pm. (Cover Tu-Th men L15,000, women free; F-Sa L20,000. M2: Piaţa Universităţii. Open Tu-Su 9pm-5am.) Hyper **Swing House,** Str. Gabroveni 30, pulls an enthusiastic crowd. Live music nightly, with weekly swing performances. (Drink min. L30,000. M2: Piaţa Unirii. Open daily 6pm-6am.) **Dubliner Irish Pub,** Bd. N. Titulescu 18, has the best Guinness south of the Carpathians. (M2,3: Piaţa Victoriei. Open daily noon-3am.) Take the last metro (11:30pm) to Semănătoarea and let the noisy crowd lead you through the maze of dorms. **R2,** on the right, followed after about 50m by **R1**—straight ahead—and **R3**—to the left. **Maxxx** is nearby; together they're the most popular discos in town during the school year (Oct. to late June). (Cover for men L15,000; women M-F free, Sa-Su L10,000. Open daily Oct. to late June 9:30pm-4am. M3: Semănătoarea and Grozăveşti.)

TÂRGU JIU

Despite a history that began in the 13th century, it is the **Constantin Brâncuşi National Cultural Assembly** (Complexul Cultural National Constantin Brăncuşi) alone that keeps the town of Târgu Jiu (TIR-goo dj-IOO) from passing almost entirely unnoticed. These world-renowned, open-air works by Brăncuşi (bran-CHOOSH), one of the world's most noted modern sculptors, make Târgu Jiu one of the most artistically rich towns in Romania. **Parcul Tineretului,** at the east end of Calea Eroilor (in the triangle formed by Str. Craiovei, Calea Bucureşti, and Str. Tudor Vladimirescu) is dominated by an impressive **Column of Infinity** (Coloana Infinitului) at the center. At the other end of Calea Eroilor, by the banks of Jiu River, lie the other three sculptures: the arched **Kissing Gate** (Poarta Săratului), **Aleea Scaunelor,** a long alley lined with 30 squat, round seats, and the **Table of Silence** (Masa Tăcerii). **Trains** run to Bucharest (5hr., 4 per day, L60,000) and Cluj-Napoca (6hr., 1 per day, L30,000). Exit the station, turn right on Bd. Republicii, turn left on Str. Unirii, and turn right on Str. Griviţa or Str. Victoriei; on the next street is the **tourist office,** OJT, Str. Eroilor 6. (Tel./fax (053) 21 40 10. Open M-F 10am-3pm.) It's connected to the excellent **Hotel Gorjul,** Str. Eroilor 6, also close to Parcul Central. (Tel. (053) 21 48 15. Singles L300,000; doubles L380,000; triples L420,000. Breakfast included.)

TRANSYLVANIA

Though the name evokes images of a dark, evil land of black magic and vampires, Transylvania (Ardeal) is a region of green hills and mountains descending gently from the Carpathians to the Hungarian Plain, dotted with towns. The vampire legends, however, have their roots in the architecture: Transylvanian buildings are tilted, jagged, and more sternly Gothic than anywhere else in Eastern Europe.

ROMANIA

CLUJ-NAPOCA

Cluj-Napoca (CLOOZH na-PO-ka) is Transylvania's unofficial capital and student center, but loses much of its vitality with the student exodus in June. Still, the large (30%) vocal Hungarian minority and lingering Hapsburg influence add flavor to the town. The 80m Gothic steeple of the Catholic **Church of St. Michael** (Biserica Sf. Mihail) pierces the skyline in **Piața Unirii. Bánffy Palace** houses the **National Museum of Art** (Muzeul Național de Artă). (Open W-Su 10am-5pm. L6000.) From Piața Unirii, head along busy Str. 21 Dec. 1989, which commemorates the victims of the 1989 revolution; or head down Bd. Eroilor to **Piața Avram Iancu,** where you'll find the newly built patriotic **statue of Avram Iancu.** For the **National Theater and Opera** (Teatrul Național și Opera Română), also in the square, buy tickets at Piața Ștefan cel Mare 14. (Tel. (064) 19 53 63. Seats L20,000, students L4000.) From Piața Unirii, take Str. Napoca to Piața Blaja, then head left up to Str. Gh. Bilașcu. There's a Japanese garden with a pond and bridge, and greenhouses with waterlilies, orchids, and palm trees at the gorgeous **Botanical Garden** (Grădină Botanica). (Open daily 9am-7pm. L4000. Useful map L3000.)

Trains (tel. (064) 19 24 75) run from Piața Mihai Viteazul to Brașov (5hr., 8 per day, L80,000); Timișoara (5hr., 8 per day, L80,000); Bucharest (7hr., 7 per day, L45,600); and Budapest (9-12hr., 4 per day, round-trip L400,000). **Buses** (tel. (064) 43 52 78) go from Str. Giordano Bruno 3 to Budapest (9hr., 4 per week, L180,000). From the train station, the bus station is a quick walk to the right and another right across a bridge. Cross the street and head down Str. Horea, which changes to Str. Gh. Doja after crossing the river; the main square, **Piața Unirii** (1km), spreads its end. The **tourist office,** on Str. Memorandumului, three blocks from Unirii, arranges **rooms.** (Tel. (064) 19 69 55. Open M-F 8am-8pm, Sa-Su 9am-12:30pm.) Take bus 3 to "Albini" to find **Hotel Onix,** Str. Albini 12. (Tel. (064) 41 40 76; fax 41 40 47. Singles L285,000; doubles L320,000. Breakfast included. Call ahead.) Follow Gh. Doja across the bridge, turn slightly left off what becomes Horea, and head up the hill to get to **Hotel Piccola Italia,** Str. Racoviță 20. (Tel. (064) 13 61 10. Singles L200,000; doubles L250,000. Call ahead.) A big indoor/outdoor **market** invades Piața Mihai Viteazul daily as long as it's light out. **Postal code:** 3400.

BRAȘOV

Established as the center of Carpathian defense, Brașov (BRA-shohv) became an international crossroads and is now an ideal starting point for excursions into the mountains. But with an exquisite city center and cable cars to nearby mountain tops, it's also a worthwhile stop in itself. **Piața Sfatului** and **Str. Republicii** are perfect for a stroll. The **History Museum** on the square used to be the city hall and courthouse; renovation should be completed by the summer of 2000. (Open Tu-Su 10am-6pm. L4000, students L1000.) Beyond the square along Str. Gh. Barițiu looms the Lutheran **Black Church** (Biserica Neagră), Romania's most celebrated Gothic church, so called because it was charred by fire in 1689. (Open M-Sa 10am-5pm. L5000.) To see the mountains without breaking a sweat, **cable cars** (telecabina) climb up Muntele Tâmpa from Aleea T. Brediceanu. Look for steep, stone steps off the main road. (L10,000, round-trip L15,000. Open M noon-6pm, Tu-F 10am-7pm, Sa-Su 10am-8pm.) To climb a road less traveled, trails on Aleea T. Brediceanu lead to the majestic **Weaver's Bastion** and other **medieval ruins.**

Frequent **trains** go to Bucharest (3-4hr., L40,000) and Cluj-Napoca (5-6hr., L70,000). Train info can be found at **CFR** on Str. Republicii. (Open M-F 8am-7pm, Sa 9am-1pm.) To get from the station to town, take bus 4 (dir: Piața Unirii; 2 rides L3000) to the main **Piața Sfatului** (10min.); descend in front of Black Church. Hotel Aro-Palace, Bd. Eroilor 9, offers free **maps** of the city. From Piața Sfatului, walk right on Str. Mureșenilor until it intersects Bd. Eroilor and turn right. **Private-room** hawkers descend on the train station; in general, they offer good rooms (US$10-15). **Hotel Postăvarul,** Politehnicii 2, shares an entrance with Hotel Corona; to get there, follow the pedestrian Str. Republicii away from Piața Sfatului and take the last right. (Tel. (068) 14 43 30. Singles L235,000; doubles L320-360,000; triples L480,000. Breakfast included.) **Postal code:** 2200.

🄴 EXCURSION FROM BRAȘOV: BRAN. It's a dark and stormy night—the perfect setting for Bran, the once home of **Vlad Țepeș Dracula** (literally Vlad the Impaler, son of Dracula), the supposed villain-hero of Bram Stoker's famed novel *Dracula*. More fiction than fact, as Prince of Wallachia, Mr. Dracula was charged with protecting the Bran pass, and had to impale some folks as part of his job. Țepeș never even lived in the **castle** at Bran; despite its lack of vampiric significance, the castle is worth a visit. (Open Tu-Su 9am-6pm. L30,000, students L20,000.) To get to Bran from Brașov, take a **trolleybus** to "Autogară 2" (officially called "Gară Bartolomeu"), where **buses** go to Bran (45min., every hr., L8000). To reach the castle, get off at the main bus stop by the sign that says "Cabana Bran Castle—500m." Then take the main road back toward Brașov and take the first right. For **tourist info,** call (068) 23 68 84. (Open daily 8am-6pm.)

TIMIȘOARA

In 1989, 105 years after becoming the first European city illuminated by electric street lamps, pleasant Timișoara (tee-mee-SHWAH-rah; pop. 327,830), Romania's westernmost city, ignited a revolution that left communism in cinders. The tourist hub revolves around **Piața Victoriei,** home to the **National Theater** (Teatrul Național) and **Opera House** (Opera Timișoara). **Metropolitan Cathedral,** across the square from the Opera, was built between 1936 and 1946 in Moldavian folk style, with a rainbow-tiled roof and 8000kg bells. An impressive **museum,** down the stairs in the front right corner of the church, downstairs displays religious artifacts. (Cathedral open 24hr. Services M-F 6pm, Su 10am and 6pm. Museum open W-Su 10am-1pm. Free.) Piața Victoriei was a gathering place for protesters during the uprising against Ceaușescu. The wooden *troika* across the street and plaques at the entrance record the sacrifices made by the young revolutionaries of December 1989. The lovely **Park of Roses** (Parcul Rozelor) is worth the walk from the center; with the Cathedral behind you, turn right, go down Bd. Loga past Str. 20 Decembrie 1989, and take any right in the next few blocks. Str. Alba Iulia travels from Piața Victoriei past shops to **Piața Libertății,** the old city center.

If you arrive by **train,** get off at **Timișoara Nord** rather than Timișoara Est. Turn left outside the station, follow Bd. Republicii to the opera, and follow Str. Alba Iulia from just to the left and up a bit to Piața Libertății; to the right is Piața Victoriei. **Trains** go from CFR Agenție de Voiaj, Piața Victoriei 2, 2nd fl. (tel. (056) 19 18 89), to Bucharest (8hr., 8 per day, L170,000) and Budapest (5hr., 2 per day, round-trip L450,000). **Colibri Travel and Tourism,** Bd. C. D. Loga 2, is near Cinema Capitol. (Tel./fax (056) 19 40 74. Open M-F 9am-5pm.) **Hotel Banatul** is on Bd. Republicii 3-5. (Tel. (056) 19 19 03; fax 19 01 30. Singles L70-120,000; doubles L120-180,000; triples L180,000. Breakfast included.) To find **Hotel Central,** Str. Lenau 6, from the Opera, take the first left off Piața Victoriei. (Tel. (056) 19 00 91. Doubles L240,000. Breakfast included.) Pick up **groceries** around **Piața Victoriei.**

ROMANIAN MOLDOVA AND BUCOVINA

Eastern Romania, which once included the neighboring Republic of Moldova, extends from the Carpathians to the Prut River. Somewhat underdeveloped today, its northern landscape rolls into green, gentle hills that contain some of Romania's most beautiful churches and villages.

SUCEAVA

Although modern Suceava (soo-chay-AH-vah) may not impress, it is a useful base for exploring the Bucovina monasteries. The ruins of the **Royal Fortress** (Cetatea de Scaun) sprawl across **Parcul Cetății,** east of Piața 22 Decembrie. Built around 1388, they remain in excellent shape. Go left on Bd. Ipătescu, right on Str. Cetății (a gravel path), down the hill, and up the path and stairs. The defenses resisted the 1476 siege of Sultan Mohammed II, conqueror of Constantinople, but not the 1675 Ottoman attacks. (Open daily 8am-9pm. L5000.) The **History Museum** (Muzeul Bucovinei Secția de Istorie), Str. Ștefan cel Mare 33, is a cut above the rest. (Open Tu-Su 8am-7pm. L6000, students L3000.) There are two **train stations** (tel. (030) 21

ROMANIA

38 97): the main **Suceava,** Str. Lorga 7, Cart. Burdujeni; and **Suceava Nord,** Str. Gării 4 Cart. Ițcani. Trains go to Bucharest (6½hr., 11 per day, L90,000); Timişoara (13½hr., 3 per day, L120,000); and Moscow (14½hr., 1 per day, L1,000,000). Buy tickets at **CFR,** Str. Bălcescu 8. (Tel. (030) 21 43 35. Open M-F 8am-8pm. International tickets 8am-2pm.) From the main station, take trolley 2 (15min., round-trip L2600) six stops to the *centru* (get off where ruins surround a stone tower); from Suceava Nord, take bus 1. The ONT **tourist office,** Str. Bălcescu 2, in the main square, arranges monastery **tours** (US$50-60 per day) and books **rooms** (US$13). (Tel. (030) 22 12 97; fax 21 47 00. Open M-F 8am-4pm.) You can also ask at **Bucovina Estur,** Str. Ștefan cel Mare 24, across the *piața* from ONT, about rooms. (Tel. (030) 22 32 59. US$12-25 per person.) **Hotel Autogară** is above the bus station. (Tel. (030) 21 60 89. L150,000 per person.) **Postal code:** 5800.

🔁 EXCURSIONS FROM SUCEAVA: BUKOVINA MONASTERIES

Bukovina's painted monasteries lie hidden among green hills and rustic farming villages. Built 500 years ago by Ștefan cel Mare and his successors, the exquisite structures serenely mix Moldavian and Byzantine architectures, Romanian soul, and Christian dogma. Getting to them on public transport can be a trial of faith; instead, try one of the tours organized by ONT (see above). Dress modestly.

VORONEȚ. Voroneț Blue (Albastru de Voroneț) is a phrase that haunts Romanian art conservationists feverishly looking for a modern version of the brilliantly colored 15th-century paint. Built in 1488, Voroneț's **frescoes** are incredible; the *Last Judgment* on the east wall is a masterpiece. (Open daily 8am-8pm. L5000, students L2500.) To reach Voroneț from Suceava, take a **train** (1¼hr., 9 per day, L13,000) or **bus** (1hr., 2 per day, L18,000) to Gura Humorului. Then turn right on Ștefan cel Mare with your back to the train station and catch the bus for Voroneț (10min., M-F 4 per day, L6000). To walk to the monastery, keep going, and after 1km go left onto Cartierul Voroneț, which goes to Voroneț (5km).

MOLDOVIȚA. Moldovița, built in 1532 and painted in 1537, is the largest of the painted monasteries, and its frescoes are among the best-preserved. Be sure to see the religious tome given by Catherine the Great. (L5000, students L1500.) From Suceava, take a **train** to Vama (1½hr., 8 per day); switch to the train to Vatra Moldoviței, 2km east of Moldovița (5th stop; 35min., 3 per day, L20,000 from Suceava).

SUCEVIȚA. Beautifully set in fortified hills, Sucevița's white walls and frescoes shine. The shade of green you see is unique to Sucevița. The west wall remains unpainted—the artist fell from the scaffolding, and his ghost prevents completion. (Open daily 6am-9pm. L5000, students L3000.) From Suceava, catch the **train** to Rădăuți (2hr., 7 per day, L1300). Turn left from the train station, follow the road right to reach the bus statio, and catch a **bus** to Sucevița (30min., M-F 4 per day until 6pm, Sa-Su 3 per day until 3pm, L15,000). The Moldovița-Rădăuți bus runs between the Sucevița and Moldovița monasteries (1hr., 1 per day, L10,000).

PUTNA. Immaculately white and beautifully simple, only one tower of Putna has survived the ravages of history, which have included fires, earthquakes, and attacks; not even the frescoes remain. The complex encompasses the marble-canopied **tomb of Ștefan cel Mare** and a **museum.** (Monastery open daily 8am-8pm; free. Museum open daily 9am-5pm. L5000, students L1500. Church open daily 9am-5pm; free.) For the scenic ride to Putna, catch direct **trains** from Suceava, 75km southeast (2½hr., 5 per day, L15,000). Exiting the platform, take a right and then a left at the first intersection and keep walking (1km).

RUSSIA (РОССИЯ)

US$1 = 26R (RUBLES)	10R = US$0.39
CDN$1 = 17R	10R = CDN$0.57
UK£1 = 41R	10R = UK£0.24
IR£1 = 35R	10R = IR£0.29
AUS$1 = 17R	10R = AUS$0.59
NZ$1 = 14R	10R = NZ$0.73
SAR1 = 4.25R	10R = SAR2.33
DM1 = 14R	10R = DM0.71

PHONE CODES | **Country code:** 7. **International dialing prefix:** 810.

Eight years after the fall of the Evil Empire, we still don't understand Russia, and it still doesn't understand us. The current paradoxes in which it exists go well beyond any of the clichés visited upon it by Western journalists. Vaguely repentant former communists man the ship of state under the standard of the market, while impoverished, outspoken pensioners long for a rosy-tinted Soviet past. Heedless of the failing provinces, cosmopolitan Moscow indiscriminately gobbles down hypercapitalism, while St. Petersburg struggles not to resemble a ghost capital. Conservative monarchists, believers in the fundamental Orthodoxy of the Russian soul, rub elbows, and none too gently, with conservative Communist-nationalists, believ-

RUSSIA

ers in Russian greatness through nuclear weapons. Neither have much affection left for the West, by whom most Russians feel profoundly betrayed.

Russia is in many ways the ideal destination for a budget traveler—inexpensive and well-served by public transportation, with hundreds of neglected monasteries, kremlins, and churches. At the same time, it is a bureaucratic nightmare that would have made Trotsky blush, and you can't exactly skip through in a day. Still, if Russia does not collapse into a group of feudal strongholds, it can offer you the world (or half the world, at least), from the capital's rousing nightlife to Lake Baikal, the world's deepest lake, and from lavishly decorated medieval cathedrals to rusted glimpses of life as it was before the Iron Curtain fell.

How much longer can you sit there without *Let's Go: Eastern Europe 2000?*

DISCOVER RUSSIA

Moscow and St. Petersburg are Russia's yin and yang. Moscow is bold, daring, overwhelming, and Eastern, grounded in the history of Russia's Bolshevik and Communist revolutionaries. St. Petersburg, on the other hand, seems oddly serene, a bastion of the West more closely tied to Peter and Catherine than Mikhail and Boris. Rivaling other great cultural capitals, **St. Petersburg** flaunts Europe's largest art collection at the Hermitage, the royal opulence of the Summer and Winter Palaces, and one of the best ballet companies in the world. Especially when the infamous White Nights descend on the city in June, the friendly, relaxed pace of St. Petersburg almost feels more Scandinavian than Russian. Relaxation, however, doesn't impede on fun; St. Pete's nightlife is the most accessible and vibrant in Russia (see p. 770). **Moscow,** on the other hand, is wilder, wackier, and most definitely Russian. From the city's graveyard of fallen statues to the ironically-named Exhibition of Soviet Economic Achievements, Moscow is haunted by its baffling past century of history. There is more to Moscow, however, than the shadows of revolution: the spires of St. Basil's are even more brilliant in real life than in photos, and the collections of the Kremlin—including the intricate Fabergé eggs—are mind-boggling. And like any good sprawling metropolis, Moscow has an insane, treacherous, wild night scene (see p. 760).

GETTING THERE AND GETTING AROUND

BY PLANE. Flying into Moscow or St. Petersburg is the easiest way to enter Russia, which boasts a not-so-reliable air system monopolized by **Aeroflot,** infamous for its disastrous safety record. Nascent alternative **Transair** services only select cities.

BY TRAIN. In a perfect world, everyone would fly into St. Petersburg or Moscow, skipping customs officials who tear apart packs and demand bribes, and avoid Belarus entirely. But it's not a perfect world, and you'll most likely find yourself on a westbound train through Belarus, in whicih case you may need a US$20-30 **transit visa,** although you can sometimes get by with a Russian one. If you wait until you reach the border, you'll likely pay more and risk missing your train. Foreigners are officially required to pay inflated Intourist prices for domestic train tickets; passports are required, and name of the buyer (printed on the ticket) will be checked against your passport on board. **Eurail** is not valid in Russia.

Train compartments come in four **classes.** The best is *lyuks* (люкс), or *2-myagky* (2-person soft; мягкий)—a place in a two-bunk cabin in the same car as second-class *kupeyny* (купейний), which has four bunks. The next class down is *platskartny* (плацкартный), an open car with 52 shorter, harder bunks. Aim for places 1-33; places 34-37 are next to the unnaturally foul bathroom, while places 38-52 are on the side of the car and get horribly hot during the summer. Women traveling alone can try to buy out a *lyuks* compartment for security, or can travel *platskartny* with the regular folk and depend on the crowds to shame would-be harassers into silence. *Platskartny* is also a good idea on the theft-ridden St. Petersburg-Moscow line, as you are less likely to be targeted there. This logic can only be taken so far; the *obshchy* class may be devoid of crooks, but you'll be traveling alongside livestock. All first- and second-class cars are equipped with samovars that dispense scalding water for soups, hot cocoa, and coffee. *Elektrichka* (commuter rail; marked on signs as пригородные поезда; *prigorodnye poezda*) has its own platforms at each station; buy tickets at the *kassa*. These trains are often packed, especially on weekends, so expect to stand.

BY BUS. Finnord buses leave for St. Petersburg four times per day from Lahti, Finland, and are cheaper than trains. Buses, slightly less expensive and less crowded than trains, are your best bet for for shorter distances. On the Hungarian **Ikarus** buses, you'll get seated in a reclining chair and can store luggage for free.

BY CAR AND BY THUMB. Like much else in Russia, **driving** is a hassle. Motorists must secure an itinerary card and a special "Autotourist" visa when securing their invitation; they are also limited to driving 300 mi. per day. Russian drivers are notoriously reckless and dangerous. Road conditions are poor, particularly at night. Gas stations, oil, antifreeze, and spare parts are all extremely rare. And the only emergency roadside help is from police, notoriously unhelpful toward foreigners (and particularly fond of Western currency). If you decide to drive despite these hassles, the speed limit in residential areas is 60km per hr., and on expressways 110km per hr. Hailing a **taxi** is indistinguishable from **hitchhiking,** and should be treated with equal caution. Most drivers who stop will be private citizens trying to make a little extra cash (despite the recent restriction on this technically illegal activity). Those seeking rides stand off the curb and hold out a hand into the street, palm down; when a car stops, riders tell the driver the destination before getting in; he will either refuse the destination altogether or ask *Skolko?* (How much?), leading to protracted negotiations. Never get into a car that has more than one person in it. While this informal system might seem dicey, officially labeled taxis can also be expensive and dangerous, with reports of kidnappings and muggings.

ESSENTIALS

DOCUMENTS AND FORMALITIES. Citizens of Australia, Canada, Ireland, New Zealand, South Africa, the UK, and the US all require a **visa** to enter Russia; visas require an **invitation** stating the traveler's itinerary and dates of travel. They are inherently difficult to get without a Russian connection. Travel agencies that advertise discounted tickets to Russia also often provide visas. **Info Travel,** 387 Harvard St, Brookline, MA 02146 (tel. (617) 566-2197; email infostudy@aol.com), provides invitations and visas to Russia from US$145. A larger but significantly more expensive operation is **Russia House,** 1800 Connecticut Ave NW, Washington, DC 20009 (US tel. (202) 986-6010), and 17 Leningradsky Prospekt, Moscow 125040 (tel. (095) 250 01 43). Invitations and visas are available at fairly exorbitant prices (to Russia from US$275; Ukraine and Belarus US$175). **Traveler's Guest House,** Bolshaya Pereyaslavskaya 50, 10th fl., 129401 Moscow, Russia (tel. (095) 971 40 59; email tgh@glas.apc.org), arranges visa invitations, will register you once you arrive, makes reservations, and gets train tickets. **Families Association (HOFA),** 5-25 Tavricheskaya, 193015 St. Petersburg, Russia (tel./fax (81) 22 75 19 92; e-mail hofa@usa.net) arranges homestays in more than 20 cities of the former Soviet Union and provides visa invitations for HOFA guests to Russia, Ukraine, and Belarus (singles US$30; doubles US$50).

If you already have an invitation, apply for the **visa** in person or by mail at a Russian embassy or consulate (single-entry, 60-day US$70 for 2-week service, US$80 for 1-week service, US$110 for 3-business-day service; double-entry visas US$105, US$125, US$145). If you have even tentative plans to visit a city, have it put on your visa. Many hotels will **register your visa** for you on arrival, as should the organizations listed above. However, they can only do that if you fly into a city where they are represented. If you enter the country elsewhere, you'll have to climb into the seventh circle of bureaucratic hell known is the central OVIR (ОВИР) office (in Moscow called UVIR—УВИР) to register. OVIR is also where you should attempt to extend your visa, but it's far better to get a visa for longer than you plan to stay.

RUSSIA

Russian Embassies at Home: Australia, 78 Canberra Ave, Griffith ACT 2603 Canberra (tel. (06) 295 90 33; fax 295 18 47); **Canada,** 285 Charlotte St, Ottawa, ON K1N 8L5 (tel. (613) 235-4341; fax 236-6342; visa tel. (613) 236-7220); **Ireland,** 186 Orwell Rd, Dublin 14 (tel. (01) 492 35 25; fax 269 83 09); **New Zealand,** 57 Messines Rd, Karori, Wellington (tel. (04) 476 61 13; fax 476 38 43); **South Africa,** Butano Building, 316 Brooks St, Menlo Park, Pretoria; P.O. Box 6743, Pretoria (tel. (012) 362 13 37; fax 362 01 16); **UK,** 6-7 Kensington Palace Gdns, London W84 QP (tel. (020) 72 29 36 28; fax 77 27 86 25); **US** (consular division), 2641 Tunlaw Rd NW, Washington, DC 20007 (tel. (202) 939-8907 or (202) 939-8913; fax (202) 483-7579).

Foreign Embassies in Russia: All embassies are located in **Moscow** (see p. 760) many consulates are also located in **St. Petersburg** (see p. 770).

Customs: Customs enforcement is arbitrary and unpredictable; one day they'll tear your pack apart, the next they'll just nod and dismiss you. At the border, politely answer the officials, but *do not* offer any information they don't specifically ask for. Upon your entrance to the country, you'll be given a **Customs Declaration Form** to declare all your valuables and foreign currency; don't lose it. Everything listed on the customs form must be on you when you leave the country. You may not export works of art, icons, old samovars (pre-electric models), or anything published before 1945. Keep receipts for any expensive or antique-looking souvenirs. You cannot bring rubles into or out of the country.

TOURIST OFFICES. Russian tourist centers exist to make money on tours and tickets, not to help confused tourists, so don't expect maps or even common courtesy. Yet trying won't hurt, and apologetic inquiries can yield unexpected results.

MONEY. The **ruble** was redenominated in 1998, losing three zeros. The old currency is gradually being fazed out, although some prices are still quoted in thousands. Government regulations require that you show your passport when you exchange money. Most **currency exchange** (*Obmen Valyuty;* Обмен Валюты) places will exchange US dollars and Deutschmarks, and some also accept French francs and British pounds. **Do not exchange money on the street.** Banks offer the best combination of good rates and security. **ATMs** (*bankomat;* банкомат) linked to all major networks and credit cards can be found all over most cities, but are highly unreliable. Big establishments now accept major **credit cards.** Main branches of banks will usually accept **traveler's checks** and grant cash advances on credit cards, most often Visa. Be aware that most establishments do not accept crumpled, torn, or written-on bills of any denomination. Russians are also wary of the old US$100 bills; bring the new Benjamins if you bring any at all. In St. Petersburg and Moscow (but nowhere else) a 5-10% **tip** is becoming customary. In both cities, expect to pay US$15-20 for a hostel bed and US$5-10 for restaurant meals

COMMUNICATION

Post: There is neither rhyme nor reason to Russia's **mail service.** Delivery can take anywhere from two weeks to eternity. **Poste Restante** will rarely, if ever, reach you in Russia. A more reliable option for **AmEx** card- and traveler's check-holders is to receive letters at AmEx travel service bureaus. Airmail **letters** to Australia, Canada, New Zealand, South Africa, the UK, and the US cost 7R; postcards cost 5R. *Zakaznoe* (special delivery; заказное) costs 8R and should take only 10 days.

Telephone: Your best bet in Russia, even for local calls, is a **phone card.** Dial 8, wait for the tone, then dial the city code. Direct **international calls** can be made from telephone offices and hotel rooms: dial 8, wait for the tone, then dial 10 and the country code. You cannot call collect, unless you use AT&T service (through the number above), which will cost your party dearly (to the US 1st min. US$8, each additional min. US$2.78). Prices for international calls vary greatly from city to city, from US$1.50 per min. (to North America) up to US$4.17. To make calls from a telephone office, buy tokens or phone cards, or simply prepay your calls (depending on the city) and use the *mezhdugorodnye* phones; be sure to press the *otvet* (reply; ответ) button when your party answers or you won't be heard. If there are no automatic phones, you must pay for your call at the counter and have it dialed for you by the operator. Calling into the country is much less frustrating.

RUSSIA

International direct dial numbers include: **AT&T,** 755 50 42 in Moscow, 325 50 42 in St. Petersburg; **Sprint,** 747 33 24 in Moscow; **Canada Direct,** 755 50 45 in Moscow, 747 33 25 in St. Petersburg; **BT Direct,** 810 800 110 10 44. When calling from another city in Russia, dial 8-095 or 8-812 before these codes; you pay for the phone call to Moscow or St. Petersburg in addition to the international connection. **Fire,** tel. 01. **Police,** tel. 02. **Ambulance,** tel. 03. Note that failure to register Global Positioning Systems (G.P.S.), cellular phones, and other radio transmission devices can result in search, seizure, and arrest; for more info, see http://travel.state.gov/travel_warnings.html.

Language: Take some time to familiarize yourself with the **Cyrillic** alphabet (see p. 949). It's not as difficult as it looks and will make getting around and getting by immeasurably easier. Once you get the hang of the alphabet, you can pronounce just about any Russian word, though you will probably sound like an idiot. Although more and more people are speaking **English** in Russia, come equipped with at least a few helpful Russian phrases.

HEALTH AND SAFETY. Reports of **crime** against foreigners are on the rise, particularly in Moscow and St. Petersburg. Although it is hard to look Russian, try not to flaunt your true nationality. Your trip will be that much more pleasant if you never have to file a crime report with the local *militsia*, who will not speak English and will not help you. Reports of mafia warfare are scaring off tourists, but unless you bring a shop for them to blow up, you are unlikely to be a target. After the recent eruption of violence in the Northern Caucasus, the Dagestan and Chechnyan regions of Russia are best avoided. Water in much of Russia is drinkable in small doses, but not in Moscow and St. Petersburg; boil it to be safe. A gamma globulin shot will lower your risk of hepatitis A (see p. 29). Check the expiration date before buying any packaged snack. For **medical emergencies,** either leave the country or go to the American Medical Centers in St. Petersburg or Moscow; these clinics have American-born and trained doctors and speak English.

ACCOMMODATIONS. The only **hostels** in Russia are in St. Petersburg and Moscow, and even those average US$18 per night. Reserve well in advance, especially in summer. Hotels offer several classes of rooms. "Lux," usually two-room doubles with TV, phone, fridge, and bath, are the most expensive. "Polu-lux" rooms are singles or doubles with TV, phone, and bath. Rooms with bath and no TV, when they exist, are cheaper. The lowest priced rooms are *bez udobstv* (без удобств), which means one room with a sink. Expect to pay 150-250R for a single in a budget hotel. As a rule, only cash is accepted as payment. In many hotels, hot water—sometimes all water—is turned on only a few hours per day. **University dorms** are a cheap alternative; some accept foreign students for US$5-10 per night. The rooms are liveable, but don't expect sparkling bathrooms or reliable hot water. Make arrangements with an institute from home. **Homestays,** often arranged through a tourist office, are often the cheapest (50-100R per night) and best option in the countryside.

FOOD AND DRINK. Russian cuisine is a medley of dishes both delectable and disgusting; tasty borscht can come in the same meal as a bit of *salo* (pig fat). As a rule, the quality of both the ingredients and the preparation improves vastly the farther south you travel. If you are stuck in the culinary wasteland of the upper latitudes, look for a Georgian or Azerbaijani restaurant for respite. The largest meal of the day, *obed* (lunch; обед), is eaten at midday. Ordering a number of *zakuski* (Russified *tapas;* закуски) instead of a main dish can save money and add variety. One can find basic Russian food on the street, at stores, or at the market. **Dietas** (диета) sell goods for people on special diets (such as diabetics); **produkty** (продукты) and **gastronoms** (гастроном) offer a variety of meats, cheeses, breads, and packaged goods. The larger **universam** (универсам) simulates a supermarket with its wide variety. The **market** (*rynok;* рынок) sells abundant fruits and vegetables, meat, fresh milk, butter, honey, and cheese. Wash and dry everything before you eat it— Russian farmers use pesticides as if they were going out of style. The **kiosks** found in every town act as mini-convenience stores, selling soda, juice, candy bars, and cookies; point to what you want. On the streets, you'll see a lot of s*hashlyki* (barbequed meat on a stick; шашлыки) and *kvas* (квас), an alcoholic dark-brown drink.

RUSSIA

Zolotoye koltso, *Russkaya*, and *Zubrovka* are the best vodkas; the much-touted *Stolichnaya* is mostly made for export. *Moskovskaya* is another known name. Among local beers, *Baltika* (Балтика) is the most popular and arguably the best.

Vendors do not provide **bags** for merchandise. You can usually buy plastic bags in stores, at markets, and on the streets, but bring your own to be safe. In stores, decide what you want, then go to a *kassa* and tell the person there the item, the price, and the *otdyel* (department; отдел) from which you are buying. The person will take your money and give you a receipt. You then take the receipt back to the *otdyel*, give it to the person working there, and they will give you what you want.

LOCAL FACTS

Time: Both St. Petersburg and Moscow are 3hr. ahead of Greenwich Mean Time (GMT; see p. 49). The rest of Western Russia is 2hr. ahead of GMT.

Climate: Both St. Petersburg and Moscow suffer excrutiatingly cold winters and sweltering summers. Spring and autumn are the best times to visit Moscow; to catch a glimpse of St. Petersburg's infamous White Nights, visit in June.

Hours: Most establishments, even train ticket offices, close for a lunch break sometime between noon and 3pm. Places tend to close at least 30 minutes earlier than they should, if they choose to open at all. "24-hour" stores often take a lunch or "technical" break and 1 day off each week.

Holidays: New Year's Day (Jan. 1); Orthodox Christmas (Jan. 7); Defenders of the Motherland (Feb. 23); International Women's Day (Mar. 8); Orthodox Easter (Apr. 11); Labor Day (May 1-2); Victory Day (May 9); Independence Day (June 12); and Great October Socialist Revolution (Nov. 7).

Festivals: In the 3rd week of June, when the sun barely touches the horizon, St. Petersburg holds a series of outdoor evening concerts as part of the **White Nights Festival.**

MOSCOW (МОСКВА)

Moscow has an audacity of place—a persistent sense of itself on the cusp of world history. Riding the crest of the recent bubble economy has returned the city to its 19th-century magnificence—Stalin's massive edifices now stand out like monsterland anachronisms amidst the restored pink-and-green of the new old city. If one keeps to the 16th-century sidestreets, it is even possible to glimpse what Napoleon saw with the city at his feet: golden domes sparkling over the great mass of Asia. But Moscow's circles, emanating from the Kremlin like the early Muscovite conquests and spiraling into a crumbling wasteland on the peripheries, mirror the condition of its residents: living on the margins of a system they don't understand and never authorized, flinging themselves into the city center only to return drab and wasted to their concrete blocks. Post-ideological, post-apocalyptic, post-whatever-the-hell-you-want, Moscow is in your face. Brutal, tiring, and not as unsafe as it is maddening, Moscow at the millennium is most definitely the end of the world.

▐▀ GETTING THERE AND GETTING AROUND

Flights: International flights arrive at **Sheremetyevo-2** (Шереметьево-2; tel. 956 46 66). Vans (look for the "автолайн" sign in front) run to M2: Rechnoy Vokzal (20min., every 10min. 7am-10pm, 10R). Or take bus 551 to M2: Rechnoy Vokzal (Речной Вокзал) or bus 517 to M7: Planyornaya (Планёрная); 10R. Most flights within the former USSR fly out of **Vnukovo** (Внуково; tel. 436 21 09), **Bikovo** (Быково; tel. 558 47 38), **Domodedovo** (Домодедово; tel. 323 85 65), or **Sheremetyevo-1** (tel. 578 23 72). Buy tickets at the *kassa* (касса) at the **Central Airport Station** (Tsentralny Aerovokzal; Центральный Аэровокзал), 2 stops on tram 23 or trolley 12 or 70 from M2: Aeroport. Express bus schedules posted outside the station. Taxis to the center will try to rip you off—in June 1999 you could bargain down to US$25.

Trains: Buying tickets in Russia can be enormously frustrating. If you don't speak Russian, you may want to buy through **Intourist** or a hotel. Russian speakers should buy tickets for the *elektrichka* (local trains) at the *prigorodniye kassa* (local ticket booths; пригородная касса) in each station. Tickets for longer trips can be purchased at the **Central Train**

Moscow Center

ACCOMMODATIONS

A Traveller's Guest House
B Galina's Flat
C American Academy of
   Foreign Languages
D Prakash Guesthouse

SEE COLOR INSERTS FOR MORE MOSCOW MAPS

TURGENEVSKAYA M
TO A (1.25km)
CHISTYE PRUDY M
TO B (800m)
ul. Myasnitskaya
Belarus
ul. Maroseyka
Moscow Choral Synagogue
KITAI-GOROD M
KITAI-GOROD M
kit. proezd
ul. Bol. Lubyanka
Mayakovsky Museum
LUBYANKA M
Lubyansky proezd
Hotel Rossiya
Moskvoretc. nab.
TO C (3km)
Moskovsky Gorodskoy Bureau Ekskursy
ul. Rozhdestvenka
KUZNETSKI MOST M
LUBYANKA M
PL. REVOLYUTSII
Ilinka ul.
St. Basil's (Pokrovsky Soboa)
Lenin's Tomb
reka Moskva
United Kingdom
Sofiykaya nab.
Kremlevskaya nab.
ul. Petrovska
Bolshoy Teatr
Kuznetsky Most
ul. Pushechnaya
Teatral Nyi pr.
PL. REVOLYUTSII M
Kazan Cathedral
RED SQ. GUM (KRASNAYA PL.)
Belltower
Assumption Cathedral
Archangel Cathedral
Stanislavsky Museum-House
TEATRALNAYA M
State Historical Museum
Lenin Museum
KREMLIN
Patriarch's Palace
Annunciation Cathedral
Armory Museum
ul. Pushkinskaya
OKHOTNY RYAD M
Central Post Office
Intourist
Manege
ul. Mokhovaya
ALEXANDROVSKI SAD M
Alexander Gardens (Aleksandrovsky Sad)
BIBLIOTEKA IM. LENINA M
BOROVITSKAYA M
TO D (8km)
Tverskoy bul.
PUSHKINSKAYA/TVERSKAYA M
ul. Bol. Bronnaya
Leontevsky per.
ul. Tverskaya
ul. Mal. Nikitsky
ul. Znamenka
ARBATSKAYA M
ARBATSKAYA M
Pushkin Museum of Fine Arts
Central Museum of the Revolution (Muzey Revolyutsii)
Ukraine
Muzey Narodnovo Iskusstva
Gogol Museum
Nikitsky bul.
American Express
Patriarch's Pond (Patriarshy Prud)
Gorky's Apartment
A. Tolstoy Museum-Apartment
Lermontov House-Museum
ul. Maj. Molchanovk
Staroconyushenny per.
Canada
Mal. Kozikhinsky per.
Chekhov's House Museum
Sadovaya Kudrinskaya bul.
ul. Spiridonova
Nikitsky bul.
ul. Bol. Nikitsky
New Zealand
ul. Povarskaya
Borisoglebsky per.
Lithuania
Mongolia
Novy Arbat
Arbat
Herzen Museum
THE ARBAT
ul. Mal. Bronnaya
Zoo
Gruzinskaya
BARRIKADNAYA M
KRASNOPRESNENSKAYA M
ul. Bol. Konjuskovskaya
ul. Konjuskovskaya
TO WHITE HOUSE (150m)
United States
Novinsky bul.
SMOLENSKAYA M
SMOLENSKAYA M

0   200 yards
0   200 meters

N

RUSSIA

Agency (Tsentralnoe Zheleznodorozhnoe Agenstvo; Центральное Железнодорожное Агенство), to the right of Yaroslavsky Vokzal. M4: Komsomolskaya. Use window 10 or 11. Complete schedules are posted to the left. *Kassa* open daily 8am-1pm and 2-7pm. After hours, try the 24-hour **Intourist** *kassa* on the 2nd floor of Leningradsky Vokzal (entrance 3, windows 19 and 20). The main domestic and international ticket office for foreigners is the **Main Ticket Office** (Intourtrans Glavnoe Zheleznodorozhnoe Agenstvo; Главное Железнодорожное Агенство), Maly Kharitonevsky per. 6 (Малый Харитоневский; tel. 262 06 04). M5: Turgenevskaya. Take a right off ul. Myasnitskaya (Мясницкая) and walk into the connected building on the right. Open daily 8am-1pm and 2-7pm. Moscow's 9 train stations are arranged around the metro's circle line (M4). **Leningradsky Vokzal** (Ленинградский), Komsomolskaya pl. 3. M1,4: Komsomolskaya. To: **St. Petersburg. Kazansky Vokzal** (Казанский), Komsomolskaya pl. 2, opposite Leningradsky Vokzal, serves the east and southeast. **Yaroslavsky Vokzal** (Ярославский), Komsomolskaya pl. 5, is the starting point for the **Trans-Siberian Railroad. Paveletsky Vokzal** (Павелецкий), Paveletskaya pl. 1, serves the Crimea and eastern Ukraine. **Rizhsky Vokzal** (Рижский) Rizhkaya pl. 79/3. To: **Rīga** (16hr.) and Estonia. **Belorussky Vokzal** (Белорусский), pl. Tverskaya Zastava. To: **Warsaw** (24hr.) and **Minsk** (9-13hr.). **Kievsky Vokzal** (Киевский), pl. Kievskovo Vokzala, sends trains to Bulgaria, Romania, Slovakia, and **Kiev** (15-17hr., US$20-30).

Public Transportation: The **Metro** is large and efficient—a masterpiece of Stalinist urban planning. There are 9 Metro lines; in *Let's Go*, "M1" indicates a stop on line 1, "M1,6" indicates a stop served by lines 1 and 6, etc. Runs daily 6am-1am. Passages between lines or stations are indicated by signs of a man walking up stairs; individual exit signs indicate street names. A station serving more than 1 line may have more than 1 name. Buy token-cards (4R) from the *kassa* inside stations. Consult the **metro maps** at the end of this book. **Bus** and **trolley** tickets are available in gray kiosks labeled "проездные билеты" and from the driver (4R). Punch your ticket when you get on, or risk a 10R fine.

Taxis: Taxi stands have a round sign with a green "T." If you don't speak Russian, you'll get ripped off, particularly if you don't know Moscow. Ask around for the going rate and agree on a price before you get in. Be sure the meter is turned on.

🛈 ORIENTATION AND PRACTICAL INFORMATION

A series of concentric rings radiates outward from the **Kremlin** (Kreml; Кремль). The outermost **Moscow Ring Road** marks the city limits, but most sights lie within the **Garden Ring** (Sadovoe Koltso; Садовое Кольцо). Main shopping streets include **Novy Arbat** (Новый Арбат), which runs west parallel to the Metro's blue lines, and **Ul. Tverskaya** (Тверская), which extends north along the green line. Familiarize yourself with the Cyrillic alphabet and orient yourself by the Metro (which stops within 15min. of anywhere in the city). **Slavyanka** (Славянка), ul. Kuznetsky most 9, sells extensive city maps (20R) in English. Other maps are likely to be outdated; check the date of publication. Also refer to the **color maps** at the back of this book.

TOURIST, FINANCIAL, AND LOCAL SERVICES

Tourist Offices: Intourservice Central Excursion Bureau, Nikitsky per. 4a (Никитский; tel. 203 75 85; fax 200 12 43). M1: Okhotny Ryad. **Intourist,** ul. Mokhovaya 13 (Моховая; tel. 292 12 78). Arranges English-language tours.

Budget Travel: Student Travel Agency Russia (STAR), ul. Baltiyskaya 9, 3rd fl. (чл. Ьелтийская; tel. 797 95 55). M2: Sokol. Open M-F 10am-6pm, Sa 11am-4pm.

Embassies: Most open M-F 9 or 9:30am-noon or 1pm; some also 1-5 or 6pm. **Australia,** Kropotkinsky per. 13 (Кропоткинский; tel. 956 60 70; fax 956 61 70). M3: Smolenskaya. **Belarus,** ul. Maroseyka 17/6 (Маросейка; tel. 923 38 38). **Canada,** Starokonyushenny per. 23 (Староконюшенный; tel. 956 66 66; fax 232 99 48). M1: Kropotkinskaya. **China** consular section, ul. Druzhby 6 (Дружбы; tel. 143 15 40). **Estonia** consular section, Kalzhny per. 8 (Калжний; tel. 290 31 78). M3: Arbatskaya. **Ireland,** Grokholsky per. 5 (Грохольский; tel. 742 09 07; fax 975 20 66). M4,5: Prospekt Mira. **Lithuania** consular section, Borisoglebsky per. 10 (Борисоглебский; tel. 291 15 01). M3: Arbatskaya. **Mongolia** consular section, Spasopeskovsky per. 711 (Спасолесковский; tel. 241 15 48). **New Zealand,** ul. Povarskaya 44 (Поварская; tel.

WE BRAKE FOR NO ONE Moscow drivers are notorious—unbelievably fast and blissfully ignorant of the gentle art of yielding to pedestrians. Should you dare venture from your curbside security onto the blacktop, they will honk, yell, and gesticulate obscenely, but they will not touch their brakes. A single day on the streets of Moscow will convince you that the subterranean underpasses are there out of dire necessity. Even when there's a light, the "walk" sign is only illuminated just long enough to allow a mad dash across the road; whereas crosswalks are islands of safety in many countries, here they're not much more than zebra lines on the road. The only time that cars *might* stop for you would be if you're female, alone, and out at night—and that's only because they think you're a prostitute. On the roads of Moscow, there are pedestrians and there are drivers. And pedestrians are most decidedly not wanted.

956 35 79; fax 956 35 83). M4,6: Krasnopresnenskaya. Open M-F 9am-5:30pm. **South Africa,** Bolshoy Strochinovsky per. 22/25 (Большой Строчиновский; tel. 230 68 69; fax 230 68 65). **UK,** Sofiyskaya nab. 14 (Софийская; tel. 956 72 00; fax 956 74 20). M1,3,8: Borovitskaya. **Ukraine,** Leontevsky per. 18 (Леонтьевский; visa tel. 229 69 22), off ul. Tverskaya. M3: Tverskaya. **US,** Novinsky 19/23 (Новинский; tel. 252 24 50; emergency tel. 230 20 01; fax 956 42 61). M6: Krasnopresnenskaya.

Currency Exchange: *Moscow Express Directory,* free in most luxury hotels, lists places to buy and cash traveler's checks. Usually only main branches of large banks will change traveler's checks or issue cash advances. Nearly every bank and hotel has an **ATM;** particularly reliable is the one in the lobby of the **Gostinitsa Intourist Hotel.**

American Express: ul. Sadovaya-Kudrinskaya 21a, Moscow 103001 (Садовая-Кудринская; tel. 755 90 24; fax 755 90 04). M2: Mayakovskaya; cross the street/parking lot ahead and turn left on Bolshaya Sadovaya (Большая Садовая), which becomes Sadovaya-Kudrinskaya. Cashes traveler's checks. Mail held. Open M-F 9am-5pm, Sa 10am-2pm. **AmEx ATM** in lobby (24hr.).

English Bookstores: Angliyskaya Kniga (Английская Книга), ul. Kuznetsky most 18 (tel. 928 20 21). M6: Kuznetsky most. Open M-F 10am-7pm, Sa 10am-6pm.

Laundromat: California Cleaners, Leninsky pr. 111/3 (tel. 956 52 84), and 12 other locations around Moscow. For free pick-up and delivery, call 497 00 05. US$2 per kg.

EMERGENCY AND COMMUNICATIONS

Emergencies: Ambulance, tel. 03. **Fire,** tel. 01. **Police,** tel. 02. Call your embassy for passport and visa problems. Call 299 11 80 to report offenses *by* the police.

Pharmacies: Leningradsky pr. 74 (Ленинградский; tel. 151 45 70). M2: Sokol. Kutuzovsky pr. 14 (Кутузовский; tel. 243 16 01). M3: Kutuzovskaya. Both open 24hr.

Medical Assistance: American Medical Center, Vtoroy Tverskoy-Yamskoy per. 10 (2-ой Тверской-Ямской; tel. 956 33 66; fax 956 23 06). M2: Mayakovskaya. US$215 per visit. Open M-F 8am-8pm, Sa 9am-5pm; 24hr. for emergencies, though it'll cost more.

Internet Access: Internet Chevignon Café, Stoleshnikov per. 14, 2nd fl. (Столэшніков пзр; tel. 733 92 06). M2: Tverskaya; walk downhill on Tverskaya, turn left onto Stoleshnikov, and enter through the Levi's shop. One drink (29R) buys 30min. of access. Open daily noon-midnight. **Partiya Internet Café** (Партия), Volgogradsky pr. 1 (Волгоградский). M6: Proletarskaya. US$3 per hr. Open daily 10am-8pm.

Telephones: Moscow Central Telegraph (see **Post Offices** below). To **call abroad,** go to the 2nd hall with telephones. Collect and calling card calls not available. Prepay at the counter for the amount of time you expect to talk. Use the *mezhdunarodnye telefony* (international telephone cabinets; международные телефоны). To Europe US$1-1.50 per min.; to the US and Australia US$2-3 per min. Open 24hr. **Local calls** require new phonecards, available at some Metro stops and kiosks.

Post Offices: Moscow Central Telegraph, ul. Tverskaya 7, uphill from the Kremlin. M1: Okhotny Ryad. **International mail** service open M-F 8am-2pm and 3-9pm, Sa 8am-2pm and 3-7pm, Su 9am-2pm and 3-7pm. Address mail to be held: Москва **103009,** До востребования (POSTE RESTANTE), SPRINGER, Jerry. **Faxes** and **telegrams** at window 1. **Letters** at window 32. Open daily 8am-10pm. **Gostinitsa Intourist Hotel post office,** ul.

Tverskaya 3/5. Address mail to be held: LENIN, Vladimir, До востребования, К-600, Гостиница Интурист, ул7 Тверская 3/5, Москва. Open M-F 9am-noon and 1-6pm. Bring unwrapped **packages** you want to send to the Intourist post office or to Myasnitskaya 26 (Мясницкая).

PHONE CODE	City code: 095. From outside Russia, dial int'l dialing prefix (see inside back cover) + 7 + 95 + local number.

■ ACCOMMODATIONS

Just about everything can be found in Moscow these days—except budget accommodations. Call a week ahead in summer. Women standing outside major rail stations rent **private rooms** (*sdayu komnatu*; сдаю комнату) or **apartments** (*sdayu kvartiru*; сдаю квартиру) for as low as 200-250R per night—haggle haggle haggle.

Traveller's Guest House, ul. Bolshaya Pereyaslavskaya 50, 10th fl. (Большая Переяслаская; tel. 971 40 59; fax 280 76 86; email tgh@glas.apc.org). M4,5: Prospekt Mira (Проспект Мира). Walk 10min. north along pr. Mira, take the 3rd right on Banny per. (Банный), and turn left at the end of the street; it's the white, 12-story building across the street. The only hostel-like accommodation in Moscow—*the* place to meet other budget travelers and get travel advice. Fluent English, spotless rooms, and kitchen facilities. Dorms US$18; singles US$36; doubles US$48-54. Laundry US$2. Airport pick-up and drop-off US$40. Russian **visa invitations** US$40. Reserve a week ahead; retain copies of all reservation forms and receipts. Check-out 11am. V, MC.

Galina's Flat, ul. Chaplygina 8, #35, 5th fl. (Чаплыгина; tel. 921 60 38). M1: Chistye Prudy; take bul. Chistoprudny (Чистопрудный), then the 1st left on Kharitonevsky per. (Харитоньевский), the 2nd right on Chaplygina, go through the courtyard, turn right, enter by the "Уникум" sign, and it's upstairs on the right. Relaxed, homey, welcoming digs. Dorm US$9; bed in a double US$11. Hot showers. Kitchen facilities. Call ahead.

American Academy of Foreign Languages, ul. Bolshaya Cheryomushinskaya 17a (Большая Черёмушинская; tel. 129 43 00; fax 123 15 00). M5: Akademicheskaya (Академическая); turn left at the Ho Chi Minh statue, walk 15min. on ul. Dmitriya Ulyanova (Дмитрия Ульянова), and turn left at the trolley tracks on Bolshaya Cheryomushinskaya. Clean rooms. Bed in a triple 100R; in a quad 80R. 2-room "lux" suites 500R for a single; 550R for a double. Half-lux suites 450R. 25% off if you call ahead.

Prakash Guesthouse, ul. Profsoyuznaya 83, kor. 1 (2nd entrance), 3rd fl., (Профсоюзная; tel. 334 82 01; fax 334 25 98; email prakash@matrix.ru). M5: Belyaevo (Беляево); take the exit nearest the last car, go all the way to the right of the tunnel, exit from the last stairway on the left, and it's the 4th building on your right. Enter from the 3rd entrance, right of the main entrance and to the rear of the building; the office is on the 2nd fl. Call ahead and they'll meet you at the Metro. Friendly if remote lodgings catering (not exclusively) to Indian guests. Arranges train tickets to St. Petersburg. All rooms with shower, toilet, and phone. Dorm US$15; singles US$30; doubles US$40. Breakfast US$6. Free **email.** Reception 7am-11pm. V, MC.

○ FOOD

Avoid the tourist-targeted venues and follow the natives to local eateries for home-cooked meals at wallet-friendly prices. Many restaurants list prices in US$ to avoid having to change their menus to keep up with inflation, but payment is usually in rubles. Scattered bread stands, increasingly rare in central Moscow but quite common at outdoor market areas, are still an excellent choice for sweet and savory pies (3-5R). Moscow's first **McDonald's** (Макдоналдс—not that you need the Cyrillic, ye seeker of the Golden Arches) continues the steady homogenization of world culture at ul. Bolshaya Bronnaya 29 (Большая Бронная; M6: Pushkinskaya).

NEAR THE KREMLIN (OFF UL. TVERSKAYA AND THE ARBAT)

Praga, Arbat 2 (tel. 290 31 37), near the corner of Novy Arbat. M3: Arbatskaya. Home of the famous "Praga" chocolate torte sold all over Moscow. The bakery next door sells delectable pastries and mini-cakes for a mere 5R each. Open daily 9am-8pm.

Moscow Bombay, Glinishchevsky per. 3 (Глинищевский; tel. 292 97 31). M6: Pushkin-skaya; walk 5min. downhill on Tverskaya and turn left on Glinishchevsky. English menu with pages of Indian and European specialties. Entrees around US$9. Students 10% off. Reservations recommended. Open daily noon-midnight. V, MC.

Evropeiskoe Bistro (Европейское Бистро), Arbat 16 (tel. 291 71 61), with an orange-and-blue awning. Cafeteria-style "Eurofood"—Russian cuisine with a snazzy name. Patio seating facilitates people-watching. Meals 150-200R. Open daily 8am-midnight.

ELSEWHERE IN MOSCOW

Guria's, Komsomolsky pr. 7/3 (Комсомольский; tel. 246 03 78), on the corner of ul. Frunze. M1,4: Park Kultury. Superb, cheap Georgian fare. Cabbage leaves stuffed with rice and meat (40R) are a must. Entrees 30-50R. Open daily noon-11pm.

Café Margarita (Кафе Маргарита), ul. Malaya Bronnaya 28 (tel. 299 65 34). M2: Maya-kovskaya; take a left on Bolshaya Sadovaya and another on Malaya Bronnaya. The house specialty is tomatoes stuffed with garlic and cheese. Hearty Russian meals 400R. Live piano music after 7pm (cover 15R). Open daily 1pm-midnight.

Zaydi i poprobuy (Зайди и попробуй), pr. Mira 124 (Мира; tel./fax 286 81 65). M5: Rizhs-kaya. Entrance on Malaya Moskovskaya ul. (Малая Московская). Cheap, tasty Russian cuisine. Meals around 150R. Open daily 11am-11:30pm.

Mama Zoya's, Sechenovsky per. 8 (Сеченовский; tel. 202 04 05). M1: Kropotkinskaya; walk 4 blocks down ul. Ostozhenka (Остроженка), turn right on Sechenovsky, turn right at the Mama Zoya's sign, and head to the basement in back. Home-style Georgian feasts with traditional live music. Entrees 35-55R. Open daily 11am-midnight.

MARKETS AND SUPERMARKETS

Your best bet for fresh fruits and veggies is a market—Georgians, Armenians, Uzbeks, and peasants cart their finest produce into the city daily. Remember to wash fruit and vegetables with bottled water. The **Central Market** (M8: Tsvetnoy Bulvar), next to the Old Circus, has reopened after its recent reconstruction. The alternative is the **Rizhsky Market** (M5: Rizhskaya). Impromptu markets (usually 10am-8pm), where produce is sold by the kg (bring your own bag), spring up around metro stations; try "Turgenevskaya," "Kuznetsky Most," "Aeroport," "Bauman-skaya," and between "Novoslobodskaya" and "Mendeleevskaya." **Eliseevsky Gas-tronom** (Елисеевский), ul. Tverskaya 14 (tel. 209 0760; M2: Tverskaya), is Moscow's most famous grocery and is as much a visual spectacle as it is a place to buy food. It has higher prices than most other groceries (if you dare demean it by calling it a grocery; open M-F 8am-9pm, Sa 10am-7pm). **Dorogomilovo** (Дорогомилого), ul. Boshaya Dorogomilovskaya 8 (Большая Дорогомиловская; M4: Kievskaya), across the park from Kievsky Vokzal, is relatively cheap and stocks Western foods. (Open M-Sa 9am-9pm, Su 9am-7pm.)

👁 SIGHTS

Moscow's sights reflect the city's strange history: the visitor can choose among 16th-century churches and Soviet-era museums, but there's little between. Russia's capital suffers from the 200 years when St. Petersburg was the tsar's seat—there are no grand palaces, and the city's art museums, though impressive, pale in comparison with St. Petersburg's Hermitage. Still, despite this gap, and despite the fact that the Soviet regime destroyed 80% of the city's pre-revolutionary splendor, the capital still packs in enough sights to occupy visitors for over a week.

RED SQUARE (KRASNAYA PL.)

There is nothing red about it; *krasnaya* meant "beautiful" long before the Communists co-opted it. Red Square (Krasnaya ploshchad; Красная площадь), a 700-meter-long lesson in history and culture, has been the site of everything from a giant farmer's market to public hangings. On one side, the **Kremlin,** the seat of the Communist Party for 70-odd years, is the historical and religious heart of Russia; on the other, **GUM,** once a market and the world's largest purveyor of Soviet "consumer goods," is now an upscale shopping mall. At one end stands **St. Basil's Cathedral;** at the other sits the **State Historical Musuem** and **Lenin's Mausoleum.** Moscow's

RUSSIA

mayor has built a church to block the largest entrance to the square, ensuring that Communist parades will never again march through.

ST. BASIL'S CATHEDRAL. There is perhaps no more familiar symbol of Moscow than St. Basil's Cathedral (Pokrovsky Sobor or Sobor Vasiliya Blazhennovo; Собор Василия Блаженного), with its crazy-quilted onion domes. Completed in 1561, it was commissioned by Ivan the Terrible to celebrate his 1552 victory over the Tatars in Kazan. The cathedral bears the moniker of a holy fool, Vasily (Basil in English), who correctly predicted that Ivan would murder his own son. The maze-like interior—unusual for Orthodox churches—is filled with complex (albeit reconstructed) frescoes. Downstairs, an exhibit traces the history of the church and Ivan's campaign against the Tatars, all in Russian. *(M3: Ploshchad Revolutsii;* Площадь Революции. *Open W-M 10am-5pm; kassa closes at 4:30pm. 75R, students 38R. Buy tickets from the kassa to the left of the entrance, then proceed upstairs.)*

LENIN'S MAUSOLEUM. Though the Party, so to speak, is finally over, and Lenin's name and face are coming down all over Moscow, his mausoleum still stands in front of the Kremlin, patrolled by several scowling guards. The line to get into this squat, red structure (Mavzoley V.I. Lenina; Мавзолей В.И. Ленина) was three hours long in its glory days, but today it has completely vanished. Entrance to the mausoleum not only grants a view of Vlad's embalmed remains, but also of the **Kremlin wall,** where Stalin, Brezhnev, Andropov, Gagarin, and John Reed (author of *Ten Days that Shook the World*) are buried. Note the balcony on top, where Russian leaders stood during the May Day and November 7 parades. *(Open Tu-Th and Sa-Su 10am-1pm. Check bags and cameras at the cloakroam in Aleksandrovsky Sad.)*

THE KREMLIN

Complex open F-W 10am-5:30pm. Armory and Diamond Fund open F-W 10-11:30am, noon-1:30, 2:30-4, and 4:30-6pm. Armory 280R, students 140R. Diamond Fund 100R. Entrance to all cathedrals 200R, students 110R; after 4pm 90R, students 45R. Cameras 30R. Buy tickets at the kassa in Alexander Gardens, on the west side of the Kremlin, and enter through Borovitskaya gate in the southwest corner. English-speaking guides offer tours at outrageous prices; don't forget to haggle. Local hotels also offer tours.

The Kremlin (Kreml; Кремль) sits geographically and historically in the center of Moscow: it's where Ivan the Terrible reigned with his iron fist; where Napoleon simmered while Moscow burned; where Stalin ruled from behind the Iron Curtain; and where the USSR was dissolved in 1991. But despite this tremendous political history, the Kremlin's magnificent churches are the real attraction. Besides the sights listed below, the only other place in the complex you can actually enter is the **Kremlin Palace of Congresses,** the square white monster built by Khrushchev in 1961 for Communist Party Congresses; today it's a summertime theater.

CATHEDRAL SQUARE. Follow the eager masses to Cathedral Square, home to the most famous gold domes in Russia. As you enter through Borovitskaya gate, the first church to the left is the **Annunciation Cathedral** (Blagoveshchensky Sobor; Благовещеиский Собор), which guards luminous icons by Andrei Rublev and Theophanes the Greek. The square **Archangel Cathedral** (Arkhangelsky Sobor; Архангельский Собор), which gleams with vivid icons and frescoes, is the final resting place for many of the tsars who ruled prior to Peter the Great, including Ivans III (the Great) and IV (the Terrible) and Mikhail Romanov. **Assumption Cathedral** (Uspensky Sobor; Успенский Собор) at the center of the square is the oldest cathedral in the Russian state. Behind it, the **Patriarch's Palace** (Patriarshy Dvorets; Патриарший Дворец) houses the **Museum of 17th-Century Russian Applied Art and Life.** To the right of the Assumption Cathedral is **Ivan the Great's Belltower** (Kolokolnya Ivana Velikovo; Колокольня Ивана Великого). Directly behind the belltower is the **Tsar Bell** (Tsar-kolokol; Царь-колокол), the world's largest; it has never rung and never will—a 1737 fire caused a piece weighing 11½ tons to crack off.

ARMORY MUSEUM AND DIAMOND FUND. The nine rooms of the Armory Museum and Diamond Fund (Oruzheynaya i Vystavka Almaznovo Fonda; Оружейная и Вьставка Алмазного Фонда), just to the left as you enter the Kremlin complex, contain all of the riches of the Russian Church and state not currently in St. Petersburg's Hermitage; marvel at the opulence of the Russian court. Room 3, on the second floor, holds the legendary **Fabergé eggs**—each opens to reveal an impossibly intricate jewelled miniature; room 6 holds thrones, crowns, and other royal necessities; and room 9 contains royal coaches and sleds. The Diamond Fund, in an annex of the Armory, has still more glitter, including a 190-carat diamond given to Catherine the Great by Gregory Orlov, a "special friend."

CHURCHES, MONASTERIES, AND SYNAGOGUES

NOVODEVICHY CONVENT AND CEMETERY. You can't miss this most famous of Moscow's monasteries (Новодевичий Монастырь), thanks to its high brick walls, golden domes, and (on Sundays) tourist buses. Tsars and nobles kept the coffers filled by exiling their well-dowried wives and daughters here when they grew tired of them. The **Smolensk Cathedral** (Smolensky Sobor; Смоленский Собор), in the center of the convent, shows off Russian icons and frescoes. As you exit the convent gates, turn right and follow the exterior wall back around to the **cemetery** (kladbishche; кладбище)—a massive pilgrimage site that cradles the graves of Gogol, Chekhov, Stanislavsky, Khrushchev, Shostakovich, Mayakovsky, Bulgakov, and other luminaries. *(M1: Sportivnaya. Take the exit out of the Metro that doesn't go to the stadium, take a right, and it's several blocks down on the left. Open W-M 10am-5:30pm; cathedrals close at 4:45pm. Closed first M of each month. Admission to grounds 25R, students 14R. Smolensk Cathedral 56R, students 30R; special exhibits 56R, students 30R. Cemetary open daily in summer 9am-7pm; in winter 9am-6pm; 20R. Cyrillic maps of cemetary 5R. Buy tickets at the small kiosk across the street from the entrance.)*

CATHEDRAL OF CHRIST THE SAVIOR. The city's most controversial landmark is the enormous, gold-domed Cathedral of Christ the Savior (Khram Khrista Spositelya; Храм Христа Спасителя), which replaced a public pool in the early 90s (amidst much controversy) when it was discovered that water vapor from the pool was damaging paintings at the nearby Pushkin Museum. After winning the battle for the site, the Orthodox Church and mayor Yury Luzhkov constructed the cathedral in a mere two years. The beautiful monolith is worth a visit, though the interior was closed in summer 1999 due to construction. *(M1: Kropotkinskaya. Between ul. Volkhonka (Волхонка) and the Moscow River.)*

MOSCOW CHORAL SYNAGOGUE. First constructed in the 1870s, the Moscow Choral Synagogue is a much-needed break from the city's ubiquitous onion domes. Though it functioned during Soviet rule, all but the bravest were deterred by KGB agents who photographed anyone who entered. Today more than 200,000 Jews officially live in Moscow, and services are increasingly well attended. The graffiti occasionally sprayed on the building serves as a sad reminder that anti-Semitism in Russia is not dead. *(Bolshoy Spasoglinishchevsky per. 10 (Большой Спасогинищевский). M5,6: Kitai-Gorod. Go north on Solyansky Proezd (Солянский Проезд) and take the first left. Open daily 9:30am-6pm; Sabbath services Sa 9am.)*

PEDESTRIAN AREAS AND PARKS

THE ARBAT. A pedestrian shopping arcade, the Arbat was once a showpiece of *glasnost* and a haven for political radicals, Hare Krishnas, street poets, and *metallisty* (heavy metal rockers). Today, the flavor of political rebellion has been replaced by the more universal taste of capitalism, including McDonald's, Baskin Robbins, and Benetton. A quick bite or a leisurely meal in one of many outdoor cafés provides the ideal venue for extensive people-watching. *(M3: Arbatskaya.)*

PUSHKIN SQUARE AND PATRIARCH'S POND. Pushkin Square (Pushkinskaya Pl.) is center of free speech in Moscow—the site of evangelizing missionary groups, amateur politicians handing out petitions, and all major Russian news organizations. Follow ul. Bolshaya Bronnaya, next to Mickey D's, down to the bottom of the hill, turn right, and follow ul. Malaya Bronnaya to **Patriarch's Pond** (Patriarshy Prud; Патриаршие Пруды), where Mikhail Bulgakov's *The Master and Margarita*

RUSSIA

begins. This region, known as the Margarita, is popular with artsy students and old men playing dominoes. *(M6: Pushkinskaya. Halfway up ul. Tverskaya from Red Square.)*

GORKY PARK. In summer, droves of out-of-towners and young Muscovites promenade, relax, and ride the roller-coaster at Moscow's **amusement park;** in winter the entire park becomes an **ice rink.** Though attractions are far outnumbered by ice cream kiosks and the rides are on their last legs, the park is a must-see for its symbolic and historical significance. *(M1,4: Park Kultury or M4,5: Oktyabrskaya. From the Park Kultury stop, cross Krimsky most. From Oktyabrskaya, walk downhill on Krimsky val. and enter through the main gate. Open daily 10am-midnight. General admission 15R. Most rides 40-70R.)*

KOLOMENSKOE SUMMER RESIDENCE. Another respite from Moscow's chaos is the tsars' summer residence on a wooded slope above the Moskva River. Peter the Great's 1702 log cabin and Bratsk Prison have been moved here from Arkhangelsk and Siberia, respectively. At the edge of the complex stands the 16th-century **Assumption Church** (Uspenskaya Sobor). *(M2: Kolomenskaya. Follow the exit signs to "к музею Коломенское." Turn right out of the Metro and walk about 400m to the main entrance gate. Grounds open daily 7am-10pm. Free.)*

IZMAYLOVSKY PARK. Rather far out, the park (Измайловский Парк) is better known for its colossal weekend **market,** Vernisazh (Вернисаж), than for its lush greenery. Arrive late Sunday afternoon, when people want to go home and are willing to make a deal. *Everything* is sold here, from carpets and samovars to military uniforms and old Soviet money to jewelry and *matryoshki*. *(M3: Izmaylovsky Park. Go left and follow the hordes. Open daily 9am-5:30pm.)*

MUSEUMS

The **Moscow Metro,** one of the most beautiful metros in the world, is worth a tour of its own. All the stations are unique, and those inside the Circle Line are quite elaborate, with mosaics, sculptures, and crazy chandeliers. It's only 4R, and you can stay as long you as like. Stations Kievskaya, Mayakovskaya, and Ploshchad Revolutsii are particularly good, as are **Komsomolskaya, Rimskaya,** and **Mendeleevksaya.**

Tretyakov Gallery (Tretyakovskaya Galereya; Третьяковская Галерея), Lavrushensky per. 10 (Лаврушенский; tel. 203 77 88), in Zamoskvareche. M7: Tretyakovskaya; turn left and then left again, take an immediate right onto Tolmachevsky per. (Толмачевский пер.), and turn right after two blocks on Lavrushensky per. A veritable treasure chest of Russian national art, mostly from the 18th and 19th centuries. The heart of the gallery is the collection of icons; its crown jewel is the 12th-century Vladimir *Virgin Mary* icon from Constantinople. 175R, students 100R. Open Tu-Su 10am-8pm.

Pushkin Museum of Fine Arts (Muzey Izobrazitelnykh Iskusstv im. A.S. Pushkina; Музей Изобразительных Искусств им. А.С. Пушкина), ul. Volkhonka 12 (tel. 203 95 78). M1: Kropotkinskaya. The second most famous art museum in Russia after the Hermitage, with collections of Impressionist, Renaissance, Egyptian, and Classical art. To the left of the main entrance is the **Museum of Private Collections,** with foreign and Russian art from the 19th and 20th centuries. Open Tu-Su 10am-7pm; *kassa* closes at 6pm. The Private Collections close 5pm. Joint ticket 150R, students 80R.

Central Museum of the Revolution (Muzey Revolyutsii; Музей Революции), ul. Tverskaya 21 (tel. 299 67 24). M6: Pushkinskaya; walk one block uphill on Tverskaya, and the gates are on the left. Covers Russian history from the Revolution to present day in exhausting detail. Open Tu, Th, and Sa 10am-6pm, W 11am-7pm, Su 10am-5pm. 10R.

State Tretyakov Gallery (Gosudarstvennaya Tretyakovskaya Galereya; Государственная Третьяковская Галерея), ul. Krymsky Val 10 (Крымский Вал; tel. 238 13 78). M1,4: Park Kultury. Opposite the Gorky Park entrance; it's the building in back, with an entrance to the right. Contemporary Russian art on the ground floor, various 19th-century artists on the second, and a retrospective of 1910-1930 Russian art at the top. Open Tu-Su 10am-8pm; *kassa* closes 7pm. 175R, students 100R.

State Historical Museum, Krasnaya pl. 1 (tel. 924 45 29). M2,3: Ploshchad Revolutsii. Across from Lenin's tomb in Red Square. Traces Russian history from the Neaderthals to the Kievan Rus dynasty to modern Russia. Open M and W-Su 11am-7pm; last entrance 6pm. Closed 1st M of each month. 120R, students 60R.

RUSSIA

AUTHORS' HOUSES

Russians take immense pride in their formidable literary history, preserving authors' houses in their original state, down to half-empty teacups on the mantlepiece. Each is guarded by a team of fiercely loyal *babushki*.

Lev Tolstoy Estate, ul. Lva Tolstovo 21 (Льва Толстого; tel. 246 94 44). M1,4: Park Kultury; walk down Komsomolsky pr., turn right at the corner on ul. Lva Tolstovo, and it's three blocks up on the left. The author lived here in the winters of 1882-1901. One of the most perfectly preserved house-museums in Moscow. Open in summer Tu-Su 10am-6pm; off-season 10am-3:30pm. Closed last F of the month. 50R, students 5R.

Gorky's Apartment, ul. Malaya Nikitskaya 6/2 (Малая Никитская; tel. 290 51 30). M3: Arbatskaya; cross Novy Arbat, turn right on Merelyakovsky per. (Мерзляковский пер.), cross the small park, and it's directly across from you. Entrance is on ul. Spiridonova to the left. A pilgrimage site more for its architectural interest (Art Nouveau) than for its collection of Maxim Gorky's possessions. Open W and F noon-7pm, Th and Sa-Su 10am-5pm. Closed last Th of the month. Free; 5-10R donation requested.

Gogol Museum (Muzey Gogolya; Музей Гоголя), Nikitsky bul. 7 (tel. 291 12 40). M3: Arbatskaya; cross Novy Arbat and take the first right on Nikitsky bul. Only two small rooms in a library, but it provides a glimpse of the brilliant writer's life and meager possessions—without costing a ruble. Open M and W-F noon-6:45pm, Sa-Su noon-3:45pm.

♫ ENTERTAINMENT

Moscow is a large, fast-paced city, and it has the entertainment options to prove it. From September to June, when Moscovite companies are in town, the city boasts good theater, ballet, and opera, along with excellent orchestras. Tickets bought in advance can be very cheap (US$2-5).

Bolshoy Teatr (Big Theater; Большой Театр), Teatralnaya pl. 1 (tel. 292 00 50). M2: Teatralnaya Pl. Home to both the opera and the world-renowned ballet companies, with consistently excellent performances. Champagne and caviar at intermission. Daily performances Sept.-June 7pm. *Kassa* open noon-7pm. Tickets 30-1000R.

Musical Operetta Theater, ul. Bolshaya Dmitrovka 6 (tel. 292 63 77), just east of the Bolshoy. M2: Teatralnaya. Operettas staged all year. Shows at 7pm. Tickets 25-150R.

Tchaikovsky Conservatory's Big and Small Halls, Triumfalnaya pl. 4/31 (tel. 229 03 78). M2: Mayakovskaya. During intermission, locals sneak into the Big Hall (Bolshoy Zal; Большой Зал) to admire its pipe organ and chandeliers. Concerts almost daily 7pm plus Su 2pm. *Kassa* in Big Hall open daily noon-7pm. Tickets from 100R. Back-row tickets for the Maly Zal (Small Hall; Малый Зал) just 5R.

Leninsky Komsomol (LENKOM), ul. Malaya Dmitrovka 6 (tel. 299 96 68). M6: Pushkinskaya. Director Mark Zakharov is well known in Russia and attracts crowds to see dramas such as *Figaro* and *Chaika* and bright Broadway-style musicals. Performances noon and 7pm. *Kassa* open daily 1-3pm and 5-7pm. Tickets around 50-150R.

Great Moscow Circus, pr. Vernadskovo 7. M1: Universitet. It was the greatest show on earth, but all the big stars defected and eventually died (ah, mortality!); now it's the greatest show in Moscow. Performances Tu-F 7pm, Sa-Su 11:30am, 3, and 7pm. *Kassa* open daily 11am-3pm and 4-7pm. Tickets from 50R.

NIGHTCLUBS AND BARS

Moscow's nightlife is the most kickin' action this side of the Volga, and certainly the most varied—not to mention the most expensive and dangerous—in Eastern Europe. While Moscow may not be New York or London, it certainly thinks it is—cover charges are usually 100R. Check the weekend editions of *The Moscow Times* or *The Moscow Tribune,* or *The Moscow Times's* Friday pull-out section, *MT Out,* for info on weekly events as well as bar and club reviews.

Propaganda, Bolshoy Zlatoustinsky per. 7 (Большой Златоустинский; tel. 924 57 32). M5,6: Kitai-Gorod; walk down ul. Maroseika and turn left on Bolshoy Zlatoustinsky per. Popular expat and local student dance bar featuring a mix of Top-40, funk, and acid jazz. Cheap beer. Cover 40R. Open Su-Th noon-2am, F-Sa noon-6am.

RUSSIA

Krizis Zhanra, per. Prechistensky 22/4 (Прзчистзнский; tel. 241 29 40). M1: Kropotkin-skaya; walk down ul. Prechistenka (Прзчистзнка) away from the Church of Christ the Savior, take the third right onto Prechistensky, walk through the gate across from the Danish Embassy, turn left, and it's the first large door on the left. One of the best places in Moscow to grab a beer. Popular with local and foreign students. Czech beers 50R. Live concerts pack in crowds daily 7-10pm. Open daily 11am-midnight.

TaxMan, Krymsky val. 6 (Крымский Вал; tel. 238 08 64). M5: Oktyabrskaya; walk downhill on Krymsky val. and it's opposite the entrance to Gorky Park. Inexpensive drinks and musical variety pack students into centrally located bar. Pool tables and an arm-wrestling table. Draft beer 40R. Varying cover for live music. Open daily noon-6am.

Sports Bar, Novy Arbat 10 (tel. 290 43 11). M3: Arbatskaya. Next to Melodiya. Paradise for Eurosport lovers, with 8 TVs at the bar and a large screen. The 2nd floor is the place to shoot pool, throw darts, and watch New Russians compare their New Cellular Phones. Live music 8-11pm; disco opens 11pm. Expensive drinks (think 100R a beer); happy hour 5-8pm features 2-for-1 beer specials. Open daily noon-6am.

⚡ EXCURSION FROM MOSCOW: SERGIEV POSAD

Possibly Russia's most famous pilgrimage point, Sergiev Posad (Сергиев Посад) attracts wandering Orthodox believers with a mass of churches huddled at its main sight, **St. Sergius's Trinity Monastery** (Troitsko-Sergieva Lavra; Троицко-Сергиева Лавра). The stunning monastery, founded around 1340, is again a religious center—the paths between the churches are dotted with monks in flowing robes. Although each church is exquisite, the opulence of Russian Orthodoxy is best visible inside the **Trinity Cathedral,** where the numerous covered heads and quickly crossing hands captivate visitors as much as the gilded Andrei Rublyov icons. *Elektrichki* (commuter trains) run to Sergiev Posad from Moscow's Yaroslavsky Vokzal (1½hr., 1-2 per hr., round-trip 25R).

ST. PETERSBURG (САНКТ-ПЕТЕРБУРГ)

In St. Petersburg, Russia suddenly becomes wide boulevards, brightly colored façades, glorious palaces, and artistic revelry. This splendor is exactly what Peter the Great intended when he founded the city in 1703 atop a drained swamp on the Gulf of Finland; the land was strategically chosen to drag Russia away from Byzantium and toward the West. But St. Petersburg was also the birthplace of the 1917 revolution, which would turn Russia decisively away from the western world. St. Petersburg's name changes reflected the currents of its history; German-sounding *Sankt Peterburg* was changed to Petrograd during WWI, which the Bolsheviks traded in for the more proletarian Leningrad in 1924, only to reclaim St. Petersburg when Lenin fell out of favor. Yet it was Leningrad that suffered the brutal 900-day siege in WWII by the Nazis, during which close to a million people died. Despite— or because of—its turbulent past, the city has proved a muse; the splendid palaces have inspired the masterpieces of Dostoevsky, Gogol, Tchaikovsky, and Stravinsky, while the seedy cafés and dark courtyards of the city's underbelly fostered the revolutionary dreams of Lenin and Trotsky. Moscow may be the embodiment of Mother Russia's bold, post-apocalyptic youth, but St. Petersburg remains the majestic and mysterious symbol of Peter's great Russian dream.

▣ GETTING THERE AND GETTING AROUND

Flights: The main airport, **Pulkovo** (Пулково), has two terminals: Pulkovo-1 for domestic and Pulkovo-2 for international flights. M2: Moskovskaya. From the metro, take bus 39 for Pulkovo-1 (30-40min.), or bus 13 for Pulkovo-2 (25-30min.). Hostels can usually arrange for you to be taken (or met) by taxi (usually US$30-40).

Trains: Tsentralnye Zheleznodorozhnye Kassy (Central Ticket Offices; Центральные Железнодорожные Кассы), Canal Griboedova 24. Foreigners must purchase domestic tickets at **Intourist** windows #100-104 and international tickets at windows #90-99 on the 2nd fl. For prices, go to ticket window #90; 4R per question. Check your ticket to see which station your train leaves from.

RUSSIA

St. Petersburg

ACCOMMODATIONS

A Hostel Holiday (HI)
B International Youth Hostel
C Petrovsky Hostel

RUSSIA

Varshavsky Vokzal (Варшавский Вокзал). M1: Baltiskaya (Балтийская). To: **Tallinn** (8hr., 1 per day, 477R); **Vilnius** (11hr., 1 per day, 822R); **Rīga** (12hr., 1 per day, 1049R); and **Warsaw** (27hr., 1 per day, 1123R).

Vitebsky Vokzal (Витебский Вокзал). M1: Pushkinskaya (Пушкинская). To: **Kiev** (26-32hr., 2 per day, 725R) and **Odessa** (36hr., 1 per day, 870R).

Moskovsky Vokzal (Московский Вокзал). M1: Pl. Vosstaniya. To: **Moscow** (6-9hr., 15 per day, 305R). Anna Karennina threw herself under a train here.

Finlyandsky Vokzal (Финляндский Вокзал). M1: Pl. Lenina (Ленина). To: **Helsinki** (5hr., 2 per day, 1134R).

Buses: nab. Obvodnovo Kanala 36 (Обводного Канала; tel. 166 5777; international info tel. 166 81 01). M4: Ligovsky pr. Take tram 19, 25, 44, or 49, or trolley 42, from the M1 stop across the canal. Facing the canal, turn right and walk two blocks. Enter through the back of the station on your right. Advance ticket booth open daily 8am-2pm and 3-8pm. Destinations in **Finland, Estonia,** and **Belarus.** (1-2 trains per day to capitals and major cities.) Baggage 2-5R extra, depending on destination.

Local Transportation: The **Metro** (Метро) runs daily 5:30am-12:30am. Four lines run from the outskirts of the city through the center. A Metro **token** (*zheton;* жетон) costs 3R. **Trolleys** 1, 5, and 22 go from pl. Vosstaniya to the bottom of Nevsky pr., near the Hermitage. **Buses, trams,** and **trolleys** run 6am-midnight; tickets (2R) are purchased from the driver. Punch them on-board; the fine for not doing so is 9R.

Taxis: Fares are flat. Never get into a cab with more than one person already in it.

☑ ORIENTATION & PRACTICAL INFORMATION

The city center lies on mainland St. Petersburg between the south bank of the **Neva River** and the north bank of the **Fontanka River. Nevsky prospekt** (Невский Проспект) runs through this downtown area; most of St. Petersburg's major sights—including the Winter and Summer Palaces, the Hermitage, and main cathedrals—are on Nevsky pr. **Moscow Train Station** (Moskovsky Vokzal; Московский Вокзал), the city's main train station, is near the midway point of Nevsky pr.; **Vitebsky Vokzal** (Виебский Вокзал), another station, is at the southern edge of the center on Liteyny pr. (Литейний пр.). East of the downtown and across the Neva sprawls **Vasilevsky Island,** the city's largest island; most of its sights are congregated on the island's eastern edge in the **Strelka** neighborhood. On the north side of the Neva and across from the Winter Palace is the historic heart of the city. North of downtown, across the Neva on the mainland, is the **Finland Train Station** (Finlyandsky Vokzal; Финляндский Вокэал); **Warsaw Train Station** (Varshavsky Vokzal; Варшавский Вокэал) is to the south of downtown. The easiest means of navigation is the **Metro.** In the center, **trolleys** 1, 5, and 22 go up and down Nevsky pr.

TOURIST AND FINANCIAL SERVICES

Tourist Office: Ost-West Contact Service, ul. Mayakovskovo 7 (Маяковского; tel. 327 34 16; fax 327 34 17). Lots of info. Open M-F 10am-6pm, Sa noon-6pm.

Budget Travel: Sinbad Travel (FIYTO), 3-ya Sovetskaya ul. 28 (3-я Советская; tel. 327 83 84; fax 329 80 19; email sindbad@ryh.spb.su; www.spb.ru/ryh). In the International Hostel. Arranges tickets, tours and adventure trips. US$5 fee for train tickets. 10-80% discounts on plane tickets. Open M-F 9:30am-8pm, Sa-Su 10am-5pm. English spoken.

Consulates: Canada, Malodetskoselsky pr. 32 (Малодетскосельский; tel. 325 84 48; fax 325 83 93). M1: Tekhnologichesky Institut. Open M-F 9:30am-1pm and 2-5pm. **UK,** pl. Proletarskoy Diktatury 5 (Пролетарской Диктатуры; tel. 325 60 36; fax 325 60 37). M1: Chernyshevskaya. Open M-F 9am-1pm and 2-5pm. **US,** ul. Furshtatskaya 15 (Фурштатская; tel. 275 17 01; 24-hour emergency tel. 274 86 92; fax 213 69 62). M1: Chernyshevskaya. Open M-F 9:15am-1pm and 2-5:30pm. Citizens of **Australia** and **New Zealand** contact their embassies in Moscow, or in emergencies the UK consulate.

Currency Exchange: Look for "Обмен валюты" (*obmen valyuty*) signs everywhere. **Central Exchange Office,** ul. Mikhailovskaya 4 (Михайловская; tel. 110 49 09). Off Nevsky pr. across from Grand Hotel Europe. M3: Gostiny Dvor. Expect a wait. Open M-F 9am-1:30pm and 3-6pm, Sa-Su 9:30am-2pm and 3-6pm. Keep receipts to change rubles back into hard currency, but it still might not be possible. Bring your passport.

RUSSIA

The drainage system in St. Petersburg hasn't changed since the city was founded, so there is no effective water purification system, making exposure to giardia very likely. Always boil tap water at least 10min., dry veggies, and drink bottled water.

EMERGENCY AND COMMUNICATIONS

Emergencies: Multilingual police office which deals specifically with crimes against foreigners is at Ligovsky Pr. 145 (24-hour hotline 164 97 87).

Pharmacies: Nevsky pr. 22. Open M-F 8am-9pm, Sa-Su 24hr. At night enter in back.

Medical Assistance: American Medical Center, ul. Serpukhovskaya 10 (Серпуховская; tel. 326 17 30; fax 326 17 31; 24-hour emergency hotline 310 96 11). M1: Tekhnologichesky Institut (Технологический Институт).

Internet Access: Tetris Internet Café (Тетрис), Chernyakhovskovo 33 (Черняховского; tel. 164 48 77; email postmaster@dux.ru; www.dux.ru). M4: Ligovsky Prospect. Exit the Metro, turn left onto Ligovsky pr. and go straight. 8OR per hr.

Telephones: Central Telephone and Telegraph, Bolshaya Morskaya ul. 3/5 (Большая Морская). Facing the Admiralty, it's right off Nevsky pr. near Dvortsovaya pl. For intercity calls, the *mezhdugorodny* (междугородный) phone booths; they take *zhetony* (tokens; жетоны) sold across from the booths (3R). Prepay phone calls in the *kassa* in the 2nd (for intercity) or 3rd (for international) halls. For long-distance calls, push 8 and wait for the tone before dialing. Open M-F 9am-12:30pm and 1-8pm, Su 9am-12:30pm and 1-5pm. **Intercity calls** can also be made from phones on the street that take the phone cards sold at the central office and kiosks. For **AT&T Direct,** call 325 50 42.

Post Office: ul. Pochtamtskaya 9 (Почтамтская). From Nevsky pr., go west on ul. Malaya Morskaya (Малая Морская), which becomes ul. Pochtamtskaya; it's about two blocks past Isaakievsky Sobor on the right. Changes money and telephones. Address mail to be held: "KAREINA, Anna, До Востребования, **190 000** Санкт-Петербург, Главпочтамт, Russia." Open M-Sa 9am-7:30pm, Su 10am-5:30pm.

PHONE CODE | City code: 812. From outside Russia dial int'l dialing prefix (see inside back cover) + 7 + 812 + local number.

ACCOMMODATIONS

Hostel "Holiday" (HI), ul. Mikhailova 1 (Михайлова; tel. 542 73 64; fax 325 85 59; email postmaster@hostelling.spb.su; www.spb.su/holiday). M1: Pl. Lenina. Exit at Finlyandsky Vokzal, turn left on ul. Komsomola (Комсомола), then right on ul. Mikhailova. Just before the river, turn left into a courtyard, then right. Visa support available (single-entry US$30). Dorms US$14; doubles US$38 per person. Breakfast included. US$1 discount for HI members; US$2 after five days. **Internet.** Check-out 11am. Call ahead.

International Youth Hostel (HI), 3-ya Sovetskaya ul. 28 (3-я Советская; tel. 329 80 18; fax 329 80 19; email ryh@ryh.spb.ru; www.spb.ru/ryh). M1: Pl. Vosstaniya. Walk along Suvorovsky pr. (Суворовский) for three blocks, then turn right on 3-ya Sovetskaya ul. A tidy hostel in a pleasant neighborhood with all the Soviet basics. Dorms US$17; ISIC holder US$18; nonmembers $19. Breakfast included. Minimal kitchen. Laundry (US$4 for 4kg). **Internet.** Check-out 11am. Curfew 1am. V, MC.

Petrovsky Hostel, ul. Baltiyskaya 26 (Балтийская; tel. 252 75 63; fax 252 40 19). M1: Narvskaya. From the Metro, turn left on pr. Stachek (Стачек) to ul. Baltiskaya and turn left. Though a little ways from the center, this is a solid, cheap option. 130R, 150R for one-night stays. Kitchen. Sheets not included. Check-in by midnight. Check-out 11am.

FOOD

St. Petersburg's menus seem to vary little, but many places harbor top-secret methods of preparing tasty old Russian classics; unfortunately menus are often only in Cyrillic. Good luck! Fast food venues are all over the city. Cafés have long been pivotal to St. Petersburg culture, inspiring Dostoevsky's frightening tales of Russian urban life and Lenin's dreams of revolution; today's cafés are mostly mainstream,

RUSSIA

holding only vague echoes of former glory. **Markets** stock tons of stuff; bargain and play hard to get. The **covered market,** Kuznechny per. 3 (Кузнечьный), just around the corner from M1: Vladimirskaya, and the **Maltsevski Rynok,** ul. Nekrasova 52 (Некрасова), at the top of Ligovsky pr. (Лиговский; M1: Pl. Vosstaniya), are the biggest and most exciting. For pre-packaged **groceries** head to **Magasin #11** (Магасин; M1, 3: Pl. Vosstaniya), Nevsky pr. 105. (Open daily 10am-10pm.)

Kafe Hutorok (Хуторок), 3-ya Sovetskaya ul. 24. M1: Pl. Vosstaniya. This café whips up great Russian food; try the cherry dumplings. Entrees 75-125R. Open 10am-11pm.

Tbilisi (Тблиси), ul. Sytninskaya 10 (Сытнинская; tel. 232 93 91). M2: Gorkovskaya. Follow the wrought-iron fence that wraps around Park Lenina away from the fortress until you see the Sytny (Сытный) market; Tblisi is behind it. Georgian delights. Entrees 40-50R. English menu. Open daily noon-11pm.

Koshkin Dom (Кошкин Дом), Liteyny pr. 23 (Литейний) and ul. Vosstaniya 2. M1: Pl. Vosstaniya. Carnivorous fun! Soups and entrees 15-50R; salads 10-25R. Open 24hr.

Bistro Maslenitsa, (Бистро Масленица), Nevsky pr. 27 (tel. 558 87 48). M2: Nevsky Prospekt. 15 ways to stuff a blini. Blini 5-25R. Open 24hr.

Green Crest (Грин Крест), Vladimirsky pr. 7 (Владимирский). M1: Vladimirskaya; M4: Dostoevskaya. "Ecological oasis in this gastronomical desert," reads the welcoming sign at the door; rabbits rejoice! Open daily 9am-11:30pm.

Tandoor (Тандур), Voznesensky pr. 2 (tel. 312 38 86). M2: Nevsky Prospekt. On the corner of Admiralteysky pr., two blocks to the left after the end of Nevsky pr. Russian boys in Aladdin costumes with golden slippers serve Indian delights. Dinner US$15-25. Lunch special noon-4pm US$10. Open daily noon-11pm.

Minutka (Минутка), Nevsky pr. 20. M2: Nevsky Prospekt. Large sandwiches for not-so-large prices. 12" subs 55-75R. Open daily 10am-10pm.

👁 SIGHTS

■ **THE HERMITAGE.** Originally a collection of 225 paintings bought by Catherine the Great in 1764, the **State Hermitage Museum** (Эрмитаж), the world's largest art collection, rivals the Louvre and the Prado in architectural, historical, and artistic significance. The **Winter Palace** (Zimny Dvorets; Зимний Дворец), commissioned in 1762, reflects the extravagant tastes of the Empress Elizabeth, Peter the Great's daughter. By the end of the 1760s, the collection amassed by the empress had become too large for the Winter Palace, and Catherine appointed Vallin de la Mothe to build the **Small Hermitage** (Maly Hermitage; Малый Эрмитаж), where she could retreat by herself or with one of her lovers. The **Big Hermitage** (Veliky Hermitage; Великий Эрмитаж) and the **Hermitage Theater** (Hermitazhny Teatr; Эрмитажный Театр) were completed in the 1780s. Stasov, a famous imperial Russian architect, built the fifth building, the **New Hermitage** (Novy Hermitage; Новый Эрмитаж), in 1851. The tsars lived with here until 1917, after which the museum complex was nationalized. Five buildings now hold the incredible collection, but it is impossible to absorb the whole museum in a day or even a week—indeed, only 5% of the three-million-piece collection is on display at any one time. Buy an indispensable English floor guide (5R) at the souvenir tables near the *kassa.*

The **Palace Square** (Dvortsovaya Ploshchad; Дворцовая Площадь), the huge windswept expanse in front of the Winter Palace, has witnessed many turning points in Russia's history; here, Catherine took the crown after overthrowing her husband, Tsar Peter III, Nicholas II's guards fired into a crowd of peaceful demonstrators on "Bloody Sunday" in 1905, leading to the 1905 revolution, and Lenin's Bolsheviks seized power from the provisional government during the storming of the Winter Palace in October 1917. *(Dvortsovaya nab. 34 (Дворцовая). M2: Nevsky Prospekt. Exiting the Metro, turn left and walk down Nevsky pr. to its end at the Admiralty. Head right onto and across Palace Square. Open M-Sa 10:30am-6pm, Su 10:30am-5pm; cashier and upper floors close 1hr. earlier. Kassa located on the river side of the building. 250R, students free. Cameras 75R. Lines can be long; come early. Students buy tickets at kassa 5.)*

RUSSIA

ST. ISAAC'S CATHEDRAL AND AROUND. Glittering, intricately-carved master-pieces of iconography await beneath the dome of **St. Isaac's Cathedral** (Isaakievsky Sobor; Исаакиевский Собор), a massive example of 19th-century civic-religious architecture. On a sunny day, the 100kg of pure gold that coats the dome shines for miles; 60 laborers died from inhaling fumes during the gilding. Some of Russia's greatest artists have worked on the murals and mosaics in the ornate interior. *(M2: Nevsky Prospekt. Exiting the Metro, turn left and walk to the end of Nevsky pr. Turn left onto Admiraltevsky pr.; the cathedral is at the corner of Admiraltevsky and Voznesensky pr. Open Tu-Su 11am-7pm; 200R, students 80R. Colonnade open 11am-6pm; 100R, students 40R. The kassa is to the right of the cathedral. Foreigners buy tickets inside the church.)*

FORTRESS OF PETER AND PAUL. Across the river from the Hermitage, the walls and golden spire of the **Fortress of Peter and Paul** (Petropavlovskaya Krepost; Петропавловская Крепость) beckon. Construction of the fortress began on May 27, 1703, a date now considered the birthday of St. Petersburg. Originally intended as a defense against the Swedes, it never saw battle as Peter I defeated the northern invaders before the bulwarks were finished. Inside, the **Peter and Paul Cathedral** (Petropavlovsky Sobor; Петропавловский Собор) glows with rosy marble walls and a breath-taking Baroque iconostasis. Before entering the main vault you will pass through the recently-restored **Chapel of St. Catherine the Martyr.** The bodies of the Romanovs—Tsar Nicholas II, his family, and their faithful servants—were entombed here on July 17, 1998, the eightieth anniversary of their murder at the hands of the Bolsheviks. **Trubetskoy Bastion** (Трубецкой Бастион), in the fortress's southwest corner, is a reconstruction of the prison where Peter the Great held and tortured his first son, Aleksei. Dostoevsky, Gorky, Trotsky, and Lenin's older brother also spent time here. *(M2: Gorkovskaya. Exiting the Metro, turn right on Kamennoostrovsky pr. (Каменноостровский), the street in front of you (there is no sign). Follow the street to the river, and cross the bridge to the island fortress. Open M and Th-Su 11am-6pm, Tu 11am-5pm; closed last Tu of month. US$3, students US$1.50; additional charges for special exhibitions. Purchase a single ticket for all museums at the kassa in the middle of the island or in the smaller kassa to the right just inside the main entrance.)*

ALEKSANDR NEVSKY MONASTERY. A major pilgrimage spot and a peaceful strolling place, **Aleksandr Nevsky Monastery** (Aleksandro-Nevskaya Lavra; Александро-невская Лавра), in 1797 became one of four Orthodox monasteries that have received the highest monastic title of *"lavra."* The 1716 **Lazarus Cemetery** (Lazarevskoye Kladbishche; Лазаревское Кладбище) is the city's oldest burial ground. The **Tikhvin Cemetery** (Tikhvinskoye Kladbishche; Тихвинское Кладбище), next to Lazarus Cemetery, is the permanent home of **Fyodor Dostoevsky, Pyotr Tchaikovsky,** and **Igor Stravinsky.** The **Church of the Annunciation** (Blagoveshchenskaya Tserkov; Благовещенская Церковь), farther along the central stone path on the left and currently under renovation, was the original burial place of the Romanovs, who were moved to Peter and Paul Cathedral in 1998. The **Trinity Cathedral** (Troitsky Sobor; Троицкий Собор), at the end of the path, is a functioning church, teeming with *babushki* energetically crossing themselves. *(M3, 4: Pl. Aleksandra Nevska. Lazarus Cemetery lies to the left of the entrance, Tihkvin to the right. Cemeteries open M-W and F-Su 10am-7pm. Cemeteries 20R, students 10R. Cathedral free. Modest dress.)*

ALONG NEVSKY PROSPEKT. The easternmost boulevard of central St. Petersburg, Nevsky pr. was constructed under Peter the Great. Keeping in line with his vision for St. Petersburg, the avenue is of epic scale, running 4.5km. The Prospekt begins at the **Admiralty** (Admiralteystvo; Адмиралтий), whose golden spire—painted black during WWII to disguise it from German artillery bombers—towers over the gardens and Dvortsovaya pl. *(M2: Nevsky Prospekt. Exit the Metro, turn left and walk to the end of Nevsky pr.)* To the left of the Admiralty as you face it, **Bronze Horseman** stands as a symbol of the city and its founder's massive will. *(M2: Nevsky Prospekt. Exiting the Metro, turn left and walk to the end of Nevsky pr.)* Farther down is the colossal **Kazan Cathedral** (Kazansky Sobor; Казанский Собор), modeled after St. Peter's in Rome. It now houses the **State Museum of the History of Religion,** which is

RUSSIA

A MUSEUM-GOER IN A STRANGE LAND Like

many museums in Eastern Europe, those in Russia charge foreigners much higher rates than natives. In desperation, some travelers don a fluffy fur hat, snarl a little, push the exact number of rubles for a Russian ticket toward the *babushka* at the *kassa*, and remain stoically mute. Go ahead and try; it might work. Once inside, don't worry about forgetting to see anything—the *babushki* in each room will make sure of that. Many museums, with floors made of precious inlaid wood, will ask visitors to don *tapochki*, giant slippers that go over your shoes and transform the polished gallery floor into a veritable ice rink. There are no guardrails—only irreplaceable imperial china—to slow your stride. Make sure your slippers fit well, or after navigating dozens of slippery wooden exhibition rooms you will meet an unfortunate end on the marble stairs.

---

not worth the rubles. *(M2: Nevsky Prospekt. Open M-Tu and Th-F 11am-6pm, Sa noon-6pm, Su 12:30-6pm; kassa closes at 5pm. Cathedral is free; museum 45R, students 22R.)*

Three blocks off Nevsky pr. up on the Griboyedov canal from the Dom Knigi, the colorful **Church of the Bleeding Savior,** a.k.a. the Savior on the Blood (Spas Na Krovi; Спас На Крови), sits on the site of Tsar Aleksandr II's 1881 assassination. Reopened after 20 years of Soviet condemnation, the church and its gorgeous mosiacs have been beautifully renovated. *(M2: Nevsky Prospekt.)* Some of the bloodiest confrontations of the February Revolution, the first stage of the 1917 Revolution, took place in **Uprising Square** (Ploshchad Vosstaniya; Площадь Восстания), the halfway point of Nevsky pr., near Moskovsky Vokzal. *(M1: Ploshchad Vosstaniya.)*

PISKAROV MEMORIAL CEMETERY. Close to a million people died during the 900 days that the German army sieged the city in WWII; the remote and chilling **Piskarov Memorial Cemetery** (Piskarovskoye Memorialnoye Kladbishche; Пискаровское Мемориальное Кладбище) is their grave. The monument reads: "No one is forgotten; nothing is forgotten." *(M1: Ploshchad Muzhestva (Площадь Мужества). Go left on the street, and at the corner, cross Nepokorennykh pr. (Непокоренных) in front and catch bus 123. Ride about 6 stops (7-10min.). The cemetery will be on the left.)*

MUSEUMS. The **Russian Museum** (Russky Muzey; Русский Музей) boasts the second-largest collection of Russian art after Moscow's Tretyakov Gallery, and the title of first public museum of Russian art (1898). *(M3: Gostiny Dvor. Down ul. Mikhailovsky past the Grand Hotel Europe. Open M 10am-5pm, W-Su 10am-6pm; kassa closes at 5pm. 140R, students 70R.)* Facing the Admiralty from across the river, **Kunstkamera Anthropological and Ethnographic Museum** (Muzey Antropologii i Etnografii—Kunstkamera; Музей Антропологии и Этнографии—Кунсткамера) is a natural history museum with a morbid twist—check out Petey's anatomical collection, featuring severed heads bathed in formaldehyde. *(Open M-F 11am-5pm. 50R, students 20R.)* Find Soviet proganda galore at the **Museum of Russian Political History** (Muzey Politicheskoy Istorii Rossii; Музей Политической Истории России), ul. Kuybysheva 2/4. *(M2: Gorkovskaya. Go down Kronverksky pr. toward the river and turn left on Kuybysheva. Open F-W 10am-6pm. 60R, students 30R.)* **Dostoevsky House** (Dom Dostoevskovo; Дом Достоевского), Kuznechny per. 5/2 (Кузнечный) is where Dostoevsky wrote *The Brothers Karamazov.* *(M1: Vladimirskaya; go around the corner to the right. Open Tu-Su 11am-6pm; kassa closes 5:30pm; closed last W of each month. 70R, students 3R.)*

♫ ENTERTAINMENT

St. Petersburg's famed White Nights lend the night sky a pale glow from mid-June to early July. In summer, lone misanthropes stroll under the illuminated night sky and watch the bridges over the Neva go up at 1:30am. Remember to walk on the same side of the river as your hotel—the bridges don't go back down until 4-5am, though some close briefly between 3 and 3:20am. The city holds a series of outdoor evening concerts as part of the **White Nights Festival;** check kiosks, posters, and the monthly *Pulse,* for more info. It is fairly easy to get tickets to world-class performances for as little as 20-30R, although many of the renowned theaters are known to grossly overcharge foreigners; buying Russian tickets from scalpers will save you money but you'll have to dress up and play Russian at the show. A monthly program in Russian is usually posted throughout the city.

THEATER, MUSIC, AND CIRCUS. The **Mariinsky Teatr** (Мариинский), a.k.a. the "Kirov," Teatralnaya pl. 1 (Театральная), where Tchaikovsky's *Nutcracker* and *Sleeping Beauty* premiered, is one of the most famous ballet halls in the world. Pavlova, Nureyev, Nizhinsky, and Baryshnikov all started here. For two weeks in June, the theater hosts the **White Nights Festival.** Tickets (15R and up) go on sale ten days in advance. (M4: Sadovaya. Tel. 114 43 44. *Kassa* open W-Su 11am-3pm and 4-7pm.) **Shostakovich Philharmonic Hall,** Mikhailovskaya ul. 2 (tel. 118 42 57; M3: Gostiny Dvor), opposite the Grand Hotel Europe, has both classical and modern concerts. **Aleksandrinsky Teatr** (Александринский Театр), pl. Ostrovskovo 2, attracts some of Russia's most famous actors and companies. (M3: Gostiny Dvor. Tel. 110 41 03. *Kassa* open daily 11am-3pm and 4-8pm.) The Russian circus, while justly famous, is not for animal rights activists; **Tsirk** (Circus; Цирк), nab. Fontanki 3, near the Russky Muzey, is Russia's oldest traditional circus. (M3: Gostiny Dvor. Tel. 314 84 78. Tickets from 10R. *Kassa* open daily 11am-4pm.)

NIGHTLIFE. During the pre-Gorbachev era, St. Petersburg was the heart of the Russian underground music scene; today, the city still hosts a large number of good clubs. Be careful when going home; cabs are usually a safe bet, but make sure your bridge isn't up. HI hostels can recommend the newest places. Check the Friday issue of *St. Petersburg Times* and *Pulse* for events. From the Metro, turn left on Ligovsky and follow it for 10min. to get to hip-happening ⬛**Metro,** Ligovsky pr. 174, and its three dance floors. (M4: Ligovsky Prospekt. Beer 35-75R per pint; mixed drinks 45-80R. Cover Su-Th 36-54R; F-Sa 54-90R. Open daily 10pm-6am.) **Mama,** (Мама), ul. Malaya Monetnaya 3b (Малая Монетная), is very hip, very young, very techno, and rages very late. (M2: Gorkovskaya. Beer 30-55R. Cover 60R. Open F-Sa 11:50pm-6am.) Go right for four blocks on pr. Chernyshevskovo (Чернышевского), then turn left on Shpalernaya and look for the small sign on the left to find the mellow **JFC Jazz Club,** Shpalernaya ul. 33 (Шпалерная). (M1: Chernyshevskaya. Tel. 272 9850. Cover 35R. Open daily 7-10pm.) You wouldn't be reading *Let's Go Europe* if we didn't tell you where to get your Guinness (35R)— **The Shamrock,** ul. Dekabristov 27 (Декабристов), is the place, across from the Mariinsky in Teatralnaya pl. (M4: Sadovaya. Open daily noon-2am.) **69 Club,** 2-aya Krasnoarmeiskaya 6 (2-ая Красноармейская), attracts both gay and straight clubbers. (M1: Technologichesky Institut. Cover 30-120R. Open Tu-Su 11pm-6am.)

⬛ EXCURSIONS FROM ST. PETERSBURG

Ride the suburban *elektrichka* trains out of St. Petersburg to witness the Russians' love of the countryside. Most residents of St. Petersburg own or share a *dacha* outside the city and go there every weekend. The tsars were no different; they, too, built country houses. Burned to the ground during the Nazi retreat, Soviet authorities restored three palaces to their original opulence.

PETERHOF (Петергоф). Formerly known as Petrodvorets (Петродворец), this is the largest and most thoroughly restored of the palaces. The entire complex at Peterhof is 300 years old, although many tsars added their own touches. The **Grand Palace** (Bolshoy Dvorets; Большой Дворец) was Peter's first home here, but his daughter, Empress Elizabeth, and then Catherine the Great greatly expanded and remodeled it with a generous portion of opulence. (Open Tu-Su 10:30am-6pm; *kassa* closes at 5pm; closed last Tu of the month. Tours 10:30am-noon and 2:45-4:15pm. 200R, students 100R. Cameras 80R. Handbags must be checked; 1R.)

Below the Grand Palace, the **Lower Gardens** are perfect for a picnic on the shores of the Gulf of Finland. (Open daily 9am-9pm. 100R, students 50R. Fountains flow May-Sept. M-F 11am-8pm, Su 11am-9pm.) Follow the sound of children's shrieks and giggles to the **"joke fountains,"** which, triggered by one misstep, splash their

RUSSIA

unwitting victims. On the other side of the garden stands the elegant **Monplaisir,** where Peter actually lived; he was the tsar with good taste. (Open Th-Tu 10:30am-6pm; closed last Th of the month. 70R, students 35R.) Next door is the **Catherine Building** (Ekaterininsky Korpus; Екатерининский Корпус), where Cathy the Great laid low while her hubby was being overthrown on her orders. (Open F-W 10:30am-6pm; closed last F of each month. 70R, students 35R.) The **Hermitage Pavilion,** in the woods of the eastern part of the lower park, is opposite Monplaisir; its 17th- and 18th-century European art is well worth seeing. (Open Tu-Su 10:30am-5pm; closed last Th of the month. 70R, students 35R.)

Take the **elektrichka** from the Baltiysky vokzal (M1: Baltiyskaya; Балтийская; 40min., every 15min., 8R). Buy tickets from the office (*prigorodnye kassa;* Пригородные касса) in the courtyard—ask for "NO-viy Peter-GOFF, too-DAH ee oh-BRAHT-nah." Get off at Novy Peterhof (sit in the first cars or you might not see the station sign until it's too late); there, hop on a shuttle to the main gates (3R).

TSARSKOYE SELO (Царское Село)/**PUSHKIN** (Пушкин). About 25km south of the city, **Tsarskoye Selo** ("Tsar's Village") surrounds Catherine the Great's summer residence, a gorgeous azure, white, and gold Baroque palace overlooking sprawling, English-style parks. The area was renamed "Pushkin" during the Soviet era—most Russians and train conductors still use that name. The Baroque Palace, named **Catherine's Palace** (Ekaterininsky Dvorets), after Elizabeth's mom Catherine I, was largely destroyed by the Nazis; each room exhibits a photograph of it in a war-torn condition. Despite this, many of the salons, especially the huge, glittering **Grand Hall** ballroom, have been magnificently restored. (Tel. 466 66 69. Open W-M 10am-5pm; closed last Monday of the month. 186R, students 92R. Photos 86R.) Bring a picnic and wander through the lovely 1400-acre **Catherine Park,** a melange of English, French, and Italian gardening styles. (Open daily 10am-8pm. 50R, students 25R; free after 6pm.) Take any **elektrichka** from Vitebsky vokzal (M1: Pushkinskaya). To buy your ticket, go to the bunker-like building behind the station to the right (tickets 6R). All trains leaving from platforms 1-3 stop in Pushkin (30min.). From the station, it's a 10-minute ride on bus 371 or 382 (2R) to its end.

PAVLOVSK (Павловск). Catherine the Great gave the park and gardens at Pavlovsk to her son Paul in 1777, perhaps because she wanted to keep her eye on him. The largest **park** of all the outlying palaces, Pavlovsk's lush, shady paths wind past wild foliage, bridges, and pavilions. (Open daily 9am-8pm. 14R, students 7R.) Paul's **Great Palace** is not as spectacular as his mother's at Tsarskoye Selo, but is nonetheless worth a visit. (Open Sa-Th 10am-5pm. 140R, students 70R.) Although visits to Pushkin and Pavlovsk can be combined in one day, a leisurely visit is more enjoyable. To reach Pavlovsk, get off at the **elektrichka** stop after Pushkin on trains leaving from platforms 1-3 at Vitebsky vokzal. To get to the palace from the train station, take bus 370, 383, or 383A. To get to Pushkin from Pavlovsk, take bus 370 or 383 from the Great Palace, or bus 473 from Pavlovsk Station (3R).

BABUSHKA BOYCOTT They push harder than anyone on the buses and metro. They bundle up to the ears on even the hottest days in scarves and winter coats, then strip down to teeny-weeny bikinis and sunbathe on the banks of the Neva. They are *babushki,* and they mean business. Technically, *babushka* means grandma, but under the Soviet system, once it became all right to be rude, Russians began using it as a generic term for elderly women. In any case, be warned: if a *babushka* gets on the bus or metro, no matter how hardy she looks, and how weak and tired you feel, surrender your seat, or prepare for the verbal pummeling of a lifetime.

SLOVAKIA (SLOVENSKO)

US$1 = 41SK (SLOVAK KORUNY)	**10SK = US$0.24**
CDN$1 = 28SK	**10SK = CDN$0.36**
UK£1 = 66SK	**10SK = UK£0.15**
IR£1 = 56SK	**10SK = IR£0.18**
AUS$1 = 27SK	**10SK = AUS$0.37**
NZ$1 = 22SK	**10SK = NZ$0.46**
SAR1 = 6.83SK	**10SK = SAR1.46**
DM1 = 22.43SK	**10SK = DM0.44**

PHONE CODES | Country code: 421. International dialing prefix: 00.

After centuries of nomadic invasions, Hungarian domination, and Soviet industrialization, Slovakia has finally emerged as an independent country. Freedom has introduced new challenges, however, as the older generation reluctantly gives way to their chic, English-speaking offspring. The nation remains in a state of generational flux between industry and agriculture, unable to muster the resources necessary for an easy Westernization and unwilling to return to its past. This leaves a strange mixture of fairy-tale traditionalism and easy-going youth, which combine with low prices to create a haven for budget travelers. From tiny villages to the busy streets of its capital, Slovakia is coming to grips with progress, as the good old days retreat to castle ruins, pastures, and the stunning Tatras above.

For more on Slovakia's wacky adventures, try *Let's Go: Eastern Europe 2000.*

DISCOVER SLOVAKIA

Slovakia is an outdoor-lover's paradise. In western Slovakia, the **Low Tatras** near **Liptovský Mikuláš** are a relatively deserted mountain range offering everything from easy day hikes in the wooded foothills to hefty over-night treks high above the tree line (p. 786). You'll have to battle with German and Slovak tourists to tackle the trails and slopes of the **High Tatras** near **Starý Smokovec,** but it'll be worth it to witness the snow-capped, tarn-laced peaks of this super-compact range, one of the best—and cheapest—mountain playlands in Europe (p. 785). Farther south, **Slov-**

enský **Raj National Park** offers miles of ravine-crossing, cliff-climbing, heart-stopping treks. For the more faint-hearted visitor to the Slovaks' favorite national park, there are many ice caves ripe for spelunking (p. 786).

GETTING THERE AND GETTING AROUND

Although Bratislava has its own airport, it is cheaper and easier to fly into Vienna's **Wien Schwechat Flughafen** (see p. 85). **ŽSR** is the national train company; every information desk has a copy of **Cestovný poriadok** (58Sk), the master schedule. Large train stations operate **BIJ-Wasteels** offices, which offer 30% discounts on tickets to European cities for those under 26. **Eurail** is not valid in Slovakia. As everywhere, you'll pay extra for an InterCity or EuroCity fast train, and if there's a boxed R on the timetable, a *miestenka* (reservation; 7Sk) is required. If you board the train without one, expect to pay a 150Sk fine. *Odchody* (departures) and *príchody* (arrivals) are posted on yellow and white signs, respectively. Reservations are sometimes required and generally recommended for *expresný* trains and first-class seats, but are not necessary for *rychlík* (fast), *spešný* (semi-fast), or *osobný* (local) trains. In many hilly regions, **ČSAD** or **SAD buses** are the best option. Except for very long trips, buy the ticket on the bus. Schedules seem designed to drive foreigners batty with their many footnotes; the most important are as follows: **X** (it actually looks like two crossed hammers), weekdays only; **a,** Saturdays and Sundays only; **r** and **k,** excluding holidays. **Numbers** refer to the days of the week on which the bus runs—1 is Monday, 2 is Tuesday, etc. *"Premava"* means including; *"nepremava"* is except; following those words are often lists of dates (day, then month). In the summer, watch out for July 5.

Road conditions in Slovakia are generally good. However, gas is expensive at US$2.75 per gallon. To travel on expressways, drivers must display a special sticker on their windshield available at border crossings for 200-400 SK. The **Auto Atlas CSFR,** sold in Slovakia, lists the telephone numbers of roadside assistance services nationwide. The national motoring club is **Ustředni Automotoklub SR,** Wolkrova 4, 851 01 Bratislava (tel. (07) 85 09 10; open M-F 7:45am-4:45pm). In Bratislava, contact 24-hour road service by dialing (07) 36 37 11. The Slovaks love to ride **bicycles; VKÚ** publishes color-coded cycling maps (70-80Sk). Bicycle rentals are available through most tourist offices. **Hitchhiking** is common among Slovaks; *Let's Go* does not recommend hitchhiking as a safe means of transportation.

ESSENTIALS

DOCUMENTS AND FORMALITIES. Citizens of South Africa and the US can visit Slovakia visa-free for up to 30 days; Canada and Ireland 90 days; and the UK 180 days. Citizens of Australia and New Zealand need a 30-day visa (single-entry US$21; double-entry US$32; 90-day multiple-entry US$52; 180-day multiple-entry US$93; transit US$21). Apply to an embassy or consulate in person or by mail; processing takes two days. Travelers must also register their visa within three days of entering Slovakia, although hotels will do this automatically. If you need a visa extension, you must notify the Office of Border and Alien Police.

Slovakian Embassies Abroad: Australia, 47 Culgoa Circuit, O'Malley, Canberra ACT 2606 (tel. (6) 290 15 16; fax 290 17 55); **Canada,** 50 Rideau Terr, Ottawa, ON K1M 2A1 (tel. (613) 749-4442; fax 749-4989); **South Africa,** 930 Arcadia St, Arcadia, Pretoria; P.O. Box 12736, Hatfield, 0028 (tel. (012) 342 20 51; fax 342 36 88); **UK,** 25 Kensington Palace Gdns, London W8 4QY (tel. (020) 72 43 08 03; fax 77 27 58 24); **US,** 2201 Wisconsin Ave NW, #250, Washington, DC 20007 (tel. (202) 965-5160; fax 965-5166; email svkem@concentric.net; www.slovakemb.com).

Foreign Embassies in Slovakia: All foreign embassies are in **Bratislava** (see p. 782).

TOURIST OFFICES. The main tourist offices are organized as the **Asociácia Informačných Centier Slovenská (AICS);** look for the green logo. The offices are invariably on a town's main square; the nearest one can be found by dialing 186. English is often spoken and accommodations can usually be secured.

MONEY. One hundred **halér** make up one Slovak **koruna (Sk). Všeobecná Úverová Banka (VÚB)** has offices in even the smallest towns and cashes **traveler's checks** for a 1% commission. Most offices give **MC** cash advances and have Cirrus/Plus/MC/Visa **ATMs,** called **Bankomat.** Many **Slovenská Sporiteľňa** bureaus handle **Visa** cash advances and have Visa **ATMs.** Leave your **AmEx** at home—it's useless in Slovakia. A very basic day in Slovakia (staying in campgrounds and shopping at grocery stores) averages US$15; a more extravagant day (hostels and restaurants) averages US$20-25. **Tipping** is common in restaurants; most people round up to a convenient number by refusing change when they pay, with 8-10% being generous.

COMMUNICATION

Post: Slovakia's postal system is efficient. *Poste Restante* mail with a "1" after the city name will arrive at the main post office. Sending an airmail **letter** to Australia, Canada, New Zealand, South Africa, UK, and the US costs 10Sk and takes 1-2 weeks.

Telephone: Local calls cost 2Sk. Even in small towns, **cardphones** are common. They sometimes refuse your card (150Sk), but they're more reliable than coin-phones. **International direct dial** numbers include: **AT&T,** 00 42 10 01 01; **Sprint,** 00 42 18 71 87; **MCI WorldPhone Direct,** 00 42 10 01 12; **Canada Direct,** 00 42 10 01 51; **BT Direct,** 080 00 44 01. **Fire,** tel. 150. **Ambulance,** tel. 155. **Police,** tel. 158.

Language: Slovak, closely related to Czech, is a tricky Slavic language, but any attempt will be appreciated. English is not uncommon among youth, but people outside the capital are more likely to speak German. You may not find any English-speakers, even in the tourist office. Russian is understood, but not always welcome. For basic phrases, see p. 949.

ACCOMMODATIONS AND CAMPING. Foreigners will often pay twice as much as Slovaks for the same room. Finding cheap accommodations in Bratislava before July is impossible, and without reservations, the outlook in Slovenský Raj and the Tatras is bleak. The tourist office, **SATUR,** or **Slovakotourist** can usually help. **Juniorhotels (HI),** although uncommon, are a step above the usual hostel. In the mountains, **chaty** (mountain huts/chalets) range from plush quarters for 400Sk to a friendly bunk and outhouse for 150Sk. **Hotel** prices fall drastically outside Bratislava and the High Tatras, and are rarely full. **Penzióny** (pensions) are less expensive than hotels. Two forms of *ubytovanie* (lodging) cater mainly to Slovaks and offer bare-bones rooms: **stadiums** and sport centers run hotels for teams, and **workers' hostels** offer hospital-like rooms with no pub and real workers. **Campgrounds** lurk on the outskirts of most towns, and many offer bungalows.

FOOD AND DRINK. Slovakia emerged from its 1000-year Hungarian captivity with a taste for paprika, spicy *gulaš,* and fine wines. The good news for vegetarians is that the national dish, *brynd°ové halusky,* is a plate of dumpling-esque pasta smothered in sheep's cheese; the bad news is that it sometimes comes with bacon. The most-favored Slovak beer is *Zlatý Ba°ant.*

LOCAL FACTS

Time: Slovakia is 1hr. ahead of Greenwich Mean Time (GMT; see p. 49).

Climate: Slovakia has a continental climate, with bitter-cold winters, very warm summers, and moderate precipitation. Spring and autumn are the best times to visit the country, although Nov.-Feb. is the best time for skiing and Aug. is the best time for hiking.

Hours: Most museums close Mondays, and theaters take a break during July and Aug. **Shops** are open M-F 9am-6pm; some close noon-2pm and some are open until noon on Saturday. **Banks** are open M-F 8am-3pm.

Holidays in 2000: Independence Day (Jan. 1); Epiphany (Jan. 6); Good Friday (Apr. 21); Easter (Apr. 23); Labor Day (May 1); Sts. Cyril and Methodius Day (July 5); Anniversary of Slovak National Uprising (Aug. 29); Constitution Day (Sept. 1); Our Lady of the Seven Sorrows (Sept. 15); All Saint's Day (Nov. 1); Christmas (Dec. 24-26).

BRATISLAVA

Perched directly between Vienna and Budapest, Bratislava is experienced most often as a passing blip—a blur of Soviet-style apartment blocks, polluted roadways, and crumbling buildings—on the way to bigger, more cosmopolitan cities. Prague continues to loom over Bratislava, reminding Slovaks of the relative disappointment of post-Czechoslovak independence. However, Bratislava's cobblestoned Old Town hosts relaxing cafés, talented street musicians, and several stunning Baroque buildings, while vineyards and castle ruins lace the outskirts of town. If nothing else, Bratislava offers visitors the thrill of an "undiscovered" city, and a glimpse into the psyche of a nation struggling to redefine itself.

▌ GETTING THERE AND GETTING AROUND

Trains: Bratislava Hlavná stanica (tel. 39 59 04), north of the city center. International tickets at counters 5-13. **Wasteels** office in front sells discounted tickets to under 26ers (see p. 62). Open M-F 8:30am-4:30pm. To: **Vienna** (1½hr., 3 per day, 248Sk); **Budapest** (2½-3hr., 7 per day, 660 Sk, Wasteels 245Sk); **Prague** (5hr., 7 per day, 350Sk); **Warsaw** (8hr., 1 per day, 1400Sk, Wasteels 342Sk); **Kraków** (8hr., 1 per day, 1080Sk, Wasteels 205Sk); and **Berlin** (10hr., 2 per day, 3600Sk, Wasteels 2497Sk).

Buses: Mlynské nivy 31 (tel. 09 84 22 22 22), east of the center. More reliable and frequent than trains for domestic transport. Check ticket for bus number (*č. aut.*) since several different buses may depart from the same stand. To: **Vienna** (1½hr., 10 per day, 400Sk); **Budapest** (4hr., 2 per day, 400Sk); and **Prague** (5hr., 8 per day, 247Sk).

Local Transportation: Daytime **trams** and **buses** (4am-11pm) cost 10Sk per ride; buy tickets at kiosks or the orange *automats* in most bus stations. **Night buses** marked with black and orange numbers in the 500s require 2 10Sk tickets; they run at midnight and 3am. Most trams pass by Nám. SNP, while most buses stop at the north base of Nový Most. The fine for joyriding is 1000Sk. **Tourist passes** are sold at some kiosks: 24-hour 45Sk, 48-hour 80Sk, 3-day 100Sk, 7-day 150Sk.

Hitchhiking: Those hitching to **Vienna** cross most SNP and walk down Viedenská cesta; though this road also travels to **Hungary** via Győr, fewer cars head in that direction. Hitchers to **Prague** take bus 121 or 122 from the center to the Patronka stop.

▌ ORIENTATION AND PRACTICAL INFORMATION

Bratislava is a proverbial stone's throw from the borders of Austria and Hungary. Avoid getting off at the **Nové Mesto** train station; it's much farther from the center than **Hlavná stanica** (Main Station). To get downtown from Hlavná stanica, head straight past the waiting buses, turn right on Šancová and left on Štefánikova; or take tram 1 to "Poštová" at **Nám. SNP** (the city center lies between Nám. SNP and the river). From there, Uršulínska leads to the tourist office. From the bus station, take trolleybus 215 to the center; or turn right on Mlynské nivy, walk 10min. to Dunajska, then follow it to Kamenné nám. (a block from the tourist office).

Tourist Offices: Bratislavská Informačná Služba (BIS), Klobučnicka 2 (tel. 54 43 37 15 and 54 43 43 70; fax 54 43 27 08; email bis@isnet.sk; www.isnet.sk/bis). Sells maps (28Sk), gives city tours, and books rooms (singles July-Aug. 300Sk, Sept.-June 900Sk) for a 50Sk fee. Open M-F 8am-7pm, Sa-Su 8:30am-1:30pm.

Embassies: Canada (honorary consulate), Kolárska 4 (tel. 36 12 77; fax 36 12 20). Open M and W 3-5pm. **South Africa,** Jančova 8 (tel. 54 41 15 82; fax 54 41 25 81). Open M-F 9am-noon. **UK,** Panská 16 (tel. 54 41 96 32; fax 54 41 00 02). **US,** Hviezdoslavovo nám. 4 (tel. 54 43 08 61; emergency (0903) 70 36 66; fax 54 41 51 48). Open M-F 8am-4:30pm.

Currency Exchange: VÚB, Gorkého 9 (tel. 59 55 79 76; fax 59 55 80 90). 1% commission on traveler's checks. **Cash advances** on V, MC. Open M-W and F 8am-5pm, Th 8am-noon. A **24-hour currency exchange machine** outside Bank Austria, Mostová 6, changes US$, DM, and UK£ into Sk for no commission. **ATMs** are all over the center.

American Express: Tatratour, Mickiewiczova 2 (tel. 52 93 28 11; fax 31 78 88). Cash 1% commission, traveler's checks 2%. Mail held. Open M-F 9am-6pm, Sa 9am-noon.

Bratislava
ACCOMMODATIONS
A Youth Hostel
B Youth Hostel Bernolak
C Pension Gremium

24-hour Pharmacy: Nám. SNP 20 (tel. 54 43 29 52), at Gorkého and Laurinská.

Internet Access: Klub Internet, Vajanského nábr. 2 (tel. 59 34 91 96). At the back of the National Museum on Múzejná. 2Sk per min. Open M-F 9am-9pm, Sa-Su noon-9am.

Post Office: Nám. SNP 35 (tel. 54 43 12 41). *Poste Restante* at counter 5. Open M-F 7am-8pm, Sa 7am-6pm, Su 9am-2pm. Address mail to be held: Thomas <u>MCCARTHY</u>, *Poste Restante*, Nám. SNP 35, **81000** Bratislava 1, Slovakia.

PHONE CODE City code: 7. From outside Slovakia, dial int'l dialing prefix (see inside back cover) + 421 + 7 + local number.

▌ ACCOMMODATIONS AND CAMPING

In July and August, several dorms open as hostels; until then, good deals are hard to find. Most cheap beds are a 20-minute walk (5-minute tram ride) from the center.

🔖 **Pension Gremium,** Gorkého 11 (tel. 54 13 10 26; fax 54 43 06 53). Central location just off Hviezdoslavovo nám. with fluffy beds, sparkling private showers, huge fans, and a popular café downstairs. Singles 890Sk; doubles 1290Sk. Breakfast included. English spoken. Only five rooms, so call ahead. Check-out 9am. V, MC.

Youth Hostel Bernolak, Bernolákova 1 (tel. 39 77 21; fax 39 77 24). From the train station, take bus 23, 74, or 218, or tram 3 to "Račianske Mýto." From the bus station, take bus 121 or 122. A friendly hostel with a disco downstairs. All rooms have baths. 300Sk per person; 10% discount with Euro26, HI, or ISIC. Check-out 9am. Open July-Sept. 15.

Výskumný Ústav Zváračský, Pionierska 17 (tel. 504 67 61). Tram 3 from train station to "Pionierska." Worker's hostel. Singles 350Sk; doubles 700Sk. Curfew midnight.

Autocamping Zlaté Piesky, Senecká cesta 2 (tel. 25 73 73), in suburban Trnávka. Take tram 2 or 4 or bus 215 from the train station to the last stop and cross the footbridge. 90Sk per tent, 100Sk per person. Bungalow doubles 650Sk; triples 900Sk.

◐ FOOD

A few restaurants serve the region's spicy meat mixtures. If all else fails, you can chow at one of the city's ubiquitous burger stands. For **groceries,** try **Tesco,** Kamenné nám. 1. (Open M-W 8am-7pm, Th-F 8am-8pm, Sa 8am-5pm, Su 9am-5pm.)

◼ **Prašná Bašta,** Zámočnícka 11 (tel. 54 43 49 57). Excellent traditional Slovak dishes 88-175Sk. Ask for the English menu. Open daily 11am-11pm.

Café London, Panská 17 (tel. 54 43 12 61), in the British Council's courtyard. Offers the respite of good, old-fashioned sandwiches (52-118Sk). Open M-F 9am-9pm.

Vegetarian Jedáleň, Laurinská 8. Cafeteria-style lunch spot popular with local businessfolk and young Slovak herbivores. Entrees 50-100Sk. Open M-F 11am-3pm.

◉ SIGHTS

Almost all of the sights worth seeing in Bratislava are located in **Old Bratislava** (Stará Bratislava), centered around **Nám. SNP.** From Nám. SNP, which commemorates the bloody Slovak National Uprising (SNP) against the fascist regime, walk down Uršulínska to **Primaciálné nám.** and the square's Neoclassical **Primate's Palace** (Primaciálný Palác), Primaciálné nám. 1, which dates from 1781. Napoleon and Austrian Emperor Franz I signed the Peace of Pressburg here in 1805. (Open Tu-Su 10am-5pm. 20Sk.) A walk to the left (as you exit the palace) down Klobučnícka leads to **Hlavné nám.;** from there, a right up Zámočnicka will bring you to the 13th-century **St. Michael's Tower** (Michalská Brána), the only preserved gateway from the town's medieval fortifications. (Open M and W-F 10am-5pm, Sa-Su 11am-6pm. 20Sk.) Retrace your steps to Hlavné nám. and set foot in the square's Old Town Hall (Stará Radnica), Hlavné nám. 1, to view the **Town History Museum** (Muzeum Histórie Mesta). You don't need a ticket to see the wonderful 1:500 model of 1945-55 Bratislava inside. (Open Tu-F 10am-5pm, Sa-Su 11am-6pm. 25Sk, students 10Sk.) From Hlavné nám., walk left down Rybárska Brána until you end up in the eastern end of **Hviezdoslavovo nám.** Continue straight down Mostová (the continuation of Rybárska Brána on the other side of the square) and turn left at the Danube to reach the **Slovak National Museum** (Slovenské Národné Muzeum), Vajanského nábr. 2, which houses local archaeological finds including casts of Neanderthal skeletons. (Open Tu-Su 9am-5pm. 20Sk, students 10Sk.) Backtrack along the Danube past Nám. Štúra to the **Slovak National Gallery,** Rázusovo nábr. 2, which displays artwork from the Gothic and Baroque periods, as well as some modern works. (Open Tu-Su 10am-6pm. 25Sk, students 5Sk.) Continue with the Danube on your left to **New Bridge** (Nový Most), whose reins are held by a giant flying saucer. (10Sk to ascend.) Turn right on Staromestská and follow it away from the river to get to **St. Martin's Cathedral** (Dóm sv. Martina), a fairly typical Gothic church where the kings of Hungary were crowned for three centuries (now undergoing renovations). Cross the highway on the far side of St. Martin's using the pedestrian overpass to view articles of a vanished population at the **Museum of Jewish Culture** (Múzeum Židovskej Kultúry), Židovská 17. (Open M-F and Su 11am-5pm. Last entry 4:30pm. 50Sk.)

Perched on a hill to the west of the city center, the four-towered **Bratislava Castle** (Bratislavský hrad) is Bratislava's defining landmark. Of strategic importance for more than a millennium, the castle's heyday came in the 18th century, when Austrian Empress Maria Theresa held court there. The castle was destroyed by fire in 1811 and by bombs during WWII; what's left today is a communist-era restoration. The view of the Danube is more impressive than the castle itself.

♫ ENTERTAINMENT

For film, concert, and theater schedules, get a copy of *Kám v Bratislave* at BIS (see **Tourist Offices,** p. 782); it's entirely in Slovak, but the info is easily deciphered.

SLOVAKIA

> ## YOU WANT FRIES WITH THAT?
> The only thing less comprehensible to Westerners than a Slovakian menu is a menu at one of Bratislava's many burger stands. A *syrový burger* (cheeseburger) costs less than a *hamburger so syrom* (hamburger with cheese) because, as the stand owner will explain with humiliatingly clear logic, a cheeseburger is made of cheese—*only* cheese. A *pressburger*, named after Bratislava's former moniker Pressburg, consists of bologna on a bun, and hamburgers are actually ham. Everything comes boiled, except, of course, the cheese.

Slovenská Filharmonia plays regularly at Palackého 2; the box office is around the corner on Medená. (Tel. 54 43 33 51. Open M-Tu and Th-F 1-7pm, W 8am-2pm.) The Filharmonia and most theaters vacation July-August. A dozen **cinemas** are scattered across the city; unfortunately, most films are dubbed into Slovak. Bratislava's sleekest twentysomethings gather at the **Alligator Club**, Laurinská 7, to hear live blues bands (daily at 7pm) and sip mixed drinks (80-120Sk). (Open M-F 10am-midnight, Sa 11am-midnight, Su 11am-10pm.) **Dubliner**, Sedlarská 6, Bratislava's *ersatz* Irish pub, has pricey Guinness (75Sk). (Open M-Sa 10am-1am, Su 11am-midnight.)

THE TATRA MOUNTAINS (TATRY)

The mesmerizing High Tatras span the border between Slovakia and Poland and are home to hundreds of addictive hiking and skiing trails along the Carpathians' highest peaks (2650m). The Tatras are one of the most compact ranges in the world, and feature sky-scraping hikes, glacial tarns, and super-deep snows.

STARÝ SMOKOVEC. Starý Smokovec (STAH-ree SMO-ko-vets) is the High Tatras' most central resort and, founded in the 17th century, one of the oldest. Cheap sleeps down the road in Horný Smokovec make it easily accessible to the budget traveler. The town is a little bland, but the town's trails are spectacular. The funicular to **Hrebienok** (1285m) leads right to the heart of hiking country; to hike it, start at the funicular station behind Hotel Grand (behind the train station) and head 30min. up the green trail. Another 20min. from Hrebienok, the green trail leads north to the foaming **Cold Waterfall** (Studeného Potoka). The eastward blue trail descends from the waterfall to **Tatranská Lomnica** (1½hr.), while the yellow trail goes down along the river to **Tatranská Lesná** (1½hr.). A TEŽ train goes from Tatranská Lomnica and Tatranská Lesná back to Starý Smokovec. The long, red **Tatranská magistrála** trail travels west from Hrebienok breaking the tree-line at chalet **Sliezsky Dom** (tel. (0969) 442 52 61; 2hr., 1670m; 240Sk per person), then zig-zagging down to **Chata Nu Popradskom Plese**, a.k.a. **Chata Kapitána Moravku** (1500m; 5½hr.; tel. (0969) 449 21 77; 170-230Sk per person) on the shore of the lake **Popradské Pleso.**

TEŽ **trains** arrive from Poprad (30min., every hr., 12Sk) at the town's lowest point, south of Hotel Grand. **Buses** to many Tatra resorts and to Zakopane, Poland (2hr., 2 per day July-Aug. and Dec.-Mar., 80Sk) stop in a parking lot just east of the train station. Facing uphill, head up the road that runs just left of the train station, then cross the main road veering left. The **Tatranská Informačná Kancelária**, in Dom Služieb, has weather info and sells hiking maps, including the crucial **VKÚ sheet 113** (70Sk). (Tel. (0969) 44 23 34 40; fax 442 31 27. Open M-F 8am-5pm, Sa 9am-1pm.) Turn right on the main road from the stations and walk 10min. to **Hotel Šport**, a mega-complex that includes a café, sauna, pool, and massage parlor. (Tel. (0969) 442 23 61; fax 442 27 19. Singles 415Sk; doubles 720Sk; triples 1015Sk. Breakfast included.) Another 15min. along the road (or 2 stops on the TEŽ toward Tatranská Lomnica), and down a short path through the trees, is **Hotel Junior Vysoké Tatry.** (Tel. (0969) 442 26 61; fax 442 24 93. Singles 230Sk; doubles 360Sk; triples 490Sk; quads 560Sk; with ISIC, singles 200Sk. 10Sk cheaper off-season; 30% MC discount. Breakfast included. Book one week ahead.) **Grocers** clutter Starý Smokovec; five are on the main road above the stations.

ŠTRBSKÉ PLESO. Placid Štrbské Pleso (Lake Štrbské; SHTERB-skay PLAY-so) is the Tatras' most-beloved **ski** resort. The town is the range's highest settlement and a great starting point for **hikes.** Just one lift runs in summer, hoisting visitors to **Chata pod Soliskom** (1840m) overlooking the lake and the expansive plains behind Štrbské Pleso. (Runs June-Sept. 8am-3:30pm. July-Aug. 85Sk, round-trip 120Sk; June and Sept. 60Sk, round-trip 85Sk.) Once at the top, hike the red trail to the peak of **Predné Solisko** (2093m). TEŽ **trains** leave hourly for **Starý Smokovec** (30min., 16Sk).

LIPTOVSKÝ MIKULÁŠ. Liptovský Mikuláš (LIP-tov-skee MEE-koo-lash) is fairly drab, but it's a good base for hiking in the **Nízke Tatry** (Low Tatras). To hike **Mt. Ďumbier,** the region's tallest peak (2043m), catch an early **bus** (20min., every hr., 10Sk) from platform 11 at the bus station to Liptovský Ján Kúpele and hike the blue trail up the Štiavnica river and onto the Ďumbierske Sedlo (saddle) by Chata (hut) generála M.R. Štefanika (5hr.). Then follow the red trail to the ridge, which leads to the summit (1½hr.). Going back down the ridge and following the red sign leads to neighboring peak **Chopok** (2024m), the second-highest in the range. At the hut there, **Kammená chata,** snag a bed (120Sk), a beer (30Sk), or a mug of tea (10Sk). From Chopok, it's a mellow walk down the blue trail to the bus stop at Jasná (1½hr.), but you may prefer the view from the chairlift (June-Sept. 8:30am-4pm; Dec.-Mar. until 3:30pm; 85Sk). **Trains** from Bratislava (4hr., 7 per day, 192Sk) are cheaper and more frequent than buses. To get to the center, follow Štefánikova toward the gas station at the far end of the bus station, then turn right onto Hodžu. The **tourist office,** Nám. Mieru 1, in the Dom Služieb complex on the northern side of the square, books rooms and sells hiking maps; ask for VKÚ sheets 122 and 123 (78Sk). (Tel. (0849) 552 24 18; fax 55 14 48; email infolm@trynet.sk. Open mid-June to mid-Sept. and mid-Dec. to Mar. M-F 8am-7pm, Sa 8am-2pm, Su noon-6pm; reduced hours off-season.) **Hotel Kriváň,** Štúrova 5, is right across the square from the tourist office. (Tel. (0849) 552 24 14; fax 552 42 43. Singles 250-350Sk; doubles 350-500Sk.)

SLOVENSKÝ RAJ

South of Poprad and on the other side of the Nízke Tatry lies the Slovenský Raj (Slovak Paradise) National Park. Fast-flowing streams have carved deep ravines into the limestone hills, while hikers and skiers have carved their own trails between tiny villages cut off from the rest of Slovakia. On the shores of manmade lake Palčmanská Maša, **Dedinky** (pop. 400) is the largest town on Slovenský Raj's southern border. The easiest way to get there is to catch the **bus** from **Poprad** (dir: Rožňava; 1hr., 6 per day, 33Sk). The bus stops at a junction 2km south of Dedinky. From the intersection, walk down the road that the bus didn't take. The road curves down into the basin and comes to an intersection. Turn right and you will to find the disused railway station and a big dam. Cross the dam, turn right, and walk 10min. to Dedinky. Pick up a copy of **VKÚ sheet 124** (70-80Sk) before entering the region, or at comfy **Hotel Priehrada** in Dedinky; the hotel also offers **camping.** (Tel. (0942) 982 12; fax 982 21. 200Sk per person; cheaper Sept. to mid-Dec. and Apr.-June. Camping 20Sk per tent, 20Sk per person. Check-out 10am in hotel, 9am in huts.) One of the nicest hikes is **Biele vody** (White Waters; 1½hr.). The hike up one of the park's many rapids involves ladders and is one-way, so there's no turning back, even for vertigo. From Hotel Priehrada in Dedinky, take the red trail to Biele Vody. The blue cascade trail will be on the left; the green trail leads back down.

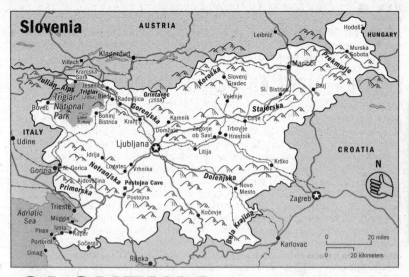

SLOVENIA (SLOVENIJA)

US$1 = 183SIT (SLOVENIAN TOLARS)	100SIT = US$0.54
CDN$1 = 123SIT	100SIT = CDN$0.80
UK£1 = 294SIT	100SIT = UK£0.33
IR£1 = 247SIT	100SIT = IR£0.40
AUS$1 = 119SIT	100SIT = AUS$0.83
NZ$1 = 97SIT	100SIT = NZ$1.01
SAR1 = 30SIT	100SIT = SAR3.25
DM1 = 99SIT	100SIT = DM1.01

PHONE CODES Country code: 386. International dialing prefix: 00.

Slovenia, the most prosperous of Yugoslavia's breakaway republics, has reveled in its independence, modernizing rapidly while turning a hungry eye toward the West. It has quickly separated itself from its neighbors, using liberal politics and a high GDP to gain entrance into highly sought-after trade and security alliances. For a country half Switzerland's size, Slovenia, on the "sunny side of the Alps," is also extraordinarily diverse: in a day, you can breakfast on an Alpine peak, lunch under the Mediterranean sun, and dine in a vineyard on the Pannonian plains.

For more coverage of Slovenia, check out *Let's Go: Eastern Europe 2000*.

DISCOVER SLOVENIA

Fashioning itself a Western European in an Eastern European's body, Slovenia doesn't quite fit in with its post-Soviet brethren. Prices are higher, locals are friendlier, and *everything* is cleaner and more efficient. Any visit to this Balkan odd-ball must start in youthful **Ljubljana** (p. 789). Planned by a prominent Central European architect, the city has the splendor and majesty of the most important Hapsburg cities and a café scene on par with Paris or Vienna. However, most visitors venture to Slovenia not for its urban escapades but for its Alpine delights. The **Julian Alps** (p. 792), while not as high as their Western cousins, are no less exciting: **Lake Bled** (p. 792) and **Lake Bohinj** (p. 792) are traversed by miles of hikes—ranging from relaxed to treacherous—in summer. In winter, both towns host very snowy, very steep, and relatively cheap skiing. For a taste of the Mediterranean, head south to Slovenia's corner of the **Istrian Peninsula** (p. 793), where you can lounge on the sun-scorched beaches of **Piran** (p. 793).

GETTING THERE AND GETTING AROUND

Slovenia is easily accessible by train, or plane. There are three international **airports,** but commercial flights all arrive at the **Ljubljana Airport,** which has regular bus service to the city 25km away. The national carrier **Adria Airways** flies to European capitals. A regular **hydrofoil** service also runs between Venice and Portorož.

Trains are cheap, clean, and reliable. Round-trip tickets are 20% cheaper than two one-way tickets. For most international destinations, travelers under 26 can get a 20% discount; check at the Ljubljana station (look for the **BIJ-Wasteels** logo). Domestic tickets are available for ISIC holders at a 30% discount. In both cases ask for a *"popust"* (discount). *"Vlak"* means train, *"prihodi vlakov"* means arrivals, and *"odhodi vlakov"* means departures. Look for trains that run *dnevno* (daily). **Buses** are roughly 25% more expensive, but run to some otherwise inaccessible places in the mountains. Tickets are sold at the station or on board; put your luggage in the passenger compartment if it's not too crowded. All large backpacks cost 200Sit extra. For those traveling by **car,** the **Automobile Association of Slovenia's** emergency telephone number is 987. *Let's Go* does not recommend **hitchhiking,** which is extremely uncommon in Slovenia. If not traveling by bus or train, most Slovenes transport themselves by **bike.** Nearly every town has a bike rental office.

ESSENTIALS

DOCUMENTS AND FORMALITIES. Australian, Canadian, Irish, New Zealand, UK, and US citizens can visit visa-free for up to 90 days. South Africans need visas (180-day single-entry or transit US$35; 180-day multiple entry US$70). Apply by mail or in person in your home country. Processing takes a few days.

Slovenian Embassies at Home: Australia, Level 6, Advance Bank Center, 60 Marcus Clarke St 2608, Canberra ACT 2601 (tel. (6) 243 48 30); **Canada,** 150 Metcalfe St, #2101, Ottawa, ON K2P 1P1 (tel. (613) 565-5781; fax 565-5783); **New Zealand,** Eastern Hutt Rd, Pomare, Lower Hutt, Wellington (tel. (644) 567 27); **UK,** Cavendish Ct 11-15, Wigmore St, London W1H 9LA (tel. (020) 74 95 77 75); **US,** 1525 New Hampshire Ave NW, Washington, DC 20036 (tel. (202) 667-5363; fax 667-4563).

Foreign Embassies in Slovenia: All embassies are located in Ljubljana (see p. 789).

TOURIST OFFICES. Tourist offices are in most major cities and tourist spots. The staff are helpful, speak English and German, provide basic information, and assist in finding accommodations. The main tourist organization in Slovenia is **Kompas.**

MONEY. The national **currency** is the Slovenian **tolar** (Sit). Currency prices are stable and set in Deutschmarks (DM). **Banks** are usually open Monday-Friday 8am-5pm and Saturday 8-11am. Some establishments charge no commission, a fact reflected by worse rates. Almost everyone accepts **credit cards,** including AmEx, but the most widely endorsed is MC. There's a 20% **Value Added Tax,** but for purchases over 9000Sit, it is refundable at the border. There is one **ATM** in Ljubljana, but they are nonexistent outside the city. You can, fortunately, withdraw money from bank tellers. Hostels average US$10-12; restaurant meals run US$4-7.

COMMUNICATION

Post: Mail is the cheap and reliable. **Post offices** are open M-F 8am-7pm and Sa 8am-noon, with night and Su service in larger cities. Airmail **letters** *(letalsko)* take 1-2 weeks to reach North America, Australia, New Zealand, and South Africa. To Australia and New Zealand, letters cost 110Sit, postcards 100Sit; US 105Sit, 95Sit; UK 100Sit, 90Sit.

Telephone: While at the post office, purchase a **magnetic phone card** (750Sit per 50 impulses, which yields 50 local calls or 90 seconds to the US). For MCI WorldPhone call 080 88 08. Similar services for other phone companies are not yet available, but should be by 2000. Operators will assist in connecting collect calls if you dial 901. Calling the US is expensive (over US$6 per min.). If you must, try the phones at the post office and pay when you're finished. Slovenia is in the midst of phone number reform; most aren't changing until January 2000, so some of the numbers in this chapter will be incorrect. **Ambulance,** tel. 112. **Fire,** tel. 112. **Police,** tel. 113.

Language: Slovene, a Slavic language, employs the Latin alphabet. Most young people speak at least some English, but the older generation (especially in the Alps) is more likely to understand German (in the north) or Italian (along the Adriatic). For a handy-dandy language chart and tips on pronounciation, see p. 949.

ACCOMMODATIONS AND CAMPING. At the height of tourist season, prices are steep, services slow, and rooms scarce. The seaside, packed as early as June, is claustrophobic in July and August. Tourists also tend to swarm to the mountains during these months. **Youth hostels** and **student dormitories** are cheap, but open only in summer (June 25-Aug. 30). **Pensions** are pricey and **hotels** impossible. The best option is **private rooms**—prices vary according to location, but rarely exceed US$30. Inquire at the tourist office or look for *Zimmer frei* or *sobe* signs on the street. **Campgrounds** can be crowded, but are generally in excellent condition.

FOOD AND DRINK. For mouth-watering homestyle cooking, try a *gostilna* or *gostišče* (interchangeable words for a restaurant, although a *gostišče* usually also rents rooms). **Vegetarians** should look for *štruklji*—sweet dumplings eaten as an entree. Fast food is not nearly as appetizing: the most popular street food in Ljubljana is horse burger. *Renski Rizling* and *Šipon* are popular white wines; *Cviček*, from the central region, and *Teran*, from the coast, are popular reds.

LOCAL FACTS

Time: Slovenia is 1hr. ahead of Greenwich Mean Time (GMT; see p. 49).

Climate Slovenia's climate varies by region: Mediterranean near the Adriatic, Alpine in the mountains, moderately continental on the eastern plains, and pleasant everywhere in summer, although snow may strew the Alps as late as June.

Hours: Business hours are M-F 8am-5pm, Sa 8am-noon.

Holidays: New Year's Day (Jan. 1-2); Culture Day (Prešeren Day; Feb. 8); Easter (Apr. 23-24); National Resistance Day (WWII; Apr. 27); Labor Day (May 1-2); National Day (June 25); Assumption (Aug. 15); Reformation Day (Oct. 31); Remembrance Day (Nov. 1); Christmas (Dec. 25); Independence Day (Dec. 26).

Festivals: The **International Jazz Festival** in Ljubljana hosts the world's best jazz musicians every June. The **International Summer Festival** in Ljubljana is a two-month (July-Aug.) extravaganza of opera, theater, and classical music.

LJUBLJANA

If you are arriving in Ljubljana (pop. 350,000) after some time in Central Europe, the prices will stop you in your carefree monetary tracks. The city has been scarred by dual architectural disasters: an 1895 earthquake and extensive Socialist urban planning. Despite the high prices and the lack of a true cosmopolitan feel, Ljubljana manages to find its niche among European capitals. A large student population ensures that bars and clubs can be found on virtually every corner, and the beautifully organized city center is worthy of the social life it houses.

GETTING THERE AND GETTING AROUND

Trains: trg O.F. 6 (tel. 291 33 32). To: **Zagreb** (2½hr., 7 per day, 2200Sit); **Trieste** (3hr., 4 per day, 2900Sit); **Munich** (6hr., 3 per day, 9000Sit); **Venice** (6hr., 3 per day, 4300Sit); **Vienna** (6hr., 2 per day, 7700Sit); and **Budapest** (9hr., 2 per day, 6300Sit).

Buses: trg O.F. 4 (tel. 134 38 38), in front of the train station. To: **Zagreb** (3hr., 4 per day, 2270Sit) and **Munich** (6hr., 3 per week, 5500Sit).

Public Transportation: Buses run to midnight. Drop 130Sit in the box beside the driver, or buy 80Sit tokens at post offices and newsstands. **Ljubljanski Potniški Promet,** in the kiosk at Slovenska cesta 55, sells one-day (280Sit) and weekly (1400Sit) passes.

▐ ORIENTATION AND PRACTICAL INFORMATION

The **train** and **bus stations** are on **trg Osvobodilne Fronte (trg O.F.).** Turn left as you exit the train station, right onto **Resljeva,** and then bear right on **Trubarjeva cesta,** which will lead you to **Prešernov trg,** the main square. After crossing the **Triple Bridge** (Tromostovje), **Old Town** (Stari Miasto) emerges at the castle hill's base; the tourist office is on the left at the corner of Stritarjeva and Miklošičeva.

Tourist Office: Tourist Information Center (TIC), Stritarjeva 1 (tel. 306 12 35; fax 133 02 44; email pcl.tic-lj@ljubljana.si). Free maps and excellent brochures in English. Open M-F 8am-7pm, Sa 9am-5pm, Su 10am-6pm. **Branch** at the train station.

Embassies and Consulates: Australia, trg Republike 3 (tel. 125 42 52; fax 126 47 21). **UK,** trg Republike 3 (tel. 125 71 91; fax 125 01 74). Both open M-F 9am-noon. **US,** Pražakova 4 (tel. 30 14 27; fax 30 14 01). Open M-F 2-4pm; Tu and Th also 9am-noon.

Currency Exchange: The best rates are in **Upimo,** Šubičeva 1 (open M-F 8am-6:30pm, Sa 8:30-1pm) or Kongresni trg 13 (open M-F 8:30-6pm). The only **ATM** is on trg Republike in the Maximarket archway next to the travel office (24hr.).

Luggage storage: At the train station; look for the *garderoba.* 180Sit per day. Open 24hr.

Internet Access: Podhod, Plečnikov trg, between Maximarket and Kongresni trg. 2 free computers at the back of club. Ask for internet card at the bar.

Post Office: Slovenska 32. *Poste Restante (poštno ležeče pošiljke)* received at Pražkova 3, parallel to trg O.F. Address mail to be held: Ricki LAKE, *Poste Restante,* Pražkova 3, **1106** Ljubljana, Slovenia. Open M-F 7am-8pm, Sa 7am-1pm.

PHONE CODE	City code: 061. From outside Slovenia, dial int'l dialing prefix (see inside back cover) + 386 + 61 + local number.

▐ ACCOMMODATIONS AND FOOD

Ljubljana is not heavily touristed by backpackers, and therefore lacks true budget accommodations. On top of that, there is a nightly **tourist tax** (185Sit). The tourist office (see above) finds private singles (2200-3500Sit) and doubles (4000-5500Sit).

Dijaški Dom Tabor (HI), Vidovdanska 7 (tel. 31 60 69; fax 32 10 60). Turn left from the train station, then right on Resljeva, left on Komenskega, and left on Vidovdanska. Clean, with a friendly staff. **Internet** access. Students 2200Sit. Breakfast 400Sit. Laundry 1000Sit. Check-out 11am. Unenforced 10pm curfew. Open June 25-Aug. 28.

Dijaški Dom Bežigrad, Kardeljeva pl. 28 (tel. 34 28 67; fax 34 28 64). Turn right at the train station and walk to the large crossroad with Slovenska. Take bus 6 (dir: Črnuče) or 8 (dir: Ježica) to "Stadion" (5min.). Continue in the direction of the bus and take the path through the park on the right. Singles 2600Sit, with shower 3000Sit; doubles and triples 1800-2600Sit per person. Open mid-June to Aug. daily; Sept.-May Sa-Su.

Autocamp Ježica, Dunajska 270 (tel. 168 39 13; fax 168 39 12). Follow directions to Dijaški dom Bežigrad (see above), but take bus 8 and get off at "Ježica." Swimming pool and tennis. 700Sit per person. Bungalows: singles 5000Sit; doubles 7600Sit.

The cheapest eateries are **cafeterias;** in the basement of Maximarket on trg Republike, a full meal costs 800Sit. (Open M-F 9am-4pm, Sa 9am-3pm.) The same basement also houses a **supermarket.** (Open M-F 9am-8pm, Sa 9am-7pm.) Also look for the huge outdoor **market** at Vodnikov trg next to the cathedral. (Open M-Sa 9am-6pm, Su 9am-2pm.) ■ **Italijanska kuhinja pri Albertu in Adrianu,** Trubarjeva 36, serves up Italian dishes for 800-1400Sit. (Open M-W 10am-10pm, Th-Sa 10am-midnight.)

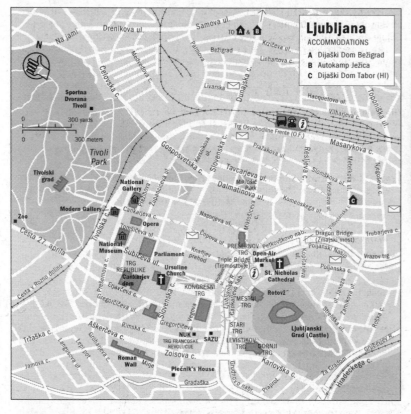

SIGHTS AND ENTERTAINMENT

The best way to see the city is to meet in front of the *rotovž* (city hall), Mestni trg 1, for the two-hour **walking tour** in English and Slovene. (June-Sept. daily 5pm; Oct.-May Su 11am. 700Sit, students 500Sit.) A short walk from the *rotovž* down Stritarjeva across the **Triple Bridge** (Tromostovje), which majestically guards the Old Town, brings you to the main square, **Prešernov trg**, with its 17th-century Neoclassical **Franciscan Church** (Frančiškanska cerkev). Cross the bridge back to the Old Town and take a left along the water; on your right, the *stolnica* (cathedral) occupies the site of an old Romanesque church dedicated by local fishermen to their patron St. Nicholas. (Closed noon-3pm.) At the end of Vodnikov trg sprawls the **Dragon Bridge** (Zmajski most), originally named after the Emperor Franz Joseph but renamed by locals due to its coat of arms. On the opposite side of Vodnikov trg, the narrow path Studentovska leads uphill to **Ljubljana Castle** (Ljubljanski Grad), which dates from at least 1144, but was almost entirely destroyed by an earthquake in 1511; what you see dates from the 16th and 17th centuries. The castle is currently under renovation. (Open daily 10am-9pm. 200Sit, students 100Sit.)

The bridge west of the castle at the beginning of Mestni trg, leads to the **former Jewish ghetto,** Židovska ulica. A left on Gosposka brings you to the **National University Library** (Narodna in Univerzitetna Knjižnica). Walk down Slovenska and turn left just past the **Ursuline Church** to reach **trg Republike,** home to the national Parliament, the colossal Maximarket, and Cankarjev *dom*, the city's cultural center. The **National Museum** (Narodni Muzej), Muzejska 1, exhibits archaeology, ethnography, and history. (Open Tu-Su 10am-6pm, Th until 8pm. 500Sit, students 300Sit.) The

Gallery of Modern Art (Moderna Galerija), Cankarjeva 15, on the corner of Prešernova, has a collection of 20th-century Slovenian art. (Open June-Aug. Tu-Sa 10am-7pm, Su 10am-1pm; Sept.-May Tu-Sa 10am-6pm. 500Sit, students 300Sit.)

The **Ljubljana International Summer Festival** (July-Aug.) is a conglomeration of opera, theater, and music performances. **Casa del Papa,** Celovška 54a, pays homage to Hemingway with its decor and latin beats from the club downstairs. (Open daily 11am-2am.) **Le Petit Café,** trg Francoske revolucije 4, is *the* student hangout in Ljubljana, placed strategically next to the university library. (Open M-F 7:30am-11pm, Sa 9am-11pm, Su noon-9pm.) **Jazz Club Gajo,** Beethovnova 8, hosts free jazz concerts 2 to 4 days each week. (Open M-F 10am-2am, Sa-Su 7pm-midnight.)

JULIJSKE ALPE (JULIAN ALPS)

The Southern Alps are not as high as their Austrian or Swiss counterparts, but they are no less beautiful. The mountains cover the northwest of Slovenia, peaking at 2864m on Mt Triglav in the heart of the Triglav National Park.

BLED. Alpine hills, snow-covered peaks, an opaque lake, and a stately castle make Bled one of Slovenia's most striking destinations. On the island in the middle of the lake, the **Church of the Assumption,** largely rebuilt in the 17th century, retains a unique pre-Romanesque apse. Get there by renting a **boat** for 1000Sit per hr., hopping on a **gondola** (round-trip 1500Sit), or even swimming. High above the water perches the picture-perfect 16th-century **Bled Castle** (Blejski grad), which houses a **museum** detailing the history of the Bled region; the official path to the castle is on Grajska cesta. (Open daily 8am-7pm. 500Sit, students 400Sit, children 250Sit.)

Trains stop in Lesce (tel. (064) 74 11 13), 5km from Bled on the Ljubljana-Salzburg-Munich line (from Ljubljana 1hr., 450 Sit); frequent **buses** (10min., 200Sit) shuttle to **Ljubljanska** (the main street) and then the **bus station,** cesta Svobode 4 (closer to the hostel and castle). **Buses** also run directly from Ljubljana (1½hr., 1 per hr., 880Slt). **Turističko društvo,** cesta Svobode 15, has maps and copies of the *Bled Tourist News.* (Tel. (064) 74 11 22; fax 74 15 55. Open July and Aug. M-Sa 8am-10pm, Su noon-6pm; June and Sept. M-Sa until 8pm; Mar.-May and Oct. M-Sa until 7pm; Nov.-Feb. M-Sa 9am-5pm; Su noon-6pm.) **Kompas Bled,** Ljubljanska cesta 4, rents mountain **bikes** and **private rooms.** (Tel. (064) 74 15 15. Bikes 500Sit per hr., 1500Sit per day.) To find a room yourself, look for *sobe* signs on Prešernova and Ljubljanska. The newly-renovated ◨**Bledec Youth Hostel,** Grajska cesta 17, is a sparkling jewel. With your back to the bus station, turn left and follow the street all the way up. (Tel. (064) 74 52 50. 2400Sit; members and students 2000Sit. Book one day ahead. Reception open summer 7am-8pm; winter until 7pm.) To get to **Camping Zaka-Bled,** cesta Svobode 13, from the bus station, walk downhill on cesta Svobode, and walk along the lake for 25min. (Tel. (064) 74 82 00; fax 74 82 02. 1240Sit per person. Check-out 3pm. Open Apr.-Oct.) Grab **groceries** at **Špecerija,** Ljubljanska 4. (Open M-Sa 7am-7pm, Su 9am-noon.) **Postal code:** 4260.

LAKE BOHINJ (BOHINJSKO JEZERO). Although only 30km southwest of Bled, Bohinjsko (BOH-heen-sko) Jezero's character is worlds away. Surrounded by the **Triglav National Park,** the glacial lake—bordered by the three towns of Ribčev Laz, Stara Fužina, and Ukanc—is Slovenia's center for alpine tourism. **Hikes** from the shores of the lake range from the casual to the nearly impossible. Trails throughout Slovenia are marked with a white circle inside a red circle; look for the blaze on trees and rocks. Pick up maps (1200-1600Sit) at the tourist office. **Triglav,** the highest point in Slovenia, is a challenging two-day journey from town. The most popular and accessible destination is **Savica Waterfall** (Slap Savica). Take a bus from Ribčev Laz to "Bohinj-Zlatorog," get off at Hotel Zlatorog, and follow the signs uphill (1hr. to the trailhead at Koča pri Savici, then 20min. to the waterfall).

Trains from Ljubljana (5 per day, 2hr.) arrive in **Bohinjska Bistrica,** 6km away from Lake Bohinj. **Buses** from Ljubljana (2¼hr., every hr., 1300Sit) stop in Bled (35min., 460Sit) and Bohinjska Bistrica (10min., 200Sit), on their way to the lake; they stop at Hotel Jezero in Ribčev Laz before continuing on to Hotel Zlatorog in Ukanc, on the other side of the lake. The **tourist office,** Ribčev Laz 48, arranges accommodations (1300-2500Sit per person, plus tourist tax) and changes money. (Tel. (064) 72 33 70; fax 72 33 30. Open July-Aug. M-Sa 7:30am-9pm, Su 9am-3pm; Apr.-June and Sept.-Oct. M-Sa 8am-7pm; Nov.-Mar. M-Sa 8am-5pm.) To **AvtoCamp Zlatorog,** Ukanc 2, take the bus to Hotel Zlatorog and backtrack a bit. (Tel. (064) 72 34 82; fax 72 34 46. July-Aug. 1600Sit; May-June and Aug.-Sept. 1000Sit.) The **Mercator supermarket** is next to the tourist office. (Open M-F 7am-7pm, Sa 7am-5pm.) **Postal code:** 4265.

ISTRIA (THE COAST)

Although Slovenia claims only 40km of the Adriatic coast, this stretch has developed its own Italian flavor, with palm trees and fishing boats dotting the shore. **Koper** is a handy jumping-off point from which to explore Venetian-tinged **Piran.**

⊡ GETTING THERE AND GETTING AROUND. Koper is the only town served by **trains;** catch one from **Ljubljana** (2¼hr., 4 per day, 1500Sit). **Buses** from **Ljubljana** go to Piran (40min., 9 per day, 380Sit) and Koper (2¼hr., 13 per day, 1730Sit); they also run from **Trieste, Italy** to Koper (45min., 17 per day, 420Sit) and Piran (1½hr., 6 per day, 780Sit). Buses from **Poreč, Croatia** (2hr., 3 per day, 1160Sit) also go to Koper. From **Venice, catamarans** speed to **Portorož,** Slovenia (F-Su, departs 8am, 2½hr.); buses connect to Koper (35min., 9 per day, 340Sit). There are nine buses a day between Koper and Piran (40min., 380Sit).

KOPER. With no beaches and too much industry, Koper is useful only as a transport hub. The **train** and **bus station** is at Kolodvorska 11 (bus tel. (066) 346 20; train tel. 312 21). The staff at **Kompas,** Pristaniška 17, arranges rooms. (Tel. (066) 27 23 46; fax 27 41 35. Open M-F 8am-7:30pm, Sa 8am-1pm.) **Dijaški Dom Koper,** Cankarjeva 5, 1km from the station, is the only youth hostel in Slovenian Istria; turn right as you exit, follow Kolodvorska cesta toward the city center, pass through Kosovelov trg, walk up Manesiceva to trg Brolo, and take a right onto Cankarjeva. (Tel. (066) 27 32 50; fax 27 31 82. 1966Sit, 1512Sit if you stay more than 3 nights, plus 83Sit tourist tax; students 10% off. Open June 15-Aug. 23.)

PIRAN. Piran (pop. 5,000) flourished under the rule of Medieval Venice, which today still sighs through the tiny town's richly colored shutters. Piran's beauty far surpasses that of its larger neighbors. Although you might be tempted to jump in the sea anywhere along the peninsula for a swim, don't miss strolling along Piran's lovely streets. Facing the sea, take a right from the bus stop along the quay to reach the central **Tartinijev trg.** The **tourist office,** Tartinijev trg 2, sells great maps (690Sit). (Tel./fax (066) 74 02 20. Open Tu-Sa 10am-5pm, Su 10am-2pm.) To book a private room, visit **Turistbiro,** Kidričevo nabr. 4 (tel. (066) 74 61 99; fax 74 61 99; email zasebne.sobe@siol.net), at the corner of Tomažičev trg. From the bus station, walk toward the tip of the peninsula until you see it. The proprietor of **Penzion-Val,** Gregorčičeva 38a (tel. (066) 745 99; fax 74 69 11), near the lighthouse, contends that he runs the best pension in Slovenia, with a bed and breakfast for only 2700Sit per person. To get there from the bus stop, keep walking toward the tip of the peninsula; you can't miss it. **Supermarket Kras** is at Zelenjavni trg. 1, with an **outdoor market** out front. (Open M-Sa 7am-8pm, Su 8am-noon.)

SPAIN (ESPAÑA)

US$1 = 158.57 PESETAS (PTAS)
CDN$1 = 105.93PTAS
UK£1 = 253.18PTAS
IR£1 = 211.27PTAS
AUS$1 = 100.95PTAS
NZ$1 = 83.62PTAS
SAR1 = 26.01PTAS
EUR€1 = 166.39PTAS

100PTAS = US$0.63
100PTAS = CDN$0.94
100PTAS = UK£0.40
100PTAS = IR£0.47
100PTAS = AUS$0.99
100PTAS = NZ$1.20
100PTAS = SAR3.84
100PTAS = EUR€0.60

PHONE CODE Country code: 34. International dialing prefix: 37.

With a history that spans over 50 constitutions and an endless array of kingdoms, controlled by Arabs, Visgoths, Germans, French, Celts, and indigenous peoples, Spain can only be described imprecisely—as a *mestizo* (mixed) culture. Nine centuries of Roman rule left the empire's imprint in irrigation techniques, architecture, language, and its trademark use of olives and grapes. The Muslim invasion of AD 711 ushered in centuries of religious toleration and the growth of classical Greek science and Eastern artistic traditions. Following the marriage of Fernando of Aragón and Isabel of Castilla and the fall of the Moorish Granada, Spain became a united Catholic dominion. Under their watchful eye, Columbus was dispatched to the New World, and the country's Jews and Moors were ruthlessly expelled. Through savvy royal matchmaking, the Spanish Empire was Europe's most powerful by the 16th century, encompassing modern-day Belgium and the Netherlands, as well as parts of Germany, Austria, Italy, and the American colonies.

Eventual Napoleonic occupation and incompetent government not only inspired Spanish colonies in the Americas to declare their independence, but also ushered in an era of nationalism and political unrest in Spain itself. Tensions arising from rapid industrialization in some areas and increasingly mounting nationalism were sparked by international depression, and erupted in the Spanish Civil War (1936-39). Aided by Hitler and Mussolini, Francisco Franco emerged from the war as the country's Fascist dictator and ruled until his death in 1975. Under King Juan Carlos I, Franco's hand-picked successor, who widely diverged from Franco politically, Spain has become a modern, stable, and democratic constitutional monarchy.

Noble flamenco dancers, graceful bullfighters, and five different spoken languages set Spain significantly apart from the rest of Europe; and draw almost 50 million tourists annually, effectively doubling the country's population. Much of the crunch comes in July and August. This fact—and Andalucía's searing heat—counsel against traveling in summer in southern Spain; choose central or northern destinations. Regardless of southern heat, Spain is a budget traveler's dream; inexpensive, politically stable; art and architecture, beaches, and nightlife all vie for supremacy. You can ski or surf, enjoy Picasso or cave paintings, dance until dawn or just chat in a plaza café. You can do Spain in one week, one month, or one year. But you must do it at least once.

For more detailed coverage of the glories of Spain, grab the scintillating and delicious *Let's Go: Spain, Portugal, and Morocco 2000*.

DISCOVER SPAIN

Begin your Spanish adventure in **Madrid** (p. 799)—soaking in its unique blend of art, architecture, and cosmopolitan life; after spending your days ogling art in its museums and your nights partaking in the dancing 'til dawn regime; take your bleary-eyed self to the austere palace of **El Escorial** (p. 809) outside the city and the twisting streets of **Toledo** (p. 810), once home to El Greco and a thriving Jewish community.

Head off into Central Spain, Don Quixote territory, to the famed university town of **Salamanca** (p. 814) and then down to Andalucía, Spain's southernmost region and the Moors' last stronghold in Spain; its center is one of the country's most beautiful and intriguing cities, **Seville** (p. 822). Delve deeper into Arab-influenced Andalucía—don't miss the stunning mosque in **Córdoba** (p. 818) and the world-famous Alhambra in **Granada** (p. 831). The region was also the breeding ground for those passionate cultural expressions—flamenco (see **Jerez,** p. 827) and bullfighting (see **Ronda,** p. 828). The tanning fields of the **Costa del Sol** stretch along the Mediterranean; join in at posh **Marbella** (p. 830). Move up along the east coast to **Valencia** to indulge in native paella and oranges (p. 836). The northeast's gem is **Barcelona** (see p. 837) one of Europe's most vibrant cities. After a tour of bizarre Modernista architecture and raging nightlife, discover the beaches of the **Costa Brava** and enchanting seaside resorts of **Tossa de Mar** (p. 849) and **Cadaqués** (p. 850); the nearby town of **Figueres** (p. 849) is home to Salvador Dalí's engaging museum/monument to himself, while close by **Girona** boasts a perfectly preserved medieval center (p. 848). Farther north is the natural haven of the **Pyrenees** (p. 850), where adventure tourism reigns. Moving westward, in the heart of the Basque Country, **San Sebastián** (p. 854) entertains with beaches and fabulous tapas bars; a daytrip away is **Bilbao** (p. 857), home of the incredible Guggenheim museum. The **Camino de Santiago** pilgrimage (p. 862) winds along the northern coast to the **Santiago de Compostela** cathedral (p. 861), the unrivaled monarch of Spanish religious monuments. Spain also offers some of the world's craziest nightlife, the most famous being the 24-hour party that is **Ibiza** (p. 860) on the Balearic Islands.

GETTING THERE AND GETTING AROUND

BY PLANE. Airports in Madrid and Barcelona handle most international flights; Seville also has a major international airport. **Iberia** serves all domestic locations and all major international cities (see **By Plane,** p. 49). **Air Europa** (US tel. (888) 238-7672 or (718) 244-6016; Spain tel. 902 30 06 00; email easyspain@g-air-europa.es; www.g-aireuropa.es) flies out of New York City and most European cities to Spain and has discounts available for those under 22.

BY TRAIN. RENFE (www.renfe.es), the Spanish centralized national rail system, has clean, punctual, reasonably priced trains with various levels of service. Its network radiates from Madrid; many small towns are not served. *Alta Velocidad Española* (AVE) trains are the fastest between Madrid-Córdoba-Seville. *Talgos* are almost as fast; *Talgo 200s* run on *AVE* rails—there are four lines from Madrid to Málaga, Algeciras, Cádiz, and Huelva. *Intercity* is cheaper and a bit dowdier, but still fairly fast. *Estrellas* are slow night trains with bunks. *Cercanías* (commuter trains) go from cities to suburbs and nearby towns. *Tranvía, semidirecto,* and *correo* trains are slower-than-slow. Trains connect with most major European cities via France. The other train company in Spain is **FEVE,** which sluggishly but dependably runs between many northern towns not served by RENFE.

Eurail is valid in Spain (US$11 reservation fee for *AVE* and *Intercity* trains). **Spain Flexipass** offers three days of unlimited travel in a two-month period (1st-class US$196, 2nd-class US$154; up to 7 additional rail-days US$40, US$32 each). **Iberic Flexipass** offers three days of unlimited first-class travel in Spain and Portugal for US$204; up to seven additional rail-days cost US$44 each. With a valid ISIC, a **Tarjeta Joven** for unlimited travel for seven consecutive days costs 19,000ptas. Buy tickets at RENFE travel offices, train stations, and authorized travel agencies.

BY BUS. In Spain, ignore romanticized versions of European train travel—**buses** are cheaper, run more frequently, and are sometimes even faster than trains. Additionally, buses are the only public transportation to and within isolated areas. Spain has many private companies instead of one national bus line, making trip planning something of an ordeal; fortunately, most cities now have centralized bus stations.

BY FERRY. Trasmediterránea ferries (24-hour. tel. 902 45 46 45; www.trasmediterranea.com) frequently shuttle between Tangier, Morocco and Tarifa, Algeciras, and Gibraltar (see p. 818). They also go to the Balearic Islands (see p. 858).

BY CAR. Rental cars cost considerably less than in other European countries. For most major international companies you must be over 24; for local companies you must be over 21. In either case, you have to have had a driver's license for at least one year, and be prepared to pay for expensive fuel. Renting from abroad is significantly less expensive than renting after you have arrived in Spain. **Speed limits** are as follows: 50 km per hr. (30 mph) in cities, 90 or 100 km per hr. (56 or 62 mph) outside cities, and 120 km per hr. (74 mph) on expressways. In residential areas the speed limit is 20 km per hr. (12 mph). Roads marked **A** for *autopista* are toll roads. *Autovías* (non-toll highways) are marked **N** and are the main highways; virtually as fast as, and more scenic than, *autopistas*. The national motoring club is **Real Automóvil Club de España** (RACE), José Abascal 10, 28003 Madrid (tel. 91 447 32 00).

BY BIKE AND BY THUMB. Spain is a very mountainous country but **biking** can be done; in tourist centers it shouldn't be hard to rent a bike, especially in the flatter southern region. **Hitchhiking** is reportedly slow and can be dangerous; hitchers say it is best in the north, along the Mediterranean coast, and in the Balearic Islands.

ESSENTIALS

DOCUMENTS AND FORMALITIES. Travelers need legal passports or visas to enter and leave Spain. A passport allows Canadian, British, New Zealand, and US citizens to remain for 90 days. Citizens of South Africa and Australia need a **visa** to enter Spain. Admission as a visitor does not include the right to **work**, which is authorized only by a work permit; entering Spain to **study** requires a special visa.

Spanish Embassies at Home: Australia, 15 Arkana St, Yarralumla, ACT 2600; mailing address: P.O. Box 9076, Deakin, ACT 2600 (tel. (02) 62 73 35 55; fax 62 73 39 18); **Canada,** 74 Stanley Ave, Ottawa, ON K1M 1P4 (tel. (613) 747-2252; fax 744-1224); **Ireland** (consulate), 17A Merlyn Park, Ballsbridge, Dublin 4 (tel. (035) 269 16 40; fax 269 18 54); **South Africa,** 169 Pine St, Arcadia, P.O. Box 1633, Pretoria 0083 (tel. (012) 344 38 75); **UK,** 39 Chesham Pl, London SW1X 8SB (tel. (020) 72 35 55 55; fax 72 59 53 92); **US,** 2375 Pennsylvania Ave NW, Washington, DC 20037 (tel. (202) 728-2332; fax 728-2308). **New Zealanders** should consult the Australian embassy.

Foreign Embassies in Spain: Embassies are in **Madrid** (see p. 802). All countries have consulates in **Barcelona** (see p. 840). **Australia, UK,** and **US** consulates are in **Seville** (see p. 824). Another **Canadian** consulate is in **Málaga;** the **South African** consulate is in **Bilbao; UK** consulates are in **Bilbao, Palma de Mallorca, Ibiza, Alicante,** and **Málaga; US** consulates are in **Málaga, Valencia, La Coruña,** and **Palma de Mallorca.**

TOURIST OFFICES. Most towns have a centrally located **Oficina de Turismo** (tourist office, fondly called *Turismo*) that distributes information on sights, lodgings, and events, plus a free map here and there. Although most don't book lodgings, many keep a list of approved establishments or can point you to a *casa particular* (private room). **Viajes TIVE,** the national chain of student travel agencies, dispenses transport info and has discount travel tickets, ISICs, and HI cards. The Spanish tourist office's comprehensive website is www.okspain.org.

Tourist Boards at Home: Canada, 2 Bloor St. W. #3402, Toronto, ON M4W 3E2 (tel. (416) 961-3131; fax 961-1992); **UK,** 22/23 Manchester Sq, London W1M 5AP (tel. (020) 74 86 80 77; fax 74 86 80 34); **US,** 666 Fifth Ave, 35th fl., New York, NY 10103 (tel. (212) 265-8822; fax 265-8864).

MONEY. The currency units are *pesetas* (ptas). Bills are in denominations of 10,000, 5000, 2000 and 1000ptas; there are 1, 5, 10, 25, 50, 100, 200 and 500ptas coins.

Tipping and Bargaining: Tipping is not very common in Spain and certainly not expected. In restaurants, all prices include service charge; tipping is optional. Happy customers can toss in some spare change—usually no more than 5%. Train, airport, and hotel porters get 100-150ptas per bag, while taxi drivers sometimes get 5-10%. Travelers can try bargaining for hostel prices in the off-season, especially in less-touristed areas.

Taxes: Spain levies a **Value Added Tax (IVA** in Spain) on all goods and services. The standard rate is 7%. Non-EU citizens who have been in the EU for fewer than 180 days can claim back these taxes at the airport (ask shops to supply you with tax return forms). Stores, restaurants, and lodgings include the IVA in their prices, unless otherwise noted.

COMMUNICATION

Post: Mailing a **postcard** or **letter** from Spain costs 155ptas to Australia, New Zealand, and South Africa; Canada and the US 115ptas; Ireland and the UK 70ptas. Airmail letters *(por avión)* take 4-7 business days to the US and Canada; it's faster to the UK and Ireland, slower to Australia and New Zealand. *Poste Restante* is called *Lista de Correos.*

Telephone: Region and city codes are included in all phone numbers and are necessary, even to call within a city. Local phone calls are 25ptas. 1000- and 2000ptas phone cards are sold by tobacconists and are most convenient. Collect calls *(cobro revertido)* are billed at steep person-to-person *(persona a persona)* rates, but may be cheaper than calls from hotels. **International direct dial** numbers: **AT&T,** 900 99 00 11; **Sprint,** 900 99 00 13; **MCI WorldPhone Direct,** 900 99 00 14; **Canada Direct,** 900 99 00 15; **BT Direct,** 900 99 00 44; **Ireland Direct,** 900 99 03 53; **Australia Direct,** 900 99 00 61; **Telecom New Zealand Direct,** 900 99 00 64; **Telkom South Africa Direct,** 900 99 00 64. **Local operator,** tel. 009. **Directory assistance,** tel. 1003. **National police,** tel. 091. **Police emergency,** tel. 092. **Medical emergency,** tel. 061.

Language: There are 5 official languages in Spain, plus plenty of dialects. Catalán is the language of choice in Catalonia, Valencian in Valencia. The Basque (Euskera) language is

SPAIN

spoken in north-central Spain, and Galician (Gallego, related to Portuguese) is spoken in the once-Celtic northwest. Spanish (Castilian, or *castellano*) is spoken everywhere. To partake of some *castellano*, peruse our spiffy language chart on p. 949.

ACCOMMODATIONS AND CAMPING. REAJ, the Spanish Hostelling International (HI) affiliate, runs 165 youth hostels year-round. **HI cards** are required and are available at youth hostels and from Spain's main national youth/travel company, TIVE. Reservations can be made through the central REAJ office (tel. 91 347 77 00; fax 91 401 81 60) or by direct calls to specific hostels. Accommodations have many aliases in Spain; each name indicates a specific type of establishment. Cheapest and barest are *hospedajes* and *casas de huéspedes*. Higher in quality are *pensiones* and *fondas*, then *hostales*, then *hostal-residencias;* these three levels are similar and are budget travel staples. The highest-priced accommodations are *hoteles*, often too expensive for budget travelers. **Campgrounds** are government-regulated and on a three-class system, rated and priced according to the quality of amenities. Tourist offices have the *Guía de Campings*, a guide to all official campgrounds in Spain.

FOOD AND DRINK. Spaniards start their day with a breakfast of coffee or hot chocolate and *bollos* (rolls) or *churros* (lightly fried fritters). Dinner (lunch to Americans) is served between 2 and 3pm, and is several courses. Supper at home is light—often a sandwich—and eaten around 9pm. Supper out—also a light meal—begins later, usually around 10pm. Some restaurants are "open" from 8am until 1 or 2am, but most only serve meals from 1 or 2 to 4pm and from 8pm until midnight. Prices for a full meal start at about 800ptas in the cheapest bar-restaurants. Many places offer a *plato combinado* (combination platter—main course and side dishes on a single plate, plus bread, and sometimes beverage—roughly 500-1200ptas) or a *menú del día* (two or three set dishes, bread, beverage, and dessert—roughly 800-1500ptas). Spain's tapas (small portions of savory meats and vegetables cooked according to local recipes) are truly tasty. *Raciones* are basically large tapas served as entrees. *Bocadillos* are filling sandwiches on hunks of thick bread. Spanish specialties include *tortilla de patata* (potato omelette), *jamón serrano* (smoked ham), *calamares fritos* (fried squid), *arroz* (rice), *chorizo* (spicy sausage), *gambas* (shrimp), *lomo* (pork), paella (steamed saffron rice with seafood, chicken, and vegetables), and gazpacho (cold tomato-based soup). Vegetarians should remember the phrase "*yo soy vegetariano*" (I am a vegetarian), and repeat it often when ordering. *Vino blanco* is white wine and *tinto* is red. Beer is *cerveza;* Mahou and Cruzcampo are the most common Spanish brands. Rioja is a renowned grape-growing region, with excellent red wines. *Sangría* is made of red wine, sugar, brandy, and fruit. *Tinto de verano* is red wine with flavored seltzer.

LOCAL FACTS

Time: Spain is 1hr. ahead of Greenwich Mean Time (GMT; see p. 49).

Climate: The northwest is rightly called "wet" Spain, with a humid, temperate climate. The interior's climate resembles that of Central Europe—long winters and, in the lowlands, hot, dry summers. The east and south coasts enjoy a Mediterranean climate. The northeast coast can be humid, but the southwest is the sweltering, especially Seville and Córdoba.

Hours: The day gets started around 9am, shops close down for a long lunch from 1:30 or 2pm until 4:30 or 5pm, when they reopen until 8pm. On Saturday, shops are usually open only in the morning, and Sunday is a day of rest for almost all places of business. Banking hours in Spain are M-F 9am-2pm; Oct.-May, banks are also open Sa 9am-1pm.

Holidays: New Year's Day (Jan. 1); Epiphany (Jan. 6); *Semana Santa* (Apr. 17-23); May Day (May 1); Corpus Christi (June 22); Feast of the Assumption (Aug. 15); National Day (Oct. 12); All Saints' Day (Nov. 1); Feast of the Immaculate Conception (Dec. 8); and Christmas (Dec. 25). Some of these religious celebrations are no longer legal holidays, but business slows anyway and sometimes stops altogether. *Semana Santa* (Holy Week), the week before Easter, sees much celebration, especially in Andalucía.

Festivals: Spain loves festivals: Mar. 2-12 is **Carnaval** nationally but **Cádiz** gets especially wild (see p. 827), **Valencia** does **Las Fallas** Mar. 12-19 (see p. 836); **Semana Santa** is a big deal just about everywhere Apr. 17-23. **Barcelona's** Festa di Sant Jordi is Apr. 23 (see p. 837); **Seville** follows *Semana Santa* with an elaborate **Feria de Abril** from late Apr.-early May (see p. 826); **Corpus Christi** is June 22 is extra fun in **Toledo** and **Granada** (see p. 810 and p. 831); **Pamplona** gets all the glory July 6-14 for **San Fermines** (Running of the Bulls; see p. 852); **La Asunción** is Aug. 16; and **Semana Grande** breaks out along the northern coast Aug. 19-27. Bullfights are part of most festivals May-Oct.

MADRID

After decades of Franco's totalitarian repression, Madrid's youth burst out laughing and crying during the 1980s, an era known as *la Movida* (the "Movement"), and they have yet to stop. The newest generation, too young to recall the Franco years, seems neither cognizant of the city's historic landmarks nor preoccupied with the future—youths have taken over the streets, shed the decorous reserve of their predecessors, and captured the present. Bright lights and a perpetual stream of cars and people blur the distinction between 4pm and 4am, and infinitely energized *madrileños* crowd bars and discos until dawn. Unlike much of the world, Madrid does not live to work, but rather works to live.

SPAIN

▟ GETTING THERE AND GETTING AROUND

Flights: Info and reservations tel. 902 40 05 00. **Aeropuerto Internacional de Barajas,** 15km northeast of Madrid. The new **Barajas metro line** connects the airport to Madrid (follow signs to the metro). Take line 8 to Mar de Cristal, switch to line 4, and change to line 2 at Goya to get to Sol, smack in the city center. Another option is the **Bus-Aeropuerto** (look for EMT signs outside), which goes to Pl. de Colón (every 15-25min. 4:45am-10pm, every hr. 10pm-1:45am, 385ptas). From the plaza (M: Colón; brown line, L4), the metro runs all over town. **Iberia,** Santa Cruz de Marcenado 2 (tel. 91 587 81 56).

Trains: Info and reservations tel. 91 328 90 20. There are 2 stations with long-distance service. **Estación Chamartín,** on Agustín de Foxá (24hr. tel. 91 328 90 20). M: Chamartín. Bus 5 departs from just beyond the lockers for Sol (45min.). To: **Barcelona** (7hr., 10 per day, 4900-6400ptas); **Lisbon** (10hr., 1 per day, 7000-10,000ptas); **Paris** (13hr., 3 per day, 7000-10,000ptas); and **Nice** (22hr., 3 per day, 14,000ptas). **Estación Atocha** (tel. 91 328 90 20). M: Atocha-Renfe. Serves Andalucía, Castilla-La Mancha, Extremadura, Valencia, Castilla y León, and El Escorial. To: **Seville** (2½hr., 18 per day, 8200ptas) and **Córdoba** (1¾hr., 15 per day, 6000ptas). The **RENFE Main Office,** C. Alcalá 44, at Gran Vía (tel. 91 534 05 05). M: Banco de España. Sells tickets for Chamartín as well as AVE and Talgo tickets. Open M-F 9:30am-8pm.

Buses: Private companies have their own stations, but most buses pass through **Estación Sur de Autobuses** (tel. 91 468 42 00), on C. Méndez Álvaro. **Estación Auto Res,** Pl. Conde de Casal 6 (tel. 91 551 72 00). M: Conde de Casal. To: **Cuenca** (2-2½hr., 1315-1600ptas); **Salamanca** (2½-3¼hr., 4 per day, 1460-2210ptas); and **Valencia** (4hr., 13 per day, 2865ptas). **Estación Empresa Larrea,** Po. Florida 11 (tel. 91 530 48 00). M: Príncipe Pío (via extension from M: Ópera). To: **Ávila** (2hr., 4 per day, 910ptas).

Public Transportation: Empresa Municipal de Transportes (**EMT**; tel. 91 406 88 10). The clean and efficient **metro** (info tel. 91 580 19 80) runs 6am-1:30am. Rides cost 130ptas; a 10-ride pass *(bonotransporte)* runs 680ptas. Pick up a free *Plano del Metro* at any ticket booth. Hold on to your ticket until you leave the metro. **Buses** run daily 6am-11:30pm and cost 130ptas per ride (10-ride *bonotransporte* pass 680ptas). Pick up the unwieldy *Plano de Los Transportes* from a newsstand (200ptas) or the free *Madrid en Autobús* from any bus kiosk. Night buses (N1-N20) run from Pl. Cibeles to the outskirts of Madrid (every 30min. 11:30pm-3am; every hr. 3-6am); see the *Plano* for details.

Taxi: Tel. 91 445 90 08 or 91 447 32 32. Base fare is 170ptas, plus 50-75ptas per km and supplements. A taxi between the city center and the airport costs about 3000ptas.

Hitchhiking: Hitchhiking, neither popular nor safe, is legal only on minor routes; the Guardia Civil de Tráfico picks up would-be highway hitchers and deposits them at nearby towns or on a bus. Try the message boards at HI hostels for ride-share offers.

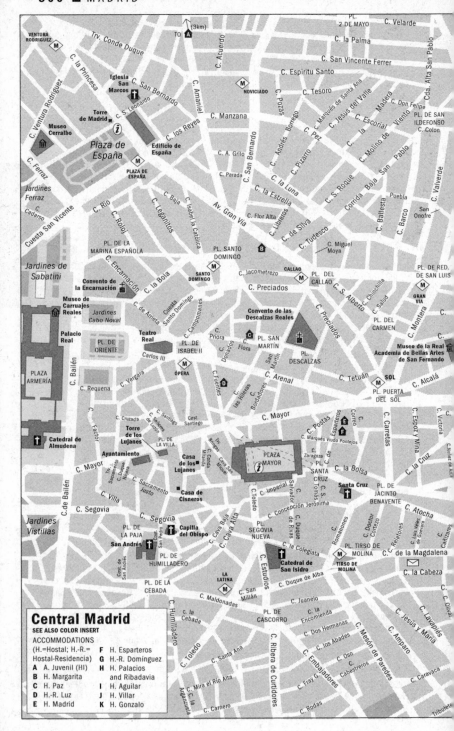

Central Madrid

SEE ALSO COLOR INSERT

ACCOMMODATIONS
(H.=Hostal; H.-R. =
Hostal-Residencia)
A A. Juvenil (HI)
B H. Margarita
C H. Paz
D H.-R. Luz
E H. Madrid

F H. Esparteros
G H.-R. Domínguez
H H. Palacios
   and Ribadavia
I H. Aguilar
J H. Villar
K H. Gonzalo

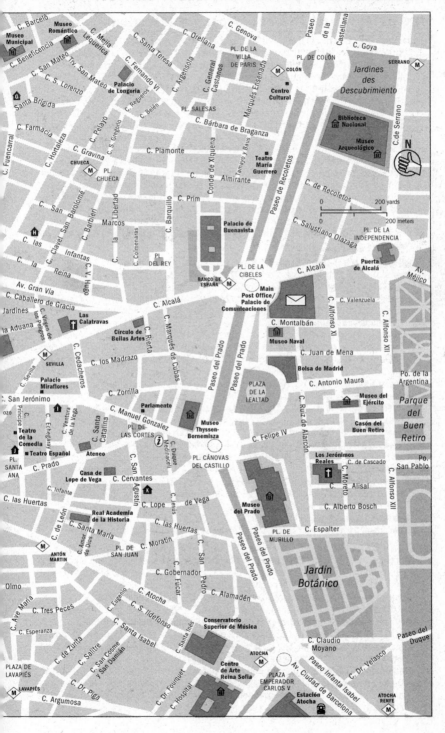

🔎 ORIENTATION AND PRACTICAL INFORMATION

Kilómetro 0 in **Puerta del Sol** ("Sol" for short) is the epicenter of the city (and the country), within walking distance of most sights. Just to the west is the **Plaza Mayor;** farther west lie the **Palacio Real** and the **Ópera** district. East of Sol lies **Huertas**—centered around **Plaza Santa Ana,** bordered by C. Alcalá to the north, Po. Prado to the east, Sol to the west, and C. Atocha to the south—a one-time literary district and today the pulse of café, theater, and museum life. The area north of Sol is bordered by the **Gran Vía,** which runs northwest to **Plaza de España.** North of Gran Vía are three club and bar-hopping districts, linked by **Calle de Fuencarral: Malasaña, Bilbao,** and **Chueca.** Beyond Gran Vía and east of Malasaña and Chueca lies modern Madrid. East of Sol, the thoroughfare **Paseo de la Castellana-Paseo de Recoletos-Paseo del Prado** splits Madrid in two, running from **Atocha** in the south to **Plaza de Castilla** in the north, passing the Prado, the fountains of **Plaza Cibeles** and **Plaza Colón.** Northwest of Sol lies **Argüelles,** an energetic neighborhood of families and students spilling over from **Moncloa,** the student district, whose center is on C. Isaac Peral.

Get a map at the tourist office and refer also to this book's **color map** of Madrid's metro. Madrid is extremely safe compared to other major European cities, but the Puerta del Sol, Pl. Dos de Mayo in Malasaña, Pl. de Chueca, and Pl. España are particularly intimidating late at night.

TOURIST AND FINANCIAL SERVICES

Tourist Offices: Municipal, Pl. Mayor 3 (tel. 91 366 54 77 or 91 588 16 36; fax 91 366 54 77). M: Sol. Indispensable maps, accommodations guides, and monthly activity guides. Open M-F 10am-8pm, Sa 10am-2pm. **Oficinas de Información,** C. Princesa 1 (tel. 91 541 23 25), off Pl. España. M: Pl. España. **Regional/Provincial Office of the Comunidad de Madrid,** Mercado Pta. de Toledo, Ronda de Toledo 1, stand 3134 (tel. 91 364 18 76). In a gallery in the plaza opposite M: Pta. de Toledo. Info, brochures, and maps on towns in the Comunidad. Open M-F 9am-7pm, Sa 9:30am-1:30pm. **Branches** at **Estación Chamartín,** the **airport,** and C. Duque Medinaceli 2 (tel. 91 429 49 51), just off Pl. Cortés (M: Sol; open M-F 9am-7pm, Sa 9am-1pm).

General Info Line: Tel. 010. 20ptas per min. Ask for *inglés* and they'll tell you anything.

Embassies: Embassies open M-F; call for hours. **Australia,** Santa Engracia 120 (tel. 91 579 04 28; fax 91 442 53 62; www.embaustralia.es). **Canada,** C. Núñez de Balboa 35 (tel. 91 431 43 00; fax 91 435 74 88; info.ic.gc.ca/tourism). M: Velázquez. **New Zealand,** Pl. de la Lealtad 2 (tel. 91 523 02 26; fax 91 523 01 71). M: Banco de España. **South Africa,** Claudio Coello 91, 6th fl. (tel. 91 436 37 80; fax 91 577 74 14). **UK,** C. Fernando El Santo 16 (tel. 91 319 02 00; fax 91 308 10 33). M: Colón. **US,** C. Serrano 75 (tel. 91 587 22 00; fax 91 587 23 03). M: Rubén Darío.

Currency Exchange: Banco Central Hispano, C. de Alcalá 49 (tel. 91 558 41 00). M: Banco de España. No commission on exchange; the best rates on AmEx checks. Open June-Aug. M-F 8:30am-2:30pm; Sept.-May M-Th 8:30am-2:30pm, F-Sa 8:30am-1pm.

American Express: Pl. Cortés 2 (tel. 91 322 55 00). M: Sevilla. 1% commission on cash exchange, 2% for traveler's checks (no commission on AmEx checks).

LOCAL SERVICES

Luggage Storage: At the **Estaciones de Chamartín** (lockers by the *consigna* area by the bus stop) and **Atocha** (to the left of the simulated rainforest). Both 400-600ptas per day. Also at the **Estación Sur de Autobuses.** 800ptas per day.

Bookstores: FNAC, C. Preciados 28 (tel. 91 595 62 00). M: Callao. Open M-Sa 10am-9:30pm, Su noon-9:30pm.

Gay and Lesbian Services: Colectivo de Gais y Lesbianas de Madrid (COGAM), C. Fuencarral 37 (tel./fax 91 523 00 70), opposite the Ministry of Justice. M: Gran Vía. English usually spoken. Open M-F 5-9pm. **GAI-INFORM** (tel. 91 523 00 70) provides info about gay associations and activities. Open daily 5-9pm.

Laundromats: Lavandería Donoso Cortés, C. Donoso Cortés 17 (tel. 91 446 96 90). M: Quevedo; walk down C. Bravo Murillo. Wash 600ptas, soap 60ptas. Open M-F 9am-2pm and 3:30-8pm, Sa 9am-2pm. **Lavandería Automática SIDEC,** C. Don Felipe 4. M: Tribunal. Wash 600ptas, soap 25ptas. Open M-F 10am-9pm.

EMERGENCY AND COMMUNICATIONS

Emergency: Tel. 092 (local police) or 091 (national police).

Crisis Lines: Rape Hotline (tel. 91 574 01 10). Open M-F 10am-2pm and 4-7pm.

Medical Assistance: In a medical **emergency,** dial 061. Or, try the **Anglo-American Medical Unit,** Conde de Aranda 1, 1st fl. (tel. 91 435 18 23). M: Serrano or Retiro. Doctors, dentists, and optometrists. Initial visit 8000ptas. Open 9am-8pm.

Internet Access: La Casa de Internet, C. Luchana 20 (tel. 91 446 55 41). M: Bilboa. 800ptas per hr. (students 600ptas). Open 10am-10pm. **Net Café,** C. San Bernardo 81 (tel. 91 594 09 99). M: San Bernardo. One drink buys 1hr. Open M-Th 6pm-2am, F-Su 4pm-3am. **Sol.Com,** Pta. del Sol 6. M: Sol. 750ptas per hr. Open daily 9am-11pm.

Post Office: Palacio de Comunicaciones (tel. 902 19 71 97), in Pl. Cibeles. M: Banco de España. Open M-F 8:30am-10pm, Sa 8:30am-8pm, Su 9:30am-1:30pm. *Lista de Correos* (*Poste Restante;* window 80) open M-F 8:30am-9:30pm, Sa 8:30am-8pm. Address mail to be held: Sam JACOBY, *Lista de Correos,* **28080** Madrid, Spain.

PHONE CODE	Spain has no city codes. From outside Spain, dial int'l dialing prefix (see inside back cover) + 34 + local number.

█ ACCOMMODATIONS AND CAMPING

For summer visits, make reservations. Expect to pay 2400ptas per person for a basic hostel bed, slightly less for a *pensión,* and a bit more in a two-star *hostal.* **Viajes Brújula,** Torre de Madrid 14, 6th fl., will book you a room (but no HI hostels) for 300ptas; you must go in person. (Tel. 91 559 97 04; fax 91 548 46 24. M: Pl. España. English spoken. Open M-F 9am-7pm.) You can also try **branches** at **Estación Atocha,** in the AVE terminal (tel. 91 539 11 73; open daily 8am-10pm); **Estación Chamartín** (tel. 91 315 78 94; open daily 7am-11:30pm); and the **airport bus terminal,** on Pl. Colón (tel. 91 575 96 80; open daily 8am-10pm). Tourist offices can provide info about the 13 or so **campsites** within 50km of Madrid.

Prices and locations in **Centro,** between Sol and the Palacio Real, are as good as it gets. The area crawls with tourists and hostels; stray several blocks away from Pta. del Sol for better deals on quieter streets. The centrally located **Huertas** district, between C. San Jerónimo and C. de las Huertas, tends to be quieter than other areas and is good for a night out. **Gran Vía** is a 24-hour parade of flashing cars, sex shops, and stack-heeled shoes; though *hostales* are everywhere, accommodations tend to be overpriced and less comfortable, and the area is not as safe as Centro or Huertas. Hard-core party pits **Malasaña** and **Chueca,** bisected by C. Fuencarral, host plenty of cheap *hostales,* but the area is noisy and can be dangerous.

EL CENTRO: SOL, ÓPERA, AND PLAZA MAYOR

▓**Hostal Paz,** C. Flora 4, 1st and 4th fl. (tel. 91 547 30 47). M: Ópera. Don't be deterred by the dark street, parallel to C. Arenal, off C. Donados or C. Hileras. Ten brilliant rooms, some overlooking a courtyard. Satellite TV, A/C, and spotless, spacious bathrooms. Singles 2500ptas; doubles 3800-4300ptas; triples 5700ptas. Laundry 1100ptas. V, MC.

Hostal-Residencia Luz, C. Fuentes 10, 3rd fl. (tel. 91 542 07 59), off C. Arenal. M: Ópera. Twelve sunny, redecorated rooms with hardwood floors, and bathrooms so sparkling you won't mind sharing. Satellite TV, fax, and public phone. Singles 2500ptas; doubles 3600ptas; triples 5500ptas. Laundry 1000ptas. 7% IVA not included.

Hostal Esparteros, C. Esparteros 12, 4th fl. (tel. 91 522 59 76). Cheap, small, comfortable rooms with either balcony or large windows. Friendly, English-speaking owner eager to share info on Madrid's history and sights. Singles 1800ptas, with shower 2200ptas; double with bath 3200; triple with shower 4400ptas. Laundry 1000ptas.

Hostal Madrid, C. Esparteros 6, 2nd fl. (tel. 91 522 00 60; fax 91 532 35 10), off C. Mayor. M: Sol. The backpacker's equivalent of a five-star hotel. Spacious rooms, all with TV, phone, A/C, large windows, and new bathrooms. Singles 5000ptas; doubles 8500ptas; triple with balcony 10,000ptas. Reservations recommended. Visa.

HUERTAS

Hostal Gonzalo, C. Cervantes 34, 3rd fl. (tel. 91 429 27 14, fax. 91 420 20 07), off C. León, which is off C. Atocha. M: Antón Martín. A budget traveler's dream: newly-renovated rooms with shiny baths, firm beds, TV, and fans in summer. Singles 4500ptas; doubles 5500ptas; one triple 7000ptas. Ask about discounts.

Hostal Villar, C. Príncipe 18, 1st-4th fl. (tel. 91 531 66 00; fax 91 521 50 73; email hvillar@arrakis.es). M: Sol; walk down C. San Jerónimo and turn right on C. Príncipe. The 1970s stormed through here, leaving in their wake 46 brown rooms with TV, phone, A/C, and slanted floors. Singles 2350-3000ptas; doubles 3400-4400ptas; triples 5500-5900ptas; quads 6000-7600ptas. V, MC.

Hostal Aguilar, C. San Jerónimo 32, 2nd fl. (tel. 91 429 59 26 or 91 429 36 61; fax 91 429 26 61). M: Sol. Clean, modern rooms, all with phone, A/C, coin-operated TV, and vast bathroom. Spartan yet elegant lounge with deep couches. Singles 3500ptas; doubles 5800ptas; triples 7500ptas; 1500ptas per additional person. V, MC.

GRAN VÍA

Hostal Margarita, Gran Vía 50, 5th fl. (tel. 91 541 91 82; fax 91 541 91 88). M: Callao. Airy and tastefully sparse rooms, with big windows, pretty little bathrooms, TVs, and telephones. Singles 3200ptas, with shower 4000ptas; doubles 5100ptas; triples 6600ptas. 20% off stays longer than a week. Laundry 1200ptas. V, MC.

MALASAÑA AND CHUECA

Hostal Palacios and **Hostal Ribadavia,** C. Fuencarral 25, 1st-3rd fl. (tel. 91 531 10 58 or 91 531 48 47). M: Gran Vía. Run by the same cheerful family. Request a room in Palacios (1st and 2nd fl.) for larger rooms with TV. Ribadavia (3rd fl.) is older but very comfortable. Singles 2500-3500ptas; doubles 3800ptas-4800ptas; triples 5500-6600ptas; one quad 7500ptas. V, MC, AmEx.

Hostal-Residencia Domínguez, C. Santa Brígida 1 (tel. 91 532 15 47). M: Tribunal; go down C. Fuencarral toward Gran Vía and turn left on C. Santa Brígida. Quiet, spartan rooms with TV. Hospitable owner ready with tips on local nightlife. Singles 1900ptas, with bath 2500ptas; doubles with bath 4000ptas. Reservations recommended.

ELSEWHERE IN MADRID

Albergue Juvenil Santa Cruz de Marcenado (HI), C. Santa Cruz de Marcenado 28 (tel. 91 547 45 32; fax 91 548 11 96). M: Argüelles; follow C. Alberto Aguilera away from C. Princesa, turn right on C. Serrano Jóve, and turn left on C. Santa Cruz de Marcenado. Modern, renovated facilities. 1300ptas, under 27 950ptas. Members only; HI cards 1800ptas. Breakfast included. Lockers 200ptas. 3-day max. stay. Reception 9am-1:30pm. Strict curfew 1:30am. Reserve ahead. Closed Dec. 25 and Jan. 1.

Camping Osuna (tel. 91 741 05 10; fax 91 320 63 65), on Av. Logroño. M: Canillejas; Cross the pedestrian overpass, walk through the parking lot, turn right along the freeway, pass under a freeway and an arch, and look for signs to the right. Hot showers, laundry, bar, and restaurant. 660ptas per person, per tent, and per car, plus 7% IVA.

◪ FOOD

In Madrid, it's not hard to fork it down without forking over too much. Between *churro*-laden breakfasts, two-hour lunches, *meriendas* (snacks), dinner, and *tapas*, it's a wonder *madrileños* get anything done at all. In the tourist-infested **Centro** area, prices run high. **Pl. Santa Ana** in **Huertas** is a favorite spot to snack, and you might actually sit next to a real Spanish person. **Calles Echegaray, Ventura de la Vega,** and **Manuel Fernández González** are also good places to hunt for budget eats. The **Lavapiés-La Latina-Atocha** area, south of Sol between C. Atocha and C. Toledo, has plenty of *menús* for around 1000ptas. Head to **Calle Santa Isabel,** by Madrid-Atocha and the Reina Sofía, for reasonably-priced *bocadillos* (sandwiches) and *tapas*. Off Gran Vía, **Calle Fuencarral** is lined with budget eateries. **Chueca** is flooded with chic restaurants and **Malasaña's** restaurants often feature adventurous menus, filled with veggie options. The area north of **Glorieta de Bilbao** in the "V" formed by **Calles Fuencarral** and **Luchana** and including **Pl. de Olavide** is swarming with bars, cafés, and restaurants. The middle-class *barrio* of **Argüelles** near the Ciudad Universitaria is replete with cheap markets and restaurants.

You can't walk a block in Madrid without tripping over at least five *cafeterías*, where a sandwich, coffee, and dessert cost around 600ptas. A full meal at a *restaurante* or *casa* costs at least 1100ptas. Note the following buzz words for a quick, cheap bite: *bocadillo* (sandwich on hard roll; 350-400ptas); *sandwich* (on sliced bread, *a la plancha* if you want it grilled; 300ptas); *croissant* (with ham and cheese; 250ptas); *ración* (a large *tapa*, served with bread; 300-600ptas); and *empanada* (a puff pastry with tuna; 200-300ptas). Fresh produce in Madrid is rare, and vegetarians may shrink a size. For a nibble, pop into any local food shop or **Rodilla,** an all-purpose food chain notable for its green decor. Get **groceries** at **%Dia, Simago,** and the glorified **Mercado de San Miguel,** on Pl. San Miguel, off the northwest corner of Pl. Mayor. (Open M-Th 9:30am-2pm and 5:30-8:30pm, F-Sa 9am-2:30pm and 5:30-9pm.) In the following listings, *restaurantes* are open daily from 1 to 4pm and 8pm to midnight unless otherwise noted.

▨ **Museo del Jamón,** C. San Jerónimo 6 (tel. 91 521 03 46), in **Centro.** M: Sol. Don't miss this or one of five other much-loved locations (also Gran Vía). Succulent Iberian ham served up in every form your piggish little heart could desire: *bocadillo, chiquito, croissant, ración* (100-600ptas). *Tapas maestro* and cold, frothy mugs of Mahou beer. Noisy by sundown. Open M-Sa 9am-12:30am, Su 10am-12:30am. V, AmEx.

Can Punyetes, C. Señores de Luzón 5 (tel. 91 542 09 21), off C. Mayor in **Centro.** M: Ópera. A neighborhood secret best known for its *tostadas* (495-775ptas). Entrees 465-1030ptas. *Menú* 1350ptas. A/C. Open M-Sa 1-5pm and 8pm-12:30am.

▨ **Casa Alberto,** C. Huertas 18 (tel. 91 429 93 56), in **Huertas.** M: Anton-Martin. Old-world interior, but the *tapas* are all-new house recipes. Try the *gambas al ajillo* (shrimp in garlic and hot peppers; 1250ptas) or the filled *canapes* (275-350ptas). V, MC.

Gula Gula, C. Infantes 5 (tel. 91 522 87 64), off C. Echegaray near C. Huertas, in **Huertas.** M: Antón Martin. Also at Gran Vía 1 (tel. 91 522 8764), near C. Accacá. So exotic that waiters/waitresses often wear bikinis. All-you-can-eat salad bar 1500ptas. *Spectáculo* Sunday at 11pm might have storytellers or drag queens. Make reservations on weekends.

La Farfalla, C. Santa María 17 (tel. 91 369 46 91), in **Huertas.** M: Antón Martín; follow C. Huertas 1 block south and look for the butterfly above the entrance. The specialty is Argentine-style grilled meat (1100-1750ptas), but don't miss the *erótica* or *exquisita* thin-crust pizza (700ptas). Open for dinner Su-Th until 3am, F-Sa until 4am. Visa.

▨ **El Estragón,** Pl. de la Paja 10 (tel. 91 365 89 82). M: **La Latina.** Uphill off C. Segovia, facing La Capilla del Obispo. Vegetarian food that will make diehard carnivores reconsider. Delicious and creative *menú* 1900ptas. Open daily 1-5pm and 8:30pm-midnight.

Museo Chicote, C. Gran Vía 12 (tel. 91 532 97 80). M: **Gran Vía.** Its deep, leather booths are deceptive—frugal meals abound. The best deals are for breakfast, with coffee and fresh house pastries (240-400ptas).

▨ **El 26 de Libertad,** C. Libertad 26 (tel. 91 522 25 22), off C. las Infantas. M: **Chueca.** Spectacular food featuring innovative and exotic Spanish cuisine. Lunchtime *menú* 1250ptas. Open M-F 1-4pm and 8pm-midnight, Sa 1-4pm and 9pm-1am.

Restaurante Zara, C. las Infantas 5 (tel. 91 532 20 74), off C. Hortaleza in **Chueca.** M: Gran Vía. Bold and beautiful locals swarm to this island of colorful Cuban cuisine. Meat entrees 700-1100ptas. Open M-F 1-4pm and 8pm-midnight. V, MC, AmEx.

La Gata Flora, C. 2 de Mayo 1 and C. San Vicente Ferrer 33 (tel. 91 521 20 20), in **Chueca.** M: Noviciado or Tribunal. Pink exterior and huge servings. *Menú* 1075ptas. Open Su-Th 2-4pm and 8:30pm-midnight, F-Sa 2-4pm and 8:30pm-1am. V, MC.

La Tarterie, C. Cardenal Cisneros 24 (tel. 91 593 85 27), right off C. Luchana, which is off Glorieta de Bilbao. M: **Bilbao.** Admire local experimental art along with tasty quiche (675ptas), salad (650ptas), or pizza (775-1050ptas).

La Crêperie, Po. Pintor Rosales 28 (tel. 91 548 23 58), in **Argüelles.** M: Ventura Rodríguez. Cherub decor is almost as sweet as their crêpes (370-805ptas). Have a meal or a snack. Open Su-Th 1:30-4:15pm and 8pm-1am; F-Sa 1:30-4:15pm.

SPAIN

Cáscaras, C. Ventura Rodríguez 7 (tel. 91 542 83 36), in **Argüelles.** M: Ventura Rodríguez. Sleek interior looks like a tortilla—which is what the restaurant serves (745-955ptas). *Tapas* and Mahou beer. Open M-F 7am-1am, Sa-Su 10am-2am. V, MC, AmEx.

◉ SIGHTS

Madrid, as large as it may seem at first, is a walker's city. A lounger's city, too—when panting for a break from the museums or a retreat from the summer's scorching heat, head for the shade at the Parque del Retiro or any sidewalk café.

EL CENTRO: SOL, ÓPERA, AND PLAZA MAYOR

PUERTA DEL SOL. Kilómetro 0—the origin of six national highways—marks the center of the city (and of the country) in the most chaotic of Madrid's plazas, with taxis, bars, and street performers galore. The statue **El Oso y el Madroño,** a bear and strawberry tree, is the symbol of the city and a universal meeting place. *(M: Sol.)*

PLAZA MAYOR. Although Juan de Herrera, the architect of El Escorial, also designed this plaza, its elegant arcades, spindly towers, and verandas are much softer. These elements, fused together for Felipe III in 1620, came to define "Madrid-style" architecture and inspired every peering *balcón* constructed thereafter. The bullfights and public executions once held here are now but ghosts haunting the plaza's lively cafés. Pl. Mayor awakens at night as *madrileños* resurface and tourists multiply. *(M: Sol; from Puerta del Sol, walk down C. Mayor.)*

CATEDRAL DE SAN ISIDRO. This 17th-century church reigned as Madrid's cathedral from the late 19th century until the Catedral de la Almudena was consecrated in 1993. *(At the intersection of C. Toledo and C. Sacramento. M: Sol; from Pta. del Sol, go down C. Mayor through Pl. Mayor, and exit onto C. Toledo. Open for mass only.)*

PLAZA DE LA VILLA. This small and quiet plaza marks the heart of what was old Madrid. The **Torre de los Lujanes,** a 15th-century building on the eastern side of the plaza, is the sole remnant of the once-lavish residence of the Lujanes family. The characteristically Hapsburg 17th-century **Ayuntamiento** was both the mayor's home and the city jail. *(M: Sol; head down C. Mayor past the Pl. Mayor and it's on your left.)*

◪THE PALACIO REAL. This amazingly luxurious palace was built for the first Bourbon King, Felipe V, to replace the burned Alcázar. It took 40 years to build, and the decoration of its 2000 rooms with 20km of tapestry dragged on for a century. The view out of the **Campo del Moro,** which runs from the palace down to the river, is straight out of a fairy tale. *(M: Ópera. Or, from Sol, go down C. Mayor past Pl. de la Villa and turn right on C. de Bailén. Open Apr.-Sept. M-Sa 9am-6pm, Su 9am-3pm; Oct.-Mar. M-Sa 9:30am-5pm, Su 9am-2pm. 850ptas, students 350ptas; with Spanish tour 950ptas, students 850ptas. W free for EU citizens.)* The palace faces **Plaza de Oriente,** a sculpture garden mostly featuring works designed for the palace roof that had to stay earthbound due to a little engineering oversight (they proved too heavy for the roof to support).

CATEDRAL DE LA ALMUDENA. Begun in 1879 and finished a century later, the cathedral's interior is a modern contrast to the gilded Palacio Real. The reason for the controversy surrounding its recent face-lift is immediately apparent: the stained-glass windows and frescoes are an almost psychedelic mix of traditional and abstract. *(M: Ópera. Or, from Sol, head down C. Mayor and it's just across C. Bailén. Open M-F 10am-1:30pm and 6-8:45pm, Su 10am-2pm and 6-8:45pm. Closed during mass.)*

HUERTAS, GRAN VÍA, MALASAÑA, CHUECA, AND ARGÜELLES

East of Pta. del Sol, the sights of **Huertas** reflect its literary ilk, from authors' houses to famous cafés. Home to Cervantes, Góngora, Quevedo, Calderón, and Moratín, the neighborhood enjoyed a fleeting return to literary prominence when Hemingway hung out here. *(M: Sol.)* **Gran Vía,** which stretches from Pl. de Callao to Pl. de España, is a sight in itself. It's the busiest street in Madrid, lined with massive skyscrapers, fast-food joints, and bustling stores. *(M: Callao and M: Pl. España.)* **Malasaña** and **Chueca** bristle with Madrid's alternative scene; this area between C. de Fuencarral and C. de San Bernardo, north of Gran Vía, boasts avant-garde architecture, chic eateries, and the city's hippest fashion. Out of the way in **Argüelles,** Goya's frescoed dome in the worthwhile **Ermita de San Antonio de la Florida** arches above his own buried corpse. *(M: Príncipe Pío; turn left on C. de Buen Altamirano, go through the park, turn left on Po. Florida, and it's at the end of the street. Open Tu-Su 10am-2pm. Free.)*

THE RETIRO AND ENVIRONS

☙**Parque del Retiro,** a top picnic and suntanning zone, was originally intended to be a *buen retiro* (nice retreat) for Felipe IV. The **Estanque Grande,** a lake in the middle of the park, has become its social center, especially on Sundays. South of the lake, the exquisite steel-and-glass **Palacio de Cristal,** built by Ricardo Velázquez, hosts art shows. A few steps south of the *estanque*, the **Palacio de Velázquez** exhibits works in conjunction with the Museo de Arte Reina Sofía. *(M: Retiro.)* Just to the west of the park, between the Retiro and the Prado, is the **Iglesia de San Jerónimo,** where Fernando and Isabel were crowned and King Alfonso XIII was married. *(Just off Po. Prado on C. Ruiz de Alarcón. Open daily 8am-1:30pm and 5-8:30pm.)*

EL PARDO

Built as a hunting lodge for Carlos I in 1547, **El Pardo** was subsequently enlarged by generations of Hapsburg and Bourbon royalty into the magnificent country palace it is today. The palace is renowned for its collection of tapestries, several of which were designed by Goya. Franco resided here from 1940-1975. Admission to the palace's **chapel** and the nearby **Casita del Príncipe** is free. *(Open Apr.-Sept. M-F 9:30am-6pm, Su 9:25am-1:40pm; Oct.-Mar. M-F 10:30am-5pm, Su 9:55am-1:40pm. Compulsory 45min. guided tour in Spanish. 650ptas, students 250ptas, W free for EU citizens. Catch bus 601 (15min., 150ptas) from in front of the Ejército del Aire building above M: Moncloa.)*

🏛 MUSEUMS

The worthwhile **Paseo del Arte** ticket grants admission to the Museo del Prado, Colección Thyssen-Bornemisza, and Centro de Arte Reina Sofía (1275ptas).

🖼 **Museo del Prado** (tel. 91 420 37 68), on Po. Prado at Pl. Cánovas del Castillo. M: Banco de España or Atocha. The nation's pride and one of Europe's finest museums. Its walls are graced by Goya's "black paintings," Velázquez's *Las Meninas,* a strong Flemish collection, with works by Van Dyck, van der Weyden, Albrecht Dürer, Pieter Brueghel the Elder, and Rubens (a result of the Spanish Hapsburgs' long reign over the Netherlands), and other works by Titian, Raphael, Tintoretto, Botticelli, Bosch, and El Greco. Open Tu-Sa 9am-7pm, Su 9am-2pm. 500ptas, students 250ptas; Sa 2:30-7pm and Su free.

🖼 **Museo Thyssen-Bornemisza** (tel. 91 369 01 51), on the corner of Po. Prado and C. San Jerónimo. M: Banco de España. This 18th-century palace houses a fabulous collection of art accumulated by generations of the Austro-Hungarian magnates. The museum surveys it all, parading canvases and sculptures from the 14th to 20th centuries. An impressive collection of works by many of the greats—including El Greco, Titian, Caravaggio, Picasso, Rothko, Hopper, Mondrian, Klee, Chagall, and Dalí—is housed here. Open Tu-Su 10am-7pm. 700ptas, students 400ptas.

🖼 **Museo Nacional Centro de Arte Reina Sofía,** C. Santa Isabel 52 (tel. 91 467 50 62), opposite Estación Atocha at the southern end of Po. Prado. M: Atocha. The centerpiece of the Reina Sofía's collection of 20th-century art is Picasso's masterpiece *Guernica,* painted to display the agony of the 2000 killed in the Nazi bombing of the Basque town of Guernica (see p. 858) for the Fascists during the Spanish Civil War. Works by Miró, Julio González, Juan Gris, Picasso, and Dalí also illustrate the essential role of Spanish artists in the Cubist and Surrealist movements. Open M and W-F 10am-9pm, Su 10am-2:30pm. 500ptas, students 250ptas; Sa after 2:30pm and Su free.

Museo de la Real Academia de Bellas Artes de San Fernando, C. Alcalá 13 (tel. 91 522 00 46). M: Sol or Seville. An excellent collection of Old Masters, surpassed only by the Prado. In the same building, the **Calcografía Real** (Royal Print and Drawing Collection) houses Goya's studio and temporary exhibitions. Both open Tu-F 9am-7:30pm, Sa-M 9:30am-2:30pm. Joint ticket M-F 400ptas, students 200ptas; Sa-Su free.

Museo de América, Av. Reyes Católicos 6 (tel. 91 549 26 41), near Av. Puerta de Hierro. M: Moncloa. This under-appreciated museum documents the cultures of America's pre-

Columbian civilizations and the effects of the Spanish conquest. Open Tu-Sa 10am-3pm, Su 10am-2:30pm. 500ptas, students 200ptas; Su free.

Monasterio de las Descalzas Reales (tel. 91 559 74 04), on Pl. Descalzas, between Pl. Callao and Pta. de Sol. M: Callao or Sol. Home to 26 Franciscan nuns and an impressive collection of religious art. Open Tu-Th and Sa 10:30am-12:45pm and 4-6pm, F 10:30am-12:45pm, Su 11am-1:45pm. 650ptas, students 250ptas. EU citizens free W.

♪ ENTERTAINMENT

The indispensible weekly *Guía del Ocio* (125ptas) carries comprehensive entertainment listings; the tourist office's *En Madrid* (free) is also helpful.

CLASSIC CAFÉS. While away an afternoon lingering over a *café con leche* and soak up a little Madrid culture in these historic cafés. **Café Gijón,** Po. Recoletos 21 (M: Colón), was designated a historic site due to a history of attracting the city's intellectuals, which eases the blow of the expensive coffee (300ptas). (Open daily 9am-1:30am.) Look pensive on leather couches in **Café Círculo de Bellas Artes,** C. Alcalá 42 (M: Banco de España; cover 100ptas) or gaze at the Palacio Real from the ritzy **Café de Oriente,** Pl. Oriente 2 (M: Ópera; open daily 8:30am-1:30am).

FILM, THEATER, AND MUSIC. The **Parque del Retiro** sometimes shows free movies at 11pm in summer. The state-subsidized *filmoteca*, in the renovated Art Deco **Ciné Doré,** C. Santa Isabel 3, is the best for repertory cinema. (Tel. 91 369 11 25; M: Antón Martín. Tickets 200-400ptas.) Subtitled films are shown in many private theaters, including **Alphaville** and **Renoir**—check the *v.o. (versión original)* listings in entertainment guides. In July and August, **Plazas Mayor, Lavapiés,** and **Villa de París** frequently host plays. **Teatro Español,** C. Príncipe 25, regularly showcases winners of the prestigious Lope de Vega award. (Tel. 91 429 62 97. M: Sol. Tickets 1500-3000ptas. Summer venue.) **Teatro de la Comedia,** C. Príncipe 14, often showcases classical Spanish theater. (Tel. 91 521 49 31. M: Sevilla. Tickets 1300-2600ptas; Th reduced price.) The **Centro Cultural de la Villa,** Pl. Colón, produces for ballet and plays in summer. (Tel. 91 575 60 80. M: Colón or Serrano. Tickets 2000ptas.) **The Suditorio Nacional,** C. Príncipe de Vergara 146, hosts the finest classical performances. (Tel. 91 337 01 00. M: Cruz del Rayo. Tickets 800-4200ptas.) **Flamenco** is tourist-oriented and expensive. If you must, try **Casa Patas,** Casa Canizares 10. (Tel. 91 369 04 96. Shows Th-Sa midnight.)

SPORTS. Spanish sports fans go ballistic for **fútbol** (soccer to North Americans). Every Sunday and some Saturdays from September and June, one of two local teams plays at home. **Real Madrid** plays at Estadio Santiago Bernabeu, Po. Castellana 104 (tel. 91 457 11 12; M: Lima). **Atlético de Madrid** plays at Estadio Vicente Calderón, C. Virgen del Puerto 67 (tel. 366 47 07; M: Pirámides or Marqués de Vadillos). **Corridas** (bullfights) are held during the Festival of San Isidro and every Sunday in summer, less frequently the rest of the year. The season lasts from March to October, signaled by posters in bars and cafés (especially on C. Victoria, off C. San Jerónimo). **Plaza de las Ventas,** C. Alcalá 237, east of central Madrid, is the biggest ring in Spain. (Tel. 91 356 22 00. M: Ventas. Tickets 450-15,200ptas.)

◩ NIGHTLIFE

Spaniards get an average of one hour less sleep than other Europeans, and *madrileños* claim to need even less than that. Proud of their nocturnal offerings (they'll say with a straight face that Paris or New York bored them), they insist that they don't retire until they've "killed the night"—and a good part of the following morning. As the sun sets, *terrazas* and *chiringuitos* (outdoor cafés/bars) spill across sidewalks all over Madrid. An average night engages several neighborhoods and countless venues—*madrileños* perhaps start in the *tapas* bars of **Huertas,** move to a first-session disco in **Malasaña,** and then continue on to **Chueca's** wild portals. **Centro's** clubs are both pricey and touristy, but multiple floors and mainstream music keep the streets lined. After-hours, head to landmark clubs in Chueca or on **Gran Vía.** For most clubs and discos, life doesn't begin until around 2am; don't be surprised if at 5:30am there's a line of people still waiting outside. The *entrada* (cover) can be as high as 2000ptas and men may be charged up to 500ptas more than women; women may not be charged at all. Bat your eyelashes, girls.

🟦 **Joy Eslava,** C. Arenal 11. M: Sol or Ópera. Three-tiered theater-turned-disco. Young crowd grooves to disco, techno, R&B, and salsa. Cover 1500-2000ptas; includes 1 drink. Open M-Th 11:30pm-dawn, F-Sa 7-10:15pm and 11:30pm-5:30am.

🟦 **Soul Kitchen,** C. Mesonero Romanos 13. M: Gran Vía or Callao. Those in the know don't get here before 4am. A revived hotspot and the only real hip-hop club in town. Cover 1000ptas, after 2am 2000ptas; includes 1 drink. Open W-Sa midnight-5:30am.

🟦 **Midday,** C. Amaniel 13. M: Noviciado. The after-hours club for Madrid's *gente guapa.* Techno and house for the extremely energized only. Open Su 9am-3pm.

Refugio, C. Dr. Cortezo 1. M: Tirso de Molina; it's the 1st door on your left. Outrageous gay men's scene, but fun for all. It's got a dark room for the shadiest of affairs. Cover 1000ptas; includes 1 drink. Open Tu-Su midnight-morning.

Kapital, C. Atocha 125, 1 block off Po. Prado. M: Atocha. One of the most extreme results of *La Movida,* this macro-*discoteca* strives to impress. Seven floors of overstimulation. Packed with glittery 20-year-olds willing to pay the 1200ptas cover (includes 1 drink). Drinks 800-1000ptas. Open Th 12:30-6am, F-Su 6-11pm and 12:30-6am.

Heaven, C. Veneras 2. M: Santo Domingo. Heavenly drag performances and underwordly industrial party for a primarily gay crowd. Cover 500-1500ptas; includes 1 drink. Drinks 650-900ptas. Open daily 1:30am-morning.

Goa After Club, C. Mesonero Romanos 13 (see above). Soul Kitchen's after-hours party; high-energy techno for the exhausted but perseverant clubber. Cover 1000ptas; includes 1 drink. Open Sa-Su 6-10am.

🔳 EXCURSIONS FROM MADRID

EL ESCORIAL. The **Monasterio de San Lorenzo del Escorial** was a gift from Felipe II to God, the people, and himself, commemorating his victory over the French at the battle of San Quintín in 1557. Near the town of **San Lorenzo,** El Escorial is filled with artistic treasures, two palaces, a church, two pantheons, and a magnificent library. *Don't* come on Monday, when the complex and most of the town shut down. To avoid crowds, enter El Escorial by the gate on the west side on C. Florida Blanca into a collection of Flemish tapestries and paintings. The adjacent **Museos de Arquitectura** and **Pintura** chronicle the construction of El Escorial and include masterpieces by Bosch, El Greco, Titian, Tintoretto, Velázquez, Zurbarán, Van Dyck, and others. The **Palacio Real,** lined with 16th-century *azulejos* (tiles), includes the **Salón del Trono** (Throne Room), Felipe II's spartan 16th-century apartments, and the luxurious 18th-century rooms of Carlos III and Carlos IV. The macabre **Panteón Real** is filled with tombs of monarchs and glitters with intricate gold-and-marble designs from 1654. (Tel. 91 890 59 03. Complex open Tu-Su Apr.-Sept. 10am-7pm; Oct.-Mar. 10am-6pm. 850ptas, students 350ptas; W free for EU citizens. Tour 950ptas.)

Autocares Herranz **buses** leave from Madrid's "Moncloa" metro station for El Escorial's **Plaza Virgen de Gracia,** the center of town (1hr., every hr., round-trip 750ptas). The Autocares Herranz office, C. Reina Victoria 3, and the bar/casino at C. Rey 27 sell tickets to Madrid. From the bus stop, exit left and turn right up C. Florida Blanca to get to the **tourist office,** C. Florida Blanca 10. (Tel. 918 90 15 54. Open M-Sa 10am-6pm.) **Trains** (tel. 918 90 07 14) also chug to Ctra. Estación, 2km from El Escorial, from Madrid's Atocha and Chamartín stations (1hr., every 20min., 790ptas); from the station, take a shuttle bus to the Pl. Virgen de Gracia.

EL VALLE DE LOS CAÍDOS. In a valley of the Sierra de Guadarrama, 8km north of El Escorial, Franco built the overpowering monument of **Santa Cruz del Valle de los Caídos** (Valley of the Fallen) as a memorial to those who gave their lives in the Civil War. Naturally, the massive granite cross was meant to honor only those who died "serving *Dios* and *España*," i.e., the Fascist Nationalists. Non-fascist prisoners of war were forced put to work building the monument, and thousands died during

SPAIN

its construction. Although Franco lies buried beneath the high altar, there is no mention of his tomb in tourist literature—testimony to modern Spain's view of the dictator. El Valle de los Caídos is accessible only via El Escorial. Autocares Herranz runs one **bus** to the monument (15min.; leaves El Escorial Tu-Su 3:15pm, returns 5:30pm; round-trip 870ptas includes admission but excludes funicular). (Open daily in summer daily 9:30am-7pm; off-season 10am-6pm. Mass daily 11am. 650ptas, students 250ptas; W free EU citizens. Funicular 350ptas.)

CENTRAL SPAIN

Castilla La Mancha, surrounding Madrid to the west and south, is one of Spain's least-developed regions; medieval cities and olive groves sprinkle the land. On the other sides of Madrid are **Castilla y León's** dramatic cathedrals; despite glorious historical architecture and history, the regions have not been as economically successful as its more high-tech, neighbors. Farther west, bordering Portugal, stark **Extremadura's** arid plains bake under intense summer sun, relieved by scattered patches of glowing sunflowers and refreshingly few tourists.

CASTILLA LA MANCHA

Cervantes chose to set Don Quijote's adventures in La Mancha (*manxa* is Arabic for parched earth) in an effort to evoke a cultural and material backwater. No fantasy of the Knight of the Sad Countenance is needed to transform the austere beauty of this battered, windswept plateau. Its tumultuous history, gloomy medieval fortresses, and awesome crags provide enough food for the imagination.

TOLEDO

Toledo (pop. 65,000) may today be marred by armies of tourists and caravans of kitsch, but this former capital of the Holy Roman, Visigoth, and Muslim empires remains a treasure trove of Spanish culture. The city's churches, synagogues, and mosques reflect a time when Spain's three religions peacefully coexisted.

🖩🖂🏠 **PRACTICAL INFO, ACCOMMODATIONS, AND FOOD. Trains** (tel. 925 22 30 99) arrive from Madrid's Estación Atocha (1½hr., 10-20 per day, 640ptas) at Po. Rosa 2, opposite the Puente de Azarquiel. Take bus 5 or 6 from the right of the station to Pl. Zocodóver (115ptas), take C. Armas downhill as it changes names and leads through the gates (Puerta Nueva de Bisagra), and cross the intersection to reach the **tourist office** (15min.). (Tel. 925 22 08 43; fax 925 25 26 48. Open M-F 9am-6pm, Sa 9am-7pm, Su 9am-3pm.) Surf the **internet** at **Scorpions,** on C. Pintor Matías Moreno. (100ptas per 6min. Open daily noon-midnight.) To get from the station to the **Residencia Juvenil San Servando (HI),** on Castillo San Servando, cross the street, turn left and turn immediately right up Callejón del Hospital; when the steps reach a road, turn right and then right again, and follow signs to the Hospital Provincial (10min.). (Tel. 925 22 45 54. 1325ptas, under 27 1125ptas. Laundry. Reception 7am-11:50pm. Curfew 12:30am. Sometimes closed—call ahead.) From Pl. Zocodóver, head up C. Sillería, go diagonally left through Pl. San Agustín, and turn right to get to **Pensión Castilla,** C. Recoletos 6. (Tel. 925 25 63 18. Singles 2200ptas; doubles with bath 3900ptas.) Next door is **Pensión Segovia,** C. Recoletos 4. (Tel. 925 21 11 24. Singles 2200ptas; doubles 3000ptas; triples 4500ptas.) **Camping El Greco,** is 1.5km from town on the road away from Madrid (C-502); take bus 7 from Pl. Zocodóver. (Tel. 925 22 00 90. 595ptas per person, 620ptas per tent, 550ptas per car; add 7% IVA tax.) Try one of Toledo's marzipan delights, or do lunch at **Restaurante El Zoco,** C. Barrio Rey 7, off Pl. Zocodóver. (*Menús* 800-1500ptas. Open daily 1:30-4pm and 8-10:30pm.) **Postal code:** 45070.

📷🎵 **SIGHTS AND ENTERTAINMENT.** Toledo's major sights (many closed on Mondays) lie within the walls; despite well-marked streets, you'll probably get lost. Southwest of Pl. Zocodóver, Toledo's grandiose **catedral** at the Arco de Palacioz,

Toledo

ACCOMMODATIONS

A Pensión Segovia
B Pensión Castilla
C Residencia Juvenil
   San Servando (HI)

boasts five naves, delicate stained glass, and unapologetic ostentatiousness. (Open July-Aug. M-Sa 10:30am-1:30pm and 3:30-7pm, Su 10:30am-1:30pm and 4-6pm; Sept.-June M-Sa closes at 6pm, Su 10:30am-1:30pm and 4-6pm. 500ptas; tickets sold at the store opposite the entrance.) Toledo's most formidable landmark, the **Alcázar,** Cuesta Carlos V 2, uphill from Pl. Zocodóver, has been a stronghold of Romans, Visigoths, Moors, and Fascists. Today, it houses a national military museum. (Open Tu-Su 9:30am-2:30pm. 200ptas; EU citizens W free.)

Greek painter Doménikos Theotokópoulos, or **El Greco,** spent most of his life in Toledo. Many of his works are displayed throughout town; on the west side of town, the **Iglesia de Santo Tomé,** on Pl. Conde, houses his famous *El entierro del Conde de Orgaz (Burial of Count Orgaz).* (Open daily 10am-7pm. 200ptas.) Downhill and to the left lies the **Casa Museo de El Greco,** C. Samuel Levi 3, with 19 works by the master. (Open Tu-Sa 10am-2pm and 4-6pm, Su 10am-2pm. 200ptas, students free; Sa and Su afternoons free for all.) The impressive and untouristed **Museo de Santa Cruz,** C. Cervantes 3, off Pl. Zocodóver, also exhibits a handful of El Grecos in its eclectic collection. (Open M 10am-2pm and 4-6:30pm, Tu-Sa 10am-6:30pm, Su 10am-2pm. 200ptas, students 100ptas.)

The simple exterior of the 14th-century **Sinagoga del Tránsito,** on C. Samuel Levi, hides an incredibly ornate interior with Mudéjar plasterwork, an intricate wooden ceiling, and Hebrew inscriptions, and now houses the **Museo Sefardí.** (Open Tu-Sa 10am-2pm and 4-6pm, Su 10am-2pm. 400ptas, students 200ptas; free Sa 4-6pm and Su.) The 12th-century **Sinagoga de Santa María la Blanca,** down the street to the right, was built as a mosque, was then used as the city's main synagogue, and in 1492 was converted to a church. (Open daily June-Aug. 10am-2pm and 3:30-7pm;

Sept.-May closes 6pm. 200ptas.) At the far western edge of the city, with great views is the Franciscan **Monasterio de San Juan de los Reyes,** commissioned by Isabel and Fernando. (Open daily 10am-2pm and 3:30-6pm; off-season until 5pm. 150ptas.)

For nightlife, try **C. Santa Fe,** east of and through the arch from Pl. Zocodóver, which brims with beer and local youths. **Zaida,** in the Centro Comercial Miradero, downhill on C. Armas, is a perennial hot spot for dancing. (Open daily 9pm-5am.) The town goes crazy for **Corpus Christi,** celebrated the eighth Sunday after Easter.

CUENCA

Cuenca (pop. 43,500) is a vertical hilltop city surrounded by two rivers and stunning rock formations. The enchanting old city safeguards most of Cuenca's unique charm, including the famed *casas colgadas* (hanging houses) that dangle high above the Río Huécar, off Pl. Mayor. Carefully cross the San Pablo bridge to **Hoz del Huécar** for a spectacular view of the *casas* and cliffs. Many of the *casas* now house museums; on Pl. Ciudad de Ronda is the excellent **Museo de Arte Abstracto Español.** (Open Tu-F and holidays 11am-2pm and 4-6pm, Sa 11am-2pm and 4-8pm, Su 11am-2:30pm. 500ptas, students 250ptas.) The perfectly square **cathedral,** in Pl. Mayor, is quite unique. (Open June-Aug. 11am-2pm and 4-6pm; Sept.-May 10:30am-2pm and 4-6pm. Free.)

Trains arrive on Po. Ferrocarril, in the new city, from Madrid's Estación Atocha (2½-3hr., 6 per day, 1375ptas) and Valencia (3-4hr., 4 per day, 1515ptas). **Buses** roll into C. Fermín Caballero, right in front of the train station, from Madrid (2½hr., 7 per day, 1315-1615ptas); Toledo (3hr., 5 per week, 1620ptas); and Barcelona (3½hr., M-Sa 1 per day, 4320ptas). From either station, go left to the first bus shelter and take bus 1 or 2 (every 30min., 1-3 per day, 85ptas) to the end to reach Pl. Mayor and the **tourist office.** (Tel. 969 23 21 19. Open daily 9am-9pm.) To reach ⊠ **Pensión Tabanqueta,** C. Trabuco 13, in the old city, head up C. San Pedro from the cathedral, which turns into C. Trabuco after Pl. Trabuco. (Tel. 969 21 12 90. Singles 2000ptas; doubles 4000ptas; triples 6000ptas.) In the new city, take C. Fermín Caballero from the bus station, turn left at the busy intersection on C. Hurtado de Mendoza and continue on Av. República Argentina to **Pensión Cuenca** at #8, 2nd fl. (Tel. 969 21 25 74. Singles 1800-2100ptas; doubles 2700-3800ptas.) Budget eateries line **C. Cervantes** and **C. República Argentina.** Grab **groceries** at **%Día,** on Av. Castilla La Mancha at Av. República Argentina. (Open M-Th 9:30am-2pm and 5:30-8:30pm, F-Sa 9am-2:30pm and 5:30-9pm.) **Postal code:** 16004.

SEGOVIA

In the 12th and 13th centuries Segovia (pop. 55,000) had more Romanesque monuments than anywhere else in Europe. Today, its remaining cathedrals and castles represent Castile at its finest—a labyrinthine town of twisted alleys filled with the aromas of *sopa castellano* (bread, egg, and garlic soup) and *cochinillo asado* (roast suckling pig).

◪ ◪◪◪ **PRACTICAL INFO, ACCOMMODATIONS, AND FOOD.** Although **trains** run frequently from the station on Po. Obispo Quesada to Madrid (2hr., 9 per day, 775ptas), **buses** are often more convenient: they depart from Po. Ezequiel González 12 for Ávila (1hr., M-F 8 per day, Sa-Su 1 per day, 555ptas); Madrid (1¾hr., every hr., 765ptas); and Salamanca (3hr., 3 per day, 1245ptas). Your first stop should be the **Municipal Tourist Office,** Pl. Mayor 10, in front of the bus stop, which has indispensable maps. (Tel. 921 46 03 34. Open daily 10am-2pm and 5-8pm.) **Kitius,** Av. Fernández Ladreda 28, has the fastest **internet** connection you've ever encountered. (Open M-Sa 9am-2pm and 5-8:30pm. 900ptas per hr.)

In summer, finding a *hostal* room can be a nightmare; book ahead and prepare to pay at least 2500ptas for a single. The **Residencia Juvenil "Emperador Teodosio" (HI),** Av. Conde de Sepúlveda, is only open to travelers in July and August, when its hotel-like doubles and triples, all with private baths, make it extremely popular. From the train station, turn right, cross the street, and walk along Po. Obispo Quesada, which becomes Av. Conde de Sepúlveda (10min.). From the bus station, turn right on C. Ezequiel González, which becomes Av. Conde Sepúlveda (10min.). (Tel. 921 44 11 11. 1450ptas, under 27 1000ptas. 3-night max. stay. Curfew varies.) **Hostal Juan Bravo,** C. Juan Bravo 12, 2nd fl., on the main thoroughfare in the old town, has bright, newly renovated rooms. (Tel. 921 46 34 13. Singles 2500-3500ptas; doubles 3800-4800ptas; triples 5000-6500ptas. V, MC.) To get to **Hostal Don Jaime,** Ochoa Ondategui 8, face away from the aqueduct stairs and it's on the first street to your left. The breakfast is fabulous (375ptas). (Tel. 921 44 47 87. Singles 3000ptas; doubles 3800ptas, with bath 5500ptas; triples with bath 6800ptas.) **Camping Acueducto,** Ctra. Nacional 601, km 112, is 2km toward La Granja. Take the Autobus Urbano from Pl. Azoguejo to Nueva Segovia (100ptas). (Tel. 921 42 50 00. 500ptas per person and per tent. Open year-round.)

Sample Segovia's famed lamb, *croquetas*, or *sopa castellana*, but steer clear of pricey Pl. Mayor and Pl. Azoguejo. Get **groceries** at **%Día,** C. Fernández Jiménez 3. (Open M-Th 9:30am-2pm and 5:30-8:30pm, F-Sa 9am-2:30pm and 5:30-9pm.) The local color of the hidden **Bar-Mesón Cueva de San Estéban,** C. Valdeláguila 15, off Pl. San Estéban and C. Escuderos, is worth seeking out. (*Menú* 900ptas. Open daily 10am-midnight.) **Postal code:** 40001.

🎫 🍴 **SIGHTS AND ENTERTAINMENT.** The **cathedral,** commissioned by Carlos I in 1525, towers above Pl. Mayor. Inside, the **Sala Capitular** displays intricate tapestries; the **museum** has a series of 17th-century paintings on marble depicting the Passion of Christ. (Open daily Apr.-Oct. 9:15am-6:45pm; Nov.-Mar. 9:30am-5:45pm. 300ptas). The **Alcázar,** a late-medieval castle and site of Isabel's coronation in 1474, dominates the northern end of the old quarter. In the **Sala de Solio** (throne room), an inscription reads: *tanto monta, monta tanto* ("she mounts, as does he"). Elevate your mind from the gutter long enough to appreciate this statement, which signified Fernando and Isabel's equal authority as sovereigns. The **Sala de Armas** holds an arsenal of medieval weaponry. From Pl. Mayor, follow C. Marques del Arco and walk through the park. (Open daily Apr.-Sept. 10am-7pm; Oct.-Mar. 10am-6pm. 400ptas.) The serpentine **roman aqueduct** commands the entrance to the old city. Constructed by the Romans around 50 BC, it is built from 20,000 blocks of granite, without any mortar holding them together. View it at its maximum height (28.9m) from Pl. del Azoguejo, or catch its profile from the steps on the left side of the plaza. This spectacular engineering feat was restored by the monarchy in the 15th century and was still in use 50 years ago. **Pl. Mayor** and its tributaries reign at night, crammed with cafés and bars; **Pl. Azoguejo** and **C. Carmen,** down near the aqueduct, are filled with bars as well. For clubs, head to **C. de Ruiz de Alda,** off Pl. Azoguejo.

🧳 **EXCURSION FROM SEGOVIA: LA GRANJA DE SAN ILDEFONSO.** The royal palace and grounds of **La Granja,** 9km southeast of Segovia, were commissioned by Philip V, the first Bourbon King. Of the four royal summer retreats (the others being El Pardo, El Escorial, and Aranjuez), this "Versailles of Spain" is by far the most extravagant. Marble, lace curtains, lavish crystal chandeliers, and a world-class collection of Flemish tapestries enliven the palace. Manicured gardens and a forest surround the palace. (Open June-Sept. Tu-Su 10am-6pm; Oct.-Mar. Tu-Sa 10am-1:30pm and 3-5pm, Su 10am-2pm; Apr.-May Tu-F 10am-1:30pm and 3-5pm, Sa-Su 10am-6pm. 650ptas, students 250ptas, W free for EU citizens.) **Buses** run to La Granja from Segovia (20min., 10-14 per day, round-trip 200ptas).

CASTILLA Y LEÓN

Castilla y León's cities emerge like islands from a sea of burnt sienna. The monuments—the majestic Gothic cathedrals, the slender Romanesque belfries along the Camino de Santiago, the intricate sandstone of Salamanca, and the proud city walls of Ávila—have emblazoned themselves as national images.

ÁVILA

Ávila (pop. 50,000), is renowned for its 2.5km of magnificently preserved 12th-century stone walls that encircle the old city. Apparently untouched by pollution or the blare of tourist traffic, Ávila makes a great daytrip from Segovia or Madrid.

◪▐▖◙ PRACTICAL INFO, ACCOMMODATIONS, AND FOOD. Trains leave the station at Av. José Antonio (tel. 920 25 02 02), for Villalba (transfer point for Segovia; 1hr., 16 per day, 980ptas); Madrid (1½-2hr., 20-25 per day, 835-1500ptas); and Salamanca (1¾hr., 3 per day, 835ptas). From the train station, take Av. José Antonio, turn right on Av. del Dieciocho, turn left on Av. Madrid, and turn left again on C. Duque de Alba to reach Pl. de Santa Teresa. The **bus station,** Av. Madrid 2 (tel. 920 22 01 54), on the northeast side of town, serves Segovia (1hr., 2-7 per day, 555ptas); Madrid (1½hr., 5-8 per day, 910ptas); and Salamanca (1½hr., 2-4 per day, 700ptas). Cross the street and follow C. Duque de Alba to reach Pl. de Santa Teresa. To continue on to Ávila's **tourist office,** Pl. Catedral 4, walk through the main gate and turn right on C. Alemania. (Tel. 920 21 13 87. Open daily 10am-2pm and 4-7pm.) Get on the **internet** at C. Estrada 12. (700ptas per hr. Open M-F 10am-2pm and 5-9pm, Sa 11am-2pm.)

Ávila's walls are brimming with comfortable and reasonably priced accommodations. The beautiful and spacious **Pensión Continental,** Pl. Catedral 6, is next to the tourist office. (Tel. 920 21 15 02; fax 25 16 91. Singles 2350ptas; doubles 3950-4800ptas; triples 5900-7200ptas. V, MC, AmEx.) **Hostal Casa Felipe,** Pl. Victoria 12, has TVs and a bar. (Tel. 920 21 39 24. Singles 2200ptas; doubles with shower 4000ptas; triples 4500ptas.) The city has won fame for its *ternera de Ávila* (veal) and *mollejas* (sweetbread). Its *yemas de Santa Teresa* or *yemas de Ávila* (local confections made of egg yolks and honey) and *vino de Cebreros* (a smooth regional wine) are also delectable. **Calle San Segundo,** off Pl. Santa Teresa, and **Plaza Victoria** are budget dining goldmines. **Restaurante El Grande,** Pl. Santa Teresa 8, is a popular family-style restaurant with outdoor seating. (*Raciones* 375-800ptas; *menú* 765ptas. Open daily noon-4pm and 8pm-midnight). **Postal code:** 05001.

▨ ▎J SIGHTS AND ENTERTAINMENT. Ávila's **medieval walls,** the oldest and best-preserved medieval walls in Spain, dating from 1090. Eighty-eight massive towers reinforce the three-meter-thick walls. To walk along the walls, start from the Puerta del Alcázar, directly before you with your back to the Pl. de la Teresa. (Open in summer Tu-Su 11am-1:30pm and 5-7:30pm; off-season Tu-Su 10:30am-3:30pm. 200ptas.) Inside the walls, the profile of the **cathedral** looming over the watchtowers is believed to have inspired Santa Teresa's metaphor of the soul as a diamond castle. (From the Pl. de la Teresa, walk through the *puerta* and turn right on C. Cruz Vieja. Open daily Apr.-Oct. 10am-1pm and 3:30-6pm; Nov.-Mar. 10am-1:30pm and 3:30-5:30pm. 250ptas.) Santa Teresa's admirers built the 17th-century **Convento de Santa Teresa** on the site of her birthplace and childhood home. (From the Pl. de Sta. Teresa, turn left on C. San Segundo, right on Po. del Rastro, and left into the Puerta de Sta. Teresa. Open daily May-Sept. 9:30am-1:30pm and 3:30-9pm; Oct.-Apr. 9:30am-1:30pm and 3:30-8:30pm.) To the right of the convent, the **Sala de Reliquias** holds Santa Teresa relics, including her right ring finger and the cord with which she flagellated herself. (Open daily 9:30am-1:30pm and 3:30-7:30pm. Free.) A short distance outside the city walls on Po. Encarnación is the **Monasterio de la Encarnación,** where Santa Teresa lived for 30 years. The mandatory 15-minute guided tour in Spanish visits Santa Teresa's tiny cell and the staircase where she had her mystical encounter with the child Jesus. (Open daily in summer 10am-1pm and 4-7pm; off-season 10am-1pm and 3:30-6pm. 150ptas.)

SALAMANCA

For centuries, the gates of Salamanca have welcomed students, scholars, rogues, royals, and saints. The bustling city is famed for its university—the oldest in Spain, and once one of the "four leading lights of the world," along with the universities of Bologna, Paris, and Oxford—and for its warm golden sandstone architecture.

PRACTICAL INFO, ACCOMMODATIONS, AND FOOD. Trains chug from Po. Estación Ferrocarril (tel. 923 12 02 02) to Ávila (2hr., 3 per day, 1100ptas); Madrid (3½hr., 4 per day, 2500ptas); and Lisbon (6hr., 1 per day, 4600ptas). **Buses** run from Av. Filiberto Villalobos 71/85 (tel. 923 23 67 17) to Ávila (1-2hr., 2-7 per day, 750ptas); Madrid (2½-3hr., 3-14 per day, 2230-2690ptas); León (3hr., 3 per day, 1675ptas); and Segovia (3hr., 1-3 per day, 1260ptas). Bus 1 (75ptas) from the train station and bus 4 from the bus station head to Gran Vía, a block from Pl. Mercado (next to the town center at Pl. Mayor). The **tourist office** is at Pl. Mayor 14. (Tel. 923 21 83 42. Open M-Sa 9:30am-2pm and 4:30-6:30pm, Su 10am-2pm and 4:30-6:30pm.) Access the **internet** at **Informática Abaco Bar,** C. Zamora 7 (150ptas per 30min.).

Reasonably priced *hostales* and *pensiones* cater to the floods of student visitors, especially off **Pl. Mayor** and **C. Meléndez. Pensión Estefanía,** C. Jesús 3-5, off Pl. Mayor, has a prime location and clean rooms. (Tel. 923 21 73 72. Singles 2000ptas; doubles with shower 3500ptas; triples 4600ptas. Showers 150ptas.) Spacious rooms and a comfy TV lounge await at **Hostal La Perla Salamantina,** Sánchez Barbero 7. Exit Pl. Mayor via Pl. Poeta Iglesias, cross the street, and take the first right. (Tel. 923 21 76 56. Singles 2000-2500ptas; doubles 3800-4800ptas.) Albetur buses shuttle **campers** from Gran Vía (every 30min.) to the four-star **Regio,** 4km toward Madrid on the Ctra. Salamanca. (Tel. 923 13 88 88. 375-425ptas per person, per tent, and per car.) **Simago,** C. Toro 82, has a downstairs **supermarket.** (Open M-Sa 9:30am-8:30pm.) Cafés and restaurants surround Pl. Mayor; full meals in cheaper back alley spots run around 1000ptas. **Restaurante El Bardo,** C. Compañía 8, between the Casa de Conchas and the Clerecía, is a traditional Spanish restaurant with veggie options and a lively bar downstairs. (Tel. 923 21 90 89. Entrees 1000-1800ptas. Open daily 10am-5pm and 7pm-1am. V, MC.) **Postal code:** 37001.

SIGHTS AND ENTERTAINMENT. The **Plaza Mayor,** designed by Alberto Churriguera, exemplifies the best of the city's famed architecture and has been called one of the most beautiful squares in Spain. Between its nearly 100 sandstone arches hang medallions with bas-reliefs of famous Spaniards, from El Cid to Franco. Walk down C. Rua Mayor to Pl. San Isidro to reach the 15th-century **Casa de las Conchas** (House of Shells), one of Salamanca's most famed landmarks, adorned by over 300 rows of scallop shells chiseled in sandstone. Go down Patio de las Escuelas, off C. Libreros (which leads south from Pl. San Isidro), to enter the **Universidad,** founded in 1218. The university's 16th-century **entry façade** is one of the best examples of Spanish Plateresque, named for the delicate filigree work of *plateros* (silversmiths). Hidden in the sculptural work lies a tiny hidden frog; legend dictates that those who can spot the frog without assistance will be blessed with good luck and even marriage. Inside the Escuelas Menores, the University Museum contains the Cielo de Salamanca, a 15th-century fresco of the zodiac. (Open M-F 9:30am-1:30pm and 4-7:30pm, Sa 9:30am-1:30pm and 4-7pm, Su 10am-2pm. 300ptas, students 150ptas.) Continue down Rua Mayor to Pl. Anaya to reach the *vieja* (old) and *nueva* (new) cathedrals. Begun in 1513 to accommodate the growing tide of Catholics, the spindly-spired late-Gothic **Catedral Nueva** weren't finished until 1733. The smaller Romanesque **Catedral Vieja** (1140) has a striking cupola with depictions of apocalyptic angels separating the sinners from the saved. The **museum** in the latter houses a Mudéjar Salinas organ, one of the oldest organs in Europe. (Cathedrals open daily Apr.-Sept. 9am-2pm and 4-8pm; Oct.-Mar. 9am-1pm and 4-6pm. *Vieja,* cloister, and museum 300ptas. *Nueva* free.) If religious zeal intrigues you, inquire at the tourist office about Salamanca's impressive **convents.**

Nightlife concentrates on **Pl. Mayor,** overflowing as far west as **San Vicente;** also check out **C. Bordadores** and **Gran Vía. Camelot,** C. Bordadores 3, is a monastery-turned-club packed with converts anxious to be defrocked. Swing to Top-40 songs at the popular **Café Moderno,** Gran Vía 75. For a more relaxed setting, **Birdland,** C. Azafranal 57, by Pl. España, features jazz. A mainly gay clientele grooves under black lights at **Submarino,** C. San Justo 27, built in an old submarine.

SPAIN

🖪 **EXCURSION FROM SALAMANCA: CIUDAD RODRIGO.** A medieval town characterized by fabulous masonry and honey-colored stone, Ciudad Rodrigo rises from the plains near the Portuguese border. The **cathedral** is the town's masterpiece; with biblical and mythological scenes illustrated in intricate stonework, the **cloister** alone justifies the trip from Salamanca. Fascinating figures festoon the columns—making love, playing peek-a-boo, or nibbling body parts. The cathedral's **museum** includes an ancient clavichord and Velázquez's *Llanto de Adam y Eva por Ariel muerto.* (Cathedral open daily 9:30am-1pm and 4-8pm; free. Cloister and museum open daily 10am-1pm and 4-6pm; 200ptas. Mandatory Spanish tour.) **Buses** arrive from Salamanca (1¼hr., 3-8 per day, 720ptas).

LEÓN

Formerly the center of Christian Spain, today León is best known for its 13th-century Gothic **cathedral** on La Pulchra Leonina, arguably the most beautiful cathedral in Spain. Its spectacular blue stained-glass windows have earned the city the nickname *La Ciudad Azul* (The Blue City) and would alone warrant a trip to León. The cathedral's **museo** includes gruesome wonders, including a sculpture depicting the skinning of a saint. (Cathedral open daily in summer 8:30am-1:30pm and 4-8pm; off-season closes at 7pm; free. Museum open M-F 9:30am-1:30pm and 4-7pm, Sa 9:30am-1:30pm; 500ptas.) The **Basílica de San Isidoro** was dedicated in the 11th century to San Isidoro de Sevilla, whose remains were brought to León while Muslims ruled the south. The corpses of countless royals rest in the **Panteón Real,** whose ceilings are covered with vibrant 12th-century frescoes. (Open July-Aug. M-Sa 9am-8pm, Su 9am-2pm; Sept.-June M-Sa 9am-1:30pm and 4-7pm, Su 9am-2pm. 400ptas.) During the "early" night, the area around **Pl. San Martín** sweats with bars, discos, and techno-pop. After 2am, the crowds stagger to **C. Lancia** and **C. Conde de Guillén,** both filled with discos and bars. **Fiestas** commemorating St. John and St. Peter are held June 21-30, as is a *corrida de toros* (bullfight).

    Trains (tel. 987 27 02 02) run from Av. Astorga 2 to Madrid (4½-5½hr., 9 per day, 3315ptas) and La Coruña (7hr., 5 per day, 3200-4400ptas). **Buses** (tel. 987 21 10 00) leave from Po. Ingeniero Saenz de Miera for Madrid (4½hr., 8-12 per day, 2610-4200ptas). Take a right as you exit the train station (or a left from the bus station) and follow Av. de Palencia, which leads across the river to Pl. Guzmán el Bueno, turns into Av. de Ordoño II, and eventually leads to the cathedral and the adjacent **tourist office**, Pl. Regla 4. (Tel. 987 23 70 82; fax 987 27 33 91. Open M-F 10am-2pm and 5-7:30pm, Sa 10am-2pm and 4:30-8:30pm, Su 10am-2pm.) The friendly proprietors at 🖪**Hostal Oviedo,** Av. Roma 26, 2nd fl., off Pl. Guzmán el Bueno, offer huge rooms. (Tel. 987 22 22 36. Singles 2000ptas; doubles 3300ptas; triples 5000ptas.) To get to the basic **Consejo de Europa (HI),** Po. Parque 2, walk with the river on your right along Av. Facultad de Veterinaria and at Pl. Toros head behind the stadium. (Tel. 987 20 02 06. 1100ptas, under 27 950ptas. Breakfast 300ptas. Open late June-Aug.) Pick up **groceries** at **Consum,** on Av. de José Antonio (open M-Sa 9:30am-6:30pm), or eat at **Calle Ancha,** on C. Generalísimo Franco between C. General Mola and C. Conde Luna (scrumptious *menús* 900-950ptas; open daily 1-4pm and 9:15pm-midnight; V, MC). **Postal code:** 24071.

BURGOS

During its 500 years as capital of Castile, Burgos (pop. 180,000) witnessed the birth of the extraordinary cathedral and Rodrigo Díaz de Vivar, better known as El Cid Campeador, the national hero of Spain. Nine centuries after El Cid's banishment, General Franco stationed his headquarters here. Today, natives share the streets with history-seeking tourists and pilgrims completing the Camino de Santiago.

🖪🖭🖰 **PRACTICAL INFO, ACCOMMODATIONS, AND FOOD. Trains** (tel. 947 20 35 60) go from the end of Av. Conde de Guadalhorce, across the river from the center (south of the river), to León (2hr., 8 per day, 2000ptas); Madrid (3½hr., 10 per day, 3000ptas); San Sebastián (4hr., 8 per day, 2400ptas); Bilbao (4hr., 5 per day, 1800ptas); and Barcelona (8hr., 12 per day, 5000ptas). Follow Av. Conde de Guadal-

SPAIN

horce across the river and take the first right on Av. Generalísimo Franco, which turns into Po. Espolón, to reach the center (10min.). **Buses** (tel. 947 28 88 55) leave C. Miranda 4, off Pl. Vega south of the river, for Bilbao (2-3hr., 8 per day, 1420ptas); Madrid (3hr., 12-15 per day, 1920ptas); León (3½hr., M-Sa 1 per day, 1700ptas); San Sebastián (3½hr., 7 per day, 1825ptas); Pamplona (3½hr., 5 per day, 1900ptas); and Barcelona (7½hr., 3-4 per day, 4960ptas). To get to the **tourist office**, Pl. Alonso Martínez 7, follow C. Madrid through Pl. Vega and across the river, then turn right on Po. Espolón, left on C. Santander, and follow the signs. (Tel. 947 20 31 25. Open M-F 9am-2pm and 5-7pm, Sa-Su 10am-2pm and 5-8pm.) The **Café Cabaret Ciber-Café** is at C. Puebla 21. (500ptas per 30min. Open Su-Th 5pm-2am, F-Sa 4pm-4am.)

Cheap hostels line the streets near **Pl. Alonso Martínez,** north of the river. To get from Pl. España to the family-run ⊠**Pensión Peña,** C. Puebla 18, 2nd. fl., take C. San Lesmes and then your third right. (Tel. 947 20 63 23. Singles 1600-1700ptas; doubles 2800-2900ptas. Laundry.) From the bus station, walk toward the center and look right before C. Valladolid to reach **Pension Dallas,** Pl. Vega 1-6. (Tel. 947 20 54 57. Singles 2000ptas; doubles 4000ptas. Showers 300ptas.) To get to **Camping Fuentes Blancas,** take the bus from Pl. España (dir: Fuentes Blancas; July to mid-Sept. 4 per day, 75ptas). (615ptas per person, per tent, and per car. Open Apr.-Sept.) **Pl. Alonso Martínez** teems with restaurants. At ⊠**La Riojana's,** C. Avellanos 10, the *menú* (900ptas) will fill the emptiest of stomachs. (Open daily noon-1am.) **Spar Supermercado,** on C. Concepción, is between C. Hospital Militar and C. San Cosme. (Open M-F 9am-2pm and 5-8pm, Sa 9am-2pm.) **Postal code:** 09070.

⊠ 🎭 **SIGHTS AND ENTERTAINMENT.** The spires of Burgos' magnificent Gothic **cathedral** rise high above the city. The 13th-century Gothic north façade appears starkly contrasts with the intricate 15th-century towers and 16th-century stained-glass dome of the **Capilla Mayor,** where parts of El Cid's body rest in peace. (Open daily 9:30am-1pm and 4-7pm. 400ptas, students 200ptas.) Opposite the cathedral stands the **Iglesia de San Nicolás,** on Pl. Santa Maria, which contains 15th- and 16th-century Hispano-Flemish paintings and altars. (Open July-Sept. M 9am-8pm, Tu-Su 9am-2pm and 4-8pm; Oct.-June Tu-F 6:30-7:30pm, Sa 9:30am-2pm and 5-7pm. Free.) Altarpieces await up C. Pozo Seco at the **Iglesia de San Esteban/Museo del Retablo.** (Open June-Sept. Tu-Sa 10:30am-2pm and 4:30-7pm, Su 10:30am-2pm; Oct.-May Sa 10:30am-2pm and 4:30-7pm, Su 10:30am-2pm. 200ptas, students 100ptas.) The 200 steps behind the museum lead to an astounding view of the red roofs of Burgos from the ruins of a medieval **castle** presiding over Burgos from high above the cathedral. By midnight, **C. Avellanos** (opposite Pl. Alonso Martínez) is at full boil. Crowds bubble over into nearby **C. Huerto del Rey,** then steam it up at *discotecas* along **C. San Juan.** Don't show up at **Besame Mucho,** off Pl. Lesmes, until after 2am.

EXTREMADURA

In a land of harsh beauty and cruel extremes, arid plains bake under an intense summer sun, relieved by scattered patches of glowing sunflowers. These lands hardened New World conquistadors such as Hernán Cortés and Francisco Pizarro, but the conquering heroes never returned to share their spoils with their native land, one of the more economically depressed regions of Spain.

MÉRIDA

Mérida (pop. 60,000) has more Roman ruins than anywhere else in Spain. This veritable "little Rome" includes aqueducts, a hippodrome, and an amphitheater, while the **Museo Romano** flaunts all the Roman memorabilia one could want. (Tel. 924 31 16 90. Open Tu-Su 10am-2pm and 5-7pm; off-season Tu-Sa 4-6pm. 400ptas, students 200ptas; Sa afternoons and Su free.) Over the wide, shallow Río Gaudiana, the large **Puente Romano** is still the main entrance to town. The 6000-seat **Teatro Romano,** a gift from Emperor Augustus to the city in 16 BC, is located in a park across the street from the museum; in summer it hosts **Teatro Clásico** performances. (Tel. 924 31 25 30. Performances July-Aug. daily at 10:45pm. Tickets 700-3500ptas.) The 16,000-seat

Anfiteatro Romano next door was inaugurated in 8 BC and hosted man-to-man gladiator combat, as well as the popular contests between men and wild animals. (Both open daily in summer 9:30am-1:45pm and 5-7:15pm; off-season schedules subject to change. Joint ticket covers these and 3 other sights. 800ptas, EU students 400ptas; Sa afternoon and Su morning free.) **Buses** arrive from Seville (3hr., 14 per day, 1600ptas); Salamanca (5hr., 4 per day, 2185ptas); and Madrid (5½hr., 8 per day, 2760-3790ptas). The **tourist office,** on C.P.M. Plano, is opposite the Museo Romano. (Tel. 924 26 32 32. Open M-F 9am-1:45pm and 5-7:15pm, Sa-Su 9:15am-1:45pm.) To get to the **Pensión El Arco,** C. Cervantes 16, follow C. Santa Eulalia up from Pl. España and turn left. (Tel. 924 31 83 21. Singles 1800ptas; doubles 3000ptas.) Outdoor cafés abound in and around the Pl. de España, but for budget eating try **EcoStop supermarket,** on C. Cabo Verde. **Café Internet,** C. Baños 25 (tel. 924 38 86 58), offers a beer and 30min. of computer use for 350ptas. **Postal code:** 06800.

SOUTHERN SPAIN (ANDALUCÍA)

Greeks, Phoenicians, and Romans colonized and traded in Andalucía, but the most enduring influences were left by Arabs, who arrived in AD 711 and bequeathed the region with far more than the flamenco music and gypsy ballads proverbially associated with southern Spain. The Moors sparked the European Renaissance by reintroducing the wisdom and science of Classical Greece and the Near East. Under Moorish rule, which lasted until 1492, Seville and Granada reached the pinnacle of Islamic arts, and Córdoba matured into the most culturally influential Islamic city. The Moors perfected a distinctly Andalusian architectural style marked by cool patios and patterns made of red brick and white stone. The dark legacy of Andalucía is its failure to progress economically; stagnant industrialization and severe drought have mired the region in indefinite recession. Still, residents retain an unshakable faith in the good life—good food, good drink, and spirited company.

✕ FERRIES TO MOROCCO

Ferries hop the Straits of Gibraltar from **Gibraltar** and **Algeciras.** From Gibraltar, **Tourafrica Int. Ltd.,** 2a Main St (tel. 776 66; fax 767 54), sails to **Tangier** (3 per week, UK£18, round-trip UK£30). From Algeciras, boats go in summer to **Ceuta** (1½hr., 30-35 per day, 1884-3002ptas) and **Tangier** (2½hr., every hr., 3200ptas per person, 20% off with Eurail; hydrofoils 1hr., 3 per day, 3900ptas).

CÓRDOBA

"Sevilla is a young girl, gay, laughing, provoking—but Córdoba…Córdoba is a dear old lady." Nowhere else do the remnants of Spain's ancient Islamic, Jewish, and Catholic heritage so visibly intermingle, a legacy reflected in Córdoba's (pop. 315,000) unique art and architecture. The playwright and philosopher Seneca settled here during the Roman occupation; the city was also home to the medieval Jewish philosopher Maimonides, who spearheaded Córdoba's political and intellectual reemergence under Islamic rule (AD 711-1263). Today, springtime festivals, flower-filled patios, and a busy nightlife still make Córdoba one of Spain's most beloved cities. The city may be a "a dear old lady," but she is far from tired.

▐ GETTING THERE AND GETTING AROUND

Flights: Córdoba Airport (tel. 957 21 41 00), on Av. del Aeropuerto.
Trains: (tel. 957 40 02 02), on Av. de América. To: **Seville** (45min.-1¼hr., 27 per day, 1065-2700ptas); **Madrid** (2-6hr., 29 per day, 3700-7100ptas); **Málaga** (2¼-3hr., 20 per day, 1650-3000ptas); **Cádiz** (2½-4hr., 7 per day, 2370-3700ptas); **Granada** (4-4½hr., 3 per day, 2130-2785ptas); **Algeciras** (5½hr., 2 per day, 2800-3300ptas); and

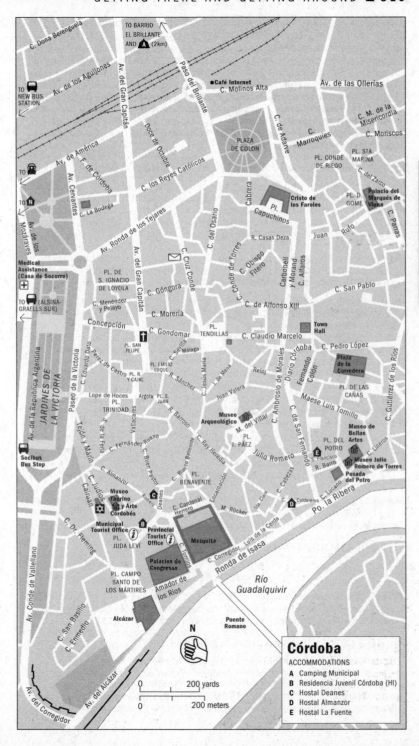

SPAIN

Córdoba

ACCOMMODATIONS

A Camping Municipal
B Residencia Juvenil Córdoba (HI)
C Hostal Deanes
D Hostal Almanzor
E Hostal La Fuente

Barcelona (10-11hr., 5 per day, 6100-8400ptas). Student discounts for all fares. For international tickets, contact **RENFE**, Ronda de los Tejares 10 (tel. 957 49 02 02).

Buses: The main station is at C. Diego Serrano 14, 1 block from Av. Medina Azahara; another station is on Av. de América, opposite the train station. **Alsina Graells Sur** (info tel. 957 40 40 40; tickets 957 27 81 00) covers most of Andalucía. To: **Seville** (2hr., 10-14 per day, 1200ptas); **Granada** (3hr., 8 per day, 1515-1635ptas); **Málaga** (3-3½hr., 5 per day, 1540ptas); and **Algeciras** (5hr., 2 per day, 2805ptas). **Bacoma** (tel. 957 45 65 14) runs to **Barcelona** (10hr., 1 per day, 7625ptas). **Socibus** (tel. 902 22 92 92) sends exceptionally cheap buses to **Madrid** (4½hr., 7 per day, 1540ptas) and departs from C. de los Sastres in front of Hotel Meliá. **Empresa Ramírez** (tel. 957 41 01 00) runs buses to nearby towns and camping sites.

⁊ ORIENTATION AND PRACTICAL INFORMATION

The modern and commercial northern half of Córdoba extends from the train station on **Avenida de América** southeast to **Plaza de las Tendillas,** the center of the city. To reach the city center from the train station, walk down Av. Cervantes, turn left on C. Concepción, and continue straight into the plaza. From the main bus station on C. Diego Serrano, exit left, make an immediate left, head to the right on Av. Medina Azahara, continue through the park, go into Pl. A Grilo, and continue down C. Concepción. The older, more touristy part of Córdoba is a medieval maze of beautiful and disorienting streets known as the **Judería** (old Jewish quarter), extending from Pl. Tendillas past the **Mezquita** and **Alcázar** to the river.

Tourist Offices: Provincial Tourist Office, C. Torrijos 10 (tel. 957 47 12 35; fax 49 17 78), in the Junta de Andalucía, on the west side of the Mezquita. Take bus 3 (from the street between the train and bus stations) along the river until the stone arch is on the right, then head 1 block up C. Torrijos. English-speaking staff with good, free maps of the monument section and info on all of Andalucía. Open M-Sa in summer 9:30am-8pm; off-season 9:30am-6pm. **Oficina Municipal de Turismo y Congresos** (tel./fax 957 20 05 22), on Pl. Juda Levi, next to the youth hostel, has Córdoba-specific info. Open June-Sept. M-Sa 8:30am-2:30pm; Oct.-May M-Sa 9am-2pm and 4:30-6:30pm.

Luggage Storage: Lockers at the train and main bus stations. 300-600ptas. Open 24hr.

Emergency: Tel. 092. **Police** (tel. 957 47 75 00), on Av. de Medina Azarah, by the main bus station. **Ambulance** (tel. 29 55 70). **Fire** (tel. 080).

Medical Assistance: Red Cross Hospital (tel. 957 42 06 66; in emergency 22 22 22), on Po. Victoria. English spoken. The Pl. Tendillas **pharmacy** has a list of night pharmacies.

Internet Access: El Navegante Café Internet, C. Llanos del Pretorio 1 (tel. 957 49 75 36), off Av. de América, near the train station. 250ptas per 15min., 350ptas per 30min., 600ptas per hr. Open daily 8am-3:30pm and 8pm-3am.

Post Office: C. Cruz Conde 15 (tel. 957 47 91 96), just north of Pl. Tendillas. Open M-F 8:30am-8:30pm, Sa 9:30am-2pm. Address mail to be held: Darth VADER, *Lista de Correos,* C. Cruz Conde 15, **14070** Córdoba, Spain.

⟋ ACCOMMODATIONS AND CAMPING

Most accommodations cluster near the train station, around the Judería, and off Pl. Tendillas. Call up to several months ahead during *Semana Santa* and summer.

▓ Residencia Juvenil Córdoba (HI) (tel. 957 29 01 66; fax 29 05 00), on Pl. Juda Levi, 2min. west of the Mezquita, in the Judería. The best place to stay in Córdoba—huge, modern, and sparkling. 1300ptas, over 26 1800ptas; nonmembers add 300ptas. Breakfast 195ptas. A/C. Check-out 10am. Check-in 1pm. Reservations recommended.

Hostal La Fuente, C. San Fernando 51 (tel. 957 48 78 27; fax 48 78 27). From the Mezquita, follow C. Corregidor Luis de la Cerda east to C. San Fernando. Relax with the friendly owners in the traditional bar or courtyard. All rooms with bath, some with TV and A/C. Singles 3000ptas; doubles 4000-5000ptas. Breakfast 275ptas. V, MC, AmEx.

Hostal Deanes, C. Deanes 6 (tel. 957 29 37 44). From the northeast corner of the Mezquita, take C. Cardenal Herrero and turn right onto C. Romero (which becomes C.

Deanes). Perfectly situated, with beautiful white walls, high ceilings, and an enormous patio. Doubles 4000ptas, with bath 5000ptas. No reservations.

Hostal Almanzor, C. Cardenal González 10 (tel./fax 957 48 54 00), at the riverside end of C. Rey Heredía, 3 blocks east of the Mezquita. Talk about luxurious. All rooms have cable TV; some have A/C and heat. Singles 1500-2500ptas, with bath 2000-3000ptas; doubles with bath 3000-4000ptas. Reception 24hr. V, MC, AmEx.

Camping Municipal, Av. Brillante 50 (tel. 957 28 21 65). From the train station, turn left on Av. de América, left on Av. Brillante, and walk uphill for 20min.; or take bus 10 or 11 from Av. Cervantes near the station. Drivers should follow signs from the train station to the Big Pryca/La Sierra Mall and Supermarket; from there, turn right, then left at the roundabout after 2 lights, and it's on the right. Public pool. 400-560ptas per tent.

◌ FOOD

Walk 5min. away from the touristy Mezquita area in almost any direction to find regional specialties—including gazpacho, *salmorejo* (a gazpacho-like cream soup topped with hard-boiled eggs and pieces of ham), and *rabo de toro* (bull's tail simmered in tomato sauce)—at reasonable prices. Try the small restaurants on **C. Doctor Fleming,** or the even cheaper eateries farther away in **Barrio Cruz Conde,** around **Av. Menéndez Pidal** and **Pl. Tendillas.** Stock up at **Supermarket Simago,** on C. Jesús María, half a block south of Pl. Tendillas. (Open M-Sa 9am-9pm.)

Mesón San Basilio, C. San Basilio 19 (tel. 957 29 70 07), to the left of the Alcázar, past Campo Santo de los Martires. The locals love it, and so will you. *Menú* 1000ptas. Open daily in summer 12:30-4pm and 8pm-midnight; off-season noon-4pm and 7-11:30pm.

El Pincantón, C. Fernández Ruano 19. From the northeast corner of the Mezquita, walk up Romero and turn left on Fernández. Take ordinary tapas, pour on *salsa picante*, and stick it in a roll for lunch (150-300ptas). Open daily 10am-2pm and 8pm-midnight.

Sociedad de Plateros, C. San Francisco 6 (tel. 957 47 00 42), between C. San Fernando and Pl. Potro. A Córdoba mainstay since 1872. Tapas 200-300ptas. Meals served M-Sa 1-4pm and 8pm-midnight; bar open until 2:30am. V, MC.

◉ SIGHTS

Built in AD 784, the **Mezquita** was intended to surpass all other mosques in grandeur. Over the next two centuries, the spectacular building was gradually enlarged, making it the largest mosque in the world at that time. Visitors enter through the arcaded courtyard **Patio de los Naranjos;** inside, 850 pink and blue marble, alabaster, and stone columns support hundreds of two-tiered, red-and-white striped arches. At the far end of the Mezquita lies the **Capilla Villaviciosa,** the first example of Caliphal vaulting, which became greatly influential in Spanish architecture. In the center, intricate gold, pink, and blue marble Byzantine mosaics—a gift from Emperor Constantine VII—shimmer across the arches of the **Mihrab,** the dome where the Muslims guarded the Quran. Although the town rallied violently against the proposed erection of a **cathedral** in the center of the mosque after the Christians conquered Córdoba in 1236, the towering **Crucero** (transept) and **Coro** (choir dome) were soon built. (Open in summer M-Sa 10am-7pm, Su 9-11am and 1:30pm-dusk; off-season M-Sa 10am-5:30pm, Su 2-5:30pm. 750ptas.)

The **Judería** (Jewish quarter) is the historic area just northwest of the Mezquita. Downhill from the Moorish arch, the small **Sinagoga,** on C. Judíos, is one of the few synagogues remaining in Spain, a solemn reminder of the 1492 expulsion of the Jews. (Open Tu-Sa 10am-2pm and 3:30-5:30pm, Su 10am-1:30pm. Free due to restoration.) Just to the south along the river is the **Alcázar,** constructed for Catholic monarchs in 1328 during the conquest of Granada. Fernando and Isabel bade Columbus farewell here, and later the building served as Inquisition headquarters (1490-1821). Its museum displays first-century Roman mosaics. (Open May-Sept. Tu-Sa 10am-2pm and 6-8pm, Su 9:30am-3pm; Oct.-Apr. Tu-Sa 10am-2pm and 4:30-6:30pm, Su 9:30am-3pm. Illuminated gardens open daily 8pm-midnight. 300ptas, students 150ptas; Friday free.) The **Museo Taurino y de Arte Cordobés,** on Pl. Maimonides, highlights the history and lore of the bullfight. (Open May-Sept. Tu-Sa 10am-2pm and 6-8pm, Su 9:30am-3pm; Oct.-Apr. Tu-Sa 10am-2pm and 5-7pm, Su 9:30am-3pm. 450ptas, students 225ptas; F free.) There is a **combined ticket** for the Alcázar, Museo Taurino y de Arte Cordobés, and the **Museo Julio Romero,** which displays Romero's sensual portraits of Córdoban women (1075ptas, students 550ptas).

ENTERTAINMENT

Pick up a free copy of *La Guía de Ocio,* a monthly guide to cultural events, at the tourist office. For flamenco, hordes of tourists flock to see the big-name dancers at the **Tablao Cardenal,** C. Torrijos 10, facing the Mezquita. (Tel. 957 48 33 20. Shows Tu-Sa 10:30pm. 2800ptasptas includes 1 drink.) Or check out **La Bolería,** C. Pedro López 3. (Tel. 957 48 38 39. Shows daily at 10:30pm. 1500ptas includes 1 drink.)

Of Córdoba's festivals, floats, and parades, **Semana Santa,** in early April, is the most extravagant. During the **Festival de los Patios,** in the first two weeks of May, the city erupts with classical music concerts, flamenco dances, and a city-wide decorated patio contest. Late May brings the **Feria de Nuestra Señora de la Salud** *("La Feria"),* a week of colorful clothing, live dancing, and nonstop drinking.

Starting the first weekend in June, the **Brillante barrio,** uphill from Av. de América, is the place to be: the air is cool, the beer is cooler, and the prices are close to zero. Take bus 10 from RENFE until 11pm; a cab should cost 500-900ptas. Or, walk up Av. Brillante to where C. Poeta Emilia Prados meets C. Poeta Juan Ramon Jiménez. Go through **Cafeteria Terra** to discover a massive open-air patio where myriad **bars** converge. From there, pubs and clubs line **Av. Brillante.**

EXCURSION FROM CÓRDOBA: MADINAT AL-ZAHRA

Built in the **Sierra Morena** by Abderramán III for his favorite wife, Azahara, this 10th-century medina was considered one of the greatest palaces of its time. The site, long thought to be mythical, was discovered in the mid-19th century and excavated in the early 20th century, and today is one of Spain's most impressive archaeological finds. (Tel. 957 32 91 30. Open May-Sept. Tu-Sa 10am-2pm and 6-8:30pm, Su 10am-2pm; Oct.-Apr. Tu-Sa 10am-2pm and 4-6:30pm, Su 10am-2pm. 250ptas, EU citizens free.) **Córdoba Vision** offers a two-hour guided visit to the site in English. (Tel. 957 23 17 34. 2500ptas.) Reaching Madinat Al-Zahra takes some effort if you don't go with an organized tour. The **0-1 bus** leaves from Av. República Argentina in Córdoba for Cruce Medina Azahara; from there you can walk 45min. to the palace. (Info tel. 957 25 57 00; or ask at the tourist office. Departs every hr. 115ptas.)

SEVILLE (SEVILLA)

Site of a Roman acropolis, capital of the Moorish empire, focal point of the Spanish Renaissance, and guardian angel of traditional Andalusian culture, Seville has yet to disappoint visitors. Jean Cocteau included it with Venice and Beijing in his trio of magical cities, and the city has inspired operas by Bizet, Mozart, and Rossini. The 16th-century maxim *"Qui non ha visto Sevilla non ha visto maravilla"*—one who has not seen Seville has not seen a marvel—remains true today.

GETTING THERE AND GETTING AROUND

Flights: Aeropuerto San Pablo (tel. 954 44 90 00), 12km from town on Ctra. Madrid. A taxi from the center of town costs about 2000ptas. **Los Amarillos** (tel. 954 41 52 01) runs a bus there from the Hotel Alfonso XIII in the Pta. Jerez (every hr., 750ptas).

Trains: Estación Santa Justa, on Av. Kansas City (tel. 954 54 02 02). Buses C1 and C2 run from just left of the station as you exit. **RENFE,** C. Zaragoza 29 (tel. 954 22 26 93), is near Pl. Nueva. Open M-F 9am-1:15pm and 4-7pm. To: **Córdoba** (45min.-1½hr., 23 per day, 2300ptas); **Madrid** (2½hr., 20 per day, 8200ptas); **Málaga** (2½hr., 5 per day, 2090ptas); **Granada** (3½hr., 5 per day, 2610ptas); **Valencia** (8½hr., 4 per day, 5300ptas); and **Barcelona** (12hr., 6 per day, 6400ptas).

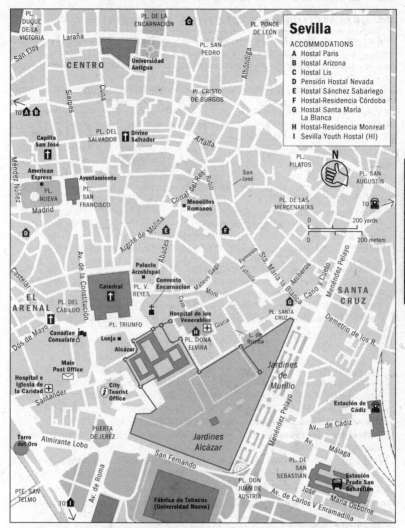

SPAIN

Sevilla

ACCOMMODATIONS

A Hostal Paris
B Hostal Arizona
C Hostal Lis
D Pensión Hostal Nevada
E Hostal Sánchez Sabariego
F Hostal-Residencia Córdoba
G Hostal Santa María
   La Blanca
H Hostal-Residencia Monreal
I Sevilla Youth Hostal (HI)

Buses: Buses from the older **Prado de San Sebastián** (tel. 954 41 71 11), on C. Manuel Vazquez Sagastizabal, serve mainly Andalucía:

Transportes Alsina Graells (tel. 954 41 88 11). To: **Córdoba** (2hr., 10 per day, 1200ptas); **Málaga** (2½hr., 10 per day, 1850ptas); and **Granada** (3hr., 9 per day, 2400ptas).

Transportes Comes (tel. 954 41 68 58). To: **Cádiz** (1½hr., 12 per day, 1300ptas).

Los Amarillos (tel. 954 41 52 01). To: **Marbella** (3hr., 3 per day, 1820ptas) and **Barcelona** (16hr., 1 per day, 8820ptas).

The newer **Plaza de Armas** (tel. 954 90 80 40), a Puente Cristo de la Expiración and C. Arjona, serves destinations outside Andalucía and Spain.

Socibus (tel. 954 90 11 60). To: **Madrid** (6hr., 15 per day, 2715ptas) and **Portugal** (1 per day, various destinations including Lagos, from 2745ptas).

Public Transportation: Buses run every 10min. 6am-11:15pm and converge on Pl. Nueva, Pl. Encarnación, and in front of the cathedral on Av. Constitución. Limited **night service** departs from Pl. Nueva (every hr. midnight-2am). **Single-ride** 125ptas, **bonobús** (10 rides with transfers) 560-650ptas. Buses C3 and C4 circle the center.

SPAIN

🛈 ORIENTATION AND PRACTICAL INFORMATION

Most of the city, including the alleyways of the old **Barrio de Santa Cruz,** lies on the east bank of the **Río Guadalquivir.** The historic and proud **Barrio de Triana** and modern, middle-class **Barrio de los Remedios** occupy the west bank. The **cathedral,** next to Barrio de Santa Cruz, is Seville's centerpiece. **Av. de la Constitución** runs alongside the cathedral. **El Centro** (downtown), a busy commercial pedestrian zone, lies north of the cathedral starting where Av. Constitución hits **Plaza Nueva.**

To get to the cathedral (near the tourist office) or Barrio Santa Cruz from the **train station** or the **Prado de San Sebastián bus station,** take bus C1 or C2. To walk from the train station to the cathedral, head right on C. José Laguillo, turn left on C. María Auxiliadora (which turns into C. Recaredo and C. Menéndez Pelayo), turn right on C. Santa María La Blanca, turn left along C. Ximénez de Enciso, and bear right on C. Rodrigo Caro (40min.). From Pr. San Sebastián, walk straight out of the station, turn left on C. Menéndez Pelayo, turn right on C. San Fernando, bear right on Av. Constitución, and the tourist office will be on your right. To get from the **Plaza de Armas bus station** to El Centro, take bus C1, C2, C3, or C4; or walk right (facing the river) three blocks and turn right on C. Alfonso XII (10min.). To walk to the cathedral, exit right onto Po. Cristobal Colón along the river, and turn left on C. Adriano, which leads to C. García Vinuesa and ends at the cathedral (20min.).

Tourist Offices: Junta de Andalucía, Av. Constitución 21B (tel. 954 22 14 04; fax 954 22 97 53), 1 block south of the cathedral. Open M-F 9am-7pm, Sa 10am-2pm and 3-7pm, Su 10am-2pm. **Branches** at the train station and Pl. Nueva.

Consulates: Australia, Federico Rubio 14 (tel. 95 422 09 71; fax 95 421 11 45); **UK,** Pl. Nueva 8B (tel. 95 422 88 75; fax 95 421 03 23); **US,** Po. Delicias 7 (tel. 95 423 18 85; fax 95 423 20 40).

American Express: Pl. Nueva 7 (tel. 954 21 16 17). Holds mail, changes money, yada yada yada. Open M-F 9:30am-1:30pm and 4:30-7:30pm, Sa 10am-1pm.

Luggage Storage: At both **bus stations** and at the **train station** (250-500ptas per day).

Laundromat: Lavandería Robledo, C. F. Sánchez Bedolla 18, 1 block west of the cathedral. Wash and dry 950ptas per 5kg. Open M-F 10am-2pm and 5-8pm.

Emergency: Tel. 091 or 092. **Police,** Av. Paseo de las Delicias 15 (tel. 954 61 54 50).

Medical Assistance: Ambulatorio Esperanza Macarena (tel. 954 42 01 05).

Internet Access: Cibercenter, C. Julio César 8, off C. Reyes Católicos. 250ptas per 15min. Open daily 9am-9pm.

Post Office: Av. Constitución 32 (tel. 954 21 64 76), opposite the cathedral. Open M-F 10am-8:30pm, Sa 9:30am-2pm. Address mail to be held: Ben HARDER, *Lista de Correos,* Av. Constitución 32, **41080** Sevilla, Spain.

PHONE CODE	Spain has no city codes. From outside Spain, dial int'l dialing prefix (see inside back cover) + 34 + local number.

🏠 ACCOMMODATIONS AND CAMPING

Rooms vanish and prices soar during *Semana Santa* and the *Feria de Abril;* reserve ahead. The narrow streets east of the cathedral in the **Barrio de Santa Cruz** are full of cheap, central hostels. The hostels on the quiet back streets around the **Pl. de Armas** bus station, mostly on C. Gravina, are generally the nicest, cheapest, and quietest accommodations in the city. The disorienting yet charming array of narrow streets around Pl. de la Encarnación in **El Centro** hosts fewer hostels.

▨ **Hostal-Residencia Córdoba,** C. Farnesio 12 (tel. 954 22 74 98), off C. Fabiola in **Santa Cruz.** From the cathedral, head all the way up C. Mateos Gago. Immaculate and spacious, with a beautiful patio. Singles 3200-7000ptas; doubles 4700-9000ptas.

▨ **Hostal Paris,** C. San Pedro Mártir 14 (tel. 954 22 98 61 or 21 96 45; fax 21 96 45), off C. Gravina near **Pl. de Armas.** Brand new, clean, and classy. All rooms with bath, A/C, and TV. Singles 3500ptas; doubles 5000-6000ptas. V, MC, AmEx.

▓ **Hostal Lis,** C. Escarpín 10 (tel. 954 21 30 88), on an alley near Pl. Encarnación in **El Centro.** Each room is decorated with its own unique Sevillian tiles. Singles 2000-3000ptas; doubles 3500-3900ptas; triples 5000-6000ptas.

Hostal Santa María La Blanca, C. Santa María la Blanca 28 (tel. 954 42 11 74), in **Santa Cruz.** A bargain for the district. Fans available upon request. Singles 1500-2000ptas; doubles 3000-4000ptas; triples 4500-6000ptas.

Hostal Sánchez Sabariego, C. Corral del Rey 23 (tel. 954 21 44 70), in **Santa Cruz.** Follow C. Argote de Molina from the right of the cathedral (as you face it) and follow signs to Hostal Sierpes. Friendly, with antique furniture. Singles 2500-3000ptas; doubles 4500-6000ptas.

Hostal-Residencia Monreal, C. Rodrigo Caro 8 (tel. 954 21 41 66), in **Santa Cruz.** Head up C. Mateos Gago from the cathedral and take your 1st right. Clean but unremarkable. Singles 2500ptas; doubles 5000-7000ptas; triples 5600-9300ptas. A/C. V, MC.

Hostal Arizona, Pedro del Toro 14 (tel. 954 21 60 42), off C. Gravina near **Pl. de Armas.** Attractive rooms. Singles 2000ptas; doubles 3000-4000ptas; triples 4500ptas.

Sevilla Youth Hostel (HI), C. Isaac Peral 2 (tel. 954 61 31 50; fax 954 61 31 58). Bus 34 from Pr. San Sebastián stops behind it just after Po. Delicias (take bus C2 or 27 from the train station or C3 from Pl. Armas to Pr. San Sebastián). Out of the way, but clean and disinfected. 1800ptas, under 27 1300ptas. Members only; sells HI cards.

Pensión Hostal Nevada, C. Gamazo 28 (tel. 954 22 53 40), in **El Arenal.** From Pl. Nueva, take C. Barcelona and turn right on C. Gamazo. Cool courtyard and leather sofas. Singles 2200-3500ptas; doubles 4000-8500ptas.

Camping Sevilla, Ctra. Madrid-Cádiz, km 534 (tel. 954 51 43 79), 12km away. From Pr. San Sebastián, take bus 70 to "Parque Alcosa" and walk 800m. Showers, market, and pool. 460ptas per person, per car, and per tent.

◖ FOOD

Seville keeps its cuisine light—it claims to be the birthplace of tapas. Popular venues for *el tapeo* (tapas-barhopping) are **Triana, Barrio Santa Cruz,** and **El Arenal.** Locals imbibe Seville's own Cruzcampo beer, a light, smooth pilsner. **Mercado del Arenal,** between C. Almansa and C. Arenal, has meat, produce, and baked goods. (Open M-Sa 9am-2pm.) **Grocery** shop at **%Día supermarket,** on C. San Juan de Ávila, on Pl. Gavídia. (Open M-F 9:30am-2pm and 6:30-9pm, Sa 9am-1pm.)

▓ **Restaurante-Bar El Baratillo/Casa Chari,** C. Pavia 12 (tel. 954 22 96 51), on a tiny street off C. Dos de Mayo in **Santa Cruz.** Ask in advance for the tour-de-force: homemade paella (2500ptas for 2). *Menú* 500ptas. Open M-F 8am-10pm, Sa noon-5pm.

Pizzería San Marco, C. Mesón de Moro 6/10 (tel. 954 21 43 90), off C. Mateos Gago in **Santa Cruz.** In a huge, 12th-century Moorish bath house. Pizzas and pastas 675-995ptas. Open Tu-Su 1:15-3:30pm and 8:15pm-12:30am, F-Sa until 1am. V, MC.

Bodega Santa Cruz, C. Rodrigo Caro 1 (tel. 954 21 32 46), in **Santa Cruz.** Take C. Mateos Gago from in front of the cathedral and it's on the 1st corner on the right. Casual and crowded, with lots of tasty tapas (175-200ptas). Open daily 8am-midnight.

Bar Cáceres, C. San José 24 in **Santa Cruz.** The best breakfast in Seville. *Desayuno de la Casa* (orange juice, coffee, ham, eggs, toast) 600ptas. Open daily 7:30am-8pm.

▓ **La Ortiga,** C. Procurador 19 (tel. 954 33 74 18), off C. Castilla in **Triana.** Enjoy organic tapas and poetry. Open M-Sa June-Aug. 8pm-12:30am; Sept.-May 5pm-12:30am.

El Rinconcillo, C. Gerona 40 or C. Alhóndiga 2 (tel. 954 22 31 83), in **El Centro.** A popular spot dating from 1670. Tapas 185-300ptas, *raciones* 225-1850ptas. V, MC.

◉ SIGHTS

THE CATHEDRAL. In order to clear space for what is today Seville's most impressive sight, Christians razed an Almohad mosque in 1401, leaving only the famed **La Giralda** minaret. That tower and its twins in Marrakesh and Rabat are the oldest and largest surviving Almohad minarets. The **cathedral** took over 100 years to complete and is the largest Gothic structure in the world. The golden **retablo mayor** (altarpiece) is one of the largest in the world. Circle the choir to view the **Sepulcro de Cristóbol Colón,** allegedly Columbus' tomb. His coffin-bearers represent grateful kings

SPAIN

of Castilla, León, Aragón, and Navarra. The cathedral's **Sacristía Mayor** museum holds Riberas, Murillos, and a glittering Corpus Christi icon. Outside, the **Patio de Los Naranjos** (orange trees) evokes the bygone days of the Arab Caliphate. *(Cathedral complex and Giralda open M-Sa 10:30am-6pm, Su 2-7pm. 700ptas, students 200ptas; Su free.)*

ALCÁZAR. The imposing 9th-century walls of the Alcázar, which faces the cathedral next to Pl. Triunfo, date from the Moorish era—as do several interior spaces, including the exquisitely carved **Patio de las Muñecas**. Of the later Christian additions to the palace, the most exceptional is the **Patio de las Doncellas** (Maid's Court), with ornate archways and complex tilework. The astonishing golden-domed **Salón de los Embajadores** is where Fernando and Isabel supposedly welcomed Columbus back when he returned from America. *(Open Tu-Sa 9:30am-7pm, Su 9:30am-5pm. 700ptas, students free. English-language audio guide 400ptas.)*

BARRIO SANTA CRUZ. King Fernando III forced Jews fleeing Toledo to live in the Barrio de Santa Cruz, now a neighborhood of winding alleys, wrought-iron gates, and fountained courtyards. Beyond C. Lope de Rueda, off C. Ximénez de Enciso, is the charming and fragrant **Plaza de Santa Cruz.** A church in Pl. Santa Cruz houses the grave of the artist Murillo, who died after falling from a scaffold while painting ceiling frescoes in a Cádiz church. Nearby, **Iglesia de Santa María la Blanca** was built in 1391 on the foundation of a synagogue and features Murillo's *Last Supper.* *(On C. Santa María la Blanca. Open M-Sa 10-11am and 6:30-8pm, Su 9:30am-2pm and 6:30-8pm.)*

LA MACARENA. This area northeast of El Centro is named not for the popular mid-90s dance, but rather for the virgin of Seville. A stretch of 12th-century **murallas** (walls) runs between the Pta. Macarena and the Pta. Córdoba on the Ronda de Capuchinos ring road. At the west end is the **Basílica Macarena,** whose venerated image of *La Virgen de la Macarena* is paraded through town during *Semana Santa.* A **treasury** within glitters with the virgin's jewels and other finery. *(On Pl. San Gil. Open daily 9:30am-1pm and 5-8pm. Basilica free. Treasury 300ptas.)* Nearby, **Convento de Santa Paula** includes a church with Gothic, Mudéjar, and Renaissance elements. *(On Pl. Sta. Paula. Open Tu-Su 10am-1pm and 4:30-6:30pm.)*

OTHER SIGHTS. Lovely tropical gardens and innumerable courtyards abound in the monstrous **Parque de María Luisa,** southeast of the city center. *(Open daily 8am-10pm.)* The expansive neighboring **Plaza de España** boasts tiled murals. The neighborhoods of **El Arenal,** west of the cathedral, and **Triana,** just across the river, were Seville's chaotic 16th- and 17th century mariners' quarters. The **Museo Provincial de Bellas Artes** in El Arenal boasts Spain's finest collection of Seville School painters (especially Murillo and Zurbarán), as well as works by foreign masters El Greco and Jan Breughel. *(Pl. Museo 9. Open Tu 3-8pm, W-Sa 9am-8pm, Su 9am-3pm. 250ptas, students and EU citizens free.)* North of Triana, visit the **Museo de Arte Contemporáneo** for works by modern art stars like Miró. *(C. Américo Vespucio 2. Open Tu-Sa 10am-10pm, Su 10am-3pm. 250ptas, EU citizens free.)*

🎵 🎭 ENTERTAINMENT AND NIGHTLIFE

BULLFIGHTS AND FESTIVALS. Get your fix of flamenco at **Los Gallos,** Pl. Santa Cruz 11, on the west edge of Barrio Santa Cruz. (Shows nightly at 9 and 11pm. Cover and 1 drink 3500ptas.) Although the cheapest place to buy **bullfight** tickets is at the ring on Po. Marqués de Contadero (tel. 954 22 35 06), if there's a line you can try the booths on C. Sierpes, C. Velázquez, or Pl. Toros (tickets 3000-13,000ptas). Seville's world-famous **Semana Santa** (Holy Week) festival, during which penitents in hoods guide bejeweled, candle-lit floats through the streets, lasts from Palm Sunday to Good Friday (Apr. 16-21). In late April, the city explodes with the six-day **Feria de Abril** (Apr. Fair), which began as a 19th-century popular revolt against foreign influence and continues today as a popular revolt against sobriety, raging through the night with circuses, bullfights, and flamenco shows.

NIGHTLIFE. Seville's reputation for gaiety is tried and true—most clubs don't get going until well after midnight, and the real fun often starts after 3am. Popular bars cluster around **Pl. Alfalfa** in El Centro, **C. Mateos Gago** near the cathedral, **C. Adriano** in El Arenal, and **C. Betis** in Triana. Down Po. Delicias near the Parque María Luisa, **Alfonso, Libano,** and **Chile** are popular *chiringuitos* (beach bars). ▓**La Carbonería,** C. Levies 18, off C. Santa María La Blanca, has a huge patio and has free nightly live music. (Open M-Sa 8pm-3:30am, Su 8pm-2:30am.) **Cervecería El Tremendo,** C. San Felipe 15, is packed with locals. (Open Th-Tu noon-4:30pm and 8pm-12:30am.) Dance the night away at popular **Catedral,** C. Cuesta del Rosario 12. (Cover 1000ptas for men; includes 1 drink. No cover for women. Open Th-Tu midnight-8am, W midnight-6am.) The liveliest gay disco in town is **Itaca,** C. Amor de Dios 25. (Open Su-Th until 5am, F-Sa until 8am.)

▓ EXCURSIONS FROM SEVILLE

CÁDIZ. Founded by the Phoenicians in 1100 BC, Cádiz (pop. 155,000) is considered the oldest inhabited city in Europe. **Carnaval** is perhaps Spain's most dazzling party (Mar. 2-12 in 2000), while the city attracts year-round with golden, pebble-strewn **beaches** that put those of its eastern neighbors to shame. **Playa de la Caleta** is the most convenient, but better sand awaits in the new city; take bus 1 from Pl. España (115ptas) and get off at Pl. Glorieta Ingeniero (in front of Hotel Victoria) to roast at the squeaky clean ▓**Playa Victoria.** Back in town, the gold-domed, 18th-century **cathedral** is considered the last great cathedral built by colonial riches. From Pl. San Juan de Dios, follow C. Pelota. (Open Tu-Sa 10am-1pm. 500ptas.) RENFE **trains** (tel. 956 25 43 01) arrive at Pl. Sevilla, off Av. Puerto, from Seville (2hr., 12 per day, 1100ptas) and Córdoba (5hr., 10-12 per day, 2325-3700ptas). From the train station, walk two blocks past the fountain, with the port on your right, and look left for **Pl. San Juan de Dios** (the old town center). Transportes Generales Comes **buses** (tel. 956 22 78 11) arrive at Pl. Hispanidad 1 from Seville (2hr., 11 per day, 1300ptas). From the bus station, walk 5min. down Av. Puerto with the port on your left and Pl. de San Juan de Dios will be after the park on your right, with the **tourist office** at #11. (Tel. 956 24 10 01. Open M-F 9am-2pm and 5-8pm.) Most *hostales* huddle around the harbor, in Pl. San Juan de Dios, and just behind it on C. Marqués de Cádiz. **Hostal Colón** is at C. Marqués de Cádiz 6. (Tel. 956 28 53 51. Singles 2000ptas; doubles 3500ptas; triples 4500ptas.)

JEREZ DE LA FRONTERA. Although unremarkable in appearance, Jerez de la Frontera (pop. 200,000) is the cradle of three staples of Andalusian culture: flamenco, Carthusian horses, and, of course, *jerez* (sherry). Most *bodegas* (wine cellars) offer tours in English, but most are closed in August. **Williams and Humbert, Ltd.,** Nuño de Cañas 1, is one of the nicest, with prize-winning Carthusian horses. (Tel. 956 34 65 39. Tours M-F 1:30pm. 400ptas, students 250ptas.) **Trains** (tel. 956 34 23 19) arrive at Pl. Estación from Cádiz (45min., 12 per day, 375ptas) and Seville (1¼hr., 12 per day, 895ptas). **Buses** (tel. 956 34 52 07) go to Arcos (45min., every hr., 225ptas); Cádiz (1hr., 19 per day, 350ptas); Seville (1½hr., 12 per day, 870ptas); and Ronda (2¾hr., 4 per day, 1270ptas). From the train station, exit right, follow C. Cartuja past the bus station, continue on C. Medina, and go left at Pl. Romero Martínez on C. Cerrón, which leads to C. Santa María, C. Lencería, and then C. Larga, to reach the **tourist office,** C. Larga 39; from the bus station, exit left and follow the directions above. (Tel. 956 33 11 50. Open June-Aug. M-F 9am-2pm and 5-8pm, Sa 10am-2pm and 5-7pm; Sept.-May M-Sa 8am-2pm and 4-7pm.) Take bus L8 from the bus station or bus L1 from Pl. Arenal (10min.) to reach the **Albergue Juvenil (HI),** Av. Carrero Blanco 30. (Tel. 956 14 39 01; fax 956 14 32 63. 1100-1800ptas, under 27 800-1300ptas; nonmembers add 300ptas. Call ahead.)

ARCOS DE LA FRONTERA. The premier *pueblo blanco* (white village) on *la ruta de los pueblos blancos*, with Roman ruins and castles at every turn, Arcos (pop. 33,000) is in essence a historic monument. Wander the winding white alleys, ruins, and hanging flowers of the **old quarter,** and marvel at the stunning view from **Pl. Cabildo.** In the square is the **Iglesia de Santa María,** a mix of Baroque, Renaissance, and Gothic styles. From C. Corregidores, Transportes Generales Comes **buses** (tel.

SPAIN

956 70 20 15) go to Cádiz (1½hr., 6 per day 675ptas); Ronda (1¾hr., 4 per day, 950ptas); and Costa del Sol (3-4hr., 1 per day, 1535-2060ptas). Los Amarillos buses (tel. 956 70 02 57) go to Jerez (15min., 19 per day, 225ptas) and Seville (2hr., 2 per day, 905ptas). To reach the old quarter from the bus station, exit left, turn left, and continue 20min. uphill on C. Muñoz Vásquez as it changes names. One block to the right is the **tourist office,** on Pl. Cabildo. (Tel. 956 70 22 64; fax 956 70 09 00. Open June-Aug. M-F 10am-2pm and 5:30-7:30pm, Sa 10am-2pm and 5-7pm, Su 10:30am-1pm; Sept.-May M-Sa 9am-2pm and 5-7pm.) **Hostal Callejón de las Monjas,** C. Dean Espinosa 4, is in the old quarter behind Iglesia de Santa María. (Tel. 956 70 23 02. Singles 3500-4500ptas; doubles 3500-4500ptas.)

RONDA. Ronda (pop. 38,000) will catch your eye and give you lots of reasons why you've got to visit here. The stomach-churning ascent is most people's first impression, but it's the effect on their hearts that's not soon forgotten. Divided in two by a 100-meter gorge, the city has long attracted forlorn artistic types—Pliny, Ptolemy, and pfriends called it "Arunda" (surrounded by mountains), German poet Rainer Maria Rilke wrote his *Spanish Elegies* here, Orson Welles had his ashes buried on a bull farm outside of town, and Hemingway loved his bullfights. The precipitous gorge, carved by the Río Guadalevín, dips below the **Puente Nuevo,** opposite Pl. España. Bullfighting aficionados charge over to Ronda's **Plaza de Toros,** Spain's oldest bullring (est. 1785) and cradle of the modern *corrida*. The **Museo Taurino** inside is filled with interesting factoids. (Open daily June-Sept. 10am-8pm; Oct.-May 10am-6pm. 400ptas.) **Trains** (tel. 95 287 16 73), Av. Alférez Provisional, near Av. Andalucía, run to Algeciras (2hr., 5 per day, 880ptas). Change at Bobadilla for Málaga (2hr., 5 per day, 1225ptas); Granada (3hr., 3 per day, 1730ptas); and Seville (3hr., 2 per day, 2155ptas). **Buses** (tel. 95 218 70 61) go from Pl. Concepción García Redondo 2, near Av. Andalucía, to Marbella (1½hr., 5 per day, 605ptas); Málaga (2½hr., 10 per day, 1075ptas); Cádiz (4hr., 3 per day, 1610ptas); and Seville (5 per day, 1285ptas). To reach the town center from the **train station,** turn right on Av. Andalucía and follow it through Pl. Merced past the **bus station** (it becomes C. San José) until it ends. Take a left on C. Jerez, and follow it past the lush park and Pl. Toros, to **Plaza de España** and the new bridge. The **tourist office** is at Pl. España 1. (Tel. 95 287 12 72. Open M-F 9am-2pm and 4-7pm, Sa-Su 10am-3pm.) **Pensión Virgen del Rocio** is at C. Nueva 18, off Pl. España. (Tel. 95 287 74 25. Singles 2200-4500ptas; doubles 3500-5300ptas. V, MC.) Some of the best restaurants line the streets around **Pl. España** and those heading to **Cra. Espinel. Postal code:** 29400.

GIBRALTAR

E.T. PHONE HOME | Gibraltar's **phone code** is 350 from the UK; 350 from the US; and 9567 from Spain. For **USA Direct,** dial 88 00; for **BT Direct,** 84 00.

Anglophiles and homesick Brits will get jolly well excited over Gibraltar's fish 'n' chips, while everyone else goes batty over the tax-free cigarettes. Britain and Spain have long contested the enclave, and there remains a massive British military presence. Despite the Rock's history and refreshingly diverse population, it's basically a tourist trap. Admire the view of Iberia and the Straits from the imposing Rock, speak some English, then scurry back to the Spanish coast. Cable cars run from the southern end of Main St to the northern tip of the massif known as **Top of the Rock,** stopping halfway up at **Apes' Den,** home to a colony of monkeys that has inhabited the Rock since before the Moorish invasion. The ruins of a Moorish wall crumble down the road from the cable car station to the south, near the spooky chambers of **St. Michael's Cave.** (Cable car every 10min. M-Sa 9:30am-5:45pm. UK£3.65 (with one-hour walk down), round-trip UK£5; includes Apes' Den and cave.)

 Buses arrive in the bordering Spanish town of **La Línea** from Algeciras (40min., 2 per hr., 225ptas); Marbella (1¾hr., 4 per day, 685ptas); Cádiz (3hr., 5 per day, 1460ptas); Málaga (3¼hr., 4 per day, 1255ptas); Granada (5-6hr., 2 per day, 2435ptas); Seville (6hr., 3 per day, 2575ptas); and Madrid (7hr., 2 per day, 3215ptas). From the bus station, walk toward the Rock; the border is 5min. away. After passing Spanish customs and Gibraltar's passport control, cross the airport tarmac and head along the highway into town (20min.) or catch bus 9 or 10 (UK£0.40 or 100ptas). The **tourist office,** in Duke of Kent House, Cathedral Sq, is across the park from the Gibraltar Museum. (Tel. 749 50; fax 749 43. Open M-F 9am-5:30pm.) To get to **Queen's Hotel,** 1 Boyd St, walk through Southport Gate, bear right, and enter around the back. (Tel. 740 00; fax 400 30. Singles UK£18-36; doubles UK£30-40; triples £54. *Let's Go* and student discount 20%. Breakfast included. Laundry. V, MC, AmEx.) **Emile Youth Hostel Gibraltar,** on Line Wall Rd., is opposite the square at the beginning of Main St. (Tel. 511 06. Dorms UK£10; singles UK£15; doubles UK£25. Breakfast included. Lockout 10:30am-4:30pm. Curfew 11:30pm.) Fish 'n' chips shops abound; for potato chips head to the **Safeway** in the Europort commercial complex. (Open M-Sa 8am-8pm.).

ALGECIRAS

Algeciras has some pleasant older areas, but most tourists see only the dingy port, which offers easy access to Gibraltar and Morocco; Moroccan migrant workers, Spanish army recruits, and tourists traffic the area day and night. RENFE **trains** (tel. 956 63 02 02) run from Ctra. Cádiz, way down C. Juan de la Cierva, to Granada (5½hr., 4 per day, 2370-2565ptas); Córdoba (5hr., 6 per day, 2485-3300ptas); Málaga (5½hr., 3 per day, 2115ptas); and Madrid (6hr., 3 per day, 5200ptas). Empresa Portillo **buses** (tel. 956 65 10 55) leave from Av. Virgen del Carmen 15 for Granada (5hr., 2 per day, 2505ptas) and the Costa del Sol; Linesur La Valenciana (tel. 956 60 34 00) runs from C. Juan de la Cierva 5 to Seville (3hr., 8 per day, 1955ptas); and Transportes Generales Comes (tel. 956 65 34 56) goes from C. San Bernardo 1 to La Línea/Gibraltar (45min., 2 per hr., 225ptas). To get from the train or bus stations to the **tourist office,** on C. Juan de la Cierva, follow C. San Bernardo/C. Juan de la Cierva along the tracks toward the port, past a parking lot on the left. (Tel. 956 57 26 36; fax 956 57 04 75. Open M-F 9am-2pm.) To get to the **ferry** port from the tourist office, continue down C. Juan de la Cierva and turn left on Av. Virgen del Carmen. Hostels cluster around **C. José Santacana,** parallel to Av. Marina one block inland. To get to 🏠**Hostal Rif,** C. Rafael de Muro 11, follow C. Santacana into the market square, bear left around the kiosk, and continue one block up C. Rafael del Muro. (Tel. 956 65 49 53. Singles 1200-1500ptas; doubles 2400ptas; quads 4800ptas.) **Hostal Residencia Versailles,** is at C. Moutero Ríos 12, off C. Cayetano del Toro. (Tel. 956 65 42 11. Singles 2500ptas; doubles 3200-3700ptas; triples 4500-4700ptas.)

COSTA DEL SOL

The coast has sold its soul to the Devil; now he's starting to collect. Artifice covers once-natural charms, as chic promenades and swanky hotels line its shore. The Costa del Sol officially extends from Tarifa in the southwest to Cabo de Gata, east of Almería; post-industrial Málaga is right in the middle. To the northeast, rocky beaches have helped to preserve some natural beauty. To the southwest, water seems to wash up on more concrete than sand, and high season bring swarms of tourists (so reserve ahead or ask about private rooms), but nothing can detract from the coast's eight months of spring and four months of summer.

MÁLAGA. In the hundred years since the Romantics discovered Málaga (pop. 531,140) the 19th-century villas have been replaced by 70s highrises and the beach is better known for its bars than untouched sand. Yet Málaga, a critical transport hub for the province, brims with all the requisite historical monuments. Guarding the east end of Po. Parque, the 11th-century **Alcazaba** structure was originally built as a fortified palace for Moorish kings. (Open W-M 9:30am-8pm.) Málaga's **cathedral,** C. Molina Lario, is a pastiche of Gothic, Renaissance, and Baroque styles. (Open M-Sa 10am-12:45pm and 4-6:45pm. 200ptas.) Diehard fans can visit Picasso's birthplace that now houses the **Picasso Foundation,** Pl. Merced. (Open M-Sa 10am-2pm and 6-9pm, Su 10am-2pm. Free.)

From **Estación de Málaga** (tel. 95 236 02 02), Explanada de la Estación, **trains** go to Córdoba (2hr., 12 per day, 2100ptas); Seville (3hr., 3 per day, 1800ptas); Madrid (4hr., 5 per day, 8000ptas); and Barcelona (13hr., 3 per day, 6700ptas). One block from the RENFE station along C. Roger de Flor, **buses,** Po. Tilos (tel. 95 235 00 61), go to Marbella (1½hr., every hr., 575ptas); Granada (2hr., every hr., 1200ptas); Algeciras (3hr., 11 per day, 1250ptas); Córdoba (3hr., 5 per day, 1500ptas); Seville (3hr., 10 per day, 2200ptas); and Madrid (7hr., 8 per day, 2800ptas). To reach the center from the bus station take bus 4 or 21; from the train station take bus 3 (115ptas). The **tourist office,** Av. Cervantes 1, is in a little gray house on Po. Parque. (Tel. 95 260 44 10; fax 95 221 41 20. Open M-F 8:15am-2:45pm and 4:30-7pm, Sa 9:30am-1:30pm.) Most budget establishments are in the old town, between Pl. Marina and Pl. Constitución. **Hostal La Palma,** C. Martínez 7, is off C. Marqués de Larios. (Tel. 95 222 67 72. Singles 2000-3000ptas; doubles 3500-5000ptas; triples 3300-4500ptas; quads 4400-6000ptas.) **Hostal Aurora,** Muro de Puerta Nueva 1, is 5min. from Pl. Constitución. (Tel. 95 222 40 04. Singles 1800-3000ptas; doubles 3000-4500ptas.) Seaside Po. Marítimo stretches toward the lively beachfront district **El Pedregalejo** (bus 11 or 40min. on foot), where restaurants specialize in fresh seafood. A **supermarket** is in **El Corte Inglés,** Av. Andalucía 4-6, opposite the post office. (Open June-Aug. M-Sa 10am-10pm; Sept.-May 10am-9:30pm.) In summer, folks crowd the bars in **El Pedregalejo** and between **C. Comedias** and **C. Granada,** which leads out of Pl. Constitución. **Postal code:** 29080.

MARBELLA. A host of international jet-setters choose five-star Marbella (pop. 100,000) to dock their yachts, park their weary jets, and live the glitzy, glam life. But it's still possible to steal away from the city with a budgeted good time. The city's controversial mayor has "cleaned up" the "marginal" elements (drug dealers, prostitutes, dogs, fellow politicians, etc.); catch it now before he sets his sights on backpackers. Although the beaches beckon with 320 days of sunshine per year, no visit to Marbella would be complete without a stroll through the **casco antiguo,** a maze of cobblestoned streets and ancient whitewashed façades. The **Museo del Grabado Español Contemporáneo,** on C. Hospital Bazán, is a treasure trove of engravings by Miró, Picasso, Dalí, Goya, and contemporary artists. (Open M-F 10:15am-2pm and 5:30-8:30pm. 300ptas.) City buses along Av. Richard Soriano (dir: San Pedro; 125ptas) bring you to chic and trendy **Puerto Banús.** Buffered by imposing white yachts, this is where it's at. With 22km of **beach,** Marbella offers a variety of sizzling settings, from below its chic promenade to **Playa de las Chapas,** 10km east via the Fuengirola bus. In the *casco antiguo* are mellow bars. Between the beach and the old town, C. Puerta del Mar is home to several gay bars. Later in the evening, the city's young 'uns head to the **Puerto Deportivo** ("The Port"), a world of disco-bars. After midnight, the action shifts to **Puerto Banús** where dancing goes until dawn. (Cover for men 2000ptas, women usually free.)

Accessible only by bus, the new **station** (tel. 95 276 44 00) atop Av. Trapiche sends **buses** to Málaga (1½hr., every 30min., 605ptas); Algeciras (1½hr., 9 per day, 760ptas); Granada (4hr., 4 per day, 1785ptas); Seville (4hr., 3 per day, 1895ptas); Madrid (7½hr., 10 per day, 3085ptas); and Barcelona (16hr., 4 per day, 8325ptas). To reach the main strip, exit and walk left, make the first right on Av. Trapiche, and follow any downhill route to the perpendicular Av. Ramón y Cajal, which becomes Av. Ricardo Soriano on the way to Puerto Banús. C. Peral curves up from Av. Ramón y Cajal around the **casco antiguo.** The **tourist office** (tel. 95 277 14 42) is on C. Glorieta de la Fontanilla. A **branch** is in the old town (tel. 95 282 35 50) on Pl. Naranjos. (Both open June-Aug. M-F 9:30am-9pm; Sept.-May M-F 9:30am-8pm, Sa 10am-2pm.) The area in the *casco antiguo* around Pl. Naranjos is packed with hostels. ◪**Hostal del Pilar,** C. Mesoncillo 4, is off either C. Peral, an extension of C. Huerta Chica, or from the bus station it is off C. San Francisco. (Tel. 95 282 99 36; email hostal@marbellascene.com. 1500-2500ptas per person; roof 1000-1500ptas.) The excellent **Albergue Juvenil (HI),** C. Trapiche 2, downhill from the bus station, is just like a proper hotel, only you can afford to stay here. (Tel. 95 277 14 91; fax 95 286 32 27. 1100-1800ptas; under 27 800-1300ptas. **Tents** outside 700ptas per person.) On the Marbella-Fuengirola bus line; ask the bus driver to stop at **Camping Marbella Playa.** (Tel. 95 277 83 91. 310-570ptas per person, 520-970ptas per tent.) A **24-hour minimarket** beckons from the corner of C. Pablo Casals and Av. Fontanilla, which intersects with Av. Ricardo Soriano. **Postal code:** 29600.

GRANADA

"Give him alms, woman! For there is nothing crueler in life than to be blind in Granada," proclaims an inscription in the spectacular red-clay Alhambra, the palace-fortress complex in the hills of Granada. The last Muslim stronghold in Spain, Granada was lost by the ruler Boabdil to Catholic monarchs Fernando and Isabel in 1492. Although the Christians torched all the mosques and the lower city, embers of Granada's Arab essence still linger; the Albaicín, an enchanting maze of Moorish houses and twisting alleys, is Spain's best-preserved Arab settlement.

▐ GETTING THERE AND GETTING AROUND

Trains: RENFE Station (tel. 958 27 12 72), Av. Andaluces. To: **Seville** (4-5hr., 5 per day, 2610ptas); **Madrid** (5-6hr., 2 per day, 3200ptas); **Algeciras** (5-7hr., 3 per day, 2375ptas); and **Barcelona** (12-13hr., 2 per day, 6400ptas).

Buses: Station on Ctra. Madrid, near C. Arzobispo Pedro de Castro. **Alsina Graells** (tel. 958 18 50 10) runs to: **Córdoba** (3hr., 9 per day, 1515ptas); **Seville** (3hr., 9 per day, 2350ptas); **La Línea/Gibraltar** (4hr., 10 per day, 2445ptas); **Algeciras** (5hr., 6 per day, 2550ptas); and **Madrid** (5hr., 10 per day, 1945ptas). **Bacoma** (tel. 958 15 75 57) goes to: **Alicante** (6hr., 5 per day, 3375ptas) and **Valencia** (8hr., 4 per day, 4910ptas).

Public Transportation: Take bus 10 from the bus station to the youth hostel, C. de Ronda, C. Recogidas, or C. Acera de Darro; or bus 3 from the bus station to Av. Constitución, Gran Vía, or Pl. Isabel la Católica. "Bus Alhambra" leaves from Pl. Nueva. All buses 120ptas, *bonobus* (15 tickets) 1000ptas. Handy free map at the tourist office.

▐ ORIENTATION AND PRACTICAL INFORMATION

The geographic center of Granada is the small **Plaza de Isabel la Católica**, the intersection of the city's two main arteries, **Calle de los Reyes Católicos** and **Gran Vía de Colón**. To reach Gran Vía and the **cathedral** from the train station, walk three blocks up Av. Andaluces to take bus 3-6, 9, or 11 from Av. Constitución; from the bus station, take bus 3. Two short blocks uphill on C. Reyes Católicos sits **Plaza Nueva**. Downhill on C. Reyes Católicos lies Pl. Carmen, site of the **Ayuntamiento** and Puerta Real. The **Alhambra** commands the steep hill up from Pl. Nueva.

Tourist Office: Oficina Provincial, Pl. Mariana Pineda 10 (tel. 958 22 66 88; fax 958 22 89 16; www.dipgra.es). From Pta. Real, turn right onto C. Angel Ganivet, then take a right 2 blocks later to reach the plaza. Open M-F 9:30am-7pm, Sa 10am-2pm.

American Express: C. Reyes Católicos 31 (tel. 958 22 45 12), between Pl. Isabel la Católica and Pta. Real. Open M-F 9:30am-1:30pm and 2-8pm, Sa 10am-2pm and 3-7pm, Su 9am-2pm.

Luggage Storage: At the train and bus stations. 400ptas. Open daily 4-9pm.

El Corte Inglés: On C. Geril (tel. 958 22 32 40). Follow C. Acera del Casino from Pta. Real onto the tree-lined road. Giant department store has everything. Clothing! Furniture! Maps! Jewelry! Nail polish! Barber shop! Bicycles! Groceries! Open M-Sa 10am-10pm.

Laundromat: C. La Paz 19. From Pl. Trinidad, take C. Alhóndiga and turn right. Wash 400ptas; dry 200ptas. Open M-F 9:30am-2pm and 4:30-8:30pm, Sa 9am-2pm.

Emergency: Tel. 092. **Police:** C. Duquesa 21 (tel. 958 24 81 00).

Medical Assistance: Clínica de San Cecilio, C. Dr. Oloriz 16 (tel. 958 28 02 00 or 958 27 20 00), on the road to Jaén. **Ambulance:** Tel. 958 28 44 50.

Internet Access: Madar Internet, C. Caldevera Nueva 12 (tel. 656 48 69 93). Open M-Sa 10am-midnight, Su noon-midnight. 400ptas per hr., students 300ptas.

Post Office: On Pta. Real, at C. Acera de Darro and C. Angel Ganinet. Open M-F 8am-9pm, Sa 9:30am-2pm. Wires money; fax service available. Address mail to be held: Anne BROWNING, *Lista de Correos*, Pta. Real, **18009** Granada, Spain.

▐◖ ACCOMMODATIONS, CAMPING, AND FOOD

Near **Pl. Nueva,** hostels line Cuesta de Gomérez, the street leading uphill to the Alhambra. The area around C. Mesones and C. Alhóndiga is close to the cathedral;

SPAIN

hostels cluster around **Pl. Trinidad,** at the end of C. Mesones as you approach from Pta. Real. Hostels are sprinkled along **Gran Vía.** Call ahead during *Semana Santa.*

■ **Hostal Residencia Britz,** Cuesta de Gomérez 1 (tel. 958 22 36 52), on the corner of Pl. Nueva. Luxurious beds and green-tiled bathrooms. Singles 2300ptas; doubles 3900ptas, with bath 5400ptas. *Let's Go* discount 6%. Laundry 600ptas. Reception 24hr. V, MC.

■ **Residencia Universitaria Antares,** C. Cetti Meriém 10 (tel. 958 22 83 13), at C. Elvira, 1 block from Gran Vía and the cathedral. Spotless and cheap, and in a great location. All rooms with balconies and sinks. Singles 1500ptas; doubles 3000ptas; triple 4500ptas.

Albergue Juvenil Granada (HI), Av. Ramón y Cajal 2 (tel. 958 27 26 38; fax 958 28 52 85). From the bus station, take bus 10 (from the train station, #11) to "El Estadio de la Juventud." 1600ptas, under 27 1300ptas; non-members 1600ptas. Reception 24hr.

Hostal Gomérez, Cuesta de Gomérez 10 (tel. 958 22 44 37) in Pl. Nueva. Clean rooms with firm beds. Multilingual owner. Singles 1600ptas; doubles 2700ptas; triple 3700ptas. Off-season *Let's Go* discount 100-200ptas. Laundry 1000ptas.

Hospedaje Almohada, C. Postigo de Zarate 4 (tel. 958 20 74 46), near the cathedral. From Pl. Trinidad, walk 1 block down C. Duquesa; it's to the right down C. Málaga (no sign; big red door). Social courtyard. Singles 1800ptas; doubles 3500ptas. Laundry.

Hostal Zurita, Pl. Trinidad 7 (tel. 958 27 50 20), near the cathedral. Beautiful rooms. Singles 1875ptas; doubles 3750-5000ptas; triples 5000-5500ptas.

Hostal Gran Vía, Gran Vía 17 (tel. 958 27 92 12), 4 blocks from Pl. Isabel la Católica. Clean, bright rooms. Singles 2500ptas; doubles 3000-4000ptas; triples 6000ptas.

Sierra Nevada, Av. Madrid 107 (tel. 958 15 00 62; fax 958 15 09 54). Take bus 3 or 10. Lots of trees. 560ptas per person, per tent, and per car. Hot showers. Open Mar.-Oct.

Cheap, tasty North African cuisine abounds near the **Albaicín,** while teahouses and cafés crowd **C. Calderería Nueva,** off C. Elvira, which leads out of the plaza. When ordering drinks, **tapas are free in Granada;** order a drink at one of the places around **Pl. Nueva** and eagerly anticipate the arrival of tasty tapas. **La Nueva Bodega,** C. Cetti Meriém 9, off C. Elvira, serves *menús* (825-1400ptas) and *bocadillos* (300ptas). (Open daily noon-midnight.) Drink and eat with the local good ol' boys at **Bodega Mancha,** C. Joaquin Costa 10, or **Bodega Castañeda,** C. Almireceros 1/3, off C. Elvira. (Both open daily 8am-4pm and 6pm-1am, Sa-Su noon-4pm and 6pm-3am.) Veggie delights await at **Naturi Albaicín,** C. Calderería Nueva 10; try the *berenjenas rellenas* (stuffed eggplant). (*Menús* 950-1150ptas. Open Sa-Th 1-4pm and 7-11pm, F 7-11pm.) Feast on immense portions of fresh seafood high on the Albaicín at **El Ladrillo II,** on C. Panaderos, off Cuesta del Chapiz. (Open daily 12:30pm-1:30am.) Stock up at the **market,** on C. San Augustín, or at **Supermercado T. Mariscal,** on C. Genil, next to El Corte Inglés. (Open M-F 9:30am-2pm and 5-9pm, Sa 9:30am-2pm.)

◉ SIGHTS

■**THE ALHAMBRA.** "If you have died without seeing the Alhambra, you have not lived." From the streets of Granada, the Alhambra appears simple, blocky, faded— but up close the fortress-palace reveals its astoundingly elaborate detail. The first Nazarite King Alhamar built the fortress **Alcazaba,** the section of the complex with the oldest recorded history. A dark, spiraling staircase leads up to a 360° view of Granada and the mountains. Follow signs to the *Palacio Nazaries* to see the stunningly ornate **Alcázar,** a royal palace built for the Moorish rulers Yusuf I (1333-1354) and Mohammed V (1354-1391), where tourists gape at dripping stalactite archways, multicolored tiles, and sculpted fountains. Fernando and Isabel respectfully restored the Alcázar after they drove the Moors from Spain, but two generations later, Emperor Carlos V demolished part of it to make way for his **Palacio de Carlos V;** although glaringly incongruous when juxtaposed with such Moorish splendor, many consider it one of the most beautiful Renaissance buildings in Spain. Over a bridge are the vibrant blossoms, towering cypresses, and streaming waterways of **El Generalife,** the sultan's vacation retreat. (*Follow C. Cuesta de Gomérez from Pl. Nueva, and be prepared to pant (20min.). Or take the Alhambra-Neptuno microbus (every 15min., 120ptas) from Pl. Isabel la Católica or Pl. Nueva. Tel. 958 22 15 03. Open Apr.-Sept. daily 8:30am-8pm;*

SPAIN

Granada

ACCOMMODATIONS
A Albergue Juvenil (HI)
B Hostal Zurita
C Hospedaje Almohada
D Hostal Gran Vía
E Residencia Universitaria Antares
F Hostal Residencia Britz
G Hostal Gomérez

El Generalife

Entrance
Shuttle Stop

ALHAMBRA
Puerta Carros
Palacio Carlos V
Puerta de la Justicia
Alcázar
Alcazaba
Puerta de las cuesta de Gomérez Granadas

Cuesta de los Chinos
C. Real
Po. Central

Río Darro

ALBAICÍN

Walls of the Albaicín

Monasterio Santa Isabel la Real
Real Cancillería

S. Ana
PL. SAN ANA
PLAZA NUEVA

Corral del Carbón
S. Domingo
PL. DEL REALEJO
C. Santiago
C. Molinos
Cta. Realejo

PL. PADRE SUÁREZ
PL. DE ISABEL LA CATÓLICA
Palacio de la Madraza
Catedral
C. Reyes Católicos
Puerta Real
PL. CARMEN
PL. NUEVA

C. Sta. Escolástica
C. Varela
C. San Matías
C. Miguel Gallnet
PL. CAMPILLO
PL. MARIANA PINEDA
C. San Jacinto

Puerta de Elvira
PL. TRIUNFO
Gran Vía de Colón

Santos Justo y Pastor
Universidad
PL. UNIVERSIDAD
S. Jerónimo

Basílica San Juan de Dios

C. San Juan de Dios
C. Santa Bárbara
Av. Fuente Nueva
C. Doctor Severo Ochoa

Av. de Murcia
PL. SAN ISIDRO
Av. Ancha de Capuchinos
C. Real Cartuja
Av. Constitución
C. Madrid

CAMPUS UNIVERSITARIO

200 yards
200 meters

N

TO A

Oct.-Mar. M-Sa 9am-5:45pm. Nighttime visits June-Sept. Tu, Th, and Sa 10-11:30pm; Oct.-May Sa 8-10pm. 1000ptas. Limited visitors per day, so arrive early. Enter the Palace of the Nazarites (Alcázar) during the time specified on your ticket, but stay as long as you like.)

THE CATHEDRAL QUARTER. Downhill from the Alhambra, the **Capilla Real** (Royal Chapel), Fernando and Isabel's private chapel, exemplifies Christian Granada. The **crypt** houses their lead caskets. The **sacristy** houses Isabel's private **art collection**, which favors 15th-century Flemish and German artists, as well as the glittering **royal jewels.** *(Open Apr.-Sept. M-Sa 10:30am-1pm and 4-7pm; Oct.-Mar. M-Sa 10:30am-1pm and 3:30-6:30pm, Su 11am-1pm. 300ptas.)* The adjacent **cathedral,** Spain's first of pure Renaissance style, was built from 1523-1704 by Fernando and Isabel on the foundation of the major Arab mosque. *(Open daily Apr.-Sept. 10:30am-1:30pm and 4-7pm; Oct.-Mar. 10:30am-1:30pm and 3:30-6:30pm. Closed Su morning. 300ptas.)*

THE ALBAICÍN. The Moors built their first fortress in this fascinating and gorgeous old Arab quarter. After the Reconquest, a small Arab population clung to the neighborhood on this hill until their expulsion in the 17th century. A labyrinth of steep slopes and dark narrow alleys, the Albaicín warrants caution at night. Take C. Acera del Darro from Pl. Nueva, climb the Cuesta del Chapiz on the left, then wander aimlessly through Muslim ramparts past whitewashed walls dripping with bright flowers. The terrace adjacent to **Iglesia de San Nicolás** affords the city's best view of the Alhambra, especially in winter, when snow adorns the Sierra Nevada. *(Bus 12 runs from beside the cathedral to C. Pagés, at the top of the Albaicín. Another Alhambra bus goes from Pl. Nueva to the top; from there, walk down C. Agua through Pta. Arabe.)*

ENTERTAINMENT AND NIGHTLIFE

The *Guía del Ocio*, sold at newsstands (100ptas), lists clubs, pubs, and cafés. The tourist office also distributes a monthly guide, *Cultura en Granada*. Tourists and locals alike flock to **Los Jardines Neptuno,** on C. Arabial, near the Neptuno shopping center at the base of C. Recogidas for **flamenco.** (Tel. 958 52 25 33. Cover 3500ptas; includes 1 drink.) A smoky, intimate setting awaits at **Eshavira** (tel. 958 20 32 62), on C. Postigo de la Cuna, in an alley off C. Azacayes, between C. Elvira and Gran Vía.

The most boisterous nightspots crowd **C. Pedro Antonio de Alarcón,** from Pl. Albert Einstein to Ancha de Gracia. The cobblestoned patio at **Taberna El 22,** Pl. Santa Gregorio 5, near Pl. Nueva at the top of C. Calderería Nueva, hosts a young and mellow throng. (Open daily noon-3pm and 9pm-3am). The seductively scented **Kasbah,** C. Calderería Nueva 4, offers silky pillows and romantic nooks. (Open daily 3pm-3am.) There's only room to wiggle at **Cine/Disco Granada 10,** C. Cárcel Baja 14, three blocks from Pl. Isabel la Católica along Gran Vía. (Cover 700-1000ptas; includes 1 drink. Open daily 9pm-4am.) **Bar-Rama,** on C. Pedro Antonio de Alarcon, is known as **"Chupitos"** for its shot-sized concoctions. (Open daily 9pm-4am.)

HIKING AND SKIING NEAR GRANADA: SIERRA NEVADA

The peaks of **Mulhacén** (3481m) and **Veleta** (3470m), the highest in Spain, sparkle with snow and buzz with tourists for most of the year. **Ski** season runs from December to April. In the rest of the year, the bare mountains are arguably less attractive, as black slate slopes are dotted by patches of yellow-green moss; nevertheless, tourists **hike, parasail,** and take **jeep tours.** Before you go, check road and snow conditions (tel. 958 24 91 19) and hotel vacancies.

EASTERN SPAIN (VALENCIA)

Valencia's rich soil and famous orange groves, nourished by Moor-designed irrigation systems, have earned its nickname, *Huerta de España* (Spain's Orchard). Dunes, sandbars, jagged promontories, and lagoons mark the grand coastline, and lovely fountains and pools grace carefully landscaped public gardens in Valencian cities. The famed Spanish rice dish paella was created somewhere in Valencia.

ALICANTE (ALACANT)

Sun-drenched Alicante (pop. 250,000) has somehow been chiseled into the most redeeming sort of resort town—dutifully entertaining, yet quietly charming. While nightlife energizes the city, Alicante's mosaic-lined waterside Explanada relaxes it at sunset. High above the rows of bronzed bodies, the ancient *castillo*, spared by Franco, guards the wicked tangle of streets in the cobblestoned *casco antiguo*.

⚅ ⌐ ☐ PRACTICAL INFO, ACCOMMODATIONS, AND FOOD. RENFE **trains** (tel. 96 592 02 02) run from **Estación Término** on Av. Salamanca, at the end of Av. Estación, to Valencia (1½hr., 12 per day, 1400-3000ptas); Madrid (4hr., 9 per day, 3200-4700ptas); and Barcelona (4½-6hr., 7 per day, 4400-6600ptas). Trains from **Estació Marina,** Av. Villajoyosa 2 (tel. 96 526 27 31), on Explanada d'Espanya, serve the Costa Blanca. **Buses** (tel. 96 513 07 00) run from C. Portugal 17 to Valencia (1980ptas); Granada (6hr., 5 per day, 3375ptas); Madrid (6½hr., 7 per day, 3000ptas); and Barcelona (8hr., 6 per day, 4700ptas). From the bus station, turn left on C. d'Italia, take the third right on Av. Dr. Gadea, and turn left at the waterfront to reach the Explanada d'Espanya and the **tourist office** at #2. (Tel. 96 520 00 00; fax 96 520 02 43. Open M-F 10am-8pm, Sa 10am-2pm and 3-8pm.) Log on the **internet** at **Battlezone,** C. Campos Vassallo 9. (300-400ptas per hr. Open June-Aug. M-Th 11am-3pm and 4:30-11pm, F-Su 11am-3pm and 4:30pm-midnight; Sept.-May reduced hours.)

For lodgings, stay away from most places along C. San Fernando and around the Església de Santa María, and opt instead for places in the newer section of town. The ⊠ **Pensión Les Monges Palace,** C. Monjas 2, is behind the Ayuntamiento, in the center of the historic district. (Tel. 96 521 50 46. Singles 2100-3200ptas; doubles 3900-5000ptas; triples 5000-6000ptas. V, MC.) **Habitaciones México,** C. General Primo de Rivera 10, off the end of Av. Alfonso X El Sabio, wins the award for nicest hostel owner. (Tel. 96 520 93 07; email mexrooms@lix.ctv.es. Singles 1900-2200ptas; doubles 3600-4200ptas; triples 6000ptas. Internet.) Take bus 21 to **camp** at Playa Mutxavista. (Tel. 96 565 45 26. 520ptas per person and per tent. Open year-round.) Try the family-run *bar-restaurantes* in the *casco antiguo*, between the cathedral and the castle steps. Buy basics at **Supermarket Mercadona,** C. Alvarez Sereix 5, off Av. Federico Soto. (Open M-Sa 9am-9pm.) **Postal code:** 03070.

▣ ⌐ SIGHTS AND ENTERTAINMENT. Complete with drawbridges, dark passageways, and hidden tunnels, the Carthaginian **Castell de Santa Bárbara** keeps silent guard over Alicante's beach. A paved road from the old section of Alicante leads to the top, but most people take the **elevator** from a hidden entrance on Av. Jovellanos, across the street from Playa Postiguet. (Castle open Apr.-Sept. 10am-7:30pm; Oct.-Mar. 9am-6:30pm; free. Elevator 400ptas.) A crowd of Valencian modernist art pieces roosts along with a few Mirós, Picassos, Kandinskys, and Calders in the **Museu de Arte del Siglo XX La Asegurada,** Pl. Santa Maria 3, at the east end of C. Mayor. (Open May-Sept. Tu-Sa 10:30am-1:30pm and 6-9pm, Su 10:30am-1pm; Oct.-Apr. Tu-Sa 10am-1pm and 5-8pm, Su 10am-1pm. Free.) Alicante's own **Playa de El Postiguet** attracts sun worshipers, as do nearby **Playa de San Juan** (take TAM bus 21, 22, or 31) and **Playa del Mutxavista** (take TAM bus 21).

Warm-weather nightlife also centers on the **Playa de San Juan;** the **Trensnochador** night train (July-Aug. F-Sa and every other Su-Th every hr. 10:30pm-6am; round-trip 150-700ptas) runs from Estació Marina to "Discotecas" and other stops along the beach, where discos are packed until dawn. Try **Penélope, Pachá, KU, KM,** and **Insomnia** (cover from 1500ptas; open nightly until 9am) at the "Disco Benidorm" stop (round-trip 650ptas). In Alicante itself, the **new port** and the old section of town, **El Barne,** overflow with students and *bar-musicales.* During the hedonistic **Festival de Sant Joan** (June 20-29), *fogueres* (symbolic or satiric effigies) are paraded around the *casco antiguo* and are then burned in a bonfire on the 24th.

VALENCIA

Stylish, cosmopolitan, and business-oriented, Valencia is a striking contrast to the surrounding orchards and mountain ranges. Parks and gardens soothe the city's congested environment, and nearby beaches complement the frenetic pace.

⚠ ▜▛ PRACTICAL INFO, ACCOMMODATIONS, AND FOOD. **Trains** arrive at C. Xàtiva 24 (tel. 96 352 02 02) from Alicante (2hr., 9 per day, 1375-3000ptas); Barcelona (4-6hr., 11 per day, 3200ptas); and Madrid (5-7½hr., 12 per day, 2890-5600ptas). From the station, follow Av. Marquéz de Sotelo to the central **Pl. Ayuntamiento.** **Buses** (tel. 96 349 72 22) go from Av. Menéndez Pidal 13 to Alicante (2¼-3hr., 9 per day, 1980ptas); Madrid (4-5hr., 2865-3165ptas); and Barcelona (4½hr., 10 per day, 2900ptas). Bus 8 (110ptas) connects to Pl. Ayuntamiento and the train station. Trasmediterránea **ferries** (tel. 902 45 46 45) sail to the Balearic Islands (see p. 858); take bus 4 from Pl. Ayuntamiento or bus 1 or 2 from the bus station. The main **tourist office,** C. Paz 46-48, has other branches at the train station and on Pl. Ayuntamiento. (Tel. 96 398 64 22. Open M-F 10am-6pm, Sa 10am-2pm. Your mother misses you: **email** her at **Agora Internet,** C. Paz 33. (400-500ptas per 30min.)

The best lodgings are around **Pl. Ayuntamiento** and **Pl. Mercado;** avoid areas around Pl. Pilar. To get from the train station to the ⚑**Pilgrim's Youth Hostel,** Pl. Hombres del Mar 25, take the metro to "Benimaclet," switch to L4 toward Av. Dr. Lluch, and get off at "Las Arenals"; the entrance is on the other side of the building. (Tel. 96 356 42 88; fax 96 355 33 08; email albergue@ran.es. With *Let's Go:* 1500-2000ptas, under 27 1000ptas. **Internet.** Reception 24hr. Reserve ahead.) To get from the train station to the spotless **Hostal-Residencia El Cid,** C. Cerrajeros 13, pass Pl. Ayuntamiento and take the second left off C. Vicente Mártir. (Tel. 96 392 23 23. Singles 1700ptas; doubles 3000-4000ptas.) **Hostal-Residencia Universal,** C. Barcas 5, is off Pl. Ayuntamiento. (Tel. 96 351 53 84. Singles 2300ptas; doubles 3600-4200ptas; triples 5100ptas.) Paella is the most famous of Valencia's 200 rice dishes; try as many as you can before leaving. To get to ⚑**Restaurante La Utielana,** Pl. Picadero dos Aguas 3, take C. Barcelonina off Pl. Ayuntamiento, turn left at the end across Pl. Rodrigo Botet, turn right on C. Procida, and go down a little alley on the left. (Seafood paella 375ptas. Open Sept.-July M-F 1:15-4pm and 9-11pm, Sa 1:15-4pm.) Get **groceries** at **El Corte Inglés,** C. Pintor Sorolla 26. (Open M-Sa 10am-9:30pm.) **Postal code:** 46080.

▨ ▟ SIGHTS AND ENTERTAINMENT. Most sights line the **Río Turia** or cluster near **Pl. Reina,** down C. San Vicente Mártir from Pl. Ayuntamiento. EMT bus 5, dubbed the **Bus Turístic,** makes a loop of old town sights (110ptas; 1-day pass 500ptas). The 13th-century **cathedral,** on Pl. Reina, was built on the site of an Arab mosque. In a fit of hyperbole (or vertigo), Victor Hugo counted 300 bell towers from the **Micalet** (cathedral tower); in reality, there are about 100. The **Museo de la Catedral** squeezes many treasures into very little space. (Cathedral open daily in summer 8am-2pm and 5-8pm; off-season closes earlier; free. Tower open daily 10am-1pm and 4:30-7pm; 200ptas. Museum open Mar.-Nov. M-F 10am-1pm and 4:30-7pm, Sa 10am-1pm; Dec.-Feb. M-Sa 10am-1pm; 200ptas.) Across the river, the **Museu Provincial de Belles Artes,** on C. Sant Pius V, next to the Jardines del Reial, displays superb 14th- to 16th-century Valencian art. (Open Tu-Su 10am-2pm and 4-7:30pm. Free.) West across the old river, the **Instituto València de Arte Moderno (IVAM),** C. Guillem de Castro 118, has works by 20th-century sculptor Julio González. (Open Tu-Su 10am-7pm. 350ptas, students 175ptas; Su free.) The city just built the massive **Ciudad de las Artes y las Ciencias** (tel. 963 52 60 23), south along the riverbed off the road to Saler, featuring an IMAX theater, an underwater city, and a performing arts center. The most popular **beaches** are **Las Arenas** and **Malvarrosa;** take bus 19 from Pl. Ayuntamiento (in summer also 20, 21, and 22). To get to the more attractive **Saler,** 14km from the center, take an Autobuses Buñol bus (tel. 96 349 14 25) from Gran Vía Germanias and C. Sueca (25min., 2 per hr., 160ptas).

Bars and pubs abound in the **El Carme** district. Follow Pl. Mercado and C. Bolsería (bear right at the fork) to **Pl. Tossal** to guzzle *agua de Valencia* (orange juice, champagne, and vodka) with the masses, then head to **Av. Blasco Ibañez** with your dancing shoes. **Caballito de Mar,** C. Eugenia Viñes 22, at Playa de Malvarrosa, is popular in summer. The most famed festival in Valencia is **Las Fallas** (Mar. 12-19), which culminates with a mass burning of gigantic (up to 30m) satirical papier-mâché effigies.

COSTA BLANCA

This "white coast" which extends from Denía through Calpe, Alicante, and Elche, derives its name from its fine, white sands. UBESA **buses** (Valencia tel. 96 340 08 55) run to Gandía (1½hr., 12 per day) and Calpe (3-3½hr., 10 per day). From Alicante buses run to Calpe (1½hr., 18 per day). **Trains** also run from Valencia to Gandía (1hr., every 30min., 495ptas). Going to **Calpe** (Calp) is like stepping into a Dalí landscape that has been mobbed by sun-seeking tourists. The town cowers beneath the **Peñó d'Ifach** (327m), a giant rock protrusion whose precipitous face drops straight to the sea. **Gandía** attracts with fine sand beaches. The **tourist office,** Marqués de Campo, is opposite the train station. (Tel. 96 287 77 88. Open June-Aug. M-F 10am-2pm and 4:30-7:30pm, Sa 10am-1pm; Sept.-May reduced hours.) La Amistad **buses** (8 per day, 105ptas) go from outside the train station in Gandía to **Platja de Piles,** 10km south, where you'll find beach, beach, and more beach. To sleep at the fantastic 🏠**Alberg Mar i Vent (HI)** in Platja, follow the signs down C. Dr. Fleming. (Tel. 96 283 17 48. 1100-1300ptas, under 27 800ptas. Sheets 300ptas. Flexible 3-day max. stay. Curfew Su-Th 2am, F-Sa 4am. Open Feb. 15-Dec. 15. Call in advance.)

NORTHEAST SPAIN

Northeastern Spain encompasses the country's most avidly regionalistic areas, as well as some of its best cuisine. **Catalunyans** are justly proud of their treasures, from mountains to beaches to hip Barcelona. The glorious **Pyrenees** line the French border, presenting a prickly face to the rest of the continent. Little-known **Navarra** basks in the limelight once a year when bulls race through the streets of Pamplona. Industrious **Aragón** packs in busy cities and the most dramatic parts of the Pyrenees. The **Basques** are fiercely regionalistic, but happily share their beautiful coasts and rich history. The **Balearic Islands** are always ready for the next party.

CATALUNYA

From rocky Costa Brava to the lush Pyrenees and chic Barcelona, Catalunya is a vacation in itself. Graced with the nation's richest resources, it is one of the most prosperous regions. Catalán is the region's official language (though most everyone is bilingual), and local cuisine is lauded throughout Spain.

BARCELONA

Paris, London, and New York have been described as *noir* cities, best captured in black and white, but Barcelona is best seen in vivid color. The 1992 Summer Olympics consummated Barcelona's recent rise to glory and won it worldwide admiration. The late 19th century welcomed brilliantly daring *Modernista* architecture; after Franco's regime ended, the city reclaimed its role as the world's premier showcase of avant-garde architecture. Today, amidst the graceful Gothic churches, a serpentine old town, wrought-iron balconies, and grand, tree-lined European avenues, Antoni Gaudí's technicolor flights of fancy battle for attention with the city's latest architectural triumphs—carefully angled and glassy-white museums and malls. An unprecedented tourist boom continues to draw in Eurail travelers; reserve early, dress well, and prepare yourself for a circus.

▐ GETTING THERE AND GETTING AROUND

Flights: El Prat de Llobregat airport (tel. 93 298 38 38), 12km southwest of Barcelona. To get to the central Pl. Catalunya, take the **Aerobus** (40min., every 15min., 485ptas) or a RENFE **train** (20min., every 30min., 315-355ptas). Late-night city **bus** EN goes to Pl. Espanya (every hr. until 2:40am, 145ptas). A **taxi** ride to the city costs 2000-3500ptas.

Trains: Estació Barcelona-Sants (tel. 93 490 02 02), on Pl. Països Catalans. M: Sants-Estació. Main domestic and international terminal. **RENFE** (tel. 93 490 02 02 or 93 490 11 22) to: **Valencia** (4hr., 15 per day, 3500-7200ptas); **Montpellier, France,** with connections to Geneva and Paris (5hr., 2 per day, 12,608-43,800ptas); **Madrid** (7-8hr., 6 per day, 4900-7000ptas); **Seville** (12hr., 4 per day, 6700-26,700ptas); and **Milan** (13hr., 1 per day, 12,608-43,800ptas). **Estació França** (tel. 93 319 64 16), on Av. Marqués de L'Argentera. M: Barceloneta. Serves a few domestic and international routes.

Buses: Estació del Nord, C. Ali-bei 80 (tel. 93 265 65 08). M: Arc de Triomf ("Nàpols" exit). **Enatcar** (tel. 93 245 25 28) buses go to: **Valencia** (4hr., 10 per day, 2690ptas) and **Madrid** (8hr., 5 per day, 2690ptas). **Sarfa** (tel. 93 265 11 58) buses serve the **Costa Brava. Linebús** (tel. 93 232 10 92) goes to **Paris** (14hr., 6 per week, 11,950ptas). **Julià Vía** (tel. 93 232 10 92) sends buses to: **Marseille** (10hr., 5 per week, 7100ptas) and **Paris** (15hr., 6 per week, 12,000ptas).

Ferries: Trasmediterránea (tel. 902 45 46 45), Estació Marítima-Moll Barcelona, Moll de Sant Bertran. M: Drassanes; follow Las Ramblas toward the Columbus monument, which points the way. In summer, boats go almost daily to the Balearic Islands (see p. 858).

Hitchhiking: Let's Go does not recommend hitchhiking. Those hitching to France often take Av. Meridiana from M: Fabra i Puig to reach highway A7. Those en route to Valencia take bus 7 from Rambla Catalunya on the Gran Vía side to the autopista ("A") from here. Hitchhiking on autopistas is illegal, but permitted on national highways ("N").

Public Transportation: Info tel. 010. Pick up a Guia d'Autobusos Urbans de Barcelona for metro and bus routes. **Buses** run 5am-10pm and cost 145ptas per ride. The **metro** runs M-Th 5am-11pm, F-Sa 5am-2am, Su 6am-midnight; buy tickets from vending machines or stations (145ptas) and hold on to them. A **T1 Pass** (795ptas) is valid for 10 rides on bus, metro, and commuter rail and can be shared; a **T-DIA Card** (575ptas) is good for one day of unlimited bus or metro travel. The **Nitbus** (160ptas) runs 10pm-4am.

Taxis: Tel. 93 330 03 00. First 6min. or 1.9km 300ptas; each additional km 110ptas.

Car Rental: Docar, C. Montnegre 18 (tel. 93 439 81 19). From 4480ptas per day, plus 23ptas per km including insurance. Open M-F 8:30am-2pm and 3:30-8pm, Sa 9am-2pm.

🎯 ORIENTATION AND PRACTICAL INFORMATION

Barcelona slopes gently upward from the harbor to the mountains. **Passeig de Colon** runs parallel to the shore; from Pg. Colón, **Las Ramblas,** the city's main thoroughfare, runs from the harbor to **Plaça de Catalunya,** the city's center. Las Ramblas is divided into five parts: **Rambla de Santa Mónica, Rambla de Caputxins, Rambla de Sant Josep, Rambla de Estudis,** and **Rambla de Canaletas.** The **Barri Gòtic** area is enclosed by Las Ramblas to the west and **Vía Laietana** to the east, and is bisected by east-west **Carrer de Ferran.** East of Vía Laietana lies the maze-like neighborhood of **La Ribera,** which borders the **Parc de la Ciutadella** and the **Estació de França train station.** Farther east is the **Vila Olímpica,** along with a shiny array of malls, discos, and hotels. West of Las Ramblas is **El Ravel,** including the shrinking red-light district. Farther west rises **Montjuïc,** a picturesque hill crammed with sights. South of Pg. Colon, a bridge leads from the **Port Vell** (Old Port) to the ultramodern malls **Moll d'Espanya** and **Maremagnum.** The gridded **L'Eixample** district, created during urban expansion, fans toward the hills from Pl. Catalunya and is split by the main shopping street **Passeig de Gràcia. Avinguda Diagonal** separates L'Eixample from **Gràcia,** a residential area farther north. The peak of **Tibidabo** to the northwest is the highest point in Barcelona. For more detail, refer to this book's **color maps** of the city and metro.

Barcelona is fairly safe, even at night, but secure your valuables while in outdoor cafés, in the Pl. Reial and Barri Gòtic, and on Las Ramblas, and be careful deep in El Ravel. Most areas with nightlife are well-policed, lit, and, for the most part, safe.

TOURIST AND FINANCIAL SERVICES

Tourist Offices: Info tel. 010, 906 30 12 82, or 93 304 34 21; www.barcelonaturisme.com. **Informacio Turistica at Plaça Catalunya,** Pl. Catalunya 17S, below Pl. Catalunya. M: Catalunya. The biggest, best, and busiest tourist office. Open daily 9am-9pm. **Branches** at Pl. Sant Jaume I (M: Jaume I), in the Barcelona-Sants train station (M: Sants-Estació), and at the airport. **Mobile info offices** dot the city in the summer.

SPAIN

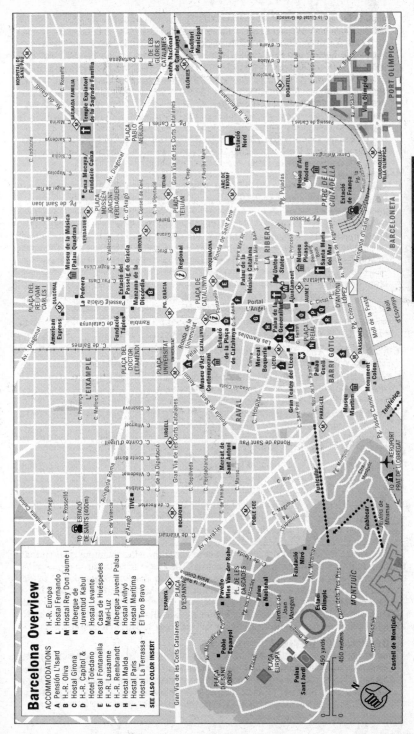

Barcelona Overview

ACCOMMODATIONS
A Pensión L'Isard
B H.-R. Oliva
C Hostal Girona
D H.-R. Capitol &
  Hotel Toledano
E Hostal Fontanella
F H.-R. Lausanne
G H.-R. Rembrandt
H Hostal Malda
I Hostal Paris
J Hostal La Terrassa

K H.-R. Europa
L Hostal Fernando
M Hostal Rey Don Jaume I
N Albergue
  Juventud Kabul
O Hostal Levante
P Casa de Huéspedes
  Mari-Luz
Q Albergue Juvenil Palau
R Hostal Avinyó
S Hostal Marítima
T El Toro Bravo

SEE ALSO COLOR INSERT

Budget Travel: Unlimited Student Travel (USIT), Rda. Universidad 16 (tel. 902 32 52 75; www.unlimited.es), 1½ blocks from Pl. Catalunya. M: Catalunya. Also at C. Rocafort 116-118, 2 blocks from M: Rocafort. Open M-F 10am-8pm, Sa 10am-1:30pm. Bring your ISIC card.

Consulates: Australia, Gran Vía Carlos III 98, 9th fl. (tel. 933 30 94 96; fax 934 11 09 04). **Canada,** Passeig de Gràcia 77, 3rd fl. (tel. 932 15 07 04; fax 934 87 91 17). **New Zealand,** Traversa de Gracia 64, 4th fl. (tel. 932 09 03 99; fax 932 02 08 90). **South Africa,** Teodora Lamadrid 7-11 (tel. 934 18 64 45; fax 934 18 05 38). **UK,** Av. Diagonal 477 (tel. 934 19 90 44; fax 934 05 24 11). **US,** Pg. Reina Elisenda 23 (tel. 932 80 22 27; fax 932 05 52 06).

Currency Exchange: ATMs give the best rates (at no commission); the next best are at **banks.** Banks open M-F 8:30am-2pm.

American Express: Pg. Gràcia 101 (24-hour tel. 900 99 44 26; fax 93 415 37 00). M: Diagonal. Entrance on C. Rosselló. Mail held. Open M-F 9:30am-6pm, Sa 10am-noon.

LOCAL SERVICES

Luggage Storage: Lockers (300-600ptas) at **Estació Barcelona-Sants** (open daily 4am-midnight); **Estació França** (open daily 6am-11pm); and **Estació del Nord** (open 24hr.).

El Corte Inglés: Pl. Catalunya 14, Av. Diagonal 471-473, and Av. Diagonal 617. Great map and everything else you've ever wanted (except that pony). Open M-Sa 10am-9:30pm.

English Bookstores: LAIE, Av. Pau Claris 85 (tel. 93 318 17 39), 1 block from the Gran Vía. M: Urquinaona or Pl. Catalunya. Open M-F 10am-9pm, Sa 10:30am-9pm. **The Bookstore,** C. La Granja 13 (tel. 93 237 95 19), in Gràcia off Travesera del Dalt. M: Lesseps. Book trade. Open M-Sa 11am-1:30pm and 2:30-7pm. Also **Cómplices;** see below.

Gay and Lesbian Services: Cómplices, C. Cervantes 2 (tel. 93 412 72 83). M: Liceu. From C. Ferrán, take C. Avinyó and then the 2nd left. Gay and lesbian bookstore with English books, and a map of gay and lesbian bars and discos. Open M-F 10:30am-8:30pm, Sa noon-8:30pm.

Laundromat: Tintoreria San Pablo, C. San Pau 105 (tel. 93 329 42 49). M: Liceu. 1200ptas per load. Open M-F 9am-1:30pm and 4-8pm.

EMERGENCY AND COMMUNICATIONS

Emergency: Medical emergencies, 061. **National police,** 091. **Local police,** 092.

Police: Las Ramblas 43 (tel. 93 301 90 60), opposite Pl. Reial and next to C. Nou de La Rambla. M: Liceu. English spoken. Open 7am-midnight.

Pharmacies: Late-night pharmacies rotate; check pharmacy windows for listings.

Hospitals: Barcelona Centro Médico (BCM), Av. Diagonal 612, 2nd fl., #14 (tel. 93 414 06 43). Coordinates referrals, especially for foreigners.

Internet Access: Email from Spain, Las Ramblas 42 and Pje. Bacardí 1 (tel. 93 481 75 75). M: Liceu. 600ptas per 30min., 1000ptas per hr.

Telephones: Pick up a **phone card** at tobacco stores, tourist offices, post offices, or some newspaper stands on Las Ramblas. **Directory assistance,** tel. 1003.

Post Office: On Pl. Antoni López (tel. 93 318 38 31), at the end of Vía Laietana, portside. M: Jaume I or Barceloneta. Fax services. Open M-F 8:30am-9:30pm. Address mail to be held: Al GORE, *Lista de Correos*, Pl. Antoni López, Barcelona **08003,** Spain.

▐ ACCOMMODATIONS AND CAMPING

Although *albergues* (hostels) and *pensiones* abound, visitors without reservations will end up scrambling for a room in summer. The **Ciutat Vella,** the area between Pl. Catalunya and the shore, including the **Barri Gòtic, Las Ramblas, El Ravel,** and **La Ribera,** offers a wealth of budget accommodations, but in July and August you *must* call ahead. **Lower Barri Gòtic** hostels are cheapest, but be careful at night; **Upper Barri Gòtic,** north of C. Portaferrisa, is pricier but safer. **L'Eixample** offers the safest, most beautiful hostels. Signs with a big "P" or "H" mark the location of hostels.

LOWER BARRI GÒTIC

Albergue de Juventud Kabul, Pl. Reial 17 (tel. 93 318 51 90; fax 93 301 40 34). M: Liceu; walk south on Las Ramblas and turn left after C. Ferrán; it's on the near right corner of the *plaça*. Legendary among European backpackers. If you're looking for sobriety, go elsewhere. TV, **internet,** and pool table. 1900ptas. Sheets 200ptas. Key deposit 1000ptas. Laundry 800ptas. Flexible 5-night max. stay. Reception 24hr.

Albergue Juvenil Palau (HI), C. Palau 6 (tel. 93 412 50 80). M: Liceu. From Las Ramblas, take C. Ferrán to C. Enseyança, which becomes C. Palau. A small, tranquil refuge in the heart of the Barri Gòtic. Common room with TV. 1600ptas. Breakfast included. Sheets 200ptas. Kitchen. Flexible 5-night max. stay. Reception 7am-3am. Curfew 3am.

Hostal Fernando, C. Ferrán 31 (tel. 93 301 79 93). M: Liceu. Sparkles with cleanliness; charms with a friendly, multilingual staff. Recently renovated. Dorms 1900ptas; doubles with bath 6000ptas; triples with bath 7000ptas. **Internet.** V, MC.

Hostal Malda, C. Pí 5 (tel. 93 317 30 02). M: Liceu. From Las Ramblas, head east on C. Portaferrissa, take the 4th right, and look for the green "Galleries Maldo" sign. One of the best deals in the area. Singles 1500ptas; doubles 3000-3500ptas; triples 4000ptas.

Hostal Paris, Cardenal Casañas 4 (tel. 93 301 37 85; fax 93 412 70 96), on Las Ramblas opposite M: Liceu. Central, with standard rooms and a common room with TV. Singles 2800ptas, with bath 5000ptas; doubles 4800ptas, with bath 6000ptas. V, MC.

Hostal Levante, Baixada de San Miguel 2 (tel. 93 317 95 65l; fax 93 317 05 26; email hostallevante@mx3.redestb.es). M: Liceu; walk down C. Ferrán, turn right on C. Avinyó, and take your 1st left. Excellent TV lounge, large windows, and knowledgeable owner. Singles 3000ptas; doubles 4600ptas, with bath 5800ptas. Reception 24hr. V, MC.

Hostal Avinyo, C. Avinyó 42 (tel. 93 318 79 45; fax 318 68 93). M: Drassanes. Unassuming entrance leads to cheery rooms. Doubles 3200ptas, with shower 4400ptas; triples 4800ptas, with bath 6600ptas; quads 6400ptas, with bath 7200ptas. V, MC.

Hostal Residencia Rembrandt, C. Portaferrisa 23 (tel./fax 93 318 10 11). M: Liceu; walk north on Las Ramblas and turn right on C. Portaferrisa. Singles 3000ptas; doubles 4800ptas, with bath 6000ptas; triples 7000ptas. Breakfast 400ptas.

Casa de Huéspedes Mari-Luz, C. Palau 4 (tel. 93 317 34 63), 1 block from Pl. Sant Jaume. M: Jaume I or Liceu. Take C. Ciutat to C. Templaris, then take the 2nd left. 1700ptas. Kitchen. Laundry 800ptas. Reservations accepted. V, MC.

Hostal-Residencia Europa, C. Boquería 18 (tel. 93 318 76 20). M: Liceu. A popular spot a few feet off Las Ramblas. Singles 3200-5800ptas; doubles 5800-7800ptas.

Hostal Layetana, Pl. Ramón Berenguer el Gran 2 (tel. 93 319 20 12). M: Jaume I; head north and it's on the left after less than a block. Singles 2500ptas; doubles 4000ptas, with bath 5600ptas; add 7% IVA. Showers 200ptas. V, MC.

Hostal Marítima, Las Ramblas 4 (tel. 93 302 31 52), down a tiny alley off the port end of Las Ramblas. M: Drassanes; follow signs to the Museo de Cera next door. Prime location. Singles 2000-2500ptas; doubles 4000-5000ptas. Laundry. Reception 24hr.

Hotel Rey Don Jaime I, C. Jaume I 11 (tel. 93 310 62 08). M: Jaume I. Rooms with bath and phone. Singles 4700ptas; doubles 6900ptas; triples 9500ptas. V, MC, AmEx.

UPPER BARRI GÒTIC

■ Hostal Fontanella, Vía Laietana 71 (tel./fax 317 59 43). M: Urquinaona; head down Vía Laietana. Floral bouquets, flowing curtains, and embroidered towels. Singles 2900-3800ptas; doubles 4800-6600ptas. Reservations with deposit. V, MC, AmEx.

■ Hotel Toledano/Hostal Residencia Capitol, Las Ramblas 138 (tel. 93 301 08 72; fax 93 412 31 42; email toledano@idgrup.ibernet.com). M: Pl. Catalunya; it's just down Las Ramblas, on the left. Rooms border on luxurious. Hostel singles 2900ptas, doubles 4600-5200ptas, triples 5900-6500ptas, quads 6800-7400ptas; hotel 3600ptas, 6900ptas, 8600ptas, 9600ptas; add 7% IVA. Reception 24hr. V, MC, AmEx.

Hostal Residencia Lausanne, Av. Portal de L'Angel 24 (tel. 93 302 11 39). M: Pl. Catalunya. Peaceful hostel almost as fancy as the imperial façade. Doubles 4500-5000ptas, with shower 7500ptas; triples with shower 8000ptas, with bath 9600ptas.

EL RAVEL

■ Pensión L'Isard, C. Tallers 82 (tel. 93 302 51 83), near MACBA, the contemporary art museum. M: Universitat; take the "Pelai" exit, go left at the end of the block, and turn left at the pharmacy. Singles 2000ptas; doubles 4000-5000ptas; triples 5400ptas.

Hostal La Terrassa, Junta de Comerç 11 (tel. 93 302 51 74; fax 93 301 21 88). M: Liceu; take C. Hospital and turn left after Teatre Romea. Small, clean rooms and social courtyard. Doubles 3600ptas, with shower 4400ptas; triples with shower 5700ptas. V, MC.

SPAIN

L'EIXAMPLE

■ **Hostal Residencia Oliva,** Pg. Gràcia 32, 4th fl. (tel. 93 488 01 62 or 93 488 17 89), at C. Diputació. M: Pg. Gràcia. Treat yourself—elegant bureaus and TVs. Singles 3200ptas; doubles 6000, with bath 7000ptas. Reservations essential.

Hostal Girona, Av. Girona 24, 1st fl. (tel. 93 265 02 59; fax 93 265 85 32). M: Urquinaona. Between C. Casp and C. Ausias Marc. Singles 3000ptas; doubles 6000ptas. V, MC.

CAMPING

El Toro Bravo (tel. 936 37 34 62), 11km south of Barcelona. Take intercity bus L95 (20-40min., 200ptas) from Pl. Catalunya or Pl. Espanya. **Filipinas** (tel. 936 58 28 95) is 1km down the road from El Toro Bravo. Both 675ptas per person, 725ptas per tent.

◘ FOOD

Barcelona's restaurants are a refreshing combo of cosmopolitan style and Catalán cuisine. For the cheapest meals, be on the lookout for 850-1050ptas *menús* posted in the restaurants on the side streets of the **Barri Gòtic.** In El Ravel, look on **C. Tallers** and **Sitges.** In mellow **Gràcia,** food is authentic; L'Eixample can be pricey, but you can try the *patisserías.* The weekly *Guía del Ocio* (125ptas at newsstands) lists more options. Be aware that many restauranteurs close up shop and take vacations in August. *Torrades* (toasted bread with olive oil, garlic, and tomato*)* are a Catalán delight not to be missed. Make your own meal at awe-inspiring **La Boqueria,** officially Mercat de Sant Josep, on Las Ramblas near the Liceu metro station. (Open M-Sa 7am-8pm.) **Champion Supermarket** is at Las Ramblas 113. (Open M-Sa 9am-9pm.) Do fast food, Spanish-style, at the ubiquitous **PANS & Co** (sandwiches 300-695ptas).

BARRI GÒTIC

■ **Els Quatre Gats,** C. Montsió 3 (tel. 93 302 41 40). M: Catalunya; go down Av. Portal de L'Angel and take your 2nd left. Picasso loved it *and* designed the menu. Delicious tapas 150-650ptas. Live music. Open Sept.-July M-Sa 9am-2am, Su 5pm-2am. V, MC, AmEx.

■ **Irati,** C. Cardenal Casanyes 17 (tel. 93 302 30 84). An excellent Basque tapas bar. Bartenders pour *sidra* (cider) from 3 ft. above the glass and parade platters of treats. Tapas 140ptas. Open Tu-Sa noon-midnight, Su noon-5pm; tapas served M-Sa noon-3pm and 7-11pm. V, MC.

Peimong, C. Templarios 6-10 (tel. 93 318 28 73). M: Liceu; take C. Ferrán off Las Ramblas to Pl. Sant Jaume, then turn right on C. Ciutat and take the 2nd right. Meat-lovers of the world unite(!) for less than 750ptas. Open Tu-Su 1-5pm and 8pm-midnight.

Juicy Jones, Cardenal Caseñao 7 (tel. 93 302 43 30). M: Liceu; go down Las Ramblas and take the 1st left. Fabulous veggie cuisine. *Menú* 1000ptas. Open daily 1pm-midnight.

Restaurante Bidasoa, C. Serra 21 (tel. 93 318 10 63). M: Drassanes; head up C. Josep Anselm Clavé and take the 3rd left. 40 years of practice have paid off. Meals 600ptas or under. Open Sept.-July Tu-Su noon-3:30pm and 8pm-midnight.

Les Quinze Nits, Pl. Reial 6 (tel. 93 317 30 75). Savory Catalán cuisine and a classy atmosphere reward those who wait (the line moves quickly). Appetizers 195-690ptas. Entrees 640-1150ptas. Open daily 1-3:45pm and 8:30-11:30pm. V, MC.

ELSEWHERE IN BARCELONA

■ **Restaurante Riera,** C. Joaquín Costa 30 (tel. 93 443 32 93), in **El Ravel.** M: Liceu or Universitat. Off C. Carme coming from Liceu, or off Ronda de Sant Antoni coming from Universitat. 3-course gorge-fest (750ptas). Open daily 1-4pm and 8-11:30pm.

Bar Restaurante Los Toreros, C. Xuclá 3-5 (tel. 93 318 23 25), between C. Fortuny and C. Carme, both off Las Ramblas in **El Ravel.** M: Catalunya. Popular tapas *menú* (2000ptas, drinks included). Open Tu-Sa 9am-midnight, Su 9am-5pm.

■ **LLuna Plena,** C. Montcada 2 (tel. 93 310 54 29), in **La Ribera.** M: Jaume I; take C. Princesa and turn left onto C. Montcada. The afternoon *menú* is a steal at 1000ptas. Very busy. Open Sept.-July Tu-Sa 1-4pm and 8-11:30pm, Su 1-4pm. V, MC.

El Glop de la Rambla, R. Catalunya 65 (tel. 93 487 00 97), in **Gràcia.** M: Pg. Gràcia. Famous for *chorizo* (sausage). Lunch *menú* 1000ptas. Open M-Sa 8am-1am, Su 11am-1am. V, MC.

Comme-Bio, Gran Vía de les Corts Catalanes 603 (tel. 93 301 03 76), in **L'Eixample.** M: Catalunya. At the corner of Corts Catalanes and Rambla Catalunya. Creative all-veggie menu. Salads, pizzas, and pastas 550-1200ptas. Open M-Sa 9am-midnight, Su noon-midnight. V, MC.

SIGHTS

Barcelona's *Modernista* treasures dominate the city. **Las Ramblas** and the lovely **Barri Gòtic** are the traditional tourist areas, but don't neglect the vibrant **La Ribera** and **El Ravel.** The upscale avenues of **L'Eixample,** the panoramic city views from **Montjuïc** and **Tibidabo,** Gaudí's **Parc Güell,** and harborside areas like **Port Olímpic** are each a delight. The **Ruta del Modernisme** pass (600ptas, students 400ptas) grants a 50% discount on entrance to Barcelona's *Modernista* masterpieces: Casa Lleó Morera, Palau Güell, Templo La Sagrada Familia, Casa Milà (La Pedrera), Palau de la Música, Casa-Museu Gaudí, Fundació Antoni Tápies, and the Museu d'Art Modern. Buy passes at the **Casa Lleó Morera,** on the corner of Pg. Grácia and C. Consedel (tel. 93 488 01 39). In summer, the air-conditioned, hop-on, hop-off **Bus Turístic** stops at 25 sights; hop on at Pl. Catalunya, in front of El Corte Inglés. (Buses run Apr.-Dec. daily every 10-30min. 9am-9:30pm. Day pass 1800ptas, 2-day 2300ptas.)

LAS RAMBLAS

This pedestrian-only median strip is a veritable urban carnival, where street performers dance, fortune-tellers survey palms, human statues shift poses, vendors sell birds and flowers, and artists sell their work. Walking the strip is in an experience in itself, but there are also some more conventional sights along the way.

ESGLÉSIA DE SANT PAU. Barcelona's oldest Romanesque church, the 10th-century Església de Sant Pau stands in stark contrast to its setting in the former red-light district, El Raval. *(C. Sant Pau 99. Open M-F 5-8pm.)*

PALAU GÜELL. Antoni Gaudí's Palau Güell has the most spectacular Gaudí interior in Barcelona. The rooftop displays his first use of covering surfaces with shards of ceramic or glass. *(C. Nou de la Rambla 3-5, 2 blocks down from Teatre Liceu, on the right. Open M-Sa 10am-2pm and 4-8pm. 400ptas, students 200ptas. Arrive early.)*

MUSEU D'ART CONTEMPORANI (MACBA). Designed by American architect Richard Meier, gleaming white MACBA's gentle curves and large, angular windows contrast with the surrounding rundown Gothic neighborhood. The museum features excellent rotating exhibits. *(Pl. dels Angels 1. M: Universitat or Catalunya. From Las Ramblas, walk north on C. Elisabets and turn right on C. Montalerge. Open M and W-F 11am-8pm, Sa 10am-8pm, Su 10am-3pm. M and Th-F 750ptas, W 375ptas; students 550ptas.)*

OTHER SIGHTS. Plaça Reial, off Las Ramblas, is known for loud evening crowds and Gaudí's street lamps. The disaster-prone opera house, **Gran Teatre del Liceu,** Las Ramblas 61, is on the corner of C. Sant Pau. Ravaged by a fire in 1994, the theater reopened in 1999. Nearby, by the *Modernista* **La Boquería** market, **Joan Miró's pavement mosaic** brightens the street. At the port end of Las Ramblas, the **Monument a Colom** towers above the city, with a confused Christopher Columbus proudly pointing toward Libya. *(Elevator open June-Sept. daily 9am-8:30pm; Oct.-Mar. M-F 10am-1:30pm and 3:30-7:30pm, Sa-Su 10am-6:30pm; Apr.-May M-F 10am-1:30pm and 3:30-7:30pm, Sa-Su 10am-7:30pm. 250ptas.)*

BARRI GÒTIC

While the weathered, narrow streets of the Barri Gòtic, such as **Carrer de la Pietat** and **Carrer del Paradis,** have preserved their medieval charm, the ever-growing tourist economy has infused a new, multilingual liveliness into the area.

PLAÇA DE SANT JAUME. Any tour should begin in the handsome Pl. de Sant Jaume, Barcelona's political center since Roman times. The square is dominated by the **Palau de la Generalitat,** seat of Catalunya's autonomous government, and the **Ajuntament,** the Spanish government's seat of power. *(Palau open 2nd and 3rd Su of each month 10am-2pm. Ajuntament open Sa-Su 10am-2pm. Free.)*

ESGLÉSIA CATEDRAL DE LA SANTA CREU. Above Pl. Seu rise the jagged spires of the 14th-century Gothic Església Catedral de la Santa Creu. Barcelona's patron saint and Christian martyr Santa Euália lies in the church **crypt.** Geese waddle around the periphery of the lovely **cloister.** *(Cathedral open daily 8am-1:30pm and 4-7pm.*

SPAIN

Coro (choral chamber) 125ptas. Cloister open daily 9am-1:15pm and 4-7pm; free. Elevator to the rooftop open M-F 9:30am-12:30pm and 4-6:30pm, Sa-Su 9:30am-12:30pm; 200ptas.)

PLAÇA DE REI. On the opposite side of the Església Catedral in Pl. de Rei is the **Palau Reial** (Royal Palace), the former royal residence. The **Museu d'Historia de la Ciutat** and **Museu Frederic Marès** now hold court here. The former chronicles the history of Barcelona, from Roman foundations to modern day; original Roman ruins are in the basement. *(On Pl. Rei, with an entrance on C. Verguer. M: Jaume I. Walk up C. Jaume I and turn right. Open June-Sept. Tu-Sa 10am-8pm, Su 10am-2pm; Oct.-May Tu-Sa 10am-2pm and 4-8pm, Su 10am-2pm. 1000ptas, students 700ptas; 1st Sa of each month 3-8pm free.)*

LA RIBERA

◪**PALAU DE LA MÚSICA CATALANA.** *Modernista* architect Lluís Domènech i Montaner designed the amazing, must-see, adjective-defying Palau de la Música Catalana. *(C. Sant Francesc de Paula 2, up Vía Laietana near the intersection of C. Ionqueres. Tel. 93 268 10 00. For performance info, see p. 846. Open M-F 10am-9pm. Mandatory tours every 30min., 10:30am-3pm; 700ptas, students 500ptas; tickets on sale from 10am.)*

◪**MUSEU PICASSO.** The museum boasts the world's best collection from Picasso's formative time, at the beginning of his Blue Period, as well as prints, ceramics, and pencil sketches by 11-year-old Pablo. The collection includes an excellent display of his Cubist interpretations of Velázquez's *Las Meninas*. *(C. Montcad 15-19. M: Jaume I; walk down C. Princesa, and C. Montcada is on the right. Open Tu-Sa 10am-8pm, Su 10am-3pm. 700ptas, students 400ptas; 1st Su of each month free.)*

OTHER SIGHTS. Ribera's narrow streets converge at the foot of the 14th-century Gothic **Església Santa María del Mar's** octagonal towers. The church once stood on the coastline of the Mediterranean, before Barcelona's mud flats were solidified and used as foundation. *(Open M-Sa 9am-1:30pm and 4:30-8pm, Su 9am-2pm and 5-8:30pm.)* Museums, art galleries, art workshops, and Baroque palaces pack the **Carrer de Montcada,** beginning behind the church.

PARC DE LA CIUTADELLA AND VILA OLÍMPICA

The peaceful **Parc de la Ciutadella** once housed the fortress in which Barcelona's influential citizens were imprisoned by Felipe V in the early 18th century. Host of the 1888 Universal Exposition, the park now harbors Gaudí and friends' wacky **Cascada** fountains, a zoo, and several museums including the eclectic **Museu d'Art Modern,** on Pl. Armes in the center of the park. *(M: Arc de Triomf. Open Tu-Sa 10am-7pm, Su 10am-2:30pm. 600ptas, students 400ptas.)* The **Vila Olímpica,** beyond the east side of the zoo, was built to house 15,000 athletes and entertain millions of tourists for the 1992 Olympics, and is today a modern-day yuppieville, home to public parks, a shopping center, and offices. Toward the Mediterranean, **Port Olímpic** flaunts Frank Gehry's huge fish sculpture, while **beaches** stretch out from the port. *(M: Ciutadella/ Vila Olímpica; walk along the waterfront on Ronda Litoral toward the 2 towers.)*

L'EIXAMPLE

The *Renaixença* of Catalán culture and the growth of Barcelona during the 19th century pushed the city past its medieval walls and into ordered modernity. The carefully designed **Eixample** (uh-SHOMP-luh) neighborhood gave rise to *passeigs* lined with high-brow shopping and fantastic must-see designs.

◪**SAGRADA FAMILIA.** Only Gaudí's genius could draw thousands of tourists to a church still being built; the architect himself guessed that the **Temple Expiadori de la Sagrada Familia** would take 200 years to complete. Gaudí lived in the complex for his last 11 years until, in 1926, he was run over by a trolley. A **museum** displays artifacts relating to the construction. *(On C. Marinara, between C. Mallorca and C. Provença. M: Sagrada Familia. Open daily Apr.-Aug. 9am-8pm; Sept.-Oct. and Mar. 9am-7pm; Jan.-Feb. and Nov.-Dec. 9am-6pm. Tours Apr.-Oct. 11:30am, 1, 4, and 6:30pm; Nov.-May 11:30am and 1pm. Church and museum 800ptas. Elevator 200ptas.)*

MANZANA DE LA DISCORDIA. A short walk from Pl. Catalunya, the odd-numbered side of Pg. Gràcia, between Aragó and Consell de Cent, is popularly known as *la*

MARVELOUS MODERNISME In the late 19th and early 20th centuries, Barcelona's flourishing bourgeoisie commissioned a new class of architects to build their houses, reshaping the face of L'Eixample with *Modernista* architecture that employed revolutionary shapes, materials, and spaces to reflect the signs and symbols of Catalunya. **Antoni Gaudí's** serpentine rooftops, warrior-like chimneys, and skeletal façades are perhaps the most famous examples of this style. A staunch regionalist, Gaudí incorporated an array of Catalán symbols and myths in his organic architecture. Gaudí designed every feature of his buildings, down to the furniture, colorful ceramic mosaics, and elaborate light fixtures that fill his boisterous buildings. Even his methods were unconventional; Gaudí designed the vault of the Colònia Güell by hanging sand bags from a wire model of the ceiling, the inversion of which perfectly balanced against structural stress. Although most of Gaudí's creations seem fantastical, they are architectural breakthroughs that have since been imitated only by advanced computer technology and mathematics. Fellow *Modernista* luminaries include **Luis Domènech i Montaner,** noted for his heavily decorated surfaces as exemplified by the Palau de la Música Catalana and Casa Lleó i Morera, and **Josep Puig i Cadafalch,** who developed an antiquarian style uniting local and foreign traditions.

manzana de la discordia (block of discord), referring to the aesthetic competition of three buildings on the block. At the **Casa Lleó i Morera,** by Domènech i Montaner, you can buy the **Ruta del Modernisme pass** and tour the interior of sprouting flowers, stained glass, and doorway sculptures. Puig i Cadafalch went for a geometric, Moorish-influenced pattern on the façade of **Casa Amatller** at #41. Gaudí's balconies ripple and tiles sparkle on **Casa Batlló** at #43. Experts and tourists alike argue as to the meaning of the façade; the most popular theory claims that it represents Catalunya's patron Sant Jordi (Saint George) slaying his dragon.

CASA MILÀ (LA PEDRERA). Many *modernisme* buffs argue that the spectacular Casa Milà apartment building popularly known as *La Pedrera* (Stone Quarry) is Gaudí's most refined work. The winding attic houses the **Espai Gaudí,** a multimedia presentation of Gaudí's life and works. New since the summer of 1999, a restored apartment awaits one floor below, exhibiting the fine, captivating interior of Gaudí homes. *(Pg. Gràcia 92. Open daily 10am-8pm. Tours M-F noon and 6pm, Sa-Su 11am. 600ptas, students 350ptas; with apartment 1000ptas.)*

MONTJUÏC

Historically, whoever has controlled Montjuïc (Hill of the Jews) has ruled Barcelona. Dozens of despotic rulers have modified the **Castell de Monjuïc,** built atop an ancient Jewish cemetery; Franco made it one of his "interrogation" headquarters. *(Take the funicular from Pl. Raquel Meller (M: Parallel) to Av. Miramar, then take the teleferic cable car (every 10min., 225ptas, round-trip 375ptas) to the top.)* The **Fonts Luminoses** (Illuminated Fountains), dominated by the huge central **Font Mágica** (Magic Fountain), are visible from Pl. Espanya up Av. Reina María Cristina. *(From M: Espanya, catch bus 50 at Av. Reina María Cristina. Runs every 10min.)* The **Palau Nacional,** behind the fountains up the stairs, was designed by Ludwig Mies van der Rohe as Germany's Expo pavilion in 1929 and now houses the Romanesque and Gothic art of the **Museu Nacional d'Art de Catalunya (MNAC).** *(Open Tu-W and F-Sa 10am-7pm, Th 10am-9pm, Su 10am-2:30pm. 800ptas, with temporary exhibits 900ptas; with youth card 50% off.)* In 1929, Barcelona inaugurated the **Estadi Olímpic de Montjuïc** farther up the hill in its bid for the 1932 Olympic games; 60 years later it was revamped for the 1992 extravaganza. *(Open daily 10am-8pm. Free.)* About 100m down Av. Miramar from the stadium is the unique **Fundació Miró,** with works from all periods of Miró's career. *(Miramar 71-75, on Pl. Neptú. Open July-Sept. Tu-W and F-Sa 10am-8pm, Th 10am-9:30pm, Su 10am-2:30pm; Oct.-June Tu-W and F-Sa 10am-7pm, Th 10am-9:30pm, Su 10am-2:30pm. 800ptas, students 450ptas.)*

PARC GÜELL

On a hill just north of Gràcia lies one of Barcelona's greatest treasures and perhaps the world's most enchanting public park. Gaudí intended Parc Güell to be a garden city, designing the multicolored dwarfish houses and sparkling ceramic-mosaic stairways for the city's elite. When only two aristocrats signed on, it became a park instead. Inside, an elegant white staircase adorned with patterned tiles and a giant, gaping salamander leads to a pavilion supported by 86 pillars and decked out by the longest park bench in the world, a tile-shard, serpentine wonder. In the midst of the park awaits the **Casa-Museu Gaudí,** the architect's former home. *(Take bus 24 from Pg. Gràcia, or take the metro to "Vallarca," walk straight down Av. L'Hospital Militar, take a left onto Baixada de la Gloria, and take the outdoor escalators uphill. Open daily May-Aug. 10am-9pm; Apr. and Sept. 10am-8pm; Mar. and Oct. 10am-7pm; Nov.-Feb. 10am-6pm; free. Museum open daily May-Sept. 10am-8pm; Oct. and Mar.-Apr. 10am-7pm; Nov.-Feb. 10am-6pm; 300ptas.)*

TIBIDABO

The name comes from the smashing view this area commands over Barcelona, the Pyrenees, the Mediterranean, and even (on clear days) Mallorca; in St. Matthew's Gospel, the devil tempts Jesus by offering him spell-binding scenery, saying "All this I will give to you *(tibi dabo)* if you fall prostrate and worship me." Ride the elevator up the nearby **Torre de Collserola** communications tower for thrills (500ptas). The **Tibibús** (270ptas) runs from Pl. Catalunya to the Torre de Collserola (every 30min.-1hr., 270ptas.); commuter **trains** (round-trip including funicular and attraction park entrance 1900ptas) go from Pl. Catalunya to Av. Tibidabo. To reach the mountaintop, take the city bus on weekdays and the **Tramvia Blau** (Blue Train) on weekends. At the top of the street, take the funicular (200ptas).

🎵 ENTERTAINMENT

For entertainment tips, pick up the *Guía del Ocio* (www.guiadelociobcn.es) at any newsstand (125ptas). The **Gran Teatre del Liceu,** Ramblas 51-59 (tel. 93 485 99 00; www.liceubarcelona.com), founded in 1847, one of the world's leading opera stages until the interior was destroyed by a fire in 1994, has reopened for the year 2000. **Palau de la Música Catalana,** C. San Francesc de Paula 2, off Vía Laietana near Pl. Urquinaona, has a variety of concerts. (See p. 844. Tel. 93 268 10 00. Tickets run 1000-26,000ptas. Box office open M-Sa 10am-9pm, Su 1hr. prior to concert.) The **Grec-Barcelona** summer festival (www.grecbcn.com) turns the city into an international theater, music, and dance extravaganza from late June to mid-August. For festival info, ask at the tourist office or contact **Institut de Cultura de Barcelona (ICUB),** Palau de la Virreina, Ramblas 99 (tel. 93 301 77 75; open M-F 10am-2pm and 4-8pm). Buy tickets through **TelEntrada** (tel. 902 10 12 12; www.telentrada.com) or the Pl. Catalunya tourist office. The *Cine* section in *Guía del Ocio* denotes subtitled **films** with *V.O. subtitulada;* other foreign films are dubbed, usually in Catalán.

Grab face paint and join **F.C. Barcelona** at the 110,000-seat stadium **Nou Camp** for **soccer.** (Tel. 93 496 36 00. Box office at C. Aristedes Maillol 12/18.) The **sardana,** Catalunya's regional dance, is a popular form of Barcelona amusement. All join hands to dance in a circle in front of the cathedral, on Pl. Sagrada Familia, or at Parc de la Ciutadella on Sundays at noon. **Fiestas** abound; for info, call 93 301 77 75. The **Festa de Sant Jordi** (St. George; Apr. 23) celebrates Catalunya's patron saint with a feast. Men give women roses, and women give men books (how progressive).

🏙 NIGHTLIFE

Nightlife in Barcelona begins with the 5pm stroll and winds down about 14 hours later. After *siesta,* the masses roll into Las Ramblas, while youngsters model the latest fashions on **C. Portal l'Angel** and **Portaferrissa.** The theater crowd lingers in cafés and tapas bars around **Liceu,** and foreign twentysomethings order *copas* in **Pl. Reial.** The well-off mature crowd cruises **L'Eixample,** while bona fide Barcelonan students head to **Gràcia.** Dinner is served between 9 and 11pm; the bar scene revs up around 10pm; and discos don't start bumping until close to 2am, when the night is still young. Along **Las Ramblas** and throughout **Ciutat Vella,** *cervecerías* and *bar-restaurantes* can be found every five steps. In **L'Eixample,** a slew of hip spots lies between **Pg. Gràcia** and **C. Aribau,** and **C. Rossell** and **C. València.** The farther from Las Ramblas, the less touristy the bar; **La Ribera** is particularly untouristed.

▓ **Les Bosc de les Fades** (tel. 93 317 26 49). M: Drassanes. Just off Las Ramblas near the water, next to the wax museum. Enter into a fairy-tale world, gnarly trees and all. Open Su-Th until 1:30am, F-Sa until 2:30am.

▓ **La Oveja Negra,** C. Sitges 5 (tel. 93 317 10 87). M: Catalunya; go down Las Ramblas, turn right on C. Tallers, and take the 1st left. The most popular tavern in town. Large *sangría* 1000ptas. Open M-Th 9am-2:30am, F 9am-3:30am, Sa-Su 5pm-3am.

Casa Almirall, C. Joaquim Costa 33. Weathered couches mark the oldest bar in Barcelona. Get your absinthe fix for 500ptas. Open daily 7pm-3am.

Schilling, C. Ferrán 23 (tel. 93 317 67 87). M: Liceu. Mixed gay and straight crowd. Beer 295ptas. Glass of wine 200ptas. Open M-F 9am-2am, Sa-Su 11am-2am.

Café d l'Opera, Las Ramblas 74 (tel. 93 317 75 85). M: Liceu. A Barcelona institution. Beer 325-560ptas. 4-person *sangría* 1690ptas. Open daily 8am-2:30am.

I COULD HAVE DANCED ALL NIGHT

At clubs bouncers can be finicky, and what's hip varies from day to day: dress well, and guys should beware ridiculously high covers. Expect to pay 500ptas for a beer and at least 800ptas for drinks at clubs, more still at Maremagnum and Port Olympic. In the **Montjuic** area, the epic **Poble Espanyol,** on Av. Marqués de Comillas, has 12 restaurants, 15 bars, three *bares-musicales*, and a few large *discotecas*. Dancing starts at around 1:30am, and usually doesn't end until 9am. (M: Pl. Espanya. Open in summer nightly; off-season Th-Sa.) The **Olympic Village** brims with 20-odd bars and clubs, but many revelers choose to dance on the port itself. Things begin at midnight and wind down at 6am. From M: Ciutadella-Vila Olímpica (L4), walk down C. Marina toward the twin towers, where there's **no cover** anywhere. Or walk down Las Ramblas and cross over the wavy bridge to get to **Maremagnum,** where there's something for everyone, though pricetags vary; explore all floors of the disco mall complex before following your ears to your hotspot of choice.

▐ EXCURSIONS FROM BARCELONA

MONTSERRAT. An hour northwest of Barcelona, the mountain of Montserrat is where a wandering 9th-century mountaineer had a blinding vision of the Virgin Mary. In the 11th century, a monastery was founded to worship the Virgin, and the site has since evolved into a major pilgrimage center. The **monastery's** ornate **basilica** is above Pl. Creu. Right of the main chapel is a route through the **side chapels** that leads to the 12th-century Romanesque **La Moreneta** (the black Virgin Mary), Montserrat's venerated icon. (Open daily in summer 9-10:30am, noon-6:15pm, and 7:30-8:30pm.) In Pl. Santa María, the **Museo de Montserrat** exhibits a sweeping range of art, from an Egyptian mummy to several Picassos. (Open daily in summer 9am-6pm; off-season 9:30am-6:30pm. 500ptas, students 300ptas.) The **Santa Cova funicular** descends from Pl. Creu to paths that wind along to ancient hermitages. (Every 20min. daily in summer 10am-1pm and 2-6pm; off-season Sa-Su only; round-trip 360ptas.) Take the **St. Joan funicular** up for more inspirational views. (Every 20min. spring through fall 10am-7pm. Round-trip 895ptas.) The dilapidated **St. Joan monastery** and **shrine** are only 20min. from the highest station. The real prize is **Sant Jerónim** (1235m), about 2hr. from Pl. Creu (1hr. from the terminus of the St. Joan funicular); take the sharp left after 45min. at the little old chapel.

FFCC **trains** (tel. 93 205 15 15) to Montserrat leave from M: Espanya in Barcelona (1hr., every hr., 1185ptas, round-trip 1855ptas); get off at Aeri de Montserrat, *not* Olesa de Montserrat. From the base of the mountain at the other end, the heart-stopping **Aeri cable car** runs up to the monastery (every 15min. 9:25am-1:45pm and 3-6:15pm; round-trip 925ptas, included in train fare). From the upper cable car station, turn left and walk to **Pl. Creu,** where there's an **info booth.** (Tel. 93 835 02 51. Open July-Sept. daily 10am-7pm; Oct.-June M-F 9am-6pm, Sa-Su 10am-7pm.)

SITGES. Forty kilometers south of Barcelona, the resort town of Sitges is famed for its prime tanning grounds, lively cultural festivals, international gay community, and wired nightlife. Long considered a watered-down Ibiza, Sitges has better beaches than the notorious Balearic hotspot, and on mainland Spain, you won't

SPAIN

find much crazier beach-oriented nightlife. The **beach** is 10min. from the train station via any street. In town, **C. Parellades** is the main tourist drag. Late-night foolhardiness clusters around **C. Primer de Maig**, which runs directly from the beach, and its continuation, **C. Marques Montroig.** The wild things are at the "disco-beach" **Atlántida,** in Sector Terramar. Shuffle your feet at **Pachá,** on Pg. Sant Didac, in nearby Vallpineda. Buses run from midnight to 4am to the two discos from C. Primer de Maig. During **Carnaval,** March 2-12 in 2000, Spaniards crash the town for a frenzy of dancing, costumes, and alcohol. **Cercanías Trains** link Sitges to Barcelona's Sants Station and M: Gràcia (40min., every 15min., 310-355ptas; last train back 10:25pm). The **tourist office,** on Pg. Vilafranca, is near the train station. From the station, turn right on C. Artur Carbonell and go downhill. (Tel. 93 894 42 51; fax 93 894 43 05. Open W-M 10am-1pm and 5:30-9pm.) If you plan to stay the night, reserve early. **Hostal Internacional** is at Sant Francesc 52. (Tel. 93 894 26 90. Doubles 5000-6000ptas.)

GIRONA (GERONA)

A world-class city patiently waiting for the world to notice, Girona (pop. 70,500) is really two cities in one: a hushed medieval masterpiece on one riverbank, and a thriving, modern city on the other. Though founded by the Romans, the city owes more to the renowned *cabalistas de Girona*, who for centuries spread the teachings of Kabbalah (mystical Judaism) in the West. Still a cultural center and university town, Girona is a magnet for artists, intellectuals, and activists.

◪◪◫ **PRACTICAL INFO, ACCOMMODATIONS, AND FOOD.** Girona is the Costa Brava's transport center: all trains between Barcelona and southern France stop here, and scores of buses travel daily to the Costa Brava. **Trains** (tel. 972 20 70 93) depart from off C. Barcelona in the new town to Figueres (45min., 21 per day, 375ptas); Barcelona (1¼hr., 21 per day, 1265ptas); Madrid (9-10½hr., 1 per day, 6000-7500ptas); and Paris (11hr., 1 per day, 16,900ptas). **Buses** (tel. 972 21 23 19) depart from just around the corner. To get to the old city from the station, head straight through the parking lot, turn left on C. Barcelona, bear right via C. Santa Eugenia to the Gran Vía de Jaume III, continue straight across to C. Nou, and cross the Pont de Pedra. The **tourist office,** Rambla Llibertat 1, is directly on the other side. (Tel. 972 22 65 75; fax 972 22 66 12. Open M-F 8am-8pm, Sa 8am-2pm and 4-8pm, Su 9am-2pm.) Get your **internet** fix at **Ciberxuxes,** C. Carme 55. (300ptas per 30min., 500ptas per hr. Open M-F 9am-1pm and 5-8pm.) The ultra-modern **Alberg-Residència Cerverí de Girona (HI),** C. Ciutadans 9, is on the street to the left directly after the Pont de Pedra. (Tel. 972 21 81 21; fax 972 21 20 23. 2275ptas, under 27 1800ptas. Members only; sells HI cards. Breakfast included. Sheets 350ptas. Laundry. Make reservations through the Barcelona office (tel. 93 483 83 63) for Aug.) The **Pensió Viladomat,** C. Ciutadans 5, next to the hostel, has clean, well-furnished rooms. (Tel. 972 20 31 76. Singles 2000ptas; doubles 4000-6500ptas.) Girona abounds with innovative Catalunyan cuisine; for excellent, inexpensive food, try restaurants along **C. Cort Reial. Café Le Bistrot,** Pujada Sant Domènec 4, packs in locals for its lunchtime *menú* (1200ptas), pizza, and crêpes (500-675ptas). (Open M-Sa 1-5pm and 7pm-1am, M-Th until 1:30am.) Pick up cheap grub at the **market** in Pl. Clave and Rubalcaba, in the new city near the river (open M-Sa 8am-1pm), or at **Supeco,** C. Sequia 10, a block from C. Nou off the Gran Vía. (Open M-Sa 9am-1:30pm and 5-8:30pm.) **Postal code:** 17070.

◪◪ **SIGHTS AND ENTERTAINMENT.** Most sights are in the old city, across the river from the train station. After crossing over the Pont de Pedra, turn left down Rambla de la Llibertat, continue on C. Argenteria, bear right across C. Cort Reial, climb the stairs, and head left to reach C. Força. **El Call,** the medieval Jewish neighborhood, begins at C. Sant Llorenç; take a right off C. Força into a narrow alleyway. A thriving community in the Middle Ages, it was virtually wiped out by the 1492 expulsion, mass emigration, conversion, and the Inquisition. The entrance to **Centre Bonastruc Ça Porta,** the site of the last synagogue in Girona (today a museum), is off C. Sant Llorenç about halfway up the hill. (Open June-Oct. M-Sa 10am-8pm, Su 10am-3pm; Nov.-May M-Sa 10am-6pm, Su 10am-2pm. Free.) Uphill on C. Força and around the corner to the right, the Gothic **cathedral** rises up a record-breaking 90 Rococo steps from the plaza below. The **Tesoro Capitular** within contains some of Girona's most precious possessions, including the **Tapis de la Creació,** a 15th-century tapestry depicting the creation story. (Both open July-Aug. Tu-Su 10am-2pm and 4-7pm; Sept.-June closed Su 4-7pm. 400ptas.)

The **Rambla** and **Pl. de Independencia** are the places to see and be seen, gossip, flirt, and dance. Some summer Fridays witness spontaneous *sardanas,* traditional Catalán dances involving 10 to 12 musicians serenading a ring of dancers. Bars near **Pl. Ferrán Catòlic** draw big crowds, but in summer, **Parc de la Devesa,** across the river from the old town and several blocks to the left, has all the cachet, and often live music as well. Artsy folk mill around bars in the old town.

■ EXCURSIONS FROM GIRONA: THE COSTA BRAVA

TOSSA DE MAR. Far from undiscovered, pretty Tossa de Mar (pop. 3800), about 40km north of Barcelona, is packed with tourists in summer. That said, the town still stands out for its **beaches,** framed by reddened cliffs; its **calas** (small bays), accessible by foot; and its small-town sincerity, long since abandoned by larger resort towns. Inside the walled **Vila Vella** (Old Town), spiraling medieval alleys lead to a tiny plaza, where the **Museu Municipal** displays 20s and 30s art and will host a special Dalí exhibit in 2000. (Open Tu-Su June-Sept. 10am-7pm; Oct.-May 10am-1pm and 3-6pm. 1000ptas.) Sarfa **buses** run to Pl. de les Nacions Sense Estat, at the corner of Av. Pelegrí and Av. Ferrán Agulló, from Girona (1hr., 1-2 per day, 615ptas) and Barcelona (3½hr., 8-9 per day, 1120ptas). The **tourist office** shares the same building. (Tel. 972 34 01 08; fax 972 34 07 12. Open mid-June to mid-Sept. M-Sa 9am-9pm, Su 10am-1pm; May to mid-June and mid-Sept. to Oct. M-Sa 10am-1pm and 4-8pm; Nov.-Apr. M-F 10am-1pm and 4-7pm, Sa 10am-1pm.) Surf the **internet** at **La LLuna,** on Av. Sant Raimon de Penyafort. (300-400ptas per 15min. Open May-Oct. daily 3pm-midnight.) ◪**Pensión Pepi,** C. Sant Miguel 10, offers cozy rooms with bath. Turn left off Av. de Pelegrí onto Maria Auxiliadora and veer right onto C. Sant Miguel. (Tel. 972 34 05 26. Singles 1400-1500ptas; doubles 3000-4000ptas. Breakfast 300ptas. V, MC.) To get to **Fonda/Can Lluna,** C. Roqueta 20, turn right off Pg. Mar onto C. Peixeteras, walk through C. Estalt, turn left at the end, and head straight. (Tel. 972 34 03 65. 1750-1900ptas per person.) **Camp** at **Can Martí** (tel. 972 34 08 51; fax 972 34 24 61), at the end of Rambla Pau Casals, off Av. Ferrán Agulló, 15min. from the station. The paella at ◪**Restaurant Marina,** C. Tarull 6, is delicious. (*Menú* 1350ptas. Open *Semana Santa*-Oct. daily 11am-11pm.) **Postal code:** 17320.

FIGUERES. In 1974, Salvador Dalí chose his native, beachless **Figueres** (pop. 37,000), 36km north of Girona, as the site to build a museum to house his works, catapulting the city to instant fame. Despite his reputation as a self-promoting fascist, his self-monument is undeniably a masterpiece—and the second most popular museum in Spain. The ◪**Teatre-Museu Dalí,** in Pl. Gala i S. Dalí, parades the artist's erotically nightmarish drawings, extraterrestrial landscapes, and bizarre installations. From the Rambla, take C. Girona, which becomes C. Jonquera, and climb the steps. (Open July-Sept. 9am-7:15pm and 10pm-12:30am; Oct.-June 6 10:30am-5:15pm and 10pm-12:30am. 1000ptas, students 800ptas.) **Trains** (tel. 972 20 70 93) run to Girona (30min., 21 per day, 375ptas) and Barcelona (1½hr., 21 per day, 1265ptas). **Buses** (tel. 972 67 33 54) truck to Girona (1hr., 4-6 per day, 475ptas); Cadaqués (1¼hr., 2-5 per day, 490ptas); and Barcelona (2¼hr., 4-6 per day, 1750ptas). The **tourist office** is on Pl. Sol. (Tel. 972 50 31 55. Open July-Aug. M-Sa 8am-9pm, Su 9am-6pm; Easter-June and Oct. M-F 8:30am-3pm and 4:30-8pm, Sa 9:30am-1:30pm and 3:30-6:30pm; Sept. and Nov.-Easter M-F 8:30am-3pm.) Get on the **internet** at **Netway,** Pl. Tarradella 14. (400ptas per 30min. Open M-F 9am-1pm and 3-7pm.) Even finding a place to sleep in Figueres can be a surreal experience, but ◪**Alberg Tramuntana (HI),** C. Anciet de Pagès 2, behind the tourist office, is cheap and chock full o' amenities. (Tel. 972 50 12 13; fax 972 67 38 08. 2000-2325ptas, under 27 1575-1800ptas. Members only; sells HI cards. Breakfast included. Sheets 350ptas. Reception daily

8am-2pm and 4-11pm. Lockout M-F 2-4pm, Sa-Su 1-7pm. Curfew midnight; in summer open for 10min. at 1, 2, 3, and 4am. Reserve in advance through the Barcelona office (tel. 93 483 83 63) or call the hostel 2-3 days ahead. V, MC, AmEx.) Buy **groceries** at **MAXOR**, Pl. Sol 5. (Open July-Sept. M-F 8am-9pm, Sa 8am-9pm; Oct.-June M-Sa 8am-8:30pm.) **Postal code:** 17600.

CADAQUÉS. The whitewashed houses and rocky beaches of Cadaqués (pop. 1800) have attracted artists, writers, and musicians—not to mention tourists—ever since Dalí built his summer home here in the 30s. The **Centre d'Art Perrot-Moore,** C. Vigilant 1, near the town center, houses a Dalí erotic fantasy room. (Open July-Aug. daily 10:30am-1:30pm and 4:30-8:30pm; Apr.-June and Sept.-Oct. M-Sa 10:30am-1:30pm and 4:30-8pm. 800ptas, students 500ptas.) **Casa-Museu Salvador Dalí,** Port Lligat, Dalí's home until 1982, is complete with a pop-art miniature Alhambra and lip-shaped sofa. Follow the signs to Port Lligat (bear right with your back to the statue of liberty) and then to the Casa de Dalí. (Open daily mid-June to mid-Sept. 10:30am-9pm; mid-Mar. to mid-June and mid-Sept. to Nov. Tu-Su 10:30am-6pm. 1200ptas, students 700ptas.) For a **beach** excursion, try the rocky **Platja Gran,** near the town center, or **Sa Concha,** 5min. away. **Buses** arrive from Figueres (1hr., 3-5 per day, 490ptas); Girona (2hr., 1-2 per day, 940ptas); and Barcelona (2½hr., 2-5 per day, 2045ptas). With your back to the Sarfa office at the bus stop, walk right along Av. Caritat Serinyana; the **tourist office,** C. Cotxe 2, is off Pl. Frederic Rahola opposite the *passeig.* (Tel. 972 25 83 15; fax 15 95 42. Open July-Aug. M-Sa 10am-2pm and 4-9pm, Su 10am-1pm; Sept.-June M-Sa 10:30am-1pm and 4-8pm.) **Hostal Cristina,** C. Riera, has newly renovated, waterfront rooms. (Tel. 972 25 81 38. Singles 2000-3000ptas; doubles 4000-8000ptas. V, MC.) **Camping Cadaqués,** Ctra. Portlligat 17, is on the left on the way to Dalí's house. (Tel. 972 25 81 26. 550ptas per person, 695ptas per tent, 550ptas per car; add 7% IVA. Open June-Sept. 15.) Pack a **picnic** from **Super Auvi,** C. Riera. (Open daily mid-July to Aug. M-Sa 8am-9pm, Su 8am-2pm; Sept. to mid-July M-Sa 8am-2pm and 4-9pm, Su 8am-2pm.) **Postal code:** 17488.

THE PYRENEES

The jagged green mountains, Romanesque churches, and tranquil towns of the Pyrenees draw hikers and high-brow skiers in search of outdoor adventures. Mist and fog obscure visibility at high altitudes, creating either a dreamy atmosphere or slightly nerve-racking driving conditions. *Ski España* lists vital statistics of all ski stations in Spain. Without a car, transport is tricky, but feasible.

VAL D'ARAN. Some of the Catalán Pyrenees' most dazzling peaks cluster around Val d'Aran, in the northwest corner of Catalunya. The Val d'Aran is best known for its chic ski resorts—the Spanish royal family's favorite slopes are those of **Baquiera-Beret.** The **Albergue Era Garona (HI),** a few kilometers away in the town of **Salardú,** is accessible by shuttle **bus** in high-season from Vielha (see below). (Tel. 973 64 52 71. 2375ptas, under 27 1800ptas. Members only; HI cards sold. Breakfast included. Sheets 350ptas.) For skiing info, contact the **Oficeria de Baquiera-Beret** (tel. 973 64 44 55; fax 973 64 44 88) or the tourist office in Vielha (tel. 973 64 01 10).

The biggest town in the valley, **Vielha** (pop. 3700) welcomes hikers and skiers to its lively streets with every sort of service outdoorsy types might desire. Only 12km from Bacquiera-Beret, shuttle **buses** connect the two in July and August (schedules at the tourist office). Alsina Graells **buses** (tel. 973 26 85 00) also run to Barcelona (5½hr., 4 per day, 3325ptas). The **tourist office,** C. Sarriulèra 6, is one block upstream from the *plaça.* (Tel. 973 64 01 10; fax 973 64 05 37. Open daily July to mid-Sept. 9am-1pm and 4-8pm; mid-Sept. to June M-Sa 10am-1pm and 4:30-7:30pm.) **Camins,** Av. Pas d'Arro 5 (tel. 973 64 24 44), can help plan outdoor adventures. Several inexpensive *pensiones* cluster at the end of C. Reiau, off Pg. Libertat (which intersects Av. Casteiro at Pl. Sant Antoni); try **Casa Vicenta** at # 3. (Tel. 973 64 08 19. Singles 2000-3000ptas; doubles 3500-4500ptas.) **Pensión Busquets,** C. Mayor 11, is in the old part of town. (Tel. 973 64 02 38. 1800-2000ptas per person.)

SWM SEEKING... Tall, dark, handsome, rich, famous, respected, powerful, and searching for life partner. Enjoys water sports (competed on the Olympic sailing team). Educated at Georgetown. Looking for that special someone—attractive, charismatic, and preferably of noble lineage—to share interests and raise a family.

His name is Felipe, the Prince of Asturias and heir to the Spanish throne. All eyes have turned to Felipe—more than 30, with two recently married older sisters—to choose the next set of genes that will contribute to the Bourbon dynasty. Whom will he choose for his queen when he takes over one of Europe's last remaining powerful monarchies? The competition is fierce. Lovely ladies from wealthy families are stalking the streets of Madrid and the slopes of the Val d'Aran, but so far there are no frontrunners. Cross your fingers and pack something nice—you could be the next Queen of Spain.

PARQUE NACIONAL DE ORDESA. The beauty of Ordesa's Aragonese Pyrenees will reduce even the most seasoned of travelers to monosyllabic stupefaction. Well-maintained trails cut across idyllic forests, jagged rock faces, snow-covered peaks, rushing rivers, and magnificent waterfalls. The **visitor center "El Parador"** is beyond the Ordesa park entrance. (Open daily June 9am-1:30pm and 4-7pm; July-Aug. 9am-1pm and 3:30-7pm; Apr.-May 9am-2pm and 3:30-6pm.) The **Soaso Circle** is the most practical hike; frequent signposts clearly mark the five-hour journey, which can be cut to a two-hour loop. If you prefer a private mountain hike, try the **Circo Cotatuero** or the **Circo Carriata.** Both are two- to three-hour hikes that can be combined into a five-hour trek. More experienced hikers might attempt the **Torla-Gavarnie** trail, a six-hour haul (one-way) all the way to Gavarnie, France.

It is easiest to enter the park through the village of **Torla,** where you can buy the indispensable *Editorial Alpina* guide (675ptas). You can reach Torla by Empresa Hudebus **bus** (tel. 974 21 32 77) from **Sabiñánigo** (55min., 1-2 per day, 355ptas), in turn accessible by La Oscense **bus** (tel. 974 35 50 60) from **Jaca** (July only; 30min., 1-2 per day, 110-185ptas) or any **train** on the Zaragoza-Huesca-Jaca line. A **bus** also shuttles between Torla and **Ordesa** (July-Aug. only; every 15min., round-trip 200ptas). Off-season, you'll have to **hike** the 8km to the entrance or cab it (tel. 974 48 62 43; 1500-2000ptas). Within the park, many **refugios** (mountain huts, usually without facilities) allow overnight stays. The 120-bed **Refugio Góriz** is a 4-hour hike from the parking lot. (Tel. 974 34 12 01. 1000ptas per person.) In Torla, ascend C. Francia one block to reach **Refugio L'Atalaya,** C. Francia 45 (tel. 974 48 60 22), and **Refugio Briet** (tel. 974 48 62 21), across the street. (Both 1000ptas per person.) Opposite Refugio L'Atalaya, **Compañia de Ordesa** (tel. 974 48 64 17) rents mountain bikes and organizes excursions. Outside Torla are **Camping Río Ara** (tel. 974 48 62 48) and **Camping San Anton** (tel. 974 48 60 63). (Both 460ptas per person, per tent, and per car. Open Apr.-Oct.) Stock up at **Supermercado Torla,** on C. Francia. (Open daily Feb.-Nov. 8am-2pm and 4-8pm; Dec.-Jan. 10am-2pm and 4-8pm.)

JACA. For centuries, pilgrims bound for Santiago would cross the Pyrenees into Spain, nest in Jaca (pop. 14,000) for the night, and be off by dawn. They had the right idea; use it as launching pad for the Pyrenees. RENFE **trains** (tel. 974 36 13 32) run from C. Estación to Zaragoza (3hr., 2 per day, 1325ptas) and Madrid (7hr., 1 per day, 4200ptas); **buses** shuttle from the station to the Ayuntamiento on the central C. Mayor. From the **bus station** on Av. Jacetania, walk through the *plaça* to C. Zocotin and go straight two blocks to reach C. Mayor. La Oscense **buses** (tel. 974 35 50 60) run to Zaragoza (2hr., 1 per day, 1460ptas) and Pamplona (2hr., 1 per day, 860ptas). The **tourist office,** Av. Regimiento de Galicia 2, is off C. Mayor. (Tel. 974 36 00 98. Open July-Aug. M-F 9am-2pm and 4:30-8pm, Sa 10am-1:30pm and 5-8pm, Su 10am-1:30pm; Sept.-June M-F 9am-1:30pm and 4:30-7pm, Sa 10am-1pm and 5-7pm.) To get to the **Albergue Juvenil de Escuelas Pias (HI),** Av. Perimetral 6, from C. Mayor, turn left on C. Regimiento de Galicia, turn left on Av. Perimetral, and turn right after the bend on the dirt driveway before the sports center. (Tel. 974 36 05 36. 1500ptas, under 27 1300ptas; nonmembers add 400ptas. Curfew midnight.) Or try **Habitaciones Martínez,** C. Mayor 53. (Tel. 974 36 33 74. Singles 1500ptas; doubles 3000ptas.)

NAVARRA

The spirit of the Navarrese emanates from the rustic Pyrenean *pueblos* on the French border to bustling Pamplona to the dusty villages in the south. Bordered by Basque Country to the west and Aragón to the east, Navarra's little-visited villages greet tourists with open arms.

PAMPLONA (IRUÑA)

Long, long ago, Pamplona's fiesta in honor of its patron saint, San Fermín, was just another religious holiday. But ever since Ernest Hemingway wrote *The Sun Also Rises*, hordes of visitors from around the world have come the week of July 6-14 to witness and experience *San Fermines*, the legendary "Running of the Bulls."

▟ ▛▞ PRACTICAL INFO, ACCOMMODATIONS, AND FOOD. RENFE **trains** (tel. 948 13 02 02) run from off Av. San Jorge to Zaragoza (2hr., 1 per day, 1565-1900ptas); San Sebastián (2hr., 2 per day, 1195-1500ptas); Madrid (5hr., 8 per day, 4200ptas); and Barcelona (6-8hr., 3 per day, 4100-5300ptas). **Buses** (tel. 948 22 38 54) go from C. Conde Oliveto, at C. Yanguas y Miranda, to San Sebastián (1hr., 7-8 per day, 780ptas); Bilbao (2hr., 4-7 per day, 1520-1535ptas); Zaragoza (2-3hr., 6 per day, 1450-1650ptas); Madrid (5hr., 4-5 per day, 3140-3300ptas); and Barcelona (5½hr., 3-4 per day, 2820ptas). From the bus station, turn left on Av. Conde Oliveto, take the second left at the Pl. Príncipe de Viana rotary on Av. San Ignacio, continue to the end of Po. Sarasate, bear right to Pl. Castillo, take C. San Nicolas, turn right on C. San Miguel, and walk through Pl. San Francisco to reach the **tourist office**, C. Eslava 1; from the train station, take bus 9 (95ptas) to the end, cut across Po. Sarasate, walk diagonally left to Pl. Castillo, and follow the directions above. (Tel. 948 20 65 40; fax 948 20 70 36. During *San Fermines* daily 10am-5pm; July-Aug. M-Sa 10am-2pm and 4-7pm, Su 10am-2pm; Sept.-June M-F 10am-2pm and 4-7pm, Sa 10am-2pm.) During *San Fermines*, **store luggage** at the Ayuntamiento, around the corner from the bus station at C. Garcia Jimenez and C. Yanguas y Miranda. (Open 24hr. 300ptas.) **Email** pals back home from the **iturNet cibercafé**, C. Iturrama 1, at C. Abejeras. (500ptas per hr. Open M-Sa 10am-2pm and 4:30-10pm; closed for *San Fermines*.)

And now, kids, a lesson in supply and demand: smart *sanferministas* book their rooms up to a year (at least two months) in advance, often paying up-front rates up to four times higher than those listed here. Beware hawkers at the train and bus stations—quality and prices vary tremendously. Check the newspaper *Diario de Navarra* for **casas particulares.** Many roomless folks find themselves forced to sleep on the lawns of the Ciudadela or on Pl. Fueros, Pl. Castillo, or the banks of the river. Be careful—if you can't store your backpack (storage fills fast), sleep on top of it. To reach **Pensión Santa Cecilia,** C. Navarrería 17, follow C. Chapitela, take the first right on C. Mercaderes, and make a 45° left. (Tel. 948 22 22 30. *San Fermines* dorms 5000ptas. Rest of year singles 2500ptas; doubles 4000ptas; triples 5600ptas. Laundry. V, MC.) **Angeles Arrondo Lizarraga Pension** is at C. Estafeta 25, 5th fl.; look for the CAMAS sign. (Tel. 948 22 18 16. *San Fermines* 4000-6000ptas per person. Rest of year singles 1500ptas; doubles 3000ptas.) Show up early during the fiesta (no reservations) to get a room at **Fonda La Montañesa,** C. San Gregorio 2. (Tel. 948 22 43 80. *San Fermines* dorms 5000ptas; rest of year 1600ptas.) To get to **Camping Ezcaba,** 7km away in Eusa, take the La Montañesa **bus** from Pl. Toros to Eusa (4 per day) to the end. (Tel. 948 33 03 15. 450ptas per person, per tent, and per car. Open June-Oct.) For cheap eats, try the areas near Pensión Santa Cecilia, above **Pl. San Francisco,** and around **Po. Ronda. Calles Navarrería** and **San Lorenzo** and **Po. Sarasate** host *bocadillo* bars. Grab **groceries** at **Vendi,** at C. Hilarión Eslava and C. Mayor. (Open during *San Fermines* M-Sa 9am-2pm; otherwise M-F 9am-2pm and 5:30-7:30pm, Sa 9am-2pm. V, MC.) **Postal code:** 31001.

▣ ▟ SIGHTS AND ENTERTAINMENT. Pamplona's rich architectural legacy gives reason enough to visit during the 51 other weeks of the year. The recently restored late 14th-century **Gothic cathedral** is at the end of C. Navarrería. (Open M-F

10am-1:30pm and 4-7pm, Sa 10am-1:30pm. Tours at 10:30, 11:30am, 12:30, and 5pm. 500ptas.) The impressive walls of the pentagonal **Ciudadela** once humbled even Napoleon; today the Ciudadela hosts free exhibits and concerts in summer. From the old quarter, pick up C. Redín at the far end of the cathedral plaza, head left along the walls past the **Portal de Zumalacárregui** and along the Río Arga, and bear left through the **Parque de la Taconera.** (Open daily 7am-10pm; closed for *San Fermines.* Free.) Throughout the year, **Pl. de Castillo** is the social heart of the city. Hemingway's favorite haunt was the **Café-Bar Iruña,** which he immortalized in *The Sun Also Rises.* (Open daily 5pm-3am.) The young and the restless booze up at bars in the *casco antiguo,* around **Calles de Jarauta, San Nicolas,** and **San Gregorio.**

> ▌❗ Although Pamplona is usually a very safe city, crime skyrockets during *San Fermines,* when some unfortunately come to the fiesta to take advantage of tourists—beware assaults and muggings. Do not roam alone at night, and take extreme care in the parks and shady streets of the *casco antiguo.*

※ **LOS SAN FERMINES (JULY 6-14).** Visitors from the world overcrowd Pamplona for one week of the year in search of Europe's greatest party. Pamplona delivers, with an eight-day frenzy of parades, bullfights, parties, dancing, fireworks, concerts, and wine. Pamplonese, uniformly clad in white garb with red sashes and bandanas, literally throw themselves into the merry-making, displaying obscene levels of both physical stamina and alcohol tolerance. The "Running of the Bulls," called the *encierro,* is the focal point of *San Fermines;* the first *encierro* of the festival takes place on July 7 at 8am and is repeated at 8am every day for the following seven days. Hundreds of bleary-eyed, hung-over, hyper-adrenalized runners flee from very large bulls as bystanders cheer from barricades, windows, balconies, and doorways. Both the bulls and the mob are dangerous; terrified runners, all convinced the bull is right behind them, flee for dear life, and react without concern for those around them. Hemingway had the right idea: don't run. Watch the *encierro* from the bullring instead; arrive around 6:45am. Tickets for the Grada section of the ring are available before 7am (M-F 450ptas, Sa-Su 600ptas). You can watch for free, but the free section is overcrowded, and it can be hard to see and breathe. If you want to participate in the bullring excitement, you can line up by the Pl. Toros well before 7:30am and run in *before* the bulls are even in sight. To watch one of the bullfights, wait in the line that forms at the bullring around 8pm every evening (from 2000ptas). As one bullfight ends, tickets go on sale for the next day. Once the running is over, the insanity spills into the streets and gathers steam until nightfall, when it explodes with singing in the bars, dancing in the alleyways, spontaneous parades, and a no-holds-barred party in Pl. Castillo, which quickly becomes Europe's biggest open-air dance floor.

ARAGÓN

In the south, sun-baked towns give way to prosperous Zaragoza, while up north the stunning snow-capped peaks of the Pyrenees peer down on tiny medieval towns. The region's harsh terrain and climate, coupled with its strategic location, have produced a martial culture known among Spaniards for its obstinacy.

ZARAGOZA

Augustus founded Zaragoza (pop. 700,000) in 14 BC, modestly naming it Caesaraugusta after himself. The city gained everlasting fame when the Virgin Mary later dropped in for a visit; it's been a pilgrimage site ever since. The massive Baroque **Basílica de Nuestra Señora del Pilar** dominates the vast **Plaza del Pilar,** defining the skyline with brightly colored tiled domes. The interior is even more incredible, with frescoes by Goya and Velázquez. Don't leave without seeing the panoramic views from one of the towers; take the elevator in the corner, on the left as you face the

Museo del Pilar, which exhibits the glittering *Joyero de la Virgen* (Virgin's jewels). (Basilica open daily 5:45am-9:30pm; free. Museum open daily 9am-2pm and 4-6pm; 200ptas. Elevator runs June-Aug. Sa-Th 9:30am-2pm and 4-7pm; Sept.-May Sa-Th 9:30am-2pm and 4-6pm; 200ptas.) The ⬛**Palacio de la Aljafería,** on C. Castillo, is the principle relic of Aragón's Moorish era. Head left on C. Coso from Pl. España as you face the *casco viejo*, continue on Conde Aranda, and turn right on Pl. Maria Agustín, then left on C. Aliaferia. (Open mid-Apr. to mid-Oct. M-W and Sa 10am-2pm and 4:30-8pm, F 4:30-8pm, Su 10am-2pm; mid-Oct. to mid-Apr. closed Sa. 300ptas, students 150ptas.) The **Museo Pablo Gargallo,** on Pl. San Felipe, houses marvelous works by one of the most innovative sculptors of the 1920s. From Pl. España, walk down C. Don Jaime I, turn left on C. Menéndez Nuñez, and walk 5min. to the plaza. (Open Tu-Sa 10am-2pm and 5-9pm, Su 10am-2pm. Free.)

Trains (tel. 976 28 02 02) run from Av. Anselmo Clavé to Madrid (3hr., 8 per day, 3100-3800ptas); San Sebastián (4hr., 2 per day, 2800ptas); Barcelona (4hr., 7 per day, 3100-3800ptas); and Valencia (6hr., 2 per day, 2475-2580ptas). Agreda Automóvil **buses** (tel. 976 22 93 43) go from Po. María Agustín 7 to Barcelona (3½hr., 15-18 per day, 1640ptas) and Madrid (3½hr., 15-18 per day, 1740ptas). From the train station, cross Av. Anselmo Clavé, head down C. General Mayandía, turn right on Po. María Agustín (which becomes Po. Pamplona and leads to Pl. Paraíso), follow Po. Independencia from the plaza to Pl. de España, and continue on C. Don Jaime I (to the right) to reach **Pl. Pilar;** from the bus station, turn right as you exit and follow the same directions. The **tourist office** is on Pl. Pilar, in the black glass cube. (Tel. 972 20 12 00; fax 972 20 06 35. Open M-Sa 10am-8pm, Su 10am-2pm. Open M-Sa 11am-2:30pm and 4:30-8pm.) Take bus 22 from the train station to reach **Albergue-Residencia Juvenil Baltasar Gracián (HI),** C. Franco y Lopez 4. (Tel. 976 55 15 04. 1425ptas, under 27 1055ptas. Curfew midnight. Reserve ahead.) **Hostal Ambos Mundos** is on Pl. Pilar 16, at C. Don Jaime I. (Tel. 976 29 97 04; fax 976 29 97 02. Singles 2500ptas; doubles 4500ptas.) ⬛**Bar Los Amigos,** C. Mártires 8, off Pl. España, has tons of cheap sandwiches (250-475ptas). (Open daily noon-3pm and 7-11pm.) Get **groceries** at **Galerías Primero,** C. San Jorge the continuation of C. Merdeo Nuñez. (Open M-Sa 9am-2pm and 5-8:30pm.) **Postal code:** 50001.

BASQUE COUNTRY (PAÍS VASCO)

The varied landscape of Basque Country resembles a nation complete unto itself, combining cosmopolitan cities, verdant hills, industrial wastelands, and quaint fishing villages; many believe that the strongly nationalistic Basques are the native people of Iberia, as their culture and language date back several millennia. Although Castilian Spanish is the predominant language, Basque *euskera* has enjoyed a resurgence of popularity. Basque cuisine is some of Iberia's finest.

SAN SEBASTIÁN (DONOSTIA)

Surrounded by gorgeous mountains, coolly elegant San Sebastián (pop. 170,000) welcomes visitors with broad boulevards, garden avenues, ornate buildings, and radiant beaches. Locals and tourists alike down *pintxos* (tapas) and drinks in the *parte vieja* (old city), which claims the most bars per square meter in the world.

▐ GETTING THERE AND GETTING AROUND

Trains: RENFE, Estación del Norte (tel. 943 28 30 89), on Po. Francia, on the east side of Puente María Cristina. To: **Pamplona** (2hr., 2-12 per day, 1500ptas); **Zaragoza** (4hr., 5 per day, 2700-3900ptas); **Madrid** (8hr., 4 per day, 4600-4800ptas); **Paris** (8-11hr., 3 per day, 11,000ptas; change at Hendaye); and **Barcelona** (9hr., 1 per day, 4700-4900ptas).

Buses: Most buses pass through the central station on Pl. Pío XII, about 13 blocks south of Av. Libertad on Av. Sancho el Sabio. Bus 28 goes to the city center from the bus station. **PESA,** Av. Sancho el Sabio 33 (tel. 902 10 12 10), goes to **Bilbao** (1¼hr., every 30min., 1060-1200ptas). **Continental Auto,** Av. Sancho el Sabio 31 (tel. 943 46 90 74), serves **Madrid** (6hr., 3-17 per day, 3685-4000ptas). From Po. Vizcaya 16, **La Roncalesa** (tel. 943

46 10 64) runs to **Pamplona** (1hr., 7 per day, 780ptas) and **Vibarsa** (tel. 902 10 13 63) serves **Barcelona** (7hr., 3-5 per day, 2450-2600ptas). **Turytrans** (tel. 943 46 23 60) serves **Paris** (11 hr., 3-5 per week, 7600-8000ptas).

☑ ORIENTATION AND PRACTICAL INFORMATION

The city center and most beaches lie on a peninsula on the west side of the **Río Urumea** (river); at the tip, the **Monte Urgulla** juts out into the bay. Inland, nightlife rages and budget accommodations and restaurants cluster in the **parte vieja**. To the south, at the base of the peninsula, is the commercial area. From the bus station, head right (north) up Av. Sancho el Sabio toward the cathedral, ocean, and *parte vieja*. East of the river are the **RENFE station** and the **Playa de la Zurriola**. Head straight from the train station, cross the Puente María Cristina (bridge), head right at the fountain for four blocks, and then left on Av. Libertad to the port; the *parte vieja* will lie to your right and the **Playa de la Concha** to your left.

Tourist Office: Centro de Atracción y Turismo (tel. 943 48 11 66; fax 943 48 11 72), on C. Reina Regente, in the Teatro Victoria Eugenia in the *parte vieja*. From the train station, turn right immediately after crossing the Puente María Cristina and turn left on C. Reina Regente at the Puerte de Zurriola. From the bus station, go down Av. Sancho el Sabio, bear right at Pl. Centenario onto C. Prim, and follow Av. Libertad left to the end. Open June-Sept. M-Sa 8am-8pm, Su 10am-1pm; Oct.-May M-Sa 9am-2pm and 3:30-7pm.

Laundromat: Lavomatique, C. Iñigo 13, off C. San Juan. Wash 575ptas; dry 400ptas. Open M-F 10am-1pm and 4-7pm, Sa-Su 10am-1pm.

Emergency: Tel. 012. **Police: Municipal** (tel. 943 45 00 00), on C. Easo.

Medical Services: Casa de Socorro, C. Bengoetxea 4 (tel. 943 44 06 33).

Internet Access: Airtel, C. Euso 25. 150ptas per 15min. Open June-Aug. M-F 9:30am-1pm and 4-7:30pm, Sa 10am-1pm; Sept.-May Sa also 4-8pm.

Post Office: C. Urdaneta, the street just south of the cathedral. *Poste Restante* at window 11. Address mail to be held: Marya SPENCE, *Lista de Correos,* C. Urdaneta, **20006** San Sebastián, Spain. Open M-F 8:30am-8:30pm, Sa 9:30am-2pm.

▐ ACCOMMODATIONS AND CAMPING

Desperate backpackers will scrounge for rooms in July and August, particularly during *San Fermines* (July 6-14) and *Semana Grande* (starts the Sunday of the week of Aug. 15); September's film festival is not much better. Budget options center in the *parte vieja* and around the cathedral. Most hostel owners know of **casas particulares**—don't be afraid to ask for help.

PARTE VIEJA

▨ **Pensión Amaiur,** C. 31 de Agosto 44, 2nd fl. (tel. 943 42 96 54). From Alameda del Boulevard, go up C. San Jerónimo to the end and turn left. Simply great. June 22-Sept. doubles 5500ptas, triples 7500ptas; Apr.-June 21 and Oct. 4000ptas, 5200ptas; Nov.-Mar. 3300ptas, 4200ptas. *Let's Go* discount 300ptas. English and French spoken.

▨ **Pensión Loinaz,** C. San Lorenzo 17 (tel. 943 42 67 14), off C. San Juan. Bright rooms and big windows. July-Aug. doubles 4200-4700ptas, triples 6200ptas; Apr.-June 3200ptas, 4500ptas; Sept.-Apr. 2700ptas, 3800ptas. *Let's Go* discount 500ptas. Laundry.

Pensión San Lorenzo, C. San Lorenzo 2 (tel. 943 42 55 16), off C. San Juan. Cozy rooms. June-Oct. 1500-2000ptas per person. Nov.-May singles 1500ptas; doubles 2800ptas; triples 3900ptas; quads 5000ptas. Kitchen.

Pensión Boulevard, Alameda del Boulevard 24 (tel. 943 42 94 05). Beautiful, modern rooms, some with balconies. In summer 2000ptas per person. Off-season singles 2500ptas; doubles 3000-4500ptas; triples 4000ptas.

OUTSIDE THE PARTE VIEJA

Albergue Juvenil la Sirena (HI), Po. Igueldo 25 (tel. 943 31 02 68; fax 943 21 40 90), to the far west. Take bus 24 from the train or bus station to Av. Zumalacárregui (in front of the San Sebastián Hotel); then take Av. Brunet toward the mountain and turn left at the end. In summer 2200ptas, under 27 1950ptas; off-season 1950ptas, 1600ptas. HI and

SPAIN

ISIC members only. Breakfast included. Sheets 385ptas. Laundry. Kitchen. Lockout 11am-3pm. Curfew June-Aug. 2am; Sept.-May Su-Th midnight, F-Sa 2am. Visa.

Pensión Urkia, C. Urbieta 12, 3rd fl. (tel. 943 42 44 36). C. Urbieta runs west along the cathedral; it's 1 block north at C. Arrasate. Lovely linens, bath, and TV. July-Sept. doubles 5300ptas; Oct.-June singles 3000ptas, doubles 3745ptas.

Pensión La Perla, C. Loiola 10, 2nd fl. (tel. 943 42 81 23), on the street directly ahead of the cathedral. Attractive rooms with polished floors, bath, and TV. July-Sept. singles 4000ptas, doubles 6000ptas; Oct.-June singles 3225ptas, doubles 3750ptas.

Camping: Camping Igueldo (tel. 943 21 45 02), 5km west. Take bus 16 (dir: Barrio de Igueldo-Campin; 2 per hr., 110ptas) from Alameda del Boulevard. June-Aug. 2889ptas for tent and 2 people, 425ptas per additional person; Sept.-May 1386ptas, 357ptas. Reception June-Aug. 8am-midnight; Sept.-May 9am-1pm and 5-9pm.

◖ FOOD

Pintxos (tapas; rarely more than 175ptas each), chased down with the fizzy regional white wine *txacoli*, are a religion here; bars in the lively old city spread an array of enticing tidbits on toothpicks or bread. The entire *parte vieja* seems to exist for no other purpose than to feed. Your first stop should to sample the to-die-for delicacies at ■**Bar La Cepa,** C. 31 de Agosto 7-9. (*Pintxos* 160-325ptas. *Bocadillos* 425-750ptas. Open daily 1pm-midnight. V, MC, AmEx.) **Bar Intza,** C. Esterlines 12, also has tasty *bocadillos* (325-550ptas). (Open Su-Th 10am-4pm and 6:30-11:30pm, later F-Sa. Open July-Oct. 15 and Nov.-May 14.) **Bar Juantxo,** C. Embeltrán 6, is a local favorite famous for its sandwiches (285-495ptas)—they sell about 1000 a day. (Open daily 8:30am-midnight.) In the *parte nueva,* ■**Tenis Ondarreta,** on Po. Peine de los Vientos, is worth the walk and the extra buck (entrees 1300-1950ptas; open M-Sa 1-4pm and 9-11pm, Su 1-4pm), while **Caravanseri Café,** C. San Bartolomé 1, east of the cathedral, has veggie options and combo plates for 675-1300ptas. (Open M-Sa 8am-12:30am, Su 10am-midnight.) **Mercado de la Bretxa,** on Alameda del Boulevard at C. San Juan, sells fresh produce. (Both open M-F 7:30am-2pm and 5-7:30pm, Sa 7:30am-2pm.) **Super Todo Todo,** on Alameda del Boulevard, is around the corner corner from the tourist office. (Open M-Sa 8:30am-9pm, Su 10am-2pm.)

◖ ♫ SIGHTS AND ENTERTAINMENT

San Sebastián's most attractive sight is the city itself. The views from **Monte Igueldo,** west of the center, are the best in town: by day, the countryside meets the ocean in a line of white and blue, and by night the flood-lit **Isla Santa Clara** (island) seems to float on a ring of light. The walk up the mountain is not too strenuous, but the weary can take a funicular. Across the bay from Monte Igueldo, **Monte Urgull,** at the northern tip of the *parte vieja* jutting out into the bay, is crowned by the over-grown **Castillo de Santa Cruz de la Mota** (castle), in turn topped by the statue of the **Sagrado Corazón de Jesús.** (Open daily June-Aug. 8am-8pm; Sept.-May 8am-6pm.) Directly below the hill, on Po. Nuevo in the *parte vieja*, the serene **Museo de San Telmo** resides in a Dominican monastery and is strewn with Basque funerary relics, a montage of Basque artifacts, El Grecos, and dinosaur skeletons. (Open Tu-Sa 10:30am-1:30pm and 4-8pm, Su 10:30am-2pm. 350ptas, students 200ptas.) Just to the west, **Plaza Constitución** features the ornate portal of **Iglesia Santa María** and numbered balconies dating from the plaza's days as a bull ring. The gorgeous **Playa de la Concha** curves along the western shore of the city; the shore turns into the smaller and steeper **Playa de Ondarreta** beyond the **Palacio de Miramar.**

The five-day **Festival de Jazz** (tel. 943 48 11 79; www.jazzaldia.com), in mid- to late July, is one of Europe's most ambitious. Movie stars and directors own the streets for a week in September during the **Festival Internacional del Cine,** one of the most important in the world (along with Venice, Cannes, and Berlin). During **Semana Grande** (Big Week; week of August 15), the city is ablaze with concerts, movies, and an international fireworks festival. At any time of year, the *parte vieja* pulls out all the stops after dark. **C. Fermín Calbetón,** three blocks in from Alameda del Boulevard, sweats in a pool of bars. **Bar Tas-Tas,** C. Fermín Calbetón 35, attracts a gener-

WHAT THE DEVIL ARE THEY TXPEAKING?

Linguists still cannot pinpoint the origin of *euskera*, though its commonalities with Caucasian and African dialects suggest that prehistoric Basques may have migrated from the Caucasus via Africa. Referred to by other Spaniards as *la lengua del diablo* (the devil's tongue), *euskera* has come to symbolize cultural self-determination. Only half a million natives, mainly in País Vasco and northern Navarra, speak the language. Franco banned *euskera* and forbade giving children Basque names (like Iñaki or Estibaliz), but since his death there has been a resurgence of everything from *euskera* TV shows to *ikastolas* (Basque schools), making it a language of the old and the young.

ous helping of international backpackers. (Open daily 3pm-3am.) Music shakes the floor at **Bars Sariketa**, C. Fermín Calbetó 23. (Open daily 5:30pm-3:30am.) **Bataplán**, on Po. Concha along the beach, is a small but mighty disco where the music starts thumping at midnight (cover 2000ptas; includes 1 drink).

EXCURSION FROM SAN SEBASTIÁN: HONDARRIBIA

Refreshingly simple Hondarribia (pop. 14,000) flaunts a silky-smooth **beach** as well as a gorgeous stone-and-timber *casco antiguo*, centered around Carlos V's imposing **palace** in Pl. Armas, that provides welcome relief from Coppertone fumes. Six kilometers up Av. Monte Jaizkibel, **Monte Jaizkibel**, the highest mountain on the Costa Cantábrica, guards the **Santuario de Guadalupe** and offer incredible views of the coast. **Boats** leave from the end of C. Domingo Egia, off La Marina (every 15min., reduced off-season, 200ptas), for the **beach** town of Hendaye, France, 5km away. Interurbanos **buses** (tel. 943 64 13 02) arrive on C. Zuluaga from San Sebastián (45min., 4 per hr., 200ptas). The **tourist office**, C. Javier Ugarte 6, is in Pl. San Cristobál. (Tel. 943 64 54 58. Open July-Aug. daily 10am-8pm; Sept.-June M-F 9am-1:30pm and 4-6:30pm, Sa 10am-2pm.) To get from the bus stop to the modern **Albergue Juan Sebastián Elcano (HI)**, Ctra. Faro, head down C. Itsasargi, bear left at the beach, turn left at the rotary, and follow the signs uphill. (Tel. 943 64 15 50; fax 943 64 00 28. 1875ptas; under 31 1250ptas. Members only; HI cards 1000-1500ptas. Breakfast included. Sheets 115ptas. 3-night max. stay when full. Reception 9am-noon and 4-7pm. Curfew midnight; doors open briefly at 1 and 2am. Call ahead.) Several **markets** spill onto **C. San Pedro,** three blocks inland from the port.

BILBAO (BILBO)

Graced with the marvelous new Guggenheim Museum, Bilbao (pop. 1,000,000) is finally overcoming its reputation as a business-minded industrial center. Though the city may not win any beauty pageants, its medieval *casco viejo*, wide 19th-century boulevards lined by grandiose buildings, and stunning brand new subway and riverwalk make this up-and-coming city well worth a stop.

PRACTICAL INFO, ACCOMMODATIONS, AND FOOD. RENFE trains
(tel. 94 423 86 23) arrive at the **Estación de Abando**, Pl. Circular 2, from Salamanca (5½-6½hr., 2 per day, 3500ptas); Madrid (5¾-9hr., 2 per day, 4200-4400ptas); and Barcelona (9½-11hr., Su-F 2 per day, 5100ptas). From Pl. Circular, head right around the station and cross the Puente del Arenal (bridge) to reach Pl. Arriaga, the entrance to the *casco viejo*. Most **bus companies** leave from the **Termibús terminal,** C. Gurtubay 1 (tel. 94 439 50 77; M: San Mamés), on the west side of town, for San Sebastián (1hr., 8-23 per day, 1100ptas); Pamplona (2hr., 4-6 per day, 1560ptas); Zaragoza (4hr., 4-6 per day, 2430ptas); and Salamanca (5hr., 1-2 per day, 3200ptas). To get there, take the metro to "Casco Viejo," exit onto Pl. Unamuno, take a right on C. Sombreria, and turn right on C. Correo. **ANSA (GETSA, VIACAR)** buses leave from C. Autonomía 17 (tel. 94 444 31 00) for Burgos (2hr., 4 per day, 1435ptas); Madrid (4-5hr., 9-15 per day, 3270ptas); and Barcelona (7hr. 3-4 per day, 4900ptas). To get there from the station, go left as you exit down C. Hurtado de Amézaga, and bear right at Pl. Zabálburu onto C. Autonomía. To reach the **tourist office**, on Pl. Arenal,

turn left after crossing the bridge from the train station. (Tel. 94 479 57 60; fax 94 479 57 61; www.bilbao.net. Open M-F 9am-2pm and 4-7:30pm, Sa 9am-2pm, Su 10am-2pm.) **Cybercafé Antxi,** C. Luis Briñas 13, is near the Termibús terminal. (300ptas per 30min. Open M-F 11am-1:30pm and 4-10:30pm.)

After crossing the Puente del Arenal toward the *casco viejo,* turn right on C. Ribera and left on C. Santa María to reach **Pensión Mendez** at #13, 4th fl. (Tel. 94 416 03 64. Singles 3000-5000ptas; doubles 4000-7000ptas; triples 6000-9000ptas.) To get from Pl. Arriaga to **Pensión Ladero,** C. Lotería 1, 4th fl., take C. Bidebarrieta and turn left onto C. Lotería. (Tel. 94 415 09 32. Singles 2500ptas; doubles 4000ptas.) **Mercado de la Ribera,** on the bank of the river as you head left from the tourist office, is the biggest indoor market in Spain. (Open mid-June to mid-Sept. M-Sa 8am-2pm; mid-Sept. to mid-June M-F 8am-2pm and 4:30-7pm, Sa 8am-2pm.) Pick up **groceries** at the massive **Simago,** Pl. Santos Juanes. (Open M-Sa 9am-9pm.) **Postal code:** 48005.

SIGHTS AND ENTERTAINMENT. Frank O. Gehry's **Guggenheim Museum Bilbao,** Av. Abandoibarra 2, can only be described as breathtaking. Lauded in the international press with every superlative imaginable, it has catapulted Bilbao straight into cultural stardom. The US$100 million building's undulating curves of glistening titanium, limestone, and glass are an absolute must-see. The museum currently hosts rotating exhibits drawn from the Guggenheim Foundation's collection. From Pl. Circular, head down Gran Vía, right across Pl. de Frederico Moyúo, and down Alameda de Recalde. (Tel. 94 435 90 80; www.guggenheim.org/bilbao.html. Open Tu-Su 10am-8pm. 800ptas, students 400ptas. Joint admission with Museo de Bellas Artes 900ptas.) From the Guggenheim, follow the Alameda de Mazarredo to the often overshadowed **Museo de Bellas Artes,** Pl. Museo 2, which hoards an impressive collection of 12th- to 20th-century art. (Open Tu-Sa 10am-8:30pm, Su 10am-2pm. 400ptas, students 200ptas; W free.)

Revelers in the *casco viejo* spill out into the streets, especially on **C. Barrencalle** (Barrenkale). Teenagers and twentysomethings also jam at **C. Licenciado Poza** on the west side of town. For a mellower scene, people-watch at the elegant 19th-century **Café Boulevard,** C. Arenal 3. (Open daily 12:15-1:30 and 7-11pm.) The massive blowout *fiesta* is **Semana Grande,** nine days beginning the weekend after Aug. 15.

EXCURSION FROM BILBAO: GUERNICA (GERNIKA). On April 27, 1937, the Nazi "Condor Legion" released an estimated 29,000kg of explosives on Guernica, obliterating 70% of a city in three hours. The nearly 2000 people who were killed in the bombings were immortalized in Pablo Picasso's stark masterpiece *Guernica,* now in Madrid's Reina Sofía gallery (see p. 807). The eerily modern city today offers little attraction aside from the **Gernika Museoa,** Foru Plaza 1, which features a moving exhibition chronicling the bombardment (open July-Aug. daily 10am-7pm; Sept.-June M-Sa 10am-2pm and 4-7pm, Su 10am-2pm), and the 2000-year-old **El Arbol** (tree), the emotional focus of the city, but it's a good daytrip for those interested in learning more about this infamous event (and seeing the ramifications it caused). **Trains** (tel. 94 625 11 82) roll in from Bilbao (45min., 315ptas).

BALEARIC ISLANDS

Every year, discos, ancient history, and beaches—especially beaches—draw nearly 2 million of the hippest Europeans to the *Islas Baleares,* 100km off the east coast of Spain. **Mallorca,** home to Palma, the islands' capital, absorbs the bulk of invaders who come to explore their limestone cliffs, orchards, and clear turquoise waters. **Ibiza,** a counter-culture haven since the 1960s, boasts an active gay community; its capital Eivissa offers what many consider the best nightlife in all of Europe. The smaller, less-touristed islands such as **Menorca** offer empty white beaches, hidden coves, and mysterious Bronze Age megaliths.

GETTING THERE AND GETTING AROUND

Flights to the islands, fast and cheap, are the easiest way to get there. Those under 26 often get discounts from **Iberia/Aviaco Airlines** (Barcelona tel. 902 40 05 00;

www.iberia.com), which flies to **Palma de Mallorca** and **Ibiza** from **Madrid** (1hr., students round-trip 25-30,000ptas); **Barcelona** (40min., students round-trip 10-20,000ptas); and **Valencia. Air Europa** (tel. 902 24 00 42) and **SpanAir** (tel. 902 13 14 15; www.spanair.com) offer budget flights to and between the islands. Most cheap round-trip **charters** include a week's stay in a hotel; some companies called *mayoristas* sell "seat-only" deals. **Ferries** to the islands serve as a secondary mode of transport. **Trasmediterránea** (tel. 902 45 46 45; www.trasmediterranea.com) departs from **Barcelona's** Estació Marítima Moll and **Valencia's** Estació Marítima for **Mallorca** and **Ibiza. Buquebus** (tel. 902 41 42 42 or 93 481 73 60; email reservas@buquebus.es) goes from **Barcelona** to **Palma** (4hr., 2 per day, 8150ptas). Book airline or ferry tickets through a travel agency in Barcelona, Valencia, or on the islands.

Within the islands, **ferries** are the most cost-efficient; they run from **Palma** to **Mahón** (6½hr., Su, 3045ptas) and **Ibiza** (2½-4½hr., 6 per week, 3330-5210ptas). **Iberia** flies from **Palma** to **Ibiza** (35min., 4 per day, 8900ptas) and **Mahón, Menorca** (35min., 4 per day, 8900ptas). All three major islands have good **bus** systems. A day's **car** rental costs around 4500ptas, **mopeds** 2700ptas per day, and **bikes** 1000ptas per day.

MALLORCA

Mallorca believes in a simple equation—more hotels + more tourists = more money. Yet amid the tourism, lemon groves and olive trees adorn the jagged cliffs of the north coast, and lazy, calm bays and caves scoop into the rest of the coast. The capital of the Balearics, **Palma** (pop. 323,000) does not shy from conspicuous consumption, but it still manages to please with its well-preserved old quarter and local flavor. The tourist office distributes a list of over 40 nearby **beaches,** many a mere bus ride from Palma; one popular choice is **El Arenal** (Platja de Palma; bus 15), 11km southeast (toward the airport). After sunning, many head to the streets around **Pl. Reina** and **La Llotja** to imbibe. **ABACO,** C. Sant Joan 1, in the Barri Gòtic near the waterfront, is the perfect place for a cocktail. (Drinks 1900-2100ptas. Open daily 9pm-2:30am.) Every Friday, the newspaper *El Día de Mundo* (125ptas) lists bars and discos. Clubbers boogie on the beaches and near **El Terreno**—a mother lode of clubs centers on **Pl. Gomila** and along **C. Joan Miró. Baccus,** around the corner on C. Lluis Fábregas 2, draws gay and lesbian hedonists until 3am. **BCM** in nearby **Magaluf** is supposedly the biggest club in Europe. (Last Playa-Sol bus 8pm. Taxi 1800ptas. Cover 2000-2500ptas. Open daily 11pm-6am.)

To get from the airport to the center, take bus 17 to **Pl. d'Espanya** (15min., every 20min., 295ptas). To continue to the **tourist office,** C. Sant Dominic 11, follow Pg. Marítim (a.k.a. Av. Juan Roca) to Av. Antoni Maura, follow C. Conquistador out of Pl. de la Reina, and continue on C. Sant Dominic. (Tel. 971 71 15 27. Open M-F 9am-8pm, Sa 9am-1:30pm.) **Branches** are in Pl. Espanya, Pl. Reina, and the airport. **Hostal Apuntadores,** C. Apuntadores 8, is in the middle of the action, less than a block from Pl. Reina. (Tel. 971 71 34 91; email apuntadores@jet.es. Singles 2400-2700ptas; doubles 3900-4700ptas.) From the port, go left on Av. Gabriel Roca and turn right on C. Argentina to reach **Hostal Cuba,** C. San Magí 1. (Tel. 971 73 81 59. Singles 2000ptas; doubles 4000ptas.) Take bus 15 from Pl. Espanya (every 8min., 175ptas) and ask to get off at Hotel Acapulco to reach the pristine and palatial **Alberg Platja de Palma (HI),** C. Costa Brava 13. (Tel. 971 26 08 92. 1500ptas; members only. Sheets 200ptas. Breakfast included. Laundry. Reception 8am-3am. Curfew Su-Th midnight, F-Sa 3am.) **Camp** at **Platja Blava,** at km 8 on the highway between Alcúdia and C'an Picafort. Take Autocares Mallorca from Pl. Espanya (2 per day, 575ptas). (Tel. 971 53 78 63. 475-575ptas per person; 1300-1530ptas per site.) **Servicio y Precios,** on C. Felip Bauzà, near Pl. Reina, has **groceries.** (Open M-F 8:30am-8:30pm, Sa 9am-2pm.)

The west coast of the Mallorca is one of the most beautiful landscapes in the Mediterranean. In **Puerto de Sóller,** a pebble and sand beach lines the small bay, where windsurfers zip back and forth. **Hotel Miramar** is at C. Marina 12. (Tel. 971 63 13 50. Singles 4900ptas; doubles 5150ptas; triples 7600ptas.) Nord Balear **buses** link Puerto de Sóller to Palma via Valldemossa (2hr., 5 per day, 450ptas).

MENORCA

Menorca's (pop. 69,000) raw beaches, rustic landscape, and well-preserved ancient monuments draw ecologists, sun worshippers, and photographers alike. Perched atop a steep bluff, **Mahón** (Maó; pop. 23,300) is the main gateway to the island. From the **airport,** take a taxi (1100ptas) to downtown Mahón. From the **ferry station,** walk left (with your back to the water) for 150m, turn right at the steps, take Portal de Mar to Costa de Sa, which becomes C. Hannover and then C. Ses Moreres, and continue straight ahead to the **tourist office,** Pl. s'Esplanada 40. (Tel. 971 36 37 90; fax 971 36 74 15; www.menorca.com. Open M-F 8:30am-7:30pm, Sa 9am-2pm.) To get to **Hostal La Isla,** C. Santa Catalina 4, take C. Concepció from Pl. Miranda. (Tel. 971 36 64 92. Singles 2300ptas; doubles 5000ptas. Visa.) To reach the sunny **Hostal Orsi,** C. Infanta 19, from Pl. s'Esplanada, take C. Ses Moreres, which becomes C. Hannover, turn right at Pl. Constitució, and follow C. Nou through Pl. Reial. (Tel. 971 36 47 51. Singles 2500ptas; doubles 4400-5000ptas; add 7% IVA. Breakfast included. V, MC.)

The more popular **beaches** outside Mahón are accessible by bus (under 30min., 50-250ptas); many of the best beaches require a vehicle, but are worth the extra hassle. Autocares Fornells **buses** (6 per day) leave C. Vasallo in Mahón for sandy **Arenal d'en Castell,** while TMSA buses (6 per day) go to touristy **Calean Porter.** Take a Transportes Menorca bus from Mahón (6 per day) for the gorgeous beaches surrounding **Son Bou.** To explore the island's flora and fauna, head to **Es Grau** via Autocares Fornells bus (3 per day) from C. Vasallo in Mahón. At **Cala Bosch,** jagged cliffs plummet into pale-blue water; take Torres bus (18 per day) from Ciutadella.

Ciutadella (Ciudadela; pop. 21,200), the other main town on Menorca, combines colorful stucco and medieval cobblestone with a tranquility that eludes Mahón, but you'll pay for it. Transportes Menorca (TMSA) **buses** shuttle between Mahón and Ciutadella (55min., 6 per day, 550ptas). The **tourist office** is at Pl. Catedral 3. (Tel. 971 38 26 93. Open M-F 8am-3pm and 4:30-8pm, Sa 10am-2pm.) **Hotel Geminis** is at C. Josepa Rossinyol 4; take C. Sud off Av. Capital Negrete (as you approach from Pl. s'Esplanada) and turn left on C. Josepa Rossinyol. (Tel. 971 38 58 96; fax 971 38 36 83. Singles 3700ptas; doubles 7500ptas. Breakfast included. Reserve early for Aug.)

IBIZA

A hippie enclave since the 60s, Ibiza's (pop. 84,000) summer camp for disco fiends and high fashion victims evokes a sense of new-age decadence. Although a thriving gay community still lends credence to its image as a "tolerant" center, the island's high price tags preclude true diversity. Oh, and Ibiza has **beaches,** too. **Eivissa** (Ibiza City) is the world's biggest 24-hour party; the show begins at sunset. Wrapped in 16th-century walls, **Dalt Vila** (High Town) hosts 20th-century urban bustle in the city's oldest buildings. Its twisting, sloping streets lead up to the 14th-century **cathedral** and superb views of the city and ocean. No beach is within quick walking distance, but **Platja de Talamanca, Platja des Duros, Platja d'en Bossa,** and **Platja Figueredes** are at most 20min. away by bike; buses also leave from Av. Isidor Macabich 20 for Platja d'en Bossa (every 30min., 125ptas). The real fun begins when the sun goes down. **Calle Virgen** is the center of gay nightlife. The island's **discos** (virtually all of which have a mixed gay/straight crowd) are world-famous and ever-changing. There is something different going every day—see *Ministry in Ibiza* or *Party Sun,* free at many hostels, bars, and restaurants. The **Discobus** runs to and from all the major hotspots (runs midnight-6:30am, 250ptas). Wild, wild **Privilege** is best known for M night "manumission" parties. (Cover from 4000ptas; includes 1 drink. Open June-Sept. M and W-Sa midnight-7am.) At **Amnesia,** on the road to San Antonio, you can forget who you are, where you're from, and who you came with at what may just be the craziest disco scene ever. (Cream parties Th; foam parties W and Su. Cover 4000-7000ptas. Open daily midnight-6am.) Both lie on the discobus route to San Antonio. Playful **Pachá,** on Pg. Perimitral, is 20min. from the port. (Cover 5000ptas; includes 1 drink. Open daily 11:15pm-7:30am.) Cap off your night with a dancing morning in **Space,** Platja de Bossa (open daily 7am-4pm), then cruise across to **Bora Bora,** on Platja de Bossa, which catches the crowd around 4pm.

The local paper *Diario de Ibiza* (www.diariodeibiza.es; 125ptas) features an *Agenda* page with everything you need to know about Ibiza. The **tourist office,** C. Antoni Riquer 2, is on the water. (Tel. 971 30 19 00; www.ibizaonline.com. Open M-F 9:30am-1:30pm and 5-7pm, Sa 10:30am-1pm.) Cheap accommodations in town are rare. The letters "CH" *(casa de huespedes)* mark many doorways; call the owners at the phone number on the door. **Hostal Residencia Sol y Brisa** is at Av. B. V. Ramón 15, parallel to Pg. Vara de Rey. (Tel. 971 31 08 18; fax 971 30 30 32. Singles 3000ptas; doubles 5000ptas.) **Hostal Residencia Ripoll** is at C. Vicente Cuervo 14. (Tel. 971 31 42 75. July-Sept. singles 3500ptas; doubles 5500ptas.) For a **supermarket,** try **Comestibles Tony,** Carrer d'Enmig 1. (Open daily 9am-2pm and 5-8pm.)

NORTHWESTERN SPAIN

Northwestern Spain is the least-visited part of the country; it's seclusion is half its charm. Rainy **Galicia** hides mysterious Celtic ruins, left when the Celts made a pit stop on its quiet beaches along the west coast. Tiny **Asturias** is tucked on the northern coast, allowing access to its dramatic Picos de Europa.

GALICIA (GALIZA)

If, as the old Galician saying goes, "rain is art," then there is no gallery more beautiful than the misty skies of northwestern Spain. Often veiled in a silvery drizzle, it is a province of fern-laden eucalyptus woods, slate-roofed fishing villages, and seemingly endless white beaches. Galicians speak *gallego,* a linguistic missing link of sorts between Castilian and Portuguese.

SANTIAGO DE COMPOSTELA

Ever since the remains of the Apostle St. James were discovered here in AD 813, Santiago has drawn pilgrims eager to bask in the beauty of one of Christianity's holiest cities. The cathedral marks the end of the *Camino del Santiago,* a 900-kilometer pilgrimage believed to halve one's time in purgatory. Today, sunburnt pilgrims, street musicians, and hordes of tourists fill Santiago's granite streets, as the city relishes its year as one of the designated Cultural Capitals of Europe for 2000.

🔲🗓🖰 PRACTICAL INFO, ACCOMMODATIONS AND FOOD. Trains (tel. 981 52 02 02) go from Itòrreo, in the southern end of the city, to León (6½hr., 2 per day, 3500ptas) and Madrid (8hr., 3 per day, 5700ptas). From the station, cross the street, bear right at the top of the stairs, take C. Hórreo to Pr. Galicia *(don't* take Av. Lugo), and go one more block to C. Bautizatos, from which **Rúa do Franco** (C. Franco), **Rúa do Vilar** (C. Vilar), and **Rúa Nova** (C. Nueva) lead to the cathedral at the city center. **Buses** (tel. 981 58 77 00) run from C. San Cayetano (30min. from downtown) to San Sebastián (6hr., 2 per day, 6910ptas); Madrid (8-9hr., 3 per day, 5040ptas); and Bilbao (9½hr., 4 per day, 6300ptas). From the station, take bus 10 or bus C Circular to reach Pr. Galicia (90ptas). The **tourist office** is on C. Vilar. (Tel. 981 58 44 00. Open M-F 10am-2pm and 4-7pm, Sa 11am-2pm and 5-7pm, Su 11am-2pm.) Check your **email** at **Nova 50,** R. Nova 50. (200ptas per hr. Open daily 9am-midnight.)

Hostels and *pensiones* cluster around **C. Vilar** and **C. Raíña** (between C. Vilar and C. Franco). **🔳Hospedaje Ramos,** C. Raíña 18, 2nd fl., above O Papa Una restaurant, is super-cozy. (Tel. 981 58 18 59. Singles 1800-2000ptas; doubles 3300-3600ptas.) From Pr. Galicia, turn right on C. Fonte San Antonio and left up the granite street to reach **Hospedaje Itatti,** Pr. Mazarelos 1. (Tel. 981 58 06 29. Singles 2000-3000ptas, doubles 3500-5000ptas. V, MC.) **Hospedaje Santa Cruz,** is at C. Vilar 42, 2nd fl. (Tel. 981 58 28 15. Singles June-Sept. 3500ptas, Oct.-May 1500ptas; doubles 4000ptas, 3000ptas.) Take bus 6 or 9 to get to **Camping As Cancelas,** C. 25 de Xullo 35, 2km from the cathedral on the northern edge of town. (Tel. 981 58 02 66. 550ptas per person, per car, and per tent.) Bars and cafeterias line old town streets, offering a variety of remarkably inexpensive *menús;* most restaurants are on R. Vilar, R. Franco, and C. Raíña. **Supermercados Lorenzo Froiz,** Pr. Toural, is one block into the old city from Pr. Galicia (open M-Sa 9am-3pm and 5-9pm). **Postal code:** 15701.

THESE BOOTS WERE MADE FOR WALKING

One night in AD 813, a hermit trudged through the hills on the way to his hermitage. Suddenly, miraculously, bright visions revealed the long-forgotten tomb of the Apostle James ("Santiago" in Spanish). Around this *campus stellae* (field of stars) the cathedral of Santiago de Compostela was built, and around this cathedral a world-famous pilgrimage was born. Since the 12th century, thousands of pilgrims have traveled the 900km of the **Camino de Santiago.** Clever Benedictine monks built monasteries to host *peregrinos* (pilgrims) along the *camino,* helping to make Santiago's cathedral the most frequented Christian shrine in the world. The scallop-edged conch shell, used for dipping in streams along the way, has become a symbol of the Camino de Santiago; the shells, tied onto weathered backpacks, make pilgrims easy to spot, as do crook-necked walking sticks and sunburned faces. Pilgrims must cover 100km on foot or horse or 200km on bike to receive *La Compostela,* a certificate of completion issued by the cathedral. Shelters along the way offer free lodging to pilgrims and stamp "pilgrims' passports" to prove that they were there. At 30km per day, walking the entire *camino* takes about a month. For inspiration along the way, keep in mind that you are joining the ranks of such illustrious pilgrims as Fernando and Isabel, Francis of Assisi, Pope John Paul II, and Shirley MacLaine. For more info, contact the **Officinal de Acogida del Peregrino,** C. Vilar 1 (tel. 981 56 24 19).

🖼 🏮 **SIGHTS AND ENTERTAINMENT.** Offering a cool, quiet sanctuary to priest, pilgrim, and tourist alike, Santiago's **cathedral** rises above lively old city center. Each of its four façades is a masterpiece from a different time period, and entrances open up onto four different plazas: Platerías, Quintana, Obradoiro, and Azabaxería. The southern **Praza de Platerías** is the oldest of the four façades; the 18th-century Baroque **Obradoiro** façade encases the Maestro Mateo's **Pórtico de la Gloria,** considered the crowning achievement of Spanish Romanesque sculpture. The revered remains of **St. James** lie beneath the high altar in a silver coffer. Inside the **museum** are gorgeous 16th-century tapestries and two poignant statues of the pregnant Virgin Mary. (Cathedral open daily 7am-9pm. Museum open June-Sept. M-Sa 10am-1:30pm and 4-7:30pm, Su and holidays 10am-1:30pm and 4-7pm; Oct.-May M-Sa 11am-1pm and 4-6pm, Su and holidays 10am-1:30pm and 4-7pm. 500ptas.) Those curious about the Camino de Santiago can head to the **Museo das Peregrinacións,** Pl. San Miguel. (Open Tu-F 10am-8pm, Sa 10:30am-1:30pm and 5-8pm, Su 10:30am-1:30pm. 400ptas, students 200ptas.)

At night, crowds looking for post-pilgrimage consumption flood cellars throughout the city. To boogie with local students, hit the bars and clubs off **Pl. Roxa** (take C. Montevo Ríos). **Casa das Crechas,** Vía Sacra 3, just off Pl. Quintana, pumps Guinness. Go dancin' at ultra-hip **Casting Araguaney,** C. Montevo Ríos 25-2, a few blocks off Pl. Galicia, in Hotel Araguaney. (Cover 500ptas. Open W-Sa 1am-6am.)

🏞 **EXCURSION FROM SANTIAGO: O CASTRO DE BAROÑA.** Nineteen kilometers south of the town of **Noya** is a little-known treasure of historical intrigue and mesmerizing natural beauty: the seaside remains of the 5th-century Celtic fortress 🖼**O Castro de Baroña.** The foundations dot the isthmus, ascending to a rocky promontory above the sea and then descending down to a crescent beach. Castromil **buses** from Santiago to Muros stop in Noya (1hr., every hr., 630ptas); Hefsel **buses** from Noya to Riveira in turn stop at O Castro—tell the driver your destination (30min., 250ptas).

RÍAS ALTAS

If Galicia is the forgotten corner of Spain, then the small *rías* of the Costa de la Muerte are the forgotten corner of Galicia. However, the beaches here are arguably the emptiest, cleanest, and loveliest in all of Spain.

LA CORUÑA (A CORUÑA). While the newer parts of La Coruña are mundane, recent massive efforts have cleaned up its *ciudad vieja* (old city) and pleasant **beaches.** Hercules allegedly erected the 2nd-century **Torre de Hércules,** now the world's oldest working lighthouse, upon the remains of an unfortunate enemy; you can climb a 237-step tunnel to the pinnacle. Take the path from the Orzán and Riazor beaches, or bus 9 or 13 (110ptas). (Open daily July-Sept. 10am-7pm; Oct.-June 10am-6pm. 250ptas.) **Trains** (tel 981 15 02 02) go from Pr. San Cristóbal to Santiago de Compostela (1hr., 19 per day, 505-635ptas) and Madrid (11hr., 1-3 per day, 5500-8700ptas). **Buses** (tel. 981 23 96 44) go from C. Caballeros, across Av. Alcalde Molina from the train station, to Santiago (1½hr., 17 per day, 800ptas); Oviedo (5hr., 4 per day, 3060ptas); and Madrid (8½hr., 6 per day, 4890-6975ptas). From the bus station, take bus 1 or 1A (110ptas) to the **tourist office**, on Dársena de la Marina. (Tel. 981 22 18 22. Open M-F 9am-2pm and 4:30-6:30pm, Sa 9am-2pm and 5-7pm, Su 10am-2pm and 5-7pm.) ◪**Hospedaje María Pita**, C. Riego de Agua 38, 3rd fl, has a homey feel. (Tel. 981 22 11 87. Doubles 2900-3210ptas.) For **groceries**, go to **Supermercados Claudio.** (Open daily 9am-3pm and 5-9pm.)

RÍAS DE CEDEIRA AND VIVERO. Where the average tourist seldom treads, ferncovered rainforests give way to soft, empty beaches. Thick mists veil the valleys of these northernmost *rías*. Seaside **Vivero's** (pop. 14,000) tiny old city huddles at the forest's edge. The nearest beach is in the resort town of **Covas,** 1km across the river; **Playa de Area** suns itself 4km away. IASA **buses** (tel. 981 56 01 03), run to El Ferrol (2hr., 6 per day, 985ptas) and La Coruña (4hr., 5 per day, 6:30am-7:30am, 1635ptas). Vivero's **tourist office** is on Av. Ramón Canosa. (Tel. 982 56 08 79. Open daily 11am-2pm and 5:30-8:30pm.) **Fonda Bossanova,** Av. Galicia 11, is one block from the bus station toward Covas. (Tel. 982 56 01 50. Singles 2000ptas; doubles 2500ptas.)

Small **Cedeira** (pop. 8500) offers pretty beaches and breathtaking scenery. The **Santuario de San Andrés de Teixido** (a steep 12km hike from town), which still hosts pagan cults with thriving rituals, overlooks the sea from 620m. **Bus** service is fairly sparse; RIALSA runs from Cedeira to El Ferrol (1hr., 7 per day, 490ptas), where other buses connect to La Coruña. To get to Vivero, take an IASA bus from C. Ezequiel Lopez 28 to Campo do Hospital (15min., 5 per day, 120ptas), then change to the Campo do Hospital-Vivero IASA bus line. Get off at the second bus stop in Cedeira for the **tourist office,** C. Ezequiel Lopez 22. (Tel. 981 48 21 87. Open July-Aug. M-Sa 10:30am-2pm and 6-9pm, Su noon-2pm; May-June and Sept. M-Sa 10:30am-2pm and 5-8pm, Su noon-2pm.) **Hostal Chelsea,** Pr. Sagrado Corazón 9, is around the corner from the first bus stop. (Tel. 981 48 23 40. Doubles 4000-4500ptas.)

ASTURIAS

Seething cliffs and hell-reaching ravines lend an epic scope to the tiny land of Asturias, tucked between Basque Country and Galicia.

PICOS DE EUROPA

God bless tectonic folding and contracting—three hundred million years ago, 'twas a mere flapping of Mother Nature's limestone bedsheet that erected the Picos de Europa, a mountain range of curious variation and chaotic beauty. Most of the area has been granted environmental protection as the **Picos de Europa National Park,** a rugged playpen for mountaineers, trekkers, and idle admirers alike. Near the **Cares Gorge** (Garganta del Cares) lie the park's most popular trails and most famous peaks. For a list of mountain **refugios** (typically cabins with bunks but not blankets) and general information on the park, contact the **Picos de Europa National Park Visitors Center** (tel. 985 84 86 14).

OVIEDO. Though Oviedo (pop. 200,000), the area's capital and transport hub, isn't necessarily the prettiest city in Spain, it provides an excellent base for exploring the mountains. ALSA **buses** (tel. 985 28 12 00) arrive in Pl. Primo de Rivera from León (2hr., 8 per day, 1010ptas); Burgos (4hr., 2 per day, 1645ptas); Madrid (6hr., 15 per day, 3740-6000ptas); and Santiago de Compostela (8hr., 3 per day, 3630ptas). C. Fray Ceferino leads from the other side of the plaza to C. Uría, where RENFE **trains** (tel. 985 24 33 64) arrive from León (2½hr., 8 per day, 925-1600ptas) and Madrid (6½-8hr., 3 per day, 4500-5800ptas). Walking down C. Uría with the station behind you, the old city is to the left; its two main plazas are **Pl. Mayor** and **Pl. de Alfonso II,** known to locals as Pl. de la Catedral and to tourists as Pl. de la **Tourist Office.** (Tel. 985 21 33 85. Open M-F 9:30am-1:30pm and 4:30-6:30pm, Sa 9am-2pm.) To get to **Residencia Juvenil Ramón Menéndez Pidal,** C. Julián Clavería 14, just off Pl. Toros, take bus 2 from C. Uría. (Tel. 985 23 20 54. 1000ptas, under 27 750ptas.) Near the cathedral are **Pensión Pomar,** C. Jovellanos 7 (tel. 985 22 27 91), and **Pensión Martinez,** C. Jovellanos 5 (tel. 985 21 53 44). (Singles 1500-2000ptas; doubles 3000-3500ptas; triples 3000-4500ptas.) Feed the big, bad wolf in you at ■**Mesón Luferca,** a.k.a. **La Casa Real del Jamón,** C. Covadonga 20—you may never have seen so many pig parts. (Open M-Sa 8:30am-midnight.) Grab **groceries** at **El Corte Inglés,** on C. General Alorza, opposite the bus station. (Open M-Sa 10am-9:30pm.)

▲ HIKING AND TREKKING. Before setting out for the mountains, load up on **maps** and other info in Oviedo. **TIVE,** C. Calvo Sotelo 5, is a budget travel agency with info on hiking and excursions. (Tel. 985 23 60 58. Open M-F 8am-3pm.) **ICONA,** C. Arquitecto Reguera 13, 2nd fl. (tel. 985 24 14 12), has trail and camping info. The **Dirección Regional de Deportes,** on Pl. España (tel. 985 27 23 47), handles referrals for outdoor sports and mountaineering. ALSA **buses** also run to from Oviedo to several other good bases from which to explore the mountains, including **Cangas de Onís** (1¼hr., 685ptas) and **Covadonga** (1¾hr., 785ptas).

SWEDEN (SVERIGE)

US$1 = 8.16KR (SWEDISH KRONOR)	1KR = US$0.12
CDN$1 = 5.52KR	1KR = CDN$0.18
UK£1= 13.33KR	1KR = UK£0.08
IR£1 = 10.93KR	1KR = IR£0.08
AUS$1 = 5.31KR	1KR = AUS$0.19
NZ$1 = 4.36KR	1KR = NZ$0.23
SAR1 = 1.34KR	1KR = SAR0.74
EUR€1 = 8.61KR	1KR = EUR€0.12

PHONE CODE Country code: 46. International dialing prefix: 009.

When the celebrated Swedish entertainer Jonas Gardell named his last hit show *På besök i Mellanmjölks Land* (On Tour in the Land of 2% Milk), he was poking fun at the Swedish concept of *lagom* (moderation). The idea implies that life should be lived somewhere between wealth and poverty, ecstasy and depression, whole milk and skim. The reputation of the *lagom* Swede results in both the complaint that Swedes are sober, boring, unemotional folk and praise for Volvo's sleek designs and Swedes' skill in international conflict resolution. Yet Sweden is, in fact, a country of dramatic extremes: even the Scandinavian weather silently defies the *lagom* stereotype; while the summer sun never sets, it seems to disappear almost entirely in the winter. Over 2400km long, Sweden stretches from the mountainous Arctic reaches of Kiruna down to the flat, temperate farmland and white-sand beaches of Skåne and Småland in the south. Dalarna, Värmland, and Norrland counties evoke images of quiet woods, folk music, and rustic country Midsummer celebration, while the capital city of Stockholm shines as a thoroughly cosmopolitan center.

The contrast of natural and geographical extremes is also in Sweden's social, political, and cultural landscape. Sweden's mythic early history of violent Viking conflict and conquest has given way to a successful experiment with egalitarian socialism and a succession of international peacekeepers: Alfred Nobel established his prizes for peaceful contributions to humanity; Raoul Wallenberg clambered over the roofs of Nazi trains to hand out Swedish passports that saved thousands of Jews from concentration camps; UN Secretary General Dag Hammarskjöld was awarded the Nobel Peace Prize posthumously; and late Prime Minister Olof Palme marched against the Vietnam War, sheltered American draft resisters, and was later assassinated for his peace efforts. Culturally, Sweden is oft thought of as the land of fiddlers and hurdy-gurdy accordions, but film director Ingmar Berman and playwright August Strindberg gained fame for their dark sophistication, and Lasse Hallström's films, like *My Life as a Dog*, reveal the wide range of Swedish humor.

DISCOVER SWEDEN

The natural starting point for any tour of Sweden is vibrant **Stockholm,** arguably one of the most attractive capitals in Europe. Gamla Stan, the city's medieval core, has not only the usual old-town winding, cobblestoned, and catacombed streets, but the stunning Royal Palace to boot (see p. 869). Don't forget a daytrip to the similarly mind-numbing **Drottingholm Palace,** home to the Swedish royal family (see p. 876). After at least two days in Stockholm, head to student country in **Uppsala,** the alleged site of early pagan activity, today just the site of shady activities on the part of its 20,000 students (see p. 882). On the western coast, Sweden's second-largest city, **Gothenburg,** counterbalances Stockholm's frenetic atmosphere with a laid-back attitude (see p. 881). Off the eastern coast in the Baltic Sea, the island of **Gotland,** rife with medieval churches, white-sand beaches, and prehistoric sites, invites travelers to bike, camp, and enjoy many of its attractions for free (see p. 877).

GETTING THERE AND GETTING AROUND

BY PLANE. Most international flights land in Stockholm, though domestic flights also connect to northern Sweden. **Transwede** (tel. (020) 22 52 25) and **SAS**, in Australia (tel. (02) 92 99 98 00); South Africa (tel. (8) 84 56 00); Sweden (tel. (020) 72 77 27); UK (tel. (0845) 60 72 77 27); US (tel. (800) 221-2350); elsewhere call Sweden +46 (8) 797 50 80), offer youth standby fares (round-trip 350kr) on flights between Stockholm and other Swedish cities. SAS also offers domestic and international "Air Pass" coupons; see p. 49. **Finnair** (US tel. (800) 950-5000) offers North Americans a similar **"Nordic Pass"** (4 coupons US$300) for flights within Scandinavia.

BY TRAIN. Statens Järnvägar (SJ), the state railway company, runs reliable and frequent trains throughout the southern half of Sweden. Seat **reservations** (15kr) are required on some trains (indicated by a R, IN, or IC on the schedule); on all others, they are recommended. Reservations are also mandatory on the new high-speed **X2000** trains (which connect to Stockholm, Gothenburg, Malmö, and Mora); they are included in the normal ticket price, but are additional for railpass holders. For reservations, call (020) 75 75 75, toll-free in Sweden. In southern Skåne, private **pågatågen** trains service Helsingborg, Lund, Malmö, and Ystad; InterRail and Scanrail passes are valid. Northern Sweden is served by two main rail routes: the coastal **Malmbanan** runs north from Stockholm through Boden, Umeå, and Kiruna to Narvik, Norway; from Midsummer (June 23-24 in 2000) to early August, the privately run **Inlandsbanan** also travels farther inland from Mora to Gällivare.

 Eurail is valid in Sweden. The *buy-in-Scandinavia* **Scanrail Pass** allows five days within 15 (1575kr, under 26 1190kr) or 21 consecutive days (2510kr, under 26 1815kr) of unlimited rail travel through Scandinavia, and free or discounted ferry rides. This differs from the *buy-outside-Scandinavia* **Scanrail Pass** (see p. 61).

BY BUS. In the north, buses may be a better option than trains. **Swebus** (tel. (08) 655 90 00) is the principal bus company, offering intercity service all over Sweden, Norway, and Denmark. **Swebus Express** (tel. (020) 64 06 40; toll-free in Sweden) services southern Sweden only. **Bus Stop** (tel. (08) 440 85 70; fax 440 85 77) reserves tickets for buses from Stockholm. Bus tickets are treated as an extension of the rail network, and can be bought from state railways as well. You can also buy tickets on the bus. If a bus is full, more will be put into service. Express buses offer discounts for children, seniors, students, and youth. Bicycles are not allowed on buses.

BY FERRY. The most common way to enter Sweden from the continent is by ferry from **Copenhagen** to **Malmö** (see p. 879) in the south. **Ystad** (see p. 880), also on the southern tip, sends boats to **Bornholm** and **Poland**. Ferries from **Gothenburg** (see p. 881), on the west coast, serve **Frederikshavn, Denmark; Kiel, Germany; and Newcastle** and **Harwich, England**. From **Stockholm** on the east coast (see p. 870), ferries run to the **Åland Islands, Gotland, Turku,** and **Helsinki**. North of Stockholm, Silja Line ferries (tel. (090) 71 44 00) connect **Umeå** and **Vaasa, Finland**.

BY CAR. By law, everyone must wear seatbelts and headlights must always be on. Road conditions are good and there is little traffic. There are no toll roads. Unleaded **gas** costs an average of US$1 per liter. When filling stations are closed, look for pumps marked "*sedel automat*," which operate after-hours. To get on the *motorväg* (highway) ask for the *påfart* (entrance); in getting off, you will be looking for an *avfart* (exit), and then probably for *parkering* (parking). **Renting** a car within Sweden averages US$40-115 per day, including VAT. Special discounts abound, particularly if you opt for a fly/drive package or if you rent for an extended period.

BY BIKE AND BY THUMB. Sweden is a biker's heaven: paths cover most of the country, particularly in the south, and you can complete a trip of Sweden on the hostel-spotted **Sverigeleden bike route.** Contact STF (see below) for info. **Hitching,** which *Let's Go* discourages, can be slow near major cities but picks up in the north.

Sweden

ESSENTIALS

DOCUMENTS AND FORMALITIES. South Africans need a **visa** for stays of any length. Citizens of Australia, New Zealand, Canada, the UK, Ireland, and the US can visit for up to 90 days without one, but this three-month period begins upon entry into any Scandinavian country; for more than 90 days in any combination of Finland, Iceland, Norway, and/or Sweden, you will need a visa.

Swedish Embassies at Home: Australia, 5 Turrana St, Yarralumla, Canberra, ACT 2600 (tel. 62 73 30 33; fax 62 73 32 98); **Canada,** 377 Dalhousie St, Ottawa, ON K1N 9N8 (tel. (613) 241-8553; fax 241-2277); **South Africa,** P.O. Box 3982, Cape Town 8000 (tel. (021) 425 39 88; fax 425 10 16); **UK**, 11 Montagu Pl, London W1H 2AL (tel. (020) 77 24 21 01; fax 79 17 64 77); **US**, 1501 M St NW, Washington, DC 20005 (tel. (202) 467-2600; fax 467-2656).

Foreign Embassies in Sweden: All located in **Stockholm** (see p. 872).

TOURIST OFFICES. Every town and nearly every village has a tourist office, which typically dispenses free maps and information. Many book private rooms, rent bikes, sell local discount cards, and change money. For more info before arriving in Sweden, contact the Swedish Tourist Board: **UK**, 11 Montagu Pl, London W1H 2AL (tel. (020) 77 24 58 68; fax 77 24 58 72); **US**, 655 Third Ave, 18th fl., New York, NY 10017 (tel. (212) 885-9760; fax 885-9764; www.gosweden.org).

MONEY. The main unit of Swedish currency is the **krona**, divided into 100 *öre*. Bills come in denominations of 20, 50, 100, and 500kr; coins come in 1 and 5kr, and 10 and 50 *öre*. Many post offices also double as banks. While commissions may vary, exchange rates remain constant; exchange money in large denominations. **Tipping** is not expected, as gratuities are generally added to the bill (add 10% for taxis). The **VAT** in Sweden is a shocking 25%. Luckily, for purchases of more than $13 in a single store during a single visit, you can receive a VAT refund of 20%.

COMMUNICATION

Post: Mailing a **postcard** or **letter** from Sweden to Australia, Canada, New Zealand, the US and South Africa costs 8kr.

Telephone: Pay phones need at least 2kr, but most accept only **phone cards** *(Telefonkort)*, available at newsstands and post offices in denominations of 30, 60, or 120 units (35kr, 60kr, and 100kr). **International direct dial** numbers include: **AT&T**, 020 79 56 11; **Sprint**, 020 79 90 11; **MCI WorldPhone Direct**, 020 79 59 22; **Australia Direct**, 020 79 90 61, **Canada Direct**, 020 79 90 15; **BT Direct**, 020 79 91 44; **Ireland Direct**, 020 79 93 53; **Telecom New Zealand Direct**, 020 79 84 31; **Telkom South Africa Direct**, 020 79 90 27. For **ambulance, fire,** or **police,** dial 112.

Language: Swedish. Almost all Swedes speak some English; most under 50 are fluent. But you can impress that special Swedish someone with a few phrases from p. 949.

ACCOMMODATIONS AND CAMPING. Youth hostels *(vandrarhem)* in Sweden cost about 100-150kr per night. The 300-odd HI-affiliated hostels run by the **Svenska Turistföreningen (STF)** are invariably top-notch (nonmembers pay 40kr extra per night). **Private hotels** are, with few exceptions, very good as well. Most hostels have kitchens, laundry, and common areas. Reception desks are usually open 8 to 10am and 5 to 7 or 10pm (reduced hours in winter). To reserve ahead, call the hostel directly or contact the STF headquarters in Stockholm (tel. (08) 463 22 70); all sell **Hostelling International (HI)** membership cards (250kr) or offer guest cards. Tourist offices often book beds in hostels for no fee, and can help find **private rooms** (100-250kr). STF also manages mountain huts in the northern wilds with 10-80 beds that cost 155-195kr in high season (nonmembers 195-245kr). Huts are popular; plan ahead. More economical hotels are beginning to offer reduced-service rooms at prices competitive with hostels, especially for groups of three or more. Many **camp-grounds** (80-110kr per site) also offer *stugor* (cottages) for around 85-175kr per person. International Camping Cards are not valid in Sweden; Swedish Camping Cards are virtually mandatory. Year-long memberships (60kr per family) are available through **Sveriges Campingvärdars Riksförbund (SCR)**, Box 255, 451 17 Uddevalla (email ck@camping.se), or at any SCR campground. You may **camp** for free for one or two nights anywhere—except gardens and farmland—as long as you respect the flora, fauna, and the owner's privacy and always pack out all garbage. Pick up the **Right (and Wrongs) of Public Access in Sweden** brochure from the STF or from tourist offices, or call the Swedish Environmental Protection Agency (tel. (08) 698 10 00).

FOOD AND DRINK. Food is very expensive in restaurants and not much cheaper in grocery stores. Rely on supermarkets and outdoor fruit and vegetable markets. Ubiquitous stands provide the most kebabs for your kronor (25-35kr for meat, rice, and veggies). **Potatoes** are the national staple; these and other dishes are invariably smothered with dill. Try tasty milk products like *messmör* (spreadable cheese) and *filmjölk*, a fluid yogurt. When you tire of groceries, seek out restaurants offering an affordable **dagens rätt** (40-60kr), a daily special including an entree, salad, bread, and drink, often all-you-can-eat and usually available only at lunch. A real

MIDSUMMER MADNESS For Midsummer (June 23-24 in 2000), Swedes emerge from the woodwork to celebrate the sun after a long and dark winter. Groups of families, villages, and amorous youngsters erect and dance around the **Midsommarstång**, a cross-shaped pole with two rings dangling from the ends. Its phallic construction symbolizes the fertilization of the soil it is staked in, and thoughts of other fertilization abound as girls place flowers under their pillows to induce dreams of their future spouses. The largest celebrations are in Dalarna, where alcohol and pickled herring flow freely and people flood the city for a two-day party. Keep Midsummer in mind while planning a trip—most transportation lines and establishments are closed.

beer *(starköl)* costs 10-15kr in stores and 30-50kr per pint in city pubs. The cheaper, weaker *lättöl* (alcohol up to 3.5%) can be purchased at supermarkets and convenience stores for 8-12kr per 0.5L. Though the drinking age is 18, bars and many night clubs have age restrictions as high as 25 (usually less strictly enforced earlier in the night); you must be 20 to buy alcohol from the state-run Systembolaget stores, which monopolize the sale of hard booze (wine from 40kr per bottle, liquor 115kr per 0.35L; open M-F; expect long lines on F).

LOCAL FACTS

Time: Sweden is 1hr. ahead of Greenwich Mean Time (GMT; see p. 49).

Climate: The best time to visit is May-Sept., when daytime temperatures average 20°C (68°F) in the south and 16°C (61°F) in the north; nights can get chilly. Bring an umbrella for frequent light rains. If you go in winter, bring heavy cold-weather gear; temperatures are frequently below -5°C (23°F). The **midnight sun** is best seen early June to mid-July.

Hours: Banks are usually open M-F 9:30am-3pm (6pm in some large cities). **Stores** stay open M-F 9am-6pm, Sa 10am-1pm. **Museums** are usually open Tu-Su 10am-4pm.

Holidays: New Year's Day (Jan. 1); Epiphany (Jan. 5-6); Easter Sunday and Monday (Apr. 23-24); Valborg's Eve (Apr. 30); May Day (May 1); Ascension Day (June 1); National Day (June 6); Whit Sunday and Monday (June 11-12); Midsummer's Eve and Midsummer (June 23-24); All Saints Eve and Day (Nov. 3-4); Christmas Eve and Day (Dec. 24-25); Boxing Day (Dec. 26); New Year's Eve (Dec. 31).

Festivals: Midsummer incites family frolicking and bacchanalian dancing around maypoles. July and Aug. bring two special festivals, the *surströmming* (rotten herring) and crayfish parties. In mid-August, the **Stockholm Water Festival** features fireworks, market stalls, and outdoor cafés. The **Water Festival** (Aug.; www.waterfestival.se) in Stockholm is an arts festival with concerts, dance, theater, food, sports, and fireworks.

STOCKHOLM

Sweden's capital is a city at peace with itself. Striking modern architecture flanks ancient castles, beautiful waterways are woven into the urban center, and young and old mingle seamlessly. The whole place seems immune to the social ills faced by every other modern city. Locals' friendliness and English-language skills make Stockholm a joy to navigate. The "Jewel of Scandinavia" lives up to its moniker: waterways wind through the city that launched ABBA and the Cardigans, and the relentless summer sun allows Stockholm's cobblestoned streets, world-class museums, chic cafés, and nightclubs to rock around the clock.

GETTING THERE AND GETTING AROUND

Flights: Arlanda Airport (tel. 797 60 00), 45km north of the city. **Flygbussar** buses (tel. 686 37 87) run between the airport and Cityterminalen (40min., every 10min. 4:25am-10pm, 60kr, public transport passes not valid). **Bus 583** runs from the airport to "J" railway stop "Märsta" (10min., 35kr or 5 coupons; SL pass valid); Centralen is 40min. farther by train. For the best deal, buy an SL pass on arrival at the Pressbyrån if you don't plan to buy a Stockholm card (see below for info on card and SL pass).

Trains: Centralstation. T-bana: T-Centralen. Info and reservations tel. (020) 75 75 75). To: **Oslo** (6hr., 2 per day, 505kr, under 25 353kr); **Copenhagen** (7-8hr., 5-6 per day, 527kr, under 25 371kr); and **Berlin** (18hr., 2 per day, 1100kr, under 25 900kr). See p. 866 for info on **reservations. Lockers** 15-35kr per 24hr. **Showers** 25kr.

Buses: Cityterminalen, upstairs from Centralstation. **Terminal Service** (tel. 762 59 97): to the airport (60kr) and to Gotland ferries (50kr). **Bus Stop** (tel. 440 85 70) handles longer routes: **Gothenburg** (7hr., 7 per day, 220-315kr, under 25 175-250kr); **Malmö** (10hr., 2 per day, 280-395kr, under 25 225-315kr); and **Copenhagen** (10hr., 1 per day, 390kr).

Ferries: All ferries are 50% with Scanrail unless otherwise noted and free with Eurail. **Silja Line,** Kungsg. 2 (tel. 22 21 40), sails overnight to **Mariehamn** (5hr., 1 per day, 99kr); **Turku (Åbo), Finland** (10-11hr., 2 per day, 275-385kr); and **Helsinki** (16 hr., 1 per day, 585kr; book ahead). To get to the terminal, take T-bana to "Gärdet" and follow "Värtahamnen" signs, or take the Silja bus (14kr) from Cityterminalen. **Viking Line** sails to **Mariehamn** (5½hr., 1 per day, round-trip 99kr); **Turku (Åbo)** (12hr., 2 per day, 222-321kr; with Scanrail 111kr); and **Helsinki** (15hr., 1 per day, 321kr). Viking Line terminal is at Stadsgården on Södermalm. T-bana: Slussen. **Destination Gotland** (tel. 20 10 20) sails to **Visby, Gotland** from Nynäshamn, 1hr. south of the city (see p. 877).

Public Transportation: SL office (tel. 600 10 00), Sergels Torg. Open M-F 7am-9pm, Sa-Su 8am-9pm. T-bana: T-Centralen. Walk-in office in basement of Centralstation open M-Sa 6:30am-11:15pm, Su 7am-11:15pm. Most in-town destinations cost 2 coupons (14kr, 1hr. unlimited bus/subway transfer). **Rabattkuponger** (95kr), books of 20 coupons, are sold at Pressbyrån news agents. The **SL Tourist Card** (Turistkort) is valid on buses, subways, commuter trains, and the trams and ferries to Djurgården (24hr. 60kr, 72hr. 120kr). **Tunnelbana** (subway; also **T-bana**) runs 5am-12:30am. After hours, it is replaced by night buses. Check schedules on bus-stop kiosks.

Taxis: Rather high fares. Try to agree on a price before you get in. 435kr from the airport to Centralstation. **Taxi Stockholm** (tel. 15 00 00) and **Taxicard** (tel. 97 00 00).

Bike Rental: Skepp & Hoj (tel. 660 57 57) on Djurgårdsbron. Bikes and rollerblades 150kr per day, 500kr per week. Open daily 9am-9pm.

Hitchhiking: Waiting on highways is illegal in Sweden. Hitchers going south take the T-bana to the gas station on Kungens Kurva in Skärholmen; those going north take bus 52 to Sveaplan and stand on Sveav. at Norrtull. *Let's Go* does not recommend hitchhiking.

■ ORIENTATION AND PRACTICAL INFORMATION

Stockholm is built on seven islands at the junction of **Lake Mälaren** to the west and the **Baltic Sea** to the east. The northern island is divided into two sections: **Norrmalm**—home to Centralstation and the shopping district on Drottningg.—and **Östermalm,** which boasts the elegant waterfront **Strandvägen** and much of the nightlife that fans out from **Stureplan Square.** The mainly residential western island, **Kungsholmen,** has the **Stadshuset** (City Hall) and grassy beaches. The southern island of **Södermalm,** formerly Stockholm's slum, hosts cafés, artists, and an extensive gay scene. Södermalm's little sister-island, **Långholmen,** is a nature preserve, while the island of **Djurgården** is a veritable nature-playground and site of the Nordiska Museet and the Vasa Museet. At the center of these five islands is **Gamla Stan** (Old Town) island, which surrounds the main street, **Västerlånggatan.** Gamla Stan's neighboring island **Skeppsholmen** (best reached via Norrmalm) harbors mostly museums. The T-bana links the islands, but you can easily walk around the center.

TOURIST, FINANCIAL, AND LOCAL SERVICES

Tourist Offices: Sweden House, Hamng. 27 (tel. 789 24 90; fax 789 24 91; email info@stoinfo.se; www.stoinfo.se), in the northeast corner of Kungsträdgården. From Centralstation, walk up Klarabergsg. to Sergels Torg (the plaza with the 50-foot glass tower) and bear right on Hamng. Books rooms for 20-50kr. Sells the **Stockholm Card** (see **Sights,** p. 874). Open June-Aug. M-F 8am-7pm, Sa-Su 9am-5pm; Sept.-May M-F 9am-6pm, Sa-Su 10am-3pm. **Hotellcentralen** (tel. 789 24 25; fax 791 86 66; email hotels@stoinfo.se), at the train station, books rooms (20-50kr) throughout Scandinavia. Comprehensive color city map 15kr. Open daily May-Sept. 7am-9pm; Oct.-Apr. 9am-6pm.

SWEDEN

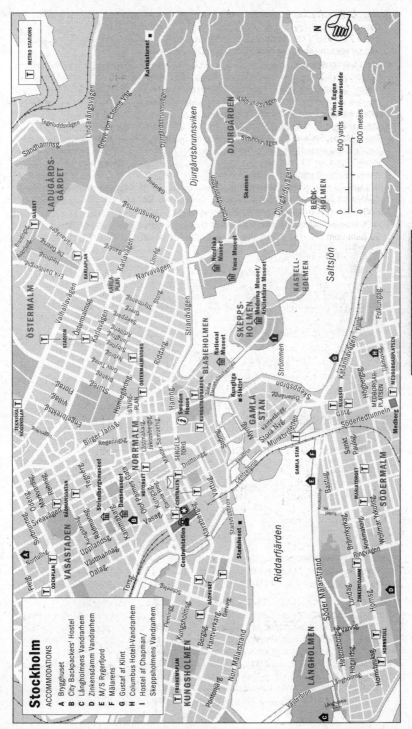

Stockholm

ACCOMMODATIONS

A Brygghuset
B City Backpackers' Hostel
C Långholmens Vandrarhem
D Zinkensdamm Vandrarhem
E M/S Rygerfjord
F Mälarens
G Gustaf af Klint
H Columbus Hotel-Vandrarhem
I Hostel af Chapman/
   Skeppsholmens Vandrarhem

METRO STATIONS

SWEDEN

Embassies: Australia, Sergels Torg 12, 11th fl. (tel. 613 29 00, in emergency 020 79 84 80; fax 24 74 14); **Canada,** Tegelbacken 4 (tel. 453 30 00; fax 24 24 91; www.canadaemb.se); **Ireland,** Ostermalmsg. 97 (tel. 661 80 05; fax 660 13 53); **South Africa,** Linnég. 76 (tel. 24 39 50, in emergency 07 08 56 75 35; fax 660 71 36; (www.southafricanemb.se). **UK,** Skarpög. 6-8 (tel. 671 90 00, in emergency 07 04 28 49 97; fax 662 99 89). **US,** Strandvagen 101 (tel. 783 53 00; fax 661 19 64).

Currency Exchange: Forex in Centralstation (tel. 411 67 34; open daily 7am-9pm), in Cityterminalen (tel. 21 42 80; open M-F 8am-8pm, Sa 8am-5pm), and in the tourist office in Sverigehuset (tel. 20 03 89). 15kr commission per traveler's check, 20kr for cash.

American Express: Norrlandsg. 21 (tel. 411 05 40). T-bana: Östermalmstorg. No fee to cash AmEx traveler's checks, 20kr for cash. Open M-F 9am-5pm, Sa 9am-1pm.

Bookstore: Akademibokhandeln, at Mäster Samuelsg. 32 (tel. 613 61 00), Sergels Torg 12 (tel. 411 59 90). Open June-Aug. M-F 9:30am-6:30pm, Sa 10am-4pm, Su noon-4pm; Sept.-May M–Sa 10am-4pm.

Gay and Lesbian Services: RFSL, the Riksförbundet för Sexuellt Likaberättigande (Swedish Federation for Sexual Equality), Sveav. 57 (tel. 736 02 13; www.rfsl.se). T-bana: Rådmansg. Features a bookstore and a café and distributes *Queer Xtra (QX),* with bar, club, and events guide. Open M-Th noon-8pm, F noon-6pm, Sa-Su 1-4pm.

EMERGENCY AND COMMUNICATIONS

Emergencies: Ambulance, fire, and **police,** tel. 112.

Pharmacy: Look for the green and white "Apotek" signs. **Apotek C. W. Scheele,** Klarabergsg. 64, at the overpass over Vasag. T-bana: T-Centralen. Open 24hr.

Medical Assistance: Tel. 463 91 00.

Internet Access: Stadsbibliotek, Odeng. 59, in the annex. T-bana: Odenplan. 20min. free. Open M-Th 11am-7pm. **Café Access** (tel. 50 83 14 89), in the basement the Kulturhuset building on Sergels Torg. 20kr per 30min. Open Sa-Su noon-5pm.

Telephones: Buy phone cards at **Pressbyrån** stores (especially at T-bana stations) for 30 (30kr), 60 (60kr), or 120 (100kr) units. **National directory assistance:** 079 75.

Post Office: Drottningg. 53 (tel. 781 46 82). Open M-F 8am-7pm, Sa 10am-3pm. Address mail to be held: Fox MULDER, *Poste Restante,* Drottningg. 53, **10110** Stockholm 1, Sweden. Also in Centralstation (tel. 781 22 98). Open 10am-7pm.

PHONE CODE	City code: 08. From outside Sweden, dial int'l dialing prefix (see inside back cover) + 46 + 8 + local number.

■ ACCOMMODATIONS AND CAMPING

Summer demands reservations, and many HI hostels limit stays to five nights. If you haven't booked ahead, arrive around 7am. Stockholm's several **boat-hostels (botels)** offer a novel solution to the compact city's space issues, but they can be cramped and noisy—request a room on the water side of the boat. **Campers** should bring insect repellent to ward off the infamous Swedish mosquitoes. If you don't have a (mandatory) **Swedish Camping Card,** either site below will sell you one for 49kr. Using an SL bus pass (or Stockholm Card) is the cheapest way to get to campsites.

Columbus Hotell-Vandrarhem, Tjärhovsg. 11 (tel. 644 17 17; fax 702 07 64; email columbus@columbus.se), in Södermalm. 3 blocks east of T-bana: Medborgarplatsen. This former brewery, prison, and plague hospital is a dream city hostel: clean, bright, and spacious. Dorms 145kr; singles 370kr and doubles 370kr. Breakfast 50kr. Affiliated hotel. Kitchen and bar. Reception 24hr. Accepts email reservations. V, MC, AmEx.

City Backpackers' Vandrarhem, Upplandsgatan 2A (tel. 20 69 20; fax 10 04 64; www.svif.se), in Norrmalm. From Centralstation, go left on Vasag. and bear right on Upplandsgaten. Super-friendly. Dorms 150-180kr; doubles 450kr. Kitchen. Laundry. Sauna. Reception June-Aug. 8am-noon and 2-7pm; Sept.-May 9am-noon and 2-7pm. V, MC.

Hostel af Chapman/Skeppsholmens Vandrarhem (HI/STF) (tel. 463 22 66; fax 611 71 55; email info@chapman.stfturist.se; www.meravsverige.nu), off Skeppsholmen—great location. From T-bana: T-Centralen, take bus 65. A fully-rigged sailing ship moored majestically off the island, in front of the less mythic (but roomier) on-shore hostel. Some non-reservable beds available daily at 7:15am. Dorms 100-130kr; doubles 300kr; nonmembers add 40kr. Breakfast 45kr. Kitchen. Laundry. Reception 24hr. Curfew on boat 3am. Accepts email reservations. V, MC, AmEx.

Zinkensdamm Vandrarhem (HI), Zinkens Väg 20 (tel. 616 81 00; fax 616 81 20; email info@zinkensdamm.swedenhotels.se), in Södermalm. From T-bana: Zinkensdamm, head south on Ringv. 3 blocks, then turn right on Zinkens Väg. Verdant, quiet, peaceful area. Comfortable, with TV, sauna, laundry, bike rental, and pub. 135kr, nonmembers 175kr. Kitchen. Reception 24hr. Accepts email reservations. V, MC.

Brygghuset, Norrtullsg. 12N (tel. 31 24 24; fax 31 02 06). From T-bana: Odenplan ("Odenplan" exit), walk two blocks north on Norrtullsg.; or walk 25min. from city center. Bright, clean rooms. Dorms 130kr; doubles 320kr. Reception daily 8am-noon and 3-10pm. Lockout noon-3pm. Curfew 2am; you can get a key for 20kr. Open June to mid-Sept.

Mälarens, Södermalarstrand, Kajplats 6 (tel. 644 43 85; fax 641 37 33; email info@icts.se; www.icts.se). T-bana: Slussen (lower exit); then walk 300m west. The classiest of the floating hostels in Söder if lots of red carpet does it for you. Dorms 150kr; doubles 390kr; quads 700kr. Breakfast 45kr. Reception 8-10am in café, in office until 11pm. Check-out 9am. Accepts email reservations. V, MC.

Långholmens Vandrarhem (HI), Kronohäktet (tel. 668 05 10; fax 720 85 75; email vandrarhem@langholmen.com), on Långholmen Island. T-bana: Hornstull; then walk north on Långholmsg., turn left onto Högalidsg., hang a right on Långholmsbron over the bridge onto Långholmen, then turn left and walk 300m. 2-4 beds per converted prison cell. 155kr; nonmembers 195kr. Breakfast 60kr. Sheets 40kr. Kitchen, café/pub, and laundry. Reception 24hr. Check-out 10am. Accepts email reservations. V, MC, AmEx.

Gustaf af Klint, Stadsgårdskajen 153 (tel. 640 40 77; fax 640 64 16, www.gustafafklint.com), in Södermalm. A former Navy ship moored 200m east of T-bana: Slussen (lower exit). Cramped dorms 120kr; cabins 140kr; doubles 320kr. Breakfast 47kr. Laundry. Key deposit 50kr. Reception in summer 24hr. V, MC.

M/S Rygerfjord, Söder Mälarstrand Kajplats 12 (tel. 84 08 30; fax 84 07 30; www.rygerfjord.se). T-bana: Mariatorget; exit towards Mariatorget, follow Torkel Knutssonsg. down to the water and look for the sign. Cozy rooms and, in summer, an on-deck bar. Dorms 145kr; doubles 330kr. Breakfast 35kr. Reception 7am-1am. Check-out 11am. V, MC.

Ängby Camping, Blackebergsv. 24 (tel. 37 04 20; fax 37 82 26; email reservation@angby-camping.se), on Lake Mälaren. T-bana: Ängbyplan; go downstairs, turn left on Färjestadsvägen, bear left at the fork, and it's at the bottom of the road. 110kr for 2 people with tent. Reception 7am-11pm in the summer; reduced in off-season. Open year-round.

Bredäng Camping (tel. 97 70 71; fax 708 72 62; www.camping.se/plats/A04), 10km southwest, near Lake Mälaren. T-bana: Bredäng. You can also take the ferry from nearby Mälarhöjdsbadet to Stockholm City Hall or Drottningholm in summer (35kr, 3-4 per day). Follow signs downstairs, past the big apartment complex, and along Stora Sällskapets Väg to the campsite (10min.). Store, laundry. 160kr per tent; 4-bed cabins with kitchen from 400kr. Reception June-Aug. 7am-11pm; reduced in off-season.

◘ FOOD

Stockholm's restaurants reflect the city's increasing ethnic diversity, but local cuisine is well worth tracking down. Your best bet is to gorge on the all-you-can-eat breakfasts offered by most hostels, and then track down a cheap *dagens rätt* lunch special served at many restaurants (45-80kr; usually served 11:30am-3pm). For **groceries,** try **Hemköp City,** at the exit from T-bana: Centralen, on Sergels Torg. (Open M-F 8am-9pm, Sa-Su 10am-9pm.) **Konsum** and **ICA** are other supermarket chains. **Hötorget Square** hosts an open-air **fruit market.** (Open M-Sa 7am-6pm.) The three-story **Kungshallen food court,** across the street at Kungsg. 44, is classier than its North American counterpart, with cafés, delis, and fast food. (Lunch or dinner 30-100kr. Open daily M-F 9am-11pm, Sa 11am-11pm, Su noon-11pm.)

Collage, Smålandsg. 2. T-bana: Östermalmstorg.; exit towards Stureplan. The ultimate budget dinner. Extensive buffet (served 6:30-9:30pm) 35kr. Get discount tickets for cheap drinks until 10pm. Dance off your dinner at the disco after 11pm (see **p. 876**).

Herman's Hermitage, Stora Nyg. 11, in Gamla Stan; **Herman's Höjdare,** Fjällg. 23A, in Söder. Superlative vegetarian fare. The Söder branch has an all-you-can-eat buffet with a view (lunch 60kr, dinner 85kr); in Gamla Stan, weekday lunch is 60kr. Söder open M-F 11am-9pm, Sa-Su noon-9pm, in summer daily until 11pm; Gamla Stan open M-F 11am-6pm, Sa-Su 11am-8pm, in summer also M-F 6-8pm.

Sandy's, branches at Kungsg. 57, Odenplan 16, and Drottiningg. 2. Let Sandy's "Starting Kick" jumpstart your morning. Coffee, fresh-squeezed OJ, yogurt with muesli, and a sandwich for 33kr. Open M-F 7:30am-7pm, Sa 11am-5pm.

Café Stensture, Trångsund 10. Use the entrance on Ankargränd to get a real feel for this medieval-prison-turned-café, which once housed the assassin of King Gustav III. Tiny tables with quaint nooks and crannies. Open daily 10am-9pm.

Pauli's Café, Dramaten 2 trappen, 2nd fl., in Nybroplan. T-bana: Östermalmstorg; then walk down Birger Jarlsg. toward the water. Upstairs in the National Theater. Summer lunch buffet of Swedish delicacies 70kr. Buffet served 11:30am-2pm.

⊙ SIGHTS

Stockholm was founded in the 13th century and became Sweden's capital in 1436. Its long history has contributed to the development of a rich cultural tradition that's even trickled down to the subway—the decorated stops constitute the longest art exhibit in the world. Serious sightseers should pick up the **Stockholm Card** (Stockholmskortet; 24-hour 199kr, 48-hour 398kr, 72-hour 498kr; available at tourist offices in Sweden House and Central Station), which covers admission to most museums and allows unlimited transportation on the subways and buses.

KUNGSHOLMEN AND STADSHUSET (CITY HALL). On the tip of Kungsholmen closest to Gamla Stan towers the regal **Stadshuset.** Jutting into the skyline at 106m, the **Stadshustornet** (City Hall Tower) offers a stunning aerial view of the downtown area. The building is emblematic of 1920s Swedish architecture and is the symbol of Stockholm. The interior boasts municipal Viking chambers; the **Blå Hallen** (Blue Hall), where the dinner party for the Nobel Prize Celebration is held; and the mosaic-tiled **Gyllene Hallen** (Gold Hall), where the Nobels, nobles, and other notables dance the rest of the night away. To cool off, take the plunge into the water off Stadshuset lawn. *(Hantverkarg. 1. T-bana: Rådhuset; then walk east on Hantverkarg. Compulsory guided tours daily June-Aug. 10, 11am, noon, and 2pm; Sept. 10am, noon, and 2pm; Oct.-May 10am and noon. 40kr. Tower open daily May-Sept. 10am-4:30pm. 15kr.)*

GAMLA STAN (OLD TOWN). *(T-bana: Gamla Stan. Or take bus 46 or 55.)* Across the water from Stadshuset and at the center of Stockholm's islands is the city's medieval core, replete with winding, cobblestoned, and catacombed streets. The main pedestrian street, **Västerlångg.,** is packed with cafés, shops, and cheesy tourist paraphernalia. On nearby **Stora Nyg.** and **Österlångg.** the commercial onslaught is a little less severe. **Tours** of the Old Town depart three times a week in summer. *(June-Aug. M, W, and F at 7pm. Meet at the Obelisk in Slottsbacken outside the palace. 50kr.)* At the top of Gamla Stan's winding streets is **Stortorget** (Town Square), where the annual **Julmarknad** (Christmas Fair) serves hot *glögg* (spiced wine) and sells handicrafts. Behind the square is the impressive **Storkyrkan** (Royal Chapel), site of royal weddings and the dramatic medieval sculpture of Stockholm's patron Saint Göran (George) slaying the dragon. *(Open daily May-Aug. 9am-6pm; Sept.-Apr. 9am-4pm. Free.)*

The crowning attraction of Gamla Stan, however, is the stunning **Kungliga Slottet** (Royal Palace), winter home of the Swedish royal family and site of the daily Changing of the Guard. You can roam through a portion of the **State Apartments,** swing by the **Skattkammaren** (Royal Treasury) to drool over royal regalia and the crown jewels (including the sword of legendary King Gustav, who unified Sweden in 1524), and visit the **armory** and **Gustav III's Antikmuseum** (Museum of Antiquities). *(All four open daily May-Aug. 10am-6pm, Sept.-Apr. Tu-Su noon-3pm. Individual tickets: State Apartments 50kr; Treasury 50kr; Armory 60kr; Museum of Antiquities 50kr. Joint ticket for all four 100kr, students 70kr. Joint ticket to Kungliga Slottet, Rosendal Palace, and Gustav III's Pavilion*

100kr, students 80kr. Changing of the Guard ceremony in summer M-Sa 12:10pm, Su 1:10pm, rest of year W and Sa at 12:10pm and Su at 1:10pm.)

SKEPPSHOLMEN AND BLASIEHOLMEN. On Skeppsholmen, the island east of Gamla Stan, the **Moderna Museet** (Modern Museum) and **Arkitekturmuseet** (Architecture Museum) are housed in adjacent buildings newly designed by the architect Rafael Moneo. Though the buildings have received mixed reviews, the Moderna's Pop Art collection is nonetheless regarded as one of Europe's finest collections of 20th-century art. *(T-bana: Kungsträdgården; then walk towards the water on Södra Blasieholm-shamner, cross the bridge to Skeppsholmen, and follow the signs. Both open in summer Tu-Th 11am-10pm, F-Su 11am-10pm; reduced hours in winter. Modern Museum 60kr, students 40kr. Architecture Museum 45kr, students 30kr. Joint ticket 80kr, students 65kr.)* On Södra Blasieholmshamnen right before you cross the bridge to Skeppsholmen, the **National Museet** (National Museum of Fine Art) has works by Rembrandt, Renoir, and Rodin, but also pays homage to national artists such as Carl Larsson, Anders Zorn, and Eugen Jansson. *(T-bana: Kungsträdgården. Open Mar.-Dec. Tu 11am-8pm, W-Su 11am-5pm; Jan.-Feb. Tu and Th 11am-8pm, W and F-Su 11am-5pm. 60kr, under 16 free.)*

DJURGÅRDEN. East of Skeppsholmen lies the island of Djurgården, a national park in the heart of the city. **Skansen** is an open-air museum featuring 150 historical buildings, handicrafts, and a zoo. The homes—extracted from different periods of Swedish history—are inhabited by actors in period costume. *(Take bus 44 or 47 from Drottningg. and Klarabergsg. in Sergels Torg, opposite T-Centralen. Park and zoo open daily June-Aug. 10am-10pm; May 10am-8pm; Sept.-Apr. 10am-4pm. Historical buildings open daily May-Aug. 11am-5pm; Sept.-Apr. 11am-3pm. 60kr.)* The **Vasa Museet** houses a mammoth wooden Vasa warship that sank on her maiden voyage in 1628, before even leaving the harbor; it was salvaged in 1961. *(Galärvarvsv. 14, Djurgården. www.vasamuseet.se. Take bus 44, 47, or 69. Open June 10-Aug. 20 daily 9:30am-7pm, Aug. 21-June 9 M-Tu and Th-Su 10am-5pm, W 10am-8pm. 60kr.)* Next door, the **Nordiska Museet** (Nordic Museum) presents an innovative exhibit on Swedish history from the Viking age to the modern era of Volvo, ABBA, and Electrolux. *(Djurgårdsvägen 6-16. Take bus 44 or 47. Open daily 10am-9pm. 60kr.)* On the far side of the island, **Prins Eugens Waldemarsudde,** home of the full-time prince, part-time painter, contains Eugens' principal works and a personal collection of Larssons, Janssons, and Zorns. The seaside grounds also have a collection of sculptures including works by Hasselberg and Rodin. *(Prins Eugen Väg 6. Take bus 47. Open June-Aug. Tu-Su 11am-5pm, Sept.-May Tu-Su 11am-4pm. 50kr.)*

♫ ENTERTAINMENT

For up-to-date info on the latest events, check out *Stockholm this Week* (published monthly), or the Swedish *DN På Stan* (free at the tourist office).

THEATER AND CONCERTS. The three stages of the national theater, **Dramaten,** Nybroplan (tel. 667 06 80), feature Swedish- and English-language performances of August Strindberg and other Scandinavian and international playwrights (80-350kr), while the **Operan** (tel. 24 82 40) offers opera and ballet (70-350kr). Cheaper student, obstructed-view, or rush tickets are often available. The **Konserthuset** at Hötorget (tel. 10 21 10) features classical music concerts from the Stockholm Philharmoniker; concerts are also held at the **Globen** arena (tel. 600 34 00; 50-300kr). Pop music venues include **Skansen** (tel. 57 89 00 05) and the stage at **Gröna Lund** (tel. 670 76 00), Djurgården's huge outdoor Tivoli amusement park. (Open late Apr. to early Sept. M-Th noon-11pm, F-Sa noon-midnight. Su noon-9pm. Tickets 125-300kr.) Check theater and concert listings in *Stockholm this Week*, then visit Sweden House or call BiljettDirekt (tel. 077 170 70 70) for tickets.

FESTIVALS. Stockholm's festivals include: the world-class **Jazz and Blues Festival** at Skansen (tel. 747 92 36; www.stockholmjazz.com); the **Stockholm Water Festival,** a week-long aqua party and carnival (mid-Aug.; tel. 10 23 03; www.waterfestival.se); the two-week **Strindberg Festival** (late Aug. or early Sept.; tel. 34 14 01; www.strindberg.stockholm.se/festivalen); and the gay and lesbian **Stockholm Pride** (late July;

tel. 33 59 55; www.stockholmpride.org). Skansen and Gamla Stan also host celebrations for many national holidays, including St. Lucia Dagen (Dec. 13), Christmas (Dec. 25), Midsummer (June 23-24), and National Day (June 6).

⬛ NIGHTLIFE

Stockholm's beautiful people and their admirers party until 5am at the many nightclubs and bars around Stureplan in **Östermalm** (T-bana: Östermalmtorg); be prepared to pay steep cover and wait in long lines. While these are the people you'll want to watch, the people with whom you'll want to mingle are across the river in **Södermalm** ("Söder"), Stockholm's answer to London's SoHo or New York's Greenwich Village. Söder is also the core of Stockholm's gay scene; pick up *QX (Queer Extra)* for entertainment and nightlife info. Expect a scene that is a little grittier and rougher around the edges, but much more relaxed, interesting, and inexpensive. Most establishments there close between 1 and 3am. The bars and cafés lining **Götgatan** make a good point of departure (T-bana: Slussen, Medborgplatsen, or Skanstull). New cafés and bars are also sprouting up in the up-and-coming neighborhoods of **Vasastaden** (T-bana: Sankt Eriksplan) and **Kungsholmen** (T-bana: Rådhuset). Stockholm's compactness and the excellent night bus service means revelers can partake of any or all of these scenes in a single night.

Alcohol is very expensive at bars (35-55kr per beer) but available cheaply (10-15kr per 0.5L of beer) at **Systembolaget** state liquor stores. (Open M-F 9am-5pm.) Lighter beer (up to 3.5% alcohol) is in supermarkets at around 10kr per beer.

Bröderna Olssons Garlic and Shots, Folkungag. 84, in Söder, across from the Columbus Hostel. T-bana: Medborgarplatsen. Electric atmosphere and funky downstairs vodka bar. Their trademark garlic-flavored beer will ensure a quickly-vacated hostel room after you stumble home. 100 esoteric shots (33kr each). Open daily 5pm-1am.

La Cucaracha, Bondeg., in Söder. T-bana: Skanstull; walk up Götg. away from the Globe Arena (giant golf ball) and turn right on Bondeg. Latin rhythms heat up a jumping dance floor after 11pm. Beer 30kr, mixed drinks 60-70kr. 23 and up. Open daily until 1am.

Pelikan, Blekingeg. 40, in Söder. T-bana: Skanstull; walk up Götg. away from the Globe Arena and right on Blekingeg. Unpretentious crowds are at the smoky, well-lit beer hall adjoining the darker and artsier **Kristallen.** Beer 37kr, mixed drinks 40-50kr. 23 and up.

Snaps, Medborgarplatsen, in the free-standing yellow house. Very popular bar and bistro with a basement dance floor (jungle, reggae, and dance music). Beer 38kr, mixed drinks 58-78kr. Women 23 and up, men 25 and up. Open M-Tu 5pm-1am, W-Sa 5pm-3am.

Tranan, Karlbergsv. 14, in Vastaden, across from T-bana: Odenplan. A young, hip (but not oppressively so) crowd gathers at this trendy, sit-down bar to hear sweet beats and sip pricey drinks. The Chemical Brothers have been known to play here as "secret guests" when in town. Beer 44kr, mixed drinks 62kr. No cover. Age 23 and up. Open 5pm-1am.

Fasching, Kungsg. 63 (tel. 21 62 67; www.fasching.se). T-bana: T-Centralen. Sweden's best for live jazz, latin, blues, funk, fusion, and world music in a funky loft-like space. Cover 70-250kr. Open 8pm-midnight. Used as a regular disco F-Sa midnight-3am.

⬛ EXCURSIONS FROM STOCKHOLM

Part of Stockholm's allure is the wonderful area surrounding it. To the west lies **Lake Mälaren,** and to the east the **skärgård** (archipelago), 24,000 islands that vary from lush (near the mainland) to barren (on the outer edge). For more info on daytrips, visit the Excursion Shop in Sweden House (see p. 870), or the kiosks on Stadshusbron, Strömkajen, or Nybroplan in Stockholm.

LAKE MÄLAREN. The Mälaren Valley is home to **Birka,** where the Vikings established the country's first city, on **Björkö.** It was also the site of Sweden's first encounter with Christianity in AD 829. Today you can visit the excavation sites, burial mounds, and a Viking museum. (1¾-hour ferry departs Stockholm from Stadshusbron, next to Stadhuset, at 10am; departs Björkö at 3:45pm. One-hour guided tour, museum admission, and round-trip ferry 200kr; available May-Sept.)

The Swedish royal family's home, **Drottingholm Palace,** is only 45min. away by ferry. The ghost of elegant Drottning (Queen) Larisa Ulrika, for whom the palace was a wedding gift, presides over lush Baroque gardens and extravagant Rococo interiors. Catch the free half-hourly tour in English of the palace's **theater** (40kr, students 10kr). **Kina Slott,** Drottningholm's Chinese pavilion, was an 18th-century royal summer cottage. (Palace open daily May-Aug. 10am-4:30pm; Sept. noon-3:30pm. 50kr, students 25kr. Pavilion open daily May-Aug. 11am-4:30pm; Sept. noon-3:30pm; Apr. and Oct. 1-3:30pm. 50kr, students 25kr. Strömma Kanalbolaget ferries depart from Stadshusbron, near the Stadshuset, mid-June to mid-Aug. every 30min. 9:30am-4pm; return every hr. 10:30am-5:30pm. 85kr round-trip. Or take the subway to T-bana: Brommaplan, then take bus 301-323.)

If you have the urge to brush shoulders with more royalty, **Gripsholm Castle** looms majestically over the bucolic hamlet of **Mariefred.** Built in 1380 on Lake Mälarens by the Lord High Chancellor Bo Jonsson Grip, the castle is adorned with portraits and its original Renaissance wall paintings and furniture. (Open May-Aug. daily 10am-4pm; Sept. Tu-Su 10am-3pm; Oct.-Dec. Sa-Su 10am-3pm; Jan.-Apr. Sa-Su noon-3pm. 50kr, students 25kr.) A short walk from the castle is **Grafikens Hus,** once the royal barn, now a print-making workshop. (Open May-Aug. daily 11am-5pm; Sept.-Apr. Sa-Su 11am-5pm. 40kr.) To get to Mariefred, take the train to Läggesta, then catch bus 303 (15kr) and ask the driver to drop you off at the castle (1hr. total).

SKÄRGÅRD. Little can compare to these tranquil islands. Longer stays in the area's 20 hostels must be booked months ahead, but the odd night may still be available on short notice. Better still, bring a tent and enjoy free camping courtesy of the law of public access (see p. 868) on almost any island except Sandhamn (some islands are also in military protection zones and are not open to foreigners). Otherwise it is easy to daytrip. The Waxholmsbolaget ferry company (tel. 679 58 30) serves even the tiniest of islands and offers the 16-day **Båtluffarkortet card** (a bargain at 275kr), good for unlimited boat travel throughout the archipelago. The excursions shop at Sweden House in Stockholm (see p. 870) sells the ferry pass and has information on hostels and camping as well as kayak and canoe rentals.

In the archipelago you can try your hand at fishing or investigate the waterways by canoe or kayak; in winter ice-skating is popular. Only an hour away from Stockholm by ferry in the archipelago is **Vaxholm,** a fortress town founded in 1647. The historic town is small enough to explore by foot, and the fortress is on a small island accessible by boat. (Ferry departs from Nybroplan in Stockholm at noon, returns 4:30pm.) **Utö** has great bike paths; bike rental and ferry packages are available from Sweden House. **Sandhamn,** three hours from Stockholm, is ideal for swimming and sailing. Another option for an afternoon of fun in the sun is **Finnhamn.** (Ferry 2¾hr.; departs Strömkajen in Stockholm daily at 9am, M-F also 10am; returns M-Th 3:45 and 6:55pm, F 1:50 and 7pm, Sa 3:10 and 5:35pm, Su 3:25pm and 6:15pm. 80kr.) On the island of **Öja,** you can puzzle your way through the labyrinth north of Landsort, which is supposed to bring good luck to fishermen. Take the *pendeltåg* from Stockholm to Nynäshamn, take bus 852 from there to Ankarudden, and hop on the ferry to Landsort (2½hr.).

GOTLAND

Gotland, 300km south of Stockholm, is Sweden's biggest island, famed for its green meadows, white sand beaches, and cobblestoned capital, Visby. While Visby's wall (the oldest medieval monument in Scandinavia) may have kept the Danes at bay, it hasn't been very successful against the tourists; luckily, the island's natural beauty provides plenty of reason to leave the hordes behind.

⬛ GETTING THERE AND GETTING AROUND. Destination Gotland ferries sail to Visby from **Nynäshamn** (just south of Stockholm; 3-5hr.) and **Oskarshamn** (north of Kalmar; 2½-4hr.). Fares are highest on weekends (215-430kr), cheaper during the week, and cheapest for early-morning and late-night departures (130-205kr, students 80-130kr); Scanrailers get 50% off. (Tel. (0498) 20 10 20. June-Aug. 2-5 per day;

Oct.-May 1 per day from each terminal.) To get to Nynäshamn from **Stockholm**, take the bus from Cityterminalen (1hr., 50kr) or the *pendeltåg* (commuter train) from Centralstation (45min., 35kr; *rabattkuponger* and SL passes valid). To get to Oskarshamn, hop on a bus (2hr., 75kr) or train from **Kalmar.** In Stockholm, **Gotland City,** Kungsg. 57A, books ferries and has tourist info. (Tel. (08) 406 15 00; fax 406 15 90. Open June-Aug. M-F 9:30am-6pm, Sa 10am-2pm; Sept.-May M-F 9:30am-5pm.)

To explore the island, pick up a bus timetable at the ferry terminal or at the Visby **bus station,** Kung Magnusväg 1 (tel. (0498) 21 41 12). Bus rides cost 11-42kr (bikes 20kr extra). If you have a few days, cycling along Gotland's extensive paths and bike-friendly motorways is the best way to explore Gotland's flat terrain.

VISBY. Once you reach Gotland, walk 10min. to the left as you exit the ferry terminal to get to the **tourist office,** Hamng. 4, which has maps of Gotland (25-65kr) and Visby (free). (Tel. (0498) 20 17 00; fax 20 17 17. Open mid-June to mid-Aug. M-F 7am-7pm, Sa-Su 8am-6pm; May to mid-June and late Aug. M-F 8am-5pm, Sa-Su 10am-4pm; Sept. M-F 8am-5pm, Sa-Su 11am-2pm; Oct.-Apr. M-F 10am-noon and 1-3pm.) **O'Hoj Cykeluthyrning,** opposite the ferry terminal, rents **bikes.** (60-110kr per day, 300-550kr per week. Open daily 7am-6pm.) The **Visby Fängelse Vandrarhem,** Skeppsbron 1, is 300m to the left as you exit the ferry terminal. You'll recognize it by the friendly barbed wire atop the walls—until Feb. 1998 this was a maximum-security prison. (Tel. (0498) 20 60 50; fax 20 51 10. Dorms 150kr; bed in a double cell 200kr. Reception M-F 11am-2pm, Sa-Su 11am-noon; call ahead to arrive at another time. Reservations recommended.) Otherwise, **Gotlands Turistcenter,** Färjeleden 3, will help you find a room. (Tel. (0498) 20 12 60; fax 21 29 20. Open June-Aug. daily 6am-10pm, 11:30pm when a late ferry comes in; Sept.-May daily 8am-6pm.) **Private rooms** inside Visby's walls cost 285kr for singles and 425kr for doubles (outside the city walls 240kr and 380kr). While in town, try to catch a local to teach you how to play **Kubb,** a Viking game that today is only played in Gotland. Oh, and don't mind the concrete sheep—they're herding traffic in the right direction. **Postal code:** 62101.

ELSEWHERE ON GOTLAND. Great daytrips from Visby include visits to the mystical monoliths on **Fårö,** off the northern tip of the island (bus 23, 2hr.); the blazing beaches of **Tofta,** about 15km south of Visby (bus 31, 30min.); and the calcified cliffs of **Hoburgen** at the island's southernmost tip (bus 11, 3hr.). The Turistcenter (see above) can also get you info on the more than 30 hostels on the island, campgrounds and bike rentals elsewhere on the island. To economize, you can also take advantage of the right of public access (see p. 868).

SOUTHERN SWEDEN

Islands and skerries line the southern coasts; the southwest **Småland** coastline, between Västervik and Kalmar, is particularly scenic, while the western **Halland** coast is scattered with small resort towns.

KALMAR

The stunning Renaissance castle **Kalmar Slott** is the site of the inception of the 1397 Kalmar Union, which attempted to unite the kingdoms of Denmark, Norway, Sweden, and Finland. This year it hosts a **Renaissance Festival** (June 30-July 2, 2000). (Open daily June-Aug. 10am-6pm; Apr.-May and Sept. 10am-4pm; Oct.-Mar. 2nd weekend of each month 11am-3:30pm. 60kr, students 30kr.) The Baroque **Kalmar Domkyrka,** on Stortorget, has the splendor of a major cathedral, but, alas, is *sans* bishop. (Open M-F 8am-7pm, Sa-Su 9am-7pm. Free organ concerts W noon.) The **Kalmar Läns Museum,** Skeppsbrog. 51, has relics from the wreckage of the 17th-century warship, **Kronan,** which met a glorious end when it sank in a 1676 battle against the Danish. (Open daily mid-June to mid-Aug. 10am-6pm; mid-Aug. to mid-June 10am-4pm. 50kr, students 20kr.) In the nearby towns, collectively dubbed **Glasriket** (Kingdom of Crystal), exquisite hand-blown crystal is made by the artisans depicted in the movie *My Life as a Dog,* such as **Orrefors** (tel. (0481) 34 19) and

Kosta Boda (tel. (0478) 345 00). Take bus 138 (1hr., 58kr) from the train station. (Both open M-F 9am-6pm, Sa 10am-4pm, Su noon-4pm.)

Trains and **buses** arrive south of town, across the bay from the castle. To get from the train station to the **tourist office**, Larmg. 6, go right on Stationsg., turn left on Ölandsg., and look left. (Tel. (0480) 153 50; fax 174 53. Open June-Aug. M-F 9am-7pm, Sa 10am-3pm, Su 1-6pm; July M-F 9am-8pm, Sa 10am-5pm; Sept.-May M-F 9am-5pm; May and Sept. M-F 9am-5pm, Sa 10am-1pm.) To get from the tourist office to the **Kalmar Vandrarhem (HI),** Rappeg. 1, on the island of Ängö, go north on Larmg., turn right on Södra Kanalg., turn left on Ängöleden, and it's on the right. (Tel. (0480) 129 28; fax 882 93. 145kr, nonmembers 185kr. Breakfast 49kr. Reception June-Aug. 8-10am and 4:30-10pm; Sept.-May until 9pm.) **Stensö Camping** is 2km south of Kalmar. (Tel. (0480) 888 03. June-Aug. 125kr; Apr. and Sept.-Oct. 100kr. Call ahead.) Restaurants cluster around **Larmtorget. Postal code:** 39101.

◪ **EXCURSION FROM KALMAR: ÖLAND.** Visible from Kalmar's coast, the island of **Öland** stretches over 100km of green fields and white sand beaches. The royal family roosts here on holiday, and Crown Princess Victoria's birthday, Victoriadagen (July 14), is celebrated island-wide. Commoners flock to the **beaches** of Löttorp and Böda in the north and Grönhögen and Ottenby in the south. **Buses** 101 and 106 go from Kalmar's train station to Öland (30-40kr). Öland's **tourist office** (tel. (0485) 56 06 00) is in Färjestaden. Sleep at **Vandrarhem Borgholm,** Rosenfors (tel. (0485) 107 56), or **Vandrarhem Böda** (tel. (0485) 220 38), on Melböda in Löttorp.

MALMÖ

Though Malmö (mahl-MER), the country's third-largest city, is often used merely as a gateway, its beautiful squares **Stortorget** and **Lilla Torg** lend the city its own appeal. In the west end, the reconstructed **Malmöhus Castle** houses the **Malmös Museer,** which documents the city's history. (Tel. (040) 34 44 00. Open daily June-Aug. 10am-4pm; Sept.-May noon-4pm. 40kr, students 20kr.) The **Form Design Center,** Lilla Torg 9, highlights Swedish design, art, and architecture. (Open Tu-F 11am-5pm, Th 11am-6pm, Sa 10am-4pm, Su noon-4pm. Free.) The **Malmö Konsthall,** St. Johannesg. 7, exhibits modern art. (Open daily 11am-5pm, W until 11pm. Free.)

The **train station** and **harbor** lie just north of the Old Town. Pilen **ferries** (tel. (040) 23 44 11) run to Copenhagen (45min., 59kr); **trains** arrive from Gothenburg (3½hr., 395kr, under 25 275kr) and Stockholm (4½-6hr., 560kr, under 25 395kr). The **tourist office** in the train station has free maps and the very useful *Malmö this Month.* (Open June-Aug. M-F 9am-7pm, Sa-Su 10am-2pm and 5-7pm; Sept.-May M-F 9am-5pm, Sa 10am-2pm.) Log on at the **Cyberspace C@fè,** Engelbrektsg. 13. (Tel. (040) 611 01 16. Open daily 10am-10pm. 22kr per 30min.) From the train station or harbor, take bus 21C to the sparkling **Vandrarhem Malmö (HI),** Backav. 18. (Tel. (040) 822 20; fax 51 06 59. 125kr; nonmembers 165kr. Breakfast 38kr. Reception 8-10am and 4-8pm.) Or **camp** in the giant Malmöhus Park for free. Your wallet will thank you for feasting at **Café Siesta,** Hjorttackeg. 1. *(Dagens rätt* M-F 50kr. Open M and Sa 10am-6pm, Tu-F 10am-midnight, Su noon-midnight.) **Postal code:** 20110.

LUND

What Oxford and Cambridge are to England, Uppsala and Lund are to Sweden. Lund University's antagonism with its scholarly northern neighbors in Uppsala has inspired countless pranks, drag shows, and drinkfests in Lund's bright streets. The town's ancient **cathedral,** St. Laurentius, is an impressive 900-year-old reminder of the time when Lund was the religious center of Scandinavia. (Open M-F 8am-6pm, W until 7pm, Sa 9:30am-5pm, Su 9:30am-6pm. Tours in English M-Sa 3pm. Free organ concerts Su 10am.) Head south to **Student Info** (www.lu.se/intsek/international/whatsup.html) at the student union (*akademiska föreningen,* or AF; open Sept.-May M-F 10am-4pm) to catch up on concerts, exhibitions, and sports events. Nearby **Kulturen,** at the end of Sankt Anneg. on Tegnerplastén, is an open-air museum with 17th- and 18th-century Swedish homes, churches, and history displays. (Open May-Sept. daily 11am-5pm; Oct.-Apr. Tu-Su noon-4pm. 40kr.)

Lund is easily accessible from Malmö on most **SJ trains** and by local **pågatågen** (10min., 30kr; railpasses valid). The **tourist office**, Kyrkog. 11, opposite the cathedral, books 175kr rooms for a 50kr fee. (Tel. (046) 35 50 40; fax 12 59 63. Open June-Aug. M-F 10am-6pm, Sa-Su 10am-2pm; Sept. and May M-F 10am-5pm, Sa 10am-2pm; Oct.-Apr. M-F 10am-5pm.) Rest your tired limbs at the delightful **HI Hostel Tåget** (The Train), Vävareg. 22, housed in authentic 1940s sleeping cars. To get there take the overpass to the park side of the station. (Tel. (046) 14 28 20; fax 32 05 68. 110kr, nonmembers 140kr. Reception daily Apr.-Oct. 8-10am and 5-8pm, Nov.-Mar. 5-7pm.) If you've missed "the train," try to find a bed in Malmö—the aging **Lundabygdens Vandrarhem** is just as far and is not on our preferred list. To get to **Källby Camping**, take bus 1 (dir: Klostergården) and ask to be let off at the campground. (Tel. (046) 35 51 88. 30kr per tent. Open mid-June to Aug.) Mårtenstorget features a fresh fruit and vegetable **market.** (Open M-Sa 7am-2:30pm.) **Mejeriet,** Stora Söderg. 64, packs a bar, movie theater, and lots of summer events into a former dairy. Hours vary with shows; call (046) 12 38 11 for info. **Postal code:** 22101.

YSTAD

Travelers just passing through en route to Bornholm often miss out on the charms of this quiet town. In town, walk down **Stora Östergatan,** a pedestrian shopping street, to hit **Stortorget,** the market square. Just south of the market square lies the ancient monastery, **Gråbrödraklostret.** (Open M-F noon-5pm, Sa-Su noon-4pm. Free.) **Ales Stenar** (Ale's Stones), a mysterious circular stone formation outside the city dating from the late Iron Age (thought to be a type of grave), is accessible during the summer via bus 322 (30min., 20-30kr). Trafiken (tel. (0411) 180 65) and Scandlines (tel. (042) 18 63 00) **ferries** leave from behind the train station for Bornholm (2½ hr., 3 per day in summer, 140kr) and Poland. **Trains** pull in from Malmö (1hr., 60kr). The **tourist office** is across the tracks from the station. (Tel. (0411) 776 81. Open mid-June to mid-Aug. M-F 9am-7pm, Sa 10am-7pm, Su 11am-6pm; mid-Aug. to mid-June M-F 9am-5pm.) The train station houses the new hostel **Vandrarhemmet Stationer.** (160kr. Breakfast 45kr. Reception June-Aug. 5-7pm and 9-10pm; Oct.-May 5-6pm.) To get to the beachfront **Vandrarhem Kantarellen** or **Sandskogens Camping,** walk east from the bus or train station along Österleden; hostel reception is on the right between Fritidsvägen and Jaktpaviljongsvägen, while camping is to the left up Jaktpaviljongsvägen (both 30min.). Or, take bus 572 from the station (5min., 8kr). (Hostel tel. (0411) 665 66; fax 109 13. 120kr, nonmembers 160kr. Reception 9-10am and 4-6pm. Kitchen. Camping tel. (0411) 192 70. 105kr.) **Postal code:** 27101.

VARBERG

Located between Gothenborg and Malmö, coastal Varberg beckons with expansive white sand beaches and the spectacular **Varberg Fortress,** overlooking the sky-blue waters of the Kattegatt. (Tours mid-June to mid-Aug. every hr. 11am-4pm. 30kr.) Just south of town, the shallow bay of **Apelviken** offers some of the best **windsurfing** and **surfing** in northern Europe. **Surfer's Paradise,** Söderg. 22, rents gear and gives tips. (Tel. (0340) 67 70 55. Call ahead.) Those who would rather explore the gorgeous **beaches** (some nude) can rent bikes at **BF Cykel,** Östra Langg. 47. (70kr per day. Open M-F 9:30am-6pm, Sa 9:30am-2pm.) **Trains** arrive from Gothenborg (1hr., 100kr, under 25 70kr) and Malmö (2½hr., 290kr, under 25 205kr). To get from the station to the **tourist office,** in Brunnsparken, walk four blocks right on Västra Vallg. (Tel. (0340) 887 70; fax 61 11 95. Open mid-June to mid-Aug. M-Sa 9am-7pm, Su 3-7pm; off-season reduced hours.) The bright rooms of **Varbergs Fästning Vandrarhem,** inside the fortress, will make you forget it was used as the Crown Jail from 1852-1931. Being locked up was never this fun (unless you're into that), nor this popular; book ahead. (Tel. (0340) 887 88. Dorms 135kr; singles 130kr. Reception open June-Aug. 8-10am and 5-9pm; Sept.-May call ahead.) If you're acquitted, there's usually room at **Skeppsgårdens Vandrarhem,** Krabbesväg 4. From the tourist office, continue down Västra Vallg., go right on Lasarettsg., then left on Knut Porses väg. (Tel. (0340) 130 35 or (070) 321 30 35; fax (0340) 103 95. 150kr. Breakfast included. Reception 8am-noon and 2-9pm.) **Apelvikens Camping** is on the beach. (Tel. (0340)

141 78; fax 875 38. Open late Mar. to Oct. 120-160kr.) The **Mignan Café**, Drottningg. 23, and **Majas Café** on Kungsg., both just off Stortorget (the main square), have fantastic breakfasts and lunch specials (40-50kr). **Postal code:** 43201.

GOTHENBURG (GÖTEBORG)

The long-time hub of Swedish industry and the country's second-largest city, Göteborg (YUH-ta-boy) is a city where culture and history aren't always on display, but university students fuel an active but easy-going café scene. *Göteborgare* think of themselves as more welcoming than their counterparts in Stockholm, whom they contemptuously call *Nollåttor* (zero-eights), after Stockholm's area code.

◪ ▐▗ PRACTICAL INFO, ACCOMMODATIONS, AND FOOD. Trains go from Nordstaden to Malmö (3½hr., 9 per day, 395kr, under 25 275kr); Stockholm (3½-6hr., 10 per day, 520kr, under 25 355kr); and Oslo (4½hr., 3 per day, 407kr, under 25 282kr). Stena Line **ferries** (tel. (031) 704 00 00; fax 85 85 95) sail to Frederikshavn, Denmark (3hr., 15 per day, 80kr) and Kiel, Germany (14hr., 820kr); SeaCat **hydrofoils** (tel. (031) 775 08 00; fax 12 60 90) to Frederikshavn (1hr. 45min., 4 per day, 100-120kr); and Scandinavian Seaways (tel. (031) 65 06 50) to Newcastle, England (22hr., 1125kr). The **tourist office**, Kungsportsplatsen 2, sells **Göteborg Cards,** which include unlimited public transit and various attractions (24-hour 75kr). From the station, cross Drottningtorget, and follow Östra Larmag. from the right of the Radisson (5min.). (Tel. (031) 61 25 00; fax 61 25 01. Open daily late June to early Aug. 9am-8pm; early June and late Aug. 9am-6pm; May M-F 9am-6pm, Sa-Su 10am-2pm; Sept.-Apr. M-F 9am-5pm, Sa 10am-2pm.) The **city library** *(stadsbibliotek),* on Götaplatsen, has free **internet.** (Open M-Th 10am-8pm, F 10am-6pm, Sa 11am-4pm.)

To reach the gorgeous **Slottskogens Hostel (STF/HI),** Vegag. 21, take tram 1 or 2 (dir: Frölunda) to "Olivedalsg." and walk uphill. (Tel. (031) 42 65 20; fax 14 21 02. Dorms 95-110kr; singles 205kr; nonmembers add 40kr. Kitchen. Sauna. Bike rental. Reception 8am-noon and 3-10pm. Check-in 3-6pm. V, MC.) The quiet **Masthuggsterrassen (SVIF),** Masthuggsterrassen 8, is perched on the harbor. Take tram 3, 4, or 9 to "Masthuggstorget," cross the square diagonally, go down Angra Långg away from the center, and look for signs. (Tel. (031) 42 48 20; fax 42 48 21; email masthuggsterrassen.vandrarhem@telia.com. 130kr. Reception 8-10am and 5-8pm. V, MC.) To reach the **Stigbergsliden Hostel (STF/HI),** Stigbergsliden 10, take tram 3 or 4 to "Stigbergstorget" and walk east down the hill. (Tel. (031) 24 16 20; fax 24 65 20; email vandrarhem.stigbergsliden@swipnet.se. Dorms 110kr; singles 205kr; doubles 260kr; nonmembers add 40kr. Reception 8-10am and 4-10pm. Check-in 4-6pm. V, MC.) Pitch your tent at **Kärralund Camping,** Olbersg. Catch tram 5 to "Welanderg.," then go east on Olbersg. (Tel. (031) 84 02 00; fax 84 05 00. 130kr per tent; rooms 110-150kr. Reception 7am-11pm.) **Matilda's,** on Kungstorget, is a farm-style kitchen that whips up top-notch sandwiches and pier (20-37kr). (Open May 31-July 3 M-F 10am-6pm, Sa 10am-4pm; July 5-30 M-F 11am-5pm.) **Postal code:** 40401.

▨ ▟ SIGHTS AND ENTERTAINMENT. To the south of Nordstaden, just across Drottningtorget (main square) and the Hamn canal, is the touristy island of **Inom Vallgraven.** One more canal farther and to the west lie **Vasastaden,** the student grotto, and **Haga,** the old city. **Kungsport Avenyn,** the city's main drag, stretches from Kungsportsplatsen all the way up to **Götaplatsen,** site of Carl Milles' famous **sculpture fountain** of Poseidon. Although the final version features a large fish squirming out of his hand, Milles' original design featured a more virile Poseidon wielding his member like a mighty trident. On the same square, the regal **Konstmuseet** houses the largest collection of Nordic art in Scandinavia as well as the **Hasselblad Center,** an excellent photo exhibition. (Open May-Aug. M-F 11am-4pm, Sa-Su 11am-5pm; Sept.-Apr. Tu and Th-F 11am-4pm, W 11am-9pm, Sa-Su 11am-5pm. 35kr.) The **Göteborgs Operan,** Lilla Bommen (box office tel. (031) 13 13 00), an opera house that mimics a ship at full mast, is en route to the **Göteborg Maritime Centrum,** which features a large number of docked ships and sailing vessels that you can board and tour. (Open daily Mar.-Apr. and Sept.-Nov. 10am-4pm; May-June and Aug. 10am-

6pm; July 10am-9pm. 35kr.) **Stadsmuseet,** Norra Hamng. 12, houses exhibits on city history, from Vikings to the city's post-industrial rebirth. (Open June-Aug. daily 11am-4pm; Sept.-Apr. Tu and Th-Su 11am-4pm, W 11am-8pm. 40kr, students 10kr.) **Göteborgs Skärgård** (Archipelago) is a summer paradise for beach-goers and sailors. The secluded beach on **Vrångö** island in the archipelago makes a good daytrip; take tram 4 to "Saltholmen," then catch a **ferry** (tel. (031) 69 64 00).

Göteborg also has a thriving theater and classical music scene—pick up *What's on in Göteborg* at the tourist office. A younger, punkish crowd gathers at the bar **Underground.** (No cover. Open Tu-Th until 3am, F-Sa until 5am, Su-M until 1am.) Nightlife also abounds on **Kungportsavenyn.** Worthwhile stops are the pub **Bryggeriet** (open F-Sa til 3am, Su-Th til 2am) and the jumping dance floor at **Havanna** (no cover; women 20 and up, men 22 and up).

CENTRAL SWEDEN

Swedes get misty-eyed just talking about the province of Dalarna, near southern Sweden and yet also a part of the northern wilderness. This popular vacation spot is Sweden's *Smultronstället*—a secret place where people go to commune with nature, with themselves, and with their significant others. Scores of Swedes spend their summer holidays here in tidy red and white farmhouses in the woods.

UPPSALA

Once a hotbed of pagan spirituality and the cradle of Swedish civilization, Uppsala is now a Nordic Oxbridge, sheltering the 20,000 students of Sweden's oldest university. Scandinavia's largest cathedral, the magnificent **Domkyrka,** where Swedish monarchs were once crowned, looms just over the river. (Open daily 8am-6pm. Tours in English June-Aug. M-Sa 1pm.) The university museum, **Gustavianum,** across from the Domkyrka, houses the **Anatomical Theater,** the site of 18th-century public human dissections. (Open May-Sept. daily 11am-4pm; Sept.-May W and F-Su 11am-4pm, Th 11am-9pm.) The debate still rages over whether **Gamla Uppsala** (Old Uppsala), 4km north of the center, was the site of a legendary pagan temple. Today, little remains save huge burial mounds of monarchs and **Gamla Uppsala Kyrka,** one of Sweden's oldest churches. (Open daily May-Aug. 9am-6pm; Sept.-Apr. 9am-4pm. Free.) Take bus 2, 20, 24, or 54 (14kr) north from Dragarbrunnsg. After exhausting Uppsala, you can hop the boat to **Skokloster,** a dazzling Baroque palace built between 1654 and 1676. (Open May-Aug. daily 11am-4pm. 60kr, students 40kr. Boat departs in summer Tu-Su 11:30am from Islandsbron on Östra Åg. and Munkg.; returns 5:15pm; round-trip 110kr.)

Trains pull in from Stockholm (40min., every hr., 65kr, under 25 50kr). To get from the station to the **tourist office,** Fyristorg 8, walk right on Kungsg., left on St. Persg., and across the bridge. (Tel. (018) 27 48 00; fax 13 28 95. Open in summer M-F 10am-6pm, Sa 10am-3pm, Su noon-2pm; in winter closed Su.) The **Basic Hotel,** Kungsg. 27, has rooms with bathroom, shower, and kitchenette. (150kr. Laundry 10kr. Reception M-F 7am-11pm, Sa-Su 8am-10pm.) For peaceful, newly renovated rooms, try **Sunnersta Herrgård (HI),** Sunnerstav. 24, 6km south of town. Take bus 20 or 50 (16kr) from Dragarbrunnsg. to Herrgårdsv., then walk two blocks behind the kiosk, and walk 50m left. (Tel. (018) 32 42 20. 160kr; nonmembers 200kr. Breakfast 60kr. Reception 8-11am and 5-9pm. Open May-Aug. V, MC.) **Fyrishov Camping,** Idrottsg. 2, off Svartbäcksg., is 2km from the city center. Take bus 4 or 6 (bus 50 or 54 at night; 10min.) to "Fyrishov." (Tel. (018) 27 49 60; fax 24 43 33. Tents 85kr; 4- to 5-bed huts June-Aug. 8 545kr. Swedish Camping Card required; buy one for 60kr. Reception 7am-10pm.) **Max and Marie,** Drottningg. 7, serves a daily veggie buffet. (55kr, students 50kr. Open M-F 11am-3pm.) Good bets after dark are **Fellini,** Svartbäcksg. 7, a loud student rock and blues bar (open M-Sa 11am-1am), and the moody **Fredman's,** with live R&B, blues, and rock Wednesday to Saturday (cover 20-100kr; open Su-Tu 5pm-1am; W-Sa 5pm-2am; age 20 and up). **Postal code:** 75101.

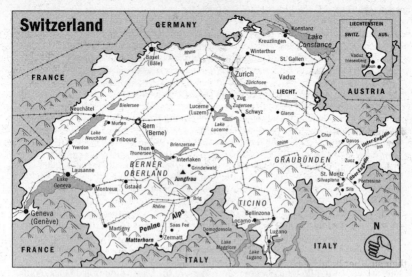

SWITZERLAND
(SCHWEIZ, SVIZZERA, SUISSE)

US$1 = 1.52SFR (SWISS FRANCS)	1SFR = US$0.66
CDN$1 = 1.02SFR	1SFR = CDN$0.98
UK£1 = 2.43SFR	1SFR = UK£0.41
IR£1 = 2.03SFR	1SFR= IR£0.49
AUS$1 = 0.98SFR	1SFR = AUS$1.02
NZ$1 = 0.80SFR	1SFR = NZ$1.25
SAR1= 0.25SFR	1SFR = SAR4.03
EUR€1= 1.60SFR	1SFR= EUR€0.62

PHONE CODE	Country code: 41. International dialing prefix: 00.

Switzerland's unparalleled natural beauty seduces hikers, skiers, bikers, paragliders, and scenery gazers from all over the globe to romp about its alpine playground. Three-fifths of the country is dominated by mountains: the Jura cover the northwest region, bordering France, while the Alps stretch gracefully across the entire lower half of Switzerland, flirting with Italy in the southern Lepontine chain and colliding with Austria in the eastern Rhaetian Alps. The rest of Switzerland is blanketed with meadows ripe for frolicking, pristine glacier lakes, and tiny hilltop hamlets as well as urban centers of culture and commerce.

The Swiss people are united by neither language nor religion, yet have managed to coexist (more or less) peacefully for centuries. As a people, they defy classification—they value their history and traditions, but not to the point that visitors can expect to see alp-horn blowing, *Lederhosen*-clad mountain men prancing about the slick Bahnhofstraße of Zurich's shopping district. While the stereotypes of Switzerland as a "Big Money" banking and watch-making mecca are true to some extent (nearly 4% of the Swiss are employed in the banking industry), its energetic youth culture belies the staid reputation that plagues Switzerland.

The Swiss, adept at welcoming tourists with open arms, have raised the hospitality industry to an art; service, food, and accommodations are consistently high-quality even at the most modest *pensions*. Although Switzerland is not known for being cheap, the thrifty traveler can always find a bargain. And in Switzerland, the best things—warm Swiss hospitality and sublime vistas—are priceless.

For the real skinny, check out *Let's Go: Austria and Switzerland 2000*.

DISCOVER SWITZERLAND

The Swiss are practically mountain goats, and with a backyard like the Alps, who wouldn't be? If you have one week, do not pass Go, head directly for **Interlaken** (p. 905), a backpacker town brimming with opportunities to participate in adventure sports like paragliding, bungee jumping, canyoning, river rafting, kayaking, and other death-defying acts as well as to waterfall hikes in the **Lauterbrunnen Valley** (p. 907). If you have two weeks, spend the first in Interlaken, then hit the Valais, with hiking as well as summer and winter skiing in **Zermatt** (p. 908) and **Saas Fee** (p. 908). If you have more time, head east to Graubünden, the most rural and wild canton, for cheap winter skiing and snowboarding as well as summer hiking in **Arosa** (p. 901). While many come to Switzerland to commune with nature, others come to commune with other backpackers: popular hotspots include **Montreux** (especially during the JazzFest; p. 893), cosmopolitan **Geneva** (p. 887), and cutting-edge, consumer-culture **Zurich** (p. 896). Backpacker getaway hostels hidden away in the hills are an up-and-coming phenomenon: explore the Swiss countryside based out of **Leysin** (p. 893), **Gryon** (p. 893), **Lugano** (p. 909), or **Locarno** (p. 910).

GETTING THERE AND GETTING AROUND

BY PLANE. Major international airports for overseas connections are located in **Bern, Geneva,** and **Zurich.** The **Basel** airport has connections to European cities.

BY TRAIN. Switzerland's public transportation system is comprehensive and efficient. Federal (**SBB, CFF**) and private **railways** connect most towns and villages. **Eurail** is valid on most intercity trains; note that it is *not* valid in the Bernese Oberland (Interlaken and the Jungfrau). **Swisspasses** are expensive, but are worth buying if you will be traveling extensively in the country, as they cover not only intercity trains but also public trams within 30 cities, yellow post buses, ferries and water taxis, and 25-50% discounts on many mountain railways and cable cars (2nd class: 4-day US$188, 8-day US$238, 15-day US$288, 1-month US$400). Two people traveling together qualify for a 40% companion discount on the second Swisspass. The **Swiss Flexipass,** valid for any three days of second-class travel within 30 days, costs US$176 and may not be worth it. **Regional Passes** (50-175SFr), available in eight different regions, can be bought in major tourist offices by holders of Eurail passes. The **Swiss Card,** sold only abroad, offers 50% off most trains and buses in Switzerland for one month (US$128). For national **rail info,** dial 157 22 22.

BY BUS AND BY FERRY. Federally run yellow **postal buses (PTT)** connect even the smallest villages (Swisspasses valid, but not Eurail). PTT stations are usually adjacent to train stations; local schedules are available at train stations as well. On most lakes, notably Lake Geneva, Lake Neuchâtel, and Lake Lucerne, **ferries** run between towns. Swisspass generally grants free passage; Eurail may get you a discount.

BY CAR. The **Association for Safe International Road Travel (ASIRT)** considers road travel (by car or bus) to be relatively safe in Switzerland. With armies of mechanized road crews ready to remove snow at moment's notice, roads at altitudes of up to 1500m generally remain open throughout winter. The **speed limit** is 50km per hr. (31mph) within cities; outside towns, the limit is 130km per hr. (81mph) on highways, 100km per hr. (62mph) on all other roads. Many small Swiss towns forbid cars to enter; some forbid only visitors' cars, require special permits, or restrict driving hours. EU citizens driving in Switzerland don't need any special documentation, just registration and a license. To rent a car, you must have had a valid driver's license for at least one year. Drivers under 25 must pay a daily "young driver" fee. Rates for all cars rented in Switzerland include an obligatory 40SFr annual **road toll**, called a *vignette*. All cars must carry a first-aid kit and a red emergency triangle. Emergency phones are located along all major highways. The **Swiss Touring Club**, rue Pierre-Fatio 9, CH-1211 Geneva 3 (tel. (022) 737 12 12) operates road patrols that assist motorists in need; dial 140 for help.

BY BIKE AND BY THUMB. Cycling, though strenuous, is a splendid way to see the country; rental at most stations is 26SFr per day (slightly more to return to another station). The **Touring Club Suisse,** Cyclo Tourisme, chemin Riantbosson 11-13, CH-1217 Meyrin (tel. (022) 785 12 22; fax 785 12 62), will send you information, maps, brochures, route descriptions, and mileage charts. In Switzerland, some men and women traveling in groups and men traveling alone **hitch** (called "autostop") beyond the range of bus or train routes.

ESSENTIALS

DOCUMENTS AND FORMALITIES. Switzerland does not require visas for nationals of Australia, Canada, the EU, New Zealand, South Africa, or the US, for stays of shorter than three months.

Swiss Embassies at Home: **Australia,** 7 Melbourne Ave, Forrest, Canberra, ACT 2603 (tel. (02) 62 73 39 77; fax 6273 3428); **Canada,** 5 Marlborough Ave, Ottawa, ON KIN 8E6 (tel. (613) 235-1837; fax 563-1394); **Ireland,** 6 Ailesbury Rd, Ballsbridge, Dublin 4 (tel. (01) 218 63 82/83; fax 283 03 44); **New Zealand,** 22 Panama St, Wellington (tel. (04) 472-1593; fax 499-6302); **South Africa** 818 George Ave, Arcadia 0083, P.O. Box 2289, 0001 Pretoria (tel. (012) 43 67 07; fax 43 67-71); Cradock Heights, 2nd fl., 21 Cradock Ave, Rosebank 2196; P.O. Box 724, Parklands 2121 (tel. (011) 442 75 00; fax 442 78 91); **UK,** 16-18 Montague Pl., London W1H 2BQ (tel. (020) 76 16 60 00; fax 77 24 70 01); **US,** 2900 Cathedral Ave, NW, Washington DC 20008-3499 (tel. (202) 745-7900; fax 387-2564).

Foreign Embassies in Switzerland: Nearly all foreign embassies are in **Bern** (p. 903). Most consulates are in **Zurich** (see p. 896).

TOURIST OFFICES. The **Swiss National Tourist Office,** marked by a standard blue "i" sign, is represented in nearly every town in Switzerland, though in smaller towns the staff may not speak English.

Tourist Boards at Home: **Canada,** 154 University Ave, Toronto, ON M5H 3Y9 (tel. (416) 971-9734; 926 East Mall, Etobicoke, ON M9B 6K1 (tel. (416) 695-2090; fax 695-2774; www.switzerlandtourism.com); **UK,** Swiss Centre, Swiss Court, London W1V 8EE (tel. (020) 77 34 19 21; fax 74 37 45 77; stlondon@switzerlandtourism.ch); **US,** 608 Fifth Ave, New York, NY 10020 (tel. (212) 757-5944; fax 262-6116).

MONEY. The Swiss monetary unit is the **Swiss Franc (SFr),** divided into 100 *centimes* (called *Rappen* in German Switzerland). Coins are issued in denominations of 5, 10, 20, and 50 *centimes* and 1, 2, and 5SFr; bills come in 10, 20, 50, 100, 500, and 1000SFr. Currency exchange is easiest at ATMs, train stations, and post offices, where rates are the same as or close to bank rates but where commissions are smaller. There is technically no need for **tipping** in Switzerland, as gratuities are already automatically factored into prices; however, it's polite to round up to the nearest 5SFr; say *Zahlen bitte* (TSAHL-en BIT-uh) to ask for the bill, then tell the waiter how much change you want back. Switzerland's vistas come at a price: if you stay in hostels and prepare most of your own food, expect to spend between US$30-65 per day. A dorm bed in a hostel averages around US$12-18, while hotel singles start at about US$18. A basic sit-down meal usually costs around US$12.

COMMUNICATION

Post: **Airmail** from Switzerland averages 7-20 days to North America, although times are more unpredictable from smaller towns. Domestic letters take 1-3 days.

Telephone: **International direct dial** numbers include: **AT&T,** 0800 89 00 11; **Sprint,** 0800 89 09 78; **MCI WorldPhone Direct,** 0800 89 02 22; **Canada Direct,** 0800 55 83

30; **BT Direct,** 0800 55 25 44; **Telkom South Africa Direct,** 0800 55 85 35. **Police,** tel. 117. **Ambulance,** tel. 144.

Languages: German, French, Italian, and Romansch. English is the most common 2nd language in Switzerland, and most urban Swiss speak it fluently. Outside of cities and among older residents, however, you may have to rely on phrasebooks. Leap right in with our language charts on p. 949, you multilingual fool, you.

ACCOMMODATIONS AND CAMPING. Like most things Swiss, accommodations are usually clean, orderly, and expensive. Wherever you stay, be sure to ask for a **guest card.** Normally, the "card" is merely a copy of your receipt for the night's lodging, sometimes available only after staying three nights or more, and grants discounts to hiking excursions, town museums, and public transportation. Most local tourist offices distribute extensive listings (the *Gastgeberverzeichnis*), and many will reserve a room for a small fee. **Hotels** are expensive (singles 50-75SFr; doubles 80-150SFr); the cheapest hotel-style accommodations have **Gasthof** or **Gästehaus** ("inn") in the name; **Hotel-Garni** also means cheap.

Renting a **private room** (*Privatzimmer)* in a family home is inexpensive (rooms start at 25-60SFr per person) and friendly. Such rooms generally include a hot water, a sink, and use of a toilet and shower. Many places rent only for longer stays, or they may levy a surcharge (10-20%) for stays of fewer than 3 nights. Slightly more expensive, **pensions** (*Pensionen)* are similar to the American and British B&B. Most places have double beds (*Doppelzimmer)*, so single travelers usually have to pay more. Continental breakfast is *de rigueur;* the classier places will add meat, cheese, and an egg. With over 1200 **campgrounds,** camping can be one of the most inexpensive ways of enjoying Switzerland. Prices average 6-9SFr per person, 4-10SFr per tent—a joyous fact in such an expensive country. You must obtain permission from landowners to camp on private property. Most sites are open in the summer only, but some 80 sites are specifically set aside for winter camping. Camping along roads and in public areas is forbidden.

FOOD AND DRINK. Switzerland's hearty cooking will keep you warm through those frigid alpine winters but will skyrocket your cholesterol. Bernese *Rösti,* a plateful of hash brown potatoes skilleted and sometimes flavored with bacon or cheese is prevalent in the German regions, as is *fondue* in the French. Try Valaisian *raclette,* made by melting cheese over a fire, then scraping it onto a baked potato and garnishing with meat or vegetables. Self-serve cafeterias and supermarkets **Migros** and **Co-op** supply the most essential Swiss culinary invention, milk chocolate (*Lindt, Toblerone,* and *Nestlé* are native favorites), on the cheap.

SKIING AND HIKING. Switzerland's 9000km of **hiking paths** range from simple foothill excursions to ice-axe-wielding glacier expeditions. Bands of white-red-white mark trails; if there are no markings, you're on an "unofficial" trail, which is not always a problem—most are well maintained. Blue-white-blue markings indicate that a trail requires special equipment, either for difficult rock climbs or glacier climbing. **Swiss Alpine Club (SAC) huts** are modest and extremely practical for those interested in trekking in higher, more remote areas of the Alps. Bunk rooms sleep 10 to 20 side by side, with blankets (no electricity or running water) provided. One night's stay without food averages 30SFr (members 20-25SFr). Membership costs 126SFr. Contact the SAC, Sektion Zermatt, Haus Dolomite, CH-3920 Zermatt, Switzerland (tel. (028) 67 26 10). The best maps to bring are the **Freytag-Berndt** and **Kümmerly-Frey** maps (around US$10), available in Swiss bookstores.

Skiing in Switzerland is often less expensive than in North America if you avoid the pricey resorts. Passes (valid for transportation to, from, and on lifts) run 30-50SFr per day and 100-300SFr per week. A week of lift tickets, equipment rental, lessons, lodging, and *demi-pension* (half-pension—breakfast plus one other meal, usually dinner) averages 475SFr. Summer skiing is no longer as prevalent as it once was, but is still available in Zermatt.

LOCAL FACTS

Time: Switzerland is 1hr. ahead of Greenwich Mean Time (GMT; see p. 49).

Climate: Switzerland is surprisingly mild; in July, temperatures can briefly reach temperatures can reach 38°C (100°F), while in Feb. they get down to -10°C (5°F). Mountainous areas are cooler and wetter the higher you get; as a rule, temperatures drop about 1.7°C (3°F) with each additional 300m. Bring warm sweaters Sept.-May; add a thick coat, hat, and gloves in winter. The lake areas, from Lake Constance down to Geneva, are very rainy.

Hours: Most **stores** in Switzerland close for lunch (noon-3pm), Sa afternoons, and all day Su. Many **museums** close M. **Banks** are open M-F 8am-12:30pm and 2-4:30pm.

Holidays: New Year's Day (Jan. 1-2); Good Friday (Apr. 5); Easter Monday (Apr. 5); Labor Day (May 1); Ascension Day (June 1); Whitmonday (June 11); Swiss National Day (Aug. 1); and Christmas (Dec. 25-26).

Festivals: Two raucous festivals are Basel's **Fasnacht** (Carnival) in Mar. and Geneva's **Escalade**. "Open-Air" music festivals occur all over Switzerland throughout the summer. A few highlights include the **Montreux JazzFest** (July), Bern's **Gurtenfestival** (mid-July), **Paléo Festival Nyon** near Geneva (late July), and the **Open-Air St. Gallen** (late June). Try heiwww.unige.ch/switzerland/culture/events.htm or www.music.ch for more info.

FRENCH SWITZERLAND

GENEVA (GENÈVE, GENF)

"I detest Geneva," muttered Napoleon in 1798, "they know English too well." They still do—two-thirds of Geneva (pop. 180,000) is either foreign-born or from elsewhere in Switzerland—but he had more to contend with than linguistic contempt, as Geneva's citizens have always had a long and belligerent tradition of battling for their political and religious independence. In 1536, Geneva welcomed a young, unknown John Calvin to its cathedral; later, aesthetes and free thinkers including Voltaire, Madame de Staël, and Rousseau lived here. Today, multinational organizations (including the Red Cross and the United Nations) continue to lend the city an international feel that contrasts strongly with the homogeneity of most Swiss towns. Indeed, many say that the only thing Geneva shares with the rest of Switzerland is its neutral foreign policy and the state religion, banking.

▐ GETTING THERE AND GETTING AROUND

Flights: Cointrin Airport (tel. 717 71 11, flight info tel. 799 31 11) is a hub for **Swissair** (tel. (0848) 80 07 00). **Bus** 10 connects to the center (15min., every 6min., 2.20SFr), while the **train** (6min., every 10 min., 4.80SFr) runs to Gare Cornavin.

Trains: Gare Cornavin, on pl. Cornavin, is the main station (www.sbb.ch). Hourly to: **Bern** (2hr., 40SFr); **Basel** (3hr., 72SFr); **Interlaken** (3hr., 65SFr); and **Zurich** (3½hr., 77SFr). Also to: **Lyon** (2hr., 6 per day, 58SFr, under 26 48SFr); **Paris** (3¾hr., 8 per day, 196SFr, under 26 166SFr); and **Milan** (4hr., 6 per day, 164SFr, under 26 132SFr). Reservations and info open M-F 8:30am-7pm, Sa 9am-5:30pm. **Gare des Eaux-Vives** (tel. 736 16 20), on the eastern edge of the city, connects to France via tram 12 (dir: Amandoliers SNCF). To: **Annecy** (1½hr., every hr., 14.50SFr) and **Chamonix** (2½hr., 4 per day, 20.40SFr).

Ferries: CGN (tel. 741 52 31) runs hugely popular routes to Lausanne and Montreux, that depart from quai du Mont-Blanc. Round-trip 47-57SFr.

Public Transportation: Transport Publics Genevois (tel. 308 34 34), next to the tourist office in Gare Cornavin, has free bus route maps. Open daily 6:15am-8pm. **1hr.** of unlimited bus travel 2.20SFr; **3 stops or fewer** 1.50SFr. **Day passes** 5SFr for 1 zone, 8.50SFr for 4. SwissPass valid on all buses; Eurailpass not valid. Buses run roughly 5:30am-midnight. Buy tickets and passes at the train station, others at automatic vendors at every stop. Stamp multi-use tickets before boarding or risk a 60SFr fine.

Taxis: Taxi-Phone (tel. 331 41 33). 6.30SFr base fare 2.70SFr per km. Taxi from airport to city 25-30SFr (15-20min.; 4 passengers max.).

SWITZERLAND

Bike Rental: Genève Roule, pl. Montbrillant 17 (tel. 740 13 43), behind the station. 28 free bikes (50SFr deposit). Nicer ones from 5SFr per day. Open daily 7:30am-9:30pm.

Hitchhiking: Hitchers headed to Germany or northern Switzerland reportedly take bus 4/44 to "Jardin Botanique"; to France, bus 4/44 to "Palettes," then line D to "St-Julien."

🚩 ORIENTATION AND PRACTICAL INFORMATION

On the southwestern shore of **Lac Léman** (Lake Geneva), the labyrinthine cobble-stoned streets and quiet squares of the *vieille ville* surround the **Cathédrale de St-Pierre** and the **university.** Banks, bistros, and boutiques line the **Rhône River** to the north. Farther north, the United Nations, Red Cross, and World Trade Organization overlook the city. Carry your **passport** with you at all times; the French border is close by, and regional buses and local trams (12 and 16) often cross it.

TOURIST, FINANCIAL, AND LOCAL SERVICES

Tourist Offices: Main office, rue du Mont-Blanc 3 (tel. 909 70 00; fax 909 70 11; www.geneve-tourisme.ch), 5min. from Cornavin toward the pont du Mont-Blanc. **May move to the central post building in 2000.** English-speaking staff books hotel rooms (5SFr fee) and offers walking tours (2hr.; June 14-Oct. 2 M-Sa 10am; Oct. 3-June 13 Sa 10am; 12SFr, students 8SFr). Pick up the indispensable *Info Jeunes.* Open mid-June to Aug. M-F 8am-6pm, Sa-Su 8am-5pm; Sept. to mid-June M-Sa 9am-6pm. In summer, Geneva's **Centre d'Accueil et de Renseignements** (CAR; tel. 731 46 47) is parked by the Metro Shopping entrance to Cornavin Station. Answers questions and posts lists of musical and theatrical performances. Open mid-June to mid-Sept. 9am-11pm.

Consulates: Australia, chemin des Fins 2 (tel. 799 91 00). **Canada,** rue du Pré-de-Bichette 1 (tel. 919 92 00). **New Zealand,** chemin des Fins 2 (tel. 929 03 50). **South Africa,** rue de Rhône 65 (tel. 849 54 54). **UK,** rue de Vermont 37 (tel. 918 24 00). **US,** World Trade Center Bldg. 2 (tel. 798 16 05; recorded info 798 16 15).

Currency Exchange: ATMs have the best rates. **Gare Cornavin** offers good rates, no commission on traveler's checks, and credit card advances (200SFr min.); also wires money. Open Apr.-Oct. 6:45am-9:30pm; Nov.-Mar. 6:45am-8pm. Western Union open daily 7am-7pm.

Gay and Lesbian Services: Dialogai, rue de la Navigation 11-13 (tel. 906 40 40). Mostly male resource group with programs from support groups to outdoor activities. Publishes *Dialogai,* a guide to French-speaking Switzerland's gay scene. Open M-Th 2-7pm.

Laundromat: En 5 Sec SA, rue Cornavin 5 (tel. 732 32 57), 2min. from Gare Cornavin. Open Su-F 7:30am-6:45pm, Sa 8am-12:30pm.

EMERGENCIES AND COMMUNICATIONS

Emergencies: Police, rue Pecolat 5 (tel. 117). **Fire,** tel. 118. **Ambulance,** tel. 144.

Pharmacy: The pharmacy at the train station has the longest regular hours. Check *Genève Agenda* for late-night pharmacies (until 9 or 11pm), or call 144 or 111 (7pm-8am).

Medical Assistance: Hôpital Cantonal, rue Micheli-du-Crest 24 (tel. 372 33 11). Bus 1 or 5 or tram 12. Call the Association des Médecins (tel. 320 84 20) for walk-in clinic info.

Internet Cafés: Café Video ROM, on pl. de Cornavin (tel. 901 16 21). 5SFr per hr. Open M-Th 11am-8:30pm, F-Sa 11am-10pm, Su 1-8:30pm. **Point 6,** rue de Vieux-Billard 7a (tel. 800 26 00). 7SFr per hr. Open 10am-midnight.

Post Office: Poste Centrale, rue de Mont-Blanc 18, 1 block from Gare Cornavin in the Hôtel des Postes. Address mail to be held: Alexa du PONT, *Poste Restante,* **CH-1211** Genève 1 Mont-Blanc, Switzerland. Open M-F 7:30am-6pm, Sa 8-11am.

PHONE CODE	City code: 022. From outside Switzerland, dial country code (41) + city code (22) + local number.

🔥 ACCOMMODATIONS AND CAMPING

You can usually find dorm beds and hostel rooms in Geneva, but hotels fill quickly, so reserve in advance. If the places listed below are booked, try one of the 50 others listed in *Info Jeunes* (free at the tourist office).

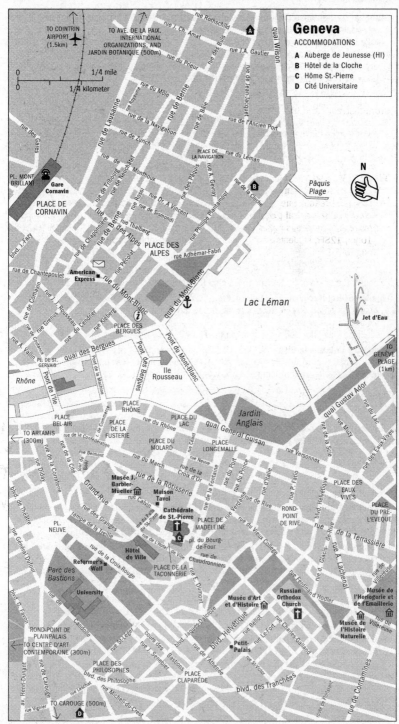

Geneva

ACCOMMODATIONS

A Auberge de Jeunesse (HI)
B Hôtel de la Cloche
C Hôme St.-Pierre
D Cité Universitaire

SWITZERLAND

Auberge de Jeunesse (HI), rue Rothschild 28-30 (tel. 732 62 60; fax 738 39 87). Walk left from the station down rue de Lausanne (15min.), turn right on rue Rothschild, and take bus 1 (dir: Wilson) to the end. A great meeting place, with CNN, library, and snack bar. Dorms 23SFr; doubles 60-70SFr; quads 99SFr. Breakfast included. Kitchen. Laundry. 5-night max. stay. Reception 6:30-10am and 4pm-midnight (in winter from 5pm). Lockout 10am-4pm (in winter 5pm). Curfew midnight. V, MC.

Cité Universitaire, av. Miremont 46 (tel. 839 22 11; fax 839 22 23). Take bus 3 (dir: Crêts-de-Champel) from "Le Popeye" on pl. de 22 Cantons, on the far right as you exit the station, to the end. Institutional housing with TV rooms, disco (open Th and Sa, free for guests), ping-pong, and small grocery shop. Dorms (July-Sept. only) 17SFr; singles 38SFr; doubles 55SFr; studios with kitchenette and bathroom 68SFr. **Internet.** Reception M-F 8am-noon and 2-10pm, Sa 8am-noon and 6-10pm, Su 9-11am and 6-10pm. For dorms only: lockout 10am-6pm and curfew 11pm. V, MC, AmEx.

Hôme St-Pierre, cours St-Pierre 4 (tel. 310 37 07; fax 310 17 27), seconds from the cathedral. Cross pont du Mont-Blanc from the station, head up rampe de la Treille, and take the 3rd right (15min.). Spectacular rooftop views and a convivial atmosphere. **Women only.** Dorms 22SFr; singles 36-45SFr; doubles 50-60SFr. Breakfast (M-Sa) 5SFr. Kitchen. Laundry 7SFr. Reception M-Sa 9am-noon and 4-8pm, Su 9am-noon. Reserve ahead. V, MC, AmEx.

Hôtel de la Cloche, rue de la Cloche 6 (tel. 732 94 81; fax 738 16 12), off quai du Mont-Blanc. A converted mansion—each room has chandeliers, antique mirrors, balconies, and TVs. Singles 50SFr; doubles 80SFr; triples 95SFr; quads 130SFr. In winter 5-10SFr discount. Breakfast 5SFr. Reception 8am-midnight. Reserve ahead. V, MC, AmEx.

Centre St-Boniface, av. du Mail 14 (tel. 322 26 00; fax 322 26 01). From the station, head right on bd. Fazy, across pont de La Coulouvrenière, and along av. du Mail (20min.). Jesuit-run center with TV room access. Singles 40SFr, some with shower and balcony. Kitchen. Reception M-F 9am-noon and 4-7pm. Reserve ahead.

Camping Pointe-à-la-Bise (tel. 752 12 96), on chemin de la Bise. Take bus 9 to "Rive," then bus E (north) to "Bise" (about 7km). 6SFr per person. No tents provided; beds are 18SFr each. Reception 8am-noon and 4-8pm. Open Apr.-Oct.

FOOD

You can find anything from sushi to paella in Geneva, but you may need a banker's salary to foot the bill. For a quick bite, **supermarkets** are on virtually every street corner, and *pâtisseries*, pasta/pizza parlors, and cafés permeate **pl. du Bourg-de-Four,** below Cathédrale de St-Pierre. The restaurant on the first floor of **Co-op,** on the corner of rue du Commerce and rue du Rhône, in the Centre Rhône Fusterie, has *Menüs* from 9.50SFr and salads for 2.30SFr per 100g. (Open M 9am-6:45pm, Tu-W, and F 8:30am-6:45pm, Th 8:30am-8pm, Sa 8:30am-5pm.)

Restaurant Manora, rue de Cornavin 4 (tel. 909 44 10), 3min. to the right of the station in the Placette department store. Huge self-serve restaurant with salads (from 4.20SFr), fruit tarts (3.20SFr), and entrees (from 11SFr). Open M-Sa 7am-9pm, Su 9am-9pm.

Le Rozzel, Grand-Rue 18 (tel. 312 42 72). Take bus 5 to pl. Neuve, then walk up the hill past the cathedral on rue Jean-Calvin to Grand-Rue. Sit outside and enjoy Breton-style *crêpes* (dinner 7-17SFr, dessert 5-12SFr). Open M-F 8am-10pm, Sa 10am-10pm. V, MC, AmEx.

Chez Costa, pl. de Rondeau 1 (tel. 300 13 66), in Carouge. Take tram 12 or 13 to "Carouge" and walk 1min. downhill. Red plush upholstery, dark wood interior, and a shaded outdoor patio. Breakfast 3-3.50SFr, steak 16-20Fr, *plat du jour* 12SFr.

La Crise, rue de Chantepoulet 13 (tel. 738 02 64). From the station, turn right on rue de Cornavin and left on rue de Chantepoulet. Healthy portions of veggie food with slender prices. Quiche and veggies 8.50SFr, soup 3.50SFr. Open M-F 6am-8pm, Sa 6am-3pm.

Auberge de Saviese, rue des Pâquis 20 (tel. 732 83 30). From Gare Cornavin, turn left onto rue de Lausanne and right on rue de Zurich, which brings you to rue des Pâquis. Load up on traditional Swiss specialties. Excellent *fondue au cognac* 19.50SFr, *raclette* with all the trimmings 29SFr. Open M-F 11:30-11pm, Sa-Su 6-11pm. V, MC, AmEx.

👁 🎵 SIGHTS AND ENTERTAINMENT

VIEILLE VILLE AND WATERFRONT. The *vieille ville*'s **Cathédrale de St-Pierre,** the navel of the Protestant world, is as austere as the day that Calvin, who preached to full houses here from 1536 to 1564, stripped it of its popish baubles. The 157-step **north tower** offers a commanding view over the old town. *(Open June-Sept. M-Sa 9am-7pm, Su 11:30am-7pm; Oct.-May Tu-Su 10am-noon and 2-5pm. Tower open July-Aug. 3SFr.)* The ruins of a Roman sanctuary, a 4th-century basilica, and a 6th-century church rest in an **archaeological site** below the cathedral. *(Open June-Sept. Tu-Su 11am-5pm; Oct.-May Tu-Sa 2-5pm. 5SFr, students 3SFr.)* Near the west end of the cathedral sits the 14th-century **Maison Tavel,** Geneva's oldest civilian medieval building, a posh, fortified urban palace that today houses a historical municipal **museum.** A few steps away is the 15th- to 17th-century **Hôtel de Ville** (Town Hall), where world leaders met on August 22, 1864 to sign the **Geneva Convention** that still governs conduct during war. The **Grand-Rue** leading away from the Hôtel de Ville is crammed with art galleries, medieval workshops, and 18th-century mansions; plaques along the street commemorate famous residents, including philosopher Jean-Jacques Rousseau, born at #40. Below the cathedral on rue de la Croix-Rouge, the lovely **Parc des Bastions** includes the **Mur des Réformateurs** (Reformers' Wall), a sprawling collection of bas-relief narrative panels and the towering figures of the Reformers themselves, including Knox, Calvin, and Cromwell. On the other side of the park, the ▣**Petit-Palais** contains works by Picasso, Renoir, Gauguin, Cézanne, and Chagall. *(Terrasse St-Victor 2, off bd. Helvétique. Take bus 17 to "Petit Palais" or 1, 3, or 5 to "Claparède." Open M-F 10am-6pm, Sa-Su 10am-5pm. 10SFr, students 5SFr.)* Farther east lie the glittering domes of the **Russian Orthodox Church,** whose interior is filled with hauntingly lovely icons, stained glass, and a heavy aroma of incense. *(Rue Toepffer. Take rue de Chaudronniers from the vieille ville.)*

As you descend toward the lake from the cathedral you will fast-forward 600 years; the streets widen, buses scuttle back and forth, and every corner sports a chic boutique or watch shop. The largest fountain in the world, the **Jet d'Eau,** down quai Gustave-Ardor on the waterfront, spews a spectacular plume of water 140m into the air (about seven tons at once). In the nearby **Jardin Anglais,** a floral clock (perhaps Geneva's most overrated attraction) pays homage to Geneva's watch industry with over 6,500 plants and the world's second-largest second hand (2.5m).

INTERNATIONAL HILL. Spectacular views of Lac Léman with Mont-Blanc in the background await in a series of garden-parks on the northern side of Geneva, up the hill behind the train station. For even better vistas, climb higher to Geneva's international city, home to myriad embassies and multilateral organizations, the highlight being the **International Red Cross.** Leave your ironic detachment at the door of its ▣**Museum,** lest it be ripped forcibly from you during a powerful tour. This fantastic museum employs images rather than rhetoric to drive home its emotional narrative of humanitarianism. *(Av. de la Paix 17. Take bus 8, F, V, or Z to "Appia" or "Ariana." Tel. 748 95 11. Open Su-M and W-Sa 10am-5pm. 10SFr, students 5SFr. Self-guided audio tours 5SFr.)* In the Red Cross's shadow stands the European headquarters of the **United Nations,** housed in the building that once sheltered the League of Nations. The guided tour of the UN is quite dull; the constant traffic of international diplomats (often in handsome non-Western dress) provides more excitement than anything the guides have to say. *(Open daily July-Aug. 9am-6pm; Apr.-June and Sept.-Oct. 10am-noon and 2-4pm; Nov.-Mar. M-F 10am-noon and 2-4pm. 8.50SFr, students 6.50SFr.)*

🎵 🎭 ENTERTAINMENT AND NIGHTLIFE

Genève Agenda, available at the tourist office, is your guide to fun, with event listings ranging from major festivals to movies. In July and August, the **Cinelac** turns Genève Plage into an open-air cinema screening mostly American films. Check listings in *Genève Agenda* for indoor cinemas ("v.o." indicates original language, with French and sometimes German subtitles; "st. ang." indicates English subtitles). There's also the biggest celebration of **American Independence Day** outside the US

FOR ART'S SAKE In the summer of 1996 a group of artists staged a sit-in demonstration at place du Bourg-de-Four just below the Cathédrale de St-Pierre. They ripped up pavement, built bonfires, and confused the hell out of tourists for six days until the city capitulated and granted them a no-rent lease for an abandoned industrial park on the left bank, now called Artamis (tel. 320 39 30; www.artamis.org). You'll find it at 12 rue de Strand, accessible by bus 2 or 10 ("Palladium"). This 10-building complex, a former run-down factory, displays high-quality graffiti and houses a mix of thriving art workshops, theaters, and fund-raising facilities as well as some of the best deals in town: an **internet café** (5SFr per hr.), a movie theater (2SFr), and bars. The Database building is a recording studio where many of the top house and jungle DJs in the area come to experiment and exchange ideas. All facilities and the main phone line (with information on performances and events) are open daily 4pm to 2am.

(July 4), and the **Fêtes de Genève** in early August is filled with international music and fireworks. **Free jazz concerts** take place in July and August at the Théâtre de Verdure in Parc de la Grange.

Summer nightlife centers around the cafés on the lakeside quays in the **Pl. du Bourg-de-Four,** below Cathédrale de St-Pierre, and the village of **Carouge** (take tram 12 to "pl. du Marché"), home to ▨**Au Chat Noir,** rue Vautier 13, a popular venue for jazz, funk, rock, salsa, and sax-moaning blues, with live concerts every night. (Open M-Th 6pm-4am, F 6pm-5am, Sa 9pm-5am, Su 9pm-4am. Concerts 9:30pm; 15SFr.) Back in the *vieille ville,* consort with the artsy patrons of the famous, chic bar **La Clémence,** pl. du Bourg-de-Four 20 (open M-Th 7am-12:30am, F-Sa 7am-1:30am), or chat merrily in the mother tongue at the friendly Irish cellar bar **Flanagan's,** rue du Cheval-Blanc 4, off Grand-Rue. (Guinness 8SFr. Live music Th-Sa 10pm-2am. Open daily 4pm-2am.) World rock pumps through the club **Abag Brasil,** 10 rue des Vieux-Grenardiers. (Open Th-Sa from 11pm.)

LAUSANNE

The story of Lausanne is a tale of two cities: the *vieille ville* is cosmopolitan and businesslike, while the lakefront at Ouchy is lazy and fairly decadent. To stroll through the 2000-year-old remains of the Roman city **Vicus de Lousanna,** take bus 2 to "Bois-de-Vaux" and follow the signs. Follow the medieval covered stairs to the hilltop to reach the Gothic **cathédrale,** consecrated in 1275 under Holy Roman Emperor Rudolph and Pope Gregory X. Climb the 200-step **tower** for a spectacular view of the city, lake, and mountains beyond. (Cathedral open daily July to mid-Sept. 7am-7pm; mid-Sept. to June 7am-5pm. Free guided tours July-Sept. 10:30, 11:15am, 3, and 3:45pm. Tower open 8:30-11:30am and 1:30-5:30pm. 2SFr.) Stretch your legs on Ouchy's main promenades, the **quai de Belgique** and **pl. de la Navigation.** The **Musée Olympique,** quai d'Ouchy 1, is a high-tech temple to modern Olympians with a smaller exhibit on the ancient games. (Open May-Sept. M-W and F-Su 9am-6pm, Th 9am-8pm; Oct.-Apr. Tu-W and F-Su 9am-6pm, Th 9am-8pm. 14SFr, students 9SFr; the idyllic grounds are free.) Another collection of note is the ▨**Collection de l'Art Brut,** Av. Bergières 11, filled with disturbing and beautiful artwork by atypical artists—institutionalized schizophrenics, peasants, and convicted criminals. The biographies of the artists are nearly as rich and fascinating as the art. Take bus 2 or 3 to "Jomini." (Open Tu-Su 11am-1pm, 2-6pm. 6SFr, students 4SFr.)

Frequent **trains** (tel. 157 22 22) arrive at pl. de la Gare 9, half-way between the *vieille ville* and the lakefront, from Montreux (20min., 9.40SFr); Geneva (50min., 20SFr); Basel (2½hr., 62SFr); and Zurich (2½hr., 67SFr). Take **Métro Ouchy** or **bus** 1, 3, or 5 to downtown. The **tourist office,** in the train station, reserves rooms (4-6SFr). (Tel. 617 73 73; www.lausanne.tourisme.ch. Open Apr.-Sept. 9am-9pm, Oct.-Mar. 9am-6pm.) To reach the large and gleaming **Jeunotel (HI),** chemin du Bois-de-Vaux 36, take bus 2 (dir: Bourdonette) to "Bois-de-Vaux," cross the street, and follow the signs. (Tel. (021) 626 02 22; fax 626 02 26. Dorms 24-31SFr; singles 42-57SFr; doubles 86-104SFr; triples and quads 34SFr per person. Reception 24hr. V, MC.) Spacious rooms compensate for run-down hallways and common baths in the **Hotel Excelsior,** chemin du Closelet 6. From the station, turn right on av. de la Gare, right on av. d'Ouchy, and left after the bridge on Closelet (5min.). (Tel. (021) 616 84 51; fax 616 84 58. Singles 60-98SFr; doubles 100-140SFr. Reception 8am-10pm.) To get to the lakeside **Camping de Vidy,** chemin du Camping 3, follow the directions above to Jeunotel and continue past it under the overpass; reception is straight across rte. de Vidy. (Tel. (021) 622 50 00; fax 622 50 01. 6.50SFr, students 6SFr; tents 7-11SFr; 1- to 4-person bungalows 54-86SFr; city tax 1.20SFr per person and 1.40SFr per car. Shower included. Reception 8am-12:30pm and 5-8pm.) Restaurants, cafés, and bars cluster around **pl. St-François** and the **vieille ville. Migros supermarket,** 2 av. de Rhodanie, is near the "Ouchy" Metro stop. (Open in spring and summer M-Sa 9am-7pm, Su 8am-9:45pm.) **Postal code:** CH-1001.

MONTREUX

Montreux is postcard Switzerland at its swanky, genteel best. The crystal-blue water of Lac Léman (Lake Geneva) and the snow-capped Alps are a photographer's dream. The gloomy 13th-century Savoy fortress, the **Château de Chillon,** on a nearby island, is one of the most visited attractions in Switzerland. It features all the comforts of home—including prison cells, a torture chamber, and a weapons room—and inspired Lord Byron's *The Prisoner of Chillon* as well as works by Rousseau, Hugo, and Dumas. Take the CGN **ferry** (11SFr, under 26 5.50SFr) or bus 1 to "Chillon" (2.60SFr). (Tel. 963 39 12. Open Apr.-Sept. 9am-6pm; Mar. and Oct. 9:30am-5pm; Nov.-Feb. 10am-4pm. 7SFr, students 5.50SFr.) Montreux's main attraction, however, is the world-famous **Montreux Jazz Festival,** one of the biggest parties in Europe, which lasts 15 days starting the first Friday in July. Write to the tourist office well in advance, call the **Jazz Boutique** ticket sellers (tel. 963 82 82; open mid-Mar. to summer), or check out www.montreuxjazz.com for info and tickets (39-99SFr). If you can find a room but no tickets, the **Jazz Off,** offers 500 hours of free, open-air concerts by new bands and established musicians.

Trains (tel. (021) 963 45 15) arrive frequently at av. des Alpes from Lausanne (20min., 9.40SFr); Geneva (1hr., 29SFr); and Bern (1½hr., 40SFr). Descend the stairs opposite the station, head left on Grand-Rue, and look to the right for the **tourist office,** on pl. du Débarcadère. (Tel. 962 84 84; fax 963 78 95; www.montreux.ch. Open June-Aug. daily 9am-7pm; Sept.-Oct. M-Sa 9am-noon and 1:30-6pm, Su 9am-noon; Nov.-Apr. M-F 9am-noon and 1:30-6pm, Sa 9am-noon.) Cheap rooms are scarce in Montreux and almost nonexistent during the jazz festival; book ahead. To get to the modern and social **Auberge de Jeunesse Montreux (HI),** passage de l'Auberge 8, walk 20min. along the lake past the Montreux Tennis Club. (Tel. 963 49 34; fax 963 27 29. Dorms 29SFr; doubles 38-42SFr; nonmembers add 5SFr. Off-season 2SFr less. Breakfast included. Lockers 2SFr deposit. Laundry 8SFr. Reception Apr.-Sept. 7-10am and 4-11pm; Oct.-Mar. 7:30-9:30am and 5-10pm. Lockout 10am-4pm. Curfew midnight; key available with a passport deposit. V, MC, AmEx.) **Hôtel Pension Wilhelm,** rue du Marché 13-15, is 3min. left up av. des Alpes and a left uphill on rue du Marché from the station. (Tel. 963 14 31; fax 963 32 85. Singles (off-season only) 65SFr; doubles 50-120SFr. Breakfast included. Reception M 7am-3pm, Tu-Su 7am-midnight. Closed Oct.-Feb. unless you call ahead.) To **camp** at **Les Horizons Bleus,** take bus 1 to "Villeneuve" and follow the lake to the left (5min.). (Tel. 960 15 47. 7SFr per person, 6-12SFr per tent; tax 0.50SFr. Cheaper in winter. Shower included. Reception 9am-12:30pm and 4-9pm.) **Migros supermarket,** av. du Casino 49, has a restaurant next door. (Open M 9am-7pm, Tu-Th 8am-7pm, F 8am-9pm, Sa 7:30am-5pm. Restaurant opens 30min. earlier M-F.) **Postal code:** CH-1820.

⚡ EXCURSIONS FROM MONTREUX: LEYSIN AND GRYON. Ranging from small (Leysin) to diminutive (Gryon), these two towns are unlikely stops on a grand tour of Europe. However, both boast idyllic locations between breathtaking mountains and fantastic hostels that are ideal places to recharge. Anglophone-friendly **Leysin** is full of once-mobile backpackers who came, saw, and stayed, bolstering a local industry catering to skiers, snowboarders, climbers, mountain bikers, paragliders, and hikers. The **tourist office,** in the Centre Sportif (tel. (024) 494 29 21), up the road to the left from the pl. du Marché, provides **hiking maps** in winter and summer, while the **guides office** (tel. (024) 494 18 46) organizes **trekking** and all activities **alpine.** Just 50m from the start of the skiing and biking trails, the ◧**Hiking Sheep Guesthouse,** in Villa La Joux, features spiffy facilities, breathtaking balconies, and a super-friendly manager. (Tel. (024) 494 35 35. June 15-Dec. 15 dorms 26SFr; doubles 33SFr. Dec. 16-June 14 dorms 30SFr; doubles 35SFr. V, MC.) To reach Leysin, take the **cog railway** from **Aigle** (30min., every hr.), accessible by **train** from Montreux (10min., 2 per hr.) and Lausanne (30min., 2 per hr.).

Tiny **Gryon** has experienced a 25% population increase in recent years (now pop. 1000), but it doesn't seem to have marred its untouched, tranquil setting. Its main draw is the **Chalet St. Martin,** a teeming pocket of Australian-Swiss enthusiasm high in the Alps. The English-speaking staff maintains a cooperative-style establishment where bohemian backpackers taking a "vacation from their vacation" have been known to stay...and stay. The hostel rents skis and videos, and has daily sign-ups for **cheese farm tours, paragliding, thermal baths,** and other daily excursions. (First night 17SFr, thereafter 15SFr; in winter, add 3SFr. **Internet.** Check-in 9am-9pm.) To reach Gryon, take the **cog railway** from **Bex** (30min., every hr., 5.60SFr; Swisspass and Eurail valid), one stop down from Aigle on the rail line. To reach the hostel from the Gryon stop, head uphill and follow the signs.

NEUCHÂTEL

Though Alexandre Dumas was referring to the unique yellow stone common to the Neuchâtel's architecture when he likened the city to a carving made out of a block of butter, his comment could easily be misinterpreted as a reference to the city's many pâtisseries. But aside from its gastronomic delights, Neuchâtel also glows with a remarkable medieval beauty. The vieille ville is centered around the pl. des Halles; the rue de Château leads from there up to the **château** and a neighboring church, **Collégiale.** (Tours of the château Apr.-Sept. M-Sa 10, 11am, 2, 3, and 4pm; M-F also noon; Su 2, 3, 4pm. Church open daily Apr.-Sept. 9am-8pm; Oct.-Mar. 9am-6:30pm. Free.) Climb the 125 steps of the **Tour des Prisons** just below the church on rue Jehanne-de-Hochberg for a stunning vista of the lake and city (or take advantage of the opportunity to lock a traveling companion in one of the tiny wooden cells instead). (Open Apr.-Sept. 8am-6pm. 0.50SFr.) Baroque music floats through the **Musée d'Art et d'Histoire,** esplanade Léopold Robert 1, on the lake behind and to the left of the tourist office. (Open Tu-Su 10am-5pm. 7SFr, students 4SFr; Th free.) Satisfy your sweet tooth at the **Wodey-Suchard Chocolate Factory,** rue de Seyon 5, behind the main bus stop on pl. Pury. (Open M 11am-6:30pm, Tu-F 6:30am-6:30pm, Sa 6:30am-5pm.) A daytrip to nearby **Cressier** will delight with wine-tasting and vineyard strolls; **trains** run hourly to Cressier (10min., 3.60SFr).

Trains run frequently to Bern (45min., 17.20SFr); Geneva (1½hr., 41SFr); Basel (1¾hr., 35SFr); and Interlaken (2hr., 41SFr). From the station, take bus 6 to the central bus stop on pl. Pury to get to the center of town. From pl. Pury, face the lake and walk two blocks to the left to reach the **tourist office,** Hôtel des Postes. (Tel. (032) 889 68 90; fax 889 62 96; www.etatne.ch. Open June-Sept. M-F 9am-7pm, Sa 9am-noon, Su 4-7pm; Oct.-May M-F 9am-noon and 1:30-5:30pm, Sa 9am-noon.) The quirky **Oasis Neuchâtel,** rue de Suchiez 35, overlooks the lake. From pl. Pury, take bus 1 (dir: Cormondrèche) to "Vauseyon"; head uphill to the right, follow rue du Suchiez up, and it's up the road on the left. (Tel. (032) 731 31 90; fax 730 37 09. Dorms 23SFr; doubles 56SFr. Breakfast included. Reception daily 8-10am and 5-9pm.) If it's full, ask for the *Hôtel Restaurant* guide at the tourist office for cheap options in nearby towns. The laid-back **Crêperie Bach et Buck,** av. du Premier-Mars 22, sells crêpes for under 10SFr. (Open M-Sa 11:30am-2pm, F-Sa also 5:30-11:30pm, Su 6-10pm.) Do some dancin' at the **Casino de la Rotonde,** fbg. du Lac 14. (Beer 3-5SFr. Cover around 10SFr. Open F-Sa 10pm-4am.) **Postal code:** CH-2001.

SWITZERLAND

GERMAN SWITZERLAND

BASEL (BÂLE)

Perched on the Rhine a stone's throw from France and Germany, Switzerland's third-largest city (rhymes with "nozzle") blends the two cultures into a distinct character of its own. Basel is home to a large medieval quarter and one of the oldest universities in Switzerland (graduates include Erasmus of Rotterdam, Bernoulli, and Nietzsche). As you wander Basel's streets, you'll encounter art from Roman times to the 20th century and be serenaded by student musicians on every corner.

🔃🔃 PRACTICAL INFO, ACCOMMODATIONS, AND FOOD. Basel has three **train stations:** the French SNCF (tel. (061) 157 22 22) and Swiss SBB stations (tel. (061) 157 22 22; 1.19SFr per min.) are on Centralbahnpl., near the Altstadt. The German DB station (tel. (061) 690 11 11) is across the Rhine down Greifeng. Frequent trains chug to Zurich (1hr., 31SFr); Bern (1¼hr., 37SFr); Geneva (3hr., 72SFr); Paris (5-6hr., 138SFr, under 26 25% off); and Munich via Stuttgart (5¼hr., 204SFr, under 26 25% off). To reach the **tourist office,** Schifflände 5, from the SBB and SNCF stations, head across the Centralbahnpl., left on Elisabethenanlage, right down Elisabethenstr., left on Freiestr., right at the Marktpl., and left at the river (20min.); from the DB station, follow Rosentalstr. (which becomes Clarastr. and then Greifeng.) over the Mittlere Rheinbrücke and turn right along the river (15min.). (Tel. (061) 268 68 68; fax 268 68 70; www.baseltourismus.ch. Open M-F 8:30am-6pm.) From Barfüsserpl., follow Steinenvorstadt to the end to reach the **Internet Center** at #79. (3SFr per 30min. Open M-W 9am-10pm, Th and Sa 9am-midnight, Su 4-10pm.)

There's only one (busy) hostel in Basel, and very few hotels even remotely approach budget status—stop reading this sentence and make a reservation *now.* If you've heeded our advice, you'll get to walk from the SBB station down Aeschengraben to St. Alban Anlage and follow the signs downhill from the tower to the **Jugendherberge (HI),** St. Alban-Kirchrain 10 (12min.). (Tel. (061) 272 05 72; fax 272 08 33. Dorms 28.60SFr; singles 69.60-79.60SFr; 2- to 3-bed rooms 39.60-49.60SFr. Jan.-Feb. 19 and Nov.-Dec. 2.50SFr less. Breakfast included. Laundry. Reception 7-10am and 2pm-midnight. Check-out 7-10am. V, MC.) The **Hotel-Pension Steinenschanze,** Steinengraben 69, has rooms with phones and TVs. From the SBB station, turn left on Centralbahnstr., follow the signs for Heuwaage (5min.), go up the ramp under the bridge, and turn left on Steinengraben. (Tel. (061) 272 53 53; fax 272 45 73. Singles 110-130SFr, under 25 with ISIC 60SFr; doubles 160-190SFr, 100SFr. Breakfast included. Students 3-night max. stay. Reception 24hr. V, MC, AmEx.) To reach **Hecht am Rhein,** Rheing. 8, cross the Mittlere Rheinbrücke and turn right on Rheing.; lone women may not feel comfortable here. (Tel. (061) 691 22 20; fax 681 07 88. Single 70-80SFr; doubles 120-130SFr. Breakfast included. V, MC, AmEx.) For **Camp Waldhort,** Heideweg 16, in Reinach, take tram 11 to "Landhof," backtrack 200m, cross the main street, and follow the signs. (Tel. (061) 711 64 29. Reception 7am-12:30pm and 2-10pm. 7SFr per person, 10SFr per tent. Open Mar.-Oct.)

Restaurants multiply on Barfüsserpl., Marktpl., and the streets between them. Migrate to **Migros** branches at Steinenvorstadt, Clarapl. 17 (open M-W and F 8am-6:30pm, Th 8am-9pm, Sa 7:30am-5pm) or Bahnhof SBB (open M-F 6am-10pm, Sa-Su 7:30am-10pm). Italian-speaking servers present tasty German fare at **Zum Schnabel,** Trillengässlein 2. (Bratwurst, *Rösti*, and salad 12.80SFr. Open M-Th 8am-midnight, Sa-Su 8am-1am. V, MC, AmEx.) **Postal code:** CH-4001.

📷🔦 SIGHTS AND ENTERTAINMENT. Most sights lie on the **Groß-Basel** (Greater Basel) side of the Rhine, on the same side as the train station. The **Münster,** Basel's medieval treasure, stands along the Rhine in the center of Groß-Basel on the site of an ancient Celtic settlement and a Roman fort. The church holds Erasmus and Bernoulli's tombs, and the **tower** boasts the best view of Klein-Basel (across the river), the Rhine, and the Black Forest. (Cathedral open in summer M-F 10am-5pm, Sa 10am-4pm, Su 1-5pm; off-season M-Sa 11am-4pm, Su 2-4pm; free. Tower 3SFr.)

SWITZERLAND

MONSTER MADNESS In 1529, Basel's residents spiritedly joined the Reformation and ousted the bishop, keeping his *crozier* (staff) as the town's emblem. The staff shares this honor with the basilisk (Basel-isk), a creature part bat, part dragon, and part rooster, which caused what may be the world's first and only public trial and execution of a chicken. In 1474, a hen allegedly laid an egg on a dung heap under a full moon, an action sure to hatch the horrible creature. The bird was tried, found guilty, and beheaded, and the egg was ceremonially burnt.

Walk away from the river up Münsterberg and turn right on Freiestr. to reach the Marktpl. and the blinding red, green, and gold **Rathaus.** Near the other end of Freiestr., on Theaterpl., the chaotic, iron-sculpted **Jean Tinguely Fountain.** Basel has an astounding 30 museums; the most interesting of the bunch is the ▨**Kunstmuseum** (Museum of Fine Arts), St. Alban-Graben 16, with an outstanding collection of works by old and new masters, including Picasso, van Gogh, and Dalí. (Open Tu-Su 10am-5pm. 7SFr, students 5SFr; first Su of the month free.) Tickets are also good at the ▨**Museum für Gegenwartskunst** (Museum of Contemporary Art), St. Alban-Rhein-weg 60, which has important pieces by Calder, Johns, Warhol, Lichtenstein, and Pollock. (Open Tu-Su 11am-5pm.) The **Fondation Beyeler,** in the suburb of Riehen, has sublime curation; the grounds are art, too. (Baelstr. 107. Take tram 6 to "Rie-hendorf." Open 10am-6pm, W 10am-8pm. 12SFr, students 9SFr.)

Basel's carnival, or **Fasnacht,** a not-to-be-missed 4am parade over 600 years in the running, commences the Monday before Lent with the Morgestraich and keeps going strong for 72 hours (Mar. 13-15, 2000). Head to **Barfüsserpl.** for an evening of bar-hopping. **Atlantis,** Klosterburg 13, is a multi-level, sophisticated bar that sways to reggae, jazz, and funk. (Concerts 10-23SFr. Open M-Th 11am-2am, F 11am-4am, Sa 5pm-4am.) **Brauerei Fischerstube,** Rheing. 45, is an old-school Biergarten adjacent to Basel's only brewery. (Beer 2.50-5.90SFr. Open M-Th 10am-midnight, F-Sa 10am-1am, Su 5pm-midnight. V, MC.)

ZURICH (ZÜRICH)

Switzerland has a bank for every 1200 people, and about half of those are in Zurich, where battalions of ballyhooed and Bally-shoed executives charge daily to the world's premier gold exchange and fourth-largest stock exchange. But there's more to Zurich than money. Ulrich Zwingli led the Swiss Protestant Reformation here in the 16th century, and revolution brewed again in 1916 when James Joyce toiled away on *Ulysses* in the city, while exile Vladimir Lenin read Marx and dreamed of revolution in another. Meanwhile, a group of raucous young artists next door calling themselves the Dadaists pushed the limits of the ridiculous at the Cabaret Voltaire. The counterculture spirit shared by these thinkers continues to run through the veins of the Altstadt and student quarter, only steps away from the rabid capitalism of the famous Bahnhofstraße shopping district.

▨ GETTING THERE AND GETTING AROUND

Flights: Kloten Airport (tel. 816 25 00). Zurich is Swissair's main hub (tel. 157 10 60). **Trains** run to the Hauptbahnhof (every 10-20min., 6SFr; Eurailpass and Swisspass valid).

Trains: Hauptbahnhof, on Bahnhofpl. To: **Basel** (1hr., 2-4 per hr., 31SFr); **Bern** (1¼hr., 1-2 per hr., 48SFr); **Geneva** (3hr., every hr., 77SFr); **Munich** (4hr., 4 per day, 91SFr); **Milan** (4½hr., every hr., 75SFr); **Salzburg** (6hr., 3 per day, 101SFr); **Venice** (6½hr., 96SFr); **Paris** (8hr., every hr., 100SFr); and **Vienna** (9hr., 3 per day, 132SFr).

Public Transportation: All public buses, trams, and trolleys run 5:30am-midnight. **Short rides** (fewer than 5 stops) 2.10SFr; **long rides** 3.60SFr. Buy a ticket before boarding and validate it in the machine or face a fine (from 50SFr). A **Tageskarte** is good for 1 day of unlimited public transport (7.20SFr). Nightbuses run F-Sa at 1, 1:30, and 2am.

Taxis: Tel. 444 44 44 or 222 22 22. 6SFr base fare and 3SFr per km.

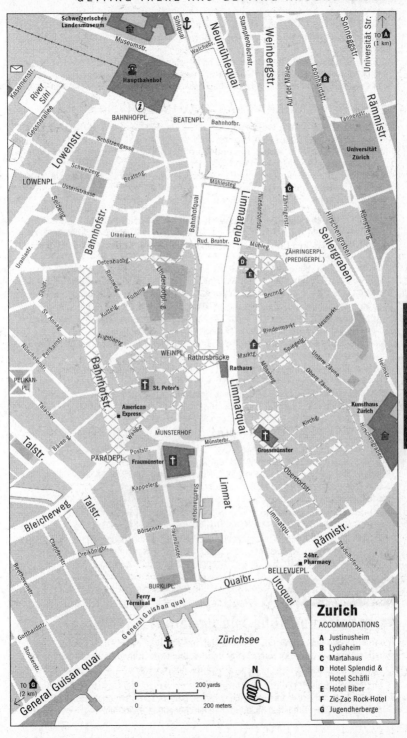

SWITZERLAND

Zurich

ACCOMMODATIONS

A Justinusheim
B Lydiaheim
C Martahaus
D Hotel Splendid &
   Hotel Schäfli
E Hotel Biber
F Zic-Zac Rock-Hotel
G Jugendherberge

Bike Rental: At the baggage counter *(Gepäckexpedition Fly-Gepäck)* in the station. 19-25SFr per day; 6SFr surcharge if you leave it at another station. Open daily 6:45am-7:45pm.

Hitchhiking: Hitchers to Basel, Geneva, Paris, or Bonn take streetcar 4 to "Werdhölzli" or bus 33 to "Pfingstweidstr."; to Lucerne, Italy, and Austria, they take streetcar 9 or 14 to "Bahnhof Wiedikon" and walk down Schimmelstr. to Silhölzli; to Munich, they take streetcar 14 or 7 to "Milchbuck" and walk to Schaffhauserstr. toward St. Gallen and St. Margarethen.

🔢 ORIENTATION AND PRACTICAL INFORMATION

The **Hauptbahnhof**, on the western bank of the **Limmat River**, sits at the top of Bahnhofstr., which overflows with bankers and well-coiffed shoppers by day but falls dead quiet by 6pm. In contrast, the university district on the hillside of the eastern bank pulses nightly with crowded bars and hip restaurants. Sprawling along the Limmat, the Altstadt is a giant pedestrian zone. The Altstadt's **Limmatquai,** which becomes Uto-Quai and Seefeldquai across the bridge from the Hauptbahnhof, is a favorite strolling destination for many residents and tourists.

TOURIST, FINANCIAL, AND LOCAL SERVICES

Tourist Offices: Main office (tel. 214 40 00; fax 215 40 44; www.zurichtourism.ch; hotel reservation service tel. 215 40 40), in the Hauptbahnhof. Open Apr.-Oct. M-F 8:30am-8:30pm, Sa-Su 8:30am-6:30pm; Nov.-Mar. M-F 8:30am-7pm, Sa-Su 8:30am-6:30pm.

Consulates: UK, Minervastr. 117 (tel. 383 65 60). Open M-F 9am-noon. **US,** Dufourstr. 101 (tel. 422 25 66). Open M-F 10am-1pm. **Australian, Canadian, Irish,** and **South African** citizens should contact embassies in Bern. **New Zealand's** consulate is in Geneva.

Currency Exchange: At the Hauptbahnhof. Cash advances on V, MC. Open daily 6:30am-10:45pm. **Credit Suisse,** Bahnhofstr. 53. 2.50SFr commission. Open M-F 9am-6pm, Th 9am-7pm, Sa 9am-4pm. **ATMs** are all over (most take MC).

American Express: Uraniastr. 14, CH-8023 (tel. 228 77 77). Mail held. **ATM.** Open M-F 8:30am-6pm, Sa 9am-1pm.

Luggage Storage: At the Hauptbahnhof. Lockers 4-8SFr per day. Luggage storage 5SFr at the *Gepäck* counter. Open daily 6am-10:50pm.

Gay and Lesbian Services: Homosexuelle Arbeitsgruppe Zürich (HAZ), Sihlquai 67, P.O. Box 7088, CH-8023 (tel. 271 22 50), offers a library, meetings, and the free newsletter *InfoSchwül.* Open Tu-F 7:30-11pm, Su noon-2pm and 6-11pm.

Laundromat: Selbstbedienung-Wäscherei (tel. 242 99 14), in the Hauptbahnhof. Wash and dry 10.20SFr per 5kg. Open daily 6am-11pm.

EMERGENCIES AND COMMUNICATIONS

Emergencies: Police, tel. 117. **Fire,** tel. 118. **Ambulance,** tel. 144; English spoken. **Medical Emergency,** tel. 261 61 00.

24-Hour Pharmacy: Theaterstr. 14 (tel. 252 56 00), on Bellevuepl.

Internet Access: Internet Café, Uraniastr. 3 (tel. 210 33 11), in the Urania Parkhaus. 5SFr per 20min. Open M 10am-6pm, Tu-Th 10am-midnight, F-Sa 10am-2am, Su 10am-11pm.

Post Office: Main Office, Sihlpost, Lagerstr. 2, just behind the station. Open M-F 7:30am-8pm, Sa 8am-4pm. Address mail to be held: Sihlpost, *Postlagernde Briefe* für Clint EASTWOOD, **CH-8021** Zürich, Switzerland. **Branches** throughout the city.

PHONE CODE	City code: 01. From outside Switzerland, call country code (41) + city code (1) + local number.

🏠 ACCOMMODATIONS AND CAMPING

The few budget accommodations in Zurich are easily accessible via Zurich's public transportation. Reserve at least a day in advance, especially during the summer.

🏨 **Justinus Heim Zürich,** Freudenbergstr. 146 (tel. 361 38 06; fax 362 29 82). Take tram 9 or 10 to "Seilbahn Rigiblick," then take the hillside tram (by the Migros) uphill to the end. Quiet, cheap, private rooms overlooking Zurich. Singles 35-60SFr; doubles 80-100SFr; triples 120-140SFr. Breakfast included. Kitchen. Reception 8am-9pm.

SWITZERLAND

Martahaus, Zähringerstr. 36 (tel. 251 45 50; fax 251 45 40). Turn left from the station, cross Bahnhofbrücke, and take the 2nd (sharp) right after Limmatquai at the Seilgraben sign. The most comfortable budget accommodations in the Altstadt. Dorms 35SFr; singles 70SFr; doubles 98SFR; triples 120SFr. Breakfast included. Reception 24hr. V, MC, AmEx.

Jugendherberge Zürich (HI), Mutschellenstr. 114 (tel. 482 35 44; fax 480 17 27). Take tram 7 (dir: Wollishofen) to "Morgantal" and backtrack 5min. along Mutschellenstr. A little cramped and crowded, but offers CNN and free nightly movies. Dorms 31SFr; doubles 90SFr; nonmembers add 5SFr. Breakfast included. Laundry. Reception 24hr. V, MC.

Foyer Hottingen, Hottingenstr. 31 (tel. 256 19 19; fax 261 93 19). Take tram 3 (dir: Kluspl.) to "Hottingerpl." to reach this impeccably clean and newly renovated house. Modern facilities and multilingual staff. Dorms (**women only** in summer) 30-40SFr; singles 65SFr; doubles 100SFr. Breakfast included. Kitchen. Reception 6am-midnight.

The City Backpacker-Hotel Biber, Niederdorfstr. 5 (tel. 251 90 15; fax 251 90 24). Cross Bahnhofbrücke in front of the station and turn right on Niederdorfstr. Well-used rooms, a party-happy rooftop deck, and a prime location for bar-hopping in a traditional Altstadt building. Dorms 29SFr (27SFr in winter); singles 65SFr; doubles 88SFr. Sheets 3SFr. Kitchen. Laundry 9SFr. **Internet** 10SFr per hr. Reception 8am-noon and 3-10pm.

Zic-Zac Rock-Hotel, Marktg. 7 (tel. 261 21 81; fax 261 21 75; email rockhotel.ch@bluewin.ch). Funky furniture, trendy lighting, and rock 'n' roll superstar names distinguish each room, all with TV and phone. Singles 65-85SFr; doubles 110-150SFr; triples 150-160SFr; quads 240SFr. Breakfast 8.50SFr. Reception 24hr.

Camping Seebucht, Seestr. 559 (tel. 482 16 12; fax 482 16 60). Take tram 11 to Bürklipl., then catch bus 161 or 165 to "Stadtgrenze." Market and café. 8.50SFr per person, 12SFr per tent. Showers 2SFr. Tents and caravans available. Reception 7:30am-noon and 3-10pm. Open May to late Sept.

⛏ FOOD

The cheapest meals in Zurich are available at *Würstli* stands (sausage and bread 5SFr). For heartier appetites, Zurich prides itself on its *Geschnetzeltes mit Rösti*, slivered veal in cream sauce with hash-brown potatoes. **Co-op Super Center,** straddling the Limmat River next to the train station, is indeed a super Co-op. (Open M-F 7am-8pm, Sa 7am-4pm.) **Migros,** Mutschellenstr. 189, is near the hostel. (Open M-F 8am-6:30pm, Sa 8am-4pm.)

Bodega Española, Münsterg. 15 (tel. 251 23 10). Delicious Catalan delights. Egg and potato tortilla dishes 15.50SFr. Enormous salads 9.50SFr. Open daily 10am-12:30am.

Hiltl, Sihlstr. 28 (tel. 227 70 00). Trade carrot sticks with the vegetarian elite at this swank restaurant. All-day salad buffet 4.60SFr per 100g (15SFr for large salad). Indian dinner buffet 4.60SFr per 100g. Open M-Sa 7am-11pm, Su 11am-11pm.

Johanniter, Niederdorfstr. 70 (tel. 251 46 00). A favorite with locals, this Swiss restaurant along Niederdorfstr. has elegant sidewalk seating. Hearty Swiss *Rösti* and noodle dishes 15-18SFr. Open Su-Th 10am-2am, F-Sa 10am-4am.

Zeughauskeller, Bahnhofstr. 28a (tel. 211 26 90), near Paradepl. This *Biergarten* serves Swiss specialties like fondue, *Rösti*, and sausage from multilingual menus. The cheapest specialties are their filling *Wurst* plates (15SFr). Open daily 11:30am-11pm.

Gran-Café, Limmatquai 66 (tel. 252 31 19). Outdoor seating and some of the cheapest meals around. Daily *Menüs* (11.80SFr) are guaranteed in 7min. or they're free. Open M-F 6am-midnight, Sa-Su 7:30am-midnight.

▦ SIGHTS

ALTSTADT. The stately causeway of capitalism known as **Bahnhofstraße** runs from the Hauptbahnhof to the head of the Zürichsee and hosts Cartier, Rolex, Chanel, and Armani. Half-way down Bahnhofstr. lies **Paradeplatz,** the town center, under which Zurich's banks reputedly keep their gold reserves. Right off Paradepl., the Gothic 13th-century Protestant **Fraumünster** contrasts with its vivid stained-glass windows designed by Marc Chagall in the 70s. The merging of Old and New Testament stories in the five windows reveals Chagall's radical personal interpretation of the texts. Near the Fraumünster, **St. Peter's Church** has the largest clock face in Europe, with a second hand nearly 4m long. The **Grossmünster,** facing off the Fraumünster from across the river, is where Ulrich Zwingli spearheaded the Reformation in German-speaking Switzerland (one of his Bibles lies in a protected case near the pulpit from which he preached). The church's twin neo-Gothic towers (added in 1786) have become a symbol of Zurich. Head up the twisting stairs to the top of one of the **towers** for a panoramic view of Zurich. *(Church open Mar. 15-Oct. 9am-6pm; Nov.-Mar. 14 10am-5pm; free. Tower open Mar.-Oct. daily 1:30-5pm, Nov.-Feb. Sa-Su 1:30-4:30pm; 2SFr.)* Down Münsterg. from the Grossmünster lies **Spiegelgasse,** lined by commemorative plaques honoring the greats, including Vladimir Illitsch Uljanow (a.k.a. "Lenin") at #14 and "Cabaret Voltaire" (former haunt of Hans Arp, Tristan Tzara, and Hugo Ball) at #3 (a funky bar; see below).

MUSEUMS. The incredible ▧**Kunsthaus Zürich,** on Rämistr., covers Western art from the 15th century to the present with an undeniable bias toward the 20th century, mixing in famous locals (including Giacometti, Segantini, and Hodler) along with the international set. *(Heimpl. 1. Take tram 3, 5, 8, or 9 to "Kunsthaus." Tel. 251 67 65. Open Tu-Th 10am-9pm, F-Su 10am-5pm. 4SFr, students 3SFr; Su free.)* The **Museum Rietberg,** in two mansions in Rieter Park, presents an exquisite collection of Asian, African, and other non-European art. The **Museum of Classical Archaeology** astounds with a basement full of replicas of nearly every great statue in the ancient world from 800 BC on, as well as Greco-Roman art on the first floor. *(Rämistr. 73. Take tram 6, 9, or 19 to "ETH." Tel. 257 28 20. Open Tu-F 1-6pm, Sa-Su 11am-5pm. Free.)* The **Schweizerisches Landesmuseum** (Swiss National Museum) contains 16th-century astrological instruments, Ulrich Zwingli's weapons from the Battle of Kappel (in which he died in 1531), and a tiny bejeweled clock, with a golden skeleton morbidly indicating the time, as well as mediocre medieval artifacts. *(Museumstr. 2. Tel. 218 65 11. Open Tu-Su 10:30am-5pm. Free. Special exhibits around 8SFr.)*

OTHER SIGHTS. Take tram 6, 9, or 10 to "ETH" uphill from the university (above the town on the Grossmünster side of the river) to reach the grave of author **James Joyce,** in the Fluntern Cemetery. Farther from town, visitors to the **Lindt and Sprüngli Chocolate Factory** are welcomed with an open box of Lindt chocolate and a movie about chocolate machines and depart with free souvenir boxes of the chocolate. *(Seestr. 204. Take S-1 or S-8 to "Kilchberg" from the Hauptbahnhof (5.40SFr) or bus 165 to "Kilchberg"; turn right out of the station, turn left down the 1st street, take an immediate right, and continue for 3min. Tel. 716 22 33. Open W-F 10am-noon and 1-4pm. All exhibits in German. Free.)*

▧ NIGHTLIFE

Niederdorfstr. rocks as the epicenter of Zurich's nightlife (although women may not want to walk alone in this area at night), and Münsterg. and Limmatquai are lined with cafés and bars. Pick up *ZüriTip* or check posters around town for hotspots. On Friday and Saturday nights in summer, **Hirschenpl.** hosts sword-swallowers and other daredevil street performers. The **Zürich Night Card,** available at the main tourist office, provides discounts on Zurich's nightlife offerings and free public transport for three consecutive evenings after 5pm (20SFr). **Casa Bar,** Münsterg. 30, is a tiny, crowded pub with first-rate live jazz. (Open daily 7pm-2am.) **Castel DADA,** Münsterg. 26, next to Casa Bar, is a lively bar and disco on the former site of the "Cabaret Voltaire." (Open Su-Th 6pm-2am, F-Sa 8pm-2am. Disco open until 4am.) Thornton Wilder and Vladimir Lenin used to get sloshed at the posh, artsy **Bar Odeon,** Limmatquai 2, on Bellevuepl. (Open Su-Th 7am-2am, F-Sa 7am-4am.)

ST. GALLEN

Book lovers gasp at the sight of St. Gallen's astounding main attraction, the **Stiftsbibliotek** (Abbey Library), a Baroque library designated a World Heritage Treasure by UNESCO. Perfectly preserved golden spines, lavishly carved and polished exotic wood bookcases, and shiny parquet enhance its collection of 140,000 volumes and

SWITZERLAND

2000 manuscripts. Umberto Eco was seen sniffing around here to get inspiration for *The Name of the Rose*. (Open Apr.-Nov. M-Sa 9am-noon and 1:30-5pm, Su 10am-noon and 1:30-4pm; Dec.-Mar. M-Sa 9am-noon and 1:30-4pm. 7SFr, students 5SFr.) The enormous windows of the Abbey's **Kathedrale St. Gallen**, founded in the 8th century but renovated in the mid-18th, let in light on the golden gate spanning the interior of the church. (Open daily 7am-6pm except during mass.) Follow the Marktplatz away from the train station to reach **Museumstraße**, which holds four museums, the largest of which are the **Historisches** and **Ethnology Museums** at #50. (All open Tu-Sa 10am-noon and 2-5pm, Su 10am-5pm. Ticket for all four 6SFr, students 2SFr.) In late June, the **Open Air St. Gallen Music Festival** features 20 live bands; past performers include the Beastie Boys, Garbage, Cypress Hill, and James Brown. (Tickets 144SFr. Tel. (071) 222 21 21.)

Trains roll to Zurich (1hr., 29SFr); Bern (2½hr., 65SFr); and Munich (3hr., 63SFr, under 26 49SFr). To get to the **tourist office**, Bahnhofpl. 1a, from the train station, head through the bus stop and past the fountain on the left; it's on the right. (Tel. (071) 227 37 37; fax 227 37 67. Tours June 12-Sept. M, W, and F 2pm; 15SFr. Open M-F 9am-noon and 1-6pm, Sa 9am-noon.) Get on the **internet** at **Media Lounge**, 10 Katerineng. (2SFr per 10min. Open M-F 9am-9pm, Sa 10am-5pm.) Perched on a hill above town, the ◙**Jugendherberge St. Gallen (HI),** Jüchstr. 25, has a terrace, jukebox, and library. Take the orange train (dir: Trogener) from the smaller Appenzeller/Trogener station to the right of the main station to "Schülerhaus"; walk uphill, turn left across the train tracks, and walk 2min. downhill. (Tel. (071) 245 47 77; fax 245 49 83. Dorms 24SFr; singles 58SFr; doubles 66SFr; nonmembers add 5SFr each. Breakfast included. Reception M-Sa 7-10am and 5-10:30pm, Su 6-10:30pm. Check-out 9am. Lockout 10am-5pm. Closed Dec. 15-Mar. 7.) **Hotel Elite,** Metzgerg. 9-11, is simple and central. (Tel. (071) 222 12 36; fax 222 21 77. Singles 60-70SFr; doubles 110SFr. Breakfast included.) A secluded rooftop awaits at **Pizzeria Testarossa,** Metzgerg. 20, up the street that is opposite the bus station on Marktpl. (Pizzas from 13SFr. Open Tu-F 10am-midnight, Sa-Su 10am-2pm and 5pm-midnight.) **Postal code:** CH-9000.

◪ **EXCURSION FROM ST. GALLEN: APPENZELL.** St. Gallen is an ideal urban base from which to hike the pastoral hills of Appenzell. **Appenzell** offers great **hiking** without the temperature extremes of Zermatt or the Ticino region. Ask at the **tourist office,** Hauptg. 4 (tel. (071) 788 96 41; www.appenzellerland-ferien.ch), next to the *Rathaus*, for a detailed trail map and hiking suggestions. The office also makes hotel reservations, books cable car excursions, and arranges **cheesemaking** tours. The ever-present aroma of Appenzeller cheese lingers around **Gasthaus Hof** (tel. (071) 787 22 10; fax (071) 787 58 83), on Landsgemeindeplatz in the center of town, a family-run restaurant that provides guest rooms in a separate house. (Dorms 28SFr; singles 65SFr, 95SFr with shower; doubles 110SFr, 130SFr with shower. Breakfast included. Check-in 11am. Restaurant open 8am-11pm.) Many hiking trails are dotted with **Gasthöfe** (guesthouses), splendid old farmhouses and restaurants for the road-weary. The rattling but prompt **Appenzellerbahn** chugs between Appenzell and **St. Gallen** twice an hour from 6am-midnight (1hr., 10SFr).

AROSA

The beautiful, secluded town of Arosa, in the canton of Graubünden, makes an effort to cater to budget-conscious **skiers** and **snowboarders** with affordable ski-and-stay packages. Developed ski trails dominate only one side of the valley; on the other, **hiking** trails stretch infinitely to isolated valleys. A free **shuttle bus** shuttles between the hottest spots in town, including the ski lifts and the **tourist office** (*Kurverein;* www.arosa.ch), which arranges hiking trips and ski lessons and makes free hotel reservations. Two large houses rule the budget accommodations scene (tel. (081) 378 84 23 for both). ◪**Haus Florentium**, a former convent buried in the woods at the top of the town, has been converted to a 150-bed party house. From the tourist office, follow the cobblestoned path down the hill, turn right at the road at the top, left at the gravel path, and right at Pension Suveran. (Dec.-Apr. 1-night stay and 2-day ski pass 140SFr; 6-night stay and 7-day ski pass 430SFr. July-

S W I T Z E R L A N D

Aug. 36SFr per night. Breakfast included.) The smaller **Haus Bellaval,** above the train station, offers basic dorms. (In winter 1-night stay and 2-day ski pass 132SFr; 6-night stay and 7-day pass 382SFr. In summer 1-night stay and 2-day hiking lift pass 53SFr.) In summer, lifts are not necessary for hiking, so the better choice (also closer to more hiking trails) is the **Jugendherberge (HI),** on Seewaldstr. Go past the tourist office, bear left down the hill, and follow the sign. (Tel./fax (081) 377 13 97. Dorms 26SFr; doubles 96SFr. Breakfast included. Reception 7-10am and 5-10pm. Curfew 10pm; key available. Open mid-June to mid-Oct. and mid-Dec. to mid-Apr.) Get groceries at the **Co-op,** before the tourist office on Poststr. (Open M-F 8am-12:30pm and 2-6:30pm, Sa 8am-4pm.) Arosa is accessible by **train** only via a scenic route from Chur (1hr., every hr., 11.80SFr), which is accessible by train from Zurich (1½hr., every hr. 4:54am-11:10pm, 38SFr).

LUCERNE (LUZERN)

Lucerne just may be the fondue pot at the end of the rainbow—the Swiss traveler's dream come true. It combines the museums, festivals, and nightlife of the cosmopolitan cities to the north with the outdoor opportunities and natural splendor of the south. The sunrise over the city's most acclaimed peak, **Mount Pilatus,** has hypnotized hikers and artists (including Twain, Wagner, and Goethe) for centuries.

🛈🛏🍴 **PRACTICAL INFO, ACCOMMODATIONS, AND FOOD. Trains** arrive at least hourly from Zurich (1hr., 22SFr); Basel (1¼hr., 31SFr); Bern (1½hr., 32SFr); Interlaken (2hr., 26SFr); Lugano (2¾hr., 55SFr); and Geneva (3hr., 70SFr). The **tourist office,** in the station, leads walking tours of major monuments. (Tel. (041) 410 71 71; fax 410 73 34. Open May-Oct. M-F 8:30am-7:30pm, Sa-Su 9am-7:30pm; Nov.-Apr. M-F 8:30am-6pm, Sa 9am-6pm, Su 9am-1pm. Tours Apr. 14 to Oct. M-Sa 9:45 am and 2pm; Nov. 4-Apr. 13 W and Sa 9:45am; 15SFr.) The train station is the cheapest place to rent a **bike** (26SFr per day). **C+A Clothing,** on Hertensteinstr. at the top of the Altstadt, has two busy terminals to satisfy your **internet** cravings. (Free. Open M-W 9am-6:30pm, Th-F 9am-9pm, Sa 8:30am-4pm.) To reach ⚑**Backpackers,** Alpenquai 42, turn right from the station onto Insenquai, which becomes Alpenquai (15min.). (Tel. (041) 360 04 20; fax 360 04 42. 21.50-26.50SFr. Sheets 2SFr. Kitchen. Reception 7:30-10am and 4-11pm.) **Hotel Löwengraben,** Löwengraben 18, at the top of the Altstadt, was a prison until 1998. From the station, head straight across the Seebrücke, turn left at Schwanenpl. on Grendelstr. and bear left onto Grabenstr., which becomes Löwengraben. (Tel. (041) 417 12 12; fax 417 12 11. Dorms 20-35SFr; doubles 90SFr.) Take bus 18 to "Jugendherberge" for the (surprise) **Jugendherberge (HI),** Sedelstr. 12. After 7:30pm, take bus 19 to "Rosenberg," continue in the direction of the bus, and bear right. (Tel. (041) 420 88 00; fax 420 56 16. Dorms May-Oct. 30.50SFr; Nov.-Apr. 28SFr. Doubles 37.50-43.50SFr. Breakfast included. Laundry 12SFr. Reception 7-10am and 2pm-midnight. V, MC, AmEx.) Take bus 2 (dir: Würzenbach) to "Verkehrshaus" to reach **Camping Lido,** Lidostr. 8. (Tel. (041) 370 21 46; fax 370 21 45. 6.50SFr per person, 3SFr per tent, 5SFr per car. Showers 0.50SFr per 3min. Reception 8am-6pm. Open Mar. 15-Oct.) The restaurant upstairs in **Migros market** on Hertensteinstr. (a good source for cheap grub itself) has full meals from 7.50SFr. (Open M-W 8am-6:30pm, Th-F 8am-9pm, Sa 8am-4pm.) **Krone,** Rösslig. 15, is a favorite for quick, cheap eats ranging from burgers to lasagna to kebabs (around 9SFr each). (*Menüs* 11SFr. Open daily 7am-7pm.) **Postal code:** CH-6000.

📷🎭 **SIGHTS AND ENTERTAINMENT.** The Altstadt is famous for its frescoed houses and oriel windows, especially those in the buildings on Hirschenpl. To get medieval, traipse along the 660-year-old **Kapellbrücke,** a famous wooden-roofed bridge that runs from left of the train station (as you exit) to the Altstadt and is ornately decorated with Swiss historical scenes. Down the river, the covered **Spreuerbrücke** is adorned with Kaspar Meglinger's eerie *Totentanz* (Dance of Death) paintings. For a magnificent view of Lucerne, climb the ramparts of the medieval city *(Musegg Mauern).* Take the trail on the far side of the wall to reach stairs up to the path along the wall; several towers have stairs to the top. East of the wall, the city mascot, the dying **Lion of Lucerne,** is carved into a cliff on Denkmalstr. Mark Twain called the 9m monument, honoring the Swiss Guard who died defending Marie Antoinette in Revolutionary Paris, "the most mournful and moving piece of stone in the world."

The **Picasso Museum,** Furreng. 21, in Am Rhyn Haus, chronicles the artist's life with 200 moving photographs taken by close friend David Duncan. Head down Rathausquai from Schwanenpl. and bear right on Furreng. (Open daily Apr.-Oct. 10am-6pm; Nov.-Mar. 11am-1pm and 2-4pm. 6SFr, students 3SFr.) Walk 15min. along the lake to reach the **Verkehrshaus der Schweiz** (Transport Museum), Lidostr. 5, which features a planetarium, IMAX shows, and a virtual-reality exhibit. (Open daily Apr. 4-Oct. 9am-6pm; Nov.-Mar. 10am-5pm. 18SFr, students 16SFr. IMAX 14SFr. 33% off with Eurail.) The **Richard Wagner Museum,** Wagnerweg 27, in Wagner's secluded sylvan home, displays the composer's original letters, scores, and instruments. Turn right from the station and walk 25min. along the lake. (Open Mar. 15-Nov. 30 Tu-Su 10am-noon and 2-5pm. 5SFr, students 4SFr.)

The Altstadt is quiet after 7pm, when the action moves to Haldenstr. and the streets near the station. **Hexenkessel,** Haldenstr. 21, going for that mock-pagan look, has a two-story cauldron of loud music and spinning DJs. (Obligatory beer 7SFr. Open daily 9pm-2:30am.) Every summer, elite crews flock to Lucerne to compete in world-class **rowing regattas;** the Swiss National Championships and the Olympic Qualifiers will be held in 2000 from July 8 to 13.

▚ **OUTDOORS AND HIKING: MT. PILATUS AND RIGI KULM.** The view of the Alps from the top of **Mt. Pilatus** (2132m), is absolutely phenomenal. For the most memorable trip, catch a boat from Lucerne to Alpnachstad (90min.), ascend by the world's steepest **cogwheel train** (48° gradient), descend by cable car to Krienz, and take the bus back to Lucerne (entire trip 77.60SFr, with Eurail or Swisspass 40SFr). With a little more time and exercise, cut down on the price by taking a train or boat to Hegiswil and hiking up to Fräkmüntegg (3hr.), a half-way point on the cable car (22SFr; 25% off with Eurail or Swisspass).

Across the sea from Pilatus soars the **Rigi Kilm.** Sunrise on the summit is a must-see for any Lucerne visitor; sunsets get good reviews, too (see Mark Twain's *A Tramp Abroad*). **Ferries** run from Lucerne to Vitzna'u, where you can catch a cogwheel train to the summit. You can also conquer Rigi on foot; it's 5hr. from Vitznau to the top, and anyone who tires out half-way can pick the train up at Rigi Kaltbad (3hr. up the hill) to drag them the rest of the way. To make sunrise viewing possible, stay at **Massenlager Rigi Kulm.** (Tel. (041) 855 03 03. Dorms 25SFr. Reception 8am-10pm.) Afterward, return by train, take the cable car from Rigi Kaltbad to Weggis, and return to Lucerne by boat (all transit costs 84SFr, with Eurail or Swisspass 42SFr).

BERN

Although Bern has been Switzerland's capital since 1848, don't expect a slick political machine. Parliament is in session only four times a year, and politics is considered part-time work. Indeed, you'll probably see more suitors than suits in Bern: the city is known instead for Toblerone, flowers, bears, and a decidedly romantic design.

▐▌▐▐ **PRACTICAL INFO, ACCOMMODATIONS, AND FOOD. Trains** (tel. (031) 157 22 22) run to Bahnhofpl. from Interlaken (50min., every hr., 25SFr); Zurich (1¼hr., 2 per hr., 48SFr); Basel (1¼hr., 2 per hr., 37SFr); Lucerne (1½hr., every hr., 32SFr); Geneva (2hr., 2 per hr., 50SFr); Milan (3½hr., 14 per day, 72SFr); Paris (4½hr., 5 per day, 92SFr); and Munich (5½hr., 4 per day, 123SFr). Under-26ers get 25% off international fares. **Bike rental** is free at **Blubike,** on Casinopl. (tel. (031) 311 leads city tours and has a free phone line to hotels. (Tel. (031) 328 12 12; fax 312 12 33. Open June-Sept. daily 9am-8:30pm; Oct.-May M-Sa 9am-6:30pm, Su 10am-5pm. Tours daily in summer; 6-23SFr.) **Embassies: Australia** Alpenstr. 29 (tel. (031) 351 01 43); **Canada,** Kirchenfeldstr. 88 (tel. (031) 352 32 00; fax 357 32 10); **Ireland,** Kirchenfeldstr. 68 (tel. (031) 352 14 42; fax 352 14 55); **South Africa,** Alpenstr. 29 (tel. (031) 350 13 13; visa fax 350 13 11); **UK,** Thunstr. 50 (tel. (031) 352 50 21); and **US,**

Jubiläumsstr. 93 (tel. (031) 351 70 11; fax 351 73 44). Check your **email** downstairs in **JäggiBücher**, in the Loeb department store at Spitalg. 47-51, on Bubenbergpl. (20min. free. Open M-W and F 9am-6:30pm, Th 9am-9pm, Sa 8am-5pm.)

To get from the station to the raucous **Jugendherberge (HI)**, Weiherg. 4, cross the tram lines, go down Christoffelg., take the road through the gates left of the Park Café, and follow the signs down to Weiherg. (Tel. (031) 311 63 16; fax 312 52 40. Dorms 20.25SFr; overflow mattresses on the floor 14SFr; nonmembers add 5SFr. Breakfast 6SFr. Laundry 6SFr. 3-night max. stay. Reception June-Sept. 7-9:30am and 3pm-midnight; Oct.-May 7-9:30am and 5pm-midnight. Check-out 9am. Curfew midnight. Reserve by fax. Closed two weeks in Jan. V, MC.) To reach the **Landhaus Hotel**, Altenbergstr. 4/6, take bus 12 (dir: Schlosshalde) to "Bärengraben" and walk down to the Aare on the left. (Tel. (031) 331 41 66; fax 332 69 04; email landhaus@spectravels.ch. Dorms 30SFr; doubles 110-140SFr. Breakfast included with doubles; with dorms 7SFr. Kitchen. Laundry 4-6SFr. **Internet**.) **Pension Martha-haus**, Wyttenbachstr. 22a, is in a quiet suburb. From the station, turn left on Boll-werk, cross Lorrainebrücke, bear right onto Victoriastr., and take the first left on Wyttenbachstr. Or, take bus 20 to "Gewerbeschule," then the first right. (Tel. (031) 332 41 35; fax 333 33 86; email martahaus@bluewin.ch. Singles 60-90SFr; doubles 95-120SFr; triples 120-150SFr. 5-10SFr less in winter. Breakfast included. Laundry 8SFr. Reception 7:30am-9pm. Reserve ahead. V, MC.) To get to **Camping Eichholz**, Strandweg 49, take tram 9 to "Wabern," backtrack 50m, and take the first right. (Tel. (031) 961 26 02. 6.90SFr, students 5.50SFr; tents 5-8.50SFr; 2-bed rooms 15SFr. Showers 1SFr. Laundry 5SFr. Open May-Sept. Reserve ahead.)

Manora, Bubenbergpl. 5a, has tasty salads, fruit, and entrees. (Open M-Sa 7am-10:30pm, Su opens 9am.) Popular with quirky types, the bustling **Café des Pyrénées**, Kornhauspl. 17, offers inventive sandwiches (calamari 6.50SFr). (Open M-F 9am-12:30am, Sa 8am-5pm.) **Café 49**, Gerechtigkeitsg. 49, a spicy, Mediterranean eatery, is tucked in a cellar in the Altstadt. (Open Tu-Sa 10am-12:30am.) Fruit and vegeta-ble **markets** sprawl daily over Bärenpl. (May-Oct. 8am-6pm) and every Tu and Sa over Bundepl. (year-round). **Postal code:** CH-3000.

▣🎜 **SIGHTS AND ENTERTAINMENT.** The massive **Bundeshaus** dominates the Aare river and hides the politicians in the **Parlamentsgebäude**. (Tel. (031) 322 85 22. Tours (45min.) every hr. 9-11am and 2-4pm when Parliament is not in session. Free.) From the state house, Kockerg. and Herreng. lead to the 15th-century Protes-tant **Münster** (cathedral). The late Gothic portal sculpture of the Last Judgment depicts the naked damned shuffling off unhappily to Hell on God's left. Climb the spire—the tallest in all of Switzerland—for a fantastic view of the Aare and beyond. (Open Easter-Oct. Tu-Sa 10am-5pm, Su 11:30am-5pm; Nov.-Easter Tu-F 10am-noon and 2-4pm, Sa until 5pm, Su 11am-2pm. Tower 3SFr.) Head down Münsterg., take a right on Hotelg. and turn left on Kramg. to reach the 13th-century **Zytglogge** (clock tower), whose figures creak to life at 4min. before the hour with a couple of pallid rooster squawks; less entertaining than the fervent oohs and aahs of the gathered tourists. (Tours of the interior May-Oct. daily 4:30pm. 6SFr.) Down Kramg. (which becomes Gerechtigkeitsg.) and across the Nydeggbrücke lie the stone-lined **Bären-graben** (bear pits), which date back to the 15th century. (Open June-Sept. daily 8am-6pm; Oct.-May Th-M 8am-6pm. 3SFr to feed the bears.)

Several **museums** cluster at **Helvetiapl.** across the Kirchenfeldbrücke (take tram 3 or 5 or walk south from the Zytglogge). The **Bernisches Historische Museum** has seven levels jam-packed with exhibits ranging from Münster artifacts to illuminated Islamic manuscripts. (Helvetiapl. 5. Open Tu-Su 10am-5pm. 5SFr, students 3SFr; Sa free.) The **Kunstmuseum** focuses on 20th-century art, including the works of Kandin-sky, Feininger, and the world's largest Paul Klee collection—room after room (2500 works) of his geometrically dreamy art. (Hodlerstr. 8-12, near Lorrainebrücke. Open Tu 10am-9pm, W-Su 10am-5pm. 6SFr, students 4SFr.) In the Altstadt, **Albert Einstein's House**, Kramg. 49, between the Zytglogge and the Münster, is where the theory of relativity was conceived (1905); today it houses his photos and letters. (Kramg. 49. Open Feb.-Nov. Tu-F 10am-5pm, Sa 10am-4pm. 3SFr, students 2SFr.)

Berner Altstadtsommer features free dance and music concerts in the squares of the Altstadt. July's **Gurten Festival** attracts big names like Bob Dylan and Björk (www.gurtenfestival.ch; contact Ticket Corner at 848 80 08 00). At night, head to the bars and cafés along **Bärenpl.**, or the city's oldest wine cellar, **Klötzlikeller Weine Stube,** Gerechtigkeitsg. 62. (3.40-5.20SFr per glass. Open Tu-Th 4pm-12:30am, F-Sa 4pm-1:30am.) The **Art Café,** Gurteng. 3, is a café by day and a smoky bar by night. (Open M-W 7am-12:30am, Th-F 7am-2:30am, Sa 8am-2:30am, Su 6pm-12:30am.)

INTERLAKEN

Located between the crystal-blue Thunersee and Brienzersee lakes at the base of the largest mountains in Switzerland, Interlaken has earned its rightful place as one of Switzerland's prime tourist attractions. Nearby adventure playgrounds and the natural beauty of its surroundings make the town a favorite backpacker haunt.

🛂🛈🛉 PRACTICAL INFO, ACCOMMODATIONS, AND FOOD. The **Westbah-nhof** (tel. (033) 826 47 50) borders the Thunersee in the center of town; the **Ostbah-nhof** (tel. (033) 828 73 19) is on the Brienzersee, 10min. from the center. **Trains** arrive at both from Bern (25SFr); Lucerne (27SFr); Zurich (62SFr); Geneva (65SFr); and Lugano (72SFr). To get from the Westbahnhof to the **tourist office,** Höheweg 37, in the Hotel Metropole, turn left on Bahnhofpl. and right on Bahnhofstr., which becomes Höheweg. (Tel. (033) 822 21 21. Open July-Aug. M-F 8am-noon and 1:30-6:30pm, Sa 8am-5pm, Su 5-7pm; Sept.-June M-F 8am-noon and 2-6pm, Sa 8am-noon.) Rent **bikes** at either train station (26-30SFr per day).

Don't let hustlers at the station pressure you into taking you to an accommodation. The ☒**Backpackers Villa Sonnenhof,** Alpenstr. 16, diagonally across Höhenmatte from the tourist office, offers spacious, airy rooms with priceless mountain views. (Tel. (033) 826 71 71; fax 826 71 72; email backpackers@villa.ch. Dorms 29-33SFr; doubles 74SFr. Add 3SFr for Jungfrau view, balcony, and bathroom. Breakfast included. Kitchen. **Internet.** Bike rental. Reception 7:30-11am and 4-9pm. Reserve ahead. V, MC, AmEx.) The **Funny Farm,** down Hauptstr. past Balmer's (see below) in nearby Matten, is more commune than youth hostel, and offers volleyball, a pool, and an outdoor bar. (Tel. (079) 652 61 27. 25SFr. Breakfast included. **Internet.**) To reach the quiet and family-run **Heidi's Garni-Hotel Beyeler,** Bernastr. 37, turn right from the Westbahnhof and bear left on Bernastr., just behind the Migros. (Tel./fax (033) 822 90 30. Dorms 20-30SFr; doubles 60-80SFr. Bike rental. V, MC.) Something like an American fraternity house, **Balmer's Herberge,** Hauptstr. 23-25, is in the village of Matten. Head left from Westbahnhof, veer right onto Bahnhofstr., turn right on Centralstr., and follow the signs. Sign in and return at 5pm, when beds are assigned (no reservations). (Tel. (033) 822 19 61; fax 823 32 61. 2- to 8-bed dorms 19-28SFr; doubles 56SFr. Overflow mattresses 13SFr. Small breakfast included. Showers 1SFr per 5min. Kitchen. Laundry. Bike rental. **Internet.** Reception in summer 6:30am-noon and 4:30-11pm; off-season 6:30-9am and 4:30-11pm.) **Camping Sackgut** is just across the river from the Ostbahnhof. (Tel. (079) 656 89 58. 14.10-22.10SFr for one person and tent. Reception 9-11am and 4-7pm. Open May-Oct.)

Many hostels serve cheap food, but you can also eat on the cheap at **Migros market,** across from Westbahnhof, or at their restaurant upstairs. (Open M-Th 7:30am-6:30pm, F 7:30am-9pm, Sa 7:30am-4pm.) Revelers head to **Buddy's,** Höheweg 33, a small, crowded English pub. (Open daily 10am-12:30am.) Drunken herds then migrate to Interlaken's oldest disco, **Johnny's Dancing Club,** Höheweg 92, downstairs in the Hotel Carlton. (Open Tu-Su 9:30pm-3am.) **Postal code:** CH-3800.

🛶 OUTDOORS AND HIKING. Interlaken's steep precipices, raging rivers, and open spaces are prime spots for such adrenaline-pumping activities as paragliding, whitewater rafting, bungee-jumping, and canyoning (which involves putting on a wetsuit and harness and rappeling and swimming down a waterfall). Competition has driven prices down, and most companies charge similar prices. **Alpin Raft** (AR; tel. (033) 823 41 00), the original company, has wild Australian guides. **Alpine Center** (AC; tel. (033) 823 55 23), the newest and smallest company, provides the most per-

SWITZERLAND

sonal service. **Adventure World,** Kirchg. 18 (AW; tel. (033) 826 77 11), is the largest company. All three companies offer **paragliding** (AR/AC 140SFr, AW 150SFr); **canyoning** (AR/AC 125SFr, AW 130SFr); **river rafting** (AR/AC 85SFr, AW 90SFr); and **skydiving** (380SFr). Alpin Raft and Adventure World also offer **bungee-jumping** (100-220SFr) and **hang gliding** (AR 155SFr, AW 170SFr), and Alpin Raft also offers **sea kayaking** on the nearby Brienzersee (54-70SFr).

Independent **Swiss Alpine Guides** (tel. (033) 822 60 00; fax 822 61 51) lead full-day ice-climbing clinics (June-Oct., 135SFr), as well as full-day glacier treks (in summer daily; 120SFr). Interlaken's winter activities include skiing, snowboarding, ice canyoning, snow rafting, and glacier skiing. Contact the **Verkehrsverein Interlaken (tourist office),** Höheweg 37 (tel. 822 21 21; fax 822 52 21) or any of the adventure companies for info. There are three **skiing** areas in the Jungfrau region (info tel. 828 71 11; www.jungfraubahn.ch; 1-day passes 52SFr, 2-day 105SFr).

> Interlaken's adventure sports industry is thrilling and usually death-defying, but accidents do happen. Be aware that on July 27, 1999, 19 adventure-seeking tourists were killed by a sudden flash flood while canyoning on the Saxeten river.

The towns closer to the mountains have more serious **hiking,** but Interlaken has a few good hikes of its own. The most worthwhile hike climbs to the **Harder Kulm.** The half-day hike reveals a striking mountainscape including the Eiger, Mönch, and Jungfrau (only the last is visible from Interlaken). From the Ostbahnhof, head toward town and take the first road bridge across the river; follow first the yellow signs and then the white-red-white *Bergweg* flashes on the rocks. From the top, signs lead back down to the Westbahnhof. A **funicular** runs from the trailhead near the Ostbahnhof to the top. (May-Oct. 2hr. up, 1½hr. down. 12.80SFr, round-trip 20SFr; 25% off with Eurailpass or SwissPass.)

🛈 EXCURSIONS FROM INTERLAKEN: THUNERSEE AND BRIENZERSEE.
Appreciate Bernese Oberland's calm waters and stark mountain peaks on a lake cruise on either the **Thunersee** (to the west) or the **Brienzersee** (to the east). Ferries on Thunersee are free with Eurail, Swisspass, and Bernese Oberland passes. Major towns on the Thunersee are **Thun** and **Spiez,** which each boast several castles. **Brienz** is the main town on the Brienzersee, filled with preserved traditional Swiss dwellings and wood-carvers galore. **Trains** run to Thun from Interlaken's Westbahnhof (13.60SFr.) and Bern (12.60SFr.); and to Spiez from Interlaken's Westbahnhof (8SFr), Bern (30min., 17.20SFr), and Thun (10min., 6.20SFr). **Boats** also connect towns on each lake. Spiez and Thun have **tourist offices** adjacent to their respective train stations (Spiez tel. (033) 654 20 20; Thun tel. (033) 222 23 40). Perhaps the best reason to visit the Thunersee is the ⏏**Swiss Adventure Hostel,** in the tiny town of Boltigen, 30min. from Spiez by train (dir: Zweissimen). This restful, wholesome alternative to the partying adventure scene in Interlaken offers the same adventure sports opportunities as Interlaken companies, with a more personal experience. If you book an adventure activity through them, your first night is free. (Tel. (033) 733 73 73; fax 733 73 74. 18-24SFr; double 68SFr. All-you-can-eat breakfast 5SFr. **Internet.** Bike rental. Two free shuttles run from Interlaken each day; call for times. V, MC.)

JUNGFRAU REGION

The most famous (and most-visited) region of the Bernese Oberland, the Jungfrau area has attracted tourists for hundreds of years with glorious hiking trails and permanently snow-capped peaks. The three most famous mountains are the **Jungfrau** (Maiden), the **Eiger** (Ogre), and the **Mönch** (Monk). Locals say that the monk protects the maiden by standing between her and the ogre, but at 4158m, she could probably beat the puny Eiger (3970m) up. From Interlaken, the valley splits at the foot of the Jungfrau: the eastern valley contains Grindelwald, with easy access to two glaciers, while the western valley (the Lauterbrunnen) hosts many smaller towns, including Wengen, Gimmelwald, Murren, and Lauterbrunnen, each with

SWITZERLAND

unique hiking opportunities. The two valleys are divided by an easily hikeable ridge. Pick up the *Lauterbrunnen/Jungfrau Region Wanderkarte* (15SFr at any tourist office) for an overview of the hikes.

GRINDELWALD. Beneath the north face of the Eiger and within walking distance of the only glaciers accessible by foot in the Bernese Oberland, Grindelwald is a cold-weather paradise for hikers, climbers, and skiers. To reach the trail leading up the side of the **Upper Glacier** *(Obere Grindelwaldgletscher)*, take the postal bus from Grindelwald (dir: Grosse Scheidegg) to "Oberslaubkule," walk uphill, and follow the "Glecksteinhütte" signs to the right. Access to the **Lower Glacier** *(Untere Grindelwaldgletscher)* is closer to town: walk up the main street away from the station, follow signs downhill to "Pfingstegg," and then follow signs up the glacial valley to "Stieregg" (4hr. round-trip). The best strenuous hike away from the glaciers leads up to **Faulhorn** (2681m). It starts from the HI hostel, heads uphill through Allflue and Waldspitz, and continues to Bachsee and the Faulhorn past beautiful highland meadows, waterfalls, and streams (5hr.). From there descend to Bussalp (2hr.) and catch a bus back to Grindelwald.

Berner-Oberlander-Bahn **trains** run from Interlaken's Ostabahnhof (9SFr). To reach the **tourist office,** in the Sport-Zentrum, turn right from the station. (Tel. (036) 854 12 12; fax 854 12 10. Open July-Aug. M-F 8am-7pm, Sa 8am-5pm, Su 9-11am and 3-5pm; Sept.-June M-F 8am-noon and 2-6pm, Sa 8am-noon and 2-5pm.) The **Jugendherberge (HI)** sits in an beautiful wooden chalet above town. Go left on the main street from the station (5-7min.), cut uphill to the right at the tiny brown sign, and turn left at the fork by the blue SJH sign. (Tel. (036) 853 10 09; fax 853 50 29. Dorms 28-30.50SFr; doubles 41.50-46SFr. Breakfast included. Bikes 15SFr per day.) The bright-blue **Mountain Hostel,** at the Grund station next to the river, is equally far, but charming. Turn right out of the station, then right on the small trail toward "Grund"; go to the bottom of the valley, bearing right at the Glacier Hotel. (Tel. (036) 853 39 00; fax 853 47 30. Dorms 32SFr; doubles 84SFr. Breakfast included.) To **camp** at **Gletscherdorf,** turn right out of the station, take the first right after the tourist office, and then the third left. (Tel. (036) 853 14 29; fax 853 31 29. 9SFr per person, 5-15SFr per tent.) Frugal gourmets shop at the **Co-op** that roosts opposite the tourist office. (Open M-F 8am-6:30pm, Sa 8am-4pm.) A **Migros supermarket** lies farther down the main street away from the station. (Open M-F 8am-noon and 1:30-6:30pm, Sa 8am-5pm.) **Postal code:** CH-3818.

LAUTERBRUNNEN. The beautiful Lauterbrunnen Valley gets its name from its 72 waterfalls that plummet down the sheer walls of the narrow, glacier-cut valley. **Lauterbrunnen Town,** which lies in the middle of the valley, is an ideal base for hiking and skiing. It also lies near the **Staubbach Falls** (280m). To reach the main hiking trail, follow the right branch of the main road as it leaves town, which eventually dwindles to a dirt trail. The first, most-touristed segment of the trail leads past the Staubbach, Spissbach, Agertenbach, and Mümenbach Falls to the greatest of them all, the **Trümmelbach Falls,** comprising 10 glacier-bed chutes that generate mighty winds and a roaring din and see water gush past at up to 20,000L per second (40min.). Explore via tunnels, footbridges, and an underground funicular. (Open July-Aug. 8:30am-6pm; Apr.-June and Sept.-Nov. 9am-5pm. 10SFr.) The trail becomes less-trafficked as it continues on to **Stechelberg** (1½hr. from Lauterbrunnen), where **cable cars** leave for Gimmelwald (7.20SFr), Mürren (14SFr), Birg (33.20SFr), and Schilthorn (48SFr), small towns throughout the Lauterbrunnen Valley; the first two are free with the Swisspass, and Eurailers get 25% off all four.

Trains connect to Lauterbrunnen Town from Interlaken's Ostbahnhof (6.20SFr); Wengen (5.60SFr); and Mürren (9.40SFr). The **tourist office,** on the main street, is 200m left of the station. (Tel. (033) 855 19 55; fax 855 36 04. Open July-Aug. M-F 8am-noon and 2-7pm, Sa 9am-noon and 3-7pm, Su 9am-3pm; Sept.-June closed Sa-Su.) To reach **Hotel Staubbach** (tel. 855 54 54; hotel@staubbach.ch; www.staubbach.ch) from the station, follow the main street towards the waterfall (400m); the hotel is on the left. The comfortable rooms, most with private bath and shower, have unobstructed views of the Staubbach Falls. (Singles 50SFr, with shower 60SFr; doubles 80-100SFr; 3- to 6-bed rooms 35-40SFr per person. 5SFr extra per person in high season. Parking and breakfast included.) **Valley Hostel** is left off the main street, down a driveway, and past the **Co-op** (open M-F 8am-noon and 2-6:30pm, Sa 8am-noon and 1:30-4pm) on the right. (Tel. (033) 855 20 08. Dorms 20SFr; double 50SFr. Kitchen. Laundry.) **Camping Jungfrau,** up the main street from the station toward the large waterfall, has cheap beds, kitchens, showers, lounges, and a store. (Tel. (033) 856 20 10; fax 856 20 20. 8-10SFr per person, 6-15SFr per tent. Dorms 20-22SFr. Laundry. Reception in summer 7am-9pm; off-season 8am-noon and 2:30-6:30pm.) **Postal code:** CH-3822.

ZERMATT AND THE MATTERHORN

A trick of the valley blocks out the great Alpine summits surrounding **Zermatt,** allowing the **Matterhorn** (4478m), orange at dawn and cloud-shrouded much of the time, to rise alone above the town. The Matterhorn is the Holy Grail for serious climbers, but only those with loads of money (around 800SFr), experience, equipment, and time to train in the area. Fortunately, miles of spectacular, well-marked paths are accessible to all visitors. No visit to Zermatt is complete without struggling up to the **Hörnlihütte,** the base camp for climbs up to the Matterhorn and a strenuous four- to five-hour hike past the tiny lake **Schwarzsee; a cable car** also runs to the Schwarzsee (20SFr, 31.50SFr round-trip). Zermatt is one of the world's best-equipped ski centers, with 245km of challenging ski runs in winter and more summer ski trails than any other Alpine resort. **Ski and boot rental** prices are fairly standard (1-day 57SFr; 10% off for youth hostelers at Roc Sports; most shops open daily 8am-noon and 2-7pm). A one-day **ski pass** in the Matterhorn area costs 58SFr.

Cars and buses are illegal in Zermatt to preserve the Alpine air—the only way in is the hourly BVZ (Brig-Visp-Zermatt) **rail line.** Connect from Visp (from Lausanne; 35SFr) or Stalden-Saas (from Saas Fee; 1hr., 31SFr). The **tourist office,** on Bahnhofpl., in the station complex, sells hiking maps (27.90SFr). (Tel. (027) 967 01 81; fax 967 01 85. Open mid-June to mid-Oct. M-F 8:30am-6pm, Sa 8:30am-7pm, Su 9:30am-noon and 4-7pm; mid-Oct. to mid-June reduced hours.) The **Snow & Alpine Center,** on Bahnhofstr., to the right from the station past the post office (open M-Sa 8am-noon and 3-7pm, Su 10am-noon and 4-7pm), houses the **Bergführerbüro** (Guides Office; tel. (027) 966 24 60; fax 966 24 69) and **Skischulbüro** (Ski School Office; tel. (027) 967 24 66). **Hotel Bahnhof,** 1min. from the station (turn left down Bahnhofstr. as you exit), offers hotel housing at hostel rates. (Tel. (027) 967 24 06; fax 967 72 16; email Hotel_Bahnhof@hotmail.com. Dorms 30SFr; singles 52-56SFr; doubles 82-88SFr. Kitchen. Laundry. Reception 8:30am-8pm. Open mid-Dec. to mid-Oct.) To reach the **Matterhorn Hostel,** turn right along Bahnhofstr., left at the church, and right after the river on Schluhmattstr. (12min.). (Tel./fax (027) 968 19 15; email matterhorn.hostel@smile.ch. 24-29SFr. Laundry. **Internet.** Reception 7:30-11am and 4-10pm. V, MC, AmEx.) **Camping Matterhorn Zermatt,** on Bahnhofstr., is 5min. to the left of the station. (Tel./fax (027) 967 39 21. 8.50-9SFr. Reception May-Sept. 8:30-10am and 5:15-7pm.) Local legend **Walliser Kanne,** on Bahnhofstr., next to the post office, serves slightly upscale Swiss fare. (Entrees 15-19SFr. Open 11:30am-2pm and 6-10pm. V, MC, AmEx.) Pick up **groceries** at **Co-op Center** opposite the station. (Open M-Sa 8:15am-12:15pm and 1:45-6:30pm, Su 4-6:30pm.) **Postal code:** CH-3920.

SAAS FEE

Nicknamed "the pearl of the Alps," Saas Fee (1800m) is in a hanging valley above the Saastal, snuggled among thirteen 4000m peaks, including the **Dom** (4545m), the second-highest mountain in Switzerland. Visitors turn their attention to the mountains and the glacial glory of the **Feegletscher.** Summer **skiers** enjoy 20km of runs, and in winter an immense network of lifts opens (day-passes 58SFr). Stores in the **Swiss Rentasport System** rents several grades of equipment (skis 28-50SFr per day, snowboards 28-38SFr, boots 15-19SFr). In summer, the **Alpine Guide's office** by the church has a selection of **climbs** and **hikes** for both amateurs and experts. (Tel. (027) 957 44 64. Open M-Sa 9:30am-noon and 3-6pm.)

Post buses run hourly to Visp (50min., 14.60SFr), where you can connect to Lausanne, and Stalden Saas (40min., 11.80SFr), which links up with Zermatt (add 31SFr). Reserve a place on the bus at least two hours ahead (call (027) 957 19 45 or stop by the station). The **tourist office,** opposite the bus station, reserves rooms (10SFr) and gives hiking advice. (Tel. (027) 958 18 58; fax 958 18 60. Open July to mid-Sept. and mid-Dec. to mid-Apr. M-F 8:30am-noon and 2-6:30pm, Sa 8am-7pm, Su 9am-noon and 3-6pm; mid-Sept. to mid-Dec and mid-Apr. to June M-Sa 8:30am-noon and 2-6pm, Su 10am-noon and 4-6pm.) Those willing to sacrifice comfort can find bargains in hotel basements. The cheapest is **Hotel Garni Imseng;** from the station, head down the main street, left of the tourist office, then turn left and pass the church. (Tel. (027) 958 12 58, fax 958 12 55. 20SFr. Sheets 5SFr. Breakfast 15SFr.) Across the street behind Hotel Feehof Garni, the subterranean dorm at the **Hotel Berghof** is a bit more spacious. (Tel. (027) 957 24 84; fax 957 46 72. 25SFr. Breakfast 10SFr. Open June-Apr.) The **Supermarkt** is on the main street near the tourist office. (Open M-Sa 8:30am-12:15pm and 2:25-6:30pm.) **Postal code:** CH-3906.

ITALIAN SWITZERLAND (TICINO)

Ever since Switzerland won the Italian-speaking canton of Ticino (Tessin in German and French) from Italy in 1512, the region has been renowned for its mix of Swiss efficiency and Italian *dolce vita*—no wonder the rest of Switzerland vacations here among the jasmine-laced villas painted the bright colors of Italian *gelato*. Lush, almost Mediterranean, vegetation, emerald lakes, and shaded castles render Ticino's hilly countryside as romantic as its famed resorts, Lugano and Locarno. The **Ticino Card,** available at tourist offices, provides three days of free or half-price travel on local boats, cable cars, and other regional transit (June 15-Oct. 15; 55SFr).

LUGANO

Lugano, Switzerland's third-largest banking center, lies in the crevassed bay between San Salvatore and Monte Brè. Warmed by a Mediterranean climate, Lugano's shady streets are lined with tiles, climbing vines, and blood-red wildflowers. The leafy frescoes of the 16th-century **Cattedrale San Lorenzo,** just below the train station, are still magnificently vivid. The national monument **Basilica Sacro Cuore,** on C. Elevezia, has frescoes ringing that altar that feature Swiss hikers walking alongside the disciples. The most spectacular fresco in town, however, is the gargantuan *Crucifixion* in the **Chiesa Santa Maria degli Angiuli,** on the waterfront to the right of the tourist office. The **Museo delle Culture Extraeuropee,** 324 V. Cortivo, on the footpath to Gandria in the Villa Heleneum, features masks, statues, and shields from New Caledonia and other distant locales. (Open Mar. 5-Oct. W-Su 10am-5pm. 5SFr, students 3SFr.) Armed with topographic **maps** and **trail guides** (sold at the tourist office, lent at the hostel), hikers can tackle **Monte Brè** (933m) or **Monte San Salvatore** (912m). Alpine guides at the **ASBEST Adventure Company,** V. Basilea 28 (tel. (091) 966 11 14), offer everything from **snowshoeing** and **skiing** (85SFr) to **paragliding** (150SFr) and **canyoning** (from 70SFr).

Trains (tel. (091) 157 22 22) run frequently to Locarno via Bellinzona (1hr., 16.40SFr); Milan (1½hr., 19SFr); Zurich (3hr., 62SFr); and Bern via Lucerne (4½hr., 77SFr). From the station, cross the Centro footbridge, take V. Cattedrale onto V. Pessina, go left on V. dei Pesci, then turn left again on Riva via Vela for the **tourist office.** (Tel. (091) 913 32 32. Open Apr.-Oct. M-F 9am-6:30pm, Sa 9am-12:30pm and 1:30-5pm, Su 10am-2pm; Nov.-Mar. M-F 9am-12:30pm and 1:30-5pm.) To reach the luxury-villa-turned-independent-hostel ⬛**Hotel Montarina,** 1 V. Montarina, walk 200m to the right from the station, cross the tracks, and walk 1min. uphill. (Tel. (091) 966 72 72; fax 966 12 13. Dorms 20SFr; singles 50-65SFr; doubles 80-120SFr. Sheets 4SFr. Laundry. Reception 8am-10pm. Open Mar.-Nov.) To reach the almost equally posh **Ostello della Gioventù (HI)** at #13, in Lugano-Savosa, exit left from the station, go down the second ramp, cross the street, go 100m uphill, catch bus 5 to "Crocifisso" (6th stop), then backtrack and turn left up V. Cantonale. (Tel. (091) 966 27 28; fax 968 23 63. Dorms 17SFr; singles 32-42SFr; doubles 46-60SFr. Sheets 2SFr.

Breakfast 7SFr. Reception 7am-12:30pm and 3-10pm. Curfew 10pm; ask for a key. Reserve ahead. Open mid-Mar. to Oct.) To **camp** at **La Palma** (tel. (091) 605 25 61) or **Eurocampo** (tel. (091) 605 21 14), take the Ferrovia-Lugano-Ponte-Tresa (FLP) train to Agno (4.40SFr), turn left from the stop and left again on V. Molinazzo. (7-7.50SFr per person, 6-10SFr per tent. Shower included. Open Apr.-Oct.)

La Tinèra, 2 V. dei Gorini, behind Credit Suisse in P. della Riforma, is a low-lit underground restaurant with great specials (13-18SFr). (Open M-Sa 8:30am-11pm. V, MC, AmEx.) **Migros supermarket,** 15 V. Pretoria, two blocks left of the post office, offers fresh pasta. (Open M-F 8am-6:30pm, Sa 7:30am-5pm.) The **Pave Pub,** riva Albertolli 1, is a self-proclaimed *museo di birra* (beer museum), with 50 different brands. (From 4SFr. Open daily 11am-1am.) **Postal code:** CH-6900.

LOCARNO

On the shores of Lake Maggiore, Locarno basks in warm near-Mediterranean breezes and bright Italian sun, with luxuriant palm trees replacing the rugged Alps. During its famous **film festival** (Aug. 2-12, 2000; www.pardo.ch), 150,000 people descend to one of the most important movie premiere events in the world. Locarno's most striking church is the **Madonna del Sasso** (Madonna of the Rock), accessible by foot or **funicular** (next to the McDonald's by the station). The orange-yellow complex includes a densely ornate sanctuary and a museum next door. (Grounds open daily 7am-9pm. Museum open Apr.-Oct. M-F 2-5pm, Su 10am-noon and 2-5pm; 2.50SFr, students 1.50SFr.) Heed the call of Locarno's lake by renting a **paddle-** or **motorboat** along the shore, or catch a **ferry** (1¼hr., 20SFr) to the botanical gardens on the nearby island of **Brissago.** (Gardens open 9am-6pm; 6SFr.) For the price of a drink (min. 5SFr), you can take the delightfully cheesy **Katja-boat** for a mini-tour of the lake. (20min. Departs from the Hotel Rosa daily 10am-1pm.)

Trains (tel. (091) 743 65 64) run from P. Stazione to Lugano (45min., 2 per hr., 28SFr); Milan (2½hr., 3 per day, 63SFr); Zurich (2¾hr., every hr., 60SFr); and Lucerne (3hr., 2 per hr., 56SFr). For Zermatt (4hr., 88SFr); Montreux (4¾hr., 74SFr); or Geneva (5¾hr., 91SFr), change in Domodossola, Italy (1¾hr., 2 per hr., 41SFr). From the station, walk diagonally right, cross V. della Stazione, continue through pedestrian V. alla Ramogna, and cross Largo Zorzi to the left to reach the **tourist office** on P. Grande, in the same building as the *Kursaal* (casino). (Tel. (091) 751 03 33; fax 751 90 70; www.lagomaggiore.com. Open July 19-Aug. 15 M-F 9am-7pm, Sa 10am-5pm, Su 10am-4pm; mid-Mar. to July 19 and Aug. 15 to mid-Oct. Sa closes 4pm; rest of year closed Sa-Su.) The **Pensione Città Vecchia,** 13 V. Toretta, has the best prices and location in town. From P. Grande, turn right on V. Toretta (*not* vigola Toretta; look for a brown sign with the *alberghi* on it) and continue to the top. (Tel./fax (091) 751 45 54; email cittavecchia@datacomm.ch. Dorms 22-24SFr; singles 33-35SFr; doubles 60-73SFr. Breakfast 4.50SFr. Check-in 1-6pm; call ahead to arrive later. Reserve ahead. Open Mar.-Oct.) From the station, turn left, follow V. alla Romogna to P. Grande, turn right on V. della Motta, bear left on V. B. Rusca past P.S. Francesco, take V. Varenna, and follow the signs to reach the **Palagiovani Youth Hostel (HI),** 18 V. Varenna. (Tel. (091) 756 15 00; fax 756 15 01. Dorms 31-38SFr; doubles 33-43SFr; off-season 2.50SFr less. Breakfast included. Laundry 6SFr. Reception in summer 8-10am and 3-11:30pm; in winter 8-10am and 4-11:30pm.)

Dining and revelry are centered on the P. Grande and the lake, both excellent areas to seek out your favorite variety of *gelato*. On the left as you exit the station, **Inova,** 1 V. della Stazione, is a huge self-serve restaurant. (Salad bar 4.90-9.90SFr. Pasta buffet 8.50SFr. Meaty menus 11.90-14.90SFr. Open M-Sa 7:30am-10pm, Su 8am-10pm.) For cheap **supermarket** fare, try **Aperto,** at the station (open daily 6am-10pm) or **Migros,** on P. Grande (open M-Sa 9am-7pm). **Postal code:** CH-6600.

⚡ EXCURSION FROM LOCARNO: ASCONA. In addition to enjoying Ascona's tropical sunshine and sparkling water, history buffs can trace the steps of the 19th-century leftist thinkers and bohemian artists who tried to establish Utopia on the mountain above, known as **Monte Verità.** The **tourist office** (tel. (091) 791 00 90; email ascona@etlm.ch; www.ascona.ch) is in the Casa Serodine, behind the Chiesa SS Pietro e Paolo. Reach Ascona by **bus** 31 from Locarno (15min., every 15min. 6:23am-midnight, 2.40SFr) or by **ferry** (1hr., 10 per day, day-pass 11SFr).

TURKEY (TÜRKİYE)

US$1 = 447,000 TL	100,000TL = US$0.22
CDN$1 = 300,201TL	100,000TL = CDN$0.33
UK£1 = 709,478TL	100,000TL = UK£0.14
IR£1 = 601,741TL	100,000TL = IR£0.17
AUS$1 = 282,504TL	100,000TL = AUS$0.35
NZ$1 = 229,311TL	1000,000TL = NZ$0.44
SAR1 =73,641TL	100,000TL = SAR1.44

PHONE CODE   Country code: 90. International dialing prefix: 00.

Merely 77 years old, Turkey is a young nation that has inherited the combined riches of Ancient Greeks and Romans, the Byzantines, and the Ottomans. Asia Minor has seen more than 10,000 years of cultural traffic, and each passing civilization has left a layer of debris for the intrepid traveler to unearth. İstanbul and the Mediterranean and Aegean Coasts have an established tourist industry that makes enjoying Turkey easy. The rest of the country awaits exploration: pristine meadows, sun-soaked beaches, cliffside monasteries, medieval churches, a wealth of archaeological treasures, and countless cups of *çay*.

Following the creation of the East Roman Empire, Constantinople (İstanbul) became the center of Greek Orthodox culture. The Selçuk Turks encroached upon the Byzantine Empire from the 11th to the 14th centuries, and the Ottomans conquered İstanbul in 1453. The Ottoman Empire, which grew to include the Balkans, North Africa, and most of the Middle East, lasted from the early 1400s to the end of WWI. A weakened military and European power play led to the decline of the empire in the late 19th century. Early 20th-century leader Mustafa Kemal (Atatürk) expelled foreign armies and established the Turkish Republic. Equating modernization with Westernization, Atatürk abolished the Ottoman Caliphate, romanized the alphabet, and set up a democratic government. Recent history is dominated by the actions of the military, which occupied Northern Cyprus in 1974, organized three coups, and spearheaded ongoing conflicts with Kurdish rebels in the southeast. Turkey made news in February 1999 with the arrest and trial of Kurdish rebel leader Abdullah Öcalan. In August 1999, a devastating earthquake struck northwestern Turkey; over 18,000 people were confirmed dead and tens of thousands left homeless, reminding that Turkey's infrastructure is still developing.

For a true Turkish delight, consult the shiny *Let's Go Turkey 2000*.

DISCOVER TURKEY

Bargain at bazaars, marvel at Ottoman palaces, and stand in awe of the Hagia Sophia in Turkey's capital, **İstanbul** (p. 915). Swing northeast to **Edirne,** the former Ottoman capital and home to the finest mosque in all of Turkey (p. 924), before starting the trek down the sparkling **Aegean Coast.** From **Çanakkale,** make daytrips to the famed battlefield of **Gallipoli** and the ruins of **Troy,** former home of that babe whose face launched a thousand ships (p. 927). Head south to party-hardy **Kuşadası** (p. 929) and take a detour to admire the unparalleled ruins of **Ephesus** (p. 930). Partake in the real after-dark fun in **Bodrum** (p. 931), where folks boogie down all night, every night, then head inland to **Aphrodisias,** near **Pamukkale,** to take in some of antiquity's best temples (p. 930). From there it's just a bit farther south to the **Mediterranean Coast** and the **Turkish Riviera,** where **Ölüdeniz,** near **Fethiye,** tempts with a secluded blue lagoon and the waterfalls of the **Butterfly Valley** (p. 933). Let yourself be drawn through **Kaş** to the eternal flame of **Olimpos** (p. 933), then desert the coast for the region of **Cappadocia** in Central Turkey. Base yourself in **Göreme,** a surreal world of underground cities and fairy chimneys (p. 935).

GETTING THERE AND GETTING AROUND

BY PLANE. Turkish Airlines (THY), Delta, and the major European airlines fly into **İstanbul,** with some flights to **Ankara** and **Antalya.** THY (www.thy.com), with offices in **New York** (tel. (212) 339-9650), **Sydney** (tel. (02) 92 99 84 00), **London** (tel. (020) 77 66 93 00), and **Cape Town,** connects over 30 Turkish cities. Domestic flights average US$80 one-way; student discounts are available.

BY TRAIN. Although trains link Turkey to Athens and Bucharest, some lines may be suspended due to political crises in the Balkans. Despite low fares, trains within Turkey are no bargain, as they are slow and follow circuitous routes. **Eurail** is not valid in Turkey; **InterRail** passes are. If you have a Eurail pass, take the train as far as Alexandroupolis in Greece, and ride the bus from there.

BY BUS. Frequent, modern, and cheap, buses connect all Turkish cities and are the best way to get around. In large cities, bus companies run free shuttles called *servis* from their town offices to the *otogar* (bus station), which is often located quite a distance away. Buy tickets from local offices or purchase them directly at the station. Many lines grant students a 10% discount. **Fez Travel,** 15 Akbıyık Cad., Sultanahmet, İstanbul (tel. (212) 516 90 24; www.feztravel.com) offers a hop-on, hop-off "backpacker bus" loop (June-Oct. US$190, under 26 US$173).

 Road travel in Turkey is considered dangerous by European and American standards. Whether taking a bus or driving, travelers should educate themselves about road conditions. Only travel on reputable bus companies such as **Ulusoy, Varan,** and **Kamil Koç,** and avoid road travel at night and in inclement weather.

BY FERRY. Multiple ferry routes run connect **Greece** and Turkey's **Aegean Coast:** boats run from **Lesvos** and **Hios** to **Çeşme; Samos** to **Kuşadası; Kos** to **Bodrum;** and **Rhodes** to **Bodrum.** Boats also arrive from **Italy:** ferries go from **Venice** to **İzmir** and **Antalya** and from **Brindisi** to **Çeşme.** For more info on ferries connecting to and from the Aegean Coast, see p. 927. Boats also connect Greece to Turkey's **Mediterranean Coast,** for example, from **Rhodes** to **Marmaris;** see p. 932. Domestic **Turkish Maritime Lines** (TML) ferries sail from **İstanbul** to **İzmir** and to destinations on the Black Sea Coast. Most ferries are comfortable and well-equipped. Fares jump sharply in July and August, but student discounts are often available. Reserve ahead, and check in at least two hours in advance. If you arrive in Turkey by boat, expect to pay a US$11 Turkish port tax. Most countries also charge a port tax for exit (US$17 in Greece).

BY DOLMUŞ AND BY CAR. Expensive shared taxis known as **dolmuş** (usually minibuses) let passengers off at any point along a fixed route; they leave whenever

TURKEY

they fill up. The **speed limit** is 50km per hr. (31mph) in cities, 90km per hr. (55mph) on highways, and 130km per hr. (80mph) on *oto yolu* (toll roads). You must have an International Driving Permit (IDP) to drive in Turkey. If you get in an accident, file a report with the **traffic police** (tel. 118). Contact the **Turkish Touring and Automobile Association** (TTOK; tel. (242) 282 81 40) for more info.

BY MOPED AND BY THUMB. Mopeds are an easy, cheap way to tour coastal areas and the countryside. Expect to pay US$20-35 per day; remember to bargain. Be sure to ask if the quoted price includes tax and insurance. Those who choose to accept the risks of **hitchhiking** generally pay half what cheap bus fare would be. The hitching signal is a waving hand or the standard thumb.

ESSENTIALS

DOCUMENTS AND FORMALITIES. Canadians and New Zealanders can stay in Turkey for up to three months without a visa; South Africans are permitted to stay visa-free for one month. Citizens of Australia, Ireland, the UK, and the US require visas; although they can be obtained from Turkish embassies, it is most convenient to get them upon arrival in Turkey. A three-month visa costs AUS$30 for Australians, UK£10 for British citizens, IR£13 for Irish citizens, and US$45 for US citizens.

Turkish Embassies at Home: Australia, 60 Muggaway, Red Hill, Canberra ACT 2603 (tel. (02) 62 95 02 27; fax 62 39 65 92); **Canada,** 197 Wurtemburg St, Ottawa, ON K1N 8L9 (tel. (613) 789-4044; fax 789-3442); **Ireland,** 11 Clyde Rd, Ballsbridge, Dublin 4 (tel. (01) 668 52 40; fax 668 50 14); **New Zealand,** 15-17 Murphy St, Level 8, Wellington (tel. (4) 472 12 90; fax 472 12 77); **South Africa,** 1067 Church St, Hatfield, Pretoria 0181 (tel. (12) 342 60 53; fax 342 60 52); **UK,** 43 Belgrave Sq, London SWIX 8PA (tel. (020) 73 93 02 02; fax 73 93 00 66); **US,** 1714 Massachusetts Ave NW, Washington, DC 20036 (tel. (202) 659-8200; fax 659-0744); consular section open M-F 10am-1pm; phones staffed 2:30-4:30pm.

Foreign Embassies in Turkey: All country embassies are listed in **Ankara** (see p. 934); consulates are in **İstanbul** (see p. 915).

MONEY. Turkey's currency, the *lira* (TL), comes in denominations of 250,000, 500,000, 1,000,000, and 5,000,000TL. Coins come in values of 500, 1000, 2500, 5000, 10,000, 50,000, 100,000, and 250,000TL. Because the *lira* suffers from sky-high inflation, *Let's Go* quotes prices in US dollars.

Tipping and Bargaining: Tip taxi drivers, hotel porters, and waiters (leave it on the table) about US$1 for good service. 15-20% tips are only required in very deluxe restaurants, where service may be included in the bill *(servis dahil)*. **Bargaining** is common at outdoor markets, at bazaars, and in some carpet and souvenir shops. Allow the seller to name a price first, counter with a lower price (less than what you intend to pay, but not less than half the seller's price), and let the fun begin!

Taxes: A 10-20% **value-added tax** *(katma değer vergisi;* KDV) is included in the prices of most goods. It can theoretically be reclaimed upon departure.

COMMUNICATION

Post: PTTs (Post, Telegraph, and Telephone offices) are well-marked by yellow signs. Some PTTs may charge a small sum for *Poste Restante.* **Airmail** from Turkey takes 1-2 weeks; mark cards and envelopes "uçak ile" and tell the vendor the letter's destination: *Avustralya, Kanada, Büyük Bretanya* (Great Britain), *İrlanda, Yeni Zelanda* (New Zealand), *Güney Afrika* (South Africa), or *Amerika.*

Telephones: Make international calls at post offices. New phones accept **phone cards** *(telekart),* available at the PTT, while old ones require tokens *(jeton).* Card phones have directions in English. For **directory assistance** in Turkey, dial 118; for an **international operator,** dial 115. **International direct dial** numbers include: **AT&T,** 00 800 122 77; **Sprint,** 00 800 144 77; **MCI WorldPhone Direct,** 00 800 111 77; **Canada Direct,** 00 800 166 77; **BT Direct,** 00 800 44 11 77; **Ireland Direct,** 00 800 353 11 77; **Austra-**

TURKEY

lia Direct, 00 800 61 11 77; and **Telkom South Africa Direct,** 00 800 27 11 77. **Emergency medical assistance,** tel. 112. **Police,** tel. 155.

Language and Customs: Turkish. English is spoken in well-touristed areas. Off the beaten track, sign language and a pocket dictionary will usually suffice. When a Turk raises his chin and clicks his tongue, he means *hayır* (no); this gesture is sometimes accompanied by a shutting of the eyes or the raising of eyebrows. *Evet* (yes) may be signalled by a sharp downward nod. It is considered rude to point your finger or the sole of your shoe towards someone. Although public displays of affection are considered inappropriate, Turks often greet one another with a kiss on both cheeks.

HEALTH AND SAFETY. The most significant **health** concerns in Turkey are parasites and other gastrointestinal ailments. Never drink unbottled or unpurified water, and be wary of food sold by street vendors (see p. 31). Always carry toilet paper; expect to encounter pit toilets. Most doctors speak some English. Signs in pharmacy windows indicate night-duty pharmacies *(nöbetçi)*. If you're caught doing **drugs** in Turkey (or are caught in the company of someone who is), you're screwed. Stories of lengthy prison sentences and dealer-informers are true; embassies are utterly helpless in all cases. Exporting **antiques** is punishable by imprisonment. Foreign **women,** especially those traveling alone, attract significant attention in Turkey. Catcalls and other forms of verbal harassment are common; physical harassment is rare. One way of deflecting unwanted attention is showing your displeasure by making a scene; try the expressions *"ayıp!"* ("shame!") or *"haydi git"* ("go away"). Holler "eem-DAHT" ("help") if the situation gets out of hand. Carry a kerchief or scarf to cover your head in mosques. The touristed parts of Turkey may be more comfortable for women travelers. Dress modestly, especially farther east. **Travel to southeastern Turkey should only be undertaken after careful consideration of the risks involved.** Some provinces are effectively in a state of civil war and under martial law as Kurdish guerillas fight for separation from Turkey.

ACCOMMODATIONS AND CAMPING. Clean, cheap accommodations are available nearly everywhere in Turkey. Basic rooms cost US$6-10 for a single and US$14-20 for a double. **Pensions** *(pansiyon)*, by far the most common form of accommodation, are often private homes with rooms for travelers; don't expect toilet paper or towels. Most Turkish towns have a **hamam,** or bathhouse, where you can get a steam bath for US$4; they schedule different times for men and women. **Camping** is popular in Turkey, and cheap campgrounds abound (around US$2 per person). Official government campsites are open from April or May to October.

FOOD AND DRINK. Staples of Turkish cuisine like *çorban salatası* (shepherd's salad), *mercimek çorbası* (lentil soup), rice pilaf, and *yoğurt* are not listed on *lokanta* (restaurant) menus; their availability is understood. *Et* is the generic word for meat: lamb is *kuzu*, veal is *dana eti*. Chicken, usually known as *tavuk*, becomes *piliç* when roasted. *Kebap*, the most famous of Turkish meat dishes, ranges from skewer *(şiş)* or spit *(döner)* broiling to oven roasting. *Köfte* are medallion-sized, spiced meatballs. Turks eat a lot of seafood; *kalamar* (squid), *midye* (mussels), and platefuls of *balık* (fish). **Vegetarians** often choose to subsist on Turkey's wide variety of *meze* (appetizers). *Dolma* are peppers, grape leaves, or eggplant stuffed with rice and served hot or cold, with or without meat. Turks serve **tea** *(çay)* hot, with sugar. **Coffee** *(kahve)* comes unsweetened *(sade)*, medium-sweet *(orta)* and sweet *(şekerli)*. Ice-cold *rakı*, an aniseed liquor, is Turkey's **national drink**. *Baklava*, a flaky pastry with nuts and soaked in honey, and Turkish Delight *(lokum)* are the most famous Turkish desserts.

LOCAL FACTS

Time Zone: Turkey is 2hr. ahead of Greenwich Mean Time (GMT; see p. 49).

Climate: The Mediterranean and Aegean coasts are extremely hot in July and August. In central and eastern Anatolia, winter is very cold and summer very hot. The Black Sea Coast, moderate almost all year, contains areas where rain falls 200 days per year.

Hours: Museums and **archaeological sites** are open Tu-Su 9am-5pm. **Banks, post offices,** and **tourist offices** are usually open 8:30am-12:30pm and 1:30-5:30pm.

Holidays and Festivals in 2000: New Year's Day (Jan. 1); National Sovereignty and Children's Day (Apr. 23); Ataturk Commemoration and Youth and Sports Day (May 1); Victory Day (Aug. 30); and Republic Day (Oct. 29). During **Ramazan** (Ramadan; Nov. 28), a 1-month fasting period, pious Muslims abstain from eating, drinking, smoking, and sex between dawn and dusk; businesses may have shorter hours, and public eating is inappropriate. During the 3-day **Şeker Bayramı** (Sugar Holiday), which marks Ramazan's conclusion, bus and train tickets and hotel rooms may be scarce. **Kurban Bayramı** (Sacrifice Holiday; Mar. 17) occurs a few months after Ramazan.

İSTANBUL

Straddling two continents and three millennia of history, İstanbul exists on an incomprehensible scale, set against a densely historic landscape of Ottoman mosques, Byzantine mosaics, and Roman masonry. The Bosphorus Straits have proven both the city's lifeline and its curse, providing a strategic location between two seas and two continents that has attracted countless sieges from covetous neighbors. Having withstood innumerable demographic shifts, wars, natural disasters, and foreign occupations, İstanbul naturally comprises a unique mix of civilizations, a composition evident not only in architecture and religious practices, but also in everyday customs. Black-veiled women link arms with their scantily clad daughters on the city's tiny, winding streets, and *nouveau riche* donning Harley Davidson boots parade past street merchants selling gold, spices, and aphrodisiacs as well as sights that double as backdrops for love scenes in Turkish pop videos.

▐ GETTING THERE AND GETTING AROUND

Flights: Atatürk Havaalanı, 30km from the city. The domestic and international terminals are connected by **bus** (every 20min. 6am-10pm). To reach **Sultanahmet,** take a Havaş **shuttle bus** from either terminal to Aksaray (every 30min., US$6), then walk 1 block south to Millet Cad. and take an Eminönü-bound **tram** to the Sultanahmet stop. Or take a **taxi** (US$4) to the Yeşilköy train station and take the commuter rail *(tren)* to the end of the line in Sirkeci. A direct **taxi** to Sultanahmet costs US$17-20. To reach **Taksim,** take the Havaş shuttle to the end of the line (45min., every 30min., US$6). To reach the airport, have a private service such as **Karasu** (tel. 638 66 01) pick you up from your hostel (US$5.50) or take the Havaş shuttle from the McDonald's in Taksim.

Buses: Esenler Otobüs Terminal (tel. 658 00 36), in Esenler, 3km from central İstanbul. Serves intercity buses. To get there, take the tram to Yusufpaşa (1 stop past Aksaray; US$0.50), walk 1min. to the Aksaray Metro station on broad Adnan Menderes Bul., and take the Metro to the *otogar* (15min., US$0.50). Most companies have **courtesy buses** *(servis)* that run to the *otogar* from Eminönü, Taksim, and elsewhere in the city (free with bus ticket purchase). Various companies serve additional international destinations. The following have good reputations; be careful when choosing a company.

Ulusoy (tel. 658 30 00; fax 658 30 10). To: **İzmir** (6hr., every hr., US$20, students US$17); **Bodrum** (8hr., 2 per day, US$23, students US$20); and **Athens** (21hr., M-Sa 1 per day, US$60, students US$51).

Varan (tel. 658 02 74). To: **Ankara** (6hr., 7 per day, US$22, students US$20) and **Bodrum** (13hr., 3 per day, US$28, students US$25.50).

Kamil Koç (tel. 658 20 00). To: **Bursa** (4hr., every 30min., US$8, students US$7.50) and **Ankara** (6hr., every hr., US$13, students US$12).

Pamukkale (tel./fax 658 22 22). To: **Pamukkale** (10hr., 6 per day, US$13-14).

Parlak Tur (tel. 658 17 55). To: **Prague** (2 days, departs Sa 4pm, US$80).

Trains: In virtually every case, it's faster and cheaper to take intercity buses.

Haydarpaşa Garı (tel. (216) 336 04 75), on the Asian side. Sends trains to Anatolia. Take the ferry (every 20min., US$0.50) from Karaköy pier 7, halfway between Galata Bridge and the Karaköy tourist office. Buy rail tickets for Anatolia can be bought in advance at the **TCDD** office upstairs. To: **Ankara** (6½-9hr., 5 per day, US$7-12).

TURKEY

Sirkeci Garı (tel. (212) 527 00 50), in Eminönü, downhill from Sultanahmet toward the Golden Horn. Sends trains to Europe. Connect to most European cities through Athens or Bucharest. Some lines may be suspended due to political crises in the Balkans. Call ahead for info and student fares. To: **Athens** (24hr., 1 per day, US$60); **Bucharest** (27hr., 1 per day, US$30); and **Budapest** (40hr., 1 per day, US$90).

Ferries: Turkish Maritime Lines (tel. 249 92 22), near Karaköy pier 7, just left of the **Haydarpaşa** ferry terminal. Look for the building with the blue awning marked *Denizcilik İşletmeleri*. Ferries leave for **Bandırma**, with train connections to **İzmir** (combination ticket US$10-25). Local ferries run primarily between Europe and Asia. Pick up a timetable *(feribot tarifesi;* US$0.60) at any pier. Fast **seabus** catamarans also run along the ferry routes. Address any questions to **Seabus Information** (tel. (216) 362 04 44).

Public Transportation: Buses serve most stops every 10min. 5am-10:30pm, less frequently 10:30pm-midnight. Signs on the front indicate destination; on the right side, major stops. **Dolmuş** (see p. 912) run during daylight hours and early evening and are found near most major bus hubs, including Aksaray and Eminönü; destinations are posted in the front window. A **tramvay** (tram) runs from Eminönü to Zeytinburnu (US$0.50); follow the tracks back to Sultanahmet even if you don't actually take it. **AKBİL** is an **electronic ticket system** that works on municipal ferries, buses, trams, seabuses, and the subway (but not *dolmuş*). A deposit of US$5 will get you a plastic tab to which you can add money in 1,000,000TL increments and which will save you 15-50% on fares. Add credit at any white IETT public bus booth with the "AKBİL *satılır*" sign (at bigger bus and tram stops); press your tab into the reader, remove it, insert a 1,000,000TL note, and press again. **Regular tickets** are not interchangeable. Tickets for trams and buses without ticket sellers are available from little white booths, while ferries and seabuses take *jeton* (tokens), available at ferry stops.

Taxis: Little yellow Fiats. Taxi drivers are even more reckless and speed-crazed than other İstanbul drivers. Be alert when catching a cab in Sultanahmet or Taksim. One light on the meter means day rate; 2 mean night rate. Check change carefully. Rides within the city center shouldn't be more than US$5.

■ ORIENTATION AND PRACTICAL INFORMATION

Waterways divide İstanbul into three sections. The **Bosphorus Strait** (Boğaz) separates Asia from Europe. Turks call the western, European side of İstanbul **Avrupa** and the eastern, Asian side **Asya.** The **Golden Horn,** a sizeable river originating just outside the city, splits Avrupa into northern and southern parts. Directions in İstanbul are usually further specified by city precinct or district. Most of the sights and tourist facilities are south of the Golden Horn, toward the eastern end of the peninsula, which is framed by the Horn and the Sea of Marmara. The other half of "Europe" is focused on **Taksim Square,** the commercial and social center of the northern European bank. Two main arteries radiate from the square: **İstiklâl Caddesi,** the main downtown shopping street, and **Cumhuriyet Caddesi.** The Asian side of İstanbul is primarily residential, but offers plenty of rewarding wandering and a more relaxed pace. Sultanahmet, Taksim, and Kadıköy (on the Asian side) are the districts that will be the most relevant for the majority visitors to the city.

TOURIST, FINANCIAL, AND LOCAL SERVICES

Tourist Office: 3 Divan Yolu (tel./fax 518 87 54), in **Sultanahmet,** in the white metal kiosk, at the north end of the Hippodrome. Open daily 9am-5pm. **Branches** in the Sirkeci train station, in the Atatürk Airport, and the Karaköy Maritime Station.

Travel Agencies: Indigo Tourism and Travel Agency, 24 Akbıyık Cad. (tel. 517 72 66; fax 518 53 33), in the heart of the hotel cluster in Sultanahmet. Sells GO 25 cards (US$5) as well as bus, plane, and ferry tickets, arranges airport shuttle service, and holds mail. Open in summer daily 8:30am-7:30pm; in winter M-Sa 9:30am-6pm.

Consulates: Australia, 58 Tepecik Yolu, Etiler (tel. 257 70 52). **Canada,** 107/3 Büyükdere Cad., Gayrettepe (tel. 272 51 74; fax 272 34 27). **Ireland** (honorary), 25/A Cumhuriyet Cad., Mobil Altı, Elmadağ (tel. 246 60 25). **New Zealand,** 100/102 Maya Akar Center, Büyükdere Cad., Esentepe (tel. 211 11 14; fax 211 04 73). **South Africa,** 106 Büyükdere Cad., Esentepe (tel. 275 47 93; fax 288 76 42). **UK,** 34 Meşrutiyet Cad.,

TURKEY

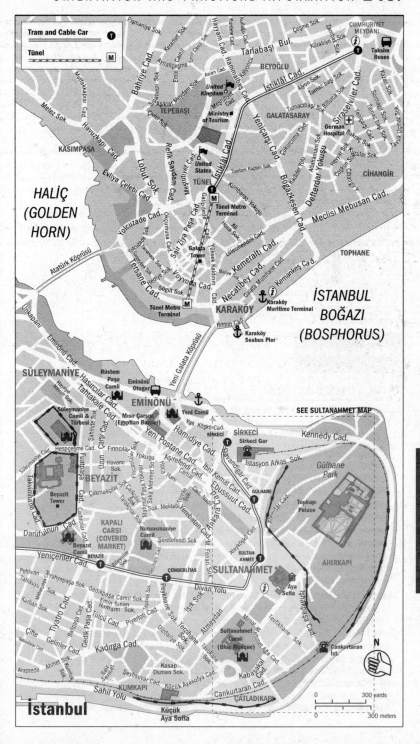

İstanbul

Tram and Cable Car ⓣ

Tünel Ⓜ

HALİÇ (GOLDEN HORN)

İSTANBUL BOĞAZI (BOSPHORUS)

CUMHURIYET MEYDANI

Taksim Buses

BEYOĞLU

TEPEBAŞI

United Kingdom

Ministry of Tourism

GALATASARAY

German Hospital

United States

TÜNEL

CIHANGIR

Tünel Metro Terminal

Galata Tower

Meclisi Mebusan Cad.

TOPHANE

Tünel Metro Terminal

KARAKÖY

Karaköy Maritime Terminal

Karaköy Seabus Pier

KASIMPAŞA

SÜLEYMANIYE

Rüstem Paşa Camii

Eminönü Otogar

EMİNÖNÜ

Yeni Camii

Mısır Çarşısı (Egyptian Bazaar)

SİRKECİ

Sirkeci Gar

İstasyon Arkas. Sok.

Kennedy Cad.

Gülhane Park

Topkapı Palace

BEYAZIT

Beyazit Tower

GÜLHANE

Hespçeşme Cad.

KAPALI CARSI (COVERED MARKET)

Nuruosmaniye Camii

Şerefefendi Sok

Beyazit Camii

SULTANAHMET

AHIRKAPI

Darülfünun Cad.

Yeniçeriler Cad.

BEYAZIT

ÇEMBERLİTAŞ

Divan Yolu

Aya Sofia

Sultanahmet Camii (Blue Mosque)

Cankurtaran İst.

Kadırga Cad.

KUMKAPI

Sahil Yolu

Küçük Aya Sofia

ÇATLADIKAPI

SEE SULTANAHMET MAP

N

TURKEY

0 ————— 300 yards
0 ————— 300 meters

Beyoğlu/Tepebaşı (tel. 293 75 40; fax 245 49 89). **US,** 104/108 Meşrutiyet Cad., Tepebaşı (tel. 251 36 02; fax 251 32 18).

Currency Exchange: *Bureaux de change* open M-F 8:30am-noon and 1:30-5pm; most charge no commission. Most **ATMs** accept all cards; banks exchange traveler's checks.

American Express: Türk Express, 4½ Cumhuriyet Cad., 3rd fl. (tel. 235 95 00), uphill from Taksim Sq. Open M-F 9am-6pm. Their office in the **Hilton Hotel lobby,** Cumhuriyet Cad. (tel. 241 02 48), helps when Türk Express is closed. Open daily 8:30am-8pm. Neither grants cash advances or accepts wired money.

English Bookstores: Kiosks at the Blue Mosque and on Aya Sofia Meydanı in Sultanahmet sell international papers. **Robinson Crusoe,** 389 İstiklâl Cad. (tel. 293 69 68).

Laundromats: Star Laundry, 18 Akbıyık Cad. (tel. 638 23 02), below Star Pension in Sultanahmet. Wash and dry US$1 per kg (2kg min.). Open daily 8am-10pm.

EMERGENCY AND COMMUNICATIONS

Emergency: Tel. 155. **Tourist Police,** at the beginning of Yerebatan Cad. in Sultanahmet (24-hour tel. 527 45 03 or 528 53 69; fax 512 76 76).

Hospitals: American Hospital, Admiral Bristol Hastanesi, 20 Güzelbahçe Sok., Nişantaşı (tel. 231 40 50). The **German Hospital,** 119 Sıraselviler Cad., Taksim (tel. 251 71 00).

Internet Access: The **Sinem Internet Café,** 16 Dr. Emin Paşa Sok. (tel. 513 62 29), in an alley off Divan Yolu by the Metro stop. US$1.80 per hr. Open daily 9am-10pm.

Post Office: The **PTT** (Post, Telegraph, and Telephone) office nearest Sultanahmet is opposite the entrance to Hagia Sophia. **Main branch,** 25 Büyük Postane Sok, in Sirkeci. Stamp and **currency exchange** services open 8:30am-7pm. Phones open 24hr. Address mail to be held: Ayşe INAN, *Poste Restante,* Merkez 3 Postane, PTT, Sirkeci, 25 Büyük Postane Sok., **5270050** İstanbul.

PHONE CODES	City codes: 212 (European side) and 216 (Asian side); you must dial the code between sides. From outside Turkey, dial int'l dialing prefix + 90 + 212/216 + local number.

◤ ACCOMMODATIONS

Budget accommodations are mainly in **Sultanahmet,** a.k.a. Tourist Central, bounded by Hagia Sophia, the Blue Mosque, and the walls of the Topkapı Palace. The sidestreets around **Sirkeci** train station and **Aksaray** offer tons of dirt-cheap hotels, but are not the most pleasant places to stay. Rates can rise by 20% in July and August.

■ **İstanbul Hostel,** 35 Kutlugün Sok. (tel. 516 93 80; fax 516 93 84), down the hill from the Four Seasons Hotel. If you had to choose a hostel floor off of which to eat, this should be it. Happy Hour 6:30-9:30pm (beer US$2). Dorms US$5; singles US$11.

■ **Sultan Hostel,** 3 Terbıyık Sok. (tel. 516 92 60; fax 517 16 26), at Fez Travel. Around the corner from Orient Hostel. Great views of the Sea of Marmara from the rooftop restaurant and bar. Happy Hour 5-8pm. Dorms US$5; singles US$9. Laundry. V, MC.

■ **Yücelt Hostel/Interyouth Hostel,** 6/1 Caferiye Cad. (tel. 513 61 50; fax 512 76 28; email info@backpackersturkey.com). Free beer until 9pm! Three included meals a day (including all-you-can-drink beer, wine, or tea). More amenities than you could list in 4 lines. Dorms US$7; singles US$16; doubles US$20. Did we mention free beer?

Moonlight Pension, 87 Akbıyık Cad. (tel. 517 54 29; fax 516 24 80). Away from the madness of the backpacker scene. Rooftop views. Dorms US$5; doubles US$16; triples US$21. Kitchen. Laundry. **Internet.**

Orient Youth Hostel, 13 Akbıyık Cad. (tel. 517 94 93; fax 518 38 94; email orienthostel@superonline.com), near Topkapı Palace. Happy Hour daily until 10pm. At night, the bar (see p. 924) receives Turkey's biggest Australian invasion since Gallipoli. Dorms US$5-5.25; doubles US$12.50. Breakfast included. **Internet.**

Side Pension/Hotel Side, 20 Utangaç Sok. (tel 517 65 90; fax 517 65 90), near the entrance of the Four Seasons Hotel. Newly renovated, this charming hotel/pension occupies two buildings by the corner of Tevfikhane Sok. and Utangaç Sok. *Pension sin-*

TURKEY

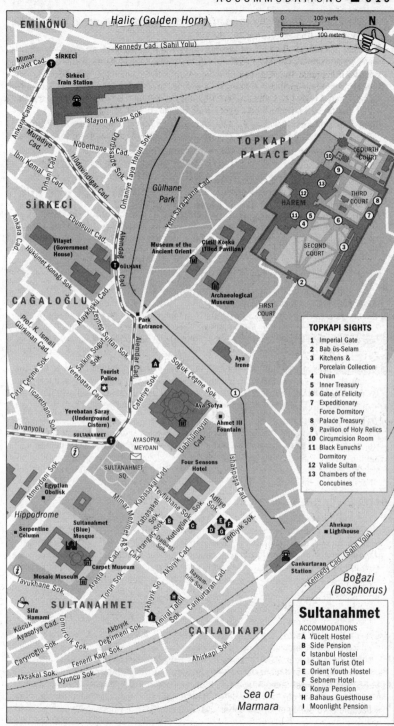

EMİNÖNÜ

Haliç (Golden Horn)

Kennedy Cad. (Sahil Yolu)

N

SİRKECİ
Sirkeci
Train Station

Istayon Arkası Sok.

TOPKAPI
PALACE

FOURTH COURT

Mimar
Kemalet Cad.
Muradiye Cad.
Ankara Cad.
İbni Kemal Cad.
Nöbethane Cad.
Darüssade Cad.
Hüdavendigar Cad.
Orhan Cad.

SİRKECİ

THIRD COURT

HAREM

Gülhane
Park

Yeni Saraçhane Cad.
Ohhaniye Tava Hatun Sok.

Ebussuut Cad.

Vilayet
(Government
House)

GÜLHANE

Museum of the
Ancient Orient

Çinili Köşkü
(Tiled Pavilion)

SECOND COURT

Ankara Cad.
Hükümet Konağı Sok.

CAĞALOĞLU

Alemdağ Cad.
Alayköşkü Sok.
Alayköşkü Sok.

Archaeological
Museum

FIRST COURT

Park
Entrance

Prof. K. İsmail
Gürkman Cad.
Salkım Söğut Sok.
Yerebatan Cad.

Tourist
Police

Aya
Irene

Soğuk Çeşme Sok.
Cafeniye Sok.

Çatal Çeşme Sok.
Çeşme Sok.
Çatal Ticarethane Sok.

Yerebatan Saray
(Underground
Cistern)

SULTANAHMET

Aya Sofya

Babıhümayun Cad.

Ahmet III
Fountain

Divanyolu

SULTANAHMET

İshakpaşa Cad.

AYASOFYA
MEYDANI

SULTANAHMET
SQ.

Four Seasons
Hotel

Egyptian
Obelisk

Armeydan Sok.

Mimar Mehmet Ağa Cad.
Kabasakal Cad.
Tevfikhane Sok.
Adliye
Sok.

Adliye
Sok.

Hippodrome

Serpentine
Column

Sultanahmet
(Blue)
Mosque

Kabasakal
Sok.
Kutluğün Sok.
Dalbastı Sok.
Akbıyık Cad.

Terbıyık Sok.

Ahırkapı
Lighthouse

Carpet Museum

Cankurtaran
Station

Mosaic Museum

Tavukhane Sok.

Arasta Sok.
Torun Sok.
Bayram-
fırın Sok.
Cankurtaran Cad.

*Boğazi
(Bosphorus)*

Kennedy Cad. (Sahil Yolu)

Sifa
Hamamı

SULTANAHMET

Akbıyık Sok.
Amiral Tafdil Sok.

Küçük
Ayasofya Sok.
Tomurcuk Sok.
Akbıyık Değirmeni Sok.
Caviroğlu Sok.
Fenerli Kapı Sok.
Aksakal Sok.
Oyuncu Sok.
Ahirkapı Sok.

ÇATLADIKAPI

*Sea of
Marmara*

TURKEY

TOPKAPI SIGHTS

1 Imperial Gate
2 Bab üs-Selam
3 Kitchens &
  Porcelain Collection
4 Divan
5 Inner Treasury
6 Gate of Felicity
7 Expeditionary
  Force Dormitory
8 Palace Treasury
9 Pavilion of Holy Relics
10 Circumcision Room
11 Black Eunuchs'
   Dormitory
12 Valide Sultan
13 Chambers of the
   Concubines

Sultanahmet

ACCOMMODATIONS

A Yücelt Hostel
B Side Pension
C Istanbul Hostel
D Sultan Turist Otel
E Orient Youth Hostel
F Sebnem Hotel
G Konya Pension
H Bahaus Guesthouse
I Moonlight Pension

0   100 yards
0   100 meters

gles US$20; doubles US$25; triples US$35. Add US$10 for bath. Hotel singles US$40; doubles US$50; triples US$60. In winter, US$5 less. V, MC.

Sebnem Hotel, 1 Akbıyık Cad. (tel. 517 66 23; fax 638 10 56; email sebnemHotel@webjump.com), next door to Hanedan Hotel. Lovely converted house with canopy beds. Singles US$30; doubles US$40. Breakfast included. **Internet.**

Bahaus Guesthouse, Akbıyık Cad., 11 Bayram Fırını Sok. (tel. 517 66 97; fax 517 66 97). A comfortable hotel with a view of the Sea of Marmara. Free backgammon courses from the owner. Singles US$20; doubles US$25-30. Breakfast included.

Konya Pansiyon (tel. 517 36 77), on Terbıyık Sok. Probably the cheapest place in the area. Quiet, tidy, and a block from Akbıyık Sok. Singles US$5; doubles US$7. Kitchen.

◖ FOOD

İstanbul's restaurants, like its clubs and bars, often stick by the golden rule that if it's well advertised or easy to find, it's not worth visiting. Poking around side-streets is always worthwhile. Sultanahmet's heavily advertised "Turkish" restaurants aren't difficult to find, but much better meals can be found on **İstiklâl Cad.** and around **Taksim.** Small Bosphorus towns such as **Arnavutköy** and **Sarıyer** (on the European side) and **Çengelköy** (on the Asian side) are the best places for fresh **fish.** Good **kebap** shops are everywhere, but quality tends to be better in residential areas. **Ortaköy** is the place to go for **baked potatoes** with all kinds of fillings. There's a **grocery** store on every corner. A large, fresh selection of produce can be found in the city's **open-air markets;** the best is the daily one in **Beşiktaş,** near Barbaros Cad.

SULTANAHMET AND DİVAN YOLU

◖ **Dârüzziyâfe** (tel. 511 84 14), behind the Sultanahmet Camii on the Hippodrome. Their specialty, *Süleymaniye çorbası* (meat and veggie soup; US$2), is a must, as is their *çilek keşkül* (strawberry pudding; US$1.50). No alcohol—they serve rosehip nectar instead. Open daily noon-11pm.

◖ **Cennet,** 90 Divan Yolu (tel. 513 14 16), on the right side of the road as you walk from Sultanahmet toward Aksaray, 3min. from the Sultanahmet tram. Watch women make *gözleme* (Anatolian pancakes). Divine cheese pancake US$1. Live Turkish music and dancing nightly. Open daily 10am-midnight. US$1 service charge per person.

Doy-Doy, 13 Şifa Hamamı Sok. (tel. 517 15 88). Easily the best and cheapest source of Sultanahmet's cheap eats, 3-story Doy-Doy keeps locals and backpackers coming back for more. Tasty *kebap* and salads (US$3.50 and under). Open daily 8:30am-late.

Pudding Shop, 6 Divan Yolu (tel. 522 29 70; fax 512 44 58). A major pit-stop on the Hippie Trail to the Far and Middle East during the 70s. Nicknamed the Pudding Shop by hippies, it was the setting for the drug deal scene in *Midnight Express.* Now clean.

İSTİKLÂL CADDESİ AND TAKSİM

◖ **Haci Baba,** 49 İstiklâl Cad. (tel. 244 18 86), has perfected a wide range of Turkish standards in its 78 years. Large, stylish dining room and a terrace overlooking the court-yard of Aya Triada. Entrees around US$7. Open daily 10am-10pm.

Afacan, on İstiklâl Cad. Two locations, one at the top end of İstiklâl Cad, by the 1st movie theater, and the 2nd at the other end, past the Galatasaray Lisesi. Seriously good *kebaps* and *dolma.* Bottom open daily 8am-11pm, top open daily 10am-midnight.

İnci Pastahanesi, 126 İstiklâl Cad. (tel. 243 24 12). Has served the neighborhood for 52 years under the same owner. The specialty is the scandalously cheap *profiterol,* a creme-filled cake smothered in chocolate sauce (US$1.20). Open daily 7am-9pm.

◖ SIGHTS

İstanbul's hosts an incomparable array of world-famous churches, mosques, palaces, and museums. Most budget travelers spend a lot of time in **Sultanahmet,** the area around the **Hagia Sophia** mosque, south of and uphill from Sirkeci. Merchants crowd the district between the **Grand Bazaar,** east of the university, and the **Egyptian Bazaar,** just southeast of Eminönü.

HAGIA SOPHIA (AYA SOFİA)

Hagia Sophia opened in December of AD 537. Covering an area of 7570 square meters and rising to a height of 55.6m, it was then the grandest building in the world. Upon entering the church and marvelling at its girth, which was even larger than King Solomon's temple in Jerusalem, Emperor Justinian I reportedly exclaimed, "Solomon, I have outdone you!" Twenty years later, an earthquake brought the dome crashing to the ground. After falling to the Ottomans in 1453, Hagia Sophia was converted into a mosque, and remained one until Atatürk established it as a museum in 1932. Hagia Sophia's austere interior amplifies its awesome size. The nave is overshadowed by the massive, gold-leaf mosaic dome. The **mihrab,** the calligraphy-adorned portal pointing toward Mecca, stands in the **apse,** a space which housed the altar during the mosque's Orthodox incarnation. The elaborate marble square in the floor marks the spot where Byzantine emperors were once crowned. The **minber,** the platform used to address the crowd at Muslim prayer, is atop the stairway to the right of the *mihrab*. The **gallery** contains Byzantine mosaics uncovered from beneath a thick layer of Ottoman plaster as well as the famed **sweating pillar,** which is sheathed in bronze. The pillar has a hole where you can insert your finger to collect the odd drop of water, believed to possess healing powers; you'll have to wait a bit, though—health isn't easy to come by. *(Museum open Tu-Su 9:30am-4:30pm. Gallery open Tu-Su 9:30-11:30am and 1-4pm. US$4.80, students free.)*

BLUE MOSQUE (12SULTANAHMET CAMİİ)

Between the Hippodrome and Hagia Sophia, the Blue Mosque, Sultan Ahmet's response to Hagia Sophia (1617), takes its name from the beautiful blue İznik tiles inside. Not nearly as large as Hagia Sophia, the mosque's internal framework of iron bars enables the entire structure to bend in earthquakes (so far, it has withstood 20). Enter from the east side through the **courtyard.** The mosque's **six minarets** are the primary source of its fame; at the time, only the mosque at Mecca had six minarets, and the thought of equalling that sacred edifice was considered heretical. Sultan Ahmet circumvented this difficulty by financing the construction of a seventh minaret at Mecca. A small stone from the **Ka'aba** at Mecca is almost invisible from the tourists' area. *(Open Tu-Sa outside of prayer times. Dress modestly: no shorts or tank tops, and women must wear head coverings. Donation requested.)* The small, square, single-domed structure in front of the Blue Mosque, **Sultan Ahmet's Tomb** (Sultanahmet'in Türbesi), contains the sultan's remains as well as those of his wife and sons, Osman II and Murat IV. The tomb's İznik tiles are well-situated for close analysis. *(Open Tu-Su 9:30am-4:30pm. US$1, students free.)*

THE HIPPODROME (AT MEYDANI)

Behind the Blue Mosque, the remains of this ancient Roman circus form a pleasant park whose tranquility defies its turbulent history. Built by the Roman Emperor Septimus Severus in AD 200, the Hippodrome was the site of chariot races and public executions. Constantine, the first Byzantine Emperor, enlarged the racetrack to 500m on each side. The tall, northernmost column with hieroglyphics is the **Egyptian Obelisk** (Dikili Taş), erected by the Pharaoh Thutmosis III in 1500 BC and brought from Egypt to Constantinople in the 4th century by Emperor Theodosius I. Farther south, the subterranean bronze stump is all that remains of the **Serpentine Column,** originally placed at the Oracle of Delphi. The southernmost column is the **Column of Constantine,** whose original gold-plated bronze tiling was looted by Crusaders during the sack of Constantinople. On the east side of the Hippodrome along Atmeydanı Sok. is the superb **Museum of Turkish and Islamic Art** (İbrahim Paşa Sarayı). The Ottoman calligraphy is particularly impressive. *(Open Tu-Su 9:30am-4:30pm. US$2, students US$1.20.)*

TURKEY

TOPKAPI PALACE (TOPKAPI SARAYI)

The main entrance is on Babıhümayun Cad., the cobblestoned street off Hagia Sophia square. Open W-M 9am-4:30pm. US$4, students free. Harem open W-M; mandatory tours every 30min. 9:30am-3:30pm. Harem US$2.50, students US$1.50.

Towering from the high ground at the tip of the old city, hidden behind walls up to 12m high, Topkapı Palace was the nerve center of the Ottoman Empire from the 15th to the 19th centuries. Topkapı offers unparalleled insight into the wealth, excess, cruelty, and artistic vitality that characterized the Ottoman Empire at its peak. Built by Mehmet the Conqueror between AD 1458 and 1465, the palace became an imperial residence under Süleyman the Magnificent. The palace is divided into a series of courts surrounded by palace walls.

FIRST AND SECOND COURTYARDS. The general public was permitted entrance via the **Imperial Gate** to the **first courtyard,** where they watched executions, traded, and viewed the nexus of the Empire's glory. At the end of the first courtyard, the capped conical towers of the **Gate of Greeting** (Bab-üs-Selam) mark the entrance to the **second courtyard.** To the right beyond the colonnade, the **Imperial kitchens,** feature distinctive conical and vaulted chimneys and house three collections of porcelain and silver. The last set of doors on the left of the narrow alley leads to the palace's world-famous **Chinese and Japanese porcelain collections.** Across the courtyard, where ostriches and eunuchs once roamed, lies the **Divan** (also known as Kubbealtı), whose window grilles, awnings, walls, and ceilings are bathed in gold leaf. The **Council Chamber,** the room closest to the Harem, retains its original classical Ottoman calligraphic decor. Abutting the Council Chamber is the plush rococo-style room in which the **Grand Vizier** once received foreign dignitaries. Next door and to the right is the **Inner Treasury,** where various cutting, bludgeoning, and hacking instruments are kept.

THIRD COURTYARD. The **third courtyard,** officially known as **Enderun** (inside), is accessible through the **Gate of Felicity.** The **Expeditionary Force Dormitory** holds a costume collection that traces the evolution of imperial costumes. Move along down the colonnade to the incredible **Palace Treasury,** where ornate gold objects, the legendary **Topkapı dagger** (essentially three giant emeralds with a knife sprouting out of them), the 86-carat **Spoonmaker's Diamond,** and much more await your ogling. Just on the other side of the courtyard is the **Pavilion of Holy Relics,** which houses the booty taken by Selim the Grim after the Ottoman capture of Egypt as well as gifts sent by the governor of Mecca and Medina upon Selim's victory. Note that this is an *extremely* sacred site to Muslims; dress appropriately.

FOURTH COURTYARD. Three passages lead into the **fourth courtyard.** If Topkapı can be thought of as the nerve center of the Ottoman Empire, then the fourth courtyard certainly qualifies as the pleasure center, as it was amongst these pavilions, gardens, and fountains that the infamous merriments and sordid garden parties occurred. From the broad marble terrace at the west end, you can take in the uninterrupted vistas of the Sea of Marmara and the Bosphorus. The **Revan Pavilion,** the building farthest from the edge of the terrace, was built in 1635 to commemorate Sultan Murat IV's Revan campaign; at the other end of the portico is the **Circumcision Room,** an octagonal chamber that overhangs the edge of the pavilion, built by Ibrahim the Mad. At the other end of the terrace stands the **Bağdat Köşku,** Murat I's monument to his capture of Baghdad in 1638. An octagonal/cruciform base supports the dome; the interior sports an amazing radial symmetry.

HAREM. The Harem's 400-plus rooms housed the sultan, his immediate family, and a small army of servants, eunuchs, and general assistants. Because it was forbidden for men other than the sultan and his sons to live here, the Harem became a source of intrigue and the subject of endless gossip. The mandatory tour proceeds to the **Black Eunuchs' Dormitory** on the left, then into the women's section of the harem, beginning with the chambers of the **Valide Sultan,** the sultan's mother. If a concubine attracted the sultan's affections or if the sultan spent a night with her, she would be promoted to nicer quarters, with concubines of her own; if she were lucky and came to carry the sultan's first son, she could become his wife.

THE ARCHAEOLOGICAL MUSEUM COMPLEX

The **tiled pavilion** was built in 1472 by Mehmet the Conqueror to view the athletic competitions below; the display covers the full spectrum of Ottoman tile-making, including some rare early İznik tiles. The smaller, cement building adjacent to the Tiled Pavilion, the **Museum of the Ancient Orient,** is rarely open; hidden inside is an excellent collection of large stone artifacts from Anatolia, Mesopotamia, and Egypt dating from the first and second millennia BC. The ▧ **Archaeology Museum** contains one of the world's great collections of Classical and Hellenistic art. *(About 150m downhill from the first courtyard of Topkapı Palace. When the palace is closed, enter the museums through Gülhane Park; a separate road next to the park ticket booths leads to the complex. Museum complex open Tu-Su 9:30am-4:30pm. US$3, students free.)*

GRAND BAZAAR (KAPALI ÇARŞISI)

Consisting of over 4000 shops, several banks, mosques, police stations, and restaurants, this enormous "covered bazaar" could be a city in itself. It began in 1461 as a modest affair during the reign of Mehmet the Conqueror, but today forms the entrance to the massive mercantile sprawl that starts at Çemberlitaş and covers the hill down to Eminönü, ending at the **Egyptian Spice Bazaar** (Mısır Çarşısı) and the Golden Horn waterfront. This colorful, chaotic, labyrinthine world combines all the best and worst of shopping in Turkey. Although the bazaar is loosely organized according to specific themes, much of it is a jumble of shops selling hookah pipes, bright baubles, copper filigree shovels, Byzantine-style icons on red velvet, Turkish daggers, embroidered pillows, amber jewelry, silver flintlock guns, musical instruments, chess sets, hand puppets, and, of course, evil-eye keychains. Through banter and barter, haggle and hassle, a day spent at the Kapalı Çarşısı is bound to tempt, titillate, and tantalize even the most experienced traveler. You'll surely get lost, so enjoy the ride. *(www.grand-bazaar.com. From Sultanahmet, follow the tram tracks 5min. toward Aksaray, walk to the mosque on your right, enter the side gate, and walk with the park on your left to the bazaar entrance. Open M-Sa 9am-7pm.)*

YEREBATAN SARAYI (UNDERGROUND CISTERN)

The underground cistern is actually a vast underground cavern whose shallow water eerily reflects the images of its 336 supporting columns, all illuminated by colored ambient lighting. Echoing sounds of dripping water and muted classical tunes will accompany your stroll across the elevated wooden walkways. Underground walkways originally linked the cistern to Topkapı Palace, but were blocked to curb rampant trafficking in stolen goods and abducted women. *(With your back to Hagia Sophia, the entrance is 175m away on the left side of Yerebatan Cad. Open daily 9:30am-5:30pm. US$3, students US$2.50.)*

SÜLEYMANİYE COMPLEX (SÜLEYMANİYE KÜLLİYESİ)

To the north of İstanbul University sits the massive and elegant **Süleymaniye Camii,** one of architect Sinan's great masterpieces, part of a larger complex that includes **tombs,** an **imaret** (soup kitchen), and several **medreses** (Islamic schools). *(From the university, head out the northwest gate to Süleymaniye Cad. From Sultanahmet, walk along the tramway (15min.). Mosque open Tu-Su 9:30am-4:30pm, except during prayers.)* Prof. Sıddık Sami Onar Sok. runs between the university and the mosque. Passing through the graveyard brings you to the superbly decorated **royal tombs** of Süleyman I and his wife, Haseki Hürrem. *(Open Tu-Su 9:30am-4:30pm. Donation requested.)* Walk along the Süleymaniye Camii's southwest side to the large arch just below the dome and enter the mosque's central courtyard through the smaller tourist entrance to the left of the main door. After removing your shoes (women should also put on a headscarf), proceed inside the vast and perfectly proportioned mosque. The stained-glass windows are the work of the master Sarhoş İbrahim (İbrahim the Drunkard).

PRINCE'S ISLANDS (ADALAR)

The craggy Prince's Islands are known to locals simply as the *Adalar* (islands). **Büyükada** is the largest and most enjoyable island, with pine-forested scenery, swimming spots, and peaceful walks. **Yörük Ali** is the main **beach** and picnicking spot. *(US$5 carriage ride from town.)* The main forms of transportation on the islands are **walking, biking,** and **horse-and-buggy rides.** The lovely ■ **Ideal Aile Pansiyon,** 14 Kadıyoran Cad. has large rooms that are more like apartments than hotel rooms. *(Tel. 382 68 57. US$16 per person.)* Ferries depart from the north side of Eminönü or Kabataş; look for "Sirkeci Adalar" signs (3-4 per day, round-trip US$2.50).

◤ HAMAMS (TURKISH BATHS)

Remember that while most İstanbul baths have either separate women's sections or women's hours, not all have designated female attendants. Women should specifically request female washers. Self service is always an option; signal your preference by showing the attendants your bar of soap and wash cloth.

■ **Çemberlitaş Hamamı,** 8 Verzirhan Cad. (tel. 522 79 74), just a soap-slide away from the Çemberlitaş tram stop. Built by Sinan in 1584, it's also one of the most beautiful. Vigorous "towel service" after the bath requires a US$1.50-3 tip. Bath US$14, with massage US$18; students US$8, US$12.

■ **Çinli Hamamı,** in Fatih, near the butcher shops at the end of Itfaiye Cad. Built for the pirate Barbarossa, this bath is excellent and authentic. It retains a few of its original İznik and Kütahya tiles. Both sections open 9am-8pm. Bath US$4; massage US$4.

Cağaloğlu Hamamı (tel. 522 24 24), on Yerebatan Cad., 2km up from Yerebatan Cistern in Sultanahmet. Scenes from *Indiana Jones* were shot in this famous *hamam*. Stone and water can tend toward the lukewarm. Men's section open daily 7am-10pm; women's section 8am-8pm. US$8 for self-service; US$30 for massage and scrubdown.

◪ NIGHTLIFE

İstanbul's nightlife varies—there are male-only *çay* houses that tend to be dingy, poorly lit, and even somewhat unsafe. Small, relaxed **café-bars,** cavernous **rock bars,** and familiar **backpacker bars** are concentrated in the Sultanahmet area. The hippest İstanbul clubs often move from unlisted spots in Taksim in the winter to unlisted summer spots throughout the city. The Beşiktaş end of **Ortaköy** is a maze of upscale hangouts; along the coastal road toward Arnavutköy are a string of open-air clubs (cover US$18-45). Bouncers are highly selective, but wander between Ortaköy and **Bebek** and try your luck. İstanbul night action is centered around **Taksim** and **İstiklâl Cad. Sultanahmet's** bars all lie within 100m of another; beer prices are standardized at US$1-1.25. Solo females should take a cab home.

■ **Jazz Spot,** at the end of Büyük Parmakkapı Sok in Taksim. A mixed group of music lovers mostly sit while live bands lay the funk on thick. Live music daily 11pm. Beer US$3. No cover June-Aug.; Sept.-May F-Sa US$10. Open 11am-4am.

■ **Mordi Café Bar,** 47 Akbıyık Cad., down the street from the Orient Hostel in Sultanahmet. Leagues above the other backpacker bars in cleanliness and ambience, this spot was recently created from a private residence. Happy Hour until 10pm.

Peyote, on İmam Adnan Sok. (tel. 293 32 62), next to Leman Kültür in Taksim. This humble spot is one of the area's cheapest venues for live music. Beer US$1.25. Live music Tu-Sa 11:30pm. F-Sa cover US$7.50; includes 1 drink. Open M-Sa 6pm-4am.

Madrid Bar, on İpek Sok., off Küçük Parmakkapı Sok., which is off İstiklâl Cad in Taksim. This small, mellow spot is popular with Turkish students and young foreigners looking for some of the cheapest pints in Taksim (US$1.25). Open 2pm-2am.

Orient Bar, 13 Akbıyık Sok. (tel. 517 94 93), in the Orient Youth Hostel in Sultanahmet. Revelry abounds in this boisterous basement bar. *Nargile* (water pipe) nights (Th and Su 9pm) attract international types, while evening belly dancing shows (M, W, F 10pm) are entertaining albeit inauthentic. Happy hour until 10pm. Open 8pm-2am.

EDİRNE

An easy *dolmuş* ride from the Greek (7km away) or Bulgarian (20km) border, Edirne once nourished the genius of Sinan, the quintessential Ottoman architect. His masterpiece, the **Selimiye Camii,** considered by many to be the finest mosque in Turkey, presides over the city with 71m minarets (the tallest in the Muslim world)

TURKEY

THE *HAMAM* EXPERIENCE

To use a *hamam*, pay the entrance fee plus additional charges for massage and *kese* (abrasive mitt). Bring your own soap and towel *(peştemal)*, or pay to borrow the bath's. Some *hamam*s allow patrons to leave valuables at the front desk or in special cubicles *(camekan)*. Men generally strip naked and wrap the *peştemal* around their waists. Turkish women frequently strip naked in the bath, but wear underwear under your *peştemal* until you can gauge the sensibilities of a given *hamam*. Some have a hot, sauna-like room where you can lie and warm yourself to the point of near-lightheadedness. After you've worked up a sweat, proceed to the warm main room, which has a large, heated stone *(göbek taşı)*. Bathe yourself at the basins lining the walls (one per person), pouring a mixture of hot and cold water over yourself using the bowl provided. Keep soapsuds clear of the basin water, and take care not to douse others. Men should never drop their *peştemal;* cleaning your lower half is tricky, but not impossible. You usually pay extra to be washed and receive a **massage** on the large, heated marble stone. Typically, masseuse and client are of the same gender; female visitors may request a female masseuse. Don't be shocked if your masseur or masseuse is only wearing underwear. The massage is sometimes harder than what most visitors expect; say *"lütfen daha yumuşak"* ("gentler please") if you are in any pain. Following the massage and *kese,* used to strip excess skin cells beyond all imagination, you will usually be sponged gently and shampooed. Once you feel you have reached optimum cleanliness, return to your cubicle, order a drink to rehydrate, and relax before returning to the dusty world outside.

and 999 windows. Its vast, ornately-decorated interior is even more impressive. Edirne's other must-see sight is the **Beyazıt Complex,** built in the late 1480s by the court architect of Beyazıt II. The centerpiece is the **Beyazıt Camii,** a beautiful, single-domed mosque surrounded by multi-domed buildings designed to be schools, storehouses, and asylums. For a long but pleasant walk to the complex, follow Horozlu Bayir Cad. from its origin near the Sukullu Hamamı across two bends of the river. Unfortunately, only one wing remains open today. (Open daily 8:30am-5:30pm. US$0.75, students free.) Back in town, Sinan's 16th-century **Sokollu Hamamı** (Turkish bath), beside the Üç Şerefeli Camii, has superior service and inspiring architecture. (Tel. (284) 225 21 93. Open daily 7am-11pm for men; 9am-6pm for women. US$2.50, with massage US$6.25.) Those less interested in cleanliness can get down and dirty when the annual **Kırkpınar Grease Wrestling Festival** comes to town in early July; call the tourist office for more info.

Buses arrive from İstanbul (3hr., every 30min., US$6.50); Bursa (Apr.-Dec. 2 per day, US$12.50); Ankara (8hr., 2 per night, US$15); and İzmir (11hr., 2 per day, US$12.50). From the *otogar,* walk across the street and take a *dolmuş* into Edirne. The **tourist office,** 17 Talat Paşa Cad., 300m from the town center, has free maps. (Tel. (284) 213 92 08. Open June-Aug. M-F 8:30am-5:30pm and occasional weekend hours; Sept.-May M-F 8:30am-5:30pm.) The wonderful **Hotel Kervansaray,** along Hürriyet Meydanı on Eski Camii, was built in the 16th century. A call to prayer resonates down the corridors at 4:30am. (Tel. (284) 225 21 95; fax 225 04 62. Singles US$30; doubles US$60; triples US$90. Breakfast included. Turkish bath. **Internet.** V, MC.) **Hotel Aksaray** is at the intersection of Maarif Cad. and Ali Paşa Ortakapı Cad. (Tel. (284) 225 39 01. Singles US$6.25; doubles US$10-15; triples US$11.25-18.75.) Don't leave town without sipping *çay* (US$0.25-0.45) at **Şera Park Café,** on Selimiye Meydanı in the park between Selimiye Camii and Eski Camii.

BURSA

In the shadow of the slopes of Mt. Uludağ, Bursa is both one of Turkey's holiest cities and a major industrial center; its fantastic examples of early Islamic architecture are also some of the most stunning in all of Turkey. The immense **Ulu Cami** stands in the center of town on Atatürk Cad. From the statue of Atatürk, head east along Atatürk Cad., bear right, and continue along Yeşil Cad. following the "Yeşil" signs to reach the gorgeous, blue-green, hilltop **Yeşil Türbe** (Green Tomb; open

TURKEY

daily 8:30am-noon and 1-5:30pm) and the onion-shaped minaret caps of the 15th-century **Yeşil Camii** across the street. *Şehade* (royal sons) are buried in tombs surrounding the **Muradiye Camii,** a testament to the early Ottoman practice of fratricide (the eldest son made a practice of killing his younger brothers to ensure a smooth succession). To reach the complex, catch a "Muradiye" *dolmuş* or bus from the Atatürk Cad./Heykel area. (Open daily 8:30am-noon and 1-5:30pm. US$0.60.) Bursa's fabled **mineral baths** are in the **Çekirge** ("Grasshopper") area west of the city. On Çekirge Cad. is the shiny ▧ **Eski Kaplıca** ("old bath"), one of the finest baths in the country, with a hot pool, a hotter pool, and a great massage room. Take bus 40 or a Çekirge *dolmuş* and ask for Eski Kaplıca. (Tel. (224) 233 93 00. Men US$7.10; women US$5.35; scrub US$5.35; massage US$5.35.)

Kamil Koç **buses** go from the terminal, 20km outside the city center, to İstanbul (3½hr., US$9); İzmir (5hr., every hr., US$9.50); Ankara (5½hr., every hr., US$10.50); Çeşme (6hr., 1 per day, US$11.50); and Kuşadası (7½hr, 9 per day, US$12). Local bus 90/A goes downtown (US$0.60). **Seabuses** (tel. (226) 812 04 99) go between İstanbul and Yalova (35min.-1hr., 14 per day, US$4-7.10), from which buses connects to Bursa (50min., every 30min., US$2.40). To get to the **tourist office,** head to the Ulu Cami side of Atatürk Cad., walk past the fountain toward the Atatürk statue, and go down the stairs on the left. (Tel. (224) 220 18 48. Open daily May-Sept. 8:30am-6pm; Oct.-Apr. 8am-5pm.) The spacious **Saray Oteli,** İnönü Cad., 1 Matbaa Çık, is at the large roundabout where İnönü Cad. meets Atatürk Cad. (Tel. (224) 221 28 20. Singles US$8; doubles US$19; triples US$23.80.) The basic but friendly **Otel Güneş** is at 75 İnebey Cad. (Tel. (224) 222 14 04. Singles US$8.30; doubles US$12; triples US$18.) ▧ **Kebapçı İskender** claims to have invented the unbeatable dish *İskender kebap* (lamb with tomato sauce, bread, and yogurt; US$4.30) in 1867; there's one branch at 7 Ünlü Cad. and another by the Cultural Center on Atatürk Bul. (Open daily 11am-9pm.) **Postal code:** 16300.

⚔ BORDER CROSSINGS: BULGARIA AND GREECE

By far the easiest way to cross into **Bulgaria** from Turkey is to take a direct bus from İstanbul. Or, for a more adventurous route, take a local bus (US$1) to **Kapıkale,** the Turkish border town, 18km west of Edirne, where two options await. A direct train goes to **Sofia** (8hr., departs daily 3:30am, US$20). Or, if you're looking for even more stories to tell the grandkids, walk or take a *dolmuş* (US$1) to the actual Turkish border, just several (hot) kilometers away from **Andreevo, Bulgaria.** Would-be crossers will have to walk (if the guards will even allow it) or hitch a ride on a bus crossing the border directly from İstanbul. Once on the other side, you have to catch a taxi from Andreevo to **Svelingrad** (16km away; no accommodations) and then another to **Plovdiv,** the closest town with direct transport to Sofia.

The easiest way to cross into **Greece** is also a direct bus from İstanbul; the border crossing between **Pazarkule** and the Greek border (open 9am-noon) is inconvenient, but feasible. From Edirne, you can either take a taxi all the way to Pazarkule (15min., US$6.25), or catch the local bus to **Karaağiç** (US$0.50) and then walk the remaining 2km to Pazarkule. Though the 1km between the Turkish and Greek border posts is a no man's land (no one may walk through without a military escort), Greek taxis usually wait at the border to ferry travelers across the stretch to **Kastanies,** from which you can make bus and train connections to elsewhere in Greece.

AEGEAN COAST

Fabulous classical ruins and a sinuous coastline concealing sublime beaches have helped transform Turkey's once tranquil Aegean coast into an increasingly popular destination. Framed by 5000-year-old mythology and history, the region's intensely rich culture offers an eye-full for photographers, archaeologists, nature-lovers, and hedonistic nomads.

FERRIES TO GREECE AND ITALY

From **Çeşme**, ferries run to **Hios, Greece** (1hr.; in summer Tu and Th-Sa; in winter Th; US$30, round-trip US$40; US$10 Greek port tax for stays longer than a day). In summer, **Turkish Maritime Lines** (tel. (232) 712 10 91) runs ferries from **Çeşme** to **Brindisi, Italy** (36hr.; M and F 11pm, Tu 11am; deck passage US$95). From **Kuşadası**, ferries head to **Samos, Greece** (in summer daily 8:30am and 4:30pm; in winter 2 per week). A $10 port tax is sometimes included in the ticket price. From Bodrum, **Bodrum Express Lines** (tel. (252) 316 40 67) runs ferries to **Kos** (1½hr., May-Sept. 1 per day) as well as hydrofoils to **Kos** (15min., 1 per day, US$21, round-trip US$24) and **Rhodes** (2¼hr, 1 per week, US$43, round-trip US$48-63).

GALLIPOLI (GELİBOLU)

The strategic position of the Gallipoli Peninsula on the Dardanelles made it the backdrop of a major Allied offensive in WWI, which sought to take Constantinople and create a Balkan front. Eighty thousand Turks and more than 200,000 soldiers of the British Empire—Englishmen, Australians, New Zealanders, and Indians—lost their lives in the blood-soaked, entrenched stalemate. This battle launched its hero **Atatürk** into his status as Turkey's founding father. It's best to visit the battlefields as a daytrip from nearby **Eceabat** or **Çanakkale. Ana-Tur,** Cumhuriyet Meydanı Özay İşhani Kat. 2, No. 30 (tel. (286) 271 58 42 or 217 07 71), in Çanakkale, and the **Down Under Travel Agency** (see Down Under Hostel, below; agency tel. (286) 814 24 31; fax 814 24 30; email d.under@mailexcite.com; tours US$13), in Eceabat, both offer **tours.** To visit on your own, take a *dolmuş* to the **Kabatep Müzesi** from Eceabat. (Tel. (286) 814 12 97. Open daily 8:30am-noon and 1-5:30pm. US$0.75.)

Gallipoli town is a more expensive and less convenient base for touring the battle-fields, but is also a relaxing destination of its own. **Çanakkale Truva** (tel. (286) 566 11 83 or 566 26 26) operates **buses** from Gallipoli to Çanakkale (US$2); Edirne (2 per day, US$5); İstanbul (16 per day, US$7.50); and İzmir (9 per day, US$9). A minibus runs every half-hour to Eceabat (30min., US$0.75). From the bus station, walk 1km with the sea to your right to reach the center of town. To reach the **Yılmaz Hotel,** 8 Liman Mevkii, walk from the **Liman Meydanı** (the main square) across the bridge next to the old watchtower. (Tel. (286) 566 12 56. Singles US$12. Breakfast included. Tours US$25.) In **Eceabat,** the **Down Under Hostel,** 39 Topçular Sok., has spotless doubles and triples with bath and a helpful, English-speaking staff. (Tel. (286) 814 10 65; fax. 814 19 00. US$5 per person. **Internet** US$4 per hr.)

ÇANAKKALE

With cheap accommodations and good bus connections, Çanakkale (pop. 60,000) is an easy base from which to explore Gallipoli and Troy. The **Grassy Castle** (Çimenlik Kalesi), 200m downstream from the harbor, is a park and naval museum. **Buses** arrive frequently from İstanbul (5hr., US$10); İzmir (5hr., US$7.50); and Bursa (5½hr., US$6.25). To get to the **tourist office,** 67 İskele Meydanı, go left from the station, take a right on Demircioğlu Cad, and follow the signs marked *Feribot* to the docks; it's on the left. (Tel./fax (286) 217 11 87. Open daily 8:30am-7:30pm.) **Anzac House,** 61 Cumhuriyet Meydanı, opposite the taxi stand, and can arrange tours of Gallipoli and Troy. (Tel. (286) 217 01 56; fax 217 29 06. Dorms US$4; singles US$8.15; doubles US$10; triples US$12. Breakfast US$1.50. **Internet** US$4 per hr.)

TROY (TRUVA)

Troy, made famous by Homer, remained under a blanket of mythology until Hein-rich Schliemann, millionaire-cum-archaeologist, uncovered the ancient city 32km south of Çanakkale, proving that the stories are more than fiction and that lovely Helen and the wooden horse are worthy of the space they take up in history books. Nine distinct strata of Bronze Age fortifications are explained in the **Excavation House.** (Site and house open daily in summer 8:30am-7:30pm; off-season 8am-5pm. US$2.50, students US$1.25.) **Anzac House** (tel. (286) 217 54 82) leads tours from Çanakkale at 9am (US$8); arrive by 8:30am and bring lots of water. Or, visit the site by taking a *dolmuş* from the *dolmuş* lot in Çanakkale (every 30min., US$0.75).

TURKEY

BERGAMA (PERGAMON)

Ancient **Pergamon,** once capital of the Roman province of Asia, then boasted the second-largest library in the world. Ruins of this great Hellenistic and Roman city dominate the hilltop. From the river (near the Pension Athena), cross the bridge, head diagonally to the right and uphill through the old town, follow the paved road until you come upon a gate, and follow the path to the right up to the temples and marble ruins of the **Acropolis.** On your way up, enjoy the breathtaking view of the Hellenistic **theater,** which once seated 10,000. Farther up, try to land three coins on top of the column inside the **wishing well** for good luck. Follow the yellow signs from Atatürk Meydanı on the west side of town to reach the famed **Asclepion,** an ancient healing center where the foremost doctor of the ancient world, native-born Galen, once worked. A marble colonnade, theater, and healing rooms remain today. (Open daily in summer 8:30am-7pm; in winter 8:30am-5:30pm. US$2.50 each, students US$1.25.) Near the river and the old part of Bergama stand the remnants of **Kızıl Avlu,** a pagan temple that became one of the Seven Churches of the Apocalypse mentioned in the Book of Revelations (Rev. 2:3: "This is where Satan has his altar"). Pergamon is across the river from the pleasant, modern town of **Bergama,** which sends buses to İzmir (1½hr., 2 per hr., US$2.75); Ankara (9hr., departs 10:30pm, US$13.75); and İstanbul (9hr., departs 11pm, US$15). From the bus station, walk 1km right on İzmir Cad. and turn left on Cumhuriyet Meydanı to reach the **tourist office.** (Tel. (232) 633 18 62. Open daily Apr.-Sept. 8:30am-5pm; Oct.-Mar. M-Sa 8:30am-5pm.) **Pension Athena,** on the road beyond İstiklâl Meydanı, boasts "Not the best, but we're trying to get there." Chalk one up for honest advertising. (Tel. (232) 633 34 20. US$5-7; 10% off with *Let's Go.* Laundry US$6.) **Postal code:** 35700.

İZMİR

İzmir (pop. 3 million), formerly **Smyrna** (reputed to be the birthplace of Homer), rose from the rubble of the 1922 Turkish War of Independence to become Turkey's third-largest city. *Çay salonular* (teahouses), the cries of children and street vendors, and a full-fledged **bazaar** (open M-Sa 8am-8pm) line the streets of Anafartalar Cad. İzmir's **Archaeological Museum,** near Konak Square, houses finds from Ephesus and other local sites. (Open Tu-Su 8:30am-5:30pm. US$2, students US$1.) In late June and early July, the **International İzmir Festival** brings Turkish and international acts to İzmir, Çeşme, and Ephesus (call the Hilton Hotel at (232) 441 60 61 for info; tickets US$5-15). Budget hotels, cheap eateries, bus company offices, and the **Basmane train station** are located around **9 Eylül Meydanı,** a rotary at the center of the Basmane district. **Buses** run from **Yeni Garaj,** İzmir's new intercity bus station, to Kuşadası (1½hr., 2 per hr., US$3); Bodrum (4hr., 2 per hr., US$7); Marmaris (5hr., every hr., US$8.75); Bursa (5hr., 2 per hr., US$7.50); Ankara (8hr., 2 per hr., US$12.50); and İstanbul (9hr., 2 per hr., US$15). Take bus 601 from the station (US$0.50, students US$0.30; buy ticket from kiosk before boarding) to the end on **Sehit Fethibey Bul.** in **Konak,** then walk up Anafartalar Cad., cross Gazi Bul. (turn right here to reach 9 Eylül Meydanı directly), and turn right on Gazi Osman Paşa Bul. to reach the **tourist office** at 1/1D Gazi Osman Paşa Bul., 30m northwest of the İzmir Hilton Hotel. (Tel. (232) 445 73 90; fax 489 92 78. Open daily in summer 8:30am-6:30pm, in winter 8:30am-5:30pm.) From there, continue down Gazi Osman Paşa Bul. and turn left on Gazi Bul. to reach 9 Eylül Meydanı. **Hotel Oba,** 1369 Sok. #27, four blocks down 1369 Sok from 9 Eylül Meydanı, is a rare find. (Tel. (232) 441 96 05; fax 483 81 98. Singles US$12; doubles US$16. Breakfast included.) **Güzel İzmir Hotel** is at 1368 Sok. #8, also near 9 Eylül Meydanı. (Tel. (232) 483 50 69. Singles US$7.50; doubles US$15; triples US$21.)

ÇEŞME

A breezy seaside village an hour west of İzmir, Çeşme has deservedly gained popularity for its cool climate, warm, crystal-clear waters, and proximity to the Greek island of Hios. With a long ribbon of clean, powder-white sand flanked by rolling rush-covered dunes, **Altınkum Beach** is one of Turkey's finest. *Dolmuş* run to Altınkum from the lot on Çarşı Cad., by the tourist office (20min., May-Oct. every

30min., US$0.75). The most impressive site in Çeşme proper is the **castle.** (Open Tu-Su 8:30am-noon and 1-5:30pm. US$1.25, students US$0.75.) **Buses** (tel. (232) 716 80 79) run from the *otogar*, just off Çarşı Cad, to İzmir (every 30min., US$2.50); Ankara (10hr., 2 per day, US$15); and İstanbul (10hr., 3 per day, US$17.50). Buy **ferry** tickets from **Ertürk Tourism and Travel Agency**, 5/8 Beyazıt Cad., next to the *kervansaray*. (Tel. (232) 712 67 68. Open daily in summer 8am-9:30pm; in winter 8am-6:30pm.) From the main gate of the *otogar*, follow Çarşı Cad. along the left side of the parking lot (marked by the Kamil Koç and Ulusoy booths) about 200m, turn right at the sea, and walk 300m to the main square in front of the castle. The **tourist office**, 8 İskele Meydanı, is across from the castle and *kervansaray*. (Tel./fax (232) 712 66 53. Open in summer M-F 8:30am-7pm, Sa-Su 8:30am-5pm; in winter M-F 8:30am-5:30pm.) **Tarhan Pension,** 9 Çarşı Sok., Musalla Mah., near the *kervansaray* (turn left after the "No Problem" café), is clean and cozy. (Tel. (223) 712 65 99. Singles US$7.50; doubles US$15; triples US$22.50. Kitchen. Laundry.) On the corner past the *kervansaray* and *hamam*, you'll find **Alim Pension,** Tarihi Türk Hamamı Yanı. (Tel. (232) 712 78 28; fax 712 83 19. Singles US$5; doubles US$10; triples US$15; quads US$20.) **Postal code:** 35930.

KUŞADASI

Kuşadası's picturesque setting on sea-sloping hills, its excellent sand beaches, and its proximity to archaeological wonders have ensured the town's place as a grand resort. While Kuşadası is swamped with tourists of all kinds, it has managed to retain its charm. The carpets and jewelry for sale at the **Grand Bazaar** and **Barbaros Hayrettin Paşa Bul.** are, contrary to the claims of shop owners, expensive, but they're free to browse (unfulfilled desires are healthy, anyway). Crowded but clean **beaches** are just a *dolmuş* ride away. **Dilek National Park,** a nature reserve 26km away, is fantastic for swimming, walking, and picnicking. (Open daily in high-season 8am-8pm; off-season 8am-5pm. US$5 per car, US$1.20 per person.) No trip to Kuşadası would be complete without seeing **Güvercinada** (Pigeon Island), the peninsula covered with everybody's favorite bird.

Buses leave from Kahramanlar Sok., about 2km from the town center. Pamukkale buses (tel. (256) 612 09 38) go to İzmir (1½hr., every hr., US$3); Bodrum (2½hr., 4 per day, US$6); Pamukkale (3½hr., 1 per day, US$7); Marmaris (4hr., 1 per day, US$9.50); Fethiye (5½hr., 1 per day, US$12); Ankara (9hr., 4 per day, US$15); and İstanbul (9hr., 6 per day, US$18). City **dolmuş** run from the lot next to the bus station to Selçuk (20min., every 15min., US$1) via Ephesus (ask to be let off). The **tourist office**, 13 Liman Cad., is at Güvercin Ada Sok, in the port area. (Tel. (256) 614 11 03; fax 614 62 95. Open M-F 8am-noon, 1:30-5:30pm.) **Ekol Travel** with **WorldSpan,** Kıbrıs Cad., 9/1 Buyral Sok, sells ferry tickets; flash *Let's Go* for 15% off. (Tel. (256) 614 92 55; fax 614 26 44. Open daily May-Nov. 8:30am-10pm; Dec.-Apr. 8:30am-5:30pm.) The fabulous ■ **Hotel Sammy's Palace,** 14 Kıbrıs Cad., will pay for your cab fare from the bus station and transport to and from Ephesus. (Tel. (256) 612 25 88; mobile tel. (532) 274 21 29; fax (256) 612 99 91; email sammy@superonline.com. Roof US$3; dorms US$5; singles US$8; doubles US$12. Laundry. **Internet.**) **The Golden Bed Pansiyon**, off Arslanlar Cad., is somewhat hard to find; follow the signs. The *pansion* also offers free transport to and from the station and Ephesus. (Tel./fax (256) 614 87 08. US$6 per person. Breakfast included. Laundry.) Take a Selçuk *dolmuş* to **camp** at **Önder,** 2km north of town on Atatürk Bul. (Tel. (256) 614 24 13. US$2.40 per person, US$1.60 per tent, US$1.60 per car.) Take the *dolmuş* heading to Selçuk and ask to be left off at Çınaraltı for exceptional food at ■ **Çınaraltı Restaurant.** The nighttime madness of the well-named **Barlar Sokak** (Bars Street) literally spills out into the streets. **Postal code:** 09400.

SELÇUK

Selçuk is the most convenient base from which to explore nearby Ephesus, and also offers several notable archaeological sites of its own. The colossal **Basilica of Saint John** lies off Atatürk Cad. on the supposed site of St. John's grave, about 400m from Sabahattındede Cad. Head the other way down Sabahattındede Cad. to reach

TURKEY

the sad remains of the **Temple of Artemis,** one of the **seven wonders of the ancient world.** (Open 8:30am-5:30pm. Free.) The stunning 14th-century İsa Bey Camii is at the foot of the hill on which the Basilica of St. John and the Ayasoluk castle stand. The **Ephesus Museum** (Efes Müzesi), directly across from the tourist office, houses a world-class collection of recent finds from Ephesus. (Open daily 8:30am-noon and 1-5:30pm. US$2.50, students free.) **Buses** run from the *otogar,* at the corner of Sabahattındede Cad. and the road just east of Atatürk Cad., to İzmir (every 30min., US$2.50); Bodrum (3hr., every 30min., US$6); Marmaris (4hr., every hr., US$7.50); Fethiye (5½hr., every 2hr., US$11.25); Ankara (9hr., 1 per day, US$15); and İstanbul (every hr., US$17.50). **Minibuses** run to Kuşadası (30min., every 30min., US$1). Beware the infamous bus station hawkers. **Trains** go to İzmir (2½hr., 7 per day, US$0.75). The **tourist office,** 35-36 Agora Çarşısı, Atatürk Mah., is on the southwest corner of Sabahattındede and Atatürk Cad. (Tel. (232) 892 63 28. Open daily 8:30am-noon and 1-5:30pm.) The spotless **All Blacks Hotel and Pension,** offers free transport to Ephesus. (Tel. (232) 892 36 57; fax. 892 94 06; email abnomads@egenet.com.tr. Singles US$6; doubles US$12; triples US$18. **Internet.**) **Australian New Zealand Pension,** 7 Prof. Miltner sok., behind the museum, offers rides to Ephesus and the beach. (Dorms US$4; rooms US$4-8; with *Let's Go* 15% off. Laundry.)

⑫ EXCURSION FROM SELÇUK: EPHESUS (EFES). Ephesus boasts a concentration of Classical art and architecture surpassed only by Rome and Athens; the ruins rank first among Turkey's ancient sites in terms of sheer size and state of preservation. On the left just before the site's main entrance is the **Vedius Gymnasium,** built in AD 150; beyond the vegetation are the horseshoe-shaped remains of the city's **stadium.** After the main entrance gate, the tree-shaded road leads straight ahead to the colonnaded **Arcadiane,** Ephesus' main drag. Uphill along the **Street of Curetes** or **Marble Road,** you'll see the imposing ruins of the **Temple of Hadrian** on the left. A little further up the hill on the left are the ruins of the exquisite **Fountain of Trajan.** The building on the left as you walk up the ramp is the **Prytaneion,** dedicated to the worship of **Vesta,** which contained an eternal flame tended by the **Vestal Virgins.** The road that runs by the top entrance leads to the **House of the Virgin Mary** (8km, 1-1½hr. on foot), where, according to pious belief, Mary lived after leaving Jerusalem. (Tel. (232) 892 64 02. Site open 8am-6pm. US$5, students free.) The easiest way to get to Ephesus from **Kuşadası** or **Selçuk** is to take advantage of the free shuttle service offered by hotels. Or, from the Kuşadası *otogar,* take a **dolmuş** to Selçuk and ask the driver to stop at Ephesus (20min., US$1). From the Selçuk *otogar,* take any *dolmuş* toward Kuşadası (5min., frequent in summer, US$0.50). **Taxis** run from Selçuk to the site ($5). The site is also an easy **walk** from Selçuk.

PAMUKKALE

Pamukkale ("Cotton Castle"), formerly ancient Hierapolis (Holy City), has been drawing the weary and the curious to its thermal springs for more than 23 centuries. A favorite getaway spot for vacationing Romans almost two millennia ago, the warm **baths** at Pamukkale still bubble away. (Open 24hr. US$3, students free.) Don't leave town without a dip in the warm fizzy waters of the **sacred fountain** at the Pamukkale Motel. (Tel. (258) 272 20 24. Pool open daily 8am-8pm. US$4 per 2hr.) Behind the Pamukkale Motel, the enormous and well-preserved **Grand Theater** dominates the **ruins of Hierapolis.** The former city bath has been converted into a spectacular **Archaeological Museum** that reopened in fall 1999. (Open Tu-Su 8am-5pm. US$1.25, students US$0.75.) **Buses** to Pamukkale stop in the center of Pamukkale Köyü; some direct buses arrive from Selçuk or Kuşadası (4½hr., 5-6 per day, US$6), but the usual route is through Denizli, where buses arrive from İzmir (3½hr., 30 per day, US$5); Kuşadası (3½hr., 5am and 5pm, US$6); Marmaris (4hr., 9 per day, US$7); Bodrum (4hr., 5 per day, US$7); and İstanbul (12hr., 7 per day, US$16). *Dolmuş* go between Denizli and Pamukkale (25min., every 30min., US$1). The **tourist office** is at the top of the hill, within the site gates. (Tel. (258) 272 20 77; fax 272 28 82. Open in summer daily 8:30am-7pm; in winter M-F 8:30am-5pm.) The **⊠Koray Hotel,** 27 Fevzi Çakmak Cad., has the food in town. (Tel. (258) 272 23 00;

TURKEY

fax 272 20 95. Singles US$10; doubles US$16; cheaper in winter.) The brand-new **Venüs Hotel** is on Namık Kemal Cad. (Tel. (258) 272 21 52. Singles US$8; doubles US$13; triples US$15.) Both hotels have swimming pools with local thermal water and offer free pick-up from Denizli.

▶ EXCURSION FROM PAMUKKALE: APHRODISIAS. Still very much under excavation, the **ruins of Aphrodisias** have not yet benefited from reconstruction, but some archaeologists predict that they will eventually eclipse Ephesus in grandeur. The highlights of a visit to Aphrodisias are the soaring Ionic columns of the **Temple of Aphrodite,** an ancient 30,000-seat **stadium,** one of the best-preserved stadiums ever excavated, and a new and well-funded **museum,** near the site entrance, which features a breathtaking collection of sculpture. (In summer site open daily 8:30am-7:30pm, museum 8:30am-6pm; in winter both close 5pm. Joint ticket US$2.40, students free.) Make the ruins a daytrip from Pamukkale; **buses** leave daily at 10am and return at 5pm (2hr., round-trip US$6.50).

BODRUM

Bodrum's nightlife is notorious, its beaches divine, and its ruins impressive. Before it became the "Bedroom of the Mediterranean," the ancient city of **Halicarnassus** was known for **Herodotus,** the "father of history," and for the 4th-century BC funerary monument to King Mausolus that was so magnificent that its **mausoleum** was declared one of the **seven wonders of the ancient world.** Unfortunately, most of the remains were either destroyed, buried beneath the modern town of Bodrum, or shipped to London's British Museum. To reach the mausoleum, turn onto Kirkateyn Sok. from Neyzen Tevfik Cad. (Open in summer Tu-Su 8am-noon and 1-5:30pm; off-season closes 5pm. US$1.60, students US$1.) Bodrum's formidable **castle,** built during the 15th and 16th centuries over the ruins of an ancient acropolis by crusaders from the Knights of St. John, now houses the **Museum of Underwater Archaeology.** (Open Tu-Su 8am-noon and 1-5pm. US$3.80, students free.) **Ali Güven's shop,** Çarşı Mah., Kosophan Sok., off Cumhuriyet Cad., is near Ziraat Bankası; Ali's famous sandals may be out of your league (US$150-200), but you can watch him craft shoes for the likes of Bette Midler, Mick Jagger, and Donna Karan. The opulent ◼**Halikarnas Disco,** on Z. Müren Cad., at the end of Cumhuriyet Cad., is 1.5km from the center of town. (Cover US$16. Beer US$3.) The club **Hadi Gari,** Cumhuriyet Cad., next to the castle, is stylin'. (Beer US$2.40. Open midnight-4am.) Options abound on **Cumhuriyet Cad.;** start shaking that tush.

From the *otogar* on Cevat Şakir Cad., Pamukkale **buses** (tel. (252) 316 13 69) go to Kuşadası (2½hr., every hr., US$6); Marmaris (3hr., every hr., US$5); İzmir (4hr., every hr., US$7); Pamukkale (5hr., 3 per day, US$7); Fethiye (5hr., 4 per day, US$7); Bursa (10hr., 3 per day, US$13); Ankara (11hr., 2 per day, US$14.50); and İstanbul (12hr., 3 per day, US$19). **Dolmuş** go from the *otogar* to Marmaris (3hr., every hr., US$6). Bodrum Express Lines (tel. (252) 316 40 67; fax 313 00 77) has offices in the *otogar* and on the left, past the castle on the right toward the sea; for info on **ferries** to Greece, see p. 927. The **tourist office,** 48 Barış Meydanı, at the foot of the castle, has room listings. (Tel. (252) 316 10 91; fax 316 76 94. Open Apr.-Oct. daily 9am-8pm; Nov.-Mar. M-F 8am-noon and 1-5pm.) To get from the *otogar* to the peaceful **Emiko Pansiyon,** Atatürk Cad., 11 Uslu Sok., follow Cevat Şakir Cad. toward the castle, turn left on Atatürk Cad., turn right after after 50m down the alley plastered with signs (including one for Emiko Pansiyon), and turn right on the street after Taşlık Sok. (Tel./fax (252) 316 55 60. US$8-10 per person. Breakfast US$2. Kitchen. Laundry.) **Uslu Pension,** 35 Cumhuriyet Cad., has great views of the sea. (Tel. (252) 313 68 46. US$7 per person.) Turn onto Atatürk Cad. from Cevat Şakir Cad. and turn left into the second alleyway for ◼**Tarçin's** tasty homemade meals. (Meals US$2-9. Open M-F 8am-6pm.) **Postal code:** 48400.

▶ EXCURSIONS FROM BODRUM: BODRUM PENINSULA. Bodrum's popularity among Turks stems largely from its location at the head of the **Bodrum Peninsula,** where traditional villages mingle with coastal vistas and dramatic crags. Explore the peninsula's greener northern coast or its drier, sandier southern coastline. Tour **boats** bound for **beaches** on the peninsula's southern coast skirt the front of the castle (depart daily 9-11am, return 5-6pm; US$12 including lunch). Tour itineraries vary widely; check the tour schedule at the dock. Popular destinations include **Kara Ada** (Black Island), where clay from deep within a cave is reputed to restore youthful beauty (US$0.60), and **Deveplajı** (Camel Beach), where the beach's namesakes offer rides (US$4 per 10min.). The northern end of the peninsula, calmer than the southern coast, has rocky beaches and deep water. **Dolmuş** depart frequently from Bodrum's *otogar* for the quiet shores of **Gölköy** and **Türkbükü**, which draw Turkish tourists and their yachts (30min., US$1); the sand paradise of **Yahşi**, the longest beach in Bodrum (30min., every 15min., US$1); the clean sand and peaceful shore of **Bağla** (40min., every 30min., US $1); and the sunken ruins of ancient **Mindos**, near **Gümüşluk's** beach (40min., US$1.40).

MEDITERRANEAN COAST

Alternately chic, garish, and remote, Turkey's Mediterranean coast stretches along lush national parks, sun-soaked beaches, and pine forests. Natural beauty and ancient ruins have made the western Mediterranean one of the most touristed regions in Turkey. By day, travelers take tranquil boat trips, hike among waterfalls, and explore submerged ruins; by night, they exchange stories over Ephesus, dance under the stars, and fall asleep in seaside *pansiyons* and treehouses.

FERRIES TO GREECE

From **Marmaris, catamarans** (1hr., May-Oct. daily, Nov.-Apr. 2 per week, round-trip US$15-30); **hydrofoils** (1hr., May-Oct. 2 per day, US$15-25); and **ferries** (when there are enough cars) all go to **Rhodes.** Make reservations the day before at a **Marmaris** travel agency; try **Yeşil Marmaris** (tel. (252) 412 64 86), on the harbor.

MARMARİS

Marmaris contains all the beach town necessities: seaside restaurants, expensive yachts, a boisterous beachfront, and decadent nighttime festivities. The city's natural harbor hosted the naval campaigns of Süleyman the Magnificent; today, boats set off for spectacular nearby coves and the Greek island of Rhodes (ask at the Interyouth Hostel about excursions). To get from the tourist office to the 16th-century **castle,** take the street to the right, turn left into the bazaar, turn right down the alley after the Sultan Restaurant, and climb to the top of the stairs. (Open Tu-Su 8:30am-noon, 1-5:30pm. US$1, students US$0.60.) It's hard to tell which is hotter in Marmaris: the burning sun or the blazing nightlife. Head to bars behind the tourist office on **Bar St. Buses** (tel. (252) 412 30 37) go from Mustafa Münir Elgin Bul. to Bodrum (3¾hr., every hr., US$6); İzmir (4½hr., every hr., US$9); Pamukkale (4½hr, every hr., US$7); Kuşadası (5hr., daily mid-June to mid-Sept., US$9); Ankara (11hr., 4 per day, US$22); İstanbul (12½hr., US$23); and Göreme (14hr., 1 per day, US$16). From the bus station, out of town on Mustafa Münir Elgin Bul., take a *dolmuş* (US$0.40) or taxi (US$3) to the central Ulusal Egemenlik Bul., which hosts the Tansaş Shopping Center and the *dolmuş* hub. The **tourist office** is 250m along Kordon Cad. (Tel. (252) 412 72 77. Open in summer daily 9am-6pm; in winter M-F 8am-5:30pm.) The hospitable ■ **Interyouth Hostel,** Tepe Mah., 42 Sok. No. 45, is deep in the bazaar; follow the signs. (Tel. (252) 412 36 87; fax 412 78 23; email interyouth@turk.net. Dorms US$5; room US$13; with ISIC or HI card US$1 off. Breakfast and dinner included. Laundry. **Internet.**) **Postal code:** 48700.

DALYAN AND KAUNOS (CAUNOS)

The cobblestoned, placid village of Dalyan seems to have grown naturally out of the nearby breezy river. Dalyan's sites are best seen on a **boat tour** that visits the ruins of ancient **Kaunos** (tel. (252) 284 28 45; open in summer 8am-7pm; in winter 9am-5pm; US$1.60, students free); **İztuzu Beach,** where endangered loggerhead turtles lay their eggs by night (open 8am-8pm; beach chair rental US$4); and local **mud baths** and **thermal springs** (open 7am-7:30pm; US$1). **Boat tour** offices are behind the **turtle statue** in town (tours US$10 including lunch). The *dolmuş* from Ortaca stops in front of the PTT. Facing the PTT, turn left, follow the road right, and go straight. The open area with the turtle statue and mosque is directly ahead. City **buses** go to Ortaca (20min., every 15min., US$0.40), where buses in turn go to Fethiye (1¼hr., US$2.40) and Marmaris (1½hr., US$2.40). With your back to the turtle statue, head into the passageway across Maraş Sok to reach the **tourist office.** (Tel. (252) 284 42 35. Open daily in summer 8:30am-noon and 1-6pm; in winter 8:30am-noon and 1-5:30pm.) From the turtle statue, walk 75m down Maraş Sok., make the second left on 10 Sok., and walk one block to find **Kristal Pension.** (Tel. (252) 284 22 63; fax 284 27 43. Singles US$7; doubles US$14. Breakfast included.)

FETHIYE

Fethiye, on a harbor ringed by pine forests and mountains, is a peaceful base for exploring nearby sights. An easy trip away are the marvelous pebble **beach** and **Blue Lagoon** in **Ölüdeniz**—the idyllic peninsula of beach is cradled in wooded hills and lapped by shining clear water. Enter from Tabiat Park, on the right of the road from Fethiye. From the *dolmuş* station, it's a 20-minute walk or a US$4.80 taxi ride to the tip. (Park and lagoon open 6:30am-9pm. US$1.20, students US$0.60.) Take a **boat** from the beach in Ölüdeniz (45min., 3 per day, US$2) to reach the tiny, turquoise, indescribably beautiful bay of **Butterfly Valley,** home to waterfalls and the nocturnal orange-and-black Jersey Tiger butterfly. Rocky paths marked by blue dots wind their way up to two waterfalls (US$1, students US$0.50). To reach Ölüdeniz from Fethiye, take a **dolmuş** from the stop near the intersection of Hastane and Atatürk Cad. (20-25min., every 10min., US$1.20). In Fethiye, **Fetur,** 50m past the tourist office on Fevzi Çakmak Cad., arranges daily tours. (Tel. (252) 614 20 34; fax 614 38 45; www.fethiye-net.com. Open daily 9am-5:30pm.)

Buses run frequently to Fethiye's *otogar* on Ölüdeniz Cad. from Marmaris (2½hr., US$4.80). If there are no *servis* shuttles to the center, cross the street and take a *dolmuş* to the PTT in town (10min., US $0.40). From there, walk down Atatürk Cad. to the **tourist office,** 1/A İskele Meydanı. (Tel./fax (252) 614 15 27. Open daily 8:30am-7pm; in winter M-F 8am-5pm.) Call for free pickup from the *otogar* to get to the fantastic **Ferah Pansiyon 2,** Karagözler Ordu Cad. No. 21. (Tel./fax (252) 614 28 16; www.BackpackingEurope.com. Dorms US$3.60; US$10-12 per room. Laundry.)

KAŞ

Sandwiched between sea and mountains, cosmopolitan Kaş is refreshingly hassle-free, its pleasant streets lined with cheap, hospitable lodgings, excellent restaurants, and fun bars. A peninsula curving around one side of the town's harbor creates a calm, rock-lined lagoon ideal for swimming. The city also serves as a gateway to the backpacker heaven of Olimpos; to get there, take any Antalya-bound bus. The *otogar,* uphill on Atatürk Cad., sends buses to Fethiye (2hr., 6 per day, US$3.60); Antalya (3hr., every 30min., US$5.40); İzmir (8-9hr., 4 per day, US$14.50-16); Ankara (11hr., 2 per day, US$17-19); and İstanbul (14-15hr., 4 per day, US$24). The **tourist office,** 5 Cumhuriyet Meydanı, is to the left as you face the back of the Atatürk statue. (Tel. (242) 836 12 38; fax 836 16 95). Open daily in summer 8am-noon and 1-7pm; in winter M-F 8am-5pm.) Budget **pansiyons** line the sidestreets to the right of Atatürk Bul. (as you head from the *otogar* to the waterfront). **Hotel Nisa** is on Hastane Cad. (Tel. (242) 836 35 81. Doubles US$12. Breakfast US$2. Kitchen. Laundry.)

OLIMPOS

Enchanting Olimpos is a true backpacker's town. Ancient ruins choked with Amazon vines become more frequent as you move away from the cluster of pensions toward the sea. Crabs, frogs, multicolored birds, lizards, and butterflies dart among the sun-dappled ruins. Wander through to discover a preserved **mausoleum** and **mosaic house.** Walk along the main path at the surf, where the best-preserved group of ruins looms over the water on a rocky cliff to the right. (Ruins and beach US$2.80, students US$1.85. Hold on to your ticket stub.) The town's other main

TURKEY

attraction is ⬛ **Chimæra,** the perpetual flame springing from the mountainside 7km away. Mythology explains the flame as the breath of the Chimæra, a mythical beast; geologists suggest natural methane gas. **Bus tours** leave Olimpos at 9:30pm (2½hr., US$2.80); ask at any hostel for details. To get to Olimpos from Kaş, take an Antalya-bound **bus** or take an hourly bus (3hr., US$3.20). Buses stop at a rest station on the main road. From there, *dolmuş* run to the tree-house-*pansiyons* (15min., every hr., US$1.15), dropping passengers off at the place of their choice. As Olimpos is classified as an archaeological site, the use of concrete is banned, so resourceful Olimpians have constructed **treehouse pansiyons,** which line the dirt road to the beach and ruins. **Şaban Pansiyon** is relaxed and welcoming, with 21 treehouses. (Tel. (252) 892 12 65. Treehouses US$7 per person; doubles US$20; **camping** US$6. Breakfast and excellent dinner included.)

CENTRAL TURKEY

While the Aegean and Mediterranean coasts suffer from rampant tourism, Central Turkey hosts some of the country's most authentic and hospitable towns, from sophisticated Ankara to the surreal underground cities of Cappadocia.

ANKARA

Though less charming than İstanbul, Ankara is unquestionably the seat of the Turkish Republic. In 1923, after the Turkish War of Independence, Atatürk planned and built this modern city overnight, more or less from scratch. Today, Ankara is an administrative metropolis and the nation's premier college town. If you catch it on a sunny summer day or busy night, you might find Ankara livelier and more engaging than its reputation might suggest.

▉▛.⬛ **PRACTICAL INFO, ACCOMMODATIONS, AND FOOD. Trains** arrive from the *otogar,* 1.5km southwest of Ulus Square on the end of Cumhuriyet Bul., from İstanbul (6½-9½hr., 6 per day, US$6-33) and İzmir (15hr., 2 per day, US$7). To get to the center, follow the covered tunnel past the last platform into the "Maltepe" station of the east-west **Ankaray subway,** which stops in Kızılay and Ulus (5-ride pass US$2.50, students US$1.50). The Ankaray also connects to the **bus terminal** (AŞTİ or *otogar*), 5km west in Söğütözü, from which buses depart frequently for İstanbul (5½hr., 9 per day, US$20.50); İzmir (8hr., 3 per day, US$18.75); and Marmaris and Bodrum (10-12hr., each 1 per day, US$21.75). The English-speaking **tourist office,** 121 Gazi Mustafa Kemal Bul., is directly outside the "Maltepe" Ankaray station. (Tel. (312) 231 55 72. Open daily 9am-5pm.) **Embassies** in Ankara include: **Australia,** 83 Nenehatun Cad., Gaziomanpaşa (tel. (312) 446 11 80); **Bulgaria,** 124 Atatürk Bul. (tel. (312) 426 74 55); **Canada,** 75 Nenehatun Cad. (tel. (312) 436 12 75); **Greece,** 9-11 Ziaürrahman Cad., Gaziomanpaşa (tel. (312) 436 88 60); **New Zealand,** 13/4 İran Cad., Kavaklıdere (tel. (312) 467 90 56); **South Africa,** 27 Filistin Sok., Gaziomanpaşa (tel. (312) 446 40 56); **UK,** 46A Şehit Ersan Cad., Çankaya (tel. (312) 468 62 30); and **US,** 110 Atatürk Bul. (tel. (312) 468 61 10). Log on at the ⬛ **Internet Center Café,** 107 Atatürk Bul. (US$1.90-2.50 per hr. Open daily 9am-11pm.)

Of the two main accommodations centers, **Ulus** is cheaper, but **Kızılay** is safer and cleaner. Head south on Atatürk Bul., take the fourth left after the McDonald's on Meşrutiyet Cad., and take the third right on Selânik Cad. to reach the peaceful **Otel Ertan,** 70 Selânik Cad, in Kızılay. (Tel. (312) 418 40 84. Singles US$13.75; doubles US$20.) To get to the **M.E.B. Özel Çağdaş Erkek Öğrenci Yurdu,** 15 Neyzen Tevfik Sok., Maltepe, from the Demirtepe Ankaray stop, walk 100m along Gazi Mustafa Kemal Bul. with the mosque to your right, take the stairs down just past the mosque, and walk up on Neyzen Tevfik Sok.; it's on the left. (Tel. (321) 232 29 54. US$7.50. June-Aug. co-ed; rest of year male students only.) In Ulus, try **Hotel Kale,** Anafartalar Cad., 13 Alataş Sok. From the equestrian statue, follow Anafartalar Cad. toward the Citadel, bear right before it becomes Hisarparkı Cad., turn left onto Şan Sok., and it's 150m head. (Tel. (321) 311 33 93. Singles US$14; doubles US$24.)

Kızılay has lots of eats; try **Ulus' Gençlik Park,** or the more posh **Hisar** or **Kavaklıdere.** In Kızılay, **Göksu Restaurant,** 22A Bayındur Sok., has excellent and fairly cheap fare. (Open 11am-midnight.) In Ulus, the classy **Çiçek Lokantası,** 12/A Çankırı Cad. has up every kind of *izgara* (grilled food). (Open daily 7am-10pm.) A Gima **supermarket** is on Anafartalar Cad. in Ulus. **Postal code:** 06443.

SIGHTS AND ENTERTAINMENT. The fantastic **Museum of Anatolian Civilizations** (Anadolu Medeniyetleri Müzesi) lies at the foot of the citadel looming over the old town. The museum is in a restored 15th-century Ottoman *han* (inn) and *bedesten* (covered bazaar) and features a world-class collection of ancient artifacts. From the equestrian statue in Ulus, walk east to the top of Hisarparkı Cad., turn right at the bottom of the Citadel steps, and follow the Citadel boundaries. (Open Tu-Su 8:30am-5:15pm. US$3, students US$2.) Don't leave town without visiting **Atatürk's mausoleum, Anıt Kabir.** The structure, nearly 1km long, houses Atatürk's sarcophagus and many personal effects. Take the subway to "Tandoğan" and follow the signs; when you reach the unmarked entrance guarded by two soldiers, the entrance is just 10min. uphill. (Open M 1:30-5pm, Tu-Su 9am-5pm. Free.)

At night, dig the many flavors of live music in the bars of **Kızılay;** pub life centers on **İnkilâp Sok.** and the livelier **Bayındır Sok.,** two and three blocks to the left of Kızılay. **S.S.K. İşhane,** on the corner of Ziya Gökalp Cad. and Selânik Cad., is packed with live music bars, including **Gölge Bar,** the most popular rock bar in town. (Cover F-Sa after 9pm US$2.50; includes 1 beer. Open daily 1pm-4am.)

CAPPADOCIA

Nowhere else on earth looks quite like Cappadocia. The unique landscape began to take shape 10 million years ago, when volcanic lava and ash hardened into a layer of soft rock called **tufa.** Rain, wind, and flooding from the Kızılırmak River shaped the tufa into a striking landscape of cone-shaped monoliths called *peribaca* ("fairy chimneys"), grouped in cave-riddled valleys and along gorge ridges. Throughout Cappadocia, other-worldly moonscapes, stairs, windows, and sentry holes have been carved into the already eerily-eroded rock.

NEVŞEHIR

Although **Nevşehir** is not especially interesting, it is the region's transport hub. Even when tickets appear to be direct to Göreme or Ürgüp, what you are really getting is probably a *servis* shuttle to Nevşehir and then a regular bus onward from there. **Dolmuş** leave frequently from outside the tourist office for Göreme and Ürgüp (US$0.40-0.75). They stop at the *otogar* on their way out of town. The *otogar* runs buses to Ankara (4hr., 12 per day, US$7.50); Bursa (9hr., 1 per day, US$13.75); İstanbul (10hr., 5 per day, US$15); İzmir (12hr., 2 per day, $15); and Bodrum (14hr., 1 per day, US$18.75). From the main bus station, Lale Cad. runs uphill on your right towards center city. From Lale Cad., outside the Göreme and Nevşehir ticket agencies, turn left at the intersection and you will see the multilingual **tourist office,** 14 Yeni Kayseri Cad. (Tel. (384) 213 36 59. Open Apr.-Nov. M-F 8am-5:30pm, Sa-Su 9:30am-5pm; Nov.-Apr. M-F 8am-5pm.) If you find yourself needing to spend the night in Nevşehir, **Şems Otel** is on Atatürk Bul. (Tel. (384) 213 35 97; fax 213 08 34. US$10 per person. Breakfast included.)

GÖREME

An ideal base for exploring Cappadocia, Göreme brims with fairy chimneys, cavehouses, and friendly locals. The city bears a ubiquitous cave theme—most bars and discos are subterranean, and *pansiyons* often have "cave" rooms.

PRACTICAL INFO, ACCOMMODATIONS, AND FOOD. Buses go via Nevşehir to Ankara (4hr., 14 per day, US$7.50); Bursa (10hr., 3 per day, US$14); Pamukkale (10hr., 6 per day, US$14); İstanbul (11hr., 8 per day 6:30-8:30pm, US$15); İzmir (11hr., 3 per day, US$15); Olimpos (12hr., 7 per day, US$19);

TURKEY

Marmaris (14hr., 5 per day, US$20); and Bodrum (14hr., 6 per day, US$19). The **bus station**, in the center of town, contains the town's only official **tourist office**, which just has lodgings info. As you exit the station, the main road is directly in front of you. The city government has set **prices** for the town's **hostels:** dorms US$5; singles US$6, with shower US$8. However, starred **hotels** can charge higher rates, and the price for singles may rise in the next year. The friendly ▨ **Köse Pansiyon** is just past and behind the PTT, on the main road just past the turn-off for the Open-Air Museum. (Tel. (384) 271 22 94; fax 271 25 77. Breakfast US$1.25.) The view from the **Kookaburra Pansiyon** (tel. (384) 271 25 49), on the hill behind the bus terminal, is fantastic. The excellent **Paradise Pansiyon** is on the road to the Open-Air Museum. (Tel./fax (384) 271 22 48. Breakfast US$1.60. Laundry US$6.) **Kaya Camping,** 5-10min. uphill from the Museum, offers superb views. (Tel. (384) 343 31 00. US$3 per person, US$1.50 per tent.) Take the first right on the road to the mosque (as you approach from the bus station) and head left up a small hill to get to **Mehmet Paşa Bar and Restaurant,** which offers mouth-watering Turkish entrees (US$5) in a restored 1826 Ottoman mansion. (Open in summer 9am-midnight.) ▨ **Café Doci@,** to the left as you exit the *otogar* (bus station), has mammoth burgers (US$4), South Park on a big-screen TV, and **internet** (US$4 per hr., after 8pm US$2). **Postal code:** 50180.

▨ ⚠ **SIGHTS AND HIKING.** One of Cappadocia's biggest draws is its **Open-Air Museum,** 1km out of Göreme on the Ürgüp road, which contains seven Byzantine churches, a convent, and a kitchen/refectory. In the 4th century, St. Basil founded one of the first Christian monasteries here, setting down religious tenets that influenced the entire Western monastic movement. The churches are laden with frescoes; the most spectacular lie within the **Dark Church** (Karanlık Kilise). To get to the museum from the bus station in Göreme, walk 100m and take a right at the first major intersection. (Open mid-June to mid-Oct. 8am-6:30pm; mid-Oct. to mid-June 8am-5:30pm. Museum US$4, students US$2. Dark Church US$7.80, students US$4.)

When good Christians die, they go to heaven; when good **hikers** die, they go to Cappadocia. Mountain ranges with spectacular views, magical fairy chimneys, and eerie rock formations are all within striking distance of Göreme. Follow the road leading to the Open-Air Museum 1km past the museum itself, take a left on the dirt road by Kaya Camping, turn left again at the next paved road, and walk 3km to reach **Sunset Point** (US$0.60, students US$0.40). From there, you can descend into the **Rose Valley,** where bizarre, multi-colored rock formations make for one of the area's better hikes. After getting lost a few times, you'll eventually end up in Çavuşin, from which you can take the Avanos-Nevşehir **bus** or the Avanos-Zelve-Göreme-Ürgüp minibus back to Göreme (M-F every 30min. until 6pm, Sa-Su every hr.) or take a **taxi** instead (US$4). Follow the canal west of the bus terminal to reach **Pigeon Valley,** whose namesakes have been hunted almost to extinction. This hike is also somewhat confusing, but ultimately you'll end up in Uçhisar. If you're short on time, consider a full-day **guided tour** of the nearby terrain; competing tour companies peddle similar products (US$25, students US$23). Try **Zemi Tours** (tel. (384) 271 25 76), with an office on the road leading from the *otogar* to the museum.

▨ **EXCURSIONS FROM GÖREME: UNDERGROUND CITIES.** Cappadocia contains almost 200 **underground cities; Kaymaklı** and **Derinkuyu** are the two largest. The cities, all carved from tufa, were designed with mind-boggling ingenuity: low, narrow passages that were easily blocked off by massive boulders hindered prospective invaders, while sudden, concealed drops foiled would-be invaders who fell to their deaths. Beware the uncharted tunnels in both cities. Red arrows lead down, blue arrows up. (Both open daily in summer 8am-7pm; off-season 8am-5:30pm. Kaymaklı US$2.50, students US$2. Derinkuyu US$2.50, students US$1.50.) From Göreme, **dolmuş** run to Nevşehir (US$0.40) and then continue on to Kaymaklı (30min. total, US$0.50) and Derinkuyu (45min. total, US$0.75).

ÜRGÜP

While Coke and Pepsi furiously compete for dominance of the cola market, Göreme and Ürgüp vie for the Cappadocian tourist industry. Ürgüp is Pepsi—not as popular, but just as good. Emerging from a collage of bizarre rock formations and early Christian dwellings interspersed among sunny vineyards and old Greek mansions, Ürgüp is the choice of the next generation. The main square, marked by an Atatürk statue, is 20m down Güllüce Cad. from the *otogar*. Bring a special friend to the co-ed **Tarihi Şehir Hamamı,** in the main square; complete bath with massage, scrub, and sauna runs US$5 per person. (Open daily 7am-11pm.) Cappadocia is one of Turkey's major viticultural regions, with its center in Ürgüp. Uphill to the right behind the Atatürk statue is the renowned **Turasan Winery,** supplier of 60% of Cappadocia's wines, which offers free tours and tastings in its rock-carved wine cellar. (Open 8am-8pm; tours available until 5pm.) Several wine shops around the main square also offer free tastings. Come nightfall put on your dancing shoes and head to **Harem Disco,** at the foot of the road to the winery. (Open daily until 4am.)

Buses head to Ankara (5hr., 13 per day, US$7.50); Pamukkale (10hr., 1 per day, US$14); İstanbul (12hr., 5 per day, US$15); İzmir (12hr., 1 per day, US$15); Kuşadası (13hr., 1 per day, US$17.50); Selçuk (13hr., 1 per day, US$17.50); Bodrum (14hr., 1 per day, US$19); Fethiye (15hr., 1 per day, US$19); and Marmaris (15hr., 1 per day, US$19). English-speaking **Aydın Altan** of **Nevtur** (tel. (384) 341 43 02) loves to answer bus-related questions. The **tourist office** is in the garden on Kayseri Cad.; follow the signs from anywhere in the city. (Tel. (384) 341 40 59. Open daily Apr.-Oct. 8am-7pm; Nov.-Mar. 8am-5pm.) ▓ **Bahçe Hostel,** opposite the *hamam*, is the town's only backpacker hostel. (Tel (384) 341 33 14; fax 341 48 78. Dorms US$5; rooms US$5-6.) **Hotel Asia Minor** is behind the Atatürk statue. (Tel. (384) 341 46 45; fax 341 27 21. US$30 per person. Breakfast included.) **Postal code:** 50400.

UKRAINE (УКРАЇНА)

US$1 = 4.50HV (HRYVNY)	1HV = US$0.22
CDN$1 = 3.02HV	1HV = CDN$0.33
UK£1 = 7.23HV	1HV = UK£0.14
IR£1 = 6.00HV	1HV = IR£0.16
AUS$1 = 2.93HV	1HV = AUS$0.33
NZ$1 = 2.39HV	1HV = NZ$0.41
SARI = 0.74HV	1HV = SAR1.31
DM1 = 2.44HV	1HV = DM0.40

PHONE CODES   **Country code:** 380. **International dialing prefix:** (8)10.

Stuck between the stubbornly nostalgic heart of Russia and a bloc of nouveau-riche EU-aspirants, vast and fertile Ukraine stumbles along on its own path. Kiev, for centuries the cradle of Russian culture, now finds itself besieged by Western Ukraine with its Uniate congregations in lavish Polish cathedrals, its bold rhetoric of Ukrainian nationalism, and its traditional affinity for Europe; on the other side is lovely Crimea, whose predominantly Russian population longs for the Motherland. East-central Ukraine, meanwhile, is an industrial wasteland and home to the infamous, still-functioning Chernobyl nuclear power plant.

There is nothing quaint or pretty about an industrial nation that has turned into a giant cluster of subsistence farmers, but it is an absolutely unique travel experience. Decades off the beaten path, "tourism" in Ukraine is like nothing in the rest of modern Europe. Quality museums in the cities cost nothing and are empty, medieval castles in the west still loom dark and unsupervised, and the Black Sea Coast, even after years of Soviet tourism, retains an untouchable natural magnificence. There are treasures here, but you'll have to find them yourself. Ukraine, with enough troubles of its own, isn't inclined to play host.

For more detailed coverage of Ukraine, refer to *Let's Go: Eastern Europe 2000*.

DISCOVER UKRAINE

Getting a visa and invitation is worth the hassle: Ukraine has numerous impressive cities, miles of Black Sea beaches, and expanses of country and villages sprawling in between, all of it untouched by tourists and ridiculously cheap. Start any trip to Ukraine in **Kiev,** the country's capital. Once the seat of the Kievan Rus dynasty, modern Kiev exists in a time warp, as if its tree-lined streets and riverside vistas were still sheltered by the Iron Curtain. Don't forget to partake in the city's *kvas* ritual to give your visit an authentically Ukrainian feel (p. 942). **Lviv,** in Western Ukraine, really is an undiscovered jewel; you have only the Ukrainian visa authorities to thank. Often touted as an eastern Kraków, Lviv feels more Polish than Ukrainian with its cobblestoned streets, Catholic churches, and pastel-colored Old Town (p. 945). Real Ukrainian fun, however, is had in **Crimea,** the Russian-speaking, breath-taking peninsula jutting into the Black Sea. **Yalta,** its centerpiece, hosts hordes of New Russians, very warm waters, and the best spear-fishing in the Black Sea (p. 946). Farther west, **Odessa,** the former party town of the USSR, still hums, just at a lower frequency. When you emerge from the alcoholic fog of an Odessan night, be sure to visit the Catacombs, the best WWII museum in Europe ((p. 946).

GETTING THERE AND GETTING AROUND

BY PLANE. Air Ukraine International (US tel. (800) 876-0114; Kiev tel. (44) 216 70 40) flies to Kiev, Lviv, and Odessa from a number of European capitals, as well as from Chicago, New York, and Washington, DC. Air France, ČSA, Lufthansa, LOT, Malév, SAS, and Swissair also fly to Kiev.

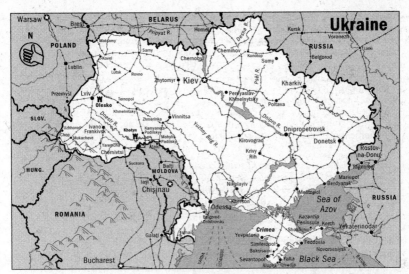

BY TRAIN. Trains are cheap, run frequently from all of Ukraine's neighbors, and are the most popular means of entering the country. When coming from a non-ex-Soviet country, expect a two-hour stop at the border. Domestically, they go everywhere and offer dirt-cheap comfort. For long-distance travel, try to buy tickets a few days in advance. If you're leaving from a town that's not the start of the train route, however, you can only obtain same-day tickets. You can also try to plead with the conductor, who will charge the cost of the ticket, pocket the money, and find you a seat. In larger towns, foreigners need to buy their tickets from a separate Intourist window, but in most towns you get to line up with the locals. On most trains within Ukraine there are two classes: *platzkart*, where you'll be crammed in with *babushki* and their baskets of fruit, and *coupé*, less crowded but still with disgusting bathrooms. When traveling between Lviv and Kiev, choose trains #92 and 91—both have special "Grand-Tour" cars (Гранд-Тур) that are even cozier (60hv).

BY BUS. In general, buses are a bit more expensive and a lot less comfortable, but are the best way to go short distances. In large cities, buy tickets at least the night before leaving at the regular ticket windows. In smaller cities, the *kasa* will start selling tickets only an hour before the bus departs. Sometimes, they'll direct you to buy the ticket from the driver.

BY FERRY. Ferries across the Black Sea are limited to a few routes from Odessa and Yalta to Istanbul. River transport is infrequent. Kiev hydrofoils go only as far as Chernihiv. The port agents know more than the Intourist offices about boats.

BY CAR, BY BIKE, AND BY THUMB. Road conditions are poor in Ukraine; one should not drive. Within cities, private **taxis** are indispensable. Both hitchhiking and cycling are uncommon in Ukraine; *Let's Go* does not recommend either as a safe mode of transportation.

ESSENTIALS

DOCUMENTS AND FORMALITIES. All foreign travelers arriving in Ukraine must have a **visa**, which requires an **invitation** from a citizen or official organization, or a tourist voucher from a travel agency. Regular single-entry visa at a Ukrainian embassy or consulate—with invitation in hand—takes up to nine days. Single entry visas cost US$30; double-entry US$80; multiple-entry US$120; these prices do not include the US$45 processing fee. Three-day rush service costs US$60 (double-entry US$120). If you need help getting an **invitation**, try Diane Sadovnikov, a former

UKRAINE

missionary living and working in Ukraine who arranges them (US$35; see p. 943). If you arrive at the Kiev airport without a visa, you can get a tourist voucher-*cum*-invitation, which will allow you to buy a visa and proceed through **customs.** Declare all valuables and foreign currency above US$1000 in order to settle your tab when leaving the country. Most foreigners must purchase a $3 per week health insurance policy for their stay in Ukraine, in addition to any other policies they already own.

Upon arrival, check into a hotel or register with the hall of nightmares that is the **Office of Visas and Registration** (OVIR; ОВИР), in Kiev, bul. Tarasa Shevchenka 34 (Тараса Шевченка), or at police stations in smaller cities, within your first three days in the country. Visas may also be extended here. **Do not lose the paper given to you when entering the country to supplement your visa;** it is required to leave. If you have a double-entry visa, you'll be given a re-entry slip (*vyezd;* въезд) upon arrival.

Ukrainian Embassies at Home: Australia (honorary consul), #3, Ground Floor, 902-912 Mt. Alexander Road, Essendon, Victoria 3040; **Canada,** 331 Metcalfe St, Ottawa, ON K2P 0J9 (tel. (613) 230-2961); **South Africa,** 398 Marais Brooklyn, Pretoria; P.O. Box 57291 Arcadia, 0007 (tel. (012) 46 19 46); **UK,** 60 Holand Park Rd, London W11 3SJ (tel. (020) 77 27 63 12; fax 77 92 17 08); **US,** 3350 M St NW, Washington, DC 20007 (tel. (202) 333-7507; fax 333-7510; ukremb.com).

Foreign Embassies in Ukraine: All foreign embassies are in **Kiev** (see p. 943).

TOURIST OFFICES. In theory, the breakup of the Soviet Union brought about the demise of the official state travel agency, **Intourist,** which was responsible for foreigners in Ukraine. In reality, they still have an office in almost every city, sometimes under another name, and offer hard-to-find train tickets. However, they're used to dealing with groups rather than individuals. Smaller tourist offices—if they exist—may be more helpful. Don't be surprised if they don't speak English.

MONEY. In September 1996, Ukraine wiped the extra zeros off most prices by replacing the **karbovanets** (Krb; a.k.a. kupon) with a new currency, the **hryvnia** (hv; plural hryvny; гривна); each hryvnia is worth 100,000 karbovantsi. Exchanging US dollars and Deutschmarks is fairly simple, since Ukrainians frequently use the two currencies themselves; *Obmin Valyut* (Обмін Валют) kiosks in the center of most cities offer the best rates. Other currencies pose difficulties. **Traveler's checks** can be changed into US dollars in many cities. **X-Change Point** (available in Kiev, Odessa, Yalta, Uzhhorod, Dnipropetrovsk, and Lviv) is a rare Renaissance thinker in the Dark Ages of Ukrainian finance—they have **Western Union** and can give Visa cash advances. Most banks give V/MC cash advances for a high commission. **Private money changers** lurk near legitimate kiosks; **do not** exchange money with them—it's illegal and they might slip you a wad of useless *karbovantsi.* There are **ATMs** in the larger cities. Although locals don't usually leave **tips,** most expats give 10% of the meal's price. Accommodations in Ukraine average US$10-12; meals run US$5-7.

COMMUNICATION

Post: Mail is cheap but slow—a minimum of 2-4 weeks from Kiev to any foreign destination). From other cities, it may never arrive, or even be picked up.

Telephones: Local calls from gray pay phones generally cost 10-30hv. The easiest way to make **international calls** is with **Utel** (Ukraine telephone). Buy a Utel **phone card** (sold at most Utel phone locations) and dial your international operator (counted as a local call). Utel phones can be found in expensive hotels, city telephone centers, and some fancy restaurants. If you don't have a calling card, order your international call at the central telephone office; estimate how long the call will take and prepay at the counter. Order intercity calls at the post office and pay up front; in some cities, pay phones marked "Міжміський" *(mizhmisky)* work with tokens, as do Utel phones. To: Moscow 0.60hv per min.; Ireland and UK 3.90hv; US 4.64hv; Australia, New Zealand, South Africa 5.76hv. Window 3 puts calls through to North America. When making an international call from a private phone, dial 8, wait for a tone, then dial 10, country code, city code, and number. **Fire,** tel. 01. **Police,** tel. 02. **Ambulance,** tel. 03. **International Direct Dial** numbers include: **AT&T,** (8) 100 11—wait for another tone after the 8; **BT Direct,** (8) 10 04 41; **Canada Direct,** (8) 100 17; **MCI,** (8) 100 13; **Sprint,** (8) 100 15.

UKRAINE

Language: Your trip will go more smoothly if you can throw around a few words of Ukrainian or Russian. In Crimea and most of east Ukraine, Russian is more common than Ukrainian; even in Kiev, most people speak Russian (although all official signs—such as those on the Metro—are in Ukrainian). In Western Ukraine, Ukrainian is preferred, and Polish is often understood. *Let's Go* uses Ukrainian names in Kiev and Western Ukraine, and Russian in the Crimea and Odeshchina. For basic Russian and Ukrainian, see p. 949.

HEALTH AND SAFETY. While Ukraine is neither violent nor politically volatile, it is poor and its people desperate. Keep your foreign profile low, watch your belongings, and don't make easy acquaintances. Travelers who have been harassed by the police say it's possible to get back on the law's good side with a US$20 bill. It's a wise idea to **register** with your embassy once you get to Ukraine. This makes the process of recovering a lost passport much quicker. **Women** traveling alone are likely to be harassed in one way or another. Ukrainian women never go to restaurants alone, so expect to feel conspicuous if you do. There is not much **racial diversity** in Ukraine today. Although non-Caucasians may experience discrimination at stores, restaurants, and hotels, the biggest problems come from the militia, which frequently stops people who they suspect to be non-Slavic.

Authorities recommend boiling water for 10min. before drinking it, and bottled water is even safer. It is extremely difficult, however, to find non-carbonated bottled water outside Kiev. Fruits and vegetables from open **markets** are generally safe, although storage conditions and pesticides make thorough washing imperative. Embassy officials declare that Chernobyl-related **radiation** poses minimal risk to short-term travelers, but the region should be given a wide berth.

ACCOMMODATIONS AND CAMPING. Not all hotels accept foreigners, and those that do often charge many times more than what a Ukrainian would pay. Hotels fall into two categories, **hotels** and **tourist bases**—called Турбаза (TOOR-bah-zah), usually part of a complex targeted at motoring tourists. Although room prices in Kiev are astronomical, singles run anywhere from 5-90hv in the rest of the country. More expensive hotels aren't necessarily nicer, and in some hotels, women lodging alone may be mistaken for prostitutes. Hotels may hold onto your passport during your stay, although you can get it back if you politely suggest you'd rather keep it with you. You will be given a *vizitka* (hotel card; візитка) to show to the hall monitor (*dezhurnaya*; дежурная; or *cherhova*; чергова) to get a key; surrender it when you leave the building. Hot water is a godsend when you find it; some places have no water at all for a few hours every day.

Private rooms can be arranged through overseas agencies or bargained for at the train station. Prices run 2-10hv per person, but conditions vary. During the summer, **university dorms** might put you up, depending on whether the *kommandant* likes you; come during business hours to see this powerful bureaucrat. A bed usually costs 2-10hv. Most cities have a **campground**, which is a remote hotel with trailers.

FOOD AND DRINK. Ukraine is not going to make your tummy happy. New, fancy restaurants are popping up to accommodate tourists and the few Ukrainians who can afford them. There are few choices between these and the *stolovaya*, dying bastions of cheap, hot food. The busier it is, the fresher the food. Most restaurateurs' reactions to **vegetarians** are hostile, and the meat-free menu rarely has more

UKRAINE

JUST FOR THE TASTE When the sun is high and the steppe is hotter than a Saharan parking lot, Aussies thirst for a *Fosters*, Czechs a *Pilsner*, and Yankees a *Bud*, but a true Ukrainian won't have anything other than a ladle of **kvas** (квас). In Kiev you'll see it served from siphons, in the provinces from rusty cisterns. The taste—kind of like beer without the hops—varies depending on the container, but it all comes down to acidic bread bubbles; the drink is based on a sourdough solution that rushes tingling into your bloodstream. It's so addictive that Kiev drinks *kvas* all summer, even in the rain, when groups of young tots, middle-aged shoppers, and love-struck teenagers huddle around toothless tap-masters, all under one leaky umbrella.

than mushrooms (*hribi*; гриби). When you ask for an entree without meat (*bez myaso*), make sure they don't just bring you another kind of meat. Produce is sold by the kilogram at **markets** (usually open 7am-5pm). Pay the cashier first for the item you want, then trade your receipt for the products at the counter.

LOCAL FACTS

Time: Ukraine is 2hr. ahead of Greenwich Mean Time (GMT).

Climate: Along the Black Sea, summers are hot and winters are mild. Inland Ukraine has a more continental climate, with bitter-cold winters and very warm summers.

Holidays: New Year's (Jan. 1); Orthodox Christmas (Jan. 7); International Women's Day (Mar. 8); Good Friday (Apr. 28); Orthodox Easter (Apr. 30); Labor Day (May 1-2); Victory Day (1945; May 9); Holy Trinity (June 18-19); Constitution Day (June 28); Independence Day (1991; Aug. 24).

Festivals: Every March, Kiev hosts international drama troupes for a two-week multilingual **theater festival.** The wildest party in Eastern Europe is in Kazantip, near Yalta (Aug.), when the entire town morphs into a **radioactive rave.**

KIEV (КИЇВ)

Once the USSR's third-largest city, Kiev doesn't seem to have quite figured out how to become a thriving capital(ist) metropolis. It should share in other newly liberated Eastern European cities' vibrancy and vivacity, but has yet to radiate progress: locals still prefer to store their money in dollars under their pillows, hesitant foreign investment and stagnant political reform are daily headlines, and visiting Americans are more likely to be shopping for wives than for tourist kitsch. However, this lull provides an untouristed environment in which to enjoy Kiev's rich (albeit crumbling) melange of medieval cathedrals and 17th-century façades.

▄ GETTING THERE AND GETTING AROUND

Flights: The international **Kiev-Borospil Airport** (Київ-Бороспіль; tel. 296 75 29) is 30min. southeast of the city. The city **bus** or a *marshrutne taksi* (маршрутне таксі) runs to MR: Livoberezhna (Лівобережна) every 2hr. Buy tickets (2.50hv) on the bus.

Trains: Kiev-Passazhyrsky (Київ-Пассажирський), Vokzalna pl. (tel. 005). MR: Vokzalna. In the main ticketing room on the 1st fl., arrivals are listed on the right, departures on the left. **Tickets** can be purchased at **Intourist,** 2nd fl. Open daily 8am-1pm, 2-7pm, and 8pm-7am. **Passports** are required to buy international tickets. If Intourist or the *kasa* claims not to have tickets, try again 6hr. and 2hr. before departure. Scalpers add 4-6hv to the price, but may have unavailable tickets. To: **Odessa** (11hr., 5 per day, 22-34hv); **Lviv** (12hr., 5 per day, 14-hv); **Minsk** (12-13hr., 1 per day, 10-47hv); **Warsaw** (15hr., 1 per day, 82hv); **Moscow** (15-17hr., 15 per day, 43-63hv); and **Simferopol** (18hr., 4 per day, 21-47hv). **Luggage storage** 2hv.

Buses: Tsentralny Avtovokzal (Центральний Автовокзал), Moskovska pl. 3 (Московська; tel. 265 04 30), is 10min. past Libidska, the last stop on the MG line. Go right and then left out of the Metro; hop on bus 4 or walk 6o the big highway and follow it to the right. To: **Minsk** (2 per day, 21hv) and **Moscow** (2 per day, 42hv). **Pivdenna** (Південна), pr. Akademyka Hlushkova 3 (Академика Глушкова; tel. 263 40 04), runs to **Odessa. Podil** (Поділ), vul. Nyzhny Val 15a (Нижній Вал), sends buses to the **Crimea.**

Public Transportation: The three intersecting lines of the **Metropoliten** are efficient but limited: blue (MB), green (MG), and red (MR). Buy tokens good on all public transport at the "Каса" *(Kasa)* for 0.30hv. "Перехід" *(perekhid)* indicates a walkway to another station, "вихід у місто" *(vykhid u misto)* an exit onto the street, "вхід" *(vkhid)* an entrance to the Metro. Buy tickets for Kiev's extensive **trams, trolleys,** and **buses** at numbered kiosks (0.30hv) or from a conductor and punch them on board to avoid a 6hv fine (or jail!).

▨ ORIENTATION AND PRACTICAL INFORMATION

Almost all attractions and services lie in western Kiev, on the right bank of the Dnipro. Two Metro stops away from the train station, the busy boulevard **Khreshchatik**

UKRAINE

(Хрещатик) satisfies most tourist needs, except housing. The center of Kiev is vul. Khreshchatik's fountained **Maydan Nezalezhnosti** (Майдан Незалежності).

Tourist Office: Kiev still lacks decent tourist offices. **Ukraine Hotel**, Tarassa Shevchaka blvd. 5, is your best bet for guidance. MB: Ploshcha Iva Tolstovo.

Embassies: Belarus, vul. Yanvarskogo Vossttanaya 6 (Январского Восстанія; tel. 290 02 01). Open M-F 10am-5pm. **Canada,** vul. Yaroslaviv Val 31 (Ярославів Вал; tel. 464 11 44). Open M-Tu and Th-F 8:30am-noon. **Latvia,** vul. Desyatynna, 4/6 (Десятинна; tel. 229 23 60). Open M-F 10am-5pm. **Russia,** pr. Kutuzova 8 (Кутузова; tel. 294 79 36). Open M-Th 9am-6pm, F 9am-5pm. **UK,** vul. Desyatynna 6 (tel. 462 00 11; fax 462 00 13). Open M-F 9am-5:30pm. **US,** vul. Yu. Kotsyubinskoho 10 (Ю. Коцюбинського; tel. 246 97 50; emergency tel. 216 38 05; fax 244 73 50; consular services fax 216 33 93). Open M-F 8:45-11:45am.

Currency Exchange: Look for "Обмін-Валют" (Obmin-Valyut) signs in windows; they have good rates but take only US$ or DM. For traveler's checks or cash advances, try a bank.

Medical Assistance: Check with the **US Embassy** (see above) for a list of safe hospitals. **Emergency Care Center,** vul. Mechnikova 1 (tel. 227 92 30).

Internet Access: Cyber Café (Кібер Кафе), Proresnaya 21 (tel. 228 05 48). 12hv per hr. Open daily 10am to whenever the last integrated user leaves.

Telephones: Myzhmisky Perehovorny Punkt (Мижміський Переговорний Пункт), at the post office, or **Telefon-Telefaks** (Телефон-Телефакс), around the corner (entrance on Khreshchatyk). Both open 24hr. Dial AT&T or MCI operators from Utel phones. Calls within Kiev (0.50hv) require phone cards. Buy Utel **phone cards** (10hv, 20hv, and 40hv) at the post office or a hotel. For more info, see p. 940.

Post Office: vul. Khreshchatyk 22, next to Maydan Nezalezhnosti. *Poste Restante* at counters 29-30. Address mail to be held: Britney SPEARS, *Poste Restante*, **252 001** Київ-1, Почтамт до Воетребоваиия, UKRAINE. Open M-Sa 8am-8pm, Su 9am-7pm.

PHONE CODE	City code: 044. From outside Ukraine, dial int'l dialing prefix (see inside back cover) + 380 + 44 + local number.

ACCOMMODATIONS AND FOOD

Accommodations in Kiev suffer from an unfortunate combination of capitalist prices and socialist quality. **Diane Sadovnikov** (Ukraine tel./fax 516 24 33; US tel./fax (757) 463-6906; email ims-travel@imb.net), a former missionary living and working in Kiev, arranges private apartments (45-75hv per person) and homestays, and makes room reservations. **Hostinitsa Druzhba** (Дружба), bul. Druzhby Narodiv 5 (Дружби Народів). Go left, then right, to exit from MB: Libidska; go straight and turn left before the overpass onto the major road, and it'll be on the left. (Tel./fax 268 33 87. Singles 55hv; doubles 112-168hv; bed in a triple 58hv.) **Grazhdanski Aviatski Institut Student Hotel,** vul. Nyzhinska 29E (Ніжіньска), is the best deal around if you don't mind the trek. From behind MR: Vokzalna, ride six or seven stops on tram 1K or 7 to "Граматна" (Hramatna). Backtrack 1½ blocks, turn right on vul. Nyzhinska, cross at the first intersection with a trolley, and follow the path into the complex. Walk diagonally to block "Д"; after passing Д on the right, the entrance lies 100m down to your right (50min. total). (Tel. 484 90 59. Singles 36hv; doubles 44hv.)

For those on a tight budget, the best option is a trip to one of Kiev's *rynki* (markets): **Bessarabsky Rynok** (Бессарабский Ринок), vul. Khreshchatik and bul. Shevchenka (Шевченка), has the best meat and produce. (Open M 7am-5pm, Tu-Su 7am-7pm.) **Supermarket 7/24,** vul. Baseyna 1/2 (Басеіна; tel. 221 58 57), behind Bessarabsky Rynok, is open, well, 24/7. ▓**Café Panorama** (Кафе Панорама), down Andriyivsky uzviz from St. Andrew's Church, past the statue and up the wooden steps to the right, serves simple beef or chicken *shashlik* for 15hv. (Open daily in summer 11am-11pm.) **Pantagruel** (Пантагрюель), vul. Lysenko 1 (Лисенко), next to MG: Zoloty Vorota, serves mouth-watering, authentic Italian food. (Entrees 16-22hv. Live music F-Sa 8-10pm. Open Su-Th 11am-11pm, F-Sa 11am-2am.)

UKRAINE

📷 🎵 SIGHTS AND ENTERTAINMENT

VULITSYA KHRESHCHATYK AND ENVIRONS. The downtown area centers around **vul. Khreshchatyk** (Хрещатик), a broad commercial boulevard built after WWII. Its southern end is at bul. Tarasa Shevchenka, where **Lenin** towers. *(Northeast of M: Ploscha Lva Tolstoho.)* Heading north past **Druzhba Theater** leads you to **Independence Plaza** (Maidan Nezalezhnosti; formerly October Revolution Square), encircled by large fountains and teeming with book vendors, musicians, and disgruntled youth. *(Just off vul. Khreshchatyk; turn left when you reach MG: Maidan Nezalezhnosti.)* Continuing north on vul. Khreshchatyk will bring you to the northern end of the street at **Khreshchaty Park,** where a monument commemorates the brave soccer players from Kiev forced to play a "death match" against the army team of the invading Germans; although they overcame their weakened condition to win the game, they were thrown into a concentration camp and died in front of a firing squad.

VOLODYMYRSKA VULITSYA: ST. SOPHIA TO VOLODIMIRSKY CATHEDRAL. Many tourists come to Kiev primarily to see the golden domes, ornate façades, and Byzantine icons of the enormous **St. Sophia Monastery Complex.** Once the cultural center of mighty Kievan Rus, today it constitutes the focal point of the increasingly complex question of Ukrainian nationalism. *(Volodymyrska vul. 24. From Independence Plaza, just northwest of MG: Maidan Nezalezhnosti, head west up Sofiyska vul. Open F-Tu 10am-5:30pm, W 10am-4:30pm. 6hv; one-hour tour 10hv; architectural museum and exhibits each 2hv extra. Cameras 10hv.)* Heading south down Volodymyrska vul. (Володимирьска) will bring you to the **Golden Gate** (Zoloty Vorota; Золоти Ворота), which has marked the city entrance since 1037. *(MR, MG: Zoloty Vorota.)* Farther south, Volodymyrska runs into bul. Tarasa Shevchenka (бул. Тараса Шевченка); turning right will bring you to the multi-domed **Volodimyrsky Cathedral,** built to commemorate 900 years of Christianity in Kiev. *(MR: Universitet. Note that turning left/east on bul. Tarasa Shevchenka instead of right would lead you back to Lenin and the southern end of vul. Khreshchatyk.)* Heading in the other direction from St. Sophia, north instead of south, leads past pl. Khmelnytskoho, a gorgeous square presided over by a statue of **Bohdan Khmelnitsky,** who led the 17th-century uprising against Polish rule, to Miklailivska pl.

ANDRIVSKY UZVIZ AND THE PODIL DISTRICT. You can take the **funicular** up to the top of the cobblestoned **Andrivsky uzviz**—and then walk down the winding road to browse its cafés and galleries. *(Funicular departs from just south of MB: Poshtova. From St. Sophia, walk north on Volodymyrska vul, bear right on Mikhailivska pl., and turn left on vul. Mikhailivska. Runs daily every 5min. 6:30am-11pm. 0.30hv.)* Next to the vendors selling Ukrainian pipes and Soviet Army hats, some independent galleries show the new and boldest work by Ukrainian artists, but most just sell touristy paintings of **St. Andrew's Cathedral,** which looms over the street (closed for renovations). Andrivsky uzviz spills out into **Kontraktova pl.,** the center of **Podil,** Kiev's city center in the 11th and 12th centuries. Just east of the *ploscha,* the ▨**Chernobyl Museum,** Provulok Zhorevii 1, uses powerful imagery to convey the magnitude of the disaster; ask to see the video of the explosion. *(Open M-Sa 10am-6pm; closed last M of the month. Free.)*

KIEV-PECHERY MONASTERY (KIEVO-PECHERSKA LAVRA). Kiev's oldest and holiest religious site is the mysterious **Kiev-Pechery Monastery** (Kievo-Pecherska Lavra; Києво-Печерська Лавра), once the center of Orthodox Christianity. Its monks were mummified and entombed in the **caves**—the most interesting part of the complex. You're only allowed to look at the monks whose palms are facing up. Buy a candle (0.50-1hv) as you enter if you want to see anything. Also on the grounds of the monastery are numerous churches, gardens, and museums. Most noteworthy are the 18th-century **Great Cave Bell Tower** (Velyka lavrska dzvinytsya; Велика лаврська дзвіниця), which offers fantastic views of the river and Kiev; and the 12th-century **Holy Trinity Church** (Troitska Nadzramna Tserkva; Троїцка надзрамна церква), the monastery's entrance. *(From MR: Arsenalna, turn left as you exit, and walk 20min. down vul. Sichnevoho Povstanyiya. Monastery complex open daily 9:30am-7pm; in winter until 6pm. Ticket for all churches and exhibitions, but excluding museums, 8hv, students*

UKRAINE

4hv. Caves open W-M 9-11:30am and 1-4pm; women should cover their heads and shoulders, while men should wear pants. Bell tower open daily 9:30am-8pm. 2.5hv, students 1hv.)

NIGHTLIFE. Club Sofia, vul. Sofiivska 7 (Софïïвська), off Maydan Nezalezhnosti, is a smoky cellar jam-packed with young artists, intellectuals, foreigners, and Ukrainians. (Open daily noon-1am.) **Al Capone,** Kostyantyniuska 26, is the boss of late night boogying. Check Club Sofia for listings of new discos.

LVIV (ЛЬВİВ)

Dear Abby,

Divorced from Poland in 1945 after 600 years of ups and down, I just went through a breakup with the USSR, for whom I had cooked and slaved for over 45 years. In spite of my age, I feel ready to be conquered by the world. I just want to be loved, admired, and remembered. My steeple-filled city center teems with energy that can't be found anywhere else in Ukraine, and, if I do say so myself, I'm fun!

Worthy and waiting, Lviv

◪ █.█ PRACTICAL INFO, ACCOMMODATIONS, AND FOOD. Trains (tel. 748 20 68) go from pl. Vokzalna (Вокзальна) to Kraków (8hr., 2 per day, 8hv); Kiev (11-16hr., 8 per day, 25hv, *coupé* 40hv); Warsaw (13hr., 1 per day, 82hv); Odessa (14hr., 3 per day, 20hv, *coupé* 40hv); Budapest (14hr., 1 per day, 211hv); Bratislava (18hr., 1 per day, 265hv); Prague (21hr., 1 per day, 383hv); and Moscow (29hr., 3 per day, *coupé* 130hv). **Tickets** are available at Intourist windows 23-25. Tram 1 runs from the train station to the Old Town; tram 6 to the north end of pr. Svobody. The main **bus station,** on vul. Stryska (Стрийська; tel. 63 24 73), on the outskirts of town, send buses to Kraków (7-9hr., 1 per day, 57hv) and Warsaw (10hr., 4 per day, 57hv). From the station, bus 18 goes to the train station, from which trams go into town. **Lviv Inturyst,** in the Hotel George, plans guided **tours.** (Tel. (0322) 72 67 40; fax 97 12 87. Open M-F 9am-5pm.) To get to the beautiful ◪**Hotel George** (Готель Жорж), pl. Mitskevycha 1, take tram 1 from the train station to "Дорошенка" (Doroshenka). Walk another block, and head right at the park to the big pink building. (Tel. (0322) 72 59 52. Singles 73-302hv; doubles 83hv. Breakfast included.) Take tram 6 from the train station to Opera, then walk away from Opera and take a right onto Tsvova (Цвова) to find **Hotel Lviv,** ul. 700-richna Lvova 7, a few blocks north of pr. Svobody. (Tel. (0322) 79 22 70. Singles 30-54hv; doubles 30-84hv.) **Mediviya** (Медивия), vul. Krakivska 17, has food cooked by Ukrainians, for Ukrainians. (Tel. (0322) 72 91 41. Open daily 10am-10pm.) **Mini Market,** vul. Doroshenka 6 (Дорошенка), is a block from the Grand Hotel. (Open 24hr.) **Postal code:** 290 000.

◪ █ SIGHTS AND ENTERTAINMENT. Before you venture into the heart of the city, a great way to introduce yourself to Lviv is to climb up to **High Castle Hill** (Vysoky Zamok; Высокий Замок); follow vul. Krivonoca (Кривоноса) from its intersection with Hotny and Halytskono and go until you pass #39, then take a left down the long shaded dirt road to wind your way up around the hill counter-clockwise. Begin a tour of the city on Pr. Svobody, dominated by the dazzlingly complex exterior of the ◪**Theater of Opera and Ballet** (Teatr Opery ta Baletu; Театра Опери та Балету). You don't have to love opera, and you don't even need a tux; you just have to go and marvel at the great space, great voices, great sets. (Tel. (0322) 72 88 60. Shows from 5hv.) Also on pr. Svobody is the impressive **National Museum** (Natsionalny Muzey; Нацiональний Музей). (Open M-W 11am-5pm, Sa-Su noon-6pm. 1hv, students 0.50hv; students free M.) The heart of the city is **pl. Rynok,** the historic market square, around which clusters a collage of richly decorated merchant homes dating from the 16th to 18th centuries. Just beyond the gaze of trident-armed Neptune statue on the 19th-century **town hall,** is pl. Katedralna (Катедральна), where the grand Polish **Catholic Cathedral** (Katolitsky Sobor; Католицкий собор) stands.

Opera, experimental drama, cheap tickets, and an artistic population make Lviv's performance halls the city's second most frequented institution after cafés. Purchase tickets at each theater's *kasa* or at the *teatralny kasy* (ticket windows;

UKRAINE

театральни каси), pr. Svobody 37. (Open M-Sa 10am-1pm and 2:30-6pm.) After the arias, stop at a club-café; try **Club-Café Lyalka** (Клуб-Кафе Ляљка), vul. Halytskoho 1 (Галицького), below the Teatr Lyalok (Puppet Theater), where shabbily-dressed artfuls do shots while arguing with the sophisticated black-clad wine-sippers. (Jazz on W. Cover F-Sa 5hv. Open M-F 1-11pm, Sa-Su 11am to 1 or 2am.)

SIMFEROPOL (СІМФЕРОПОЛЬ)

God made the Crimea, and all Simferopol (sim-fer-ROH-pul) got was a lousy train station. **Trains** run from ul. Gagarina (Гагарина; tel. (0652) 005) to Odessa (14hr., 1 per day, 20hv); Kiev (15hr., 4 per day, 45hv); Moscow (28hr., 4 per day, 70hv); Lviv (32hr., 1 per day, 35hv); and Minsk (35hr., 3 per week, 70hv). **Buses** for Yalta leave from the train station (2hr., 2 per hr., 4.65hv), but most other buses leave from the bus station, accessible from the train station by trolleys 2 (more direct) and 6 via the city center. The best place to sleep is on the train out of town, but if you have a layover, you can stay at the central **Gostinitsa Ukraina** (Украина), ul. Rozy Lyuksemburg 7-9. (Tel. (0652) 51 01 65. Singles 41-92hv; doubles 60-110hv.)

YALTA (ЯЛТА)

The gaudy Yalta waterfront, with its hot dog vendors and computerized astrology stands, dashes any illusion that this is still the city of Chekhov, Rachmaninov, and Tolstoy. Enjoy Yalta for what it is: a lovely, historical city weathering the storm of capitalism the best it can. If **Anton Chekhov** is your deity of choice, Yalta is your Mecca, or at least Medina. The author lived here for the last five years of his tuberculosis, and you can practically retrace his every step from monuments and plaques. At ul. Kirova 112, you can explore the **house** he built, the **garden** he planted, and the **museum** about him. Take trolleybus 1 to Pionerskaya (Пионерская), cross the street, and walk up the hill. (Open Tu-Su 10am-5:15pm. 10hv, students 5hv.) Ask at the campground about **hikes** up to the **Uchan Su Waterfall. Buses** (tel. (0654) 34 20 92) leave from Moskovskaya ul. 57 for Simferopol (2hr., every 30min., 4.50hv); across the way is the **trolleybus station**, which sends more comfortable trolleys to the Simferopol train station (2½hr., 4.25hv). From either station, take trolleybus 1 uphill to Sovetskaya pl. (Советская), then get off and walk two blocks toward the sea. **Intourist**, ul. Drazhinskovo 50, is in Hotel Yalta. (Open daily 9am-5pm.) The prices at Yalta's beachside hotels have increased dramatically and may continue to do so. Book ahead. Bus station *babushki* often offer great deals on **private rooms** (from 20hv). **Hostinitsa Krym** (Крым), Moskovskaya ul. 1/6, is central. (Tel. (0654) 32 60 01; reservations tel. 32 78 73. Singles 33hv; doubles 45hv; triples 55hv; 1st night add 2.55hv. Shower 2.25hv.) To get to **Motel-Camping Polyana Skazok** (Поляна Сказак), ul. Kirova 167 (Кірова), take bus 11, 26, or 27 from the bus station to "Поляна Сказок," then go uphill (20min.). (Tel. (0654) 39 52 19. No tents. 2-person bungalow 30hv; motel doubles 50-65hv.) **Café Siren** (Сирень), ul. Roosevelta 4 (Рузвелта) has Russian grub. (Meals 5-6hv. Open daily 8am-9pm.)

EXCURSIONS FROM YALTA. Only an hour's **hike** or a 15-minute **boat** ride away from Yalta, **Livadia** hosted the imprecisely named **Yalta Conference,** when Churchill, Roosevelt, and Stalin met in February 1945 at Tsar Nicholas II's summer palace to hash out postwar territorial claims. The **Great Palace** (Veliky Dvorets; Великий Дворец) is worth the visit regardless of historical significance. (Open in summer daily 10am-6pm; in winter Th-Tu 10am-4pm. 8hv, students 6hv.) **Buses** 26 and 27 run to Livadia from **Yalta** (10min., every 30-40min., 0.85hv).

ODESSA (ОДЕССА)

With the help of luck, Catherine the Great's patronage, and its location on the sea, Odessa long ago became an important port with all the attendant prosperity and corruption. The party town of the former USSR still hums, just at a lower frequency. With a history of Jewish mobsters, Odessa has taken to post-Soviet crime like a swan to water, becoming one of the parent cities of the Russian mafia.

UKRAINE

▨ ▟.▛ PRACTICAL INFO, ACCOMMODATIONS, AND FOOD. Trains go from pl. Privokzalnaya (Привокзальная), at the south end of ul. Pushkinskaya, to Kiev (12hr., 2 per day, 46hv); Simferopol (13hr., 1 per day, 26hv); Lviv (16hr., 1 per day, 45hv); and Moscow (26hr., 3 per day, 121hv). Trams 2, 3, and 12 run along ul. Preobrazhenskaya to ul. Deribasovskaya. **Buses** go from ul. Dzerzhinskovo 58 (Дзержинского) to Kiev (12hr., 4 per day, 35hv) and Simferopol (8hr., 2 per day, 26hv); take tram 5 from the train station or 15 from downtown. Both stop four blocks from the station. Buy tickets at the station at least the night before. **Morskoy Vokzal** (Морской Вокзал), ul. Suvorov 12 (Суворов) sends **ferries** unpredictably to Yalta (8-14 per year, 130hv) and Istanbul (1-2 days, 3 per week, US$75-90). **Eugenik Travel** in Morskoy Vokzal arranges tours and sells ferry tickets. (Open daily 9am-6pm.) **Private rooms** are cheap (US$5 per person), but you'll be lucky to get anything near the center. Take tram 3 or 12 from the train station to the downtown hotels, all near noisy ul. Grecheskaya and ul. Deribasovskaya. Charming **Pasazh** (Пасаж), ul. Preobrazhenskaya 34, is next to the real Pasazh. (Tel. (0482) 22 48 49. Singles 40-75hv; doubles 64-138hv.) Or sleep at **Spartak** (Спартак), ul. Deribasovskaya 25. (Tel. (0482) 26 89 23. Singles 45-86hv; doubles 60-90hv.) The **Privoz mega-market** (Привоз), Privoznaya ul., is near the train station. **Postal code:** 270 015.

▨ ♫ SIGHTS AND ENTERTAINMENT. Street culture centers on **ul. Deribasovskaya,** inhabited by jazz musicians, mimes, and young hipsters. Take a left on ul. Rishelevskaya from the end of the street to find the **Museum of the Black Sea Fleet** (Muzey morskovo flotu; Музей морского флота), ul. Lanzheronovskaya 6 (Ланжероновская), and its collection of ship models. (Open F-W 10am-3pm. 5hv. Russian tour 10hv.) Also a left off ul. Deribasovskaya onto ul. Yekaterinskaya, the statue of the **Duc de Richelieu,** the city's founder, stares down the **Potemkin Stairs** (Potomkinski skhody; Потемкинская Лестница) toward the shiny port, **Morskoy Vokzal.** Director Sergei Eisenstein used the stairs in his 1925 silent epic *Battleship Potemkin,* and the name stuck. At the top of the steps, shady **Primorsky bul.** offers prime people-watching space.Odessa's main rock source was directly underground, so construction led to the creation of the world's longest series of ▨**catacombs.** During the Nazi occupation, the resistance was based here, and the city has set up an excellent **museum** in their honor. Eugenik Travel (see above) organizes tours in English (3hr., 50hv.). The farther from the center you go, the cleaner the **beaches;** most are reachable either by public transport or walking. Trolley 5 goes to **Delfin** (Дельфин), on the edge of the park, and **Arkadiya** (Аркадия); tram 17 and 18 go to **Golden Shore** (Zolotoy Berig; Золотой Берег); **Lanzheron** (Ланжерон) and **Vidrada** (Видрада) are a pleasant walk from Odessa through Park Shevchenko.

The **Opera and Ballet Theater** (Teatr Opery i Baleta; Театр Оперы и Балета), at the end of ul. Rishelevskaya, has shows Sunday at noon, and evening performances (W-Su) at 6pm. Buy tickets in advance from the ticket office to the right of the theater. (Open M-F 10:30am-5pm, Sa-Su 10:30am-4pm. 15-25hv, US$3-35 when a major act comes to town.) Odessa, the party town of the former USSR, truly never sleeps. The restaurants, cafés, and bars on **ul. Deribasovskaya** hop all night with beer, vodka, and music ranging from Euro-techno to Slavic folk. ▨**Gambrinus** (Гамбринус), at #31, downstairs at the intersection with ul. Zhukova (Жукова). is a historical landmark. (Open daily 10am-11pm.)

UKRAINE

APPENDIX

GLOSSARY

addition (F): check
aérogare (F): air terminal
agora (Gr): a level city square; marketplace
albergue (S): youth hostel
Altstadt (G): old city
apse: nook beyond the altar of a church
arrondisement (F): district of city
auberge de jeunesse (F): youth hostel
autobus (G): bus
autoroute (F): motorway
ayuntamiento (S): city hall
Bahnhof (G): train station
billet (F): ticket
boulangerie (F): bakery
Brücke (G): bridge
caff (B): diner-style restaurant
calle (S): street
camping (F): campsite
campo (I): square
capote (F): condom
carnet (F): packet
carrer (S): street
casco antiguo (S): old city
casco viejo (S): old city
cave (F): wine cellar
çay (T): tea
centre commercial (F): shopping plaza
centre ville (F): town center
(el) centro (S): city center
cerveza (S): beer
chambres d'hôtes (F): bed and breakfasts
charcuterie (F): shop selling cooked meats
ciudad nueva (S): new city
ciudad vieja (S): old city
ciudad vella (S): old city
con bagno (I): (room) with private bath
confiserie (F): candy store
correspondence (F): connection
corso (I): principal street or avenue
dégustation (F): tasting (i.e., wine tasting)
dolmus (T): shared taxis
domatia (Gr): room in private home
droit(e) (F): right (i.e., right-hand side)
duomo (I): cathedral
entrée (F): appetizer
essence (F): gasoline
est (F): east
estación (S): station
fermo posta (I): *Poste Restante*
ferrovia (I): railways
formidable (F): terrific

foyer (F): student dorm
Fremdenverkehrsamt (G): tourist office
gabinetto (I): toilet, WC
gare (F): train station
gare routière (F): bus station
gauche (F): left (i.e., left-hand side)
gîte d'étape (F): hostel
grilli (Fi): fast-food stand
hamam (T): bathhouse
Hauptbahnhof (G): main train station
hebdomadaire (F): weekly
Hlavní nádraží (C): train station
hospedajes (S): cheap accommodation
hostal (S): hostel
hôtel de ville (F): town hall
iglesia (S): church
Innenstadt (G): city center
Jugendherberge: youth hostel
kaamos (Fi): polar night
kahuila (Fi): café
Kauppatori (Fi): Market Square
kesähotelli (Fi): summer hotels
Kirche (G): church
laverie (F): laundromat
leoforeo (Gr): bus
Mairie (F): mayor's office
marché (F): outdoor market
marché aux puce (F): flea market
Marktplatz (G): marketplace
Mehrbettzimmer (G): dorm
Mensa (G): university cafeteria
midi (F): noon
minuit (F): midnight
monnaie (F): change
museo (S): museum
nádraží (C): station
Neustadt (G): new city
nord (F): north
ouest (F): west
office de tourisme (F): tourist office
olut (Fi): beer
ostello (I): youth hostel
otogar (T): bus station
paella (S): rice dish with seafood, meat, and vegetables
panini (I): sandwiches
palazzo (I): palace
paleochora (Gr): old town
pansiyon (T): typical accommodation
parque (S): park
paseo (S): promenade (abbreviated *po.*)
passeig (S): promenade (abbreviated *pg.*)
pâtisserie (F): pastry shop

pensione (S): room in private home
pensao (P): cheap accommodation
plaça (S): square
place (F): square
plage (F): beach
plat (F): main course
plateia (Gr): town square
Platz (G): square
playa (S): beach
plaza (S): square
pleio (Gr): ferry
piazza (I): city square
piazzale (I): large open square
pintxos (S): appetizers; snacks
Platz (G): square
pont (F): bridge
préservatif (F): condom
primi (I): first course (usually pasta)
ravintola (Fi): restaurant
Privatzimmer (G): room in a private home
retkeilymaja (Fi): youth hostel
S-Bahn (G): short-distance commuter rail
secondi (I): second course (usually meat or fish)
souvlaki (Gr): shish kebab
spiaggia (I): beach
spotted dick (B): steamed sponge pudding with raisins
stazione (I): station
Straße (G): street
Straßenbahn (G): streetcar; tram
sud (F): south
syndicat d'initiative (F): tourist office
tabacs (F): all-purpose newsstand
Tageskarte (G): "day card"; pass valid for one day
tapas (S): appetizers; snacks
taverna (Gr): restaurant or tavern
télécarte (F): phone card
télépherique (F): cable car lift
torvet (D): main square
train à grande vitesse or TGV (F): super-fast train
turismo (S): tourist office
U-Bahn (G): subway; metro
via (I): street
viale (I): street
vicolo (I): alley, lane
vieille ville (F): old city
vino (S): wine
Zug (G): train

B=British, C=Czech, D=Danish, F=French, Fi=Finnish, G=German, Gr=Greek, I=Italian, P=Portugese, S=Spanish, T=Turkish

LANGUAGES

GERMAN

Consonants are the same as in English, except for *c* (pronounced *k*); *j* (pronounced *y*); *k* (pronounced, even before *n*); *p* (nearly always pronounced, even before *f*); *qu* (pronounced *kv*); *s* (pronounced *z* at the beginning of a word); *v* (pronounced *f*); *w* (pronounced *v*); *z* (pronounced *ts*). The ß, or *ess-tsett*, is a double *s*. Pronounce *sch* as *sh*. Vowels are pronounced as follows: *a* as in "father"; *e* as the a in "hay" or the indistinct vowel sound in "uh"; *i* as the ee in "cheese"; *o* as in "oh"; *u* as in "fondue"; *y* as the oo in "boot"; *au* as in "sauerkraut"; *eu* as the oi in "boil." With *ei* and *ie,* pronounce the last letter as a long English vowel—*heiße* is HIGH-ssuh; *viele* is FEEL-uh.

FRENCH

Don't pronounce any final consonants except *l, f,* or *c;* an *e* on the end of the word, however, means that you should pronounce the final consonant sound, e.g., *muet* is mew-AY but *muette* is mew-ET. Nor should you pronounce the final *s* in plural nouns. *J* is like the *s* in "pleasure." *C* sounds like a *k* before *a, o,* and *u;* like an *s* before *e* and *i*. A *ç* always sounds like an *s*. Vowels are short and precise: *a* as the o in "mom"; *e* as in "help" (é becomes the a in "hay"); *i* as the ee in "creep"; *o* as in "oh." *Ui* sounds like the word "whee." *U* is a short, clipped oo sound; hold your lips as if you were about to say "ooh," but say ee instead. *Ou* is a straight OO sound. With few exceptions, all syllables receive equal emphasis.

ITALIAN

There are seven vowel sounds in standard Italian: *a* as in "father," *i* as the ee in "cheese," *u* as the oo in "droop," *e* either as ay in "bay" or eh in "set," and *o* both as oh in "bone" and o as in "off." *H* is always silent, *r* always rolled. *C* and *g* are hard before a, o, or u, as in *cat* and *goose*, but they soften into ch and j sounds, respectively, when followed by i or e, as in *ciao* (chow; "goodbye") and *gelato* (jeh-LAH-toh; "ice cream"). *Ch* and *gh* are pronounced like k and g before i and e, as in *chianti* (ky-AHN-tee) and *spaghetti* (spah-GEHT-tee). Pronounce *gn* like the ni in onion, as in *bagno* (BAHN-yoh; "bath"). *Gli* is like the lli in million, so *sbagliato* ("wrong") is said "zbal-YAH-toh." When followed by a, o, or u, *sc* is pronounced as sk, as in *scusi* (SKOO-zee; "excuse me"); when followed by an e or i, sh as in *sciopero* (SHOH-pair-oh).

SPANISH

Spanish pronunciation is very regular. Vowels are always pronounced the same way: *a* as in "father"; *e* as in escapade; *i* as the ee in "eat"; *o* as in "oat"; *u* as in "boot"; *y*, by itself, as *ee*. Consonants are the same as in English except for: *j* and soft *g* (before "e" or "i"), pronounced like an *h*; *ll*, like the y in "yes"; *ñ*, as in "cognac"; *rr* (trilled "r"); *h* is always silent; *x* retains its English sound; *z* and soft *c* ("th"). The stress in Spanish words falls on the last syllable, unless the word ends in a vowel, "s," or "n," or has an accent.

THE GREEK ALPHABET

GREEK	ROMAN	GREEK	ROMAN	GREEK	ROMAN	GREEK	ROMAN
Α, α	A, a	Η, η	I, i; E,e	Ν, ν	N, n	Τ, τ	T, t
Β, β	V, v	Θ, θ	Th, th	Ξ, ξ	X, x	Υ, υ	Y, y; I, i
Γ, γ	G, g; Y, y	Ι, ι	I, i	Ο, ο	O, o	Φ, φ	F, f
Δ, δ	D, d	Κ, κ	K, k	Π, π	P, p	Χ, χ	Ch, ch; H, h
Ε, ε	E, e	Λ, λ	L, l	Ρ, ρ	R, r	Ψ, ψ	Ps, ps
Ζ, ζ	Z, z	Μ, μ	M, m	Σ, σ, ς	S, s	Ω, ω	O, o

THE CYRILLIC ALPHABET

CYR.	ENGLISH	CYR.	ENGLISH	CYR.	ENGLISH	CYR.	ENGLISH
А, а	a ("ah")	И, и	i ("ee")	Р, р	r	Ш, ш	sh
Б, б	b	Й, й	y	С, с	s	Щ, щ	shch
В, в	v	К, к	k	Т, т	t	Ъ, ъ	(hard—no sound)
Г, г	g	Л, л	l	У, у	u ("oo")	Ы, ы	y ("pit")
Д, д	d	М, м	m	Ф, ф	f	Ь, ь	(soft—no sound)
Е, е	ye or e	Н, н	n	Х, х	kh ("ch")	Э, э	eh
Ё, ё	yo ("aw")	О, о	o ("aw")	Ц, ц	ts	Ю, ю	yoo
Ж, ж	zh ("j")	П, п	p	Ч, ч	ch	Я, я	yah
З, з	z						

APPENDIX

ENGLISH	FRENCH	SPANISH	GERMAN	ITALIAN
THE BASICS				
hello	bonjour	hola	hallo	buongiorno / buona sera / buona notte
goodbye	au revoir	adios / hasta luego	Auf Wiedersehen (f.) Tschüß (inf.)	arrivederci (f.) ciao (inf.)
please	s'il vous plaît	por favor	bitte	per favore
thank you / you're welcome	merci / je vous en pris (f.) de rien (inf.)	gracias / de nada	danke / bitte	grazie / prego
yes / no	oui / non	sí / no	ja / nein	sì / no
excuse me / sorry	Excusez-moi / Je suis désolé.	perdón	Entschuldigung / Verzeihung	scusi / mi dispiace
How are you?	Comment ça va?	¿Como está?	Wie geht es Ihnen?/ Wie geht es Dir?	Come sta (f.)/stai (inf.)?
Fine / well.	Ça va.	Así así. / Bien.	Mir geht es gut.	Sto bene.
Do you speak English?	Parlez-vous anglais?	¿Habla inglés?	Sprechen Sie Englisch?	Parla inglese?
What's your name? My name is...	Comment vous appelez-vous? Je m'appelle...	¿Cómo se llama? Me llamo...	Wie heißen Sie? Ich heiße...	Come si chiama? Mi chiamo...
Sorry? / Please repeat	Pardon? / Répétez, s'il vous plaît.	¿Perdón?	Bitte / Können Sie das wiederholen?	Potrebbe ripetere?
I don't understand	Je ne comprends pas.	No entiendo.	Ich verstehe nicht.	Non capisco.
How do you say...?	Comment ça se dit...en français?	¿Cómo se dice...en español?	Wie sagt man...auf Deutsch?	Come si dice...?
How much...?	Ça coûte combien?	¿Cuánto cuesta...?	Wie viel kostet...?	Quanto costa...?
Help! / Stop!	Au secours! / Arrêtez!	¡Socorro! / ¡Déjame!	Hilfe! / Hör auf!	Aiuto! / Ferma!
DIRECTIONS				
Where is...?	Où est...?	¿Dónde está...?	Wo ist...?	Dov'è...?
straight ahead	toute droite	derecho	gerade aus	sempre diritto
(to the) right / left	(à) droite / gauche	(a la) derecha / izquierda	(nach) rechts / links	(a) destra /sinistra
near / far	loin / proche	cerca / lejos	nahe / weit	lontano / vicino
I'm lost.	Je me suis égaré (m.) / égarée (f.).	Estoy perdido (m.) / perdida (f.).	Ich habe mich verirrt.	Mi sono perso (m.)/ persa (f.)
town center/old city	vieille ville	el centro	Altstadt	il centro
post office	la poste	correos	Post	posta
the police	la police	la policia	die Polizei	la polizia
the hospital	l'hôpital	el hospital	Krankenhaus	l'ospedale
a doctor	un médecin	un doctór	Arzt	dottore
telephone	téléphone	teléfono	Telefon	telefono
bathroom	les toilettes/la salle de bain	el baño	Toilette	il bagno
TRANSPORTATION				
bus station	la gare routière	estación de autobús	Zentrale Omnibusbahnhof (ZOB)	stazione di autobus
train station	la gare	estación de tren	Bahnhof	stazione
arrival /departure	arrivée / départ	llegada / salida	Ankunft / Abfahrt	l'arrivo / la partenza
ticket / supplement	billet / supplément	billete / suplemento	Fahrkarte / Zuschlag	biglietto / supplemento
platform / track	voie	anden / vía	Bahnsteig / Gleis	binario
entrance / exit	entrée / sortie	entradas / salida	Eingang / Ausgang	l'ingresso / l'uscita
seat reservation	réservation de place	reserva	Sitzplatzreservierung	prenotazione posti
timetable	horaire	horario	Fahrplan	orario
berth / couchette	place couchée / couchette	cama / cabina de lit-eras	Bettplatz / Liegeplatz	letto / cuccetta
I would like a one-way (round-trip) ticket to...	Je voudrais un billet (aller-retour) pour...	Quisiera un billete ida (de ida y vuelta) a...	Ich möchte eine einfache Fahrkarte (Rückfahrkarte) nach...	Vorrei un biglietto solo andata (andata e ritorna) per...
first / second class	première / deuxième class	primera / segunda clase	erste / zweite Klasse	prima / seconda classe
left luggage	consigne	consigna	Schliessfächer (lockers)	deposito bagagli

ENGLISH	FRENCH	SPANISH	GERMAN	ITALIAN
What time does the train / bus / ferry leave?	A quelle heure le train / car / bac part?	¿Cuándo sale el tren / autobús / barca de pasaje?	Um wieviel Uhr fährt der Zug / der Autobus / die Fähre ab?	A che ora parte il treno / l'autobus / il traghetto?
Do you stop at...?	Vous arrêtez à...?	¿Para en/a...?	Halten Sie...?	Ferma a...?
bus stop (tram stop)	arrêt d'autobus (arrêt de tramway)	parada de autobus	Bushaltestelle (Straßenbahnhaltestelle)	fermata dell'autobus
car	voiture	coche	Auto/Wagen	macchina/automobile
taxi	taxi	taxi	Taxi	tassì

ACCOMMODATIONS

hotel	l'hôtel	el hotel	Hotel	albergo
hostel	auberge de jeunesse	hostal / albergue	Jugendherberge	ostello
guesthouse	(no equivalent)	pensión	Gasthof/Gästehaus	(no equivalent)
I'd like a single / double.	Je voudrais une chambre simple / pour deux.	Quisiera un cuarto simple / un doble.	Ich möchte ein Einzelzimmer / Doppelzimmer	Vorrei una càmera sìngola / doppia.
camping	camping	camping	Campingplatz	campèggio
I'd like to make a reservation.	Je voudrais faire une réservation.	Quisiera hacer una reserva.	Ich möchte eine Reservierung machen.	Vorrei fare una prenotazione.

TIME AND NUMBERS

yesterday	hier	ayer	gestern	ieri
today	aujourd'hui	hoy	heute	oggi
tomorrow	demain	mañana	morgen	domani
day after tomorrow	lendemain	(no equivalent)	übermorgen	dopodomani
morning	matin	mañana	Morgen	mattina
afternoon	après-midi	tarde	Nachmittag / Abend	pomeriggio
What time does it open / close?	A quelle heure ça ouvre / ferme?	¿A que hora abre / cierre?	Um wieviel Uhr öffnet / schließt es?	A che ora si apre / chiude...?
Monday, Tuesday, Wednesday, Thursday, Friday, Saturday, Sunday	lundi, mardi, mercredi, jeudi, vendredi, samedi, dimanche	lunes, martes, miércoles, jueves, viernes, sábado, domingo	Montag, Dienstag, Mittwoch, Donnerstag, Freitag, Samstag/ Sonnabend, Sonntag	lunedì, martedì, mercoledì, giovedì, venerdì, sabato, domenica
one	un	uno	eins	uno
two	deux	dos	zwei	due
three	trois	tres	drei	tre
four	quatre	cuatro	vier	quattro
five	cinq	cinco	fünf	cinque
six	six	seis	sechs	sei
seven	sept	siete	sieben	sette
eight	huit	ocho	acht	otto
nine	neuf	nueve	neun	nove
ten	dix	diez	zehn	dieci
eleven	onze	once	elf	undici
twelve	douze	doce	zwölf	dodici
twenty	vingt	veinte	zwanzig	venti
thirty	trente	treinta	dreißig	trenta
forty	quarante	cuarenta	vierzig	quaranta
fifty	cinquante	cinquenta	fünfzig	cinquanta
sixty	soixante	seseta	sechzig	sessanta
seventy	soixante-dix	setenta	siebzig	settanta
eighty	quatre-vingt	ochenta	achtzig	ottanta
ninety	quatre-vingt-dix	noventa	neunzig	novanta
one hundred	cent	cien	hundert	cento
one thousand	mille	mil	tausend	mille

ENGLISH	BULGARIAN	PRONOUNCED	CZECH	PRONOUNCED
hello	Добър ден	DOH-bur den	Dobrý den	DO-bree den
goodbye	Добиждане	doh-VIZH-dan-eh	Na shledanou	nah SLEH-dah-noh-oo
please	Извинете	eez-vi-NEH-teh	Prosím	PROH-seem
thank you	Благодаря	blahg-oh-dahr-YAH	Děkuji	DYEH-koo-yih
yes / no	Да / Не	dah / neh	Ano / ne	AH-no / neh
sorry / excuse me	съжалявам	sahz-ha-LYA-vahm	Promiňte	PROH-mihn-teh
Do you speak English?	Говорите ли Английски?	go-VO-rih-te li an-GLIS-keeh	Mluvíte anglicky?	MLOO-vit-eh ahng-GLIT-ski
I don't understand.	Не разбирам.	neh rahz-BIH-rahm	Nerozumím.	neh-rohz-oo-MEEM
Help!	Помощ!	PO-mosht	Pomoc!	poh-MOTS
Where is...?	Къде е?	kuh-DEH eh	Kde?	k-DEH
left / right / straight ahead	отляво / отдясно / направо	ot-LYAH-vo / ot-DYAHS-no / na-PRA-vo	vlevo / vpravo / rovně	LEH-vah / PRAH-vah
What time does [the train / bus / boat] (depart / arrive)?	В колко часа (заминава / пристига) [влакът / автобус / фериборт]?	V kol-ko cha-sah (za-mee-NAH-va / prih-STEE-ga) [VLA-kat / af-toe-BUS / feh-ree-bot]	Kdy (odjíždí / přijíž) [vlak / autobus / loď]?	k-DEE (ot-yeezh-dee / pree-yeezh) [vlahk / OUT-oh-boos / loadge]
today / tomorrow / yesterday	Днес / утре / вчера	dness / oo-treh / VCHEH-rah	dnes / zítra	dness / ZEE-tra
I'd like a (one-way / round-trip) ticket.	Искам един билет (отиване/отиване и връщане).	EES-kahm eh-DEEN bee-LEHT (oh-TEE-va-neh / oh-TEE va-neh ee VRIH-shta-neh)	Rád/Ráda bych (jen tam /zpáteční) jízdenku do...	rahd / rahd-ah bikh (yen tam / SPAH-tech-nyee) YEEZ-denkoo DOH...
How much is it?	Колко Струва?	KOHL-ko STROO-va	Kolik stojí?	KOH-lihk STOH-yee
hostel	общежитие	ob-shteh-zhit-yeh	mládežnická noclehárna	mla-dezh-nit-ska nots-le-har-na
hotel	хотел	hotel	hotel	ho-TELL
camping	лагеруване	lageruvane	kemping	KEM-ping
I'd like a (single / double) room.	Искам (самостоятелна / за двама) стая.	EES-kahm (sa-mo-sto-YA-tel-na / za DVA-ma) STA-ya	Máte volné (jed-nolůžkový / dvoulůžkový) pokoj.	MAH-te VOL-nee (YED-no-loosh-ko-vee / DVOH-loosh-ko-vee) PO-koy

ENGLISH	FINNISH	PRONOUNCED	GREEK	PRONOUNCED
hello	hei	hey	Γεια σας	YAH-sas
goodbye	näkemiin	NA-kay-meen	αντιο	an-DEE-oh
please	pyydän	BU-dan	Παρακαλω	pah-rah-kah-LO
thank you	kiitos	KEE-tohss	Ευχαριστω	ef-hah-ree-STO
yes / no	kyllä / ei	EW-la / AY	Ναι / Οχι	NEH / OH-hee
sorry / excuse me	anteeksi	ON-take-see	Συγνομη	seeg-NO-mee
Do you speak English?	Puhutteko englantia?	POO-hoot-teh-kaw ENG-lan-ti-ah?	Μιλας αγγλικα?	mee-LAHS ahn-glee-KAH?
I don't understand.	En ymmärrä.	ehn OOM-ma-ruh.	Δεν καταλαβαινω.	dhen kah-tah-lah-VEH-no.
Help!	Apua!	AH-poo-ah	βοηθεια!	vo-EETH-ee-ah!
Where is...?	Missä on...?	MEESS-ah OWN	Που ειναι...?	pou-EE-neh...?
left / right / straight ahead	vasen / oikea / suoraan	VAHSS-en / OY-kay-ah / SOOA-rahn	αριστερα / δεξια / ευθεια / ορτοδος	a-ree-stair-AH / dek-see-AH / or-tho-DOX-os
What time does [the train / bus / boat] (depart / arrive)?	Mihin aikaan [juna / bussi / laiva] (lähtee / saapuu)	ME-hin EYE-ka-ahn [yoo-na / BOOSE-ee / LIVE-a] (leh-tee/SAA-poo-oo)?	Τι ωρα (φευγει/φτα νει) [το τρενο / του λεωφορειου / το καραβι]?	tee OR-ah (feev-yee / ftah-nee) [toe TRAY-no / too lee-oh-for-EE-oo / toe kah-RAH-vee]
today / tomorrow / yesterday	tänään / huomenna / eilen	YEH-nehhn / HOOA-main-na/EYE-lane	σημερα/αυριο/χθες	SEE-mer-a / AV-ree-o / k-THES
I'd like a (one-way / round-trip) ticket.	Saisinko (menolipun / menopaluulipun).	SAY-sing-koah (MAY-no-LIP-poon / MAY-no-PAH-looo-LIP-poon)	Θα ηθελα (μονο / εισιτηριο / εισιτηριο με επιστροφη).	tha ETH-eh-la (mo-NO ee-see-TEE-ree-o /ee-see-TEE-ree-o me eh-pee-stro-FEE)
How much does it cost?	Paljonko tämä maksaa?	PA-lee-onk-o teh-meh MOCK-sah	ποσο κανει?	PO-so KAH-nee
hostel	retkeilymaja	rett-keh-eel-oo-my-ah	ξενωναζ νεοτητοζ	zee-NO-naz nee-OH-tee-toes
hotel	hotelli	ho-TELL-ee	ξενοδοχειο	zee-no-do-hee-oh
camping	leirintäalue	leiry-teh-rah-ah-loo-eh	καμπιγκ	KAHM-ping
I'd like a (single / double) room?	Haluaisin (yhden / kah-den) hengen huoneen.	HAH-loo-eye-seen (oo-den / kah-den) hen-gen hoo-oh-neen	Θελω ενα (μονο / διπλο) δωματιο	THEEL-oh EE-na (mon-OH / dee-PLO) doh-MA-tee-oh

DANISH	PRONOUNCED	DUTCH	PRONOUNCED	ESTONIAN	PRONOUNCED
goddag / hej	go-DAY / HI	hallo	hallo	tere	TEH-re
farvel / hejhej	fah-VEL / HI-hi	tot ziens	tote-zines	head aega	hed AEH-gah
vær så venlig	VAIR soh VEN-li	alstublieft	ALST-oo-bleeft	palun	PA-lun
tak	TACK	dank u wel	dahnk oo vel	tänan	TEH-nan
ja / nej	ya / nye	ja / nee	ya / nay	jaa / ei	yah / ay
undskyld	UN-scoold	excuseert u mij	ex-koo-ZEERT oo my	Vabandage	vah-pan-TAGE-euh
Taler du engelsk?	TAY'-luh dou ENG'-elsk	Spreekt u engels?	spreehkt oo ENG-elz	Kas te räägite inglise keelt?	Kas te RA-A-gite ING-lise keelt
Jeg forstår ikke.	yai for-STOR IG-guh	Ik begrijp u niet.	ik bih-GHRIPE oo neet	Ma ei saa aru.	ma ee sa AH-roo
Hjælp!	yelp	help!	help	Appi!	APP-pi
Hvor er?	voa' air	Var iz...?	var iz	Kus on...?	kuhs on
til venstre / til højre / lige ud	till VEN-struh / till HOY-ruh / lee oothe	links / rechts/ rechtdoor	links / hrechts / hrecht-doer	vasakul / paremal / otse edasi	VA-sa-cul / PA-ray-mal / AWT-seh AY-duh-see
Hvornår (går / ankommer) [toget / bussen / båden]?	vor-NOR (gore / AN-kom-ma) [TOE'-et / BOOSE-en / BOTHE-en]?	Hoe laat (vertrekt / arriveert) de [trein /bus / kom] ?	hoo laht (ver-TREKhT / ah-ree-VEERT) der [trine / boose / kom]	Mis kell (lähels / saabub) [rong / buss /paat]?	meese kell (LA-helss / SAH-boob) [hrong / bus /paht]?
i dag / i morgen / i går	ee-DAY / ee-MORN / ee-GORE	vandaag / morgen /gisteren	von-DAHG / MOR-khun / KHIST-urn	täna / eile / homme	TEN-ah / EYHL / OH-may
Jeg vil gerne ha en (enkelbillet / tur-retur billet) til ...	YAI vil' GAIR-nuh ha een (EHN-kul-bill-ETT / TOOR-re-TOOR bill-ETT) till...	Ik wil graag (een enkele reis / een retour).	ik vil khrahk ayn (ENG-ker-lur rays / ayn ruh-toor)	Palun, (üheotsa / edasi-tagasi) piletit	PA-loon (EW-heh-awt-sah / Eh-da-see-TA-ga-see) PEE-let-it
Hvad koster det?	va KOS'-tor dey	Wat kost dit?	vot kost dit	Kui palju?	kwee PAL-you
vandrerhjem	VAN-drar-yem	jeugdherberg	YOOKHT-hair-bairkh	ühiselamu	ew-hee-sel-a-moo
hotel	ho-TELL	hotel	ho-TELL	hotell	ho-TELL
campingplads	CAM-ping-plass	kamperen	KAM-per-en	laagriplats	LAH-gree-plats
Jeg ønsker et (enkeltværelse / dobbeltværelse).	YAI URN-ska it (EHN-kult-vair-ELL-sih / DOP-ult-vair-ELL-sih)	Ik wil graag een (een- / twee-) per-sonskamer.	ik vil khrahk ayn (AYN- / TVAY-) pair-sones-kah-mer	Ma sooviksin(ühe-list /kahelist).	ma SOO-vik-sin (EW-hel-ist / KA-hel-ist)

HUNGARIAN	PRONOUNCED	LATVIAN	PRONOUNCED	LITHUANIAN	PRONOUNCED
jó napot	YOH naw-pot	labdien	LAHB-dyen	Labądien	Lah-bah-DEE-yen
szia	SEE-ya	Uz redzēšanos	ooz red-zee-shun-wass	viso gero	VYEE-so GYEH-ro
kérem	KAY-rem	lūdzu	LOOD-zuh	Prašau	prah-SHAU
köszönöm	KUR-sur-num	paldies	PAHL-dee-yes	Ačiu	AH-chyoo
igen / nem	EE-gen / nem	jā / nē	yah / ney	Taip / Ne	TAY-p / neh
sajnálom	shoy-na-lawm	atvainojos	AHT-vine-wa-ywoss	Atsiprašau	ahts-yi-prah-SHAoo
Beszél angolul?	BES–el AWN-gohlul	Vai Jūs runājat angliski	vie yoose ROO-na-yaht AHN-glee-skee	Ar Jūs kalbate angliškai?	ahr yoose KAHL-bah-te AHNG-lish-kigh
Nem értem	NEM AYR-tem	Es nesaprotu	ehs NEH-sa-proh-too	Aš nesuprantu.	ahsh ne-soo-pran-too
Segítség!	SHEH-gheet-shayg	Palīdzājiet!	PAH-leedz-ayee-et	Gelbėkite!	GYEL-beh-kyi-te
Hol van...?	hole von	Kur ir...?	kuhr ihr	Kur yra...?	koor ee-RAH
bal / jobb / elöre	ball / yobe / eh-LEW-ray	kreisi/labi/pa taisno	kray-sih/lah-bih/ puh-TICE-nwah	į kairę/ dešinę/ važiuokite pirmyn	EE kigh-reh / EE deh-shi-neh / vazh-yo-kee-tay PEER-meen
Mikor (indul / érkesik) [vonat / busz-komp].	MEE-kawr (EEN-dool / AIR-keh-zik) [VO-nawt / boose / komp]	Kad (atiet / pienākt) [vilciens / autobuss / prā-mis].	cud (uh-tyat / pyah-nahkt) [VILLT-see-anss / OW-to-boose / prah-miss]	Kada (atvyksta / išvyksta) [traukinys / autobusas / lai-vas]?	ka-DAH (aht-vyook-sta / EESH-vooksta) [trav-KEEN-oose /OW-toe-bus / LIVE-us]
ma / holnap / teg-nap	ma / OLE-nap / teg-nap	šodien / rīt / vakar	SHWA-dee-ahn/ reet / VAH-kahr	šiandien / vakar/ rytoj	SHYEN-dien / VAA-car / ree-TOY
Szeretnék egy (jegyet csak oda / returjegyet).	SEH-rett-nake edge (YED-jet chok AW-daw / rih-toor-YED-jet).	Es vēlos (vienā virzienā / turp un atpakal) bileti.	ess VAIH-lywoss (VYA-na VIR-zeea-na / toorp oon AHT-pa-kal) bee-let-ee	Aš norėčiau bilieta į vieną /abi puses.	ahsh no-RYEH-chi-aoo vien-ah /ah-bee POO-sess
Mennyibe kerül?	menyeebeh keh rewl	Cik maksā?	sikh MAHK-sah	Kiek kainuoja?	KEE-yek KYE-new-oh-yah
szálló	SA-lo	jaunieđu viesnīca	yow-nya-duh vyess-nee-tsah	jaunimo viešbutis	YAWN-ee-mo VYESH-boo-teese
szálloda	SA-lo-da	viesnīca	vyess-nee-tsah	viešbutis	VYESH-boo-teese
kemping	KEM-ping	kempings	kem-ping	kemping	kem-ping
Szeretnék egy (egyágyas / kétágyas) szobát	SEH-rett-nake edge (EDGE-ah-dyosh / KAY-tah-dyosh) SAW-baat.	Es vēlos istabu (vienai / divām) personām.	ess VAIH-lywoss IH-stah-boo (VYA-nye / DIH-vahm) PAIR-swa-huhm	Aš norėčiau kam-bario (vienviečio / dviviečio).	ahsh no-RYEH-chi-aoo KAHM-bah-rio (vyen-VYEEA-chyo /dvyee-VYEEA-chyo)

ENGLISH	NORWEGIAN	PRONOUNCED	POLISH	PRONOUNCED
hello	hallo	hah-LOH	cześć	tcheshch
goodbye	morna	morn-ah	do widzenia	doh vee-DZHEN-ya
please	vær så god	VAIR-seh go	proszę	PROH-sheh
thank you	takk	TAHK	dziękuję	jeng-KOO-yeh
yes / no	Ja / Ikke or Ne	yah / IK-eh, nay	tak / nie	tak / nyeh
sorry / excuse me	unnskyld	OON-shool	Przepraszam	psheh-PRAH-sham
Do you speak English?	Snakker du engelsk?	SNA-kuh doo ENG-elsk	Czy Pan(i) mówi po anglicki?	tcheh PAHN (-ee) MOO-vee poh an-GLITS-kee
I don't understand.	Jeg forstår ikke.	yai four-STOR IK-eh	Nie rozumiem	nyeh roh-ZOO-myem
Help!	Hjelpe!	YELP-eh	Na pomoc!	nah POH-motz
Where is...?	Hvor er...?	VOR air...?	Gdzie jest...?	gdzheh yest
left / right / straight ahead	til venstre / til høyre / rett frem.	till VEN-struh / till HOY-ruh / reht frem	lewo / prawo / prosto	leh-vo / prah-vo / pross-toh
What time does [the train / bus / boat] (depart / arrive)?	Når (går / kommer) [toget / bussen / båten]?	nor (gore / COMB-air) TOE-geh / BOOSE-en / BOAT-en	O której godzinie (przy-chodzi / odchodzi) [pociąg / autobus]?	POHT-shawng / OW-toh-boos
today / tomorrow / yesterday	i dag / morgen / i går	ee DAHG / ee MORN / ee GORE	dzis / jutro / wczoraj	dzeess / yeeoo-tro / VCHORE-eye
I'd like a (one-way / round-trip) ticket.	Jeg vil gjerne ha (enkelt-billet / tur-retur)	YAI vill YAR-na ha (ENG-kult-bill-LET / TOOR rih-TOOR)	Poproszę bilet (w jedną stronę / tam i z pow-rotem)	poh-PROH-sheh BEE-leht (VYEHD-nawng STROH-neh / tahm ee spoh-VROH-tehm)
How much does it cost?	Hvor mye koster det?	VOR MEW-eh KOST-er deh?	Ile to kosztuje?	EE-leh toh kosh-TOO-yeh
hostel	vandrerhjem	VON-druh-yem	schronisko młodzieżowe	schrhon-isk-oh mwod-zyeh-zhoh-veh
hotel	hotell	ho-TELL	hotel	ho-tell
camping	camping	CAM-ping	kemping	kem-ping
I'd like a (single / double) room?	Jeg vil gjerne ha et (enkeltrom / dobbel-trom)	YAI vill YAIR-na ha ett (ENG-kult-room / DUB-elt-room)	Chicia(a) bym pokój (jednoosbowy / dwuo-sobowy)	KHTS-HAHW(a) bihm POH-kooy (yehd-noo-soh-BOH-vih /dvohoo-soh-BOH-vih)

ENGLISH	SERBO-CROATIAN	PRONOUNCED	SLOVAK	PRONOUNCED
hello	zdravo	ZDRAH-vo	dobrý deň	DOH-bree dyeny
goodbye	doviđenja	do-vee-JEHN-ya	do videnia	doh vidyen-nyiah
please	molim	MO-leem	prosím	PROH-seem
thank you	hvala vam	HVAH-la vahm	dakujem	dyak-uh-yem
yes / no	da / ne	da / neh	áno / nie	AA-no / nyieh
sorry / excuse me	oprostite	aw-PROSS-tee-tay	prepáčte	preh-padch-tyeh
Do you speak English?	Govorite li engleski?	GO-vor-i-teh lee eng-LEH-ski	Hovoríte po anglicky?	HO-voh-ree-tyeh poh ahn-glits-kih
I don't understand.	Ne razumijem.	neh ra-ZOO-mi-yem	Nerozumiem.	nyeh-ro-zuh-miehm
Help!	U pomoć!	OO pomoch	Pomoc!	po-mots
Where is...?	Gdje je?	g-DYEH YEH	Kde je?	gdyeh yeh
left / right / straight ahead	lijevo / desno / ravno	LYEH-vo / DESS-no / RAV-no	vlavo / vpravo / rovno	vlyah-vo / vprah-vo / rohv-no
What time does [the train / bus / boat] (depart / arrive)?	Kada [vlak/autobus/brod] (polazil/dolazil)?	KAH-da [vlok/ow-TOE-boose/brod] (poh-la-zil/doh-la-zil)	Kedy (odchádza / prichádza) [vlak / auto-bus/loč]?	keh-dee (wode-chahdz-ah / pree-chahdz-ah) [vlahk / ow-toe-bus / loatch]
today / tomorrow / yesterday	danas / sutra / jučer	DA-nass / SOO-tra/YOO-chay	dnes / zajtra / včera	dnyes / zye-tra / fcheh-rah
I'd like a (one-way / round-trip) ticket to...	Htio bih (u jednom smjerna / povratna karta) za...	HTEE-o beeh (oo YEH-dnom smee-YEH-roo / POV-rat-na KAR-ta) zah...	Prosím si... (jednos-merny / spiatočný) lís-tok.	PROH-seem sih (yed-no-smair-nee / spee-ya-tok-nee) lease-tok
What does it cost?	Koliko to košta?	KO-li-koh toh KOH-shta	Coto stojí?	KOH-to STOH-yee
hostel	omladinsko prenoćište	om-la-din-skoh preh-no-chish-teh	turistická ubytovňa mládeže	too-rist-ih-kah oo-bit-ov-nya mlah-deh-zhe
hotel	hotel	hotel	hotel	ho-tell
camping	camping	cam-ping	kemping	kem-ping
I'd like a (single / double) room?	Želio bih (jednokrevetnu / dvokrevetnu) sobu.	ZHEL-i-o bih (yed-no-KREH-vet-noo / dvoh-KREH-vet-noo) SO-bu	Potrebujem (jed-nolôžkovú izbu / izbu pre dve osoby)	po-tre-bu-yem (yed-no-loozh-ko-voo iz-buh) (iz-buh preh dveh oh-so-bih)

PORTUGUESE	PRONOUNCED	ROMANIAN	PRONOUNCED	RUSSIAN	PRONOUNCED
olá	oh-LAH	bună ziua	BOO-nuh zee-wah	добрый день	DOH-brih DYEN
adeus	ah-DAY-oosh	la revedere	la reh-veh-deh-reh	До свидания	dah svee-DA-nya
por favor	pur fah-VOR	Vă rog	vuh rohg	пожалуйсто	pa-ZHA-loo-sta
obrigado(-a) (m./f.)	oh-bree-GAH-doo/da	Mulţumesc	mool-tsoo-MESK	спасибо	spa-SEE-bah
sim / não	seeng / now	da / nu	dah / noo	да / нет	dah / nyet
desculpe	dish-KOOL-peh	Scuzaţi-mă	skoo-ZAH-tzee muh	извините	eez-vee-NEET-yeh
Fala inglês?	FAH-lah een-GLAYSH?	Vorbiţi englezeşte?	vor-BEETZ ehng-leh-ZESH-teh	Вы говорите по английски?	vih go-vo-REE-tyeh po ahn-GLEE-ske?
não compreendo	now kompreeAYNdoo	Nu înţeleg	noo ihn-TZEH-lehg	Я не понимаю	ya nee pa-nee-MA-yoo
Socorro!	so-ko-RO!	Ajutor!	AH-zhoot-or	Помогите!	pah-mah-ZHEE-tyeh
Onde é que é ...?	OHN-deh eh keh eh	Unde...?	OON-deh	Где...?	g-dye
esquerda / direita /em frente	ish-CARE-da / dee-RAY-ta / ayn FRAIN-teh	stânga / dreapta / drept înainte	stoong-gah / DRAY-ahp-ta / DREPT oon-EYE-een-tay	налево / направо / прямо	na-LYEV-ah / na-PRA-va / PRYA-moh
A que horas (parte / chega) o [combóio / camioneta / barco]?	ah keh AW-rahsh (PAR-teh / cheh-gah) oh kohn-BOY-oo / kam-yoo-NET-ah / bar-koh	La ce oră (pleacă / soseşte) [trenul / autobuzul / vaporul]?	la-CHAY orr-uh (PLAYUH-ker / so-SESH-teh) [tray-nool / OW-toe-booze-ool / va-poe-rool]	В котором часу [поезд / автобус / корабль] (приезжаем / уезжает)?	V kah-tor-um cha-soo [poy-yezd / af-toe-boose / kah-rah-bil] (pree-yeh-zhy-yet / oo-yeh-zhy-yet)
hoje / amanhã / ontem	OH-zheh / ah-ming-YAH / ohn-tane	astăzi / mâine / ieri	AHSS-teuh-zi/MUH-ee-neh / YAIR-ee	сегодня / завтра /вчера	see-VOD-nya / ZAHF-tra / fchee-RAH
Queria um bilhete (simples / de ida e volta)	kay-ree-ah um bee-YEH-teh (seem-plays / deh EE-da ee VOL-ta)	Aş dori un bilet (dus / dus întors)	AHSH doe-ree oon bee-LET (doose / doose uhn-torse)	Можно билет (в один конец / туда и обратно)	MWOZH-nuh beel-yet (v ah-DEEN kah-NYETS / too-DAH ee ah-BRAHT-na)
Quanto custa?	KWAHN-too KOOSH-tah?	Cât costă?	kiht KOH-stuh	Сколько стоит?	SKOHL-ka STOH-yet?
pousada de juventude	poh-ZA-da deh zhoo-vain-TOO-deh	pensiune	pen-SYOO-neh	общежитие	ahb-ZHAZH-eet-na
Hotel	ot-TEL	hotel / motel	hotel / motel	гостиница	gah-STEE-nyit-sa
campismo	cahm-peez-mo	camping	CAM-ping	жить в палатках	ZHEET v PA-lat-kach
Tem um quarto individual / duple?	tem om-KWAR-toe een-DE-vee-DU-ahl / DOO-play?	Aş dori o cameră cu (un loc / două locuri).	AHSH doe-ree oh cah-meh-ruh koo (oon lok / DOE-uh LOK-oor-ee).	Я бы хотел номер на (одного / двоих)	yah kah-TYEL bee NAW-meer na (AHD-na-vo / dvah-EEK)

SLOVENE	PRONOUNCED	SWEDISH	PRONOUNCED	TURKISH	PRONOUNCED
idravo	ee-drah-voh	Goddag / Hej då	go-DOG / HEY-daw	merhaba	MEHR-hah-bah
na svidenje	nah SVEE-den-yeh	adjö	a-DYEUH	İyi günler.	eee-YEE goon-lehr
prosim	PROH-seem	vär så snälla	VAIR so SNELL-uh	lütfen	LEWT-fen
hvala	HVAA-lah	tack	talk	teşekkur ederim	tesh-ekur edeh-rim
ja /ne	yah / neh	ja / nej	yah / ney	evet / hayır	EH-vet / HI-yuhr
oprostite	oh-proh-stee-teh	förlåt	fer-LOTT	affedersiniz	ahf-feh-DER-see-neez
Govorite anglesko?	go-vo-REE-te ang-LEH-shko	pratar du engelska?	PROH-ter doo ENG-ell-skuh?	İngilizçe biliyor musunuz?	EEN-gee-leez-jeh bee-lee-YOR-moo-su-nooz
Ne razumem	neh rah-ZOO-mehm	Jag förstår inte.	YAW fir-SHTOOR IN-tuh	Anlamadım.	ahn-luh-mah-dim
Na pomoč!	na poh-MOTCH!	Hjälp!	yelp!	İmdat!	EEEm-Daht!
Kje je...?	kyeh yeh...?	Var är... ?	varr air...	...nerede?	NEHR-eh-deh
na levi / na desni / naravnost	na leh-vee / na des-nee / nar-ow-nost	vänster / höger / rakt fram	VENN-ster / HEUR-ger / rakt FRAHM	sol / sağ / doğru	sohl / sa-a / doh-oo
Ob kateri uri [vlak / avtobus / ladja] (odpelje / pripelje)	op ka-teh-ree oo-ree [wlahk / AW-toe-bus / lad-ya](ot-PEL-yeh / prip-el-geh)	När (avgår / kommer) [tåget / bussen / båten]?	NAIR (AHV-gore / KOM-mar) [TOE-get / BOOSE-en / BO-ten]	[Otobüs / Tren / Vapur] ne zaman (kalkar / gelir)	[oh-toe-boose / tren / va-POOR] neh za-mahn (kal-kar / geh-leer)
danes / jutri / včeraj	DAH-ness / YOU-tree / WCHEH-ray	idag / imorgon / igår	ee-DOG / ee-MOR-on/ee-GOR	bügün / yarın / dün	boo-goon / yahr-un / doon
Rad bi (enosmerno / povratno) vozo-vnico.	rat bih za (EH-no-smer-no / po-VRUT-no) voh-ZOW-nih-tso	Jag vil gärna ha en (enkelbiljett / retur-biljett)	YAW vil-YAIR-nuh-ha en (EN-kul-bill-yet / re-TOOR-bill-yet)	(sırf gidiş / gidiş-dönüs) bir bilet istiyorum	(serf gi-DEESH / der-NYOOSH) beer be-LET i-STEE-yo-rum
Koliko to stane?	koh-lee-koh toh stah-neh	Hur mycket kostar det?	hoor-MOOK-eh KOST-ar day?	...ne kadar?	neh kah-dar?
mladinski dom	mla-dinsk-ih dom	vandrarhem	VON-dra-hem	gençlik yurdu	gench-LIK YOOR-du
hotel	hoh-tel	hotell	ho-TELL	otel	oh-tell
autokamp	ow-toe-kamp	campingplats	CAM-ping-plots	kamp yeri	camp yair-ee
Rad/Rada (m/f) bi (enoposteljno/dvo-posteljo) sobo	raht/RA-da bee (en-o-POST-el-nyo /dvoh -POST-el-nyo) so-bo.	Jag vil gärna ha ett (enkelrum / dub-belrum)?	YAW vil-YAIR-nuh-ha et (EHN-kel-room / DOO-bel-room)	(Tek/çift) kişilik bir oda istiyorum.	(Tehk/cheeft) keesh-eee-leek beer aw-dah ee-STEE-yo-rum.

TIMELINE

ANCIENT CIV.

2500-1300 BC: Minoan civilization in Crete

2500-500 BC: Early Greek civilization

500-100 BC: Classical and Hellenistic Greece

509 BC: beginning of Roman Republic

146 BC - AD 192: Imperial Rome

293: Diocletian splits Roman Empire between East and West

312-337: Constantine the Great reunites Roman Empire with new capital at Byzantine (later known as Constantinople). Christianity becomes the new Roman state religion.

360-450: Huns invade Russia and Europe; Visigoths, Vandals, and other "barbarians" attack HRE.

480: Death of last legitimate Roman Emperor, Julius Nepos; Theodoric and Ostrogoths invade Italy and effectively signal the fall of the empire.

EARLY MIDDLE AGES

527-565: Byzantine emperor Justinian the Great recaptures North Africa, southern Spain, and Italy. The Justinian Code, the most influential legal text in European history, revises Roman laws.

622-650: Islam spreads through Middle East, North Africa, and Asia Minor.

719: Arabs complete their conquest of Spain.

790: Vikings begin to attack the British Isles.

800: Charlemagne is crowned Holy Roman Emperor by the Pope. The Carolingian Empire, which stretches from the Adriatic to the Baltic, combines Orthodox Christianity, Roman administration, and Frankish military might.

843: Following the death of Charlemagne's son, Louis the Pious, the Carolingian Empire is divided amongst his three sons, disintegrating centralized power and leading to the rise of local lords.

867-1059: Macedonian dynasty rules Byzantine Empire and starts to recover lands from Muslims.

962: Otto I founds new Holy Roman Empire in Germany.

996: Hugh Capet takes the French throne; Capetian dynasty of France is founded.

HIGH MIDDLE AGES

1066: Harold of the Saxons is defeated at the Battle of Normandy by William I of Normandy

1095-99: Pope Urban II calls for the freeing of the Holy Land from Muslim occupation; Jerusalem recaptured by First Crusade.

1095-1291: Holy Wars: the seven Crusades

1215: England's King John forced to sign the Magna Carta, the "great charter" guaranteeing the rights of the English nobility

1233: Spanish Inquisition begins

1223-1241: Genghis Khan invades Russia; Mongols invade Kiev, Silesia, Poland, and Hungary.

1284-97: Wales defeated by England's Edward I; Scots rebel.

1299: Ottoman Empire founded in Turkey

THE RENAISSANCE

1325: beginning of Renaissance in Italy

1337-1452: Hundred Years War between England and France. The English win early battles, but are eventually expelled from southwestern France.

1347-52: The Black Plague sweeps across Europe. 25 million die, between one-half and one-third of Europe's population. Episodes will recur through 1771.

1356: Bohemian king Charles IV's "Golden Bull" edict officially recognizes various German princes and kings as rulers; the empire breaks up into a number of large kingdoms and duchies.

1378-1417: The Great Schism: Popes fight for control of the Roman Catholic Church in Avignon, France and Rome. The election of an Italian cardinal finally during the Council fo Constance ends the schism, but papal authority remains weak.

1450: Florence becomes the center of the Renaissance. Invention of printing press in Germany by Johannes Gutenberg.

1453: The Byzantine Empire falls to the Ottomans with the fall of Constantinople; the Turks rename it Istanbul.

1455-85: English War of the Roses between houses of York and Lancaster. Henry Tudor (of Lancaster; a.k.a. Henry VII) defeats his opponents and inagurates the Tudor dynasty in England.

1462-1505: Ivan III (the Great) rules as the first tsar in Russia; he expands to the north and west and drives out the Mongols.

1469: Ferdinand of Aragon and Isabella of Castile marry to unite Spain

1490s: beginning of the Age of Exploration

1516-56: Charles V becomes heir to the Spanish and Hapsburg (Germany and Austria) crowns. Enters into dynastic struggles with Francis I of France and Henry VIII

REFORMATION AND COUNTERREFORMATION

1517: Reformation begins in Germany with Martin Luther's *95 Theses;* Luther is excommunicated in 1521. By the end of the decade, the Holy Roman Empire was divided.

1520-66: height of Ottoman Empire under Süleyman I (the Magnificent)

1527: Holy Roman Empire attacks Rome, imprisons Pope Clement VII; end of Italian Renaissance

1534: Henry VIII divorces Catherine of Aragon, breaks with the church of Rome, and declares himself head of the Protestant Church in England; beginning of the English Reformation

1536-41: Reformation reaches Norway, Denmark, then Scotland

1543: Copernicus' *Concerning the Revolutions of the Celestial Spheres,* which rejects the Aristotelian view of the universe in favor of a heliocentric one, is published.

1545-1563: Council of Trent, keystone of the Counterreformation, upholds justification by faith, confirms the truth of the Scripture, reaffirms the seven sacraments and the Eucharist.

1547: Ivan IV (the Terrible) becomes tsar of Russia and battles with Boyars (nobles) for power

1553: Death of Edward VI (successor to King Henry VII); his successor, Queen (Bloody) Mary I, restores the Catholic Church in England

1555: Peace of Augsburg: Charles V grants the princes of Germany the right to establish the religion of their own people, whether Catholic or Protestant

1556: Holy Roman Emperor Charles V divides power between brother Ferdinand I (Austrian Hapsburg lands) and son Philip II (Spain, Netherlands). Spain is the greatest power in Europe.

1558-1603: Reign of Queen Elizabeth I following death of Mary I; restores Protestant Church

1572: Saint Bartholomew's Day Massacre of French Huguenots in Paris

1587: Mary, Queen of Scots, is executed.

1588: The Spanish Armada is defeated by the English; Spain no longer dominates Europe.

WARS OF RELIGION

1594: Henry IV crowned King of France, establishes Bourbon dynasty, and ends French wars of religion. Henry's Edict of Nantes (1598) grants limited toleration to French Huguenots.

1600: Danish astronomer Tycho Brahe moves to Prague and works with Johannes Kepler, who postulates three laws of planetary motion in line with the Copernican view.

1610-43: Louis XII of France is guided by chief minister Cardinal Richelieu, who preaches *raison d'état* (reason of state), placing the needs of the national above elite privelege.

1616-33: Galileo is condemned by the pope for teaching that the sun is at the center of the universe, and is then condemned by the Inquisition

1618-1648: Thirty Years' War: Struggle between the Roman Catholic and Hapsburg Holy Roman Empire and German Protestant towns. The Peace of Westphalia (1648) grants the member-states of the Holy Roman Empire full sovereignty. Germany's population is cut in half due to war and pestilence. Spain acknowledges the independence of the Netherlands.

SCIENTIFIC REVOLUTION

1637: Descartes' *Discourse on Method* starts with the assertion that "I think, therefore I am" *(cogito, ergo sum);* "Cartesian" thinking breaks the world down into parts.

1640-88: Frederick William, the Great Elector of Brandenburg-Prussia, inherits a weakened collection of territories, but develops them into an efficient state bureaucracy based in military might.

1642-60: England plunges into civil war between Cavaliers (Loyalists to King Charles I) and Roundheads (Parliament). After Charles I is executed (1649), Oliver Cromwell dissolves the Rump Parliament and declares himself Lord Protector (1653). After his death (1658), Charles II takes the throne, restoring the Stuart line (1660).

1643: Louis XIV, the Sun King, becomes King of France, though chief minister Cardinal Mazarin exerts real power until 1661. Colbert, Louis' chief minister for finance, builds up the navy, reforms legal codes, and establishes national academies of culture. France, the richest and most populous European state, becomes the greatest nation in Europe; French replaces Latin as the universal European tongue. Louis' dynastic wars that will continue through 1715.

1653: Thomas Hobbes' *Leviathan* suggests that individuals find refuge from the brutal state of nature by giving up their rights to an absolute ruler in exchange for safety and security.

1682-1725: Peter I (the Great) in Russia campaigns to westernize Russia and introduces great military reforms (conscription, meritocracy, military schools). After the Battle of Poltava (1709), Russia gradually replaces Sweden as the dominant power in the Baltics.

1685: Louis XIV revokes the Edict of Nantes of 1598.

1687: Isaac Newton's *Principia* lays the foundation for modern science, synthesizing the previous scientific theories of Galileo, Descartes, Kepler, et. al.

1688: Glorious Revolution in England: Catholic James II flees to France and William, Prince of Orange, and Mary, James' daughter, ascend to the throne with very little bloodshed. The Declaration of Rights (1689) asserts the fundamental principles of constitutional monarchy.

1690: John Locke's *An Essay Concerning Human Understanding* postulates that each person is a *tabula rasa* (blank slate) at birth and thus that all knowledge is sensory.

1700-1800: Industrial Revolution kicks off in Northern England: invention of steam engine, spinning mill, spinning jennys. Factory manufacturing becomes a symbol of the industrial age.

1700-1747: beginning of the Enlightenment; *philosophes* celebrate reason, directly reflect the influence of Scientific Revolution. 1748-1778: High Enlightenment; inaugurated by Montesquieu's *The Spirit of the Laws,* ends with the deaths of Voltaire and Rousseau. 1779-1800: late Enlightenment; move from emphasis on reason to human emotions; also features experiments in the free market and enlightened despotism.

AGE OF ENLIGHTENMENT

1700-1721: Great Northern War: Saxony, Poland, Brandenburg-Prussia, Hannover, Denmark, and Russia ally to attack Sweden; Sweden loses lands in Germany, Poland, the the Baltics

1701-1714: War of the Spanish Succession: upon Hapsburg Charles II's death, Austria and Britain fight France and Germany to keep Louis XIV's son, Philip V, off the Spanish throne. The Treaty of Utrecht (1713) allows him to rule but prevents him from merging his empire with France. Spain cedes half of Italy and the Spanish Netherlands to Austria. France, weakened and financially burdened by Louis' dynastic wars, is no longer the preeminent power on the continent.

1707: The Act of Union joins England, Scotland, and Wales in the United Kingdom of Great Britain

1740-1786: Frederick II's (the Great) "enlightened" reforms enhance the efficiency of the Prussian absolutist state. The Prussian and Austrian states vie for power.

1740-1748: War of the Austrian Succession: Frederick II invades and wins Hapsburg Silesia.

1751-1770s: Denis Diderot's *Encyclopedia*, the greatest work of the Enlightenment, is published; it constitutes the first attempt at a compilation of all the world's knowledge

1756-1763: Seven Years' War: Austria and France put aside longstanding differences aside to join forces against Prussia and Britain. Battle spreads to North America, the Caribbean, and India.

1762: Jean-Jacques Rousseau's *The Social Contract* imagines a social contract in which the individual gives up his freedom to the "general will" in exchange for safety and security.

1772-95: Poland is carved up between Austria, Prussia, and Russia over the course of three partitions (1772, 1793, 1795).

1780s: "Enlightened despots" Maria Theresa and son Joseph II of Austria abolish serfdom and improve conditions of rural life; Catherine the Great clarifies the rights of the Russian nobility, although there is virtually no change in the life of the masses. Critics in France condemn the king for despotism, elite privilege, and high taxes to finance foreign wars and the court.

FRENCH REVOLUTION AND NAPOLEON

1789: French Revolution: The third estate of the Estates-General declares itself a "National Assembly" (June 20) and takes the so-called Tennis Court Oath to demand limits on the king's authority (June 23). Crowds storm the Bastille (July 14). The National Assembly formally abolishes the "feudal regime" (August 4) and authors a declaration of rights and a new constitution.

1791-93: Louis XVI tries to flee France, but is caught at the border; the Revolution enters a second, more radical phase. The monarchy is overthrown and is replaced by a republic.

1793: Louis XVI is tried and hanged. The Jacobin-dominated government collapses into a dictatorship that brings on "the Terror," famed for its use of the guillotine. The Committee of Public Safety, led by Maximilien Robespierre, executes all perceived counter-revolutionaries.

1794-99: Moderate Jacobins and others, afraid they might be next to be "purged," overthrow the dictatorship and establish the "Directory," a second try at representative government. Robespierre is guillotined. High society returns to France, but instability remains.

1799: Sieyès and Napoleon Bonaparte overthrow the Directory and found the Consulat (1799).

1799-1814: After designating himself "consul for life" (1802) and then emperor (1804), Napoleon loses a disastrous naval defeat to Great Britain at the Battle of Trafalgar (1805), but gains significant lands on the continent. He abolishes the Holy Roman Empire, dismembers Prussia, and captures Hapsburg Vienna. The Napoleonic Code (1804) defines property rights, declares all people equal before the law, and affirms the freedoms of religion and work. After wars with Britain and Spain, his Grand Army is disastrously defeated in Russia (1812). Russia, Prussia, Britain, and Austria allied forces sweep into Paris, and Napoleon abdicates (1814).

1814: Bourbon rule is restored in France with Louis XVIII. The Treaty of Paris leaves France with its lands as of November 1792.

INDUSTRIAL REVOLUTION

1800-1850: The Industrial Revolution, born in England in the 18th century, spreads throughout Western Europe. Life expectancy, population, and urbanization all rise.

1815-1848: Liberal revolts in Spain, Portugal, Italy, Germany, and Poland.

1825-55: Reign of Nicholas I in Russia. The Decembrist revolt during his accession (1825) fails.

1830: The "July Revolution" in France places liberal Louis-Philippe on the throne rather than continuing with the Bourbon dynasty, encouraging liberal and nationalist movements elsewhere.

1830-50: origins of socialism and experimentation with utopian societies

1831: Belgium wins autonomy from the Netherlands;

1832: Greece's independence is recognized by the Turks

1832-46: The British Reform Act of 1832 grants one out of every five adult male citizens suffrage. Additional reforms abolish slavery and limited child labor (1833).

1837-1901: Queen Victoria of Britain leads the Victorian Age of reform

1848-49: "a springtime of nationalities": Prussians, Austrians, Germans, Italians, Poles, Czechs, Hungarians, and South Slavs demand liberalist and nationalist reforms. The February Revolution in France ends with the abdication of Louis-Philippe and the declaration of the Second French Republic; Louis Napoleon Bonaparte, Napoleon's nephew, is elected president. Only Britain and Russia remain untouched by revolution.

1851: Louis Napoleon dissolves the National Assembly, stages a coup, and declares himself Emperor Napoleon III. He furthers centralized French economic and political power and oversees the rebuilding of Paris.

NATIONAL UNIFICATION

1853-56: Crimean War: Russians, British-French-Piedmontese, and Austrian troops clash over Russian influence of Constantinople; Russia capitulates

1855-81: Reign of Tsar Alexander II; the tsar abolishes serfdom in Russia (1861).

1859: Charles Darwin's *On the Origin of Species* professes the theory of natural selection

1859-70: unification of Italy, led by Victor Emmanuel II, Camillo Cavour, Giuseppe Mazzini, and Giuseppe Garibaldi

1866-1871: Otto von Bismarck, appointed Prime Minister of Prussia under Frederick William. Bismarck unifies the new German Empire, including lands acquired in the Austro-Prussian War (1866) and Franco-Prussian War (1870-71; includes Alsace-Lorraine).

1867: Dual Monarchy of Austria-Hungary is created. The British Reform Bill of 1867 grants the vote to the head of each household, doubling the number of voters in Britain.

INDUSTRIALIZATION AND IMPERIALISM

1870-1914: Second Industrial Revolution and rapid industrialization: inventions include electricity, the sewing machine, the telephone, and the automobile; living standards rise dramatically.

1880-1914: Age of Imperialism: Asia and the scramble for Africa

1882: Germany, Austria-Hungary, and Italy form the Triple Alliance to unite against Russian conquests; the system alliances later contributes to WWI

1890s: Sigmund Freud develops the method of psychoanalysis

1905: Albert Einstein's *Special Theory of Relativity* is published. France and Britain, previously steadfast rivals, join Russia in the Triple Entente alliance. Norway gains independence from Sweden. The First Moroccan Crisis tests English-French resolve in light of German demands in French-dominated Morocco. In the Russian Revolution of 1905, troops fire on marchers on "Bloody Sunday"; the tsar is forced to grant a parliament and the promise of civil rights.

1908: Bosnian Crisis: Austro-Hungarian government announces annexation of Bosnia-Herzegovina, in violation of the 1878 Congress of Berlin. Russia is outraged, but unwilling to go to war.

1909-11: Second Moroccan Crisis: France establishes a virtual protectorate in Morocco, in violation of the Algeciras agreements of 1906; appeases Germany with territory in the French Congo.

WORLD WAR I

1914: Austro-Hungarian Archduke Francis Ferdinand is assassinated in Sarajevo by Serb nationalists (June 28). Austria hands Serb officials a lengthy ultimatum (July 23); when all points are not met, it declares war on Serbia (July 28). World War I breaks out between Austro-Hungary and Germany (Italy remains neutral) and France, Britain, and Russia.

1917: The United States enters the war on the Allied side (April). Russia withdraws from the war after October Revolution, in which the Bolsheviks seize power; the Treaty of Brest-Litovsk yields lands to Germany.

1918: WWI ends with Allied victory.

1918-21: Civil war breaks out in Russia between the Bolsheviks and Mensheviks; the Bolsheviks, led by Lenin and Trotsky, are victorious. The Communist International is founded to assist revolutions in other countries.

1919: The "Big Four" at the Treaty of Versailles (Orlando of Italy, Lloyd George of Britain, Clemenceau of France, and Wilson of the US) assigns blame to Germany; the weak new Weimar Republic is forced under the "war guilt clause" to assume the financial burden of the war. Germany, Austria-Hungary, and Russia all lose extensive territories. The idealistic League of Nations is formed by US President Wilson to arbitrate future international disputes, but is not ratified by the US or Russian governments.

INTERWAR YEARS

1920: Adolf Hitler rises to the head of the nationalist German Workers' Party, which he renames the National Socialist German Workers' (Nazi) Party.

1921-23: German inflation spirals out of control. The American Dawes Plan (1924) extends the schedule for the payment of war reparations; the German economy improves.

1922: The Union of Soviet Socialist Republics is created, including Russia, Belarus, and Ukraine. "Duce" Benito Mussolini becomes prime minister of the first fascist government, in Italy. The Irish Free State is formed; Northern Ireland remains a part of the UK.

1923: French and Belgian troops occupy the mine-rich Ruhr Valley to force reparation payments from the Germans; they withdraw after nine months.

1924: death of Lenin

1925: Hitler's *Mein Kampf (My Struggle)* is published, predicting that Germany will rearm, then conquer *Lebensraum* (living space) at the expense of "inferior" Slavic peoples.

1927: Dictator Joseph Stalin assumes power in Russia; his arrests and "purges" target rivals and opponents. German economy collapses.

1929: Stock market crash on Wall Street exacerbates European economic woes. German Prime Minister Gustav Stresemann dies in the same month, heightening political instability and lending to the rise of the Nazis.

1930: Nazis and Communists gain seats in the German Reichstag, although Social Democrats retain the plurality.

1930s: Dictatorships exist in Portugal, Spain, Germany, Italy, Austria, Hungary, Yugoslavia, Greece, Turkey, Bulgaria, Romania, Poland, Lithuania, Latvia, Estonia, and the USSR. Only France, Switzerland, Britain, Ireland, Benelux, Scandinavia, and Czechoslovakia remain democracies.

1931: King Alfonso XIII of Spain is overthrown; Spain becomes a republic

1932: The Nazi Party becomes the largest in the Reichstag.

1933: Hitler is appointed chancellor, forming the 17th and last Weimar government. The Enabling Act extends the "emergency" powers of the Nazi Party and transfers power from the legislative to the executive branch. Hitler bans all parties but the Nazis and implements a totalitarian state.

1935-36: The Nuremberg Laws strip Jews of citizenship and force them to wear Stars of David as identification. Hitler defies the Treaty of Versailles by beginning steady rearmament and moving into the demilitarized Rhineland. Hitler signs a pact forming the "Axis" with Mussolini and the "Anti-Comintern" (Anti-Communist) Pact with Japan.

1936-39: The Spanish Civil War pits loyalists against nationalists, led by General Francisco Franco, and is perceived as a struggle against international fascism. Britain, Ireland, and France support the loyalists but remain neutral; German and Italian aid to Franco's troops proves decisive.

1938: *Kristallnacht* (Night of Broken Glass): Nazis destroy Jewish stores and homes throughout Germany, and beaten and imprison thousands of Jews. Hitler declares the unification *(Anschluß)* of Austria and Germany. At the Munich Conference, the other Great Powers appease Hitler with the Sudetenland and other lands in exchange for no further expansion.

1939: Hitler signs a non-aggression pact with Russia. The Nazis invade Czechoslovakia and then Poland, initiating WWII. Hitler unveils his "final solution: the annihilation of Jews in Europe.

1940: The Nazis capture Paris and set up the puppet Vichy government. Hitler contemplates invading Britain, but is put off by Nazi defeat in the Battle of Britain.

1941: The US enters the war after the bombing of Pearl Harbor by the Japanese. The Nazis renege on their non-aggression pact by invading Russia; German troops freeze in the freezing winter.

1941-45: Six million Jews die in the Holocaust

1943: The tide turns in favor of the Allies, as German troops go on the defensive in the Soviet Union and North Africa. The Allies invade southern Italy; Mussolini signs an armistice, and Allies continue to fight the Germans in Italy.

1944: D-day (June 6): Allied troops invasion on the coast of Normandy. By August, the Allies take Paris and de Gaulle's government is recognized.

1945: Yalta Conference (February): Churchill, Roosevelt, and Stalin formulate the UN, plan the final defeat and occupation of Nazi Germany, and determine spheres of influence in post-war Europe; Stalin promises free elections throughout Eastern Europe. Adolf Hitler commits suicide (April). Potsdam Conference: Churchill, Truman, and Stalin set up four occupation zones (the fourth for the French) in Germany, Berlin, Austria, and Vienna.

1946-1990: decolonialization of Africa, the Middle East, the Indian subcontinent, and SE Asia

1948-49: US airlift to Berlin; beginning of the Cold War between the USSR and the US

1949: The Soviet-occupied zone of East Germany becomes the German Democratic Republic; the American, British, and French zones in the West become the German Federal Republic. Twelve nations sign the North Atlantic Treaty Organization (NATO) to counter Soviet aggression.

1953: death of Stalin

1955-64: After winning the power struggle in Russia, Nikita Khrushchev offers brief respite from the censorship of the Stalinist era, but the Communist Party retains power

1956: Soviet intervention crushes the Hungarian Uprising against Communism. Suez Canal Crisis: Nasser of Egypt announces nationalization of the Suez Canal, demanding an end to British and French colonialism

1961: construction of the Berlin Wall between East and West

1962: the Cuban Missile Crisis bring the US and the Soviet Union to the brink of nuclear war

1967: creation of the European Community (including France, Benelux, Italy, and West Germany), which eliminates tariffs between partners; they are later joined by other powers (Britain, Denmark, and Ireland in 1973; Greece in 1981; Spain and Portugal in 1986; Eastern Germany in 1990; Austria, Sweden, and Finland in 1995)

1968: Soviets clamp down on the reformist "Prague Spring" in Czechoslovakia

1970s: Greece, Portugal, and Spain undergo democratization following the collapse of the Greek government and the deaths of the Portuguese and Spanish dictators Salazar and Franco

1985: head of state Mikhail Gorbachev initiates bold economic and political reforms in the USSR

1989: The fall of the Berlin Wall (November), symbolizing the fall of communism in Eastern Europe, the "Velvet Revolution" of Czechoslovakia, the violent overthrow of dictator Ceausescu in Romania, and the fall of Communist regimes in Bulgaria, Romania, and Albania symbolize the fall of the Iron Curtain.

1991: Boris Yeltsin is elected President of the "Russian Federation" and moves to initiate a Russian market economy. A failed coup d'état accelerates the collapse of the USSR; the republics one by one begin to declare their independence. Gorbachev resigns (December 25).

1992: Treaty of Maastricht: 12 members of the EC and six other European states forge a European Economic Area, eliminating national barriers for the movement of goods and services, workers, and capital

1995: The fall of the Communists in Yugoslavia leads to civil war between Croats, Muslims, and Serbs.

VISUAL ART IN EUROPE

CLASSICAL: ANTIQUITY TO AD 500

430 BC: Parthenon Frieze
410 BC: *Goddess of Victory*
320 BC: Lysippus, *Head of Alexander the Great*
200 BC: *Venus de Milo*
40: Triumphal Arch of Tiberius
80: Roman Colosseum
115: *Trajan's Column*
130: Pantheon
200-305: Roman catacomb paintings

MEDIEVAL: 500-1150

510-520: mosaics and *S. Apollinare in Classe* in Ravenna
698: Lindisfarne Gospels
800: Gospels of Charlemagne
802: Aachen cathedral
1015: bronze doors of Hildesheim cathedral
1080: Bayeux tapestry

GOTHIC: 1150-1300

1150: Nôtre-Dame in Paris started
1194: Chartres cathedral
1248: Saint-Chapelle in Paris

RENAISSANCE: 1385-1520

1415-16: Donatello, *St George*
1420-36: dome of Florence cathedral
1432-34: van Eyck, *Ghent altarpiece, Marriage of the Arnolfini*
1440: Fra Angelico, *The Annunciation*
1446: King's College Chapel in Cambridge begun
1485: Botticelli, *The Birth of Venus*
1495: da Vinci, *The Last Supper* in Milan
1502: Bramante, *Tempietto* in Rome; da Vinci, *Mona Lisa*
1504: Dürer, *Adam and Eve* engraving
1508-12: Michelangelo, *Sistine Chapel ceiling* in the Vatican
1512-14: Raphael, *The nymph Galatea*
1515: Grünewald, *Isenheim Altarpiece*

MANNERISM: 1520-1615

1550: Palladio, *Villa Rotunda*
1555-58: Tintoretto, *St. George and the dragon*
1568: Pieter Bruegel the Elder, *Peasant Wedding*

BAROQUE: 1600-1740

1627-28: Rubens, *Virgin and Child enthroned with saints*
1645-52: Bernini, *The ecstasy of St. Teresa*
1655-58: Rembrandt van Rijn, *Self-Portrait*
1656: Velázquez, *Las Meninas*
1660-80: Louis XIV's Palace at Versailles, designed by Bernini
1675-1710: Wren, *St. Paul's Cathedral* in London

ROCOCO: 1710-70

1719: Watteau, *Fête in a Park*
1760: Fragonard, *The park of the Villa d'Este, Tivoli*

NEOCLASSICISM: 1760-1840

1761: Mengs, *Parnassus*
1793: David, *Death of Marat*
1814: Ingres, *La Grande Odalisque*

ROMANTICISM: 1800-1850

1807: Friedrich, *The Cross in the Mountains*
1830: Delacroix, *Liberty Leading the People*
1842: Turner, *Steamer in a Snowstorm*

IMPRESSIONISM: 1867-86

1876: Renoir, *Dance at the Moulin de la Galette*
1882: Manet, *A Bar at the Folies-Bergère*
1884: Monet, *Haystacks at Giverny*
1884-86: Seurat, *Sunday Afternoon on the Island of La Grande Jatte*

POST-IMPRESSIONISM: 1880-1900

1879-82: Cézanne, *Still Life*
1889: van Gogh, *Yellow Wheat and Cypruses, Room at Arles*
1891-1902: Gauguin, series of paintings in Tahiti
1893: Munch, *The Scream*
1906-26: Monet, *Water Lilies*

FAUVISM: 1897-1911

1905: Matisse, *Woman with the Hat*
1908: Matisse, *The Dinner Table*

AVANT-GARDE GEOMETRICAL EXPERIMENTS: 1905-1925

1912: Kandinksy, *With Black Arch*
1918: Malevich, *White on White*
1921: Mondrian, *Composition in Red, Yelllow and Blue*

CUBISM: 1907-1914

1907: Picasso, *Les Demoiselles d'Avignon*
1911: Braque, *Man with a Guitar*
1912: Picasso, *Violin and Grapes*

DADAISM: 1905-1920

1917: Duchamp, *Fountain*
9999: Mix France Art Dog

SURREALISM: 1907-1923

1929: Magritte, *The Treachery of Images ("Ceci n'est pas une pipe")*
1931: Dali, *The Persistence of Memory*

POP ART: 1950-70

1963: Oldenburg, *Soft Fur Good Humors*

APPENDIX

INDEX

GO AWAY

LET'S GO GUIDEBOOKS

NEW FOR 2000:
Let's Go: China
Let's Go: Israel
Let's Go: Middle East
Let's Go: Peru & Ecuador

**30 ultimate
budget roadtrip
handbooks**

LET'S GO MAP GUIDES

The perfect map companion or weekend guide.

- New York
- London
- Paris
- Florence
- Los Angeles
- New Orleans
- Rome
- Seattle

- Prague
- Berlin
- Chicago
- Madrid
- Amsterdam
- Boston
- San Francisco
- Washington, D.C.

NEW FOR 2000:
- Sydney
- Hong Kong

Visit our web site www.letsgo.com

Next time, make your *own* hotel arrangements.

Yahoo! Travel

Do You YAHOO!?

©1999 Yahoo! Inc.

READER QUESTIONNAIRE

Name: _____

Address: _____

City: _____ **State:** _____ **Country:** _____

ZIP/Postal Code: _____ **E-mail:** _____ **How old are you?** ____

And you're...?   in high school   in college   in graduate school
     employed   retired   between jobs

Which book(s) have you used? _____

Where have you gone with Let's Go? _____

Have you traveled extensively before? yes no

Had you used Let's Go before? yes no   **Would you use it again?** yes no

How did you hear about Let's Go? friend   store clerk   television
    review   bookstore display
    ad/promotion   internet   other: _____

Why did you choose Let's Go? reputation   budget focus   annual updating
    wit & incision   price   other: _____

Which guides have you used? Fodor's Cognoscenti Maps Frommer's $-a-day
    Lonely Planet Moon Guides Rick Steve's
    Rough Guides UpClose other: _____

Which guide do you prefer? Why? _____

Please rank the following in your Let's Go guide: (1=needs improvement, 5=perfect)

packaging/cover 1 2 3 4 5	food 1 2 3 4 5	maps 1 2 3 4 5	
cultural introduction 1 2 3 4 5	sights 1 2 3 4 5	directions 1 2 3 4 5	
"Essentials" 1 2 3 4 5	entertainment 1 2 3 4 5	writing style 1 2 3 4 5	
practical info 1 2 3 4 5	gay/lesbian info 1 2 3 4 5	budget resources 1 2 3 4 5	
accommodations 1 2 3 4 5	up-to-date info 1 2 3 4 5	other: _____ 1 2 3 4 5	

How long was your trip? one week two wks. three wks. a month 2+ months

Why did you go? sightseeing adventure travel study abroad other: _____

What was your average daily budget, not including flights? _____

Do you buy a separate map when you visit a foreign city? yes no

Have you used a Let's Go Map Guide? yes no **If you have, which one?** _____

Would you recommend them to others? yes no

Have you visited Let's Go's website? yes no

What would you like to see included on Let's Go's website? _____

What percentage of your trip planning did you do on the web? _____

What kind of Let's Go guide would you like to see? recreation (e.g., skiing) phrasebook
    spring break adventure/trekking first-time travel info Europe altas

Which of the following destinations would you like to see Let's Go cover?
    Argentina Brazil Canada Caribbean Chile Costa Rica Cuba
    Morocco Nepal Russia Scandinavia Southwest USA other: _____

Where did you buy your guidebook? independent bookstore college bookstore
    travel store Internet chain bookstore gift other: _____

Please fill this out and return it to **Let's Go, St. Martin's Press,** 175 Fifth Ave., New York, NY 10010-7848. All respondents will receive a free subscription to **The Yellow-jacket,** the Let's Go Newsletter. You can find a more extensive version of this survey on the web at http://www.letsgo.com.

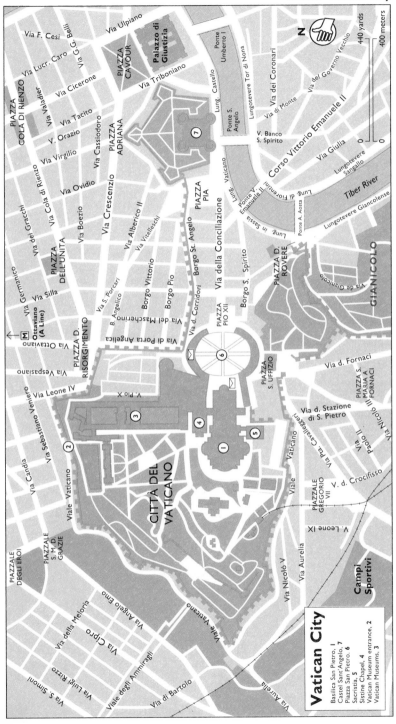

Vatican City

Basilica San Pietro, 1
Castel Sant'Angelo, 7
Piazza San Pietro, 6
Sacristia, 5
Sistine Chapel, 4
Vatican Museum entrance, 2
Vatican Museums, 3

N

440 yards

400 meters

CITTÀ DEL VATICANO

Tiber River

GIANICOLO

Campi Sportivi

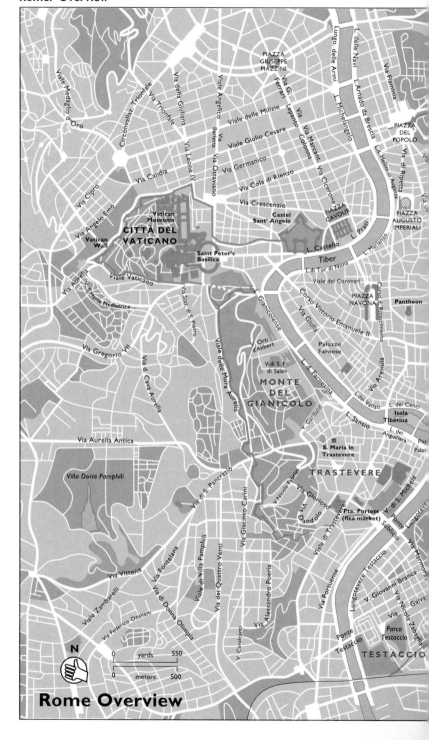

Rome Overview

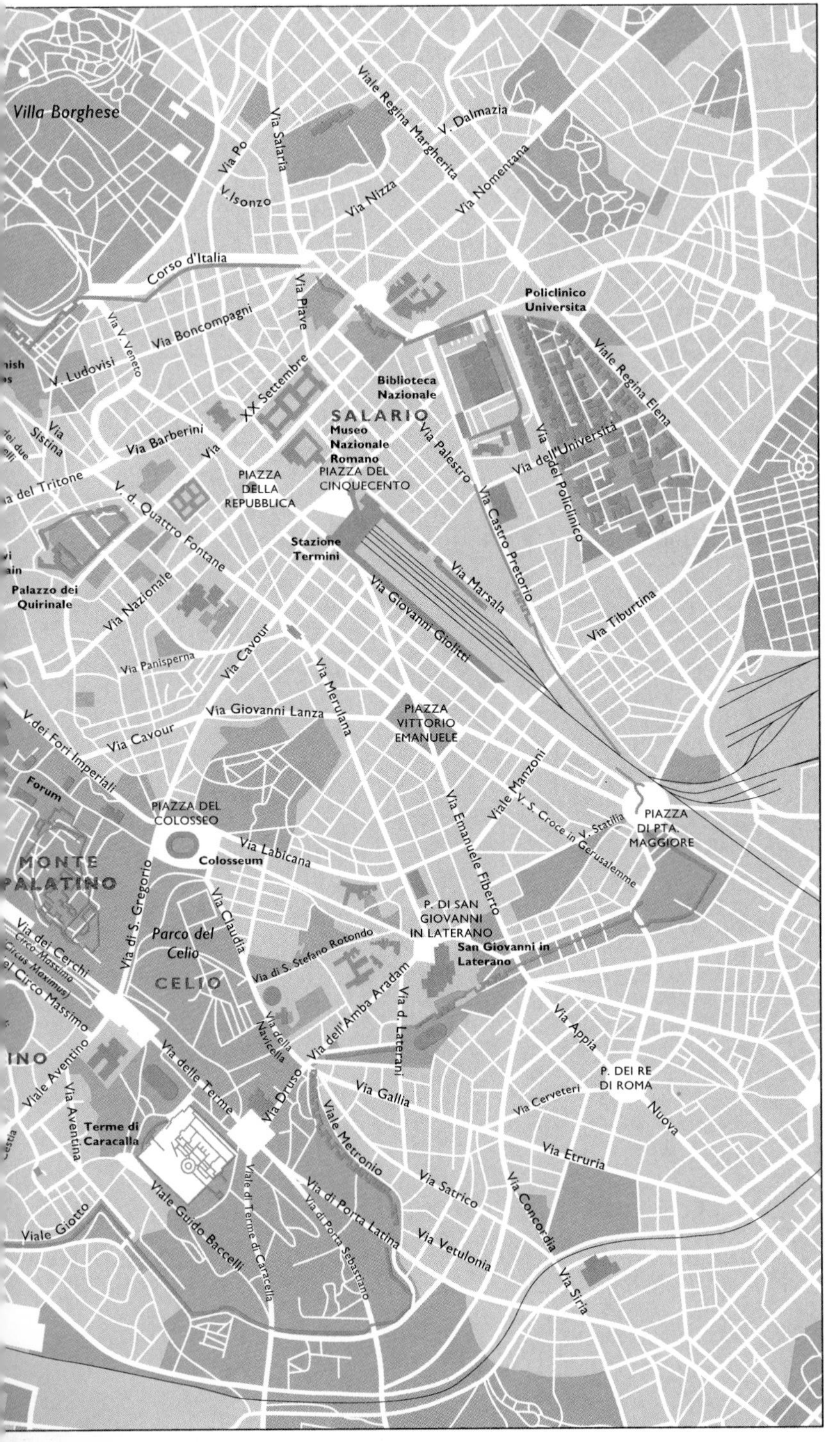
Villa Borghese
Via Po
Via Salaria
Viale Regina Margherita
V. Dalmazia
V. Isonzo
Via Nizza
Via Nomentana
Corso d'Italia
Via Piave
Via V. Veneto
Via Boncompagni
V. Ludovisi
Policlinico
Universita
Viale Regina Elena
Biblioteca
Nazionale
XX Settembre
SALARIO
Museo
Nazionale
Romano
Via Palestro
Via dell'Università
Via del Policlinico
Via Sistina
Via Barberini
Via
PIAZZA
DELLA
REPUBBLICA
PIAZZA DEL
CINQUECENTO
Via Castro Pretorio
del Tritone
V. d. Quattro Fontane
Stazione
Termini
Via Marsala
Palazzo dei
Quirinale
Via Nazionale
Via Giovanni Giolitti
Via Tiburtina
Via Panisperna
Via Cavour
Via Merulana
Via Giovanni Lanza
PIAZZA
VITTORIO
EMANUELE
V. dei Fori Imperiali
Via Cavour
Forum
PIAZZA DEL
COLOSSEO
Viale Manzoni
V. S. Croce in Gerusalemme
V. Statilia
PIAZZA
DI PTA.
MAGGIORE
Via Labicana
Colosseum
MONTE
PALATINO
Via Emanuele Filiberto
Via di S. Gregorio
Via Claudia
Parco del
Celio
P. DI SAN
GIOVANNI
IN LATERANO
Via dei Cerchi
Circo Massimo
(Circus Maximus)
Via del Circo Massimo
Via di S. Stefano Rotondo
San Giovanni in
Laterano
CELIO
Via della Navicella
Via dell'Amba Aradam
Via d. Laterani
Via Appia
INO
Viale Aventino
Via Aventina
Via delle Terme
Via Druso
P. DEI RE
DI ROMA
Via Gallia
Via Cerveteri
Nuova
Viale Metronio
Terme di
Caracalla
Via Etruria
Via Satrico
Viale di Terme di Caracalla
Via di Porta Latina
Via di Porta Sebastiano
Via Concordia
Viale Guido Baccelli
Viale Giotto
Via Vetulonia
Via Siria

Rome Transport

TO YOUTH HOSTEL

FLAMINIO

F-LINE
A-LINE

LEPANTO

PIAZZA DEL POPOLO

A-LINE

OTTAVIANO

MOSCA

81 492

PIAZZA RISORGIMENTO

PIAZZA CAVOUR

32

64

PIAZZA COLONNA

St. Peter's Basilica

Via d. Conciliazione

Castel Sant'Angelo

Tiber

Viale dei Coronari

34

Stazione S. Pietro

Corso Vittorio Emanuele II

PIAZZA NAVONA

Pantheon

116

CAMPO DEI FIORI

LARGO ARGENTINA

V. d. Plebescito

MONTE DEL GIANICOLO

Teatro Marcello

Isola Tiberina

Via Aurelia Antica

TRASTEVERE

60

PIAZZA SONNINO

Porta Portese

Via di villa Pamphili

Via dei Quattro Venti

Via G. Barrilli

Via Alessandro Poerio

Viale di Trastevere

PIRAMIDE

Via F. Ozanam

Parco Testaccio

TESTACCIO

13

N

Stazione Trastevere

Gianicolense

Circonvallazione

LLA BORGHESE

BOLOGNA

Via Po

Via S. Filia

Via Nizza

Via Nomentana

Viale Regina Margherita

·60·

·490·

dei Brassili

Corso d'Italia

·490·

Via Piave

Viale del Policlinico

·490·

116

POLICLINICO

NA

Via V. Veneto

Via Boncompagni

Via Piemonte

V. Castro Pretoria

Via XX Settembre

SALARIO

CASTRO PRETORIO

Viale Regina Elena

BERINI

·60·492·

Via Sistina

·60·492·

Via Barberini

Via Volturno

Via Gotto

·492·

B-LINE

REPUBBLICA

V. d'Quattro Fontane

P. D. CINQUECENTO

P. D. REPUBBLICA

A-LINE

64 110

170 714

·70·

Via Pretoriano

Via Lollis

Stazione Termini

TERMINI

·492·

Via Marsala

Via Tiburtino

·64·70·170·

Via Nazionale

Via Cavour

B-LINE

·70·

70

Via Giovanni Giolitti

Via Giov. Lanza

CAVOUR

Via Cavour

P. VITT. EMANUELE

VITTORIO

Via Merulana

Via Manzoni

P. PORTA MAGGIORE

·13·

man rum

COLOSSEO

Via Labicana

·714·

Viale Manzoni

MANZONI

Colosseum

Via di S. Giovanni in Laterano

·13·

Via Statilia

·13·

A-LINE

ALATINO

Via di S. Gregorio

V. Claudia

S. Giovanni in Laterano

Via la Spezia

·81·

·81·628·

B-LINE

CELIO

117

Via di S. Stefano Rotondo

·81·673·

218

Via dell'Amba Aradam

Via di Laterani

·81·673·714·

S. GIOVANNI

Via Aosta

Via Monza

Via Taranto

·13·81·673·

CIRCO MASSIMO

·628· V. delle Terme

Via della Navicella

·673·

Via Gallia

·218·673·

Via Appia Nuova

Via Magna Grecia

RE DI ROMA

Via Druso

Via Metronio

Via Magna Grecia

Via Cerveteri

Terme Di Caracalla

Viale Guido Baccelli

Viale di Terme di Caracalla

·673·

Via Satrico

·628·

Via Concordia

Via Etruria

PONTE LUNGO

·71·

Via di Porta Latina

Via di Porta Sebastiano

·218·

·218·

Via Vetulonia

Via Vescia

673

Via Latina

Via Ivrea

Giotto

stazione stiense

·715·

Porta S. Sebastiano

TO CATACOMBS

Porta S. Appia Antica

·638·

0   1/2 mile

0   500 meters

TO LAURENTINA

Central Rome

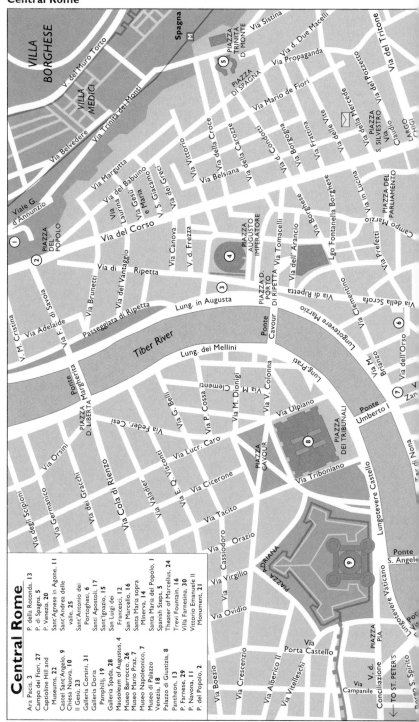

VILLA BORGHESE

VILLA MEDICI

Spagna Ⓜ

Via Sistina

Via del Tritone

PIAZZA TRINITÀ D. MONTE

Ⓢ

Via d. Due Macelli

Via Propaganda

PIAZZA DI SPAGNA

Via Mario de Fiori

Via del Pozzetto

Via del Muro Torto

V. del Muro Torto

PIAZZA S. SILVESTRO

Via della Mercede

LARGO CHIGI

Via Claudio

Via Belvedere

Via Trinità dei Monti

Via Margutta

Via del Babuino

Laurina

Via Gesù e Maria

V. S. Giacomo

Via dei Greci

Via Vittorio

Via B. della Croce

Via della Carozze

Via della Vite

Via d. Condotti

Via Bocca di Leone

Via Borgogna

Via Frattina

Via delle Vite

Via in Lucina

PIAZZA DEL PARLAMENTO

Viale G. d'Annunzio

Ⓛ

PIAZZA DEL POPOLO

Ⓜ

Via del Corso

Via Belsiana

Campo Marzio

Via Canova

Via Brunetti

Via di Vantaggio

Via del Vantaggio

Ripetta

V. d. Frezza

PIAZZA AUGUSTO IMPERATORE

Ⓓ

Via Tomacelli

Via dell'Arancio

Via Borghese

Lgo Fontanella Borghese

Via Prefetti

Via di Ripetta

Passeggiata di Ripetta

Lung. in Augusta

PIAZZA D. PORTO DI RIPETTA

Ⓒ

Via di Ripetta

Via della Scrofa

V. M. Cristina

Via Adelaide

Via F.

Ponte Cavour

Lungotevere Marzio

Via Clementino

Ⓕ

Tiber River

Lung. dei Mellini

Lung. Prati

Via dell'Orso

Ⓖ

Via M. Brianzo

Ⓘ

PIAZZA D. LIBERTÀ

Via Feder. Cesi

Via Clement

Via M. Dionigi

Via V. Colonna

Via Ulpiano

Ponte Umberto I

Via di Nona

Zan

Via Orsini

Via G. Belli

Via P. Cossa

PIAZZA CAVOUR

Via degli Scipioni

Via Germanico

Via dei Gracchi

Via Cola di Rienzo

Via Valadier

Via E. Q. Visconti

Via Lucr. Caro

Ⓗ

PIAZZA DEI TRIBUNALI

Via Tiburtino

Lungotevere Castello

Via Cicerone

Via Tacito

Via Cassiodoro

Via Orazio

Via Virgilio

Via Ovidio

PIAZZA ADRIANA

Ⓘ

Ponte S. Angel

Via Cassiodoro

Via Crescenzio

Via Boezio

Via Alberico II

Via Vitelleschi

Lungotevere Vaticano

Via Porta Castello

PIAZZA PIA

Via Conciliazione

V. d. Spirito

Po

S. Spirito

Via Campanile

← TO ST. PETER'S

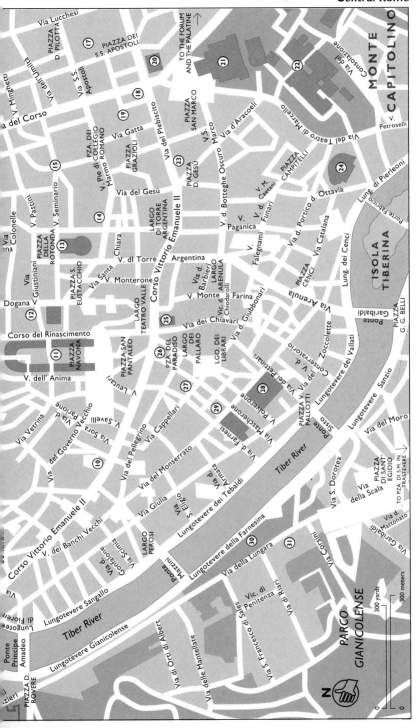

MONTE CAPITOLINO

Via Lucchesi

Via Umiltà

PIAZZA D. PILOTTA

PIAZZA DEI S.S. APOSTOLI

Via S.S. Apostoli

a del Corso

TO THE FORUM AND THE PALATINE

V. del Consolazione

V. Petroselli

Via Minghetti

Via Gatta

PZA. DEI COLLEGIO Marmo ROMANO

PIAZZA GRAZIOLI

Via del Plebiscito

PIAZZA SAN MARCO

V.S. Marco

Via d'Aracoeli

Via del Teatro di Marcello

Lung. di Pierleoni

Via Pastini

V. Seminario

V. Pie di

Via del Gesù

PIAZZA D. GESÙ

V. d. Botteghe Oscure

V. M. Caetani

V. d. Funari

PIAZZA CAMPITELLI

Via d. Portico d. Ottavia

Via Catalana

ISOLA TIBERINA

Porte Fabricio

Colonelle

V. Via

PIAZZA DELLA ROTONDA

Chiara

V. Santa

LARGO DI TORRE ARGENTINA

Corso Vittorio Emanuele II

V. Paganica

V. Falegnami

Lung. dei Cenci

PIAZZA CENCI

Ponte Garibaldi

PIAZZA G. G. BELLI

Via Giustiniani

PIAZZA S. EUSTACCHIO

V. di Torre   Argentina

V. Monterone

Via d. Barbieri

LARGO ARENULA

V. Monte Farina

Vic. d. Chiodaroli

Via Arenula

Dogana

Corso del Rinascimento

LARGO TEATRO VALLE

Via dei Chiavari

LGO DEI LIBRARI

V. d. Giubbonari

V. d. Conservatorio

Lungotevere dei Vallati

V. dell' Anima

PIAZZA NAVONA

PIAZZA SAN PANTALEO

PZA. DEL PARADISO

LARGO DEI PALLARO

Via dei Pettinari

V. d. Zoccolette

Lungotevere Sanzio

Via del Moro

V. Leutari

V. Savelli

Via del Governo Vecchio

Via Sora

Vicolo Vecchio

Via Cappellari

Via Masherone

V. Polverone

PIAZZA V. PALLOTTI

Ponte Sisto

Via S. Dorotea

PIAZZA DI SANT' EGIDIO

Via della Scala

TO PZA. D.I S.M. IN TRASTEVERE

Via Verrina

Via d. Pellegrino

Via del Monserrato

Via d. Farnesi

Tiber River

Via d. Parione

Via Giulia

Via S. Eligio

Via d. Armata

Lungotevere dei Tebaldi

Via d. Mattonato

Via Garibaldi

Corso Vittorio Emanuele II

V. dei Banchi Vecchi

LARGO PEROSI

Via d. Scimia

Via d. Gonfalone

Ponte Mazzini

Lungotevere della Farnesina

Lungotevere della Lungara

Via Corsini

PARCO GIANICOLENSE

Ponte Principe Amadeo

PIAZZA D. ROVERE

Lungotevere Sangallo

Tiber River

Lungotevere Gianicolense

Via di Orti di Alberi

Via delle Mantellate

Vic. di Penitenza

Via di Riari

Via S. Francesco di Sales

Vic. di Sales

300 yards

300 meters

N

Rome: Villa Borghese

Via Giovannelli
Giovanni Paisiello
Via S. Mercadante
Via P. Raimondi
PIAZZALE DEI RAIMONDI
Via dei Daini
Via dell'Uccelliera
Viale dell'Uccelliera
Via P. Raimondi
Galleria Borghese
Viale Museo Borghese
V. Puttaci
PIAZZA E. SIENKIEWICZ
Via di S. Teresa
Via Po
Corso d'Italia
V. Puglia
V. Romagna
Via Sardegna
Via Sicilia
Via Boncompagni
Via Quintina
Via Piemonte
200 yards
200 meters
Via Toscana
Via Marche

GIARDINO ZOOLOGICO
Zoologico
VILLA BORGHESE
Viale del Giardino
Via Ulisse Aldrovandi
Viale dei Cavalli Marini
Viale P. Canonica
Viale dell'Aranciera
PIAZZA DI SIENA
Viale Casina di Raffaello
Pineta
Viale Goethe
V. di S. Paolo del Brasile
PIAZZALE BRASILE
Porta Pinciana
Via Pinciana
Via Vittorio Veneto
Via Emilia
Via Aurora
Via Porta Pinciana
Via Ludovisi
Via Liguria

Galleria Naz. d'Arte Moderne
Via Omero
Viale delle Belle Arti
Museo Naz. di Villa Giulia
PIAZZALE PAOLA BORGHESE
Via Bernadotte
PIAZZALE DEL FIOCCO
V. F. Laguardia
PIAZZALE D. CANESTRE
V. Magnolie
GALOPPATOIO
Viale Valadier
PIAZZALE DEI MARTIRI
Viale Galoppatoio
Viale del Muro Torto
VILLA MEDICI
Via del Babuino
Spagna
A LINE

V. di Villa Giulia
V. di S. Eugenio
Via Flaminia
Via Flaminia
VILLA STROHL FERN
VILLA RUFFO
Viale Madama
V. Washington
Flaminio
PIAZZALE FLAMINIO
Viale d. Belvedere
Viale Trinità dei Monti
Via del Babuino
Via del Corso
PIAZZA AUGUSTO IMPERATORE
Via Vittoria
Via della Croce
Via V. A. Canova

PIAZZA DELLA MARINA
V. D. A. Azuni
V. G. Pisanelli
V. Romanosi
V. Disavola
Via Savoia
PIAZZA DEL POPOLO
Via Brunetti
Via del Vantaggio
Via Ripetta
Lungo. in Augusta

Lungotevere delle Navi
Ponte d. Risorg
Fiume Tevere
Ponte G. Matteotti
Lungo, Arnaldo da Brescia
Ponte Nenni
Ponte Margherita
Lungo. d. Mellini
PIAZZA D. LIBERTÀ
Via Fed. Cesi
Via G. Belli

PIAZZA MONTE GRAPPA
Lungotevere delle Armi
Viale Giuseppe Mazzini
Viale della Milizie
PIAZZA DELLE CINQUE GIORNATE
Lungo. Michelangelo
Via Settembrini
Via Giulio Cesare
A LINE
Via degli Scipioni
Lepanto
Via Pompeo Magno
Via dei Gracchi
Via Valadier
PIAZZA COLA DI RIENZO
Via Marc. Colonna
Via Ezio
Via Boerio
Via E. Q. Visconte

N

Villa Borghese

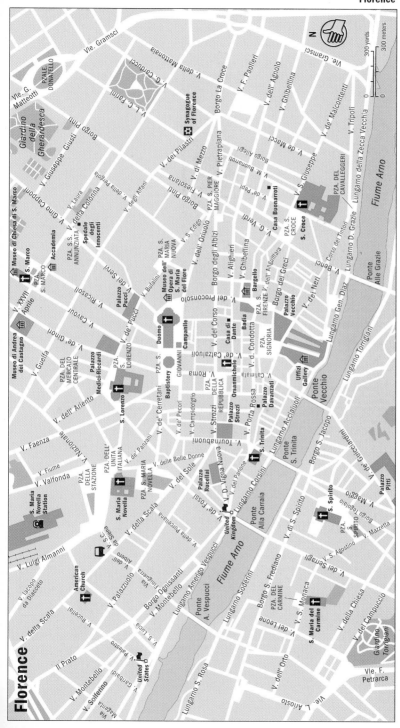

Venice

Venice

TO MAINLAND

Ponte
della Libertà

CANNARE

Rio di S. Girolamo

Rio del Battello

CAMPO
DEL GHETTO

Canale di Cannareggio

C. Riello

R. terrà
Leonard

Lista di Spagna

CAMPO
SAN
GEREMIA

Canal Grande

Ponte
Scalzi

Riva d. Biasio

Lista d. Bari

SANTA CR

Fondamenta di Santa Lucia

F. d. S. Simeon Piccolo

Rio Marin

CAM
DE
MOR

Corte
Canal

Canale di Chiara

C. d. Lacca

R. di

Rio della Saccherre

CAMPO
S. ROCCO

Canale Scomenzera

Rio

F. Minotto

CAMPO
DI SAN
MARGHERITA

Rio terra dei Pensieri

Nuovo

Rio Foscari

Rio d. Santa Margherita

Rio di S. Barnaba

Calle
Avogaria

Rio d. Ognissonti

Fondamenta della Zattere

DORSODU

Canale della Giudecca

Venice

Amex, **3**
Campo dei Frari, **10**
Campo S. Giorgio, **12**
Campo SS. Giovanni e Paolo, **13**
Campo San Salvaatore, **7**
Church of S. Maria Della Salute, **9**
Church of S. Maria Formosa, **14**
Church of San Zaccaria, **11**
Gallerie dell' Accademia, **8**
Hospital (Ospedale Civili), **20**
IYHF, **4**
Palazzo Ducale (Doge's Palace), **6**
Piazza San Marco, **5**
Piazzale Roma, **18**
Ponte Rialto, **21**
Post Office, **2**
Questura di Venezia, **19**
Teatro Goldoni, **15**
Tourist Office (APT),
  Piazza San Marco, **16**
Tourist Office (APT),
  Stazione S. Lucia, **17**
Train Station, **1**

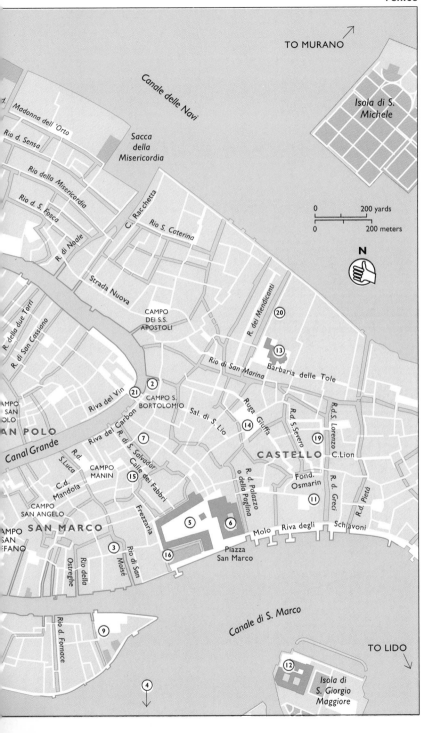

Milan

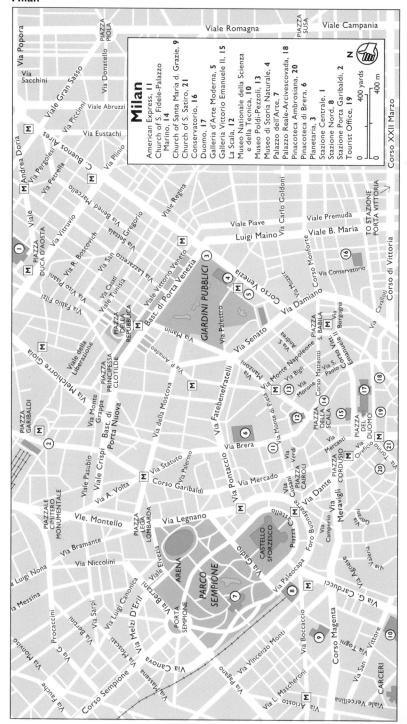

Milan

American Express, 11
Church of S. Fidele-Palazzo
Marino, 14
Church of Santa Maria d. Grazie, 9
Church of S. Satiro, 21
Conservatorio, 16
Duomo, 17
Galleria d'Arte Moderna, 5
Galleria Vittorio Emanuele II, 15
La Scala, 12
Museo Nazionale della Scienza
e della Tecnica, 10
Museo Poldi-Pezzoli, 13
Museo di Storia Naturale, 4
Palazzo dell'Arte, 7
Palazzo Reale-Arcivescovada, 18
Pinacoteca Ambrosiana, 20
Pinacoteca di Brera, 6
Planetaria, 3
Stazione Centrale, 1
Stazione Nord, 8
Stazione Porta Garibaldi, 2
Tourist Office, 19

400 yards
400 m

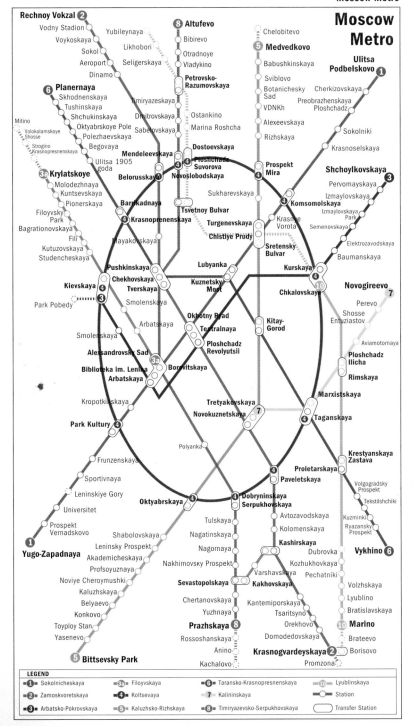

Moscow Metro

Moscow

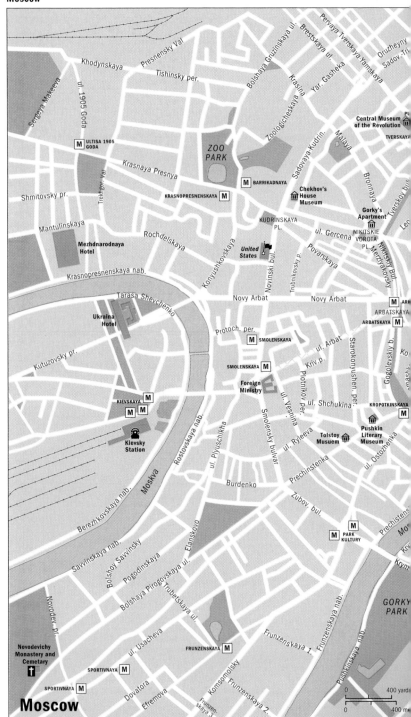

Khodynskaya

Presnensky Val

Tishinsky per.

ul. 1905 Goda

Sergeya Makeeva

Bolshaya Gruzinskaya ul.

Brestskaya ul.

Pervaya Tverskaya-Yamskaya

Oruzheyny

Sadov.-Tri

M ULTISA 1905 GODA

Krasnaya Presnya

Krasina

Yar. Gasheka

Zoologicheskaya

Central Museum of the Revolution 🏛

PL

TVERSKAYA

Trekhtor. val

Shmitovsky pr.

ZOO PARK

Sadovaya-Kudrin.

Malaya

M BARRIKADNAYA

Chekhov's House Museum 🏛

Bronnaya

Tverskoy bu

KRASNOPRESNENSKAYA **M**

KUDRINSKAYA PL.

Gorky's Apartment 🏛

NIKITSKIE VOROTA PL.

Leon

Mantulinskaya

Rochdelskaya

ul. Gercena

Nikitsky Bul.

Merzlyakovsky

Mezhdnarodnaya Hotel

Konyushkovskaya

United States 🚩

Novinski bul.

Povarskaya

Trubnikovsky p.

Krasnopresnenskaya nab.

Tarasa Shevchenko

Novy Arbat

Novy Arbat

M ARB

ARBATSKAYA

Ukraina Hotel

Protoch. per.

ARBATSKAYA **M**

Kutuzovsky pr.

M SMOLENSKAYA

ul. Arbat

Starokonyushen. per.

Gogolevsky b.

Ko

Kriv.p.

SMOLENSKAYA **M**

Plotnikov per.

ul. Shchukina

KROPOTKINSKAYA

mashk

KIEVSKAYA **M**

Foreign Ministry

ul. Vesnina

Pushkin Literary Museum 🏛

M

M **M**

Rostovskaya nab.

Smolensky buvar

ul. Ryleeva

Tolstoy Museum 🏛

ul. Ostozhenka

Kievsky Station 🚂

ul. Plyuschikha

Prechistenka

Burdenko

Zubov. bul.

Prechisten

Mo

Berezhkovskaya nab.

Moskva

Savvinskaya nab.

Bolshoy Savvinsky

Pogodinskaya

Elanskovo

M PARK KULTURY

M

Kru

Krym

Novodev. pr.

Bolshaya Pirogovskaya ul.

Trubetskaya ul.

Frunzenskaya nab.

GORKY PARK

Novodevichy Monastery and Cemetary ✝

ul. Usacheva

FRUNZENSKAYA **M**

Frunzenskaya 1.

Pushkinskaya nab.

SPORTIVNAYA **M**

SPORTIVNAYA **M**

Dovatora

Efremova

Komsomolsky

Frunzenskaya 2.

Frunzen-skaya 3.

0   400 yards

0   400 me

Moscow

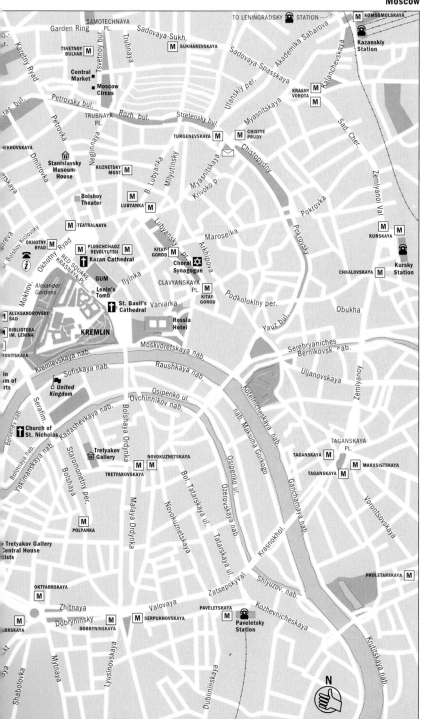

Московское Метро

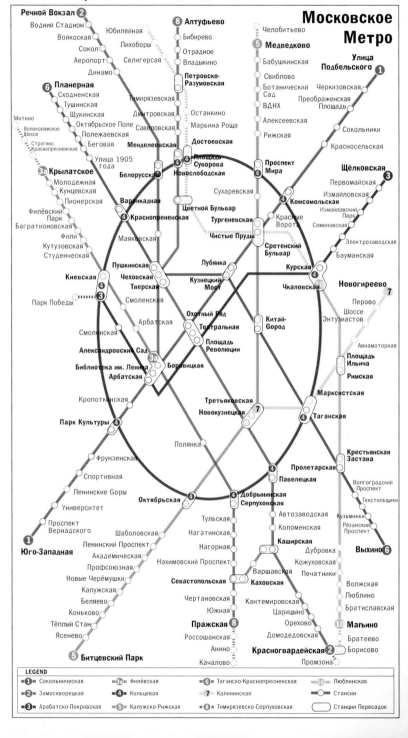

Московское Метро

Речной Вокзал ②
Водний Стадион
Юбилейная
Войковская
Лихоборы
Сокол
Аэропорт
Селигерсая
Динамо

Планерная ⑥
Сходненская
Тушинская
Щукинская
Октябрьское Поле
Полежаевская
Беговая

Митино
Волоколамское Шоссе
Строгино Краснопресненская

Крылатское ③а
Молодежная
Кунцевская
Пионерская
Филёвский Парк
Багратионовская
Фили
Кутузовская
Студенческая

Бибирево
Отрадное
Владыкино

Петровско-Разумовская

Тимирязевская
Дмитровская
Савёловская

Менделеевская

Белорусская ②

Баррикадная
Краснопресненская ④

Останкино
Марьина Роща

Достоевская

Площадь Суворова ④
Новослободская

Сухаревская

Цветной Бульвар
Тургеневская

Чистые Пруды

Маяковская

Пушкинская
Чеховская
Тверская

Смоленская

Алтуфьево ⑧

Челобитьево
Медведково ⑤
Бабушкинская
Свиблово
Ботанический Сад
ВДНХ
Алексеевская
Рижская

Проспект Мира

Комсомольская

Красные Ворота

Сретенский Бульвар

Лубянка
Кузнецкий Мост

Киевская ④
Парк Победы ③

Арбатская

Смоленская

Александровский Сад
Библиотека им. Ленина
Арбатская
Боровицкая ③а

Кропоткинская

Охотный Ряд
Театральная

Площадь Революции

Китай-Город

Улица Подбельского ①
Черкизовская
Преображенская Площадь
Сокольники
Красносельская

Щёлковская ③
Первомайская
Измайловская
Измайловский Парк
Семеновская
Электрозаводская
Бауманская

Курская ④
Чкаловская
Новогиреево ⑦
Перово
Шоссе Энтузиастов
Авиамоторная
Площадь Ильича
Римская
Марксистская

Третьяковская
Новокузнецкая ⑦
Таганская ④

Парк Культуры ④

Полянка

Крестьянская Застава
Волгоградский Проспект
Текстильщики
Кузьминки
Рязанский Проспект

Фрунзенская
Спортивная
Ленинские Горы
Университет
Проспект Вернадского

Юго-Западная ①

Октябрьская ④

Тульская
Нагатинская
Нагорная

Добрынинская ④
Серпуховская

Автозаводская
Коломенская

Павелецкая ④

Пролетарская

Шаболовская
Ленинский Проспект
Академическая
Профсоюзная
Новые Черёмушки
Калужская
Беляево
Коньково
Тёплый Стан
Ясенево

Битцевский Парк ⑤

Нахимовский Проспект
Севастопольская
Чертановская
Южная

Пражская ⑧
Россошанская
Анино
Качалово

Каширская
Варшавская
Каховская
Кантемировская
Царицыно
Орехово
Домодедовская

Красногвардейская ②
Промзона

Дубровка
Кожуховская
Печатники
Волжская
Люблино
Братиславская

Марьино ⑩
Братеево
Борисово

LEGEND

■①■	Сокольническая	■③а■	Филёвская	■⑥■	Таганско-Краснопресненская	■⑩■	Люблинская
■②■	Замоскворецкая	■④■	Кольцевая	7	Калининская	■○■	Станции
■③■	Арбатско-Покровская	■⑤■	Калужско-Рижская	■⑧■	Тимирязевско-Серпуховская	▭	Станции Пересадок

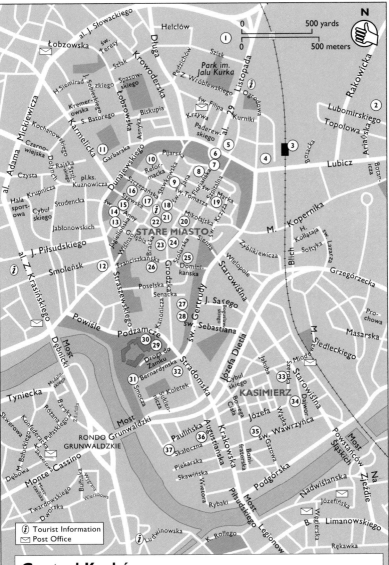

Central Kraków

Akademia Ekonomiczna, 2
Almatur Office, 24
Barbican, 6
Bernardine Church, 32
Bus Station, 4
Carmelite Church, 11
Cartoon Gallery, 9
City Historical Museum, 17
Collegium Maius, 14
Corpus Christi Church, 35
Czartoryski Art Museum, 8
Dominican Church, 25
Dragon Statue, 31

Filharmonia, 12
Franciscan Church, 26
Grunwald Memorial, 5
Jewish Cemetery, 33
Jewish Museum, 34
Kraków Głowny Station, 3
Monastery of the
 Reformed Franciscans, 10
Muzeum Historii Fotografii, 23
Orbis Office, 19
Pauline Church, 37
Police Station, 18
Politechnika Krakowska, 1

St. Andrew's Church, 28
St. Anne's Church, 15
St. Catherine's Church, 36
St. Florian's Gate, 7
St. Mary's Church, 20
St. Peter and Paul Church, 27
Stary Teatr (Old Theater), 16
Sukiennice (Cloth Hall), 21
Town Hall, 22
University Museum, 13
Wawel Castle, 29
Wawel Cathedral, 30

(i) Tourist Information
✉ Post Office

Prague

Prague

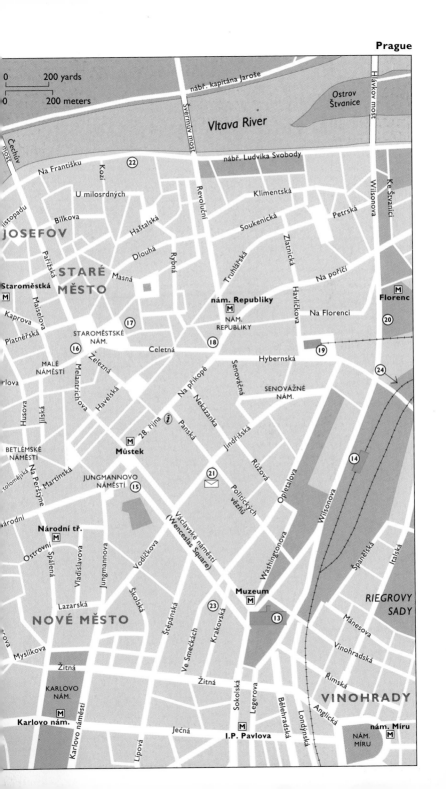

Central Budapest

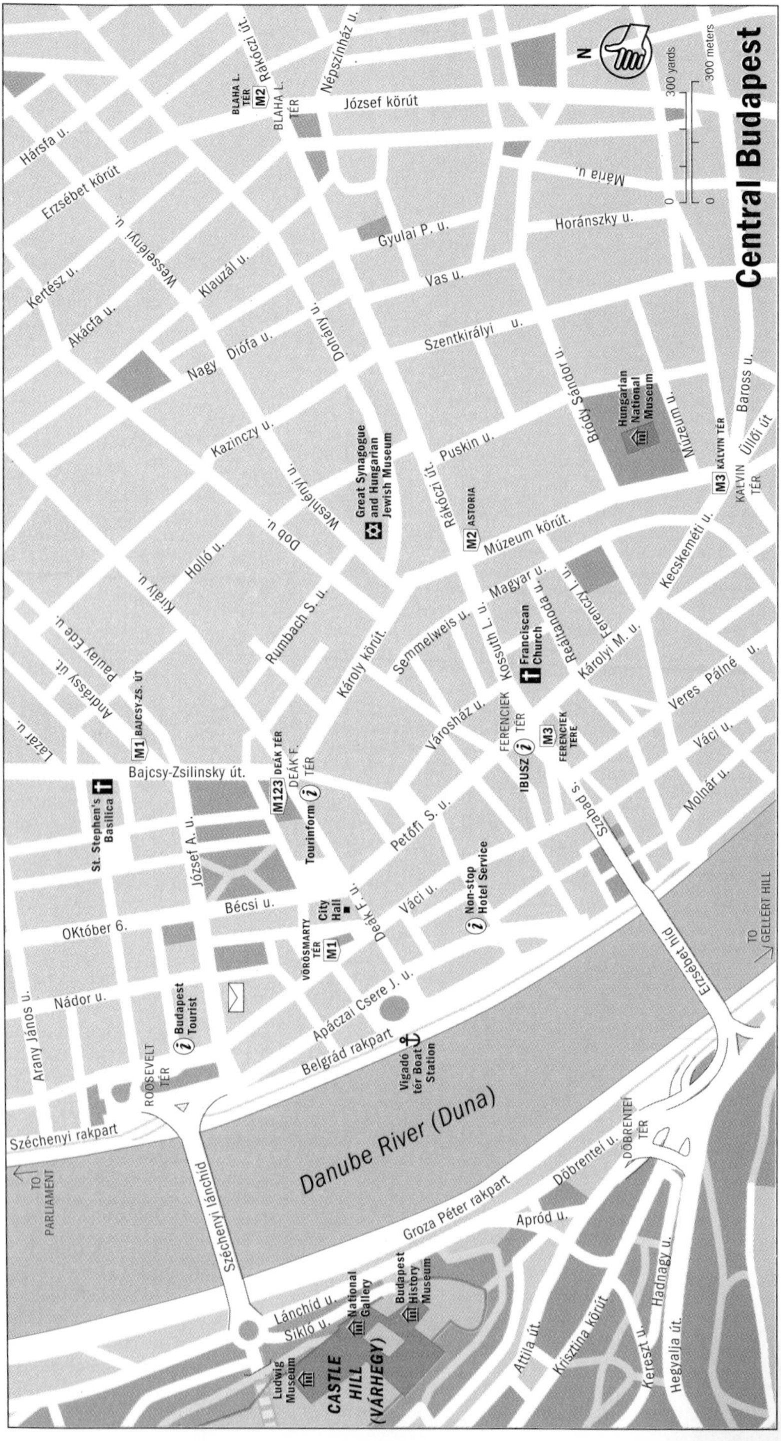

Central Budapest

N

300 yards
300 meters

Streets and places (labels on map):

Hársfa u.
Erzsébet körút
Wesselényi u.
Kertész u.
Akácfa u.
BLAHA L. TÉR
M2
BLAHA L. TÉR
Rákóczi út
Népszínház u.
József körút
Mária u.
Horánszky u.
Gyulai P. u.
Vas u.
Klauzál u.
Diófa u.
Dohány u.
Szentkirályi u.
Nagy
Kazinczy u.
Puskin u.
Wesselényi u.
Great Synagogue and Hungarian Jewish Museum
Rákóczi út
ASTORIA
M2
Múzeum körút.
Hungarian National Museum
Bródy Sándor u.
Múzeum u.
M3 KÁLVIN TÉR
KÁLVIN TÉR
Baross u.
Üllői út
Holló u.
Dob u.
Király u.
Pauláy Ede u.
Rumbach S. u.
Károly körút.
Semmelweis u.
Kossuth L. u.
Magyar
Ferenczy u.
Reáltanoda u.
Kecskeméti u.
Andrássy út
BAJCSY-ZS. ÚT
M1
Lázár u.
Bajcsy-Zsilinsky út.
DEÁK TÉR
DEÁK F. TÉR
M123
Franciscan Church
Károlyi M. u.
Veres Pálné
St. Stephen's Basilica
Tourinform (i)
Petőfi S. u.
Városház u.
FERENCIEK TÉR
IBUSZ (i)
M3
FERENCIEK TERE
Váci u.
József A. u.
Bécsi u.
Molnár u.
OKtóber 6.
Deák F. u.
VÖRÖSMARTY TÉR
City Hall
M1
Váci u.
Non-stop Hotel Service (i)
Szabad s.
Nádor u.
Arany János u.
ROOSEVELT TÉR
Budapest Tourist (i)
Apáczai Csere J. u.
Belgrád rakpart
Vigadó tér Boat Station
TO GELLÉRT HILL
Erzsébet híd
Széchenyi rakpart
TO PARLIAMENT
Széchenyi lánchíd
Danube River (Duna)
Groza Péter rakpart
Apród u.
Döbrentei u.
DÖBRENTEI TÉR
Lánchíd u.
National Gallery
Budapest History Museum
Siklo u.
Attila út
Krisztina körút
Hadnagy u.
KeresZt u.
Hegyalja út
Ludwig Museum
CASTLE HILL (VÁRHEGY)

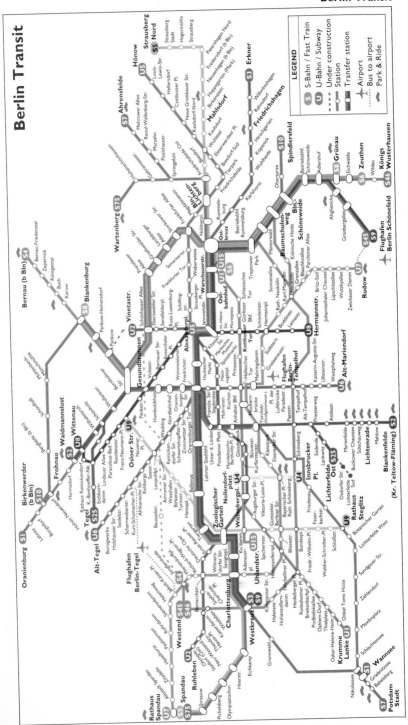

Berlin Transit

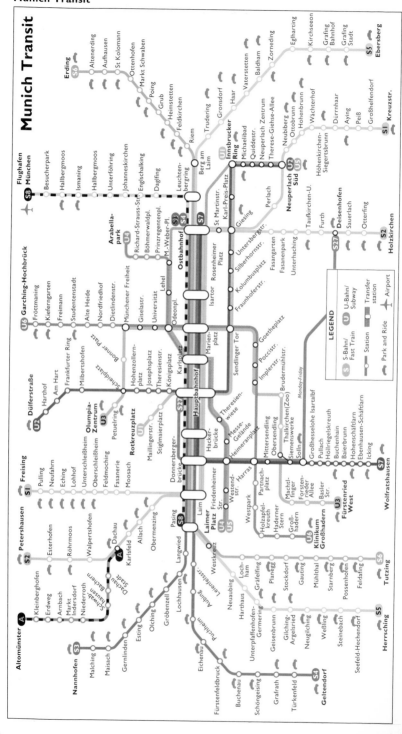

Munich Transit

Hamburg Transit

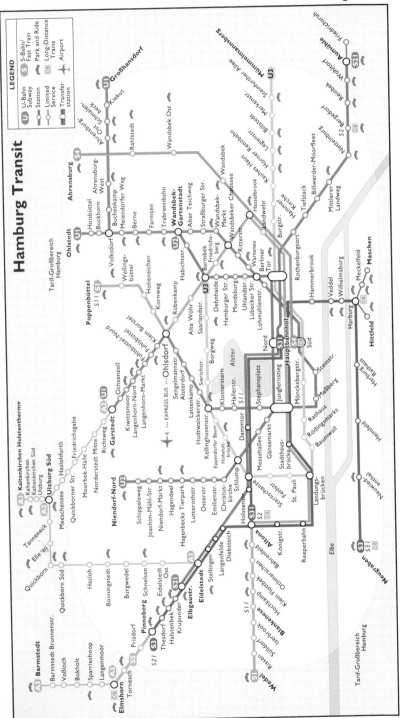

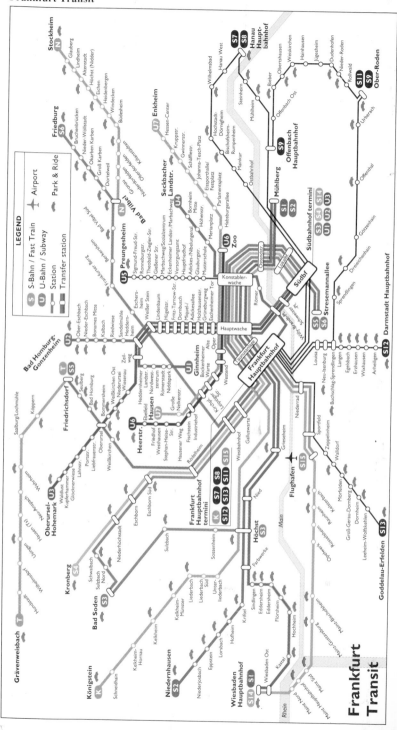

Frankfurt Transit